Brukner & Khan's

Clinical Sports

Medicine

FOURTH EDITION

*We dedicate this fourth edition to the Clinical Sports Medicine community—to each
clinician, educator, and policy maker committed to improving health through
the power of physical activity.*

Brukner & Khan's

Clinical Sports Medicine

FOURTH EDITION

BRUKNER
BAHR
BLAIR
COOK
CROSSLEY
McCONNELL
McCRORY
NOAKES
KHAN

The McGraw·Hill Companies

Sydney New York San Francisco Auckland
Bangkok Bogotá Caracas Hong Kong
Kuala Lumpur Lisbon London Madrid
Mexico City Milan New Delhi San Juan
Seoul Singapore Taipei Toronto

First published 1993
Second edition 2001
Revised second edition 2002
Third edition 2006
Revised third edition 2009

Text © 2012 McGraw-Hill Australia Pty Ltd
Additional owners of copyright are acknowledged in on-page credits.

Every effort has been made to trace and acknowledge copyrighted material. The authors and publishers tender their apologies should any infringement have occurred.

i○ 0 6612597

National Library of Australia Cataloguing-in-Publication Data
Author: Brukner, Peter.
Title: Brukner & Khan's Clinical Sports Medicine / Peter Brukner,
                    Karim Khan.
Edition: 4th ed.
ISBN: 9780070998131 (hbk.)
Notes: Includes index.
                    Previous ed.: Clinical Sports Medicine, 2007.
Subjects: Sports medicine.
                    Sports injuries.
Other Authors/Contributors:
                    Khan, Karim.
Dewey Number: 617.1027

Published in Australia by
McGraw-Hill Australia Pty Ltd
Level 2, 82 Waterloo Road, North Ryde NSW 2113
Publisher: Fiona Richardson
Senior production editor: Yani Silvana
Production editor: Jess Ní Chuinn
Publishing and digital manager: Carolyn Crowther
Editorial coordinator: Fiona Collison
Copy editor: Jill Pope
Illustrator: Vicky Earle (anatomical figures)
Proofreader: Mary-Jo O'Rourke
Indexer: Russell Brooks
Cover design: Georgette Hall
Internal design: David Rosenmeyer
Typeset in 9/11.5 pt Scala by Midland Typesetters, Australia
Printed in China on 80gsm matt art by iBook Printing Ltd

Foreword to the first edition (1993)

Sport in Australia is ingrained in the national consciousness more widely, deeply, and indelibly than almost anywhere else in the world. When a prominent sportsperson sustains a sporting injury, either traumatically or from overuse, becomes excessively fatigued, or fails to live up to expectations, this assumes national importance. It is even more relevant nowadays with greater individual participation in sporting activities. The same type of problems occur for recreational athletes, middle-aged people wanting to become fit, or older people wishing to sustain a higher level of activity in their later years.

In *Clinical Sports Medicine* the authors take sport and exercise medicine out of the realm of the elite athlete and place it fairly and squarely where it belongs—as a subspecialty to serve everyone in the community who wishes to be active.

The book is organized in a manner that is sensible and usable. The chapters are arranged according to the anatomical region of the symptom rather than diagnostic categories. This results in a very usable text for the sports physician, general/family practitioner, physiotherapist, masseur, or athletic trainer whose practice contains many active individuals.

Practical aspects of sports medicine are well covered—care of the sporting team and concerns that a clinician might have when traveling with a team. In all, this is an eminently usable text which is timely in its production and will find an important place among clinicians involved in the care of active individuals.

JOHN R SUTTON MD, FRACP
Professor of Medicine, Exercise Physiology and Sports Medicine
Faculty of Health Sciences
University of Sydney
Past President, American College of Sports Medicine

This foreword was written by the late Professor John Sutton before his untimely death in 1996; it is retained in this textbook out of profound respect for this champion of the integration of science, physical activity promotion, and multidisciplinary patient care.

Foreword to the fourth edition

Humans were not designed to sit at desks all day and in front of televisions all evening, and this physical inactivity is related to a host of health-related issues. Increasing physical activity is one very powerful way to mitigate many of the health issues we face today, and programs such as the Healthy People 2020 initiative and the Exercise is Medicine campaign encourage individuals to remain active throughout their lifetime.

As people become more involved in sport and exercise, sports medicine becomes increasingly important, and *Clinical Sports Medicine* has understandably become what we in the US refer to as the "PDR" (Physicians' Desk Reference) of sports medicine. For my UK colleagues the translation is "BNF" (British National Formulary). This text is extremely comprehensive, covering fundamental principles of biomechanics, diagnosis and treatment, regional musculoskeletal injuries, and medical problems. The text also addresses those practical issues of sports medicine that are often missing from other texts, such as dealing with athletic teams, covering endurance events, and working with the elite athlete.

The organization of the text makes it remarkably easy to use, including such features as color-coded book sections, flow diagrams to reinforce concepts, and tables that clearly organize information. Vicky Earle's anatomical drawings are truly among the best in the business. All these features put an astounding wealth of information at the reader's fingertips. This information has been assembled by a group of over 100 experienced and world-class physical therapists, physicians, and scientists. These co-authors provide up-to-date references when available, and clearly state when evidence is lacking.

This updated, fourth edition includes 200 new photos/graphics and 13 new chapters on current topics, including Integrating evidence into clinical practice, Principles of activity promotion, and Medical emergencies in sport. The editors continue to add to the clinically relevant topics with one of my favorites being what I call "How to manage the patient who has seen everyone and wants a cure from you!" (Chapter 41).

An innovative and exciting addition to this edition is the integration of the *Clinical Sports Medicine* masterclasses that allow you, through videos and podcasts on the *Clinical Sports Medicine* website, to learn directly from the experts. These masterclasses, which will be updated regularly, provide a remarkably dynamic component to the text.

It is exciting to watch *Clinical Sports Medicine* evolve substantially with each edition. The editors' focus of this text is to "help clinicians help patients" and they have clearly hit their mark. This book is an absolute must-have for any sports medicine professional.

Professor Irene Davis, PT, PhD, FACSM, FAPTA, FASB
Director, Spaulding National Running Center
Department of Physical Medicine and Rehabilitation
Harvard Medical School
Spaulding-Cambridge Outpatient Center
Cambridge, MA, USA

Brief contents

Part C   Special groups of participants

Part D   Management of medical problems

Part E   Practical sports medicine

Contents

PART A   Fundamental principles

Contents

Contents

Contents

PART B   Regional problems

Contents

Contents

Contents

Contents

Contents

PART D Management of medical problems

Contents

PART E   Practical sports medicine

Contents

"Helping clinicians help patients" has been the clear focus of *Clinical Sports Medicine* from its inception. This fourth edition (CSM4) builds unashamedly on its 20-year history. Twenty-year history? The more than 100 contributing authors average 15 years of practical experience each, so you are holding well over 1500 years of distilled clinical wisdom in your hand!

If you will permit us some level 5 evidence (expert opinion—see all-new Chapter 3), CSM4 provides clinicians in sports and exercise medicine and physiotherapy/physical therapy at least five major benefits:

- The wholehearted commitment from leading clinical faculty from all over the English-speaking world means that CSM4 provides the reader with an authoritative text—you can trust these authors.
- At 1270 pages and 67 chapters, CSM4 already carries 25% more pages than the best-selling third edition. Our ruthless editing to focus on clinical relevance means this edition contains 40% new material. CSM4 provides a comprehensive base for your clinical library. We provide some specific examples below.
- With more than 1000 color images (photos and graphics), the book paints a million words (1000 pictures each painting 1000 words!) over and above its 1270 pages! More than 200 of those images are new to this edition—customized for CSM4's learners—further extending the book's clarity and usability.
- Every copy of CSM4 comes with a code that gives you online access to more than four hours of assessment and treatment video and audio material. Called *Clinical Sports Medicine* masterclasses, this material is integrated with the text and will be free of charge to book owners for 12 months from registration at www.clinicalsportsmedicine.com. You have "the expert in the room."
- Reflecting the expanding evidence base for our field, we include an introduction to evidence-based practice (Chapter 3). All authors aimed to incorporate the best available level of evidence via text, tables, and current references. The online content of CSM4 will benefit from regular updates, adding further to the usefulness of this text for busy clinicians.

In short, CSM4 provides excellent value as an authoritative clinical foundation for physiotherapists, medical practitioners, osteopaths, massage therapists, podiatrists, sports/athletic trainers, sports therapists, fitness leaders, and nurses. It has also proven popular for students in sports physiotherapy, medicine, and human movement studies/kinesiology.

Editors and authors

As the task of editing a book of this magnitude was beyond the two of us, the CSM4 reader now benefits from the wisdom and productivity of seven sports and exercise medicine greats—Roald Bahr, Steven Blair, Jill Cook, Kay Crossley, Jenny McConnell, Paul McCrory, and Timothy Noakes.

The quality of our chapter authors, representing more than 14 countries, grows with each edition. Among our all-star cast, we are particularly grateful to Håkan Alfredson, Elizabeth Arendt, Carl Askling, Kim Bennell, John Drezner, Richard Frobell, Per Holmich, Mark Hutchinson, Gwen Jull, Pekka Kannus, Ben Kibler, Nicola Maffulli, Lorimer Moseley, George Murrell, Kevin Singer, and Willem van Mechelen.

New chapters

The new chapters in this edition are:

Chapter 1 Sports and exercise medicine: addressing the world's greatest public health problem

Chapter 3 Integrating evidence into clinical practice to make quality decisions

Chapter 4 Sports injuries: acute

Chapter 5 Sports injuries: overuse

Chapter 16 Principles of physical activity promotion for clinicians

Chapter 23 Wrist pain

Chapter 24 Hand and finger injuries

Chapter 28 Hip-related pain

Chapter 45 Military personnel

Chapter 47 Medical emergencies in the sporting context

Chapter 48 Sudden cardiac death in sport

Chapter 52 Renal symptoms during exercise

Chapter 54 Exercise to treat neurological diseases and improve mental health

A plethora of new, clinically relevant content

Here is just a sampler of new approaches to specific "hot topics" with a few of the contributing authors:

- The all-new Chapter 28 Hip-related pain clarifies the concept of **femoroacetabular impingement (FAI)**, its diagnosis and management
- The latest **concussion** guidelines based on the Zurich consensus meeting (with Paul McCrory)
- A fully revamped discussion of **neck pain** (with Gwen Jull)
- Further tips on management of **tendinopathies** (with Jill Cook, Hakan Alfredson, and Ben Kibler)
- Discussion of whether **ACL injuries** should be managed operatively or conservatively (with Richard Frobell and Liza Arendt)
- A revolution in **pain science** and its implications for clinical practice (with Lorimer Moseley)
- How to prevent **hamstring problems** from being a major burden—prevention and treatment strategies (with Carl Askling and Anthony Schache)
- A practical approach to **leg pain**, including compartment pressure testing (with Mark Hutchinson and a demonstration on the masterclasses website)
- How to manage **the patient who has seen everyone**—and now wants a miracle cure from you (with Jim Macintyre)
- Prevention of sudden **cardiac death** and a practical approach to **sports cardiology** (with Jon Drezner and Sanjay Sharma)
- **Exercise in the heat** as well as **prevention of hyponatremia** (with Tim Noakes)
- **Drugs**—based on latest WADA guidelines

We could have made this list much longer but instead we use a toll-free part of the *Clinical Sports Medicine* masterclasses website (www.clinicalsportsmedicine.com) to take you on a tour.

No single profession has all the answers required to treat the ill or injured sportsperson and to provide exercise advice as needed. CSM4 was created by a champion team of co-authors and critical reviewers tremendously committed to the vision of "Helping clinicians help patients." We are confident that whatever your training, *Clinical Sports Medicine* fourth edition will reinforce and refine existing knowledge and techniques, and introduce useful new approaches for your clinical practice as well as for your teaching of our wonderful vocation. Enjoy this first hybrid print and digital *Clinical Sports Medicine*.

Peter Brukner

OAM, MBBS, DRCOG, FACSP, FASMF, FACSM, FFSEM

Sports physician

Head, Sports Medicine and Sports Science, Liverpool Football Club, UK

Founding Partner, Olympic Park Sports Medicine Centre, Melbourne, Australia

Associate Professor, Centre for Health, Exercise and Sports Medicine, The University of Melbourne

Honorary Fellow, Faculty of Law, The University of Melbourne

Adjunct Professor, School of Human Movement Studies, The University of Queensland

Adjunct Professor, Liverpool John Moores University, UK

Visiting Associate Professor, Stanford University, USA 1997

Executive Member, Australian College of Sports Physicians 1985–2000

President, Australian College of Sports Physicians 1991–92, 1999–2000

Board of Trustees, American College of Sports Medicine 2000–02

State and Federal Council Member, Sports Medicine Australia 1984–90

Team physician

Socceroos, 2007–10, Asian Cup Finals 2007, World Cup Finals 2010

Australian Olympic Team, Atlanta 1996, Sydney 2000

Australian Commonwealth Games teams, Edinburgh 1986, Kuala Lumpur 1998

Australian team, World Student Games, Edmonton 1983, Kobe 1985, Zagreb 1987

Australian Athletics team 1990–2000, World Championships Tokyo 1991, Gothenburg 1995, Seville 1999

Australian team, World Cup Athletics, Havana 1992

Australian Mens Hockey team 1995–96

Australian team, World Swimming Championships, Madrid 1986

Melbourne Football Club (AFL) 1987–90

Collingwood Football Club (AFL) 1996

Editorial boards

Clinical Journal of Sport Medicine

The Physician and Sportsmedicine

Current Sports Medicine Reports

British Journal of Sports Medicine

Editor

Sport Health 1990–95

Co-author

Food for Sport 1987

Stress Fractures 1999

Drugs in Sport—What the GP Needs to Know 1996, 2000

The Encyclopedia of Exercise, Sport and Health 2004

Essential Sports Medicine 2005

Clinical Sports Anatomy 2010

Awards

Medal of the Order of Australia 2006

Inaugural Honour Award, *Australian College of Sports Physicians* 1996

Citation Award, *American College of Sports Medicine* 2000

Karim Khan

MD, PhD, MBA, FACSP, FSMA, DipSportMed, FACSM, FFSEM(Hon)

Sports physician

Professor, University of British Columbia, Vancouver, Canada (Department of Family Practice and School of Kinesiology); Associate Member, Departments of Physical Therapy, and Orthopaedics

Executive Associate Director, Centre for Hip Health and Mobility, Vancouver, Canada

Principal Fellow with title Professor, School of Physiotherapy, The University of Melbourne, Melbourne, Australia

Visiting Professor, School of Human Movement Studies, The University of Queensland, Brisbane, Australia

Clinical Professor, Centre for Musculoskeletal Studies, School of Surgery, University of Western Australia, Perth, Australia

Exercise is Medicine Committee, American College of Sports Medicine

Medical Education Committee, American College of Sports Medicine 2002–04

Research Evaluation Committee, American College of Sports Medicine 2005–07

Scientific Subcommittee, Aspetar Hospital, Doha, Qatar 2011–

Team physician

Olympic Games Sydney 2000, Basketball Competition Venue

Australian Women's Basketball (The Opals) 1991–96

The Australian Ballet Company 1991–96

The Australian Ballet School 1991–96

Australian team, World Student Games 1993

Australian team, Junior World Cup Hockey 1993

Editorial boards

BMJ (International Advisory Board) 2008–

Scandinavian Journal of Medicine and Science in Sport 2007–

British Journal of Sports Medicine (North American Editor) 2005–07

Journal of Science and Medicine in Sport 1997–2001

Year Book of Sports Medicine 2008–10

Clinical Journal of Sport Medicine 2003–06

Editor-in-chief

British Journal of Sports Medicine 2008–

Sport Health 1995–97

Co-author

Physical Activity and Bone Health 2001

The Encyclopedia of Exercise, Sport and Health 2004

Selected awards

Prime Minister's Medal for Service to Australian Sport 2000

Sports Medicine Australia Fellows' Citation for Service 2005

Honorary Fellowship, Faculty of Sports and Exercise Medicine (Ireland) 2011

Roald Bahr PhD

Professor of Sports Medicine, Norwegian School of Sport Sciences, Oslo Sports Trauma Research Center; Chair, Department of Sports Medicine, Olympic Training Center, Norway

Steven Blair, PED

Professor, Department of Exercise Science and Epidemiology and Biostatistics, Public Health Research Center, University of South Carolina, USA

Jill Cook PhD, GradCertHigherEd, GradDipManip, BAppSci (Phty)

Professor and Principal Research Fellow, Department of Physiotherapy, School of Primary Health Care, Monash University, Melbourne, Australia

Kay Crossley BAppSci(Physio), PhD

Physiotherapist, Olympic Park Sports Medicine Centre, Melbourne, Australia; Associate Professor, School of Health and Rehabilitation Sciences, The University of Queensland; Principal Research Fellow, Dept

Mechanical Engineering and Physiotherapy, The University of Melbourne; Australian Olympic Team Physiotherapist, Sydney 2000

Jenny McConnell AM, FACP, BAppSci(Physio), GradDipManTher, MBiomedEng

Director, McConnell and Clements Physiotherapy, Sydney, Australia; Visiting Senior Fellow, Centre for Health, Exercise and Sports Medicine, The University of Melbourne, Australia

Paul McCrory MBBS, PhD, FRACP, FACSP, FFSEM, FACSM, FASMF, GradDipEpidStats

Associate Professor, Centre for Health, Exercise and Sports Medicine, The University of Melbourne, Australia; Brain Research Institute, Florey Neurosciences Institutes, The University of Melbourne; Australian Centre for Research into Sports Injury and its Prevention (ACRISP)—an IOC Research Centre Collaboration

Timothy Noakes OMS, MBChB, MD, DSc, FACSM(Hon), FFSEM (UK)

Sports Physician and Exercise Physiologist, Discovery Health Professor of Exercise and Sports Science, University of Cape Town and Sports Science Institute of South Africa, Cape Town, South Africa

Co-authors

Jason Agosta BAppSc (Podiatry)

Podiatrist, private practice, East Melbourne; Podiatrist, Essendon Football Club and Melbourne Storm (Rugby League)

Håkan Alfredson MD, PhD

Orthopaedic Surgeon, Professor Sports Medicine Unit, University of Umeå, Sweden

Hashel Al Tunaiji MBBS, MSc

Sport Medicine Physician; Postdoctoral Fellow, Centre for Hip Health and Mobility, University of British Columbia (UBC), Vancouver, Canada; Family Medicine, UBC, Abu Dhabi, United Arab Emirates

Julia Alleyne BHSc(PT), MD, CCFP, FACSM, DipSportMed(CASM)

Associate Clinical Professor; Chair Sport Medicine Fellowship, Department of Family and Community Medicine, University of Toronto; Medical Director, Sport CARE, Women's College Hospital, Toronto; Chair, Education Commission FIMS; Canadian Olympic Committee, Medical Staff, Salt Lake City 2002, Turin 2006, Beijing 2008, Vancouver 2010, Chief Medical Officer London 2012

Jock Anderson MBBS, FRANZCR, FRACSP(Hon)

Associate Professor, University of New South Wales; Member International Skeletal Society and Australasian Musculoskeletal Imaging Group; Director of Medical Imaging at Sydney 2000 Olympic and Paralympic Games; Director of Medical Imaging for Rugby World Cup, Australia 2003

Elizabeth Arendt MD, FACSM

Orthopaedic Surgeon; Professor, Vice Chair Department of Orthopaedic Surgery, University of Minnesota, USA; Past Team Physician USA Soccer and USA Women's Hockey; Task Force on Women's Issues, NCAA Medical Safeguards Committee; Current chair of AAOS Women's Health Issues Advisory Board

Maureen C. Ashe BScPT, MSc, PhD

Assistant Professor, University of British Columbia; Family Practice, Vancouver, Canada

Carl Askling PhD, PT

Vice-President, Swedish Sports Trauma Research Group; Swedish School of Sport and Health Sciences and Department of Molecular Medicine and Surgery, Karolinska Institutet, Stockholm, Sweden

Christian Barton PT, PhD

Research Supervisor, Queen Mary University of London, Centre for Sports and Exercise Medicine

Simon Bell FRCS, FRACS, FAOrthA, PhD

Associate Professor, Monash University and Melbourne Shoulder and Elbow Centre, Orthopaedic Surgery, Melbourne, Australia; Head of the Upper Limb Unit, Orthopaedic Department, Division of Surgery, Monash Medical Centre, Monash University; President of the Victorian Shoulder and Elbow Society; Senior Research Fellow, Centre for Health, Exercise and Sports Medicine, The University of Melbourne

Kim Bennell BAppSc(Physio), PhD

Professor, Centre for Health, Exercise and Sports Medicine, Department of Physiotherapy, The University of Melbourne

Chris Bradshaw MBBS, FACSP

Head Physician, Olympic Park Sports Medicine Centre, Geelong Campus; Team Physician, Geelong Football Club (AFL); Former Team Physician Fulham Football Club (EPL), Track and Field Australia, Olympic Games, Sydney 2000; ACSP Board of Censors, Board of Examiners

Shane Brun PhD

Associate Professor, Musculoskeletal and Sports Medicine, Clinical Skills Unit, School of Medicine and Dentistry, James Cook University, Townsville, Australia

Dennis Caine PhD

Professor, University of North Dakota, Department of Physical Education, Exercise Science and Wellness, Grand Forks, USA; Associate Editor, *British Journal of Sports Medicine*

Nick Carter MB ChB, MRCP

Consultant in Rheumatology and Rehabilitation, Medical Defence Services, Medical Rehabilitation Centre, Headley Court, UK

Navin Chandra MRCP, MBBS, BSc

Cardiology Specialty Registrar, Cardiology, London Deanery, North-West Thames, London, UK

Jacqueline Close MBBS, MD, FRCP, FRACP

Consultant Geriatrician, Prince of Wales Hospital, Department of Geriatric Medicine, Sydney, Australia; Principal Research Fellow, Neuroscience Research Australia; Conjoint Associate Professor, The University of New South Wales

Phil Coles BAppSc(Physio), MSc(Sports Physio)

Head of Physical Therapies Department, Liverpool Football Club, UK; APA Titled Sports Physiotherapist; CSP

Natalie Collins BPhysio(Hons I), PhD

NHMRC Postdoctoral Research Fellow, Department of Mechanical Engineering, The University of Melbourne; Physiotherapist, Olympic Park Sports Medicine Centre, Melbourne, Australia

Wendy L. Cook MD, MHSc, FRCPC

Geriatrician, Clinical Instructor, Division of Geriatric Medicine, Faculty of Medicine, University of British Columbia, Vancouver, Canada

Randall Cooper BPhysio, MPhysio, FACP

Specialist Sports Physiotherapist, Olympic Park Sports Medicine Centre, Melbourne, Australia; Physiotherapist, Australian Winter Olympics team, Torino, Italy 2006

Sallie Cowan BAppSci(Physio), GradDipManipTher, PhD

Senior Research Fellow, Musculoskeletal Physiotherapist, School of Physiotherapy, The University of Melbourne, Australia

Gavin Davis MBBS, FRACS (Neurosurgery)

Associate Professor Neurosurgery, Cabrini Hospital, Melbourne, Australia; Chairman, Department of Surgical Specialties, Cabrini Hospital; Consultant Neurosurgeon, Austin and Box Hill Hospitals; University of Notre Dame, Australia

Jennifer Davis PhD

Canadian Institutes of Health Research Postdoctoral Fellow; Health Economist/Epidemiologist, University of British Columbia, Centre for Clinical Epidemiology and Evaluation, School of Population and Public Health, Vancouver, Canada

Tony J Delaney RFD, MBBS, FACSP

Sports Physician, Narrabeen Sports and Exercise Medicine Clinic, Academy of Sport, Sydney; Visiting Senior Specialist, Sports Medicine Clinic, 1st Health Support Battalion, Holsworthy Military Area and Fleet Base East Health Centre, New South Wales, Australia; Chair, Australian Defence Force Sports, Rehabilitation and Musculoskeletal Consultative Group; Past Senior Medical Officer, 1st Commando Regiment

Jon Drezner MD

Associate Professor, Department of Family Medicine, University of Washington, Seattle, USA; Vice-President, American Medical Society for Sports Medicine; Team Physician, Seattle Seahawks and UW Huskies

Jiri Dvorak MD

FIFA Chief Medical Officer; Senior Consultant, Spine Unit, Schulthess Clinic Zurich; Associate Professor Neurology, University of Zurich, Switzerland

Lars Engebretsen MD, PhD

Professor, Department of Orthopaedic Surgery, Oslo University Hospital and Faculty of Medicine, University of Oslo and Oslo Sports Trauma Research Center, Norway; Head Physician Norwegian Olympic Center (Olympiatoppen); Head Scientific Activities, International Olympic Committee (IOC); Past President ESSKA

Peter J. Fazey PT, MT, FACP

Specialist Musculoskeletal Physiotherapist, The Centre for Musculoskeletal Studies, School of Surgery, Faculty of Medicine, Dentistry and Health Sciences, University of Western Australia; President of the Australian College of Physiotherapists

Bruce B. Forster MSc, MD, FRCPC

Professor and Head, Department of Radiology, Faculty of Medicine, University of British Columbia, Vancouver, Canada; Regional Medical Director, Medical Imaging, Vancouver Coastal Health

Richard Frobell PhD

Assistant Professor, Department of Orthopedics, Medical Faculty, Lund University, Sweden

Andrew Garnham MBBS, FACSP

Conjoint Clinical Senior Lecturer, School of Exercise and Nutrition Sciences, Deakin University, Burwood, Australia; Past President of the Australasian College of Sports Physicians

Robert Granter BSocSci, AdDipRemMass(Myotherapy)

Soft Tissue Therapist, Victorian Institute of Sport, Melbourne, Australia; Head of Massage Therapy Services, Australian Olympic Team 1996 and 2000; Head of Massage Therapy Services, Melbourne 2006 Commonwealth Games

Peter T. Gropper MD, FRCSC

Clinical Professor, Department of Orthopedic Surgery, University of British Columbia, Vancouver, Canada

Callista Haggis, MAP

Research Consultant, Centre for Hip Health and Mobility, University of British Columbia, Vancouver, Canada

Peter Harcourt MBBS, DipRACOG, FACSP, FSMA

Sports Physician; Medical Director, Victorian Institute of Sport; Australian Olympic Games Medical Team 1992–2004; Head, Commonwealth Games Medical Team, 2006

Matthew Hislop MBBS, MSc, FACSP

Sport and Exercise Medicine Physician, Brisbane Sports and Exercise Medicine Specialists, Brisbane, Australia; Joint Team Physician, Brisbane Broncos (NRL); Team Physician, Reds Rugby Academy

Sandy Hoffmann, MD, FACSM, CAQ

Associate Clinical Professor Sports Medicine, Idaho State University; Team Physician, Idaho State University, Pocatello, Idaho, USA

Per Holmich MD

Orthopaedic Surgeon, Associate Research Professor, Copenhagen University Hospital, Arthroscopic Center Amager; Associate Professor of Anatomy, University of Copenhagen, Denmark

Karen Holzer MBBS, FACSP, PhD

Sports Physician, Melbourne, Australia; NHMRC Senior Research Fellow, Department of Respiratory Medicine, Royal Melbourne Hospital; Australian Team Doctor, World Track and Field Championships, Helsinki 2005, and Olympic Games, Beijing 2008

Mark R. Hutchinson MD, FACSM

Professor of Orthopaedics and Sports Medicine and Head Team Physician, University of Illinois at Chicago, Chicago, Illinois; Head Team Physician, WNBA Chicago Sky; Volunteer Event Physician, LaSalle Bank Chicago Marathon, Chicago, Illinois, USA

Zafar Iqbal MBBS, BSc, DCH, DRCOG, MRCGP, MSc(SEM), DipPCR

First Team Doctor, Liverpool FC; Sports and Exercise Medicine Physician, Liverpool, UK

Gwendolen Jull MPhysio, PhD, FACP

Professor, Division of Physiotherapy, School of Health and Rehabilitation Sciences, The University of Queensland, Brisbane, Australia

Pekka Kannus MD, PhD

Chief Physician, Injury and Osteoporosis Research Center, UKK Institute, Tampere, Finland; Associate Professor (Docent) of Sports Medicine, University of Jyväskylä, Finland; Visiting Professor, Department of Orthopedics and Rehabilitation, University of Vermont College of Medicine, Burlington, Vermont, USA

Jon Karlsson MD, PhD

Professor of Orthopaedics and Sports Traumatology, Senior Consultant, Professor, Sahlgrenska University Hospital, Department of Orthopaedics, Gothenburg, Sweden

Joanne Kemp BAppSci(Physio), MSportsPhysio

APA Sports Physiotherapist; Principal Physiotherapist and Director, Bodysystem Physio, Hobart, Tasmania, Australia; PhD Candidate, The University of Melbourne, Australia

W. Ben Kibler MD, FACSM

Medical Director, Lexington Clinic Sports Medicine Center, The Shoulder Center of Kentucky, Section of Orthopedic Surgery, Lexington Clinic, Lexington, KY, USA

Mary Kinch HDST(PhysEd), BAppSc(Physio)

Physiotherapist, Olympic Park Sports Medicine Centre, Melbourne, Australia; APA Titled Sports Physiotherapist; Clinical Pilates Physiotherapist

Zoltan Kiss MBBS, FRACP, FRANZCR, DDU

Senior Fellow (Hon), Faculty of Medicine, Dentistry and Health Sciences, The University of Melbourne, Australia; Consultant Radiologist, Melbourne, Australia

Michael S. Koehle MD, MSc, CCFP, DipSportMed(CASM)

Sport Physician, Clinical Assistant Professor, Allan McGavin Sports Medicine Centre, Department of Family Practice, University of British Columbia, Vancouver, Canada

Jonas Kwiatkowski, BSc

Research Assistant, Vancouver General Hospital, Centre for Hip Health and Mobility, Vancouver, Canada

Andrew Lambart BAppSc(Physio)

Physiotherapist, Olympic Park Sports Medicine Centre, Melbourne, Australia; Team Physiotherapist, Hawthorn Football Club (AFL); Australian Olympic Team Physiotherapist, Athens 2004

Theresa Lee, PhD, MBBS (Hons 1), FRANZCR

Consultant Radiologist, PRP Diagnostic Imaging, Sydney, Australia

Mark Link MD, FACC, FHRS

Professor of Medicine, Tufts University School of Medicine, Tufts Medical Center, Cardiac Arrhythmia Center, Boston, MA, USA

Teresa Liu-Ambrose PhD, PT

Assistant Professor, University of British Columbia, School of Rehabilitation Sciences, Division of Physical Therapy; Head, Exercise and Cognitive Function Unit, Centre for Hip Health and Mobility, Vancouver, Canada

Zuzana Machotka MPhysio(Musc and Sports), BPhysio

Clinical Researcher/Physiotherapist, International Centre for Allied Health Evidence, University of South Australia, Adelaide, Australia; Australian Paralympic Winter Team

Jim Macintyre MD, MPE, FACSM, DipSportsMed

Primary Care Sports Medicine, Center of Orthopedic and Rehabilitation Excellence, Jordan Valley Medical Center, West Jordan, Utah

Erin M Macri BSc(Kin), MPT

Registered Physical Therapist; Masters of Science Candidate in Experimental Medicine, University of British Columbia, Centre for Hip Health and Mobility, Vancouver, Canada

Nicola Maffulli MD, MS, PhD, FRCS(Orth)

Professor of Sports and Exercise Medicine, Consultant Trauma and Orthopaedic Surgeon, Queen Mary University of London, Barts and The London School of Medicine; Centre for Sports and Exercise Medicine, Mile End Hospital, London, UK

Michael Makdissi BSc(Hons), MBBS, PhD, FACSP

Sports Medicine Physician, Olympic Park Sports Medicine Centre, Melbourne, Australia; NHMRC Training Fellowship, Melbourne Brain Centre, Florey Neurosciences Institute, The University of Melbourne, Australia

Chris Milne BHB, MBChB, DipObst, DipSportsMed, FRNZCGP, FACSP

Sports Physician, Anglesea Sports Medicine, Hamilton; Olympic Team Physician, New Zealand

Hayden Morris MBBS, DipAnat, FRACS

Orthopaedic Surgeon, Olympic Park Sports Medicine Centre, Melbourne, Australia

Lorimer Moseley PhD

Professor of Clinical Neurosciences and Chair of Physiotherapy, University of South Australia, Adelaide, Australia; Visiting Senior Research Fellow, Neuroscience Research Australia

George Murrell MBBS, DPhil

Professor and Director, Department of Orthopaedic Surgery, St George Hospital Campus, The University of New South Wales, Sydney, Australia

Babette Pluim MD, PhD, MPH, FFSEM (UK, Ire)

Sports Medicine Physician, Royal Netherlands Lawn Tennis Association, Amersfoort, the Netherlands;

Deputy Editor, British Journal of Sports Medicine

Joel M. Press MD

Professor, Physical Medicine and Rehabilitation, Feinberg/Northwestern School of Medicine; Medical Director, Spine and Sports Rehabilitation Centers, Rehabilitation Institute of Chicago, USA; Reva and David Logan Distinguished Chair of Musculoskeletal Rehabilitation

Michael Pritchard BMedSci, MBBS (Hons), FRACS (Orth)

Orthopaedic Surgeon, St Johns Hospital, Hobart, Australia

Douglas Race BPE, MA candidate

Research Technician, Bone Health Research Group, Department of Orthopedic Engineering, University of British Columbia, Vancouver, Canada

Stephan Rudzki MBBS, GradDipSportSc, MPH, PhD, FACSP

Brigadier, Australian Defence Force, Joint Health Command; Director General Army Health Services, Canberra, Australia

Anthony Schache BPhysio(Hons), PhD

Physiotherapist, Olympic Park Sports Medicine Centre and Richmond Football Club (AFL), Melbourne, Australia; Research Fellow, Hugh Williamson Gait Laboratory, Royal Children's Hospital, Melbourne and Centre for Health Exercise and Sports Medicine, The University of Melbourne, Australia

Alex Scott BSc(PT), PhD, RPT

Assistant Professor, Department of Physical Therapy, University of British Columbia, Vancouver, Canada

Sanjay Sharma BSc, MD, FRCP, FESC

Professor, St George's University of London, Department of Cardiovascular Sciences, London, UK; Medical Director, London Marathon; Consultant Cardiologist for Cardiac Risk in the Young; Cardiology Advisor for the English Institute of Sport, Lawn Tennis Association and English Rugby League

Catherine Sherrington MPH, BAppSc, PhD

NHMRC Senior Research Fellow, Musculoskeletal Division, The George Institute for Global Health, Sydney, Australia

Karin Grävare Silbernagel PT, ATC, PhD

Postdoctoral Researcher, Spencer Laboratory, Department of Mechanical Engineering, University of Delaware, USA

Kevin P. Singer PhD, PT

Physiotherapist; Professor and Head of the Centre for Musculoskeletal Studies, School of Surgery, The University of Western Australia, Perth, Australia

Meena M. Sran BSc(PT), MPhysioSt(Manips), PhD

Researcher and Physiotherapist, BC Women's Hospital and Health Centre, Movement Essentials Physiotherapy; Vice-President, International Organization of Physical Therapists in Women's Health, Vancouver, Canada

Cameron Stuart BASc

Research Assistant, Centre for Hip Health and Mobility, University of British Columbia, Vancouver, Canada

Hasan Tahir BSc, MBBS, Dip SEM, FRCP

Consultant Physician in Acute Medicine and Rheumatology, Whipps Cross University Hospital NHS Trust; Department of Rheumatology, Clinical Lead for Acute Medicine, Biological Therapies and Research; Professor of Medicine, St Matthew's University Hospital, London, UK

Larissa Trease BMedSci(Hons), MBBS(Hons), FACSP

Sport and Exercise Medicine Physician, Olympic Park Sports Medicine Centre, Melbourne, Australia; Chief Medical Officer, Australian Paralympic Team, Beijing 2008.

Michael Turner MB BS, MD, FFSEM (UK and Ireland)

Chief Medical Adviser, Lawn Tennis Association, UK

Willem van Mechelen MD, PhD, FACSM, FECSS

Department Head of Public and Occupational Health, Co-director EMGO Institute, VU University Medical Center, Amsterdam, The Netherlands

Evert Verhagen PhD

Assistant Professor, VU University Medical Center, EMGO Institute for Health and Care Research, Department of Public and Occupational Health, Amsterdam, The Netherlands

Bill Vicenzino PhD, MSc, BPhysio, GradDipSportPhysio

Professor of Sports Physiotherapy and Head of Physiotherapy, School of Health and Rehabilitation Sciences, The University of Queensland, Brisbane, Australia

Nick Webborn MBBS

Sports Physician and Medical Adviser to the British Paralympic Association; The Sussex Centre for Sport and Exercise Medicine, University of Brighton, Eastbourne, UK

Charlotte Yong-Hing MD

Department of Radiology, Vancouver General Hospital, University of British Columbia, Canada

Vanessa Young BSc, MBChB (Otago)

Wellington Hospital, Wellington, New Zealand; International Exchange Scholar 2010, Centre for Hip Health and Mobility, Vancouver, Canada

Other contributors

Alex Bennett MRCP, PhD

Consultant Rheumatologist, Defence Medical Rehabilitation Centre, Headley Court, UK

Mario Bizzini PT, PhD

Research Associate, FIFA—Medical Assessment and Research Centre (F-MARC) and Schulthess Clinic, Zurich, Switzerland

Michael Bresler MD

Section Chief, Department of Musculoskeletal MRI, Vice Head for Clinical Operations, Assistant Professor of Radiology, University of Illinois College of Medicine, University of Illinois Medical Center, Chicago, II, USA

Malcolm Collins PhD

Chief Specialist Scientist, South African Medical Research Council; Associate Professor, UCT/MRC Research Unit for Exercise Science and Sports Medicine, Department of Human Biology, Faculty of Health Sciences, University of Cape Town, South Africa

Emma Colson BAppSc(Physio), GradDipManipPhysio

APA Sports and Musculoskeletal Physiotherapist, Topbike Physio, Melbourne, Australia

Robert Jan de Vos MD, PhD

Sports Physician (Registrar), The Hague Medical Centre, Department of Sports Medicine, Leidschendam, The Netherlands

Angie Fearon PhD Candidate, BAppSc(Phyiso), MPhysio

Australian National University, College of Medicine, Biology and the Environment; The Canberra Hospital, Trauma and Orthopaedic Research Unit, Canberra, Australia

Scott Fraser BSc, PT, DipSport Physiotherapy

Allan McGavin Sports Medicine and Physiotherapy Centre, War Memorial Gym, University Boulevard, Vancouver, Canada

Nick Gardiner BSc(Hons) Sports Therapy, PGCHE, MSST

BSc Sports Therapy Course Leader at London Metropolitan University(LMU); Founder of Fit For Sport, Sports Therapy and Injury Clinic, London, UK

Pierre Guy MD, MBA

Associate Professor and Clinician-Scientist/Orthopedic Surgeon, Department of Orthopaedics, Center for Hip Health and Mobility, University of British Columbia, Vancouver, Canada

Astrid Junge PhD

Head of Research, FIFA—Medical Assessment and Research Centre (F-MARC) and Schulthess Clinic, Zurich, Switzerland

Carol Kennedy BScPT, MClSc(manip), FCAMPT

Treloar Physiotherapy Clinic, Vancouver, Canada

Syx Langemann BFA

Blackframe Studios Photography, Vancouver, Canada

Moira O'Brien FRCPI, FFSEM, FFSEM(UK), FTCD, FECSS, MA

Professor Emeritus of Anatomy, Trinity College Dublin, Ireland; Osteoporosis and Sports Medicine Consultant at Euromedic Dundrum, Rockfield Medical Campus, Ballaly, Dundrum, Dublin; President, Irish Osteoporosis Society

John Orchard BA, MD, PhD, FACSP, FACSM, FFSEM (UK)

Sports Physician, Adjunct Associate Professor, University of Sydney, School of Public Health, Sydney, Australia

Nadia Picco

Senior Graphic Designer, Digital Printing and Graphic Services, The Media Group, University of British Columbia, Vancouver, Canada

Cyrus Press MD

Chief Resident, University of Illinois Medical Center, Department of Orthopaedic Surgery, Chicago, II, USA

Craig Purdam MSports Physio

Head of Physical Therapies, Australian Institute of Sport, Canberra, Australia; Olympic Team Physiotherapist 1984–2000; Adjunct Professor, University of Canberra; APA Specialist Sports Physiotherapist

Ann Quinn PhD, MSc, BAppSc, DipEd, DipNutr.

Peak Performance Specialist; Director, Quintessential Edge, London, UK

Aaron Sciascia MS, ATC, NASM-PES

Program Coordinator, Lexington Clinic Sports Medicine Center; Coordinator of The Shoulder Center of Kentucky, USA

Ian Shrier MD, PhD, DipSportMed, FACSM

Associate Professor, Department of Family Medicine, McGill University; Centre for Clinical Epidemiology and Community Studies, SMBD-Jewish General Hospital, Montreal, Quebec, Canada; Past-President, Canadian Academy of Sport and Exercise Medicine

Andy Stephens BAppSci(Physio)

Physiotherapist, Olympic Park Sports Medicine Centre, Melbourne, Australia

Kent Sweeting BHlthSc(Pod)(Hons)

Podiatrist and Director, Performance Podiatry and Physiotherapy; Lecturer, Queensland University of Technology, School of Public Health, Brisbane, Australia

Paul Thompson MD, FACC, FACSM

Medical Director of Cardiology and The Athletes' Heart Program, Preventive Cardiology, Hartford Hospital, Connecticut, USA

Susan White MBBS(Hons), FACSP, FASMF

Sports Physician, Olympic Park Sports Medicine Centre, Melbourne, Australia; Chief Medical Officer, Swimming Australia; Member, Medical Commission, Australian Olympic Committee; Medical Director Australian Team, Youth Olympic Games 2010

The illustrator

Vicky Earle B Sc (AAM), MET, Cert TBDL

Medical Illustrator, The Media Group, University of British Columbia, Vancouver, Canada

Vicky is a highly experienced medical illustrator who has been involved in the design and production of a wide variety of surgical procedural and medical illustrations that have been used in journals, books, conferences, lectures, and legal presentations. Her keen interest in *Clinical Sports Medicine* stems not only from a great appreciation of the human body and its capabilities, but also from a decade of racing experience as a championship rower and paddler—and knowing first-hand the many injuries that accompany these activities.

Acknowledgments

No need to apologize, let me look at what needs to be done. Immediate email response from an extremely busy co-author when asked to contribute to this fourth edition.

This completely updated print and online resource is unashamedly founded on the previous three editions. To date, this text has satisfied more than 80 000 clinicians and provided core material for students who focus on the care of active people in Australia, New Zealand, Africa, Asia, Europe, and the Americas. Japanese readers have their own translation. The overwhelming support for this clinically based textbook means we are particularly indebted to our partners in all previous editions.

Specific thanks for the fourth edition go to chapter co-authors listed with their affiliations on pages xxxvi–xli. Expert co-authors provide the crucial innovation and timeliness that *Clinical Sports Medicine* users demand. We are both humbled and privileged to be sharing cover authorship with seven amazing colleagues and friends—Drs Cook, Crossley, McConnell, Bahr, Blair, McCrory, and Noakes (ladies first, of course). We would love to have listed more names on the cover but the designer overruled us on that one! A further 109 co-authors made this book happen. It takes a community to create *Clinical Sports Medicine*—and we are grateful for every single member of that hardworking international community.

Because this edition fully embraces digital media, we especially acknowledge those co-authors who contributed to this innovation. Particular thanks go to Dr Mark Hutchinson, and the team in Chicago, for providing critical and substantial content for the online masterclasses.

Vicky Earle has gained international recognition for her artwork; thank you for continuing to translate clinical innovation in ways that jump to life for users. The University of British Columbia (Department of Family Practice—Faculty of Medicine as well as Faculty of Education) provided essential support (KK), as did the Olympic Park Sports Medicine Centre, The University of Melbourne and Liverpool Football Club (PB). *Clinical Sports Medicine* benefits from the continuity, consistency, and integration honed over two decades, and from the expertise and freshness of cutting-edge international chapter authors. We seek out the world's best and we appreciate their responding to our calls! It has been a pleasure to work with every member of the *Clinical Sports Medicine* 4th edition team.

We give special thanks to our publishing team, who efficiently developed Brukner and Khan dreaming into the book you hold in your hands: publishing director Nicole Meehan, who has been a visionary leader; publishers Elizabeth Walton and Fiona Richardson; production editors Yani Silvana and Jess Ní Chuinn; and freelance editor Jill Pope. McGraw-Hill's support of all our crazy ideas has allowed us to generate a few good ones; thanks for your judgment and filtering! Within the authors' multi-faceted production team in three countries, Zuzana Machotka and Callista Haggis earn special thanks—for their skill, attention to detail, and good humor even under pressure. Finally, axiomatically, the most profound thanks we reserve for our long-suffering friends and families: Diana and Heather, we both know that words are not enough!

Guided tour of your book

The principal text in its field, this fourth edition of *Clinical Sports Medicine* continues to provide readers with quality, up-to-date content. The engaging material has been contributed by leading experts from around the world. Look out for these key features, which are designed to enhance your learning.

Integrated learning resources

New to this edition is the *Clinical Sports Medicine* website containing masterclasses with video and audio content.

The authors have worked with specialists to film key clinical procedures, including video clips demonstrating physical examinations, key rehabilitation exercise programs, and joint injections. Much of this video content has been commissioned for this edition.

 www.clinicalsportsmedicine.com.

Wherever this icon appears in the book, go to the website to view a video or listen to a podcast. Access is via the pincode card located in the front of the book.

For easy reference, a summary of the online content (where relevant) is given at the end of each chapter.

> *CLINICAL SPORTS MEDICINE*
> MASTERCLASSES
>  www.clinicalsportsmedicine.com
>
> - Listen to the interview with chapter authors.
> - See demonstration of biomechanical assessment.
> - See a demonstration of the original low-Dye technique augmented with reverse sixes and calcaneal slings anchored to the lower leg.
>
> RECOMMENDED WEBSITES
> Barton CJ, Bonanno D, Menz HB. Development and evaluation of a tool for the assessment of footwear characteristics: www.ncbi.nlm.nih.gov/pmc/articles/PMC2678108/?tool=pubmed

First-class content

As with previous editions the emphasis is on treatment and rehabilitation. The chapters in Part B, which address regional problems, are heavily illustrated with clinical photos, relevant imaging, and anatomical illustrations.

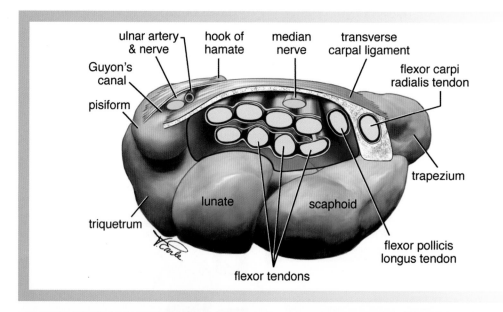

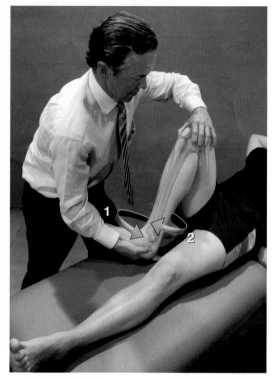

The list of **world-renowned contributors** has grown even longer in this edition and brings a truly global perspective to the book.

Practice pearls are a valuable feature that provide clinical tips and important information to keep in the forefront of your mind.

In the large majority of hamstring strains, the injured muscle is biceps femoris (reported as 76–87%).[5] Semimembranosus injury is uncommon; semitendinosus injury is rare.

The importance of **evidence-based practice** is emphasized with a new chapter on this topic. In addition, there is a comprehensive list of references at the end of every chapter.

Chapter 3

Integrating evidence into clinical practice to make quality decisions

with CATHERINE SHERRINGTON

Randomized trials are for clinicians who are uncertain as to whether they are right or not—and I am certain I am right.   Sir Ian Chalmers, quoting an unnamed orthopedic surgeon

This chapter opens with an exercise we use to introduce the concept of evidence-based practice to final-year students in human movement sciences/ kinesiology (i.e. non-clinicians). If you are an experienced clinician or an expert on evidence-based practice you may want to skip over this chapter!

The "case" for the students to consider involves Mrs J, a 55-year-old woman. Students are told she presents with persistent knee pain due to osteo-arthritis. The students are given the information in the box (below) and are asked to suggest a treatment for Mrs J.

In our student exercise we call for a vote and every year the first ballot results in option 1 (surgery) receiving about 80% of the votes! We then lead an open-class discussion and emphasize that the quality of the data should carry more weight than the clinical training of the person providing the advice. Students

---

Co-authors

Jason Agosta BAppSc (Podiatry)
Podiatrist, private practice, East Melbourne; Podiatrist, Essendon Football Club and Melbourne Storm (Rugby League)

Håkan Alfredson MD, PhD
Orthopaedic Surgeon, Professor Sports Medicine Unit, University of Umeå, Sweden

Hashel Al Tunaiji MBBS, MSc
Sport Medicine Physician; Postdoctoral Fellow, Centre for Hip Health and Mobility, University of British Columbia (UBC), Vancouver, Canada; Family Medicine, UBC, Abu Dhabi, United Arab Emirates

Julia Alleyne BHSc(PT), MD, CCFP, FACSM, DipSportMed(CASM)
Associate Clinical Professor; Chair Sport Medicine Fellowship, Department of Family and Community Medicine, University of Toronto; Medical Director, Sport CARE, Women's College Hospital, Toronto; Chair, Education Commission FIMS; Canadian Olympic Committee, Medical Staff, Salt Lake City 2002, Turin 2006, Beijing 2008, Vancouver 2010; Chief Medical Officer London 2012

Jock Anderson MBBS, FRANZCR, FRACSP(Hon)
Associate Professor, University of New South Wales; Member International Skeletal Society and Australasian Musculoskeletal Imaging Group; Director of Medical Imaging at Sydney 2000 Olympic and Paralympic Games; Director of Medical Imaging for Rugby World Cup, Australia 2003

Elizabeth Arendt MD, FACSM
Orthopaedic Surgeon; Professor, Vice Chair Department of Orthopaedic Surgery, University of Minnesota, USA; Past Team Physician USA Soccer and USA Women's Hockey; Task Force on Women's Issues, NCAA Medical Safeguards Committee; Current chair of AAOS Women's Health Issues Advisory Board

Maureen C. Ashe BScPT, MSc, PhD
Assistant Professor, University of British Columbia; Family Practice, Vancouver, Canada

Carl Askling PhD, PT
Vice-President, Swedish Sports Trauma Research Group; Swedish School of Sport and Health Sciences and Department of Molecular Medicine and Surgery, Karolinska Institutet, Stockholm, Sweden

Christian Barton PT, PhD
Research Supervisor, Queen Mary University of London, Centre for Sports and Exercise Medicine

Simon Bell FRCS, FRACS, FAOrthA, PhD
Associate Professor, Monash University and Melbourne Shoulder and Elbow Centre, Orthopaedic Surgery, Melbourne, Australia; Head of the Upper Limb Unit, Orthopaedic Department, Division of Surgery, Monash Medical Centre, Monash University; President of the Victorian Shoulder and Elbow Society; Senior Research Fellow, Centre for Health, Exercise and Sports Medicine, The University of Melbourne

Kim Bennell BAppSc(Physio), PhD
Professor, Centre for Health, Exercise and Sports Medicine, Department of Physiotherapy, The University of Melbourne

Chris Bradshaw MBBS, FACSP
Head Physician, Olympic Park Sports Medicine Centre, Geelong Campus; Team Physician, Geelong Football Club (AFL); Former Team Physician Fulham Football Club (EPL), Track and Field Australia, Olympic Games, Sydney 2000; ACSP Board of Censors, Board of Examiners

Shane Brun PhD
Associate Professor, Musculoskeletal and Sports Medicine, Clinical Skills Unit, School of Medicine and Dentistry, James Cook University, Townsville, Australia

Dennis Caine PhD
Professor, University of North Dakota, Department of Physical Education, Exercise Science and Wellness, Grand Forks, USA; Associate Editor, British Journal of Sports Medicine

xxxvi

Women and activity-related issues across the lifespan   **Chapter 43**

REFERENCES

1. Abramovitz BA, Birch LL. Five-year-old girls' ideas about dieting are predicted by their mothers' dieting. *J Am Diet Assoc* 2000;100(10):1157–63.
2. Wang Q J, Alen M, Nicholson P et al. Growth patterns at distal radius and tibial shaft in pubertal girls: a 2-year longitudinal study. *J Bone Miner Res* 2005;20(6):954–61.
3. Bailey DA, Heather AD, McKay HA et al. Calcium accretion in girls and boys during puberty: a longitudinal analysis. *J Bone Miner Res* 2000;15(11): 2245–50.
4. Bailey DA, Wedge JH, McCulloch RG et al. Epidemiology of fractures of the distal end of the radius in children as associated with growth. *J Bone Joint Surg Am* 1989;71A(8):1225–31.
5. Faulkner RA, McCulloch RG, Fyke SL et al. Comparison of areal and estimated volumetric bone density values between older men and women. *Osteoporos Int* 1995;5(4):271–5.
6. Torstveit MK, Sundgot-Borgen J. Participation in leanness sports but not training volume is associated with menstrual dysfunction: a national survey of 1276 elite athletes and controls. *Br J Sports Med* 2005;5(41):141–7.
7. Thomis M, Claessens AL, Lefevre J et al. Adolescent growth spurts in female gymnasts. *J Pediatr* 2005;146(2):239–44.
8. Warren MP, Brooks-Gunn J, Fox RP et al. Osteopenia in exercise-associated amenorrhea using ballet dancers as a model: a longitudinal study. *J Clin Endocrinol Metab* 2002;87(7):3162–8.
9. Bennell KL, Malcolm SA, Thomas SA et al. Risk factors for stress fractures in track and field athletes – a twelve-month prospective study. *Am J Sports Med* 1996;24(6):810–18.
10. Loud KJ, Gordon CM, Micheli LJ et al. Correlates of stress fractures among preadolescent and adolescent girls. *Pediatrics* 2005;115(4):e399–406.
11. Frankovich RJ, Lebrun CM. Menstrual cycle, contraception, and performance. *Clin Sports Med* 2000;19(2):251–71.
12. Janse de Jonge XA. Effects of the menstrual cycle on exercise performance. *Sports Med* 2003;33(11):833–51.
13. Bryant M, Cassidy A, Hill C et al. Effect of consumption of soy isoflavones on behavioural, somatic and affective symptoms in women with premenstrual syndrome. *Br J Nutr* 2005;93(5):731–9.
14. Wyatt KM, Dimmock PW, O'Brien PM. Selective serotonin reuptake inhibitors for premenstrual

syndrome. *Cochrane Database Syst Rev* 2009;4(4): CD001396.
15. Yonkers KA, Brown C, Pearlstein TB et al. Efficacy of a new low-dose oral contraceptive with drospirenone in premenstrual dysphoric disorder. *Obstet Gynecol* 2005;106(3):492–501.
16. Steiner M, Hirschberg AL, Bergeron R et al. Luteal phase dosing with paroxetine controlled release (CR) in the treatment of premenstrual dysphoric disorder. *Am J Obstet Gynecol* 2005;192(2):352–60.
17. Benagiano G, Carrara S, Filippi V. Safety, efficacy and patient satisfaction with continuous daily administration of levonorgestrel/ethinylestradiol oral contraceptives. *Patient Prefer Adherence* 2009;3: 131–43.
18. Krishnan S, Kiley J. The lowest-dose, extended-cycle combined oral contraceptive with continuous ethinyl estradiol in the United States: a review of the literature on ethinyl estradiol 20 µg/levonorgestrel 100 µg + ethinyl estradiol 10 µg. *Int J Womens Health* 2010;2:235–9.
19. Wanichsetakul P, Kamudhamas A, Watanaruangkovit P et al. Bone mineral density at various anatomic bone sites in women receiving combined oral contraceptives and depot-medroxyprogesterone acetate for contraception. *Contraception* 2002;65(6):407–10.
20. Rome E, Ziegler J, Secic M et al. Bone biochemical markers in adolescent girls using either depot medroxyprogesterone acetate or an oral contraceptive. *J Pediatr Adolesc Gynecol* 2004;17(6):373–7.
21. De Souza MJ. Menstrual disturbances in athletes: a focus on luteal phase defects. *Med Sci Sports Exerc* 2003;35(9):1553–63.
22. Prior JC, Vigna YM. Ovulation disturbances and exercise training. *Clin Obstet Gynecol* 1991;34(1): 180–90.
23. Williams NI, Bullen BA, McArthur JW et al. Effects of short-term strenuous endurance exercise upon corpus luteum function. *Med Sci Sports Exerc* 1999;31(7): 949–58.
24. Petit MA, Prior JC, Barr SI. Running and ovulation positively change cancellous bone in premenopausal women. *Med Sci Sports Exerc* 1999;31(6):780–7.
25. Malina RM, Spirduso WW, Tate C et al. Age at menarche and selected menstrual characteristics in athletes at different competitive levels and in different sports. *Med Sci Sports* 1978;10(3):218–22.
26. Nattiv A, Puffer JC, Green GA. Lifestyles and health risks of collegiate athletes: a multi-centre study. *Clin J Sport Med* 1997;7(4):262–72.

931

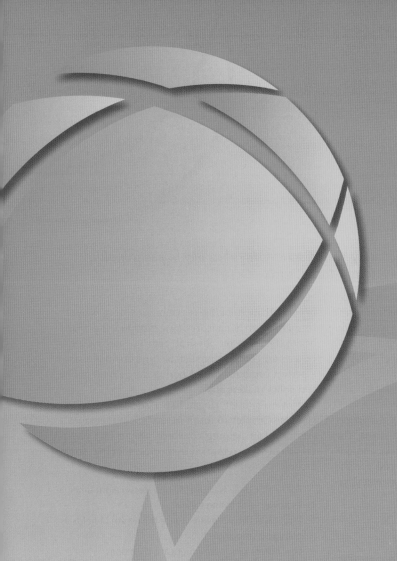

Part A

Fundamental principles

Sports and exercise medicine: addressing the world's greatest public health problem

with JENNIFER DAVIS and STEVEN BLAIR

Exercise in the prevention of coronary heart disease: today's best buy in public health.
Jeremy Morris, 1994

The three previous editions of *Clinical Sports Medicine* focused on how to practice sports and exercise medicine. This chapter takes us back one step to "why?" Why practice sports and exercise medicine?

The burden of physical inactivity and sedentary behavior

Where to start? Surf the web, read any magazine, look around you as you walk down the street. The problem of physical inactivity is not subtle, and this chapter aims to provide a launching pad for the sports clinician—a key agent in the war against physical inactivity.

The one trillion dollar argument (US alone!)

The year 2000 seems like antiquity, but even then physical inactivity cost the US $1 trillion annually.[1] This information gained enormous exposure and the fundamental data and methods that underpin those calculations still apply. Methods to analyze economic burden of disease have been refined,[2] updated, and expanded[3] to include many additional costs. Thus, the costs of physical inactivity can only have increased in the past decade (Table 1.1). Note that a week of physical *inactivity* is estimated to incur the same health costs as a week of smoking.[4]

Physical fitness—more health benefits than smoking cessation or weight loss

Having identified that physical inactivity is a problem, we can look for a solution. How can the problem of physical inactivity be addressed? Physical activity! It is known that physical fitness provides more health benefits than smoking cessation or losing weight.[5] Numerous systematic reviews expound the many health benefits of physical activity, but systemic reviews are complex, predictable, and unemotional—a perfect combination for boring the general public and policy makers alike.

However, brief slogan-like ("sticky") messages (see also Chapter 16 for more on "sticky messages") are useful in helping convince people that physical activity is a remarkable medical therapy. Some include:

- For health, daily walking (30 minutes) is eight times as powerful as losing weight.
- Physical activity provides twice the health benefits as giving up smoking.[5, 6]
- Low fitness kills more Americans than does 'smokadiabesity'—smoking, diabetes, and obesity *combined*.[7]

These sticky messages reflect data from Steven Blair's epidemiological study at the Cooper Institute in Texas (Fig. 1.1).[5] Note that "attributable fraction" refers to the proportion of deaths in the *population* that are due to the specific risk factor. It differs from "individual level" risk profiling.

The molecular mechanisms that explain the health benefits of physical activity

Experimental and mechanistic data shows how physical activity promotes health at the cellular and subcellular level. Some examples of exercise-induced health benefits at the molecular level that many patients find interesting and that can help motivate some are shown in the box opposite.

Table 1.1 Conditions precipitated by physical inactivity and resulting health care costs in the US

Unhealthy condition	Annual cost of condition in US$
Hypertriglyceridemia Hypercholesterolemia Hyperglycemia Insulin resistance Increased thrombosis Increased resting blood pressure Increased risk of myocardial ischemia Increased incidence of lethal ventricular arrhythmias Decreased cardiac stroke volume and maximal cardiac output	286.5 billion
Obesity	238 billion
Type 2 diabetes	98 billion
Breast and colon cancer	107 billion for all cancers
Osteoporosis	6 billion
Sarcopenia	300 billion for all disabilities
Back pain	28 billion
Gallstone disease	5 billion
Decreased psychological wellbeing	(cost not known)
Total	**1000 billion = 1 trillion**

ADAPTED FROM BOOTH ET AL.[1]

This was published in 2000 so is likely to be an *underestimate* today.

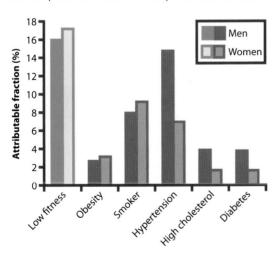

Figure 1.1 Attributable fractions (%) for all-cause deaths in 40 842 (3333 deaths) men and 12 943 (491 deaths) women in the Aerobics Center Longitudinal Study. The attributable fractions are adjusted for age and each other item in the figure
BLAIR[5]

Examples of exercise-induced health benefits at the molecular level

Preventing type 2 diabetes
Running on a treadmill stimulates key enzymes for energy sensing/signaling, including an important one called AMP kinase (AMPK). This protein helps remove fatty acids during muscular contraction and limits fatty acid biosynthesis. Exercise also enhances muscle membrane glucose transport capacity by recruiting a critical transport protein, GLUT-4, to the sarcolemma and T tubules where the protein can be active. Increasing the expression of GLUT-4 in skeletal muscle can be considered a crucial way of "mopping" glucose out of the bloodstream and into muscle and, hence, reducing the demand for insulin.[8]

Brain function
1. Both resistance training and endurance (aerobic) training can improve brain function. Convincingly,

continued

continued

the improvement in brain function can be shown using functional magnetic resonance imaging (fMRI) (Fig.1.2).

2. Animal studies show that improvements in brain function arise through improved blood flow and via particular hormones, including insulin-like growth factor 1 (IGF-1) and "brain derived neurotrophic factors" (BDNF).

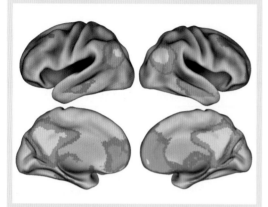

Figure 1.2 Sophisticated contemporary brain imaging, including functional MRI and "connectivity" mapping (illustrated), demonstrates that brain function improves with exercise training

Putting it all together—the economic imperative

"Exercise—the best buy in public health" concluded Jeremy Morris. A recent success story? Not at all! That was the title of a 1994 paper![9] The evidence has piled up since then: personal, regional, and national economic benefits accrue to those who are physically active.[6, 10] But how can we encourage adoption of this most powerful behavior—physical activity as medicine!

Practical challenges

Physical activity was not a societal burden when survival depended on it. Because we have engineered physical activity out of contemporary society, sedentary behavior is an easier choice. Similarly, poverty in various forms can make it very difficult for an individual to be active. Although clinicians are an important part of the team that promotes physical activity, society will need to make a concerted effort at various levels. This multilevel approach has been codified as the socioecological model of behavior change (Fig. 1.3).[11]

Consider the difference in likelihood of physical activity for Roald in Norway and a nameless inhabitant of a mythical urban wasteland. Roald's government provides tax benefits for healthy behavior and he lives close to a large forest with attractive walking paths. He can ride to work safely on a dedicated bike lane. His community promotes free public cross-country skiing by grooming and lighting the paths. His friends consider skating to be a great social activity. All levels of school-age children do at least 30 minutes of exercise each day as part of the school curriculum. All five elements of the socioecological model are working toward Roald and his family having an active lifestyle.

The darkest hour is just before the dawn

This chapter is written in a spirit of optimism. The human race has faced major challenges previously in public health and this problem—physical inactivity—is remediable. The remainder of this book is dedicated to keeping people active by preventing and treating musculoskeletal conditions in those who want to be active and by prescribing therapeutic exercise for those who have medical conditions.[12]

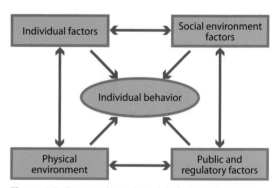

Figure 1.3 Socioecological model of physical activity

RECOMMENDED WEBSITES

British Journal of Sports Medicine: www.bjsm.bmj.com
Exercise is Medicine: www.exerciseismedicine.org
International Society of Physical Activity and Health:
www.ispah.org

RECOMMENDED READING

Blair SN. Physical inactivity: the biggest public health problem of the 21st century. *Br J Sports Med* 2009;43(1):1–2.

Booth FW, Chakravarthy MV, Gordon SE, Spangenburg EE. Waging war on physical inactivity: using modern molecular ammunition against an ancient enemy. *J Appl Physiol* 2002;93(1):3–30.

REFERENCES

1. Booth FW, Gordon SE, Carlson CJ et al. Waging war on modern chronic diseases: primary prevention through exercise biology. *J Appl Physiol* 2000;88(2):774–87.
2. Katzmarzyk PT, Janssen I. The economic costs associated with physical inactivity and obesity in Canada: an update. *Can J Appl Physiol* 2004;29(1):90–115.
3. Davis JC, Marra CA, Robertson MC et al. Economic evaluation of dose-response resistance training in older women: a cost-effectiveness and cost-utility analysis. *Osteoporos Int* 2011;22(5):1355–66.
4. Khan KM, Davis JC. A week of physical inactivity has similar health costs to smoking a packet of cigarettes. *Br J Sports Med* 2010;44(6):395.
5. Blair SN. Physical inactivity: the biggest public health problem of the 21st century. *Br J Sports Med* 2009;43(1):1–2.
6. Muller-Riemenschneider F, Reinhold T, Nocon M et al. Long-term effectiveness of interventions promoting physical activity: a systematic review. *Prev Med* 2008;47(4):354–68.
7. Khan KM, Tunaijia H Al. As different as Venus and Mars: time to distinguish efficacy (can it work?). *Br J Sports Med* 2011;45(10):759–60.
8. Booth FW, Chakravarthy MV, Gordon SE et al. Waging war on physical inactivity: using modern molecular ammunition against an ancient enemy. *J Appl Physiol* 2002;93(1):3–30.
9. Morris JN. Exercise in the prevention of coronary heart disease: today's best buy in public health. *Med Sci Sports Exerc* 1994;26(7):807–14.
10. Muller-Riemenschneider F, Reinhold T, Willich SN. Cost-effectiveness of interventions promoting physical activity. *Br J Sports Med* 2009;43(1):70–6.
11. Sallis J, Owen N. Ecological models. In: Glanz K, Lewis F, Rimer B (eds). *Health behavior and health education*. San Francisco: Jossey-Bass, 1997:403–24.
12. Khan KM, Weiler R, Blair SN. Prescribing exercise in primary care. *BMJ* 2011;343:d4141.

Chapter 2

Sports and exercise medicine: the team approach

You may have the greatest bunch of individual stars in the world, but if they don't play together, the club won't be worth a dime.   Babe Ruth

Sports and exercise medicine includes:

- injury prevention, diagnosis, treatment, and rehabilitation
- management of medical problems
- exercise prescription in health and in chronic disease states
- the needs of exercising in special subpopulations
- the medical care of sporting teams and events
- medical care in situations of altered physiology, such as at altitude or at depth
- performance enhancement through training, nutrition, and psychology
- ethical issues, such as the problem of drug abuse in sport.

Because of the breadth of content, sports and exercise medicine lends itself to being practiced by a multidisciplinary team of professionals with specialized skills who provide optimal care for the athlete and improve each other's knowledge and skills.[1-7] The adage that a "champion team" would always beat a "team of champions" applies to sports and exercise medicine. This team approach can be implemented in a multidisciplinary sports and exercise medicine clinic or by individual practitioners of different disciplines collaborating by cross-referral.

The sports and exercise medicine team

The most appropriate sports and exercise medicine team depends on the setting. In an isolated rural community, the sports and exercise medicine team may consist of a family physician or a physiotherapist/physical therapist alone. In a populous city, the team may consist of:

- physiotherapist/physical therapist
- sports physician
- massage therapist
- exercise specialist for exercise prescription
- athletic trainer
- orthopedic surgeon
- radiologist
- podiatrist
- dietitian/nutritionist
- psychologist
- other professionals such as osteopaths, chiropractors, exercise physiologists, biomechanists, nurses, occupational therapists, orthotists, optometrists
- coach
- fitness adviser.

In the Olympic polyclinic, an institution that aims to serve all 10 000 athletes at the games, the sports medicine team includes 160 practitioners (Table 2.1).

Multiskilling

The practitioners in the team have each developed skills in a particular area of sports and exercise medicine. There may also be a considerable amount of overlap between the different practitioners. Practitioners should aim to increase their knowledge and skills in areas other than the one in which they received their basic training. This "multiskilling" is critical if the practitioner is geographically isolated or is traveling with sporting teams.

The concept of multiskilling is best illustrated by example. When an athlete presents with an

Table 2.1 The clinical team structure for the preparation in advance of the 2012 London Summer Olympic Games

Administration/organization
(health professional background in brackets)

- Chief Medical Officer (sports and exercise medicine)
- medical manager (nursing)
- polyclinic manager (nursing)
- 4×"cluster" venue managers—serving multiple venues (nursing or hospital/health services management)

(In addition, for the Games themselves, 30 additional venue medical managers provide administrative/organizational support.)

Clinical consulting

Leads in each of:
- sports and exercise medicine
- physical therapies (including oversight for massage, chiropractic, osteopathy)
- polyclinic (emergency medicine–trained clinical director—with support from dentistry and podiatry)
- emergency medicine
- imaging
- pharmacy
- veterinary

(In addition, for the 3-week period of the Games themselves, 3000 additional clinicians volunteer.)

overuse injury of the lower limb, the podiatrist or biomechanist likely has the best knowledge of the relationship between abnormal biomechanics and the development of the injury, in clinical biomechanical assessment, and in possible correction of any biomechanical cause. However, it is essential that other practitioners, such as the sports physician, physiotherapist/physical therapist and sports/athletic trainer, all have a basic understanding of lower limb biomechanics and are able to perform a clinical assessment. Similarly, in the athlete who presents complaining of excessive fatigue and poor performance, the dietitian is best able to assess the nutritional state of the athlete and determine if a nutritional deficiency is responsible for the patient's symptoms. However, other practitioners such as the sports physician, physiotherapist/physical therapist, or trainer must also be aware of the possibility of nutritional deficiency as a cause of tiredness, and be able to perform a brief nutritional assessment.

The sports and exercise medicine model

The traditional medical model (Fig. 2.1) has the physician as the primary contact practitioner with subsequent referral to other clinicians.

The sports and exercise medicine model (Fig. 2.2 overleaf) is different. The athlete's primary professional contact is often with a physiotherapist/physical therapist; however, it is just as likely to be a trainer,

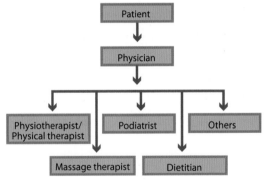

Figure 2.1 The traditional medical model

physician, or massage therapist. It is essential that all practitioners in the health care team understand their own strengths and limitations, and are aware of who else can improve management of the patient.

The challenges of management

The secret of success in sports and exercise medicine is to take a broad view of the patient and his or her problem. The narrow view may provide short-term amelioration of symptoms but will ultimately lead to failure. An example of a narrow view is a runner who presents with shin pain, and is diagnosed as having a stress fracture of the tibia, and is treated with rest until free of pain. Although it is likely that in the short term the athlete will improve and return to activity, there remains a high likelihood of recurrence

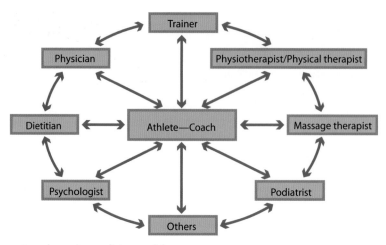

Figure 2.2 The sports and exercise medicine model

of the problem on resumption of activity. The clinician must always ask "Why has this injury/illness occurred?" The cause may be obvious—for example, recent sudden doubling of training load—or it may be subtle and, in many cases, multifactorial.

The greatest challenge of sports and exercise medicine is to identify and correct the *cause* of the injury/illness. The runner with shin pain arising from a stress fracture may have abnormal biomechanics, inappropriate footwear, a change of training surface, or a change in quantity or quality of training. In medicine, there are two main challenges—diagnosis and treatment. In sports and exercise medicine, it is necessary to diagnose both the problem and the cause. Treatment then needs to be focused on both these areas.

Diagnosis

Every attempt should be made to diagnose the precise anatomical and pathological cause of the presenting problem. Knowledge of anatomy (especially surface anatomy) and an understanding of the pathological processes likely to occur in athletes often permit a precise diagnosis. Thus, instead of using a purely descriptive term such as "shin splints," the practitioner should attempt to diagnose which of the three underlying causes it could be—stress fracture, chronic compartment syndrome, or periostitis—and use the specific term. Accurate diagnosis guides precise treatment. However, some clinical situations do not allow a precise anatomical and pathological diagnosis. For example, in many cases of low back pain, it is clinically impossible to differentiate between potential sites of pathology. In situations

such as these, it is necessary to monitor symptoms and signs through careful clinical assessment and correct any abnormalities present (e.g. hypomobility of an intervertebral segment) using appropriate treatment techniques.

Diagnosis of the presenting problem should be followed by diagnosis of the cause of the problem. The US orthopedic surgeon Ben Kibler has coined the term "victim" for the presenting problem, and "culprit" for the cause.[8] Diagnosis of the cause often requires a good understanding of biomechanics, technique, training, nutrition, and psychology. Just as more than one pathological process may contribute to the patient's symptoms, a combination of factors may cause the problem.

As with any branch of medicine, diagnosis depends on careful clinical assessment, which consists of obtaining a history, performing a physical examination, and organizing investigations. The most important of these is undoubtedly the history; unfortunately, this is often neglected. It is essential that the sports clinician be a good listener and develop skills that enable him or her to elicit the appropriate information from the athlete. Once the history has been taken, an examination can be performed. It is essential to develop examination routines for each joint or region and to include in the examination an assessment of any potential causes.

Investigations should be regarded as an adjunct to, rather than a substitute for, adequate history and examination.[9] The investigation must be appropriate to the athlete's problem, and provide additional information; it should only be performed if it will affect the diagnosis and/or treatment.

Treatment

Ideally, treatment has two components—treatment of the presenting injury/illness and treatment to correct the cause. Generally, the majority of sports and exercise medicine problems will not be corrected by a single form of treatment. A combination of different forms of treatment will usually give the best results. Therefore, it is important for clinicians to be aware of the variety of treatments available and to appreciate when their use may be appropriate. It is also important for clinicians to develop as many treatment skills as possible or, alternatively, ensure access to others with particular skills. It is essential to evaluate the effectiveness of treatment constantly. If a particular treatment is not proving to be effective, it is important firstly to reconsider the diagnosis (Chapter 41). If the diagnosis appears to be correct, other treatments should be considered.

Meeting individual needs

Every patient is a unique individual with specific needs. Without an understanding of this, it is not possible to manage the athlete appropriately. The patient may be an Olympic athlete whose selection depends on a peak performance at forthcoming trials, or he or she may be a non-competitive business executive whose jogging is an important means of coping with everyday life, or a club tennis player whose weekly competitive game is as important as a Wimbledon final is to a professional. Alternatively, the patient may be someone to whom sport is not at all important but whose low back pain causes discomfort at work.

The cost of treatment should also be considered. Does the athlete merely require a diagnosis and reassurance that there is no major injury? Or does the athlete want twice-daily treatment in order to be able to play in an important game? Treatment depends on the patient's situation, not purely on the diagnosis.

The coach, the athlete, and the clinician

The relationship between the coach, the athlete, and the clinician is shown in Figure 2.3. The clinician obviously needs to develop a good relationship with the athlete. A feeling of mutual trust and confidence

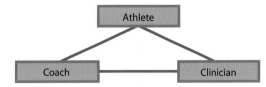

Figure 2.3 The relationship between the coach, the athlete, and the clinician

will lead to the athlete feeling that he or she can confide in the clinician and the clinician feeling that the athlete will comply with advice.

As the coach is directly responsible for the athlete's training and performance, it is essential to involve the coach in clinical decision making. Unfortunately, some coaches have a distrust of clinicians; however, it is essential for the coach to understand that the clinician is also aiming to maximize the performance and health of the athlete. When major injuries occur, professional athletes' agents will be involved in discussions. Involving the coach in the management plan is essential for athlete compliance. The coach will also be valuable in supervising the recommended treatment or rehabilitation program. In addition, discussion with the coach may help to establish a possible technique-related cause for the injury. Ethical issues that arise with respect to patient confidentiality are discussed in Chapter 67.

"Love thy sport" (and physical activity!)

To be a successful sports and exercise clinician it is essential to be an advocate for physical activity. A good understanding of a sport confers two advantages. Firstly, if clinicians understand the physical demands and technical aspects of a particular sport, it will improve their understanding of possible causes of injury and also facilitate development of sport-specific rehabilitation programs. Secondly, it will result in the athlete having increased confidence in the clinician. The best way to understand the sport is to attend training and competition, and ideally to participate in the sport. Thus, it is essential to be on site, not only to be available when injuries occur, but also to develop a thorough understanding of the sport and its culture.

📄 RECOMMENDED READING

Batt ME, Maryon-Davis A. Sport and exercise medicine:
    a timely specialty development. *Clin J Sport Med*
    2007;17(2):85–6.
Blair SN. Physical inactivity: the biggest public health
    problem of the 21st century. *Br J Sports Med*
    2009;43(1):1–2.
Cullen M, Batt ME. Sport and exercise medicine in the
    United Kingdom comes of age. *Br J Sports Med*
    2005;39(5):250–1.
Noakes TD. The role of the faculty of sports and exercise
    medicine for public health and elite athlete care.
    Br J Sports Med. 2010 Nov;44(14):998–1001.

📋 REFERENCES

1. Brukner PD, Crossley KM, Morris H et al.
    Recent advances in sports medicine. *Med J Aust*
    2006;184(4):188–93.
2. Blair SN. Physical inactivity: the biggest public
    health problem of the 21st century. *Br J Sports Med*
    2009;43(1):1–2.
3. Robison S. Sports and exercise medicine—a bright
    future? *Scott Med J* 2010;55(2):2.
4. Batt ME, Maryon-Davis A. Sport and exercise medicine:
    a timely specialty development. *Clin J Sport Med*
    2007;17(2):85–6.
5. Cullen M, Batt ME. Sport and exercise medicine in
    the United Kingdom comes of age. *Br J Sports Med*
    2005;39(5):250–1.
6. Harland RW. Essay: Sport and exercise medicine—a
    personal perspective. *Lancet* 2005;366 Suppl 1:S53–4.
7. Hahn A. Sports medicine, sports science: the
    multidisciplinary road to sports success. *J Sci Med Sport*
    2004;7(3):275–7.
8. Kibler WB, Sciascia A. Current concepts: scapular
    dyskinesis. *Br J Sports Med* 2010;44(5):300–5.
9. Coris EE, Zwygart K, Fletcher M et al. Imaging in
    sports medicine: an overview. *Sports Med Arthrosc*
    2009;17(1):2–12.

Chapter 3

Integrating evidence into clinical practice to make quality decisions

with CATHERINE SHERRINGTON

Randomized trials are for clinicians who are uncertain as to whether they are right or not—and I am certain I am right. Sir Ian Chalmers, quoting an unnamed orthopedic surgeon

This chapter opens with an exercise we use to introduce the concept of evidence-based practice to final-year students in human movement sciences/kinesiology (i.e. non-clinicians). If you are an experienced clinician or an expert on evidence-based practice you may want to skip over this chapter!

The "case" for the students to consider involves Mrs J, a 55-year-old woman. Students are told she presents with persistent knee pain due to osteo-

arthritis. The students are given the information in the box (below) and are asked to suggest a treatment for Mrs J.

In our student exercise we call for a vote and every year the first ballot results in option 1 (surgery) receiving about 80% of the votes! We then lead an open-class discussion and emphasize that the quality of the data should carry more weight than the clinical training of the person providing the advice. Students

Which evidence carries most weight?

You are asked to advise Mrs J, a 55-year-old woman with knee osteoarthritis, as to whether or not knee arthroscopy is a good idea. You have your own personal opinion, and you obtain the following four pieces of further information. Which of the four options carries the most weight with you? Would you advise that surgery is a good idea?

1. Dr X, an expert knee surgeon, advises in favor of surgery because "I have done hundreds of these operations and *obtained good or excellent results in over 90% of them.*" The surgeon offers you and your friend the phone numbers of patients who can provide testimonials. You call a few of these patients and they all vouch for surgery.

2. A published study of cases done by another surgeon, Dr Y, shows that 75% of patients who have had this type of surgery reported improvements. Overall *75% of patients had an "excellent or good" outcome*. Patients were recruited and interviewed two years after the surgery.

3. A published study examined patients who had presented with knee pain to a specialist in osteoarthritis two years earlier. One group of patients had undergone arthroscopic surgery, the other had not. *Patients who had undergone surgery reported playing more golf and tennis than those who had not undergone arthroscopic surgery.* The paper concluded that surgery was associated with superior outcomes compared to conservative management.

4. A physiotherapy student obtained ethics approval to attend doctors' offices and recruit patients with knee osteoarthritis. The surgeon decided to allocate patients randomly to either "surgery" or "no surgery." Two years later, the student interviewed the patients again and found that *both groups of patients* (those who had had surgery and those who had not) *had similar levels of pain and function.* Both groups had pain scores of around 50 out of 100 where 100 is severe pain.

review the options and many begin to see the limitations of options 1, 2, and 3. The evidence in option 4 is designed to mimic an important randomized trial that addressed this question.[1] (We deliberately avoid the word "randomized" as students are sensitized to this being important, even before they really understand study design.)

The aim of this introduction to the course is for students to link quality of evidence and decision making. This sounds axiomatic, but our experience over many years reinforces that at first students fail to distinguish "evidence" from "eminence." Students find this practical exercise much more meaningful than a soporific lecture on "research methods." Students are then primed to engage with the literature with a view to making "quality decisions" together with patients.

Life before evidence-based practice

Clinicians trained after the year 2000 might be surprised that the term "evidence-based medicine" first appeared in 1991.[2] Professor Paul McCrory describes that dark period before as a time of "eminence-based practice" but he jests. Nevertheless, a certain amount of clinical training relied on wisdom passing down from mentor to mentor. When clinical trials were few, the opinionated veteran was king. This is understandable in an emerging field.

Sackett and the McMaster contribution

Dr David Sackett and colleagues from McMaster University[3-5] described a pedagogical approach to evidence-based practice (Fig. 3.1). This type of health care reflects "the conscientious, explicit and judicious use of current best evidence in making decisions about the care of individual patients. Evidence-based practice integrates individual clinical expertise with the best available clinical evidence from systematic research."[5] Since the mid 1990s, evidence-based practice has been facilitated by the Cochrane Collaboration (www.cochrane.org), which conducts and publishes high-quality systematic reviews of randomized trials of effects of interventions to address a wide range of health problems.

Applying Sackett's approach to the case of Mrs J (boxed item p. 11), we note that many patients with that clinical presentation have been encouraged to have immediate arthroscopy, based on "expert opinion." They have not been provided with the full range of options that have been evaluated in research. Armed with the information that is freely available through

'Evidence-based practice' is the integration of best research evidence with clinical expertise and patient values—Dave Sackett

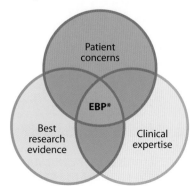

Figure 3.1 Schematic illustration of how clinical skills, evidence from research, and patient desire should overlap to provide the "quality decision" for the patient * evidence-based practice

PubMed, the "best evidence" is that a well-conducted randomized controlled trial (RCT), systematic review, or meta-analysis (Fig. 3.2) suggests that arthroscopy is no better than placebo. The pieces of evidence provided in options 1 to 3 in the boxed item on page 11 represent a much lower level of evidence—data with much greater potential for bias and, hence, potentially flawed conclusions. However, "evidence" is not synonymous with randomized trials alone. If there is a question about clinical prognosis, or patient experiences, the best evidence comes from other study designs.[6] (See also Recommended reading.)

Different study designs provide different quality evidence (Fig. 3.2). The levels in this figure map

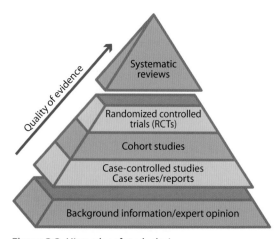

Figure 3.2 Hierarchy of study designs

closely, but not perfectly, to the Oxford "levels of evidence" shown in Table 3.1. We use the Oxford levels of evidence in this book.

Table 3.1 Levels of evidence

Level of evidence	Study design
Level 1	Systematic review of homogenous RCTs, individual RCT with narrow confidence interval
Level 2	Individual cohort study or low-quality RCT
Level 3	Individual case-control studies, non-consecutive cohort study
Level 4	Case series
Level 5	Expert opinion

This seems obvious—so what is the problem?

Evidence-based practice has intrinsic appeal; however, execution is the challenge. There are not enough individual RCTs, let alone systematic reviews or meta-analyses, to provide a body of evidence for every clinical encounter. For example, your patient might be an elite athlete who earns over US $150 000 per week; however, unfortunately, the relevant RCT was conducted in recreational athletes whose only reward was pleasure.

Also, clinical trials only provide data on "average effects" of interventions; your clinical experience means you can adjust those average effects to estimate what might happen in an individual patient. For example, a highly motivated individual might be expected to do better than average with an exercise intervention—where compliance is important.

In your office, you need to marry three things— the patient's wishes, the clinical evaluation you performed to make a diagnosis, and the evidence (Fig. 3.1). These elements were all part of Sackett's original definition of evidence-based practice.[7] Unfortunately, some "radical" advocates of pseudo-evidence-based practice forget the importance of the patient's wishes and your clinical evaluation, and they focus purely on the evidence component. If given license, those folk (usually non-practicing) disempower clinicians who work with real people; these radicals devalue clinicians' previous experience and patient wishes. If you are a clinician, don't be disempowered. Embrace evidence-based practice as additional value for your patients.

Evidence-based practice helps you distinguish evidence from propaganda (advertisement), probability from certainty, data from assertions, rational belief from superstitions, and, ultimately, science from folklore.[8]

By incorporating new evidence, your skills are continually updated—you are not stuck in a time warp where you practice today as you did in your year of graduation!

In summary, the health professions combine the art of caring for people with the best that science has to offer. The healing part can be likened to the community "shaman"—or healer. The patient's perspective and wishes are critical to reaching a "quality decision." The days of paternalism should be behind us. And remember that the plural of "anecdote" is not "data"![9]

In summary, the purpose of this chapter is to provide a perspective on evidence-based practice and to encourage interested readers to follow up with their own searches on the topic. Use the Recommended reading below. Evidence-based practice and clinical reasoning form key parts of the curriculum for students in all health disciplines; this chapter is not meant to provide a comprehensive text for that! Enjoy your evidence-based practice classes and remember that the key is to integrate clinical acumen with the evidence to meet the patient's needs (Fig. 3.1)! That way you'll make quality clinical decisions!

⊕ RECOMMENDED WEBSITES

Centre for Evidence-Based Medicine: www.cebm.net

The Cochrane Collaboration: www.cochrane.org

📄 RECOMMENDED READING

Herbert R, Jamtvedt G, Mead J et al. *Practical evidence-based physiotherapy.* Edinburgh: Elsevier, 2005.

📑 REFERENCES

1. Kirkley A, Birmingham TB, Litchfield RB et al. A randomized trial of arthroscopic surgery for osteoarthritis of the knee. *N Engl J Med* 2008;359(11):1097–107.

2. Guyatt G. Evidence-based medicine. *ACP Journal Club* 1991;A-16:144.

3. Sackett DL. Evidence-based medicine. *Lancet* 1995;346(8983):1171.

4. Sackett DL, Rosenberg WM. On the need for evidence-based medicine. *Health Econ* 1995;4(4):249–54.

5. Sackett DL, Straus S, Richardson WM et al. *Evidence-based medicine: how to practice and teach EBM.* London: Churchill Livingstone, 2000.

6. Herbert R, Jamtvedt G, Mead J et al. *Practical evidence-based physiotherapy.* Edinburgh: Elsevier, 2005.

7. Sackett DL, Rosenberg WM, Gray JA et al. Evidence-based medicine: what it is and what it isn't. *BMJ* 1996;312(7023):71–2.

8. Dawes M, Summerskill W, Glasziou P et al. Sicily statement on evidence-based practice. *BMC Med Educ* 2005;5(1):1.

9. McCrory P. Research realpolitik. *Br J Sports Med* 2002;36(1):1.

Chapter 4

Sports injuries: acute

There are a lot of myths about my injuries. They say I have broken every bone in my body. Not true. But I have broken 35 bones. I had surgery 14 times to pin and plate. I shattered my pelvis. I forget all of the things that have broke.   Evel Knievel

Sports injuries can occur during any sporting activity, event, or training session. Injuries can affect a variety of musculoskeletal structures such as muscles, ligaments, and bones. They can be classified by location, type, body side, and injury event.

An injury may be categorized as being either an acute injury or an overuse injury depending on the mechanism of injury and the onset of symptoms (Table 4.1). This chapter will review acute injuries, while the subsequent chapter (Chapter 5) will describe overuse injuries.

Acute injuries may be due to extrinsic causes (such

Table 4.1 Classification of sporting injuries

Site	Acute injuries	Overuse injuries (Chapter 5)
Bone	Fracture	Stress fracture
	Periosteal contusion	"Bone strain," "stress reaction"
		Osteitis, periostitis
		Apophysitis
Articular cartilage	Osteochondral/chondral fractures	Chondropathy (e.g. softening, fibrillation, fissuring,
	Minor osteochondral injury	chondromalacia)
Joint	Dislocation	Synovitis
	Subluxation	Osteoarthritis
Ligament	Sprain/tear (grades I–III)	Inflammation
Muscle	Strain/tear (grades I–III)	Chronic compartment syndrome
	Contusion	Delayed onset muscle soreness
	Cramp	Focal tissue thickening/fibrosis
	Acute compartment syndrome	
Tendon	Tear (complete or partial)	Tendinopathy (includes paratenonitis, tenosynovitis,
		tendinosis, tendonitis)
Bursa	Traumatic bursitis	Bursitis
Nerve	Neuropraxia	Entrapment
		Minor nerve injury/irritation
		Altered neuromechanical sensitivity
Skin	Laceration	Blister
	Abrasion	Callus
	Puncture wound	

as a direct blow) as a result of contact with another player or equipment, or intrinsic causes (such as a ligament sprain or muscle tear). As shown in Table 4.1, acute injuries may be classified according to the particular site injured (e.g. bone, cartilage, joint, ligament, muscle, tendon, bursa, nerve, skin) and the type of injury (e.g. fracture, dislocation, sprain, or strain).

Bone

Fracture

Fractures may be due to direct trauma such as a blow, or indirect trauma such as a fall on the outstretched hand or a twisting injury. Fractures may be closed, or open (compound), where the bony fragment punctures the skin.

Fractures are classified as transverse, oblique, spiral, or comminuted (Fig. 4.1). Another type of fracture seen in athletes, particularly children, is the avulsion fracture, where a piece of bone attached to a tendon or ligament is torn away.

The clinical features of a fracture are pain, tenderness, localized bruising, swelling, and, in some cases, deformity and restriction of movement. Fractures are managed by anatomical and functional realignment. Non-displaced or minimally displaced fractures can be treated with bracing or casting. Displaced fractures require reduction and immobilization. A displaced, unstable fracture requires surgical stabilization.

There are a number of possible complications of fracture. These include:

- infection
- acute compartment syndrome
- associated injury (e.g. nerve, vessel)
- deep venous thrombosis/pulmonary embolism
- delayed union/non-union
- mal-union.

Infection is most likely to occur in open (compound) fractures. Prophylactic antibiotic therapy is required in the treatment of any open fracture.

Occasionally a fracture may cause swelling of a muscle compartment that is surrounded by a non-distensible fascial sheath, usually in the flexor compartment of the forearm or the anterior compartment of the lower leg. This condition—acute muscle compartment syndrome—causes pain out of proportion to the fracture, pain on passive stretch, pulselessness, and paresthesia. This may require urgent fasciotomy, that is, release of the tight band of tissue surrounding the muscle compartment.

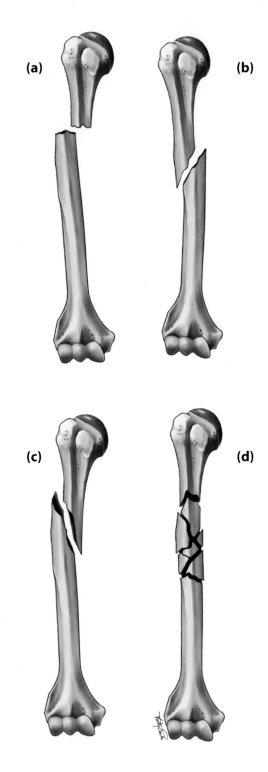

(a) **(b)**

(c) **(d)**

Figure 4.1 Types of fracture **(a)** transverse **(b)** oblique **(c)** spiral **(d)** comminuted

Occasionally, deep venous thrombosis and pulmonary embolism may occur after a fracture, especially a lower limb fracture. This should be prevented by early movement and active muscle contraction. Delayed union, or mal-union of a fracture causes persistent pain and disability that may require bone grafting, with or without internal fixation.

The problems of immobilization are discussed in Chapter 13. If immobilization is required for fracture healing, muscle wasting and joint stiffness will occur. Muscle wasting can be reduced by the use of electrical muscle stimulation and by isometric muscle contractions. Joint stiffness can be reduced by the use of limited motion braces instead of complete immobilization, or by the use of surgical fixation, which allows early movement.

Growth plate fractures in children and adolescents present a particular problem. These fractures are reviewed in Chapter 42.

Soft tissue injury, such as ligament or muscle damage, is often associated with a fracture, and may cause more long-term problems than the fracture itself. Thus it is important to address the soft tissue components of any bony injury. Specific fractures that are common in athletes are discussed in Part B (Chapters 17–41).

Periosteal injury

Acute periosteal injuries are uncommon. Like fractures, they can be extremely painful. Examples of periosteal injury include the condition known as a "hip pointer," an injury to the periosteum of the iliac crest caused by a direct blow, and periosteal injury of the tibia resulting from a blow from a kick, stick, or ball.

Articular cartilage

Articular cartilage lines the ends of long bones. It provides a low-friction gliding surface, acts as a shock absorber, and reduces peak pressures on underlying bone.[1] These injuries are far more common than was previously realized. Increased participation in recreational and competitive sports has now been linked to a growing risk of articular cartilage injuries, especially concerning the knee.[2] These injuries if left untreated can result in premature osteoarthritis of the joint and in turn affect activities of daily living.[1, 2]

With the advent of MRI and arthroscopy, it is now possible to distinguish three classes of articular cartilage injuries (Fig. 4.2):

1. disruption of the articular cartilage at its deeper layers with or without subchondral bone damage, while the articular surface itself remains intact (Fig. 4.2a).
2. disruption of the articular surface only (Fig. 4.2b).
3. disruption of both articular cartilage and subchondral bone (Fig. 4.2c).

Prognosis is related to the depth the injury extends toward the underlying bone.[1] Factors affecting return to sport include age, duration of symptoms, number of previous injuries, associated injuries, lesion type, size, and location.[2]

Articular cartilage may be injured by acute shearing injuries such as dislocation and subluxation. Common sites of chondral and osteochondral injuries are the superior articular surface of the talus, the

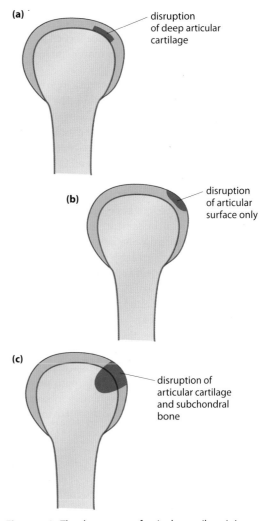

(a) disruption of deep articular cartilage

(b) disruption of articular surface only

(c) disruption of articular cartilage and subchondral bone

Figure 4.2 The three types of articular cartilage injury

femoral condyles, the patella, and the capitellum of the humerus. Osteochondral injuries may be associated with soft tissue conditions such as ligament sprains and complete ruptures (e.g. anterior cruciate ligament injury). As an initial X-ray is often normal, the clinician must maintain a high index of suspicion of osteochondral damage if an apparently "simple joint sprain" remains painful and swollen for longer than expected. These injuries should be investigated with MRI. Arthroscopy may be required to assess the degree of damage and to remove loose fragments or to perform chondroplasty (smooth loose edges of damaged articular cartilage).

Acute damage to articular cartilage is present in association with complete ligament ruptures[3] and may predispose to premature osteoarthritis.[1, 2, 4] Therefore, every attempt should be made to restore the smooth surface of the articular cartilage. Immobilization has a detrimental effect on articular cartilage but continuous passive movement may help counter this effect.

Articular cartilage has a limited capacity to regenerate or repair due to its avascular nature. The larger the lesion or defect the lower the probability of healing.[2] Treatment aims to restore the structural integrity and function. This is important in athletes whose joints are required to withstand significant stresses during their sport. Currently a range of interventions exist to encourage cartilage repair. Interventions can be broadly classified into bone marrow stimulation techniques, joint debridement and drilling, autologous chondrocyte implantation, and osteochondral transplantation (mosaicplasty).[1] Great debate continues as to which treatment approach for symptomatic chondral and osteochondral defects is most effective. Research is required on the long-term effects of the various treatment options.

It is important to identify articular cartilage injuries in children and adolescents before skeletal maturity. Chondral lesions, either diagnosed after MRI or during arthroscopic procedure, are more prevalent than meniscal or ligamentous injuries in skeletally immature patients admitted to hospital following acute knee trauma.[5]

Joint

Dislocation/subluxation

Dislocation of a joint occurs when trauma produces complete dissociation of the articulating surfaces of the joint. Subluxation occurs when the articulating

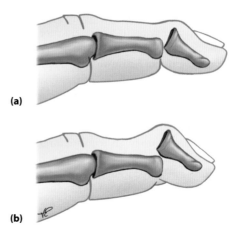

(a)

(b)

Figure 4.3 (a) Subluxation and **(b)** dislocation of a joint

surfaces remain partially in contact with each other (Fig. 4.3).

The stability of a joint depends on its anatomy. The hip is relatively stable because it has a deep ball and socket configuration, whereas the shoulder is far less stable because it has a small area of bony contact. Less stable joints (such as the shoulder and fingers) are more likely to dislocate. More stable joints (such as the hip, elbow, ankle, and subtalar joints) require much greater forces to dislocate and are, therefore, more likely to be associated with other injuries (e.g. fractures, nerve and vascular damage). All dislocations and subluxations result in injuries to the surrounding joint capsule and ligaments.

Complications of dislocations include associated nerve damage (e.g. axillary nerve injury in shoulder dislocations) and vascular damage (e.g. brachial artery damage in elbow dislocations). All dislocations should be X-rayed to exclude an associated fracture.

Dislocated joints, in most cases, can be reduced relatively easily. Occasionally muscle relaxation is required and this is achieved either by the use of an injected relaxant such as diazepam or by general anesthetic. After reduction, the joint needs to be protected to allow the joint capsule and ligaments to heal. Where possible, early protected mobilization is encouraged. Subsequent muscle strengthening gives the joint increased stability. Management of common dislocations (e.g. shoulder dislocation) is detailed in Part B.

Ligament

The stability of a joint is increased by the presence of a joint capsule of connective tissue, thickened at points of stress to form ligaments. Ligaments are made up

A

of closely packed collagen fibers and provide passive joint stability.[6] Load is transferred in the direction of the ligament from bone to bone. Injuries occur when a ligament is under excessive load.

Ligament injuries range from mild injuries involving the tearing of only a few fibers to complete tears of the ligament, which may lead to instability of the joint. Ligament injuries are divided into three grades (Fig. 4.4). A grade I sprain represents some stretched fibers but clinical testing reveals normal range of motion on stressing the ligament. A grade II sprain involves a considerable proportion of the fibers and, therefore, stretching of the joint and stressing the ligament show increased laxity but a definite end point. A grade III sprain is a complete tear of the ligament with excessive joint laxity and no firm end point. Although grade III sprains are often painful, they can also be pain-free as sensory fibers are completely divided in the injury.

The management of acute ligament sprains is summarized in Figure 4.5 overleaf. The initial management consists of first aid to minimize bleeding and swelling (Chapter 13). For grade I and grade II sprains, treatment aims to promote tissue healing, prevent joint stiffness, protect against further damage, and strengthen muscle to provide additional joint stability. The healing of collagen in a partial ligament tear takes several months.[7, 8] However, depending on the degree of damage, return to sport may be possible sooner than this, especially with protection against further injury.

A recent review of the evidence on acute ankle sprains demonstrated a period of at least six weeks to three months before ligament healing occurred.[9] From six weeks to one year, 31% of subjects continued to have objective mechanical laxity and subjective ankle instability. Therefore protection for return to physical activity and sport should be considered because of the moderate risk of re-injury with continual instability.

The treatment of a grade III sprain may be either conservative or surgical. For example, the torn medial collateral ligament of the knee and the torn lateral ligament of the ankle may be treated conservatively with full or partial immobilization. Alternatively, the two ends of a torn ligament can be reattached surgically and the joint then fully or partially immobilized for approximately six weeks. In certain instances (e.g. anterior cruciate ligament rupture), torn ligament tissue is not amenable to primary repair and surgical ligament reconstruction may be required (Fig. 32.10 on page 651).

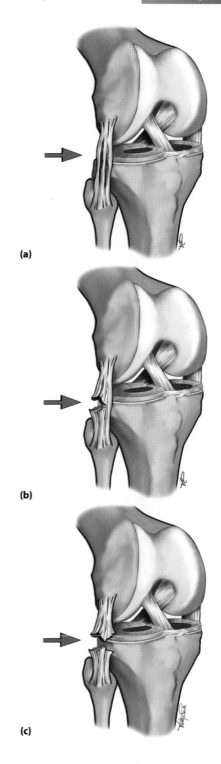

(a)

(b)

(c)

Figure 4.4 Ligament sprains (a) grade I (b) grade II (c) grade III

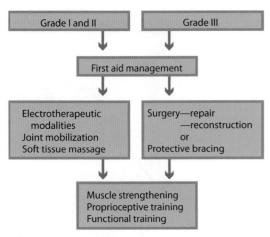

Figure 4.5 Management of acute ligament sprains

A number of tissue engineering interventions aim to restore normal function and minimize further joint injury. Examples include the use of growth factors, gene transfer and gene therapy, cell therapy, and the use of scaffolding materials.[6,10] However, further research is required on the effectiveness of these interventions.

Muscle

Muscle injuries are among the most common injuries in sports. The frequency of muscle injuries ranges from 10% to 55% of all sustained sporting injuries and includes muscle strains/tears and contusions.[11]

Strain/tear

Muscles are strained or torn when some or all of the fibers fail to cope with the demands placed upon them. Muscles that are commonly affected are the hamstrings, quadriceps, and gastrocnemius; these muscles are all biarthrodial (cross two joints) and thus more vulnerable to injury. A muscle is most likely to tear during sudden acceleration or deceleration.

Muscle strains are classified into three grades (Fig. 4.6). A grade I strain involves a small number of muscle fibers and causes localized pain but no loss of strength. A grade II strain is a tear of a significant number of muscle fibers with associated pain and swelling. Pain is reproduced on muscle contraction. Strength is reduced and movement is limited by pain. A grade III strain is a complete tear of the muscle. This is seen most frequently at the musculotendinous junction.

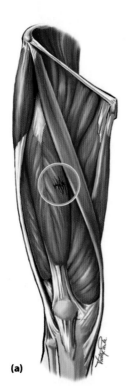

(a)

(b)

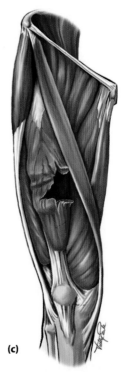

(c)

Figure 4.6 Muscle strains (a) grade I (b) grade II (c) grade III

The healing of muscle injuries can be divided into three phases which are similar to those in ligament injury healing (Fig. 4.7).

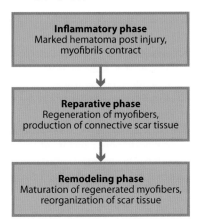

Figure 4.7 The three phases of muscle injury healing

Acute management of muscle strains should involve:[11, 12]

- early ice and compression
- a short period of immobilization (depending on severity and limited to the first few days after the injury only)
- early gentle mobilization and range of motion exercises (depending on severity and within pain limits; avoid aggressive stretching techniques)
- early gentle massage of the affected muscle (massage may be best avoided for the first 24–48 hours depending on severity).

Early mobilization in severe cases can cause re-rupture at the original muscle injury point and therefore accurate assessment of severity is essential. Re-ruptures cause the greatest amount of time lost from sporting activity.[11]

MRI scans and ultrasound can be helpful in the elite athlete but should not replace important clinical assessment. Early return to activity and sport can be considered in the elite athlete.[12] However, return to sport should be determined by extent of muscle strain, muscle group, and demands of the sport placed on the individual athlete.

A number of factors predispose to muscle strains:

- inadequate warm-up
- insufficient joint range of motion
- excessive muscle tightness
- fatigue/overuse/inadequate recovery
- muscle imbalance[13]
- previous injury

- faulty technique/biomechanics
- spinal dysfunction.

Most muscle strains are preventable. Methods of injury prevention are discussed in Chapter 9.

The use of nonsteroidal anti-inflammatory drugs (NSAIDs) in the early stages of muscle strain continues to be widely debated. The analgesic properties of NSAIDs are not significantly better than paracetamol for musculoskeletal injury.[14] However, there are more adverse effects associated with NSAIDs and therefore using paracetamol rather than an NSAID is suggested.[14]

Contusion

A muscle contusion usually results from a direct blow from an opposition player or firm contact with equipment in collision sports, such as football, basketball, and hockey. The blow causes local muscle damage with bleeding. The most common site of muscle contusions is the front of the thigh in the quadriceps muscle. This injury is known as a "cork thigh," "charley horse," and also "dead leg."

Management of contusion includes minimization of bleeding and swelling, followed by stretching and strengthening. Although most of these injuries are relatively minor and do not limit participation in sport, a severe contusion may occasionally result in a large amount of bleeding, especially if the player continues in the game after sustaining the injury. Heat, alcohol, and vigorous massage increase bleeding after a contusion and must be avoided.

Athletes playing sports with a high risk of contusions in a specific area, such as the thigh in some football codes, should consider the use of protective equipment such as padding. The athlete must weigh up the benefit of reducing injury risk versus the reduction in mobility that may result from wearing the equipment.

Myositis ossificans

An occasional complication of a muscle hematoma is myositis ossificans. This occurs when the hematoma calcifies. The incidence is highest in high-contact sports, such as the various football codes. Although myositis ossificans is most common following more severe muscle contusions, it may also occur in relatively minor cases. Hemophilia and other bleeding disorders are risk factors.[11] Myositis ossificans should be suspected in any muscle contusion that does not resolve in the normal time frame. An X-ray or ultrasound performed 10 to 14 days after the injury may show an area of calcification. Management of myositis ossificans is conservative and recovery is usually slow.

Cramp

Muscle cramps are painful involuntary muscle contractions that occur suddenly and can be temporarily debilitating. Muscle cramp either during or immediately after exercise is commonly referred to "exercise associated muscle cramping" (EAMC). EAMC can be defined as "painful, spasmodic and involuntary contraction of skeletal muscle that occurs during or immediately after exercise."[15] The most common site of muscle cramps is the calf.

The etiology of EAMC remains unclear. A leading theory ascribes its etiology to altered neuromuscular control.[15, 16] This theory is based on cramping occurring with repetitive muscle contraction after which increased excitatory and decreased inhibitory signals to the a-motor neuron develop. With continual muscle contraction, excessive excitation results in a cramp. This accounts for immediate effectiveness of inhibitory techniques such as stretching of the muscle or electrical stimulation methods. The fact that elite soccer players rarely cramp during normal 90-minute games but commonly suffer cramps when extra time is played would appear to support the excessive muscle contraction theory.

The treatment of cramps is aimed at reducing muscle spindle and motor neuron activity by reflex inhibition and afferent stimulation. Passive stretching reduces muscle electromyographic activity within 10 to 20 seconds, resulting in symptomatic relief. Passive tension should be applied to the affected muscle for 20 to 30 seconds or until fasciculation ceases, after which the muscle can gradually return to normal length. The effectiveness of passive stretching in treating EAMC offers further support for the hypothesis that abnormal spinal reflex activity is associated with EAMC, rather than a systemic disturbance, such as dehydration or electrolyte depletion.[15]

There are no proven strategies for the prevention of exercise-induced muscle cramp but regular muscle stretching, correction of muscle balance and posture, adequate conditioning for the activity, mental preparation for competition, and avoidance of provocative drugs may all be beneficial. Other strategies such as incorporating plyometrics or eccentric muscle strengthening into training programs, maintaining adequate carbohydrate reserves during competition,

or treating myofascial trigger points require further investigation.[17]

Tendon

Complete or partial tendon ruptures may occur acutely (Fig. 4.8). Normal tendons consist of tight parallel bundles of collagen fibers. Injuries to tendons generally occur at the point of least blood supply (e.g. with the Achilles tendon usually 2 cm [0.75 in.] above the insertion of the tendon) or at the musculotendinous junction.

A tendon rupture occurs without warning, usually in an older athlete without a history of injury in that particular tendon. The two most commonly ruptured tendons are the Achilles tendon and the supraspinatus tendon of the shoulder. The main objective of the treatment of tendon injuries is to restore full motion and function. Partial tears are characterized by the sudden onset of pain and by localized tender-

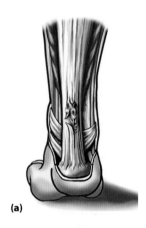

(a)

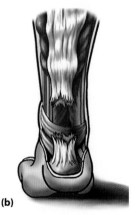

(b)

Figure 4.8 Tendon rupture **(a)** partial **(b)** complete

ness but they may be difficult to distinguish from tendinopathy (Chapter 5).

When investigation is indicated, ultrasound and MRI can be useful. Both modalities can distinguish between a partial or complete tendon rupture and overuse tendinopathy. Generally, acute tendon rupture requires surgical treatment followed by progressive rehabilitation.

Bursa

The body contains many bursae situated usually between bony surfaces and overlying tendons. Bursae are flat sacs of synovial membrane that contain synovial fluid. They are located where moving structures are in close proximity (such as between tendon and bone, muscle and bone, and ligament and bone) and facilitate movement by minimizing friction in these areas.

Most injuries to bursae are associated with overuse (Chapter 5), but occasionally a direct fall onto a bursa may result in acute traumatic bursitis due to bleeding into the bursa. The management of acute hemorrhagic bursitis involves the application of ice and compression. Aspiration may be indicated if the condition does not resolve.

Nerve

Major nerve injuries are unusual in athletes. However, a few nerves are relatively exposed and susceptible to injury from a direct blow. The nerves most often injured in this way are the ulnar nerve at the elbow, and the common peroneal nerve at the neck of the fibula. Specific peripheral nerve injuries can be associated with particular sports (e.g. radial nerve palsy with arm wrestling). The various codes of football, hockey, baseball, and winter activities are associated with higher risk for these injuries.[18]

The immediate symptoms are tingling, numbness, and pain in the distribution of the nerve. In minor nerve injuries the symptoms usually diminish quickly but in more severe injuries there will be persistent pain in the area of the distribution of the nerve. Occasionally in severe injuries there will be paralysis or weakness of the muscles innervated by that nerve, in addition to sensory loss in the sensory distribution of the nerve. While this paralysis is present the area should be supported in a brace or cast. This injury, known as "neuropraxia," usually resolves spontaneously but slowly.

There is increasing awareness that minor nerve injury is a common accompanying feature of many injuries. These nerve injuries are detected clinically by changes in neuromechanical sensitivity and may make a significant contribution to the patient's symptoms. The concept of neuromechanical sensitivity is discussed more fully in Chapter 6.

Skin

Acute skin injuries are common in contact sports. Possible damage to underlying structures, such as tendons, muscles, blood vessels, and nerves, should always be considered. Open wounds may be abrasions, lacerations, or puncture wounds. The principles of treatment of all open wounds are shown in Table 4.2.

Table 4.2 Principles of treatment of all open wounds

Principle	Details
1. Stop any associated bleeding	Apply a pressure bandage directly to the injured part and elevate it. If the wound is open and clean, bring the wound edges together using adhesive strips or sutures. A contaminated wound should not be closed.
2. Prevent infection	Remove all dirt and contamination by simple irrigation. Extensively wash and scrub with antiseptic solution as required as soon as possible. If the wound is severely contaminated, prophylactic antibiotic therapy should be commenced (e.g. flucloxacillin 500 mg orally four times a day). If anaerobic organisms are suspected (e.g. wound inflicted by a bite), add an antibiotic such as metronidazole (400 mg orally three times a day).
3. Immobilization (where needed)	This applies when the wound is over a constantly moving part (e.g. the anterior aspect of the knee). Certain lacerations (e.g. pretibial lacerations) require particular care and strict immobilization to encourage healing.
4. Check tetanus status	All contaminated wounds, especially penetrating wounds, have the potential to become infected with *Clostridium tetani*. Tetanus immunization consists of a course of three injections over 6 months given during childhood. Further tetanus toxoid boosters should be given at 5 to 10 year intervals. In the case of a possible contaminated wound, a booster should be given if none has been administered within the previous 5 years.

REFERENCES

1. Bhosale AM, Richardson JB. Articular cartilage: structure, injuries and review of management. *Brit Med Bull* 2008;87:77–95.

2. Mithoefer K, Hambly K, Della Villa S et al. Return to sports participation after articular cartilage repair in the knee: scientific evidence. *Am J Sports Med* 2009;37 Suppl 1:167S–76S.

3. Engebretsen L, Fritts HM. Osteochondral lesions and cruciate ligament injuries. MRI in 18 knees. *Acta Orthop Scand* 1993;64:434–6.

4. Myklebust G, Bahr R. Return to play guidelines after anterior cruciate ligament surgery. *Br J Sports Med* 2005;39(3):127–31.

5. Oeppen RS, Connolly SA, Bencardino JT et al. Acute injury of the articular cartilage and subchondral bone: a common but unrecognized lesion in the immature knee. *AJR* 2004; 182(1):111–7.

6. Woo SLY, Abramowitch SD, Kilger R et al. Biomechanics of knee ligaments: injury, healing, and repair. *J Biomech* 2006;39(1):1–20.

7. Frank C. Ligament healing: current knowledge and clinical applications. *J Am Acad Orthop Surg* 1996;4:74–83.

8. Frank C, Shrive N, Hiraoka H et al. Optimisation of the biology of soft tissue repair. *J Sci Med Sport* 1999;2(3):190–210.

9. Hubbard TJ, Hicks-Little CA. Ankle ligament healing after an acute ankle sprain: an evidence-based approach. *J Athl Train* 2008;43(5):523–9.

10. Warnke PH. In-vivo tissue engineering of biological joint replacements. *Lancet* 2010;376(9739):394–6.

11. Jarvinen TAH, Jarvinen TLN, Kaariainen M et al. Muscle injuries: optimising recovery. *Best Prac Res Clin Rheumatol* 2007;21(2):317–31.

12. Orchard JW, Best TM, Mueller-Wohlfahrt H-W et al. The early management of muscle strains in the elite athlete: best practice in a world with a limited evidence basis. *Br J Sports Med* 2008;42(3):158–9.

13. Croisier J-L, Ganteaume S, Binet J et al. Strength imbalances and prevention of hamstring injury in professional soccer players: a prospective study. *Am J Sports Med* 2008;36(8):1469–75.

14. Paoloni JA, Milne C, Orchard JW et al. Non-steroidal anti-inflammatory drugs in sports medicine: guidelines for practical but sensible use. *Br J Sports Med* 2009;43:863–65.

15. Schwellnus MP. Cause of exercise associated muscle cramps (EAMC)–altered neuromuscular control, dehydration or electrolyte depletion? *Br J Sports Med* 2009;43(6):401–8.

16. Schwellnus MP. Muscle cramping in the marathon: aetiology and risk factors. *Sports Med* 2007;37(4–5):364–7.

17. Bentley S. Exercise-induced muscle cramp. Proposed mechanisms and management. *Sports Med* 1996;21(6):409–20.

18. Toth C, McNeil S, Feasby T. Peripheral nervous system injuries in sport and recreation: a systematic review. *Sports Med* 2005;35(8):717–38.

Chapter 5

Sports injuries: overuse

And he's got the icepack on his groin there, so possibly not the old shoulder injury.
Ray French, British TV sports commentator

Overuse injuries present three distinct challenges to the clinician—diagnosis, understanding of why the injury occurred, and treatment. Diagnosis requires taking a comprehensive history of the onset, nature, and site of the pain along with a thorough assessment of potential risk factors; for example, training and technique. Careful examination may reveal which anatomical structure is affected. It is often helpful to ask patients to perform the maneuver that produces their pain.

The skilled clinician must seek a cause for every overuse injury. The cause may be quite evident, such as a sudden doubling of training quantity, poor footwear, or an obvious biomechanical abnormality, or may be more subtle, such as running on a cambered surface, muscle imbalance, or leg length discrepancy. The causes of overuse injuries are usually divided into extrinsic factors such as training, surfaces, shoes, equipment, and environmental conditions, or intrinsic factors such as age, gender, malalignment, leg length discrepancy, muscle imbalance, muscle weakness, lack of flexibility, and body composition. Possible factors in the development of overuse injuries are shown in Table 5.1.

Treatment of overuse injuries will usually require addressing of the cause as well as specific additional elements such as activity modification, specific exercises to promote tissue repair, soft tissue massage, and pharmacologic agents where appropriate (Chapter 13).

Bone stress

Bone stress reactions, which can develop into stress fractures, are fatigue failure injuries of the bone.

Table 5.1 Overuse injuries: predisposing factors

Extrinsic factors	Intrinsic factors
Training errors	Malalignment
• excessive volume	• pes planus
• excessive intensity	• pes cavus
• rapid increase	• rearfoot varus
• sudden change in type	• tibia vara
• excessive fatigue	• genu valgum
• inadequate recovery	• genu varum
• faulty technique	• patella alta
Surfaces	• femoral neck
• hard	anteversion
• soft	• tibial torsion
• cambered	Leg length discrepancy
Shoes	Muscle imbalance
• inappropriate	Muscle weakness
• worn out	Lack of flexibility
Equipment	• generalized muscle
• inappropriate	tightness
Environmental conditions	• focal areas of muscle
• hot	thickening
• cold	• restricted joint range of
• humid	motion
Psychological factors	Sex, size, body composition
Inadequate nutrition	Other
	• genetic factors
	• endocrine factors
	• metabolic conditions

Stress fractures account for 0.7% to 20% of all sports medicine clinic injuries.[1] Track-and-field athletes have the highest incidence of stress fractures compared with other athletes.[1-3] There is a continuum of bone response to stress that ranges from mild (bone strain) to severe (stress fracture) (Fig. 5.1). The clinical features of bone strain, stress reaction, and stress fractures are summarized in Table 5.2. Different sites of stress fractures are associated with particular sporting activities (Fig. 5.2).

Mechanism

In a normal environment, musculoskeletal integrity is maintained by a balance of fatigue damage with remodeling activity, stimulated by normal repetitive low-intensity loading forces.[3] The rate of remodeling responds to the loads through the bone, which includes the forces transferred from surrounding muscle activity. High levels of bone stress, through an increase in activity, may lead to higher rates of fatigue damage where the remodeling response may not be able to cope. This then manifests clinically as a bone stress injury.

Overload stress can be applied to bone through two mechanisms:

1. the redistribution of impact forces resulting in increased stress at focal points in bone
2. the action of muscle pull across bone.

Such overload leads to osteoclastic activity that surpasses the rate of osteoblastic new bone formation, resulting in temporary weakening of bone. If physical activity is continued, trabecular microfractures result and these cause early bone marrow edema seen on MRI scanning. In most cases, bone responds to these microfractures by forming periosteal new bone for reinforcement. However, if the osteoclastic activity continues to exceed the rate of osteoblastic new bone formation, eventually a full cortical break occurs.[2] A summary of the histological changes resulting from bone stress is displayed in Figure 5.3.

Risk factors

There has been considerable research investigating the association between bone stress injuries and various risk factors (Table 5.3). Two important risk factors are (i) a rapid increase or change in the load on the bone (rapid change in volume or intensity of training), and (ii) an energy imbalance between calories expended and taken in. Energy imbalance

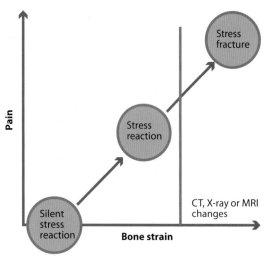

Figure 5.1 The continuum of bone stress: from silent stress reaction through to stress fracture. Stress fracture is detected by changes on X-ray, CT scan or MRI

Table 5.2 Continuum of bony changes with overuse

Clinical features	Bone strain	Stress reaction	Stress fracture
Local pain	Nil	Yes	Yes
Local tenderness	Nil	Yes	Yes
X-ray appearance	Normal	Normal	Abnormal (periosteal reaction or cortical defect in cortical bone, sclerosis in trabecular bone)
MRI appearance	May show increased high signal	Increased high signal	Increased high signal ± cortical defect
Radioisotopic bone scan appearance	Increased uptake	Increased uptake	Increased uptake
CT scan appearance	Normal	Normal	Features of stress fracture (as for X-ray)

Site of stress fracture	Associated sport/activity
Coracoid process of scapula	Trapshooting
Scapula	Running with hand weights
Humerus	Throwing; racquet sports
Olecranon	Throwing; pitching
Ulna	Racquet sports (esp. tennis); gymnastics; volleyball; swimming; softball; wheelchair sports
Ribs—1st	Throwing; pitching
Ribs—2nd–10th	Rowing; kayaking
Pars interarticularis	Gymnastics; ballet; cricket fast bowling; volleyball; springboard diving
Pubic ramus*	Distance running; ballet
Femur—neck	Distance running; jumping; ballet
Femur—shaft	Distance running
Patella	Running; hurdling
Tibia—plateau	Running
Tibia—shaft	Running; ballet
Fibula	Running; aerobics; race-walking; ballet
Medial malleolus×	Running; basketball
Calcaneus	Long-distance military marching
Talus	Pole vaulting
Navicular	Sprinting; middle-distance running; hurdling; long jump; triple jump; football
Metatarsal—general	Running; ballet; marching
Metatarsal—2nd base	Ballet
Metatarsal—5th	Tennis; ballet
Sesamoid bone—foot	Running; ballet; basketball; skating

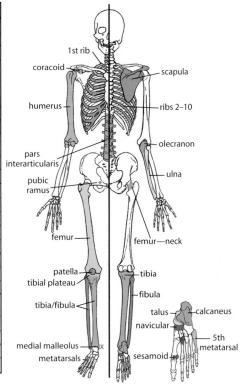

Figure 5.2 Stress fractures: site and common associated activity

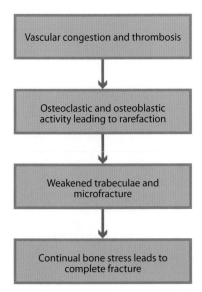

Figure 5.3 The histological changes resulting from bone stress

The flow chart in Figure 5.3 reads:

Vascular congestion and thrombosis

↓

Osteoclastic and osteoblastic activity leading to rarefaction

↓

Weakened trabeculae and microfracture

↓

Continual bone stress leads to complete fracture

Table 5.3 Risk factors associated with the development of bone stress injuries

Risk factor	Data associated with bone stress injuries
Training	>32 km/week[5]
	Rapid change
Surfaces	Hard or cambered surfaces[6]
Physical characteristics	Narrow bone width[7]
	Less muscle[8]
	Increased hip external rotation[7]
	Leg length discrepancy[8]
Weight	Low lean mass
Gender	Female (×1.2–10)
	Female athlete triad—osteoporosis, menstrual irregularity, disordered eating[4]

causes menstrual irregularity (loss of luteal hormone pulsatility) and impaired bone health.[4] This topic is covered more fully in Chapter 43.

Skeletal sites

The bones most commonly affected by stress fracture are the tibia, metatarsals, fibula, tarsal navicular, femur, and pelvis.[1, 9, 10] A list of sites of stress fractures and the likely associated sports or activities is shown in Figure 5.2.

Clinical diagnosis

The typical history of a stress fracture is that of localized pain which comes on during or after exercise, and persists or increases if exercise is continued. It is also important to take a risk factor history such as enquiring if there has been a recent change in training volume or intensity, change of equipment such as running shoes, or change of training surface. An assessment of energy balance is essential, particularly in the female athlete, as is a menstrual history and questions related to eating disorders.

The physical examination typically reveals local tenderness over the involved bone when the bone is relatively superficial (e.g. tibia, fibula, metatarsals). Diagnosis of stress fractures of the femur and pars interarticularis present more of a challenge. Specific tests such as the fulcrum test (femur) and single-legged hyperextension (pars) can be used.

Potential risk factors should be assessed as part of the physical examination. These include leg length discrepancy, femoral neck anteversion, muscle weakness, and excessive subtalar pronation.

Imaging diagnosis

Imaging plays a significant role in the diagnosis. Imaging options include plain radiography, bone scan, CT, MRI, and, more recently, ultrasound (US). The diagnostic features of a stress fracture are shown in Table 5.4.

Table 5.4 Diagnostic features of a stress fracture

- localized pain and tenderness over the fracture site
- a history of a recent change in training or taking up a new activity
- X-ray appearance often normal[12] or there may be a periosteal reaction (Fig. 5.4)
- abnormal appearance on MRI (Fig. 5.5), radioisotopic bone scan (scintigraphy) (Fig. 5.6)[13, 14] or CT scan (Fig. 5.7)

Plain radiographs have poor sensitivity and may not detect stress injury until the injury has developed along the bone stress continuum.[11, 12] Although some old textbooks suggested that stress fractures become visible on plain radiograph after two to six weeks, prospective studies prove that some stress fractures remain invisible on plain radiography. Radiographic changes, when present, include subtle focal periosteal bone formation (Fig. 5.4) or, later, frank cortical defects.

In countries where clinicians have ready access to MRI, this is generally the first line investigation of bone stress injuries. MRI is sensitive in detecting pathophysiological changes in soft tissue, bone, and marrow associated with bone-related stress injuries. It can reveal abnormalities in these structures before plain radiographic changes and has comparable sensitivity to a bone scan.[11] Other advantages of MRI for bone imaging are its multiplanar capability (which helps the clinician precisely define the location and extent of injury), lack of exposure to ionizing

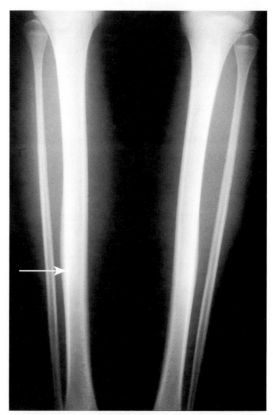

Figure 5.4 X-ray showing periosteal new bone formation indicative of a stress fracture

radiation, and significantly less imaging time than a three-phase bone scan.

The typical MRI appearance of a stress fracture shows periosteal and marrow edema plus or minus the actual fracture line (Fig. 5.5). Several fat-suppression techniques such as short tau inversion recovery are used to maximize the sensitivity of MRI in bone stress injuries.[13]

Radioisotopic bone scan was the most important diagnostic test for athletic stress fractures in the 1990s.[13] The technical aspects of this modality are outlined in Chapter 12. The appearance of a bone stress injury on bone scan is a focal area of increased uptake (Fig. 5.6).

Note that bone scan lacks specificity for stress fractures—bony abnormalities such as tumors, especially osteoid osteoma, and osteomyelitis have similar appearances. It may also be difficult to precisely localize the site of the area of increased uptake.

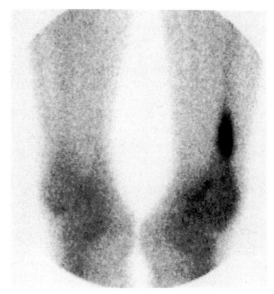

Figure 5.6 Stress fracture: radioisotopic bone scan appearance   COURTESY OF ZS KISS

Increased uptake can occur in nonpainful sites, indicating subclinical accelerated remodeling. As with plain film, CT scan, and MRI, imaging appearance returns to normal after clinical resolution because of ongoing bony remodeling.[13]

CT is less sensitive than a bone scan or MRI in the early detection of bone-related stress injury.[11, 12] However, it more sensitive than both radiographs or MRI for the detection of cortical fracture lines. CT is thus well suited to demonstrate stress fractures of the sacrum, pars interarticularis, tarsal navicular, and longitudinal stress fractures of the tibia.[11]

The CT scan will clearly image the fracture (Fig. 5.7 overleaf) and differentiate between a stress fracture (positive bone scan, clear fracture line) and a stress reaction (positive bone scan and negative CT scan). The CT can also distinguish a bone stress injury from other causes of hot bone scans such as osteoid osteoma and osteomyelitis.

Ultrasound has some potential in the diagnosis of stress fracture but it is not ready for routine clinical use.[12]

Low-risk and high-risk stress fracture

Stress fractures can be classified as low-risk or high-risk. Low-risk fractures generally require no treatment other than rest.

Low-risk stress fractures include femoral shaft, medial tibia, ribs, ulna shaft, and first through fourth

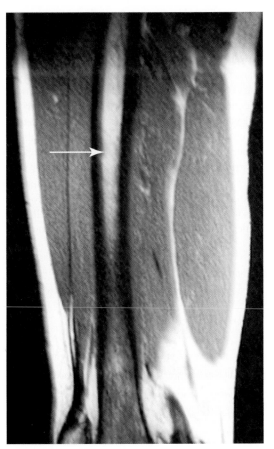

Figure 5.5 MRI of a stress fracture showing bony edema (white)

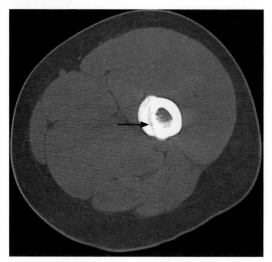

Figure 5.7 CT of a stress fracture showing a cortical defect (arrowed)

General principles of stress fracture treatment

The treatment of stress fractures generally requires avoidance of the precipitating activity. The majority of stress fractures heal within six weeks of beginning relative rest. The return to sport after clinical healing of a stress fracture should be a gradual process to enable the bone to adapt to an increased load (Chapter 15). When activities of daily living are pain-free and there is no tenderness on bony palpation, then weight-bearing exercise can be gradually increased, firstly walking, then jogging, then running at increased speeds.

Fitness should be maintained by cross-training. This could include swimming, cycling, or water running. This period of rehabilitation is also an opportune time to correct any identified risk factors. This might involve modification of the training plan to ensure graduated increase in load, correction of mechanical abnormalities with the use of orthoses, and ensuring adequate energy intake.

Some specific treatments have been suggested to accelerate bone healing (electrical and ultrasound stimulation, pharmacologic agents such as pamidronate) or to enable the athlete to return to activity more quickly (pneumatic leg brace); however, more evidence is required as to their efficacy and safety.[3]

Healing is assessed clinically by the absence of local tenderness and functionally by the ability to perform the precipitating activity without pain. It is not useful to attempt to monitor healing with X-ray or radioisotopic bone scan.[1] CT scan appearances of healing stress fractures can be deceptive as in some cases the fracture is still visible well after clinical healing has occurred.[14] Figure 5.8 shows the

metatarsals—all of which have a favorable natural history. These sites tend to be on the compressive side of the bone and respond well to activity modification. Low-risk stress fractures are less likely to recur, become a non-union, or have a significant complication should they progress to complete fracture.

High-risk stress fractures do not have an overall favorable natural history. With delay in diagnosis or with less aggressive treatment, high-risk stress fractures tend to progress to non-union or complete fracture, require operative management, or recur in the same location. High-risk stress fracture locations include the femoral neck, the anterior tibial diaphysis, the medial malleolus, the talus, the tarsal navicular, the proximal fifth metatarsal, and the sesamoid bones of the foot (Table 5.5).

Table 5.5 Stress fractures that require specific treatment other than rest

Stress fracture	Treatment
Femoral neck	Undisplaced: initial bed rest for 1 week, then gradual weight-bearing Displaced: surgical fixation
Talus (lateral process)	Non-weight-bearing cast immobilization for 6 weeks, or surgical excision of fragment
Navicular	Non-weight-bearing via cast immobilization or boot immobilization for 6–8 weeks
Metatarsal—2nd base	Non-weight-bearing for 2 weeks; partial weight-bearing for 2 weeks
Sesamoid bone of the foot	Non-weight-bearing for 4 weeks
Metatarsal—5th base[a]	Cast/boot immobilization or percutaneous screw fixation
Anterior tibial cortex	Non-weight-bearing on crutches for 6–8 weeks, or intramedullary screw fixation

(a) This is not a Jones fracture, which is an acute fracture (Chapter 40)

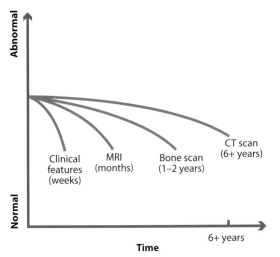

Figure 5.8 MRI, bone scan, and CT scan return to their normal appearance well after clinical union occurs

relationship between imaging appearance and the various stages of bone stress.

Osteitis and periostitis

Osteitis (impaction trauma or primary inflammation of bone) and periostitis (abnormal histological appearance of periosteal collagen) are also considered overuse injuries. The condition known as "osteitis pubis" occurs in the pubic bones of the pelvis and is characterized by deep-seated pain and tenderness of the symphysis pubis with generalized increased uptake on the radioisotopic bone scan. The exact pathogenesis of this injury remains in debate (see also Chapter 29).

Periostitis or tenoperiostitis (pain at the tendinous attachment to bone) occurs commonly, mainly at the medial border of the tibia, a condition often known as "shin splints." In this condition, tenderness along the medial border of the tibia corresponds with an area of increased uptake on bone scan.

The treatment of periostitis (or tenoperiostitis) consists of local symptomatic therapy as well as unloading the muscle contraction on the periosteum. In the shin, strain may be reduced by altering the biomechanics through controlling excessive pronation. Soft tissue therapy and stretching may also be effective.

Apophysitis

Bony injury may occur at the attachment of the strong, large tendons to the growth areas; this condition is called "apophysitis." The most common examples are Osgood-Schlatter disease at the attachment of the patellar tendon to the tibial tuberosity and Sever's disease at the attachment of the Achilles tendon to the calcaneus. A full description of apophysitis is given in Chapter 42.

Articular cartilage

Overuse injury can affect the articular cartilage lining of joints, particularly in osteoarthritis. Changes range from microscopic inflammatory changes to softening, fibrillation, fissuring, and ultimately to gross visible changes. In younger people, this pathology can arise at the patella (patellofemoral syndrome), but it is important to note that the pain of patellofemoral syndrome can occur in the presence of normal joint surfaces. This very common condition is discussed in Chapter 33.

Joint

Inflammatory changes in joints associated with overuse are classified as synovitis or capsulitis. Examples of these problems are the sinus tarsi syndrome of the subtalar joint and synovitis of the hip joint.

Impingement syndromes occur when a bony abnormality, either congenital or acquired, causes two bony surfaces to impinge on each other (e.g. femoro-acetabular impingement at hip, posterior impingement at ankle), or impinge on a structure passing between them (e.g. supraspinatus tendon in shoulder) causing damage to that structure. Treatment requires either removal of the structural abnormality or modification of biomechanics to relieve the impingement.

Ligament

Overuse injuries of ligaments are uncommon and may be more associated with skeletally immature athletes. Overuse ulnar collateral ligament injuries of the elbow occur in young baseball pitchers.[15, 16]

Muscle

Overuse muscle injuries are commonly attributed to muscle imbalances. Imbalances can lead to changes in muscle length and strength between the antagonist and agonist muscles, which can affect the overall muscle function. Muscle weakness, inflexibility, and poor muscle endurance can affect sporting performance through abnormal movement patterns. Muscle imbalances coupled with fatigue can lead to muscle injury.

Focal tissue thickening/fibrosis

Focal tissue thickening or fibrosis can be defined as repetitive microtrauma caused by overuse that damages muscle fibers. This is thought by some to lead to development of adhesions between muscle fibers and the formation of cross-linkages in fascia (Fig. 5.9). Muscle imbalances are commonly associated with muscle overuse injuries.

Clinically, the changes may be palpated as firm, focal areas of tissue thickening, with taut, thickened bands arranged in the direction of the stress, or as large areas of increased muscle tone and thickening.

These lesions may cause local pain or predispose other structures, such as tendons, to injury due to a reduction in the ability of the tissue to elongate under stretch or eccentric load. This will also compromise the ability of the affected muscle to contract and relax rapidly.

These minor muscle injuries, which occur frequently in association with hard training, may respond to regular soft tissue therapy, strengthening, and stretching (Chapter 13). Prevention of these injuries is discussed in Chapter 9.

Chronic compartment syndrome

Chronic compartment syndrome refers to the intermittent and reversible pathologic elevation of compartment pressures following exertion.[17] The condition usually affects the lower leg but may also occur in the forearm in the sports of tennis, rock climbing and weightlifting.[18]

The muscles of the lower leg are divided into a number of compartments by fascial sheaths, which are relatively inelastic thickenings of collagenous tissue. Exercise raises the intracompartmental pressure and may cause local muscle swelling and accumulation of fluid in the interstitial spaces. The tight fascia prevents expansion. This impairs the blood supply and causes pain with exertion. Compression of neurological structures may also contribute to the clinical presentation. A vicious cycle may occur (Fig. 5.10). Muscle hypertrophy may also precipitate chronic compartment syndrome.

The main symptom of chronic compartment syndrome is pain that commences during activity and ceases with rest. This differs from other overuse injuries such as tendinopathies, where pain may be present with initial exercise, then diminish as the affected area warms up, only to return following cessation of activity. Compartment pressures may be measured both at rest and during pain-provoking exercise. Compartment pressure testing is described in Chapter 12.

Treatment of chronic compartment syndrome initially involves soft tissue therapy[19] and correction of biomechanical abnormalities where possible. If this fails, surgical treatment may be required—fasciotomy (release of the fascia) or fasciectomy (removal of the fascia).

Muscle soreness

Soreness accompanies muscle strains. A particular type of muscle soreness known as "delayed onset

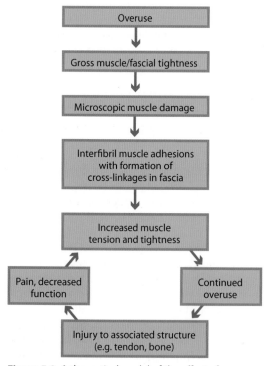

Figure 5.9 A theoretical model of the effect of overuse on muscle tissue

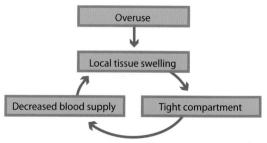

Figure 5.10 The development of increased muscle compartment pressure

muscle soreness" (DOMS) develops 24 to 48 hours after unaccustomed high-intensity physical activity. It appears to be more severe after eccentric exercise (involving muscle contraction while muscle is lengthening), such as downhill running.

Typically soreness arises within the first day after exercise and peaks at approximately 48 hours after exercise.[20] DOMS results in temporary decrease in muscle force production, increase in passive tension, and increase in muscle soreness which may be accompanied with localized swelling.[20, 21]

Variable results have been shown with preventative approaches such as the use of vitamin C and E, and protein supplements.[21] It occurs less in those who train regularly, although even trained individuals may become sore after an unaccustomed exercise bout.

Treatment of DOMS could include massage, active recovery, contrast baths, cryotherapy, electrotherapy (TENS, ultrasound), hyperbaric oxygen therapy, compression garments, and stretching.[20–22] Nonsteroidal anti-inflammatory drugs (NSAIDs) may improve muscle soreness but not necessarily muscle function or sporting performance. Additionally, repeated use over extended periods may have detrimental effects on muscle repair and adaptation to training.[21, 22]

Tendon
with JILL COOK, CRAIG PURDAM
Tendon overuse injury (tendinopathy)
Tendon overuse injuries provide a major proportion of the sports clinician's workload. The clinical presentation is straightforward in many cases—the patient presents with tendon pain during or after activity (Table 5.6). Loading tests demonstrate increased pain with increased load and palpation can localize tendon pain accurately (e.g. to a focal region of the Achilles tendon). In the 1980s, the underlying pathology was often referred to as "tendonitis"—this was associated with a belief that cellular inflammation contributed to the pathological process. A large number of histopathological studies in the 1990s indicated that inflammatory cells were absent in patients who underwent surgery for tendon pain. The pathological findings at surgery were consistent with "tendinosis." The boxed item (overleaf) illustrates tendon pathology—"tendinosis"—at the anatomical level (Fig. 5.11 overleaf) and at two microscopic levels (Figs 5.12, 5.13 overleaf). The pathology is also summarized in Table 5.7 on page 35.

Table 5.6 Clinical presentation of patients with overuse tendon pain (tendinosis)

- Pain some time after exercise or, more frequently, the following morning upon rising.
- It can be pain free at rest and initially becomes more painful with use.
- Athletes can "run through" the pain or the pain disappears when they warm up, only to return after exercise when they cool down.
- The athlete is able to continue to train fully in the early stages of the condition; this may interfere with the healing process.
- Examination reveals local tenderness and/or thickening.
- Frank swelling and crepitus may be present, although crepitus is more usually a sign of associated tenosynovitis (it is not "inflammatory fluid").

A contemporary model of a continuum of tendon pathology
Tendon authorities Jill Cook and Craig Purdam have proposed that tendon pathology should be considered as a continuum.[23] They contend that the dichotomy of "normal" and "degenerative tendinosis" is too simplistic. Importantly, their three-part classification has implications for treatment, and so it is summarized here and illustrated (Fig. 5.14 on page 36).

Stage 1. Reactive tendinopathy
This refers to the non-inflammatory response of tendon cells and matrix proteins to an acute tensile or compressive overload. Tendon cells become activated and may proliferate in this stage—they become more prominent, and produce repair proteins, especially proteoglycans. This results in a short-term thickening of a portion of the tendon that reduces stress. This differs from normal tendon adaptation to tensile load that generally occurs through tendon stiffening with little change in thickness.

Reactive tendinopathy is seen clinically in the acutely overloaded tendon and is more common in the younger person. It also arises when there is direct trauma to a tendon.

At this stage, both ultrasound and MRI show mild fusiform swelling—greater tendon diameter. The change in imaging appearance is mainly derived from the increase in bound water within the matrix proteins (proteoglycans).

Tendinosis: what is it?

This box illustrates the pathology found at end-stage tendinopathy—when symptoms have been present for at least three months. The illustration (Fig. 5.11) is based on pathological specimens (Figs 5.12, 5.13) obtained at surgery for chronic sports-related tendon pain.

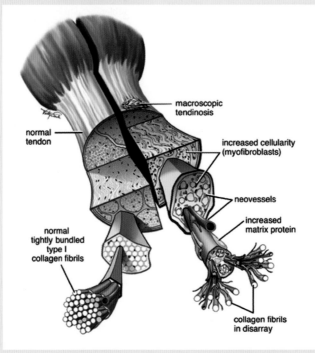

Figure 5.11 The contrasting features of normal tendon (left side) and tendinosis (right side). Characteristic features at this macroscopic level are the collagen fibers of different sizes in disarray, abnormal cell numbers (decreased and increased), abnormally prominent blood vessels, and an increase in matrix proteins

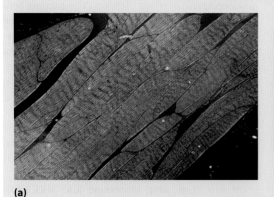
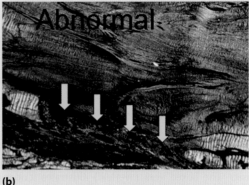

(a)   (b)

Figure 5.12 Under polarized light microscopy (a) normal tendon has tightly bundled parallel collagen fibrils with a characteristic golden reflectivity (b) a specimen from a patient with chronic patellar tendinopathy showing collagen fibril separation and frank discontinuity (arrows) within some fibrils

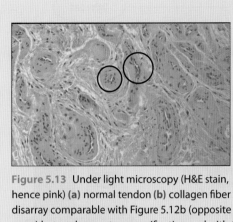

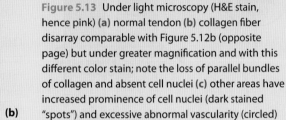

Figure 5.13 Under light microscopy (H&E stain, hence pink) **(a)** normal tendon **(b)** collagen fiber disarray comparable with Figure 5.12b (opposite page) but under greater magnification and with this different color stain; note the loss of parallel bundles of collagen and absent cell nuclei **(c)** other areas have increased prominence of cell nuclei (dark stained "spots") and excessive abnormal vascularity (circled)

Table 5.7 Five elements of normal tendon compared with the characteristic elements of end-stage tendon overuse injury

Tendon element	Normal tendon	Changes that occur in response to excessive tendon loading
Cells—tenocytes	Tendon cells are spindle-shaped, and nuclei cluster in longitudinal chains on microscopy	Tissue has proliferation of cells with abnormally rounded nuclei (Fig. 5.13c) and areas with fewer than normal cell numbers (Fig. 5.13b)
Ground substance or "matrix" proteins	The ground substance in the matrix is minimal and is not visible when stained for light microscopic viewing	Increased amount of ground substance/matrix proteins which stain and are visible under light microscopy
Collagen	Linear and tightly bundled and has a characteristic crimp under polarized light	Disrupted—both longitudinally and in its bundles (Fig. 5.13b)
Nerves	Minimal intratendinous nerves, some innervation of connective tissue in and around the tendon	Abnormal ingrowth of nerves (mostly sympathetic) and a preponderance of neuropeptides
Vessels	Minimal vascularity when examined histologically or by using ultrasound	Prominent vessels histologically or using ultrasound (Fig. 5.13c)

Stage 2. Tendon dysrepair

This describes a worsening tendon pathology with greater matrix breakdown. Tendon cells are more prominent and take on a rounded appearance (chondrocytic); myofibroblasts appear. Protein production increases—both matrix proteoglycans and collagen. As a result of these changes, collagen separates and the matrix becomes somewhat disorganized. The disruption of the matrix may allow for some ingrowth of vessels and nerves.

This is seen clinically in overloaded tendons in the young but it may appear across a spectrum of ages and loading environments. The transition from the previous stage may be difficult to detect clinically but imaging will reveal more focal changes of hypoechogenicity on ultrasound. There may be a mild increase

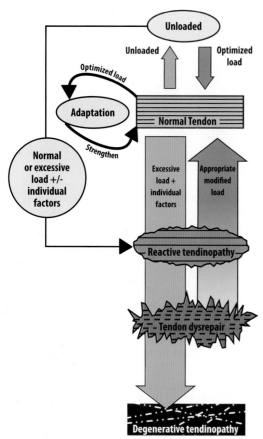

Figure 5.14 The Cook–Purdam model to help clinicians understand the relationship between load/unloading and the several stages of tendon pathology

REDRAWN FOR *CLINICAL SPORTS MEDICINE* WITH PERMISSION FROM *BRITISH JOURNAL OF SPORTS MEDICINE*[23]

in vascularity on color or Doppler ultrasound. MRI reveals a swollen tendon with increased signal.

Stage 3. Degenerative tendinopathy

This is the stage that is present in patients who undergo surgery for chronic tendon pain—it is the "end stage" of tendon overuse injury. The matrix and cell changes described in Stages 1 and 2 progress so that areas of apoptosis (absent cell nuclei due to cell death) are evident. Large areas of matrix are disordered and filled with vessels, matrix breakdown products, and little collagen. The tendon is now heterogenous— degenerative pathology is interspersed between other stages of pathology and normal tendon.

Clinicians see this pathology in older patients (who may not be particularly active) and also in young athletes who can accelerate development of pathology with substantial and repeated tendon load. Another common presentation is the middle-aged, recreationally active person with focal tendon swelling and pain (e.g. mid-Achilles region).

In this stage, compromised matrix and vascular changes can be very obvious on ultrasound scans as hypoechogenic regions with few reflections from collagen fascicles. Larger vessels are usually prominent on Doppler ultrasound (Chapter 37). MRI shows increased tendon size and intratendinous signal. The changes are more focal than spread throughout the tendon.

Other terms associated with overuse tendon injuries

Although the most-used clinical label for tendon overuse injuries is "tendinopathy" as above, and used in specific chapters of this book (i.e. Achilles tendinopathy), the terms "paratenonitis," "partial tear," and "tendonitis" need definition.

Paratenonitis

This term includes peritendonitis, tenosynovitis (single layer of areolar tissue covering the tendon) and tenovaginitis (double-layered tendon sheath). This occurs in situations where the tendon rubs over a bony prominence (e.g. flexor hallucis tendinopathy at the medial malleolus) and/or where repeated movement directly irritates the paratenon. Uncommonly, it can coexist with partial tears and tendinosis.

Partial tear

The term "partial tear of a tendon" should be reserved for a macroscopically evident subcutaneous partial tear of a tendon. This is an uncommon acute—not overuse—injury, at least in the Achilles and patellar tendon (see Chapter 4). The pathology found in partial tears is that of tendinosis.

Tendonitis

"Tendonitis" refers to inflammation of the tendon itself and, despite the former popularity of the diagnostic label, has rarely been shown to occur histologically. This may be because tissue is not obtained from tendons in humans who have only had tendon pain for a short time (days). Tendonitis may occur in association with paratendonitis. True inflammatory tendonitis may underpin the tendinopathies associated with the inflammatory arthritides.

Bursa

The body contains many bursae situated usually between bony surfaces and overlying tendons. Their role is to facilitate movement of the tendon over the bony surface. Overuse injuries in bursae are quite common, particularly at the subacromial bursa, the greater trochanteric bursa, and the retrocalcaneal bursa separating the Achilles tendon from the calcaneus. Overuse pathologies affecting bursae commonly couple with other local pathologies such as tendinopathies and impingement syndromes.[24, 25]

All bursae are susceptible to injury. Typically injuries to bursae are overuse injuries resulting from excessive shearing and/or compressive forces.[26, 27] Common bursal presentations in the sporting population include iliotibial band friction syndrome (frequently seen in runners, cyclists, and endurance sports),[27, 28] sub-acromial bursitis (commonly seen in overhead athletes),[29] trochanteric bursitis proposed to be linked to gluteus minimus and/or medius injury and/or weakness,[25] and retrocalaneal bursitis, which is often associated with insertional Achilles.[30]

Symptoms include localized pain and swelling and typically increase with activity. Conservative approaches to treatment are often trialed first.

Treatment involves removal of irritating loads, reduction of inflammation, and a progressive return to pain-free activity. Specific treatments include ice, electrical stimulation, iontophoresis, and gentle stretching. Once initial inflammation subsides, a stretching and strengthening program for the surrounding tissues and muscles can commence. NSAIDs are widely prescribed for these conditions, and corticosteroid injections, often guided by ultrasound, are considered where conservative approaches have failed.

Nerve

Nerve entrapment syndromes occur in athletes as a result of swelling in the surrounding soft tissues or anatomical abnormalities. These may affect the suprascapular nerve, the posterior interosseous, the ulnar and median nerves in the forearm, the obturator nerve in the groin, the posterior tibial nerve at the tarsal tunnel on the medial aspect of the ankle, and, most commonly, the interdigital nerves, especially between the third and fourth toes, a condition known as Morton's neuroma. This condition is not a true neuroma but rather a nerve compression. These nerve entrapments occasionally require surgical decompression.[31]

Chronic mild irritation of a nerve may result in damage manifested by an increased neuro-mechanical sensitivity. These may be the primary cause of the patient's symptoms or may contribute to symptoms. This concept is discussed more fully in Chapter 6.

Skin

The skin's integrity is constantly challenged by athletic activity, weather conditions, and pathogenic organisms.

Blisters

The skin of many athletes is subjected to friction-related forces and this is compounded by perspiration.[32, 33] Exposure to shearing and compressive forces can lead to mechanical separation of the epidermal cell layers. Hydrostatic pressure causes further separation and allows plasma-like fluid or sweat into the space to form a blister.[33] The repair process starts 24 hours post-incident and blisters generally heal in approximately five days.[33] Blisters may occur at any site of friction with an external source, such as shoes or sporting equipment.

Blisters are common in marathon runners, race walkers, triathletes, hikers, and in military populations. Foot blisters are painful and can have an impact on sporting performance. Type of sock, race, previous hiking or military experience, and known orthopedic foot conditions predict the development of foot blisters in the military population.[32]

Foot blisters can be prevented by wearing-in new shoes, wearing socks, and smearing petroleum jelly over the sock at sites of friction. Strategies to prevent blisters also serve to prevent callus. Symptomatic callus can be pared down with a scalpel blade, taking care not to lacerate the normal skin.

At the first sign of a blister, the aggravating source should be removed and either adhesive tape applied over the blistered area or blister pads be applied. Blister pads prevent blisters by acting as a barrier between skin and shoe.

Treatment of blisters involves prevention of infection by the use of antiseptics, and protection with sticking plaster. Fluid-filled blisters may be punctured and drained.

Infections

Almost any cutaneous infection can afflict athletes; however, their activities place these individuals at higher risk to develop and subsequently transmit their skin ailment to competitors. Athletes acquire infections as a result of their interaction with other athletes and with the environment in which they compete. An athlete's skin is often macerated from sweating, which promotes common infections in sports including bacterial, fungal, and viral infections; however, parasites can also afflict the athlete.[34]

Dermatitis

An athlete's skin suffers repeated exposure to trauma, heat, moisture, and numerous allergens and chemicals. These factors combine with other unique and less well-defined genetically predisposing factors in the athlete's skin to cause both allergic contact dermatitis and irritant contact dermatitis. As with other cases of contact dermatitis, these eruptions in athletes present as a spectrum from acute to subacute to chronic dermatitis. Recognizing the unique environmental irritants and allergens encountered by athletes is paramount to facilitate appropriate therapy and prevention.[35]

Skin cancers

Although not technically overuse injuries, we include skin cancer here as it is a critical pathology and sports and exercise clinicians are in a position to save lives by being aware of this condition, which has greater incidence in certain sports.[36] Ultraviolet light exposure is the most important risk factor for cutaneous melanoma and nonmelanoma skin cancers. Nonmelanoma skin cancer includes basal cell carcinoma and squamous cell carcinoma. Constitutive skin color and genetic factors, as well as immunological factors, play a role in the development of skin cancer.

But it's not that simple ...

Although it is important to have a good understanding of the conditions outlined in this chapter and in Chapter 4, three important additional components are necessary for successful management of patients with sporting injuries.

Pain: where is it coming from?

The pain your patient feels at a particular site may not necessarily be emanating from that site. It is essential to understand the concept of "referred pain," which is the topic of Chapter 6.

Masquerades

There are many medical conditions whose presentation may mimic a sporting injury. While many of these conditions are relatively rare, it is nevertheless important to keep them at the back of your mind. If the clinical pattern does not seem to fit the obvious diagnosis, then think of the conditions that may masquerade as sporting injuries. These are described in Chapter 7.

The kinetic chain

Every athletic activity involves movements of joints and limbs in coordinated ways to perform a task. These activities include running, jumping, throwing, stopping, and kicking. The tasks may include throwing a ball, hitting a ball, kicking a ball, jumping over an object, or propelling the body through air or water. Individual body segments and joints, collectively called "links," must be moved in certain specific sequences to allow efficient accomplishment of the tasks.

The sequencing of the links is called the "kinetic chain" of an athletic activity.[37] Each kinetic chain has its own sequence but the basic organization includes proximal to distal sequencing, a proximal base of support or stability, and successive activation of each segment of the link and each successive link. The net result is generation of force and energy in each link, summation of the developed force and energy through each of the links, and efficient transfer of the force and energy to the terminal link.

Injuries or adaptations in some areas of the kinetic chain can cause problems not only locally but distantly, as distal links must compensate for the lack of force and energy delivered through the more proximal links. This phenomenon, called "catch-up," is both inefficient in the kinetic chain, and dangerous to the distal link because it may cause more load or stress than the link can safely handle. These changes may result in anatomical or biomechanical situations that increase injury risk, perpetuate injury patterns, or decrease performance. For example, a tennis player with stiffness of the lumbar spine may overload the rotator cuff muscles while serving to generate sufficient power and, thus, develop a tear of the rotator cuff muscles.

These deficits in the kinetic chain must be identified and corrected as part of the treatment and rehabilitation process. We will be constantly returning to the theme of the kinetic chain throughout the following chapters.

REFERENCES

1. Brukner PD, Bennell KL, Matheson GO. *Stress fractures.* Melbourne: Blackwells Scientific Asia, 1999.

2. Diehl JJ, Best TM, Kaeding CC. Classification and return-to-play considerations for stress fractures. *Clin Sports Med* 2006;25(1):17–28.

3. Rome K, Handoll HHG, Ashford R. Interventions for preventing and treating stress fractures and stress reactions of bone of the lower limbs in young adults. *Cochrane Database Syst Rev* 2009(2):CD000450.

4. Manore MM, Kam, LC, Loucks, AB. The female athlete triad: components, nutrition issues, and health consequences. *J Sports Sci* 2007;25 (1):S61–71.

5. Macera CA. Lower extremity injuries in runners: advances in prediction. *Sports Med* 1992;13:50–7.

6. Johanson MA. Contributing factors in microtrauma injuries of the lower extremity. *J Back Musculoskelet Rehabil* 1992;2:12–25.

7. Giladi M, Milgrom C, Simkin A et al. Stress fractures and tibial bone width. A risk factor. *J Bone Joint Surg* 1987;69-B:326–9.

8. Bennell KL, Malcolm SA, Thomas SA et al. Risk factors for stress fractures in track and field athletes: a 12-month prospective study. *Am J Sports Med* 1996;24:810–18.

9. Brukner PD, Bradshaw C, Khan KM et al. Stress fractures: a series of 180 cases. *Clin J Sport Med* 1996;6(2):85–9.

10. Baquie P, Brukner PD. Injuries presenting to an Australian Sports Medicine Centre: a 12-month study. *Clin J Sport Med* 1997;7(1):28–31.

11. Datir AP. Stress-related bone injuries with emphasis on MRI. *Clin Radiol* 2007;9:828–36.

12. Moran DS. Imaging of lower extremity stress fracture injuries. *Sports Med (Auckland)* 2008;38(4):345–56.

13. Fredericson M, Jennings F, Beaulieu C, Matheson GO. Stress fractures in athletes. *Top Magn Reson Imaging* 2006;17:309–25.

14. Khan KM, Fuller PJ, Brukner PD et al. Outcome of conservative and surgical management of navicular stress fracture in athletes. Eighty-six cases proven with computerized tomography. *Am J Sports Med* 1992;20(6):657–66.

15. Harada M, Takahara M, Mura N et al. Risk factors for elbow injuries among young baseball players. *J Shoulder Elbow Surg* 2010 Jun;19(4):502–7.

16. Parks ED, Ray TR. Prevention of overuse injuries in young baseball pitchers. *Sports Health: A Multidisciplinary Approach* 2009;1:514.

17. van Zoest WJF, Hoogeveen AR, Scheltinga MRM et al. Chronic deep posterior compartment syndrome of the leg in athletes: postoperative results of fasciotomy. *Int J Sports Med* 2008;29(5):419–23.

18. Piasecki DP, Meyer D, Bach BR. Exertional compartment syndrome of the forearm in an elite flatwater sprint kayaker. *Am J Sports Med* 2008;36(11):2222–5.

19. Blackman PG, Simmons LR, Crossley KM. Treatment of chronic exertional anterior compartment syndrome with massage: a pilot study. *Clin J Sport Med* 1998;8:14–17.

20. Herbert RD, de Noronha M. Stretching to prevent or reduce muscle soreness after exercise. *Cochrane Database Syst Rev* 2007(4):CD004577.

21. Howatson G, van Someren KA. The prevention and treatment of exercise-induced muscle damage. *Sports Med* 2008;38(6):483–503.

22. Barnett A. Using recovery modalities between training sessions in elite athletes: does it help? *Sports Med* 2006;36(9):781–96.

23. Cook JL, Purdam CR. Is tendon pathology a continuum? A pathology model to explain the clinical presentation of load-induced tendinopathy. *Br J Sports Med* 2009;43(6):409-16.

24. Koh ES, Lee JC, Healy JC. MRI of overuse injury in elite athletes. *Clin Radiol* 2007;62(11):1036–43.

25. Kong A, Van der Vliet A, Zadow S. MRI and US of gluteal tendinopathy in greater trochanteric pain syndrome. *Eur Radiol* 2007;17:1772–83.

26. Benjamin M, Kaiser E, Milz S. Structure-function relationships in tendons: a review. *J Anat* 2008;212:211–28.

27. Hariri S, Savidge E, Reinold MM et al. Treatment of recalcitrant iliotibial band friction syndrome with open iliotibial band bursectomy: indications, technique, and clinical outcomes. *Am J Sports Med* 2009;37(7):1417–24.

28. Ellis R, Hing W, Reid D. Iliotibial band friction syndrome—a systematic review. *Man Ther* 2007;12(3):200–8.

29. Seroyer ST, Nho SJ, Bach BR et al. Shoulder pain in the overhead throwing athlete. *Sports Health: A Multidisciplinary Approach* 2009;1:108–20.

30. Werd MB. Achilles tendon sports injuries: a review of classification and treatment. *J Am Podiatr Med Assoc* 2007;97(1):37–48.

31. Banky J, McCrory PR. Mouthguard use in Australian football. *J Sci Med Sport* 1999;2(1):20–9.

32. Van Tiggelen D, Wickes S, Coorevits P, Dumalin M, Witvrouw E. Sock systems to prevent foot blisters

and the impact on overuse injuries of the knee joint. *Mil Med* 2009;174(2):183–9.

33. Yavuz M, Davis BL. Plantar shear stress distribution in athletic individuals with frictional foot blisters. *J Am Podiatr Medl Assoc* 2010;100(2):116–20.

34. Adams BB. Skin infections in athletes. *Dermatol Nurs* 2008;20(1):39–44.

35. Kockentiet B, Adams BB. Contact dermatitis in athletes. *J Am Acad Dermatol* 2007;56(6):1048–55.

36. Harrison SC, Bergfeld WF. Ultraviolet light and skin cancer in athletes. *Sports Health* 2009;1(4):335–40.

37. Kibler WB. Determining the extent of the functional deficit. In: Kibler WB, Herring SA, Press JM (eds). *Functional Rehabilitation of Sports and Musculoskeletal Injuries*. Gaithersburg, MD: Aspen Publishers, 1998: 16–19.

Chapter 6

Pain: why and how does it hurt?

with G LORIMER MOSELEY

Then, [Mr Hammerhead Shark], his shirt covered in blood, spun around and hit his knee on the table, at which point he swore and yelled "My knee! My knee!," the whole time unfussed about the hammer stuck in his neck.   G Lorimer Moseley. *Painful yarns. Metaphors & stories to help understand the biology of pain.* Canberra: Dancing Giraffe Press, 2007

Even the simplest biological organisms can protect themselves from threatening stimuli—by altering their path of movement away from the source of the threat.[1] As evolution has honed us into more and more sophisticated creatures, we have also honed this fundamental capacity to protect ourselves from threat. Indeed, humans have very sophisticated methods of protection, perhaps none more sophisticated than pain. This chapter includes:

- some examples of the "fearful and wonderful complexity" of pain, which are conveyed by
  - proposing a contemporary definition of pain that is contrary to conventional definitions but which integrates the huge amount of research that has been undertaken since our conventional definitions were established
  - introducing the idea of nociception and describing some of what is known about the biological mechanisms that underpin nociception
  - providing a conceptual framework with which to make sense of pain within the context of clinical practice
- a very practical clinical approach to considering referred pain when managing patients.

What is pain?

Almost everyone experiences pain. Those who do not experience pain as the rest of us know it are at a distinct disadvantage in life and are likely to die young without living fast. Pain is an unpleasant sensory and emotional experience that is felt in the body and that

COURTESY OF MALCOLM WILLETT

motivates us to do something to escape it. These two characteristics of pain—its unpleasantness and its anatomical focus—are what makes it such an effective protective device. Pain alerts us to tissue damage or the threat thereof. Pain makes us seek attention. Pain changes our behavior. Pain stops us competing, keeps us seeking a cure, and compels us to prioritize pain relief above almost everything else. In fact, if the brain concludes that there is something more important than protecting a body part, then it makes the executive decision to *not* produce pain. Therein lies the key to really understanding pain—it is as simple and as difficult as this—if *the brain* concludes that a body part is in danger and needs protecting, and you, the organism, ought to know about it, then *the brain* will make that body part hurt.[2]

This concept of pain integrates a vast body of basic, applied, and clinical research. It differs greatly from conventional theories, which have changed little since the seventeenth century when Rene Descartes was ridiculed for suggesting that we were not made from four bodily humors.[3]

 The critical concept is that pain is not a measure of tissue damage, but an indicator of the brain's conviction about the need to protect certain tissue.

To better understand pain as the protective output of the brain, not as a marker of tissue damage, let us consider several contrasts between the two models (Table 6.1).

What is nociception?

Nociception is not pain. "Nociception" refers to the detection, transmission, and processing of noxious stimuli. A noxious stimulus is one that is actually or potentially damaging. The neurons that detect noxious stimuli and transmit a nociceptive message to the spinal cord are called "nociceptors" ("danger receptors"). Nociceptors are high-threshold neurons, which means that a stimulus needs to be of sufficient intensity to evoke a response. The intensity of the stimulus is usually approaching or surpassing that which is damaging to the tissue in which the neuron

resides. Nociceptors are thinner than other peripheral neurons and many of them are not myelinated. They fall into two classes—C fibers (unmyelinated, slow conducting neurons) and Aδ fibers (myelinated, slow conducting neurons). Although all nociceptors are C or Aδ neurones, not all C and Aδ fibers are nociceptors (see Meyer et al.[4] for review).

Nociceptors are located in almost all the tissues of the body (with the notable exception of the brain). This network of neurons can be considered a very thorough surveillance system. Of course, the surveillance function of the peripheral nervous system is much more comprehensive than nociceptors alone—however, nociceptors are always surveying the anatomical landscape for dangerous events. All such events fall into one or more of three categories—thermal, chemical, or mechanical. Thus, nociceptors have specialized receptors that are cold-sensitive, hot-sensitive, chemosensitive, or mechanosensitive. In addition to these high-threshold neurons, humans have low-threshold neurons that are solely interested in one modality or another, such as thermosensitive Aβ fibers, which inform brainstem areas of even tiny fluctuations in tissue temperature—fluctuations that are well within a safe operating range. In contrast to low-threshold single-modal neurons, nociceptors are bimodal or multimodal. That is, they are responsive to thermal and mechanical input, or to thermal, mechanical, and chemical input. These nociceptors, situated in the tissues of the body, are called primary nociceptors (see Bevan[5] and Butler & Moseley[6] for reviews).

Table 6.1 Contrasts between pain as a protective output of the brain and pain as a marker of tissue damage

Pain as a protective output of the brain	Pain as a marker of tissue damage
Pain is in consciousness.	Damage is in the body.
One can *not* be in pain and not know about it.	One can be severely damaged and not know about it.
No brain, no pain.	No body, no damage.
Pain is affected by who is in the area.	Damage is not.
Pain is affected by what else is at stake.	Damage is not.
Pain is affected by beliefs.	Damage is not (well, not directly).
Pain can occur in a body part that does not exist.	Damage cannot.
Pain can occur in a body part that is not damaged.	Damage can occur in a body part that is not painful.
Pain can occur without activation of nociceptors (see below).	Damage cannot (excepting local anesthetic or pre-injury nociceptor death).

Primary nociceptors are also different from other peripheral neurons in that they project to neurons in the dorsal horn of the spinal cord, not to thalamic or cortical structures. The neurons with which primary nociceptors synapse in the spinal cord are called "secondary" or "spinal" nociceptors and the synapse is open to modulatory input from other peripheral inputs and to descending input (see below). That the nociceptive system is polymodal and has a "relay station" in the spinal cord raises two very important issues.

That primary nociceptors are multimodal and only project as far as the spinal cord clearly shows that the nociceptive system, *per se*, is not able to transmit modality-specific information. That is, the nociceptive system does not tell the brain that something is "dangerously hot," or "dangerously cold," or "dangerously squashed." Rather, the nociceptive system has the apparently simple task of telling the brain that something is "dangerous." It is the non-nociceptive inputs that provide critical information about the nature of the danger. The polymodal characteristic also means that, if a stimulus is both dangerously hot and dangerously squashing, it evokes quicker firing of primary nociceptors, which effectively tells the spinal nociceptor that something is "doubly dangerous." To consider a clinical example, if a primary nociceptor is activated by chemicals released by an inflammatory event and the tissues are then poked and prodded, the addition of a mechanical input to the chemical input will increase firing of nociceptors.

That primary nociceptive input is open to modulation at the spinal relay station means that other peripheral input can decrease noxious input. Peripheral input at the spinal relay station is from interneurons that are activated by activation of wide diameter peripheral neurons (Aβ fibers) from the same or adjacent areas. This is why one can, for example, "rub it better" or, in a more sophisticated way, put TENS on it. In fact, TENS was born from Melzack and Wall's famous gate control theory of 1965.[7] Moreover, the spinal relay station can be modulated by descending input from suprapinal structures and it is this descending input that arguably represents a more important and potent modulatory influence.[8]

State-dependent sensitivity of primary nociceptors
Primary nociceptors become sensitized in the presence of chemical irritants. The most common

chemical irritants are generated by the tissues themselves when they are injured. Together, these tissues are called "inflammatory soup" because there are many chemicals involved and the exact ingredients of any particular soup is individual. Figure 6.1 depicts typical inflammation-mediated sensitization of primary nociceptors. This "peripheral sensitization" is exactly that—nociceptors become responsive to stimuli that are not normally evocative. One

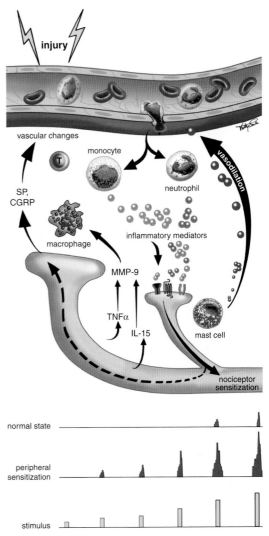

Figure 6.1 A simplified illustration of the connection between nerve terminals and vasculature. The green (normal) and red (sensitized) bars depict nociceptor responses to test stimuli (yellow bars). When there is peripheral sensitization (red bars), even tiny stimuli evoke responses

obvious example is that of sunburn—sunburnt skin hurts when you get into a shower of 40°C (104°F) because nociceptors are sensitized sufficiently to be activated by a thermal stimulus 4–5°C (7–9°F) cooler than that which would normally be required. That peripherally sensitized tissues are heat-sensitive is a very important phenomenon for the reasoning clinician because, as will be mentioned later, centrally sensitized tissue is not heat-sensitive. Therefore, if one has concluded that there is a peripheral problem and one can heat the culprit tissues to 42°C, one can confirm the conclusion, or question it, by determining whether the tissues are more sensitive in the presence of thermal stimuli that would normally be too cool to activate nociceptors (see also Fig. 6.2).

Another aspect of sunburn, the reddening of the skin, is an important aspect of peripheral sensitization. Reddening of the skin is a sign of neurogenic

inflammation (see also Figs 6.1 & 6.2). When nociceptors are activated, an impulse is transmitted along every branch of the nociceptor. If an impulse transmits "in the wrong direction" and arrives at another terminal branch, then it causes the release of chemicals that in themselves are inflammatory and cause vasodilation.[4] This mechanism is responsible for the flare that occurs around a skin wound or scratch. It is an important mechanism if the nociceptor is being activated proximally (e.g. in the dorsal root ganglion or in the spinal cord), because it means that the tissues become inflamed even though the problem is not in the tissues.

State-dependent sensitivity of spinal nociceptors

When spinal nociceptors are active for some time, they too become sensitized. Many biological processes that can contribute to "central sensitization"

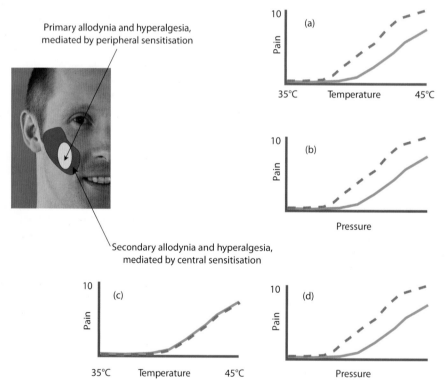

Figure 6.2 Peripheral and central sensitization. Presuming an injury within the lightly shaded zone, the presence of inflammation in the area and activation of primary nociceptors will lead to peripheral sensitization. This will manifest as primary allodynia and hyperalgesia, as represented by a shift in the thermal pain threshold so that pain is evoked at lower temperatures than normal (**a**), and a similar shift in the mechanical pain threshold so that pain is evoked at lower pressures than normal (**b**). If central sensitization ensues, the surrounding area, here represented by the dark shaded zone, will become mechanically sensitive (**d**) but will *not* be thermally sensitive (**c**)

have been uncovered. (In-depth discussion is beyond the scope of this chapter; however, there are several resources that discuss central sensitization in more detail listed at the end of this chapter.) The manifestation of central sensitization is mechanical sensitivity beyond the area of injury and peripheral sensitization (Fig. 6.2). In short, central sensitization means that the spinal cord "upregulates" nociceptive input at the spinal cord (see Woolf & Salter,[8] Doubell, Mannion & Woolf,[9] and Fields & Basbaum[10] for reviews). This has implications for the biopsychosocial model of pain perception which is outlined in Chapter 20 (Fig. 20.2, on page 315).

The brain decides

As was emphasized earlier, pain emerges from the brain and reflects the brain's evaluation of threat to body tissue and the need for action. Spinal nociceptors are important informants in this regard, but, ultimately, nociception is neither sufficient nor necessary for pain (see Table 6.1 on page 42). Modern conceptual models of pain highlight this critical role of the brain. One framework that makes this clear is that of cortical representations (see Butler & Moseley[6] for a clinician-friendly review). According to this framework, an individual will experience, for example, ankle pain, when a network of brain cells, distributed across the brain, is activated. That network of brain cells, then, is considered the neural representation of that individual's ankle pain. As it is a unique and distributed network, one might call it a neurotag.[6] Each of the brain cells that constitute this ankle pain neurotag also contributes to other neurotags, and activation, or otherwise, of this ankle pain neurotag is open to modulation at every synapse of every constituent brain cell. This brings an enormous complexity to the neurophysiology of pain, although pain is simply one expression of the neurophysiology of consciousness, which no one fully understands.

This conceptual framework means that anything that is represented by that individual's brain, *and* which provides credible evidence about the danger to which the ankle is currently exposed, should modulate activity of the ankle pain neurotag. In more clinical terms, anything that provides credible information about the likely danger level should modulate ankle pain. Credible information may relate to likely consequences of damage—for example, ankle damage is more dangerous to a top-level dancer than it is to an archer, a fact that will upregulate the ankle

pain neurotag. However, a top-level dancer might have the long-held belief that her body is indestructible, which would downregulate the ankle pain neurotag. Credible information might relate to other sensory cues—for example, damaging one's ankle on the bend in the final of a 200 m race in front of a screaming crowd may very well lead to those same cues upregulating the ankle pain neurotag when those sensory cues occur again. Clearly, this neural complexity has clear implications for rehabilitation, in that the neuroscience of pain and protection suggests that rehabilitation of this individual with ankle pain is not complete until the athlete has been exposed to every credible byte of information that implies danger to the ankle.

Hopefully you can now appreciate why Descartes' idea, that we have pain receptors in the tissues and pain signals are transmitted to the brain,[3] is inadequate (although popular). The simplicity of Descartes' idea is seductive, but it simply does not hold up. If, as a clinician or patient, one is to accept the true complexity of pain as evidenced by a huge amount of experimental and clinical literature and as conceptualized by the representation framework, then one must also accept that activity in primary nociceptors is one of many contributors to pain. The truly modern-day clinician should be open to non-tissue contributions (i.e. central sensitization or central downregulation) and be alert to evidence of their influence.

Charles Darwin suggested that young scientists should write down the results that do not support their current beliefs because these are the results they are most likely to forget.[11] Perhaps clinicians should do the same. With regard to pain, this would mean writing it down when the same mechanical input flares a condition one day and not the next, when pain is worse in competition than it is in training, when strength, endurance, control, and flexibility are exemplary but the sportsperson still tweaks a hamstring running at 90%. Some such findings might be squeezed into a Descartian framework, but, arguably, they fit more easily into a modern knowledge-based framework.

The brain corrects the spinal cord

The brain has several hundred projections to the spinal nociceptor. Projections originate throughout the brain and have both facilitatory and inhibitory effects. Structures within the brainstem (e.g. the periaqueductal gray [PAG matter]) are important relay stations between the brain and the spinal nociceptor[12,13]. The effect of such a powerful modulatory capacity is, not surprisingly, powerful modulation.

There are many experiments that have investigated how the brain modulates the spinal nociceptors. We can easily summarize them here using the same language as above: once the brain evaluates the true danger level and need for action, it corrects the spinal cord by either inhibiting spinal nociceptors or facilitating them.

Going back to the example of ankle pain, on a neurophysiological level, activation of the brain's ankle pain neurotag sends a copy to a virtual comparator,

which also receives a copy of the ascending spinal nociceptive input. The two inputs are compared and the comparator sends a correction to the midbrain and thence to the distal terminal of the spinal nociceptor (Fig. 6.3).

This kind of feedback loop is embedded in theoretical and experimental investigations of many aspects of human physiology. For example, in motor control the idea of reafference and sensory–motor feedback loops is well established—a motor command is thought to generate an efferent copy that is then compared to sensory feedback of the movement

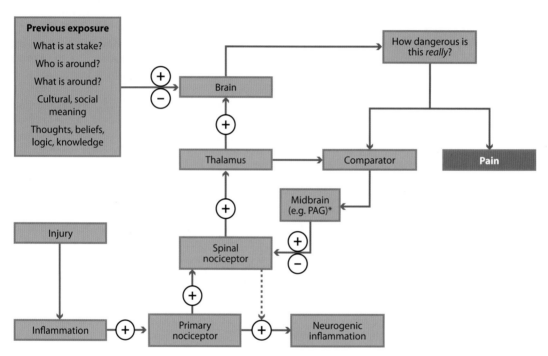

* PAG (periaqueductal gray matter)

Figure 6.3 Feedback loops within the nociceptive system and the endpoint of pain: injury excites primary nociceptors. Injury-induced inflammation activates and sensitizes primary nociceptors (peripheral sensitization). Activation of nociceptors causes neurogenic inflammation in nearby areas and excites spinal nociceptors. Spinal nociceptors project to thalamic nuclei, which then project to the brain. A complex evaluative process occurs within the brain, whereby every byte of information that provides credible evidence about the actual danger faced by the tissues in question is able to upregulate or downregulate the pain neurotag. This process permits the brain to determine "How dangerous is this *really*?" The final "decision" leads to activation of the pain neurotag and pain emerges into consciousness. Simultaneously, as though a bifurcation of a single neural output, the determined danger level is sent to a "comparator," where it is used as a reference for the spinal nociceptor input. This comparator then modulates midbrain structures and thence in turn the spinal nociceptor to "correct" its activation level. Thus, descending modulation can be facilitatory or inhibitory. The broken line from spinal nociceptor towards neurogenic inflammation refers to the possibility of tissue inflammation evoked by descending facilitation. That is, excessive facilitation of the spinal nociceptor in the absence of primary nociceptor activity activates the primary nociceptor antidromically, which induces neurogenic inflammation in the periphery.

(from proprioceptors), and any discrepancy between the predicted and actual outcome is used to correct the motor command.[14]

> If the brain concludes that the need to protect tissues is greater than spinal nociceptor activity would suggest, it will facilitate the spinal nociceptor. If the brain concludes the need to protect is less than spinal nociceptor activity would suggest, it will inhibit the spinal nociceptor.

The effects of such correction will be different if the spinal cord itself is sensitized. That is, if non-tissue factors are increasing the brain's evaluation of danger to a particular tissue, such that the brain upregulates the spinal cord, it has the capacity to maintain, or indeed instigate, central sensitization. There is potential here for a vicious cycle of increasing nociception → increased perceived danger → increased descending facilitation → increased nociception. Thus, it is all the more important for the clinician to evaluate *every* factor that is contributing to the perception of threat to tissues.

When pain persists, the brain changes

In much the same way that spinal nociceptors adapt to become more sensitive, so too do the brain cells that underpin pain[15-18] (see Wand et al.[19] for review of cortical changes in people with pain). That is, the more the pain neurotag is active, the better it gets at being active. This manifests in more and more advanced hyperalgesia and allodynia, extended across modalities and exhibiting "over-generalization." Over-generalization refers to that phenomenon in which pain begins to be evoked by more innocuous stimuli, in different contexts, and under different circumstances. Spreading pain, unpredictable pain, and pain less and less related to tissue activity are cardinal signs of cortical changes.

The full mechanisms and manifestations of cortical sensitivity are not as well understood as the changes in the spinal nociceptor are understood, but they are, at least theoretically, likely to be of far more widespread impact for the clinician and patient. Suffice it to say that the complexity of pain and the adaptability of the nervous system mean that the modern clinician needs to think well beyond the tissues when dealing with anyone in pain. Indeed, common changes in the sensitivity of the nociception/pain system can be mediated at various levels of the neuraxis (Table 6.2).

Treating someone in pain—a complex system requires a comprehensive approach

This chapter is not designed to provide a comprehensive guide to treating the patient in pain. Instead, here is suggested an approach to rehabilitation that integrates at least some of the complexity of the human, and targets aspects of normal and altered physiology associated with pain (Fig. 6.4 overleaf). The model is most established for the management of people in chronic pain.[2] This is extremely relevant to sports and exercise medicine as (i) active people often present with these symptoms, and (ii) our discipline is gaining an increasing reputation for helping patients with chronic pain syndromes. Because the biological mechanisms that underpin pain are the same for acute and chronic pain, although with increasing sensitivity as pain persists, the model is applicable across patient groups.

Table 6.2 Clinical patterns of increased sensitivity to peripheral stimuli and possible underlying mechanisms.

Clinical manifestation	Possible underlying cause
Mechanical allodynia: mechanical stimuli that do not normally evoke pain now do.	Peripheral sensitization, central sensitization, cortical modulation
Thermal allodynia: heat pain threshold is decreased.	Peripheral sensitization, cortical modulation
Hyperalgesia: normally painful stimuli are now more painful.	Peripheral sensitization, central sensitization, cortical modulation
Primary hyperalgesia	Hyperalgesia attributed to peripheral sensitization
Secondary hyperalgesia	Hyperalgesia attributed to central sensitization

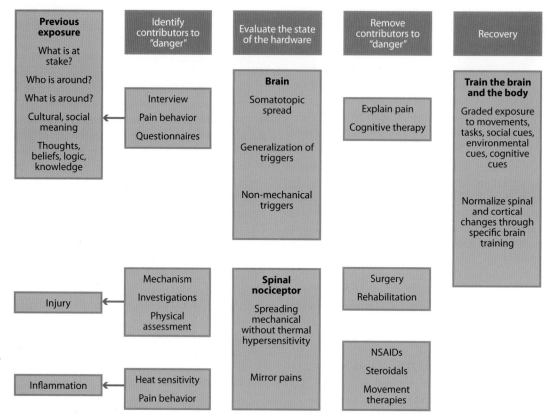

Figure 6.4 Major contributions to pain and their clinical implications.
The left column lists the major contributions to the brain's evaluation of danger to tissues, which determines pain and descending modulation. The second column suggests mechanisms with which to assess the major contributions, thereby identifying key triggers. The middle column suggests signs of spinal and cortical sensitization, so as to determine the state of the nociceptive system. The fourth column suggests approaches to minimize the impact of the triggers that have been identified. (Note that this extends beyond physical approaches to include cognitive and educational approaches.) The final column recommends avenues to recovery. (Note the emphasis on training both the body and the brain, via specific techniques and graded exposure to physical and non-physical triggers.)

Clinical approach to referred pain— often neglected in clinical teaching

As outlined above, pain and nociception are not the same thing. That pain does not exist in the tissues, but is created by the brain, is clearly demonstrated by referred pain. In referred pain, an error occurs in the brain's processes that determine where, exactly, it should hurt. That is, the location of the nociceptive input is "misread" by the brain. Perhaps the most famous and clinically recognized example of referred pain is pain in the neck or left arm when the heart is in fact in danger. Another common example is leg pain when the nociceptive input arises from a structure in the back. See the box opposite and Table 6.3

for examples of referred pain often encountered in the sports and exercise medicine clinic.

It is important to keep in mind that there is always a reason for pain. That pain is the end-point of a complex, danger-relevant processing system means that, when the tissue that hurts seems normal, we need to look elsewhere rather than presume the patient is not really in pain. So just because the pattern of pain does not fit a recognized diagnosis, to conclude that the pain does not exist is to conclude that your patient is lying. A key theme of this chapter is that when considering what it means to "look elsewhere" we must remain open to the possibility that non-noxious triggers are dominating the pain state.

Four case scenarios—referred pain is a common culprit!

- A patient presents with a long history of intermittent dull occipital headache. The patient is thoroughly investigated for eye problems and the presence of intracranial pathology. All tests are normal.
- A patient presents with a history of an ache in the right shoulder that is difficult to localize and is associated with pain on the medial aspect of the upper arm. There is some neck stiffness and tightness in the trapezius muscle.
- A 35-year-old executive complains of episodes of sharp left-sided chest pain related to activity. The patient has already undergone extensive cardiological investigations that were all normal.
- A young sportsperson presents with a history of recurrent episodes of buttock and hamstring pain. There is no history of an acute tear and the patient describes the pain as deep-seated and dull with occasional sharp cramping in the hamstring. Examination of the hamstring shows some mild tenderness but full stretch and strength.

All of the above clinical presentations are common in sports and exercise medicine practice. All these patients are experiencing referred pain. Unless this is recognized, treatment will be unsuccessful.

With regard to referred pain, "looking elsewhere" means to consider that the brain is wrongly locating the pain and that there is a noxious contributor elsewhere. This does not mean we randomly select tissues to assess. Rather, there is a mountain of clinical data, and an ever-growing body of neuroanatomical data, that provide common patterns, and mechanisms, of referred pain. The dominant mechanisms are radicular referred pain and somatic referred pain.

Radicular pain

Radicular pain (a topic that is commonly taught to undergraduate health professionals) is pain associated with nerve root compression or irritation. It has the characteristic quality of sharp, shooting pain in a relatively narrow band, known as "a dermatome" (Fig. 6.5). If the radicular pain is associated with compression of the nerve root, it is usually accompanied by neurological abnormalities (e.g. paresthesia corresponding to a dermatomal distribution, muscle weakness). Irritation of the dorsal root ganglion can evoke a similar distribution of pain, although the shooting pain may be delayed for several seconds and often reverberates (see Butler & Moseley[6] for more on this). That nerve root irritation and dorsal root ganglion irritation evoke pain in the area normally supplied by the affected nerve is intuitively sensible. The spinal neurons that convey the danger message have no method by which to differentiate where along the primary nociceptor the activity was generated. (A helpful metaphor for explaining this to patients is that of the Paris–London express train—normally, this train is a non-stop service, so the station master at London knows that the number of passengers disembarking in London reflects the number of passengers boarding in Paris. However, if

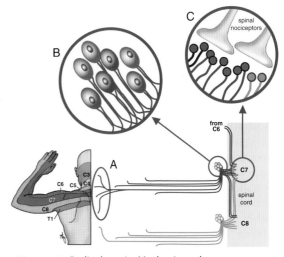

Figure 6.5 Radicular pain. Mechanisms that can contribute to radicular pain by convergence of multiple incoming nociceptors. Radicular pain within the peripheral supply of a single spinal segment can occur via convergence of multiple branches of single nociceptors (**A**), or within the dorsal root ganglion of that peripheral nerve (**B**). Pain within adjacent spinal nerve root territory can occur via convergence within the dorsal horn, where projections from levels below or above can terminate alongside those from the spinal segment concerned (**C**)

something is wrong along the line, perhaps at Calais, such that the train stops there to pick up passengers, the station master in London will *wrongly* conclude that there are more people than usual boarding at Paris.)

Somatic pain

The other type of referred pain (which residents generally are not familiar with when they begin their sports and exercise medicine rotation) is often called somatic referred pain. The mechanisms that underpin somatic referred pain are not as structurally simple as radicular referred pain, because the "disrupted transmission" occurs within the central nervous system, perhaps at the dorsal horn in the spinal cord (e.g. where visceral and musculoskeletal afferents converge, such as is the case with left arm pain evoked by cardiac problems, or where immune mechanisms form functional connections with contralateral spinal nociceptors such as might evoke "mirror pains" at the identical site on the opposite limb), in the thalamus, or in the brain. One can conceptualize somatic referred pain as the brain attempting to localize the pain in response to ambiguous input. This means that the boundaries of pain are not precisely marked, that the pain can move, and that there is a large amount of variability between individuals. Two structures that are widely held to be common contributors to somatic referred pain are myofascial trigger points and joints.

Somatic pain associated with "trigger points"

Trigger points are present in all patients with chronic musculoskeletal pain and are thought to reflect sensitization of nociceptive processing in the central nervous system (Fig. 6.2). Dr Janet Travell first published on myofascial pain in 1942, so it is not surprising that new data challenge her initial theories about the mechanisms that underpin soft tissue pain. Together with David Simons, she defined a trigger point as "a discrete, focal, hyperirritable spot in a taut band of muscle."[20] The spots are painful on compression and can produce referred pain, referred tenderness, motor dysfunction, and autonomic phenomena. Trigger points are classified as being "active" or "latent" depending on their clinical characteristics.

An active trigger point is associated with pain at rest. It is tender to palpation with a referred pain pattern that is similar to the patient's pain complaint. When stimulated, an active trigger point sets off a "local twitch response" in the affected muscle. A local twitch response is defined as "a transient visible or palpable contraction or dimpling of the muscle and skin." Evaluation of the electromyographic activity of the trigger point reveals unique, prolonged, and rapid motor end-plate activity.[21]

Patients with active trigger points present with persistent regional pain. It is usually related to activity,

although it can be constant. Occasionally it is worse at night and can interfere with sleep. It is frequently associated with muscle shortening and decreased range of motion. The most common areas affected (with the site of the trigger points in brackets) are the head and neck (upper trapezius, sternocleidomastoid muscles), shoulder girdle (supraspinatus, infraspinatus), low back and pelvis (quadratus lumborum, gluteal muscles), and hamstring region (gluteal, piriformis). These patterns clearly reflect central convergence of peripheral inputs, which further implicates the central nervous system in their generation and contribution to a pain state.

Elimination of myofascial trigger points is an important component of the management of chronic musculoskeletal pain. Suggested methods of eliminating trigger points include the cold and stretch technique advocated by Travell and Simons,[20] application of various physical therapy modalities, soft tissue techniques such as myofascial release and ischemic pressure, and injections of local anesthetic or corticosteroid.

We have found ischemic pressure and dry needling to be the most effective (Chapter 13). Although these techniques are widely used, the mechanisms that underpin their effects are not well understood—they could involve modulation of nociceptive mechanisms at a peripheral, spinal, thalamic, or cortical level. Indeed, they could even involve high-order mechanisms associated with the emergence of pain itself. This is a field where clinical practice may change as new evidence emerges, or new evidence may underscore the validity of current clinical practice.

Somatic pain from joints

Examples of somatic pain from joints are pain in the hamstring and buttock associated with nociceptive input from the anulus fibrosus of the intervertebral disk or the apophyseal joint, and pain around the shoulder, which may be associated with nociceptive input from structures in the cervical spine. That somatic pain can be referred from a joint provides the critical rationale for joint mobilization.[22]

Recognizing somatic referred pain

Somatic referred pain is a static, dull ache that is hard to localize. It is not accompanied by neurological abnormalities. Clearly the possibility of somatic referred pain should be considered in any patient presenting with pain that is dull and poorly localized and where the physical assessment does not identify tissues within the painful zone to be primary nociceptive contributors. This is not a trivial task because painful areas become sensitive areas through the usual processes of neurogenic inflammation and central sensitization. Understanding the neurobiology of acute and chronic pain should greatly enhance the precision and interpretation of assessment—particularly when pain is chronic. Critically, patients with somatic referred pain have been mislabeled as "crackpots" by clinicians who are only familiar with radicular pain. Clinicians unfamiliar with the biology of nociception and pain assume, incorrectly, that the patient is malingering.

Because somatic referred pain often reflects the brain's attempt to *best* localize a noxious event in the presence of ambiguous or conflicting information, the location of the pain often moves, even to the point of "jumping sides." Fields of referred pain from particular segments overlap greatly, both within and between individuals. Therefore, mapping of these areas of pain distribution (sclerotomes) should only be used as a guide.

Clinical assessment of referred pain

The possibility that some or all of the patient's pain may be referred from another source should be considered in all cases of musculoskeletal pain. Features of pain that suggest it is more likely to be referred include:

- a dull, aching nature
- poorly localized
- deep-seated
- movement from point to point
- less local tenderness than expected
- longstanding pain
- a failure to respond to local treatment.

While it is not possible to map out distinct patterns of referred somatic pain, there are common sites of referred pain that tend to emanate from particular regions. These sites are shown in Table 6.3 overleaf. The examination of any patient presenting with pain in one of these regions must include an examination of all possible sites of nociceptive input.

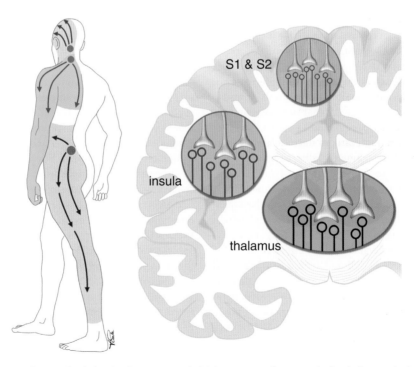

Figure 6.6 Somatic (non-radicular) pain. Convergence in higher centres, for example the thalamus, the insula and the primary (S1) and secondary (S2) somatosensory areas, can result in pain referred in non-radicular patterns, for example within a limb or body segment or 'quadrant'

Table 6.3 Common sites of referred pain

Site of referred pain	Source of pain
Occipital headache	Upper cervical spine TrPs in upper trapezius, sterncleidomastoid
Shoulder	Lower cervical, upper thoracic spine TrPs in supraspinatus, infraspinatus
Lateral elbow	Lower cervical (C5–6), upper thoracic spine TrPs in forearm extensor muscles, supinator, and triceps
Chest wall	Thoracic spine TrPs in pectoral major, intercostals muscles
Sacroiliac region, loin, flank	Thoracolumnbar junction (L4–5) TrPs in quadratus lumborum
Groin	Sacroiliac joint, thoracolumbar junction, upper lumbar spine TrPs in adductors, gluteal muscles
Buttock, hamstring	Lumbar spine, sacroiliac joint TrPs in gluteal muscles and piriformis
Lateral knee/thigh	Lumbar spine TrPs in tensor fascia lata. gluteus minimus

TrPs = trigger points

The aim of clinical assessment is to reproduce the referred pain by stressing the hypothesized nociceptive driver. This is achieved by local palpation if the source is muscle, by passive or active joint movement (physiological or accessory) if the source is joint, or by increasing neuromechanical sensitivity if the source is neural. Inability to reproduce the referred pain does not necessarily exclude the diagnosis of referred pain.

Any significant abnormality of joints, muscle, or neural structures at a site that is a possible contributor to referred pain should be noted. The best means of confirming this is to treat the abnormality (e.g. restore full motion to the joint, eliminate active trigger points, or restore normal neural mechanosensitivity) and then determine the effect on the pain.

Consider a patient presenting with low back pain with contributions from joint, muscle, and neural structures. This patient later develops unilateral buttock and upper hamstring pain in addition to the low back pain. It is dull and aching in quality and is poorly localized. On local examination, there is diffuse minimal local tenderness with good hamstring stretch and strength. Assessment of possible sources of this patient's hamstring and buttock pain involves a neuromechanical sensitivity test (the slump test) to assess the contribution of neural structures, palpation of the joints of the lumbar spine to assess the possible joint contribution, and palpation

of the paravertebral and gluteal muscles to assess the presence of active trigger points and taut bands. Any abnormalities found on assessment are then treated and the effect on the patient's symptoms and functional activity reviewed.

Clinical summary

Pain is a complex experience that serves to motivate us to protect the tissues of our body. Primary nociceptors serve as an "always on" surveillance system that alerts the brain to dangerous or potentially dangerous stimuli. This danger message is processed in the spinal cord, then in the thalamus, and then in the brain. Pain emerges from the brain into consciousness if the brain decides that tissue is in fact in danger and it needs to be protected. Anything that relates to the brain's evaluation of danger to body tissue will modulate pain. The brain modulates the spinal cord to upregulate or downregulate activity of the spinal nociceptor. Moreover, as pain persists, the mechanisms that subserve nociception become more sensitive. The brain can refer pain to an area that is not in fact in danger if there is a disruption in the peripheral nervous system (radicular referred pain) or in the central nervous system (somatic referred pain). Clinical assessment should engage with the complexity of pain and consider referred pain patterns and non-tissue contributions to a pain state.

RECOMMENDED READING

Butler D, Moseley GL. *Explain pain*. Adelaide: NOI Group Publishing, 2003.

McMahon SB, Koltzenburg M, eds. *Wall and Melzack's textbook of pain*. 5th edn. London: Elsevier 2006.

Moseley GL. A pain neuromatrix approach to patients with chronic pain. *Man Ther* 2003;8(3):130–140.

Moseley GL. *Painful yarns. Metaphors and stories to help understand the biology of pain*. Canberra: Dancing Giraffe Press, 2007.

Moseley GL. Reconceptualising pain according to modern pain science. *Phys Ther Rev* 2007;12(3):169–78.

Schaible HG, Del Rosso A, Matucci-Cerinic M. Neurogenic aspects of inflammation. *Rheum Dis Clin North Am* 2005;31(1):77–101,ix.

Tracey I, Mantyh PW. The cerebral signature and its modulation for pain perception. *Neuron* 2007;55(3):377–91.

REFERENCES

1. Jennings HS. Studies on reactions to stimuli in unicellular organisms. *J Physiol* 1897;21(4–5):258–322.

2. Moseley GL. Reconceptualising pain according to modern pain science. *Phys Ther Rev* 2007;12(3):169–78.

3. Descartes R. *L'Homme*. Paris, 1644.

4. Meyer R, Ringkamp M, Campbell JN, Raja SN. Peripheral mechanisms of cutaneous nociception. In: McMahon SB, Koltzenburg M, eds. *Wall and Melzack's textbook of pain*. 5th edn. London: Elsevier, 2006:3–35.

5. Bevan S. Nociceptive peripheral neurons: cellular properties. In: Wall P, Melzack R, eds. *Wall and Melzack's textbook of pain*. 4th edn. Edinburgh: Churchill Livingstone, 1999:85–103.

6. Butler D, Moseley GL. *Explain pain*. Adelaide: NOI Group Publishing, 2003.

7. Melzack R, Wall PD. Pain mechanisms: a new theory. *Science* 1965;150(699):971–9.

8. Woolf CJ, Salter M. Plasticity and pain: the role of the dorsal horn. In: McMahon SB, Koltzenburg M, eds. *Wall and Melzack's textbook of pain*. 5th edn. London: Elsevier, 2006:91–107.

9. Doubell TP, Mannion RJ, Woolf CJ. The dorsal horn: state-dependent sensory processing, plasticity and the generation of pain. In: Wall P, Melzack R, eds. *Wall and Melzack's textbook of pain*. 4th edn. Edinburgh: Churchill Livingstone, 1999:165–81.

10. Fields HL, Basbaum AI. Central nervous system mechanisms of pain modulation. In: Wall P, Melzack R, eds. *Wall and Melzack's textbook of pain*. 4th edn. Edinburgh: Churchill Livingstone, 1999:309–29.

11. Darwin F. *The life and letters of Charles Darwin, including an autobiographical chapter*. London: John Murray, 1887.

12. Giesler GJ, Liebeskind JC. Inhibition of visceral pain by electrical stimulation of the periaqueductal gray matter. *Pain* 1976;2(1):43–8.

13. Tracey I, Ploghaus A, Gati JS et al. Imaging attentional modulation of pain in the periaqueductal gray in humans. *J Neurosci* 2002;22(7):2748–52.

14. Von Holst H. Relations between the central nervous system and the peripheral organs. *Br J Animal Behav* 1950;2:89–94.

15. Apkarian AV, Bushnell MC, Treede RD, Zubieta JK. Human brain mechanisms of pain perception and regulation in health and disease. *Eur J Pain* 2005;9(4):463–84.

16. Apkarian AV, Grachev ID, Krauss BR, Szeverenyi M. Imaging brain pathophysiology in chronic CRPS pain. In: Harden RN, Baron R, Janig W, eds. *Progress in pain research and management*. Seattle: IASP Press, 2001:209–26.

17. Baliki MN, Geha PY, Apkarian AV. Spontaneous pain and brain activity in neuropathic pain: functional MRI and pharmacologic functional MRI studies. *Curr Pain Headache Rep* 2007;11(3):171–7.

18. Baliki MN, Geha PY, Apkarian AV, Chialvo DR. Beyond feeling: chronic pain hurts the brain, disrupting the default-mode network dynamics. *J Neurosci* 2008;28(6):1398–403.

19. Wand BM, Parkitny L, O'Connell NE et al. Cortical changes in chronic low back pain: current state of the art and implications for clinical practice. *Man Ther* 2011 Feb;16(1):15–20.

20. Simons DG, Travell JG, Simons LS. *Travell and Simons' myofascial pain and dysfunction: the trigger point manual, upper half of body*. Vol 1. 2nd edn. Baltimore: Williams & Wilkins, 1999.

21. Gerwin RD. Myofascial pain and fibromyalgia: diagnosis and treatment. *J Back Musculoskelet Rehabil* 1998;11(3):175–81.

22. Gross A, Miller J, D'Sylva J et al. Manipulation or mobilisation for neck pain. *Cochrane Database Syst Rev* (1):CD004249.

A

Chapter 7

Beware: conditions masquerading as sports injuries

with NICK CARTER

This is a wise maxim, "to take warning from others of what may be to your own advantage."
Terence. *Heautontimoroumenos*, Act i. Sc. 2, 36 (210), circa 185 BC

Not every patient who presents to the sports and exercise medicine clinician has a sports-related condition. Sports and exercise medicine has its share of conditions that must not be missed—"red flag" conditions that may appear at first to be rather benign. The patient with the minor "calf strain" may have a deep venous thrombosis; the young basketball player who has been labeled as having Osgood-Schlatter disease may actually have an osteosarcoma. In this chapter we:

* outline a clinical approach that should maximize your chances of recognizing a condition that is "masquerading" as a sports-related condition
* describe some of these conditions and illustrate how they can present.

How to recognize a condition masquerading as a sports injury

As always, the key to recognizing that everything is not as the first impression might suggest is a thorough history and a detailed physical examination. If you do not recognize a masquerading condition from the history and examination, it is unlikely you will order the appropriate investigations to make the diagnosis. For example, if a patient presents with tibial pain and it is, in fact, due to hypercalcemia secondary to lung cancer, a bone scan of the tibia looking for stress fracture will usually not help with the diagnosis, but a history of weight loss, occasional hemoptysis, and associated abdominal pain may. In a basketball player with shoulder pain, the history of associated arm tightness and the physical finding of prominent superficial veins are more important

clues to axillary vein thrombosis than would be a gray-scale ultrasound scan looking for rotator cuff tendinopathy.

If there is something about the history and examination that does not fit the pattern of the common conditions, then consider alternative, less common conditions. You must ask yourself, "Could this be a rare condition or unusual manifestation?" Then other options are entertained, and the appropriate diagnosis can be conceived. Thus, successful diagnosis of masquerading conditions requires recognition of a discrepancy between the patient's clinical features and the typical clinical pattern.

Conditions masquerading as sports injuries

Table 7.1 lists some of the conditions that may masquerade as sports and exercise medicine conditions. These are outlined below.

Bone and soft tissue tumors

Primary malignant tumors of bone and soft tissues are rare, but when they occur it is most likely to be in the younger age group (second to third decade). Osteosarcomata can present at the distal or proximal end of long bones, more commonly in the lower limb, producing joint pain. Patients often recognize that pain is aggravated by activity and hence present to the sports and exercise medicine clinic. The pathological diagnosis of osteosarcoma is dependent on the detection of tumor-producing bone and so an X-ray may reveal a moth-eaten appearance with new bone formation in the soft tissues and lifting of the

Table 7.1 Conditions that may masquerade as sports and exercise medicine conditions

Bone and soft tissue tumors	Vascular
Osteosarcoma	Venous thrombosis (e.g. deep venous thrombosis, axillary vein thrombosis)
Synovial sarcoma	Artery entrapment (e.g. popliteal artery entrapment)
Synovial chondromatosis	Peripheral vascular disease
Pigmented villonodular synovitis	**Genetic**
Rhabdomyosarcoma	Marfan syndrome
Osteoid osteoma	Hemochromatosis
Ganglion cyst	**Granulomatous diseases**
Rheumatological	Tuberculosis
Inflammatory monoarthritis	Sarcoidosis
Inflammatory polyarthritis	**Infection**
Inflammatory low back pain (e.g. sacroiliitis)	Osteomyelitis
Enthesopathies (e.g. psoriatic, reactive arthritis)	Septic arthritis
Disorders of muscle	Shingles
Dermatomyositis	Lyme disease
Polymyositis	**Regional pain syndromes**
Muscular dystrophy	Complex regional pain syndrome
Endocrine	Fibromyalgia/myofascial pain syndrome
Dysthyroidism	
Hypercalcemia	
Hypocalcemia	
Hyperparathyroidism	
Diabetes	
Cushing's syndrome	
Acromegaly	

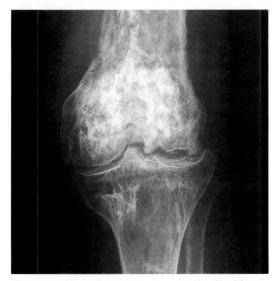

Figure 7.1 X-ray of an osteosarcoma in the distal femur

periosteum (Fig. 7.1). In young patients, the differential diagnosis includes osteomyelitis. It is recommended that any child or adolescent with bone pain be X-rayed. Surgery is the preferred treatment.

Synovial sarcomata frequently involve the larger lower joints, such as the knee and ankle. Patients present with pain, often at night or with activity, maybe with instability and swelling.

Trauma may result in hemorrhage into a rhabdomyosarcoma. In patients with hematomata that are slow to resolve, or where the history of trauma does not fit with the clinical signs, the clinician should consider this alternative diagnosis.

Malignant tumors (e.g. of the breast, lung, and prostate) may metastasize to bone. Patients may not recognize that a previously treated malignancy could be related to their limb pain. Breast carcinoma may also present as a frozen shoulder. An accurate history is, therefore, central to making an accurate diagnosis. Red flag signs for malignancy or infection include prominent night pain, often being woken at night with pain, fever, loss of appetite, weight loss, and malaise. Patients exhibiting these symptoms should be examined and investigated thoroughly to determine the cause.

Synovial chondromatosis and pigmented villon-odular synovitis[1] are benign tumors of the synovium found mainly in the knee; they present with mechanical symptoms.

Osteoid osteoma (Fig. 7.2a) is a benign bone tumor that often presents as exercise-related bone pain and tenderness and is, therefore, frequently misdiagnosed as a stress fracture. The bone scan appearance is also similar to that of a stress fracture, although the isotope uptake is more intense and widespread. This condition is characterized clinically by the presence of night pain and by the abolition of symptoms with the use of aspirin. The tumor has a characteristic appearance on CT scan (Fig. 7.2b) with a central nidus.

Ganglion cysts are lined by connective tissue, contain mucinous fluid, and are found mainly around the wrist, hand, knee, and foot. They may be attached to a joint capsule or tendon sheath, and may have a connection to the synovial cavity. They are usually asymptomatic, but can occasionally cause pain and cosmetic deformity (see Chapter 23).[2]

Rheumatological conditions
Rheumatological conditions are dealt with in greater detail in the section on multiple joint problems (Chapter 55). Patients with inflammatory musculoskeletal disorders frequently present to the sports and exercise medicine clinic with their condition masquerading as a traumatic or mechanical condition. Low back pain of ankylosing spondylitis, psoriatic enthesopathy[3] presenting as patellar tendinopathy, or flitting arthritis in early rheumatoid arthritis are common examples.

Effective management of sportspeople presenting with musculoskeletal complaints requires a structured history, physical examination, and definitive diagnosis to distinguish soft tissue problems from joint problems, and an inflammatory syndrome from a non-inflammatory syndrome. Clues to a systemic inflammatory etiology include constitutional symptoms, morning stiffness, elevated acute-phase reactants, and progressive symptoms despite modification of physical activity. The mechanism of injury or lack thereof is also a clue to any underlying disease. In these circumstances, a more complete work-up is reasonable, including radiographs, MR imaging, and laboratory testing for autoantibodies.[4]

In patients presenting with an acutely swollen knee without a history of precipitant trauma or patellar tendinopathy without overload, the clinician may be alerted to the possibility that these could be inflammatory in origin. Prominent morning joint or back stiffness, night pain, or extra-articular manifestations of rheumatological conditions (e.g. skin rashes, nail abnormalities—Fig. 7.3), bowel disturbance, eye

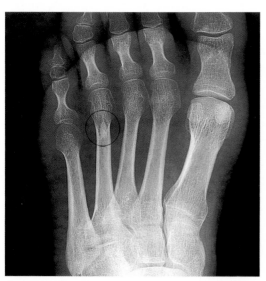

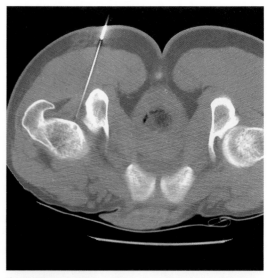

Figure 7.2 Osteoid osteoma **(a)** X-ray of an osteoid osteoma

(b) CT scan of an osteoid osteoma about to undergo radioablation therapy

Figure 7.3 Typical appearance of nails in a patient with psoriatic arthropathy

involvement (conjunctivitis, iritis) or urethral discharge may all provide clues.

Inflammation of entheses (e.g. in lateral elbow pain, patellar tendinopathy [Fig. 7.4], insertional Achilles tendinopathy, and plantar fasciitis) is almost universal among those with HLA (human leukocyte antigens) B27-related, seronegative (for rheumatoid factor) arthropathies. Enthesopathy is usually associated with other joint or extra-articular involvement, although a subgroup exists with enthesitis as the sole presentation.

Disorders of muscle

Dermatomyositis and polymyositis are inflammatory connective tissue disorders characterized by proximal limb girdle weakness, often without pain. Dermatomyositis, unlike polymyositis, is also associated with a photosensitive skin rash in light-exposed areas

(hands and face). In the older adult, dermatomyositis may be associated with malignancy in approximately 50% of cases. The primary malignancy may be easily detectable, or it may be occult. In the younger adult, weakness may be profound (e.g. inability to rise from the floor); however, in the early stages it may manifest only as under-performance in training or competition.

Dermatomyositis and polymyositis may also be associated with other connective tissue disorders such as systemic lupus erythematosus or systemic sclerosis, and muscle abnormality is characterized by elevated creatine kinase levels and electromyographic (EMG) and muscle biopsy changes.

Endurance sportspeople may complain of myalgia and fatigue that is out of proportion with their training schedule. The differential diagnosis to explain these symptoms is broad. Mitochondrial myopathies, although uncommon, may present with cramping and muscle pain.[5] Consider myoglobinuria in these patients. Referral to a specialist neurologist for investigations and diagnosis will be necessary.[6]

Regional limb girdle dystrophies, such as limb girdle dystrophy and facio-scapulo-humeral dystrophy, may also present with proximal limb girdle weakness in young adults. These are also associated with characteristic EMG changes.

Endocrine disorders

Disorders of thyroid function may present with a variety of rheumatological conditions.[7] Proximal muscle weakness with elevated creatine kinase and fibromyalgia may develop with hypothyroidism. Hyperthyroidism is associated with thyroid acropachy (soft tissue swelling and periosteal bone

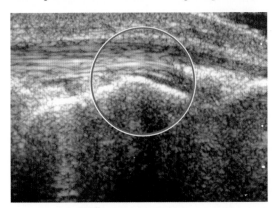
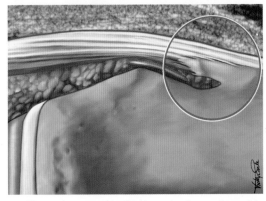

Figure 7.4 Calcification (circled) of the distal portion of the patellar tendon near the tibial insertion in a patient with psoriatic arthropathy **(a)** Sagittal midline ultrasound scan **(b)** Anatomical depiction with arrow pointing to proximal tibial articular surface for orientation

changes), adhesive capsulitis, and also painless proximal muscle weakness.[4] Hyperparathyroidism may be associated with the deposition of calcium pyrophosphate in joints. Patients may develop acute pseudogout or a polyarticular inflammatory arthritis resembling rheumatoid arthritis. X-rays of the wrists or knees may demonstrate chondrocalcinosis of the menisci or triangular fibrocartilage complex (Fig. 7.5).

Adhesive capsulitis or septic arthritis may be the presenting complaint in patients with diabetes mellitus, and those with other endocrine disorders such as acromegaly may develop premature osteoarthritis or carpal tunnel syndrome. Patients with hypercalcemia secondary to malignancy (e.g. of the lung), or other conditions such as hyperparathyroidism, can present with bone pain as well as constipation, confusion, and renal calculi. A proximal myopathy may develop in patients with primary Cushing's syndrome or after corticosteroid use.

Vascular disorders

Patients with venous thrombosis or arterial abnormalities (Fig. 7.6) may present with limb pain and swelling aggravated by exercise. Calf, femoral, or axillary veins are common sites for thrombosis. While a precipitant cause may be apparent (e.g. recent surgery or air travel), consider also the thrombophilias such as the antiphospholipid syndrome, or deficiencies of protein C, protein S, antithrombin III, or factor V Leiden.

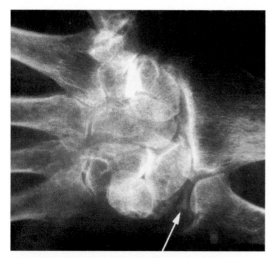

Figure 7.5 Chondrocalcinosis of the triangular fibrocartilage in calcium pyrophosphate dihydrate deposition disease

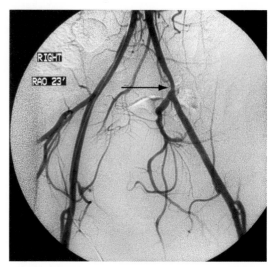

Figure 7.6 Angiogram showing common iliac artery stenosis

The claudicant pain of peripheral vascular disease is most likely to be first noticed with exercise, and so patients may present to the sports and exercise medicine clinician. Remember also that arteriopathy can occur in patients with diabetes. Various specific vascular entrapments are also found, such as popliteal artery entrapment, which presents as exercise-related calf pain, and thoracic outlet syndrome.

Genetic disorders

Marfan syndrome is an autosomal dominant disorder of fibrillin characterized by musculoskeletal, cardiac, and ocular abnormalities (see also Chapter 48).[8] Musculoskeletal problems are common due to joint hypermobility, ligament laxity, scoliosis, or spondylolysis. In patients with the Marfanoid habitus, referral for echocardiography and ophthalmological opinion should be considered, as sudden cardiac death (Chapter 48) or lens dislocation may result.

Hemochromatosis is an autosomal recessive disorder of iron handling, which results in iron overload. Patients may present with a calcium pyrophosphate arthropathy, with characteristic involvement of the second and third metacarpophalangeal joints and hook-shaped osteophytes seen on X-ray of these joints. While ferritin levels are raised in patients with hemochromatosis, it is important to remember that ferritin may also be elevated in sportspeople taking iron supplements, or in response to any acute inflammatory illness.[9] Fasting transferrin levels and detection of the HFE gene (the hemochromatosis gene) are central to the diagnosis of inherited hemochromatosis.

Granulomatous diseases

Tuberculosis is a granulomatous mycobacterial infection. Musculoskeletal involvement includes chronic septic arthritis and Pott's spine fracture.

Patients with acute sarcoidosis can present with fevers, lower limb (commonly) rash, and ankle swelling. The rash of erythema nodosum (Fig. 7.7) may be mistaken for cellulitis, and antibiotics have frequently been prescribed in error. The diagnosis is easily made by chest X-ray, which shows changes of bilateral hilar lymphadenopathy. (The differential diagnosis of bilateral hilar lymphadenopathy includes tuberculosis and lymphoma.) Chronic sarcoidosis is a systemic disorder involving the lungs, central nervous system, skin, eyes, and musculoskeletal system. Patients can present with chronic arthropathy together with bone cysts, or with bone pain due to hypercalcemia.

Infection

Bone and joint infections, while uncommon, may have disastrous consequences if the diagnosis is missed. Bone pain in children, worse at night or with activity, should alert the clinician to the possibility of osteomyelitis. Bone infection near a joint may result in a reactive joint effusion.

Septic arthritis is rare in the normal joint. However, in arthritic, recently arthrocentesed or diabetic joints, sepsis is much more common. Rapid joint destruction may follow if sepsis is left untreated.

Even though *Staphylococcus aureus* is the causative organism in more than 50% of cases of acute septic joints, it is imperative that joint aspiration for Gram stain, and culture and blood cultures are taken before commencement of antibiotic treatment. Once-

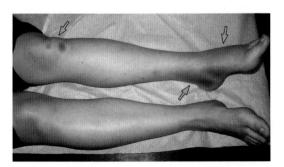

Figure 7.7 Erythema nodosum in acute sarcoidosis
PHOTO COURTESY OF RAHEEM B KHERANI

only or repeated joint lavage may be considered in patients receiving intravenous antibiotic treatment. The immunocompromised patient may present with a chronic septic arthritis. In this situation, tuberculosis or fungal infections should be considered. In suspected cases of septic arthritis, the patient should be admitted to hospital.[10]

Another cause of arthritis is Lyme disease, a common arthropod-borne infection in some countries including the US. Hallmarks of Lyme disease are erythema migrans, disruption of electrical conduction of cardiac muscle, the development of neurological abnormalities, and episodes of arthritis. Intermittent episodes of arthritis occur several weeks or months after infection and, despite adequate antibiotic therapy, symptoms persist in 10% of patients with arthritis. The severity of arthritis can range from mild to moderate inflammation of the joints and tendons months after infection, to a chronic, debilitating osteoarthropathy complete with destruction of cartilage and erosion of bone within a few years in a subset of these individuals. In severe cases, the highly inflammatory aspects of Lyme arthritis can lead to cartilage and bone erosion with permanent joint dysfunction. The diagnosis of Lyme disease is clinical, and serological tests should be used to confirm the clinical diagnosis.[11]

Pain syndromes

Complex regional pain syndrome type I is a post-traumatic phenomenon characterized by localized pain out of proportion to the injury, vasomotor disturbances, edema, and delayed recovery from injury. The vasomotor disturbances of an extremity manifest as vasodilation (warmth, redness) or vasoconstriction (coolness, cyanosis, mottling).[12] Early mobilization, use of motor imagery, and avoidance of surgery are important keys to successful management (see also Chapter 6).

Myofascial pain syndromes develop secondary to either acute or overuse trauma. They present as regional pain associated with the presence of one or more active trigger points (Chapter 6).

Fibromyalgia is a chronic pain syndrome characterized by widespread pain, chronic fatigue, decreased pain threshold, sleep disturbance, psychological distress, and characteristic tender points. It is often associated with other symptoms including irritable bowel syndrome, dyspareunia, headache, irritable bladder, and subjective joint swelling and pain. Fibromyalgia is diagnosed on the examination finding of 11 of 18 specific tender point sites in a patient with widespread pain. Chronic fatigue syndrome has many similarities to fibromyalgia[10] and may be the same disease process. It may present as excessive post-exercise muscle soreness, but is always associated with excessive fatigue. There is evidence that exercise improves global wellbeing in women with this condition.[13]

📄 RECOMMENDED READING

Abraham P, Chevalier JM, Leftheriotis G et al. Lower extremity arterial disease in sports. *Am J Sports Med* 1997;25(4):581–4.

Abraham P, Saumet JL, Chevalier JM. External iliac artery endofibrosis in athletes. *Sports Med* 1997;24(4):221–6.

Damron TA, Morris C, Rougraff B et al. Diagnosis and treatment of joint-related tumors that mimic sports-related injuries. *Instr Course Lect* 2009 Jan 15;833–47.

Gisselbaek M, Kirchoff R, Jorgensen U. Osteoid osteoma as a cause of hip pain in a young athlete. *Scand J Med Sci Sports* 1998;8:50–1.

Jennings F, Lambert E, Fredericson M. Rheumatic diseases presenting as sports-related injuries. *Sports Med* 2008;38(11):917–30.

Panni AS, Milano G, Luciana L. Two cases of extra-articular synovial chondromatosis in sportsmen. *J Sports Traumatol* 1994;16:31–8.

Pommering TL, Wroble RR. Septic arthritis of the shoulder. Treating an atypical case. *Phys Sportsmed* 1996;24(5):75–85.

Wnorowski DC. When tumors pose as sports injuries. *Phys Sportsmed* 1998;26(2):98–103.

Cohen NP, Gosset J, Staron RB et al. Vertebral sarcoidosis of the spine of a footbal player. *Am J Orthop* 2003;30:371

Onga T, Yamamoto T, Akisue T et al. Biceps tendinitis caused by an osteochondroma in the bicipital groove: a rare cause of shoulder pain in a baseball player. *Clin Orthop Relat Res* 2005;431:241–4

Wiliams EV, Windless P, Blease S et al. Chronic groin pain in an athlete: an unusual presentation. *Br J Sports Med* 1998;32:182–3.

📋 REFERENCES

1. Sharma H, Rana B, Mahendra A, Jane MJ, Reid R. Outcome of 17 pigmented villonodular synovitis (PVNS) of the knee at 6 years mean follow-up. *Knee* 2007;14(5):390–4.

2. Beaman FD, Peterson JJ. MR imaging of cysts, ganglia, and bursae about the knee. *Radiol Clin North Am* 2007; 45(6):969–82, vi.

3. Paul C, Ortonne JP. Psoriasis evaluation in clinical practice: systematic review and expert opinion. *J Eur Acad Dermatol Venereol* 2010;24 Suppl 2:1.

4. Jennings F, Lambert E, Fredericson M. Rheumatic diseases presenting as sports-related injuries. *Sports Med* 2008;38(11):917–30.

5. Varadhachary AS, Weihl CC, Pestronk A. Mitochondrial pathology in immune and inflammatory myopathies. *Curr Opin Rheumatol*;22(6):651–7.

6. Testa M, Navazio FM, Neugebauer J. Recognition, diagnosis, and treatment of mitochondrial myopathies in endurance athletes. *Curr Sports Med Rep* 2005;4(5):282–7.

7. Sahin G, Korkmaz C, Isiksoy S, Yalcin AU. Autoimmune hypothyroidism and lupus-like syndrome. *Rheumatol Int*;30(4):519–21.

8. Callewaert B, Malfait F, Loeys B et al. Ehlers-Danlos syndromes and Marfan syndrome. *Best Pract Res Clin Rheumatol* 2008;22(1):165–89.

9. Zotter H, Robinson N, Zorzoli M et al. Abnormally high serum ferritin levels among professional road cyclists. *Br J Sports Med* 2004;38(6):704–8.

10. Mathews CJ, Kingsley G, Field M et al. Management of septic arthritis: a systematic review. *Ann Rheum Dis* 2007;66(4):440–5.

11. Nardelli DT, Callister SM, Schell RF. Lyme arthritis: current concepts and a change in paradigm. *Clin Vaccine Immunol.* 2008;15(1):21–34.

12. Daly AE, Bialocerkowski AE. Does evidence support physiotherapy management of adult complex regional pain syndrome type one? A systematic review. *Eur J Pain* 2009;13(4):339–53.

13. Kelley GA, Kelley KS, Hootman JM et al. Exercise and global well-being in community-dwelling adults with fibromyalgia: a systematic review with meta-analysis. *BMC Public Health*;10:198.

Chapter 8

Clinical aspects of biomechanics and sporting injuries

with CHRISTIAN BARTON, NATALIE COLLINS, and KAY CROSSLEY*

Dana Way (biomechanist) is a fundamental part of our team—if you're not using a biomechanics and video review, you're at a huge disadvantage in Olympic-level competition.
Athletics Canada head coach, Alex Gardiner

The term "biomechanics" can be used in a variety of ways. In this book, biomechanics refers to the description, analysis, and assessment of human movement during sporting activities.[1] There are skeletal, muscular, and neurological considerations when describing biomechanics. This chapter focuses on the actual movement occurring in the body segments (technically known as "kinematics"), rather than the forces that are driving the movement ("kinetics"). Our approach can be referred to as "subjective biomechanical analysis." We aim to describe movement such as running, squatting, or the tennis serve as it appears to visual observation. This reflects how clinicians assess and treat, and it can be done without expensive laboratory equipment.

The aims of this chapter are to:

- outline the basics of "ideal" lower limb biomechanics for the novice
- explain the ideal biomechanics with running
- describe lower limb biomechanical assessment in the clinical setting
- outline how to clinically assess footwear
- review the best available evidence associating biomechanical factors with injuries, as well as sharing clinical opinions as to which technical factors in sports contribute to specific injuries
- discuss how to manage biomechanical abnormalities detected in the assessment

---

* We thank Jason Agosta who contributed the biomechanics elements in the first three editions of *Clinical Sports Medicine*

- review the biomechanics of other common activities—cycling, throwing, swimming, tennis, volleyball, and waterpolo.

We address lower limb and upper limb biomechanics separately for the learner's convenience; however, the experienced clinician will consider the close relationship between the upper and lower limbs during a variety of functional tasks.

"Ideal" lower limb biomechanics—the basics

Here we discuss ideal structural characteristics, including available joint range of motion, and stance position. Note that each individual has his or her own mechanical make-up due to structural characteristics (anatomy), and may never achieve the "ideal" position or biomechanical function.

A guide to lower limb joint ranges of motion when in neutral positions is shown in Table 8.1 overleaf. The anatomical planes of the body are shown in Figure 8.1 overleaf.

Lower limb joint motion

The hip joint is formed between the femoral head and the acetabulum. The ball-and-socket structure of this joint permits motion in all three planes.

The knee joint is formed between the tibial plateau and the femoral condyles. Primarily a hinge joint, the knee allows flexion and extension in the sagittal plane. The knee also permits some rotation in the transverse plane. This secondary motion is particularly important to allow the knee to lock into an

Table 8.1 A guide to lower limb joint ranges of motion when in neutral positions

Joint	Plane	Assessment position	Available range
Hip	Sagittal	Supine Prone	Flexion = 120° Extension = 20°
	Frontal	Supine	Abduction = 40°; adduction = 25°
	Transverse	Supine/prone ± hip flexion/ extension	Internal rotation = 45°; external rotation = 45°
Knee	Sagittal	Supine	Flexion = 135°; Extension = 0°
	Frontal		None
	Transverse	Full extension 70° flexion	None 45° rotation
Foot and ankle (triplanar)[a]	Sagittal	Supine	Plantarflexion = 45°; Dorsiflexion = 20°
	Frontal		Supination = 45–60°; Pronation = 15–30°
First MTP	Sagittal	Supine	Plantarflexion = 45°, Dorsiflexion = 70°

(a) Refers to combined motion of the talocrural, subtalar, midtarsal, and metatarsal break joints

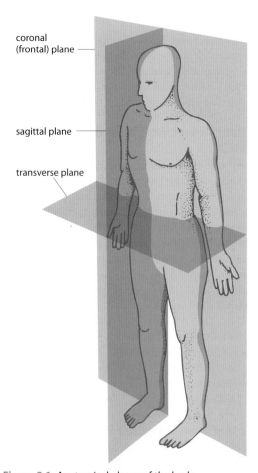

coronal
(frontal) plane

sagittal plane

transverse plane

Figure 8.1 Anatomical planes of the body

extended position for stance stability, and to unlock when moving into flexion for shock absorption.

The ankle joint (between the shank and rearfoot) consists primarily of two articulations, the *talocrual joint* and the *subtalar joint (STJ)*. The *talocrual joint* is formed between the talus and the mortise of the tibia and fibula malleoli. Its axis of motion is predominantly in the frontal plane, which allows dorsiflexion and plantarflexion motion in the sagittal plane[2] (Fig. 8.2).

The *subtalar joint* is formed between the calcaneus and talus. The three articular facets of the subtalar joint allow for complex triplanar motions of pronation and supination. The axis of motion runs posteriorly and inferiorly in the sagittal plane (40–50°), and laterally in the transverse plane (20–25°)[2] (Fig. 8.3a–d). During pronation, the subtalar joint axis provides primarily eversion, which is combined with dorsiflexion and abduction (Fig. 8.3d). During supination, the subtalar joint axis provides primarily inversion, which is combined with plantarflexion and adduction (Fig. 8.3c).

The *midtarsal joint* is formed between the midfoot and rearfoot, and consists of two articulations, the *calcaneocuboid joint* and the *talonavicular joint*. These articulations provide two joint axes. The oblique axis allows large amounts of sagittal plane (dorsiflexion/plantarflexion) motion and transverse plane (abduction/adduction) motion, while the longitudinal axis allows small amounts of coronal plane (eversion and inversion) motion (Fig. 8.4a,b on page 64).

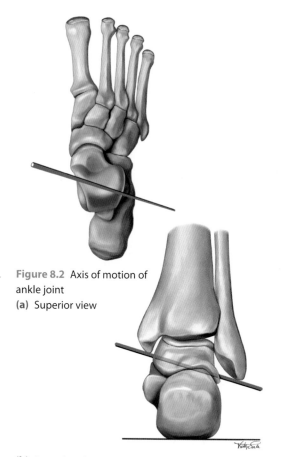

Figure 8.2 Axis of motion of ankle joint
(a) Superior view

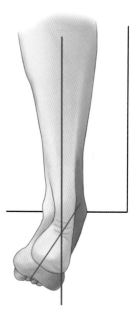

(b) Superior view. Angle between axis of motion of subtalar joint and longitudinal axis of the rearfoot is approximately 15°

(c) Supination at subtalar joint with 20° calcaneal inversion

(b) Posterior view

Importantly, the orientation between these two axes allows the role of the foot to change during weight-bearing. As the rearfoot everts, the two axes become more parallel, unlocking the foot and allowing it to conform to the surface and/or absorb the ground reaction force (GRF). Conversely, as the

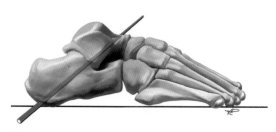

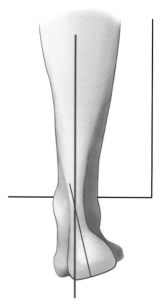

Figure 8.3 Axis of motion of subtalar joint
(a) Lateral view. Angle of inclination approximately 50° to transverse plane

(d) Pronation at subtalar joint with 10° calcaneal inversion

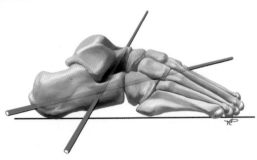

Figure 8.4 Oblique and longitudinal axis of midtarsal joint

(a) Lateral view

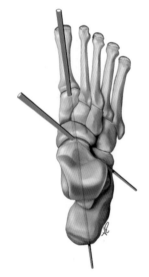

(b) Superior view

rearfoot inverts, the two axes converge, locking the foot into a supinated position and allowing it to function as a rigid lever for propulsion.[2]

The *metatarsal break* (Fig. 8.5) is formed between the distal tarsal bones of the midfoot (cuneiforms and cuboid) and the five metatarsal bones (forefoot). The axis of motion for these joints runs primarily in the transverse plane in an oblique direction (Fig. 8.5 a and b). This leads primarily to sagittal plane motion (flexion/extension), although some coronal plane motion occurs medially (adduction, Fig. 8.5c) and laterally (fifth ray, Fig. 8.5c).

The *first metatarsophalangeal joint* is formed between the head of the first metatarsal and the base of the proximal phalanx. The primary motion that occurs at this joint is in the sagittal plane (flexion/extension). In particular, extension of this joint

is essential to optimize function of the windlass mechanism during gait (Fig. 8.6).

Ideal neutral stance position

To examine stance position, have the patient adopt a normal, comfortable, standing posture. Ideal neutral stance occurs when the joints of the lower limbs and feet are symmetrically aligned, with the weight-bearing line passing through the anterior superior iliac spine, the patella, and the second metatarsal (Fig. 8.7 on page 66).

When the feet are in a symmetrical position, the subtalar (talocalcaneal) joint is neither pronated nor supinated, and the midtarsal joint (talonavicular and calcaneocuboid joints) is maximally pronated so that the first and second metatarsal heads are in contact with the ground. The long axis of the forefoot through the second metatarsal is perpendicular to the bisection of the heel (Fig. 8.8 on page 66) and in line with the tibial tuberosity. The ankle joint is neither plantarflexed nor dorsiflexed, and the tibia is perpendicular to the supporting surface in the sagittal

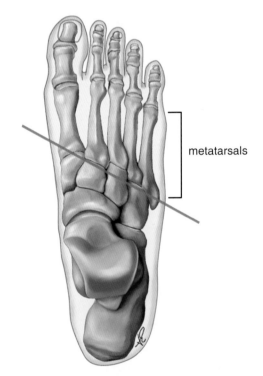

metatarsals

Figure 8.5 (a) The metatarsal break—the joint between the distal tarsal bones of the midfoot (cuneiforms and cuboid) and the five metatarsal bones (forefoot)

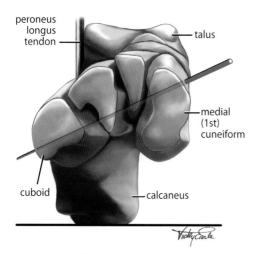

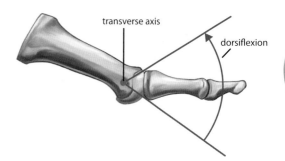

Figure 8.6 Motion of the hallux around the transverse axis of the first metatarsophalangeal joint

Figure 8.5 (cont.) (b) The metatarsal break (frontal plane). The axis of motion runs as shown (green rod)

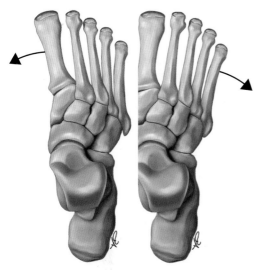

Coronal plane motion at the metatarsal break showing that the forefoot can **(c)** adduct and **(d)** abduct

and frontal plane. The knee is fully extended (but not hyperextended) and in slight valgus alignment. The hips are in a neutral position (neither internally nor externally rotated, neither flexed nor extended). The left and right anterior superior iliac spines of the pelvis are level. A slight anterior tilt of the pelvis is normal. More specific objective descriptions of ideal alignment are outlined in the assessment section.

Figure 8.7 The alignment of the lower limb in neutral position. The weight-bearing line runs through the anterior superior iliac spine, patella, and second metatarsal. The calcaneus is in line with the tibia, and the forefoot is perpendicular to the calcaneus

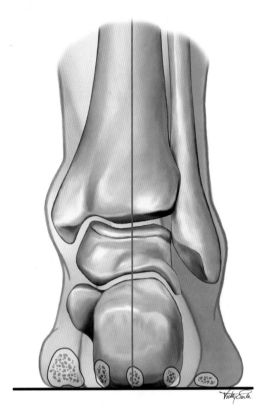

Figure 8.8 Normal relationship between the forefoot and rearfoot when the foot is in neutral stance

"Ideal" biomechanics with movement—running

As injury mechanisms for many overuse injuries are associated with suboptimal lower limb biomechanics, the clinician must know how to assess lower limb biomechanics during running. We focus first on the heel strike pattern of running, as this is the predominant pattern for the majority of runners.[3] We then consider how biomechanics are altered when running with a forefoot strike pattern.

Although we focus on ideal running biomechanics, ideal walking biomechanics are similar to heel strike running patterns outlined below. The most important biomechanical feature that distinguishes running from walking is the airborne or "float" phase of running, where neither foot is in contact with the ground.[2] Additionally, vertical ground reaction forces during running are double those of walking,[2, 4] the pelvis is in greater anterior tilt,[5] and sagittal plane excursions of the knee and hip are increased. Ultimately, this leads to greater stress on structures of the lower limb.

The heel strike pattern of running can be split into five phases (Fig. 8.9), each of which will be discussed below.

Loading (heel strike to foot flat)

With the leg swinging toward the line of progression, and the foot supinated, the rearfoot (heel) contacts the ground in slight inversion (0 to 5°).[2, 6–8] At heel strike, the pelvis is level, in slight anterior tilt (10°), and internally rotated; the hip is externally rotated (5 to 10°) and flexed (30°); and the knee is flexed (10°). Due to the laterally directed line of the ground reaction force produced by heel strike, a cascade of events occurs to assist shock absorption. Firstly, the rearfoot begins to evert; this is accompanied by tibial and femoral (hip) internal rotation, and hip adduction. This is combined with knee flexion, which peaks at around 45°, and hip flexion of approximately 35° as a result of the ground reaction force line passing posterior and anterior to the hip and knee, respectively.[9, 10] Each of these motions is controlled by eccentric muscle activity which helps to dissipate the ground reaction forces. In addition, there may be contralateral pelvic drop, although this should be minimal (approximately 5°).[10] The gluteal musculature should actively control this motion and further dissipate the ground reaction forces.

Initial rearfoot eversion also results in more parallel alignment of the midtarsal joints (i.e. calcaneocuboid and talonavicular), causing them to unlock.[2] Importantly, this allows the forefoot to make solid contact with the ground at foot flat[11] and allows the foot to adapt during loading to potential uneven or unstable terrain.[2]

Although motions that comprise foot pronation are normal, they should not be excessive (i.e. hyperpronation). Excessive motion places strain on structures designed to control foot pronation, such as the plantar fascia, tibialis posterior muscle, and intrinsic foot musculature.[2] Excessive pronation also increases medial ground reaction forces, accentuating more proximal motion at the knee, hip, and pelvis, and increasing load on ligamentous and muscular structures responsible for proximal control.[2]

The clinician should carefully note proximal motion during this early phase of stance. Excessive contralateral pelvic drop and or hip adduction/internal rotation may increase strain on structures required to control it, such as the iliofemoral band, gluteal musculature, tensor fascia lata muscle, and hip adductors. Additionally, this may also place increased

(a) Walking

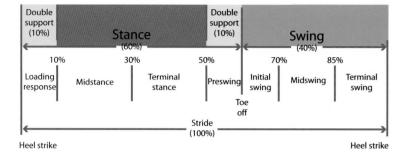

(b) Running

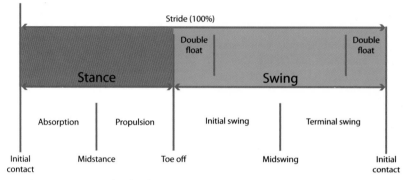

Figure 8.9 Gait cycle with phases and individual components
ADAPTED FROM DUGAN AND BHAT[2]

or altered loading on the lumbar spine, tibiofemoral joint, and patellofemoral joint. Any excessive anterior tilting of the pelvis may place excessive strain on the lumbar spine and/or hamstring musculature.

Conversely, inadequate pronation or excessive supination leads to an excessive or prolonged laterally directed ground reaction force,[2] resulting in a less mobile foot and poorer shock absorption capacity. This may be associated with lower limb stress fractures,[12] or may increase the incidence of lateral ankle sprain and chronic ankle instability.[13, 14]

Midstance (foot flat to heel off)

The beginning of midstance is indicated by the forefoot making contact with the ground, normally in a neutral transverse plane position (i.e. not abducted or adducted).[6] Lower limb biomechanical function during midstance involves a transition from biomechanics required for shock absorption following loading, to biomechanics required for propulsion. During this time, the ankle moves toward maximal dorsiflexion (approximately 20°) to allow forward motion of the tibia and the center of mass to pass

over the stance leg.[15] At the same time, the hip and knee are moving from flexion toward extended positions, assisting forward motion of the body's center of mass.

Maximal foot pronation followed by maximal ankle dorsiflexion should be reached immediately after the body's center of mass has passed anterior to the stance limb.[11] Peak rearfoot eversion should reach approximately 10°,[6, 16] and peak forefoot abduction approximately 5°.[6] The rearfoot then begins to invert and the forefoot adducts, causing the foot to supinate, and the tibia and femur to externally rotate.[11]

There are a number of things for the clinician to consider during this phase. Excessive pronation, or a delay/failure to transition from shock absorption to propulsion actions by the lower limb, may be detrimental to a number of structures. Firstly, this will place excessive strain on structures responsible for controlling pronation and increase the risk of conditions such as plantar fasciitis, Achilles and tibialis posterior tendinopathies, proximal tibialis posterior periostitis, or tibial stress fractures due to excessive pull of the tibialis posterior and long flexors. Also, continued instability of the foot may lead to development of first metatarsophalangeal joint abnormalities, including exostoses and hallux valgus, sesamoid pain, and/or excessive interdigital compression (Morton's neuroma). If left untreated, over time this instability may also lead to metatarsal or sesamoid stress fractures.

More proximally, excessive or prolonged pronation also result in abnormal transverse and frontal plane motion at the hip and knee due to a delay in external rotation. Ultimately, this may place excessive strain on many structures such as the patellofemoral joint, patellar tendon (both conditions discussed in Chapter 33), iliofemoral band (Chapter 34), and musculature that controls this motion. Conversely, the same proximal anomalies may result due to inadequate pelvic and hip control. The source of the biomechanical dysfunction may need to be determined through further structural and functional tests (see assessment section).

Propulsion (heel off to toe off)

Following heel off, the foot continues to supinate. Importantly, as this occurs, inversion of the rearfoot causes the transverse tarsal joint axes to converge.[2] This convergence of joint axes causes the midfoot to lock into position, creating a rigid lever.[2]

Concurrently, the stance limb continues to externally rotate, the hip reaches maximal extension of between 0 and 10°,[5, 15, 17] and the knee flexes once more due to hamstring muscle contraction.[15, 17] Additionally, acceleration of the stance limb is provided through plantar flexion at the ankle, produced by the gastrocnemius and soleus complex.[18] This same gastrocnemius and soleus activity, along with the tibialis posterior, continues to actively assist supination of the foot, and maintain its function as a rigid lever.[2] Passively, rigidity of the foot is supported by the "windlass mechanism" (i.e. increased tension of the plantar fascia due to extension of the metatarsals) which pulls the calcaneus and metatarsal heads together[2] (Fig. 8.10). By toe off, the rearfoot should be inverted to approximately 10°, and the forefoot adducted approximately 5°.[6]

Failure of normal propulsion causes an inefficient gait pattern. This can limit performance and predispose to injury for several reasons. First, the peroneal musculature may be forced to work harder to stabilize the medial and lateral columns of the foot, which can lead to stress fracture of the fibula.

Second, impaired supination may lead to toe off via the lateral rays instead of the first ray. This may compress the transverse arch of the foot excessively,

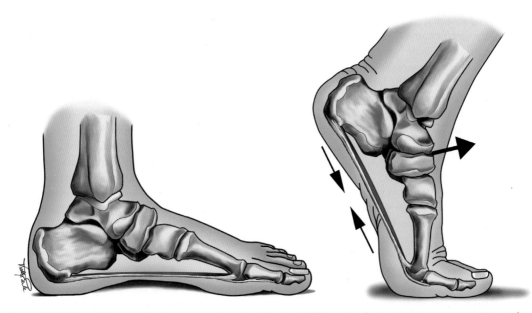

Figure 8.10 The windlass mechanism comes into play after heel off. Metatarsal extension increases tension on the plantar fascia, and forces the transverse tarsal joint into flexion, which increases stability at push off

and lead to interdigital nerve compression (Morton's neuroma), and risk of lateral ray stress fracture.

Third, and more proximally, reduced propulsion from the stance limb may increase reliance on the swing phase to produce forward momentum. To achieve this, the hip flexors—rectus femoris and iliopsoas—will generate more rapid hip flexion, increasing the potential for tendinopathies. To compensate for impaired propulsion, pelvic and trunk rotation may increase, which increases strain on spinal structures.

Initial swing

Following ipsilateral toe off, the body is thrust into the first "float" phase, where neither limb is in contact with the ground. Rectus femoris and iliopsoas muscle activity continue the forward momentum of the now swinging limb.[19] As the limb advances, the pelvis moves with it, thrusting the hip into abduction and external rotation, which are in turn controlled by the hip adductors.[19] The tibialis anterior contracts to begin dorsiflexing the foot in preparation for terminal swing.[19] While these motions continue, they are aided by the addition of a new stable support when the contralateral limb strikes the ground and commences its own *loading* phase. Continuation of normal swing at this time relies on the ability of the contralateral gluteal musculature to dissipate the ground reaction force produced by this event and prevent the pelvis dropping on the swing side. Failure to do so will increase the work required by the hip and knee flexors to clear the swinging limb, possibly leading to overuse.

Terminal swing

Following contralateral toe off, the body is thrust into the second "float" phase. During this time, the ipsilateral swinging hip reaches maximal flexion (approximately 30°),[5, 9] being brought under control by the hamstring and gluteal musculature.[19] The same hamstring activity slows the rapidly extending knee in preparation for heel strike. At the same time, the hip adductors, which have been working eccentrically to control abduction of the swinging limb, begin to work concentrically to adduct the hip and bring it toward the midline.[19]

Angle and base of gait

The angle of gait is the angle between the longitudinal bisection of the foot and the line of progression (Fig. 8.11). The normal angle of gait is approximately

10° abducted from the line of progression in walking. Abducted gait describes an angle of gait greater than 10°. The angle of gait reflects the hip and tibial transverse plane positions. The base of gait is the distance between the medial aspect of the heels (Fig. 8.12a, b overleaf). A normal base of gait is approximately 2.5–3.0 cm.

Changes from the normal angle and base of gait may be secondary to structural abnormalities or, more commonly, as compensation for another abnormality. For example, a wide base of gait may be necessary to increase stability. As running velocity increases, the angle and base of gait decrease. With faster running, the angle of gait approaches zero and foot strike is on the line of progression. This limits deviation of the center of mass as the lower limbs move beneath the body, thus allowing more efficient locomotion (Fig. 8.12b).

Influence of gait velocity

Increased gait velocity influences a number of biomechanical factors. As gait velocity is increased, greater emphasis is placed on the swinging actions of the upper limbs, trunk, and lower limbs to produce forward momentum.[2] This difference has significant implications for the flexibility and eccentric muscle control requirements of these structures (e.g. ipsilateral hamstring strain during late swing). Greater

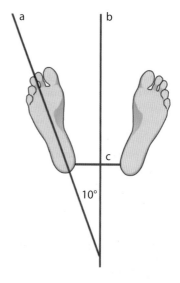

Figure 8.11 The angle of gait is the angle between **(a)** the long axis at the foot and **(b)** the line of progression. **(c)** Base of gait is the distance between the medial aspect of the heels

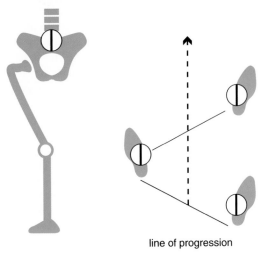

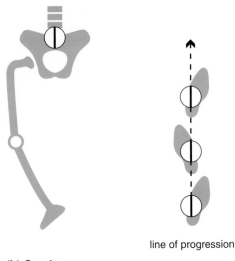

line of progression

Figure 8.12 Angle and base of gait
(a) Walking

(b) Running

line of progression

excursion of the proximal joints (knee, hip, and pelvis) also occurs with increased velocity, placing increased reliance on eccentric muscle control.[19, 20] At the foot and ankle, the bones making up the rearfoot, midfoot, and forefoot all reduce their excursions in all three planes with increased velocity.[21] This indicates the need for stiffer joint structures with increased speed and a greater demand on intrinsic foot musculature control.[21]

In slower running, the stance phase takes longer than the swing phase. As running speed increases, stance phase and flight phase times approach each other, until the stance phase becomes shorter than the swing phase in sprinting[2] (Fig. 8.13).

Additionally, as running velocity increases, foot strike patterns may be altered. As mentioned previously, foot strike patterns are similar between slow running and walking for most individuals (Fig. 8.14). During faster running (striding), the foot may strike with the heel and forefoot simultaneously prior to toe off, or may strike with the forefoot initially followed by heel lowering to the surface prior to toe off. In sprinting, weight-bearing is maintained on the forefoot from contact to toe off, although the heel may lower to the supporting surface at midstance. In some individuals, this pattern can commence even at slower running speeds, or immediately on initiation of a run. In particular, habitual barefoot runners often have a natural forefoot strike pattern regardless of velocity.[3]

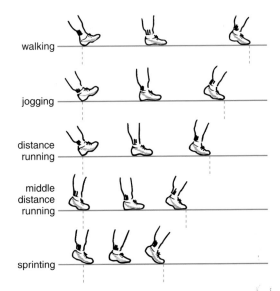

Figure 8.13 Pattern of the stance phase during different speeds of walking and running

Comparing heel and forefoot strike patterns

Changing from a heel strike to a forefoot strike pattern has significant implications for lower limb biomechanics and assessment. Most importantly, it has implications for biomechanical relationships between segments, as well as shock loading. Firstly, forefoot strike patterns result in slight plantar flexion of the foot at impact, followed by dorsiflexion as the heel lowers to the ground.[2] This means

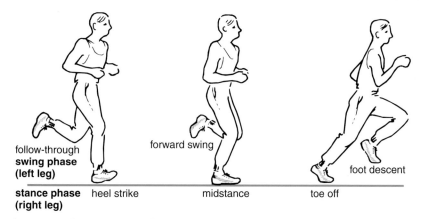

follow-through
**swing phase
(left leg)**

forward swing

foot descent

stance phase   heel strike   midstance   toe off
(right leg)

Figure 8.14 The swing and stance phases of running

that the ankle joint is more compliant and able to absorb ground reaction forces in the sagittal plane, leading to a reduction in vertical ground reaction force and loading rates following foot strike.[3, 6] These reduced loading rates may have implications for injury management and prevention,[3] since injuries such as plantar fasciitis and tibial stress fractures have recently been linked to higher loading rates in rearfoot strikers.[22, 23]

Recent evidence linking loading rates to lower limb injury has led to a growing popularity for running barefoot or with a minimalistic shoe. The rationale for this is that running in the modern running shoe inhibits the natural forefoot strike pattern due to its increased heel height associated with the addition of cushioning.[3] However, there is currently an absence of empirical evidence to support any recommendation that making this change would be successful in reducing injury rates. Regardless, habitual strike patterns should be considered during any biomechanical assessment, especially when assessing patients where excessive ground reaction force is considered a possible cause (e.g. plantar fasciitis or stress fracture).

Forefoot running significantly affects motion of the rearfoot and forefoot. Specifically, rearfoot eversion excursion is significantly higher, while eversion magnitude is significantly less in forefoot strikers.[6] Additionally, the rearfoot predominantly inverts during early stance during a forefoot strike pattern, whereas it everts during a rearfoot strike pattern.[6] As would be expected, striking the ground with the forefoot first leads to increased forefoot motion (abduction and dorsiflexion).[6] The implications of these

differences should be considered during any biomechanical evaluation.

Influence of fatigue on running biomechanics

Frequently, a patient will complain of pain that only occurs following prolonged activity. For example, an individual with patellofemoral pain (Chapter 33) may report no pain during the early stages of a run, but may need to cease running due to severe pain after 5 kilometers (3 miles). This can make clinical assessment difficult, since the condition may result from faulty biomechanics that only occur with fatigue. For example, excessive hip adduction during running in the individual with patellofemoral pain may occur due to poor gluteal muscle endurance. Therefore, the clinician should evaluate functional biomechanics both at baseline and following fatigue and/or onset of pain. In the clinical setting, this means scheduling the appointment so that the patient can be seen before and immediately after a run.

Lower limb biomechanical assessment in the clinical setting

This section aims to help the junior clinician develop a routine for efficient lower limb biomechanical assessment. There is no "single" best way to assess biomechanics, and the experienced clinician will vary his or her assessment depending on the clinical presentation.

For this example, consider the patient to have patellofemoral pain—a condition that warrants assessment of the entire kinetic chain.

PRACTICE PEARL

Two guiding principles will help guide a comprehensive yet speedy assessment

1   Examine from distal to proximal (start at the foot and then examine proximally to the pelvis and trunk).

2   Examine the patient in "static stance" first, before increasingly challenging him or her with "functional" tests, before moving to fully "dynamic" or "sport-specific" tests as appropriate (see Fig. 8.15 for concept of the hierarchy). These terms are explained below.

Thorough biomechanical assessment may require the patient to stand, walk, run, land on two feet, and land on one leg only. Assessment during "function" (playing sports, executing certain sporting activities

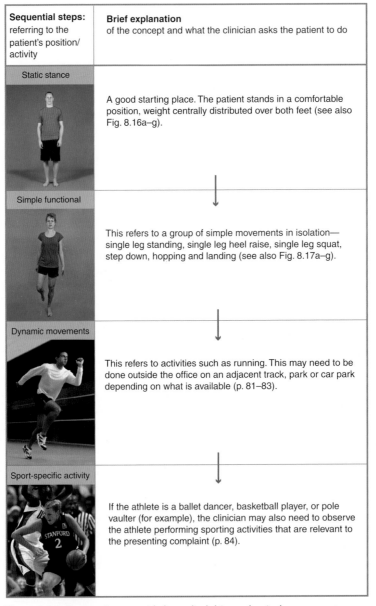

Sequential steps: referring to the patient's position/activity	Brief explanation of the concept and what the clinician asks the patient to do
Static stance	A good starting place. The patient stands in a comfortable position, weight centrally distributed over both feet (see also Fig. 8.16a–g).
Simple functional	This refers to a group of simple movements in isolation— single leg standing, single leg heel raise, single leg squat, step down, hopping and landing (see also Fig. 8.17a–g).
Dynamic movements	This refers to activities such as running. This may need to be done outside the office on an adjacent track, park or car park depending on what is available (p. 81–83).
Sport-specific activity	If the athlete is a ballet dancer, basketball player, or pole vaulter (for example), the clinician may also need to observe the athlete performing sporting activities that are relevant to the presenting complaint (p. 84).

Figure 8.15 An overview to guide lower limb biomechanical assessment (see also the detailed Figs 8.16, 8.17 and 8.18 on pages 73–82)

such as a kick or a pirouette) may also be relevant. We explain each of these steps in the order that many experienced clinicians perform the assessment. The major elements in the assessment are:

- structural ("static") biomechanical assessment (Fig. 8.16)
- functional lower limb tests—single-leg stance, heel raise, squat, and landing (Fig. 8.17 on pages 79–82)
- assessment of a patient's running biomechanics ("dynamic assessment") (Fig. 8.18 on page 82)
- detailed sport-specific tests as indicated by the above tests and the clinical presentation.

Structural ("static") biomechanical assessment

The clinician performs the assessment of static stance by critically viewing the foot, ankle, knee, and pelvis (Fig. 8.16a). This procedure is elaborated in sequence below and also demonstrated on the *Clinical Sports Medicine* masterclasses ("Biomechanical assessment").

WWW **www.clinicalsportsmedicine.com**

Foot—static assessment

Inspect the foot subjectively (Does it look abnormal?), quantify posture using the six-item Foot Posture Index on page 74, and also pay attention to first metatarsophalangeal joint range of motion (below) (Fig. 8.16b).

Foot Posture Index

The Foot Posture Index (FPI) is a rapid, quantitative measure of static foot biomechanics where each of six items is given a score between –2 and +2. It reflects foot posture at the rearfoot, midfoot, and forefoot—as well as giving an overall impression of foot type. It requires no equipment and takes two minutes for experienced clinicians to complete[24, 25] (Table 8.2 overleaf).

Additional background information about the FPI, including definitions and pictures of various foot types for each item, are shown in the user guide and manual[28] which can be seen on the *Clinical Sports Medicine* masterclasses.

WWW **www.clinicalsportsmedicine.com**

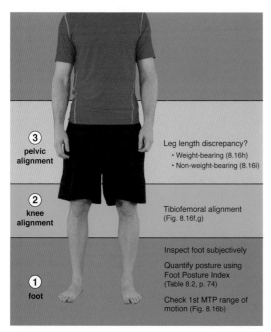

Figure 8.16 Static assessment of the lower limb
(a) With the patient in this comfortable position, static stance examination begins at the foot. The examiner then assesses the ankle, knee, and hip/pelvis

(b) Focused foot examination includes subjective examination (Does the foot look normal?), performing the Foot Posture Index (Table 8.2 overleaf), and assessing first MTP joint dorsiflexion MTP (shown)

Table 8.2 The Foot Posture Index[24]

Each of the six items in the FPI is scored as −2 (highly supinated), −1 (supinated), 0 (neutral), +1 (pronated), or +2 (highly pronated); this leads to sums between −12 (highly supinated) and +12 (highly pronated).[26]

Talar head palpation

The talar head is palpated on the anterior aspect of the ankle. If the head can be felt equally on the medial and lateral side, a neutral score (0) is given. If greater prominence is felt medially, a pronated score is given (+1 if greater prominence felt medially; +2 if *only* medial prominence is felt); if greater prominence is felt laterally, a supinated score is given (−1 if greater prominence felt laterally; −2 if *only* lateral prominence is felt).

Supra and infra lateral malleolar curvature

A neutral score for this item is given if the curves above and below the lateral malleolus are equal. If the curve above the malleolus is flatter, a pronated score is given (+2 defined by completely flat); if the curve below the malleolus is flatter, a supinated score is give (−2 defined by completely flat).

Calcaneal frontal plane position

A neutral score is given if the rearfoot is perpendicular to the floor. A more valgus rearfoot relative to the floor is given a pronated score (+2 defined by >5°); a more varus rearfoot relative to the floor is given a supinated score (−2 defined by <5°).

Bulging in the region of the talonavicular joint (TNJ)

A neutral score is given if the skin immediately superficial to the TNJ is flat. If the TNJ is bulging, a pronated score is given (+2 defined by marked bulging); if the TNJ area is concave (indented), a supinated score is given (−2 defined by marked concavity).

Height and congruence of the medial longitudinal arch

A neutral score is given if the arch shape is uniform and similarly shaped to the circumference of a circle. If the arch is flattened and lowered, a pronated score is given (+2 defined by the mid-portion of the arch making contact with the floor); if the arch is high, a supinated score is give (−2 defined by an acutely angled posterior end of the arch).

Abduction/adduction of the forefoot on the rearfoot

A neutral score is given when the forefoot can be seen equally on the medial and lateral side when viewed from behind the axis of the rearfoot. If more of the forefoot is visible laterally than medially, a pronated score is given (+2 defined by only lateral forefoot being visible); if more of the forefoot is visible medially than laterally, a supinated score is given (−2 defined by only medial forefoot being visible).

The average total FPI score for the normal healthy population is 2.4 (i.e. slightly pronated).[27] Considering this, scores of 0 to +5 are considered neutral. A score of +6 to +9 is considered pronated, ≥+10 is considered highly pronated, −1 to −4 is considered supinated, and −5 to −12 is considered highly supinated.

Note that, as with any clinical skill, training and experience are important. The clinician should rate at least 30 individuals with a broad range of foot types before applying the FPI clinically.[29–31]

Jack's test for first metatarsophalangeal (MTP) joint range (plantar fascia integrity)

The clinician can rapidly assess the first MTP joint and also the integrity of the plantar fascia using "Jack's test"[32] (Fig. 8.16b). The normal range of first MTP joint dorsiflexion motion should be around 50° relative to the floor. As the first ray dorsiflexes, tightening of an intact plantar fascia should cause the rearfoot to invert. If the rearfoot does not move, it suggests poor plantar fascia integrity, which can result in inadequate supination during the propulsive phase of gait. Additionally, increased resistance to or a reduction in motion may result from the presence of a valgus aligned forefoot.[33] Both these structural issues can be corrected using orthoses, taping, and/or corrective exercise.

Ankle dorsiflexion—static assessment

Accurate ankle dorsiflexion in weight-bearing using an inclinometer (Fig. 8.16c, d) provides a more useful measure of range of motion at this important joint than does a rough assessment when the patient is lying on a treatment couch or doing a lunge (Fig. 8.16e). This ankle biomechanical assessment is best done with the knee both flexed and extended (Fig. 8.16c, d). Normal ankle dorsiflexion range with the knee flexed is 45°, and with the knee extended is 40°.[30] We recommend that clinicians have an inclinometer readily available (Fig. 8.16e)—this cheap instrument adds accuracy to measurements and actually reduces assessment time.

If the ankle dorsiflexion range differs in those two positions by more than 5°, it suggests there is limitation of dorsiflexion with the knee extended; this points to gastrocnemius tightness. If excessive foot pronation is required to achieve normal ankle dorsiflexion range (i.e. 45°) with the knee bent, excessive pronation is likely during functional activities such as running.

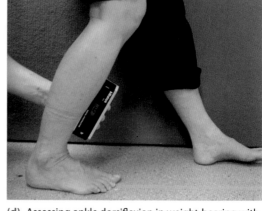

(d) Assessing ankle dorsiflexion in weight-bearing with the knee bent (flexed)

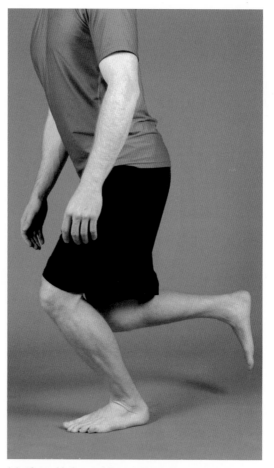

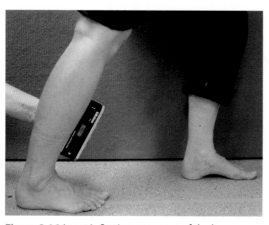

Figure 8.16 (cont.) Static assessment of the lower limb—ankle range of motion
(c) Assessing ankle dorsiflexion in weight-bearing with the knee straight/extended

(e) The ankle lunge (shown) is a common clinical measure of ankle dorsiflexion but provides less information than can quickly be obtained using an inclinometer (Figs 8.16c, d)

An alternative way of measuring ankle dorsi-flexion is to have the patient perform a lunge (as in Figure 8.16d alone). This popular method compares one side with the other, and does not identify gastrocnemius tightness as the cause of the limitation if there are bilateral problems.

Tibiofemoral alignment at the knee—static assessment

Tibiofemoral joint alignment may reflect genu varum (Fig. 8.16f) or valgum (Fig. 8.16g) and this can also be measured using an inclinometer. This measure compares favorably to the "gold standard" radiographic measure.[34]

Leg length and pelvic alignment—static assessment

Weight-bearing leg length is assessed using a measuring tape to rapidly compare the distance from the floor to the anterior superior iliac spine (ASIS) on each side (Fig. 8.16h).

A difference between sides of greater than 1 cm is clinically meaningful, and its source needs to be identified. Asymmetry in foot posture (i.e. a more pronated foot on the shorter side) may indicate a "functional leg length difference"—the patient functions as if there is a leg length difference when anatomically the legs are of equal length.

Asymmetry in foot posture in the absence of a weight-bearing leg length difference may indicate a "structural leg length difference" (i.e. the leg is longer on the more pronated side). The latter can be tested by also measuring leg length non-weight-bearing (i.e. lying supine).

Non-weight-bearing assessment of leg length is performed with the patient supine. The distance from the ASIS to the medial malleolus is measured on each side, ensuring that the femur is in neutral rotation (Fig. 8.16i).

The purpose of leg length assessment in both weight-bearing and non-weight-bearing states is to determine whether there is any discrepancy and, if so, whether it is due to pelvic asymmetry, thigh/leg structure, and/or foot posture. Knowing this

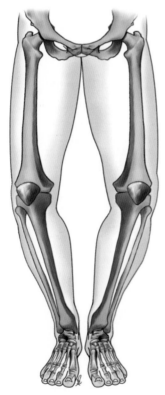

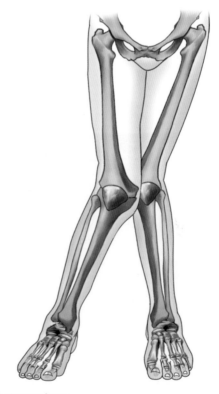

Figure 8.16 (cont.) Static assessment of the lower limb—alignment at the knee

(f) Genu varum

(g) Genu valgum

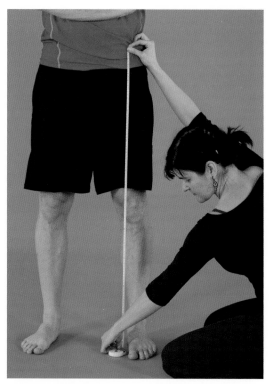

Figure 8.16 (cont.) Static assessment of the lower limb—leg length

(h) Weight-bearing—with the patient standing, the height of the anterior superior iliac spine (ASIS) from the floor is measured on each side to calculate leg length

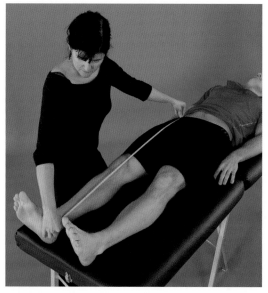

(i) Non-weight-bearing assessment of leg length is performed with the patient supine

allows the clinician to manage the discrepancy appropriately.

Summary of static assessment

The "static" biomechanical assessment of the foot, ankle, knee, and pelvic alignment provides a substantial amount of valuable clinical information and can be completed in less than five minutes. Possible mechanisms that underpin common clinical observations are tabled overleaf (Table 8.3) and discussed on the *Clinical Sports Medicine* masterclasses.

WWW   **www.clinicalsportsmedicine.com**

Functional lower limb tests—single-leg stance, heel raise, squat, and landing from a jump

The next step is to assess simple functional movements (Fig. 8.17a–e on pages 79–81). The patient should do these tests both with and without sporting footwear where appropriate. This will help the clinician determine whether the individual's footwear is detrimental, beneficial, or has no effect on functional biomechanics.

Single-leg stance with progressions—functional assessment

The single-leg stance test begins to challenge lower limb balance and proprioception. Inability to maintain the single-leg stance position is likely to carry over to suboptimal biomechanics during sporting activity. The patient performs this test with (i) eyes open, (ii) eyes closed, and (iii) challenged further by also performing a single-heel raise (Fig. 8.17a). Depending on the balance requirements for the individual, once balance can be maintained in single-leg stance for at least 20 seconds, balance can be assessed using more challenging activities, including variations in surfaces and ability to adapt to perturbations.

Single-leg heel raise (with a focus on tibialis posterior function)—functional assessment

Tibialis posterior is an under-recognized contributor to normal lower limb biomechanics—it has a particularly important role in control of foot pronation, and it helps stabilize the plantar arch during activity. Through its attachments to the navicular, cuneiforms,

Table 8.3 Common lower limb biomechanical observations, possible mechanisms, and confirmatory assessments

Observation	Possible mechanisms	Confirmatory assessments
Excessive or asymmetrical pelvic or trunk movement (frontal, transverse, sagittal planes)	Inadequate ROM (hip)	ROM tests: clinical/inclinometer; figure "4" test (Fig. 28.11c)
	Leg length discrepancy (structural or functional)	Leg length evaluation (weight-bearing and non-weight-bearing) (Fig. 8.16h, i) Foot Posture Index (Table 8.2; Fig. 8.16b)
	Inadequate strength (abdominals, lumbopelvic muscles, hip abductors)	Manual muscle tests
	Altered neuromotor control (hip abductors, lumbopelvic muscles)	Biofeedback
	Decreased muscle length (hamstrings, rectus abdominus, rectus femoris)	Muscle length tests
	Lumbar spine / sacro iliac joint stiffness/pain	Joint palpation
Increased hip adduction/femoral internal rotation	Structural (femoral anteversion)	Radiographic—MRI, X-ray Clinical assessment
	Inadequate ROM (hip)	ROM tests: clinical/inclinometer; figure "4" test (Fig. 28.11c)
	Inadequate strength (hip external rotators, abductors)	Manual muscle test (Figs 28.3a, b); clinical strength (hand-held dynamometer)
	Altered neuromotor control (hip external rotators, hip abductors)	Biofeedback
Increased apparent knee valgus	Structural (genu varum, tibial varum, coxa varum)	Radiographic—MRI, X-ray Clinical assessment—goniometer, inclinometer
	Inadequate ROM (hip)	ROM tests: clinical (Fig. 28.3c) / inclinometer; figure "4" test (Fig. 28.11c)
	Inadequate strength (hip external rotators, hip abductors, quadriceps, hamstrings)	Manual muscle test; clinical strength (hand-held dynamometer) Active gluteal and tensor fascia lata trigger points
	Altered neuromotor control (hip external rotators, hip abductors, lumbopelvic muscles)	Biofeedback Active gluteal and tensor fascia lata trigger points
Ankle equinus	Inadequate ROM (ankle)	ROM tests (Fig. 8.16c–e)
	Tight gastrocnemius	ROM tests with knee extended (Fig. 8.16c)

Observation	Possible mechanisms	Confirmatory assessments
Excessive or prolonged foot pronation	Pronated foot type	Foot Posture Index (Table 8.2; Fig. 8.16b)
	Impaired windlass mechanism	Jack's test (Fig. 8.16b)
	Tibialis posterior weakness	Single-leg heel raise; manual muscle test; inability to form arch
	Ankle equines	Ankle dorsiflexion measures (Fig. 8.16c–e)
	Leg length discrepancy (structural or functional)	Leg length evaluation (weight-bearing and non-weight-bearing) (Fig. 8.16h, i)
Excessive or prolonged foot supination	Supinated foot type	Foot Posture Index (Table 8.2; Fig. 8.16b)
	Chronic ankle instability	Ankle ligament integrity tests
	Leg length discrepancy (structural or functional)	Leg length evaluation (weight-bearing and non-weight-bearing) (Fig. 8.16h, i)
Reduced propulsion	Impaired windlass mechanism	Jack's test (Fig. 8.16b)
	Tibialis posterior weakness	Single-leg heel raise; manual muscle test; inability to form arch
	Pronated foot type	Foot Posture Index (Table 8.2; Fig. 8.16b)

ROM = range of motion

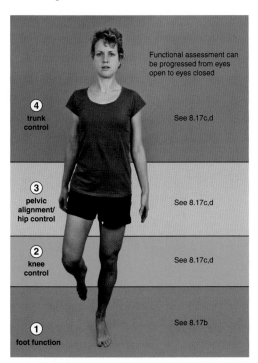

Figure 8.17 Functional assessment of the lower limb
(a) Single-leg stance to evaluate alignment and control

(b) The heel raise. Look for (i) inability to rise through the medial arch (tibialis posterior weakness), and (ii) failure of the heel to invert

cuboid, and bases of the second to fourth metatarsals, tibialis posterior inverts the subtalar joint. It is a primary dynamic stabilizer of the foot against eversion forces, and is also important for propulsion.

The single-leg heel raise (Fig. 8.17b) is a simple functional test that tests the ability of tibialis posterior to resupinate the foot during propulsion of gait. Tibialis posterior muscle weakness will manifest as inability to rise up through the medial aspect of the foot and invert the rearfoot toward the end of the heel raise. (Note that the same procedure can be prescribed as a therapeutic exercise when deficits are observed—this may initially require the use of support.)

If tibialis posterior problems are suspected, the "arch form" test can be used to evaluate the intrinsic control of the tibialis posterior during stance of gait. The patient is instructed to gently lift up the inside arch while pushing the first metatarsophalangeal joint into the ground. The clinician can monitor performance by placing a finger underneath the joint to ensure sufficient downward pressure. The patient should be able to maintain this for ten seconds. This procedure also provides a therapeutic exercise when deficits are observed. Note that the arch form test would not necessarily be part of a routine rapid biomechanical assessment—it provides additional information should the clinical setting warrant the test.

Single-leg squat to assess knee, hip, and trunk muscle function

The continuum of activities from single-leg squat (at approximately 45° knee flexion), step-down, hopping, to landing provides a logical progression to the lower limb biomechanical assessment. There are many variations for performing a single-leg squat, including depth (knee flexion angle), arm position (crossed, hands on hips, no constraints), and posture of the unsupported leg (in front, behind). It is prudent for the clinician to have a consistent approach to these variations. In our examples, we use the 45° and 60° squat angles and have the patient's arms crossed, unsupported leg in front (Fig. 8.17c, d).

Assessment of hip and trunk function

Five main observations may indicate altered hip or trunk muscle function. The first four can be observed from in front of the patient; the fifth is an overall assessment (Table 8.1).

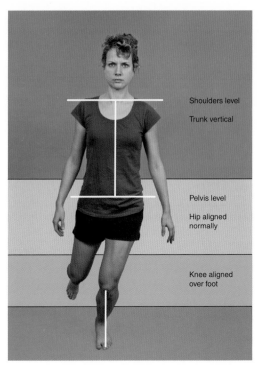

Shoulders level

Trunk vertical

Pelvis level

Hip aligned normally

Knee aligned over foot

Figure 8.17 (cont.) Functional assessment of the lower limb—single-leg squat
(c) Good form

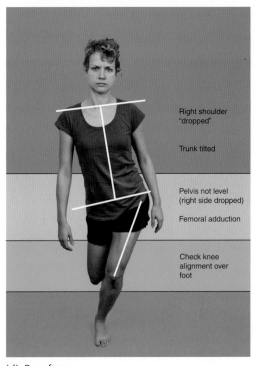

Right shoulder "dropped"

Trunk tilted

Pelvis not level (right side dropped)

Femoral adduction

Check knee alignment over foot

(d) Poor form

Trunk

Also referred to as a "Trendelenberg sign," trunk lean (and/or rotation) toward the stance leg may be an adaptation to altered control of hip abduction/rotation or trunk lateral flexion/rotation. This may be observed as a more lateral position of the shoulder, relative to the hip (Table 8.3 and Fig. 8.17d).

Pelvis/hip

Altered control of hip abduction/rotation or trunk lateral flexion/rotation may present as either (i) inability to maintain a level pelvis, or (ii) ipsilateral shift of a level pelvis. Both presentations may be observed as a lateral hip (ASIS) relative to the knee (hip adduction), and may also be referred to as a "Trendelenberg sign" (Table 8.3 and Fig. 8.17d).

Knee

Does the center of the knee remain over the center of the foot? If the knee deviates toward a more medial position (relative to the foot), this is an indication of increased hip internal rotation and/or adduction, and appears as a knee valgus (apparent knee valgus) posture. Increased hip internal rotation/adduction may result from altered control of hip muscles (e.g. hip external rotators) (Table 8.3).

Overall impression

An individual with altered hip/trunk muscle function may exhibit global signs, such as poor quality of movement or coordination, inability to squat to the desired depth, increased speed of activity, or inability to maintain balance.

Landing—specific considerations

There are a number of ways to evaluate single-leg and double-leg landing biomechanics in the clinical setting. The clinician should determine what is appropriate taking into account the individual's sporting requirements and injury history. It may be more appropriate to evaluate single-leg landing if a higher functioning sportsperson presents with a lower limb injury, such as our example of the patient with patellofemoral pain. The single-leg landing may be the best way to identify biomechanical deficiencies such as increased knee abduction, and decreased knee, hip, and trunk flexion.

Conversely, in individuals recovering from injury and/or surgery, double-leg landing may be a more appropriate test, so that healing tissue does not receive excessive stress. It may also be important to evaluate landing performance both pre- and post-exercise, since fatigue is associated with increased knee abduction and reduced knee flexion during landing.[35, 36]

We suggest evaluating both double-leg and single-leg landing using a drop landing assessment from a 30 cm high platform (Fig. 8.17e–g). The clinician should observe the landing pattern for signs of reduced knee and hip flexion, and/or an abnormally erect landing posture. Knee valgus is another movement to observe. Maximum knee valgus should reach approximately 10° for females and 5° for males for both tests from this height.[37] Excessive valgus and/or the presence of a heavy landing pattern involving minimal knee, hip, and trunk flexion increases risk for future knee injury or re-injury, such as non-contact anterior cruciate ligament injuries (Chapter 32).

As with running and squatting assessment, video footage can be used for more in-depth analysis of

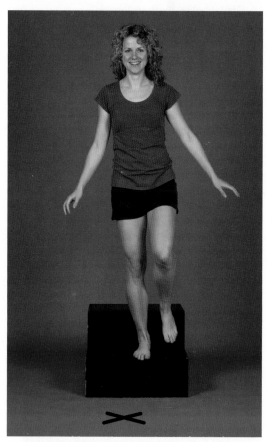

Figure 8.17 (cont.) Functional assessment of the lower limb
(e) Starting position for single leg landing

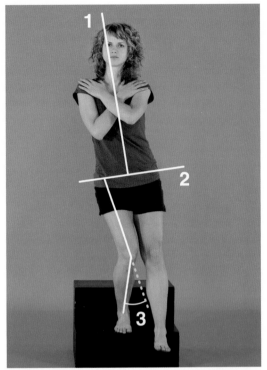

Figure 8.17 (cont.) Functional assessment of the lower limb

(f) View from the front

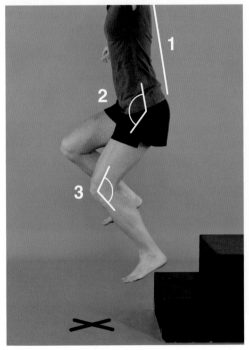

(g) View from the side

double-leg and single-leg landing. The clinician can use slow-motion replay and computer software packages to gain a more accurate picture of the degree of knee valgus during landing.

Dynamic movement assessment (e.g. running biomechanics)

A key to clinical biomechanical assessment is careful observation of functional movement (Fig. 8.18). Running is a component of many sports, and the clinician should have an effective method to assess for biomechanical problems associated with running. As a clinician, look for obvious deviations from the ideal running pattern, and use this to guide further assessment and treatment decisions. Common deviations and possible implications to injury are outlined in the "Ideal biomechanics with movement—running" section earlier in this chapter. If possible, observe sportspeople participating in their sport. If necessary, sport-specific skills can be broken down into component movements to simplify observation in the clinic. Furthermore, functional clinical tests outlined in this chapter may provide insight into

Figure 8.18 Dynamic movements are an important part of the lower limb biomechanical assessment

biomechanics during more sport-specific tasks when they cannot be evaluated in the clinical setting. For example, excessive hip adduction during the completion of a single-leg squat may be indicative of excessive hip adduction during running and landing.

To detect suboptimal biomechanics with the naked eye takes years of training and experience. Video analysis can provide valuable information from multiple views, and can assist the clinician greatly. This is usually done by having the patient run on a treadmill; reflective markers can be added to identify anatomical landmarks and bony alignment. Video footage can then be slowed on a replay, and this may reveal otherwise hidden anomalies. A number of computer software programs (e.g. Dartfish, SiliconCoach) can also assist with this analysis. The source of any biomechanical anomalies may be further investigated by a thorough clinical assessment.

Sport-specific assessment

Detailed sport-specific assessment is outside the scope of this chapter. Specific injuries associated with certain sport biomechanics are listed in Table 8.4 overleaf. The principles for sport-specific lower limb assessment (and biomechanical assessment for upper limb too) are:

- to understand the normal biomechanics in the sport and the normal range
- to view the sportsperson in action, both fresh and when the patient is fatigued
- to perform formal biomechanical assessment in a laboratory with reflective markers, which may be helpful both for diagnosis and for the purpose of rehabilitating the patient.

Summary of the lower limb biomechanical assessment

To iterate how we opened this section, there is no single way to perform the lower limb biomechanical assessment; it varies by clinical specialty (e.g. physiotherapy, podiatry, medicine, soft tissue therapy, nurse). Also, the clinical problem influences the order of the assessment, and the relative emphasis on various elements. In this introductory chapter, we ignored the tests used to assess aggravating activities which help identify a link between activity and injury. For teaching purposes, we deliberately outlined a simple procedure that would apply for a patient with patellofemoral pain.

Clinical assessment of footwear—the Footwear Assessment Tool

Footwear assessment is a vital component of the lower limb biomechanical evaluation. The Footwear Assessment Tool is a free, 6-item template to guide the clinician in assessing footwear.[38] It is illustrated on http://tiny.cc/sw1k8 and is reproduced on the *Clinical Sports Medicine* masterclasses.

 www.clinicalsportsmedicine.com

The following items are key.

Fit

Consider length, width, and depth because an inadequately sized shoe can compress the foot and cause joint compressions (e.g. Morton's neuroma) or restrict normal foot function.

General structure

The three elements of structure that need to be assessed are pitch (heel height), last shape, and the forefoot flexion point.

Pitch (heel height)

The pitch of a shoe influences sagittal plane motion during gait. A low pitch (flat shoe) is not suitable for an individual with structural ankle equinus (limited ankle dorsiflexion), as it will lead to even greater compensatory foot pronation to augment step/stride length.

Last

Last shapes accommodate varying foot types. A straight last (0 to 5°) accommodates a more pronated foot better, whereas a curved last (>15°) may optimize gait efficiency in a supinated foot (Fig. 9.10c).

Forefoot sole flexion point

The sole flexion point should line up with the first metatarsophalangeal joint. If the flexion point of the shoe is too proximal, stability is impaired. If the flexion point is too distal, it will impair normal sagittal plane motion of the first metatarsophalangeal joint.

Motion control properties

Motion control is particularly important for excessive pronators. Footwear properties that influence motion control include the presence or absence of a multiple density sole, heel counter stiffness, midfoot torsional and sagittal stability, and type of fixation (e.g. lacing).

Table 8.4 Sport-specific technique faults that experienced clinicians believe are associated with increased risk of specific injuries (level 5 evidence)

Sport	Technique	Injury
Tennis	Excessive wrist action with backhand	Extensor tendinopathy of elbow
	Service contact made too far back (i.e. ball toss not in front)	Flexor tendinopathy of elbow
Swimming	Insufficient body roll Low elbow on recovery Insufficient shoulder external rotation	Rotator cuff tendinopathy
Diving	Shooting at the water too early (backward dives)	Lumbar spine injuries
Cycling	Incorrect handlebar and seat height	Thoracic/lumbar spine injuries
	Toe-in/toe-out on cleats	Iliotibial band friction syndrome, patellofemoral pain syndrome
Weightlifting (Olympic)	Bar position too far in front of body in clean or jerk phase	Lumbar spine injuries Sacroiliac joint injuries
Weightlifting (power lifting)	Grip too wide on bar in bench press	Pectoralis major tendinopathy
	Toes pointing forward on squatting	Patellofemoral pain syndrome, medial meniscus injury
Javelin	Elbow "dropped"	Medial elbow pain
	Poor hip drive	Thoracic/lumbar spine dysfunction
Triple jump	"Blocking" on step phase	Sacroiliac joint/lumbar spine injuries, patellar tendinopathy, sinus tarsi syndrome
High jump	Incorrect foot plant	Patellar tendinopathy, sinus tarsi syndrome, fibular stress fracture
Pole vault	Too close on take-off	Lumbar spine injuries (e.g. spondylolysis)
	Late plant	Ankle impingement, talar stress fracture, shoulder impingement
Running	Anterior pelvic tilt	Hamstring injuries
	Poor lateral pelvic control	Iliotibial band friction syndrome
Cricket bowling	Mixed side-on/front-on action	Pars interarticularis stress fracture
Baseball pitching	Opening up too soon	Anterior shoulder instability, elbow medial collateral ligament sprains, osteochondritis of radiocapitellar joint
	Dropped elbow "hanging"	Rotator cuff tendinopathy
Gymnastics	Excessive lumbar hyperextension on landing	Pars interarticularis stress fracture
	Tumble too short (insufficient rotation)	Anterior ankle impingement
Rowing	Change from bow side to stroke side	Rib stress fractures
Ballet	Poor turnout	Hip injuries, medial knee pain
	"Sickling" *en pointe*	Second metatarsal stress fracture

These properties can be quantified using the "Motion Control Properties Scale" outlined below (Table 8.5). Scores range from 0 to 11, with 11 indicating the highest level of motion control.

Cushioning

Although evidence is limited, footwear cushioning is thought to be important for the prevention of lower limb stress fractures, particularly in more active populations.[39] Footwear components to consider include sole density, inner soles, and the presence or absence of cushioning systems such as air and gel pockets. However, the presence of cushioning in the heel may have implications for the pitch of the shoe (i.e. increase heel height), with subsequent undesirable influences on foot strike patterns (i.e. inhibit forefoot striking).[3]

Wear patterns

The wear pattern of a shoe can provide insight into the biomechanics of gait. Medial tilt of the upper, medial compression of the midsole (Fig. 8.19a), and greater medial than lateral wear of the outsole (Fig. 8.19b) indicate excessive pronation. Lateral tilt of the upper, lateral compression/collapse of the midsole, and greater lateral than medial wear of the outsole reflect excessive supination.

Conditions related to suboptimal lower limb biomechanics

Conventional wisdom has linked suboptimal lower limb biomechanics with various injuries, but there is a lack of prospective empirical evidence to confirm that biomechanical factors increase risk for lower limb injuries.[40] Thus, for now, most biomechanical "risk factors" have only level 3 to 5 evidence (see Chapter 3 for more on levels of evidence).

Table 8.6 overleaf lists common lower limb injuries, common clinical considerations, and evidence to support these considerations. It contains the "best available evidence" at January 2011.

The topic of biomechanical risk factors is discussed further in Chapter 9, and in Part B of this book, which covers specific conditions.

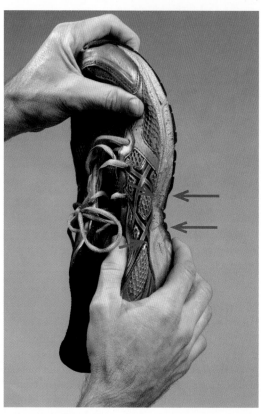

Figure 8.19 Shoe wear patterns—running shoe
(a) With medial compression of the upper

Table 8.5 Motion Control Properties Scale

Item	Score			
	0	1	2	3
Midsole density layers	Single density		Dual density	
Fixation (upper to foot)	None	Alternative to laces (e.g. strap, Velcro, zip)	Laces (at least 3 eyelets)	
Heel counter stiffness	No heel counter	Minimal	Moderate	Rigid
Midfoot sagittal stability	Minimal	Moderate	Rigid	
Midfoot torsional stability	Minimal	Moderate	Rigid	

Minimal = >45°; moderate = <45°; rigid = <10°

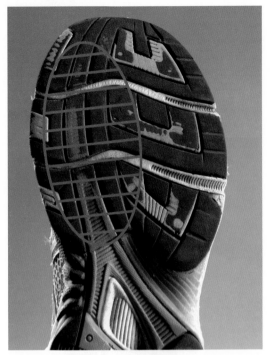

Figure 8.19 (cont.) (b) With excessive pronation there is greater wear on the medial (shaded) than the lateral sole

Management of lower limb biomechanical abnormalities

The next major theme of this chapter introduces management strategies to address biomechanical problems. There is increasing evidence about the role of therapies such as foot orthoses, footwear, taping, and exercise to improve a patient's biomechanics. This section provides a background perspective and specific chapters in Part B address specific conditions. Here we focus mostly on interventions that affect the foot and lower leg.

Foot orthoses

Foot orthoses—in-shoe devices—are used extensively in sports and exercise medicine to optimize lower limb function.[76] In this section we:

- review the various types of orthoses available
- introduce the debate about their mechanism of action
- highlight that there is high-quality evidence for their effectiveness
- share three main approaches to deciding how to fit an orthotic for a specific patient.

Types of foot orthoses

Foot orthoses range in material from soft or flexible to semirigid devices, and may be prefabricated or custom-fabricated. Prefabricated or "off-the-shelf" foot orthoses (Fig. 8.20a overleaf) are usually fabricated from materials such as EVA (ethyl-vinyl acetate), polyurethane, cork, or rubber. The devices' generic shape can be customized a little to the individual via heat molding or the addition of wedges or heel raises. Prefabricated orthoses provide a quick and cheap intervention but their limited potential for customization and inability to achieve total plantar contact may restrict their use in some patients.

Custom-fabricated foot orthoses (Fig. 8.20b) are manufactured from a three-dimensional representation of the individual's foot using plaster impressions or laser-scanning devices. Custom foot orthoses may accommodate specific structural anomalies more effectively than prefabricated orthoses. Most often, custom foot orthoses are manufactured from polypropylene and carbon-fiber composites. As such, they are generally more rigid than prefabricated orthoses, and are often perceived to more effectively optimize biomechanical control. Their prescription requires a higher level of expertise and specific equipment.

In the sports and exercise medicine setting, a podiatrist will typically prescribe custom-fabricated foot orthoses, which will be manufactured in a laboratory. The prescription will typically contain information regarding materials to be used, extent of accommodative postings, and shoe fit. In the laboratory, a solid model of the foot is manufactured from the three-dimensional representation. Additional material is added to provide the appropriate level (degrees) of control. The material of choice is then vacuum-pressed onto the model, and covered to suit the individual.

To date, no study has identified an advantage for custom-fabricated devices over prefabricated orthoses when managing lower limb conditions.[76] The following factors should influence the recommendation for a particular type of orthotic:

- If the patient wears a wide range of footwear during training and competition, the custom-fabricated orthotic has an advantage as it can be designed to fit a wide range of footwear; prefabricated devices may need to be modified to fit into specific footwear.
- If the patient participates in sports that involve repetitive landing, a more soft or flexible device minimizes the risk of arch discomfort or blistering.

Table 8.6 Best available evidence[a] for the association between common lower limb overuse injuries and biomechanics (as at January 2011)

Injury/condition	Associated lower limb biomechanical risk factor	Injury/condition	Associated lower limb biomechanical risk factor
Sesamoiditis	Supinated foot type[41, 42] Pronated foot type Forefoot valgus, plantar flexed first ray[42] Decreased ankle DF/ankle equinus[42] Limited first ray range of motion	Iliotibial band friction syndrome	Increased hip adduction (dynamic [e.g. running])[71] Increased knee IR (dynamic [e.g. running])[71] Increased knee flexion at heel strike[72] Increased velocity of knee IR (dynamic [e.g. running])[72] Increased maximal foot inversion[72]
Plantar fasciitis	Pronated foot type[23, 43, 44] Decreased ankle DF/ankle equinus[43, 45, 46] Increased ankle DF[23] Supinated foot type[47] Leg length difference[47]	Adductor tendinopathy	Decreased total hip rotation (IR, ER)[73]
		Metatarsal stress fractures	Pronated foot type[12] Increased subtalar joint inversion[48] Supinated foot
Achilles tendinopathy	Increased subtalar joint inversion[48] Increased ankle DF[49] Decreased gastrocnemius length[48] Supinated foot type[50] Pronated foot type[50, 51]	Tarsal stress fractures	Increased subtalar joint inversion[48]
		Navicular stress fractures	Pronated foot type Ankle equinus
Lateral ankle sprain, chronic ankle instability	Prolonged pronation[52] Decreased ankle DF[53] Increased first metatarsophalangeal joint extension [52, 54] Increased ankle inversion at heel strike[13, 14]	Fibular stress fractures	Supinated foot type Pronated foot type
		Tibial stress fractures	Supinated foot type[12]
Peroneal tendinopathy	Supinated foot type[55]	Femoral stress fractures	Supinated foot type[12] Decreased subtalar joint inversion[48]
Medial shin pain (medial tibial stress syndrome, shin splints)	Pronated foot type[56, 57, 58] Increased ankle PF[59] Supinated foot type[60] Decreased ankle DF/ankle equinus[61] Decreased hip IR[62]	Unspecified lower limb stress fractures	Pronated foot type[48] Supinated foot type[48] Increased hip ER[74] Leg length difference[75]
Patellar tendinopathy	Decreased quadriceps and hamstrings flexibility[63] Anteriorly tilted patella[64] Pronated foot type Supinated foot type		
Patellofemoral pain syndrome	Pronated foot type[65] Hypermobile patella[66] Decreased quadriceps flexibility[66] Increased hip IR (passive and dynamic)[65] Decreased knee flexion (dynamic [e.g. jump-landing])[65] Increased knee abduction moment[67] Increased Q angle[68] (p.693) Increased hip adduction (dynamic [e.g. running])[69] Decreased hamstrings flexibility[70]		

Green = supported by prospective findings

Orange = supported by case-control or retrospective findings

Black = no/inconclusive evidence, clinical opinion

DF = dorsiflexion; PF = plantarflexion; IR = internal rotation; ER = external rotation

(a) Evidence is included from the highest quality studies (i.e. if there is evidence from a prospective study, evidence from case-control studies are not included)

Figure 8.20 Orthoses
(a) Prefabricated or "off-the-shelf" orthoses

(b) Custom-fabricated or casted orthoses

Furthermore, many sportspeople do not tolerate large degrees of arch support from orthoses; in these circumstances, it is often helpful to reduce the arch contour.

- The difference in cost may be an important determinant for some patients, although the more expensive custom orthotic also has greater durability. It is not unusual for a custom orthotic to last five years or more.
- There is generally a several-week interval between fitting and supply of custom orthoses, particularly when they are manufactured off-site. Once the patient has the orthotic, there may be a further "wearing-in" period to prevent adverse effects. This means that there may be a delay in attaining the full therapeutic benefits of the intervention. (It may be appropriate to prescribe a prefabricated device for the interim period.)
- Other considerations include the patient's body mass (e.g. greater weight requires a rigid orthotic to influence greater forces) and personal preference.

Mechanism of action—an unfinished story

Traditional dogma was that foot orthoses controlled foot motion and, thus, improved biomechanical efficiency and balanced loads on structures more appropriately. However, this is now in dispute. Some studies indicate that foot orthoses can influence foot motion,[77–79] while others show that they impart no systematic effects on foot motion.[80, 81]

Alternative paradigms relating to shock absorption and neuromuscular effects[82] include:

- that the cushioning effect of orthoses attenuates the impact force that occurs when the foot hits the ground[83–85]
- that the input provided by foot orthoses through their total contact with the plantar surface of the foot stimulates the neuromuscular system, which may reduce muscle activity and fatigue, and optimize performance.[86–88]

This is an exciting area of investigation which we will follow closely over the next few years.

Orthoses are effective—high-quality evidence is accumulating

Irrespective of how foot orthoses exert their clinical effects, evidence from systematic reviews (level 1) and controlled clinical trials (level 2) supports their use in a variety of conditions related to suboptimal lower limb biomechanics (Table 8.7). (See Chapter 3 for a discussion of levels of evidence.)

Three contemporary approaches for fitting an orthotic

Although evidence is accumulating that specific types of orthoses are effective in specific settings to treat specific clinical conditions, it is still difficult to recommend a "gold standard" approach to prescribing orthoses. This part of our clinical approach remains an art based on limited science—as it is in many situations across healthcare. Thus, the clinician should integrate the research findings that provide support for some approaches (see below) and also take into account the clinical assessment findings, previous clinical experience with the condition and the type of patient, as well as the patient's preferred orthotic type. This integration is consistent with the three-pronged approach to evidence-based practice (Chapter 3; Fig. 3.1 in particular).

Table 8.7 Best available evidence for the use of foot orthoses in the management of common lower limb conditions

Condition	Type of orthotic	Level of evidence	Reference
Prevention			
Lower limb overuse conditions (stress fractures, ankle sprains, foot and ankle problems)	Prefabricated, custom-fabricated	1	Collins[76]
Stress fractures (femoral, tibial, unspecified)	Custom-fabricated, shock-absorbing	1	Rome,[39] Snyder[89]
Treatment			
Patellofemoral pain syndrome	Prefabricated	1	Barton[90]
Chronic musculoskeletal pain associated with pes cavus	Custom-fabricated	1	Burns[91]
Achilles tendinopathy	Custom-fabricated	2	Mayer[92]
Plantar fasciitis	Prefabricated	2	Baldassin,[93] Landorf,[94] Martin,[95]
	Custom-fabricated	2	Baldassin,[93] Landorf,[94] Lynch,[96] Martin,[95] Rome,[97] Roos[98]
Lower limb overuse conditions (varied)	Custom-fabricated	2	Trotter[99]
Lateral ankle sprain/chronic ankle instability	Custom-fabricated	3	Guskiewicz,[100] Orteza[101]
Medial shin pain (medial tibial stress syndrome, shin splints)	Prefabricated	3	Louden[102]
Sesamoiditis	Custom-fabricated	5	Sammarco,[103] ACFAOM[104]
Peroneal tendinopathy	Custom-fabricated	5	ACFAOM[104]
Patellar tendinopathy	Custom-fabricated	5	ACFAOM[104]
Iliotibial band friction syndrome	Custom-fabricated	5	ACFAOM[104]

Green = supported by systematic reviews or randomized controlled trials

Orange = supported by nonrandomized studies and case series

Black = expert opinion, clinical guidelines

The traditional approach—Root and the goal of "subtalar joint neutral"

Merton Root developed the functional foot orthotic in the 1950s and 1960s.[105] He proposed that subtalar joint neutral served as a standard position to evaluate structural relationships in the foot[105] and that this position represented normal foot alignment during the midstance and heel-off phases of gait.[106] Unfortunately, the alignment measures proposed by Root are unreliable, and the subtalar joint is not in neutral during midstance.[106] Nevertheless, this approach to casting orthoses has been associated with many successful clinical outcomes, and it remains one of the most common ways of prescribing orthoses.[107]

Treatment direction test

Professor Bill Vicenzino[108] proposed a "treatment direction test" (TDT) to prescribe and apply foot orthoses for lower limb musculoskeletal disorders that have a biomechanical association. The TDT complements the "tissue-stress model" of McPoil and Hunt,[106] in that it seeks to identify symptomatic tissues under excessive loads, and reduce these loads using an external physical modality. This may consist of adhesive strapping tape, temporary felt orthoses, or prefabricated foot orthoses with or without add-on wedges. The modality is selected based on what the clinician identifies as an aberrant movement pattern, such as excessive or prolonged pronation.

The quality and pain-free quantity of a patient-specific aggravating activity is assessed with and without the external modality. For example, the single-leg squat is suitable to assess a patient with patellofemoral pain, while a heel raise is more appropriate for Achilles tendinopathy. An improvement in the quality of movement or an increase in pain-free repetitions of at least 75% indicates a high likelihood of success with subsequent prescription of orthoses. The reliability and validity of the TDT is under review.

Comfort

Nigg et al.[87] proposed that comfortable devices (orthoses, footwear) that support the skeleton's preferred movement path could reduce muscle activity and the resulting fatigue, and thus improve performance. Vicenzino and colleagues[109] proposed a model of prescription for prefabricated foot orthoses based on patient comfort. Once the patient reports comfort, the clinician can further modify the device to improve pain-free performance of an aggravating functional

A team approach: correcting biomechanics with exercises and functional retraining

In this box, we emphasize that clinicians working together can better address biomechanical factors than a single clinician working alone

Exercises and functional retraining should always be considered when managing lower limb biomechanical issues. Exercises and functional retraining are expanded in Chapters 14 and 15; here we want to emphasize the team approach. All clinicians in sports and exercise medicine should appreciate the influence of muscle imbalance on biomechanical abnormalities. Thus, excessive tightness of muscles such as the psoas, tensor fascia lata, hip adductors, hamstrings, and gastrocnemius can be addressed using exercises such as static stretches and proprioceptive neuromuscular facilitation (PNF), in conjunction with other modalities such as soft tissue therapy, heat, or dry needling. Muscle weakness or uncoordination requires strengthening and retraining exercises (Chapter 15):

- Dysfunction of the abdominals, gluteus medius and minimus, hip external rotators, vastus medialis obliquus, and tibialis posterior should be considered in the patient with suboptimal lower limb biomechanics. Although non-weight-bearing exercises may be used initially, they should be progressed to functional weight-bearing positions as soon as possible.
- Once optimal static muscle activation has been achieved, exercises can be progressed by adding lower limb movements, resistance (e.g. dumbbells, resistance bands), or stability challenges (e.g. Swedish balls, single-limb stance).
- Motor control exercises of the hip and foot are useful to promote optimal alignment of the lower limb in the sagittal, frontal, and transverse planes, as well as ideal muscle recruitment patterns.
- Exercises that incorporate the lower limb in its closed kinetic chain function include the single-leg squat, single-leg heel raise, single-leg stance, and arch form.

- The next stage involves integration of this new control into functional activities, such as running, landing, or sport-specific skills. Small components of the overall movement should be incorporated initially, along with specific instruction and feedback. These movements may need to be performed slowly, to allow them to be integrated successfully into the functional activity (Chapter 15).

Attend to the entire kinetic chain

It is important to consider the potential causes and effects of suboptimal biomechanics on the entire neuromusculoskeletal system. For example:

- Ankle joint stiffness may contribute to altered biomechanics during gait, or may occur as a consequence of calf muscle imbalance.
- Joint pain or stiffness can be addressed with active or passive mobilization of peripheral or vertebral joints, or Mulligan's "Mobilisation with Movement."[115]
- Increased neural mechanosensitivity can be managed with appropriate exercises, as well as correction of possible causes such as spinal hypomobility.

Other interventions aimed at reducing pain (such as pharmacotherapy, electrotherapy, and acupuncture) may facilitate optimal performance of exercises (Chapter 13).

Last resort! Training modifications

If these interventions fail to optimize lower limb biomechanics, the clinician may need to investigate other options. This is particularly the case with structural anomalies. It may be necessary for the sportsperson to reduce training load, incorporate cross-training, or even modify his or her technique to ensure maximal training benefits while minimizing potential for injury. A Cochrane review found evidence that modification of training schedules by reducing running frequency, distance, or duration significantly reduced the incidence of overuse injuries.[116]

task, all the time aiming to maintain comfort. The first clinical trial to utilize this method reported greater than 80% success with orthoses over a one-year period.[110]

Irrespective of the long-term outcome of this branch of research, comfort should always be an important consideration for all foot orthoses prescribed. If the device is not comfortable, there is the risk of skin blistering and new foot pain. Also, any device that is perceived to be uncomfortable is likely to lead to poor patient compliance.

Footwear as a therapy rather than as a cause of injury!

When considering any intervention addressing suboptimal lower limb biomechanics, the potential influence of footwear should be considered (see also "Clinical assessment of footwear" above). Consider how the current footwear influences the patient's condition, how footwear interacts with other treatment (e.g. foot orthoses), and whether altering footwear characteristics can help treat the condition.

Fit
Footwear fit is particularly important when prescribing orthoses. If an orthotic is added to a shoe that has inadequate room, it may result in forefoot pain or limit the time the orthotic is worn. Remember that sportspeople often wear a range of shoes in training and competition—check all of them!

General structure
One particularly important consideration in the case of ankle equinus is the pitch of the shoe (heel height, discussed above). Structural equinus may be compensated for by prescribing new footwear with greater heel height, or adding a heel lift to existing footwear. Conversely, if the clinician aims to change the patient's foot strike pattern from a rearfoot strike to a forefoot strike (e.g. to reduce lower limb shock loading), it may pay to lower the pitch.

Motion control properties
If the patient's shoe has suboptimal motion control (e.g. minimal heel counter stiffness) leading to excessive foot pronation, shoe replacement may be the best treatment. Footwear with greater heel counter stiffness, midfoot sole rigidity, adequate lacing (Fig 8.21a, b), and possibly a multiple density sole (i.e. increased density on the medial aspect of the shoe) may prevent excessive foot motion. Footwear support can also be enhanced by

education on how to complete loop lacing (see Fig. 8.21 for instructions and details). Such changes in relation to footwear may reduce the need for foot orthoses.

Taping
Adhesive strapping tape (Chapter 13) is a temporary intervention to address lower limb biomechanical issues. Anti-pronation tape (Fig. 8.22) is commonly used to treat plantar fasciitis (Chapter 40) and patellofemoral pain (Chapter 33).

This type of taping—anti-pronation tape—has both biomechanical and neuromuscular effects

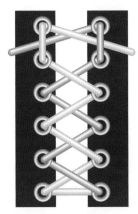

Figure 8.21 (a) Lock-lacing to prevent heel slippage—lace the shoe normally until the second set of eyelets. Then feed the laces into the top eyelet on the same side. Now cross each lace over, and feed through the loop formed between the first and second eyelet on the opposite side. Laces should then be pulled and tied as normal

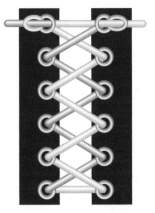

(b) Loop to create a snug fit—after lacing, put each lace end back through the last hole to create a small loop on the top side of the shoe. Then thread each loose end through the loop on the opposite side and tighten

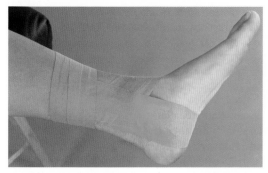

Figure 8.22 Anti-pronation taping as invented by podiatrist Dr Ralph Dye
(a) Low-Dye taping–straps to reduce subtalar joint motion

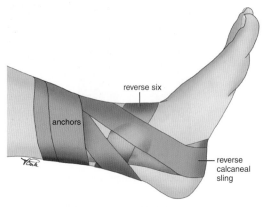

reverse six

anchors

reverse calcaneal sling

(b) Augmented low-Dye taping adds reverse sixes (purple) and calcaneal slings (green) anchored to the lower leg[111]

during static and dynamic tasks.[112] Specifically, it increases navicular and medial longitudinal arch height, reduces tibial internal rotation and calcaneal eversion, alters patterns of plantar pressure, and reduces activity of particular leg muscles.[112]

Techniques such as patellar taping may also alleviate symptoms associated with patellofemoral joint biomechanics.[113, 114] It is important to be aware of skin breakdown associated with prolonged use of tape (particularly in sportspeople involved in vigorous activity), and to implement appropriate strategies to prevent this.

Biomechanics of cycling
with EMMA COLSON

Cycling is unique due to the combination of extreme postural inertia of the upper and lower body together with excessive, repetitive load on the lower limbs. A competitive road cyclist sits in the same position for 25–35 hours per week and cycles at a rate of

80–120 rpm, thus performing in excess of 150 000 lower limb repetitions per week. There are four main Olympic cycling disciplines—road, track, mountain bike, and BMX. Within some of these disciplines, there are different events with different athlete types in competition (sprint, endurance, and a mixture of both). There are also a huge variety of recreational cyclists.

As most kilometers are done on road bikes, we present below the set-up basics of a road bike.

Set-up and positioning on the bike
Factors that the clinician must take into account when assessing bike set-up include seat height, seat fore/aft position, and reach. When assessing set-up, always ensure the cyclist has warmed up first.

Seat height
Incorrect seat height has several sequelae. If the seat is too high, power is diminished because lower limb muscles must work beyond their optimal length–tension range. Also, there is excess stress on the posterior structures (hamstrings, gastrocnemius, and posterior knee joint capsule). Furthermore, compensatory excessive hip extension causes loss of the stable pelvic core.[117] In this situation, the rider often rocks the pelvis from side to side to maintain stability on the bicycle, and this fatigues structures such as the adductors, gluteals, spine, and even upper body musculature.

Conversely, a low seat increases knee flexion throughout the pedal cycle and increases patellofemoral and suprapatellar bursal loading.[118] It also places the hamstring, gluteal, and gastrocnemius muscles in a suboptimal length–tension relationship.[117]

Measurement
- Foot at bottom stroke (Fig. 8.23a). With the elite cyclist, measurements are a guide, but in the end this is the desired "look."
- In-seam measurement (Fig. 8.23b). A useful rough guide is the Le Mond method first described by US cyclist Greg Le Mond. This measurement multiplied by a factor of 0.88 will roughly approximate the measurement of the center-to-top height (see Fig. 8.23c).
- Center-to-top measurement (Fig. 8.23c). This height should be equal to the in-seam measurement multiplied by 0.88 (Le Mond method).

Figure 8.23 Measurement of seat height
(a) Elite rider extension of stroke

(c) Center-to-top measuring

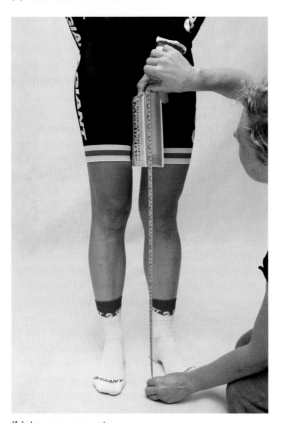

(b) In-seam measuring

Variations to seat height measurement will depend on:

- seat type and weight distribution
- cleat position—movement fore or aft will effectively alter leg length
- cleat stack height—will affect relative leg length
- personal preference—excessively plantarflexed riders might like a high seat
- seat fore/aft—a set-back seat may need to be lower
- crank length—smaller cranks will require a higher seat
- shoe thickness—thicker soles increase relative leg length
- rider experience—for the recreational cyclist or one new to the sport, the first priority is the ability to safely dismount, so this type of cyclist might ride with the seat at lower than optimum height.

Seat fore/aft position

Fore/aft position is important for knee loading.[118] A seat too far forward will result in increased patellofemoral compression forces. The seat fore/aft position also affects hip flexion and gluteal–hamstring muscle length. If the seat is too far back, the hamstring and gluteal muscles will be overlengthened, which appears to inhibit force production. If the seat is too far forward, the knees become more flexed, the hips more extended, and the muscles of the lower limb are at a less than optimal length–tension relationship. In addition, the more upright position is less aerodynamic.

Seat inclination can also be varied from 0° of anterior tilt (i.e. a "flat" seat) to about 15°; inclination beyond this angle causes the rider to slip off the seat. Traditionally, it has been recommended that the seat be flat. A biomechanical study suggested that 10–15° of anterior inclination reduces low back pain.[119] Further study of this matter is required.

Measurement
- Plumb bolt method for saddle fore/aft measurement (Fig. 8.24). Here the bike is level and the plumb bolt is dropped from the posterior part of the tibial tuberosity to land either over the pedal axis or behind it. Landing in front of the axis will result in increased patellofemoral joint loading.

Figure 8.24 Measurement of seat fore/aft position—plumb bolt over axis

The amount of seat set-back is a personal choice and will relate to the following:
- rider size—a larger cyclist will be more comfortable further back
- hip flexibility—a cyclist with poor hip range will need to be further forward
- bike handling—moving behind the bottom bracket may lighten the front end a little, which could feel unbalanced and less stable for a road bike but allow a mountain biker to lift the front and push the front wheel into corners more
- event type—time trial and triathlon cyclists are usually very far forward, as they lean down and stretch out in front of the bike into an extreme aerodynamic position; this sort of riding is not comfortable for long-distance endurance training
- rider stability and flexibility—a cyclist needs flexibility and also stability to sustain a set-back seat position; this comes with years of cycling experience and can be assisted by specific exercises.

Reach
Reach measurement probably has the most variability with set-up. There is no measurement for reach as it will depend on rider flexibility, experience, comfort, desired bike-handling and desired aerodynamics. In Figure 8.25, it is clear that the same setting of reach can look right if the cyclist has the flexibility and control to maintain the position (Fig. 8.25a), or look wrong if the cyclist is stiff or unable to maintain the desired position (Fig. 8.25b).

Measurement
- Bar reach and drop—good positioning (Fig. 8.25a). With good positioning, the set-up allows the cyclist to attain an anteriorly tilted pelvis, a flat unkinked back, retracted scapulae, unlocked elbows, and relaxed upper limbs.
- Bar reach and drop—poor positioning (Fig. 8.25b). Poor positioning results when, for the same settings as those used in Figure 8.25a, the cyclist has poor flexibility through the pelvis, hip, and hamstrings. This pulls the cyclist backward and makes the bike reach look too extreme.

Variations to reach will be dependent on the type of cycling. Track riders and time trial cyclists will be very stretched out, whereas a mountain biker will be more upright, reflecting less aerodynamic demand and more focus on handling and maneuverability.

A

Figure 8.25 Measurement of bar reach and drop
(a) Good positioning

(b) Poor positioning

Cranks

Crank size is proportionate to trochanteric height (leg length). In general, the issue is really only for small riders. Riders under about 165 cm (5 ft 5 in.) should be on cranks of 170 cm length or less. Very small riders of 160 cm (5 ft 3 in.) or less could be better on 167.5 or even 165 cm cranks. If there is any issue of knee problems in a smaller cyclist, this is one point to give early consideration to. Conversely, very tall riders should be on 175 cm cranks and those over 180 cm (6 ft) might consider 177.5 cm cranks. Crank size seems unimportant for people of average height.

Cleats/pedal interface

Cleats are the most finicky part of elite cycling. Effective force transference, and hence less injury potential, is gained with a cleat with a low stack height. This places the foot closer to the pedal.

Float has become a popular and controversial part of cleat design. The desired outcome of float is motion that allows the cyclist to move the foot unrestrained if required. Getting out of the seat is one such example. If the foot were fixed rigidly to the pedal, the knee would be strained excessively. Float, however, should not be confused with slop. "Slop" is undesired motion of the foot while applying power to the pedals. Hence, a good cleat design has a midpoint that the foot will sit at most of the time, with a small amount of force required to move off that midpoint.

Cleat positioning

- Fore/aft. The cleat should allow the base of the first metatarsal to sit over the pedal axis. This facilitates maximum leverage though the foot (Fig. 8.26a).
- Medial and lateral. Most cleats allow adjustment toward the inside or outside of the shoe. Riders with narrow hips would place the cleats to the maximum outside position, thus allowing their legs to be close together—mimicking their standing alignment. Riders with wide hips or a wide natural stance would do the opposite.
- Rotation. In general, the feet should be pointing straight ahead. However, if the cyclist has a natural toe-out position, then the cleat needs to be rotated in to accommodate that. Many cyclists ride quite comfortably hitting the crank with their heel slightly on each pedal stroke.

Figure 8.26 (a) Cleat position. Note the therapist's thumb is over the base of the first metatarsal, which lines up with the center point of the pedal spindle

Figure 8.26 (cont.) (b) Limb alignment. Note the alignment of the hip, knee, and ankle

The main aim of cleat setting is to align the hip, knee, and ankle (Fig. 8.26b). However, should the natural stance of the cyclist be poorly aligned, the cleats will need to be set to allow for this.

Pedal and cleat systems mostly go together. The size of the pedal platform might be relevant for very tall cyclists who find smaller cleat systems too unstable. Similarly, very small riders might find a large pedal platform reduces their foot leverage.

Cyclists with narrow hips may also have problems with the increased Q angle of some pedal systems that are set a long way out from the crank. This situation is aggravated by a wide bottom bracket (on many mountain bikes) and also cranks that angle outward at the pedal end.

Seats

Comfort on the seat is imperative to endurance cycling. Seats should be set horizontal, as mentioned above. A slight downward tilt can be useful with aerobar use or for someone with limited hip motion. Seats should be narrow enough to allow the legs to pedal freely without impingement (Fig. 8.27).

Shoes

Many road shoes have a poor foot bed and may require the addition of an orthotic, especially for riders with pronation. Also assess the different shoe shapes. Recreational cyclists riding "street wear" bike shoes sacrifice rigidity, and will overload the knees if they do any substantial distance in them.

Handlebars

Handlebars come in different shapes and sizes. The addition of aerobars to a road bike without any adjustment to seat position will probably create overstretching and neck problems.

Bike set-up in other forms of cycling

Other forms of riding follow this basic bicycle set-up, but some aspects are altered because of the specifics of the sport.

In mountain biking, the aerodynamic positioning is less important than control (depending on the

Figure 8.27 Seat width. Note how the narrow seat allows the cyclist's legs to drop down unimpeded

technical difficulty of the course). Thus, the rider is more upright, and maneuverability of the bicycle becomes paramount. Hence, the frames tend to be small in comparison to the rider, and reach is often shortened to make the front end easier to position and lift over objects.

For the same reason, trick/trial bikes look ridiculously small for the rider.

For downhill mountain biking, power generation is not as important as stability and control, so the seat is positioned to maintain a center of gravity as low as possible. Downhill cyclists usually have another bike with a "correct" seat set-up for fitness training, as distance training with their competition bike set-up would predispose to knee problems.

For time trial, track sprinting and triathlons, the relative height of the seat to handlebars is sometimes increased to improve aerodynamics. These cyclists need good flexibility and excellent stability. Aerobars are added in triathlons to enhance aerodynamics. Triathletes tend to ride with the seat positioned higher and further forward than recommended, and hence "toe" more (i.e. paddle using the toe rather than dipping the heel to plantar grade). This most likely increases the contribution of their quadriceps at the expense of underutilization of the hamstring, gastrocnemius, and gluteal muscles.[117] Anecdotally, triathletes report that their hamstrings feel better for the running section after using this position in the ride.

Aerodynamics and wind resistance

Wind resistance is the primary retarding force in road cycling.[120] The single most important factor in reducing the effect of wind resistance is the front-on surface area that the cyclist exposes to the wind. This becomes particularly important for the cyclist involved in time trial events. The rider must be able to position the pelvis in an anterior tilt to flatten out the lumbar spine and so reduce his or her front-on surface area. It appears that there is a metabolic cost for the cyclist to attain such a position, but this is far outweighed by the aerodynamic power savings.[121]

Road bikes are designed with this ideal in mind, and hence an inability to attain an aerodynamic posture can result in injuries. Physical assessment and rehabilitation of the road cyclist should be directed toward the cyclist attaining an efficient aerodynamic posture without placing strain on his or her body to do so. This requires flexibility, strength, and motor control. Should the cyclist be unable to control a posture to fit the bike, then the setting of the bicycle needs to be modified to ensure injury-free cycling.

Pedaling technique

Motion of the pedal stroke needs to appear (and sound) smooth and continuous. Trying to create an upstroke can be injurious to the cyclist. Cleats aid proprioception, to stop the foot falling off the pedal during high-intensity pedaling.[122]

An upstroke utilizes the psoas and hamstrings at their less than optimal length–tension range, and so will destabilize the pelvis, providing an ineffective base for generation of leg muscle power. The last "up" phase of the pedal cycle is very short. It corresponds to the power phase of the opposite pedal in steady-state riding. The momentum of the ascending leg and drive of the opposite leg create a negative torque situation that drives the ascending leg through to the top stroke.

Assessment

The practitioner needs to understand the cycling discipline of the injured athlete. Cyclist experience, phase of training program, and current goals must be established. As always, the history of the injury is important, with special attention to recent crashes, equipment modifications, training spikes, or training variations. The important components of the physical assessment are:

- body type and size—big sprinters will have very different issues to small hill climbers; very small females are often riding equipment designed for much larger people
- physical alignment (or malalignment) and how that might relate to the injury
- flexibility and stability—to attain the on-bike posture (Fig. 8.28 overleaf), the cyclist needs to be flexible through:
  - arm overhead
  - thoracic spine
  - pelvis anterior tilt
  - hamstrings in tilt position
  - gluteals/hips (tightness here will affect knee tracking)
  - iliotibial band
  - knee range
  - ankle dorsiflexion range.

The cyclist also needs the appropriate muscle strength to hold the on-bike position (Fig. 8.28), and

Figure 8.29 Strengthening exercises for cyclists (a) Scapular strengthening exercises. Cyclists with neck problems should strengthen the scapular retractors while maintaining an anterior pelvic tilt

Figure 8.28 Cyclist in "on-bike" posture. Maintenance of this posture requires both flexibility and stability. The ability to deliver power in the posture requires dissociation of the hips from a stable pelvis and trunk

dissociation of the hip motion from the pelvis and trunk to deliver power.

Strength imbalances in cycling can result in the overloading of one leg or other regions of the body. Assessment should be made of right versus left leg, the lower nerve roots, the vastus medialis obliquus, gluteus maximus, gluteus medius, erector spinae, pelvic floor, transversus abdominis, pelvic floor, the upper body stabilizers (the retractor group), and also single-leg balance and control.

Rehabilitation

The key to the management of cycling injuries is to identify and treat the cause. It is important for the cyclist to continue riding, in a modified form, if at all possible.

Rehabilitation exercises should, as much as possible, mimic the on-bike demands. Hence, working the body while maintaining an on-bike anterior tilt position is useful. Examples of important rehabilitation exercises for the cyclist are shown in Figure 8.29.

Conclusion

An appreciation of the postural/biomechanical and physical demands of the sport of cycling will enhance the practitioner's ability to diagnose and manage cycling injuries.

Upper limb biomechanics
with W. BEN KIBLER

Correct biomechanics are as important in upper limb activities as they are in lower limb activities. For example, repeated throwing places tremendous stresses on the upper limb, especially the shoulder and elbow joints.[1,2,3] Throwing, however, is a "whole body activity," involving the transfer of momentum from body to ball.

The biomechanics of throwing

Throwing is a whole body activity that commences with drive from the large leg muscles and rotation of the hips, and progresses through segmental rotation of the trunk and shoulder girdle. It continues

A

Figure 8.29 (cont.) (b) Gluteal strengthening exercise. A weak gluteal muscle can be worked in this on-bike position. Thus, the rehabilitation aims of stability (holding the pelvis in single-leg stance), strengthening of the gluteals, and rehearsing dissociation of the limb from the pelvis are incorporated

(c) High box step-ups. Strength imbalances in the right quadriceps are addressed in this high stepping activity. The cyclist maintains an anterior tilt to mimic the on-bike position

with a "whip-like" transfer of momentum through elbow extension and through the small muscles of the forearm and hand, transferring propulsive force to the ball.

The skilled clinician should assess both the scapulohumeral and the truncal mechanics in a throwing sportsperson. The role of the scapula in throwing is discussed in more detail below, and the back, trunk, and hips serve as a center of rotation and a transfer link from the legs to the shoulder.

Throwing can be divided into four phases:

1. preparation/wind-up   } 80% time sequence
2. cocking   }
3. acceleration   2% time sequence
4. deceleration/follow-through   18% time sequence

Wind-up

Wind-up (Fig. 8.30 overleaf) establishes the rhythm of the pitch or throw. During wind-up, the body rotates so that the hip and shoulders are at 90° to the target. The major forces arise in the lower half of the body and develop a forward-moving "controlled fall." In pitching, hip flexion of the lead leg raises the center of gravity. The wind-up phase lasts 500–1000 milliseconds. During this phase, muscles of the shoulder are relatively inactive.

Cocking

The cocking movement (Fig. 8.31 overleaf) positions the body to enable all body segments to contribute to ball propulsion. In cocking, the shoulder moves into abduction through full horizontal extension and then into maximal external rotation. When the scapula is maximally retracted, the acromion starts to elevate. With maximal external rotation, the shoulder is "loaded," with the anterior capsule coiled tightly in the apprehension position, storing elastic energy. The internal rotators are stretched.[124] At this stage, anterior joint forces are maximal and can exceed 350 newtons (N).

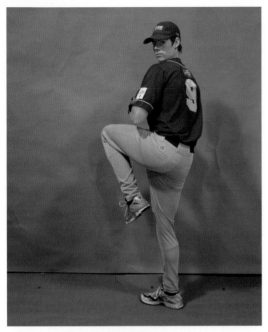

Figure 8.30 Throwing—wind-up

Figure 8.31 Throwing—cocking

Toward the end of cocking, the static anterior restraints (anterior inferior glenohumeral ligament and anterior inferior capsule) are under the greatest strain. Because of the repetitive nature of throwing,

these structures can become attenuated and lead to subtle instability.[125] In the trunk, tensile forces increase in the abdomen, hip extensors, and spine, with the lead hip internally rotating just prior to ground contact.

The cocking phase ends with the planting of the lead leg, with the body positioned for energy transfer through the legs, trunk, and arms to the ball. This phase also lasts 500–1000 milliseconds. The wind-up and cocking phases together constitute 80% of the duration of the pitch (approximately 1500 milliseconds).

Shoulder cocking continues with the counter-clockwise rotation of the pelvis and trunk (when viewed from above), which abruptly places the arm behind the body in an externally rotated position.

Lateral trunk flexion determines the degree of arm abduction. When viewed in the coronal plane, the relative abduction of the humerus to the long axis of the trunk is a fairly constant 90–100°, regardless of style. The overhand athlete leans contralaterally, while the side-arm or submarine thrower actually leans toward the throwing arm. Rotation of the trunk also aids in abduction. Although the muscles of the shoulder produce little abduction during the early cocking phase of a well-executed throw, the peri-scapular muscles are quite active. The force couple between the upper trapezius and serratus anterior initiates acromial elevation, and the lower trapezius maintains elevation at abduction angles greater than 65°.

Acceleration

The acceleration phase (Fig. 8.32) is extremely explosive. It consists of the rapid release of two forces—the stored elastic force of the tightly bound fibrous tissue of the capsule, and forceful internal rotation from the internal rotators (subscapularis, pectoralis major, latissimus dorsi, teres major). This generates excessive forces at the glenohumeral articulation[126] and, thus, the cuff musculature remains highly active to keep the humeral head enlocated in the glenoid.

Large muscles outside the rotator cuff are responsible for the subsequent acceleration of the arm. This includes muscles of the anterior chest wall, as well as the muscles and fascia that surround the spine. The critical role of the muscles controlling scapulothoracic motion—scapular positioning and stabilization against the thorax—is discussed below.

At the shoulder, acceleration is the shortest phase of the throwing motion, lasting only 50 milliseconds

Figure 8.32 Throwing—acceleration

Figure 8.33 Throwing—deceleration/follow-through

(2% of the overall time). In both the acceleration and the late-cocking phases, muscle fatigue (which is accelerated if there is mild instability due to attenuated static restrains) can lead to loss of coordinated rotator cuff motion and, thus, decreased anterior shoulder wall support.

The acceleration phase concludes with ball release, which occurs at approximately ear level. The movements involved in acceleration place enormous valgus forces on the elbow, which tends to lag behind the inwardly rotating shoulder.

Deceleration/follow-through

Not all the momentum of the throw is transferred to the ball. In the deceleration/follow-through phase (Fig. 8.33), very high forces pull forward on the glenohumeral joint following ball release, which places large stresses on the posterior shoulder structures. During this time, both intrinsic and extrinsic shoulder muscles fire at significant percentages of their maximum, attempting to develop in excess of 500 N to slow the arm down. The force tending to pull the humerus out of the shoulder socket can exceed 500 N (roughly equivalent to 135 kg [300 lb]). The eccentric contraction of the rotator cuff external rotators decelerates the rapid internal rotation of the shoulder, as does eccentric contraction of the scapular stabilizers and posterior deltoid fibers. In

the properly thrown pitch, the spine and its associated musculature have a significant role as a force attenuator.

Toward the end of the pitching motion, the torso, having decelerated so the arm could acquire kinetic energy in the arm acceleration phase, begins to rotate forward. The forward rotation of this larger link segment helps to reacquire some of this energy. This theoretically reduces the burden on the serratus anterior and other stabilizers, which are attempting to eccentrically maintain the position of the scapula and maintain the humeral head within the glenoid.

In addition to the high stresses on the posterior shoulder structures, this phase places large stresses on the elbow flexors that act to limit rapid elbow extension. This phase lasts approximately 350 milliseconds and constitutes approximately 18% of the total time.

The role of the trunk in throwing is clear. When trunk motion is inhibited, or the potential ground reaction force reduced, throwing velocity is markedly lower. In one study, with a normal overhead throw rated at 100%, peak velocities dropped to 84% when a forward stride was not allowed, and dropped to 63.5% and 53.1% when the lower body and lower body plus trunk were restricted, respectively.[127] Peak ball-release velocities attained by water polo players are approximately half the velocity that a thrown baseball might reach on land where a ground reaction force can be generated.

Normal biomechanics of the scapula in throwing

In recent years, the importance of the scapula in normal throwing biomechanics has been increasingly recognized. For optimal shoulder function, and to decrease injury risk, the scapula must move in a coordinated way (Fig. 8.34). This section outlines Ben Kibler's[128] description of the role of the scapula in throwing (Table 8.8). If the clinician understands the normal scapular biomechanics, he or she will then be able to detect abnormal scapular biomechanics in patients with upper limb injuries (for clinical implications of abnormal shoulder biomechanics, see Table 8.9 opposite).

Table 8.8 Scapular function in normal shoulder mechanics

1. provides a stable socket for the humerus
2. retracts and protracts along the thoracic wall
3. rotates to elevate the acromion
4. provides a base for muscle attachment
5. provides a key link in the kinetic chain.

The scapula provides a stable socket for the humerus

In normal shoulder function, the scapula forms a stable base for glenohumeral articulation. The glenoid is the socket of the ball-and-socket glenohumeral joint. Thus, the scapula must rotate as the humerus moves, so that the center of rotation of the glenohumeral joint remains optimal throughout the throwing or serving motion. This coordinated movement keeps the angle between the glenoid and the humerus within the physiologically tolerable or "safe zone," which extends about 30° of extension or flexion from neutral. In this range, there is maximal "concavity/compression" of the glenohumeral joint, and the muscle constraints around the shoulder are also enhanced. The maximal concavity/compression results from the slightly negative intra-articular pressure of the normal joint, with optimal positioning of the glenoid in relation to the humerus, and coordinated muscle activity.

The scapula must retract and protract along the thoracic wall

In the cocking phase of throwing (as well as in the tennis serve and swimming recovery), the scapula retracts (see above). Once acceleration begins, the scapula protracts smoothly laterally and then anteriorly around the thoracic wall to keep the scapula in a normal position relative to the humerus and also to dissipate some of the deceleration forces that occur in follow-through.

The scapula rotates to elevate the acromion

As almost all throwing and serving activities occur with a humerus-to-spine angle of between 85° and 100° of abduction, the scapula must tilt upward to clear the acromion from the rotator cuff.

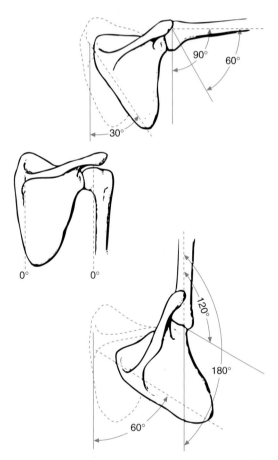

Figure 8.34 Normal scapulothoracic rhythm allows the scapula to rotate upwardly during abduction, bringing the glenoid fossa directly under the humeral head to lend stability to the glenohumeral joint

The scapula provides a base for muscle attachment

Stabilizing muscles attach to the medial, superior, and inferior borders of the scapula to control its position and motion. The extrinsic muscles (deltoid, biceps, and triceps) attach along the lateral aspect of the scapula and perform gross motor activities of the glenohumeral joint. The intrinsic muscles of the rotator cuff (supraspinatus, infraspinatus, and subscapularis) attach along the entire surface of the scapula and work most efficiently with the arm between 70° and 100° of abduction. In this position, they form a "compressor cuff" enlocating the humeral head into the socket.

The scapula provides a key link in the kinetic chain

The scapula links the proximal-to-distal sequencing of velocity, energy, and forces that optimize shoulder function. For most shoulder activities, this sequencing starts at the ground. Individual body segments, or links, move in a coordinated way to generate, summate, and transfer force through various body segments to the terminal link. This sequencing is termed the "kinetic chain." Large proximal body segments provide the bulk of the force.

The scapula is pivotal in transferring the large forces and high energy from the legs, back, and trunk to the arm and the hand. Forces generated in the proximal segments are transferred efficiently and are regulated as they go through the funnel of the shoulder when the scapula provides a stable and controlled platform. The entire arm rotates as a unit around the stable base of the glenohumeral socket.

Thus, the scapula performs various interrelated functions to maintain the normal glenohumeral path and provide a stable base for muscular function. Abnormalities in scapular function that predispose to injury are discussed below.

Abnormal scapular biomechanics and physiology

The scapular roles can be altered by many anatomical factors to create abnormal biomechanics and physiology, both locally and in the kinetic chain (Table 8.9).

Table 8.9 Alterations to scapular function

Scapular function alteration	Effect on scapular function
Anatomical factors	
Cervical spine lordosis	Excessive scapular protraction—leads to impingement with elevation
Thoracic spine kyphosis	Excessive scapular protraction—leads to impingement with elevation
Shoulder asymmetry (i.e. drooping of the shoulder or "tennis shoulder")	Impingement/impaired muscle function and fatigue
Injuries of scapula, clavicle	Alters orientation of scapula, length of clavicular strut Painful conditions that inhibit muscle function
Abnormalities in muscle function	
Overuse, direct trauma, glenohumeral causes (instability, labral lesions, arthrosis)	Muscle weakness or force couple imbalances—serratus anterior and lower trapezius are particularly susceptible. Can be a non-specific response to a variety of glenohumeral pathologies (this can be seen as analogous to the knee, in that weakness of the vastus medialis obliquus can result in the patellofemoral syndrome)
Glenohumeral inflexibility, posterior (capsular or muscular)	Limits smooth glenohumeral joint motion and limits wind-up, so that the glenoid and scapula get pulled forward and inferiorly by the moving arm, leading to excessive protraction, which, in turn, holds the scapula and, importantly, the acromion inferiorly and, thus, makes it prone to impingement
Nerve injury (causes less than 5% of abnormal muscle function in shoulder problems)	Long thoracic nerve—serratus anterior, inhibited Accessory nerve—trapezius function inhibited

Clinical significance of scapular biomechanics in shoulder injuries

Abnormal shoulder biomechanics can compromise normal shoulder function. This observation has been given various descriptive titles, such as "scapulothoracic dyskinesis," "floating scapula," and "lateral scapular slide." The clinician must recognize that these are merely titles for the same phenomenon—abnormal scapular function. We provide examples of how abnormal biomechanics can cause shoulder and elbow problems.

Lack of full retraction of the scapula on the thorax destabilizes the cocking point and prevents acceleration out of a fully cocked position. Lack of full scapular protraction increases the deceleration forces on the shoulder and alters the normal safe zone between the glenoid and the humerus as the arm moves through the acceleration phase. Too much protraction because of tightness in the glenohumeral capsule causes impingement as the scapula rotates down and forward. These cumulatively lead to abnormalities in concavity/compression due to the changes in the safe zone of the glenohumeral angle.

Loss of coordinated retraction/protraction in throwing opens up the front of the glenohumeral joint and, thus, provides an insufficient anterior bony buttress to anterior translation of the humeral head. This increases shear stress on the rest of the anterior stabilizing structure—the labrum and glenohumeral ligaments—which further decreases the stability of the glenoid for the rotating humerus.

Lack of acromial elevation leads to impingement in the cocking and follow-through phases. Impingement can also occur secondary to painful shoulder conditions that inhibit the function of the serratus anterior and lower trapezius muscles. As these muscles normally act as a force couple to elevate the acromion, their inhibition commonly causes impingement. Thus, detecting and, if necessary, reversing serratus anterior and trapezius inhibition is an important step in treating shoulder conditions.

If the scapula is unstable, the lack of an anchor affects the function of all scapular muscles. Muscles without a stable origin cannot develop appropriate or maximal torque and are predisposed to suffering muscular imbalance. If the scapula is truly unstable on the thoracic wall, as in spinal accessory nerve palsies or in extremely inhibited muscles, then the muscle origins and insertions are effectively reversed and the distal end of the muscle becomes the origin. The scapula is then pulled laterally by the muscle, which contracts from the more stable distal humeral end rather than from the proximal scapular end. A further problem of the unstable scapula is that it does not provide a stable base for glenohumeral rotation during link sequencing. Therefore, the arm works on an unstable platform and loses mechanical efficiency.

One of the most important scapular biomechanical abnormalities is the loss of the link function in the kinetic chain. The kinetic chain permits efficient transfer of energy and force to the hand. The scapula and shoulder funnel forces from the large segments—the legs and trunk—to the smaller, rapidly moving small segments of the arm.

Scapular dysfunction impairs force transmission from the lower to the upper extremity. This reduces the force delivered to the hand, or creates a situation of "catch-up" in which the more distal links have to overwork to compensate for the loss of the proximally generated force. The distal links have neither the size, the muscle cross-sectional area, nor the time in which to develop these larger forces efficiently. For example, a 20% decrease in kinetic energy delivered from the hip and trunk to the arm necessitates an 80% increase in muscle mass or a 34% increase in rotational velocity at the shoulder to deliver the same amount of resultant force to the hand. Such an adaptation would predispose to overload problems.

This explains why injuries apparently unrelated to the upper limb (e.g. decreased push-off due to Achilles tendinopathy, decreased quadriceps drive after a muscle strain, or decreased segmental trunk rotation secondary to thoracic segmental hypomobility) can affect upper limb throwing mechanics and predispose to further, or more serious, upper limb injury.

Changes in throwing arm with repeated pitching

Repeated throwing causes adaptive changes to gradually develop in the shoulder and elbow. Changes occur in flexibility, soft tissue/muscle strength, and bony contour.

At the shoulder, long-term throwing athletes have increased range of external rotation. This arises because of the repeated stress to the anterior capsule in the cocking phase and stretch or breakdown in the anterior static stabilizers of the shoulder joint (the inferior glenohumeral ligaments). This may compromise the dynamic balance that exists between shoulder function and stability. The combination of increased shoulder external rotation range of motion and breakdown of the static stabilizers may lead to anterior instability of the shoulder and secondary impingement.

The normal strength ratio of internal rotators to external rotators is approximately 3:2; however, in throwers this imbalance is exaggerated and, over time, lack of external rotation strength may increase vulnerability to injury. These dynamic changes in the shoulder joint highlight the need for a structured exercise program to prevent or correct muscle imbalances.

Throwing also produces structural changes at the elbow. Due to the valgus stress applied in the throwing action, there is a breakdown of the medial stabilizing structures (medial collateral ligament, joint capsule, flexor muscles). This leads to the development of an increased carrying angle at the elbow.

Less frequently, the eccentric overload on elbow structures causes anterior capsular strains, posterior impingement, or forearm flexor strains and, subsequently, a fixed flexion deformity.

Common biomechanical abnormalities specific to pitching

One of the most common biomechanical problems is caused by the pitcher "opening up too soon." Normally the body rotates out of the cocking phase when the arm is fully cocked (externally rotated). If the body opens up too soon, the arm lags behind and is not fully externally rotated. This results in increased stress to the anterior shoulder structures and an increased eccentric load to the shoulder external rotators. It also results in increased valgus stress at the elbow.

The other common abnormality seen in pitchers is known as "hanging," which is a characteristic sign of fatigue. Decreased shoulder abduction leads to dropping of the elbow and a reduction in velocity. There is an associated increase in the likelihood of injury, particularly to the rotator cuff as well as to the shoulder joint and the elbow. It is normally related to excessive intensity, frequency, or duration of activity.

The type of pitch is determined by the spin imparted onto the ball by the hands and fingers at ball release. The normal follow-through involves forearm pronation. In "breaking" pitches, the forearm is relatively supinated at release and then pronates. "Breaking" pitches are associated with an increased risk of injury.

Some pitchers incorrectly forcefully supinate against the normal pronation of follow-through.

Biomechanics of swimming

Swimming relies on propulsion through the water using both the upper and lower limbs.[129] Approximately 90% of propulsion is generated by the upper limbs. The forward propulsive forces must overcome the drag force of the water. Therefore, when swimming front crawl (freestyle), the swimmer tries to maintain as horizontal a position as possible. If the head and shoulders are high in the water and the hips and legs are lower, or there is excessive side-to-side movement, there is an increased drag effect.

In freestyle, butterfly, and backstroke there are two phases of the stroke—the pull-through and the recovery. In simple terms, the pull-through involves adduction and internal rotation of the shoulder as the elbow flexes and then extends. The recovery phase involves abduction and external rotation of the shoulder, again followed by elbow flexion and then extension.

In all four competitive swimming strokes, swimmers do not simply pull the arm straight through the water. For example, pull-through is S-shaped in freestyle. Not all of the underwater phase of the stroke contributes to propulsion. In all strokes the beginning of propulsion, or catch point, begins approximately one-third of the way through the underwater phase. This represents the arm position where the elbow is above the hand. Understanding swimming biomechanics can aid stroke proficiency and minimize risk of injury.

Swimming biomechanics and shoulder pain

Shoulder pain is extremely common among swimmers and is usually due to impingement and rotator cuff tendinopathy. Traditionally, anatomical factors were thought to cause impingement but it now appears that it is largely due to muscle weakness, dynamic muscle imbalance, and biomechanical faults.

If the scapular stabilizing muscles are weak and the short scapulohumeral muscles tight, there will be insufficient scapular protraction and lateral rotation during the swimming stroke and, thus, a tendency for rotator cuff impingement. This problem is exacerbated if cervical and thoracic hypomobility is present. Dynamic imbalance between the internal and external shoulder rotators may also promote impingement in the pull-through phase of a stroke, as the internal rotators are often excessively (>3:2 ratio) strong in swimmers.

Swimmers strive to have a long stroke as this improves propulsion, but the resultant prolonged shoulder adduction and internal rotation may lead to hypovascularity of the supraspinatus muscle and increased risk of tendinopathy. This is exacerbated if hand paddles are used. Therefore, the stroke may need to be shortened to decrease injury risk. Other technique factors that predispose to impingement are an excessively straight arm during the recovery phase and insufficient body roll. Body roll also increases the efficiency of forward propulsion in freestyle and backstroke by allowing the shoulder to act in a more neutral position relative to the coronal plane, balancing the adductors and abductors.

To prevent shoulder injury in a swimmer, the practitioner should:

- ensure that the swimmer has adequate strength and control of the scapular stabilizing muscles
- ensure that the internal to external rotator strength ratio is normal (for the sport)[130]
- ensure the swimmer stretches the scapulohumeral muscles, including the infraspinatus, teres minor, and subscapularis muscles
- correct cervical and thoracic hypomobility.

When assessing swimming technique to prevent injury, the practitioner should look for good elbow height during the recovery phase of the stroke and adequate body roll. (A bilateral breathing pattern increases body roll.)

Common technical errors in specific swimming strokes that predispose to injury are shown in Table 8.10.

Biomechanics of tennis

Tennis places great stress on the shoulder and elbow. The shoulder receives maximal loads during the serve and overhead strokes, and rotator cuff impingement may arise from a mechanism parallel to that in throwers and swimmers. The tennis service begins with 90° abduction and external rotation in the cocking phase. The shoulder then moves rapidly from external to internal rotation and from abduction into forward flexion. The deceleration or follow-through phase is controlled by the external rotators. Impingement is exacerbated by increased internal rotation of the shoulder in forward flexion. Over 50% of the total kinetic energy and total force generated

Table 8.10 Common technical errors in specific swimming strokes that predispose to injury

Swimming stroke	Common technical error that predisposes to shoulder injury
Butterfly	Entering the arms into the water too far outside the line of the shoulders or with the arms too close together
Backstroke	Pull-through with elbows extended, which results in a straight pull-through instead of an S-shaped pull-through Insufficient body roll
Freestyle	A line of pull-through that crosses far beyond the midline Striving for too much length in the stroke Insufficient body roll
Breaststroke	Excessive elbow extension

in the tennis serve is created by the lower legs, hips, and trunk.

In many tennis serving motions, the feet and body are actually off the ground when this rotation reaches its maximum peak. The entire stable base of the arm, in this situation, rests on the scapula rather than on the feet or the ground. Therefore, stability of the scapula in relationship to the entire moving arm is the key point at this important time in the throwing sequence.

If we compare the biomechanics of serving to those of pitching, we find that the forces transmitted to the shoulder are lower in serving, as the tennis racquet dissipates much of the impact force. This enables the tennis player to serve more than 100 times daily, whereas the pitcher can only pitch approximately every fourth day. Because of the racquet, tennis serving requires a smaller range of internal/external rotation than pitching. Nevertheless, shoulder instability may develop over time.

Tennis biomechanics and elbow pain

Elbow pain (Chapter 22) is extremely common among tennis players. This may be due to the dominant activity of the wrist extensors. Poor backhand technique is a major predisposing factor.[131] The role of racquets in the development of increased force through the elbow is discussed in Chapter 9. Commencing tennis late in life also appears to be a risk factor for elbow pain.

Tennis racquets

Tennis racquets can play an important role in injury and, although they could be categorized as a factor in tennis biomechanics, we discuss them in Chapter 9.

Biomechanics of other overhead sports

Any sport involving overhead activity may lead to the development of shoulder and elbow problems. Many of the principles of biomechanics discussed above apply to these sports. Water polo and volleyball provide the clinician with some specific challenges.

Water polo

Water polo players are particularly susceptible, as the sport involves a combination of swimming and throwing. Shoulder impingement commonly occurs in association with anterior instability. Instability may be atraumatic or traumatic (e.g. as a result of a block). Water polo players are susceptible to imbalance between internal and external rotators and they may have poor scapular control. Prevention of injury may be enhanced by prophylactic strengthening of the external rotators and scapular stabilizers.

Water polo players have a restricted throwing action due to the large ball size, the presence of the water, and the lack of a base of support. This leads to poor throwing biomechanics—shoulder stabilizers must generate more forces and there is reduced elbow angular acceleration. They may attempt to overcome this by angling their bodies to become more horizontal in the water when shooting, thus enabling them to throw with the shoulder at 90° of abduction, reducing the likelihood of impingement.

Volleyball

The overhead spike in volleyball is associated with a high incidence of shoulder injury. The technique is similar to the throwing action. There is limitation in the amount of follow-through available with a spike due to the proximity of the net. Another potential hazard for the "spiker" is that the spike may be blocked by an opponent. Internal and external rotator muscle balance must be maintained to prevent injury, and the practitioner should also ensure that sportspeople have adequate scapular control.

An injury that is unique to volleyball, and results from specific biomechanics in association with an anatomical predisposition, is suprascapular nerve entrapment at the spinoglenoid notch.[132] Players who use the "float" serve and who have a suprascapular nerve that turns sharply after passing through the spinoglenoid notch are predisposed to traction-induced palsy of the suprascapular nerve (see Fig. 21.28 and page 373 in Chapter 21).

CLINICAL SPORTS MEDICINE
MASTERCLASSES
[W] www.clinicalsportsmedicine.com

- Listen to the interview with chapter authors.
- See demonstration of biomechanical assessment.
- See a demonstration of the original low-Dye technique augmented with reverse sixes and calcaneal slings anchored to the lower leg.

RECOMMENDED WEBSITES

Barton CJ, Bonanno D, Menz HB. Development and evaluation of a tool for the assessment of footwear characteristics: www.ncbi.nlm.nih.gov/pmc/articles/PMC2678108/?tool=pubmed

RECOMMENDED READING

Barton CJ, Bonanno D, Menz HB. Development and evaluation of a tool for the assessment of footwear characteristics. *J Foot Ankle Res* 2009;23(2):10.

Kaufman KR, Brodine SK, Shaffer RA, Johnson CW, Cullison TR. The effect of foot structure and range of motion on musculoskeletal overuse injuries. *Am J Sports Med* 1999;27(5):585–93.

Lang LM, Volpe RG, Wernick J. Static biomechanical evaluation of the foot and lower limb: the podiatrist's perspective. *Man Ther* 1997;2(2):58–66.

Mellion MB, Burke ER. Bicycling injuries. *Clin Sports Med* 1994;13:1–258.

Neely FG. Biomechanical risk factors for exercise-related lower limb injuries. *Sports Med* 1998;26:395–413.

Werner SL, Plancer KD. Biomechanics of wrist injuries in sports. *Clin Sports Med* 1998;17:407–20.

Whiting W, Zernicke R. *Biomechanics of musculoskeletal injury* 2nd edn. Champaign, Il: Human Kinetics, 2008.

Yates B, White S. The incidence and risk factors in the development of medial tibial stress syndrome among naval recruits. *Am J Sports Med* 2004;32(3):772–80.

REFERENCES

1. Winter DA. *Biomechanics and motor control of human movement*. 4th edn. Hoboken, New Jersey: John Wiley & Sons, 2009.
2. Dugan SA, Bhat KP. Biomechanics and analysis of running gait. *Phys Med Rehabil Clin N Am* 2005;16(3):603–21.
3. Lieberman DE, Venkadesan M, Werbel WA et al. Foot strike patterns and collision forces in habitually barefoot versus shod runners. *Nature* 2010;463(7280):531–5.
4. Nilsson J, Thorstensson A. Ground reaction forces at different speeds of human walking and running. *Acta Physiol Scand* 1989;136(2):217–27.
5. Franz JR, Paylo KW, Dicharry J et al. Changes in the coordination of hip and pelvis kinematics with mode of locomotion. *Gait Posture* 2009;29(3):494–8.
6. Pohl MB, Buckley JG. Changes in foot and shank coupling due to alterations in foot strike pattern during running. *Clin Biomech (Bristol, Avon)* 2008;23(3):334–41.
7. Mann RA, Baxter DE, Lutter LD. Running symposium. *Foot Ankle* 1981;1(4):190–224.
8. Williams KR. Biomechanics of running. *Exerc Sport Sci Rev* 1985;13:389–441.
9. Ferber R, Davis IM, Williams DS, 3rd. Gender differences in lower extremity mechanics during running. *Clin Biomech (Bristol, Avon)* 2003;18(4):350–7.
10. Riley PO, DellaCroce U, Kerrigan DC. Effect of age on lower extremity joint moment contributions to gait speed. *Gait Posture* 2001;14(3):264–70.
11. Rodgers MM. Dynamic foot biomechanics. *J Orthop Sports Phys Ther* 1995;21(6):306–16.
12. Simkin A, Leichter I, Giladi M, Stein M, Milgrom C. Combined effect of foot arch structure and an orthotic device on stress fractures. *Foot Ankle* 1989;10(1):25–9.
13. Monaghan K, Delahunt E, Caulfield B. Ankle function during gait in patients with chronic ankle instability compared to controls. *Clin Biomech (Bristol, Avon)* 2006;21(2):168–74.
14. Drewes LK, McKeon PO, Paolini G et al. Altered ankle kinematics and shank-rear-foot coupling in those with chronic ankle instability. *J Sport Rehabil* 2009;18(3):375–88.
15. Winter DA. Moments of force and mechanical power in jogging. *J Biomech* 1983;16(1):91–7.
16. Stackhouse CL, Davis IM, Hamill J. Orthotic intervention in forefoot and rearfoot strike running patterns. *Clin Biomech (Bristol, Avon)* 2004;19(1):64–70.
17. Riley PO, Dicharry J, Franz J et al. A kinematics and kinetic comparison of overground and treadmill running. *Med Sci Sports Exerc* 2008;40(6):1093–100.
18. Adelaar RS. The practical biomechanics of running. *Am J Sports Med* 1986;14(6):497–500.
19. Ounpuu S. The biomechanics of walking and running. *Clin Sports Med* 1994;13(4):843–63.
20. Winter DA, Bishop PJ. Lower extremity injury. Biomechanical factors associated with chronic injury to the lower extremity. *Sports Med* 1992;14(3):149–56.

A

21. Nester CJ. Lessons from dynamic cadaver and invasive bone pin studies: do we know how the foot really moves during gait? *J Foot Ankle Res* 2009;2:18.

22. Milner CE, Ferber R, Pollard CD et al. Biomechanical factors associated with tibial stress fracture in female runners. *Med Sci Sports Exerc* 2006;38(2):323–8.

23. Pohl MB, Hamill J, Davis IS. Biomechanical and anatomic factors associated with a history of plantar fasciitis in female runners. *Clin J Sport Med* 2009;19(5):372–6.

24. Redmond AC, Crosbie J, Ouvrier RA. Development and validation of a novel rating system for scoring standing foot posture: the Foot Posture Index. *Clin Biomech (Bristol, Avon)* 2006;21(1):89–98.

25. Chuter VH. Relationships between foot type and dynamic rearfoot frontal plane motion. *J Foot Ankle Res* 2010;3:9.

26. Redmond AC, Crosbie J, Ouvrier RA. Development and validation of a novel rating system for scoring standing foot posture: the Foot Posture Index. *Clin Biomech (Bristol, Avon)* 2006;21(1):89–98.

27. Redmond AC, Crane YZ, Menz HB. Normative values for the Foot Posture Index. *J Foot Ankle Res* 2008;1(1):6.

28. Redmond AC. The foot posture index: easy quantification of standing foot posture. Available at http://courses.ki.se/fpi_manual-formatted_august_2005v2_1_.pdf?node=202687, 2005.

29. Cornwall MW, McPoil TG, Lebec M et al. Reliability of the modified Foot Posture Index. *J Am Podiatr Med Assoc* 2008;98(1):7–13.

30. Barton CJ, Bonanno D, Levinger P et al. Foot and ankle characteristics in patellofemoral pain syndrome: a case control and reliability study. *J Orthop Sports Phys Ther* 2010;40(5):286–96.

31. Evans AM, Copper AW, Scharfbillig RW et al. Reliability of the foot posture index and traditional measures of foot position. *J Am Podiatr Med Assoc* 2003;93(3):203–13.

32. Jack EA. Naviculo-cuneiform fusion in the treatment of flat foot. *J Bone Joint Surg Br* 1953;35–B(1):75–82.

33. Glasoe WM, Allen MK, Ludewig PM. Comparison of first ray dorsal mobility among different forefoot alignments. *J Orthop Sports Phys Ther* 2000;30(10):612–20; discussion 621–3.

34. Hinman RS, May RL, Crossley KM. Is there an alternative to the full-leg radiograph for determining knee joint alignment in osteoarthritis? *Arthritis Rheum* 2006;55(2):306–13.

35. Jacobs CA, Uhl TL, Mattacola CG et al. Hip abductor function and lower extremity landing kinematics: sex differences. *J Athl Train* 2007;42(1):76–83.

36. Chappell JD, Herman DC, Knight BS et al. Effect of fatigue on knee kinetics and kinematics in stop-jump tasks. *Am J Sports Med* 2005;33(7):1022–9.

37. Herrington L, Munro A. Drop jump landing knee valgus angle; normative data in a physically active population. *Phys Ther Sport* 2010;11(2):56–9.

38. Barton CJ, Bonanno D, Menz HB. Development and evaluation of a tool for the assessment of footwear characteristics. *J Foot Ankle Res* 2009;2:10.

39. Rome K, Handoll HH, Ashford R. Interventions for preventing and treating stress fractures and stress reactions of bone of the lower limbs in young adults. *Cochrane Database Syst Rev* 2005(2):CD000450.

40. van Gent RN, Siem D, van Middelkoop M et al. Incidence and determinants of lower extremity running injuries in long distance runners: a systematic review. *Br J Sports Med* 2007;41(8):469–80; discussion 480.

41. Dennis KJ, McKinney S. Sesamoids and accessory bones of the foot. *Clin Podiatr Med Surg* 1990;7(4):717–23.

42. Dedmond BT, Cory JW, McBryde A Jr. The hallucal sesamoid complex. *J Am Acad Orthop Surg* 2006;14(13):745–53.

43. Riddle DL, Pulisic M, Pidcoe P, Johnson RE. Risk factors for plantar fasciitis: a matched case-control study. *J Bone Joint Surg Am* 2003;85-A(5):872–7.

44. Irving DB, Cook JL, Young MA et al. Obesity and pronated foot type may increase the risk of chronic plantar heel pain: a matched case-control study. *BMC Musculoskelet Disord* 2007;8:41.

45. Kibler WB, Goldberg C, Chandler TJ. Functional biomechanical deficits in running athletes with plantar fasciitis. *Am J Sports Med* 1991;19(1):66–71.

46. Messier SP, Pittala KA. Etiologic factors associated with selected running injuries. *Med Sci Sports Exerc* 1988;20(5):501–5.

47. Warren BL. Anatomical factors associated with predicting plantar fasciitis in long-distance runners. *Med Sci Sports Exerc* 1984;16(1):60–3.

48. Kaufman KR, Brodine SK, Shaffer RA et al. The effect of foot structure and range of motion on musculoskeletal overuse injuries. *Am J Sports Med* 1999;27(5):585–93.

49. Mahieu NN, Witvrouw E, Stevens V et al. Intrinsic risk factors for the development of achilles tendon overuse injury: a prospective study. *Am J Sports Med* 2006;34(2):226–35.

50. McCrory JL, Martin DF, Lowery RB et al. Etiologic factors associated with Achilles tendinitis in runners. *Med Sci Sports Exerc* 1999;31(10):1374–81.

51. Ryan M, Grau S, Krauss I et al. Kinematic analysis of runners with achilles mid-portion tendinopathy. *Foot Ankle Int* 2009;30(12):1190–5.

52. Willems T, Witvrouw E, Delbaere K et al. Relationship between gait biomechanics and inversion sprains: a prospective study of risk factors. *Gait Posture* 2005;21(4):379–87.

53. Willems TM, Witvrouw E, Delbaere K et al. Intrinsic risk factors for inversion ankle sprains in male subjects: a prospective study. *Am J Sports Med* 2005;33(3):415–23.

54. Willems TM, Witvrouw E, Delbaere K et al. Intrinsic risk factors for inversion ankle sprains in females—a prospective study. *Scand J Med Sci Sports* 2005;15(5):336–45.

55. Brandes CB, Smith RW. Characterization of patients with primary peroneus longus tendinopathy: a review of twenty-two cases. *Foot Ankle Int* 2000;21(6):462–8.

56. Willems TM, De Clercq D, Delbaere K et al. A prospective study of gait related risk factors for exercise-related lower leg pain. *Gait Posture* 2006;23(1):91–8.

57. Yates B, White S. The incidence and risk factors in the development of medial tibial stress syndrome among naval recruits. *Am J Sports Med* 2004;32(3):772–80.

58. Bennett JE, Reinking MF, Pluemer B et al. Factors contributing to the development of medial tibial stress syndrome in high school runners. *J Orthop Sports Phys Ther* 2001;31(9):504–10.

59. Hubbard TJ, Carpenter EM, Cordova ML. Contributing factors to medial tibial stress syndrome: a prospective investigation. *Med Sci Sports Exerc* 2009;41(3):490–6.

60. Wen DY, Puffer JC, Schmalzried TP. Lower extremity alignment and risk of overuse injuries in runners. *Med Sci Sports Exerc* 1997;29(10):1291–8.

61. Tweed JL, Campbell JA, Avil SJ. Biomechanical risk factors in the development of medial tibial stress syndrome in distance runners. *J Am Podiatr Med Assoc* 2008;98(6):436–44.

62. Moen MH, Bongers T, Bakker EW et al. Risk factors and prognostic indicators for medial tibial stress syndrome. *Scand J Med Sci Sports* 2010;June 18 epub.

63. Witvrouw E, Bellemans J, Lysens R et al. Intrinsic risk factors for the development of patellar tendinitis in an athletic population. A two-year prospective study. *Am J Sports Med* 2001;29(2):190–5.

64. Tyler TF, Hershman EB, Nicholas SJ et al. Evidence of abnormal anteroposterior patellar tilt in patients with patellar tendinitis with use of a new radiographic measurement. *Am J Sports Med* 2002;30(3):396–401.

65. Boling MC, Padua DA, Marshall SW et al. A prospective investigation of biomechanical risk factors for patellofemoral pain syndrome: the Joint Undertaking to Monitor and Prevent ACL Injury (JUMP-ACL) cohort. *Am J Sports Med* 2009;37(11):2108–16.

66. Witvrouw E, Lysens R, Bellemans J et al. Intrinsic risk factors for the development of anterior knee pain in an athletic population. A two-year prospective study. *Am J Sports Med* 2000;28(4):480–9.

67. Myer GD, Ford KR, Barber Foss KD et al. The incidence and potential pathomechanics of patellofemoral pain in female athletes. *Clin Biomech (Bristol, Avon)* 2010;25(7):700–7.

68. Messier SP, Davis SE, Curl WW et al. Etiologic factors associated with patellofemoral pain in runners. *Med Sci Sports Exerc* 1991;23(9):1008–15.

69. Barton CJ, Levinger P, Menz HB, Webster KE. Kinematic gait characteristics associated with patellofemoral pain syndrome: a systematic review. *Gait Posture* 2009;30(4):405–16.

70. Patil S, White L, Jones A, Hui AC. Idiopathic anterior knee pain in the young. A prospective controlled trial. *Acta Orthop Belg* 2010;76(3):356–9.

71. Noehren B, Davis I, Hamill J. ASB clinical biomechanics award winner 2006 prospective study of the biomechanical factors associated with iliotibial band syndrome. *Clin Biomech (Bristol, Avon)* 2007;22(9):951–6.

72. Miller RH, Lowry JL, Meardon SA et al. Lower extremity mechanics of iliotibial band syndrome during an exhaustive run. *Gait Posture* 2007;26(3):407–13.

73. Verrall GM, Slavotinek JP, Barnes PG et al. Hip joint range of motion restriction precedes athletic chronic groin injury. *J Sci Med Sport* 2007;10(6):463–6.

74. Giladi M, Milgrom C, Simkin A et al. Stress fractures. Identifiable risk factors. *Am J Sports Med* 1991;19(6):647–52.

75. Korpelainen R, Orava S, Karpakka J et al. Risk factors for recurrent stress fractures in athletes. *Am J Sports Med* 2001;29(3):304–10.

76. Collins N, Bisset L, McPoil T et al. Foot orthoses in lower limb overuse conditions: a systematic review and meta-analysis. *Foot Ankle Int* 2007;28(3):396–412.

77. Eng JJ, Pierrynowski MR. The effect of soft foot orthotics on three-dimensional lower-limb kinematics during walking and running. *Phys Ther* 1994;74(9):836–44.

78. McCulloch MU, Brunt D, Vander Linden D. The effect of foot orthotics and gait velocity on lower limb kinematics and temporal events of stance. *J Orthop Sports Phys Ther* 1993;17(1):2–10.

79. Novick A, Kelley DL. Position and movement changes of the foot with orthotic intervention during the loading response of gait. *J Orthop Sports Phys Ther* 1990;11(7):301–12.

80. Brown GP, Donatelli R, Catlin PA et al. The effect of two types of foot orthoses on rearfoot mechanics. *J Orthop Sports Phys Ther* 1995;21(5):258–67.

81. Stacoff A, Reinschmidt C, Nigg BM et al. Effects of foot orthoses on skeletal motion during running. *Clin Biomech (Bristol, Avon)* 2000;15(1):54–64.

82. Mills K, Blanch P, Chapman AR et al. Foot orthoses and gait: a systematic review and meta-analysis of literature pertaining to potential mechanisms. *Br J Sports Med* 2010;44(14):1035–46.

83. Bobbert MF, Yeadon MR, Nigg BM. Mechanical analysis of the landing phase in heel-toe running. *J Biomech* 1992;25(3):223–34.

84. Hohmann E, Wortler K, Imhoff AB. MR imaging of the hip and knee before and after marathon running. *Am J Sports Med* 2004;32(1):55–9.

85. Nigg BM. Impact forces in running. *Curr Opin Orthop* 1997;8(6):43–7.

86. Nawoczenski DA, Janisse DJ. Foot orthoses in rehabilitation—what's new. *Clin Sports Med* 2004;23(1):157–67.

87. Nigg BM, Nurse MA, Stefanyshyn DJ. Shoe inserts and orthotics for sport and physical activities. *Med Sci Sports Exerc* 1999;31(7 Suppl):S421–8.

88. Nigg BM. The role of impact forces and foot pronation: a new paradigm. *Clin J Sport Med* 2001;11(1):2–9.

89. Snyder RA, DeAngelis JP, Koester MC et al. Does shoe insole modification prevent stress fractures? A systematic review. *HSS J* 2009;5(2):92–8.

90. Barton CJ, Munteanu SE, Menz HB et al. The efficacy of foot orthoses in the treatment of individuals with patellofemoral pain syndrome: a systematic review. *Sports Med* 2010;40(5):377–95.

91. Burns J, Landorf KB, Ryan MM et al. Interventions for the prevention and treatment of pes cavus. *Cochrane Database Syst Rev* 2007(4):CD006154.

92. Mayer F, Hirschmuller A, Muller S et al. Effects of short-term treatment strategies over 4 weeks in Achilles tendinopathy. *Br J Sports Med* 2007;41(7):e6.

93. Baldassin V, Gomes CR, Beraldo PS. Effectiveness of prefabricated and customized foot orthoses made from low-cost foam for noncomplicated plantar fasciitis: a randomized controlled trial. *Arch Phys Med Rehabil* 2009;90(4):701–6.

94. Landorf KB, Keenan AM, Herbert RD. Effectiveness of foot orthoses to treat plantar fasciitis: a randomized trial. *Arch Intern Med* 2006;166(12):1305–10.

95. Martin JE, Hosch JC, Goforth WP et al. Mechanical treatment of plantar fasciitis. A prospective study. *J Am Podiatr Med Assoc* 2001;91(2):55–62.

96. Lynch DM, Goforth WP, Martin JE et al. Conservative treatment of plantar fasciitis. A prospective study. *J Am Podiatr Med Assoc* 1998;88(8):375–80.

97. Rome K, Gray J, Stewart F et al. Evaluating the clinical effectiveness and cost-effectiveness of foot orthoses in the treatment of plantar heel pain: a feasibility study. *J Am Podiatr Med Assoc* 2004;94(3):229–38.

98. Roos E, Engstrom M, Soderberg B. Foot orthoses for the treatment of plantar fasciitis. *Foot Ankle Int* 2006;27(8):606–11.

99. Trotter LC, Pierrynowski MR. The short-term effectiveness of full-contact custom-made foot orthoses and prefabricated shoe inserts on lower-extremity musculoskeletal pain: a randomized clinical trial. *J Am Podiatr Med Assoc* 2008;98(5):357–63.

100. Guskiewicz KM, Perrin DH. Effect of orthotics on postural sway following inversion ankle sprain. *J Orthop Sports Phys Ther* 1996;23(5):326–31.

101. Orteza LC, Vogelbach WD, Denegar CR. The effect of molded and unmolded orthotics on balance and pain while jogging following inversion ankle sprain. *J Athl Train* 1992;27(1):80–4.

102. Loudon JK, Dolphino MR. Use of foot orthoses and calf stretching for individuals with medial tibial stress syndrome. *Foot Ankle Spec* 2010;3(1):15–20.

103. Sammarco VJ, Nichols R. Orthotic management for disorders of the hallux. *Foot Ankle Clin* 2005;10(1):191–209.

104. American College of Foot and Ankle Orthopedics and Medicine. Prescription custom foot orthoses practice guidelines, 2011 (www.acfaom.org).

105. Root ML. Development of the functional orthosis. *Clin Podiatr Med Surg* 1994;11(2):183–210.

106. McPoil TG, Hunt GC. Evaluation and management of foot and ankle disorders: present problems and future directions. *J Orthop Sports Phys Ther* 1995;21(6):381–8.

107. Landorf K, Keenan AM, Rushworth RL. Foot orthosis prescription habits of Australian and New Zealand podiatric physicians. *J Am Podiatr Med Assoc* 2001;91(4):174–83.

108. Vicenzino B. Foot orthotics in the treatment of lower limb conditions: a musculoskeletal physiotherapy perspective. *Man Ther* 2004;9(4):185–96.

109. Vicenzino B, Collins N, Crossley K et al. Foot orthoses and physiotherapy in the treatment of patellofemoral pain syndrome: a randomised clinical trial. *BMC Musculoskelet Disord* 2008;9(1):27.

110. Collins N, Crossley K, Beller E et al. Foot orthoses and physiotherapy in the treatment of patellofemoral pain syndrome: randomised clinical trial. *BMJ* 2008;337:a1735.

111. Dye RW. A strapping. *J Natl Assoc Chiropodists* 1939;29:11–12.

112. Franettovich M, Chapman A, Blanch P et al. A physiological and psychological basis for anti-pronation taping from a critical review of the literature. *Sports Med* 2008;38(8):617–31.

113. Aminaka N, Gribble PA. A systematic review of the effects of therapeutic taping on patellofemoral pain syndrome. *J Athl Train* 2005;40(4):341–51.

114. Overington M, Goddard D, Hing W. A critical appraisal and literature critique on the effect of patellar taping: is patellar taping effective in the treatment of patellofemoral pain syndrome? *New Zealand Journal of Physiotherapy* 2006;34:66–80.

115. Mulligan BR. *Manual therapy–"NAGS," "SNAGS," "MWM'S" etc.* 4th edn. Wellington: Plane View Services, 1999.

116. Yeung EW, Yeung SS. Interventions for preventing lower limb soft-tissue injuries in runners. *Cochrane Database Syst Rev* 2001;(3):CD001256.

117. Brown DA, Kautz SA, Dairaghi CA. Muscle activity patterns altered during pedaling at different body orientations. *J Biomech* 1996;29(10):1349–56.

118. McLean B, Blanch P. Bicycle seat height: a biomechanical consideration when assessing and treating knee pain in cyclists. *Sport Health* 1993;11:12–15.

119. Salai M, Brosh T, Blankstein A et al. Effect of changing the saddle angle on the incidence of low back pain in recreational bicyclists. *Br J Sports Med* 1999;33(6):398–400.

120. Faria IE. Energy expenditure, aerodynamics and medical problems in cycling – an update. *Sports Med* 1992;14(1):43–63.

121. Gnehm P, Reichenbach S, Altpeter E et al. Influence of different racing positions on metabolic cost in elite cyclists. *Med Sci Sports Exerc* 1997;29(6):818–23.

122. Capmal S, Vandewalle H. Torque-velocity relationship during cycle ergometer sprints with and without toe clips. *Eur J Appl Physiol Occup Physiol* 1997;76(4):375–9.

123. Arroyo J, Hershon S, Bigliani L. Special considerations in the athlete throwing shoulder. *Orthop Clin North Am* 1997;28:69–78.

124. Herrington L. Glenohumeral joint: internal and external rotation range of motion in javelin throwers. *Br J Sports Med* 1998;32(3):226–8.

125. Kvitne RS, Jobe FW, Jobe CM. Shoulder instability in the overhand or throwing athlete. *Clin Sports Med* 1995;14(4):917–35.

126. Cavallo RJ, Speer KP. Shoulder instability and impingement in throwing athletes. *Med Sci Sports Exerc* 1998;30(4):S18–25.

127. Toyoshima S, Hoshikawa T, Miyashita M et al. Contribution of the body parts to throwing performance. In: Nelson RC, Morehouse CA, eds. *Biomechanics IV*. Baltimore: University Park Press, 1974:169–74.

128. Kibler WB. The role of the scapula in athletic shoulder function. *Am J Sports Med* 1998;26(2):325–37.

129. Troup JP. The physiology and biomechanics of competitive swimming. *Clin Sports Med* 1999;18(2):267–85.

130. Bak K, Magnusson SP. Shoulder strength and range of motion in symptomatic and pain-free elite swimmers. *Am J Sports Med* 1997;25(4):454–9.

131. Knudson D, Blackwell J. Upper extremity angular kinematics of the one-handed backhand drive in tennis players with and without tennis elbow. *Int J Sports Med* 1997;18(2):79–82.

132. Ferretti A, De Carli A, Fontana M. Injury of the suprascapular nerve at the spinoglenoid notch – the natural history of infraspinatus atrophy in volleyball players. *Am J Sports Med* 1998;26(6):759–63.

Chapter 9

Principles of injury prevention

with ROALD BAHR

Intellectuals solve problems; geniuses prevent them. Albert Einstein

The 2000s saw a remarkable acceleration in the focus on sports injury prevention; athletes in the second decade of this century benefit from the knowledge that interventions can prevent major knee and ankle injuries. Improving uptake remains a challenge, as in all areas of preventive health.

In this book, we use the term "prevention" synonymously with "primary prevention."[1] Examples of primary prevention include health promotion and injury prevention among those who have never had an injury (e.g. ankle braces being worn by an entire team, even those without previous ankle sprain). "Secondary prevention" refers to early diagnosis and intervention to limit the development of disability or reduce the risk of re-injury. We refer to this as "treatment" (e.g. early RICE treatment of an ankle sprain, see Chapter 13). Finally, "tertiary prevention" is the focus on rehabilitation to reduce and/or correct an existing disability attributed to an underlying disease. We refer to this as "rehabilitation" (Chapter 15); in the case of a patient who has had an ankle sprain, this would refer to wobble board exercises and graduated return to sport after the initial treatment for the sprain. The proactive clinician will initiate injury prevention strategies, give prevention advice during consultations where treatment is being sought, and devise in-season strategy planning sessions with coaches and during screening of athletes (Chapter 62).

This chapter begins with a widely-used model of how sports injuries occur. This is a very useful guide to ways to prevent sport injuries in a systematic matter. From there, we direct the reader to review the importance of correct biomechanics of sports for injury prevention as outlined in Chapter 8. Then, we discuss other important factors that may assist in the prevention of injury:

- warm-up
- stretching
- taping and bracing
- protective equipment
- suitable equipment
- appropriate surfaces
- appropriate training.

Systematic injury prevention

Willem van Mechelen et al.[2] provided the now classic conceptual model for prevention of sports injuries (Fig. 9.1). First, identify the magnitude of the problem and describe it in terms of the incidence and severity of sports injuries. If you are responsible for a team, this involves recording all injuries within the squad, as well as training and match exposure. Second, identify the risk factors and injury mechanisms that

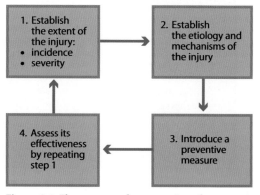

Figure 9.1 The sequence for prevention of sports injuries FROM VAN MECHELEN ET AL.[2]

play a part in causing those sports injuries. For the practitioner, this involves systematic examination of sportspeople and their training and competition program (see below). The third step is to introduce measures that are likely to reduce the future risk and/or severity of sports injuries, based on the etiologic factors and the injury mechanisms identified in the second step. Finally, the effect of the measures must be evaluated by repeating the first step. In the research setting, preventive efforts are best evaluated using a randomized controlled trial (RCT) design. For the clinician responsible for a team, continuous surveillance of the injury pattern within the team will reveal whether changes occur in the injury risk.

Clinicians who want to prevent injuries in a systematic way could base their approach on the updated model by Meeuwisse et al. to describe the potential causative factors for injury.[3] This model was also expanded by Bahr and Holme[4] and Bahr and Krosshaug[5] (Fig. 9.2). The model not only takes into account the multifactorial nature of sports injuries, but also the time sequence of events leading to injuries.

First, it considers the internal risk factors—factors that may predispose or protect the sportsperson from injury. This includes sportsperson characteristics, factors such as age, maturation, gender, body composition, and fitness level. One factor that has been consistently documented to be a significant predictor is previous injury—almost regardless of the injury type studied. Internal factors such as these interact to predispose to or protect from injury.

Internal risk factors can be modifiable and non-modifiable, and both are important from a prevention point of view. Modifiable risk factors may be targeted by specific training methods. Non-modifiable factors (such as gender) can be used to target intervention measures to those athletes who are at increased risk. An example of the clinical relevance of gender in sports injury and prevention is the higher predisposition of injury to the anterior cruciate ligament (ACL) in female athletes compared with males.[6]

Female athletes in most team sports are at up to six times greater risk of sustaining an ACL tear than their male counterparts. Therefore, it makes sense to target training programs to prevent ACL tears toward women in sports like soccer, basketball, and team handball, while the lower risk among men may not justify such interventions (Chapter 32).

The second group of risk factors is the external factors sportspeople are exposed to, for example, floor friction in indoor team sports, snow conditions in alpine skiing, a slippery surface (on a running

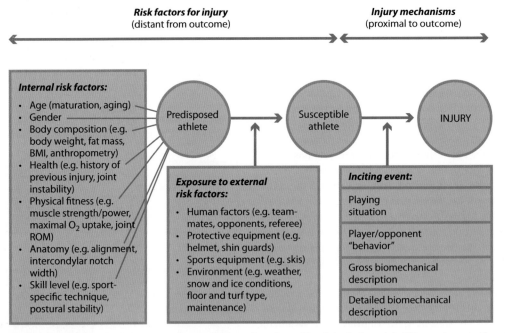

Figure 9.2 A comprehensive injury causation model based on the epidemiological model of Meeuwisse et al.[3] and modified by Bahr & Krosshaug[5]

BMI = body mass index; ROM = range of motion

tr.

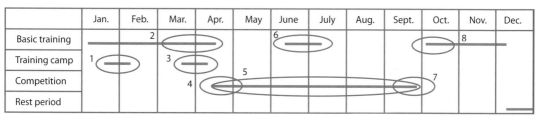
A

track), very cold weather, or inappropriate footwear. Exposure to such external risk factors may interact with the internal factors to make the athlete more or less susceptible to injury. When intrinsic and extrinsic risk factors act simultaneously, the sportsperson is at far greater risk of injury than when risk factors are present in isolation.

The final link in the chain of events is the inciting event, which is usually referred to as the injury mechanism—what we see when watching an injury situation. Again, it may be helpful to use a comprehensive model to describe the inciting event, which accounts for the events leading to the injury situation (playing situation, player and opponent behavior), as well as to include a description of whole body and joint biomechanics at the time of injury (Chapter 8).[5]

Each injury type and each sport has its typical patterns, and for team medical staff it is important to consult the literature to reveal the typical injuries and their mechanisms for the sport in question. However, one limitation of the model is that it is not obvious how the team's training routine and competitive schedule can be taken into consideration as potential causes, and the model has therefore traditionally mainly been used to describe the causes of acute injuries. For overuse injuries, the inciting event can sometimes be distant from the outcome. For example, for a stress fracture in a long-distance runner, the inciting event is not usually the single training session when pain became evident, but the training and competition program he or she has followed over the previous weeks or months.

For clinicians, this model can be used to identify potential causes of injury. The key questions to ask are: Who is at increased risk? Why? And how do injuries typically occur? When caring for a defined group of sportspeople, such as a soccer team or an alpine skiing team, this can be done using a systematic risk management approach. Individual risk factors (and protective factors) can be mapped during the pre-season physical examination (e.g. history of previous injury, malalignment) or tested as part of the team's fitness testing program (e.g. strength, flexibility, neuromuscular control). Then it is possible to do a risk analysis to document the parts of the season when sportspeople are at the greatest risk of sustaining injuries as a result of the training or competitive programs (Fig. 9.3). Examples of situations in which

	Jan.	Feb.	Mar.	Apr.	May	June	July	Aug.	Sept.	Oct.	Nov.	Dec.
Basic training		2				6					8	
Training camp	1		3									
Competition				4	5					7		
Rest period												

Figure 9.3 Risk profile. Examples of periods of season when a college basketball team may be at particular risk of injury. The comments below concern the risk periods that are circled:

1. Change of time zone, off-court training surface, climate, and altitude during training camp in Colorado. Emphasis on defensive stance training and quick lateral movements could lead to several groin injuries (Chapters 28 and 29). Athletes should not increase the amount or intensity of training too much.
2. Transition to greater amount of on-court training and intensity, combined with several practice games. Floor surface quite hard. Risk of lower limb injuries such as Achilles tendinopathy, medial tibial stress syndrome.
3. New training camp to fine-tune players before beginning the competitive season; practice games on unusually slippery courts. Competition to avoid being cut from the squad leads to increased intensity during training and competition.

4. The beginning of the competitive season. A higher tempo and a packed competitive schedule to which the athlete is unaccustomed. Risk of overuse injury (e.g. patellar tendinopathy, tibial stress fracture) compounded by heavy academic program leads to additional fatigue.
5. High risk of acute injuries during the competitive season, and a tough competition schedule at full intensity.
6. Interposed period of hard basic training, with strength exercises to which the athlete is not accustomed, and plyometric training increases risk of tendinopathy and muscle strain.
7. The end of the competitive season. Worn out and tired players? This is an important time to treat low-level "grumbling" injuries aggressively. Waiting for the injury to heal with "rest" alone is not recommended.
8. Transition to basic training period with running on trails.

risk increases are when sportspeople switch from one training surface to another (e.g. from grass to gravel) or to new types of training (e.g. at the start of a strength training period).

This type of analysis provides an excellent basis for planning injury prevention measures, particularly for overuse injuries. The analysis is based on the idea that the risk of injuries is greater during transitional periods, and that each stage has certain characteristics that may increase risk. The risk profile usually varies from sport to sport. Healthcare personnel responsible for teams or training groups should do this type of analysis in collaboration with the coaches and athletes and create a plan for relevant preventive measures based on the risk analysis.

Warm-up

Warm-up prepares the body for exercise. The type of exercise to be performed determines the type of warm-up. The most effective warm-up consists of both general and specific exercises. General exercises may include jogging, general stretching, and resistance exercises. Specific exercises include stretches and movements appropriate for the particular activity about to be undertaken.

The possible benefits of warm-up prior to physical activity include:[7–9]

- increased blood flow to muscles
- increased oxyhemoglobin breakdown, with increased oxygen delivery to muscles
- increased circulation leading to decreased vascular resistance
- increased release of oxygen from myoglobin

- enhanced cellular metabolism
- reduced muscle viscosity leading to smoother muscle contraction and increased mechanical efficiency
- increased speed of nerve impulses
- increased sensitivity of nerve receptors
- decreased activity of alpha fibers and sensitivity of muscles to stretch
- decreased number of injuries due to increased range of motion
- decreased stiffness of connective tissue leading to decreased likelihood of tears
- increased cardiovascular response to sudden strenuous exercise
- increased relaxation and concentration.

There is no data on which to prescribe intensity and duration of a warm-up. Thus, it may make sense to allow sportspeople to determine their warm-up individually. In team sports, there can be a regimen with a built-in period of "free warm-up." One guideline for the intensity of the warm-up is to produce some mild sweating without fatigue. The effect of a warm-up lasts approximately 30 minutes, so it is important not to warm up too early.[7]

Several clinical studies, including a recent high-quality randomized trial,[10] have shown that structured warm-up programs designed to prevent injuries can reduce injury risk by 50% or more. However, it is not known whether it is the physiological effects of the warm-up program as described above that confers the effect on injury risk, or whether the reduced risk results from training effects on strength, neuromuscular control, technique, or other factors.

Stretching for prevention and performance
with IAN SHRIER

The ability to move a joint smoothly throughout a full range of movement is an important component of good health. There is a hereditary component to general flexibility, and specific joints or muscles may become stiff as a result of injury, overactivity, or inactivity. Many clinicians have long believed that increased flexibility attained through stretching decreases injuries, minimizes and alleviates muscle soreness, and improves performance. However, research by Peter Magnusson and others has illuminated the effects of stretching;[11–20] this has led some to challenge the dogmas that stretching prevents injury and improves performance.

Timing of stretching is critical! Pre-exercise or outside exercise?

A critical concept that is underemphasized in health professionals' training is that stretching before exercise is a different intervention from stretching outside periods of exercise.[21] In fact, the effects are similar to weight-lifting. For example, an acute bout of weight-lifting or stretching will cause an immediate decrease in strength, power, and endurance.[22] However, if one weight-lifts or stretches for weeks, there is an increase in strength, power, and endurance.[22] With respect to injury, *pre-exercise* stretching in isolation (with or without warm-up) does not decrease overall injury rates.[23-25] However, a meta-analysis of the three studies (conducted on the military and on fire fighters) that included a stretching component not immediately prior to exercise suggested that *regular* stretching resulted in approximately 32% reduction in injuries.[21]

Food for thought—stretching specificity and potential mechanisms of action

Despite the above studies, several unanswered questions remain. First, it is possible that a specific pre-exercise stretching program does prevent a particular injury type (e.g. stretching the hamstrings to prevent hamstring strains) even though overall injury rates are unaffected. If this were true, then pre-exercise stretching would also be likely to cause other injuries, presumably through the loss of strength, power, and endurance. Second, Witvrouw et al.[26] have raised an interesting hypothesis that pre-exercise stretching may be more important for preventing injury in sports that have a high intensity of stretch-shortening cycles (e.g. football, basketball) than in sports with relatively low demands on the muscle tendon stretch-shortening cycle (e.g. jogging, cycling, swimming). Although this hypothesis has been challenged, based on an extrapolation of existing basic science data,[27] there are no good studies in this area and it should be a high priority for research.

Finally, some have argued that, in addition to the type of sport, the effects of stretching are dependent on the population (e.g. elite athletes), duration of stretch, type of stretch, presence of warm-up, and timing of the stretching (e.g. post-exercise). With all the possible combinations of the above factors, the debate on the "stretching prevents injury" hypothesis is not likely to go away (although hopefully it will become more focused), and clinicians have no choice but to extrapolate the current evidence in order to make a decision.[28] That said, it does seem that there is a consensus that pre-exercise stretching reduces performance on tests of physical capacity, whereas regular stretching improves performance on tests of physical capacity.[22] How these changes affect performance in sports depends on the sport.[29] For example, although tests of performance suggest that a karate kick would have less force after stretching, stretching may increase the range of motion enough to allow the fighter to actually hit the opponent's head—and a kick that hits the head represents a better performance than a kick that misses the head.

The roles of different types of stretching

Athletes commonly perform three different types of stretching exercises—static, ballistic, and proprioceptive neuromuscular facilitation (PNF). More recently, some authors have also discussed "dynamic" stretching. However, the description of dynamic stretching usually given seems to be one of warming up rather than stretching,[30] and therefore it is not described here.

Static stretching

In static stretching, the stretch position is assumed slowly and gently and held for 30–60 seconds.[8] The athlete should not experience any discomfort in the stretched muscle. As the position is held, tension from the stretch becomes strong enough to initiate the inverse myotatic stretch reflex with subsequent muscle relaxation. The muscle can then be stretched a little further, again without discomfort. This increased stretch should also be held for approximately 30 seconds, then relaxed. If, during either stage of the stretch, there is a feeling of tension or pain, overstretching is occurring and this may cause injury. The athlete should ease off to a more comfortable position. Of the different types of stretches, static stretch produces the least amount of tension, and is theoretically the safest method of increasing flexibility.

Ballistic stretching

In a ballistic stretch, the muscle is stretched to near its limit, then stretched further with a bouncing movement. The disadvantage of this stretch is that the quick bouncing causes a strong reflex muscle contraction. Some people believe that stretching a muscle against this increased tension heightens the chances of injury. Therefore, this technique is not commonly used, except in gymnastics, ballet, and dance.

Proprioceptive neuromuscular facilitation stretching

PNF stretching is performed by alternating contraction and relaxation of both agonist and antagonist muscles. Although PNF stretching was originally based on the belief that muscle relaxation is increased after both agonist contraction and antagonist muscle contraction, research has shown this is not correct, and EMG activity is actually increased.[31, 32]

There are a number of different PNF stretching techniques (Fig. 9.4 overleaf). PNF stretching may produce greater flexibility gains than other stretching techniques. Its major disadvantage is that there is a tendency to overstretch. PNF stretches should ideally be performed with a partner who is aware of the potential dangers of the technique.

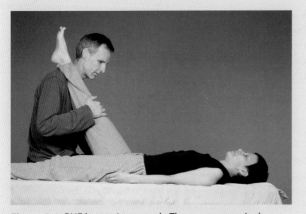

Principles of stretching

The basic principles of stretching are as follows:

- Warm-up prior to stretching.
- Stretch gently and slowly.
- Stretch to the point of tension but never pain.

A general stretching program involving stretches of the major muscle groups is shown in Figure 9.5. Specific stretches related to specific injuries are shown in the relevant chapters in Part B.

Figure 9.4 PNF hamstring stretch. The partner passively stretches the hamstring to the onset of discomfort. The athlete then performs isometric hamstring contraction against the partner's shoulder. The partner then passively stretches the hamstring further to the point of discomfort

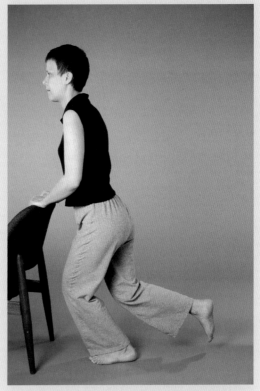

Figure 9.5 General stretching program
(a) Gastrocnemius. Pushing against a wall or fence with leg straight out behind, feeling a gentle calf stretch

(b) Soleus. Supported by a wall or fence with knee flexed, bring leg to be stretched underneath body and lunge forward, again feeling a gentle steady calf stretch

(e) Groin. Sitting on the floor with the knees flexed, soles of feet together and the back kept straight, gently push the outside of the knees towards the ground until a stretch is felt in the groin

(c) Calf (general). With the toes supported on a step or gutter, allow the heel to drop beneath the level of the toe. Allow gravity to impart a gentle stretch

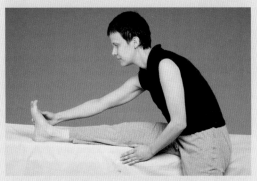

(d) Hamstrings. With the leg supported on a beam or bench and keeping the leg straight, gently bend forward at the hips until a stretch is felt at the hamstring. Do not bend the back in order to get the chest closer to the knee; rather, bend at the hips, keeping the back straight

(f) Groin. Sitting on the floor with the legs straight and the hips abducted, bend forward at the hips until a stretch is felt in the groin. By bending toward either leg, this can be used to stretch the hamstrings

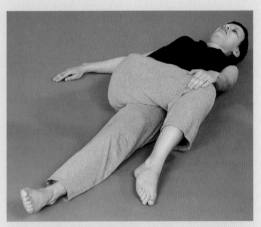

(i) Lower back. Lying on the ground or a bed, bend up one knee and rotate towards the opposite side until the knee touches the floor. Keep the shoulders flat on the ground. A gentle stretch should be felt in the lower back

(g) Quadriceps. In a standing position, pull the heel to the buttock until a stretch is felt at the front of the thigh. The stretch can be increased if necessary by pressing the hips forward. Attempt to keep the knees together and do not rotate at the pelvis

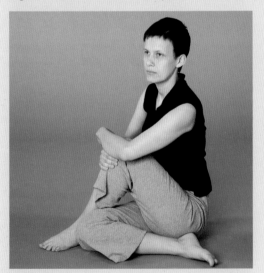

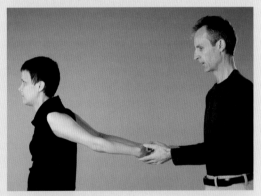

(j) Pectoral girdle. Standing or in a seated position, clasp both hands behind the back and straighten the elbows. A partner then lifts the hands gently. Keep the back straight. A stretch should be felt in the front of the shoulder and in the chest

(h) Gluteals/piriformis (left). Sitting on the floor, bend the left leg up in front. Place the left heel over the thigh of the right leg and pull the left knee towards the chest, until a stretch is felt in the left gluteal region. Attempt to keep both buttocks square on the ground

A

(k) Triceps. Lifting the arm into maximum flexion and abduction, bend the elbow to its fully flexed position. Then, placing the opposite hand on the elbow, pull across and back until a stretch is felt in the triceps and shoulders

(l) Levator scapulae. Place the chin on the chest and then rotate the head away from the side to be stretched. Then apply a stretch with the hand on the side of the head. A stretch should be felt in the neck and shoulder

Taping and bracing

Taping (or strapping) and bracing are used to restrict undesired, potentially harmful motion and allow desired motion. There are two main indications for the use of tape and braces:

- Prevention—taping is used as a preventive measure in high-risk activities (e.g. basketball players' ankles).
- Rehabilitation—taping is used as a protective mechanism during the healing and rehabilitation phase.[33, 34]

Although taping and bracing are used in injury management of conditions in numerous joints, they have not been proven to be effective for primary injury prevention in the shoulder, elbow, knee, and spinal joints. However, there is good evidence to suggest that bracing may prevent re-injuries in sportspeople with a history of a previous ankle sprain.

Taping

There are many different tapes and bandages available for use by sportspeople. However, when the purpose is to restrict undesired motion, only adhesive, non-stretch (rigid) tape is appropriate (Fig. 9.6). Elastic tape is inappropriate for restricting motion. Good tape should be adhesive, strong, non-irritant, and easily torn by the therapist.

Tape is ideally applied over joints where skin sliding can be limited to one direction. The joints most suitable for taping are the ankle, wrist, finger, acromioclavicular joint, and the first metatarsophalangeal joint. As well as providing mechanical support, tape

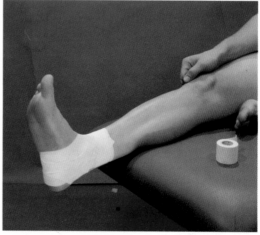

Figure 9.6 Taping application—an example of ankle taping

may enhance proprioception. Guidelines for tape application are given below.

Preparation

- The athlete and the therapist should be in a comfortable position for tape application.
- Tailor the taping to the needs of the individual and the sport being played. It is important to provide support but not to restrict essential movement.
- Injured ligaments should be held in a shortened position during taping. Ligaments that have not previously been injured should be held in neutral position.
- Shave body hair, preferably at least eight hours prior to tape application to avoid skin irritation.
- Clean skin, and remove grease and sweat.
- Apply an adhesive skin spray prior to taping, especially if sweating is likely to reduce the adhesiveness of the tape.
- Use an underwrap if a skin allergy exists.
- Take care with the use of non-stretch tape around swollen joints.
- Use tape of appropriate width.

Application

- Use anchors proximally and distally, as tape adheres better to itself than to skin.
- Unroll the tape before laying it on the skin, to ensure correct tension.
- Apply even pressure.
- Overlap the previous tape by one-half, to ensure strength and even application.
- Smooth out all folds and creases, to prevent blisters and lacerations.
- If discomfort is present after tape application, adjust the tape.

Removal

- Remove tape carefully with the use of tape cutters or tape scissors.

Complications

Complications of tape application include reduced circulation from tight taping, skin irritation due to mechanical or allergic phenomena, and decreased effectiveness of tape with time. Tape provides substantial material support but, as with any material, it does have a threshold where it fails.[35] It may be necessary to reapply tape at a suitable break during the sporting activity (e.g. at half-time). Tape application requires practice to perfect technique.

Bracing

Bracing has several advantages over taping. A sportsperson can put a brace on by himself or herself and, although the initial cost of a brace may be high, a good-quality, strong brace lasts a considerable time and may prove to be cheaper than repeated taping.

Bracing has a number of disadvantages. These include:

- possible slipping of the brace during use
- the weight of the brace
- problems with exact sizing
- the risk of the brace wearing out at an inopportune moment.

It may be necessary for braces to be custom-made.

A number of different types of braces are available. Heat-retaining sleeves are commonly used in the treatment of many chronic inflammatory conditions. These sleeves are usually made out of neoprene. The neoprene support offers increased warmth and comfort over the affected area and may improve proprioception; however, it provides little or no mechanical support. The sleeves are available for most joints and muscles. Increased mechanical support can be gained by the use of harder material or the addition of straps or laces. Some braces are used only to restrict movement (e.g. a hinged knee brace; Fig. 9.7).[36-38]

Braces can be custom-made by molding thermoplastic material over the affected part. Such splints are commonly used on the hand and wrist, particularly over the first carpometacarpal joint after a Bennett's fracture, or at the first metacarpophalangeal joint after a hyperextension sprain or ulnar collateral ligament sprain (Fig. 9.8).

Protective equipment

Protective equipment has been designed to shield various parts of the body against injury without interfering with sporting activity. Protective equipment can also be used on return to activity after injury in situations where direct contact may aggravate the injury.

Helmets are mandatory in certain sports (e.g. motor racing, motor cycling, cycling, ice hockey, horse riding, American football; Fig. 9.9). In other sports (e.g. rugby football, skateboarding), the use of helmets is not universally accepted. The role of helmets and face shields[39] in protection against head injuries is discussed in Chapter 17.

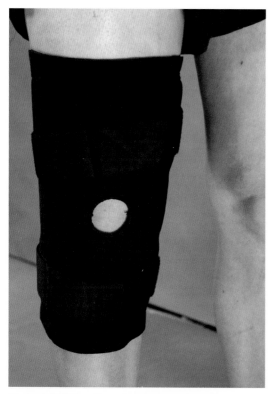

Figure 9.7 Hinged knee brace

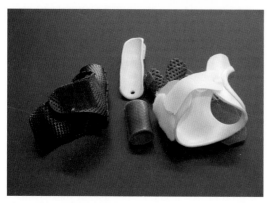

Figure 9.8 Molded braces

Other commonly worn protective equipment includes mouth-guards in most collision sports; shoulder pads in American and rugby football; chest, forearm, and groin protectors in ice hockey; knee pads when playing on artificial surfaces or while rollerblading; wrist guards in rollerblading and snowboarding; and shin pads in soccer and hockey. It is important that protective equipment fits correctly. Protective equipment may provide a psychological benefit by increasing a player's confidence.

Figure 9.9 Helmets

Suitable equipment

Running shoes (also see Chapter 8), football boots, ski boots, and tennis racquets are important elements that contribute to, or prevent, sports injuries.

Running shoes

As detailed in Chapter 8, the clinician must be able to assess foot type and advise sportspeople on the type of shoe most suited to their needs. The optimum shoe to prevent injuries is one that matches the runner's specific mechanical features.

Several features of shoes may affect foot function. The heel counter, the upper rear part of the shoe, should be made of rigid, firm plastic to assist in rearfoot stability.[40]

Forefoot flexibility (Fig. 9.10a) must be adequate to allow easy motion of the foot flexing at toe-off. With a rigid sole, the calf muscles may need to perform extra work in order to plantarflex the foot during propulsion.

The midsole of the shoe is probably the most important feature. Midsoles are usually made of ethylene vinyl acetate (EVA), which is light and is a good shock absorber. The most important feature of the midsole is that it should not be too hard or too soft. Midsoles that are too soft permit excessive mobility.

Figure 9.10 Characteristics of a running shoe
(a) Forefoot flexibility

(b) Midsole: dual density. Medial side of the midsole is harder than the lateral side. This promotes stability

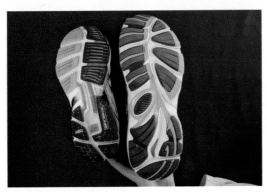

(c) Last shape. The shoe on the left is straight, while the shoe on the right is curved

Runners requiring control of excessive motion should use a midsole of dual density that is harder on the medial aspect of the foot (Fig. 9.10b). Runners requiring extra shock absorption should choose a shoe

with a soft midsole that still provides lateral stability. Maximum impact forces vary little in magnitude between soft and hard midsoles, but the maximal forces occur at a later stage in the soft shoes.

Midsoles that are flared promote rapid and excessive pronation of the foot, and should be avoided. This negative aspect of lateral flaring outweighs the advantage of decreased impact forces.

Last construction refers to the method used to join the upper of the shoe to the midsole. Shoes are generally slip lasted, where the upper is sewn together and glued directly to the sole. This promotes shoe flexibility but may reduce stability.

Last shape (straight or curved) may offer a range of shoes to fit an individual, and give comfort to different foot types (Fig. 9.10c). There is no evidence to support the commonly held view that the shape of a shoe influences foot function.

A summary of the recommended features of the running shoe for different foot types is shown in Table 9.1.

 There is no optimal running shoe *per se* but certain shoes are optimal for an individual.

Running spikes

Poorly designed running spikes may contribute to foot and lower limb injuries; however, there is a dearth of published literature in this field. The majority of running spikes are designed so that the spike plate is plantargrade in relation to the heel. When running on a flat surface, the heel lift is negligible and, thus, the heel is lower than the forefoot, which is called "negative heel" (Fig. 9.11). This phenomenon is the opposite of a heel "raise," as used in the treatment of Achilles problems.

When running in spikes, the runner strikes the ground on the forefoot and midfoot with the heel off the ground. The heel does not usually make contact with the ground while running at or near top speed.

Table 9.1 Shoe features appropriate for different foot types

Shoe features	Excessive pronator	Normal	Excessive supinator
Heel counter	Rigid	Rigid	Rigid
Forefoot flexibility	Yes	Yes	Yes
Midsole density	Hard dual density	Intermediate	Soft
Last construction	Combination	Slip or combination	Slip
Shape of last	Straight or slightly curved	Slightly curved	Curved or slightly curved

Figure 9.11 Running spikes with negative heel (left) compared with modified heel lifted with EVA material (right)

Figure 9.12 Football boots
(a) Midsole cushioned boot

(b) Thermoplastic outsole with cleats designed to enhance rotation

However, at lesser speeds, as the body weight moves over the foot, the foot lowers to the ground with little stability because of the negative heel.

The calf muscles may be subject to greater eccentric load due to the negative heel lift, as the tibia is required to dorsiflex over the foot through a greater range. In addition, the small heel provides little stability for the eccentric lowering of the heel by the calf muscles. These factors may predispose to the development of Achilles tendinopathy and shin pain in runners, as well as increasing the amount of compensatory pronation and midtarsal joint dorsiflexion. Running spikes may be modified to provide more stability by increasing the heel lift and balancing the shoe (Fig. 9.11).

Football boots

Football boots (Fig. 9.12) require all the features of a good running shoe in addition to features that will allow kicking and rapid changes of direction, particularly on soft surfaces.

The construction of many types of football boots provides inadequate support for the lower limb. Common structural features found in football boots and the problems associated with each particular feature are summarized in Table 9.2.

The ideal football boot should be of adequate foot depth in the upper, have a rigid heel counter, have sufficient forefoot flexibility, have a wide sole, and be slightly curved in shape, and the "stops" or cleats should be placed to allow adequate forefoot flexibility.

Ski boots

Generally, ski boots have become stiffer. However, a stiff ski boot does not allow adequate compensatory

Table 9.2 Problems associated with certain structural features of football boots

Structural features	Associated problems
Soft heel counter	Decreased rearfoot support
Narrow sole (width)	Decreased stability Skin lesions—blisters
Curved shape	Decreased stability / poor fit
Rigid sole	Decreased forefoot flexibility
Shallow upper	Decreased stability / poor fit
"Stop"/cleat placement	Often at point of forefoot flexibility Sometimes causes pain under first metatarsophalangeal joint

movement at the midtarsal and subtalar joint, and places additional stress on the bones and joints of the lower limb. More advanced skiers require stiff boots. Ski boots should be individually fitted; boots are available that allow individual molding to the shape of the skier's foot.

During skiing, control is maintained by pronating the foot to edge the downhill ski into the slope. Skiers with excessive pronation (Chapter 8) will be required to internally rotate their tibia further to maintain edge control, potentially leading to greater stress on medial knee structures and the patellofemoral joint.

Excessive foot pronation may be corrected with an orthosis placed in the ski boot to restore the foot to a neutral position. As the degree of correction possible with orthoses is limited by boot fit, additional control is sometimes required by the use of canting or wedging of the underside of the boot. These changes to the boot may affect the release mechanism of the binding.

Most equipment-related skiing injuries occur when the ski acts as a lever to turn or twist the lower leg, and many can be prevented with appropriate binding release. Beginners are particularly at risk as they have relatively tighter bindings and boots and bindings of lower quality than intermediate level skiers.[41, 42]

Tennis racquets
with BABETTE PLUIM

In tennis, the impact between ball and racquet produces a significant amount of force. How much force reaches the tennis player's arm depends on how fast the player swings the racquet, the speed of the incoming ball, where on the racquet face the ball is struck, the qualities of the racquet, the string tension, and the stroke mechanics.

Each racquet has an area where the initial shock is at a minimum—the center of percussion or "sweet spot." When the ball is hit in the sweet spot, the shot feels good. If the ball is not hit in the sweet spot, there is increased shock transmitted to the hand, wrist, and elbow.

The major factor in the etiology of tennis-related elbow pain is incorrect stroking technique, especially the one-handed backhand drive. However, the characteristics of the racquet may also contribute. The older style wooden racquets were heavy and flexible, both of which reduced shock on impact. The modern wide-body racquets are lighter and stiffer in order to generate increased power, but these racquets do not absorb the shock of impact as well as wooden racquets.

There are a number of ways of altering the tennis racquet to reduce the shock at impact and lessen the force transmitted to the player's arm:

- lower string tension
  - use gut or high-quality synthetic string
  - use a thinner string
- increase flexibility of the racquet
- increase the size of the racquet head
- increase the weight (add lead tape to head and handle)
- increase the grip size (Fig. 9.13).

The tennis player should choose the largest comfortable grip size (Fig. 9.13). A larger grip size prevents the player gripping the racquet too tightly. Players should also be encouraged to loosen their grip on the racquet. It is only necessary to squeeze firmly on the grip during the acceleration phase of the stroke.

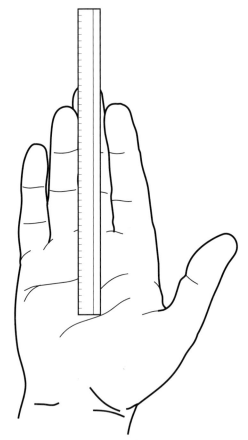

Figure 9.13 Grip size. Optimal racquet grip circumference should equal the distance from the proximal palmar crease to the tip of the ring finger

Appropriate surfaces

with JOHN ORCHARD

The surface on which sportspeople play is under the spotlight, as it may be a major contributor to injury risk through excessive shoe–surface traction. This possibility was proposed as a mechanism for ACL rupture in European handball as early as 1990,[43] and has later been examined in a large, epidemiological study where the ACL injury rate was compared between two different floor types—wooden floors (parquet, generally having lower friction) and artificial floors (generally having higher friction).[44] These results indicated that the risk of ACL injury among female team handball players is higher on high-friction artificial floors than on wooden floors. However, other factors also play a significant role for shoe-surface friction, principally shoe type and floor maintenance.

In Australian Rules football, Orchard et al.[45] noted the greater rate of ACL injuries in the northern (warmer) climes. Although it was tempting to attribute this to drier weather, and thus ground hardness,[46] that hypothesis was not supported by data from American football teams where games were played on natural grass. Further analysis of both the Australian and the US data suggested that the type of grass itself and, thus, the tightness of the thatch may influence ACL risk; the more northern Australian venues had types of grass that permitted excessive shoe–surface traction (Fig. 9.14).

(b) Kikuyu grass, also showing a thick thatch layer

(c) Rye grass surface, showing a minimal thatch layer. This is probably a safer surface than the others, as the blades or cleats of the football boot are less likely to be "gripped" by the surface

Figure 9.14 Four different types of grasses that provide the surface for Australian Rules football and have been associated with different rates of ACL injury.
(a) Bermuda ("couch") grass surface, showing a thick thatch layer between grass leaves and soil

(d) Annual blue grass surface, showing a moderate thatch layer

WITH PERMISSION FROM *BR J SPORTS MED*[45]

According to turf authority McNitt,[47] perennial rye grass is associated with lower shoe–surface traction than Kentucky blue grass or bermuda grass because it creates less thatch. These studies suggest that rye grass generally offers a safer surface with respect to ACL injuries for football than some other grasses.

To prevent all possible injuries, it is important to consider playing surface hardness because of its association with overuse injuries such as stress fractures, shin pain, and tendinopathy. A hard surface such as concrete generates greater force through the musculoskeletal system than a forgiving surface such as grass. Sporting activities can generate extremely high loads that may, or may not, be modulated by the surface. Maximal impact forces during walking have been shown to approach twice body weight; during running three to four times; and during jumping five to 12 times.[48]

Appropriate training

The clinician should understand different elements of training and their possible relationship to injury. This facilitates obtaining a full training history from an injured athlete or learning about the longer term training strategy from a coach. This makes it possible to determine where training error occurred and to take active steps to prevent this recurring. This chapter reviews the principles of training with a view to how injury can be prevented. The reader is directed to other sources for detailed outlines of the various types of training.

Principles of training

"Training" is the pursuit of activity that will ultimately lead to an increase in performance in a given sport. A number of general principles of training apply to all sports:

* periodization
* specificity
* overload
* individuality.

Periodization

Periodization is an important component of all training programs, in both the long term and the short term. Training can be divided into three distinct phases: conditioning (preparation), pre-competition (transitional), and competition.

The conditioning phase emphasizes developing aerobic and anaerobic fitness, strength, and power. Often during this period, the sportsperson is "training tired" and if required to compete would probably perform poorly. During the pre-competition phase of training, the emphasis switches from pure conditioning to technique work. During the competition phase, the emphasis is on competitive performance while maintaining basic conditioning (Table 9.3).

In many sports (e.g. basketball, football, hockey), a four- to six-month competition season is usual. In some instances, a sportsperson is required to undertake two periods of competition in the one year. A suggested program for athletes in these types of sports is shown in Figure 9.15. In other instances, the competition period may last as long as eight to 10 months and conditioning work must extend into the competitive season. However, the same principles of training apply. The athlete should aim for a peak performance at a predetermined time in a competitive season, such as a specific championship or final.

To ensure complete recovery from the physical and mental stress of competition, adequate time should be allowed between the end of one season and the start of the next. This period may last four to six weeks.

In the intermediate time frame, it is important to introduce easy weeks into the training program; these give the sportsperson time to recover (Chapter 10) and diminish risk of injury. During these easy weeks, the volume and intensity of training may be decreased and the opportunity may be taken to test the athlete's progress in the form of a time trial, mini-competition, or practice match. The optimal spacing of these easy weeks is probably every third or fourth week.

Table 9.3 Different types of training are performed during the three phases of the yearly cycle

Training phase	Aerobic training	Anaerobic training	Plyometrics training	Weight training	Technique training	Competition
Preparation/conditioning	+++	++	++	+++	+	−
Transitional/pre-competition	++	+++	++	++	+++	−
Competition	+	+	−	+	++	+++

(a) Team sports (e.g. basketball) with five to six month season

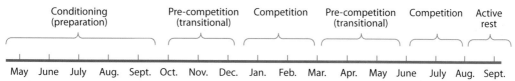

(b) Eighteen-month program for an athlete who wishes to peak twice in that period

Figure 9.15 Periodization of training

In the short term, the training program must allow for adequate recovery between training sessions. For example, an athlete whose training program involves weight training, aerobic and anaerobic training as well as technique work might plan to combine aerobic work with a weight session and technique work with an anaerobic session. A suggested program for such an athlete is shown in Table 9.4.

Overload

Overload is a variable that athletes and coaches manipulate to allow the athlete to perform work at a greater intensity, or to perform a greater volume of work at a given intensity, or to decrease recovery time between efforts of a given volume and intensity.

Overload principles include the following:

- Apply stress to the body over and above that which is normally encountered.
- If increased stress is not excessive and adequate adaptation time is allowed, the work capacity of the athlete will be increased ("supercompensation").
- Allow adequate recovery time to produce a training effect.

Table 9.4 Suggested three-weekly cycle for a track and field athlete[a]

Week	1	2	3
Monday	Jog Weights	Jog Weights (pyramid)	Jog Test bench press Light weights
Tuesday	Interval	6 × 120 m Technique Plyometrics	2 × 150 m (timed) Technique
Wednesday	Jog Weights	Jog Weights (pyramid)	Jog Test power clean Light weights
Thursday	Interval (e.g. 4 × 300 m) Plyometrics	400 m + 300 m + 200 m + 100 m Technique	1 × 300 m (timed) Technique
Friday	Jog Weights	Jog Weights	Jog Gymnastics Swim
Saturday	Interval (e.g. 6 × 100 m)	4 × 200 m	6 × 20 m
Sunday	Rest	Rest	Rest

(a) For example, a pole vaulter, whose training requires aerobic and anaerobic training, weight training, plyometrics, and technique work. The third week of the cycle is a "recovery week."

- Increase training load by changing the volume (quantity or duration) or the intensity (quality) of training.
- Only increase volume *or* intensity at any particular time (increases in volume should precede increases in intensity).
- Progress new training activities slowly so as not to cause injury to muscle groups and joints unaccustomed to that activity.
- Titrate overload to maximally improve performance without incurring injury (this is an art!).
- Monitor the athlete closely for signs of decreased performance or overtraining (Chapter 57).

Guide to aerobic training

Aerobic training effects occur while maintaining a heart rate of between 70% and 85% of the maximum heart rate.

Maximum heart rate is estimated by subtracting the age of the sportsperson from 220; for example, a 30-year-old sportsperson has a maximum heart rate of approximately 190 (220 – 30). The ideal range of heart rate for a 30-year-old to gain an aerobic effect would, therefore, be between 135 and 160 beats per minute.

Specificity

Specificity refers to the principle of directing training to performance in the athlete's given sport. It is important, therefore, to identify the most important components of fitness for each particular sport and to tailor the sportsperson's training toward improving these particular components. There is no advantage for a power athlete in doing large amounts of endurance training, nor for an endurance athlete to spend considerable time on strength training. Some sports (e.g. football) require both strength and endurance training.

Individuality

As individual differences between sportspeople are great, training must be tailored to the individual's needs. Individuals differ in their tolerance of particular training loads, response to specific training stimuli, speed of recovery, psychological make-up, nutritional intake, and lifestyle habits. Individual responses to training are influenced by previous training history, age, current state of fitness, and genetic make-up.

Training methods

Types of training include endurance or aerobic training, anaerobic training, strength and power training, speed training, agility training, specific skill training, and cross-training.

Aerobic training

Aerobic training is performed to increase aerobic capacity or fitness. Aerobic capacity is measured by the maximum oxygen consumption, better known as the VO_2max—the maximum amount of oxygen an individual is able to utilize in one minute per kilogram of body weight. This can be measured in the laboratory. A simpler, but less exact, method known as "the predicted VO_2max" is estimated by measuring the heart rate at a specific workload. This predicted VO_2max is commonly performed in health and fitness centers. Alternatively, the rating of perceived exertion (RPE) can be measured at a series of submaximal workloads so that the maximal workload predicted to occur at a maximal RPE of 20 units can be estimated. Although the athlete is unable to monitor oxygen consumption directly during training, he or she can monitor heart rate or RPE, both of which correlate well with oxygen consumption during submaximal activity. Thus, heart rate or RPE can be used to monitor intensity of aerobic training (see box).

Anaerobic training

Anaerobic exercise utilizes the anaerobic (oxygen-independent, i.e. without the need for oxygen) metabolism of glucose to produce energy. This pathway utilizes ATP as its energy substrate and, as a result, produces less energy per molecule of glucose utilized than does aerobic exercise.

Anaerobic training improves the capacity to maintain a high rate of power production for short durations of exercise at very high intensities. This requires that muscle recruitment and muscle contractile function be better maintained after training so that the onset of fatigue is delayed. This may result in part from increased efficiency of the body's anaerobic metabolism, while also improving its tolerance of lactic acidosis. The level of discomfort experienced in training correlates well with measured serum lactate concentrations. Physiologists and coaches regularly measure blood lactate concentrations during training to assess progress. This usually occurs in submaximal exercise, where the blood lactate level is plotted against speed of movement (e.g. swimming, rowing, running, cycling). However, many other variables

The Central Governor Model (CGM) for the limits of performance

The concept of maximum oxygen consumption (VO_2max) and lactic acidosis limiting athletic performance is currently undergoing critical evaluation.[49–51] The "classical" model of Hill, which still enjoys support among a substantial number of exercise physiologists, suggests that:

1. Progressive muscle hypoxia limits maximal exercise performance. As a result, the main determinant of exercise performance is the heart's ability to supply sufficient blood (and oxygen) to the exercising muscles.

2. Anaerobiosis (lack of muscle oxygen) secondary to the inability further to increase the cardiac output (producing a "plateau" in cardiac output) explains the onset of lactate production by skeletal muscle at the "anaerobic threshold."

3. Mitochondrial adaptation in the exercising muscles, associated with an increased ability of the heart to pump a larger cardiac output, are the exclusive biological changes that explain changes in performance with endurance training.

This model has been challenged by the contemporary, but certainly not universally accepted, model of Timothy Noakes, the South African physician and exercise physiologist. Noakes' data refute the classical model. Instead, he proposes that skeletal muscle recruitment and contractile function are regulated by a hierarchy of controls (conceptually "the central governor") specifically to prevent damage to any number of different organs.[51–60] He argues that, according to the Hill model in which a plateau in cardiac output precedes the development of skeletal muscle anaerobiosis and lactic acidosis, the first organ to be threatened by the plateau in cardiac output would be the heart, not skeletal muscle. The plateau in cardiac output would prevent any further increase in blood flow to the heart, leading to myocardial ischemia, the onset of chest pain (angina pectoris), and heart failure. He also provides evidence that this was, in fact, the belief of the early exercise physiologists, including Hill in England and Dill at the Harvard Fatigue Laboratory in the United States, and was a central component of their teachings. Since Hill understood that the heart could not survive a prolonged period of ischemia, he conceived the presence of a "governor" in either the heart or the brain that would reduce heart function and spare the heart by causing a "slowing of the circulation" as soon as myocardial ischemia developed. Noakes and colleagues have extended this interpretation to suggest that the governor exists in the central nervous system, hence it is called the central governor, and that it responds to multiple sensory inputs from all the organs in the body (Figure 9.16 overleaf). In response to those inputs, the central governor regulates the number of motor units that can be recruited in the exercising limbs on a moment-to-moment basis, reducing or limiting the number that can be recruited when their continued recruitment, necessary to maintain the work output or exercise intensity, threatens whole-body homeostasis. Hence Noakes writes that "during maximal exercise, progressive myocardial ischemia preceding skeletal muscle anaerobiosis must be thwarted, so that neither the heart nor the skeletal muscle develop irreversible rigor and necrosis with fatal consequences." The reader is directed to the publications that summarize this argument to date.[51–53, 55–60]

probably contribute to the superior performance after "anaerobic" training.

Irrespective of the theoretical background that underpins the physiology, the most efficient method of increasing anaerobic fitness is to undertake a form of intermittent exercise or interval training. Interval training involves a number of bouts of exercise separated by periods of rest or recovery. The principle of such training is to achieve a level of lactic acidosis with one individual effort and then allow the body to recover from its effects before embarking on another bout of exercise. There is scope for enormous variation in the intensity and duration of the exercise bouts and the duration of the recovery period.

Anaerobic training will also reset the central governor mechanism, perhaps teaching the governor that it can allow a slightly higher exercise intensity without risking a catastrophic bodily failure. In addition, anaerobic training will also increase the ability of the skeletal muscle fibers to produce more force. There is growing interest in the concept that differences in skeletal muscle contractility may modify athletic performance by determining the shortest possible duration the foot is in contact with the ground. This is because faster running requires

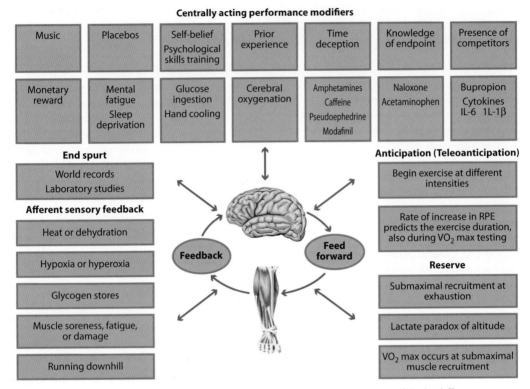

Centrally acting performance modifiers

Music	Placebos	Self-belief Psychological skills training	Prior experience	Time deception	Knowledge of endpoint	Presence of competitors
Monetary reward	Mental fatigue Sleep deprivation	Glucose ingestion Hand cooling	Cerebral oxygenation	Amphetamines Caffeine Pseudoephedrine Modafinil	Naloxone Acetaminophen	Bupropion Cytokines IL-6 1L-1β

End spurt

World records
Laboratory studies

Afferent sensory feedback

Heat or dehydration

Hypoxia or hyperoxia

Glycogen stores

Muscle soreness, fatigue, or damage

Running downhill

Feedback

Feed forward

Anticipation (Teleoanticipation)

Begin exercise at different intensities

Rate of increase in RPE predicts the exercise duration, also during VO_2 max testing

Reserve

Submaximal recruitment at exhaustion

Lactate paradox of altitude

VO_2 max occurs at submaximal muscle recruitment

Figure 9.16 The central governor responds to multiple sensory input from all organs of the body[59]

shorter foot contact times and hence greater skeletal muscle contractility and the recruitment of a greater number of muscle fibers.[61] In contrast, skeletal muscle contractility may be impaired in certain disease states.[62]

Interval training must be activity-specific. It is also important to note that interval training is only one component of an athlete's training, often undertaken in conjunction with an aerobic program. Because of its increased intensity, the potential for injury or accelerated chronic fatigue while undertaking interval training is relatively greater than for aerobic training.

Strength and power training

Muscular strength is the amount of force that may be exerted by an individual in a single maximum muscular contraction. Power is the maximum amount of work an individual can perform in a given unit of time. Both of these qualities are inherent to many athletic pursuits; therefore, the development of muscular strength and power is an important component of training.

Isotonic strength training

Isotonic strength training is a commonly utilized strength technique:

- It may be concentric (in which the muscle shortens as it contracts to move a weight) or eccentric (in which the muscle contracts as it lengthens) or utilize a combined movement.

Three different resistance training techniques

1. Isotonic (same rate of contraction) exercise: resistance to movement is constant and the speed of movement is varied.
2. Isokinetic (same speed of movement) exercise: a muscle group contracts to move through a range of motion at a constant speed with variable resistance. To achieve this, the resistance must be increased as the movement progresses (i.e. with an isokinetic machine).
3. Isometric (same length, i.e. muscle doesn't change length) exercise: maximal muscular contraction against immovable resistance.

- Resistance can be provided by free weights, rubber bands, pulleys, weight machines, or the individual's own body weight.
- Examples include the bench press, the dumbbell curl, the power squat, and the calf raise.

Advantages of isotonic strength training over isometric and isokinetic techniques:

- It tends to be more functional, natural movements than other forms of strength training.
- The athlete can observe the work being done as the weight is lifted.
- It may be performed over a full range of movement or, alternatively, over a specific limited range of movement.
- The athlete/coach can measure the amount of weight lifted and the number of repetitions performed.

Potential dangers of isotonic strength training include the following:

- Athletes require adequate supervision in the gymnasium.
- Athletes should never attempt to lift a maximal weight without a "spotter"—an assistant who is able to help the athlete if problems arise.
- Isotonic machines such as Keiser equipment may provide a safe alternative to free weights, but these machines limit the range of motion and are unable to provide truly constant resistance through the lift.

Isotonic exercises, in which the body weight of the individual is used as resistance, are also safer than free weights and are often more convenient to perform. Exercises such as sit-ups, push-ups, and chin-ups can be done almost anywhere and require no supervision. However, it is difficult to increase the resistance of the exercise, and the only way to increase the effort is to increase the number of repetitions performed.

Isokinetic and isometric strength training

Because of the need for specialized equipment, the use of isokinetic training by athletes is usually limited to rehabilitation from injury (Chapter 15). Isometric training is usually discouraged because it develops strength in a very small range of motion; however, it is used in rehabilitation after injury where range of motion may be restricted.

Olympic-type weight-lifting

Olympic-type weight-lifting is often used as part of a strength training program. Olympic lifting involves the lifting of a weight from the floor to a position above the ground. The Olympic-type lifts are the power clean, snatch, and clean and jerk. These lifts exercise a greater number of muscle groups than conventional weight-lifting, exercising them both concentrically and eccentrically. The potential for injury is high, and athletes must learn correct lifting techniques before attempting large weights. It is advisable to wear a weight belt to prevent back injuries. Because of the explosive nature of the lift, Olympic-type lifting is an excellent means for improving power as well as strength.

Plyometric training

Another technique of increasing power is plyometric training. Plyometric exercises (plyometrics) use the natural elastic recoil elements of human muscle and the neurological stretch reflex to produce a stronger, faster muscle response. Plyometrics is a form of resistance training that combines a rapid eccentric muscle contraction followed by a rapid concentric contraction to produce a fast forceful movement. It must be performed in conjunction with a resistance training program, as athletes need to have minimum basic strength levels before commencing plyometrics.

There are a number of plyometric exercises available. They include hopping and bounding drills, jumps over hurdles, and depth jumps. All of these activities emphasize spending as little time as possible in contact with the ground. Because of the explosive nature of the exercise, plyometrics has a great potential for injury and, therefore, an athlete's plyometrics program should be carefully supervised. This form of exercise can cause delayed onset muscle soreness (Chapter 4). Plyometric training should only be performed when the athlete is fresh, and the volume of work should be built up gradually. The training surface must be firm, but forgiving, such as sprung basketball floors. When technique begins to deteriorate, the exercise should be stopped.

Speed training

Running speed, a largely inherited ability, is an important component of many sports. Athletes can, however, develop speed by improving muscular power and strength, thus increasing stride length and cadence, as well as by improving technique, which increases the efficiency of ground coverage. Therefore, running speed can be increased by undertaking resistance and power training as well as by performing running drills. These drills may include high knees, heel to buttock, and overspeed work (e.g. downhill running).

Agility training

Agility and rapid reflexes are inherited characteristics. However, like speed, they can be improved somewhat by training and, thus, are included in training programs of all sports. There is an increasing emphasis on agility training for exercise prescription among seniors, to prevent falls.[58] Examples of specific agility exercises include the classic military stepping exercises and figure of eight running. These exercises should be sport-specific whenever possible.

Specific skill training

Sports have specific skills that require training in order to achieve a high level of efficiency. A proportion of training time must be devoted to developing these specific skills, preferably with the aid of a coach. Often, skill training requires the repetition of explosive movements and, therefore, has a high risk of injury. To prevent injury, a proportion of skill training should be done at an intensity level below normal competition conditions.

Cross-training

To prevent injury it may be beneficial to reduce the amount of weight-bearing exercise. Cross-training enables the athlete to maintain aerobic fitness while reducing stress on weight-bearing joints, muscles, and tendons.

In athletes with a chronic condition such as articular cartilage damage to a weight-bearing joint, cross-training may be used to reduce the impact load while maintaining adequate training volume. Similarly, in a patient returning to sport from an overuse injury (such as a stress fracture), cross-training can reduce the risk of recurrence.

Runners may wish to introduce one to two sessions per week of activities such as cycling, swimming, or water-running. These alternative work-outs can mirror the athlete's usual training session (e.g. interval training, aerobic, or anaerobic training).

Adequate recovery

Adequate recovery is essential if the athlete is to benefit fully from training and prevent injuries from occurring. This is discussed in the next chapter (Chapter 10).

A

RECOMMENDED READING

Arnason A, Engebretsen L, Bahr R. No effect of a video-based awareness program on the rate of soccer injuries. *Am J Sports Med* 2005 Jan;33(1):77–84.

Bahr R, Engebretsen L. *Sports injury prevention.* Chicheseter: Wiley Blackwell, 2009.

Bahr R, Maehlum S. *Clinical guide to sports injuries: an illustrated guide to the management of injuries in physical activity.* Champaign, Il: Human Kinetics Publishers, 2004.

Barbic D, Pater J, Brison RJ. Comparison of mouth guard designs and concussion prevention in contact sports: a multicenter randomized controlled trial. *Clin J Sport Med* 2005;15(5):294–8.

Emery CA, Cassidy JD, Klassen TP et al. Effectiveness of a home-based balance-training program in reducing sports-related injuries among healthy adolescents: a cluster randomized controlled trial. *CMAJ* 2005 Mar 15;172(6):749–54.

McHugh MP. Injury prevention in professional sports: protecting your investments. *Scand J Med Sci Sports* 2009;19:751–2.

Maffulli N, Longo UG, Gougoulias N et al. Long-term health outcomes of youth sports injuries. *Br J Sports Med* 2010;44:21–5.

Murphy DF, Connolly DA, Beynnon BD. Risk factors for lower extremity injury: a review of the literature. *Br J Sports Med* 2003;37(1):13–29.

Noakes TD, Peltonen JE, Rusko HK. Evidence that a central governor regulates exercise performance during acute hypoxia and hyperoxia. *J Exp Biol* 2001;204(Pt 18):3225–34.

Noakes TD, St Clair Gibson A, Lambert EV. From catastrophe to complexity: a novel model of integrative central neural regulation of effort and fatigue during exercise in humans. *Br J Sports Med* 2004;38(4):511–14.

Noakes TD, St Clair Gibson A. Logical limitations to the "catastrophe" models of fatigue during exercise in humans. *Br J Sports Med* 2004;38(5):648–9.

St Clair Gibson A, Noakes TD. Evidence for complex system integration and dynamic neural regulation of skeletal muscle recruitment during exercise in humans. *Br J Sports Med* 2004;38(6):797–806.

Lambert EV, St Clair Gibson A, Noakes TD. Complex systems model of fatigue: integrative homoeostatic control of peripheral physiological systems during exercise in humans. *Br J Sports Med* 2005;39(1):52–62.

Noakes TD, St Clair Gibson A, Lambert EV. From catastrophe to complexity: a novel model of integrative central neural regulation of effort and fatigue during exercise in humans: summary and conclusions. *Br J Sports Med* 2005;39(2):120–4.

Noakes TD. *Lore of running.* 4th edn, Human Kinetics Publishers, Champaign, Il. 2003.

Olsen OE, Myklebust G, Engebretsen L et al. Exercises to prevent lower limb injuries in youth sports: cluster randomized controlled trial. *BMJ* 2005 26;330(7489):449.

Shrier I. Does stretching help prevent injuries? In: MacAuley D, Best T, eds. *Evidence-based sports medicine.* 2nd edn. Malden: Blackwell Publishing, 2007: 36–58.

Thacker SB, Stroup DF, Branche CM et al. Prevention of knee injuries in sports. A systematic review of the literature. *J Sports Med Phys Fitness* 2003;43(2): 165–79.

Verhagen E, van der Beek A, Twisk J et al. The effect of a proprioceptive balance board training program for the prevention of ankle sprains: a prospective controlled trial. *Am J Sports Med* 2004;32(6):1385–93.

Yeung EW, Yeung SS. Interventions for preventing lower limb soft-tissue injuries in runners. *Cochrane Database Syst Rev* 2001;(3):CD001256.

REFERENCES

1. Vaz D, Santos L, Carneiro AV. Risk factors: definitions and practical implications. *Rev Port Cardiol* 2005;24(1):121–31.
2. van Mechelen W, Hlobil H, Kemper HC. Incidence, severity, aetiology and prevention of sports injuries. A review of concepts. *Sports Med* 1992;14(2):82–99.
3. Meeuwisse W, Tyreman H, Hagel B et al. Dynamic model of etiology in sport injury: the recursive nature of risk and causation. *Clin J Sport Med* 2007;17(3):215–19.
4. Bahr R, Holme I. Risk factors for sports injuries—a methodological approach. *Br J Sports Med* 2003;37(5):384–92.
5. Bahr R, Krosshaug T. Understanding injury mechanisms: a key component of preventing injuries in sport. *Br J Sports Med* 2005;39(6):324–9.
6. Alentorn-Geli E, Myer GD, Silvers HJ et al. Prevention of non-contact anterior cruciate ligament injuries in soccer players. Part 1: Mechanisms of injury and underlying risk factors. *Knee Surg Sports Traumatol Arthrosc* 2009;17(7):705–29.
7. Green JP, Grenier SG, McGill SM. Low-back stiffness is altered with warm-up and bench rest: implications for athletes. *Med Sci Sports Exerc* 2002;34(7):1076–81.

8. Rosenbaum D, Hennig EM. The influence of stretching and warm-up exercises on Achilles tendon reflex activity. *J Sports Sci* 1995;13(6):481–90.

9. Stewart IB, Sleivert GG. The effect of warm-up intensity on range of motion and anaerobic performance. *J Orthop Sports Phys Ther* 1998;27(2):154–61.

10. Olsen OE, Myklebust G, Engebretsen L et al. Exercises to prevent lower limb injuries in youth sports: cluster randomised controlled trial. *BMJ* 2005;330(7489):449.

11. Magnusson SP. Passive properties of human skeletal muscle during stretch maneuvers. A review. *Scand J Med Sci Sports* 1998;8(2):65–77.

12. Magnusson SP, Aagaard P, Larsson B et al. Passive energy absorption by human muscle-tendon unit is unaffected by increase in intramuscular temperature. *J Appl Physiol* 2000;88(4):1215–20.

13. Magnusson SP, Aagaard P, Nielson JJ. Passive energy return after repeated stretches of the hamstring muscle-tendon unit. *Med Sci Sports Exerc* 2000;32(6):1160–4.

14. Magnusson SP, Aagard P, Simonsen E et al. A biomechanical evaluation of cyclic and static stretch in human skeletal muscle. *Int J Sports Med* 1998;19(5):310–16.

15. Magnusson SP, Simonsen EB, Aagaard P et al. Mechanical and physical responses to stretching with and without preisometric contraction in human skeletal muscle. *Arch Phys Med Rehabil* 1996;77(4):373–8.

16. Magnusson SP, Simonsen EB, Aagaard P et al. Viscoelastic response to repeated static stretching in the human hamstring muscle. *Scand J Med Sci Sports* 1995;5(6):342–7.

17. Magnusson SP, Simonsen EB, Aagaard P et al. A mechanism for altered flexibility in human skeletal muscle. *J Physiol* 1996;497 (Pt 1):291–8.

18. Magnusson SP, Simonsen EB, Dyhre-Poulsen P et al. Viscoelastic stress relaxation during static stretch in human skeletal muscle in the absence of EMG activity. *Scand J Med Sci Sports* 1996;6(6):323–8.

19. Halbertsma JPK, Goeken LNH. Stretching exercises—effect on passive extensibility and stiffness in short hamstrings of healthy subjects. *Arch Phys Med Rehabil* 1994;75(9):976–81.

20. Halbertsma JPK, Mulder I, Goeken LNH et al. Repeated passive stretching: acute effect on the passive muscle moment and extensibility of short hamstrings. *Arch Phys Med Rehabil* 1999;80(4):407–14.

21. Shrier I. Meta-analysis on preexercise stretching. *Med Sci Sports Exerc* 2004;36(10):1832; author reply 1833.

22. Shrier I. Does stretching improve performance? A systematic and critical review of the literature. *Clin J Sport Med* 2004;14(5):267–73.

23. Herbert RD, Gabriel M. Effects of stretching before and after exercising on muscle soreness and risk of injury: systematic review. *BMJ* 2002;325(7362):468.

24. Pope RP, Herbert RD, Kirwan JD et al. A randomized trial of preexercise stretching for prevention of lower-limb injury. *Med Sci Sports Exerc* 2000;32(2):271–7.

25. Shrier I. Stretching before exercise does not reduce the risk of local muscle injury: a critical review of the clinical and basic science literature. *Clin J Sport Med* 1999;9(4):221–7.

26. Witvrouw E, Mahieu N, Danneels L et al. Stretching and injury prevention: an obscure relationship. *Sports Med* 2004;34(7):443–9.

27. Shrier I. Stretching perspectives. *Curr Sports Med Rep* 2005;4(5):237–8.

28. Shrier I. Stretching before exercise: an evidence based approach. *Br J Sports Med* 2000;34(5):324–5.

29. Shrier I. When and whom to stretch? Gauging the benefits and drawbacks for individual patients. *Phys Sportsmed* 2005;33(3):22–6.

30. Herman SL, Smith DT. Four-week dynamic stretching warm-up intervention elicits longer-term performance benefits. *J Strength Cond Res* 2008;22(4):1286–97.

31. Markos PD. Ipsilateral and contralateral effects of proprioceptive neuromuscular facilitation techniques on hip motion and electro-myographic activity. *Phys Ther* 1979;59(11):1366–73.

32. Moore MA, Hutton RS. Electro-myographic investigation of muscle stretching techniques. *Med Sci Sports Exerc* 1980;12(5):322–9.

33. Bahr R, Lian O, Bahr IA. A twofold reduction in the incidence of acute ankle sprains in volleyball after the introduction of an injury prevention program: a prospective cohort study. *Scand J Med Sci Sports* 1997;7(3):172–7.

34. Verhagen E, van der Beek A, Twisk J et al. The effect of a proprioceptive balance board training program for the prevention of ankle sprains: a prospective controlled trial. *Am J Sports Med* 2004;32(6):1385–93.

35. Bragg RW, Macmahon JM, Overom EK et al. Failure and fatigue characteristics of adhesive athletic tape. *Med Sci Sports Exerc* 2002;34(3):403–10.

36. Beynnon BD, Ryder SH, Konradsen L et al. The effect of anterior cruciate ligament trauma and bracing on knee proprioception. *Am J Sports Med* 1999;27(2):150–5.

37. Fleming BC, Renstrom PA, Beynnon BD et al. The influence of functional knee bracing on the anterior cruciate ligament strain biomechanics in weightbearing and nonweightbearing knees. *Am J Sports Med* 2000;28(6):815–24.

38. Swirtun LR, Jansson A, Renstrom P. The effects of a functional knee brace during early treatment of patients with a nonoperated acute anterior cruciate ligament tear: a prospective randomized study. *Clin J Sport Med* 2005;15(5):299–304.

39. Benson BW, Mohtadi NG, Rose MS et al. Head and neck injuries among ice hockey players wearing full face shields vs half face shields. *JAMA* 1999;282(24):2328–32.

40. Wilk BR, Fisher KL, Gutierrez W. Defective running shoes as a contributing factor in plantar fasciitis in a triathlete. *J Orthop Sports Phys Ther* 2000;30(1):21–8; discussion 29–31.

41. Finch CF, Kelsall HL. The effectiveness of ski bindings and their professional adjustment for preventing alpine skiing injuries. *Sports Med* 1998;25(6):407–16.

42. Natri A, Beynnon BD, Ettlinger CF et al. Alpine ski bindings and injuries. Current findings. *Sports Med* 1999;28(1):35–48.

43. Strand T, Tvedte R, Engebretsen L et al. [Anterior cruciate ligament injuries in handball playing. Mechanisms and incidence of injuries]. *Tidsskr Nor Laegeforen* 1990;110(17):2222–5.

44. Olsen OE, Myklebust G, Bahr R. Effect of floor type on injury risk in team handball. *Scand J Med Sci Sports* 2003;13(5):299–304.

45. Orchard JW, Chivers I, Aldous D et al. Rye grass is associated with fewer non-contact anterior cruciate ligament injuries than bermuda grass. *Br J Sports Med* 2005;39(10):704–9.

46. Orchard J. Is there a relationship between ground and climatic conditions and injuries in football? *Sports Med* 2002;32(7):419–32.

47. McNitt A, Waddington D, Middour R. Traction measurement on natural turf. In Hoerner E, ed. *Safety in American football*. American Society for Testing and Materials, 1997;145–55.

48. Whiting WC, Zernicke RF. *Biomechanics of musculoskeletal injury*. Champaign, Il: Human Kinetics, 2006.

49. Noakes TD. 1996 J. B. Wolffe Memorial Lecture. Challenging beliefs: *ex Africa semper aliquid novi*. *Med Sci Sports Exerc* 1997;29:571–90.

50. Noakes TD. Maximal oxygen uptake: "classical" versus "contemporary" viewpoints: a rebuttal. *Med Sci Sports Exerc* 1998;30(9):1381–98.

51. Noakes TD, St Clair Gibson A, Lambert EV. From catastrophe to complexity: a novel model of integrative central neural regulation of effort and fatigue during exercise in humans. *Br J Sports Med* 2004;38(4):511–14.

52. Noakes TD, Peltonen JE, Rusko HK. Evidence that a central governor regulates exercise performance during acute hypoxia and hyperoxia. *J Exp Biol* 2001;204(Pt 18):3225–34.

53. Noakes TD, St Clair Gibson A. Logical limitations to the "catastrophe" models of fatigue during exercise in humans. *Br J Sports Med* 2004;38(5):648–9.

54. Noakes TD. Physiological factors limiting exercise performance in CFS. *Med Sci Sports Exerc* 2004;36(6):1087.

55. Noakes TD, St Clair Gibson A, Lambert EV. From catastrophe to complexity: a novel model of integrative central neural regulation of effort and fatigue during exercise in humans: summary and conclusions. *Br J Sports Med* 2005;39(2):120–4.

56. Lambert EV, St Clair Gibson A, Noakes TD. Complex systems model of fatigue: integrative homoeostatic control of peripheral physiological systems during exercise in humans. *Br J Sports Med* 2005;39(1):52–62.

57. St Clair Gibson A, Noakes TD. Evidence for complex system integration and dynamic neural regulation of skeletal muscle recruitment during exercise in humans. *Br J Sports Med* 2004;38(6):797–806.

58. Liu-Ambrose T, Khan KM, Eng JJ et al. Resistance and agility training reduce fall risk in women aged 75 to 85 with low bone mass: a 6-month randomized, controlled trial. *J Am Geriatr Soc* 2004;52(5):657–65.

59. Noakes TD. Time to move beyond a brainless exercise physiology: the evidence for complex regulation of human exercise performance. *Appl Physiol Nutr Metab* 2011;36(1):23–35.

60. Noakes TD. Is it time to retire the A.V. Hill model? A rebuttal to the article by Professor Roy Shephard. *Sports Med* 2011;41(4): 263–77.

61. Nummela AT, Keränen T, Mikkelsson LO. Factors related to top running speed and economy. *Int J Sports Med* 2007;28(8): 655–61.

62. Rae DE, Noakes TD, San Juan AF et al. Excessive skeletal muscle recruitment during strenuous exercise in McArdle patients. *Eur J Appl Physiol* 2010;110(5):1047–55. Epub 2010 Aug 4.

Chapter 10

Recovery

Recovery underway—ice bath filling, beer in hand.   Tweet by @jmsenger (John Senger)

In recent years, there has been an increased emphasis on recovery following bouts of heavy training or competition, and the possible means by which recovery can be enhanced. There are a number of situations where enhancing recovery can be helpful for the sportsperson.

The athlete may have to perform again in a few hours' time, such as running a heat of an event in the morning and then the final later in the day. Occasionally in tournaments, individuals or teams have to compete twice in one day. A tennis player may have to play a singles match and then a doubles match a few hours later, or a team sport athlete may have a number of games in a day as part of a weekend round robin tournament. Even though playing another high-intensity competition the same day is the exception rather than the rule, it is not uncommon to have to play on consecutive days or at least two or three times a week. Full recovery is obviously very important.

Even for those playing weekly, it is important to be fully recovered as quickly as possible, to enable the athlete to train effectively during the week. In all these situations, recovery from exhaustive activity is important, and coaches and conditioning staff have, in recent times, implemented post-game programs to enhance recovery.

Overall, the aim is to maximize performance and minimize potential for injury at the next event. The specific objectives in the recovery process are:

- restoration of function
- neuromuscular recovery
- tissue repair
- resolution of muscle soreness
- psychological recovery.

Unfortunately, there is limited research into the various recovery methods. Current research has a number of limitations:

- poor study design
    - often not randomized
    - lacks appropriate control populations
- small numbers
    - increased likelihood of chance findings
    - difficulty finding statistical benefit
    - confusing statistical and clinical benefits
- optimum regimen unknown for most techniques
- different sports having different requirements
- underlying mechanisms unclear/speculative
- indirect outcome measures.

A number of methods are commonly used to hasten the recovery process. These include:

- warm-down (active recovery)
- cold water immersion (ice baths)
- massage
- compression garments
- lifestyle factors
- nutrition
- psychology.

Warm-down or active recovery

Most serious sportspeople perform a warm-down or active recovery following the conclusion of intense exercise. The length of warm-down generally varies with the level of the participant's activity, but ranges from 5 to 15 minutes. Running athletes generally perform a walk or walk/jog regime, while swimmers will usually use their customary stroke but at a slow pace. This is usually followed by stretching of the muscles used in training or competition.

The evidence for the effectiveness of active recovery is conflicting, with studies showing positive effects,[1, 2] no change,[3, 4] and even in one study a negative effect on peak power and lactate levels.[5]

Despite the lack of clear evidence, the practice of active recovery following strenuous exercise is almost universally conducted in high-level sport.

Deep-water running

Deep-water running involves "running" in the deep end of a swimming pool using a buoyancy vest. This technique can be used to maintain fitness during recovery from lower limb injury (Chapter 15), and as a form of cross-training to reduce impact, with the aim of reducing overuse injuries (Chapter 9). Its use has also been advocated as part of the recovery program either immediately after the bout of strenuous exercise or the following day. Reilly et al. showed that a regimen of deep-water running for three consecutive days after intense exercise reduced muscle soreness and appeared to speed up the restoration of muscle strength.[6]

Cold water immersion (ice baths)

The use of cold water immersion (CWI) or, as it is popularly known, "ice baths," has become common among sportspeople attempting to enhance the recovery process. There are numerous different regimes used and, again, the evidence for their efficacy is conflicting.

The scientific rationale underpinning CWI for recovery after sport is yet to be determined.[7] CWI has a cooling effect on body tissues, based on a physical heat loss to the surrounding environment. It is also associated with a peripheral vasoconstrictive response, reduced perfusion, and a decrease in edema formation. While CWI has a significant effect on skin temperature, it is not clear whether intramuscular temperature is also cooled. Sudden exposure to CWI results in "cold shock" with associated increase in heart rate, blood pressure, respiratory minute volume, and metabolism.[7] Patients with a history of cardiac problems, particularly arrhythmias, should avoid CWI. There is also evidence of increased oxidative stress and free radical formation, which may be detrimental.

The majority of scientific studies show an improvement in restoration of physical performance after CWI.[8, 9] It is also thought to have a positive psychological effect and, anecdotally, players invariably report that they believe these techniques help their recovery.

There is much variation in the preferred method of CWI. The simplest and easiest method involves the athlete standing waist deep in an ice bath (2–10°C). Initially, the most popular form of immersion involved one minute in followed by one minute out of the bath. This was repeated two or three times. More recently, a regime of five minutes standing in the ice bath has become the most favored. The ideal temperature of the bath is also not clear, but ice bath temperatures in the range of 10–15°C are the most commonly used.

Contrast baths, alternating warm and cold baths for one minute each, repeated three or four times, have also been used, but do not appear to give any added advantage of CWI.[10]

Massage

Regular soft tissue therapy contributes to soft tissue recovery from intense athletic activity. Intense training causes prolonged elevation of muscle tone in both the resting and the contractile states. This is often felt as muscle "tightness" by sportspeople and occurs particularly during periods of adaptation to increased volume and intensity of training.

It is thought that hard training and "abnormal tone" have numerous effects. These may impair the delivery of nutrients and oxygen to the cells and slow the removal of metabolites. They may contribute to biomechanical abnormalities, particularly if muscle tightness is asymmetrical. Increased tone also limits the extensibility and shock absorbency of soft tissue and thus predisposes the tissue to strain. Fatigue associated with hard training also impairs proprioceptive mechanisms and may directly trigger nociceptors.

Intense training also causes irritation of previously inadequately treated soft tissue lesions. Repetitive microtrauma of these lesions may cause bulky connective tissue to develop, which further compromises muscle function and flexibility. Fascial tissue may become less pliable due to cross-linkages developing. Active trigger points that result from heavy training may reduce muscle strength. These problems can impair training and competition and can progress to injury if they are not resolved.

Although not entirely clear, soft tissue therapy is thought to work by reducing excessive post-exercise muscle tone, increasing muscle range of motion, increasing the circulation and nutrition to damaged tissue, and deactivating symptomatic trigger points. As well as improving soft tissue function, regular soft tissue therapy provides the opportunity for the thera-pist to identify any soft tissue abnormalities, which, if untreated, could progress to injury.

A review of the scientific evidence regarding the efficacy of soft tissue therapy for recovery of skeletal muscle from strenuous exercise concluded that there was little support for the use of massage to improve physical performance, but some evidence that it will lead to a reduction in post-exercise soreness and delayed onset muscle soreness (DOMS).[11] There was no agreement on the type, duration, and timing of the post-exercise massage.

Compression garments

Compression garment such as lower limb tights (Fig. 10.1) and below-knee socks are widely advocated as recovery aids. Players are advised to put the tights on soon after the finish of their event and leave them on for the next 24 hours. Most research has shown a significant reduction in post-event muscle soreness with the use of compression garments, but there is little evidence that the use of the garments aids performance.[12, 13]

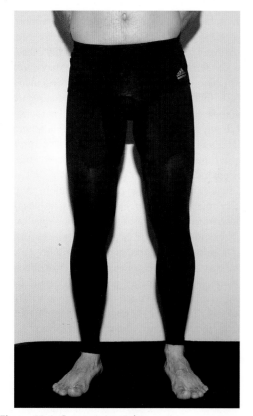

Figure 10.1 Compression tights

Lifestyle factors

Adequate rest and sleep are thought to be important in the recovery process, although there has been little research into this area. It has been shown that sleep loss following a match can interfere with perform-ance at training the next day; however, any loss of sleep is likely to be compensated for the next night.[14]

It is traditional in certain sports to overindulge in alcohol following a competition. This can have a sig-nificant negative effect on recovery. Studies in cyclists showed that muscle glycogen storage was impaired when alcohol was consumed immediately after exer-cise and displaced carbohydrate intake from the recov-ery diet.[15] It is likely, however, that the most important effects of alcohol intake on glycogen resynthesis are indirect—by interfering with the athlete's ability, or interest, to achieve the recommended amounts of carbohydrate required for optimal glycogen restora-tion.[16] A recent study showed a significant reduction in muscle function during recovery from eccentric-induced muscle damage after alcohol intake.[17]

Nutrition

Nutrition aids recovery from intense exercise by replenishing glycogen stores and by providing neces-sary protein and water.

Recovery encompasses a complex range of proc-esses that include:

- refueling the muscle and liver glycogen (carbohydrate) stores
- replacing the fluid and electrolytes lost in sweat
- manufacturing new muscle protein, red blood cells, and other cellular components as part of the repair and adaptation process
- allowing the immune system to handle the damage and challenges caused by the exercise bout.

Glycogen replacement

Glycogen is the major energy source for muscular activity (Chapter 38). Training depletes muscle and liver glycogen stores. Repetitive bouts of activity can cause profound glycogen depletion, and impair sporting performance.

The major dietary factor in post-exercise refueling is the amount of carbohydrate consumed. Depending on the fuel cost of the training schedule or the need to fuel up to race, a serious sportsperson may need to consume 7–12 g of carbohydrate per kg body weight each day (350–840 g per day for a 70 kg athlete) to ensure adequate glycogen stores.

In the immediate post-exercise period, sports-people are encouraged to consume a carbohydrate-rich snack or meal that provides 1–1.2 g of carbohydrate per kg body weight within the first hour of finishing, as this is when rates of glycogen synthesis are greatest. This is especially important if the time between prolonged training sessions is less than eight hours. The type and form (meal or snack) of carbohydrate that is suitable will depend on a number of factors, including the sportsperson's overall daily carbohydrate and energy requirements, gastric tolerance, access and availability of suitable food options, and the length of time before the next training session. Table 10.1 gives examples of snacks providing at least 50 g of carbohydrate.

In general, the immune system is suppressed by intensive training, with many parameters being reduced or disturbed during the hours following a work-out. This may place sportspeople at risk of succumbing to an infectious illness during this time. The most recent evidence points to carbohydrate as one of the most promising nutritional immune protectors. Ensuring adequate carbohydrate stores before exercise, and consuming carbohydrate during and/or after a prolonged or high-intensity work-out, has been shown to reduce the disturbance to immune system markers. The carbohydrate reduces the stress hormone response to exercise, thus minimizing its effect on the immune system, as well as supplying glucose to fuel the activity of many of the immune system white cells.

Protein replacement

Intense exercise results in breakdown of muscle tissue. Intake of protein in recovery meals is recommended to enhance net protein balance, tissue repair, and adaptations involving synthesis of new proteins.

Prolonged and high-intensity exercise causes a substantial breakdown of muscle protein. During the recovery phase, there is a reduction in catabolic (breakdown) processes and a gradual increase in anabolic (building) processes, which continues for at least 24 hours after exercise. Early intake after exercise (within the first hour) of essential amino acids from good-quality protein foods helps to promote the increase in protein rebuilding. Consuming food sources of protein in meals and snacks after this "window of opportunity" will further promote protein synthesis, although the rate at which it occurs is less.

Although research is continuing into the optimal type (e.g. casein, whey), timing, and amount of protein needed to maximize the desired adaptation from the training stimulus, most agree that both resistance and endurance athletes will benefit from consuming 10–20 g of high-quality protein in the first hour after exercise. Table 10.2 lists a number of everyday foods that provide approximately 10 g of protein.

Co-ingestion of carbohydrate and protein

The co-ingestion of protein with carbohydrate will increase the efficiency of muscle glycogen storage when the amount of carbohydrate ingested is below the threshold for maximum glycogen synthesis, or when feeding intervals are more than one hour apart. The effectiveness of protein to enhance muscle glycogen

Table 10.1 Carbohydrate-rich recovery snacks (50 g CHO portions)

- 700–800 mL sports drink
- 2 sports gels
- 500 mL fruit juice or soft drink
- 300 mL carbohydrate loader drink
- 2 slices toast/bread with jam or honey or banana topping
- 2 cereal bars
- 1 cup thick vegetable soup + large bread roll
- 115 g (1 large or 2 small) cake-style muffins, fruit buns or scones
- 300 g (large) baked potato with salsa filling
- 100 g pancakes (2 stack) + 30 g syrup

from an Australian Institute of Sport fact sheet

Table 10.2 Foods providing approximately 10 g of protein

Animal foods	Plant-based foods
• 40 g cooked lean beef/ pork/lamb	• 120 g tofu
• 40 g skinless cooked chicken	• 4 slices bread
• 50 g canned tuna/ salmon or cooked fish	• 200 g baked beans
• 300 mL milk/glass of Milo	• 60 g nuts
• 200 g tub yoghurt	• 2 cups pasta/3 cups rice
• 300ml flavored milk	• 0.75 cup cooked lentils/ kidney beans
• 1.5 slices (30 g) cheese	
• 2 eggs	

from an Australian Institute of Sport fact sheet

storage appears limited to the first hour after supplementation. It has been shown that glycogen storage during the first 40 minutes of recovery after exercise was twice as fast after a carbohydrate–protein feeding than after an isoenergetic carbohydrate feeding, and four times faster than after a carbohydrate feeding of the same carbohydrate concentration.[18] This trend also continued following the second feeding two hours into recovery.

The co-ingestion of protein with carbohydrate during recovery also increases protein synthesis, and results in a more positive whole-body net protein balance compared with drinks matched for total carbohydrate.[19] Table 10.3 provides a list of carbohydrate-rich snacks that also provide at least 10 g of protein.

Rehydration

Large amounts of fluid may be lost during exertion, particularly with increasing intensity and in hot or humid conditions. It can be difficult for sportspeople to maintain fluid balance in certain environmental conditions. Athletes should weigh themselves before and after exercise and replace the weight lost with water.

The majority of sportspeople finish training or competition sessions with some level of fluid deficit. Many fail to drink sufficient volumes of fluid to restore fluid balance. As a fluid deficit incurred

Table 10.3 Nutritious carbohydrate–protein recovery snacks (contain 50 g CHO + valuable source of protein and micronutrients)

- 250–300 mL liquid meal supplement
- 300 g creamed rice
- 250–300 mL milkshake or fruit smoothie
- 600 mL low fat flavored milk
- 1–2 sports bars (check labels for carbohydrate and protein content)
- 1 large bowl (2 cups) breakfast cereal with milk
- 1 large or 2 small cereal bars + 200 g carton fruit-flavored yoghurt
- 220 g baked beans on 2 slices of toast
- 1 bread roll with cheese/meat filling + large banana
- 300 g (bowl) fruit salad with 200 g fruit-flavored yoghurt
- 2 crumpets with thickly spread peanut butter + 250 mL milk
- 300 g (large) baked potato + cottage cheese filling + glass of milk

from an Australian Institute of Sport fact sheet

during one session has the potential to negatively impact on performance during subsequent training sessions, sportspeople need to incorporate strategies to restore fluid balance, especially in situations where there is a limited amount of time before their next training session.

Athletes should aim to consume 125–150% of their estimated fluid losses in the 4–6 hours after exercise. The recommendation to consume a volume of fluid greater than that lost in sweat takes into account the continued loss of fluid from the body through sweating and obligatory urine losses.

Fluid replacement alone will not guarantee rehydration after exercise. Unless there is simultaneous replacement of electrolytes lost in sweat, especially sodium, consumption of a large volume of fluid may simply result in large urine losses. The addition of sodium, either in the drink or the food consumed with the fluid, will reduce urine losses and thereby enhance fluid balance in the post-exercise period. Further, sodium will also preserve thirst, enhancing voluntary intake. As the amount of sodium considered optimal for re-hydration (50–80 mmol/L) is in excess of that found in most commercially available sports drinks, sportspeople may be best advised to consume fluids after exercise with everyday foods containing sodium.

There is considerable individual variation in sodium concentration of sweat. It may be important in high-level athletes to identify those with high sweat sodium content, and therefore sweat testing may be performed. This is performed with the use of a patch fixed to the forearm during activity (Fig. 10.2). Those with high sodium content may require additional sodium supplementation before and after activity.

In considering the type of fluids needed to achieve their rehydration goals, sportspeople should also consider the length of time before their next session, the degree of the fluid deficit incurred, taste preferences, daily energy budget, as well as their other recovery goals. With the latter, athletes can simultaneously meet their refueling, repair, and some of their re-hydration goals by consuming fluids that also provide a source of carbohydrate and protein (e.g. flavored milk, liquid meal supplement).

Psychology

As the nervous system controls cardiovascular function, respiration, and metabolism during and after exercise, psychological factors play an important role in recovery.

Figure 10.2 Sweat testing

The function of the autonomic nervous system

After exercise, the nervous system, which functions by releasing neurotransmitters, may be substantially fatigued. The efferent cells of the peripheral nervous system are categorized into those that control skeletal muscle (somatic nerves) and those that control glands, cardiac muscle, and smooth muscle found in the walls of body organs such as the gastrointestinal tract, the blood vessels, and airways (autonomic nerves).

Autonomic nerves themselves are divided into sympathetic and parasympathetic nerves, according to both anatomical and physiological differences. Some organs receive input from both sympathetic and parasympathetic nerves.

Effect of exercise on the autonomic nervous system

The sympathetic nervous system controls the "fight or flight" reaction, which is characterized by an adrenalin rush, tachycardia, increased cardiac output, and bronchodilation. At the same time, blood is shunted away from the gastrointestinal organs to enhance muscle blood flow. Liver glycogen stores are used up to provide blood glucose.

After exercise, this automatic effect should be reversed to allow muscles to relax and to replenish body stores of glycogen. If there is insufficient recovery of the nervous system, the sportsperson may remain sympathetically aroused. This manifests as increased resting heart rate, muscle tiredness, and insomnia. Sympathetic overarousal may delay absorption of nutrients from the gastrointestinal tract, as well as elevating the metabolic rate. Over time, the sympathetic nervous system can become exhausted, and the patient develops bradycardia, an inability to utilize glycogen, and a diminution in work capacity. This psychological state parallels depression.

Techniques that aid psychological recovery

Sportspeople who have a good understanding of their arousal level are generally calm and stable. They, thus, tend to place less stress on their autonomic nervous system. Specific techniques can lower arousal level. These include the use of soft tissue therapy, spas, warm baths and showers, flotation tanks, music, visualization and relaxation tapes. As recovery is vital for optimal performance, coaches should be encouraged to incorporate recovery time into athletes' schedules.

REFERENCES

1. Gill ND, Beaven CM, Cook C. Effectiveness of post-match recovery strategies in rugby players. *Br J Sports Med* 2006;40(3):260–3.

2. Suzuki M, Umeda T, Nakaji S et al. Effect of incorporating low intensity exercise into the recovery period after a rugby match. *Br J Sports Med* 2004;38(4):436–40.

3. Andersson H, Raastad T, Nilsson J et al. Neuromuscular fatigue and recovery in elite female soccer: effects of active recovery. *Med Sci Sports Exerc* 2008;40(2):372–80.

4. Dawson B, Cow S, Modra, S et al. Effects of immediate post-game recovery procedures on muscle soreness, power and flexiblity levels over the next 48 hours. *J Sci Med Sport* 2005;8(2):210–21.

5. Spencer M, Bishop D, Dawson B et al. Metabolism and performance in repeated cycle sprints: active versus passive recovery. *Med Sci Sports Exerc* 2006;8(1):1492–9.

6. Reilly T, Cable NT, Dowzer CN. The efficacy of deep water running. In: McCabe PT, ed. *Contemporary ergonomics*. London: Taylor & Francis, 2002:162–6.

7. Bleakley CM, Davison GW. What is the biochemical and physiological rationale for using cold-water immersion in sports recovery? A systematic review. *Br J Sports Med* 2010;44:179–87.

8. Vaile J, O'Hagan C, Stefanovic B et al. Effect of cold water immersion on repeated cycling performance and limb blood flow. *Br J Sports Med* 2011;45(10):825–9.

9. Montgomery PG, Pyne DB, Hopkins WG et al. The effect of recovery strategies on physical performance and cumulative fatigue in competitive basketball. *J Sports Sci* 2008;26(11):1135–45.

10. Ingram J, Dawson B, Goodman C et al. Effect of water immersion methods on post-exercise recovery from simulated team post exercise. *J Sci Med Sport* 2009;12(3):417–21.

11. Best TM, Hunter R, Wilcox A et al. Effectiveness of sports massage for recovery of skeletal muscle from strenuous exercise. *Clin J Sports Med* 2008;18(5):446–60.

12. Kraemer WJ, Flanagan SD, Comstock BA et al. Effects of a whole body compression garment on markers of recovery after a heavy resistance workout in men and women. *J Strength Cond Res* 2010;24(3):804–14.

13. Duffield R, Cannon J, King M. The effects of compresion garments on recovery of muscle performance following high-intensity sprint and plyometric exercise. *J Sci Med Sport* 2010;13(1):136–40.

14. Reilly T, Piercy M. The effects of partial sleep deprivation on weight-lifting performance. *Ergonomics* 1994;37:107–15.

15. Burke LM, Collier GR, Davis PG et al. Muscle glycogen storage after prolonged exercise: effect of the frequency of carbohydrate feedings. *Am J Clin Nutr* 1996;64:115–19.

16. Burke LM, Kiens B, Ivy JL. Carbohydrates and fat for training and recovery. *J Sports Sci* 2004;22(1):15–30.

17. Barnes MJ, Mundel T, Stannard SR. Acute alcohol consumption aggravates the decline in muscle performance following strenuous eccentric exercise. *J Sci Med Sport* 2010;13(1):189–93.

18. Ivy JL, Goforth HW Jr, Damon BM et al. Early postexercise muscle glycogen recovery is enhanced with a carbohydrate-protein supplement. *J Appl Physiol* 2002;93(4):1337–44.

19. Howarth KR, Moreau NA, Phillips SM et al. Coingestion of protein with carbohydrate during recovery from endurance exercise stiumulates muscle protein synthesis in humans. *J Appl Physiol* 2009;106:1394–402.

Chapter 11

Principles of diagnosis: clinical assessment

There is no more difficult art to acquire than the art of observation. William Osler

The importance of making an accurate, pathological diagnosis cannot be overemphasized. This chapter addresses what physicians call the history and physical examination and what physiotherapists/physical therapists consider the subjective and objective assessment. Chapter 12 addresses investigations.

Far too often, sporting injuries are given descriptive labels such as "swimmer's shoulder" or "tennis elbow." These terms do not represent diagnoses. Accurate pathological diagnosis is essential for several reasons:

1. It enables the clinician to explain the problem and the natural history of the condition to the athlete, who will want to know precisely for how long he or she will be affected. A patient may present with an acute knee injury, but the diagnosis of anterior cruciate ligament tear has markedly different implications from the diagnosis of minor meniscal injury.
2. It enables optimum treatment. Numerous conditions have similar presentations but markedly different treatments. For example, consider the differences in treatment between lateral ligament sprain of the ankle and osteochondral fracture of the talus, patellofemoral joint syndrome and meniscal tear, hamstring tear and hamstring pain referred from the lumbar spine.
3. It enables optimum rehabilitation prescription. For example, rehabilitation after shin pain due to stress fracture will be more gradual than that after identical shin pain due to chronic compartment syndrome.

 When a patient presents with an overuse injury, an accurate pathological diagnosis must be supplemented by assessment of the etiologic factors underlying the condition, otherwise the injury is likely to be slow to recover and highly likely to recur.

Etiologic factors include training error, malalignment, faulty technique, and inappropriate equipment. An important etiologic factor can sometimes be identified by examining the entire "kinetic chain."

Occasionally, it may be impossible to make a precise pathological diagnosis. For example, in a patient with low back pain, the exact source of the pain is often difficult to isolate. In such cases, it is still possible to exclude certain causes of low back pain (e.g. spondylolysis) and identify abnormalities such as areas of focal tenderness, altered soft tissue consistency, or abnormalities of range of motion. Treatment then aims to correct these abnormalities. How treatment affects symptoms and signs can help determine how each particular abnormality contributes to the overall picture.

Making a diagnosis

Diagnosis relies on taking a careful history, performing a thorough physical examination, and using appropriate investigations. There is a tendency for clinicians to rely too heavily on sophisticated investigations and to neglect their clinical skills.[1]

Keys to accurate diagnosis in patients presenting with apparent musculoskeletal pain include:

- whether the symptoms are of musculoskeletal origin (Chapter 7)
- possible local causes of the patient's symptoms

- sites that could be referring pain to the site of the symptoms (Chapter 6)
- the relevant kinetic chain (e.g. the back and lower limb in a shoulder injury of a tennis player)
- biomechanics (Chapter 8)
- other possible causative factors (e.g. metabolic).

History

History remains the keystone of accurate diagnosis; it will provide the diagnosis in the majority of cases. At the conclusion of taking the history, it is important to consider the differential diagnosis and the possible etiologic factors. Then proceed to a thorough, focused examination.

The following principles need to be considered when taking a history.

Allow enough time

The patient must feel that the clinician has time available to allow the story to unfold, otherwise important symptoms will not surface.[2] In addition to the details of the injury, there must be time to take the history of the training program or diet as appropriate. Look into possible causes of injury. As a minimum, 30 minutes is required to assess a patient with a new injury; however, in complex chronic cases up to one hour may be necessary.

Be a good listener

The clinician must let the story unravel. Appropriate body language and focus on the patient (not the medical record) help this.[3] The sports clinician is in the fortunate position that many patients have good body awareness and are generally able to describe symptoms very well. When seeing inactive patients for exercise prescription, take the time to listen to their goals and fears (Chapter 16).

Know the sport

It is helpful to understand the technical demands of a sport when seeing a sportsperson, as this engenders patient confidence. More importantly, knowledge of the biomechanics and techniques of a particular sport can assist greatly in both making the primary diagnosis and uncovering the predisposing factors.

Circumstances of the injury

The first task in history taking is to determine the exact circumstances of the injury. Most patients will be able to describe in considerable detail the mechanism of injury. In acute injuries, this is the single

most important clue to diagnosis. For example, an inversion injury to the ankle strongly suggests a lateral ligament injury, a valgus strain to the knee may cause a medial collateral ligament injury, and a pivoting injury accompanied by a "pop" in the knee and followed by rapid swelling suggests an anterior cruciate ligament injury.

Obtain an accurate description of symptoms

An accurate description of the patient's symptoms is essential. Common musculoskeletal symptoms include pain, swelling, instability, and loss of function.

Pain

Consider the characteristics of the patient's pain:

1. Location: Note the exact location of pain. A detailed knowledge of surface anatomy will enable you to determine the structures likely to be involved. If the pain is poorly localized or varies from site to site, consider the possibility of referred pain.
2. Onset: Speed of onset helps determine whether the pain is due to an acute or overuse injury. Was the onset of pain associated with a snap, crack, tear, or other sensation?
3. Severity: Severity may be classified as mild, moderate, or severe. Assess the severity of the pain immediately after the injury and also subsequently. Was the patient able to continue activity?
4. Irritability: This refers to the level of activity required to provoke pain and how long it subsequently takes to settle. The degree of irritability is especially important, because it affects how vigorously the examination should be performed and how aggressive the treatment should be.
5. Nature: This refers to the quality of the pain. It is important to allow patients to describe pain in their own words.
6. Behavior: Is the pain constant or intermittent? What is the time course of the pain? Is it worse on waking up or does it worsen during the day? Does it wake the patient at night?
7. Radiation: Does the pain radiate at all? If so, where?
8. Aggravating factors: Which activity or posture aggravates the pain?
9. Relieving factors: Is the pain relieved by rest or the adoption of certain postures? Do certain activities

relieve the pain? Is the pain affected by climatic changes (e.g. cold weather)?

10. Associated features: These include swelling, instability, sensory symptoms such as pins and needles, tingling, or numbness, and motor symptoms, such as muscle weakness.

11. Previous treatment: What was the initial treatment of the injury? Was ice applied? Was firm compression applied? Was the injured part immobilized? If so, for how long? What treatment has been performed and what effect did that treatment have on the pain?

Swelling

Immediate swelling following an injury may indicate a severe injury such as a fracture or major ligament tear accompanied by hemarthrosis. Record the degree of swelling—mild, moderate, or severe—and subsequent changes in the amount of swelling.

Instability

Any history of giving way or feeling of instability is significant. Try to elicit the exact activity that causes this feeling. For example, in throwing, does the feeling of instability occur in the cocking phase or the follow-through?

Function

It is important to know whether the athlete was:

- able to continue activity without any problems immediately after the injury happened
- able to continue with some restriction
- unable to continue.

Note subsequent changes in function with time.

History of a previous similar injury

If the sportsperson has had a previous similar injury, record full details of all treatment given, response to each type of treatment, and whether any maintenance treatment or exercises have been performed following initial rehabilitation. Previous injury is a major risk factor for recurrence.[4]

Other injuries

Past injuries may have contributed to the current injury; for example, an inadequately rehabilitated muscle tear that has led to muscle imbalance and a subsequent overuse injury. Because of the importance of spinal abnormalities as a potential component of the athlete's pain (Chapter 6), the patient should always be questioned about spinal symptoms, especially pain and stiffness in the lower back or neck. Past or present injuries in body parts that may at first seem unrelated to the present injury may also be important. For example, a hamstring injury in a throwing athlete can impair the kinetic chain leading to the shoulder, alter throwing biomechanics and, thus, contribute to a rotator cuff injury.

General health

Is the patient otherwise healthy? The presence of symptoms such as weight loss and general malaise may suggest a serious abnormality (e.g. a tumor). It must be remembered that musculoskeletal symptoms are not always activity-related (Chapter 7).

Work and leisure activities

Work and leisure activities can play a role in both the etiology and subsequent management of an injury. For example, a patient whose job involves continual bending or who enjoys gardening may aggravate his or her low back pain. It is important to know about these activities and to ascertain whether they can be curtailed.

Consider why the problem has occurred

Predisposing factors should be considered not only in overuse injuries but also in medical conditions and in acute injuries. In an athlete suffering from exercise-induced asthma, symptoms may occur only during important competition if there is an underlying psychological component. Alternatively, the asthma may occur only at a particular time of the year or at a particular venue if allergy is present.

An athlete with an acute hamstring tear may have a history of low back problems or, alternatively, a history of a previous inadequately rehabilitated tear. Recurrence can only be prevented by eliminating the underlying cause.

Training history

In any overuse injury, a comprehensive training history is required. This is best done as a weekly diary, as most sportspeople train on a weekly cycle (Chapter 9). It should contain both the quantity and quality of training, and describe any recent changes. Note the total amount of training (distance or hours depending on the sport) and training surfaces. Continual activity on hard surfaces or a recent change in surface may predispose to injury. In running sports, pay particular attention to footwear (Chapter 9). For both training and competition shoes, note the shoe type, age, and the wear pattern. Record recovery activities such as massage, spa/sauna, and hours of sleep.

Equipment

Inappropriate equipment may predispose to injury (Chapter 9). For example, a bicycle seat that is set too low may contribute to patellofemoral pain.

Technique

Patients should discuss technique problems that either they, or their coach, have noted. Faulty technique may contribute to injury. For example, a "wristy" backhand drive may contribute to extensor tendinopathy at the elbow.

Overtraining

Symptoms such as excessive fatigue, recurrent illness, reduced motivation, persistent soreness, and stiffness may point to overtraining as an etiologic factor (Chapter 9).

Psychological factors

Injury can be caused or exacerbated by a number of psychological factors that may relate to sport (i.e. pressure of impending competition) or may concern personal or business life. The clinician needs to consider this possibility and approach it sensitively.

Nutritional factors

Inadequate nutrition can predispose to the overtraining syndrome and may play a role in the development of musculoskeletal injuries. In an athlete presenting with excessive tiredness (Chapter 57), a full dietary history is essential.

History of exercise-induced anaphylaxis

Exercise-induced anaphylaxis (EIA) and food-dependent exercise-induced anaphylaxis (FDEIA) are rare but potentially life-threatening clinical syndromes in which association with exercise is crucial. This is a clinical syndrome in which anaphylaxis occurs in conjunction with exercise. Given the rarity of the condition, our current understanding relies on case studies only.[5, 6]

Determine the importance of the sport to the athlete

The level of commitment to the sport, which will not necessarily correlate with the athlete's expertise, has a bearing on management decisions. Be aware of the athlete's short- and long-term future sporting commitments, to schedule appropriate treatment and rehabilitation programs.

Examination

A number of general principles should be followed in an examination.[7] At the conclusion of the examination, the differential diagnosis and possible predisposing factors should be considered. If the practitioner is certain of the diagnosis and of the predisposing factors, then counseling and treatment can begin. However, in many cases, further information may be required and the practitioner must decide what, if any, investigations may be needed.

The general principles to be followed in an examination are outlined below.

Develop a routine

Use a specific routine for examining each joint, region, or system, as this forms a habit and allows you to concentrate on the findings and their significance, rather than thinking of what to do next. In Part B, we outline a routine for examining each body part.

Where relevant, examine the other side

With some aspects of the examination (e.g. ligamentous laxity or muscle tightness), it is important to compare sides using the uninjured side as a control.

Consider possible causes of the injury

Try to ascertain the cause of the injury. It is not sufficient to examine the painful area only (e.g. the Achilles tendon). Examine joints, muscles, and neural structures proximal and distal to the injured area, seeking predisposing factors (e.g. limited dorsiflexion of the ankle, tight gastrocnemius–soleus complex, lumbar facet joint dysfunction).

Attempt to reproduce the patient's symptoms

It is helpful to reproduce the patient's symptoms if possible. This can be achieved both by active and/or passive movements and by palpation either locally or, in the case of referred pain, at the site of referral. It may require you to send the patient for a run or some other test of function prior to examination (see below).

Assess local tissues

Assess the joints, muscles, and neural structures at the site of pain for tenderness, tissue feel, and range of motion.

Assess for referred pain

Assess the joints, muscles, and neural structures that may refer to the site of pain (Chapter 6).

Assess neural mechanosensitivity

Neural mechanosensitivity (Chapter 6) should be assessed using one or more of the neurodynamic tests (on page 150).

Examine the spine

Many injuries have a spinal component to the pain or dysfunction. The presence of abnormal neural mechanosensitivity suggests a possible spinal component. In lower limb injuries, examine the lumbar spine and the thoracolumbar junction. In upper limb injuries, examine the cervical and upper thoracic spines. In particular, it is important to seek hypomobility of isolated spinal segments, as this may contribute to distant symptoms.

Biomechanical examination

As biomechanical abnormalities are one of the major causes of overuse injuries, it is essential to include this examination in the assessment of overuse injuries (Chapter 8). The biomechanical examination of the lower limb is illustrated in Chapter 8.

Functional testing

If a particular maneuver reproduces the patient's pain, then have the patient perform that maneuver in an attempt to understand why the pain has occurred. This can sometimes be done in the office (e.g. a deep squat) or it may be necessary to watch the athlete perform the activity at a training venue, for example, a long jumper taking off, or a gymnast performing a backward walkover. Video analysis may be helpful.

The examination routine
Inspection

It is important to observe the individual walking into the office or walking off the field of play, as well as inspecting the injured area. Note any evidence of deformity, asymmetry, bruising, swelling, skin changes, and muscle wasting. There may, however, be a degree of asymmetry due to one side being dominant, such as the racquet arm in a tennis player.

Range of motion testing (active)

Ask the athlete to perform active range of motion exercises without assistance. Look carefully for restriction of range of motion, the onset of pain at a particular

point in the range, and the presence of abnormal patterns of movement. In many conditions, such as shoulder impingement or patellofemoral pain, the pattern of movement is critical to making a correct diagnosis.

If a patient's pain is not elicited on normal plane movement testing, examine "combined movements" (i.e. movements in two or more planes). By combining movements and evaluating symptom response, additional information is gained to help predict the site of the lesion. Other movements, such as repeated, quick or sustained movements, may be required to elicit the patient's pain.

Range of motion testing (passive)

Passive range of motion testing is used to elicit joint and muscle stiffness. Injury may be the cause of joint stiffness. Alternatively, stiffness may already have been present and predisposed to injury by placing excessive stress on other structures (e.g. a stiff ankle joint can predispose to Achilles tendinopathy). Range of motion testing should include all directions of movement appropriate to a particular joint, and should be compared both with normal range and the unaffected side. Overpressure may be used at the end of range to elicit the patient's symptoms.

Palpation

Palpation is a vital component of examination, and precise knowledge of anatomy, especially surface anatomy, optimizes its value. At times it is essential to determine the exact site of maximal tenderness (e.g. in differentiating between bony tenderness and ligament attachment tenderness after a sprained ankle). When palpating soft tissues, properties of the soft tissue that need to be assessed include:

- resistance
- muscle spasm
- tenderness.

Palpate carefully and try to visualize the structures being palpated. Commence with the skin, feeling for any changes in temperature or amount of sweating, infection, or increased sympathetic activity. When palpating muscle, assess tone, focal areas of thickening or trigger points, muscle length, and imbalance.

It is important not only to palpate the precise area of pain, for example, the supraspinatus tendon attachment, but also the regions proximal and distal to the painful area, such as the muscle belly of the trapezius muscle. Determine whether tenderness is focal or diffuse. This may help differentiate between, for example, a stress fracture (focal tenderness) and periostitis (diffuse tenderness).

To palpate joints correctly, it is important to understand the two different types of movement present at a joint. Physiological movements are movements that patients can perform themselves. However, in order to achieve a full range of physiological movement, accessory movements are required.

Accessory movements are the involuntary, inter-articular movements, including glides, rotations, and tilts, that occur in both spinal and peripheral joints during normal physiological movements. Loss of these normal accessory movements may cause pain, altered range, or abnormal quality of physiological joint movement. Palpation of the spinal and peripheral joints is based on these principles. An example of palpation of accessory movements involves postero-anterior pressure over the spinous process of the vertebra, producing a glide between that vertebra and the ones above and below.

Ligament testing

Ligaments are examined for laxity and pain. Specific tests have been devised for all the major ligaments of the body. These involve moving the joint to stress a particular ligament. This may cause pain or reveal laxity in the joint. Laxity is graded into +1 (mild), +2 (moderate), and +3 (severe). Pain on stressing the ligament is also significant and may indicate, in the absence of laxity, a mild injury or grade I ligament sprain. A number of different tests may assess a single ligament: for example, the anterior drawer, Lachman's, and pivot shift tests all test anterior cruciate ligament laxity.

Strength testing

Muscles or groups of muscles should be tested for strength and compared with the unaffected side. Muscle weakness may occur as a result of an injury, (e.g. secondary to a chronic joint effusion), or may be a predisposing factor toward injury.

Testing neural mechanosensitivity

Advances in the understanding of neural mechano-sensitivity have led to improved awareness of why pain occurs in chronic overuse injuries and pain syndromes. Changes in neural mechanosensitivity are an important component of these disorders (Chapter 6).

Just as restrictions of the normal mechanics of joints and muscles may contribute to symptoms, restriction of the normal mechanics of the nervous system may

also produce pain. Certain movements require considerable variations in nerve length. Neurodynamic testing examines restriction of these normal mechanics and their effect on the patient's symptoms. Treatment aims to restore normal nerve mechanics.

Neurodynamic tests produce systematic increases in neural mechanosensitivity by successive addition of movements that increase neural mechanosensitivity. The tests may provoke the presenting symptoms or, alternatively, other symptoms such as pins and needles, or numbness. The amount of resistance encountered during the test is also significant, especially when compared with the uninjured side. The assessment of symptom production and resistance may be affected by each step in the neurodynamics test (Figs 11.1–11.4). This may give an indication of the location of the abnormality.

The main neurodynamic tests are:

- straight leg raise (SLR) (Fig. 11.1)
- slump test (Fig. 11.2)
- neural Thomas test (Fig. 11.3, on page 152)
- upper limb neurodynamics test (ULTT) (Fig. 11.4, on page 153).

A summary of the tests, the methods, user guidance, normal responses and variations of each test is shown in Table 11.1 on page 155.

A neurodynamic test can be considered positive if:

- it reproduces the patient's symptoms
- the test response can be altered by movements of different body parts that alter neural mechanosensitivity
- differences in the test occur from side to side and from what is considered normal.

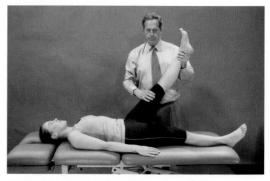

Figure 11.1 Straight leg raise

(a) Patient lies supine. The examiner places one hand under the Achilles tendon and the other above the knee. The leg is lifted perpendicular to the bed with the hand above the knee, preventing any knee flexion

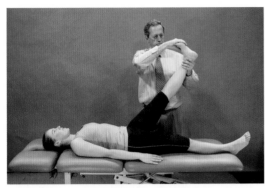

Figure 11.1 (cont.) (b) Dorsiflexion of the ankle is added. Eversion and toe extension may sensitize this test further. Other variations can be added (Table 11.1 page 155)

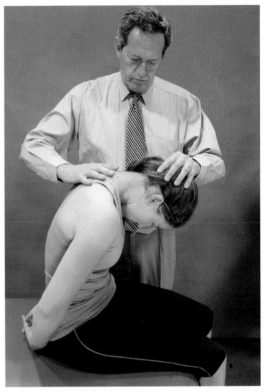

(b) Patient is asked to put chin on chest and overpressure is applied

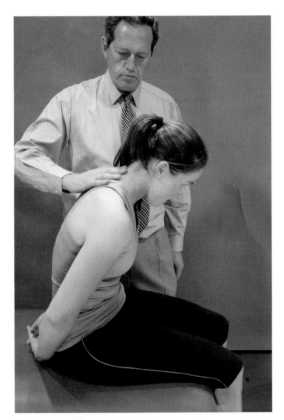

Figure 11.2 Slump test
(a) Patient slumps forward and overpressure is applied. The sacrum should remain vertical

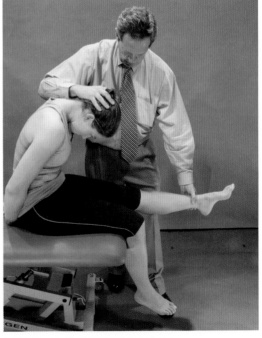

(c) Patient actively extends one knee

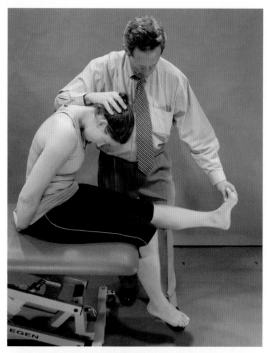

(d) Patient actively dorsiflexes the ankle and overpressure may be applied

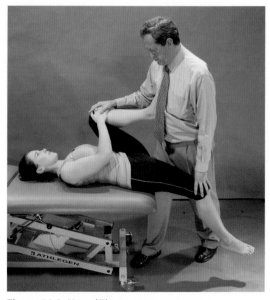

Figure 11.3 Neural Thomas test
(a) Patient lies supine over the end of the couch in the Thomas position

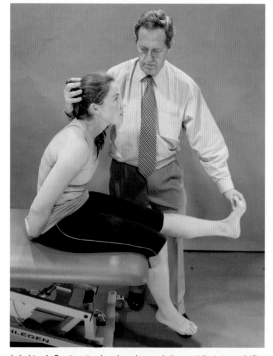

(e) Neck flexion is slowly released. Steps (d), (e), and (f) are repeated with the other knee. Other variations can be added (Table 11.1 page 155)

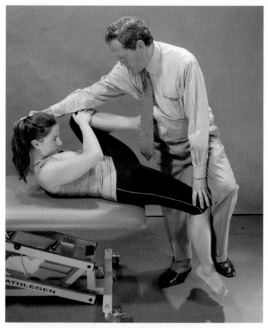

(b) Patient's neck is passively flexed by the examiner, then the examiner passively flexes the patient's (right) knee with his leg

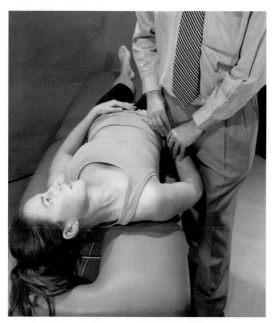

Figure 11.4 Upper limb neurodynamics test
(a) Patient lies supine close to the edge of the couch.
Neck is laterally flexed away from the side to be tested

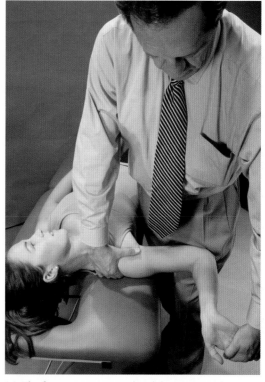

(c) The forearm is supinated and the wrist and fingers extended

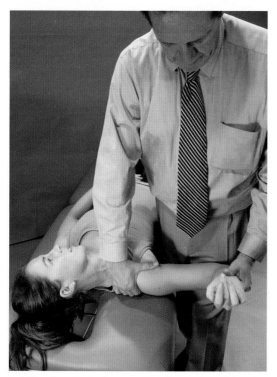

(b) The shoulder is depressed by the examiner's hand (left) and the arm abducted to approximately 110° and externally rotated

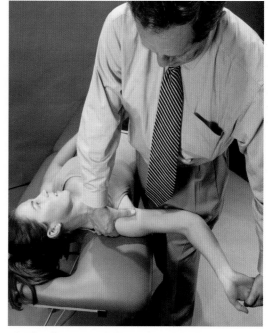

(d) The elbow is extended to the point of onset of symptoms

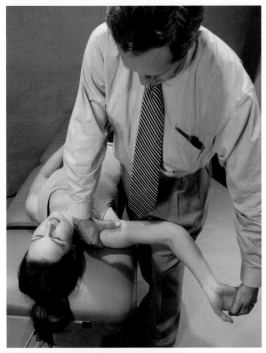

(e) The neck position returns to neutral and is then laterally flexed towards the side of the test. Any change in symptoms is noted. Other variations can be added (Table 11.1)

Neurodynamic tests are non-specific but form an extremely useful part of the examination. Abnormalities of neural mechanosensitivity should lead the clinician to examine possible sites of abnormality, especially the spine. Neurodynamic tests can also be used as a treatment procedure. This is discussed in Chapter 13.

Spinal examination

Clinical experience suggests that spinal abnormality (e.g. hypomobility) can present in various ways. The presentation may be as pain or injury and this may occur either locally (at the spine) or distantly. Examples for both upper limb and lower limb spinal abnormalities are given in Table 11.2. The pathophysiology underlying these concepts has been discussed in Chapter 6.

In patients presenting with upper limb pain, the cervical and upper thoracic spines must be examined. Examine the lumbar spine (including the thoracolumbar junction) in any patient presenting with lower limb pain. An abnormal neurodynamic test strongly indicates a spinal component to the pain.

However, a negative neurodynamic test does not exclude the possibility of a spinal component.

Begin examining the relevant area of the spine by assessing range of movement with the patient standing. The patient should then lie prone on a firm examination table so the examiner can palpate the vertebrae centrally over the spinous processes and laterally over the apophyseal joints to detect any hypomobility and/or tenderness. Hypomobility or tenderness at a level appropriate to that of the patient's symptoms indicate the site is a possible source of referred pain (Chapter 6).

After detecting spinal abnormality on examination, perform a trial treatment (Chapter 13) and then reassess the patient's symptoms and signs. If there is a change in the pain and/or range of movement, then this strongly suggests that the spine is contributing to the symptoms.

Occasionally, palpation of a particular site in the spine will actually reproduce the patient's symptoms distant from the spine. It is important to understand that, even if the symptoms are not produced by palpation of the spine, this does not rule out the possibility of a spinal component.

Biomechanical examination

The role of abnormal biomechanics in the production of injuries, especially overuse injuries, is discussed in Chapter 8. Because abnormal biomechanics can contribute to any overuse injury, all clinicians need to perform a biomechanical examination.

As with other components of the examination, it is important to develop a routine for the assessment of biomechanical abnormalities. A routine for the assessment of lower limb biomechanics is illustrated in Chapter 8.

Technique

Faulty technique is another common cause of injury. A list of technique faults associated with particular injuries is shown in Table 5.1 on page 25. While the clinician cannot be aware of all techniques in various sports, he or she should be able to identify the common technique faults in popular activities (e.g. pelvic instability while running, faulty backhand drive in tennis). Clinicians should seek biomechanical advice and assistance with assessment from the athlete's coach or a colleague with expertise in the particular area. Video analysis with slow motion or freeze frame may be helpful.

Equipment

Inappropriate equipment predisposes to injury (Chapter 9). Inspect the sportsperson's equipment (e.g. running shoes, football boots, tennis racquet, bicycle, helmet).

Table 11.1 Neurodynamic tests

Test	Method	Indications	Normal response	Variations
Straight leg raise (Fig. 11.1)	Patient lies supine Leg extended Clinician lifts leg	Leg pain Back pain Headache	Tightness and/or pain in posterior knee, thigh, and calf	Ankle dorsiflexion Ankle plantarflexion/inversion Hip adduction Hip medial rotation Passive neck flexion
Slump test (Fig. 11.2)	Patient sitting Slumps Neck flexion Knee extension Ankle dorsiflexion Release neck flexion	Back pain Buttock pain Leg pain	Upper thoracic pain Posterior knee pain Hamstring pain	Leg abduction (obturator nerve) Hip adduction Hip medial rotation Ankle and foot alterations
Neural Thomas test (Fig. 11.3)	Patient lies supine Hip extension Neck flexion Knee flexion	Groin pain Anterior thigh pain	Quadriceps pain and/or tightness	Hip abduction/adduction Hip medial/lateral rotation
Upper limb neurodynamics test (Fig. 11.4)	Patient supine toward side of couch Cervical contralateral flexion Shoulder girdle depression Shoulder abducted to 110° and externally rotated Forearm supination Wrist/fingers extended Elbow extended	Arm pain Neck/upper thoracic pain Headache	Ache in cubital fossa Tingling in thumb and fingers	Forearm pronation Wrist deviation Shoulder flexion/extension Add straight leg raise

Table 11.2 Examples of how spinal abnormality can manifest locally or distantly, with either pain or injury in the upper limb and lower limb

Presentation	Local manifestation	Distant manifestation
Upper limb		
Pain	Hypomobility of C5–6 joint presenting as neck pain	Hypomobility of C5–6 joint presents as elbow pain
Injury		Hypomobility of C5–6 joint predisposing to lateral elbow tendinopathy in a tennis player
Lower limb		
Pain	Hypomobility of L5–S1 joint presenting as lumbosacral pain	Hypomobility of L5–S1 joint presents as buttock and hamstring pain
Injury		Hypomobility of L5–S1 joint predisposing to a hamstring tear in a sprinter

📄 RECOMMENDED READING

Murtagh J. *General practice*. 4th edn. Sydney: McGraw-Hill, 2007.

📋 REFERENCES

1. Khan K, Tress B, Hare W et al. 'Treat the patient, not the X-ray': advances in diagnostic imaging do not replace the need for clinical interpretation. *Clin J Sport Med* 1998;8:1–4.

2. Vernec A, Shrier I. A teaching unit in primary care sports medicine for family medicine residents. *Acad Med* 2001;76:293–6.

3. Ruusuvuori J. Looking means listening: coordinating displays of engagement in doctor–patient interaction. *Soc Sci Med* 2001;52:1093–108.

4. Orchard JW. Intrinsic and extrinsic risk factors for muscle strains in Australian football. *Am J Sports Med* 2001;29:300–3.

5. Barg W, Medrala W, Wolanczyk-Medrala A. Exercise-induced anaphylaxis: an update on diagnosis and treatment. *Curr Allergy Asthma Rep* 2011;11(1):45–51.

6. Robson-Ansley P, Toit GD. Pathophysiology, diagnosis and management of exercise-induced anaphylaxis. *Curr Opin Allergy Clin Immunol* 2010;10:312–17.

7. Plastaras CT, Rittenberg JD, Rittenberg KE et al. Comprehensive functional evaluation of the injured runner. *Phys Med Rehabil Clin North Am* 2005;16: 623–49.

Chapter 12

Principles of diagnosis: investigations including imaging

with BRUCE FORSTER, ZOLTAN KISS, JOCK ANDERSON, THERESA LEE, and CHARLOTTE YONG-HING

Treat the patient, not the X-ray.   James M Hunter

This chapter includes seven principles that may help clinicians maximize the utility of investigations, and which laboratory and special investigations add detail to the sports and exercise medicine diagnosis.

Investigations

Appropriate investigations can confirm or exclude a diagnosis suggested by the history and physical examination but should never be a substitute for careful history taking and a comprehensive examination (Chapter 11).

1. Understand the meaning of test results

The sports clinician should be able to interpret investigation results and not rely blindly on the investigation report. A clinician who knows that about a quarter of asymptomatic elite jumping athletes have ultrasound abnormalities in their patellar tendons can reassure the patient that the imaging finding is not an indication for surgery. This is an example of a false positive investigation. Many such examples exist.

2. Know how soon changes can be detected by investigations

To detect certain abnormalities, the timing of an investigation may need to be appropriate. A female gymnast must have hormone levels tested in the second half of her menstrual cycle to detect low progesterone levels in luteal deficiency. Likewise, there is nothing to be gained by repeating a radioisotopic bone scan or a CT scan to assess fracture healing two months after diagnosing a lumbar pars interarticularis defect in a tennis player.

3. Only order investigations that will influence management

It is inappropriate to perform extensive (and expensive) investigations to confirm an already obvious diagnosis. If a stress fracture is seen on a plain X-ray, there is rarely anything to be gained from an MRI scan.

4. Provide relevant clinical findings on the requisition

Accurate and complete clinical information on requisition forms helps to avoid imaging and reporting errors.[1] When particular X-ray views are required they should be requested. If you cannot remember the names of certain views, write that down on the request forms—the radiographer will generally know and, if not, the radiologist will! It is often helpful to call the radiologist in advance to discuss the best way to image a patient. Remember that weight-bearing views are important to assess suspected osteoarthritis at the hip, knee, and ankle. "Functional" views (with the patient placing the joint in the position of pain) are useful for anterior and posterior impingement of the ankle (Chapter 39).

5. Do not accept a poor quality test

Inappropriate views or investigations performed on inferior equipment can lead to more diagnostic confusion than no investigation at all.

6. Develop a close working relationship with investigators

Optimizing communication between colleagues improves the quality of the service.[1] Regular clinical-radiological rounds or case presentations should be encouraged. Digital imaging and telemedicine have made this much easier.

7. Explain the investigations to the patient

Give the patient an understanding of the rationale behind each investigation. A sportsperson who complains of persistent ankle pain and swelling several months after an ankle sprain may need an X-ray and MRI. If the patient is merely told that an X-ray is necessary to exclude bony damage, he or she might become confused when told that the X-ray is normal but that further investigations are required to exclude bony or osteochondral damage. Also, be sure to alert patients who are going for a minimally invasive procedure (e.g. MR arthrogram) that this will require an "injection." It is helpful to give the patient a leaflet explaining the investigation, how long it will take, and when he or she should be reviewed with the results of the investigation.

Radiological investigation

Plain X-ray

Despite the availability of sophisticated imaging, plain film radiography often provides diagnostic information about bony abnormalities, such as fractures, dislocations, dysplasia, and calcification (Fig. 12.1).[2]

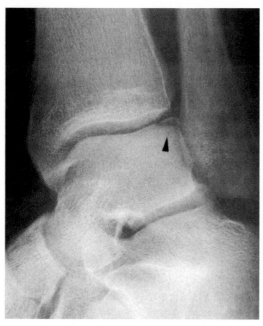

Figure 12.1 X-ray of an osteochondral fracture of the talar dome

COURTESY OF IF ANDERSON

Correctly positioning the patient is vital for a useful X-ray. A minimum of two perpendicular views is required to evaluate any bone adequately. Complex joints such as the ankle, wrist, or elbow may require additional or specialized views. Weight-bearing or "stress" views may give further information.

Computed tomographic (CT) scanning

CT scanning (Fig. 12.2) allows cross-sectional imaging of soft tissue, calcific deposits, and bone.

CT scanning is particularly useful in evaluation of the spine, fractures in small bones, and fractures in anatomically complex regions, such as the ankle, foot, or pelvis. CT scanners are capable of providing high-resolution reconstructions of the imaging data in any plane.

CT arthrography is performed after an injection of radio-opaque contrast medium into the joint cavity—most commonly the shoulder or ankle. This procedure is becoming superseded by MR arthrograms (MRA) with gadolinium (see below). The disadvantage of CT scanning is the significant radiation dose, especially in children.

Magnetic resonance imaging (MRI)

MRI (Fig. 12.3) is based on the number of free water protons present within a tissue sample. When a patient is placed in a strong magnetic field, the free water protons align with the external magnetic field. In MRI, a series of radiofrequency (RF) pulses are applied to the tissue sample, which causes the

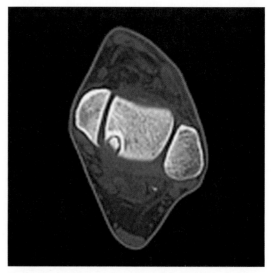

Figure 12.2 CT scan of an osteochondral fracture of the talar dome

MRI is not dependent on ionizing radiation and is not invasive. Compared with CT scanning, it is less capable of defining bone details and detecting small areas of calcification, but it is nevertheless very useful at revealing occult bony abnormalities,[4-6] and its superior contrast resolution allows the detection of subtle soft tissue changes. This latter property, together with its multiplanar scanning capability, is most valuable in detecting spinal disk/root abnormalities, avascular necrosis, and bone marrow tumors, and in evaluating soft tissue masses. MRI is commonly used to assess internal derangement of joints.[7, 8]

There are a few strict contraindications to MRI (e.g. certain brain aneurysm clips, neurostimulators, cardiac pacemakers) but, contrary to popular medical opinion, patients with metallic orthopedic hardware and metallic surgical clips outside the brain, in place for more than six weeks, can be safely scanned.

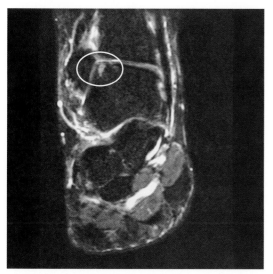

Figure 12.3 MRI of an osteochondral fracture (circled) of the talar dome. The plain X-rays and CT were normal

protons to change their alignment relative to the external magnetic field. The energy released during this realignment of protons is used to create the image.

A pulse sequence is a specific series of RF pulses or gradient changes that result in excitation and realignment of water protons in a predictable fashion, allowing for the creation of an image. Spin echo (SE), gradient echo (GRE), and inversion recovery (IR) sequences are the basic types of sequences used in musculoskeletal imaging.[3] T1-weighted, T2-weighted, proton density, and short T1 inversion recovery (STIR) sequences are often taken (Table 12.1). Fat-suppressed and fat-saturated sequences can also be taken.

MRI can be overly sensitive to abnormal tissue signals and thus provide false positive results. In asymptomatic athletes in numerous studies, MR images are consistent with significant injury although none exists.[9, 10] This emphasizes the need for the appropriate selection of patients for investigation, and careful clinical–imaging correlation.[1] As with any medical investigation, errors can occur; ideally, images should be read by an experienced musculoskeletal MRI radiologist.

Ultrasound scan (for diagnosis)

High-resolution ultrasound scanning (Fig. 12.4 overleaf) with 10–12 megahertz (MHz) probes is a painless

Table 12.1 Different MRI images

Image	Signal intensity	Clinical use
T1-weighted image	Fat: bright Muscle: intermediate Water, tendons and fibrocartilage: dark	Good for anatomical detail, bone marrow Lacks sensitivity in detecting soft tissue injury Good for meniscal pathology
T2-weighted image	Water: bright Fat: intermediate Muscle, fibrocartilage: dark	Good for most soft tissue injury, especially tendons
Proton density (PD)	Fat: bright Calcium, tendons, fibrocartilage: dark Water: intermediate	Good for menisci and ligaments
Short T1 inversion recovery (STIR)/ fat saturated T2 sequence	Water: very bright Fat, muscle, fibrocartilage: dark	Good for bone marrow and soft tissue pathology

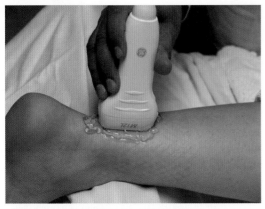

Figure 12.4 (a) Probe position for Achilles tendon ultrasound scan (longitudinal)

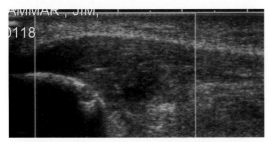

(b) Gray-scale ultrasound scan of the patellar tendon

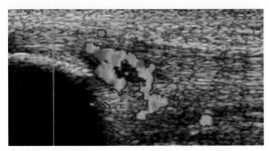

(c) Color Doppler ultrasound scan of the patellar tendon

method of imaging tendons, muscles, and other soft tissues without exposing the patient to any radiation. Other advantages include its dynamic nature, its short examination time, and its ability to guide therapeutic injection under real time. Disadvantages include the less graphic images, the fact that it is more operator-dependent with respect to image quality than any other modality, and the fact that it cannot penetrate tissues to show deeper structures, such as shoulder/ hip labra or anterior cruciate ligaments/menisci. The most commonly examined areas are large tendons (e.g. the Achilles, patellar, and rotator cuff tendons),

and the muscles of the thigh and calf. Ultrasound can also demonstrate muscle tear, hematoma formation, or early calcification, and may be useful in localizing foreign bodies.

Ultrasound scanning is able to distinguish complete tendon rupture from other tendon abnormalities (e.g. tendinopathy). As with MRI, ultrasound imaging of elite athletes reveals morphological "abnormalities" that are not symptomatic and do not appear to predict imminent tendon pain.[11]

Real-time ultrasound examination during active movement (dynamic ultrasound) is particularly helpful in the evaluation of shoulder impingement. In recent years, color Doppler ultrasound has gained popularity in sports and exercise medicine for the assessment of tendons, as innovative research suggested that the abnormal flow detected using the color Doppler feature provided a better guide as to whether tendons were painful or not.[12] Although this had been the case in cross-sectional studies,[13] longitudinal studies have failed to show that color Doppler ultrasound findings of vascularity predict changes in symptoms.[13–15] Also, exercise affects the level of vascularity.[16] Also, in several studies, ablation of this abnormal flow using the sclerosing agent polidocanol was shown to reduce tendon pain.[17,18] The use of ultrasound to help guide injection is discussed in Chapter 13.

Radioisotopic bone scan

Radioisotopic bone scan (scintigraphy) (Fig. 12.5) is a highly sensitive but non-specific nuclear medicine investigation used to detect areas of increased blood flow (inflammation, infection) and bone turnover (fractures and other bone lesions, including tumors). This was used much more widely before the advent of MRI for sports and exercise medicine imaging.

Radioisotopic bone scans are useful for the detection of stress fractures and osteochondral lesions[19–21] but give little information regarding soft tissue and involve significant radiation exposure. Bone scans are particularly useful when seeking subtle fractures such as the hook of the hamate, as these can be overlooked when using CT scans or MRI.

Single photon emission computed tomography (SPECT) techniques are also used in sports and exercise medicine, particularly in the detection of stress fractures of the pars interarticularis of the lumbar spine.

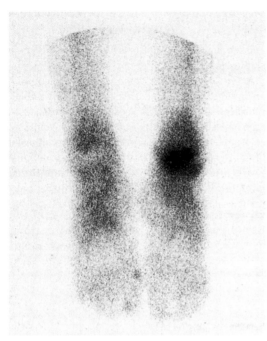

Figure 12.5 Radioisotopic bone scan of an osteochondral fracture of the talar dome
COURTESY OF IF ANDERSON

Neurological investigations

Electromyography

Electromyography (EMG) measures muscle activity by recording action potentials from the contracting fibers, either by using surface electrodes or by inserting needle electrodes into the muscle. After an electrical stimulus is applied to muscle, the type of response provides information regarding the nature of the dysfunction.

Nerve conduction studies

Motor and sensory nerve conduction studies aim to recognize and localize peripheral nerve abnormalities. After a stimulus (either electrical or mechanical) is applied to a distant part of the nerve, electrical action potentials are measured. Characteristic changes in the amplitude or velocity of action potential conduction reflect abnormalities of nerve function (e.g. demyelination or axonal damage).

Neuropsychological testing

Neuropsychological testing is used to assess the severity of and recovery from minor head injury. The specific techniques used are discussed in Chapter 17.

Muscle assessment

Compartment pressure testing

Intracompartmental pressures are measured at rest and during exercise using a Stryker catheter (Fig. 12.6). In doing so, the patient exercises the muscles of the specific compartment either to exhaustion or until symptoms are reproduced. Post-exercise resting pressure is monitored for five minutes. The diagnosis of compartment, pressure syndrome is confirmed when the compartment pressures reach a diagnostic threshold during and after exercise (Chapter 35).

Cardiovascular investigations (see Chapters 48, 49)

Electrocardiography (ECG), exercise stress tests, and echocardiography are important investigations in sports and exercise medicine. They are discussed in the context of cardiac conditions in Chapters 48 and 49.

Respiratory investigations

Pulmonary function tests

A number of simple tests of ventilatory capacity, such as forced expiratory volume in one second

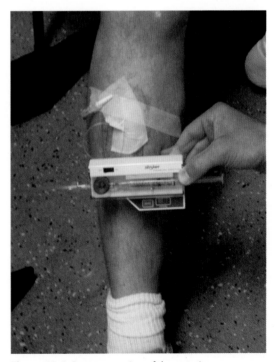

Figure 12.6 Pressure testing of the anterior compartment of the lower limb

(FEV$_1$) and forced vital capacity (FVC), require relatively simple apparatus. Coupled with arterial blood gas measurements, these tests provide information on the mechanical characteristics of the ventilatory pump and the adequacy of pulmonary gas exchange. Carbon monoxide transfer indicates the gas exchange mechanisms and may detect subtle changes in function. More sophisticated techniques enable measurement of lung compliance, peripheral airway disease, airway reactivity, mucociliary clearance, respiratory muscle function, and work of breathing.

Bronchial provocation challenge tests used in the diagnosis of exercise-induced bronchospasm (EIB) are discussed fully in Chapter 50.

The diagnosis

As a result of careful clinical assessment (Chapter 11) and the judicious use of investigations, the diagnosis should be evident. The next step is to discuss the diagnosis, the possible causes of the problem, and an outline of the treatment program with the patient. Muscle charts and models of particular joints can assist the sportsperson to understand the condition. Internet links can often provide the athlete with a lot of information; this will be appreciated.

Once the diagnosis is made and a clear explanation given to the patient, it is time to consider what treatment is appropriate for the condition. Chapter 13 provides an overview of current treatment alternatives.

🌐 RECOMMENDED WEBSITES

MyPacs radiology reference case manager: www.mypacs.net

European Society of Radiology teaching database: www.eurorad.org

American College of Radiology website: www.acr.org/ac

📄 RECOMMENDED READING

Anderson J, Read J. *Atlas of imaging in sports medicine.* Sydney: McGraw-Hill, 2nd edn, 2007.

Anderson J. *An atlas of radiography for sports injuries.* Sydney: McGraw-Hill, 2000.

Cooper R, Allwright S, Anderson J. *Atlas of nuclear imaging in sports medicine.* Sydney: McGraw-Hill, 2003.

Greenspan A. *Orthopedic imaging: a practical approach.* Lippincott, Williams & Wilkins; 5th edn, 2010.

Kremkau FW. *Sonography: principles and instruments.* Saunders, 8th edn, 2011.

Shelly MJ, Hodnett PA, MacMahon PJ et al. MR imaging of muscle injury. *Magn Reson Imaging Clin N Am* 2009;17(4):757–73.

📑 REFERENCES

1. Cohen, MD. Accuracy of information on imaging requisitions: does it matter? *J Am Coll Radiol* 2007;4:617-621.

2. Taljanovic MS, Hunter TB, Fitzpatrick KA et al. Musculoskeletal magnetic resonance imaging: importance of radiography. *Skeletal Radiol* 2003;32:403–11.

3. Spritzer CE. Impact of magnetic resonance imaging in sports medicine. In: Garrett WE, Speer KP, Kirkendall DT, eds. *Principles and practice of orthopaedic sports medicine.* Philadelphia: Lippincott, Williams & Wilkins, 2000.

4. Bencardino J, Rosenberg ZS, Delfaut E. MR imaging in sports injuries of the foot and ankle. *Magn Reson Imaging Clin N Am* 1999;7:131–49, ix.

5. Ascenti G, Visalli C, Genitori A et al. Multiple hypervascular pancreatic metastases from renal cell carcinoma: dynamic MR and spiral CT in three cases. *Clin Imaging* 2004;28:349–52.

6. Gaeta M, Minutoli F, Scribano E et al. CT and MR imaging findings in athletes with early tibial stress injuries: comparison with bone scintigraphy findings and emphasis on cortical abnormalities. *Radiology* 2005;235:553–61.

7. Mohan BR, Gosal HS. Reliability of clinical diagnosis in meniscal tears. *Int Orthopedics* 2007. 31(1):57–60.

8. Rosas HG, De Smet AA. Magnetic resonance imaging of the meniscus. *Top Magn Reson Imaging* 2009. 20(3):151–73.

9. Miniaci A, Mascia AT, Salonen DC et al. Magnetic resonance imaging of the shoulder in asymptomatic professional baseball pitchers. *Am J Sports Med* 2002;30:66–73.

10. Zanetti M, Pfirrmann CW, Schmid MR et al. Patients with suspected meniscal tears: prevalence of abnormalities seen on MRI of 100 symptomatic and 100 contralateral asymptomatic knees. *AJR Am J Roentgenol.* 2003;181(3):635–41.

11. Cook JL, Khan KM, Harcourt PR et al. Patellar tendon ultrasonography in asymptomatic active athletes reveals hypoechoic regions: a study of 320 tendons. Victorian Institute of Sport Tendon Study Group. *Clin J Sport Med* 1998;8:73–7.

12. Weinberg EP, Adams MJ, Hollenberg GM. Color Doppler sonography of patellar tendinosis. *Am J Roentgenol* 1998;171:743–4.

13. Zanetti M, Metzdorf A, Kundert HP et al. Achilles tendons: clinical relevance of neovascularization diagnosed with power Doppler US. *Radiology* 2003;227:556–60.

14. Khan KM, Forster BB, Robinson J et al. Are ultrasound and magnetic resonance imaging of value in assessment of Achilles tendon disorders? A two year prospective study. *Br J Sports Med* 2003;37:149–53.

15. Reiter M, Ulreich N, Dirisamer A et al. Colour and power Doppler sonography in symptomatic Achilles tendon disease. *Int J Sports Med* 2004;25:301–5.

16. Cook JL, Kiss ZS, Ptasznik R et al. Is vascularity more evident after exercise? Implications for tendon imaging. *Am J Roentgenol* 2005;185:1138–40.

27. Alfredson H, Ohberg L. Neovascularisation in chronic painful patellar tendinosis—promising results after sclerosing neovessels outside the tendon challenge the need for surgery. *Knee Surg Sports Traumatol Arthrosc* 2005;13:74–80.

18. Alfredson H, Ohberg L. Sclerosing injections to areas of neovascularisation reduce pain in chronic Achilles tendinopathy: a double-blind randomised controlled trial. *Knee Surg Sports Traumatol Arthrosc* 2005;13: 338–44.

19. Shikare S, Samsi AB, Tilve GH. Bone imaging in sports medicine. *J Postgrad Med* 1997;43:71–2.

20. Ishibashi Y, Okamura, Y, Otsuka, H et al. Comparison of scintigraphy and magnetic resonance imaging for stress injuries of bone. *Clin J Sport Med* 2002;12: 79–84.

21. Groshar D, Gorenberg M, Ben Haim et al. Lower extremity scintigraphy: the foot and ankle. *Semin Nucl Med* 1998;28:62–77.

Chapter 13

Treatments used for musculoskeletal conditions: more choices and more evidence

with ROBERT GRANTER

The good physician treats the disease; the great physician treats the patient who has the disease. William Osler

Treatment begins when the patient first presents with symptoms. But the boundary between the end of treatment and the start of rehabilitation is blurry. In many conditions that are managed conservatively (e.g. hamstring muscle strain, tendinopathy), the exercises that are started for "treatment" also contribute to the rehabilitation process. If one were required to make a distinction, it might be that the treatment techniques are often used in acute to subacute presentations, and rehabilitation commences when clinical presentation stabilizes, which can be anywhere from subacute to chronic.

This book discusses therapies that apply to both "treatment" and "rehabilitation" in just one of the relevant chapters. For example, manual therapy is covered in this chapter, even though it can be an important part of ongoing rehabilitation. On the other hand, exercise prescription (resistance exercises, proprioceptive training, flexibility training, and activities that combine these elements), an essential "treatment" of musculoskeletal conditions, is covered in Chapter 15.

Evidence for treatment effectiveness is continually changing

This chapter provides the essential background for treatments that are referred to in Part B, "Regional problems." Here specific treatments are defined and described, the levels of evidence for their effectiveness are reported, and a clinical perspective is provided for their use in musculoskeletal medicine.

There has been a remarkable explosion of evidence to support treatments in sport and exercise medicine in the past decade (see box). In 2010 alone, new

sports medicine treatment evidence was published in the *New England Journal of Medicine*,[1] *Journal of the American Medical Association (JAMA)*,[2] *BMJ*, and the *Lancet*.[3]

> **Just a small sample of high-quality research published during a small window of time (2010). This provides an increasingly stronger foundation for treatment in sports and exercise medicine.**
>
> Frobell RB, Roos EM, Roos HP et al. A randomized trial of treatment for acute anterior cruciate ligament tears. *N Engl J Med* 2010; 363: 331–42.
>
> Emery CA, Kang J, Shrier I et al. Risk of injury associated with body checking among youth ice hockey players. *JAMA* 2010;303:2265–72.
>
> de Vos RJ, Weir A, van Schie HT et al. Platelet-rich plasma injection for chronic Achilles tendinopathy: a randomized controlled trial. *JAMA* 2010;303: 144–9.
>
> Coombes K, Bisset L, Vicenzino B. Efficacy and safety of corticosteroid injections and other injections for management of tendinopathy: a systematic review of randomised controlled trials. *Lancet* 2010;376(9754):1751–67.
>
> Cooper R, Kuh D, Hardy R; Mortality Review Group; FALCon and HALCyon Study Teams. Objectively measured physical capability levels and mortality: systematic review and meta-analysis. *BMJ* 2010 Sep 9;341:c4467. doi: 10.1136/bmj.c4467.
>
> Bleakley CM, O'Connor SR, Tully MA et al. Effect of accelerated rehabilitation on function after ankle sprain: randomised controlled trial. *BMJ* 2010;340:c1964. doi: 10.1136/bmj.c1964.

Nevertheless, we remind the reader that there has been no randomized controlled trial evidence suggesting that, when jumping from an airplane, using a parachute provides superior outcomes to jumping without one.[4] All evidence of harm to those who jumped without a parachute has been in retrospective case series (level 4 evidence; Fig. 13.1). As clinicians, we should take note of the evidence that has been gathered but celebrate that our craft remains as much art as science.

Part of the art of musculoskeletal medicine is ensuring that patients can benefit from the appropriate elements of a large menu of available treatments. This chapter discusses this menu according to the following subheadings:

- acute management
- immobilization and early mobilization
- therapeutic drugs
- blood and blood products
- heat and cold
- electrotherapy
- extracorporeal shock wave therapy
- manual therapy
- acupuncture and dry needling
- hyperbaric oxygen therapy
- surgery.

The clinician should evaluate the effectiveness of each type of treatment by comparing symptoms and signs before and after treatment (i.e. both immediately after treatment and again at the next visit). This enables the clinician to choose the most appropriate mode of treatment for the specific injury and the specific individual. It also allows the clinician to change

Figure 13.1 Skydiving. There is only level 4 evidence (case reports) to suggest that wearing a parachute is associated with outcomes superior to those when not wearing one when jumping from an airplane

modalities or allows opportunity for further investigation in presentations that are not improving.

Acute management

The most important time in the treatment of acute soft tissue injuries is in the 24 hours immediately following injury. When soft tissue is injured, blood vessels are usually damaged too. Thus, blood accumulates around damaged tissue and compresses adjoining tissues, which causes secondary hypoxic injury and further tissue damage. Consequently, every effort should be made to reduce bleeding at the site of injury. The most appropriate method of doing this is summarized by the letters RICE:

R   **R**est
I   **I**ce
C   **C**ompression
E   **E**levation

Rest

Whenever possible following injury, the athlete should cease activity, to decrease bleeding and swelling. For example, with a thigh contusion, bleeding will be increased by contraction of the quadriceps muscle during running. Where necessary, complete rest can be achieved with the use of crutches for a lower limb injury or a sling for upper limb injuries. Immobilizing or resting the injured extremity helps prevent further damage by reducing further injury, reducing hematoma and thereby reducing size of the scar in injured soft tissue.[5]

Ice

Immediately after injury, ice is principally used to reduce tissue metabolism.[6] Early ice application has been associated with significantly reduced hematoma, less inflammation and tissue necrosis, and somewhat accelerated early regeneration in muscle tissues.[5, 7, 8] Ice is also used in the later stages of injury treatment as a therapeutic modality. Ice can be applied in a number of forms, as shown in Table 13.5 on page 182.

Standard application of ice after soft tissue injury consists of 20 minutes of continuous ice treatment performed every two hours for at least six hours following injury.[7, 9, 10] Additionally, intermittent ice application has shown to be more effective than continuous ice application in reducing pain on activity immediately after ankle sprain.[9] An intermittent application includes 10 minutes of ice followed by a 10-minute rest and then reapplied for a further 10 minutes, every two hours over the initial 24 to 48 hours.

Ice should not be applied where local tissue circulation is impaired (e.g. in Raynaud's phenomenon, peripheral vascular disease) or to patients who suffer from a cold allergy. Other adverse effects of prolonged ice application are skin burns and nerve damage.[11]

Compression

Compression of the injured area with a firm bandage reduces bleeding and, therefore, minimizes swelling. Compression should be applied both during and after ice application. The width of the bandage applied varies according to the injured area.

The bandage should be applied firmly, but not so tightly as to cause pain. Bandaging should start just distal to the site of bleeding, with each layer of the bandage overlapping the underlying layer by one-half. It should extend to at least a hand's breadth proximal to the injury margin.

Elevation

The rationale for elevation stems from the fundamental principles of physiology and traumatology. Specifically, the elevation of an injured extremity above the level of the heart results in a decrease in hydrostatic pressure and, subsequently, reduces the accumulation of interstitial fluid.[5] Elevation can be achieved by using a sling for upper limb injuries and by resting lower limbs on a chair, pillows, or bucket. It is important to ensure that the lower limb is above the level of the pelvis.

In the first 72 hours following injury, HARM-ful factors should be avoided:

H **H**eat and heat rubs: Heat may increase the bleeding at the injured site. Avoid hot baths, showers, saunas, heat packs, and heat rubs.
A **A**lcohol: A moderate consumption of alcohol after eccentric-based leg exercises has shown to significantly increase the loss of dynamic and static quadriceps strength.[12] Alcohol may mask pain and severity of injury and therefore increase the risk of re-injury.[13] To minimize exercise-related losses in muscle function and to accelerate recovery, avoidance of alcohol post-injury is paramount.
R **R**unning/moderate activity: Running or any form of moderate activity can cause further damage at the injury site.
M **M**assage/vigorous soft tissue therapy: Vigorous massage should be avoided in the first 24 to 48 hours. It could cause further bleeding and swelling to the injury site.

Immobilization and early mobilization

Immobilization has beneficial effects in the early phase of muscle regeneration and is crucial for fracture healing. However, lengthy immobilization has detrimental effects; it causes joint stiffness, degenerative changes in articular cartilage, osteopenia, muscle atrophy, weakness, and stiffness.

A short period of immobilization following muscle injury is beneficial and should be limited to the first few days after the injury only.[5] This allows the scar tissue to gain the required strength against contractile forces. Additionally, restricting mobilization to a period of less than one week minimizes the adverse effects seen with immobility such as muscle atrophy, loss of muscle extensibility, and strength.[14]

Re-injury is common when active mobilization is begun too early after substantial musculoskeletal injury.[5] Avoiding re-injury is important, as re-injury can account for the greatest time lost from sporting activity.

If early active mobilization is begun immediately after a moderate soft tissue injury, a larger connective tissue scar can develop.[8] In contrast, immobilization appears to provide the new granulation tissue with greater tensile strength to withstand the forces created by generated muscle forces.[5, 8]

Complete immobilization is primarily required for acute fractures. Certain stress fractures (e.g. tarsal navicular fractures) also require immobilization. Occasionally in severe soft tissue injuries, it may be helpful to immobilize the injured area for up to 48 hours to limit pain and swelling.

Immobilization can be obtained through the use of rigid braces, air splints, taping, thermoplastic materials or, most commonly, with the use of a plaster cast. Despite the poor strength of plaster cast compared to the more rigid fiberglass cast, the low cost and supreme molding properties keep plaster cast clinically popular.[15]

Plaster casts have the disadvantages of being relatively heavy, prone to damage, and not water-resistant. For undisplaced fractures and immobilization of soft tissue injuries, fiberglass casts are preferred. Fiberglass casting material is light, strong, and waterproof. A waterproof underwrap is available that enables the athlete to bathe without the need to protect the cast. This allows those with lower limb casts to exercise in water to maintain fitness.

Protected mobilization

Mobilization has numerous tissue benefits.[16] One way to achieve early, but safe, mobilization is by "protected mobilization." This term refers to the use of protective taping or bracing to prevent movement in a direction that would cause excessive stress on an injured structure. For example, a hinged knee brace prevents valgus strain in a second degree medial collateral ligament injury. Non-injured structures are allowed to move (i.e. the knee joint continues to function), and this feature distinguishes protected mobilization from complete immobilization. This allows enough movement to prevent stiffness, maintain muscle strength, and improve the nourishment of the articular cartilage, while still protecting the damaged ligament.

After the short initial immobilization period, the mobilization of the injured skeletal muscle should be started gradually (i.e. within the limits of pain) as soon as possible. Early mobilization induces more rapid and intensive capillary ingrowth into the injured area, better regeneration of muscle fibers, and more parallel orientation of the regenerating myofibers in comparison to immobilization.[5, 8, 16]

Continuous passive motion

Continuous passive motion is currently a part of patient rehabilitation regimens after a variety of orthopedic surgical procedures. It can enhance the joint healing process, and has shown to stimulate chondrocyte PRG4 metabolism in laboratory studies.[17]

Therapeutic drugs

The sports medical team plays an important role in preparing and maintaining an athlete at peak performance. Every attempt is made to promote both the health and the performance of a player. Therapeutic drugs can help accelerate rehabilitation, and as a result can allow a quicker return to sport post injury. In addition, therapeutic drugs can allow a player to continue their sport while injuries are healing, which is especially relevant at a professional level of sport.

Recent studies have investigated the use of therapeutic drugs and nutritional supplements by athletes during sporting competitions.[18–22] These studies have shown an average use of 1.7 supplements per athlete and 0.8 medications per athlete during competition in track and field events, and 0.63 medications per player per match among international soccer players.[18, 20, 21] Additionally, 61% and 54% of Canadian athletes used some form of medication during the Atlanta and Sydney Olympics respectively.[18, 20, 21] The most frequently used therapeutic drugs included nonsteroidal anti-inflammatory drugs (NSAIDs), respiratory drugs, and various analgesics.

This section discusses a range of therapeutic drugs including analgesics, NSAIDs, corticosteroids, nitric oxide, and antidepressants. Various methods of drug delivery, including iontophoresis, corticosteroid, and anesthetic injections, as well as therapies such as sclerosing therapy and prolotherapy, are discussed. Interventions for articular cartilage and osteoarthritis including hyaluronic acid therapy, glucosamine sulfate, and chondroitin sulfate use are also discussed.

Analgesics

The RICE approach, mentioned above, can provide nonpharmaceutical pain relief in the acute phase of some sporting injuries. Although the RICE approach is important in the early stage of tissue healing, it may not always provide adequate pain relief. Analgesic drugs are often then considered. The term "analgesic" translates from the Greek *an* (without) and *algos* (pain). Therefore an analgesic is used to relieve pain or achieve analgesia.

Analgesics are used in the acute phase immediately after injury to reduce pain. Subsequent use depends on the degree and duration of pain. Pain reduction during rehabilitation may facilitate movement. Aspirin (ASA), paracetamol (acetominophen), and codeine are the most commonly used analgesics, either singly or in combination.

Aspirin

At low dosages (250–300 mg), aspirin (or acetylsalicylic acid [ASA]) has an analgesic and antipyretic effect. At higher dosages aspirin also has an anti-inflammatory effect, but these dosages are associated with a significant incidence of adverse effects, particularly of the gastrointestinal system. We advise against the use of aspirin in acute injuries because it inhibits platelet aggregation and, thus, may increase bleeding associated with the injury.

Paracetamol

Paracetamol (acetaminophen) has an analgesic and antipyretic effect but has no influence on the inflammatory process and no effect on blood clotting, and is ineffective in intense pain.[23] It is recommended that adult oral doses of paracetamol for the treatment of pain or fever be 650–1000 mg every four hours as needed and up to a maximum daily dose of 4 g.[23] At a single dose of 1000 mg, paracetamol reaches its ceiling effect in adults and a further increase to this does not increase its analgesic effects but does, however, increase its toxicity levels.

Since the first synthesis of paracetamol in 1878 by Morse, its method of action has not been well understood. However, recent laboratory studies have demonstrated that the analgesic effects of paracetamol are the result of the involvement of the cannabinoid system.[23, 24] The cannabinoid system involves a group of neuro-modulatory lipids and their associated receptors, which have influence over physiological processes such as appetite, pain sensation, mood, and memory. It is thought the cannabinoid-1 receptors, which are primarily located in the central nervous system, are involved in the analgesic effects of paracetamol.

The involvement of this system may now explain some of the strange adverse effects that can be associated with the use of paracetamol, such as mood swings and appetite suppression. These effects are not associated with other analgesics and NSAIDs. The incidence of adverse effects is comparable to placebo.[25] It is thus safe for use in acute sports injuries at up to 3–4 g/day.[26]

Codeine

Codeine is a more potent analgesic. It is a narcotic analgesic and was formerly listed as a banned substance by the International Olympic Committee (Chapter 66). This ban was lifted in the mid-1990s.

Topical analgesics

Topical analgesics are used extensively by athletes and are known as "sports rubs," "heat rubs" and "liniments." Most commercially available topical analgesics contain a combination of substances such as menthol, methyl salicylate, camphor, and eucalyptus oil.

The majority of topical analgesics act as skin counterirritants. Most products contain two or more active ingredients that produce redness, dilate blood vessels, and stimulate pain and temperature receptors. The type and intensity of the effect depends on the particular counterirritant, and its concentration, dosage, and method of application. The exact mechanism of action of counterirritants is unknown.

Counterirritants should not be used to replace a proper warm-up as they do not penetrate to deeper muscles, but they may be of use as an adjunct to warm-up. Counterirritants may irritate the skin, causing burning and pain on application, redness, and itchiness, and they occasionally cause blistering or contact dermatitis. They are not appropriate around the groin, mouth, or eye regions, and they should not be used on broken skin.

Counterirritants often include a variety of herbal compounds such as capsaicin, camphor, menthol, salicylates, and eucalyptus oil. Table 13.1 outlines the proposed uses and mechanisms of action of these compounds.

Previously, the mechanism of action of counterirritants was proposed to be via the stimulation of sensory receptors to dampen painful stimuli.[27, 29, 30] However, more recent evidence has demonstrated that their mechanism of action is related to their effect on specific ion channels known as the transient receptor potential (TRP) channels.[28, 31] These ion channels are thermosensitive (i.e. sensitive to extreme heat or cold). When TRP channels are activated, calcitonin gene-related peptide (CGRP), substance P (SP), and other inflammatory neurotransmitters are released. This causes local irritation and an inflammatory response.

Symptoms such as pain, burning, itching, and redness in the skin are due to excitation and sensitization of A delta (Aδ)- and C-fiber nociceptors. Prolonged activation of these nociceptors results in a depletion of presynaptic neurotransmitters. This is thought to give rise to the analgesic properties of counterirritants. It is important to note that counterirritants lower or increase the temperature activation of TRP channels. This explains the cooling and heating effects of heat rubs and ice gels.[27, 28] Figure 13.2 shows a summary of the mechanism of action of counterirritants.

Nonsteroidal anti-inflammatory drugs (NSAIDs)

Nonsteriodal anti-inflammatory drugs (NSAIDs) are drugs with analgesic, anti-inflammatory, and antipyretic properties. The term "nonsteroidal" is used to distinguish this class of drugs from steroids, which, among other effects, produce similar anti-inflammatory effects.

Generally, the use of NSAIDs is well accepted in conditions where excessive inflammation is the prime cause of the patient's symptoms (e.g. bursitis); however, the role of NSAIDs in the treatment of other acute and overuse conditions is widely debated.

Table 13.1 Common counterirritants: uses and mechanism of action

Counterirritant	Description	Uses	Mechanism of action
Menthol	Derived from peppermint or other mint oils	• Cough suppressant • Analgesic • Cooling effect	Binds to TRPV3 and k-opioid receptors[27, 28]
Salicylates	Derived from the bark of the willow tree	• Analgesic • Anti-acne • Antipyretic agent • Cooling effect	Binds to TRPA1[27, 29]
Camphor	A sweet smelling compound derived from the wood of the camphor laurel tree (*Cinnamomum camphora*)	• Decongestant • Cough suppressant • Antipruritic agent • Analgesic • Heating effect	Binds to TRPV3 receptors[28]
Capsaicin	The active component in chilli peppers	• Appetite stimulation • Heating effect • Analgesic • Others (treatment of gastric ulcers, rheumatoid, shingles)	Binds to TRPV1 receptors[27–29]
Eucalyptus oil	Distilled oil from the leaf of the eucalyptus tree, native to Australia	• Decongestant • Anti-inflammatory • Analgesic • Antibacterial agent	Binds to TRPM8[28]

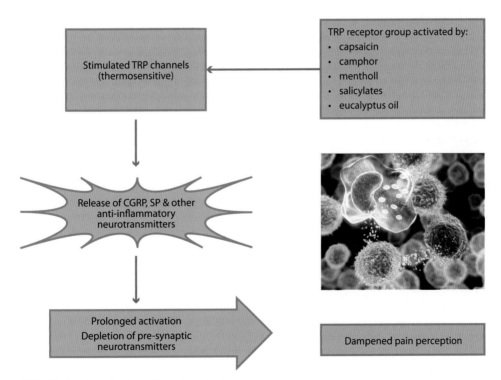

Figure 13.2 Mechanism of action of counterirritants

The most common NSAIDs include aspirin, ibuprofen, diclofenac, and naproxen, and at low doses they are available over the counter, making them popular drugs among the general population as well as athletes, especially in terms of self-medicating. These NSAIDs are frequently associated with adverse effects, especially on the stomach, and as a result a different type of NSAID, the COX-2 inhibitor, which reduces the risk of stomach adverse effects, came into use over the past two decades. However, their association with cardiovascular adverse effects has led to some of these drugs being removed from the market.

The frequency of administration of NSAIDs varies between the different drugs and is related to their half-life (Table 13.2).

Use in sport

Recent studies on the use of NSAIDs in sport have demonstrated an alarming rate of use. A summary of these studies and their findings are displayed in Table 13.3.

Mechanism of action

Inflammation occurs at the site of acute injury. A local soft tissue injury such as a ligament tear causes the release of arachidonic acid from cell walls. Arachidonic acid is converted by a number of enzymes, in particular cyclo-oxygenase (COX), to prostaglandins, thromboxane, and prostacyclins. These substances mediate the inflammatory response.

The mechanisms of action of NSAIDs are through the inhibition of the COX system (Fig. 13.3 on page 172). Inhibition of the COX-converting enzyme, specifically through inhibition of prostaglandin, prostacyclins, and thromboxane synthesis, induces anti-inflammatory, analgesic, antithrombotic, and antipyretic effects.[35]

Efficacy

In spite of the widespread clinical use of NSAIDs, there are no convincing research data proving their effectiveness in the treatment of acute soft tissue injuries. Most studies lacked a placebo group and compared the effectiveness of one NSAID with another.[36] They do not appear to be any more effective than simple analgesics in the management of acute muscle injuries.[37, 38] The lack of scientific support for the use of NSAIDs in acute injury may reflect biological reality, or may be due to the methodological difficulties in performing randomized placebo-controlled trials in the diverse range of acute sporting injuries.

A summary of the use of NSAIDs based on research evidence is shown in Table 13.4 overleaf.

Adverse effects

NSAIDs are absorbed by the digestive system, and after entering the blood stream, are metabolized in the liver and later excreted by the kidneys. Adverse effects are associated with the gastrointestinal tract, cardiovascular systems, and kidney function.[40] Susceptibility increases with prolonged use.[26, 39, 41]

In general, the NSAIDs have minimal adverse effects; the most common are gastrointestinal symptoms, especially epigastric pain, nausea, indigestion, and heartburn. There appears to be considerable individual variation of adverse effect profiles among the different NSAIDs.

The risk of dyspeptic adverse effects can be lowered by using the minimum effective dose, taking the drug with or immediately after food or milk, or by the use of antacids. Alcohol, cigarettes, and coffee may aggravate the dyspepsia. To our knowledge, frank peptic ulceration with the short-term use of NSAIDs has not been reported among sportspeople. Occult bleeding may contribute to iron depletion in

Table 13.2 Commonly used NSAIDs

Drug	Some trade names	Usual dose (mg)	Half-life	Daily doses
Acetylsalicylic acid (ASA)	Aspirin	650	30 mins	3–4
Celecoxib	Celebrex	100–200	11–12 hours	1–2
Diclofenac	Voltaren	25–50	1–2 hours	2–3
Ibuprofen	Brufen, Motrin, Advil	400	1–2.5 hours	3–4
Meloxicam	Mobic	7.5–15	20–24 hours	1
Naproxen	Naprosyn, Anaprox	250–1000	12–15 hours	1–2

Table 13.3 Prevalence of NSAIDs use in sport

Study	Sport/event	Findings
Gorski 2009[32]	2008 Brazil Ironman Triathlon (3.8 km swim, 180 km cycle, 42.2 km run)	• 327 athletes in study • 59.9% reported using NSAIDs in the preceeding three months • 48.5% without medical prescription • Most athletes unaware of adverse effects • Pre-race used mostly for treatment of injuries • During event used mostly for pain relief and injury prevention
Wharam 2006[33]	2004 New Zealand Ironman triathlon (3.8 km swim, 180 km cycle, 42.2 km run)	• 330 athletes in study • 30% reported NSAIDs use • NSAIDs use was related to the incidence of hyponatremia • NSAIDs users had significantly higher plasma K, urea, and creatinine, and lower Na levels
McAnulty 2007[34]	Western States endurance run (160 km)	• 60 athletes in study • Plasma cytokines x2–3 higher in users of NSAIDs • NSAIDs users had significant amount of delayed onset muscle soreness (DOMS) day 1 post race • NSAIDs use during race did not alleviate muscle damage or DOMS and increased oxidative stress markers
Huang 2006[18]	Atlanta and Sydney Olympic Games (1996 & 2000)	• 257 Canadian athletes in study • Most commonly used drugs were NSAIDs • NSAIDs use was 33% of athletes in Atlanta and 38% in Sydney • The use of NSAIDs was highest in softball (60%) in Atlanta and gymnastics (100%) in Sydney
Taioli 2007[19]	Italian Professional Football/Soccer League (season 2003–04)	• 743 athletes in study • 92.6% of players reported the use of NSAIDs in previous year • 86.1% current users of NSAIDs • 22% of players used NSAIDs for >60 days/year
Tscholl 2009[21]	FIFA World Cups (2002 & 2006)	• 2944 team physicians' reports on players' medication intake • NSAIDs were the most frequently prescribed substances • Constituted 46.5% (2002), and 47.7% (2006) of all medications used • >50% of players used NSAIDs at least once during a tournament and 30.8% prior to a match • On average, 22.9% of the players used NSAIDs in two out of three matches • 10.6% of the players used NSAIDs for every match • >10% of the players used at least 2 forms of NSAIDs and some players used up to 5 different types • The use of COX-2 inhibitors decreased significantly from 2002 to 2006
Tscholl 2010[20]	International Association of Athletics Federations World Championships (multiple championship data from 2003 to 2004)	• Analysis of 3887 doping control forms • 27.3% of athletes used NSAIDs • Athletes in power and sprint disciplines reported using more NSAIDs • Significant increase in use with age

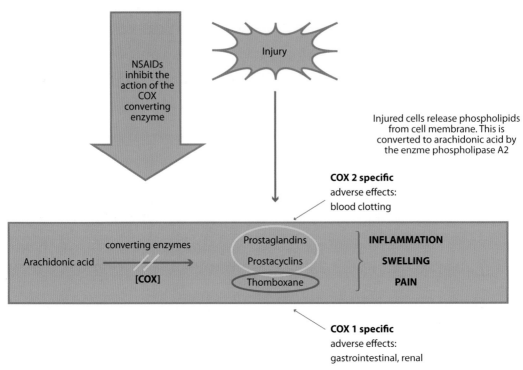

Figure 13.3 Mechanism of action of NSAIDs

Table 13.4 Guidelines for use of NSAIDs[35, 38–40]

Injury site	Use of NSAIDs (benefit/debatable/adverse effects)
Ligament injury	Adverse effect: • Continued pain (seen in acute ankle injuries [>6 months continued pain and instability])
Tendon injury	Debatable: • Chronic tendinopathy has an inflammatory component • May be useful in acute presentations for pain relief (use simple analgesics first)
Bone injury (fracture/stress fracture)	Adverse effect: • Delay bone consolidation • Avoid especially in the first few weeks of fracture and with stress fractures Possible benefit: • Reduce incidence of myositis ossificans and ectopic bone formation post-prosthetic joint surgery; whether this benefit translates to sports injuries is unknown
Muscle injuries (contusion, strain, DOMS)	Possible adverse effect in prolonged use: • Inhibits protein synthesis, affects remodeling and regeneration phase by reducing myofibroblast proliferation • Has demonstrated increased creatine kinase when taken prior to endurance sport events, in turn increasing the extent of muscle injury post event
Impingement syndromes and bursitis	Benefit: • Pain relief if required for shoulder bursitis, de Quervain's, trochanteric bursitis (rare, most lateral hip pain is gluteal tendinopathy), ITBFS, Morton's neuroma

athletes. The clinician should be wary of prescribing long-term use of these drugs in iron-depleted sportspeople.

Other occasional adverse effects include asthma, allergic rhinitis, rashes, tinnitus, deafness, headache, and confusion. The NSAIDs have a number of important drug interactions with anticoagulants, antihypertensives, diuretics, and peripheral vasodilators. Older patients with a history of hypertension, congestive heart failure, or coronary artery disease are at particular risk of adverse cardiovascular events with NSAIDs. Patients with impaired renal function are at risk of fluid retention, hyperkalemia (increased serum potassium level), and hypertension.

Prolonged use of NSAIDs is associated with harmful effects in terms of cell metabolism and growth.[33, 39] NSAIDs have proved to inhibit or decrease the synthesis of extracellular matrix, including collagen turnover and muscle regeneration, and therefore can affect the strength of healing tissue.[33, 42]

Overall NSAIDs can delay healing in acute ligament, muscle, and tendon injuries.[22, 26, 33, 35, 40, 43] This is thought to be due to their detrimental effect on the cell regeneration phase, as NSAIDs can cause increased fibrosis at the site of injury.[43] With an increase in fibrosis, weakness at the injury site can develop. Fibrosis increases with prolonged use.[34, 42] Slower muscle and ligament recovery increases the risk of re-injury.

Therefore, even though NSAIDs may prove to be beneficial in the short term with their analgesic and anti-inflammatory effects, an increased risk of re-injury could potentially impede athletic performance. More studies are needed to investigate the effectiveness of NSAIDs, particularly in the management of overuse injuries. In the meantime, the precise criteria for the use of NSAIDs in the management of sporting injuries remain a matter for debate.

Things to consider when prescribing NSAIDs are shown in the box, and a simple guide to the use of NSAIDs is shown in Figure 13.4 overleaf.

COX-2 inhibitors

Selective COX-2 inhibitors were introduced in 1999, promising the same anti-inflammatory and analgesic effects as their traditional counterparts but with reduced gastrointestinal adverse effects.[40, 44] Reduced gastrointestinal effects occurred through inhibition of COX 1, which has shown to be associated with the upkeep of stomach mucosal lining.[40, 44]

Clinical considerations when prescribing NSAIDs

- The use of paracetamol should be considered for acute and chronic musculoskeletal pain, due to its similar analgesic effects but lower adverse effects than NSAIDs.
- NSAIDs should be avoided in the first 48 hours post injury.
- Excessive inflammation, after the initial 48 hours, may warrant use of NSAIDs.
- Long-term use (>5 days) should be avoided.
- NSAIDs should be limited to minimal dose and minimal duration.
- If NSAIDs are required for longer than 5 days, revisit assessment and diagnosis.
- Use gastro-protective agents for patients at high risk of gastrointestinal problems (e.g. co-administer gastroprotective agents such as misoprosol, H_2 antagonist).
- There is no evidence that prophylactic use of NSAIDs decreases injury risk or improves athletic function.
- Figure 13.4 overleaf gives a simple guide to the use of NSAIDs.[39]

After introduction of these selective COX-2 inhibitors (featured in many "-coxib" drugs such as celecoxib), there was an increase in vascular thrombotic events. COX-2 inhibitors were found to disturb the prostacylin–thromboxane balance, which affects vascular homeostasis.[40, 44] By 2004 Valdecoxib and rofecoxib were taken off the market, as these drugs specifically were associated with a high number of vascular accidents through the increase in thromboxane.[44]

Currently, COX-2 inhibitors such as celecoxib are widely used particularly in those who have had dyspeptic adverse effects with the use of the traditional NSAIDs.

Ketorolac tromethamine (Toradol, Acular)

Ketorolac tromethamine is a potent analgesic and anti-inflammatory medication that can be administered orally, intravenously, and intramuscularly. It acts by blocking the synthesis of prostaglandins in the cyclo-oxygenase pathway.[45]

A survey of US National Football League teams revealed that 28 out of the 30 teams that responded to the survey used ketorolac with 93% game-day usage.[46] Adverse effects include headache, vasodilatation, asthma, bleeding, and kidney dysfunction.

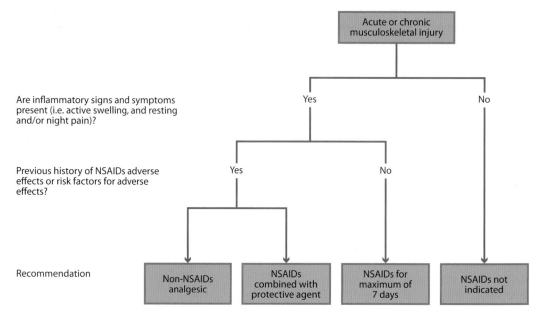

Figure 13.4 Decision tree for the prescription of NSAIDs to athletes with an acute or chronic musculoskeletal injury
FROM WARDEN[39]

Of particular concern in the sporting context is the bleeding tendency.

Topical anti-inflammatory agents

In light of the recent trials demonstrating the harmful cardiovascular effects of some NSAIDs, in addition to the ongoing gastrointestinal concerns, especially with prolonged use, an increased interest in and use of topical NSAIDs has resulted.[26][27] Topical analgesics can achieve similar analgesic effects to oral formulations without the systematic adverse effects and safety concerns.[27] Topical administration of NSAIDs has several benefits over their oral counterparts. These include lower systemic absorption and hence lower adverse effects, and effective localized analgesic and anti-inflammatory effects.[47]

A number of topical anti-inflammatory products are available. These include benzydamine, adrenocortical extract, indomethacin, and diclofenac gel. Traditionally these topical drugs have been administered through creams, gels, and sprays, which often required three to four applications per day. More recently, anti-inflammatory drugs have been applied through a patch which releases the drug over 24 hours.

There is some evidence of their efficacy. One recent systematic review assessed the effectiveness of topical NSAIDs against a placebo control for chronic musculoskeletal pain.[48] Populations included were predominately knee osteoarthritis. Typical NSAIDs were used for the search strategy, including dicoflenac, ibuprofen, and naproxen. This review identified 25 randomized control trials (RCTs). Minimal adverse events were identified with the highest complication rate found in one study of 6% associated with cutaneous rash. Overall, this review found topical NSAIDs were effective and safe in treating chronic musculoskeletal conditions for a period of two weeks.

One recent RCT on the effects of ibuprofen topical gel on muscle soreness resulting from unaccustomed exercise found that it was not effective on DOMS after exercise.[49] This trial included 106 participants of varying ages. Exclusion criteria included occupations that required heavy lifting or strenuous activity, or participation in weight or resistance training programs for the past six months. Subjects performed elbow and knee flexor exercises of 80% (6 sets of 10 reps) of 1RM (repetition maximum).

Corticosteroids

The use of corticosteroids, which are potent anti-inflammatory drugs, is controversial due to the incidence of adverse effects and concern regarding the effect of corticosteroids on tissue healing. Corticosteroids may be administered either by local injection, orally, or by iontophoresis. We found no randomized controlled trials of iontophoresis for sports medicine conditions.

A goal of the use of local corticosteroid injection is to reduce pain and inflammation sufficiently to allow a strengthening program to commence. Corticosteroid injections should be considered a "bridge" treatment that provides immediate symptomatic relief while the underlying cause of the problem is addressed with definitive, disease-modifying therapy.

Local injection for various pathologies

Local injection of corticosteroid agents maximizes the concentration at the site of the injury and minimizes the risk of adverse effects associated with systemic administration. Clinicians often use local injection of corticosteroids in conditions that include bursitis, paratenonitis, tenosynovitis, joint synovitis, osteoarthritis, chronic muscle strain, and trigger points. Conditions such as subacromial, olecranon, pre-patellar, and retrocalcaneal bursitis may be resistant to standard physiotherapy/physical therapy combined with NSAIDs.

Intra-articular injections, particularly into weight-bearing joints, must be approached with considerable caution because of possible long-term damage to articular cartilage. They should be performed only when the condition has proven refractory to treatments such as physiotherapy and NSAIDs. Rheumatologists have long used corticosteroids intra-articularly in acute monoarticular exacerbations of osteoarthritis. An acute attack of gouty arthritis may also respond well to aspiration and corticosteroid injection as part of the overall management.

Apophyseal joint injections have been used in the management of patients with back pain and who have only a short-term response to manual therapy, but the efficacy of such treatment at the lumbar spine is no better than placebo.[50] Controversy surrounds the use of injectable corticosteroid into the epidural space.

The role of corticosteroids in the treatment of tendon conditions was systematically reviewed in 2010.[3] As tendinopathy is not associated with inflammatory cells (Chapter 4), corticosteroid therapy is generally falling out of favor for this condition.[3] In lateral elbow pain, corticosteroid injections decrease the likelihood of good outcomes at six months and beyond compared with a "wait and see" approach.[51] See individual regional chapters (Part B) for specific treatment recommendations.

Some clinicians recommend the injection of trigger points with corticosteroid. Soft tissue therapy, dry needling, or local anesthetic injection appear to be equally as effective.

Adverse effects of corticosteroid injections include the potential systemic effects of absorbed cortisone, and local effects of injection. Corticosteroids inhibit collagen synthesis and tenocyte-fibroblast cell activity, and thus may impair tissue repair.[52, 53] As deleterious effects of corticosteroids appear to be dose-related, repeated injections are discouraged.

The main adverse effect of corticosteroid injection, apart from the possible damage to articular cartilage and tendon, is infection. This is a rare occurrence and should be prevented by the use of strict aseptic technique, particularly when performing intra-articular injections. The presence of an overlying skin infection is a contraindication to injection.

Corticosteroid injections commonly cause a short-term exacerbation of symptoms, a phenomenon known as "post-injection flare." This may commence soon after injection and usually subsides within 24 hours. This phenomenon is thought to be due to a crystalline synovitis, and is considered by some to be a positive sign of a favorable outcome to the treatment. Patients should always be warned that this may occur.

Corticosteroid injections have the reputation of being a particularly painful procedure, but this can be minimized by adding local anesthetic (0.5–1.0 mL 1% lignocaine [lidocaine]) to the injection. The abolition of pain after the local anesthetic injection may be diagnostically significant.

Traditionally, patients have been advised to rest and minimize activity for three to seven days following corticosteroid injection.

There are a number of different forms of injectable corticosteroid available. They include hydrocortisone, betamethasone, methylprednisolone, and triamcinalone. The main differences are in the speed of onset and half-life of action. There is no convincing evidence that their efficacy differs.

Oral corticosteroids

Despite their effectiveness as an anti-inflammatory agent, clinicians have traditionally been reluctant to use oral corticosteroids for the treatment of musculoskeletal inflammation, probably because of potential adverse effects.[54] The most common conditions for which they are used are acute cervical or lumbar radiculopathy/diskogenic pain, osteitis pubis, adhesive capsulitis (frozen shoulder), and chronic tendinopathies.

Possible complications include avascular necrosis of the femoral head.[55] However, the use of short courses (5–7 days) of oral prednisolone (25–50 mg) appears to be associated with minimal detrimental effects.

Note that the use of oral corticosteroids is still banned by the International Olympic Committee in competition.

Iontophoresis

Iontophoresis is a process by which drugs can be transmitted through the intact skin via electrical potential. Drugs such as corticosteroids, salicylates, local anesthetics, and NSAIDs can thus be administered locally without the traumatic effects of injection, with no pain for the patient, no infection risk, and fewer systemic adverse effects.[56, 57]

This process has been shown to deliver the drugs through skin and subcutaneous tissue, and has been in use since the 1950s.[56] In this way, the drug can reach tissue that may have markedly reduced vascularity (e.g. a bursa or tendon).

The results of well-controlled studies suggest that iontophoresis with diclofenac or salicylates improves symptoms in lateral epicondylitis. Iontophoresis with corticosteroid appears to give rapid-onset analgesia in both lateral epicondylitis and plantar fasciitis. Short-term iontophoresis (two weeks) improves pain and facilitates rehabilitation.[58]

Physiotherapists sometimes use iontophoresis to treat inflammatory conditions such as plantar fasciitis, lateral epicondylitis, rotator cuff and Achilles tendinopathy, and bursitis presentations.[56, 57] A recent laboratory study found that iontophoresis could facilitate the transmission of dexamethasone (a synthetic glucocorticoid steroid) into subcutaneous human tissue.[56] This study reported that some subjects appeared to have good effects, while others showed minimal improvement. This may highlight that iontophoresis may have an individual treatment response.

A systematic review on iontophoresis included 11 articles focusing on common musculoskeletal inflammatory conditions, including plantar fasciitis, epicondylitis, Achilles tendinopathy, and carpal tunnel syndrome.[57] This review found that the internal validity of most of these studies was compromised in some way, leaving results at high risk of bias. It concluded that research on iontophoresis

was limited and called for further studies. In addition to this review, an RCT (level 2 evidence) reported positive effects for iontophoresis in conjunction with low-Dye taping for plantar fasciitis.[59] In light of this finding, iontophoresis may currently be best used as an adjunct treatment in the treatment of inflammatory musculoskeletal conditions.

Nitric oxide donor

Glyceryl trinitrate (GTN), or nitroglycerin, is a nitric oxide donor used for over 100 years as a vasodilator and for symptomatic treatment of angina. The mechanism of action of organic nitrates is through the production of nitric oxide, a highly reactive free radical that is an important mediator in many physiological and pathophysioogical processes.

One action of nitric oxide is to stimulate collagen synthesis by wound fibroblasts, so it is proposed that nitric oxide may modulate tendon healing by stimulating fibroblasts to repair collagen. Thus, organic nitrates such as GTN may be viewed as prodrugs of endogenous nitric oxide, an endothelial cell-derived relaxing factor. Transdermal GTN patches are a simple way of applying and dosing nitric oxide.

Paoloni et al. provided level 2 evidence that use of nitric oxide donor (GTN patches applied locally 1.25 mg/day) was an effective treatment for non-insertional Achilles, supraspinatus and lateral elbow tendinopathy.[60–2] About 20% more patients prescribed the GTN patches were asymptomatic at six months than control group participants who received "best-practice" care (i.e. rehabilitation alone) (Fig. 13.5).

A recent RCT (level 2 evidence) included 40 subjects with non-insertional Achilles tendinopathy.[63] Both groups received standard physiotherapy treatment and one group incorporated the use of a daily GTN patch at a dose of 2.5 mg/24 h. This study found conflicting results to the Paoloni study in that at six months there was no significant difference in pain or disability scores between groups. Headaches occurred in 4 (20%) of subjects.

Another RCT (level 2 evidence) included 154 subjects with lateral epicondylosis, divided into four groups.[64] All four groups performed wrist extensor strengthening and stretching exercises. The groups included one control and three GTN patch groups of different pharmaceutical strengths (0.72 mg/24 h; 1.44 mg/24 h; 3.6 mg/24 h). This trial, in contrast to the previous RCT on lateral epicondylosis, did not demonstrate significant findings for the use of GTN

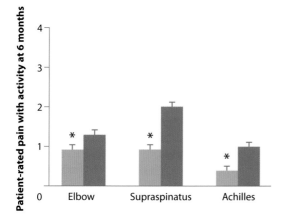

Glyceryl trinitrate (GTN) group   Placebo group

* indicates p<0.05 (i.e. statistically significant)

Figure 13.5 At six months GTN patches provided outcomes superior to those from the placebo patch for three different tendinopathies (elbow, shoulder, and Achilles)[60–62]

patches over traditional rehabilitation programs. Furthermore, headaches were linked to increased dosage.

A systematic review of three trials found some evidence that topical GTN is more effective than placebo for rotator cuff disease in the short term among patients with acute symptoms (<7 days duration).[65]

While GTN appears to offer short-term benefits up to six months in the treatment of lateral epicondylosis, at five years there does not appear to be significant clinical benefits when compared with patients undertaking a standard tendon rehabilitation program alone.[66] This is in contrast to findings of continued benefits at long-term follow-up described in the literature for patients with Achilles tendinopathy treated with GTN.[67] Thus, the long-term effectiveness of GTN requires further investigation.

Sclerosing therapy

Hakan Alfredson and his Swedish colleagues used sclerosant therapy to treat tendinopathy. With the use of ultrasound in conjunction with color Doppler (CD) and histological analysis, there was a relationship with vasculo-neural ingrowth around tendons and pain, which was not found in control subjects.[68] Injection of local anesthetic into these vasculo-neural structures has demonstrated instant short-term pain relief in Achilles tendinopathy, further strengthening

the hypothesis that these neuro-vascular structures are associated with pain in chronic tendinopathy.[68]

Furthermore, histological analysis has found sensory nerves and corresponding neuropeptides, substance P and calcitonin gene-related peptide, associated with these structures. Prostoglandin was not found, which would indicate that there was no inflammatory mediated response. As a result, it has been proposed that, by applying sclerosing techniques to these structures, the pain in chronic tendinopathy should resolve.

Polidocanol, a substance which has been in use for many years in the treatment of varicose veins, is considered a safe drug with minimal adverse effects.[69] Polidocanol has both a sclerosing effect and a local anesthetic effect. Its proposed mechanism in treating tendinopathy is still unclear, but it is thought to either destroy neovessels or have an effect on local nerves.[68] In the box (below) is a protocol, proposed by the Swedish group, for polidocanol injections used for sclerosing therapy for chronic pain tendinopathies.

Prolotherapy

Prolotherapy, an injection-based treatment of chronic musculoskeletal pain, has grown in popularity and has received significant recent attention.[70]

Prolotherapy (proliferative injection therapy) involves a series of injections, at the site of prolonged soft tissue injury, in order to stimulate a pro-inflammatory response. Prolotherapy is useful in the treatment of joint and ligament instabilities, where increased strength of connective tissue is required. Prolotherapy injections produce dense

---

Protocol for sclerosing therapy using polidocanol[67]

Procedure
Dose: 5 mg/ mL to 10mg/mL
0.1–0.2 mL of solution is injected into each neovessel/ nerve area outside of the tendon

Post injection
First 2 weeks: No strenuous activity; short walks and cycling allowed
After 2 weeks: Return to previous activity level
6 to 8 weeks: Gradual return to sport. Follow-up required and reassessment on ultrasound and color Doppler performed if pain and reduced function continues. Patients are given an option of re-injection with the same protocol as above if not satisfied with results at 6 to 8 weeks.

fibrous tissue to strengthen the attachments of ligaments, tendons, joint capsules, and other fascial structures.[70, 71] The action of prolotherapy is thus in contrast to anti-inflammatory interventions such as corticosteroid injections. Corticosteroid injections are thought to produce rapid short-term effects, whereas prolotherapy aims to produce significant long-term effects.

The choice of prolotherapy technique varies for different treating conditions, severities, and practitioner preference.[70] A small volume of an irritant solution is injected at multiple sites on painful ligament and tendon insertions, and in adjacent joint spaces. The most commonly used prolotherapy solutions are purported to act in different ways—dextrose 10% by osmotic rupture of cells, phenol-glycerine-glucose (P2G) by local cellular irritation, and sodium morrhuate by chemotactic attraction of inflammatory mediators. Adverse effects can involve bleeding and pain at the site of injection.

A number of case series and a few RCTs have reported benefits of prolotherapy in terms of pain and clinical outcomes. Clinical presentations that may benefit from prolotherapy include knee osteoarthritis, chronic low back pain, lateral epicondylosis, plantar fasciitis, hip adductor tendinopathy, Achilles tendinopathy, and sacroiliac joint dysfunction.[70–4] At this stage, prolotherapy seems to be better suited as an adjunct therapy, and can be more effective alongside a well-structured, specific exercise program to strengthen around the injured area.

Glucosamine sulfate and chondroitin sulfate

Glucosamine sulfate and chondroitin sulfate are compounds extracted from animal products that have been used in various forms for osteoarthritic symptoms in Europe for more than a decade. They are absorbed from the gastrointestinal tract and appear to be capable of increasing proteoglycan synthesis in articular cartilage. Whether or not they are effective, and in whom, remains controversial.

A meta-analysis showed that, compared with placebo, glucosamine, chondroitin, and their combination do not reduce joint pain or have an impact on narrowing of joint space.[75]

No study so far has found any serious adverse effects from either glucosamine or chondroitin. The most common adverse effects are increased intestinal gas and softened stools.

Hyaluronic acid therapy (Hyalgan, Synvisc, Ostenil, Orthovisc)

Hyaluronic acid is a polysaccharide member of the family of glycosaminoglycans. It is a naturally occurring substance in the body and is primarily found in synovial fluid and articular cartilage. It has a major role in joint homeostasis, by maintaining synovial fluid viscosity and by stimulating cell function activities in the extracellular matrix of cartilage.[76–8] In osteoarthritic joints, hyaluronic acid concentration levels and average molecular weight have been shown to be decreased. This decrease could account for the increase in joint susceptibly to cartilage injury and further deteriorative processes.[78] Figure 13.6 summarizes hyaluronic acid's mechanisms of action and its effects on osteoarthritis.

Hyaluronic acid is obtained either from animals (rooster combs), or humans, or is genetically engineered. It has been given as an intra-articular injection for patients with osteoarthritis of the knee. The usual course of treatment involves a series of 3–5 injections into the joint at weekly intervals.

The effectiveness of hyaluronic acid for knee osteoarthritis is comparable with NSAIDs and corticosteroid injections.[76, 79–83] The advantage of hyaluronic acid over corticosteroids is reduced systemic adverse effects. Hyaluronic acid demonstrates a favorable safety profile, with adverse effects largely related to the local injection itself (e.g. pain at injection site for up to 72 hours). Unlike corticosteroids (which can provide immediate short-term relief but can have questionable long-term outcomes), hyaluronic acid aims to elicit favorable long-term outcomes by restoring viscoelestacity to synovial fluid, encouraging normal hyaluronic acid synthesis, and reducing further joint deterioration. This in turn decreases pain and increases function of the affected joint.

In recent years, hyaluronic acid intra-articular injection therapy has gained popularity as a conservative measure for the treatment for knee osteoarthritis for pain relief and improved function.[78] The evidence base for hyaluronic acid injection therapy in other areas such as the hip, shoulder, ankle, and trapezio-metacarpal joint continues to build.[77, 84] Long-term results—greater than 5 years—for the use of hyaluronic acid for osteoarthritis are limited, and its effectiveness in treating osteoarthritis in joints other than the knee is not known. However, with its promising initial results, routine use of hyaluronic

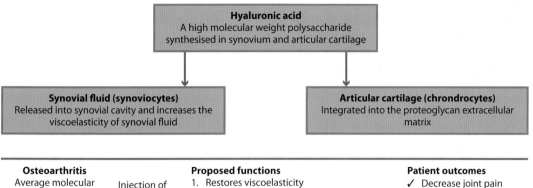

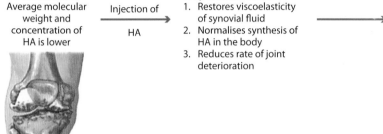

Figure 13.6 Hyaluronic acid: mechanism of function

FROM MEI-DAN ET AL.[77] AND MIGLIORE ET AL.[78]

acid injection therapy for traumatic cartilage injuries in sports medicine could become a possibility.

Antidepressants

Antidepressants, especially the tricyclics and the selective serotonin reuptake inhibitors (SSRIs), are widely used in the treatment of chronic pain. Originally, the therapeutic effect of these drugs was thought to be related to their antidepressant properties, but their analgesic efficacy at doses below those needed for a reduction of depression and their relatively rapid effect suggest another mechanism of action. They can also improve sleep, which can be a boon to patients with chronic pain.

Treatment should commence with a low (amitryptyline, 10 mg) bedtime dosage, which is titrated slowly upward depending on patient response. Adverse effects vary, and include excess daytime sedation, dry mouth, constipation, weight gain, and, in older patients, urinary retention. Antidepressants can be administered in conjunction with other analgesics and anti-inflammatory medications.

There is limited evidence for the use of tricyclic antidepressants in chronic musculoskeletal pain,[85] but more convincing evidence in fibromyalgia.[86-8]

Local anesthetic injections

Local anesthetic pain-killing injections are part of professional contact sports such as football. The aim of such injections is to lower the rate of players missing matches through injury. The most common injuries that are treated in this way are acromioclavicular joint sprains, finger and rib injuries, and iliac crest hematoma.

Clinicians expert in these injections recommend against intra-articular injections to the knee, ankle, wrist, joints of the foot, and to the pubic symphysis and major tendons of the lower limb. In one physician's six-year case series, local anesthetic was used for 268 injuries (about 10% of players each week).[89] These injections were associated with four major complications (chronic tendinopathies, bursal infection, worsening ligament tears, and osteolysis of the distal clavicle).

Local anesthetics are known to be myotoxic. Procaine is the least toxic, and bupivacaine (Marcain) the most. Changes can be seen within five minutes of injection, with typical appearances of hypercontracted myofibrils, followed by lytic degeneration of striated muscle sarcoplasmic reticulum, and myocyte edema and necrosis over the next 1-2 days.

Fortunately, the myoblasts and connective tissue are undamaged, meaning the muscle can regenerate in 3–4 weeks.[90, 91] Such basic science evidence seems to conflict with current clinical practice of injecting muscle injuries with local anesthetic. Practitioners should consider this and remain judicious with their use.

Local anesthetic injections are increasingly being performed under ultrasound control.[92] Players requesting injections should be made well aware of the possible complications. The joints affected by long-term injury sequelae of professional football (such as increased rates of osteoarthritis of the knee [in particular], hip, ankle, and lumbar spine) are not the joints associated with injuries for which local anesthetic is commonly used.

To enable the benefit and risk profile of local anesthetic injections to be better understood, it has been argued that professional football competitions make local anesthetics legal only with compulsory notification.

Traumeel

Traumeel is a preparation of traditional healing herbs containing arnica, belladonna, calendula, chamomile, millefolium, heparin, St John's wort, and echinacea. It is not diluted to the extent of most homeopathic preparations, meaning a certain concentration of the original substances remains.

According to the manufacturers, the mechanism of action of Traumeel appears to be the result of modulation of the release of oxygen radicals from activated neutrophils, and inhibition of the release of inflammatory mediators (possibly interleukin-1 from activated macrophages) and neuropepetides.

In an *in vitro* study,[93] Traumeel inhibited secretion of pro-inflammatory cytokines IL-1β, TNF-α, IL-8 from T-cells and monocytes without toxic adverse effects. There are few RCTs using Traumeel. In one study among Chilean elite athletes,[94] Traumeel was compared with diclofenac in the management of tendon pain. A three-armed RCT compared Traumeel (n=89) v Diclofenac (n=87) v Placebo (n=76). Mean pain reductions (VAS) were 5.2, 3.6 and 1.4 respectively (p<0.001). Return to play (days) was 20.3, 24.6 and 30.6 (p<0.001). Further studies will be required to reproduce these findings in other conditions.

Bisphosphonates

Bisphosphonates are used mainly in the management of postmenopausal osteoporosis to prevent fragility fractures; however, recently there has been considerable interest in their use to prevent or accelerate healing of stress fractures and fractures. Pamidronate, zoledronate, and ibandronic acid have been used for this purpose.

Bone is constantly remodeling to adapt to load, under the control of osteocytes, osteoblasts, and specialised phagocytic cells called osteoclasts. Bisphosphonates are toxic to osteoclasts and thus have a net anabolic action.[95]

Before treatment with these drugs, it is necessary to measure renal function, and serum calcium and phosphate, as there is a risk of potentiation of hypocalcemia and hypophosphatemia. Patients should also be warned of flu-like symptoms (amenable to paracetamol). Bisphosponates are contraindicated in women of childbearing age, given evidence of teratogenicity in animal studies,[96] and long-term use has been associated with atypical stress fractures of the femur in older people.[97]

Stress fracture prevention was examined in an RCT of 324 Israeli infantry recruits, and found to be ineffective.[98] In a case series of five female college athletes with stress fractures, four were able to return to play within one week of treatment with intravenous pamidronate, presumably due to the bone analgesic effects of bisphosphonates.[99] At this point in time, endocrinologists would generally advise against using this medication for management of stress fractures. Its use in sports medicine remains "off label" and experimental.

Blood and blood products
with ROBERT JAN DE VOS

Autologous blood injections
Human blood contains many growth factors, in particular platelet-rich growth factor which may have a positive effect on healing of bone, tendon, or muscle injuries. In autologous blood injections (ABI), blood is drawn from an arm vein and injected directly into the injured part, usually under ultrasound guidance. The amount of blood injected depends on the size of the tendon.

This procedure has been used mainly in tendinopathies. Two studies have shown an improvement in lateral epicondylitis of the elbow ("tennis elbow," extensor tendinopathy).[100, 101]

Platelet-rich plasma
Platelet-rich plasma (PRP) is the product derived when autologous whole blood is centrifuged to

separate a preparation with a very high platelet and plasma content. The preparation is rich in both plasmatic and platelet α-granule derived growth factors, as well as many thousands of other substances.[102]

A PRP injection is similar to an autologous blood injection, with the only difference being that a larger amount of blood is withdrawn from an arm vein. The blood is then placed into a tube, which in turn is placed into a centrifuge, which spins many thousand times a minute, for various lengths of time depending on the protocol. At this point, the cells in the blood have separated from the fluid component of blood (plasma) into the three main cell types—red blood cells, white blood cells, and platelets. The platelets are then selectively removed and used for injection. In this way, the theoretical benefit is that a greater concentration of platelets is delivered into the damaged body part than if whole blood was given alone (approximately 2–10 times greater concentration).

Many different versions of PRP are described depending on the duration, force, and number of spins. The plasma can be manipulated to have a moderate (2–3 times baseline whole blood) or high (6–8 times) yield of platelets, and can also be leukocyte-rich or -depleted. Few trials have examined the relative merits of different preparations, and nor is there a universally agreed nomenclature.[102]

Laboratory results suggested that the application of PRP can increase tendon collagen synthesis and vascularity, and that it may be a good treatment option for tendon injuries.[103]

There have been several case reports and cohorts in humans examining the efficacy of PRP treatment. In a retrospective comparison, Sanchez et al.[104] reported faster healing of ruptured Achilles tendons compared to matched cases. However, there is one small RCT that showed no benefit of local PRP application at short-term and one-year follow-up in patients with a ruptured Achilles tendon.[105] Two studies described a series of patients with patella tendinopathy treated with PRP.[106, 107] There was statistically significant improvement in pain scores at six months, but no difference in pain score compared to exercise therapy.

There is one positive cohort study in Achilles,[108] one case series in arthroscopic rotator cuff repair[109] and one case series in ACL reconstruction.

Two studies showed positive results in elbow tendinopathy.[110, 111] One small comparative study[110] showed short-term benefit compared to local anesthesia injections, and one good quality RCT[111] reported

excellent results after a PRP injection, but the control group received corticosteroid injections—these are detrimental to the long-term outcome of elbow tendinopathy.[3]

Only one RCT of high methodological quality has been published. De Vos et al.[2] performed a prospective, double-blind RCT in a single center, comparing 27 patients with Achilles tendinopathy in each group with either a single PRP injection or a placebo saline injection. Both groups also performed eccentric loading exercises. There was no difference in outcomes between groups.

In conclusion, there remain many unanswered questions in this field regarding a possible optimum usage of PRP, and large scale RCTs need to be performed before their clinical efficacy can be established (Chapter 3).[2]

Heat and cold
Cryotherapy

Cryotherapy is the application of ice for therapeutic purposes. It is one of the most common treatment modalities used in the initial management of acute musculoskeletal injuries.[6] In an acute inflammatory presentation, cryotherapy aims to decrease edema through vasoconstriction, and reduce secondary hypoxic injury by lowering the metabolic demand of injured tissues.[6, 8] Localized analgesia is thought to occur when the skin temperature drops below 15°C, because of decreasing nerve conduction velocity.[7, 9, 112] In subacute presentations, ice application is thought to bring about similar analgesic effects, allowing earlier return to sport. The different methods of using cryotherapy are outlined in Table 13.5 overleaf.

A combination of ice and exercise has previously shown to be more effective than ice alone for acute ankle sprain injuries.[6] Cryotherapy could have detrimental effects on performance because of a reduction in the conduction velocity of other, non-nociceptive fibers. This can lead to reduced muscle torque, which could alter movement patterns and increase the risk of injury.[7] However, evidence has shown that cryotherapy does not negatively affect joint position sense.[7]

Ice massage, as described for medial tibial stress syndrome, may be performed using ice in a polystyrene cup.[113] Ice is massaged into the painful area using overlapping circular or longitudinal strokes. The massage usually continues until the skin is numb to fine touch. This is thought to be a period of 7–10 minutes.[113] This is often repeated several times a day.

Table 13.5 Superficial cold modalities used for treating sports-related injuries

Modality	Description	Special concerns	Temperature	Duration	Exercise during application	Expense
Reusable cold packs	Durable plastic packs containing silica gel that are available in many sizes and shapes	Apply a towel between the bag and skin to avoid nerve damage or frostbite	≤15°C (59°F)	20–30 min	No	Inexpensive
Endothermal cold packs	Packets are squeezed or crushed to activate: convenient for emergency use	Single use only	20°C (68°F)	15–20 min	No	Expensive
Crushed ice bags	Crushed ice molds easily to body parts	Apply a towel between the bag and skin to avoid nerve damage or frostbite	0°C (32°F)	5–15 min	No	Inexpensive
Vapocoolant sprays	Easily portable therapy for regional myofascial pain syndrome, acute injuries, pain relief, and in rehabilitation with spray and stretch techniques	Intermittently spray the area for <6 sec to avoid frostbite	Varies depending on duration of treatment	Multiple brief sprays	Spray <6 sec and stretch to increase range of motion	Expensive
Ice water immersion	Whenever uniform cold application to an extremity is desired	Carries the most risk of hypersensitivity reactions; restrict amount of extremity immersion	0°C (32°F)	5–10 min	Allows motion of the extremity during treatment	Inexpensive
Ice massage	Used to produce analgesia: freeze water in a foam cup, then peel back cup to expose the ice; massage area as often as needed	Apply for short intervals to avoid frostbite; avoid excess pressure	0°C (32°F)	5–10 min	Can allow supervised, gentle, stretching during analgesia	Inexpensive
Refrigerant inflatable bladders	When cold and compression are needed	Avoid excess compression	10–25°C (50–77°F)	Depends on temperature	No	Expensive
Thermal cooling blankets	To provide constant temperature, such as after surgery	Scrutinize temperature settings	10–25°C (50–77°F)	Depends on temperature	No	Expensive
Contrast baths	Transition treatment between cold and heat for a subacute injury, sympathetic mediated pain, stiff joints	Do not use in acute setting due to potential to increase blood flow	Hot bath 40.5°C (105°F) Cold bath 15.5°C (60°F)	4 min hot, 1 min cold	Allows motion of the extremity during treatment	Inexpensive

Superficial heat

Appropriate warm-up (Chapter 9) and superficial heat may contribute to improved treatment of soft tissue injuries. Stimulated warm muscles absorb more energy than do unstimulated muscles.[8] The indications, contraindications and adverse effects of superficial heat therapy are shown in Table 13.6. Heat should not be applied in the first 24 hours following an acute injury.

Heat can be applied in a number of different ways

Table 13.6 Features of electrotherapeutic and thermal modalities

Modality	Effects	Clinical indications	Contraindications	Danger
Cryotherapy (ice)	Decreases pain Decreases swelling/ bleeding (vasoconstriction) Decreases cellular metabolism	Muscle spasm Trigger point pain Acute swelling/edema Inflammation Heat illness Contusion (e.g. cork thigh) Acute injuries Pre- and post-massage	Cold hypersensitivity Raynaud's phenomenon Circulatory insufficiency	Ice burns Anesthesia (masks pain) Increased edema after prolonged use Superficial nerve damage
Superficial heat	Pain relief Increases local blood flow	Pain Muscle spasm Cervical pain Chronic pain and swelling	Sensory changes Circulatory problems Heat injury Hypersensitivity or hyposensitivity to heat	Increased bleeding and swelling (if used in first 48 hours after acute injury) Burns
Ultrasound	*Thermal* Increases local blood flow Increases cellular metabolism Increases extensibility of connective tissue Decreases pain	Muscle spasm Contusion Localized inflammation and pain (e.g. ligament sprains, muscle strains)	Pregnancy Acute phase of injury Deep venous thrombosis Acute infection Pacemaker Should not be used over open epiphyses, broken skin, major nerves, cranium, fractures, eyes, gonads, malignancies or post-radiotherapy areas Myositis ossificans (early stages)	Burns Tissue damage
Ultrasound	*Non-thermal* Micro massage Increases cell permeability Decreases pain	Acute injuries	Malignancy Open epiphyses Pacemaker	Tissue damage
TENS	*High frequency* Pain relief (immediate and short term) Muscle stimulation	Decreases acute pain and muscle spasm	Over carotid sinus Cardiac pacemaker Sensory deficit Bleeding disorders Epilepsy Over malignant sites	Removal of protective influence of pain

continues

Table 13.6 Features of electrotherapeutic and thermal modalities *(continued)*

Modality	Effects	Clinical indications	Contraindications	Danger
TENS *continued*	*Low frequency* Latent pain relief	Muscle re-education Trigger points Acupuncture points Muscle spasm Chronic pain		
Interferential stimulation	Pain relief Decreases edema and swelling Muscle stimulation Increases cellular activity	Acute soft tissue injuries Swelling/edema Muscle spasm Pain, especially deep (e.g. acute knee, ankle, shoulder injuries)	Use over carotid sinus Cardiac pacemaker Sensory deficit Arterial disease Deep venous thrombosis Pregnancy Local infection Malignant tumor	Electrical burns may occur (due to increased skin resistance)
High-voltage galvanic stimulation	Pain relief Decreases swelling/edema Decreases inflammation Muscle stimulation	Pain Muscle spasm Swelling/edema Muscle inhibition Inflammation (e.g. tendinopathy) Post-operative muscle disuse atrophy	Sensory deficit Increased skin resistance Broken skin As for TENS	
Laser	Pain relief Decreases muscle spasm Increases cell regeneration Decreases inflammation	Localized, superficial pain and inflammation Trigger points Superficial ligaments and tendon injuries Superficial wound healing Directly over the eye	Pregnancy Patients receiving photosensitive medication Malignancies Infants	Retinal damage with prolonged exposure Gastrointestinal symptoms with treatment of chronic pain
Magnetic field therapy	Decreases swelling and edema Decreases inflammation	Acute soft tissue injury Edema (e.g. acute joint sprain, contusion)	Pregnancy Tuberculosis	

including warm showers and baths, warm whirlpools, and heat packs. These are summarized in Table 13.7. Heat packs are canvas bags filled with hydrophilic silicone gel stored in hot water and wrapped in towels. They are then applied for 15 minutes.

Contrast therapy

Contrast baths (referred to in the literature as contrast therapy) are commonly used as a treatment modality to address swelling/edema. They are also used for recovery purposes. Contrast baths consist of cold (cryotherapy) and heat applied either to an injured body part or through body immersion, and this repeated in an alternating fashion. Contrast baths have previously shown effects through change of blood flow, reduced local inflammation, local vasoconstriction and vasodilation, reduced edema, reduced pain and muscle stiffness.[114] However, the exact physiological process that results in these effects is not well understood.

A recent systematic review[114] aimed to assess the effectiveness of contrast therapy. This review identified 12 RCTs, all of small sample size. All studies differed in their application and protocol for contrast

Table 13.7 Heat modalities

Modality	Description	Special concerns	Temperature	Duration	Exercise during application
Heat packs	Vigorous heating for superficial injuries; mild effects reduce muscle spasm in deeper tissues	Layers of towel must be placed between hot pack and skin to avoid burns Severely impaired skin sensation Avoid open wounds Avoid in acute presentations	149°F (65°C)	5 min, then check for mottled erythema	No
Fluidotherapy	Vigorous heating, ideal for hand or foot; allows high temperature without discomfort	Systemic infectious diseases (treatment may increase core body temperature and thus contribute to a fever) Malignancies Avoid open wounds Severely impaired skin sensation	35–45°C (95–113°F)	10–30 min	Yes
Hydrotherapy	Whirlpool tanks combine thermal, pressure, and buoyancy effects of water	Care with "fear of water" patients Ensure adequate hydration levels prior to hydrotherapy Open wounds require waterproof dressing	35.5–40.5°C (95.9–104.9°F)	10–20 min	Gravity-free exercise
Radiant heat	Heat from infra-red lamp; no discomfort of weight, good for treating large areas	Protect eyes if used for facial applications	Depends on intensity, distance from source	Up to 20 min	No

therapy. Alternating heat and cold temperatures ranged from 38°C to 42°C for heat and 8°C to 15°C for cold; duration of therapy ranged from 6 to 31 minutes; hot–cold time ratios ranged from 2:1 to 10:1. Across the 12 RCTs, there was some evidence that contrast therapy could reduce creatine kinase (CK) levels and blood lactate concentration, thereby showing some evidence that this therapy can aid in muscle recovery. There was no consensus on whether hot or cold should be initiated or finished with.

Creatine kinase has shown to be produced in response to skeletal muscle damage after strenuous exercise[115] and an increase in blood lactate concentrate has shown to relate to exercise threshold.[116]

A standard protocol for contrast therapy for an injured part could be hot bath immersion for 4 minutes, followed by a cold bath with ice and water for 1–2 minutes. This could be repeated three to seven times. A cold bath should be used to finish to encourage vasoconstriction.

Electrotherapy

A large number of different electrotherapeutic modalities are available for the treatment of sporting injuries. Their use varies widely between therapists and is based on clinical experience, rather than scientific evidence. Although electrotherapeutic modalities are claimed to decrease inflammation and promote healing, there is only limited evidence as yet to support many of these claims. In any case, such modalities should not be relied on as the sole form of treatment. A summary of the different electro-therapeutic modalities, their clinical indications, contraindications, and adverse effects is shown in Table 13.6.

Ultrasound
with NICK GARDINER

Ultrasound is one of the most frequent electrother-apy modalities used by physiotherapists today.[117–19] Therapeutic ultrasound aims to produce an effect on the body's tissues, as opposed to diagnostic ultrasound, which is used for imaging purposes. Ultrasound is commonly used for localized superficial conditions such as muscle strains, tendinopathies, and bursitis, and for treatment of scar tissue.[117, 120] Ultrasound can produce both thermal and non-thermal effects.[121] The effects, clinical indications, contraindications, and adverse effects of ultrasound therapy are shown in Table 13.6.

Ultrasound can be used over a wide range of intensities, frequencies and treatment times. Dosage parameters vary among ultrasound studies, and this can partly explain the conflicting evidence for its use. Dosage parameters are important to address in ultrasound studies, as a substantial variation in one factor, such as intensity (which can range from 0.1 to 3.0 w/cm²), can affect the ultrasound machine's output and hence its overall therapeutic effect.

Ultrasound has a pro-inflammatory effect—by stimulating mast cells, platelets, and white blood cells.[122] This could explain why studies assessing the anti-inflammatory effects of ultrasound have found no effects.[119] One review reports that ultrasound has been shown to have an enhancing effect for inflam-matory, proliferative, and remodeling stages of tissue healing.[119] During the proliferative phase (scar pro-duction), ultrasound has a stimulatory effect on fibroblasts, endothelial cells, and myofibroblasts.[119] During the remodeling phase, ultrasound aids col-lagen orientation, which may improve the tensile strength of scar tissue.[119]

Ultrasound may have more effect on dense colla-genous tissues (such as ligament and tendons). The higher the protein content in a tissue, the higher the ultrasound absorption (Fig. 13.7). Cartilage and bone can reflect normal ultrasound and therefore ultra-sound is contraindicated directly over these struc-tures.[119] Studies focusing on muscle contusions and DOMS have shown no effect.[119, 122]

As with any electrotherapy modality, ultrasound is rarely used alone and is often used as an adjunct treatment for a variety of musculoskeletal condi-tions.[117, 121]

One study has shown that, out of 33 ultrasound machines that were used in physiotherapy practices, only 32.3% were correctly calibrated.[118] Additionally, two (6%) did not work at all. Use of uncalibrated equipment may cause harmful adverse effects.

Phonophoresis
Phonophoresis is the use of ultrasound therapy in com-bination with a pharmacological coupling medium, usually either an analgesic or anti-inflammatory medi-cation. Phonophoresis facilitates transdermal drug delivery such as hydrocortisone, salicylic acid, and

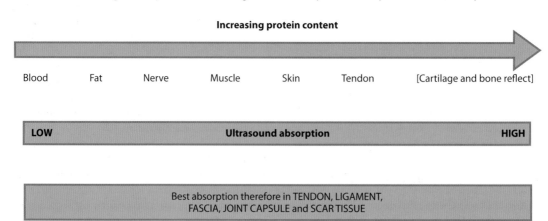

Figure 13.7 Ultrasound absorption characteristics
FROM WATSON[119]

lignocaine (lidocaine) and is used for pain management, soft tissue swelling, and soft tissue inflammation.[120, 121] The clinical effect of this method of treatment is unknown.

LIPUS (low-intensity pulsed ultrasound machine)

High-intensity ultrasound and conventional physiotherapy ultrasound machines have been shown to have detrimental effects on bony healing.[123] Low-intensity (<0.1 W/cm²) pulsed ultrasound (LIPUS) (Fig. 13.8) has been used successfully in the treatment of acute fractures, as well as those that show delayed or non-union.[123–25] The mechanism of action of LIPUS is not through its thermal effects, but through its influences on the cell membrane and cellular activity.[123]

LIPUS is performed using a stationary treatment head over the fracture site. The low intensity of the treatment means there is no risk of tissue damage. LIPUS is introduced daily for 20 minutes, in contrast to traditional ultrasound practice, which is usually for no more than 5 minutes, no more than three times a week.

A recent review on LIPUS reports that LIPUS at 1.5 mHz, pulsed at 1 kHz with 30 mW/cm² applied for 20 minutes per day can accelerate bony healing in tibial, radial, and scaphoid fractures by up to 40%.[123] *In vivo* and *in vitro* laboratory studies have shown LIPUS has positive effects on all stages of bony healing (inflammatory, soft callus, hard callus formation) by enhancing the bone mineralisation process (ultrasound stimulates osteocalcin, alkaline phosphatase, VEGF, and MMP-13).[123]

LIPUS stimulates specific mechanoreceptors (integrins), present on various cell types which are associated with fracture healing.[123] Integrin activation

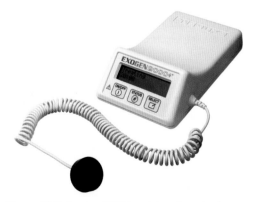

Figure 13.8 Exogen 2000 low-intensity pulsed ultrasound machine

stimulates various enzyme pathways which are directly related to COX-2 and prostaglandin release.[123] COX-2 and prostaglandin are essential components for bone mineralization and endochondral ossification associated with fracture healing.[123] Evidence is emerging that LIPUS can accelerate healing of an acute fracture, minimize delayed healing, and stimulate healing processes in non-union presentations.[123]

TENS (Transcutaneous electrical nerve stimulation)

Transcutaneous electrical nerve stimulation (TENS) is a non-invasive, analgesic electrotherapeutic modality. It is used to relieve nociceptive, neuropathic, and musculoskeletal pain.[126–8] Pulsed electrical currents are produced by a portable, battery-operated generator and applied across intact surfaces of the skin via conducting pads. Conducting pads can be self-adhesive carbon rubber or gel electrodes.[129] Mild electrical burns and minor skin irritations are rare but can occur with its use.[126]

Jones et al. 2009[126] describe three types of TENS (Table 13.8 overleaf).

High-frequency currents generated by a portable stimulating unit are administered via conducting pads (electrodes) placed on the intact surface of the skin. Research into the effectiveness of TENS treatment in patients with both acute (mainly postoperative) pain and chronic pain has produced conflicting results.[127] Some patients obtain good pain relief, some respond initially but then become tolerant, and others fail to respond at all.

Two recent Cochrane systematic reviews have focused on the effectiveness of TENS for chronic pain.[127, 128, 130] "Chronic" was defined as pain lasting greater than three months. The first review identified four RCTs evaluating TENS for chronic low back pain and found conflicting results for its use.[130] With small sample sizes and varying TENS dosage parameters, TENS effectiveness was inconclusive. Chronic pain presentations in the second review included myofascial, knee osteoarthritic, rheumatological wrist, and temporomandibular joint pain.[128] This review found some support for the analgesic properties of TENS but concluded further research into its use was needed. Both reviews suggested that TENS could be best used as an adjunct therapy.

Acupuncture-like TENS (AL-TENS) describes high-intensity low-frequency currents passed across the surface of the skin to elicit strong but comfortable phasic muscle contractions at sites myotomally

Table 13.8 TENS techniques

	Physiological intention	Clinical technique
Conventional TENS	Selective activation of large-diameter non-noxious afferents to elicit segmental analgesia	Low-intensity/high-frequency TENS at site of pain to produce "strong but comfortable TENS paraesthesiae." Administer whenever in pain
Acupuncture-like TENS	Activation of small-diameter (motor) afferents to elicit extrasegmental analgesia	High-intensity/low-frequency TENS over muscles, acupuncture points, or trigger points to produce "strong but comfortable muscle contractions." Administer for 15–30 minutes at a time
Intense TENS	Activation of small-diameter afferents to elicit peripheral nerve blockade and extrasegmental analgesia	High-intensity/high-frequency TENS over nerves arising from painful site to produce "maximum tolerable (painful) TENS paresthesia." Administer for a few minutes at a time

ADAPTED FROM JONES ET AL.[126]

related to the origin of the pain.[131] AL-TENS appears to be mediated through the release of endorphins within the central nervous system. This form of TENS is often used to stimulate trigger points or acupuncture points. The indications and contraindications for TENS are shown in Table 13.6.

Interferential stimulation

Interferential stimulation is a form of TENS in which two alternating medium-frequency currents are simultaneously applied to the skin. The two sinusoidal currents become superimposed on each other, where they intersect and cause wave interference, which in turn results in a modulated frequency equal to the difference in frequency of the two original waves (beat frequency).

Interferential therapy stimulates muscle in a similar manner to normal voluntary muscle contraction. It has an effect on pain similar to conventional TENS and has varying effects on circulation depending on the frequency used. Vasodilation occurs at frequencies of 90–100 Hz, whereas at low frequencies of 0–10 Hz, muscle stimulation occurs to assist removal of fluid in venous and lymph channels. The clinical indications and contraindications for interferential stimulation are shown in Table 13.6.

High-voltage galvanic stimulation

High-voltage galvanic stimulation (HVGS) is also a form of TENS and has two distinct specifications. It transmits voltage greater than 100 V and it has a twin-peaked monophasic current with a high peak but low average current.

The treatment is not actually galvanic but is called galvanic due to its monophasic current. The low average current density results in minimal charge build-up on the electrodes, thus minimizing the possibility of chemical burns. There are two methods of HVGS application. Pads or a probe are used over muscles requiring stimulation or local painful sites.

The clinical indications and contraindications for HVGS are shown in Table 13.6.

Low-voltage galvanic stimulation

Low-voltage stimulators were the earliest forms of electrical stimulation used for pain relief. They stimulate innervated or denervated muscles and can also be used as a medium for iontophoresis.

There are three types of currents—faradic (now rarely used), sinusoidal, and galvanic (direct). Wave forms can deliver high average currents to produce chemical and thermal responses. However, this modality is more likely to cause thermal and chemical burns.

Neuromuscular stimulators

Neuromuscular electrical stimulators (NMES) are primarily used to maintain strength and flexibility, minimize atrophy during the healing process, and re-educate weak or poorly controlled muscles. They are similar to conventional TENS units and the units are interchangeable. The difference lies in the fact that the NMES have an interruption (on–off) mode in the current to allow the muscle to contract for a set period of time and then relax. This prevents fatigue and maximizes strengthening. NMES is used to improve muscle control in situations where active control is reduced (e.g. vastus medialis obliquus, and scapular retraction muscles).

Point stimulators

Point stimulators or hyperstimulation analgesia are a form of electroacutherapy, similar to acupuncture except that the points are stimulated with electrical current instead of needles. Small electrodes deliver current to a well-defined focal region which is perceived by the patient as a stinging sensation. It is thought that pain may be modulated when noxious stimuli cause descending tract inhibition.

Laser

Low-level laser therapy (LLLT) is a non-invasive, safe modality used for the treatment of musculoskeletal pain. LLLT has been shown to improve a range of outcomes in neck pain, tendinopathies (elbow and Achilles), and chronic joint disorders such as knee osteoarthritis.[132-5] The clinical indications and contraindications of laser are shown in Table 13.6.

There are two methods of application of LLLT: point treatment and scanning techniques for larger areas. Outputs which vary from 1 to 500 mW for continuous applications and wavelengths which vary from 400 nm within visible red light to 1064 nm within the infrared spectrum must be considered for appropriate treatment dosages. The effects of LLLT are dosage-dependent and, as such, the World Association of Laser Therapy (WALT) has developed guidelines for systematic reviews to ensure consistent reporting of treatment parameters.[136]

Recent systematic reviews have highlighted that the effectiveness of LLLT is dosage-dependent.[132-5] Local steroid injections negate the anti-inflammatory and cell stimulatory effects of LLLT and, as such, LLLT may not be as effective following steroid injection.[137]

LLLT has shown to modulate the inflammatory process by inhibiting the release of prostaglandins, reducing tumor necrosis factor alpha (TNFα), interleukin (IL1), and COX-2 levels.[133] Unlike anti-inflammatory drugs, which can have a negative effect on the proliferative and remodeling stages of healing, LLLT has the ability to improve repair with a stimulatory effect on collagen through fibroblast and collagen fiber production.[133, 138] Anti-inflammatory effects have been demonstrated for high LLLT doses (7.5 J/cm², in the first 72 hours post injury), whereas stimulatory effects to promote healing have been demonstrated at lower doses (2 J/cm²).[133, 138]

Research evidence continues to emerge for LLLT. One recent trial demonstrated that LLLT, applied before high-intensity exercise in professional athletes, can decrease muscle damage by reducing creatine kinase blood levels and increasing lactate removal.[139] Another trial coupled LLLT with eccentric exercises in the treatment of chronic Achilles tendinopathy in recreational sportspeople.[140] This trial found a significant improvement in pain levels, morning stiffness, and ankle range of motion compared to eccentric exercises with sham LLLT.

Diathermy

Microwave and short-wave diathermies use high-frequency electromagnetic waves to create heat in superficial muscles.

These electromagnetic waves are strongly reflected from metal surfaces, which can cause metal to overheat. Therefore, for safety reasons, diathermy should be applied on a wooden plinth or stool; it is also contraindicated over metal implants, cardiac pacemakers, and hearing aids. As with other forms of electrotherapy, microwave and short-wave diathermies are contraindicated for malignancy, pregnancy, and epilepsy.

Preliminary findings from a recent clinical trial have demonstrated that pulsed short-wave diathermy (PSWD) can increase blood flow, and skin temperature in healthy subjects.[141] An increase in vascular circulation and tissue temperature can lead to increased nutrition and oxygen at the injured area, with associated increase in removal of metabolic waste. These effects could explain the reduction in pain and swelling following application of PSWD. Additionally, a recent RCT has found significant reductions in synovial sac thickness, via ultrasound assessment, in osteoarthritic knees with correlated to significant reductions in knee pain.[142]

Magnetic therapy

Magnetic therapy is a widely used treatment, particularly in those with chronic pain. There are two ways in which magnetic therapy is delivered—pulsed electromagnetic fields (PEMF), using an alternating current through a coil applicator, and static magnetic fields (SMF). Magnetic therapy, both PEMF and SMF, is used for a variety of clinical presentations including neuropathies, inflammatory conditions, mechanical musculoskeletal pain, fibromyalgic pain, rheumatic pain, and post-surgical pain, and for wound healing purposes.[143, 144]

A variety of SMF products are available. These include magnetic bracelets and jewelry; magnetic braces and straps for wrists, ankles, knees, and lumbar area; shoe insoles; mattresses; and magnetic blankets.[145, 146] All methods of application are considered safe and non-invasive. Adverse effects are rare, although redness of the skin at the site of application can occur.[146]

Research into the mechanisms of action of magnetic therapy is limited and inconsistent.[147] Two main theories have been proposed. The first theory is that magnetic therapy can cause vasodilation and a general increase in blood flow at the injury site.[146] It is assumed that increased blood flow will lead to increased oxygen delivery to tissues, which in turn will provide analgesia and accelerate tissue healing.[145]

The second theory suggests that magnetic therapy may reduce pain by changing cell membrane potentials, thereby reducing the outputs of nociceptors.[146] Systematic reviews into the effectiveness of PEMF and SMF continue to be conflicting and inconclusive.[143, 144, 146, 148, 149] The clinical indications and contraindications of magnetic field therapy are shown in Table 13.6.

Studies investigating the use of static magnets to minimize DOMS have found no differences in pain, range of movement, or muscle force production compared to controls in healthy subjects.[145, 150] In the clinical presentation of subacromial shoulder impingement, one RCT has found no difference between PEMF compared with controls.[151] However, in this trial both groups received a generic exercise program and both significantly improved from baseline, which could negate the measurable effects of PEMF.

Another RCT assessed the effects of PEMF on patient outcomes after arthroscopic surgery, specifically on the articular cartilage of the knee.[152] PEMF was applied at 1.5 mT for 6 hours per day for the first 90 days post surgery. This trial found a significant decrease in NSAID usage and a significantly better subjective functional outcome at 3-year follow-up compared with control. Further studies focusing on magnetic therapy in terms of effects on articular cartilage are warranted.

Extracorporeal shock wave therapy

Extracorporeal shock wave therapy (ESWT) has become a promising treatment for a variety of tendinopathies where conservative measures have failed.[153–5] ESWT has been used in studies of tendinopathy at the shoulder, Achilles, and elbow as well as in plantar fascia and shin pain.[154, 156, 157]

Extracorporeal shock wave therapy is a non-invasive, safe technique[155] (Fig. 13.9). Although rare, reported adverse effects include transient pain, reddening of the skin, nausea, and neurological symptoms such

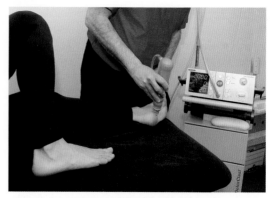

Figure 13.9 Extracorporeal shock wave therapy machine

as tingling and numbness.[158, 159] Contraindications to ESWT include application over open growth plates, implanted metal, malignancies, and pregnancy.

There are two main types of ESWT; high- and low-level energy. High-energy ESWT is painful and is used in conjunction with local anesthetic. It is often applied in a single dose with energy levels greater than 0.6 mJ/m².[155] Low-energy ESWT uses energy levels of less than 0.08 mJ/m² and requires multiple treatments over a period of time.[155] The use of local anesthetic is variable with low-energy applications.

The mechanism of action of ESWT is still unclear. One theory is that the repeated "shock wave" results in local microtrauma, creating neovascularization.[153, 155] As a result, the new blood vessels promote tissue healing. Another theory is that the stimulation of an acute inflammatory response in a chronic inflammatory environment can promote healing.[160] As a new inflammatory reaction is considered beneficial after ESWT, anti-inflammatory medications should not be used after treatment.

ESWT is a dose-dependent modality.[153, 155, 157–9] Therefore, as with all electrotherapy modalities, inconsistent results in the literature can be partly explained by variations in treatment parameters. To date, studies have been variable in use of local anesthetics, energy levels, number and frequency of treatments, as well as method of application and localization (ultrasound-guided versus clinician-guided). Further exploration of optimal ESWT settings, timing of treatment, number of sessions, and follow-up treatments is needed.

Manual therapy

Manual (manipulative) therapy is a "hands on" physical intervention which encompasses a variety of treatment techniques. It focuses on reducing pain, increasing range of motion, and improving relaxation of soft tissue and joint structures. Manual therapy may also hasten tissue healing, increase tissue extensibility, facilitate movement and improve overall physical function. There are a variety of specific manual therapy techniques including:

- massage
- soft tissue mobilization
- connective tissue techniques
- myofascial release
- cranial sacral techniques
- joint mobilizations and manipulations
- visceral mobilizations
- muscle energy techniques.

The discipline of manual therapy relies on careful clinical assessment and particular attention to identifying abnormalities of tissue texture, tenderness, pain, and restricted movement. Manual therapy is used to correct these abnormalities. Each abnormality detected in the clinical assessment must be considered as a possible contributor to the patient's symptoms and signs.

Attention is focused on tissue texture, tenderness, pain, and restricted movement. Reassessment should always be performed after a manual therapy technique. Reassessment allows the clinician to evaluate the effectiveness of a treatment and assess whether it promotes a desired effect. It is essential that each technique is explained to and agreed by the patient, to encourage relaxation and thereby achieve maximum benefit from the treatment.

Manual therapy can be applied to joints, muscles (including tendons and fascia), and neural structures. This section focuses on some different types of manual therapy used in the treatment of abnormalities of each of these structures as shown below:

1. joints:
    - mobilization
    - manipulation
    - traction
2. muscles:
    - soft tissue therapy
    - muscle energy techniques
3. neural structures:
    - neural stretching.

Joint mobilization

Mobilization is a passive movement technique applied to a spinal or peripheral joint in which an

oscillatory movement is performed within the control of the patient, who can prevent the movement if desired (Fig. 13.10).

Mobilization aims to restore full range of motion to a joint that is noted to be stiff and/or painful on clinical examination. Reduced range of motion (stiffness) may result from restriction of either physiological movements of the joint or accessory movements of the joint.

Physiological joint movements are those that can be performed actively by the patient. For example, physiological movements at the shoulder are flexion/extension, abduction/adduction, and internal/external rotation.

Accessory movements cannot be performed voluntarily by the patient. Although the range of movement is small, a full range of accessory movements is essential for normal active and passive joint movements. The clinician can detect loss of an accessory movement by observing or palpating restriction in normal joint range of motion. Accessory movements in the shoulder include posteroanterior and anteroposterior movement, longitudinal movements (both superiorly and inferiorly), and lateral movement.

Mobilization is commonly performed at the vertebral joints. The exact physiological mechanism

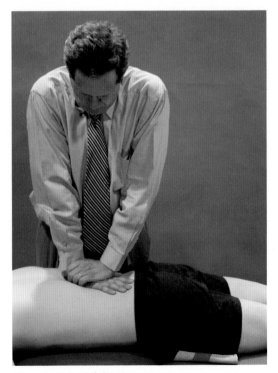

Figure 13.10 Mobilization

by which mobilization exerts a beneficial effect on these joints is uncertain but may include:

- an effect on the hydrostatics of the intervertebral disk and intervertebral bodies
- activation of type I and II mechanoreceptors in the capsule of the apophyseal joint
- alteration of the activity of the neuromuscular spindle in the intrinsic muscles
- assistance in the pumping effect on the venous plexus of the vertebral segment.

Common mobilizing techniques

A large number of mobilizing techniques are available to the clinician. These include those recommended by Maitland, Kaltenborn, Cyriax, McKenzie, and others.[161-4]

Maitland techniques involve mobilization in either physiological or accessory ranges of motion using rhythmic, oscillating movements.[163] Numerous RCTs have been performed, with the majority of high-quality trials demonstrating mobilization to be an effective treatment for spinal pain.[165-7] Mobilization appears to be particularly effective when combined with other treatments such as soft tissue and muscle stabilizing techniques,[168] and with exercise therapy.[165, 169]

Grades of mobilization

When using mobilizing techniques, treatment may begin with a gentle grade of movement, particularly if there is local pain and tenderness. The intensity of the treatment may gradually increase until normal movement is restored. For a stiff, pain-free joint, more vigorous mobilization may be performed from the commencement of treatment.

Maitland describes different types of mobilization at different ranges of movement and different amplitudes (Table 13.9). Treatment grade depends on whether pain or stiffness is the main problem. In painful joints, grades I and II are most commonly used (Fig. 13.11). In pain-free stiff joints, grades III and IV are used. Often when treating painful joints,

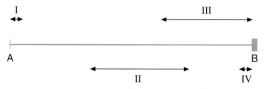

Figure 13.11 Grades of mobilization (A: beginning of range of movement; B: end of range of movement)

Table 13.9 Grades of mobilization

Grade	Degree of mobilization
I	Small amplitude movement performed at the beginning of range
II	Large amplitude movement performed within the free range but not moving into any resistance or stiffness
III	Large amplitude movement performed up to the limit of range
IV	Small amplitude movement performed at the limit of range

initial grade I and grade II treatment will improve the patient's pain-free range and eventually allow grade III and IV movements to be performed in subsequent treatment sessions.

Indications and contraindications for mobilization

Any joint in which there is pain or stiffness on physiological and/or accessory movements can be treated with mobilization. Contraindications to mobilization are:

- local malignancy
- local bony infection (e.g. osteomyelitis, tuberculosis)
- fractures
- spinal cord compression
- cauda equina compression
- inflammatory arthritis conditions (active stage).

Joint manipulation

Manipulation is a sudden movement or thrust of small amplitude performed at high speed at the end of joint range, such that the patient is unable to prevent the movement. Manipulation is performed primarily at the intervertebral joints, but may also be performed at peripheral joints.

Manipulation can be an effective method of treatment.[170-2] There is some evidence from systematic reviews that manipulation techniques can be effective in the treatment of neck pain and headaches.[167, 173, 174] Inconsistent findings are seen for its use in various presentations of low back pain.[165, 173]

Manipulation is associated with considerable risks if performed inappropriately or with faulty technique. In the case of cervical manipulations, serious risks can include stroke and neurological deficits. Therefore manipulation should only be performed by fully qualified practitioners who have had formal training in manipulative skills.

Indications and contraindications for manipulation

There are two main indications for manipulation. The first is a stiff, pain-free joint that has been mobilized to the full extent of range possible. The second is an acute, locked joint such as a cervical apophyseal joint.

The contraindications for manipulation are:

- all the contraindications for mobilization
- vertebral artery insufficiency (test prior to cervical manipulation; Chapter 20)
- rheumatoid arthritis of the atlanto-occipital and C1–2 joints
- spondylolisthesis (if symptoms arise from the slip)
- acute nerve root compression
- children whose epiphyseal plates have not closed
- joint instability
- pregnancy (last trimester)
- recent "whiplash" injury
- hemophilia.

Joint traction

Traction which involves intermittent or sustained pressure in a direction to distract joint surfaces can be used to treat patients with spinal pain; it is often used as an adjunct treatment by a variety of health professionals. Spinal traction is proposed to result in distraction of the vertebral bodies or facet joints, widening of the intervertebral foramen, tensioning of ligamentous structures, and stretching of the spinal musculature.[175] Theories on the analgesic effects of traction include stimulation of mechanoreceptors resulting in inhibition of reflex muscle spasm, and changes in vertebral disc mechanics.[175–7]

Acknowledging the wide range of treatment parameters which can be used with this modality, there is some evidence that traction may be effective in the treatment of mechanical neck pain when used on an intermittent setting.[175] However, research evidence is yet to support its effectiveness for lumbar spinal pain.[175–9]

Types of traction

Traction has been used for the treatment of spinal disorders for centuries. In the 19th century, traction beds were used to treat scoliosis, back pain, rickets, and spinal deformity. Traction corsets, chairs, and body suspension apparatus were also developed.[177] By the 20th century, traction became a popular

treatment for chronic low back pain and neck pain, and is still used for these presentations today.

Traction may be applied in a variety of ways:

- mechanical/motorized (motorized by a pulley system which applies the traction force)
- manual (applied by a therapist)
- self/auto (patient administered where traction force is applied by grasping various pulleys and bars)
- gravitational (patient is fixed to a tilt table/bed and inverted)
- underwater (patient is fixed proximally perpendicularly to water level and traction applied distally).

Traction can be applied at different duration settings including—continuous (hours to days), sustained (20 to 60 minutes), and intermittent (alternating cycles of a few seconds to minutes).[177] The direction of traction force can be axial (caudad to cephalad), positional (patient determined), and in various spinal positional biases (flexion, extension, lateral flexion).[177] Traction can also be performed in a variety of positions including lying, sitting, and suspended.

Adverse effects associated with traction include nerve impingement, which has a higher risk when traction is applied with heavy loads (greater than 50% total body weight), respiratory constraints from harnesses, increased pain, aggravation of neurological symptoms, and increase in blood pressure, particularly with gravitational traction.[176]

Absolute contraindications include:[177]

- spinal malignancy
- spinal cord compression
- local infection (osteomyelitis, disciitis)
- osteoporosis
- inflammatory spondyloarthritis
- acute fracture
- uncontrolled hypertension
- severe cardiorespiratory or respiratory disease
- aortic or iliac aneurysm
- pregnancy.

Soft tissue therapy

Soft tissue therapy, also known as massage therapy, is a very popular clinical treatment for abnormalities such as:

- increased muscle tone/tension
- myofascial trigger points, active or latent
  - refer pain in a regular pattern
  - inhibit local muscle contraction
- palpably abnormal thickening of connective tissue.

In this section, we touch on the biological rationale for soft tissue therapy in musculoskeletal medicine, provide an overview of several key soft tissue techniques, which are used as specific treatments in Part B, and alert the reader to some self-treatment options.

Any assessment of soft tissue must identify regions of abnormal tension and focal abnormalities such as trigger points by range of motion testing and precise, systematic palpation.

Soft tissue abnormalities may be a cause of pain and, importantly, may adversely affect neuromuscular control. Areas of increased muscle tone, connective tissue thickening, and pain-producing or inhibitory trigger points[180] may reduce muscle power and endurance and lead to abnormal muscle activation. As such, soft tissue therapy may play an important role in correcting the inhibition of healthy activation patterns.[181]

As described in Chapter 6, it is important to look for both proximal and distal contributions to the patient's pain. Pain may refer directly to the site (e.g. from spinal structures or myofascial trigger points). Similarly, pain may develop indirectly from altered muscle activation patterns caused by the inhibitory effect of inflammation, active trigger points, and pain behavior.

Position of treatment

For successful soft tissue therapy, the "target tissue" should be placed in an ideal position, either under tension or laxity. The advantages of treating soft tissue in a position of stretch include:

- Focal sites of abnormality, taut bands, or areas of increased tension will often become more easily palpable.
- Myofascial trigger points may become more clearly evident and refer more dramatically in positions of stretch.
- Positions of increased neural mechanosensitivity will often facilitate palpation of the soft tissue abnormalities that contribute to improved neural mechanics.
- There is enhanced effectiveness of rupturing abnormal cross-linkages between collagen fibers.

Digital ischemic pressure

Digital ischemic pressure describes the application of direct pressure perpendicular to the skin towards the center of a muscle with sufficient pressure to evoke a

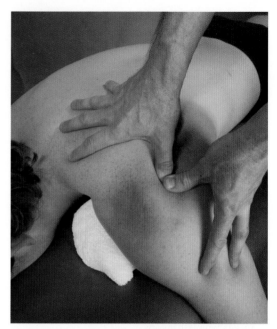

Figure 13.12 (a) Digital ischemic pressure to the infraspinatus trigger point using the therapist's thumb

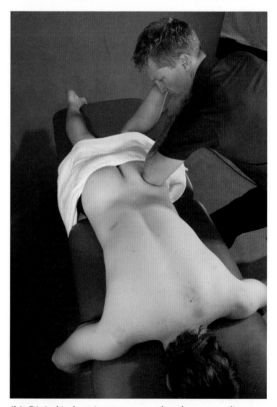

(b) Digital ischemic pressure to the gluteus medius trigger point using the therapist's elbow

temporary ischemic reaction (Fig. 13.12). The aims of this technique are to stimulate the tension-monitoring receptors within muscle to reduce muscle tone, to provide an analgesic response in soft tissue by eliciting a release of pain-mediating substances, and to deactivate symptomatic trigger points.

Digital ischemic pressure may be performed by either using the therapist's thumb (Fig. 13.12a), elbow (Fig.13.12b), or a hand-held device such as a T-shaped bar.

Sustained myofascial tension

Sustained myofascial tension is performed by applying a tensile force with the thumb, braced digits, or forearm (Fig. 13.13) in the direction of greatest fascial restriction, or in the direction of elongation necessary for normal function. The aim of this technique is to restore the optimal length of tissue in the exact location where abnormal structural thickening is present.

By inducing a prolonged tensile force, the aim is to rupture abnormal cross-linkages between collagen fibers that limit the ability of connective tissue to elongate. The cross-linkages form as a result of the inflammatory response to acute or overuse injury.

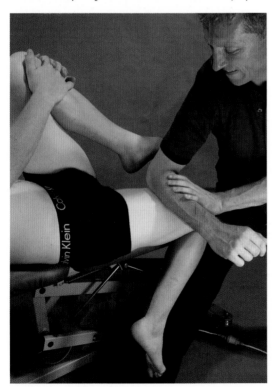

Figure 13.13 Sustained myofascial tension

Tension is developed in the tissue by blocking or anchoring one thumb proximal or distal to the lesion, and moving the other thumb or braced digit through the region of dysfunction to impart a shear force. Greater shear force can be imparted by using passive or active joint movement in conjunction with local tissue contact,

Depth of treatment

Granter and King developed a grading system for depth of soft tissue therapy (Table 13.10).

The scale of treatment depth is based on the patient's level of pain (I–IV) and the therapist's sense of resistance to palpation (A–C). Post-acute lesions are first treated without pain to gauge the response to treatment without a sense of tissue resistance, that is, to IA depth. Progression of treatment would be to IB and then IIB about one week after the injury. A chronic lesion requires deep pressure, such as IIC progressing to IIIC. This grading system permits clinicians to record depth of treatment consistently.

Combination treatment

Following soft tissue techniques that are aimed at restoring muscle length, sustained stretching can be performed to maximize the goal of restoring muscle length.

Maximum benefits of soft tissue treatment arise when used as an adjunct to therapy. Correction of muscle strength and length issues as well as regaining neurodynamic balance should be addressed. Sporting technique should also be considered to gain maximum benefit from intervention and reduce further injury susceptibility

Table 13.10 Granter–King scale for grading the depth of soft tissue therapy

Pain grade (P)	Patient's perception of pain
I	No pain perceived
II	Commencement of pain
III	Moderate level of pain
IV	Severe level of pain (seldom used)

Resistance grade (R)	Therapist's perception of tissue resistance
A	No sense of tissue resistance
B	Onset of tissue resistance
C	Moderate tissue resistance

Lubricants

Many soft tissue techniques require a lubricant applied to the skin to aid both patient comfort and the therapist's ability to palpate the tissue for abnormalities. There should be sufficient lubricant to prevent excessive resistance, particularly when palpating areas with large amounts of hair. Irritation of hair follicles may result in contact dermatitis.

With techniques such as sustained myofascial tension, skin contact should be maximal; therefore, no lubricant (or a dense cream) is required. As repetitive movements are not used in this technique, there is little risk of irritation to hair follicles.

Vacuum cupping

The aim of vacuum cupping is to stretch soft tissue. Oil is applied to the skin to contain the negative pressure created in the cup by a vacuum pump. In the vacuum, the soft tissue is "drawn" upwards, thereby stretching the soft tissue in a regulated, sustained stretch. The cup contains a one-way valve that allows the pump to be removed.

Vacuum cupping has been used in, for example, anterior compartment syndrome of the lower limb, thickening of the medial aponeurosis of the soleus, and muscle tightness in the iliotibial band.

Cupping can cause significant capillary rupture and damage to the periosteum if used with excessive vacuum or with incorrect placement. The skin color should be monitored closely and the cup removed if the skin becomes more deeply rose-colored than normal reactive hyperemia. Generally the longer a cup is left *in situ* or the more vacuum is applied, the more bruising that can develop, and this should be explained to the patient prior to treatment.

Initial application should be for 15 seconds at a degree of suction such that the patient does not perceive a stretch in the tissue. The procedure can be repeated. Subsequent application can progress to a duration of 90 seconds at a degree of vacuum suction where comfortable tissue stretch is perceived by the patient.

Self-treatment

The patient can work on his or her own soft tissue using various techniques designed to reduce muscle tone/tension and deactivate symptomatic myofascial trigger points (Fig. 13.14). Self-treatment can be undertaken daily and should not cause a pain response that is excessive, which would adversely affect training, or result in an increase in symptoms.

Figure 13.14 Self-treatment: treating the gluteus medius with a tennis ball

Typically, self-treatment would involve the application of a sustained force (digital ischemic pressure) to the identified lesion, with pressure sustained until tone/tension reduces and pain or referred symptoms resolve.

Muscle energy techniques

Muscle energy techniques are gentle modalities used in the treatment of pathology around the spine and pelvis.[182] Muscle energy techniques are performed under patient-control, and involve isometric and isotonic contractions which are specifically directed and controlled by the therapist.[183] Muscle energy techniques are based on the principle that optimal static and dynamic body posture should be symmetrical. Therefore muscle energy techniques are indicated when asymmetry, restriction, or tenderness of the musculoskeletal system is observed.

Muscle energy techniques aim to improve a patient's overall function, including sporting performance, by addressing muscle and joint imbalances.[182, 183] For example, a moderately severe hamstring muscle tear may result in an adaptive posterior rotation of the ilium on the sacrum. Local treatment of the hamstring muscle tear may assist in healing of the tear, but may not correct the adaptive change in the pelvis. Thus, further problems may arise.

Treatment involves the therapist applying a counterforce while the patient performs voluntary muscle contractions of varying intensity, in a precise direction.[182] Proposed clinical benefits are thought to be through the Golgi tendon organs, which produce relaxation of local musculature.[183] As such, muscle energy techniques utilize the concept of reciprocal innervations, in which contraction of agonist muscles inhibits the antagonist muscle via a reflex response. Additionally, contraction of facilitated muscle in a lengthened position may also activate the Golgi tendon organ and may also result in reflex muscle inhibition. Therefore there is potential for both the agonist and antagonist muscles to relax and therefore improve asymmetries and muscle imbalances.

Treatment techniques can vary in reference to muscles contracted short of or into resistance, degree of patient effort (moderate, maximum), single versus multiple contractions, direction of force, whether a muscle stretch is incorporated directly after technique, and whether muscle energy techniques are used alone or as an adjunct treatment.

Although muscle energy techniques are commonly used by musculoskeletal therapists, there is limited evidence to support its effectiveness in the treatment of spinal dysfunction. However, there is emerging evidence that muscle energy techniques can improve cervical range of motion and hamstring length in asymptomatic patients, and reduce pain levels in non-specific lumbar pelvic pain presentations.[182, 184–6]

Neural stretching

The nervous system needs to adapt to mechanical loads. It can do this through elongation, sliding, cross-section change, angulation, and compression.[187] However, when the nervous system cannot cope under loads, it can lead to neural edema, ischemia, fibrosis, and hypoxia—all of which can alter neurodynamics.[187] This change in neurodynamics may make a significant contribution to the patient's symptoms and signs in certain injuries (Chapter 6). Unless these abnormalities are corrected in addition to other soft tissue abnormalities associated with the injury, full recovery, as indicated by full pain-free range of motion, may not occur.

"Neural tension" was a term used in the past to describe peripheral nervous system dysfunction, but was thought to only address the mechanical aspects of the dysfunction.[187] Nowadays terms such as "neurodynamics" and neuromechanical sensitivity are employed to describe the biomechanical, physiological, and structural dysfunction of the nervous system.[187]

Neural stretching (mobilization) is a treatment modality, which address the nervous system. Neural stretches aim to restore dynamic balance of the nervous system.[187] Proposed benefits include facilitation of nerve gliding, decrease in nerve adherence, dispersion of noxious fluids, increased neural vascularity, and improved axoplasmic flow.[187]

These stretches are adaptations of the neurodynamic tests (Chapter 11). The two most commonly used neural stretches are adaptations of the upper limb neurodynamic test (Fig. 13.15) and the slump test (Fig. 13.16).

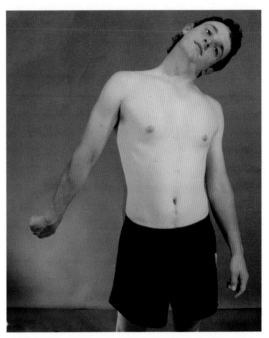

Figure 13.15 Upper limb neurodynamics test stretch. Athlete adopts the position illustrated. The degree of stretch can be increased by shoulder depression

Figure 13.16 Slump stretch. Athlete adopts the position illustrated. The degree of stretch can be increased by forward flexion of the trunk

A systematic review evaluated the effectiveness of neural mobilizations and found that, even though the studies reported positive effects, low methodological quality and the small number of studies provide limited evidence for their use.[181] However, these stretches can often be helpful in the treatment of conditions in which neurodynamics are abnormal, and variations of these tests may be used for both diagnosis and treatment.

Particular care must be taken in acute or irritable conditions, as neural stretches may aggravate the patient's symptoms. Stretches should always begin gently, and gradually increase under the close supervision of an experienced clinician. As with other methods of treatment, neural stretches alone are rarely sufficient to correct all abnormalities present. They can be particularly effective in longstanding, chronic conditions where increased neural mechanosensitivity is common.

Acupuncture

In traditional Chinese medicine "meridians" and the flow of vital energy, "qi," form the theoretical basis for acupuncture. Acupuncture is a medical tradition dating back to the most ancient times in China, and the stimulation of acupuncture points is thought to correct and rebalance the flow of qi, thereby restoring health. The word "acupuncture" is derived from the Latin word *acus* (the needle) and means "puncturing of bodily tissue for the relief of pain."

Acupuncture is performed by inserting fine needles of various lengths and diameters into acupuncture points located all over the body. The needles are inserted to various depths, rotated, and either immediately withdrawn or left in place. The needles may also be stimulated electrically (electroacupuncture), or by moxibustion (application of heat to acupuncture points by burning moxa, the dried leaves of *Artemisia vulgaris*).

The mechanism of action of acupuncture is uncertain, but it is thought that there are multiple processes contributing to its overall effect. The "gate control" of pain, in which stimulation of one part of the body may block pain from other parts of the body, together with the release of endogenous opioids may account for its analgesic effects.[188] The autonomic nervous system may also play an important role in mediating the acupuncture effect. In addition, acupuncture causes the body to release endorphins from the pituitary gland and other organs that may block signals in the pain pathways.

There have been several recent reviews on the use of acupuncture for painful conditions.[188–94] One review, specifically focusing on pain studies, concluded that the use of acupuncture for the treatment of pain was unclear.[188]

Two reviews evaluated the Cochrane database of systematic reviews on traditional Chinese medicine techniques and acupuncture alone respectively.[189–90] The first found acupuncture reviews were inconclusive for a variety of presentations (musculoskeletal pain, mental health and addictive disorders, gynecological conditions, stroke, nausea and vomiting, and other), which could be accounted for by poor methodological quality and heterogeneity between individual studies.[190]

The second review agreed with this finding for pain presentations, but did find evidence to support its use for nausea and vomiting related to chemotherapy and postoperative pain, as well as for headache.[189] Agreeing with this, another review found evidence to support its use peri-operatively for postoperative pain management, the majority of which was for abdominal surgery.[192]

A review focusing on osteoarthritis of the knee found evidence to support acupuncture for improved pain and functional outcomes.[193] Another review found that acupuncture compared to no treatment or acupuncture used as an adjunct treatment was supported by the evidence for non-specific chronic low back pain.[194]

Another review focused on acupuncture as a treatment for sport fatigue.[191] Sport fatigue was defined as fatigue occurring after intense training for a period of time or fierce competition in athletes, leading to absence of the original competitive levels. Although this review reported some evidence that acupuncture could be a useful treatment, no search strategy was presented and therefore this review may not have captured all relevant literature on which to form firm conclusions.

Additionally, preliminary evidence has shown that acupuncture into painful acupuncture points may be useful to reduce the effects of DOMS and may have an effect on perceived exertion scores on 20-km cycling performance.[195, 196]

Dry needling

Karel Lewit in 1979 first studied and observed that analgesic effects of local anesthetic injection into painful myofascial trigger points appeared to be from the needle penetration itself, rather than the anesthetic alone.[197–9] He described this observation as the "needle effect." Since then the practice of inserting solid needles for pain relief purposes has been termed "dry needling."

Dry needling, as defined by Huguenin, involves multiple advances of an acupuncture-type needle into the muscle in the region of a trigger point, aiming to reproduce the patient's symptoms, visualize local twitch responses, and achieve relief of muscle tension and pain.[200]

In sports and exercise medicine, the use of dry needling is becoming more widespread, and is used in the treatment of both acute and chronic musculoskeletal conditions (Fig. 13.17). It is theorized that trigger points can become active in response to muscle overload and/or muscle injury.[201]

Usually, there is increased resistance to the needle in the area of the trigger point compared to the surrounding "normal" muscle. If resistance and pain are not encountered at the first attempt, it may be necessary to draw back slightly and move the needle around to find the trigger point and produce a local twitch response. A local twitch response seems to be associated with a bigger treatment effect, and this should be explained to the patient.[200, 201]

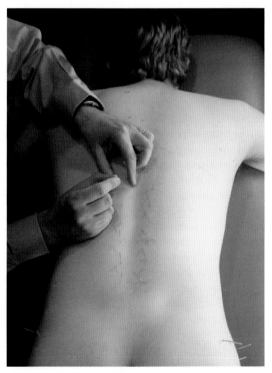

Figure 13.17 Dry needling

Adverse effects associated with dry needling include post-treatment soreness, which seems to occur in the first 24 hours after the treatment.[200] Application of heat and stretching exercises seem to minimize this soreness.[200] Therefore patient selection is important, especially in patients with needle phobias, as some may not tolerate this form of treatment. Contraindications to dry needling include bleeding disorders, active infection, blood-borne diseases, allergies to metal, unstable epilepsy, and the third trimester of pregnancy. Additionally, extreme care should be taken when dry needling near the lungs, to avoid causing a pneumothorax.

The most commonly used dry needling technique involves inserting the needle into the taut band and leaving it in place for a few minutes. Alternatively, one can introduce the needle into the taut band within the muscle and then repeatedly move the needle in and out of the muscle (but not back through the skin), constantly trying to find points within the band that reproduce the patient's pain and also produce a "twitch" response.

When the needle makes contact with the trigger point, the patient feels an acute pain of varying intensity at the site of insertion, or in the area of pain referral, or both. Frequently, a twitch response occurs in the muscle when contact is made. Initially, the needle may be grasped by the muscle, followed by gradual relaxation and lengthening of the muscle.

Dry needling of a number of trigger points can be done at each treatment session. Usually after the first treatment session, pain relief lasts three to four days. Then following each subsequent session, the duration of the pain relief is longer. Up to three or four treatment sessions may be required initially to eliminate the trigger point. A single trigger point should not be needled more than twice in a week.

Following dry needling, there will be some residual local pain and tenderness. If the needling has elicited a particularly painful response, then it is helpful to apply a heat pack to the area for 10 minutes after treatment. Following dry needling treatment, it is important to passively stretch the affected muscles to maximize the increased range of motion.

Several studies have compared dry needling with injection of local anesthetic and various other substances. There is some evidence that dry needling can be just as effective.[202, 203]

Two recent reviews have evaluated its effectiveness for pain relief purposes in active trigger points and for non-specific low back pain respectively.[201, 204]

Included studies were limited by low methodological quality, small sample sizes, varying treatment parameters (depth and location of needles, number of treatment sessions), and differing control groups used. However, although the current evidence was inconsistent and limited, dry needling did appear useful as an adjunct treatment.

One study, using a single-blinded same-control design, found that dry needling of an active infraspinatus trigger point in shoulder pain did significantly increase ipsilateral shoulder range of movement and pain pressure thresholds both locally and distally (over anterior deltoid and extensor carpi radialis longus muscles).[205] This suggests that dry needling can have more than just a local effect, and adds to the evidence that active trigger points can refer pain.

Another recent study has assessed the effect of dry needling on sportspeople with posterior thigh pain referred from gluteal trigger points.[206] Dry needling did not improve objective measures of range of movement or muscle pain, but did significantly improve perceived muscle tightness during running in both dry needling and control groups. In this study, the control group used a placebo needle with a blunt end that did not penetrate the skin.

Hyperbaric oxygen therapy

Hyperbaric oxygen therapy refers to a medical procedure that has been in existence since the 1960s.[207] Hyperbaric oxygen therapy can be described as breathing 100% oxygen intermittently under increased pressure while in a treatment chamber (i.e. at greater than atmospheric pressure).[208] It is usually performed within a therapeutic hyperbaric chamber and can consist of one or multiple treatment sessions.

Hyperbaric oxygen therapy is widely accepted as a primary treatment for decompression sickness, air embolism, and carbon monoxide poisoning. It also appears to improve recovery after severe burns and crush injuries, and is used in wound management.[208]

Adverse reactions are rare and can be related to the increased pressure in air-filled cavities (e.g. middle ear, sinuses, dental fillings), and increased air density which can cause respiratory distress. Additionally, claustrophobia should also be considered. Contraindications to hyperbaric oxygen therapy include untreated pneumothorax, severe airway problems, uncontrolled epilepsy, and some chemotherapeutics.[208]

Hyperbaric oxygen therapy has not been shown to have a beneficial effect in the treatment of ankle sprains[209] and DOMS.[210] Hyperbaric oxygen therapy did not improve sports performance and could potentially impair sporting ability.[211, 212]

Surgery

Despite the many advances in the non-operative management of sports injuries, surgery has a major role to play in the management of both acute injuries and overuse injuries. Surgery is used to remove, repair, reconstruct, and realign damaged tissue. Sports surgery can be classified as arthroscopic surgery or open surgery.

Arthroscopic surgery

Arthroscopy involves the introduction of a fiber-optic telescope into a joint space to provide diagnostic information and afford the opportunity to undertake minimally invasive surgery. It is a well-established procedure for the knee, shoulder, elbow, ankle, and hip, and, more recently, the wrist.

Arthroscopy utilizes a light source to illuminate the joint and a video camera to capture the image, which is then displayed on one or more screens. The arthroscope is introduced through a standard portal, while another portal or portals are used to introduce operating instruments. The location of portals is important, to minimize the risk of damage to vessels and nerves. A number of instruments are available for use in arthroscopic procedures.

Arthroscopy can be carried out under local, regional or, often, general anesthesia as a day procedure. The main areas of interest to be viewed through the arthroscope are the articular surfaces, the synovium, and the intra-articular structures (such as the meniscus and cruciate ligaments of the knee, the glenoid labrum, the rotator cuff tendons of the shoulder, and the acetabular labrum of the hip). In most joints, the majority of the articular surfaces can be viewed. Assessment of stability can be aided by combining a direct view of the joint with maneuvers that place the joint under stress.

Common procedures performed through the arthroscope include removal of loose bodies within the joint, separation of and removal of the torn part of a meniscus, repair of a torn structure (such as a peripheral tear of the meniscus, a labral detachment in the shoulder), or dividing a tight structure (such as the glenohumeral joint capsule in the shoulder or scar tissue in the knee). More complex reconstructive joint procedures (anterior cruciate ligament recon-struction, rotator cuff repair) can be performed with the aid of an arthroscope.

Arthroscopy has a low complication rate. There is a small incidence of infection and delayed portal healing. Occasionally, arthroscopy can produce a persistent joint reaction manifesting as prolonged joint effusion, persistent pain, and muscle wasting. Whether this is due to the arthroscopy itself or to the underlying joint pathology is sometimes difficult to determine. Complex regional pain syndrome type 1 may occasionally develop after arthroscopy.

Open surgery

The open surgical treatment of sports-related prob-lems includes surgery related to acute trauma and surgery for the treatment of overuse injuries. Surgery after an acute injury aims to recreate the pre-injury anatomy by the repair of damaged tissues. This may require internal fixation for an unstable fracture, or repair of torn ligaments or tendons. If repair of the damaged tissue is not possible, a reconstructive pro-cedure may be performed (e.g. anterior cruciate liga-ment reconstruction).

Following an acute injury, the sportsperson may develop chronic problems (such as instability) that may require surgical repair or reconstruction. Chronic ligamentous or capsular inadequacy may develop following an injury or as a gradual process. Surgery may be required to tighten the stretched tissue, either by moving the attachment of the tissue, or by a shortening procedure (such as plication, reefing, or shifting).

Overuse injuries that have failed to respond to conservative measures are sometimes managed by surgical tissue release, division, or excision. Excision may be performed if impingement is present, or if degenerative change has led to tissue necrosis. In nerve compression, decompression or transposition of the nerve may be required. Stress fractures that fail to heal (non-union) are treated by fixation or bone graft.

With all surgical procedures—arthroscopic or open—the surgery must be considered as only a part of the treatment. Adequate post-surgical rehabilita-tion is equally as important as the procedure itself. Rehabilitation following injury and surgery is dis-cussed in Chapter 15.

🌐 RECOMMENDED WEBSITES

The *British Medical Journal*'s Clinical Evidence site: www.clinicalevidence.com/ceweb/conditions/msd/msd.jsp.

📄 RECOMMENDED READING

Boyling JD, Jull GA. *Grieve's modern manual therapy. The vertebral column*. 3rd edn. Edinburgh: Churchill Livingstone, 2004.

Cameron MH. *Physical agents in rehabilitation*. Philadelphia, PA: WB Saunders, 1999.

Hunter G. Specific soft tissue mobilization in the management of soft tissue dysfunction. *Man Ther* 1998; 3(1): 2–11.

Jarvinen TA, Jarvinen TL, Kaariainen M, Kalimo H, Jarvinen M. Muscle injuries: biology and treatment. *Am J Sports Med* 2005; 33(5): 745–64.

Kaltenborn FM. *Manual therapy of the extremity joints*. Oslo: Bokhandel, 1975.

Kannus P, Parkkari J, Jarvinen T, Jarvinen T, Jarvinen M. Basic science and clinical studies coincide: active treatment approach is needed after a sports injury. *Scand J Med Sci Sports* 2003;13:150–4.

Maitland GD. *Vertebral manipulation*. 5th edn. London: Butterworths, 1986.

McKenzie R. *The lumbar spine: mechanical diagnosis and therapy*. Waikane: Spinal Publications, 1981.

Refshauge K, Gass E. *Musculoskeletal physiotherapy: Clinical science and evidence-based practice*. 2nd edn. Oxford: Butterworth-Heinemann, 2004.

Simons DG, Travell JG, Simons LS. *Myofascial pain and dysfunction. The trigger point manual*. 2nd edn. Baltimore, MA: Williams & Wilkins, 1999.

Weerapong P, Hume PA, Kolt GS. The mechanisms of massage and effects on performance, muscle recovery and injury prevention. *Sports Med* 2005;35(3):235–56.

📑 REFERENCES

1. Frobell RB, Roos EM, Roos HP et al. A randomized trial of treatment for acute anterior cruciate ligament tears. *New Eng J Med* 2010;363:331–42.

2. de Vos RJ, Weir A, van Schie HT et al. Platelet-rich plasma injection for chronic Achilles tendinopathy: a randomized controlled trial. *JAMA* 2010;303(2):144–9.

3. Coombes K, Bisset L, Vicenzino B. Efficacy and safety of corticosteroid and other injections in the management of tendinopathy: a systematic review of randomised controlled trials. *Lancet* 2010;376(9754):1751–67.

4. Smith GC, Pell JP. Parachute use to prevent death and major trauma related to gravitational challenge: systematic review of randomised controlled trials. *BMJ* 2003;327(7429):1459–61.

5. Järvinen TAH, Järvinen TLN, Kääriäinen M et al. Muscle injuries: optimising recovery. *Best Prac Res Clini Rheumatol* 2007;21(2):317–31.

6. Bleakley C, McDonough S, MacAuley D. The use of ice in the treatment of acute soft-tissue injury. *Am J Sports Med* 2004;32(1):251–61.

7. Bleakley CM, O'Connor S, Tully MA et al. The PRICE study (protection rest ice compression elevation): design of a randomised controlled trial comparing standard versus cryokinetic ice applications in the management of acute ankle sprain [ISRCTN13903946]. *BMC Musc Dis* 2007;8:125–32.

8. Jarvinen TAH, Jarvinen TLN, Kaariainen M et al. Muscle injuries: biology and treatment. *Am J Sports Med* 2005;33(5):745–64.

9. Bleakley CM, McDonough SM, MacAuley DC. Cryotherapy for acute ankle sprains: a randomised controlled study of two different icing protocols. *Br J Sports Med* 2006;40(8):700–5.

10. MacAuley D. Ice therapy: how good is the evidence? *Int J Sports Med* 2001;22(5):379–84.

11. Moeller JL, Monroe J, McKeag D. Cryotherapy-induced common peroneal nerve palsy. *Clin J Sport Med* 1997;7(3):212–16.

12. Barnes MJ, Mundel T, Stannard SR. Acute alcohol consumption aggravates the decline in muscle performance following strenuous eccentric exercise. *J Sci Med Sport* 2010;13(1):189–93.

13. Suter PM, Schutz Y. The effect of exercise, alcohol or both combined on health and physical performance. *Int J Obes* 2008;32(S6):S48–52.

14. Jarvinen MJ, Lehto MUK. The effects of early mobilisation and immobilisation on the healing process following muscle injuries. *Sports Med* 1993;15(2):78–89.

15. Stewart T, Cheong W, Barr V et al. Strong and light plaster casts? *Injury* 2009;40(8):890–93.

16. Kannus P, Parkkari J, Järvinen TLN et al. Basic science and clinical studies coincide: active treatment approach is needed after a sports injury. *Scand J Med Sci Sports* 2003;13(3):150–4.

17. Nugent-Derfus GE, Takara T, O'Neill JK et al. Continuous passive motion applied to whole joints stimulates chondrocyte biosynthesis of PRG4. *Osteo Cartilage* 2007;15(5):566–74.

A

18. Huang SH, Johnson K, Pipe AL. The use of dietary supplements and medications by Canadian athletes at the Atlanta and Sydney Olympic Games. *Clin J Sport Med* 2006;16:27–33.

19. Taioli E. Use of permitted drugs in Italian soccer players. *Br J Sports Med* 2007;41:439–41.

20. Tscholl P, Alonso JM, Dolle ÃG et al. The use of drugs and nutritional supplements in top-level track and field athletes. *Am J Sports Med* 2009;38(1):133–40.

21. Tscholl P, Feddermann N, Junge A et al. The use and abuse of painkillers in international soccer. *Am J Sports Med* 2009;37(2):260–5.

22. Tscholl P, Junge A, Dvorak J. The use of medication and nutritional supplements during FIFA World Cups 2002 and 2006. *Br J Sports Med* 2008;42:725–30.

23. Bertolini A, Ferrari A, Ottani A et al. Paracetamol: new vistas of an old drug. *CNS Drug Rev* 2006;12(3–4): 250–75.

24. Dani M, Guindon J, Lambert C et al. The local antinociceptive effects of paracetamol in neuropathic pain are mediated by cannabinoid receptors. *Eur J Pharmacol* 2007;573(1–3):214–15.

25. Toms L, Derry S, Moore AR et al. Single dose oral paracetamol (acetaminophen) with codeine for postoperative pain in adults. *Coch Data Syst Rev* 2009;1.

26. Derman EW. Pain management in sports medicine: use and abuse of anti-inflammatory and other agents. *Sth African Fam Prac* 2010;52(1):27–32.

27. Stanos SP. Topical agents for the management of musculoskeletal pain. *J Pain Symp Manage* 2007;33(3):342–55.

28. Vriens J, Nilius B, Vennekens R. Herbal compounds and toxins modulating TRP channels. *Curr Neuropharm* 2008;6(1):79–96.

29. Mason L, Moore AR, Edwards JE et al. Systematic review of efficacy of topical rubefacients containing salicylates for the treatment of acute and chronic pain. *BMJ* 2004;328(7446):95.

30. Mason L, Moore RA, Derry S et al. Systematic review of topical capsaicin for the treatment of chronic pain. *BMJ* 2004;328(7446):991.

31. Li Wan, Po A. PJ Practice checklist: Topical analgesics. *Pharm J* 1996.

32. Gorski T, Cadore EL, Pinto SS et al. Use of Nonsteroidal anti-inflammatory drugs (NSAIDs) in triathletes: prevalence, level of awareness, and reasons for use. *Br J Sports Med* 2011;45(2):85–90.

33. Wharam PC, Speedy DB, Noakes TD et al. NSAID use increases the risk of developing hyponatremia during an Ironman triathlon. *Med Sci Sports Exerc* 2006;38(4):618–22.

34. McAnulty S, McAnulty L, Nieman D et al. Effect of NSAID on muscle injury and oxidative stress. *Int J Sports Med* 2007;28(11):909–15.

35. Paoloni JA, Milne C, Orchard J et al. Non-steroidal anti-inflammatory drugs in sports medicine: guidelines for practical but sensible use. *Br J Sports Med* 2009;43(11):863–5.

36. Radi Z, Khan N. Effects of cyclooxygenase inhibition on bone, tendon, and ligament healing. *Inflam Res* 2005;54(9):358–66.

37. Rahusen FTG, Weinhold PS, Almekinders LC. Nonsteroidal anti-inflammatory drugs and acetaminophen in the treatment of an acute muscle injury. *Am J Sports Med* 2004;32(8):1856–9.

38. Derman E, Schwellnus M. Pain management in sports medicine: use and abuse of anti-anflammatory and other agents. *Sth African Fam Prac* 2010;52(1):29–32.

39. Warden SJ. Prophylactic misuse and recommended use of non-steroidal anti-inflammatory drugs by athletes. *Br J Sports Med* 2009;43(8):548–9.

40. Ziltener JL, Leal S, Fournier PE. Non-steroidal anti-inflammatory drugs for athletes: an update. *Ann Phys Rehab Med* 2010;53(4):278–88.

41. Kroenke K, Krebs EE, Bair MJ. Pharmacotherapy of chronic pain: a synthesis of recommendations from systematic reviews. *Gen Hosp Psych* 2009;31(3):206–19.

42. Smith C. Timing of NSAID treatment after muscle injury or training. *CME* 2008;26(7):350–5.

43. Alaranta A, Alaranta H, Helenius I. Use of prescription drugs in athletes. *Sports Med* 2008;38(6):449–63.

44. De Carli A, Volpi P, Pelosini I et al. New therapeutic approaches for management of sport-induced muscle strains. *Adv Ther* 2009;26(12):1072–83.

45. Dietzel D, Hedlund E. Injections and return to play. *Curr Pain Headache Rep* 2005;9(1):11–16.

46. Tokisk JM, Powell ET, Schlegel TF et al. Ketorolac use in the National Football League. *Phys Sportsmed* 2002;30(9):19–25.

47. Marnett LJ. The COXIB experience: a look in the rearview mirror. *Ann Rev Pharmacol Toxicol* 2009;49(1):265–90.

48. Mason L, Moore RA, Edward JE et al. Topical NSAIDs for chronic musculoskeletal pain: systemic review and meta-analysis. *BMC Musculoskelet Disord* 2004;5:28.

49. Hyldahl RD, Keadle J, Rouzier PA et al. Effects of ibuprofen topical gel on muscle soreness. *Med Sci Sports Exerc* 2010;42(3):614–21.

50. Bogduk N. A narrative review of intra-articular corticosteroid injections for low back pain. *Pain Med* 2005;6(4):287–96.

51. Scott A, Khan KM. Corticosteroids: short-term gain for long-term pain? *Lancet* 2010;376(9754):1714–15.

52. Scutt N, Rolf C, Scutt A. Glucocorticoids inhibit tenocyte proliferation and tendon progenitor cell recruitment. *J Orth Res* 2006;24(2):173–82.

53. Wong MW, Tang YY, Lee SK et al. Effect of dexamethasone on cultured human tenocytes and its reversibility by platelet-derived growth factor. *J Bone Joint Surg Am* 2003;85-A(10):1914–20.

54. Brukner P, Nicol A. Use of oral corticosteroids in sports medicine. *Curr Sports Med Rep* 2004;3:181–3.

55. Gebhard KL, Maibach HI. Relationship between systemic corticosteroids and osteonecrosis. *Am J Clin Dermatol* 2001;2(6):377–88.

56. Gurney AB, Wascher DC. Absorption of dexamethasone sodium phosphate in human connective tissue using iontophoresis. *Am J Sports Med* 2008;36(4):753–9.

57. Hamann H, Hodges M, Evans B. Effectiveness of iontophoresis of anti-inflammatory medications in the treatment of common musculoskeletal inflammatory conditions: a systematic review. *Phys Ther Rev* 2006;11(3):190–4.

58. Bolin DJ. Transdermal approaches to pain in sports injury management. *Curr Sports Med Rep* 2003;2: 303–09.

59. Osborne HR, Allison GT. Treatment of plantar fasciitis by LowDye taping and iontophoresis: short term results of a double blinded, randomised, placebo controlled clinical trial of dexamethasone and acetic acid. *Br J Sports Med* 2006;40(6):545–9.

60. Paoloni JA, Appleyard RC, Nelson J et al. Topical nitric oxide application in the treatment of chronic extensor tendinosis at the elbow: A randomized, double-blinded, placebo-controlled clinical trial. *Am J Sports Med* 2003;31(6):915–20.

61. Paoloni JA, Appleyard RC, Nelson J et al. Topical glyceryl trinitrate treatment of chronic noninsertional achilles tendinopathy. A randomized, double-blind, placebo-controlled trial. *J Bone Joint Surg Am* 2004;86(5):916–22.

62. Paoloni JA, Appleyard RC, Nelson J et al. Topical glyceryl trinitrate application in the treatment of chronic supraspinatus tendinopathy: a randomized, double-blinded, placebo-controlled clinical trial. *Am J Sports Med* 2005;33(6):806–13.

63. Kane TPC, Ismail M, Calder JDF. Topical glyceryl trinitrate and noninsertional achilles tendinopathy. *Am J Sports Med* 2008;36(6):1160–3.

64. Paoloni JA, Murrell GA, Burch RM et al. Randomised, double-blind, placebo-controlled clinical trial of a new topical glyceryl trinitrate patch for chronic lateral epicondylosis. *Br J Sports Med* 2009;43(4):299–302.

65. Cumpston M, Johnston RV, Wengier L et al. Topical glyceryl trinitrate for rotator cuff disease. *Coch Data Syst Rev* 2009(3):CD006355.

66. McCallum SD, Paoloni JA, Murrell GA. Five-year prospective comparison study of topical glyceryl trinitrate treatment of chronic lateral epicondylosis at the elbow. *Br J Sports Med* 2011;45(5):416–20.

67. Paoloni JA, Murrel GA. Three-year followup study of topical glyceryl trinitrate treatment of chronic noninsertional Achilles tendinopathy. *Foot Ankle Int* 2007;28(10):1064–8.

68. Alfredson H, Öhberg L, Zeisig E et al. Treatment of midportion Achilles tendinosis: similar clinical results with US and CD-guided surgery outside the tendon and sclerosing polidocanol injections. *Knee Surg Sports Traum Arth* 2007;15(12):1504–9.

69. Ceulen RPM, Bullens-Goessens YIJM, Pi-Van De Venne SJA et al. Outcomes and side effects of duplex-guided sclerotherapy in the treatment of great saphenous veins with 1% versus 3% polidocanol foam: results of a randomized controlled trial with 1-year follow-up. *Dermatol Surg* 2007;33(3):276–81.

70. Rabago D, Slattengren A, Zgierska A. Prolotherapy in primary care practice. *Primary Care* 2010;37 (1):65–80.

71. Cusi M, Saunders J, Hungerford B et al. The use of prolotherapy in the sacroiliac joint. *Br J Sports Med* 2010;44(2):100–4.

72. Choi H, McCartney M, Best TM. Treatment of osteitis pubis and osteomyelitis of the pubic symphysis in athletes: a systematic review. *Br J Sports Med* 2011;45(1):57–64.

73. Rabago D, Best TM, Zgierska AE et al. A systematic review of four injection therapies for lateral epicondylosis: prolotherapy, polidocanol, whole blood and platelet-rich plasma. *Br J Sports Med* 2009;43(7):471–81.

74. Yelland MJ, Sweeting KR, Lyftogt JA et al. Prolotherapy injections and eccentric loading exercises for painful Achilles tendinosis: a randomised trial. *Br J Sports Med* 2011;45(5):421–8.

75. Wandel S JP, Juni P, Tendal B et al. Effects of glucosamine, chondroitin, or placebo in patients with osteoarthritis of hip or knee: network meta-analysis. *BMJ* 2010(Sep 16);341:C4675.

A

76. Bellamy N, Campbell J, Robinson V et al. Viscosupplementation for the treatment of osteoarthritis of the knee. *Cochrane Database Syst Rev* 2005;18(2):CD005321.

77. Mei-Dan O, Kish B, Shabat S, M et al. Treatment of osteoarthritis of the ankle by intra-articular injections of hyaluronic acid: a prospective study. *J Am Podiatr Med Assoc* 2010;100(2):93–100.

78. Migliore A, Granata M. Intra-articular use of hyaluronic acid in the treatment of osteoarthritis. *Clin Inter Aging* 2008;3(2):365–9.

79. Aggarwal A, Sempowski IP. Hyaluronic acid injections for knee osteoarthritis. Systematic review of the literature. *Can Fam Physician* 2004;50:249–56.

80. Anandacoomarasamy A, March L. Current evidence for osteoarthritis treatments. *Ther Adv Musc Dis* 2010;2(1):17–28.

81. Arrich J, Piribauer F, Mad P et al. Intra-articular hyaluronic acid for the treatment of osteoarthritis of the knee: systematic review and meta-analysis. *Can Med Assoc J* 2005;172(8):1039–43.

82. Conrozier T, Vignon E. Is there evidence to support the inclusion of viscosupplementation in the treatment paradigm for patients with hip osteoarthritis? *Clin Exp Rheumatol* 2005;23(5):711–16.

83. Lo GH, LaValley M, McAlindon T et al. Intra-articular hyaluronic acid in treatment of knee osteoarthritis: a meta-analysis. *JAMA* 2003;290(23):3115–21.

84. Qvistgaard E, Christensen R, Torp-Pedersen S et al. Intra-articular treatment of hip osteoarthritis: a randomized trial of hyaluronic acid, corticosteroid, and isotonic saline. *Osteo Cart* 2006;14(2):163–70.

85. Moulin DE. Systematic drug treatment for chronic musculoskeletal pain. *Clin J Pain* 2001;17:S86–93.

86. O'Malley PG, Balden E, Tomkins G et al. Treatment of fibromyalgia with antidepressants. a meta-analysis. *J Gen Int Med* 2000;15(9):659–66.

87. Tofferi JK Jackson JJ, O'Malley PG. Treatment of fibromyalgia with cyclobenzaprine: a meta-analysis. *Arthritis Rheum* 2004;51(1):9–13.

88. Goldenberg DL. Pharmacological treatment of fibromyalgia and other chronic musculoskeletal pain. *Best Pract Res Clin Rheumatol* 2007;21(3):499–511.

89. Orchard J. Benefits and risks of using local anaestheic for pain relief to allow early return to play in professional football. *Br J Sports Med* 2002;36:209–13.

90. Zink W Graf BM. Local anaesthetic myotoxicity. *Reg Anesth Pain Med* 2004;29:333–40.

91. Hogan Q, Dotson R, Erickson S et al. Local anesthetic myotoxicity: a case and review. *Anesthesiology* 1994;80(4):942–7.

92. James P, Barbour T, Stone I. The match day use of ultrasound during professional football finals matches. *Br J Sports Med* 2010;44(16):1149–52.

93. Porozov S, Cahalon L, Weiser M et al. Inhibition of Il-1β and TNF-α secretion from resting and activated human immunocytes by the homeopathic medication Traumeel S. *Clin Dev Imm* 2004;11(2):143–9.

94. Orizola AJ, Vargas F. The efficacy of Traumeel S versus diclofenac and placebo ointment in tendinous pain in elite athletes: a randomised controlled trial. *Med Sci Sports Exerc* 2007;39(5):s79.

95. Drake MT Clarke BL, Khosla S. Bisphosphonates: mechanism of action and role in clinical practice. *Mayo Clin Proc* 2008;83(9):1032–45.

96. McNicholl DM, Heaney LG. The safety of bisphosphonate use in pre-menopausal women on corticosteroids. *Curr Drug Saf* 2010;5(2):182–7.

97. Black DM, Kelly MP, Genant HK et al. Bisphosphonates and fractures of the subtrochanteric or diaphyseal femur. *N Engl J Med* 2010;362:1761–71.

98. Milgrom C, Finestone A, Novack V et al. The effect of prophylactic treatment with risedronate on stress fracture incidence among infantry recruits. *Bone* 2004;35:418–24.

99. Stewart GW, Brunet ME, Manning MR et al. Treatment of stress fractures in athletes with intravenous pamidronate. *Clin J Sport Med* 2005;15(2):92–4.

100. Connell DA, Ali KE, Ahmad M et al. Ultrasound-guided autologous blood injection for tennis elbow. *Skeletal Radiol* 2006;35(6):371–7.

101. Edwards SG, Calandruccio JH. Autologous blood injections for refractory lateral epicondylitis. *J Hand Surg Am* 2003;28(2):272–8.

102. Ehrenfest DMD, Rasmussen L, Albrektsson T. Classification of platelet concentrates: from pure platelet-rich plasma (P-PRP) to leucocyte- and platelet-rich fibrin (L-PRF). *Trends Biotechnol* 2009;27(3):158–67.

103. de Mos M, van der Windt AE, Jahr H et al. Can platelet-rich plasma enhance tendon repair? A cell culture study. *Am J Sports Med* 2008;36(6):1171–8.

104. Sanchez M, Anitua E, Azofra J et al. Comparison of surgically repaired Achilles tendon tears using platelet-rich fibrin matrices. *Am J Sport Med* 2007;35(2):245–51.

105. Schepull T, Kvist J, Norrman H et al. Autologous platelets have no effect on the healing of human achilles tendon ruptures: A randomized single-blind study. *Am J Sports Med* 2011;39(1):38–47.

106. Kon E, Filardo G, Delcogliano M et al. Platelet-rich plasma: new clinical application. A pilot study for the treatment of jumper's knee. *Injury* 2009;40: 598–603.

107. Filardo G, Kon E, Della Villa S et al. Use of platelet-rich plasma for the treatment of refractory jumper's knee. *Int Orthop* 2010 Aug;34(6)909–15.

108. Gaweda K, Tarczynska M, Kryzanowski W. Treatment of achilles tendinopathy with platelet-rich plasma. *Int J Sports Med* 2010;31(8):577–83.

109. Randelli PS, Arrigoni P, Cabitza P et al. Autologous platelet rich plasma for arthroscopic rotator cuff repair. A pilot study. *Dis Rehab* 2008;30:1584–9.

110. Mishra, A Pavelko T. Treatment of chronic elbow tendinosis with buffered platelet-rich plasma. *Am J Sports Med* 2006;34:1774–8.

111. Peerbooms JC, Sluimer J, Bruijn DJ et al. Positive effect of an autologous platelet concentrate in lateral epicondylitis in a double-blind randomized controlled trial. *Am J Sports Med* 2010;38(2):255–62.

112. Herrera E, Sandoval MC, Camargo DM et al. Motor and sensory nerve conduction are affected differently by ice pack, ice massage, and cold water immersion. *Phys Ther* 2010;90(4):581–91.

113. Tolbert TA, Binkley HM. Treatment and prevention of shin splints. *Strength Condit J* 2009;31(5):69–72.

114. Hing WA, White SG, Bouaaphone A et al. Contrast therapy—A systematic review. *Phys Ther Sport* 2008;9(3):148–61.

115. Brancaccio P, Maffulli N, Limongelli FM. Creatine kinase monitoring in sport medicine. *Br Med Bull* 2007;81–2(1):209–30.

116. Chmura J, Nazar K. Parallel changes in the onset of blood lactate accumulation (OBLA) and threshold of psychomotor performance deterioration during incremental exercise after training in athletes. *Intl J Psychophysiol* 2010;75:287–90.

117. Chipchase LS, Trinkle D. Therapeutic ultrasound: clinician usage and perception of efficacy. *Hong Kong Physio J* 2003;21(1):5–14.

118. Ferrari CB, Andrade MAB, Adamowski JC et al. Evaluation of therapeutic ultrasound equipments performance. *Ultrasonics* 2010;50(7):704–9.

119. Watson T. Ultrasound in contemporary physiotherapy practice. *Ultrasonics* 2008;48(4):321–9.

120. Wong RA, Schumann B, Townsend R et al. A survey of therapeutic ultrasound use by physical therapists who are orthopaedic certified specialists. *Phys Ther* 2007;87(8):986–94.

121. Mitragotri S. Innovation: Healing sound: the use of ultrasound in drug delivery and other therapeutic applications. *Nature Rev Drug Disc* 2005;4(3):255–60.

122. Aytar A, Tuzun EH, Eker L et al. Effectiveness of low-dose pulsed ultrasound for treatment of delayed-onset muscle soreness: a double-blind randomized controlled trial. *Isokine Ex Sci* 2008;16(4):239–47.

123. Pounder NM, Harrison AJ. Low intensity pulsed ultrasound for fracture healing: a review of the clinical evidence and the associated biological mechanism of action. *Ultrasonics* 2008;48(4):330–8.

124. Warden SJ. A new direction for ultrasound therapy in sports medicine. *Sports Med* 2003;33(2):95–107.

125. Warden SJ, McKeeken JM. Ultrasound usage and dosage in sports physiotherapy. *Ultrasound Med Biol* 2002;28(8):1075–80.

126. Jones I, Johnson MI. Transcutaneous electrical nerve stimulation. *Contin Educ Anaesth Crit Care Pain* 2009;9(4):130–5.

127. Khadilkar A, Milne S, Brosseau L. Transcutaneous electrical nerve stimulation (TENS) for chronic low-back pain. *Coch Data Syst Rev* 2005(3):CD003008.

128. Nnoaham KE, Kumbang J. Transcutaneous electrical nerve stimulation (TENS) for chronic pain *Coch Data Syst Rev* 2008(3):CD003222.

129. Scudds RJ, Scudds RA, Baxter GD et al. Transcutaneous electrical nerve stimulation for the treatment of pain in physiotherapy practices in Hong Kong and the United Kingdom—a survey of usage and perceived effectiveness compared with other pain relieving modalities. *Hong Kong Physio J* 2009;27(1):11–20.

130. Khadilkar A, Odebiyi DO, Brosseau L et al. Transcutaneous electrical nerve stimulation (TENS) versus placebo for chronic low-back pain (review). *Coch Data Syst Rev* 2008(4):CD003008.

131. Bjordal JM, Johnson MI, Ljunggreen AE. Transcutaneous electrical nerve stimulation (TENS) can reduce postoperative analgesic consumption. A meta-analysis with assessment of optimal treatment parameters for postoperative pain. *Eur J Pain* 2003;7(2):181–88.

132. Bjordal JM, Couppe C, Chow RT et al. A systematic review of low level laser therapy with location-specific doses for pain from chronic joint disorders. *Aus J Physio* 2003;49:107–16.

133. Bjordal JM, Johnson M, Iversen V et al. Low-level laser therapy in acute pain: a systematic review of possible mechanisms of action and clinical effects in randomized placebo-controlled trials. *Photomed Laser Surg* 2006;24(2):237–47.

134. Bjordal JM, Lopes-Martins RAB, Iversen VV. A randomised, placebo controlled trial of low level laser therapy for activated Achilles tendinitis with microdialysis measurement of peritendinous prostaglandin E2 concentrations. *Br J Sports Med* 2006;40(1):76–80.

135. Chow RT, Barnsley L. Systematic review of the literature of low-level laser therapy (lllt) in the management of neck pain. *Lasers Surg Med* 2005;37:46–52.

136. World Association of Laser Therapy (WALT). Standards for the design and conduct of systematic reviews with low-level laser therapy for musculoskeletal pain and disorders. *Photomed Laser Surg* 2006;24(6):759–60.

137. Lopes-Martins RAB, Albertini R et al. Steroid receptor antagonist mifepristone inhibits the anti-inflammatory effects of photoradiation. *Photomed Laser Surg* 006;24(2):197–201.

138. Bjordal JM, Lopes-Martins RAB, Joensen J et al. A systematic review with procedural assessments and meta-analysis of low level laser therapy in lateral elbow tendinopathy (tennis elbow). *BMC Musculoskelet Disord* 2008;9:75.

139. Leal Junior E, Lopes-Martins R, Baroni B et al. Effect of 830 nm low-level laser therapy applied before high-intensity exercises on skeletal muscle recovery in athletes. *Lasers Med Sci* 2009;24(6):857–63.

140. Stergioulas A, Stergioula M, Aarskog R et al. Effects of low-level laser therapy and eccentric exercises in the treatment of recreational athletes with chronic Achilles tendinopathy. *Am J Sports Med* 2008;36(5):881–7.

141. Al-Mandeel MM, Watson T. The thermal and nonthermal effects of high and low doses of pulsed short wave therapy (PSWT). *Physiother Res Int* 2010;15(4):199–211.

142. Jan M-H, Chai H-M, Wang C-L et al. Effects of repetitive shortwave diathermy for reducing synovitis in patients with knee osteoarthritis: an ultrasonographic study. *Phys Ther* 2006;86(2):236–44.

143. Colbert AP, Wahbeh H, Harling N et al. Static magnetic field therapy: a critical review of treatment parameters. *eCAM* 2009;6(2):133–9.

144. Eccles NK. A critical review of randomized controlled trials of static magnets for pain relief. *J Altern Comp Med* 2005;11(3):495–509.

145. Mikesky AE, Hayden MW. Effect of static magnetic therapy on recovery from delayed onset muscle soreness. *Phys Ther Sport* 2005;6(4):188–94.

146. Pittler MH, Brown EM, Ernst E. Static magnets for reducing pain: systematic review and meta-analysis of randomized trials. *Can Med Assoc J* 2007;177(7): 736–42.

147. McKay JC, Prato FS, Thomas AW. A literature review: the effects of magnetic field exposure on blood flow and blood vessels in the microvasculature. *Bioelectromagnetics* 2007;28(2):81–98.

148. Laakso L, Lutter F, Young C. Static magnets – what are they and what do they do? *Rev Bras Fisioter* 2009;13(1):10–23.

149. Markov M. Magnetic field therapy: a review. *Electromag Biol Med* 2007;26:1–23.

150. Reeser JC, Smith DT, Fischer V et al. Static magnetic fields neither prevent nor diminish symptoms and signs of delayed onset muscle soreness. *Arch Phys Med Rehab* 2005;86(3):565–70.

151. Aktas I, Akgun K, Cakmak B. Therapeutic effect of pulsed electromagnetic field in conservative treatment of subacromial impingement syndrome. *Clin Rheumatol* 2007;26:1234–39.

152. Zorzi C, Dall'Oca C, Cadossi R et al. Effects of pulsed electromagnetic fields on patients' recovery after arthroscopic surgery: prospective, randomized and double-blind study. *Knee Surg Sports Traumatol Arth* 2007;15(7):830–4.

153. Rompe JD, Maffulli N. Repetitive shock wave therapy for lateral elbow tendinopathy (tennis elbow): a systematic and qualitative analysis. *Br Med Bull* 2007;83(1):355–78.

154. Schmitz C, DePace R. Pain relief by extracorporeal shockwave therapy: an update on the current understanding. *Urol Res* 2009;37(4):231–4.

155. van Leeuwen MT, Zwerver J, van den Akker-Scheek I. Extracorporeal shockwave therapy for patellar tendinopathy: a review of the literature. *Br J Sports Med* 2009;43(3):163–8.

156. Rompe JD, Cacchio A, Furia JP et al. Low-energy extracorporeal shock wave therapy as a treatment for medial tibial stress syndrome. *Am J Sports Med* 2010;38:125–32.

157. Vavken P, Holinka J, Rompe JD et al. Focused extracorporeal shock wave therapy in calcifying

tendinitis of the shoulder: a meta-analysis. *Sports Health: A Multidisciplinary Approach* 2009;1(2):137–44.

158. Buchbinder R, Green S, Youd JM et al. Shock wave therapy for lateral elbow pain (review). *Coch Data Syst Rev* 2005(4):CD003524.

159. Thomson C, Crawford F, Murray G. The effectiveness of extra corporeal shock wave therapy for plantar heel pain: a systematic review and meta-analysis. *BMC Musc Dis* 2005;6(1):19.

160. Zimmermann R, Cumpanas A, Miclea F et al. Extracorporeal shock wave therapy for the treatment of chronic pelvic pain syndrome in males: a randomised, double-blind, placebo-controlled study. *Eur Urol* 2009;56:418–24.

161. Cyriax J. *Textbook of orthopaedic medicine*. 6th edn. London: Bailliere Tindall, 1975.

162. Kaltenborn F. *Manual therapy of the extremity joints*. Oslo, Bokhandel, 1975.

163. Maitland GD. *Vertebral manipulation*. 5th ed. London: Butterworths, 1986.

164. McKenzie R. *The lumbar spine: mechanical diagnosis and therapy*. Waikane: Spinal Publications, 1981.

165. Bronfort G, Haas M, Evans R et al. Evidence-informed management of chronic low back pain with spinal manipulation and mobilization. *Spine J* 2007;8(1): 213–25.

166. Sran MM. To treat or not to treat: new evidence for the effectiveness of manual therapy. *Br J Sports Med* 2004;38:521–5.

167. Vernon H, Humphreys K, Hagino C. Chronic mechanical neck pain in adults treated by manual therapy: a systematic review of change scores in randomized clinical trials. *J Manip Physiol Ther* 2007;30(3):215–27.

168. Hoving JL, Koes BW, de Vet HC et al. Manual therapy, physical therapy, or continued care by general practitioner for patients with neck pain. *Ann Intern Med.* 2002;136:713–22.

169. Jull GP, Trott P, Potter HP et al. A randomized controlled trial of exercise and manipulative therapy for cervicogenic headache. *Spine* 2002;27(17):1835–43.

170. Aure OF, Hoel Nilsen J, Vasseljen O. Manual therapy and exercise therapy in patients with chronic low back pain: a randomized, controlled trial with 1-year follow-up. *Spine* 2003;28(6):525–31.

171. Cleland JA, Childs MJD, McRae M et al. Immediate effects of thoracic manipulation in patients with neck pain: a randomized clinical trial. *Manual Ther* 2005;10(2):127–35.

172. Mior S. Manipulation and mobilization in the treatment of chronic pain. *Clin J Pain* 2001;17:S70–6.

173. Ernst E, Canter PH. A systematic review of systematic reviews of spinal manipulation. *J R Soc Med* 2006;99(4):192–6.

174. Walser RF, Meserve BB, Boucher TR. The effectiveness of thoracic spine manipulation for the management of musculoskeletal conditions: a systematic review and meta-analysis of randomized clinical trials. *J Man Manip Ther* 2009;17(4):237–46.

175. Graham N, Gross A, Goldsmith C. Mechanical traction for mechanical neck disorders: a systematic review. *J Rehab Med* 2006;38(3):145–52.

176. Clarke JMA, van Tulder MP, Blomberg SMDP et al. Traction for low back pain with or without sciatica: an updated systematic review within the framework of the cochrane collaboration. *Spine* 2006;31(14):1591–9.

177. Gay RE, Brault JS. Evidence-informed management of chronic low back pain with traction therapy. *Spine J* 2008;8(1):234–42.

178. Graham N, Gross A, Goldsmith C et al. Mechanical traction for neck pain with or without radiculopathy. *Coch Data Syst Rev (3)* 2008;3:CD006408.

179. Macario A, Pergolizzi JV. Systematic literature review of spinal decompression via motorized traction for chronic discogenic low back pain. *Pain Pract* 2006;6(3):171–8.

180. Gerwin R, Shannon S, Hong C-Z et al. Interrater reliability in myofascial trigger point examination. *Pain* 1997;69:65–73.

181. Lucas KR, Polus BI, Rich PA. Latent myofascial trigger points: their effects on muscle activation and movement efficiency. *J Bodywork Move Ther* 2004;8(3):160–6.

182. Selkow N, Grindstaff T, Cross K et al. Short-term effect of muscle energy technique on pain in individuals with non-specific lumbopelvic pain: a pilot study. *J Man Manip Ther* 2009;17(1):E14–18.

183. Chaitow L. *Muscle energy techniques: advanced soft tissue techniques*. 3rd ed. Elsevier Health Sciences, 2006.

184. Burns DK, Wells MR. Gross range of motion in the cervical spine: the effects of osteopathic muscle energy technique in asymptomatic subjects. *J Am Osteopath Assoc* 2006;106(3):137–42.

185. Smith M, Fryer G. A comparison of two muscle energy techniques for increasing flexibility of the hamstring muscle group. *J Bodywork Mov Ther* 2008;12(4):312–17.

186. Wilson E, Payton O, Donegan-Shoaf L, Dec K. Muscle energy technique in patients with acute lower back

pain: a pilot clinical trial. *J. Orthop Sports Phys Ther* 2003;33:502–12.

187. Ellis RF, Hing WA. Neural mobilization: a systematic review of randomized controlled trials with an analysis of therapeutic efficacy. *J Man Manip Ther* 2008;16(1):8–22.

188. Madsen MV, Gotzsche PC, Hrobjartsson A. Acupuncture treatment for pain: systematic review of randomised clinical trials with acupuncture, placebo acupuncture, and no acupuncture groups. *BMJ* 2009; 338:a3115.

189. Ernst E. Acupuncture: What does the most reliable evidence tell us? *J Pain Symp Man* 2009;37(4):709–14.

190. Manheimer E, Wieland S, Kimbrough E et al. Evidence from the Cochrane Collaboration for traditional Chinese medicine therapies. *J Altern Comp Med* 2009;15(9):1001–14.

191. Sun D-l, Zhang Y, Chen D-l. Research progress in sports fatigue prevented and treated by acupuncture. *J Acupunc Tuina Sci* 2009;7(2):123–28.

192. Sun Y, Gan TJ, Dubose JW et al. Acupuncture and related techniques for postoperative pain: a systematic review of randomized controlled trials. *Br J Anaesth.* 2008;101(2):151–60.

193. White A, Foster NE, Cummings M et al. Acupuncture treatment for chronic knee pain: a systematic review. *Rheumatology* 2007:46(3):384–90

194. Yuan JP, Purepong NM, Kerr DPP et al. Effectiveness of acupuncture for low back pain: a systematic review. *Spine* 2008;33(23):E887–900.

195. Dhillon SM. The acute effect of acupuncture on 20-km cycling performance. *Clin J Sport Med* 2008;18(1): 76–80.

196. Itoh K, Ochi H, Kitakoji H. Effects of tender point acupuncture on delayed onset muscle soreness (DOMS) – a pragmatic trial. *Chin Med* 2008;3(1):14.

197. Lewit K. The needle effect in the relief of musculoskeletal pain. *Pain* 1979;6:83.

198. Simons DG. Clinical and etiological update of myofascial pain from trigger points. *J Musc Pain* 1996;4(1):93–122.

199. Simons DG, Dommerholt J. Myofascial pain syndrome—trigger points. *J Musc Pain* 2007;15(1): 63–79.

200. Huguenin LK. Myofascial trigger points: the current evidence. *Phys Ther Sport* 2004;5(1):2–12.

201. Tough EA, White AR, Cummings TM et al. Acupuncture and dry needling in the management of myofascial trigger point pain: a systematic review and meta-analysis of randomised controlled trials. *Eur J Pain* 2009;13(1):3–10.

202. Garvey TA, Marks MR, Wiesel SW. A prospective, randomised, double-blind evaluation of trigger-point injection therapy for low-back pain. *Spine* 1989;14:962–4.

203. Hong C. Lidocaine injection versus dry needling to myofascial trigger point: the importance of the local twitch response. *Am J Phys Med Rehab* 1994;73(4):256–263

204. Furlan AD, van Tulder M, Cherkin D et al. Acupuncture and dry-needling for low back pain: an updated systematic review within the framework of the Cochrane collaboration. *Spine* 2005;30(8): 944–63.

205. Hsieh Y-LP, Kao MJ, Kuan TS et al. Dry needling to a key myofascial trigger point may reduce the irritability of satellite MTrPs. *Am J Phys Med Rehab* 2007;86(5):397–403.

206. Huguenin L, Brukner PD, McCrory P et al. Effect of dry needling of gluteal muscles on straight leg raise: a randomised, placebo controlled, double blind trial. *Br J Sports Med* 2005;39(2):84–90.

207. D'agostino-Dias M, Fontes B, Poggetti RS et al. Hyperbaric oxygen therapy: types of injury and number of sessions – a review of 1506 cases. *Undersea Hyperb Med* 2008;35(1):53–60.

208. Mortensen CR. Hyperbaric oxygen therapy. *Curr Anaes Crit Care* 2008;19:333–7.

209. Borromeo CN, Ryan JL, Marchetto PA et al. Hyperbaric oxygen therapy for acute ankle sprains. *Am J Sports Med* 1997;25(5):619–25.

210. Staples JR, Clement DB, Taunton JE et al. Effects of hyperbaric oxygen on a human model of injury. *Am J Sports Med* 1999;27(5):600–5.

211. Kawada S, Fukaya K, Ohtani M et al. Effects of pre-exposure to hyperbaric hyperoxia on high-intensity exercise performance. *J Strength Cond Res* 2008;22(1):66–74

212. Rozenek R, Fobel BF, Banks JC et al. Does hyperbaric oxygen exposure affect high-intensity, short-duration exercise performance? *J Strength Cond Res* 2007;21(4):1037–41.

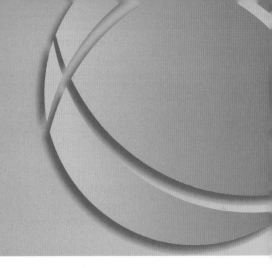

Chapter 14

Core stability

with SALLIE COWAN

Annika Sorenstam's 500 daily sit-ups are famous.
EJ Clair, Junior Editor *Pacific Northwest Golf Magazine*

In recent years, an understanding of the concept of core stability has changed the way in which we rehabilitate our patients. This book uses the term "core stability" but there are many other interchangeable terms (Table 14.1). The musculoskeletal core of the body includes the spine, hips and pelvis, proximal lower limb, and abdominal structures.

We use the term "stability" rather than "strength" because strength is just one component of the dynamic stability required. Dynamic stabilization refers to the ability to utilize strength and endurance and motor control in a functional manner through all planes of motion and action despite changes in the centre of gravity.[1] A comprehensive strengthening or facilitation of these core muscles has been advocated as a preventive, rehabilitative, and performance-enhancing program for various lumbar spine and musculoskeletal injuries.

The stability of the lumbopelvic region is crucial, to provide a foundation for limb movement, to support loads, and to protect the spine.[2] Nearly 30 years ago, Panjabi[2] described an innovative model of spinal stabilization that still serves as an appropriate model of understanding core stability today. The model incorporates a passive subsystem, an active subsystem, and a neural control system (Fig. 14.1).

The passive subsystem consists of bony and ligamentous structures of the spine. While passive components of the system are integral components of spinal stability, on their own they are unable to bear much of a compressive load[3, 4] and offer most restraint toward the end of range. Thus the active subsystem is vital to allow for support of the body mass and additional loads associated with dynamic activity.[2, 5] The active subsystem consists of the muscles that attach directly and indirectly to the spinal column; this system, however, is only as good as the system that drives it—the control subsystem.[6] The control system must sense the requirements of stability and plan strategies to meets these demands—thus activating muscles at the right time, in the right amount, and in the right sequence; it then must turn these muscles

Table 14.1 Terms used to describe core stability

Lumbar/lumbopelvic stabilization
Dynamic stabilization
Motor control
Neuromuscular training
Neutral spine control
Muscular fusion
Trunk stabilization
Core strengthening

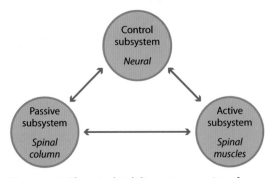

Figure 14.1 The spinal stability system consists of three subsystems: passive spinal column, active spinal muscles, and neural control unit   FROM PANJABI[2]

off appropriately. Thus, Panjabi contends that these three subsystems are interdependent components of the spinal stabilization system, with one subsystem capable of compensating for deficits in another.

The muscles that make up the active subsystem—often referred to as the "core"—include the abdominals in the front, paraspinals and gluteals in the back, diaphragm as the roof, pelvic floor and hip girdle musculature as the bottom, and hip abductors and rotators laterally.[6] All these muscles have direct or indirect attachments to the extensive thoracolumbar fascia and spinal column, which connect the upper and lower limbs.

A major advance in our understanding of how muscles contribute to lumbar stabilization came from recognizing the difference between local and global muscles.[7] Global (dynamic, phasic) muscles

are the large, torque-producing muscles, such as the rectus abdominis, external oblique, and the thoracic part of lumbar iliocostalis, which link the pelvis to the thoracic cage and provide general trunk stabilization as well as movement.

Local (postural, tonic) muscles are those that attach directly to the lumbar vertebrae and are responsible for providing segmental stability and directly controlling the lumbar segments during movement. These muscles include the lumbar multifidus, psoas major, quadratus lumborum, the lumbar parts of iliocostalis and longissimus, transversus abdominis, the diaphragm, and the posterior fibers of internal oblique (Fig. 14.2).

The neural subsystem has the complex task of maintaining stability by continually monitoring and adjusting the tension in these muscles. In addition

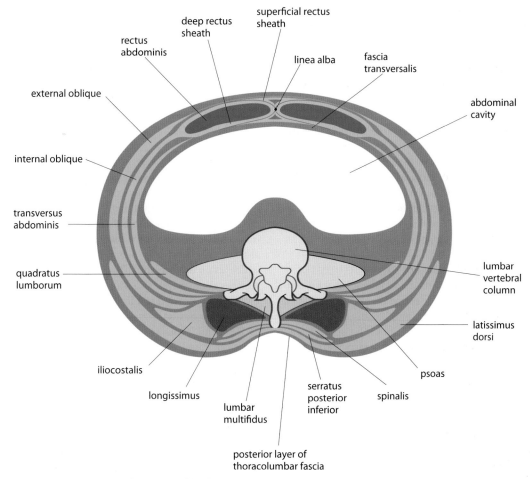

Figure 14.2 Cross-sectional anatomy of the lumbar spine

to providing segmental stability (local muscles), the neural subsystem must also allow for desired joint movement (global muscles) to occur.[2, 5]

Spinal instability occurs when either of these components is disturbed. Instability can result from tissue damage (e.g. disk injury), insufficient muscle strength or endurance, or poor motor control or, often, a combination of all three factors. *Gross instability* is true displacement of vertebrae, such as with traumatic disruption of two out of three vertebrae, whereas *functional instability* is a relatively increased range of the neutral zone (the range in which internal resistance from active muscular control is minimal).[8] Active stiffness or stability can be achieved through muscular co-contraction.[9]

Whereas previously the major emphasis in rehabilitation had been to strengthen the global muscles (e.g. the use of sit-ups as a treatment for low back pain), we now understand that both groups of muscles must be working efficiently. We have also come to realize that strength is not the only, nor indeed the most important, quality of the muscle. Muscle activation, coordination, and endurance may be more important than strength, and any rehabilitation program should reflect this.

Anatomy

Stability and movement are critically dependent on the coordination of all the muscles surrounding the lumbar spine. Even though recent research has advocated the importance of a few muscles in particular (transversus abdominis and multifidus), all core muscles are needed for optimal stabilization and performance.[10] To achieve muscular co-contraction, precise neural input and output is needed.[11]

Osseous and ligamentous structures

Passive stiffness is imparted to the lumbar spine by the osseoligamentous structures. Functional instability may be caused by injury to any of these structures. The posterior elements of the spine include the pedicle, lamina, and pars interarticularis. These structures are, in fact, flexible. However, too much load causes failure, typically at the pars. The intervertebral disk is composed of the anulus fibrosus, nucleus pulposus, and the end plates. Compressive and shearing loads can cause injury, initially to the end plates, and ultimately to the anulus such that posterior disk herniations result. Weak muscular control can cause excessive external loads on the disk, thus causing a vicious cycle where the disk no

longer provides optimal passive stiffness or stability. The spinal ligaments provide little stability in the neutral zone. Their more important role may be to provide afferent proprioception of the lumbar spine segments.[12]

The thoracolumbar fascia

The thoracolumbar fascia (TLF) plays an important role in spinal stability, working as a retinacular strap of the muscles of the lumbar spine. It consists of three layers—the anterior, middle, and posterior. The posterior layer has the most important role in supporting the lumbar spine and abdominal musculature.

The transversus abdominis has large attachments to the middle and posterior layers of the TLF.[6] The posterior layer of the TLF consists of two laminae—a superficial lamina with fibers passing downward and medially, and a deep lamina with fibers passing downward and laterally. The aponeurosis of the latissimus dorsi muscle forms the superficial layer. In essence, the TLF provides a link between the lower limb and the upper limb,[13] with the interaction between intraabdominal pressure and fascial tension being critical for spinal stability.[6] With contraction of the muscular contents, the TLF acts as an activated proprioceptor, like a back belt providing feedback in lifting activities.

Paraspinals

There are two major groups of the lumbar extensors—the erector spinae and the so-called local muscles (rotators, intertransversi, multifidi). The erector spinae in the lumbar region are composed of two major muscles—the longissimus and iliocostalis. These are actually primarily thoracic muscles which act on the lumbar region via a long tendon that attaches to the pelvis. This long moment arm is ideal for lumbar extension and for creating posterior shear with lumbar flexion.[4]

Deep and medial to the erector spinae muscles lie the local muscles. The rotators and intertransversi muscles do not have a great moment arm. It is likely that they represent length transducers or position sensors of a spinal segment by way of their rich composition of muscle spindles. The multifidi pass along two or three spinal levels. They are theorized to work as segmental stabilizers. Due to their short moment arms, the multifidi are not involved much in gross movement. The multifidi have been found to be atrophied in individuals with low back pain.[14]

A

Quadratus lumborum

The quadratus lumborum is a large, thin, quadrangular-shaped muscle that has direct insertions to the lumbar spine. There are three major components or muscular fascicles to the quadratus lumborum—the inferior oblique, superior oblique, and longitudinal fascicles. Both the longitudinal and superior oblique fibers have no direct action on the lumbar spine. They are designed as secondary respiratory muscles to stabilize the twelfth rib during respiration. The inferior oblique fibers of the quadratus lumborum are a weak lateral flexor of the lumbar vertebrae. McGill believes the quadratus lumborum is a major stabilizer of the spine, typically working isometrically.[15]

Abdominals

The abdominal muscles serve as a vital component of the core. The transversus abdominis, the deepest of the abdominal muscles, has received particular attention. Its fibers run horizontally around the abdomen, and when it contracts bilaterally it reduces the circumference of the abdominal wall, flattening the lower region to increase the intrabdominal pressure and tension in the thoracolumbar fascia. Isolated activation of the transversus abdominis is achieved through "hollowing in" of the abdomen.[6] As well, the transversus abdominis has been shown to activate in a feed-forward fashion prior to limb movement, theoretically to stabilize the lumbar spine. Patients with low back pain have delayed activation of the transversus abdominis,[1] as have individuals with chronic groin pain.[16]

The internal oblique forms the middle layer of the abdominal wall and has similar fiber orientation to the transversus abdominis, and thus contributes to the support of the abdominal contents and the modulation of the intra-abdominal pressure. However, the fiber orientation of the internal oblique and, more so, of the external oblique means that they have major functions in controlling trunk movement, as well as imparting functional stability to the lumbar spine.[15]

The rectus abdominis is a paired, strap-like muscle of the anterior abdominal wall. Contraction of this muscle predominantly causes flexion of the lumbar spine. Many fitness programs incorrectly emphasize rectus abdominis and internal oblique development, thus creating an imbalance with the relatively weaker external oblique.[17]

Hip girdle musculature

The hip musculature plays a major role in all dynamic activities, particularly those in upright stance,

stabilization of the trunk/pelvis, and in transferring force from the lower extremities to the pelvis and spine.[18] Poor endurance and delayed firing of the hip extensor (gluteus maximus) and abductor (gluteus medius) muscles have been noted in individuals with lower extremity instability,[19] knee pain,[20] or low back pain.[21] Nadler et al. demonstrated a significant asymmetry in hip extensor strength in female athletes with reported low back pain.[22] In a prospective study, Nadler et al. demonstrated a significant association between hip strength imbalance of the hip extensors measured during the pre-participation physical examination, and the occurrence of low back pain in female athletes over the ensuing year.[23] Overall, the hip appears to play a significant role in transferring forces from the lower extremities to the pelvis and spine, acting as one link within the kinetic chain.

The psoas major is a long, thick muscle whose primary action is flexion of the hip. However, based on its attachment sites into the lumbar spine, it has the potential to aid in spinal biomechanics. The psoas muscle has three proximal attachment sites—the medial half of the transverse processes from T12 to L5, the intervertebral disk, and the vertebral body adjacent to the disk.[19] However, it is not likely that the psoas provides much stability to the lumbar spine except in increased lumbar flexion.[4] Increased stability requirements or a tight psoas may concomitantly cause increased compressive injurious loads to the lumbar disks.

Diaphragm and pelvic floor

The diaphragm serves as the roof of the core, with the pelvic floor forming the base. The diaphragm and pelvic floor contribute to spinal stability primarily through their role in generating intra-abdominal pressure and by restricting movement of the abdominal viscera.[6] Recent studies have indicated that individuals with sacroiliac pain have impaired recruitment of the diaphragm and pelvic floor.[24] Ventilatory challenges on the body may cause further diaphragm dysfunction and lead to more compressive loads on the lumbar spine.[25] Thus, diaphragmatic breathing techniques may be an important part of a core strengthening program. Furthermore, the pelvic floor musculature is coactivated with transversus abdominis contraction.[26]

Assessment of core stability

While there is no single measure of core stability, a few simple tests will provide an indication of the endurance of certain key muscle groups. The four tests advocated are the prone and lateral bridges, and the torso flexor and extensor endurance tests. The bridge tests are functional in that they assess strength, muscle endurance, and how well the athlete is able to control the trunk by the synchronous activation of many muscles.[27]

The prone bridge (Fig. 14.3) is performed by supporting the body's weight between the forearms and toes; it primarily assesses the anterior and posterior core muscles. Failure occurs when the patient loses neutral pelvis and falls into a lordotic position with anterior rotation of the pelvis.

The lateral bridge (Fig. 14.4) assesses the lateral core muscles. Failure occurs when the patient loses the straight posture and the hip falls towards the table.

Testing of the torso flexors (Fig. 14.5) can be done by timing how long the patient can hold a position of seated torso flexion at 60°. Failure occurs when the torso falls below 60°.

The endurance of the torso extensors (Fig. 14.6) can be tested with the patient prone. Failure occurs when the upper body falls from horizontal into a flexed position.

McGill[4] has published normative data for the lateral, flexor, and extensor tests for young, healthy individuals and this is shown in Table 14.2.

McGill has further shown that the relationship of endurance among the anterior, lateral, and posterior musculature is upset once back troubles begin, and this persists long after symptoms have resolved.

Figure 14.3 Prone bridge. Patients support themselves on the forearms, with the pelvis in the neutral position and the body straight

Figure 14.4 Lateral bridge. Legs are extended and the top foot placed in front of the lower foot for support. Patients support themselves on one elbow and their feet while lifting their hips off the floor to create a straight line over their body length. The uninvolved arm is held across the chest with the hand placed on the opposite shoulder

Figure 14.5 Flexor endurance test. The patient sits at 60° with both hips and knees at 90°, arms folded across the chest with the hands placed on the opposite shoulder, and toes secured under toe straps or by the examiner

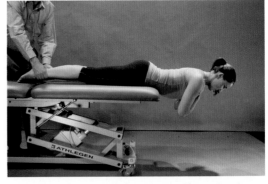

Figure 14.6 Extensor endurance test. The patient is prone over the edge of the couch with the pelvis, hips, and knees secured. The upper limbs are held across the chest with the hands resting on the opposite shoulders

Table 14.2 Mean endurance times in seconds and flexion/extension ratio in young, healthy subjects (mean age 21 years)[4]

	Men	Women
Extension	161	185
Flexion	136	134
Right side bridge	95	75
Left side bridge	99	78
Flexion/extension ratio	0.84	0.72

Typically, the extensor endurance is diminished relative to flexor endurance (e.g. flexion/extension ratio >1.0) and lateral musculature.[4]

The single-legged squat exercise (Fig. 14.7) is also used as an indicator of lumbopelvic–hip stability. The single-legged squat is functional, requires control of the body over a single weight-bearing lower limb, and is frequently used clinically to assess hip and trunk muscular coordination and/or control.

Ultrasound imaging is also used as an assessment technique.

Figure 14.7 Single-legged squat exercise

Exercise of the core musculature

Exercise of the core musculature is more than trunk strengthening.[10] In fact, motor relearning of inhibited muscles may be more important than strengthening in patients with low back pain. In athletic endeavors, muscle endurance appears to be more important than pure muscle strength.[28]

The overload principle advocated in sports medicine is a nemesis in the back. In other words, the progressive resistance strengthening of some core muscles, particularly the lumbar extensors, may be unsafe to the back. In fact, many traditional back strengthening exercises may also be unsafe. For example, Roman chair exercises or back extensor strengthening machines require at least torso mass as resistance, which is a load often injurious to the lumbar spine.[3]

Traditional sit-ups are also unsafe because they cause increased compression loads on the lumbar spine.[29] Pelvic tilts are utilized less often than in the past because they may increase spinal loading. In addition, all these traditional exercises are non-functional.[4] In individuals suspected of having instability, stretching exercises should be used with caution, particularly ones encouraging end-range lumbar flexion. The risk of lumbar injury is greatly increased when the spine is fully flexed and with excessive repetitive torsion.[30] Exercise must progress from training isolated muscles to training as an integrated unit to facilitate functional activity.

The neutral spine has been advocated by some as a safe place to begin exercise.[31] The neutral spine position is a pain-free position that should not be confused with assuming a flat back posture. It is said to be the position of power and balance. However, because functional activities move through the neutral position, exercises should be progressed to non-neutral positions.

Decreasing spinal and pelvic viscosity

Spinal exercises should not be done in the first hour after awakening due to the increased hydrostatic pressures in the disk during that time.[32] The cat/camel (Fig. 14.8 overleaf) and the pelvic translation exercises are ways to achieve spinal segment and pelvic accessory motion prior to starting more aggressive exercises. As well, improving hip range of motion can help dissipate forces from the lumbar spine. A short aerobic program may also be implemented to serve as a warm-up. Fast walking appears to cause less torque on the lower back than slow walking.[33]

Figure 14.8 Cat/camel exercise

Use of biofeedback and real-time ultrasound in retraining core control

Pressure biofeedback units are used to help facilitate the activation of the multifidi and transversus abdominis.[6] Verbal cues may also be useful to facilitate muscle activation. For example, abdominal "hollowing" is performed by transversus abdominis activation; abdominal "bracing" is performed by co-contraction of many muscles including the transversus abdominis, external obliques, and internal obliques. However, most of these isolation exercises of the transversus abdominis are in non-functional positions. When the trained muscle is "awakened," exercise training should quickly shift to functional positions and activities.

The use of real-time ultrasound imaging has become increasingly popular as a means of assessing muscle size and activity during the rehabilitation process. Most emphasis has been on the assessment of muscle size and muscle activation in the transversus abdominis and multifidus muscles. These measures have been shown to be valid.[34]

Ultrasound imaging may improve treatment from two perspectives—as a measure of muscle dysfunction and outcome, and as a tool for provision of feedback. There is some evidence that the use of ultrasound to both guide treatment and assess outcome has been successful in monitoring multifidus[35] and transversus abdominis function[36] with positive clinical outcomes in patients with chronic low back pain.

Accurate feedback is critical for skill learning, and feedback with ultrasound imaging may increase the quality of training, particularly for the group of patients who find it difficult to activate these muscles. Several studies using ultrasound imaging in the training of muscle control in patients with low back pain have reported positive outcomes.[35] However, whether the outcome with inclusion of ultrasound was improved above that which could be achieved without ultrasound feedback has not been established.

Stabilization exercises

Stabilization exercises can be progressed from a beginning level to more advanced levels. There are many different programs published; however, the general principles are common to all. Initially the motor skill (e.g. activation of transversus abdominis and multifidus) must be learned, but ultimately the activation must become automatic without conscious effort when performing the patient's sporting activity.

Rehabilitation of these muscles takes place in three distinct stages:

1. formal motor skill training
2. functional progression
3. sport-specific training.

Most clinicians agree that a motor relearning approach, especially teaching patients to activate their deep stabilizing muscles (transversus abdominis and multifidus), is the first stage of the program. Richardson et al.[6] advocate a segmental stabilization approach focusing on the co-contraction of transversus abdominis and multifidus, and also stressing the importance of the pelvic floor musculature. The most significant motor skill that is linked to the stability of these two muscles is the action of abdominal "drawing in" (Fig. 14.9).

The aim is for the patient to use the correct muscles in response to the command "draw in your abdominal wall without moving your spine or pelvis and hold for 10 seconds while breathing normally." The four-point kneeling position (Fig. 14.10) is the best position to teach the patient the action. Ask the patient to take a relaxed breath in and out and

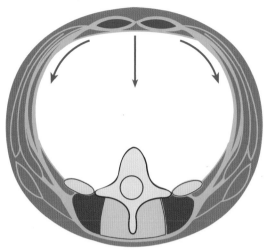

Figure 14.9 Diagrammatic representation of the muscle contraction of "drawing in" of the abdominal wall with an isometric contraction of the lumbar multifidus

Figure 14.10 The four-point kneeling position

then draw the abdomen up toward the spine without taking a breath. The contraction must be performed in a slow and controlled manner. At the same time, the patient contracts the pelvic floor and slightly anteriorly rotates the pelvis to activate the multifidi. Assessment of optimal recruitment of these muscles can be done through palpation or with the use of biofeedback or ultrasound imaging. Once the contraction has been achieved, the patient should commence breathing in a slow and controlled manner, holding the contraction for 10 seconds.

Once the action is understood by the patient, the formal test is conducted with the patient lying prone and using a pressure biofeedback unit. The patient lies prone with arms by their side, and the pressure biofeedback unit is placed under the abdomen, with

the navel in the center and the distal edge of the pad in line with the right and left anterior superior iliac spines. The pressure pad is inflated to 70 mmHg and allowed to stabilize. The patient is again instructed to breathe in and out and then, without breathing in, to slowly draw in the abdomen so that it lifts up off the pad, keeping the spinal position steady. Once the contraction has been achieved, the patient should commence normal relaxed breathing. The contraction is held for 10 seconds and the procedure repeated up to 10 times.

A successful performance of the test reduces the pressure by 6–10 mmHg. This pressure change indicates that the patient is able to contract the transversus abdominis into its shortened range independently of the other abdominal muscles. Once the abdominal drawing-in technique is successfully learned in the prone position, the patient is encouraged to continue the exercise while in the sitting and standing positions. Richardson et al.[6] describe this process of segmental stabilization as a three-stage exercise model—Stage 1, local segmental control; Stage 2, closed-chain segmental control; Stage 3, open-chain segmental control (Fig 14.11 overleaf), which forms the building blocks for the development of joint protection mechanisms.

Others have a different approach to the drawing-in exercise. McGill advocates bracing of the spine,[4] which activates all the abdominal musculature and extensors at once. This is usually performed with the patient in a standing position, by simultaneously contracting the abdominal musculature and the extensors. Bracing activates all three layers of the abdominal musculature, not just the transversus abdominis.

Once the patient has learned to stabilize the lumbopelvic region with the above isometric exercises to create a functional muscle corset, he or she can progress towards dynamic stabilization. McGill advocates early incorporation of his "big three" exercises into the program.[4] These are outlined below:

1. Curl-ups for the rectus abdominis (Fig. 14.12 overleaf). The rectus abdominis is most active during the initial elevation of the head, neck, and shoulders. The lumbar spine should stay in neutral. The exercise can be advanced by asking the patient to raise the elbows a couple of centimeters.

2. Side bridge exercises for the obliques, quadratus lumborum, and transversus abdominis (Fig. 14.13 overleaf). Abdominal bracing is also required.

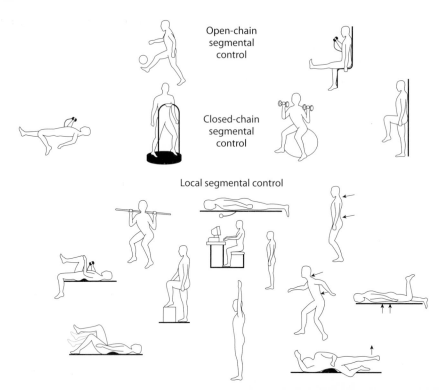

Open-chain
segmental
control

Closed-chain
segmental
control

Local segmental control

Figure 14.11 The segmental stabilization model for the prevention and treatment of low back pain
FROM RICHARDSON[37]

The exercise can be advanced initially by placing the free arm along the side of the torso, and subsequently by straightening the legs.

3. Bird dog exercise (Fig. 14.14). Leg and arm extensions in a hands–knees position, eventually leading to the "bird dog" exercise for the back extensors.

Figure 14.13 Side bridges
(a) In the beginning, position the patient on the side supported by the elbow and hip. The free hand is placed on the opposite shoulder pulling it down

Figure 14.12 Curl-ups. Patient lies supine with the hands supporting the lumbar region. Do not flatten the back to the floor. One leg is bent with the knee flexed to 90°. Do not flex the cervical spine. Leave the elbows on the floor while elevating the head and shoulders a short distance off the floor

(b) The torso is straightened until the body is supported on the elbow and feet

Figure 14.14 Bird dog exercise. The bird dog position is with hands under the shoulders and knees directly under the hips. Initially, simply lift one hand or knee a couple of centimeters off the floor. The patient can progress to raising the opposite hand and knee simultaneously, then raising one arm or leg at a time and then raising the opposite arm and leg simultaneously, as shown

Other frequently used exercises include the clam (Fig. 14.15) and the bridge (Fig. 14.16). It is important to avoid incorrect techniques (Fig. 14.16c).

Many clinicians base their progressive exercises on Saal and Saal's seminal dynamic lumbar stabilization efficacy study (Table 14.3).[38]

Sahrmann also describes a series of progressive lower abdominal muscle exercises (Table 14.4 overleaf).[17]

Table 14.3 Stabilization and abdominal program described by Saal[31]

Finding neutral position
Sitting stabilization
Prone gluteal squeezes
Supine pelvic bracing
Pelvic bridging progression
Quadruped
Kneeling stabilization
Wall slide quadriceps strengthening
Position transition with postural control
Curl-ups
Dead bugs
Diagonal curl-ups
Straight leg lowering

Functional progression

The initial basic strengthening exercises described above are initiated on the ground. The exercises must progress to positions of function, from a stable ground environment to a progressively less stable environment, and movements must increase in complexity.[27] In other words, the sportsperson must progress from muscle activation and strengthening to a program of dynamic stabilization.

Figure 14.15 Clam

(b) Supine bridging with leg extension

Figure 14.16 Bridging
(a) Supine bridging

(c) Incorrect bridging technique

Table 14.4 Sahrmann's lower abdominal exercise progression[17]

Position	Exercise
Base position	Supine with knee bent and feet on floor; spine stabilized with "navel to spine" cue
Level 0.3	Base position with one foot lifted
Level 0.4	Base position with one knee held to chest and other foot lifted
Level 0.5	Base position with one knee held *lightly* to chest and other foot lifted
Level 1A	Knee to chest (>90° of hip flexion) held actively and other foot lifted
Level 1B	Knee to chest (at 90° of hip flexion) held actively and other foot lifted
Level 2	Knee to chest (at 90° of hip flexion) held actively and other foot lifted and slid on ground
Level 3	Knee to chest (at 90° of hip flexion) held actively and other foot lifted and slid *not* on ground
Level 4	Bilateral heel slides
Level 5	Bilateral leg lifts to 90°

Several important principles must be applied to exercise progression. These include dynamic exercises, multiplanar exercises, balance, proprioception, power exercises (plyometrics), sport specificity, and motor programming.

When the sportsperson has first mastered proper activation and control of the lumbopelvic region, he or she should progress from a stable surface to a labile surface. Eventually, external input can be added to challenge the athlete even more (Fig. 14.17).

Secondly, exercises must be performed in all planes. While sagittal (sit-ups, lunges) and frontal plane (side-walking, side bridges) exercises are popular, the transverse/rotational plane is frequently neglected.

Thirdly, proprioceptive training should be incorporated (Fig. 14.18). Balance-board or dura-disk training improves proprioception in all the joints, tendons, and muscles, not just those at the ankle.

Plyometrics should also be incorporated (Fig. 14.19) as jumping exercises require a strong and stable core. Advancement to a physioball (Fig. 14.20 on page 222) can be done at this stage (Table 14.5 on page 223).

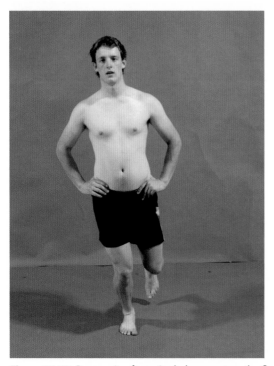

Figure 14.17 Progression from single-leg squat on the floor to a single-leg squat on a dura disk

A

Figure 14.19 Plyometric exercises. These exercises should be multiplanar and upgraded to include labile surfaces
(a) Preparing for take-off

Figure 14.18 Proprioceptive training using a balance board
(a) Balance board with both legs

(b) Balance board on single leg

(b) Explosive movement

Figure 14.19 (cont.) (c) Maintaining good core control

Figure 14.20 Use of physioball
(a) Leg lift seated on ball

(d) Absorbing forces on landing with knee flexion and activation of deep abdominal muscles

(b) Bird dog or superman on ball

(c) Push-ups

Figure 14.20 (cont.) (d) Bridging on ball

(e) Plant on the ball, moving hips forward

(f) Hamstring pull in

Table 14.5 Physioball exercises for the core

Abdominal crunch
Balancing exercise while seated
Superman prone exercise
Modified push-up
Pelvic bridging

Core strengthening for sports

Core training programs for sports are widely used by strengthening and conditioning coaches at the collegiate and professional levels. An example of Vern Gambetta's program is provided in Table 14.6.[39]

Different fitness programs incorporate various aspects of core strengthening and may be a useful way to maintain compliance in many individuals (Table 14.7).

Table 14.6 Advanced core program used by Vern Gambetta[39]

Body weight and gravitational loading—push-ups, pull-ups, rope climbs
Body blade exercises
Medicine ball exercises—throwing and catching
Dumbbell exercises in diagonal patterns
Stretch cord exercises
Balance training with labile surfaces
Squats
Lunges

Table 14.7 Fitness programs utilizing core strengthening principles

Pilates
Yoga (some forms)
Tai-chi
Feldenkrais
Somatics
Matrix dumbbell program

Efficacy of core strengthening exercise

Core strengthening programs have not been well researched for clinical outcomes. Studies are hampered by the lack of consensus on what constitutes a core strengthening program. For example, some studies describe remedial neuromuscular retraining, some describe sport-specific training, and others describe functional education. No randomized controlled trial (RCT) has been conducted on the efficacy of core strengthening. Most studies are prospective, uncontrolled case series.

Prevention of injury and performance improvement

In 2001, Nadler et al. attempted to evaluate the occurrence of low back pain before and after incorporation of a core strengthening program.[23] The core strengthening program included sit-ups, pelvic tilts, squats, lunges, leg presses, dead lifts, hang cleans, and Roman chair exercises. Although the incidence of low back pain decreased by 47% in male athletes, this was not statistically significant. In female athletes, the overall incidence of low back pain slightly increased despite core conditioning. This negative result may have been due to the use of some unsafe exercises (e.g. Roman chair extensor training).[6, 40] In addition, the exercises chosen for this study included only frontal and sagittal plane movements, which may have affected the results. Future studies incorporating exercises in the transverse plane may help to solve the issue surrounding core strengthening exercise and low back pain.

A study comparing core stability measures between male and female sportspeople and their incidence of lower extremity injury found that reduced isometric hip abductor and external rotation strength were predictors of injury. From this, the authors claimed that "core stability has an important role in injury prevention."[41] While the findings of this study may be important, core stability was not measured.[42]

Another study found a rehabilitation program consisting of progressive agility and trunk stabilization exercises was more effective than a program emphasizing isolated hamstring stretching and strengthening, in promoting return to sports and preventing injury recurrence in sportspeople suffering an acute hamstring strain.[43]

Treatment of low back pain

The first study conducted of a core stability program was an uncontrolled prospective trial of "dynamic lumbar stabilization" for patients with lumbar disk herniations creating radiculopathy.[38] The impact of therapeutic exercise alone was difficult to ascertain in this study, due to other non-operative interventions being offered, such as medication, epidural steroid injections, and back school. The exercise training program was well outlined and consisted of a flexibility program, joint mobilization of the hip and the thoracolumbar spinal segments, a stabilization and abdominal program (see Table 14.3), gym program,

and aerobic activity. Successful outcomes were achieved in 50 of 52 (96%) individuals. The described dynamic lumbar stabilization program resembles the current concept of a core stability program without the higher level sport-specific core training. Several other authors have since described similar programs.[44, 45] More recently, Tsao and Hodges[36] have shown that delayed activity of transversus abdominis in individuals with low back pain can be changed (and maintained after 6 months) with training.

Effectiveness in sports injuries

To date, the only studies to have shown a positive benefit of core stability training in the management of sporting injuries are Sherry and Best's study[43] on the treatment of hamstring strains, and a study by Holmich et al.[46] on the rehabilitation of sportspeople with chronic groin pain which incorporated some stability training into its program. However, a number of other sporting pathologies theoretically would benefit from this mode of training. These include stress fractures of the pars interarticularis of the lumbar spine, a common injury among cricket fast bowlers and other sports that involve repetitive hyperextension and rotation. The positive results from O'Sullivan et al.'s study[45] in non-sporting patients with spondylolysis would suggest that core stability training may be effective in this condition. Lumbar instability seen commonly in gymnasts is another condition for which theoretically a core stability program may be helpful. Many physiotherapists now incorporate an element of core stability training in the rehabilitation of a wide variety of lower limb injuries.

Conclusion

The concept of core stability has a theoretical basis in the treatment and prevention of various musculoskeletal conditions. However, other than studies in the treatment of low back pain, research is severely lacking. With the advancement in knowledge of motor learning theories and anatomy, core stability programs appear to be on the cusp of innovative new research.

A

📄 RECOMMENDED READING

Akuthota V, Nadlet S. Core strengthening. *Arch Phys Med Rehabil* 2004; 85: S86–92.

Bliss LS, Teeple P. Core stability: the centerpiece of any training program. *Curr Sports Med Rep* 2005; 4: 179–83.

Bogduk N. *Clinical anatomy of the lumbar spine and sacrum.* 3rd edn. New York: Churchill Livingstone, 1997.

McGill S. *Low back disorders: evidence-based prevention and rehabilitation.* Champaign, Il: Human Kinetics, 2002.

Richardson C, Jull G, Hodges P et al. *Therapeutic exercise for spinal segmental stabilization in low back pain.* 2nd edn. Edinburgh: Churchill Livingstone, 2004.

Sahrmann S. *Diagnosis and treatment of movement impairment syndromes.* St Louis: Mosby, 2002.

Sherry M, Best T, Heiderscheit B. The core: where are we and where are we going? *Clin J Sport Med* 2005; 15: 1–2.

📋 REFERENCES

1. Hodges PW, Richardson CA. Inefficient muscular stabilization of the lumbar spine associated with low back pain. *Spine,* 1996;21(22):2640–50.
2. Panjabi MM. *The* stabilizing system of the spine. Part 1. Function, dysfunction, adaptation and enhancement. *J Spinal Disord* 1992;5(5):383–9.
3. Lucas DB Bresler B. *Stability of the ligamentous spine.* San Francisco: Biomechanics Laboratory, University of California, 1961.
4. McGill S. *Low back disorders: evidence-based prevention and rehabilitiation.* Champaign, Il: Human Kinetics, 2002.
5. McGill SM, Grenier S, Kavcic N et al. Co-ordination of muscle activity to assure stability of the lumbar spine. *J Electromyogr Kinesiol* 2003;13:353–9.
6. Richardson CA, Hodges PW, Hides JA. *Therapeutic exercise for spinal segmental stabilization in low back pain—scientific basis and clinical approach.* 2nd edn. Edinburgh: Churchill Livingstone, 2004.
7. Bergmark A. Stability of the lumbar spine: a study in mechanical engineering. *Acta Orth Scand,* 1989;230 (Supp):20–4.
8. Panjabi MM, Clinical Instability and low back pain. *J Electromyogr Kinesiol* 2003;13(4):371–9.
9. Porterfiled J, DeRosa C. *Mechanical low back pain: perspectives in functional anatomy.* 2nd edn. Philadelphia: WB Saunders, 1998.
10. Akuthota V, Nadlet S. Core strengthening. *Arch Phys Med Rehab* 2004;85:S86–92.
11. Ebenbichler GR, Oddsson LA, Kollmitzer J et al. Sensory-motor control of the lower back: implications for rehabilitation. *Med Sci Sports Exerc* 2001;33(11) 1889–98.
12. Solomonow M. Introduction to surface electromyography. *J Electromyogr Kinesiol* 1998;8(5):347.
13. Vleeming A, Pool-Goudzwaard AL, Stoeckart R et al. The posterior layer of the thoracolumbar fascia. Its function in load transfer from the spine to legs. *Spine* 1995;20(7):753–8.
14. Hides JA, Richardson CA, Jull GA. Multifidus muscle recovery is not automatic after resolution of acute, first-episode low back pain. *Spine* 1996;21(23):2763–9.
15. McGill S. Low back stability: from formal description to issues for performance and rehabilitation. *Exerc Sport Sci Rev* 2001;29(1):26–31.
16. Cowan SM, Schache A, Brukner P et al. Delayed onset of transversus abdominus in long-standing groin pain. *Med Sci Sports Exerc* 2004;36(12):2040–5.
17. Sahrmann S. *Diagnosis and treatment of movement impairment syndromes.* St Louis: Mosby, 2002.
18. Lyons K, Perry J, Gronley JK et al. Timing and relative intensity of hip extensor and abductor muscle action during level and stair ambulation. *Phys Ther* 1983;63(10):1597–605.
19. Beckman SM, Buchanan TS. Ankle inversion injury and hypermobility—effect on hip and ankle muscle electromyography onset latency. *Arch Phys Med Rehab* 1995;76(12):1138–43.
20. Cowan SM, Crossley KM, Bennell KL. Altered hip and trunk muscle function in individuals with patellofemoral pain. *Br J Sports Med* 2009;43: 584–8.
21. Devita P, Hunter PB, Skelly WA. Effects of a functional knee brace on the biomechanics of running. *Med Sci Sports Exerc* 1992;24(7):797–806.
22. Nadler SF, Malanga GA, DePrince M et al. The relationship between lower extremity injury, low back pain, and hip muscle strength in male and female collegiate athletes. *Clin J Sport Med* 2000;10(2):89–97.
23. Nadler SF, Malanga GA, Feinberg JH et al. Relationship between hip muscle imbalance and occurrence of low back pain in collegiate athletes: a prospective study. *Am J Phys Med Rehabil* 2001;80(8):572–7.
24. O'Sullivan PB, Beales DJ, Beetham JA et al. Altered motor control strategies in subjects with sacroiliac joint pain during the active straight leg raise test. *Spine* 2002;27(1):E1–8.
25. McGill S, Sharratt MT, Seguin JP. Loads on spinal tissues during simultaneous lifting and ventilatory challenge. *Ergonomics* 1995;38(9)1772–92.

26. Sapsford RR, Hodges PW, Richardson CA et al. Co-activation of the abdominal and pelvic floor muscles during voluntary exercises. *Neurourol Urodyn* 2001;(1):31–42.

27. Bliss LS, Teeple P. Core stability: the centerpiece of any training program. *Curr Sports Med Rep* 2005;4:179–83.

28. Taimela S, Kankaanpaa M, Luoto S. The effect of lumbar fatigue on the ability to sense a change in lumbar position. A controlled study. *Spine* 1999;24(13):1322–7.

29. Juker D, McGill S, Kropf P et al. Quantative intramuscular myoelectric activity of lumbar portions of psoas and the abdominal wall during a wide variety of tasks. *Med Sci Sports Exerc* 1998;30(2): 301–10.

30. Farfan HF, Cossette JW, Robertson GH et al. The effects of torsion on the lumbar intervertebral joints: the role of torsion in the production of disc degeneration. *J Bone Joint Surg* 1970;52(3):468–97.

31. Saal JA. Dynamic muscular stabilization in the nonoperative treatment of lumbar pain syndromes. *Orthop Rev* 1990;9(8):691–700.

32. Adams MA, Dolan P, Hutton W. Diurnal variations in the stresses on the lumbar spine. *Spine* 1987;12(2): 130–7.

33. Callaghan JP, Patla A, McGill S. Low back three-dimensional joint forces, kinematics, and kinetics during walking. *Clin Biomech* 1999;14(3):203–16.

34. Hodges PW. Ultrasound imaging in rehabilitation. Just a fad? *J Orth Sports Phys Ther* 2005;35:333–7.

35. Hides JA, Stokes MJ, Saide M et al. Evidence of lumbar multifidus muscle wasting ipsilateral to symptoms in patients with acute/subacute low back pain. *Spine* 1994;19(2):165–72.

36. Tsao H, Hodges P. Persistence of improvements in postural strategies following motor control training in people with recurrent low back pain. *J Electromyogr Kinesiol* 2008;18(4): 559–67.

37. Richardson CA, Jull GA. Muscle control-pain control. What exercises would you prescribe? *Man Ther* 1995;1(1):2–10

38. Saal JA, Saal JS. Nonoperative treatment of herniated lumbar intervertebral disc with radiculopathy. An outcome study. *Spine* 1989;14(4):431–7.

39. Gambetta V. The core of the matter. *Coach Manage* 2002;10:5.

40. Kollmitzer J, Ebenbichler GR, Sabo A et al. Effects of back extensor strength straining versus balance training on postural control. *Med Sci Sports Exerc* 2000;32(10):1770–6.

41. Leetun DT, Ireland ML, Willson JD et al. Core stability measures as risk factors for lower extremity injury in athletes. *Med Sci Sports Exerc* 2004;36(6):926–34.

42. Sherry MA, Best TM, Heiderscheit B. The core: where are we and where are we going? *Clin J Sport Med* 2005;15:1–2.

43. Sherry MA, Best TM. A comparison of 2 rehabilitation programs in the treatment of hamstring strains. *J Orth Sports Phys Ther* 2004;34:116–25.

44. Manniche C, Lundberg E, Christensen I. Intensive dynamic back exercises for chronic low back pain: a clinical trial. *Pain* 1991;47(1):53–63.

45. O'Sullivan PB, Phyty GD, Twomey LT et al. Evaluation of specific stabilizing exercise in the treatment of chronic low back pain with radiologic diagnosis of spondylolysis or spondylolisthesis. *Spine* 1997;22(24):2959–67.

46. Holmich P, Uhrskov P, Ulnits L et al. Effectiveness of active physical training as treatment for long-standing adductor-related groin pain in athletes: randomised trial. *Lancet* 1999;353: 439–43.

Chapter 15

Principles of rehabilitation

There are a lot of good memories, and because I was injured, during the rehab, I met my wife. The tennis was very good but the injuries were good for something too.   Richard Krajicek

Sports rehabilitation begins as soon as possible after the initial treatment of an acute injury. As discussed in Chapter 13, treatment techniques are frequently used in acute to subacute presentations, and focused on pain relief before the rehabilitation phase begins. Rehabilitation focuses on return to sports participation, and aims to return the sportsperson to their pre-injury level of performance. Once the athlete has successfully returned to sport, rehabilitation can adopt a preventive approach.

Exercise programs often form a large component of an athlete's rehabilitation. Exercise programs typically aim to address the following components:

- muscle activation and motor control
- muscle strength, power, endurance
- flexibility (joints and muscles)
- proprioception
- cardiovascular fitness
- functional exercises
- sports-specific skills
- correction of biomechanical abnormalities.

These components are discussed in this chapter. Figure 15.1 displays an example model of the integration of individual components into a progressive rehabilitation program. This chapter also describes the keys to a successful rehabilitation program, the components of exercise programs for rehabilitation, as well as discussing stages and progression of rehabilitation, monitoring of rehabilitation programs, and the psychological aspects involved with rehabilitation.

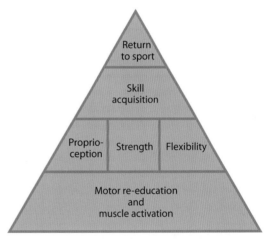

Figure 15.1 Integration of individual components into a progressive rehabilitation program

Keys to a successful rehabilitation program

Sports medicine is readily classified as a science; however, devising a successful rehabilitation program should be considered an art. Skilful rehabilitation cannot be replaced by a recipe approach, as each individual brings his or her own personality and lifestyle factors to the therapy room. Some sportspeople have considerable career or job commitments, whereas others are full-time professionals. Some have good support from their family and peers, whereas others do not. Furthermore, each individual has different post-injury sporting goals, levels of skill, and degrees of competitiveness, all of which influence the rehabilitation program.

Once the diagnosis has been made (Chapters 11 and 12) and initial treatment instituted (Chapter 13), the therapist performs a comprehensive baseline assessment from which to measure progress. An appropriate, individualized rehabilitation plan can then be formulated. Keys to a successful rehabilitation program involves giving adequate explanation, providing precise prescription, making the most of available facilities and equipment, and beginning as soon as possible.

Explanation

The rehabilitation plan should be explained to the sportsperson with realistic, approximate time frames. It should be emphasized that the time frames are only approximate and not "promises." It is important to set both short-term goals (e.g. the removal of a brace or the commencement of jogging) and long-term goals (e.g. such as return to sport).

It is also important to explain the rationale behind the program, to improve compliance. This is only possible if the therapist has first formulated a working diagnosis and a hypothesis as to why the injury occurred. For example, if lack of flexibility contributed to an injury, the therapist should explain their rational when incorporating an ongoing program to gradually improve the athlete's flexibility beyond their pre-injury level. Similarly, if dynamic joint instability was thought to be a precipitating factor, or a result of injury, rehabilitation could emphasize muscle control and strengthening, and this would need to be explained to the athlete.

Provide precise prescription

During the rehabilitation program, the therapist must emphasize correct exercise technique and carefully apply principles for the progression and limitation of exercises and activities. Furthermore, learning styles often vary between individuals. Some sportspeople may be visual learners, whereas others may need to "feel" the movement or exercise to understand how to perform it correctly. Others may learn through detailed explanation or through a combination of visual and auditory cues. Therefore, when prescribing exercises, it may be more effective to explain and demonstrate the desired movement or exercise in a variety of ways.

The therapist should constantly monitor and provide feedback to the athlete, particularly when performing the exercise(s) for the first time. Constant monitoring will allow the therapist to assess whether a program requires immediate modification. The importance of close supervision is paramount, to allow an athlete to gain maximum benefit from the exercises and to avoid injuries from performing exercises incorrectly. Number of repetitions and sets of exercises should not be recipe-based but should be assessed, to avoid injuries associated with fatigue and/or over-compensation.

Make the most of the available facilities

Therapists should be confident enough to be able to use several pieces of equipment for rehabilitation purposes. Successful rehabilitation programs take into account the individual, and therefore often have multiple components such as strength, flexibility, and sports-specific skills. If facilities such as a gymnasium, pool, or biofeedback devices are available, the rehabilitation program may take advantage of some, or all, of these facilities. If there is limited equipment and/or facilities are not available, exercise bikes, rubber tubes, steps, and free weights can be used within a relatively confined space. Additionally, functional exercises which take advantage of body position and body weight for resistance and grade of difficulty can be incorporated.

Begin as soon as possible

The rehabilitation program should start as early as possible, once the acute clinical presentation is stable. Pain, inflammation, swelling, or joint effusion must be controlled in the early stages, as they can inhibit optimal function and lead to pain inhibition. Rest from aggravating activities, ice, electrotherapeutic modalities, and analgesic medications are often utilized in these early stages (Chapter 13).

Understanding the pathophysiology, phases, and time frames of soft tissue healing following an injury can improve the therapist's ability to construct a successful rehabilitation program and avoid the risk of further injury. Starting rehabilitation early can avoid the detrimental effects of muscle atrophy and de-conditioning.

Components of exercise programs for rehabilitation

Muscle conditioning

There are four main components of muscle conditioning:

- muscle activation and motor control
- muscle strength

- muscle power
- muscle endurance.

Each of these components is necessary to varying degrees in both activities of daily living and sport. Each component may be affected by injury and, therefore, must be assessed and focused on for rehabilitation and preventative purposes.

Muscle activation and motor control

Muscle activation and motor control are crucial, but often overlooked, aspects of muscle conditioning. Motor control relates to how the central nervous system organizes the musculoskeletal system to create coordinated and skilled movements. In other words, motor control incorporates muscle activation with neural input to gain the desired movement and/or skill. Perception, motor planning, motor execution, and feedback are all important parts of the process and need to be considered in rehabilitation. Repeated practice of a movement adds to learning and leads to the development of skill. Without practice and feedback through this system, optimal muscle activation and motor control cannot be achieved. Therefore, practice of correct movement patterns with multiple feedback opportunities, such as visual and auditory feedback, will aid in enhancing muscle activation, motor control, and ultimately rehabilitation and injury prevention.

Injury can cause pain and swelling, both of which have been demonstrated to have an inhibitory effect on a muscle's function.[1-4] Quadriceps inhibition has been observed in several knee pathologies including anterior cruciate ligament, patellofemoral joint, and meniscal injuries.[3 4] Increasing knee joint effusion has shown to affect peak ground reaction force, knee force angles, and knee extensor overall movement on single leg drop landing.[4]

Artificially induced medial knee pain has been shown to decrease extensor movement and muscle activation in the quadriceps and hamstring muscles during lunging and walking tasks.[5 6] This indicates that nociceptive input can alter muscle activity and motor control, leading in turn to increased forces across a joint surface. This can increase the risk of injury to that joint. Altered muscle activation in the shoulder has been associated with a variety of shoulder injuries.[7]

Both passive and active structures around the joint are responsible for its overall stability. At lower loads, passive structures can be adequate in providing joint stability.[4] However, with increasing weight-bearing loads, such as during sporting activity where joint forces are greater, the roles of muscle activation and motor control are paramount to minimize joint injury. For example, ongoing quadriceps weakness compromises joint stability and increases injury risk and joint degenerative changes.[4]

Muscle activation and motor control are particularly important in the rehabilitation of injuries of the shoulder region (Chapter 21), low back (Chapter 26), hip, groin and pelvis (Chapters 28, 29), and knee (Chapters 32, 33). To demonstrate the role of motor control, we give two examples, the shoulder and the pelvis, in the box overleaf.

Muscle conditioning must commence with teaching the patient how to activate an inhibited muscle. For example, following an anterior cruciate ligament reconstruction, the quadricep muscles are inhibited, and the patient is taken through a series of progressive exercises that result in a solid isometric contraction being achieved. This is essential before other forms of muscle conditioning can be commenced.

It is important to understand the difference between local and global muscles.[3] Global muscles are the large, torque-producing muscles, whereas local muscles are responsible for local stability. In recent years there has been increased understanding of the importance of the local muscles in providing joint stability.

Rehabilitation of these incorrect motor patterning syndromes relies on careful assessment of the pattern of movement, the individual strength and function of the involved muscles, and the flexibility of the muscles and joints. As this abnormal movement pattern has developed over a lengthy period, it is necessary for the patient to learn a new movement pattern. This takes time and patience. The movement should be broken down into its components, and the patient must initially learn to execute each component individually. Eventually, the complete correct movement will be learned.

Lack of flexibility in muscles and muscle groups may prevent correct execution of a particular movement. This tightness should gradually be corrected. In addition, weak, poorly functioning muscles require specific, localized strengthening, initially in isolation. Various methods are used to assist the patient to isolate the particular muscle or muscle groups. These include palpation of the muscle by the patient or therapist, verbal feedback from the therapist, the

Examples to demonstrate the role of motor control

Shoulder

Chronic shoulder impingement is one of the most common causes of chronic nontraumatic shoulder pain in the overhead sportsperson. Shoulder impingement is linked to reduced muscle activity and poor motor control.[7][8] A number of underlying pathologies have been linked to impingement: these include glenohumeral instability, rotator cuff and bicep pathology, reduced glenohumeral rotation, and reduced scapular muscle activity.[8] All of these can lead to excessive humeral translation and reduce the quality of movement, control, and function of the scapular stabilizer muscles.[9]

Current rehabilitation protocols include exercises aimed at the restoration of scapular muscle activity and motor control.[9] A specific focus is placed on the position and movement of the scapula throughout the exercise. Often poor motor control around the scapula is associated with an anterior tilt, a relative downward rotation, and a degree of internal rotation of the scapular.[9] An altered static position of the scapula does relate to a loss of dynamic scapular control.[9]

Weight-bearing through the upper limbs during sport does occur. However, it is more functional when an athlete is able to play with hands free in space to perform such task as throwing, catching, pitching, or swinging a racquet/bat. Weight-bearing exercises for rehabilitative purposes are incorporated to facilitate proprioceptive feedback, and muscle co-contraction, and to increase dynamic joint stability.[10]

For the throwing athlete, rehabilitation needs to progress to sports- or skill-specific unrestricted arm exercises before return to sport is considered.

During shoulder re-education, scapular stabilization is begun in isolation without glenohumeral movements (Chapter 21). Exercises in some degree of elevation are introduced when adequate movement patterns are established. Gradual loading, such as with free weights, is introduced with strict adherence to the correct movement pattern. When recommencing sport drills, the athlete should commence with simple activities or drills and gradually progress to more complex activities. Eventually, the athlete should return to sport using the new movement.

Pelvis

The pelvis provides another example of the problem of abnormal movement patterns. Lack of pelvic control (in any of the planes of the pelvis) while running places increased stress on lower limb muscles and tendons. This may lead to overuse injuries (e.g. hamstring injuries associated with excessive anterior pelvic tilt).

It is important to assess the whole biomechanical chain, as has been seen in patellofemoral joint pain populations. Evidence has linked dysfunction in hip and trunk control to patellofemoral joint pain.[3] For example, dysfunction in the gluteus medius can result in contralateral dropping of the pelvis, promoting internal rotation at the hip, leading to an increased genu valgus and Q angle at the knee.[3] This leads to an increase in lateral forces in the patellofemoral joint.

use of a mirror, muscle stimulation, and biofeedback. Applying strapping tape to the skin when the patient is in a desired position may help to increase postural awareness. This may facilitate correct muscle contraction and inhibit overuse of muscle groups. Initially, the movement should not be resisted, as resistance may cause the patient to compensate or return to the previous movement pattern.

The starting position of the exercise should facilitate the movement. For example, pelvic tilt exercises should be commenced lying supine. As timing, strength, and endurance improve, the patient progresses to kneeling and standing, and eventually incorporates the correct pelvic position into functional exercises (e.g. step-downs, pulley work, jogging).

The supervision of a stability program requires skill and patience from the therapist. It is important that the patient understands the concept of stability and what you are trying to achieve. Many sportspeople, in particular, are accustomed to *strengthening* their global muscles and have difficulty with the concepts of stability training. Many people also have poor body awareness and have difficulty isolating the necessary muscles. Pressure biofeedback can be extremely useful in this education process.

Other techniques used to facilitate muscle activation and motor control are listed below:[5]

- Visualization of the correct muscle action. The therapist should demonstrate and describe the muscle action to the patient. Anatomical illustrations of the muscles involved are an effective teaching aid.

- Use of instructions that cue the correct action. Phrases such as "pull your navel up toward your spine" can be used to cue the patient to the muscle action (transversus abdominis) required.

- Focus on precision. The patient has to concentrate and focus on the precise muscle action to be achieved. It should be stressed that activation of these muscles is a gentle action. Other muscles should remain relaxed during this localized exercise.

- Facilitation techniques. Show the patient how to feel the muscle contracting.

Muscle strength training

Muscle strength is the muscle's ability to exert force. Strength training can be used to enhance athletic performance, improve musculoskeletal health, and correct muscle imbalances.[11] Strength training is often used in rehabilitation when weaknesses compromises function and sport performance. This is particularly true following periods of immobilization, or injury, and in pain presentations.

Muscle hypertrophy and increase in strength are dependent on five biochemical and physiological factors that are all stimulated and enhanced by conditioning:

- increased glycogen and protein storage in muscle
- increased vascularization
- biochemical changes affecting the enzymes of energy metabolism
- increased number of myofibrils
- recruitment of neighboring motor units.

Strength gains can be seen quickly, even before physiological hypertrophy occurs. The initial strength gain in response to exercise is thought to be related to increased neuromuscular facilitation (i.e. the nervous system enhances the motor pathways so that the muscle group becomes more neurologically efficient).[11-13] Neural adaptations facilitate changes in coordination and learning that enhance the recruitment and activation of muscles during a strength task.[11]

The following factors will help maximize strength gains during rehabilitation:

- adequate warm-up to increase body temperature and metabolic efficiency
- good quality, controlled performance of the exercise
- pain-free performance of exercise

- use of slow, controlled exercise initially, with little or no resistance, to develop a good base for neural patterning to occur
- comprehensive stretching program to restore/maintain full range of motion
- muscle strengthening throughout the entire range of motion available.

Additionally, evidence demonstrates a cross-over effect when one limb is trained; strength gains will also be recorded in the contralateral limb.[11, 12] This phenomenon is termed "central adaptation," and may reflect the stabilizing or bracing role the contralateral limb may perform.

Types of exercise

The three main types of exercise used in muscle conditioning are:

- isometric
- isotonic
- isokinetic.

Additionally, exercises can be classified as either open chain or closed chain.

Isometric exercise

An isometric exercise occurs when a muscle contracts without associated movement of the joint on which the muscle acts. Isometric exercises are often the first form of strengthening exercise used after injury, especially if the region is excessively painful or if the area is immobilized. These exercises are commenced as soon as the sportsperson can perform them without pain.

Isometric exercises are used when a muscle is too weak to perform range of motion exercises, in conditions where other forms of exercise are not possible (such as patellar dislocation and shoulder dislocation), or when isometric contraction is required in activities (e.g. stabilizing). Isometric exercises can minimize muscle atrophy associated with immobilization and injury by maintaining or improving static strength, minimizing swelling via the muscle pump action, and enhancing neural and proprioceptive inputs to the muscle.

Ideally, isometric exercises are held for 5 seconds with a rest of 10 seconds. They can be performed frequently during the day in sets of 10 repetitions. The number of sets will vary at different stages of the rehabilitation program. If an athlete has difficulty, exercises may be performed against resistance or against an immovable object. It is important to remember that the quality of exercise is more important than the quantity.

Isometric exercises should be carried out at multiple angles if possible, as strength gain can be specific to the angle of exercise. The athlete should progress from submaximal to maximal isometric exercise slowly within the limitations of pain and function. When significant isometric effect is tolerated at multiple joint angles, dynamic exercises may begin.

An example of an isometric exercise for the lower limb is shown in Figure 15.2.

Isotonic exercise

Isotonic exercises are performed when the joint moves through a range of motion against a constant resistance or weight. Isotonic exercises may be performed with free weights, such as dumbbells or sandbags (Fig. 15.3).

Free weights encourage natural movement patterns and require muscle coordination and joint stability in all planes of movement, and therefore may transfer strength gains more readily to the playing field.[14] With free weights it is possible to simulate athletic activities as the body position can be varied.

Isotonic exercises may be:

* concentric—a shortening isotonic contraction in which the origin and insertion of the muscles approximate. Individual muscle fibers shorten during concentric contraction
* eccentric—a lengthening isotonic contraction where the origin and insertion of the muscles separate. The individual muscle fibers lengthen during eccentric contraction.

Concentric and eccentric exercises for the quadriceps are shown in Figure 15.4.

The intramuscular force produced per motor unit during an eccentric contraction is larger than that during a concentric contraction.[12] Eccentric contractions may generate high tension within the series elastic component, which consists of connective tissue and the actin–myosin cross-bridges in muscles. It has been observed that eccentric exercise results in higher rates of delayed onset muscle soreness (DOMS) and even muscle damage if used inappropriately.[15, 16] Consequently, eccentric programs should commence at very low levels and progress gradually to higher intensity and volume. The use of eccentric exercise programs may help prevent recurrence of musculotendinous injuries.

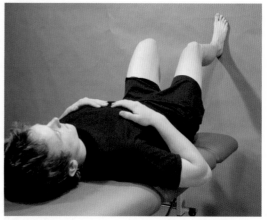

Figure 15.2 Isometric co-contraction of hamstrings, gluteals, and quadriceps muscles with patient pushing foot into wall

Figure 15.3 Isotonic exercises **(a)** Dumbbell

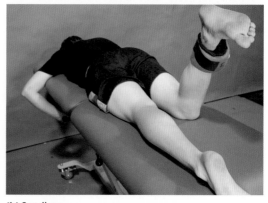

(b) Sandbag

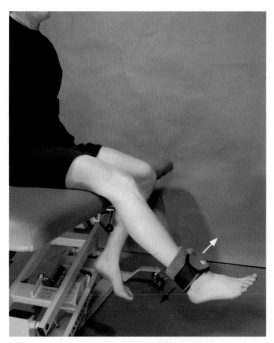

Figure 15.4 Concentric (white arrow) and eccentric (black arrow) exercises—quadriceps

Eccentric training has been advocated in the rehabilitation of tendon injuries, due to the proposed facilitation of tendon remodeling through promotion of collagen fibers within the injured tendon.[16-18] There is evidence that Achilles and patellar tendinopathies respond well to an eccentric rehabilitation program.[15, 16] Emerging evidence has also found benefits in lateral elbow tendinopathies.[16, 17, 19]

However, not all tendon injuries benefit from eccentric exercises. Specifically, eccentric exercises have shown poor success rates for insertional Achilles tendinopathy compared to mid-tendon clinical presentations.[16] Therefore, the site of tendon pathology should be considered when prescribing eccentric exercises.

Isokinetic exercises

Isokinetic exercises are performed on devices at a fixed speed with a variable resistance that is totally accommodative to the individual throughout the range of motion. The velocity is, therefore, constant at a preselected dynamic rate, while the resistance varies to match the force applied at every point in the range of motion. This enables the patient to perform more work than is possible with either constant or variable resistance isotonic exercise.

Isokinetic testing can highlight imbalances, such as scapular muscle imbalances in overhead athletes with chronic impingement signs.[8] A number of isokinetic devices are available and include the Ariel, Biodex, Cybex, KinCom, Lido, and Merac machines. However, these machines are costly, which may explain why they are more commonplace in research than in clinical settings. A recent study found comparable benefits of isokinetic versus a standard exercise program for a chronic low back pain population.[20]

Open chain and closed chain exercises

An open kinetic chain exercise often involves single joint movement performed in a non-weight-bearing position where the distal extremity freely moves through space.[21] Closed kinetic chain exercises involve multiple joints and are performed in weight-bearing positions with a fixed distal extremity. Closed kinetic exercises are thought to be more functional, provide more proprioceptive feedback, and cause less sheer joint forces than open kinetic chain exercises.[21]

Although some studies promote closed kinetic chain exercises over open kinetic exercises,[21, 22] others advocate that both types of exercises play beneficial roles in rehabilitation, especially in regards to anterior cruciate rehabilitation and patellofemoral pain.[23-25] Proposed advantages and disadvantages of open and closed kinetic exercise are shown in Table 15.1 overleaf.

An example of these exercises are shown in Figure 15.5a, b (overleaf). Figure 15.5c (overleaf) shows an example of open (right arm) and closed (left arm) chain exercises for the shoulder girdle. Closed chain upper limb exercises are particularly useful during the early recovery period from shoulder surgery (Chapter 21). Excessive mobility and compromise of static stability within the glenohumeral joint has been linked to capsular, labral, and musculotendinous injuries in throwing athletes.[26] The positive benefits of closed kinetic chain exercises, performed under load-bearing positions, are thought to stimulate joint receptors and facilitate muscle co-contractions around the shoulder and therefore enhance joint stability.[8, 26]

Muscle power training

Muscle power is the muscle's rate of doing work. It is equivalent to explosive strength such as measured in a single leg hop test or a vertical jump test. As seen in strength training, the initial power gains observed

Table 15.1 Advantages and disadvantages of open and closed chain exercises

	Advantages	Disadvantages
Open chain exercises	Decreased joint compression Can exercise in non-weight-bearing positions Able to exercise through increased ROM Able to isolate individual muscles	Increased joint translation Decreased functionality
Closed chain exercises	Decreased joint forces in secondary joints (e.g. less patellofemoral force with squat) Decreased joint translation Increased functionality	Increased joint compression Not able to exercise through increased ROM Not able to isolate individual muscles

ROM = range of motion.

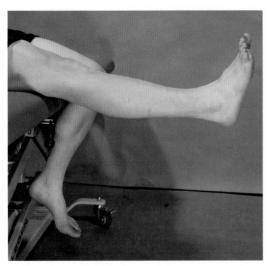

Figure 15.5 Open and closed chain exercises
(a) Open chain knee extension with the foot moving freely

(b) Closed chain knee extension with the feet immobile

(c) Open chain (right arm) and closed chain (left arm) exercises on unstable surface

with power training result in improvements in neuromuscular performance as seen on EMG muscle activity.[27] Specifically, initial improvements in power can be at attributed to improved muscle coordination between agonist and antagonist muscles.

When injury has decreased muscle power or when the athlete's sport includes periods of explosive power, the rehabilitation program should incorporate power exercises. Commonly, power-focused exercises are incorporated into the later stage of rehabilitation due to the potential of re-injury. Power exercises may include:

* fast-speed isotonic or isokinetic exercises (concentric and/or eccentric)
* increased speed of functional exercises (e.g. faster reverse calf raise, drop squat)
* plyometric exercises (e.g. hopping, bounding).

Power exercises often involve functional and sports-specific exercises. Exercises should be made appropriate to the athlete's sport to gain optimal benefits (e.g. bounding for a sprinter, jump and land for a basketballer).

Muscle endurance training

Muscle endurance is the muscle's ability to sustain contraction or perform repeated contractions. Endurance training can be thought of as the deliberate act of exercising to increase stamina and endurance, and encompasses a variety of exercise durations and intensities.

The aim of endurance training is to increase the capacity to sustain repetitive, high-intensity, low-resistance exercise such as running, cycling, and swimming.[28] Adaptations to endurance training include an increase in maximal oxygen uptake (VO_2 max) and an increased ability of skeletal muscle to generate energy via oxidative metabolism.[28 29]

The long-term consequences of prolonged endurance training have been debated in recent years, with proposed cardiovascular risks associated with cardiac fatigue.[30 31] However, a recent study of young Olympic athletes who were subjected to extreme uninterrupted endurance training over prolonged periods (up to 17 years) found that endurance training was not associated with significant changes in left ventricular morphology, deterioration in left ventricular function, or occurrence of cardiovascular symptoms or events.[32]

Endurance sports include long-distance running (greater than 5 km), cross-country skiing, cycling, rowing, and triathlon. However, a variety of sports, such as the various codes of football, swimming, and middle-distance running, require a combination of strength and endurance. Successive bouts of strength and endurance training can result in fatigue and reduced sporting performance. Therefore, care should be taken in incorporating the different components of conditioning into rehabilitation programs.

Means of incorporating endurance exercise into a rehabilitation program include riding a stationary bike, swimming, and specific low-load, high-repetition isotonic or isokinetic gym-based exercises or circuit training.

Cardiovascular fitness

The maintenance of cardiovascular fitness is often an essential component of the rehabilitation process. No matter what type of injury the sportsperson has sustained, exercises to maintain cardiovascular fitness are often incorporated as soon as possible.

In injuries to the lower limb that require a period of restricted weight-bearing activity, cardiovascular fitness may be maintained by performing activities such as cycling, or water exercises. Depending on the athlete's particular sport, this may include a combination of endurance, interval, anaerobic, and power work.

It is important to maintain alternative training methods for cardiovascular fitness, to encourage motivation and compliance with general fitness goals.

Flexibility
with IAN SHRIER

Regaining or maintaining full flexibility of joints and soft tissues is an essential component of the rehabilitation process. Following injury, musculotendinous flexibility often decreases as a result of spasm of surrounding muscles. Inflammation, pain and/or stiffness can limit joint range of motion, and the normal extensibility of the musculotendinous unit can be compromised. This may result in dysfunction of adjacent joints and soft tissues. For example, the lumbar spine may be restricted in range of motion and the paraspinal muscles may spasm following knee or hip surgery, especially after periods of restricted mobilization.

Adequate soft tissue extensibility after injury is essential to encourage pain-free range of movements. Stretching muscles and joints is one way of improving tissue and joint extensibility. The principles of stretching are discussed in Chapter 9.

Joint range of motion

Joint range of motion is often limited with injury. Pain from an injury can inhibit normal muscle function around a joint, and swelling and inflammation can increase intra-articular pressure. Both these factors can limit joint range of motion.

Prolonged reduced range of motion, such as that associated with immobilization, can result in adverse changes in articular cartilage, as well as adaptive tightening of the joint capsule and pericapsular tissues (ligaments, muscles, and tendons).

There is considerable variation in the amount of reduced joint range of motion that occurs following injury or immobilization. Joint range of motion may be influenced by the individual sportsperson's collagen make-up and past injury history. Athletes with a known tendency to develop stiffness require intensive preventive measures early into rehabilitation (e.g. early mobilization and range of movement exercises).

Wherever possible, early restoration of range of motion should be an important component of the rehabilitation process. Continuous passive motion equipment and manual techniques for joint mobilization can be used in the initial stages and are discussed in Chapter 13.

Passive exercises

Passive exercises allow a joint to be moved through the available range of motion without effort from the athlete. This is often accomplished by the therapist moving the joint through the range (refer to Fig. 15.6). Passive exercises may be used to regain range of motion when active exercises are too painful to perform or when end of range is restricted. Active-assisted exercises are where an athlete can perform relatively passive exercises with some muscle activity. These exercises can be performed with the help of the contralateral limb, such as shown for the knee in Figure 15.7, or with the help of a pulley system. These exercises can be progressed as the athlete reduces the amount of support the contralateral limb provides.

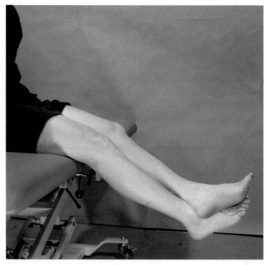

Figure 15.7 Active-assisted exercise—the left leg rests on the right, which takes the left leg through a range of motion

Active exercises

Active range of motion exercises are used to regain or maintain range of motion and function. They can be commenced as soon as possible, often within the limits of pain. Exercises are performed by the individual athlete. An example of an active range of motion exercise for the knee is shown in Figure 15.8. Exercises can be progressed to increase the range of motion, without increasing the athlete's symptoms.

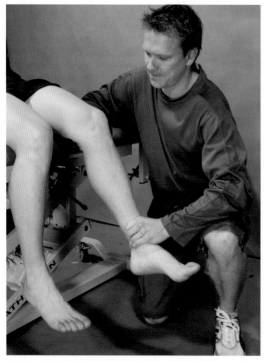

Figure 15.6 Passive exercises—the therapist passively moves the joint through a range of motion

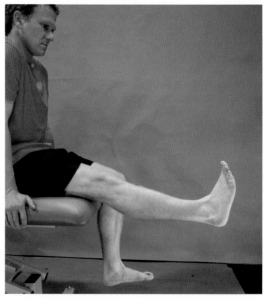

Figure 15.8 Active exercise—knee extension/flexion

In the early stages, ice and/or electrotherapeutic modalities may follow the exercise to minimize post-exercise inflammation, pain, and swelling.

Musculotendinous flexibility

The physical demands of sport place an athlete into extreme positions where a certain amount of flexibility is required. An athlete is susceptible to injury if they lack flexibility. Table 15.2 highlights some examples where lack of flexibility may be associated with specific injuries.

Stretching exercises are performed to increase flexibility. The acute effects of stretching seem to be related to the lengthening of the musculotendinous unit.[33] Traditionally, stretching has been the primary method of restoring normal flexibility. However, if the muscle tightness is secondary to neural restriction or trigger points, these may prevent stretching from being effective. Therefore, the spinal and trigger point contribution to muscle tightness should be assessed (Chapter 11), and treated with effective techniques (e.g. pressure techniques, dry needling, and others (Chapter 13)), in conjunction with an appropriate stretching program.

Stretching is often promoted as having a number of beneficial effects[34, 35], although not all of the following have been appropriately studied:

- increases muscle and joint flexibility
- increases muscle relaxation
- decreases muscle soreness
- improves circulation
- helps prevent excessive adhesion
- promotes a flexible, strong scar.

There are three main types of stretching: static, ballistic, and proprioceptive neuromuscular facilitation.

Table 15.2 Tight muscle(s) and possible associated injuries

Tight muscles	Possible associated injury
Sternocleidomastoid	Cervical apophyseal joint injuries
Psoas	Lumbar apophyseal joint, hamstring injuries
Quadriceps vastus group	Patellar tendinopathy
Vastus lateralis, iliotibial band, tensor fascia lata	Patellofemoral syndrome
Soleus	Achilles tendinopathy

These are described in Chapter 9. These stretches are typically incorporated into rehabilitation at various stages. A stretching program should be designed for the individual, taking into consideration the nature and stage of the injury, the athlete's sport and the athlete's abilities and deficits. Below are some recommendations for effective stretching.

Recommendations for effective stretching

- A gentle warm-up before stretching increases tissue temperature and facilitates stretching. This may include activities such as jogging or cycling.
- As with warm-up, superficial or deep heat modalities may be applied to the area prior to stretching to increase tissue temperature.
- Cryotherapy may reduce pain and muscle spasm and thereby enhance the overall stretch of a muscle in the initial stages after an injury, even though the temperature is decreased (i.e. opposite to heat).
- Athletes should be carefully instructed regarding the correct stretching position, as incorrect positioning may cause injury.
- Different muscles seem to require different durations of stretch.[36] In general, a slow sustained stretch should be held for a minimum of 10–15 seconds and progressed for 1 minute or longer. The athlete should feel stretch in the appropriate area.
- As the athlete's flexibility improves increases in intensity, duration, frequency, and type of stretch can be considered.
- Stretching should always be pain-free i.e. "tightness" without pain.

Traditionally, stretching has been the primary method of restoring normal flexibility and has been widely promoted for injury prevention and performance enhancing for sporting activity. Some authors have suggested stretching does not prevent injury in otherwise healthy individuals.[37] However, others have noted that it is important to differentiate between pre-exercise stretching (where stretching does not appear to prevent injury)[38], and regular stretching outside periods of exercise (where there is some clinical and basic science evidence suggesting stretching may prevent injury).[39, 40] Additionally, stretching does not seem to reduce the effects of delayed onset of muscle soreness.[41]

Furthermore, the acute effects of stretching can cause temporary strength deficits and hence reduce sporting performance.[42] This deficit seems to be associated with stretches performed for more than

60 seconds, while stretches of shorter duration may have less significant deficits.[42] As traditional stretching routines are performed during warm-up sessions prior to playing sport, the amount of time athletes stretch should be taken into consideration.

The role of stretching in rehabilitation may have more of an effect in select patients compared to healthy individuals. Stretching four times per day compared to once per day shortened time to return to activity for hamstring injuries from 15.0 days to 13.3 days.[43] However, strengthening for lateral elbow tendinopathy (Chapter 22)[44] and groin pain[45] (Chapter 29) was much more effective than stretching. Whether stretching plus strengthening is superior to strengthening alone has never been studied, and there are theoretical reasons why it may be superior or inferior.[40]

The dangers of stretching

Regardless of which type of stretching is used, over-stretching and subsequent injury can occur. This depends on the intensity, duration, and velocity of the stretch, as well as the number of movements performed in a given period. These factors should be closely monitored, and progressed gradually as the rehabilitation program proceeds. Stretching should not be performed into pain. Specific stretching may be contraindicated in some situations; for example, in hypermobility syndromes where one would generally not want to increase tissue compliance. In addition, one would not want to stretch the anterior capsule in the presence of anterior instability of the shoulder in baseball pitchers, although some clinicians have advocated for stretching of the posterior capsule.

Ballistic stretches significantly increase tendon flexibility and elasticity and have been promoted for end-stage rehabilitation for tendon injuries.[8] However, ballistic stretching involves eccentric contractions during the stretch phase, which may result in soreness or injury, and therefore care should be taken when incorporating such stretches. Table 15.3 provides a safety checklist for ballistic stretching.

Proprioception

The term "proprioception" is derived from the Latin word *proprius* meaning "one's own" and the word "perception." Therefore proprioception relates to how the body perceives and maintains itself in space. Sensory feedback from peripheral mechanoreceptors is mediated in the central nervous system and is responsible for providing information concerning joint position, motion, vibration, and pressure.[46]

Table 15.3 The following procedures could be followed to reduce the risk of injury with ballistic stretching:

- the athlete is thoroughly warmed up
- it is preceded by slow static stretching
- it is only introduced in the advanced stages of a stretching program
- it is taught carefully and performed with accuracy and care
- it is performed slowly and in a controlled manner, gradually increasing speed.

Proprioception maintains joint stability through the feedback of position and movement sense, and assists in coordination of movement.[47] [48] Evidence has also shown that proprioceptive deficits in the pelvis and trunk can affect knee dynamic stability and increase the risk of knee injury, especially in females.[46] There is evidence to suggest that proprioception can significantly improve after a warm-up that incorporates some stretching exercises, but may diminish with muscle fatigue and injury.[49]

It has been observed that in benign hypermobility syndrome, which affects females more than males, proprioception can be significantly impaired.[47] This could partly explain the painful joint presentations in this population. A proprioceptive-focused rehabilitation program, consisting of walking exercises (e.g. on heels, backwards), balance board, and mini-trampoline exercises, has been shown to reduce pain levels in this group.[47] This information could translate to athletes who require extreme flexibility for their sport (such as ballet dancers and gymnasts) and who may present with painful hypermobile joints (e.g. extreme hyperextension of the knee and back). Treatment may involve pain relief where preceeding rehabilitation may focus on proprioceptive and balance to improve joint stability.

In acute and overuse soft tissue injuries, long-term changes in proprioception and motor control often result.[48] These can be caused by the partial and complete disruption of joint and ligament receptors. Additionally, partial disruption to receptors can lead to altered afferent information to the central nervous system.[48] Ultimately this can lead to reduced postural control, reduced maximal strength, and altered muscle reaction time in response to external stimuli.[48]

Ankle sprains are common in sport, with 40% resulting in re-injury even though objective mechanical stability tests may appear normal prior to injury.[50] Normally, proprioceptive input from joint position sense, and motion sense received from mechanoreceptors, will cause a reflex neural muscular activation, especially in response to perturbation. Following an ankle sprain, a ligament has the potential for adequate healing; however, mechanoreceptor disruption can reduce the joint position and motion sense around the ankle joint. This has been observed with poor motor control on walking heel strike after ankle injury, with an associated increase in risk of re-injury.[50] Additionally, it has been observed that there is a delayed peroneal longus reaction time in response to sudden inversion forces following ankle inversion sprain.[50]

Proprioceptive rehabilitation can involve balance exercises such as single-leg stance, plyometric exercises, agility exercises, and sport-specific exercises. Equipment that may be used to challenge the athlete's proprioception and balance include rocker boards (Fig. 15.9a), dura disks (Fig. 15.9b), Swiss balls (Fig. 15.9c), and mini-trampolines (Fig. 15.9d).

Figure 15.9 Proprioceptive aids
(a) Rocker board

(c) Swiss ball

(b) Dura disk

(d) Mini-trampoline

Proprioceptive-focused rehabilitation programs have shown improvements in re-injury rate and episodes of "giving way" in ankle and knee injuries.[48] Detailed progression of lower limb proprioceptive exercises is shown in the box below.

Ankle taping has been advocated to enhance pro-prioception by providing an increase in cutaneous feedback. Taping techniques are widely used following sporting injuries for rehabilitation and return to sport purposes. However, current evidence is limited to support the effectiveness of taping.

Functional exercises

Once reasonable levels of motor control, strength, power, endurance, flexibility, and proprioception have been achieved, the athlete can be gradually introduced to the functional activities that form the basis of his or her sport. These activities can prepare the athlete physically and mentally for the demands of the sport. Depending on the nature of the activity, functional exercises can enhance other components of the rehabilitation program.

Basic functional activities (e.g. walking, jogging, striding) can commence early in the rehabilitation program and are gradually progressed. They may be performed alone or in the company of teammates.

Agility drills relevant to the sport can also be gradually introduced. They can initially be performed in isolation and progressed with sporting equipment (e.g. a basketball or hockey stick). As the athlete's functional level improves, drills may be performed with a teammate or within team training. Functional exercises are often supplemented with progressive strength, power, endurance, flexibility, and motor control exercises that become more sport-specific. An example of the progression of functional exercises for an athlete recovering from a serious lower limb injury is shown in the box below.

Sport skills

Once adequate muscle conditioning, flexibility, motor control, and proprioception have been attained, sport skills should be incorporated into a rehabilitation program, often in the later stages. With graduated

---

Progression of lower limb neuromuscular exercises

Progression of neuromuscular exercises
Partial weight-bearing
- Walking with support (crutches) ensuring correct heel–toe movement
- Seated with feet on rocker board, forward/backward rocking for 2 minutes pain-free, first with both legs, then with one leg

Full weight-bearing
- Multiaxial rocker or dura disk (both legs)
  — 2–3 minutes each way circling
  — Attempt to balance for 15 seconds, rest 10 seconds
  — Progressively increase complexity—arms out in front of body
    – arms crossed
    – eyes closed
    – knee bends
    – other leg swinging
    – bounce/catch ball
- Balance on mini-trampoline
  — Same progression as above
  — Hop and land
  — Hop and land with one-quarter turn and return
  — Progress to half turn, three-quarter turn and full turn
  — Rhythmical hopping, alternatively placing toe forward and sideways

— Rhythmical hopping across a line, forward/backward, sideways
- Jumping
  — Various patterns
- Hopping without rebounder
  — Alternatively two hops on one leg, two hops on other leg
- Skipping
  — On spot, both legs, forward/backward/sideways
  — Single leg, two hops on one leg, two hops on other leg
- Advanced tasks
  — Walk/run across a steep hill each way
  — Run sideways up and down hill, each way
  — Walk along balance beam, then bounce and throw ball while walking
  — Sideways step-ups, gradually increasing height of step
- Running drills
  — Straight
  — Backward
  — Sideways
  — Circle (5 m diameter)
  — Cutting 90°
  — Zigzag through cones set at 45°

An example of the progression of functional exercises for an athlete recovering from a serious lower limb injury

1. Walking
2. Jogging
   (a) Jog 200 m, walk 200 m
   (b) Increase jog to 400 m, walk nil
   (c) Increase jog to 1500 m
   (d) Increase jog to 3 km
3. Running
   (a) Increase pace during 3 km; run intermittently for 100 m at a time (surge)
4. Sprint
   (a) Accelerate for 20 m, half-pace for 40 m, decelerate for 30 m
   (b) Repeat up to 10 times
   (c) Gradually increase pace to 60, 70, 80, 90 and 100%
5. Figure of eight
   (a) Run large (25 m) figure of eight, 5 times
   (b) Gradually increase speed
   (c) Progress to smaller (15 m, 10 m, 5 m) figures
6. Agility drills
   (a) 45° zigzag slowly increasing speed
   (b) 90° cutting
   (c) Run around square (forward, sideways, backward)
   (d) Side to side (e.g. across tennis court)

return to training, the athlete relearns the various motor patterns necessary for their sport.

For tissues that have not been subjected to performance level stress for an extended period of time, progression should be gradual—through sports-specific tasks of increasing difficulty. The athlete can begin with basic sports skills (such as kicking a football) and then progress to more sports-specific skills (such as kicking for a goal or to a teammate on the run).

An athlete can only progress to skills training if there is no increase in the signs and symptoms of the injury following training. If there is any exacerbation of symptoms, the task should be reassessed and modified.

Sport skills should be incorporated into all rehabilitation programs. Performing sport-related activities can increase an athlete's motivation and maintain sporting skill levels.

Examples include a tennis player recovering from a knee injury hitting shots while seated in a wheelchair, a basketballer dribbling with the opposite arm following shoulder dislocation, and a footballer jogging and stretching with the rest of the team while recovering from a hamstring injury.

In the later stages of rehabilitation, particular attention should be placed on proper sporting technique, to reduce the risk of re-injury from incorrect techniques. Incorrect techniques may be compensatory from the initial injury, or from reduced practice and training time. Therefore, appropriate sport skills should be introduced prior to return to full training or sport. Examples of progressive sport skills programs for a basketball player and a tennis player returning after serious lower limb injury are shown in the boxes below and overleaf.

Return to sport skills program after lower limb injury: basketball player

Individual drill
Defensive stance
- Stationary
- Side to side
- Pivoting
Dribbling
- Forward/backward
- Side to side
- Zigzag
- Cross-overs
Shooting
- Foul shots (no jump)
- Dribble and shoot (no jump)
- Dribble, jump shot, rebound alone
Lay ups
- Alone
Rebounding
- Post moves
- High post
- Low post
Team drills
- Set play
- One on one
- Half court play
- Full court scrimmage
- Match practice
- Match (off bench)
- Match (start)

Return to sport skills program after lower limb injury: tennis player

Ground strokes
- Forehand, backhand, gradually increase time from 5–20 minutes

Serving
- Service action without ball, 10 repetitions
- Half pace serves, 10 repetitions
- Gradually increase 50% to 100% serves, 10 repetitions
- Gradually increase repetitions to 40 with break after each set of 20

Overhead shots
- Slow at first, 15 repetitions
- Gradually increase speed

Match practice
- Initially 15 minutes
- Gradually progress to one set, two sets, full match

Hydrotherapy

Hydrotherapy or pool therapy is a form of treatment widely used in the treatment of sporting injuries. It may be used in conjunction with other forms of rehabilitation, or as the sole form of rehabilitation.

Specific therapeutic exercises can be performed to rehabilitate the injured part. These exercises may be aimed at relief of pain or muscle spasm, relaxation, or restoration of full joint movement. Hydrotherapy exercises may result in increased muscular strength, power, and endurance, as well as improvement of functional level, including coordination and balance.

Hydrotherapy may be beneficial in acute or overuse injuries. In acute injuries, the warmth and buoyancy of the water induces relaxation, reduces pain, and encourages early movement. Isometric exercises can commence against the buoyancy of the water.

Range of motion exercises may be easily performed and may be assisted by buoyancy. It is also possible to use hydrotherapy wearing the appropriate splint required for treatment. Exercises may be assisted by floats to aid buoyancy.

Strength exercises may also be performed in the water. These may be isometric or isotonic (both concentric and eccentric). Graded progressive exercises can be devised utilizing buoyancy, varied speed of movement and movement patterns, varied equipment, and by altering the length of the lever arm creating turbulence.

Deep-water running

Deep-water running, or aqua running, consists of simulated running in the deep end of a pool, aided by a flotation device (vest or belt) that maintains the head above water (Chapter 10). The form of running in the water is patterned as closely as possible after the pattern used on land, but therapists should be aware that, for most sportspeople, deep-water running provides a new stress to the body: hence the risk of a new injury caused by deep-water running is increased. Athletes should therefore undergo a conditioning phase of deep-water running to lessen the risk of injury. The participant may be held in one location by a tether cord or by the force of a wall jet, or may actually run through the water. As there is no contact with the bottom of the pool, impact is eliminated.

A greater physiological response in terms of maximum oxygen uptake and heart rate can be obtained by adhering strictly to proper technique. The water line should be at the shoulder level, and the mouth should be comfortably out of the water without having to tilt the head back. The head should be straight, not down. The body should assume a position slightly forward of the vertical, with the spine maintained in a neutral position.[51] Arm and leg motion should be identical to that used on land.

Studies have shown that in spite of slightly lower heart rates (80–95%) and maximum oxygen uptake (83–89%) for a given level of perceived exertion, deep-water running elicits a sufficient cardiovascular response to result in a training effect. Several possible explanations exist for the differences in metabolic response to deep-water running and land-based running. Differences in muscle use and activation patterns contribute to these differences in exercise response. Furthermore, as weight-bearing is eliminated but replaced with resistance, larger muscle groups of the lower extremities perform relatively less work, and the upper extremities perform comparatively more work than they would during land-based exercise.[52]

There are three methods for grading deep-water running exercise intensity—heart rate, rating of perceived exertion, and cadence. Work-out programs are typically designed to reproduce the work the athlete would do on land and incorporate long runs as well as interval–speed training. The heart rate response is used primarily during long runs. Rating of perceived exertion and cadence are most often used for interval sessions.[51]

Correction of biomechanical abnormalities

Biomechanical abnormalities are an important pre-disposing factor to injury, especially overuse injuries. Normal upper and lower limb biomechanics associated with walking, running, and throwing are discussed in Chapter 8. Biomechanical examination should form part of the injury assessment, especially in overuse injury presentations. When an abnormality is detected, the clinician must determine whether the abnormality is contributing to the injury, either directly or indirectly. This requires the clinician to have a good understanding of the biomechanics and the pathology of the injury within the specific sporting environment. For example, the nature of injuries and the biomechanics associated with skiing would be different from those associated with swimming.

If abnormal biomechanics is contributing to an injury, its correction is a vital part of treatment, rehabilitation, and prevention. An athlete should not be allowed to return to the same activity that produced the overuse injury without addressing the causative factors. Otherwise the risk of re-injury is high, and subsequent rehabilitation and return to sport may not be as time-efficient or successful.

Abnormal biomechanics may be due to a structural abnormality, such as genu valgum, and may be difficult to correct. Therefore an assessment should be carefully made in regards to compensation strategies that the athlete may have developed over time that may have contributed to the injury. These strategies would then need to be addressed within the rehabilitation program. Muscle weakness, muscle imbalance, poor motor control, and/or poor sporting technique can also contribute to an injury. A number of treatment options are available to address these components. Muscle stretching, muscle strengthening and motor control exercises, taping, padding, shoe modifications, and orthoses (casted or non-casted) are just some interventions that may be incorporated into a rehabilitation program.

Stages of rehabilitation

Rehabilitation can be divided into four stages according to the athlete's level of function.

Initial stage

Flexibility and range of motion exercises should be commenced as early as possible, to improve soft tissue extensibility and joint range. It is important to consider the pathophysiology of tissue healing, and initially limit load to the injured area. Frequent gentle range of motion exercises (passive or active) can be commenced within the limits of pain. Manual techniques, heat or ice, and electrotherapeutic modalities may be useful adjuncts. Focus also on appropriate muscle conditioning exercises in a pain-free range of motion. It is important to assess accurately the level at which the athlete is able to perform an exercise correctly without exacerbation of signs and symptoms.

In the early stages, exercises should progress from muscle activation to maximal isometric exercises, then to multiple angle exercises and short arc exercises. Isometric and short arc strength gains will transfer to the isotonic and isokinetic programs in the intermediate phase. Performing the exercises frequently will improve endurance. Initially, exercises may be performed in a non-weight-bearing or partial weight-bearing position, and then can progress to a functional weight-bearing position as tolerated.

Resistance may be introduced with the incorporation of isometric and short arc exercises with the use of light weights and elastic devices (such as rubber bands or tubing).

A focus on stability and motor control is an essential component of the initial stage, to establish a solid foundation for successful progression through the rehabilitation stages. Exercises can then be progressed with range of motion, resistance, and motor control with correct movement patterns.

Simple proprioception and balance exercises, such as single-leg stance, are often introduced early to increase an athlete's awareness around the injured area. Motor control exercises, such as side stepping, and grapevine stepping (Fig. 15.10), are often incorporated in the initial stages to progress the proprioception and balance exercises with movement control.

At this stage, functional activities may be limited to the pool or stationary bicycle to maintain cardiovascular fitness and muscular endurance.

Intermediate/Preparticipation stage

The intermediate stage can begin when the sportsperson is able to perform activities of daily living, and has good range of motion, and reasonable strength throughout that range that is relatively pain free.

Flexibility exercises for the injured and adjacent areas should be performed regularly. Ongoing soft tissue therapy may also prove beneficial. When possible, a variety of different stretching techniques should be performed on the same area. Exercises, in this stage, can be performed through the full range of motion available around the injured area. Therapists

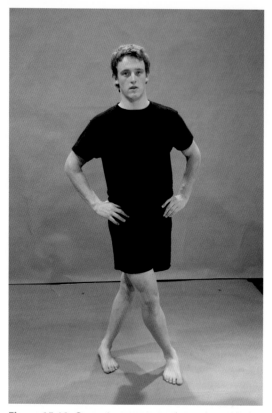

Figure 15.10 Grapevine step. Lateral stepping with the trailing leg going over the leading leg, then under the leading leg

should be mindful that the tensile strength of the healing tissue is still compromised, and progress is dependent on the athlete's signs and symptoms.

Strength gains are made by increasing resistance and number of repetitions. Endurance gains are made by increasing the overall work load and progressing cardiovascular endurance exercises. Power exercises may be slowly introduced in the later part of this stage by incorporating a speed element to resistance exercises; care must be taken to avoid injury.

Functional exercises should be introduced as soon as possible to start preparing the athlete for return to sport. Progression through supervised walking, jogging, striding, and initial agility work acts can easily be progressed into sport-specific activities in the advanced stage. A gradual increase in load allows time for adaptation and minimizes risk of re-injury. This can initially involve alternate day activity, with a gradual increase in volume and subsequent increases in frequency and intensity. Only one parameter should be increased at a time.

To increase motivation through the rehabilitation process, it may be possible for the athlete to undertake modified sport-specific activities. In the case of lower limb injuries, a tennis player could stand at the net hitting volleys, a hockey player could hit without running, and a basketball player could shoot from a set distance.

During the intermediate stage, the rehabilitation program may incorporate a variety of exercises, depending on the availability of equipment. Free weights, machines, pulleys, and rubber tubing may all be integrated into the program, with a variety of exercises performed using this equipment. Pool, exercise bike, stair climber, and isokinetic devices may be used if available. Close supervision and assessment of exercises are important in this stage to again avoid the risk of re-injury and encourage appropriate movement patterns.

Advanced stage

To reach the advanced stage of rehabilitation, the athlete must have gained adequate strength and endurance with full flexibility and range of motion. Activities of daily living should produce little or no symptoms or signs. Proprioceptive, agility and functional exercises can be progressed from the initial and intermediate stages, and the athlete should be able to tolerate a reasonable exercise work load. General cardiovascular fitness and endurance should have been maintained at a reasonable level. This stage introduces a graduated return to sporting activity while progressing the existing rehabilitation program. This stage of rehabilitation should correspond to the healing tissue entering the remodeling/maturation phase.

The athlete progresses through a sequence of functional activities required for the sport. This may include building up from jogging to striding to hopping to bounding, and agility skills of increasing complexity, intensity, and volume. These activities are often performed initially in isolation and then slowly integrated into a more realistic sports environment. This may involve the introduction of equipment (such as a ball or racquet) and then performing activities with a teammate. Further progression occurs with the introduction of team drills and increased skills practice.

In the advanced stage, muscle conditioning should be specific to the sporting activity required. For example, an emphasis on power for sprinters and lifters and endurance for distance runners is essential to be able to progress the athlete to the next rehabilitation stage—return to sport. Sport-specific positioning can be incorporated to enhance the gains of rehabilitation to the particular sport (such as wall sits for the skier, and prone bench pulleys for the swimmer).

Particular attention must be devoted to the athlete's biomechanics. If incorrect technique was implicated as a possible cause for the original injury (Chapter 8), the coach and therapist must ensure that the athlete relearns the correct technique. Alternatively, the athlete may develop compensation in their technique as a result of the initial injury. Unconscious guarding or protective mechanisms may continue and result in altered movement patterns. Video analysis may help both in assessment and for feedback purposes.

The athlete is usually participating in between 70% and 90% of normal training load by the later part of the advanced stage. As well as regaining the necessary muscle conditioning, flexibility, and function to facilitate return to sport, this stage of the rehabilitation program aims to restore the athlete's confidence. The athlete may fear injury recurrence, lack of full return of skills, or permanent residual disability. Athletes may be particularly apprehensive about performing the activity that caused the original injury. These fears may gradually subside with support from the therapist and a well-programmed return to sport. However, psychological effects may need to be addressed further and this is discussed later in this chapter (on page 247).

Return to sport

The following criteria should be used when determining whether an athlete is ready to return to full sporting activity:

- time constraints for soft tissue healing have been observed
- pain-free full range of movement
- no persistent swelling
- adequate strength and endurance
- good flexibility
- good proprioception and balance
- adequate cardiovascular fitness
- skills regained
- no persistent biomechanical abnormality
- athlete psychologically ready
- coach satisfied with training form.

There are a number of relative contraindications to return to sport. These include:

- persistent recurrent swelling—which indicates a joint is not ready for activity, although some minor degree of swelling may be tolerated
- joint instability—which may be controlled by brace or tape and good muscle control
- loss of joint range of motion—some of which may be acceptable in some joints and this needs to be assessed
- lack of full muscle strength—where strength of at least 90% of the contralateral side is recommended (strength of 80% of the contralateral limb may be acceptable in long-term ligamentous injury as long as there are no functional deficits).

Table 15.4 Progression of rehabilitation

Stage	Functional level	Sport	Management
Initial	Poor	Nil Substitute activities (e.g. swimming, cycling)	RICE Stretch/range of motion exercises Isometric exercises Stability program/Fitness maintenance
Intermediate/ Preparticipation	Good	Isolated skills (e.g. basketball shooting)	Stretch/range of motion exercises Strength Neuromuscular exercises Agility exercises Stability program/Fitness maintenance
Advanced	Good	Commence sport- specific agility work Skills Game drills	Strength, especially power Neuromuscular exercises Stability program Functional activity
Return to sport	Good	Full	Continue strength/power work, flexibility

It is vital to emphasize to the athlete that rehabilitation does not stop when he or she returns to sport. Therapists should be aware that collagen maturation and remodeling may continue for up to 12 months post injury. An athlete should not be considered completely rehabilitated until he or she has completed a full season of sport successfully following injury.

Secondary prevention

As the primary risk factor for an injury is a history of a previous similar injury, it is essential to pay constant attention to the vulnerable area. For example, athletes with a history of ankle sprain(s) should incorporate specific ankle strengthening exercises and proprioceptive training into their gym program on a regular basis. Similarly, athletes with a history of a muscle injury (e.g. hamstring strain) should continue to actively strengthen the muscle (e.g. eccentric hamstring exercises), and maintain muscle flexibility.

Progression of rehabilitation

There are several different parameters that the therapist may manipulate to progress the athlete's program to a level at which return to sport is possible. These parameters are:

- type of activity
- duration of activity
- frequency of activity/rest
- intensity of activity
- complexity of activity.

Type of activity

In the early stages of the rehabilitation program, activities that do not directly stress the injured area may be of most benefit. These activities can improve the stability and strength around the injured area indirectly. For example, tennis players may practice ground strokes in a set position following ankle injury, and swimmers may cycle after shoulder impingement injury as an upper limb weight-bearing exercise, as well as maintaining their cardiovascular fitness. Later in the intermediate and advanced stages, activities may specifically involve the injured area and will test its integrity. Additionally, incorporating functional and sports-specific activities around the injured area prepares the athlete for a safer return to sport.

Duration of activity

Once the activity tests the integrity of the injured area, the time spent performing that activity may be increased gradually. For example, the time spent jogging can be gradually increased. The total duration of the rehabilitation program may also increase in duration. For example, in the early stages, a program may be short in duration and performed several times per day. This may then be progressed to incorporate more exercises, which therefore increases the duration, and it can be performed once to twice a day, and so on.

Frequency

An integral part of the rehabilitation program is recovery (Chapter 10). Recovery allows tissues to adapt to the stress of exercise and reduces the risk of overload leading to injury. For example, a runner with Achilles tendinopathy may initially run every third day, then every second day, then two out of every three days, and ultimately return to their previous level of running six or seven days per week. On non-running days, the same athlete may cross-train and incorporate other forms of fitness exercises such as swimming or cycling, or focus on other elements of rehabilitation such as muscle strengthening. These elements may continue well after an athlete returns to sport successfully, as a preventive strategy.

Intensity

As the athlete progresses through the rehabilitation program, the intensity (speed and power) of an activity can increase. For example, a rehabilitation program for a sprinter may involve progression from half pace to three-quarter pace to full pace. Race starts are often incorporated in the advance stage of rehabilitation.

Complexity of activity

The athlete can progress from simple to more complex, demanding, sport-specific activities. For example, a basketballer may progress from dribbling slowly in a straight line to introducing turns at increasing speeds, and a tennis player may progress from ground strokes only to incorporating overhead shots and rallying drills.

Monitoring rehabilitation programs

The therapist should customize each rehabilitation program by taking into account the individual differences between athletes, which in turn can improve compliance, minimize the effects of incorrect techniques, and reduce the risk of re-injury. The program should be closely monitored initially and progressively, to increase safety by providing opportunities of modification, based on subjective and objective assessment findings.

A number of parameters can be regularly monitored. These include:

- pain and tenderness
- range of motion
- swelling
- heat and redness
- ability to perform exercises and functional activities
- number of repetitions and sets of exercises until fatigue.

If adverse effects occur, the program should not be progressed. Assessment should be made as to whether to reduce or to continue a program at the same level. Additionally it may be one, or only a few, components of a program which result in adverse effects, and these may need to either be modified or omitted until progression can be made safely.

Psychology

with ANN QUINN

Dealing with injury can be one of the toughest opponents an athlete may have to face. The manner in which individuals deal with the injury varies greatly. Some athletes adjust to the stressful event with little difficulty, whereas others are devastated by the experience.

Injured athletes experience a variety of responses following an athletic injury. These may include irrational thoughts and beliefs; attacks on self-image and self-esteem; feelings of helplessness, anger, and depression; and uncertainty surrounding the future. These are in addition to the psychological impact that the injury has on the individual's future performance.

The injury recovery process is thus a complex combination of many psychological factors that determine each athlete's response to the injury, and thus to his or her confidence and duration of recovery. The whole person, not just the injury, should be the focus of treatment. The purpose of this section is to provide the sports and exercise medicine team with an understanding of the emotional reactions to injury, and then focus on practical strategies and guidelines that the medical team can employ to facilitate recovery from injury and improve patient compliance.

Emotional responses to injury

Athletes' emotional responses after injury and during rehabilitation have been examined extensively in the literature. There is considerable consistency among the quantitative studies—elevated negative emotion is reported at initial post-injury assessments compared with pre-injury levels[53, 54] and the intensity of negative mood reduces over time,[55-58] with duration of injury determining the persistence of negative emotions.[58] Elevated levels of depression, anger, tension, and frustration are the most frequently reported emotions.[56, 58] However, Brewer et al.[59] noted that athletes retain a "positive emotion profile" after injury, despite elevated levels of negative emotion.

Negative emotions at the time of injury are influenced by low self-esteem, long duration of injury, and a medical professional rating of low "athletic function." During rehabilitation, slow progress in recovery and the experience of daily hassles predicted negative emotions, while active coping and intensity of effort in rehabilitation predicted vigor.[60] Some evidence has also indicated that negative emotion has a detrimental effect on athletes' adherence to rehabilitation programs.[61] In contrast, vigor was a significant predictor for both athletes' confidence and time to recovery.[62]

Psychological strategies to facilitate recovery

Psychological skills have been shown to benefit the injured athlete by promoting and maintaining a positive mind-set, focusing on healing occurring within the injured body part, and decreasing stress and anxiety through positive visualizations and self-talk.[63-65] The sports and exercise medicine team can assist greatly with these strategies. They can begin by educating athletes about their injuries and rehabilitation, and increase effective communication and active listening. Through setting short-term goals and giving strategies to cope with pain, they can help athletes to increase their compliance to rehabilitation, and they can also help to provide social support and encourage positive self-belief.[66] Some practical guidelines and strategies are outlined below for the sports and exercise medicine team.

Make sure the athlete fully understands the injury, why it happened, and the rehabilitation program

The first thing an athlete will need to do is to process the injury—why it occurred, and what exactly has happened. Many athletes have indicated that they did not fully understand what was expected of them, or the exact nature of the injury, and many of them were not even confident of their treatment.[57] It is thus imperative that the clinician or physiotherapist gives a detailed explanation in simple language that the athlete understands. If the clinician is still awaiting scans and is unable to accurately predict the length of injury, that should be explained rather than perhaps underestimating the predicted length of recovery, because underestimating recovery may lead to more negative states at later stages of rehabilitation.

Once the injury is accurately diagnosed, educating the injured athlete about the physiological nature of the recovery will help the athlete to better understand the program ahead. Sometimes at this stage, an athlete's focus narrows due to pain and fear about consequences of the injury and possibility of recurrence. It is thus important to take the time to fully explain the recovery steps ahead and to reassure them.

Effective listening—listen to what the athlete really is saying

Take the time to really listen to the athlete—what he or she is saying and, importantly, what he or she might not be saying. Athletes are dealing with all sorts of frustration at this time. Players with high self-esteem and good concentration are more able to control their frustration levels and have a positive outlook, which helps them focus on the rehabilitation tasks they are required to perform. As a result, they have a more rapid recovery from injury.

There are many pressures to deal with during rehabilitation. These pressures include the worry of missing important events or being permanently replaced, and the risk of financial loss; there may be added pressures from teammates. Injuries that result from malice from opponents, from a mistake by a teammate or from a lack of professionalism (such as not warming up or not following the doctor's instructions) may cause a player to develop high levels of frustration. Whatever the frustration, the best thing the clinician can do is to be there and to listen to them; they can also help players identify and confront views that they may have about their future.

It has also been found that written emotional disclosure is effective in enhancing psychological rehabilitation, by contributing to a greater personal understanding of the injury event and attenuating athletes' grief-related response.[67]

Athletes really need the reassurance that they still belong to the team and that their coaches and teammates care about what happens to them, both as athletes and as individuals.[68]

Establish short-term and long-term rehabilitation goals

The athlete, coach, physiotherapist, clinician, and other members of the athlete's team should collaborate to make the plans for a successful return. Goal setting is crucial to allow a stepwise approach, and to ensure that the player concentrates on immediate treatment goals rather than becoming anxious about the long-term goal. The goals should relate to:

- the amount and types of treatment to be used
- the appropriate intensity, frequency, and duration of the rehabilitation exercises (the range of movement, strength, and endurance activities)
- the number of rehabilitation sessions per day and per week that will be needed for full recovery
- a realistic date to return to competition.[69]

This time out of competition is also a great opportunity for athletes to work with the coach to critically assess their current skills and set goals for skill improvement.[69] They may not be able to physically do the skills at this time, but they can mentally train and visualize their success. It is also an excellent time to work on further developing their mental skills (e.g. concentration, relaxation), and setting some goals in other areas of their life such as family, school or career, and fun. Often, full-time athletes have difficulty occupying themselves when injured, so this is the perfect time to put lots of other exciting goals in place. It is also important that athletes record and monitor their progress and reward all their achievements on the road to recovery. This also provides an excellent motivation to reflect back later and see how far they have progressed.

Social support

Social support comes in many forms—listening support, emotional support, emotional challenge, task appreciation, task challenge, reality confirmation, tangible assistance, and personal assistance. A review of the research suggests that social support plays a role in whether athletes successfully cope with the stress of a severe injury, and evidence exists to suggest that athletes need strong supportive people behind them to encourage their return, and that social support was positively related to adherence.[70] However, the research has not demonstrated the strong support for the role of social support in adherence behavior that has been reported in the health literature.[71, 72] Nevertheless, as Quinn[62] found in her study, being a team athlete is a significant predictor of a faster recovery. In a more recent study, Bone and Fry[73] found that when severely injured athletes perceive that their athletic trainers provide strong social support they are more likely to believe in their rehabilitation programs. It is thus recommended that the sports and exercise medicine team ensures that social support is nurtured through all members of the team. Likewise, family and friends should provide important emotional support immediately following injury.

Staying positive

Positive self-talk has been shown to be positively associated with adherence to rehabilitation programs[74] and with faster healing times.[75] Likewise, vigor has been found to be a significant predictor of a faster recovery.[62] Encouraging athletes to keep positive and maintain their high energy and spirit does help to ensure them a quicker recovery. Although they cannot control the fact that they are injured, they can direct and control their thoughts about it and remain focused on the positives of all they can do during this time. An optimistic state of mind, along with powerful, positive affirmations said passionately, help to keep injured athletes focused and energized.

Imagery

Mental imagery has been shown to be a very effective tool to enhance rehabilitation, increase confidence, and facilitate recovery rates.[63, 64] Through the use of pictures and videos, symbolic learning and psychoneuromuscular processes are reinforced.

Imagery can be used in many ways throughout rehabilitation. These include:

- pain management
    - using imagery to practice dealing with expected pain
    - using imagery as a distraction
    - imagining the pain dispersing
    - using imagery to block the pain
- healing—to see and feel the healing
- cognitive imagery—to learn and properly perform the rehabilitation exercises
- treatment—imagining treatment and promoting recovery

- motivational imagery—to enhance mental toughness, help maintain concentration and foster a positive attitude
- recovery—to imagine being fully functional and active
- performance
    - mental rehearsal
    - feeling ready and confident to return
    - competing successfully on return and staying injury-free.

Coping strategies

Athletes do not adopt a one-dimensional approach to coping,[76] but respond to the stress of injury using a varied arsenal of coping strategies including problem-focused coping (finding out information and learning new skills to manage the problem) or emotion-focused coping (e.g. releasing pent up emotions, managing hostile feelings, meditating, relaxing); others use avoidance strategies. Many athletes show a preference for problem-focused coping.[77] Some, however, have chosen to adopt techniques in which they mask their genuine emotions and display socially desirable behaviors.[75] However, long-term acting, inhibition, and suppression have been linked with poor psychological and physical rehabilitation outcomes, including fatigue, hypertension, and a weakened immune system.[78]

To facilitate healthy psychological recovery from injury, injured athletes should be encouraged to explore all their emotions, and to actively engage in periodical emotional disclosure rather than remaining stoic; they should work with their rehabilitation team to identify practical strategies to best help them cope with the stress of their injury.

Relaxation

Relaxation training has been found to be another important psychological intervention, to reduce pain and tension in injured areas and to release psychological distress.[79] The stress of being injured may increase muscle tension in the injured areas,[80] and it may also increase perception of pain.[79] Autogenic training can help individuals reduce anxiety, irritability, and fatigue. This intervention also helps individuals to modify their reactions to pain, to increase their ability to deal with stress, and to reduce sleep disorders.[81] In addition, the use of relaxation techniques during injury recovery facilitates mind–body awareness and control and should be a part of all injury recovery programs.

Confidence to return to competition

For some athletes, the suggestion of returning to their sport brings doubts, fears, and anxieties. Despite assurance from trainers, physicians, and coaches, these athletes do not feel ready to return. As psychological recovery is a highly subjective phenomenon, it ultimately rests with the perceived confidence of the injured athlete to be able to meet the physical demands of full competition. Quinn[62] found that, during injury recovery, the best mood state predictor of confidence was vigor. Overall, it was confidence and being confident of being successful that were among the best predictors of confidence on recovery. Among the best predictors of a faster recovery time were confidence of recovering in the estimated time, experiencing fewer hassles, progress, and more vigor. Most importantly, athletes, coaches, and the medical team must be very patient and take the time needed to recover.

Podlung and Eklund[82] found that perceptions of success centered on (but were not limited to) a return to pre-injury levels and attaining pre-injury goals, staying on the "right" path, creating realistic expectations of post-injury performance, and remaining uninjured.

Other strategies

There are many other strategies that can be used:

- Provide recovery timetables. Follow up frequently with encouragement and small doses of information.
- An effective strategy for injured athletes is to talk to other athletes who have successfully recovered from the same injury. This will provide some insight and help the athlete to know what to expect during recovery.
- Provide motivational articles to read (e.g. Lance Armstrong's[83] book, *It's not about the bike: my journey back to life*, and Andre Agassi's autobiography *Open*).
- Make sure that 30 repetitions means 30 repetitions. Doing twice what the physiotherapist sets will not get an athlete back twice as fast. The reality is that overdoing rehabilitation may have a huge detrimental effect.
- Encourage athletes to keep in close touch with their teammates, friends, and coaches. Many athletes disappear when they are injured, which can lead to feelings of isolation and increase the likelihood of mood and adherence problems. Keep them involved by having them complete their rehabilitation exercises at the same time and place as the team. Also get them involved in the organization of the club/sport, helping out on competition days, and making the most of the opportunity to analyze competitors and do some match statistics.
- Encourage athletes to use the time to do something they have always wanted to do (such as learning a language or photography), so they keep busy and make something positive of their time off.

Conclusion

Injury recovery is one of the most testing times in sport; however, with planning and support from the medical team, family, friends, coaches, and teammates, athletes can successfully return to their sport in the minimum time. The sports and exercise medicine team is in the best position to educate and empower athletes to use psychological interventions to enhance the recovery process. These skills used during rehabilitation will help to motivate athletes to adhere to rehabilitation, and will increase speed of recovery, control anxiety levels, and enhance self-confidence.

REFERENCES

1. Arendt-Nielsen L, Sluka KA, Nie HL. Experimental muscle pain impairs descending inhibition. *Pain* 2008;140(3):465–71.

2. Graven-Nielsen T, Lund H, Arendt-Nielsen L et al. Inhibition of maximal voluntary contraction force by experimental muscle pain: A centrally mediated mechanism. *Muscle Nerve* 2002;26(5):708–12.

3. Cowan SM, Crossley KM, Bennell KL. Altered hip and trunk muscle function in individuals with patellofemoral pain. *Br J Sports Med* 2009;43:584–8.

4. Palmieri-Smith RM, Kreinbrink J, Ashton-Miller JA et al. Quadriceps inhibition induced by an experimental knee joint effusion affects knee joint mechanics during a single legged drop landing. *Am J Sports Med* 2007;35(8):1269–75.

5. Henriksen M, Alkjaer T, Simonsen EB et al. Experimental muscle pain during a forward lunge—the effects on knee joint dynamics and electromyographic activity. *Br J Sports Med* 2009;43:503–7.

6. Henriksen M, Alkjaer T, Lund H et al. Experimental quadriceps muscle pain impairs knee joint control during walking. *J Appl Physiol* 2007;103(1):132–9.

7. Kibler W, Sciascia A. Rehabilitation of the athlete's shoulder. *Clin Sports Med* 2008;27(4):821–31.

8. Cools AM, Declercq G, Cagnie B et al. Internal impingement in the tennis player: rehabilitation guidelines. *Br J Sports Med* 2008;42:165–71.

9. Kibler WB, Sciascia AD, Uhl TL et al. Electromyographic analysis of specific exercises for scapular control in early phases of shoulder rehabilitation. *Am J Sports Med* 2008;36(9):1789–98.

10. Escamilla RF, Yamashiro K, Paulos L et al. Shoulder muscle activity and function in common shoulder rehabilitation exercises. *Sports Med* 2009;39(8): 663–85.

11. Folland JP, Williams AG. The adaptations to strength training. *Sports Med* 2007;37(2):145–68.

12. Gabriel DA, Kamen G, Frost G. Neural adaptations to resistive exercise: mechanisms and recommendations for training practices. *Sports Med* 2006;36(2):133–49.

13. Jensen JL, Marstrand PCD, Nielsen JB. Motor skill training and strength training are associated with different plastic changes in the central nervous system. *J Appl Physiol* 2005;99(4):1558–68.

14. Cotterman ML, Darby LA, Skelly WA. Comparison of muscle force production using the Smith machine and free weights for bench press and squat exercises. *J Strength Cond Res* 2005;19(1):169–76.

15. Roig M, O'Brien K, Kirk G et al. The effects of eccentric versus concentric resistance training on muscle strength and mass in healthy adults: a systematic review with meta-analysis. *Br J Sports Med* 2009;43:556–68.

16. Rees JD, Wolman RL, Wilson A. Eccentric exercises; why do they work, what are the problems and how can we improve them? *Br J Sports Med* 2009;43:242–6.

17. Woodley BL, Newsham-West RJ, Baxter GD. Chronic tendinopathy: effectiveness of eccentric exercise. *Br J Sports Med* 2007;41:188–98.

18. Visnes H, Bahr R. The evolution of eccentric training as treatment for patellar tendinopathy (jumper's knee): a critical review of exercise programmes. *Br J Sports Med* 2007;41:217–23.

19. Tyler TF, Thomas GC, Nicholas SJ et al. Addition of isolated wrist extensor eccentric exercise to standard treatment for chronic lateral epicondylosis: a prospective randomized trial. *J Should Elbow Surg* 2010;19(6):917–22.

20. Sertpoyraz F, Eyigor S, Karapolat H et al. Comparison of isokinetic exercise versus standard exercise training in patients with chronic low back pain: a randomized controlled study. *Clin Rehab* 2009;23(3):238–47.

21. Stensdotter A-K, Hodges PW, Mellor R et al. Quadriceps activation in closed and in open kinetic chain exercise. *Med Sci Sports Exerc* 2003;35(12):2043–7.

22. Bakhtiary AH, Fatemi E. Open versus closed kinetic chain exercises for patellar chondromalacia. *Br J Sports Med* 2008;42:99–102.

23. Tagesson S, Öberg B, Good L et al. Comprehensive rehabilitation program with quadriceps strengthening in closed versus open kinetic chain exercise in patients with anterior cruciate ligament deficiency a randomized clinical trial evaluating dynamic tibial translation and muscle function. *Am J Sports Med* 2008;36(2):298–307.

24. Beynnon BD, Johnson RJ, Abate JA et al. Treatment of anterior cruciate ligament injuries, Part I. *Am J Sports Med* 2005;33(10):1579–602.

25. Witvrouw E, Danneels L, Van Tiggelen D et al. Open versus closed kinetic chain exercises in patellofemoral pain: a 5-year prospective randomized study. *Am J Sports Med* 2004;32(5):1122–30.

26. Reinold MM, Gill TJ, Wilk KE et al. Current concepts in the evaluation and treatment of he shoulder in overhead throwing athletes, Part 2: Injury prevention and treatment. *Sports Health* 2010;2(2):101–15.

27. Kyrolainen H, Avela J, McBride JM et al. Effects of power training on muscle structure and neuromuscular performance. *Scand J Med Sci Sports* 2005;15:58–64.

28. Nader GA. Concurrent strength and endurance training: from molecules to man. *Med Sci Sports Exerc* 2006;38(11):1965–70.

29. Burgomaster KA, Howarth KR, Phillips SM et al. Similar metabolic adaptations during exercise after low volume sprint interval and traditional endurance training in humans. *J Physiol* 2008;586(1):151–60.

30. Whyte GP, George K, Sharma S et al. Cardiac fatigue following prolonged endurance exercise of differing distances. *Med Sci Sports Exer* 2000;32(6):1067–72.

31. Sahlén A, Rubulis A, Winter R et al. Cardiac fatigue in long-distance runners is associated with ventricular repolarization abnormalities. *Heart Rhythm* 2009;6(4):512–19.

32. Pelliccia A, Kinoshita N, Pisicchio C et al. Long-term clinical consequences of intense, uninterrupted endurance training in Olympic athletes. *J Am Coll Cardiol* 2010;55(15):1619–25.

33. Guissard N, Duchateau J. Neural aspects of muscle stretching. *Ex Sport Sci Rev* 2006;34(4):154–8.

34. Gleim GW, McHugh MP. Flexibility and its effect on sports injury and performance. *Sports Med* 1997;24:289–99.

35. Woods K, Bishop P, Jones E. Warm-up and stretching in the prevention of muscular injury. *Sports Med* 2007;37(12):1089–99.

36. Shrier I, Gossal K. Myths and truths of stretching: individualized recommendations for healthy muscles. *Phys Sportsmed* 2000;28(8):57–63.

37. Small K, Mc Naughton L, Matthews M. A systematic review into the efficacy of static stretching as part of a warm-up for the prevention of exercise-related injury. *Res Sports Med* 2008;16:213–31.

38. Shrier I. Stretching before exercise does not reduce the risk of local muscle injury: a critical review of the clinical and basic science literature. *Clin J Sport Med* 1999;9(4):221–7.

39. Shrier I. Does stretching help prevent injuries? In: MacAuley D, Best T, eds. *Evidence-based sports medicine.* London: Blackwell Publishing, 2007.

40. Shrier I. Stretching perspectives. *Curr Sports Med Rep* 2005;4(5):237–8.

41. Herbert RD, de Noronha M. Stretching to prevent or reduce muscle soreness after exercise. *Coch Data Syst Rev* 2007;(4):CD004577..

42. Rubini EC, Costa ALL, Gomes PSC. The effects of stretching on strength performance. *Sports Med* 2007;37(3):213–24.

43. Malliaropoulos N, Papalexandris S, Papalada A et al. The role of stretching in rehabilitation of hamstring

injuries: 80 athletes follow-up. *Med Sci Sports Exerc* 2004;36(5):756–9.

44. Svernlov B, Adolfsson L. Non-operative treatment regime including eccentric training for lateral humeral epicondylalgia. *Scand J Med Sci Sports* 2001;11(6): 328–34.

45. Holmich P, Uhrskou P, Ulnits L et al. Effectiveness of active physical training as treatment for long-standing adductor-related groin pain in athletes: randomised trial. *Lancet* 1999;353(9151):439–43.

46. Zazulak BT, Hewett TE, Reeves NP et al. The effects of core proprioception on knee injury. *Am J Sports Med* 2007;35(3):368–73.

47. Sahin N, Baskent A, Cakmak A et al. Evaluation of knee proprioception and effects of proprioception exercise in patients with benign joint hypermobility syndrome. *Rheumatol Int* 2007;28(10):995–1000.

48. Zech AM, Hubscher L, Vogt W et al. Neuromuscular training for rehabilitation of sports injuries: a systematic review. *Med Sci Sports Exerc* 2009;41(10): 1831–41.

49. Bartlett MJ, Warren PJ. Effect of warming up on knee proprioception before sporting activity. *Br J Sports Med* 2002;36:132–4.

50. Hughes T, Rochester P. The effects of proprioceptive exercise and taping on proprioception in subjects with functional ankle instability: A review of the literature. *Phys Ther Sport* 2008;9(3):136–47.

51. Wilder RP, Cole AJ, Becker BE. Aquatic strategies for athletic rehabilitation. In: Kibler WB, Herring SA, Press JM, eds. *Functional rehabilitation of sports and musculoskeletal injuries.* Gaithersburg, MD: Aspen Publishers, 1998:109–26.

52. Wilder RP, Brennan DK. Physiological responses to deep water running in athletes. *Sports Med* 1993;16(6):374–80.

53. Leddy MH, Lambert MJ, Ogles BM. Psychological consequences of athletic injury among high-level competitors. *Res Quart Exerc Sport* 1994;65 (4): 347–4.

54. Smith AM, Stuart MJ, Wiese-Bjornstal DM et al. Competitive athletes: Preinjury and postinjury mood state and self-esteem. *Mayo Clinic Proc* 1993;68: 939–47.

55. McDonald SA, Hardy CJ. Affective response patterns of the injured athlete: an exploratory analysis. *Sport Psych* 1990;4:261–74.

56. Quackenbush N, Crossman J. Injured athletes: a study of emotional responses. *J Sport Behav* 1994;17(3): 178–87.

57. Quinn AM. The psychological factors involved in the recovery of elite athletes from long term injuries. Unpublished PhD, University of Melbourne, Melbourne. 1996.

58. Smith M, Scott SG, O'Fallon WM et al. The emotional responses of athletes to injury. *Mayo Clinic Proc* 1990;65:38–50.

59. Brewe BW, Linder DE, Phelps CM. Situational correlates of emotional adjustment to athletic injury. *Clin J Sport Med* 1995; 5:241–5.

60. Quinn AM, Fallon BJ. The change in psychological characteristics and reactions of elite athletes from injury onset until full recovery. *J App Psych* 1999;11:210–29.

61. Daly JM, Brewer BW, Van Raalte JL et al. Cognitive appraisal, emotional adjustment, and adherence to rehabilitation following knee surgery. *J Sport Rehab* 1995;4:23–30.

62. Quinn AM, Fallon BJ. The predictors of recovery time. *J Sport Rehab* 2000;9:62–76.

63. Driediger M, Hall CR, Callow N. Imagery use by injured athletes: a qualitative analysis. *J Sports Sci* 2006;24(3):261–71.

64. Green L. The use of imagery in the rehabilitation of injured athletes. In Pargman D, ed. *Psychological basis of sport injuries.* 2nd ed. Morgantown, WV: Fitness Information Technology; 1999. 235–51.

65. Ievleva L, Orlick T. Mental links to enhanced healing: an exploratory study. *Sport Psych* 1991; 5:25–40.

66. Christakou,A. Lavallee D. Rehabilitation from sports injuries: from theory to practice. *Perspect Public Health* 2009;129(3):120–6.

67. Mankad A, Gordon S. Psycholinguistic changes in athletes' grief response to injury after written emotional disclosure. *J Sports Rehab* 2010;19(3):328–42.

68. Fisher AC. Adherence to sports injury rehabilitation programmes. *Sports Med* 1990;9(3):151–8.

69. Gould D, Petlichkoff LM, Prentice B et al. Psychology of sports injuries. *Gatorade Sports Science Institute Sports Science Exchange Roundtable* 2000;11(2):40.

70. Udry E. Coping and social support among injured athletes following surgery. *J Sports Ex Psych* 1997;19: 71–90.

71. Bianco T, Eklund RC. Conceptual considerations for social support research in sport and exercise settings. The case of sport injury. *J Sport Ex Psych* 2001;23:85–107.

72. Udry E. Social Support: Exploring its roles in the context of athletic injuries. *J Sports Rehab* 1996; 5:151–63.

73. Bone JB, Fry MD. The influence of injured athletes' perceptions of social support from certified athletic trainers on their beliefs about rehabilitation. *J Sport Rehab* 2006;15(2):156–67.

74. Scherzer CB, Brewer BW, Cornelius AE et al. Psychological skills and adherence to rehabilitation after reconstruction of the anterior cruciate ligament. *J Sport Rehab* 2001;10 (3):165–72.

75. Mankad A, Gordon S, Wallman K. Perceptions of emotional climate among injured athletes. *J Clin Sports Psych* 2009;3:1–14.

76. Hall AK. The role of coping in rehabilitation from sports injury: the application of an integrated approach. Unpublished PhD, University of Melbourne, Melbourne. 2005.

77. Udry E, Gould D, Bridges D et al. Down but not out: athlete responses to season ending injuries. *J Sport Ex Psych* 1997;19:229–48.

78. Ashkanasy NM, Zerbe WJ, Härtel CEJ. Managing emotions in a changing workplace. In. Ashkanasy N, Zerbe WJ, Härtel CEJ, eds. *Managing emotions in the workplace* (p. 3–22). Armonk, NY: M.E. Sharpe, Inc. 2002.

79. Shaffer SM, Wiese-Bjornstal DM. Psychosocial intervention strategies in sports medicine. In Richard R, Wiese-Bjornstal DM, eds. *Counseling in sports medicine* (pp.41–54). Champaign, Il: Human Kinetics. 1999.

80. Ievleva L, Orlick T. Mental paths to enhanced recovery from a sports injury. In Pargman D, ed. *Psychological bases of sport injuries* (p. 199–220). Morgantown, WV: Fitness Information Technology. 1999.

81. Davis M, Eshelman R, McKay M. *The relaxation & stress reduction workbook* 4th ed. Oakland, CA: New Harbinger Publications, Inc. 1995.

82. Podlog L. Eklund RC. High-level athletes' perceptions of success in returning to sport following injury. *Psych Sport Exerc* 2009;10(5):535–44.

83. Armstrong L, Jenkins S. *It's not about the bike: my journey back to life.* New York: G.P. Putnam's Sons, 2000.

84. Agassi A. *Open: an autobiography.* New York: Knopf Doubleday Publishing Group, 2009.

Chapter 16

Principles of physical activity promotion for clinicians

with VANESSA YOUNG

The road to hell is paved with good intentions.   Samuel Johnson, 1775

Success story: Moving from inactivity to independence at age 72 years

Mrs L* is a 72-year-old woman who lives alone. Three months ago, she fell and broke her hip at home. This led to her having a total hip replacement (because of existing

ISTOCKPHOTO

Figure 16.1 Mrs L and her granddaughter both enjoy the independence that Mrs L gained from her physical activity program

* Patient details have been anonymized and image is not a true likeness

hip arthritis), an inpatient rehabilitation stay, and some time attending outpatient physical therapy. In addition to her history of osteoarthritis, she has stable hypertension, hyperlipidemia, and well controlled type 2 diabetes.

As Mrs L had a previously inactive lifestyle, she is slowly incorporating exercise into her routine. Her physical activity goals are to improve her balance, improve her blood pressure, and maintain her weight. She feels that increasing her physical activity will improve the osteoarthritis-associated pain, and provide more opportunities for social interactions. She commenced walking her granddaughter to school to promote both her own health, and also her granddaughter's. She started to monitor her activity level by wearing a pedometer; her initial goal was to reach 4000 steps per day. She attended a seniors' strength and balance class twice a week at the recreation center to reduce her risk of falls. Mrs L has attended group medical visits for older adults with diabetes, which ensures regular follow-up and provides social and clinical support.

…

Six months later, Mrs L reports increased confidence when moving about and completing activities of daily living, decreased pain, improved range of motion, and better quality sleep. She has been able to reduce her dose of antihypertensive medication.

As outlined in Chapter 1, an active lifestyle decreases mortality and the risk of many chronic conditions, including diabetes, heart disease, stroke, and breast and colon cancers. Health professionals are in an important position to provide advice on health promotion behaviors, such as physical activity. In a survey of 7238 people in Sweden, 76% of respondents thought healthcare professionals had a responsibility to promote physical activity in patients.[1] Exercise counseling is effective in promoting an active lifestyle,[2,3] and adherence to exercise prescriptions is as good as adherence to other treatments for chronic diseases (65%).[4] However, most health professionals feel pressured for time and under-qualified to prescribe physical activity.[5,6] Also, some clinicians are skeptical about giving lifestyle advice because they feel that repeating advice is often futile because patients do not change their behavior.[7]

This chapter identifies the appropriate "target audience," and provides a background on how to recommend activity for health promotion. This chapter links to Chapter 60, which provides summaries of exercise prescriptions for specific conditions.

Who should receive exercise counseling?

"Physical activity is not for everyone!" This is not true! Actually physical activity is beneficial for everyone, but not everyone is at the appropriate stage of enlightenment to realize it! Thus, identifying individuals who wish to incorporate more physical activity into their lifestyle is a critical step, rather than launching into a "one-size fits all" activity promotion program. Sedentary individuals with chronic medical problems and those at high risk should look to physical activity as medicine—it will decrease risk of injury and treat chronic disease. Although certain people may not reach the recommended levels of physical activity, all individuals are recommended to be physically active. Adapting physical activity recommendations to an individual's ability level provides multiple benefits to those with pre-existing medical conditions, and in high-risk patient groups.

Addressing physical activity in routine clinical consultations (in the same manner as has been done to influence smoking cessation) helps to identify patients who wish to incorporate a physical activity lifestyle change. Single questions to measure the level of physical activity as a brief intervention in every patient encounter have been trialed.[8,9] Physical activity should be considered a "vital sign" and can be routinely incorporated into electronic medical record patient registration forms.[10] If appropriate, opportunistic advice such as mentioning the benefits of exercise will establish a platform for further discussions on this topic in later consultations.[11]

Are there medical contraindications to being active?

Patient questionnaires help the clinician determine whether there are contraindications to specific activities. One questionnaire is the Physical Activity Readiness, or PAR-Q (Fig. 16.2). This initial screening form indicates whether a further medical assessment is required, which may involve completion of the PAR-Medx. However, these do not have to be completed prior to patients starting an exercise program.

The American College of Sports Medicine (ACSM)'s exercise prescription guidelines (8th ed)[12] recommend that no medical consultation before exercise is necessary for healthy adults, provided that they have no cardiovascular disease risk factors or symptoms of cardiovascular disease. In these individuals,

Physical Activity Readiness
Questionnaire - PAR-Q
(revised 2002)

PAR-Q & YOU

(A Questionnaire for People Aged 15 to 69)

Regular physical activity is fun and healthy, and increasingly more people are starting to become active every day. Being more active is very safe for most people. However, some people should check with their doctor before they start becoming much more physically active.

If you are planning to become much more physically active than you are now, start by answering the seven questions in the box below. If you are between the ages of 15 and 69, the PAR-Q will tell you if you should check with your doctor before you start. If you are over 69 years of age, and you are not used to being very active, check with your doctor.

Common sense is your best guide when you answer these questions. Please read the questions carefully and answer each one honestly: check YES or NO.

YES	NO	
☐	☐	**1. Has your doctor ever said that you have a heart condition and that you should only do physical activity recommended by a doctor?**
☐	☐	**2. Do you feel pain in your chest when you do physical activity?**
☐	☐	**3. In the past month, have you had chest pain when you were not doing physical activity?**
☐	☐	**4. Do you lose your balance because of dizziness or do you ever lose consciousness?**
☐	☐	**5. Do you have a bone or joint problem (for example, back, knee or hip) that could be made worse by a change in your physical activity?**
☐	☐	**6. Is your doctor currently prescribing drugs (for example, water pills) for your blood pressure or heart condition?**
☐	☐	**7. Do you know of any other reason why you should not do physical activity?**

If you answered

YES to one or more questions

Talk with your doctor by phone or in person BEFORE you start becoming much more physically active or BEFORE you have a fitness appraisal. Tell your doctor about the PAR-Q and which questions you answered YES.

- You may be able to do any activity you want—as long as you start slowly and build up gradually. Or, you may need to restrict your activities to those which are safe for you. Talk with your doctor about the kinds of activities you wish to participate in and follow his/her advice.
- Find out which community programs are safe and helpful for you.

NO to all questions

If you answered NO honestly to all PAR-Q questions, you can be reasonably sure that you can:

- start becoming more physically active—begin slowly and build up gradually. This is the safest and easiest way to go.
- take part in a fitness appraisal—this is an excellent way to determine your basic fitness so that you can plan the best way for you to live actively. It is also highly recommended that you have your blood pressure evaluated. If your reading is over 144/94, talk with your doctor before becoming more physically active.

DELAY BECOMING MUCH MORE ACTIVE:

- if you are not feeling well because of a temporary illness such as a cold or a fever—wait until you feel better; or
- if you are or may be pregnant—talk to your doctor before your start becoming more active.

PLEASE NOTE: If your health changes so that you then answer YES to any of the above questions, tell your fitness or health professional. Ask whether you should change your physical activity plan.

Informed use of the PAR-Q: The Canadian Society for Exercise Physiology, Health Canada, and their agents assume no liability for persons who undertake physical actvity, and if in doubt after completing this questionnaire, consult your doctor prior to physical activity.

No changes permitted. You are encouraged to photocopy the PAR-Q but only if you use the entire form.

NOTE: If the PAR-Q is being given to a person before he or she participates in a physical activity program or a fitness appraisal. This section may be used for legal or administrative purposes.

'I have read, understood and completed this questionnaire. Any questions I had were answered to my full satisfaction.'

NAME ______________________

SIGNATURE ______________________ DATE ______________________

SIGNATURE OF PARENT ______________________ WITNESS ______________________
or GUARDIAN (for participants under the age of age of majority

Note: This physical activity clearance is valid for a maximum of 12 months from the date it is completed and becomes invalid if your condition changes so that you would answer YES to any of the seven questions.

© Canadian Society for Exercise Physiology Sponsored by: Health Canada Santè Canada continued other side ...

Figure 16.2 The PAR-Q questionnaire

exercise tests can be expensive and difficult to interpret. Routine testing is also unnecessary as the rate of cardiovascular complications induced by exercise in individuals who are normally fit is low.

Exercise screening prior to starting a physical activity program is advised in:

1. men aged 45 or older and women 55 and older
2. those with more than two cardiovascular disease risk factors
3. individuals with signs or symptoms of coronary artery disease
4. those with known cardiac, pulmonary, or metabolic disease[12] (ACSM guidelines, 8th ed, 2010).

Assertive screening, where individuals are screened for the participants' benefit and not the providers', also has a role in some individuals (e.g. in elderly patients with no acute medical conditions). This allows older adults to participate in exercise programs without feeling as though the risks of doing so significantly outweigh the benefits,[13] especially as older adults report that frailty or poor health commonly prohibit them from taking part in regular activity.[14] Physical activity reduces the very risk factors that are incorrectly considered to mitigate against exercising (Table 16.1)![15]

Table 16.1 Risk factors that are reduced by exercise

Diabetes	Decreases HbA1c by 0.8%
Dyslipidemia	Increases HDL 2.5%
Hypertension	Decreases BP by 3.4/2.4 mmHg
Cigarette smoking	Increased abstinence at 3 and 12 months
Obesity	Mean weight loss 6.7 kg at 1 year
Psychosocial health	Decreased depression, anxiety, hostility, somatization and stress

ADAPTED FROM METKUS ET AL.[15]

Executing the prescription

Bess Marcus teaches us that all individuals are ready for some form of education about exercise—but we must customize the prescription to their level of readiness for change.[16, 17] Individuals who are interested in increasing their activity are suitable candidates for specific exercise prescriptions. The goal is to elicit a behavior change to incorporate increased activity into the patient's lifestyle, resulting in attainment of the individual's goals.

Figure 16.3 Bess Marcus is one of the pioneers of tailoring physical activity interventions to patients' readiness for change. This 2nd edition of her excellent book (with LeighAnn Forsyth) provides a practical manual for exercise prescription in any setting

REPRINTED WITH PERMISSION OF HUMAN KINETICS, CHAMPAIGN, ILLINOIS. WWW.HUMANKINETICS.COM

Compliance with recommendations from health professionals is complex; however, it can be significantly improved if the patient–clinician interaction is optimized. Patients report increased satisfaction about the clinician–patient appointment when they have motivational counseling to tailor a physical activity program,[18] and patients actually seek advice and anticipate discussions that address lifestyle changes from health professionals during routine consultations.[7, 19]

Practical steps with the consultation

Helping the patient identify benefits of exercise is one way of personalizing the exercise prescription. Such benefits may include an improved sense of health and wellbeing, achieving and/or maintaining a healthy body weight, and increasing opportunities for social interactions.

The likelihood of a successful lifestyle change also increases by brainstorming barriers to exercise with the patient, and also strategies that increase confidence to overcome these.[20] These may include functional issues such as access limitations, beliefs of physical limitations, physical barriers such as bad weather, fatigue, competing demands/priorities, and boredom.[18]

Health professionals should assist the patient with setting positive goals. For example, appropriately treating musculoskeletal conditions results in improved ability to conduct activities of daily living, mitigates cardiovascular disease risk factors leading to improved blood pressure and cholesterol readings, increases aerobic capacity resulting in enjoying the ability to play tennis or run a half-marathon. The SMART goal framework, often used in organizational management,[21] is a useful structure to communicate clear intentions of a behavioral change:[22]

S **S**pecific
M **M**easurable
A **A**chievable/**A**ttainable
R **R**elevant
T **T**ime-based

An even shorter question to test usefulness of goals is "how and when?." Without these elements, goals are nothing more than "good intentions" and *the road to hell is paved with good intentions* (the quote that opens this chapter).

Goals should be reviewed regularly and revised as needed.

Documentation of the exercise prescription allows the patient to monitor his or her progress toward goals, and reinforces the importance of the physical activity lifestyle change. In addition, it serves as a motivating reminder of exercise recommendations from a health professional.[23] If the patient commits publicly to the goal, there is a much greater chance of sticking to the commitment than if he or she does not commit publicly.[24]

Exercise guidelines

An individual's preferred activities should be identified and incorporated into their lifestyle. It is important to establish how much activity occurs during the usual tasks of daily living. A patient's current level of activity must be identified, and further activity is recommended in addition to this.

Activities that decrease the amount of sedentary behavior (i.e. watching TV, sitting at a desk) are also recommended. It should be emphasized that even a small increase in activity is beneficial. Many evidence-based guidelines have been established, with overlapping recommendations. For sedentary individuals, those aged >65 or those with a background of chronic illness, the advice is to "start low, go slow" by gradually increasing the amount of activity over time. The ACSM[12] recommends that healthy

adults younger than 65 years of age undertake the "basic exercise prescription" advocated in the box below.

Exercise prescriptions are individualized recommendations of "doses" or amounts of activity. They commonly include components of aerobic, load-bearing (i.e. resistance), and flexibility exercises. These types of exercise can be further defined by their recommended intensity, frequency, and duration. These factors vary according to the individual's health status and goals.

Aerobic activity

Moving large muscles in a rhythmic pattern for a sustained period of time is called aerobic (or endurance) activity. Examples include walking/hiking, jogging/running, cycling, and swimming. This type of exercise increases cardiovascular and respiratory fitness by encouraging the body to adapt to the physiological stresses placed on these systems. Hence, increasing aerobic activity modifies cardiovascular disease risk factors.

The amount of aerobic activity refers to duration (length of time), frequency (how often), and intensity (a measure of work rate or how strenuous an activity is). Moderate or vigorous intensity aerobic activity is recommended.

Almost certainly, 60 minutes of accumulated physical activity daily results in greater health benefits than 30 minutes of the same activity, but the inflection point where the health benefits per minute of activity is maximal remains undetermined.[25] The dose–response relationship between many aspects of health and physical activity is unclear. However,

---

The ACSM's[12] basic exercise prescription

- Aerobic exercise, 30 minutes (or more) of moderate and/or vigorous activity on a minimum of 5 days per week and at least 2 resistance training sessions per week.
  - This should be in addition to the routine activities of daily living which are light intensity or less than 10 minutes duration.
  - Moderate/vigorous activity >10 minutes duration can be counted toward the recommendation.
  - The resistance training (muscle strengthening) should consist of 8–12 repetitions and 2–4 sets of exercises for each of the major muscle groups; these should be undertaken a minimum of twice a week.

individuals who do not demonstrate an improvement in aerobic endurance, yet nonetheless strive to meet physical activity recommendations, still reap the benefits of increased activity, particularly in terms of primary prevention. There is a dose–response relationship whereby moderate intensity exercise is sufficient for achieving health benefits; however, vigorous intensity exercise leads to further benefits. The greatest magnitude of effect is seen in individuals who are sedentary and then become active; there is postulated to be a smaller benefit in active individuals who then become more active.[26, 27] Health-related benefits are reached in low-intensity, longer-duration activities, whereas high-intensity, short-duration activities increase cardiorespiratory fitness.

Defining intensity

Aerobic intensity[12] is traditionally based on %VO_2 max, which is a measure of the maximum amount of oxygen uptake. Measurement of VO_2 max is a maximal exercise test done using open circuit spirometry in a controlled environment. As this is not always practical, submaximal tests (e.g. treadmill tests, timed walk tests) may be done to predict VO_2 max.

Intensity can be discussed in relative and absolute terms. Relative intensity is the amount of effort based on an individual's level of fitness, such as the "rating of perceived exertion" (RPE), or heart rate. Absolute intensity is a standard measure of effort based on energy expenditure, or metabolic equivalents (METs—metabolic equivalents of task).

Heart rate is a useful measure of intensity, assuming that it has a linear relationship with oxygen consumption in aerobic exercise. The maximum heart rate is traditionally estimated using the equation HR_{max} = 220−age. But, for young, healthy individuals, a maximal exercise test may be performed which will give a true HR_{max}. The ACSM recommends an intensity of 70–85% HR_{max} which approximates to 50–70% VO_2 max.[12] The HR_{max} is not useful for prescribing low-intensity exercise, as it may result in the target heart rate being below the resting heart rate.

Intensity can also be measured by energy expenditure, or multiples of metabolic activity relative to the amount of energy used at rest per minute (METs). However, VO_2 max decreases with age and different individuals exert varying amounts of effort with the same tasks. Light-intensity activity is usually less than 3.0 METs, moderate intensity activity 3.0–5.9 METs, and vigorous intensity activity more than 6.0 METs.

Table 16.2 shows activities in terms of METs. Energy expenditure may vary between individuals doing the same activity, as illustrated in Table 16.2.

The rating of perceived exertion, such as Borg's scale,[29] is a "subjective rating of overall exertion, taking into account personal fitness, environmental conditions and fatigue," which is used to monitor how close an individual is to maximal exertion. In addition, it may be used in certain individuals where heart rate is not an appropriate marker for intensity, for example, in those on beta blockers. This is a guideline to monitor individuals' progress as, unsurprisingly, it has large inter-individual variability. Moderate exercise is rated 11–15 on Borg's rated perceived exertion (RPE) scale. Table 16.3 shows a diagram of this 6–20 scale.

In practice, a moderate intensity can be reached by advising patients that they should still be able to talk while exercising, but be working hard enough that they feel as though they are breathing harder. This "talk test" can be used as a marker of intensity as it is closely related to the ventilatory threshold,[30] which is also a marker of ischemia in cardiovascular disease.[31]

For those who are sedentary, exercise should be introduced and increased gradually.[15] For example, walk for 5 minutes every day at first, then increase the time by 10 minutes a day, then slowly increase speed to promote maintenance and minimize the risk of injuries.

Table 16.2 Energy expenditure of commonly referenced METs versus METs measured in Kozey et al., 2010[28]

Activity	MET values from study*	Reference MET values
Ascending stairs	9.6	5
Descending stairs	4	3
Gardening	3.6	4.5
Mowing the lawn	3.2	3.5
Vacuuming	3.3	3.5
Walking (1.56m/s, 3% grade)	5.6	6
Walking (1.56m/s, on the flat)	4.5	3.8
Basketball	8.3	4.5
Tennis	9.0	7

Table 16.3 Borg's original "ratings of perceived exertion" (RPE) scale

Rating	Perceived level of exertion
6	No exertion at all
7	Extremely light
8	
9	Very light
10	
11	Light
12	
13	Somewhat hard
14	
15	Hard (heavy)
16	
17	Very hard
18	
19	Extremely hard
20	Maximal exertion

Risk of injury is low in active people compared with inactive people. However, as active people do more activity at a vigorous intensity, they often have a higher rate of injury compared with inactive people. Gradually increasing the amount of exercise decreases musculoskeletal injuries and minimizes the risk of a sudden cardiac event.

Resistance training

Resistance training[12, 32] (i.e. load-bearing exercise) makes activities of daily living easier, and leads to systemic benefits such as improved balance and cognition, increased bone density, and cardiovascular benefits. In addition, it helps inactive individuals to build muscle strength, endurance, and power before commencing aerobic exercise.

Body weight, dynamic machines, and free weights can all provide resistance exercise. Varying intensity (how much weight), frequency (how often), and repetitions (number of times a weight is lifted) tailors the exercise prescription for the patient.

In the "basic exercise prescription for health" (primary prevention), individuals should undertake 2–3 sets of 8–12 repetitions of resistance exercises twice weekly (Table 16.4). Examples of resistance exercises that involve all of the main muscle groups (arms, shoulders, chest, abdomen, back, legs, thighs) are illustrated in Figure 16.4 overleaf.

There should be 2 to 3 minute rest intervals between each set and 48 hours between training sessions for the same muscle group to increase muscular fitness. Training different muscle groups on separate days of the week may improve adherence to recommendations, as it leads to a more flexible program. In doing a number of sets for a particular muscle group, different exercises may be used to vary sets. For example, a set of bench presses and then a set of tricep dips can be used to train the pectoral muscles. To maintain muscular fitness, training muscle groups once a week at the same intensity will suffice.

Exercises should be controlled, rhythmic, and of moderate–slow speed throughout a full range of motion. The breathing pattern should be natural and should avoid the Valsalva maneuver as it causes an increase in systolic and diastolic blood pressures. Breath should be exhaled in lifting and inhaled in lowering. Concentric and eccentric muscle action should be active in lifting and lowering respectively.

Resistance exercises should be repeated until it would be difficult to do another repetition with good form and technique; this is called the "repetition

Table 16.4 Resistance exercises classified by body region (diagrams of each of these are shown in Fig. 16.4 overleaf)

Chest and shoulders	Upper and lower back	Abdominal region	Arm region	Hips and thighs	Leg region
• Bench press • Shoulder shrugs • Seated (overhead) press • Upright row	• Back extension • Latissimus pull-down • Bent-over row	• Bent knee curl-up • Reverse sit-up	• Arm curl • Triceps pull-down	• Leg curl • Seated leg press • Half-squat • Side leg raises	• Heel raise (rising up on toes)

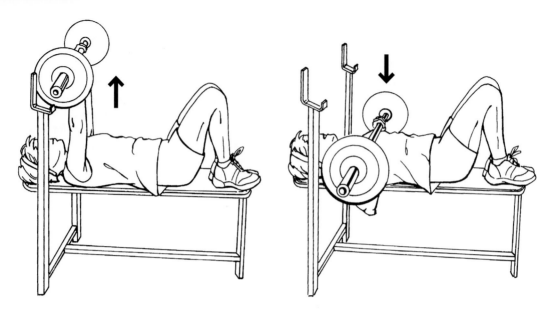

Figure 16.4 Examples of resistance exercises that involve all of the main muscle groups (arms, shoulders, chest, abdomen, back, legs, thighs)
(a) Bench press

(b) Shoulder shrugs

(c) Seated (overhead) press

(d) Upright row

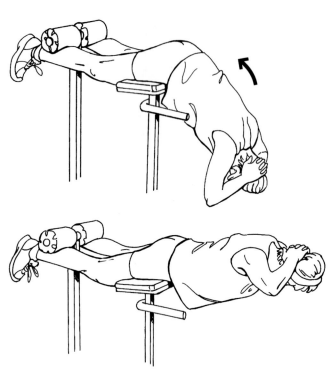

(e) Back extension

(f) Latissimus pull-down

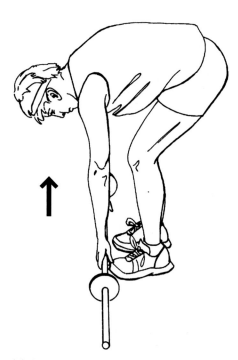

(g) Bent-over row

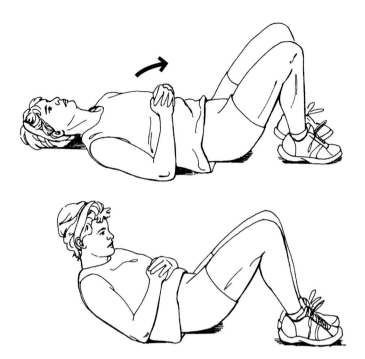

(h) Bent knee curl-up

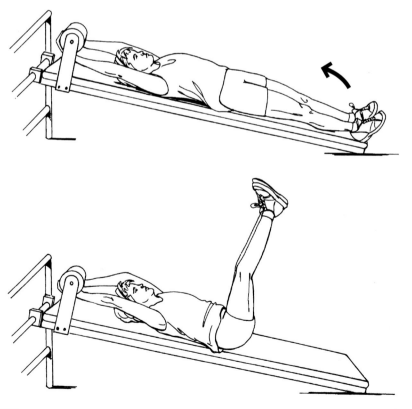

(i) Reverse sit-up

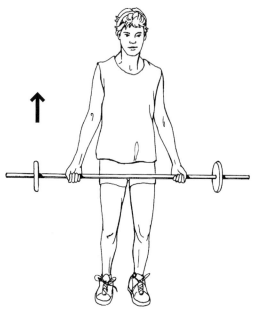

(j) Arm curl

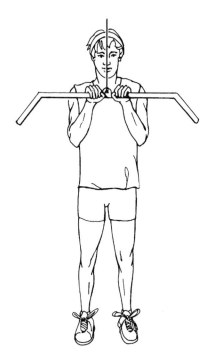
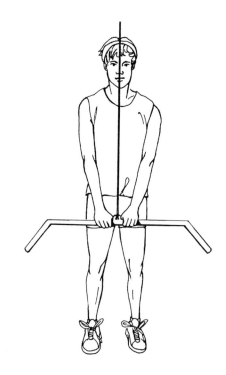

(k) Triceps pull-down

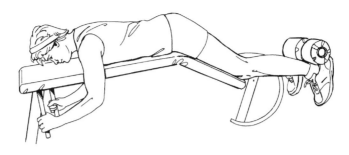

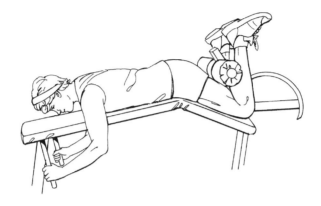

(l) Leg curl

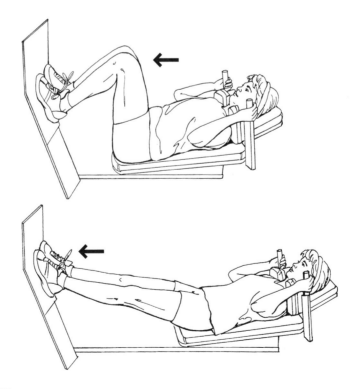

(m) Seated leg press

(n) Half-squat

(o) Side leg raises

(p) Heel raise (rising up on toes)

maximum." This is the point where the muscle is fatigued. Continuing to lift until muscle failure increases the possibility of injury. The appropriate weight for fatigue to occur in 8–12 repetitions can be determined from a percentage of the one repetition maximum (1RM). Determining a repetition maximum is done by:

1. warming up—with several submaximal repetitions
2. determining the 1RM (or multiple RM) within 4 trials with rest periods of 3 to 5 minutes between trials. This can be done by selecting an initial weight approximating 50–70% capacity and increasing the weight until the repetition cannot be completed.

Muscle strength and mass increases in response to stimuli, so weight should be increased to maintain an 8–12 RM. Conversely, if an individual cannot perform 8 repetitions, the weight should be decreased. Older adults should commence at a lower intensity (30–40% 1RM) and increase the number of repetitions per set to 10–15. The intensity should be altered more slowly than in young, healthy individuals. When the older adult is conditioned, it is appropriate to modify the intensity to 8–12 RM.

Although static and dynamic machines provide variation, free weights optimize proprioceptive feedback, and lead to greater muscle development.[33] Multiple joint exercises (e.g. chest press) are preferable to single joint exercises (e.g. biceps curl) as they target multiple muscle groups. Agonists and antagonists (opposing muscle groups) should also be trained together to help avoid imbalances and injury. As with aerobic activity, intensity should start low and gradually progress to allow for physiological adaptation. Loads of more than 40% of 1RM increase strength and function in untrained people.[34]

Flexibility
Warm-ups and cool-downs allow the body to adapt physiologically to a level of physical activity. The warm-up is usually 5–10 minutes of lower intensity activity that is similar to the type of activity that is about to occur. ACSM guidelines suggest 10 minutes of stretching following a warm-up or cool-down to maintain a full range of motion and improve physical function.

Proprioceptive neuromuscular facilitation, static and dynamic stretching improve flexibility. Stretching should be done for at least 4 repetitions involving all major muscle groups to the limit of discomfort in a range of motion where tightness is felt, but no further. Static stretches should be held for 15–60 seconds. For proprioceptive neuromuscular facilitation, a 6-second contraction should be followed by a 10- to 30-second assisted stretch.

Follow-up
Follow-up is useful to monitor and evaluate goals, reinforce health benefits, and provide encouragement. Individuals who have been advised to increase their levels of activity should be reviewed regularly. This is particularly important for those who have chronic diseases (e.g. congestive heart failure) where it may be pertinent to be aware of any increase in severity of symptoms.[35] People with chronic diseases may require more advice or cautious adjustments in their program for the first couple of months before transitioning to unsupervised training.[36] Chapter 60 gives specific exercise prescription examples for this population.

An overlooked element of motivation
How would marketing experts sell physical activity? Heath and Heath, the authors of *Made to stick*,[37] share a 6-part acronym for SUCCESS. Importantly, it is based on empirical psychology experiments! Powerful messages are (**S**) simple, (**U**) unexpected, (**C**) concrete, (**C**) credible, (**E**) emotional, and (**S**) stories. In their world, the clinical story packs more punch than the systematic review (see Chapter 3 for more on evidence-based practice and systematic reviews).

How do we apply this to giving exercise advice? To make our advice "stick," clinicians need to suggest activities that the patient enjoys. A pedometer can help to provide a step goal to increase physical activity levels by more than 2000 steps per day.[38] Media campaigns promoting 10 000 steps per day[39] can add weight to the efforts of individual clinicians.

Greater success can occur when the clinicians' efforts are embedded within multiple interventions and within a socioecological support framework. In an ideal model, community-based approaches would provide social support, as well as access to parks and recreation services. Built environments (e.g. bike lanes) can also facilitate physical activity. Patients would be supported by group medical visits, and physicians would adopt a chronic care model focusing on lifestyle interventions with interdisciplinary teams. Health promotion can also be supported by workplace initiatives, as well as public health and education policies. Today's world provides the opportunity for internet resources and email prompting to promote physical activity.[40, 41] The box below discusses behavior change.

Summary

Your goal is to inspire exercise. Four key steps are to:

1. ask every patient about their current level of activity and exercise
2. discover
   (a) whether they interested in modifying their lifestyle and/or starting an exercise program
   (b) where are they on the stages of change
3. advise accordingly—if the patient is healthy, provide exercise advice. If the patient is not healthy, consider screening first, then give advice on exercise. Remember, "start low, go slow." Increase amount gradually over time
4. follow-up—review and revise exercise prescription.

A discussion of behavior change—turning theory into practice

Translation of intention into behavior is a challenge for all health professionals and exercise advocates. There are various models for identifying how likely a patient is to adopt exercise behavior. Of these, the transtheoretical model has the most evidence as a mechanism of intervention.[42] The premise is that people dynamically cycle and progress through four key stages—pre-contemplation, contemplation, action, and maintenance—before developing a habit.[43] Self-efficacy and decisional-balance are important mediators to assist progress through this cycle.[44] Increasing levels of self-efficacy (or self-confidence) correlate with progression through the stages. The person's decision as to whether to exercise or not depends on the relative cons and pros (or costs versus benefits) at that stage of change. In the pre-contemplation stage, for example, the perceived cons of activity outweigh the pros. As the individual progresses through the stages, the pros and cons will equalize, and in the maintenance phase, then the pros of incorporating a physical activity lifestyle change will be greater than the cons. Motivational counseling— where clinicians help patients to identify the benefits of physical activity, barriers to adopting a lifestyle change to increase physical activity, and set appropriate goals—assists patients to progress through the stages of change.[3] Identifying an individual's stage of change may be done using a simple questionnaire (e.g. as shown in Figure 16.5).[45]

Stages of change

Moderate physical activity includes such activities as walking, gardening, and heavy housecleaning. For moderate activity to be regular, it must add up to a total of **30 or more minutes per day** and be done **at least 5 days per week**. For example, you could take a 30-minute walk or take a 10-minute walk, rake leaves for 10 minutes and climb stairs for 10 minutes, adding up to a total of 30 minutes. Physical activity can add up to give you **Get moving** health rewards!

Find your personal starting point

For each question below, please mark Yes or No.

	Yes	No
1. I currently participate in moderate physical activity.	A. ⚪	B. ⚪
2. I intend to increase my participation in moderate physical activity in the next 6 months.	C. ⚪	D. ⚪
3. I currently engage in **regular** moderate physical activity.	E. ⚪	F. ⚪
4. I have been participating in moderate physical activity **regularly** for the past 6 months	G. ⚪	H. ⚪
5. In the past, I have been **regularly** physically active in moderate activities for a period of at least 3 months.	I. ⚪	J. ⚪

SCORING INSTRUCTIONS TO DETERMINE YOUR STAGE OF CHANGE:

Determine your stage of readiness and refer to the enclosed stage-based handouts.
- If line **B** and **D** are checked. **STAGE 1—Precontemplation:** currently has no intenion of being active
- If line **B** and **C** are checked. **STAGE 2—Contemplation:** not active, but intends to be soon
- If line **A** and **F** are checked. **STAGE 3—Preparation:** trying but not yet regularly active
- If line **A, E** and **H** are checked. **STAGE 4—Action:** regularly active, but for less than 6 months
- If line **A, E** and **G** are checked. **STAGE 5—Maintenance:** regularly active for 6 months or more
- If line **I** is checked, you may be in **Relapse**

Figure 16.5 Stages of change questionnaire

RECOMMENDED WEBSITES

Exercise is Medicine: www.exerciseismedicine.org

Physical activity guidelines for Americans:
www.health.gov/paguidelines

RECOMMENDED READING

American College of Sports Medicine. *ACSM's Guidelines for exercise testing and prescription*. 8th edn. Hagerstown, MD: Lippincott Williams and Wilkins, 2009.

Warburton DE, Charlesworth S, Ivey A et al. A systematic review of the evidence for Canada's physical activity guidelines for adults. *Int J Behav Nutr Phys Act* 2010;7:39.

REFERENCES

1. Leijon ME, Stark-Ekman D, Nilsen P et al. Is there a demand for physical activity interventions provided by the health care sector? Findings from a population survey. *BMC Public Health* 2010;10:34.

2. Elley CR, Kerse N, Arroll B et al. Effectiveness of counselling patients on physical activity in general practice: cluster randomised controlled trial. *Br Med J (Clin Res Ed)* 2003;326(7393):793.

3. Kallings LV, Leijon M, Hellenius ML et al. Physical activity on prescription in primary health care: a follow-up of physical activity level and quality of life. *Scand J Med Sci Sports* 2008;18(2):154–61.

4. Kallings LV, Leijon ME, Kowalski J et al. A. Self-reported adherence: a method for evaluating prescribed physical activity in primary health care patients. *J Phys Act Health* 2009;6(4):483–92.

5. Kennedy MF, Meeuwisse WH. Exercise counselling by family physicians in Canada. *Prev Med* 2003;37(3):226–32.

6. Douglas F, Torrance N, van Teijlingen E et al. Primary care staff's views and experiences related to routinely advising patients about physical activity. A questionnaire survey. *BMC Public Health* 2006;6:138.

7. Jennings GL. Hypertension and adherence to physical activity programs—a sticky matter! *Br J Sports Med* 2010;44(14):994–7.

8. Milton K, Bull FC, Bauman A. Reliability and validity testing of a single-item physical activity measure. *Br J Sports Med* 2011;45(3):203–8.

9. Rose SB, Elley CR, Lawton BA et al. A single question reliably identifies physically inactive women in primary care. *N Z Med J* 2008;121(1268):U2897.

10. Sallis RE. Exercise is medicine and physicians need to prescribe it! *Br J Sports Med* 2009;43(1):3–4.

11. Fox K, Biddle S, Edmunds L et al. Physical activity promotion through primary health care in England. *Br J Gen Pract* 1997;47(419):367–9.

12. American College of Sports Medicine. *ACSM's Guidelines for exercise testing and prescription*. 8th edn. Hagerstown, MD: Lippincott Williams and Wilkins, 2009.

13. Campbell AJ. Assertive screening: health checks prior to exercise programmes in older people. *Br J Sports Med* 2009;43(1):5.

14. Rhodes RE, Martin AD, Taunton JE et al. Factors associated with exercise adherence among older adults. An individual perspective. *Sports Med* 1999;28(6):397–411.

15. Metkus TS Jr, Baughman KL, Thompson PD. Exercise prescription and primary prevention of cardiovascular disease. *Circulation* 2010;121(23):2601–4.

16. Marcus BH, Selby VC, Niaura RS et al. Self-efficacy and the stages of exercise behavior change. *Res Q Exerc Sport* 1992;63(1):60–6.

17. Marcus BH, Forsyth L. *Motivating people to be physically active*. 2nd edn. Human Kinetics, 2009.

18. Pinto BM, Goldstein MG, DePue JD et al. Acceptability and feasibility of physician-based activity counseling. The PAL project. *Am J Prev Med* 1998;15(2):95–102.

19. Albright CL, Cohen S, Gibbons L et al. Incorporating physical activity advice into primary care: physician-delivered advice within the activity counseling trial. *Am J Prev Med* 2000;18(3):225–34.

20. Rhodes RE, Plotnikoff RC. Understanding action control: predicting physical activity intention-behavior profiles across 6 months in a Canadian sample. *Health Psychol* 2006;25(3):292–9.

21. Doran GT. There's a S.M.A.R.T. way to write management's goals and objectives. *Manage Rev* 1981(November):35–6.

22. Schut HA, Stam HJ. Goals in rehabilitation teamwork. *Disabil Rehabil* 1994;16(4):223–6.

23. Swinburn BA, Walter LG, Arroll B et al. The green prescription study: a randomized controlled trial of written exercise advice provided by general practitioners. *Am J Public Health* 1998;88(2):288–91.

24. Cialdini R. Harness the science of persuasion. *Harv Bus Rev* 2001(October):72–9.

25. Mikus CR, Earnest CP, Blair SN et al. Heart rate and exercise intensity during training: observations from the DREW Study. *Br J Sports Med* 2009;43(10):750–5.

26. Lollgen H, Bockenhoff A, Knapp G. Physical activity and all-cause mortality: an updated meta-analysis

with different intensity categories. *Int J Sports Med* 2009;30(3):213–24.

27. Haskell WL. J.B. Wolffe Memorial Lecture. Health consequences of physical activity: understanding and challenges regarding dose–response. *Med Sci Sports Exerc* 1994;26(6):649–60.

28. Kozey SL, Lyden K, Howe CA et al. Accelerometer output and MET values of common physical activities. *Med Sci Sports Ex.* 2010;42(9):1776–84.

29. Borg GA. Psychophysical bases of perceived exertion. *Med Sci Sports Ex* 1982;14(5):377–81.

30. Foster C, Porcari JP, Anderson J et al. The talk test as a marker of exercise training intensity. *J Cardiopulm Rehabil Prev* 2008;28(1):24–30.

31. Meyer K, Samek L, Pinchas A et al. Relationship between ventilatory threshold and onset of ischaemia in ECG during stress testing. *Eur Heart J* 1995;16(5): 623–30.

32. American College of Sports Medicine. ACSM position stand. Progression models in resistance training for healthy adults. *Med Sci Sports Ex* 2009;41(3):687–708.

33. Schick EE, Coburn JW, Brown LE et al. A comparison of muscle activation between a Smith machine and free weight bench press. *J Strength Cond Res* 2010;24(3):779–84.

34. Onambele-Pearson GL, Breen L, Stewart CE. Influence of exercise intensity in older persons with unchanged habitual nutritional intake: skeletal muscle and endocrine adaptations. *Age (Dordr)* 2010;32(2):139–53.

35. Braith RW, Beck DT. Resistance exercise: training adaptations and developing a safe exercise prescription. *Heart Fail Rev* 2008;13(1):69–79.

36. Bredahl TV, Puggaard L, Roessler KK. Exercise on prescription. effect of attendance on participants' psychological factors in a Danish version of Exercise on Prescription: a study protocol. *BMC Health Serv Res* 2008;8:139.

37. Heath C, Heath D. *Made to stick*. New York: Random House, 2007.

38. Bravata DM, Smith-Spangler C et al. Using pedometers to increase physical activity and improve health: a systematic review. *JAMA* 2007;298(19):2296–304.

39. Tudor-Locke C, Bassett DR Jr. How many steps/day are enough? Preliminary pedometer indices for public health. *Sports Med* 2004;34(1):1–8.

40. Trost SG, Owen N, Bauman AE et al. Correlates of adults' participation in physical activity: review and update. *Med Sci Sports Ex* 2002;34(12):1996–2001.

41. Marcus BH, Ciccolo JT, Sciamanna CN. Using electronic/computer interventions to promote physical activity. *Br J Sports Med* 2009;43(2):102–5.

42. Rhodes RE, Pfaeffli LA. Mediators of physical activity behaviour change among adult non-clinical populations: a review update. *Int J Behav Nutr Phys Act* 2010;7:37.

43. Prochaska JO, DiClemente CC, Norcross JC. In search of how people change. Applications to addictive behaviors. *Am Psychol* 1992;47(9):1102–14.

44. Marcus BH, Simkin LR. The transtheoretical model: applications to exercise behavior. *Med Sci Sports Ex* 1994;26(11):1400–4.

45. Marcus BH, Forsyth LH. *Motivating people to be physically active*. Champaign, Il: Human Kinetics, 2003:21.

Part B

Regional
problems

Chapter 17

Sports concussion

with PAUL McCRORY, MICHAEL MAKDISSI, GAVIN DAVIS, and MICHAEL TURNER

You get a concussion, they've got to take you out of the game. So if you can hide it and conceal it as much as possible, you pay for it the next day, but you'll be able to ... stay in the game. Washington Redskins fullback Mike Sellers

Although head injuries are common in all contact sports, the vast majority of head injuries are minor. Sports in which minor head injuries are seen include football, boxing, gymnastics, horse riding, and martial arts. The incidence ranges from 0.25–4 per 1000 player hours of exposure in professional team sports. Amateur horse jumping jockeys have the highest concussion rate of any sport (95 concussions per 1000 player hours of exposure), followed by professional jumps and flat jockeys.

Head injuries of all levels are a medical emergency because they can prove fatal. Severe head injuries are discussed in Chapter 47. The clinician's role in the management of acute head injuries is to (i) recognize the problem, (ii) ensure immediate resuscitation, and (iii) transfer the injured sportsperson to the appropriate facility. In this chapter we discuss:

- definition of concussion
- prevention of concussion
- clinically relevant pathophysiology
- management of the concussed sportsperson
- complications of concussion
- return-to-play issues.

The chapter helps the reader to learn to diagnose and manage concussions in sport using the Sport Concussion Assessment Tool 2 (SCAT2)[1] (Fig. 17.2 on pages 283–286) and the Pocket SCAT2[2] (Fig. 17.3 on page 287).

We emphasize the SCAT2 tools, as they result from 10 years of collaboration by global experts who met most recently at the 3rd International Consensus Conference on Concussion in Sport held in Zurich in November 2008 (Fig. 17.1).

COVER REPRODUCED WITH PERMISSION FROM BJSM

Figure 17.1 The most recent international consensus meeting on concussion was held in Zurich, Switzerland, 2008 and the proceedings published in the *British Journal of Sports Medicine* in May 2009. http://bjsm.bmj.com/content/43/Suppl_1[3]

The SCAT tools (Figs 17.2 and 17.3) and Consensus statement[3] have been used internationally to assist clinicians and sportspeople reach "quality decisions" (Chapter 3) about return to play (RTP) following concussion.

Definition of concussion

"Concussion" is the term commonly used to describe a subtype of head injury. It is worth noting that the terms "concussion" and "mild traumatic brain injury" refer to entirely different injury constructs and the terms cannot be used interchangeably. While concussion is a subset of MTBI, the converse is not true.

Many publications on concussion refer to the Glasgow Coma Scale as a means of classifying traumatic brain injury (TBI). This is a validated and widely used measure of conscious state used in the assessment of TBI. Its primary role is in the measurement of serial change in neurological status post injury, which is critical in determining the need for further intervention. It also has a secondary role in determining the prognosis of TBI by subdividing the spectrum of injury into mild, moderate, and severe TBI based on an assessment at 6 hours post injury. The scale, however, does not encompass sport concussion, because of the mild nature of the symptoms involved and the fact that many concussion symptoms affecting conscious state are completely resolved by 6 hours.

The 3rd International Consensus Conference on Concussion in Sport re-affirmed the definition of sports concussion reached previously by experts at earlier meetings (see box).[3–5]

> **Definition of concussion**
>
> Concussion is defined as a complex pathophysiological process affecting the brain, induced by traumatic biomechanical forces. Several common features that incorporate clinical, pathologic, and biomechanical injury constructs that may be utilized in defining the nature of a concussive head injury include the following:
>
> 1. Concussion may be caused either by a direct blow to the head, face, neck or elsewhere on the body with an "impulsive" force transmitted to the head.
> 2. Concussion typically results in the rapid onset of short-lived impairment of neurologic function that resolves spontaneously.
> 3. Concussion may result in neuropathological changes, but the acute clinical symptoms largely reflect a functional disturbance rather than a structural injury.
> 4. Concussion results in a graded set of clinical symptoms that may or may not involve loss of consciousness. Resolution of the clinical and cognitive symptoms typically follows a sequential course; however, it is important to note that in a small percentage of cases, post-concussive symptoms may be prolonged.
> 5. No abnormality on standard structural neuroimaging studies is seen in concussion.

Prevention of concussion

There is no good clinical evidence that currently available protective equipment will prevent concussion, although mouth-guards have a definite role in preventing dental and orofacial injury.[6–8] Biomechanical studies have shown a reduction in impact forces to the brain with the use of head gear and helmets, but these findings have not been translated to show a reduction in concussion incidence in published randomized controlled trials. For skiing and snowboarding, there are a number of studies to suggest that helmets provide protection against head and facial injury, and hence should be recommended for participants in alpine sports. In specific sports such as cycling, motor, and equestrian sports, protective helmets may prevent other forms of head injury (e.g. skull fracture) that are related to falling on hard road surfaces, and these may be an important injury-prevention issue for those sports.[6]

Consideration of rule changes to reduce head injury incidence or severity may be appropriate where a clear-cut mechanism is implicated in a particular sport. An example of this is in football (soccer) where research studies demonstrated that upper limb to head contact in heading contests accounted for approximately 50% of concussions.[9] Rule changes also may be needed in some sports (e.g. rugby) to allow an effective off-field medical assessment to occur without compromising the athlete's welfare, affecting the flow of the game, or unduly penalizing the player's team. It is important to note that rule enforcement may be a critical aspect of modifying injury risk in these settings, and that referees play an important role in this regard.

The major concern with the recommendation for helmet use in sport is the phenomenon known as "risk compensation," whereby helmeted athletes change their playing behavior in the misguided belief that the protective equipment will stop all injury. Risk compensation is where the use of protective equipment results in behavioral change such as the adoption of more dangerous playing techniques, which can result in a paradoxical increase in injury rates. This may be a particular concern in child and adolescent athletes, where head injury rates are often higher than in adult athletes.[10]

The competitive/aggressive nature of sport which makes it fun to play and watch should not be discouraged. However, sporting organizations should be encouraged to address violence that may increase concussion risk. Fair play and respect should be supported as key elements of sport.[11]

The initial impact: applied pathophysiology

Neurological dysfunction in concussion is transient, even though the athlete has sustained a significant impact to the brain. More severe forms of diffuse brain injury involve shearing forces to the brain, which cause pathological damage. Although the pathophysiology of concussion remains poorly understood, the current consensus is that it reflects a disturbance of brain function, rather than a structural injury. Research in animal models of concussion suggest that linear acceleration or rotational shearing forces may result in short-lived neurochemical, metabolic, or gene-expression changes.

The concussed athlete, although conscious and without obvious focal neurological signs, may have impaired higher cortical function (e.g. impaired short-term memory). These subtle cognitive changes may only be detected by neuropsychological testing (discussed later in this chapter). While there are no gross structural changes on traditional imaging, newer imaging techniques (e.g. functional MRI) and EEG studies demonstrate prolonged alterations in brain activation patterns following concussion. The clinical significance of these results remains unclear. Subtle functional deficits are also suggested by recent work on saccadic eye movement abnormalities in the setting of TBI. These have been used as markers in other neurological diseases (e.g. Huntingdon's disease) and can be measured relatively easily. Studies of TBI suggest that increased saccadic latency may be a sensitive and stable biomarker of the functional disturbance that occurs in concussion in the absence of structural injury.[12]

Following a blow to the head, the athlete's conscious state may be altered. This may vary from simply being stunned to a significant loss of consciousness. Memory is typically affected in a concussive episode. A period of retrograde amnesia (i.e. loss of memory of events prior to the incident), or anterograde amnesia (i.e. loss of memory of events after the incident) may follow minor head injury. The duration

of amnesia does not indicate the severity of the concussive episode.

The ability to think clearly, concentrate on tasks, and process information is also affected. Concussive symptoms such as headache, dizziness, blurred vision, and nausea may also be present.

Frequently, in episodes of mild concussion (often called "bell ringers"), the athlete will be dazed or stunned for a period of seconds only and continue playing. The other players and coaches may be unaware that a concussive episode has occurred. Alert medical and training staff should closely observe the actions of a player who has received a knock to the head for any signs of impaired performance.

Management of the concussed athlete

Patient management is discussed in the on-field setting and with respect with return to sport.

On-field management

Every sportsperson who sustains a head injury is at risk of having a structural brain injury (e.g. brain contusion). One of the critical roles of the initial medical assessment is to examine the player neurologically for such injuries. However, it is not possible on the sidelines to absolutely exclude structural brain injury, especially when a player may have ongoing cognitive impairment that limits examination, or where structural injury (e.g. subdural hematoma) may take time to develop post injury. See Chapter 47 for emergency management of head injuries.

Clinical features that may raise concerns of structural head injury include:

- the mechanism of injury, particularly if there is a high velocity of impact or collision with an unyielding body part (e.g. head to knee impact), or where the injury involves a vertical fall (e.g. fall from a horse, spear tackle in rugby)
- immediate and/or prolonged loss of consciousness
- evidence of a skull fracture and/or bleeding or cerebrospinal fluid (CSF) leak from ears/nose
- examination finding of a focal neurological deficit
- seizure
- progression of any clinical features over time. Any deterioration in clinical state, in particular, worsening headache, nausea, or vomiting, or deterioration in conscious state should raise suspicion of a structural head injury and warrant urgent investigation. Similarly, structural head injury should be kept in

mind in any case where symptoms persist beyond 10 days.

A player with a suspected structural head injury requires immediate transport to a hospital with a neurosurgical unit, and an urgent computerized tomography (CT) brain scan to exclude intracranial pathology (e.g. hemorrhage, swelling), and to exclude/manage any associated cervical spine injury.

It is essential that all team physicians who have an on-field injury management role in their sport have formal training and certification in both first aid and trauma management. Depending on the country concerned there may be regional differences in certification and accreditation courses; some of the best known include Advanced Trauma Life Support (ATLS), Emergency Management of Severe Trauma (EMST), Pre-Hospital Emergency Care Course (PHECC), Pre-Hospital Trauma Life Support (PHTLS), and the British Association of Immediate Care Course (BASICS). This list is not exhaustive; all these courses deliver the skill set required to appropriately and safely manage acute injuries. A medical degree alone is insufficient training in this regard. The initial priorities when confronted by an acutely injured sportsperson are the basic principles of first aid. The simple mnemonic DR ABC may be a useful aide-memoire:

D	**Danger**	Ensure that there are no immediate environmental dangers that may potentially injure the patient or treatment team. This may involve stopping play in a football match or marshalling cars on a motor racetrack.
R	**Response**	Is the patient conscious? Can the patient talk?
A	**Airway**	Ensure a clear and unobstructed airway. Remove any mouth-guard or dental device that may be present.
B	**Breathing**	Ensure the patient is breathing adequately.
C	**Circulation**	Ensure an adequate circulation.

Once the basic first aid aspects of care have been achieved and the patient stabilized, consideration of removal of the patient from the field to an appropriate facility for further assessment is necessary. At this time, careful assessment for the presence of a cervical spinal cord or other injury is necessary. If an alert patient complains of neck pain, has evidence of neck tenderness or deformity, or has neurological signs suggestive of a spinal injury, then neck bracing and transport on a suitable spinal frame are required. If the patient is unconscious, then a cervical injury should be assumed until proven otherwise. Airway protection takes precedence over any potential spinal injury. In this situation, the removal of helmets or other head protectors should only be performed by individuals trained in this aspect of trauma management.

The clinical management of a concussed athlete may involve the treatment of a disorientated, confused, unconscious, uncooperative, or convulsing patient. The immediate treatment priorities remain the basic first aid principles of ABC—airway, breathing, circulation. Once this has been established and the patient stabilized, a full medical and neurological assessment examination should follow. On-site physicians are in an ideal position to initiate the critical early steps in an athlete's care, to ensure optimal recovery from a head injury. Typically, with an athlete who is conscious, without a spinal cord injury, and with a medical doctor present at the side lines, the more detailed assessment of the injured athlete would occur in the medical rooms where a quiet and unhurried environment exists. In some situations, where no doctor is present, removal to a hospital emergency department is the correct approach.

When examining a concussed sportsperson, a full neurological examination is important. Because the major management priorities at this stage are to establish an accurate diagnosis and exclude a catastrophic intracranial injury, this part of the examination should be particularly thorough. Having determined the presence of a concussive injury, the patient needs to be serially monitored until full recovery ensues. In the acute situation following a TBI of any severity, conscious state is the key element to assess initially. This is what is measured in the Glasgow Coma Scale and is included in the SCAT2 assessment tool.

Once severe brain or cervical spine injury have been excluded, then the most important components of concussion management include:

- confirming the diagnosis (which includes differentiating concussion from other pathologies, such as post-traumatic headaches and structural head injuries)
- determining when the player has fully recovered, so that he or she can safely return to competition.

See the supporting podcast discussing these issues in *Clinical Sports Medicine* masterclasses at www. clinicalsportsmedicine.com.

Confirming the diagnosis

Symptoms and signs

Common symptoms of concussion include headache, nausea, dizziness and balance problems, blurred vision or other visual disturbance, confusion, memory loss, and a feeling of slowness or fatigue (Table 17.1). Many of these symptoms in isolation are not specific to concussion; nevertheless, a diagnosis of concussion should be suspected in any player who presents with any of these symptoms following a collision or direct trauma to the head.

When performing an on-field assessment, it is suggested that elements of the PocketSCAT2 (Fig. 17.3 on page 287) be utilized as a quick means of making such assessment.

Clinical features that are more specific to a diagnosis of concussion include: loss of consciousness (LOC), concussive convulsions, confusion or attention deficit, memory disturbance, and balance disturbance. These features, however, may not be present in all cases and, in some cases, may present in a delayed fashion.

If a concussion is suspected, the player should be removed from the playing environment, with appropriate care of the cervical spine, and evaluated in a place free from distraction (e.g. medical room). When the diagnosis of concussion is obvious (e.g. loss of consciousness, confusion), the player should be medically assessed, including the use of the SCAT2 form (Fig. 17.2 on pages 283–6), and must be monitored regularly for signs of deterioration or other warning signs of a potential underlying structural brain injury. When the diagnosis is uncertain, a standard protocol for assessment should be followed. The assessment as per the SCAT2 form should be used and focus on:

- symptom checklist
- tests of cognitive function (e.g. Maddock's questions, Standardized Assessment of Concussion [SAC])
- tests of balance function.

Any player with symptoms and/or evidence of a disturbance of cognitive function (e.g. LOC, balance disturbance, disorientation, or cognitive deficit) can be considered to have a concussive injury. Once concussion is medically diagnosed, the player should be removed from the game or training and not return to play on that day.

For practical purposes, the Pocket SCAT2 can be utilized on-field or on the sideline to screen for concussion and, once concussion is diagnosed, the player can be removed to the medical room where the full SCAT2 assessment tool can be administered. If the diagnosis of concussion is confirmed following assessment, then the player should not be returned to play on the day. In addition to post injury assessment, it is recommended that the SCAT2 be used for pre-season baseline testing. This is helpful for interpreting the post-concussion test score as it provides an objective record of possible change.

Table 17.1 Symptoms and signs of concussion

Symptoms	Signs
Headache	Loss of consciousness or impaired conscious state
Dizziness	Poor coordination or balance
Nausea or vomiting	Concussive convulsion or impact seizure
Unsteadiness or loss of balance	Gait unsteadiness or loss of balance
Confusion	Slow to answer questions or follow directions
Unaware of period, opposition, score of game	Easily distracted, poor concentration
Feeling "dinged," stunned, or "dazed"	Displaying unusual or inappropriate emotions
Seeing stars or flashing lights	Vacant stare or glassy eyed
Ringing in the ears	Slurred speech
Double vision or blurred vision	Personality changes
	Inappropriate playing behavior
	Significantly decreased playing ability
	Double vision or blurred vision

Does amnesia associate with injury severity?

There is renewed interest in the role of post-traumatic amnesia and its role as a surrogate measure of injury severity. Post-traumatic amnesia can be separated into retrograde amnesia (loss of memory of events prior to the injury), and anterograde amnesia (loss of memory of events post injury). Virtually all concussed sportspeople will have a period of amnesia, however brief, whether they were unconscious or not.

 In broad terms, the duration of post-traumatic amnesia does not reflect the severity of mild TBI (concussion). This contrasts with moderate to severe TBI, where post-traumatic amnesia is a prognostic factor and should be assessed in all cases.

Note that retrograde amnesia varies depending on when it is measured after injury; thus, it is a particularly poor indicator of injury severity.

 The burden and duration of the clinical post-concussive symptoms may be more important than the presence or duration of amnesia alone. The overall clinical management and return to play depend on the presence and recovery of all symptoms and signs.

Does an acutely concussed athlete need to go to hospital or have urgent neuroimaging?

The treating clinician may face the decision of whether the athlete should be referred on to a hospital emergency facility or for urgent neuroimaging. In general terms, an uncomplicated concussion does not need routine neuroimaging. Imaging, however, has a role in the exclusion of suspected intracranial injury. Apart from "cookbook"-type approaches, referral to such a center depends on the experience, ability, and competence of the physician at hand. If the team physician happens to be a neurologist or neurosurgeon experienced in concussion management, then the clinical referral pathways will be different from those of a family practitioner called to assist at a football match after an injury has occurred. The overall approach should be "when in doubt, refer."

There are a number of indications that may suggest the need for urgent imaging or hospital referral (see box).

Other diagnostic tests such as biomarkers, EEG, and functional MR brain scanning (fMRI) do not have a role in the early diagnosis and management

Indications for urgent imaging or hospital referral

Any player who has or develops the following:

- Fractured skull
- Penetrating skull trauma
- Deterioration in conscious state following injury
- Focal neurological signs
- Confusion or impairment of consciousness >30 minutes
- Loss of consciousness >5 minutes
- Persistent vomiting or increasing headache post injury
- Any convulsive movements
- More than one episode of concussive injury in a match or training session
- Where there is assessment difficulty (e.g. an intoxicated patient)
- All children with head injuries
- High-risk patients (e.g. hemophilia, anticoagulant use)
- Inadequate post injury supervision
- High-risk injury mechanism (e.g. high-velocity impact, missile injury)

of a concussion injury, except in an experimental context.[13] Structural neuroimaging (such as CT and MRI) does not clinically add to a diagnosis of concussion; however, these have an important role in informing about more significant injuries.

How should acute concussion be graded?

There is no reliable or scientifically validated system of grading the severity of sports-related concussion. At the present time, there are at least 45 published anecdotal severity scales. The danger is that sportspeople and/or their coaches may "shop around" for a scale that is not in their best medical interests. At the end of the day, good clinical judgment should prevail over written guidelines. At the First International Conference on Concussion in Sport (Vienna, 2001) the expert committee endorsed no specific grading system for concussion, but recommended that combined measures of recovery should be used to assess injury severity and guide individual decisions on return to play (RTP).[5] This was re-endorsed at the Prague 2004 meeting[4] and the Zurich 2008 meeting.[3]

Determining when the player can return safely to competition

Return-to-play decisions remain difficult. Expert consensus guidelines recommend that players should *not* return to competition until they have recovered *completely* from their concussive injury. Currently, however, there is no single gold standard measure of brain disturbance and recovery following concussion. Instead, clinicians must rely on indirect measures to inform clinical judgment. In practical terms, this involves a multifaceted clinical approach, which includes assessment of symptoms, signs (such as balance), and cognitive function.

Return to play on the day of injury

There is substantial controversy regarding the safety of RTP on the day of the injury. The Zurich consensus group reaffirmed the previous general management principle that *no* return to play on the day should be contemplated for a concussed athlete. It was acknowledged, however, that certain professional sports (e.g. American football) have published evidence suggesting that mild cases of concussion can safely RTP on the day of injury. It must be noted that this situation is supported by immediate and expert medical care by experienced personnel, emergent neuroimaging, and immediate access to neuropsychological testing. As a result, this really is only applicable at the highest levels of professional sport, where recovery can be rapidly assessed and management decisions made. There is also published evidence in high school and college sportspeople that RTP on the day of injury results in delayed and prolonged cognitive deterioration. As a result, same day RTP should not be attempted with young (<18 years) athletes, even if participating in professional sport. It is not within the scope or expertise of a physiotherapist, trainer, or other non-medical person to manage a concussive injury or determine the timing of return to play.

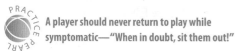 A player should never return to play while symptomatic—"When in doubt, sit them out!"

Return to play during the subsequent week

Whether or not to allow the concussed patient to return to training and then competition is one of the most difficult decisions the sports physician must make. In minor cases of concussion, where all symptoms resolve quickly and there is no amnesia, no sign of cortical dysfunction, nor evidence of impairment of short-term memory or information processing, the player may be allowed to return once recovered. Neuropsychological testing may be used to confirm full recovery. A player permitted to return to play should be closely observed for any signs of impaired function. A multifaceted clinical approach is used to manage players in the week following injury. In practical terms, this involves five sequential steps:

1. a period of cognitive and physical rest to facilitate recovery
2. monitoring for recovery of post-concussion symptoms and signs
3. the use of neuropsychological tests to estimate recovery of cognitive function
4. a graduated return to activity with monitoring for recurrence of symptoms
5. a final medical clearance before resuming full contact training and/or playing.

Period of cognitive and physical rest to facilitate recovery

Early rest is important to allow recovery following a concussive injury. Physical activity, physiological stress (e.g. altitude and flying), and cognitive loads (e.g. studying, video games, or computer work) can all worsen symptoms and possibly delay recovery following concussion. Players should be advised to rest from these activities in the early stages after a concussive injury, especially while symptomatic (see "Concussion injury advice," p. 4 of SCAT2). Similarly, the use of alcohol, narcotic analgesics, anti-inflammatory medication, or sedatives can exacerbate symptoms following head trauma, delay recovery, or mask deterioration; these should also be avoided. Specific advice should also be given on avoidance of activities that place the individual at risk of further injury (e.g. driving).

The cornerstone of concussion management is physical and cognitive rest until symptoms resolve, and then a graded program of exertion prior to medical clearance and return to play. The recovery and outcome of concussion may be modified by a number of factors that may require more sophisticated management strategies. The Zurich consensus panel agreed that a range of "modifying" factors may influence the investigation and management of concussion and, in some cases, may predict the potential for prolonged or persistent symptoms. These modifiers would also be important to consider in a detailed concussion history and are outlined in Table 17.2.

When these modifying influences are present, simple RTP advice may be inappropriate. It may be wise to consider additional investigations including

Table 17.2 Factors that influence whether investigation or more sophisticated management (e.g. referral to a physician with expertise in concussion management) is indicated

Factors	Modifier
Symptoms	Number Duration (>10 days) Severity
Signs	Prolonged LOC (>1min) Amnesia
Sequelae	Concussive convulsions
Temporal	Frequency—repeated concussions over time Timing—injuries close together in time "Recency"—recent concussion or TBI
Threshold	Repeated concussions occurring with progressively less impact force or slower recovery after each successive concussion
Age	Child and adolescent (<18 years old)
Co- and pre-morbidities	Migraine Depression or other mental health disorders Attention deficit hyperactivity disorder (ADHD) Learning disabilities Sleep disorders
Medication	Psychoactive drugs Anticoagulants
Behavior	Dangerous style of play
Sport	High-risk activity Contact and collision sport High sporting level

formal neuropsychological testing, balance assessment, and neuroimaging. It is envisioned that athletes with such modifying features would be managed in a multidisciplinary manner coordinated by a physician with specific expertise in the management of concussive injury.

Monitoring for recovery of post-concussion symptoms and signs

The symptoms of concussion are dynamic and evolve over time. It is important that players who are suspected of having a concussion be monitored over time to assess for delayed symptom onset. Monitoring of post-concussion symptoms and signs can be facilitated by the use of the SCAT2.

Use of neuropsychological tests to estimate recovery of cognitive function

Cognitive deficits associated with concussion are typically subtle and may exist in a number of domains. Common deficits that follow concussion in sport include reduced attention and ability to process information, slowed reaction times, and impaired memory.

The use of neuropsychological tests in the management of concussion overcomes the reliance on subjective symptoms, which are known to be poorly recognized and variably reported, and allows detection of cognitive deficits, which have been observed to outlast symptoms in many cases of concussion.

There are a number of levels of complexity of cognitive testing, including:

- formal neuropsychological testing
- screening computerized cognitive test batteries
- basic paper-and-pencil evaluation (i.e. SCAT2).

Formal neuropsychological testing remains the clinical best practice standard for the assessment of cognitive function.[14] Formal testing is logistically impractical for routine use following concussive injuries, but is recommended in any case where there is uncertainty about recovery, or in difficult cases (e.g. prolonged recovery).

Screening computerized cognitive tests provide a practical alternative for the assessment of cognitive recovery. Ideally, the tests should be compared to the individual's own pre-injury baseline. A number of screening computerized cognitive test batteries have been validated for use following concussion in sport and are readily available. These include test platforms such as CogState Sport (www.cogstate.com/go/sport), ImPACT (www.impacttest.com), Headminder (www.headminder.com), and the US military tool Automated Neuropsychological Assessment Metrics (ANAM) (www.armymedicine.army.mil/prr/anam.html).

Screening computerized cognitive tests are strongly encouraged in the routine management of concussion in sports with a high risk of head injury (e.g. football codes). Computerized tests provide a quick, valid, and reliable measure of cognitive recovery following a concussive injury. Furthermore, routine use of computerized screening tests in

B

the pre-season facilitates screening of players for cognitive deterioration over time.

Basic paper-and-pencil cognitive tests (e.g. SCAT2, Fig. 17.2) are the quickest and simplest of the cognitive screening tests; however, they are the least sensitive to subtle cognitive changes that accompany concussion.[3] In cases where the concussion has resulted in brief symptoms and clinically the player has recovered well, basic paper-and-pencil cognitive tests can be used to provide an estimate of cognitive function. The use of a basic paper-and-pencil evaluation should be combined with a conservative RTP approach, and careful monitoring of symptoms as the player progresses through a graduated RTP program.

Overall, it is important to remember that neuropsychological testing is only one component of assessment, and therefore should not be the sole basis of management decisions. Neuropsychological testing does not replace the need for a full history, and clinical and neurological examination.

Graduated return to activity

Following a concussive injury, players should be returned to play in a graduated fashion once clinical features have resolved and cognitive function returned to baseline. When considering RTP, the athlete should be off all medications at the time of considering commencement of the rehabilitation phase or at the final medical assessment. Overall, a more conservative approach (i.e. longer time to return to sport) should be used in cases where there

is any uncertainty about the player's recovery "if in doubt, sit them out."

In accordance with current consensus guidelines, there is no mandatory period of time that a player must be withheld from play following a concussion. However, at minimum, a player must be symptom-free at rest and with exertion, and have returned to baseline level of cognitive performance.

The Zurich consensus statement[3] recommends a stepwise graduated RTP protocol (Table 17.3). If a player remains asymptomatic for 24 hours at level 1, they may progress to level 2. They are allowed to advance provided that they remain asymptomatic. Using this protocol, an athlete should take approximately a week before returning to normal game play. If any symptoms surface during the progression, players should drop back to the previous level in which they were asymptomatic for a further 24 hours attempting to progress.

A final medical clearance before resuming full contact training and/or playing

A player who has suffered from a concussive injury must not be allowed to return to play before having a medical clearance. In every case, the decision regarding the timing of return to training should be made by a medical doctor with experience in concussive injuries. This assessment is multidimensional and based on evidence of resolution of the athlete's symptoms, physical signs, and cognitive deficit. Ideally, concussed players should be examined by an experienced medical practitioner with the decision about return

Table 17.3 Graduated return-to-play protocol

Rehabilitation stage	Functional exercise at each stage of rehabilitation	Objective at each stage
1. No activity	Complete physical and cognitive rest	Recovery
2. Light aerobic exercise	Walking, swimming, or stationary cycling keeping intensity <70% HR max. No resistance training	Increase heart rate
3. Sport-specific exercise	Skating drills in ice hockey, running drills in soccer. No head impact activities	Add movement
4. Non-contact training drills	Progression to more complex training drills (e.g. passing drills in hockey and football)	Exercise, coordination, and cognitive load
5. Full contact practice	Following medical clearance, participate in normal training activities	Restore confidence and assess functional skills by coaching staff
6. Return to play	Normal game play	

Reproduced with permission from Table 1: Zurich consensus statement[3] in *British Journal of Sports Medicine*

to play based on the clinical findings and, if possible, neuropsychological testing. In general, a more conservative approach (i.e. longer time to return to sport) is used in cases where there is any uncertainty about the player's recovery "if in doubt, sit them out."

In a number of contact sports, such as boxing and rugby football, authorities have legislated for a mandatory exclusion period from competition for concussed players. While the intent of such a policy is praiseworthy, an arbitrary exclusion period is hard to justify scientifically, as each episode of concussion requires individual evaluation. For some players the period of exclusion will be too long, and for other players not long enough. More importantly, the assumption that a player has recovered simply because a prescribed period of time has passed has the potential to lead to premature return to play and resultant problems.

The risk of premature return to play and concussion sequelae

There are several risks of premature return to play.

Risk of further injury

The principal concern of premature return to play of a concussed athlete is that, because of the impaired cognitive function (e.g. slowed information processing, reduced attention), the athlete will sustain further injury (either concussive or other) when returning to a dangerous playing environment.

Second impact syndrome

Second impact syndrome (SIS) is frequently mentioned in the concussion literature but surprisingly has little scientific evidence for its existence. It is a term used to describe the potential catastrophic consequences resulting from a second concussive blow to the head before an individual has fully recovered from the symptoms of a previous concussion. The second head injury is believed to result in loss of cerebrovascular auto-regulation, which in turn leads to brain swelling secondary to increased cerebral blood flow. Mortality in this condition approaches 100%.

The evidence that repeated concussion is a risk factor for SIS has been critically reviewed, and published cases of SIS were classified as definite, probable, possible, or not SIS according to four criteria.[15] Seventeen published cases of SIS were identified from the literature. None were classified as "definite" SIS, five were considered to be "probable" SIS, and 12 were classified as "not" SIS primarily because there was an absence of a witnessed second impact. In addition, the veracity of teammate recall of concussive episodes, which is often the basis of a "first impact" in such cases, was shown to be unreliable. Based on these results, the investigators concluded that there is a lack of evidence to support the claim that the second impact is a risk factor for diffuse cerebral swelling. In this paper, the central issue was whether repeated concussion was a risk factor for cerebral swelling, which is the putative definition of SIS. There is published evidence that acute (and delayed) brain swelling may occur following a single blow to the head, in association with a structural injury such as a subdural hematoma and also in disorders of calcium channels, suggesting a possible genetic basis for some of these cases. Such events are virtually only seen in children and adolescents.

Concussive convulsions

A variety of immediate motor phenomena (e.g. tonic posturing) or convulsive movements may accompany a concussion. Although dramatic, these clinical features are generally benign and require no specific management beyond the standard treatment of the underlying concussive injury. These dramatic phenomena are a non-epileptic manifestation of concussion.[16]

Prolongation of symptoms

If a player recommences playing while symptomatic, post-concussive symptoms may be prolonged. This may also increase the chance of developing "post-concussive syndrome," in which fatigue, difficulty in concentration, and headaches persist for some time, often months, following the original injury. These patients should undergo formal neuropsychological testing as well as an MRI brain scan. If these tests are normal, there is no specific treatment other than rest and reassurance. Return to sport is not advisable while symptoms are present as exercise appears to prolong the condition.

Chronic traumatic encephalopathy

Recent publications have suggested that US footballers may suffer similar medical risks as boxers. Pathological case reports and cross-sectional surveys have suggested that retired NFL footballers, who have had recurrent concussions during their sporting careers, disproportionately suffer from mild cognitive impairment, depression, and other mental health problems. What is becoming increasingly clear from a number of diverse lines of research is that a small percentage of footballers seem to suffer chronic or long-term sequelae from sports-related head injury. At this time, very little is known about what type, frequency, or amount of trauma is necessary to induce the accumulation of these pathological proteins in the brain and, more importantly, why only a small number of athletes are at risk for chronic traumatic encephalopathy. Nevertheless, this concern should reinforce the need for conservative management strategies designed to ensure player safety.

Mental health issues

Mental health issues (such as depression) have been reported as a long-term consequence of traumatic brain injury, including sports-related concussion. Neuroimaging studies using fMRI suggest that a depressed mood following concussion may reflect an underlying pathophysiological abnormality consistent with a limbic–frontal model of depression. All players with ongoing symptoms or a prolonged clinical course should be screened for depression using standard clinical tools (e.g. Hospital Anxiety and Depression Scale [HADS], Beck Depression Inventory [BDI]).

Children and concussion in sport

The SCAT2 is appropriate for use in children and adolescents older than 10 years of age. Children younger than 10 years old report different symptoms, so age and developmentally appropriate evaluation is recommended.[17] An additional consideration in assessing the child or adolescent sportsperson with a concussion is that, in the clinical evaluation by the healthcare professional, there may be the need to include both patient and parent input, as well as teacher and school input when appropriate.

The decision to use neuropsychological testing is broadly the same as the adult assessment paradigm.

However, timing of testing may differ in order to assist planning in school and home management (and may be performed while the patient is still symptomatic). If cognitive testing is performed, it must be developmentally sensitive until late teen years due to the ongoing cognitive maturation that occurs during this period which, in turn, makes the utility of comparison to either the person's own baseline performance or to population norms limited. In this age group, it is more important to consider the use of trained neuropsychologists to interpret assessment data, particularly in children with learning disorders and/or ADHD who may need more sophisticated assessment strategies.

Children should not be returned to practice or play until clinically completely symptom-free, which may require a longer time frame than for adults. In addition, the concept of "cognitive rest" is highlighted, with special reference to a child's need to limit exertion with activities of daily living and to limit scholastic and other cognitive stressors (e.g. text messaging, video games) while symptomatic. School attendance and activities may also need to be modified to avoid provocation of symptoms.

Because of the different physiological response and longer recovery after concussion and specific risks (e.g. diffuse cerebral swelling) related to head impact during childhood and adolescence, a more conservative return-to-play approach is recommended. It is appropriate to extend the amount of time of asymptomatic rest and/or the length of the graded exertion in children and adolescents. It is not appropriate for a child or adolescent sportsperson with concussion to return to play on the same day as the injury, regardless of the level of athletic performance. Concussion modifiers apply even more to this population than to adults and may mandate more cautious RTP advice.

SCAT2

Sport Concussion Assessment Tool 2

Name

Sport/team

Date/time of injury

Date/time of assessment

Age   Gender   M   F

Years of education completed

Examiner

What is the SCAT2?[1]

This tool represents a standardized method of evaluating injured athletes for concussion and can be used in athletes aged from 10 years and older. It supersedes the original SCAT published in 2005[2]. This tool also enables the calculation of the Standardized Assessment of Concussion (SAC)[3,4] score and the Maddocks questions[5] for sideline concussion assessment.

Instructions for using the SCAT2

The SCAT2 is designed for the use of medical and health professionals. Preseason baseline testing with the SCAT2 can be helpful for interpreting post-injury test scores. Words in Italics throughout the SCAT2 are the instructions given to the athlete by the tester.

This tool may be freely copied for distribtion to individuals, teams, groups and organizations.

What is a concussion?

A concussion is a disturbance in brain function caused by a direct or indirect force to the head. It results in a variety of non-specific symptoms (like those listed below) and often does not involve loss of consciousness. Concussion should be suspected in the presence of **any one or more** of the following:
- Symptoms (such as headache), or
- Physical signs (such as unsteadiness), or
- Impaired brain function (e.g. confusion) or
- Abnormal behaviour.

Any athlete with a suspected concussion should be REMOVED FROM PLAY, medically assessed, monitored for deterioration (i.e., should not be left alone) and should not drive a motor vehicle.

Symptom Evaluation

How do you feel?

You should score yourself on the following symptoms, based on how you feel now.

	none	mild		moderate		severe	
Headache	0	1	2	3	4	5	6
"Pressure in head"	0	1	2	3	4	5	6
Neck Pain	0	1	2	3	4	5	6
Nausea or vomiting	0	1	2	3	4	5	6
Dizziness	0	1	2	3	4	5	6
Blurred vision	0	1	2	3	4	5	6
Balance problems	0	1	2	3	4	5	6
Sensitivity to light	0	1	2	3	4	5	6
Sensitivity to noise	0	1	2	3	4	5	6
Feeling slowed down	0	1	2	3	4	5	6
Feeling like "in a fog"	0	1	2	3	4	5	6
"Don't feel right"	0	1	2	3	4	5	6
Difficulty concentrating	0	1	2	3	4	5	6
Difficulty remembering	0	1	2	3	4	5	6
Fatigue or low energy	0	1	2	3	4	5	6
Confusion	0	1	2	3	4	5	6
Drowsiness	0	1	2	3	4	5	6
Trouble falling asleep (if applicable)	0	1	2	3	4	5	6
More emotional	0	1	2	3	4	5	6
Irritability	0	1	2	3	4	5	6
Sadness	0	1	2	3	4	5	6
Nervous or Anxious	0	1	2	3	4	5	6

Total number of symptoms (Maximum possible 22)

Symptom severity score
(Add all scores in table, maximum possible: 22 x 6 = 132)

Do the symptoms get worse with physical activity?   Y   N
Do the symptoms get worse with mental activity?   Y   N

Overall rating
If you know the athlete well prior to the injury, how different is the athlete acting compared to his / her usual self? Please circle one response.

no different   very different   unsure

Figure 17.2 Sport Concussion Assessment Tool (SCAT).[3] The SCAT has no copyright restrictions and can be photocopied from this book or downloaded free from www.bjsm.bmj.com   *continues*

Cognitive & Physical Evaluation

1 **Symptom score** (from page 1)
22 **minus** number of symptoms   of 22

2 **Physical signs score**
Was there loss of consciousness or unresponsiveness?   Y   N
If yes, how long?   minutes
Was there a balance problem/unsteadiness?   Y   N

Physical signs score (1 point for each negative response)   of 2

3 **Glasgow coma scale (GCS)**

Best eye response (E)
No eye opening	1
Eye opening in response to pain	2
Eye opening to speech	3
Eyes opening spontaneously	4

Best verbal response (V)
No verbal response	1
Incomprehensible sounds	2
Inappropriate words	3
Confused	4
Oriented	5

Best motor response (M)
No motor response	1
Extension to pain	2
Abnormal flexion to pain	3
Flexion/Withdrawal to pain	4
Localizes to pain	5
Obeys commands	6

Glasgow Coma score (E + V + M)   of 15

GCS should be recorded for all athletes in case of subsequent deterioration.

4 **Sideline Assessment – Maddocks Score**
"I am going to ask you a few questions, please listen carefully and give your best effort."

Modified Maddocks questions (1 point for each correct answer)
At what venue are we at today?	0	1
Which half is it now?	0	1
Who scored last in this match?	0	1
What team did you play last week/game?	0	1
Did your team win the last game?	0	1

Maddocks score   of 5

Maddocks score is validated for sideline diagnosis of concussion only and is not included in SCAT 2 summary score for serial testing.

5 **Cognitive assessment**
Standardized Assessment of Concussion (SAC)
Orientation (1 point for each correct answer)
What month is it?	0	1
What is the date today?	0	1
What is the day of the week?	0	1
What year is it?	0	1
What time is it right now? (within 1 hour)	0	1

Orientation score   of 5

Immediate memory
"I am going to test your memory. I will read you a list of words and when I am done, repeat back as many words as you can remember, in any order."

Trials 2 & 3:
"I am going to repeat the same list again. Repeat back as many words as you can remember in any order, even if you said the word before."

Complete all 3 trials regardless of score on trial 1 & 2. Read the words at a rate of one per second. Score 1 pt. for each correct response. Total score equals sum across all 3 trials. Do not inform the athlete that delayed recall will be tested.

List	Trial 1	Trial 2	Trial 3	Alternative word list		
elbow	0 1	0 1	0 1	candle	baby	finger
apple	0 1	0 1	0 1	paper	monkey	penny
carpet	0 1	0 1	0 1	sugar	perfume	blanket
saddle	0 1	0 1	0 1	sandwich	sunset	lemon
bubble	0 1	0 1	0 1	wagon	iron	insect
Total						

Immediate memory score   of 15

Concentration
Digits Backward:
"I am going to read you a string of numbers and when I am done, you repeat them back to me backwards, in reverse order of how I read them to you. For example, if I say 7-1-9, you would say 9-1-7."

If correct, go to next string length. If incorrect, read trial 2. One point possible for each string length. Stop after incorrect on both trials. The digits should be read at the rate of one per second.

				Alternative digit lists		
4-9-3	0	1	6-2-9	5-2-6	4-1-5
3-8-1-4	0	1	3-2-7-9	1-7-9-5	4-9-6-8
6-2-9-7-1	0	1	1-5-2-8-6	3-8-5-2-7	6-1-8-4-3
7-1-8-4-6-2	0	1	5-3-9-1-4-8	8-3-1-9-6-4	7-2-4-8-5-6

Months in Reverse Order:
"Now tell me the months of the year in reverse order. Start with the last month and go backward. So you'll say December, November ... Go ahead"

1 pt. for entire sequence correct

Dec-Nov-Oct-Sept-Aug-Jul-Jun-May-Apr-Mar-Feb-Jan   0   1

Concentration score   of 5

[1] This tool has been developed by a group of international experts at the 3rd International Consensus meeting on Concussion in Sport held in Zurich, Switzerland in November 2008. The full details of the conference outcomes and the authors of the tool are published in British Journal of Sports Medicine, 2009, volume 43, supplement 1.
The outcome paper will also be simultaneously co-published in the May 2009 issues of Clinical Journal of Sports Medicine, Physical Medicine & Rehabilitation, Journal of Athletic Training, Journal of Clinical Neuroscience, Journal of Science & Medicine in Sport, Neurosurgery, Scandinavian Journal of Science & Medicine in Sport and the Journal of Clinical Sports Medicine.

[2] McCrory P et al. Summary and agreement statement of the 2nd International Conference on Concussion in Sport, Prague 2004. British Journal of Sports Medicine. 2005; 39: 196-204

[3] McCrea M. Standardized mental status testing of acute concussion. Clinical Journal of Sports Medicine. 2001; 11: 176-181

[4] McCrea M, Randolph C, Kelly J. Standardized Assessment of Concussion: Manual for administration, scoring and interpretation. Waukesha, Wisconsin, USA.

[5] Maddocks, DL; Dicker, GD; Saling, MM. The assessment of orientation following concussion in athletes. Clin J Sport Med. 1995;5(1):32–3

[6] Guskiewicz KM. Assessment of postural stability following sport-related concussion. Current Sports Medicine Reports. 2003; 2: 24-30

Figure 17.2 (cont.) Sport Concussion Assessment Tool (SCAT)

6 Balance examination

This balance testing is based on a modified version of the Balance Error Scoring System (BESS)[6]. A stopwatch or watch with a second hand is required for this testing.

Balance testing
"I am now going to test your balance. Please take your shoes off, roll up your pant legs above ankle (if applicable), and remove any ankle taping (if applicable). This test will consist of three twenty second tests with different stances."

(a) Double leg stance:
"The first stance is standing with your feet together with your hands on your hips and with your eyes closed. You should try to maintain stability in that position for 20 seconds. I will be counting the number of times you move out of this position. I will start timing when you are set and have closed your eyes."

(b) Single leg stance:
"If you were to kick a ball, which foot would you use? [This will be the dominant foot] Now stand on your non-dominant foot. The dominant leg should be held in approximately 30 degrees of hip flexion and 45 degrees of knee flexion. Again, you should try to maintain stability for 20 seconds with your hands on your hips and your eyes closed. I will be counting the number of times you move out of this position. If you stumble out of this position, open your eyes and return to the start position and continue balancing. I will start timing when you are set and have closed your eyes."

(c) Tandem stance:
"Now stand heel-to-toe with your **non-dominant foot** in back. Your weight should be evenly distributed across both feet. Again, you should try to maintain stability for 20 seconds with your hands on your hips and your eyes closed. I will be counting the number of times you move out of this position. If you stumble out of this position, open your eyes and return to the start position and continue balancing. I will start timing when you are set and have closed your eyes."

Balance testing – types of errors
1. Hands lifted off iliac crest
2. Opening eyes
3. Step, stumble, or fall
4. Moving hip into > 30 degrees abduction
5. Lifting forefoot or heel
6. Remaining out of test position > 5 sec

Each of the 20-second trials is scored by counting the errors, or deviations from the proper stance, accumulated by the athlete. The examiner will begin counting errors only after the individual has assumed the proper start position. **The modified BESS is calculated by adding one error point for each error during the three 20-second tests. The maximum total number of errors for any single condition is 10.** If a athlete commits multiple errors simultaneously, only one error is recorded but the athlete should quickly return to the testing position, and counting should resume once subject is set. Subjects that are unable to maintain the testing procedure for a minimum of **five seconds** at the start are assigned the highest possible score, ten, for that testing condition.

Which foot was tested: Left   Right
(i.e. which is the **non-dominant** foot)

Condition	Total errors
Double Leg Stance (feet together)	of 10
Single leg stance (non-dominant foot)	of 10
Tandem stance (non-dominant foot at back)	of 10
Balance examination score (30 **minus** total errors)	of 30

7 Coordination examination

Upper limb coordination
Finger-to-nose (FTN) task: "I am going to test your coordination now. Please sit comfortably on the chair with your eyes open and your arm (either right or left) outstretched (shoulder flexed to 90 degrees and elbow and fingers extended). When I give a start signal, I would like you to perform five successive finger to nose repetitions using your index finger to touch the tip of the nose as quickly and as accurately as possible."

Which arm was tested: Left   Right

Scoring: 5 correct repetitions in < 4 seconds = 1
Note for testers: Athletes fail the test if they do not touch their nose, do not fully extend their elbow or do not perform five repetitions. Failure should be scored as 0.

Coordination score   of 1

8 Cognitive assessment
Standardized Assessment of Concussion (SAC)

Delayed recall
"Do you remember that list of words I read a few times earlier? Tell me as many words from the list as you can remember in any order."

Circle each word correctly recalled. Total score equals number of words recalled.

List		Alternative word list		
elbow	candle	baby	finger
apple	paper	monkey	penny
carpet	sugar	perfume	blanket
saddle	sandwich	sunset	lemon
bubble	wagon	iron	insect

Delayed recall score   of 5

Overall score

Test domain	Score
Symptom score	of 22
Physical signs score	of 2
Glasgow Coma score (E + V + M)	of 15
Balance examination score	of 30
Coordination score	of 1
Subtotal	**of 70**
Orientation score	of 5
Immediate memory score	of 5
Concentration score	of 15
Delayed recall score	of 5
SAC subtotal	**of 30**
SCAT2 total	**of 100**
Maddocks Score	**of 5**

Definitive normative data for a SCAT2 "cut-off" score is not available at this time and will be developed in prospective studies. Embedded within the SCAT2 is the SAC score that can be utilized separately in concussion management. The scoring system also takes on particular clinical significance during serial assessment where it can be used to document either a decline or an improvement in neurological functioning.

Scoring data from the SCAT2 or SAC should not be used as a stand alone method to diagnose concussion, measure recovery or make decisions about an athlete's readiness to return to competition after concussion.

Figure 17.2 (cont.) Sport Concussion Assessment Tool (SCAT)   *continues*

285

Athlete Information

Any athlete suspected of having a concussion should be removed from play, and then seek medical evaluation.

Signs to watch for

Problems could arise over the first 24-48 hours. You should not be left alone and must go to a hospital at once if you:
- Have a headache that gets worse
- Are very drowsy or can't be awakened (woken up)
- Can't recognize people or places
- Have repeated vomiting
- Behave unusually or seem confused; are very irritable
- Have seizures (arms and legs jerk uncontrollably)
- Have weak or numb arms or legs
- Are unsteady on your feet; have slurred speech

Remember, it is better to be safe.
Consult your doctor after a suspected concussion.

Return to play

Athletes should not be returned to play the same day of injury. When returning athletes to play, they should follow a stepwise symptom-limited program, with stages of progression. For example:
1. rest until asymptomatic (physical and mental rest)
2. light aerobic exercise (e.g. stationary cycle)
3. sport-specific exercise
4. non-contact training drills (start light resistance training)
5. full contact training after medical clearance
6. return to competition (game play)

There should be approximately 24 hours (or longer) for each stage and the athlete should return to stage 1 if symptoms recur. Resistance training should only be added in the later stages.
Medical clearance should be given before return to play.

Tool	Test domain	Time	Score			
		Date tested				
		Days post injury				
SCAT2	Symptom score					
	Physical signs score					
	Glasgow Coma score (E + V + M)					
	Balance examination score					
	Coordination score					
SAC	Orientation score					
	Immediate memory score					
	Concentration score					
	Delayed recall score					
	SAC Score					
Total	SCAT2					
Symptom severity score (max possible 132)						
Return to play			☐Y ☐N	☐Y ☐N	☐Y ☐N	☐Y ☐N

Additional comments

Concussion injury advice (To be given to concussed athlete)

This patient has received an injury to the head. A careful medical examination has been carried out and no sign of any serious complications has been found. It is expected that recovery will be rapid, but the patient will need monitoring for a further period by a responsible adult. Your treating physician will provide guidance as to this timeframe.

If you notice any change in behaviour, vomiting, dizziness, worsening headache, double vision or excessive drowsiness, please telephone the clinic or the nearest hospital emergency department immediately.

Other important points:
- Rest and avoid strenuous activity for at least 24 hours
- No alcohol
- No sleeping tablets
- Use paracetamol or codeine for headache. Do **not** use aspirin or anti-inflammatory medication
- Do **not** drive until medically cleared
- Do **not** train or play sport until medically cleared

Clinic phone number

Patient's name

Date/time of injury

Date/time of medical review

Treating physician

Contact details or stamp

SCAT2 SPORT CONCUSSION ASSESMENT TOOL 2 | PAGE 4

Figure 17.2 (cont.) Sport Concussion Assessment Tool (SCAT)

Pocket SCAT2

Concussion should be suspected in the presence of **any one or more** of the following: symptoms (such as headache), or physical signs (such as unsteadiness), or impaired brain function (e.g. confusion) or abnormal behaviour.

1. Symptoms

Presence of any of the following signs & symptoms may suggest a concussion.

- Loss of consciousness
- Seizure or convulsion
- Amnesia
- Headache
- "Pressure in head"
- Neck Pain
- Nausea or vomiting
- Dizziness
- Blurred vision
- Balance problems
- Sensitivity to light
- Sensitivity to noise
- Feeling slowed down
- Feeling like "in a fog"
- "Don't feel right"
- Difficulty concentrating
- Difficulty remembering
- Fatigue or low energy
- Confusion
- Drowsiness
- More emotional
- Irritability
- Sadness
- Nervous or anxious

2. Memory function

Failure to answer all questions correctly may suggest a concussion.

"At what venue are we at today?"
"Which half is it now?"
"Who scored last in this game?"
"What team did you play last week/game?"
"Did your team win the last game?"

3. Balance testing

Instructions for tandem stance

*"Now stand heel-to-toe with your **non-dominant** foot in back. Your weight should be evenly distributed across both feet. You should try to maintain stability for 20 seconds with your hands on your hips and your eyes closed. I will be counting the number of times you move out of this position. If you stumble out of this position, open your eyes and return to the start position and continue balancing. I will start timing when you are set and have closed your eyes."*

Observe the athlete for 20 seconds. If they make more than 5 errors (such as lift their hands off their hips; open their eyes; lift their forefoot or heel; step, stumble, or fall; or remain out of the start position for more that 5 seconds) then this may suggest a concussion.

Any athlete with a suspected concussion should be **IMMEDIATELY REMOVED FROM PLAY**, urgently assessed medically, should not be left alone and should not drive a motor vehicle.

Figure 17.3 Pocket Sport Concussion Assessment Tool 2 (SCAT2).[3] The Pocket SCAT2 has no copyright restrictions and can be photocopied from this book or downloaded free from www.bjsm.bmj.com

CLINICAL SPORTS MEDICINE
MASTERCLASSES
W www.clinicalsportsmedicine.com

Listen to the podcast with chapter author Paul McCrory
which covers:

- confirming the diagnosis (includes differentiating
  concussion from other pathologies, such as post-
  traumatic headaches and structural head injuries)
- determining when the player has fully recovered so
  that he/she can safely return to competition.

RECOMMENDED WEBSITES

BJSM online: Podcast: Concussion Update—Part 3, 6 Aug
2009. Available: http://bjsm.bmj.com/

Thinkfirst: www.thinkfirst.ca

CDC HeadsUp program: www.cdc.gov/concussion/

RECOMMENDED READING

Alla S, Sullivan SJ, Hale L et al. Self-report scales/checklists
for the measurement of concussion symptoms:
a systematic review. *Br J Sports Med* 2009;43 Suppl 1:
i3–12.

Collie A, Maruff P, Darby D. Computerized
neuropsychological testing in sport. *Br J Sports Med*
2001;35:297–302.

Guskiewicz KM. Balance assessment in the management
of sport-related concussion. *Clin Sports Med*
2011;30(1):89–102.

Guskiewicz KM, Mihalik JP. Biomechanics of sport
concussion: quest for the elusive injury threshold.
Exerc Sport Sci Rev 2011;39(1):4–11.

Guskiewicz KM, Marshall SW, Bailes J et al. Recurrent
concussion and risk of depression in retired
professional football players. *Med Sci Sports Exerc*
2007;39(6):903–9.

Makdissi M, Darby Dl, Maruff P et al. Natural history
of concussion in sport: markers of severity and
implications for management. *Am J Sports Med*
2010;38:464–71.

Makdissi M. Is the simple versus complex classification
of concussion a valid and useful differentiation? *Br J
Sports Med* 2009;43 Suppl 1:i23–27.

McCrory P, Meeuwisse W, Johnston K et al. Consensus
statement on concussion in sport: the 3rd International
Conference on Concussion in Sport held in Zurich,
November 2008. *Br J Sports Med* 2009;43 Suppl 1:
i76–90.

McCrory P. Who should retire after repeated concussions?
In: MacAuley D, Best T, eds. *Evidence based sports
medicine*. London: British Medical Journal; 2007.

Putukian M, Aubry M, McCrory P. Return to play after
sports concussion in elite and non-elite athletes?
Br J Sports Med 2009;43 Suppl 1:i28–31.

Schneider KJ, Emery CA, Kang J et al. Examining Sport
Concussion Assessment Tool ratings for male and
female youth hockey players with and without a history
of concussion. *Br J Sports Med* 2010;44(15):1112–7.

Shehata N, Wiley JP, Richea S et al. Sport Concussion
Assessment Tool: baseline values for varsity collision
sport athletes. *Br J Sports Med* 2009; 43(10):730–4.

REFERENCES

1. Sport Concussion Assessment Tool 2. *Br J Sports Med*
   2009;43:i85–88.

2. Pocket SCAT 2. *Br J Sports Med* 2009;43:i89–90.

3. McCrory P, Meeuwisse W, Johnston K et al. Consensus
   statement on concussion in sport: The 3rd International
   Conference on Concussion in Sport held in Zurich,
   November 2008. *Br J Sports Med* 2009;43 Suppl 1:
   i76–90.

4. McCrory P, Johnston K, Meeuwisse W et al. Summary
   and agreement statement of the 2nd International
   Conference on Concussion in Sport, Prague 2004.
   Br J Sports Med 2005;39(4):196–204.

5. Aubry M, Cantu R, Dvorak J et al. Summary and
   agreement statement of the First International
   Conference on Concussion in Sport, Vienna 2001.
   Recommendations for the improvement of safety and
   health of athletes who may suffer concussive injuries.
   Br J Sports Med 2002;36(1):6–10.

6. Benson BW, Hamilton GM, Meeuwisse WH et al.
   Is protective equipment useful in preventing
   concussion? A systematic review of the literature.
   Br J Sports Med 2009;43 Suppl 1:i56–67.

7. Labella CR, Smith BW, Sigurdsson A. Effect of
   mouthguards on dental injuries and concussions in
   college basketball. *Med Sci Sports Exerc* 2002;34(1):41–4.

8. Barbic D, Pater J, Brison RJ. Comparison of mouth
   guard designs and concussion prevention in contact
   sports: a multicenter randomized controlled trial.
   Clin J Sport Med 2005;15(5):294–8.

9. Andersen TE, Arnason A, Engebretsen L et al.
   Mechanisms of head injuries in elite football. *Br J
   Sports Med* 2004;38(6):690–6.

10. Hagel B, Meeuwisse W. Risk compensation: a "side
    effect" of sport injury prevention? *Clin J Sport Med*
    2004;14(4):193–6.

11. Shaw NH. Bodychecking in hockey. *CMAJ*
    2004;170(1):15–6; author reply 16, 18.

12. Carpenter R. The saccadic system: a neurological microcosm. *Adv Clin Neurosci Rehab* 2004;4: 6–8.

13. Davis GA, Iverson GL, Guskiewicz KM et al. Contributions of neuroimaging, balance testing, electrophysiology and blood markers to the assessment of sport-related concussion. *Br J Sports Med* 2009;43 Suppl 1:i36–45.

14. Echemendia RJ, Herring S, Bailes J. Who should conduct and interpret the neuropsychological assessment in sports-related concussion? *Br J Sports Med* 2009;43 Suppl 1:i32–5.

15. McCrory PR, Berkovic SF. Second impact syndrome. *Neurology* 1998;50(3):677–83.

16. McCrory PR, Berkovic SF. Concussive convulsions. Incidence in sport and treatment recommendations. *Sports Med* 1998;25(2):131–6.

17. Purcell L. What are the most appropriate return-to-play guidelines for concussed child athletes? *Br J Sports Med* 2009;43 Suppl 1:i51–5.

B

Chapter 18

Headache

with PAUL McCRORY

I'm very brave generally, he went on in a low voice: only today I happen to have a headache.
Tweedledum in Lewis Carroll's *Through the looking-glass*, 1871

Headache has been called "the most common complaint of humanity," affecting approximately two-thirds of the population. Athletes suffer from the same causes of headache as non-athletes. In addition, there are several causes of headache that relate directly to exercise. Numerous attempts have been made to classify the different types of headache. Headaches can be classified into seven groups, the first four of which are seen commonly, and the second three less commonly:

1. headache associated with viral illness (e.g. respiratory infections, sinusitis, influenza)
2. vascular headaches (e.g. migraine, cluster headache)
3. cervical headache (e.g. referred from joints, muscles, and fascia of the cervical region)
4. tension headache or muscle contraction headache
5. intracranial causes (e.g. tumor, hemorrhage, subdural hematoma, meningitis)
6. exercise-related headache (e.g. benign exertional headache, "footballers' migraine")
7. other causes (e.g. drugs, psychogenic, post-spinal procedure, post-traumatic).

Exercise-related and post-traumatic headache are of particular concern in sportspeople. While it is usually possible to differentiate between the groups, headaches of mixed type occur commonly.

The International Headache Society (IHS) (website at end of chapter), in conjunction with the World Health Organization (WHO), has proposed an overall classification for headache.[1] While this classification system is used mainly for research purposes, it nevertheless provides a framework to assist in clinical management.

Headache in sport

Although a few published studies have documented that headache is a frequent complaint in sportspeople (occurring in up to 85% of American footballers), relatively little systematic research or attempts at classifying sport-related headache have occurred to date.[2] The IHS headache classification is problematic when applied in this setting and is of little use to the practicing clinician. Kernick and Goadsby have proposed a simplified organizational system that is of greater relevance when treating professional and amateur sportspeople:[3]

1. a recognized headache syndrome (e.g. migraine) coincidental to sporting activity
2. a recognized headache syndrome (e.g. migraine) induced by sporting activity
3. headache arising from mechanisms that occur during sport or exertion
   (a) headache related to changes in cardiovascular parameters
   (b) headache related to trauma
   (c) headache arising from structures in the neck
4. headache arising from mechanisms specific to an individual sport (e.g. goggle headache).

While this approach somewhat reflects the limited published data in the field, its classification does not fit easily either into the IHS categories nor into a sports physician's clinical framework. As such, this new classification may need further conceptual development and validation through formal epidemiological studies.

Clinical approach to the patient with headache

The majority of headaches do not require medical assessment. However, certain symptoms may indicate the presence of more serious abnormalities and require medical assessment. These symptoms are:

- new or unaccustomed headache
- atypical headache
- stiff neck or meningeal signs
- systemic symptoms (e.g. fever, weight loss, malaise)
- neurological symptoms (e.g. drowsiness, weakness, numbness of limbs)
- local extracranial symptoms (e.g. ear, sinus, teeth)
- changes in the pattern of headache
- headache increasing over a few days
- sudden onset of severe headache
- headaches that wake the patient up during the night or in the early morning
- chronic headache with localized pain.

The clinical approach to the sportsperson complaining of headache is shown in Figure 18.1. The practitioner should carry out the following:

1. Exclude possible intracranial causes. These include hemorrhage, tumor, infection, and subdural hematoma. If an intracranial abnormality is suspected as a result of a full neurological examination, imaging of the brain with CT or MRI may be indicated.
2. Exclude headache associated with a viral illness. The presence of common illnesses that may provoke headache should be excluded. These include respiratory tract infection, sinusitis, and influenza.
3. Exclude drug-induced headaches. Many commonly used drugs can provoke headache, including
   - alcohol
   - analgesics (e.g. aspirin [ASA], codeine)
   - antibiotics and antifungals
   - antihypertensives (e.g. methyldopa)

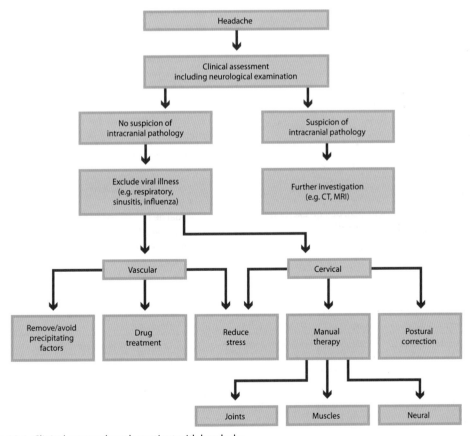

Figure 18.1 Clinical approach to the patient with headache

- caffeine
- corticosteroids
- cyclosporin
- dipyridamole
- indomethacin
- monoamine oxidase inhibitors (MAOIs)
- nicotine
- nitrazepam
- nitrous oxide
- oral contraceptives
- sympathomimetics
- theophylline
- vasodilators.

4. Exclude exercise-related headache.
5. Differentiate between vascular, tension, and cervical causes. The majority of headaches are either due to vascular causes (such as migraine) or referred from the joints and/or muscles of the neck. Classic vascular and cervical headaches each have distinctive features (Table 18.1), although frequently features of both types may be present. Tension headaches may occur unrelated to cervical injury or dysfunction, and tend to be of a low-grade daily headache presentation. In some cases, external stress is important in both their genesis and continuity.

History

 The clinical history is the most important component of the assessment of the athlete with headache.

The location of the headache is typically frontal or temporal in migrainous headaches, and occipital in cervical headaches. However, cervical headaches may also present as retro-orbital or temporal headaches.

Sudden onset of severe headache may indicate a cerebral hemorrhage or migraine, while cervical headaches typically have a more gradual onset. A recent history of a blow to the head may also be relevant. Recent exposure to possible precipitating factors (such as particular foods) should be noted if migraine is suspected.

Migrainous headaches are typically severe, as are headaches associated with meningeal irritation due to hemorrhage or meningitis. Cervical headaches are usually less severe. A throbbing pain is typical of a vascular headache, while a dull ache is more typical of a cervical headache.

The behavior of a headache in both the short term and long term is important. Migrainous headaches typically occur episodically. The frequency of these attacks should be noted. Migraines usually have a finite duration (hours), whereas cervical headache can last for days. The presence of any neck and arm symptoms should also be noted. Brief episodes of headache associated with exercise may indicate benign exertional headache. It is important to note whether specific motions such as neck movement easily irritate the headache. This is particularly relevant for manual therapy treatment.

Headache aggravated by neck movements may indicate a cervical cause for the headache. Exercise

Table 18.1 Clinical features of vascular and cervical headaches

Features	Vascular headache	Cervical headache
Age of onset	10–40 years	20–60 years
Onset	Fast	Slow
Site	Frontal or temporal	Occipital (usually), retro-orbital, or temporal
Side	Unilateral/bilateral	Unilateral
Type of pain	Throbbing	Dull ache
Constancy	Episodic	Constant
Time course	Hours	Days
Neurological symptoms	Common (e.g. visual disturbances, nausea)	Occasionally (e.g. paresthesia)
History of trauma	Rare	Common (e.g. whiplash)
Triggers	Food, drugs, stress	Trauma, posture
Treatment	Avoid precipitating factors Drugs Stress reduction	Manual therapy Stress reduction Postural correction

usually aggravates headaches of all types. Migraine is usually relieved by sleep.

Prior to the onset of migrainous headaches, there may be associated visual or sensory symptoms (migraine with aura). Nausea and vomiting are also commonly associated with migrainous headaches and usually follow the headache episode. The presence of neurological symptoms or systemic symptoms, such as weight loss and malaise, may be indicative of a more serious cause of headache.

Associated upper or lower respiratory tract symptoms, symptoms of sinusitis, temporomandibular joint problems, or influenza-like symptoms may indicate an association with one of these conditions. The presence of neck pain or stiffness should also be noted.

A past history of head trauma, even if relatively minor, may be significant, as subdural hematoma may present some time after the trauma. Previous problems such as encephalitis or major systemic illnesses should be recorded.

Whether the athlete is taking any medications (e.g. oral contraceptive pill) or recreational drugs (e.g. nicotine, alcohol, caffeine) should also be noted.

An assessment of life stresses is an important part of the history. These include personal relationships, work pressures, and problems related to the athlete's sporting activity. (See also the biopsychocial model, Chapter 20.)

 Stress aggravates both vascular and, particularly, cervical headache. An assessment of life stresses is an important part of the history.

Examination

In all patients presenting with headache, a full neurological examination is required and the skull and cervical spine must always be particularly examined. Depending on the presence or absence of specific symptoms in the history, the examination should consist of some or all of:

- general appearance
- mental state
- speech
- skull examination
- cervical spine examination
- gait and stance
- pupils and fundi
- special senses (e.g. smell, vision, hearing)
- other cranial nerves
- motor system
- sensory system
- general examination.

Vascular headaches

Vascular headaches include migraine, cluster headache, toxic headache, exertional headache, and some types of post-traumatic headache. Vascular headaches affect at least one-fifth of the population at some time during their lives. Common to all these headaches is a tendency toward extracranial vascular dilatation manifested by the throbbing headache phase of a particular attack. Vasoconstriction may also be evident and responsible for the painless sensory phenomena prior to the onset of head pain.

Vascular headaches usually begin early in life, often at puberty or in the second decade. There may be a familial tendency (50%). The headache usually begins early in the morning and reaches high intensity within two hours. It may last for a number of hours. Headaches usually resolve within a day but can recur daily or several times a week. There may be an increased frequency of occurrence in certain seasons, especially during spring.

Marked variations in headache frequency are seen within individuals. After menopause, headaches are usually diminished but in some women they may become more frequent and severe. The use of medications (such as vasodilators, hormone replacement therapy, or the oral contraceptive pill) may exacerbate an underlying tendency towards vascular headaches.

Migraine

Migraine with and without aura (i.e. vascular headache occurring with and without neurological symptoms) present a difficult management problem, particularly in sportspeople who develop migraine headaches after exercise. Approximately 20% of migraineurs experience migraine precipitated by exercise. Although most people think of migraine as headache alone, the true migraine sufferer usually notices a spectrum of symptoms, including nausea, vomiting, diarrhea, and weight gain. They may notice a prodromal period with evidence of endocrine disturbance (e.g. fluid retention). In the typical migraine attack with aura, painless sensory neurological symptoms such as visual disturbances (e.g. scotomas), paresthesia, vertigo, hemiplegia, and ophthalmoplegia may precede the headache.

The type of neurological symptoms that develop vary depending on which part of the intracranial vascular tree is affected by the disturbance. In migraine with aura, occipital branches of the vascular tree may be affected and visual symptoms such as flashing lights and scotoma predominate. In a rare form of migraine seen in children—known as vertebrobasilar migraine—brain stem abnormalities such as behavioral disturbances and even death have been described.

The IHS criteria for the diagnosis of migraine without aura are shown in Table 18.2.

Clinical features

Patients describe migraine headache pain as sharp and intense. It is often throbbing, beating, or pulsing, although occasionally the pain is steady. Commonly, it begins in the temple or forehead on both sides. When it starts on one side, it may spread to the other side. If the headache is intense, it may spread to the occiput and even change to a muscle-contraction type of headache. Occasionally the vascular headache begins at the back of the head and moves forward.

Many patients do not spontaneously volunteer their visual or sensory symptoms, either because they fail to link them with their headache or because they are hesitant to share the hallucinatory experiences. Occasionally patients may suffer the sensory phenomena without the headache developing. The common neurological accompaniments to migraine with aura are visual. Patients speak of bright colored or white objects (stars, edges, angles, balls) often to one side of the visual field. These objects may shine or flicker and may move across the visual field, leaving in their wake darkness or a scotoma.

Table 18.2 The International Headache Society (IHS) criteria for the diagnosis of migraine without aura (IHS 1.1)[1]

A.	At least five attacks fulfilling criteria B–D below
B.	Headache attacks lasting 4–72 hours (untreated or unsuccessfully treated)
C.	Headache has at least two of the following characteristics:
	1. unilateral location
	2. pulsating quality
	3. moderate or severe pain intensity
	4. aggravation by or causing avoidance of routine physical activity (e.g. walking or climbing stairs)
D.	During headache at least one of the following:
	1. nausea and/or vomiting
	2. photophobia and phonophobia
E.	Not attributed to another disorder

The visual symptoms usually last about 20 minutes and most often clear before the sensory, cognitive, or headache symptoms begin.

Sensory symptoms are usually described as tingling, pricking, or pins and needles. These commonly commence in the face or fingers, and gradually spread up the limb or over the same side of the body. Vertigo, dysphasia, diplopia, confusion, and amnesia are less commonly reported. Headache most often follows the neurological symptoms but may precede or accompany them.

Nausea, vomiting, and dizziness are common during or after the attack. After the headache, diuresis, diarrhea, euphoria, or a surge of energy are commonly described. The typical features associated with migraine are:

- precipitating factors (such as tiredness, stress or release from stress [e.g. "weekend migraine"])
- character and location of headache
- periodicity
- presence of migraine accompaniments (e.g. visual, gastrointestinal symptoms)
- relief with anti-migraine therapy (e.g. sumatriptan).

Precipitating factors in migraine

A number of precipitating factors are commonly found in association with migraine headaches. These are:

- endocrine changes (e.g. premenstrual or menstrual, oral contraceptive pills, pregnancy, puberty, menopause, hyperthyroidism)
- metabolic changes (e.g. fever, anemia)
- rhinitis
- change in temperature or altitude
- change in activity
- alcohol (especially red wine)
- foods (e.g. chocolate, cheese, nuts, hot dogs)
- drugs (e.g. glyceryl trinitrate [nitroglycerin], nitrates, indomethacin)
- blood pressure changes
- sleep—too much or too little.

Treatment

Most patients choose to lie quietly in a dark room during a migraine attack. Sleep often terminates the attack. The primary method of active treatment is pharmacological. High-dose aspirin (ASA) (900–1200 mg) is the drug of choice for the acute treatment of migraine. Other acute agents such as sumatriptan (intramuscular or intranasal[4]) or ergot preparations may be used as second-line therapy. Frequent sufferers of migraine may find prophylactic drug therapy necessary and reasonably effective. An important part of the management of the migraine sufferer is to identify and avoid precipitating factors. Traditional herbal remedies (such as feverfew) may be helpful.

It is critical in the management of migraine and other forms of headache that the use of repeated doses of simple analgesia alone be avoided. One of the consequences of the overuse of analgesic medication is the so-called "analgesic rebound headache," which becomes a self-generating headache requiring increasing doses of analgesia. Analgesic rebound headache, once established, is extremely difficult to treat and usually requires a specialist headache neurological clinic. For this reason, the use of simple analgesics in headache treatment should be limited to a maximum of three days per week. Treatment of the headache should be directed at the cause of the problem, not simply pain management.

Cluster headache

Cluster headache is also known as "histamine headache," "migrainous neuralgia," and "Horton's headache." It is five times more common in men than in women. This form of headache may be distinguished from other vascular headaches by the typical nature of the history. The pain typically occurs in attacks and is an intense burning or "boring" sensation. The attacks frequently begin in middle age and may be precipitated by alcohol. On the affected side there may be associated rhinorrhea, nasal obstruction, perspiration, and conjunctival injection. A partial Horner's syndrome is often seen. There is usually no family history. Patients are usually disabled during a cluster headache.

Patients with cluster headache are usually extremely sensitive to vasodilating agents. Oral glyceryl trinitrate (nitroglycerin) has been used as a provocative test for this condition.

Treatment depends on the age and health of the patient and the timing of attacks. Acute attacks may be aborted by inhalation of 100% oxygen at 7 L per minute. The mechanism of this relief is unclear. Headache prophylaxis may be necessary. Methysergide may be used in younger patients, and either prednisolone or lithium or both in older patients. Generally, the use of these medications requires specialist input due to the adverse-effect profile. Ergot preparations may also be used.

Cervical headache

"Cervical headache" or "cervicogenic headache" are terms used to describe headache caused by abnormalities of the joints, muscles, fascia, and neural structures of the cervical region. There are a number of classifications for cervical or cervicogenic headache, with differing criteria for physical dysfunction. These criteria are summarized in Table 18.3.

Mechanism

The mechanism of production of headache from abnormalities in the cervical region is variable. It may be primarily referred pain caused by irritation of the upper cervical nerve roots. This may be due to damage to the atlantoaxial joint or compression of the nerves as they pass through the muscles. Headache emanating from the lower cervical segments probably originates from irritation of the posterior primary rami, which transmit sensation to the spinal portion of the trigeminocervical nucleus.

Table 18.3 Current criteria for physical dysfunction in headache classification

International Headache Society[1]	International Association for the Study of Pain	Antonaci and Sjaadstad et al.[5]
Resistance to or limitation of passive neck movements	Reduced range of motion in the neck	Restriction of range of movement in the neck
Changes in neck muscle contour, texture, or tone, or response to active stretching or contraction	–	–
Abnormal tenderness in neck muscles	–	Pressure over the ipsilateral upper cervical or occipital region reproduces headache

FROM KERNICH ET AL.[3]

Commonly, pain may also be referred to the head from active trigger points (Fig. 18.2). Frontal headaches are associated with trigger points in the suboccipital muscles, while temporal headaches are associated with trigger points in the upper trapezius, splenius capitis and cervicis, and sternocleidomastoid muscles.

Clinical features

History

A cervical headache is typically described as a steady dull ache, often unilateral but sometimes bilateral. It can be intermittent or constant in nature, depending on specific factors contributing to the headache such as mechanical factors, chronicity of the condition, or psychosocial or pain disorder overlay. The patient describes a pulling or gripping feeling or, alternatively, may describe a tight band around the head. The headache is usually in the suboccipital region and is commonly referred to the frontal, retro-orbital, or temporal regions.

Cervical headache is usually of gradual onset. The patient often wakes with a headache that may improve during the day. Alternatively, it may be brought on later in the day as a result of occupational factors such as repetitive movements or sustained postures. Cervical headaches may be present for days, weeks, or even months. There may be a history of acute trauma (such as a whiplash injury sustained in a motor accident) or repetitive trauma (e.g. associated with work or a sporting activity).

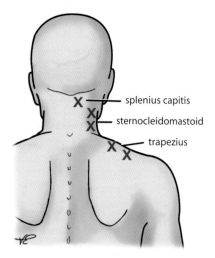

splenius capitis
sternocleidomastoid
trapezius

Figure 18.2 Sites of trigger points causing cervical headache

Cervical headache is often associated with neck pain or stiffness and may be aggravated by neck or head movements, such as repetitive jolting when traveling in a car or bus. It is often associated with a feeling of light-headedness, dizziness, and tinnitus. Nausea may be present, but vomiting is rare. The patient often complains of impaired concentration, an inability to function normally, and depression. Poor posture is often associated with a cervical headache. This may be either a contributory factor or an effect of a headache. The abnormal posture typically seen with cervical headache is rounded shoulders, head-forward posture with extension through the upper cervical spine, and protruded chin. This results in shortening and increased tone through the upper cervical extensor muscles and weakness of the cervical flexor muscles (Chapter 20).

Examination

Examination of the patient with suspected cervical headache involves systematic examination of the joints, muscles, and neural structures of the cervical region, as well as assessment of cervical posture. As with any musculoskeletal examination, one of the aims of the examination is to reproduce the patient's symptoms. It is important to remember that abnormalities of a number of different structures may contribute to the patient's pain.

Common joint abnormalities found on examination of the patient with cervical headache include stiffness and tenderness over the upper cervical (C1–2, C2–3) joints. Tenderness may be maximal centrally, especially where bilateral pain is present, or unilaterally over the apophyseal joints if unilateral pain is present. It is not uncommon for abnormalities of the lower cervical joints to be present as well.

On examination of the muscles of the cervical region, it is common to find increased tone and muscle shortening in the suboccipital and erector spinae muscles. There is often associated weakness in the cervical flexors. Active trigger points are frequently present, particularly in the suboccipital, sternocleidomastoid, and trapezius muscles.

Impaired motor control in cervical flexor and extensor muscles is not uncommon in patients with cervicogenic headache. Jull and others have developed the craniocervical flexion test (CCFT) (Fig. 20.6) to assess the deep flexor muscles.[6]

A neural component of the patient's headache is suspected if upper limb neurodynamic testing reproduces the patient's pain (Chapter 6).

Treatment

Treatment of the patient with cervical headache requires correction of the abnormalities of joints, muscles, and neural structures found on examination, as well as correction of any possible precipitating factors such as postural abnormalities or emotional stress.

Treatment of cervical intervertebral joint abnormalities involves mobilization or manipulation of the C1–2 and C2–3 joints.

A comprehensive exercise program includes motor control exercises for the cervical flexor and extensor muscles and stretching of any short cervical extensor muscles if indicated on assessment. An assistive strap can be used to target specific cervical segments in range of motion exercises (Chapter 20).

Soft tissue therapy to the muscles and the fascia of the cervical region is aimed at releasing generally tight muscles and fascia (commonly the cervical extensors). Active trigger points can be treated with spray and stretch techniques, or dry needling (Chapter 13).

Cervical muscle retraining is beneficial alone and in combination with manual therapy in reducing the incidence of cervicogenic headache.[7] This includes retraining of the deep cervical flexors (Fig. 18.3), extensors, and scapular stabilizers.

Postural retraining is an essential part of treatment. The patient must learn to reduce the amount of upper cervical extension by retracting the chin and lengthening the spine toward a neutral position (Chapter 20). Identification and reduction of sources of stress to the patient should be incorporated in the treatment program.

Figure 18.3 Retraining of the deep cervical flexors (see also Fig. 20.12 on page 330)

PHOTO COURTESY OF PROFESSOR GWENDOLEN JULL

Exercise-related causes of headache

Primary exertional headache

Benign exertional headache has been reported in association with weightlifting, running, and other sporting activities. The IHS criteria include that the headache:

A. is a pulsating headache fulfilling criteria B and C
B. is lasting from 5 minutes to 48 hours
C. is brought on by and occurring only during or after physical exertion
D. is not attributed to another disorder.

The onset of the headache is with straining and Valsalva maneuvers, such as those seen in weightlifting and competitive swimming. The major differential diagnosis is subarachnoid hemorrhage, which needs to be excluded by the appropriate investigations.

It has been postulated that exertional headache is due to dilatation of the pain-sensitive venous sinuses at the base of the brain, as a result of increased cerebral arterial pressure due to exertion. Studies of weightlifters have shown that systolic blood pressure may reach levels above 400 mmHg and diastolic pressures above 300 mmHg with maximal lifts.

A similar type of headache is described in relation to sexual activity and has been termed primary headache associated with sexual activity (with subdivisions of preorgasmic headache and orgasmic headache) (IHS 4.4).

The management of this condition involves either avoiding the precipitating activity or drug treatment (e.g. indomethacin 25 mg three times a day). In practice, the headaches tend to recur over weeks to months and then slowly resolve, although in some cases they may be lifelong.

Exertional migraine

Exertional migraine shows the typical pattern of migraine with exertion as the precipitating factor. Most patients with this condition describe the migraine beginning immediately after exercise, more frequently when the exercise has been vigorous. Exertional migraine is often severe and may be worse in hot weather. Treatment is based on standard migraine treatment.

Post-traumatic headache

Trauma to the head and neck in sport may lead to the development of headache. The initiating traumatic

B

event may not necessarily be severe. The IHS diagnostic criteria for post-traumatic headache are shown in Table 18.4.

There are a number of specific subtypes of post-traumatic headaches.

Post-traumatic migraine

Post-traumatic migraine may be seen in sports such as soccer, where repetitive heading of the ball gives rise to the term "footballer's migraine."[8, 9] Even mild head trauma can induce migraine. One particular syndrome that is recognized in the setting of minor head blows is migrainous cortical blindness. This disturbing condition often raises fear of serious cerebral injury but tends to resolve over 1–2 hours.

Extracranial vascular headache

There is a tendency to develop periodic headaches at the site of head or scalp trauma. These headaches may share a number of migrainous features, although at times they can be described as "jabbing" pains.

Dysautonomic cephalalgia

Dysautonomic cephalalgia occurs in association with trauma to the anterior triangle of the neck, resulting in injury to the sympathetic fibers alongside the carotid artery. This results in autonomic symptoms such as Horner's syndrome, and excessive sweating associated with a unilateral headache. Propranolol

has been used with some success in the management of this condition.

External compression headache

External compression headache (IHS 13.10), formerly known as "swim goggle headache," presents with pain in the facial and temporal areas produced from wearing excessively tight face masks or swimming goggles. It is commonly seen in swimmers and divers. In divers, this may be referred to as "mask squeeze," and is seen on descent to depth as the effects of pressure reduce the air space inside the mask. It is believed to be due to continuous stimulation of cutaneous nerves by the application of pressure.

High-altitude headache

High-altitude headache (IHS 10.1.1) is a well-recognized accompaniment of acute mountain sickness, which occurs within 24 hours of ascent to altitudes above 23 000 m. The headaches are vascular in nature and are seen in unacclimatized individuals. Typically these are associated with other physiological effects of altitude, or they may be an early manifestation of acute mountain sickness. The treatment is to descend to lower altitude, although pharmacological interventions such as acetazolamide, ibuprofen, and sumatriptan may be used.

Table 18.4 The International Headache Society (IHS) criteria for the diagnosis of acute post-traumatic headache (IHS 5.1.1)

Mild head injury	Moderate or severe head injury
A. Headache, no typical characteristics known, fulfilling criteria C and D	A. Headache, no typical characteristics known, fulfilling criteria C and D below

B. Head trauma with all the following:
  1. Either no loss of consciousness, or loss of consciousness of <30 minutes' duration
  2. Glasgow Coma Scale (GCS) ≥13
  3. Symptoms and/or signs diagnostic of concussion
	B. Head trauma with at least one of the following:
	  1. Loss of consciousness for >30 minutes
	  2. Glasgow Coma Scale (GCS) <13
	  3. Post-traumatic amnesia for >48 hours
	  4. Imaging demonstration of a traumatic brain lesion (cerebral hematoma, intracerebral and/or subarachnoid hemorrhage, brain contusion, and/or skull fracture)

C. Headache develops within 7 days after head trauma	C. Headache develops within 7 days after head trauma or after regaining consciousness following head trauma

D. One or other of the following:
  1. Headache resolves within 3 months after head trauma
  2. Headache persists but 3 months have not yet passed since head trauma
	D. One or other of the following:
	  1. Headache resolves within 3 months after head trauma
	  2. Headache persists but 3 months have not yet passed since head trauma

Hypercapnia headache

Hypercapnia headache (IHS 10.1.2) or "diver's headache" is a vascular type of headache thought to be due to carbon dioxide accumulation during "skip" breathing. The arterial pCO_2 level is usually increased above 50 mmHg in the absence of hypoxia. Divers are also prone to headaches from other causes, such as cold exposure, muscular or temporomandibular joint pain from gripping the mouthpiece too tightly, cervicogenic headaches from incorrect buoyancy technique, middle ear and sinus barotrauma, and cerebral decompression illness.

RECOMMENDED WEBSITES

International Headache Society: http://ihs-classification.org/en/

RECOMMENDED READING

Boyling JD, Jull GA, eds. *Grieve's modern manual therapy*. 3rd edn. Edinburgh: Churchill Livingstone, 2004.

Fricton J, Velly A, Ouyang W et al. Does exercise therapy improve headache? A systematic review with meta-analysis. *Curr Pain Headache Rep.* 2009 Dec;13(6): 413-9.

Jensen S. Neck related causes of headache. *Aust Fam Physician* 2005;34(8):635-9.

Kernick DP, Goadsby PJ. Guidance for the management of headache in sport on behalf of the Royal College of General Practitioners and the British Association for the Study of Headache. *Cephalagia* 2011 Jan;31(1): 106-11.

McCrory P. Headaches and exercise. *Sports Med* 2000;30:221-9.

Sallis RE, Jones K. Prevalence of headaches in footballers. *Med Sci Sports Exerc* 2000;32(11):1820-4.

Turner J. Exercise-related headache. *Curr Sports Med Rep* 2003;2:15-17.

REFERENCES

1. Sarchielli P. XI Congress of the International Headache Society. September 13-16, 2003, Rome, Italy. *Expert Opin Pharmacother* 2004;5(4):959-75.
2. Nadelson C. Sport and exercise-induced migraines. *Curr Sports Med Rep* 2006;5(1):29-33.
3. Kernick DP, Goadsby PJ. Guidance for the management of headache in sport on behalf of The Royal College of General Practitioners and The British Association for the Study of Headache. *Cephalalgia* 2011 Jan;31(1):106–11.
4. McCrory P, Heywood J, Ugoni A. Open label study of intranasal sumatriptan (Imigran) for footballer's headache. *Br J Sports Med* 2005;39(8):55244.
5. Antonaci F, Sjaastad O. Cervicogenic headache: a real headache. *Curr Neurol Neurosci Rep* 2011;11(2):149–55.
6. Jull G, Falla D, Treleaven J, eds. *A therapeutic exercise approach for cervical disorders* 3rd edn. Edinburgh: Churchill Livingstone, 2004.
7. Jull G, Trott P, Potter H et al. A randomized controlled trial of exercise and manipulative therapy for cervicogenic headache. *Spine (Phila Pa 1976)* 2002;27(17):1835–43; discussion 1843.
8. Matthews WB. Footballer's migraine. *Br Med J* 1972;2(5809):326–7.
9. Mainardi F, Alicicco E, Maggioni F et al. Headache and soccer: a survey in professional soccer players of the Italian "Serie A." *Neurol Sci* 2009;30(1):33–6.

Chapter 19

Facial injuries

I was trying to move it while it was still fresh. I know that once it sets it's harder.
Steve Nash commenting on trying to align his nasal fracture during an
NBA Western Conference Final Game

Injuries to the face in sport usually result from direct trauma. After reviewing clinical assessment and soft tissue injury management, this chapter outlines management of injuries to the nose, ear, eye, teeth, and facial bones.

Functional anatomy

The bones of the face are shown in Figure 19.1. As most of these bones are subcutaneous, they are easily examined. Examination should include palpation of the forehead and supraorbital rims for irregularities and contour deformities.

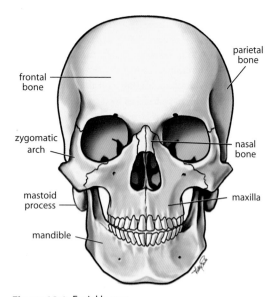

Figure 19.1 Facial bones

The orbit is a cone-shaped cavity formed by the union of seven cranial and facial bones. The orbital margin consists of the supraorbital ridge above, the infraorbital margin below, the zygomatic arch laterally, and the nasal bone medially. The recess formed protects the eye from a blow from a large object. A smaller, deformable object such as a squash ball may, nevertheless, compress the eyeball and cause a "blow-out" fracture of the orbit.

The zygomatic arch of the malar bone creates the prominence of the cheek. Fractures in this region may cause flattening of the cheek and a palpable irregularity in the inferior orbital margin.

The maxilla forms the upper jaw. Its superior surface helps create the floor of the orbit and the inferior surface forms the major part of the hard palate. Mobility of the hard palate, determined by grasping the central incisors, indicates a maxillary fracture.

The lower jaw consists of the horseshoe-shaped mandible. The mandible is made up of body, angle, and ramus, which are easily palpated. The coronoid process can be palpated by a direct intraoral approach. The gingiva overlying the alveolar ridge may be lacerated in mandibular body fractures.

Clinical assessment

Facial injuries[1] are frequently associated with profuse bleeding. While it is important to control the bleeding, it is also vital to fully assess the underlying structures. All head and neck injuries should be considered closed head injuries. Cervical spine precautions should be taken if the patient is unconscious or has neurological deficits or cervical spine tenderness.

The airway is particularly vulnerable to obstruction because of bleeding, structural compromise of bony structures (e.g. mandible), or dislodged teeth, tooth fragments, or dental appliances. The practical steps to assess facial injuries are as follows:

- Ascertain the mechanism of injury and locate the source of the patient's pain.
- Check for blurred vision, diplopia, concussion, or cerebrospinal fluid leakage.
- Inspect the nasal septum for hematomas and nasal obstruction.
- Inspect the external ear for hematomas.
- Observe facial asymmetry or structural depressions.
- Look for a sunken eye globe suggestive of a blow-out fracture.
- Observe lacerations or deep abrasions overlying suspected fractures.

Palpate facial bones (orbital rims, nasal bones, temporomandibular joints) for significant tenderness, crepitus, numbness, or contour irregularities. Midface instability or crepitus may be demonstrated by stabilizing the forehead with one hand while gently pulling on the maxillary incisors with the other gloved hand. Bimanual palpation along the mandible and maxilla (one gloved hand palpating intraorally) will uncover instability, irregularity, or tenderness.

Assess extraocular eye movements and cranial nerves III, IV, and VI by having the patient keep his or her chin in a fixed position while tracking the examiner's finger movements in all four quadrants. If the patient is able to track the movements without reporting diplopia, acute extraocular nerve entrapment caused by an orbital blow-out fracture can be ruled out. An inability to raise the eyebrow or wrinkle the forehead following laceration to the eyebrow suggests injury to the temporal branch of the facial nerve on that side. Reduced sensation over the skin below the eye in the distribution of the infraorbital nerve may be associated with a blow-out fracture of the orbit. The nerve distribution includes the upper gum and lip.

If the patient is unable to open his or her mouth, or exhibits severe pain along the lateral aspect of the cheek or jaw when attempting to open the mouth, a fracture of the mandible or zygoma must be considered. With the mouth open, the oral cavity should be assessed to rule out damage to the teeth, and lacerations in the intraoral mucosa or tongue. Locate fractured or missing teeth, when possible, to avoid accidental aspiration. When asked to close the mouth, the patient's sense of malocclusion suggests

a significant fracture of the mandible, maxilla, or palate.

Leakage of cerebrospinal fluid (CSF) following a blow to the nose (CSF rhinorrhea) may indicate a fracture of the base of the anterior cranial fossa. CSF is a clear discharge and the patient may report a salty taste in the mouth. If there is doubt about the origin of a nasal discharge associated with trauma, the discharge should be tested with a urinary dipstick for glucose. CSF is positive for glucose.

A list of common conditions and conditions not to be missed is shown in Table 19.1 overleaf.

Soft tissue injuries

Contusions and lacerations to the face and scalp are prevalent in sports such as football, ice hockey, martial arts, and racquet sports.[1] Examination should include palpation of the underlying bone to detect bony tenderness. Neurological examination is required if there is a history of loss of consciousness or suspected skull fracture.

Begin immediate management with ice and pressure to reduce local swelling. Control bleeding with direct pressure over the wound using sterile gauze. A player with a bleeding wound must be removed from the field of play immediately, as there is concern that the presence of blood may increase the risk of hepatitis B or human immunodeficiency virus (HIV) infection for other players (Chapter 56).

After removing the athlete from the field of play, examine the laceration closely under good light. Further cleaning and removal of foreign bodies may be required. If necessary, infiltrate a local anesthetic agent to adequately clean the wound. The local anesthetic used should be 1% or 2% lignocaine (lidocaine) containing adrenalin (epinephrine) 1:100 000 to provide some vasoconstriction as well as analgesia.

Lacerations longer than 0.25–0.5 cm (0.1–0.2 in.) should be closed if they appear clean. Closure may be obtained by suturing or by taping with adhesive strips (steristrips). Steristrips are ideal for small wounds; however, persistent bleeding or excessive sweating may prevent adhesion. To overcome this, tincture of benzoin (Friar's Balsam) may be applied to increase adhesiveness. Adequate dressings are required to keep the adhesive strips in place, especially if the player is returning to the field. Scalp wounds often bleed profusely. Small wounds can be controlled with local pressure; however, larger ones require suturing.

If facial lacerations require suturing, use 5/0 or 6/0 nylon. It is important that the skin edges are

Table 19.1 Facial injuries in sport

Category	Common	Less common	Not to be missed
Facial soft tissue	Contusion Laceration		
Nose	Fracture of nasal bones Epistaxis	Fracture of nasal septum Septal hematoma	
Ear	Contusion ("cauliflower ear") Otitis media Otitis externa	Laceration Ruptured tympanic membrane	Fractured petrous temporal bone Torn auditory nerve
Eye	Corneal abrasion Corneal foreign body Conjunctival foreign body Subconjunctival hemorrhage Eyelid laceration	Chemical burns Vitreous hemorrhage Retinal hemorrhage Retinal edema Hyphema	Corneal laceration Retinal detachment Lens dislocation Blow-out fracture of the orbit Optic nerve injury Injury to lacrimal system
Teeth	Enamel chip fracture Luxated tooth Avulsed tooth	Crown fracture	
Facial bones	Temporomandibular joint sprain or malalignment	Fractured maxilla Fractured mandible	

healthy. Pieces of devitalized skin should be debrided. Take care to approximate the skin edges carefully while suturing. Remove sutures after five days and place adhesive strips over the wound for a further week. The wound should be kept dry for at least 48 hours.

An alternative to suturing is skin stapling. Staples must be covered if the player is returning to the field to prevent them from being accidentally torn out or from injuring another player in a collision. Another alternative is the use of histoacryl glue.

Deep wounds require closure in appropriate layers. Deep forehead and scalp lacerations involve damage to the galea aponeurotica. This layer should be closed with interrupted 5/0 absorbable sutures prior to skin closure.

Lacerations of the eyebrow and lip require strict anatomical approximation. Eyebrow hair should not be shaved. In lacerations involving the vermilion border of the lip, accurate alignment is obtained by placing the first suture at the mucocutaneous junction.

Full thickness lacerations of the lip require a three layer closure, preferably performed by a plastic surgeon. The oral mucosa is closed first, then the orbicularis oris layer, and finally skin. Deep intraoral lacerations should be closed with 3/0 silk sutures, which should remain in place for one week.

All patients with potentially contaminated wounds should receive tetanus prophylaxis (if indicated) and the wound should be cleaned meticulously. The question of prophylactic oral antibiotic therapy is controversial and depends on the depth and the location of the laceration.

Bite wounds to the face may be contaminated by another player's saliva, and there is debate over whether they should be closed or left to heal by second intention. Many clinicians prescribe broad-spectrum antibiotics that include coverage for anaerobes (such as amoxicillin/clavulanate 500 mg three times daily or 875 mg twice daily, or doxycycline 100 mg twice daily in the event of penicillin allergy for 3–5 days). Due to cosmetic concerns, wounds on the face could be closed depending on the level of contamination and the comfort level of the clinician. It is important that clinicians follow local antibiotic guidelines in making prophylaxis decisions, and for the choice of the most appropriate antibiotics. If signs of infection appear, treatment with intravenous antibiotics is reasonable providing there are no signs of abscess formation.

Human bite wounds also raise the issue of viral contamination—hepatitis and HIV. Any patient negative for anti–hepatitis B antibodies who is bitten by an individual positive for hepatitis B antigen should receive both hepatitis B immune globulin (HBIG) and hepatitis B vaccine. The risk for transmitting HIV through saliva is extremely low, but is of concern if there is blood in the saliva. Counseling regarding post-exposure HIV prophylaxis is appropriate in this setting.

Nose

Nasal injuries are common in contact sports such as football and boxing.

Epistaxis (nosebleed)

Nasal hemorrhage occurs frequently in association with nasal injuries. It usually arises from the nasal septum, which receives its blood supply from branches of the internal and external carotid arteries. In most cases, the bleeding arises from a rich plexus of vessels in the anterior part of the septum, known as "Little's area" or "Kiesselbach's area" (Fig. 19.2).

Initial management consists of prolonged direct digital pressure on the lower nose for up to 20 minutes, compressing the vessels on the nasal septum with the patient sitting upright. Cold compresses over the bridge of the nose promote vasoconstriction. If bleeding continues, apply cotton wool soaked in adrenalin (epinephrine) 1:1000 to the nasal septum. If the bleeding site can be located, it can be cauterized with silver nitrate applicators (cotton swabs soaked in 4% trichloracetic acid).

If bleeding persists, specialist referral is indicated. The nose will usually be packed with 1 cm (0.5 in.) ribbon gauze impregnated with bismuth iodoform petroleum paste (BIPP) and left for 48 hours. Post-nasal packing may be required if the bleeding

originates from the back of the nose. In the rare cases that bleeding persists despite these local measures, maxillary artery or anterior ethmoidal artery ligation may be indicated.

Nasal fractures

Fractures of the nose are usually caused by a direct blow. Symptoms and signs of nasal fracture include pain, epistaxis, swelling, crepitus, deformity, and mobility of the nose. Nasal distortion may *not* be obvious once soft tissue swelling develops. Initial management is directed toward controlling the nasal hemorrhage. An associated laceration should be sutured with 6/0 nylon and requires prophylactic antibiotic therapy. The nasal passages should be examined to exclude a septal hematoma (see below) and patients should be advised to return if they notice increased pain or develop a fever.

X-rays are probably not required as undisplaced fractures require no treatment and displaced fractures are clinically obvious. Displaced nasal fractures may require reduction. There are two indications for reduction of fractures—obstruction of the nasal passages, and cosmetic deformity.

In young athletes, displaced fractures are almost always reduced because of a tendency toward increased sinus infections and a decrease in the size of the nasal passage. Attempts at immediate reduction of nasal fractures are associated with a risk of arterial damage and severe acute hemorrhage. Thus, contrary to Steve Nash's beliefs (chapter opening quote), it is preferable to delay fracture reduction and refer the patient to a surgeon within seven days of the injury. When the soft tissue swelling has settled sufficiently, reduction, if necessary, can be carried out under general anesthesia.

Many sportspeople decide to delay reduction of their nasal fracture, provided there is no obstruction to the nasal passages, until a more convenient time such as the end of a season or at the time of retirement from contact sports.

Septal hematoma

Septal hematoma is an important condition that can complicate what seems to be a trivial nosebleed. A septal hematoma is caused by hemorrhage between the two layers of mucosa covering the septum. The presenting complaint is either nasal obstruction or nasal pain. The patient may be febrile, and nasal examination reveals a cherry-like structure (the dull red swollen septum) that occludes the nasal passages. Treatment of a large septal hematoma involves

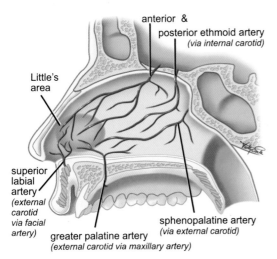

anterior & posterior ethmoid artery *(via internal carotid)*

Little's area

superior labial artery *(external carotid via facial artery)*

greater palatine artery *(external carotid via maxillary artery)*

sphenopalatine artery *(via external carotid)*

Figure 19.2 Little's (Kiesselbach's) area

evacuation of the clot using a wide-bore needle or a small incision, followed by nasal packing to prevent recurrence of the hematoma. Antibiotic prophylaxis should be given to prevent development of a septal abscess and subsequent cartilage necrosis.

Ear

Ear injuries in sport are not common. The most frequent injury is a contusion to the ear known as an "auricular hematoma."

Auricular hematoma

This injury occurs mainly in rugby scrums, boxing, or wrestling as a result of a shearing blow. Recurrent contusions result in hemorrhage between the perichondrium and the cartilage. This may eventually develop into a chronic swelling, commonly known as "cauliflower ear." An acute hematoma (Fig. 19.3) should be treated initially with ice and firm compression, but may need to be drained by aspiration under strict aseptic conditions. A pressure dressing (cotton wool soaked in collodion) is then applied and is carefully packed against the ear to follow the contours of

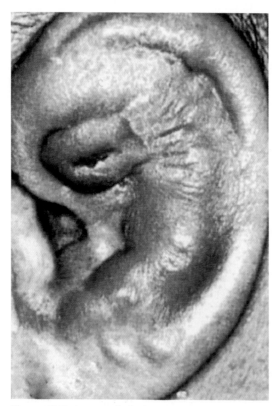

Figure 19.3 Acute auricular hematoma

the outer ear. This is bandaged firmly. The ear must be examined daily to assess progress. Return to non-contact sports can be immediate, but headgear or a helmet is required for return to contact sport. Rugby forwards frequently wear headgear which protects their ears as a preventive measure.

Lacerations

Lacerations to the ear require careful cleansing and suture. As lacerations located between the scalp and the ear are easily missed, this area should always be examined, especially if there is a history of the ear being pulled forward. Tears of the auricular cartilage should be carefully aligned and sutured with absorbable 5/0 sutures. The perichondrium should be closed as a separate layer. Prophylactic oral antibiotic therapy is recommended.

Perforated eardrum

A blow across the side of the head may occasionally injure the eardrum. Pain, bleeding from the ear, or impaired hearing suggest tympanic membrane rupture. These ruptures usually heal spontaneously. Prophylactic antibiotic therapy (amoxycillin [amoxicillin] 250–500 mg 8 hourly if not allergic to penicillin) should be administered. It is important to keep the ear dry while a perforation is present. In sports where significant pressure changes occur, such as platform diving, scuba diving, and high-altitude mountain climbing, athletes should not return to play until the tympanic membrane has healed. Athletes participating in water sports, such as swimming and water polo, should use custom-fabricated ear plugs to maintain a dry ear canal. Dry land athletes may return to play as soon as any vertigo has resolved.[1]

A severe blow across the head may fracture the skull and cause inner ear bleeding. Discharge from the ear (otorrhea) may signal a neurosurgical emergency and, thus, patients should be referred immediately for specialist treatment.

Otitis externa

Otitis externa is the most common ear condition affecting competitive swimmers. It is generally caused by bacteria, although fungal infection can also contribute. Symptoms include earache, pruritus, discharge, and impaired hearing. On examination, there may be discharge in the ear and local redness along the external auditory meatus. There may be tragal tenderness and pain on tragal pull.

Management involves careful aural toilet combined with topical antibiotic and corticosteroid ear drops. The patient should, preferably, abstain from swimming until fully recovered, and avoid rubbing or drying the ear until after the infection has cleared. The use of earplugs in this condition is controversial. They may traumatize the ear canal and predispose the swimmer to infection.

 Recurrent attacks of otitis externa may be prevented by instillation of alcohol ear drops (e.g. 5% acetic acid in isopropyl alcohol [Aquaear]) after each swimming session.

Eye

Eye injuries occur most commonly in stick sports, racquet sports (especially squash), and contact sports.[2] All eye injuries, even those that appear to be minor, require thorough examination. All serious eye injuries should be referred immediately to an ophthalmologist. The indications for immediate referral to an ophthalmologist are shown in the box.

Athletes with a previous history of impaired vision in one or both eyes, or previous eye trauma or surgery should be evaluated by an ophthalmologist prior to participating in a high-risk sport.

Indications for immediate referral to a specialist ophthalmologist

Symptoms
Severe eye pain
Persistent blurred or double vision
Persistent photophobia

Signs
Suspected penetrating injury (corneal laceration, pear-shaped pupil)
Hyphema
Embedded foreign body
No view of fundus (suspected vitreous hemorrhage or retinal detachment)
Markedly impaired visual acuity: 6/12 or less
Loss of part of visual field

Assessment of the injured eye

To assess the injured eye, it is important to understand the anatomy. The anatomy of the eye is shown in Figure 19.4.

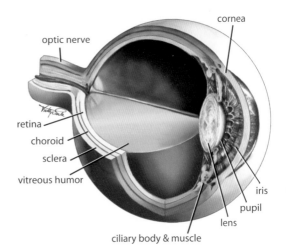

Figure 19.4 Anatomy of the eye

For a thorough assessment of the injured eye, an eye injuries kit (Fig. 19.5) is very useful and can be carried as part of the "physician's bag" (Chapter 63). The kit includes a small mirror, a pencil torch, an ophthalmoscope, a sterile solution for irrigation, local anesthetic eye drops (e.g. amethocaine), fluorescein, antibiotic drops and ointments, cotton buds, contact lens lubricant and case, eye patches, tape, and a Snellen chart to assess visual acuity.

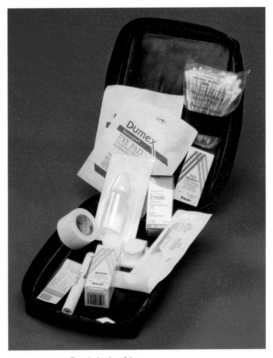

Figure 19.5 Eye injuries kit

The history of the eye injury provides useful diagnostic information. Seek to discover the history of the mechanism of injury. Were glasses, contact lenses, or a protective device being worn at the time of injury? Note any previous eye injury or problems. Ask about symptoms such as pain, blurred vision, loss of vision, flashing lights, and diplopia (double vision).

Test the visual acuity of each eye using a Snellen chart, with and without glasses or contact lenses. If a Snellen chart is not available, use pages of a newspaper with variable print sizes as an approximate assessment of visual acuity. On the sporting arena, a scoreboard can be used to test distant vision.

Inspect the eyelids for bruising, swelling, or laceration. Note any obvious foreign body, hemorrhage, or change in pupil size.

If pain or photophobia due to the injury prevent examination of the eye, instil a drop of a sterile topical anesthetic agent (such as amethocaine) to assist examination.

Inspect the cornea for foreign material and abrasions. Fluorescein staining will help reveal areas of corneal ulceration or foreign bodies. Evert the upper lid to exclude the presence of a subtarsal foreign body.

Test eye movements in all directions. A restriction in any direction or the presence of diplopia may indicate orbital fracture. Compare the size, shape, and light reaction of the pupil with the uninjured eye. An enlarged, poorly reacting pupil may be present after injury to the iris. A pear-shaped pupil suggests the presence of a full thickness corneal or scleral laceration (penetrating injury).

Inspect the anterior chamber for the presence of blood—hyphema (Fig. 19.6).

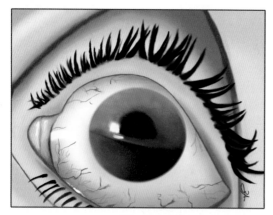

Figure 19.6 Hyphema—note the fluid level in the anterior chamber

 Ophthalmoscopic examination should routinely be performed to inspect the lens, vitreous humor, and retina.

The absence of a red reflex on ophthalmoscopic examination may be due to a corneal opacity, a lens opacity (cataract), intraocular bleeding, or a retinal detachment. Failure to visualize the fundus may be a sign of vitreous hemorrhage, which can result from a retinal tear. Contusion of the retina may produce retinal edema, seen as areas of pallor (and thickening) as well as retinal hemorrhage.

Radiological examination of the orbit is indicated in all cases of traumatic eye injury with diplopia, and in cases where an intraocular or intraorbital foreign body is suspected.

Corneal injuries: abrasions and foreign body

Corneal injuries in sport include abrasion, foreign body, and, less commonly, alkali burn.

Corneal abrasion, one of the most frequent injuries to the eye during sport, occurs as a result of a scratch from either a fingernail or foreign body. The patient complains of pain, a sensation of a foreign body being present in the eye, and, if the central cornea is involved, blurred vision.

A topical anesthetic drop should be instilled to assist in corneal examination. Fluorescein staining will help locate corneal abrasions or foreign bodies. Evert the upper lid to exclude a subtarsal foreign body.

Treatment of corneal abrasions includes the instillation of antibiotic eye drops (e.g. chloramphenicol), and padding of the eye (Fig. 19.7). If pain and photophobia are severe, add a topical mydriatic (e.g. 2% homatropine). A local anesthetic agent should never be used for pain relief as it can delay healing and result in further damage.

Corneal foreign bodies can be removed with a cotton-tip applicator by an appropriately trained practitioner. If the foreign body is more deeply embedded, the patient should be referred to an ophthalmologist for its removal. Rust rings, which occasionally remain after metallic foreign bodies have been embedded in the cornea, require removal by an ophthalmologist. Antibiotic eye ointment should be administered following foreign body removal, and the eye padded for 24 hours until the corneal epithelium has healed.

If an athlete has sustained an alkali burn (from line markings), irrigate the eye copiously for 20 minutes

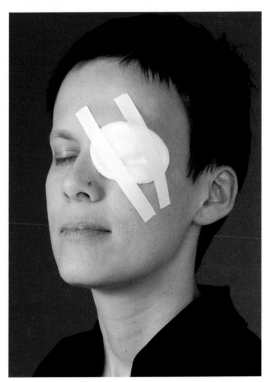

Figure 19.7 Eye padding

with sterile saline or tap water and instil a local anesthetic agent to assist this. The player should be seen as soon as possible by an ophthalmologist.

Subconjunctival hemorrhage

Trauma to the conjunctiva may cause subconjunctival hemorrhage—a bright red area in the white conjunctiva. Unless the hemorrhage is extensive, or visual symptoms or photophobia are present, it is not clinically important. Blood pressure should be measured to exclude hypertension. The subconjunctival hemorrhage may, however, obscure a perforation of the globe. If this is suspected, the patient should be referred to an ophthalmologist. In most cases, however, the patient merely requires reassurance.

Eyelid injuries

In all injuries to the eyelids, the eye also needs to be examined to exclude ocular injury. Direct trauma to the eyelids may cause a large amount of bruising, which should be treated with cold compresses in the first 24 hours. Hemorrhage may spread subcutaneously across the midline to the other eye. A coexisting orbital fracture needs to be excluded in these patients.

Lacerations of the eyelid require meticulous primary repair. Each anatomical layer (conjunctiva, tarsal plate, and skin) should be repaired separately by an ophthalmic surgeon.

Trauma near the medial canthus may lacerate the upper or lower lacrimal canaliculus (tear duct). If this is not repaired, the patient may have permanent watering of the eye. Such injuries require ophthalmological referral for microscopic suturing of the cut ends of the canaliculus.

Hyphema

Bleeding into the anterior chamber of the eye results from ruptured iris vessels and may only be visible with slit lamp examination. More significant bleeds present with a clear layer in the anterior chamber, visible after the blood settles (Fig. 19.6). In hyphemas of small volume, visual acuity may be unaffected. Associated injuries may occur and all patients with a hyphema should be referred to an ophthalmologist.

The aim of treatment of hyphema is to prevent further bleeding, which may, in turn, result in uncontrollable glaucoma or blood staining of the cornea. The patient needs to rest in bed while the hemorrhage clears, usually over three to five days. Aspirin and other anti-inflammatory medications should be avoided, as these may provoke further bleeding.

Lens dislocation

Blunt trauma may result in varying degrees of lens displacement. Partial dislocation causes few symptoms. Complete lens dislocation results in blurred vision. A common sign of lens dislocation is a quivering of the iris when the patient moves the eye. Iritis and glaucoma are possible sequelae of lens dislocation. Immediate ophthalmological referral is required. Surgical removal of the displaced lens may be indicated.

Vitreous hemorrhage

Bleeding into the vitreous humor signifies damage to the retina, choroid, or ciliary body. Ophthalmoscopic examination reveals loss of the red reflex and a hazy appearance. Treatment generally consists of bed rest, but more severe cases may require removal of the blood and vitreous humor.

Retinal hemorrhage

Injury to the retina can result from a direct blow to the eye or a blow to the back of the head. Valsalva maneuvers (e.g. in weightlifting) may also produce retinal edema and hemorrhage. The patient may remain asymptomatic if peripheral areas of the retina are affected; however, central retinal damage blurs vision. On ophthalmoscopic examination, central retinal edema appears as a white opacity that partially obscures the retinal vessels. Boxers may develop atrophic macular holes and loss of central vision as a result of recurrent contusive injuries.

Retinal detachment

Retinal detachment may result from any blunt or perforating trauma, and may occur months or even years after the initial injury. The patient complains of flashes of light or the appearance of a "curtain" spreading across the field of vision. Ophthalmoscopic examination reveals elevation and folding of the detached retina, which trembles with each eye movement. Immediate referral for surgical treatment is indicated. An unusual case of retinal detachment in sport occurred in a swimmer who received an accidental blow to the goggles.[3]

Orbital injuries

Blow-out fracture of the orbit results from direct trauma such as a fist, cricket ball, baseball,[4] or squash ball (Fig. 19.8). Compression of the globe and orbital

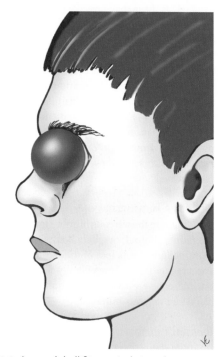

Figure 19.8 A squash ball fits precisely into the eye socket

contents produces a fracture in the weakest part of the orbit, the orbital floor. Contents of the orbit may herniate through the defect. The patient typically presents with a periorbital hematoma, a protruding or sunken eye, double vision on upward gaze, and numbness of the cheek. Double vision on upward gaze is due to the entrapment of the inferior rectus muscle in the fracture.

A detailed examination of the eye must be performed to exclude intraocular injuries such as hyphema, lens dislocation, or ruptured globe. If an orbital fracture is suspected, X-ray should be performed. The X-ray may not show the fracture but may demonstrate some clouding of the maxillary sinus. CT examination is used to confirm the fracture.

Antibiotic therapy should be commenced immediately and the patient referred to an ophthalmologist. Surgery may be required to release the trapped muscle and repair the bony defect.

Prevention of eye injuries

Athletes with certain eye problems should avoid contact sports altogether. These problems include:

- functionally only one eye
- severe myopia
- Marfan syndrome
- previous retinal detachment.

For squash, protective eye wear must be worn by people who have either only one good eye, amblyopia (lazy eye), recent eye surgery, history of preretinal detachment conditions, or diabetic retinopathy. Protective eye wear should meet the Australian Standard AS4066 1992 or the US Standard ASTM F803.

Contact lenses offer no protection against eye trauma. Hard contact lenses are not suitable for sporting activity and should never be used in contact sport. Soft lenses appear to be reasonably safe in contact sport. One of the most common "crises" in injury management is a lost contact lens. The athlete will complain that the contact lens is no longer in its correct position and cannot be located. Usually the lens has been displaced and with careful examination can be located elsewhere on the eye, often at the lower lid. Occasionally, the lens is displaced completely from the eye and lost on the playing surface. Those who wear contact lenses during sport should always carry a spare pair of contact lenses or a pair of protective spectacles as a back-up.

Those sportspeople who cannot or do not like to wear contact lenses can use protective goggles made of polycarbonate, which are available for most prescriptions. These polycarbonate goggles are also used as eye protection in sports with a high risk for eye injuries. The most obvious examples of these are squash and racquetball, where the size of the ball enables it to enter the orbit and compress the globe. The routine use of closed goggles is strongly recommended.

Certain sports require protection not only of the eye but of the other facial structures. In sports such as American football, ice hockey, cricket, and lacrosse, protective helmets and faceguards should also provide adequate eye protection. Because of the profound effects of major eye injury, we encourage sportspeople and sport-governing bodies to be proactive in promoting and enforcing the use of eye protection where indicated.[5]

Teeth

Collisions with opponents during contact sports are the most common cause of dental injuries. Direct blows from equipment such as hockey sticks and bats may also injure teeth.

Thorough examination of the oral cavity should be carried out in all cases of facial trauma, to detect injuries to the teeth. If a chipped or avulsed tooth cannot be found, chest and abdominal X-ray may be required to locate the missing fragment.

Enamel chip fractures are not painful and require non-urgent dental referral. Crown fractures that expose the dentine are painful when exposed to air, heat, or cold and require urgent dental referral. A severe crown injury exposing the dental pulp requires immediate dental referral. The fractured tooth fragment should be retained in milk.

Occasionally, a forceful blow causes a tooth or teeth to be luxated or moved. These teeth should be repositioned in their original site using firm finger pressure, and subsequently splinted with aluminium foil prior to dental referral.

Tooth avulsion may also occur as a result of a direct blow. The tooth may be saved by quick and appropriate action.[6] The critical time is in the first 15 minutes following the injury. An avulsed tooth should be retrieved and handled by the crown. If dirty, it should be irrigated with sterile saline solution or milk, or sucked clean under the tongue. Debris should not be scraped off the root. If the patient is conscious and alert, the tooth should then be reimplanted and splinted. It is essential to confirm that the labial and lingual surfaces of the tooth are in proper position by comparison with the adjacent teeth. When the tooth has been implanted into the proper position, the patient should be asked to bite on sterile gauze and be transported immediately for dental treatment. If the patient is not fully alert, the tooth can be stored in a suitable medium such as a glass jar, paper cup, or sealable plastic bag containing sterile saline or fresh milk, preferably skim milk, for transport, and the patient immediately referred to a dentist. With suitable storage, the tooth may be successfully reimplanted by the dentist within two hours of the injury.

Prevention of dental injuries

Most dental injuries can be prevented or reduced in severity by the wearing of an effective mouth-guard. Evidence suggests that athletes who do not wear mouth-guards are at 1.6—1.9 times the risk of orofacial injury compared with mouth-guard users.[7] The standard "one size fits all" mouth-guard has limited effectiveness, and a custom-made mouth-guard fitted by a dentist should be worn in sports where the risk of dental injury is high. In youth sports, parents, as well as coaches, should take responsibility for ensuring that competitors wear mouth-guards.[8] Sports such as basketball, baseball, and soccer have a higher rate of dental injuries than many parents and athletes realize. Medical personnel should encourage mouth-guard use in these sports, in addition to the traditional contact sports such as American football, rugby, ice hockey, and wrestling.

Bimaxillary mouth-guards are also available to cover both the upper and lower teeth. These tend to make breathing and speech difficult, and are not popular with sportspeople.

Mouth-guards should be kept in a plastic box and regularly rinsed with an antiseptic mouthwash. They should not be allowed to overheat, as they will deform.

Fractures of facial bones

In sport, facial fractures may result from blows by implements such as bats or sticks, equipment such as skis,[9] and from collision injuries. Mountain biking is a sport that causes a significant proportion of facial injuries. Eye wear[10] and face shields[11] can protect against facial injuries.

Symptoms and signs range from pain, swelling, laceration, and bruising to gross deformity.

Examination may reveal facial asymmetry, discoloration, or obvious deformity. The bite should be examined for malocclusion. Bimanual examination of the facial bones may show areas of discontinuity and mobility. If maxillary fracture is suspected, the upper teeth can be grasped to determine evidence of excessive movement of the upper jaw and midface. Opening and closing the jaw may reveal pain, limitation, or deviation with mandibular injuries.

Initial management of facial fractures is directed toward maintenance of the patient's airway. In mandibular body fractures and maxillary fractures, this may require emergency manual reduction. Associated head and cervical spine injuries should be excluded. The oral cavity requires inspection for bleeding or dental damage.

Fractures of the zygomaticomaxillary complex

Zygomaticomaxillary complex fractures (Fig. 19.9) occur from a direct blow to the cheek such as from a fist, hockey stick, or baseball. Signs include swelling and bruising, flatness of the cheek, and mandibular function disturbance. If associated with an orbital fracture, there may be concomitant diplopia, numbness of the affected cheek, limitation of ocular movement, and asymmetry of the eyes.

Surgical treatment consists of closed or open reduction under general anesthesia. Unstable fractures require fixation. Associated orbital fractures are treated by open reduction and reconstruction of the orbital floor.

Maxillary fractures

Maxillary fractures usually result from a direct crushing blow to the middle portion of the face, such as from a hockey stick, a baseball, or collision. They are classified as Le Fort I, II, and III fractures depending on whether the nasal or cheek bones are involved. Le Fort I fractures result in the separation of the maxilla from the nasal-septal structures and the pterygoid plates. Clinically, Le Fort I fractures are identified when the entire maxilla moves as a separate unit. Le Fort II fractures separate the maxilla and the nasal complex from the orbital and zygomatic structures. On clinical examination, the maxilla and nose move together as one unit. Le Fort III fractures separate the maxillary, zygomatic, nasal, and orbital structures from the cranial base (Fig. 19.10).[12]

Maxillary fractures are often accompanied by cranial damage, obstruction of the nasal airway, edema of the soft palate, hemorrhage into the sinuses, and disturbance of the contents of the orbit. CSF rhinorrhea may occur, indicating fracture of the cribriform plate. Reduced sensation in the infraorbital region is common.

Examination findings include lengthening of the face, midface mobility, malocclusion of the bite, and periorbital bruising. Initial treatment is aimed at protecting the airway—the conscious patient should sit leaning forward. This should be followed by rapid

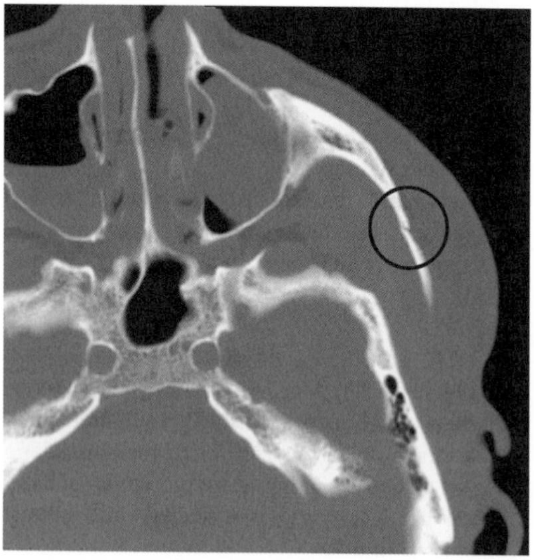

Figure 19.9 CT scan confirming a fractured zygomatic arch; plain radiography did not detect the fracture

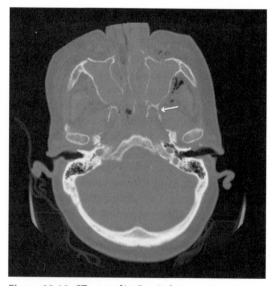
Figure 19.10 CT scan of Le Fort III fracture (arrow)

transfer for definitive diagnosis and treatment. Surgical treatment involves reduction and fixation with wires, screws, or a plate.

Mandibular fractures

Fracture of the mandible is one of the most common facial fractures in sport and usually results from a direct blow. The most common fracture sites are the mandibular angle and the condyle. The mandible usually breaks in more than one place as a result of the trauma, and these fractures usually occur on opposite sides of the midline. Fractures may be displaced or undisplaced.

Undisplaced fractures

Minor mandibular fractures are painful, tender, and swollen. These are managed conservatively with analgesia and rest. The patient should eat soft food only for up to four weeks as symptoms resolve.

Displaced mandibular fractures

Displaced mandibular fractures are severe injuries that result from considerable force. Alveolar (tooth-bearing) fractures are the most common type. These fractures range from single-tooth fractures or avulsions to complete segment mobility. The clinical diagnosis is obvious when two or more teeth move as a unit.

Inspection may reveal malalignment of teeth and bruising to the floor of the mouth. Palpation reveals malocclusion, tenderness, and defects along the lower border of the mandible. Paresthesia or anesthesia of the lower lip and chin suggest damage to the inferior alveolar nerve.

Initial treatment includes maintenance of the airway in a forward-sitting position with the patient's hands supporting the lower jaw. A jaw bandage can be used in comminuted or badly displaced fractures. The bandage needs to be applied with caution, as it may compromise the airway by causing backward displacement of the mandible. A cervical collar can be used as an alternative. A concussed or unconscious patient should be placed in a lateral position with head tilt and jaw support after the mouth has been cleared of any dislodged teeth or tooth fragments. Occasionally, the tongue may need to be held forward to maintain an open airway.

Most displaced mandibular fractures require closed reduction and intermaxillary fixation for four to six weeks. If adequate closed reduction cannot be achieved, then open reduction and internal fixation

are required. A fracture of one condyle usually does not require immobilization except to control pain. Active jaw exercises should be commenced as soon as pain permits.

During the period of intermaxillary fixation, the sportsperson may perform mild exercises such as stationary bike riding and light weightlifting. Resumption of contact sport should be delayed until at least one to two months after the jaws are unwired. Earlier resumption is possible when internal fixation has been used. The use of a protective polycarbonate facial shield may offer some protection if early return to play is contemplated.

Patients with mandibular fractures, who are eating soft food or have their jaws wired, must be referred to a dietitian for advice on suitable liquid meals and foods suitable for vitamizing.

Temporomandibular injuries

Blows to the mandible can produce a variety of temporomandibular joint (TMJ) injuries. Trauma to the jaw while the mouth is open occasionally produces TMJ dislocation. Other injuries include hemarthrosis, meniscal displacement, and intracapsular fracture of the head of the condyle.

Examination of the injured TMJ may reveal limitation of opening, pain, and malocclusion. Dislocation of the TMJ causes inability to close the mouth. A dislocated TMJ may be reduced by placing both thumbs along the line of the lower teeth as far posteriorly as possible and applying downward and backward pressure. Longstanding dislocations may require general anesthesia for reduction. Management of TMJ dislocation includes rest with limitation of mouth opening for up to seven to 10 days, a soft diet, and analgesics such as aspirin. Contact sport should be avoided for up to two weeks depending on the symptoms. Boxers should not attempt sparring for at least six weeks.

Chronic temporomandibular pain

Chronic TMJ problems are sometimes referred to as "temporomandibular joint dysfunction" or "myofascial pain dysfunction syndrome." This syndrome appears to affect males more than females, with a peak incidence in the early twenties. Patients complain of pain, limitation of movement, clicking, and locking of the TMJ. Treatment should include assessment by a dentist to exclude any malocclusion problem, and physiotherapy evaluation with a view to manual therapy; exercise therapy can be invaluable.

Prevention of facial injuries

Protective equipment has been designed for sports where facial injury is a risk (Chapter 9). Properly designed helmets have reduced the incidence of facio-maxillary injuries. Ideally, helmets should be individually fitted for each athlete. Helmets are designed for a single impact or multiple impacts. Single-impact helmets (such as most pushbike and motorbike helmets) must be discarded after the user has had a fall.

📄 RECOMMENDED READING

Heimme MR, Murphy MA. Ocular injuries in basketball and baseball: what are the risks and how can we prevent them? *Curr Sports Med Rep* 2008;7(5):284–8.

MacEwen CJ, McLatchie GR. Eye injuries in sport. *Scott Med J* 2010;55(2):22–4.

Mourouzis C, Koumoura F. Sports-related maxillofacial fractures: a retrospective study of 125 patients. *Int J Oral Maxillofac Surg* 2005;34;635–8.

Reehal P. Facial injury in sport. *Curr Sports Med Rep* 2010;9(1):27–34.

Roccia F, Diaspro A, Nasi A, Berrone S. Management of sport-related maxillofacial injuries. *J Craniofac Surg* 2008;19(2):377–82.

Pieper P, St. Mars T, Valdez AM. Epidemiology and prevention of sports-related eye injuries. *J Emerg Nurs* 2010;36(4):359–61.

Youn J, Sallis RE, Smith G, Jones K. Ocular injury rates in college sports. *Med Sci Sports Exerc* 2008;40(3):428–32.

📋 REFERENCES

1. Romeo SJ, Hawley CJ, Romeo MW et al. Facial injuries in sports—a team physician's guide to diagnosis and treatment. *Phys Sportsmed* 2005;33(4):45–53.
2. Drolsum L. Eye injuries in sports. *Scand J Med Sci Sports* 1999;9:53–6.
3. Killer HE, Blumer BK, Rust ON. Avulsion of the optic disc after a blow to swimming goggles. *J Pediatr Ophthalmol Strabismus* 1999;36:92–3.
4. Vinger PF, Duma SM, Crandall J. Baseball hardness as a risk factor for eye injuries. *Arch Ophthalmol* 1999;117:354–8.
5. Jones NP. Eye injuries in sport: where next? *Br J Sports Med* 1998;32:197–8.
6. Ranalli DN. Dental injuries in sports. *Curr Sports Med Rep* 2005;4(1):12–17.
7. Knapik JJ, Marshall SW, Lee RB et al. Mouthguards in sport activities history, physical properties and injury prevention effectiveness. *Sports Med* 2007;37(2):117–44.
8. Diab N, Mourino AP. Parental attitudes towards mouthguards. *Pediatr Dent* 1997;19:455–60.
9. Gassner R, Ulmer H, Tuli T at al. Incidence of oral and maxillofacial skiing injuries due to different injury mechanisms. *J Oral Maxillofac Surg* 1999;57:1068–73.
10. Webster DA, Bayliss GV, Spadaro JA. Head and face injuries in scholastic women's lacrosse with and without eyewear. *Med Sci Sports Exerc* 1999;31:938–41.
11. Asplund C, Bettcher S, Borchers J. Facial protection and head injuries in ice hockey: a systematic review. *Br J Sports Med* 2009;43(13):993–9.
12. Ranalli DN, Demas PN. Orofacial injuries from sport—Preventive measures for sports medicine. *Sports Med* 2002;32(7):409–18.

Chapter 20

Neck pain

with ERIN MACRI, MEENA SRAN, and GWENDOLEN JULL

Living the past is a dull and lonely business; looking back strains the neck muscles, causing you to bump into people not going your way. American novelist Edna Ferber

This chapter considers acute and chronic soft tissue conditions that cause neck pain. Severe neck injuries are considered in Chapter 47.

The surface anatomy of the neck is shown in Figure 20.1. Structures of the neck that are likely to cause pain are the zygapophyseal joints, cervical disks, the ligaments and muscles of the neck, and neural structures.

Clinical perspective

Neck pain is considered within a biopsychosocial model where, collectively, account is taken of biological factors, any psychological reactions (e.g. anxiety, fear), and social factors (e.g. home or family situation, access to healthcare, occupational factors) that may contribute to the disorder and potentially

influence recovery (Fig 20.2 overleaf).[1, 2] This model fits well within the framework of the World Health Organization's Interational Classification of Functioning, Disability and Health (ICF) domains where impairments, activity, and participation limitations are considered within the context of a person's overall health and quality of life.[3] The biopsychosocial approach to healthcare, within the framework of the ICF, is a very relevant model for the individual with a neck pain disorder.[4]

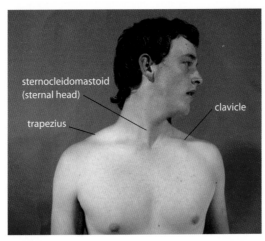

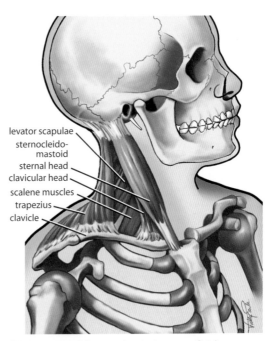

Figure 20.1 Anatomy of the neck
(a) Surface anatomy of the neck from in front

(b) Anatomy of the anterior neck—superficial

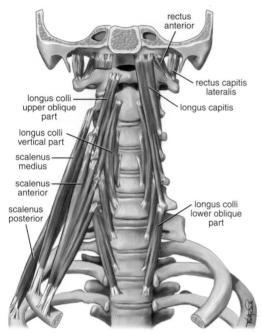

rectus
anterior

rectus capitis
lateralis

longus capitis

longus colli
upper oblique
part

longus colli
vertical part

scalenus
medius

scalenus
anterior

scalenus
posterior

longus colli
lower oblique
part

(c) Anatomy of the anterior neck—deep cervical
musculature

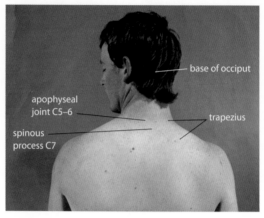

base of occiput

apophyseal
joint C5–6

spinous
process C7

trapezius

(d) Surface anatomy of the neck from behind

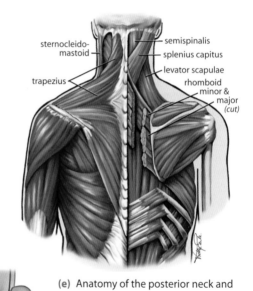

sternocleido-
mastoid

trapezius

semispinalis

splenius capitus

levator scapulae

rhomboid
minor &
major
(cut)

(e) Anatomy of the posterior neck and
scapulothoracic region

rectus capitis
posterior minor

semispinalis
capitis

splenius capitis

sternocleidomastoid

trapezius

superior oblique

inferior oblique

rectus capitis
posterior major

longissimus capitis

semispinalis cervicis

multifidus

semispinalis capitis
(cut)

splenius capitis
(cut)

(f) Anatomy of the posterior neck—
deep cervical musculature

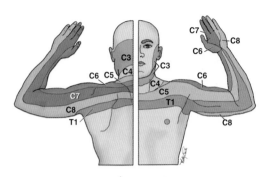

(g) Dermatomal distribution for the cervical spine

and manual therapy, is effective in the treatment of mechanical neck pain.[4, 7, 8]

Effective management of individuals with neck pain requires a thorough history and physical examination, sound clinical reasoning to develop an effective approach to treatment, as well as a collaborative therapeutic relationship between the patient and therapist. Rapport building and education are vital in helping patients both to accept short-term treatment planning and to participate diligently in long-term management of their condition, toward return to normal function and participation in their sport, work, and recreation, and, importantly, prevention of recurrent episodes.

Many people suffer from chronic or recurrent bouts of neck pain[5] and impairments may persist, even after symptoms have resolved.[6] This underscores the importance of seeking treatment; systematic reviews (Chapter 3) indicate that multimodal treatment, including specific therapeutic exercise

Assessing patients with neck pain

History

Knowledge of the duration and time course of neck pain, mechanisms of injury, and factors that may

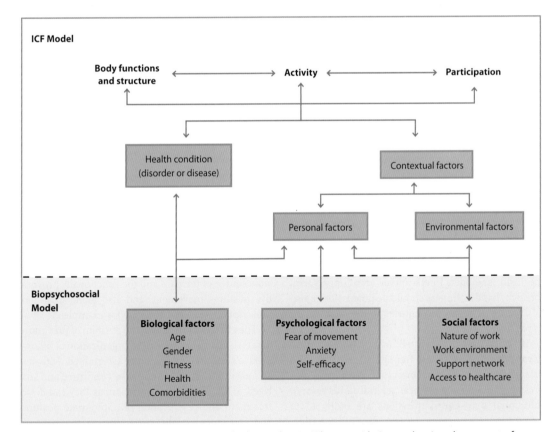

Figure 20.2 The biopsychosocial model as applied to neck pain. When considering neck pain, take account of biological factors, psychological reactions (e.g. anxiety, fear), and social factors (e.g. home or family situation, access to healthcare, occupational factors) that may contribute to the disorder and potentially influence recovery.[1, 2]

underlie or perpetuate an insidious onset of neck pain provide the foundation for a comprehensive understanding of the patient and their neck disorder. The onset and severity of the patient's symptoms are important in determining the extent of injury. Onset may have been sudden (either due to external trauma or an abnormal movement) or delayed (following trauma—it is common in whiplash injuries for patients to report onset of pain that evening or the next day[9]). Alternatively, onset may be insidious, possibly a result of repetitive movements or prolonged abnormal postures relating to sport or occupation. (See Chapter 11 for tips on taking a comprehensive history to assess musculoskeletal disorders.)

Symptoms and their behavior

The neck is a particularly complex part of the body and the clinician must be careful not to overlook the possibility of symptoms of more serious comorbidities beyond soft tissue damage (e.g. concussion, traumatic brain injury, non-cervical causes of dizziness, acute onset severe headaches, post-traumatic syringomyelia, other spinal cord involvement). Specific mandatory questions when assessing the patient with a cervical spine disorder include those relating to general health and "red flag" conditions. Pertinent to cervical disorders, questions also include those for the "5 Ds" (dizziness, diplopia, dysphagia, dysarthria, drop attacks) and other questions pertaining to vertebrobasilar insufficiency or craniovertebral ligament instability (e.g. nausea, perioral paresthesia, tinnitus, "lump in the throat," dizziness or syncope with turning, looking up, or holding sustained positions) as relevant to the patient's presentation.

Determine the location of the symptoms—is the pain in the upper or lower cervical regions, primarily central, right-sided or left-sided, or is there a generalized ache? Any radiation of the pain to the head, shoulder, interscapular area, upper arm, forearm, hand or fingers should be noted. (Refer also to Chapter 21 regarding injuries to the shoulder or upper arm.)

If headaches are reported, ask additional questions regarding intensity, frequency, duration, and progression (e.g. if acute onset, and severe and progressing, emergency medical referral is necessary). Additional open-ended questions are indicated to investigate other symptoms (e.g. dizziness, vertigo, tinnitus, unusual sensory symptoms).

The patient's choice of descriptors for their symptoms may also give an indication of the pathoanatomical source or physiological mechanism of pain. For example, severe lancinating pain referred in a dermatomal distribution (Fig. 20.1g) suggests nerve root compression and neuropathic pain. Any associated symptoms in the upper arm (such as pins and needles, numbness, or weakness) may also relate to nerve compression or irritation.

Individuals with neck pain may report dizziness or lightheadedness in association with their neck pain.

Like headaches, dizziness can arise from a variety of sources, and the clinician must be able to identify when these symptoms require further medical investigation prior to initiating conservative treatment.

Dizziness can be cervicogenic, vasculogenic, cerebellar, or vestibular in origin (e.g. labyrinthine or vestibular nerve injury), or may relate to other systems entirely (e.g. postural hypotension, cardiac, post-illness, neurological). Cervicogenic dizziness is often described as a feeling of lightheadedness, unsteadiness, disequilibrium, or imbalance. If symptoms are benign and non-cervicogenic, consider referring to a vestibular therapist.

Determine how easily the pain is aggravated—"irritability." If the condition is irritable, the pain may be aggravated very easily or by relatively minor movements, and may take several minutes to hours to ease. The degree of irritability influences the extent of the examination (limited or full) and the intensity of treatment.

The diurnal pattern of symptoms can help determine if the condition is primarily inflammatory (pain likely worse in the morning and constant in nature) or mechanical (generally worse with specific movements or activities, might be worse in the evening, intermittent in nature).

Aggravating and easing factors inform on the possible source of the pain and the functionally provocative postures/movement, and also guide treatment prescription. (See box opposite for examples.)

The effect of lying down, the position of maximum comfort, and the number and organization of pillows used to sleep at night should be ascertained. Activities and positions reported should be confirmed and analyzed in the physical examination, as they can direct treatment and re-education of appropriate postures and movements/skills pertaining to the patient's sport or work.

If the pain cannot be reduced or abolished through positioning or specific activities, the clinician should

B

- If reading aggravates pain, it may indicate that prolonged flexion is aggravating the intervertebral disk or posterior cervical structures;[10] this would also lead the clinician to investigate the fatigability of the cervical extensors.
- If looking up (extension) aggravates the pain, it may suggest zygapophyseal joint involvement.[11, 12]
- If talking on the telephone (lateral flexion) produces ipsilateral pain, it may indicate compression of structures exiting the foramen or zygapophyseal compression.
- Pain with contralateral lateral flexion may indicate a stretch irritation of mechanosensitive neural structures.

consider non-mechanical factors that may be contributing to the pain. Aggravating and easing factors also provide information about the patient's pain-coping strategies (e.g. high reliance on medication or passive treatment modalities or, conversely, continues activities and copes with the pain).

Occupational factors

Enquiry about the patient's sport(s), hobbies, and occupation and their relationship to the patient's neck pain provides the clinician with vital information regarding typical postures and movements and loads that the neck is being subjected to, that may be contributing to the patient's ongoing symptoms. Such information guides the long-term objectives of treatment and highlights where further investigation is needed (ergonomic evaluation of work station, biomechanical analysis of cycling style or tennis serving mechanics). The Patient Specific Functional Scale (PSFS)[13] (see next section) asks the patient to nominate activities which are restricted because of neck pain, and can also help guide further investigations regarding specific biomechanical factors contributing to the current condition. It also informs the clinician of the patient's perceived level of disability.

Outcome measures

There are numerous outcome measures recommended for people with neck pain. Three commonly used measures are the Numeric Pain Rating Scale (NPRS), Neck Disability Index (NDI),[14] and the PSFS.[13] Outcome measures assist the clinician to understand base-line presentation, as well as to evaluate the course of recovery throughout treatment. In addition, in the case of whiplash injuries in particular, high initial ratings of pain and disability predict protracted recovery,[6, 15–18] further emphasizing the value for use of such scales.[19]

The NPRS is an easy tool for quantifying self-reported pain levels and measuring changes in pain over time. Patients are asked to rate their pain on a scale between 0 and 10 where 0 is "no pain" and 10 is "the worst pain imaginable." An initial pain score of greater than 5 has almost six times the risk of ongoing pain or disability at follow-up compared with scores less than 5.[18]

The NDI contains 10 items regarding functional abilities and symptoms. The questionnaire is easy to complete. Each item has a five-point scale and the score is summed and converted to a percentage.[14, 20] The minimal detectable change is 19.6 percentage points, while the minimum clinically important change for the NDI is 19 percentage points.[21]

The PSFS asks patients to nominate at least three activities they are currently experiencing difficulty with as a result of their condition. For each activity, patients rate their ability to perform these activities, with 0 being "completely unable" and 10 being "able to complete the task at their full, pre-injury level."[4, 13] In patients with cervical radiculopathy, the PSFS has better construct validity, reliability and responsiveness than the NDI,[22] although both are equally able to detect change over time.[13] The minimal detectable change for the PSFS is 2.1, and the minimum clinically important change is 2.0.[22]

Physical examination

The history guides the clinician to the structures that may be producing the patient's symptoms and thus directs the physical examination. The goal of examination is to determine whether the pain is primarily coming from articular, muscular, or neural structures, to guide treatment. As with any soft tissue injury, all three structures may be involved to some extent. Perform a neurological examination if symptoms are reported in the arm below the level of the shoulder. In addition to examining for a structural source of pain, also examine the function of the region to identify impairments in the sensorimotor system resulting from pain, to identify postural or other muscle function drivers of the disorder. While examination focuses on the cervical and upper thoracic spines and axio-scapular region (Chapter 25), do not neglect the craniomandibular complex, which may be contribute to and/or result from the current episode of neck pain (Chapter 19). The examination involves the following:

1. Observation
   (a) static posture of the spine and axio-scapular region in sitting and standing: all three planes
   (b) dynamic postures (relevant sports- or activity-related functional movements that aggravate symptoms)
2. Active range of motion
   (a) upper cervical flexion (Fig. 20.3a)
   (b) lower cervical flexion (Fig. 20.3b)
   (c) upper cervical extension (Fig. 20.3c)
   (d) lower cervical extension (Fig. 20.3d)
   (e) lateral flexion
   (f) rotation
   (g) combined movements (Fig. 20.3e)
   (h) shoulder girdle—Apley's scratch test (hand behind back, hand behind head)
3. Manual examination
   (a) manual provocation tests

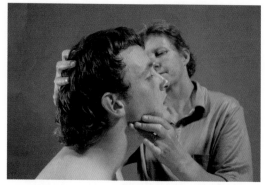

(c) Active movement—upper cervical extension with chin protruding

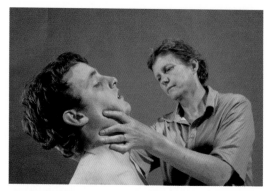

(d) Active movement—lower cervical extension with upper cervical spine in neutral or flexion

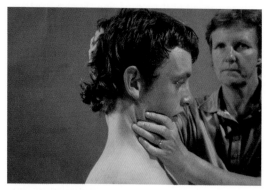

Figure 20.3 Examination of the patient with neck pain—range of motion
(a) Active movement—upper cervical flexion

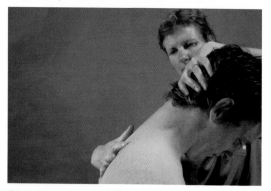

(b) Active movement—lower cervical flexion

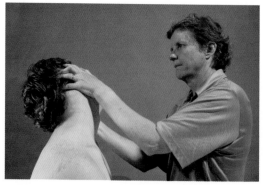

(e) Combined movements, using a combination of flexion or extension and lateral flexion or rotation, may reproduce pain or other symptoms. The movements can be adapted to be more specific for the upper cervical spine with upper cervical flexion or extension. Overpressure may be applied as shown

(b) passive physiological intervertebral movements

(c) cervical flexion rotation test (Fig. 20.4)

(d) stability tests, including craniovertebral ligaments

(e) Spurling's test

(g) palpation

4. Tests of muscle function

(a) cervical flexors (Fig. 20.5 on page 321)

(b) cervical extensors (Fig. 20.6 on page 322)

(c) axio-scapular muscles (Fig. 20.7 on page 323)

5. Tests of the nervous system

(a) conductive tests (Chapter 11)

(b) neural mobility and provocation tests (Chapter 11)

6. Tests of cervical somatosensory function

(a) cervical position sense—joint position error
    (Fig. 20.8 on page 324)

(b) balance—standing balance, dynamic balance

(c) eye movement control—smooth pursuit

7. Additional special tests

(a) vertebrobasilar insufficiency

(b) additional tests in the presence of dizziness.

Observation

Begin the physical examination by observing the patient's static and dynamic postures. Static posture is examined in all three planes and is evaluated in

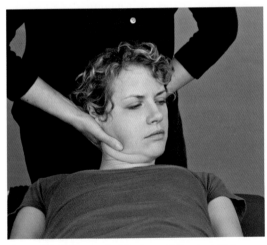

Figure 20.4 The cervical flexion rotation test. The patient is positioned in a supine position, hands resting on the abdomen, with the head beyond the end of the treatment table, supported by the clinician. The clinician brings the patient's neck passively into full flexion, then assesses passive rotation range of motion of the C1–2 joint, taking care not to move into painful range.[25] A visually estimated reduction in 10° to one side is considered a positive test result, with a minimum detectable change of 7°.[26]

both sitting and standing. Posture assessment must include the orientation of the lumbopelvic region, thoracic spine, and axio-scapular region, as well as head and neck orientation. In assessment of dynamic postures, observe how the patient walks into your office and removes his or her coat. Have the patient demonstrate any specific tasks he or she currently finds painful or difficult. Take note of the patient's willingness to move, quality and ease of movement, and objective indicators of discomfort. Assess overall muscle tone, bulk, and symmetry. Hypertrophy may be present in chronic conditions; muscle wasting may be suggestive of deconditioning or neurological involvement; a crease in the skin at the back of the neck may reflect a localized instability. Note any deformities, scars, swelling, skin changes, temperature differences, or any other relevant abnormalities.

Active range of motion

Evaluate range of motion of the upper and lower cervical spines and cervicothoracic region. Measure range of motion, and assess quality of movement and any symptoms that are produced. "Quality" refers to fluidity and ease of movement and the course of the trajectory in a given plane. For example, when assessing side flexion, stiffness or altered somatosensory function may result in combined movements (side flexion with some rotation), rather than pure side flexion in a frontal plane. If the stiffness is in the upper cervical spine, the rotation may be in a contralateral direction, whereas in the lower cervical region, it may be ipsilateral.

Where possible, measure pure planar movements, as these are more reliable than combined movements. Check for any aberrant eye movements such as nystagmus, closed eyes during movement, or altered tracking (i.e. not looking in the direction of head movement). It is normal to look to the right with the eyes when turning the head and neck to the right. Looking elsewhere is not uncommon for people with neck dysfunction. Closing the eyes may be a strategy to reduce sensations of vertigo or dizziness during head movements.

If range of motion is decreased, determine what is limiting the movement. Is the pain only at end of range, or is it painful throughout movement? Is movement ceased before the onset of symptoms? Is fear of causing further pain or harm stopping the patient from moving through full range? Location of the symptoms during specific movements may begin to identify the source of the pain (e.g. ipsilateral neck pain during side flexion may indicate zygapoph-yseal joint involvement). In some cases the clinician may wish to follow up with passive range of motion to further assess movement. Apley's scratch test (scratching one's back while reaching over the head with one hand and behind the back with the other hand) is a quick screen for the upper extremities to rule out involvement, although more complete assessment is indicated if this test reveals limited range, pain provocation, or other abnormalities.

Manual examination

Assessment of the neck includes tests of both stability and mobility. Manual provocation tests (discrete segmental postero-anterior glides [PAs]) can help identify painful segments. Passive physiological intervertebral movements further localize the segment(s) with altered mobility. Spurling's test (extending the neck, rotating the head, then applying downward pressure on the head) assesses the effect of closing down the intervertebral foramen on symptoms that may be related to a sensitive nerve root. The cervical flexion rotation test is a validated test to localize hypomobility at the C1–2 segment[23, 24] (see Fig. 20.4). The craniocervical ligaments are examined individually as indicated, specifically the transverse ligament, tectorial membrane, and alar ligament.

Tests of muscle function

Neck pain and injury can change neck and axio-scapular muscle function. These include re-organization of motor control strategies, changes in muscle properties, and reductions in muscle strength and endurance (see Falla et al. for review[30]). In relation to motor control, changes occur in muscles' patterns of activation and thus function. For example, in the cervical flexor group, activity of the deep cervical muscles (longus capitis and colli) is reduced in the presence of neck pain, while activity in the superficial cervical muscles (sternocleidomastoid, anterior scalene muscles) is increased.[31, 32] This altered pattern is evident in both prescribed tasks and functional activities,[33, 34] and occurs in neck disorders of both insidious and traumatic origin.[35, 36]

Impaired deep muscle activity has significance for the support and control of injured or pathological cervical segments. In addition, greater co-activation of the neck flexors and extensors occurs in association with neck pain,[37] and such increased co-activation has been demonstrated in functional tasks such as typing.[34] There are also changes in the muscles'

temporal behavior (relative timing of activation), such that the neck flexor muscles lose their feed-forward activation in response to perturbations induced by arm movements.[38] This makes cervical segments more vulnerable to unprotected loading. The neck muscles also lose strength and become more fatigable.[39] Notably, they lose their endurance capacity not only at maximum contractions but also at lower contraction intensities,[40] which is very relevant for functional activities of the neck.

There is objective muscle biopsy proof that fiber types change within the neck flexors and extensors.[41] There is an increased proportion of type IIC transitional fibers, consistent with a transformation of slow-twitch oxidative type-I fibers to fast-twitch glycolytic type-IIB fibers, which fits with muscles' loss of endurance capacity. Muscle atrophy occurs in individuals with chronic neck pain disorders,[42, 43] and widespread fatty infiltrate in the flexor and extensor muscles has been identified using T1 MR imaging, particularly in the deep muscles of those with chronic whiplash associated disorders.[44, 45] It appears that fatty infiltrate is a feature of chronic whiplash, but not of chronic insidious-onset neck pain,[46, 47] which suggests there might be differences in pathophysiological mechanisms between these two neck pain groups.

The axio-scapular muscles are common sites of tenderness but, importantly, poor function of the shoulder girdle may overload cervical structures and contribute to the pain state. The upper trapezius attaches to the cranium and ligamentum nuchae, and the levator scapulae attaches directly to the upper four cervical segments. Normal upper limb function induces both compressive loads and movement in the cervical segments.[48, 49] Poor scapular mechanics and muscle control may adversely increase these loads and strains. Additionally, specific morphological and histological changes have been shown in the upper trapezius muscle in association with pain.[50, 51] Electromyographic studies have revealed greater fatigability of the upper trapezius[52] and changed patterns of trapezius behavior in functional tasks in individuals with neck pain disorders.[34, 53]

Assessment of cervical flexors

The first stage of assessment evaluates aspects of motor control. The cranio-cervical flexion test (CCFT) assesses the activation and isometric endurance capacity of the deep longus capitis and colli muscles, and their interaction with the superficial sternocleidomastoid and anterior scalene muscles during the performance of five progressive stages of increasing cranio-cervical flexion range (for review see Jull et al.[54]) The test is a low-load test performed in supine lying with the patient guided to each stage by feedback from a pressure sensor (Stabilizer, Chattanooga USA) placed behind the neck (Fig. 20.5). When longus colli contracts, there is a slight flattening of the cervical curve, which is measured by the pressure sensor as an increase in pressure. The change in pressure registered by the pressure sensor essentially quantifies the deep neck flexor muscles'

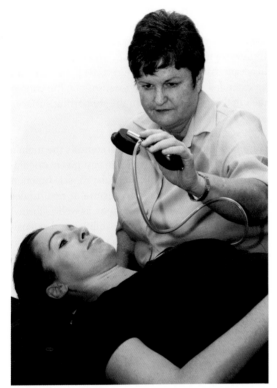

performance. With a baseline pressure of 20 mmHg, the patient attempts to progressively target 2 mmHg increments for a potential total of five stages, to a maximum 30 mmHg, using an appropriate cranio-cervical flexion action (rather than retraction).

The sternocleidomastoid and anterior scalene muscles flex the neck but not the head. Inappropriate activity in these two muscles is observed and palpated. The endurance capacity of the deep neck flexors is tested at functionally relevant low contractile intensities, at pressure targets that the patient can achieve with the appropriate movement pattern.[54] Asymptomatic individuals can target and maintain the contraction at the third or higher stages of the test, whereas individuals with neck pain can usually only achieve stages one or two.

Once the altered motor behavior has been re-educated and as the patient's pain level permits, assessment is progressed to test cervical flexor strength and endurance using a head lift test while maintaining a cranio-cervical flexion position. This is a test predominantly of the sternocleidomastoid and anterior scalene muscles, which provide over 80% of the cervical flexion torque.[55, 56] The deep neck flexors are too weak to cope with the level of load if the patient's chin protrudes when attempting to lift or hold the head position.[57]

Assessment of cervical extensors

Testing of the cervical extensors is guided by knowledge of the morphological change in these muscles in neck disorders. Extension is tested at the cranio-cervical and the cervical regions (C2–7).[58] The

Figure 20.5 (a) The cranio-cervical flexion test
The pressure sensor is placed suboccipitally and inflated to 20 mmHg. The patient is instructed to keep the superficial muscles relaxed and flex the upper cervical spine with a gentle nodding action, maintaining each target position, in increments of 2 mmHg, for 10 seconds (to a maximum of 30 mmHg). The therapist analyses the quality of cranio-cervical flexion movement through each stage of the test. Each stage should be performed with increasing ranges of flexion, which will not be observed if the patient substitutes with a retraction action. Any excessive use of the superficial flexors is observed or palpated
PHOTO COURTESY OF PROFESSOR GWENDOLEN JULL

(b) The face of the pressure sensor showing the marked 2 mmHg increments that the patient targets with craniocervical flexion

patient lies prone, propped on elbows, with the cranio-cervical region in a neutral position. While all extensors work in this position to support head mass, cranio-cervical extension (chin lift and lower) and rotation (30–40°) are tested to bias work towards the sub-occipital extensors and rotators respectively. Cervical extension is tested with the cranio-cervical region maintained in a neutral position (Fig. 20.6). The neutral head position is designed to take the

Figure 20.6 Testing cervical extensors. Note the maintenance of the cranio-cervical region in a neutral position in the test of cervical extension

emphasis from the superficial extensors attaching to the cranium with the aim of ensuring work of the deeper cervical group (semispinalis cervicis/multifidus).[59] In these tests, the quality, precision, and range of movement are assessed in tandem with patient reports of fatigue.

The second phase of testing is a more conventional measure of endurance using a modified Biering-Sorensen test[60] and is used when the patient's pain permits. The patient lies prone with their head supported over the end of the couch, such that the cranio-cervical and cervical regions are in a neutral position. Support is released and the time that the patient can hold the head/neck position without deviation is recorded. The test can be made more efficient (timewise) if a light weight (e.g. 1 kg) is placed on the head and baseline values are recorded. The test can be extended to the thoracic extensors by the patient raising their shoulders from the supporting surface.

Axio-scapular muscles

An interaction of muscle actions controls the mobile scapulae three-dimensionally at any given orientation. Clinical assessment of scapular muscle function involves analysis of scapular posture at rest, under light load, and with arm movement, as well as formal tests of the muscles' contractile abilities and extensibility as indicated. Variations in scapular orientation are common, and a process of examination is necessary to disentangle normal variations from scapular dysfunction contributing to the patient's neck pain. There are several potentially relevant shoulder girdle dysfunctions.[61]

A common presentation is observation of a downwardly rotated scapula (ski-slope appearance of line of the nape of the neck), which signals poor function of the three portions of the trapezius. The medial border of the scapula may be slightly winged (weakness of serratus anterior) and the inferior border prominent (excessive anterior tilt; weak lower trapezius). Resting tone of muscles such as the levator scapulae and rhomboids may be increased if compensating for poor upper trapezius function, and the muscles are often palpably tender.

An indication of a direct relationship between scapular posture, poor axio-scapular muscle function, and the neck pain syndrome can be gained from the response to a simple test.[58] The patient's baseline range and pain in cervical rotation is assessed, the clinician manually corrects scapular position and the patient repeats the cervical rotation movement

(Fig. 20.7). An improvement in range and pain and a reduction in palpable tenderness of the levator scapulae signal a role of scapular muscle dysfunction in the cervical pain state.

In further evaluation of dynamic control using the example of a downwardly rotated scapula, light isometric resistance to shoulder abduction (arm by the side) will subtly increase the scapular downward rotation if the upper trapezius is weak. Impaired trapezius and serratus anterior muscle function is revealed by a reduced ability to upwardly rotate, posteriorly tilt, and externally rotate the scapula during full arm elevation, and poor eccentric control with arm lowering. The endurance capacity of the scapular muscle synergy is tested in prone lying under low load, relevant to their postural function, using a modified Grade 3 muscle test for the lower trapezius.[62] The patient's scapula is passively placed in a neutral position on the posterior chest wall and the patient holds the position. The pattern of muscle activity is analyzed by observation and palpation, and signs of fatigue (tremor or loss of position) are noted. The capacity of the axio-scapular muscles to fix the scapula to the chest wall in a neutral postural position is also tested under load in the quadruped position. Substantial winging of the medial border of the scapula is an indication of poor axio-scapular muscle control, particularly of the serratus anterior muscle.

Length tests of axio-scapular muscles may be indicated for muscles such as levator scapulae, scalenes, and upper trapezius (if an upwardly rotated scapula is evident), as are length tests for pectoralis major and minor in the presence of a protracted scapula.

Muscle length tests should not be performed

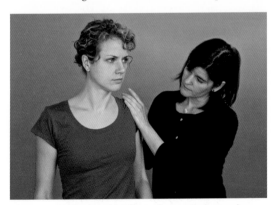

Figure 20.7 Testing the effect of corrected scapular position on range and pain in cervical rotation. Improved range and reduced pain indicates a role for aberrant scapular posture in the neck pain disorder

when the neck pain is acute or in the presence of any mechanosensitive neural tissue (notably scalenes and upper trapezius) as testing may also aggravate the neck disorder in these circumstances.

Muscle-length tests involve elongating a muscle by stabilizing at the origin and passively lengthening across the muscle to its insertion point. The goal is to evaluate whether a postural anomaly is being caused in part by altered muscle length or tone (as compared to, for example, stiff joints, weakness, or poor postural awareness).

Tests of the nervous system

As part of a comprehensive cervical spine assessment, conductive tests will include reflex testing, myotomal testing, and dermatomal examination (Chapter 11 e.g. upper limb neurodynamics test). Upper limb neurodynamics tests and nerve palpation can identify peripheral nerve mechanosensitivity.[63]

Tests of cervical somatosensory function

The somatosensory system is one of three components contributing to postural control (i.e. the control of both static and dynamic postural equilibrium)—the other two systems being the vestibular and visual systems. Cervicogenic dizziness can be caused by altered afferent input from the cervical spine in the presence of pain or impairment. Essentially similar to motion sickness, dizziness or nausea occurs in the presence of conflicting input between somatosensory (i.e. cervical afferent input), visual, and vestibular systems.[64]

The cervical muscles, and especially the suboccipital msucles, contain a high percentage of muscle spindles per gram of muscle, which relay somatosensory information to the central nervous system.[65, 66, 67] These afferents are important in the control of head and neck position. In addition, these afferents are intricately involved in linking information from the visual and vestibular systems.

In the presence of pain or impairment in the cervical spine, it is therefore not uncommon for patients to present with changes in the function of the somatosensory system, particularly after a whiplash injury. It has further been shown that if a patient reports dizziness in association with their neck pain the results of these tests of somatosensory function are even more pronounced.[68, 69, 70]

Three clinical tests for cervical somatosensory function are joint position sense (test of relocation error), standing balance, and eye movement control. Joint position error can be measured easily in a clinical setting by assessing the accuracy with which a patient returns to their natural head posture following a movement in any plane. The patient sits in a chair positioned 90 cm from a wall and a pre-calibrated target is attached to the wall.[71] A laser is attached to a head band that is mounted on the patient's head (Fig. 20.8a). The target is positioned on the wall, the center of which corresponds to the patient's neutral starting position. The patient closes his or her eyes, rotates the head fully to the right (Fig. 20.8b), then returns as closely as possible to the neutral position (Fig. 20.8c). The test is repeated at least three times in each direction. The distance of the laser light in the relocated position is measured from the original target position. An error of greater than 7.1 cm indicates impairment.[72] In addition to this measurement, the clinician notes any altered movement strategies or any searching for the neutral position.

Balance can be measured both statically and dynamically. Static balance is assessed by testing the patient's ability to stand in narrow stance (feet together). Tests are progressed as indicated from eyes open to eyes closed, from a firm surface to a soft surface such as dense foam, 10 cm thick. Stance positions are held for 30 seconds. Further test progression could include tandem stance or single-leg stance on a firm surface, again eyes open then eyes closed.[64] The clinician notes the quality of balance (e.g. increased sway) or failure to maintain the position for the 30 seconds. Dynamic balance tests could include the Dynamic Gait Index, the 10 m walk with head turns, or a step test.[64] Normative data for these tests varies with age.

There is not yet an objective test for clinically measuring smooth pursuit. However, qualitatively the clinician can assess eye movement control by watching the patient's eyes follow an object such as the clinician's finger through all visual fields while sitting with the head in a neutral position, noting any saccadic movements or production of dizziness. The test is then repeated with the trunk rotated 45° (the head remains in neutral) to see if a change in neck position affects eye movement control.[72] Additional tests for the visual system include gaze stability (moving the head while focused on a stationary target), saccadic movements (alternating gaze quickly between two targets), and eye–head coordination (a combination of looking to a target followed by moving the head to the same target).[64] These qualitative tests are similar to assessments of visual systems

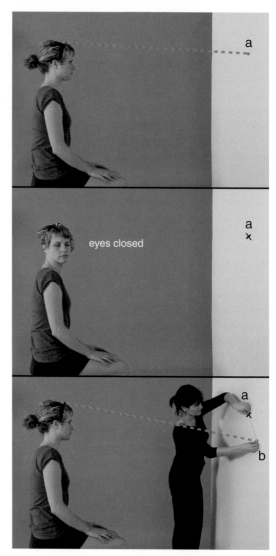

Figure 20.8 Testing cervical kinesthetic sense—joint position error

in neurological populations such as people who have had a stroke or persons with vestibular disorders.

There are no unique clinical tests for cervicogenic dizziness. Tests are generally provocative in nature and involve various combinations of the somatosensory, vestibular, and visual systems. Therefore it is a differential diagnosis, and requires a ruling-out of various other causes.[73] Use of a series of tests (including tests of the cervical somatosensory system, vestibular system, and other tests such as Rhomberg's test) can help rule out involvement of various systems, and if tests where only neck movements cause dizziness are positive, then one can commence treatment with a working hypothesis of cervicogenic dizziness. If tests of any of the other systems are positive, referral for appropriate investigations is warranted.

Vertebrobasilar insufficiency

Vertebral artery testing is generally performed in conjunction with appropriate questioning in the history, as a screen for the presence of symptoms possibly relating to risk of vertebrobasilar insufficiency. The testing is used as a premanipulative screen, and is also used when assessing dizziness to rule out vertebrobasilar insufficiency as a potential cause of the dizziness. In theory, a positive test (i.e. reproduction of symptoms such as dizziness, nausea, or nystagmus with sustained rotation or extension) could indicate vertebrobasilar compromise. A positive test indicates a contraindication to high-velocity thrust and end-range manual therapy techniques to minimize risk for development of ischemia, stroke, or damage to the vertebrobasilar complex.

However, clinical provocative tests for vertebrobasilar insufficiency have been shown to have poor validity and low sensitivity.[74–78] Case studies have been documented where vertebrobasilar insufficiency testing has been negative despite later adverse events.[75, 78] Attempts have been made to develop more sensitive tests in clinical settings (such as portable Doppler ultrasound), but to date such tests have not been shown to be reliable.[79]

Early signs of vertebral artery pathology may be commonly nothing more than neck or head pain, which may on initial assessment be misdiagnosed as mechanical neck pain.[75, 78] In the presence of positive findings on vertebrobasilar insufficiency testing, cervical manipulation is contraindicated. Even with negative findings, it is advisable to avoid using manipulation initially or in circumstances where the patient presents with an unexplained change in neck symptoms.[75] Beyond this, clinicians should consider assessment results and make an evidence-informed risk–benefit analysis.[78] The patient should always be included in treatment planning decisions regarding use of high-velocity manipulations.

Radiology

Radiological considerations are discussed in the box below.

Is C-spine X-ray degeneration associated with neck pain?

Regardless of injury, degenerative changes begin at a young age (early 20s) and correlate well with age.[27] In the older patient, osteoarthritis may be evident in the zygapophyseal joints. Risk of injury and/or pain is increased in people with pre-existing foraminal narrowing, such as in spondylosis/stenosis.[28, 29]

Importantly, however, degeneration of the cervical spine, as seen radiologically, does not correlate well with clinical findings of neck pain.[2] Nevertheless, in cases of trauma to the cervical spine, damage can be seen in soft tissues as well as cartilage of zygapophyseal joints.[27] This could eventually lead to radiographic findings of single-level degenerative changes, in comparison with multisegmental changes typically seen with aging (Fig. 20.9).

Most patients presenting with neck pain do not require diagnostic imaging. However, X-rays should be performed according to the Canadian c-spine rules (see Chapter 47). In the presence of hard neurological findings (suggesting nerve root involvement), CT scans or MRI can determine the extent of the pathology (see Chapter 12).

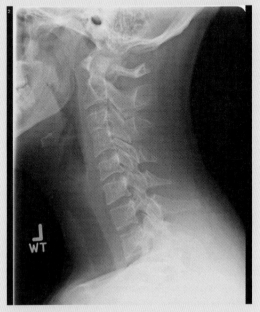

Figure 20.9 Degeneration of the cervical spine does not correlate well with clinical findings of neck pain

Treatment of neck pain

Effective management of the sportsperson or any member of the community with neck pain relies on a careful and thorough assessment as outlined above. Treatment strategies will depend on the diagnosis, acuity of the injury, severity and irritability of the condition, the nature of movement and muscle function impairments, and on the patient's goals and stated wishes (Chapter 3).

There are a number of different treatments available (Chapter 13). Physical therapies include postural re-education, therapeutic exercise, manual therapy, soft tissue techniques, neural tissue mobilization, and other pain relieving techniques such as dry needling and transcutaneous electrical stimulation (TENS). As most cervical injuries recover well with conservative treatment, it is rare that more invasive approaches (such as radiofrequency neurotomy or facet block injections) are required. These forms of treatment should only be considered in extreme cases of high-level persistent pain and protracted recovery where investigations confirm a local pain driver. In cases where there is a more widespread pain disorder or complicated psychosocial overlay, it may be advisable to avoid such invasive procedures.

Patients with neck pain often present with a complex set of physical findings, including articular dysfunction, deficits in muscle coordination and control, focal areas of increased muscle tone with trigger points, muscle shortening (or lengthening, as in trapezius), and reduced strength and endurance.[1, 53, 80–82] Treatment aims to relieve pain and restore normal joint range, muscle control, endurance, strength, and length, with the overall goal of restoring the patient's normal function and participation in sport, work, and social activities. Selection of specific treatment modalities is directed by current research, but equally relies on sound clinical reasoning, the experience of the clinician, and the unique features and goals of the patient being treated.[83]

PRACTICE PEARL

Multimodal treatment is the best approach to managing neck pain.

Education

Effective rehabilitation cannot be delivered in the absence of education to ensure the patient understands the nature of their pain or condition, agrees to the treatment plan, and diligently takes part in their recovery process.

Congruent with the notion that multimodal treatment is the best approach to managing neck pain,[4, 7, 8] a Cochrane review of 10 trials of patient education (only two of which were rated as high-quality) found that education, when delivered in isolation, was not an effective treatment for neck pain.[84]

Posture

Patients with mechanical neck pain typically have a postural component to their condition. Posture may be a contributing factor to the patient's current episode, for example, poor posture at a work station may lead to onset of neck pain over time. Alternatively, postural changes may follow the onset of pain or injury, such as when weakness of the neck musculature or altered postural awareness reduces the patient's ability to maintain good posture.

Postural abnormalities may be either adaptive (e.g. adopting certain positions in order to achieve relief of pain, for example, a patient may hold their elbow bent and arm by their side in the presence of a sensitive peripheral nerve), or maladaptive (the patient tends to slouch with head-forward posture, resulting in extension in the upper cervical region, which aggravates the painful facet joints). In either case, it is important to identify postural abnormalities that may be contributing to, or easing, current symptoms. By doing so, the clinician can help the individual find effective postures for symptom control and healing in the early stages of rehabilitation, as well as improve posture in the long term, and so minimize risk of future recurrence. In some patients, posture is the primary cause of their pain—the "cervical postural syndrome."

The cervical postural syndrome is characterized by a typical posture of protruding chin and increased upper cervical lordosis (Fig. 20.10). The patient often has reduced thoracic extension, rounded shoulders, short pectoral muscles, restricted shoulder movements, and forward carriage of the head. The patient may complain of either a burning or aching pain across the shoulders and neck, or suboccipital pain around the attachment of the trapezius and the upper cervical extensors.

Pain is aggravated by prolonged static postures and is typically relieved by movement. It may be seen in sportspeople such as cyclists or baseball catchers, whose sport requires them to adopt prolonged postures. Similar problems occur in the workplace, among people working at a computer, painters, and production line workers. Examination

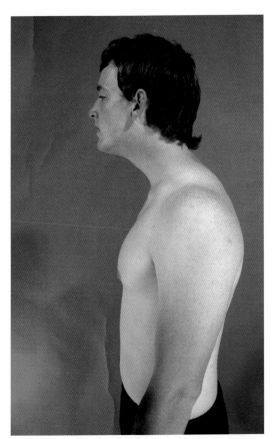

Figure 20.10 Poor cervical posture showing the chin protruding and increased upper cervical lordosis

Postural correction begins with education. Long-term postural improvements require buy-in by the patient, who must be diligent. In addition to education, treatment addresses the specific deficits, so may include a combination of specific exercises, manual therapy, soft tissue techniques, neural tissue mobilization, or other pain-relieving techniques.

Taping can provide proprioceptive feedback for patients with postural problems in the initial stages of re-education (Fig. 20.11). Biofeedback may be helpful on an intermittent basis in improving the patient's body awareness, and could include mirrors, photographs, video analysis (especially for dynamic postures such as running, throwing a ball, or other sport specific task), or EMG biofeedback. In addition to treatment aimed at intrinsic factors, give consideration to the patient's environment through ergonomic assessment of work stations or sports equipment (e.g. bicycle alignment).

usually reveals hypomobility of the lower cervical and upper thoracic regions with hypertonicity and the presence of trigger points in the muscles. There is weakness of the deep neck flexors and serratus anterior, as well as the mid and lower trapezius and/or rhomboids. However, protective/adaptive postures may be in response to adverse nerve mechanosensitivity, with reduced mobility evident in the upper limb neurodynamic tests.

To develop a treatment plan, the clinician must first assess whether the patient is able to correct posture with cueing alone. In patients who are unable to correct their posture, look for a reason why this is the case. Reasons include poor patterns of postural muscle use, muscle "tightness" (e.g. short or hypertonic suboccipital muscles), poor body awareness, unwillingness due to pain, and the presence of regional joint stiffness. Identifying the specific reasons for poor posture will direct the treatment approach.

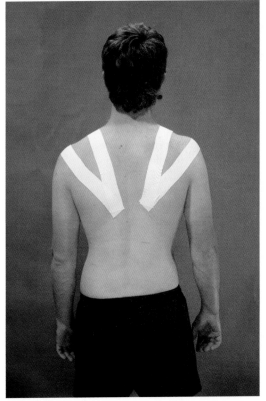

Figure 20.11 An example of taping for improved scapular positioning

Exercise therapy

Exercise is a vital component of the treatment of the patient with neck pain.

Exercise alone has beneficial effects, but superior effects come when exercise is combined with manual therapy.[85]

Clinicians should prescribe exercises carefully, with the patient's unique assessment findings guiding decision making regarding exercise selection and dosage. Several types of exercise are often employed in the rehabilitation of the patient with neck pain, including rehabilitation of muscle function, muscle lengthening exercises, and active exercise, to restore cervical range of movement.

Therapeutic exercise for the muscle system is prescribed in two stages, based on increasing knowledge of the changes in muscle behavior and function with neck pain, and the specificity of effect of exercise methods:[32, 86, 87]

- Stage 1 is concerned with rehabilitation of muscle control. It aims to improve the control capacity of the deep postural muscles, train the coordination between the layers of the neck muscles and axio-scapular muscles, and train muscle control within functional and work activities.
- Stage 2 addresses muscle strength and endurance and is commenced once the altered behavior between the deep and superficial neck muscles and axio-scapular muscles has been addressed.

As the goal of therapeutic exercise is to restore normal motor control, function, and quality of movement, the exercises should challenge the patient, yet be performed with correct technique and without aggravation of symptoms, especially in the acute stages of recovery. Pain can inhibit the motor learning process.[88] The neck flexors, extensors, and axio-scapular muscles may all require attention, and exercise prescription is based on assessment findings.

Motor control exercises

Neck flexors

Stage 1 training for the neck flexor muscles addresses any altered behaviors between the deep and superficial muscles and the low-level endurance capacity of the deep neck flexors for their role in segmental support and control of posture. Often the patient needs to learn the correct movement of cranio-cervical flexion in the supine position in preparation for training the

low-level endurance of the deep flexors for their functional role. This can be achieved by practice using a large excursion of head rotation from extension to flexion. The patient gains feedback of the correct movement by feeling the back of the head sliding up and down the bed (Fig. 20.5), rather than just pressure on the back of the head if a poor retraction pattern is used. The movement can be facilitated with appropriate eye movement. The patient trains to perform the movement with appropriate deep muscle activity and palpates the superficial sternocleidomastoid and anterior scalene muscles to ensure that they are relaxed throughout the entire excursion of movement (Fig. 20.12a on page 330).

Once the correct movement is attained, the endurance of the deep neck flexors is trained. This is facilitated by the use of the pressure sensor placed behind the neck (Fig. 20.6) which, together with self-palpation for relaxed sternocleidomastoid and anterior scalene muscles, informs the patient of their ability to perform and hold a contraction of the deep neck flexors. The patient practices with the feedback under the clinician's supervision, but also learns the sensation of the movement and holding contraction so that they can practice at home without the external feedback.[58] Formal training should continue until the patient can perform 10 repetitions of 10 second holds at each of the five pressure increments from the baseline of 20 mmHg to the maximum of 30 mmHg.

Functional training should also commence immediately so that, in the motor learning process, the patient can perform multiple repetitions of the muscle contraction conveniently during the day. The deep neck flexors are activated when the patient assumes an upright neutral postural position[87] and this can be augmented by the patient attempting to lift the base of their skull off the top of their neck in a neck lengthening maneuver.[89, 90] Retraining spinal posture incorporating good lumbopelvic position and control[91] is a vital aspect of any exercise program for neck pain disorders.

Once this goal for the deep neck flexors has been achieved, the exercise program is progressed to Stage 2 to train neck flexor endurance and strength at progressive contraction intensities. This is achieved by progressively increasing the gravitational load of a head lift exercise. Initially, the patient sits on a chair placed close to a wall with the head resting on the wall. The position of cranio-cervical flexion is preset by sliding the back of the head up the wall, and then head weight is supported just off the wall (Fig. 20.12b). The position is held up to a maximum of 10 seconds (aim for 10 repetitions). Control of chin position is essential. The load is increased by progressively moving the chair further from the wall and ultimately changing the position to supine with the support of two pillows. Strengthening is progressed as appropriate to the individual patient's requirement for work or sport (compare strength requirements for office workers versus sports such as wrestling, rugby, American football, and other contact sports). In addition to formal strength training, correct interaction between the deep and superficial flexors is trained throughout range of movement, particularly the antigravity control of head extension or any combined movement that the patient requires functionally for work.

Neck extensors

Stage 1 training for the neck extensors is commenced either in the prone on elbows or the quadruped position, depending on the patient's ability to control scapular/trunk posture. The patient trains the movements of cranio-cervical extension and rotation and cervical extension (C2–7) until they can perform three sets of 10 repetitions through a full excursion of movement without fatigue (Fig. 20.7). Instructing the patient to read an imaginary book (eye focus down) while he or she curls the head and neck backward maintains the cranio-cervical region in a neutral position and facilitates the desired cervical extension. Stage 2 training involves adding load, notably to the cervical extension exercise. Progressive weights (commencing with 0.5 kg) can be attached to headgear (e.g. a bike helmet) for this purpose if neck specific resistance equipment is not available.

Axio-scapular muscles

Stage 1 training focuses initially on improving the activation and endurance capacity of the trapezius and serratus anterior muscles, as well as re-educating the axio-scapular muscles functionally to provide adequate scapular stability in posture and during arm movements. In the motor relearning phase, the lower portion of trapezius can be targeted with the patient in a side-lying position (rather than prone [for ease of practice at home]) with the arm supported on pillows in approximately 140° elevation (Fig. 20.12c). The patient practices drawing the scapula diagonally across the chest wall and holding the position for 10 seconds (10 repetitions). The serratus anterior is formally trained with a scapular protraction exercise,

either in a standing against a wall or in a prone on elbows position. Concomitantly, patients learn and train to hold their scapulae in a neutral position on the chest wall in sitting and standing postures. Once patients can control "ideal" static scapular posture, the scapular control is re-educated for functions requiring less than 30° elevation (control of the scapula in a neutral position), during arm movement through range and, importantly, in sport- or occupation-specific arm postures and movements.

Stage 2 training introduces load, but emphasis must be placed on control of both spinal and scapular posture in any free-weight or equipment-based exercise. Strengthening exercises should commence with light loads, concentrating on spinal and scapular control with both concentric and eccentric arm loading. Strengthening exercises also include task specificity—a focus on specific upper limb movements that are relevant to the individual's work or sport. Load is progressed, but the emphasis is always placed on control of scapular and spinal posture and, indeed, all body segments.

Stretching

Muscle stretching exercises are often prescribed for patients with neck pain, stiffness, and reduced range of movement, but should only be included when indicated by the assessment findings and with due consideration to why a muscle is apparently tight or the movement limited.

> Muscle stretching is not indicated when the apparent "tightness" of the muscle is a protective response for neural tissue mechanosensitivity (upper trapezius and scalene muscles), acute pain, potential segmental instability, or marked segmental pathology.

The upper trapezius may have tender areas with a feeling of tightness reported by the patient, but in the presence of a downwardly rotated scapula, the muscle is lengthened rather than shortened. In this latter situation, levator scapulae may be tight. While stretching the levator scapulae may give temporary relief of pain or tightness, permanent change in length and reduction of tone is likely only achieved when function is restored to the tripartite trapezius and serratus anterior muscles. Muscles that may require lengthening exercises in association with poor scapular postural position are the pectoralis minor and major muscles.

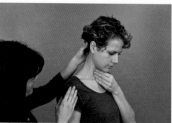

Figure 20.12 (a) Training the deep cervical flexors in the initial motor relearning stage. The patient concentrates on performing the correct movement and palpates to ensure no dominant activity in the superficial flexors. Inner range contractions are held to improve endurance capacity of these muscles at contraction intensities in line with those required in sitting and standing postures. The pressure biofeedback is used only to teach the patient the holding contraction and to monitor progression of the exercise

(b) Head lifts from the wall. Note the patient must control the cranio-cervical flexion position in this initial strengthening exercise in Stage 2 training

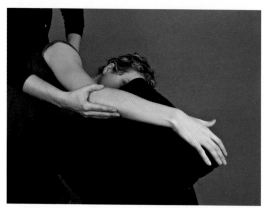

(c) Side-lying scapular setting for the early training of the lower trapezius muscle in the motor relearning stage

Range of motion exercises

Range of motion exercises are typically dynamic in nature and aim to move the cervical spine, thoracic spine, and/or upper extremities through functional planes of movement. Range of motion exercises have several indications—to assist pain control, to provide assurance to the patient that it is safe to move, to prevent loss of range of motion secondary to disuse, to improve joint mobility, and to maintain gains in motion achieved with manual therapy treatment. Active exercises should produce minimal or negligible pain and be designed to target the hypomobile segments/regions as much as possible. For example, practicing rotation in neck flexion will better target a restriction of C1–2 rotation. The use of assistive straps (Fig. 20.13) as advocated by Mulligan will helps focus the movement to specific cervical segments.[92] Combined arm elevation and cervical rotation will help mobilize the cervico-thoracic region. Carefully designed exercises will have better effect.

330

Figure 20.13 Mulligan self-applied rotation mobilization with a self-assistive strap

Active range of motion exercises can be performed using 5–10 repetitions several times per day.

Manual therapy

Manual therapy is indicated as a treatment method for neck pain in situations where the joint and related structures are believed to be a source of pain, and also where joint play is limited (i.e. hypomobility). Hypomobility in the cervical segments can be caused by local muscle spasm, localized swelling, or fibrous adhesions. Hypermobility could be related to local

soft tissue damage. Manual examination can reasonably accurately identify the segmental level responsible for a patient's complaint.[93, 94] Manual therapy is not indicated for hypermobile joints, except as a gentle approach to manage pain.

 Techniques generally fall under the categories of mobilization or manipulation.

A recent Cochrane review of 27 studies found moderate-quality evidence to support the use of both mobilization and manipulation for subacute and chronic neck pain[95]. There was low-quality evidence to support thoracic manipulation for acute neck pain, and low-quality evidence suggesting that mobilization techniques were of similar benefit to acupuncture in treating pain and function.[7] Thoracic spine manipulation in conjunction with exercise may speed recovery from non-specific neck pain over exercise alone.[95]

Clinicians today have many theoretical models and clinical approaches to guide specific choice of technique (e.g. Maitland, Kaltenborn, Mulligan, McKenzie approaches). Choice of technique depends on the examination findings, patho-anatomical diagnosis, clinician's skills and experience, patient wishes, and response to treatment. In the clinic, it is important to continuously evaluate effectiveness of a given technique by assessing effect on symptoms, clinical findings, and function.

A number of different mobilization techniques are used in the treatment of neck pain, including purely passive mobilization and passive mobilization in association with active movement. Possible progressions of passive mobilization include a change in the position in which the joint is mobilized, the grade of mobilization, the speed and amplitude of the technique, the amount of compression, and the use of combined movements.

A highly irritable condition should be treated with techniques that do not aggravate the condition. It is often helpful to begin with accessory movements performed in a neutral position or a position of ease, short of discomfort.

Progressive grades of mobilization or manipulation can be used in non-irritable conditions if loss of motion and increased tissue resistance are the primary problems. Sustained natural apophyseal glides (SNAGs)[96] are an effective treatment for cervicogenic dizziness, and they also improve pain levels and disability. These findings were maintained at

12-week follow-up.[97] Similar techniques are effective as a self-applied technique in the management of cervicogenic headache of C1–2 origin.[98]

Manipulation

A manipulation may be performed to reduce pain and restore joint mobility. Pre-screening for indicators of vascular compromise, including holding the neck in the manipulation position, should be performed prior to cervical spine manipulations. Cervical manipulation has not been shown to be more effective (in terms of speed of recovery) than mobilization on patients with neck pain of less than three months' duration, an important consideration given the very rare but inherent risks associated with cervical manipulations.[99] In addition, the results of preliminary studies regarding the alternative use of thoracic manipulations suggest that the use of cervical manipulations may be unnecessary.[95] Having stated this, the choice of manipulative techniques in recent years has moved away from riskier end-of-range cervical rotation positions and tends to be more localized, thus reducing stress at the vertebral artery.[100]

Soft tissue techniques

Soft tissue techniques may be used for the treatment of increased local muscle tone or trigger points, muscle shortening, scar tissue adhesions, fascial thickening or tightness, edema, or pain. They may be beneficial in helping the patient relax prior to performing joint mobilizations or manipulations. However, it is important to maintain perspective regarding the use of soft tissue techniques. These techniques may assist with short-term palliative treatment; however, they should only constitute a small part of the management program. To date there is limited evidence that these techniques address symptoms in the long term or correct impairments. Techniques should be carefully selected and used as an adjunct to modalities such as exercise and manual therapy, to address long-term rehabilitation objectives.

Neural tissue mobilization

Increased neural mechanosensitivity may be detected by neurodynamic tests such as the upper limb neurodynamic tests or passive neck flexion (Chapter 11). These tests apply a longitudinal mechanical stimulus to test the compliance of the nerve trunks to changes in their anatomical course.[101] If neurodynamic tests reproduce the patient's typical symptoms, and the patient reports tenderness on palpation of the affected peripheral nerves, peripheral nerve sensitization may be present.[102] In this case, direct neural tissue gliding techniques can be trialed in conjunction with treatment of the interfacing structures (i.e. joints, muscles, fascia, and skin).[63] Neural tissue mobilization techniques must be used with due caution in the presence of positive signs for impaired nerve conduction that might suggest nerve compression/denervation.

Biomechanical studies support current trends away from using neural stretching techniques, or "tensioners," toward prescription of techniques which move the nerve—"sliders."[103] Sliders use combinations of movements to lengthen a nerve bed across one joint while shortening the nerve bed of an adjacent joint, resulting in maximum nerve excursion with minimal nerve strain.[103, 104] This is a particularly beneficial approach with highly irritable nerves.[103] With peripheral nerve sensitization (Chapter 6), neural glides (Chapter 13) can help reduce neural tissue sensitivity and restore neural tissue mobility.

Dry needling

Needling techniques such as acupuncture (traditional Chinese or Western practice) and intramuscular stimulation are becoming more popular as a treatment adjunct, especially for patients who have chronic neck pain. Available evidence suggests acupuncture and electroacupuncture may improve pain compared with "wait and see" and certain sham treatments, although some studies have found no difference between conventional points compared to non-specific points on the neck.[105, 106, 107] There may also be a small but significant reduction in disability.[105] A systematic review concluded that there was an overall lack of rigorous evidence to support whether or not dry needling of trigger points was effective.[108] Research is also limited in the area of intramuscular stimulation, with two studies involving cervical spine myofascial pain reporting improvements in pain;[109, 110] one of these also showed improvement in cervical range of motion and depressive symptoms following treatment.[110]

Stress management

Comprehensive treatment is provided within a biopsychosocial approach (Fig. 20.2) which involves stepping back and recognizing the whole person. Following neck injuries, especially if the mechanism of injury was traumatic, it is not uncommon to identify a myriad of psychosocial features that may have contributed to, or are a direct result of, the patient's current presentation. Stress may lead to increased muscle tension and postural abnormalities that can accentuate physical findings in the cervical spine. Breathing patterns may change, resulting in increased use of the accessory muscles of respiration, compounding stresses on muscles already shown to be overactive following neck injuries. In major traumatic injuries, patients may report nightmares or have fears of returning to their previous activities (e.g. a roofer who fell and now is fearful of climbing ladders; a pilot who is now very anxious when flying).

Response to pain and injury varies widely among individuals (Chapter 6), and psychological features may be a driver of persistent pain or may moderate the effect of physical treatments. Stressors are numerous and are far beyond the scope of this chapter. Developing the skills to identify the many factors influencing a patient's recovery is crucial. Stress management or targeted psychological management may play an important role in the treatment of some patients with neck pain. Widely used relaxation techniques include breathing exercises, yoga, meditation, and relaxation massage. In some cases, referral to a health psychologist for cognitive behavioral therapy may be indicated.

Neck pain syndromes

Most neck pain is regarded as non-specific in the absence of radiological evidence of relevant pathoanatomy. However, commonly recognized "syndromes" causing neck pain include the cervical postural syndrome (described above), acute wry neck, acceleration–deceleration injury, acute nerve root pain, and stingers/burners in the athletic population.

Acute wry neck

The acute wry neck is characterized by a sudden onset of sharp neck pain with protective deformity and limitation of movement. It typically occurs either after a sudden, quick movement or on waking. There may have been unusual movements or prolonged abnormal postures prior to the onset of pain. The zygapophyseal joint and the diskogenic wry neck are the two most common types of acute wry neck. They can usually be differentiated by the history and examination.

Zygapophyseal wry neck

The zygapophyseal wry neck occurs more frequently in children and young adults, most commonly at the C2–3 level.[111] It is commonly associated with a sudden movement resulting in sharp pain. Locking of C0–1 or C1–2 may involve some trauma, in which case the craniovertebral ligaments should be assessed. The patient typically presents with an antalgic posture—usually lateral flexion away from the side of the damaged joint and slight flexion. The patient is unable to correct the abnormal posture due to pain and muscle spasm.

Active movements are markedly limited due to muscle spasm. Soft tissue techniques, joint mobilization, and/or manipulation can be effective. Lateral flexion, or manual traction in the line of the deformity are often the first techniques employed. Ice, heat, ultrasound or electrotherapeutic modalities may be an effective adjunct to treatment. Range of motion may not be fully restored immediately following manual therapy, possibly due to the presence of muscle spasm or swelling. A home exercise program should be prescribed including gentle range of motion and motor control exercises, and advice should be given regarding activities to avoid and also sleep hygiene, to encourage optimal cervical spine support.

Diskogenic wry neck

The diskogenic wry neck usually has a more gradual onset than the zygapophyseal wry neck; it classically occurs when waking after a long sleep in an abnormal posture. It tends to occur in an older age group (e.g. middle-aged adults) and pain is often felt in the lower cervical or upper thoracic region. Pain often feels deep and the patient typically presents with a lateral flexion deformity with some rotation and possibly flexion. There may be some radiation of pain to the medial scapular region[112] and the patient may have a history of degenerative joint disease in the lower cervical spine.

It is important to differentiate this condition from a locked zygapophyseal joint, as treatment that is appropriate for the zygapophyseal wry neck (such as manipulation) may seriously aggravate the diskogenic wry neck.

Treatment of the diskogenic wry neck often begins in a position of ease with gentle manual therapy techniques such as segmental rotation or cervical traction. Temporary use of a soft collar may provide some relief. Soft tissue techniques and electrotherapeutic modalities may be beneficial in the very early stages of treatment for managing pain or muscle spasm. Postural retraining and motor control exercises should begin as soon as they can be tolerated.

Acceleration–deceleration injury

Acute acceleration/deceleration injury to the cervical spine is a common injury in motor vehicle accidents (MVA). It can also occur in sports when the cervical spine is suddenly extended in contact with the ground or by a direct blow from an opponent. This syndrome is commonly known as "whiplash," or "whiplash associated disorders." Whiplash is described by the Quebec Task Force as "an acceleration–deceleration mechanism of energy transfer to the neck. It may result from rear-end or side-impact motor vehicle collisions, but can also occur with diving or other mishaps. The impact may result in bony or soft-tissue injuries (whiplash injury), which in turn may lead to a variety of clinical manifestations (whiplash associated disorders [WAD])."[9]

The mechanism of injury that results in a whiplash type of injury from an MVA involves two factors—force vector and a change in velocity—and the entire event typically lasts no more than 450 ms. In fact, in MVAs the injury is believed to occur more specifically somewhere between 60 and 100 ms following initial impact.

The lower cervical spine and upper thoracic spine experience extension, while the upper cervical spine experiences flexion, resulting in a non-physiological "S" shape through the neck. Rather than gliding and extending physiologically, an abnormal axis of rotation results in joint compression, often at the C5–6 and C2–3 zygapophyseal joints. Since postural reflexes typically take about 100 ms to respond, and voluntary responses about 250 ms, the cervical spine is passively subjected to the insulting forces with no ability to actively protect itself.[113–117]

As a result of research into the mechanics of whiplash injury, clarification has also emerged regarding the threshold for injury which influences current beliefs regarding "low-velocity impacts." Specifically, symptoms have been reported with a change in velocity of as little as 8 km/hr in "rear-end" directed vectors.[113]

The most common symptoms of whiplash include neck pain, headache, and decreased neck mobility, and would thus be graded as WAD I or II according to the Quebec Task Force classification system.[9, 118, 119]

If there are hard neurological signs, WAD III is the grade assigned. Occasionally, this mechanism of injury results in cervical spine fracture (Chapter 47), in which case it is classified as WAD IV.[9]

The patient may not feel pain immediately post injury; however, symptoms may increase gradually in the 48 hours following injury.[9] Muscles, joints (including ligaments), and neural tissue may all be affected. Early mobilization is recommended in the management of acute whiplash, including education and spinal range of motion exercises within a comfortable range. After the acute phase, treatment should focus on increasing function and return to normal activity as soon as possible. A multimodal approach to treatment including therapeutic exercise, manual therapy, and education is the best-evidence approach to effective and timely recovery from WAD.[4, 7, 8]

Cervicogenic headache

Cervicogenic headaches (headaches secondary to a cervical musculoskeletal disorder) constitute approximately 14–18% of all frequent intermittent headaches[120, 121] and are classically accompanied by neck pain and stiffness.[122, 123] The reader is encouraged to read Chapter 18 regarding the many varieties of headaches, as a patient with neck pain caused by trauma may present with headache; however, the headache is not necessarily cervicogenic.[124, 125] Effective treatment relies on accurate diagnosis of the source of the headache.[126–128]

Cervicogenic headache is associated with movement relating to joint and muscle impairment.[35] Research has shown that the flexion rotation test is a valid and reliable test for diagnosing cervicogenic headache of C1–2 origin (Fig. 20.4), with high sensitivity and specificity.[24, 128] Results of this test are not influenced by age, gender, sleep postures, or hand dominance; however, pain lower in the neck may influence results.[129]

Acute nerve root pain

Acute cervical nerve root pain is characterized by moderate-to-severe arm pain which is irritable. Neck pain may or may not be a feature. The pain is aggravated by movements of the cervical spine that reduce the size of the intervertebral foramen (ipsilateral extension, rotation, cervical compression, Spurling's test[130]) or any movement or posture that increases tension on the nerve root (cervical contralateral side flexion, ipsilateral shoulder depression, arm movements such as shoulder abduction or elbow extension). The pain may be eased by cervical flexion or positions that decrease tension on the nerve root (e.g. arm cradled or overhead). There may be associated sensory symptoms, such as pins and needles, paresthesia and muscle weakness, and possibly altered reflexes. In the presence of signs of impaired conduction, further medical investigation should be conducted to rule out space-occupying lesions such as a large disk injury. Nerve root pain may occur as the result of compromise of the intervertebral foramen due to the presence of osteophytes (zygapophyseal or uncovertebral joints), disk changes, spondylosis, or inflammation of a nearby structure. Modified mechanosensitivity tests should be performed with caution if the clinician suspects nerve root compression/denervation, and nerve palpation may be used to assess sensitivity.

Treatment consists of techniques that open up the foramen; however, care must be taken as this condition is usually irritable. High-velocity manipulation is contraindicated. Sustained traction in the position of ease can be effective. Neural tissue mobilizations such as "sliders" may be helpful, and can be applied indirectly (e.g. opposite arm) if the patient cannot tolerate the affected side. Treatment should include discussion of sleeping positions, and typical postures such as sitting should be assessed; corrective cues should be given to minimize strain on the nerve bed. Pain relief is a primary aim of management in the acute stage. Local measures to reduce pain and inflammation include ice, heat, and electrotherapeutic modalities. The patient frequently requires adequate analgesic medication. Muscular deficits and other impairments can be treated as soon as possible (using modified positions if necessary); however, pain relief is the immediate and primary aim.

Stingers or burners

The "stinger" or "burner" phenomenon is seen frequently in American football and rugby, and less often in other contact sports. The player experiences transient upper extremity burning-type pain that may also be accompanied by paresthesia and/or weakness. Symptoms may be localized to the neck or may radiate to the arm and hand. There are two mechanisms of injury that can cause a neuropraxia—tensile (traction) and compressive:

- Downward displacement of the shoulder with concomitant contralateral side flexion of the neck can result in a traction injury to either the cervical nerve root or the brachial plexus.

- More commonly, cervical extension and ipsilateral side flexion can result in a compression-type injury; a direct blow to the brachial plexus may also result in a compressive injury.[131, 132]

The symptoms are usually transient, but persistent neurological dysfunction and recurrent stingers may occur.

Most stingers/burners are thought to involve the upper trunk (C5, C6) of the brachial plexus, although it is often difficult to localize the source of the injury. One study showed that footballers with recurrent or chronic burner syndromes had nerve root compression in the intervertebral foramina secondary to disk disease.[131] A high incidence of cervical canal stenosis was found in this group.

Assessment of an acute stinger involves first ruling out more serious injury such as spinal cord or brain involvement, fracture, or vascular injury.[133] On-field spinal precautions should be used in the presence of neck pain, positive neurological findings, or loss of consciousness.[132] Consideration can be given to clearing the athlete with no previous history of stingers to return to play immediately if symptoms resolve quickly with associated full range of motion, normal neurovascular findings, and negative Spurling's test. However, in the presence of any positive findings or impairments, the player should not return to the game, and should be further assessed and monitored over the following days. Diagnostic imaging should be requested in the presence of positive neurological findings or if fracture or instability are suspected.[132] The athlete should be excluded from sport until the symptoms resolve fully.[134] For serious injuries, refer to Chapter 47 regarding appropriate first aid and urgent care.

In most uncomplicated stingers, symptoms usually resolve over a varying period of time from minutes to days. Treatment should be aimed at specific findings on assessment.[132] A gentle exercise program that does not bring on typical symptoms may be started early on, with care to avoid positions that might aggravate the nerve. As in all cases of nerve damage, there will be an element of the recovery that is simply time- and rest-dependent, and treatment cannot speed this process (with the exception of avoiding aggravating positions that might delay recovery further). In the event of recurrent stingers, consideration may have to be given to removing the player from contact sports altogether.[133, 134]

Conclusion

Non-specific neck pain can arise under both traumatic and non-traumatic conditions.

 A best-evidence approach to treatment includes careful assessment of the patient and treatment with a multimodal approach.

Education, correction of sport or workplace drivers of abnormal strain, manual therapy, and therapeutic exercise are the main approaches to management. Management is set within a biopsychosocial model and consideration must be given to additional psychosocial factors influencing pain and treatment outcome when indicated. In rare instances where assessment findings suggest involvement of other systems (such as neurological, vestibular, or vascular), further investigations are warranted.

📄 RECOMMENDED READING

Butler D. *The sensitive nervous system*. Adelaide: NOI Group Publications, 2000.

Jull G, Sterling M, Falla D et al. *Whiplash, headache and neck pain: research based directions for physical therapies*. Edinburgh: Elsevier–Churchill Livingstone, Edinburgh, 2008.

Kristjansson E, Treleaven J. Sensorimotor function and dizziness in neck pain: implications for assessment and management. *J Orthop Sports Phys Ther* 2009;39(5):364–77.

Standaert CJ, Herring SA. Expert opinion and controversies in musculoskeletal and sports medicine: stingers. *Arch Phys Med Rehabil* 2009;90(3):402–6.

Rihn JA, Anderson DT, Lamb K et al. Cervical spine injuries in American football. *Sports Med* 2009;39(9):697–708.

Hall CM, Brody LT. *Therapeutic exercise: moving toward function*. Philadelphia: Lippincott Williams & Wilkins, 2005.

Moseley GL. *Painful yarns: metaphors and stories to help understand the biology of pain*. Canberra: Dancing Giraffe Press, 2007.

📄 REFERENCES

1. Jull G, Sterling M. Bring back the biopsychosocial model for neck pain disorders. *Man Ther* 2009;14(2):117–18.

2. Haldeman S, Carroll L, Cassidy JD. Findings from the bone and joint decade 2000 to 2010 task force on neck pain and its associated disorders. *J Occup Environ Med* 2010;52(4):424–7.

3. World Health Organization. *International Classification of Functioning, Disability and Health (ICF)*. Geneva: World Health Organization, 2010.

4. Childs JD, Cleland JA, Elliott JM et al. Neck pain: clinical practice guidelines linked to the International Classification of Functioning, Disability, and Health from the Orthopedic Section of the American Physical Therapy Association. Erratum appears in J Orthop Sports Phys Ther. 2009 Apr;39(4):297]. *J Orthop Sports Phys Ther* 2008;38(9):A1–34.

5. Carroll LJP, Hogg-Johnson SP, van der Velde GDC et al. Course and prognostic factors for neck pain in the general population: results of the bone and joint decade 2000–2010 task force on neck pain and its associated disorders. *Spine* 2008;33(4S) (Supplement):S75–82.

6. Sterling M, Jull G, Vicenzino B et al. Physical and psychological factors predict outcome following whiplash injury. *Pain* 2005;114(1–2):141–8.

7. Gross A, Miller J, D'Sylva J et al. Manipulation or mobilisation for neck pain: a Cochrane review. *Man Ther* 2010;15(4):315–33.

8. Hoving JL, de Vet HCW, Koes BW et al. Manual therapy, physical therapy, or continued care by the general practitioner for patients with neck pain: long-term results from a pragmatic randomized clinical trial. *Clin J Pain* 2006;22(4):370–7.

9. Spitzer WO, Skovron ML, Salmi LR et al. Scientific monograph of the Quebec Task Force on Whiplash-Associated Disorders: redefining "whiplash" and its management. *Spine* 1995;20(8 Suppl):S1–73.

10. McKenzie R, May S. *The cervical and thoracic spine. mechanical diagnosis and therapy*. Raumati Beach, New Zealand: Spinal Publications, 2006.

11. Kitagawa T, Fujiwara A, Kobayashi N et al. Morphologic changes in the cervical neural foramen due to flexion and extension: in vivo imaging study. *Spine* 2004;29(24):2821–5.

12. Cusick JF, Pintar FA, Yoganandan N. Whiplash syndrome: kinematic factors influencing pain patterns. *Spine* 2001;26(11):1252–8.

13. Westaway MD, Stratford PW, Binkley JM. The patient-specific functional scale: validation of its use in persons

with neck dysfunction. *J Orthop Sports Phys Ther* 1998;27(5):331–8.

14. Vernon H, Mior S. The Neck Disability Index: a study of reliability and validity.[Erratum appears in *J Manipulative Physiol Ther* 1992 Jan;15(1):followi]. *J Manipulative Physiol Ther* 1991;14(7):409–15.

15. Scholten-Peeters GG, Bekkering GE, Verhagen AP et al. Clinical practice guideline for the physiotherapy of patients with whiplash-associated disorders. *Spine* 2002;27(4):412–22.

16. Kamper SJ, Rebbeck TJ, Maher CG et al. Course and prognostic factors of whiplash: a systematic review and meta-analysis. *Pain* 2008;138(3):617–29.

17. Sterling M, Jull G, Kenardy J. Physical and psychological factors maintain long-term predictive capacity post-whiplash injury. *Pain* 2006;122(1–2):102–8.

18. Walton DM, Pretty J, MacDermid JC et al. Risk factors for persistent problems following whiplash injury: results of a systematic review and meta-analysis. *J Orthop Sports Phys Ther* 2009;39(5):334–50.

19. Leigh TA, Smith C, Wade B et al. *Clinical practice guidelines for the physiotherapy treatment of whiplash associated disorders.* University of British Columbia, 2004.

20. Vernon H. The neck disability index: patient assessment and outcome monitoring in whiplash. *J Musculoskel Pain* 1996;4:95–104.

21. Cleland JA, Childs JD, Whitman JM. Psychometric properties of the Neck Disability Index and Numeric Pain Rating Scale in patients with mechanical neck pain. *Arch Phys Med Rehabil* 2008;89(1):69–74.

22. Cleland JA, Fritz JM, Whitman JM et al. The reliability and construct validity of the Neck Disability Index and patient specific functional scale in patients with cervical radiculopathy. *Spine* 2006;31(5):598–602.

23. Takasaki H, Hall T, Oshiro S et al. Normal kinematics of the upper cervical spine during the Flexion-Rotation Test – in vivo measurements using magnetic resonance imaging. *Man Ther* 2011;16(2):167–71.

24. Hall TM, Robinson KW, Fujinawa O et al. Intertester reliability and diagnostic validity of the cervical flexion-rotation test. *J Manipulative Physiol Ther* 2008;31(4):293–300.

25. Smith K, Hall T, Robinson K. The influence of age, gender, lifestyle factors and sub-clinical neck pain on the cervical flexion-rotation test and cervical range of motion. *Man Ther* 2008;13(6):552–9.

26. Hall T, Briffa K, Hopper D et al. Long-term stability and minimal detectable change of the cervical flexion-

rotation test. *J Orthop Sports Phys Ther* 2010;40(4):225–9.

27. Uhrenholt L, Hauge E, Charles AV et al. Degenerative and traumatic changes in the lower cervical spine facet joints. *Scand J Rheumatol* 2008;37(5):375–84.

28. Panjabi MM, Maak TG, Ivancic PC et al. Dynamic intervertebral foramen narrowing during simulated rear impact. *Spine* 2006;31(5):E128–34.

29. Kelly JD, Aliquo D, Sitler MR et al. Association of burners with cervical canal and foraminal stenosis. *Am J Sports Med* 2000;28(2):214–7.

30. Falla D, Farina D. Neural and muscular factors associated with motor impairment in neck pain. *Curr Rheumatol Rep* 2007;9(6):497–502.

31. Falla DL, Jull GA, Hodges PW. Patients with neck pain demonstrate reduced electromyographic activity of the deep cervical flexor muscles during performance of the craniocervical flexion test. *Spine* 2004;29(19):2108–14.

32. Jull GA, Falla D, Vicenzino B et al. The effect of therapeutic exercise on activation of the deep cervical flexor muscles in people with chronic neck pain. *Man Ther* 2009;14(6):696–701.

33. Falla D, Bilenkij G, Jull G. Patients with chronic neck pain demonstrate altered patterns of muscle activation during performance of a functional upper limb task. *Spine* 2004;29(13):1436–40.

34. Johnston V, Jull G, Darnell R et al. Alterations in cervical muscle activity in functional and stressful tasks in female office workers with neck pain. *Eur J Appl Physiol* 2008;103(3):253–64.

35. Jull G, Amiri M, Bullock-Saxton J et al. Cervical musculoskeletal impairment in frequent intermittent headache. Part 1: Subjects with single headaches. *Cephalalgia* 2007;27(7):793–802.

36. Jull G, Kristjansson E, Dall'Alba P. Impairment in the cervical flexors: a comparison of whiplash and insidious onset neck pain patients. *Man Ther* 2004;9(2):89–94.

37. Lindstrøm R, Schomacher J, Farina D et al. Association between neck muscle coactivation, pain, and strength in women with neck pain *Man Ther* 2011;16(1):80–6.

38. Falla D, Jull G, Hodges PW. Feedforward activity of the cervical flexor muscles during voluntary arm movements is delayed in chronic neck pain. *Exp Brain Res* 2004;157(1):43–8.

39. Falla D, Rainoldi A, Merletti R et al. Myoelectric manifestations of sternocleidomastoid and anterior scalene muscle fatigue in chronic neck pain patients. *Clin Neurophysiol* 2003;114(3):488–495.

40. O'Leary S, Falla D, Jull G et al. Muscle specificity in tests of cervical flexor muscle performance. *J Electromyogr Kinesiol* 2007;17(1):35–40.

41. Uhlig Y, Weber BR, Grob D et al. Fiber composition and fiber transformations in neck muscles of patients with dysfunction of the cervical spine. *J Orthop Res* 1995;13(2):240–9.

42. Kristjansson E. Reliability of ultrasonography for the cervical multifidus muscle in asymptomatic and symptomatic subjects. *Man Ther* 2004;9(2):83–8.

43. McPartland JM, Brodeur RR, Hallgren RC. Chronic neck pain, standing balance, and suboccipital muscle atrophy—a pilot study. *J Manipulative Physiol Ther* 1997;20(1):24–9.

44. Elliott J, Jull G, Noteboom JT et al. Fatty infiltration in the cervical extensor muscles in persistent whiplash-associated disorders: a magnetic resonance imaging analysis. *Spine* 2006;31(22):E847–55.

45. Elliott J, O'Leary S, Sterling M et al. MRI findings of fatty infiltrate in the cervical flexors in chronic whiplash. *Spine (Phila Pa 1976)* 2010 Apr 20;35(9):948–54.

46. DeLoose V, Oord MVd, Keser I et al. MRI study of the morphometry of the cervical musculature in F-16 pilots. *Aviat Space Environ Med* 2009;80(8):727–31.

47. Elliott J, Sterling M, Noteboom JT et al. Fatty infiltrate in the cervical extensor muscles is not a feature of chronic, insidious-onset neck pain. *Clin Radiol* 2008;63(6):681–7.

48. Behrsin JF, Maguire K. Levator scapulae action during shoulder movement. A possible mechanism of shoulder pain of cervical origin. *Aust J Physiother* 1986;32(2):101–6.

49. Takasaki H, Hall T, Kaneko S et al. Cervical segmental motion induced by shoulder abduction assessed by magnetic resonance imaging. *Spine* 2009;34(3):E122–6.

50. Kadi F, Waling K, Ahlgren C et al. Pathological mechanisms implicated in localized female trapezius myalgia. *Pain* 1998;78(3):191–6.

51. Larsson S, Alund M, Cai H et al. Chronic pain after soft-tissue injury of the cervical spine: trapezius muscle blood flow and electromyography at static loads and fatigue. *Pain* 1994;57(2):173–80.

52. Falla D, Farina D. Muscle fiber conduction velocity of the upper trapezius muscle during dynamic contraction of the upper limb in patients with chronic neck pain. *Pain* 2005;116(1–2):138–45.

53. Nederhand MJ, Hermens HJ, Ijzerman MJ et al. Cervical muscle dysfunction in chronic whiplash-associated disorder grade 2: the relevance of the trauma. *Spine* 2002;27(10):1056–61.

54. Jull G, O'Leary S, Falla D. Clinical assessment of the deep cervical flexor muscles: the Craniocervical Flexion Test. *J Manip Physiol Ther* 2008;31(7):525–33.

55. O'Leary S, Jull G, Kim M et al. Cranio-cervical flexor muscle impairment at maximal, moderate, and low loads is a feature of neck pain. *Man Ther* 2007 12(1):34–9.

56. Vasavada AN, Li S, Delp SL. Influence of muscle morphology and moment arms on moment-generating capacity of human neck muscles. *Spine* 1998;23(4):412–22.

57. Harris K, Heer D, Roy T et al. Reliability of a measurement of neck flexor muscle endurance. *Phys Ther* 2005;85(12):1349–55.

58. Jull G, Sterling M, Falla D et al. *Whiplash, headache and neck pain: research based directions for physical therapies.* Edinburgh: Elsevier UK, 2008.

59. Elliott J, O'Leary S, Cagnie B et al. Muscle functional magnetic resonance imaging of cervical extensor muscles during different cervical extension exercises. *Arch Phys Med Rehabil* 2010;91 1418–22.

60. Lee H, Nicholson LL, Adams RD. Cervical range of motion associations with subclinical neck pain. *Spine* 2004;29(1):33–40.

61. Sahrmann SA. *Diagnosis and treatment of movement impairment syndromes.* St. Louis: Mosby, 2002.

62. Kendall F, McGeary E, Provance P. *Muscles: testing and function.* 4th edn. Baltimore: Williams and Wilkins, 1993.

63. Butler DS. *Mobilisation of the nervous system.* Melbourne: Churchill Livingstone, 1994.

64. Kristjansson E, Treleaven J. Sensorimotor function and dizziness in neck pain: implications for assessment and management. *J Orthop Sports Phys Ther* 2009;39(5):364–77.

65. Boyd-Clark LC, Briggs CA, Galea MP. Muscle spindle distribution, morphology, and density in longus colli and multifidus muscles of the cervical spine. *Spine* 2002;27(7):694–701.

66. Kulkarni V, Chandy MJ, Babu KS. Quantitative study of muscle spindles in suboccipital muscles of human foetuses. *Neurol India* 2001;49(4):355–9.

67. Liu J-X, Thornell L-E, Pedrosa-Domellöf F. Muscle spindles in the deep muscles of the human neck: a morphological and immunocytochemical study. *J Histochem Cytochem* 2003;51(2):175–86.

68. Treleaven J, Jull G, LowChoy N. Smooth pursuit neck torsion test in whiplash-associated disorders:

B

relationship to self-reports of neck pain and disability, dizziness and anxiety. *J Rehabil Med* 2005;37(4):219–23.

69. Treleaven J, Jull G, Lowchoy N. Standing balance in persistent whiplash: a comparison between subjects with and without dizziness. *J Rehabil Med* 2005;37(4):224–9.

70. Treleaven J, Jull G, LowChoy N. The relationship of cervical joint position error to balance and eye movement disturbances in persistent whiplash. *Man Ther* 2006;11(2):99–106.

71. Roren A, Mayoux-Benhamou M-A, Fayad F et al. Comparison of visual and ultrasound based techniques to measure head repositioning in healthy and neck-pain subjects. *Man Ther* 2009;14(3):270–7.

72. Tjell C, Tenenbaum A, Sandström S. Smooth pursuit neck torsion test- a specific test for whiplash associated disorders? *J Whiplash and Rel Dis* 2002;1:9–24.

73. Karlberg M, Johansson R, Magnusson M et al. Dizziness of suspected cervical origin distinguished by posturographic assessment of human postural dynamics. *J Vestib Res* 1996;6(1):37–47.

74. Thomas LC, Rivett DA, Bolton PS. Pre-manipulative testing and the use of the velocimeter. *Man Ther* 2008;13(1):29–36.

75. Childs JD, Flynn TW, Fritz JM et al. Screening for vertebrobasilar insufficiency in patients with neck pain: manual therapy decision-making in the presence of uncertainty. *J Orthop Sports Phys Ther* 2005;35(5): 300–6.

76. Arnold C, Bourassa R, Langer T et al. Doppler studies evaluating the effect of a physical therapy screening protocol on vertebral artery blood flow. *Man Ther* 2004;9(1):13–21.

77. Zaina C, Grant R, Johnson C et al. The effect of cervical rotation on blood flow in the contralateral vertebral artery. *Man Ther* 2003;8(2):103–9.

78. Kerry R, Taylor AJ. Cervical arterial dysfunction: knowledge and reasoning for manual physical therapists. *J Orthop Sports Phys Ther* 2009;39(5): 378–87.

79. Thomas LC, Rivett DA, Bolton PS. Validity of the Doppler velocimeter in examination of vertebral artery blood flow and its use in pre-manipulative screening of the neck. *Man Ther* 2009;14(5):544–9.

80. Sterling M, Jull G, Wright A. The effect of musculoskeletal pain on motor activity and control. *J Pain* 2001;2:135–45.

81. Jull G. Deep cervical flexor muscle dysfunction in whiplash. World congress on whiplash-associated disorders. Vancouver, B.C. *J Musculoskel Pain* 2000;8:143–54.

82. Ettlin T, Schuster C, Stoffel R et al. A distinct pattern of myofascial findings in patients after whiplash injury. *Arch Phys Med Rehabil* 2008;89(7):1290–3.

83. Jull G, Moore A. The primacy of clinical reasoning and clinical practical skills. *Man Ther* 2009;14(4):353–4.

84. Haines T, Gross AR, Burnie S et al. A Cochrane review of patient education for neck pain. *Spine J* 2009;9(10):859–71.

85. Miller J, Gross A, D'Sylva J et al. Manual therapy and exercise for neck pain: a systematic review. *Man Ther* 2010;15:334–54.

86. Falla D, Jull G, Hodges P et al. An endurance-strength training regime is effective in reducing myoelectric manifestations of cervical flexor muscle fatigue in females with chronic neck pain. *Clin Neurophysiol* 2006;117(4):828–37.

87. Falla D, Jull G, Russell T et al. Effect of neck exercise on sitting posture in patients with chronic neck pain. *Phys Ther* 2007;87(4):408–17.

88. Boudreau S, Romaniello A, Wang K et al. The effects of intra-oral pain on motor cortex neuroplasticity associated with short-term novel tongue-protrusion training in humans. *Pain* 2007;132:169–78.

89. Fountain FP, Minear WL, Allison PD. Function of longus colli and longissimus cervicis muscles in man. *Arch Phys Med Rehabil* 1966;47:665–9.

90. Vitti M, Fujiwara M, Basmajian JV et al. The integrated roles of longus colli and sternocleidomastoid muscles: an eletromyographic study. *Anat Rec* 1973;177:471–84.

91. Caneiro J, O'Sullivan P, Burnett A et al. The influence of different sitting postures on head/neck posture and muscle activity. *Man Ther* 2010;15 54–60.

92. Mulligan B. *Self treatments for back, neck, and limbs, a new approach.* Wellington: Plane View Press, 2003.

93. Jull G, Bogduk N, Marsland A. The accuracy of manual diagnosis for cervical zygapophysial joint pain syndromes. *Med J Aust* 1988;148(5):233–6.

94. Phillips DR, Twomey LT. A comparison of manual diagnosis with a diagnosis established by a uni-level lumbar spinal block procedure. *Man Ther* 2000; 1:82–87.

95. Cleland JA, Mintken PE, Carpenter K et al. Examination of a clinical prediction rule to identify patients with neck pain likely to benefit from thoracic spine thrust manipulation and a general cervical range of motion exercise: multi-center randomized clinical trial. *Phys Ther* 2010;90(9):1239–50.

96. Mulligan BR. *Manual therapy: NAGS, SNAGS, MWMs etc. 5th Edn.* Wellington, NZ: Plane View Services, 2006.

97. Reid SA, Rivett DA, Katekar MG et al. Sustained natural apophyseal glides (SNAGs) are an effective treatment for cervicogenic dizziness. *Man Ther* 2008;13(4):357–66.

98. Hall T, Chan H, Christensen L et al. Efficacy of a C1–C2 self-sustained natural apophyseal glide (SNAG) in the management of cervicogenic headache. *J Orthop Sports Phys Ther* 2007;37(3):100–7.

99. Leaver AM, Maher CG, Herbert RD et al. A randomized controlled trial comparing manipulation with mobilization for recent onset neck pain. *Arch Phys Med Rehabil* 2010;91(9):1313–8.

100. Hing WA, Reid DA, Monaghan M. Manipulation of the cervical spine. *Man Ther* 2003;8(1):2–9.

101. Elvey R, Hall T. Neural tissue evaluation and treatment. In: Donatelli R, ed. *Physical therapy of the shoulder.* New York: Churchill Livingstone, 1997: 131–52.

102. Schmid AB, Brunner F, Luomajoki H et al. Reliability of clinical tests to evaluate nerve function and mechanosensitivity of the upper limb peripheral nervous system. *BMC Musculoskelet Disord* 2009; 10:11.

103. Coppieters MW, Butler DS. Do 'sliders' slide and 'tensioners' tension? An analysis of neurodynamic techniques and considerations regarding their application. *Man Ther* 2008;13(3):213–21.

104. Coppieters MW, Hough AD, Dilley A. Different nerve-gliding exercises induce different magnitudes of median nerve longitudinal excursion: an in vivo study using dynamic ultrasound imaging. *J Orthop Sports Phys Ther* 2009;39(3):164–71.

105. Leaver AM, Refshauge KM, Maher CG et al. Conservative interventions provide short-term relief for non-specific neck pain: a systematic review. *J Physiother* 2010;56(2):73–85.

106. Trinh K, Graham N, Gross A et al. Acupuncture for neck disorders. *Spine* 2007;32(2):236–43.

107. Sahin N, Ozcan E, Sezen K et al. Efficacy of acupuncture in patients with chronic neck pain—a randomised, sham controlled trial. *Acupunct Electrother Res* 2010;35(1–2):17–27.

108. Tough EA, White AR, Cummings TM et al. Acupuncture and dry needling in the management of myofascial trigger point pain: a systematic review and meta-analysis of randomised controlled trials. *Eur J Pain* 2009;13(1):3–10.

109. Chu J. Twitch-obtaining intramuscular stimulation (TOIMS): long term observations in the management of chronic partial cervical radiculopathy. *Electromyogr Clin Neurophysiol* 2000;40(8):503–10.

110. Ga H, Koh H-J, Choi J-H et al. Intramuscular and nerve root stimulation vs lidocaine injection to trigger points in myofascial pain syndrome. *J Rehabil Med* 2007;39(5):374–8.

111. Grieve G. *Common vertebral joint problems.* New York: Churchill Livingstone, 1988.

112. Cloward RB. Cervical diskography. A contribution to the etiology and mechanism of neck, shoulder and arm pain. *Ann Surg* 1959;150:1052–64.

113. Human head and neck kinematics after low velocity rear-end impacts – understanding "whiplash" (SAE paper 952724). *Proceedings of the 39th Stapp Car Crash Conference (P–299)*; 1995 Nov 8–10, 1995; San Diego, CA. Society of Automotive Engineers (Biodynamic Research Corporation Online). Warrendale, PA.

114. Analysis of human test subject kinematic responses to low velocity rear-end impacts. *SAE International Congress & Exposition*; 1993 March 10–5, 1993; Detroit, MI. Society of Automotive Engineers (Biodynamic Research Corporation Online). Warrendale, PA.

115. BC Whiplash Initiative: *PMRF's whiplash-associated disorders – a comprehensive syllabus*: Physical Medicine Research Foundation, 1998.

116. Chen C, Lu Y, Kallakuri S et al. Distribution of A-delta and C-fiber receptors in the cervical facet joint capsule and their response to stretch. *J Bone Joint Surg Am* 2006;88(8):1807–16.

117. Yoganandan N, Pintar FA, Stemper BD et al. Biomechanics of side impact: injury criteria, aging occupants, and airbag technology. *J Biomech* 2007;40(2):227–43.

118. Balla J, Iansek R. Headaches arising from disorders of the cervical spine. In: Hopkins A, ed. *Headache. Problems in diagnosis and management.* London: Saunders, 1988:241–67

119. Stovner LJ. The nosologic status of the whiplash syndrome: a critical review based on a methodological approach. *Spine* 1996;21(23):2735–46.

120. Pfaffenrath V, Kaube H. Diagnostics of cervicogenic headache. *Funct Neurol* 1990;5(2):159–64.

121. Nilsson N. The prevalence of cervicogenic headache in a random population sample of 20–59 year olds. *Spine* 1995;20(17):1884–8.

122. Sjaastad O, Fredriksen T, Pfaffenrath V. Cervicogenic headache: diagnostic criteria. The Cervicogenic

Headache International Study Group. *Headache* 1998;38:442–5.

123. Zito G, Jull G, Story I. Clinical tests of musculoskeletal dysfunction in the diagnosis of cervicogenic headache. *Man Ther* 2006;11(2):118–29.

124. Radanov B, Di-Stefano G, Augustiny K. Symptomatic approach to posttraumatic headache and its possible implications for treatment. *Eur Spine J* 2001;10: 403–407.

125. Drottning M, Staff PH, Sjaastad O. Cervicogenic headache (CEH) after whiplash injury. *Cephalalgia* 2002;22(3):165–71.

126. Hall T, Briffa K, Hopper D et al. Long-term stability and minimal detectable change of the cervical flexion-rotation test. *J Orthop Sports Phys Ther* 2010;40(4):225–9.

127. Becker WJ. Cervicogenic headache: evidence that the neck is a pain generator. *Headache* 2010;50(4): 699–705.

128. Oginces M, Hall T, Robinson K et al. The diagnostic validity of the cervical flexion-rotation test in C1/2-related cervicogenic headache. *Man Ther* 2007;12(3):256–62.

129. Smith K, Hall T, Robinson K. The influence of age, gender, lifestyle factors and sub-clinical neck pain on the cervical flexion-rotation test and cervical range of motion. *Man Ther* 2008;13(6):552–9.

130. Takasaki H, Hall T, Jull G et al. The influence of cervical traction, compression, and Spurling test on cervical intervertebral foramen size. *Spine* 2009;34(16):1658–62.

131. Levitz CL, Reilly PJ, Torg JS. The pathomechanics of chronic, recurrent cervical nerve root neurapraxia. The chronic burner syndrome. *Am J Sports Med* 1997;25(1):73–6.

132. Rihn JA, Anderson DT, Lamb K et al. Cervical spine injuries in American football. *Sports Med* 2009;39(9):697–708.

133. Standaert CJ, Herring SA. Expert opinion and controversies in musculoskeletal and sports medicine: stingers. *Arch Phys Med Rehabil* 2009; 90(3):402–6.

134. Weinberg J, Rokito S, Silber JS. Etiology, treatment, and prevention of athletic "stingers." *Clin Sports Med* 2003;22(3):493–500.

B

Chapter 21

Shoulder pain

with W. BEN KIBLER, GEORGE A. C. MURRELL, and BABETTE PLUIM

> *This was an arthroscopic and, as much as possible, noninvasive procedure. With aggressive rehabilitation, I expect to be back in form for the Shark Shootout [in December 2009].*   Confident golfer Greg Norman after having an arthroscopic superior labral repair (SLAP lesion) and a partial rotator cuff repair (October 2009)

> *Having made the decision to have surgery in September in order to facilitate my playing the Shark Shootout, I am disappointed. At the same time, I understand it would not be prudent to rush my return to competitive golf.*   Norman's new plan was to return to practice in February 2010 and competition in the following months

Adapted from various sources including www.shark.com

In recent years, there have been many advances in the assessment and treatment of shoulder pain. In this chapter we review:

- functional anatomy
- key features of the clinical history
- how to conduct a swift and effective physical examination
- investigations
- treatment of important shoulder conditions
- prescription for practical shoulder rehabilitation.

 A swift and effective physical examination and prescription for practical shoulder rehabilitation can be seen in the *Clinical Sports Medicine* masterclasses at www.clinicalsportsmedicine.com.

Functional anatomy—static and dynamic

The glenohumeral joint is an inherently unstable shallow ball and socket joint, often described as the equivalent of a golf ball (head of humerus) on a tee (glenoid). In fact, the relationship between the humeral head and the glenoid cavity more accurately parallels a sea lion balancing a ball on its nose. Thus, effective shoulder function and stability require both static constraints—the glenohumeral ligaments, glenoid labrum, and capsule—and dynamic constraints, predominantly the rotator cuff and scapular stabilizing muscles (Fig. 21.1).

Static stabilizers

The main static stabilizers of the shoulder in the functional position (abducted) are the anterior and posterior bands of the inferior glenohumeral ligament. They are attached to the labrum, which, in turn, attaches directly to the margin of the glenoid fossa. The anterior band of the inferior glenohumeral ligament prevents anterior translation, and the posterior band prevents posterior translation of the humeral head. The superior margin of the anterior band of this ligament attaches to the glenoid fossa anteriorly at the two o'clock position. When the arm is placed into abduction and external rotation, this broad ligamentous band rotates anteriorly to prevent subluxation of the joint.[1] Shoulder stability is also enhanced by the glenoid labrum, a ring of fibrous tissue attached to the rim of the glenoid, which expands the size and depth of the glenoid cavity. It increases the superior–inferior diameter of the glenoid by 75% and the anterior–posterior diameter by 50%.

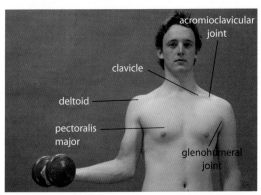

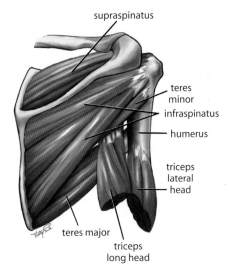

Figure 21.1 Anatomy of the shoulder region
(a) Surface anatomy from the front

(c) Rotator cuff musculature from behind

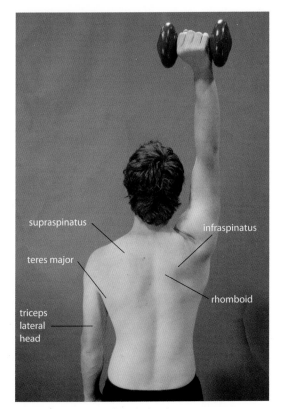

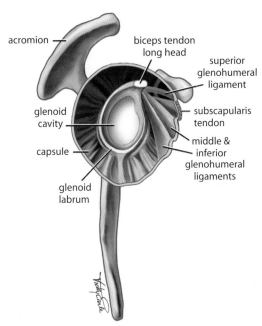

(d) Ligaments and muscles of the glenoid

(b) Surface anatomy from behind

Dynamic stabilizers

The dynamic stabilizers of the glenohumeral joint are the rotator cuff muscles,[2] which act in co-contraction to seat the humeral head in the glenoid. The rotator cuff muscles, principally the supraspinatus and, to a lesser extent, the infraspinatus, teres minor, and subscapularis, counteract the action of the deltoid (which elevates the humeral head) by preventing the head of the humerus from moving superiorly when the arm is raised.

Scapulohumeral rhythm

The scapular stabilizers also play an important role in shoulder joint movement. Normal shoulder function requires smooth integration of movement, not only

343

at the glenohumeral joint but also at the scapulothoracic, acromioclavicular, and sternoclavicular joints. This integrated movement is referred to as "scapulohumeral rhythm." Adequate scapulohumeral rhythm is required to achieve full upper limb elevation.

Scapulohumeral rhythm is the smooth integration and coordination of scapulothoracic, acromioclavicular, sternoclavicular, and glenohumeral joint movement, resulting in normal shoulder girdle movement.

Scapulohumeral rhythm should be smooth, coordinated, and symmetrical. Disturbed scapulohumeral rhythm manifests as altered or jerky movement.[3-5] This may be as a result of injury to the shoulder girdle or may have been a predisposing factor to injury. Abnormalities of scapulohumeral rhythm are most commonly due to weakness and/or poor motor control of the scapular stabilizers (with or without weakness of the rotator cuff muscles), shortening of the scapulohumeral muscles, or involuntary adaptation to avoid a painful arc.[6]

Full upper limb elevation requires upward rotation of the scapula, which ensures that the coracoacromial arch is removed from the path of the greater tuberosity of the elevating humerus, thus avoiding potential impingement. Scapular control also enhances joint stability at greater than 90° of abduction by placing the glenoid fossa under the humeral head, where stability is assisted by the action of the deltoid muscle.

The muscles controlling the scapula are:

- trapezius (all three portions)
- serratus anterior (upper and lower portions)
- rhomboids
- levator scapulae
- pectoralis minor.

These muscles work in coordinated patterns called "force couples" to control three-dimensional scapular motion.[7] The main upward rotation force couple involves the upper trapezius coordinating with the lower trapezius/serratus anterior. Anterior/posterior tilt and rotation involve the upper trapezius/pectoralis minor force coupled with the serratus anterior/lower trapezius. A stable scapula provides a base for the muscles arising from the scapula and acting on the humerus, allowing them to maintain their optimal length–tension relationship. Experienced clinicians emphasize adequate strengthening and retraining of the scapula stabilizers following shoulder injury.

Clinical perspective

A practical approach to shoulder pain

Because numerous structures can cause shoulder pain, we suggest narrowing the problem down to one or more of the following six "categories" of shoulder pain:

- rotator cuff
- instability
- labral injury
- stiffness
- acromioclavicular (AC) joint pathology
- referred pain.

Rotator cuff muscles and tendons

Injuries to the rotator cuff muscles and tendons may be acute, chronic, or acute on chronic. Acute injuries include muscle strains, and partial or complete tendon tears. Overuse injuries include tendinopathy. An example of an acute on chronic injury is a complete rotator cuff tendon tear in a previously degenerative tendon. Sportspeople with rotator cuff tendon injuries present with shoulder pain and difficulty with overhead activities.

Shoulder instability

Pain resulting from instability may arise from the anterior, posterior, or superior shoulder capsule and labrum, and from the periscapular muscles. Instability may result from changes to passive structures such as ligament, capsule or labrum (i.e. hypermobility), or it can be caused by poor motor control (i.e. dynamic instability).

Labral injury

Glenoid labral lesions may occur either as an acute injury or from overuse. Instability may be obvious clinically in patients with recurrent episodes of dislocation or subluxation. In many cases, however, instability may initially cause relatively minor symptoms, such as impingement or joint pain.

Shoulder stiffness

Hypomobility may be secondary to trauma, including surgery, or from injury to the cervical nerve roots or brachial plexus. It may occur spontaneously in middle age—a condition termed "idiopathic adhesive capsulitis" or "frozen shoulder."

Acromioclavicular joint pathology

Pain is usually localized over the acromioclavicular joint.[8]

Referred pain

Pain can refer to the shoulder from the cervical spine, the upper thoracic spine, and associated soft tissues (see also Chapter 20). Similarly, shoulder dysfunction can lead to trapezial fatigue or may radiate into the neck, behind the scapula, the upper arm, forearm, or, less commonly, the wrist and hand.

Diagnosis of shoulder pain in the sportsperson requires taking a thorough history, performing a thorough examination, and organizing appropriate investigations. A list of possible causes of shoulder pain is shown in Table 21.1.

History

Endeavor to determine the *exact* site of the patient's pain; this can be difficult. Although acromioclavicular joint pain and bicipital pain are well localized, the pain of most other shoulder pathologies is more diffuse. The onset of shoulder pain may be either acute (e.g. a dislocation, subluxation, or rotator cuff tear), or insidious (e.g. rotator cuff tendinopathy).

Identify the position of the shoulder at the time of injury. If the arm was wrenched backward while in a vulnerable position, it suggests anterior dislocation or subluxation. A fall onto the point of the shoulder can cause acromioclavicular joint injury. In chronic shoulder pain, the activity or position that precipitates the patient's pain should be noted (such as the cocking phase of throwing or the pull-through phase of swimming).

Note the severity of the pain, aggravating and easing factors, and the effect of the pain on activities of daily living and sporting activity. Night pain is very common in rotator cuff dysfunction and adhesive capsulitis.

Sensory symptoms such as numbness or pins and needles should be noted, as should any episodes of "dead arm" (in a baseball pitcher this suggests labral injury). Assess upper limb strength. He or she may report catching and locking, or inability to develop normal speed in the action.

Inquire as to past or present problems elsewhere in the kinetic chain, such as knee or ankle sprains or lower back pain. Also, clarify exact physiotherapy for previous local or distant problems. Look for predisposing factors (e.g. a training diary may reveal excessive load on the region).

Examination

A complete examination involves:

1. Observation
   (a) from the front
   (b) from behind (Fig. 21.2a overleaf)
2. Active movements
   (a) arm elevation—watch scapular motion and position[6] (Fig. 21.2b overleaf)

Table 21.1 Causes of shoulder pain

Common	Less common	Not to be missed
Rotator cuff	Rotator cuff	Tumor (bone tumors in the young)
• Strain	• Tear	Referred pain
• Tendinopathy	• Calcific tendinopathy	• Diaphragm
Glenohumeral dislocation	Adhesive capsulitis (frozen shoulder)	• Gall bladder
Glenohumeral instability	Biceps tendonitis	• Perforated duodenal ulcer
Glenoid labral tears	Nerve entrapment	• Heart
Referred pain	• Suprascapular	• Spleen (left shoulder pain)
• Cervical spine	• Long thoracic	• Apex of lungs
• Thoracic spine	Fracture	Thoracic outlet syndrome
• Myofascial structures	• Scapula	Axillary vein thrombosis
Fracture of clavicle	• Neck of humerus	
Acromioclavicular (AC) joint sprain	• Stress fracture of coracoid process	
Other muscle tear	Levator scapulae syndrome	
• Pectoralis major	Glenohumeral joint arthritis	
• Long head of biceps	Brachial plexus	
	Neuropraxia ("burner")	
	Neuritis (viral)	

(b)   external rotation with elbows at side (Fig. 21.2c)
(c)   external rotation at 90° of abduction (Fig. 21.2d)
(d)   internal rotation (Fig. 21.2e)
(e)   horizontal flexion (Fig. 21.2f)

3. Passive movements
(a) to (e) as for active movements (above)

4. Resisted movements

 These tests are most reliable when performed with the shoulder in a position of stabilized retraction— this maximizes rotator cuff strength capability.[9]

(a)   external rotation (Fig. 21.2g)
(b)   subscapularis lift-off test—Gerber's test (Fig. 21.2h page 348)
(c)   deltoid (Fig. 21.2i page 348)
(d)   supraspinatus (Fig. 21.2j page 348)
(e)   upper cut[10] (Fig. 21.2k page 348)

5. Palpation
(a)   acromioclavicular joint
(b)   rotator cuff tendon
(c)   bicipital groove

6. Special tests
(a)   acromioclavicular joint—modified O'Brien's test (Fig. 21.2l page 349)

(b)   scapular corrective maneuvers—scapular assistance test (SAT) (Fig. 21.2m page 349)
(c)   scapular corrective maneuvers—scapular retraction test (SRT)[6, 9] (Fig. 21.2n page 349)
(d)   lateral slide test (LST)[11] (Fig. 21.2o page 349)
(e)   impingement—Neer test (Fig. 21.2p page 350)
(f)   impingement—Hawkins/Kennedy test (Fig. 21.2q page 350)
(g)   instability—load and shift test (Fig. 21.2r page 350)
(h)   instability—apprehension, augmentation, relocation test (Fig. 21.2s page 351)
(i)   inferior—sulcus sign (Fig. 21.2t page 351)
(j)   superior labral anterior to posterior (SLAP) lesion—dynamic labral shear (DLS)[10] (Fig. 21.2u page 351)
(k)   SLAP lesion—O'Brien's test (Fig. 21.2v page 351)
(l)   specific palpation for trigger points (Fig. 21.2w page 352)
(m)   neural dynamics—upper limb neurodynamics test (Chapter 11)
(n)   cervical spine (Chapter 20)

A rapid screening examination is shown in the box (p. 352).

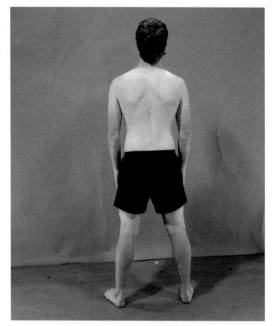

Figure 21.2 Examination of the patient with shoulder pain
(a) Observation from behind. Look for wasting or asymmetry of shoulder height, scapular position, and muscle bulk

(b) Active movements—elevation. Watch for prominence of the medial scapular border. This indicates loss of scapular control, which is called "scapular dyskinesis"

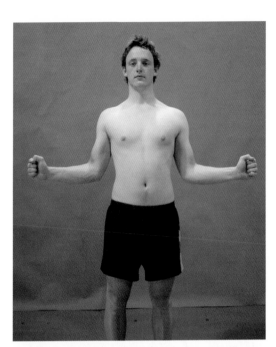

(c) Active movements—external rotation with elbows at side

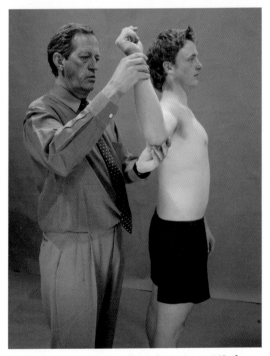

(d) Active movements—external rotation at 90° of abduction

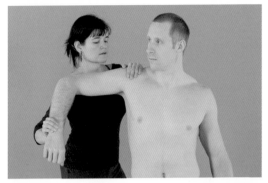

(e) Active movements—internal rotation. With the arm at 90° abduction, stabilize the scapula and rotate the arm in internal/external rotation to tightness. This test is superior to the traditional "reach up behind the back test," which has seven degrees of freedom, only one of which is glenohumeral rotation

(f) Active movements—horizontal flexion. Acromioclavicular joint injury may be painful with this movement

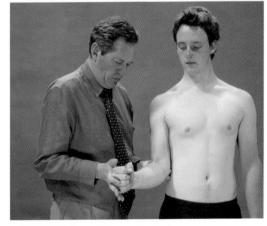

(g) Resisted movements—external rotation. Commence in the modified neutral position to isolate muscles

B

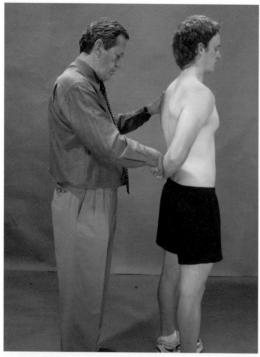

(h) Resisted movements—subscapularis lift-off test (Gerber's test). Push away from the spine against resistance

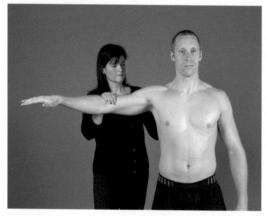

(i) Resisted movements—deltoid. Resisted abduction at 90° with the arm in neutral rotation

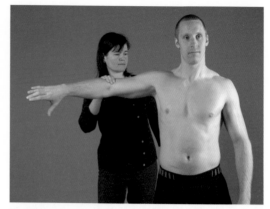

(j) Resisted movements—"empty can" position (90° of abduction, 30° of horizontal flexion and full internal rotation). This test may indicate supraspinatus abnormalities. Repeat with a retracted scapula. Improved strength with scapular retraction indicates that the rotator cuff is not injured but is weak due to scapular dyskinesis

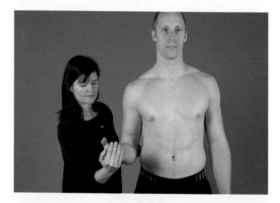

(k) Upper cut. From the starting position (top panel), the patient is asked to perform an "upper cut" punch while the examiner resists as shown (lower panel). Pain or a painful pop over the anterior shoulder represents a positive test

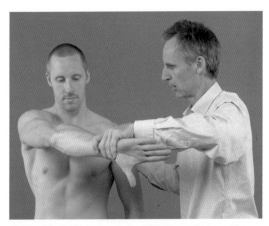

(l) Modified O'Brien's test for AC joint pathology. The test is positive for AC joint pathology when the patient's pain is reproduced in the position shown

(n) Scapular corrective maneuvers—scapular retraction test (SRT). The examiner stabilizes the medial scapular border as the arm is elevated (shown) or externally rotated. Relief of impingement symptoms is a positive test

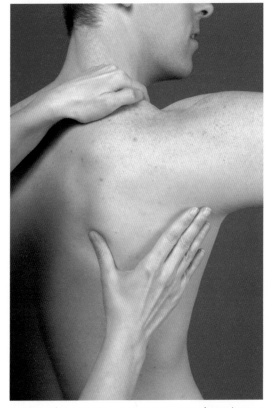

(m) Scapular corrective maneuvers—scapular assistance test (SAT). One hand is placed on the upper trapezius, the other on the inferior medial scapular border. The examiner assists scapular upward rotation as the arm is elevated. A positive test reduces impingement signs and symptoms and indicates that scapular control is required as part of rehabilitation

(o) Lateral slide test. In the starting position (position 1, top panel), the inferomedial angle of the scapula is marked on both the injured and non-injured side with an X. The distance from the reference point on the spine to the medial border of the scapula is measured on both sides. In positions 2 and 3 (middle and lower panels), distances are again measured from the medial border of the scapula to the fixed reference point on the spine. Asymmetry of greater than 1.5 cm represents an abnormality and this is most commonly found in position 3 (lower panel)

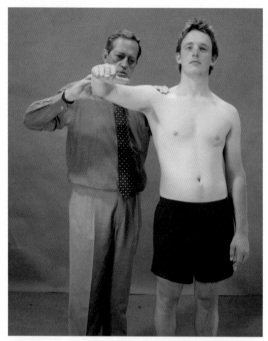

(p) Special tests—impingement (Neer test). The aim is to elicit pain while moving the greater tuberosity under the acromion

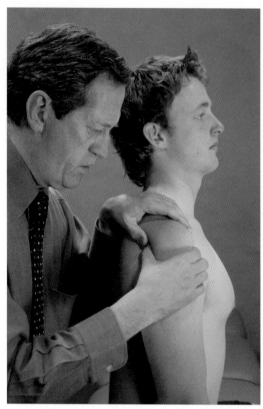

(r) Special tests—instability (load and shift test, or "drawer test"). The right humeral head is grasped with the right hand, while the left hand stabilizes the scapula. The right hand loads the joint to ensure concentric reduction and then applies anterior and posterior shearing forces. The direction and translation can be graded using a scale of 0–3

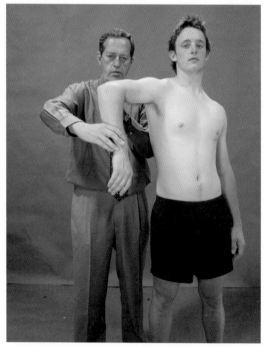

(q) Special tests—impingement (Hawkins/Kennedy test). The shoulder is placed in 90° of forward flexion and then forcibly internally rotated

B

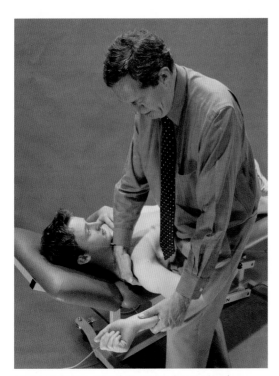

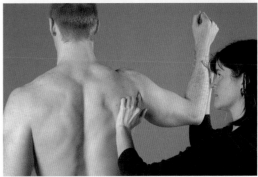

(s) Special tests—instability (apprehension and relocation test). With the patient supine, the arm is taken into abduction and external rotation. The test can be augmented by pushing the humeral head anteriorly from behind. The relocation test is performed by pushing posteriorly on the upper part of the humerus. The relocation test is positive if the apprehension or pain are relieved

(u) SLAP lesion—dynamic labral shear (DLS). In the starting position (top panel) the arm is externally rotated to tightness. The examiner applies a shear load to the joint (lower panel) by maintaining external rotation and horizontal abduction and lowering the arm from 120° to 60° of abduction. Reproduction of pain or a painful click or catch during that maneuver represents a positive test

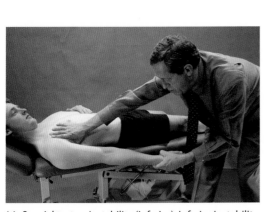

(t) Special tests—instability (inferior). Inferior instability is tested with the examiner placing inferior traction onto the shoulder joint. A positive test is when the humeral head is translated inferiorly such that a visible sulcus appears between the acromion and the humeral head (the "sulcus sign")

(v) Special tests—SLAP lesion (O'Brien's test). The patient's shoulder is held in 90° of forward flexion, 10° of horizontal adduction, and maximal internal rotation. The examiner holds the patient's wrist and resists the patient's attempt to horizontally adduct and forward flex the shoulder

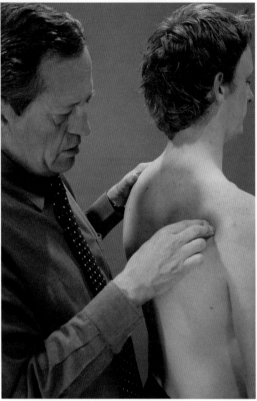

(w) Assessment of trigger points (e.g. infraspinatus)

Rapid shoulder screening examination

1. Observation from the front and back (Fig. 21.2a)
2. Kinetic chain screening—one leg stability series[12]
3. Elevation of arms in forward flexion, 3–5 times, to observe for scapular dyskinetic movement
4. Palpation and the modified O'Brien's test for acromioclavicular joint pain (Fig. 21.2l)
5. Palpation of the bicipital groove
6. Passive external rotation (restriction may indicate frozen shoulder or arthritis)
7. Impingement signs in internal and external rotation (for impingement and rotator cuff pathology) and with the scapular assistance test (SAT)
8. Power of external rotation and of the supraspinatus (for rotator cuff tear)[13]
9. Dynamic labral shear (DLS) for superior labral anterior to posterior (SLAP) lesion—(Fig. 21.2u)
10. Apprehension, augmentation, relocation signs if suspected instability (Fig. 21.2s)

Shoulder investigations
with BRUCE FORSTER

We discuss the principles of shoulder investigations (including diagnostic arthroscopy), as they are a critical element of efficient management of the patient with shoulder pain.

X-ray

Plain X-rays are important in the diagnosis of shoulder abnormalities. Routine views (AP with internal and external rotation, and axillary lateral) provide a good overview of the region. A "true" AP view is useful for assessing joint space narrowing (i.e. arthritis). In cases of trauma, an adequate axillary view may not be possible and it is mandatory to obtain a true lateral film to exclude dislocation. The conditions that can be identified on plain films are:

- calcific tendinopathy
- glenohumeral joint arthritis
- impingement (sclerosis of anterior and/or lateral acromion, sclerosis of greater tuberosity)
- proximal humeral head migration (severe rotator cuff dysfunction)
- fractures.

Special views have been described to evaluate instability and impingement. Supraspinatus outlet views and down-tilted acromial films are obtained to evaluate impingement. In cases of instability, special views (such as the West Point view or the Stryker notch view) are used to better detect Bankart and Hill-Sachs' lesions.

Arthrography

Detailed anatomical information is obtained when arthrography (joint injected with dye) is combined with CT of the shoulder (CT arthrogram) or MR arthrography (see below). This examination gives excellent detail of capsular attachments and of the labrum. Small avulsion fractures of the glenoid rim (Bankart lesion) and the humeral head (Hill-Sachs' lesion) are clearly defined.

Ultrasound

High-resolution ultrasound, in the hands of an experienced operator, is a reliable non-invasive technique for imaging the rotator cuff and adjacent muscles, the bursae, and the long head of the biceps muscle. The examination may be performed as a static or dynamic investigation. Tendon swelling, thickening of the bursa, abnormal fluid collection, or calcific tendinopathy may be detected, as may a partial or complete rotator cuff tear. It is important to define the size and location of the tear, and if there is any supraspinatus muscle atrophy (indicating a chronic and usually irreparable rotator cuff tear). If there is a partial thickness tear, it is important to determine the thickness of the tear—as a percentage of the thickness of the tendon—as tears over 50% usually progress and are less likely to respond to non-operative treatment. It is also important to determine if the partial thickness tear is on the bursal side, undersurface, or intrasubstance. A dynamic examination performed while the patient is actively abducting the shoulder may confirm the presence of impingement (see tendinopathy management).

 High-resolution ultrasound, in the hands of an experienced operator, is a reliable non-invasive technique for imaging the rotator cuff and adjacent muscles, the bursae, and the long head of biceps muscle.

Magnetic resonance imaging

MRI allows multiplanar, non-invasive examination of the shoulder and is used to detect a rotator cuff tear. Bone detail is not defined as well as with CT, and examination with shoulder movement is not possible. MR arthrogram with contrast is well suited to evaluate labral tears or instability.

 MR arthrogram with contrast is well suited to evaluate labral tears or instability.

Diagnostic arthroscopy

Arthroscopy of the shoulder, as well as being therapeutic, can provide useful diagnostic information. Shoulder arthroscopy permits inspection of the glenohumeral joint and the subacromial space. Arthroscopy of the glenohumeral joint cavity is particularly useful as it:

- enables inspection of the glenoid labrum for evidence of a Bankart lesion or a SLAP lesion
- permits assessment of the state of the articular cartilage
- will demonstrate the presence of a Hill-Sachs' lesion
- allows inspection of the shoulder capsule and synovium (a red synovium and thickened capsule are characteristic of adhesive capsulitis)
- will identify a drive-through sign for laxity

- permits inspection of the undersurface of the rotator cuff tendons, the biceps tendon, and the subacromial bursa
- enables inspection and probing of the bursal surface of the rotator cuff.

Arthroscopy of the subacromial space allows assessment of:

- bursitis
- coracoacromial ligament ossification (spur formation)
- lateral spurs
- os acromionale
- bursal side rotator cuff tears
- full thickness rotator cuff tears.

An examination under anesthesia (EUA) performed in conjunction with arthroscopy may sometimes be helpful to assess the presence, direction, and severity of shoulder laxity, and to assess shoulder range of motion.

It is important to remember that these sophisticated investigations are only an adjunct to the clinical findings. In many cases of shoulder pain, the clinical findings provide sufficient information to diagnose the cause of the shoulder pain.

Impingement

"Impingement" is a confusing term. Despite its popularity as a diagnosis, rotator cuff impingement is actually a clinical sign. The exact pathophysiology of impingement is not completely clear, although current thinking is that the syndrome begins as an overuse injury[14] with tendinopathy of supraspinatus, especially on its undersurface near biceps (this is the location of highest stress). Our unpublished data suggest that pain from tendinopathy is likely due to increased nerve density in the tendon. Pain causes secondary rotator cuff muscle dysfunction, leading to proximal humeral head migration, and subsequent subacromial bursitis. The additional pain caused by the bursitis leads to increased dysfunction and impingement, which leads to ossification of the coracoacromial ligament (i.e. bone spur). On X-ray these changes are often described as "evidence of impingement." Large spurs can cause bursal side damage to the rotator cuff. To summarize, younger sportspeople will present with undersurface tendinopathies and tears, bursal side changes with more chronic overuse, and intrasubstance tears with more severe tendinopathy.

At least nine specific diagnoses may be associated with the signs and symptoms of impingement.[15-17] These are outlined in the box.

Shoulder impingement may be:

- external
  - primary
  - secondary
- internal.

The clinical features, appropriate investigations, and treatment are summarized in Figure 21.3.

Diagnoses associated with rotator cuff impingement

- Subacromial bone spurs and/or bursal hypertrophy
- Acromioclavicular joint arthrosis and/or bone spurs
- Rotator cuff disease
- Superior labral injury
- Glenohumeral internal rotation deficit (GIRD)
- Glenohumeral instability
- Biceps tendinopathy
- Scapular dyskinesis
- Cervical radiculopathy

Primary external impingement

Abnormalities of the superior structures may lead to encroachment into the subacromial space from above. The undersurface of the acromion may be abnormally beaked, curved, or hooked (Fig. 21.4). These abnormalities result from either a congenital abnormality (os acromiale) or osteophyte formation. Other abnormalities that tend to occur in older age groups include thickening of the coracoacromial arch or osteophyte formation on the inferior surface of the acromioclavicular joint.[18]

Secondary external impingement

Encroachment into the subacromial space from above in younger sportspeople may also occur as a result of excessive angulation of the acromion due to inadequate muscular stabilization of the scapula. The muscles responsible for stabilization and motion of the scapula can become deficient, either because their activation in force couples is altered, or because their strength balance is altered. These deficiencies result in failure to control scapulohumeral rhythm, which results in abnormal scapular movement.

	External		Internal (glenoid)
	Primary	**Secondary**	
Etiology	Outlet obstruction ➡ Rotator cuff dysfunction	Instability ➡ Rotator cuff dysfunction	Repetitive microtrauma (± instability) ➡ Rotator cuff dysfunction
Location of impingement	Subacromial	Subacromial	Posterior–superior glenoid
Age at presentation (years)	>35	<35	<35
Presentation	Anterior and/or lateral shoulder pain with overhead activity	Anterior and/or lateral shoulder pain with overhead activity	Posterior and/or anterior shoulder pain with abduction/external rotation
Impingement tests	++	+	+/–
Apprehension test	–	+/–	+/–
Relocation test	–	+/–	+/–
Radiographs	Anterior acromial spurring, AC arthritis, greater tuberosity sclerosis/cysts	–	–
Initial treatment	Relative rest, NSAIDs, rotator cuff and periscapular strengthening	Relative rest, NSAIDs, rotator cuff and periscapular strengthening	Relative rest, NSAIDs, rotator cuff and periscapular strengthening
Surgical treatment	Open or arthroscopic subacromial decompression (ASD)	Stabilization procedure +/– ASD	Stabilization procedure +/– ASD

Figure 21.3 Impingement subtypes, their features, and management

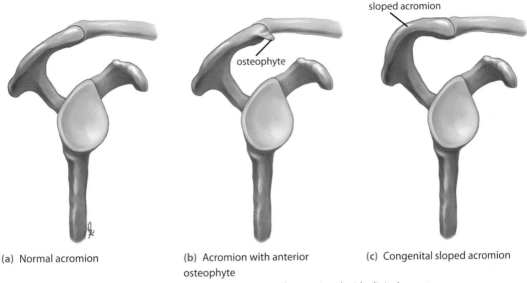

sloped acromion

osteophyte

B

(a) Normal acromion

(b) Acromion with anterior osteophyte

(c) Congenital sloped acromion

Figure 21.4 Acromial shapes. Abnormalities are not necessarily associated with clinical symptoms

The anterior tilt and excessive internal rotation create more narrowing of the subacromial space via anteroinferior movement of the acromion, and may result in impingement symptoms (Fig. 21.5). This is exacerbated by excessive tightness of the pectoralis minor, which pulls the scapula into a protracted position.[19–21]

The rotator cuff tendons are also liable to be weakened following large volumes of load (e.g. through resistance in swimming or throwing). Imbalance between the elevators of the humeral head (deltoid) and the humeral head stabilizers (rotator cuff muscles) may lead to the humeral head moving superiorly with deltoid contraction, forcing it against the undersurface of the rotator cuff tendons and narrowing the space through which the rotator cuff tendons pass.

To effectively treat shoulder pain associated with impingement, it is essential to recognize the specific factor(s) contributing to the impingement (Fig. 21.6 overleaf)—it is not sufficient merely to diagnose shoulder impingement.

In any sportsperson presenting with impingement, it is important to consider superior labral injury or instability. Expert clinical opinion suggests that these may lead to the development of impingement via several mechanisms. Unless instability is recognized and treated, impingement symptoms are likely to persist.

Figure 21.5 Lack of scapular stabilization results in excessive rotation and protraction of the scapula with glenohumeral movement. This causes inferior movement of the acromion

Internal impingement

Internal or glenoid impingement occurs mainly in overhead sportspeople during the late cocking stage of throwing (extension, abduction, and external rotation),

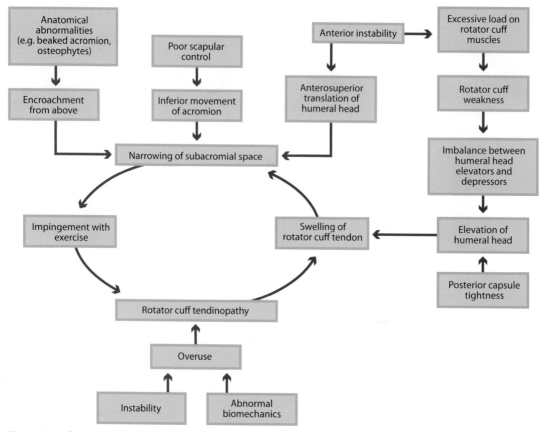

Figure 21.6 Factors involved in the development of external impingement

when impingement of the undersurface of the rotator cuff occurs against the posterosuperior surface of the glenoid (Fig. 21.7). This is normally a physiological occurrence; however, it may become pathologic in the overhead sportsperson due to repetitive trauma/overuse, and injury to the superior labrum.

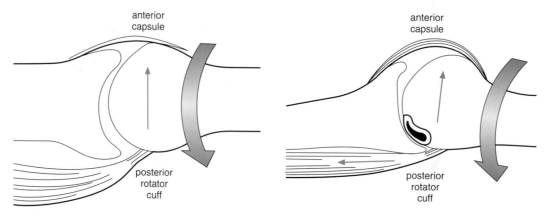

Figure 21.7 Internal impingement
(a) Superior view of an abducted, externally rotated shoulder demonstrates anterior displacement of the humeral head with anterior capsular laxity

(b) Impingement of the supraspinatus and infraspinatus tendons on the posterosuperior glenoid rim occurs with further anterior translation and posterior angulation (horizontal extension) of the humerus

Rotator cuff injuries

Rotator cuff tendinopathy

In rotator cuff tendinopathy, the tendons become swollen and hypercellular, the collagen matrix is disorganized and the tendon weaker, and there is an increase in vasculature and nerve density. Studies in running rats and in human swimmers suggest the major determinant of the onset of tendinopathy is the volume (e.g. distance swum, time running) of work. Apoptosis (programmed cell death) and associated pathways are increased in overuse tendinopathy (Fig. 21.8).[22]

Calcification may occur in any of the rotator cuff tendons but it is most often seen in the supraspinatus tendon.[23] The cause of this calcification is undetermined and it can be asymptomatic. Pain is often severe at rest, with movements, and at night. Deposits of calcium may be seen on plain X-ray and on ultrasound.

 PRACTICE PEARL Calcium deposits are sometimes seen as an incidental finding. In any tendon, calcification is not synonymous with clinical symptoms.

Clinical features

The sportsperson with rotator cuff tendinopathy complains of pain with overhead activity such as throwing, swimming, and overhead shots in racquet sports. Activities undertaken at less than 90° of abduction are usually pain-free. There may also be a history of associated symptoms of instability, such as recurrent subluxation or episodes of "dead arm." Night pain is common.

On examination, there may be tenderness over the supraspinatus tendon proximal to or at its insertion into the greater tuberosity of the humerus. Active movement may reveal a painful arc on abduction between approximately 70° and 120°. Internal rotation is commonly reduced. Rotator cuff strength should be measured with the scapula adequately stabilized.

Symptoms can be reproduced with impingement tests (Figs 21.2p, q) as well as with end-range passive flexion. Pain will also occur with resisted contraction of the supraspinatus, which is best performed with resisted upward movement with the shoulder joint in 90° of abduction, 30° of horizontal flexion and internal rotation (Fig. 21.2j).

PRACTICE PEARL Symptoms can frequently be relieved or lessened by the scapular assistance test (SAT) (Fig. 21.2m). This test helps identify those patients who will respond favorably to scapular stabilization exercises.

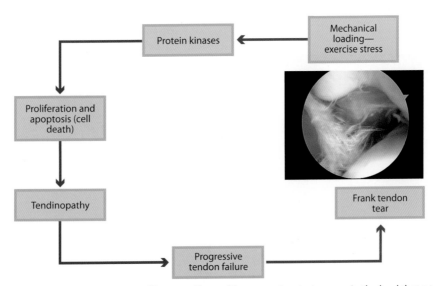

Figure 21.8 A schematic representation of how tendinopathies may arise. An increase in the load that a tendon experiences activates protein kinases, which increases the rate of tendon cell turnover (proliferation as well as apoptosis). Increased cell turnover results in excessive matrix remodelling and a tendon that is weaker and more prone to rupture

ADAPTED FROM MURRELL GA. UNDERSTANDING TENDINOPATHIES. *BR J SPORTS MED* 2002;36:392–3

The investigation of choice in rotator cuff tendinopathy is MRI. This may also identify a partial tear of the rotator cuff (Fig. 21.9).[24] Ultrasound can rule out a full-thickness tear, define a partial thickness tear, identify a thickened subacromial bursa, and rule in or out "impingement" of the bursa under the lateral acromion as the arm is abducted.

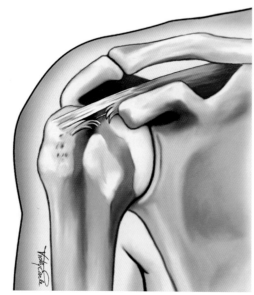

Figure 21.9 Rotator cuff tendinopathy
(a) Pathology generally begins on the inferior surface of the tendon

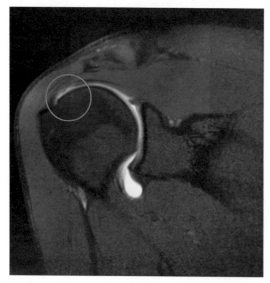

(b) MR arthrogram shows high signal contrast (white) corresponding to a partial supraspinatus tendon tear

Treatment of rotator cuff tendinopathy

Treatment of rotator cuff tendinopathy should be considered in two parts. The first part is to treat the tendinopathy itself. The patient should avoid the aggravating activity, and apply ice locally. There is no level 2 evidence (Chapter 3) to support nonsteroidal anti-inflammatory drugs (NSAIDs), ultrasound, interferential stimulation, laser, magnetic field therapy, or local massage. There *is* level 2 evidence to support nitric oxide donor therapy (glyceryl trinitrate[25] [GTN] patches applied locally at 1.25 mg/day),[26] and for a single corticosteroid injection.[27] Glyceryl trinitrate patches come in varying doses—a 5 mg patch should be cut in quarters and applied for 24 hours at a time and then replaced (Fig. 21.10); a 2 mg patch would best be cut in half and applied similarly. Successful outcomes occurred at three to six months. A corticosteroid injection into the subacromial space (Fig. 21.11) may reduce the sportsperson's symptoms sufficiently to allow commencement of an appropriate rehabilitation program.

The second part of treatment should be the correction of associated abnormalities. These include glenohumeral instability, muscle weakness or incoordination, soft tissue tightness, impaired scapulohumeral rhythm, and training errors. The treatment of scapulohumeral rhythm abnormalities is considered on pages 377–8.

Decreased rotator cuff strength or imbalance also predispose to the development of tendinopathy. Treatment involves strengthening of the external rotators as they are usually relatively weak compared

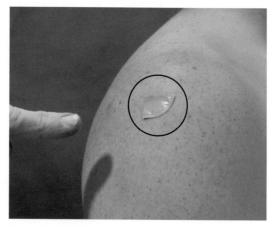

Figure 21.10 Nitric oxide donor therapy—glyceryl trinitrate (GTN) patches applied locally at 1.25 mg/day to the site of maximal tenderness. Patches remain on the skin for 24 hours and are then replaced[26]

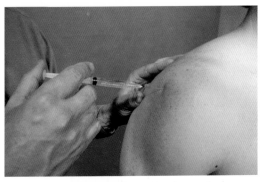

Figure 21.11 Subacromial injection. One technique is to insert the needle from the posterolateral aspect of the acromion in an anterior and superior direction toward the coracoid process

with the internal rotators. Itoi examined symptomatic and asymptomatic rotator cuff tears using single photon emission computed tomography (SPECT), and showed that symptomatic patients were firing the trapezius, whereas asymptomatic patients were firing the lateral deltoid.[28] An exercise program to strengthen the rotator cuff muscles is described on pages 382–3.[29]

Posterior capsular tightness is commonly associated with decreased internal rotation and reduced rotator cuff strength. Stretching of the posterior capsule is helpful (Fig. 21.12).

While correction of these factors may improve tendinopathy, there is no level 2 evidence to support any particular rehabilitation strategy or regimen for managing supraspinatus tendinopathy. This provides fertile ground for novel clinical research.

Abnormalities along the kinetic chain must also be identified and corrected. In addition, training errors, including overuse (Chapter 9), and technique faults such as in throwing or swimming (Chapter 8), should be corrected with the aid of a coach.

Management of calcific tendinopathy can be difficult. If there is a defined calcific lesion that is still fluid in nature, instant relief may be obtained by aspiration under ultrasound guidance. Mature calcific lesions may be disrupted by extracorporeal shock wave therapy (also called "lithotripsy") (Chapter 13).[30–33] We have found ultrasound-guided identification (with a breast biopsy needle) and arthroscopy removal to be very effective.[34]

Rotator cuff tears
Complete and partial tears of the rotator cuff tendon are commonly seen in older sportspeople who present with shoulder pain during activity. These patients

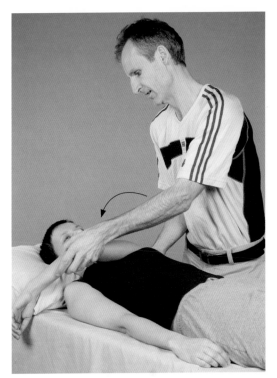

Figure 21.12 Posterior shoulder capsular stretching **(a)** Motion is mainly between the scapular and thoracic wall, which exacerbates scapular slide

(b) Exercise with the scapula stabilized allows stretch at an appropriate location often complain of an inability to sleep on the affected shoulder. Examination reveals positive impingement signs, and sometimes weakness on supraspinatus testing. Diagnosis is confirmed on MRI or ultrasound. If the tear is small and of partial thickness, treatment may be conservative. Full thickness rotator cuff tears in young sportspeople require surgical repair. In older people, treatment should be guided by the patient's symptoms and level of function.

Glenoid labrum injuries

Clinically relevant anatomy

The glenoid labrum is a ring of fibrous tissue attached to the rim of the glenoid. It expands the size and depth of the glenoid cavity, thus increasing the stability of the glenohumeral joint. It also plays a role in proprioception, aiding in muscular control, and it acts as a washer, spreading loads equally over the interface[35] (Fig. 21.13).

The labrum varies in size and shape and has a

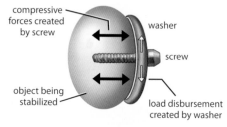

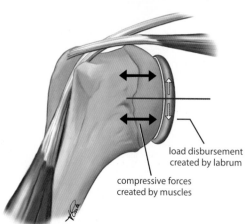

Figure 21.13 The glenoid labrum contributes to proprioception and stability. Ben Kibler compares the stability role with that of a washer (top panel). Like a washer, the deformable labrum (bottom panel), expands the depth and increases the size of the glenoid to increase stability of the interface. The labrum helps to spread load over the glenohumeral joint

wedge-shaped appearance in cross-section. The labral attachment is generally continuous with the edge of the glenoid and blends directly into the articular surface. Occasionally the attachment is meniscoid, with the free edge extending over the rim of the glenoid onto the articular surface. This can sometimes be mistaken for a tear but is a normal anatomical variant.

The labrum is the primary attachment site for the shoulder capsule and glenohumeral ligaments. The superior aspect of the glenoid labrum also serves as the attachment site for the tendon of the long head of the biceps muscle. Injuries to the glenoid labrum are divided into superior labrum anterior to posterior (SLAP) and non-SLAP lesions, and further into stable and unstable lesions.[36, 37] SLAP lesions are injuries to the labrum that extend from anterior to the biceps tendon to posterior to the tendon. Snyder et al.[38] have divided these injuries into four types (Fig. 21.14).

SLAP lesions are either stable or unstable, depending on whether the majority of the superior labrum and the biceps tendon are firmly attached to the glenoid margin. Non-SLAP lesions include degenerative, flap, and vertical labral tears,[38] as well as unstable lesions such as Bankart lesions.

 Definitions: When experts in the field refer to "SLAP" lesion, they mean the most common type of "labral tear." Trainees should consider the terms synonymous.

Making the diagnosis

The diagnosis of a glenoid labral tear relies on eliciting a history of an appropriate mechanism of injury, clinical assessment, and appropriate investigations.

The most common mechanism of injury to the superior glenoid labrum is excessive traction on the labrum through the long head of biceps (e.g. carrying or dropping and catching a heavy object). Throwing injuries occur due to a combination of peel-back traction of the biceps on the labrum in shoulder cocking, abnormal posterosuperior humeral head translation in cocking due to glenohumeral internal rotation deficit, and excessive scapular protraction.[15–17] Patients complain of pain localized to the posterior or posterior–superior joint line, especially in abduction. Pain in the shoulder is exacerbated by overhead and behind-the-back arm motions. Popping, catching, or grinding may also be present.

On examination, there may be tenderness over the anterior aspect of the shoulder and pain on resisted biceps contraction. Although a number of specific tests have been described for SLAP lesions, the DLS

Types of slap lesion

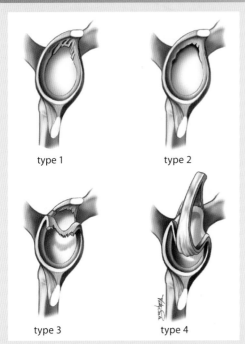

type 1   type 2

type 3   type 4

Figure 21.14 Four types of SLAP lesions have been described:

In type 1, the attachment of the labrum to the glenoid is intact but there is evidence of fraying and degeneration

Type 2 lesions involve detachment of the superior labrum and tendon of the long head of biceps from the glenoid rim

In type 3 injuries, the meniscoid superior labrum is torn away and displaced into the joint but the tendon and its labral rim attachment are intact

In type 4 lesions, the tear of the superior labrum extends into the tendon, part of which is displaced into the joint along with the superior labrum

(dynamic labral shear) test (Fig. 21.2u) is reliable, has a high sensitivity and specificity, and has predictive value and a high likelihood ratio.[10]

Plain radiography is usually unremarkable. MR arthrography yields greater detail of intra-articular shoulder structures than does conventional MRI (Fig. 21.15).[39] MR arthrography is particularly useful for the detection and assessment of not only glenoid labral tears, but also small loose bodies, or cartilage flaps. Interpretation of MR arthrograms of the shoulder is best performed by a radiologist with particular

expertise in the area, as interpretation is complicated by a wide range of normal anatomical variants. The static MRI is well complemented by dynamic tests such as the dynamic labral shear (DLS, Fig. 21.2u) which provide a context for interpreting the clinical importance of the MRI. Interestingly, a comparison of MRI and clinical findings found a combination of clinical tests to be more sensitive than MRI.[19, 40] Often a clear obvious history is sufficient and MRI examination is unnecessary.

PRACTICE PEARL
If the patient does *not* have a good history consistent with a labral tear *and* has a positive DLS test, the MRI signal changes in the labrum are likely not clinically relevant.

Treatment

Conservative management is usually unsuccessful in all but the most minor SLAP lesions in younger sportspeople. Unstable SLAP lesions (types 2 and 4) should be repaired arthroscopically by reattaching the labrum to the glenoid. For stable SLAP lesions (types 1 and 3) and stable non-SLAP lesions, arthroscopic debridement to eliminate mechanical irritation is usually adequate. Unstable non-SLAP lesions, such as a Bankart lesion (which may occur together with a SLAP lesion), should be treated with arthroscopic fixation.[41] In patients 50 years or older, surgical repair of SLAP lesions does not yield additional

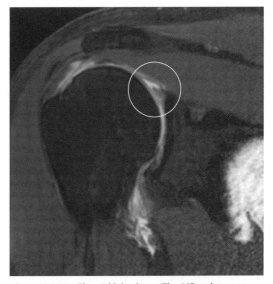

Figure 21.15 Glenoid labral tear. The MR arthrogram reveals the torn labral tissue (circle) surrounded by the high-signal arthrographic contrast medium

B

benefit over conservative treatment and therefore should be avoided.

Some sportspeople with isolated superior labral tears do well with conservative (non-operative) care, particularly those who do not participate in overhead sports. Treatment generally consists of NSAIDs and physical therapy, with a focus on scapular stabilization exercises and a stretching program for the posterior capsule. Since SLAP lesions are best characterized arthroscopically, it is difficult to determine the exact type of SLAP lesion that will respond best to non-operative care.[42]

Specific exercises can be prescribed based on the mechanism of injury, clinical findings, and diagnosed type of lesion if known. (For example, with a compressive injury, caution should be used with weight-bearing exercises. Conversely, heavy weights should be avoided early on with traction injuries.) The clinician should also be aware if the long head of biceps tendon is involved.

Goals of conservative care are to restore range of motion, neuromuscular control, dynamic stability, and proprioception, and ultimately restore full strength, power, and endurance (see p. 376 for details on shoulder rehabilitation principles).[43] If non-operative treatment is successful, the athlete can expect full return to sport within 3–6 months.[42]

 Labral lesions are frequently associated with shoulder instability and this must be addressed as part of the management.

Dislocation of the glenohumeral joint

Anterior dislocation

One of the most common traumatic sports injuries is acute dislocation of the glenohumeral joint (Fig. 21.16a). In almost all cases, this is an anterior dislocation and it results from the arm being forced into excessive abduction and external rotation. Most anterior dislocations damage the attachment of the labrum to the anterior glenoid margin (Bankart lesion). There may also be an associated fracture of the anterior glenoid rim (bony Bankart lesion) or disruption of the glenohumeral ligaments. A compression fracture of the humeral head posteriorly (Hill-Sachs' lesion) or tearing of the posterior or superior labrum may also be present.

 Most anterior dislocations damage the attachment of the labrum to the anterior glenoid margin (Bankart lesion). There may also be an associated fracture of the anterior glenoid rim (bony Bankart lesion) or disruption of the glenohumeral ligaments.

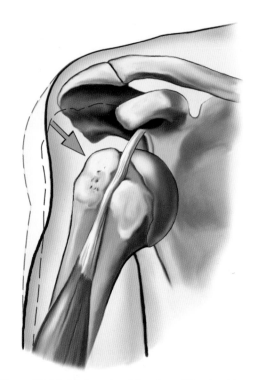

Figure 21.16 (a) Anterior dislocation of the shoulder disrupts the joint capsule plus/minus the stabilizing ligaments

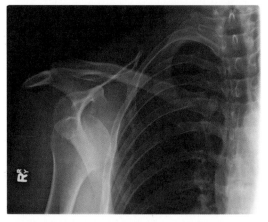

(b) Typical radiographic appearance—the humeral head sits medially over the scapula

The history is usually one of acute trauma, either direct or indirect, associated with sudden onset of acute shoulder pain. A patient may describe a feeling of the shoulder "popping out."

On examination, the dislocated shoulder has a characteristic appearance with a prominent humeral head and a hollow below the acromion. There is a loss of the normal smooth contour compared with the uninjured side. Anterior dislocations of the glenohumeral joint are occasionally associated with damage to the axillary nerve, resulting in impaired sensation on the lateral aspect of the shoulder and deltoid weakness. This should be assessed in any acute dislocation.

Management of first time anterior dislocation

In a hospital setting, the dislocated shoulder should be X-rayed (Fig. 21.16b) prior to reduction, as a fracture may be present. In most cases, however, this is not practical and the dislocation should be reduced as soon as possible. In these cases, a post-reduction film should be obtained.

The sooner the dislocated shoulder is reduced, the easier it usually is to reduce. There are a number of methods to relocate the humeral head onto the glenoid cavity. One method is demonstrated in Figure 21.17.

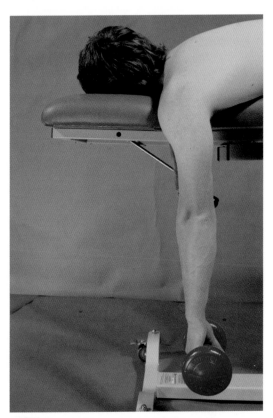

Figure 21.17 Position of patient with anterior dislocation of the shoulder to allow reduction of the shoulder. A small weight may be held in the hand to facilitate reduction

Injection of 10–15 mL of xylocaine into the joint can reduce pain and muscle spasm and aid reduction.

Management of a sportsperson who dislocates their shoulder for the first time is controversial (see box overleaf).

Arthroscopic stabilization

Arthroscopic Bankart repair is currently the most popular surgical procedure. Following a Bankart repair, the patient may commence pendular movements with the arm within 24 hours and maintain the arm in a sling for 3–4 weeks. Once the initial pain from the procedure has subsided, active external rotation movements, to just short of the limit of rotation achieved on the operating table, are commenced. Active internal rotation exercises can be gradually introduced as pain subsides. By six weeks, active strengthening can commence. Return to full sport is often achieved at three months.[49]

Recurrent dislocation and Bankart repair

Shoulder dislocations in young sportspeople have a high rate of recurrence, leading to chronic shoulder instability. Because of this high incidence of recurrent dislocation, arthroscopy should be considered after shoulder dislocation in the younger sportsperson. If a Bankart lesion is found at arthroscopy, this should be repaired, either arthroscopically or as an open surgical procedure.

Following a Bankart repair, the patient may commence pendular movements with the arm within 24 hours, and maintain the arm in a sling for three to four weeks. Once the initial pain from the procedure has subsided, active external rotation movements, to just short of the limit of rotation achieved on the operating table, are commenced. It may be helpful to place the arm in a splint in some abduction and external rotation to limit the amount of anterior capsular shortening. Active internal rotation exercises can be gradually introduced as pain subsides. By six weeks, active strengthening can commence. Return to full sport is often achieved at three to four months.[49]

Posterior dislocation of the glenohumeral joint

Acute traumatic posterior dislocation is far less common than anterior dislocation. It occurs either as a result of direct trauma or due to a fall on the outstretched arm that is in some degree of internal rotation or adduction. It may also be caused by a fit of any cause (e.g. electric shock, epileptic fit).

First-time shoulder dislocation: conservative or surgical treatment?

Traditional management of anterior shoulder dislocations consisted of a reduction of the glenohumeral joint and immobilisation, followed by physical therapy to restore the range of shoulder motion and strength. This traditional management approach is being challenged however, due to the high rate of recurrence, especially in young sportspeople.

Historically, first-time anterior shoulder dislocations were managed by immobilization in a sling in **internal rotation** for a period ranging from 2–6 weeks, followed by physical therapy. Does the length and position of post-reduction immobilization matter? Level 1 evidence indicates that recurrent instability is *not* affected by the duration of immobilization in internal rotation (IR).[43] Hovelius et al.[44] followed a large cohort of patients who were randomly assigned to immobilization in IR for up to a week or 3–4 weeks and found no difference in the recurrence rate at two, five or 10 years follow-up.

Some clinicians have advocated immobilization in a position of 30° **external rotation** (ER), rather than the traditional internal rotation. Clinical MRI studies showed that placing the shoulder in ER after a first-time traumatic anterior shoulder dislocation significantly improved the position of the labroligamentous lesion on the glenoid rim.[45] However, there is a lack of high-quality comparative studies on which to base decision-making, and only level 2 evidence that it may be reduced by immobilization in ER. A recent Cochrane review on conservative management of traumatic anterior shoulder dislocations by Handoll et al.[46] concluded that there was insufficient evidence to make any recommendations for practice.

Studies[47] report 72–95% recurrence in patients under 20 years of age, 70–82% recurrence between the ages of 20 and 30 years, and 14–22% in patients older than 50 years.[4, 18, 29–34]

A Cochrane review evaluating the level 1 evidence of non-operative versus operative treatment of acute first-time shoulder dislocations concluded that early surgical intervention was warranted in young adults (aged less than 30 years) engaged in highly demanding physical activities.[48] There was a 75% reduction of relative risk for subsequent instability in the surgical group in this high-risk patient population.

There is now considerable evidence to consider primary stabilization as an option for treatment in the high-risk group, less than 25 years of age. This is based not only on recurrences but improved quality of life outcomes. Early surgical repair in young patients (15–25 years) should be the treatment of choice because it reduces recurrence rates from 80–90% to 3–15% and improves overall quality of life.[47] In patients aged 25–40 years, an initial trial of non-operative management is reasonable because their risk of re-dislocation is much lower (20–30%). Patients over 40 years of age should be managed non-operatively due to a low recurrence rate of 10–15%, but associated injuries such as rotator cuff tears, bone defects, and neurological injury must be addressed.[47]

Inspection of the patient's shoulder may reveal loss of the normal rounded appearance at the front of the shoulder. The arm is held in internal rotation and adduction. The cardinal sign is limitation of external rotation. Suspicion of a posterior dislocation should be based on the mechanism of injury, and the presence of pain and impaired function.

 The cardinal sign of posterior dislocation is limited external rotation. Suspicion of this diagnosis should be based on the mechanism of injury, and the presence of pain and impaired function.

Posterior dislocation can easily be overlooked in the AP X-ray. X-ray must include a true lateral or, if possible, axillary view.

The shoulder is reduced by applying traction forward with forward pressure on the humerus.

 Posterior dislocation can easily be overlooked in the AP X-ray. X-ray must include a true lateral or, if possible, axillary view.

Shoulder instability
Anterior instability
Anterior glenohumeral instability may be post-traumatic (as a result of an acute episode of trauma causing anterior dislocation or subluxation), or atraumatic, or a combination (for instance, an acute traumatic episode in a lax shoulder).

In differentiating between the two types of anterior instability, the history is the most useful factor. In post-traumatic instability, the patient usually reports a specific incident that precipitated the problem. This is commonly a moderately forceful abduction and external rotation injury. Following this episode, however, the patient reports that the shoulder has never returned to normal. In many post-traumatic types of instability, a true dislocation may not have occurred and the symptoms are related to recurrent subluxation.

The atraumatic type of abnormality is common in people with capsular laxity—including sportspeople, especially those involved in repeated overhead activities such as baseball pitchers, javelin throwers, swimmers, and tennis players.

Clinical features

The symptoms of anterior instability include recurrent dislocation or subluxation, shoulder pain, and episodes that patients describe as having a "dead arm." Pain usually arises from impingement of the rotator cuff tendons, with recurrent anterior translation of the humeral head and recurrent "silent subluxation." This is aggravated by the eventual weakening of the rotator cuff muscles which, in turn, fail to depress the humeral head adequately. The recurrent episodes of impingement result in a rotator cuff tendinopathy (Fig. 21.6).

Anterior shoulder pain in association with post-traumatic anterior instability may be due to "catching" of a labral detachment. This pain and sensation of "catching" may be reproduced on anterior drawer or load and shift testing (Fig. 21.2r).

The episodes of subluxation and dislocation usually increase in frequency. Occasionally, a stage is reached where relatively minor activities such as yawning or rolling over in bed may result in a subluxation or dislocation.

On examination, note the presence of any generalized ligamentous laxity. A sulcus sign (Fig. 21.2t) upon downward traction on the arm points to the diagnosis of generalized ligamentous laxity. The amount of external rotation at the shoulder should also be noted. Full assessment of the power of all the primary and secondary muscles controlling the shoulder should be performed to exclude any neurological deficit. Tenderness may be present anteriorly (related to damage to the anterior structures) or posteriorly (if there has been significant traction injury). Pay particular attention to supraspinatus strength

with older adults, as supraspinatus tears commonly occur with a shoulder dislocation in patients over the age of 50 years.

The patient is asked which position causes symptoms or dislocation. With anterior instability, this is usually in abduction and external rotation. The degree of anterior shoulder laxity can then be assessed with the load and shift drawer test (Fig. 21.2r). The apprehension–augmentation–relocation test (Fig. 21.2s) is also an indicator of anterior instability and has greater inter- and intra-observer reliability than all other tests for shoulder instability.[4] If instability is present, these positions will cause either pain or apprehension. The presence of apprehension is a more specific indicator of traumatic anterior instability than pain.[4, 50] If the examiner pushes the humeral head forward, this may aggravate the sportsperson's apprehension and confirm the diagnosis of anterior instability (augmentation test). Conversely, posterior pressure on the humeral head may reduce apprehension (relocation test). If the degree of instability is relatively minor and apprehension is not perceived in this position, then an alternative method of examination is firstly to perform the anterior drawer test (Fig. 21.2r) and then, while maintaining the humeral head subluxated anteriorly, bring the arm into abduction and external rotation.

Investigations

Investigations may be useful in demonstrating some of the associated features of instability, such as the Hill-Sachs' lesion (Fig. 21.18 overleaf) or the Bankart lesion (Fig. 21.19 overleaf). Appropriate plain X-rays (Fig. 21.18b) or CT scans (Fig. 21.19b) may demonstrate these lesions. MRI will reliably demonstrate the presence of bony lesions, as well as soft tissue abnormalities of the labrum, the capsule, and the associated tendons. However, an X-ray is usually all that is necessary to demonstrate traumatic anterior instability.

Treatment

First-time dislocation is discussed above. Here, we outline management of instability. As outlined earlier, a traditional sling should not be used to manage instability.

Traumatic instability

In sportspeople, particularly those whose dominant throwing arm is involved, the underlying mechanical

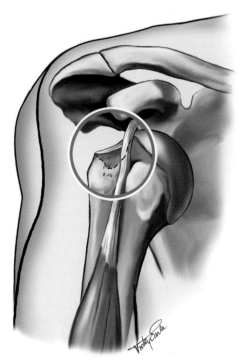

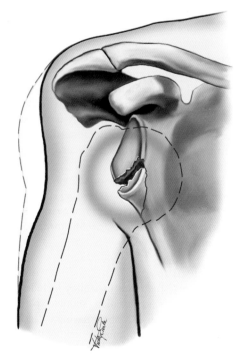

Figure 21.18 (a) Hill-Sachs' lesion showing where the humeral head has impacted on the glenoid rim

Figure 21.19 (a) Bankart lesion showing a fragment of bone separated from the glenoid rim

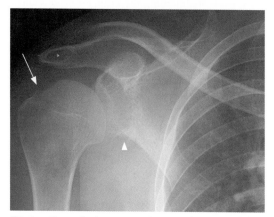

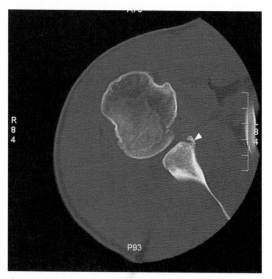

(b) A radiograph showing a Hill-Sachs' lesion (arrow) and a Bankart lesion (arrowhead)

(b) CT scan of a bony Bankart lesion (arrowhead). CT may show this pathology where it is undetected by plain radiography

lesion should be corrected. Arthroscopic Bankart repair is now the standard treatment for recurrent anterior dislocation. Other mechanical problems such as a tear in the rotator cuff may also be corrected. If an extremely large Hill-Sachs' lesion is present, a procedure such as bone grafting may be necessary. Tendon transfer and other non-anatomical procedures, such as the Magnusson-Stack and Putti-Platt procedures, are not recommended for sportspeople as they invariably lead to a loss of external rotation and reduced shoulder power.

Atraumatic instability

In treating atraumatic instability, intensive reha-bilitation involves strengthening of the dynamic stabilizers (rotator cuff muscles) and scapular sta-bilizing muscles, with particular emphasis on the muscles opposing the direction of the instability (see pp. 376–83). Modification of sporting activity may also be helpful. If conservative measures fail, surgery should be considered. This usually involves a capsu-lar shift procedure.

Posterior instability

The most common type of posterior instability seen in sportspeople is an atraumatic type that is part of a multidirectional instability. Often, in these patients, the shoulder may be voluntarily posteriorly sublux-ated. In this group of patients, there is usually a marked posterior drawer (Fig. 21.2r).

Most patients with atraumatic posterior instability can be treated by strengthening of the posterior sta-bilizing muscles. If these measures fail, then surgery should be considered.

As a result of dislocation or subluxation, the pos-terior labrum may be torn, resulting in a type of post-traumatic posterior instability. If this is symptomatic, surgical correction of the underlying damage may be indicated.

Multidirectional instability

Multidirectional instability of the glenohumeral joint involves a combination of two or three insta-bilities—anterior, posterior, and inferior. Most com-monly, multidirectional instability is an atraumatic type of instability, often associated with generalized ligamentous laxity throughout the body. However, it may also result from repetitive trauma, especially at the extremes of motion or, rarely, from a direct blow.

Generalized ligamentous laxity can be assessed by examination of the wrists, thumbs, elbows, and knees to determine the presence of hyperextensibil-ity. On examination of the shoulder, the presence of instability in the anterior or posterior direction may be assessed by the anterior and posterior drawer tests (Fig. 21.2r). Inferior laxity is determined by inferior traction on the arm as it is held by the side. An inferior subluxation of the glenohumeral joint will be shown by the presence of a "sulcus sign" under the acromion, as shown in Figure 21.2t.

A major characteristic of multidirectional instabil-ity is that pain in translation occurs in the mid-ranges of motion. This indicates a prominent role of altered muscle activation. Lower trapezius and serratus anterior activity is decreased, and pectoralis minor and lattissimus dorsi increased, creating a posi-tion of scapular protraction and glenoid tilting.[19, 20] Frequently the symptoms and pain can be alleviated by placing the scapula in stabilized retraction.

Relief of symptoms and decreased translation will point to the need for a therapeutic exercise program for the scapular and shoulder stabilizers. Stretching of the muscles around the shoulder joint should be avoided. If multidirectional instability fails to respond to conservative measures, surgical treat-ment may be attempted. However, the results of sur-gical treatment, particularly in those patients with generalized ligamentous laxity, are not as good as in post-traumatic instability.[51]

Adhesive capsulitis ("frozen shoulder")

Glenohumeral joint stiffness is not uncommon after significant trauma (e.g. a fracture or surgery). It may also follow an injury to the neural structures in the neck or it may occur spontaneously.

The age group in which spontaneous shoulder stiffness, commonly referred to as "adhesive cap-sulitis," occurs is between 40 and 60 years of age. Idiopathic adhesive capsulitis more commonly affects the left shoulder and is more prevalent in women than men (1.3:1). Adhesive capsulitis is more common in patients with diabetes, and there is also an association with thyroid disorders.

The diagnosis of shoulder stiffness is relatively easy to make by evaluating passive external rotation with the elbow at the side. Care should be taken to stabilize the scapula when examining for shoulder stiffness as significant range of motion can occur at the scapulothoracic articulation (the anterior scapula with the posterior thorax—ribs 2–7). Surgical or post-traumatic surgical stiffness usually resolves within 12 months, and surgical intervention is rarely neces-sary. Symptomatic physiotherapy may be valuable.

Treatment

Idiopathic adhesive capsulitis is a self-limiting con-dition that resolves, on average, over 1.5 years. One management option, therefore, is to wait for it to resolve on its own. There is no evidence that physio-therapy, injections, or drugs change the outcome.

Arthroscopic capsular release to divide the thick-ened shoulder capsule and an early aggressive super-vised range of motion program are effective at restoring motion and relieving pain.[52, 53] The results from this procedure are not as good in patients with diabetes.

Fracture of the clavicle

Fracture of the clavicle is usually caused by either a fall onto the point of the shoulder (e.g. in horse riding or cycling), or by direct contact with opponents in sports such as football.

Middle-third clavicular fracture

The clavicle usually fractures in its middle third, with the outer fragment displacing inferiorly and the medial fragment superiorly. It is extremely painful. On examination, there is localized tenderness and swelling, and the bony deformity may be palpated. With clavicular shortening or angulation, the scapula will assume a protracted position.

X-ray reveals the fracture. There has been a change in perspective about imaging clavicle fractures, as it is sometimes difficult to assess the true clavicle position on plain X-ray. Thus, overlap and shortening need to be carefully monitored for the first 3–4 weeks of non-operative management because significant deformity can occur.

Treatment

The principles of treatment are to provide pain relief. Clavicle fractures almost always heal in four to six weeks. However, often the ends overlap and the clavicle is foreshortened. A foreshortened clavicle is associated with significant functional deficits. A figure-of-eight bandage is designed to prevent foreshortening and has significant theoretical advantages over a sling or collar and cuff. During this time the patient should perform self-assisted shoulder flexion to a maximum of 90° to prevent stiffness of the glenohumeral joint.[54]

These fractures are best managed conservatively and usually heal well. Early surgical fixation is indicated if there is compromise of the skin by bony fragments or foreshortening of greater than 1–2 cm (0.5–1 in.). Occasionally, non-union of a fracture of the clavicle may occur with a fibrous pseudoarthrosis forming. This is treated surgically by open reduction and internal fixation with a dynamic compression plate and bone chips[28] to ensure the length of the clavicle is maintained.

Distal clavicle fractures

Distal clavicle fractures comprise 12–15% of all clavicle fractures. Many of these fractures involve disruption of the acromioclavicular and/or coracoclavicular ligaments. These fractures are more prone to non-union and delayed union. Classification for these fractures is shown in Table 21.2.

Generally, fractures medial to the ligament attachments have greater displacement of fracture fragments, and this is associated with increased risk of delayed union or non-union if treated non-operatively.

Minimally displaced fractures distal to the coracoclavicular ligament attachments (type I) may be treated with a sling for comfort, and early range of motion and isometric strengthening exercises. If displacement is present, then rehabilitation should progress slowly, with active range of motion exercises introduced only when pain resolves and healing has begun radiographically.

Treatment of the more medial (type II) fractures is more controversial. As there is a high rate of non-union, surgical treatment is often recommended. Distal intra-articular fractures (type III), if stable, should be treated non-surgically as they tend to heal with minimal dysfunction.

 The treatment of distal clavicle fractures in the immature adult is different from that in the adult.

Even fractures that present with significant displacement are stable, and will eventually heal in an anatomical position. This is due to the fact that, although the fracture is medial to the coracoclavicular ligament attachment, the periosteal envelope remains attached to the coracoclavicular ligaments. The hematoma and subsequent new bone formation stimulated by the periosteum result in remodeling and complete union.

Table 21.2 The American Shoulder and Elbow Society Classification of distal clavicle fractures

Type	Pathology
I	Fracture distal to coracoclavicular ligaments with little displacement
IIa	Fracture medial to coracoclavicular ligaments
IIb	Fracture between coracoclavicular ligaments
III	Intra-articular fracture without ligament disruption

Acromioclavicular joint conditions

Acute acromioclavicular joint injuries

The acromioclavicular joint is another common site of injury in sportspeople who fall onto the point of the shoulder.

Stability of the acromioclavicular joint is provided by a number of structures (Fig. 21.20). In order of decreasing importance, these are:

- the coracoclavicular ligament comprising the conoid and trapezoid ligaments.
- the acromioclavicular ligaments
- the joint capsule.

A modified classification system by Rockwood describes six different types of acromioclavicular joint injuries (Fig. 21.21 overleaf):[55]

- Type I injury corresponds to sprain of the capsule of the joint and is characterized clinically by localized tenderness and pain on movement, especially horizontal flexion.
- Type II injuries correspond to a complete tear of the acromioclavicular ligaments with sprain of the coracoclavicular ligaments. On examination, as well as localized tenderness, there is a palpable step deformity.
- Type III and V injuries consist of complete tears of the coracoclavicular ligaments, the conoid and

trapezoid. In type III and V injuries, a marked step deformity is present (Fig. 21.22 page 371). Type V injuries can be distinguished from type III injuries radiographically by the amount of displacement.

- Type IV injuries are characterized by posterior displacement of the clavicle.
- Type VI injuries have an inferiorly displaced clavicle into either a subacromial or subcoracoid position.

Type V injuries can be distinguished from type III injuries radiographically by the amount of displacement. A type V injury has between three and five times greater coracoclavicular space than normal, whereas a type III injury has 25–100% greater coracoclavicular distance than the uninjured side. Type V injury typically involves much greater soft tissue injury and includes damage to the muscle, fascia, and occasionally the skin.

Types IV, V and VI injuries also have complete rupture of all the ligament complexes and are much rarer injuries than types I, II and III.[56]

Management is based on the general principles of management of ligamentous injuries. Initially, ice is applied to minimize the degree of damage and the injured part is immobilized in a sling for pain relief. This may be for two to three days in the case of type I injuries, or up to six weeks in severe type II or type III injuries. Isometric strengthening exercises should be commenced once pain permits. Return to sport is possible when there is no further localized tenderness and a full range of pain-free movement has been regained. The sportsperson may feel more comfortable on return to sport if the acromioclavicular joint is taped (Fig. 21.23 page 371).

The major functional problems in a high grade (III–IV) injury result from loss of strut function to stabilize the scapula, glenohumeral joint, and arm, and 73% of type III acromioclavicular separations show an alteration of scapular mechanics.[57] Thus, much more consideration should be given to reconstruction in those patients exhibiting altered scapular mechanics.

> The treatment of type III injuries is controversial. Historically, most of these injuries have been treated surgically. However, most clinicians now consider conservative management to be equally effective.

Surgery is clearly indicated for type IV, V, and VI injuries and those type III injuries that fail to respond adequately to conservative management.[56, 58]

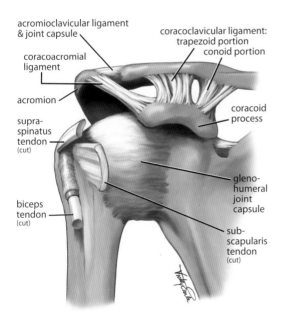

acromioclavicular ligament & joint capsule

coracoclavicular ligament: trapezoid portion, conoid portion

coracoacromial ligament

acromion

supra-spinatus tendon (cut)

coracoid process

gleno-humeral joint capsule

biceps tendon (cut)

sub-scapularis tendon (cut)

Figure 21.20 The acromioclavicular joint

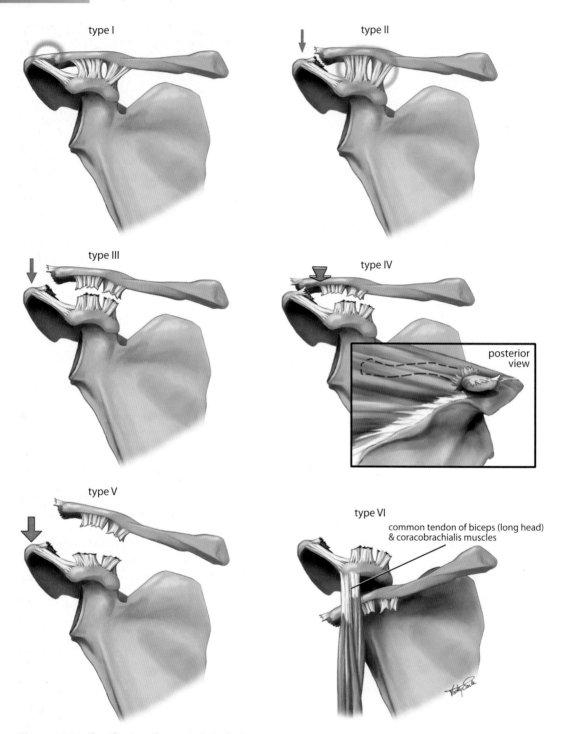

type I

type II

type III

type IV

posterior view

type V

type VI

common tendon of biceps (long head) & coracobrachialis muscles

Figure 21.21 Classification of acromioclavicular joint injuries

Figure 21.22 Marked step deformity at the acromioclavicular joint in type III injury

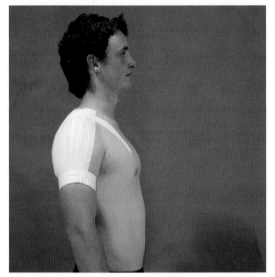

Figure 21.23 Taping after acromioclavicular joint injury

Chronic acromioclavicular joint pain

Chronic acromioclavicular joint pain may occur as a result of repeated minor injuries to the acromioclavicular joint, or following a type II or type III injury. This can damage the fibrocartilaginous meniscus situated within the acromioclavicular joint.

Another cause of chronic acromioclavicular joint pain—osteolysis of the outer end of the clavicle—is seen occasionally, especially in weightlifters performing large numbers of bench presses. X-ray in this condition shows a "moth-eaten" appearance of the distal end of the clavicle (Fig. 21.24). Horizontal flexion is painful. Rotator cuff impingement may occur due to the abnormal scapular position that results from loss of the clavicle strut. Treatment consists of physical

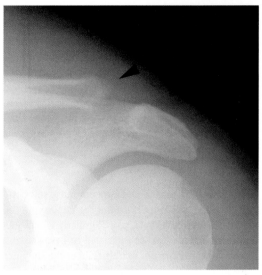

B

Figure 21.24 Osteolysis of the outer end of the clavicle, showing a "moth-eaten" appearance

therapy, including electrotherapeutic modalities and mobilization, combined with muscle strengthening.

Osteoarthritis of the acromioclavicular joint may occur as a result of recurrent injuries. This is characterized by a typical X-ray appearance with sclerosis and osteophyte formation (Fig. 21.25).

Acromioclavicular joint pain is usually localized over the joint. Symptoms may be reproduced by acromioclavicular joint compression using the

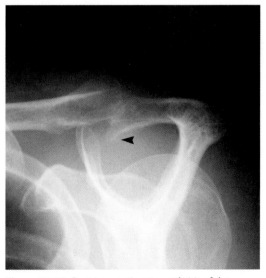

Figure 21.25 Post-traumatic osteoarthritis of the acromioclavicular joint showing a spur and bony irregularity on the acromion

modified O'Brien's test (Fig. 21.2l) or cross-arm adduction. An injection of local anesthetic and corticosteroid into the acromioclavicular joint can confirm the diagnosis and provide effective symptom relief.

Persistent acromioclavicular joint pain may require arthroscopic distal clavicle excision.[59, 60] The surgeon must take care not to disrupt the ligamentous attachments to the distal clavicle. More than 5 mm resection alters the joint loads and removes the bony attachments.[60]

Referred pain

The joints of the cervical and upper thoracic spine frequently refer pain to the shoulder region, even in the absence of neck or thoracic pain. Similarly, a malfunctioning shoulder often has associated periscapular and trapezial (i.e. neck) pain. Examination of the shoulder must therefore include an examination of the cervical and upper thoracic spine (see Chapter 20).

Muscles and fascia in the neck, upper thoracic, and scapular regions may also contribute to shoulder pain. Active trigger points can be found in any of the muscles of the neck and shoulder; however, those that commonly contribute to shoulder pain are in the trapezius, infraspinatus, levator scapulae, and rhomboids (Fig. 21.26). Soft tissue techniques (Fig. 21.27) and dry needling can be used to treat trigger points.

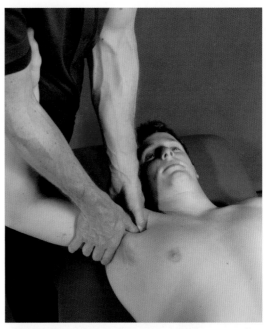

Figure 21.27 Several soft tissue techniques are used in clinical practice to treat shoulder pain
(a) Ischemic pressure to the pectoralis major

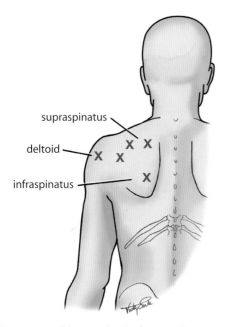

Figure 21.26 Trigger points in the trapezius, infraspinatus, levator scapulae, and rhomboids may refer pain to the shoulder

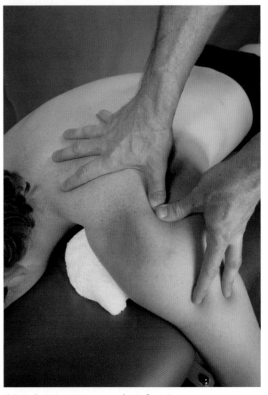

(b) Ischemic pressure to the infraspinatus

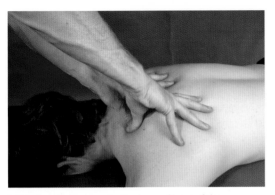

(c) Ischemic pressure to the lower fibers of the trapezius

The contribution of neural structures to the patient's shoulder pain can be assessed by the upper limb neurodynamic test (Chapter 11). The test is considered positive with reproduction of the patient's symptoms or restricted mobility compared with the non-painful side. Neural glides (Chapter 13) may help reduce neural tissue sensitivity and restore mobility.

Less common causes of shoulder pain

Biceps tendinopathy

The long head of the biceps tendon that passes from the superior lip of the glenoid through the bicipital groove in the humerus is susceptible to overuse injury. This occurs particularly in sportspeople performing a large volume of weight training (such as bench presses and "dips"). This injury is not common but it is often incorrectly diagnosed when, in fact, referred pain or rotator cuff tendinopathy are producing pain in the biceps region.

Palpation of the region may show local tenderness of the biceps tendon, either in the bicipital groove close to its attachment to the glenoid, or at the musculotendinous junction. Pain may be reproduced by passive stretching of the biceps or by using the upper cut[9] test (Fig. 21.2k).

No form of treatment has been shown to be of benefit for biceps tendinopathy/fraying.

Rupture of the long head of the biceps

Rupture of the loaded long head of the biceps muscle may occur in the older sportsperson and is usually accompanied by immediate sharp pain and a tearing sensation.

The deformity is obvious—the muscle is detached from its proximal attachment and bunches up in the distal arm. The deformity is accentuated by contraction of the biceps. Often there is little ongoing pain. Surprisingly, biceps strength is almost fully maintained. Imaging is via MRI or ultrasound.[61]

Those who do not rely on their upper arm in sport are generally satisfied with reassurance and require no definitive treatment. In those who perform power sports, surgery may be indicated.

Pectoralis major tears

Pectoralis major tears may be partial ruptures (grades I–II) or complete (grade III). Complete rupture occurs at the site of its insertion in the humerus. This is usually seen in weight training, especially when performing a bench press. The typical history is of sudden onset of pain on the medial aspect of the upper arm. Examination reveals localized tenderness and swelling. Resisted contraction of the pectoralis major is weak and may be painful.

A partial tear is treated conservatively with ice and a strengthening program over a period of four to six weeks. A complete tear should be treated by surgical repair of the muscle.[62]

It is usually possible to differentiate between a partial and a complete tear clinically. Ultrasound or MRI examination may assist in this differentiation.

Subscapularis muscle tears

Tears of the subscapularis muscle can occur with sudden forceful external rotation or extension applied to the abducted arm. There is usually no associated instability. The main complaint is pain; range of motion may be maintained.

On examination, the patient has increased passive external rotation with the shoulder adducted at the side, weakness of internal rotation and a positive lift-off sign (Fig. 21.2h).

MRI and ultrasound will confirm the diagnosis. Treatment should be acute surgical repair.

Nerve entrapments

Shoulder pain may arise from entrapments to:

- the suprascapular nerve
- the long thoracic nerve
- the axillary nerve.

Suprascapular nerve

The most common entrapment is of the suprascapular nerve.[63] The suprascapular nerve is derived from the upper trunk of the brachial plexus formed by the roots of the C5 and C6 nerves. The course of the nerve is shown in Figure 21.28. The nerve passes downward beneath the trapezius to the superior border of the scapula. Here it passes through the suprascapular notch. The roof of this notch is formed by the transverse scapular ligament. After passing through the notch, the nerve supplies the supraspinatus muscle as well as articular branches to both the glenohumeral and acromioclavicular joints. The nerve then turns around the lateral edge of the base of the spine of the scapula (the spinoglenoid notch) to innervate the infraspinatus muscle. Entrapment of the suprascapular nerve may occur at either the suprascapular notch or the spinoglenoid notch.

The patient usually complains of pain that is deep and poorly localized. It is often felt posteriorly and laterally in the shoulder, or referred to the arm, neck, or upper anterior chest wall. The patient may describe shoulder weakness.

On examination, there may be wasting of the supraspinatus and/or infraspinatus muscles, accompanied by weakness on abduction and external rotation. Tenderness over the suprascapular notch may also be present.

The site of entrapment in cases of combined supraspinatus and infraspinatus weakness is the suprascapular notch. The nerve may be stretched and kinked in this position by extremes of scapular motion associated with the throwing action. It may also occur in tennis players who complain of a weakness and lack of control over backhand volleys. Diagnosis is made on the clinical symptoms and confirmed by

an abnormal electromyogram (Chapter 12). Surgical decompression of the nerve at the site of entrapment is occasionally required.

Isolated infraspinatus weakness and wasting may occur when the suprascapular nerve is trapped at the spinoglenoid notch. This condition has been seen in volleyball players who use the "float" serve[64] and in weight lifters. It can also arise due to a cyst that results from superior glenoid labral tears compressing the nerve. Treatment should be directed to repairing the labral tear.

Long thoracic nerve

The long thoracic nerve is formed from the roots of the C5, C6, and C7 nerves. The nerve passes behind the brachial plexus to perforate the fascia of the proximal serratus anterior, passing medial to the coracoid with branches throughout the length of the serratus anterior. Long thoracic nerve palsy causes paralysis of the serratus anterior, with winging of the scapula. The nerve may be injured by traction on the neck or shoulder, or by blunt trauma. Isolated long thoracic nerve palsy may also follow viral illnesses.

Clinical features include pain and limited shoulder elevation. Patients may complain of difficulty in lifting weights or an uncomfortable feeling of pressure from a chair against a winged scapula while sitting. They may also develop secondary impingement due to poor scapular control.

The most striking feature on examination is winging of the scapula when pushing against a wall with both hands.

Electromyographic studies will confirm the diagnosis.

Initial treatment is conservative and most patients will recover fully. Surgical tendon transfer may occasionally be required.

Axillary nerve compression

Axillary nerve compression, or quadrilateral space syndrome, is an uncommon condition caused by compression of the posterior humeral circumflex artery and axillary nerve or one of its major branches in the quadrilateral space. The quadrilateral or quadrangular space is located over the posterior scapula in the subdeltoid region and consists of the teres minor superiorly, teres major inferiorly, the long head of triceps medially, and the surgical neck of the humerus laterally. The axillary nerve and the posterior humeral circumflex artery pass through the space at a level inferior to the glenohumeral joint capsule.[65]

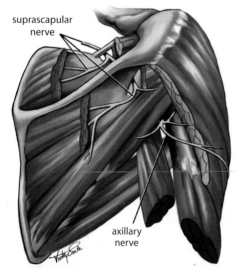

suprascapular nerve

axillary nerve

Figure 21.28 Course of the suprascapular nerve

Quadrilateral space syndrome is seen in throwing sportspeople and is characterized by poorly localized posterior shoulder pain, paresthesia over the lateral aspect of the shoulder and arm, and deltoid and teres minor weakness. The condition may occur secondary to abnormal fibrous bands, although traumatic causes have been described. Diagnosis is by electromyography or subclavian arteriogram, although this is associated with some risk. Treatment is initially conservative. Occasionally, surgical exploration is required.

Axillary nerve injuries can also occur with anterior dislocation of the shoulder and by blunt trauma to the anterior lateral deltoid muscle.[66]

Thoracic outlet syndrome

The term "thoracic outlet syndrome" refers to a group of conditions that result from compression of the neurovascular structures that course from the neck to the axilla through the thoracic outlet (Fig. 21.29). The brachial plexus and subclavian vessels are especially susceptible to compression because of their proximity to one another in the thoracic outlet. The most common site of compression is the costoclavicular space between the clavicle and the first rib (costoclavicular syndrome).[67, 68] Other sites of compression are the triangle between the anterior scalene muscle, the middle scalene muscle, and the upper border

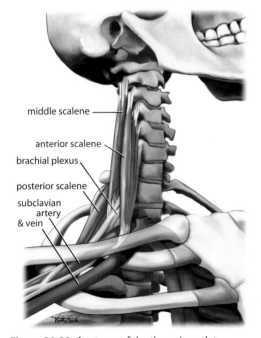

middle scalene

anterior scalene

brachial plexus

posterior scalene

subclavian artery & vein

Figure 21.29 Anatomy of the thoracic outlet

of the first rib (anterior scalene syndrome); and the angle between the coracoid process and the pectoralis minor insertion (hyperabduction syndrome or pectoralis minor syndrome).

This condition occurs in overhead sportspeople.[69] Poor posture with drooping shoulders and scapular protraction can decrease the diameter of the cervico-axillary canal, causing thoracic outlet syndrome symptoms. Congenital anatomical abnormalities including complete cervical rib, incomplete cervical ribs with fibrous bands, fibrous bands from the transverse process of C7, and clavicular abnormalities can all compress the neurovascular structures. Complete cervical ribs are rare but, if present, are often bilateral. However, only 10% of patients with cervical ribs have thoracic outlet syndrome symptoms. Thoracic outlet syndrome symptoms may be caused by shortening of the scalene muscles secondary to active trigger points.

Traumatic structural changes that can cause thoracic outlet syndrome include fractures of the clavicle and/or first rib, pseudoarthrosis of the clavicle, malunion of clavicle fractures, exuberant callus formation, and a crush injury of the upper thorax. Thoracic outlet syndrome symptoms are common in patients with chronic scapular dyskinesis. They have tight pectoralis minor, scalene, and upper trapezius muscles, with weak serratus anterior and lower trapezius muscles; this causes excessive anterior tilt and protraction.

 While patients with thoracic outlet syndrome occasionally present with a pure arterial, venous, or neurogenic picture, most often the picture is mixed.

The patient with thoracic outlet syndrome may complain of pain in the neck or shoulder, or numbness or tingling involving either the entire upper limb or the forearm and hand. The patient may state that the arm feels weak or easily fatigued. There may be venous engorgement or coolness of the involved arm.

Physical signs may be absent.

Various clinical tests have been proposed to assist in the diagnosis of this condition. A patient with arterial compression may have a positive Adson's test. The patient begins the test with the head laterally rotated to the side of the symptoms and extended. The patient then abducts the involved arm and inspires deeply. A positive test obliterates the radial pulse and reproduces symptoms. The sensitivity of this test can be greatly increased by the use of Doppler flow patterns during the maneuver. The most sensitive provocation test is the Roos hyperabduction/external rotation test, in which the patient opens and closes his or her hands for 1–3 minutes with elbows bent and arms abducted to 90° and externally rotated in an attempt to reproduce the symptoms. Evaluation of scapular motion and position can help to rule scapular dyskinesis in or out.

Treatment

Treatment for any subset of thoracic outlet syndrome focuses on the specific area compromised. However, certain treatments apply to all forms of thoracic outlet syndrome. Correction of drooping shoulders, poor posture, and poor body mechanics is vital. The patient should be taught proper positioning while sitting, standing, and lying down. Physical therapy should address pectoral and scalene stretching, trigger point treatment, soft tissue mobilization of restricted tissues, scapular mobilization, and scapulothoracic mobility. Joint mobilization of the first rib can restore accessory motion of the sternoclavicular and acromioclavicular joints. Therapeutic exercise, education, and manual therapy can correct forward head posture. Thoracic extension and brachial plexus neuromobility exercises are added as tolerated.

Surgical consultation and treatment is warranted for patients who have neurogenic thoracic outlet syndrome that does not respond to aggressive non-surgical management and for patients who have vascular compromise or thrombus formation. Arterial compression caused by a complete cervical rib is usually treated by first rib resection.

Axillary vein thrombosis ("effort" thrombosis)

Axillary vein thrombosis is also known as "effort" thrombosis because of its frequent association with repetitive vigorous activities or with blunt trauma that results in direct or indirect injury to the vein. The eponymous name, Paget-von Schrötter syndrome, is falling out of favor. The axillary vein can be compressed at various sites along its path, most significantly in the costoclavicular space. Compression most often occurs when the patient hyperextends the neck and hyperabducts the arm simultaneously, or when the patient assumes a military brace position with a backward thrust of the shoulders. Compression can also occur between the clavicle and the first rib, the costocoracoid ligament and first rib, or the subclavian muscles and first rib.

Patients complain of dull, aching pain, numbness or tightness, and heaviness of the upper arm and shoulder, along with fatigue, after activities involving the extremity.

On examination, the entire upper extremity will be swollen, the skin may be mottled and cold, and superficial veins may be prominent.

The diagnosis is confirmed on venography.

 In axillary vein thrombosis, the entire upper extremity will be swollen, the skin may be mottled and cold, and superficial veins may be prominent.

Treatment involves rest and anticoagulant therapy. Most patients make a full recovery and are able to resume sporting activities.[70]

Fractures around the shoulder joint

Stress fractures around the shoulder joint are uncommon. Stress fracture of the coracoid process is associated with the sport of trapshooting. Patients with this stress fracture have localized tenderness over the coracoid process and a focal area of abnormality on MRI or isotopic bone scan.

Scapular fractures are usually due to a crushing force, either a fall on the shoulder or direct violence. Examination reveals marked tenderness and swelling. X-rays should be taken to exclude other associated injuries, such as a rib fracture, dislocated shoulder, or dislocated sternoclavicular joint. Scapular fractures usually heal well, even if they are displaced. A broad arm sling is worn for comfort, and active movements are commenced as soon as pain permits.

Fracture of the neck of the humerus is caused by a fall on the outstretched hand or direct violence. It is seen in adolescents, young adults, and the elderly. Fractures involving more than two fragments displaced by more than 1 cm (0.5 in.) or associated with shoulder dislocation require surgical assessment. Minimally displaced or angulated fractures may be treated conservatively. Impacted fractures heal rapidly and can be supported in a broad arm sling. Displaced fractures are best treated in a collar and cuff that allows gravity to correct any angulation. For the first two weeks the arm should be kept in a sling under a shirt. After two weeks, pendular movement exercises of the shoulder joint should be commenced. From four weeks, a collar and cuff may be worn outside the clothes and gradually removed in stages over the following two weeks.

An unusual fracture is seen among throwing athletes.[71] These athletes can sustain a closed external

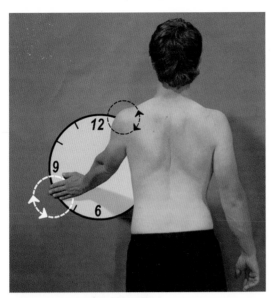

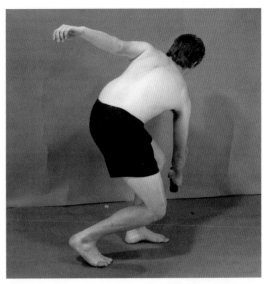

B

Figure 21.32 Scapular exercises

(a) Scapular clock—the patient envisions a clock tattooed on the injured shoulder then places the arm against a wall (as shown) or on a ball which may be rolled against the wall or on a table/couch. The patient then moves the shoulder in the direction of 12 o'clock, 3 o'clock or 6 o'clock, which facilitates scapula elevation, retraction, and depression, respectively

(c) Lawn mower—starting position. This exercise simulates pulling the starting cord of a lawn mower. It can be commenced with large amounts of trunk rotation and lower limb extension to guide shoulder motion. Early in rehabilitation, it is done without weights; dumbbells (shown) and tubing can be used to progress the exercise

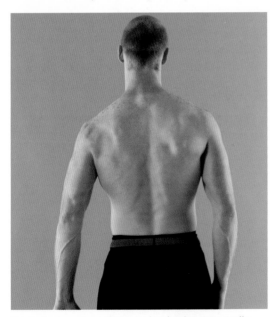

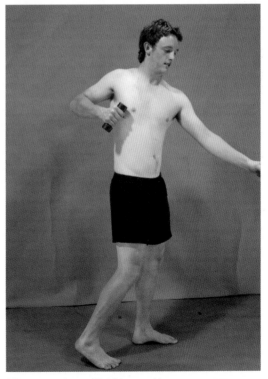

(b) Low row—the patient pushes back isometrically with the arm in no more than 10° of extension. The patient is instructed to "push back with your entire arm and slide your scapula down at the same time"

(d) Lawn mower—finishing position

379

(e) Inferior glide—starting position

joint mobilizations, proprioceptive neuromuscular facilitation patterns, and passive stretching. The pace of progression should be relatively slow in the healing phases, but may be more vigorous after three to six weeks. Sleeper stretches (Fig. 21.33b) are very effective in achieving and maintaining glenohumeral rotation.

Figure 21.33 Exercises for abduction and improved glenohumeral rotation
(a) Wand exercise for active-assisted range of motion. The patient assists his right shoulder abduction by pushing the wand with his left hand

activation patterns. Therefore, the thrower's shoulder should be rehabilitated at the 90° position to allow for the normal motor patterns to be recreated. This is the physiological angle for length-dependent motor patterns. Furthermore, at 90° of abduction, the inferior glenohumeral ligamentous constraints become taut in this position and, thus, contribute maximally to control of the instant center of rotation.

Practice

Aim to achieve 90° of abduction early in the rehabilitation process by reducing pain from impingement or other sources as quickly as possible. Maintain scapular stabilizer strength so that acromial elevation clears the acromion from the rotator cuff. Tendinopathy should be minimized to allow the tendons to slide under the coracoacromial arch. In operative cases, the subacromial space should be cleared of impediments to abduction, such as calcific deposits, bone spurs, or excessively thick bursal tissue. When performing surgical reconstruction for shoulder stability, the surgeon must ensure that 90° of abduction can be obtained on the operating table. (This will allow early achievement of 90° of abduction without undue stress on the ligaments.) This is analogous to ensuring full extension of the knee in anterior cruciate ligament reconstructions. Specific exercises to achieve 90° of abduction include active-assisted wand maneuvers (Fig. 21.33a), gentle

(b) Sleeper stretch—lying in the position shown, the patient stretches the posterior capsule

Closed chain rehabilitation

Principle

The predominant method of muscle activation around the shoulder articulation is a closed chain activity emphasizing co-contraction force couples at the scapulothoracic and glenohumeral joint. This results in proper scapulohumeral rhythm, and allows the rotator cuff to work as a "compressor cuff," conferring concavity–compression and a stable instant center of rotation. Closed chain activity also simulates the normal proprioceptive pathways that exist in the throwing motion, and allows feedback from the muscle spindles and Golgi tendon organs in their proper anatomical positions. Closed chain activity replicates the normal ball and socket kinematics, minimizing translation in the mid-ranges of motion. Finally, by decreasing deltoid activation, these activities decrease the tendency for superior humeral migration if the rotator cuff is weak.

Open chain activities, which involve agonist–antagonist force couples and generate force for the shoulder and the kinetic chain, are also seen around the shoulder articulation but are of secondary importance. They require deltoid and other extrinsic muscle activation, create shear forces at the glenohumeral joint and require large ranges of motion. Exercises to simulate these activities should be instituted later in rehabilitation, as they produce larger forces and require greater motions than the shoulder can tolerate early in rehabilitation. Closed chain rehabilitation provides a stable scapular base and early rotator cuff strength, which allows open chain activities.

Practice

The exercises are started at levels below 90° of abduction in the early phases of rehabilitation to allow for healing of the tissues.[11, 73] They may be started at 45° of abduction and 60° of flexion and then proceed to 90° of abduction as tolerated. The hand is placed against some object, such as a table, ball, or wall, and resistance is generated through the activities of the scapula and shoulder. When the arm can be safely positioned at 90° of abduction, it is placed in either abduction or flexion and a specific progression is started.

The closed chain activities are first started with scapular stabilization. Patterns of retraction and protraction of the scapula are started in single planes, then progress to elevation and depression of the entire scapula, then selective elevation of the acromion (Fig. 21.34).

The next progression is on to rotator cuff activity. Joint compression with contraction into the shoulder joint is followed by "clock" exercises, in which the hand is moved to the various positions on the clock face, ranging from eight o'clock to four o'clock

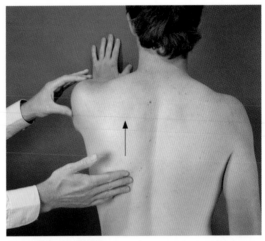

Figure 21.34 Scapular exercises
(a) Scapular elevation

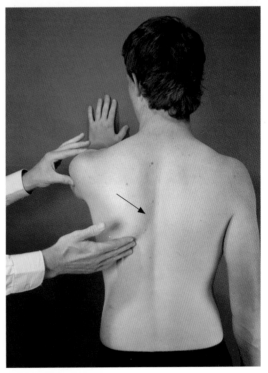

(b) Scapular retraction

(Fig. 21.32a). This allows for rotation of the humerus with the arm at 90° of abduction, which replicates rotator cuff activity throughout all components of the rotator cuff. These activities are first done against fixed resistance, such as a wall, and then moved to movable resistance, such as a ball or some other movable implement. These exercises may be done early in the rehabilitation phase, as they do not put shear on the joint and they allow rotator cuff muscles to be activated without being inhibited by pain or deltoid overactivity.

Closed chain progressions may be used in later phases of rehabilitation. They include various types of push-ups (wall leans, knee push-ups, and regular push-ups; Fig. 21.35) and scaption exercises (Fig. 21.36).

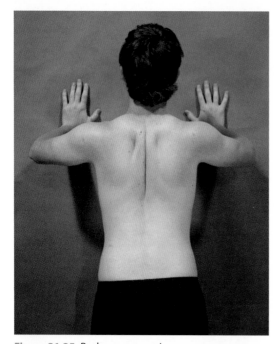

Figure 21.35 Push-up progressions
(a) Wall push-ups

(b) Knee push-ups

Figure 21.36 Scaption exercises (see also *Clinical Sports Medicine* masterclasses online)

 WWW **These are demonstrated in the *Clinical Sports Medicine* masterclasses at www.clinicalsportsmedicine.com.**

Plyometric exercises
Principle

Most athletic activities involve development of power. Power is the rate of doing work and, therefore, has a time component. For most sports, this time component is relatively rapid. Plyometric activities develop the sportsperson's ability to generate power by producing a stretch-shortening cycle in which the muscle is eccentrically stretched and slowly loaded. This pre-tensioning phase is followed by a rapid concentric contraction to develop a large amount of momentum and force. Because these exercises develop a large amount of strain in the eccentric phase of the activity, and force in the concentric phase of the activity, they should be done when complete anatomical healing has occurred. Similarly, because large ranges of motion are required, full range of motion should be obtained before the plyometric activities are started. These stretch-shortening activation sequences are part of the normal force-dependent patterns that are present in skilled sportspeople.

Practice

Plyometrics should be done for all body segments involved in the activity, and not just the shoulder. Hip rotation, knee flexion and extension, and trunk rotation are all power activities that require plyometric activation. Plyometric activities for the lower extremity can be done in the early phases of rehabilitation, but plyometric exercises for the upper extremity should be instituted in later phases. Many different activities and devices can be utilized in plyometric exercises.

Rubber tubing is a very effective plyometric device (Fig. 21.37). The arm or leg can be positioned exactly in the position of the athletic activity and then the motion can be replicated by use of the rubber tubing. Balls are also excellent plyometric devices. The weight of the ball creates a pre-stretch as the ball is caught and creates resistance for contraction forces (Fig. 21.38). Light weights can also be used for plyometric activities, but caution must be used in using heavier weights in a plyometric fashion due to the forces applied on the joint. Plyometric activities with

Figure 21.38 Throwing and catching a basketball against a mini-trampoline

larger weights can be done more easily in the lower extremity than the upper extremity. By reproducing these stretch-shortening cycles at positions of physiological function, these plyometric activities also stimulate proprioceptive feedback to fine-tune the muscle activity patterns. Plyometric exercises are the most appropriate open chain exercises for functional shoulder rehabilitation.

Rotator cuff exercises

Principle

The rotator cuff muscles act as a unit in functional shoulder activities. Because many pathological conditions contribute to rotator cuff overload, selective isolated rotator cuff exercises are frequently not successful in relieving the clinical symptoms.

Practice

Rotator cuff muscles should be rehabilitated as an integrated unit, rather than as individual muscles. They do not work in isolation in shoulder function, and the anatomical positions and motions that are used for testing are not seen in shoulder function. Because they require a stabilized scapula to provide a stable base of muscle origin, and because individual rotator cuff activity creates shear across the glenohumeral joint, early rotator cuff exercises should be done in a closed chain fashion.

Closed chain rotator cuff strengthening exercises redevelop the composite rotator cuff effectively and that isolated rotator cuff exercises are not commonly needed in later stages of rehabilitation. An effective progression of rotator cuff activation exercises includes progression from close chain to open chain methods, arm position from horizontal to vertical to diagonal, and exercise speed from low to high.[3]

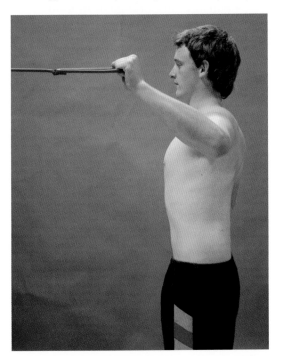

Figure 21.37 Rubber tubing plyometric exercises. The tubing creates an eccentric stretch and offers resistance to concentric contraction

If rotator cuff deficits are still observed in the later phases of rehabilitation, isolated rotator cuff exercises can be prescribed. If prescribed, individual rotator cuff exercises should be incorporated into an integrated conditioning program.

A useful clinical sign for deficiencies in rotator cuff rehabilitation is exacerbation of clinical symptoms when rotator cuff exercises are started. This can most likely be traced to abnormalities in other parts of the kinetic chain, most commonly the scapular stabilizers.

Putting it all together—specific rehabilitation protocols

Many different therapeutic exercises can be used to fulfill each of the above principles. The protocol should address the functional deficits identified and should follow a general sequence as described above, although exact details will be based on the patient's clinical presentation and the therapist's skill and imagination. Adherence to this program requires patient education and guidance from the physician and physiotherapist on the techniques of rehabilitation. Most of the physiotherapy can be done by home programs once the exercises have been taught appropriately. Physiotherapy office visits are used for assessment of achievement of the individual goals for the rehabilitation sequence, instruction in the exercises to be done in the next phase, and specific guidance as to goals to achieve for the next rehabilitation phase. Modalities such as ice, electrotherapeutic modalities, ultrasound, and heat are very rarely indicated after the initial stages of pain reduction.

This protocol assumes, if surgery has been performed, stable repair of the labrum, capsule, or rotator cuff, and ability to achieve 90° of abduction without impingement or excessive capsular stretch at the time of the operation. The time frame depends on the severity of the injury or extent of the surgical procedure(s). The rehabilitation goal is to progress postoperative labral repairs, shoulder reconstructions, and acromioplasties to 90° of passive or active-assisted abduction by three weeks, and rotator cuff repairs to 90° of passive or active-assisted abduction by four to six weeks.

Acute phase

The goals of the acute phase are:

- tissue healing
- reduction of pain and inflammation

- re-establishment of non-painful range of motion below 90° of abduction
- retardation of muscle atrophy
- scapular control
- maintenance of fitness in other components of the kinetic chain.

Tissue healing

Tissue healing is a combination of:

- rest
- short-term immobilization
- modalities
- surgery.

Reduction of pain and inflammation

Aggressive treatment is used to control pain, to decrease muscle atrophy and scapular instability due to serratus and/or trapezius inhibition. This is done through:

- analgesic medications (with due consideration to the negative effects of NSAIDs on tendon healing)
- electrotherapeutic modalities
- ice or cold compression devices
- posture and positioning.

Re-establishment of range of motion

The range of motion should be started in pain-free arcs, kept below 90° of abduction, and may be passive or active-assisted. The degree of movement is guided by the stability of the operative repair. Range of motion should be re-established by:

- pendulum exercises
- manual capsular stretching and cross-fiber massage
- T-bar or ropes and pulleys.

Retardation of muscle atrophy

Isometric exercises, with the arm below 90° of abduction and 90° of flexion, should be done in patients with labral or capsular repair, but not in those with rotator cuff repairs.

Scapular control

The exercises to maintain scapular control include:

- isometric scapular pinches and scapular elevation
- low row (Fig. 21.32b)
- closed chain weight shifts, with hands on table and the shoulders flexed less than 60° and abducted less than 45°
- tilt board or circular board weight shifts with the same limitations (Fig. 21.39).

Figure 21.39 Closed chain weight shift using tilt board

Maintainenance of fitness in rest of kinetic chain

Exercises to maintain fitness in the rest of the kinetic chain include:

- aerobic exercises such as running, bicycling, or stepping
- anaerobic agility drills
- lower extremity strengthening by machines, squat exercises, or open chain leg lifts
- elbow and wrist strengthening by isometric exercises or rubber tubing
- flexibility exercises for areas of tightness
- integration of the kinetic chain by leg and trunk stabilization on a ball, employing rotational and oblique patterns of contraction (Fig. 21.40).

Criteria for movement out of the acute phase

The criteria for movement out of the acute phase include:

- progression of tissue healing (healed or sufficiently stabilized for active motion and tissue loading)
- passive range of motion at 66–75% of opposite side
- minimal pain
- manual muscle strength in non-pathological areas of 4+/5
- achievement of scapular asymmetry of less than 1.5 cm (0.6 in.)
- kinetic chain function and integration.

Recovery phase

The goals of the recovery phase are:

- normal active and passive shoulder and glenohumeral range of motion
- improved scapular control

Figure 21.40 Plyoball hip and trunk rotation exercise

- normal upper extremity strength and balance
- normal shoulder arthrokinetics in single and then multiple planes of motion
- normal kinetic chain and force generation patterns.

Normal range of motion

Normal active and passive shoulder and glenohumeral range of motion is achieved by:

- active-assisted motion above 90° of abduction with wand
- active-assisted, then active, motion in internal and external rotation, with scapula stabilized so that glenohumeral rotation is normalized without substitution movements from the scapula.

Scapular control

Scapular control is improved by:

- scapular proprioceptive neuromuscular facilitation patterns
- closed chain exercises at 90° of flexion, 90° of abduction, scapular retraction/protraction and scapular elevation/depression (Fig. 21.34)
- modified push-ups (Fig. 21.35)

- regular push-ups
- ball catch and push exercises (Fig. 21.38)
- dips (Fig. 21.32)
  - clock
  - low row
  - lawn mower.

Upper extremity strength and balance
Normal upper extremity strength and balance are achieved by:

- glenohumeral proprioceptive neuromuscular facilitation patterns
- closed chain exercises at 90° of flexion then 90° of abduction, using the glenohumeral depressors and glenohumeral internal/external rotators
- forearm curls
- isolated rotator cuff exercises
- machines or weights for light bench presses, military presses and pull-downs. The resistance should initially be light, then progress as strength improves. Emphasis is placed on proper mechanics, proper technique, and joint stabilization.

Normal shoulder arthrokinetics
Normal shoulder arthrokinetics is achieved by:

- range of motion exercises with arm at 90° of abduction—this is the position where most throwing and serving activities occur; the periarticular soft tissues must be completely loose and balanced at this position
- muscle activity at 90° of abduction—normal muscle firing patterns must be re-established at this position, both in organization of force generation and force regulation patterns, and in proprioceptive sensory feedback; closed chain patterns are an excellent method to re-establish the normal neurological patterns for joint stabilization
- open chain exercises, including mild plyometric exercises, which may be built upon the base of the closed chain stabilization to allow normal control of joint mobility.

Normal kinetic chain and force generation
Normal kinetic chain and force generation patterns are achieved by:

- normalization of all inflexibilities throughout the kinetic chain
- normal agonist–antagonist force couples in the legs using squats, plyometric depth jumps, lunges, and hip extensions

- trunk rotation exercises with medicine ball or tubing
- integrated exercises with leg and trunk stabilization, rotations, diagonal patterns from hip to shoulder, and medicine ball throws
- rotator cuff strength of 4+/5 or higher
- normal kinetic chain function.

Functional phase
The goals of the functional phase are:

- to increase power and endurance in the upper extremity
- to increase normal multiple-plane neuromuscular control—locally, regionally, and in the entire kinetic chain
- instruction in rehabilitation activities
- sport-specific activity.

Power and endurance in upper extremity
Power is the rate of doing work. Work may be done to move the joint and the extremity, or it may be done to absorb a load and stabilize the joint or extremity. Power has a time component and, for shoulder activity, quick movements and quick reactions are the dominant ways of doing work. These exercises should, therefore, be done with relatively rapid movements in planes that approximate normal shoulder function (i.e. 90° of abduction in shoulder, trunk rotation, and diagonal arm motions, rapid external/internal rotation). The exercises include:

- diagonal and multiplanar motions with rubber tubing (Fig. 21.37), light weights, small medicine balls, and isokinetic machines
- plyometrics—wall push-ups (Fig. 21.35a), corner push-ups, weighted ball throws, and tubing. Tubing and medicine balls are very effective plyometric devices.

Multiple-plane neuromuscular control
The force-dependent motor firing patterns should be re-established. No subclinical adaptations, such as "opening up" (trunk rotation too far in front of shoulder rotation), three-quarter arm positioning on throwing, or excessive wrist snap should be allowed. Help in this area can be obtained by watching pre-injury videos or by using a knowledgeable coach in the particular sport. Special care must be taken to integrate all of the components of the kinetic chain completely, to generate and funnel the proper forces to and through the shoulder.

Rehabilitation

The sportsperson who is injured while playing a sport will most often return to the sport with the same sports demands. The body should be healed from the symptomatic standpoint and should be prepared for resuming the stresses inherent in playing the sport. The aim of rehabilitation is to restore:

- flexibility—general body flexibility, with an emphasis on sport-specific problems (shoulder internal rotation and elbow extension in the arm, low back, hip rotation, and hamstrings in the legs)
- strength—appropriate amounts and locations of strength for force generation, trunk rotation strength for sport-specific activities (quadriceps/hamstring strength for force generation, trunk rotation strength, strength balance for the shoulder)
- power—rapid movements in appropriate planes with light weights
- endurance—mainly anaerobic exercises due to short duration, explosive, and ballistic activities seen in throwing and serving. These exercises should be based on the periodization principle of conditioning.

Sport-specific activity

Functional progressions of throwing or serving must be completed before the sportsperson can return to competition. These progressions will gradually test all of the mechanical parts of the throwing or serving motion. Very few deviations from normal parameters of arm motion, arm position, force generation, smoothness of all of the kinetic chain, and pre-injury form should be allowed, as most of these adaptations will be biomechanically inefficient. The sportsperson may move through the progressions as rapidly as possible.

Criteria for return to play

The criteria for return to play include:

- normal clinical examination
- normal shoulder arthrokinetics
- normal kinetic chain integration
- completed progressions.

CLINICAL SPORTS MEDICINE MASTERCLASSES

www.clinicalsportsmedicine.com

- How to conduct a swift and effective physical examination.
- Prescription for practical shoulder rehabilitation.
- Demonstration of key shoulder exercises.

REFERENCES

1. Pagnani MJ, Warren RF. Stabilizers of the glenohumeral joint. *J Shoulder Elbow Surg* 1994;3(3):173–90.
2. Ainsworth R, Lewis JS. Exercise therapy for the conservative management of full thickness tears of the rotator cuff: a systematic review. *Br J Sports Med* 2007;41(4):200–10.
3. Kibler WB, Uhl TL, Maddux JW et al. Qualitative clinical evaluation of scapular dysfunction: a reliability study. *J Shoulder Elbow Surg* 2002;11(6):550–6.
4. Tzannes A, Paxinos A, Callanan M et al. An assessment of the interexaminer reliability of tests for shoulder instability. *J Shoulder Elbow Surg* 2004;13(1):18–23.
5. Uhl TL, Kibler WB, Gecewich B et al. Evaluation of clinical assessment methods for scapular dyskinesis. *Arthroscopy* 2009;25(11):1240–8.
6. Kibler WB, Ludewig PM, McClure P et al. Scapular Summit 2009: Introduction. July 16, 2009, Lexington, Kentucky. *J Orthop Sports Phys Ther* 2009;39(11): A1–A13.
7. Cools AM, Declercq GA, Cambier DC et al. Trapezius activity and intramuscular balance during isokinetic exercise in overhead athletes with impingement symptoms. *Scand J Med Sci Sports* 2007;17(1):25–33.
8. Walton J, Mahajan S, Paxinos A et al. Diagnostic values of tests for acromioclavicular joint pain. *J Bone Joint Surg Am* 2004;86–A(4):807–12.
9. Kibler WB, Sciascia AD, Uhl TL et al. Electromyographic analysis of specific exercises for scapular control in early phases of shoulder rehabilitation. *Am J Sports Med* 2008;36(9):1789–98.
10. Kibler BW, Sciascia AD, Hester P et al. Clinical utility of traditional and new tests in the diagnosis of biceps tendon injuries and superior labrum anterior and posterior lesions in the shoulder. *Am J Sports Med* 2009;37(9):1840–7.
11. Kibler WB, McMullen JM. Scapular dyskinesis and its relation to shoulder pain. *J Am Acad Orthop Surg* 2003;11(2):142–51.
12. Kibler WB, Press J, Sciascia A. The role of core stability in athletic function. *Sports Med* 2006;36(3):189–98.
13. Murrell GA, Walton JR. Diagnosis of rotator cuff tears. *Lancet* 2001;357(9258):769–70.

B

14. Sein ML, Walton J, Linklater J et al. Shoulder pain in elite swimmers: primarily due to swim-volume-induced supraspinatus tendinopathy. *Br J Sports Med* 2010;44:105–13.

15. Burkhart SS, Morgan CD, Kibler WB. The disabled throwing shoulder: spectrum of pathology Part I: pathoanatomy and biomechanics. *Arthroscopy* 2003;19(4):404–20.

16. Burkhart SS, Morgan CD, Kibler WB. The disabled throwing shoulder: spectrum of pathology Part II: evaluation and treatment of SLAP lesions in throwers. *Arthroscopy* 2003;19(5):531–9.

17. Burkhart SS, Morgan CD, Kibler WB. The disabled throwing shoulder: spectrum of pathology Part III: the SICK scapula, scapular dyskinesis, the kinetic chain, and rehabilitation. *Arthroscopy* 2003;19(6):641–61.

18. Ogawa K, Yoshida A, Inokuchi W et al. Acromial spur: relationship to aging and morphologic changes in the rotator cuff. *J Shoulder Elbow Surg* 2005;14(6):591–8.

19. Ludewig PM, Reynolds JF. The association of scapular kinematics and glenohumeral joint pathologies. *J Orthop Sports Phys Ther* 2009;39(2):90–104.

20. Ludewig PM, Phadke V, Braman JP et al. Motion of the shoulder complex during multiplanar humeral elevation. *J Bone Joint Surg Am* 2009;91(2):378–89.

21. Phadke V, Camargo PR, Ludewig PM. Scapular and rotator cuff muscle activity during arm elevation: A review of normal function and alterations with shoulder impingement. *Rev Bras Fisioter* 2009;13(1):1–9.

22. Yuan J, Murrell GA, Wei AQ et al. Apoptosis in rotator cuff tendonopathy. *J Orthop Res* 2002;20(6):1372–9.

23. Uhthoff HK, Loehr JW. Calcific tendinopathy of the rotator cuff: pathogenesis, diagnosis, and management. *J Am Acad Orthop Surg* 1997;5(4):183–91.

24. Miller D, Frost A, Hall A et al. A 'one-stop clinic' for the diagnosis and management of rotator cuff pathology: getting the right diagnosis first time. *Int J Clin Pract* 2008;62(5):750–53.

25. Cumpston M, Johnston RV, Wengier L et al. Topical glyceryl trinitrate for rotator cuff disease. *Cochrane Database Syst Rev* 2009;(3):CD006355.

26. Paoloni JA, Appleyard RC, Nelson J et al. Topical glyceryl trinitrate application in the treatment of chronic supraspinatus tendinopathy: a randomized, double-blinded, placebo-controlled clinical trial. *Am J Sports Med* 2005;33(6):806–13.

27. Blair B, Rokito AS, Cuomo F et al. Efficacy of injections of corticosteroids for subacromial impingement syndrome. *J Bone Joint Surg Am* 1996;78(11):1685–9.

28. Shinozaki N, Sano H, Omi R et al. Differences in muscle activities during shoulder elevation in patients with symptomatic and asymptomatic rotator cuff tears: analysis using positron emission tomography. *American Academy of Orthopaedic Surgeons Annual Meeting*; 2010; New Orleans.

29. Miller P, Osmotherly P. Does scapula taping facilitate recovery for shoulder impingement symptoms? A pilot randomized controlled trial. *J Man Manip Ther* 2009;17(1):E6–13.

30. Gerdesmeyer L, Wagenpfeil S, Haake M et al. Extracorporeal shock wave therapy for the treatment of chronic calcifying tendonitis of the rotator cuff: a randomized controlled trial. *JAMA* 2003;290(19): 2573–80.

31. Harniman E, Carette S, Kennedy C et al. Extracorporeal shock wave therapy for calcific and noncalcific tendonitis of the rotator cuff: a systematic review. *J Hand Ther* 2004;17(2):132–51.

32. Moretti B, Garofalo R, Genco S et al. Medium-energy shock wave therapy in the treatment of rotator cuff calcifying tendinitis. *Knee Surg Sports Traumatol Arthrosc* 2005;13(5):405–10.

33. Peters J, Luboldt W, Schwarz W et al. Extracorporeal shock wave therapy in calcific tendinitis of the shoulder. *Skeletal Radiol* 2004;33(12):712–8.

34. Kelly MJ, Lam PH, Briggs L et al. Ultrasound-guided placement of a localization wire for arthroscopic treatment of calcific tendinitis. *78th Annual Meeting of the American Academy of Orthopaedic Surgeons*; 2011; San Diego.

35. Veeger HE, van der Helm FC. Shoulder function: the prefect compromise between mobility and stability. *J Biomech* 2007;40:2119–29.

36. Wilk KE, Reinold MM, Dugas JR et al. Current concepts in the recognition and treatment of superior labral (SLAP) lesions. *J Orthop Sports Phys Ther* 2005;35(5):273–91.

37. Rhee YG, Lee DH, Lim CT. Unstable isolated SLAP lesion: clinical presentation and outcome of arthroscopic fixation. *Arthroscopy* 2005;21(9):1099.

38. Snyder SJ, Banas MP, Karzel RP. An analysis of 140 injuries to the superior glenoid labrum. *J Shoulder Elbow Surg* 1995;4(4):243–8.

39. Applegate GR, Hewitt M, Snyder SJ et al. Chronic labral tears: value of magnetic resonance arthrography in evaluating the glenoid labrum and labral-bicipital complex. *Arthroscopy* 2004;20(9):959–63.

40. Liu SH, Henry MH, Nuccion S et al. Diagnosis of glenoid labral tears—a comparison between magnetic resonance imaging and clinical examinations. *Am J Sports Med* 1996;24(2):149–54.

41. Fabbriciani C, Milano G, Demontis A et al. Arthroscopic versus open treatment of Bankart lesion of the shoulder: a prospective randomized study. *Arthroscopy* 2004;20(5):456–62.

42. Edwards SL, Lee JA, Bell JE et al. Nonoperative treatment of superior labrum anterior posterior tears: improvements in pain, function and quality of life. *Am J Sports Med* 2010;38(7):1456–61.

43. Kuhn JE. Treating the initial anterior shoulder dislocation—an evidence-based medicine approach. *Sports Med Arthrosc* 2006;14:192–8.

44. Hovelius L, Augustini BG, Fredin H et al. Primary anterior dislocation of the shoulder in young patients. A ten-year prospective study. *J Bone Joint Surg Am* 1996;78:1677–84.

45. Itoi E, Sashi R, Minagawa H et al. Position of immobilization after dislocation of the glenohumeral joint. A study with use of magnetic resonance imaging. *J Bone Joint Surg Am* 2001;83-A:661–7.

46. Handoll HH, Hanchard NC, Goodchild L et al. Conservative management following closed reduction of traumatic anterior dislocation of the shoulder. *Cochrane Database Syst Rev* 2006;1:CD004962.

47. Boone JL, Arciero RA. First-time anterior shoulder dislocations: has the standard changed? *Br J Sports Med* 2010;44:355–360.

48. Handoll HH, Almaiyah MA, Rangan A. Surgical versus non-surgical treatment for acute anterior shoulder dislocation. *Cochrane Database Syst Rev* 2004;1:CD004325.

49. Cox CL, Kuhn JE. Operative versus nonoperative treatment of acute shoulder dislocation in the athlete. *Curr Sports Med Rep* 2008;7(5):263–68.

50. Speer KP, Hannafin JA, Altchek DW et al. An evaluation of the shoulder relocation test. *Am J Sports Med* 1994;22(2):177–83.

51. Plancher KD, Lipnick SL. Analysis of evidence-based medicine for shoulder instability. *Arthroscopy* 2009;25(8):897–908.

52. Warner JJ, Allen A, Marks PH et al. Arthroscopic release for chronic, refractory adhesive capsulitis of the shoulder. *J Bone Joint Surg* 1996;78A(12):1808–16.

53. Diwan DB, Murrell GA. An evaluation of the effects of the extent of capsular release and of postoperative therapy on the temporal outcomes of adhesive capsulitis. *Arthroscopy* 2005;21(9):1105–13.

54. Pujalte GGA, Housner JA. Management of clavicle fractures. *Curr Sports Med Rep* 2008;7(5):275–80.

55. Bradley JP, Elkousy H. Decision making: operative versus nonoperative treatment of acromioclavicular joint injuries. *Clin Sports Med* 2003;22(2):277–90.

56. Turnbull JR. Acromioclavicular joint disorders. *Med Sci Sports Exerc* 1998;30(4 Suppl):S26–32.

57. Gumina S, Carbone S, Postacchini F. Scapular dyskinesis and SICK scapula syndrome in patients with type III acromioclavicular dislocation. *Arthroscopy* 2009;25:40–45.

58. Ceccarelli E, Bondi R, Alviti F et al. Treatment of acute grade III acromioclavicular dislocation: a lack of evidence. *J Orthop Traumatol* 2008;9(2):105–8.

59. Kay SP, Dragoo JL, Lee R. Long-term results of arthroscopic resection of the distal clavicle with concomitant subacromial decompression. *Arthroscopy* 2003;19(8):805–9.

60. Debski RE, Fenwick JA, Vangura A, Jr et al. Effect of arthroscopic procedures on the acromioclavicular joint. *Clin Orthop Relat Res* 2003(406):89–96.

61. Zanetti M, Weishaupt D, Gerber C et al. Tendinopathy and rupture of the tendon of the long head of the biceps brachii muscle: evaluation with MR arthrography. *AJR Am J Roentgenol* 1998;170(6):1557–61.

62. Petilon J, Carr DR, Sekiya JK et al. Pectoralis major muscle injuries: evaluation and management. *J Am Acad Orthop Surg* 2005;13(1):59–68.

63. Bayramoglu A, Demiryurek D, Tuccar E et al. Variations in anatomy at the suprascapular notch possibly causing suprascapular nerve entrapment: an anatomical study. *Knee Surg Sports Traumatol Arthrosc* 2003;11(6):393–98.

64. Ferretti A, De Carli A, Fontana M. Injury of the suprascapular nerve at the spinoglenoid notch—the natural history of infraspinatus atrophy in volleyball players. *Am J Sports Med* 1998;26(6):759–63.

65. Feinberg JH, Nadler SF, Krivickas LS. Peripheral nerve injuries in the athlete. *Sports Med* 1997;24(6):385–408.

66. Krivickas LS, Wilbourn AJ. Peripheral nerve injuries in athletes: a case series of over 200 injuries. *Semin Neurol* 2000;20(2):225–32.

67. Atasoy E. Thoracic outlet syndrome: anatomy. *Hand Clin* 2004;20(1):7–14,v.

68. Brantigan CO, Roos DB. Etiology of neurogenic thoracic outlet syndrome. *Hand Clin* 2004;20(1):17–22.

69. Richardson AB. Thoracic outlet syndrome in aquatic athletes. *Clin Sports Med* 1999;18(2):361–78.

70. Chaudhry MA, Hajarnavis J. Paget-von Schrotter syndrome: primary subclavian-axillary vein thrombosis in sport activities. *Clin J Sport Med* 2003;13(4):269–71.

71. Ogawa K, Yoshida A. Throwing fracture of the humeral shaft. An analysis of 90 patients. *Am J Sports Med* 1998;26(2):242–6.

72. Kibler WB. The role of the scapula in athletic shoulder function. *Am J Sports Med* 1998;26(2):325–37.

73. Kibler WB. Rehabilitation of rotator cuff tendinopathy. *Clin Sports Med* 2003;22(4):837–47.

74. Kibler WB, McMullen J, Uhl T. Shoulder rehabilitation strategies, guidelines, and practice. *Orthop Clin North Am* 2001;32(3):527–38.

Chapter 22

Elbow and arm pain

with ALEX SCOTT, SIMON BELL, and BILL VICENZINO

*In 2000, the injuries really started to kick in and my elbow gave me a lot of problems.
At the end of the year I had to take 20 months off before I could come back into the game.*
Richard Krajicek, former professional tennis player and 1996 Wimbledon Champion

Use of the upper limb in sport demands a well-functioning elbow. In addition, injuries in this region may interfere with the patient's everyday activities. It is impossible to think of "elbow pain" without imagining a tennis player or a golfer with tendinopathy. But other important conditions can also cause elbow and arm symptoms. We outline the clinical approach to elbow pain under the following headings:

- lateral elbow pain, with a particular focus on extensor tendinopathy
- medial elbow pain
- posterior elbow pain
- acute elbow injuries
- forearm pain
- upper arm pain.

Lateral elbow pain

The lateral elbow is the most common site of pain about the elbow (Fig. 22.1). Some diagnoses that need be considered are tennis elbow, referred pain from the cervical and upper thoracic spine, synovitis of the radiohumeral joint, radiohumeral bursitis, osteochondritis dissecans of the capitellum and radius, or a combination thereof (Table 22.1).

If your patient is between 30 and 60 years with local lateral elbow pain, with or without some spread into the forearm, but no pain in the neck, arm, and beyond the wrist, then "tennis elbow" is the likely diagnosis. Although evocative, the term "tennis elbow" is unsatisfactory as it gives little indication of pathology; in fact, sports medicine clinicians are more likely to see this condition in non-tennis

players than in tennis players. The term "lateral epicondylitis" is not accurate, as the primary pathology in chronic cases is not inflammatory as implied by the suffix "itis." The term "epicondylosis" is also not accurate, as not all patients present with degenerative

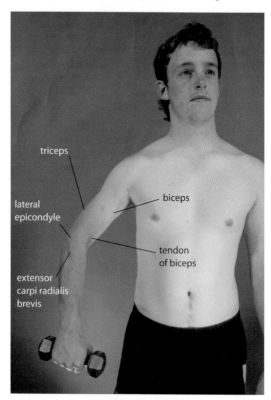

Figure 22.1 Anatomy of the lateral elbow
(a) Surface anatomy of the lateral elbow

mass, but it never extends into the hand and fingers, or proximally into the arm. The onset of pain is often insidious but may be acute. There may have been recent changes in training, technique, duties, or equipment used in sport or work.

The severity of pain ranges from relatively trivial pain to an almost incapacitating pain that may keep the patient awake at night. It is important to note whether the pain is aggravated by relatively minor everyday activities (e.g. picking up a cup) or whether it requires repeated activity (e.g. playing tennis, brick-laying) to become painful.

Pain in the lateral aspect of the forearm may implicate entrapment of the posterior interosseous nerve or irritation of other neural structures. If pain is closely related to the activity level, it is more likely to be of a mechanical origin. If pain is persistent, unpredictable, or related to posture, consider a source of pain from other anatomical structures, non-musculoskeletal pathologies, or abnormal central nervous system functioning (consider complex regional pain states). Lateral elbow tendinopathy is typically painful with gripping or wrist extension, whereas referred pain may be provoked by prolonged postures, such as lengthy periods seated at a desk or in a car. Associated sensory symptoms (e.g. pins and needles) also suggest a neural component. Presence of neck, upper thoracic, or shoulder pain should be noted, especially when symptoms extend beyond the lateral elbow and forearm.

Often by the time the patient presents to the sports medicine clinician, he or she has undergone a variety of treatments. It is important to note the response to each of these treatments.

An activity history should also be taken, noting any recent change in the level of activity. In tennis players, note any change in racquet size, grip size, or string tension, and whether or not any comment has been made regarding the patient's technique. This is also relevant to occupations involving manual tool handling tasks.

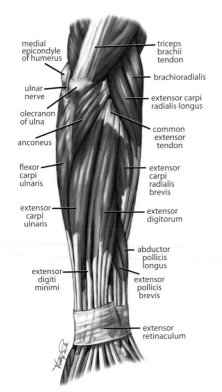

medial epicondyle of humerus — triceps brachii tendon — brachioradialis — ulnar nerve — extensor carpi radialis longus — olecranon of ulna — common extensor tendon — anconeus — flexor carpi ulnaris — extensor carpi radialis brevis — extensor carpi ulnaris — extensor digitorum — abductor pollicis longus — extensor digiti minimi — extensor pollicis brevis — extensor retinaculum

(b) Anatomy of the lateral elbow from behind

changes as implied by the suffix "osis" (Chapter 5). "Lateral elbow tendinopathy" or "lateral elbow pain" are more general terms which do not assume a given pathology or an exact source of symptoms and thus better reflect the clinical situation.

Clinical assessment

History

Begin by eliciting the characteristics of the patient's lateral elbow pain. The diffuse pain of extensor tendinopathy is typically located about the lateral epicondyle and proximal forearm. Occasionally the pain may radiate into the forearm extensor muscle

Table 22.1 Causes of lateral elbow pain

Common	Less common	Not to be missed
Extensor tendinopathy	Synovitis of the radiohumeral joint	Osteochondritis dissecans
Referred pain	Radiohumeral bursitis	• Capitellum
• Cervical spine	Posterior interosseous nerve	• Radius (in adolescents)
• Upper thoracic spine	entrapment (radial tunnel syndrome)	
• Neuro-myofascial		

B

Examination

Examination involves:

1. Observation from the front
2. Active movements
   (a) elbow flexion/extension
   (b) supination/pronation
   (c) wrist flexion (forearm pronated) (Fig. 22.2a)
   (d) wrist extension
3. Passive movements
   (a)–(d) as above
4. Resisted movements
   (a) wrist extension (Fig. 22.2b)
   (b) extension at the third metacarpophalangeal joint (Fig. 22.2c)
   (c) grip test (Fig. 22.2d)
5. Palpation
   (a) lateral epicondyle (Fig. 22.2e)
   (b) extensor muscles (Fig. 22.2f)

6. Special tests
   (a) neurodynamic tests
   (b) cervical spine examination (Chapter 20)
   (c) thoracic spine examination (Chapter 25)
   (d) periscapular soft tissues (Fig. 22.2g)

(c) Resisted muscle testing—extension at third metacarpophalangeal joint

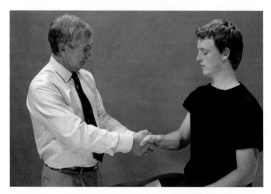

(d) Resisted muscle testing—grip strength. Attempt to reproduce pain

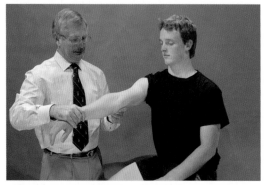

Figure 22.2 Examination of the patient with lateral elbow pain
(a) Active movement—wrist flexion with forearm fully pronated

(b) Resisted muscle testing—patient resists the clinician's pressure by extension of the wrist

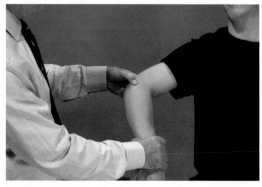

(e) Palpation—lateral epicondyle. Attempt to locate painful site distal to lateral epicondyle

(f) Palpation—extensor muscles. Pincer grip is used with passive flexion and extension to provide exact feel of damaged tissue

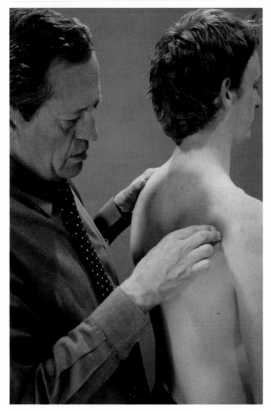

(g) Periscapular soft tissues—palpation of active trigger points and changes in muscle tone and length in the periscapular soft tissues

Investigations

Investigations are usually not performed in the straightforward case of lateral elbow pain. However, in longstanding cases, plain X-ray (AP and lateral views) of the elbow may show osteochondritis

dissecans, degenerative joint changes, or evidence of heterotopic calcification.

Grey scale and power Doppler ultrasound examination may prove to be a useful diagnostic tool. Ultrasound may demonstrate the degree of tendon or ligament damage[1] as well as the presence of a bursa, while power Doppler may show neovascularity.[2] The lack of both ultrasound and power Doppler findings in longstanding cases should prompt the practitioner to investigate other possible causes of the pain.

Lateral elbow tendinopathy

Lateral elbow tendinopathy is a a common sports medicine condition.

Clinically relevant pathology

It is conventional wisdom that the extensor carpi radialis brevis tendon is the most common tendon to become a problem; however, it has been suggested that the extensor digitorum (or extensor carpi ulnaris) may be implicated if the middle finger extension test is more provocative than the wrist extension test.[3] The tendon may be affected at its origin[4] or mid-substance. The latter is characterized on light microscopy as an excess of both fibroblasts and blood vessels.[5-7] The vessels appear consistent with what Alfredson calls "neovessels,"[8] pathologists call "angiogenesis," and Nirschl called "angiofibroblastic hyperplasia."[6] This abnormal tissue has a large number of nociceptive fibers, which may explain why the lesion can cause such intense pain. With continued use, the lesion may extend into microscopic partial tears.[9] Conversely, a tear may be the primary abnormality with degenerative change being secondary. A summary of the putative processes leading to the development of extensor tendinopathy is shown in Figure 22.3 overleaf.

With manual tasks that require wrist stabilization (such as gripping), or wrist extension movements, a considerable load may be placed on the extensor carpi radialis brevis tendon. The highest stresses occur in the extensor carpi radialis brevis tendon when the elbow is extended and the forearm pronated, which is the most provocative position in which to reproduce pain and test grip force. Not only is grip strength reduced in lateral elbow tendinopathy, but there is also evidence that the gripping mechanism is compromised, with those affected tending to grip in a flexed wrist position compared with controls.[10] Surprisingly, this abnormal gripping action was also present on the unaffected elbow side in unilateral

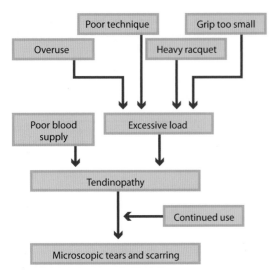

Figure 22.3 Processes leading to the development of extensor carpi radialis brevis tendinopathy

tendinopathy, inferring central neural mechanisms at play.[11] Consistent with these findings are reductions in reaction time and speed of movement that are bilaterally present in unilateral tendinopathy.[10, 12] Most intriguingly, tendinosis-like tissue changes can also be triggered bilaterally in response to unilateral overuse, as documented in a recent animal model.

Clinical features

Lateral elbow tendinopathy occurs in association with many tasks that involve loaded and repeated gripping and/or wrist extension actions/activities. These tasks includes sports (such as tennis, squash, and badminton) as well as occupational and leisure pursuits (such as carpentry, bricklaying, sewing, and knitting). Computer use has been shown to be associated with the development of this condition.[13] The peak incidence is between the ages of 40 and 50 years; however, the condition may affect any age group, although other conditions should be considered more carefully the further the patient is from this age group.

There are two distinct clinical presentations of lateral elbow tendinopathy. The most common is an insidious onset of pain, which occurs 24–72 hours after unaccustomed activity involving repeated wrist extension. This occurs typically after a person spends the weekend engaged in manual activity (such as laying bricks, using a screwdriver, or after prolonged sewing or knitting). In the tennis player, it may occur following the use of a new racquet, playing with wet

heavy balls, or overhitting, especially hitting into the wind. It also occurs when the player is hitting "late" (getting into position slowly), so that body weight is not transferred correctly and the player relies excessively on the forearm muscles for power.

The other clinical presentation is a sudden onset of lateral elbow pain associated with a single instance of exertion involving the wrist extensors (e.g. lifting a heavy object), or in tennis players attempting a hard backhand with too much reliance on the forearm and not enough on the trunk and legs. The insidious onset is thought to correspond to microscopic tears within the tendon, whereas the acute onset may correspond to larger macroscopic tears of the tendon.

On examination, insertional versus mid-substance lesions are differentiated by the site of maximal tenderness, with the latter being approximately 1–2 cm (0.5–1 in.) distal to the lateral epicondyle. Palpation of the entire tendon and the associated muscle(s) provide valuable information on tissue tightness or hypersensitivity, which is useful in guiding treatment.

Typically, the pain is reproduced by resisted wrist extension, especially with the elbow extended and forearm pronated. Resisted extension of the middle finger is also painful (Fig. 22.2c).

The upper limb neurodynamic or neural provcation test, especially with radial nerve bias, may reproduce lateral elbow pain or show restriction of movement compared with the other side. In either situation, this may implicate a neural component to the pain. Examination of the cervical spine frequently detects decreased range of movement, especially lateral flexion. Palpation of the cervical and upper thoracic spine may show stiffness and tenderness both centrally and over the apophyseal joint on the side of the pain, usually around the C5–6 level. Active trigger points can occur in the periscapular soft tissues (Fig. 22.2g). In chronic cases, it is not uncommon to find decreased joint play in the elbow joints.

Treatment

No single treatment has proven to be totally effective, and it is most likely that the patient is best served through a combination of different treatments selected on the basis of the patient's clinical presentation[14] and informed by current best evidence.

The basic principles of treating soft tissue injuries apply, with a specific focus on addressing the grip strength deficit and coordination impairments of the upper limb and the wrist. These deficits are best addressed through exercise. There must be control of pain (e.g. ice, analgesic medications, relative rest, electrotherapy), encouragement of the healing process, restoration of any flexibility deficit, correction of any predisposing factors, and a gradual return to activity. Treatment of any spinal or neural dysfunctions often speeds up resolution[15] and is highly recommended if there is concomitant neck pain, which has been shown to be associated with poorer outcomes.[16, 17] It is helpful to think of exercise as the key to managing this condition, with other treatments being adjunctive, mainly to resolve pain and facilitate tissue healing.

Exercises for strengthening and coordination

We recommend progressively graduated exercise to:

* improve strength and endurance capacity (Fig. 22.4)
* normalize flexibility of the forearm muscles (Fig. 22.5)
* improve coordination (Fig. 22.6).[18]

It is unknown how much pain should be experienced during exercise without compromising resolution, but experience indicates that it should be

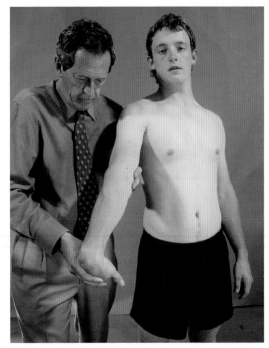

Figure 22.5 Stretching the extensor carpi radialis brevis tendon

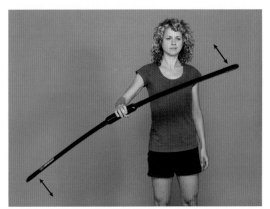

Figure 22.6 Coordination exercise focusing on supination/pronation at an early stage in rehabilitation of lateral elbow tendinopathy. The patient oscillates the body blade with the shoulder in a position that approximates the scapular plane

Figure 22.4 Strengthening exercises for wrist extensors. Exercises can be isometric, concentric (black arrow), eccentric (white arrow), or functional

minimized through careful selection of load and type of exercise. For example, in very painful elbows, isometric low load exercise (with taping and/or mobilization with movements) (Fig. 22.7 overleaf) to improve endurance should be favored initially, and progressed in load and complexity (concentric, eccentric) as pain subsides, to emphasize strengthening.

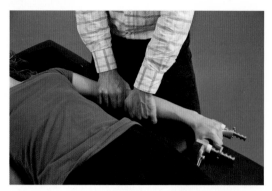

Figure 22.7 Mobilization with movement

Exercise is supported by clinical trials[19, 20] and, in one particular study,[17] long-term benefits and prevention of recurrence were seen in patients who had previously failed common treatments such as corticosteroid injections and oral medications.

Electrotherapeutic modalities

The application of electrotherapeutic modalities such as laser, extracorporeal shock wave therapy (ESWT), TENS, and ultrasound are often advocated and commonly used in practice for these conditions, despite mixed evidence on their effectiveness. In some part related to this mixed evidence is the fundamental issue of what constitutes an appropriate dosage, which can be challenging to the practitioner. For example, laser administered at a wavelength of 904 nm (but not 820 nm or 1064 nm) offers short-term pain relief and a reduction in disability, either applied in isolation or in combination with exercise.[21]

A modality where a perplexing situation arises is ESWT, which is effective at some sites of tendinopathy, but not for lateral elbow tendinopathy,[22] although the issue of dose for this modality has perhaps not been adequately explored. Interestingly, TENS, which is a scientifically developed modality for the reduction of pain, has only recently been considered in clinical trials of tennis elbow.[23] Practitioners should be aware that dosage plays an important role in delivering beneficial outcomes;[24] high frequencies (e.g. 85–110 Hz) and pulse durations of approximately 200 microseconds delivered at a strong but sub-noxious intensity are recommended.

 PRACTICE PEARL Therapeutic ultrasound (i.e. not diagnostic ultrasound) has very little evidence to support its use in treatment of lateral elbow tendinopathy.[25]

A recent clinical trial showed that, while ultrasound reduced pain over time, as did the comparator laser treatment, the patients did not rate their condition as being sufficiently improved afterward, in the short term.[26]

Manual therapy

There is evidence of benefit with elbow mobilization with movement[27] (Fig. 22.7), in combination with exercise[28] and with the addition of cervical and thoracic spine treatment to elbow treatment.[29]

 PRACTICE PEARL Specific manual therapy applied to the joints or soft tissues of the elbow and forearm is beneficial for lateral elbow tendinopathy.

Cervical mobilization (Fig. 22.8), thoracic mobilization, and neural tissue mobilization (Fig. 22.9) are commonly used as adjuncts to other forms of treatment.

Transverse frictions are frequently advocated at the site of the lesion; however, there is little evidence that these are beneficial and some evidence that the outcomes are less effective than supervised exercise when frictions are combined with Mill's manipulation, which is a small-amplitude high-velocity thrust performed at end of elbow extension while the wrist and hand are flexed.[29–31]

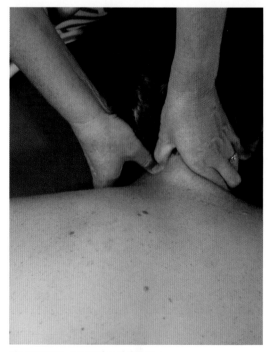

Figure 22.8 Cervical mobilization

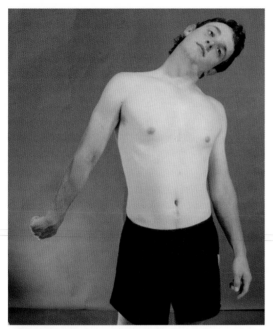

Figure 22.9 Neural tissue mobilization positioned at end of range

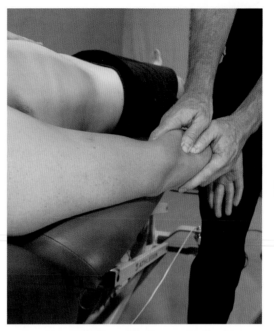

Figure 22.10 Soft tissue techniques
(a) Sustained longitudinal pressure to the extensor carpi radialis brevis muscle in the position of maximum elbow extension and wrist flexion

There is little evidence to support the use of digital ischemic pressures and myofascial massage, although it may be trialed to judge if the individual patient will benefit from its application. A critical aspect of such soft tissue manual therapy techniques is targeting them to areas exhibiting increased resistance, tightness, or thickening to digital pressure in the absence of severe pain. In this situation, the tissues are usually placed under various conditions of stretch while digital pressure is applied, either sustained (Fig. 22.10a) or longitudinally directed in motion (Fig. 22.10b).

These techniques usually produce pain during application; however, this pain should be within the patient's tolerance, not severe, and not outlast the treatment. The presence of severe pain and very little or no resistance, tightness, or thickening are contraindications to high force/load soft tissue techniques.

Trigger points

In patients with lateral elbow pain, active trigger points associated with muscle shortening are frequently found in the forearm extensor muscles—brachioradialis, extensor carpi radialis longus, extensor carpi radialis brevis, extensor digitorum, extensor carpi ulnaris, extensor digiti minimi and anconeus, as well as in the periscapular area. Digital ischemic

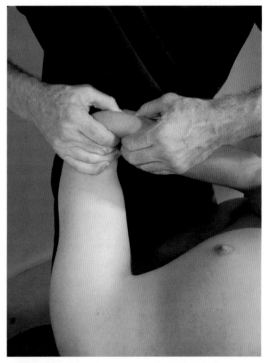

(b) Digital ischemic pressure to deep muscle fibers in the shortened position pressure or dry needling of these trigger points may help resolution of the condition.

Acupuncture

There is some evidence of short-term (two to eight weeks) benefit with the use of acupuncture for lateral elbow pain.[32]

Bracing and taping

Counterforce bracing (Fig. 22.11) increases forearm extensors, stretching pain tolerance, but it does not appear to influence neuromuscular parameters such as strength or proprioception of these muscles.[33] If a brace is to be used, it should demonstrably reduce pain on gripping or on resisted tests of wrist and middle finger extension. In these cases, the brace should be worn during the performance of pain pro-vocative tasks, such as on returning to an aggravating activity like tennis. The brace should be correctly applied, which is approximately 10 cm (4 in.) below the elbow joint. Tensioning the brace up to 50 N has been found to be beneficial.[33]

A deloading taping technique can improve pain-free gripping.[34] Our clinical experience indicates that it is very useful in patients who have severe pain and pain at night (Fig. 22.12).

Iontophoresis

There is insufficient evidence from clinical trials to support or refute the use of corticosteroids delivered by iontophoresis.

Figure 22.12 The diamond tape technique
(a) The anchor point X marks the site from which the tape is tensioned longitudinally (along the solid lined arrow) and laid onto the skin. The skin should be pulled toward the site of pain (dotted line arrow)
FROM VICENZINO ET AL.[34]

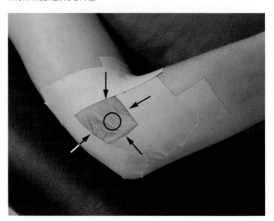

(b) Note the overlapping ends of the tape and the orange-peel effect on the skin with the diamond tape, resulting in a translation of skin away from the tape toward the site of pain (O) as shown by the broken-line arrows

Corticosteroid injection

The use of corticosteroid injection in the treatment of lateral elbow tendinopathy requires careful consid-eration because the best evidence to date indicates that, while it is very effective in the short term (i.e. >80% success rate), there are unfavorable conse-quences later (i.e. >6–12 weeks)—such as signifi-cantly delayed recovery and 62% greater recurrences than if the patient was advised to adopt a wait-and-see approach.[35, 36] Thus, it is prudent to consider using this injection within a more comprehensive manage-ment framework as illustrated in Figure 22.13.

Figure 22.11 Counterforce brace

Prior to any injection, the clinician should fully inform the patient of likely short- and long-term outcomes, as adopting a wait-and-see policy will result in approximately 80% success rate at 12 months.[37] When corticosteroid and local anesthetic agents are injected, the aim should be *around* the extensor carpi radialis brevis tendon, directly over the point of maximal tenderness, but not into the tendon substance itself.

PRACTICE PEARL

A comprehensive program for management of lateral elbow pain (Fig. 22.13) would include first implementing a graduated progressive exercise program over 8 weeks, pain relief if required, ergonomic advice, and activity modification. [37]

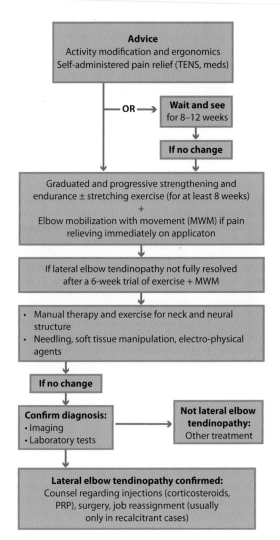

Advice
Activity modification and ergonomics
Self-administered pain relief (TENS, meds)

— OR →

Wait and see
for 8–12 weeks

↓

If no change

Graduated and progressive strengthening and endurance ± stretching exercise (for at least 8 weeks)
+
Elbow mobilization with movement (MWM) if pain relieving immediately on applicaton

If lateral elbow tendinopathy not fully resolved after a 6-week trial of exercise + MWM

• Manual therapy and exercise for neck and neural structure
• Needling, soft tissue manipulation, electro-physical agents

If no change

Confirm diagnosis:
• Imaging
• Laboratory tests

Not lateral elbow tendinopathy:
Other treatment

Lateral elbow tendinopathy confirmed:
Counsel regarding injections (corticosteroids, PRP), surgery, job reassignment (usually only in recalcitrant cases)

Figure 22.13 Treatment algorithm

Nitric oxide donor therapy

Initial studies of lateral elbow, Achilles, and supraspinatus tendinopathies provided level 2 evidence that nitric oxide donor therapy (glyceryl trinitrate [GTN] patches applied locally 1.25 mg/day) improved outcomes within three to six months[38] (Fig. 22.14). One mechanism by which this treatment might work is through enhanced collagen synthesis. However, a recent dose-ranging clinical trial for lateral elbow tendinopathy failed to confirm the initial findings, and highlighted that type of exercise (strengthening as opposed to stretching) is a significant consideration.[39]

Pragmatically, the practitioner and patient need to be aware that 4–5% of patients using a GTN patch will develop headaches or skin rash that are severe enough to discontinue treatment, and that this seems to be dose-dependent. Thus it is important to carefully meter the dose and monitor the response.

Botulinum toxin

Historically used for neuromuscular conditions, botulinum toxin (Botox) injection is a new and unproven treatment for tendinopathy. There is evidence that it produces short-term improvement in pain when compared to placebo;[36, 40] however, it is important to counsel the patient prior to the treatment that there will be a high likelihood (92% at 8 weeks post injection)[41] of an extensor muscle lag.

Autologous blood injection

It has been suggested that the introduction of autologous blood or platelet-rich plasma (in which autologous blood is first concentrated via centrifugation and isolation of the platelet fraction) may re-initiate

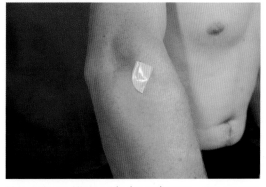

Figure 22.14 Nitric oxide donor therapy—one-quarter of a 0.5 mg/24 hr glyceryl trinitrate (GTN) patch in place over the most tender site of extensor tendinopathy

or enhance a presumably deficient inflammation–repair response, thereby promoting healing. There is conflicting evidence, with one high-quality trial showing no difference from a placebo,[36] two others showing superiority to corticosteroid injection,[42, 43] and a number of case series indicating it is beneficial in the short term[44] and long term.[45]

Correct predisposing factors

Probably the most important factor to be avoided is excessive or unaccustomed activity. In tennis players, a major cause is a faulty backhand technique with the elbow leading (Fig. 22.15). Other technique faults that may predispose to the development of extensor tendinopathy include excessive forearm pronation while attempting to hit top-spin forehands and excessive wrist flick (flexion) movement while serving. Correction of these faults requires assistance of a qualified tennis coach. Other factors, such as racquet type, grip size, string tension, court surface, and ball weight, may influence the amount of shock imparted to the elbow (Chapter 9). A mid-sized, graphite racquet with a large "sweet spot" and a grip size that feels comfortable should be used. Care should be taken to avoid using racquets with excessively large or, especially, small grips.

Surgery

Surgery might be considered occasionally in the case with a long history (e.g. >18 months) of severe lateral elbow pain that is recalcitrant to the treatment strategies outlined above. Surgery is varied, but most approaches involve some degree of excision of the degenerative tissue within the common extensor/extensor carpi radialis brevis tendon and release of the tendon from the lateral epicondyle. A recent systematic review has concluded that there is a dearth of quality evidence to recommend one surgical approach over others.[46]

Return to activity

As with all soft tissue injuries, it is important to return gradually to activity following treatment. The tennis player should initially practice backhand technique without a ball, then progress slowly from gentle hitting from the service line to eventually hitting full length shots (Chapter 15). Depending on the severity of the condition and the length of the rehabilitation program, this graduated return should take place over a period of three to six weeks.

Figure 22.15 Backhand technique
(a) Incorrect

(b) Correct

Other causes of lateral elbow pain

Other causes of lateral elbow pain may occur in isolation or in conjunction with the previously mentioned conditions.

Radiohumeral bursitis is occasionally seen in sportspeople. This may be distinguished from extensor tendinopathy by the site of tenderness, which is over the radiohumeral joint and distal to the lateral epicondyle, maximally over the anterolateral aspect of the head of the radius. The presence of this bursitis may be confirmed on ultrasound examination. Injection with a corticosteroid agent is the most effective form of treatment.

Osteochondritis of the capitellum or radial head may occur in younger sportspeople (Chapter 42) involved in throwing sports. This is a significant condition as it can cause an enlarged, deformed capitellum that may predispose to the development of osteoarthritis. The treatment of this condition involves avoidance of aggravating activities.

The lateral elbow is a common site of referred pain, especially from the cervical and upper thoracic spine and periscapular soft tissues. Most patients with chronic lateral elbow pain are likely to have some component of their pain emanating from the cervical and thoracic spine (Chapter 20). Any associated abnormalities of the cervical and thoracic spine should be treated and the patient's signs reassessed immediately after treatment. If there is a noticeable difference, this may indicate a significant component of referred pain.

Medial elbow pain

Patients who present with medial elbow pain can be considered in two main groups. One group has pain associated with excessive activity of the wrist flexors. This is the medial equivalent of extensor tendinopathy, with a similar pathological process occurring in the tendons of pronator teres and the flexor group. This condition can be referred to as "flexor/pronator tendinopathy."

The second group of patients have medial elbow pain related to excessive throwing activities. Throwing produces a valgus stress on the elbow that is resisted primarily by the anterior oblique portion of the medial collateral ligament of the elbow and secondarily by the stability of the radiocapitellar joint. Repetitive throwing, especially if throwing technique is poor (Chapter 9), leads to stretching of the ligament and a degree of valgus instability. A fixed flexion deformity of the elbow may develop as a result of scarring of the medial collateral ligament. Subsequently, there may be some secondary impingement of the medial tip of the olecranon onto the olecranon fossa, producing a synovitis or loose body formation. With valgus stress, the compressive forces may also damage the radio-capitellar joint. Several of these pathological entities may be present in combination.

In children and adolescents, repetitive valgus stress may result in damage to the medial epicondylar epiphysis with pain and tenderness in this region. This usually responds to a period of rest followed by a gradual return to throwing activity, but may progress to avulsion with continued activity. This condition, commonly known as "little leaguer's elbow," is considered in Chapter 42. The causes of medial elbow pain are shown in Table 22.2.

Flexor/pronator tendinopathy

This condition is not as common as its lateral equivalent; it accounts for 9–20% of all epicondylalgia diagnoses.[47] It is seen especially in golfers ("golfer's elbow") and in tennis players who impart a lot of top spin on their forehand shot. The primary pathology exists in the tendinous origin of the forearm flexor muscles, particularly in the pronator teres tendon.[48] Ultrasound is sensitive and specific for detecting clinically defined medial epicondylitis, with focal hypoechoic areas of tendinosis being the most common finding, followed by partial tears (i.e. these are identical to lateral epicondylalgia ultrasound findings).

On examination, there is usually localized tenderness just at or below the medial epicondyle, with pain on resisted wrist flexion and resisted forearm pronation (Fig. 22.16 overleaf).

Treatment is along the same lines as treatment of extensor tendinopathy (Fig. 22.13). Particular attention should be paid to the tennis forehand or the golf swing technique. Due to its close proximity to the medial epicondyle, the ulnar nerve may become irritated or trapped in scar tissue. This should be treated with neural mobilization.

Medial collateral ligament sprain

Sprain of the medial collateral ligament of the elbow may occur as an acute injury, or as the result of

Table 22.2 Causes of medial elbow pain

Common	Less common	Not to be missed
Flexor/pronator tendinopathy	Ulnar neuritis	Referred pain
Medial collateral ligament sprain	Avulsion fracture of the medial	
• Acute	epicondyle (children and adolescents)	
• Chronic	Apophysitis (children and adolescents)	

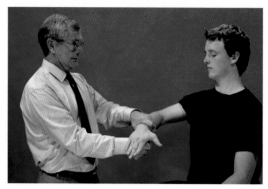

Figure 22.16 Medial elbow pain reproduced with resisted wrist flexion and forearm pronation

Figure 22.17 (a) Assessment of integrity of the medial collateral ligament

chronic excessive valgus stress due to throwing. It occurs particularly in baseball pitchers and javelin throwers. The repeated valgus stress, especially in throwers who "open up too soon" (i.e. become front-on too early in the throwing motion), leads initially to microtearing and inflammation of the ligament, then scarring and calcification and, occasionally ligament rupture. The biomechanics of throwing is discussed in Chapter 8.

On examination, there is localized tenderness over the ligament and mild instability on valgus stress (Fig. 22.17a). There are often associated abnormalities, such as a flexion contracture of the forearm muscles, synovitis and loose body formation around the tip of the olecranon, as well as damage to the radiocapitellar joint. However, many throwers demonstrate a flexion contracture without concurrent medial collateral ligament pathology.[49]

Treatment in the early stages of the injury involves modification of activity, correction of faulty technique, local electrotherapeutic modalities (possibly as for lateral elbow tendinopathy, as little research exists for the medial equivalent), and soft tissue therapy to the medial ligament. Medial strapping of the elbow may offer additional protection (Fig. 22.17b). Specific muscle strengthening should be commenced, concentrating on the forearm flexors and pronators (Fig. 22.18). Advanced pathology may require arthroscopic removal of loose bodies and bony spurs. Occasionally, significant instability develops and requires ligament reconstruction; this should be avoided if possible, as the results of surgery are often disappointing.

Ulnar neuritis

The ulnar nerve pierces the intermuscular septum in the middle of the upper arm then passes deep to

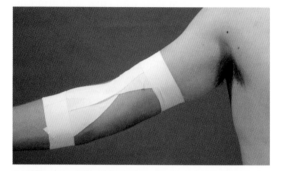

(b) Elbow stability tape

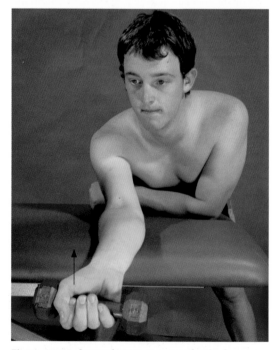

Figure 22.18 Strengthening exercises for the forearm flexors and pronators

the medial head of the triceps muscle to locate in a superficial groove (the ulnar sulcus) between the olecranon and the medial epicondyle. It then enters the forearm between the humerus and the ulnar heads of the flexor carpi ulnaris muscle.

Inflammation of the ulnar nerve can occur as a result of a combination of any of four factors:[50]

1. Traction injuries to the nerve may occur because of the dynamic valgus forces of throwing, especially when combined with valgus instability of the elbow.
2. Progressive compression can occur at the cubital tunnel secondary to inflammation and adhesions from repetitive stresses, or where the nerve passes between the two heads of the flexor carpi ulnaris due to muscle overdevelopment secondary to resistance weight-training exercises.
3. Recurrent subluxation of the nerve can occur due to acquired laxity from repetitive stress or direct trauma.
4. Irregularities within the ulnar groove (such as spurs) commonly result from overuse injuries in throwers.

The patient presents with posteromedial elbow pain and sensory symptoms such as pins and needles or numbness along the ulnar nerve distribution on the ulnar border of the forearm and the ulnar one and a half fingers. The nerve may be tender behind the medial epicondyle (Fig. 22.19), and tapping over the nerve may reproduce symptoms in some cases. Placing the elbow in maximum flexion, the forearm in pronation and the wrist in full extension for one minute may reproduce medial elbow pain and tingling/numbness in the ring and little finger if ulnar neuritis is present. Patients with clinical features of ulnar nerve involvement should undergo nerve conduction studies.[47] Reports of a snapping sensation

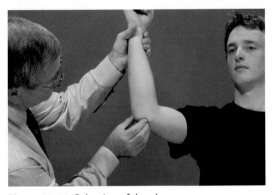

Figure 22.19 Palpation of the ulnar nerve

should lead to the suspicion of ulnar nerve subluxation, which can be confirmed with dynamic ultrasound examination.[51]

Treatment of ulnar neuritis depends on the initiating factor:

1. Traction injuries related to valgus instability from throwing are best served by treating the instability to reduce the ongoing irritation of the ulnar nerve.
2. If adhesions are felt to be present, treatment may include local soft tissue therapy to the nerve in the ulnar groove, to mobilize soft tissue that may be compressing or tethering the nerve and restricting its free movement. Neural mobilisation is often beneficial.
3. Recurrent subluxation of the ulnar nerve should be referred to a neurologist or neurosurgeon experienced in managing this condition in active individuals. Management will depend on the degree of symptoms, electrophysiological evidence of nerve injury, and local management expertise (in relation to nerve transposition surgery).
4. Bony irregularities may be amenable to arthroscopic debridement.

Posterior elbow pain

The main causes of posterior elbow pain are olecranon bursitis, triceps tendinopathy, and posterior impingement. Gout should always be considered.

Olecranon bursitis

Olecranon bursitis may present after a single episode of trauma or, more commonly, after repeated trauma, such as falls onto a hard surface affecting the posterior aspect of the elbow. This is commonly seen in basketball players "taking a charge." It is also seen in individuals who rest their elbow on a hard surface for long periods of time when it is known as "student's elbow." The olecranon bursa is a subcutaneous bursa that may become filled with blood and serous fluid (Fig. 22.20 overleaf).

Treatment consists initially of NSAIDs, rest, and firm compression. If this fails, aspiration of the contents of the bursa and injection with a mixture of corticosteroid and local anesthetic agents are usually effective. The needle should be inserted at an oblique angle to reduce the risk of sinus formation. Although this is considered a straightforward procedure among experienced clinicians, there is a trend to use ultrasound imaging support to increase the accuracy of needle insertion. If recurrent bursitis

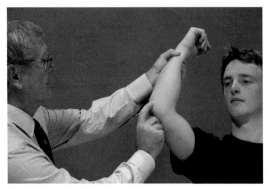

Figure 22.20 Olecranon bursa
(a) Palpation site of bursa

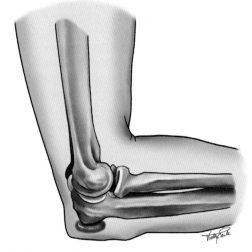

(b) Olecranon bursitis

does not respond to aspiration and injection, surgical excision of the bursa is required.

Occasionally, olecranon bursitis can become infected. This is a serious complication that requires immediate drainage, strict immobilization, and antibiotic therapy. Osteomyelitis and septic arthritis can follow. Excision of the bursa is occasionally required.

Triceps tendinopathy

Tendinopathy at the insertion of the triceps onto the olecranon is occasionally seen. Standard conservative measures for treatment of tendinopathy should be used. Soft tissue therapy including self-massage with a styrofoam roll, and dry needling to reduce excessive tightness of the triceps musculotendinous complex may be helpful.

Posterior impingement

Posterior impingement is probably the most common cause of posterior elbow pain. It occurs in two situations. In the younger sportsperson there is the "hyperextension valgus overload syndrome." Repetitive hyperextension valgus stress to the elbow results in impingement of the posterior medial corner of the olecranon tip on the olecranon fossa. Over time this causes osteophyte formation, exacerbating the impingement and leading to a fixed flexion deformity.

In the older patient, the most common cause is early osteoarthritis, which often predominantly affects the radiocapitellar joint. Generalized osteophytes form through the elbow. Impingement of these osteophytes posteriorly results in posterior pain. The main clinical feature in sportspeople with posterior impingement is a fixed flexion deformity of some degree and posterior pain with forced extension (Fig. 22.21).

Physiotherapy may include strategies to minimize hyperextension forces such as taping or bracing, along with a strength and flexibility program, and graduated return to sport or activity. If conservative measures fail, arthroscopic removal of the impinging posterior bone and soft tissue is very effective in relieving symptoms and improving extension.

Acute elbow injuries

Acute elbow injuries include fractures, dislocations, and ligament or tendon ruptures.

Investigation

Given the nature of an acute elbow injury, radiography is often used as an initial assessment. In an

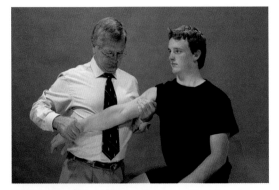

Figure 22.21 Posterior impingement. The elbow is forced into end-range extension. If posterior pain is produced, then posterior impingement is present

attempt to reduce unnecessary use of such investigations, which are not without implications to both the patient and the healthcare system, an assessment protocol has been developed.[52, 53] Patients who cannot fully extend their elbow after injury should be referred for X-ray, because there is a 50% chance of fracture. Those who are fully able to extend the elbow are unlikely to have a fracture, although they should be followed up in 7–10 days if symptoms have not resolved.

Fractures

As the complication rate for elbow fractures is higher than with fractures near other joints, it is essential that fractures in this region are recognized and treated early and aggressively. Unstable fractures, usually those associated with displacement, should be referred early for orthopedic management. When the articular or cortical surface has less than 2 mm (0.1 in.) of vertical or horizontal displacement, the fracture can be regarded as stable and treated conservatively.[54]

The most common complication of elbow fractures is stiffness, particularly loss of terminal extension. Prompt diagnosis and treatment that includes an early rehabilitation program can help avoid this outcome. Thus, treatment of elbow fractures must be aggressive. Surgically stabilizing an adult elbow fracture allows early commencement of a postoperative range of motion program.

A stable fracture that involves no significant comminution, displacement, or angulation may be treated conservatively. In adults, immobilizing the arm for a few days, even up to a week, is generally well tolerated. Then the arm should be placed in a removal splint and early motion commenced. The fracture should be protected for a further six to eight weeks, with early and frequent radiographic checks to ensure the reduction stays anatomical.

The other main complication of elbow fractures, particularly in high-energy injuries, is heterotopic ossification. This usually appears within the first month after surgery and plateaus after four to six months. Traumatized elbows that are forcefully or passively manipulated may also be at greater risk of this complication.[55] Therefore, gentle, active assisted range of motion and pain-free stretching exercises are preferred. Mobilization with movements, applied correctly in a pain-free manner, may be helpful in restoring motion.[27] Heterotopic bone formation has also been associated with elbow fractures treated surgically between one and five days after injury or

treated with multiple surgical procedures. Thus, surgery should be performed in the first 24 hours after injury or after five to seven days.

Long-term follow-up of bicolumnar fractures of the distal humerus, capitellum/trochlear fractures, or elbow fracture-dislocations is recommended. A five year study has shown that 75 of 139 patients with elbow fractures exhibit radiographic evidence of moderate to severe arthrosis.[56] This is not the case for fractures of the olecranon and radial head.

Supracondylar fractures

Supracondylar fractures are more common around the age of 12 years than in adults. They often occur from a fall on an outstretched arm, either from a height or from a bicycle. Because they are rotationally unstable and have a high rate of neurovascular complications, these fractures should be regarded as an orthopedic emergency.

For fractures that are unstable, displaced, or that cannot be reduced without jeopardizing the blood supply, the treatment of choice is closed reduction in the operating room under general anesthesia. Percutaneous pins placed across the fracture maintain the reduction and prevent late slippage. The arm is initially placed in a splint and then several days later in a cast. The pins are removed after four to six weeks. Stiffness is typically not a problem in children recovering from fractures.

Olecranon fractures

Olecranon fractures occur from a fall onto an outstretched hand or from direct trauma to the elbow.

If the fracture is non-displaced and stable, the patient should be able to extend the arm against gravity. Treatment consists of immobilizing the arm for two to three weeks in a posterior splint, then in a removable splint and a range-of-motion program commenced.

If the patient is unable to extend the elbow against gravity or if radiographs show significant displacement, open reduction with internal fixation by tension-band wiring is preferred. Early motion is started within one week of surgery.

Radial head fracture

The most common fracture around the elbow in sportspeople is the radial head fracture, almost always resulting from a fall onto an outstretched hand.

Most radial head fractures are minimally displaced or non-displaced (type 1) and are very difficult to see on radiographs. Sometimes the only clue is the fat pad sign, which appears as a triangular radiolucency just in front of the elbow joint. Early aspiration, splinting with an easily removable device, and early commencement of a range of motion program yields excellent results. Complete healing can be expected within six to eight weeks.

For displaced radial head fractures (type 2), surgical intervention with operative fixation or excision is preferred. Comminuted fractures (type 3) are treated by excision. Type 4 fractures occur in the presence of a dislocation and can be very unstable. They always require surgical treatment.

Dislocations
Posterior
The most serious acute injury to the elbow is posterior dislocation of the elbow. This can occur either in contact sports or when falling from a height such as while pole vaulting. There is often an associated fracture of the coronoid process or radial head. The usual mechanism is a posterolateral rotatory force resulting from a fall on an outstretched hand with the shoulder abducted, axial compression, forearm in supination then forced flexion of the elbow.[57]

The major complication of posterior dislocation of the elbow is impairment of the vascular supply to the forearm. Assessment of pulses distal to the dislocation is essential. If pulses are absent, reduction of the dislocation is required urgently. Reduction is usually relatively easy. With the elbow held at 45°, the clinician stabilises the humerus by gripping the anterior aspect of the distal humerus, and traction is placed longitudinally along the forearm with the other hand (Fig. 22.22). The elbow usually reduces

Figure 22.22 Technique for reduction of posterior dislocation of the elbow

with a pronounced clunk. If vascular impairment persists after reduction, urgent surgical intervention is required.

Following reduction, the stability of the collateral ligaments should be assessed (Fig. 22.17a). A post-reduction X-ray should also be performed. Small fractures of the coronoid process or undisplaced fractures of the radial head only require conservative treatment with support in a sling for two to three weeks. Large coronoid fractures, however, may result in chronic instability and should be reduced and fixed surgically. Large fractures of the radial head may be difficult to manage but in most cases can be internally fixed. Occasionally, a large fracture of the capitellum may occur. This also requires internal fixation. Sometimes a piece of bone becomes trapped in the joint after reduction. This needs to be excluded with good-quality post-reduction X-rays.

Long-term loss of extension is frequently a problem following elbow dislocation. Immediate active mobilization under supervision has been shown to result in less restriction of elbow extension with no apparent increase in instability.[58] Professional sportspeople with a simple dislocation with no associated fracture or instability are able to return to sport relatively quickly after an accelerated rehabilitation program. Verrall described three cases of stable dislocations in professional footballers who returned to sport after 13, 21 and seven days respectively with no further complications.[59] Joint mobilization (Fig. 22.23) may be required as part of the treatment. Surrounding muscles should also be strengthened. Elbow stability taping should be applied on return to sport (Fig. 22.17b).

Heterotopic ossification occasionally occurs following elbow dislocation. The use of nonsteroidal anti-inflammatory drugs (NSAIDs) for a period of three months following the injury may reduce the incidence of this complication.

Some patients may develop chronic instability of the elbow following an acute dislocation. This is classically posterior lateral instability. If symptoms are unacceptable, then a reconstruction of the lateral ulnar collateral ligament may be indicated.

Other dislocations
Elbow dislocations in directions other than posterior occur occasionally. These are often associated with severe ligamentous disruption, and patients should be referred to an orthopedic surgeon immediately.

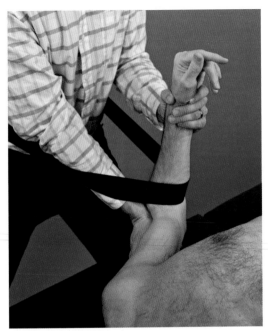

Figure 22.23 Examples of mobilisation with movement techniques that use a glide out of the plane of extension to improve extension

(a) Sustained lateral glide applied through a belt while assisted active extension is performed

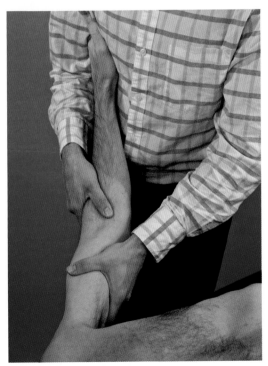

(b) Sustained internal rotation[27]

Acute rupture of the medial collateral ligament

Acute rupture of the medial collateral ligament may occur in a previously damaged ligament or in a normal ligament subjected to extreme valgus stress (e.g. elbow dislocation). The degree of instability should be assessed by applying valgus stress to the elbow at 30° of flexion (Fig. 22.17a). If complete disruption is present with associated instability, surgical repair of the ligament is required. Incomplete tears should be treated with protection in a brace and muscle strengthening for a period of three to six weeks, followed by graduated return to sport.

Tendon ruptures

Acute avulsion of the biceps or triceps tendons from their insertions is a rare condition.

Rupture of the biceps tendon insertion occurs predominantly in young or middle-aged males engaged in strength activities (e.g. weightlifting). Partial ruptures are more painful than complete ruptures, due to mechanical irritation of the remaining intact tendon. Early surgical repair of complete ruptures would be expected to lead to better outcomes, as complete rupture of tendons leads to degenerative processes due to the loss of mechanical load.

Rupture of the triceps tendon occurs most commonly with excessive deceleration force, such as during a fall or by a direct blow to the posterior aspect of the elbow. Partial and complete triceps ruptures are seen in American National Football League linemen. Partial tears tend to heal well without surgery.

Acute complete ruptures at the insertion of either of these tendons should be treated surgically.

Forearm pain

Fracture of the radius and ulna

The bones of the forearm are commonly injured by a fall on the back or front of the outstretched hand. It is usual for both bones to break, although a single bone may be fractured in cases of direct violence or in fractures of the distal third where there is no shortening.

A displaced fracture is usually clinically obvious. X-rays should be taken for post-reduction comparison and for exclusion of a concurrent dislocation. Two types of dislocation occur—the Monteggia injury (fractured ulna with dislocated head of the radius at the elbow joint) and the Galeazzi injury (fractured

B

radius with dislocated head of the ulna at the wrist joint).

In children, angulation of less than 10° is acceptable. Other fractures should be reduced under local or general anesthesia depending on the age of the child. The usual position for immobilization is in pronation, although in proximal radial fractures and in Smith's fractures at the wrist, the forearm should be held in supination. The plaster should extend above the elbow and leave the metacarpophalangeal joints free. Depending on the age of the child, immobilization should last four to six weeks. The position should be checked by X-ray every one to two weeks depending on stability.

In adults, perfect reduction of radial and ulnar fractures is necessary to ensure future sporting function. Most of these fractures are significantly displaced and require internal fixation by plate and screw. Depending on the accuracy of the reduction, either a cast or crepe bandage support is required postoperatively for 8–10 weeks. Isolated fracture of the ulna is treated conservatively by an above-elbow cast in mid-pronation for eight weeks. Monteggia and Galeazzi injuries are usually displaced and should be referred to an orthopedic surgeon for reduction.

Stress fractures

Stress fractures of the forearm bones occur occasionally in sportspeople involved in upper limb sports (e.g. baseball, tennis, swimming). Treatment involves rest and correction of the possible predisposing factors, such as faulty technique.

Entrapment of the posterior interosseous nerve (radial tunnel syndrome)

The radial nerve divides into the superficial radial and the posterior interosseous nerve at the level of the radiocapitellar joint (Fig. 22.24). The posterior interosseous nerve passes distal to the origin of the extensor carpi radialis brevis and enters the arcade of Frohse. Prior to entering the arcade, it gives off branches to the extensor carpi radialis brevis and supinator muscles. The arcade is a semicircular fibrous arch at the proximal head of the supinator muscle, which begins at the tip of the lateral epicondyle and extends downward, attaching to the medial aspect of the lateral epicondyle. The posterior interosseous nerve then emerges from the supinator muscle distally, where it divides into terminal branches that innervate the medial extensors. Compression of the

posterior interosseous nerve may occur at one of four sites:

* fibrous bands in front of the radial head
* recurrent radial vessels
* arcade of Frohse
* tendinous margin of the extensor carpi radialis brevis muscle.

It is often difficult to differentiate between extensor tendinopathy and the early stages of posterior interosseous nerve entrapment. Posterior interosseous nerve entrapment is seen in patients who repetitively pronate and supinate the forearm, whereas extensor tendinopathy is more frequently associated with repetitive wrist extension. Symptoms of posterior interosseous nerve entrapment include paresthesia in the hand and lateral forearm, pain over the forearm extensor mass, wrist aching, and middle or upper third humeral pain.

Maximal tenderness is over the supinator muscle, four finger-breadths below the lateral epicondyle (distal to the area of maximal tenderness in extensor tendinopathy). Reproduction of symptoms by manual palpation of these local structures, and the relief of such palpation-induced symptoms by injection of local anesthetic, should be considered as part of the physical examination.[61] Nerve entrapment also causes

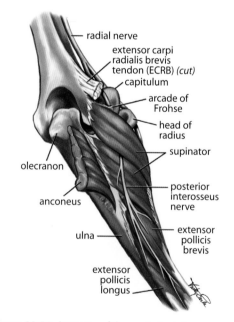

Figure 22.24 Anatomy of the posterior interosseous nerve[60]

marked pain on resisted supination of the forearm with the elbow flexed to 90° and the forearm fully pronated. Another sign is pain with resisted extension of the middle finger with the elbow extended, although this can be positive in extensor tendinopathy as well. Neurodynamic tests may reproduce the patient's symptoms and nerve conduction studies may be performed to confirm the diagnosis.

Treatment consists of soft tissue therapy over the supinator muscle at the site of entrapment and neural tissue mobilisation, along with exercises targeting strength and endurance deficits in the forearm muscles. If this is unsuccessful, decompression surgery may be required.

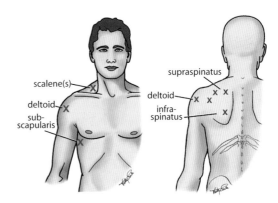

Figure 22.25 Myofascial trigger points around the shoulder region that refer pain to the upper arm

Forearm compartment pressure syndrome

Forearm compartment pressure syndromes have been described in kayakers, canoeists, motor cyclists (popularly termed "arm pump" in motor cross), and weight-training athletes. The flexor compartment is most usually affected. Symptoms include activity-related pain that is relieved by rest. Diagnosis requires compartment pressure testing (Chapter 11). Treatment consists of local soft tissue therapy. Surgical fasciotomy may be required.

Upper arm pain

An aching pain in the upper arm is a common complaint, especially among manual workers (e.g. bricklayers, carpenters) and sportspeople. The most common cause is myofascial pain, but stress fracture of the humerus needs to be considered.

Myofascial pain

A dull non-specific pain in the upper arm is most likely to be myofascial in nature. The most common source of the upper arm pain is trigger points in and around the infraspinatus muscle (Fig. 22.25). Firm palpation of these trigger points often reproduces the patient's pain. The cervical spine and glenohumeral joint need to be assessed for their possible involvement, and treatment directed accordingly.

Treatment consists of heat, and digital ischemic pressure or dry needling to the trigger points.

Attention should also be paid to the lower cervical and upper thoracic to mid-thoracic spine. Increased muscle tone and trigger points may be found in the paraspinal muscles, and hypomobility of the intervertebral segments may be present. These abnormalities must also be treated with heat and soft tissue techniques.

Stress reaction of the humerus

Stress reactions and fractures of the humerus have been described in baseball pitchers, tennis players, javelin throwers, bodybuilders, and weightlifters. In a group of symptomatic elite tennis players, MRI of the humerus demonstrated bone marrow edema and/or periostitis, and the extent of imaging changes was related to the severity and duration of symptoms.[62] Most of the fractures occurred in adolescents and were associated with a recent increase in activity. In a number of cases, the diagnosis was made retrospectively when an acute fracture occurred and the patient acknowledged symptoms leading up to the acute episode.

Recommended treatment follows the general principles of management of simple stress fractures, involving avoidance of the aggravating activity until symptom-free and no local tenderness, then gradual resumption of the activity.

CLINICAL SPORTS MEDICINE
MASTERCLASSES

[W] www.clinicalsportsmedicine.com

Listen to the podcast with chapter authors Vicenzino and Scott. They provide practical tips on:

- confirming the diagnosis of lateral elbow pain
- choosing among the many treatment options.

RECOMMENDED READING

Vicenzino B, Hing W, Rivett D, Hall T. *Mobilisation with movement: the art and the science.* Sydney: Churchill Livingstone, 2011.

REFERENCES

1. Clarke AW, Ahmad M, Curtis M et al. Lateral Elbow Tendinopathy. *Am J Sports Med* 2010;38(6):1209–14.
2. du Toit C, Stieler M, Saunders R et al. Diagnostic accuracy of power Doppler ultrasound in patients with chronic tennis elbow. *Br J Sports Med* 2008;42(11): 872–6.
3. Fairbank SM, Corlett RJ. The role of the extensor digitorum communis muscle in lateral epicondylitis. *J Hand Surg Br* 2002;27B(5):405–9.
4. Milz S, Tischer T, Buettner A et al. Molecular composition and pathology of entheses on the medial and lateral epicondyles of the humerus: a structural basis for epicondylitis. *Ann Rheum Dis* 2004;63(9):1015–21.
5. Coonrad RW, Hooper WR. Tennis elbow—its course, natural history, conservative and surgical management. *J Bone Joint Surg Am* 1973;55(6):1177–82.
6. Nirschl RP, Pettrone FA. Tennis elbow: the surgical treatment of lateral epicondylitis. *J Bone Joint Surg Am* 1979;61(6):832–9.
7. Kraushaar BS, Nirschl RP. Tendinosis of the elbow (tennis elbow) – Clinical features and findings of histological, immunohistochemical, and electron microscopy studies. *J Bone Joint Surg Am* 1999;81(2): 259–78.
8. Alfredson H, Ohberg L, Forsgren S. Is vasculo-neural ingrowth the cause of pain in chronic Achilles tendinosis? An investigation using ultrasonography and colour Doppler, immunohistochemistry, and diagnostic injections. *Knee Surg Sports Traumatol Arthrosc* 2003;11(5):334–8.
9. Regan W, Wold LE, Coonrad R et al. Microscopic histopathology of chronic refractory lateral epicondylitis. *Am J Sports Med* 1992;20(6):746–9.
10. Bisset LM, Russell T, Bradley S et al. Bilateral sensorimotor abnormalities in unilateral lateral epicondylalgia. *Arch Phys Med Rehabil* 2006;87(4): 490–5.
11. Andersson G, Forsgren S, Scott A et al. Tenocyte hypercellularity and vascular proliferation in a rabbit model of tendinopathy: contralateral effects suggest the involvement of central neuronal mechanisms. *Br J Sports Med* 2011;45(5):399–406.
12. Pienimaki TT, Kauranen K, Vanharanta H. Bilaterally decreased motor performance of arms in patients with chronic tennis elbow. *Arch Phys Med Rehabil* 1997;78(10):1092–95.
13. Waugh EJ, Jaglal SB, Davis AM. Computer use associated with poor long-term prognosis of conservatively managed lateral epicondylalgia. *J Orthop Sports Phys Ther* 2004;34(12):770–80.
14. Coombes BK, Bisset L, Vicenzino B. A new integrative model of lateral epicondylalgia. *Br J Sports Med* 2009;43(4):252–8.
15. Cleland JA, Flynn TW, Palmer JA. Incorporation of manual therapy directed at the cervicothoracic spine in patients with lateral epicondylalgia: a pilot clinical trial. *J Man Manip Ther* 2005;13(3):143–51.
16. Smidt N, Lewis M, van der Windt D et al. Lateral epicondylitis in general practice: course and prognostic indicators of outcome. *J Rheumatol* 2006;33(10): 2053–2059.
17. Pienimaki T, Karinen P, Kemila T et al. Long-term follow-up of conservatively treated chronic tennis elbow patients. A prospective and retrospective analysis. *Scand J Rehabil Med* 1998;30(3):159–66.
18. Coombes B, Bisset L, Connelly L et al. Optimising corticosteroid injection for lateral epicondylalgia with the addition of physiotherapy: a protocol for a randomised control trial with placebo comparison. *BMC Musculoskelet Disord* 2009;10(1):76.
19. Pienimäki TT, Tarvainen TK, Siira PT et al. Progressive strengthening and stretching exercises and ultrasound for chronic lateral epicondylitis. *Physiother* 1996;82(9):522–30.
20. Svernlov B, Adolfsson L. Non-operative treatment regime including eccentric training for lateral humeral epicondylalgia. *Scand J Med Sci Sports* 2001;11(6): 328–34.
21. Bjordal JM, Lopes-Martins RAB, Joensen J et al. A systematic review with procedural assessments and meta-analysis of low level laser therapy in lateral elbow tendinopathy (tennis elbow). *BMC Musculoskelet Disord* 2008;9:75.
22. Staples MP, Forbes A, Ptasznik R et al. A randomized controlled trial of extracorporeal shock wave therapy

B

for lateral epicondylitis (tennis elbow). *J Rheumatol* 2008;35(10):2038–46.

23. Chesterton LS, van der Windt DA, Sim J et al. Transcutaneous electrical nerve stimulation for the management of tennis elbow: a pragmatic randomized controlled trial: the TATE trial (ISRCTN 87141084). *BMC Musculoskelet Disord* 2009;10:156.

24. Bjordal JM, Johnson MI, Ljunggreen AE. Transcutaneous electrical nerve stimulation (TENS) can reduce postoperative analgesic consumption. A meta-analysis with assessment of optimal treatment parameters for postoperative pain. *Eur J Pain* 2003;7(2):181–8.

25. van der Windt DA, van der Heijden GJ, van den Berg SG et al. Ultrasound therapy for musculoskeletal disorders: a systematic review. *Pain* 1999;81(3):257–71.

26. Oeken O, Kahraman Y, Ayhan F et al. The short-term efficacy of laser, brace, and ultrasound treatment in lateral epicondylitis: A prospective, randomized, controlled trial. *J Hand Ther* 2008;21(1):63–8.

27. Vicenzino B, Hing W, Rivett D et al. *Mobilisation with movement: the art and the science.* Sydney: Churchill Livingstone, 2011.

28. Bisset L, Beller E, Jull G et al. Mobilisation with movement and exercise, corticosteroid injection, or wait and see for tennis elbow: randomised trial. *BMJ* 2006;333(7575):939–41.

29. Vicenzino B, Cleland JA, Bisset L. Joint manipulation in the management of lateral epicondylalgia: a clinical commentary. *J Man Manip Ther* 2007;15(1):50–6.

30. Stasinopoulos D, Stasinopoulos I. Comparison of effects of Cyriax physiotherapy, a supervised exercise programme and polarized polychromatic non-coherent light (Bioptron light) for the treatment of lateral epicondylitis. *Clin Rehabil* 2006;20(1):12–23.

31. Verhaar JA, Walenkamp G, van Mameren H et al. Local corticosteroid injection versus cyriax-type physiotherapy for tennis elbow. *J Bone Joint Surg* 1996;78B(1):128–32.

32. Bisset L, Paungmali A, Vicenzino B et al. A systematic review and meta-analysis of clinical trials on physical interventions for lateral epicondylalgia. *Br J Sports Med* 2005;39(7):411–22.

33. Ng G. The effects of forearm brace tension on neuromuscular performance in subjects with lateral humeral epicondylosis: a review. *Int Sportmed J* 2005;6(2):124–29.

34. Vicenzino B, Brooksbank J, Minto J et al. Initial effects of elbow taping on pain-free grip strength and pressure pain threshold. *J Orthop Sports Phys Ther* 2003;33(7):400–7.

35. Scott A, Khan KM. Corticosteroids: short-term gain for long-term pain? *Lancet*; 376(9754):1714–5.

36. Coombes BK, Bisset L, Vicenzino B. Efficacy and safety of corticosteroid injections and other injections for management of tendinopathy: a systematic review of randomised controlled trials. *Lancet* 2010;376(9754):1751–67.

37. Bisset L, Smidt N, van der Windt DA et al. Conservative treatments for tennis elbow—do subgroups of patients respond differently? *Rheumatology* 2007;46(10):1601–5.

38. Murrell GA. Using nitric oxide to treat tendinopathy. *Br J Sports Med* 2007;41(4):227–31.

39. Paoloni JA, Murrell GA, Burch R et al. Randomised, double blind, placebo controlled, multicentre dose-ranging clinical trial of a new topical glyceryl trinitrate patch for chronic lateral epicondylosis. *Br J Sports Med* 2009;43:399–302.

40. Espandar R, Heidari P, Rasouli MR et al. Use of anatomic measurement to guide injection of botulinum toxin for the management of chronic lateral epicondylitis: a randomized controlled trial. *CMAJ* 2010;182(8):768–73.

41. Vicenzino B, Coombes BK. A single botulinum toxin injection at a precise anatomic point on the forearm reduces pain at rest, compared to placebo injection in patients with chronic refractory lateral epicondylitis. *Evid Based Med* 2010;15(5):149–50.

42. Peerbooms JC, Sluimer J, Bruijn DlJ et al. Positive effect of an autologous platelet concentrate in lateral epicondylitis in a double-blind randomized controlled trial. *Am J Sports Med* 2010;38(2):255–62.

43. Kazemi M, Azma K, Tavana B et al. Autologous blood versus corticosteroid local injection in the short-term treatment of lateral elbow tendinopathy: a randomized clinical trial of efficacy. *Am J Phys Med Rehabil* 2010;89(8):660–7

44. Rabago D, Best T, Zgierska A et al. A systematic review of four injection therapies for lateral epicondylosis: prolotherapy, polidocanol, whole blood and platelet rich plasma. *Br J Sports Med* 2009 Jul;43(7):471–81.

45. Mishra A, Pavelko T. Treatment of chronic elbow tendinosis with buffered platelet-rich plasma. *Am J Sports Med* 2006;34(11):1774–8.

46. Karkhanis S, Frost A, Maffulli N. Operative management of tennis elbow: a quantitative review. *Br Med Bull* 2008;88(1):171–88.

47. Ciccotti MC, Schwartz MA, Ciccotti MG. Diagnosis and treatment of medial epicondylitis of the elbow. *Clin Sports Med* 2004;23(4):693–705.

48. Park GY, Lee SM, Lee MY. Diagnostic value of ultrasonography for clinical medial epicondylitis. *Arch Phys Med Rehabil* 2008;89(4):738–42.

49. King J, Brelsford HJ, Tullos HS. Analysis of the pitching arm of the professional baseball pitcher. *Clin Orthop Relat Res.* 1969;67:116–23.

50. Frostick SP, Mohammad M, Ritchie DA. Sport injuries of the elbow. *Br J Sports Med* 1999;33(5):301–11.

51. Jacobson JA, Jebson PJL, Jeffers AW et al. Ulnar nerve dislocation and snapping triceps syndrome: diagnosis with dynamic sonography—report of three cases. *Radiology* 2001;220(3):601–5.

52. Richard MJ, Messmer C, Wray WH et al. Management of subluxating ulnar nerve at the elbow. *Orthopedics* 2010;33(9):672.

53. Appelboam A, Reuben AD, Benger JR et al. Elbow extension test to rule out elbow fracture: multicentre, prospective validation and observational study of diagnostic accuracy in adults and children. *BMJ* 2008;Dec 9;337:a2428.

54. Shapiro MS, Wang JC. Elbow fractures—treating to avoid complications. *Phys Sportsmed* 1995;23(4):39–50.

55. Ellerin BE, Helfet D, Parikh S et al. Current therapy in the management of heterotopic ossification of the elbow: a review with case studies. *Am J Phys Med Rehabil* 1999;78(3):259–71.

56. Guitton TG, Zurakowski D, van Dijk NC et al. Incidence and risk factors for the development of radiographic arthrosis after traumatic elbow injuries. *J Hand Surg Am* 2010;35(12):1976–80.

57. O'Driscoll SW, Morrey BF, Korinek S et al. Elbow subluxation and dislocation. *Clin Orthop Rel Res* 1992(280):186–97.

58. Ross G, McDevitt ER, Chronister R et al. Treatment of simple elbow dislocation using an immediate motion protocol. *Am J Sports Med* 1999;27(3):308–11.

59. Verrall GM. Return to Australian rules football after acute elbow dislocation: a report of three cases and review of the literature. *J Sci Med Sport* 2001;4(2):245–50.

60. Konjengbam M, Elangbam J. Radial nerve in the radial tunnel: anatomic sites of entrapment neuropathy. *Clin Anat* 2004;17(1):21–5.

61. Sarhadi NS, Korday SN, Bainbridge LC. Radial tunnel syndrome: diagnosis and management. *J Hand Surg* 1998;23(5):617–19.

62. Lee JC, Malara FA, Wood T et al. MRI of stress reaction of the distal humerus in elite tennis players. *Am J Roentgenol* 2006;187(4):901–4.

Chapter 23

Wrist pain

with ANDREW GARNHAM, MAUREEN ASHE, and PETER GROPPER

All this year I've been wanting to avoid surgery with different treatments but evidently the injury is more serious. The recovery time is prolonged but it depends on many factors that can't be measured today. Juan Martin Del Potro, Argentinian tennis player and US Open Champion 2009, announcing surgery for a wrist flexor tendon injury.* May, 2010 quoted in Guardian.co.uk.

The wrist is frequently injured during sport.[1] Distal radial fractures are the most common fracture seen in emergency departments,[2] and scaphoid fractures are the most common carpal fracture.[3] Men are more likely to sustain a hand or wrist injury;[4] children and adolescents are more likely to have a wrist injury compared with adults.[5] Injuries to the wrist range from acute traumatic fractures (such as occur during football, hockey, and snowboarding) to overuse conditions (which occur in racquet sports, golf, and gymnastics). If wrist injuries are not treated appropriately at the time of injury, they can lead to future impairments that can affect not only sporting endeavors but also activities of daily living.[6]

In this chapter we address two common clinical scenarios:

- the acute wrist injury (usually as a result of a fall onto the outstretched hand)
- the longer-term (chronic, or subacute) wrist pain that has developed gradually with or without a clear history of a past injury.

Acute wrist injuries

The wrist joint has multiple axes of movement—flexion–extension and radial–ulnar deviation occur at the radiocarpal joints, and pronation–supination occurs at the distal radioulnar joint (in conjunction with the proximal radioulnar joint). These movements provide mobility for hand function.

Injuries to the wrist often occur due to a fall on the outstretched hand (FOOSH). In sportspeople, the most common acute injuries are fractures of the distal radius or scaphoid, or damage to an intercarpal ligament. Intercarpal ligament injuries are becoming more frequently recognized and, if they are not treated appropriately (e.g. including surgical repair where indicated), may result in long-term disability. The causes of acute pain in this region are shown in Table 23.1 overleaf.

The anatomy of the wrist is complex (Fig. 23.1 overleaf). It is helpful to know the surface anatomy of the scaphoid tubercle, hook of hamate, pisiform, Lister's tubercle, and anatomical snuffbox. The bony anatomy consists of a proximal row (lunate, triquetrum, pisiform) and a distal row (trapezium, trapezoid, capitate, hamate), which are bridged by the scaphoid bone. Normally, the distal carpal row should be stable; thus, a ligamentous injury here can greatly impair the integrity of the wrist. The proximal row permits more intercarpal movement to allow wrist flexion/extension and radial and ulnar deviation. Here a ligamentous injury disrupts important kinematics between the scaphoid, lunate, and triquetrum, resulting in carpal instability with potential weakness and impairment of hand function.

History

It is essential to determine the mechanism of the injury causing wrist pain. A fall on the outstretched

---

* Del Potro returned to competition nine months after surgery.

Table 23.1 Causes of acute wrist pain

Common	Less common	Not to be missed
Distal radius fracture (often intra-articular in the athlete)	Fracture of hook of hamate	Carpal dislocation
	Triangular fibrocartilage complex tear	Anterior dislocation of lunate
Scaphoid fracture	Distal radioulnar joint instability	Perilunar dislocation
Wrist ligament sprain/tear	Scapholunate dissociation	Traumatic ulnar artery aneurysm or thrombosis (karate)
• Intercarpal ligament		
• Scapholunate ligament		
• Lunotriquetral ligament		

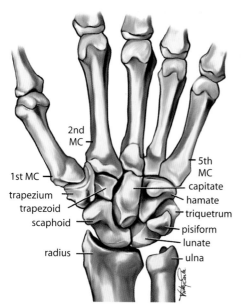

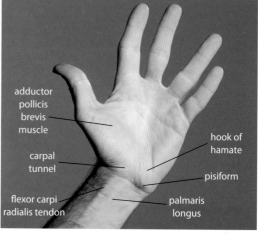

(c) Surface anatomy, volar view

Figure 23.1 Anatomy of the wrist
(a) Carpal bones (MC = metacarpal)

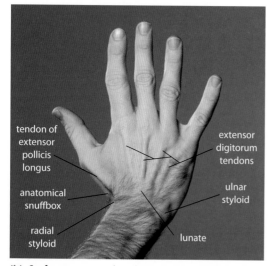

(b) Surface anatomy, dorsal view

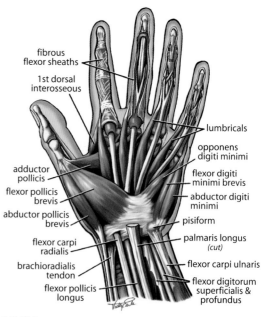

(d) Volar aspect

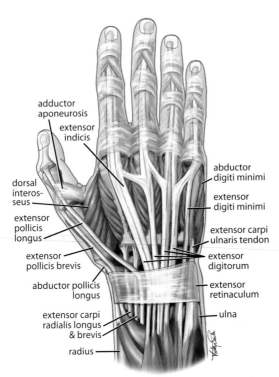

adductor aponeurosis

extensor indicis

dorsal interosseus

extensor pollicis longus

extensor pollicis brevis

abductor pollicis longus

extensor carpi radialis longus & brevis

radius

abductor digiti minimi

extensor digiti minimi

extensor carpi ulnaris tendon

extensor digitorum

extensor retinaculum

ulna

B

(e) Dorsal aspect

Table 23.2 Clinical distinction between dorsal and volar pain in acute wrist pain

Causes of dorsal wrist pain	Causes of volar wrist pain
Scaphoid fracture	Carpal instability
Scaphoid impaction syndrome	Hook of hamate fracture
Fracture dislocation of carpus	
Lunate fracture	
Distal radius fracture	
Scapholunate ligament tear	
Kienböck's disease (acute onset)	
Lunotriquetral ligament tear	
Distal radioulnar joint injury	
Carpometacarpal dislocation	

hand may be severe enough to fracture the scaphoid or distal radius, or damage the intercarpal ligaments and/or triangular fibrocartilage complex. These injuries are commonly encountered in high-velocity activities such as snowboarding,[7] rollerblading,[8, 9] or falling off a bike. A patient may fracture the hook of hamate while swinging a golf club,[10] tennis racquet, or bat, or while striking a hard object (e.g. the ground). Rotational stress to the distal radioulnar joint, and forced ulnar deviation and rotation may tear the triangular fibrocartilage complex. It is very useful to determine the site of the pain; the causes of volar pain are different from those of dorsal wrist pain (Table 23.2). Other important aspects of the history may include:

- hand dominance
- occupation (computer-related, manual labor, food service industry)
- degree of reliance on hands in occupation/recreation
- history of past upper extremity fractures, including childhood fractures/injuries
- history of osteoarthritis, rheumatoid arthritis, thyroid dysfunction, diabetes
- any unusual sounds (e.g. clicks, clunks, snaps)

- recurrent wrist swelling, which raises the suspicion of wrist instability
- musician (number of years playing, hours of practice per week, change in playing, complex piece, etc.)
- gardening, crafts, hobbies.

Examination
Examination involves:

1. Observation (Fig. 23.2a overleaf)
2. Active movements
   (a) flexion/extension
   (b) supination/pronation
   (c) radial/ulnar deviation (Fig. 23.2b overleaf)
3. Passive movements
   (a) extension (Fig. 23.2c overleaf)
   (b) flexion (Fig. 23.2d overleaf)
4. Palpation
   (a) distal forearm (Fig. 23.2e overleaf)
   (b) radial snuffbox (Fig. 23.2f overleaf)
   (c) base of metacarpals
   (d) lunate (Fig. 23.2g overleaf)
   (e) head of ulna (Fig. 23.2h overleaf)
   (f) radioulnar joint
5. Special tests
   (a) hamate/pisiform (Fig. 23.2i overleaf)
   (b) Watson's test for scapholunate injury (Fig. 23.2j on page 418)
   (c) stress of triangular fibrocartilage complex (Fig. 23.2k on page 418)

(d) ulnar fovea sign for foveal disruption and ulnar triquetral ligament injury (Fig. 23.2l on page 418)

(e) grip—Jamar dynamometer (may be contraindicated if a maximal effort is not permitted [e.g. after tendon repair])

(f) dexterity—Purdue pegboard (Fig. 23.2m on page 419)

(g) dexterity—Moberg pick-up test

(h) sensation—Semmes Weinstein monofilament testing

(i) sensation—temperature

(j) nerve entrapment—Tinel's sign

6. Standardized rating scales

Figure 23.2 Examination of the patient with an acute wrist injury

(a) Observation. Inspect the wrist for obvious deformity suggesting a distal radial fracture. Swelling in the region of the radial snuffbox may indicate a scaphoid fracture. Inspect the hand and wrist posture, temperature, color, muscular wasting, scars, normal arches of the hand

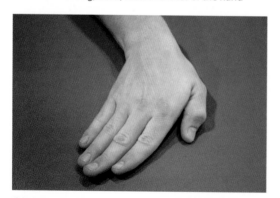

(b) Active movement—radial/ulnar deviation. Normal range is radial 20° and ulnar 60°. Pain and restriction of movement should be noted. Always compare motion with that of the other hand

(c) Range of motion—the "prayer position." Normal range of motion in wrist extension is 70°

(d) Range of motion—the "reverse prayer position." Normal range of motion in wrist flexion is 80°–90°

B

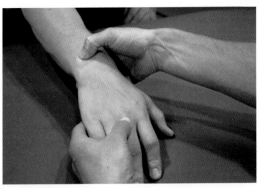

(e) Palpation—the distal forearm is palpated for bony tenderness or deformity

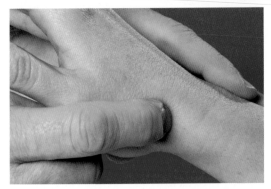

(f) Palpation—radial snuffbox. The proximal snuffbox is the site of the radial styloid, the middle snuffbox is the site of the scaphoid bone, while the distal snuffbox is over the scaphotrapezial joint

(g) Palpation—the lunate is palpated as a bony prominence proximal to the capitate sulcus. Lunate tenderness may correspond to a fracture. On the radial side of the lunate lies the scapholunate joint, which may be tender in scapholunate ligament sprain. This is a site of ganglion formation

(h) Palpation—head of ulna and ulnar snuffbox. Swelling and tenderness over the dorsal ulnar aspect of the wrist is present with fractures of the ulnar styloid. Distal to the ulnar head is the ulnar snuffbox. The triquetrum lies in this sulcus and can be palpated with the wrist in radial deviation. Tenderness may indicate triquetral fracture or triquetrolunate injury. The triquetrohamate joint is located more distally. Pain here may represent triquetrohamate ligament injury

(i) Palpation—the pisiform is palpated at the flexor crease of the wrist on the ulnar side. Tenderness in this region may occur with pisiform or triquetral fracture. The hook of hamate is 1 cm (0.5 in.) distal and radial to the pisiform. Examination may show tenderness over the hook or on the dorsal ulnar surface

Several valid and reliable assessment scales can quantify function of the wrist specifically, or the upper extremity, after an injury. These include the Patient Rated Wrist Evaluation (PRWE),[11, 12] the Disability of the Arm, Shoulder and Hand (DASH and Quick DASH),[13, 14] and the Mayo wrist score measurements.[15] The Mayo and DASH scores can conveniently be completed online at the following website for various orthopedic scores (www.orthopaedicscore.com).

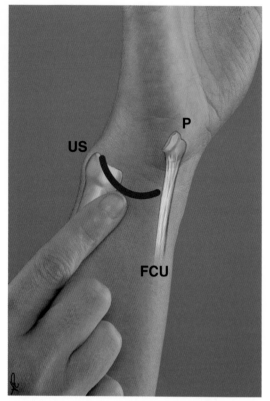

(j) Special test—Watson's test for scapholunate instability. The examiner places the thumb on the scaphoid tuberosity as shown with the wrist in ulnar deviation. The wrist is then deviated radially with the examiner placing pressure on the scaphoid. If the athlete feels pain dorsally (over the scapholunate ligament) or the examiner feels the scaphoid move dorsally, then scapholunate dissociation is present

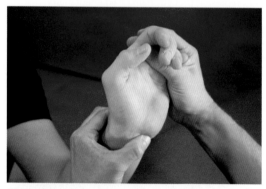

(k) Special test—triangular fibrocartilage complex integrity. The wrist is placed into dorsiflexion and ulnar deviation and then rotated. Overpressure causes pain and occasionally clicking in patients with a tear of the triangular fibrocartilage complex

(l) Ulnar fovea sign for foveal disruption and ulnar triquetral ligament injury. The ulnar styloid process is easily palpated with the forearm in neutral rotation. The fovea lies between the ulnar styloid (US) process and the flexor carpi ulnaris (FCU) tendon. Distally it is bounded by the pisiforn (P) bone and proximally by the volar surface of the ulnar head, which in this photo is under the examiner's finger pulp. The tip of the examiner's index finger points to the location of the fovea

Investigations
Plain radiography

Following trauma, routine radiograph views should include a PA with the wrist neutral as well as PAs with both radial and ulnar deviation. If ligament injury is suspected, also obtain a PA view with clenched fist. A straight lateral view of the wrist, with the dorsum of the distal forearm and the hand forming a straight line, permits assessment of the distal radius, the lunate, the scaphoid, and the capitate and may reveal subtle instability. Undisplaced distal radial and scaphoid fractures, however, are often difficult to see

on initial radiographs; clinical suspicion of fracture warrants investigation with other modalities (see "Special imaging studies" below).

The normal PA view is shown in Figure 23.3a. Inspect each bone in turn. Note the line joining the proximal ends of the proximal row of the carpus and the "C" shape of the midcarpal joint (Gilula's arcs). If these lines are not smooth, a major abnormality is present. Assess the size of the scapholunate gap and look for scaphoid flexion (the signet ring sign) as these are signs of scapholunate instability.

The lateral radiograph of the normal wrist can be seen in Figure 23.3b. The proximal pole of the lunate fits into the concavity of the distal radius, and the

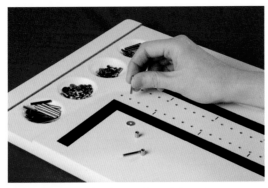

(m) Special test—Purdue pegboard dexterity test. This measures dexterity for activities that involve gross movements of the hands, fingers, and arms, and also those that require "fingertip" dexterity

convex head of the capitate fits into the distal concavity of the lunate. These bones should be aligned with each other and with the base of the third metacarpal. A clenched fist PA view should be taken if scapholunate instability is suspected. This is indicated by a widened gap of 3 mm (0.1 in.) or greater between the scaphoid and lunate on the PA view; however, this may not present until some time after a scapholunate tear.

PRACTICE PEARL   Scapholunate instability cannot be ruled out on initial plain radiographs, as it may take some months for the scaphoid and lunate to separate significantly radiographically.

Special imaging studies

The combination of the complex anatomy of the wrist and subtle wrist injuries that can cause substantial morbidity has led to the development of specialized wrist imaging techniques. Special scaphoid views should be requested if a scaphoid fracture is suspected. A carpal tunnel view with the wrist in dorsiflexion allows inspection of the hook of hamate and the ridge of the trapezium. For suspected mechanical pathology (such as an occult ganglion, an occult fracture, non-union, or bone necrosis), several modalities are useful (e.g. ultrasonography, radionuclide bone scan, CT scan, MRI).

Ultrasonography is a quick and accessible way to assess soft tissue abnormalities such as tendon injury, synovial thickening, ganglions, and synovial cysts.

Bone scans have high sensitivity and low specificity; thus, they can effectively rule out subtle fractures.

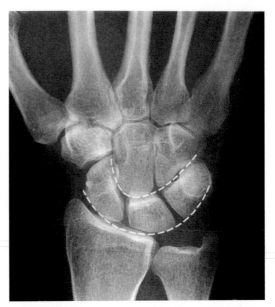

Figure 23.3 Radiograph of the wrist
(a) PA view—Gilula's arcs

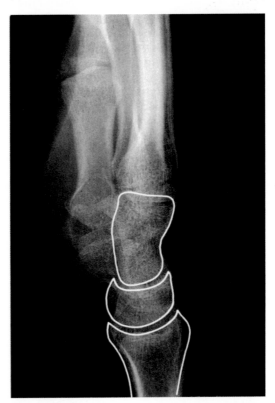

(b) Lateral view

419

MRI may be equally sensitive to and more specific than a bone scan. CT scanning is particularly useful for evaluating fractures that are difficult to evaluate fully on plain films, but MRI can also provide information about soft tissue injuries. Thus, a complete scapholunate ligament tear is more effectively identified with MRI than with CT.

Arthrography of the wrist is no longer used as an investigative tool except in combination with MRI—"MR arthrogram" or MRA.

If all imaging results are negative but clinically significant wrist pain persists, the clinician should refer the patient to a specialist for further evaluation.

Fracture of the distal radius and ulna

Distal radial fractures (Fig. 23.4) are very common peripheral fractures.[2] As the force required to fracture young adults' bones is great, sportspeople may simultaneously incur an intra-articular fracture and ligamentous strain or rupture. The higher the forces involved (e.g. in high-velocity sports), the greater the likelihood of a complex injury involving articular structures. Thus, thorough assessment of ligamentous injury is essential when fractures occur.

Initial treatment of the fracture is anatomical reduction and immobilization for up to six weeks in a cast that covers the distal half of the forearm, the wrist, and the hand, leaving the metacarpophalangeal joints free.[16] Radiographs are required every two weeks during healing to ensure that satisfactory reduction is maintained.

Inaccurate reduction, articular surface angulation, radial inclination, or inadequate restoration of length all require early internal fixation with fixed angle-volar plating.[16, 17] While it is sometimes not possible to achieve perfect reduction because of dorsal comminution, every effort should be made to restore anatomical alignment to avoid ongoing functional impairment. Overall, there is a trend to more aggressive treatment using volar plating, and this has led to improved functional outcomes, especially in the young active adult.

Fracture of the scaphoid

Carpal fractures account for many hand/wrist fractures. The most common carpal fracture involves the scaphoid;[4] the usual mechanism is a fall on the outstretched hand. As the patient's pain may settle soon after the fall, he or she may not present to a clinician until some time after the injury.

The key examination finding is tenderness in the anatomical snuffbox (Fig. 23.2f on page 417). This may be accompanied by swelling and loss of grip strength. Snuffbox tenderness should be compared with the other wrist, as some degree of tenderness is normal. Swelling in the snuffbox should also be sought. A more specific clinical test for scaphoid fracture is pain on axial compression of the thumb toward the radius or direct pressure on the scaphoid tuberosity with radial deviation of the wrist.

Plain radiographs with special scaphoid views will usually demonstrate the fracture (Fig. 23.5). If a scaphoid fracture is suspected clinically but the radiograph is normal, a fracture cannot be ruled out. MRI is an ideal diagnostic test for an acute injury that may be cost-saving in some settings.[15] Bone scan also has excellent sensitivity for scaphoid fracture. Note that it can take 24 hours for the injury to be revealed on MRI or bone scan.

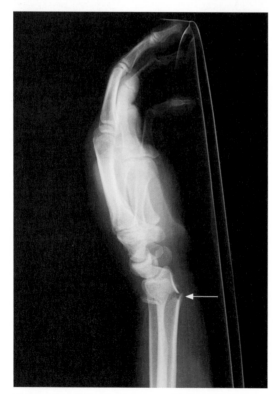

Figure 23.4 Colles' fracture, a specific type of distal radial fracture

 If a scaphoid fracture is suspected clinically but the radiograph is normal, a fracture cannot be ruled out.

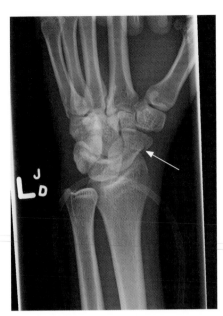

Figure 23.5 A subtle scaphoid fracture

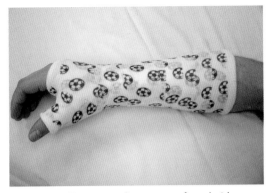

Figure 23.6 Two types of treatment of scaphoid fractures
(a) Cast immobilization

B

In cases where these imaging modalities are not available, the wrist should be immobilized for 12 days as if a fracture were present, and followed by clinical examination and repeat radiograph.

Note that scaphoid fracture is the most commonly missed fracture leading to litigation. If there is no bony damage, scapholunate instability should also be considered (see below).

Traditional treatment of stable and unstable scaphoid fractures

A stable scaphoid fracture should be immobilized for eight weeks in a scaphoid cast extending from the proximal forearm to, but not including, the interphalangeal joint of the thumb (Fig. 23.6a). On removing the cast, re-evaluate the fracture clinically and radiologically. As with all fractures, clinical union precedes radiological union and determines readiness to return to sport. Absence of pain on palpation, and comfort when the wrist is rotated and angulated by the examiner indicate clinical union. Radiological union of the scaphoid should occur before finally discharging the patient from follow-up. Overall, in excess of 90% of scaphoid fractures heal without problems.

Unstable, angulated (>15–20°) or significantly displaced fractures (diastasis in the fracture gap >1.5 mm) require immediate percutaneous fixation (Fig. 23.6b) or open reduction and internal fixation.

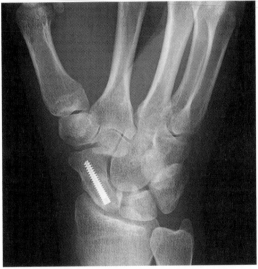

(b) Surgical fixation. This is increasingly being used for uncomplicated scaphoid fractures (see also box overleaf)

Emerging treatment of stable scaphoid fractures

By early 2011, new data emerged surrounding the management of "routine" scaphoid fractures—the undisplaced or minimally displaced fracture. Until then, meta-analyses indicated that there was no evidence to determine whether non-surgical or surgical management was superior. However, publication of four new randomized controlled trials (RCTs) in 2007 and 2008 led Buizje and colleagues to conclude in a 2010 meta-analysis that surgical treatment provides superior functional outcome and requires less time off work (see box overleaf).[18] Surgical treatment, however, was associated with a higher rate of complications

The case for surgical management of uncomplicated scaphoid fracture

Study or subgroup	Operative			Conservative				Std. mean difference
	Mean	SD	Total	Mean	SD	Total	Weight	IV, random, 95% CI
Arora	4	4.2	21	13	14.1	23	17.6%	−0.83 [−1.45, −0.21]
Dias	3.9	1	39	5.2	1.8	42	31.3%	−0.88 [−1.33, −0.42]
McQueen	6.3	7.9	23	12.3	19.2	24	20.0%	−0.40 [−0.98, 0.18]
Vinnars	4.5	1	40	5	1.5	35	31.1%	−0.39 [−0.85, 0.06]
TOTAL (95% CI)			123			124	100.0%	−0.62 [−0.89, −0.36]

Heterogeneity: Tau^2 = 0.00; Chi^2 = 3.16; df = 3 (P = 0.37); I^2 = 5%
Test for overall effect: Z = 4.62 (P <0.00001)

Key data from the meta-analysis of 4 key papers indicating that that surgical treatment ("operative" column, 123 patients) provide a superior functional outcome and requires less time off work than conservative management (124 patients). The table indicates that the overall mean advantage to the surgical group was 38% (reflected by the standard mean difference of −0.62 (with confidence intervals that do not cross 0).

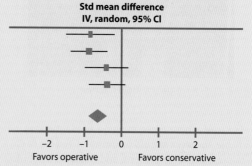

Std mean difference
IV, random, 95% CI

−2   −1   0   1   2
Favors operative   Favors conservative

Figure 23.7 This is a "forest plot" and each orange square summarizes the results from one study. The orange diamond represents the overall result—taking all studies into account. As the confidence intervals do not cross 0, there is a significant difference between treatments which favor surgery
REPRODUCED FROM BUIZJE[18] WITH PERMISSION

(25% compared with 9%) and, surprisingly, a greater prevalence of scaphotrapezial osteoarthritis. Both of these downsides of surgery were not statistically significantly different between the groups.

Complications of scaphoid fracture

Because the blood supply to the scaphoid originates distally (Fig. 23.8.a), flow to the proximal pole can be diminished, which can then be at risk of necrosis after a fracture (Fig. 23.8b). Scaphoid fractures also have a risk of delayed union or non-union. Non-union and osteonecrosis can occur on their own or can occur in combination.

If there is clinical evidence of incomplete union when the cast is removed, the fracture should be immobilized for a further four to six weeks. The clinical signs of healing are:

- scaphoid is non-tender to palpation
- there is no pain when the wrist is twisted and force is placed through the scaphoid.

Further immobilization beyond this time is unlikely to prove beneficial.

CT scan is the investigation of choice to detect non-union, but MRI can be used if CT is not available.

Contemporary management of nonunion

Contemporary treatment of scaphoid non-union requires management by a specialist hand or orthopedic trauma surgeon. Simple non-unions may be treated with fixation alone or fixation with bone graft (if there is a deformity or there has been bone resorption); ostenecrosis or osteonecrosis with combined non-union may require a vascularized bone graft.[19]

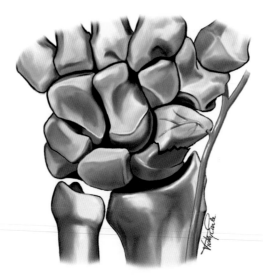

Figure 23.8 **(a)** Blood vessels around the scaphoid. The artery to the scaphoid enters via the distal pole, so fractures at the waist of the scaphoid compromise blood flow to the proximal fragment

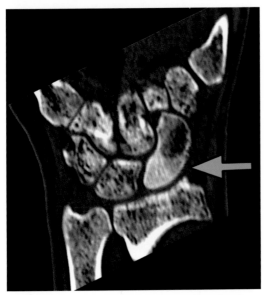

(b) Wrist CT scan showing the characteristic sclerotic appearance of avascular necrosis (arrowhead, mirroring (a) above) in the proximal pole of the scaphoid

Post-immobilization wrist rehabilitation

Following successful treatment of a scaphoid fracture, the patient is invariably left with a stiff wrist joint and wasted muscles. Mobilization and strengthening of the wrist and other stiff structures should

begin immediately after cast removal. Post-fracture, it is prudent to ensure there has been no ligamentous involvement by using the clenched-fist radiograph or MR plus/minus arthroscopy if clinical suspicion is high. If the wrist is intact, the athlete may be able to return to certain activities using a protective device. Compression tubing (Fig. 23.9a) worn under the protective splint reduces edema and improves comfort. Different sports have different rules about what constitutes an "allowable" protective cast (Fig. 23.9b).

Fracture of the hook of hamate

B

Fracture of the hook of hamate may occur while swinging a golf club,[10, 20, 21] tennis racquet, or baseball bat. The fracture is especially likely to occur when the golf club strikes the ground instead of the ball, forcing the top of the handle of the club against the hook of the hamate of the top hand (Fig. 23.10a overleaf). This mechanism may compress the superficial and deep terminal branches of the ulnar nerve, producing both sensory and motor changes.

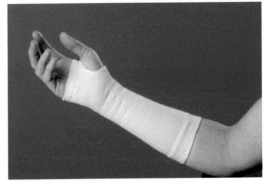

Figure 23.9 Following a scaphoid fracture, the athlete may wear compression tubing underneath a protective cast
(a) Compression tubing

(b) Protective cast

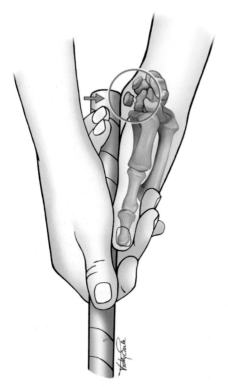

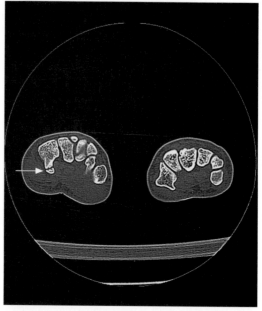

(b) CT scan of a fracture of the hook of hamate

Figure 23.10 Fracture of the hook of hamate
(a) Possible mechanism—when the golf club is
suddenly decelerated (e.g. hitting the ground), the grip
is forced against the hook of hamate

Symptoms include reduced grip strength and
ulnar wrist pain. Examination reveals volar wrist tenderness over the hook of hamate.

Routine radiographs of the wrist do not image
the fracture and even the classic "carpal tunnel view"
with the wrist in dorsiflexion is an insensitive test.
CT scan (Fig. 23.10b) and MRI (Fig. 23.10c) are the
best imaging tools.

This fracture often fails to heal with immobilization; most sports medicine cases of the fracture
are actually stress fractures that present late. In
some sportspeople (e.g. baseball players), the hook of
hamate fracture is likely to be a completed stress fracture not due to acute trauma. If diagnosis is delayed,
or the fracture fails to heal clinically within four
weeks of immobilization, current surgical practice
is excision of the fractured hook followed by wrist
immobilization for three weeks (in preference to
open reduction and internal fixation).[10, 22, 23] The pain

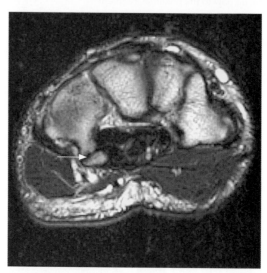

(c) MRI scan of a fracture of the hook of hamate

only dissipates slowly, but the patient can usually
resume sport six weeks after surgery.

Dislocation of the carpal bones

There are a number of different types of dislocation
of the carpal bones, mostly involving the lunate. They
are the uncommon end-stage of severe ligament disruption. Failure to recognize them generally results
in disastrous consequences.

Anterior dislocation of the lunate

The lunate may dislocate anteriorly because of forced dorsiflexion when the sportsperson falls onto the outstretched hand, or the carpus and hand may dislocate dorsally on the lunate, leading to perilunar dislocation. Pain is usually severe and deformity obvious.

Plain radiograph reveals the dislocation best in the lateral view with the lunate tilted volarly and not articulating with the capitate.

Treatment of anterior dislocation of the lunate is open reduction and primary ligament repair, followed by cast immobilization for eight weeks. Anterior lunate dislocation may be associated with median nerve compression and paresthesia in the radial three and a half digits. This requires surgical decompression.

Perilunar dislocation of the lunate

Perilunar dislocation is occasionally associated with a fractured waist of the scaphoid when the lunate remains with the radius and the capitate is dislocated dorsally. This complex injury is often overlooked—the diagnosis is difficult to make.

Perilunar dislocation requires treatment by a hand and wrist surgeon, as long-term instablity and radiographic wrist arthritis can occur.[24]

Scapholunate dissociation

Pain and dysfunction at the wrist can be disabling. A complex composition of different joint surfaces with multiple ligamentous attachments contributes to the challenges faced when trying to understand wrist pain and dysfunction. Thus, a thorough assessment of range of motion and ligamentous stability is essential to rule out serious threats to the architectural integrity of the wrist and hand. Fortunately, most wrist traumatic events do not lead to significant capsuloligamentous or bony structural failure, which means the injury can be treated conservatively. However, a minor ligamentous structural injury or failure can progress; if not identified and managed correctly in the early stages, there is the potential for significant structural failure leading to a chronic impairment.

Scapholunate dissociation is due to scapholunate ligament tear and loss of secondary restraints (Fig. 23.11a). Rotatory subluxation of the scaphoid may occur as a result of disruption of its ligamentous attachments due to acute trauma (e.g. a fall on the dorsiflexed hand). Examination reveals tenderness 2 cm (1 in.) distal to Lister's tubercle on the radial

side of the lunate. There may be little, or no, swelling. The key examination maneuver is Watson's test (Fig. 23.2j). If the test causes pain or reveals dorsal

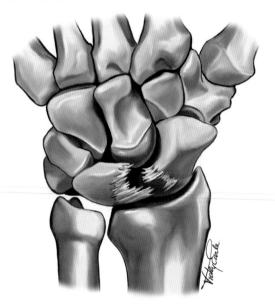

Figure 23.11 Scapholunate dissociation
(a) Coronal graphic shows a tear of the dorsal component of the scapholunate ligament

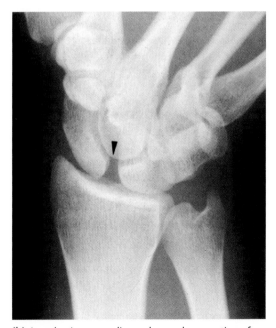

(b) In a classic case, radiograph reveals separation of the scaphoid and lunate (arrowhead). This can be a late sign, so normal radiography does not rule out this condition

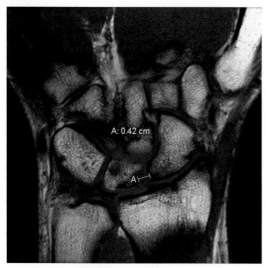

(c) MRI shows that the scapholunate interval diastasis (A) is 4.2 mm (0.14 in.). The upper limit of normal is 3 mm (0.1 in.)

movement of the scaphoid, scapholunate instability is present.

Conventional radiographic views may not show any abnormality, but stress films, such as the clenched fist PA view, may reveal a gap greater than 3 mm (0.1 in.) between the scaphoid and lunate (Fig. 23.11b). A lateral radiograph may show an increased volar flexion of the distal pole of the scaphoid and dorsiflexion of the lunate. If these tests are negative but the injury is suspected clinically, MRI is indicated (Fig. 23.11c).

Treatment of scapholunate dissociation is open reduction and repair of the ligaments and internal fixation. The patient must accept that any surgical repair will result in permanent reduction in wrist motion. Hence, minor dissociations in the presence of normal movement probably should not be repaired.

Subacute onset and chronic wrist pain

When a patient presents with subacute onset or chronic wrist pain, the clinician should consider whether the pain may be a manifestation of a systemic condition (e.g. metabolic disorder, spondyloarthropathy [Chapter 55]). The clinician should rule out an uncommon presentation of radiating pain from a more proximal problem (such as a herniated cervical disk).

A detailed history will reveal whether the problem stems from an overuse condition (e.g. tenosynovitis)

or from an acute injury that has not been correctly diagnosed or treated. Some patients suffer only minor discomfort at the time of an initial injury and fail to seek attention at that time. Acute injuries are discussed above.

The location of wrist pain narrows down the diagnosis of subacute onset wrist pain. Determine whether the wrist pain is essentially dorsal, volar, radial, or ulnar (Table 23.3), as this is the first step to determining the differential diagnosis.

History

A thorough history of the onset of pain and the circumstances surrounding the onset will provide the best clues to a previous acute injury. Factors that aggravate the pain provide useful information as to which structures are involved in chronic wrist pain.

Pain after repeated movement, with stiffness after a period of rest, suggests an inflammatory condition such as tenosynovitis. Pain aggravated by weight-bearing activities, such as gymnastics or diving, suggests bone or joint involvement. A history of joint clicking may be associated with carpal instability, triangular fibrocartilage tears, or extensor carpi ulnaris subluxation. Characteristic night pain, with or without paresthesia, is found in carpal tunnel syndrome. Associated neck or elbow symptoms suggest referred pain.

Examination

Inspection may reveal a ganglion on the dorsum of the wrist. Swelling over the radial styloid may indicate de Quervain's tenosynovitis. Muscle wasting of the thenar or hypothenar eminence is found in the late stages of median or ulnar nerve compression respectively.

Palpate the wrist to detect tenderness and to determine whether the pathology appears to be extra-articular (i.e. soft tissue) or articular. Examine the radial side of the lunate closely (Fig. 23.2g). Tenderness is present in scapholunate ligament sprain. On the ulnar side of the lunate lies the triquetrolunate ligament. Tenderness and an associated click on radial and ulnar deviation of the wrist may occur with partial or complete tears of this ligament. On the volar aspect of the wrist, palpate the tuberosity of the trapezium as a bony prominence at the base of the thenar eminence (Fig. 23.12a).

Additional tests may be performed to diagnose overuse injuries. Restricted wrist movements and pain on passive stretching of the tendons is associated

Table 23.3 Causes of subacute onset wrist pain according to location of pain. More common causes are listed first

Dorsal	Volar	Ulnar	Radial
Ganglion	Scaphoid aseptic necrosis	Triangular fibrocartilage	Scaphoid fracture (missed)
Intersection syndrome	Stenosing tendinopathies	complex tears	Non-union of scaphoid
Kienböck's disease	Flexor carpi ulnaris	Ulnar impaction syndrome	fracture
Dorsal pole of lunate and	tendinopathy	Distal radioulnar joint	De Quervain's tenosynovitis
distal radius impingement	Flexor carpi radialis	instability	Scaphoid impaction
(gymnasts)	tendinopathy	Carpal instability	syndrome
Posterior interosseous nerve	Carpal tunnel syndrome	Scapholunate dissociation	Intersection syndrome
entrapment	Ulnar tunnel syndrome	Ulnar nerve compression	Flexor carpi radialis
Inflammatory arthropathy	Pisotriquetral degenerative	(cyclists, golfers)	tendinopathy
Degenerative joint disease	joint disease	Flexor carpi ulnaris	Dorsal pole of lunate
Extensor carpi ulnaris	Avascular necrosis of the	tendinopathy	impingement on distal
tendinopathy	capitate (weightlifters)	Extensor carpi ulnaris	radius (gymnasts)
Extensor carpi ulnaris	Extensor pollicis longus	tendinopathy	Scapholunate dissociation
subluxation	impingement/rupture	Extensor carpi ulnaris	
Injuries to distal radial	(gymnasts)	subluxation	
epiphysis (children)		Distal radioulnar joint	
Extensor pollicis longus		impaction syndromes	
impingement on Lister's		(golfers)	
tubercle (occasional		Scaphoid impaction	
rupture)		syndrome	

with tenosynovitis. Tenosynovitis of the abductor pollicis longus and extensor pollicis brevis (de Quervain's disease) may be confirmed by Finkelstein's test (Fig. 23.12b). Tinel's sign is positive if carpal tunnel syndrome is present (Fig. 23.12c overleaf). Tears of the triangular fibrocartilage complex can be detected using the "press test" (Fig. 23.12d overleaf).[25]

Extra-articular conditions

Many conditions can cause subacute and chronic wrist pain; clinical assessment can provide insight into whether this is due to extra-articular (soft tissue) conditions, or articular (bone or joint) conditions. Common extra-articular conditions include de Quervain's tenosynovitis, intersection syndrome, ganglia, impingement syndromes, and tendinopathies.

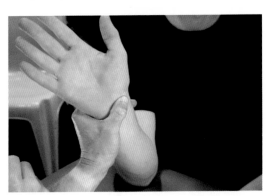

Figure 23.12 Additional examination of the patient with wrist pain of gradual onset
(a) Palpation—tuberosity of the trapezium at the base of the thenar eminence. Tenderness proximal to the tuberosity may be associated with flexor carpi radialis tendinopathy. Tenderness distal may indicate injury to the carpometacarpal ligament of the thumb

(b) Special test—Finkelstein's test to detect de Quervain's disease. The thumb is placed in the palm of the hand with flexion of the metacarpophalangeal and interphalangeal joints while the examiner deviates the wrist in the ulnar direction

(c) Special tests—Tinel's test. Tapping over the median nerve at the wrist produces tingling and altered sensation in the distribution of the median nerve in carpal tunnel syndrome

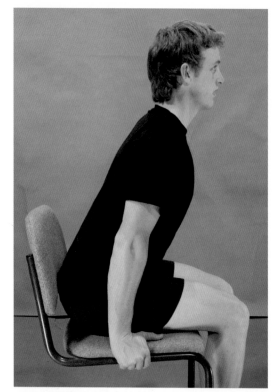

(d) Special tests—press test (or "sitting hands" test). Attempting to raise body weight from a chair reproduces the pain of the triangular fibrocartilage complex injury

De Quervain's tenosynovitis

De Quervain's tenosynovitis is an inflammation of the synovium of the abductor pollicis longus and extensor pollicis brevis tendons as they pass in their synovial sheath in a fibro-osseous tunnel at the level

of the radial styloid (Fig. 23.13). This is the most common radial-sided tendinopathy in sportspeople and occurs particularly with racquet sports, ten-pin bowlers, rowers, and canoeists. The left thumb of a right-handed golfer is particularly at risk because of the hyperabduction required during a golf swing.

There is local tenderness and swelling, which may extend proximally and distally along the course of the tendons. In severe cases, crepitus may be felt. A positive Finkelstein's test is diagnostic (Fig. 23.13b) but not pathognomonic, because flexor carpi radialis tendinopathy also causes a positive test.

Treatment includes splinting, local electrotherapeutic modalities, stretches, and graduated strengthening. Patients often find a pen build-up (a rubber addition to enlarge the diameter of the pen) useful as this reduces the stretch on the extensor tendons. An injection of corticosteroid and local anesthetic into the tendon sheath usually proves helpful.[26] In rare cases, surgical release is necessary.

One study that pooled the results of seven investigations concluded that cortisone alone cured 83% of cases, injection and splinting cured 61%, and splinting alone cured 14%. It is of note that no patients gained symptom reduction from rest and NSAIDs.[27] Unfortunately, the original studies did not compare

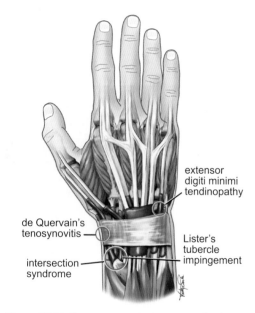

Figure 23.13 Some extra-articular causes of pain around the wrist
(a) Sites of pain where tendons pass through fibro-osseous tunnels

injection to another form of treatment; thus, further studies are needed to determine the most effective treatment for this condition.

Intersection syndrome

Intersection syndrome is a bursitis that occurs at the site where the abductor pollicis longus and extensor pollicis brevis tendons cross over the extensor carpi radialis tendons just proximal to the extensor retinaculum (Fig. 23.14). It may be due to friction at the site of crossing, or it may arise from tenosynovitis of the two extensor tendons within their synovial sheath. This condition is sometimes called "oarsmen's wrist" because of its common occurrence in rowers;[28] however, it is also seen in canoeists, and in weight-training and racquet sports. Windy conditions commonly provoke this condition in canoeists.

Tenderness is found dorsally on the radial side, with swelling and crepitus a short distance proximal to the site of maximal tenderness in de Quervain's disease (Fig. 23.13).

Treatment involves relative rest, and early intervention with corticosteroid injection into the bursa if there is no response. Surgical decompression is rarely necessary. For rowers, other considerations include reducing the amount of rowing, and changing the size of the oar and/or rowing technique.[28]

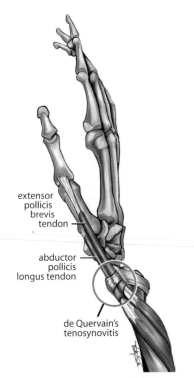

extensor pollicis brevis tendon

abductor pollicis longus tendon

de Quervain's tenosynovitis

(b) Graphic view of the radial styloid showing the thickening and edema of the first extensor compartment tendons in de Quervain's tenosynovitis

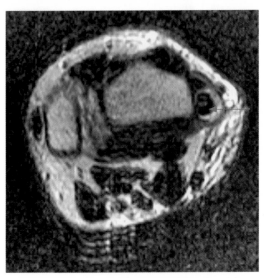

(c) MRI of the region reveals increased signal and the thickened tendon the thickened tendon and fluid in the sheath of abductor pollicis longus (arrow)

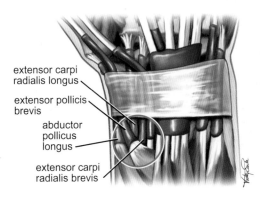

extensor carpi radialis longus

extensor pollicis brevis

abductor pollicus longus

extensor carpi radialis brevis

Figure 23.14 Sites of pain and mechanisms of intersection syndrome. Causes of intersection syndrome include inflammation at the site where the abductor pollicis longus and extensor pollicis brevis cross the wrist extensors (extensor carpi radialis brevis and longus) and tenosynovitis of the wrist extensors themselves

Ganglions

Ganglions occur in sportspeople of any age. They are a synovial cyst communicating with the joint space (Fig. 23.15). They most often present as a relatively painless swelling. They occur in several common sites on both the dorsal and volar aspects of the wrist, most commonly the scapholunate space, presumably as a result of previous ligamentous trauma. They may also be intracapsular, or even intra-osseous.

The patient's main complaint is of intermittent wrist pain and reduced movement. Swelling may be visible intermittently or not at all, and so should not be relied upon to make the diagnosis. Ultrasonography is a useful investigation; however, T2-weighted MRI highlights ganglion cysts (Fig. 23.15b) and is the investigation of choice. The sportsperson must be reassured that the ganglion is benign.

Treatment is only indicated for a symptomatic ganglion. When symptoms persist, aspiration and/or corticosteroid infiltration are at least temporarily effective and can be performed under ultrasound guidance where this is feasible. Some persistent symptomatic ganglions require surgery. Without complete removal, the lesion returns rapidly.

Impingement syndromes

A number of impingement syndromes may cause wrist pain:

- Scaphoid impaction syndrome may occur because of repetitive hyperextension stresses (e.g. in weightlifting, gymnastics). This mechanism is also responsible for avascular necrosis of the capitate in weightlifters.
- Impaction of the dorsal pole of the lunate on the distal radius is seen in gymnasts.
- The extensor pollicis longus may impinge on Lister's tubercle and occasionally ruptures.
- Triquetrohamate impingement syndrome may result from forced wrist extension and ulnar deviation (e.g. in racquet sports, gymnastics).
- Radial styloid impaction syndrome can result from repeated forced radial deviation, especially among golfers.
- Patients with these syndromes present with localized tenderness and are treated with rest and a protective brace. Occasionally, corticosteroid injection or surgical exploration may be helpful.

Tendinopathies around the wrist

Any of the flexor and extensor tendons around the wrist may become painful with excessive activity. On

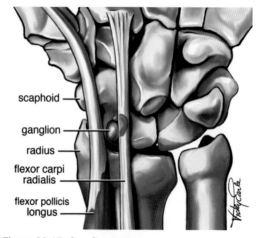

Figure 23.15 Ganglion cyst
(a) Graphic view of the dorsum of the wrist showing the ganglion arising from the joint

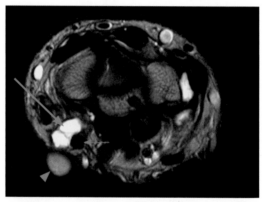

(b) MRI shows the bilobed high-signal ganglion (larger arrow) surrounding the tendon of flexor carpi radialis (small arrow) and very close to the patient's site of pain (the MR-compatible marker placed over the skin, arrowhead)

examination, there is tenderness and occasionally swelling and crepitus.

The principles of treating tendinopathies apply; management should include attention to biomechanics (ergonomics), relative rest, ice, progressive strengthening, and functional rehabilitation.[25]

Injuries to the distal radial epiphysis

Injuries to the distal radial epiphysis occur frequently in young elite gymnasts. Fractures may occur but overuse injury to the epiphysis is more common. The gymnast complains of pain and limitation of dorsiflexion. Examination reveals minimal swelling and tenderness about the distal radial epiphysis with no signs of tendinopathy, synovial cysts, or joint dysfunction.

Common radiographic findings include widening of the growth plate, cystic changes (usually of the metaphyseal aspect of the epiphyseal plate), and haziness in the normal radiolucent area of the epiphyseal plate when compared with the asymptomatic side. If there is narrowing of the growth plate, the possibility of a Salter Harris V stress fracture must be considered (Chapter 42).

Prevention by alteration of the training program is the best means of managing this condition. Once pain is present, avoidance of aggravating activities is required; however, the condition can take months to settle. There should be particular attention to strengthening of the forearm flexors, as incorrect weight-bearing through an excessively extended wrist is a major causative factor.

Articular causes of subacute and chronic wrist pain

Common articular causes of subacute and chronic wrist pain include triangular fibrocartilage complex (TFCC) tears, Kienböck's disease and injuries to the distal radial epiphysis.

Triangular fibrocartilage complex tear

The triangular fibrocartilage complex lies between the ulna and the carpus. It is the major stabilizer of the distal radioulnar joint. The "complex" consists of the triangular fibrocartilage, ulnar meniscus homolog, ulnar collateral ligament, numerous carpal ligaments, and the extensor carpi ulnaris tendon sheath. The triangular fibrocartilage complex is a common site of ulnar wrist pain. Compressive loads to the wrist, especially if accompanied by ulnar deviation (e.g. in gymnastics, diving, golf, racquet sports), may tear the central portion of the cartilage. It can also be disrupted after a distal radial–ulnar fracture and after disruption to the distal radioulnar joint.

Examination reveals tenderness and swelling over the dorsal ulnar aspect of the wrist, pain on resisted wrist dorsiflexion and ulnar deviation (Fig. 23.2k on page 418), a clicking sensation on wrist movement and reduced grip strength. The "press test"[29] may be helpful (Fig. 23.12d). The patient creates an axial ulnar load by attempting to lift his or her weight up off a chair using the affected wrist. A positive test replicates the presenting symptom.

High-quality MRI can image the triangular fibrocartilage complex and this is an increasingly popular investigation for ulnar-sided wrist pain.[30] Estimates of sensitivity and specificity are about 60% and 90% respectively,[31] which suggests that a negative MRI should not be used to rule out the condition if it is clinically suspected. Ultrasonography shows promise for matching MRI in the detection of triangular fibrocartilage complex lesions.[32]

Treatment may include protective bracing, strengthening when able, heat and/or electrotherapy modalities for pain. Arthroscopy permits accurate diagnosis and excision of any torn cartilage if required. If the ulna is longer than the radius (positive ulnar variance), it impinges on the triangular fibrocartilage and predisposes it to tearing. It may be necessary to shorten the ulna as well as excising the torn fibrocartilage.[33]

Distal radioulnar joint instability

The thickened dorsal and volar aspects of the triangular fibrocartilage act as the dorsal and volar ligaments of the distal radioulnar joint. Subluxation of the ulnar head occurs because of avulsion of these ligaments. It may be either volar or dorsal. Dorsal subluxation of the ulnar head associated with a tear of the volar radioulnar ligament is more common and may be due to repetitive or forceful pronation in contact sports, tennis, or gymnastics. Dorsal displacement of the ulnar styloid process during pronation may be detected on true lateral radiograph. Treatment requires repair of the triangular fibrocartilage complex.[34]

Kienböck's disease

Kienböck's disease is avascular necrosis of the lunate, possibly because of repeated trauma. This can present as chronic dorsal or volar wrist pain in a sportsperson who has repeated impact to the wrist. It is most common in those aged in their twenties. There is localized tenderness over the lunate and loss of grip strength.

Radiographs may show a smaller lunate of increased radio-opacity but false negatives can occur, so clinical suspicion warrants further investigation with isotopic bone scan or MRI.

The clinical impression is that in the acute stage, immobilization may be therapeutic, whereas in chronic cases surgery is often required. The evidence base regarding treatment of this condition is limited.[35]

Missed acute injuries presenting with articular chronic wrist pain

Conditions that may mimic gradual onset wrist pain include scaphoid fracture and scapholunate dissociation (see above). Chronic scapholunate dissociation should always be considered in patients with persistent pain and/or clicking (p. 425).

Numbness and hand pain

Patients may present with wrist numbness or paresthesia. This suggests a neurological pathology, most likely carpal tunnel syndrome or ulnar nerve compression.

Carpal tunnel syndrome

The median nerve may be compressed as it passes through the carpal tunnel along with the flexor digitorum profundus, flexor digitorum superficialis, and flexor pollicis longus tendons (Fig. 23.16). This condition is characterized by burning volar wrist pain with numbness or paresthesia in the distribution of the median nerve (thumb, index finger, middle finger, and radial side of the ring finger). Nocturnal paresthesiae are characteristic. The pain can radiate to the forearm, elbow, and shoulder. Tinel's sign may be elicited by tapping over the volar aspect of the wrist (Fig. 23.12c).

The most important aspects in diagnosis are the history and physical examination; however, nerve conduction studies can help confirm the diagnosis and may predict how the patient will respond to surgery.[36] Diabetes mellitus should be excluded as it is a risk factor for carpal tunnel syndrome.

Mild cases may be treated conservatively with NSAIDs and splinting.[37–39] A single corticosteroid injection may provide temporary relief[39, 40] but persistent cases require surgical treatment.[41] Surgery may be either open or endoscopic, and systematic

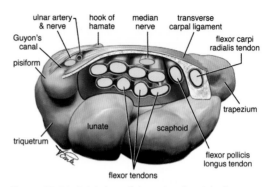

Figure 23.16 Axial view of the wrist, showing the median nerve trapped in the carpal tunnel and the location of the ulnar nerve

reviews to date show no difference between the two techniques for symptom relief.[42]

Ulnar nerve compression

The ulnar nerve may be compressed at the wrist as it passes through Guyon's canal. This injury is most commonly seen in cyclists due to supporting body weight over a long duration ride[43] because of poor bike fit or a failure to use several relaxed handlebar grip positions. It also occurs in karate players, and a recent study highlighted the risk of hand neurovascular changes in baseball players, especially catchers, from repeated trauma associated with catching a ball.[44] Within Guyon's canal, the nerve lies with the ulnar artery between the pisiform bone on the ulnar side and the hamate radially (Fig. 23.16).

Symptoms include pain and paresthesia to the little finger and ulnar side of the fourth finger. Weakness usually develops later.

Non-surgical treatment involves splinting, NSAIDs, and changes in the cyclist's grip on the handlebars (Chapter 8). Surgical exploration of Guyon's canal may be required.

CLINICAL SPORTS MEDICINE
MASTERCLASSES

🆆 www.clinicalsportsmedicine.com

- Video demonstration of wrist examination.
- Discussion of the approach to interpretation of imaging in the painful wrist.
- Podcast relating to the management of scaphoid fractures.

📖 REFERENCES

1. Rettig AC. Athletic injuries of the wrist and hand. Part I: traumatic injuries of the wrist. *Am J Sports Med* 2003;31(6):1038–48.

2. Venditolli PA, Sonia J, Davison KS et al. Descriptive study of osteoporotic fractures and hip fracture risk evaluation of subjects with past minor fractures. *J Bone Joint Surg Br* 2005;87-B:309.

3. Phillips TG, Reibach AM, Slomiany WP. Diagnosis and management of scaphoid fractures. *Am Fam Physician* 2004;70(5):879–84.

4. Hill C, Riaz M, Mozzam A et al. A regional audit of hand and wrist injuries. A study of 4873 injuries. *J Hand Surg Br* 1998;23(2):196–200.

5. Parmelee-Peters K, Eathorne SW. The wrist: common injuries and management. *Prim Care* 2005;32(1): 35–70.

6. Dekker R, Groothoff JW, van der Sluis CK et al. Long-term disabilities and handicaps following sports injuries: outcome after outpatient treatment. *Disabil Rehabil* 2003;25(20):1153–7.

7. Chow TK, Corbett SW, Farstad DJ. Spectrum of injuries from snowboarding. *J Trauma* 1996;41(2):321–5.

8. Heller DR, Routley V, Chambers S. Rollerblading injuries in young people. *J Paediatr Child Health* 1996;32(1):35–8.

9. Ellis JA, Kierulf JC, Klassen TP. Injuries associated with in-line skating from the Canadian hospitals injury reporting and prevention program database. *Can J Public Health* 1995;86(2):133–6.

10. Aldridge JM, 3rd, Mallon WJ. Hook of the hamate fractures in competitive golfers: results of treatment by excision of the fractured hook of the hamate. *Orthopedics* 2003;26(7):717–19.

11. Joy CM, Robert SR, Allan D et al. Responsiveness of the short form-36, disability of the arm, shoulder, and hand questionnaire, patient-rated wrist evaluation, and physical impairment measurements in evaluating recovery after a distal radius fracture. *J Hand Surg* 2000;25(2):330–40.

12. MacDermid JC, Turgeon T, Richards RS et al. Patient rating of wrist pain and disability: a reliable and valid measurement tool. *J Orthop Trauma* 1998;12(8):577–86.

13. Beaton DE, Katz JN, Fossel AH et al. Measuring the whole or the parts? Validity, reliability, and responsiveness of the Disabilities of the Arm, Shoulder and Hand outcome measure in different regions of the upper extremity. *J Hand Ther* 2001;14(2):128–46.

14. The Institute for Work and Health. The DASH Outcome Measure, 2010, www.dash.iwh.on.ca/.

15. Buijze GA, Ring D. Clinical impact of united versus nonunited fractures of the proximal half of the ulnar styloid following volar plate fixation of the distal radius. *J Hand Surg Am* 2010;35(2):223–7.

16. Glickel SZ, Catalano LW, Raia FJ et al. Long-term outcomes of closed reduction and percutaneous pinning for the treatment of distal radius fractures. *J Hand Surg Am* 2008;33(10):1700–5.

17. Handoll HH, Huntley JS, Madhok R. Different methods of external fixation for treating distal radial fractures in adults. *Cochrane Database Syst Rev* 2008(1):CD006522.

18. Buijze GA, Doornberg JN, Ham JS et al. Surgical compared with conservative treatment for acute nondisplaced or minimally displaced scaphoid fractures: a systematic review and meta-analysis of randomized controlled trials. *J Bone Joint Surg Am* 2010;92(6):1534–44.

19. Handoll HH, Watts AC. Bone grafts and bone substitutes for treating distal radial fractures in adults. *Cochrane Database Syst Rev* 2008(2):CD006836.

20. Jacobson JA, Miller BS, Morag Y. Golf and racquet sports injuries. *Semin Musculoskelet Radiol* 2005;9(4):346–59.

21. Theriault G, Lachance P. Golf injuries. An overview. *Sports Med* 1998;26(1):43–57.

22. Scheufler O, Radmer S, Erdmann D et al. Therapeutic alternatives in nonunion of hamate hook fractures: personal experience in 8 patients and review of literature. *Ann Plast Surg* 2005;55(2):149–54.

23. Scheufler O, Andresen R, Radmer S et al. Hook of hamate fractures: critical evaluation of different therapeutic procedures. *Plast Reconstr Surg* 2005;115(2):488–97.

24. Forli A, Courvoisier A, Wimsey S et al. Perilunate dislocations and transscaphoid perilunate fracture-dislocations: a retrospective study with minimum ten-year follow-up. *J Hand Surg Am* 2010;35(1):62–8.

25. Skirven T. Clinical examination of the wrist. *J Hand Ther* 1996;9(2):96–107.

B

26. Peters-Veluthamaningal C, van der Windt DA, Winters JC et al. Corticosteroid injection for de Quervain's tenosynovitis. *Cochrane Database Syst Rev* 2009;3):CD005616.

27. Richie CA, 3rd, Briner WW, Jr. Corticosteroid injection for treatment of de Quervain's tenosynovitis: a pooled quantitative literature evaluation. *J Am Board Fam Pract* 2003;16(2):102–6.

28. McNally E, Wilson D, Seiler S. Rowing injuries. *Semin Musculoskelet Radiol* 2005;9(4):379–96.

29. Lester B, Halbrecht J, Levy IM et al. "Press test" for office diagnosis of triangular fibrocartilage complex tears of the wrist. *Ann Plast Surg* 1995;35(1):41–5.

30. Berna-Serna JD, Martinez F, Reus M et al. Wrist arthrography: a simple method. *Eur Radiol* 2006;16(2):469–72.

31. De Smet L. Magnetic resonance imaging for diagnosing lesions of the triangular fibrocartilage complex. *Acta Orthop Belg* 2005;71(4):396–8.

32. Keogh CF, Wong AD, Wells NJ et al. High-resolution sonography of the triangular fibrocartilage: initial experience and correlation with MRI and arthroscopic findings. *AJR Am J Roentgenol* 2004;182(2):333–6.

33. Tomaino MM, Weiser RW. Combined arthroscopic TFCC debridement and wafer resection of the distal ulna in wrists with triangular fibrocartilage complex tears and positive ulnar variance. *J Hand Surg Am* 2001;26(6):1047–52.

34. Ozer K. A new surgical technique for the ligament reconstruction of the trapeziometacarpal joint. *Tech Hand Up Extrem Surg* 2006;10(3):181–6.

35. Innes L, Strauch RJ. Systematic review of the treatment of Kienböck's disease in its early and late stages. *J Hand Surg Am* 2010;35(5):713–17,717.e1–4.

36. Schrijver HM, Gerritsen AA, Strijers RL et al. Correlating nerve conduction studies and clinical outcome measures on carpal tunnel syndrome: lessons from a randomized controlled trial. *J Clin Neurophysiol* 2005;22(3):216–21.

37. Dincer U, Cakar E, Kiralp MZ et al. The effectiveness of conservative treatments of carpal tunnel syndrome: splinting, ultrasound, and low-level laser therapies. *Photomed Laser Surg* 2009;27(1):119–25.

38. Milo R, Kalichman L, Volchek L et al. Local corticosteroid treatment for carpal tunnel syndrome: a 6-month clinical and electrophysiological follow-up study. *J Back Musculoskelet Rehabil* 2009;22(2):59–64.

39. Popescu S, Poenaru D, Galbeaza G et al. Conservative treatment for carpal tunnel syndrome. *Mædica – a Journal of Clinical Medicine* 2008:249–53.

40. Wong SM, Hui AC, Lo SK et al. Single vs. two steroid injections for carpal tunnel syndrome: a randomized clinical trial. *Int J Clin Pract* 2005;59(12):1417–21.

41. Hui AC, Wong S, Leung CH et al. A randomized controlled trial of surgery vs steroid injection for carpal tunnel syndrome. *Neurology* 2005;64(12):2074–8.

42. Thoma A, Veltri K, Haines T et al. A systematic review of reviews comparing the effectiveness of endoscopic and open carpal tunnel decompression. *Plast Reconstr Surg* 2004;113(4):1184–91.

43. Capitani D, Beer S. Handlebar palsy—a compression syndrome of the deep terminal (motor) branch of the ulnar nerve in biking. *J Neurol* 2002;249(10):1441–5.

44. Ginn TA, Smith AM, Snyder JR et al. Vascular changes of the hand in professional baseball players with emphasis on digital ischemia in catchers. *J Bone Joint Surg Am* 2005;87(7):1464–9.

Chapter 24

Hand and finger injuries

with ANDREW GARNHAM, MAUREEN ASHE, PETER GROPPER, and DOUGLAS RACE

Graeme Smith, the South Africa cricket captain, sustained a fracture to the fourth finger of his left hand that could put him out of the upcoming home Test series against India. Smith sustained the injury when he was hit by a Shoaib Akhtar bouncer. Smith broke his right middle finger during the 2010 Indian Premier League, while a fractured little finger on his left hand kept him out of the recent series in India in February. Mitchell Johnson broke Smith's right hand twice during South Africa's home and away series against Australia in 2008–09.
Compiled from ESPN Cricinfo (www.espncricinfo.com), November 2010

Sport-related injuries account for up to 15% of all hand injuries seen in accident and emergency departments.[1] Although the majority of hand and finger injuries require minimal treatment, some are potentially serious and require immobilization, precise splinting, or even surgery. Finger injuries are often neglected by sportspeople with the expectation that they will resolve spontaneously. This means that the patient often presents too late for effective treatment. The importance of early assessment and management must be stressed so that long-term deformity and functional impairment can be avoided. Many hand and finger injuries require specific rehabilitation and

appropriate protection on resumption of sport. Joints in this region do not respond well to immobilization; therefore, full immobilization should be minimized. The causes of pain in this region are shown in Table 24.1.

The anatomy of this area is demonstrated in Figure 24.1 overleaf.

Clinical evaluation
History
The mechanism of injury is the most important component of the history of acute hand injuries. A direct, severe blow to the fingers may result in a

Table 24.1 Causes of hand and finger pain

Common	Less common	Not to be missed
Metacarpal fracture	Bennett's fracture	Potential infection (e.g. human bite)
Phalanx fracture	Dislocation of the MCP joint	Avulsion of long flexor tendons
Dislocation of the PIP joint	Dislocation of the DIP joint	
Mallet finger	Radial collateral ligament sprain, first MCP joint	
Ulnar collateral ligament sprain/tear, first MCP joint	Sprain of the DIP joint	
Sprain of the PIP joint	Stress fractures	
Laceration	Glomus tumor	
Infections		
Subungual hematoma		

PIP = proximal interphalangeal; DIP = distal interphalangeal; MCP = metacarpophalangeal

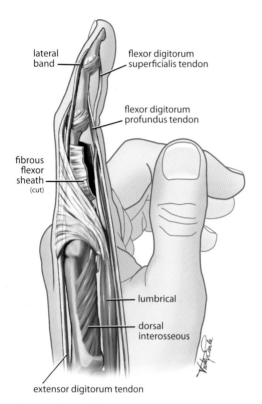

lateral band

flexor digitorum superficialis tendon

flexor digitorum profundus tendon

fibrous flexor sheath (cut)

lumbrical

dorsal interosseous

extensor digitorum tendon

Figure 24.1 Anatomy of the metacarpals and fingers
(a) Metacarpals and fingers

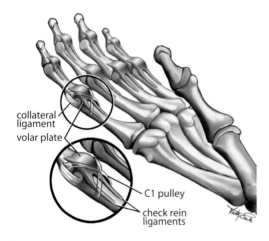

collateral ligament

volar plate

C1 pulley

check rein ligaments

(b) The volar plate

fracture, whereas a blow to the point of the finger may produce an interphalangeal dislocation, joint sprain, or long flexor or extensor tendon avulsion. A punching injury often results in a fracture at the base of the first metacarpal or to the neck of one of

the other metacarpals, usually the fifth. An avulsion of the flexor digitorum profundus tendon, usually to the fourth finger, is suggested by a history of a patient grabbing an opponent's clothing while attempting a tackle. Associated features such as an audible crack, degree of pain, swelling, bruising, and loss of function should also be noted.

Examination

Carefully palpate the bones and soft tissues of the hand and fingers, looking for tenderness. The examiner should always be conscious of what structure is being palpated at any particular time. The joints should be examined to determine active and passive range of movement and stability. Stability should be tested both in an anteroposterior direction, and with ulnar and radial deviation to assess the collateral ligaments. The cause of any loss of active range of movement should be carefully assessed and not presumed to be due to swelling.

Normal range of motion for the second to fifth digits is approximately 80° of flexion at the distal interphalangeal (DIP), 100° of flexion at the proximal interphalangeal (PIP), and 90° of flexion at the metacarpophalangeal (MCP) joint. A common injury site that can be overlooked is the volar plate, a thick fibrocartilagenous tissue that reinforces the phalangeal joints on the palmar or volar surface (Figs 24.1b).

The extensor tendons of the hand are often divided into six compartments. At the wrist on the dorsal side of the hand, the tendons are encased in synovial sheaths as they pass under the extensor retinaculum (Fig. 23.13). When palpating in the most radial compartment—compartment one—the examiner identifies abductor pollicis longus and extensor pollicis brevis, the tissues involved in de Quervain's tenosynovitis. Lister's tubercle is located on the dorsal surface of the distal end of the radius. The extensor pollicis longus angles sharply around the bony prominence, and the tendon can be damaged or even ruptured after a serious wrist fracture. The anatomical snuffbox is composed of the extensor pollicis longus and brevis and abductor pollicis longus. The floor of the snuffbox is the scaphoid and the scaphotrapezial joint. Clinically, this is a significant region for several reasons. Tenderness may suggest scaphoid fracture. The deep branch of the radial arterial passes through as well as the superficial branch of the radial nerve; consequently, if a cast or splint is applied too tightly, it can lead to numbness in the thumb.

Examination involves:

1. Observation and sensation testing as per the wrist (Fig. 23.2a, page 416). Special note should be made of the hand arches and any deformities at the proximal or distal interphalangeal joints.
   (a) hand at rest (Fig. 24.2a)
   (b) hand with clenched fist (Fig. 24.2b)
2. Active movements—fingers (all joints)
   (a) flexion
   (b) extension
   (c) abduction
   (d) adduction
3. Active movements—thumb
   (a) flexion
   (b) extension
   (c) palmar abduction (Fig. 24.2c)
   (d) palmar adduction (Fig. 24.2d)
   (e) opposition (Fig. 24.2e)
4. Resisted movements (tendons)
   (a) flexor digitorum profundus (Fig. 24.2f overleaf)
   (b) flexor digitorum superficialis (Fig. 24.2g overleaf)
   (c) extensor tendon (Fig. 24.2h overleaf)

5. Special test
   (a) ulnar collateral ligament of the first MCP joint (Fig. 24.2i overleaf)
   (b) IP joint collateral ligaments

Investigations

Routine radiographs of the hand include the PA, oblique and lateral views. All traumatic finger injuries should be X-rayed. Ideally, "dislocations" need to be radiographed before reduction to exclude fracture,

B

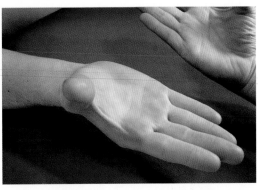

(c) Thumb movement—palmar abduction

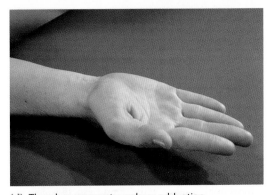

(d) Thumb movement—palmar adduction

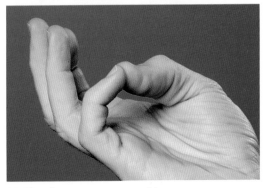

(e) Thumb movement—opposition

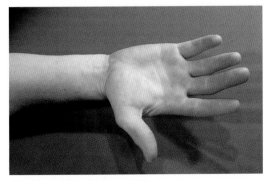

Figure 24.2 Examination of fingers
(a) Attitude of hand at rest

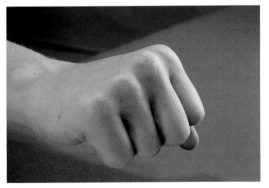

(b) Attitude of hand with clenched fist

437

(f) Tendon integrity—flexor digitorum profundus. The patient flexes the DIP joint with the PIP joint held in extension

(h) Tendon integrity—extensor tendon. The patient extends the PIP joint with the MCP joint in extension

(g) Tendon integrity—flexor digitorum superficialis. The patient flexes the PIP joint with the DIP joints of other fingers held in extension

(i) Special test—the ulnar collateral ligament of the thumb is tested with 10° of flexion at the first MCP joint

and after reduction to confirm relocation. Even when pre-reduction radiographs are not performed because reduction has occurred on the field, post-reduction films should be obtained after the game. Care should be taken with lateral views to isolate the affected finger to avoid bony overlap. The use of more sophisticated investigation techniques is usually not required.

Principles of treatment of hand injuries

The functional hand requires mobility, stability, sensitivity, and freedom from pain. It may be necessary to obtain stability by surgical methods. However, conservative rehabilitation is essential to regain mobility and long-term freedom from pain. Treatment and rehabilitation of hand injuries is complex. As the hand is unforgiving of mismanagement, practitioners who do not see hand injuries regularly should ideally refer patients to an experienced hand therapist, or at least obtain advice while managing the patient.[2]

Inflammation and swelling are obvious in the hand and fingers. During the inflammatory phase, the therapist must aim to reduce edema and monitor progress by signs of redness, heat, and increased pain. During the regenerative phase (characterized by proliferation of scar tissue), the therapist can use supportive splints and active exercises to maintain range of motion. During remodeling, it is appropriate to use dynamic and serial splints, and active and active assisted exercises, in addition to heat, stretching, and electrotherapeutic modalities.[3]

Control of edema

Control of edema can be achieved through splinting, compression, ice, elevation, and electrotherapeutic modalities. Splinting needs to be in the intrinsic plus position, with the wrist in 30° of dorsiflexion, the MCP joints flexed to 70° and the PIP joint extended to 0° with the thumb abducted (Fig. 24.3). Splints are

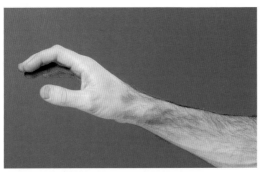

Figure 24.3 The "intrinsic plus" position for splinting of hand injuries—30° of wrist dorsiflexion, 70° of MCP flexion and minimal PIP flexion

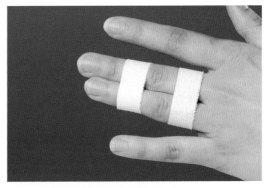

Figure 24.4 Buddy taping of fingers

B

periodically removed to allow exercise. Fist-making exercises are used to maintain joint movement and to help remove edema. During exercise, the hand should be elevated. Short frequent exercise periods are optimum.

Compression in the hand can be achieved with a number of compression gloves and by using a Coban elastic bandage—a 2.5 cm (1 in.) size is appropriate for fingers. If appropriate, active tendon gliding and range of motion exercises in combination with elevation can assist in the reduction of swelling. Electrotherapeutic modalities can be useful in the control of edema.

Exercises

Exercises may be active, active assisted, or resisted. Tendon lacerations or ruptures are generally treated by protocols determined by the surgical technique and preferences of the treating surgeon. A full description of the protocols is beyond the scope of this chapter and the reader is referred elsewhere. Exercise prescription for other injuries includes:

- blocking exercises, which isolate the muscle being used by immobilizing appropriate joints with the other hand
- composite flexion exercises (e.g. tendon gliding exercises)
- extension exercises
- active assisted exercises in which the patient takes a joint through the full range of motion and then the therapist assists in gaining slightly greater range with overpressure.

Taping and splinting

The most commonly used method of taping is "buddy taping" (Fig. 24.4). Its role is to provide a vehicle for active assisted exercise. The uninjured digit provides additional stability and encourages full range of motion.

In the acute phase of injury, static splints are used to reduce edema. Dynamic splints can also be used in the repair phase of injury to provide some force along joints and encourage increased range of motion (Fig. 24.5 overleaf). With dynamic splinting, the splint should be worn with less tension for a longer period.

Fractures of the metacarpals

Fracture of the base of the first metacarpal

Fractures of the base of the first metacarpal commonly occur because of a punch connecting with a hard object, such as an opponent's head, or a fall on the abducted thumb. There are two main types of fracture—the extra-articular transverse fracture of the base of the first metacarpal about 1 cm (0.5 in.) distal to the joint (Fig. 24.6a overleaf), and a Bennett's fracture dislocation of the first carpometacarpal joint (Fig. 24.6b overleaf).

The transverse fracture near the base of the first metacarpal results in the thumb lying flexed across the palm. Reduction of this fracture involves extension of the distal segment of the metacarpal. This fracture can usually be immobilized in a short arm spica cast.

A Bennett's fracture dislocation of the first carpometacarpal joint occurs as a result of axial compression when the first metacarpal is driven proximally, shearing off its base. A small medial fragment of the metacarpal remains attached to the strong volar ligament and the main shaft of the metacarpal is pulled proximally by the unopposed pull of the abductor pollicis longus muscle.

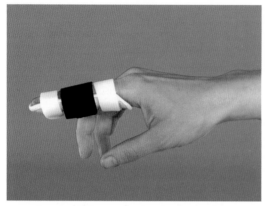

Figure 24.5 Two types of splints used to treat fixed flexion deformity

(a) Dynamic (also known as "belly gutter") splint. This simple finger gutter splint has a "belly." It is usually put on half an hour before bed with gentle tension on the strap over the PIP joint. This provides a progressive, mild, end-range stretch into extension overnight

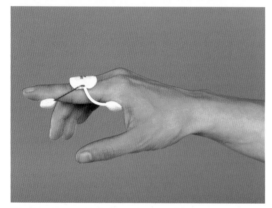

(b) A commercial dynamic (spring) finger-based PIP extension splint

A patient with a Bennett's fracture should be referred to a hand surgeon. Treatment requires closed reduction and percutaneous Kirschner wire fixation, together with cast immobilization for four to six weeks.

On removal of the cast, mobilization of the surrounding joints is required and, if early return to sport is required, a protective device should be worn. Persons not engaging in contact sport find soft neoprene braces (Fig. 24.7) supportive and comfortable after a Bennett's fracture and other common hand injuries. These are not replacements for firmer splints and braces that might be needed when trauma can be anticipated.

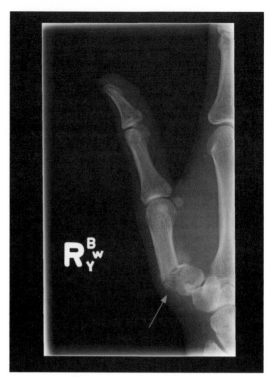

Figure 24.6 Fractures of the base of the first metacarpal

(a) Healing transverse fracture

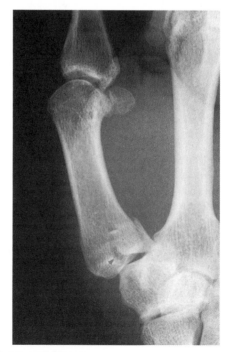

(b) Bennett's fracture

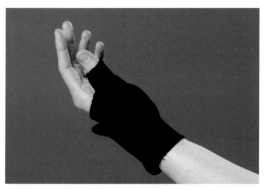

Figure 24.7 Soft neoprene splints can provide support during rehabilitation after a hand injury

Fractures of the other metacarpals

Fractures of the second to fifth metacarpals may also occur as the result of a punch. These fractures are most commonly seen in the fourth and fifth metacarpals, and have been referred to as "boxer's fracture."

The fracture is usually accompanied by considerable flexion deformity of the distal fragment which results in a characteristic "dropped knuckle" appearance.

However, this deformity results in surprisingly little functional disability (Figs 24.8, 24.9).

The acceptable angulation for fractures of the neck of the fourth and fifth metacarpals is up to 30° as long as there is little rotational deformity. Up to 10° angulation is acceptable in the second and third metacarpals. However, prominence of the metacarpal head in the palm of the hand may be a problem for tennis players and other sportspeople who require a firm grip.

Treatment involves splinting or casting in a position of 90° of flexion of the MCP joints to prevent shortening of the collateral ligament and subsequent stiffness (Fig. 24.10). Check that this position does not displace the fracture. The splint may be removed

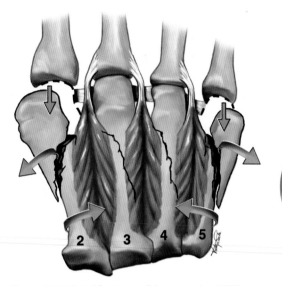

Figure 24.9 Spiral fractures of the second and fifth metacarpals (border digits) are more unstable than those of the third and fourth metacarpals, as only one side of the border metacarpals is supported by the strong, deep transverse intercarpal ligaments

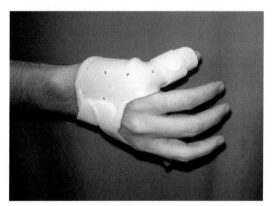

Figure 24.10 Treatment splint for fracture of the fifth metacarpal

after two to three weeks and sport resumed immediately with protection.

Intra-articular fractures of the metacarpals require anatomical correction. In displaced fractures, this usually involves Kirschner wiring. Long spiral fractures of the metacarpal shaft may require internal fixation or percutaneous pinning if they are angulated or rotated. Check for rotation of finger fractures clinically by having the patient clench his or her fist, not by using radiographs. If fractures are undisplaced, they can be immobilized in a gutter splint with flexion of the MCP joint.[4]

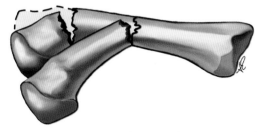

Figure 24.8 In metacarpal fractures, the more proximal the fracture, the more the knuckle will drop

Fractures of phalanges
Proximal phalanx fractures
Fractures of the proximal phalanx may lead to functional impairment due to the extensor and flexor tendons coming into contact with callus and exposed bone.

To control and reduce the fracture under ring block, the MCP joint should be flexed to 70°. The PIP joint is then flexed and longitudinal traction applied in line with the shaft of the distal fragment to oppose the fracture. However, this is often difficult. The fracture is immobilized with the wrist slightly extended and at 70° of flexion of the MCP joints. These fractures require weekly radiographs to ensure movement has not occurred. If further stability is needed, the adjacent finger can be buddy taped. The splint is removed after three to four weeks and buddy taping continued. Motion is essential at three to four weeks. Unstable fractures require urgent surgical referral.

Rotational deformity of phalangeal fractures may not be obvious in extension, so the fingers should be examined end on with PIP and DIP flexion to reveal any deformity present. All malrotated fractures need open reduction and possibly internal fixation.

Middle phalanx fractures
Fractures of the middle phalanx involve cortical bone. Generally oblique or transverse, these fractures heal slowly. The central slip of the extensor tendon attaches dorsally to the base of the bone, and the flexor digitorum inserts on the volar surface more distally. Because of this anatomy, fractures *distal* to the flexor tendon attachment result in flexion of the proximal fragment and extension of the distal fragment.

Stable fractures are immobilized in a splint for three weeks in 70° of MCP joint flexion and 0° of PIP joint flexion. When the splint is removed, range of motion exercises are begun.

Unstable fractures, or intra-articular fractures involving more than 25% of the PIP joint surface, require open reduction and internal fixation. Small-caliber Kirschner wires are used and range of motion exercises are begun as soon as fixation is considered to be stable.

Volar plate avulsion fracture can occur at the PIP joint following a hyperextension injury. This injury is very common, and usually ignored owing to an unawareness of the potential consequences. The anatomical appearance and the radiographic appearance are shown in Figure 24.1b on page 436 and in

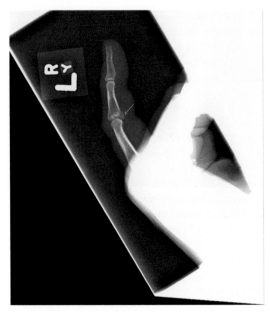

Figure 24.11 Radiograph confirms the subtle nature of a volar plate avulsion

Figure 24.11. At present, non-randomized controlled trials have compared early mobilization with splinting and found that mobilization has led to good functional outcomes.[5]

Distal phalanx fractures
Fractures of the distal phalanx are usually caused by crushing injuries, such as fingers being jammed between a fast-moving ball and a stick or a bat. They are usually non-displaced.

Often a splint and compression dressing will provide adequate treatment for non-displaced fractures. Much of the pain associated with these fractures can be due to subungual hematoma. Significant subungual hematoma requires nail bed exploration and excision, as the nail bed is often disrupted. In this case, surgical repair may be required to prevent future nail deformity. This represents a compound fracture and should be treated as such. Perforation of the nail to drain a subungual hematoma is contraindicated in this instance as it converts a closed fracture to a compound fracture. Most distal phalangeal fractures heal in four to six weeks.

Dislocation of the metacarpophalangeal joints
Dorsal dislocation of the MCP joints of the fingers is uncommon, and usually occurs in the index finger

or thumb. It has been called the "irreducible disloca-tion" because the metacarpal head is pushed through the volar plate of the MCP joint and caught between the lumbrical and long flexor tendons with a button-holing effect. Suspect this injury when examination reveals hyperextension of the involved MCP joint with ulnar deviation of the finger overlapping the adjacent finger.

An attempt to reduce the dislocation may be made by increasing the deformity and pushing the proximal phalanx through the tear in the volar plate. However, open reduction is usually required. The MCP joint is usually stable after reduction in 30° of MCP flexion, and early movement can be commenced in a dorsal splint allowing full flexion but preventing the last 30° of MCP joint extension. The immobilization is main-tained for five to six weeks. Associated osteochon-dral fractures require open reduction and internal fixation.

Dislocations of the finger joints

Dislocations of the PIP joint

Dorsal PIP joint dislocations are the most common hand dislocation. They usually result from a hyperex-tension stress with some degree of longitudinal com-pression, such as may occur in ball sports. This may produce disruption of both the volar plate and at least one collateral ligament. Ideally, radiographs should precede treatment to confirm the diagnosis and exclude an associated fracture. In practice, reduction often occurs on or beside the playing area.

Reduction is maintained in a splint that allows full PIP flexion but blocks the final 15° of PIP extension for 10 days (Fig. 24.12), followed by active flexion exercises and buddy taping. If left untreated, a hyper-extension deformity and instability may develop.

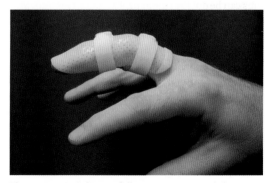

Figure 24.12 Splinting following a PIP joint dislocation. This dorsal block splint allows flexion but stops full extension at the PIP joint

Radiography must be performed after reduction. As discussed above in the section on middle phalanx fractures, all of these fractures must be tested for instability. More commonly, these patients develop a fixed flexion deformity (90%).

Swelling should be managed using an elastic pressure bandage, soft tissue treatment, and electro-therapeutic modalities.

If radiographs reveal a fracture of the volar lip of the middle phalanx involving more than one-third of the joint surface, open reduction and internal fixa-tion is required to restore stability.

Volar dislocations of the PIP joint are uncommon and are often resistant to closed reduction. There is almost always an associated rupture of one or more collateral ligaments along with disruption of the extensor central slip insertion. This injury predis-poses to the development of a boutonnière (button-hole) deformity and should be treated with a splint, holding the PIP joint of the affected finger in exten-sion for six weeks while encouraging DIP movement, or with surgical repair.

Dislocations of the DIP joint

Dislocations of the DIP joint usually occur dorsally and are commonly associated with a volar skin laceration. The injury is most often due to a ball hitting the finger and causing hyperextension. Reduction is achieved by traction and flexion. The joint should be splinted for three weeks in 10° of flexion. Collateral ligament inju-ries are rare. Flexor tendon function must be assessed as avulsion can occur with this injury.

The less common volar dislocation occurs in asso-ciation with a fracture and usually involves damage to the extensor tendon. This presents with the mallet finger deformity. Thus, all mallet fingers must be radiographed to exclude fracture. If volar dislocation has occurred, open repair is indicated.

Ligament and tendon injuries

Sprain of the ulnar collateral ligament of the first MCP joint

Injury to the ulnar collateral ligament of the thumb is one of the most common hand injuries seen in sport-speople. It is known colloquially as "skier's thumb" and usually results from forced abduction and hyper-extension of the MCP joint. The mechanism of injury is characteristic. The patient may complain of weak-ness of thumb–index (tip) pinch grip (Fig. 24.13a overleaf).

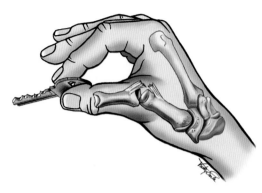

Figure 24.13 Complete ligament tear of the first MCP joint

(a) Pinching is affected

(b) Protective splint worn during return to sport

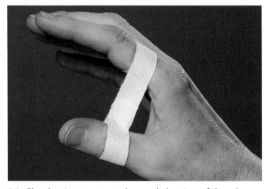

(c) Check rein to prevent hyperabduction of thumb

Examination reveals swelling and tenderness over the ulnar aspect of the first MCP joint. Before testing stability, radiography should be performed to exclude an avulsion fracture. Stability of the ligament is tested by stressing the joint in a radial direction (Fig. 24.2i). Pain occurs with both complete and partial tears of the ulnar collateral ligament.

If the injured thumb deviates 10–20° further than the non-injured side and there is no clear end feel, then complete disruption of the ligament is likely.

Deviation within 10–20° of the non-injured side indicates a partial tear of the ulnar collateral ligament. This should be treated with immobilization in a splint with the MCP joint in slight flexion for six weeks. Further protective splinting is required during return to sport and may be required for up to 12 months (Fig. 24.13b). The thumb may also be taped with the index finger, which acts as a less secure check rein to prevent hyperabduction (Fig. 24.13c).

A complete tear of the ulnar collateral ligament (Stener lesion) requires surgical repair because of interposition of the extensor hood (Fig. 24.14). A displaced avulsion fracture of the base of the proximal phalanx also requires open reduction and internal fixation with Kirschner wires. Residual volar or lateral subluxation of the proximal phalanx on the metacarpal head is also an indication for surgery, as is a chronic injury to the ulnar collateral ligament with functional instability, pain, and weakness of thumb–index pinch grip. After surgery, the thumb is placed in a thumb spica cast for four to six weeks followed by protective splinting during sporting activity for a further three months.

Injuries to the radial collateral ligament of the first MCP joint

Injuries to the radial collateral ligament of the thumb are not as common as those to the ulnar collateral ligament; however, complete ruptures can be as disabling as those of the ulnar collateral ligament. Deviation of greater than 10–20° more than on the non-injured side with ulnar stress indicates a complete tear. As there is no soft tissue caught between the two ends of the ligament, six weeks' cast immobilization is the treatment of choice.

Capsular sprain of the first MCP joint

Capsular sprains of the first MCP joint are an extremely common injury in ball-handling sports. They result from a hyperextension injury and are prone to recurrence. Treatment involves active rehabilitation and protection of the joint from hyperextension. This is achieved with the use of a thermoplastic brace over the dorsal aspect of the MCP joint.

PIP joint sprains

The collateral ligaments of the PIP joints are commonly injured as a result of a sideways force. Partial

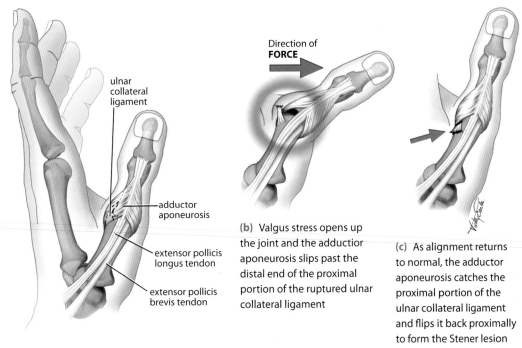

ulnar collateral ligament

adductor aponeurosis

extensor pollicis longus tendon

extensor pollicis brevis tendon

Direction of **FORCE**

(b) Valgus stress opens up the joint and the adductior aponeurosis slips past the distal end of the proximal portion of the ruptured ulnar collateral ligament

(c) As alignment returns to normal, the adductor aponeurosis catches the proximal portion of the ulnar collateral ligament and flips it back proximally to form the Stener lesion

B

(a) Anatomy

Figure 24.14 Mechanism of formation of a Stener lesion of the thumb

tears of the collateral ligament are painful but remain stable on lateral stress. Complete tears show marked instability with lateral stress. This injury also includes hyperextension stress to the volar plate, which may avulse its insertion from the base of the metacarpal.

Partial and complete tears should be treated by 10 days of splinting, buddy taping, swelling management, and active exercises. Complete tears of the collateral ligament should ideally be treated with surgical repair, although in most cases conservative management provides an adequate result.[6]

Mallet finger

Mallet finger is a flexion deformity resulting from avulsion of the extensor mechanism from the DIP joint. It commonly results from a ball striking the extended fingertip, forcing the DIP joint into flexion while the extensor mechanism is actively contracting. This produces disruption or stretching of the extensor mechanism over the DIP joint. This is seen in baseball catchers, fielders, football receivers, cricketers, and basketball players.

Examination reveals tenderness over the dorsal aspect of the distal phalanx and an inability to actively extend the DIP joint from its resting flexed position.

If left untreated, a chronic mallet finger type deformity develops (Fig. 24.15a overleaf). This flexion deformity is caused by the unopposed action of the flexor digitorum profundus tendon.

Radiography must be performed to exclude an avulsion fracture of the distal phalanx or injury and subluxation to the DIP joint. The avulsion fracture is only considered significant if greater than one-third of the joint surface is involved. Any volar subluxation requires open reduction and internal fixation to correct the joint position (the subluxation). A fracture dislocation of the epiphyseal plate may occur in children. Most of these injuries are type II epiphyseal injuries and closed management is preferred.

Treatment of uncomplicated mallet finger involves splinting the DIP joint in slight hyperextension for a period of up to eight weeks, with regular monitoring. The splint is then worn for an additional six to eight weeks while engaging in sporting activity and at night. Treatment is reinstituted at any sign of recurrence of a lag. The splint may be made of metal or plastic and applied to either the volar or dorsal surface (Fig. 24.15b overleaf); patients with dorsal splints maintain pulp sensation. The finger should be kept dry and examined regularly for skin slough and maceration.

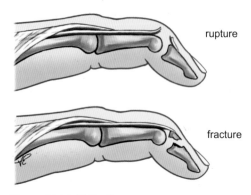

rupture

fracture

Figure 24.15 Mallet finger

(a) Mechanism of deformity—rupture or avulsion

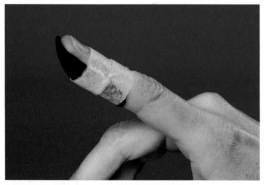

(b) "Stack" splint. A dorsal splint can also be used

When treating mallet finger, emphasize to the patient that the joint must be kept in hyperextension at all times during the eight weeks, even when the splint is removed for cleaning. If a patient is not prepared to do this, then the joint should not be splinted. The consequences of not splinting are a chronic mallet finger–type flexion deformity with osteophyte formation and degeneration of the DIP surface.

Boutonnière deformity

The boutonnière deformity results from disruption of the central slip of the extensor digitorum communis tendon at its insertion at the base of the middle phalanx, which allows migration of the lateral bands in a volar and proximal direction. This disruption allows the middle phalanx to be pulled into flexion by the flexor digitorum superficialis. It may arise from blunt trauma over the dorsal aspect of the PIP joint, or acute flexion of the joint against active resistance (such as occurs in ball sports). The PIP joint herniates through the central slip tear. The

deformity is often absent at initial presentation but develops some time later in the untreated case. The classic deformity consists of hyperextension of the DIP joints with a flexion deformity of the PIP joint (Fig. 24.16).

Early examination findings may include flexion deformity of the PIP joint and point tenderness over the dorsal slip of the middle phalanx. The patient will lack full extension of the PIP joint. Radiography may occasionally reveal an avulsion fracture from the middle phalanx. The patient can often extend the PIP joint initially. Boutonnière deformity always follows a volar PIP dislocation.

Any acute PIP joint injury showing any lag of extension in conjunction with point tenderness over the base of the middle phalanx should be regarded as an acute extensor tendon rupture. Treatment of choice, even if the lag is less than 30°, is to splint the finger with the PIP joint in full extension while allowing active flexion of the DIP joint for six weeks. On return to sport, protective splinting is continued for a further six to eight weeks or until a full pain-free range of flexion and extension is present. Associated avulsion fractures of the middle phalanx involving greater than one-third of the joint surface require open reduction and internal fixation if displaced.

In longstanding injuries, there may already be a fixed flexion deformity of the PIP joint. This may be treated with a dynamic splint (Fig. 24.5a) that gradually extends the joint to a neutral position, or a "joint jack" (Fig. 24.5b). Surgery may be indicated if this is unsuccessful.

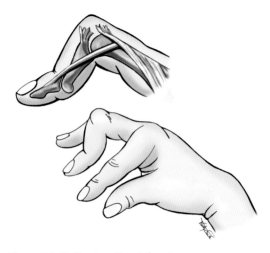

Figure 24.16 Boutonnière deformity

Avulsion of the flexor digitorum profundus tendon

This injury is most commonly seen in the ring finger and may be caused by the sportsperson grabbing an opponent's clothing, resulting in the distal phalanx being forcibly extended while the sportsperson is actively flexing. The patient often feels a "snap." The condition is often referred to as "Jersey finger."

Examination may reveal the finger assuming a position of extension relative to the other fingers. There is an inability to actively flex the DIP joint of the affected finger. Radiography should be performed to exclude an associated avulsion fracture of the distal phalanx. The bone fragment may be seen volar to the middle phalanx or PIP joint. A lump may be palpated more proximally in the finger corresponding to the avulsed tendon.

Treatment is urgent surgical repair with reattachment of the profundus tendon to the distal phalanx. This must take place within 10 days of the injury.

Lacerations and infections of the hand

Lacerations to the fingers and hand occur frequently in sport as a result of contact with equipment such as the undersurface of a football boot. All lacerations have the potential to become infected and should, therefore, be thoroughly cleaned with an antiseptic solution and observed closely for signs of infection.

Tetanus toxoid should also be administered where appropriate (Chapter 56).

A particular concern is a laceration of the hand, often over the MCP/PIP joint, caused by teeth, usually from a punch to the mouth. These injuries should always be assumed to be contaminated and an immediate course of a broad-spectrum antibiotic should be commenced. The wound should not be closed.

Lacerations over volar DIP or PIP joints may represent compound dislocations. If this has occurred, the joint has been contaminated and the patient requires hospital admission for surgical debridement and repair. Otherwise septic arthritis may follow.

Overuse conditions of the hand and fingers

Important but sometimes overlooked are the overuse problems associated with the hand. These include trigger finger, and other small joint injuries that are commonly seen in rock climbers.[7–9] Trigger finger is caused by a tenosynovitis in the flexor tendon that is large enough to be impeded by the proximal A1 (annular) pulley located at the base of the finger.

Conservative treatment involves splinting and local treatment to reduce the enlarged tendon. Corticosteroid injection is often advocated first, and then surgical release of the impeded A1 pulley.[10, 11]

📖 REFERENCES

1. Hill C, Riaz M, Mozzam A et al. A regional audit of hand and wrist injuries. A study of 4873 injuries. *J Hand Surg Br* 1998;23(2):196–200.

2. Ridha H, Crerar-Gilbert A, Fleming A. The use of Tegaderm for finger buddy-strapping: a dressing with many advantages. *Ann R Coll Surg Engl* 2008;90(6):525.

3. Oetgen ME, Dodds SD. Non-operative treatment of common finger injuries. *Curr Rev Musculoskelet Med* 2008;1(2):97–102.

4. Paulius K, Maguina P, Mejia A. Ultrasound-guided management of hand fractures. *Orthopedics* 2008;31(12).

5. Body R, Ferguson CJ. Best evidence topic report. Early mobilisation for volar plate avulsion fractures. *Emerg Med J* 2005;22(7):505.

6. Konecny J, Martinkova J, Kabela M et al. Laser in treatment of finger sprains. *Proceedings of IALMS 2007 Conference: Laser Florence the Laser Medicine World* 2007:106–8.

7. Schoffl VR, Schoffl I. Finger pain in rock climbers: reaching the right differential diagnosis and therapy. *J Sports Med Phys Fitness* 2007;47(1):70–8.

8. Schoffl VR, Schoffl I. Injuries to the finger flexor pulley system in rock climbers: Current concepts. *J Hand Surg Am* 2006;31A(4):647–54.

9. Schweizer A. Lumbrical tears in rock climbers. *J Hand Surg Br* 2003;28(2):187–9.

10. Peters-Veluthamaningal C, Winters JC, Groenier KH et al. Corticosteroid injections effective for trigger finger in adults in general practice: a double-blinded randomised placebo controlled trial. *Ann Rheum Dis* 2008;67(9):1262–6.

11. Nimigan AS, Ross DC, Gan BS. Steroid injections in the management of trigger fingers. *Am J Phys Med Rehabil* 2006;85(1):36–43.

Chapter 25

Thoracic and chest pain

with KEVIN SINGER and PETER FAZEY

A perceptive clinician elicits often scant objective signs and interprets them correctly, but the easiest way to the diagnosis is to think of it. NE Shaw *J Bone Joint Surg.* 1975;57B:412

Thoracic pain

As with neck pain (Chapter 20) and low back pain (Chapter 26), it is frequently difficult for the clinician to make a precise diagnosis in patients with pain in the region of the thoracic spine, given the interplay between the thorax, upper limb, neck, low back, and the cardiorespiratory and visceral systems. Perhaps the most common musculoskeletal problems are disorders of the thoracic intervertebral joints and the numerous rib articulations, as this region of the spine is primarily required to contribute stability to the axial skeleton. Injury to the intervertebral disk, the facet joints (also named zygapophyseal joints), or other nociceptive structures of the thoracic spine may contribute local or referred pain. Clinical presentation of these, often articular, problems is varied, with combinations of pain and altered motion the dominant feature involving one or more intervertebral segments or rib joints. There may be associated abnormalities of the paraspinal and periscapular muscles, as well as increased neural mechanosensitivity (Chapter 6). Thoracic intervertebral joint problems frequently refer pain to the lateral or anterior chest wall. Prolapse of a thoracic intervertebral disk is rare in sportspeople; however, it may be under-reported given the often diffuse symptoms that arise.[1, 2] Cross-sectional imaging studies are often necessary to rule out this diagnosis.

In adolescents, the most common cause of pain in the area of the thoracic spine is Scheuermann's disease, a disorder of the growth plates of the thoracic vertebral end-plates associated with an accentuated lower thoracic kyphosis. A list of the causes of pain in the region of the thoracic spine is shown in Table 25.1. The surface, muscle, and cross-sectional anatomy of this area are shown in Figure 25.1 overleaf.

Vague symptoms must alert the astute clinician to consider the possibility of visceral origins, as convergence of pain pathways may mimic somatic disorders. The literature reporting occult pain presentations of thoracic-like pain encourages caution when assessing an individual with unresolved, at times over-investigated, symptoms.[3, 4]

Assessment

History

The patient often complains of pain between or around the scapulae. The pain may be central,

Table 25.1 Causes of thoracic pain

Common	Less common	Not to be missed
Intervertebral joint sprain	Fracture of the rib posteriorly	Cardiac causes
• Disk	Thoracic disk prolapse	Peptic ulcer
• Zygapophyseal joints	T4 syndrome	Tumor (e.g. carcinoma of the breast,
Paraspinal muscle strain	Herpes zoster	secondary deposits)
Costovertebral joint sprain		
Scheuermann's disease (adolescents)		

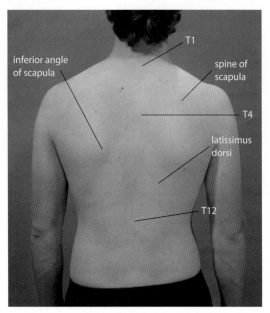

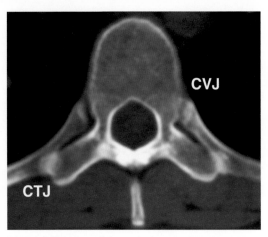

(c) Axial CT image of the typical motion segment from the lower thoracic region. The most accessible rib articulation for palpation and mobilization is the costotransverse joint (CTJ), with the costovertebral joint (CVJ) attached firmly to the lateral margin of the vertebral body

Figure 25.1 Anatomy of the thoracic spine region (a) Surface anatomy

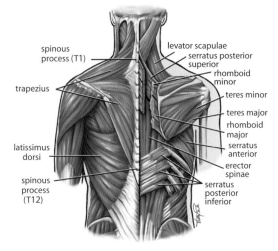

(b) Muscles of the thoracic spine region

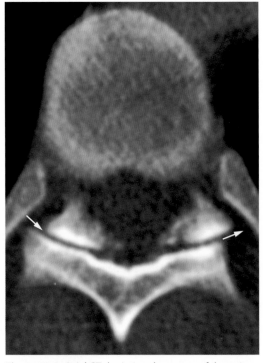

Figure 25.2 Axial CT depicting the nature of thoracic zygapophyseal joint translation in response to induced segmental rotation

unilateral or bilateral, and may have commenced suddenly (as a result of a specific movement) or have been of gradual onset (without a discernable precipitating incident). Symptoms may be elicited by any active movement—particularly rotation (Fig. 25.2) or lateral flexion.[5]

The T4–8 segments show greater ranges of axial motion compared with the stiffer upper and lower segments.[6] Any associated sensory symptoms such as paresthesias or numbness should be noted.

Although dermatomal patterns are more predictable in the thoracic region, symptoms may depart from such conventions. Vague pain noted in the region of the shoulder may relate to disturbance of the cervico-thoracic junction and, similarly, buttock, hip, or inguinal region symptoms may have a low thoracic origin.[5] The behavior of symptoms relative to activity or diurnal variation can assist in classification of the condition (Fig. 25.3).

On establishment of a musculoskeletal cause of symptoms, the clinician should consider aspects of the clinical presentation relative to SINS (Severity, Irritability, Nature and Stage) to inform clinical management and decision making:

- Severity of the condition helps determine the vigor of any prescribed activity or physical treatment.
- Irritability, or ease of aggravation, relates to the volume of prescribed activity or physical treatment.
- Nature relates to the type of condition (e.g. fracture, instability, neurological).
- Stage is relative to an acute, subacute, or chronic classification.

In the thoracic region, careful consideration needs to be given to the potential for non-musculoskeletal causes. Pertinent "red flags" include systemic illness, malignancy, unexplained weight loss, fever, and night pain; the clinician should consider these during the history-taking. Imaging studies may be required to rule out suspected pathology.

Physical examination

Examination of the thoracic spine region involves assessment of range of motion and mobility of each intervertebral segment, as well as careful palpation of the paraspinal and periscapular soft tissue. Examination of the lower cervical and upper lumbar spine should also be included, as should neurological examination for altered mechano-sensitivity. In some cases where symptoms of radiculopathy present, conduction studies may need to be considered. The examination should include the following:

1. Observation (Fig. 25.4a overleaf)
   (a) swelling
   (b) muscle spasm
   (c) postural asymmetry
   (d) skin changes (sweating or erythema may suggest an autonomic response)
   (e) deformity (scoliosis, increased kyphosis, or other deviations from normal spinal curvature)
2. Active movements. Active movements are assessed in the cardinal planes for range of motion, symptom reproduction, and aberrant patterns of movement that may be antalgic or indicative of dysfunction. Combinations of these movements in two planes may help determine tissue source of symptoms[7] (Fig. 25.5 on page 453). A consistent pattern in which a movement that stretches the symptomatic area produces symptoms which are increased by the addition of movement in another plane that also has a stretch effect may suggest an extra-articular source of symptoms (myofascial, nerve, joint capsule), while a pattern consistent with symptoms primarily on compressive movements may indicate an intra-articular source. Mixed patterns may suggest multiple tissue sources.
   (a) flexion
   (b) extension
   (c) rotation (Fig. 25.4b overleaf)
3. Palpation. Soft tissue is palpated for tenderness, swelling, spasm and trigger points, while bony and chondral structures are assessed for tenderness and deformity and motion anomalies.
   (a) soft tissue
   (b) spinous processes (Fig. 25.4c overleaf)
   (c) zygapophyseal
   (d) costotransverse joints and, indirectly, the costovertebral joints
   (e) paraspinal muscles (Fig. 25.4d overleaf)
   (f) sternal, chondral and clavicular joints
4. Special tests
   (a) springing of the ribs (Fig. 25.4e overleaf)
   (b) maximal inspiration
   (c) cough/sneeze

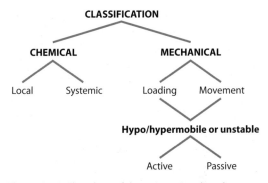

Figure 25.3 Flowchart of thoracic region disorders. Classification facilitates the differential diagnosis and better outcomes through prescription of condition-specific treatment

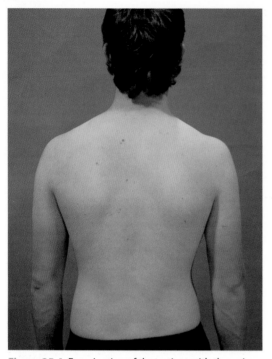

(d) neural tissue provocation tests (slump test)
(e) cervical spine examination (Chapter 20)
(f) lumbar spine examination (Chapter 26)
(g) muscle strength testing

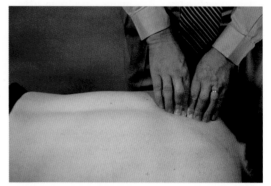

(c) Palpation—spinous processes

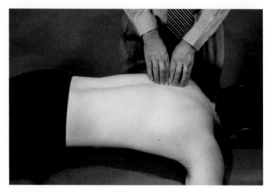

(d) Palpation—paraspinal muscles. Palpate for tightness and the presence of taut bands and active trigger points

Figure 25.4 Examination of the patient with thoracic pain
(a) Observation—any scoliosis or kyphosis should be noted

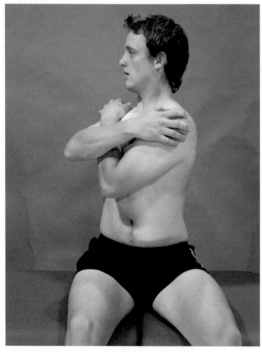

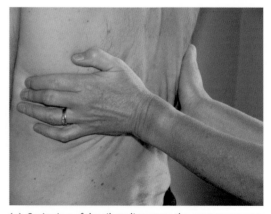

(e) Springing of the ribs adjacent to the costotransverse joints and costochondral junction

(b) Active movement—rotation

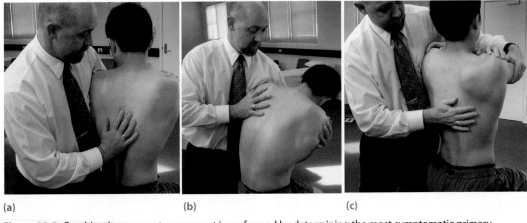

(a) **(b)** **(c)**

Figure 25.5 Combined movement assessment is performed by determining the most symptomatic primary movement; this movement is then repeated in the two extremes of another plane. For example, the primary symptomatic movement of axial plane left rotation **(a)** is subsequently performed in two positions in the sagittal plane—flexion **(b)** and extension **(c)**.

Investigations

Plain X-ray of the thoracic spine region is not routinely indicated as it usually adds little to the clinical picture. It may, however, demonstrate the presence of intervertebral growth plate abnormalities indicative of Scheuermann's disease, or show the presence of a secondary neoplastic disorder affecting the thoracic spine or ribs. CT and MRI scans may be indicated to exclude serious pathology in the presence of red flags such as unexplained weight loss or nocturnal pain. These imaging modalities may assist in confirmation of a thoracic intervertebral disk prolapse or the staging of neoplastic disease. Atypical pain patterns unresponsive to routine management should also signal the need for investigation, even in the young sportsperson.

Thoracic intervertebral joint disorders

Intervertebral joint injuries involving the intervertebral disks, rib articulations, and zygapophyseal joints are the most common cause of pain in this region. They may be of sudden or gradual onset. Examination may reveal hypomobility of one or more intervertebral segments associated with local tenderness over the spinous processes, the zygapophyseal joints, the costotransverse joints, or the surrounding paravertebral muscles. However, on occasion, pain rather than stiffness may be the main presenting feature.

Treatment aims to restore full mobility by mobilization or manipulation techniques (Fig. 25.6).

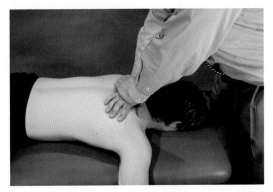

Figure 25.6 Posteroanterior mobilization (central) of the thoracic spine

Soft tissue therapy and graded specific exercise may be required to restore normal function in the paravertebral and periscapular muscles (Fig. 25.7 overleaf).

Passive techniques used include digital ischemic pressure and sustained myofascial tension. Trigger points in the paraspinal muscles are common and may be treated with appropriate soft tissue techniques. Considerable variation in joint anatomy often presents at the transitional junctions of the spine and, particularly, at the thoracolumbar junction;[8] these variations may contribute to subtle differences in segmental mechanics and injury patterns. While some zygapophyseal joints display remarkable asymmetry, others may show a morphology that acts to constrain motion. In this case hypomobility should not be perceived as unusual (Fig. 25.8 overleaf).

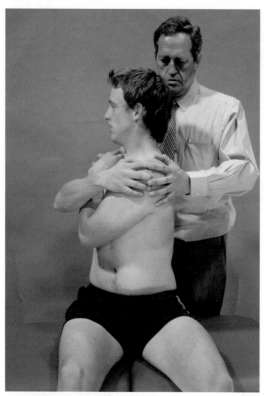

Figure 25.7 Stretching exercises

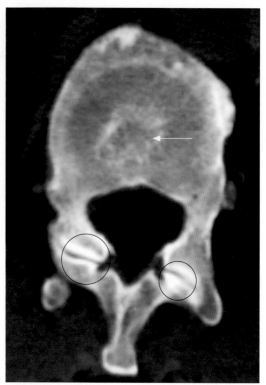

Figure 25.8 Zygapophyseal joint abnormalities
(a) Axial CT scan highlighting marked zygapophyseal joint tropism (circled). Evidence of a central Schmorl's node is noted within the end plate (arrow)

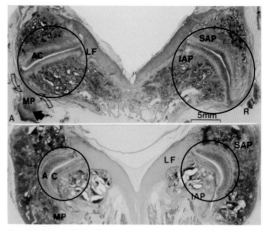

(b) Horizontal histological section (100 μm) through the zygapophyseal joints of the thoracolumbar junction to demonstrate variations in articular morphology from asymmetric (top image) to an enclosing morphology that constrains motion (lower image)

However, it is acknowledged that the transitional segments between the thoracic and lumbar regions are disposed to severe strain or injury during overload, and these segments account for the highest incidence of trauma, particularly from high-energy sports (skiing, equestrian events, jet ski, motorcross).[9]

Costovertebral and costotransverse joint disorders

Disorders of the rib articulations include inflammatory spondyloarthropathies (such as ankylosing spondylitis), degenerative change (such as osteoarthritis), and mechanical joint sprains. Costotransverse joint problems are associated with localized tenderness and restricted mobility of the joints. This is often evident on deep inspiration and active movement, as the ribs rotate in a predictable pattern relative to thoracic motion. Treatment may include mobilization of the costotransverse joints, which will have a modest influence also on the deeper costovertebral articulations. On occasion, a corticosteroid injection into the involved joint(s) may be considered when they have been unresponsive to standard management. This procedure should be performed under radiological guidance. A common problem of these small synovial joints is derangement of intra-articular synovial fold inclusions that occupy the periphery of the internal joint cavity (Fig. 25.9). These conditions are usually amenable to mobilizations or manipulation.[10]

Scheuermann's disease

Scheuermann's disease is the most common cause of pain in the thoracic spine region in adolescents. It is characterized by an accentuated low thoracic kyphosis arising from multiple vertebral end-plate irregularities involving four or more vertebral bodies (Fig. 25.10).

This condition is described in Chapter 42. Accentuated kyphosis may also arise from habitual training postures which involve loading into flexion.[11]

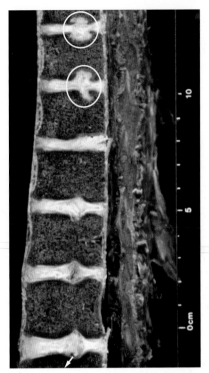

Figure 25.10 Multiple end-plate lesions (Schmorl's nodes) evident within the lower thoracic vertebral bodies (circles) typical of Scheuermann's disease

Extended training periods in one posture (e.g. cycling) tend to be associated with adaptive changes, and modification to training postures may need to be considered when recommending long-term management.

Thoracic intervertebral disk prolapse

Prolapse of a thoracic intervertebral disk is a rare condition that may be under-reported in the community.[1, 3, 12] The segments that tend to be most commonly involved are the larger disks of the lower thoracic segments (Fig. 25.11 overleaf).

The clinical presentation involves local back pain with radicular pain radiating in the distribution of the affected thoracic spinal nerve(s). However, it must be noted that referral of symptoms arising from a thoracic disk prolapse often does not follow a characteristic referral pattern, which may confuse the diagnosis.[2, 13]

T4 syndrome

Occasionally, patients present with diffuse arm pain and sensory symptoms such as bilateral paresthesias

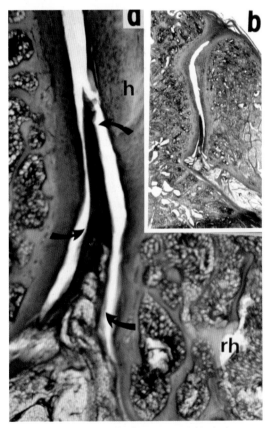

Figure 25.9 Costovertebral joint synovial inclusions. Horizontal histological section (100 μm) through the dorsal region of a costovertebral joint to demonstrate a long fibro-fatty synovial inclusion within the joint cavity. Entrapment of these innervated inclusions may contribute to localized thoracic pain, which can be relieved through manipulation

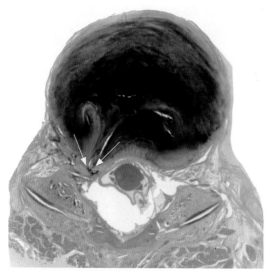

Figure 25.11 Thoracic disk prolapse
(a) Hematoxylin and eosin (H&E) stained horizontal section at T10–11 depicting a posterolateral prolapse of the intervertebral disk (arrows). Such prolapses are most common in the lower thoracic segments given the greater volume and height of these disks

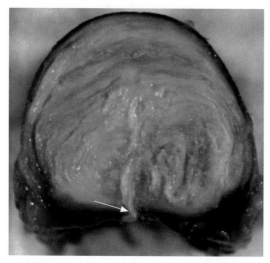

(b) Macroscopic horizontal section of a T11–12 disk to demonstrate a midline annular fissure and small central prolapse (arrow), which is a common presentation for thoracic disk lesions

in the hands, generalized headache, and inter-scapular tightness which is attributed to intervertebral joint problems around the upper thoracic region. This vague constellation of symptoms has been labeled the T4 syndrome. Although not verified clinically,

it may be speculated that symptoms arise from an involvement of the sympathetic nervous system. Examination often reveals hypomobility of the upper to middle thoracic segments together with shoulder protraction. Restoration of full mobility to these joints by mobilization or manipulation may relieve the symptoms.

Postural imbalance of the neck, shoulder and upper thoracic spine

Another common clinical presentation of the thoracic region is the tendency for specific muscle tightness which accentuates the forward head and protracted shoulder posture. Farfan coined the phrase "tired neck syndrome" to highlight the interaction of temporomandibular joint dysfunction, headache, and shoulder and interscapular pain. Selective strengthening of shoulder girdle retractors, particularly the inferior trapezius, and stretching of tight muscles contribute to the management of this problem.[14]

Chest pain

Chest pain occurs not infrequently in sportspeople, usually due to musculoskeletal causes. In mature athletes, the possibility that pain is of cardiac origin must be considered. This possibility is increased in the presence of associated symptoms such as palpitations or shortness of breath, or when there is a family history of cardiac disease. Other causes of chest pain include peptic ulceration, gastroesophageal reflux, chest infection, and malignancy.

The most common cause of chest pain in the young sportsperson under 35 years is referred pain from the cervical or thoracic spine. Thus, patients presenting with anterior or lateral chest wall pain require a thorough examination of the cervicothoracic spine and thorax.

A list of the possible causes of chest pain in sportspeople is presented in Table 25.2. The surface anatomy of this region is shown in Figure 25.12.

It may be difficult to distinguish between chest pain of cardiac origin and pain referred from the thoracic spine. They may both be unilateral and related to exercise. The clinical features of these two causes of chest pain in the athlete are considered in Table 25.3 on page 458.

Major trauma to the chest wall is a medical emergency (Chapter 47). Injuries sustained in contact sport commonly affect the ribs, resulting in either bruised or fractured ribs. These may lead to secondary dysfunction of the thoracic zygapophyseal joints,

Table 25.2 Causes of chest pain in the sportsperson

Common	Less common	Not to be missed
Rib trauma	Costochondritis	Cardiac causes
• Fracture	Sternocostal joint sprain	Peptic ulceration
• Contusion	Intercostal muscle strain	Gastroesophageal reflux
Referred pain from the thoracic spine	Rib stress fracture	Pneumothorax
Sternoclavicular joint disorders	Fractured sternum	Herpes zoster
	Side strain	Pulmonary embolism

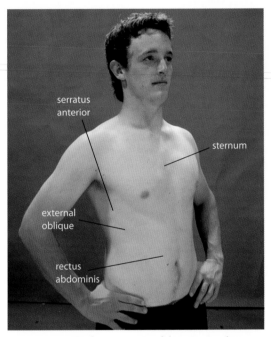

serratus
anterior

sternum

external
oblique

rectus
abdominis

Figure 25.12 Surface anatomy of the anterior chest

Assessment

History

A history of trauma to the chest wall will lead the clinician to suspect a rib injury. In the absence of trauma, the history should distinguish between musculoskeletal conditions and other cardiac, gastrointestinal, and respiratory causes. It is important to elicit the type of pain and the location of the pain. Associated symptoms such as palpitations, shortness of breath, and sweating may indicate that the pain is cardiac in nature. A history of productive cough may suggest the pain is of respiratory origin, while symptoms of reflux and relief of pain with acid-suppressing medication may indicate that gastroesophageal reflux or peptic ulceration may be the cause of the pain.

Pain aggravated by deep inspiration or coughing may be musculoskeletal in nature or indicative of a respiratory problem. Associated thoracic and, to a lesser extent, cervical or lumbar pain may suggest the thoracic spine or rib joints as possible sources of the patient's chest pain. An increase in pain with trunk rotation might add to this suspicion.

Examination

Examination of the patient with chest wall pain should include palpation of the painful area and of possible sites of referral, especially the thoracic spine. Examination of the thoracic spine has been described earlier in this chapter. The cardiovascular and respiratory systems must always be examined. The abdomen should be examined for sources of referred pain.

Investigations

If there has been significant rib trauma, a chest X-ray should be performed to exclude the presence of a pneumothorax. Specific rib views may be necessary to detect rib fractures. Chest X-ray will indicate cardiac size and may reveal evidence of respiratory

which can cause persistence of pain. Sternoclavicular and costochondral joint injuries are not uncommon. Intercostal muscle strains have been considered a cause of chest wall pain but, on close clinical examination, many patients with this presentation are actually suffering from referred pain from the thoracic spine. Stress fractures of the ribs are uncommon but seen in sports such as rowing, tennis, golf, gymnastics, and baseball pitching where rapid torsion loads are common. The etiology of chest wall muscle injury from violent overload is exemplified by fast bowlers, who induce a rapid alternation between muscle lengthening followed by rapid eccentric contraction during delivery. This action can result in a strain injury at the rib or costal cartilage insertion of the internal oblique muscle over the lower four ribs.

Table 25.3 Comparison of clinical features of chest pain of cardiac origin and chest pain referred from the thoracic spine

Feature	Referred pain from thoracic spine	Myocardial ischemia
Age	Any age, especially 20–40 years	Older, with increased possibility with increased age
History of injury	Sometimes	No
Site and radiation	Spinal and paraspinal, arms, lateral chest, anterior chest, substernal, iliac crest	Retrosternal, parasternal, jaw, neck, inner arms, epigastrium, interscapular
Type of pain	Dull, aching, occasionally sharp. Severity related to activity, site and posture. Sudden onset and offset	Constricting, vice-like ("clenched-fist" sign); may be burning. Gradual onset and offset
Aggravation	Deep inspiration, postural movement of thorax, certain activities (e.g. slumping or bending, walking upstairs, lifting, sleeping, or sitting for long periods)	Exercise, activity, heavy meals, cold, stress, emotion
Relief	Maintaining erect spine, lying down, firm pressure on back (e.g. leaning against wall)	Rest. Glyceryl trinitrate (GTN)
Associations	Chronic poor posture, employment requiring constant posture such as at a keyboard or computer	Cardiac risk factors such as family history, obesity, smoking, dyspnea, nausea, tiredness, pallor, sweating, vomiting

infection. Nuclear imaging may be required to detect stress fractures or other reactive bony conditions.

Electrocardiography and other cardiac investigations including a stress ECG/EKG and an echocardiograph may be performed if there is clinical suspicion of cardiac dysfunction. Gastroscopy may be indicated if peptic ulceration or reflux are suspected.

Rib trauma

A direct blow to the chest may result in trauma to the ribs. This may range from bruising to an undisplaced or displaced rib fracture. Typically, the patient complains of pain aggravated by deep inspiration or coughing. Examination reveals local tenderness over one or more ribs.

A pneumothorax or, rarely, a hemopneumothorax, may occur as a result of a rib fracture. Any sportsperson with rib trauma must undergo a respiratory examination to exclude these conditions. It is also important to consider trauma to underlying structures such as the liver, spleen and kidneys. Injuries to these organs are considered in Chapter 47.

X-ray may be performed to confirm the presence of a rib fracture, although it is not essential as treatment is symptomatic. Injury to the upper four ribs is unusual as they are somewhat protected. The lower

two ribs are likewise rarely fractured as they are not attached to the sternum.

Treatment of a rib fracture consists of analgesia and encouragement of deep breathing to prevent localized lung collapse. A fractured rib can be extremely painful. It continues to be painful and tender to palpation for at least three weeks. Bruised ribs may also be painful and tender for up to three weeks.

Return to sport for athletes with an undisplaced rib fracture is appropriate when pain settles. Protective padding or splints may be used in contact sports after a rib injury. The use of local anesthesia, either at the site of injury or as an intercostal nerve block, is usually not particularly effective and has the risk of causing a pneumothorax.

Contusion of the costochrondral joints can be painful; local treatment consists of cold therapy, strapping to splint the region, or corticosteroid injection.

Referred pain from the thoracic spine

Referred pain from the thoracic spine is probably the most common cause of chest wall pain in the young sportsperson. There may be a history of associated thoracic spine pain. On examination there is usually marked tenderness and stiffness, either centrally over the spinous processes of the thoracic vertebrae or, more commonly, over the thoracic zygapophyseal or costovertebral joints on the same side as the chest pain. There is also often associated tenderness in the soft tissues surrounding the thoracic spine, especially the paravertebral muscles. Active trigger points may develop and contribute to the referred pain. However, referred pain may not follow predictable patterns, and this requires the clinician to explore symptoms and to rule out visceral disorders and, conversely, unusual symptom patterns.[5, 13]

Local treatment aims to restore full range of motion of the involved thoracic intervertebral segments by mobilization or manipulation (Fig. 25.6). Soft tissue therapy to surrounding areas may be helpful. This includes digital ischemic pressure to painful sites, and sustained myofascial tension where chronic muscle and soft tissue tightness is established.

Sternoclavicular joint problems

The sternoclavicular joint is the sole articulation between the upper extremity and the axial skeleton. The joint itself is diarthrodial, with an articular disk interposed between the two bones. The articular surface of the medial clavicle is much greater than the sternal articular surface. Only about 25% of the medial clavicle's surface articulates with the sternum at any one time, making the sternoclavicular joint the joint with the least bony stability in the body.

The integrity of the joint comes from the strong surrounding ligaments, including the anterior, posterior, superior, and inferior sternoclavicular ligaments, and the interclavicular, costoclavicular, and intra-articular disk ligaments (Fig. 25.13). The epiphysis of the medial clavicle is the last to ossify and fuse, at around 18 and 25 years of age respectively. Another feature of this joint is the number of vital structures located directly posterior to the joint. These include the subclavian veins and artery, the trachea, the esophagus, and the mediastinum.

The sternoclavicular joint can be injured by a direct blow or, more commonly, indirectly from a blow to the shoulder. Simultaneous injuries of the acromioclavicular and sternoclavicular joints are reasonably common.[15–17]

Traumatic injuries of the sternoclavicular joint can be divided into first- and second-degree sprains involving the joint capsule, subluxations and dislocations involving rupture of the sternoclavicular and/or costoclavicular ligaments, and fractures of the medial clavicle. Subluxations and dislocations are further divided into anterior (more common; Fig. 25.14 overleaf) and posterior (more dangerous).

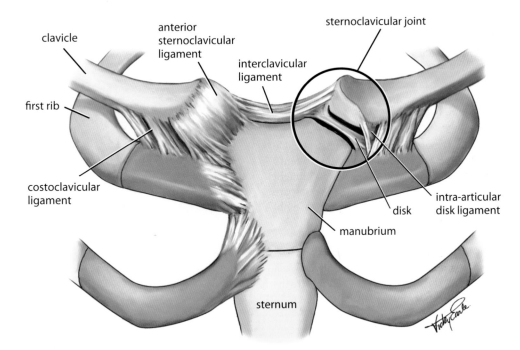

Figure 25.13 Anatomy of the sternoclavicular joint

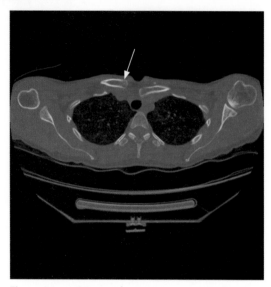

Figure 25.14 CT scan of anterior sternoclavicular joint dislocation showing clear asymmetry between the dislocated side (arrow) and the normal articulation

Patients present with local pain and swelling depending on the severity of the injury. Anterior subluxations can be treated symptomatically by a figure-of-eight bandage for one to two weeks. Anterior dislocations can be reduced with lateral traction on the abducted arm and direct pressure over the medial clavicle. Dislocations are immobilized for three to four weeks in a clavicular strap. If, after closed reduction, the joint redislocates, a period of observation is appropriate. Many patients remain asymptomatic.

Posterior dislocations are potentially dangerous because of the close proximity of vital structures behind the joint.[18–20] Closed reduction should be performed under general anesthesia as soon as possible after the injury. Traction is applied to the patient's abducted arm, and the medial clavicle is brought forward manually or with a towel clip. Reductions are generally stable and are held with a figure-of-eight strap for four weeks.

Costochondritis

Costochondritis occurs at the plane joints between the sternum and ribs. It is characterized by activity-related pain and tenderness localized to the costochondral junction over one or several of the T3–5 segments. Tietze's syndrome describes a painful inflammation of usually a single costochondral joint, although the sternoclavicular joint may involved.[21]

Treatment of costochondritis consists of non-steroidal anti-inflammatory drugs (NSAIDs), local physiotherapy and gentle mobilization of the costochondral joints. This can be an extremely difficult condition to treat. Corticosteroid injection to the costochondral junction may be of some assistance in refractory cases.

Stress fracture of the ribs

Stress fracture of the ribs has been reported with a number of sports (rowing, tennis, golf, gymnastics, baseball) and is due to excessive muscle traction at the muscular attachments to the ribs.[22, 23]

Stress fracture of the first rib is seen in baseball pitchers and appears to occur at the site of maximal distraction between the upward and downward muscular forces on the rib. This stress fracture tends to heal poorly.

Anterolateral stress fractures of the ribs (Fig. 25.15), mainly the fourth and fifth ribs, are commonly seen in rowers. This stress fracture is thought to be due to excessive action of the serratus anterior muscle. The concept of excess rib cage compression, coupled with excessive isometric thoracic muscle contraction in the beginning of the drive phase in rowing, has been proposed as the mechanism.[24]

The biomechanics of the pitching or rowing action should be assessed and discussed with the coach and sportsperson to determine the possible cause(s) and changes to technique where indicated.

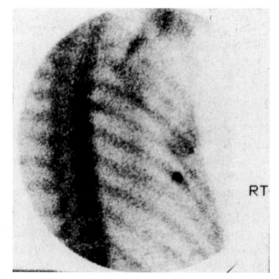

Figure 25.15 Isotopic bone scan of a stress fracture of the ribs

Side strain

Side strain is the condition described as internal oblique muscle tear at the rib or costal cartilage insertion.[25, 26] This injury in sportspeople, is particularly prevalent among cricket fast bowlers, javelin throwers, rowers, and ice hockey players. Patients with side strain present have sudden pain and point tenderness in the region of the lower costal margin. Tears have a predilection for the insertion of the eleventh rib, followed by the tenth and ninth ribs.

Cricketers, rowers, swimmers, and golfers are postulated to be susceptible to side strain due to sudden eccentric contraction of the internal oblique muscle after muscle lengthening that occurs during bowling, rowing, swimming, and driving. This injury is a major problem in cricket fast bowlers and is almost always found in the non-bowling arm.[25]

Although side strain can be diagnosed clinically, imaging plays a pivotal role in the assessment and management of these injuries. The MRI findings of tearing of muscle fibers from the ribs with acute edema and hemorrhage are shown in Figure 25.16. Ultrasound will also demonstrate these injuries. Radiologists should be alert to a complementary pathology—stripping of the rib periosteum occurs in a significant proportion of cases.

Treatment involves resting and strengthening the affected area followed by a graduated return to activity. A fast bowler will need 4–6 weeks before returning to high-level activity.

Re-injury is a particular problem. Up to 30% of first-class cricket fast bowlers with this injury suffer recurrence; the majority of these occurred within 2 years of the initial injury.

Conclusion

Disorders of the thoracic region in sportspeople can be complex, given the interactions between musculo-

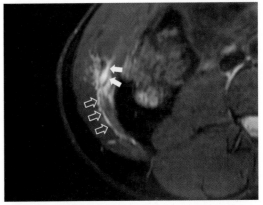

Figure 25.16 MRI (axial proton density image with fat saturation) of a side strain injury of the right internal oblique muscle. Focal grade II tearing of the internal oblique muscle is demonstrated (solid arrows) just below the muscle attachment to the periosteum of the undersurface of the tenth rib. Intermuscular haemorrhage (open arrows) tracks between the internal and external oblique muscles

skeletal and visceral systems, and their convergence in innervation. Athletic training and competition impose unique strains on the thorax and thoracic spine, particularly during the important skeletal development years; this may give rise to a variety of stress or overuse responses. In considering a differential diagnosis, the clinician needs to consider the biomechanics of the activity, common soft tissue and joint disorders, and to be aware of the potential for occult symptoms masquerading as musculoskeletal problems.

RECOMMENDED READING

Anderson J, Read J. *Atlas of imaging in sports medicine.* 2nd edn. Sydney: McGraw-Hill Education, 2007.

Lee D. *The thorax: an integrated approach.* Orthopedic Physical Therapy Products, 2003

Giles L, Singer KP. *Clinical anatomy and management of thoracic spine pain.* Oxford: Butterworth-Heinemann, 2000.

REFERENCES

1. Benson MK, Byrnes DP. The clinical syndromes and surgical treatment of thoracic intervertebral disc prolapse. *J Bone Joint Surg Br* 1975;57B(4):471–7.

2. Singer KP, Edmondston J. Introduction. The enigma of the thoracic spine. In: Giles L, Singer KP, eds. *Clinical anatomy and management of thoracic spine pain.* Oxford: Butterworth-Heinemann, 2000:3–13.

3. Papadakos N, Georges H, Sibtain N et al. Thoracic disc prolapse presenting with abdominal pain: case report and review of the literature. *Ann R Coll Surg Engl* 2009 91(5):W4–6

4. Groen GJ, Stolker RJ. Thoracic neural anatomy. In: Giles L, Singer KP, eds. *Clinical anatomy and management of thoracic spine pain.* Oxford: Butterworth-Heinemann, 2000:114–41.

5. Maigne JY. Cervicothoracic and thoracolumbar spinal pain syndromes. In: Giles L, Singer KP, eds. *Clinical anatomy and management of thoracic spine pain.* Oxford: Butterworth-Heinemann, 2000:157–68.

6. Gregersen GG, Lucas DB An in vivo study of the axial rotation of the human thoracolumbar spine. *J Bone Joint Surg* 1967;49A(2):247–62.

7. Edwards BC, *Manual of combined movements.* 2nd edn. Oxford: Butterworth-Heinemann, 1999.

8. Singer KP, Malmivaara A. Pathoanatomical characteristics of the thoracolumbar junction region. In: Giles L, Singer KP, eds. *Clinical anatomy and management of thoracic spine pain.* Oxford: Butterworth-Heinemann, 2000:100–13.

9. Reinhold M, Knop C, Beiss R et al. Operative treatment of 733 patients with acute thoracolumbar spinal injuries: comprehensive results from the second, prospective, internet-based multicentre study of the Spine Study Group of the German Association of Trauma Surgery. *Eur Spine J* 2010;19:1657–76.

10. Bogduk N, Jull G. The theoretical pathology of acute locked back: a basis for manipulative therapy. *Man Med* 1985;1:78–82.

11. Ashton-Miller JA. Thoracic hyperkyphosis in the young athlete: a review of the biomechanical issues. *Curr Sports Med Rep* 2004;3(1):47–52.

12. Wood KB, Garvey TA, Gundry C et al. Magnetic resonance imaging of the thoracic spine. Evaluation of asymptomatic individuals. *J Bone Joint Surg* 1995;77A:1631–8.

13. Whitcomb DC, Martin SP, Schoen RE et al. Chronic abdominal pain caused by thoracic disc herniation. *Am J Gastroenterol* 1995;90:835–7.

14. Farfan H. The tired neck syndrome. In: Giles L, Singer KP, eds. *Clinical anatomy and management of thoracic spine pain.* Oxford: Butterworth-Heinemann, 2000:171–6.

15. Bicos J, Nicholson GP. Treatment and results of sternoclavicular joint injuries. *Clin Sports Med* 2003;22:359–70.

16. Garretson RB III, Williams GR Jr. Clinical evaluation of injuries to the acromioclavicular and sternoclavicular joints. *Clin Sports Med* 2003;22:239–54.

17. Wroble RR. Sternoclavicular injuries. Managing damage to an overlooked joint. *Phys Sportsmed* 1995;23(9):19–24, 26.

18. Williams CC. Posterior sternoclavicular joint dislocation. *Phys Sportsmed* 1999;27(2):105–13.

19. Kiroff GK, McClure DN, Skelley JW. Delayed diagnosis of posterior sternoclavicular joint dislocation. *Med J Aust* 1996;164:242–3.

20. Mirza AH, Alam K, Ali A. Posterior sternoclavicular dislocation in a rugby player as a cause of silent vascular compromise: a case report. *Br J Sports Med* 2005;39(5):e28.

21. Gregory P, Biswas AC, Batt ME. Musculoskeletal problems of the chest wall in athletes. *Sports Med* 2002;32 (4):235–50.

22. Brukner PD, Bennell KL, Matheson GO. *Stress fractures.* Melbourne: Blackwell Scientific, 1998.

23. Hopper MA, Tirman P, Robinson P Muscle injury of the chest wall and upper extremity. *Sem Musculoskel Radiol* 2010;14:122–30.

24. Vinther A, Kanstrup L, Christiansen E et al. Exercise-induced rib stress fractures: potential risk factors related to thoracic muscle co-contraction and movement pattern. *Scand J Med Sci Sports* 2006;16:188–96.

25. Connell DA, Jhamb A, James T. Side strain: a tear of internal oblique musculature, *AJR* 2003;181:1511–17.

26. Obaid H, Nealon A, Connell D. Sonography of side strain, *AJR* 2008;191:W264–W267.

Chapter 26

Low back pain

with JOEL PRESS and JIRI DVOŘÁK

It's nothing major but it's just something I can't play with right now. Professional golfer Michelle Wie speaking about her lumbar disk injury, which caused her to drop out of an LPGA tournament in November, 2010. Quoted by Beth Ann Baldry from *Golfweek*

Low back pain is an extremely common symptom in both the general population and also among sportspeople. In this chapter we outline some salient epidemiological data and detail a clinical perspective of managing low back pain before discussing the evaluation and treatment of back pain.

Epidemiology

Back pain affects up to 85% of the population at some time in their lives. The vast majority (90%) improve over a three-month period, but nearly 50% will have at least one recurrent episode. The estimated annual cost of low back pain in the US is over US$40 billion. Low back pain is the most common disability in those under the age of 45, and the most expensive health care problem in those between the ages of 20 and 50. Back problems account for a significant percentage (25% in the US) of workers compensation claims, although the incidence of work-related low back pain varies considerably among countries (e.g. it is much lower in Scandinavia than in the US).

Considerable research has been undertaken investigating the risk factors for low back pain; these are summarized in Table 26.1.

Clinical perspective

As with neck pain, it is often not possible to make a precise anatomical and pathological diagnosis. However, this does not prevent management and treatment. In the majority of cases of low back pain, the principles of management depend on careful assessment to detect any abnormality, and then appropriate treatment to correct that abnormality. The anatomy

Table 26.1 Risk factors associated with low back pain (LBP)

Risk factor	Evidence
Age	Increased risk until age 50, then relative risk decreases in men but increases in women
Gender	Multiparous women
Obesity	Unclear
Height	Unclear
Posture	No association with lordosis or leg length discrepancy
Smoking	Strong association with LBP and sciatica
Physical work	Increased risk in those whose work involves bending, twisting or heavy physical labor Increased risk of LBP and sciatica with exposure to vibration Coal miners have fewer disk protrusions than other occupations Low risk of LBP in farmers
Sedentary occupation	Increased risk when seated Driving a motor car may cause LBP or herniated disk Jobs involving all standing or all sitting show higher incidence of LBP than those with changing positions
Increased fitness	Some evidence that good isometric endurance of back muscles may be associated with reduced LBP
Psychological factors	Stress, anxiety, depression associated with work-related LBP

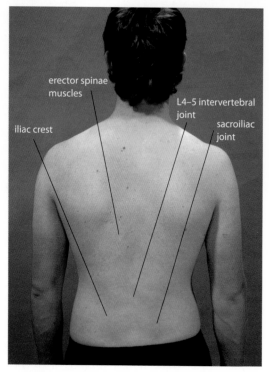

Figure 26.1 Anatomy of the low back
(a) Surface anatomy

of the low back is shown in Figure 26.1. The lumbar spine pain generators are listed in Table 26.2.

Conditions causing low back pain in which a definitive diagnosis can be made

There are a small number of conditions causing low back pain in which a definitive diagnosis can be made. These constitute considerably less than 10% of patients presenting with low back pain. The rest of the patients presenting with low back pain may be grouped together as having "somatic" low back pain.

Fractures related to direct trauma, such as a transverse process fracture or compression fracture of the vertebra, occur infrequently in the lumbar spine. Significant soft tissue injury is usually associated with these fractures.

It is usually also possible to make a definitive diagnosis in those patients presenting with nerve root compression who have typical lancinating pain radiating to the leg in a narrow band, with or without accompanying back pain. Sensory symptoms or muscle weakness (or both) are also present. Reflexes are often abnormal. Nerve root compression in the sportsperson is usually due to herniation of disk material from the nucleus pulposus of the intervertebral disk.

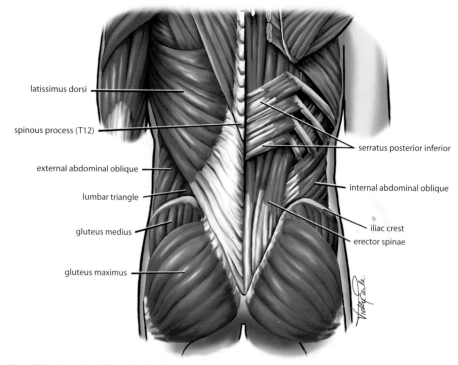

(b) Muscles of the lower back from behind

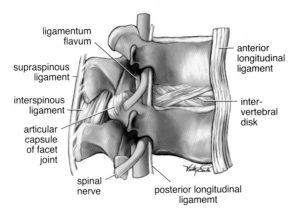

(c) The intervertebral segment

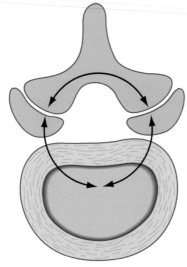

(d) The three-joint complex consisting of the intervertebral disk and the two zygapophyseal (facet) joints

Table 26.2 Lumbar spine pain generators

- Nucleus pulposus
- Anulus fibrosus
- Facet joints
- Ligaments
- Muscles
- Nerve
- Synovium

Spondylolysis or stress fracture of the pars interarticularis is seen in sports involving repeated hyperextension plus or minus rotation, such as gymnastics, skiing, fast bowling (cricket), weightlifting, throwing sports, and tennis. A spondylolisthesis or slipping of one vertebra on another may occur in sportspeople with bilateral pars defects. Spinal canal stenosis is rare in young and middle-aged sportspeople, but may occasionally be seen in older sportspeople. It is characterized by diffuse pain in the buttocks or legs aggravated by walking and relieved by rest.

Abnormalities of the hip joint such as labral tears and rim lesions may present as low back pain, and a thorough examination of the hip joint should be included in the assessment of the patient with low back pain.

Somatic low back pain

Any of the nociceptive (pain-producing) structures of the lumbar spine may cause low back pain. These structures include the vertebral venous plexus, dura mater, ligaments of the vertebral arches, muscles and their fascia, vertebral bodies, laminae, apophyseal joints, and the anulus fibrosus of the intervertebral disk.

Provocation techniques have demonstrated that damage to the intervertebral disks and the apophyseal joints are the most common causes of low back pain. With low back pain of lengthy duration, a number of factors contribute to the overall clinical picture. These may include abnormalities of the ligaments of the intervertebral joints, muscles, and fascia, as well as neural structures.

For many years, the disk was thought to have no sensory innervation. However, it is now recognized that the outer one-third to one-half of the posterior anulus fibrosus has a nerve supply. Previously, only two types of disk injury were recognized. One was herniation or rupture, in which the contents of the nucleus pulposus extruded through a tear in the anulus fibrosus into the spinal canal to impinge on structures such as the nerve root. The other was disk degeneration identified on X-ray as a narrowing of the disk space accompanied by osteophyte formation.

The disks may, however, be a source of pain without complete rupture or degeneration. There are two specific entities that may cause disk pain— torsional injury of the anulus fibrosus and compression injury.

Excessive rotational or torsional stress (Fig. 26.2 overleaf) may damage the apophyseal joint, the anulus fibrosus, or both. The anulus fibrosus is most vulnerable to a combination of axial rotation and forward flexion, which corresponds to the clinical situation of lifting in a bent and rotated position. Repeated torsional injuries to the anulus fibrosus may produce

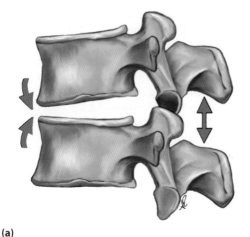

(a)

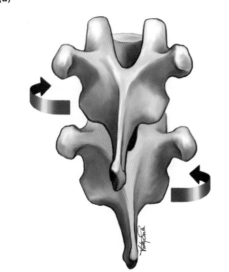

(b)

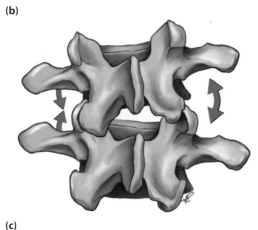

(c)

Figure 26.2 Segmental motion: **(a)** flexion/extension (sagittal plane motion); **(b)** torsion (transverse plane motion); **(c)** side-bending (frontal plane motion)

radial fissures, which can be seen on diskography. The location of these fissures corresponds to the tracks along which nuclear material is found to herniate. This suggests that previous torsional injuries of the anulus fibrosus may predispose to nuclear herniation. A tear in the anulus is thought to provoke an inflammatory response with chemical stimulation of the nociceptors. This pathological process explains the common presentation of a patient with poorly localized back pain that may be referred to the lower limb and which is aggravated by any movement of the lumbar spine, especially rotation and flexion.

Compression injuries arise as a result of excessive weight-bearing and are initiated by fractures of the vertebral end plate. As a result of this end-plate fracture, the matrix of the nucleus pulposus may be exposed to the circulation of the vertebral body. This may lead to degradation of the nucleus and increased load on the anulus. If the degradation process of the nucleus reaches the outer third of the anulus fibrosus, it is likely to produce pain. There may be both chemical and mechanical irritation of the pain receptors. These disk injuries may cause local, deep-seated low back pain as well as referred somatic pain (Chapter 6) to the buttock and lower leg.

The other common site of damage is the apophyseal joint. Possible causes of pain from the apophyseal joint include subchondral fractures, capsular tears, capsular avulsions, and hemorrhage into the joint space.

It may be possible to differentiate clinically between disk and apophyseal joint injury. Differences in pain-provoking activities (flexion with disk injuries and extension in apophyseal joint injuries) and differences in the sites of maximal tenderness (centrally with disk injuries and unilaterally with apophyseal joint injuries) may assist. However, this clinical differentiation is not always reliable and should be used only as a guide. Frequently the two conditions coexist.

Disk and apophyseal joint injuries may be associated with hypomobility of one or more intervertebral segments (Fig. 26.1c). The assessment of the mobility of each intervertebral segment is a major component of the examination of the sportsperson with low back pain. Correction of segmental hypomobility forms an important part of the treatment program.

Less commonly, low back pain may be associated with hypermobility. Generalized hypermobility is usually not symptomatic, but an isolated hypermobile segment may be significant clinically as an indicator of the presence of structural lumbar instability.

B

Trigger points frequently make a significant contribution to a patient's back pain. These may not have been the original problem, but they can become the main source of pain. Trigger points thought to be commonly associated with low back pain include quadratus lumborum, erector spinae, and gluteal. As a result of the associated muscle tightness, it may be impossible to treat the underlying joints adequately until the trigger points are eliminated and the shortened muscles returned to their normal length.

Abnormalities of joints, muscles, and neural structures may contribute significantly to the pain. In low back pain of relatively recent onset, the greatest contribution to the pain is usually from the joints. In longstanding cases of low back pain, there may be considerable contributions from the muscles and neural structures. Each of these components must be assessed clinically, and any abnormalities must be treated. Following treatment, the signs need to be reassessed to determine the effectiveness of each treatment.

A list of the causes of low back pain is shown in Table 26.3.

Functional (clinical) instability in low back pain

Stability of the lumbar intervertebral segments is principally provided by osseous and ligamentous restraints. However, without the influence of neuromuscular control, the segments are inherently unstable upon movement. Therefore, a combination of muscle forces and passive structures are utilized to dynamically stabilize the ligamentous spine under various demands of daily living and athletic activity.

It is important that the definition of stability includes the concept of control, rather than just hypermobility or increased displacement and range of movement, as it has been historically, although this will be the case in some conditions (e.g. spondylolisthesis).

The concept of core stability is discussed in Chapter 14. It is important to remember the difference between local and global muscles. Global (dynamic, phasic) muscles are the large, torque-producing muscles, such as rectus abdominis, external oblique, and the thoracic part of lumbar iliocostalis, which link the pelvis to the thoracic cage and provide general trunk stabilization as well as movement.

Local (postural, tonic) muscles are those that attach directly to the lumbar vertebrae and are responsible for providing segmental stability and directly controlling the lumbar segments during movement. These muscles include the lumbar multifidus, psoas major, quadratus lumborum, the lumbar parts of iliocostalis and longissimus, transversus abdominis, the diaphragm, and the posterior fibers of internal oblique (Fig. 14.2).

There is now considerable evidence to show that the function of at least two of these local muscles—lumbar multifidus and transversus abdominis—is impaired in patients with low back pain. Research has shown a significant reduction in segmental lumbar multifidus cross-sectional area in patients with acute first-episode unilateral back pain.[1-3] It has also been shown that lumbar multifidus demonstrated greater fatigability relative to other parts of the erector spinae in patients with chronic low back pain compared with

Table 26.3 Causes of low back pain

Common	Less common	Not to be missed
Somatic injury	Intervertebral disk prolapse	Malignancy
• Intervertebral disk	• Acute nerve root compression	• Primary
• Apophyseal joint	Spondylolisthesis	• Metastatic
Sacroiliac joint injury/inflammation	Lumbar hypermobility	Osteoid osteoma
Paravertebral and gluteal muscle	Stress fracture of the pars	Multiple myeloma
trigger points	interarticularis (spondylolysis)	Severe osteoporosis
	Spinal canal stenosis	
	Vertebral crush fracture	
	Hip joint pathology	
	Fibromyalgia	
	Rheumatological causes	
	Gynecological causes	
	Gastrointestinal causes	
	Genitourinary causes	

a normal population. Additionally, lumbar multifidus will not spontaneously increase its cross-sectional size post–acute injury, perhaps giving an insight into one of the reasons for recurring low back pain. However, the work of Hides et al.[1] demonstrated that a localized lumbar multifidus exercise program will significantly increase the cross-sectional area of the muscle.

The timing of onset of activity of transversus abdominis has been shown to be delayed in sufferers of chronic low back pain compared with individuals who have never experienced back pain.[4, 5] No significant change was detected between the two groups in any other muscle of the abdominal wall, suggesting that the local stabilizing abdominal muscles have a "feed-forward mechanism" to protect the lumbar spine during loading. This is not dissimilar to the hypothesized role of the vastus medialis obliquus on the patella (Chapter 33).

Other muscles are also affected in patients with low back pain. Seventy-five per cent of patients with radiating low back pain were shown to have abnormal EMG findings in the medial spine extensor muscles.[6] McGill and colleagues found deficiencies in spinal extensor muscle endurance, as well as flexion/extension and lateral/extensor ratios.[7]

It is unclear whether these deficiencies in muscle strength, endurance, and activation are the cause or the effect of low back pain. Nevertheless these deficits need to be addressed as part of any comprehensive rehabilitation program in those with low back pain.

History

The aim of the history in a patient with low back pain is to determine the location of the pain, its mechanism of onset, its degree of irritability, any radiation to the buttocks or legs, the aggravating and relieving factors, the presence of any associated features including sensory and motor symptoms, and any previous history of back problems, and response to treatment in the past. Factors that aggravate and relieve the pain, such as flexion/extension, and how easily the pain is aggravated are important in determining the type and intensity of treatment. Potentially serious symptoms that must be noted include:

- cauda equina symptoms (e.g. bladder or bowel dysfunction)
- spinal cord symptoms (e.g. difficulty walking, tripping over objects)

- sensory symptoms (e.g. pins and needles, paresthesia)
- motor symptoms (e.g. muscle weakness)
- systemic symptoms (e.g. weight loss, malaise)
- night pain.

The use of standardized outcome self-reporting measures, such as the Oswestry or Roland-Morris questionnaires, is also recommended as a way of quantifying the effects of low back pain.

Examination

Examination of the patient with low back pain includes assessment of pattern, timing and range of movement, detection of stiffness and tenderness in muscles and joints, and detection of neurological abnormalities or evidence of neural irritation.

1. Observation
   (a) from behind (Fig. 26.3a)
   (b) from the side (Fig. 26.3b)
2. Active movements
   (a) flexion (Fig. 26.3c)
   (b) extension (Fig. 26.3d)
   (c) lateral flexion (Fig. 26.3e on page 470)
   (d) combined movements—quadrant position (Fig. 26.3f on page 470)
   (e) single-leg extension (Fig. 26.3g on page 470)
3. Passive movements
   (a) overpressure may be applied at the end of range of active movements
   (b) muscle length (e.g. psoas, hamstring, gluteals)
   (c) hip quadrant (Chapter 28)
4. Palpation
   (a) spinous processes (Fig. 26.3h on page 470)
   (b) transverse processes
   (c) apophyseal joints
   (d) sacroiliac joint (Fig. 26.3i on page 471)
   (e) iliolumbar ligament
   (f) paraspinal muscles (Fig. 26.3j on page 471)
   (g) quadratus lumborum (Fig. 26.3k on page 471)
   (h) gluteal muscles
5. Special tests
   (a) straight leg raise/slump test (Chapter 11)
   (b) prone knee bend/femoral slump (Chapter 11)
   (c) sacroiliac joint test
   (d) neurological examination

Investigations

In the management of most cases of low back pain, investigations are not required. However, there are certain clinical indications for further investigation.

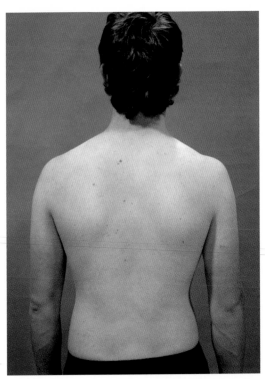

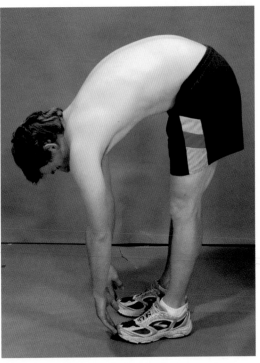

B

(c) Active movement—flexion. Look at symmetry of movement on both sides of the back, range of movement, and, if restricted, whether it is due to pain or stiffness

Figure 26.3 Examination of the patient with low back pain
(a) Observation from behind. Look for scoliosis, tilt, rotation, or asymmetrical muscle development. View the position of the spinous processes

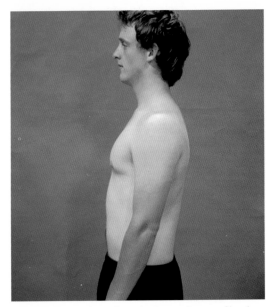

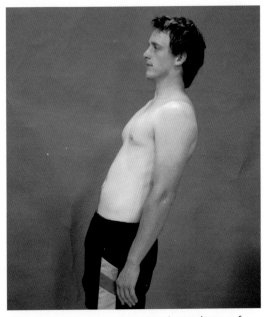

(b) Observation from the side. Assess degree of lumbar lordosis

(d) Active movement—extension. Assess degree of lumbar extension and any symptoms provoked. Patient should maintain pelvis in neutral

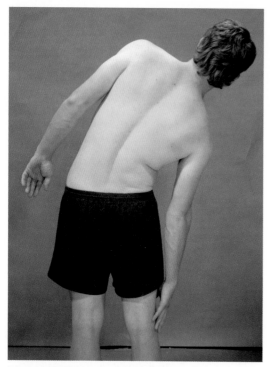

(e) Active movement—lateral flexion

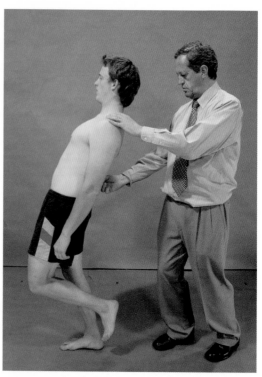

(g) Single leg extension

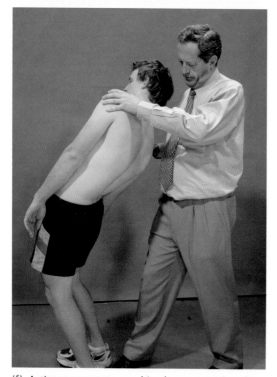

(f) Active movement—combined movement (quadrant position—extension, lateral flexion, rotation)

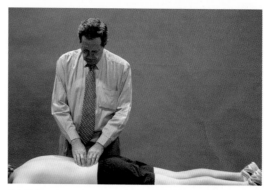

(h) Palpation—intervertebral joints. Palpate over spinous processes, apophyseal joints, and transverse processes. Assess degree of tenderness and amount of accessory posteroanterior movements

X-ray should be performed if traumatic fracture, stress fracture, spondylolisthesis, or structural lumbar instability are suspected. It is also advisable to X-ray those patients whose low back pain is not responding to treatment or where sinister abnormality may be suspected. Radioisotopic bone scan may be helpful in cases of suspected stress fracture of the pars interarticularis (spondylolysis).

B

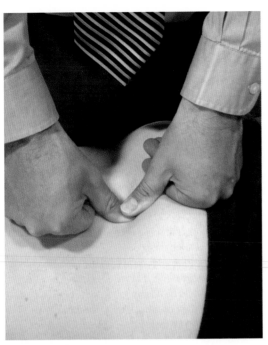

(i) Palpation—sacroiliac region. Palpate over the sacroiliac joints and iliolumbar ligaments

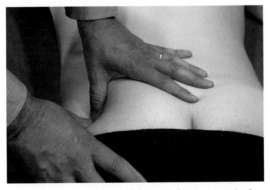

(j) Palpation—muscles and fascia. Palpate paraspinal and gluteal muscles for generalized increase in muscle tone and focal areas of tissue abnormality, including active trigger points

CT scanning is commonly performed in cases of suspected nerve root compression, but usually adds little to the clinical picture unless specific neurological signs are present. Disk protrusions and disk bulges are commonly seen in asymptomatic patients and the CT scan, unlike MRI, is unable to provide any further information on the internal structure of the intervertebral disk. However, spinal canal stenosis and facet joint arthropathy are well defined on

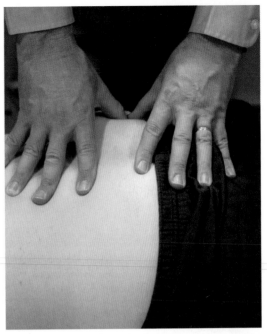

(k) Palpation—quadratus lumborum between the iliac crest and the rib cage

CT scanning. The presence of a pars interarticularis defect may also be confirmed on CT scanning.

In the investigation of patients with low back pain, MRI can be used to image the internal structure of the disk. Degenerated disks that have lost fluid have a characteristic appearance on MRI (Fig. 26.4 overleaf). MRI may confirm the presence of an annular tear in the disk and provide information about the vertebral end plate. The clinician must be wary, however, of placing too much emphasis on this investigation, as an abnormality shown on MRI may not necessarily be responsible for all or any of the patient's pain. It has been shown that a centralizing or peripheralizing pain pattern is a better indicator of internal disk disruption than an abnormality on MRI.[8]

Myelography is mentioned in older texts but since the introduction of MR imaging (non-invasive) myelography is seldom indicated.

Diskography is performed by injecting dye into the nucleus pulposus of the intervertebral disk. Reproduction of the patient's symptoms increases the likelihood that the disk is the source of pain. Diskography also gives an indication of the internal structure of the disk. Although diskography is the only imaging test for diskogenic pain, psychological factors can significantly alter the result of these tests (see biopsychosocial model of pain, Chapter 6).

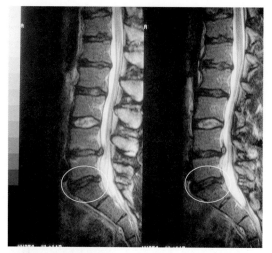

Figure 26.4 Two slices of MRI of an intervertebral disk showing decreased fluid (shown as dark coloration) in the disk at L4/5 and L5/S1 level. (There is also a small herniation at L4/5)

Severe low back pain

The majority of patients with low back pain present with mild-to-moderate pain. A small group of patients present with acute onset of severe low back pain. The aim of initial management of these patients is to reduce the pain and inflammation as rapidly as possible. When this is done, the management of these patients relies on the same principles as those with mild-to-moderate low back pain.

Acute onset of severe low back pain in the absence of nerve root signs may be due either to an acute tear of the anulus fibrosus of the disk or to an acute locked apophyseal joint.

Clinical features of severe acute low back pain

Acute low back pain is usually of sudden onset and is often triggered by a relatively minor movement such as bending to pick up an object. This minor incident may be more indicative of fatigue or lack of control, rather than tissue overload. The pain may increase over a period of hours due to the development of inflammation. Patients with chronic low back pain may also have acute exacerbations that may become more frequent and require less to initiate over time.

The pain is usually in the lower lumbar area and may be central, bilateral, or unilateral. It may radiate to the buttocks, hamstrings, or lower leg. Sharp, lancinating pain in a narrow band down the leg is radicular pain and is associated with nerve root irritation, commonly as a result of intervertebral disk prolapse. More commonly, the pain is referred to the buttock and hamstring and is somatic in nature, with the patient complaining of a deep-seated ache.

The patient with acute, sudden onset of low back pain often adopts a fixed position and movements are severely restricted in all directions. Palpation of the lumbar spine reveals areas of marked tenderness with associated muscle spasm.

Management of severe acute low back pain

- Encourage the patient to adopt the position of most comfort. This position varies considerably and may be lying prone, supine or, commonly, side-lying with a degree of lumbar flexion.
- Movements that aggravate pain should be avoided, whereas movements that reduce or have no effect on pain should be encouraged.
- Bed rest in the position of most comfort may be continued for up to 48 hours depending on the amount of pain. Bed rest longer than 48 hours has been shown to be detrimental.[9]
- Taping of the low back (Fig. 26.5) can markedly reduce acute back pain and allow quicker functional restoration.
- Analgesics may control the pain and reflex muscle spasm. Nonsteroidal anti-inflammatory drugs (NSAIDs) may help reduce inflammation.
- Electrotherapeutic modalities (e.g. TENS, interferential stimulation, and magnetic field therapy) may be helpful in reducing pain and muscle spasm in the acute stage. However, if access to these modalities in the acute stage requires any degree of travel, then bed rest alone may be preferable.
- Exercise in a direction away from the movement that aggravates the patient's symptoms should be commenced as early as possible. For those patients in whom flexion aggravates their symptoms, extension exercises should be performed (Fig. 26.6).
- The degree of extension should be determined by the level of pain. Initially, lying prone may be sufficient. Later, extension of the lumbar spine by pushing up onto the elbows may be possible. Eventually, further extension with straight arms can be achieved.
- Exercises should be immediately discontinued if peripheral symptoms develop.
- Prolonged posture involving flexion (such as sitting) should be avoided.

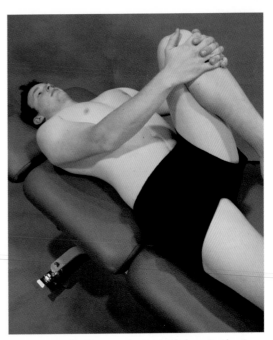

Figure 26.7 Flexion exercises—single knee to chest

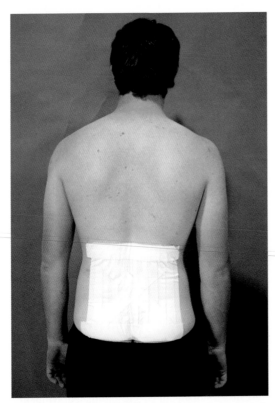

Figure 26.5 Taping technique used in the treatment of severe acute low back pain

Figure 26.6 Extension exercises—the amount of extension varies according to pain

In patients for whom extension movements aggravate their pain, flexion exercises (Fig. 26.7) or rotation (away from pain) exercises should be performed. For these patients, prolonged posture involving extension (such as standing with excessive lumbar lordosis) should be avoided.

Manual therapy has only a limited role in the treatment of severe low back pain. Gentle mobilization

techniques (e.g. posteroanterior [PA] mobilization), may be performed and the patient's response closely monitored. If there is any deterioration of symptoms, mobilization should be immediately ceased. The mobilization should be performed in the position of comfort adopted by the patient. Manipulation should not be attempted in the presence of marked muscle spasm. Similarly, gentle (grade I) soft tissue therapy may be helpful in relieving pain and muscle spasm. Traction has not been found to be helpful in patients with acute low back pain.

Mild-to-moderate low back pain

Once the acute phase (up to 48 hours) of severe low back pain has passed, with reduction in pain and muscle spasm, more intensive therapy can be commenced. Those patients whose initial presentation is with mild-to-moderate low back pain do not require such a period of rest, and treatment can commence immediately.

 Intervertebral joints, paraspinal muscles, and local nerves may all contribute to the patient's low back pain and must be identified and corrected.

The initial injury is most likely to be joint-related (e.g. a disk or apophyseal joint). However, in response to the injury, there may be associated muscle irritation and spasm, as well as neural irritation. Altered movement patterns, secondary to the initial injury, may result in the development of focal areas of increased muscle tone and trigger points. Various neural structures (nerve root or peripheral nerve) may be damaged at the initial injury. As a result, increased neural mechanosensitivity may develop. The longer the duration of the injury, the greater the contribution to the pain from muscle and neural structures.

Clinical features

Patients with mild low back pain complain of an aching pain that may be constant or intermittent. The pain may be central, unilateral, or bilateral, and is often described by the patient as a "band across the lower back." The pain may be aggravated by certain movements, such as flexion, extension, or combined movements. There may be associated somatic pain in the buttock and/or hamstring.

On examination, there is usually reduced range of motion of the lumbar spine, commonly flexion or extension. In patients with unilateral pain, there is often reduced lateral flexion. Any increased neural mechanosensitivity can be demonstrated by aggravation of the pain or reduction of range of motion with the slump test or straight leg raise (Chapter 11).

On palpation, there may be marked tenderness over the spinous processes or laterally over the apophyseal joints and transverse processes. The most typical finding in these patients is of hypomobility of one or more intervertebral segments. Depending on the severity and duration of the pain, there will be associated muscle spasm as well as focal areas of increased muscle tone and trigger points in the paravertebral and gluteal muscles.

If the muscles are very taut, palpation of the region is best performed with the patient side-lying. The muscles can be palpated using landmarks such as the transverse processes and spinous processes to identify specific muscles and ligaments. Focal areas of muscle abnormality that on palpation reproduce the patient's pain (rather than a region of diffuse muscle spasm) are likely to respond well to soft tissue therapy. These lesions feel tight but are compressible, unlike the lesions of chronic tissue thickening that have a more solid feel.

Treatment of mild-to-moderate low back pain

The treatment of non-osseous lesions causing low back pain is based on the same principles as the treatment of soft tissue injuries elsewhere in the body.

1. Identify and eliminate possible causes (e.g. poor posture, abnormal biomechanics).
2. Reduce pain and inflammation.
3. Restore full range of pain-free movement.
4. Achieve optimal flexibility and strength.
5. Maintain fitness.

There is no one treatment that is appropriate for all cases of low back pain. The ideal treatment regimen requires an integrated approach. To monitor the effectiveness of each type of treatment, it is necessary to reassess the objective clinical signs following treatment. This will reveal which treatment is most appropriate. The type of treatment depends, to a certain extent, on the degree of low back pain present and its irritability. Irritable lesions must be treated carefully so as not to aggravate pain. Lesions of low irritability, however, may be treated more aggressively with little risk of aggravating the symptoms.

Correction of predisposing factors

Correction of the factors causing low back pain is the most important component of the treatment program. This may be sufficient both to alleviate current symptoms and also to prevent recurrence. If the cause is not identified and eliminated, symptoms may persist and the likelihood of recurrence is high.

In sportspeople, correction of abnormal biomechanics that may predispose to low back pain (such as running with an excessive lordosis or lack of pelvic stability) is required. Correction of these factors is discussed in the rehabilitation section later in this chapter. Other possible causative factors include poor posture while sitting or standing, poor lifting techniques, working in stooped positions, or sleeping on a bed with poor support.

Pharmacological treatment

There is some evidence that NSAIDs are effective for short-term symptomatic relief in patients with low back pain.[10] However, it is unclear whether NSAIDs are more effective than simple analgesics such as paracetamol (acetaminophen). There is no evidence that any one type of NSAID is more effective than another. There is no place for the long-term use of NSAIDs, because of their lack of effectiveness and their significant incidence of adverse effects.

Mobilization and manipulation

Mobilization and manipulation (Chapter 13) may have two positive effects on the patient with a soft tissue injury to the lumbar spine. They act to reduce pain (Chapter 13) and also to restore movement to the hypomobile intervertebral segments detected on examination. This often involves joints at more than one level and, commonly, maximal stiffness is actually found in the level above or below the joint producing the patient's symptoms. Mobilization techniques used in the treatment of low back pain include:

- PA central (Fig. 26.8a)
- PA unilateral (Fig. 26.8b)
- rotations
- transverse vertebral pressure.

PA central mobilization and rotations are used in patients with central or bilateral pain. PA unilateral mobilization, rotations and, occasionally, transverse techniques are used if the pain is unilateral. The grade of mobilization technique used depends on the irritability of the condition and the amount of tenderness and stiffness. The most commonly used manipulation technique in the treatment of low back pain is rotation (Fig. 26.9).

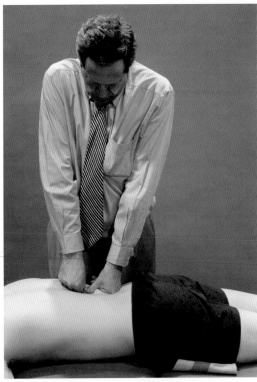

(b) PA unilateral—Thumbs are placed over the apophyseal joints

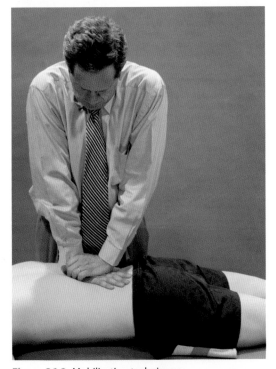

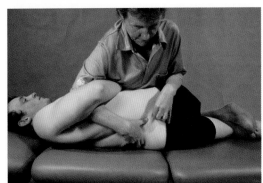

Figure 26.9 Manipulation—rotation. With the patient positioned as shown, the therapist exerts a short sudden forward thrust on the ilium while maintaining strong counterpressure on the shoulder. This position can be used for manipulation or mobilization

Figure 26.8 Mobilization techniques
(a) PA central—The therapist performs an oscillating movement over the spinous processes using thumbs or heels of the hands. Elbows are extended and pressure is exerted through the shoulders and arms

Soft tissue therapy

Abnormalities of the muscles and fascia are found in association with low back pain. The longer the low back pain has been present, the more widespread and severe are these abnormalities. Tender focal areas of abnormal tissue may be palpated.

Treatment of these areas consists of grade I transverse gliding, grade II sustained longitudinal pressure on the taut bands emanating away from the focal lesion, and sustained ischemic pressure (grade III) on the painful focal lesion (Fig. 26.10). After each treatment, the patient should be taken through the full range of pain-free motion for assessment and muscle stretch.

In more chronic pain, structural thickening in the fibers of lumbar multifidus and longissimus are seen. Less commonly involved are the intertransverserii and the quadratus lumborum. Palpation may reveal taut bands up to 1 cm (0.5 in.) in diameter about the L4–5 apophyseal joint within the lumbar multifidus muscle. In lean sportspeople, these bands may be rope-like. In stocky sportspeople, there may be gross muscle thickening that is palpable even through the thick fascial layers of the region.

Treatment is aimed at eliminating these abnormal areas of muscle tissue and, therefore, restoring normal function. Techniques used include grade II to III digital ischemic pressure to the focal lesions and grade III transverse gliding. Sustained myofascial tension techniques may also help.

In addition to assessment and treatment of the extensor muscles, attention should be paid to the flexor muscles. Tightness in the flexor muscles, commonly associated with hyperlordosis, may result in the antagonist extensors becoming excessively tight.

Dry needling

Longstanding cases of low back pain are characterized by the presence of multiple active trigger points. The most common sites are the paraspinal muscles from the mid-thoracic region to the sacrum, quadratus lumborum, and the gluteal muscles, especially gluteus medius. Dry needling to inactivate these trigger points (Fig. 26.11) reduces pain and muscle tightness, thus facilitating mobilization and manipulation of the underlying joints and, ultimately, exercise rehabilitation.[11]

Neural mobilization

Abnormal neural mechanosensitivity is often found in patients with low back pain. Neurodynamic tests such as the slump test and straight leg raise are often restricted and may aggravate the patient's symptoms.

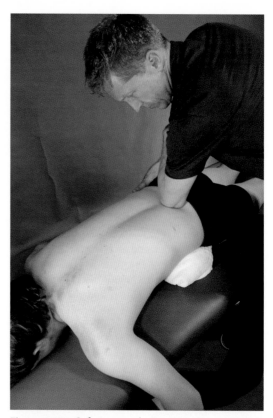

Figure 26.10 Soft tissue techniques
(a) Sustained ischemic pressure at each segmental level

(b) Sustained ischemic pressure using the knuckles to the quadratus lumborum in the position of sustained stretch

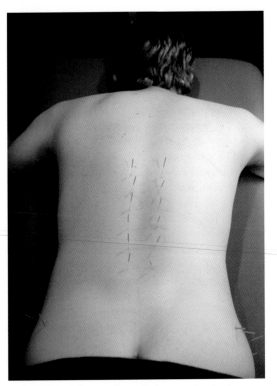

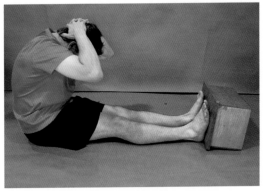

B

Figure 26.12 Neural mobilization—slump stretch. Patient adopts the position illustrated. To increase the degree of the stretch, the trunk is flexed at the hips until discomfort is felt. This position should be held for at least 10 seconds and then further trunk flexion may be performed, again to the point of onset of discomfort

Figure 26.11 Dry needling of trigger points in the paraspinal and gluteal muscles

Correction of joint and soft tissue abnormalities frequently results in an improvement in neural mechanosensitivity and in neural range of motion. This can be further improved by incorporating neural mobilizing techniques, such as slump mobilizing (Fig. 26.12), into the treatment program. Neural mobilizing should be performed with considerable caution under close supervision of an experienced clinician. Excessive use may aggravate the patient's symptoms.

Traction

Intermittent traction, performed manually or with the aid of weights or a machine, may be an effective pain-relieving technique in patients with nerve root irritation or radicular signs and symptoms, but does not play a major role in the treatment of mild-to-moderate low back pain. No high-quality studies exist on the efficacy of traction for low back pain.

Muscle energy techniques

Muscle energy techniques may be helpful in the treatment of patients with low back pain. These are discussed in Chapter 13.

Exercise therapy

Exercise therapy is an essential component of the treatment of the patient with low back pain.[12] Exercise therapy acts to help restore and maintain full range of motion, as well as providing additional mechanical support to the low back. Exercises include stretching, range of motion, strengthening, and stability exercises. Exercise therapy is discussed further in the section on rehabilitation later in this chapter.

Chronic low back pain

Occasionally, patients with low back pain due to soft tissue abnormalities fail to respond to the treatment methods above. For those patients, it is important to consider alternative diagnoses, such as lumbar instability or stress fracture. The presence of undetected predisposing factors, such as abnormal biomechanics, should also be considered.

There are a number of interventional techniques available for the treatment of the patient with persistent low back pain who fails to respond to an appropriate, correctly administered treatment program. Some clinicians argue that this should occur once the pain has become chronic (i.e. of three months' duration).

When compared with target-specific diagnoses achieved through accurate local anesthetic injections done under image intensifier, our ability to make a specific joint or disk diagnosis using clinical skill or imaging is very limited. Findings on examination that have traditionally been found to have significance, lack reliability and validity.

Interventional pain management in chronic back pain follows a logical process:

1. Obtain a target-specific diagnosis.
2. Treat the diagnosis according to evidence-based medicine.
3. If the diagnosis is neuropathic pain, or unable to be made, or if the pain ails the treatment, then block the pain pathway at the spinal cord level with spinal cord stimulation by intrathecal pump.

Diagnosis

The identifiable causes of chronic low back pain are:

- facet joints
- sacroiliac joints
- internal disk disruption (not disk bulges/prolapses etc.).

These areas can be diagnosed by the use of specific blocks.

Facet joint pain can be diagnosed with medial branch blocks. These involve using an image intensifier to place a needle onto the medial branch that supplies a facet joint and injecting local anesthetic onto the nerve. To block one joint, two nerves must be blocked; to block two joints, three nerves must be blocked. The patient then completes a pain chart and, if the pain goes away for several hours, the clinician can be approximately 60% sure of the diagnosis. A control block with a different local anesthetic is then done. If there is concordant pain relief, then the diagnostic confidence is approaching 90%.[13] Note that facet joint injections lack diagnostic and therapeutic validity.

Sacroiliac joint pain can be diagnosed with a sacroiliac joint injection, which some clinicians would combine with a deep interosseous joint injection. The data here are not as rigorous as for medial branch blocks but, with a control block, diagnostic confidence approaching 90% can again be achieved.

Disk pain is diagnosed differently. The most accurate test available is a pain provocation test, called provocative diskography. When performed according to the International Spine Intervention Society's guidelines, this is a relatively comfortable procedure. The posterior column (facet and sacroiliac joints) should first have been excluded as the cause of pain by the above methods. An MRI is then performed. If the disks are pristine, it is inappropriate to perform a diskogram, and one should look elsewhere for a diagnosis. If there is evidence of disk disease, especially high-intensity zones of type 1 or type 2 modic changes, then proceeding with diskography is reasonable if the patient's pain warrants the risk of infection.

Treatment

Once a diagnosis has been made, appropriate treatment can be undertaken. Facet joint or sacroiliac joint pain can be treated by radiofrequency neurotomy. This technique has a 90% chance of 60% pain relief and a 60% chance of 90% pain relief for lumbar facet pain.[14, 15] In the sacroiliac joint, there is evidence for a 60% chance of more than 50% pain relief, with a 30% chance of 90% pain relief.[16]

Some people advocate prolotherapy for sacroiliac joint problems. Evidence for this is currently inconclusive.

There are various percutaneous treatment options for diskogenic pain. The best data support the use of intradiskal electrothermal therapy (IDET);[17] however, the data that support IDET are mixed and even the best study shows it may be effective for only very selected patients with low back pain.[17] There is level 2 evidence (Chapter 3) for nucleoplasty in disk pain.

Epidural injections with a long-acting local anesthetic plus/minus a corticosteroid are a treatment for radicular leg pain, not a treatment for low back pain.

Despite the fact that over 250 000 lumbar fusions are performed annually in the US, there is no level 1 evidence to support this operation for diskogenic back pain.[18, 19]

Spinal surgery should only be performed when there is a specific indication. These indications are:

- nerve root compression resulting in persistent
  - bladder or bowel symptoms
  - radicular pain
  - sensory or motor abnormalities despite adequate conservative management
- persistent pain due to instability of a single intervertebral segment.

Acute nerve root compression

Acute nerve root compression is usually the result of an acute disk prolapse, when the contents of the nucleus pulposus of the intervertebral disk are extruded through a defect in the anulus fibrosus into the spinal canal. There they may irritate the nerve root (Fig. 26.13), either by direct mechanical compression by the nuclear material, or as a result of the chemical irritation caused by the extrusion.

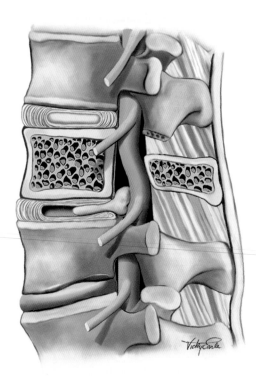

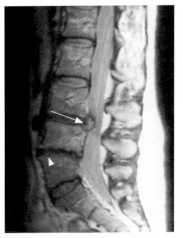

B

(c) Sagittal MRI showing prominent posterior L3–4 disk bulging (arrow) and cauda equina compression. The L4–5 disk (arrowhead) is also abnormal but not protruding

Figure 26.13 Disk extrusion compressing nerve root
(a) Spinal cord compression from severe disk prolapse

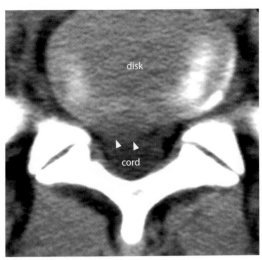

disk

cord

(b) Axial CT scan. Arrowheads point to the border between the bulging disk (anterior) and the compressed cord (posterior)

In the older sportsperson, nerve roots may be compressed by osteophytes formed as part of a degenerative process.

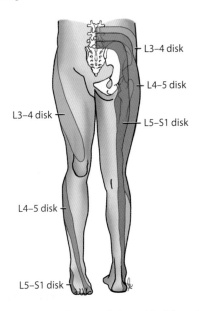

L3–4 disk

L4–5 disk

L3–4 disk

L5–S1 disk

L4–5 disk

L5–S1 disk

(d) Common areas of pain radiation with disk prolapse at the L3–4, L4–5, and L5–S1 levels

Prolapse usually occurs in disks that have been previously damaged by one of the processes mentioned above. This explains why frequently a minor movement, such as bending over to pick up an object off the floor, may cause such an apparently severe injury. Disk prolapse usually occurs between the ages of 20 and 50 years and is more common in males than females. The L5–S1 disk is the most commonly prolapsed disk and L4–5 the next most common.

Clinical features

Typically, a patient with a disk prolapse presents with acute low back pain or radicular leg pain (or both) following a relatively trivial movement usually involving flexion. On occasions, the presentation may be painless, with weakness or sensory symptoms only. The symptoms depend on the direction of the extrusion. Posterior protrusions are more likely to cause low back pain with later development of leg pain, whereas posterolateral protrusions may cause radicular symptoms without low back pain. Typical radicular symptoms include sharp shooting pain in a narrow band accompanied by pins and needles, numbness, and weakness. Pain is often aggravated by sitting, bending, lifting, coughing, or sneezing. Pain is usually eased by lying down, particularly on the asymptomatic side, and is often less after a night's rest.

On examination, the patient often demonstrates a lean to one side, usually, although not always, away from the side of pain. This is a protective scoliosis. Examination may be difficult if there is severe pain and irritability. Straight leg raise is usually limited (less than 30° in severe cases) and all active movements, particularly flexion, are usually restricted. Palpation usually reveals acute muscle spasm with marked tenderness; however, occasionally it may be unremarkable. A neurological examination should always be performed when pain extends past the buttock fold or there are subjective sensory/motor changes.

Treatment

In the acute phase, the most appropriate treatment is rest in bed in a position of maximum comfort with administration of analgesics and NSAIDs. The patient should lie as much as possible and avoid sitting. Extension exercises (Fig. 26.6) should be commenced as soon as possible. However, if exercises cause an increase in peripheral symptoms, they should be ceased.

Mobilization techniques should be performed with great care. Rotations may be effective but should be performed gently, as patients with disk prolapse may be made considerably worse with aggressive mobilization. Manipulation is contraindicated in conditions with acute neurological signs and symptoms.

Traction is often helpful in the treatment of acute disk prolapse with distal symptoms. However, it is not uncommon for the patient to experience considerable pain relief while undergoing traction, only to have increased symptoms after treatment.

A transforaminal epidural injection of corticosteroid may help if there is no significant improvement in symptoms and signs with rest.

Surgery may be required if neurological signs persist or worsen. If bowel or bladder symptoms are present, emergency surgery—microsurgical decompression—may be necessary. An open laminectomy or percutaneous diskectomy using a needle aspiration technique may be performed.

As the acute episode settles, it is important to restore normal pain-free movement to the area with localized mobilization and stretching. Following restoration of range of movement, active stabilization exercises should be performed. This is discussed later in this chapter. Postural advice, including correction of poor lifting techniques and adjustment of sporting technique, where necessary, is most important.

Stress fracture of the pars interarticularis

Stress fractures of the pars interarticularis (spondylolysis) (Fig. 26.14a) was initially thought to be congenital, but is probably an acquired overuse injury. It occurs in young sportspeople involved in sports that require episodes of hyperextension, especially if combined with rotation.[15] Sports in which this injury is commonly seen include gymnastics, fast bowling (cricket), tennis, rowing, dance, weightlifting, wrestling, pole vaulting, and high jump, as well as throwing activities such as baseball pitching, javelin, discus, and hammer throw.

The fracture usually occurs on the side opposite to the one performing the activity (i.e. left-sided fractures in right-handed tennis players).

Clinical features

Although stress fractures of the pars interarticularis are occasionally asymptomatic, patients usually complain of:

- unilateral low backache, occasionally associated with somatic buttock pain
- pain that is aggravated by movements involving lumbar extension—the athlete may describe a single episode of hyperextension that precipitated the pain.

On examination:

- pain is produced on extension with rotation and on extension while standing on the affected leg (Fig. 26.3g)

- there is often an excessive lordotic posture with associated spasm of the hamstring muscles
- palpation reveals unilateral tenderness over the site of the fracture.

In cases with recent onset of pain, X-ray may not demonstrate the fracture. In longstanding cases, the typical "Scotty dog" appearance of a pars defect is demonstrated on the 45° oblique X-ray. When a pars defect is suspected clinically but plain X-ray is normal, an isotopic bone scan, single photon emission computed tomography (SPECT) scan (Fig. 26.14b), or MRI should be performed. The latter is the most widely used investigation for this condition in most countries. Even when the X-ray demonstrates a pars defect, a SPECT scan should be performed to confirm the presence of an active stress fracture.

Patients with a positive SPECT scan result should then undergo reverse gantry CT scanning to image the fracture (Fig. 26.14c). The patient should be monitored during the healing process, both clinically and by repeat CT scan of the fracture. MRI (Fig. 26.14d overleaf) is a popular investigation for demonstrat-

ing a pars fracture but may not be as sensitive as a combination of a SPECT and CT scan.

Treatment

There is considerable variation in the recommended treatment for pars stress fractures. Almost all clinicians agree on the need for restricting the athletic activity responsible for the pain, stretching the hamstring and gluteal muscles, and strengthening the

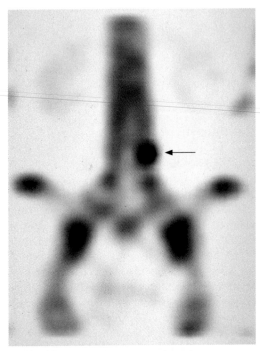

(b) SPECT scan showing increased uptake

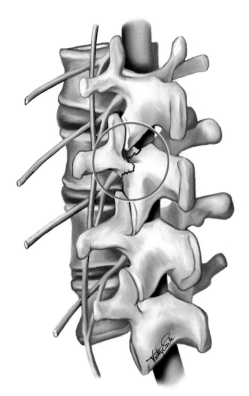

Figure 26.14 Stress fracture of the pars interarticularis
(a) Side view

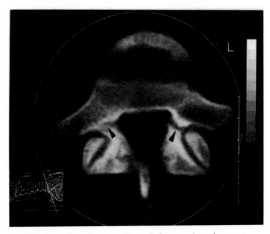

(c) CT scan showing previous (left arrow) and recent (right arrow) fractures

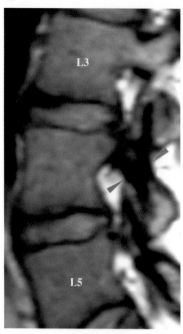

(d) MRI scan showing pars interarticularis stress fracture   COURTESY OF DR CRAIG ENGSTROM

abdominal and back extensor muscles as soon as these can be performed pain-free. However, the use of rigid anti-lordotic bracing is debated.

It is the stage and site of the defect rather than the type of treatment that determines healing of the bony defect.[20] Pars defects can be divided into early, progressive, and terminal stages.

The early stage is characterized by focal bony absorption or a hairline defect on radiographic appearance. In the progressive stage, the defect is wide and small fragments are present. Sclerotic change indicates the terminal stage of development. In most cases of early stage defects, radiographic union will be achieved; however, radiographic union will only be achieved in approximately half the progressive stage cases and virtually none of the cases with sclerotic changes.

A unilateral defect is more likely to heal than bilateral defects. There is also an improved rate of union in defects at L4 compared with defects at L5 and in lesions closer to the vertebral body.

Therefore, it is important to make an early diagnosis and commence a treatment program consisting of rest from sport and rehabilitation.

We believe that there should not be a set period of time for a treatment program, but that the patient should undergo a rehabilitation program initially involving pain-free progressive exercises but not aggravating activity (i.e. lumbar extension and rotation). When the aggravating maneuvers are pain-free and there is no local tenderness, a gradual progressive resumption of the aggravating activity over a period of four to six weeks should be conducted using pain as a guide.

O'Sullivan et al.'s landmark study[21] of the effectiveness of a specific exercise program emphasizing training of the transversus abdominis and multifidus in adults with spondylolysis and spondylolisthesis showed dramatic differences in pain scores and improved function that was maintained for 30 months compared with a control group who were treated with general fitness training, supervised exercise, modalities, and trunk flexion exercises. A core stability training program (Chapter 14) should be included in the treatment program.

As with any overuse injury, it is important to identify the cause or causes, and to correct them if possible. Technique adjustments should be made to limit the amount of hyperextension and, if necessary, a brace can be used during sporting activity.

This injury is extremely common among young fast bowlers in cricket. Fast bowlers use one of three techniques—side-on, front-on, or a mixed technique where the lower half of the body is front-on and the upper half side-on. It is this latter combined technique that appears to be associated with the development of stress fractures of the pars interarticularis.[22] The bowler and coach should be advised to change to either a side-on or front-on technique.

Spondylolisthesis

Spondylolisthesis refers to the slipping of part or all of one vertebra forward on another (Fig. 26.15a). The term is derived from the Greek *spondylos*, meaning "vertebra," and *olisthanein*, meaning "to slip or slide down a slippery path."

Spondylolisthesis is often associated with bilateral pars defects that usually develop in early childhood and have a definite family predisposition. Pars defects that develop due to athletic activity (stress fractures) rarely result in spondylolisthesis.

Spondylolisthesis is most commonly seen in children between the ages of 9 and 14. In the vast majority of cases it is the L5 vertebra that slips forward on the S1. The spondylolisthesis is graded according to the degree of slip of the vertebra. A grade I slip denotes that a vertebra has slipped up to 25% over the body of the vertebra underlying it; in a grade II slip, the displacement is greater than 25%; in a grade III slip, greater than 50%; and in a grade IV slip, greater than 75%. Lateral X-rays best demonstrate the extent of vertebral slippage (Fig. 26.15b).

Clinical features

Grade I spondylolisthesis is often asymptomatic and the patients may be unaware of the defect. Patients with grade II or higher slips may complain of low back pain, with or without leg pain. The back pain is aggravated by extension activities.

On examination, there may be a palpable dip corresponding to the slip. Associated soft tissue abnormalities may be present. In considering the treatment of this condition, it is important to remember that the patient's low back pain is not necessarily being caused by the spondylolisthesis.

Treatment

Treatment of sportspeople with grade I or grade II symptomatic spondylolisthesis is usually nonsurgical. Most cases of acute unilateral spondylolytic lesions heal over the course of a suitable treatment program, and 50% of acute bilateral lesions that are diagnosed early resolve using similar methods.[23]

A treatment program may include:

- rest from aggravating activities combined with abdominal and extensor stabilizing exercises and hamstring stretching
- antilordotic bracing that involves the application of a thoracolumbar spinal orthosis for 3–6 months to reduce lumbar lordosis
- mobilization of stiff joints above or below the slip on clinical assessment; gentle rotations may be helpful in reducing pain; manipulation should not be performed at the level of the slip.

A treatment plan may include three months of brace wearing (for more than 20 hours per day) while not participating in any sporting activities, followed by three months of brace wearing while performing select sporting activities.[24] Athletes with grade I or grade II spondylolisthesis may return to sport after treatment when they are pain-free on extension and have good spinal stabilization. If the symptoms recur, activity must be ceased.

Athletes with grade III or grade IV spondylolisthesis should avoid high speed or contact sports. Treatment is symptomatic. It is rare for a slip to progress; however, if there is evidence of progression, spinal fusion surgery should be performed. If a patient continues

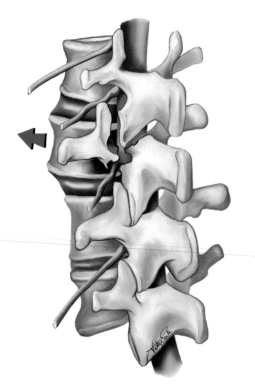

Figure 26.15 Grade I spondylolisthesis and pars defect **(a)** Side view

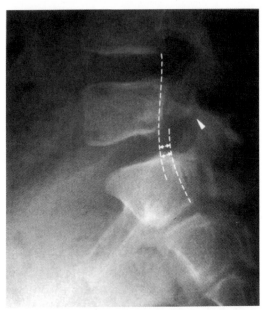

(b) X-ray (single arrow shows the defect; dotted lines show the method of measuring slippage)

to experience symptoms after a 6-month non-surgical treatment period, they should be considered for surgical treatment. Other indications for surgery include growing children with a slip of greater than 50%.[23]

Lumbar hypermobility

The majority of cases of low back pain are associated with hypomobility of one or more intervertebral segments. However, occasionally, hypermobility of an intervertebral segment may be detected on clinical assessment.

This hypermobility may be associated with a general hypermobility syndrome affecting all vertebral and peripheral joints. It is important to recognize this hypermobility syndrome because an isolated segment of reduced mobility in a generally hypermobile spine may have clinical significance.

Structural lumbar instability

The finding of an isolated hypermobile intervertebral segment may be indicative of lumbar instability. Recognition of this condition is important as it will not respond to the mobilization and manipulation techniques used to restore pain-free movement in most patients with low back pain. Treatment of lumbar instability involves retraining and strengthening of the spinal extensors and the abdominal muscles to increase stability. Any hypomobility of surrounding intervertebral segments causing pain should be treated with mobilization.

Sacroiliac joint disorders

Sacroiliac joint disorders are an important cause of low back and buttock pain, and are discussed fully in Chapter 27.

Rehabilitation following low back pain

Low back pain is usually mechanical in nature. Therefore, to eliminate and prevent recurrence of low back pain, biomechanical modification is required to reduce or eliminate the stress or stresses that are responsible for, or aggravating, the back pain. This may be a sustained mechanical stress (e.g. prolonged sitting with poor posture) or an intermittent stress (e.g. running with excessive lumbar lordosis).

Rehabilitation of the sportsperson with low back pain involves two main principles:

1. Modify activities to reduce stress to the lumbar spine. These activities include posture, activities of daily living, and sporting technique.

2. Correct predisposing biomechanical abnormalities that may be due to
   (a) generalized muscle weakness
   (b) tight muscles
   (c) poor muscle control.

The best results in the management of low back pain appear to come with a combination of therapies.[25] It is important to remember that spinal exercises should not be done in the first hour after waking, due to the increased hydrostatic pressures in the disk during that time.[26]

Posture

Prolonged poor posture places excessive strain on pain-provoking structures of the lumbar spine. Poor posture can occur while sitting, standing, or lying.

Adopting a slouched position while sitting (Fig. 26.16a) is extremely common. The correct position is shown in Figure 26.16b. A firm, straight-backed chair provides more support than a soft armchair or couch. The use of a lumbar roll encourages correct posture by increasing the lumbar lordosis. The lumbar roll should be placed just above the belt line in the hollow of the back (Fig. 26.16c).

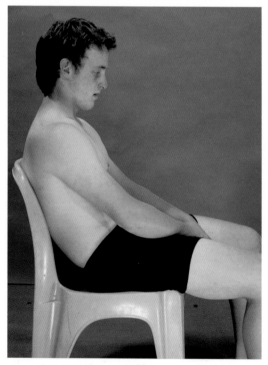

Figure 26.16 Sitting posture
(a) Slouched

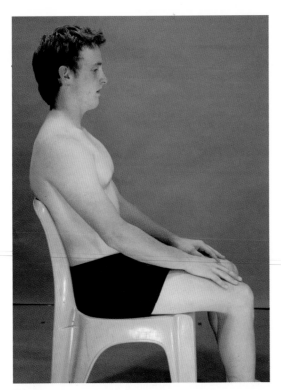

(b) Correct

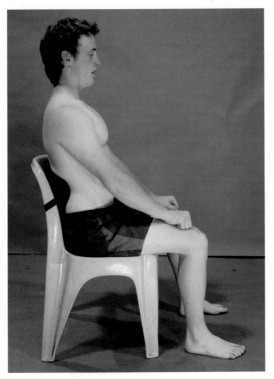

(c) Sitting with lumbar roll

Standing with a hyperlordotic posture (Fig. 26.17a overleaf) will also place excessive strain on the structures of the lumbar spine. The correct standing position should be adopted (Fig. 26.17b overleaf). When lying, the patient needs a firm, comfortable mattress. If the bed has a tendency to sag, the mattress should be placed on the floor.

Daily activities

For those people for whom excessive or prolonged lumbar flexion aggravates their low back pain, care must be taken to avoid such activities. Patients required to perform a task low down should lower themselves to the level required while maintaining the back as vertical as possible. The patient should be advised to avoid lifting as much as possible but, when unavoidable, correct technique should be used (Fig. 26.18 overleaf). There is some evidence that the key factor is the distance the object is from the body, rather than an absolutely correct technique.[5] Care should also be taken when the patient is required to pick up a relatively light object. Often patients with low back pain take great care when lifting heavy objects, but fail to brace their lumbar spine while picking up light objects. Activities that require prolonged bending and twisting, such as vacuuming, are best avoided or modified if they produce low back pain.

Sporting technique

Poor technique in sporting activities may increase stress on the structures of the lumbar spine. The technique should be assessed with the aid of a coach, and any necessary corrections made under supervision. Poor muscle control or weakness may contribute to the technique fault and are discussed in the next section.

Biomechanical abnormalities (such as excessive anterior or lateral pelvic tilt with running) are common predisposing factors to the development of low back pain. These factors may increase stress on the lumbar spine. Unless corrected, recurrence of the sportsperson's low back pain is likely.

Core stability

Impaired core stability with delayed onset of action of the transversus abdominis muscle has been shown to be associated with low back pain.

An important component of rehabilitation of patients with low back pain is to correct deficiency of core

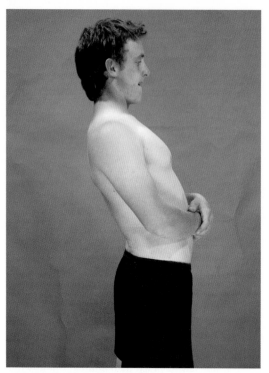

Figure 26.17 Standing posture
(a) Hyperlordotic

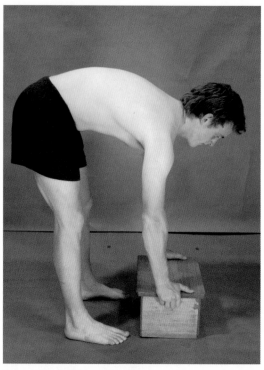

Figure 26.18 Lifting technique
(a) Incorrect

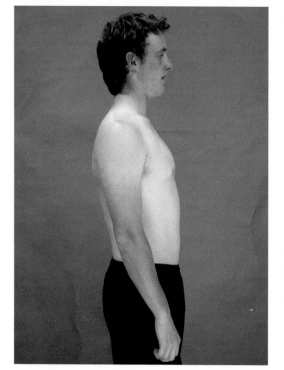

(b) Correct

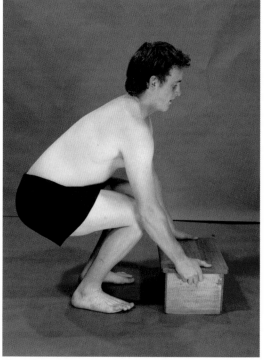

(b) Correct

stability. A core stability program is described in Chapter 14.

Once activation of the spine stabilizers (transversus abdominis and lumbar multifidus) has been achieved, global muscle strengthening should commence. In patients with low back pain, particular emphasis should be placed on strengthening the gluteal and hamstring muscles.

Adequate gluteal strength is required for pelvic control. Lack of pelvic control may lead to anterior tilting of the pelvis and increased stress on the lumbar spine. It is important that the gluteal muscles are activated during lifting and bending. Gluteal strengthening exercises should be performed while controlling pelvic movement (Fig. 26.19). The single-leg squat (Fig. 26.20 overleaf) is an excellent rehabilitation exercise combining motor control and strengthening.

Specific muscle tightness

Specific muscle tightness or shortening is commonly found in association with low back pain. Commonly shortened muscles include the erector spinae, psoas, iliotibial band, hip external rotators, hamstrings, rectus femoris, and gastrocnemius. Tightness of these muscles affects the biomechanics of the lumbar

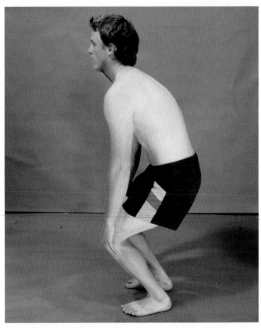

(b) Bending with gluteals but using lumbar flexion

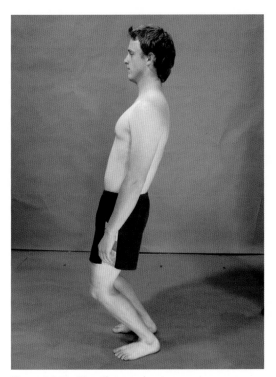

Figure 26.19 Gluteal strengthening
(a) Bending at the knee without using gluteals

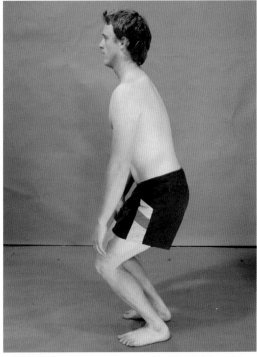

(c) Bending with gluteals and braced lumbar spine—this is the recommended exercise

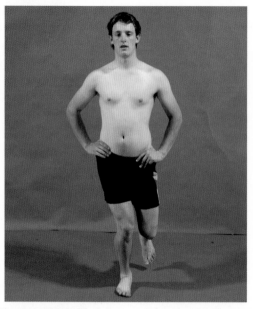

Figure 26.20 Single-leg squat—gluteal strengthening and motor control

spine. These tight muscles should be corrected as part of the rehabilitation program. The various techniques are shown in Figure 26.21.

Muscle tightness may be corrected by the use of therapist-assisted exercises, home exercises, soft tissue therapy to the muscles, and dry needling of trigger points.

Conclusion

The clinical approach to the sportsperson with low back pain is relatively straightforward. It involves initial assessment of abnormalities of the joints, muscles, and neural structures. These abnormalities are then systematically corrected by the use of manual therapy techniques. Associated with this correction of abnormalities, a comprehensive rehabilitation program must be performed, including correction of any biomechanical factors that place increased stress on the lumbar spine in the particular sportsperson. This requires individual assessment of abnormalities of technique, muscle weakness, muscle tightness, or

Muscle	Self-exercise	Assisted exercise	Myofascial release
Erector spinae	stretch here		Patient is side-lying. Therapist's wrists are crossed over each other to provide traction.
Psoas	or back vertical		Therapist's hand is over the psoas. Hip is extended from the flexed position.
Iliotibial band		Patient is side-lying and facing away. Hip is extended and adducted.	Patient is side-lying and facing away. Therapist uses elbow/forearm to perform release.

Figure 26.21 Techniques used to treat tightness of individual muscles

poor muscle control. There is now considerable evidence that inability to use the stabilizing muscles, transversus abdominis and lumbar multifidus, are important features of patients with low back pain, and a specific rehabilitation program must be instituted to correct these deficits. Low back pain provides another example of the integrated approach required in the management of sporting injuries.

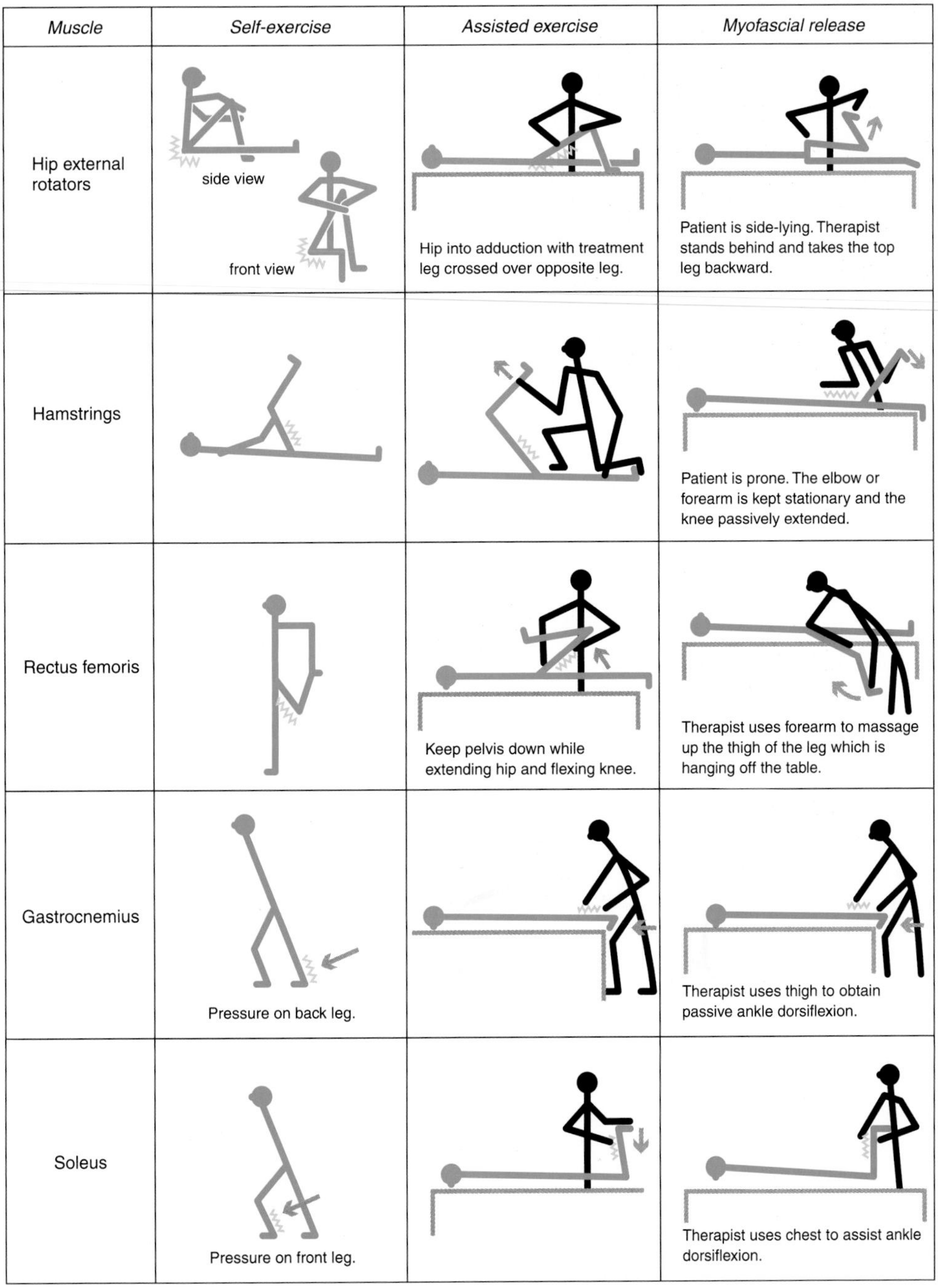

B

Muscle	Self-exercise	Assisted exercise	Myofascial release
Hip external rotators	side view / front view	Hip into adduction with treatment leg crossed over opposite leg.	Patient is side-lying. Therapist stands behind and takes the top leg backward.
Hamstrings			Patient is prone. The elbow or forearm is kept stationary and the knee passively extended.
Rectus femoris		Keep pelvis down while extending hip and flexing knee.	Therapist uses forearm to massage up the thigh of the leg which is hanging off the table.
Gastrocnemius	Pressure on back leg.		Therapist uses thigh to obtain passive ankle dorsiflexion.
Soleus	Pressure on front leg.		Therapist uses chest to assist ankle dorsiflexion.

Figure 26.21 (cont.) Techniques used to treat tightness of individual muscles

⊕ RECOMMENDED WEBSITES

An educational tool about low back pain can be found at www.lowbackpain.tv

🗎 RECOMMENDED READING

Bogduk N. *Clinical anatomy of the lumbar spine and sacrum.* 4th edn. Edinburgh: Churchill Livingstone, 2005.

Dvorak J, Dvorak V, Gilliar W et al. eds. *Musculoskeletal manual medicine.* Stuttgart, Germany: Georg Thieme Verlag, 2008.

Licciardone JC, Brimhall AK, King LN. Osteopathic manipulative treatment for low back pain: a systematic review and meta-analysis of randomized controlled trials. *BMC Musculoskelet Disord* 2005;6:43–54.

Maitland GD. *Vertebral manipulation.* 5th edn. London: Butterworths, 1986.

Nadler SF, Malanga GA, DePrince M et al. The relationship between lower extremity injury, low back pain, and hip muscle strength in male and female collegiate athletes. *Clin J Sport Med* 2000;10(2):89–97.

Richardson C, Jull G, Hodges P et al. *Therapeutic exercise for spinal segmental stabilization in low back pain.* 2nd edn. Edinburgh: Churchill Livingstone, 2004.

🗒 REFERENCES

1. Hides JA, Stokes MJ, Saide M et al. Evidence of lumbar multifidus muscle wasting ipsilateral to symptoms in patients with acute/subacute low back pain. *Spine (Phila Pa 1976)* 1994;19(2):165-72.
2. Carlson C. Axial back pain in the athlete: pathophysiology and approach to rehabilitation. *Curr Rev Musculoskelet Med* 2009;2(2):88–93.
3. Freeman MD, Woodham MA, Woodham AW. The role of the lumbar multifidus in chronic low back pain: a review. *PM R* 2010;2(2):142–6.
4. Hodges PW, Richardson CA. Inefficient muscular stabilization of the lumbar spine associated with low back pain. A motor control evaluation of transversus abdominis. *Spine (Phila Pa 1976)* 1996;21(22):2640–50.
5. Hodges PW, Richardson CA. Delayed postural contraction of transversus abdominis in low back pain associated with movement of the lower limb. *J Spinal Disord* 1998;11(1):46–56.
6. Sihvonen T, Lindgren KA, Airaksinen O et al. Movement disturbances of the lumbar spine and abnormal back muscle electromyographic findings in recurrent low back pain. *Spine (Phila Pa 1976)* 1997;22(3):289–95.

7. McGill S. *Low back disorders: evidence-based prevention and rehabilitation.* Champaign, IL: Human Kinetics, 2002.
8. Donelson R, Aprill C, Medcalf R et al. A prospective study of centralization of lumbar and referred pain. A predictor of symptomatic discs and anular competence. *Spine (Phila Pa 1976)* 1997;22(10):1115–22.
9. Deyo RA, Diehl AK, Rosenthal M. How many days of bed rest for acute low back pain? A randomized clinical trial. *N Engl J Med* 1986;315(17):1064–70.
10. Kuijpers T, van Middelkoop M, Rubinstein SM et al. A systematic review on the effectiveness of pharmacological interventions for chronic non-specific low-back pain. *Eur Spine J* 2011 Jan;20(1):40–50.
11. Furlan AD, van Tulder M, Cherkin D et al. Acupuncture and dry-needling for low back pain: an updated systematic review within the framework of the cochrane collaboration. *Spine (Phila Pa 1976)* 2005;30(8):944–63.
12. Shen FH, Samartzis D, Andersson GB. Nonsurgical management of acute and chronic low back pain. *J Am Acad Orthop Surg* 2006;14(8):477–87.
13. Lord SM, Barnsley L, Bogduk N. The utility of comparative local anesthetic blocks versus placebo-controlled blocks for the diagnosis of cervical zygapophysial joint pain. *Clin J Pain* 1995;11(3):208–13.
14. Dreyfuss P, Halbrook B, Pauza K et al. Efficacy and validity of radiofrequency neurotomy for chronic lumbar zygapophysial joint pain. *Spine (Phila Pa 1976)* 2000;25(10):1270–7.
15. van Kleef M, Barendse GA, Kessels A et al. Randomized trial of radiofrequency lumbar facet denervation for chronic low back pain. *Spine (Phila Pa 1976)* 1999;24(18):1937–42.
16. Yin W, Willard F, Carreiro J et al. Sensory stimulation-guided sacroiliac joint radiofrequency neurotomy: technique based on neuroanatomy of the dorsal sacral plexus. *Spine (Phila Pa 1976)* 2003;28(20):2419–25.
17. Pauza KJ, Howell S, Dreyfuss P et al. A randomized, placebo-controlled trial of intradiscal electrothermal therapy for the treatment of discogenic low back pain. *Spine J* 2004;4(1):27–35.
18. Carragee EJ. The surgical treatment of disc degeneration: is the race not to the swift? *Spine J* 2005;5(6):587–8.
19. Deyo RA, Nachemson A, Mirza SK. Spinal-fusion surgery—the case for restraint. *N Engl J Med* 2004;350(7):722–6.
20. Brukner P, Bennell K, Matheson G. *Stress fractures.* Melbourne: Blackwells Scientific Asia, 1999.

21. O'Sullivan PB, Phyty GD, Twomey LT et al. Evaluation of specific stabilizing exercise in the treatment of chronic low back pain with radiologic diagnosis of spondylolysis or spondylolisthesis. *Spine (Phila Pa 1976)* 1997;22(24):2959–67.

22. Elliot B, Hardcastle P, Burnett A. The influence of fast bowling and physical factors on radiologic features in high performance young fast bowlers. *Sports Train Med Rehabil* 1992;3:113–30.

23. Tsirikos AI, Garrido EG. Spondylolysis and spondylolisthesis in children and adolescents. *J Bone Joint Surg Br* 2010;92(6):751–9.

24. Leone A, Cianfoni A, Cerase A et al. Lumbar spondylolysis: a review. *Skeletal Radiol* 2011;40(6):683–700.

25. Geisser ME, Wiggert EA, Haig AJ et al. A randomized, controlled trial of manual therapy and specific adjuvant exercise for chronic low back pain. *Clin J Pain* 2005;21(6):463–70.

26. Green JP, Grenier SG, McGill SM. Low-back stiffness is altered with warm-up and bench rest: implications for athletes. *Med Sci Sports Exerc* 2002;34(7):1076–81.

B

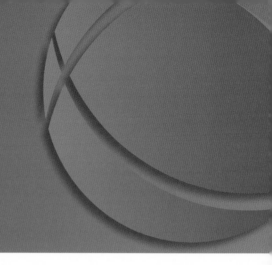

Chapter 27

Buttock pain

I can't hit a ball more than 200 yards. I have no butt. You need a butt if you're going to hit a golf ball. Dennis Quad, American actor and producer

Buttock pain is most commonly seen in athletes involved in kicking or sprinting sports. It can occur in isolation or it may be associated with low back or posterior thigh pain. Buttock pain or injuries such as pressure sores are also common in wheelchair athletes. Diagnosis of buttock pain can be difficult, as pain may arise from a number of local structures in the buttock or can be referred from the lumbar spine or sacroiliac joint (SIJ). The causes of buttock pain are shown in Table 27.1. The anatomy of the buttock region is shown in Figure 27.1.

Clinical approach

When assessing a patient with buttock pain, the clinician should attempt to determine whether the pain

is local or referred. Clues can be obtained from the nature and location of the athlete's pain. Examination may then identify which of the local or the potential pain-referring structures are causing the buttock pain. Investigation is of limited usefulness in the assessment of the patient with buttock pain.

History

A deep aching diffuse pain that is variable in site is an indication of referred pain. Buttock pain associated with low back pain suggests lumbar spine abnormality. Buttock pain associated with groin pain may suggest SIJ or hip involvement.

When the patient is easily able to localize pain of a fairly constant nature, the source is more likely to

Table 27.1 Causes of buttock pain

Common	Less common	Not to be missed
Referred pain	Quadratus femoris injuries	Spondyloarthropathies
• Lumbar spine	Piriformis conditions	• Ankylosing spondylitis
• Sacroiliac joint	• Impingement	• Reiter's syndrome (reactive
Hamstring origin tendinopathy	• Muscle strain	arthritis)
Ischiogluteal bursitis	Fibrous adhesions around sciatic	• Psoriatic arthritis
Myofascial pain	nerve	• Arthritis associated with
	Prolapsed intervertebral disk	inflammatory bowel disease
	(Chapter 26)	Malignancy
	Chronic compartment syndrome of	Bone and joint infection
	the posterior thigh	
	Stress fracture of the sacrum	
	Proximal hamstring origin avulsion	
	Apophysitis/avulsion fracture	
	• Ischial tuberosity (children)	
	Gluteus medius tendinopathy	
	(Chapter 28)	

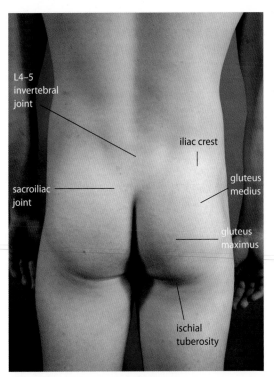

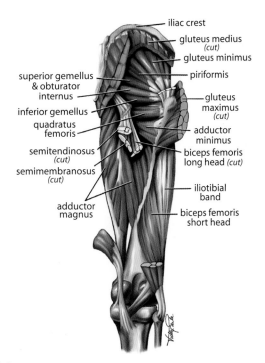

be in the buttock region itself. Pain constantly localized to the ischial tuberosity is usually due to either tendinopathy at the origin of the hamstring muscles or ischiogluteal bursitis. Pain and tenderness more proximally situated and medial to the greater trochanter may be from the piriformis muscle.

Pain aggravated by running, especially sprinting, is not diagnostic, as most conditions causing buttock pain may be aggravated by sprinting. Increased local pain on prolonged sitting may be an indication that ischiogluteal bursitis is the cause of the problem, although lumbar spine problems can be aggravated by sitting.

The timing of the buttock pain is important in establishing the nature of the diagnosis. Inflammatory pains such as those experienced in sacroiliitis as part of a spondyloarthropathy are typically worst in the morning and improve with light exercise. Such "morning stiffness" lasts at least 30 minutes. Other features that strongly suggest the presence of a spondyloarthropathy include associated enthesopathy such as Achilles tendinopathy or plantar fasciitis and multiple joint problems.

Figure 27.1 Anatomy of the buttocks
(a) Surface anatomy

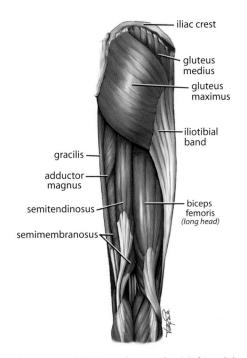

(b) Muscles of the buttock: superficial (left) and deep (right)

Examination

The slump test is an important part of the examination in attempting to differentiate between local and referred pain. However, not all cases of referred pain will have a positive slump test result. The lumbar spine should always be carefully examined, particularly for evidence of hypomobility or hypermobility of one or more intervertebral segments.

1. Observation
   (a) from behind (Fig. 27.2a)
   (b) from the side
2. Active movements—lumbar spine (Chapter 26)
   (a) flexion
   (b) extension
   (c) lateral flexion
   (d) combined movements
3. Active movements—hip joint
   (a) flexion/extension (Fig. 27.2b)
   (b) abduction/adduction
   (c) internal/external rotation
4. Passive movements
   (a) hip movements
   (b) hip quadrant—pain provocation test (Fig. 27.2c)
   (c) external rotator stretch (Fig. 27.2d)
   (d) hip extension (Fig. 27.2e)

5. Resisted movements
   (a) hip internal rotation (Fig. 27.2f)
   (b) hip external rotation (Fig. 27.2g)
   (c) knee flexion (Fig. 27.2h)
6. Palpation
   (a) sacroiliac joint (Fig. 27.2i)
   (b) gluteal muscles (Fig. 27.2j on page 496)
   (c) ischial tuberosity

(b) Active movement—hip flexion/extension

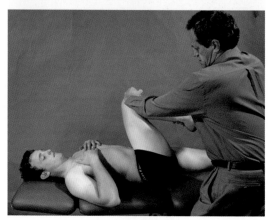

(c) Passive movement—hip quadrant (pain provocation test). The hip joint is placed into the quadrant position, which consists of flexion, adduction and internal rotation

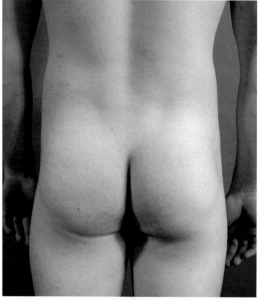

Figure 27.2 Examination of the patient with buttock pain

(a) Observation from behind may detect asymmetrical muscle wasting. Observation from the side may detect the presence of a lumbar lordosis or anterior pelvic tilt

(d) Muscle stretch—external rotators

(d)   sacrotuberous ligament

(e)   iliolumbar ligament

(f)   anterior superior iliac spines

7. Special tests

    (a)   slump test (Fig. 27.2k overleaf)

    (b)   lumbar spine examination (Chapter 26)

    (c)   sacroiliac tests

        (i)   stork test (Fig. 27.2l overleaf)

        (ii)   active straight leg raise (ASLR) (Fig. 27.2m overleaf)

        (iii)   Patrick or FABER test—flexion, abduction, external rotation (Fig. 27.2n on page 497)

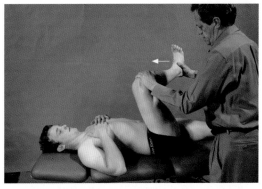

(g) Resisted movement—external rotation. Resisted external rotation from a position of internal rotation is used to isolate the piriformis muscle

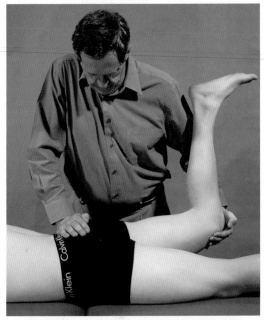

(e) Passive movement—hip extension. With the examiner's hand stabilizing the pelvis, the hip is passively extended

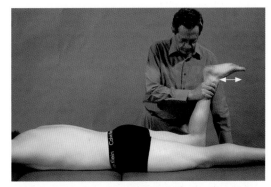

(h) Resisted movement—knee flexion. This should be performed both concentrically and eccentrically to reproduce hamstring origin pain

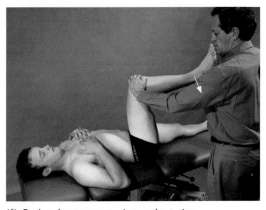

(f) Resisted movement—internal rotation

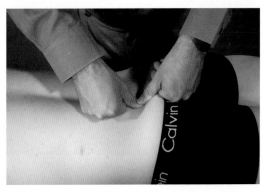

(i) Palpation—sacroiliac joint. The patient should be palpated in a posteroanterior direction over the region of the SIJ. This area also includes the iliolumbar ligament

B

495

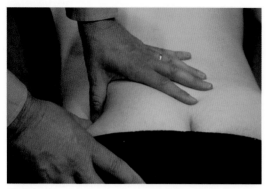

(j) Palpation—buttock. The patient should be lying prone with a pillow under the knee to place the hip into slight passive extension and relax the hip extensor muscles. Palpate from the hamstring origin across to the greater trochanter. Palpation of the gluteus medius, piriformis, and the external rotators should be performed in varying degrees of hip rotation

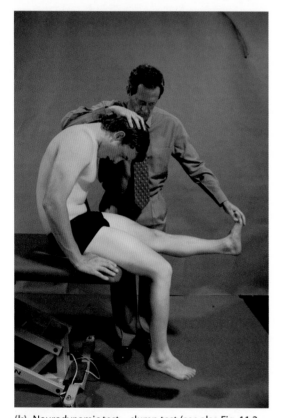

(k) Neurodynamic test—slump test (see also Fig. 11.2 on page 151). Reproduction of the patient's buttock pain in the starting position shown and relieving the pain with cervical extension is consistent with a positive slump test

(l) Stork test. The pelvis should not anteriorly/posteriorly/laterally tilt nor rotate in the transverse plane as the weight is shifted to the supporting limb

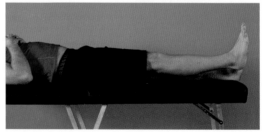

(m) Active straight leg raise (ASLR). This test involves the patient lying supine and lifting his leg to a height of 5cm

Investigations

A plain X-ray may demonstrate a stress fracture of the pars interarticularis, which may refer pain to the buttock. Spondylolisthesis may be evident. The presence of spondylolisthesis does not necessarily mean, however, that the slip is causing the patient's pain (Chapter 26).

X-ray may also show degenerative changes in the SIJ in the older athlete. Inflammatory sacroiliitis with loss of definition of the SIJ strongly suggests

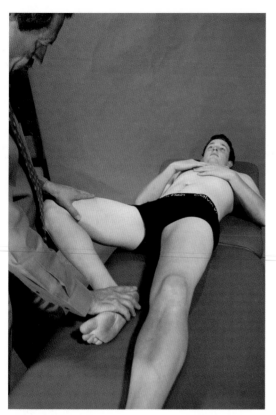

(n) FABER test—flexion, abduction, external rotation. Pain in the buttock with this test is suggestive of sacroiliac origin

a spondyloarthopathy. A recent consensus statement of rheumatologists and radiologists notes that a clear presence of bone marrow edema on MRI is essential for defining active sacroiliitis.[1]

X-rays of the ischial tuberosity in cases of chronic hamstring origin tendinopathy are usually normal; however, occasionally erosions can be demonstrated. In the adolescent, apophysitis or avulsion of the ischial tuberosity may be demonstrated.

Isotopic bone scan may show increased uptake in the region of the SIJ, or identify a stress fracture of the ischium, sacrum, or pubic ramus. Soft tissue ultrasound examination or MRI may image an enlarged or inflamed ischiogluteal bursa, or show evidence of chronic scarring at the hamstring origin.

Blood tests may indicate the presence of systemic disease. Useful screening tests are a full blood examination looking for a raised white cell count (suggesting possible infection), and erythrocyte sedimentation rate (which may be elevated in the presence of an inflammatory condition) (Chapter 55).

Referred pain from the lumbar spine

Buttock pain may be referred from the lumbar spine in the presence or absence of low back pain. Any of the somatic, innervated structures of the lumbar spine may refer pain to the buttock. Abnormalities are found most often in the intervertebral disks and the apophyseal joints. Spondylolysis and spondylolisthesis may also cause buttock pain.

The patient usually gives a history of a diffuse ache in the buttock that may vary in severity. The slump test (Fig. 27.2k) may reproduce the buttock pain with relief of pain on cervical spine extension. It has been shown that 80% of normal individuals reporting a sensory response from the slump test have relief of this response with cervical extension.[2]

A positive slump test result indicates increased neural mechanosensitivity. This may be due to damage to the nerve itself, or it may be secondary to lumbar spine abnormalities. Failure of the slump test to reproduce the patient's buttock pain does not necessarily rule out the possibility of referred pain as the cause of pain. Normative data on the slump test demonstrates that buttock pain is not a normal response to the slump test in healthy individuals.[2]

Palpation of the lumbar spine may reveal areas of tenderness and hypomobility of intervertebral segments. The best means of assessing whether a lumbar spine abnormality is the cause of buttock pain is to improve mobility of the stiff segments by mobilization or manipulation, and to reassess the symptoms and signs, both immediately after treatment and prior to the next treatment.

Local areas of buttock tenderness may occur with referred pain. In cases of longstanding referred pain, soft tissue abnormalities are usually found, especially in the gluteal muscles, external rotators, and lumbar multifidus. These include taut fibrous bands within muscles, and general muscle tightness. Active trigger points may refer pain in a characteristic distribution.

The treatment of lumbar disorders has been described in Chapter 26 and requires an integrated approach. Local electrotherapy can reduce pain and inflammation. Mobilization or manipulation may restore full mobility to stiff intervertebral segments. Soft tissue therapy and dry needling may be used to treat chronic muscle thickening both around the lumbar vertebrae and in the gluteal region. Specific stretching of the gluteal muscles and hip external rotators should be commenced if there is any evidence of tightness.

Neural mobilization such as the slump stretch should be included if there is evidence of restriction, but they should be used with caution. A recent systematic review found inconclusive evidence for the use of slump stretching for low back pain.[3] The patient should be shown an exercise program involving stretching and strengthening of the muscles supporting the lumbar spine (Chapter 26).

Sacroiliac joint disorders

The concept of the SIJ as a pain generator is now well established.[4] However, the evaluation and treatment of SIJ dysfunction remains controversial. One issue is the broad categorization and terminology utilized for the anatomical etiologies of the pain by various health professionals. Controversy also exists because of the complex anatomy and biomechanics of the SIJ.

There is no specific symptom or cluster of symptoms, nor any specific examination technique, that is both sensitive and specific for the diagnosis of SIJ abnormalities. However, two recent studies have demonstrated that positive findings on a combination of pain provocation and motion palpation tests reliably indicate SIJ dysfunction.[5, 6]

There are no imaging studies that distinguish the asymptomatic from the symptomatic patient.[4] Traditionally, local anesthetic blocks were considered the gold standard for diagnosing the SIJ as a source of pain.[7] However, it is possible that anesthetic diffuses out of the joint in some cases and may affect surrounding ligaments and nerve roots, including the lumbosacral trunk. This may reduce the specificity of SIJ anesthetic blocks as a diagnostic tool.[8]

In patients with low back pain, the prevalence of sacroiliac pain, diagnosed by local anesthetic blocks, is 15%.[9, 10] The incidence may be even higher in high level sportspeople. One study showed an incidence of over 50% in elite rowers.[11]

Functional anatomy

The SIJ is diarthrodial (synovial anterior and fibrous posterior). Its joint surfaces are reciprocally shaped but not congruent, have a high friction coefficient, and have two large elevations allowing interdigitation with the reciprocal surface. Age changes begin to occur on the iliac side of the joint as early as the third decade. The joint surface irregularities increase with age and seem to be related to weight-bearing. The capsule becomes more thickened and fibrous

with age. The ligaments of the SIJ are shown in Figure 27.3.[12]

SIJ motion is best described as a combination of flexion and extension, superior and inferior glide, and anterior and posterior translation. SIJ motion is minimal, with approximately 2.5° of rotation and 0.7 mm (0.3 in.) of translation,[7] and it is best regarded as a stress-relieving joint in conjunction with the pubic symphysis.

In the normal gait cycle, combined movements occur conversely in the right and left innominate bones, and function in connection with the sacrum and spine. Throughout this cycle, there is also rotatory motion at the pubic symphysis, which is essential for normal motion through the joint. In static stance, when one bends forward and the lumbar spine regionally extends, the sacrum regionally flexes, with the base moving forward and the apex moving posteriorly. During this motion, both innominates go into a motion of external rotation and out-flaring. This combination of motion during forward flexion is referred to as nutation of the pelvis. The opposite occurs in extension and is called counternutation.

SIJ dysfunction refers to an abnormal function (e.g. hypomobility or hypermobility) at the joint, which places stresses on structures in or around it. Therefore, SIJ dysfunction may contribute to lumbar, buttock, hamstring, or groin pain.

The precise etiology of sacroiliac dysfunction is uncertain. Osteopaths describe a number of dysfunctions associated with hypomobility, including:

- innominate shears, superior and inferior
- innominate rotations, anterior and posterior
- innominate in-flare and out-flare
- sacral torsions, flexion and extension
- unilateral sacral lesions, flexion and extension.

Vleeming and colleagues[13] have described their integrated model of joint dysfunction. It integrates structure (form and anatomy), function (forces and motor control), and the mind (emotions and awareness). Integral to the biomechanics of SIJ stability is the concept of a self-locking mechanism. The ability of the SIJ to self-lock occurs through two types of closure—form and force.

Form closure describes how specifically shaped, closely fitting contacts provide inherent stability independent of external load. Force closure describes how external compression forces add additional stability. The fascia and muscles within the region provide significant self-bracing and self-locking to the SIJ and

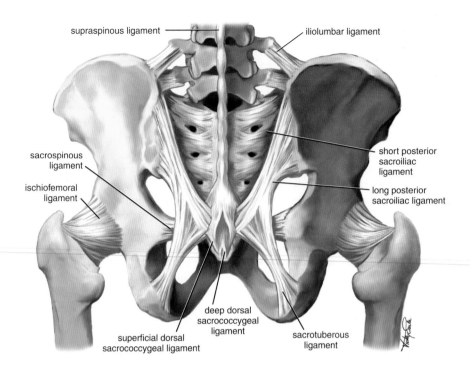

(a)

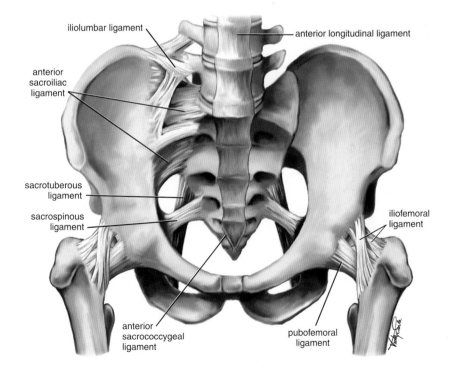

(b)

Figure 27.3 Ligaments of the sacroiliac joint
(a) posterior view **(b)** anterior view

its ligaments through their cross-like anatomical configuration. As shown in Figure 27.4, this is formed ventrally by the external abdominal obliques, linea alba, internal abdominal obliques, and transverse abdominals; dorsally the latissimus dorsi, thoracolumbar fascia, gluteus maximus, and iliotibial tract contribute significantly. The fibers of the internal oblique and transversus abdominus muscles are orientated perpendicular to the SIJ and are hence best positioned to provide force closure.[14, 15]

Vleeming et al. further proposed that the posterior layer of the thoracolumbar fascia acted to transfer load from the ipsilateral latissimus dorsi to the contralateral gluteus maximus.[13] This load transfer is thought to be critical during rotation of the trunk, helping to stabilize the lower lumbar spine and pelvis.

A connection has also been shown between the biceps femoris muscle and the sacrotuberous ligament, allowing the hamstring to play an integral role in the intrinsic stability of the SIJ. The biceps femoris, which is frequently found to be shortened on the side

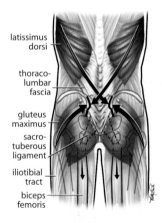

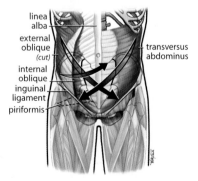

Figure 27.4 The cross-like configuration demonstrating the force closure of the sacroiliac joint

of the SIJ dysfunction, may act to compensate to help stabilize the joint.

Clinical features

The patient with SIJ pain classically describes low back pain below L5. The pain is usually restricted to one side but may occasionally be bilateral. SIJ disorders commonly refer to the buttock, groin, and posterolateral thigh. Occasionally, SIJ pain refers to the scrotum or labia.

Broadhurst[16] describes a clinically useful description of pelvic/SIJ dysfunction. Clinically, the patient has deep-seated buttock pain, difficulty in negotiating stairs, and problems rolling over in bed, with a triad of signs—pain over the SIJ, tenderness over the sacrospinous and sacrotuberous ligaments, and pain reproduction over the pubic symphysis.

Precipitating factors for the development of SIJ disorders may include muscle imbalance between the hip flexors and extensors or between the external and internal rotators of the hip, leg length imbalance, and biomechanical abnormalities (such as excessive subtalar pronation).

The physical examination should begin by observation of the sportsperson both statically and dynamically. The patient should be evaluated in standing, supine, and prone positions, and symmetry assessed in the heights of the iliac spines, anterior superior iliac spines, posterior superior iliac spines, ischial tuberosities, gluteal folds, and greater trochanters, as well as symmetry of the sacral sulci, inferior lateral angles, and pubic tubercles.

Leg length discrepancy should be assessed. True leg length discrepancies will generally cause asymmetry and pain, whereas a functional leg length discrepancy is usually the result of SIJ and/or pelvic dysfunction. Dynamic observation may reveal a decrease in stride length with walking, leading to a limp, or a Trendelenburg gait due to reflex inhibition of the gluteus medius.

Muscle strength and flexibility should be assessed. Full assessment of the hips and lumbar spine should also be performed. The presence of trigger points in surrounding muscles, particularly gluteus medius, should be noted. Palpation over the SIJ may reveal local tenderness.

Numerous clinical tests have been described to assess SIJ function; however, individually these tests are often unreliable. Positive findings on multiple SIJ tests are a more reliable indication of SIJ dysfunction.[5, 6] Some of the more popular tests include standing and seated flexion tests, the stork test (Fig. 27.2l), the ASLR test (Fig. 27.2m), and the Patrick or FABER test (Fig. 27.2n).

The ASLR test is thought to test the quality of load transfer through the lumbopelvic region.[17] This test involves the patient lying supine and lifting his or her leg to a height of 5 cm. A subjective feeling of heaviness in the leg, and observations of excessive abdominal muscle bracing and altered respiratory patterns may indicate SIJ instability. A positive ASLR test is recorded if these observations improve with manual compression of the ilia.[17]

There is no specific gold standard imaging test to diagnose SIJ dysfunction due to the location of the joint and overlying structures that make visualization difficult.[4]

Treatment

To reflect the complex nature of the SIJ and its surrounding structures, a multitude of treatment techniques have been advocated and described in the literature. In an athletic population, treatment should focus on the entire abdomino-lumbo-sacro-pelvic-hip complex, addressing articular, muscular, neural, and fascial restrictions, inhibitions, and deficiencies.[4]

Initial treatment may focus on symptom relief but ultimately treatment should address the underlying pathology. For example, if a true leg length discrepancy is assessed, then shoe inserts may be appropriate to distribute loads evenly across the pelvis.[12]

Core stability training (Chapter 14) should be included. One study has suggested that the clinical benefits incurred with training the transversus abdominis muscle may be due to significantly reduced laxity in the SIJ.[18] Exercise rehabilitation is an integral part of recovery from SIJ dysfunction. Pelvic or SIJ dysfunction should be considered with the lumbar spine in any program designed to improve the overall control of the lumbopelvic area.

Stretching and soft tissue therapy are useful in correcting pelvic/SIJ imbalance. The most common soft tissue abnormalities found with unilateral anterior tilt are tight psoas and rectus femoris muscles. A technique to reduce psoas tightness is shown in Figure 27.5.

Muscle energy techniques (Chapter 13) may also be helpful, as may osteopathic-, chiropractic-, and physiotherapy-based manipulation techniques. These techniques are often used to address altered gait mechanics and spine malalignment issues. Sacroiliac belts may be useful in the initial phases

Figure 27.5 Soft tissue therapy—psoas. Sustained longitudinal pressure is applied to the psoas muscle fibers, superior to the inguinal ligament, with the hip initially flexed and slowly moved into increased extension

of management, but not in the long term. Once soft tissue abnormalities have been resolved, contributing factors such as posture, lifestyle habits, or training errors should also be addressed, to prevent recurrence.

If these manual techniques fail to control the sacroiliac pain, injection therapy may prove useful. A combination of local anesthetic and corticosteroid agents may be injected into the region of the SIJ, as shown in Figure 27.6 overleaf, preferably under fluoroscopic or ultrasound guidance. Sclerosants are occasionally used when hypermobility is present, sometimes referred to as prolotherapy.

Prolotherapy usually involves the injection of a sclerosing agent into the extra-articular ligaments, such as the dorsal interosseous ligament. The aim of prolotherapy is to reduce pain by reducing excessive joint movement (refer to Chapter 13 for more information). A recent prospective case study reported significant improvements in subjective and clinical outcomes at a two-year follow-up, after three

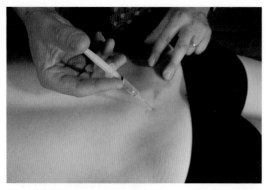

Figure 27.6 Corticosteroid injection to the region of the SIJ. Injection is directed inferolaterally

prolotherapy injections were administered six weeks apart.[19]

Iliolumbar ligament sprain

The iliolumbar ligament extends from the transverse process of the fifth lumbar vertebrae to the posterior part of the iliac crest. Sprain of this ligament may cause sacroiliac pain, particularly at its iliac attachment. It is almost impossible, however, to differentiate clinically between pain from this ligament and pain from the SIJ and its associated ligaments.

Slouching involves a combined movement of posterior pelvic tilt and lumbar spine forward flexion. The dorsal spinal muscles are thought to have a protective role both statically and dynamically around the lumbar spine and pelvis during this position.[20] However, in the case of muscle fatigue, wasting, or delayed muscle response (such as in the presence of pain), the forces impact on passive structures such as the iliolumbar ligament, and therefore make it susceptible injury.[20] Consequently sportspeople should be advised to avoid slouching in the presence of low back injury/pain to avoid further injury.

There is level I evidence that the iliolumbar ligament, as well as the other extra-articular SIJ ligaments (sacrospinous, sacrotuberous, dorsal, and ventral sacroiliac) may sometimes be a source of pain in provocative SIJ tests.[8] Therefore, in addition to their biomechanical roles, these ligaments should be considered as a potential source of pain. The same study concluded that corticosteroid injections may diffuse within these ligaments, providing pain relief.[8] Injection of a mixture of local anesthetic and corticosteroid agents to the insertion of the iliolumbar ligament at the iliac crest may also be effective.

Useful techniques to mobilize the soft tissues and joints of this region are shown in Figures 27.7 and 27.8. These can be combined with passive hip extension.

Hamstring origin tendinopathy

Tendinopathy of the hamstring origin may occur near the ischial tuberosity after an acute tear that is inadequately treated or, more commonly, as a result of overuse.[21] It is frequently seen in sprinters and middle- to long-distance runners. It is often difficult to treat and is characterized by lower gluteal pain which is aggravated with sporting activity, especially sprinting and acceleration with running.

There may be a sudden onset of sharp pain; however, more often there is an insidious onset after a session of sprinting. On examination, there is local tenderness with pain on hamstring stretch and resisted contraction around the ischial tuberosity. The lesion may be found at the attachment

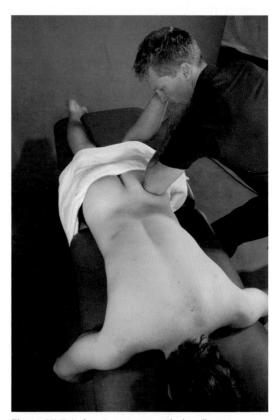

Figure 27.7 Ischemic pressure with the elbow to the origin of the hip external rotators and associated passive internal and external rotation of the hip

Figure 27.8 Ischemic pressure with the elbow to the hip abductors in the position of increased neural mechanosensitivity

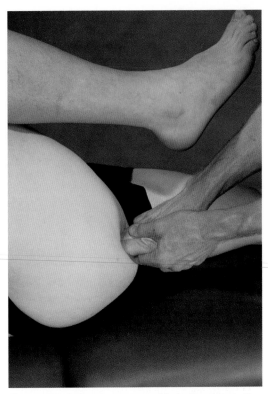

B

Figure 27.9 Ischemic pressure with the knuckles to the hamstring origin in the position of increased length

site, within the tendon, or at the musculotendinous junction. The slump test may reproduce the pain, but cervical extension makes little or no difference to the degree of pain. Pain can also be reproduced around the ischial tuberosity after prolonged sitting.

MRI is more sensitive than ultrasound investigations in diagnosis and ruling out other pathologies.[22] In one surgical study of 90 sportspeople, semi-membranosis involvement was most commonly found on MRI.[23]

Initial treatment of this condition should include soft tissue therapy (Fig. 27.9), specifically deep transverse friction to the area of palpable abnormality after reduction of inflammation with ice and nonsteroidal anti-inflammatory drugs (NSAIDs). Initial friction treatment should be relatively light. As the inflammation settles, treatment can be more vigorous.

Abnormalities within the musculotendinous unit can be treated with stretching, sustained myofascial tension, and dry needling if trigger points are present. An exercise program incorporating progressive eccentric hamstring and core stability exercises is integrated late in rehabilitation.[21]

Percutaneous corticosteroid injection can relieve symptoms but may not give long-lasting results.[21 22] Recalcitrant cases may benefit from a course of shock wave treatment to the region,[24] or injection of autologous blood.

Surgical intervention may be considered only when conservative measures have failed.[21] Tenotomy of the semimembranosis muscle, 3–4 cm distal to the origin, may have good functional outcomes and return to sport after 2–12 months.[23]

In longstanding cases of hamstring origin tendinopathy, there will be marked muscle tightness and weakness of the hamstring muscles, which may be corrected by stretching and progressive strengthening (Chapter 31). Successful rehabilitation also requires stretching of the shortened antagonist muscles such as psoas and rectus femoris.

Fibrous adhesions

Occasionally, in cases of chronic tendinopathy of hamstring origin, fibrous adhesions develop and irritate the sciatic nerve as it descends from medial to lateral just above the ischial tuberosity and then passes under the biceps femoris muscle. This condition has been termed the "hamstring syndrome."[25]

Hamstring syndrome is characterized by poorly localized buttock pain which radiates distally to the popliteal fossa.[26] Pain from sitting or hamstring stretching is caused by traction, compression, and/or irritation of the sciatic nerve.

Adhesions around the sciatic nerve may fail to respond to manual therapy, particularly if they have been present for some time. On these occasions, exploration of the sciatic nerve may be required with division of the adhesions and bands of fibrous tissue.[21, 26]

Ischiogluteal bursitis

The ischiogluteal bursa lies between the hamstring tendon and its bony origin at the ischial tuberosity. This bursa occasionally becomes inflamed. It may exist in isolation or in conjunction with hamstring origin tendinopathy.

Clinically, it is almost impossible to differentiate between ischiogluteal bursitis and hamstring origin tendinopathy, as both may present as pain aggravated by sitting or sprinting, and both are associated with local tenderness and pain on muscle contraction. One indication that ischiogluteal bursitis may be the diagnosis is that deep friction therapy fails to relieve the pain.

Ultrasound examination may reveal a fluid-filled bursa. In this case, an injection of corticosteroid and local anesthetic agents into the bursa may be appropriate. As a result of pain-induced muscle inhibition, there is usually associated hamstring muscle weakness that requires comprehensive rehabilitation.

Myofascial pain

The gluteus medius and piriformis muscles are two of the most common sites at which trigger points develop. Active trigger points in these muscles may present as buttock and/or posterior thigh pain (Fig. 27.10). These muscles are often shortened as a result of pain (Fig. 27.2d).

Careful palpation of these muscles should be performed, palpating for taut bands and exquisitely tender points that may be just tender locally or may refer pain distally into the posterior thigh. Dry needling may be an effective treatment method that can result in immediate analgesic effects and lengthening of the muscles with increased hip rotation and hamstring stretch on re-assessment.[27–29] Electrotherapy,

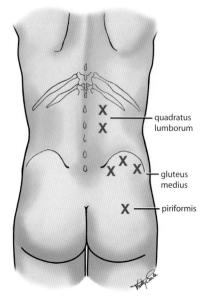

Figure 27.10 Site of trigger points that commonly refer pain to the buttock

such as ultrasound, may also be useful treatment adjunct.[30]

It is important to remember that trigger points are a secondary phenomenon. There is some evidence that there is a relationship between trigger points and joint dysfunction, mechanical low back pain, SIJ dysfunction, biomechanical abnormalities of the lower limbs, and psychological stress.[28, 30]

In an athletic population, muscle imbalances, muscle weakness, fatigue, and/or injury can contribute to the development of active trigger points.[28] This can be related to high training loads, reduced game fitness, and concurrent injuries. Therefore the clinician needs to be aware of the possible underlying causes, and aim to address these issues to enhance management and for injury prevention purposes.

Less common causes

Quadratus femoris injury

The quadratus femoris (QF) muscle originates at the ischial tuberosity and inserts onto the quadrate tubercle on the femur. Its main action involves external rotation and adduction of the hip. Additionally the QF can act as a stabiliser of the hip joint. Due to its close proximity to the origin of the hamstring muscles, QF injuries are often misdiagnosed as hamstring pathology.[31–33] Only a few cases of QF injury have been reported in the literature, mainly in sports such as badminton and tennis.[32, 33]

Clinically, athletes can present with buttock pain, or groin pain, or both. Hip pain has also been described.[31] Symptoms can radiate down the posterior thigh due to sciatic nerve irritation from a resultant hematoma.[31, 32] Pain can be aggravated by sporting activity such as running, hip stretches (flexion and adduction), and sitting.

Palpation around the ischial tuberosity and along the muscle onto its insertion on the femur can reproduce pain.[31–33] Hip flexion, and internal and external rotation can also reproduce pain. Investigations may not pick up any abnormalities on X-ray or ultrasound; however, MRI may show the correct diagnosis.[31]

Treatment for QF strains can include electrotherapy (TENS), a hip-stretching routine, and a progressive hip rotator strengthening program.[31–33] Return to sport can be anywhere from five weeks to three months.

Stress fracture of the sacrum

Sacral stress fractures are rare but occur most frequently in female distance runners. They may be associated with osteopenia secondary to menstrual and/or eating disorders, such as seen in the female athletic triad (Chapter 43).

Athletes describe unilateral non-specific low back, buttock, or hip pain exacerbated by weight-bearing activity, without a history of trauma.[34, 35] Palpation often reveals an exquisitely tender area on the sacrum. The diagnosis of stress fracture may be confirmed with bone scan or MRI, but may not always been sensitive in the early phases.[36, 37]

Treatment consists of non-weight-bearing until free of pain (one to two weeks), then a gradual increase in activity—initially non-weight-bearing (e.g. swimming, cycling, water running), and then graduated weight-bearing. Athletes may not be pain-free until six months and return to sport may not be possible until eight months post-diagnosis.[35] However, a closely monitored and structured rehabilitation program focusing on slow progression of increasing loads can accelerate return to sport in 7 to 8 weeks.[35]

Piriformis conditions

The piriformis muscle arises from the anterior surface of the sacrum and passes posterolaterally through the sciatic notch to insert into the upper border of the greater trochanter. The sciatic nerve exits the pelvis through the sciatic notch and descends immediately in front of the piriformis muscle. In 10% of the population, anatomical variations result in the sciatic nerve passing through the piriformis muscle (Fig. 27.11).[38] Two piriformis conditions are commonly seen in sportspeople—impingement and muscle strain.

Piriformis syndrome

Although known as the "piriformis syndrome," this would be better referred to as "piriformis impingement."[39] It results from pressure on the sciatic nerve, usually as a result of its aberrant course through, or above, the piriformis muscle. This condition presents as local and referred pain, and abnormal neurological symptoms in the posterior thigh and calf. Conservative treatment can consist of NSAIDs, botulinum toxin injections, stretching, acupuncture and dry needling, and soft tissue therapy, and can

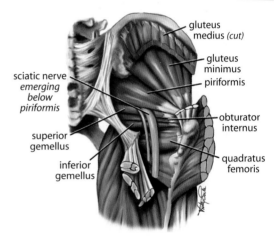

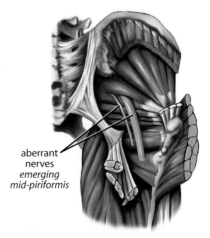

Figure 27.11 Course of the sciatic nerve in the buttock
(a) Normal

(b) Aberrant

include an adjunct core stability exercise program.[40] Surgery may be required.

Piriformis muscle strain

Piriformis muscle strain may be acute, which is often associated with muscle spasm, or chronic and may be associated with chronic muscle shortening, such as seen in long-distance walkers and runners.[41] Athletes may complain of deep buttock pain aggravated by sitting (especially greater than 20 minutes),[41] climbing stairs, squats, and internal rotation of the leg such as in cross-legged sitting.

On examination, there is often tenderness, either in the belly of the piriformis or, more distally, near its insertion into the greater trochanter. Spasm—a sausage-like palpable area—of the piriformis may also be felt. Passive internal hip rotation is reduced, and resisted abduction with the hip adducted and flexed may reproduce the pain over the piriformis. Pain may also be reproduced by resisted external rotation with the hip and knee flexed, beginning from a position of internal rotation so that end range is tested (Fig. 27.2g). Chronic cases may reveal muscle atrophy. The hip joint should be excluded as a source of symptoms.

Treatment can involves stretching of the external rotators (Figs 27.12a, b), strengthening of the hip muscles (rotators, abductors, and adductors), electrotherapeutic modalities (e.g. ultrasound, laser, high-voltage galvanic stimulation), muscle energy techniques, and soft tissue therapy to the tender area in the piriformis muscle. Longitudinal gliding combined with passive internal hip rotation (Fig. 27.12c) can be an effective technique, as is transverse gliding and sustained longitudinal release with the patient side-lying. Acupuncture and dry needling may also be considered.

Posterior thigh compartment syndrome

Posterior thigh compartment syndrome is an unusual condition that presents with the typical symptoms of a compartment syndrome—that is, pain increasing with exercise and a feeling of tightness. Posterior thigh compartment syndrome has been reported in a basketball player following a biceps femoris muscle strain, and after complete hamstring avulsion injury.[42, 43]

Pain is typically in the buttock and posterior thigh, and treatment involves range of movement exercises, massage therapy and, occasionally, surgery. Limited fasciectomy involving the ischial tuberosity and upper 5 cm (2 in.) of the posterior fascia can be performed. It is important to diagnose early and commence

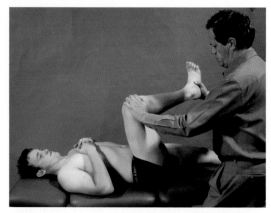

Figure 27.12 Treatment of tight piriformis muscle **(a)** Muscle stretch—hip external rotators. The hip is placed into flexion, adduction and then alternated into external and internal rotation

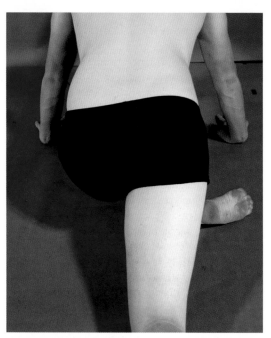

(b) Muscle stretch—external rotators

appropriate management in a time-efficient manner to avoid adverse effects such as nerve injury.

Proximal hamstring avulsion injuries

Proximal hamstring avulsion injuries can occur when the hip is forced into flexion with the knee relatively fixed at full extension, which has been cited in water skiers.[44, 45] Other mechanisms of injury include direct trauma, falling injuries, and doing the "splits." Subjectively, a popping or tearing sensation

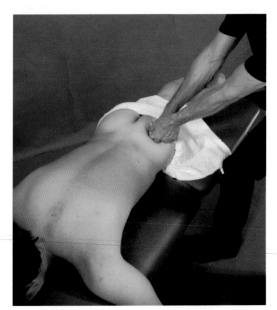

(c) Soft tissue therapy—piriformis. Sustained longitudinal pressure to the belly of the piriformis muscle, initially in passive external rotation and then moving into internal rotation

in the gluteal and proximal posterior thigh region are reported; this is followed by an inability to weight-bear.[44, 45] Aggravating factors include knee extension, weight-bearing, and sitting.

After several days, there is often a significant amount of swelling and bruising extending down the posterior thigh toward the popliteal fossa. Active knee flexion often reveals a significant deformity when performed in the prone position.[44] Chronic conditions can reveal a slow-to-resolve hematoma, which complicates the healing and encourages the scarring process.[45] Irritation of the sciatic nerve can result, prolonging functional impairment.

X-rays are often nonsignificant. Ultrasound and/or MRI can aid diagnosis, with MRI being more sensitive to the extent of the injury.[44, 45]

Conservative treatment includes off-loading the hamstrings by non-weight-bearing on crutches, gentle compression, and RICE (refer to Chapter 13 for more information). Once the sportsperson can mobilize comfortably without crutches, range of movement exercises, and progressive strengthening exercises can begin.

Surgery is indicated for acute presentations in the young and highly active populations. A complete hamstring group retraction of greater than 2 cm, seen on MRI, can also be an indication for surgery.[44]

In chronic presentations, continual hamstring tightness, muscle atrophy, and prolonged functional deficits can also indicate the need for surgery.[45] Surgery for the treatment of hamstring avulsion injuries has shown good results.[44, 46]

Apophysitis/avulsion fracture of the ischial tuberosity

Avulsion fracture of the ischial tuberosity is similar in presentation to muscle avulsion injury, but is more commonly seen in adolescents where, instead of the hamstring muscle tearing, muscle traction separates a fragment of bone from its origin at the ischial tuberosity. This fragment of bone is clearly demonstrated on plain X-ray (Fig. 27.13).

Management of this condition is generally conservative. The patient should be treated as for a severe (grade III) tear of the hamstring muscle (Chapter 31). However, if there is marked separation (greater than 2.5 cm [1 in.]) of the fragment, then surgery is indicated. There have been a number of reports of this injury in adults. The results of late surgical repair have been good.[47, 48]

Conditions not to be missed

Buttock pain may be the presenting symptom of systemic disorders, most commonly, sacroiliitis associated with spondyloarthropathies, such as ankylosing spondylitis.

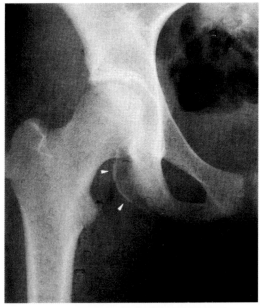

Figure 27.13 Avulsion of the ischial tuberosity

RECOMMENDED READING

Bogduk N. *Clinical anatomy of the lumbar spine and sacrum.* 4th edn. Edinburgh: Churchill Livingstone, 2004.

Brolinson PG, Kozar AJ. Sacroiliac joint dysfunction in athletes. *Curr Sports Med Rep* 2003;2(1):47–56.

Vleeming A, Mooney V, Dorman T et al. eds. *Movement, stability and low back pain: the essential role of the pelvis.* Edinburgh: Churchill Livingstone, 1997.

REFERENCES

1. Rudwaleit M, Jurik AG, Hermann KA et al. Defining active sacroiliitis on magnetic resonance imaging (MRI) for classification of axial spondyloarthritis: a consensual approach by the ASAS/OMERACT MRI group. *Ann Rheum Dis* 2009;68:1520–7

2. Walsh J, Flatley M, Johnston N et al. Slump test: sensory responses in asymptomatic subjects. *J Man Manip Ther* 2007;15(4):231–8.

3. Ellis RF, Hing WA. Neural mobilization: A systematic review of randomized controlled trials with an analysis of therapeutic efficacy. *J Man Manip Ther* 2008;16(1).

4. Brolinson PG, Kozar AJ. Sacroilliac joint dysfunction in athletes. *Curr Sports Med Rep* 2003;2(1):47–56.

5. Hancock M, Maher C, Latimer J et al. Systematic review of tests to identify the disc, SIJ or facet joint as the source of low back pain. *Eur Spine J* 2007;16(10): 1539–50.

6. Arab AM, Abdollahi I, Joghataei MT et al. Inter- and intra-examiner reliability of single and composites of selected motion palpation and pain provocation tests for sacroiliac joint. *Man Ther* 2009;14(2):213–21.

7. Bogduk N. *Clinical anatomy of the lumbar spine and sacrum.* 4th ed. Edinburgh: Churchill Livingstone, 2004.

8. Berthelot J-M, Labat J-J, Le Goff B et al. Provocative sacroiliac joint maneuvers and sacroiliac joint block are unreliable for diagnosing sacroiliac joint pain. *Joint Bone Spine* 2006;73(1):17–23.

9. Maigne JY, Aivaliklis A, Pfeffer F. Results of sacroiliac joint double block and value of sacroiliac joint pain provocation tests in 54 patients with low back pain. *Spine* 1996;21:1889–92.

10. Schwartzer AC, April CD, Bogduk N. The sacroiliac joint in chronic low back pain. *Spine* 1992;20(1):31–7.

11. Timm KE. Sacroiliac joint dysfunction in elite rowers. *J Orthop Sports Phys Ther* 1999;29:288–93.

12. Cohen SP. Sacroiliac joint pain: a comprehensive review of anatomy, diagnosis, and treatment. *Anesth Analg* 2005;101(5):1440–53.

13. Vleeming A, Mooney V, Dorman T et al. eds. *Movement, stability and low back pain: the essential role of the pelvis.* Edinburgh: Churchill Livingstone, 1997.

14. Hoek van DGA, Snijders CJ, Stoeckart R et al. A biomechanical model on muscle forces in the transfer of spinal load to the pelvis and legs. *J Biomech* 1999;32:927–33.

15. Snijders CJ, Ribbers MT, de Bakker HV et al. EMG recordings of abdominal and back muscles in various standing postures: validation of a biomechanical model on sacroiliac joint stability. *J Electromyo Kinesiol* 1998;8:205–14.

16. Broadhurst NA. Sacroiliac dysfunction as a cause of low back pain. *Aust Fam Phys* 989;18(6):623–8.

17. O'Sullivan PB, Beales DJ, Beetham JA et al. Altered motor control strategies in subjects with sacroiliac joint pain during the active straight-leg-raise test. *Spine* 2002;27(1):E1–8.

18. Richardson CA, Snijders CJ, Hides JA et al. The relation between the tranversus abdominus muscles, sacroiliac joint mechanics, and low back pain. *Spine* 2002;27:399–405.

19. Cusi M, Saunders J, Hungerford B et al. The use of prolotherapy in the sacroiliac joint. *Br J Sports Med* 2010;44:100–4.

20. Snijders CJ, Hermans PFG, Niesing R et al. Effects of slouching and muscle contraction on the strain of the iliolumbar ligament. *Man Ther* 2008;13(4):325–33.

21. Fredericson M, Moore W, Guillet M et al. High hamstring tendinopathy in runners. *Phys Sportsmed* 2005;33(5).

22. Zissen MH, Wallace G, Stevens KJ et al. High hamstring tendinopathy: MRI and ultrasound imaging and therapeutic efficacy of percutaneous corticosteroid injection. *Am J Roentgenol* 2010;195(4):993–8.

23. Lempainen L, Sarimo J, Mattila K et al. Proximal hamstring tendinopathy. *Am J Sports Med* 2009;37(4):727–34.

24. Cacchio A, Rompe JD, Furia JP et al. Shockwave therapy for the treatment of chronic proximal hamstring tendinopathy in professional athletes. *Am J Sports Med* 2011;39(1):146–53.

25. Puranen J, Orava S. The hamstring syndrome. A new diagnosis of gluteal sciatic pain. *Am J Sports Med* 1988;16(5):517–21.

26. Young IJ, van Riet RP, Bell SN. Surgical release for proximal hamstring syndrome. *Am J Sports Med* 2008;36(12):2372–8.

27. Srbely JZ, Dickey JP, Lee D et al. Dry needle stimulation of myofascial trigger points evokes

segmental anti-nociceptive effects. *J Rehab Med* 2010;42(5):463–8.

28. Huguenin L, Brukner PD, McCrory P et al. Effect of dry needling of gluteal muscles on straight leg raise: a randomised, placebo controlled, double blind trial. *Br J Sports Med* 2005;39(2):84–90.

29. Kalichman L, Vulfsons S. Dry needling in the management of musculoskeletal pain. *J Am Board Fam Med* 2010;23(5):640–6.

30. Srbely JZ, Dickey JP, Lowerison M et al. Stimulation of myofascial trigger points with ultrasound induces segmental antinociceptive effects: a randomized controlled study. *Pain* 2008;139(2):260–6.

31. O'Brien SD, Bui-Mansfield LT. MRI of quadratus femoris muscle tear: another cause of hip pain. *Am J Roentgenol* 2007;189(5):1185–9.

32. Peltola K, Heinonen OJ, Orava S et al. Quadratus femoris muscle tear: an uncommon cause for radiating gluteal pain. *Clin J Sport Med* 1999;9(4):228–30.

33. Willick SE, Lazarus M, Press JM. Quadratus femoris strain. *Clin J Sport Med* 2002;12:130–31.

34. Rodrigues LMR, Ueno FH, Filho ESV et al. Sacral stress fracture in a runner: a case report. *Clinics* 2009;62(11):1127–9.

35. Knobloch K, Schreibmueller L, Jagodzinski M et al. Rapid rehabilitation programme following sacral stress fracture in a long-distance running female athlete. *Arch Orth Traum Surg* 2007;127(9):809–13.

36. Fredericson M, Moore W, Biswal S. Sacral stress fractures: magnetic resonance imaging not always definitive for early stage injuries. *Am J Sports Med* 2007;35(5):835–9.

37. Lilley D. Swim, run ride. A case study of elite triathlete Simon Thompson: a complicated history of hamstring pain and stress fracture of the sacrum. *Sport Health* 2007;25(3):22–3.

38. Beaton LE, Anson BJ. The relation of the sciatcic nerve and of its subdivision to the piriformis muscle. *Anat Rec* 1937;70(supp 1):1–5.

39. Rich BSE, McKeag D. When sciatica is not disk disease. Detecting piriformis syndrome in active patients. *Phys Sportsmed* 1992;20(10):105–15.

40. Cramp F, Bottrell O, Campbell H et al. Non-surgical management of piriformis syndrome: a systematic review. *Phys Ther Rev* 2007;12(1):66–72.

41. Boyajian-O'Neill LA, McClain RL, Coleman MK et al. Diagnosis and management of piriformis syndrome: an osteopathic approach. *J Am Osteopath Assoc* 2008;108(11):657–64.

42. Mallo GC, Stanat SJC, Al-Humadi M et al. Posterior thigh compartment syndrome as a result of a basketball injury. *Orthopedics* 2009;32(12):923–5.

43. Kwong Y, Patel J. Spontaneous complete hamstring avulsion causing posterior thigh compartment syndrome. *Br J Sports Med* 2006;40:723–4.

44. Sallay PI. Diagnosis, classification and management of acute proximal hamstring avulsion injuries. *Op Tech Sports Med* 2009;17(4):196–204.

45. Abebe ES, Moorman CT, Garrett WE. Proximal hamstring avulsion injuries: injury mechanism, diagnosis and disease course. *Op Tech Sports Med* 2009;17(4):205–9.

46. Pombo M, Bradley JP. Proximal hamstring avulsion injuries: a technique note on surgical repairs. *Sports Health* 2009;1(3):261–4.

47. Cross MJ, Vandersluis R, Wood D et al. Surgical repair of chronic complete hamstring tendon rupture in the adult patient. *Am J Sports Med* 1998;26(6):785–8.

48. Servant CTJ, Jones CB. Displaced avulsion of the ischial apophysis: a hamstring injury requiring internal fixation. *Br J Sports Med* 1998;32:255–7.

Chapter 28

Hip-related pain

with JOANNE KEMP, KAY CROSSLEY, ANTHONY SCHACHE, and MIKE PRITCHARD

Bo says he felt his hip come out of the socket, so he popped it back in, but that's just impossible, no one's that strong.   Bo Jackson's trainer after the American football and baseball All-Star dislocated his hip when tackled during the 1990 NFL playoffs

Until recently, the hip joint was not thought to be a significant cause of problems in the athletic population, although hip disorders have long been recognized in the pediatric population (Perthes disease, slipped femoral epiphysis) and older people (osteoarthritis). It was not until the advent of, firstly, MRI, and then hip arthroscopy, that it was realized that the incidence of hip labral and acetabular rim pathology was high, and that anatomical variants such as femoroacetabular impingement (FAI) were a common underlying cause of groin pain.

Hip pain is a common cause of activity restriction in sportspeople. Hip and groin pain is the third most common injury reported in the Australian Football League (AFL),[1] accounting for between 5 and 15% of all football-related injuries;[2] it is also prevalent in many other sports, including tennis, football of all codes, and hockey.

The likelihood of a sportsperson sustaining an injury to the hip joint can be increased by the demands of the sport, in particular, sports that require repetitive hip flexion, adduction, and rotation.[2–4] Hip joint injury can also be caused by the inherent individual anatomical variations within the joint, such as FAI or developmental dysplasia of the hip (DDH).[5–11]

The range of motion of the hip is critical in determining the likelihood of intra-articular damage during sporting activity. The demands of range of motion vary between all sporting activities and the levels of activity. As range of motion decreases, the risk of impingement-related damage increases, especially with contact sports.

Intra-articular hip pathologies contribute to both a reduced ability to participate in sporting or physical activities as well as pain and also reduced function during activities of daily living. There is also considerable evidence that hip pathologies are strong contributors to hip, groin, and pelvic pain in young adults.[12, 13]

Burnett et al.[14] demonstrated that 92% of patients with an arthroscopically confirmed labral tear complained of moderate to severe groin pain. Philippon et al.[10] described labral tears and FAI in 100% of professional National Hockey League (NHL) ice hockey players presenting for hip arthroscopy or the treatment of longstanding hip and groin pain. Injury to the ligamentum teres of the hip has been cited as the third most common cause of hip and groin pain in the sportsperson.[15–17]

In this chapter, we:

- review the functional anatomy of the hip
- provide a clinical approach to assessment of what is often a longstanding problem
- detail the pathologies and management of the many important conditions that are now recognized to cause pain around the hip region.

This chapter should be read in conjunction with the chapter on groin pain (Chapter 29).

Functional anatomy and biomechanics

The hip has three functions:

- It allows mobility of the lower limb.
- It transmits loads between the upper body, trunk, and lower limb.
- It also provides a stable base in weight-bearing activities.

The anatomical structure of the hip allows it to perform these functions.

The hip joint is supported by a number of dynamic and passive supports—these include its bony morphology, passive restraints such as capsule and ligaments, and a complex system of interplaying muscle groups. The biomechanics of the hip joint are generally under-reported in the literature and so are poorly understood. An appreciation of the functional anatomy of the hip and the role of the various structures surrounding the hip will assist in this understanding (Fig. 28.1).

Morphology

The hip joint (femoroacetabular joint) is a tri-planar synovial joint, formed by the head of femur inferiorly and the acetabulum superiorly. The acetabulum sits within the bony pelvis and is normally anteverted (forward-facing) by approximately 23°[18] (Fig. 28.2a overleaf). The acetabulum also faces inferiorly and laterally.

The head and neck of the femur are also anteverted—this refers to the most superior aspect of the femoral head and the femoral neck (Fig. 28.2b overleaf). This angle is normally between 10° and 15° in adults. The head of femur also faces superiorly and medially. A reduction in either femoral or acetabular anteversion is considered to increase the risk of hip pathology.

The relationship between the head and neck of the femur, called the head–neck offset, is also very important when discussing the hip joint. This refers to the difference between the greatest diameter of the spherical femoral head and the diameter of the neck measured around the femoral neck axis in any plane (Fig. 28.2c overleaf) and is normally approximately 20 mm in people without hip pain.[8] A reduced head–neck offset[19] (also referred to as a cam lesion) is considered to increase the risk of hip pathology and will be discussed in detail below.

The morphological structure of the hip joint allows the hip to achieve its three planes of movement, being flexion and extension, adduction and abduction, and external and internal rotation.

Acetabular labrum

The acetabulum forms the socket of the hip joint, and is lined with articular cartilage. The acetabular labrum (Fig. 28.3 on page 513) is a ring of fibrocartilage and dense connective tissue which is attached

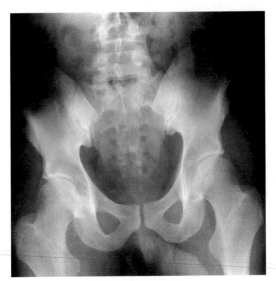

Figure 28.1 Anatomy of the hip and groin area
(a) Plain X-ray of the pelvis

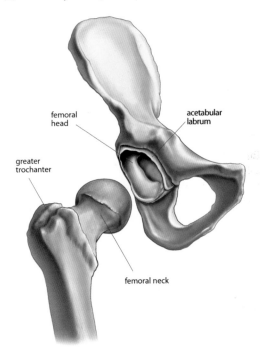

(b) The hip joint

to the bony acetabular rim. The acetabular labrum is thinnest in its anterior aspect.

The blood supply of the labrum enters though the adjacent joint capsule. Only the outer one-third of the labrum is vascularized.[20] Nocioceptive free nerve endings are distributed throughout the acetabular labrum, suggesting a pain-producing capacity.[21, 22]

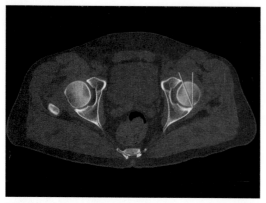

Figure 28.2 (a) CT showing acetabular anteversion[18]

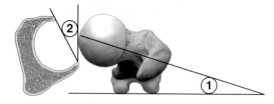

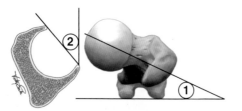

(b) Transverse views of a normal hip (upper figure) and a dysplastic hip (lower figure)[19]
(1) Angle of torsion—rotation of the femoral neck relative to the shaft (transcondylar axis), normally 10–15° of anteversion. Dysplastic hips usually have increased angle
(2) Acetabular anteversion angle—the anterior direction of the acetabulum, is normally 20–40° of anteversion. Dysplastic hips usually have increased angle but it may be decreased

The acetabular labrum has several functions. These are primarily to deepen the acetabulum, to distribute the contact stress of the acetabulum over a wider area (increasing contact area by 28%)[23] and assisting in synovial fluid containment and distribution.[22–24]

Ligaments of the hip

The transverse acetabular ligament (Fig. 28.3) traverses the acetabular notch, connecting the anterior and posterior edges of the labrum. The deepest layer of labral tissue blend into this ligament. The

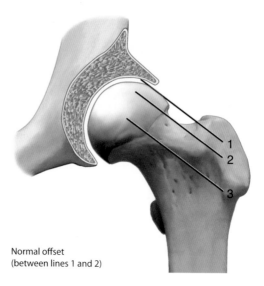

Normal offset
(between lines 1 and 2)

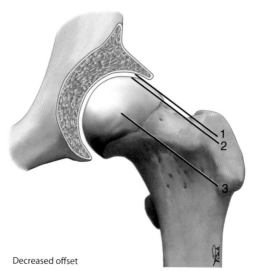

Decreased offset

(c) Femoral head–neck offset[19]
The head–neck offset is the distance between the most superior aspect of the femoral head (line 1) and the femoral neck (line 2). Line 3 is first drawn through the long axis of the neck, then parallel lines are drawn representing the superior aspect of the femoral head (line 1) and the femoral neck (line 2). The offset is the distance between lines 1 and 2. A decreased offset (lower figure) leads to reduced clearance and subsequent impingement

transverse acetabular ligament is under greatest load in weight-bearing, widening the acetabular notch and placing the transverse acetabular ligament under a tensile load.[24]

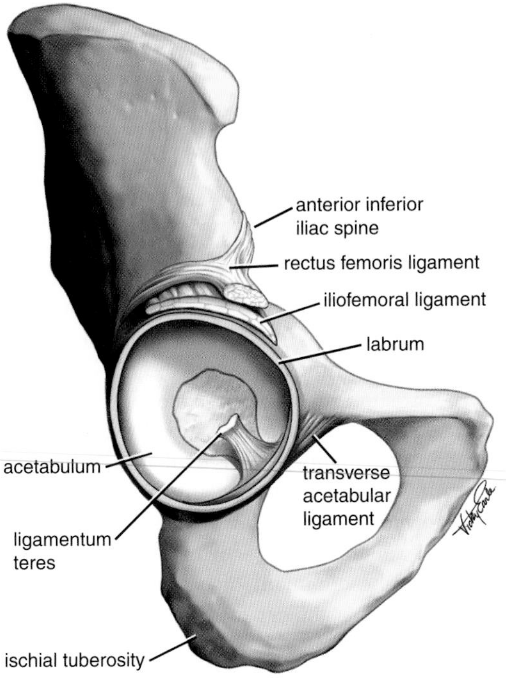

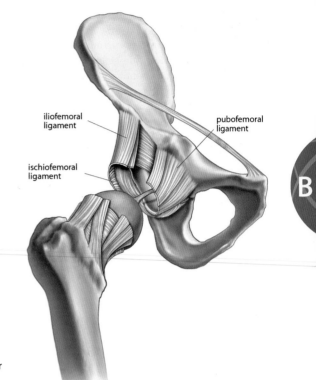

anterior inferior
iliac spine

rectus femoris ligament

iliofemoral ligament

labrum

acetabulum

transverse
acetabular
ligament

ligamentum
teres

ischial tuberosity

Figure 28.3 Transverse acetabular ligament, acetabular labrum, and ligamentum teres (resected)

iliofemoral
ligament

pubofemoral
ligament

ischiofemoral
ligament

B

Figure 28.4 Capsular ligaments of the hip

The ligamentum teres (Fig. 28.3) is an intra-articular ligament, arising from the fovea of the head of the femur, becoming triangular in shape, with an anterior and posterior branch, which insert into the anterior and posterior aspect of the transverse acetabular ligament respectively.[25] It is covered by the synovium within the hip.[15]

The ligamentum teres is also rich in free nerve endings, which are mechanoreceptors.[26] The ligamentum teres was originally thought to be a histological vestige which becomes redundant early in childhood; however, it is now assumed that the ligamentum teres plays an important proprioceptive role, especially in weight-bearing activities.[15]

The iliofemoral ligament (Y ligament of Bigelow) reinforces the anterior capsule and originates from the anterior iliac spine, fanning into an inverted Y shape to insert into the intertrochanteric line (Fig. 28.4). It is taut in hyperextension and also provides stability in relaxed standing.

The pubofemoral ligament arises from the anterior surface of the pubic ramus and inserts into the intertrochanteric fossa (Fig. 28.4). It is taut in abduction and extension, and also reinforces the anterior capsule.

The ischiofemoral ligament arises from the posterior surface of the acetabular rim and labrum, and extends into the femoral neck just proximal to the greater trochanter (Fig. 28.4). Its fibers run in a spiral pattern and are also taut in hyperextension.

The iliofemoral, pubofemoral, and ischiofemoral ligaments act to restrain hyperextension, which is of particular relevance in relaxed standing.

Chondral surfaces

Both articular surfaces of the hip are lined with articular cartilage. These chondral surfaces rely upon adequate function of the synovium and movement of synovial fluid within the joint to provide nutrition, because articular cartilage is avascular. As both the acetabular labrum and ligamentum teres have been reported to attach to the synovium, they may also play a role in the nutrition and normal function of articular cartilage within the hip joint.

Joint stability and normal muscle function

The bony morphology, acetabular labrum, ligamentum teres, other ligaments, and capsule of the hip joint all provide passive stability to the hip joint. Dynamic stability is provided by a complex inter-play between various muscles surrounding the hip joint. The concept of deep hip stabilizers, the "hip rotator cuff," has been present for some years,[27] but has grown in popularity in recent years. In particular, the primary hip stabilizers are thought to provide a posterior, medial, and inferior force on the femur to control the position of the head of femur within the acetabulum. Ultimately, the dynamic control provided by the deep hip stabilizers has potential to minimize stress on vulnerable structures, such as the antero-superior acetabular labrum, and the anterosuperior acetabular rim (Fig. 28.5).

Recent reports have described the roles of hip muscles, with respect to muscle morphology, primary action of joint movement, and lines of action in relation to the axes of joint movement[27-29] (Fig. 28.6). Some muscles have greater capacity to generate torque over larger ranges of motion (prime movers), while other muscles are better placed to act as dynamic hip joint stabilizers.

Detailed descriptions of muscle morphology have increased the understanding of the potential roles of individual muscles to act as dynamic hip stabil-izers.[29] Muscles with a larger physiological cross-sectional area (PCSA) relative to muscle fiber length (MFL) (i.e. PCSA [cm²] : MFL [cm] >1.0) generate large forces over small length changes and, hence, are considered to be joint stabilizers[29] (Table 28.1). In contrast, those muscles with smaller PCSA rela-tive to muscle fiber length (i.e. PCSA [cm²] : MFL [cm] <1.0) are considered to be "prime movers" of a joint. Generally the hip muscles tend to act as either joint stabilizers or prime movers. However, there are two muscles with both large PCSA and large MFL (gluteus maximus and adductor brevis), which sug-gests that these muscles are required to act as both stabilizers and prime movers.

The six short hip external rotators (SHER) (obtu-rator internus and externus, superior and inferior gemellus, quadratus femoris and piriformis) have the capacity to provide hip joint compression and, hence, dynamic stability during most weight-bearing and non-weight-bearing activities.[28, 30] The gluteus medius is the dominant hip abductor, and is the primary lateral stabilizer of the hip during one-leg stance activities.[29]

For the patient with hip pain and/or pathology, the clinician should also consider the lines of actions for each of the deep hip stabilizers.[28] For example, although all of the SHER have capacity to provide

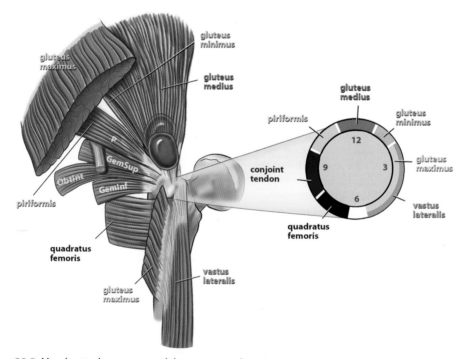

Figure 28.5 Muscle attachments around the greater trochanter

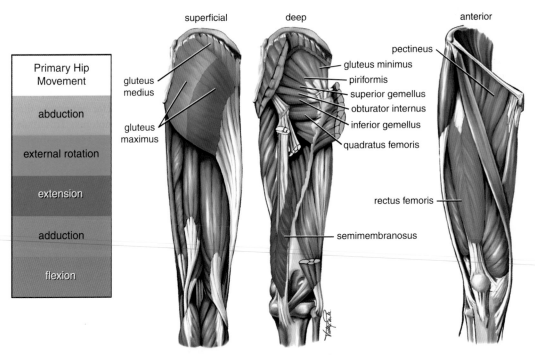

Figure 28.6 Muscles around the hip showing their primary direction of movement

Table 28.1 Hip muscles with primary function as hip stabilizer—primary and secondary actions[a]

Stabilizers (PCSA [cm²] : MFL [cm] >1.0)	Primary action	Secondary action
Gluteus maximus	Extension External rotation	Adduction
Gluteus medius	Abduction	Extension External rotation (posterior fibers) Internal rotation (anterior fibers)
Gluteus minimus	Abduction	Flexion External rotation (posterior fibers) Internal rotation (anterior fibers)
Piriformis	External rotation	Abduction
Quadratus femoris	External rotation	Adduction
Obturator internus	External rotation	
Inferior gemellus	External rotation	
Superior gemellus	External rotation	
Obturator externus		External rotation Adduction
Pectineus	Adduction	Internal rotation
Semimembranosus	Extension	
Rectus femoris	Flexion	Abduction

[a] Primary action and line of action in relation to axis of movement of hip joint in the anatomical position[28, 29]

dynamic hip stability in the anatomical position, the quadratus femoris also has a line of action that is inferomedial. Therefore it has a greater capacity to resist superior translation of the hip. Similarly, the gluteus maximus and four SHERs (piriformis, gemellus inferior and superior, obturator internus) have a line of action that is posteromedial, and may be able to resist anterior force of the hip.[31]

In contrast, although the gluteus medius is an important lateral stabilizer of the hip, its line of action is both medial and superior[28] making it the greatest contributor to both medial and superior hip contact force during walking.[31] Furthermore, the anterior fibers of gluteus medius and minimus become hip internal rotators when the hip is flexed.[32, 33] The relevance of these factors to the rehabilitation of the patient with hip pain and pathology is described below.

Clinical perspective: making sense of a complex problem

Pain related to the hip joint is commonly seen in athletic populations. Of sportspeople with longstanding adductor-related groin pain, 94% have radiological signs of FAI.[34] Of sportspeople with hip and groin pain, 22% have labral tears and 55% of people with mechanical symptoms of the hip have confirmed labral pathology.[19]

However, despite this prevalence, hip-related pain and associated pathologies have not been well managed in the athletic population until recently. Weir et al.[34] reported a mean duration of hip and groin pain in sportspeople of 22 weeks, with the maximum duration 250 weeks (5 years), while many other studies report symptom duration of greater than 2 years.[19] Byrd and Jones[16] reported an average of 7 months from initial assessment, and multiple other diagnoses being made, before a definitive diagnosis of hip pathology was made.

Hip pain also commonly coexists with other groin-related pathology, such as adductor symptoms, iliopsoas symptoms and pubic symptoms. This makes definitive diagnosis and provision of appropriate management programs difficult and often multifactorial[35] (see also Chapter 29).

Causes of hip injuries and pain are shown in Table 28.2. Hints for differentiating hip pain from lateral thigh pain are shown in the box below.

Femoroacetabular impingement

Femoroacetabular impingement (FAI) describes a morphological variant seen in approximately 20% of the general population—it is not in itself pathology.[12] There are three types of FAI described.

Hints for differentiating hip joint and lateral thigh pain

- Groin or anterior pain plus loss of range of movement, clicks, or catching generally means joint pathology.
- Lateral thigh pain plus full range of movement (once muscle spasm is taken into account) generally means lateral soft tissue structures.
- Both groin and lateral pain plus some joint restruction/signs generally means both.

Table 28.2 Causes of hip injuries/pain

Common	Less common	Not to be missed
Anterior pain		
Synovitis	Os acetabulare	Synovial chondromatosis
Labral tear	Ligament teres tear	Avascular necrosis of head of
Chondropathy	Stress fracture	femur
Osteoarthritis	Hip joint instability (hypermobility or developmental dysplasia of the hip)	Slipped capital/upper femoral epiphysis (SUFE)
	Traction apophysitis (AIIS—rectus femoris; ASIS—sartorius; lesser trochanter—iliopsoas)	Perthes Tumor
Lateral pain		
Greater trochanter pain syndrome	Referred pain from lumbar spine	Fracture of neck of femur
Gluteus medius tears and tendinopathy		Nerve root compression Tumor
Trochanteric bursitis		

The first type is impingement due to a cam lesion (Fig. 28.7b), sometimes referred to as a Ganz lesion. This describes the reduction in femoral head–neck offset described previously, which results in additional bone being seen at the head–neck junction. This additional bone is also referred to as the "bump." Cam lesions are most commonly seen on the anterior, superior, or anterosuperior aspect of the femoral neck, and are seen in 78% of people with FAI.[36]

The second type of FAI seen is referred to as "pincer impingement" (Fig. 28.7c). This refers to bony change seen in the acetabulum and is seen in 42% of people with FAI.[36] This can either manifest

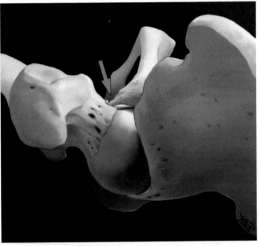

(c) Pincer lesion—bone spur extends from the acetabular surface

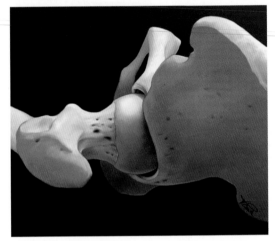

Figure 28.7 Hip joints with and without femoroacetabular impingement (FAI)

(a) Hip without FAI

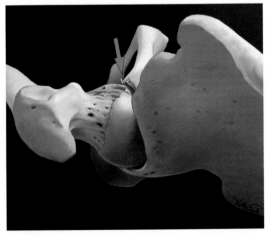

(b) Cam lesion
Additional bone arises as a "bump" from the femoral surface

as a deep acetabulum, which is most commonly seen anteriorly,[12, 37] or as a retroverted acetabulum, which leads to an apparent deeper anterior acetabular wall.

The third type of FAI seen is the mixed presentation where both cam and pincer lesions are seen; this is seen in 88% of people with FAI.[36]

It is unclear whether the development of cam deformity is due to overactivity at the epiphyseal plate between the femoral head and neck during periods of rapid growth in adolescents caused by repetitive torsional forces at the hip; or whether it is due to genetic tendencies. There is now some evidence that FAI has a familial pattern, with siblings being three times more likely to have FAI than controls.[38]

 FAI in itself is not a pathology, it is simply a variation of bony structure within the normal range seen.[38–40] Of the 20% of the population with FAI, only 23% of these people complain of hip pain.[36]

FAI, however, can result in pathology causing pain when the hip joint is placed into a position of impingement in a repetitive fashion during sporting activities, or in a single major traumatic incident such as a motor vehicle accident, or a large fall when the hip is in the position of impingement. The incidence of radiological signs of FAI in sportspeople with longstanding adductor-related groin pain has recently been reported as being 94%.[34]

The most common position of impingement is flexion with internal rotation and sometimes adduction.[2, 10, 39, 40] With most cam and pincer lesions located on the anterior or superior aspect of the hip, these positions are most likely to bring these surfaces together and cause impingement.

Several authors have postulated an association between FAI and an increased likelihood of developing other intra-articular hip pathologies—these primarily being labral tears, chondropathy, and ultimately osteoarthritis of the hip.[5, 6, 8, 11, 38]

> As there is no conclusive evidence at this stage that indicates that all sportspeople with morphological features of FAI will develop hip pathology, prophylactic surgery to correct deformities in athletes who do not have signs of hip pathology is not recommended.

The early identification of FAI in sportspeople with hip and groin pain is essential. Unfortunately, there is no gold standard in clinical diagnosis of FAI. Clinical signs that are often reported to indicate the presence of FAI include reduced range of hip internal rotation, particularly when the hip is flexed, and a positive FADIR (flexion, adduction, internal rotation) test.

Positive FADIR testing is common in FAI-related damage and radiological examination is required. Plain radiographs can be useful and, generally, a correctly centered plain AP view of the pelvis, along with extended lateral femoral neck X-rays taken at 45° and 90°—the "Dunn views"—will indicate the presence of the morphological features of FAI when read by an experienced radiologist (Fig. 28.8).

Sportspeople who present with FAI and have hip or groin pain should be encouraged to avoid the position of impingement as much as possible. This position of impingement is usually flexion, internal rotation and adduction, or any combination of these (Fig. 28.9). This may involve activity modification

Figure 28.9 Hip impingement during football

on a day-to-day basis, as well as during athletic pursuits. For example, in footballers, this may involve playing in a different position which requires less time changing direction and getting down low to the ball. It may also involve reducing the time spent on the field. Maximizing dynamic neuromotor control around the hip also assists in achieving this goal.

Factors that may contribute to the development of hip-related pain

Certain factors may contribute to the development of hip-related pain. These factors all alter the loads on the hip joint, thus placing structures within and around the hip joint under duress, which may eventuate in pain. These contributing factors can be classed as either extrinsic or intrinsic factors.

Extrinsic factors

Extrinsic factors include the type of sports played, particularly those involving repeated combined hip flexion, abduction and adduction, and loaded rotational or twisting movements. Extrinsic factors may

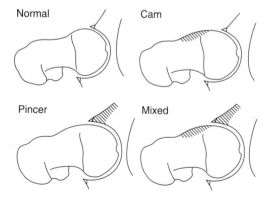

Figure 28.8 Radiological appearances of the types of FAI

also include the volume of sport and activity under-taken, footwear worn, and type of surface played upon. Of these extrinsic factors, the type of sport and volume of load undertaken are probably the most important when evaluating the sportsperson with hip-related pain.

Repeated hip flexion, abduction and adduction, and rotation and twisting are reported throughout the literature as influencing the likelihood of the develop-ment of hip pathology. The clinician must examine these loads in detail and modify them accordingly for sportspeople who experience hip-related pain.

Intrinsic factors

Intrinsic factors can also influence the development of hip pain and pathology. These factors may also alter loads within the joint, predisposing the hip to injury. Intrinsic factors are considered as either "local" or "remote," and both must be considered for comprehensive assessment of the sportsperson with hip-related pain. Identifying these factors via thor-ough assessment is essential if the clinician is to suc-cessful modify the loads within the joint to protect potentially vulnerable structures.

Local factors

The following local factors may contribute to the development of hip-related pain. These are shown Table 28.3 overleaf.

Reduced hip flexion

Reduced hip flexion may indicate the presence of FAI. In sportspeople with hip pain, this must be assessed to ensure the sportsperson has adequate range of hip flexion to meet the demands of the sport, particularly sports that involve repetitive end-range flexion (e.g. football, gymnastics).

Hip flexion can be assessed reliably in supine position, with the contralateral thigh stabilized with a seatbelt (Fig. 28.10a on page 521), using either a goniometer or inclinometer. Any pain experienced at the end range of flexion must be noted.

Reduced hip internal rotation

Reduced range of hip internal rotation may also indi-cate the presence of morphological changes such as FAI, slipped upper femoral epiphysis (SUFE), Perthes, or dysplasia that may predispose the sport-sperson to hip pathology. Many sports demand certain ranges of hip internal rotation, and these ranges must be established if a sportsperson is to

participate in the sport without the risk of hip pain. This should be assessed in both a neutral range of hip flexion, and at 90° of hip flexion.

This range can be assessed reliably with either an inclinometer or goniometer, with the patient prone for hip neutral, and sitting for 90° of flexion, with the contralateral thigh stabilized (Fig. 28.10b on page 521).

Reduced hip extension

Reduced hip extension may predispose to hip pain, as it is possible that loads are placed on the anterior margins of the joint as the sportsperson attempts to gain more range during the end stage of stance in running and gait. The anterior margins of the joint are considered to be highly vulnerable to injury, and must be protected from overload. Hip extension range of motion can be measured reliably in supine position at the end of the plinth, with an inclinom-eter (Fig. 28.10c on page 521).

Increased femoral adduction/internal rotation during functional tasks

Increased femoral adduction and/or internal rotation during functional tasks may place the hip in a posi-tion of impingement, thus increasing loads on vulner-able joint margins such as the acetabular labrum and acetabular chondral rim. This is especially important for the patient with lost range of motion.

Increased femoral adduction motion should be assessed in both static and dynamic activities, such as a single-leg squat, walking, and running. Videotaping the sportsperson performing functional tasks may assist the clinician in identifying increased adduc-tion/internal rotation (Fig. 28.10d on page 521).

Remote factors

The following remote factors may contribute to the development of hip-related pain.

Proximal factors

Increased pelvic tilt and/or lumbar hyperextension may increase the load on the anterior margins of the hip, due to the more distal placement of the anterior acetabular rim. This increased load may be a source of increased hip pain and eventually anterior hip pathology. The clinical assessment of pelvic symme-try and lumbar spine is outlined in Chapter 26.

Inadequate control of the lumbopelvic segments may result in a number of asymmetries, which alter the loads on the hip joint. In particular, lateral pelvic

Table 28.3 Local factors that can contribute to the development of hip-related pain

Factor	Possible mechanisms—structural	Possible mechanisms—functional	Confirmatory assessments
Reduced hip flexion range of motion	Cam lesion Pincer impingement Dysplasia		Plain X-ray AP pelvis Dunn view 45°/90° Positive FADIR
Reduced hip internal rotation range of motion	Acetabular retroversion Reduced femoral head–neck offset (cam lesion) Pincer impingement Femoral retroversion Osteoarthritis changes (osteophytes)		Plain X-ray AP pelvis Dunn view 45°/90°
		Reduced strength hip internal rotators Tight gluteals and piriformis Muscle spasm	Hand-held dynamometry Muscle length tests
Reduced hip extension range of motion	Acetabular anteversion Dysplasia		Plain AP X-ray
		Tightness hip flexors, quadriceps Reduced hip extensor strength Posterior pelvic tilt	Muscle length tests Hand-held dynamometry, and manual muscle tests
Increased femoral adduction/internal rotation motions	Developmental dysplasia of the hip Acetabular or femoral anteversion		Plain X-ray AP pelvis Dunne view
		Reduced hip abductor strength Reduced hip extensor strength Reduced hip external rotator strength Reduced neuromotor control/proprioception	Hand-held dynamometry, and manual muscle tests Single-leg balance challenge, and force platform

tilt may increase load on both the lateral and medial structures of the hip joint, due to the increased adductor and internal rotation moment seen on the stance leg.

Control of the hip and lumbopelvic control can be assessed using the single-leg squat (Chapter 8), other single-leg activities, and gait- or sports-specific activities. In some cases, the sportsperson should also be videotaped while running, particularly when fatigued, as altered control may become more pronounced. The demands on the lumbopelvic region for the individual's sport must be considered, as this may predispose certain athletic groups to fatigue and subsequently altered load on the hip joint.

Distal factors

Increased subtalar pronation may lead to an increase in tibial internal rotation. This may lead to an overload on the iliotibial band and the lateral structures of the hip. Increased iliotibial band tension leads to increased compression over the greater trochanter, and the development of gluteus medius and minimus

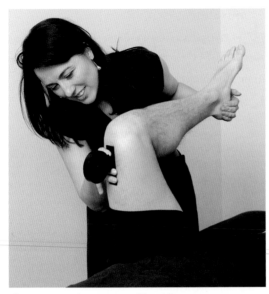

Figure 28.10 Assessment of local factors
(a) Measurement of hip flexion range of motion (using a simple inclinometer)

(b) Measurement of hip internal rotation range of motion in sitting

(c) Hip extension range of motion

(d) Increased femoral adduction and internal rotation moment

tendinopathy, and trochanteric bursitis. Increased tibial internal rotation may also create increased internal rotation of the femur, thus heightening load on the hip, particularly in sportspeople with an increased risk of impingement. The clinical assessment of the subtalar joint is outlined in Chapter 40.

Adequate range of ankle dorsiflexion during the stance phase of gait is essential in order to minimize excessive loads further up the kinetic chain. If this movement is limited, the gait pattern may be altered to achieve onward forward propulsion of the sportsperson. One adaptation commonly seen is an increase in hip adduction and rotation at the middle of the stance phase of gait. This may increase load on the hip joint in similar ways to those outlined above. The clinical assessment of ankle dorsiflexion range of motion is outlined in Chapter 38.

Clinical assessment

History

It is important to obtain a full history from the patient prior to undertaking a physical examination or obtaining any investigations. This history should include:

- age, general health, past medical history (including presence or absence of childhood conditions such as "clicky hips," slipped upper femoral epiphysis (SUFE) or infantile dysplasia) and medications

- weight and height (BMI)—BMI >25 can increase severity of symptoms of osteoarthritis and tendinopathy, as well as increase joint loads
- exact mechanism of injury (if known), including onset as sudden or insidious
- time since onset of symptoms
- pattern of symptoms since onset (worsening, improving or not changing)
- family history—there may be a genetic predisposition to FAI and osteoarthritis of the hip[38]
- presence of mechanical symptoms such as locking, clicking, or giving way—suspect labral or possibly ligamentum teres pathology
- location of pain—hip pathology may present as groin, lower back, lateral hip, buttock, or thigh pain,[41] and secondary sources of pain such as muscle spasm may be present, complicating the assessment
- nature of pain (intensity, severity, constancy, time of day, latency)—will provide clues as to presence of inflammation, synovitis, bursitis, or tendinopathy in addition to intra-articular pathology
- neurological signs and low back pain—the lumbar spine can refer pain to the hip and should be eliminated as a potential primary source of pain
- aggravating factors—be specific regarding position of hip and potential for impingement during these activities, how long it takes for these activities to provoke pain, and latent pain
- current level of activity (frequency and intensity of lower limb loading)—tendon-related pain may need to be assessed over a period of three days
- factors easing pain—be specific regarding positions of ease as well as time required for pain to ease
- current sporting history—including level of sport (community, state, national, and position played within the team); certain positions will place the hip under more load, such as midfield in AFL football
- previous sporting history—certain sports played may increase the likelihood of a hip injury (e.g. dancing, gymnastics, martial arts, tennis, hockey)
- desired level of future sporting activity—this is important to establish in order to determine level of intervention as well as future risk of injury
- activities of daily living—including occupation, length of time spent sitting, amount of hip flexion and rotation and degree of manual labor within occupation, family situation including the presence of young children
- any past treatment, including investigations, conservative treatment, or surgical intervention.

Examination

 Examination of the hip is in the *Clinical Sports Medicine* masterclasses at www.clinicalsportsmedicine.com.

Examination involves:

1. Observation
   (a) standing
      (i) general lower limb alignment
      (ii) femoral alignment
      (iii) pelvic symmetry
      (iv) muscle tone and symmetry
   (b) walking
      (i) pain
      (ii) limp
      (iii) lateral pelvic stability—Trendelenburg sign
   (c) supine
      (i) leg length
2. Active movements
   (a) hip flexion/extension
   (b) hip abduction/adduction
   (c) hip internal/external rotation at both neutral and 90° flexion
   (d) bent knee fall-out
3. Passive movements
   (a) adductor muscle stretch (Fig. 28.11a)
   (b) anterior impingement test (hip quadrant)—flexion, adduction, internal rotation (Fig. 28.11b)
   (c) internal rotation at 90° flexion
   (d) flexion, abduction, and external rotation (FABER or Patrick's test) (Fig. 28.11c)
   (e) quadriceps muscle stretch
   (f) psoas muscle stretch/impingement (Thomas position) (Fig. 28.11d overleaf)
4. Tests of muscle function
   (a) adductor squeeze test (Fig. 28.11e overleaf)
   (b) hand-held dynamometry of hip muscle strength bilaterally
      (i) flexion/extension
      (ii) adduction/abduction
      (iii) internal/external rotation
   (c) Real-time ultrasound assessment of deep hip stabilizers and deep core
   (d) de-rotation test[42] (Fig. 28.11f overleaf)
5. Palpation
   (a) adductor muscles/tendons/entheses
   (b) pelvis including pubis symphysis, ischial tuberosities, proximal hamstring attachment
   (c) iliopsoas in muscle belly and at anterior hip joint (Fig. 28.11g overleaf)

(d)   superficial hip abductors including tensor fascia lata, gluteus medius, superior gluteus maximus

(e)   greater trochanter and tendons of gluteus medius and minimus

6. Functional movements

(a)   single-leg squat (Fig. 28.11h on page 525)

(b)   hopping (to reproduce pain)

(c)   forward hop

(d)   step up and down on the affected leg (observe stability, pain level, and pain location) (Fig. 28.11i on page 525)

(e)   side step up and down on the affected leg

(f)   hip hitch (in neutral, internal, and external rotation), keeping the knee extended (Fig. 28.11j on page 525)

(g)   kicking (if appropriate)

(h)   balance and proprioception

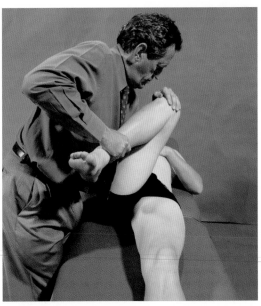

(b) Passive movement—anterior impingement (hip quadrant: flexion, adduction, and internal rotation—FADIR). This is a combined movement that is performed if hip range of motion is normal in single planes

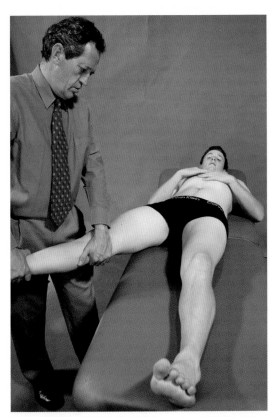

Figure 28.11 Examination of the patient with hip-related pain

(a) Passive movement—adductor muscle stretch

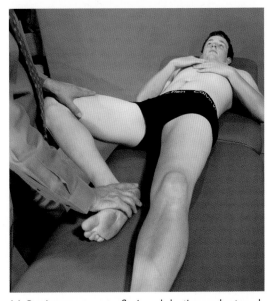

(c) Passive movement—flexion, abduction, and external rotation (FABER or Patrick's test). Range of motion, apart from extreme stiffness/laxity, is not that relevant. Some caution needs to be exercised, as it is possible to sublux an unstable hip in this position. Pain felt in the groin is very non-specific. Pain in the buttock is more likely to be due to sacroiliac joint problems. However, pain felt over the greater trochanter suggests hip joint pathology

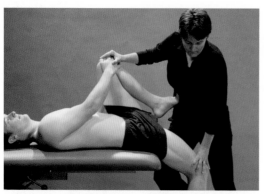

(d) Passive movement—psoas stretch (Thomas position). Pain in the hip being stretched suggests psoas abnormality. Pain in the hip being compressed can be significant for anterior impingement of the hip joint

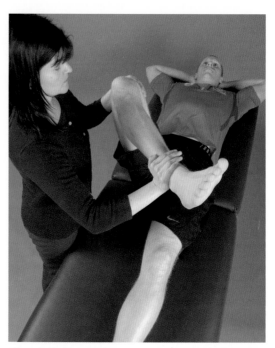

(f) De-rotation test
In 90° flexion, the hip is taken into external rotation, and the patient asked to return the leg to the axis of the table against resistance. The test result is positive when the usual pain is reproduced

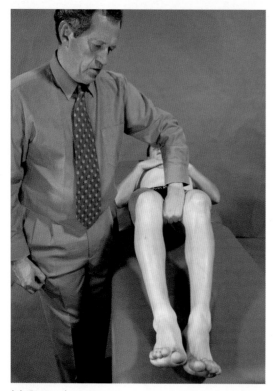

(e) Resisted movement—squeeze test. Examiner places fist between knees as shown. Patient then adducts bilaterally against the fist

 We emphasize that each individual clinician needs to develop his or her own technique for examining this joint. Between the masterclasses online and this outline, you see a range of options you can incorporate into your practice.

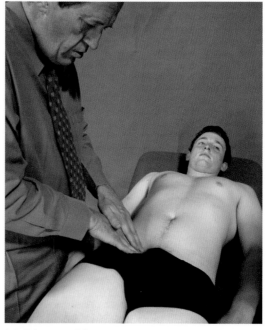

(g) Palpation of iliopsoas in muscle belly and at anterior hip joint

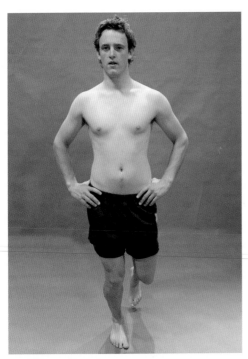

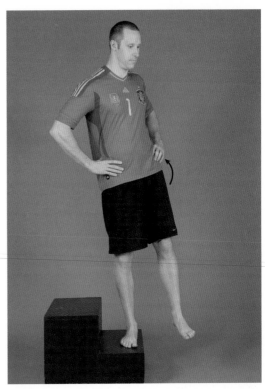

B

(h) Functional movements—single-leg squat. Note pain, degree of femoral adduction and internal rotation, and lateral pelvic stability—Trendelenburg sign

(j) Hip hitch (in neutral, internal and external rotation), keeping the knee extended

Investigations

X-ray, MRI, and ultrasonography are the mainstay of imaging for diagnosis of hip pathology. Plain X-rays are often overlooked by clinicians, but usually should be the first investigation ordered as they can provide valuable information. FAI can often be seen on an AP view of the pelvis and Dunn views of the hip (Fig. 28.8). Similarly these X-rays can also guide the clinician to the presence of osteoarthritis, and abnormalities in morphology such as acetabular dysplasia, acetabular retroversion or anteversion, the presence of os acetabulare, and not-to-be-missed pathologies such as a slipped upper femoral epiphysis, Perthes disease, tumors, fractured neck of femur, and avascular necrosis. Unfortunately a plain radiograph does not provide information about soft tissue injuries such as labral, chondral, or ligamentum teres pathology.

CT scans are generally not utilized as a diagnostic tool for hip pathology, as most diagnostic information is usually obtained by clinical examination, a plain radiograph, and MRI. However, surgeons will often obtain specific CT scans preoperatively to

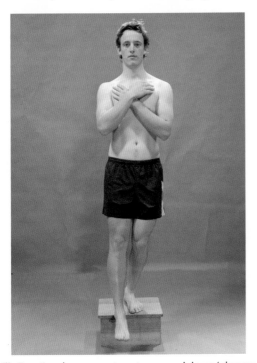

(i) Functional movements—step up and down (observe stability, pain) assist them in planning surgery for the treatment of FAI. The POD (Pritchard–O'Donnell) "position of discomfort" protocol CT gives surgeons specific three-dimensional images (Fig. 28.12) providing information regarding impingement sites, femoral head–neck morphology and version, acetabular overhang and version, and joint space loss anterosuperiorly. Surgeons may obtain specific CT scans preoperatively to assist them in planning surgery for the treatment of FAI.

MRI is commonly used in the diagnosis of soft tissue injuries of the hip. Pathologies such as labral tears, ligamentum teres tears, tendon and bursae pathology and, occasionally, chondral defects may be seen on an MRI scan. Unfortunately the sensitivity and specificity of MRI to these injuries is not high, and false-negative results are often noted.

Due to the depth of the joint, diagnostic ultrasound is not especially useful for the diagnosis of intra-articular hip pathology; however, it can be useful in determining the presence of bursae of the greater trochanter or iliopsoas tendon, and tendinopathy of these regions. Real-time ultrasound can be used to assess the function of the deep lumbar and hip stabilizing muscles.

Diagnostic injections of local anesthetic are used frequently in the hip to determine the presence of intra-articular pathology of the hip. These are generally performed under imaging guidance. A reduction in symptoms following an injection generally confirms the presence of intra-articular pathology, although a negative response does not necessarily indicate that no pathology is present, and further investigation and management may still be warranted.

Labral tears

Tears of the acetabular labrum (Fig. 28.13) are seen commonly in the athletic population, with 22% of sportspeople with groin pain having labral tears, and 55% of patients with mechanical symptoms and hip pain having labral tears.[19, 22, 43-45] The etiology of labral tears is well described in the literature.

The presence of both FAI[5, 8, 10, 37, 46] and developmental dysplasia of the hip (DDH)[47, 48] has been repeatedly shown to increase the risk of a labral tear. This is thought to be due to impingement of the labrum in the presence of FAI and increased shear forces on the outer joint margins including the labrum, in the presence of DDH.

The prevalence of labral tears in the US and Europe is greatest anteriorly.[19, 22, 43, 49] Various causes for the high number of anterior labral tears have

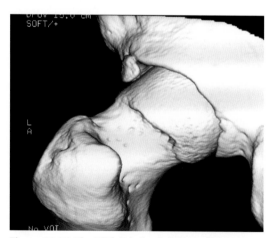

Figure 28.12 The POD (Pritchard–O'Donnell) "position of discomfort" protocol CT gives surgeons specific 3-dimensional images providing information regarding impingement sites, femoral head–neck morphology and version, acetabular overhang and version, and joint space loss anterosuperiorly

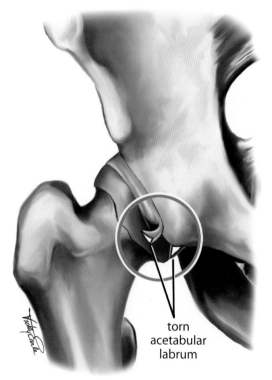

torn acetabular labrum

Figure 28.13 Labral tear
(a) Pathology

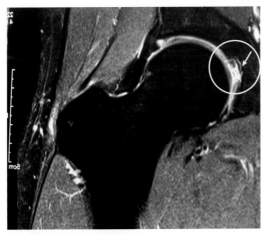

(b) MR arthrogram (MRA)
with gadolinium contrast leaking through a labral tear
(circle)

been postulated, including reduced thickness of the labrum anteriorly, the prevalence of FAI lesions seen anteriorly resulting in anterior impingement, and common functional activities, especially those with repetitive twisting and pivoting of the hip.[10]

The reduced bony support seen anteriorly in the hip due to the anteverted position of the acetabulum, which results in higher shear forces on anterior soft tissue structures, is also a likely cause of labral pathology. It has been shown that in the last 20–30% of the stance phase of gait, and in more than 5° of hip extension, increased forces are placed on anterior soft tissue structures by the head of femur.[19, 50]

Tears of the acetabular labrum are usually classified as type I or type II tears.[22, 51] Type I is described as a detachment of the labrum from the articular hyaline cartilage at the acetabular rim. Type II is described as cleavage tears within the substance of the labrum. The location of these tears relative to the vascularization of the labrum must be considered when establishing the potential for healing of the tear, and the most appropriate type of intervention.

The identification of labral tears in patients remains difficult. The patient often complains of mechanical symptoms such as locking, clicking, catching, and giving way. The location of pain is usually reported to be within the anterior hip or in the anterior groin region, although some patients report pain in the posterior buttock.

Clinical examination is also difficult, as most clinical tests have poor sensitivity and specificity regarding the type and location of pathology, although the

FADIR (Fig. 28.11b) and FABER (Fig. 28.11c) are often described as being appropriate for the diagnosis of labral pathology.

Radiological investigations remain unreliable, with MRA the only investigation having a reasonable degree of sensitivity and specificity[19] (Fig. 28.13b).

Labral tears are often suspected, but not confirmed until patients present for hip arthroscopy, which remains the gold standard for diagnosis of labral pathology.[19, 22]

Sportspeople with labral pathology may respond to conservative management, and this should usually be trialed prior to undergoing surgery, except possibly in those patients with large bumps who are engaging in activity that demands more range of motion than the sportsperson safely achieves before impingement. Management should be directed to unloading the damaged labrum, which is almost always anterior and/or superior.

Repetitive hip flexion, adduction or abduction, and rotation at the end of range should be avoided through activity modification. Improving hip joint neuromotor control via activation of the deep stabilizing muscles, initially in an unloaded and then a progressively loaded manner, appears to assist in the unloading of the labrum.

Gait retraining may also be undertaken to minimize excessive hip extension at the end of stance phase of gait, as increased hip extension has been demonstrated to increase the loads on anterior hip joint structures.[52] Neuromotor control of the hip should be maximized and any remote factors influencing the mechanics of the hip should be addressed.

Ligamentum teres tears

Tears of the ligamentum teres (Fig. 28.14 overleaf) are seen frequently in sportspeople undergoing hip arthroscopy, and are being reported more frequently in the literature. Studies have found up to 70% of sportspeople undergoing hip arthroscopy for FAI and labral tears also have tears of the ligamentum teres.[10] Tears of the ligamentum teres are classified as:

- type I—a partial tear
- type II—a complete rupture
- type III—a degenerate ligament.[53]

The mechanism of injury for ligamentum teres most commonly involves forced flexion and adduction, and often internal or external rotation.[53] Twisting motions and hyperabduction injuries have also been reported to cause a tear to this ligament.

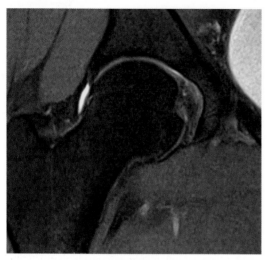

Figure 28.14 Ligament teres tear

Figure 28.15 Position from which to internally and externally rotate the hip in the ligamentum teres test

With the likelihood of the ligamentum teres playing a large proprioceptive and stabilization role of the hip becoming increasing recognized, the prompt diagnosis and management of these injuries in the sportsperson is essential. Likewise, any surgical procedure that sacrifices the ligamentum teres through open dislocation should be carefully considered.

The symptoms of a ligamentum teres tear appear to be similar to other intra-articular hip pathologies, with most patients complaining of deep groin and/or medial/anterior thigh pain, catching, reduction in range of motion, and night pain.[53, 54]

Clinically these patients will also often present with significant increased tone of the adductor muscle group, and an injured ligamentum teres when touched with a radiofrequency probe intra-operatively can generate an adduction moment force powerful enough to reduce the hip while in traction.[55] These patients also present with reduced strength of the hip external rotators and extensors.

There are presently no established radiological or clinical tests that reliably identify tears of the ligamentum teres, and hip arthroscopy is the gold standard in diagnosis of these tears. However, Pritchard et al. have recently developed a clinical test that may have clinical utility.[56]

The test aims to place the femoral head and neck into a position that avoids bony and soft tissue impingement, while placing traction on the ligamentum teres by moving the hip through a full range of internal and external rotation.

The test is performed with the patient's hip flexed to full flexion without tilting of the pelvis (Fig. 28.15).

The hip is then extended by 30 degrees. From this position (full flexion minus 30 degrees), the hip is moved into full abduction and then adducted 30 degrees (full abduction minus 30 degrees). The hip is then internally and externally rotated through full range. The presence of pain is considered a positive test.

Often ligamentum teres pathology is not confirmed until a sportsperson presents for surgery, but it should be suspected in episodes involving the mechanism of injury mentioned above. The principles of management of ligamentum teres pathology are similar to those for labral pathology, with a particular emphasis on regaining neuromotor control, excellent proprioception, and avoiding positions that place the ligament under most stress through activity modification.

The sportsperson with a ligamentum teres injury often presents with extremely overactive long adductors, which can be a source of considerable additional discomfort. This should also be managed with appropriate myofascial techniques, trigger point dry needling, and *gentle* stretching.

Synovitis

Synovitis (Fig. 28.16) is often seen in sportspeople with other intra-articular hip pathology—whether FAI, labral tears, ligamentum teres tears or chondropathy. One surgical study found synovitis coexisting in 70% of sportspeople with hip joint pathology.[2] It is rarely seen as a primary entity. Synovitis can cause considerable pain in the hip joint, with night pain and pain at rest being common presentations.

Synovitis is a concern to the clinician because of the pain and the associated changes in muscle

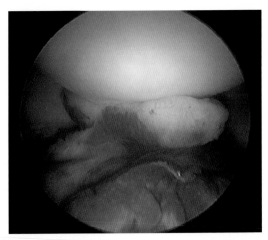

Figure 28.16 Synovitis

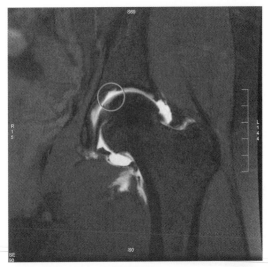

Figure 28.17 (a) Chondral lesion (acetabular side)

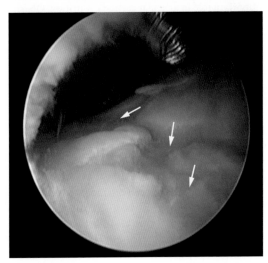

(b) Arthroscopic view of severe chondral damage secondary to FAI

activation that are seen around the hip in the presence of pain. In addition, the implications of synovial dysfunction on cytokine production, nutrition, and hydration of articular cartilage, which may already show signs of chondropathy, are significant for the long-term health of the hip joint.

Management should be aimed to addressing the other coexisting pathology, restoring normal neuromotor control around the hip, modifying loads, and also anti-inflammatory treatment such as oral non-steroidal anti-inflammatory drugs (NSAIDs) or intra-articular injection.

Chondropathy

Changes to the chondral surfaces of the hip are often seen in conjunction with other hip pathologies (Fig. 28.17). It is well reported that the presence of FAI,[5, 6, 11, 39] decreased acetabular anteversion,[7] labral pathology,[19, 48] and developmental dysplasia of the hip (DDH)[6, 7, 48] will lead to an increased risk of chondropathy and ultimately osteoarthritis of the hip. In patients with significant labral pathology, chondral loss is often up to 70% of the full thickness—or Outerbridge grade III or IV.[57]

A study examining hip pathology in AFL footballers found that full-thickness chondral loss of >30% of the acetabular depth anteriorly was found in 52% of players, who also all had labral tears and FAI.[2] It is also proposed that the presence of longstanding synovitis may also affect the nutrition of chondral surfaces, possibly exacerbating chondral damage.

The majority of chondral lesions are seen on the anterior or superior aspect of the acetabular rim, at the chondrolabral junction.[2, 57] This is not surprising

considering that this is also the location for the majority of cam and pincer lesions, and the majority of labral tears.

Developmental dysplasia of the hip (DDH) also involves a reduction in the bony coverage of the femoral head by the acetabulum; thus the anteriorly directed forces of the femoral head will be concentrated on a smaller surface area on the anterior aspect of the joint.

The clinical diagnosis of chondropathy may be confirmed with plain radiographs, although early chondral changes will not visible. MRI may identify earlier chondral lesions, although the extent of chondropathy is often only evident on hip arthroscopy.[2, 57]

Chondropathy is difficult to manage and may be difficult to confirm in the early stages without arthroscopic confirmation. If suspected, the management again is similar to that of labral pathology, as the majority of chondral lesions of the hip occur in the anterior aspect of the acetabular rim at the chondrolabral junction. As such, this region should be unloaded in the same fashion as labral pathology, with an emphasis on regaining normal neuromotor control of the hip. Recent evidence has shown atrophy in inferior gluteus maximus and hypertrophy in gluteus medius in osteoarthritis, with atrophy also occurring in gluteus medius in severe osteoarthritis.[58, 59]

Attempts to minimize synovitis should also be made, as the synovium and synovial fluid play an important role in articular cartilage nutrition. Obesity and lack of exercise aggravate the symptoms of osteoarthritis. The outcomes of hip arthroscopy for individuals with significant chondral loss are generally worse than for those with no chondral loss.[10, 17, 60, 61] Where chondral surface damage is found, conservative measures should be attempted first, and in some cases the sportsperson should be counseled to modify the amount of weight-bearing activities they undertake.

Rehabilitation of the injured hip

Rehabilitation of the injured hip requires careful consideration of the interplay between pain and loading (including progression of exercises and activities). Importantly, due to its role in all activities of daily living, including simple activities such as sit-to-stand, standing, and walking, it is hard to "rest" the hip. It is vital that the patient and the clinician have a good understanding around monitoring joint loads and the loading response.

The general principles of management of hip pathology are straightforward and consistently reported in the small amount of literature available concerning rehabilitation of the hip.[10, 19, 62–65] Unfortunately there is no evidence available other than clinical commentaries that evaluate the effectiveness of particular principles of rehabilitation of the hip.

The three most commonly reported principles of rehabilitation are shown in the box.

This section discusses each of these general principles, and then applies them to commonly seen conditions of the hip. We then outline the application of these principles of management to patients post–hip arthroscopy surgery.

Unloading and protecting damaged or potentially vulnerable structures

The most effective way to unload and protect specific structures of the hip varies slightly for different pathology, based on the understanding of the functional anatomy and biomechanics of the hip. When addressing the loads on structures outlined below, the principles of management of neuromotor control and remote factors should also be applied. Managing the load of the hip can be particularly difficult as the sportsperson has to walk about simply for activities of daily living. Thus it is vital that their ability to walk, stand, and perform everyday activities such as getting in and out of a chair is managed in such a way that these activities do not aggravate the underlying pathology.

Restoration of normal dynamic and neuromotor control

Restoration of dynamic and neuromotor control around the hip follows the same principles as other joints.

Phase 1: Deep hip stabilizer retraining

The short hip external rotator (SHER) muscles are those with the greatest capacity to provide dynamic stabilization of the hip (see above). Retraining of these deep hip stabilizers may be undertaken in the early stages of rehabilitation. As it does with other pain conditions,[66, 67] clinical observation indicates that pain appears to inhibit effective activation of the SHER muscles. Therefore, pain must be well controlled.

The initial step involves educating the patient in the role of the SHER muscles to provide dynamic hip stability, and the location and actions of these muscles. The second step involves facilitating independent

---

Three key principles of rehabilitation

1. Unload and protect damaged or potentially vulnerable structures within and around the joint.
2. Restore normal dynamic and neuromotor control around the hip joint.
3. Address other remote factors that may be altering the function of the kinetic chain.

contraction of these muscles. This is often best commenced in 4-point kneeling (Fig. 28.18a), where the patient is taught to activate the SHER muscles and then perform an isometric external rotation contraction against minimal resistance. The aim is to produce a low-level tonic hold of these muscles. In this position (90° hip flexion), the contribution from the larger external rotator (gluteus maximus) is reduced (see the section about joint structure and muscle function earlier in this chapter), thus enabling more specificity of activation for the SHER muscles.

Both the patient and the clinician must be confident that the deep hip stabilizers are activated and a real-time ultrasound machine may assist with providing feedback. Progression of the retraining includes providing different levels of resistance, number of repetitions, and speed of movements. Other progressions include increasing the amount of hip flexion, and decreasing the support (i.e. lifting one hand) to increase the balance demands and challenge to lumbopelvic stability.

Further progressions include activation of the deep hip stabilizers (Fig. 28.18b) in a variety of degrees of hip range of motion and in various functional positions as the activity of the sportsperson demands, and can be assessed using a real-time ultrasound in these varying positions. For example, a sportsperson who performs regularly in positions of hip flexion such as a deep squat should ultimately perform muscle activation in this position.

Phase 2: Gluteus maximus retraining

Gluteus maximus plays an important role in generating extension and external rotation torque, and has the potential to provide hip stabilization by resisting anterior hip force.[28, 31] Facilitation of independent gluteus maximus contraction may be best commenced prone (Figs 28.19a, b overleaf), where the patient is taught to perform an isometric external rotation contraction against minimal resistance (low-level tonic hold of these muscles). As with the SHER muscles, feedback may assist in ensuring that the muscle is activated. Since the gluteus maximus is more superficial, feedback may be provided by palpation, surface EMG biofeedback, or real-time ultrasound machine.

The activation of the gluteus maximus should be undertaken in a variety of degrees of hip range of motion determined by the functional demands the athlete's activity requires, and can be assessed using

Figure 28.18 Deep hip stabilizer strengthening exercises
(a) Activation of the SHER muscles in 4-point kneel with theraband and resistance. The degree of difficulty can be progressed by decreasing or increasing the level of resistance, changing the speed of activation and increasing the number of repetitions. The challenge to the core can also be increased by lifting one hand off the floor in this position, and the degree of hip flexion or extension, and abduction or adduction can be altered based on the needs of the sportsperson

(b) Progression of activation of deep hip stabilizers into a closed chain position, ensuring adequate deep hip external rotators, gluteus maximus, lateral pelvic, and core stability

a real-time ultrasound in these varying positions. For example, hip abduction and external rotation, or hip adduction and internal rotation for a sportsperson who performs cutting maneuvers, or in hip flexion for a sportsperson who is required to perform in a deep squatting position. It should be then progressed from open chain to closed chain and then functional positions.

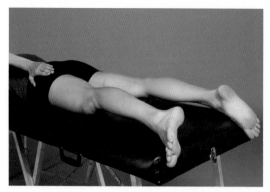

Figure 28.19 Gluteus maximus retraining exercises—examples of activation of gluteus maximus, in combination with SHER muscles in prone. Real-time ultrasound assessment can also be undertaken in this position

(a) Prone—knee extension

(b) Knee flexion

Phase 3: Generalized strengthening exercises

Generalized hip strengthening exercises should only be commenced when the patient and clinician are confident that the key stabilizing muscles can be activated and the activation maintained. During this phase, the aim is to restore muscle function (strength, endurance) and proprioception. This phase remains low-impact (Fig. 28.20a). Exercises should initially be undertaken with specific activation of the deep stabilizers prior to commencing the exercise. This ensures that the sportsperson has adequate control of the hip prior to placing it under load, which will assist in protecting vulnerable or damaged structures within the hip.

Generalized hip strengthening exercises should be undertaken, based on clinical assessment. For example, hip abductors (predominantly gluteus medius) should be targeted for those with reduced hip abduction strength.

Strengthening exercises need to be targeted to the needs of the individual, progressed according to patient responses, and targeted to the sporting/physical requirements. For example, a sportsperson who regularly jumps and lands (such as a netballer or gymnast) should incorporate these actions into their rehabilitation program (Fig. 28.20b).

Exercises are frequently commenced in prone (to ensure specificity and isolation of muscle activations) or in 4-point kneeling and then progressed into functional/weight-bearing positions, bilaterally and then unilaterally (Figs 28.20c–e).

Phase 4: Functional and sports-specific activity

Once good neuromotor control of the deep hip stabilizers and global hip muscles has been regained, functional and sport-specific activities should be assessed, and then undertaken, both to retrain these

Figure 28.20 Generalized hip strengthening exercises **(a)** An example of low-impact functional retraining of deep hip stabilizers, ensuring adequate activation of these muscle groups in a challenging situation without excessive impact or load through vulnerable hip structures

B

(b) A jumping and landing task ensuring adequate activation of deep hip, lateral pelvic, and core stabilizers at take-off and landing

movement patterns but also ensure the sportsperson can cope with these activities without failing.

Any retraining of functional activities should focus on pre-activation of the deep hip stabilizers, adequate control of the lumbar spine and pelvis during the activity, and correct alignment of the femur during weight-bearing tasks (Fig. 28.21 overleaf).

Retraining of hip stabilizers should be performed in the positions that place the hip at greatest risk of overload, such as direction change and pivoting, deep squatting, and kicking. They should also be undertaken in a repeated fashion, again to ensure the sportsperson does not fail in a controlled environment.

Criteria for returning to sport

The decision regarding a patient's readiness to return to sport is made using clinical judgment of the individual's functional capacity. In the absence of robust scientific evidence, the following criteria are suggested:

- performance on the one-leg hop test (or other single-leg functional tests) at least 90% of the uninjured side (if unilateral symptoms)

(c) and (d) Two examples of later-stage functional activities with concurrent SHER muscle activation, core activation, and functional balance and proprioceptive challenges

(e) Examples of later-stage functional exercises incorporating deep hip and core stability with proprioceptive and neuromotor control retraining

- performance on strength tests at least 90% of the uninjured side (if unilateral symptoms)
- performance on strength test indicates balance of muscle strength (e.g. external rotation strength similar to internal rotation strength; flexion similar to extension, abduction similar to adduction).

Address other remote factors that may be altering the function of the kinetic chain

As outlined previously, a number of remote factors (e.g. lumbopelvic control) are likely to influence the rehabilitation of hip pain and pathology. Therefore, all potential contributing factors should be addressed and treated appropriately.

Surgical management of the injured hip

Hip arthoscopy is the gold standard for the diagnosis of early chondral, labral, or ligamentum teres pathology, and has indications ranging from diagnostic purposes through to removal of loose bodies, labral tears, chondral lesions, FAI, version abnormalities, and dysplasia.

Hip arthroscopy has evolved substantially over the last 10 years, with improved technique and dedicated instrument design. It is now commonly performed to manage intra-articular hip pathologies, including labral tears.[68] Hip arthroscopy has revolutionized hip surgery, since this minimally invasive procedure is associated with considerably less morbidity than open procedures.

Open surgical indications include femoral and acetabular osteotomies for dysplasia and for treatment of unusual FAI morphology. Internationally, the number of hip arthroscopy procedures now performed is growing rapidly, with 30 000 procedures performed in 2008, with this number expected to increase by 15% annually.[69]

The basic principles of arthroscopic hip surgery are to treat damaged tissues to allow the healing process to be maximized. This often involves debridement of the irreparable tissue, and stimulation of a

Figure 28.21 Retraining of functional activities—single-leg hop for distance

healing response. The joint is assessed for mechanical optimization to assist with healing and help prevent further damage through mechanical insult. Range of motion is critical in this assessment.

Clinically, patients presenting for hip arthroscopy surgery tend to be grouped into two categories:

- those diagnosed with soft tissue pathology resulting from bony morphological variations, requiring reshaping on one or both sides of the joint to increase the available range of motion prior to impingement
- those not requiring bony intervention but presenting with soft tissue injuries requiring intervention.

The first group includes patients with FAI which may be cam, pincer, or mixed impingement. This group have coexisting labral pathology, ligamentum teres pathology, or chondral lesions.

 Incidental findings of FAI-related morphology without typical associated pain need no intervention, merely education and observation.

The second group includes those with soft tissue pathologies, but without morphological change requiring surgical intervention. Soft tissue pathologies include labral pathology, ligamentum teres pathology, chondral lesions, synovial pathology, loose bodies, crystalline hip arthropathy, infection, and any combination of these. Patients with these lesions may have co-existing issues such as dysplasia or hypermobility which predispose them to such injuries, but do not require surgical intervention. This group also includes patients with essentially normal morphology but who undergo a massive single episode of excessive range (usually rotation) which causes trauma to the associated soft tissues.

Hip arthroscopy is a demanding procedure with a steep learning curve requiring advanced training. Debridement of labrum, ligamentum teres, and chondral surfaces require less recovery time and less rehabilitation than more complex procedures (e.g. labral refixation and associated rim excision, and femoral head–neck reshaping for cam deformity).

The body of evidence examining outcomes following hip arthroscopy is growing rapidly, although most studies are case series (level IV) evidence. The majority of the literature focuses on outcomes following surgery for FAI, labral pathology, chondropathy, or combined pathology.

Three systematic reviews have examined outcomes following hip arthroscopy.[60, 61, 70] They each concluded that short-term outcomes are generally promising for hip arthroscopy treatment of FAI and labral pathology, although outcomes are generally poorer if significant chondropathy is observed; further long-term studies are required.

Ten-year outcome studies examining outcomes in hip arthroscopy have reached similar conclusions to the systematic reviews, mostly finding good outcomes unless significant chondral loss is present, with a number of those with significant chondral loss eventually progressing to joint replacement surgery.[17, 71, 72] These studies looked at all pathologies, and are somewhat limited by the enormous change in surgical technique that has occurred in the last decade.

Two specific studies looked at outcomes of hip arthroscopy in elite sportspeople.[2, 10] The populations included were AFL footballers and NHL ice hockey players, both of which have a high rate of hip and groin pain. Both studies examined FAI and labral pathology and found good short-term outcomes, patient satisfaction, and return-to-sport levels, although each study was limited by the short follow up of two years. Further longer term follow-up in sportspeople needs to be undertaken in order to conclusively understand the outcomes of these procedures in sportspeople.

Rehabilitation following hip arthroscopy

Rehabilitation following hip arthroscopy has been described in the literature in a number of clinical commentaries, and essentially follows the same conservative principles of management outlined above.[62, 64, 73] The individual pathology treated during hip arthroscopy must be considered when designing a postoperative rehabilitation program to ensure the hip is adequately unloaded and protected while healing. This generally involves a period of partial-weight-bearing as tolerated on crutches until a pain-free normal gait pattern is achieved.

Generally osteochondroplasties performed for the correction of FAI must be protected for at least six weeks, as should microfracture surgery performed for chondral defects.

Labral debridement and repairs should be protected for 4–6 weeks, ensuring the sportsperson avoids potential positions of impingement through activity modification and normalization of neuromuscular control around the hip.

Injuries to the ligamentum teres should be protected for six weeks by avoiding end-range positions that place the ligament under stress, and ensuring excellent neuromotor and proprioceptive control around the hip.

During this initial protective phase, the sportsperson should commence active rehabilitation of the deep hip stabilizers, initially in an isolated fashion, and then progressing into functional activity in a safe manner. During this time the therapist should also address any overactivity of the secondary stabilizers such as the long adductors, the proximal gluteals, tensor fascia lata, and the hip flexors.

Once this protective phase is complete, the sportsperson should undertake a dynamic rehabilitation program ensuring full strength of all muscle groups around the hip, normal function of the whole kinetic chain, and sport-specific activity. A full assessment of the muscle strength and function around the hip using real-time ultrasound and hand-held dynamometry at this time can also assist in providing targeted exercise programs to address any ongoing residual deficits in strength or muscle activation. Generally most sportspeople return to full sport between three and five months postoperatively following hip arthroscopy, although this varies depending on the level and type of sport played, as well as the specific pathology and surgery performed.

Os acetabulare

An os acetabulare (or os acetabuli) is defined as "a separated fragment of bone at the rim of the hip socket." They have traditionally been regarded as an unfused secondary ossification centre. The orientation of the cartilaginous growth plate is more *parallel* to the joint surface (Figs. 28.22 a, b).

 In sportspeople, an os acetabulare is seen in conjunction with FAI and is thought to be a fatigue fracture (Figs 28.22c, d).

The separation line is *perpendicular* to the joint surface. Similar fatigue fractures had previously been described in severely dysplastic hips.

In a study of 495 patients treated surgically for FAI,[74] a large osseous fragment at the anterolateral rim was found in 18 hips. All patients presented radiographically with a femoral head showing an aspherical extension producing a "cam" impingement. Sixteen hips had a retroverted acetabulum, indicating anterior overcover. Preoperative MRIs confirmed a fragment composed of labrum, articular cartilage,

and bone. The gap between the stable acetabulum and the rim fragment had a vertical orientation. All patients had been exposed to a physically demanding profession or contact sport, and in 15 hips no memorable traumatic episode was present. The mechanism

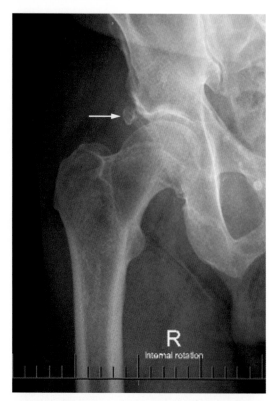

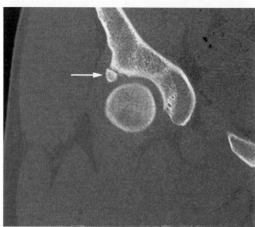

Figure 28.22 Os acetabulare (arrows)
(a) X-ray **(b)** CT scan of true os acetabulare showing orientation of the cartilaginous growth plate is more *parallel* to the joint surface

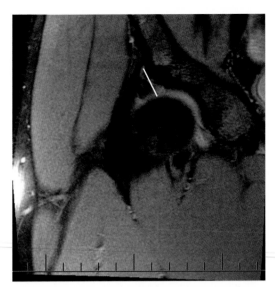
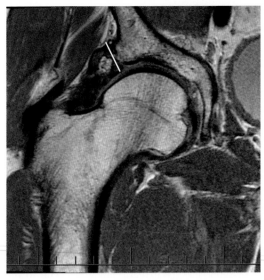

(c) and (d) are MRIs of os acetabulare due to fatigue fracture. Note the separation line *perpendicular* to joint surface

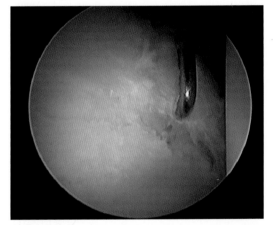
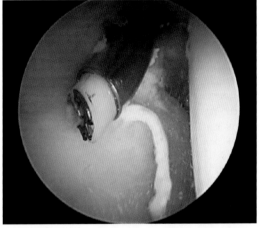

(e) The labrum and articular cartilage can be damaged at the site of the os acetabulare and can be unstable to probe

(f) Toothpaste-like calcific debris may be removed from the labrum

leading to this acetabular rim fragment is thought to be fatiguing due to femoro-acetabular impingement. The aspheric portion of the head is jammed into the acetabulum and with time causes a stress fracture of the area of overcoverage of the anterior acetabulum.

The treatment of symptomatic os acetabulare is commonly achieved during hip arthroscopy. During acetabular rim assessment, the labrum and articular cartilage is probed. It is common for the labrum and articular cartilage to be damaged at the site of the os acetabulare (Fig. 28.22e) and can be unstable to

probe. During labral takedown and rim excision, the os acetabulare is removed, and the labrum refixed to the rim of the acetabulum. If the fragment of bone is very large, removal may result in insufficient bony coverage. In these cases, refixing of the fragment is preferred.

Occasionally, toothpaste-like calcific debris (Fig. 28.22f) similar to calcific tendinopathy of the shoulder is removed from the labrum, and is thought to represent a response to labral injury, which can mimic os acetabulare on plain X-ray.

Lateral hip pain
with ANGIE FEARON

Lateral hip pain is a common presentation particularly among distance runners and women over the age of 40. Traditionally lateral hip pain was thought to be due to trochanteric bursitis. However, it appears that tendinopathy of the gluteus medius and/or minimus and bursa pathology probably co-exist. The term "greater trochanter pain syndrome" (GTPS) is now used to describe this condition.[75, 76]

Greater trochanter pain syndrome (GTPS)

The anatomy of the greater trochanter and its associated tendons and bursae is shown in Figure 28.23. There are two bursae around the greater trochanter. The gluteus medius bursa lies beneath the tendon of the gluteus medius and medial to the greater trochanter. The trochanteric bursa is lateral to the greater trochanter.

Gluteus medius tendinopathy presents with tenderness to palpation of the gluteus medius muscle, and can be triggered by sudden falls, prolonged weight-bearing on one extremity for long periods, activity overuse, or sporting injuries. Most commonly, this situation is observed in middle-aged women who have commenced unaccustomed exercise (e.g. vigorous walking or joining a gymnasium).

Patients report pain over the greater trochanter which may extend into the lateral thigh, and even the lateral leg. The pain tends to be episodic but worsening over time. Frequently, pain lying on the affected side at night is the most distressing symptom, although pain with, or following, weight-bearing activities is likely to be identified. As with other tendon problems, the cumulative load over three days needs to be drawn from the patient in order to identify the aggravating factors.

Palpation of the greater trochanter produces the "jump sign"—the person nearly leaps off the bed. Range of movement tests for flexion, adduction, abduction, and the rotations in 0° and 90° flexion are normal or slightly increased, although muscle spasm may affect these. The FABER test is frequently positive, while Ober's test (Chapter 34) may or may not be positive.

Resisted external rotation and abduction muscles tests are reported to aid with the diagnosis; however there is very limited evidence to support this. The de-rotation test (Fig. 28.11f) may assist.

The step up and down test (Fig. 28.11i) may help differentiate between tendinopathy, tears, and hip osteoarthritis. Those with more severe GTPS report higher levels of pain with stepping up forwards onto the step, and down sideways off the step. Those with less severe presentation have pain with the hip hitch with external and/or internal rotation. A report of groin pain with these activities is likely if the person has hip joint pathology (e.g. chondropathy, osteoarthritis) in addition to lateral hip pain.

A Trendelenburg gait, and weakness may be present. Differentiating between pain inhibition and true weakness is important. These symptoms specifically affect runners, possibly due to the tilting of the pelvis with running.

Diagnostic ultrasound can be performed to determine if fluid is present in the bursa or thickening exists about the bursa, and to look for echogenic changes that are consistent with tendinopathy and tears.[77, 78] Magnetic resonance imaging (MRI) demonstrates tendinopathy and tears of the gluteus medius[79, 80] (Fig. 28.24).

Treatment

The principles of treating GTPS are similar to the treatment of other tendinopathies:

- Control pain by minimizing the compression on the greater trochanter and managing the load on the tendons.
- Strengthen the gluteal muscles.[81]
- Treat the comorbidities.[82]

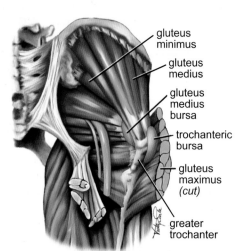

gluteus minimus

gluteus medius

gluteus medius bursa

trochanteric bursa

gluteus maximus (cut)

greater trochanter

Figure 28.23 The anatomy of the greater trochanter and its associated tendons and bursae

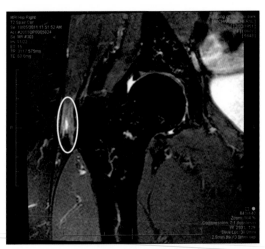

Figure 28.24 MRI appearances of gluteus medius abnormalities

(a) Tendinopathy

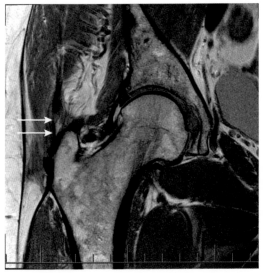

(b) Tendon tear

Managing pain

In the acute phase, treatment of GTPS consists of relative rest, ice, iliotibial band soft tissue work to improve compliance, taping, gaining good gluteal muscle control, and NSAIDs and paracetamol. Patients should be checked for hip abduction and rotation control in activities of daily living (e.g. getting out of a chair, climbing stairs, and standing). As the patient improves, sport-specific activities such as running, jumping, and hopping should be analyzed. Runners should avoid banked tracks or roads

with excessive camber when resuming their running program.

Shock wave therapy has been shown to be effective in the treatment of GTPS.[81, 83]

Recalcitrant cases may respond to a local corticosteroid injection. A peritendinous ultrasound-guided corticosteroid injection has been shown to be an effective treatment of gluteus medius tendinopathy; 72% of the patients showed a clinically significant improvement in pain level, which was defined as a reduction in the VAS pain score of ≥30%.[84] However, another study demonstrated that less than 50% of subjects had a positive outcome three months after the injection.[81]

It is essential that a corticosteroid injection is only regarded as one part of the treatment—as a means to reduce pain and enable the patient to commence a muscle strengthening and postural control program, which is the key to the treatment process.

Strengthening the gluteal (and other lower leg/trunk) muscles

The following exercises are designed to enhance the control and strength of the gluteal muscles in people with GTPS, and can be taught in addition to lumbopelvic control work (Chapter 14). Importantly, in people with GTPS, positions of hip adduction may be associated with increased pain and hence exercises such as "clams" into hip adduction may be best avoided.

In prone, with the leg slightly abducted, knee flexed 90°, the patient is instructed to medially and laterally rotate their hip within pain limits. Gaining excellent control of this movement through range—including lateral rotation—provides both concentric and eccentric activity of gluteus medius and minimus muscles in an unloaded situation. This exercise should be repeated in varying degrees of hip flexion (prone over pillows or a bolster), as this targets the anterior fibers of gluteus minimus and medius and the middle fibers of gluteus medius. Progression of this exercise is to add ankle weights (using response to load as a guide).

Hip extension and abduction in prone over pillows (hip flexion) and/or bilateral bridging (knees and feet apart to reduce hip adduction) is also useful (Fig. 28.18 on page 531).

Hip abduction strengthening should be avoided in the initial stages of GTPS because it provokes symptoms. Hip abduction should only be commenced when the patient has good control of the deep hip stabilizers, and it should commence in positions of hip abduction initially. As the acute stage resolves, hip abductor strengthening is important and may be achieved in the aquatic environment.

As the patient gains control and strength of gluteal muscles, the clinician should progress the difficulty of exercises. Options include single-leg standing with contralateral hand on a bench or backing against a wall (Fig. 28.25a) to gain static pelvic control, progessing to no assistance (Fig. 28.25b), and more challenging balance exercises (Fig. 28.25c). Rubber-band type (resistance) exercises need to be introduced very carefully, and the response monitored carefully. Pilates-style sliding boards have also been used (Fig. 28.25d).

Treat the comorbidities

Hip-related comorbidities (e.g. osteoarthritis, labral tears) frequently coexist with GTPS, and they should be addressed as outlined above.[82] Furthermore, referred pain from the spine should be assessed and treated as appropriate.

Gluteus medius tendon tears

Gluteus medius and minimus tendon tears are common in older patients. This can be confirmed on MRI[85] (Fig. 28.24b). In patients where the tear remains symptomatic despite conservative management, various surgical options are currently available. Up to 60% obtain relief from an arthroscopic bursectomy, although some patients will go on to a repair of the tendon.[86, 87]

 Examination of the hip is in the *Clinical Sports Medicine* masterclasses at www.clinicalsportsmedicine.com.

(a)

B

(c)

(b)

(d)

Figure 28.25 Examples of exercises that provide increasingly greater challenges to improve strength and control of gluteal muscles

REFERENCES

1. Orchard J, Seward H. 2008–2009 AFL injury report, www.afl.com.au/injury%20report/tabid/13706/default.aspx.

2. Singh PJ, O'Donnell JM. The outcome of hip arthroscopy in Australian Football League players: a review of 27 hips. *Arthroscopy* 2010;26(6):743–9.

3. Crawford MJ, Dy CJ, Alexander JW et al. The biomechanics of the hip labrum and the stability of the hip. *Clin Orth Rel Res* 2007(465):16–22.

4. Stähelin L, Stähelin T, Jolles BM et al. Arthroscopic offset restoration in femoroacetabular cam impingement: accuracy and early clinical outcome. *Arthroscopy* 2008; 24(1):51–7.

5. Beck M, Kalhor M, Leunig M et al. Hip morphology influences the pattern of damage to the acetabular cartilage. Femoroacetabular impingement as a cause of early osteoarthritis of the hip. *J Bone Joint Surg Br* 2005;87(7):1012–18.

6. Domayer SE, Mamisch TC, Kress I et al. Radial dGEMRIC in developmental dysplasia of the hip and in femoroacetabular impingement: preliminary results. *Osteoarth Cart* 2010;18(11):1421–8.

7. Hapa O, Yüksel HY, Muratli HH et al. Axial plane coverage and torsion measurements in primary osteoarthritis of the hip with good frontal plane coverage and spherical femoral head. *Arch Orth Trauma Surg* 2010;130(10):1305–10.

8. Ito K, Minka Ii MA, Leunig M et al. Femoroacetabular impingement and the cam-effect. A MRI-based quantitative anatomical study of the femoral head–neck offset. *J Bone Joint Surg Br* 2001;83(2):171–6.

9. McCarthy JMD, Noble PP, Aluisio FV et al. Anatomy, pathologic features, and treatment of acetabular labral tears. [Report]. *Clin Orth Rel Res* 2003;406(1):38–47.

10. Philippon MJ, Weiss DR, Kuppersmith DA et al. Arthroscopic labral repair and treatment of femoroacetabular impingement in professional hockey players. *Am J Sports Med* 2010;38(1):99–104.

11. Tanzer M, Noiseux N. Osseous abnormalities and early osteoarthritis: the role of hip impingement. *Clin Orthop Relat Res* 2004(429):170–7.

12. Ganz R, Parvizi J, Beck M et al. Femoroacetabular impingement: a cause for osteoarthritis of the hip. *Clin Orth Rel Res* 2003(417):112–20.

13. Parvizi J, Bican O, Bender B et al. Arthroscopy for labral tears in patients with developmental dysplasia of the hip: a cautionary note. *J Arthroplasty* 2009;24(6 Suppl):110–13.

14. Burnett RSJ, Della Rocca GJ, Prather H et al. Clinical presentation of patients with tears of the acetabular labrum. *J Bone Joint Surg Am* 2006;88(7):1448–57.

15. Bardakos NV, Villar RN. The ligamentum teres of the adult hip. *J Bone Joint Surg Br* 2009;91(1):8–15.

16. Byrd JW, Jones KS. Hip arthroscopy in athletes. *Clin Sports Med* 2001;20(4):749–61.

17. Byrd JWT, Jones KS. Prospective analysis of hip arthroscopy with 10-year followup. *Clin Orth Rel Res* 2010;468(3):741–6.

18. Stem E, O'Connor M, Kransdorf M et al. Computed tomography analysis of acetabular anteversion and abduction. *Skel Radiol* 2006;35(6):385–9.

19. Lewis CL, Sahrmann SA. Acetabular labral tears. *Phys Ther* 2006;86(1):110–21.

20. Petersen W, Petersen F, Tillmann B. Structure and vascularization of the acetabular labrum with regard to the pathogenesis and healing of labral lesions. *Arch Ortho Trauma Surg* 2003;123(6):283–8.

21. Kim SJ, Choi NH, Kim HJ. Operative hip arthroscopy. *Clin Orthop Relat Res* 1998(353):156–65.

22. Narvani AA, Tsiridis E, Tai CC et al. Acetabular labrum and its tears. *Br J Sports Med* 2003;37(5):207–11.

23. Ferguson SJ, Bryant JT, Ganz R et al. The acetabular labrum seal: a poroelastic finite element model. *Clin Biomech* 2000;15(6):463–8.

24. Konrath GA, Hamel AJ, Olson SA et al. The role of the acetabular labrum and the transverse acetabular ligament in load transmission in the hip. *J Bone Joint Surg Am* 1998;80(12):1781–8.

25. Rao J, Zhou YX, Villar RN. Injury to the ligamentum teres. Mechanism, findings, and results of treatment. *Clin Sports Med* 2001;20(4):791–9.

26. Leunig M, Beck M, Stauffer E et al. Free nerve endings in the ligamentum capitis femoris. *Acta Orth Scand* 2000;71(5):452–4.

27. Norkin C, Levangie P. *Joint structure and function.* Philadelphia: F.A. Davis Company 1983.

28. Neumann DA. Kinesiology of the hip: a focus on muscular actions. *J Orth Sports Phys Ther* 2010;40(2):82–94.

29. Ward SR, Winters TM, Blemker SS. The architectural design of the gluteal muscle group: implications for movement and rehabilitation. *J Orth Sports Phys Ther* 2010;40(2):95–102.

30. Levangie PK, Norkin CC. *Joint structure and function. A comprehensive analysis.* 4th edn rev. United States: F.A. Davis Company 2005.

31. Correa TA, Crossley KM, Kim HJ et al. Contributions of individual muscles to hip joint contact force in normal walking. *J Biomech* 2010;43(8):1618–22.

32. Delp SL, Hess WE, Hungerford DS et al. Variation of rotation moment arms with hip flexion. *J Biomech* 1999;32(5):493–501.

33. Blemker SS, Delp SL. Three-dimensional representation of complex muscle architectures and geometries. *Ann Biomed Eng* 2005;33(5):661–73.

34. Weir A, de Vos RJ, Moen M et al. Prevalence of radiological signs of femoroacetabular impingement in patients presenting with long-standing adductor-related groin pain. *Br J Sports Med* 2011;45(1):16–19.

35. Bradshaw CJ, Bundy M, Falvey E. The diagnosis of longstanding groin pain: a prospective clinical cohort study. *Br J Sports Med* 2008;42(10):551–4.

36. Allen D, Beaulé PE, Ramadan O et al. Prevalence of associated deformities and hip pain in patients with cam-type femoroacetabular impingement. *J Bone Joint Surg Br* 2009;91(5):589–94.

37. Siebenrock KA, Schoeniger R, Ganz R. Anterior femoro-acetabular impingement due to acetabular retroversion. Treatment with periacetabular osteotomy. *J Bone Joint Surg Am* 2003;85(2):278–86.

38. Pollard TCB, Villar RN, Norton MR et al. Femoroacetabular impingement and classification of the cam deformity: the reference interval in normal hips. *Acta Orthop* 2010;81(1):134–41.

39. Bardakos NV, Vasconcelos JC, Villar RN. Early outcome of hip arthroscopy for femoroacetabular impingement: the role of femoral osteoplasty in symptomatic improvement. *J Bone Joint Surg Br* 2008;90(12):1570–5.

40. Byrd JWT, Jones KS. Arthroscopic femoroplasty in the management of cam-type femoroacetabular impingement. *Clin Orth Rel Res* 2009;467(3):739–46.

41. Mitchell B, McCrory P, Brukner P et al. Hip joint pathology: clinical presentation and correlation between magnetic resonance arthrography, ultrasound, and arthroscopic findings in 25 consecutive cases. *Clin J Sport Med* 2003;13(3):152–6.

42. Lequesne M, Mathieu P, Vuillemin-Bodaghi V et al. Gluteal tendinopathy in refractory greater trochanter pain syndrome: diagnostic value of two clinical tests. *Arthritis Rheum* 2008;59(2):241–6.

43. McCarthy JC, Noble PC, Schuck MR et al. The watershed labral lesion: its relationship to early arthritis of the hip. *J Arthroplasty* 2001;16(8 Suppl 1):81–7.

44. McCarthy JC, Noble PC, Schuck MR et al. The role of labral lesions to development of early degenerative hip disease. *Clin Orth Rel Res* 2001(393):25–37.

45. Narvani AA, Tsiridis E, Kendall S et al. A preliminary report on prevalence of acetabular labrum tears in sports patients with groin pain. *Knee Surg Sports Traumatol Arthrosc* 2003;11(6):403–8.

46. Martin RL, Enseki KR, Draovitch P et al. Acetabular labral tears of the hip: Examination and diagnostic challenges. *J Orth Sports Phys Ther* 2006;36(7):503–15.

47. Dorrell JH, Catterall A. The torn acetabular labrum. *J Bone Joint Surg Br* 1986;68(3):400–3.

48. McCarthy JC, Lee JA. Acetabular dysplasia: a paradigm of arthroscopic examination of chondral injuries. *Clin Orth Rel Res* 2002(405):122–8.

49. Farjo LA, Glick JM, Sampson TG. Hip arthroscopy for acetabular labral tears. *Arthroscopy* 1999;15(2):132–7.

50. Lewis CL, Sahrmann SA, Moran DW. Anterior hip joint force increases with hip extension, decreased gluteal force, or decreased iliopsoas force. *J Biomech* 2007;40(16):3725–31.

51. Seldes RM, Tan V, Hunt J et al. Anatomy, histologic features, and vascularity of the adult acetabular labrum. *Clin Orth Rel Res* 2001(382):232–40.

52. Lewis CL, Sahrmann SA, Moran DW. Effect of hip angle on anterior hip joint force during gait. *Gait Posture* 2010;32(4):603–7.

53. Gray AJR, Villar RN. The ligamentum teres of the hip: an arthroscopic classification of its pathology. *Arthroscopy* 1997;13(5):575–8.

54. Byrd JWT, Jones KS. Diagnostic accuracy of clinical assessment, magnetic resonance imaging, magnetic resonance arthrography, intra-articular injection in hip arthroscopy patients. *Am J Sports Med* 2004;32(7):1668–74.

55. O'Donnell JM, Haviv B, Tikva P et al. Outcome of arthroscopic debridement of the isolated ligament teres tear. *ISHA Annual Scientific Meeting*. Cancun, Mexico, 2010.

56. Bates D, O'Donnell JM, Pritchard M et al. Assessment of a test to identify presence of ligamentum teres pathology *Submitted for publication*.

57. McCarthy JC, Lee JA. Hip arthroscopy: indications, outcomes, and complications. *J Bone Joint Surg Am* 2005;87(5):1138–45.

58. Grimaldi A, Richardson C, Durbridge G et al. The association between degenerative hip joint pathology and size of the gluteus maximus and tensor fascia lata muscles. *Man Ther* 2009;14(6):611–17.

59. Grimaldi A, Richardson C, Stanton W et al. The association between degenerative hip joint pathology and size of the gluteus medius, gluteus minimus and piriformis muscles. *Man Ther* 2009;14(6):605–10.

B

60. Baldwin KD, Harrison RA, Namdari S et al. Outcomes of hip arthroscopy for treatment of femoroacetabular impingement: a systematic review. *Curr Orth Prac* 2009;20(6):669–73.

61. Bedi A, Chen N, Robertson W et al. The management of labral tears and femoroacetabular impingement of the hip in the young, active patient. *Arthroscopy* 2008;24(10):1135–45.

62. Enseki KR, Martin R, Kelly BT. Rehabilitation after arthroscopic decompression for femoroacetabular impingement. *Clin Sports Med* 2010;29(2):247–55.

63. Shindle MK, Domb BG, Kelly BT. Hip and pelvic problems in athletes. *Op Tech Sports Med* 2007;15(4):195–203.

64. Stalzer S, Wahoff M, Scanlan M. Rehabilitation following hip arthroscopy. *Clin Sports Med* 2006;25(2):337–57.

65. Tyler TF, Nicholas SJ, Campbell RJ et al. The association of hip strength and flexibility with the incidence of adductor muscle strains in professional ice hockey players. *Am J Sports Med* 2001;29(2):124–8.

66. Hodges PW, Richardson CA. Inefficient muscular stabilisation of the lumbar spine associated with low back pain: a motor control evaluation of transversus abdominus. *Spine* 1996;21:2640–50.

67. Hodges PW, Mellor R, Crossley K et al. Pain induced by injection of hypertonic saline into the infrapatellar fat pad and effect on coordination of the quadriceps muscles. *Arthritis Rheum* 2009;61(1):70–7.

68. Philippon MJ, Stubbs AJ, Schenker ML et al. Arthroscopic management of femoroacetabular impingement: osteoplasty technique and literature review. *Am J Sports Med* 2007;35(9):1571–80.

69. Millenium Research Group. US markets for arthroscopy devices 2009. www.mrg.net

70. Robertson WJ, Kadrmas WR, Kelly BT. Arthroscopic management of labral tears in the hip: a systematic review of the literature. *Clin Orthop Relat Res* 2007;455:88–92.

71. Byrd JWT, Jones KS. Hip arthroscopy for labral pathology: prospective analysis with 10-year follow-up. *Arthroscopy* 2009;25(4):365–68.

72. Byrd JWT, Jones KS. Hip arthroscopy in athletes: 10-year follow-up. *Am J Sports Med* 2009;37(11):2140–3.

73. Philippon MJ, Christensen JC, Wahoff MS. Rehabilitation after arthroscopic repair of intra-articular disorders of the hip in a professional football athlete. *J Sport Rehab* 2009;18(1):118–34.

74. Martinez AE, Li SM, Ganz R et al. Os acetabuli in femoro-acetabular impingement: stress fracture or unfused secondary ossification centre of the acetabular rim? *Hip Int* 2006;16(4):281–6.

75. Karpinski MR, Piggott H. Greater trochanteric pain syndrome. A report of 15 cases. *J Bone Joint Surg Br* 1985;67(5):762–3.

76. Strauss EJ, Nho SJ, Kelly BT. Greater trochanteric pain syndrome. *Sports Med Arthrosc* 2010;18(2):113–19.

77. Connell DA, Bass C, Sykes CA et al. Sonographic evaluation of gluteus medius and minimus tendinopathy. *Eur Radiol* 2003;13(6):1339–47.

78. Fearon AM, Scarvell JM, Cook JL et al. Does ultrasound correlate with surgical or histologic findings in greater trochanteric pain syndrome? A pilot study. *Clin Orthop Relat Res* 2010;468(7):1838–44.

79. Kingzett-Taylor A, Tirman PF, Feller J et al. Tendinosis and tears of gluteus medius and minimus muscles as a cause of hip pain: MR imaging findings. *Am J Roentgenol* 1999;173 1123–6.

80. Blankenbaker DG, Ullrick SR, Davis KW et al. Correlation of MRI findings with clinical findings of trochanteric pain syndrome. *Skeletal Radiol* 2008;37(10):903–9.

81. Rompe JD, Segal NA, Cacchio A et al. Home training, local corticosteroid injection, or radial shock wave therapy for greater trochanter pain syndrome. *Am J Sports Med* 2009;37(10):1981–90.

82. Sayegh F, Potoupnis M, Kapetanos G. Greater trochanter bursitis pain syndrome in females with chronic low back pain and sciatica. *Acta Orthop Belg* 2004;70(5):423–8.

83. Furia J, Rompe JD, Maffulli N. Low-energy extracorporeal shock wave therapy as a treatment for greater trochanteric pain syndrome. *Am J Sports Med* 2009;37(9):1806–13.

84. Labrosse JM, Cardinal E, Leduc BE et al. Effectiveness of ultrasound-guided corticosteroid injection for the treatment of gluteus medius tendinopathy. *AJR Am J Roentgenol* 2010;194:202–6.

85. Cvitanic O, Henzie G, Skezas N et al. MRI diagnosis of tears of the hip abductor tendons (gluteus medius and gluteus minimus). *AJR Am J Roentgenol* 2004;182:137–43.

86. Lequesne M, Djian P, Vuillemin V et al. Prospective study of refractory greater trochanter pain syndrome. MRI findings of gluteal tendon tears seen at surgery. Clinical and MRI results of tendon repair. *Joint Bone Spine* 2008;75(4):458–64.

87. Voos JE, Shindle MK, Pruett A et al. Endoscopic repair of gluteus medius tendon tears of the hip. *Am J Sports Med* 2009;37(4):743–7.

Chapter 29

Groin pain

with PER HOLMICH and CHRIS BRADSHAW

I've had groin issues in the past and came back a couple of times too early so instead of missing two weeks you end up missing a month. It's important to take your time and make sure you're over 100 per cent ready. And I think for me it has something to do with my hips being tight. When your hips are tight, then the groin has a tendency to overcompensate and that's why you see all the hip surgeries in goalies, it's all related. National Hockey League goalie Jean-Sebastien Giguere appreciating the link between groin pain and hip problems (December 2010, www.theglobeandmail.com)

Groin pain is an extremely common presentation in sports and exercise medicine, particularly in footballers, yet it is poorly understood. The anatomy of the region is complex; the load on this region is extremely high in sports that involve rapid change of direction and kicking, and the hip joint itself is not a superficial joint and therefore is hard to examine.

Acute injuries to this region are relatively common and usually involve a partial tear of one of the adductor muscles. Longstanding groin pain is also extremely common, and presents much more of a clinical challenge.

With the advent of MRI and hip arthroscopy, it has become clear that problems associated with the hip joint are far more common than originally thought. The hip plays an important role in groin pain (Chapter 28). The hip can be the primary cause of the athlete's groin pain,[1] or an underlying hip abnormality such as femoroacetabular impingement can be a significant contributing factor to the development of another groin pathology.

Before we explore the interrelationship further, it is important to understand the anatomy of the groin.

Anatomy

The groin region can be thought of as where the abdomen meets the lower limbs via the pelvis.

Understanding the groin region requires an appreciation of the anatomy of the musculoskeletal, digestive, and urogenital systems. Important structures in the groin region include the lower abdominal muscles and abdominal viscera, the inguinal canal and its contents, the pubic bones and the pubic symphysis, the hip adductor muscles, and pelvic viscera and genitalia. The iliopsoas, sartorius, rectus femoris, and the hip joint itself are also common sources of groin pain.

The anatomy of the groin area is pictured in Figure 29.1.

The anatomy of the groin region is complex. The pubic symphysis is a secondary cartilaginous joint which connects the two pubic rami. It is supported by ligaments superiorly and inferiorly—by the superior pubic ligament and the arcuate pubic ligament respectively. The two pubic bones are separated by a fibrocartilaginous disc.

The pubic symphysis is the site of numerous musculotendinous attachments which act to dynamically stabilize the anterior pelvis. These muscles include the abdominals (primarily the rectus abdominis) and the hip adductors (pectineus, gracilis, adductor longus, adductor brevis, and adductor magnus). The lateral border attachment of the rectus abdominis is in close proximity to the superficial inguinal ring. This may explain the overlap of

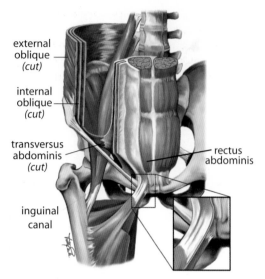

external oblique (cut)

internal oblique (cut)

transversus abdominis (cut)

rectus abdominis

inguinal canal

Figure 29.1 Anatomy of the hip and groin area
(a) Muscles of the abdominal wall

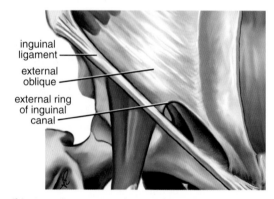

inguinal ligament

external oblique

external ring of inguinal canal

(b) Normal anatomy at the site of "sports hernias".
Compare with pathology (Fig. 29.10 on page 569)

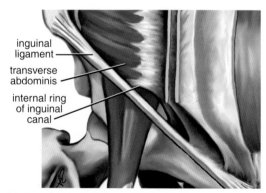

inguinal ligament

transverse abdominis

internal ring of inguinal canal

(c) Deep layers revealing transversus abdominis muscle showing usual site of tears

insertional rectus abdominis pathology with inguinal hernia symptoms.

The rectus abdominis and adductor longus attachments around the pubic symphysis are thought to blend and maintain stability of the anterior pelvis. A high-quality review[2] has highlighted emerging anatomical evidence that:

- the proximal attachment of adductor longus may be predominantly muscular rather than fibro-tendinous as previously thought
- the internal oblique and the transversus abdominis muscles are more commonly attached medially into the distal rectus sheath rather than directly into the pubis
- an extension of the fascia of the adductor longus muscle and a continuation of the rectus abdominis sheath combine to form a communicating aponeurotic structure, anterior to the pubic symphysis. This demonstrates a direct link between the adductor longus and rectus abdominis, as well as an indirect link between transversus abdominis and internal oblique via the rectus abdominis sheath.

It has also been shown that there is an intimate relationship between this aponeurotic structure (and therefore the adductor longus and rectus abdominus tendons) with the symphysis pubis capsular structures and disk.[3]

These anatomical findings have several clinical implications. Firstly, these findings indicate that pain provocation or stress tests do not load a single anatomical structure in isolation. They also help to explain why chronic groin pain presentations often have diffuse poorly localized symptoms, inconsistent clinical findings, and varied responses to management.

These findings also have implications for rehabilitation; the use of a functional approach to rehabilitation that addresses not only local structures but global core stability may be more appropriate than isolated unidimensional exercises.

Finally, these findings highlight that surgery aimed at disrupting this connection, such as an adductor tenotomy, may not have the best long-term clinical outcomes.

The close relationship of the pubic symphysis with the sacroiliac joints within the pelvic ring allows for shock absorption and transfer of load through this system. Therefore any injury or imbalance (such as reduced mobility in the lumbar spine or hip) may potentially affect the efficiency of this system.

Prevalence

Groin pain and injury are common with sports that involve kicking, rapid acceleration and deceleration, and sudden change of direction.

Currently there is no universal definition or classification of athlete groin injury/pain; therefore care must be taken in translating rates of injury reported in the literature. Additionally, the nature of injury is often poorly reported (e.g. acute versus chronic; traumatic versus overuse). Also, groin injury is often only recorded when a sportsperson misses a training session or match. Therefore the prevalence of groin injury may be underestimated, as those sportspeople who continue to train and play through injury often are not recorded.

The two most common sports associated with groin injury and longstanding pain are soccer and Australian Rules football, which both require players to run fast and kick across the body. Longstanding groin pain is also a major concern in basketball, American football, rugby, field hockey, skating, tennis, and basketball.[4–6]

Epidemiological studies have reported the following:

- Groin strain accounted for 10% of all injuries in elite Swedish ice hockey players.[7]
- The incidence of groin strains in a single National Hockey League team was 3.2 strains per 1000 player game exposures[8] and account for approximately 10 to 11% of all injuries.[5]
- In the 1997 to 2000 professional Australian Football League (AFL) season, the incidence of groin strains was 3.3 injuries per club per season and accounted for 11.9 matches missed per club per season.[9] Hamstring strains were reported with the highest incidence, closely followed by anterior cruciate ligament injuries and groin strains.
- Over a 2-year period, semi-professional Rugby League players were followed and assessed for groin injury.[10] All 100 players did not have a previous history of groin injury. Calculated risk of groin injury over the 2 years was high, at 23%, with 2.4 per 1000 hour training sessions and/or games missed. Additionally 70% of those injured had a duration of symptoms greater than seven weeks.
- Over seven consecutive European professional soccer seasons (2001/2 to 2007/8) groin injuries accounted for 1.1/1000 hours training sessions and/or games missed.[11] Match injuries were significantly higher compared with training injuries. It was calculated that 27% of groin injuries were traumatic in nature, and

73% were caused from overuse. 7.2 groin injuries were calculated per club per season.
- Over one amateur soccer season in Norway, consisting of 508 players, 10% of athletes incurred a groin injury.[12] There was a rate of 0.6 groin injuries/1000 playing hours, and 0.3 groin injuries/1000 training hours.

Risk factors

Currently, studies on risk factors for groin pain are limited to a handful of sports (e.g. AFL, ice hockey, rugby, soccer). It is difficult to compare the findings of risk factor studies because of the lack of a universal definition of groin pain. Risk factors identified in studies should take into account the demands of specific sports (e.g. athletic demands, velocities, contact versus non-contact sports, loading forces on the musculoskeletal structure). A systematic review of risk factors for groin strain injury identified very few prospective studies.[13] However, this review found a previous history of groin injury, greater abductor to adductor strength ratios, and decreased pre-season sport-specific training to be risk factors for groin injury. Additionally, core muscle weakness may increase injury risk. However, as the evidence in the literature is conflicting,[8, 14–19] debate continues on the importance and relevance of adductor strength and length, as well as age and sporting expertise or experience.

Soccer players with a previous hamstring injury, groin injury, and knee joint trauma are two to three times more likely to suffer an identical injury in the following season.[20] A prospective study, observing 508 amateur soccer players, reported that previous acute groin injury, reduced external rotation, pain on external rotation of the hip, pain on iliopsoas palpation, and reduced adductor, iliopsoas, and rectus abdominus strength were risk factors for groin pain.[12] In the same study, age and jump test performance were factors for groin injury.

Holmich found that having had a previous groin injury almost doubles the risk of developing a new groin injury, and playing at a higher level almost triples the risk of developing a groin injury.[16]

Acute injuries around the groin can settle quickly; however, resultant altered biomechanical loads can predispose the sportsperson to further injury. Rushed or inadequate rehabilitation can increase the risk of re-injury dramatically. The hip joint can be subjected to forces of up to eight times body weight during running;[21] therefore a small change in load transfer and acceptance around the pelvis can result in injury. Therefore, altered biomechanics can lead to injury, or increase the likelihood of an existing injury becoming longstanding.

Clinical overview

Due to the anatomical complexity of the region, there is often significant overlap in the signs and symptoms of different diagnoses of groin pain. Adding to this complexity, sportspeople often present with vague symptoms of insidious onset which allows them to continue to train and play with pain. As a result, athletic groin pain has a tendency to develop into a chronic presentation, and sportspeople can often return to sport before completing an adequate rehabilitation period.

Non-specific exercise-related groin pain has been given many different "diagnostic" labels; by far the most popular have been "osteitis pubis" (UK, Europe, and Australia) and "athletic pubalgia" (North America). The term "osteitis pubis" was originally used to describe an infective or inflammatory complication of suprapubic surgery.[22] It was subsequently used to describe the syndrome of exercise-related groin pain associated with radiographic bony changes at the symphysis pubis and/or increased uptake on radionuclide bone scan in the pubic symphysis.

More recently, "osteitis pubis" has become an umbrella term for all exercise-related groin pain in

sportspeople. However, as longstanding groin pain is rarely inflammatory in nature, and the finding of increased uptake on bone scan is not universal, this term seems inappropriate. The term is both inaccurate with regard to pathology, and confusing as it means different things to different people.

Other "diagnoses" of longstanding exercise-related groin pain include adductor tendinopathy/enthesopathy, iliopsoas dysfunction, posterior inguinal wall deficiency, sportsperson's hernia, sports hernia, tear of external oblique aponeurosis, "Gilmore's groin," and chronic adductor muscle strain. However, even though some clinicians believe that all longstanding groin pain in sportspeople has a single specific diagnosis, this is unlikely.

The causes of groin pain are shown in Table 29.1.

Local overload causing failure of various structures

Longstanding groin pain can be the end result of a number of different pathologies. By the time pain has been experienced for several months, a number of pathologies may be present; they often coexist and may contribute to other pain presentations. The fundamental etiology of groin pain involves mechanical *overload* within and around the pelvic region (i.e. due to sport) leading to failure under altered loads of local tissues—muscle, tendon, fascial sheath, or bone, either alone or in combination.

Table 29.1 Causes of longstanding groin pain

Common	Less common	Not to be missed
Adductor-related	Stress fracture	Slipped capital femoral epiphysis
• Tendinopathy/enthesopathy	• Neck of femur	Perthes' disease (adolescents)
• Myofascial tightness	• Pubic ramus	Intra-abdominal abnormality
Iliopsoas-related	• Acetabulum	• Prostatitis
• Neuromyofascial tightness	Nerve entrapment	• Urinary tract infections
• Tendinopathy	• Obturator	• Gynecological conditions
• Bursitis	• Ilioinguinal	Spondyloarthropathies
Abdominal wall–related	• Genitofemoral	• Ankylosing spondylitis
• Posterior inguinal wall weakness	Referred pain	Avascular necrosis of head of femur
• Tear of external oblique aponeurosis	• Lumbar spine	Tumors
• "Gilmore's groin"	• Sacroiliac joint	• Testicular
• Rectus abdominis tendinopathy	Apophysitis	• Osteoid osteoma
Pubic bone–related	• Anterior superior iliac spine	
• Pubic bone stress	• Anterior inferior iliac spine (adolescents)	
Hip joint		
• Chondral lesion		
• Labral tear		

Holmich et al. have previously introduced the concept of "diagnostic entities" when assessing sportspeople presenting with longstanding groin pain, to encourage thorough, reliable, and standardized physical examinations.[4] This concept is based on the examination and reproduction of the athlete's groin pain through palpation, and length and strength tests.[4, 23]

The three most common entities assessed in a population of 207 athletes included adductor-related, iliopsoas-related, and abdominal-related pain.[4] Iliopsoas-related pain was more common in running and in female athletes. Adductor-related pain was more common in football and in male athletes. Interestingly, adductor-related pain was observed to be rare in the female athlete. This could be due to the anatomical variation of a wider pelvis, which may make the female athlete more susceptible to hip- and iliopoas-related presentations.

We propose four clinical entities be considered for sportspeople presenting with longstanding groin pain (Table 29.2).

More than one entity is often present by the time the problem is recognized or medical attention is sought, as most sportspeople continue to train and play with discomfort and within pain limits. Figure 29.2 depicts sites of commonly associated pathologies. Multiple clinical entities were assessed in more than one-third of the athletes in the Holmich study.[4] Adductor- and iliopsoas-related pain was found to be high in coexistence. Additionally, abdominal-related pain was observed to be more

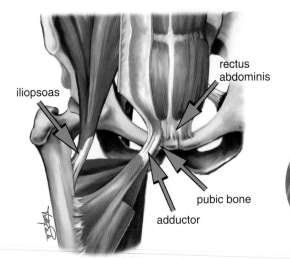

Figure 29.2 Overlapping clinical entities in longstanding groin pain in sportspeople

often a secondary entity, suggesting that abdominal-related pain often comes at a cost of other injuries/pathologies.

An example of a case study on how multiple entities develop over time is shown in the box overleaf.

What role does bone stress play?

Whether pubic bone stress causing groin pain is an entity that arises *de novo* or whether it must be preceded by failure of the local stabilizing structures (e.g. adductors, iliopsoas, abdominal wall) continues to be a controversial topic in sports and exercise medicine. Australian sports physician Geoff Verrall found

Table 29.2 Four clinical entities that may be involved in longstanding groin pain

Clinical entity	Adductor-related[23]	Iliopsoas-related[23]	Abdominal wall–related[24]	Pubic bone stress–related[25]
Pathological elements likely to underpin the entity	Musculotendinous injuries Enthesopathy Neuromyofascial Pubic symphysis instability Hip ligamentum teres pathology Rectus abdominis lesions*	Neuromyofascial tightness Iliopsoas tendinopathy Lumbar spine abnormalities Reduced range of hip movement Hip "cuff" weakness Iliopsoas bursitis (uncommon)	Posterior inguinal wall weakness Conjoint tendon tear External oblique aponeurosis tear Lumbar pathology Rectus abdominis lesions*	Stress reaction or stress fracture of the pubic bone Rectus abdominis and adductor muscle imbalance Sacroiliac joint pathology Reduced range of hip movement Pubic symphysis instability

*any of rectus abdominis tears, overuse injury, and enthesopathy

How multiple clinical entities may develop

A soccer player develops an overuse problem in the adductor region, and gradually the pain is concentrated at the adductor longus insertion at the inferior pubic bone. After a period of continued soccer playing, the iliopsoas muscle becomes painful as well. It becomes a little tight and develops tender points. The tendon insertion is thicker on ultrasound examination. The player now has two causes of pain in the groin region.

Late in a match, as a result of not being able to control the pelvis properly because of the painful adductors and the iliopsoas not working properly, the player develops a small avulsion/lesion of the conjoint tendon affecting the inguinal canal, leading to signs of an "incipient hernia."

The original cause of overuse of the adductors (or iliopsoas, lower abdominals, etc.) could be a range of problems (such as muscular pelvic instability, decreased range of motion in the hip joint for a number of reasons, generalized poor physical condition compared to the level of physical activity, pain/injury elsewhere leading to compensatory movements affecting the pelvis, and so on). The player also might have some dysfunction related to the low back/thoracolumbar region or the sacroiliac joint.

MRI evidence of bone marrow edema in a large percentage (77%) of footballers presenting with long-standing groin pain and associated pubic symphysis tenderness.[25] He proposed that pubic bone stress was a possible cause of the symptoms. However, 54% of his cohort without groin pain also demonstrated bone marrow edema.

Another Australian sports physician, Greg Lovell, demonstrated that MRI evidence of bone marrow edema was also found in asymptomatic elite junior football (soccer) players.[26] Moreover the development of groin pain was correlated to a significant increase in training loads rather than MRI findings.

In another study, Schilders et al.[27] injected a local anesthetic and steroid into the enthesis (origin) of the adductor longus muscle at the pubic cleft in competitive athletes presenting with adductor-related groin pain. All athletes had immediate pain relief. Those athletes who did not have MRI evidence of enthesis involvement had favorable one-year follow-up results, with no recurrence episodes. Of those athletes who did have MRI evidence, 94% had recurrence of groin pain at a mean of five weeks post injections. This may suggest that favorable results are more common in those athletes without MRI evidence of enthesis involvement.

A follow-up study focusing on recreational athletes found that there was no correlation between evidence of enthesis involvement and one-year follow-up results.[27] This could highlight the ability for recreational athletes to modify their activity more readily than competitive athletes and therefore the opportunity to minimize recurrence rates compared with elite athletes.

Danish surgeon Per Holmich believes that pubic bone stress arises because bending and/or torsional forces acting through the pelvis have become unbalanced.[28] He contends that at least one of his three "primary" diagnostic entities generally precedes pubic bone stress and, thus, suggests that clinical assessment and treatment focus on those entities.

Factors that increase local bone stress

A number of factors lead to stress on the pubic bones and an excess of one or more of these stressors, or an imbalance between them, may lead to pubic bone stress (Fig. 29.3).

Abnormalities in the joints and muscles around the groin and pelvic region may increase the mechanical stress placed on the pubic region, such as:

- limited hip range of motion,[8, 14, 15, 18, 19] which may be due to

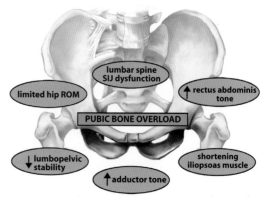

Figure 29.3 Factors leading to pubic bone overload

- intra-articular hip pathology (e.g. femoroacetabular impingement, labral tear, chondral lesion)
- joint capsule tightness
- extra-articular myofascial tightness (e.g. gluteal muscle tightness associated with trigger points)
- increased adductor muscle tone
  - after an acute adductor strain
  - due to chronic tightness (associated with adductor muscle trigger points)
- increased rectus abdominis tone
- iliopsoas muscle shortening often associated with hypomobility of upper lumbar intervertebral joints
- lumbar spine/sacroiliac joint dysfunction
  - hypomobile intervertebral joint(s)
  - sacroiliac joint stiffness
- decreased lumbopelvic stability
  - reduced transversus abdominis activation— transversus abdominis provides compression of the pelvic ring anteriorly, contributing to the mechanical stability of the joint
- impaired pelvic floor muscle function—the pelvic floor muscles contribute to tension of the pelvic ring.

Core stability and its role

There is a definite interaction between the lower extremities and the pelvic girdle. Wilson et al. have previously defined core stability as the ability of the lumbopelvic hip complex to prevent buckling and to return to equilibrium after perturbation.[29]

Core stability (Chapter 14) relies on the surrounding muscles, ligaments, bones, and fascial connection, to respond to stimuli and movement in a feed-forward feed-back fashion via the nervous system. It is clear that, when there is weakness within the system such as "poor lumbopelvic stability" or poor proximal control, this factor lends itself to reduced lower extremity function and increased risk of injury.[29–31]

Contraction of the transversus abdominis and pelvic floor muscles (both primary core stability muscles) increases the stability of the pelvic ring, specifically around the sacroiliac joints.[32] As there is a strong connection within the pelvic ring, this finding would also have an effect on the pubic symphysis. Furthermore, the fibers of transversus abdominis and internal oblique are perpendicular to the sacroiliac joint and as such are thought to serve as an internal pelvic belt.[33, 34]

Delayed onset of contractions of transversus abdominis has been observed in Australian Rules players with longstanding groin pain compared with asymptomatic controls during an active straight leg raise activity.[35] Using diagnostic ultrasound techniques, significantly smaller transversus abdominis thickness has been observed in both low back pain and longstanding groin pain populations.[36, 37] To this effect, core stability rehabilitation exercises have been incorporated into the management of longstanding groin pain in sportspeople, as well as being used for preventative purposes.

The adductors play a major role in dampening the contraction of the gluteus medius after the propulsion phase of running. They also work synergistically with the hip abductors to maintain the stability of the pelvis during the stance phase. Thus, pelvic stability is required to prevent excessive eccentric load on the adductors.

Role of the gluteal muscles

There is a frequent clinical association between groin pain (e.g. adductor, psoas) and tightness of the gluteal muscles (especially gluteus medius). Gluteus medius trigger points are commonly found in patients with groin pain, and treatment of the trigger points (dry needling, digital pressure) frequently dramatically reduces the adductor signs. The cause of this association is uncertain, but it may be related to limited hip range of motion.

Role of the hip joint

Hip pathology is a common cause of groin pain[38, 39] and we encourage you to read Chapter 28. Bradshaw et al. found that, in a series of 218 consecutive patients with groin pain seen in a sports medicine clinic in London, hip joint pathology accounted for nearly 50% of the final diagnoses.[1]

Common diagnoses included acute labral tears and impingement syndromes, with cam impingements outnumbering pincer impingements.[21] In the follow-up cohort, those who suffered hip pathologies tended to present later and were overrepresented in the group of patients who had failed to return to their pre-injury level of activity. This was particularly true of osteochondral injury. Hip injury was very common in straight line activities and twisting activities (such as racquet sports and hockey).

In another study, 94% of sportspeople with longstanding adductor-related groin pain had radiological signs of femoroacetabular impingement,[40] but there was no correlation with clinical signs, and no difference between the symptomatic and non-symptomatic.

However, in another study 22% of sportspeople with hip and groin pain had labral tears.[41] Burnett et al. demonstrated that 92% of patients with arthroscopically confirmed labral tears complained of moderate to severe groin pain.[42] Philippon et al. described the presence of labral tears and femoroacetabular impingement in 100% of professional National Hockey League (NHL) ice hockey players presenting for hip arthroscopy for the treatment of longstanding hip and groin pain.[43]

Injury to the ligamentum teres of the hip has been cited as the third most common cause of hip and groin pain in the sportsperson.[44-46]

Hip pathology also commonly coexists with other groin-related pathology, such as adductor symptoms, iliopsoas symptoms, and pubic symptoms (Fig. 29.4). This makes definitive diagnosis and provision of appropriate management programs difficult and often multifactorial.[1] Failure to recognize and correct abnormalities such as femoroacetabular impingement present in patients with other groin pathologies (e.g. adductor, psoas) may be an important factor in failed conservative management and the high rate of recurrence.

Clinical approach

It is important to appreciate the anatomy of the hip and groin, and undertake a careful history and examination. The clinical approach can be difficult as the anatomy around this region is complex, and often multiple pathologies coexist.[5] Pain may be difficult to localize and may be accompanied by vague symptoms. An insidious onset of unknown origin may also cloud the clinical presentation.

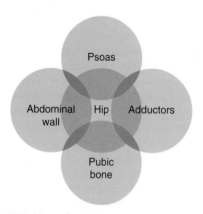

Figure 29.4 Hip and groin pain—interaction between different pathologies

History

The sportsperson experiences an insidious onset of groin pain, which is usually felt in one or both proximal pubic bones, and/or one or both proximal adductors, but may be centered on the lower abdomen or inguinal regions. The pain frequently starts in one region and is unilateral, and then spreads to other regions and can become bilateral. The pain is aggravated by exercise, with running, twisting/turning, and kicking being the most challenging activities. The sportsperson and coach usually notice a decrease in sports performance.

The pain in sportspeople with longstanding groin pain typically presents initially following activity and is accompanied by stiffness, particularly the next morning. The pain and stiffness then gradually lessen with daily activities and warm-up for the next training session or match. When the condition becomes worse, pain is present immediately upon exercise.

Nonsteroidal anti-inflammatory drugs (NSAIDs) tend to decrease pain but provide no cure. Short periods of rest reduce the severity of the symptoms, but on resumption of normal sporting activities the pain returns to its original intensity and severity. The natural history is one of progressive deterioration with continued activity until symptoms prevent participation in the activity.

The localization of the pain is important to determine which structure may be causing the pain. Adductor-related pain is located medially in the groin—centered primarily at the attachment of the adductor longus tendon to the pubic bone. Iliopsoas-related pain is located more centrally in the groin and proximal thigh.

The type of activity that aggravates the pain may be a clue to the primary site of the problem. Side-to-side movements, twisting and turning activities which aggravate the pain suggest adductor-related pain. Straight-line running or kicking suggest iliopsoas problems. Pain with sit-ups may suggest an inguinal-related pain. Note that these clinical observations are guidelines rather than hard-and-fast rules.

Pain that becomes progressively worse with exercise may suggest a stress fracture, bursitis, or nerve entrapment. A history of associated pain such as low back or buttock pain indicates that the groin pain may be referred from another site (such as the lumbar spine, the sacroiliac joint, or the thoracolumbar junction).

A full training history should be taken to determine if any recent changes in training (such as a generalized increase in volume or intensity, or the introduction of a new exercise or increase in a particular component of training) may have led to the development of the groin pain.

Examination

Each region of the groin that has the potential to produce groin pain must be examined. Examination involves:

1. Observation
   (a) standing
   (b) walking (Fig. 29.5a)
   (c) supine
2. Active movements
   (a) hip flexion/extension
   (b) hip abduction/adduction*
   (c) hip internal/external rotation
   (d) lumbar spine movements (Chapter 26)
   (e) abdominal flexion*
3. Passive movements
   (a) adductor muscle stretch (Fig. 29.5b overleaf)*
   (b) internal rotation
   (c) quadriceps muscle stretch
   (d) psoas muscle stretch—Thomas position (Fig. 29.5c overleaf)
4. Resisted movements
   (a) hip flexion—Thomas position (Fig. 29.5d overleaf)
   (b) unilateral hip adduction
   (c) "squeeze test" (bilateral hip adduction) (Fig. 29.5e overleaf)—(also see box, p. 556–8)
   (d) abdominal flexion (Fig. 29.5f overleaf)
5. Palpation
   (a) adductor muscles/tendons* (Fig. 29.5g on page 555)
   (b) pubic symphysis/ramus* (Fig. 29.5h on page 555)
   (c) rectus abdominis*
   (d) iliopsoas*
6. Special tests
   (a) pelvic symmetry
   (b) lumbar spine (Chapter 26)
   (c) sacroiliac joint (Chapter 27)
   (d) hip anterior impingement test (hip quadrant) (Fig. 29.5i on page 555)
   (e) Thomas position with added neural mechanosensitivity (Fig. 29.5j on page 555)
   (f) FABER test (Fig. 29.5k on page 556)
   (g) cough impulse – palpate abdominally (Fig. 29.5l on page 556) or through scrotum
   (h) Trendelenberg test

Note: Those physical examination tests that Holmich advocates in the "quick groin examination" are marked with an asterisk; they proved reliable when tested within and among examiners.[47]

 A sign that helps clinicians assess severity of the condition is the "crossover sign."

A positive crossover sign means that the patient's typical groin pain is reproduced when one of the provocation tests (e.g. passive hip abduction, resisted hip adduction, resisted hip flexion in Thomas position) is performed on the *contralateral* side to the symptoms. A positive crossover sign suggests substantial functional impairment and the clinical implication is that the player is very unlikely to be able to run, train, or play.

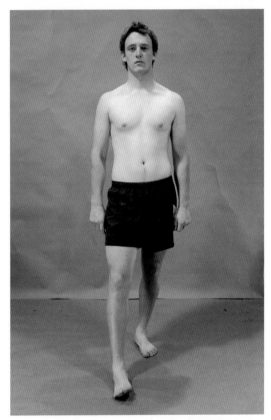

Figure 29.5 Examination of the patient with hip/groin pain
(a) Observation—patient walking. Assess lower limb alignment from in front, particularly for evidence of excessive internal or external hip rotation and muscle wasting. Assess lumbar postural abnormalities from the side

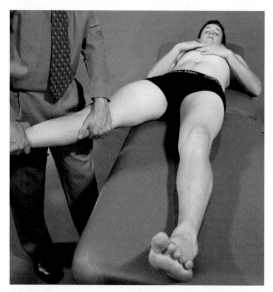

(b) Passive movement—adductor muscle stretch

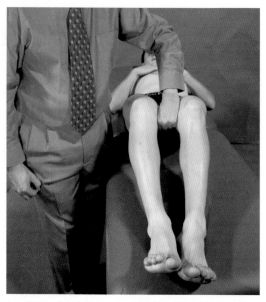

(e) Resisted movement—adductor squeeze. Examiner places fist between knees as shown. Patient then adducts bilaterally against the fist. Different angles of hip and knee flexion are used. (See box pages 556–8, for more information about adductor squeeze test.)

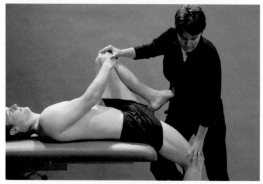

(c) Passive movement—psoas stretch (Thomas position). Pain in the hip being stretched suggests psoas abnormality. Pain in the hip being compressed can be significant for anterior impingement of the hip joint

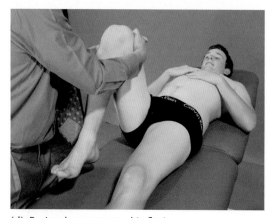

(d) Resisted movement—hip flexion

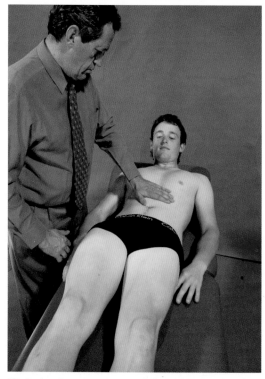

(f) Resisted movement—trunk flexion. Resisted sit-up is performed

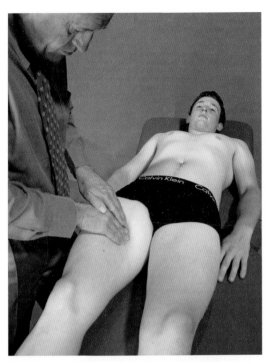

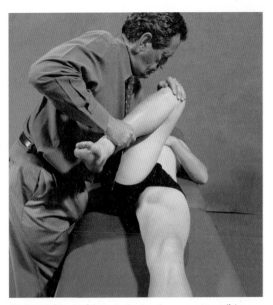

(i) Special test—hip anterior impingement test (hip quadrant). Hip is flexed to 90° flexion, then adduction and internal rotation added

(g) Palpation—adductor muscles/tendons. Start distally in the muscle belly palpating for tenderness, tightness, and trigger points. Then move proximally to palpate attachment to pubic bone.

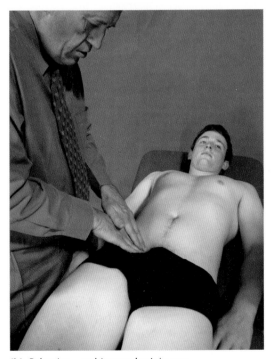

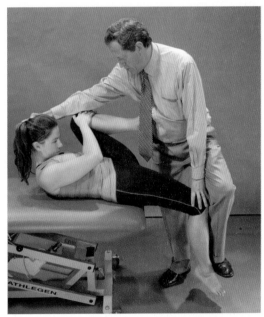

(j) Special test—Thomas position with added neural mechanosensitivity. Patient is initially placed in the iliopsoas stretch position. The neural mechanosensitivity is slowly increased by addition of cervical and upper thoracic flexion, then passive knee flexion. This test will always cause some discomfort and tightness. It is clinically significant if the patient's pain is reproduced, then reduced when the tension is taken off

(h) Palpation—pubic symphysis/ramus

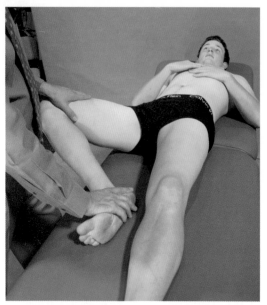

(k) Passive movement—flexion, abduction and external rotation (FABER or Patrick's test)

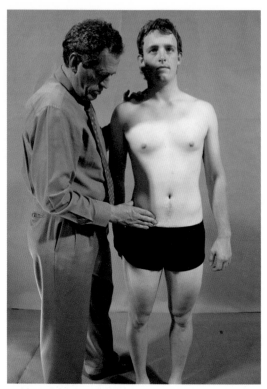

(l) Special tests—cough impulse. The patient stands and the examiner feels for a cough impulse at the sites of direct and indirect inguinal hernias. The examiner should then invaginate the scrotum and ask the patient to cough. Note dilation of the ring and discomfort

Adductor squeeze test

The most commonly used test in the assessment of groin pain is the adductor squeeze test. It is not specific for loading a specific anatomical structure; rather it is a test of load tolerance, and "willingness" to generate and subject the groin region to load. Note that pain-induced inhibition may be a significant contributor to the reduced score. The site of reported pain may be a clue to the structures suffering from excessive load and/or abnormal pathology.

Patients squeeze their knees together as hard as they can. Pain and weakness are then subjectively assessed. The adductor squeeze test is commonly performed in three positions (Fig. 29.6):

1. Legs extended, neutral rotation (Fig. 29.6a)—thought to be more specific for the adductor muscles
2. 45° hip flexion and 90° knee flexion (Fig. 29.6b)

3. 90° hip flexion, thighs vertical, knees relaxed, feet off the plinth (Fig. 29.6c).

The test can be performed subjectively with the examiner's fist placed between the knees and the strength assessed manually. While Holmich et al.[47] reported only moderate reliability in manually assessing the strength ("strong," "intermediate," or "weak") of a maximal bilateral hip adduction contraction among primarily young adult male soccer players, it is useful to obtain objective measures of hip adductor strength.

This is commonly performed with either a sphygmomanometer or dynamometer. Both methods have been shown to have good reliability[48–50] and provide an objective measure which can be monitored, or at least compared to a baseline in the event of an acute or gradual onset chronic injury.

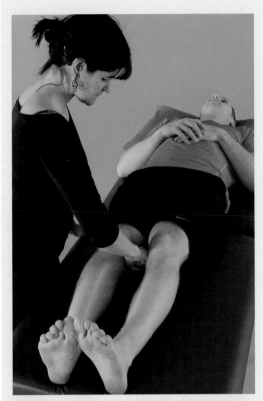

Figure 29.6 Adductor squeeze test—performed in three positions
(a) Legs extended, neutral rotation. Patients attempt to internally rotate their femurs to generate more power. Neutral rotation must be maintained

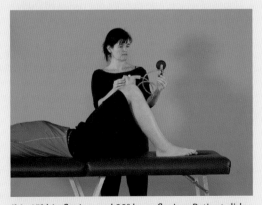

(b) 45° hip flexion and 90° knee flexion. Patient slides one heel towards buttock until medial malleolus level with opposite knee medial joint line, then flexes opposite knee to same range

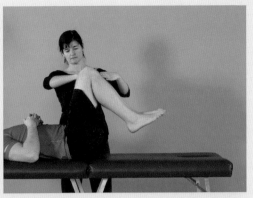

(c) 90° hip flexion, thighs vertical, knees relaxed, feet off the plinth

The patient (rather than the practitioner) places a sphygmomanometer between the knees, thus ensuring it is in a comfortable position and more likely to be consistently placed in the same position, and then squeezes the cuff as hard possible. The highest pressure displayed on the sphygmomanometer dial (to the nearest 5 mmHg), and the site and side of any groin pain experienced during the test are recorded.[48]

The second technique to objectively measure adductor strength is with a hand-held dynamometer.[49–51] The dynamometer is slightly more accurate than the sphygmomanometer but is significantly more expensive, and probably a sphygmomanometer is adequate.

A number of studies have shown a positive correlation between groin pain and a positive adductor squeeze test. Verrall et al., in a study investigating AFL players, reported that assessing the presence or absence of pain on the squeeze test is specific (88%) in identifying longstanding groin pain (tenderness at the pubic symphysis and superior pubic rami for 6 weeks).[53]

Football players with groin pain produced significantly less force on the squeeze test when compared with asymptomatic players.[48, 52, 53] It cannot be determined whether the significantly reduced maximal force production on the squeeze test is because of muscle weakness or pain inhibition (or both). Likewise, the cause or effect relationship between reduced strength on the squeeze test and the presence of longstanding groin pain is yet to be demonstrated.

Crow et al.[51] and Engebretsen et al.[12] both found that adductor squeeze dynamometer strength was reduced prior to onset of groin injury. The adductor squeeze test is now commonly used to monitor footballers during a season in an attempt to identify those at risk of developing groin pain. The study also found reduced adductor strength, measured manually, to be predictive of groin injury in footballers.

Weekly measurements with sphygmomanometer or dynamometer are taken, and any drop in strength value of >5–10% compared with pre-season non-injured values should alert the clinician to the possibility of groin pain developing, and consideration should be given to both reducing the physical training load and commencing treatment.[51]

Absolute values vary, but one study showed mean sphygmomanometer pressures at 0° and 30° hip flexion of >210 mmHg in patients without groin pain, and <185 mmHg in those with groin pain.[48] Allowing for measurement error and variation, a threshold of 200 mmHg may be useful clinically. A combination of this 200 mm threshold and reduction of >5% may be appropriate criteria.

Investigations

Investigations should be considered only after a thorough clinical assessment has been undertaken. The clinician should have a working diagnosis, which can then be further strengthened by the use of imaging techniques. Imaging techniques can aid in excluding pathologies (e.g. osteoarthritis), facilitating prognostic evaluations, and guide the direction of management.

Pelvic radiography may reveal characteristic changes at the symphysis of pubic-related groin pain, hip joint abnormality (e.g. femoroacetabular impingement) (Chapter 28), or stress fracture of the neck of the femur or pubic ramus.

Ultrasound has been used to detect inguinal hernias.[54] but its use is controversial. Ultrasound can be helpful in the assessment of muscles and tendons.[55, 56] Herniography is unreliable in detecting sports hernias.

Radionuclide bone scan shows a characteristic pattern of increased uptake in pubic-related groin pain ("osteitis pubis") and may confirm a suspected stress fracture in those cases where an X-ray fails to demonstrate the fracture.

MRI is very helpful for imaging the hip joint, especially to detect hip labral tears. It is the investigation of choice in pubic-related groin pain and stress fracture of the neck of the femur.

In terms of muscle injuries around the pelvis and hip, MRI can highlight disruption of musculotendinous margins and retracted muscles.[57] MRI can differentiate between musculotendinous injuries and tendon avulsion injuries, which has an impact on management options—namely, surgical interventions.[57]

An imaging study of subjects presenting with groin pain found 98% had positive findings on MRI that could be suggestive of cause of groin pain.[58] Compared with surgical results, MRI had good sensitivity and specificity for rectus abdominis and adductor tendon injury, and these two clinical entities were the most common.

A review on diagnosis in sportspeople presenting with longstanding groin pain. This review revealed the following results for imaging studies:[55]

- Abnormalities were found on X-ray in 76% of sportspeople with a history of groin pain, compared with 45% in controls.
- Significant changes have been observed in the sacroiliac joint(s) on X-ray, which can be suggestive of the involvement of the whole pelvic ring in longstanding groin pain presentations.
- 50% of sportspeople demonstrated positive signs on herniography on the asymptomatic side compared with 84% on the symptomatic side. This may suggest either poor sensitivity of herniography or the global involvement of the abdominal/inguinal region. Additionally, one reviewed study demonstrated that only 27% of hernias were detected on herniography.
- Increased abnormalities have been observed on the symptomatic side at the site of the adductor tubercle on bone scan. However, bone scans have shown poor validity and therefore have questionable usage in longstanding groin pain presentations.
- Abnormalities have been consistently found at the adductor tendons on MRI when groin pain was experienced for longer than one year. However, this was not consistently seen in groin pain of lesser duration. This could be suggestive of adductor tendinopathy having a secondary, progressive nature.
- A secondary cleft, interpreted as adductor microtear at symphyseal enthesis on MRI, has been observed in 70% and 88% of sportspeople presenting with

longstanding groin pain in two studies. Both studies observed no signs of secondary cleft in their matched control groups, suggesting this finding had good validity.

- Abnormalities have been consistently observed at the adductor enthesis on the symptomatic side on ultrasound investigations. Abnormalities were found to be easily detectable when the same anatomical site was compared to the asymptomatic side.
- On ultrasound investigation, normal inguinal canal could be diagnosed when some canal closure was observed under "stress." Abdominal wall deficiency could be diagnosed when an increase in cross-sectional area was observed. Additionally, an association was observed between increased groin pain and bilateral abdominal wall deficiency. Interestingly, there was no correlation with side of wall deficiency and side of groin symptoms.
- Pubic bone marrow edema has shown strong correlation with groin pain symptoms in one study but not in another. Additionally, one study observed bone marrow edema in both groin pain groups and matched controls. This could be suggestive of a normal bone process in relation to high intensity athletic training.
- Attenuation was observed in the abdominal wall musculofascial layers in 90% of groin pain subjects. 100% of positive findings correlated to side of symptoms.

Acute adductor strains

Adductor muscle strains are a common injury in sports that involve sudden changes of direction and are characterized by a history of the sportsperson feeling a "pull" or a strain in the groin region. They are more likely to occur in pre-season training.[59] It is important for the clinician to localize the injury to the muscle belly, tendomuscular junction or bony attachment, as management and prognosis can differ depending on site of injury.

Adduction of the hip involves six muscles, including adductor longus, magnus, brevis, and gracilis, pectineus, and obturator externus.[5] Within an open-chain environment, these muscles act as adductors of the hip, whereas in a closed-chain environment their function changes to more of a stability role of the hip on the pelvis.

In acute presentations the pain is usually well localized, either to the belly or the proximal musculo-tendinous junction of one of the adductor tendons near their origin on the inferior pubic ramus. It is

well established that the adductor longus muscle is the most frequently injured adductor muscle.[3-5] Examination often reveals localized tenderness, pain on passive abduction, and pain on resisted adduction or combined flexion/adduction.

Current evidence supports initial conservative treatment with exercise therapy for adductor-related groin pain in sportspeople.[5, 60, 61] A progressive strengthening program around the hip, pelvis, and abdominals seems to have most effect.[5, 61]

Treatment usually commences with initial reduction of bleeding and swelling using the RICE (rest, ice, compression, exercise) regimen (Chapter 10). Due to concerns that early stretching may predispose to the development of chronic tendinopathy, stretching does not play a significant role in the management of adductor muscle strains.

Progressive strengthening exercises should not be commenced until at least 48 hours after injury. The rehabilitation program for acute adductor strains corresponds to the basic adductor rehabilitation program described below, once the acute signs have settled.

Recurrent adductor muscle strain

Recurrent adductor muscle strains are common.[51] A review of 1292 hockey players found that those with a past history of groin pain had double the risk of injury. For a veteran player, the risk increased to five times that of a rookie.[15] This may be due to inadequate rehabilitation of the initial injury, resuming sport too quickly, or not resolving associated problems such as lumbar spine stiffness, hip restrictions, core stability, or pelvic imbalances. If untreated, these injuries can lead to chronic exercise-related groin pain.

Adductor-related groin pain

Longstanding adductor-related groin pain is localized medially in the groin and may radiate down along the adductor muscles. The key examination features that distinguish this clinical entity from others are maximal tenderness at the adductor tendon insertion and pain with resisted adduction (squeeze test) (Fig. 29.5e and box pages 556–8). Weakness of the adductor muscles is common, and palpation of the adductor longus insertion at the pubic bone reveals tenderness. Generally, increased muscle tone with trigger points along the adductor longus is often found as well. The pubic symphysis is frequently tender, but this does not help to differentiate the four clinical entities (Table 29.2).

Historically many of these patients were diagnosed as having an "adductor tendinopathy." A true tendinopathy is quite unusual, and an enthesopathy with associated adductor myofascial tightness is the more common clinical scenario.

Early warning signs

Unfortunately most patients with adductor-related groin pain continue to train and play until pain prevents them from running. When the condition has reached that stage, a lengthy period of rest and rehabilitation is usually required. However, if early warning signs are heeded, appropriate measures may prevent the development of the full-blown syndrome. These early clinical warning signs are (from most common to least common):

- tightness/stiffness during or after activity with nil (or temporary only) relief from stretching
- loss of acceleration
- loss of maximal sprinting speed
- loss of distance with long kick on run
- vague discomfort with deceleration.

Treatment

Traditional treatment for most types of groin pain was "rest;" however, this usually resulted in a return of symptoms on resumption of activity. Compared with rest and passive electrotherapy, active rehabilitation provides more than 10 times the likelihood of pain-free successful return to sport.[62] The treatment protocol outlined below combines the latest research evidence with the authors' experience.[60–63]

Five basic principles underpin a treatment regimen:

1. Ensure that exercise is performed without pain.
2. Identify and reduce the sources of increased load on the pelvis.
3. Improve lumbopelvic stability.
4. Strengthen local musculature using proven protocols.
5. Progress the patient's level of activity on the basis of regular clinical assessment.

These are outlined below.

Ensure that exercise is performed without pain

The first and most important step is for the patient to cease training and playing in pain. *Pain-free exercise* is absolutely crucial for this rehabilitation program.

If pain is experienced during any of the rehabilitation activities, or after them, that activity should be reduced or ceased altogether. Experienced clinicians use absence of pain on the key provocation tests (e.g. squeeze test and Thomas test position) as a guide to progress the rehabilitation program and minimize the mechanical stress on injured tissues (see progression of program below).

Identify and reduce the sources of increased load on the pelvis

As discussed previously, it is essential to identify and reduce the sources of increased load on the pubic bones. This may involve:

- reducing adductor muscle tone and guarding with soft tissue treatment (Fig. 29.7a) and/or dry needling
- correcting iliopsoas muscle shortening with local soft tissue treatment (Fig. 29.7b), neural mobilization (Fig. 29.7c), and mobilization of upper lumbar intervertebral joints (Chapter 26)

Figure 29.7 Treatment techniques used in adductor-related pain

(a) Soft tissue therapy—sustained myofascial tension to the adductor muscle group

(b) Soft tissue therapy—sustained myofascial tension to the iliopsoas muscle. The hip should be slowly passively extended from the flexed position shown to increase the tension

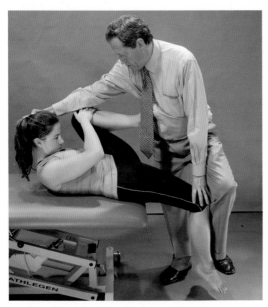

(c) Neural mobilization—Thomas position. Commence in the iliopsoas stretch position, then add passive cervical/upper thoracic tension, and then passive knee flexion to elicit a stretch

- reducing gluteus medius muscle tone and myofascial shortening with soft tissue treatment and/or dry needling
- identifying and correcting any hip joint abnormality (Chapter 28)
- mobilizing stiff intervertebral segments (Chapter 26)
- improving core stability (Chapter 14), especially activation of transversus abdominis and anterior pelvic floor muscles.

Improve lumbopelvic stability

Research has demonstrated a delayed onset of action,[35] and reduced thickness[37] of transversus abdominis activity in patients with longstanding groin pain, suggesting that impaired core or lumbopelvic stability (Chapter 14) plays a role in the development of this condition.

In our clinical experience, a core stability program has proven to be an important component of the rehabilitation program for longstanding groin pain. This program has been described in Chapter 14.

Strengthen local musculature using proven protocols

Once pain has settled and muscle shortening has been corrected in the adductor, iliopsoas, and gluteal muscles, then a graduated pain-free muscle strengthening program can be commenced. A randomized clinical trial found an active training program aimed at improving muscle strength and coordination of the muscles acting on the pelvis, in particular the adductor muscles, was more effective in the treatment of a group of sportspeople with longstanding groin pain than a physiotherapy program consisting of laser, TENS, friction massage, and stretching without active training.[62] This program is described in the box (overleaf). A similar pre-season adductor muscle strengthening program reduced the incidence of adductor muscle strains in ice hockey players who were identified as at risk.[5, 64]

Progress the patient's level of activity on the basis of regular clinical assessment

The aim of the graded exercise program is to gradually increase the load on the pubic bones and surrounding tissues. Once the patient is pain-free (see above), pain-free walking can begin and be gradually increased in speed and distance.

Exercise rehabilitation program for longstanding groin pain in sportspeople[17]

This program consists of static and dynamic exercises aimed at improving the muscles stabilizing the pelvis and the hip joints, in particular the adductor muscles. The program consists of two parts:

- Module 1: Two-week familiarization program—adductor activation
- Module 2: More demanding exercises with heavier resistance training, and balance and coordination. The training program is performed three times a week and the exercises from Module 1 are performed on the days in between the treatment days. The total length of the training period is 8–12 weeks. Sports activities are not allowed in the treatment period. Pain-free bike riding is allowed. After 6 weeks, pain-free jogging is allowed. Return to sport is allowed when neither treatment nor jogging causes any pain.

Stretching of the adductor muscles is not advised, but stretching of the other lower extremity muscles, particularly the iliopsoas, is recommended.

Module 1: Static and dynamic exercises (2-week base training program)

Static

1. (a) Adduction for 30 seconds against a soccer ball placed between the feet when lying in the supine position with the knees fully extended and the first toe pointing straight upwards (Fig. 29.8a).
   (b) Adduction for 30 seconds against a soccer ball placed between the knees when lying in the supine position with the knees and the hips flexed at 45° and the feet flat on the floor pointing straight ahead (Fig. 29.8b).

Exercises 1(a) and (b) should be repeated 10 times with 15 second recovery periods between each contraction. The force of the adduction should be just sufficient to reach the point where pain begins.

Dynamic

   (c) Sit-ups from the supine position with the hip and knee joints flexed at 45° and the feet against the floor. The sit-ups are performed as a straight abdominal curl and also with a quarter twist towards the opposite knee. Five sets of 10 with 15 second recovery periods.

   (d) In the same starting position as for the sit-ups but clamping a soccer ball between the knees, the player does a combination of a sit-ups while pulling the ball towards the head. The exercise is performed rhythmically and with accuracy to gain balance and coordination. Five sets of 10 with 15 second recovery periods.

   (e) Wobble board training for 5 minutes.

   (f) Adductor lateral slide. Using a sliding board with an extremely smooth surface (or a very smooth floor) and wearing a low-friction sock on the sliding foot, one foot is positioned next to the sliding board and the other foot on the board parallel to the first one. The foot on the board slides out laterally and is then pulled back to the starting position. The foot should be pressed against the surface through the whole exercise with as much force as tolerated within the patient's threshold of pain (Fig. 29.8c overleaf). Perform continuously for 1 minute with each leg in turn.

   (g) Forward slide. The same procedure is also done with the foot on the board placed in a 90° angle to the foot outside the board. Perform continuously for 1 minute with each leg in turn.

All the above exercises should be commenced carefully, and the number of sets and range of motion gradually increased, respecting pain and exhaustion.

Module 2: Dynamic exercises

This entire module is done twice at each training session for three training sessions per week with a day in between. Module 1 is done on alternate days, so players are training a total of six days per week. Exercises 2(a) to (e) are done as five sets of 10 repetitions.

2. (a) Lying on one side with the lower leg stretched and the upper leg bent and placed in front of the lower leg, the lower leg is moved up and down, pointing the heel upwards.
   (b) Lying on one side with the lower leg bent and the upper leg stretched, the upper leg is moved up and down, pointing the heel upwards.

(c) Begin by standing at the end of a high couch and then lie prone so that the torso is supported by the couch. The hips are at the edge of the couch at 90° of flexion and the feet are on the floor. From this position, both hips are slowly extended so both legs are lifted to the greatest possible extension of hips and spine; legs are then lowered together.

(d) Standing abduction/adduction using ankle pulleys. Begin with a low weight and gradually increase the weight but keep it submaximal.

(e) Standing on one leg, the knee of the supporting leg is flexed and extended rhythmically and in the same rhythm, swinging both arms back and forth independently ("cross-country skiing on one leg") (Fig. 29.8d overleaf). The non-weight-bearing leg is not moved. The balance and position are kept accurately, and the exercise is stopped when this is no longer possible. Progression of the exercise is obtained by holding a 1 kg (2.2 lb) weight in each hand.

(f) "Fitter" training for 5 minutes.

(g) Standing on the sliding board, side-to-side skating movements on the sliding board are done as five sets of 1 minute training periods with 15 second recovery.

Practical tips

- Supervision is important—the patient should be instructed by a physiotherapist, a physician, an athletic trainer, or another qualified person who has been trained in the details of the program.
- Exercises such as 1(d) and 2(e) are very important, especially at the end of the training period, but they are technically difficult.
- The athletes can do the program at home or at the gym or the fitness club, but we recommend physiotherapist supervision for three to four times within the first 2 weeks, and after that a visit every 10–14 days to check the technique and ensure progression.
- Patience is the key to success.
- Patients often make good progress in the first few weeks, but symptoms can plateau from that period until the 6–9 week period, when there is a positive "breakthrough."
- It is important to use pain as a guide to how much to do. Muscle soreness similar to that after a regular practice in the sports field is not a problem, but if the patient experiences pain from the injury, the intensity of the exercises should be adjusted.
- Pain medication including NSAIDs should be avoided.
- Athletes should continue with some of the exercises on a regular basis (one to two times a week) for at least a year after total recovery and return to sport.
- The athlete must appreciate that successful rehabilitation of chronic groin pain takes a minimum of 8–12 weeks.

Figure 29.8 Static and dynamic exercises to improve the muscles stabilizing the pelvis and the hip joints
(a) Static exercise—adduction for 30 seconds against a soccer ball placed between the feet

(b) Static exercise—adduction for 30 seconds against a soccer ball placed between the knees when lying in the supine position with the knees and the hips flexed at 45°

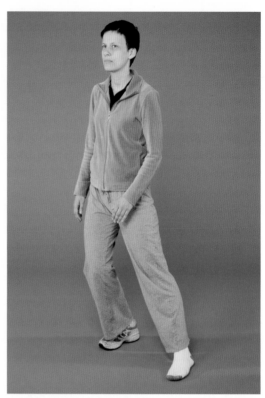

(c) Static exercise—adductor lateral slide. The foot on the slippery surface slides out laterally and is then pulled back to the starting position in contact with the surface and with as much force as tolerable

(d) Dynamic exercise—cross-country skiing on one leg. Note that the non-weight-bearing leg is not moved

The criteria for when the patient may return to running are when:

- brisk walking is pain-free
- resisted hip flexion in the Thomas position is pain-free
- there is no "crossover" sign (p. 553)
- there is minimal adductor guarding.

Various progressive running regimens can be used. One effective program is described here:[63]

- 100 m run-throughs with 10 m acceleration and deceleration phases with walk recovery. Patient should commence with six to eight repetitions on alternate days. Key criteria (adductor guarding, squeeze test) should be assessed immediately after each session and again the next morning. The running program can be progressed further by replacing walk recovery with jog recovery. The aim should be to build up to 20 × 100 m run-throughs and jog back.
- Lateral running (gradual change of direction such as figure eight) can be commenced when the above running program is completed pain-free, the hip flexion test is still pain-free with no crossover sign, there is no adductor guarding, and the squeeze test is pain-free. Figure-of-eight running should commence slowly with very gradual change of direction, then gradually increase both speed and sharpness of change of direction.

In kicking sports, short stationary kicking can be commenced when hip flexion tests are pain-free without crossover. The player may gradually increase the kicking distance and then start shorter kicking on the run. The last stage in the kicking program is long kicks at full pace and kicking around the body.

Key clinical signs suggestive of "excessive loading" during rehabilitation

The therapist must continually guard against the player "overdoing" rehabilitation. The following signs appear to suggest excessive loading and deterioration during rehabilitation:

- pain on passive hip abduction
- adductor muscle "guarding" with increased muscle tone on passive combined hip external rotation and abduction
- pain and weakness with resisted adductor contraction
- pain on the squeeze test (Fig. 29.5e)

- pain on resisted hip flexion (Fig. 29.5d)
- pain on resisted hip flexion and adduction in the Thomas test position
- positive crossover sign.

Other non-surgical treatments

Compression shorts have been advocated for those with mild pain who insist on continuing to train and play, and for those returning to sport after rehabilitation.[65–67] The shorts substantially reduce pain when worn during exercise.[68] The mechanism of action of compression shorts remains unclear.

Failure of conservative management

Conservative management as outlined above might fail for a number of reasons. These include:

- incorrect diagnosis (hip joint pathology, hernia, stress fracture, referred pain)
- inadequate period of rest
- poor compliance
- exercising into pain
- inappropriate progressions
- inadequate core stability
- persistent lumbar intervertebral hypomobility
- persistent adductor guarding.

Surgery

If persistent adductor shortening/guarding is a problem that does not respond to soft tissue treatment and/or dry needling, a partial adductor tendon release may help.[69, 70] Abolition of the patient's symptoms and signs with a trial injection of local anesthetic is advocated by some as an indication that the release will be successful in alleviating symptoms.

One technique advocated is to release the superficial section of the normal adductor longus tendon at a point distal to the insertion. It is postulated that this may have the effect of transferring stress from the superficial section of the tendon to the stress-shielded deeper portion.[71] Anecdotally, these patients often make a quick recovery and return to high-level sport after four to six weeks.

Iliopsoas-related groin pain

The iliopsoas muscle is the strongest flexor of the hip joint. The iliopsoas muscle is shown in Figure 29.9 overleaf. It arises from the five lumbar vertebrae and the ilium, and inserts into the lesser trochanter of the femur. It is occasionally injured acutely; however, it frequently becomes tight when there is neural

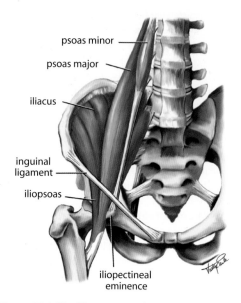

psoas minor

psoas major

iliacus

inguinal
ligament

iliopsoas

iliopectineal
eminence

Figure 29.9 The iliopsoas muscle

restriction, lumbar, pelvic, and groin pain, restriction in range of movement at the hip, lumbar and sacral regions, or poor lumbopelvic dynamic stability.

Epidemiology

The iliopsoas muscle is frequently injured during kicking activities. Kicking is an asymmetrical, ballistic task that combines hip flexion with lumbar rotation. The asymmetrical nature of kicking can lead to muscle imbalance and injury. A recent study measured the cross-sectional area, on MRI, of the iliopsoas and quadratus lumborum muscles in a group of AFL players.[72] This study found that asymmetries were common in AFL players. Cross-sectional area was consistently greater on the ipsilateral iliopsoas muscle and contralateral quadratus lumborum. Interestingly, this finding did not correlate to the number of injuries, thereby suggesting this may be a normal adaption to the demands of the sport.

In a study by Holmich et al., iliopsoas-related pain was by far the most common secondary clinical entity in athletes presenting with longstanding groin pain.[4] This suggests that, even when iliopsoas is not thought of as the primary entity to an athlete's pain presentation, a routine assessment of iliopsoas should be included in a routine assessment. Treatment for positive findings such as tightness, weakness, or pain should be incorporated into management.

Clinical concepts

Iliopsoas problems include tendinosis, snapping tendon, bursitis, tears, and avulsion injuries. Due to the close proximity of the iliopsoas bursa and tendon, injury or inflammation in the bursa should be carefully differentiated from tendon dysfunction. Whether or not iliopsoas tendinopathy and bursitis contribute substantially to exercise-related groin pain remains unclear. Most case reports associate these conditions with hip surgery and with rheumatological conditions (e.g. polymyalgia rheumatica). The thin-walled iliopsoas bursa commonly communicates with the hip joint, therefore associated restricted range of movement and/or hip pain may accompany iliopsoas pathology.

Iliopsoas problems often occur as overuse injuries resulting from excessive or repetitive hip flexion, such as kicking. Sportspeople often present with a poorly localized ache that is usually described as a deep ache, or a sensation of snapping/clicking in one side of the groin. Pain is often reproduced on palpation, stretch, and muscle strength tests. Pain or a snapping sensation is sometimes felt as the iliopsoas tendon flicks over the iliopectineal eminence and lesser trochanter when the hip is extended from the flexed and often abducted position.

There are two key clinical signs that point to the iliopsoas as the source of groin pain. The first, tenderness of the muscle in the lower abdomen, relies on palpation of the iliopsoas muscle, which is difficult in its proximal portion, deep within the pelvis. Nevertheless, the skilled examiner may detect tenderness more distally, particularly in thin sportspeople, by palpating carefully just below the inguinal ligament, lateral to the femoral artery and medial to the sartorius muscles.[47] Elevation of the ipsilateral leg or passive hip flexion can make palpation easier.

The second key clinical sign that helps distinguish the iliopsoas from other sources of groin pain is pain and tightness on iliopsoas stretch (best performed in the Thomas test position) that is exacerbated on resisted hip flexion in the stretch position (Fig. 29.5d). Frequently, the further addition of passive cervical flexion and knee flexion (Fig. 29.5j) aggravates the pain, indicating a degree of neural restriction through the muscle.

A recent study has found that normative values for hip extension in the Thomas test position is approximately 10.6° via the use of an inclinometer.[73] Therefore the clinician should be suspicious of iliopsoas or hip involvement if a sportsperson presents with a significantly lower range. It is important to examine the lumbar spine, as there is frequently an association between iliopsoas tightness and hypomobility of the upper lumbar spine from which the muscle originates. Furthermore, the close proximity of the sacroiliac joint and the hip joint itself should be taken into consideration, and assessed as possible primary or secondary involvement in the pain presentation.

Strength testing may be performed with the sportsperson in the supine position and the hip maximally flexed.[47] The thigh is then extended against the athlete's maximal resistance (Fig. 29.5d). Pain and/or weakness compared with the other side may be detected.

Treatment

Treatment of iliopsoas-related groin pain is similar to that of adductor-related groin pain (above) but with an increased emphasis on soft tissue treatment of the iliopsoas (Fig. 29.7b) and iliopsoas stretching (Fig. 29.5c) with the addition of a neural component (Fig. 29.5j). Often, mobilization of the lumbar intervertebral joints (Chapter 26) at the origin of the iliopsoas muscles markedly decreases the patient's pain.

Abdominal wall–related groin pain

The subject of "hernias" as a common cause of groin pain in sportspeople is controversial. While true inguinal hernias are relatively rare in this population, other conditions similar to hernias have been described and have come in and out of favor as common causes of groin pain. These include terms such as "sportsman's hernia," "footballer's hernia," "inguinal insufficiency," "conjoint tendon tear," "hockey player's groin," and "Gilmore's groin." Many of these entities are probably describing the same or similar clinical conditions, and all seem to respond to similar surgical treatment.

Some descriptions of sports hernia include abnormalities of the rectus abdominis muscle, avulsion of part of the internal oblique muscle fibers from the pubic tubercle, tearing within the internal oblique muscle, and abnormality in the external oblique muscle and its aponeurosis.[74]

Posterior inguinal wall weakness (sports hernia, sportsman's hernia)

A significant group of patients with groin pain, usually male football players, present with a long history of gradually worsening, poorly localized pain aggravated by activity, especially kicking. These patients have been classified as having inguinal insufficiency, footballer's hernia, or sportsman's hernia. This diagnosis is popular in soccer players in the UK and Europe. This presentation is uncommon in women, and in women other diagnoses should be thoroughly explored.[70]

Various authors have described slightly different pathologies, including a tear in the transversalis or external oblique fascia, a tear in the external oblique aponeurosis, a tear in the conjoined tendon, a separation of the inguinal ligament from the conjoined tendon, and tearing of the conjoined tendon from the pubic tubercle.[75-81] Some or all of these pathologies may lead to dilation of the external inguinal ring.

A number of contributing factors have been suggested. The condition is commonly bilateral, suggesting that a congenital posterior inguinal wall deficiency may be present.[82] Intense sporting activity, particularly involving kicking, places increased downward stress on the conjoined tendon, and causes muscle fatigue.[83] An increase in intra-abdominal pressure during sport increases stress on the transversalis fascia fibers of the posterior inguinal wall.[84]

The onset of pain is usually insidious, but it may also present as an acute injury followed by chronic pain. The pain initially tends to occur after or near the end of activity. As the condition progresses, the pain worsens and occurs earlier in activity. The pain is usually located in the posterior inguinal floor inside the external ring. It may also radiate to the testicle, adductors, or laterally in the upper thigh. The pain is usually aggravated by sudden movement, and is aggravated by sneezing, coughing, sexual activity, and the Valsalva maneuver. Symptoms have a tendency to settle after prolonged absence from sporting activity, only to recur when high-intensity exercise is resumed.

On examination, maximal tenderness is usually over the pubic tubercle. The most helpful diagnostic sign is dilation and/or discomfort to palpation of the external inguinal ring after invagination of the scrotum (Fig. 29.5l). Peritoneograms are used in Scandinavia to confirm the diagnosis in some cases, but these tests have generally gone out of favor elsewhere. There is some evidence that ultrasound examination[54] and MRI[85] may be able to detect these hernias.

Surgery is the most popular treatment for this condition. The most common procedure is a Bassini hernia repair, paying added attention to identification and repair of tears in the transversalis fascia or other structures. Most surgeons also insert a polypropylene mesh. This procedure can be performed as an open operation or laparoscopically.[81, 86, 87]

Muschaweck et al. describe an open suture repair, called the "minimal repair" technique.[88] With this mesh-free technique, the defect of the posterior wall of the inguinal canal is not enlarged, the suture is nearly tension-free and the patient can, therefore, return to full training and athletic activity within the shortest time. The genital branch of the genitofemoral nerve is often resected because of "damage." At four weeks post surgery, 75.8% of the 129 athletes in their study had returned to pre-injury sports activity.[88]

Taylor et al.[24] and Meyers et al.[70] in the US, and Biedert et al.[89] in Switzerland have reported a procedure in which they performed a broad surgical reattachment of the inferolateral edge of the rectus abdominis muscle with its fascial investment to the pubis and adjacent anterior ligaments.[24] The operation is similar to a Bassini hernia repair, with the main difference being a focus on attachment of the rectus abdominis muscle fascia to the pubis, rather than protection of the inguinal floor near the internal ring.[70] A number of the patients in these studies also had an adductor release.

If tenderness at the attachment of the inguinal ligament is present, laparoscopic release of the ligament may be effective. This procedure is currently common in the UK.[90]

Reports of results of surgery are generally very positive, but in our experience there is a relatively high rate of recurrence of symptoms. It is unclear whether this is because of an incorrect diagnosis or recurrence of the problem.

Theoretically, a rehabilitation program consisting of strengthening of the abdominal obliques, transversus abdominis, adductors, and hip flexors should help in this condition, and a trial of such a program may be worthwhile before resorting to surgery.[91] No scientific evidence exists as to the efficacy of such a program, or any surgical treatment.

Gilmore's groin

A similar condition to sports hernia has been described by Gilmore and is known as "Gilmore's groin."[92–94] Gilmore describes an injury involving a torn external oblique aponeurosis, causing dilatation of the superficial inguinal ring, a torn conjoint tendon (common tendon of insertion of the internal

oblique and transversus abdominis muscles), and a dehiscence between the inguinal ligament and the conjoint tendon. Gilmore advocates surgical repair of the defect with a reported 96% of his patients returning to sport within 15 weeks.[92]

Laparoscopic inguinal ligament release

One of the more recent innovations in the surgical management of chronic groin pain is the laparoscopic inguinal ligament release. Developed in Leicester by a general surgeon, and also known as the "Lloyd release," the technique involves a laparoscopic release of the inguinal ligament and related structures from the pubic tubercle.[90]

Clinical indications for the surgery are chronic groin pain not responding to conservative management, and tenderness on the medial attachment of the inguinal ligament to the pubis. When visualized laparoscopically, the anatomy around the pubic tubercle is very similar to a conjoined tendon attachment, with the rectus abdominis, conjoint tendon, inguinal ligament, fascia lata, adductor longus, and pectineus all contributing to the raphe of tissue attaching to the tubercle.

The surgical approach is via two small portals adjacent to the umbilicus. The peritoneum is dissected away to reveal the anatomy around the inguinal region. Using a thermal instrument, and using the inguinal ligament as an anatomical guide, the raphe of tissue is undermined away from its attachment to the pubic tubercle. The technique is similar to that of a common extensor origin release for the treatment of lateral epicondylosis, and, as such, no formal tenotomy is performed. The defect in the peritoneum is repaired using a synthetic mesh, and the laparoscopic portals are closed.

Recovery from the surgery is rapid, with the patient often returning to their previous level of activity within four weeks. In the treatment of pubic overload, it may be a more anatomical solution than the sportsman's hernia repairs and related inguinal surgery.

Tear of the external oblique aponeurosis (hockey groin)

A condition involving a tear of the external oblique aponeurosis and superficial inguinal ring has been described in elite ice hockey players.[95, 96] These players all complained of a muscular type of pain of gradual onset, exacerbated by ipsilateral hip extension and contralateral torso rotation. The discomfort

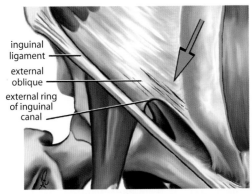

inguinal ligament

external oblique

external ring of inguinal canal

Figure 29.10 External oblique muscle showing usual site of tears

is often worse in the morning, specifically during hip extension from a sitting position, as in getting up from a bed or chair. Pain is felt mostly during the propulsion phase of skating (the first few strides) and during the slapshot motion. It is consistently located on the opposite side to the player's forehand shot. The dull ache may radiate to the scrotum, hip, and back.

On examination there are no consistent findings, although the superficial inguinal ring may be tender and/or dilated. Imaging studies are consistently negative. Various conservative therapies have been attempted without success and the definitive treatment is surgery involving repair of the torn external oblique aponeurosis. The ilioinguinal nerve is often trapped in scar tissue. If so, neurectomy is performed. Postoperatively, the patients are advised to avoid skating for four weeks, then slowly allowed to return to activity over the next six to eight weeks.

Inguinal hernia

Inguinal hernias occur in sportspeople as in the general population. They can be either direct or indirect. Small hernias may become painful as a result of exertion. Symptoms may include a characteristic dragging sensation to one side of the lower abdomen aggravated by increased intra-abdominal pressure (e.g. coughing). On examination, there is occasionally an obvious swelling, and there may be a palpable cough impulse. Treatment consists of surgical correction of the defect.

Rectus abdominis injuries

Abnormalities of the rectus abdominis occur at its tendinous insertion into the superior ramus of the pubis. The anatomy of the rectus abdominis lends itself to a direct link to the adductor longus muscle through its aponeurotic attachment over the pubic synthesis.[3] Additionally, the insertion of the oblique abdominal muscles and the transversus abdominis add to its possible role in lumbopelvic stability. Therefore close examination of the adductor muscles and core stability should be undertaken to ensure successful management strategies are considered and incorporated.

The rectus abdominis, along with the other abdominal muscles, is commonly injured via direct blows to the abdomen or from repetitive trunk movements (rotations or flexion/extension).[97] Additionally, rectus abdominis abnormalities may occur as the result of an acute strain while lifting, or as an overuse injury associated with excessive abdominal contractions (e.g. sit-ups).

Rectus abdominis strains have been reported to be common in tennis players.[98] The mechanism of injury in this population is thought to be associated with the cocking phase of the service motion, where eccentric loads are sustained followed by forced contraction of the contralateral side. Therefore careful assessment of the serve (via video analysis) should be incorporated in these athletes.

On examination, there is tenderness at the insertion of the rectus abdominis into the superior pubic ramus. Pain is aggravated by active contraction (such as a sit-up). If available, real-time ultrasound may be a useful diagnostic tool. Due to the close proximity of the inguinal canal opening, inguinal hernias should also be considered. The pelvic floor should be considered when insertional rectus abdominis abnormalities are found, as there may be a close link between the two structures.[58]

Treatment consists of correction of soft tissue dysfunction, and a gradual strengthening program. Sport-specific exercises that highlight eccentric control and lumbopelvic stability should be incorporated. Some clinicians advocate an injection of corticosteroid and local anesthetic agents into the area of attachment in recalcitrant cases, but this approach is losing favor in tendinopathies in general. If injection is tried, it should be accompanied by active rehabilitation.

Pubic bone stress–related groin pain

Historically it has been thought that athletic groin pain can arise from bony stress around the pubic symphysis, hence the term "osteitis pubis." That "diagnosis" was associated with typical radiographic and radionuclide imaging appearances. The radiographic features are the typical "moth-eaten" appearance along the margins of the pubic symphysis (Fig. 29.11a) with asymmetrical bony erosions, osteophytes, sclerotic bony margins, and subchondral bone cysts. The radionuclide bone scan shows increased uptake on the delayed static images over the pubic tubercle (Fig. 29.11b).

CT scanning is also a sensitive investigation for displaying abnormalities of the bony architecture, such as cystic changes and perisymphysis erosions (Fig. 29.11c). In more recent times, MRI has shown bone marrow edema in the body of the pubis (Fig. 29.11d).[25]

The significance of the bone marrow edema in sportspeople (mainly men) with longstanding groin pain is presently a topic of great interest and vigorous debate. As mentioned previously, Verrall et al.[25] have shown that bone marrow edema is present on MRI in a large percentage (77%) of footballers presenting with longstanding groin pain that is associated with pubic symphysis tenderness and a positive squeeze test. However, 54% of non-symptomatic footballers also demonstrated bone marrow edema on MRI. They proposed that pubic bone stress was a possible cause of the symptoms and signs such as the squeeze test, but their subsequent research showed

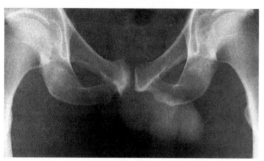

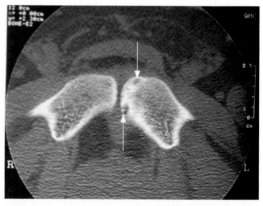

Figure 29.11 Imaging appearance of pubic bone stress–related longstanding groin pain (traditionally described as "osteitis pubis")
(a) X-ray showing the characteristic moth-eaten appearance

(c) Appearance on CT scan, showing degenerative cyst formation and erosions, with widening of the anterior margins of the symphysis

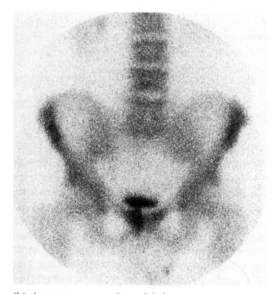

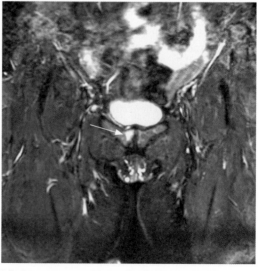

(b) Appearance on radionuclide bone scan

(d) Appearance on T2-weighted MRI, showing bony edema (arrow) in the body of the pubis only moderate levels of sensitivity[53] of the squeeze test when correlated with clinical and MRI criteria.

PRACTICE PEARL Abnormalities in all imaging modalities are seen in sportspeople who have no history of groin pain.

Nevertheless, the presence of bone marrow edema elsewhere in the body is considered significant. For example, on MRI it is characteristic of the bone bruises associated with serious knee injuries (Chapter 32).

In addition to the central cleft or cavity frequently noted in the fibrocartilaginous symphysis pubis, a secondary symphyseal cleft may be seen extending laterally from the central cleft in patients with groin pain. The secondary cleft, best seen on coronal STIR (Short T1 Inversion Recovery) MRI views, demonstrates fluid signal intensity, and is continuous with the central cleft (Fig. 29.11e) extending to the inferior margin of the pubic ramus and into the enthesis of the adductor and gracilis muscles.[99] A secondary cleft could develop as a result of chronic maceration of the central fibrocartilage owing to abnormal stress in the pelvic ring.

Injection into the central cleft confirmed the MRI findings by demonstrating flow of the dye into the secondary cleft. Injection of corticosteroid and local anesthetic into the central cleft was successful in abolishing pain in patients with groin pain and secondary cleft seen on MRI.[100] However, there was a significant recurrence of pain in the following months. The relevance of the secondary symphyseal cleft remains unclear and requires further investigation.

The pubic bones are subjected to considerable forces by the various pelvic structures mentioned above. It may be that pubic bone abnormalities are the cause of pain in a small group of patients, or they may simply be a sign of increased bone stress when the other clinical entities (e.g. adductor-related) are affected.

Treatment

In addition to the management of factors that contribute to pubic overload, a variety of treatments have focused on the symphysis pubis and bony abnormalities.

The use of corticosteroids both as a local injection into the symphysis pubis[101] and in oral form (25–50 mg/day for 7 days) has been anecdotally helpful, but no controlled trial has been reported. We have found a short (5–7 days) course of oral prednisolone (50 mg/day) helpful in settling pain, thus enabling the patient to commence the rehabilitation program earlier.

Dextrose prolotherapy injections have been shown to be helpful in one study.[102] Monthly injections of 12.5% dextrose and 0.5% lignocaine (lidocaine) into the adductor origins, suprapubic abdominal insertions, and symphysis pubis were given until resolution of symptoms. An average of 2.8 treatments were required.

Three- to six-monthly courses of intravenous injection of the bisphosphonate pamidronate were found to be helpful in one report of three cases.[103]

Some physicians are advocating the use of extracorporeal shock wave therapy, but there is no evidence to support this.

Surgery has been advocated by some clinicians. In the chronic stage of the condition, where imaging shows erosions and cystic changes in the pubic symphysis (Fig. 29.11c), surgical exploration and debridement of the symphysis may be indicated.[104] Symphyseal wedge resection[105] is out of favor as it can give rise to progressive sacroiliac arthrosis and ultimately posterior pelvic instability requiring major pelvic stabilization.[106] Arthrodesis of the pubic symphysis by bone grafting and a compression plate has been used successfully in patients with proven pubic instability.[107]

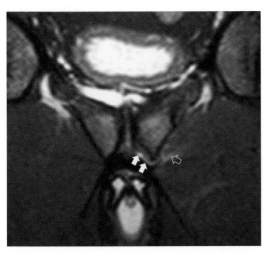

(e) MRI of the pubic symphysis at a point just posterior to the adductor longus insertion. Symphyseal degenerative changes and a "secondary cleft" sign (solid white arrows) are demonstrated. Note the reactive oedema tracking through the cleft and into the adjacent obturator externus muscle (white open arrow)

Less common injuries

Obturator neuropathy

Obturator neuropathy is a fascial entrapment of the obturator nerve as it enters the adductor compartment. Obturator neuropathies have been reported to occur in Australian Rules football and rugby. It has distinct clinical features that separate it from other causes of groin pain.[108, 109]

Obturator neuropathy presents as exercise-related groin pain, which initially is concentrated on the proximal groin, but with increasing exercise radiates towards the distal medial thigh. There may be associated weakness or a feeling of a lack of propulsion of the limb during running, but numbness is very rarely reported. At rest, examination findings can be nonspecific, with pain on passive abduction of the hip, and pain and weakness on resisted hip adduction. The ipsilateral pubic tubercle is often tender. The essential component of the physical examination is to exercise the patient to a level that reproduces his or her symptoms, and then immediately examine the patient. This examination will reveal weakness of resisted adduction and numbness over the distal medial thigh.

Bone scan in this condition often shows increased uptake over the ipsilateral pubic tubercle, frequently called "osteitis pubis" by the reporting radiologist. The diagnosis is confirmed by needle EMG (electromyogram), which shows chronic denervation patterns of the adductor muscle group.

Conservative treatment of this condition, including sustained myofascial tension massage over the adductor compartment, neural stretches, spinal mobilization, and iliopsoas soft tissue techniques, is generally unsuccessful.

The definitive treatment of this condition is surgical. An oblique incision is made in the proximal groin. The plane between the adductor longus and pectineus is identified and dissected, revealing the obturator nerve under the fascia over the adductor brevis. This fascia is divided and the nerve is freed up to the level of the obturator foramen. The fascial anatomy (Fig. 29.12) here is very important, with the fascia of the adductor longus curving around the muscle medially and passing back deep to the muscle to become the fascia over the adductor brevis, which is thought to be responsible for the fascial entrapment of the obturator nerve. Postsurgical management includes wound management, soft tissue techniques, and a graduated return to full activity over a period of four to six weeks.

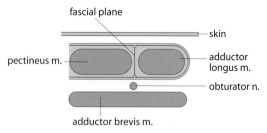

Figure 29.12 Obturator neuropathy—fascial arrangements

Other nerve entrapments

A number of superficial nerves in the groin may become entrapped and should be considered as possible causes of groin pain. The ilioinguinal nerve supplies the skin around the genitalia and inside of the thigh, and may produce pain as a result of entrapment. The genitofemoral nerve innervates an area of skin just above the groin fold. The lateral cutaneous nerve of the thigh is the most common nerve affected. This nerve supplies the outside of the thigh. This condition is known as "meralgia paresthetica." This condition is described in Chapter 30.

Diagnosis of pudendal nerve entrapment requires the presence of the following criteria—pain in the territory of the pudendal nerve from the anus to the penis or clitoris, pain being predominantly experienced while sitting, pain that does not wake the patient at night, pain that has no objective sensory impairment, and pain that is relieved by diagnostic pudendal nerve block.[110]

Treatment of these conditions is usually not necessary as they often spontaneously resolve. Meralgia paresthetica is sometimes treated with a corticosteroid injection at the site where the nerve exits the pelvis, 1 cm (0.5 in.) medial to the anterior superior iliac spine. Occasionally, the nerve needs to be explored surgically and the area of entrapment released.

Stress fractures of the neck of the femur

Stress fracture of the neck of the femur is another cause of groin pain. The usual history is one of gradual onset of groin pain, which is poorly localized and aggravated by activity. Examination may show some localized tenderness; however, often there is relatively little to find other than pain at the extremes of hip joint movement, especially internal rotation. X-ray may demonstrate the fracture if it has been present for a number of weeks but this investigation should not be relied on to rule out the condition; isotopic bone scan and MRI (Fig. 29.13) are the most sensitive tests.

Stress fractures of the neck of the femur occur on either the superior or tension side of the bone, or on the inferior or compression side (Fig. 29.14). Stress fractures of the superior aspect of the femoral neck should be regarded as a surgical emergency and treated with either urgent internal fixation or strict

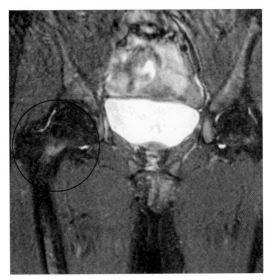

Figure 29.13 MRI showing stress fracture of the neck of the femur

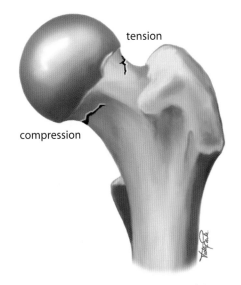

Figure 29.14 Stress fractures of the neck of the femur—superior or tension fracture on the superior aspect of the femoral neck, and inferior or compression fracture on the inferior side

bed rest. The concern is that such stress fractures have a tendency to go on to full fracture, which compromises the blood supply to the femoral head.

Stress fractures of the inferior surface of the femoral neck are more benign and can be treated with an initial period of non-weight-bearing rest followed by a period of weight-bearing without running. They require at least six weeks of rest and usually considerably longer. Following the period of rest, a further six weeks of progressive loading will take the patient back to full training. Biomechanical (Chapter 8), nutritional, and endocrine risk factors (Chapter 43) should be assessed and treated as appropriate.

Stress fracture of the inferior pubic ramus

Stress fracture of the inferior pubic ramus, especially in distance runners, is an important differential diagnosis of adductor tendinopathy. There is usually a history of overuse and localized tenderness, which is not aggravated by passive abduction or resisted adduction. In this condition, pain is often referred to the buttock.

A stress fracture may not be visible on plain X-ray for several weeks, whereas a radionuclide bone scan will demonstrate a focal area of increased activity within hours (Fig. 29.15) and an MRI will show a focal area of bone edema. As with any stress fracture, etiological factors must be considered. Stress fractures of the inferior pubic ramus in females may be associated with reduced bone density, low initial aerobic fitness, and nutritional insufficiency. Prolonged amenorrhea is also linked with this stress fracture (Chapter 43).

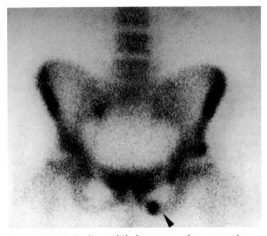

Figure 29.15 Radionuclide bone scan demonstrating stress fracture of the inferior pubic ramus

Treatment consists of relative rest from aggravating activities (such as running) until there is no longer any local tenderness. Fitness should be maintained with swimming or cycling, with gradual return to weight-bearing over a number of weeks. Predisposing factors such as a negative energy intake, muscular imbalance, or biomechanical abnormality also need assessment and intervention.

Preventive strategies can be incorporated, especially in the female military population. Strategies may include pre-training interventions focusing on improving aerobic fitness to reduce fatigue fractures, and calcium and vitamin D supplementation.[111, 112] Female recruits who report no menses in the year prior to recruitment should also be observed closely.[112]

Referred pain to the groin

The possibility of referred pain to the groin should always be considered, especially when there is little to find on local examination. A common site of referral to the groin is the sacroiliac joint, and this should always be assessed in any examination of a patient with groin pain. The sacroiliac joint, may also refer pain to the scrotum in males and labia in females. The assessment and treatment of sacroiliac problems have been discussed in Chapter 27.

The lumbar spine may refer pain to the groin. The lumbar spine and thoracolumbar junction should always be examined in a patient with groin pain. Neurodynamic tests, such as the slump and neural Thomas test position should be performed as part of the assessment (Chapter 11). Variations such as the addition of adduction or hip rotation may reproduce the patient's pain.

A positive neurodynamic test result requires further evaluation to determine the site of the abnormality. The position of reproduction of pain can be used to correct neural tightness by neural mobilization. Active trigger points may also refer to the groin and should be treated with soft tissue therapy.

REFERENCES

1. Bradshaw CJ, Bundy M, Falvey E. The diagnosis of longstanding groin pain: a prospective clinical cohort study. *Br J Sports Med* 2008;42(10):851–4.

2. Robertson BA, Barker PJ, Fahrer M et al. The anatomy of the pubic region revisited: implications for the pathogenesis and clinical management of chronic groin pain in athletes. *Sports Med* 2009;39(3):225–34.

3. Robinson P, Saleh F, Grainger A et al. Cadaveric and MRI study of the musculotendinous contributors to the capsule of the symphysis pubis. *Am J Roentgenol* 188(5):W440–5

4. Hölmich P. Long-standing groin pain in sportspeople falls into three primary patterns, a 'clinical entity' approach: a prospective study of 207 patients. *Br J Sports Med* 2007;41:247–52.

5. Tyler TF, Silvers HJ, Gerhardt MB et al. Groin injuries in sports medicine. *Sports Health* 2010;2(3):231–6.

6. Hureibi KA, McLatchie GR. Groin pain in athletes. *Scottish Med J* 2010;55(2):8–11.

7. Pettersson M, Lorentzon R. Ice hockey injuries: a four year prospective study of a Swedish elite ice hockey team. *Br J Sports Med* 1993;27(4): 251–4.

8. Tyler TF, Nicholas SJ, Campbell RJ et al. The association of hip strength and flexibility with the incidence of adductor muscle strains in professional ice hockey players. *Am J Sports Med* 2001;29(2):124–8.

9. Orchard J, Seward H. Epidemiology of injuries in the Australian Football League, seasons 1997–2000. *Br J Sports Med* 2002;36(1):39–44.

10. O'Connor D. Groin injuries in professional rugby league players: a prospective study. *J Sports Sci* 2004;22(7):629–36.

11. Werner J, Hagglund M, Walden M et al. UEFA injury study: a prospective study of hip and groin injuries in professional football over seven consecutive seasons. *Br J Sports Med* 2009;43(13):1036–40.

12. Engebretsen AH, Myklebust G, Holme I et al. Intrinsic risk factors for groin injuries among male soccer players. *Am J Sports Med* 2010;38(10):2051–7.

13. Maffey L, Emery C. What are the risk factors for groin strain injury in sport? *Sports Med* 2007;37(10):881–94.

14. Arnason A, Sigurdsson SB, Gudmundsson A et al. Risk factors for injuries in football. *Am J Sports Med* 2004;32(1 suppl):S5–16.

15. Emery CA, Meeuwisse WH. Risk factors for groin injuries in hockey. *Med Sci Sports Exerc* 2001;33(9):1423–33.

16. Hölmich P, Larsen K, Krogsgaard K et al. Exercise program for prevention of groin pain in football players: a cluster-randomized trial. *Scand J Med Sci Sports* 2010;20(6):814–21.

17. Ibrahim A, Murrell G, Knapman P. Adductor strain and hip range of movement in male professional soccer players. *J Orth Surg* 2007;15(1):46–9.

18. Verrall GM, Hamilton IA, Slavotinek JP et al. Hip joint range of motion reduction in sports-related chronic groin injury diagnosed as pubic bone stress injury. *J Sci Med Sport* 2005;8(1):77–84.

19. Witvrouw E, Danneels L, Asselman P. Muscle flexibility as a risk factor for developing muscle injuries in male professional soccer players. *Am J Sports Med* 2003;31:41–6.

20. Hagglund M, Waldan M, Ekstrand J. Previous injury as a risk factor for injury in elite football: a prospective study over two consecutive seasons. *Br J Sports Med* 2006;40(9):767–72.

21. Anderson K, Strickland SM, Warren R. Hip and groin injuries in athletes. *Am J Sports Med* 2001;29(4):521–33.

22. Adams RJ, Chandler FA. Osteitis pubis of traumatic etiology. *J Bone Joint Surg* 1953;35:685–96.

23. Holmich P, Renstrom PA, Saartok T. Hip, groin and pelvis. In: Kjaer M, Krogsgaard M, Magnusson P et al. eds. *Textbook of sports medicine*. Massachusetts: Blackwell Scientific 2003:616–37.

24. Taylor DC, Meyers WC, Moylan JA et al. Abdominal musculature abnormalities as a cause of groin pain in athletes. Inguinal hernias and pubalgia. *Am J Sports Med* 1991;19:239–42.

25. Verrall GM, Slavotinek JP, Fon GT. Incidence of pubic bone marrow oedema in Australian rules football players: relation to groin pain. *Br J Sports Med* 2001;35:28–33.

26. Lovell G, Galloway H, Hopkins W et al. Osteitis pubis and assessment of bone marrow edema at the pubic symphysis with MRI in an elite junior male soccer squad. *Clin J Sport Med* 2006;16:117–22.

27. Schilders E, Bismil Q, Robinson P et al. Adductor-related groin pain in competitive athletes. Role of adductor enthesis, magnetic resonance imaging, and entheseal pubic cleft injections. *J Bone Joint Surg Am* 2007;89(10):2173–8.

28. Holmich P, Renstrom P, Sartok T. Hip, groin and pelvis. In: Kjaer M, Krogsgaard M, Magnusson P, et al. eds. *Textbook of sports medicine*. Massachusetts: Blackwell Scientific, 2003:616–37.

B

29. Willson JD, Ireland ML, Davis I. Core strength and lower extremity alignment during single leg squats. *Med Sci Sports Exerc* 2006;38(5):945–52.

30. Lederman E. The myth of core stability. *J Bodyw Mov Ther* 2010;14(1):84–98.

31. Leetun DT, Ireland ML, Willson JD et al. Core stability measures as risk factors for lower extremity injury in athletes. *Med Sci Sports Exerc* 2004;36(6):926–34.

32. Richardson C, Snijders CJ, Hides JA et al. The relation between the transversus abdominis muscles, sacroiliac joint mechanics, and low back pain. *Spine* 2002;27(4):399–405.

33. Hoek van DGA, Snijders CJ, Stoeckart R et al. A biomechanical model on muscle forces in the transfer of spinal load to the pelvis and legs. *J Biomech* 1999;32:927–33.

34. Snijders CJ, Ribbers MT, de Bakker HV et al. EMG recordings of abdominal and back muscles in various standing postures: validation of a biomechanical model on sacroiliac joint stability. *J Electromyo Kinesiol* 1998;8:205–14.

35. Cowan SM, Schache AG, Brukner P. Delayed onset of transverse abdominus in long-standing groin pain. *Med Sci Sports Exerc* 2004;36:2040–5.

36. Ferreira P, Ferreira ML, Hodges PW. Changes in recruitment of the abdominal muscles in people with low back pain: ultrasound measurement of muscle activity. *Spine* 2004;29(22):2560–6.

37. Jansen J, Weir A, Dénis R et al. Resting thickness of transversus abdominis is decreased in athletes with longstanding adduction-related groin pain. *Man Ther* 2010;15(2):200–5.

38. Ganz R, Parvizi J, Beck M et al. Femoroacetabular impingement: a cause for osteoarthritis of the hip. *Clin Orth Rel Res* 2003(417):112–20.

39. Parvizi J, Bican O, Bender B et al. Arthroscopy for labral tears in patients with developmental dysplasia of the hip: a cautionary note. *J Arthroplasty* 2009;24(6 Suppl):110–13.

40. Weir A, de Vos RJ, Moen M et al. Prevalence of radiological signs of femoroacetabular impingement in patients presenting with long-standing adductor-related groin pain. *Br J Sports Med* 2011;45(1):6–9.

41. Lewis CL, Sahrmann SA. Acetabular labral tears. *Phys Ther* 2006;86(1):110–21.

42. Burnett RSJ, Della Rocca GJ, Prather H et al. Clinical presentation of patients with tears of the acetabular labrum. *J Bone Joint Surg Am* 2006;88(7):1448–57.

43. Philippon MJ, Weiss DR, Kuppersmith DA et al. Arthroscopic labral repair and treatment of femoroacetabular impingement in professional hockey players. *Am J Sports Med* 2010;38(1):99–104.

44. Bardakos NV, Villar RN. The ligamentum teres of the adult hip. *J Bone Joint Surg Br* 2009;91-B(1):8–15.

45. Byrd JW, Jones KS. Hip arthroscopy in athletes. *Clin Sports Med* 2001;20(4):749–61.

46. Byrd JWT, Jones KS. Prospective analysis of hip arthroscopy with 10-year followup. *Clin Orth Rel Res* 2010;468(3):741–46.

47. Hölmich P, Hölmich LR, Bjerg AM. Clinical examination of athletes with groin pain: an intraobserver and interobserver reliability study. *Br J Sports Med* 2004;38(4):446–51.

48. Malliaras P, Hogan A, Nawrocki A et al. Hip flexibility and strength measures: reliability and association with athletic groin pain. *Br J Sports Med* 2009;43(10):739–44.

49. Mens JMA, Vleeming A, Snijders CJ et al. Reliability and validity of hip adduction strength to measure disease severity in posterior pelvic pain since pregnancy. *Spine* 2002;27:1674–9.

50. Fulcher ML, Hanna CM, Raina Elley C. Reliability of handheld dynamometry in assessment of hip strength in adult male football players. *J Sci Med Sport* 2010;13(1):80–84.

51. Crow JF, Pearce AJ, Veale JP et al. Hip adductor muscle strength is reduced preceding and during the onset of groin pain in elite junior Australian football players. *J Sci Med Sport* 2010;13(2):202–04.

52. Mens J, Inklaar H, Koes BW et al. A new view on adductor related groin pain. *Clin J Sport Med* 2006;16(1):15–19.

53. Verrall GM, Slavotinek JP, Barnes PG et al. Description of pain provocation tests used for the diagnosis of sports-related chronic groin pain: relationship of tests to defined clinical (pain and tenderness) and MRI (pubic bone marrow oedema) criteria. *Scand J Med Sci Sports* 2005;15(1):36–42.

54. Orchard JW, Read JW, Neophyton J et al. Groin pain associated with ultrasound finding of inguinal canal posterior wall deficiency in Australian Rules footballers. *Br J Sports Med* 1998;32:134–39.

55. Jansen JA, Mens JM, Backx FJ et al. Diagnostics in athletes with long-standing groin pain. *Scand J Med Sci Sports* 2008;18(6):679–90.

56. Hölmich P, Bachmann Nielsen M. Ultrasound findings in adductor related groin pain. *Ultraschall Med* 2006;27(6):509–11.

57. Lischuk AW, Dorantes TM, Wong W et al. Imaging of sports-related hip and groin injuries. *Sports Health* 2010;2:252–61.

58. Zoga AC, Kavanagh EC, Omar IM et al. Athletic pubalgia and the sports hernia: MR imaging findings. *Radiology* 2008;247(3):797–807.

59. Morelli V, Smith V. Groin injuries in athletes. *Am Family Phys* 2001;64(8):1405–12.

60. Jansen J, Mens MA, Backx N. Treatment of longstanding groin pain in athletes; a systematic review. *Scand J Med Sci Sports* 2008;18:263–74.

61. Machotka Z, Kumar S, Perraton L. A systematic review of the literature on the effectiveness of exercise therapy for groin pain in athletes. *Sports Med Arth RehabTher Technol* 2009;1(1):5.

62. Holmich P, Uhrskou P, Kanstrup IL. Effectiveness of active physical training as treatment for long-standing adductor-related groin pain in athletes: randomised trial. *Lancet* 1999;353:439–43.

63. Hogan A. *A rehabilitation program for osteitis pubis in football.* Adelaide: OP Publications 2006.

64. Tyler TF, Nicholas SJ, Campbell RJ et al. The effectiveness of a preseason exercise program to prevent adductor muscle strains in professional ice hockey players. *Am J Sports Med* 2002;30(5):680–83.

65. Batt ME, McShane JM, Dillingham MF. Osteitis pubis in collegiate football players. *Med Sci Sports Exerc* 1995;27:629–33.

66. Fricker PA, Taunton JE, Ammann W. Osteitis pubis in athletes. *Sports Med* 1991;12(4):266–79.

67. Ruane JJ, Rossi TA. When groin pain is more than "just a strain": navigating a broad differential. *Phys Sportsmed* 1998;26:78.

68. McKim K, Taunton JE. The effectiveness of compression shorts in the treatment of athletes with osteitis pubis. *NZ J Sports Med* 2001;29(4):70–73.

69. Akemark C, Johansson C. Tenotomy of the adductor longus tendon in the treatment of chronic groin pain in athletes. *Am J Sports Med* 1992;20:640–43.

70. Meyers WC, Foley DP, Garrett WE et al. Management of severe lower abdominal or inguinal pain in high-performance athletes. *Am J Sports Med* 2000;28(1):2–8.

71. Orchard JW, Cook JL, Halpin N. Stress-shielding as a cause of insertional tendinopathy: the operative technique of limited adductor tenotomy supports this theory. *J Sci Med Sport* 2004;7(4):424–8.

72. Hides J, Fan T, Stanton W et al. Psoas and quadratus lumborum muscle asymmetry among elite Australian Football League players. *Br J Sports Med* 2010;44(8):563–7.

73. Ferber R, Kendall K, McElroy L Normative and critical criteria for iliotibial band and iliopsoas muscle flexibility. *J Ath Train* 2010;45(4):344.

74. Caudill P, Nyland J, Smith C et al. Sports hernias: a systematic literature review. *Br J Sports Med* 2008;42(12):954–64.

75. Fredberg U, Kissmeyer-Nielsen P. The sportsman's hernia—fact or fiction? *Scand J Med Sci Sports* 1996;6:201–4.

76. Hackney RG. The sports hernia: a cause of chronic groin pain. *Br J Sports Med* 1993;27(1):58–62.

77. Kemp S, Batt ME. The 'sports hernia'. A common cause of groin pain. *Phys Sportsmed* 1998;26(1):36–44.

78. Kumar A, Doran J, Batt ME. Results of inguinal canal repair in athletes with sports hernia. *J R Coll Surg Edinb* 2002;47(3):561–5.

79. Lovell G. The diagnosis of chronic groin pain in athletes: a review of 189 cases. *Aust J Sci Med Sport* 1995;27:76–9.

80. Malycha P, Lovell G. Inguinal surgery in athletes with chronic groin pain: The 'sportsman's' hernia. *Aus NZ J Surg* 1992;62:123–5.

81. Srinivasan A, Schuricht A. Long-term follow-up of laproscopic preperitoneal hernia repair in professional athletes. *J Laparoendosc Adv Surg Tech* 2002;12(2):101–6.

82. Simonet WT, Saylor HL, Sim L. Abdominal wall muscle tears in hockey players. *Int J Sports Med* 1995;16:126–8.

83. Hemmingway AE, Herrington L, Blower AL. Changes in muscle strength and pain in response to surgical repair of posterior abdominal wall disruption followed by rehabilitation. *Br J Sports Med* 2003;37(1):54–8.

84. Polglase AL, Frydman GM, Farmer KC. Inguinal surgery for debilitating chronic groin pain in athletes. *Med J Aust* 1991;155:674–7.

85. van den Berg JC, de Valois JC, Go PM et al. Detection of groin hernia with physical examination, ultrasound, and MRI compared with laparoscopic findings. *Invest Radiol* 1999;34(12):739–43.

86. Genitsaris M, Goulimaris I, Sikas N. Laparoscopic repair of groin pain in athletes. *Am J Sports Med* 2004;32(5):1238–42.

87. Susmallian S, Ezri T, Elis M et al. Laproscopic repair of "sportsman's hernia" in soccer players as treatment of chronic inguinal pain. *Med Sci Monit* 2004;10(2):CR52–4.

88. Muschaweck U, Berger L. Minimal repair technique of sportsmen's groin: an innovative open-suture repair to treat chronic inguinal pain. *Hernia* 2010;14(1):27–33.

89. Biedert RM, Warnke K, Meyer S. Symphysis syndrome in athletes. Surgical treatment for chronic lower abdominal, groin, and adductor pain in athletes. *Clin J Sport Med* 2003;13:278–84.

B

90. Mann CD, Sutton CD, Garcea G et al. The inguinal release procedure for groin pain: initial experience in 73 sportsmen/women. *Br J Sports Med* 2009;43(8):579–83.

91. Johnson JD, Briner Jr WW. Primary care of sports hernia. *Phys Sportsmed* 2005;33(2):35–9.

92. Brannigan AE, Kerin MJ, McEntee GP. Gilmore's groin repair in athletes. *J Orthop Sports Phys Ther* 2000;30(6):329–32.

93. Gilmore J. Groin pain in the soccer athlete: Fact, fiction, and treatment. *Clin Sports Med* 1998;17(4):787–93.

94. Lacroix VJ, Kinnear DG, Mulder DS et al. Lower abdominal pain syndrome in national hockey league players: a report of 11 cases. *Clin J Sport Med* 1998;8(1):5–9.

95. Brown RA, Mascia A, Kinnear DG et al. An 18-year review of sports groin injuries in the elite hockey player: clinical presentation, new diagnostic imaging, treatment, and results. *Clin J Sport Med* 2008;18(3):221–6.

96. Irshad K, Feldman LS, Lavoie C et al. Operative management of "hockey groin syndrome": 12 years of experience in National Hockey League players. *Surgery* 2001;130(4):764–6.

97. Johnson R. Abdominal wall injuries: rectus abdominis strains, oblique strains, rectus sheath hematoma. *Curr Sports Med Rep* 2006;5(2):99–103.

98. Maquirriain J, Ghisi JP, Kokalj AM. Rectus abdominis muscle strains in tennis players. *Br J Sports Med* 2007;41(11):842–8.

99. Brennan D, O'Connell MJ, Ryan M et al. Secondary cleft sign as a marker of injury in athletes with groin pain: MR image appearance and interpretation. *Radiology* 2005;235(1):162–7.

100. O'Connell MJ, Powell T, McCaffrey NM et al. Symphyseal cleft injection in the diagnosis and treatment of osteitis pubis in athletes. *Am J Roentgenol* 2002;179(4):955–9.

101. Holt MA, Keene JS, Graf BK et al. Treatment of osteitis pubis in athletes. Results of corticosteroid injections. *Am J Sports Med* 1995;23(5):601–6.

102. Topol GA, Reeves KD, Hassanein KM. Efficacy of dextrose proplotherapy in elite male kicking-sport athletes with groin pain. *Arch Phys Med Rehabil* 2005;86(4):697–702.

103. Maksymowych WP, Aaron SL, Russell AS. Treatment of refractory symphysitis pubis with intravenous pamidronate. *J Rheumatol* 2001;28(12):2754–7.

104. Mulhall KJ. Osteitis pubis in professional soccer players: A report of outcome with symphyseal curettage in cases refractory to conservative management. *Clin J Sport Med* 2002;12:179–81.

105. Grace JN, Sim FH, Shives TC et al. Wedge resection of the symphysis pubis for the treatment of osteitis pubis. *J Bone Joint Surg Am* 1989;71A:358–64.

106. Moore RSJ, Stover MD, Matta JM. Late posterior instability of the pelvis after resection of the symphysis pubis for the treatment of osteitis pubis. A report of two cases. *J Bone Joint Surg Am* 1998;80A:1043–8.

107. Williams PR, Thomas DP, Downes EM. Osteitis pubis and instability of the pubic symphysis: when nonoperative measures fail. *Am J Sports Med* 2000;28(3):350–5.

108. Bradshaw C, McCrory P, Bell S et al. Obturator nerve entrapment: a cause of groin pain in athletes. *Am J Sports Med* 1997;25(3):402–8.

109. Brukner P, Bradshaw C, McCrory P. Obturator neuropathy. A cause of exercise-related groin pain. *Phys Sportsmed* 1999;27(5):62–73.

110. Labat JJ, Riant T, Robert R et al. Diagnostic criteria for pudendal neuralgia by pudendal nerve entrapment (Nantes criteria). *Neurourol Urodyn* 2008;27(4):306–10.

111. Lappe J, Cullen D, Haynatzki G et al. Calcium and vitamin D supplementation decreases incidence of stress fractures in female navy recruits. *J Bone Min Res* 2008;23(5):741–9.

112. Shaffer RA, Rauh MJ, Brodine SK et al. Predictors of stress fracture susceptibility in young female recruits. *Am J Sports Med* 2006;34(1):108–15.

Chapter 30

Anterior thigh pain

with ZUZANA MACHOTKA

As strong as my legs are, it is my mind that has made me a champion.
Michael Johnson, four times Olympic Gold Medal winner who suffered from
a very publicized quadriceps strain

The anterior thigh (Fig. 30.1) is the site of common sporting injuries such as quadriceps muscle contusion and strain of the quadriceps muscle. Referred pain from the hip, sacroiliac joint (SIJ) and lumbar spine can also cause anterior thigh pain.[1] Stress fracture of the femur is an uncommon, but important diagnosis. The causes of anterior thigh pain are shown in Table 30.1 overleaf.

Clinical approach

History

The two most important aspects of the history of a patient with anterior thigh pain are the exact site of the pain and the mechanism of injury. The site of the

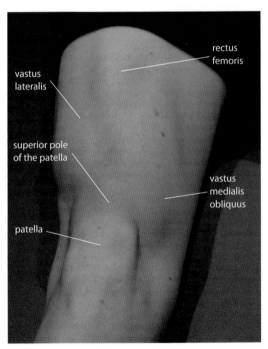

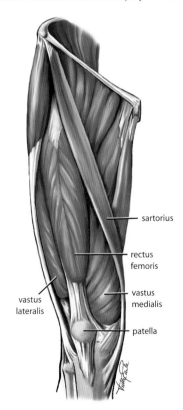

Figure 30.1 Anatomy of the anterior thigh
(a) Surface anatomy

(b) Muscles of the anterior thigh

579

Table 30.1 Causes of anterior thigh pain

Common	Less common	Not to be missed
Quadriceps muscle contusion ("cork thigh," "charley horse," "dead leg")	Referred pain	Slipped capital femoral epiphysis
	• upper lumbar spine	Perthes' disease
	• sacroiliac joint	Tumor (e.g. osteosarcoma of the femur)
Quadriceps muscle strain	• hip joint	Acute compartment syndrome of the
• distal rectus femoris	Stress fracture of the femur	thigh
• proximal rectus femoris	Sartorius muscle strain	
Myositis ossificans	Gracilis strain	
	Avulsion of the apophysis of rectus femoris	
	Nerve entrapment	
	• lateral cutaneous nerve	
	• femoral cutaneous nerve	

pain is usually well localized in cases of contusion or muscle strain. Contusions can occur anywhere in the quadriceps muscle but they are most common anterolaterally and in the vastus medialis obliquus. Muscle strains generally occur in the midline of the thigh anteriorly.

The mechanism of injury may help differentiate between the two conditions. A contusion is likely to be the result of a direct blow, whereas a muscle strain usually occurs when an athlete is striving for extra speed when running or extra distance when kicking. In contact sports, however, the athlete may have difficulty recalling the exact mechanism of injury.

Whether the athlete was able to continue activity, the present level of function, and the degree of swelling are all guides to the severity of the condition. Determine whether the RICE regimen was implemented initially and whether there were any aggravating factors (such as a continued activity). Gradual onset of poorly localized anterior thigh pain in a distance runner worsening with activity may indicate stress fracture of the femur. If the pain is variable and not clearly localized, and if specific aggravating factors are lacking, consider referred pain. Bilateral pain suggests the pain is referred from the lumbar spine.

Examination

In anterior thigh pain of acute onset, the diagnosis is usually straightforward, and examination can focus on local structures. In anterior thigh pain of insidious onset, diagnosis is more difficult and examination should include sites that refer pain to the thigh—the lumbar spine, SIJ, and hip.

The aim of the examination is to determine the exact site of the abnormality and to assess range of motion and muscle strength. Functional testing may be necessary to reproduce the symptoms.

1. Observation
   (a) standing
   (b) walking
   (c) supine
2. Active movements
   (a) hip flexion
   (b) knee flexion
   (c) knee extension
3. Passive movements
   (a) hip and knee (e.g. hip quadrant)
   (b) muscle stretch (e.g. quadriceps) (Fig. 30.2a)
4. Resisted movements
   (a) knee extension (Fig. 30.2b)

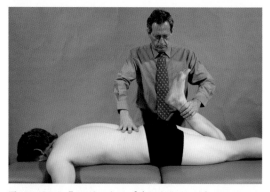

Figure 30.2 Examination of the patient with anterior thigh pain

(a) Passive movement—quadriceps stretch. A passive stretch of the quadriceps muscles is performed to end of range. Passive hip extension may be added to increase the stretch on the rectus femoris, which may reproduce the patient's pain

    (b)   straight-leg raise

    (c)   hip flexion (Fig. 30.2c)

5. Functional tests

    (a)   squat (Fig. 30.2d)

    (b)   jump

    (c)   hop

    (d)   kick

6. Palpation

    (a)   quadriceps muscle (Fig. 30.2e overleaf)

7. Special tests

    (a)   femoral stress fracture (Fig. 30.2f overleaf)

    (b)   neurodynamic testing (Fig. 30.2g overleaf)

    (c)   lumbar spine (Chapter 26)

    (d)   SIJ (Chapter 27)

    (e)   knee jerk reflex

Investigations

Investigations are usually not required in sportspeople with anterior thigh pain. If a quadriceps contusion fails to respond to treatment, X-ray may demonstrate myositis ossificans. This is usually not evident until at least three weeks after the injury. Ultrasound examination or MRI will confirm the presence of a hematoma, and may demonstrate early evidence of calcification.

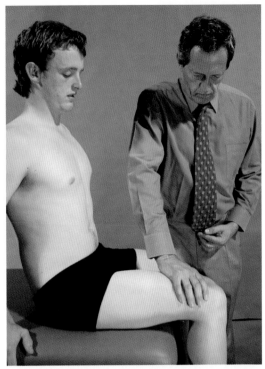

(c) Resisted movement—hip flexion

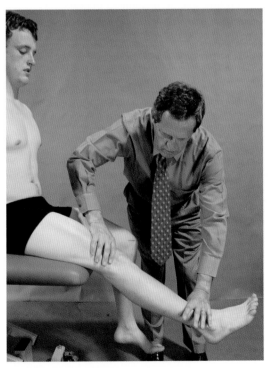

(b) Resisted movement—knee extension.
With the hip and knee flexed to 90°, the knee is extended against resistance

(d) Functional movements—squat.
If the previous activities have failed to reproduce the patient's pain, functional movements should be used to reproduce the pain. These may include squat, hop, or jump

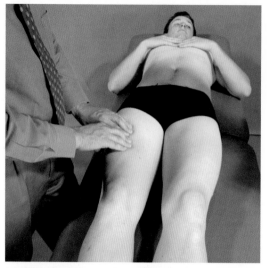

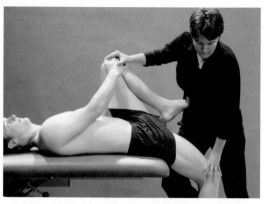

(g) Special tests—neurodynamic test (modified Thomas test). The patient is placed in the psoas stretch position. Cervical and upper thoracic flexion is added and then the clinician passively bends the patient's knee (using his or her own leg). Reproduction of the patient's symptoms indicates a neural contribution

(e) Palpation.
The anterior thigh is palpated for tenderness, swelling, and areas of focal muscle thickening. A focal defect in the muscle belly may be palpated, especially with active muscle contraction

If a stress fracture of the femur is suspected, plain X-ray is indicated. If this is normal, MRI is the investigation of choice.

When thigh pain is associated with restricted or painful hip motion, imaging is indicated. Although hip pathology most often refers to the groin (Chapter 28), it can refer to the anterior, and occasionally lateral, thigh. In adults, osteoarthritis is a likely diagnosis; in adolescents, consider a slipped capital femoral epiphysis (Chapter 42) or avulsion fracture.

Quadriceps contusion

If the patient suffered a direct blow to the anterior thigh, and examination confirms an area of tenderness and swelling with worsening pain on active contraction and passive stretch, thigh contusion with resultant hematoma is the most likely diagnosis. In severe cases with extensive swelling, pain may be severe enough to interfere with sleep.

Quadriceps contusion is an extremely common injury and is known colloquially as a "charley horse," "cork thigh," or "dead leg." It is common in contact sports such as football and basketball. In sports such as field hockey, lacrosse, and cricket, a ball traveling at high speed may cause a contusion.

Assess the severity of the contusion to determine prognosis (which can vary from several days to a number of weeks off sport) and plan appropriate treatment. The degree of passive knee flexion after 24 hours is a clinical indicator of the severity of

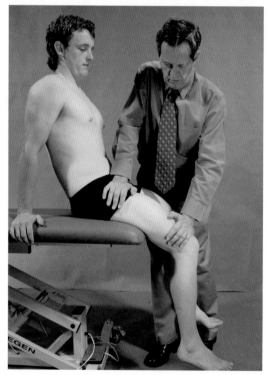

(f) Special tests—for the presence of a femoral stress fracture. This is performed with pressure over the distal end of the femur. Reproduction of the patient's pain may be indicative of a femoral stress fracture

the hematoma. For optimal treatment and accurate monitoring of progress, it is important to identify the exact muscle involved. MRI will show significant edema throughout the involved muscle (Fig. 30.3).

Blood from contusions of the lower third of the thigh may track down to the knee joint and irritate the patellofemoral joint.

Treatment

The treatment of a thigh contusion can be divided into four stages:

- Stage 1—control of hemorrhage
- Stage 2—restoration of pain-free range of motion
- Stage 3—functional rehabilitation
- Stage 4—graduated return to activity.

A summary of the types of treatment appropriate for each stage is shown in Tables 30.2 and 30.3 overleaf. Progression within each stage, and from one stage to the next, depends on the severity of the contusion and the rate of recovery.

The most important period in the treatment of a thigh contusion is in the first 24 hours following

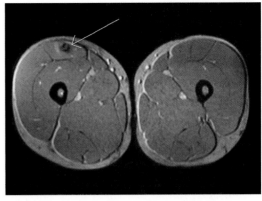

Figure 30.3 MRI appearance of severe hematoma (arrow) of the vastus intermedius muscle

the injury. A player who suffers a thigh contusion should be removed from the field of play and receive the RICE regimen (Chapter 13). If full weight-bearing is painful for the sportsperson, crutches can help unload the muscle and it emphasizes the serious nature of the condition.

Table 30.2 Grading and treatment of quadriceps contusion

Grading	Clinical features	Treatment
Mild	May or may not remember incident Usually can continue activity Sore after cooling down or next morning May restrict full ROM (stretch) (by 5–20%) Tender to palpation Minimal loss of strength	Ice, stretch, and bandage for first 24–48 hours Then should regain full ROM and start functional strengthening—bike, running, swimming Strengthening may be required Soft tissue therapy and electrotherapy are effective
Moderate	Usually remembers incident but can continue activity although may stiffen up with rest (e.g. half-time or full-time) Moderate restriction of ROM (by 20–50%) Some pain on restricted contraction Tender to palpation May have tracking Usually FWB, but often limp	See Table 30.3 overleaf
Severe	Usually remembers incident May not be able to control rapid onset of swelling/bleeding Very restricted ROM (loss of >50%) Difficulty with FWB Tender over large area (tracking) Obvious bleeding Functional loss of strength	Ice regularly over 2–3 days Stretches (active after 2–3 days) No massage/ultrasound No overpressure with passive stretching for 7–10 days

ROM = range of motion; FWB = full weight-bearing.

Table 30.3 Treatment of moderate quadriceps contusion or grade II muscle strain

Stage	Aim	Weight-bearing	RICE	Electrotherapy	Soft tissue therapy	Stretching	Strengthening
1	Control of hemorrhage	Crutches if unable to FWB	RICE, compression to include knee joint if lower third of thigh (Fig. 30.4)	Electrical stimulation Magnetic field therapy Laser if superficial Pulsed ultrasound	Contraindicated	Gentle stretch to onset of pain (Fig. 30.5a)	Static muscle contraction if possible
2	Restore and maintain pain-free ROM and muscle strength	Progress to PWB and FWB as tolerated	Maintain compression bandage when limb is dependent. Ice after exercise	As for stage 1 Higher dosages for thermal effect (ultrasound)	Grade I–II longitudinal gliding away from site of injury Grade II transverse gliding away from site of injury	Increase stretches	Static muscle contraction inner range through range (Fig. 30.6a on page 586) Stationary exercise: bike Pool (walk/swim/kick) Concentric and eccentric exercise (Fig. 30.6b on page 586)
3	Functional rehabilitation	FWB		Usually not required	Longitudinal gliding Transverse gliding	Maintain stretch (Fig. 30.5b)	All stage 2 exercises gradually increasing repetitions, speed and resistance Include pulleys, rebounder, profitter, wall squats, step-downs (Fig. 30.6c on page 586) Hop/jumping, running Increase eccentric exercises
4	Gradual return to sports				Myofascial tension in knee flexion (Fig. 30.7 on page 587)		Kicking action with pulleys Multidirectional activities Figure of eight Jumping Plyometrics Graduated specific sporting activities Must complete full training before return to sport Heat-retaining brace may be helpful

PWB = partial weight-bearing; FWB = full weight-bearing; ROM = range of motion.

In the acute management of a thigh contusion, ice should be applied in a position of maximal pain-free quadriceps stretch (Fig. 30.4). Immobilizing the knee in 120 degrees of flexion immediately after injury and for the first 24 hours may be beneficial.[2,3] This is done by bandaging the entire lower limb. The patient then mobilizes with crutches

After the restriction, active pain-free isometric exercises can be started and the use of crutches continues until the athlete is able to resume full athletic activity. It is important that this management technique is not recommended for severe contusions. This technique may reduce time away from sport, improve pain-free range of movement, and reduce the rate of re-injury.[3]

The patient must be careful not to aggravate the bleeding by excessive activity, alcohol ingestion, or the application of heat.

Loss of range of motion is the most significant finding after thigh contusion, and range of movement must be regained in a gradual, pain-free progression before return to athletic activity is considered.

After a moderate-to-severe contusion, there is a considerable risk of re-bleed in the first 7–10 days. Therefore, care must be taken with stretching, electrotherapy, heat, and massage. The patient must be careful not to overstretch. Stretching should be pain-free.

Soft tissue therapy is contraindicated for 48 hours following contusion. Subsequently, soft tissue therapy may be used, but great care must be taken not to aggravate the condition. Treatment must be light and it must produce absolutely no pain (Fig. 30.7 on page 587). Excessively painful soft tissue therapy will cause bleeding to recur and is never indicated in the treatment of contusion.

Figure 30.5 Quadriceps stretching exercises
(a) Standard quadriceps stretch while standing. It is important to have good pelvic control and not to lean forward while performing the stretch

(b) Passive stretch.
The tension of the stretch can be altered by adding hip extension

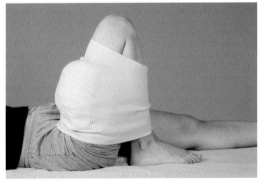

Figure 30.4 RICE treatment of an acute thigh contusion in a position of maximal pain-free stretch

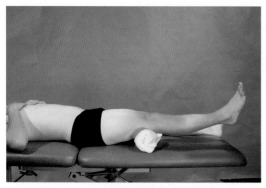

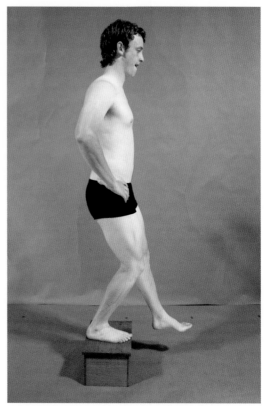

Figure 30.6 Quadriceps strengthening exercises
(a) Active quadriceps exercises. Initially inner range quadriceps strengthening is performed with a rolled towel under the knee as shown. The range is slowly increased, depending on symptoms, until through-range quadriceps contraction can be performed pain-free

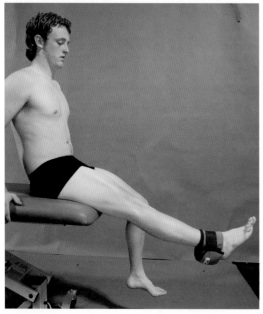

(c) Functional exercises
A variety of functional exercises can be performed in the late stage of rehabilitation: squats, wall squats, step-downs (illustrated), shuttle. Most of these involve both eccentric and concentric contraction of the quadriceps

(b) Resisted quadriceps
Concentric and eccentric exercises are performed against gradually increased resistance. Knee extension involves concentric contraction of the quadriceps muscle, while lowering the foot from extension involves eccentric quadriceps contraction

It has been suggested that athletes in high-risk sports should consider wearing thigh protection routinely.[4] Players such as ruckmen in Australian Rules football, forwards in basketball, and running backs in American football[5] may sustain a series of minor contusions during the course of a game. These appear to have a cumulative effect and may impair performance later in the game. Protective padding helps to minimize this effect.

Acute compartment syndrome of the thigh

Intramuscular hematoma of the thigh after a blunt contusion may result in high intracompartment pressures and a diagnosis of compartment syndrome of the thigh. Symptoms often include pain and paresthesia, and occur with intra-compartmental pressures greater than approximately 20 mmHg.[6] Pressures of greater than 30 mmHg over a duration of more than six hours can lead to irreversible damage.[6]

Unlike other acute compartment syndromes, this condition does not usually need to be treated by surgical decompression. This recommendation is based

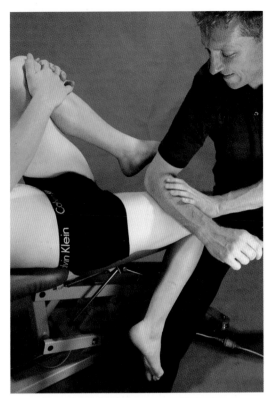

Figure 30.7 Soft tissue therapy—sustained myofascial tension in the position of maximal hip extension and knee flexion

B

on clinical evidence from cases where surgery was performed. When the muscle was viewed during surgery, there was no evidence of necrotic tissue. Also, there were no subsequent adverse effects of the compartment syndrome, such as restricted motion or loss of function.[6] In a case study of an amateur soccer player who sustained a high impact injury from an opposing player,[5] conservative treatment included rest from any lower limb activity for the first 48 hours, followed by gentle range of motion exercises of the hip and knee. This routine was slowly progressed over the following months and the athlete returned to soccer after six months.[6]

Myositis ossificans

Occasionally after a thigh contusion, the hematoma calcifies. This is known as "myositis ossificans" and can usually be seen on a plain X-ray a minimum of three weeks after the injury. If there is no convincing history of recent trauma, the practitioner must rule out the differential diagnosis of the X-ray—bone tumor (Chapter 7).[7, 8]

In myositis ossificans, osteoblasts replace some of the fibroblasts in the healing hematoma one week following the injury and lay down new bone over a number of weeks. After approximately six or seven weeks, this bone growth ceases. At this stage, a lump is often palpable. Slow resorption of the bone then occurs, but a small amount of bone may remain.

Why some contusions develop calcification is not known. Incidence rates range from 9% to 20% in athletes with a thigh contusion.[7] The more severe the contusion, the more likely is the development of myositis ossificans.[7] *Intra*muscular contusions appear to be more susceptible than *inter*muscular. Inappropriate treatment of the contusion, such as heat or massage, may increase the risk of myositis ossificans arising.[9] The risk is especially high if the contusion results in prone knee flexion of less than 45° two to three days after the injury. Thus, particular care should be taken when managing these severe contusions. A significant re-bleed may also result in the development of myositis ossificans. The incidence of myositis ossificans appears to be increased when a knee effusion is present.

Symptoms of developing myositis ossificans include an increase in morning pain and pain with activity. Patients often also complain of night pain. On palpation, the developing myositis ossificans has a characteristic "woody" feel. Initial improvement in range of motion ceases with subsequent deterioration.

Once myositis ossificans is established, there is very little that can be done to accelerate the resorptive process. Treatment may include local electrotherapy to reduce muscle spasm and gentle, painless range of motion exercises. Shock wave therapy has been suggested to improve function.[10]

Indomethacin, which reduces new bone formation,[8] has been prescribed as a preventative measure in high-risk presentations.[7] Corticosteroid injection is absolutely contraindicated in this condition. Surgery is contraindicated in the early stages and only considered when the margins of the ectopic bone are smooth on investigations, suggesting bone maturity.[7]

Quadriceps muscle strain

Strains of the quadriceps muscle usually occur during sprinting, jumping, or kicking. In football, quadriceps strains are often associated with over-striding when decelerating during running, or under-striding during the deceleration phase of the kicking leg when kicking a football on the run.[11] Fatigue, weakness, and muscle imbalances can impact on performance, and are therefore risk factors for muscle strains.

Strains are seen in all the quadriceps muscles but are most common in the rectus femoris, which is more vulnerable to strain as it passes over two joints—the hip and the knee.

> The most common site of strain is the distal musculotendinous junction of the rectus femoris (see below). Management of this type of rectus femoris strain and of strains of the vasti muscles is relatively straightforward; rehabilitation time is short. Strains of the proximal rectus are not as straightforward and are discussed on page 589.

Distal quadriceps muscle strain

Like all muscle strains, distal quadriceps strains (Fig. 30.8a) may be graded into mild (grade I), moderate (grade II), or severe, complete tears (grade III). The athlete feels the injury as a sudden pain in the anterior thigh during an activity requiring explosive muscle contraction. There is local pain and tenderness and, if the strain is severe, swelling and bruising.

Grade I strain is a minor injury with pain on resisted active contraction and on passive stretching. An area of local spasm is palpable at the site of pain. An athlete with such a strain may not cease activity at the time of the pain, but will usually notice the injury after cooling down or the following day.

Moderate or grade II strains cause significant pain on passive stretching as well as on unopposed active contraction. There is usually a moderate area of inflammation surrounding a tender palpable lesion. The athlete with a grade II strain is generally unable to continue the activity.

Complete tears of the rectus femoris occur with sudden onset of pain and disability during intense activity. A muscle fiber defect is usually palpable when the muscle is contracted. In the long term, they resolve with conservative management, often with surprisingly little disability.

Treatment

The principles of treatment of a quadriceps muscle strain are similar to those of a thigh contusion. The various treatment techniques shown in Table 30.3 are also appropriate for the treatment of quadriceps strain; however, depending on the severity of the

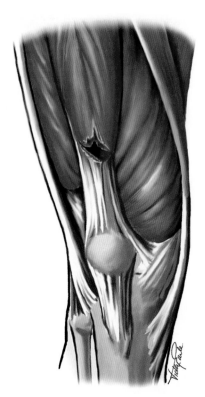

Figure 30.8 There are two types of quadriceps strains
(a) The more common occurs at the distal musculotendinous junction of rectus femoris and has a better prognosis

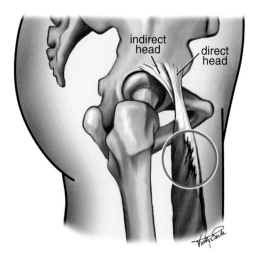

(b) The less common occurs in the proximal rectus femoris and takes longer to recover
ADAPTED FROM HASSELMAN ET AL. P.495

strain, progression through the various stages may be slower.

Although loss of range of motion may be less obvious than with a contusion, it is important that the athlete regain pain-free range of movement as soon as possible. Loss of strength may be more marked than with a thigh contusion and strength retraining requires emphasis in the rehabilitation program. As with the general principles of muscle rehabilitation, the program should commence with low-resistance, high-repetition exercise. Concentric and eccentric exercises should begin with very low weights.

General fitness can be maintained by activities such as swimming (initially with a pool buoy) and upper body training. Functional retraining should be incorporated as soon as possible. Full training must be completed prior to return to sport. Unfortunately, quadriceps strains often recur, either in the same season, or even a year or two later.[12]

Proximal rectus femoris strains

With the advent of MRI, a second type of rectus femoris strain injury was recognized occurring proximally, apparently within the belly of the muscle (Fig. 30.8b). This has been termed a "bull's-eye" lesion[13] (Fig. 30.9) and seems to contradict the basic tenet that muscle strain occurs at the muscle–tendon junction.

Cadaveric[14] and MRI[15] studies of symptomatic and asymptomatic individuals showed that the proximal tendon of the rectus femoris muscle has two components—the direct (straight) and indirect (reflected) heads (Fig. 30.8b). The tendon of the direct head originates from the anterior inferior iliac spine; the tendon of the indirect head arises from the superior acetabular ridge and the hip joint capsule, initially deep to the direct head.[14, 15] The two heads then form a conjoined tendon. As it progresses along the muscle it flattens out, laterally rotates, and migrates to the middle of the muscle belly. This has been termed the "central tendon."

Complete tears are uncommon, which is thought to be due to the extreme length of the musculo-tendinous junction (approximately two-thirds of the muscle belly).[15] Diagnosis is often difficult, because the pathology is deep and the physical assessment findings are non-specific.

In three series of proximal thigh strains,[13, 16, 17] the average time to presentation was 5–7 months.

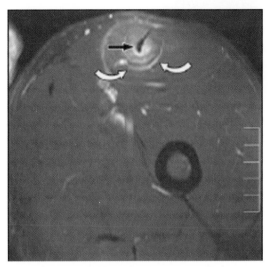

Figure 30.9 MRI of the proximal rectus femoris musculotendinous junction

(a) MRI of a proximal rectus femoris tear in a 19-year-old man shows the characteristic "bull's-eye" sign; this is made up by a halo of increased signal (white signal highlighted by white arrows) around the deep tendon (black tendon highlighted with a black arrow)

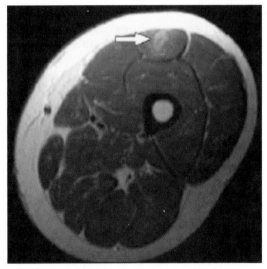

(b) A comparable MRI of a similar injury, which differs only in the tendon having a low-signal intensity inside the bright halo (arrow). This is consistent with fatty atrophy in the tendon—the results of the injury having occurred a reasonable time in the past (chronic)

Patients complained of a tender anterior thigh mass and/or weakness and pain with activities such as running and kicking. Initial injury was described as a "deep tearing sensation." The anterior thigh mass may be associated with muscle retraction.[15]

These signs and symptoms are likely to be due to the indirect and direct heads of the proximal tendon acting independently, creating a shearing phenomenon, in contrast to what occurs in the normal rectus femoris.[1] Unlike typical strains which present as focal lesions on MRI, rectus femoris proximal musculotendinous junction injuries have a longitudinal distribution of increased signal along the tendon (Fig. 30.9).[15]

Treatment

Management of proximal rectus femoris strains depends on the severity of the injury and the athletic demands of the individual. Conservative management aimed at symptom relief and avoidance of re-injury is recommended for grade I and II strains. Surgical intervention is typically reserved for grade III strains, which can involve resection of scar tissue. One series diagnosed on MRI[18] showed an average return to full training in professional footballers after a comprehensive rehabilitation program of 27 days for central tendon lesions, compared to nine days for peripheral rectus femoris strains and 4–5 days for strains of the vasti muscles.

Differentiating between a mild quadriceps strain and a quadriceps contusion

Occasionally, it may be difficult to distinguish between a minor contusion and a minor muscle strain; however, the distinction needs to be made as an athlete with a thigh strain should progress more slowly through a rehabilitation program (Table 30.3) than should the athlete with a quadriceps contusion. The athlete with thigh strain should avoid sharp acceleration and deceleration movements in the early stages of injury. Some of the features that may assist the clinician in differentiating these conditions are shown in Table 30.4. MRI or ultrasonography may also help differentiate the two conditions.

Less common causes
Stress fracture of the femur

Femoral stress fractures can occur around the femoral neck, intertrochanteric and subtrochanteric regions, and the femoral shaft.[19] Stress fractures in the femur can occur following anterior cruciate ligament (ACL) surgery using transfemoral fixation, and are associated with accelerated rehabilitation programs.[20] Stress fracture of the shaft of the femur, although uncommon, should be suspected in an athlete, especially a distance runner, who complains of a dull ache, poorly localized in the anterior thigh.

Risk factors for developing femoral stress fractures include training errors, hard training surfaces, and poor footwear.[19] Intrinsic risk factors include leg length discrepancies, and excessive foot pronation or supination.

Pain may be referred to the groin or knee, and the

Table 30.4 Distinguishing features of minor quadriceps contusion and grade I quadriceps muscle strain

Diagnostic features	Quadriceps contusion	Grade I rectus femoris muscle strain
Mechanism	Contact injury	Non-contact
Pain onset	Immediate or soon after	After cool-down (next day)
Behavior of pain (24 hours post trauma)	Improves with gentle activity	Painful with use
Location	Usually lateral or distal	Rectus femoris muscle belly (proximal or middle third)
Bruising/swelling	May be obvious early	May be absent or delayed
Palpation findings	Tenderness more obvious, lump may feel ovoid or spherical, becomes progressively harder	May be difficult to find, or may be a small area of focal tenderness with a characteristic ring of inflammation surrounding it. Muscle spasm in adjacent fibers proximally and distally
Effect of gentle stretch	May initially aggravate pain	Not associated with pain
Strength testing	No loss of strength except pain inhibition	Loss of strength (may need eccentric or functional testing to reproduce pain)

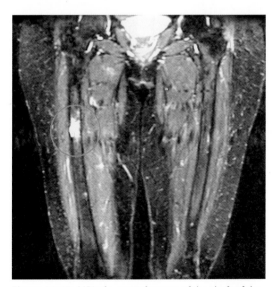

athlete may present with an antalgic gait (especially in the case of femoral neck stress fractures[21]).

PRACTICE PEARL

There may be tenderness over the shaft of the femur that can be aggravated if the patient sits with the leg hanging over the edge of a bench, particularly if there is downward pressure placed on the distal femur, the so-called "hang test" or "fulcrum test" (Fig. 30.2f).

Because X-ray is limited in detecting changes in bone structure, isotopic bone scan or MRI (Fig. 30.10) is usually required to make the diagnosis.

Treatment depends on location and type of fracture, and generally involves rest from painful activities, and maintenance of fitness by cycling or swimming for at least four weeks. Predisposing factors such as excessive training, biomechanical abnormality and, in females, menstrual disturbance should be sought, and corrected where possible. Surgery is indicated where a fracture has become displaced. When the hang test is completely negative (on average after seven weeks), it is thought to be safe to return to sport gradually.[22]

Stress fractures are more prevalent among female athletes, particularly if they have insufficient calorie intake (Chapter 43). Sports nutritionist input is an important part of the management plan.[19, 23, 24]

Female military recruits have susceptibility to lower limb stress fractures when entering with poor aerobic fitness and a history of amenorrhea (Chapter 45).[25] Prevention strategies include identifying recruits with limited aerobic fitness and including nutritionist advice for recruits with menstrual issues.

Lateral femoral cutaneous nerve injury ("meralgia paresthetica")

Lateral cutaneous nerve of thigh injury, also known as "meralgia paresthetica," can be a cause of anterolateral thigh pain. The lateral femoral cutaneous nerve is a purely sensory nerve and originates from the lumbar plexus (L2, L3). The nerve runs along the lateral border of the psoas major muscle, across the iliacus muscle, and exits the abdomen under the inguinal ligament close to the anterior superior iliac spine (ASIS). It then crosses the sartorius muscle and divides into an anterior and a posterior branch. The posterior branch pierces the fascia lata and runs distally, supplying the skin of the lateral thigh from the greater trochanter to the mid-thigh region. The anterior branch supplies the skin approximately 10 cm below the inguinal ligament and distally to the proximal knee.

This nerve is susceptible to injury via blunt trauma around the ASIS and the anterior thigh, especially in contact sports such as rugby.[26] Repeated falls from a balance beam in gymnasts may cause injury.[27] Obesity, pregnancy, and surgical procedures around the nerve are risk factors for nerve injury, irritation, and entrapment.[5, 28] Repeated hip flexion and extension during sporting activity (e.g. gymnastics) can irritate the nerve.[26]

Entrapment can occur around the ASIS between the ilium and the inguinal ligament. Symptoms include pain, numbness, and paresthesia of the anterolateral thigh without loss of reflex or motor control.[27, 28] Sporting activity can aggravate symptoms.[26, 29] Tight-fitting garments and athletic compression garments can lead to symptoms. Entrapment as a result of wearing weight belts in scuba divers has also been reported.[27]

Treatment is often conservative, with a period of rest until symptoms have resolved. Anti-inflammatory medications can be beneficial in the early phases.[28] If symptoms do not settle quickly, other interventions such as local anesthetic injection can be trialed. Thigh and hip pads can be used as preventive strategy in high contact sports.[26] If conservative treatment fails, surgical decompression of the nerve is indicated.[30]

Figure 30.10 MRI of a stress fracture of the shaft of the femur

Femoral nerve injury

The femoral nerve passes between the psoas major and the iliacus muscles and exits the abdomen deep to the inguinal ligament through the femoral canal. In the upper thigh, the nerve gives off motor branches to the quadriceps, sartorius, and pectineus muscles. The sensory branches supply the skin of the anterior thigh. The femoral nerve then continues distally as the saphenous nerve.

Injury to the nerve can occur secondary to hyperextension of the hip, such as seen in gymnasts, dancers, football players, basketball players, and long jumpers.[26, 27] Gymnasts and dancers performing maneuvers that involve extreme hip extension coupled with knee flexion are susceptible to injury of the femoral nerve.[27]

Previously, injury was thought to be due to traction placed on the nerve. However, it is now thought to be secondary to strain of the iliopsoas muscle, where a local hematoma causes compression of the nerve.[26, 27] Psoas bursitis can also lead to compression and irritation.[27]

Pain is often located around the inguinal region. Reduced power of the knee extensors and/or reduced knee jerk may also be present.[26, 27] Sometimes, despite motor changes, sensation can be normal.[27] Conservative treatment is normally trialed first until symptoms settle. Return to sport is possible when strength in the lower limb is regained.

Referred pain

Referred pain may arise from the hip joint, the SIJ, the lumbar spine (especially upper lumbar) and neural structures. Patients with referred pain may not have a history of injury and may have few signs suggesting local abnormalities. An increase in neural mechanosensitivity may suggest that referred pain is a contributing to thigh pain. The modified Thomas test (Fig. 30.2g) is the most specific neurodynamic test for a patient with anterior thigh pain.

If the modified Thomas test reproduces the patient's anterior thigh pain, and altering the neural mechanosensitivity (e.g. passive knee flexion/extension) affects the pain, the lumbar spine and psoas muscle should be examined carefully. Any area(s) of abnormality should be treated, and both the local signs (e.g. reproduction of pain with functional testing) and neurodynamic tests should be repeated to assess any changes. As with any soft tissue injury, local and referred factors may combine to produce the patient's symptoms. Commonly there is hypomobility of the upper lumbar intervertebral segments on the affected side, associated with a tight psoas muscle. Mobilization of the hypomobile segments will often significantly reduce symptoms. Deep soft tissue treatment to the psoas muscle may also be effective (Fig. 30.11).

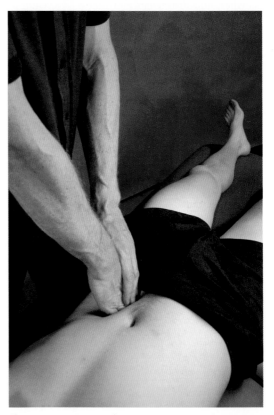

Figure 30.11 Deep soft tissue treatment to the psoas muscle

REFERENCES

1. Lesher JM, Dreyfuss P, Hager N et al. Hip joint pain referral patterns: a descriptive study. *Pain Med* 2008;9(1):22–5.
2. Guillodo Y, Saraux A. Treatment of muscle trauma in sportspeople (from injury on the field to resumption of the sport). *Ann Phys Rehabil Med* 2009;52(3):246–55.
3. Aronen JG, Garrick JG, Chronister RD et al. Quadriceps contusions: clinical results of immediate immobilization in 120 degrees of knee flexion. *Clin J Sport Med* 2006;16:383–7.
4. Gerrard DF. The use of padding in rugby union. An overview. *Sports Med* 1998;25:329–32.
5. Diaz JA, Fischer DA, Rettig AC et al. Severe quadriceps muscle contusions in athletes—a report of three cases. *Am J Sports Med* 2003;31(2):289–93.
6. Riede U, Schmid MR, Romero J. Conservative treatment of an acute compartment syndrome of the thigh. *Arch Orthop Trauma Surg* 2007;127:269–75.
7. King JB. Post-traumatic ectopic calcification in the muscles of athletes: a review. *Br J Sports Med* 1998;32:287–90.
8. Sodl JF, Bassora R, Huffman GR et al. Traumatic myositis ossificans as a result of college fraternity hazing. *Clin Orthop Relat Res* 2008;466(1):225–30.
9. Danchilk JJ, Yochum TR, Aspergren DD. Myositis ossificans traumatica. *J Manip Physiol Ther* 1993;16:605–14.
10. Buselli P, Coco V, Notarnicola A et al. Shock waves in the treatment of post-traumatic myositis ossificans. *Ultrasound Med Biol* 2010;36(3):397–409.
11. Beatty K, McIntosh A, Savage T et al. Biomechanics of the running drop punt kick with respect to the development of quadriceps strains. *Sports Health* 2007;25:18–23.
12. Orchard JW. Intrinsic and extrinsic risk factors for muscle strains in Australian football. *Am J Sports Med* 2001;29:300–3.
13. Hughes C, Hasselman CT, Best TM et al. Incomplete, intrasubstance strain injuries of the rectus femoris muscle. *Am J Sports Med* 1995;23:500–6.
14. Hasselman CT, Best TM, Hughes C et al. An explanation for various rectus femoris strain injuries using previously undescribed muscle architecture. *Am J Sports Med* 1995;23:493–9.
15. Gyftopoulos S, Rosenberg ZS, Schweitzer ME et al. Normal anatomy and strains of the deep musculotendinous junction of the proximal rectus femoris: MRI features. *Am J Roentgenol* 2008;190(3):W182–6.
16. Rask MR, Lattig GJ. Traumatic fibrosis of the rectus femoris muscle. *JAMA* 1972;221:268–9.
17. Temple HT, Kuklo TR, Sweet DE et al. Rectus femoris muscle tear appearing as a pseudotumor. *Am J Sports Med* 1998;26:544–8.
18. Cross TM, Gibbs N, Houang MT et al. Acute quadriceps muscle strains: magnetic resonance imaging features and prognosis. *Am J Sports Med* 2004;32(3):710–19.
19. Breugem SJM, Hulscher JBF, Steller P. Stress fracture of the femoral neck in a young female athlete. *Eur J Trauma Emerg Surg* 2009;35:192–5.
20. Arriaza R, Señaris J, Couceiro G et al. Stress fractures of the femur after ACL reconstruction with transfemoral fixation. *Knee Surg Sports Traumatol Arthrosc* 2006;14(11):1148–50.
21. Lee CH, Huang GS, Chao KH et al. Surgical treatment of displaced stress fractures of the femoral neck in military recruits: a report of 42 cases. *Arch Orthop Trauma Surg* 2003;123(10):527–33.
22. Johnson AW, Weiss CB, Wheeler DL. Stress fractures of the femoral shaft in athletes—more common than expected. A new clinical test. *Am J Sports Med* 1994;22:248–56.
23. Okamoto S, Arai Y, Hara K et al. A displaced stress fracture of the femoral neck in an adolescent female distance runner with female athlete triad: a case report. *Sports Med Arthrosc Rehabil Ther Tech Technol* 2010;2:6.
24. Prather H, Hunt D. Issues unique to the female runner. *Phys Med Rehabil Clin N Am* 2005;16:691–709.
25. Shaffer RA, Rauh MJ, Brodine SK et al. Predictors of stress fracture susceptibility in young female recruits. *Am J Sports Med* 2006;34(1):108–15.
26. Lorei MP, Hershman EB. Peripheral nerve injuries in athletes. Treatment and prevention. *Sports Med* 1993;16(2):130–47.
27. Kaufman MS, Domroese ME. Peripheral nerve injuries of the proximal lower limb in athletes. In Herring SA, Akuthota V, Kaufman MS, eds. *Nerve and vascular injuries in sports medicine.* New York: Springer 2009;161–70.
28. Toussaint CP, Perry EC, Pisansky MT et al. What's new in the diagnosis and treatment of peripheral nerve entrapment neuropathies. *Neurol Clin* 2010;28(4):979–1004.
29. Ulkar B, Yildiz Y, Kunduracioğlu B. Meralgia paresthetica: a long-standing performance-limiting cause of anterior thigh pain in a soccer player. *Am J Sports Med* 2003;31(5):787–9.
30. Benezis I, Boutaud B, Leclerc J et al. Lateral femoral cutaneous neuropathy and its surgical treatment: a report of 167 cases. *Muscle Nerve* 2007;36(5):659–3.

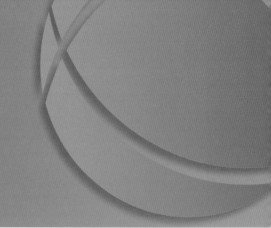

Chapter 31

Posterior thigh pain

with CARL ASKLING and ANTHONY SCHACHE

It comes on suddenly like a cyclist getting a puncture. It was like someone getting up and slapping me around the face. Derek Redmond describing the hamstring injury he suffered in the 1992 Olympic 400 m semi-final. Redmond famously got up and hobbled the remaining 250 meters of the race with the aid of his father

Pain in the "hamstring region" can prove very frustrating for recreational and amateur athletes and may even be career threatening for professional sportspeople. Hamstring muscle strains are the most common cause of posterior thigh pain, but referred pain to this area is also common.

The average number of days until return to sport for hamstring injuries ranges from 8 to 25 days.[1] The incidence of recurrence is high. Up to one-third of hamstring injuries will recur, with the greatest risk being during the initial two weeks following return to sport.[2]

This chapter focuses on:

- the relevant anatomy, which is critical to diagnosis, prognosis, and management
- the clinical distinction between the major pathologies that cause posterior thigh pain
- the increasingly appreciated role for diagnostic imaging for this injury
- treatment approaches for the two types of acute hamstring injuries and for referred pain
- the indications for considering early or late surgical treatment
- how to make the, often difficult, return-to-play decision
- preventing the rightfully feared setback—hamstring strain recurrence.

Functional anatomy

The hamstring muscle group (Fig. 31.1) consists of three main muscles—biceps femoris, semimembranosus, and semitendinosus. Biceps femoris has two heads—a long head and a short head. The long head is innervated by the tibial portion of the sciatic nerve (L5, S1–3), whereas the short head is innervated by the common peroneal portion (L5, S1–2).

The proximal hamstring complex (Fig. 31.1c) is a common site of much pathology and it has an intricate

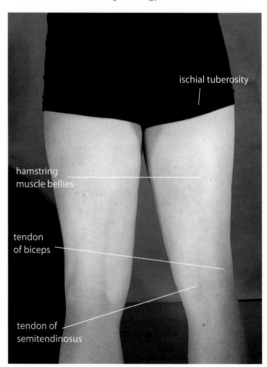

Figure 31.1 Anatomy of the posterior thigh
(a) Surface anatomy

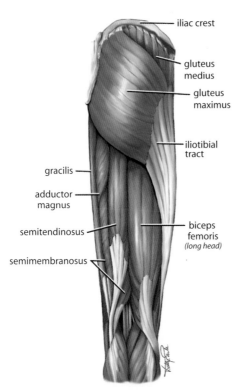

iliac crest

gluteus medius

gluteus maximus

iliotibial tract

gracilis

adductor magnus

semitendinosus

semimembranosus

biceps femoris (long head)

(b) Muscles of the posterior thigh

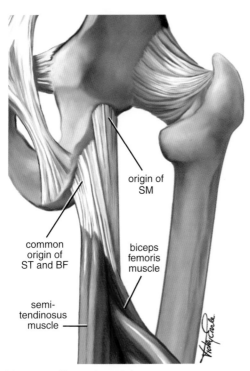

origin of SM

common origin of ST and BF

biceps femoris muscle

semi-tendinosus muscle

(c) Proximal hamstring origin

architecture.[3] The long head of biceps femoris and semitendinosus share a common proximal tendon that arises from the medial facet of the ischial tuberosity. Semitendinosus muscle fibers originate from the ischial tuberosity and the medial aspect of the common tendon; muscle fibers from the long head of bicep femoris originate from the lateral aspect of the common tendon approximately 6 cm (2¼ in.) below the ischial tuberosity. The proximal semimembranosus tendon arises from the lateral facet of the ischial tuberosity and, moving distally, extends medially, passing ventral (deep) to the semitendinosus/biceps femoris long head common proximal tendon.

The short head of biceps femoris arises from the linea aspera and thus only functions on the knee joint. Semitendinosus inserts onto the anteromedial surface of the proximal tibia (as part of the pes anserine muscle group), whereas semimembranosus inserts onto the medial tibial epicondyle (Fig. 34.10b on page 726). Biceps femoris long head and short head form a common distal tendon that has several insertions, including the lateral femoral epicondyle, fibula head, popliteus tendon, and arcuate popliteal ligament (Fig. 34.1b on page 715).[4]

The posterior portion of the adductor magnus functions as if it were a "hamstring" due to its anatomical alignment and innervation. Adductor magnus is a strong hip extensor muscle, especially when the hip is flexed; it is innervated by the tibial portion of the sciatic nerve, like the majority of the hamstring group.

Clinical reasoning

The key to effective management of posterior thigh pain is correct diagnosis. The clinician must determine whether the injury to the posterior thigh is an acute muscle strain or pain referred from elsewhere (e.g. lumbar spine). This can be challenging.

In healthy individuals, a strain to a large muscle group such as the hamstrings is the result of substantial force. The sportsperson typically recalls precisely when the incident occurred, and whether a significant force was applied to the muscle. The incident may be related to an eccentric contraction (e.g. sprinting) or it may be associated with an excessive stretch (e.g. ballet dancing).

PRACTICE PEARL

Clinicians should be reticent to diagnose an acute muscle strain in the absence of a convincing history of injury. Without a strong history of injury, consider referred pain.

Tethering of neural structures and fascial strains in the posterior thigh can also occur as an incident; however, skillful examination will reveal whether the injury has a neuromechanical or fascial component. Although the clinical examination for referred pain may not be different from a low-grade strain, the absence of evidence of muscle injury on MRI (10–20% of posterior thigh pain presentations[5-7]) should make the clinician highly suspicious of a referred cause of pain.

The causes of posterior thigh pain are listed in Table 31.1.

History

Because there are different causes of posterior thigh pain, the clinician should use the history to develop a differential diagnosis, which can then be refined further with a physical examination that is then appropriately structured. Important points that experienced clinicians consider are shown in the box. This list is *not* the complete history.

Of the points in the box, point 5—the ability to walk pain-free within 1 day of the injury—and point 11—whether it is a recurrent problem—are particularly important.

Some important points that experienced clinicians consider in the history of the patient with posterior thigh pain

1. Level of activity
   (a) Has a change in training coincided with injury?
   (b) Is there an adequate base of training?
2. Occupation/lifestyle
   (a) What factors other than sport could be aggravating the condition (e.g. prolonged sitting at work, repetitive bending over with young children)?
3. Incident
   (a) Yes—consider strain, fascial/neural trauma.
   (b) No—consider overuse, referred pain, alternative abnormality.
4. Progress since injury
   (a) Slow—indicates a more severe injury.
   (b) Erratic—strain is being aggravated by activity or injury is not a strain.
5. Ability to walk pain free within 1 day following injury[8]
   (a) Yes—sign of better prognosis
   (b) No—suggests longer rehabilitation time (4 times more likely to require >3 weeks to return to AFL football compared with those who could walk pain-free within a day).

Table 31.1 Causes of posterior thigh pain

Common	Less common	Not to be missed
Hamstring muscle strains	Referred pain	Tumors
• Type I	• Sacroiliac joint	• Bone tumors
• Type II	Tendinopathy	Vascular
• Recurrent	• Biceps femoris	• Iliac artery endofibrosis
Hamstring muscle contusion	• Semimembranosus/semitendinosus	
Referred pain	Bursitis	
• Lumbar spine	• Semimembranous	
Neural structures	• Ischiogluteal	
• Gluteal trigger points	Fibrous adhesions	
	"Hamstring syndrome" (Chapter 27)	
	Chronic compartment syndrome of the posterior thigh	
	Apophysitis/avulsion fracture of the ischial tuberosity (in adolescents)	
	Nerve entrapments	
	• Posterior cutaneous nerve of the thigh	
	• Sciatic	
	Adductor magnus strains	
	Myositis ossificans, hamstring muscle	

6. Aggravating factors
   (a) Incident-related: useful for specificity of
       rehabilitation (e.g. acceleration injuries require
       acceleration in the rehabilitation program).
   (b) Non-incident-related: eradication or
       modification for recovery and prevention (e.g.
       sitting at a computer causing back/hamstring
       pain requires ergonomic modification).
7. Behavior with sport
   (a) Increases with activity; worse after—
       inflammatory pathology.
   (b) Starts with minimal or no pain, builds up with
       activity but not as severe after—claudicant,
       either neurological or vascular.
   (c) Sudden onset—mechanical (e.g. strain).
8. Night pain
   (a) Sinister pathology.
   (b) Inflammatory condition.
9. Site of pain
   (a) Posterior thigh and/or lower back—lumbar
       referral or neuromotor/biomechanical mediator.
   (b) Buttock, sacroiliac joint without lower back
       symptoms—gluteal trigger points.
   (c) Ischial: tendinopathy/bursitis/apophysitis/
       avulsion.
10. Presence of neurological symptoms
    (a) Nerve involvement.
11. Recurrent problem
    (a) Extensive examination and rehabilitation
        required.

**(b) History of prior biceps femoris injury is
a strong predictor of risk of recurrence
(20 times more likely among football players
who had had such an injury within the
previous 12 months).[8]**

Examination

The examination further refines the distinction
between local injury (i.e. acute muscle strain),
referred pain, or other unusual causes. A practical
approach to assess various factors that commonly
cause posterior thigh pain is outlined below.

1. Observation
   (a) standing (Fig. 31.2a)
   (b) walking
   (c) lying prone
2. Active movements
   (a) lumbar movements
   (b) hip extension
   (c) knee flexion (active prone knee bend)
   (d) active knee extension (Fig. 31.2b overleaf)
3. Passive movements
   (a) hamstring muscle stretch (Fig. 31.2c overleaf)
4. Resisted movements
   (a) knee flexion in isolation
   (b) hip extension in isolation
   (c) combined contraction single-leg bridge
       (Fig. 31.2d overleaf)
5. Functional tests
   (a) running
   (b) kicking
   (c) sprint starts
6. Palpation
   (a) hamstring muscles (Fig. 31.2e overleaf)
   (b) ischial tuberosity
   (c) gluteal muscles (Fig. 31.2f on page 599)
7. Special tests
   (a) neurodynamic test: slump test (Fig. 31.2g on
       page 599)

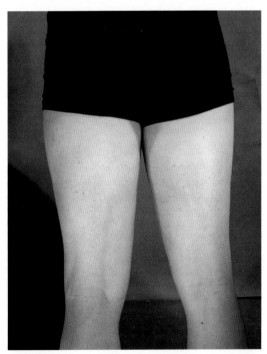

Figure 31.2 Examination of the patient with posterior
thigh pain

(a) Observation. Look for wasting, bruising, or
swelling of the posterior thigh. Observation of gait is
also important. Observation of the lumbar spine may
show the presence of an excessive lordosis or relative
asymmetry. A lateral view may demonstrate excessive
lumbar lordosis, or anterior pelvic tilt

(b) lumbar spine examination (Chapter 26)
(c) sacroiliac joint (Chapter 27)
(d) assessment of lumbopelvic stability
     (Chapter 14)
(e) biomechanical analysis

 See biomechanical analysis in *Clinical Sports Medicine* masterclasses at www.clinicalsportsmedicine.com.

(d) Combined contraction—single-leg bridge. A widely used "quick" clinical assessment of hamstring resisted contraction is the single-leg bridge. This can be done with the knee fully extended or flexed to 90° (or any angle in between these two positions).

(b) Active movement—active knee extension. The hip is actively flexed to 90° with the knee initially at 90° also. The knee is then slowly extended until pain is felt and then to the end of range

(c) Passive movement—hamstring muscle stretch. The leg is raised to the point where pain is first felt and then to the end of range, pain permitting. Movement should be compared with the uninjured side

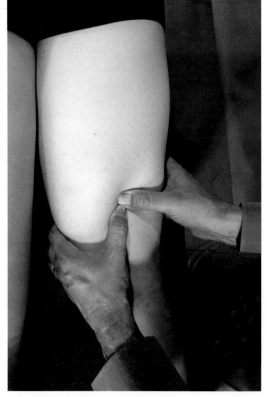

(e) Palpation. Palpate carefully bearing the underlying anatomy in mind to determine the location of an acute muscle strain (e.g. medial vs. lateral hamstring, proximal vs. distal)

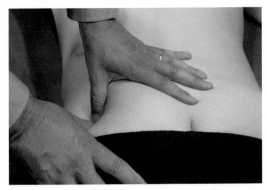

(Fig. 31.3b), and at times, computerized tomography. MRI is the most popular option (especially for the elite-level athlete) because it is non-invasive and capable of providing high-resolution images.

> **PRACTICE PEARL** MRI can help identify injury location, contribute to determining the likely prognosis, and help predict recurrence for certain injuries. This is a major new step in clinical care in the 2010s.

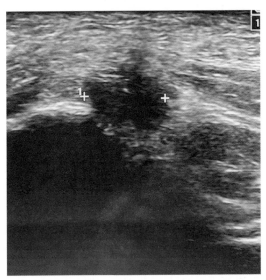

(f) Palpation—gluteal muscles. Palpate the gluteal muscles for trigger points that are taut bands, which are usually exquisitely tender locally and may refer pain into the hamstring muscle

Figure 31.3 Imaging of hamstring injuries
(a) Ultrasound showing hypoechoic area (between electronic calipers, +)

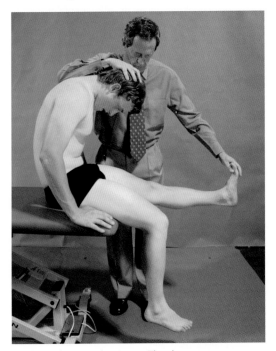

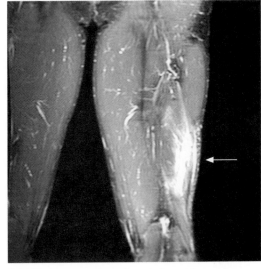

(g) Special tests—slump test. The slump test (Chapter 11) is an essential part of the examination of the patient with posterior thigh pain. It helps the clinician differentiate between hamstring muscle injuries and referred pain to the hamstring region from the lumbar spine

Investigations

Investigations of posterior thigh pain can be very useful, but clinicians must interpret these findings together with the rest of the examination. Appropriate imaging may include ultrasound (Fig. 31.3a), MRI

(b) MRI demonstrating edema in hamstring region consistent with biceps femoris muscle tear

Integrating the clinical assessment and investigation to make a diagnosis

Table 31.2 summarizes elements of the history, physical examination, and investigations that point to whether the diagnosis is likely to be an acute hamstring muscle injury, or referred pain to the posterior thigh.

Acute hamstring muscle strains

Before outlining type I and type II hamstring injuries, the epidemiologies of these injuries are outlined together. As the differentiation of acute hamstring injuries into two types has only occurred in the past few years, it is not possible to provide separate epidemiological data with confidence.

 In the large majority of hamstring strains, the injured muscle is biceps femoris (reported as 76–87%).[5] Semimembranosus injury is uncommon; semitendinosus injury is rare.

Epidemiology

Acute hamstring strains are common injuries in many popular sports, including the various football codes, field hockey, cricket, and track and field. For example, hamstring strains are the most common injury in Australian Rules football, constituting 15% of all injuries, with an incidence rate of six injuries per club (approximately 40 players) per season, and a prevalence rate of 21 missed matches per club per season.[9] Similarly, in British soccer, hamstring strains make up 12% of all injuries, with an incidence rate averaging five injuries per club per season, resulting in 15 matches and 90 days missed.[10, 11] The average injury causes the loss of three to four matches.[9, 12]

Hamstring injuries in ballet have not been captured as well as in football codes, but estimates of lifetime prevalence of hamstring injury are as high as 51% (34% acute, 17% overuse).[13]

With respect to epidemiology of recurrence, acute hamstring strains have the highest recurrence rate of any injury, a rate of 34% in Australian Rules football[9] and 12% in British soccer.[12]

Types of acute hamstring strains

There are at least two distinctly different types of acute hamstring strains (type I and type II), distinguished by different injury situations. The more common, type I, hamstring strains occur during high-speed running[7, 12, 14–19] (Fig. 31.4a). Type II hamstring strains occur during movements leading to extensive lengthening of the hamstrings when in more hip flexion, such as high kicking, sliding tackle, sagittal split; these may occur at slow speeds (Fig. 31.4b).[13–17] These are often seen in gymnasts and ballet dancers.

Type I strains (the high-speed running type) usually involve the long head of biceps femoris, most commonly at the proximal muscle–tendon junction

Table 31.2 Clinical features of hamstring muscle tear and referred hamstring pain

Clinical feature	Acute hamstring strain (type I or II)	Referred pain to posterior thigh
Onset	Sudden	May be sudden onset or gradual feeling of tightness
Pain	Moderate to severe	Usually less severe, may be cramping or "twinge"
Ability to walk	Disabling—difficulty walking, unable to run	Often able to walk/jog pain-free
Stretch	Markedly reduced	Minimal reduction
Strength	Markedly reduced contraction with pain against resistance	Full or near to full muscle strength against resistance
Local signs	Hematoma, bruising	None
Tenderness	Marked focal tenderness	Variable tenderness, usually non-specific
Slump test	Negative	Frequently positive
Trigger points	May have gluteal trigger points	Gluteal trigger points that reproduce hamstring pain on palpation or needling
Lumbar spine/ SIJ signs	May have abnormal lumbar spine/SIJ signs	Frequently have abnormal lumbar spine/SIJ signs
Investigations	Abnormal ultrasound/MRI	Normal ultrasound/MRI

Figure 31.4 (a) Sprinting is the classic activity that causes type I hamstring strains

(b) Type II hamstring strains occur with maximal stretching (e.g. dancer's sagittal split and soccer kicking)

(Fig. 31.5a overleaf).[14, 17] In contrast, type II injuries (the stretching type) are typically located close to the ischial tuberosity and involve the proximal free tendon of semimembranosus (Fig. 31.5b overleaf).[13, 20] The proximal free tendon of semimembranosus has a length of more than 10 cm; thus the stretching type of hamstring strain can in fact be considered a tendon injury.[21]

Type I strains (high-speed running type) generally cause a more marked acute decline in function but typically require a shorter rehabilitation period than the type II stretching type of hamstring strains (Fig. 31.6 overleaf).[20] The injury mechanism and location give important information about the prognosis of the injury.[13–17, 20, 22] The injury location can be determined both by maximal pain palpation and by

MRI during the first two weeks after injury occurrence. The closer the site of maximum pain palpation to the ischial tuberosity, the longer the rehabilitation period.[14, 16, 17] MRI should always be obtained when a total rupture is suspected.

Type I acute hamstring strain: sprinting-related

Although there are a variety of sports skills that can potentially heavily load the hamstrings (e.g. kicking, twisting, jumping, hurdling), sprinting is the most commonly reported mechanism of type I acute hamstring muscle strain.[7, 12, 18, 19]

Why do hamstrings fail during sprinting? Case studies suggest that hamstrings are most vulnerable to injury during the terminal swing phase of

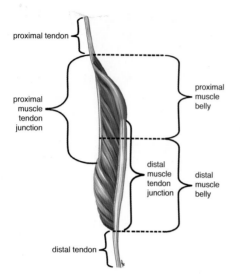

Figure 31.5 (a) Type I strains (the high-speed running type) are mainly located to the long head of biceps femoris and typically involve the proximal muscle–tendon junction[17]

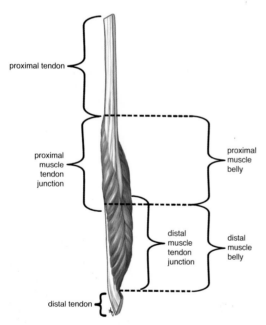

(b) Type II injuries (the stretching type) are typically located close to the ischial tuberosity and involve the proximal free tendon of semimembranosus[16]

sprinting,[23, 24] a time in the stride cycle where they are highly activated as they work eccentrically to decelerate the swinging tibia and control knee extension[25] in preparation for foot strike.

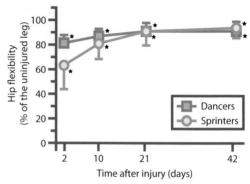

Figure 31.6 Comparison of hamstring injuries in sprinters (type I) and dancers (type II)[20]
(a) Hip flexibility (range of motion) of the injured leg expressed as a percentage of the uninjured leg in the sprinters (n = 18) and dancers (n = 15). The sprinters' injuries (type I) resulted in more reduction in flexibility, but similar times to return to near pre-injury flexibility levels

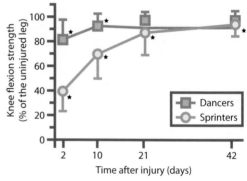

(b) Knee flexion strength in the injured leg expressed as a percentage of the uninjured leg in the sprinters (n = 18) and dancers (n = 15) showing markedly increased reduction in strength in the sprinters' injuries (type I)

Patients who present with type I acute hamstring strain typically complain of sudden onset of pain in the hamstring region that usually stops them. On examination, careful palpation and testing usually locates the injury in the long head of biceps femoris, often the proximal muscle–tendon junction.[14, 17]

If imaging is deemed necessary (e.g. if presence of type I acute hamstring strain is unclear on clinical grounds), MRI (Fig. 31.7) is the recommended imaging modality because it is non-invasive and of high resolution. The only disadvantage may be its cost. MRI can be helpful in accurately identifying

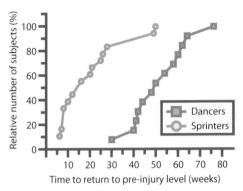

(c) Relative number of subjects in each group plotted against the corresponding time, in *weeks*, to return to pre-injury level of performance (n = 18 for the sprinters type I, n = 13 for the dancers type II) demonstrating the prolonged rehabilitation time for type II injuries

the location of the injury (semimembranosus versus biceps femoris long head versus semitendinosus; distal versus proximal) and the type of tissue involved (muscle fiber, tendon, muscle–tendon junction) rather than relying on palpation.

Both the size [5, 16, 17] and location[16, 17] of the lesion on MRI can be used to help predict prognosis. MRI can also be useful for determining the likelihood of recurrence (i.e. larger lesions tend to be associated with greater risk of recurrence).[26, 27] MRI should always be done when a total rupture is suspected.

Type II acute hamstring strain: stretch-related (dancers)

Type II acute hamstring strains more commonly occur in sports that necessitate large amplitude movements and ballistic limb actions, such as ballet

dancing and gymnastics. The common mechanism of injury in these instances is an excessive stretch into hip flexion.

In contrast to type I injuries, the stretching type injuries typically are located close to the ischial tuberosity and involve the proximal free tendon of semimembranosus.[16, 22] This can be shown on MRI (Fig 31.8).

Although type II hamstring strains can cause a less dramatic acute limitation than type I strains, their rehabilitation period is often longer than that of type I strains.[20] It is important to directly inform the sportsperson that the rehabilitation is likely to be prolonged. Unrealistically optimistic information only reinforces the disappointment and frustration of the injured sportsperson. The sportsperson can often do quite demanding rehabilitation training early on, as long as pain-provoking exercises are avoided. Passive stretching and heavy-load exercises seem to aggravate the stretch type of hamstring injuries by increasing pain.

Management of hamstring injuries

Factors related to the prognosis of hamstring injuries are shown in the box overleaf.

There is very little scientific evidence on which to base the management of hamstring injuries. According to a recent systematic review,[30] only three randomized controlled trials have evaluated the efficacy of a particular intervention for the rehabilitation of acute hamstring strains.[31–33] Consequently, much of the approach described below is on the basis of clinical experience. The management of acute hamstring strains is summarized in Table 31.3 overleaf.

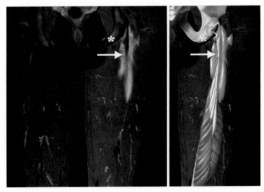

Figure 31.7 MRI showing type I hamstring injury

Figure 31.8 MRI shows the site of the type II injury close to the ischial tuberosity

Factors relating to the prognosis of hamstring injuries

The following factors have been shown to be associated with increased length of time to return to play (RTP):

- Time (days) to walk at normal pace pain-free has been shown to be significantly associated with RTP time (>1 day = 4 times more likely to take >3 weeks). Combining this with a past history of hamstring injury within 12 months resulted in a 93% chance of taking longer than 3 weeks to return in elite AFL footballers.[8]
- Days to jog pain-free is the strongest predictor of time to RTP[7]
    - 1–2 days = <2 weeks to RTP
    - 3–5 days = significantly longer than 2 weeks to RTP
    - >5 days = significantly longer than 4 weeks to RTP
- MRI-negative "hamstring strains" are associated with relatively rapid time to RTP and are relatively common (10–20%).[1, 5–7]
- The more proximal (closest to the ischial tuberosity in a biceps femoris injury) the site of maximal tenderness, the more prolonged the time to return to pre-injury level.[16]
- Injury to the proximal free tendon of biceps femoris is associated with a very long return to pre-injury level in sprinters (more than twice as long as those not involving the proximal free tendon).[16]
- A "kicking" or "slow-stretching" mechanism of injury is associated with a much more prolonged return to pre-injury level than a high-speed running mechanism, even though initial signs and symptoms may actually present as far less severe.[20]
- Length of tear (>60 mm) and cross-sectional area (>55% of total) on MRI are correlated with prolonged return to play.[5, 6, 28, 29]

Rehabilitation programs require a basic structure, but should never be a "recipe." Treat each case on its merits. The management guideline (Table 31.3) captures many experienced clinicians' recommendations.[1, 34]

Progression through phases of the rehabilitation program must not be time-dependent. Sometimes what initially appears to be rather minor injury can take an extended period to fully recover, and vice versa. Progression must be based on successfully achieving key functional and/or clinical criteria (see box on page 606).

Table 31.3 Management of hamstring injury

First 48 hours
RICE (rest, ice, compression, elevation)
Early pain-free muscle contractions (Fig. 31.9)

Subsequent
Stretching
• Hamstrings (Fig. 31.10 on page 607)
• Antagonist muscles
– Quadriceps
– Iliopsoas
Neural mobilizing (Fig. 31.11 on page 607)
Soft tissue treatment
• Hamstrings (Fig. 31.12a, b on pages 607–608)
• Gluteal trigger points (Fig. 31.13 on page 608)
Strengthening
• Hamstrings (Fig. 31.14 on page 609)
(a) Standing single-leg hamstring catches with theraband
(b) Single-leg bridge catch
(c) Single-leg ball rollouts
(d) Bridge walk-out
(e) Nordics
(f) Single-leg dead lifts with kettle bell
(g) Yo-yo
(h) Askling's gliding (Fig. 31.15 on page 610)
• Gluteals and adductor magnus (Fig. 31.16 on page 611)
Neuromuscular control exercises (Figs 31.17 and 31.18 on page 612)
Spinal mobilization
Cross-training bike
Running program
Sprinting technique drills
Advanced agility drills
Sport-specific training drills

Acute management phase

Acute injuries should always be assessed thoroughly before any treatment is administered. The fundamental objective of the acute management phase is to facilitate myofiber regeneration and to minimize fibrosis. If strategies aimed at minimizing scar tissue formation are instituted immediately, this may reduce the chances of injury recurrence.

RICE

Traditionally, the most common treatment in the first few days following type I acute hamstring strain is the rest, ice, compression, elevation (RICE) program. For example, applying ice for 10–15 minutes using a cold pack, every three to four hours, for the first few days until acute symptoms settle. Compression can be achieved in between times via an elastic bandage or tubigrip stocking.

Muscle activation

Although RICE is the recommended initial approach, recent research in cell therapy and tissue engineering is indicating an additional role for controlled and monitored exercise (or muscle contraction) regimens. Muscle contraction promotes angiogenesis (i.e. the formation of new blood vessels and the expansion of existing vascularity) and in doing so increases the likelihood of delivering muscle-derived stem cells to the injured region. These cells are likely derived from the vascular endothelium and offer great potential for providing long-term myofiber regeneration. Note that "mechanotherapy" also provides a scientific underpinning for early muscle contraction.[35]

In this light, the commencement of frequent (e.g. 3–4 times per day) low-grade pain-free muscle contractions (e.g. simple isometric hamstring contractions or active prone knee bends) immediately following injury would appear advantageous (Fig. 31.9). Such muscle contractions could be done immediately prior to the application of ice.

Medical therapies

Despite the widespread use of nonsteroidal anti-inflammatory drugs (NSAIDs) in the treatment of hamstring injuries, the two randomized controlled studies[8, 36] failed to show beneficial effects of NSAIDSs compared with analgesics or placebo on acute muscle strain injuries. It is likely that simple analgesics are just as effective, and do not have the long-term risks on skeletal muscle and the gastrointestinal system associated with NSAIDs.

One study showed favorable results with intramuscular corticosteroid injection in American football players with acute hamstring injuries.[37] Previously, the use of corticosteroids in acute muscle strains had been clearly contraindicated because they were thought to delay elimination of hematoma and necrotic tissue, as well as retarding muscle regeneration. There are concerns regarding the retrospective nature of the National Football League (NFL) study and lack of control group, so we caution against the use of corticosteroids in this situation, particularly as there have been no further studies confirming these results

There is increasing interest in the use of growth factors to accelerate healing after muscle and tendon

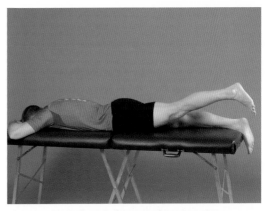

Figure 31.9 Early pain-free muscle contraction
(a) Single-leg hip extension exercise with whole leg a few centimeters (1 in.) off the plinth

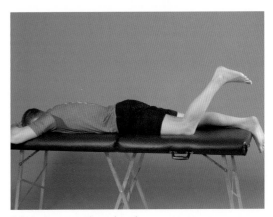

(b) Active prone knee bends

injury.[38] Animal studies have demonstrated clear benefits in terms of accelerated healing. There are various methods of delivery of the growth factors—all involving the release of growth factors from platelets. These include plasma-rich platelets (PRP) and autologous blood.[39] Clinical studies in humans are very limited at this stage, but are promising in some settings.

The combined injection of Traumeel S and Actovegin, a deproteinized calves' blood hemodialysate, immediately after a hamstring muscle injury and again at day 2 and day 4 post-injury to the area of the muscle strain and the lumbar spine, is common practice in sports medicine in Germany. It is becoming increasingly popular among elite sportspeople elsewhere, despite the lack of any controlled trials supporting its use.[38, 40]

In summary, there is limited scientific evidence to support the use of any medication in the management of hamstring muscle injuries.

Criteria for progression to subacute phase

Once the sportsperson is pain-free with walking, and sufficient force can be generated without pain on resisted hamstrings contraction, then jogging can commence and gradually increase.

In the case of high-speed running type of injuries, it is common that the sportsperson experiences a considerable improvement 4–6 days after the injury is sustained with respect to pain, strength, and flexibility. This is a potentially dangerous feeling, because the healing process is in its initial stages, and the risk for re-injury is high since the injured tissue is less able to absorb energy.

The criteria for progression to the subacute phase are shown in the box below.

Subacute/conditioning phase

Stretching

The role of targeted hamstring stretching in the rehabilitation of hamstring strain injury should be considered on an individual basis (Fig. 31.10). There is some evidence to suggest that rate of recovery can be increased with an increased daily frequency of hamstring stretching exercises.[33] Consequently, to prevent long-term loss of range of motion (e.g. perhaps from significant scar tissue), a controlled stretching program can be instituted. However, in our clinical experience, most sportspeople regain their normal range of motion without the need for excessive or aggressive hamstring stretching regimens.

It may be more important to focus on stretching of other structures. For example, tight hip flexor muscles may place the sportsperson at increased risk of hamstring strain.[41, 42]

Soft tissue treatment

A comprehensive clinical examination of the lumbar spine, sacroiliac, and buttock regions should be instituted at an early stage to assess whether not these regions have any contribution to the presenting injury. For example, Cibulka et al.[31] reported that mobilization of the sacroiliac joint was of some benefit in the treatment of acute hamstring strains.

Neural mobility restriction is frequently present in hamstring injuries secondary to bleeding around the sciatic nerve. Neural mobilizing exercises should be performed to reduce adhesions. Neural mobilizing can be performed in the hamstring stretch position (Fig. 31.10b) by adding gentle cervical flexion (Fig. 31.11).

Criterion-related rehabilitation of hamstring muscle strains

Phase	Key criteria
1. Begin running and active rehab (i.e. begin subacute/conditioning phase)	• Pain-free walking
	• Adequate force with resisted muscle contraction
2. Return to full activities (i.e. begin functional phase)	• Complete resolution of any symptoms with maximal resisted muscle contraction
	• Equivocal tenderness upon palpation (left = right)
	• Full and symptom-free range of movement/flexibility (left = right)
	• Successful completion of a structured running program (i.e. time for middle 20 meter portion of running program (page 613); time comparable to previously determined time for maximum effort recorded when uninjured)
	• Successful completion of appropriate rehabilitation exercises
	• Successful completion of controlled functional (sports-related) tasks, specific to original injury mechanism
3. Return to play	• Successful completion of sufficient period of normal training activities (e.g. one full week) with no adverse reaction of any clinical and/or functional signs and symptoms
	• Additional tests (isokinetic strength testing, Askling's H-test on page 614)

Figure 31.10 Hamstring stretches
(a) Hamstring stretch with contralateral knee flexion. The lower leg can be placed in different degrees of external and internal rotation to maximize the effectiveness of the stretch

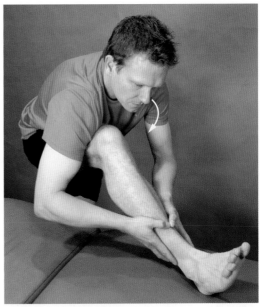

Figure 31.11 Neural mobilizing.
Neural mobilizing can be performed in the hamstring stretch position (Fig. 31.10b) by adding gentle cervical flexion

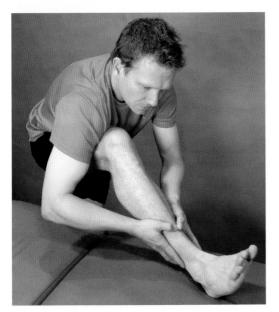

(b) Hamstring stretch with bent knee results in maximal stretch to the upper hamstrings

Soft tissue techniques can be used in the treatment of hamstring strains. Digital ischemic pressure and sustained myofascial tension (Figs 31.12a, b overleaf) are used, gently at first and then more vigorously. Longitudinal massage along the muscle may assist in scar reorganization. Abnormalities of the gluteal muscles may be associated with hamstring strains. These regions may be treated in a side-lying position using elbow ischemic pressure with the tissue on stretch and the muscle contracting (Fig. 31.13 overleaf).

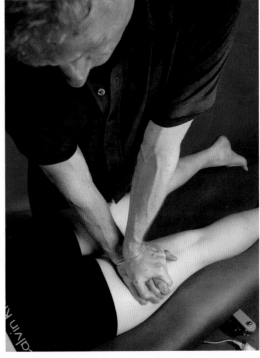

Figure 31.12 Soft tissue techniques in the treatment of hamstring injuries
(a) Sustained compression force to hamstring

B

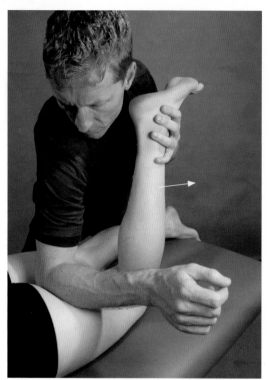

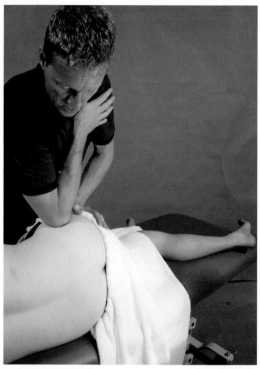

(b) Sustained myofascial tension combined with passive knee extension. The hand or the elbow (illustrated) is kept stationary and the release is performed by passively extending the knee (arrow)

Figure 31.13 Treatment of the gluteal region in a side-lying position using elbow ischemic pressure with the muscle contracting

Strengthening for hamstring muscles

Strengthening is an essential component of the rehabilitation and prevention of hamstring injuries. Muscle strengthening should be specific for deficits in motor unit recruitment, muscle bulk, type of contraction (e.g. eccentric/concentric) and ability to develop tension at speed.

Most hamstring researchers believe that the strains occur when the hamstring muscle group are extensively lengthened, especially in the stretching type of injury,[16, 22] but also in the sprinting type strains.[25, 41] It is also generally accepted that retraining needs to be specific to muscle function.[43–46]

Based on this concept, training programs for prevention and rehabilitation of hamstring injuries should include exercises emphasizing eccentric muscle contractions and extensive lengthening. Since three of the four hamstring muscles span two joints, both hip and knee joint positions need attention. When prescribing exercises, it is recommended to use exercises that involve simultaneous hip and knee flexion.

Numerous exercises fulfill these criteria and we recommend:

- standing single-leg hamstring catches with theraband (Fig. 31.14a)
- single-leg bridge catch (Fig. 31.14b)
- single-leg ball rollouts (Fig. 31.14c)
- bridge walk-outs (Fig. 31.14d)
- Nordic drops (Fig. 31.14e)
- single-leg dead lifts with dumb bell (Fig. 31.14f overleaf)
- yo-yo (Fig. 31.14g overleaf).

One study has confirmed the efficacy of Nordic drops in developing hamstring strength.[47] Other studies have shown that Nordic exercises were effective in preventing recurrence of hamstring injury (see below).[48, 49]

The Nordic strengthening program shown in Table 31.4 overleaf is based on the Mjolsnes and Arnason studies.[47, 48] It is designed for a 5–10 week pre-season training program. Introduce this with at least a day between sessions, as the eccentric load can cause delayed onset muscle soreness (DOMS). Adjust

(d) Bridge walk-outs

Figure 31.14 Strengthening exercises
(a) Standing single-leg hamstring catches with theraband

(b) Single-leg bridge catch

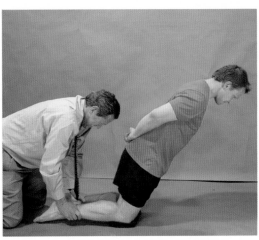

(e) Nordic eccentric hamstring exercise (drops)—
patients allow themselves to fall forward and then resist the fall for as long as possible using their hamstrings

(c) Single-leg ball rollouts

the load in response to any soreness to encourage compliance. If the program is performed in-season, then one session per week is appropriate.

Another exercise that imposes high loads during extensive lengthening of the hamstring is the so-called "Askling's gliding exercise," described below and shown in the CSM masterclass video (see Fig. 31.15 overleaf). This exercise can be used early in the rehabilitation phase, but should be used with caution (pain-free) because of the high loads exerted on the hamstrings.

 Askling's gliding exercise is shown in *Clinical Sports Medicine* masterclasses at www.clinicalsportsmedicine.com.

(f) Single-leg dead lifts with dumbbell

Figure 31.15 Askling's gliding exercise

(g) Yo-yo machine

Table 31.4 Pre-season training protocol for Nordic hamstring exercises

Week	Sessions per week	Sets and repetitions
1	1	2 × 5
2	2	2 × 6
3	3	3 × 6–8
4	3	3 × 8–10
5–10	3	3 sets, 12, 10, 8 repetitions[a]

ROM = range of motion

[a] Load is increased as subject can withstand the forward fall longer. When managing to withstand the whole ROM for 12 repetitions, increase load by adding speed to the starting phase of the motion. The partner can also increase loading further by pushing at the back of the shoulders

The exercise starts in a neutral position with all the body weight on the front leg. The gliding (backwards of the other leg) starts and goes on until a position is reached where the sportsperson is not able to go further because of pain, weakness, or limited flexibility. The upper body should be flexed forward during the gliding of the leg backwards.

This exercise is intended to be mainly an eccentric one, and therefore the movement returning to the neutral position should be supported by both the arms pulling on a hand rail. For the exercise to be progressive, movement velocity of the gliding can be increased. It is very important to perform the exercise with high concentration and not allow pain. A suitable training session might consist of 3 sets with 3 repetitions, repeated twice a week.

Generally, low-grade or minor hamstring injuries or first-time injuries progress quickly; therefore functional strength may be adequate to allow return to sport. Functional exercises could be added to ongoing training and include an exercise such as bridge walk-outs (Fig. 31.14d).

More severe or recurrent injuries require more extensive strength work and high-level eccentric load (e.g. theraband catches in standing, Nordic drops, single-leg dead lifts with a weight).

Eccentric muscle training results in muscle damage and delayed onset muscle soreness in those unaccustomed to it. Therefore, any eccentric strengthening program should allow adequate time for recovery, especially in the first few weeks.

Strengthening for hamstring synergists

Rehabilitation must not be restricted to the hamstring alone—it must also include the muscles that assist the activity of the hamstring. The gluteal muscles contribute at least 50% to isometric hip extension.[50] If gluteal strength is inadequate the hamstring muscles can be overloaded and susceptible to injury. This is especially true during sprinting activities.

The gluteus maximus acts during running to control trunk flexion of the stance leg, decelerate the swing leg, and extend the hip.[51] Any alteration in gluteus maximus activation, strength, or endurance places greater demand on the hamstrings. Overall the gluteus maximus provides powerful hip extension when sprinting, and the hamstrings help to transfer the power between the hip and knee joints.[52]

To improve gluteus maximus activation, strength, and endurance it is important to initially teach good motor patterns (coordinated, well-timed movement). Isolating the gluteus maximus from hamstring exercises should be an early priority. Progression can be made through bridging exercises (Fig. 31.16a). In the final stages, reintegrate the gluteus maximus with the hamstrings with exercises such as single-leg dead-lifts and lunges.[52, 53]

The adductor magnus is also an important hip extensor. Therefore, strengthening of the hamstring group should always include specific work to ensure adequate gluteal and adductor magnus conditioning (Fig. 31.16).[53]

Neuromuscular control exercises

Neuromuscular control of the lumbopelvic region, including anterior and posterior pelvic tilt, may be needed to promote optimal function of the

(b) Squat

(c) Split squat

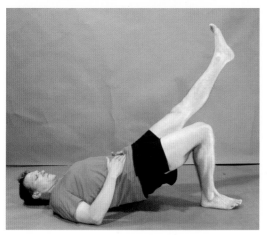

Figure 31.16 Gluteals and adductor magnus strengthening exercises
(a) One-legged bridging

hamstrings in sprinting and high-speed skilled movement. Changes in pelvic position can lead to changes in length–tension relationships or force–velocity relationships.[32]

A rehabilitation program focusing on progressive agility, neuromuscular control, and lumbopelvic stability exercises (Fig. 31.17 overleaf) was more

Figure 31.17 Lumbopelvic stability exercises—single leg balance. A quarter squat can be added

effective in preventing injury recurrence than exercises involving a more traditional stretching and simple strengthening exercise program.[32]

It is also important to consider motor control exercises for deep lumbar spine stabilizers (e.g. multifidus). Such exercises can involve isolated activations in prone lying; then progress to functional postural control exercises against gravity (e.g. sit to stand by flexing trunk forward at the hip and maintaining optimal lumbar spine lordotic angle).[54, 55]

Advanced neuromuscular control exercises for the lumbopelvic region and entire lower extremity are discussed in Chapter 14. Exercises might include side stepping, grape-vine stepping, single-leg stand windmill touches (Fig. 31.18), fast feet drills etc.[32]

Functional progression

Early commencement of a progressive running program is an important part of a rehabilitation program following a hamstring muscle injury.

 Athletes rehabilitating from hamstring strain should run on a day on/day off basis.

The basic principles of the running program and an example are shown in the two boxes opposite.

Criteria to progress to return-to-sport phase

Once the following criteria are met, the rehabilitation can progress to the next stage—the return to competition phase:

Figure 31.18 Neuromuscular control exercise
Single-limb balance windmill touches with dumbbells. Begin in (a) single-limb stance position with dumbbells overhead and perform windmill motion under control with end position of (b) touching dumbbell to floor

Basic principles of the running program for rehabilitation following a hamstring injury

1. A formal running program could commence when the sportsperson is comfortable running at approx. 50% intensity (e.g. is able to do a submaximal stride without pain). Prior to this, running would likely comprise jogging, progressing to some low-grade fartlek-type running.
2. Sportspeople rehabilitating from hamstring strain should run on a day on/day off basis (thus three runs per week). The advantage of a day off is that the clinician can assess key signs and symptoms and thus make a judgment as to whether the person has coped with or reacted adversely to the load. The structure and intensity of the next running session can then be planned accordingly.
3. It is advisable to intermingle the running program with intervals (e.g. repetitions 150 meters/200 meters at tolerable intensity) rather than using the running program as the only type of running done at all stages of the rehabilitation process. Start with the structured running program, determine the pace the sportsperson can handle without pain, then do a few sessions of repetition running, return to the running program and reassess pain-free pace etc. Finish with the running program to ensure the intensity of the mid-20 m is close to what you know the sportsperson could do prior to the injury.
4. The warm-up prior to running should start with jogging, then progress to footwork and agility drills.[32]
5. Sprinting technique drills should be included in the rehabilitation program (e.g. as part of warm-up). A purpose-developed sprint technique training program has been shown to result in a significant improvement in lower joint position sense, in a test position similar to the range of movement of the lower limb during the late swing and early stance phase of running gait.[56] Poor movement discrimination ability has been shown to be related to susceptibility to future hamstring strain injury in Australian Rules football players.[57]
6. Sport-specific training drills[58] should also be added in the late stages of rehabilitation.

- absence of clinical signs (e.g. full power with contraction, normal ROM, tenderness with palpation equal to uninjured side)

Progressive hamstring running program

1. 2 km jog
2. 2 km varying pace up to 75% of maximum
3. Run-throughs—accelerate 40 m, constant speed 20 m (in 3.5 seconds), decelerate 40 m (×3)

35 m	20 m	35 m (×3)
30 m	20 m	30 m (×3)
25 m	20 m	25 m (×3)
20 m	20 m	20 m (×3)
15 m	20 m	15 m (×3)

4. Run-throughs—accelerate 40 m, constant speed 20 m (in 2.5 seconds), decelerate 40 m (×3)

35 m	20 m	35 m (×3)
25 m	20 m	25 m (×3)
20 m	20 m	20 m (×3)
15 m	20 m	15 m (×3)
10 m	20 m	10 m (×3)

5. Running out to catch ball—uncontested (×5)
6. Running out to catch ball—contested (×5)
7. Running and picking up ball—contested (×5)

- successful completion of running program (i.e. 20 m time comparable to previously determined time recorded when uninjured)
- successful completion of appropriate rehabilitation exercises
- successful completed at least two normal duration training sessions at maximal exertion.

In severe or recurrent cases, isokinetic dynamometer assessment may be helpful. Key parameters include hamstring length at which peak torque is developed, and concentric/eccentric hamstring strength ratio.[59]

Return-to-competition/sport phase

It is extremely difficult to decide when the sportsperson is ready to return to sport after a hamstring strain.[1, 2, 32] This difficulty may be the reason that there is a conspicuously high injury recurrence rate, particularly within a few weeks after the return.[18, 60] This vulnerability to strain persists, although gradually reduces, for many weeks following return to play.[9]

Return-to-sport rehabilitation programs that only rely on subjective measures such as "pain-free movements" may result in deficits in neuromuscular control, strength, flexibility, ground reaction force attenuation and production, and lead to asymmetries between the legs during normal athletic movements.[52] These deficits and deficiencies could persist into sport practice and competition, and ultimately increase the risk of re-injury and limit athletic performance.

A criteria-based approach to rehabilitation that includes objective and quantitative tests has the potential to identify deficits and address them in a systematic progression (i.e. algorithm) during the stages of returning to sport. However, further research is needed (i.e. prospective, retrospective, and training studies) to validate the criteria-based progressions in each phase:

- completion of progressive running program
- full range of movement (equal to uninjured leg)
  - slow passive[61, 62]
  - active straight-leg raises[63]
- pain-free maximal isometric contraction
- full strength (equal or almost equal to uninjured leg)
  - measured by manual testing, hand-held dynamometer, or isokinetic machine
  - 90%[64]–95% [65, 66] of eccentric strength of uninjured leg

- functional tests
  - sprinting from a standing start
  - abrupt changes of pace during run
  - side stepping
  - bending to catch ball at full speed (if appropriate for the sport)
- successful completion of a full week of maximal training.

Askling's H-test is a complement to the clinical examination before return to sport.[67] Notably, this active test must not be performed before the time of rehabilitation at which all clinical tests, including those of passive flexibility, indicate complete recovery (see box below).

 Askling's hamstring apprehension test (H-test) is shown in *Clinical Sports Medicine* masterclasses at www.clinicalsportsmedicine.com.

It does not appear that MRI appearance is a good indicator of readiness to return to play. Abnormalities

Askling's hamstring apprehension test (H-test)

During the test, the subject should be positioned on a bench in a supine position with the contralateral leg and the upper body stabilized with straps (Fig. 31.19). A knee brace ensures full knee extension of the tested leg, and the foot of the tested leg should be kept slightly plantarflexed. No warm-up exercises are to be performed before the test. The uninjured leg is tested before the injured leg. The instruction to the subject is to perform a straight-leg raise as fast as possible to the highest point without taking any risk of injury. A set of three consecutive trials are performed, preceded by one practice trial with submaximal effort. After the three active test trials, the subject is to estimate experience of insecurity and pain on a VAS scale, from 0 to 100. In the study by Askling et al.[67] the athletes noted an average insecurity estimation of 52 for the injured leg and 0 for the uninjured leg.

The new active test seems to be sensitive enough to detect differences both in active flexibility and in insecurity after acute hamstring strains at a time when the commonly used clinical examination fails to reveal injury signs. If insecurity persists, the test should be repeated until no insecurity is reported. The athlete is then allowed to return to sport.

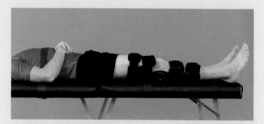

Figure 31.19 Askling's hamstring apprehension test
(a) Starting position

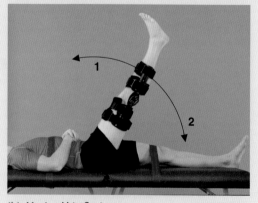

(b) Maximal hip flexion

on MRI tend to persist well after sportspeople are back to full sport.[5]

The length of time until return to sport is proportional to the severity of the injury. In most cases a sportsperson with a mild hamstring strain would achieve the return-to-play criteria (page 606) in 12–18 days if optimally treated (Table 31.3).

A practical tip to reduce the incidence of recurrence is to restrict game time when first returning from hamstring injury to minimize fatigue. In this way, return to sport can be progressed.

It is important to persist with a well-structured strength and neuromuscular control exercise program after return to sport, to lessen the likelihood of recurrence. This should be continued until there are no longer any significant asymmetries or hamstring/quadriceps ratio deficits. These sessions must be carefully scheduled to allow recovery time before exposure to high-risk activity.

Risk factors for acute hamstring strain

Risk factors for acute hamstring strain are discussed here because patients rarely present for "primary prevention"—to avoid hamstring injuries before they have one. Some risk factors may be mitigated. Risk factors for acute hamstring strains may be intrinsic (person-related) or extrinsic (environment-related) factors (as they are with all injuries [Chapters 4 and 5]). There have been two published systematic reviews on this topic to date.[68, 69]

Factors that appear to predict risk of hamstring strain are discussed below. Other factors have been evaluated, but do not appear to be risk factors; these include body mass index (BMI),[18, 70, 71] height,[18, 70–73] weight,[18, 70, 71, 73] and functional performance tests (e.g. countermovement jump, 40 m sprint tests, Nordic hamstring strength test, hamstring length measurement).[71]

Intrinsic risk factors

Age
A number of studies have shown that sportspeople of older age are at increased risk of acute hamstring strain, even when the confounding factor of previous injury is removed.[70–74] Australian Rules footballers aged 23 years or more were almost four times as likely as younger players to sustain an acute hamstring strain during the season.[72]

Older sportspeople may be at heightened risk due to increased body weight and reduced hip flexor

flexibility.[42] It has also been speculated that the high risk of older sportspeople to acute hamstring strain is related to degenerative changes at the lumbosacral junction.[75]

Past history of injury
Past history of injury is a critical factor for the development of a/another hamstring injury.

A prior history of acute hamstring strain is a significant risk for future injury.[70, 71, 73, 74] In comparison to injury-free sportspeople, those with a past history of hamstring injury do not appear to display appreciable differences in running mechanics;[76, 77] however, they do display differences in musculotendon morphology (differences in muscle volume, presence of scar tissue)[78] and contraction mechanics.[79]

It may be that the presence of scar tissue creates abnormally high rates of localized tissue strains in the immediately adjacent muscle fibers, and thus the risk of further injury.[77] Therefore strategies to reduce the development of scar tissue following initial injury are critical in terms of minimizing future risk of re-injury.

Sportspeople with a history of injury to other areas of the lower limb also have an increased likelihood of acute hamstring strain. These include:

- knee—major knee injury (e.g. anterior cruciate ligament [ACL] reconstruction, patellar dislocation)[26, 73]
- groin—history of osteitis pubis (bone marrow edema on MRI)[73]
- calf muscle strain[74]
- lumbar spine—"major" injury (i.e. episode which required radiological investigation with a specific recorded clinical diagnosis).[73]

Hamstring strength
Numerous studies have evaluated whether strength quantified via an isokinetic dynamometer is a risk factor for hamstring strain. While, intuitively, reduced muscle strength would appear to predispose to hamstring strain, the evidence is mixed. Such conflicting findings may relate to the difficulty in quantifying muscle strength in a systematic manner (i.e. what type of contraction [isometric, concentric, eccentric], what strength parameter or index to measure [peak torque, knee angle at which peak torque occurs, hamstring/quadriceps ratio, hamstring to hip flexor ratio, strength asymmetry], as well as the level of motivation of the sportspeople).

Current evidence indicates that knee flexor peak torque is not a risk factor for hamstring strain.[57, 63, 80] Increased knee extensor torque was a risk factor for hamstring strain in one study[57] but not in other studies.[63, 80, 81]

Hamstring to quadriceps ratio has also been extensively investigated. A reduced hamstring to quadriceps ratio (i.e. weaker hamstrings and/or stronger quadriceps muscles) has been shown to be a risk factor for hamstring strain in some studies[57, 59, 81, 82] but not in other studies.[63, 80]

Other factors

Other intrinsic risk factors for acute hamstring strain which have only limited supporting evidence include (but are not limited to):

- ethnicity[12, 73]
- reduced ankle dorsiflexion lunge range of motion[19]
- reduced quadriceps flexibility[19, 62]
- poor lower limb joint position sense.[57]

There is conflicting evidence regarding whether or not reduced hamstring flexibility (e.g. assessed via the active and/or passive knee extension test) is a risk factor for hamstring strain. Most studies indicate that reduced hamstring flexibility is not a risk factor;[19, 70–72] however, two studies have reported the opposite.[61, 62]

Extrinsic risk factors

Fatigue

It has long been speculated that fatigue is a risk factor for an acute hamstring strain, but there is very little evidence to support or refute this claim. Verrall et al.[7] found that 85% of acute hamstring strains occurred after the first quarter of a competitive match or after the first 15 minutes of a training session. Furthermore, Woods et al.[12] found that 47% of their acute hamstring strains occurred towards the end (during the final third) of the first and second halves of a match. Such observations suggest fatigue may be a factor, but further research is required.

Player position

There is limited evidence that different playing positions is associated with higher risk of hamstring strain. Goalkeepers have a significantly lower risk for hamstring strain than outfield players in soccer,[12] and rugby forwards have a reduced risk of hamstring strains compared with backs.[18] In American football, the speed position players, such as the wide receivers

and defensive secondary, as well as players on the special teams units, are most commonly injured.[83]

Prevention of hamstring strains

A recent Cochrane systematic review concluded that there is insufficient evidence from randomized controlled trials to draw conclusions on the effectiveness of interventions used to prevent hamstring injuries in people participating in football or other high-risk activities for these injuries.[84] However, some recent studies have suggested that Nordic exercises, a balance program, and soft tissue therapy may help prevent hamstring injuries.

Nordic drops and other eccentric exercises

There is evidence from a number of studies[48, 49, 85] that an eccentric strengthening program can reduce the incidence of hamstring injury. In Petersen's study,[49] there was a significant reduction (approximately three-fold) in the "total" number of hamstring injuries (i.e. new plus recurrent injuries), and a significant reduction (approximately seven-fold) in the number of recurrent injuries for the intervention group, which undertook a 10-week progressive pre-season eccentric training program of Nordic exercises (Fig. 31.14e on page 609) followed by a weekly seasonal program. There was also an approximate 2.5-fold reduction in number of new hamstrings injuries in the intervention group, but this did not reach statistical significance.

Arnason's study also showed a reduction in hamstring injuries with a Nordic exercise program.[48] An eccentric/concentric strengthening program using a prone leg curl machine in soccer players also prevented hamstring injuries.[85]

Two other studies have looked at the effect of Nordic exercises and shown a minimal positive effect in one study,[19] and no effect in the other.[86] However, both these studies suffered from poor compliance, which may explain the differences between their studies and those that showed a positive effect.

Balance exercises/proprioception training

Proprioceptive exercises or balance training may be an effective strategy for preventing hamstrings injuries.[87–89] A positive effect was found in one study,[89] whereas two other studies failed to show any effect.[87, 88]

In the German study,[89] 24 elite female soccer players of a German premier league soccer team performed an additional soccer-specific proprioceptive multistation training program over three years. Progression in level of difficulty from easy to complex was a main feature of the exercises. The duration of each exercise was between 15 and 30 seconds.

The exercises that were implemented were:

1. single-foot stand on right and left foot
2. jump forward in single-foot stand with flexed knee at landing and balancing
3. jump backward in single-foot stand and balancing
4. row jumping single foot
5. row jumping bipedal
6. obstacle course forward and backward
7. obstacle course sideways
8. bipedal jumping on forefoot
9. sideways jumping in single-legged stand
10. sitting on a wobble board with balancing torso
11. jumping forward over a line, landing with flexed knees, and balancing
12. standing on both hands and feet with diagonal balancing.

All exercises were performed with no additional weight; that is, players had to bear only their own body weight on one or two legs or all extremities depending on the exercise. In addition, balance training was implemented in soccer-specific match-play training on balance boards.

At the end of the three-year proprioceptive balance training intervention, non-contact hamstring injury rates were reduced from 22.4 to 8.2/1000 hours. Furthermore, the more minutes of balance training performed, the lower the rate of hamstring injuries.

Soft tissue therapy

Hoskins and Pollard[90] demonstrated that a soft tissue therapy program reduced the incidence of lower limb muscle strains, but not specifically hamstring strains, in a group of semi-elite AFL footballers. Treatment for the intervention group was individually determined and could involve manipulation/mobilization and/or soft tissue therapies to the spine and extremity. Minimum scheduling was one treatment per week for six weeks, one treatment per fortnight for three months, and then one treatment per month for the remainder of the season (three months).

No positive effect on hamstring injury prevention was found with stretching plus warm-up/cool-down.[91]

Another way of preventing hamstring injuries is to identify those at high risk of injury and modify their activity accordingly. Players can be regularly monitored during the season (e.g. following games) for signs of adverse reaction to load (e.g. palpation, pain/weakness with isometric maximum voluntary contraction [MVC] tests).

A promising clinical approach for the high-risk athlete

One test that may be helpful in screening or monitoring the state of a player's hamstrings during the season is an isometric maximum voluntary contraction (MVC). In this test the player is positioned with his or her hips and knees flexed to 90° and both heels resting on a firm plinth of adjustable height (Fig. 31.20). The cuff of a digital sphygmomanometer is pre-inflated to 10 mmHg and placed under one heel. The player pushes their heel into the cuff as hard as possible by flexing their knee without lifting their buttocks off the ground. The contraction is held for three seconds, and the peak pressure recorded. The process is repeated for the opposite leg.

The test is performed weekly one or two days post-match and any reduction in MVC is taken as a warning sign, and training load is reduced until the test returns to normal values.[92] This test may be particularly useful in those who have had a previous hamstring injury and are therefore at risk of a recurrence.

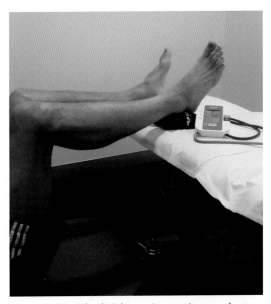

Figure 31.20 Schache's hamstring maximum voluntary contraction (MVC) test. The set-up used to measure an isometric maximum voluntary contraction (MVC) of the hamstrings with the digital sphygmomanometer

Referred pain to posterior thigh

The possibility of referred pain should always be considered in the athlete presenting with posterior thigh pain. Hamstring pain may be referred from the lumbar spine, the sacroiliac joint, or from soft tissues (e.g. the proximal fibers of the gluteus maximus and, especially, gluteus medius and the piriformis muscle) (Fig. 31.21). Often, there is a history of previous or current low back pain.

The slump test (Fig. 31.2g) should be used to detect neural mechanosensitivity. The test is positive when the patient's hamstring pain is reproduced with knee extension during neck flexion and subsequently relieved by neck extension. Examination may reveal reduced range of movement of the lumbar spine, tenderness and/or stiffness of lumbar intervertebral joint(s), or tenderness over the area of the sacroiliac joint.

A positive slump test is strongly suggestive of a referred component to the patient's pain. However, a negative slump test does not exclude the possibility of referred pain, and the lumbar spine should

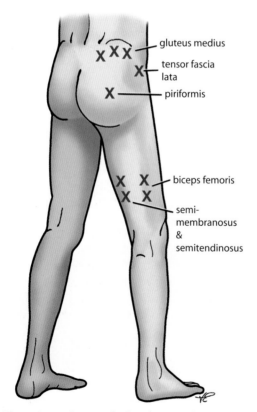

Figure 31.21 Pattern of referred pain to the hamstrings from trigger points

gluteus medius

tensor fascia lata

piriformis

biceps femoris

semi-membranosus & semitendinosus

be carefully examined to detect any intervertebral segment hypomobility. The slump stretch (Fig. 31.2g) has been advocated as a method of treatment of hamstring pain in Australian Rules footballers.[95]

Trigger points

Trigger points are common sources of referred pain to both the buttock (Chapter 27) and posterior thigh. The most common trigger points that refer pain to the mid-hamstring are in the gluteus minimus, gluteus medius, and piriformis muscles. The clinical syndrome associated with posterior thigh pain without evidence of hamstring muscle injury on MRI and reproduction of the patient's pain on palpation of gluteal trigger points is now well recognized and extremely common.[93]

The clinical features are described in Table 31.2 on page 600. The patient often complains of a feeling of tightness, cramping, or "twinge," or a feeling that the hamstring is "about to tear." On examination, there may be some localized tenderness in the hamstring although it is usually not focal, and there is restriction in hamstring and gluteal stretch. Firm palpation of the gluteal muscles will detect tight bands that contain active trigger points, which when firmly palpated are extremely tender, refer pain into the hamstring and elicit a "twitch response."

Treatment involves deactivating the trigger point either with ischemic pressure using the elbow (Fig. 31.22a) or dry needling (Fig. 31.22b). Following the local treatment, the tight muscle groups—the gluteals and hamstrings—should be stretched.

Lumbar spine

The lumbar spine is a source of pain referral to the posterior thigh. Unfortunately, it is difficult to distinguish between sources based on the behavior and distribution of the pain. Pain may be referred from the disk, zygoapophyseal joints, muscles, ligaments, or any structure that can produce pain locally in the lumbar spine.[94]

Nerve root compression may also be a cause of hamstring pain. Diagnostic blocks and provocation injections have been advocated to isolate sources of pain in the lumbar spine. However, in the clinical setting, this is often not possible. It is important to examine the lumbar spine carefully (Chapter 26). This will assist in the identification of the lumbar spine as a source of hamstring pain. Remember also that the lumbar spine may be a cause of lumbar pain indirectly. For example, the lumbar spine may cause a biomechanical block to hip extension, resulting in overload of the sacroiliac joint and referred pain to the hamstring group.

True nerve root compression is usually more definitive in its presentation. The patient may have associated neurological symptoms, such as numbness and loss of foot eversion. The management of these injuries usually involves an extended period of rest and, in certain cases, an epidural injection. In extreme cases, surgical decompression of the nerve root may be warranted.

Spondylolisthesis and spondylolysis (Chapter 26) have both been associated with hamstring pain and tightness.[96] Examination findings of positive lumbar quadrant tests or single-leg standing lumbar extension are suggestive of these conditions; these spinal pathologies can be confirmed on MRI or CT scan. Stabilization programs are the treatment of choice, as the deep abdominal muscles are deficient in people with back pain as a result of spondylolisthesis and spondylolysis.[97] In severe cases, clinicians have resorted to corticosteroid injection (+/− neuroablation using pulsed radiofrequency) under X-ray control into the deficient pars interarticularis.[98] This has low-level evidence in its support; however, it may reduce pain from spondylolysis.

 Not all lumbar-spine associated hamstring pain is due to sport-related loading of the lumbar spine.

The lumbar spine can cause pain as a result of prolonged sitting or bending forward. Sportspeople in sedentary occupations should be aware that sitting posture is a cause of injury to the hamstring. Travel involving prolonged sitting prior to training and competition may cause injury. Prolonged sitting results in sustained lumbar flexion, whereas running requires good lumbar extension. Requiring the lumbar spine to "switch" from one position to the other can cause problems. Care should be undertaken to limit prolonged sitting and to provide adequate lumbar support.

Sacroiliac complex
Sacroiliac joint abnormalities can refer pain into the hamstring or cause indirect pain in the hamstring similar to the lumbar spine. Problems of the sacroiliac joint are discussed in Chapter 27.

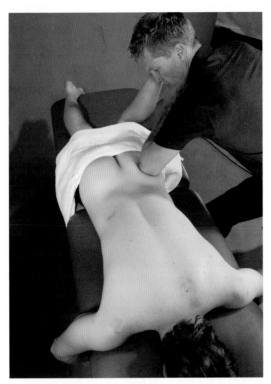
Figure 31.22 Treatment of gluteal trigger points
(a) Elbow pressure

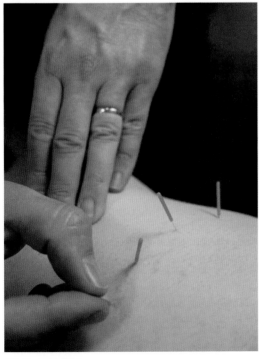
(b) Dry needling

Other hamstring injuries

Avulsion of the hamstring from the ischial tuberosity

Avulsion of the hamstring from the ischial tuberosity is seen in two groups of patients—adolescents who, instead of sustaining a hamstring muscle tear, tear their hamstring from its bony attachment at the ischium, and older people, who often have a history of chronic tendinopathy.

Sportspeople aged about 14–18 years are prone to avulsions of the ischial apophysis. Any young adult presenting with an incident of acute severe hamstring pain should be treated as if he or she has an avulsion until proven otherwise. Plain X-ray, CT scan, or MRI may be used to identify the avulsion. According to the literature, a separation of greater than 2 cm (1 in.) requires open reduction and internal fixation.[99] Separations of less than 2 cm (1 in.) are often managed conservatively, requiring 8–12 weeks' rest. However, some caution should be exercised with conservative management, as these sportspeople can be left with decreased power in their hamstrings, which limits future sporting performance. Occasionally, there is neurological involvement associated with this injury.[99]

In adults, complete rupture of the ischial origin of the hamstring muscles is relatively rare.[100, 101] The injury results from a sudden forceful flexion of the hip joint when the knee is fully extended and the hamstring muscles powerfully contracted. The most common activities associated with the rupture are waterskiing and power lifting. If treated with prompt surgery, the final functional results are good.

Common conjoint tendon tear

A significant and complex hamstring injury involving a full-thickness disruption through both the conjoint tendon of the hamstring muscle complex and the proximal musculotendinous junction of both the biceps femoris long head and semitendinosus muscles has recently been described in a footballer[102] (Fig. 31.23). The injury was successfully managed via surgical repair. The player resumed full football training activities approximately 16 weeks post surgery and was completely symptom-free.

Upper hamstring tendinopathy

Tendinopathy of the proximal hamstring tendon or "high hamstring tendinopathy" is increasingly being recognized as an important cause of chronic pain in the active population. Patients usually present with

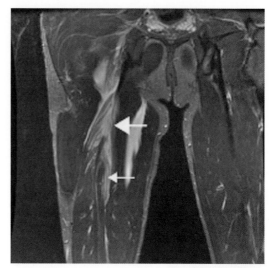

Figure 31.23 Coronal STIR (short TI inversion recovery) image through the proximal right hamstring muscle complex demonstrates discontinuity of the conjoint tendon (large arrow) compatible with full thickness disruption. The tendon tear commences 9.5 cm distal to the ischial tuberosity with the defect measuring 3.5 cm in maximal craniocaudal dimension. Note the grade 2 strains pattern of edema in the muscle fibers of semitendinosus (small arrow), which arises from the medial aspect of the conjoint tendon
FROM SCHACHE ET AL. RUPTURE OF THE CONJOINT TENDON AT THE PROXIMAL MUSCULOTENDINOUS JUNCTION OF THE BICEPS FEMORIS LONG HEAD: A CASE REPORT. *KNEE SURG SPORTS TRAUMATOL ARTHROSC* 2008;16:797–802

subacute onset of deep buttock or thigh pain that is exacerbated by repetitive activity (such as long distance running) and often is aggravated by sitting, stretching, and progressive strengthening. MRI is more sensitive overall than ultrasound in the diagnosis of these abnormalities.

Initial treatment in clinical practice should include progressive strengthening. A significant number of patients, however, fail to respond to this conservative regimen. The use of ultrasound-guided injections of corticosteroid and local anesthetic has been shown to be safe and effective in reducing pain in the short term, but is associated with a high recurrence rate when used in isolation.[103] This procedure should be performed in conjunction with a progressive strengthening program to achieve optimal results and avoid recurrent injury.

Shock wave treatment has recently been shown to be effective in the treatment of high hamstring tendinopathy.[104]

Lower hamstring tendinopathy

Lower hamstring tendinopathy is often the result of large amounts of resisted flexion knee exercises. It also occurs in sprinters. The pain pattern is inflammatory and the pain is localized to the tendons of the hamstring group. Posterior capsular pain should be differentiated from tendinopathy. Pain associated with knee hyperextension (such as in kicking) is usually capsular. Management consists of appropriate rehabilitation, focusing on biomechanical defects. Taping may help to reduce load.

Less common causes

Nerve entrapments

The hamstring group is supplied by the tibial branch of the sciatic nerve except for the short head of the biceps femoris, which is supplied by the peroneal branch of the sciatic nerve. These nerves arise from the lumbosacral plexus, specifically from the roots of L5, S1 and S2.

Nerve damage can occur at a variety of sites, resulting in pain in the posterior thigh. Compression of the nerve roots of the sacral plexus often results in pain in the hamstring group. Usually this is distinguished from other conditions by the identification of associated neurological symptoms, such as alteration in sensation, loss of the Achilles reflex, or weakness in muscles not in the hamstring group (such as the ankle evertors).

The sciatic nerve may be damaged or compressed at any point along its pathway as a result of direct impact or pelvic trauma. Compression of the nerve at the level of the piriformis has been described as an alternative cause of sciatica.[105] However, work by McCrory and Bell suggests that it is not only the piriformis but also the other hip external rotators that may cause compression of the sciatic nerve.[106]

The peripheral nerves of the body may also be a source of posterior thigh pain. The posterior cutaneous nerve of the thigh and the inferior cluneal nerve supply the skin over the posterior thigh. The posterior cutaneous nerve of the thigh has been described as the source of pain in piriformis syndrome as an alternative to the sciatic nerve.[106] If symptoms do not extend below the knee and there is no associated loss of neurological function in the structures supplied by the sciatic nerve, then the posterior cutaneous nerve of the thigh should be considered.

Ischial bursitis

It is often difficult to distinguish between high hamstring tendinopathy and ischial bursitis. Both conditions present as inflammatory pain at the origin of the hamstring muscle. An inflamed bursa is not readily palpated; however, sportspeople tend to complain of pain when sitting on hard surfaces where the ischium is under pressure. Ultrasound or MRI can confirm the presence of a fluid-filled bursa.

Anti-inflammatory medications combined with ice and rest are of limited benefit. Corticosteroid injections can be performed under X-ray control, but the results are not always satisfactory.

Adductor magnus strains

Adductor magnus strains are rare but, when they do occur, behave similarly to a hamstring strain. The mechanism tends to be more of a rotatory action of eccentric internal rotation on one hip. Prognosis tends to be far better than for hamstring strains; therefore, it is important to differentiate it from strains in the hamstring. The key to differentiating this condition is careful palpation to elicit the precise location of the tissue damage. Side-lying on the affected leg allows that hamstring group to fall laterally, so that ready access can be made to the adductor magnus.

Compartment syndrome of the posterior thigh

Although nowhere near as common as lower leg compartment syndromes, the posterior thigh can be affected by a compartment syndrome. Patients present with dull pain, stiffness, cramps, and weakness of the posterior thigh during and after training.[107] Two groups of patients with this syndrome are seen—endurance sportspeople without a history of trauma, and sportspeople with a history of hamstring injury.

Conservative management has not been successful, and posterior fasciotomy of the thigh appears to be an effective treatment.[107]

Vascular

Endofibrosis of the external iliac artery usually produces pain in the lateral and anterior thigh. However, in some cases, pain may be experienced in the posterior thigh. This condition is associated with cycling[108] and has been observed in triathletes. The pain is claudicant in nature. Pain may arise after 15–20 minutes of exercise but usually ceases immediately with the cessation of exercise.

On examination, a bruit is heard during the exercise that causes the pain. Diagnosis may be confirmed with echography or arteriography. If the condition is affecting performance, then treatment is either surgical or balloon dilation of the area where the artery is narrowed.

REFERENCES

1. Heiderscheit BC, Sherry MA, Silder A et al. Hamstring strain injuries: recommendations for diagnosis, rehabilitation, and injury prevention. *J Orth Sports Phys Ther* 2010;40(2):67–81.

2. Orchard J, Best TM, Verrall GM. Return to play following muscle strains. *Clin J Sport Med* 2005;15(6):436–41.

3. Battermann N, Appell HJ, Dargel J et al. An anatomical study of the proximal hamstring muscle complex to elucidate muscle strains in this region. *Int J Sports Med* 2011;32(3):211–5.

4. Tubbs RS, Caycedo FJ, Oakes WJ et al. Descriptive anatomy of the insertion of the biceps femoris muscle. *Clin Anat* 2006;19(6):517–21.

5. Connell DA, Schneider-Kolsky ME, Hoving JL et al. Longitudinal study comparing sonographic and MRI assessments of acute and healing hamstring injuries. *Am J Roentgenol* 2004;183(4):975–84.

6. Gibbs NJ, Cross TM, Cameron M et al. The accuracy of MRI in predicting recovery and recurrence of acute grade one hamstring muscle strains within the same season in Australia Rules football players. *J Sci Med Sport* 2004;7(2):248–58.

7. Verrall GM, Slavotinek JP, Barnes PG et al. Diagnostic and prognostic value of clinical findings in 83 athletes with posterior thigh injury – comparison of clinical findings with magnetic resonance imaging documentation of hamstring muscle strain. *Am J Sports Med* 2003;31(6):969–73.

8. Warren P, Gabbe BJ, Schneider-Kolsky M et al. Clinical predictors of time to return to competition and of recurrence following hamstring strain in elite Australian footballers. *Br J Sports Med* 2010;44(6):415–19.

9. Orchard J, Seward H. Epidemiology of injuries in the Australian Football League, seasons 1997–2000. *Br J Sports Med* 2002;36(1):39–44.

10. Hawkins RD, Fuller CW. A prospective epidemiological study of injuries in four English professional football clubs. *Br J Sports Med* 1999;33(3):196–203.

11. Hawkins RD, Hulse MA, Wilkinson C et al. The association football medical research programme: an audit of injuries in professional football. *Br J Sports Med* 2001;35(1):43–7.

12. Woods C, Hawkins RD, Maltby S et al. The Football Association Medical Research Programme: an audit of injuries in professional football – analysis of hamstring injuries. *Br J Sports Med* 2004;38(1):36–41.

13. Askling C, Lund H, Saartok T et al. Self-reported hamstring injuries in student-dancers. *Scand J Med Sci Sports* 2002;12(4):230–35.

14. Askling C, Thorstensson A. Hamstring muscle strain in sprinters. *New Studies in Athletics* 2008;23:67–79.

15. Askling C, Tengvar M, Saartok T et al. Sports related hamstring strains – two cases with different etiologies and injury sites. *Scand J Med Sci Sports* 2000;10(5):304–7.

16. Askling CM, Tengvar M, Saartok T et al. Acute first-time hamstring strains during slow-speed stretching – clinical, magnetic resonance imaging, and recovery characteristics. *Am J Sports Med* 2007;35:1716–24.

17. Askling CM, Tengvart M, Saartok T et al. Acute first-time hamstring strains during high-speed running – a longitudinal study including clinical and magnetic resonance imaging findings. *Am J Sports Med* 2007;35(2):197–206.

18. Brooks JHM, Fuller CW, Reddin DB. Incidence, risk, and prevention of hamstring muscle injuries in professional rugby union. *Am J Sports Med* 2006;34(8):1297–306.

19. Gabbe BJ, Bennell KL, Finch CF et al. Predictors of hamstring injury at the elite level of Australian football. *Scand J Med Sci Sports* 2006;16(1):7–13.

20. Askling C, Saartok T, Thorstensson A. Type of acute hamstring strain affects flexibility, strength, and time to return to pre-injury level. *Br J Sports Med* 2006;40(1):40–4.

21. Woodley SJ, Mercer SR. Hamstring muscles: architecture and innervation. *Cells Tissues Organs* 2005;179(3):125–41.

22. Askling CM, Tengvar M, Saartok T et al. Proximal hamstring strains of stretching type in different sports – injury situations, clinical and magnetic resonance imaging characteristics, and return to sport. *Am J Sports Med* 2008;36(9):1799–804.

23. Heiderscheit BC, Hoerth DM, Chumanov ES et al. Identifying the time of occurrence of a hamstring strain injury during treadmill running: a case study. *Clin Biomech* 2005;20(10):1072–8.

24. Schache AG, Wrigley TV, Baker R et al. Biomechanical response to hamstring muscle strain injury. *Gait Posture* 2009;29(2):332–8.

25. Chumanov E, Heiderscheit B, Thelen D. Hamstring musculotendon dynamics during stance and swing phases of high-speed running. *Med Sci Sports Exerc* 2011;43(3):525–32.

26. Koulouris G, Connell DA, Brukner P et al. Magnetic resonance imaging parameters for assessing risk of

B

recurrent hamstring injuries in elite athletes. *Am J Sports Med* 2007;35(9):1500–6.

27. Verrall GM, Slavotinek JP, Barnes PC et al. Assessment of physical examination and magnetic resonance imaging findings of hamstring injury as predictors for recurrent injury. *J Orth Sports Phys Ther* 2006;36(4):215–24.

28. Slavotinek JP, Verrall GM, Fon GT. Hamstring injury in athletes: using MR imaging measurements to compare extent of muscle injury with amount of time lost from competition. *Am J Roentgenol.* 2002;179:1621–8.

29. Schneider-Kolsky ME, Hoving JL, Warren P et al. A comparison between clinical assessment and magnetic resonance imaging of acute hamstring injuries. *Am J Sports Med* 2006;34:1008–15.

30. Mason DL, Dickens V, Vail A. Rehabilitation for hamstring injuries. *Cochrane Data Syst Rev* 2007(1):CD004575.

31. Cibulka MT, Rose SJ, Delitto A et al. Hamstring muscle strain treated by mobilizing the sacroiliac joint. *Phys Ther* 1986;66(8):1220–3.

32. Sherry MA, Best TM. A comparison of 2 rehabilitation programs in the treatment of acute hamstring strains. *J Orth Sports Phys Ther* 2004;34(3):116–25.

33. Malliaropoulos N, Papalexandris S, Papalada A et al. The role of stretching in rehabilitation of hamstring injuries: 80 athletes follow-up. *Med Sci Sports Exerc* 2004;36(5):756–9.

34. Petersen J, Hölmich P. Evidence-based prevention of hamstring injuries in sport. *Br J Sports Med* 2005;39:319–23.

35. Khan KM, Scott A. Mechanotherapy: how physical therapists' prescription of exercise promotes tissue repair. *Br J Sports Med* 2009;43(4):247–52.

36. Reynolds JF, Noakes TD, Schwellnus MP. Non-steroidal anti-inflammatory drugs fail to enhance healing of acute hamstring injuries treated with physiotherapy. *S Afr Med J* 1995;85:517–22.

37. Levine WN, Bergfeld JA, Tessendorf W et al. Intramuscular corticosteroid injection for hamstring injuries. A 13-year experience in the National Football League. *Am J Sports Med* 2000;28(3):297–300.

38. Linklater JM, Hamilton B, Carmichael J et al. Hamstring injuries: anatomy, imaging, and intervention. *Semin Musculoskelet Radiol* 2010;14(2):131–61.

39. Hamilton B, Knez W, Eirale C et al. Platelet rich plasma for acute muscle injury. *Acta Orthop Belg* 2010;76(4):443–8.

40. Orchard JW, Best TM, Mueller-Wohlfahrt HW et al. The early management of muscle strains in the elite athlete: best practice in a world with a limited evidence basis. *Br J Sports Med* 2008;42(3):158–9.

41. Chumanov ES, Heiderscheit BC, Thelen DG. The effect of speed and influence of individual muscles on hamstring mechanics during the swing phase of sprinting. *J Biomech* 2007;40(16):3555–62.

42. Gabbe BJ, Bennell KL, Finch CF. Why are older Australian football players at greater risk of hamstring injury? *J Sci Med Sport* 2006;9(4):327–33.

43. Aagaard P, Simonsen EB, Trolle M et al. Specificity of training velocity and training load on gains in isokinetic knee joint strength. *Acta Physiol Scand* 1996;156(2):123–9.

44. Brockett CL, Morgan DL, Proske U. Human hamstring muscles adapt to eccentric exercise by changing optimum length. *Med Sci Sports Exerc* 2001;33(5):783–90.

45. Proske U, Morgan DL, Brockett CL et al. Indentifying athletes at risk of hamstring strains and how to protect them. *Clin Exp Pharmacol Physiol* 2004;31(8):546–50.

46. Seger JY, Thorstensson A. Effects of eccentric versus concentric training on thigh muscle strength and EMG. *Int J Sports Med* 2005;26(1):45–52.

47. Mjolsnes R, Arnason A, Osthagen T et al. A 10-week randomized trial comparing eccentric vs. concentric hamstring strength training in well-trained soccer players. *Scand J Med Sci Sports* 2004;14:311–17.

48. Arnason A, Andersen TE, Holme I et al. Prevention of hamstring strains in elite soccer: an intervention study. *Scan J Med Sci Sports* 2008;18:40–8.

49. Petersen J, Thorborg K, Nielsen M et al. Eccentric strength training is effective in preventing hamstring injuries in football: a cluster-randomised trial including 942 football players. *Knee Surg Sports Traumatol Arthr* 2010;18 (Supplement 1):S56.

50. Waters RL, Perry J, McDaniels JM et al. The relative strength of the hamstrings during hip extension. *J Bone Joint Surg* 1973;56(a)(8):1592–7.

51. Lieberman DE, Raichlen DA, Pontzer H et al. The human gluteus maximus and its role in running. *J Experiment Biol* 2006;209(11):2143–55.

52. Mendiguchia J, Brughelli M. A return-to-sport algorithm for acute hamstring injuries. *Phys Ther Sport* 2011;12(1):2–14.

53. Brughelli M, Cronin J. Preventing hamstring injuries in sport. *Strength Condition J* 2008;30(1):55–64.

54. Hides JA, Lambrecht G, Richardson CA et al. The effects of rehabilitation on the muscles of the trunk following prolonged bed rest. *Eur Spine J* 2011;20(5):808–18.

55. Hides JA, Stanton WR, McMahon S et al. Effect of stabilization training on multifidus muscle cross-sectional area among young elite cricketers with low back pain. *J Orth Sports Phys Ther* 2008;30(3):101–8.

56. Cameron ML, Adams RD, Maher CG et al. Effect of the HamSprint Drills training programme on lower limb neuromuscular control in Australian football players. *J Sci Med Sport* 2009;12(1):24–30.

57. Cameron M, Adams R, Maher C. Motor control and strength as predictors of hamstring injury in elite players of Australian football. *Phys Ther Sport* 2003;4(4):159–66.

58. Verrall GM, Slavotinek JP, Barnes PG. The effect of sports-specific training on reducing the incidence of hamstring injuries in professional Australian Rules football players. *Br J Sports Med* 2005;39(6):363–8.

59. Croisier JL, Ganteaume S, Binet J et al. Strength imbalances and prevention of hamstring injury in professional soccer players – a prospective study. *Am J Sports Med* 2008;36(8):1469–75.

60. Waldén M, Hägglund M, Ekstrand J. UEFA Champions League study: a prospective study of injuries in professional football during the 2001–2002 season. *Br J Sports Med* 2005;39(8):542–6.

61. Bradley PS, Portas MD. The relationship between preseason range of motion and muscle strain injury in elite soccer players. *J Strength Cond Res* 2007;21(4):1155–9.

62. Witvrouw E, Danneels L, Asselman P et al. Muscle flexibility as a risk factor for developing muscle injuries in male professional soccer players – a prospective study. *Am J Sports Med* 2003;31(1):41–6.

63. Henderson G, Barnes CA, Portas MD. Factors associated with increased propensity for hamstring injury in English Premier League soccer players. *J Sci Med Sport* 2010;13(4):397–402.

64. Drezner JA. Practical management: Hamstring muscle injuries. *Clin J Sport Med* 2003;13(1):48–52.

65. Croisier J-L. Factors associated with recurrent hamstring injuries. *Sports Med* 2004;34(10):681–95.

66. Croisier J-L, Forthomme B, Namurois M-H et al. Hamstring muscle strain recurrence and strength performance disorders. *Am J Sports Med* 2002;30(2):199–203.

67. Askling CM, Nilsson J, Thorstensson A. A new hamstring test to complement the common clinical examination before return to sport after injury. *Knee Surg Sports Traumatol Arthrosc* 2010;18(12):1798–803.

68. Foreman TK, Addy T, Baker S et al. Prospective studies into the causation of hamstring injuries in sport: a systematic review. *Phys Ther Sport* 2006;7(2):101–9.

69. Prior M, Guerin M, Grimmer K. An evidence-based approach to hamstring strain injury: a systematic review of the literature. *Sports Health* 2009;1(2):154–64.

70. Arnason A, Sigurdsson SB, Gudmundsson A et al. Risk factors for injuries in football. *Am J Sports Med* 2004;32(1 suppl):5–16S.

71. Engebretsen AH, Myklebust G, Holme I et al. Intrinsic risk factors for hamstring injuries among male soccer players: a prospective cohort study. *Am J Sports Med* 2010;38(6):1147–53.

72. Gabbe BJ, Finch CF, Bennell KL et al. Risk factors for hamstring injuries in community level Australian football. *Br J Sports Med* 2005;39(2):106–10.

73. Verrall GM, Slavotinek JP, Barnes PG et al. Clinical risk factors for hamstring muscle strain injury: a prospective study with correlation of injury by magnetic resonance imaging. *Br J Sports Med* 2001;35(6):435–9.

74. Orchard JW. Intrinsic and extrinsic risk factors for muscle strains in Australian football. *Am J Sports Med* 2001;29(3):300–3.

75. Orchard JW, Farhart P, Leopold C. Lumbar spine region pathology and hamstring and calf injuries in athletes: is there a connection? *Br J Sports Med* 2004;38(4):502–4.

76. Lee MJC, Reid SL, Elliott BC et al. Running biomechanics and lower limb strength associated with prior hamstring injury. *Med Sci Sports Exerc* 2009;41(10):1942–51.

77. Silder A, Thelen DG, Heiderscheit BC. Effects of prior hamstring strain injury on strength, flexibility, and running mechanics. *Clin Biomech* 2010;25(7):681–86.

78. Silder A, Heiderscheit B, Thelen D et al. MR observations of long-term musculotendon remodeling following a hamstring strain injury. *Skel Radiol* 2008;37(12):1101–9.

79. Silder A, Reeder SB, Thelen DG. The influence of prior hamstring injury on lengthening muscle tissue mechanics. *J Biomech* 2010;43(12):2254–60.

80. Bennell K, Wajswelner H, Lew P et al. Isokinetic strength testing does not predict hamstring injury in Australian Rules footballers. *Br J Sports Med* 1998;32(4):309–14.

81. Orchard J, Marsden J, Lord S et al. Preseason hamstring muscle weakness associated with hamstring muscle injury in Australian footballers. *Am J Sports Med* 1997;25(1):81–5.

82. Yeung SS, Suen AMY, Yeung EW. A prospective cohort study of hamstring injuries in competitive sprinters: preseason muscle imbalance as a possible risk factor. *Br J Sports Med* 2009;43(8):589–94.

83. Elliott MC, Zarins B, Powell JW et al. Hamstring muscle strains in professional football players. A 10-year review. *Am J Sports Med* 2011;39(4): 843–50.

84. Goldman EF, Jones DE. Interventions for preventing hamstring injuries. *Coch Data Syst Rev* 2010; 20(1): CD006782.

85. Askling C, Karlsson J, Thorstensson A. Hamstring injury occurrence in elite soccer players after preseason strength training with eccentric overload. *Scand J Med Sci Sports* 2003;13:244–50.

86. Engebretsen AH, Myklebust G, Holme I et al. Prevention of injuries among male soccer players. A prospective, randomized intervention study targeting players with previous injuries of reduced function. *Am J Sports Med* 2008;36(6):1052–60.

87. Söderman K, Werner S, Pietilä T et al. Balance board training: prevention of traumatic injuries of the lower extremities in female soccer players? A prospective randomized intervention study. *Knee Surg Sports Traumatol Arthrosc* 2000;8(6):356–63.

88. Emery CA, Rose MS, McAllister JR et al. A prevention strategy to reduce the incidence of injury in high school basketball: a cluster randomized controlled trial. *Clin J Sport Med* 2007;17(1):17–24.

89. Kraemer R, Knobloch K. A soccer-specific balance training program for hamstring muscle and patellar and achilles tendon injuries: an intervention study in premier league female soccer. *Am J Sports Med* 2009;37:1384–93.

90. Hoskins W, Pollard H. The effect of a sports chiropractic manual therapy intervention on the prevention of back pain, hamstring and lower limb injuries in semielite Australian Rules footballers: a randomized controlled trial. *BMC Musculoskel Dis* 2010;11:64–75.

91. Van Mechelen W, Hlobil H, Kemper HC et al. Prevention of running injuries by warm-up, cool-down, and stretching exercises. *Am J Sports Med* 1993;21(5):711–19.

92. Schache AG, Crossley KM, Macindoe IG et al. Can a clinical test of hamstring strength identify football players at risk of hamstring strain? *Knee Surg Sports Traumatol Arthrosc* 2010;19(1):38–41.

93. Huguenin L, Brukner PD, McCrory P et al. Effect of dry needling of gluteal muscles on straight leg raise: a randomised, placebo controlled, double blind trial. *Br J Sports Med* 2005;39(2):84–90.

94. Bogduk N. *Clinical anatomy of the lumbar spine and sacrum.* 4th edn. Edinburgh: Elsevier Churchill Livingstone, 2004.

95. Kornberg C, Lew P. The effect of stretching neural structures on grade one hamstring injuries. *J Orth Sports Phys Ther* 1989;10(12):481–7.

96. Barash HL, Galante JO et al. Spondylolisthesis and tight hamstrings. *J Bone Joint Surg* 1970;52A(7): 1319–28.

97. O'Sullivan PB, Twomey L, Allison GT. Dynamic stabilization of the lumbar spine. *Clin Rev Phys Rehab Med* 1997;9(3 & 4):315–30.

98. Misaggi B, Gallazzi M, Colombo M et al. Articular facets syndrome: diagnostic grading and treatment options. *Eur Spine J* 2009;18 Suppl(1):49–51.

99. Servant CTJ, Jones CB. Displaced avulsion of the ischial apophysis: a hamstring injury requiring internal fixation. *Br J Sports Med* 1998;32:255–7.

100. Cross MJ, Vandersluis R, Wood D et al. Surgical repair of chronic complete hamstring tendon rupture in the adult patient. *Am J Sports Med* 1998;26(6):785–8.

101. Klingele KE, Sallay PI. Surgical repair of complete proximal hamstring tendon rupture. *Am J Sports Med* 2002;30(5):742–7.

102. Schache AG, Koulouris G, Kofoed W et al. Rupture of the conjoint tendon at the proximal musculotendinous junction of the biceps femoris long head: a case report. *Knee Surg Sports Traumatol Arthrosc* 2008;16:797–802.

103. Zissen MH, Wallace G, Stevens KJ et al. High hamstring tendinopathy: MRI and ultrasound imaging and therapeutic efficacy of percutaneous corticosteroid injection. *AJR Am J Roentgenol* 2010;195(4):993–8.

104. Cacchio A, Rompe JD, Furia JP et al. Shockwave therapy for the treatment of chronic proximal hamstring tendinopathy in professional athletes. *Am J Sports Med* 2011;39(1):146–53.

105. Puranen J, Orava S. The hamstring syndrome. A new diagnosis of gluteal sciatic pain. *Am J Sports Med* 1988;16(5):517–21.

106. McCrory P, Bell S, Bradshaw C. Nerve entrapment of the lower leg, ankle and foot in sport. *Sports Med* 2002;32(6):371–91.

107. Orava S, Rantanen J, Kujala UM. Fasciotomy of the posterior femoral muscle compartment in athletes. *Int J Sports Med* 1998;19(1):71–5.

108. Abraham P, Saumet JL, Chevalier JM. External iliac artery endofibrosis in athletes. *Sports Med* 1997;24(4):221–6.

Chapter 32

Acute knee injuries

with RICHARD FROBELL, RANDALL COOPER, HAYDEN MORRIS, and ELIZABETH ARENDT

As for the rupture there is no missing it. I didn't so much hear it but the "pop" like a thick elastic giving way reverberated through [my] body. It's distinct—it's clear what's happened. http://tiny.cc/u04gg

For many sportspeople, the most fearful injury is that of the acute knee—it can spell the end of a professional career. Even for recreational sportspeople, an acute knee injury may be the catalyst for early arthritis. Acute knee injuries are common in all sports that require twisting movements and sudden changes of direction, especially the various types of football, basketball, netball, and alpine skiing.

Functional anatomy

The knee joint can be divided into two parts—the tibiofemoral joint with its associated collateral ligaments, cruciate ligaments, and menisci; and the patellofemoral joint, which obtains stability from the medial and lateral retinaculum, and the large extensor mechanism tendons (quadriceps and patellar tendons) which encase the patella distally before its insertion on the proximal tibia. Most commonly we refer to the tibiofemoral joint as the knee joint. The anatomy of the knee joint is shown in Figure 32.1.

The two cruciate ("cross") ligaments, anterior and posterior, are often referred to as the "crucial" ligaments, because of their importance in providing knee stability. They are named anterior and posterior in

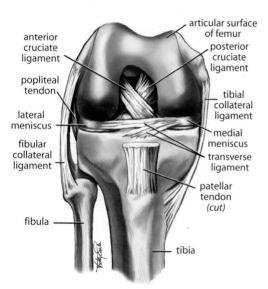

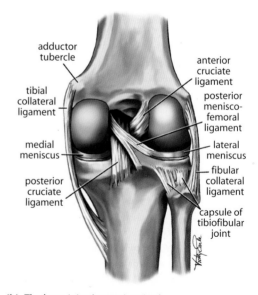

Figure 32.1 Anatomy of the knee joint

(a) The knee joint (anterior view)

(b) The knee joint (posterior view)

relation to their attachment to the tibia. The anterior cruciate ligament (ACL) prevents forward movement of the tibia in relation to the femur, and controls rotational movement of the tibia under the femur. The posterior cruciate ligament (PCL) prevents the femur from sliding forward off the tibial plateau.

The ACL is essential for control in pivoting movements. If the ACL is not functional, the tibia may rotate under the femur in an anterolateral direction, such as when a sportsperson attempts to land from a jump, pivot, or stop suddenly. The PCL stabilizes the body (femur) above the tibia. In its absence, the femur wants to shift forward on the tibia. This shift forward is accentuated when one tries to run down an incline or descend stairs.

The two collateral ligaments—the medial and the lateral—provide medial and lateral stability to the knee joint. The superficial medial collateral ligament (MCL) is extra-capsular. The deep layer, or coronary ligament, attaches to the joint margins and has an attachment from its deep layer to the medial meniscus. The MCL prevents excessive medial opening (i.e. valgus) of the tibiofemoral joint.

The lateral collateral ligament (LCL) is a narrow strong cord; it has no attachment to the lateral meniscus. It prevents lateral opening of the tibia on the femur during varus stress; it also stabilizes the upright knee in single-leg stance phase of gait.

The medial and lateral menisci are intra-articular and attach to the capsule layer at the level of the joint line. The menisci buffer some of the forces placed through the knee joint, and protect the otherwise exposed articular surfaces from damage. By increasing the concavity of the tibia, they help stabilize the knee. As the menisci contribute to joint lubrication and nutrition. it is important to preserve as much of them as possible after injury.

Clinical perspective

The acute knee injury of greatest concern to the sportsperson is the tear of the ACL. Meniscal injuries are common among sportspeople, either in isolation or combined with a ligament injury (e.g. combined with injury of the MCL or ACL). The articular cartilage of the knee is often damaged in association with ligament or meniscal injuries, which, depending on the size and/or location, can accelerate the development of arthritis.[1]

Acute knee injuries occurring in sport are listed in Table 32.1.

Does this patient have a significant knee injury?

Whether the patient has a significant injury is critical. To ascertain this, consider the following elements of the patient's story:

- the mechanism of injury (low energy force or high energy force)
- the amount of pain and disability at the time of injury
- the presence and timing of onset of swelling—which may be a clue to hemarthrosis (joint bleeding)
- the degree of disability on presentation to the clinician
- patient-specific vulnerabilities (previous injury, medical comorbidities that can affect bone and/ or tendon health).

In the majority of cases, an acute knee injury can be diagnosed with an appropriate history and examination. The main goals of assessment are:

- to determine which structures have been damaged
- to determine the extent of damage to each structure
- to determine the degree of joint/limb disability to provide safe and timely initial management.

Table 32.1 Causes of acute knee pain[(a)]

Common	Less common	Not to be missed
Medial meniscus tear	Patellar tendon rupture	Fracture of the tibial plateau
MCL sprain	Quadriceps tendon rupture	Avulsion fracture of tibial spine
ACL sprain (rupture)	Acute patellofemoral contusion	Osteochondritis dissecans (in
Lateral meniscus tear	LCL sprain	adolescents)
Articular cartilage injury	Bursal hematoma/bursitis	Complex regional pain syndrome
PCL sprain	Acute fat pad impingement	type 1 (post injury)
Patellar dislocation	Avulsion of biceps femoris tendon	Quadriceps rupture
	Dislocated superior tibiofibular joint	

[(a)] All these conditions may occur in isolation or, commonly, in association with other conditions

History

It is absolutely critical to ask the patient to tell his or her own story of the injury. The quote that opens this chapter provides a great example of how lucid a patient can be. Once the patient has explained what happened, the practitioner may elicit additional aspects of the history.

Important components of the history include:

- a description of the precise mechanism of injury and the subsequent symptoms (e.g. pain and "giving way")
- a demonstration by the patient if possible, on the uninjured knee, of the stress applied at the time of injury
- the location of pain—pain associated with cruciate ligament injuries is often poorly localized (or emanates from the lateral tibial plateau); pain from injuries to the collateral ligaments is usually fairly well localized
- the severity of pain—this does not always correlate with the severity of the injury, although most ACL injuries are usually painful immediately.

The degree and time of onset of swelling can reflect either intra-articular or extra-articular injury and, thus, provide an important clue to the injured structure (see Table 32.2). Intra-articular swelling (e.g. hemarthrosis) is usually voluminous (obvious) and develops within one or two hours of the injury.

The causes of hemarthrosis are:

- major ligament rupture
  - ACL
  - PCL
- patellar dislocation
- osteochondral fracture
- peripheral tear of the meniscus—more common medially
- acute fat pad impingement
- bleeding diathesis (rare).

Lipohemarthrosis (fat and blood in the joint) is caused by an intra-articular fracture. Lipohemarthrosis presents in a similar manner to hemarthrosis.

An effusion that develops after a few hours or, more commonly, the following day represents reactive synovitis and is a feature of meniscal and chondral injuries. There is usually little effusion with collateral ligament injuries.

If a patient volunteers having heard a "pop," a "snap," or a "tear," the injury should be considered an ACL tear until proven otherwise.

Patients presenting with a sensation of something having "moved" or "popped out" in the knee should not be assumed to have suffered a patellar dislocation. This symptom is more commonly associated with an ACL rupture. There may be associated "clicking" or "locking," and this is often seen with meniscal injuries.

"Locking" is classically associated with a loose body or displaced meniscal tear. Locking does not mean locked in one knee position; the term is used when significant loss of passive range of motion is present, especially loss of full extension. It is helpful to ask the patient in what "position" the knee locks. If the patient reports that the knee locks when it is straight, and does not bend, this usually is a manifestation of patellofemoral pain and injury—the kneecap is unable to engage in the groove secondary to pain.

The symptom of "giving way" can occur with instability, such as in ACL deficiency. Instability may also occur with meniscal tears, articular cartilage damage, patellofemoral pain (Chapter 33) and severe knee pain. In the latter cases of knee *pain* instability, a careful history will reveal more of a "jack-knife" (collapsing) phenomenon in flexion rather than a true "giving way" in extension.

Patients with recurrent patellar dislocation and those with loose bodies in the knee can describe similar sensations. If a patient reports feeling unstable on steps, this is most often a reflection of quadriceps weakness and/or pain, and rarely represents true kneecap instability.

The comprehensive history will also include:

- the initial management of the injury
- the degree of disability

Table 32.2 Time relationship of swelling to diagnosis

Immediate (0–2 hours) (hemarthrosis)	Delayed (6–24 hours) (effusion)	No swelling
ACL rupture	Meniscus	MCL sprain (superficial)
Patellar dislocation	Smaller chondral lesion	
Major chondral lesion		

- a history of previous injury to either knee or any previous surgery
- the patient's age, occupation, type of sport and leisure activities, and the level of sport played.

If the patient is a good historian, the diagnosis will be obvious in most cases.

Examination

Each structure that may be injured must be examined. Important clues to diagnosis include the presence or absence of effusion or hemarthrosis, the range of motion, and tests of the ligaments and menisci.

 Knee examination is demonstrated in detail in the *Clinical Sports Medicine* masterclasses at www.clinicalsportsmedicine.com.

Examination includes:

A. Observation
1. standing
2. walking
3. supine (Fig. 32.2a)

B. Active movements
1. flexion
2. extension
3. straight-leg raise

C. Passive movements
1. flexion (Fig. 32.2b)
2. extension (Fig. 32.2c)

D. Palpation
1. patellofemoral joint (including patellar and quadriceps tendons, medial and lateral retinaculum)
2. MCL
3. LCL
4. medial joint line (Fig. 32.2d overleaf)
5. lateral joint line
6. posterior structures (e.g. hamstring tendons, Baker's cyst, gastrocnemius origins)—best done in the prone position

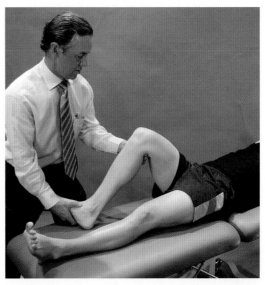

(b) Passive movement—flexion
Assess range of motion, end feel, and presence of pain

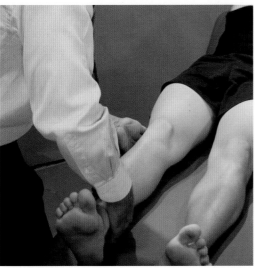

Figure 32.2 Examination of the patient with an acute knee injury
(a) Observation—supine. Look for swelling, deformity, and bruising

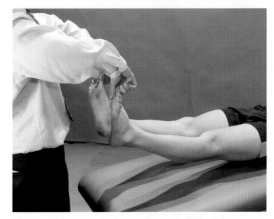

(c) Passive movement—extension. Hold both legs by the toes, looking for fixed flexion deformity or hyperextension in ACL or PCL rupture. Overpressure may be applied to assess end range. This procedure may provoke pain in meniscal injuries

E. Special tests
1. presence of effusion (Fig. 32.2e)
2. stability tests
    (a) MCL (Fig. 32.2f)
    (b) LCL (Fig. 32.2g)
    (c) ACL
        (i)   Lachman's test (Figs 32.2h–k)
        (ii) anterior drawer test (Fig. 32.2l overleaf)
        (iii) pivot shift test (Fig. 32.2m overleaf)
    (d) PCL
        (i)   posterior sag (Fig. 32.2n overleaf)
        (ii) reverse Lachman's test
        (iii) posterior drawer test (Fig. 32.2o overleaf)
        (iv) external rotation test—active and passive
    (e) patella
        (i)   medial and lateral patella translation (or mobility)
3. flexion/rotation
    (a) McMurray's test (Fig. 32.2p on page 633)
    (b) Apley's grind test
4. patellar apprehension test (Fig. 32.2q on page 633)
5. patellofemoral joint (Chapter 33)

6. functional tests
    (a) squat test (helps to assess functional valgus collapse of knee)
    (b) hop test
    (c) pelvic bridge/plank arrow (helps assess core strength)

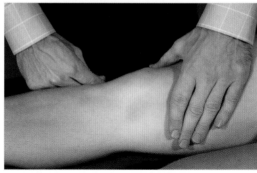

(e) Special tests—presence of effusion
Manually drain the medial subpatellar pouch by stroking the fluid in a superior direction. Then "milk" the fluid back into the knee from above on the lateral side while observing the pouch for evidence that fluid is reaccumulating. This test is more sensitive than the "patellar tap." It is important to differentiate between an intra-articular effusion and an extra-articular hemorrhagic bursitis

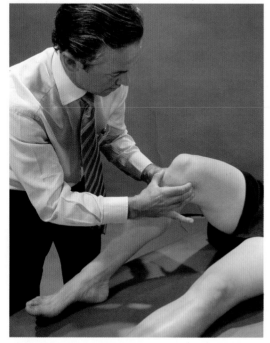

(d) Palpation—medial joint line
The knee should be palpated in 30° of flexion

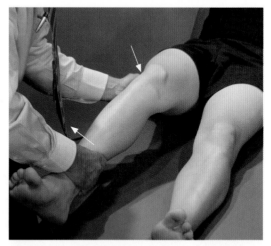

(f) Stability test—MCL
This is tested first with the knee in full extension and then also at 30° of flexion (illustrated). The examiner applies a valgus force, being careful to eliminate any femoral rotation. Assess for onset of any pain, extent of valgus movement, and feel for end point. If the knee "gaps" at full extension, there must be associated posterior cruciate injury

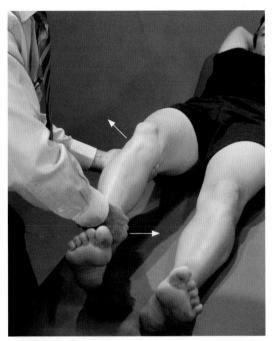

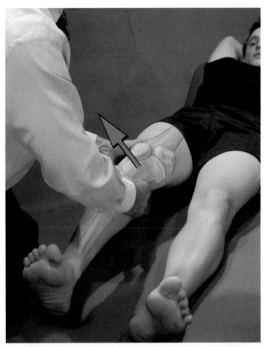

B

(g) Stability test—LCL
The LCL is tested in a similar manner to the MCL except with varus stress applied

(h) Stability test—Lachman's test
Lachman's test is performed with the knee in 15° of flexion, ensuring the hamstrings are relaxed. The examiner draws the tibia forward, feeling for laxity, and assessing the quality of the end point. Compare with the uninjured side

Lachman's test

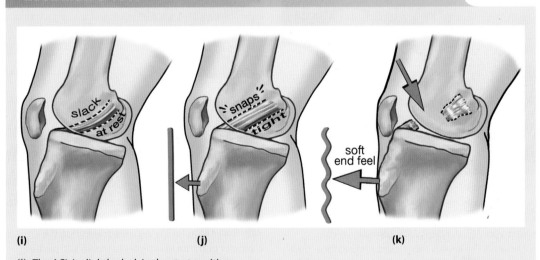

(i)   **(j)**   **(k)**

(i) The ACL is slightly slack in the start position
(j) When the ACL is intact, the ligament snaps tight and the examiner senses a "firm"/"sudden" end feel
(k) When the ACL is ruptured, the Lachman's test results in a "softer"/"gradual" end feel

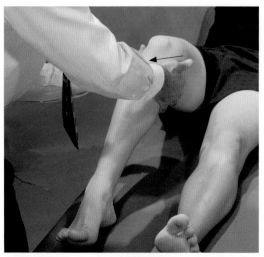

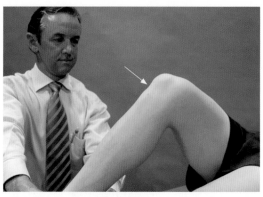

(n) Stability test—posterior sag
With both knees flexed at 90° and the patient relaxed, the position of the tibia relative to the femur is observed. This will be relatively posterior in the knee with PCL deficiency

(l) Stability test—anterior drawer test
This is performed with the knee in 90° of flexion and the patient's foot kept stable. Ensure the hamstrings are relaxed with the index finger on the femoral condyles. The tibia is drawn anteriorly and assessed for degree of movement and quality of end point. The test can be performed with the tibia in internal and external rotation to assess anterolateral and anteromedial instability respectively

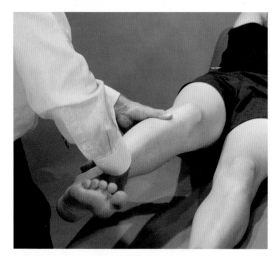

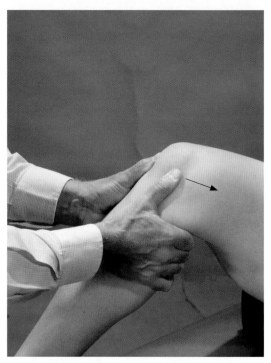

(m) Special test—pivot shift test
With the tibia internally rotated and the knee in full extension, a valgus force is applied to the knee. In a knee with ACL deficiency, the condyles will be subluxated. The knee is then flexed, looking for a "clunk" of reduction, which renders the pivot shift test positive. Maintaining this position, the knee is extended, looking for a click into subluxation, which is called a "positive jerk test"

(o) Stability test—posterior drawer test
With the knee as for the anterior drawer test, the examiner grips the tibia firmly as shown and pushes it posteriorly. Feel for the extent of the posterior movement and quality of end point. The test can be repeated with the tibia in external rotation to assess posterolateral capsular integrity

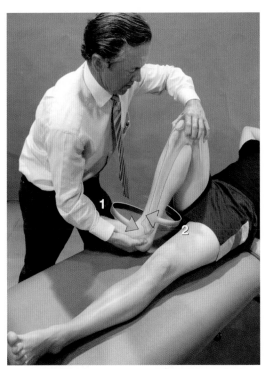

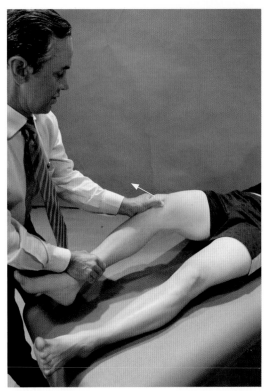

B

(p) Flexion/rotation test—McMurray's test
The knee is flexed and, at various stages of flexion, internal and external rotation of the tibia are performed. The presence of pain and a palpable "clunk" is a positive McMurray's test and is consistent with meniscal injury. If there is no clunk but the patient's pain is reproduced, then the meniscus may be damaged or there may be a patellofemoral joint abnormality

(q) Special tests—patellar apprehension test
The knee may be placed on a pillow to maintain 20–30° of flexion. Gently push the patella laterally. The test is positive if the patient develops apprehension with a sensation of impending dislocation

Investigations

X-ray

Clinicians often wonder whether or not to perform an X-ray in cases of an acute knee injury. More than 90% of radiographs ordered to evaluate knee injuries are normal. A set of decision criteria known as "the Ottawa knee rule" was developed in an adult emergency medicine setting in the mid-1990s (Table 32.3).[2] Also, surgeons always wish to see preoperative films so there are no intraoperative surprises.

The main aim of performing an X-ray in cases of moderate and severe acute knee injuries is to detect a fracture:

- a tibial avulsion fracture associated with an ACL or PCL injury
- a tibial plateau fracture following a high-speed knee-loading injury
- an osteochondral fracture after patellar dislocation.

Table 32.3 Criteria for knee X-ray based on Ottawa knee rule[a]

A knee radiograph is indicated after trauma only when at least one of the following is present:
- patient age more than 55
- tenderness at the fibular head
- tenderness over the patella
- inability to flex the knee to 90° (this captures most hemarthrosis, fractures)
- inability to weight-bear for four steps at the time of the injury and when examined.

To these, we suggest a high index of suspicion for:
- high-speed injuries
- children or adolescents (who may avulse a bony fragment instead of tearing a cruciate ligament)
- if there is clinical suspicion of loose bodies.

[a] The Ottawa knee rule was designed for use in the emergency department setting

Magnetic resonance imaging (MRI)

MRI is reliable, safe, and accurate in the diagnostic work-up of acute knee injuries. Even when a ligament disruption is diagnosed by physical examination, MRI can add value by demonstrating the extent of associated injury to cartilage and meniscus. Patellar injury and quadriceps tendon injury can also be assessed.

MRI should never be ordered in the absence of a thorough history and physical examination.

MRI findings that are not clinically relevant should be interpreted with caution. For example, meniscus tears were recently shown to be present in a relatively high proportion of asymptomatic knees.[3] Thus, such an injury presenting on MRI but not associated with relevant clinical features might be a "red herring" (irrelevant) not in need of treatment.

MRI can be very useful when a primary patellar dislocation is suspected clinically. MRI can help to detect osteochondral avulsion fractures that require surgical assessment. As the avulsed fragment swells (and deteriorates), there is a limited window of time for surgical fixation of the fragment. Usually it needs to be identified and treated within 10–14 days of the injury.

The advent of MRI brought the discovery that significant knee injuries are associated with edema in the subchondral region. This phenomenon is known as a bone bruise or bone marrow lesion (BML). Clinically, a bone bruise is associated with pain, tenderness, swelling, and delayed recovery. The presence of a bone bruise indicates substantial articular cartilage damage,[4, 5] but the clinical relevance of a bone bruise is still to be determined.

The role for diagnostic arthroscopy

In the developed world, arthroscopy is rarely used for diagnosis. However, in rare cases, when the clinical picture is unclear and the patient has persistent pain and swelling not responding to other treatment alternatives, diagnostic arthroscopy may be useful. It is then used to confirm the presence or absence of pertinent intra-articular pathology. This can be particularly useful in cases of cartilage injury; MRI is imperfect in revealing cartilage damage. Performing a knee arthroscopy for pain without other objective signs or symptoms is not advocated.

Ultrasound examination

In the setting of an acute knee injury, a complete patellar tendon rupture will be obvious clinically. High-quality ultrasound examination can demonstrate partial tears of this tendon. Ultrasound examination can also detect the size and location of bursal swelling, and differentiate intra- from extra-articular swelling if necessary.

Meniscal injuries

Acute meniscal tears occur when the shear stress generated within the knee in flexion and compression, combined with femoral rotation, exceeds the meniscal collagen's ability to resist these forces.[6] The medial meniscal attachment to the medial joint capsule decreases its mobility, thereby increasing its risk for injury compared with the more mobile lateral meniscus.[7]

Degenerative meniscal tears occur in the older population frequently without an inciting event and also without symptoms.[3]

The different types of meniscal tear are shown in Figure 32.3.

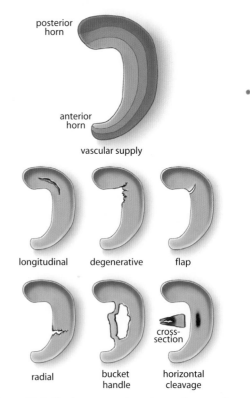

Figure 32.3 Meniscus tear orientation and zones of vascularity; these drawings are of a medial meniscal tear

Clinical features

The history can provide a mechanism and a sense of the severity of meniscal tears. The clinical features are as follows:

- The most common mechanism of meniscal injury is a twisting injury with the foot anchored on the ground; this rotational force is often caused by another player's body.
- The twisting component may be of comparatively slow speed. This type of injury is commonly seen in football and basketball players.
- The degree of pain associated with an acute meniscal injury varies considerably.
- Some patients may describe a tearing sensation at the time of injury.
- A small meniscal tear may cause no immediate symptoms; it may become painful and cause knee swelling over 24 hours.
- Small tears may also occur with minimal trauma in the older sportsperson as a result of degenerative change of the meniscus.
- Patients with more severe meniscal injuries (e.g. a longitudinal ["bucket handle"] tear) present with more severe symptoms. Pain and restriction of range of motion occur soon after injury. Intermittent locking may occur as a result of the torn flap, the "bucket handle," impinging between the articular surfaces. This may unlock spontaneously with a clicking sensation. This often occurs in association with ACL tears. In these patients, a history of locking may be due to either the ACL or the meniscal injury.

On examination, the signs of a meniscal tear include:

- joint line tenderness (palpated with the knee flexed at 45–90°)
- joint effusion—this is usually present, although absence of an effusion does not necessarily rule out meniscal damage
- pain—usually present with knee hyperflexion (such as squatting), especially with posterior horn tears
- restricted range of motion of the knee joint—this may be due to the torn meniscal flap or the effusion.

 These tests are demonstrated in the *Clinical Sports Medicine* masterclasses at www. clinicalsportsmedicine.com.

The flexion/rotation (McMurray's) test (Fig. 32.2p) is positive when pain is produced by the test, and a clunk is heard or felt that corresponds to the torn flap being impinged in the joint. However, it is not necessary to have a positive McMurray's test (i.e. a clunk) to make a diagnosis of a torn meniscus. The hyperflexion portion of the McMurray's test provokes pain in most meniscal injuries.

Pain produced by flexion and external rotation is often indicative of medial meniscal damage, whereas pain on internal rotation indicates lateral meniscal pain. Asking patients where they feel pain during hyperflexion maneuvers gives a suggestion of the location of the tear—medial or lateral.

MRI is the investigation of choice. This can aid management if the MRI shows either a complex tear (rather than minimal damage) or, more rarely, a peripheral meniscus tear. If meniscal tearing is minimal and stable without displacement, clinical progress remains the best measure of non-operative management. Peripheral meniscus tears, depending on the length of the tear, may be fixed surgically.

Treatment

The management of meniscal tears varies depending on the severity of the condition. At one end of the spectrum, a small tear or a degenerative meniscus tear, presenting with pain but not with mechanical symptoms such as locking or range of motion (ROM) restriction, should initially be treated non-surgically.[8]

On the other hand, a large painful "bucket handle" tear causing a locked knee requires urgent arthroscopic surgery. The majority of meniscal injuries fall somewhere between these two extremes, and the decision on whether to proceed immediately to arthroscopy must be made on the basis of the severity of the symptoms and signs, as well as the demands of the sportsperson.

 In the challenging situation where a patient has both early osteoarthritis and a meniscal tear, physical examination features and MRI together can help predict which patients might benefit from arthroscopic surgery.

The highest likelihood of benefit from arthroscopic partial menisectomy is in patients with clinical findings of increasing pain (as distinct from stable pain) as well as locking, when these were complemented by MRI findings of a displaced meniscal tear but no marrow lesions.[9]

Table 32.4 overleaf provides some clinical guidance for choosing either non-surgical or surgical treatment.

Table 32.4 Clinical features of meniscal injuries that may affect prognosis

Factors that may indicate non-surgical treatment is likely to be successful	Factors that may indicate surgery will be required
Symptoms develop over 24–48 hours following the injury	Severe twisting injury, sportsperson is unable to continue playing
Minimal injury or no recall of specific injury	
Able to weight-bear	Locked knee or severely restricted ROM
Minimal swelling	Positive McMurray's test (palpable clunk)
Full range of movement with pain only at end of ROM	Pain on McMurray's test with minimal knee flexion
Pain on McMurray's test only in inner range of flexion	Presence of associated ACL tear
Previous history of rapid recovery from similar injury	Little improvement of clinical features after three weeks of non-surgical treatment
Early degenerative changes on plain radiographs	

ROM = range of motion

Non-surgical management of meniscal injuries

Non-surgical management of relatively minor meniscal injuries is often successful, particularly in a person whose sport does not involve twisting activities. The principles of non-surgical management are the same as those following partial menisectomy (Table 32.5), although the rate of progress may vary depending on the clinical features.

The criteria for return to sport following meniscal injury, treated surgically or non-surgically, are shown below. If appropriate rehabilitation principles have been followed, then the criteria will usually all be satisfied:

- absence of effusion
- full range of movement
- normal quadriceps and hamstring function
- normal hip external rotator function
- good proprioception
- functional exercises performed without difficulty
- training performed without subsequent knee symptoms
- simulated match situations undertaken without subsequent knee symptoms.

Surgical management of meniscal injuries

The aim of surgery is to preserve as much of the meniscus as possible. Some meniscal lesions are suitable for repair by arthroscopic meniscal suture. The decision as to whether or not to attempt meniscal repair is based on several factors. Repair is favored if:

- the tear occurred recently (within weeks)
- the patient is younger
- the knee is stable
- the tear is peripheral.

As the outer one-third of the meniscus rim has a blood supply, tears in this region can heal.

The tear with the best chance of a successful repair is an acute longitudinal tear in the peripheral one-third of the meniscus in a young patient.[10] Degenerative, flap, horizontal cleavages, and complex meniscal tears are poor candidates for repair.[7] Young patients have a higher success rate of healing the meniscus. Peripheral meniscus tears in otherwise stable knees without concomitant ligament damage have a reduced success rate.

Partial tears may require removal of the damaged flap of the meniscus. Patients with degenerative tears with no or minimal cartilage wear are less symptomatic than those patients with concomitant cartilage damage.

Rehabilitation after meniscal surgery

Rehabilitation should always commence prior to surgery, and in some cases surgery can be avoided because "prehabilitation" leads to full recovery. For patients scheduled for surgery, it is important to:

- reduce pain and swelling with the use of electrotherapeutic modalities and gentle range of motion exercises
- maintain strength of the quadriceps, hamstrings, and hip abductor and extensor muscles
- protect against further damage to the joint (patient may use crutches if necessary)
- explain the surgical procedure and the postoperative rehabilitation program to the patient.

The precise nature of the rehabilitation process depends on the extent of the injury and the surgery performed (Table 32.5). Arthroscopic partial menisectomy is usually a straightforward procedure followed by a fairly rapid return to activity; some sportspeople

Table 32.5 Rehabilitation program for both non-surgical management of meniscal injury and following arthroscopic partial meniscectomy

Phase	Goal of phase	Time post injury	Physiotherapy	Exercise program	Functional/sport-related activity
Phase 1	Control swelling Maintain knee extension Knee flexion to 100°+ 4/5 quadriceps strength 4+/5 hamstring strength	0–1 week	Cryotherapy Electrotherapy Compression Manual therapy Gait re-education Patient education	Gentle ROM (extension and flexion) Quadriceps/VMO setting Supported (bilateral) calf raises Hip abduction and extension Hamstring pulleys/rubbers Gait re-education drills Light exercise bike	Progress to FWB and normal gait pattern
Phase 2	Eliminate swelling Full ROM 4+/5 quadriceps strength 5/5 hamstring strength	1–2 weeks	Cryotherapy Electrotherapy Compression Manual therapy Gait re-education Exercise modification and supervision	ROM drills Quadriceps/VMO setting Mini-squats and -lunges Leg press (double, then single leg) Step-ups Bridges (double-, then single-leg) Hip abduction and extension with rubber tubing Single-leg calf raises Gait re-education drills Balance and proprioceptive drills (single leg)	Swimming (light kick) Exercise bike Walking
Phase 3	Full ROM Full strength Full squat Dynamic proprioceptive training Return to running and restricted sport-specific drills	2–3 weeks	Manual therapy Exercise/activity modification and supervision	As above—increase difficulty, repetitions and weight where appropriate Jump and land drills Agility drills	Running Swimming Road bike Sport-specific exercises (progressively sequenced) (e.g. running forwards, sideways, backwards, sprinting, jumping, hopping, changing direction, kicking)
Phase 4	Full strength, ROM, and endurance of affected limb Return to sport-specific drills and restricted training and match play	3–5 weeks	As above	High-level sport-specific strengthening as required	Return to sport-specific drills, restricted training and match play

FWB = full weight-bearing; ROM = range of motion; VMO = vastus medialis obliquus

with a small isolated medial meniscal tear are ready to return to sport after four weeks of rehabilitation.

The rehabilitation process usually takes longer if there has been a more complicated tear of the meniscus, especially if the lateral meniscus is injured.

The presence of associated abnormalities (such as articular cartilage damage or MCL or ACL tears) also slows down the rehabilitation process.

If the sportsperson returns to play before the knee is properly rehabilitated, he or she may not experience difficulty during the first competition, but may be prone to develop recurrent effusions and persistent pain.

A successful return to sport after meniscal knee surgery should not be measured by the time to play the first match but, rather, the time to play the second!

Close monitoring is essential during post-menisectomy rehabilitation, while the remaining meniscus and underlying articular cartilage slowly increase their tolerance to load-bearing activities. Constant reassessment after progressively more difficult activities should be performed by the therapist monitoring the rehabilitation program. The development of increased pain or swelling should result in the program being slowed or revised accordingly.

Medial collateral ligament (MCL) injury

Injury to the MCL usually occurs as a result of a valgus stress to the partially flexed knee. This can occur in a non-contact mechanism such as downhill skiing, or in contact sports when an opponent falls across the knee from lateral to medial. MCL tears are classified on the basis of their severity into grade I (mild, first degree), grade II (moderate partial ruptures, second degree) or grade III (complete tears, third degree).

In patients with a grade I MCL sprain, there is local tenderness over the MCL on the medial femoral condyle or medial tibial plateau but usually no swelling. When a valgus stress is applied at 30° of flexion, there is pain but no laxity (Fig. 32.2f on page 630). Ligament integrity is intact.

A grade II MCL sprain is produced by a more severe valgus stress. Examination shows marked tenderness, sometimes with localized swelling. A valgus stress applied at 30° of knee flexion causes pain. Some laxity (typically <5 mm [<0.05 in.]) is present

but there is a distinct end point. The knee is stable at full extension; ligament integrity is compromised but intact throughout its length.

A grade III tear of the MCL results from a severe valgus stress that causes a complete tear of the ligament fibers. The patient often complains of a feeling of instability and a "wobbly knee." The amount of pain is variable and frequently not as severe as one would expect given the nature of the injury.

On examination of a grade III tear, there is tenderness over the ligament, and valgus stress applied at 30° of flexion reveals gross laxity without a distinct end point. A minor valgus instability is usually also found at full extension. This test may not provoke as much pain as incomplete tears of the ligament, because of complete disruption of the nociceptive fibers of the ligament.

Grade III MCL injuries are frequently associated with a torn ACL, but rarely associated with medial meniscus injury. The presentation of medial joint-line tenderness and lack of full extension is more a reflection of MCL injury. The lateral meniscus is more at risk because the mechanism of injury typically opens the medial side and compresses the lateral side.

While swelling is uncommon in grade I sprains, it may occasionally be seen with grade II injuries. In grade III sprains there is associated capsular tearing (deep and superficial fibers) and fluid escapes; some degree of swelling is common although a tense effusion is not present.

Distal MCL injuries have a tendency to recover more slowly than proximal lesions.

Treatment

A hinged knee brace (Fig. 32.4a) provides support and protection to the injured MCL for a period of 4–6 weeks, during which time the sportsperson undertakes a comprehensive rehabilitation program. The brace with the exercises promote early healing of the ligament and any associated capsular injury.

In one study,[11] there were no differences between patients with grade III MCL injuries that were treated non-surgically (i.e. bracing) and those treated surgically; thus non-surgical treatment is recommended. A typical rehabilitation program for milder MCL injuries (grade I and mild grade II) is shown in Table 32.6 overleaf. The exercises used in knee rehabilitation are shown in Figures 32.5 on pages 642–645 and 32.6 on page 646.

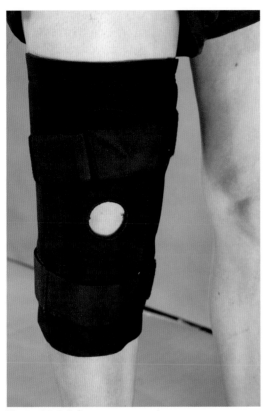

(b) Limited motion knee brace

Figure 32.4 Splints
(a) Hinged knee brace

The more severe MCL injury (the severe grade II or grade III tear) could be treated in a limited motion knee brace (Fig. 32.4b) and requires a longer period of rehabilitation as shown in Table 32.7 on page 641.

Anterior cruciate ligament (ACL) tears
The overall annual incidence of ACL tears was 81 per 100 000 inhabitants aged 10–64 years in Europe.[12] More than 200 000 ACL reconstructions at a cost of over $2 billion are performed annually in the US.[13-18]

ACL injuries occur most frequently in sports involving pivoting and sudden deceleration (e.g. football, basketball, netball, soccer, European team handball, gymnastics, downhill skiing). The incidence rate of ACL tears is between 2.4 and 9.7 times higher in female athletes competing in similar activities.[19, 20]

Although ACL tears can occur in isolation, this is relatively uncommon. More frequent are those occurring in combination with associated injuries, such as meniscal tears, articular cartilage injuries, or MCL injuries. Principally, all ACL injures have associated bone marrow lesions (BML) that are visible on MR images and form a footprint of the injury mechanism.[4]

 As the torn ACL is only one part of a more complex problem in most ACL injured knees, the diagnosis "ACL injury" may underplay the severity of an acute knee injury.

Clinical features
The majority of ACL tears occur in a non-contact situation, when the sportsperson is landing from a jump, pivoting, or decelerating suddenly. The jumping mechanism is more likely to be associated with an accompanying meniscal injury.[21]

It is common for this knee injury to result from an action that the injured sportsperson has performed repeatedly in his or her career, often a simple maneuver. Video analysis has shown that, at times, a trivial contact with another body part, such as a touch to the shoulder or hand, can precede the injury.

Table 32.6 Rehabilitation of a mild MCL injury (see Figs 32.5 and 32.6)

Phase	Goal of phase	Time post injury	Physiotherapy treatment	Exercise program	Functional/sport-related activity
Phase 1	Control swelling Knee flexion to 100°+ Allow +20° extension 4/5 quadriceps strength 4+/5 hamstring strength	0–1 week	Cryotherapy Electrotherapy Compression Manual therapy Gait re-education Patient education	Gentle ROM (flexion mainly) Quadriceps/VMO setting Supported (bilateral) calf raises Hip abduction and extension Hamstring pulleys/rubbers Gait re-education drills	Progress to FWB and normal gait pattern
Phase 2	Eliminate swelling Full flexion ROM Allow +10° extension 4+/5 quadriceps strength 5/5 hamstring strength Return to light jogging	1–2 weeks	Cryotherapy Electrotherapy Compression Manual therapy Gait re-education Exercise modification and supervision	ROM drills Quadriceps/VMO setting Mini-squats and lunges Leg press (double-, then single-leg) Step-ups Bridges (double-, then single-leg) Hip abduction and extension with rubber tubing Single-leg calf raises Gait re-education drills Balance and proprioceptive drills (single-leg)	With hinged knee brace Straight line jogging Swimming (light kick) Road bike
Phase 3	Full ROM Full strength Full squat Dynamic proprioceptive training Return to running and restricted sport-specific drills	2–4 weeks	Manual therapy Exercise/activity modification and supervision	As above—increase difficulty, repetitions and weight where appropriate Jump and land drills Agility drills	Progressive running Swimming Road bike Sport-specific exercises (progressively sequenced) (e.g. running forwards, sideways, backwards, sprinting, jumping, hopping, changing direction, kicking)
Phase 4	Full strength, ROM, and endurance of affected limb Return to sport-specific drills and restricted training and match play	3–6 weeks	As above	High-level sport-specific strengthening as required	With hinged knee brace Return to sport-specific drills, restricted training and match play

FWB = full weight-bearing; ROM = range of motion; VMO = vastus medialis obliquus

Table 32.7 Rehabilitation of a moderate-to-severe MCL injury (see Figs 32.5 and 32.6)

Phase	Time post injury	Goal of phase	Physiotherapy treatment	Exercise program	Functional/sport-related activity
Phase 1	0–4 weeks	Control swelling Knee flexion to 90°+ Allow +30° extension 4/5 quadriceps strength 4+/5 hamstring strength	Limited motion knee brace (limited 0–30°) Cryotherapy Electrotherapy Compression Manual therapy Gait re-education Patient education	Exercises done in brace Gentle flexion ROM Extension ROM to 30° only Quadriceps/VMO setting Supported (bilateral) calf raises Hip abduction and extension Hamstring pulleys/rubbers Gait drills	Initially NWB/PWB Progress to FWB Walking (normal gait pattern)
Phase 2	4–6 weeks	FWB Eliminate swelling Full ROM 4+/5 quadriceps strength 5/5 hamstring strength	Removal of brace 4–6 weeks Cryotherapy Electrotherapy Compression Manual therapy Gait re-education Exercise modification and supervision	ROM drills Quadriceps/VMO setting Mini-squats and lunges Leg press (double-, then single-leg) Step-ups Bridges (double-, then single-leg) Hip abduction and extension with rubber tubing Single-leg calf raises Gait re-education drills Balance and proprioceptive drills (single-leg)	Swimming (light kick) Road bike Walking
Phase 3	6–10 weeks	Full ROM Full strength Full squat Dynamic proprioceptive training Return to light jogging Return to running and restricted sport-specific drills	Manual therapy Exercise/activity modification and supervision	As above—increase difficulty, repetitions and weight where appropriate Jump and land drills Agility drills	Straight line jogging with hinged knee brace (no earlier than 6 weeks) Running Swimming Road bike Sport-specific exercises (progressively sequenced) (e.g. running forwards, sideways, backwards, sprinting, jumping, hopping, changing direction, kicking)
Phase 4	8–10/12 weeks	Full strength, ROM and endurance of affected limb Return to sport-specific drills and restricted training and match play	As above	High level of sport-specific strengthening as required	With hinged knee brace for first 2–4 weeks Return to sport-specific drills, restricted training and match play

FWB = full weight-bearing; NWB = non-weight-bearing; PWB = partial weight-bearing; ROM = range of motion; VMO = vastus medialis obliquus

B

Figure 32.5 Knee rehabilitation
(a) Quadriceps drills—isometric contraction

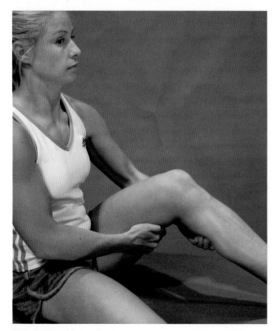

(b) Assisted knee flexion
Place hands behind the thigh and pull the knee into flexion

(c) Double-leg calf raise
Progression of the double-leg calf raise should incorporate an increase in range, sets and repetition, and speed of movement. The eccentric component should be emphasized

(d) Bridging
This is used to develop both core muscular strength and proprioception

(e) Bridging with Swiss ball
A Swiss ball may be used to progress the exercise

B

(f) Hip extension—with rubber tubing

(g) Hip abduction with rubber tubing

(h) Rubber tubing eccentric stride catch—standing

(i) Lunge—performed as shown
Progression involves a combination of increasing the
number of sets and repetitions, increasing the depth of
the lunge, and finally by holding additional weight

(j) Double-leg quarter squat

(l) Arabesque single-leg squat

(k) Single-leg half squat
All squat exercises should be pain-free. The squat may be aided by the use of a Swiss ball. Particular attention must be given to technique, and control of the pelvis, hip, and knee. Progression of the squat is similar to that of progression of the leg press exercise

(m) Rebounder—jogging
Jogging and bounding are common rebounder exercises

644

(n) Static proprioceptive hold/throwing ball
Ball throwing or "eyes closed" exercises can provide an excellent functional challenge

B

(p) Dura disk balance

(o) Wobble board

The typical features of the history include the following:

- The patient often describes an audible "pop," "crack," or feeling of "something going out and then going back."
- Most complete tears of the ACL are extremely painful, especially in the first few minutes after injury.
- Sportspeople are initially unable to continue their activity. Occasionally pain will limit further activity and this is usually associated with a large tense hemarthrosis. Occasionally, swelling is minimal or delayed.

- At times the sportsperson tries to recommence the sporting activity and feels instability or a lack of confidence in the knee. Occasionally the sportsperson may resume playing and suffer an acute episode of instability.

Most sportspeople with an ACL tear present to a clinician between 24 and 48 hours following the injury. At this stage it may be difficult to examine the knee. The best time to examine a patient with this condition is in the first hour following the injury, before the development of a tense hemarthrosis, which limits the examination. After a few days, when the swelling has started to settle and the pain is less intense, the examination usually becomes easier to perform.

After ACL rupture, these examination findings are typical:

- restricted knee range of movement
- widespread mild tenderness
- lateral joint tenderness. This is likely due to the impact pain from the collision of tibia and femur at the time of injury occurring in the valgus position
- medial joint line tenderness may be present if there is an associated medial meniscus injury.

 The Lachman's test is positive in ACL disruption and is the most useful test for this condition.

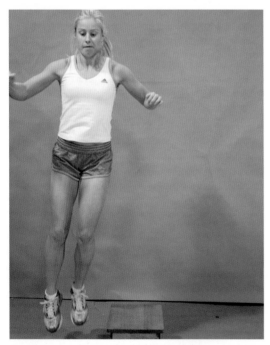

Figure 32.6 Functional activities
(a) Jump and land from block. This exercise may be used to replicate functional movements in many sports. Begin the exercise from a small height and jump without rotation. This exercise can be progressed by increasing the height of the jump and rotating 90° during the jump

(c) Carioca exercises—cross-over stepping exercise

(b) Plyometric jumps over block—lateral
Plyometric exercises should only be included in the later stages of rehabilitation. Each plyometric exercise should be sport-specific

(d) Figure-of-eight running

The Lachman's test[22] (Figs 32.2h–k) is a core competency for clinicians who see patients with knee injuries. The Lachman's test is judged on both the degree of anterior translation and the quality of the end feel (Figs 32.2j and 32.2k). With an effusion, often the maximum anterior tibial excursion is restricted, but the quality of the endpoint is indistinct.

The Lachman's test is demonstrated in the *Clinical Sports Medicine* **masterclasses at www.clinicalsportsmedicine.com.**

A positive pivot shift (or jerk) test (Fig. 32.2m) is diagnostic of ACL deficiency, but it requires the patient to have an intact MCL and iliotibial band, as well as the ability to extend the knee almost to full extension. In cases of acute injuries, especially with associated injury (e.g. meniscal tear), the pivot shift test is difficult to perform as the patient is unable to relax sufficiently.

The anterior drawer test (Fig. 32.2l) is usually positive in ACL tears; however, it is the least specific test. It should always be compared with the other side, as often there is a degree of anterior tibial translation with this test, which is quite variable within the population.

X-ray of the knee should be performed when an ACL tear is suspected. Although radiographs are often normal, it may reveal an avulsion of the ligament from the tibia or a "Segond" fracture (anterior–lateral capsular avulsion)[23] at the lateral margin of the tibial plateau (Fig. 32.7); this is pathognomonic of an ACL rupture. Experienced clinicians and radiologists may also detect signs of increased joint fluid on plain radiographs.

MRI may be useful in demonstrating an ACL injury (Fig. 32.8) when the diagnosis is uncertain clinically. However, MRI should be used mainly to detect associated meniscal tears and cartilage injuries when these injuries are suspected clinically.

Surgical or non-surgical treatment of the torn ACL?

The optimal treatment of the torn ACL is not known and there are several areas of controversy regarding the management of ACL injuries. These include the relative merits of non-surgical versus surgical management, the use of braces to prevent ACL injury or control the ACL deficient knee, whether surgery should be performed immediately after the injury or should be delayed, whether a delayed reconstruction is to be performed weeks, months, or even years after injury, the relative merits of the various surgical techniques, and the benefit of different rehabilitation programs.

One study[26] compared the results of a surgical and a non-surgical treatment strategy. In this study, 121 patients aged 18–35 with acute ACL injuries were randomly divided into two treatment groups: rehabilitation plus early ACL reconstruction, or rehabilitation alone with the possibility of a later ACL reconstruction if this was deemed necessary. Professional sportspeople and those who did not regularly practice sport

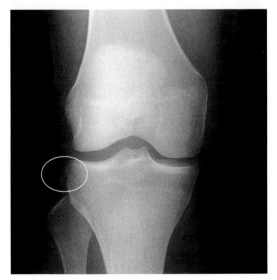

Figure 32.7 X-ray showing a Segond fracture

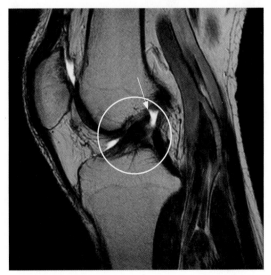

Figure 32.8 MRI of ACL (circled) showing the precise location of the tear (arrow)

What is a bone marrow lesion (BML)

A post-traumatic bone marrow lesion (BML) is only visible on MRI and accompanies an ACL injury in 80–98% of cases.[4, 24] The most common site is the lateral femoral condyle (Fig. 32.9a, b) and the lateral tibial condyle. The BML is most likely caused by impaction between the posterior aspect of the lateral tibial plateau and the lateral femoral condyle during displacement of the joint at the time of the injury. The presence of a BML indicates impaction trauma to the articular cartilage.[5]

The degree to which BMLs result in permanent injury to the cartilage continues to be investigated. At present it is not clear whether the presence of a BML is significant in the long term. Whether patients with a BML are more prone to osteoarthritis is hotly debated; one report indicated there was no difference in the longer term outcome between those with and without a post-traumatic BML.[25] Whether the presence of a BML should slow the rehabilitation process is also not clear, but most clinicians favor a non-surgical course of treatment in this regard, and limit pounding activities for three months post–bone bruise.

were excluded from the study, whereas competitive sportspeople on a sub-professional level and recreational sportspeople were included in the trial.

After two years, there were no differences in terms of knee function reported by the patient, return to sports, or surgical treatment of meniscus injury between the groups. Only 40% of the group treated with initial rehabilitation needed to have an ACL reconstruction. Thus, rehabilitation with experienced physiotherapists produced the same results at two years as did both early and universal surgical reconstruction.[26]

There is recent evidence that well-structured and extensive rehabilitation is crucial for patients with ACL injury. However, rehabilitation alone is not sufficient for approximately 50% who are likely to need surgery in order to cope with their injury. Little is known about individual factors related to a good treatment outcome, and thus the decision on selecting patients for surgery or rehabilitation is difficult.

Early-phase instability at rest (i.e. within the first three months of injury) was not a good predictor of the need for later surgical treatment, whereas instability after three months was a relatively good predictor.[27] Other possible factors include:

- the age of the patient
- the degree of instability in function

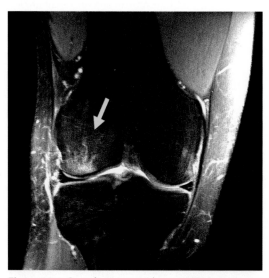
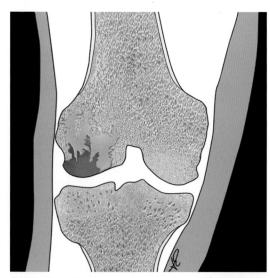

Figure 32.9 Bone bruising, evident on MRI, is an important diagnostic and prognostic feature often associated with ACL injury

(a) AP coronal MRI of a lateral femoral condyle bone marrow edema in association with an ACL rupture. In radiology exams, this is considered pathognomonic of an ACL rupture until proven otherwise

(b) The pathological appearance of a lateral femoral condyle bone marrow edema in association with an ACL tear

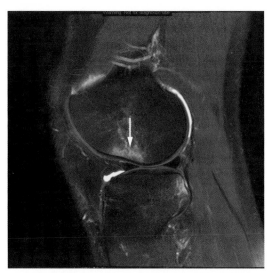

(c) Sagittal MRI appearance of the femoral condyle bone marrow lesion

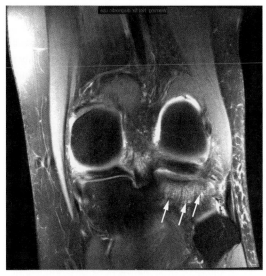

(d) The tibial plateau often also suffers bone marrow edema; posterolateral tibial bruising (arrowheads in this coronal MRI) is also pathognomonic of ACL injury

- a repairable meniscus tear
- associated knee injuries (e.g. MCL tear, meniscal tear)
- the patient's desire to return to jumping and pivoting sports
- the patient's occupation (e.g. firefighter, police).

Because there is limited evidence in determining who will benefit from what treatment, most decisions are made in consensus between the treating clinician and the patient, and are based on empiric knowledge rather than scientific evidence.

The degree of instability may be assessed by a number of parameters.[28] Instability at rest (i.e. at clinical examination of the knee) is not a reliable indicator of the functional instability experienced by the patient. However, as recurrent episodes of "giving way" indicate functional instability, this is likely to be a reliable indication of disability and a predictor of increased likelihood of needing surgery.

PRACTICE PEARL

For patients presenting with a history of episodes of the knee "giving way" or a history of instability in function despite adequate strength, an ACL reconstruction is recommended.

Many surgeons would advocate ACL reconstruction in patients with concomitant meniscal injuries (>50% prevalence) that could be repaired, but scientific data to support this is lacking.

The decision is also influenced by the demands placed on the knee. A young sportsperson who wishes to return to a pivoting sport (such as football or basketball) is more likely to need an ACL reconstruction than a sportsperson who is prepared to confine activity to those sports that do not involve a large amount of twisting, turning, and pivoting. However, some patients in the former category do perform well two years after rehabilitation alone.[26]

It is likely that repeated episodes of "giving way" increase the risk of developing knee osteoarthritis, but there is no scientific evidence to support that an ACL reconstruction reduces the incidence of future osteoarthritis. A recent report did not reveal any differences in the frequency of osteoarthritis between surgically reconstructed and non-surgically treated patients 10 years after ACL injury.[29]

Another important factor to assess is the likelihood of the patient adhering to a comprehensive, time-consuming rehabilitation program. If the patient indicates a lack of willingness to undertake appropriate rehabilitation, treatment may not be successful. It is also important that the result of an ACL reconstruction is dependent on a successful postoperative rehabilitation. Other factors to consider are the cost of surgery and rehabilitation, and the amount of time off work.

Surgery is recommended for sportspeople wishing to participate in a high-speed sport with constant change of direction and pivoting. Rehabilitation without surgery has, however, been shown to be a very good alternative also for this patient category, and could be increasingly used as the first treatment of choice. As with other conditions, a trial of non-surgical management does not rule out the possibility of later surgery when indicated.

Surgical treatment

There are numerous surgical techniques used in the treatment of ACL injuries. As ACL tears are usually in-substance tears and therefore not suitable for primary repair, reconstruction of the ACL is the surgical treatment of choice. Numerous methods of ACL reconstruction have been described.

ACL reconstructions are performed "arthroscopically aided" through small incisions. Arthroscopic surgery utilizes small incisions to help visualize the inside of the joint and facilitate tunnel placement of the ACL graft. Depending on the type of graft, incisions to harvest the graft and secure tunnel access for graft fixation are made as well.

Patient information about what happens during ACL reconstruction surgery is provided in the box. This is also available as a downloadable PDF file at www.clinicalsportsmedicine.com.

Type of graft

The aim of an ACL reconstruction is to replace the torn ACL with a graft that reproduces the normal kinetic functions of the ligament. In most cases, an autogenous graft, taken from around the knee joint, is used.

Autograft

The most common grafts used are the bone–patellar tendon–bone (BTB) autograft involving the central third of the patellar tendon, and a four-strand hamstring (semitendinosus +/– gracilis tendons) graft using the ipsilateral limb. Other autograft choices include the quadriceps tendon, and autografts from the contralateral limb. Graft choice depends on a number of factors, including surgeon competency, and his or her familiarity with the various techniques.

Among orthopedic surgeons, there is considerable debate on graft choice—in particular patellar tendon versus hamstring tendon. A systematic review published in 2004 showed no difference between the two techniques as assessed by failure rate, knee range of motion, isokinetic strength, and arthrometer testing of knee laxity.[30]

Each case should be considered on its merits, taking into account some of the differences in

potential postoperative issues. For example, after patellar tendon ACL reconstruction, pain with kneeling is common with up to 50% of patients reporting such pain.

Patients who have a hamstring graft ACL reconstruction have decreased end-range knee flexion power. The incisions used for hamstring grafts are smaller and more cosmetic.

Potential problems need to be addressed in the rehabilitation program and for that reason we advocate rehabilitation regimens with different emphases for the two types of surgery.

Allograft

Other graft options include allografts (the transplantation of cadaver tissue such as ligaments or tendons). Allografts are associated with a low risk of infection, including viral transmission (HIV and hepatitis C), despite careful screening and processing; however, they have been used successfully for many years and are associated with decreased morbidity, and patients return to their daily activities more quickly.

It has been suggested that allografts may also be associated with earlier return to sport; however, there is little evidence to support this theory.[24] The incorporation of allograft tissue appears to take at least as long as autograft tissue and arguably longer; therefore, many consider delaying the return to full sporting activities for eight to nine months.

Recently published literature suggests a higher failure rate with the use of allografts in young active patients returning early to high-demand sporting activities.[31] The reason for this higher failure rate is unclear. It could be due to graft material properties (sterilization processes used, graft donor age, storage of the graft).

Allograft surgery may be more often associated with ill-advised earlier return to sport by the sportsperson because of a faster perceived physiological recovery, when the graft is not biologically ready to be loaded and stressed during sporting activities. Further research in this area is necessary.

When should surgery be performed

The timing of ACL reconstruction after an acute injury has come under review. Traditionally, and with very little evidence in support, ACL reconstructions were performed as soon as practical after the injury. However, there is evidence that delaying the surgery may decrease the postoperative risk of arthrofibrosis (see below).[32] Initial reports suggested three weeks

What happens during ACL reconstructive surgery

The surgical reconstruction technique of an ACL tear involves harvesting the tendon (patellar or hamstring, Fig. 32.10a) through a small incision, and threading the tendon through tunnels drilled in the bones. The most crucial part of the operation is the points of entry of the tibial and femoral tunnels, and then the fixation of the graft.

The tibial attachment should be in the center of the previous anterior cruciate attachment (at the level of the inner margin of the anterior portion of the lateral meniscus). The femoral attachment is to the so-called isometric point. This is a position in the intercondylar notch on the femur at which the graft is at a fixed tension throughout the range of knee movement.

Once the graft attachment areas have been delineated and prepared, the graft is fixed by one of a variety of different methods. These methods include interference screw fixation (Fig. 32.10b), staples, or the tying of sutures around fixation posts. The better the quality of graft fixation, the more rehabilitation can be advanced in the first weeks after surgery. Improvement in the quality of graft fixation is a major reason for advancement of rehabilitation in the first weeks after ACL surgery, as it is the weakest link in the first six to eight weeks after ACL reconstruction surgery.

B

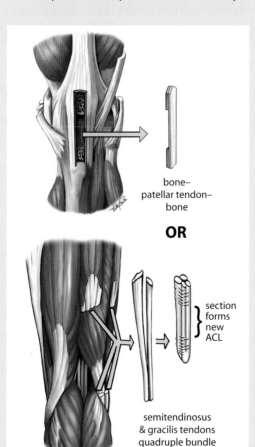

bone–
patellar tendon–
bone

OR

semitendinosus
& gracilis tendons
quadruple bundle
section forms new ACL

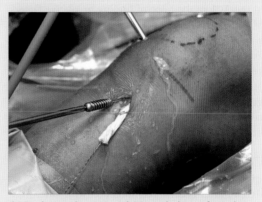

(b) Replacing the ruptured ACL with the graft tendon tissue; interference screw shown

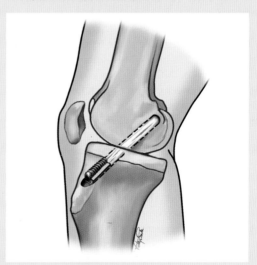

Figure 32.10 The key steps in the process of ACL reconstruction

(a) Harvesting graft tissue for the patellar tendon (top panel) or semimembranosus and gracilis tendon ("hamstring graft") ACL reconstruction

(c) After surgery—the knee with the new graft or "neoligament" in place

as the appropriate delay in surgery, but now focus is more on the condition of the knee, rather than the actual time. The injured knee should have little or no swelling, have near full range of motion, and the patient should have a normal gait.

More important than a specific timing is, however, the actual need to perform a reconstruction. Since it was recently shown that several ACL-injured sportspeople performed equally well after rehabilitation alone as did those treated with ACL reconstruction, the timing of surgery needs to be carefully considered. The option of delaying surgery until it has been proven to be needed is evidence-based and should increasingly be used in the clinical setting.

A recent study[33] studied preoperative factors for knee function two years after reconstructive surgery of the ACL in the hope of finding predictive factors of who does well after ACL reconstruction. Results showed preoperative quadriceps muscle weakness and meniscus injuries have significant negative consequences for the mid-term (two-year) functional outcome after ACL reconstruction. The authors suggested that ACL reconstruction not be performed before quadriceps muscle strength of the injured limb is at least 80% that of the uninjured limb.[33]

Combined injuries

Injuries of the ACL rarely occur in isolation; most ACL injuries occur in combination with other injuries. The presence and extent of associated injuries may affect the way in which the ACL injury is managed.

Associated injury to the MCL (grades II–III) poses a particular problem due to the tendency to develop stiffness after this injury. Most orthopedic surgeons initially treat the MCL injury in a knee brace for a period of 4–6 weeks, during which time the sportsperson undertakes a comprehensive rehabilitation program (Table 32.8). This allows for early healing of the ligament injury and any potential capsular injury, reducing the risk of chronic valgus instability.

Rehabilitation after ACL injury

Traditionally, most rehabilitation principles have been evaluated as postoperative rehabilitation protocols due to the frequent use of ACL reconstruction as the treatment of choice. Recently, however, rehabilitation alone, performed according to a protocol similar to that used postoperatively, has been shown to provide similar two-year outcomes to the combination of ACL reconstruction plus rehabilitation.[26]

Thus, rehabilitation may be performed in a similar setting regardless of whether additional reconstructive surgery is performed or not.

Rehabilitation after ACL injury has changed dramatically in recent years, resulting in greatly accelerated rehabilitation programs.[34] The major change over the past few years is the incorporation of a core stability program, along with increased emphasis on proprioceptive and balance exercises. These exercises have been used in successful ACL prevention programs (Fig. 32.6). Despite the widespread acceptance of these elements into rehabilitation programs, the two randomized trials have not shown convincing evidence of their efficacy.[35, 36]

The rehabilitation program is shown in Table 32.8. The time frames in the table are a guideline only and must be adjusted depending on the progress of the individual patient. It is essential to rehabilitate each patient individually, taking into consideration the extent of damage to the knee (e.g. articular cartilage damage), the patient's adherence to the exercise program, the amount of knee stiffness (which varies considerably between patients), and the eventual functional aims of the patient (e.g. daily activities, high-level sport).

The patient must be taught to monitor the signs and symptoms around the knee following each workout. Ice may need to be applied if pain, inflammation, or swelling is present.

The timing of return to sport depends on several different factors, including the nature of the sport, the therapist's and coach's opinions, and the confidence of the patient.

Most surgeons consider that ACL graft maturation takes up to six months, and most advocate a six-month return to sport as an initial guideline. Beyond this temporal guideline, functional testing should be used to help assess readiness to return to sport.

Functional tests include agility tests, the standing vertical jump and the "Heiden hop." The patient performs the "Heiden hop" by jumping as far as possible using the uninjured leg, landing on the injured leg. Sportspeople with good function are able to land solid with a single hop, to "stick it." Those with functional disability step further or take another small hop. Another way of testing function is by incorporating sport-specific drills.

Isokinetic testing may be used to evaluate muscle strength. Quadriceps and hamstring strength should approximate those of the uninjured leg. In the light of all these factors and the varying progress of different

Table 32.8 Rehabilitation following ACL reconstruction (see Figs 32.5 and 32.6)

Phase	Goal of phase	Time post surgery	Physiotherapy treatment	Exercise program	Functional/sport-related activity
Prehabilitation (preoperative rehabilitation)	No/minimal swelling Restore full ROM, particularly extension General 4+/5 lower limb strength or better Patient education—anatomy, surgical procedure, rehabilitation commitment, and goal setting	N/A	Cryotherapy Electrotherapy Compression Manual therapy Gait re-education Exercise modification and supervision	Dependent on ability of patient In early stages, follow the exercise program from phase 1 and progress to phase 2 If patient has high level of function, start with exercise program from phase 2 and progress weights and repetitions as appropriate	Walking Bike riding Swimming (light kick and no breaststroke)
Phase 1	PWB–FWB Eliminate swelling 0–100° ROM 4+/5 quadriceps strength 5/5 hamstring strength	0–2 weeks	Cryotherapy Electrotherapy Compression Manual therapy Gait re-education Patient education	Gentle flexion ROM Extension ROM to 0° Quadriceps/VMO setting Supported (bilateral) calf raises Hip abduction and extension Hamstring pulleys/rubbers Gait drills	Nil
Phase 2	No swelling Full knee hyperextension Knee flexion to 130°+ Full squat Good balance and control Unrestricted walking	2–12 weeks	Cryotherapy Electrotherapy Compression Manual therapy Gait re-education Exercise modification	ROM drills Quadriceps/VMO setting Mini squats and lunges Leg press (double-leg, then single-leg) Step-ups Bridges (double-leg, then single-leg) Hip abduction and extension with rubber tubing Single-leg calf raises Gait re-education drills Balance and proprioceptive drills (single-leg)	Walking Exercise bike

continues

B

Table 32.8 Rehabilitation following ACL reconstruction (see Figs 32.5 and 32.6) *continued*

Phase	Goal of phase	Time post surgery	Physiotherapy treatment	Exercise program	Functional/sport-related activity
Phase 3	Full ROM Full strength and power Return to jogging, running, and agility Return to restricted sport-specific drills	3–6 months	Manual therapy Exercise/activity modification and supervision	As above—increase difficulty, repetitions, and weight, where appropriate Jump and land drills Agility drills	Straight line jogging Swimming (light kick) Road bike Straight line running at 3 months Progressing to sport-specific running and agility (progressively sequenced) (e.g. running forwards, sideways, backwards, sprinting, jumping, hopping, changing directions, kicking)
Phase 4	Return to sport	6–12 months	As above	High-level sport-specific strengthening as required	Progressive return to sport (e.g. restricted training, unrestricted training, match play, competitive match play)

FWB = full weight-bearing; PWB = partial weight-bearing; ROM = range of motion; VMO = vastus medialis obliquus

athletes and the sport to which they are returning, the time for return to sport after ACL injury may vary from four to 12 months.

The use of a brace on return to sport is not necessary but may help the sportsperson's confidence. The use of a functional brace in the later stages of rehabilitation and on return to sport has not been shown to help.[37, 38] There is some evidence that wearing a neoprene compression sleeve improves proprioception after ACL reconstruction,[39] but there are conflicting reports. Some sporting codes have restrictions on the type of brace and material that can be used.

The research into the effectiveness of various rehabilitation techniques has generally been of poor quality and thus limited conclusions can be drawn. The Orthopedic Section of the American Physical Therapy Association recently published clinical practice guidelines, including the level of supporting evidence, for treatment of knee sprains based on an international classification of functional disability.[40] Van Grinsven and colleagues have proposed an evidence-based rehabilitation program[41] suggesting an accelerated protocol without postoperative bracing, in which reduction of pain, swelling and inflammation, regaining range of motion, and strength and neuromuscular control are the most important aims.

Considerations in rehabilitation after ACL reconstruction

Management principles of rehabilitation after ACL reconstruction have changed as surgical techniques have changed. There is a better understanding of the initial graft strength and the strength of various graft fixation techniques. There is no difference in joint laxity or clinical outcome at two years post-surgery between those who underwent accelerated rehabilitation and those with a non-accelerated program.[42]

Without an open arthrotomy, the extensor mechanism is better preserved with reduced joint adhesions. The principle of complete immobilization has been replaced with protected mobilization, with a resultant dramatic decrease in stiffness and increase in range of motion of the knee joint. This has allowed earlier commencement of a strengthening program and rapid progression to functional exercises.

The average time for rehabilitation after ACL reconstruction to return to sport has been reduced from around 12 months to six to nine months before the injured individual can regain sporting activity. The importance of early return to sports in relation to later osteoarthritis development needs to be determined.

Rehabilitation must occur from the time of injury, not from the time of surgery, which may be days, weeks, or months later if needed at all.[43] The initial management aims to reduce pain, swelling, and inflammation, thus reducing the amount of intra-articular fibrosis and resultant loss of range of motion, strength, and function.

Immediately after injury, treatment should commence, including interferential stimulation, ultrasound, and TENS, as well as strengthening exercises for the quadriceps, hamstring, hip extensor, hip abductor, and calf muscles. Pain-free range of motion exercises should also be performed.

This period is also an opportunity for explanation of the hospital protocol and the progression and goals of the rehabilitation program. The therapist should set a realistic goal, taking into consideration the individual patient. It is helpful to provide a written explanation. If necessary, the knee brace to be used postoperatively should be fitted and the use of crutches taught.

Immediately following surgery, weight-bearing status is largely determined by concomitant injuries (e.g. meniscal repair). Isolated ACL reconstructions are typically treated as weight-bearing as tolerated, using a brace and/or crutches until adequate quadriceps muscle strength is restored. Instructions should be given regarding the use of crutches, as the patient will progress from limited weight-bearing to full weight-bearing during the first two weeks.

The rehabilitation programs for patellar tendon and hamstring tendon graft ACL reconstructions are slightly different, due to the need to prevent the particular complications associated with each type of reconstruction.

Potential problems with the patellar tendon graft are kneeling pain, patellar tendinosis, and/or reduced patella mobility (see below). Therefore, attention must be paid to this area during the rehabilitation program with the use of soft tissue therapy to the patellar tendon, accompanied by a strengthening program for the tendon, and patellar taping (Chapter 33) to prevent patellofemoral and fat pad problems.

The hamstring graft should be treated as though the patient has had a hamstring tear (Chapter 31), with an appropriately paced rehabilitation program to restore full range of motion and strength.

Problems encountered during ACL rehabilitation

Universal problems that are not treatment-dependent

Low back pain

Low back pain is not uncommon in the early stages of the rehabilitation program, possibly due to the use of crutches, an altered gait pattern, and altered sleep patterns. It usually occurs in patients who have a prior history of low back pain.

Problems in non-surgically treated patients

Instability

The main problem that may occur in the rehabilitation of non-surgically treated patients is remaining functional instability. All non-surgically treated patients should have a scheduled appointment with the treating clinician within the first three months of injury. When there are complaints of symptomatic instability or lack of trust in their knee due to instability despite a successful rehabilitation program, an ACL reconstruction could be recommended. This is especially true for patients still wishing to resume sporting activities.

Symptomatic meniscal tears

Another problem that may increasingly occur among non-surgically treated patients is a symptomatic meniscal tear. Unlike those undergoing ACL reconstruction, the non-surgically treated patient does not routinely undergo surgery for meniscal tears associated with their initial injury. Some of these meniscal tears remain asymptomatic, some might heal, but some develop to be symptomatic. It is important to differentiate between symptoms related to the injured meniscus and symptoms related to the ACL injury, and to treat the symptomatic injury. When such problems are encountered, the best option is to let an experienced orthopedic surgeon assess the injury and discuss treatment alternatives with the patient.

Problems in surgically treated patients

Apart from surgical complications (e.g. infection, deep venous thrombosis, graft harvest site morbidity), a number of secondary problems may occur during the postoperative rehabilitation process.

Patellar region pain

Patellofemoral pain may occur on the injured or the uninjured side. Patients may present with typical symptoms of patellofemoral pain (Chapter 33) but often do not comment on the presence of anterior knee pain, as they assume that it is part of the normal process following surgery.

 The patient should always be asked about symptoms at the front of the knee and the patellofemoral joints should be examined at each visit.

A number of different factors predispose to the development of patellofemoral pain. Commonly, the lateral structures around the patellofemoral joint, especially the lateral retinaculum and the iliotibial band, are tight. Weakness of the vastus medialis obliquus or proximal gluteal muscles may also be an important component, as may an altered gait pattern, typically associated with excessive subtalar pronation.

It has been widely advocated that open chain exercises should be avoided in post–ACL rehabilitation programs, as they were thought to place increased force on the maturing graft. However, recent biomechanical studies have shown that both open and closed chain exercises produce similar peak strains on a graft. Clinical studies suggest that both play a beneficial role in the early rehabilitation of the reconstructed knee.[44, 45]

Closed chain activities such as squats and lunges can cause patellofemoral problems. These patellofemoral problems occur not only with patellar tendon graft reconstructions but also with hamstring tendon graft reconstructions.

The infrapatellar fat pad may be damaged by the arthroscope and can be the source of considerable discomfort after ACL reconstruction. Taping techniques (Chapter 33) can be used to unload the fat pad.

Another complication of patellar tendon ACL reconstruction is inferior displacement of the patella (patella baja) due to traction on the patella by tight infrapatellar soft tissue structures. Patellar tendinopathy (Chapter 33) is also seen following ACL reconstruction, especially with patellar tendon grafts.

A common finding in patients with chronic ACL insufficiency and reconstruction is severe trochlea chondral damage. One theory is an increased use of quadriceps strengthening exercises during the postoperative rehabilitation, at a time when quadriceps coordination may be compromised.

Lower limb stiffness

Stiffness in the foot and ankle commonly occurs as a result of a period of non-weight-bearing and the wearing of a brace. Tightness of the Achilles tendon is common. These problems may not be recognized until the patient returns to running. Full range of motion of these joints should be maintained early in the rehabilitation program, with mobilization and stretching, in addition to active plantarflexion and dorsiflexion exercises.

Soft tissue stiffness (arthrofibrosis)

The rehabilitation program and its rate of progression are influenced by the intrinsic tissue stiffness or laxity of the patient. This depends on the nature of the patient's collagen and appears to correlate with generalized ligamentous stiffness or laxity throughout the body.

Patients with stiff soft tissues may develop a large bulky scar with adhesions after ACL reconstruction. These patients are usually slow to regain full flexion and extension, and the knee may require passive mobilization by the therapist. Patients tend to have tight lateral structures around a stiff patellofemoral joint. This is known as "arthrofibrosis," or "stiff knee syndrome."[46]

Treatment involves encouraging active movement, early passive mobilization, massage, and encouraging early activity. Efforts to control swelling are critical. It may help to remove the brace earlier than usual in these patients. Severe cases may require arthroscopic scar resection as well as a vigorous rehabilitation program.

 PRACTICE PEARL Delaying reconstructive surgery until all signs of the hemarthrosis have resolved and full range of motion has been regained (in particular full extension) reduces the incidence of arthrofibrosis.

Soft tissue laxity

The group of patients classified as having "loose" soft tissue are characterized by generalized increased ligamentous laxity. These patients tend to rapidly gain good range of motion in extension and flexion. They are treated by prolonging the time in the brace to prevent hyperextension, and restricting the range available.

Range of motion exercises are discouraged, mobilization is contraindicated, and full extension work is reduced to avoid stretching the graft. The rehabilitation program is slowed in these patients to allow time for the graft to develop as much scar tissue as possible.

Outcomes after ACL treatment

While the general consensus among the surgical and sporting communities is that those sustaining an ACL injury make a full recovery after ACL reconstructive surgery, research findings suggest otherwise. Four main outcome measures are used to determine the success or failure of ACL treatment:

- the patient's own perspective of (self-reported) knee function
- return to pre-injury sporting activities
- re-injury rate
- prevalence of osteoarthritis.

Self-reported knee function

The recommended assessment of outcome after ACL injury has changed over the last 15 years. Traditionally, outcome was obtained by an observer, often using a scoring scale such as the Lysholm knee scoring scale,[47] the Cincinnati Knee Ligament Rating Scale,[48] or the International Knee Documentation Committee (IKDC).[49]

It is well known that treating surgeons underestimate symptoms and overestimate function when compared with the patient's own opinion. This was also confirmed after ACL reconstruction in a study from 2001.[50] Thus, the patient's own perspective of knee function has been in focus over the last two decades and the use of validated self-administered questionnaires has been promoted.

Data from large samples of ACL reconstruction patients can be obtained from registries, mainly from Sweden, Norway, and Denmark. There are large improvements in self-reported knee function over the first two years after surgery.

In a recent report from the Swedish ACL registry with data from more than 2000 individuals, however, self-reported knee-related quality of life, knee pain, and knee symptoms were much worse after ACL reconstruction[51] compared with an age-matched community-based sample.[52]

Little is known about self-reported knee function after non-surgical treatment. In a randomized controlled trial comparing surgical and non-surgical treatment strategies, no differences were found between the two treatment arms after two years. The results were comparable to those previously reported after ACL reconstruction.[26]

Two years after injury, ACL-injured patients report worse outcomes than an age-matched community-based sample, which indicates that none of the current treatment options succeed in restoring full knee function from the patients' perspective.

Return to sport

One of the major aims of treatment of ACL injury is to restore the knee and to get the sportsperson back in pre-injury activity. This is also the main argument for surgical treatment. Reports of return to sports following ACL injury do not use a consistent definition and thus results should be interpreted with some caution. One frequent source of misinterpretation is that the definition of return to pre-injury activity is vague and includes one, and sometimes two, levels below the actual pre-injury activity level on a 10 graded scale.

Following ACL reconstruction, there is a large variation in reports on the rate of return to sport, with variations from 65% to 88% being able to return to sport within the first year.[53-56] In a meta-analysis of 392 patients, 72% (n=281) had returned to their pre-injury activity level two years after ACL reconstruction.[57]

A recent report on national elite soccer players showed a rate of return to sport of 94% after ACL reconstruction.[58] The authors speculate that one of the main contributing factors might be the extraordinary care and rehabilitation provided by the team physiotherapists in these professional soccer clubs.

In contrast, another recent publication showed that only 63% of National Football League (NFL) sportspeople returned to NFL game play at an average of 10.8 months after ACL surgery.[59] A success rate around 70% is not excellent for a surgical treatment option, but it should be noted that some of these sportspeople do not return to sports for reasons other than knee problems. The proportion of such individuals is, however, not well described.

Among patients treated non-operatively, the rate of return to sports varies even more widely than among those treated surgically. Scientific reports suggest a range from 19% to 82% for return to pre-injury activity.[1, 26, 27, 60]

Thus, there is no firm data to support that return to pre-injury sport is more likely after ACL reconstruction than after non-surgical treatment. However, individuals active on a professional or sub-professional level often lack the possibility to wait and see, and thus most undergo surgery.

Sportspeople who successfully return to sport after non-operative treatment could represent a group gaining functionally stable knees without a fully restored stability at rest. Factors associated with success after non-surgical treatment need to be better explored.

There is some evidence that those returning to pre-injury sports after ACL injury may stop playing earlier than their non-injured counterparts.[61-63] In the only study in which the reduction in sport participation can be related to a control group, Roos et al.[60] found that only 30% of those who had ACL injury were active after three years compared with 80% of controls, and that after seven years none of the elite injured players were active regardless of the type of treatment.

In addition, previously injured sportspeople retire at a higher rate than sportspeople without previous ACL injury.[1] The reason for this may be that many of the sportspeople who return to sport experience significant knee problems such as instability, reduced range of motion, and/or pain.[62]

Re-injury rate

In most studies, among those treated with ACL reconstruction, the incidence of graft failure is generally of the order of 3–6%.[64, 65] There is some evidence from a meta-analysis that the failure rate may be lower in patellar tendon autografts,[66] although another systematic review failed to show a difference.[30]

There is an increased risk of rupture of the contralateral ACL in patients who have already had an ACL injury. This may be particularly true for females.[67]

Data from non-surgically treated individuals are lacking, but "giving way" is likely to occur with a higher frequency than graft ruptures. A "give way" episode might produce a trauma similar to the original trauma and thus cause additional meniscus damage, cartilage lesions, and collateral ligament injury. The importance of such re-injuries needs to be investigated.

Following ACL injury, there may also be an increased risk of other knee injuries (e.g. meniscal, articular cartilage injury) due to the nature of the sporting activity. Re-injury appears to be most likely in the first 12 months after surgery.[30]

Osteoarthritis

ACL rupture is associated with a significant risk of the development of osteoarthritis, with reports suggesting a frequency of osteoarthritis in 20–50% of individuals 10–15 years after injury.[68, 69] Although it was recognized that ACL injuries treated non-operatively were associated with an increased risk of osteoarthritis, it had been hoped that ACL reconstruction, by restoring knee anatomy and reducing instability, would eliminate, or substantially reduce, the incidence of osteoarthritis. At this time, however, there is no evidence that ligament reconstruction prevents the future development of osteoarthritis.[62, 63, 70–72]

Long-term follow-up studies of patients who have undergone ACL reconstruction with more modern techniques have shown that nearly all patients develop radiological signs of osteoarthritis after 15–20 years.[62, 68, 73] Many of these patients are, however, asymptomatic.

The mechanisms driving osteoarthritis development are not well understood, but the traumatic impact suffered by the subchondral bone, the cartilage, and the meniscus has been suggested as a potential initiator of the disease.[74] The extent of the traumatic impact can be visualized by MRI where post-traumatic bone marrow lesions (BML)—a footprint of the injury mechanism—occur with practically all ACL tears.[4] BML are strongly associated with articular cartilage damage, chondrocyte apoptosis, and osteocyte death.[5]

Meniscal injury is found in 75% of cases of ACL tears and these injuries are also suggested to predispose the development of osteoarthritis.[75]

A related, important sports medicine question is, "Does returning to active sport increase the likelihood of developing osteoarthritis, or does it bring this event on more quickly?" No studies have evaluated this phenomenon, but it is reasonable to assume that intense weight-bearing activity involving pivoting would accelerate the degenerative process, compared with someone who remains sedentary or takes up a non-weight-bearing sport (e.g. cycling, swimming).

We and others[1, 76] propose that sportspeople who have undergone an ACL reconstruction should receive advice about the likelihood of developing osteoarthritis, and the possibility that returning to active sports participation will accelerate its development. Many professional and dedicated sportspeople may decide to continue their sport in spite of that advice, but it is the duty of health professionals to enable them to make an informed decision.

Gender difference

Because of the increased prevalence of ACL injuries in female athletes, researchers have studied the possible differences in outcome after ACL reconstruction between males and females. The majority of studies show increased postsurgical laxity in females, but previous studies reported no difference in graft failure, activity level, or subjective or functional assessment.[53, 77–81]

However, a recent study of several thousand patients from the Swedish ACL registry who had been treated with ACL reconstruction showed significant gender differences in the self-reported outcome one and two years after surgery.[51] The authors reported that female patients showed worse outcomes than male patients before surgery, and at one and two years after ACL reconstruction, and the authors suggested that possible sex differences should be analyzed in future studies on evaluation after ACL injury/reconstruction. Thus it is possible that previous reports were underpowered and that a clinically important gender difference might exist.

Mechanism of ACL injury as a step toward prevention

As 60–80% of ACL injuries occur in non-contact situations, it seems likely that the appropriate prevention efforts are warranted. In ball sports, two common mechanisms cause ACL tears:

- a cutting maneuver[82–84]
- one-leg landing.

Cutting or sidestep maneuvers are associated with dramatic increases in the varus–valgus and internal rotation moments, as well as deceleration.

The typical ACL injury occurs with the knee externally rotated and in 10–30° of flexion when the knee is placed in a valgus position as the sportsperson takes off from the planted foot and internally rotates their upper body with the aim of suddenly changing direction (Fig. 32.11a overleaf).[85, 86] The ground reaction force falls medial to the knee joint during a cutting maneuver and this added force may tax an already tensioned ACL and lead to failure. Similarly, in the landing injuries the knee is close to full extension.

High-speed activities such as cutting or landing maneuvers require eccentric muscle action of the quadriceps to resist further flexion. It is hypothesized that vigorous eccentric quadriceps muscle action may play a role in disruption of the ACL. Although this normally may be insufficient to tear the ACL, it may be that the addition of a valgus knee position and/or rotation could trigger an ACL rupture.

One question that is often asked is why the ACL tears in situations and maneuvers that the sportsperson has performed many times in the past. Frequently, there is some external factor that renders the person susceptible. The sportsperson could be off balance, be pushed or held by an opponent, be trying to avoid collision with an opponent, or have adopted an unusually wide foot position. These perturbations may contribute to the injury by causing the sportsperson to plant the foot so as to promote unfavorable lower extremity alignment; this may be compounded by inadequate muscle protection and poor neuromuscular control.[86] Fatigue and loss of concentration may also be relevant factors.

What has become recognized is that unfavorable body movements in landing and pivoting can occur, leading to what has become known as the "functional valgus" or "dynamic valgus" knee—a pattern of knee collapse where the knee falls medial to the hip and foot. This has been called by Ireland the "position of no return," but perhaps it should be termed the "injury-prone position" since there is no proof that one cannot recover from this position (Fig. 32.11b).[87] Intervention programs aimed at reducing the risk of ACL injury are based on training safer neuromuscular patterns in simple maneuvers such as cutting and jump-landing activities.

The mechanism of ACL injury in skiing is different from that in jumping, running, and cutting sports such as football and basketball. In skiing, most ACL injuries result from internal rotation of the tibia with the knee flexed greater than 90°, a position that occurs when a skier who is falling backwards catches the inside edge of the tail of the ski.[88] Intervention programs in skiing are aimed at increasing the skier's awareness of patterns that are injurious to the knee, and giving alternative strategies in the hope of avoiding these patterns altogether.

PHOTO COURTESY OF ODD-EGIL OLSEN, OSLO SPORTS TRAUMA RESEARCH CENTER

Figure 32.11 Abnormal positions that may lead to ACL injury
(a) The typical position during the cutting maneuver which leads to ACL injury

Why do females tear their ACLs at three times the rate of males

The rate of non-contact ACL injury among female sportspeople is considerably higher (×2–8) than that in males at comparable risk (exposure) and in comparable activities. At present, four main areas are being investigated to explain this discrepancy:

1. anatomical
2. hormonal
3. shoe–surface interface
4. neuromuscular.

Anatomical differences
A number of anatomical differences between women and men have been proposed as contributing factors to the greater rupture rates of ACLs in females. These differences in females include:

- smaller size and different shape of the intercondylar notch[89, 90]
- smaller ACL within the smaller notch[91, 92]
- wider pelvis and greater Q angle
- greater ligament laxity.[93]

	muscles involved	Position of safety	body position	body position	Point of "no return"	muscles involved
back			normal lordosis	forward flexed, rotated opposite side		
hips	extensors abductors gluteals		flexed neutral abduction adduction, neutral rotation	adduction internal rotation		flexors adductors iliopsoas
knee	flexors hamstring		flexed	less flexed, valgus		extensors quadriceps
tibial rotation	plantar flexors		neutral	internal or external		dorsiflexors
landing pattern	gastrocnemius posterior tibialis		both feet in control balanced	one foot out of control unbalanced		peroneals tibialis anterior

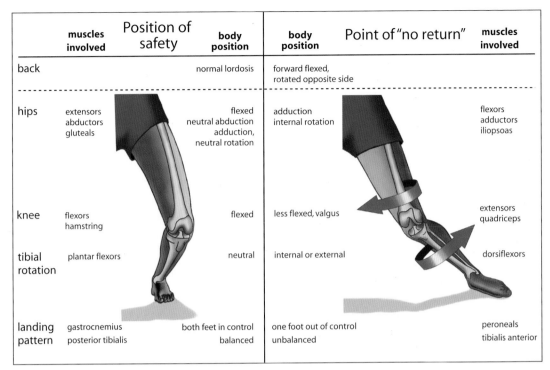

(b) The positions of safety and of "no return"

Hormonal differences

Females have a unique hormonal cycle, and estrogen has long been implicated as a risk factor in the higher ACL injury rates in females. Estrogen receptors can be detected in the human ACL;[94] relaxin receptors are found on female but not male ACLs.[95] Research examining a possible relationship between phase of the menstrual cycle and ACL injury has shown conflicting results.[92, 96–101]

If estrogen level is a risk factor, it is not likely at the material level of ligament strength, as mechanical tests of ligament failure have not shown any difference in strength between ligaments in two studies of different animal models when levels of estrogen were modified.[102, 103] One study utilized an animal model with a similar menstrual cycle as humans, and showed no difference in the material properties of the ACL with and without a two-year estrogen exposure.[104]

If hormones have a role to play in ACL injury risk, most researchers believe they are mediated through

Although anatomical differences may play a role in ACL injury risk, since there is little that one can change in one's anatomy, focus has turned to that which may be able to be changed.

the neuromuscular system and that a direct relationship is unlikely.[92, 105]

Shoe–surface interface

The shoe–surface interface can be affected by a number of factors. In team handball, a higher friction coefficient rate led to an increase in ACL tears.[106, 107] A higher rate of ACL injuries was found in footballers who wore cleats placed on the peripheral margin of the sole with a number of smaller pointed cleats positioned interiorly.[108] An uneven playing surface may also be a factor. A difference in rainfall or the type of grass may also contribute to alterations in the shoe–surface interface (Chapter 9).[109]

Neuromuscular factors

The balance of muscle power and recruitment pattern between the quadriceps and hamstring muscles is crucial to functional knee stability. Controlling the rotation of the limb under the pelvis in pivoting and landing is critical to controlling knee stability, and reducing or eliminating the functional valgus knee. Quadriceps contraction increases ACL strain between 10° and 30° of flexion. An eccentric quadriceps muscle contraction can produce forces beyond those required for ACL tensile failure.[110]

The hamstrings, in contrast, are ACL agonists, so any weakness, increased flexibility, or delayed motor signal to the hamstrings may increase the susceptibility to ACL injury.[111] Female sportspeople rely more on their quadriceps muscles than males do, and they respond to anterior tibial translation by activating their quadriceps first rather than their hamstrings.[112] Males, given a similar force, activate their hamstrings first to dynamically stabilize their knee, thus preventing displacement of the tibia on the femur.[113] This difference in the timing of muscle firing patterns has been thought to be related to the increased risk of injury in females. This study, along with the work of Hewett et al.[114] that shows that females are more "quadriceps dominant" than males, has led to the concept of a quadriceps dominant limb being a risk factor for serious knee injury, including injury to the ACL.

In addition to muscle strength and firing patterns, females land from a jump or pivot with less hip and knee flexion than do males.[114] This is what Hewett et al. refer to as "ligament dominance."[115] Training more flexion at the knee and hip in landing maneuvers has been shown to reduce valgus moments at the knee.

Risk equation

Uhorchak et al.[93] showed that a combination of female gender, decreased notch width, increased body mass index (BMI), and generalized joint laxity were strong predictors of ACL injuries. This gives firm support to the notion of a "risk equation," where no one factor predicts injury, but injury risk can be increased with the combination of certain factors. The risk factors for non-contact ACL injuries have been well-reviewed.[92, 122]

Prevention programs

Given the importance of neuromuscular factors in the etiology of ACL injuries, numerous programs have aimed to improve neuromuscular control during standing, cutting, jumping, and landing.[115-120] The components of the neuromuscular training programs are:

1. balance training
2. landing with increased flexion at the knee and hip
3. controlling body motions, especially in deceleration and pivoting maneuvers
4. some form of feedback to the sportsperson during training of these activities.

Table 32.9 and Figure 32.12 provide an example of a neuromuscular training program for European handball.

A meta-analysis[121] of the six published prevention programs demonstrated an overall positive effect in reducing ACL injuries, with a total of 29 ACL injuries in the prevention group compared with 110 in the control group. Three of the six programs showed significant reduction, while two of the remaining three demonstrated positive trends and reduced odds ratios.

Table 32.9 ACL prevention program[105]

Week	Exercises
Floor exercises	
1	Running and planting, partner running backwards and giving feedback on the quality of the movement, change position after 20 seconds
2	Jumping exercise: right leg, right leg over to left leg, left leg and finishing with a two-foot landing with flexion in both hips and knees
3	Running and planting (as in week 1), now doing a full plant-and-cut movement with the ball, focusing on knee position (Fig. 32.12a)
4	Two players together, two-leg jump forward and backwards, 180° turn and the same movement backwards; partner tries to push the player out of control but still focusing on landing technique
5	Expanding the movement from week 3 to a full plant-and-cut that then incorporates a jump shot with two-legged landing
Mat exercises	
1	Two players each standing on one leg on the mat, throwing to each other (Fig. 32.12b)
2	Jump shot from a box (30–40 cm [~1 ft] high) with a two-foot landing with flexion in hip and knees
3	"Step" down from box with one-leg landing with flexion in hip and knee
4	Two players both standing on balance mats trying to push partner out of balance, first on two legs, then on one leg
5	The players jump on a mat, catching the ball, then take a 180° turn on the mat
Wobble board exercises	
1	Two players standing two-legged on the board, throwing to each other
2	Squats on two legs, then on one leg
3	Two players throwing to each other, one foot each on the board
4	One foot on the board, bouncing the ball with eyes shut
5	Two players, both standing on balance boards trying to push partner out of balance, first on two legs, then on one leg (Fig. 32.12c)

Figure 32.12 Examples of ACL prevention exercises
(a) Floor exercise

(c) Wobble board exercise

The conclusion from this meta-analysis was that prevention programs may be effective provided that plyometrics, balance, and strengthening exercises are incorporated into the training program; that the training is performed more than once a week; and that the program continues for at least six weeks. The component of the programs which correlated best with ACL injury reduction was high-intensity plyometric movements that progressed beyond footwork and agility.[121]

The FIFA 11+ program
with MARIO BIZZINI and ASTRID JUNGE

The International Federation of Association Football (FIFA) has developed an injury prevention program known as "FIFA 11+" which is based on the same principles. In Norwegian female footballers the FIFA 11+ reduced severe injuries, overuse injuries, and injuries overall.[123] Compliance with the injury prevention program was high when it served as the warm-up program.[124] The FIFA 11+ is shown in Figure 32.13 overleaf.

Although the mechanism of ACL injury in skiing is different, neuromuscular conditioning also successfully prevents ACL injury.[88] Ski injury prevention

(b) Mat exercise

11+ A complete warm-up program

The "11+" injury prevention program was developed by an international group of experts based on their practical experience with different injury prevention programs for amateur players aged 14 or older. It is a complete warm-up package and should replace the usual warm-up prior to training. Youth football teams using "11+" as a standard warm-up had a significantly lower risk of injuries than teams that warmed-up as usual. Teams that performed "11+" regularly, at least twice a week, had 37% fewer training injuries and 29% fewer match injuries.[123]

Figure 32.13 The FIFA 11+ poster can be downloaded from www.fifa.com/medical/

The FIFA 11+ has three parts—Part I: running exercises at a slow speed combined with active stretching and controlled partner contacts; Part II: six sets of exercises, focusing on core and leg strength, balance, and plyometrics/agility, each with three levels of increasing difficulty; and Part III: running exercises at moderate/high speed combined with planting/cutting movements.

Field set up: The course is made up of six pairs of parallel cones, approximately 5–6 meters apart. Two players start at the same time from the first pair of cones, jog along the inside of the cones and do the various exercises on the way. After the last cone, they run back along the outside. On the way back, speed can be increased progressively as players warm up.

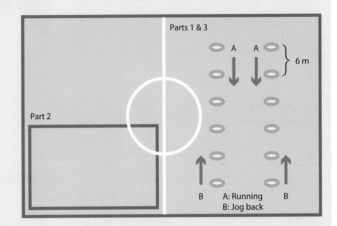

PART 1: RUNNING EXERCISES

1 RUNNING **STRAIGHT AHEAD**
Jog straight to the last cone. Make sure you keep your upper body straight, your hip, knee and foot aligned. Do not let your knee buckle inwards. Run slightly more quickly on the way back. 2 sets.

2 RUNNING **HIP OUT**
Jog to the first cone, stop and lift your knee forward. Rotate your knee to the side and put your foot down. At the next cone repeat the exercise on the other leg. Repeat until you reach the other side of the pitch. 2 sets.

3 RUNNING **HIP IN**
Jog to the first cone, stop and lift your knee to the side. Rotate your knee forward and put your foot down. At the next cone repeat the exercise on the other leg. Repeat until you reach the other side of the pitch. 2 sets.

4 RUNNING **CIRCLING PARTNER**
Jog to the first cone. Shuffle sideways towards your partner, shuffle an entire circle around one another (without changing the direction you are looking in), then shuffle back to the first cone. Repeat until you reach the other side of the pitch. 2 sets.

5 RUNNING **JUMPING WITH SHOULDER CONTACT**
Jog to the first cone. Shuffle sideways towards your partner. In the middle, jump sideways towards each other to make shoulder-to-shoulder contact. Land on both feet with your hips and knees bent. Shuffle back to the first cone. Repeat until you reach the other side of the pitch. 2 sets.

6 RUNNING **QUICK FORWARD AND BACKWARD SPRINTS**
Run quickly to the second cone then run backward quickly to the first cone, keeping your hips and knees slightly bent. Repeat, running two cones forward and one cone backward until you reach the other side of the pitch. 2 sets.

PART 2: STRENGTH PLYOMETRICS BALANCE
All exercises have three levels of increasing difficulty. Players should begin with level 1, which is presented here.

Only when an exercise can be performed without difficulty for the specified duration and number of repetitions should the player progress to the next level.

 Levels 2 and 3 of exercises 7 to 12 are presented on www.fifa.com/medical.

7.1 THE BENCH—STATIC

Starting position: Lie on your front, support your upper body with your forearms, elbows directly under your shoulders. **Exercise**: Lift up your upper body, pelvis and legs until your body is in a straight line from head to foot. Pull in stomach and gluteal muscles and hold the position for 20–30 seconds. 3 sets. **Important**: Do not sway or arch your back. Do not move your buttocks upwards.

7.2 ALTERNATE LEGS

7.3 ONE LEG LIFT AND HOLD

8.1 SIDEWAYS BENCH—STATIC

Starting position: Lie on your side with the knee of your lowermost leg bent to 90 degrees. Support yourself on your forearm and lowermost leg, elbow of supporting arm directly under shoulder. **Exercise**: Lift pelvis and uppermost leg until they form a straight line with your shoulder and hold the position for 20–30 seconds. Repeat on other side. 3 sets. **Important**: Keep pelvis stable and do not let it tilt downwards. Do not tilt shoulders, pelvis or leg forward or backward.

8.2 RAISE AND LOWER HIP

8.3 WITH LEG LIFT

9.1 HAMSTRINGS—BEGINNER

Starting position: Kneel with knees hip-width apart; partner pins your ankles firmly to the ground with both hands. **Exercise**: Slowly lean forward, while keeping your body straight from the head to the knees. When you can no longer hold the position, gently take your weight on your hands, falling into a press-up position. 3–5 repetitions. **Important**: Do exercise slowly at first, but speed up once you feel more comfortable.

9.2 INTERMEDIATE

9.3 ADVANCED

10.1 SINGLE-LEG STANCE—HOLD THE BALL

Starting position: Stand on one leg, knee and hip slightly bend and hold the ball in both hands. **Exercise**: Hold balance and keep body weight on the ball of your foot. Hold for 30 seconds, repeat on the other leg. Exercise can be made more difficult by lifting the heel from the ground slightly or passing the ball around your waist and/or under your other knee. 2 sets on each leg. **Important**: Do not let your knee buckle inwards. Keep your pelvis horizontal and do not let it tilt to the side.

10.2 THROWING BALL WITH PARTNER

10.3 TEST YOUR PARTNER

11.1 **SQUATS** WITH TOE RAISE

Starting position: Stand with feet hip width apart, hands on your hips. **Exercise**: Slowly bend hips, knees and ankles until your knees are flexed to 90 degrees. Lean upper body forward. Straighten upper body, hips and knees and stand up on your toes. Slowly lower down again, and straighten up slightly more quickly. Repeat for 30 seconds. 2 sets. **Important**: Do not let your knee buckle inwards. Lean upper body forward with a straight back.

11.2 WALKING LUNGES

11.3 LEG SQUATS

12.1 **JUMPING**—VERTICAL JUMPS

Starting position: Stand with your feet hip-width apart, hands on your hips. **Exercise**: Slowly bend hips, knees and ankles until your knees are flexed to 90 degrees. Lean upper body forward. Hold this position for 1 second, then jump as high as you can, and straighten whole body. Land softly on the balls of your feet. Repeat for 30 seconds. 2 sets. **Important**: Jump off both feet. Land gently on the balls of both feet with your knees bent.

12.2 LATERAL JUMPS

12.3 BOX JUMPS

PART 3: RUNNING EXERCISES

13 RUNNING—**ACROSS THE PITCH**

Run approx 40 m across the pitch at 75–80% of maximum pace, then jog the rest of the way. Keep your upper body straight. Your hip, knee and foot are aligned. Do not let your knees buckle inwards. Jog easily back. 2 sets.

14 RUNNING—**BOUNDING**

Take a few warm-up steps then take six to eight high bounding steps with a high knee lift and then jog the rest of the way. Lift the knee of the leading leg as high as possible and swing the opposite arm across the body. Keep your upper body straight. Land on the ball of the foot with the knee bent and spring. Do not let your knee buckle inwards. Jog back easily to recover. 2 sets.

15 RUNNING—**PLANT AND CUT**

Jog 4–5 steps straight ahead. Then plant on the right leg and cut to change direction to the left and accelerate again. Sprint 5–7 steps (80–90% of maximum pace) before you decelerate and plant on the left foot and cut to change direction to the right. Do not let your knee buckle inwards. Repeat the exercise until you reach the other side of the pitch, then jog back. 2 sets.

The key point of the program is to use the proper technique during all of the exercises. Pay full attention to correct posture and good body control, including straight leg alignment, knee-over-toe position and soft landings. The FIFA 11+ should be completed as a standard warm-up at least two to three times a week; it should take approximately 20 minutes to complete.

See the instructional video of each exercise on www.fifa.com/medical. The poster and a detailed manual can be downloaded from that website in numerous languages.

programs teach skiers to recognize and respond with appropriate strategies to dangerous situations and to avoid potentially compromising positions.[111]

Factors not yet fully explored include the role of individual sportsperson compliance, failure to comply with neuromuscular training (i.e. how quickly do we forget what we learn?), and what is the ideal age to teach these techniques (i.e. does age matter?). Do all sportspeople benefit from these intervention techniques or can we identify the "at-risk" sportsperson and train that person differently? These are the questions on which interventionists will be focusing future direction and research.

ACL rupture among children with open physes

ACL injuries are common in children and adolescents.[125] Traditionally, surgical reconstruction of the ACL in children with open physes has not been recommended due to the risk of growth abnormalities resulting from surgical violation of the physes. There are, however, also concerns that non-operative or delayed operative management risks meniscal and/or cartilage injuries, leading to premature degenerative disease. Thus there are conflicting opinions on how to treat ACL-injured children, and scientific data to support either option is insufficient.

There is increasing clinical evidence that the risk of damage to the physes is minimal, especially with the various surgical techniques currently available to minimize physeal trauma. Most surgeons currently recommend ACL reconstruction in younger patients with open growth plates although scientific evidence is lacking.

When treating the adolescent patient approaching skeletal maturity surgically, choice of graft fixation typically is similar to adults, although often one tries to avoid having a metal screw directly at the physes. The graft used is typically hamstring tendon.

In the younger patients, techniques are used to minimize the damage to the physes.[126] These include using only soft tissue for graft choice (such as hamstrings) to avoid a bone plug in the tunnel at the growth plate. Auto-patella graft is also rarely chosen as it potentially disrupts the apophyseal growth plate at the patellar tendon tibial attachment site. This is the last region of the tibial physis to close in developing adolescents.

Tunnels are made smaller in diameter than in adults, and on the tibia they are slightly more vertical or central through the tibial physis. This reduces the risk of asymmetric growth of the remaining tibia. On the femur the growth plate is avoided altogether and the "over the top" technique of ACL graft placement is used. These techniques can be individualized to meet the needs of the surgeon and the patient, depending on the age and maturation of the patient.

Posterior cruciate ligament (PCL) tears

The posterior cruciate ligament (PCL) is the primary restraint to posterior drawer, and the secondary restraint to external rotation. Isolated sectioning of the PCL results in an increased posterior translation of the knee under a posterior tibial load. This increase in laxity is relatively small at full extension and is most pronounced at 90° of flexion. Only small rotatory or valgus/varus laxity results from isolated PCL injury.

Up to 60% of PCL injuries involve disruption of the posterolateral structures. The primary stabilizers are the lateral collateral ligament (LCL) and the popliteus complex. They provide varus and external rotatory stability to the knee respectively. When both the PCL and posterolateral structures are cut, posterior laxity is significantly increased.[127]

Tears of the PCL do not appear to be as common as of the ACL, due partly to the greater strength of the PCL. However, the condition is likely underdiagnosed.

PCL injuries are often associated with meniscal and chondral injury. The incidence of associated meniscal tears varies from 16% to 28%. Longitudinal tears of the anterior horn of the lateral meniscus are the most common. There is also a high incidence of radial tears in the middle or posterior lateral meniscus.[128]

The incidence of significant chondral damage with isolated PCL injury was not thought to be as high as with ACL injury, but a recent study showed chondral damage in 52% of those with PCL tears, with lesions of grade III or more found in 16%.[128]

Clinical features

The mechanism of PCL injury is usually a direct blow to the anterior tibia with the knee in a flexed position (i.e. dashboard injury). This can be from contact with an opponent or equipment, or falling onto the hyperflexed knee. Hyperextension may also result in an injury to the PCL and posterior capsule.

The patient complains of poorly defined pain, mainly posterior, sometimes involving the calf. On examination, there is usually minimal swelling, as the PCL is an extrasynovial structure. The posterior drawer test (Fig. 32.2(o)) is the most sensitive test for PCL deficiency. This is performed in neutral, and internal and external rotation. A posterior sag of the tibia (Fig. 32.2n), and pain and laxity on a reverse Lachman's test may be present. PCL rupture is particularly disabling for downhill skiers, who rely on this ligament for stability in the tucked up position adopted in racing.

PCL tears are graded I, II, and III on the position of the medial tibial plateau relative to the medial femoral condyle at 90° of knee flexion (the posterior drawer position). The tibia normally lies approximately 1 cm (0.4 in.) anterior to the femoral condyles in the resting position. In grade I injuries the tibia continues to lie anteriorly to the femoral condyles but is slightly diminished (0–5 mm [0–0.2 in.] laxity). In grade II injuries the tibia is flush with the condyles (5–10 mm [0.2–0.4 in.] laxity). When the tibia no longer has a medial step and can be pushed beyond the medial femoral condyle (>10 mm [>0.4 in.] laxity), it is classified as a grade III injury.[129]

It is important to distinguish between an isolated PCL injury and a combined PCL and posterolateral corner injury. In isolated PCL tears, there is a decrease in tibial translation in internal rotation due primarily to the influence of the MCL.[130]

X-ray should be performed to exclude a bony avulsion from the tibial insertion of the PCL (best seen on lateral tibial radiographs). If a bony ligament avulsion is present, acute surgical repair is undertaken.

Stress radiographs provide a non-invasive measure of sagittal translation compared with the uninjured knee. It is considered that more than 7–8 mm (>0.3 in.) of posterior translation is indicative of a PCL tear.

MRI has a high predictive accuracy in the diagnosis of the acute PCL injury,[131] but a lesser accuracy in chronic injuries. If an injury to the posterolateral corner is suspected, MRI can be helpful; however, to view this region properly a specific imaging protocol is usually required. When the MRI requisition states that injury to the posterolateral corner is suspected, the radiologist can optimize the imaging protocol.

Treatment

PCL rupture can generally be managed non-surgically with a comprehensive rehabilitation program. A suggested program emphasizing intensive quadriceps exercises is shown in Table 32.10 overleaf. More severe injuries (grade III) should be immobilized in extension for the first two weeks.

Results show that patients with isolated PCL tears have a good functional result despite ongoing laxity, after an appropriate rehabilitation program. Regardless of the amount of laxity, half of the patients in one large study returned to sport at the same or higher level, one-third at a lower level, and one-sixth did not return to the same sport.[132]

Surgical reconstruction is indicated when the PCL injury occurs in combination with other posterolateral structures or where significant rotatory instability is present.

Lateral collateral ligament (LCL) tears

LCL tears are much less common than MCL tears. They are usually due to a severe, high-energy, direct varus stress on the knee and are graded in a similar fashion to MCL sprains. Differential diagnosis may be an avulsion of the biceps femoris tendon. Clinicians should be aware that local tenderness on the posterolateral corner of the knee may also occur with ACL tears.

Complete tears of the LCL are usually associated with other instabilities (such as PCL rupture), and may result in posterolateral rotatory instability of the knee. These tears are best treated by acute surgical repair in conjunction with repair of other damaged ligaments. Late or delayed reconstruction of the LCL is difficult and results are poor.

A varus knee with lateral and/or posterolateral instability is associated with worse results. An osteotomy is necessary for surgical treatment of this ligament injury, with or without a reconstruction of the ligament itself.

Articular cartilage damage

Since the introduction of arthroscopy and MRI, considerable insight has been gained into the role of articular cartilage (chondral) damage as a cause of symptoms and signs in the knee joint. Articular cartilage damage may occur as an isolated condition in which chondral or subchondral damage is the primary pathology, or in association with other injuries, such as ligamentous instability resulting from a MCL, ACL, or PCL injury, or patellar dislocations. Articular cartilage damage may also be seen in association with meniscal injury and patellar dislocation.

Classification

Chondral injury is graded according to the Outerbridge classification and more recently the International Cartilage Repair Society (ICRS) grading system

Table 32.10 Rehabilitation of a PCL tear (see Figs 32.5 and 32.6)

Phase	Goal of phase	Time post injury	Physiotherapy treatment	Exercise program	Functional/sport-related activity
Phase 1	PWB–FWB Eliminate swelling 0–100° ROM 4+/5 quadriceps strength 5/5 hamstring strength	0–2 weeks	Cryotherapy Electrotherapy Compression Manual therapy Gait re-education Patient education	Gentle flexion ROM Extension ROM to 0° Quadriceps/VMO setting Supported (bilateral) calf raises Hip abduction and extension Hamstring pulleys/rubbers Gait drills	Nil
Phase 2	No swelling Full ROM 4+/5 quadriceps strength 5/5 hamstring strength	2–4 weeks	Cryotherapy Electrotherapy Compression Manual therapy Gait re-education Exercise modification	ROM drills Quadriceps/VMO setting Mini-squats and -lunges Leg press (double-, then single-leg) Step-ups Bridges (double-, then single-leg) Hip abduction and extension with rubber tubing Single-leg calf raises Gait re-education drills Balance and proprioceptive drills (single-leg)	Walking Exercise bike
Phase 3	Full ROM Full strength and power Return to jogging, running, and agility Return to restricted sport-specific drills	4–6 weeks	Manual therapy Exercise/activity modification and supervision	As above—increase difficulty, repetitions, and weight where appropriate Jump and land drills Agility drills	Straight line jogging Swimming (light kick) Road bike Straight line running Progressing to sport-specific running and agility (progressively sequenced) (e.g. running forwards, sideways, backwards, sprinting, jumping, hopping, changing directions, kicking)
Phase 4	Return to sport	6–10 weeks	As above	High-level sport-specific strengthening as required	Progressive return to sport (e.g. restricted training, unrestricted training, match play, competitive match play)

FWB = full weight-bearing; PWB = partial weight-bearing; ROM = range of motion; VMO = vastus medialis obliquus

(Tables 32.11 and 32.12). Articular cartilage damage varies from gross, macroscopically evident defects in which the underlying bone is exposed (grade IV), to microscopic damage that appears normal on arthroscopy but is soft when probed (grade I).

Articular cartilage damage in the knee has both short-term and long-term effects. In the short term, it causes recurrent pain and swelling. In the longer term, it accelerates the development of osteoarthritis.

Treatment
Various methods have been used to encourage healing of articular cartilage defects.[133]

Microfracture (bone marrow stimulation)
Microfracture (less commonly known as bone marrow stimulation) is the most frequently used technique for treating small symptomatic lesions of the articular cartilage in the knee.[134] The procedures are technically straightforward, and the costs are low compared with those of other treatment modalities. Microfracture involves perforation of the subchondral plate to recruit mesenchymal stem cells from the bone marrow space into the lesion.

The mesenchymal stem cells are able to differentiate into fibrochondrocytes, which contribute to fibrocartilage repair of the lesion. However, the overall concentration of the mesenchymal stem cells is quite low and declines with age. The formation of a stable blood clot that maximally fills the chondral

defect is important, and it has been correlated with the success of bone marrow stimulation procedures.

Reparative fibrocartilage consists of type-I, type-II, and type-III collagen in varying amounts. The fibrocartilage does not resemble the surrounding hyaline cartilage and has less type-II collagen.

The postoperative regimen after microfracture is demanding and has been reported to be a critical aspect of the ultimate efficacy.[135] Patients with a femoral condylar lesion are initially treated with continuous passive motion with a 0° to 60° range of motion for six weeks postoperatively. The patient typically remains non-weight-bearing with the use of crutches for six weeks.

Patients who have undergone microfracture of a patellar or trochlear defect are allowed to bear weight as tolerated postoperatively, but knee motion is restricted by a brace allowing movement from 0° to 40°. Continuous passive motion is initiated immediately and used, within this arc of motion, for approximately six to eight hours daily. At two months, unrestricted motion is typically allowed and closed chain exercises are initiated.

Short-arc closed chain concentric and eccentric muscle strengthening is effective and protects the patellofemoral articulation. Typically, a return to full activities is permitted at three months after a full, painless range of motion is achieved

There are various adjuncts to improve the stability of the clot. These include various growth factors as well as hyaluronic acid viscosupplementation.

Platelet-rich plasma
There has been a remarkable increase in the use of platelet-rich plasma to facilitate healing in a variety of pathological musculoskeletal conditions. The theoretical advantage of this autologous blood product rests in the concentrated platelets and associated quantity of platelet-derived growth factor and other mitogenic factors that may promote the healing of chondral injuries.

Despite these encouraging preliminary results, however, to our knowledge, no clinical studies have proven the efficacy of platelet-rich plasma injection for focal chondral injuries of the knee.

Autologous osteochondral transplantation
Autologous osteochondral mosaicplasty, sometimes referred to as "OATS" (osteoarticular transfer system), is an effective method for resurfacing osteochondral defects of the knee.[133] The technique

Table 32.11 Outerbridge classification of chondral defects

1. Softening
2. <1 cm (<0.4 in.) partial thickness lesion
3. >1 cm (>0.4 in.) defect, deeper
4. Subchondral bone exposed

Table 32.12 International Cartilage Repair Society (ICRS) classification of chondral defects

1. Superficial lesions
   A. Soft indentation
   B. Superficial fissures or cracks
2. Lesions <50% cartilage depth
3. A. Lesions >50% depth
   B. Down to calcified layer
   C. Down to but not through subchondral bone
   D. Blisters
4. Very abnormal into subchondral bone

involves transplantation of multiple small cylindrical autogenous osteochondral plugs harvested from the less weight-bearing periphery of the articular surface of the femoral condyle; these are transferred to create a congruent and durable resurfaced area in the defect.

The procedure offers several advantages over other repair techniques, including transplantation of viable hyaline cartilage, a relatively brief rehabilitation period, and the ability to perform the procedure in a single operation.

The limitations of autologous osteochondral mosaicplasty include donor site morbidity, and a limited availability of graft that can be harvested from the patellofemoral joint or the zone adjacent to the intercondylar notch.

The outcomes of autologous mosaicplasty for symptomatic chondral defects have been encouraging, and the procedure has been used with success.[136]

Osteochondral allograft transplantation

Osteochondral allograft transplantation is a cartilage resurfacing procedure that involves transplantation of a cadaver graft consisting of intact, viable articular cartilage and its underlying subchondral bone into the defect. The size, depth, and location of the defect are all critical factors in the tailoring of the donor graft.

Advantages to the use of osteochondral allografts include the ability to achieve precise surface architecture, immediate transplantation of viable hyaline cartilage as a single-stage procedure, the potential to replace large defects or even hemicondyles, and no donor site morbidity. Use of a large dowel osteochondral transplant in this capacity eliminates the dead space that is encountered between the smaller cylindrical grafts that are used with autologous mosaicplasty.

Limitations of osteochondral allografting include limited graft availability, high cost, risk of immunological rejection, possible incomplete graft incorporation, potential for disease transmission, and the technically demanding aspects of machining and sizing the allograft.

Autologous chondrocyte implantation

Autologous chondrocyte implantation, originally described in 1994, is an innovative, novel technique to restore cartilage cells into full-thickness chondral defects. The primary theoretical advantage of auto-

logous chondrocyte implantation is the development of hyaline-like cartilage rather than fibrocartilage in the defect, presumably leading to better long-term outcomes and longevity of the healing tissue. However, the procedure is not without limitations.

Autologous chondrocyte implantation involves a minimum of two operations, one for tissue harvest and the other for cell implantation. Furthermore, autologous chondrocyte implantation is technically demanding, and complications related to the periosteal graft have been reported.

Cell-based and scaffold treatment

Although cell-based therapies for inducing cartilage regeneration, such as autologous chondrocyte implantation, have demonstrated progress, the results have not been highly predictable or reproducible. In addition, limitations have included a requirement for a two-stage procedure and a technically demanding operation that fails to provide structural support for cells during the postoperative healing and incorporation phase.

So-called second-generation techniques in which harvested autologous chondrocytes are delivered on absorbable scaffolds that support the cells during the preimplantation culturing and postoperative healing phases have evolved. Essential properties of these scaffolds include biocompatibility and biodegradability through safe biomechanical pathways at suitable time intervals.

In the matrix-associated chondrocyte implantation procedure, chondrocytes are incorporated into a porcine type-I/III collagen membrane. One surface has a relatively higher density of collagen fibers that creates a smooth low-friction surface, while the other has a rough appearance because of larger interstices between the collagen fibers to allow for seeding of chondrocytes.

Hyaluronan-based scaffolds deliver the autologous chondrocytes in a scaffold of hyaluronan derivatives. Advantages of these procedures over autologous chondrocyte implantation include a more even cell distribution, avoidance of periosteal harvest and implantation, and increased technical ease without the need for suturing to adjacent articular cartilage.[137]

Tissue-engineered collagen matrices seeded with autologous chondrocytes

Tissue-engineered collagen matrices seeded with autologous chondrocytes provide a promising new technology with which to address chondral lesions of the knee.[133] This procedure involves harvesting of the autologous chondrocytes from non-weight-bearing aspects of the knee in a manner analogous to conventional autologous chondrocyte implantation. The cells are then loaded onto a type-I bovine collagen honeycomb matrix and are cultured *ex vivo*.

In distinction to second-generation techniques, however, the cell-scaffold construct is subsequently subjected to mechanical stimulation with the use of a proprietary bioreactor that applies hydrostatic pressure to the chondrocytes for a minimum of seven days. A lack of mechanical stimulation may be responsible for chondrocyte dedifferentiation and inferior mechanical properties, and the application of a mechanical load stimulates chondrocytes to produce increased amounts of type-II collagen, aggrecan, and other critical components of a hyaline extracellular matrix.

Summary of treatments for articular cartilage defects

There is currently considerable debate as to the efficacy of the various treatments and as yet no consensus on optimal treatment has been reached.[133] There is a lack of high-quality studies (Table 32.13).

Table 32.13 Grades of recommendation for cartilage repair procedures

	Grade[a]
Marrow stimulation procedures	B
Adjuncts to marrow stimulation	I
Platelet-rich plasma	I
Autologous osteochondral transplantation	B
Osteochondral allograft transplantation	B
Autologous chondrocyte implantation	C
Hyaluronan-based scaffolds seeded with autologous chondrocytes	I
Tissue-engineered collagen matrices seeded with autologous chondrocytes	I

[a]A = good evidence (level 1 studies with consistent findings) for or against intervention; B = fair evidence (level 2 or 3 studies with consistent findings) for or against intervention; C = poor-quality evidence (level 4 or 5 studies with consistent findings) for or against intervention; I = insufficient or conflicting evidence not allowing a recommendation for or against intervention. (Chapter 3 has more on "levels of evidence.")

Although short-term reduction of symptoms has been shown with these treatments, long-term reduction of arthritic disability has not been shown. Success also varies according to size and location of the articular lesion and between treatments. As yet, no method of treatment has been able to reproduce true hyaline cartilage with its complex layered structure.

Other methods of reducing stress on the damaged articular cartilage include correction of biomechanical abnormalities, attention to ensure symmetry of gait, and the use of a brace to control any instability. Pool running may also be helpful, and the mini-trampoline is used in the early stages of running and agility work to reduce load-bearing. Proprioceptive exercises and strength exercises are also important.

Acute patellar trauma

Acute trauma to the patella (e.g. from a hockey stick or from a fall onto the kneecap) can cause a range of injuries from fracture of the patella to osteochondral damage of the patellofemoral joint with persisting patellofemoral joint pain. In some sportspeople, the pain settles without any long-term sequelae.

If there is suspicion of fracture, X-ray should be obtained. It is important to be able to differentiate between a fracture of the patella and a bipartite patella, which is a benign finding. A skyline view of the patella should be performed in addition to normal views.

If there is no evidence of fracture, the patient can be assumed to be suffering acute patellofemoral inflammation. This can be difficult to treat. Treatment consists of nonsteroidal anti-inflammatory drugs (NSAIDs), local electrotherapy (e.g. interferential stimulation, TENS), and avoidance of aggravating activities such as squatting or walking down stairs. Taping of the patella may alter the mechanics of patellar tracking and therefore reduce the irritation and pain (Chapter 33). If taping provides symptom relief, rehabilitation and altered loading by strengthened quadriceps could be beneficial.

Fracture of the patella

Patellar fractures can occur either by direct trauma, in which case the surrounding retinaculum can be intact, or by indirect injury from quadriceps contraction, in which case the retinaculum and the vastus muscles are usually torn.

Undisplaced fractures of the patella with normal function of the extensor mechanism can be managed non-surgically, initially with an extension splint. Over the next weeks as the fracture unites, the range of flexion can be gradually increased and the quadriceps strengthened in the inner range.

Fractures with significant displacement, where the extensor mechanism is not intact, require surgical treatment. This involves reduction of the patella and fixation, usually with a tension band wire technique. The vastus muscle on both sides also needs to be repaired. The rehabilitation following this procedure is as for an undisplaced fracture.

Patellar dislocation

Patellar dislocation occurs when the patella is displaced laterally, leaving its confines within the trochlea groove of the femoral condyle. Acute patellar dislocation may be either traumatic with a history of a traumatic force, followed by development of a hemarthrosis, or atraumatic, which usually occurs in young girls with associated ligamentous laxity. Often the latter do not have a history of significant trauma, and the dislocation is accompanied by mild-to-moderate swelling.

The medial patellofemoral ligament is the primary stabilizer against lateral patellar translation, providing between 53% and 67% of the medial soft tissue restraint.[138] It lies deep to the vastus medialis muscle, and attaches from the posterior part of the medial epicondyle, to the superomedial aspect of the patella, the under-surface of the vastus medialis, and the quadriceps tendon. Anatomically, the medial patellofemoral ligament acts as a passive check to prevent the patella from extreme lateral displacement.[139]

It has been suggested that, in the majority of patellar dislocation cases, the medial patellofemoral ligament is disrupted. It has also been estimated that the redislocation rate after primary patellar dislocation managed non-operatively is 15–44%.[139]

Primary patellar dislocations may also cause an osteochondral avulsion fracture, which sometimes requires surgery. Due to the limited time to intervene, caused by swelling of the avulsed fragment making it impossible to fit for fixation, a semi-urgent MRI could be recommended in young patients with a primary patellar dislocation. A shell-formed bony fragment indicating an osteochondral avulsion may be detected on plain radiographs but is easily missed, resulting in a failure to repair the injury.

Clinical features

Patients with traumatic patellar dislocation usually complain that, on twisting or jumping, the knee suddenly gave way with the development of severe pain. Often the patient describes a feeling of something "moving" or "popping out." Swelling develops almost immediately. The dislocation usually reduces spontaneously with knee extension; however, in some cases this may require some assistance or regional anesthesia (e.g. femoral nerve block).

A number of factors predispose to dislocation of the patella:

- femoral anteversion
- shallow femoral groove (trochlea dysplasia)
- genu valgum
- loose medial retinaculum
- tight lateral retinaculum
- vastus medialis dysplasia
- increased quadriceps vector (Q angle)
- patellar alta
- excessive subtalar pronation
- patellar dysplasia
- general hypermobility.

The main differential diagnosis of an acute patellar dislocation is an ACL rupture. Both conditions have similar histories of twisting, an audible "pop," a feeling of something "going out," and subsequent development of hemarthrosis.

On examination, there is usually a gross effusion, marked tenderness over the medial border of the patella, and a positive lateral apprehension test when attempts are made to push the patella in a lateral direction. Any attempt to contract the quadriceps muscle aggravates the pain, and the patient often finds a painless rest in full extension. X-rays, including anteroposterior, lateral, skyline, and intercondylar views, should be performed to rule out osteochondral fracture or a loose body.

Treatment

Treatment of traumatic patellar dislocation is somewhat controversial.[140] Most first-time dislocations should be treated non-operatively. However, there are a number of indications for surgery.

A systematic review by Stefancin and Parker[141] advocated surgery in the presence of an osteochondral fracture, substantial disruption of the medial patellar stabilizers, or a laterally subluxated patella with normal alignment of the contralateral knee. It also advocated surgery for a second dislocation, or in patients not improving with appropriate rehabilitation.

Medial patellofemoral ligament reconstructive surgery has increasingly become the surgical procedure of choice. A review suggested this procedure may provide favorable clinical and radiological outcomes for patients with patellar instability.[140] However, a critical appraisal of the papers reviewed highlighted a number of methodological limitations, which means that any conclusions made from these papers should be interpreted with caution.[140]

The principles of rehabilitation after medial patellofemoral ligament reconstruction are similar to those guiding rehabilitation after other ligamentous reconstructions of the knee, such as ACL.[142]

The most important aim of rehabilitation after patellofemoral dislocation is to reduce the chances of a recurrence of the injury. As a result, the rehabilitation program is lengthy and emphasizes core stability, pelvic positioning, vastus medialis obliquus strength, and stretching of the lateral structures when tight. A suggested rehabilitation program is shown in Table 32.14 overleaf.

The most helpful recent addition to patellofemoral rehabilitation is increased emphasis on core stability. Similar to ACL intervention exercises, rotational control of the limb under the pelvis is critical to knee and kneecap stability.

Bracing could be helpful for these patients in combination with extensive rehabilitation. The patellar brace usually has a hole for the patella and a lateral rim to prevent lateral dislocation. Bracing does not prevent recurrent instability but can be helpful for those with symptomatic instability.

Less common causes

Patellar tendon rupture

The patellar tendon occasionally ruptures spontaneously. This is usually in association with a sudden severe eccentric contraction of the quadriceps muscle, which may occur when a sportsperson stumbles, or when attempting a powerful take-off maneuver (e.g. long-jump event in track-and-field competition). There may have been a history of previous corticosteroid injection into the tendon. A previous history of patellar tendinopathy is uncommon.

Patients complain of a sudden onset of pain over the patellar tendon accompanied by a tearing sensation, and they are unable to stand. On examination, there is a visible loss of fullness at the front of the knee, as the patella is retracted proximally. The knee extensor mechanism is no longer intact and knee extension cannot be initiated from the straight-leg position.

Surgical repair of the tendon is needed and must be followed by intensive rehabilitation. Full recovery takes six to nine months and there is often some residual disability.

Quadriceps tendon rupture

Quadriceps tendon rupture is less common than patellar tendon rupture. The most usual presentation is a non-contact, dramatic, acute injury while landing from a jump or changing direction suddenly. The sportsperson, more commonly male, usually falls, and is unable to continue with the activity (e.g. basketball or volleyball). The immediate differential diagnosis includes ACL rupture, patellar dislocation, and patellar tendon rupture.

Examination reveals a defect above the region of the patella. The patient is unable to contract the extensor apparatus. Palpation should reveal the distinction from patellar tendon rupture. Imaging such as MR or US can be performed as a preoperative workup and to assess other structures.

Management requires complex surgical repair and extensive rehabilitation. Most surgeons advocate partial weight-bearing for six weeks post-operatively. The player must consider six months as a reasonable target for return to play (i.e. generally the next season). Players have returned to sport after this injury, but there must be a major focus on general strengthening, not only on rehabilitating the extensor mechanism.

Bursal hematoma

Occasionally, an acute bursal hematoma or acute prepatellar bursitis occurs as a result of a fall onto the knee. This causes bleeding into the pre-patellar bursa and subsequent inflammation.

The hematoma usually settles spontaneously with firm compression bandaging.

If the hematoma does not settle, it should be aspirated and the bloodstained fluid removed. Anti-inflammatory medication (e.g. NSAIDs) may also be appropriate. This injury is often associated with a skin wound (e.g. abrasion) and therefore may become infected. Adequate skin care is essential. If the bursa recurs, then aspiration followed by injection of a corticosteroid agent may be required. If non-surgical treatment fails, arthroscopic excision of the bursa is indicated.

Table 32.14   Rehabilitation program following patellar dislocation (see Figs 32.5 and 32.6)

Phase	Goal of phase	Time post injury	Physiotherapy treatment	Exercise program	Functional/sport-related activity
Phase 1	Control swelling Maintain knee extension Isometric quadriceps strength	0–2 weeks	Extension splint (removal dependent on surgeon/physician) Cryotherapy Electrotherapy PFJ taping Manual therapy	Quadriceps drills (supine) Bilateral calf raises Foot and ankle Hip abduction	Progress to FWB
Phase 2	No swelling Full extension Flexion to 100° 4+/5 quadriceps strength 5/5 hamstring strength	2–6 weeks	Cryotherapy Electrotherapy Compression Manual therapy Gait re-education Exercise modification	ROM drills Quadriceps/VMO setting Mini-squats and -lunges Bridges (double-, then single-leg) Hip abduction and extension with rubber tubing Single-leg calf raises Gait re-education drills Balance and proprioceptive drills (single-leg)	Walking Exercise bike
Phase 3	Full ROM Full strength and power Return to jogging, running, and agility Return to restricted sport-specific drills	6–8 weeks	Manual therapy Exercise/activity modification and supervision	As above—increase difficulty, repetitions, and weight, where appropriate Single-leg squats Single-leg press Jump and land drills Agility drills	Straight line jogging Swimming (light kick) Road bike Straight line running Progressing to sport-specific running and agility (progressively sequenced) (e.g. running forwards, sideways, backwards, sprinting, jumping, hopping, changing directions, kicking)
Phase 4	Return to sport	8–12 weeks	As above	High-level sport-specific strengthening as required	Progressive return to sport (e.g. restricted training, unrestricted training, match play, competitive match play)

FWB = full weight-bearing; PFJ = patellofemoral joint; ROM = range of motion; VMO = vastus medialis obliquus

Fat pad impingement

Acute fat pad impingement (often incorrectly referred to as "Hoffa's syndrome") usually occurs as a result of a hyperextension injury. As the fat pad is the most sensitive part of the knee, this condition may be extremely painful.[143] There may be an inferiorly tilted lower pole of the patella predisposing to injury. On examination, tenderness is distal to the patella but beyond the margin of the patellar tendon. A hemarthrosis may be present.

An acute fat pad impingement can be extremely difficult to treat. The basic principles of treatment are a reduction of aggravating activities, electrotherapeutic modalities to settle inflammation, and resumption of range of movement exercises as soon as possible. Taping of the patella may help in reducing the amount of tilt and impingement (Chapter 33). If non-surgical management is not successful, arthroscopic joint lavage and resection of the fat pad may help.

Fracture of the tibial plateau

Tibial plateau fracture (Fig. 32.14) is seen in high-speed injuries such as falls while skiing, wave-jumping, or horse-riding. This condition needs to be excluded when diagnosing collateral ligament damage with instability. The patient complains of severe pain and inability to weight-bear. Fractures are associated with a lipohemarthrosis, which can be detected on a horizontal lateral X-ray by the presence of a fat–fluid level. CT scan can help define the fracture.

Minimally displaced fractures should be treated by six weeks of non-weight-bearing in a hinged knee brace (Fig. 32.4a). Displaced fractures or fractures with unstable fragment(s) require internal surgical fixation. Displaced vertical split fractures may be fixed percutaneously during arthroscopy.

Tibial plateau fractures are commonly associated with meniscal or ACL injuries. In these cases arthroscopic assessment is required. Following recovery from a tibial plateau fracture, weight-bearing activity may need to be reduced, as the irregular joint surface predisposes to the development of osteoarthritis.

Superior tibiofibular joint injury

Acute dislocation of the superior tibiofibular joint occurs occasionally as a result of a direct blow. The patient complains of pain in the area of the joint and may be aware of obvious deformity. The lateral popliteal nerve may be damaged with this injury.

Sprain of the tibiofibular joint is more common. The patient complains of local pain aggravated by movement and, on examination, there is local tenderness and some anteroposterior instability. Treatment consists of rest and local electrotherapeutic modalities. Rarely, a chronic instability of the superior tibiofibular joint develops; this may require surgical stabilization.

Ruptured hamstring tendon

Spontaneous rupture of one of the distal hamstring tendons at the knee occurs occasionally during sprinting. Sudden onset of pain is localized to either the biceps femoris tendon or the semitendinosus tendon. Pain and weakness are present with resisted hamstring contraction.

A recent report suggested that rupture of the semitendinosus tendon could be successfully treated non-operatively.[144] In the few cases of biceps femoris tendon rupture reported, all but one was treated surgically.[145]

Coronary ligament sprain

The "coronary ligament" is the name given to the deep portion of the fibrous joint capsule attached to the periphery of each meniscus and connected to the adjacent margin of the tibia.

A sprain of the coronary ligament may occur as a result of a twisting injury. These sprains may be difficult to differentiate from a meniscal injury.

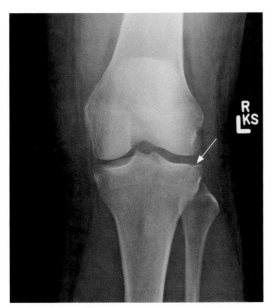

Figure 32.14 X-ray of a tibial plateau fracture

There is no joint effusion associated with this injury and usually minimal joint line swelling. There is, however, joint line tenderness and McMurray's test may be painful.

MRI interpreted by an experienced radiologist should provide a non-invasive diagnosis; however, if this fails to clarify the situation, arthroscopy may be required to differentiate coronary ligament sprains from meniscal tears. At arthroscopy, the only abnormality is occasional localized hemorrhage, and treatment is difficult. Coronary ligament sprain is often associated with a grade I MCL sprain.

CLINICAL SPORTS MEDICINE MASTERCLASSES
www.clinicalsportsmedicine.com

- Links outlined in the chapter and detailed instruction in physical examination of the patient with an acute knee injury.

RECOMMENDED WEBSITES

The University of Minnesota Orthopaedics' Sports Medicine Institute: www.sportsdoc.umn.edu

Important information websites for ACL prevention are:

- Oslo Sports Trauma Research Center: www.ostrc.no
- Cincinnati Children's Hospital Medical Center: www.cincinnatichildrens.org/svc/prog/sports-med/human
- Santa Monica Sports Medicine Federation: www.aclprevent.com/aclprevention.htm
- Vermont Ski Safety: www.vermontskisafety.com

REFERENCES

1. Myklebust G, Bahr R. Return to play guidelines after anterior cruciate ligament surgery. *Br J Sports Med* 2005;39(3):127–31.
2. Stiell IG, Greenberg GH, Wells GA et al. Prospective validation of a decision rule for the use of radiography in acute knee injuries. *JAMA* 1996;275(8):611–15.
3. Englund M, Guermaz IA, Gale D et al. Incidental meniscal findings on knee MRI in middle-aged and elderly persons. *N Engl J Med* 2008;359(11):1108–15.
4. Frobell RB, Roos HP, Roos EM et al. The acutely ACL injured knee assessed by MRI: are large volume traumatic bone marrow lesions a sign of severe compression injury? *Osteoarthritis Cartilage* 2008;16(7):829–36.
5. Johnson DL, Urban WP, Caborn DN et al. Articular cartilage changes seen with magnetic resonance imaging-detected bone bruises associated with acute anterior cruciate ligament rupture. *Am J Sports Med* 1998;26(3):409–14.
6. DeHaven KE, Bronstein RD. Arhroscopic medial meniscus repair in he athlete. *Clin Sports Med* 1997;16:69–86.
7. Pyne S. Current progress in meniscal repair and postoperative rehabilitation. *Curr Sports Med Reports* 2002;1:265–71.
8. Herrlin S, Hållander M, Wange P et al. Arthroscopic or conservative treatment of degenerative medial meniscal tears: a prospective randomised trial. *Knee Surg Sports Traumatol Arthrosc* 2007;15(4):393–401.
9. Suter LG, Fraenkel L, Losina E et al. Medical decision making in patients with knee pain, meniscal tear, and osteoarthritis. *Arthritis Rheum* 2009;61(11):1531–38.
10. Rodeo SA. Instructional course lectures, the American Academy of Orthopaedic Surgeons – arthroscopic meniscal repair with use of the outside-in technique. *J Bone Joint Surg Am* 2000;82:127–41.
11. Indelicato PA. Isolated medial collateral injuries in the knee. *J Am Acad Orthop Surg* 1995;3(1):9–14.
12. Frobell RB, Lohmander LS, Roos HP. Acute rotational trauma to the knee: poor agreement between clinical assessment and magnetic resonance imaging findings. *Scand J Med Sci Sports* 2007;17(2):109–14.
13. Ball S, Haddad FS. The impact of an acute knee clinic. *Ann R Coll Surg Engl* 2010;92(8):685–8.
14. Cooper MT, Kaeding C. Comparison of the hospital cost of autograft versus allograft soft-tissue anterior cruciate ligament reconstructions. *Arthroscopy* 2010;26(11):1478–82.
15. Fu FH, Kowalchuk D. Cost analysis comparing single-bundle and double-bundle anterior cruciate ligament (ACL) reconstruction. *Am J Sports Med* 2009;37(9):e1.
16. Gottlob CA, Baker CL, Pellissier JM et al. Cost effectiveness of anterior cruciate ligament reconstruction in young adults. *Clin Orthop Relat Res* 1999;367:272–82.
17. Paxton ES, Kymes SM, Brophy RH. Cost-effectiveness of anterior cruciate ligament reconstruction: a preliminary comparison of single-bundle and double-bundle techniques. *Am J Sports Med* 2010;38(12):2417–25.
18. Spindler KP, Wright RW. Clinical practice. Anterior cruciate ligament tear. *N Engl J Med* 2008;359(20):2135–42.

19. Agel J, Arendt E, Bershadsky B. Anterior cruciate ligament injury in national collegiate athletic association basketball and soccer: a 13 year review. *Am J Sports Med* 2005;33(4):524–30.

20. Alentorn-Geli E, Myer GD, Silvers HJ et al. Prevention of non-contact anterior cruciate ligament injuries in soccer players. Part 1: Mechanisms of injury and underlying risk factors. *Knee Surg Sports Traumatol Arth* 2009;17(7):705–29.

21. Paul JJ, Spindler KP, Andrish JT et al. Jumping versus nonjumping anterior cruciate ligament injuries: A comparison of pathology. *Clin J Sport Med* 2003;13(1):1–5.

22. Logan MC, Williams A, Lavelle J et al. What really happens during the Lachman test? *Am J Sports Med* 2004;32(2):369–75.

23. Segond P. Recherches cliniques et expérimentales sur les épanchements sanguins du genou par entorse. *Progres Med* 1879;7:297–99, 319–21, 40–41.

24. Beynnon BD, Johnson RJ, Abate JA et al. Treatment of anterior cruciate ligament injuries, part 2. *Am J Sports Med* 2005;33(11):1751–67.

25. Hanypsiak BT, Spindler KP, Rothrock CR et al. Twelve-year follow-up on anterior cruciate ligament reconstruction: long-term outcomes of prospectively studied osseous and articular injuries. *Am J Sports Med* 2008;36(4):671–7.

26. Frobell RB, Roos EM, Roos HP et al. A randomized trial of treatment for acute anterior cruciate ligament tears. *New Engl J Med* 2010;363:331–42.

27. Kostogiannis I, Ageberg E, Neuman P et al. Clinically assessed knee joint laxity as a predictor for reconstruction after an anterior cruciate ligament injury: a prospective study of 100 patients treated with activity modification and rehabilitation. *Am J Sports Med* 2008;36(8):1528–33.

28. Eitzen I, Moksnes H, Snyder-Mackler L et al. Functional tests should be accentuated more in the decision for ACL reconstruction. *Knee Surg Sports Traumatol Arthrosc* 2010;18(11):1517–25.

29. Meuffels DE, Favejee MM, Vissers MM et al. Ten year follow-up study comparing conservative versus operative treatment of anterior cruciate ligament ruptures. A matched-pair analysis of high level athletes. *Br J Sports Med* 2009;43(5):347–51.

30. Spindler KP, Kuhn JE, Freedman KB et al. Anterior cruciate ligament reconstruction autograft choice: bone-tendon-bone versus hamstring: does it really matter? A systematic review. *Am J Sports Med* 2004;32(8):1986–95.

31. Borchers JR, Pedroza A, Kaeding C. Activity level and graft type as risk factors for anterior cruciate ligament graft failure: a case-control study. *Am J Sports Med* 2009;37(12):2362–7.

32. Shelbourne KD, Patel DV. Timing of surgery in anterior cruciate ligament-injured knees. *Knee Surg Sports Traumatol Arthrosc* 1995;3:148–56.

33. Eitzen I, Holm I, Risberg MA. Preoperative quadriceps strength is a significant predictor of knee function two years after anterior cruciate ligament reconstruction. *Br J Sports Med* 2009;43(5):371–6.

34. Shelbourne KD, Nitz P. Accelerated rehabilitation after anterior cruciate ligament reconstruction. *Am J Sports Med* 1990;18(3):292–9.

35. Cooper RL, Taylor NF, Feller JA. A randomised controlled trial of proprioceptive and balance training after surgical reconstruction of the anterior cruciate ligament. *Res Sports Med* 2005;13:217–30.

36. Liu-Ambrose T, Taunton JE, MacIntyre D et al. The effects of proprioceptive or strength training on the neuromuscular function of the ACL reconstructed knee. *Scan J Med Sci Sports* 2003;13:115–23.

37. McDevitt ER, Taylor DC, Miller MD et al. Functional bracing after anterior cruciate ligament reconstruction: a prospective, randomized, multi-center study. *Am J Sports Med* 2004;32:1887–92.

38. Risberg MA, Holm I, Steen H et al. The effect of knee bracing after anterior cruciate reconstruction: a prospective, randomized study with two years' follow up. *Am J Sports Med* 1999;27:76–83.

39. Kuster MS, Grob K, Kuster M et al. The benefits of wearing a compression sleeve after ACL reconstruction. *Med Sci Sports Exerc* 1999;31(3):368–71.

40. Logerstedt DS, Snyder-Mackler L, Ritter RC et al. Knee stability and movement coordination impairments: knee ligament sprain. *J Orthop Sports Phys Ther* 2010;40(4):A1–37.

41. van Grinsven S, van Cingel RE, Holla CJ et al. Evidence-based rehabilitation following anterior cruciate ligament reconstruction. *Knee Surg Sports Traumatol Arthrosc* 2010;18(8):1128–44.

42. Beynnon BD, Uh BS, Johnson RJ et al. Rehabilitation after anterior cruciate ligament reconstruction: a prospective, randomized, double-blind comparison of programs administered over 2 different time intervals. *Am J Sports Med* 2005;33(3):347–59.

43. Shelbourne KD, Klootwyk TE, DeCarlo MS. Rehabilitation program for anterior cruciate ligament reconstruction. *Sports Med Arthrosc Rev* 1997;5:77–82.

44. Fleming BC, Oksendahl H, Beynnon BD. Open- or closed-kinetic chain exercises after anterior cruciate ligament reconstruction? *Exerc Sport Sci Rev* 2005;33(3):134–40.

45. Perry MC, Morrissey MC, King JB et al. Effects of closed versus open kinetic chain knee extensor resistance training on knee laxity and leg function in patients during the 8- to 14-week post-operative period after anterior cruciate ligament reconstruction. *Knee Surg Sports Traumatol Arthrosc* 2010;13(5):357–69.

46. Eakin CL. Knee arthrofibrosis: prevention and management of a potentially devastating condition. *Phys Sportsmed* 2001;29(3):31–42.

47. Tegner Y, Lysholm J. Rating systems in the evaluation of knee ligament injuries. *Clin Orthop Relat Res* 1985;198:43–9.

48. Noyes FR, Barber SD, Mooar LA. A rationale for assessing sports activity levels and limitations in knee disorders. *Clin Orthop Relat Res* 1989;246:238–49.

49. Hefti F, Müller W, Jakob RP et al. Evaluation of knee ligament injuries with the IKDC form. *Knee Surg Sports Traumatol Arthrosc* 1993;1(3–4):226–34.

50. Roos EM. Outcome after anterior cruciate ligament reconstruction—a comparison of patients' and surgeons' assessments. *Scand J Med Sci Sports* 2001;11(5).

51. Ageberg E, Forssblad M, Herbertsson P et al. Sex differences in patient-reported outcomes after anterior cruciate ligament reconstruction: data from the Swedish knee ligament register. *Am J Sports Med* 2010;38(7):1334–42.

52. Paradowski PT, Bergman S, Sundén-Lundius A et al. Knee complaints vary with age and gender in the adult population. Population-based reference data for the Knee injury and Osteoarthritis Outcome Score (KOOS). *BMC Musculoskelet Disord* 2006;7:38.

53. Corry IS, Webb JM, Clingeleffer AJ et al. Arthroscopic reconstruction of the anterior cruciate ligament. A comparison of patellar tendon autograft and four-strand tendon autograft. *Am J Sports Med* 1999;27:444–54.

54. Feller JA, Webster KE. A randomized comparison of patellar tendon and hamstring tendon anterior cruciate ligament reconstruction. *Am J Sports Med* 2003;31(4):564–73.

55. Gobbi A, Tuy B, Mahajan S et al. Quadrupled bone–semitendinosus anterior cruciate ligament reconstruction: a clinical investigation in a group of athletes. *Arthroscopy* 2003;19:691–9.

56. Siegel MG, Barber-Westin SD. Arthroscopic-assisted outpatient anterior cruciate ligament reconstruction using the semitendinosus and gracilis tendons. *Arthroscopy* 1998;14:268–77.

57. Biau DJ, Tournoux C, Katsahian S. ACL reconstruction: a meta-analysis of functional scores. *Clin Orthop Relat Res* 2007;458:180–7.

58. Waldén M, Hägglund M, Magnusson H et al. Anterior cruciate ligament injury in elite football: a prospective three-cohort study. *Knee Surg Sports Traumatol Arthrosc* 2011;19(1):11–19.

59. Shah VM, Andrews JR, Fleisig GS et al. Return to play after anterior cruciate ligament reconstruction in National Football League athletes. *Am J Sports Med* 2010;38(11):2233–9.

60. Roos H, Ornell M, Gardsell P et al. Soccer after anterior cruciate ligament injury: an incompatible combination? A national survey of incidence and risk factors and a 7 year follow up of 310 players. *Acta Orthop Scand* 1995;66:107–12.

61. Fink C, Hoser C, Hackl W et al. Long term outcome of operative or non-operative treatment of anterior cruciate ligament rupture: is sports activity a determining variable? *Int J Sports Med* 2001;22:304–9.

62. Myklebust G, Holm I, Maehlum S et al. Clinical, functional, and radiologic outcome in team handball players 6 to 11 years after anterior cruciate ligament injury: a follow-up study. *Am J Sports Med* 2003;31(6):981–9.

63. von Porat A, Roos EM, Roos H. High prevalence of osteoarthritis 14 years after an anterior cruciate ligament tear in male soccer players: a study of radiographic and patient relevant outcomes. *Am Rheum Dis* 2004;63(3):269–73.

64. Salmon L, Russell V, Musgrove T et al. Incidence and risk factors for graft rupture and contralateral rupture after anterior cruciate ligament reconstruction. *Arthroscopy* 2005;21(8):948–57.

65. Wright RW, Dunn WR, Amendola A et al. Risk of tearing the intact anterior cruciate ligament in the contralateral knee and rupturing the anterior cruciate ligament graft during the first 2 years after anterior cruciate ligament reconstruction: a prospective MOON cohort study. *Am J Sports Med* 2007;35(7):1131–4.

66. Freedman KB, D'Amato MJ, Nedeff DD et al. Arthroscopic anterior cruciate ligamant reconstruction: a meta-analysis comparing patellar tendon and hamstring tendon autografts. *Am J Sports Med*. 2003;31(1):2–11.

67. Shelbourne KD, Gray T, Haro M. Incidence of subsequent injury to either knee within 5 years after anterior cruciate ligament reconstruction with patellar tendon autograft. *Am J Sports Med* 2009;37(2):246–51.

68. Oiestad BE, Holm I, Aune AK et al. Knee function and prevalence of knee osteoarthritis after anterior cruciate ligament reconstruction: a prospective study with 10 to 15 years of follow-up. *Am J Sports Med* 2010;38(11):2201–10.

69. Lohmander LS, Englund PM, Dahl LL et al. The long-term consequence of anterior cruciate ligament and meniscus injuries: osteoarthritis. *Am J Sports Med* 2007;35(10):1756–69.

70. Feller JA. Anterior cruciate ligament rupture: is osteoarthritis inevitable? *Br J Sports Med* 2004;38: 383–4.

71. Fithian DC, Paxton EW, Stone ML et al. Prospective trial of a treatment algorithm for the management of the anterior cruciate ligament injured knee. *Am J Sports Med* 2005;33(3):335–46.

72. Lohmander LS, Ostenberg A, Englund M et al. High prevalence of knee osteoarthritis, pain, and functional limitations in female soccer players twelve years after anterior cruciate ligament injury. *Arthritis Rheum* 2004;50:3145–52.

73. Øiestad BE EL, Storheim K, Risberg MA. Knee osteoarthritis after anterior cruciate ligament injury: a systematic review *Am J Sports Med* 2009 Jul;37(7):1434–43.

74. Lohmander LS, Roos H. Knee ligament injury, surgery and osteoarthrosis. Truth or consequences? *Acta Orthop Scand* 1994;65(6):605–9.

75. Meunier A, Odensten M, Good L. Long-term results after primary repair or non-surgical treatment of anterior cruciate ligament rupture: a randomized study with a 15-year follow-up. *Scand J Med Sci Sports* 2007;17(3):230–7.

76. Brukner P. Return to play. A personal perspective. *Clin J Sport Med* 2005; 15(6):459–60.

77. Barber-Westin SD, Noyes F, Andrews M. A rigorous comparison between sexes of results and complications after anterior cruciate reconstruction. *Am J Sports Med* 1997;25:514–25.

78. Ferrari JD, Bach BRJ, Bush-Joseph CA et al. Anterior cruciate ligament reconstruction in men and women: an outcome analysis comparing gender. *Arthroscopy* 2001;17:588–96.

79. Gobbi A, Domzalski M, Pascual J. Comparison of anterior cruciate ligament reconstruction in male and female athletes using the patellar tendon and hamstring autografts. *Knee Surg Sports Traumatol Arthrosc* 2004;12:534–9.

80. Noojin FK, Barret GR, Hartzog CW et al. Clinical comparison of intra-articular anterior cruciate ligament reconstruction using autogenous semitendinosus and gracilis tendons in men versus women. *Am J Sports Med* 2000;28:783–9.

81. Salmon LJ, Refshauge KM, Russell VJ et al. Gender differences in outcome after anterior cruciate ligament reconstruction with hamstring tendon autograft. *Am J Sports Med* 2006;34(4):621–9.

82. McLean SG, Huang X, Su A et al. Sagittal plane biomechanics cannot injure the ACL during sidestep cutting. *Clin Biomech (Bristol, Avon)* 2004;19(8): 828–38.

83. McLean SG, Huang X, van den Bogert AJ. Association between lower extremity posture at contact and peak knee valgus moment during sidestepping: implications for ACL injury. *Clin Biomech (Bristol, Avon)* 2005;20(8):863–70.

84. McLean SG, Walker K, Ford KR et al. Evaluation of a two dimensional analysis method as a screening and evaluation tool for anterior cruciate ligament injury. *Br J Sports Med* 2005;39(6):355–62.

85. Olsen OE, Myklebust G, Engebretsen L et al. Injury mechanisms for anterior cruciate ligament injuries in team handball: a systematic video analysis. *Am J Sports Med* 2004;32(4):1002–12.

86. Teitz CC. Video analysis of ACL injuries. In: Griffin LY, ed. *Prevention of noncontact ACL injuries.* Rosemont, Ill: American Academy Orthopedic Surgeons, 2001, pp 87–92.

87. Ireland ML. Anterior cruciate ligament injuries in young female athletes. *Your Patient & Fitness* 1996;10(5): 26–30.

88. Ettlinger CF, Johnson RJ, Shealy JE. A method to help reduce the risk of serious knee sprains incurred in alpine skiing. *Am J Sports Med* 1995;23:531–7.

89. LaPrade RF, Burnett QM. Femoral intercondylar notch stenosis and correlation to anterior cruciate ligament injuries: a prospective study. *Am J Sports Med* 1994;22:198–203.

90. Souryal TO, Freeman TR. Intercondylar notch size and anterior cruciate ligament injuries in athletes – a prospective study. *Am J Sports Med* 1993;21:535–9.

91. Griffin LY, Albohm MJ, Arendt EA et. al. Understanding and preventing noncontact anterior cruciate ligament injuries: a review of the Hunt Valley II meeting, January, 2005. *Am J Sports Med* 2006;34(9):1512–32.

92. Renstrom P, Ljungqvis tA, Arendt EA et al. Non-contact ACL injuries in female athletes: an International Olympic Committee current concepts statement. *Br J Sports Med* 2008;42(6):394–412.

B

93. Uhorchak JM, Scoville CR, Williams GN et al. Risk factors associated with noncontact injury of the anterior cruciate ligament: a prospective four year evaluation of 859 West Point cadets. *Am J Sports Med* 2003;31:831–42.

94. Liu S, al-Shaikh R, Panossian V et al. Primary immunolocalization of estrogen progesterone target cells in the human anterior cruciate ligament. *J Orth Res* 1996;14(4):526–33.

95. Hame SL, Oakes DA, Markolf KL. Injury to the anterior cruciate ligament during alpine skiing: a biomechanical analysis of tibial torque and knee flexion angle. *Am J Sports Med* 2002;30(4):537–40.

96. Arendt EA, Agel J, Dick R. Anterior cruciate ligament injury patterns among collegiate men and women. *J Athl Train* 1999;34:86–92.

97. Beynnon BD, Bernstein I, Belislea et al. The effect of estradiol and progesterone on knee and ankle laxity. *Am J Sports Med* 2005;33(9):1298–304.

98. Moller-Nielsen J, Hammar M. Women's soccer injuries in relation to the menstrual cycle and oral contraceptive use. *Med Sci Sports Exerc* 1989;21(2):126–9.

99. Myklebust G, Maehlum S, Holm I et al. A prospective cohort study of anterior cruciate ligament injuries in elite Norwegian team handball. *Scand J Med Sci Sports* 1998;8(3):149–53.

100. Slauterbeck JR, Fuzie SF, Smith MP et al. The menstrual cycle, sex hormones and anterior cruciate ligament injury. *J Athl Train* 2002;37(3):275–8.

101. Wojtys EM, Huston LJ, Boynton MD et al. The effect of the menstrual cycle on anterior cruciate ligament injuries in women as determined by hormone levels. *Am J Sports Med* 2002;30(2):182–8.

102. Seneviratne A, Attia E, Williams RJ et al. The effect of estrogen on ovine anterior cruciate ligament fibroblasts: cell proliferation and collagen synthesis. *Am J Sports Med* 2004;32(7):1613–18.

103. Strickland SM, Belknap TW, Turner SA et al. Lack of hormonal influences on mechanical properties of sheep knee ligaments. *Am J Sports Med* 2003;31(2):210–15.

104. Wentorf FA, Sudoh K, Moses C et al. The effects of estrogen on material and mechanical properties of the intra- and extra-articular knee structures. *Am J Sports Med* 2006;34(12):1948–52.

105. Griffin LY, Albohm MJ, Arendt EA et al. Update on ACL injury prevention: theoretical and practical considerations. *Am J Sports Med* 2006;34(9):1512–32.

106. Myklebust G, Engebretsen L, Braekken IH et al. Prevention of anterior cruciate ligament injuries in female team handball players: a prospective intervention study over three seasons. *Clin J Sport Med* 2003;13:71–8.

107. Olsen OE, Myklebust G, Engebretsen L et al. Relationship between floor type and risk of ACL injury in team handball. *Scand J Med Sci Sports* 2003;13(5):299–304.

108. Lambson RB, Barnhill BS, Higgins RW. Football cleat design and its effect on anterior cruciate ligament injuries. *Am J Sports Med* 1996;24(2):155–9.

109. Orchard J, Seward H, McGivern J et al. Intrinsic and extrinsic risk factors for anterior cruciate ligament injury in Australian footballers. *Am J Sports Med* 2001;29(2):196–200.

110. Woo SL-Y, Debski RE, Withrow JD et al. Biomechanics of knee ligaments. *Am J Sports Med* 1999;27(4):533–43.

111. Boden BP, Griffin LY, Garrett WE Jr. Etiology and prevention of noncontact ACL injury. *Phys Sportsmed* 2000;28(4):53–60.

112. Huston LJ, Wojtys E. Neuromuscular performance characteristics in elite female athletes. *Am J Sports Med* 1996;24:427–36.

113. Griffin LY. Noncontact ACL injuries: is prevention possible? *J Musculoskel Med* 2001;18:507–16.

114. Hewett TE, Lindenfield TN, Riccobene JV et al. The effect of neuromuscular training on the incidence of knee injury in female athletes. A prospective study. *Am J Sports Med* 1999;27:699–706.

115. Hewett TE, Myer TD, Ford KR. Reducing knee and anterior cruciate ligament injuries among female athletes: a systematic review of neuromuscular training interventions. *J Knee Surg* 2005;18:82–8.

116. Heidt RS, Sweeterman LM, Carlonas RL et al. Avoidance of soccer injuries with pre-season conditioning. *Am J Sports Med* 2000;28(5):659–62.

117. Mandelbaum BR, Silvers HJ, Watanabe DS et al. Effectiveness of a neuromuscular and proprioceptive training program in preventing anterior cruciate ligament injuries in female athletes: 2-year follow-up. *Am J Sports Med* 2005;33(7):1003–10.

118. Myklebust G, Engebretsen L, Braekken IH et al. Prevention of anterior cruciate ligament injuries in female team handballers: a prospective study over three seasons. *Clin J Sport Med* 2003;13:71–8.

119. Petersen W, Braun C, Bock W et al. A controlled prospective case-control study of a prevention training program in female team handball players: the German experience. *Arch Orthop Trauma Surg* 2005;125(9):614–21.

120. Sodermann K, Werner S, Pietila T et al. Balance board training: prevention of traumatic injuries of the lower extremities in female soccer players? A prospective randomized intervention study (A). *Knee Surg Sports Arthosc* 2000;8(6):356–63.

121. Hewett TE, Ford KR, Myer GD. Anterior cruciate ligament injuries in female athletes. Part 2, a meta-analysis of neuromuscular interventions aimed at injury prevention. *Am J Sports Med* 2006;34(3): 490–8.

122. Boden BP, Sheehan FT, Torg JS et al. Noncontact anterior cruciate ligament injuries: mechanisms and risk factors. *J Am Acad Orthop Surg* 2010;18(9):520–7.

123. Soligard T, Myklebust G, Steffen K et al. Comprehensive warm-up programme to prevent injuries in young female footballers: cluster randomised controlled trial. *BMJ* 2008;337(Dec 9; a2469. doi: 10.1136/bmj.a2469).

124. Soligard T, Nilstad A, Steffen K et al. Compliance with a comprehensive warm-up programme to prevent injuries in youth football. *Br J Sports Med* 2010;44:787–93.

125. Shea KG, Apel PJ, Pfieffer RP. Anterior cruciate ligament injury in paediatric and adolescent patients. *Sports Med* 2003;33(6):455–71.

126. Bales CP, Guettler JH, Moorman CT III. Anterior cruciate ligament injuries in children with open physes: evolving strategies of treatment. *Am J Sports Med* 2004;32(8):1978–85.

127. Harner CD, Hoher J. Evaluation and treatment of posterior cruciate ligament injuries. *Am J Sports Med* 1998;26(3):471–82.

128. Hamada M, Shino K, Mitsuoka T et al. Chondral injury associated with acute isolated posterior cruciate ligament injury. *Arthroscopy* 2000;16:59–63.

129. Wind WM, Jr, Bergfeld JA, Parker RD. Evaluation and treatment of posterior cruciate ligament injuries: revisited. *Am J Sports Med* 2004;32(7):1765–75.

130. Bergfeld JA, McAllister DR, Parker RD et al. The effects of tibial rotation on posterior translation in knees in which the posterior cruciate ligament has been cut. *J Bone Joint Surg Am* 2001;83:1339–43.

131. Gross ML, Groiver JS, Bassett LW et al. Magnetic resonance imaging of the posterior cruciate ligament: clinical use to improve diagnostic accuracy. *Am J Sports Med* 1992;20:732–7.

132. Shelbourne KD, Davis TJ, Patel DV. The natural history of acute, isolated, nonoperatively treated posterior cruciate ligament injuries. A prospective study. *Am J Sports Med* 1999;27(3):276–83.

133. Bedi A, Feeley BT, Williams R Jr. Management of articular cartilage defects of the knee. *J Bone Joint Surg Am* 2010;92(4):994–1009.

134. Mithoefer K, Williams R Jr, Warren RF et al. Chondral resurfacing of articular cartilage defects in the knee with the microfracture technique. Surgical technique. *J Bone Joint Surg Am* 2006;88(Suppl 1, Part 2): 294–304.

135. Steadman JR, Ramappa AJ, Maxwell RB et al. An arthroscopic treatment regimen for osteoarthritis of the knee. *Arthroscopy* 2007;23:948–55.

136. Hangody L, Dobos J, Baló E et al. Clinical experiences with autologous osteochondral mosaicplasty in an athletic population: a 17-year prospective multicenter study. *Am J Sports Med* 2010;38(6):1125–33.

137. Kon E, Gobbi A, Filardo G et al. Arthroscopic second-generation autologous chondrocyte implantation compared with microfracture for chondral lesions of the knee: prospective nonrandomized study at 5 years. *Am J Sports Med* 2009;37:33–41.

138. Bicos J, Fulkerson JP, Amis A. The medial patellofemoral ligament. *Am J Sports Med* 2007;35: 484–92.

139. Smith TO, Walker J, Russell N. Outcomes of medial patellofemoral ligament reconstruction for patellar instability: a systematic review. *Knee Surg Sports Traumatol Arthrosc* 2007;15(11):1301–14.

140. Smith TO, Song F, Donell ST et al. Operative versus non-operative management of patellar dislocation. A meta-analysis. *Knee Surg Sports Traumatol Arthrosc* 2011;19(6):988–98.

141. Stefancin JJ, Parker RD. First-time traumatic patellar dislocation: a systematic review. *Clin Orthop Relat Res* 2007;455:93–101.

142. Fithian DC, Powers CM, Khan N. Rehabilitation of the knee after medial patellofemoral ligament reconstruction. *Clin Sports Med* 2010;29(2):283–90.

143. Dye SF, Vaupel GL, Dye CS. Conscious neurosensory mapping of the internal structures of the human knee without intra-articular anesthesia. *Am J Sports Med* 1998;26(6):773–7.

144. Adejuwon A, McCourt P, Hamilton B et al. Distal semitendinosus tendon rupture: is there any benefit of surgical intervention? *Clin J Sport Med* 2009;19(6):502–4.

145. Kusma M, Seil R, Kohn D. Isolated avulsion of the biceps femoris insertion—injury patterns and treatment options: a case report and literature review. *Arch Orthop Trauma Surg* 2007;127(9):777–80.

Chapter 33

Anterior knee pain

with KAY CROSSLEY, JILL COOK, SALLIE COWAN, and JENNY McCONNELL

In 1996, the world 1 ranked player Steffi Graf experienced "inflammation" in her left patellar tendon at Wimbledon and later in the same year she defaulted a semifinal match at Leipzig—the first withdrawal in her career. In February 1997, she defaulted in the Pan Pacific Open due to reaggravating that injury. On 10 June 1997, she underwent left knee surgery. She won only four of her career total 107 titles after that surgery; she retired in August 1999 aged 30.

Anterior knee pain is the most common presenting symptom in many physiotherapy and sports physician practices.[1, 2] It contributes substantially to the 20–40% of family practice consultations that relate to the musculoskeletal system.[3] The anatomy of the anterior knee is depicted in Figure 33.1.

In this chapter, we:

- outline the clinical approach to assessing the patient with anterior knee pain, particularly with a view to distinguishing the common conditions—patellofemoral pain and patellar tendinopathy
- detail contemporary management integrating high-level evidence with the best of clinical experience (see Chapter 3 for levels of evidence)

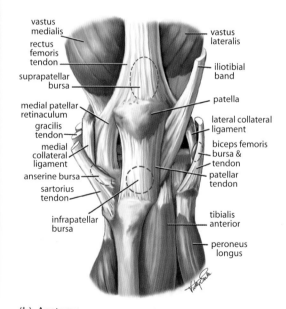

Figure 33.1 Anatomy of the anterior knee
(a) Surface anatomy

(b) Anatomy

- discuss less common causes of anterior knee pain such as fat pad impingement, which may mimic features of both patellofemoral pain and patellar tendinopathy.

Clinical approach

Distinguishing between patellofemoral pain and patellar tendinopathy as a cause of anterior knee pain can be difficult. Rarely, both conditions may be present. Causes of anterior knee pain are listed in Table 33.1.

History

There are a number of important factors to elicit from the history of a sportsperson with the presentation of "anterior knee pain." These include the specific location of the pain, the nature of aggravating activities, the history of the onset and the behavior of the pain, as well as any associated clicking, "giving way," or swelling.

Although it may be difficult for the patient with anterior knee pain to be specific about the location of the pain, this symptom often provides an important clue as to which structure is affected. For example, retropatellar or peripatellar pain suggests that the patellofemoral joint (PFJ) is a likely culprit, lateral pain localized to the lateral femoral epicondyle increases the likelihood of iliotibial band friction syndrome as the diagnosis (Chapter 34), and inferior patellar pain implicates the patellar tendon or infrapatellar fat pad. The patient who presents with bilateral knee pain is more likely to have patellofemoral pain or tendinopathy than an internal derangement of both knees.

The type of activity that aggravates the anterior knee pain also aids diagnosis. Consider two contrasting scenarios that a patient may report as causing pain at the infrapatellar region. In one case, precipitating activities, such as basketball, volleyball, high jumps, long jumps, or triple jumps that involve repetitive loading of the patellar tendon suggest the diagnosis of patellar tendinopathy. On the other hand, if a freestyle swimmer reported pain following tumble turning or vigorous kicking in the pool, where there had been no eccentric load on the tendon but a forceful extension of the knee, the practitioner should suspect an irritated fat pad. The mechanism of injury and the aggravating features are critical to accurate diagnosis.

The onset of typical patellofemoral pain is often insidious but it may present secondary to an acute traumatic episode (e.g. falling on the knee), or following another knee injury (e.g. meniscal, ligament) or knee surgery. The patient presents with a diffuse ache, which is usually exacerbated by loaded activities, such as ascending or descending stairs or running. Sometimes patellofemoral pain is aggravated by prolonged sitting ("movie-goer's knee"), but sitting tends to also aggravate pain of patellar tendinopathy so it is not diagnostic of patellofemoral pain. Pain during running that gradually worsens is more likely to be of patellofemoral origin, whereas pain that occurs at the start of activity, settles after warm-up and returns after activity is more likely to be patellar tendinopathy. Table 33.2 overleaf is an aid to differentiating patellofemoral pain and patellar tendinopathy; however, these conditions can coexist.

A history of recurrent crepitus may suggest patellofemoral pain. A feeling that the patella moves laterally at certain times suggests patellofemoral instability. An imminent feeling of "giving way" may be associated with patellar subluxation, patellofemoral pain, or meniscal abnormality. Although frank, dramatic giving way is usually associated with anterior cruciate ligament instability (Chapter 32), giving way is not uncommon in anterior knee pain presentations because of muscle weakness, or inhibition secondary to pain.

Table 33.1 Causes of anterior knee pain

Common	Less common	Occasionally seen/specific populations	Not to be missed
Patellofemoral pain	Fat pad impingement	Sinding-Larsen–Johansson lesion	Referred pain from the hip
Patellar tendinopathy	Synovial plica	Tenoperiostitis of upper tibia	Osteochondritis dissecans
	Pre-patellar bursitis	Stress fracture of the patella	Slipped capital femoral epiphysis
	Quadriceps tendinopathy	Osgood-Schlatter lesion	Perthes' disease
	Infrapatellar bursitis		Tumor (especially in the young)
	Patellofemoral instability		

Table 33.2 Comparison of the clinical features of patellofemoral pain and patellar tendinopathy

Signs	Patellofemoral pain	Patellar tendinopathy
Onset	Running (especially downhill), steps/stairs, hills Any weight-bearing activities involving knee flexion (e.g. distance running)	Activities involving jumping and/or changing direction (e.g. basketball, volleyball, high jump, netball, bounding, ballet, climbing stairs)
Pain	Non-specific or vague May be medial, lateral, or infrapatellar Aggravated by activities that load the PFJ	Usually at the inferior pole of patella Aggravated by jumping and early- to mid-squat
Inspection	Generally normal or VMO wasting	Generalized quadriceps wasting
Tenderness	Usually medial or lateral facets of patella May be tender in infrapatellar region May have no pain on palpation due to areas of patella being inaccessible	Commonly inferior pole of patellar tendon attachment Occasionally at distal attachment to tibial tuberosity Rarely in midtendon
Swelling	May have small effusion with either suprapatellar or infrapatellar swelling	Rare Tendon may be increased in thickness
Clicks/clunks	Occasional	No
Crepitus	Occasionally under patella	No
Giving way	Due to subluxation or (occasionally) quadriceps inhibition	Occasionally due to quadriceps inhibition
Knee range of motion	Usually normal May be decreased in severe cases	Usually normal No pain with overpressure
Quadriceps contraction in extension	Note quality of movement Usually not painful	Some cases are painful
PFJ movement	May be restricted in any direction Commonly restricted medial glide due to tight lateral structures	May have normal PFJ biomechanics In combined problem will have PFJ signs
VMO	May have obvious wasting, weakness, or more subtle deficits in tone and timing	May have generalized quadriceps weakness
Functional testing	Squats, stairs may aggravate PFJ taping should decrease pain	Decline squats aggravate pain PFJ taping has less effect

PFJ = patellofemoral joint; VMO = vastus medialis obliquus

A history of previous knee injury or surgery may be important; patellofemoral pain is a well-recognized complication of posterior cruciate ligament injury and anterior cruciate ligament reconstruction (Chapter 32). After ACL reconstruction using bone–patellar tendon–bone grafts (page 651), patellar tendinopathy is common.

An injury that is associated with pain and/or an effusion may result in inhibition of the vasti (reduced magnitude and onset of timing on EMG). This inhibition appears to be more profound in the vastus medialis obliquus (VMO), especially at smaller knee effusion volumes.[4, 5] Preferential inhibition of the VMO has the potential to set up an imbalance in the medial and lateral forces on the patella, predisposing to patellofemoral pain.[6] Significant knee swelling is rare in primary anterior knee pain and generally suggests additional intra-articular abnormality. However, a small effusion may be present with patellofemoral pain.

Previous treatment and the patient's response to that treatment should be noted. If treatment was unsuccessful, it is essential to determine whether the failure was due to incorrect diagnosis, inappropriate treatment, or poor patient adherence (see also Chapter 41, "Longstanding symptoms").

Examination

The primary aim of the clinical assessment is to determine the most likely cause of the patient's pain. It is critical to reproduce the patient's anterior knee pain, as location of tenderness and aggravating factors are key to the differential diagnosis. This is usually done with either a double- or single-leg squat (Fig. 33.2c overleaf). A squat done on a decline[7] makes the test more specific to the patellar tendon. It is essential to palpate the anterior knee carefully to determine the site of maximal tenderness.

 The knee examination is highlighted in the *Clinical Sports Medicine* masterclasses at www. clinicalsportsmedicine.com.

Examination includes:

1. Observation
   (a) standing (Fig. 33.2a)
   (b) walking
   (c) supine (Fig. 33.2b overleaf)
2. Functional tests
   (a) double- then single-leg squat (Fig. 33.2c overleaf)
   (b) step-up/step-down
   (c) jump/hop
   (d) lunge
   (e) double- then single-leg decline squat
3. Palpation
   (a) patella—medial and lateral facets (Fig. 33.2d overleaf)
   (b) medial/lateral retinaculum
   (c) patellar tendon
   (d) infrapatellar fat pad and inferior pole of patella (Fig. 33.2e overleaf)
   (e) tibial tubercle
   (f) effusion—swipe test, ballotment test
4. Patellofemoral joint assessment
   (a) mobility of patella
      (i) superior glide
      (ii) inferior glide
      (iii) medial glide (Fig. 33.2f on page 689)
      (iv) lateral glide—look for apprehension
   (b) dynamic assessment of patellar position
   (c) assessment of vasti function

5. Flexibility and range of motion
   (a) lateral soft tissue structures
   (b) quadriceps
   (c) hamstring
   (d) iliotibial band
   (e) gastrocnemius
   (f) soleus
   (g) knee flexion/extension
   (h) tibial rotation
   (i) hip and lumbar spine range of motion—all planes
6. Special tests (to exclude other pathology)
   (a) examination of knee joint with respect to acute injury (Chapter 32)
   (b) examination of hip joint (Chapters 28 and 29)
   (c) examination of lumbar spine (Chapter 26)
   (d) neurodynamic tests (neural Thomas test, slump test, prone bent knee test)

 Special tests 6a, b, and c are shown in the *Clinical Sports Medicine* masterclasses at www. clinicalsportsmedicine.com.

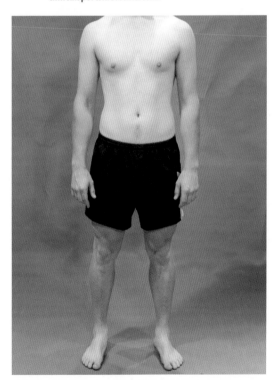

Figure 33.2 Examination of the anterior knee
(a) Observation—standing. Observe the patient from the front to examine lower limb alignment including femoral torsion, patellar alignment, and any signs of muscle wasting

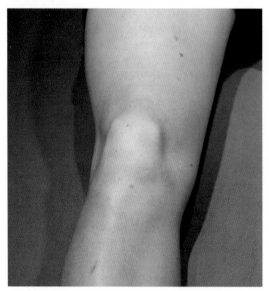

(b) Observation—supine.
Observe for lower limb alignment, effusion, position of the patella, and any evidence of patella tilt or rotation

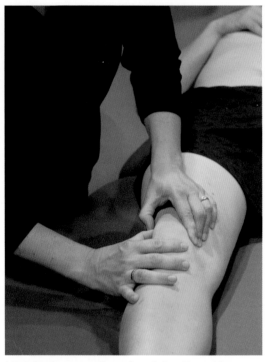

(d) Palpation—patella, and medial and lateral facets are palpated for tenderness

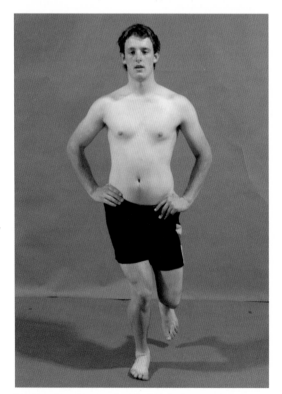

(c) Functional test—double-/single-leg squat.
If the patient's pain has not already been reproduced, functional tests such as squat, lunge, hop, step-up, step-down, or eccentric drop squat should be performed

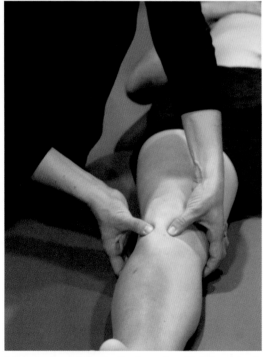

(e) Palpation—infrapatellar fat pad and inferior pole of patella

diagnosis of patellar tendinopathy.[9] However, in asymptomatic sportspeople or those with symptoms from another source in the anterior knee, the patellar tendon can have regions of "abnormal" imaging,[10–12] and the clinician should be wary of using imaging findings diagnostically.

> **WWW** Imaging in anterior knee pain is discussed in the *Clinical Sports Medicine* masterclasses at www. clinicalsportsmedicine.com.

Patellofemoral pain

In this section we:

- define the condition and underscore its significance
- review clinically relevant functional anatomy
- alert the clinician to predisposing factors and how to identify them—this may prove critical for effective long-term treatment
- summarize the results of randomized controlled trials (RCTs) that have added high-quality evidence to guide clinical treatment.

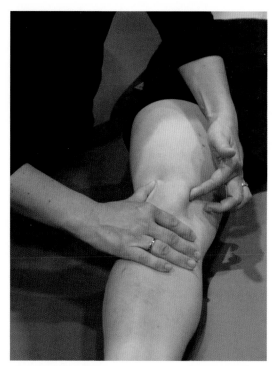

(f) Patellofemoral joint assessment—mobility of the patella—medial glide

Investigations

Imaging may be used to confirm a clinical impression obtained from the history and examination. Structural imaging includes conventional radiography, ultrasound, CT, and MRI. Occasionally, radionuclide bone scan is indicated to evaluate the "metabolic" status of the knee (e.g. after trauma, in suspected stress fracture).

The majority of patients with patellofemoral pain syndrome require either no imaging, or plain radiography consisting of a standard AP view, a true lateral view with the knee in 30° of flexion, and an axial view through the knee in 30–40° of flexion. Plain radiography can detect bipartite patella, apophyseal changes at the patellar tendon attachments, and osteoarthritis, as well as rule out potentially serious complications such as tumor or infection. Although CT and three-dimensional CT have been used to assess the PFJ morphology, MRI is gaining increasing popularity as an investigation of patellofemoral pain and the unstable patella, because of its capacity to image the patellar articular cartilage.[8]

MRI displays high signal abnormality in patellar tendinopathy. Ultrasound hypoechogenicity and excessive vascularity also indicate a potential

What is patellofemoral pain syndrome?

 Patellofemoral pain syndrome (PFPS) is the preferred term used to describe pain in and around the patella.

Synonyms for PFPS include "patellofemoral joint syndrome," "anterior knee pain," and "chondromalacia patellae." PFPS is an "umbrella" term used to embrace all peripatellar or retropatellar pain in the absence of other pathologies. Since the cause of the pain may differ between patients, it is appropriate to review the potential sources of patellofemoral pain.[13]

Numerous structures in the PFJ are susceptible to overload. A number of extra- and intra-articular components of the knee can generate neurosensory signals that ultimately result in the patient feeling pain (Chapter 6). Patellofemoral articular cartilage cannot directly be a source of nociception, as it is avascular and aneural. However, a cartilage lesion may lead to chemical or mechanical synovial irritation, edema, or erosion—all of which can result in pain.[14, 15]

Peripatellar synovitis, in the absence of obvious cartilage damage, must be considered one of the main causes of PFPS.[16] Soft tissues such as the lateral retinaculum have been implicated as a potent source of noxious input.[17–21] Another highly potent source of noxious input is the infrapatellar fat pad, which is highly innervated and is intimately related to the mechanically and chemically sensitive synovium.[22–24]

The PFPS may predispose to the development of patellofemoral osteoarthritis.

The PFPS has traditionally been considered to be a self-limiting condition. However, it may predispose to the development of patellofemoral osteoarthritis. Therefore, the condition should not be abandoned to "benign neglect" in the hope that its natural history is one of resolution.

Functional anatomy

At full extension, the patella sits lateral to the trochlea. During flexion, the patella moves medially and comes to lie within the intercondylar notch until 130° of flexion, when it starts to move laterally again.[23] The patella's mediolateral excursion is actively controlled by the quadriceps muscles, particularly the VMO and vastus lateralis components. With increasing knee flexion, a greater area of patellar articular surface comes into contact with the femur, thus offsetting the increased contact load that occurs with flexion. Loaded knee flexion activities subject the PFJ to forces ranging from 0.5 times body weight for level walking to seven to eight times body weight for stair climbing.[24] Balanced activity in the VMO and vastus lateralis are required to maintain optimal alignment and tracking of the patella within the femoral trochlea, and any change to this balance may change the magnitude and distribution of PFJ stress.

Factors that may contribute to pain

PFPS is likely to be initiated by increased or unaccustomed PFJ loads. Factors that influence PFJ load can be considered in two categories—extrinsic and intrinsic. During physical activities, the extrinsic load is created by the body's contact with the ground (ground reaction force) and is therefore moderated by body mass, speed of gait, surfaces, and footwear. The number of loading cycles and frequency of loading are also important. During weight-bearing activities, any increase in the amount of knee flexion increases the PFJ load. Therefore, when an individual experiences an increase in the magnitude of the PFJ load (e.g. higher training volume, increased speed of running), this may overload the PFJ structures sufficiently to initiate pain. (Hill/stair running and bounding *can* overload the PFJ structures but are much more likely to promote patellar tendon pain!)

Intrinsic factors can influence both the magnitude and the distribution of the PFJ load. Distribution of load is conceptualized as movement of the patella within the femoral trochlea—patella tracking. Intrinsic factors that can influence patella tracking may be considered "remote" or "local" (Fig. 33.3). Considering the patient as a whole, remote factors that affect patella tracking include femoral internal rotation, apparent knee valgus, tibial rotation, subtalar pronation, and muscle flexibility (all discussed below).[25] Local factors that influence patella movement include patella position, soft tissue tension, and neuromuscular control of the medial and lateral components of the vasti.[26]

So how does an increase in PFJ load result in patellofemoral pain? Dye[27] described a concept whereby injury to the PFJ musculoskeletal tissues results from supraphysiological loads—either a single maximal load or lower magnitude repetitive loads. Injury to these tissues initiates a cascade of events encompassing inflammation of the peripatellar synovium through to bone stress. Thus, a number of different pain-sensitive structures can give rise to the conscious sensation of patellofemoral pain (Chapter 6).[27]

Increased femoral internal rotation

Increased knee valgus

Assess subtalar pronation

Figure 33.3 Carefully observe the patient for key factors that contribute to PFPS (Table 33.3 overleaf)

Therefore, when the initial subjective and objective examinations are completed and the diagnosis of PFPS is confirmed, the clinician should assess the contribution of various extrinsic and intrinsic factors to the development of patellofemoral pain.

Although the history provides some valuable information pertaining to extrinsic factors, clinical examination is usually required to evaluate the key intrinsic contributing factors (remote and local) (Fig. 33.3). This comprehensive assessment is crucial in the planning of the treatment.

Remote intrisic factors

Remote intrinsic factors that may contribute to patellofemoral pain developing (see also Chapter 8) are:

* increased femoral internal rotation
* increased apparent knee valgus
* increased tibial rotation
* pronated foot type
* inadequate flexibility.

It is important to assess the patient in static postures as well as functional activities. Some factors may become more obvious during specific functional tasks, such as the step-down or single-leg squat, where the postural demands are high. Once a potential contributing factor has been identified, the clinician must investigate the mechanisms that may require intervention (Table 33.3 overleaf).

Increased femoral internal rotation

Increased femoral internal rotation is associated with patellofemoral pain[28] and may contribute to its development.[29] Clinical observation of the patient in standing reveals internally rotated femurs, often manifesting as "squinting patellae"—the patellae both face medially. During gait (walking or running), further internal rotation of the thigh can often be observed and may be visualized as an apparent knee valgus. Similar observations are noted during the step-down or single-leg squat test.

Increased apparent knee valgus

Genu valgum (Fig. 8.16g on page 76), or an increased Q angle, can be observed in standing and is often exaggerated during gait, possibly associated with a midstance valgus thrust. Additionally, increased hip adduction/internal rotation or a lateral pelvic drop during the step-down and single-leg squat (potentially owing to weakness of the gluteus

medius) results in an increase in apparent knee valgus posture. Apparent increased knee valgus or hip adduction,[29] and increased Q angle[30] and knee abduction moment[31] are all associated with development of patellofemoral pain.

Increased tibial rotation

Increased structural or functional tibial rotations can affect PFJ loads directly and also through transferred rotations to the femur. Tibial rotations are strongly coupled with the motion of the subtalar joint. Although there is little data on the assessment or treatment of structural tibial rotation in isolation, experienced clinicians often address functional rotation in association with femoral or subtalar rotations (see treatment outline, below).

Pronated foot type

A pronated foot type has been associated with patellofemoral pain and may contribute to its development.[29] Subtalar pronation can be observed in standing and during gait. The assessment of the extent and significance of this motion is described in Chapter 8.

Inadequate flexibility

Inadequate flexibility, or reduced compliance of the musculotendinous unit, may be observed in all the muscles that affect knee movement. Aberrations in pelvis and hip motion may be influenced by muscles such as the tensor fascia lata (and its iliotibial band), rectus femoris, and the hamstring, whereas knee function may be affected by the quadriceps,[32] hamstring, and gastrocnemius.

Local intrinsic factors

Local intrinsic factors that can contribute to the development of patellofemoral pain are:

* patella position
* soft tissue contributions
* neuromuscular control of the vasti.

Patella position

Clinical examination provides valuable information on the structural and functional relationships of the PFJ (Table 33.4 overleaf). The clinician should carefully assess passive and active movement of the patella in all directions (medial [Fig. 33.2f], lateral, superior, inferior, rotations). Although the tests for patella position are not functional and may not be repeatable,[33, 34] clinical examination of the patella

Table 33.3 Remote factors that can contribute to patellofemoral pain syndrome and their possible mechanisms

Factor	Possible mechanisms	Confirmatory assessments
Increased femoral internal rotation	Structural: • femoral anteversion Inadequate strength: • hip external rotators • hip abductors	Hip imaging—MRI, X-ray Clinical assessment Manual muscle test or hand-held dynamometer
	Altered neuromotor control: • hip external rotators • hip abductors	Biofeedback
	ROM deficits: • hip	ROM tests: • clinical inclinometer • figure "4" test or FABER (Fig. 28.11c)
Increased knee valgus	Structural: • genu varum • tibial varum • coxa varum	Radiographic—long leg X-ray Clinical—goniometer/inclinometer
	Inadequate strength: • hip external rotators • hip abductors • quadriceps • hamstrings	Manual muscle test Clinical strength—hand-held dynamometer Active gluteal and TFL trigger points (Fig. 27.10)
	Altered neuromotor control: • hip external rotators • hip abductors • lumbopelvic muscles	Biofeedback Active gluteal and TFL trigger points (Fig. 27.10)
	ROM deficits: • hip	ROM tests: • clinical (Fig. 28.3c)/inclinometer • figure "4" test or FABER (Fig. 28.11c)
Subtalar pronation		See Chapter 40
Muscle flexibility	Quadriceps/rectus femoris Hamstrings TFL/iliotibial band Gastrocnemius	See Chapter 30 See Chapter 31 See Chapter 34 See Chapter 36

ROM = range of motion; TFL = tensor fascia lata

position remains a useful tool for clinical decision making.

Soft tissue contributions

The contribution of the superficial and deep soft tissues to the PFJ mechanics can, in part, be obtained from the structural and functional assessments of patella position. Further information is available through palpation to gain an impression of the compliance of the lateral and medial soft tissues. Clinical assessment of the soft tissues is summarized in Table 33.4 and Figure 33.4 overleaf.

Neuromuscular control of the vasti

Clinical examination of the vasti (medial and lateral components) provides considerable insight into their function (Table 33.4, Fig. 33.5 overleaf). Frank muscle wasting and weakness may be obvious, but apparently normal muscle bulk does not ensure normal function. It is important also to assess the timing of the VMO contractions to ensure they are synchronous with the rest of the quadriceps mechanism, as delayed onset of VMO relative to vastus lateralis may be an indication of patellofemoral pain syndrome.[35] The vasti should be assessed in a number of positions

Table 33.4 Local factors that can contribute to patellofemoral pain

Factor	Clinical observation	
	Structural	Functional (with quadriceps contraction)
Patella position		
Lateral displacement	Patella displaced laterally, closer to the lateral than medial femoral condyle Restricted medial glide (Fig. 33.2f)	Patella moves laterally
Lateral tilt	Difficult to palpate lateral border, high medial border Lateral tilt increases with passive medial glide	Patella tilts laterally
Posterior tilt	Inferior patella pole displaced posteriorly Often difficult to palpate due to infrapatellar fat pad	Inferior pole moves further posteriorly A "dimple" may appear in the infrapatellar fat pad
Rotation	Long axis of the patella is not parallel with the long axis of the femur	Increase in rotation
Patella alta	High-riding patella	N/A
Soft tissue contributions		
Tight lateral structures	Lateral patella displacement or tilt Palpation of lateral structures (Fig. 33.4)	Lateral patella displacement or tilt (see above)
Compliant medial structures	Lateral patella displacement or tilt	Lateral patella displacement or tilt
Overall hypermobility	N/A	Increased patella mobility in all directions
Vasti neuromuscular control		
Reduced activity of quadriceps (general)	Reduced muscle bulk of quadriceps	Reduced muscle strength
Delayed onset of VMO relative to VL	Reduced muscle bulk of VMO	Delayed onset of VMO relative to VL Assess in functional positions Biofeedback can assist (Fig. 33.5 overleaf)
Reduced magnitude of VMO relative to VL	Reduced muscle bulk of VMO	Poor quantity/quality of VMO Assess in functional positions Biofeedback can assist
Altered reflex response	Reduced muscle bulk of VMO	Tendon tap

N/A = not applicable; VL = vastus lateralis; VMO = vastus medialis obliquus

or activities, including those that are functionally relevant to the patient.

Treatment of patellofemoral pain
An integrated approach to management of a patient with patellofemoral pain includes:

- reduction of pain
- addressing extrinsic contributing factors
- addressing intrinsic contributing factors
  - remote factors
  - local factors.

Because the PFPS may predispose to the development of patellofemoral osteoarthritis, treatments should aim not only to reduce pain and symptoms, but also to address all contributing factors.

Treatment of anterior knee pain is discussed with Kay Crossley in the *Clinical Sports Medicine* masterclasses at www.clinicalsportsmedicine.com.

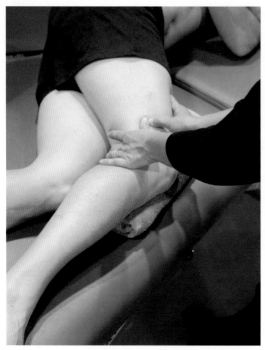

Figure 33.4 Clinical assessment of lateral soft tissue contribution. The iliotibial band and lateral retinacular structures are palpated for any reduced compliance

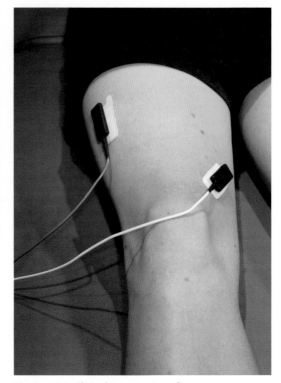

Figure 33.5 Clinical examination of neuromotor control of the vasti. The quality (amount and timing) of the vastus medialis obliquus and vastus lateralis component of the quadriceps can be assessed in a number of positions, including supine, sitting, and standing. In these positions the patient is asked to contract the quadriceps. The clinician can either observe or palpate the quality of the contraction in these positions. A surface EMG biofeedback (illustrated) may be used to provide useful information to the clinician on the relative contribution of the vasti during quadriceps contractions across the various positions

Immediate reduction of pain

The first priority of treatment is to reduce pain. Rest from aggravating activity usually suffices but it may require ice, a short course of acetaminophen (paracetamol) (rarely), or techniques such as mobilization (Fig. 33.6). Taping (Fig. 33.7) should have an immediate pain-relieving effect; when it does, this strongly suggests that the diagnosis is PFPS.

Addressing extrinsic contributing factors

Although the patient should reduce the load on the PFJ initially, it is essential that as rehabilitation progresses, any extrinsic factors that may have been placing excessive load on the PFJ (e.g. training, shoes, surfaces) be addressed.

Addressing intrinsic contributing factors

The clinician should have ascertained whether any intrinsic factors may have contributed to the patient's pain. Potential culprits should be addressed immediately. Treatment should be based on clinical assessment and, thus, must be individualized for each person. Remote intrinsic factors may be addressed

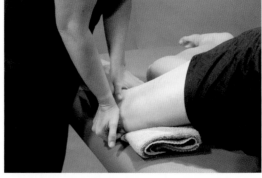

Figure 33.6 Mobilization of the patella (supine or side-lying)

through hip muscle retraining,[36, 37] improving musculotendinous compliance, or foot orthoses. Local intrinsic factors may be addressed with techniques such as patella taping or bracing, improving lateral soft tissue compliance, generalized quadriceps strengthening, or vasti retraining.

Patella taping

The aim of taping is to correct the abnormal position of the patella in relation to the femur. Although patella taping reduces patellofemoral pain substantially and immediately,[38–43] the precise mechanism of the effect is still being investigated. In the short term, patella taping speeds the onset timing of the VMO relative to the vastus lateralis;[38, 44] but its effect on magnitude of vasti muscle activation is inconclusive.[39, 40, 45, 46] Patella taping also improves knee function during gait.[40, 47] Taping is an effective interim measure to relieve patellofemoral pain while other contributing factors (e.g. VMO dysfunction, altered hip control) are being corrected.

A commonly used technique involves taping the patella with a medial glide (Fig. 33.7a). It may also require correction of abnormal lateral tilt (Fig. 33.7b), rotation (Fig. 33.7c overleaf) or inferior tilt (Fig. 33.7d overleaf). The taping is performed with rigid strapping tape. It is important that the clinician recognizes a posteriorly displaced inferior pole of the patella, as taping the patella too low increases the patient's symptoms. Taping to "unload" the fat pad [effectively to "lift" the patella away from the fat pad] can be also be used, either alone or in conjunction with the above techniques (see page 707, "Fat pad irritation/impingement" for more details; Fig. 33.15 on page 708).

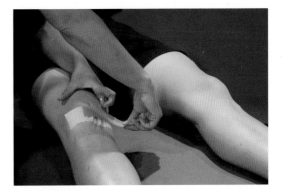
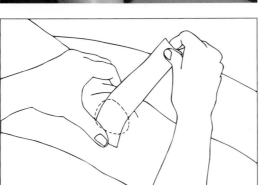
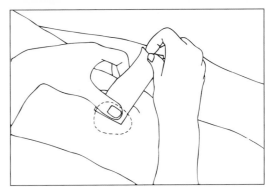

Figure 33.7 Patella taping techniques
(a) Patella taping (medial glide). Tape is applied to the lateral aspect of the patella. The patella is glided medially and the tape is anchored to the skin over the medial aspect of the knee. When taping is completed, skin creases should be evident on the inside of the knee, indicating adequate tension on the patella

(b) Patella taping (correction of lateral tilt). Tape is applied to the medial aspect of the patella and secured to the soft tissue on the inner aspect of the knee

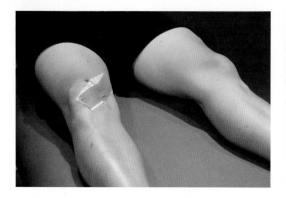

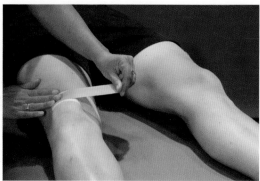

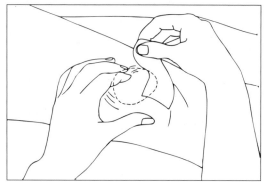

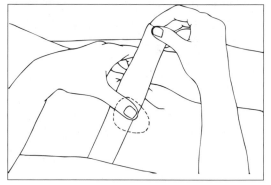

(c) Patella taping (correction of rotation).
Tape is applied to the inferior pole of the patella and taken medially and superiorly to rotate the patella

(d) Patella taping (correction of inferior tilt).
Tape is applied across the superior pole of the patella with sufficient firmness to elevate the inferior pole

Taping tips

Patella taping effects should be assessed immediately using a pain-provoking activity such as a single- or double-leg squat. If the tape has been applied correctly, the post-taping squat is less painful. If all or some pain persists, the tape should be altered, possibly including a component for tilt or rotation or both. If patella tape does not make a substantial (at least 50%) reduction in patients' pain, then the initial diagnosis should be revisited.

If patients are able to perform strengthening exercises pain-free without tape, then exercises alone will usually correct the abnormality. Most people, however, require tape to perform the exercises and, initially, to continue their sporting activities. Acute cases of patellofemoral pain may initially need tape applied 24 hours a day until the condition settles. The tape time is then gradually reduced.

Adverse skin reactions can occur beneath the rigid tape. Therefore, the area to be taped should be shaved and a protective barrier applied beneath the rigid strapping tape, to reduce both the reaction to the zinc oxide in the tape adhesive and the reaction to shearing stresses on the skin. This can be achieved with adhesive gauze tape (Hypafix or Fixomull) applied to the area to be taped. A protective barrier or plastic skin can also be used in patients with extremely sensitive skin. If skin irritation still occurs, the patient must be advised to remove the tape. Treatment with a hydrocortisone cream may be necessary. Patients with fair skin seem to have particularly sensitive skin and need to be monitored closely.

Braces

There are some commercially available braces (Fig. 33.8) that maintain medial glide. Patella braces reduce patella displacement, increase patella contact area,[48] and reduce the PFJ stress[49] in individuals with patellofemoral pain. However, a randomized controlled trial of such a brace did not find any benefit of the brace over a "sham" knee sleeve or a general quadriceps strengthening program.[50] Braces are less specific than taping and do not specifically address tilt or rotation; however, they may have a role in those patients who are unable to wear tape or who suffer recurrent patella subluxation or dislocation.

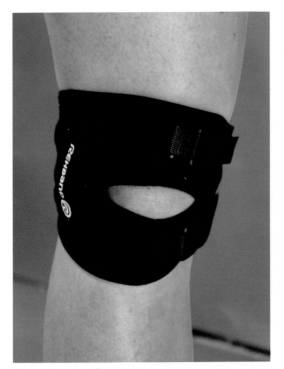

Figure 33.8 Patella stabilizing brace

Improving lateral soft tissue compliance

Stretching tight lateral structures such as the lateral retinaculum is beneficial. This is best done in a side-lying position with the knee flexed. The therapist glides the patella medially using the heel of the hand for a sustained stretch (Fig. 33.6). Other simple stretching techniques can be performed by the patient.

Vasti retraining

Vasti retraining programs have been shown to reduce patellofemoral pain [51, 52] and enhance VMO activation, relative to vastus lateralis.[38] The first step in a VMO training program is for the patient to learn to contract the muscle. The patient should palpate the VMO while contracting their quadriceps in various degrees of knee flexion and/or in different activities to determine which position gives the best contraction. A dual channel biofeedback machine may also be used. The patient needs to have minimal patellofemoral pain before these exercises can become effective, otherwise muscle action may be inhibited. Therefore, taping may be required to relieve the pain and allow contractions to occur. The patient should attempt to recruit the VMO to contract before the rest of the quadriceps.

Current evidence suggests that the VMO cannot be exercised in isolation and that no exercise appears to be preferential for activation of the VMO. Therefore, for each patient it is important to find and use the training position where the patient can attain a consistent VMO activation.

Initially, VMO exercises may commence in sitting with the knee at 90°, the foot on the floor, and the patient palpating the VMO to facilitate muscle activation. A dual channel biofeedback machine or, in some cases, a muscle stimulator may assist the process. To ensure that the vasti are trained in positions that they are required to function in, the patient should begin training in a weight-bearing position and perform functional exercises with steadily increasing load and difficulty as soon as possible. The final aim of training is to achieve a carryover from functional exercises to functional activities. The patient should perform small numbers of exercises frequently throughout the day. A series of graded VMO exercises is demonstrated in Figure 33.9 overleaf.

Generalized strengthening exercises

Even in the absence of other interventions (e.g. taping, bracing), a generalized quadriceps strengthening program may be effective in relieving patellofemoral pain and reducing disbility.[50] The available evidence does not support the effectiveness of one exercise regimen over another. However, a number of patients are unable to restore pain-free function of their PFJ without specific retraining of the vasti.

Retraining hip function

Retraining the hip abductors and external rotators is thought to stabilize the lateral pelvis and to control internal hip rotation. Such strengthening programs have been associated with pain reduction in patients with patellofemoral pain.[53] These exercises may be performed initially in non-weight-bearing positions and then progressed to weight-bearing positions (Fig. 33.9a). As soon as it is possible and practical, the patient must be taught to activate the hip abductors and external rotators, in combination with the VMO, during combined exercises (Fig. 33.9b). The emphasis of all retraining exercises will be on maintaining the activation of these muscles and correct alignment of the hip (i.e. neutral rotation) during weight-bearing flexion tasks (e.g. lunge, step-up, and step-down, Fig. 33.9c). Some patients may require retraining of their movement patterns during functional or potentially aggravating activities.[54]

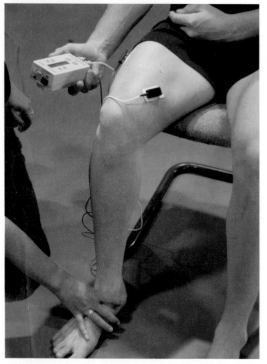

Figure 33.9 Vastus medialis obliquus (VMO) training exercises
(a) VMO exercise—seated

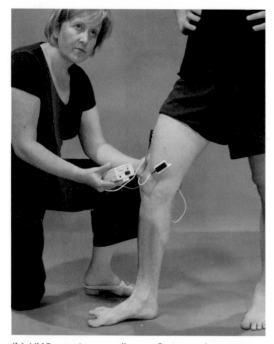

(b) VMO exercise—small range flexion and extension movements

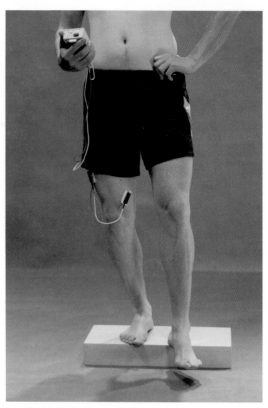

(c) VMO exercise—weight-bearing flexion tasks (step-up/step-down)

Improving musculotendinous compliance

Attention must also be paid to improving the compliance of the hip flexors, quadriceps, hamstring, and calf muscles as well as the iliotibial band through stretches, soft tissue techniques (Fig. 33.10), or dry needling. Restoration of optimal muscle and fascial length is the goal. Transverse friction and transverse gliding should be applied to focal regions of thickening. Sustained myofascial tension (myofascial release) is the technique of choice to correct fascial thickening and shortening (Fig. 33.10).

In-shoe foot orthoses

Prefabricated in-shoe foot orthoses, combined with active retraining of the extrinsic muscles of the foot, improve pain and physical function in people with patellofemoral pain.[52] Although the mechanism underpinning the clinical effects are unclear, it appears that both neuromuscular and mechanical factors need to be considered when prescribing in-shoe foot orthoses.[55] A clinical decision-making paradigm has been proposed to assist with orthotic

Figure 33.10 Soft tissue therapy—myofascial release of the iliotibial band)

prescription for people with patellofemoral pain.[56] (See also Chapter 8 for more about orthoses.)

Pain reduction during aggravating activities with either anti-pronation taping or an orthotic may indicate which patients are more likely to have a favorable response to an orthotic.[57, 58] Older people with less severe pain and a more mobile midfoot are more likely to experience success with orthoses intervention.[56]

Additionally, the clinician might consider customized foot orthoses or changing footwear; the efficacy of these interventions is not known. These interventions are discussed in Chapters 8 and 9.

Evidence base for physical interventions

A number of randomized clinical trials have assessed the efficacy of physical interventions for patello-femoral pain (Table 33.5).[59] Although these trials reflect some aspects of clinical practice, mostly the interventions are not individualized to the patients' needs. Furthermore, some studies have evaluated one aspect of intervention in isolation. These studies have enabled the assessment of a single treatment strategy, but the study results may not be generalizable to clinical scenarios. Therefore, while the evidence base for conservative therapies for patellofemoral pain is increasing in quality and quantity,[59] clinicians need to individualize their treatment approaches, thus targeting the treatment to their patient's presentations and requirements.

Treatment options that have gained popularity more recently (e.g. hip muscle retraining, gait retraining) have not yet been evaluated in high-quality controlled clinical trials. Table 33.5 summarizes evidence of the evaluation of physical interventions for patellofemoral pain (see Chapter 3 for more about evidence).

Surgery—to be avoided

Surgery is now much less commonly used in this condition than it was 30 years ago. This is probably due to the availability of evidence-based, exercise-based,

Table 33.5 Best available evidence for conservative interventions for patellofemoral pain

Intervention	Level of evidence	Reference
Multimodal intervention	1	Collins [59]
Taping	1	Warden [97]
Foot orthoses	2	Collins [98]; Eng [99]
Hip muscle retraining	2	Nakagawa [100]
Strengthening exercises	2	Herrington [101]; Song [102]; Thomee [103]; Van Linschoten [104]; Witvrouw [105, 106]
Mobilisation	2	van den Dolder [107]
Acupuncture	2	Jensen [108]
Gait retraining	4	Noehren [109]
Pharmacology	5	Australian Acute Musculoskeletal Pain Guidelines Group [110]
Bracing	1	Warden [97]
Stretching	2	Mason [111]
Manipulation	2	Stakes [112]

Green = supported by meta-analyses (systematic reviews) or randomized controlled trials; orange = supported by nonrandomized studies and case series; black = expert opinion, clinical guidelines; red = insufficient evidence; current evidence is contrary to common clinical consideration

physical interventions. To date, there has been no randomized controlled trial showing the effectiveness of surgical treatments such as chondroplasty or lateral release for patellofemoral pain. Thus, at a time when systematic reviews (level 1 evidence) argue for physical therapies for this condition, it would appear that such avenues should be tried repeatedly and with various expert therapists before being abandoned in favor of surgery, which is very much lacking in evidence. Poor surgical outcomes have been reported, and often patellofemoral pain is worsened after surgery.[60]

Patellofemoral instability

Before discussing the causes of and treatments for patellofemoral instability, we need to clearly define the term. As is also the case at the shoulder, "instability" is not a synonym for "dislocation." Instability refers to excessive joint range of motion (and is often referred to as "subluxation"). Patellofemoral instability may be primary (colloquially referred to as patellar subluxation), or secondary (meaning that the instability is due to previous acute patellar dislocation (see Chapter 32 for information on acute dislocation).

Primary patellofemoral instability

Factors that predispose to primary patellofemoral instability include patella alta (a patella that is located more superiorly than normal), trochlear dysplasia, and generalized ligamentous laxity. Patients usually describe sensations of instability (patella moving or slipping), and the pattern of tenderness around the patella may be either similar to patellofemoral pain or more generally distributed. Examination reveals patella hypermobility with apprehension and pain when the patella is pushed laterally by the examiner.

Treatment

Treatment of patellofemoral instability parallels that of patellofemoral pain. The aim of acute management is to reduce pain and swelling. Patella taping in combination with a knee extension brace may provide temporary immobilization after an initial episode. The patient may use crutches for either partial- or non-weight-bearing. Rehabilitation requires a VMO retraining program as outlined for patellofemoral pain (above) to be commenced as soon as possible.

PRACTICE PEARL Rehabilitation to improve active support for the patellofemoral joint is paramount, as dominant predisposing factors (bony morphology and ligamentous laxity) cannot be addressed easily.

In acute situations, biofeedback and/or electrical stimulation may be required as an adjunct to vasti retraining. Taping (and/or bracing) may be part of long-term management. It is also essential to address any proximal and distal contributing factors (Fig. 33.3, Tables 33.3 and 33.4). maximize trunk and lower limb muscle strength and endurance, and provide advice regarding avoiding aggravating activities.

Surgery is rarely indicated. Surgical approaches aim to correct the predisposing factors, and one technique used arthroscopic medial plication. Bony realignment procedures including "trochleaplasties" have largely lost popularity in Scandinavia and Australia but are performed in the US and elsewhere. These interventions often do not have favorable outcomes; thus they should only be considered if a properly managed conservative program fails. If the sportsperson does choose surgery, an intensive rehabilitation program is vital.

Secondary patellofemoral instability

Secondary instability results from a primary dislocation episode (see Chapter 32 for initial management) that is likely to have arisen because of rupture of the medial patellofemoral ligament. This ligament is the main static restraint to lateral patella translation. Individuals with persistent patellofemoral instability after an acute dislocation may require additional investigations. Radiographs may reveal evidence of osteochondral damage to the articular surface of the patella and femur as well as predisposing anatomical abnormalities.

Arthroscopy may be required to remove a loose osteochondral fragment, and, if appropriate, the medial patellofemoral ligament may need reconstruction.[61] As with surgery for primary instability, surgery for secondary instability also requires aggressive rehabilitation. Rehabilitation for secondary patellofemoral instability follows the same guidelines as for primary patellofemoral instability.

Patellar tendinopathy

There have been substantial advances in understanding the histopathology, imaging, conservative and surgical outcomes in patellar tendinopathy in the past decade. However, successful management of the sportsperson with patellar tendinopathy remains a major challenge for the practitioner and patient.

Nomenclature

Patellar tendinopathy was first referred to as "jumper's knee" due to its frequency in jumping sports (e.g. basketball, volleyball, and high, long and triple jumps).[62] However, the condition also occurs in sportspeople who change direction, and may occur in sportspeople who do not perform either jumping or change of direction. The term "patellar tendonitis" is a misnomer as the pathology underlying this condition is not an inflammatory "tendonitis."[63] On balance, "patellar tendinopathy" is probably the most appropriate general label for this condition.[64]

Pathology and pathogenesis of patellar tendinopathy

Normal tendon is white and glistening but the patellar tendon of patients undergoing surgery for patellar tendinopathy contains abnormal tissue adjacent to the lower pole of the patella (Fig. 33.11). Under the light microscope, symptomatic patellar tendons do not consist of tight parallel collagen bundles, but

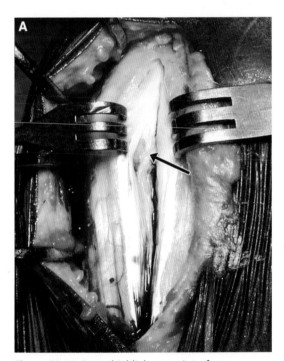

Figure 33.11 Arrow highlights a region of grey tendinosis within the otherwise glistening white patellar tendon. Skin and subcutaneous fat have been retracted   REPRINTED WITH PERMISSION OF SAGE PRESS FROM SHELBOURNE KD ET AL. RECALCITRANT PATELLAR TENDINOSIS IN ELITE ATHLETES. *AM J SPORTS MED* 2006;34 (7):1141–6

instead are separated by a large amount of ground substance that gives them a disorganized and discontinuous appearance. There are clefts in the matrix and occasional necrotic collagen fibers with small vessel ingrowth. This histopathological picture, which is called "tendinosis," (Chapter 5 on page 34) is identical in tendons with both macroscopically evident partial tears and those without.[65] These regions of tendon degeneration correspond with areas of increased signal on MRI and hypoechoic regions on ultrasound.[63]

Clinical features

The clinical features of patellar tendinopathy are outlined in Table 33.2. The patient complains of anterior knee pain aggravated by activities such as jumping, changing direction, and decelerating. The most common site of tendinopathy is the deep attachment of the tendon to the inferior pole of the patella. Distal lesions are less common and midsubstance lesions are rarely reported.[66] The tendon is tender on palpation at the inferior pole, occasionally extending into the body of the tendon. There is frequently associated thickening of the tendon. The most effective position for palpation is shown in Figure 33.12 overleaf. Expert clinicians also assess possible precipitating factors, such as weakness of the lower limb musculature including calf, quadriceps, and gluteal muscles, and shortening or increased tone of the gastrocnemius/soleus, quadriceps, and hamstring muscles.

It is important to reproduce the patient's pain on examination. Functional activity, such as a squat or hop, reproduces the pain, and these tests are superior to palpation as a method for monitoring recovery. An additional method of monitoring the clinical progress of patellar tendinopathy is the use of the Victorian Institute of Sport Assessment VISA-P questionnaire (Table 33.6 overleaf).[67, 68] This simple questionnaire takes less than five minutes to complete and patients are able to complete it themselves.

Investigations

Ultrasound examination and MRI are the investigations of choice in patellar tendinopathy, although these imaging modalities do not have 100% sensitivity and specificity for the condition[69] (Fig. 33.13 on page 704). Ultrasound examination with Doppler (Fig. 33.13b) to assess vascularity in and around the tendon is more sensitive than MRI.[9]

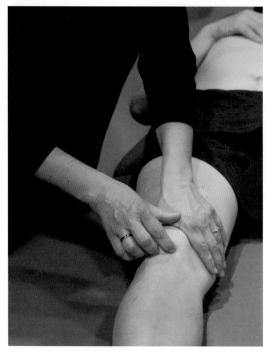

Figure 33.12 Palpation of the patellar tendon. Pressure on the superior pole of the patella tilts the inferior pole, allowing more precise palpation of the tendon origin

Treatment

Treatment of patellar tendinopathy requires patience and a multifaceted approach, which is outlined in the box on page 704. It is essential that the practitioner and patient recognize that tendinopathy that has been present for months may require a considerable period of rehabilitation before symptoms disappear (Chapter 5).

Conservative management of patellar tendinopathy requires appropriate strengthening and motor control exercises, load reduction, correcting biomechanical errors, and soft tissue therapy. More invasive treatments include injection with substances that either affect the vessels (sclerotherapy with polidocanol), or theoretically improve tendon repair (platelet-rich plasma [PRP] injections) or matrix structure (prolotherapy). Surgery is only indicated after a considered and lengthy conservative program has failed.

This section outlines the physical therapy approach of targeted exercise therapy, correction of factors that might be contributing to excessive load on the tendon, and soft tissue treatment, before out-lining medical treatments including medication, injections, and surgery.

Relative load reduction—modified activity and biomechanical correction

There are numerous ways of reducing the load on the patellar tendon without resorting to complete rest or immobilization. Relative rest means that the patient may be able to continue playing or training if it is possible to reduce the amount of jumping or sprinting, or the total weekly training hours. Some continued load on the tendon is critical to maintain tendon integrity and absolute rest is contraindicated.

Strengthening and correcting biomechanics to improve the energy-absorbing capacity of the limb should be directed at both the affected musculotendinous unit, and the hip and ankle. The ankle and calf are critical in absorbing the initial landing load that reduces the load transmitted to the knee.[70] Biomechanical studies reveal that only about 40% of landing energy is transmitted proximally.[71] Thus, the calf complex must function well to prevent more load than necessary transferring to the patellar tendon.

Better landing techniques can decrease patellar tendon load. Compared with flat-foot landing, forefoot landing generates lower ground reaction forces and, if this technique is combined with a large range of hip or knee flexion, vertical ground reaction forces can be reduced by a further 25%.[71] Landing with weight further forward that uses all available dorsiflexion may also decrease patellar tendon load.[72, 73]

Biomechanical correction requires assessment of both anatomical and functional shortcomings. Anatomical variants that can contribute to patellar tendinopathy include limited ankle dorsiflexion and hallux rigidus. There are numerous functional biomechanical abnormalities. Inflexibility of the hamstring, quadriceps, and calf muscles, as well as restricted ankle range of motion, are likely to increase the load on the patellar tendon. Hamstring shortening (decreased sit and reach test) is associated with an increased prevalence of patellar tendinopathy. Weakness of the gluteal, quadriceps, and calf muscles leads to fatigue and aberrant movement patterns that may alter forces acting on the knee during activity. Therefore, proximal and distal muscles also need assessment in patients with patellar tendinopathy.

Strengthening

There are at least six reports of effective strengthening exercises for patellar tendinopathy.[7, 74-78] These

Table 33.6 Victorian Institute of Sport Assessment (VISA) questionnaire (English version, this is available in numerous languages)

1. For how many minutes can you sit pain-free?   POINTS

   0 min | | | | | | | | | | | 100 min [ ]
        0 1 2 3 4 5 6 7 8 9 10

2. Do you have pain walking downstairs with a normal gait cycle?   POINTS

   Strong severe pain | | | | | | | | | | | No pain [ ]
        0 1 2 3 4 5 6 7 8 9 10

3. Do you have pain at the knee with full active non-weight-bearing knee extension?   POINTS

   Strong severe pain | | | | | | | | | | | No pain [ ]
        0 1 2 3 4 5 6 7 8 9 10

4. Do you have pain when doing a full weight-bearing lunge?   POINTS

   Strong severe pain | | | | | | | | | | | No pain [ ]
        0 1 2 3 4 5 6 7 8 9 10

5. Do you have problems squatting?   POINTS

   Unable | | | | | | | | | | | No problems [ ]
        0 1 2 3 4 5 6 7 8 9 10

6. Do you have pain during or immediately after doing 10 single-leg hops?   POINTS

   Strong severe pain | | | | | | | | | | | No pain [ ]
        0 1 2 3 4 5 6 7 8 9 10

7. Are you currently undertaking sport or other physical activity?   POINTS [ ]

   0 ☐ Not at all
   4 ☐ Modified training ± modified competition
   7 ☐ Full training ± competition but not at same level as when symptoms began
   10 ☐ Competing at the same or higher level as when symptoms began

8. Please complete EITHER A, B, or C in this question.
   - If you have no pain while undertaking sport please complete Q8A only.
   - If you have pain while undertaking sport but it does not stop you from completing the activity, complete Q8B only.
   - If you have pain that stops you from completing sporting activities, please complete Q8C only.

   A. If you have no pain while undertaking sport, for how long can you train/practice?   POINTS

   [ ] Nil [ ] 1–5 min [ ] 6–10 min [ ] 11–15 min [ ] >15 min [ ]
      0   7   14   21   30

   OR

   B. If you have some pain while undertaking sport, but it does not stop you from completing your training/practice, for how long can you train/practice?   POINTS

   [ ] Nil [ ] 1–5 min [ ] 6–10 min [ ] 11–15 min [ ] >15 min [ ]
      0   4   10   14   20

   OR

   C. If you have pain that stops you from completing your training/practice, for how long can you train/practice?   POINTS

   [ ] Nil [ ] 1–5 min [ ] 6–10 min [ ] 11–15 min [ ] >15 min [ ]
      0   2   5   7   10

   TOTAL SCORE [ ] /100

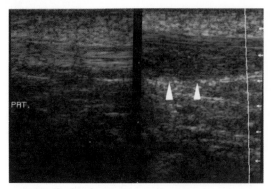

Figure 33.13 Ultrasound and MRI images of patellar tendinopathy in athletes
(a) Ultrasound image (normal [left] and thickened tendon regions). Arrowheads point to the posterior/deep edge of the patellar tendon

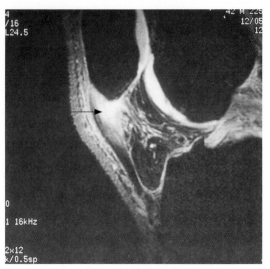

(c) MRI (appearance of patellar tendinopathy)

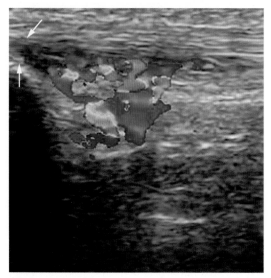

(b) Ultrasound image with color Doppler showing abnormal vascularity (blue and red signal) near the junction of the patellar tendon and the patella (arrowhead)

> ### Overview of management of patellar tendinopathy
>
> - A patient presenting with persistent painful patellar tendinopathy for the first time may require 3–6 months to recover. A patient with a longstanding history may require 6–12 months to return, pain-free, to competition without recurrence.
> - Relative tendon unloading is critical for treatment success. This is achieved by activity modification assisted by biomechanical correction.
> - Progressive strengthening is the treatment of choice. Effective exercise prescription requires thorough assessment of the patient's functional capacity and a skilful approach to increasing demand on the tendon.
> - After successful patellar tendon surgery, it takes between 6 and 12 months to return to full competitive sport. Thus, the treating physician must be sure that an appropriate conservative treatment program has failed before suggesting a tendon needs surgery.

can be divided into two groups—those reporting eccentric exercises on a decline board and those using other exercises.

Three papers suggested that exercise-based interventions such as squatting, isokinetics, and weights reduce the pain of patellar tendinopathy.[74, 75, 79] Studies have investigated the effectiveness of exercise on a 25° decline board (Fig. 33.14a)—a method specifically loading the extensor mechanism of the knee by increasing the moment arm of the knee.[76] Two trials reported improvements in pain, function, and

return to sport with exercise, although time frames for improvement varied.[7, 77] Compared with surgery, eccentric exercise on a decline board provided similar outcomes at 12 months.[78] Other studies have investigated heavy load strengthening and report equally good results.[80] Importantly, strengthening exercises when sportspeople are competing gave no improvement in pain or jump performance among the treatment group compared with those who undertook no exercise.[81, 82] This information can be used within

Table 33.7 Strengthening program for treatment of patellar tendinopathy

Timing	Type of overload	Activity
0–3 months	Strength and strength endurance	Hypertrophy and strengthen the affected muscles Focus attention on all anti-gravity muscles
3–6 months	Power and speed endurance	Weight-bearing speed-specific loads
6+ months	Combinations dependent on sport (e.g. load, speed)	Sport-specific rehabilitation

an educational context when working with a sports-person who is reluctant to modify his or her training regimen.

An effective strength program embraces the principles outlined in Table 33.7. Commonly prescribed exercises are illustrated in Figure 33.14. When and how a strengthening program should begin is discussed in the box overleaf.

Soft tissue therapy

A popular treatment for patellar tendinopathy is the use of friction; however, this lacks a logical theoretical construct. Studies that compared soft tissue therapy/transverse friction with other treatments demonstrated little benefit in reducing pain.[79, 83] Digital ischemic pressure and sustained myofascial tension to tight muscles or trigger points in the quadriceps, hamstring, and calf muscles can be performed.

(b) Lunge

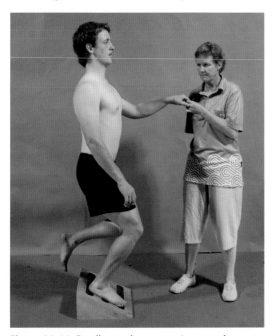

Figure 33.14 Patellar tendon eccentric strength training exercises
(a) Single-leg squat on decline board

(c) Lunge with weights

When should patellar tendon strengthening begin?

Therapists often have concerns as to when and how they should begin a strengthening program. Even sportspeople with the most severe cases of patellar tendinopathy should be able to begin some weight-based strength and other exercises (such as calf strength and isometric quadriceps work) in standing. However, the sportsperson who has not lost a lot of knee strength and bulk can progress quickly to the speed part of the program.

Both pain and the ability of the musculotendinous unit to do the work should guide the amount of strengthening to be done. If pain is a limiting factor, then the program must be modified so that the majority of the work occurs without aggravating symptoms within 24 hours of the exercise. A subjective clinical rating system, such as the VISA questionnaire (Table 33.6), administered at about monthly intervals, will help both the therapist and the patient measure progress.

If pain is under control, it is essential to monitor the ability of the limb to complete the exercises with control and quality. Exercises should only be progressed if the previous work load is easily managed, pain is controlled, and function is satisfactory.

Sportspeople with patellar tendinopathy tend to "unload" the affected limb to avoid pain, so they commonly have not only weakness but also abnormal motor patterns that must be reversed. Strength training must graduate quickly to incorporate single-leg

exercises (Fig. 33.14) as the sportsperson can continue to unload the affected tendon when exercising using both legs. Thus, exercises that target the quadriceps specifically (such as single-leg extensions) may have a place in the rehabilitation of patellar tendinopathy. Similarly, when the sportsperson is ready, increase the load on the quadriceps by having the patient stand on a 25° decline board to do squats. Compared with squatting on a flat surface, this reduces the calf contribution during the squat.

The therapist should progress the regimen by adding load and speed and then endurance to each of those levels of exercise. Combinations such as load and speed, or height and load, then follow. These end-stage exercises can provoke tendon pain, and are only recommended after a prolonged rehabilitation period, and when the sport demands intense loading. In several sports, it may not be necessary to add potentially aggravating activities such as jump training to the rehabilitation program, whereas in volleyball, for example, it is vital.

Finally, the overall exercise program must correct aberrant motor patterns such as stiff landing mechanics (discussed above) and pelvic instability. For example, weight-bearing exercises must be in a functionally required range, and the pelvis position must be monitored and controlled at all times. The common errors in rehabilitation strength programs are listed in Table 33.8.

Table 33.8 Why rehabilitation programs fail at various stages

Early failure	Late failure
Insufficient strength training	Failure to monitor the patient's symptoms
Progression of rehabilitation program too rapid	Rehabilitation and strength training end on return to training, instead of continuing throughout the return to sport
Inappropriate loads during rehabilitation (too little, too much)	No speed rehabilitation
	Plyometrics training performed inappropriately, not tolerated, or unnecessary

Cryotherapy

Cryotherapy (e.g. ice) is a popular adjunct to treatment; however, if the patient finds no clinical benefit from this modality, there is no rationale for persisting.

Pharmacotherapy

Studies of pharmacotherapy in the treatment of patellar tendinopathy are limited to phoresis, as few studies have investigated oral medications. The use of aprotinen in tendinopathy has some evidence, but is not recommended because of possible anaphylaxis after injection. Recently, the use of aprotinen during cardiac surgery has been discontinued because of increased risk of adverse effects. In one study, iontophoresis with corticosteroid improved outcome compared with phonophoresis, suggesting it may introduce corticosteroid into target tissue more effectively than phonophoresis.[84]

The model for tendinopathy proposed by Cook and Purdam (Chapter 5, Fig. 5.14 on page 36) suggests that early-stage (reactive) tendinopathy could respond to medications that reduce cell activity and protein production.[85] Ibuprofen, doxycycline, and green tea are hypothesized to improve pain and pathology in tendinopathy. In later stages of pathology, injection therapies may be more relevant.

Injection therapy

Neovascularization (Fig. 33.13b) is a cornerstone of degenerative tendon pathology and is the target of treatment by Alfredson and Ohberg.[86] In a high-quality randomized control trial of elite athletes with patellar tendinopathy, investigators found that sclerosing injections with polidocanol resulted in a significant improvement in knee function and reduced pain.[87]

Corticosteroid injections have been compared to placebo, and corticosteroid improved symptoms so much so that all 12 athletes who had placebo injection subsequently had corticosteroid injections. However, 50% of athletes in the corticosteroid group failed to recover and were referred to surgery.[88]

Blood injection therapy (autologous blood, platelet-rich plasma) has been used clinically, but there are few controlled trials. Compared with standard physiotherapy treatment, platelet-rich plasma had similar outcomes at six months.[89]

Surgery

The first randomized trial that compared surgical treatment and conservative management of patellar tendinopathy was published in 2006.[90] There was no significant difference in outcome between groups; thus, surgical intervention provided no benefit over conservative management. Consequently, the clinical implication is that surgery is not a "quick fix" for patellar tendinopathy.[90]

There is no consensus as to the optimal surgical technique to use, with surgeons performing either a longitudinal or a transverse incision over the patellar tendon, and generally excising abnormal tissue. Some surgeons excise the paratenon, while others suture it after having performed a longitudinal tenotomy and

excision of the tendinopathic area. There has been some enthusiasm for possible arthroscopic debridement of the anterior portion of the fat pad adjacent to the patellar tendon, and results published to date appear similar to those of patients undergoing open surgery.[91, 92]

A systematic review of 10 studies of surgery for patellar tendinopathy reported that techniques, rehabilitation, and outcomes varied considerably; poorer outcomes were reported for surgery that involved the patella, when the peritendon was closed, and when immobilization was standard after surgery.[93]

We recommend surgery only after a thorough, high-quality conservative program has failed. Surgeons must advise patients that, while symptomatic benefit is very likely, return to sport at the previous level cannot be guaranteed (60–80% likelihood).[91, 94] Time to return to the previous level of sport, if achieved at all, is likely to take between six and 12 months.[91, 94]

Partial patellar tendon tear

The term "partial tear" refers to a sudden significantly painful episode, which may be associated with disability; this corresponds to a tear of an area of pathology in the patellar tendon. If the partial tear is very large, causes major disability, and shows no improvement in two to three weeks, early surgery may be justified to stimulate some healing response in the tendon.

A small partial tear of the patellar tendon is often diagnosed by ultrasonography and is difficult to differentiate from an area of tendinosis. Alternatively, it may be an incidental finding on ultrasound examination. This type of partial tear is part of the continuum of tendinosis and can be managed conservatively. The indication for surgery of a small partial tear is failed conservative management.

Less common causes
Fat pad irritation/impingement (insidious onset)

We distinguish insidious onset of fat pad pain from the condition first described by Hoffa in 1903. Hoffa referred to a relatively uncommon condition where the infrapatellar fat pad was impinged between the patella and the femoral condyle due to a *direct blow* to the knee. More commonly, fat pad irritation occurs with repeated or uncontrolled hyperextension of the knee. The condition can be extremely painful and debilitating, as the fat pad is one of the most pain-sensitive structures in the knee.[13]

The insidious onset often goes unrecognized. The pain is often exacerbated by extension maneuvers, such as straight-leg raises and prolonged standing, so it needs to be recognized early so that appropriate management can be implemented.

Clinical findings include localized tenderness (at the inferior pole of the patella, deep to the tendon) and puffiness in the fat pad with the inferior pole of the patella appearing to be (or actually being) displaced posteriorly. Pain may be reproduced with active knee extension, passive overpressure in extension, or during squats. Contracting the quadriceps with the knee extended may aggravate the pain during the acute phase. There may be VMO weakness. Patients often have hyperextension of the knees (genu recurvatum) associated with increased anterior pelvic tilt. Thus, treatments should be based on the assessments outlined in the section "Factors that may contribute to pain" (p. 691) and directed to improve the control, strength, and endurance of local (vasti) proximal and distal muscles, as well as retraining to avoid uncontrolled and excessive terminal knee extension maneuvers.

A popular clinical approach consists of treating the inferiorly tilted patella by taping across the superior surface of the patella, to lever the inferior pole forward and relieve impingement of the fat pad (Fig. 33.7d). Unloading of the fat pad may be required to relieve the symptoms further.

To unload the fat pad, a "V" tape is placed below the fat pad, with the point of the "V" at the tibial tubercle coming wide to the medial and lateral joint lines. As the tape is being pulled towards the joint line, the skin is lifted towards the patella, thus shortening the fat pad (Fig. 33.15). Muscle training and improving lower limb biomechanics are the basis of clinical management. Our clinical impression is that surgery should be avoided if possible. To date, there have been no randomized controlled trials of surgery for this condition.[95]

Osgood-Schlatter lesion

Osgood-Schlatter lesion is an osteochondrosis (Chapter 42) that occurs at the tibial tuberosity in girls and boys as they approach puberty. It is much more common among boys (at about age 13–15 years, but these ages vary) than girls (age about 10–12); it results from excessive traction on the soft apophysis of the tibial tuberosity by the powerful patellar tendon.

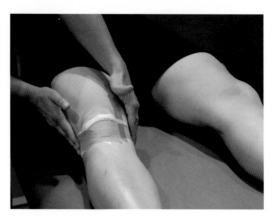

Figure 33.15 Fat pad unloading tape. Tape is applied in a "V" from the tibial tuberosity to the joint lines. The fat pad region is pinched to unload the fat pad while applying the tape. This tape is often combined with taping of the superior pole of the patella (Fig. 33.7d) in the treatment of fat pad impingement. This elevates the inferior pole of the patella

It occurs in association with high levels of activity during a period of rapid growth and is associated with a change in the tendon. Longitudinal imaging of the tendon in adolescents without pain shows that the attachment transitions to a normal attachment through a structure that can be interpreted as osteochondritic.[96] As with all tendon-related pain, the clinician must be careful not to make a diagnosis based only on imaging findings.

Treatment consists of reassurance that the condition is self-limiting. Whether or not to play sport depends on the severity of symptoms. Children with mild symptoms may wish to continue to play some or all sport; others may choose some modification of their programs. If the child prefers to cease sport because of pain, that decision should be supported. However, the amount of sport played does not seem to affect the time taken for the pain to disappear.

Sinding-Larsen–Johansson lesion

Sinding-Larsen–Johansson is a rare lesion; it is one of the group of osteochondroses found in adolescents (Chapter 42). It is an unimportant differential diagnosis in young patients with pain at the inferior pole of the patella. Treatment is outlined in Chapter 42.

Quadriceps tendinopathy

Pain arising at the quadriceps tendon at its attachment to the patella occurs mainly in older sportspeople, and in weightlifters as the quadriceps tendon is loaded more in a deeper squat. It is characterized by tenderness along the superior margin of the patella and pain on resisted quadriceps contraction. Treatment follows the same principles as treatment of patellar tendinopathy. Differential diagnosis is suprapatellar pain of PFJ origin and bipartite patella. Ruptures of the entire quadriceps attachment to the patella are not uncommon and require surgery and extensive rehabilitation.

Bursitis

There are a number of bursae around the knee joint; these are shown in Figure 33.16. The most commonly affected bursa is the pre-patellar bursa. Pre-patellar bursitis ("housemaid's knee") presents as a superficial swelling on the anterior aspect of the knee. This must be differentiated from an effusion of the knee joint.

Acute infective pre-patellar bursitis, common in those who kneel a lot, should be identified and treated quickly.

Infrapatellar bursitis can cause anterior knee pain that may mimic patellar tendinopathy; this bursa forms part of an enthesis organ of the distal insertion and, thus, can be challenging to treat.

Treatment of mild cases of bursitis includes non-steroidal anti-inflammatory drugs (NSAIDs). More severe cases require aspiration and infiltration with a corticosteroid agent and local anesthesia, followed by appropriate treatment of the enthesis if appropriate.

Synovial plica

The importance of the synovial plica, a synovial fold found along the medial edge of the patella (Fig. 33.17), has been a matter of considerable debate. An inflamed plica may cause variable sharp pain located anteriorly, medially, or posteriorly. The patient may complain of sharp pain on squatting. On examination, the plica is sometimes palpable as a thickened band under the medial border of the patella. It should only be considered as the primary cause of the patient's symptoms when the patient fails to respond to appropriate management of patellofemoral pain. In this case, and in the presence of a tender thickened band, arthroscopy should be performed and the synovial plica removed.

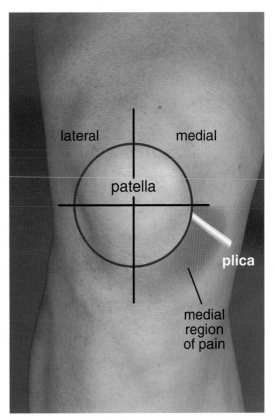

Figure 33.17 Synovial plica
(a) Medial synovial plica presents with pain in the region highlighted (red). A band of tissue may be palpable (+/- tender) running from the medial patella to the epicondylar region (blue).

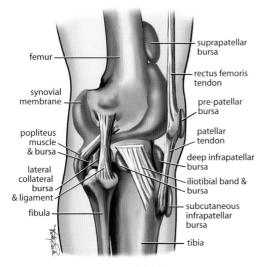

Figure 33.16 Bursae around the knee joint

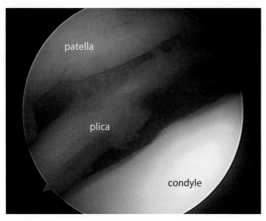

(b) A frayed, thickened synovial plica photographed at arthroscopy. It becomes sandwiched between the patella (above) and the femoral condyle (below)

CLINICAL SPORTS MEDICINE
MASTERCLASSES
www.clinicalsportsmedicine.com

- How to perform a knee examination.
- Discussion about anterior knee pain with Kay Crossley.
- Discussion of imaging in anterior knee pain.

REFERENCES

1. Taunton JE, Ryan MB, Clement DB et al. A retrospective case-control analysis of 2002 running injuries. Br J Sports Med 2002;36:95–101.
2. Baquie P, Brukner P. Injuries presenting to an Australian sports medicine centre: A 12-month study. Clin J Sport Med 1997;7(1):28–31.
3. van Middelkoop M, van Linschoten R, Berger M et al. Knee complaints seen in general practice: active sport participants versus non-sport participants. BMC Musculoskelet Disord 2008;9(1):36.
4. Torry MR, Decker MJ, Viola RW et al. Intra-articular knee joint effusion induces quadriceps avoidance gait patterns. Clin Biomech 2000;15(3):147–59.
5. Hodges PW, Mellor R, Crossley K et al. Pain induced by injection of hypertonic saline into the infrapatellar fat pad and effect on coordination of the quadriceps muscles. Arthritis Rheum 2009;61(1):70–7.
6. Elias JJ, Kilambi S, Cosgarea AJ. Computational assessment of the influence of vastus medialis obliquus function on patellofemoral pressures: model evaluation. J Biomech 2010;43(4):612–17.
7. Purdam CR, Jonsson P, Alfredson H et al. A pilot study of the eccentric decline squat in the management of painful chronic patellar tendinopathy. Br J Sports Med 2004;38(4):395–7.
8. Elias DA, White LM. Imaging of patellofemoral disorders. Clin Radiol 2004;59(7):543–57.
9. Warden SJ, Kiss ZS, Malara FA et al. Comparative accuracy of magnetic resonance imaging and ultrasonography in confirming clinically diagnosed patellar tendinopathy. Am J Sports Med 2007;35(3):427–36.
10. Cook JL, Khan KM, Kiss ZS et al. Reproducibility and clinical utility of tendon palpation to detect patellar tendinopathy in young basketball players. Br J Sports Med 2001;35:65–9.
11. Cook JL, Khan KM, Kiss ZS et al. Asymptomatic hypoechoic regions on patellar tendon ultrasound: a 4-year clinical and ultrasound followup of 46 tendons. Scand J Med Sci Sports 2001;11:321–7.
12. Shalaby M, Almekinders LC. Patellar tendinitis: the significance of magnetic resonance imaging findings. Am J Sports Med 1999;27(3):345–9.
13. Dye SF, Vaupel GL, Dye CS. Conscious neurosensory mapping of the internal structures of the human knee without intra-articular anesthesia. Am J Sports Med 1998;26(6):773–7.
14. Insall J, Falvo KA, Wise DW. Chondromalacia patellae. A prospective study. J Bone Joint Surg Am 1976;58(1):1–8.

15. Fulkerson JP. Diagnosis and treatment of patients with patellofemoral pain. *Am J Sports Med* 2002;30(3): 447–56.

16. Fulkerson JP, Gossling HR. Anatomy of the knee joint lateral retinaculum. *Clin Orthop Rel Res* 1980;153:183–8.

17. Fulkerson JP, Tennant R, Jaivin JS et al. Histologic evidence of retinacular nerve injury associated with patellofemoral malalignment. *Clin Orthop Rel Res* 1985;197:196–205.

18. Sanchis-Alfonso V, Rosello-Sastre E, Monteagudo-Castro C et al. Quantitative analysis of nerve changes in the lateral retinaculum in patients with isolated symptomatic patellofemoral malalignment. *Am J Sports Med* 1998;26(5):703–9.

19. Sanchis-Alfonso V, Roselló-Sastre E. Immunohistochemical analysis for neural markers of the lateral retinaculum in patients with isolated symptomatic patellofemoral malalignment. *Am J Sports Med* 2000;28(5):725–31.

20. Witoński D, Wągrowska-Danielewicz M. Distribution of substance-P nerve fibers in the knee joint in patients with anterior knee pain syndrome. A preliminary report. *Knee Surg Sports Traumatol Arthrosc* 1999;7(3):177–83.

21. Duri ZAA, Aichroth PM, Dowd G. The fat pad. *Am J Knee Surg* 1996;9(2):55–66.

22. Tsirbas A, Paterson RS, Keene GCR. Fat pad impingement: a missed cause of patellofemoral pain? *Aust J Sci Med Sport* 1990;December:24–26.

23. Fulkerson JP. *Disorders of the patellofemoral joint.* 3rd edn. Baltimore: Williams & Wilkins, 1997.

24. Matthews LS, Sonstegard DA, Henke JA. Load bearing characteristics of the patello-femoral joint. *Acta Orthop Scand* 1977;48(5):511–16.

25. Powers CM. The influence of altered lower-extremity kinematics on patellofemoral joint dysfunction: a theoretical perspective. *J Orthop Sports Phys Ther* 2003;33(11):639–46.

26. Grelsamer RP, Weinstein CH. Applied biomechanics of the patella. *Clin Orthop Rel Res* 2001;389:9–14.

27. Dye SF, Vaupel GL. The pathophysiology of patellofemoral pain. *Sports Med Arthrosc Rev* 1994;2:203–10.

28. Barton CJ, Levinger P, Menz HB et al. Kinematic gait characteristics associated with patellofemoral pain syndrome: a systematic review. *Gait Posture* 2009;30(4):405–16.

29. Boling MC, Padua DA, Marshall SW et al. A prospective investigation of biomechanical risk factors for patellofemoral pain syndrome. *Am J Sports Med* 2009;37(11):2108–16.

30. Messier SP, Davis SE, Curl WW et al. Etiologic factors associated with patellofemoral pain in runners. *Med Sci Sports Exerc* 1991;23(9):1008–15.

31. Myer GD, Ford KR, Barber Foss KD et al. The incidence and potential pathomechanics of patellofemoral pain in female athletes. *Clin Biomech* 2010;25(7):700–7.

32. Witvrouw E, Bellemans J, Lysens R et al. Intrinsic risk factors for the development of patellar tendinitis in an athletic population. *Am J Sports Med* 2001;29(2):190–5.

33. Watson CJ, Propps M, Galt W et al. Reliability of McConnell's classification of patellar orientation in symptomatic and asymptomatic subjects. *J Orthop Sports Phys Ther* 1999;29(7):386–93.

34. McConnell J. Reliability of McConnell's classification of patellar orientation in symptomatic and asymptomatic subjects – invited commentary. *J Orthop Sports Phys Ther* 1999;29(7):388–91.

35. Van Tiggelen D, Cowan S, Coorevits P et al. Delayed vastus medialis obliquus to vastus lateralis onset timing contributes to the development of patellofemoral pain in previously healthy men. *Am J Sports Med* 2009;37(6):1099–105.

36. Ireland ML, Wilson JD, Ballantyne BT et al. Hip strength in females with and without patellofemoral pain. *J Orthop Sports Phys Ther* 2003;33:671–6.

37. Tyler TF, Nicholas SJ, Mullaney MJ et al. The role of hip muscle function in the treatment of patellofemoral pain syndrome. *Am J Sports Med* 2006;34(4):630–6.

38. Cowan SM, Bennell KL, Hodges PW. Therapeutic patellar taping changes the timing of vasti muscle activation in people with patellofemoral pain syndrome. *Clin J Sport Med* 2002;12:339–47.

39. Ng GYF, Cheng JMF. The effects of patellar taping on pain and neuromuscular performance in subjects with patellofemoral pain syndrome. *Clin Rehabil* 2002;16(8):821–7.

40. Salsich GB, Brechter JH, Farwell D et al. The effects of patellar taping on knee kinetics, kinematics, and vastus lateralis muscle activity during stair ambulation in individuals with patellofemoral pain. *J Orthop Sports Phys Ther* 2002;32:3–10.

41. Wilson T, Carter N, Thomas G. A multicenter, single-masked study of medial, neutral, and lateral patellar taping in individuals with patellofemoral pain. *J Orthop Sports Phys Ther* 2003;33:437–48.

42. Christou EA. Patellar taping increases vastus medialis oblique activity in the presence of patellofemoral pain. *J Electromyogr Kinesiol* 2004;14(4):495–504.

43. Aminaka N, Gribble P. A systematic review of the effects of therapeutic taping on patellofemoral pain syndrome. *J Athl Train* 2005;40(4):341–51.

44. Gilleard W, McConnell J, Parsons D. The effect of patellar taping on the onset of vastus medialis obliquus and vastus lateralis muscle activity in persons with patellofemoral pain. *Phys Ther* 1998;78(1):25–32.

45. Cowan SM, Hodges PW, Crossley KM et al. Patellar taping does not change the amplitude of electromyographic activity of the vasti in a stair stepping task. *Br J Sports Med* 2006;40(1):30–4.

46. Cerny K. Vastus medialis oblique/vastus lateralis muscle activity ratios for selected exercises in persons with and without patellofemoral pain syndrome. *Phys Ther* 1995;75(8):672–83.

47. Powers CM, Landel R, Sosnick T et al. The effects of patellar taping on stride characteristics and joint motion in subjects with patellofemoral pain. *J Orthop Sports Phys Ther* 1997;26(6):286–91.

48. Powers CM, Ward SR, Chan L-D et al. The effect of bracing on patella alignment and patellofemoral joint contact area. *Med Sci Sports Exerc* 2004;36(7):1226–32.

49. Powers CM, Ward SR, Chen Y et al. The effect of bracing on patellofemoral joint stress during free and fast walking. *Am J Sports Med* 2004;32(1):224–31.

50. Lun VMY, Wiley Preston J, Meeuwisse WH et al. Effectiveness of patellar bracing for treatment of patellofemoral pain syndrome. *Clin J Sport Med* 2005;15(4):235–40.

51. Crossley K, Bennell K, Green S et al. Physical therapy for patellofemoral pain. A randomized, double-blinded, placebo controlled study. *Am J Sports Med* 2002;30(6):857–65.

52. Collins N, Crossley K, Beller E et al. Foot orthoses and physiotherapy in the treatment of patellofemoral pain syndrome: randomised clinical trial. *BMJ* 2008;337:a1735.

53. Davis IS, Powers C. Patellofemoral pain syndrome: proximal, distal, and local factors. An international research retreat. *J Orthop Sports Phys Ther* 2010;40(3):A1–48.

54. Noehren B, Scholz J, Davis I. The effect of real-time gait retraining on hip kinematics, pain and function in subjects with patellofemoral pain syndrome. *Br J Sports Med* 2011;45(9):691–6.

55. Franettovich M, Chapman A, Blanch P et al. Continual use of augmented low-Dye taping increases arch height in standing but does not influence neuromotor control of gait. *Gait Posture* 2010;31(2):247–50.

56. Vicenzino B, Collins N, Cleland J et al. A clinical prediction rule for identifying patients with patellofemoral pain who are likely to benefit from foot orthoses: a preliminary determination. *Br J Sports Med* 2010;44(12):862–6.

57. Vicenzino B. Foot orthotics in the treatment of lower limb conditions: a musculoskeletal physiotherapy perspective. *Man Ther* 2004;9(4):185–96.

58. Barton CJ, Menz HB, Crossley KM. Clinical predictors of foot orthoses efficacy in individuals with patellofemoral pain. *Med Sci Sports Exerc* 2011;43(9):1603–10.

59. Collins NJ, Bisset LM, Crossley KM, et al. Efficacy of non-surgical interventions for anterior knee pain: systematic review and meta-analysis of randomised trials. *Sports Med* in press (2012).

60. Gecha SR, Torg JS. Clinical prognosticators for the efficacy of retinacular release surgery to treat patellofemoral pain. *Clin Orthop Rel Res* 1990;253:203–8.

61. Schöttle PB, Fucentese SF, Romero J. Clinical and radiological outcome of medial patellofemoral ligament reconstruction with a semitendinosus autograft for patella instability. *Knee Surg Sports Traumatol Arthrosc* 2005;13(7):516–21.

62. Blazina ME, Kerlan RK, Jobe FW et al. Jumper's knee. *Orthop Clin North Am* 1973;4(3):665–78.

63. Khan KM, Bonar F, Desmond PM et al. Patellar tendinosis (jumper's knee): findings at histopathologic examination, US, and MR imaging. *Radiology* 1996;200(3):821–7.

64. Maffulli N, Khan KM, Puddu G. Overuse tendon conditions. Time to change a confusing terminology. *Arthroscopy* 1998;14:840–3.

65. Khan KM, Cook JL, Bonar F et al. Histopathology of common tendinopathies: update and implications for clinical management. *Sports Med* 1999;27:393–408.

66. Maffulli N, Binfield PM, Leach WJ et al. Surgical management of tendinopathy of the main body of the patellar tendon in athletes. *Clin J Sport Med* 1999;9(2):58–62.

67. Visentini PJ, Khan KM, Cook JL et al. The VISA score: an index of severity of symptoms in patients with jumper's knee (patellar tendinosis). *J Sci Med Sport* 1998;1(1):22–8.

68. Khan KM, Maffulli N, Coleman BD et al. Patellar tendinopathy: some aspects of basic science and clinical management. *Br J Sports Med* 1998;32:346–55.

69. Cook JL, Khan KM, Kiss ZS et al. Prospective imaging study of asymptomatic patellar tendinopathy in elite junior basketball players. *J Ultrasound Med* 2000;19(7):473–9.

70. Richards DP, Ajemian SV, Wiley JP et al. Knee joint dynamics predict patellar tendinitis in elite volleyball players. *Am J Sports Med* 1996;24(5):676–83.

71. Cook JL, Khan KM, Kiss ZS et al. Patellar tendinopathy in junior basketball players: a controlled clinical and ultrasonographic study of 268 patellar tendons in players aged 14–18 years. *Scand J Med Sci Sports* 2000;10(4):216–20.

72. Edwards S, Steele JR, McGhee DE et al. Landing strategies of athletes with an asymptomatic patellar tendon abnormality. *Med Sci Sports Exerc* 2010;42(11):2072–80.

73. Malliaras P, Cook JL, Kent P. Reduced ankle dorsiflexion range may increase the risk of patellar tendon injury among volleyball players. *J Sci Med Sport* 2006;9(4):304–9.

74. Jensen K, Di Fabio RP. Evaluation of eccentric exercise in treatment of patellar tendinitis. *Phys Ther* 1989;69(3):211–16.

75. Cannell LJ, Taunton JE, Clement DB et al. A randomised clinical trial of the efficacy of drop squats or leg extension/leg curl exercises to treat clinically diagnosed jumper's knee in athletes: pilot study. *Br J Sports Med* 2001;35:60–4.

76. Purdam CR, Cook JL, Hopper DM et al. Descriminative ability of functional loading tests for adolescent jumper's knee. *Phys Ther Sport* 2003;4:3–9.

77. Young MA, Cook JL, Purdam CR et al. Eccentric decline squat protocol offers superior results at 12 months compared with traditional eccentric protocol for patellar tendinopathy in volleyball players. *Br J Sports Med* 2005;39(2):102–5.

78. Bahr R, Fossan B, Loken S et al. Surgical treatment compared with eccentric training for patellar tendinopathy (jumper's knee). A randomized, controlled trial. *J Bone Joint Surg Am* 2006;88(8):1689–98.

79. Stasinopoulos D, Stasinopoulos I. Comparison of effects of exercise programme, pulsed ultrasound and transverse friction in the treatment of chronic patellar tendinopathy. *Clin Rehabil* 2004;18(4):347–52.

80. Kongsgaard M, Kovanen V, Aagaard P et al. Corticosteroid injections, eccentric decline squat training and heavy slow resistance training in patellar tendinopathy. *Scand J Med Sci Sports* 2009;19(6):790–802.

81. Fredberg U, Bolvig L, Andersen NT. Prophylactic training in asymptomatic soccer players with ultrasonographic abnormalities in achilles and patellar tendons. *Am J Sports Med* 2008;36(3):451–60.

82. Visnes H, Hoksrud A, Cook J et al. No effect of eccentric training on jumper's knee in volleyball players during the competitive season. *Clin J Sport Med* 2005;15(4):227–34.

83. Wilson J, Sevier T, Helfst R et al. Comparison of rehabilitation methods in the treatment of patellar tendinitis. *J Sport Rehabil* 2000;9:304–14.

84. Pellecchia GL, Hamel H, Behnke P. Treatment of infrapatellar tendinitis: a combination of modalities and transverse friction massage versus iontophoresis. *J Sport Rehabil* 1994;3:135–45.

85. Cook JL, Purdam CR. Is tendon pathology a continuum? A pathology model to explain the clinical presentation of load-induced tendinopathy. *Br J Sports Med* 2009;43(6):409–16.

86. Alfredson H, Öhberg L. Neovascularization in chronic painful patellar tendinosis—promising results after sclerosing neovessels outside the tendon challenge the need for surgery. *Knee Surg Sports Traumatol Arthrosc* 2005;13(2):74–80.

87. Hoksrud A, Öhberg L, Alfredson H et al. Ultrasound-guided sclerosis of neovessels in painful chronic patellar tendinopathy. *Am J Sports Med* 2006;34(11):1738–46.

88. Fredberg U, Bolvig L, Pfeiffer-Jensen M et al. Ultrasonography as a tool for diagnosis, guidance of local steroid injection and, together with pressure algometry, monitoring of the treatment of athletes with chronic jumper's knee and Achilles tendinitis: a randomized, double-blind, placebo-controlled study. *Scand J Rheumatol* 2004;33(2):94–101.

89. Filardo G, Kon E, Della Villa S et al. Use of platelet-rich plasma for the treatment of refractory jumper's knee. *Int Orthop* 2010;34(6):909–15.

90. Bahr R, Fossan B, Løken S, et al. Surgical treatment compared with eccentric training for patellar tendinopathy (Jumper's Knee). A randomized, controlled trial. *J Bone Joint Surg Am* 2006;88(8):1689–98.

91. Coleman BD, Khan KM, Kiss ZS et al. Open and arthroscopic patellar tenotomy for chronic patellar tendinopathy: a retrospective outcome study. *Am J Sports Med* 2000;28(2):193–90.

92. Willberg L, Sunding K, Ohberg L, et al. Treatment of Jumper's knee: promising short-term results in a pilot study using a new arthroscopic approach based on

imaging findings. *Knee Surg Sports Traumatol Arthrosc* 2007;15(5):676–81.

93. Kaeding CC, Pedroza AD, Powers BC. Surgical treatment of chronic patellar tendinosis: a systematic review. *Clin Orthop Rel Res* 2007;455:102–6

94. Coleman BD, Khan KM, Maffulli N et al. Studies of surgical outcome after patella tendinopathy: clinical significance of methodological deficiencies and guidelines for future studies. *Scand J Med Sci Sports* 2000;10:2–11.

95. Saddik D, McNally EG, Richardson M. MRI of Hoffa's fat pad. *Skelet Radiol* 2004;33(8):433–44.

96. Ducher G, Cook J, Spurrier D et al. Ultrasound imaging of the patellar tendon attachment to the tibia during puberty: a 12-month follow-up in tennis players. *Scand J Med Sci Sports* 2010;20(1):e35–40.

97. Warden SJ, Kiss ZS, Malara FA, et al. Comparative accuracy of magnetic resonance imaging and ultrasonography in confirming clinically diagnosed patellar tendinopathy. *Am J Sports Med* 2007;35(3): 427–36.

98. Collins N, Crossley K, Beller E, et al. Foot orthoses and physiotherapy in the treatment of patellofemoral pain syndrome: randomised clinical trial. *BMJ* 2008;337:a1735.

99. Eng JJ, Pierrynowski MR. Evaluation of soft foot orthotics in the treatment of patellofemoral pain syndrome. *Phys Ther* 1993;73(2):62-8; discussion 68–70.

100. Nakagawa TH, Muniz TB, Baldon Rde M, et al. The effect of additional strengthening of hip abductor and lateral rotator muscles in patellofemoral pain syndrome: a randomized controlled pilot study. *Clin Rehabil* 2008;22(12):1051–60.

101. Herrington L, Al-Sherhi A. A controlled trial of weight-bearing versus non-weight-bearing exercises for patellofemoral pain. *J Orthop Sports Phys Ther* 2007;37(4):155–60.

102. Song CY, Lin YF, Wei TC, et al. Surplus value of hip adduction in leg-press exercise in patients with patellofemoral pain syndrome: a randomized controlled trial. *Physical Therapy* 2009;89(5):409–18.

103. Thomee R. A comprehensive treatment approach for patellofemoral pain syndrome in young women. *Physical Therapy* 1997;77(12):1690–1703.

104. van Linschoten R, van Middelkoop M, Berger MY, et al. Supervised exercise therapy versus usual care for patellofemoral pain syndrome: an open label randomised controlled trial. *BMJ* 2009;339:b4074.

105. Witvrouw E, Danneels L, Van Tiggelen D, et al. Open versus closed kinetic chain exercises in patellofemoral pain: a 5-year prospective randomized study. *Am J Sports Med* 2004;32(5):1122–30.

106. Witvrouw E, Lysens R, Bellemans J, et al. Open versus closed kinetic chain exercises for patellofemoral pain—A prospective, randomized study. *Am J Sports Med* 2000;28(5):687–94.

107. van den Dolder PA, Roberts DL. Six sessions of manual therapy increase knee flexion and improve activity in people with anterior knee pain: a randomised controlled trial. *Aust J Physiother* 2006;52(4):261–4.

108. Jensen R, Gothesen O, Liseth K, et al. Acupuncture treatment of patellofemoral pain syndrome. *J Altern Complement Med* 1999;5(6):521–7.

109. Noehren B, Scholz J, Davis I. The effect of real-time gait retraining on hip kinematics, pain and function in subjects with patellofemoral pain syndrome. *Br J Sports Med* 2011;45(9):691–6

110. Australian Acute Musculoskeletal Pain Guidelines Group. *Evidence-based management of acute musculoskeletal pain.* Brisbane: Australian Academic Press Pty. Ltd., 2003.

111. Mason M, Keays SL, Newcombe PA. The effect of taping, quadriceps strengthening and stretching prescribed separately or combined on patellofemoral pain. *Physiother Res Int* 2011;16(2):109–19.

112. Stakes NO, Myburgh C, Brantingham JW et al. A prospective randomized clinical trial to determine efficacy of combind spinal manipulation and patella mobilization compared to patella mobilization alone in the conservative management of patellofemoral pain syndrome. *J Am Chiroprac Assoc* 2006;43(7): 11–8.

Chapter 34

Lateral, medial, and posterior knee pain

I retired because I had a knee injury, my cartilage was wearing out, it was painful and I couldn't put in the four hours of practice each day that I needed to. Guy Forget, former French professional tennis player

Although acute knee injuries and anterior knee pain are very common presentations in sports medicine practice, patients presenting with lateral, medial, or posterior knee pain can also provide challenges to the practitioner.

Lateral knee pain

Pain about the lateral knee (Fig. 34.1) is a frequent problem, especially among distance runners and cyclists. The most common cause of lateral knee pain is iliotibial band friction syndrome (ITBFS) which is an overuse injury. Training errors and biomechanical

abnormalities can precipitate ITBFS. Patellofemoral syndrome (Chapter 33) may also present as lateral knee pain. In the older active person, degeneration of the lateral meniscus or lateral compartment osteo-arthritis should be considered.

The biceps femoris tendon may cause pain as it passes posterolaterally to the knee and inserts into the head of the fibula; this occurs in sprinters and footballers. Injuries of the superior tibiofibular joint

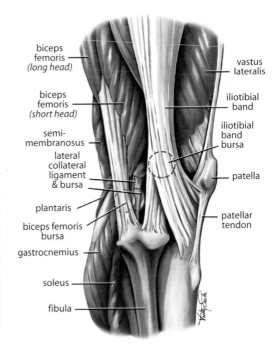

Figure 34.1 Lateral aspect of the knee
(a) Surface anatomy

(b) Anatomy of lateral aspect of the knee

may cause lateral knee pain. Lateral knee pain may be referred from the lumbar spine. The causes and differential diagnoses of lateral knee pain are shown in Table 34.1.

Clinical approach

As with acute knee injuries (Chapter 32) history and physical examination are the key to an accurate diagnosis.

History

A history of overuse suggest ITBFS or biceps femoris tendinopathy. If there is a history of excessive downhill running or running on an uneven surface, ITBFS may be implicated. If the pain occurs with sprinting or kicking activities, biceps femoris tendinopathy is more likely. Lateral knee pain following knee or ankle injury may indicate the superior tibiofibular joint or lateral meniscus as the site of injury.

The pain associated with biceps femoris tendinopathy flares up on initial activity and then starts to settle with warming up; it usually recurs following cessation of activity or the next day. When left untreated, pain persists during exercise and the athlete may not be able to continue with sporting activity. Iliotibial band (ITB) pain usually does not settle with ongoing activity and can be associated with local swelling.

Pain on sudden twisting or a history of giving way or locking may indicate degenerative lateral meniscus problems. Pain associated with excessive lateral pressure syndrome increases with activity. In active individuals who are over 50 years old, lateral compartment osteoarthritis should be considered.

The presence of back pain may suggest referred pain from the lumbar spine. Associated neurological symptoms such as weakness and paresthesia in the lower leg may indicate common peroneal nerve entrapment.

Examination

Full assessment of the ligaments of the knee (Chapter 32) should be included in the examination. Biomechanical examination should also be performed.

 A detailed knee examination can be seen in the *Clinical Sports Medicine* masterclasses at www. clinicalsportsmedicine.com

1. Observation
   (a) standing
   (b) walking
   (c) supine
   (d) side-lying
2. Active movements
   (a) knee flexion
   (b) knee extension
   (c) repeated knee flexion (0–30°) (Fig. 34.2a)
   (d) tibial rotation
3. Passive movements
   (a) knee flexion/extension
   (b) tibial rotation (Fig. 34.2b)
   (c) superior tibiofibular joint
       (i) accessory glides (Fig. 34.2c)
   (d) muscle stretches
       (i) ITB (Ober's test) (Fig. 34.2d)
       (ii) quadriceps
       (iii) hamstring
4. Resisted movements
   (a) knee flexion (Fig. 34.2e)
   (b) tibial rotation
5. Functional movements
   (a) hopping
   (b) squat/single-leg squat
   (c) jumping

Table 34.1 Causes of lateral knee pain

Common	Less common	Not to be missed
Iliotibial band friction syndrome	Patellofemoral syndrome	Common peroneal nerve injury
Lateral meniscus abnormality	Osteoarthritis of the lateral	Slipped capital femoral epiphysis
• Minor tear	compartment of the knee	Perthes' disease
• Degenerative change	Excessive lateral pressure syndrome	
• Cyst	Biceps femoris tendinopathy	
	Superior tibiofibular joint sprain	
	Synovitis of the knee joint	
	Referred pain	
	• Lumbar spine	
	• Neuromechanical sensitivity	

6. Palpation
   (a) lateral femoral epicondyle (Fig. 34.2f overleaf)
   (b) lateral joint line
   (c) lateral retinaculum
   (d) lateral border of patella
   (e) superior tibiofibular joint
   (f) biceps femoris tendon
   (g) gluteus medius
7. Special tests
   (a) full knee examination (Chapter 32)
      (i) effusion (Fig. 34.2g overleaf)
      (ii) McMurray's test (Fig. 34.2h overleaf)
   (b) neurodynamic tests
      (i) prone knee bend
      (ii) slump (Fig. 34.2i overleaf)
   (c) lumbar spine (Chapter 26)
   (d) biomechanical assessment (Chapter 8)
      (Fig. 34.2j on page 719)

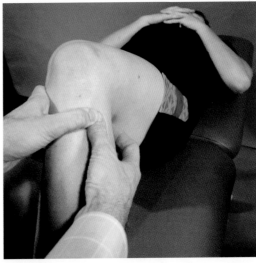

(c) Passive movements—accessory anteroposterior glide to superior tibiofibular joint

Figure 34.2 Examination of the patient with lateral knee pain

(a) Active movements—repeated flexion from 0° to 30°. This may reproduce the patient's pain if ITBFS is the cause. It can be performed in a side-lying position (illustrated), standing or as a squat

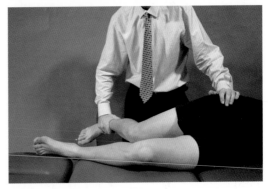

(d) Passive movement—ITB stretch
This is performed in a side-lying position with the hip in neutral rotation and knee flexion. The hip is extended and then adducted. If the ITB is tight, knee extension will occur with adduction (Ober's test)

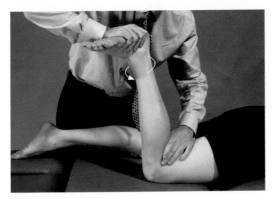

(b) Passive movements—tibial rotation
This is performed in knee flexion to assess superior tibiofibular joint movement

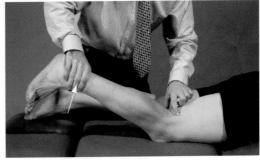

(e) Resisted movement—knee flexion
Concentric or eccentric contractions may reproduce the pain of biceps femoris tendinopathy

717

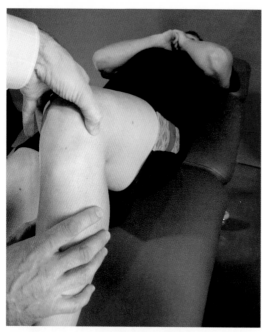

(f) Palpation—lateral femoral epicondyle

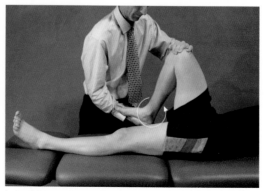

(h) Special tests—McMurray's test
The knee is flexed and, at various stages of flexion, internal and external rotation of the tibia are performed. The presence of pain and a palpable "clunk" are a positive McMurray's test and are consistent with meniscal injury. If there is no "clunk" but the patient's pain is reproduced, then the meniscus may be damaged or there may be patellofemoral joint abnormality

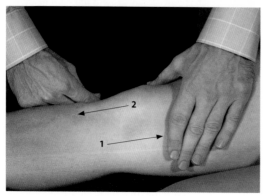

(g) Special test—knee effusion
Manually drain the medial subpatellar pouch by stroking the fluid in a superior direction. (1) Then "milk" the fluid back into the knee from above (2) while observing the pouch for reaccumulating fluid

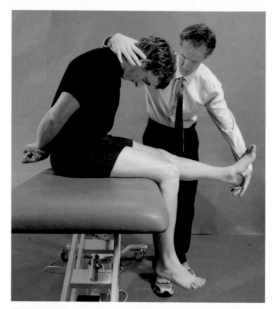

(i) Special tests—slump test

Investigations

Although the majority of younger patients with lateral knee pain do not require investigations, MR imaging can be useful in cases of persistent lateral knee pain when a degenerative lateral meniscus is suspected. It is also indicated if there is a clinical suspicion of lateral compartment osteoarthritis. X-ray has poor sensitivity for osteoarthritis. When imaging is not readily available, a diagnostic local anesthetic injection can be used to differentiate local soft tissue pain (e.g. ITBFS) from intra-articular or referred pain.

Iliotibial band friction syndrome

Iliotibial band friction syndrome (ITBFS) is an overuse injury presenting as lateral knee pain that is exacerbated by sporting activity. It is commonly seen in runners, cyclists, military recruits, and endurance

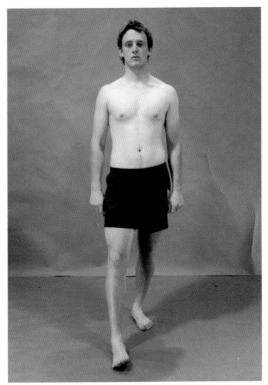

(j) Special tests—biomechanical assessment
Full lower limb biomechanical assessment should
be performed while standing, walking, and lying.
Abnormal pelvic movements (e.g. excessive lateral tilt)
should be noted

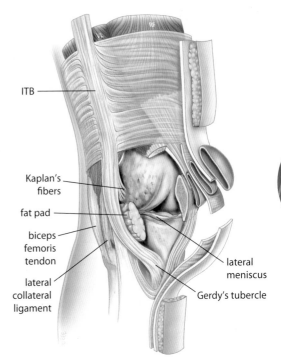

Figure 34.3 Anatomy of the iliotibial band insertion

VL = VASTUS LATERALIS; RF = RECTUS FEMORIS; ITB = ILIOTIBIAL BAND
FROM FRANKLIN-MILLER A. ET AL. *CLINICAL SPORTS ANATOMY.*
MELBOURNE: MCGRAW-HILL, 2010; P. 269

athletes.[1–4] Incidence rates in running range from
1.6% to 12% and 1% to 5.5% in military populations.[3]
In cycling, ITBFS accounts for 15% to 24% of overuse
injuries.[3]

Anatomy

Traditionally ITBFS was considered to be the result of
friction, between the ITB and the underlying lateral
epicondyle of the femur. This friction was thought to
contribute to local inflammation and irritation of an
anatomical bursa lying between the tendon and the
lateral epicondyle.[5] However, recent studies do not
support the presence of an anatomical bursa around
the lateral femoral epicondyle.[2, 4] Instead of a bursa,
it has been proposed that a richly innervated and vascularized layer of fat and connective tissue separates
the ITB from the lateral femoral epicondyle, and this
could be the likely source of pain seen in ITBFS.[2, 4]

The ITB itself is not a discrete band but a
lateral thickening of the circumferential fascia
lata that envelops the whole thigh like a stocking
(Fig. 34.3).[1, 2, 4] The ITB inserts along the length of the
femur down the linea aspera via the lateral intermuscular septum.[1, 2, 4]

Proximally, the tensor fascia lata muscle inserts
into the ITB, as does a substantial portion of the
gluteus maximus muscle.

Distally, the ITB crosses the lateral femoral epicondyle and is connected to that epicondyle by strong
fibrous bands. The ITB continues, acting like a
lateral ligament, from the lateral femoral epicondyle
to insert onto the patella and Gerdy's tubercle on the
tibia (Fig. 34.3). The ITB can also project onto the
fibula. This anatomical orientation of the ITB demonstrates the close relationship between the ITB
and the knee and hip complex and its role in lateral
stability.

Movement of the ITB around the lateral femoral
epicondyle is restricted by its strong fibrous band
attachments. However, altering tension of the fascia
lata and hip musculature can result in compressive forces around the lateral femoral epicondyle.[2, 4]

Therefore pain may result with compressive loads rather than being due to transverse frictional forces.

ITB biomechanics

The ITB plays a role in stability around the hip with its role in hip joint centering through its tensioning effect. In hip adduction and flexion, an increase in pressure around the greater trochanter has been reported.[1] This pressure is further increased by knee flexion. The same pressure is reduced in hip abduction, and knee extension. This role is supported by surgical studies that have shown that ITB lengthening can lead to favorable outcomes in trochanteric bursitis presentations.[1]

It was originally thought that ITBFS was associated with repetitive knee flexion and extension movement. However, a biomechanical study found no significant difference in sagittal knee movements between an ITBFS population and matched controls.[5] This suggests other planes of motion may be more relevant. For example, an increase in tibial internal rotation can augment compressive forces around the lateral femoral epicondyle by moving the ITB's distal attachment to the tibia more medially.[6]

Tibial internal rotation may result from poor proximal control (increased hip adduction/internal rotation), genu valgus, and/or poor rear foot mechanics. An increase in hip adduction, especially during the loading phase of running, increases the eccentric demand on the hip abductors.[6]

Runners with ITBFS can have significant weakness of their hip abductors in the affected limb,[7] and decreased ability of the hip abductors to eccentrically control abduction.[8] There is also often weakness in knee flexion and knee extension, with decreased braking forces.[9]

Weakness and fatigue can result in increased compressive forces around the lateral femoral epicondyle and therefore lead to ITBFS. Neural feedback from the richly innervated fat and connective tissue between the ITB and lateral femoral epicondyle may result in decreased tension in the hip abductors to reduce these compressive loads.[2] This can lead to hip muscle imbalances and altered biomechanics.

Clinical features

Clinically, a sportsperson with ITBFS typically complains of an ache over the lateral aspect of the knee which is aggravated by running or cycling. The pain often develops at about the same distance/time during activity. Longer training sessions, downhill running, or cambered courses are often aggravating factors.

On examination, tenderness is elicited over the lateral femoral epicondyle 2–3 cm (~1 in.) above the lateral joint line (Fig. 34.2f). Crepitus and local swelling may also be felt. Repeated flexion/extension of the knee may reproduce the patient's symptoms.

Ober's test (Fig. 34.2d) often reveals ITB tightness and may produce a burning sensation. Tightness may be secondary to shortening of the tensor fascia lata and/or gluteus maximus muscles proximally, or excessive development of the vastus lateralis, placing increased tensile load on the ITB.

Imaging is not usually required to confirm the diagnosis of ITBFS. Both ultrasound and MRI can show thickening of the ITB over the lateral femoral condyle and often a fluid collection deep to the ITB at the same site.[10]

Treatment

Treatment of ITBFS should address not only local symptoms, but also foot and especially hip biomechanics for more favorable long-term results. Although pathology is felt distally, treatment should be focused proximally.

Local treatment includes ice and electrotherapy applied to the area around the lateral femoral epicondyle. Nonsteroidal anti-inflammatory drugs (NSAIDs) may be helpful in the initial stages. Corticosteroid injection (Fig. 34.4) has traditionally been used to inject the "bursa." The inconsistent results from these injections can be attributed to a misunderstanding of the pathology. Corticosteroid injection can be helpful in reducing pain and this facilitates the patient undertaking rehabilitation exercises.

Figure 34.4 Corticosteroid injection if used, is aimed deep to the ITB tendon—between it and the underlying lateral femoral epicondyle

Soft tissue treatment to the proximal ITB (Figs 34.5a, b), dry needling (Fig. 34.5c) and self massage with a foam roll (Fig. 34.5d) all help to reduce muscle tension and tone in the ITB.

Stretching (Fig. 34.6 overleaf) is routinely proposed as a treatment for ITBFS. However, because the ITB inserts into the entire length of the femur via the lateral intermuscular septum, stretching exercises may have a limited effect on the ITB itself. Stretching may have some effect on reducing the tension in the tensor fascia lata.[2, 4] Stretching of the gluteus maximus muscle may prove more beneficial because of its close relationship to the ITB.

Tightness of the gluteal muscles and tensor fascia lata are commonly associated with ITBFS. The presence of trigger points in the tensor fascia lata, gluteus minimus, and gluteus medius may contribute to ITBFS. Gluteal trigger point dry needling (Fig. 34.5e

overleaf) and ischemic pressure can reduce the tension and relieve local pressure around the lateral femoral epicondyle.

Strengthening of the hip external rotators (Fig. 34.7a overleaf) and abductors (Fig. 34.7b overleaf) is an important component of the treatment to correct the underlying weakness and fatigability of these muscles.

Surgery to release the ITB may be indicated if conservative management fails. Methods used include excision of a triangular area of the ITB from the area overlying the lateral condyle when the knee is in a 30° position,[11] transection of the posterior half of the width of the ITB over the lateral condyle,[12] Z-lengthening of the iliotibial band,[13] and distal detachment and multiple puncture.[14]

B

Figure 34.5 Treating tight myofascial structures
(a) Sustained myofascial tension to the proximal ITB

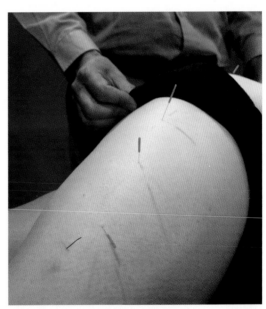

(c) Dry needling to ITB trigger points

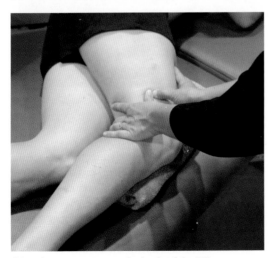

(b) Ischemic pressure to the body of the ITB

(d) Foam roll self-massage to the ITB

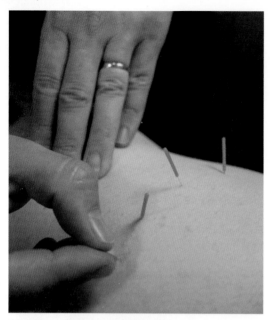

(e) Dry needling to gluteal trigger points

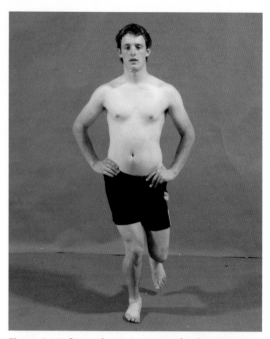

Figure 34.7 Strengthening exercises for the external hip rotators and abductors
(a) Exercise involves the patient standing on one leg and slowly performing a squat maintaining pelvic stability

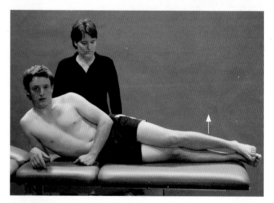

(b) Hip abduction in side-lying

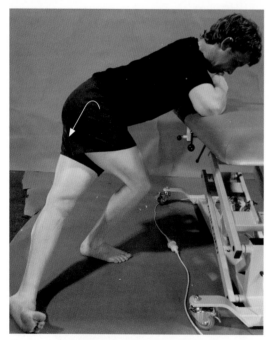

Figure 34.6 ITB stretch—the ITB on the left side is being stretched. The symptomatic leg is extended and adducted across the uninvolved leg. The patient exhales and slowly flexes the trunk laterally to the opposite side until a stretch is felt on the side of the hip

Lateral meniscus abnormality

The lateral meniscus is more circular than the medial one, which is more C-shaped (Fig. 32.3 on page 634). The lateral meniscus is loosely connected to the lateral joint capsule and, to some degree, communicates with the posterior cruciate ligament. Acute meniscal injuries are discussed in Chapter 32.

A discoid (disk-shaped) lateral meniscus is an anatomical abnormality reported in children. A discoid meniscus can present as chronic "snapping knee syndrome," can be asymptomatic, and may be an incidental finding on MRI later on in life.[15] What risk is associated with this abnormality, especially in active adolescent and adult populations, remains unclear. When symptomatic (i.e. painful, presence of joint effusion, symptoms of clicking and locking), it is often associated with a meniscal tear, which is then treated arthroscopically.[15]

In children and early adolescents, diagnosing meniscal injury can be difficult because of vague subjective findings and difficulty in localizing pain.[16] This can result in delayed diagnoses and increase chronicity. Meniscal injury in children is more common than previously thought, and is under-diagnosed.[16]

Tenderness along the lateral joint line with associated joint effusion and a positive McMurray's test is indicative of meniscal injury. X-ray can rule out differential diagnoses such as osteochondritis dissecans, and osteochondral and tibial plateau fractures.[15, 16] MRI is useful, but can be associated with false positives.[16] Treatment is based on the athlete's age, duration of symptoms, area of meniscal pathology (vascular areas compared with non-vascular) and number of associated injuries (such as cruciate ligament tear).

In adults degeneration of the lateral meniscus can also present as a gradual onset of lateral knee pain, and is often associated with quadriceps muscle atrophy.

If a runner presents complaining of lateral knee pain that comes on after 20 minutes of running and is aggravated by running up hills, the practitioner should not automatically assume that the patient has ITBFS—the problem may relate to a degenerative meniscus.

Careful physical examination should help distinguish the lateral meniscal degeneration from ITBFS conditions.

A lateral meniscus injury is often tender along the joint line, 2–3 cm below the site of tenderness in ITBFS (at the lateral femoral epicondyle). McMurray's test in full flexion (Fig. 34.2h) should also help to distinguish the conditions, as it should be positive when a meniscal injury is present and negative in cases of ITBFS.

A degenerative meniscus can present as a painful or non-painful lump at the lateral joint line. This is not an ITB bursa. If there is doubt as to the correct diagnosis, MRI is the investigation of choice.

Osteoarthritis of the lateral compartment of the knee

Lateral knee pain can also be caused by degeneration of the lateral tibial plateau; this can be associated with meniscal injury, knee malalignment (e.g. valgus malalignment), and obesity.[17, 18] Early in the disease, the patient may give a history of increasing knee pain with activity and stiffness after a period of rest.

As the disease progresses, the patient may start to experience pain at night that may disturb sleep, and morning stiffness, usually lasting less than half an hour. In the early stages, examination may only reveal a small effusion.

A useful investigation is a weight-bearing plain X-ray. This has greater sensitivity than views taken with the patient supine.

Initial treatment of osteoarthritis includes symptomatic relief with analgesia and NSAIDs if required, modification of activity, and exercise prescription, together with weight loss if indicated. Intra-articular hyaluronic acid supplements (viscosupplements) have a similar efficacy to NSAIDs, and the patient does not have to take tablets daily.[19, 20]

Functional motor control assessment focusing on load distribution such as single-leg squat, stair negotiation and gait, can identify biomechanical contributing factors. Early identification of these factors may delay or even prevent further degeneration.

Patients with severe clinical symptoms may require unicompartmental[21] or, eventually, total knee replacement.

Excessive lateral pressure syndrome

Excessive lateral pressure syndrome (lateral patellar compression syndrome) occurs when there is excessive pressure on the lateral patellofemoral joint resulting from a tight lateral retinaculum. The lateral retinaculum is not one distinct anatomical structure, but is composed of three layers. There is a deep fascia layer (not attached to the patella), an intermediate layer (composed of the ITB and the quadriceps aponeurosis and their attachments to the patella), and the deepest layer is the joint capsule.[22] Therefore an increase in pressure around the lateral retinaculum will affect the joint capsule, the patellofemoral joint, the ITB, and the quadriceps muscles. This can lead to bone strain on the lateral patella, inflammation of the lateral retinaculum, and ITBFS.

Eventually the increased bone strain on the lateral patella may lead to development of a vertical stress fracture or even separation of the lateral patellar fragment. This must be differentiated radiologically from a congenital bipartite patella. The separated fragment is in the superolateral aspect of the patella. MRI has been used to image this condition.[23]

Initial treatment of excessive lateral pressure syndrome consists of patellofemoral mobilization and soft tissue therapy to the lateral retinaculum. Taping techniques rarely help. Surgical lateral retinacular release or even removal of the lateral patellar fragment is occasionally required.[24]

Biceps femoris tendinopathy

Biceps femoris tendinopathy occurs with excessive acceleration and deceleration activities, and is often associated with running and cycling. As with most tendinopathies, it does not initially restrict sporting activity and therefore has a high risk of chronicity when not recognised early. Pain is described around the posterolateral knee and often settles after activity. Morning stiffness post exercise is often reported.

The pain can be produced with resisted flexion, especially with eccentric contractions (Fig. 34.2e) and on palpation of the tendon as it inserts onto the fibula. It is often associated with tightness of the hamstring and gluteal muscles. Stiffness of the lumbar spine and poor core stability may contribute to hamstring tightness.

Both MRI and ultrasound examination may help confirm the diagnosis.

Treatment is based on the general principles of the treatment of tendinopathy—load modification, soft tissue therapy (Fig. 34.8), and strengthening, especially eccentric strengthening of the hamstrings (Fig. 34.9). Strengthening of the hip muscles, specifically the gluteus maximus, may also prove useful.[25]

In rare cases, failed conservative measures mean surgical approaches may be considered. Surgical approaches include stripping of the paratenon, removal of degenerative tissue, and other repair techniques for torn tendons.[26]

Superior tibiofibular joint injury

The superior tibiofibular joint comprises the articulation between the lateral condyle of the tibia and the fibular head. The joint capsule is strengthened by superior anterior and posterior ligaments.[27, 28]

The superior tibiofibular joint plays a role in tibiofemoral joint stability through its surrounding anatomical structures, which include the lateral collateral ligament, arcuate ligament, popliteofibular ligament, biceps femoris tendon, and popliteus muscle.[28] The

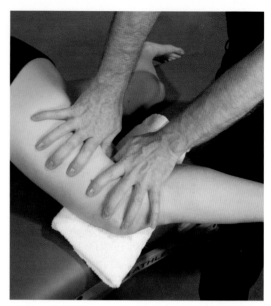

Figure 34.8 Soft tissue therapy in the treatment of biceps femoris tendinopathy. Ischemic pressure at the musculotendinous junction (shown) and muscle belly can be effective

Figure 34.9 Eccentric strengthening exercises in the treatment of biceps femoris tendinopathy. Drop-and-catch is performed in prone positions (Chapter 31). This may be progressed to include hip flexion (i.e. patient lying over the end of the bed)

superior tibiofibular joint externally rotates during ankle dorsiflexion and is thought to dissipate torsional stresses from the ankle.[28] When injured, the superior tibiofibular joint can affect knee and ankle function and can be a source of lateral knee pain.

Superior tibiofibular joint injury may result from direct trauma resulting in subluxation or dislocation of the fibula. The superior tibiofibular joint can also be sprained during twisting injuries. The mechanism of injury is often described as a combination of rotation and knee flexion (e.g. pivoting, cutting) and has been reported in sports such as rugby, soccer, skiing and the various forms of martial arts.[29] Additionally, superior tibiofibular joint injuries can be secondary to severe ankle injuries. In the older sportsperson, osteoarthritis of the superior tibiofibular joint can accompany knee arthritis; this can be confirmed on imaging.[27]

Dislocation of the joint

In the presence of a dislocation, the sportsperson may present with a prominent head of fibula, lateral knee pain, and swelling around the superior tibiofibular joint. The athlete may report "popping" or "clicking." Pain may be exacerbated by ankle movements and weight-bearing activities.

It is important to immediately assess for and rule out peroneal nerve injury.[27] A severe superior tibiofibular joint injury can be associated with popliteus tendon injury, which may be an isolated injury or part of a more complex posterolateral corner injury. Associated posterolateral corner injuries should be recognized early, as the knee becomes unstable in full extension. There is often an accompanying anterior or posterior cruciate ligament injury. Unrecognized or untreated posterolateral instability can lead to failures of repairs of the anterior or posterior cruciate ligaments, and chronic knee instability.[27]

Acute and painful subluxations can be managed conservatively with immobilization (for 2–3 weeks), followed by a progressive strengthening program of the hamstring and calf muscles.[29]

Joint sprain

In a superior tibiofibular joint sprain, pain may be local or may refer distally along the lateral calf. The joint is often tender, especially directly over the head of the fibula, and passive movement of the joint may be restricted by hamstring (biceps femoris) and peroneal muscle spasm. With these muscles relaxed, excessive movement may be detected on passive gliding (Fig. 34.2c). Excessively mobile joints are more difficult to treat and can be associated with generalized hypermobility, especially in the female sportsperson. Predisposing factors, such as excessive pronation, which place greater torsional forces through the joint, should be assessed, and may require correction.

Manual mobilization can be an effective treatment for a stiff tibiofibular joint. Strengthening of the muscles around the knee, especially the tibial rotators, may help stabilize the joint, reduce pain, and improve function.

For patients with chronic pain or instability that impairs function, surgical options include arthrodesis, fibular head resection,[30] and proximal tibiofibular joint capsule reconstruction. A gracilis autograft can lead to subjective improvements and could aid return to sport;[29] however, strength may continue to be reduced.

Referred pain

Pain may refer from the lumbar spine to the lateral aspect of the knee. Referred pain is usually a dull ache and is poorly localized. The slump test (Fig. 34.2i) may be positive. The lumbar spine should be examined in sportspeople presenting with atypical lateral knee pain.

Medial knee pain

Pain about the medial knee (Fig. 34.10) is less common than anterior and lateral knee pain. The causes of medial knee pain are shown in Table 34.2 overleaf.

Patellofemoral pain syndrome

In most cases of medial knee pain, the pain is actually anteromedial and is most frequently due to patellofemoral pain syndrome. The patellofemoral joint

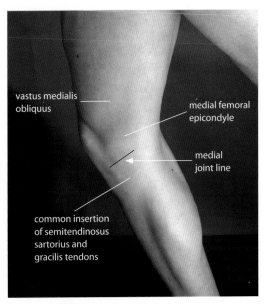

Figure 34.10 Medial aspect of the knee
(a) Surface anatomy

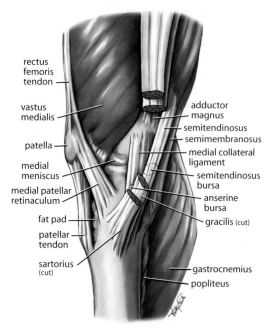

rectus
femoris
tendon

vastus
medialis

patella

medial
meniscus

medial patellar
retinaculum

fat pad

patellar
tendon

sartorius
(cut)

adductor
magnus

semitendinosus
semimembranosus

medial collateral
ligament

semitendinosus
bursa

anserine
bursa

gracilis (cut)

gastrocnemius

popliteus

(b) Anatomy   ADAPTED FROM THE *CIBA COLLECTION OF MEDICAL
ILLUSTRATIONS*, REPRODUCED BY COURTESY OF CIBA-GEIGY LIMITED,
BASEL, SWITZERLAND. ALL RIGHTS RESERVED

commonly refers pain to the medial aspect of the knee.

Recent studies suggest that the medial patellofemoral ligament may play a significant role in medial knee pain associated with patellofemoral syndrome.[31, 32] This ligament is located 2 cm proximal and parallel to the medial joint line. Medial patellofemoral ligament reconstruction as a pain-relieving surgery has been described.[32]

Patellofemoral pain syndrome (PFPS) is discussed in Chapter 33.

Medial meniscus abnormality

In the young adult patient, a small tear of the medial meniscus may cause a synovial reaction and medial knee pain (Fig. 34.11). In the older patient, gradual degeneration of the medial meniscus can present as gradual-onset medial knee pain. The clinical scenario is similar to that described for a lateral meniscal abnormality (page 722).

The sportsperson is generally aged over 35 years, and complains of "clicking" and pain with certain twisting activities, such as getting out of a car, rolling over in bed, changing direction, and cutting and pivoting movements during sporting activity. Examination reveals joint line tenderness and a positive McMurray's test (Fig. 34.2h). MRI is the investigation of choice.

Treatment is as for an acute meniscal injury (Chapter 32). Conservative management is warranted but, if this fails, surgical intervention—arthroscopic—may be required. Complete meniscectomies are contraindicated because, with a partial meniscectomy, the remaining uninjured portion of the medial meniscus can continue to contribute to shock absorption.[33] Complete meniscectomies are associated with osteoarthritis.

Osteoarthritis of the medial compartment of the knee

Osteoarthritis of the knee generally affects sportspeople over the age of 50 years, but has also been reported in adolescents and young adults.[34, 35]

Table 34.2 Causes of medial knee pain

Common	Less common	Not to be missed
Patellofemoral syndrome	Synovial plica (Chapter 32)	Tumor (in the young)
Medial meniscus	Pes anserinus	Slipped capital femoral epiphysis
• Minor tear	• Tendinopathy	Referred pain from the hip
• Degenerative change	• Bursitis	Perthes' disease
• Cyst	Medial collateral ligament	
	• Grade I sprain/bursitis	
	• Pellegrini-Stieda lesion	
	Osteoarthritis of the medial	
	compartment of the knee	
	Referred pain	
	• Lumbar spine	
	• Hip joint	
	• Neural mechanosensitivity	

are normal, MRI can distinguish the two conditions using specific articular cartilage sequences, including the technique of delayed gadolinium-enhanced MRI of cartilage (dGEMRIC), which estimates cartilage quality.[36] (See Chapter 32, page 635 for discussion of this issue.)

Identifying and monitoring athletes at a high risk of osteoarthritis provides an opportunity for prevention and disease-modifying interventions. Assessment of family history, previous knee injuries, muscle imbalances (specifically quadriceps weakness), lower limb biomechanics, and body weight can be incorporated into a screening assessment. Preventative lower limb specific rehabilitation programs reduce the risk of lower limb injuries.[37–39]

Initial management of osteoarthritis includes symptomatic relief with analgesia and modification of activity. Exercise prescription, and weight optimization should be addressed early.[20]

A randomized clinical trial found that a custom-made, valgus-producing functional knee (unloader) brace provided significant benefit in this population of patients aged in their 60s.[40] Biomechanical studies have shown that these braces maintain condylar separation.[41]

Viscosupplementation for chondroprotection with hyaluronic acid (e.g. Orthovisc, Supatrz, Hyalgan, Synvisc) given as a series of intra-articular injections can provide beneficial effects on pain, function and patient global assessment, especially at the 5th to 13th week post-injection period.[19, 42] However, further research is needed to establish their long-term effectiveness.[43]

If clinical symptoms are persistent and severe, referral is warranted. Surgical intervention may include high tibial osteotomy, unicompartmental replacement, and total knee replacement. However, early surgical intervention to prevent osteoarthritis has not been shown to be superior to conservative treatments,[34] with some surgeries being linked to the development of early degenerative changes in young adults (e.g. ACL reconstruction).[44, 45]

Pes anserinus tendinopathy/bursitis

The pes anserinus ("goose's foot") is the combined tendinous insertion of the sartorius, gracilis, and semitendinosus tendons at their attachment to the tibia (Fig. 34.10b). The area is richly innervated as each muscle (sartorius, gracilis, semitendinosus) is supplied by a different nerve (femoral, obturator, and tibial respectively). The primary action of

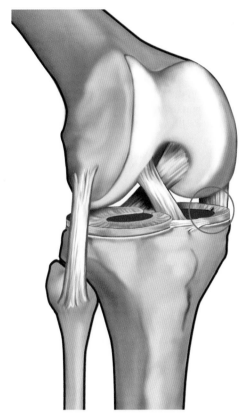

Figure 34.11 Medial meniscus tear—a common cause of medial knee pain

Osteoarthritis affects not only the articular cartilage, but also the subchondral bone and the synovium. Ligamentous, meniscal, and chondral injury, and also repetitive joint loading, can predispose to osteoarthritis.[34, 35]

Risk factors for developing premature arthritis include obesity, sports participation, previous knee injury, and genetic predisposition.[34, 35] Obesity in children, specifically, a body mass index (BMI) above the 95th percentile for height and weight ratios (for 2- to 19-year-olds), has been linked to increased risk of musculoskeletal injury.[34, 35]

Sportspeople participating in power sports such as wrestling, boxing, weight-lifting, and team sports such as soccer, basketball, and football have a higher incidence of premature knee arthritis.[34, 35] Other sports (e.g. cross-country skiing, walking, swimming) have a lower incidence of osteoarthritis.[34]

In the early stages, it is very difficult to distinguish medial compartment osteoarthritis clinically from medial meniscal injury. If weight-bearing X-rays

these muscles is to flex the knee; however, they also play an important stability role by resisting valgus strain.[46, 47]

The risk of injury to the pes anserinus is increased with excessive valgus stress. Excessive valgus stress can be the result of collateral ligament instability, meniscal pathology, muscle imbalances, or valgus knee deformity.[47]

The pes anserinus bursa lies between the pes anserinus insertion and the periosteum, and may become inflamed as a result of overuse. The pes anserinus tendons themselves can also be compressed or irritated, resulting in a tendinopathy. Pes anserinus tendinopathy/bursitis is uncommon; however, it may occur in swimmers (particularly breaststrokers), cyclists, and runners.

The clinical presentation is characterized by localized tenderness and swelling close to the medial joint line, and can mimic medial meniscus pathology. Active contraction or stretching of the medial hamstring muscles can reproduce pain. Investigations such as MRI and ultrasound can aid in diagnosis and help exclude other pathologies.[48]

Initial treatment follows the general principles of tendinopathy/bursitis management. Ultrasound-guided corticosteroid injection into the bursa can be effective in reducing pain.[48] For long-term resolution, biomechanical factors and muscle imbalances that can influence valgus forces need to be addressed.

Pellegrini-Stieda syndrome

Pellegrini-Stieda syndrome is a disruption of the femoral origin of the medial collateral ligament with calcification at the site of injury. It can be a difficult lesion to assess before radiological changes become evident. It may follow direct trauma or, less frequently, a grade II or III sprain of the medial collateral ligament. Note that imaging abnormalities exist in asymptomatic individuals.[49]

Pellegrini-Stieda syndrome is an important cause of knee stiffness. The patient complains of difficulty straightening the leg and twisting. Examination reveals marked restriction in joint range of motion with a tender lump in the proximal portion of the medial collateral ligament.

Treatment consists of active mobilization of the knee joint and infiltration of a corticosteroid agent to the tender medial collateral ligament attachment if pain persists. Surgery may be indicated in the presence of significant bone formation and persistent symptoms (pain and stiffness).[50]

Medial collateral ligament grade I sprain

A grade I medial collateral ligament sprain or bursitis often presents without a history of any major trauma. The medial collateral ligament can also become inflamed as a result of activities that put a constant valgus strain on the knee, such as swimming breaststroke. This condition is commonly referred to as "breaststroker's knee" and is actually a first-degree sprain of the medial collateral ligament, or inflammation of the medial collateral ligament bursa due to excessive stress.

Posterior knee pain

Accurate and specific diagnosis of pain about the posterior knee (Fig. 34.12) may be difficult. Posterior knee pain is a common site of referred pain from the lumbar spine and from the patellofemoral joint. Alternatively, local structures (e.g. popliteus, biceps femoris tendon) may cause posterior knee pain. A knee effusion is a common cause of pain and tightness of the back of the knee. The causes of posterior knee pain are shown in Table 34.3.

Clinical evaluation

History

Posterior knee pain precipitated by acceleration or deceleration (e.g. downhill running, kicking, sprinting) is likely to be biceps femoris or popliteus tendinopathy. Pain described as a poorly localized dull ache not directly related to activity suggests it may be referred. The presence of low back pain or patellofemoral symptoms provides a diagnostic clue. A previous acute knee injury may have caused an effusion with the development of a Baker's cyst.

Examination

In the examination of the posterior aspect of the knee, it is important to differentiate between local and referred causes of pain. The slump test (Fig. 34.2i) may indicate whether the pain is referred from the lumbar spine or neural structures. It is also important to detect the presence of an effusion, as this may be the cause of the posterior knee pain.

1. Observation
   (a) standing (Fig. 34.13a overleaf)
   (b) prone
2. Active movements
   (a) flexion
   (b) extension
   (c) tibial rotation

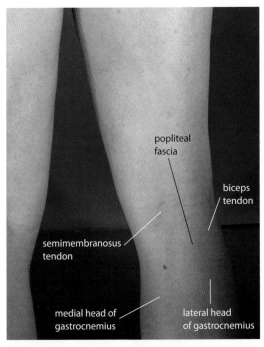

popliteal
fascia

biceps
tendon

semimembranosus
tendon

medial head of
gastrocnemius

lateral head
of gastrocnemius

femur

plantaris
(cut)

adductor
magnus
tendon

gastroc-
nemius
lateral
head
(cut) &
bursa

gastrocnemius
medial head
(cut)
& bursa

joint capsule

lateral
collateral
ligament &
bursa

oblique
popliteal
ligament

semimem-
branosus
bursa
& tendon
(cut)

biceps
femoris
bursa &
tendon
(cut)

medial
collateral
ligament

popliteus

fibula

tibia

(b) Anatomy ADAPTED FROM THE *CIBA COLLECTION OF MEDICAL ILLUSTRATIONS*, REPRODUCED BY COURTESY OF CIBA-GEIGY LIMITED, BASEL, SWITZERLAND. ALL RIGHTS RESERVED

Figure 34.12 Posterior aspect of the knee
(a) Surface anatomy

Table 34.3 Causes of posterior knee pain

Common	Less common	Not to be missed
Knee joint effusion	Popliteus tendinopathy	Deep venous thrombosis
Referred pain	Baker's cyst	Claudication
• Lumbar spine	Gastrocnemius tendinopathy	Posterior cruciate ligament sprain
• Patellofemoral joint		
• Neural mechanosensitivity		
Biceps femoris tendinopathy		

3. Passive movements
   (a) flexion
   (b) extension (with adduction and abduction)
   (c) tibial rotation
   (d) muscle stretch—hamstrings
4. Resisted movements
   (a) knee flexion
   (b) knee flexion in external tibial rotation (Fig. 34.13b overleaf)
   (c) external tibial rotation (Fig. 34.13c overleaf)
5. Palpation (Fig. 34.13d overleaf)
   (a) hamstring tendons
   (b) popliteus
   (c) joint line
   (d) gastrocnemius origin
6. Special tests
   (a) knee effusion
   (b) examination of knee joint (Chapter 32)
   (c) neurodynamic test—slump test (Fig. 34.2i on page 718)
   (d) examination of lumbar spine (Chapter 26)
   (e) biomechanical examination (Chapter 8)
   (f) squat

Investigations

Investigations may not always add to the clinical diagnosis for posterior knee pain in a sportsperson, and may not be appropriate. However, ultrasound may be used to confirm the presence of a Baker's cyst and to identify a tendinopathy. MRI or arthroscopy are the investigations of choice if the initial diagnosis does not respond to treatment.

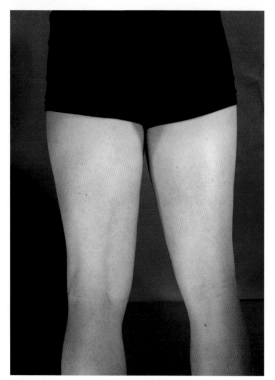

Figure 34.13 Examination of patient with posterior knee pain

(a) Observation—standing. Obvious swelling or fullness of the posterior aspect of the knee joint suggests a Baker's cyst. Inspection may reveal a biomechanical abnormality

(b) Resisted movements—knee flexion in external tibial rotation. Resisted contraction of the popliteus tendon

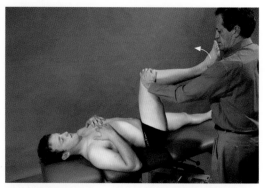

(c) Resisted movement—popliteus. With the patient supine, hips and knees flexed to 90° and the leg internally rotated, the patient is asked to "hold it there" while the examiner applies an external rotation force

(d) Palpation. This should be performed with the knee in flexion. Tenderness can be elicited over the hamstring tendons (shown), gastrocnemius origin, or popliteus. It is helpful for the patient to gently contract and relax individual muscles that are being palpated in order for the examiner to precisely pinpoint the site of pain

Popliteus tendinopathy

The popliteus muscle arises from the postero-medial border of the proximal tibial metaphysis and travels proximally beneath the lateral head of the gastrocnemius to insert onto the lateral femoral condyle. It also has attachments to the fibula and the posterior horn of the lateral meniscus.

The popliteus tendon limits external and internal rotation, knee varus stresses, and anterior translation of the femur (acts with the quadriceps and posterior cruciate ligament).[51] Additionally, the popliteus has a role in unlocking the knee during initial flexion from an extended position, and aids retraction of the posterior horn of the lateral meniscus to minimize compressive forces during knee flexion.

With its role in knee stability, the popliteal tendon could be thought of as the fifth ligament of the knee,[51] therefore should be assessed of tibial rotation during a routine knee stability assessment.

Pain associated with the popliteus region may arise from the popliteus muscle, its tendon, or the popliteus–arcuate ligament complex. Due to their close proximity, differentiation is difficult.

Isolated popliteal muscle injuries are rare. Popliteal muscle injuries associated with lateral meniscus and posterior cruciate ligament injuries are more common.[51, 52] Posterior lateral instability is often associated with some degree of popliteal pathology.

Twisting activities can result in popliteal injuries. Impingement of the popliteus tendon can occur with knee rotational instabilities (e.g. following posterior capsule–arcuate ligament strain), and overuse injuries are often associated with repetitive or prolonged acceleration/deceleration activities (e.g. downhill running).

Sportspeople typically present with posterior knee pain and may report some instability. The main clinical finding is tenderness on palpation along the proximal aspect of the tendon (Fig. 34.13d). With the athlete prone, palpation should begin near the posterolateral corner medial to the biceps tendon and then progress along the medial joint line. Resisted knee flexion in external tibial rotation may reproduce the athlete's pain (Fig. 34.13b).

Garrick and Webb[53] describe a test for the popliteus with the patient supine, hips and knees flexed to 90°, and the leg internally rotated. The patient is asked to "hold it there" while the examiner applies an external rotation force (Fig. 34.13c). It is important that the clinician assesses both active and passive tibial rotation.

Excessive rotation may be a result of repeated strain to the area. Knee flexion and extension range of motion at the end of range may be limited, and also may reproduce pain. Lower limb biomechanics should be assessed in terms of varus, valgus, and rotational forces around the knee.

Soft tissue techniques and mobilization may improve any restriction of tibial rotation or knee flexion or extension. Rehabilitation should focus on strengthening of the tibial rotators (Fig. 34.14) and hamstring muscles. Any weakness or fatigue in the quadriceps can add excessive strain on the popliteus and should be addressed (e.g. with an eccentric strengthening program).

Patients who fail to respond to initial treatment may benefit from corticosteroid injection posteriorly into the point of maximal tenderness, or into the popliteus itself guided by ultrasound.[54, 55]

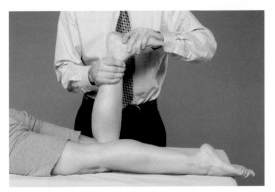

Figure 34.14 Strengthening of the tibial rotators. This may be performed against manual resistance (illustrated), with pulleys, rubber tubing resistance, or with isokinetic machines

Gastrocnemius tendinopathy

The origin of the medial gastrocnemius at the posterior femoral condyle is occasionally susceptible to painful overuse injuries, especially in runners. This may result from excessive hill running or a rapid increase in mileage.

Examination may reveal local tenderness and associated trigger points in the medial gastrocnemius muscle belly. Pain may be reproduced on resisted knee flexion, calf raises with the knee in extension, jumping, and hopping. Occasionally, stretching the gastrocnemius muscle can reproduce the athlete's pain. Possible biomechanical factors should be assessed including muscle imbalances around the hip, knee and ankle. Knee stability, footwear, and foot function should also be assessed.

Initial treatment may consist of activity modification, ice, electrotherapy, and local and generalized soft tissue therapy. A graduated stretching/strengthening program (Chapter 36) should be incorporated to ensure positive long-term results.

Baker's cyst

A Baker's cyst (popliteal cyst) can be defined as "a synovial fluid filled mass located in the popliteal fossa."[56] The mass is often an enlarged bursa located beneath the medial gastrocnemius or semimembranosis muscles or both. It can be thought of as a chronic knee joint effusion (Fig. 34.15 overleaf) that herniates between the two heads of the gastrocnemius.

In children, the mass is often isolated, asymptomatic, and resolves spontaneously. In adults, the mass almost always communicates with the knee joint and is secondary to intra-articular pathology.[56]

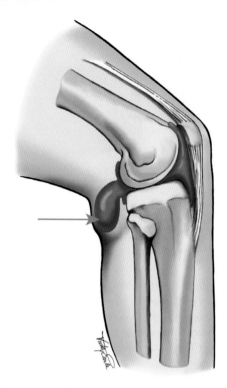

Figure 34.15 Baker's cyst (arrowed)—knee joint effusion herniating posteriorly; usually secondary to degenerative or meniscal pathology

Intra-articular pathology includes meniscal tears (most common), ACL deficiencies, cartilage degeneration, and arthritis. The size of the mass may fluctuate.

Observation of an athlete's knee in standing often reveals a palpable, swollen, tender mass over the posteromedial joint line. End-of-range knee flexion may be restricted and painful. Deep squats and kneeling

may also produce posterior knee pain. Due to its high association with intra-articular pathologies, a full assessment of the knee is warranted.

X-ray may be of little use in the assessment of Baker's cyst, but may rule out other pathologies (e.g. calcification, loose bodies). Ultrasound can visualize the cyst; however, it cannot assess intra-articular structures, which may be the underlying cause.[56]

MRI will both confirm the presence of the cyst and may identify the underlying intra-articular cause; it is considered the gold standard.[56, 57] Aspiration can differentiate between inflammatory, infectious, and mechanical etiologies.

Occasionally the cyst may rupture, leading to lower leg swelling simulating venous thrombosis. A ruptured cyst usually displays a "crescent sign"— an ecchymotic ("bruised") area around the malleoli.

Initial treatment should involve addressing the underlying cause (e.g. meniscal tear). Aspiration together with steroid injection may be useful in the short term.[56, 58] Surgery may be indicated in symptomatic athletes presenting with a large, symptomatic mass. However, unless the underlying pathology is addressed, it is more than likely the mass will reform.

Other causes of posterior knee pain

Deep venous thrombosis usually presents as calf pain (Chapter 36) but may occasionally present as posterior knee pain. It usually occurs after surgery or following a period of immobilization.

Claudication can occasionally present as posterior knee pain. It can occur in young adults, not only in the older person.

Popliteal artery entrapment syndrome usually presents as calf pain (Chapter 36).

📄 RECOMMENDED READING

Beals RK. The iliotibial tract: a review. *Curr Orthop Prac* 2009;20(1):87–91.

Ellis R, Hing W, Reid D. Iliotibial band friction syndrome—a systematic review. *Man Ther* 2007;12(3):200–8.

Fredericson M, Wolf C. Iliotibial band syndrome in runners. *Sports Med* 2005;35(5):451–9.

📄 REFERENCES

1. Beals RK. The iliotibial tract: a review. *Curr Orthop Prac* 2009;20(1):87–91.

2. Fairclough J, Hayashi K, Toumi H et al. Is iliotibial band syndrome really a friction syndrome? *J Sci Med Sport* 2007;10(2):74–6.

3. Ellis R, Hing W, Reid D. Iliotibial band friction syndrome—a systematic review. *Man Ther* 2007;12(3):200–8.

4. Falvey EC, Clark RA, Franklyn-Miller A et al. Iliotibial band syndrome: an examination of the evidence behind a number of treatment options. *Scand J Med Sci Sports* 2010;20:580–7.

5. Orchard J, Fricker PA, Abud AT et al. Biomechanics of iliotibial band friction syndrome in runners. *Am J Sports Med* 1996;24(3):375–9.

6. Noehren B, Davis I, Hamill J. Prospective study of the biomechanical factors associated with iliotibial band syndrome. *Clin Biomech* 2007;22(9):951–6.

7. Fredericson M, Cookingham CL, Chaudhari AM et al. Hip abductor weakness in distance runners with iliotibial band syndrome. *Clin J Sport Med* 2000;10:169–75.

8. Fredericson M, Wolf C. Iliotibial band syndrome in runners. *Sports Med* 2005;35(5):451–9.

9. Messier SP, Edwards DG, Martin DF et al. Etiology of iliotibial band friction syndrome in distance runners. *Med Sci Sports Exerc* 1995;27(7):951–60.

10. Nishimura G, Yamato M, Tamai K et al. MR findings in iliotibial band syndrome. *Skeletal Radiol* 1997;26(9):533–7.

11. Martens M, Librecht P, Burssens A. Surgical treatment of the iliotibial band friction syndrome. *Am J Sports Med* 1989;17(5):651–4.

12. Drogset JO, Rossvoll I, Grontvedt T. Surgical treatment of iliotibial band friction syndrome. A retrospective study of 45 patients. *Scand J Med Sci Sports* 1999;9:296–8.

13. Richards DP, Alan Barber F, Troop RL. Iliotibial band Z-lengthening. *Arthroscopy* 2003;19(3):326–9.

14. Zenz P, Huber M, Obenaus CH et al. Lengthening of the iliotibial band by femoral detachment and multiple puncture. A cadaver study. *Arch Orthop Trauma Surg* 2002;122(8):429–31.

15. Kocher MS, Klingele K, Rassman SO. Meniscal disorders: normal, discoid, and cysts. *Orthop Clin North Am* 2003;34(3):329–40.

16. Willis RB. Meniscal injuries in children and adolescents. *Op Tech Sports Med* 2006;14(3):197–202.

17. Sharma L, Song J, Felson DT et al. The role of knee alignment in disease progression and functional decline in knee osteoarthritis. *JAMA* 2001;286(2):188–95.

18. Brouwer GM, Tol AWV, Bergink AP et al. Association between valgus and varus alignment and the development and progression of radiographic osteoarthritis of the knee. *Arth Rheum* 2007;56(4):1204–11.

19. Altman RD, Moskowitz R. Intraarticular sodium hyaluronate (Hyalgan) in the treatment of patients with osteoarthritis of the knee: a randomized clinical trial. *J Rheumatol* 1998;25:2203–12.

20. Petrella RJ, Bartha C. Home based exercise therapy for older patients with knee osteoarthritis: a randomized clinical trial. *J Rheumatol* 2000;27(9):2215–21.

21. Squire MW, Callaghan JJ, Goetz DD et al. Unicompartmental knee replacement. A minimum 15 year followup study. *Clin Orthop* 1999;367:61–72.

22. Merican AM, Amis AA. Anatomy of the lateral retinaculum of the knee. *J Bone Joint Surg Br* 2008;90-B(4):527–34.

23. Shellock FG, Stone KR, Crues JV. Development and clinical application of kinematic MRI of the patellofemoral joint using an extremity MR system. *Med Sci Sports Exerc* 1999;31(5):788–91.

24. Panni AS, Tartarone M, Patricola A et al. Long-term results of lateral retinacular release. *Arthroscopy* 2005;21(5):526–31.

25. Chance-Larsen K, Littlewood C, Garth A. Prone hip extension with lower abdominal hollowing improves the relative timing of gluteus maximus activation in relation to biceps femoris. *Man Ther* 2010;15(1):61–5.

26. Longo UG, Garau G, Denaro V et al. Surgical management of tendinopathy of biceps femoris tendon in athletes. *Disabil Rehabil* 2008;30(20–22):1602–7.

27. Forster BB, Lee JS, Kelly S et al. Proximal tibiofibular joint: an often-forgotten cause of lateral knee pain. *AJR Am J Roentgenol.*2007;188(4):W359–66.

28. Scott J, Lee H, Barsoum W et al. The effect of tibiofemoral loading on proximal tibiofibular joint motion. *J Anat* 2007;211(5):647–53.

B

29. Maffulli N, Spiezia F, Oliva F et al. Gracilis autograft for recurrent posttraumatic instability of the auperior tibiofibular joint. *Am J Sports Med* 2010;38(11):2294–8.

30. Sekiya JK, Kuhn JE. Instability of the proximal tibiofibular joint. *J Am Acad Orthop Surg* 2003;11(2):120–8.

31. Luhmann SJ, Schoenecker PL, Dobbs MB et al. Adolescent patellofemoral pain: implicating the medial patellofemoral ligament as the main pain generator. *J Child Orthop* 2008;2:269–77.

32. Fithian DC, Powers CM, Khan N. Rehabilitation of the knee after medial patellofemoral ligament reconstruction. *Clin Sports Med* 2010;29:283–90.

33. Bedi A, Kelly NH, Baad M et al. Dynamic contact mechanics of the medial meniscus as a function of radial tear, repair, and partial meniscectomy. *J Bone Joint Surg Am* 2010;92(6):1398–408.

34. Nicholson S, Dickman K, Maradiegue A. Reducing premature osteoarthritis in the adolescent through appropriate screening. *J Pediat Nurs* 2009;24(1):69–74.

35. Bout-Tabaku S, Best TM. The adolescent knee and risk for osteoarthritis—an opportunity or responsibility for sport medicine physicians? *Curr Sports Med Rep* 2010;9(6):329–31

36. Bashir A, Gray ML, Hartke J et al. Nondestructive imaging of human cartilage glycosaminoglycan concentration by MRI. *Magn Reson Med* 1999;41: 857–65.

37. Olsen O-E, Myklebust G, Engebretsen L et al. Exercises to prevent lower limb injuries in youth sports: cluster randomised controlled trial. *BMJ* 2005;330(7489):449.

38. Twomey D, Finch C, Roediger E et al. Preventing lower limb injuries: is the latest evidence being translated into the football field? *J Sci Med Sport* 2009;12(4): 452–6.

39. Pasanen K, Parkkari J, Pasanen M et al. Neuromuscular training and the risk of leg injuries in female floorball players: cluster randomised controlled study. *Br J Sports Med* 2008;42(10):802–5.

40. Kirkley A, Webster-Bogaert S, Litchfield RB et al. The effect of bracing on varus gonarthrosis. *J Bone Joint Surg Am* 1999;81A:539–48.

41. Komistek RD, Dennis DA, Northcut EJ et al. An in vivo analysis of the effectiveness of the osteoarthritic knee brace during heel-strike of gait. *J Arthroplasty* 1999;14:738–42.

42. Bellamy N, Campbell J, Robinson V et al. Viscosupplementation for the treatment of osteoarthritis of the knee. *Cochrane Database Syst Rev* 2005;18(2):CD005321.

43. Zhang W, Moskowitz RW, Nuki G et al. OARSI recommendations for the management of hip and knee osteoarthritis, Part II: OARSI evidence-based, expert consensus guidelines. *Osteoarth Cart* 2008;16(2): 137–62.

44. Kessler MA, Behrend H, Henz S et al. Function, osteoarthritis and activity after ACL-rupture: 11 years follow-up results of conservative versus reconstructive treatment *Knee Surg Sports Traumatol Arthrosc* 2008;16:442–8.

45. Oiestad BE, Engebretsen L, Storheim K et al. Knee osteoarthritis after anterior cruciate ligament injury. *Am J Sports Med* 2009;37(7):1434–3.

46. Rennie WJ, Saifuddin A. Pes anserine bursitis: incidence in symptomatic knees and clinical presentation. *Skeletal Radiol* 2005;34(7):395–8.

47. Alvarez-Nemegyei J. Risk factors for pes anserinus tendinitis/bursitis syndrome: a case control study. *J Clin Rheumatol* 2007;13(2):63–5.

48. Finnoff JT, Nutz DJ, Henning PT et al. Accuracy of ultrasound-guided versus unguided pes anserinus bursa injections. *PM R* 2010;2(8):732–9.

49. Niitsu M, Ikeda K, Iijima T et al. MR imaging of Pellegrini-Stieda disease. *Radiat Med* 1999;17: 405–9.

50. Theivendran K, Lever CJ, Hart WJ. Good result after surgical treatment of Pellegrini-Stieda syndrome. *Knee Surg Sports Traumatol Arthrosc* 2009;17(10):1231–3.

51. LaPrade RF, Wozniczka JK, Stellmaker MP et al. Analysis of the static function of the popliteus tendon and evaluation of an anatomic reconstruction. *Am J Sports Med* 2010;38(3):543–9.

52. Guha AR, Gorgees KA, Walker DI. Popliteus tendon rupture: a case report and review of the literature. *Br J Sports Med* 2003;37(4):358–60.

53. Garrick JG, Webb DR. *Sports injuries: diagnosis and management.* Philadelphia: WB Saunders, 1990.

54. Petsche TS, Selesnick FH. Popliteal tendinitis. Tips for diagnosis and management. *Phys Sportsmed* 2002;30(8):27–31.

55. Smith J, Finnoff JT, Santaella-Sante B et al. Sonographically guided popliteus tendon sheath injection: techniques and accuracy. *J Ultrasound Med* 2010;29(5):775–82.

56. Fritschy D, Fasel J, Imbert J-C et al. The popliteal cyst. *Knee Surg Sports Traumatol Arthrosc* 2006;14:623–8.

57. Muche JA, Lento PH. Posterior knee pain and its causes: a clinician's guide to expediting diagnosis. *Phys Sportsmed* 2004;32(3):23–30.

58. Di Sante L, Paoloni M, Ioppolo F et al. Ultrasound-guided aspiration and corticosteroid injection of Baker's cysts in knee osteoarthritis a prospective observational study. *Am J Phys Med Rehab* 2010;89(12):970–5.

Chapter 35

Leg pain

with MARK HUTCHINSON, CHRIS BRADSHAW, and MATT HISLOP

He beat everybody on one leg. Kenny Perry, US professional golfer, referring to
Tiger Woods playing with two stress fractures in the left tibia in the 2008 US Open

The leg, defined as the anatomic region below the knee but above the ankle, is a common site of complaints among sportspeople, particularly in distance runners. The term "shin splints" is commonly used by runners as a nondescript reference of their leg pain; the term was also used by health professionals to describe the pain along the medial border of the tibia commonly experienced by runners or to describe shin pain in general. Neither use of the term is pathologically precise. There are multiple unique causes with defined pathophysiologies that should lead the clinician to a more specific diagnosis of leg pain in sportspeople. A more accurate and specific diagnosis allows for targeted treatment. Therefore the term "shin splints" should be abandoned in favor of a more specific, anatomical, and diagnostic terminology.

This chapter focuses on four major pathologies that cause leg pain:

- medial tibial stress fracture
- anterior tibial cortical stress fracture
- medial tibial stress syndrome
- chronic compartment syndromes.

Clinical perspective

Leg pain in sportspeople generally involves one or more of several pathological, anatomically specific processes:

- *Bone stress.* A continuum of increased bone damage exists from bone strain to stress reaction and stress fracture.
- *Vascular insufficiency.* This includes a reduction in arterial inflow (such as popliteal artery entrapment) or vascular outflow (due to venous insufficiency), thrombotic disease, or vascular collapse (due to elevated intracompartmental pressures).
- *Inflammation.* Inflammation develops at the insertion of muscles, or along the tendons. Periosteal changes at the tibialis posterior and soleus, and fascial changes at the medial border of the tibia may be due to traction or a variation of the stress injury to bone.
- *Elevated intracompartment pressure.* The lower leg has a number of muscle compartments, each enveloped by a thick, inelastic fascia. The muscle compartments of the lower leg are shown in Figure 35.1. As a result of overuse/inflammation, these muscle compartments may become swollen and painful, particularly if there is excessive fibrosis of the fascia.
- *Nerve entrapment.*

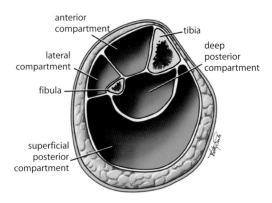

Figure 35.1 Cross-section of lower leg
(a) The various muscle compartments

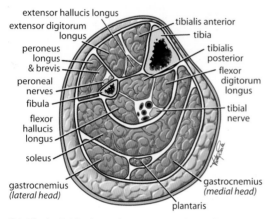

extensor hallucis longus
extensor digitorum longus
peroneus longus & brevis
peroneal nerves
fibula
flexor hallucis longus
soleus
gastrocnemius (lateral head)

tibialis anterior
tibia
tibialis posterior
flexor digitorum longus
tibial nerve
gastrocnemius (medial head)
plantaris

(b) The individual muscles, nerves, and vessels

The differentiation between these processes and the narrowing of the differential diagnosis begin with historical clues, are narrowed by clinical examination findings, and confirmed with specific targeted imaging or clinical tests (Table 35.1). Two or three of these conditions may exist simultaneously. For instance, it is not uncommon to have a stress fracture develop in a patient with chronic periostitis; periostitis or stress fracture may lead to intracompartmental swelling and tip a patient on the edge of symptomatic exertional compartment syndrome over the edge. This interrelationship is demonstrated in Figure 35.2. These co-existing conditions are generally managed differently, which explains the continued leg pain in patients when only one condition has been addressed. The less common differential diagnoses for leg pain include tendinopathy, nerve

entrapment, vascular claudication, neurogenic claudication, deep venous thrombosis (DVT), infection (osteomyelitis, cellulitis), metabolic bone disease, and tumors of bone and soft tissues, which may, in rare cases, effect prognosis and outcome of leg pain in sportspeople.

Role of biomechanics

Clinical experience suggests that abnormal biomechanics predisposes some individuals to pain on the anterior or medial border of the tibia (shin pain). Both extremes of foot type can contribute to the incidence of shin pain in sportspeople (Chapter 8). A rigid, cavus foot has limited shock absorption, thus increasing the impact pressure on the bone. In sportspeople with excessive pronation, the muscles of the superficial (soleus) and deep compartments (tibialis posterior, flexor hallucis longus, and flexor digitorum longus) are placed at a relatively lengthened position and are required to contract eccentrically harder and longer to resist pronation after heel strike. On toe-off, these muscles must contract concentrically over a greater length to complete the transition to a supinated foot, creating a rigid lever for push off. With fatigue, these muscles fail to provide the normal degree of shock absorption. The chronic traction at the muscles' origins can, in turn, lead to chronic medial tibial stress syndrome (historically termed "shin splints"). In chronic cases, this mechanism can contribute to the presentation of stress fractures or deep compartment syndromes.

The sportsperson with excessive pronation may also develop lateral shin pain or stress injuries of the fibula. Pronation of the fixed foot leads to internal tibial rotation. With repetitive excessive pronation, the tibia and fibula are exposed to repetitive rotational (torque) stresses. These stresses are transferred across the fibula, tibia, and proximal and distal tibiofibular articulations. Based on these biomechanical stresses, overuse can lead to stress reactions or stress fracture not only of the tibia but also of the fibula.

Motor imbalance can also lead to stress injuries in the lower extremity. Tight calf muscles, which commonly result from hard training, restrict ankle dorsiflexion and increase the tendency for excessive pronation, leading to increased internal rotation of the tibia. Posterior tibial tendon weakness or deficiency can likewise contribute to foot pronation. Ankle instability secondary to chronic ankle sprains cause the sportsperson to overuse the peroneal tendons to compensate for ankle stability. This

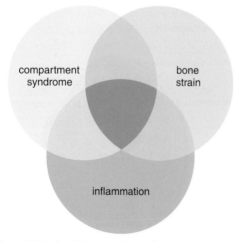

compartment syndrome

bone strain

inflammation

Figure 35.2 Possible interrelationship between the pathological sources of leg pain

Table 35.1 The clinical characteristics and imaging features of common causes of shin pain in sportspeople

Site	Pain	Effect of exercise	Associated features	Tenderness	Investigations
Bone stress reaction or stress fracture	Localized Acute or sharp Subcutaneous medial tibial surface or fibula	Constant or increasing Worse with impact	Exacerbated by therapeutic ultrasound	Subcutaneous medial tibial surface or fibula	X-ray may be negative • Look for callus or periosteal reaction Bone scan shows focal uptake (non-specific) MRI can stage severity and define prognosis but is also non-specific
Medial tibial stress syndrome	Diffuse pain on posteromedial border of tibia Variable intensity	Decreases as sportsperson warms up and stretches	Worse in the morning and after exercise Pes planus	Posteromedial edge of tibia at muscular insertions	X-rays negative Bone scan shows diffuse uptake MRI shows diffuse edema and periosteal thickening
Chronic exertional compartment syndrome	No pain at rest Ache, tightness, gradually building with exertion	Specific onset variable between sportspeople; usually 10–15 minutes into exercise Decreases with rest	Occasional muscle weakness or dysfunction with exercise Paresthesia of nerve in affected compartment is possible	None at rest Anterior and lateral more common with exertion Occasionally related to palpable muscle herniation (superficial peroneal nerve)	X-rays negative Bone scans negative Exertional compartment pressure testing is diagnostic Exertional MRI or infrared oxygen assessment may be diagnostic
Popliteal artery entrapment	Pain in calf with exertion; not anterolateral "Atypical compartment syndrome"	Worse with exertion especially active ankle plantar flexion	Pulses may be diminished with active plantar flexion (assessed by palpation or Doppler ultrasound)	Rarely in proximal calf	X-rays negative MRI may reveal hypertrophic or abnormal insertion of medial gastrocnemius MR arteriography with provocative maneuvers is diagnostic
Muscle–tendon injuries • Strains • Tendinopathy	Pain at pathologic site with resisted stretch	Pre-participation stretching usually helps	Symptoms respond to NSAIDs and ice	Pain can be at muscle belly, muscle tendon junction, tendon, or tendon insertion	Rarely required X-rays usually negative MRI gives best view of soft tissue pathology

B

overuse can be just enough to send a sportsperson with borderline compartment syndrome over the brink to symptomatic complaints. To clearly understand biomechanics and have a foundation on which to create a differential diagnosis of leg pain, a complete knowledge of lower leg anatomy is essential (Figs 35.1, 35.3). When the presentation is atypical, the possibilities must be expanded to include a broad differential diagnosis for potential causes of leg pain in sportspeople (Table 35.2).

History

Taking a good history is essential for correct diagnosis of sportspeople with leg pain. Asking the right questions should narrow the diagnosis. Clarifying the pain complaints and assessing the involved mechanism are key to the history. The history should be thorough and assess the presence of associated features with the pain, such as paresthesias or muscle hernia.[1] A complete history should include a broad review of systems to discover other facets, such as metabolic, prior surgical procedures, developmental problems, contributing medical issues, and social issues such as smoking. When the diagnosis does not classically fit the simple pain screen, a broader differential should be considered.

The key questions and the responses that may give a clue to the diagnosis are outlined in the box on page 740.

Examination

In the examination of the patient with leg pain, it is important to palpate the site of maximal tenderness and assess the consistency of soft tissue. At rest, the physical examination for certain diagnoses (specifically, chronic exertional compartment syndrome) is often unrewarding and the patient may be completely asymptomatic. The astute clinician will ask the sportsperson to reproduce the pain or symptoms via exertion or impact. This can be done on the sportsperson's playing surface, on a treadmill, or in and about the clinician's office by having the sportsperson run stairs or run around the block. A complete examination should be sequential, repeated the same way

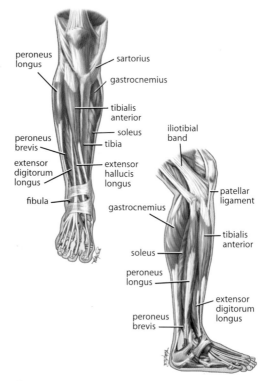

Figure 35.3 The leg

(a) Surface anatomy of the leg

(b) Anatomy of the lower leg from the front (left) and lateral aspect (right) ADAPTED FROM THE CIBA COLLECTION OF MEDICAL ILLUSTRATIONS, REPRODUCED BY COURTESY OF CIBA-GEIGY LIMITED, BASEL, SWITZERLAND, ALL RIGHTS RESERVED

Table 35.2 Causes of leg pain

Common	Less common	Not to be missed
Muscle strains/ruptures	Referred pain from spine	Tumors (osteosarcoma, osteoid
Abrasions and contusions	Chronic compartment syndrome—	osteoma)
Stress fracture	superficial posterior	Infection (osteomyelitis, cellulitis)
• Medial tibia	Vascular insufficiency/claudication	Acute compartment syndrome
• Anterior tibia*	Deep vein thrombosis (DVT)	(Chapter 47)
Medial tibial stress syndrome	(Chapter 36)	Chronic transition to acute
Chronic compartment syndrome	Popliteal artery entrapment	compartment syndrome
• Anterior	(Chapter 36)	Chronic ankle injuries and
• Lateral (peroneal)	Femoral endarteritis	Maisonneuve fracture
• Deep posterior	Atherosclerotic disease	
	Superficial peroneal nerve entrapment	
	Periosteal contusion	
	Muscle herniations	
	Baker's cysts (referred) or ganglion	*Rare and unusual*
	cysts	Syphilis
	Osgood-Schlatter's disease	Sickle cell anemia
	Pes anserine bursitis	Hyperparathyroidism
	Proximal tibiofibular subluxation	Sarcoidosis
	Acute fracture	Rickets
	Stress fracture	Paget's disease
	• Fibula	Erythema nodosum
	Achilles tendinopathy	
	Electrolyte and metabolic disturbances	
	• Dehydration cramping	

*Anterior tibial cortex stress fractures (page 747) are less common than medial tibial stress fractures but included in this column because of their clinical significance

with each patient and include observation, analysis of muscle function and range of motion, anatomically directed palpation, functional testing, and diagnosis-specific testing (Fig. 35.4 on pages 741–3).

1. Observation: assess lower limb alignment (varus/valgus, tibial torsion, pes planus) swelling, bruising, asymmetry.
   (a) standing (Fig. 35.4a overleaf)
   (b) walking—assess gait mechanics (forwards, backwards, on toes, on heels).
   (c) lying
2. Active movements: assess motor function and range of motion.
   (a) plantarflexion/dorsiflexion: check pulses in full plantar or dorsiflexion. If they are diminished, consider popliteal artery entrapment.
   (b) inversion/eversion
   (c) flexion and extension of the knee—puts the gastrocnemius/soleus complex in a contracted or relaxed position

3. Passive movements: assess true joint range of motion. May exacerbate pain in compartment syndromes.
   (a) plantarflexion (Fig. 35.4b overleaf)
   (b) dorsiflexion (Fig. 35.4c overleaf)
   (c) inversion/eversion
4. Resisted movements: assess motor function. May exacerbate pain in muscle strains and tendinopathy.
   (a) plantarflexion/dorsiflexion
   (b) inversion/eversion
5. Functional tests
   (a) hopping (Fig. 35.4d on page 742)—requires motor strength and landing skills. Rigid landing on heels exacerbates the pain of stress fracture
   (b) jumping
   (c) running—may bring on pain of exertional compartment syndrome or popliteal artery entrapment symptoms. Sportspeople should always reproduce symptoms
   (d) stair-climbing

Key diagnostic questions

Question	Clinical significance of response
Was there an acute onset of pain?	Fractures and tendon ruptures are usually acute traumatic events. In sportspeople, the acute onset of pain may be preceded by low-grade chronic pain of a stress fracture or tendinopathy.
Is there a history of injury or prior leg pains?	Old fractures or injuries can lead to scar tissue, stiffness, and pain.
Is the pain worse with impact?	Stress fractures are classically exacerbated with impact. Medial tibial stress syndrome and muscle strains may also be made worse with loading and resistance.
Is the pain worse with exertion?	Pain absent at rest that presents with exertion is classic for exertional compartment syndrome. Nonetheless, popliteal artery entrapment can have a similar presentation with posterior rather than anterior or lateral pain.
Does the pain improve with warm-up and stretching?	Medial tibial stress syndrome and muscle strains frequently improve with pre-participation stretching while stress fractures and exertional compartment syndrome generally do not.
Does the pain get worse with stretching or resistance?	Providing resistance to the muscle tendon units, including their origins and insertions, should exacerbate symptoms related to medial tibial stress syndrome and muscle tendon strains and tendinopathy.
Where is the pain? Is the pain focal? Is the pain diffuse?	The anatomic site of pain is the best physical clue to diagnosis. Focal pain over bone should raise suspicion of a stress fracture; focal pain over the muscle–tendon is likely to be a muscle strain or tendinopathy; diffuse pain over the posteriomedial border of the tibia is likely to be medial tibial stress syndrome.
Is there swelling with the pain? Is it diffuse? Is it focal?	Localized swelling is possible with a contusion, a stress fracture, or muscle herniation. Diffuse swelling may indicate more significant injury, vascular problems such as a DVT, or diffuse inflammatory problems. Medial tibial stress syndrome may have palpable swelling about muscle insertions on the posterior medial border of the tibia.
Is there electrical shooting pain? Is there weakness with the pain? Is there numbness with the pain?	Electrical shooting pain, dermatomal loss of sensation, and sclerotomal loss of motor power usually indicate nerve injury, entrapment, or radiculopathy. Always check the lumbar spine.
Does the pain get better with ice or non-steroidal anti-inflammatories (NSAIDs)?	Pathologies associated with inflammation should improve with cold therapy and anti-inflammatories. Osteoid osteomas (a benign bone tumor) have significant response to aspirin.
Is there pain at night?	Pain that wakes a patient up at night should raise concern about tumors.

6. Palpation: Evaluate pain distribution, warmth, swelling, pitting edema, posterior cords, or the presence of crepitus with motion

   (a) tibia (Fig. 35.4e overleaf)—focal pain indicates stress fracture; diffuse pain over posterior medial border of tibia indicates medial tibial stress syndrome

   (b) fibula—the entire fibula should be palpated to identify focal pain related to a stress fracture; severe eversion/external rotation ankle sprains may injure the syndesmotic connection between the tibia and fibula and be associated with a proximal fibula fracture (Maisonneuve fracture)

   (c) gastrocnemius, plantaris, and soleus muscles (Fig. 35.4f overleaf)—look for muscle strains and ruptures; tennis leg is a partial rupture of the medial head of the gastrocnemius or plantaris

   (d) gastrocnemius–soleus aponeurosis (Fig. 35.4g overleaf)—assess for swelling and focal tenderness, which may indicate tendinosis or bursititis

   (e) superficial and deep posterior compartment (Fig. 35.4h on page 743)

   (f) anterior and lateral compartment—post-exertion palpation may reveal tenseness in exertional compartment syndrome or palpable localized mass due to muscle herniation

7. Special tests

   (a) stress fracture test (Fig. 35.4i on page 743)—vibration may exacerbate pain associated with a stress fracture. Applying a vibrating tuning fork along the subcutaneous border of the tibia is a convenient and inexpensive test easily applied in the training room or office; pain may also be exacerbated with the use of therapeutic ultrasound

   (b) biomechanical examination (Chapter 8).

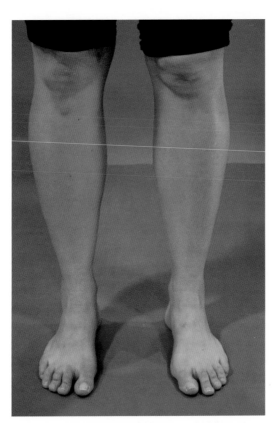

Figure 35.4 Examination of the patient with leg pain
(a) Observation—standing. Assess lower limb alignment, swelling, bruising, and any evidence of subperiosteal hematoma

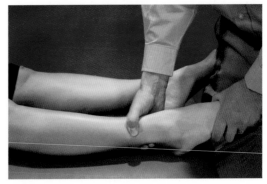

(b) Passive movement—plantarflexion
This may be restricted in anterior compartment syndrome

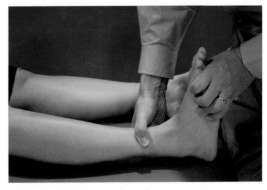

(c) Passive movement—dorsiflexion
Measure the degree of passive dorsiflexion compared with the other side

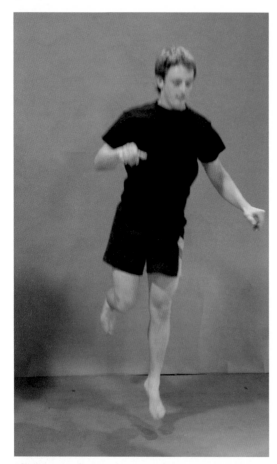

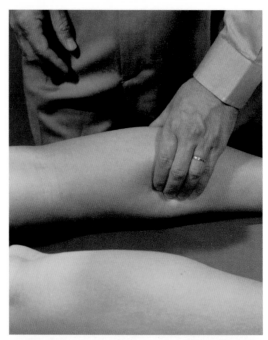

(f) Palpation—soleus muscle belly. A pincer grip is used

(d) Functional tests—hopping. If pain has not been reproduced, ask the patient to perform repeated movements, such as hopping, running, or performing calf raises

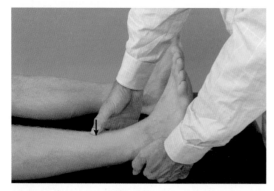

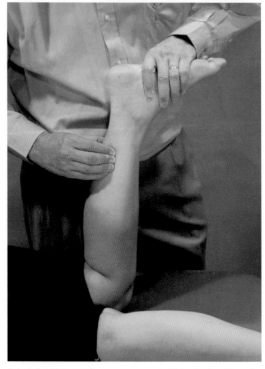

(e) Palpation—tibia. Palpate for the exact site of focal tenderness. Determine if pain is diffuse, focal, or multifocal. Bony irregularity or subtle swelling may occur along the medial tibial border with medial tibial stress syndrome or stress fractures

(g) Palpation—soleus aponeurosis. Palpate for sites of tenderness and associated taut bands that may be a precipitating factor in the development of inflammatory shin pain

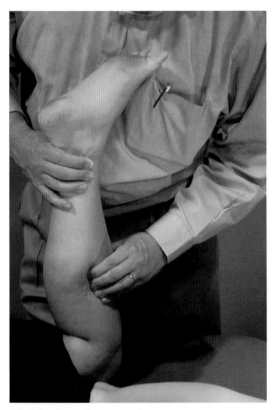

(h) Palpation—deep posterior compartment
This is palpated through the relaxed overlying muscles. In compartment pressure syndrome, the entire compartment feels tight in contrast to the localized tissue tightness of chronic muscle strain. Muscle or fascial hernias are occasionally found. The superficial posterior compartment should also be palpated

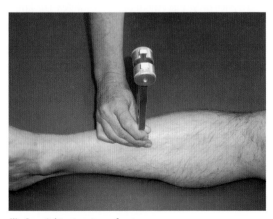

(i) Special test—stress fracture
Percussing, using a tuning fork or applying ultrasound over the site of tenderness, can provoke pain in the presence of a stress fracture

Investigations

After taking the history and performing the physical examination, extended work-up should target the most likely diagnosis. Imaging options include radiographs, MRI, CT scan, angiography, ultrasound, and nuclear medicine scans. Routine radiography is rarely clearly positive in the diagnosis of leg pain. Careful inspection may reveal a subtle radiolucent line indicating a stress fracture. An X-ray performed two to three weeks after the onset of pain may reveal periosteal reaction or a more obvious radiolucent line. However, X-ray has low sensitivity for stress fractures generally and in this location in particular.

Historically, radioisotopic bone scan was the next test in line to confirm the presence of a stress fracture or medial tibial stress syndrome. Bone scans are sensitive but not particularly specific. For stress fractures, a discrete, focal area of increased uptake is seen on either the tibia or fibula (Fig. 35.5a). In chronic medial tibial stress syndrome, the bone scan may show patchy areas of increased uptake along the medial border of the tibia (Fig. 35.5b overleaf). The absence of uptake does not preclude the diagnosis of medial tibial stress syndrome. No identifiable

B

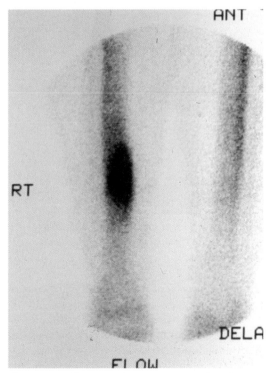

Figure 35.5 Characteristic appearances on imaging
(a) Stress fracture

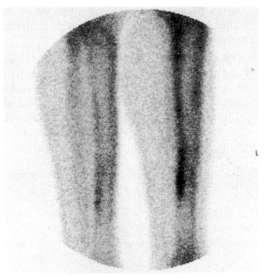

(b) Medial tibial stress syndrome

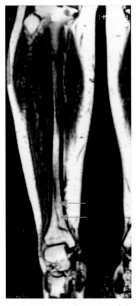

(c) MRI appearance of stress fracture of the tibia showing fracture line (arrows) in the presence of marrow edema

changes on bone scan are associated with compartment syndrome.[2]

MRI has been advocated as the investigation of choice in patients with leg pain on the basis of its sensitivity to evaluate bony lesions, marrow changes, soft tissue injuries, and correlate these findings with clinical symptoms.[3] Typically, a stress fracture appears on MRI as an area of periosteal edema (Fig. 35.5c). The

severity of injury documented on MRI (bone edema only, unicortical radiolucent line, or bicortical radiolucent line) has been directly correlated with healing time.[4, 5] Medial tibial stress syndrome appears with a broader area of edema with thickening of the posterior medial periosteum, or multiple small stress injuries of the bone. The MRI may also confirm the diagnosis of a muscle strain, muscle herniation, as well as benign (lipoma, cysts, osteoid osteoma) and malignant tumors. MR arteriography with dynamic plantarflexion is the test of choice to confirm popliteal artery entrapment syndrome (Chapter 36). The role of MRI in the diagnosis of compartment syndromes is still unclear.[3, 4, 6, 7] Pre- and post-exertional MRI scans may reveal intracompartmental edema confirming the diagnosis of exertional compartment syndrome; however, this is an expensive way to confirm this diagnosis when more cost-efficient tests are available.

 Intracompartment pressure measurement (Chapter 12, Fig. 12.6) is considered the gold standard in confirming the diagnosis of chronic exertional compartment syndrome in the sportsperson.

Pre- and immediate post-exertion measurements are essential to confirm the diagnosis. Devices used to measure the pressure include a wall blood pressure monitor with intravenous tubing and a three-way stop-cock (Whiteside's technique), the transducer and pump used for an arterial line, laboratory systems, and hand-held devices. In each case, the fascia is punctured percutaneously with either a hollow-bore needle or a needle with a side-port, followed by measurements via that device or by placement of a slit catheter. The latter two are more reproducible.

 The anatomy of the compartments and approaches for pressure testing are shown in the *Clinical Sports Medicine* masterclasses at www.clinicalsportsmedicine.com.

The anterior compartment is relatively easy to find. The deep posterior compartment or, if present, the tibialis posterior compartment may be more difficult, but is usually accessed posterior to the posteromedial edge of the tibia. Some experts recommend ultrasound to guide catheter placement;[8] however, we have not encountered any problems without using ultrasound assistance. The normal compartment pressures are 0–10 mmHg. Positive pressures include at-rest or exertional pressures over 25 mmHg or elevation of at-rest pressures greater than 10 mmHg with exertion. Pressures from 10–20 mmHg or elevated pressures that decrease with exercise are considered inconclusive. Other authors have promoted the use of non-invasive methods such as near-infrared spectroscopy, and results are promising but require further validation before general use.[7]

A summary of the recommended techniques with the appropriate exercises to produce pain is shown in Table 35.3.

Additional work-up for more atypical causes of leg pain include:

- EMG/nerve conduction studies
  - peripheral nerve entrapments & metabolic neuropathy
- Ankle/brachial index
  - vascular claudication
- Venous Doppler
  - deep venous thrombosis
- Laboratory
  - CBC (complete blood count) with differential—infection or osteomyelits
  - ESR (erythrocyte sedimentary rate)—inflammation, rheumatologic conditions
  - sickle cell preparation—sickle cell anemia
  - urine analysis with uromyoglobin—rhabdomyolyis

- CPK (creatine phosphokinase), myoglobin—rhabdomyolysis, myopathy
- PT (prothrombin time), APTT (activated partial thromboplastin time)—deep venous thrombosis
- D-dimer—deep venous thrombosis
- metabolic panel—hypokalemia, hypocalcemia, hypomagnesium, etc
- T_3 (triiodothyronine), T_4 (thyroxine), TSH (thyroid stimulating hormone)—thyroid myopathy.

Medial tibial stress fracture

Stress fractures are more commonly a cause of leg pain in sportspeople in impact, running, and jumping sports. Overall limb and foot alignment as well as limb length discrepancy may also play a role. Runners with stress fractures have a reduced cortical strength, a reduced cross-sectional area of cortical bone (thinner cortices) and reduced muscle cross-sectional area compared with sportspeople without a history of stress fractures.[9]

The incidence of stress fractures is increased with play on more rigid, unforgiving surfaces.

Approximately 90% of tibial stress fractures affect the posteromedial aspect of the tibia; the most common site is near the junction of the middle and distal thirds.

Table 35.3 Compartment pressure testing

Compartment	Location of catheter	Exacerbating exercise	Compartment pressures (n = 10 mmHg, post exercise 5 min)
Deep posterior	Junction of lower and middle third of tibia Aim deep posteriorly just behind the posteromedial tibial border	Treadmill/running Stairs Run/jump Pulleys in PF/DF Repeated case raises Isokinetic PF with IV/EV Sport-specific challenges	>25 mmHg post exercise or an increase of >10 mmHg compared with resting baseline
Superficial posterior	Aim more posteriorly from deep posterior entry into medial gastrocnemius or soleus	Treadmill Stairs Repeated calf raises	Same as above
Anterior	Mid-belly of tibialis anterior Anterior to intermuscular septum (halfway between fibula and anterior border of tibia)	Repeated DF Treadmill/running Stairs Sport-specific challenges	Same as above
Lateral (peroneal)	Mid-belly of peroneals Posterior to intermuscular septum	Repeated IV/EV Treadmill/running Stairs	Same as above

Ankle movements: PF = plantarflexion; DF = dorsiflexion; IV = inversion; EV = eversion.

Proximal metaphyseal stress fractures may be associated with more time loss from sports, as they do not respond as well to the functional bracing that allows earlier return to play. We discuss anterior tibial stress fracture—a far more sinister condition—in a separate section below (page 747).

Assessment

For a routine posteromedial stress fracture, a classic case presentation includes the following:

- Pain is of gradual onset, and is aggravated by exercise; there is often a recent history of an increase in training intensity.
- Pain may occur with walking, at rest, or even at night.
- Examination shows localized tenderness over the tibia.
- Biomechanical examination may show a rigid, cavus foot incapable of absorbing load, an excessively pronating foot causing excessive muscle fatigue, or a leg length discrepancy.
- The medial border of the tibia is tender to palpation. (Occasionally, a stress fracture of the posterior cortex produces symptoms of calf pain (Chapter 36) rather than leg pain.)
- Bone scan and MRI appearances of a stress fracture of the tibia are shown in Figures 35.5a and 35.5c. MRI scan is of particular value, as the extent of edema and cortical involvement has been directly correlated with the expected return to sport.[5]
- A CT scan may also demonstrate a stress fracture (Fig. 35.6).

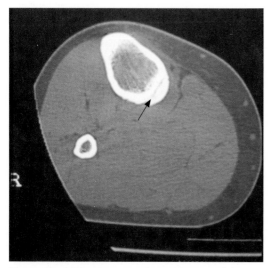

Figure 35.6 CT appearance of stress fracture of the tibia

Treatment

Prior to initiating treatment or during the treatment plan, it is important to identify which factors precipitated the stress fracture. The most common cause is an acute change in training habits, such a significant increase in distance over a short period of time, beginning double practice days after laying off of training for a season, or a change to a more rigid playing surface. Athletic coaches can play a key role in modifying training patterns to reduce the risk of these injuries.

Shoe wear, biomechanics, and repetitive impact sports such as running and gymnastics have also been implicated. Systematic reviews have determined that the use of custom semirigid orthotics leads to lower incidence of stress fractures in sportspeople and military recruits.[10]

In women, reduced bone density may be a contributing factor. All female sportspeople with a first stress fracture should be screened for the female athlete triad (Chapter 43).

Recent research has focused on reducing the vertical loading rate and ground reactive force by modifying stride length, gait retraining, and running speed.[11–15] This research concludes that a softer running style attained through gait training, a shorter stride length which reduces the stress at impact, slower running speeds that reduce the stress at impact, and reduced mileage which reduces the number of impacts can all have a preventive effect against the development of stress fractures.

The classic treatment plan is as follows:

- Initial period of rest (sometimes requiring a period of non-weight-bearing on crutches for pain relief) until the pain settles.
- The use of a pneumatic brace (Air-Stirrup Leg Brace [Aircast]) has markedly reduced return to activity time compared with "standard" recovery times in two of three studies[16, 17] and compared with a "traditional treatment" group in the third.[18] In this latter study, the brace group returned to full unrestricted activity in an average of 21 days compared with 77 days in the traditional group. The brace should extend to the knee, as the mid-leg version may actually increase the stress across a midshaft stress fracture. Routine use of this treatment modality implies rest and full-time use for one to two weeks. During that time, the sportsperson should notice excellent pain control while in the brace. If this positive response is achieved, then the sportsperson is allowed

to gradually return to impact activities and play in the brace. If pain returns, the period of rest is extended. As long as the pain is well controlled, the sportsperson is allowed to return to full athletic participation in the brace. Most sportspeople will complete their competitive season using the brace, as complete healing may not occur while they are still loading the leg, with or without the brace. Using this plan, there has been no reported cases of progression to complete catastrophic fracture of the tibia.

- If pain persists, continue to rest from sporting activity until the bony tenderness disappears (four to eight weeks).
- Once the patient is pain-free when walking and has no bony tenderness, gradually progress the quality and quantity of the exercise over the following month.
- Cross-training with low-impact exercises including swimming, cycling, and water running maintains conditioning and reduces risk of recurrence.
- Pain associated with soft tissue thickening distal to the fracture site can be treated by soft tissue techniques.
- General principles of return to activity following overuse injury should be followed (Chapter 15).

Prevention of recurrence

To prevent recurrence, it is important to:

- determine whether excessive training and biomechanics precipitated the stress fracture
- ensure adequate calorie balance, as inadequate caloric intake is a risk factor for stress fractures (see Chapter 43 on the female athlete triad).

Alternative treatments including electrical stimulation and low-intensity pulsed ultrasound have shown in case studies to have a beneficial effect on the speed of stress fracture healing in limited populations (professional and Olympic sportspeople) where a rapid return to sport is vital.[19, 20] However, a meta-analysis of randomized control trials in 2008 failed to show conclusive evidence of benefit.[21] A pilot study suggested that the use of the intravenous bisphosphonate pamidronate may decrease the time away from sport.[19] However, these studies provided level 4 evidence (case series only). The use of bisphosphonates in women during childbearing years is contraindicated.

Stress fracture of the anterior cortex of the tibia

PRACTICE PEARL

Stress fractures of the anterior cortex of the midshaft of the tibia need to be considered separately, as they are prone to delayed union, non-union, and complete fracture.[20]

Stress fracture of the anterior cortex of the medial third of the tibia presents with diffuse dull pain aggravated by physical activity. The bone is tender at the site of the fracture and there may be periosteal thickening (a palpable lump) if the symptoms have been present for some months. Isotopic bone scan (Fig. 35.7a overleaf) shows a discrete focal area of increased activity in the anterior cortex. The radiographic appearance at this stage shows a defect in the anterior cortex, which is termed "the dreaded black line" (Fig. 35.7b overleaf). This appearance is due to bony resorption and is indicative of non-union.

The mid-anterior cortex of the tibia is vulnerable to non-union for two reasons—the area has a relatively poor blood supply, and it is also an area under tension due to the morphologic bowing of the tibia. Excessive anterior tibial bowing is often noted in association with this fracture. In general, the prognosis for these resistant stress injuries is guarded, with an elevated risk of delayed union or non-union. One study presented some success with the use of pneumatic air braces in this population, thus avoiding the need for surgery.[22] However, the average return to unrestricted activities was 12 months with this form of treatment. Other options for treatment include pulsed electromagnetic stimulation, surgical excision and bone grafting, and transverse drilling at the fracture site. Chang and Harris described five cases treated with intramedullary tibial nailing;[23] they had two excellent results and three good results.

Treatment

Our current treatment protocol is as follows:

- immediate application of a pneumatic brace
- stopping anti-inflammatory medications and smoking
- thorough screening for associated nutritional, biomechanical, and nutritional risk factors
- for all elite level sportspeople, application of electrical or ultrasonic bone stimulation
- if no progress by four to six months, intramedullary nailing with or without bone grafting, debridement, or drilling is recommended.

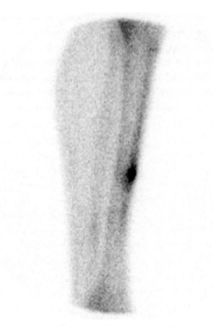

Figure 35.7 Stress fracture of the anterior tibial cortex **(a)** Bone scan appearance

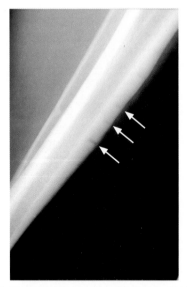

(b) Plain X-ray appearance of multiple "dreaded black lines"

Medial tibial stress syndrome

As noted previously, there has been a tendency in the past to categorize all shin pain, especially that which is not a stress fracture, under the term "shin splints."[24] Indeed, shin splints is more of a vague symptom sportspeople describe for leg pain most commonly along the posterior medial border of their tibia. With the advent of imaging techniques such as isotope bone scan, CT, and MRI, we are now able to make more precise anatomical and pathological diagnoses of patients with leg pain.

The most descriptive term that accounts for the painful traction phenomenon on the medial aspect of the leg more common in runners is *medial tibial stress syndrome* or medial tibial traction stress syndrome.

Note that studies have failed to demonstrate evidence of inflammatory cells in this condition and the authors concluded that that the underlying pathology may be similar to stress injury of bone.[25, 26]

The patient with medial tibial stress syndrome complains of diffuse pain along the medial border of the tibia (the junction of the lower third and upper two thirds of the tibia), which usually decreases with warming up. More focal pain should alert the examiner to the possibility of a true stress fracture. The sportsperson can often complete the training session but pain gradually recurs after exercise and is worse the following morning. Historically the tibialis posterior was thought to be the source of the pain, but more recently the soleus and flexor digitorum longus have been implicated.[27] The incidence of medial tibial stress syndrome has been reported to be between 4% and 35% in military personnel and sportspeople.[26, 27]

Risk factors

A number of factors may contribute to the increased stress and traction on the posterior medial aspect of the tibia. These include excessive pronation (flat feet), training errors, shoe design, surface type, muscle dysfunction, fatigue, and decreased flexibility.[28] Other risk factors that have been reported include female gender, higher body mass index (BMI), greater internal and external rotation of the hip, increased calf girth, and a history of previous stress fractures or use of orthotics.[26, 29] The biomechanics of medial tibial stress syndrome relates to the sequence of events that occurs with walking and running.[30] During midstance, foot pronation provides shock absorption and an accommodation to the varied terrain. The medial soleus is the strongest plantar flexor and invertor of the foot. The soleus muscle eccentrically contracts to resist pronation. Excessive pronation due to pes planus or overuse combined with repetitive impact loading leads to chronic traction over its insertion onto the periosteum on the posterior medial border

B

of the tibia, leading directly to medial tibial traction stress syndrome and medial tibial stress syndrome.

Metabolic bone health may also contribute. Sportspeople with pain related to medial tibial stress syndrome were found to have lower bone mineral density at the affected region compared with control and athletic control subjects.[31] Bone mineral density was also decreased on the unaffected side in subjects with unilateral symptoms. These sportspeople regained normal bone mineral density after recovery from their symptoms.[32] Reduced bone density or bone conditioning to stress may contribute to the increased risk of medial tibial stress syndrome seen in female military recruits. A study examining possible risk factors for the development of medial shin pain in military recruits showed that females were three times as likely to develop the syndrome.[33] Beyond gender, no other risk factors of statistical significance were noted, but increased hip range of motion (both internal and external rotation), and lower lean calf girth were associated with medial shin pain in the male recruits.[33]

Radiographs are routinely negative with medial tibial stress syndrome; however, with careful inspection some periosteal reaction can be seen in rare patients, and localized swelling can be seen in others. Isotopic bone scan may show patchy, diffuse areas of increased uptake along the medial border of the tibia as shown in Figure 35.5b. This is in contrast to stress fractures, which should show focal uptake. In early stages, however, the bone scan appearance may also be normal. MRI was found to have similar sensitivity and specificity to isotope bone scan.[7] Interestingly there were a number of abnormal bone scan and MRI appearances in the asymptomatic control group in that study.[7]

Treatment

Most sportspeople will present with a long history of complaints, having tried a number of home remedies, stretches, medicines, or cold treatment. Assessing previous treatments in terms of what provided relief and what exacerbated the problem is beneficial. While heat or whirlpool may improve flexibility and warm up the muscles, it also increases the circulation to the region, which can increase symptoms of inflammation.

The foundation of treatment is based on symptomatic relief, identification of risk factors, and treating the underlying pathology. Symptomatic treatment begins with rest, ice, and analgesia if needed.

Switching to pain-free cross-training activities (such as swimming or cycling) can keep the sportsperson active. Craig has suggested that no current method of treatment is better than rest alone; yet she still suggests that the use of shock-absorptive insoles is promising.[27, 34] In resistant cases, immobilization and protected weight-bearing may be necessary to rest the chronic tension placed on the soleus insertion with repeated weight-bearing.

A critical facet of treatment is based on a careful assessment of foot alignment and gait mechanics. Taping techniques are only effective if they control foot pronation. Permanent relief can occasionally be achieved through appropriate shoe wear and the application of cushioned orthotics (for shock absorption assistance) with a semi-rigid medial arch support (to support the pronated foot). We have found positive results in our patients, at least in the initial phase, by treating them with the same knee high pneumatic splint that we use for stress fractures (Air-Stirrup Leg Brace, Aircast, New Jersey, USA).

Alternative modalities can be effective in relieving pain and should be considered. The entire calf muscle should be assessed for areas of tightness or focal thickening that can be treated with appropriate soft tissue techniques (Chapter 35). Digital ischemic pressure should be applied to the thickened muscle fibers of the soleus, flexor digitorum longus, and tibialis posterior adjacent to their bony attachment, avoiding the site of periosteal attachment, which may prove too painful (Fig. 35.8a overleaf). The effect may be enhanced by adding passive dorsiflexion and plantarflexion while digital ischemic pressure is applied. Transverse friction should be used on focal regions of muscle thickening in the soleus and flexor digitorum longus. Abnormalities of the tibialis posterior may be treated through the relaxed overlying muscles. Sustained myofascial tension can be applied parallel to the tibial border, releasing the flexor digitorum longus, and along the soleus aponeurosis in the direction of normal stress with combined active ankle dorsiflexion (Fig. 35.8b overleaf). Vacuum cupping techniques can be effective but it is important to remain clear of the tibial border to avoid causing capillary damage (Fig. 35.8c overleaf).

Physical therapy programs have focused on motor strengthening and flexibility, especially proprioceptive neuromuscular facilitation (PNF) stretching. Electrical stimulation, iontophoresis, and ultrasound have been attempted with mixed results. Prolotherapy (injection with agents intended

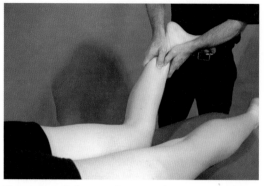

Figure 35.8 Soft tissue therapy in the treatment of inflammatory shin pain

(a) Digital ischemic pressure to the medial soleus aponeurosis and flexor digitorum longus. This can be performed with passive and active dorsiflexion

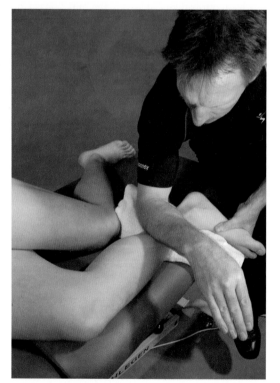

(b) Sustained myofascial tension along the soleus aponeurosis in the direction of normal stress combined with active ankle dorsiflexion

(c) Vacuum cupping

to accelerate the healing process), and platelet-rich plasma injections have also been performed but very little quality research is available to validate their efficacy. In resistant cases, surgical release (with or without periosteal tissue resection or ablation) of the superficial and posterior compartments off their conjoined insertion onto the posteromedial border of the tibia can be performed with a projected success rate of 70% improvement in high-performance elite sportspeople.[24, 35]

Chronic exertional compartment syndrome

Compartment syndrome is defined as increased pressure within a closed fibro-osseous space, causing reduced blood flow and reduced tissue perfusion, which subsequently lead to ischemic pain and possible permanent damage to the tissues of the compartment.[36] It may be acute, chronic (exertional), or convert from chronic to acute. Chronic exertional compartment syndrome (CECS) with stress fractures, and medial tibial stress syndrome are key components of the differential diagnosis of leg pain in sportspeople, especially in distance runners and those sportspeople in aerobic training. The syndrome is frequently bilateral. When the pain is in the calf, the clinician should also consider popliteal artery entrapment syndrome in the differential diagnosis (Chapter 36).

Pathogenesis

Even though, classically, exertional compartment syndrome was felt to be an ischemic phenomenon like acute compartment syndrome, the exact etiology of chronic exertional compartment syndrome is still unclear. Repetitive overuse followed by associated inflammation may lead to fibrosis and therefore reduced elasticity of the fascia surrounding the muscle compartments. As a result, when the patient exercises, the muscles attempt to expand but are unable to do so.

Biopsies have revealed abnormally thickened, non-compliant fascia. A series of biopsies at the fascial–periosteal interface revealed varying degrees of fibrocytic activity, chronic inflammatory cells, and vascular proliferation as well as a decrease in collagen irregularity, suggesting an attempt at remodeling.[37]

As a result of this stiffened, abnormal fascial compartment, when the patient exercises, the muscle attempts to expand but is resisted by a less compliant fascia. This results in increased pressure, soft tissue ischemia, and, therefore, pain.

Although ischemia is likely to play a role this has not been substantiated. It is probable that, within a tight fascial compartment, the normal consequence of metabolic activity during exercise would lead to an increase in pressure sufficient to compromise tissue perfusion at the capillary level. Birtles et al.[38] induced similar symptoms to those of compartment syndrome by restricting venous flow during exercise.

In a more recent biopsy study, Edmundsson et al[39] noted that, when patients with chronic exertional compartment syndrome had muscle biopsies at the time of their fascial release, laboratory analysis revealed lower capillary density, lower number of capillaries around muscle fibers, and lower density of capillaries per muscle fiber area.

Researchers concluded that the reduced microcirculation capacity was a likely contributor to the development of, or secondary to, the chronic exertional compartment syndrome. There is, however, conflicting evidence via nuclear magnetic resonance spectroscopy studies,[40] MIBI perfusion imaging,[41] and T2-weighed and arterial spin-labeling MRI studies.[41]

Clinical features

Typical clinical features of chronic exertional compartment syndrome are the absence of pain at rest, and increasing achy pain and a sensation of tightness with exertion. Symptoms usually resolve or significantly dissipate within several minutes of rest.

Rarely, sportspeople develop paresthesias or motor weakness with exertion.

At rest, physical examination is usually unremarkable. When the patient aims to reproduce the symptoms with exertion, the examiner may be able to palpate the increased tension in the compartment. There may be a muscle bulge or small herniation.

The most common compartment involved is the anterior compartment, presenting with anterolateral pain with exertion. The other two common compartments are the lateral compartment, which may present with paresthesias in the distribution of the superficial peroneal nerve to the dorsum of the foot, and the deep posterior compartment, usually associated with posteromedial tibial pain. Involvement of the superficial posterior compartment is quite rare.

Investigations

Investigations and screening should always include an assessment of limb and foot alignment, evaluation of the biomechanical demands of the specific sport including court surface and shoe-wear, a history of previous injuries or trauma, and a screen for overlapping pathology such as stress fractures, medial tibial stress syndrome, and metabolic and nutritional factors. In one study, diabetes mellitus was implicated as a risk factor for developing chronic exertional compartment syndrome.[42] Radiographs are frequently obtained as an inexpensive screening tool for associated bone pathology.

The definitive diagnosis is made on the basis of intracompartmental pressure measurements (Table 35.3). The use of near-infrared spectroscopy has shown promise as a non-invasive alternative but it is expensive and has not yet become commonly used.[7] In a comparison study using near-infrared spectroscopy compared with MRI and intracompartmental pressure measurements, van den Brand[7] argued that the sensitivity of near-infrared spectroscopy (85%) was superior to both MRI and intracompartmental pressure measurements (both 77%).

More recently, Williams et al. and associates have suggested that nonpainful neurosensory testing can be performed using a Pressure Specified Sensory Device pre- and post-exertion; this can guide the clinician regarding the presence of chronic exertional compartment syndrome or the efficacy of previous release.[43] Other investigators have looked more deeply into advanced imaging techniques including Tc-99m tetrofosmin single photon emission

CT, and a novel dual birdcage coil and in-scanner MRI protocol to assist with making a diagnosis using non-invasive means.[44, 45] Nonetheless, intra-compartmental pressure measurements remain the gold standard.

Deep posterior compartment syndrome

Deep posterior compartment syndrome typically presents as an ache in the region of the medial border of the tibia or as chronic calf pain. Beware the multiple other causes of calf pain including popliteal artery entrapment syndrome (Chapter 36). The deep posterior compartment contains the flexor hallucis longus, flexor digitorum longus, and tibialis posterior (Fig. 35.1). Occasionally, a separate fascial sheath surrounds the tibialis posterior muscle, forming an extra compartment that may provoke symptoms independent of the other compartments.

Active, passive, or resisted motion of these muscles may exacerbate pain. The patient describes a feeling of tightness or a bursting sensation. Pain increases with exercise. There may be associated distal symptoms (e.g. weakness, pins and needles on the plantar aspect of the foot), which may be indicative of tibial nerve compression. Small muscle hernias occasionally occur along the medial or anterior borders of the tibia after exercise.

On examination, there may be tenderness along the medial aspect of the tibia; however, this is often relatively mild. Due to the deep nature of the compartment, palpable fascial tightness is less obvious in comparison with anterior or lateral compartment syndromes. Nonetheless, the experienced clinician may be able to discern the difference between palpable tightness in the deep compartment and fascial thickening and induration found in association with medial tibial stress syndrome.

Routinely all four compartments should be measured pre- and post-exertion in sportspeople suspicious for chronic exertional compartment syndrome. To measure deep posterior compartment pressures, the needle or catheter is inserted from the medial aspect through two layers of fascia aiming posterior to the tibia (Fig. 35.9). Exercises including running or jumping, stair-climbing, use of pulleys in plantar-flexion and dorsiflexion or repeated calf raises, or isokinetic resistance machines can be used to exacerbate complaints. Routinely, we ask patients to run five minutes into their pain to ensure a valid test. It is important to reproduce the patient's pain, otherwise the test is not considered valid.

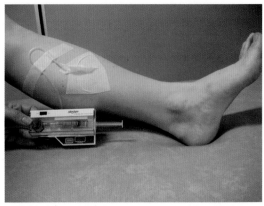

Figure 35.9 Compartment pressure testing—deep posterior compartment. The Stryker catheter is inserted into the deep posterior compartment

Post-exertional measurements must be obtained immediately after ceasing exercise and may be repeated again after 10 minutes. Normal compartment pressures are regarded as being between 0 and 10 mmHg. For the diagnosis of chronic compartment syndrome, maximal pressure during exercise of greater than 25 mmHg, an elevation of pressures greater than 10 mmHg, or a resting post-exercise pressure greater than 25 mmHg is necessary (Table 35.3). If the elevated pressure takes more than 5 minutes to return to normal, this may also be significant.

Treatment

Treatment of isolated deep posterior exertional compartment syndrome usually begins with a conservative regimen of reduced exercise and deep massage therapy. Careful analysis of all contributing factors and overlapping diagnoses must be considered. Longitudinal release work with passive and active dorsiflexion is performed to reduce fascial thickening (Fig. 35.10). Transverse frictions are used to treat chronic muscular thickening. Dry needling of the deep muscles or prolotherapy may also be helpful. Assessment and correction of any biomechanical abnormalities, especially excessive pronation, must be included.

Isolated deep posterior exertional compartment syndrome is uncommon and may be confused with medial tibial stress syndrome, popliteal artery entrapment syndrome, vascular claudication, and stress fractures. Indeed it is not surprising that initial treatment is the same as that for medial tibial stress syndrome. Unfortunately, if associated diagnoses or contributing factors cannot be identified

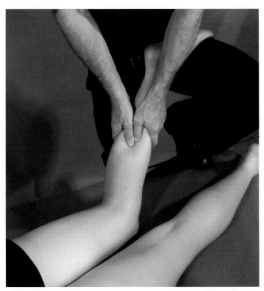

Figure 35.10 Soft tissue therapy in the treatment of deep posterior compartment syndrome—longitudinal release to reduce fascial thickening. Active or passive dorsiflexion improves the release

and if pressures are elevated, symptoms are usually refractory to treatment, and surgical release may be necessary.

The surgical approach is along the posterior medial edge of the tibia and may be performed through one or two small incisions. The saphenous vein lies directly along the path to the fascial insertion onto the posteromedial border of the tibia. Extreme care must be used to control all bleeding at the time of surgery, as injury to one of the branches is common and increases the risk of postoperative hematoma or cellulitis.[46]

Some authors have suggested a benefit of fasciectomy (removal of a portion of fascial tissue) over fasciotomy (simple incision) due to concerns that the fascial insertion and sheath reforms.[8] They argue that this periosteal stripping serves an added role of treating any associated medial tibial stress syndrome, as well as assuring release of any anatomic variations of tibialis posterior compartments. Due to the extensive nature of the procedure, which requires longer incisions and the increased risk of complications, we recommend this extensive approach only in revision cases. In addition, in patients who have positive anterior or lateral compartment pressures but only borderline pressures in the deep compartment, recommendations to restrict releases and treatment to the affected compartment are prudent. This approach

may avoid the increased complication risk that occurs when releasing the posterior compartments.[46]

Anterior and lateral exertional compartment syndromes

The anterior compartment contains the tibialis anterior, extensor digitorum longus, extensor hallucis longus, and peroneus tertius muscles, as well as the deep peroneal nerve; the lateral (peroneal) compartment contains the peroneus longus and brevis tendons as well as the superficial peroneal nerve. For anterior compartment pathology, pain during exertion is felt just lateral to the anterior border of the shin, and paresthesias may present in the first web space. For lateral compartment pathology, pain is palpated just anterior to the fibula, and paresthesias may occur over the dorsum of the foot. The intermuscular septum (raphe) between the two compartments can be visualized in thin individuals by looking for the indentation of skin when you squeeze the soft tissues between the anterior border of the tibia and fibula.

Clinical examination at rest is usually normal, or there may be palpable generalized tightness of the anterior or lateral compartment with focal regions of excessive muscle thickening. It is also important to assess the plantar flexors, especially the soleus and gastrocnemius. If these antagonists are tight, they may predispose to anterior compartment syndrome. Muscle herniation may be palpable with exertion, most commonly occurring 5–7 cm (2–3 in.) proximally to the distal tip of the fibula where the superficial peroneal nerve penetrates the lateral compartment fascia. Diagnosis of anterior and lateral exertional compartment syndrome is confirmed with pre- and post-exertional compartment testing (Table 35.3).

Treatment

Treatment is based on the same principles as for the deep posterior compartment. All contributing factors should be assessed and treated. Lowering the heel in the sportsperson's shoe or orthotics may reduce the load of the anterior muscles and alleviate pain. Sustained myofascial tension techniques combined with passive and active plantarflexion may restore fascial flexibility (Fig. 35.11a overleaf). Focal regions of muscular thickening should be treated with transverse friction or dry needling. In addition, because the anterior and lateral compartments are superficial, vacuum cupping may be attempted (Fig. 35.11b overleaf). Accurate cup placement is required to avoid capillary and periosteal damage. It is also

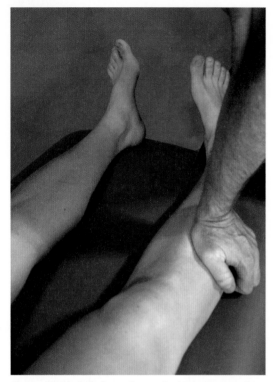

Figure 35.11 Soft tissue therapy in the treatment of anterior compartment syndrome
(a) Sustained myofascial tension with active or passive plantarflexion

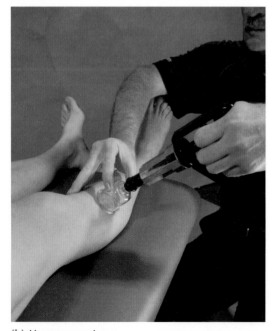

(b) Vacuum cupping

helpful to treat tightness of the posterior compartment (antagonist muscles) with sustained myofascial tension (grade III) combined with passive and active dorsiflexion.

Unfortunately, when the diagnosis is pressure positive and there are no obvious precipitating factors, conservative treatment frequently fails, and surgical release is required. Fasciectomy is rarely necessary, as success rates with anterior and lateral compartment releases with minimal incision, and percutaneous and endoscopically assisted releases approach 90%. Newer equipment including balloon catheters and endoscopic vein harvesting retractors have been used to make endoscopic assisted techniques even safer.[47] Special care is essential to visualize the superficial peroneal nerve at the time of surgery to avoid iatrogenic injury.

Acute compartment syndromes are usually associated with trauma. Intracompartmental pressures are significantly elevated and do not subside with rest. Emergency surgical release is essential to avoid ischemic injury to the extremity. This emergency is covered more completely in Chapter 47; however, it is important to be aware of a number of case reports in which acute anterior compartment syndromes were brought on by exercise and overuse.[48, 49] In many of these cases the patient or sportsperson continued to exercise through the initial pain that may have represented an exertional compartment syndrome which would have otherwise gone away with rest. When pain does not settle in an appropriate time frame, conversion of an exertional compartment syndrome to an acute compartment syndrome should be considered.

Outcomes of surgical treatment of exertional compartment syndrome

Fasciotomy with or without fasciectomy is the standard surgical treatment for both anterior and deep posterior compartment syndromes. The majority of patients undergoing this procedure (80–90%) have a satisfactory result, with many being able to return to their previous level of sport.[50] However, there is a significant percentage that either fail to improve after surgery or, after a period of improvement, have a recurrence of symptoms. Some studies suggest that failure and recurrences are more common in the deep posterior compartment,[50, 51] possibly due to failure to release the tibialis posterior compartment,[50] while another study showed a more negative outcome with the anterior compartment releases.

Micheli et al. compared outcomes by gender and noted a slightly decreased rate of successful outcomes in female patients.[52]

In a study of 18 patients who underwent revision surgery,[53] increased pressure was found only in a localized area at the site of the scar in 60% of patients, whereas 40% had high pressures throughout the compartment. They found that the exuberant scar tissue was thicker, denser, and more constricting than was the original fascia. Eight of the 18 patients had entrapment of the superficial peroneal nerve with numbness and paresthesia over the dorsum of the foot with exertion (a positive Tinel's sign) and localized tenderness over the nerve, exacerbated by active dorsiflexion and eversion, as well as passive inversion and plantar flexion. All those with peroneal nerve entrapment had a good result from the revision surgery, whereas only 50% of those without nerve entrapment had a satisfactory outcome.

Slimmon et al.[54] reported a 60% excellent or good outcome after a minimum of two years in 50 patients who underwent fasciectomy. Of the 50 patients, 58% were exercising at a lower level than before the injury, and, of those, 36% cited the return of their compartment syndrome or the development of a different lower leg compartment syndrome as the reason for the reduction in exercise levels.

The foundation of a successful surgical result begins with a proper anatomic diagnosis. Care is important to confirm the diagnosis preoperatively with intracompartmental pressure measurement, as well as treating any associated or contributing factors.

Surgery should target the specific anatomical pathology. Avoiding the release of all four compartments in every patient—unless preoperative testing provides definitive indication—reduces the risk of surgical complications. Meticulous control of intra-operative bleeding will reduce the risk of postoperative hematoma and cellulites. Due to the extensive subcutaneous dissection, postoperative cellulitis or infection is more common than some other procedures. Perioperative antibiotics and postoperative cryotherapy can reduce this risk. If identified in the postoperative period, the surgeon should have a relatively low threshold to return to the operating room and perform early irrigation.

The absolute indication for fasciectomy in contrast to fasciotomy is not clear, as the former may increase the risk of bleeding and postoperative stiffness. Perhaps the most common complication is postoperative stiffness, which can be avoided by early and aggressive postoperative mobilization.

Rehabilitation following compartment syndrome surgery

The following protocol is recommended:[2]

- Perioperative antibiotics and cryotherapy to reduce complications of infection, hematoma, and cellulites.
- Range of motion exercises of the knee and ankle in the immediate postoperative period. Full plantar and dorsiflexion is encouraged.
- Three to five days of limited weight-bearing on crutches, then full weight-bearing as tolerated.
- Once the wounds have healed, a strengthening program including cycling and swimming should commence.
- Gradual return to light jogging at about 4–6 weeks after surgery.
- Full sports participation is anticipated at 6–8 weeks if one compartment released, and 8–12 weeks if both legs and multiple compartments released.
- The sportsperson should be pain-free with 90% strength regained prior to full sports participation.

Less common causes

Stress fracture of the fibula

Stress fractures of the fibula are not seen as frequently as stress fractures of the tibia. As the fibula plays a minimal role in weight-bearing, this stress fracture is usually due to muscle traction or torsional forces placed through the bone. In the sportsperson with excessive subtalar pronation, the peroneal muscles are forced to contract harder and longer during toe-off. Examination may reveal local tenderness and pain in springing the fibula proximal to the site of the stress fracture.

This injury is usually not as painful on weight-bearing as is stress fracture of the tibia. It is treated symptomatically with rest from activity until bony tenderness settles. Due to poorer rotational control, knee-high pneumatic braces may not be as effective as on the tibia. There should then be a gradual increase in the amount of activity. Soft tissue abnormalities should be corrected. This injury is often associated with a biomechanical abnormality such as excessive pronation or excessive supination.

Referred pain

Referred pain is not a common cause of leg pain in sportspeople but should be considered in cases with persistent and atypical pain. Pain may be referred from the lumbar spine, proximal nerve entrapment, the knee joint (Baker's cyst, meniniscal cysts), the superior tibiofibular joint (instability or ganglion cyst), and, occasionally, the ankle joint (instability, Maisonneuve fracture).

Nerve entrapments

Within the leg itself, nerve entrapment of either the superficial peroneal nerve in the lateral compartment or the deep peroneal nerve in the anterior compartment can occur due to trauma or a tight brace or cast. Fascial entrapment at the level of the fibular head is also seen occasionally.

The tibial nerve in the deep posterior compartment is less commonly involved with entrapment but can be injured with trauma. Pain and sensory changes may occur. The diagnosis is suggested by the presence of motor or sensory changes, and is confirmed with nerve conduction studies performed pre and post exercise. Surgery may be required to alleviate these conditions.

Vascular pathologies

Popliteal artery entrapment syndrome usually presents with calf pain and is therefore more fully described in Chapter 36; however, it may rarely present as pain in the anterior compartment.[55] It can be misdiagnosed as anterior compartment syndrome as they both present with claudicant-type pain. However, the pain from popliteal artery entrapment disappears immediately on cessation of exercise, whereas compartment syndrome pain often persists for approximately 30 minutes as an aching sensation.

While deep venous thrombosis is most commonly posterior, chronic venous stasis changes can occur anteriorly and may be evidence of systemic disease.

Developmental issues

Juvenile tibia vara (Blount disease) usually presents due to deformity rather than pain.

Osgood-Schlatter's disease is a traction apophysitis at the insertion of the patellar tendon onto the tibial tuberosity; it is seen commonly among adolescent sportspeople. Patients usually present with pain and tenderness at the tibial tuberosity (Chapter 42).

"Growing pains" may affect the leg and are usually a diagnosis of exclusion. Intermittent achy pain exacerbated by periods of active growth with completely negative imaging and work-up are characteristic. The youngest reported patient treated with

surgical release for pressure positive chronic exertional compartment syndrome was 12 years old and it is unclear whether this patient would have grown out of the problem at maturity.

Periosteal contusion

Periosteal contusion occurs as a result of a direct blow from a hard object such as a football boot. It can be extremely painful at the time of injury; however, the pain usually settles relatively quickly. Persistent pain may occur because of a hematoma having formed under the periosteum. There will be local tenderness and bony swelling. Treatment consists of rest and protection.

Combined fractures of the tibia and fibula, and isolated fractures of the tibia

Various patterns of tibia, fibula, or combined tibia and fibula fractures can cause leg pain. These patterns range from complete to incomplete fractures, stress fractures, open or closed fractures, simple or comminuted fractures, to displaced and non-displaced fractures. In sport, combined fractures of the tibia and fibula may be related to indirect violence in landing from a jump onto a twisted foot but may also occur with direct trauma in collision sports. Pain is the most common clinical finding. Weight-bearing is virtually impossible with a displaced fracture of the tibia.

Management

When managing combined fractures of both the tibia and fibula, treatment is primarily guided by the stability and fracture pattern of the tibia. Structurally the tibia is responsible for 90% of the load across the leg. Its stability is of primary importance. Open fractures in which the bone is exposed or has punctured the skin are orthopedic emergencies. The wound must be aggressively irrigated, usually in the operating room, and the patient should be started on appropriate antibiotic therapy.

With careful scrutiny, many closed tibial fractures can be treated conservatively but angulation *must* be minimal (see Practice pearl opposite—surgical management). Specifically, minimal angulation is defined as less than 5° to 10° in the frontal plane, 10° to 15° of anterior/posterior bowing on the lateral view, and 3° to 7° of rotation deformity.

If closed management is appropriate, immobilize the limb in an above-knee plaster with the knee slightly flexed and the ankle in 90° of dorsiflexion. Elevate the limb for 3–7 days until swelling subsides.

It is imperative that check X-rays are viewed by the clinician weekly for the first few weeks to ensure that there is not progressive angulation of the fracture. At 6–8 weeks the patient may be able to switch into a hinged knee cast.

Bony union requires 8 to 12 weeks, and 16 to 20 weeks are required for consolidation. The length of time required for complete healing to occur has led some surgeons to proceed with surgical fixation, which can allow earlier mobilization and return to play in some fractures.

Physiotherapy after removal of the plaster is aimed at regaining full range of knee flexion and quadriceps muscle strength. Activities such as swimming can be resumed immediately after removal of the plaster, but multidirectional running sports must wait until range of movement and muscle strength have returned to normal.

Note that there is a strong trend toward early surgical fixation of unstable tibial fractures, with intramedullary nailing. This allows sportspeople earlier weight-bearing, and earlier conditioning activities and return to sport; it also obviates the risk of potential malunion.

Isolated fibula fractures

Twisting or a direct blow can cause an isolated fracture of the fibula. The patient may report only local tenderness. The ankle and knee joints must be carefully examined for associated injuries. A Maisonneuve injury comprises an unstable ligamentous ankle injury, tearing of the syndesmosis and the interosseous membrane connecting the tibia and fibula, and a proximal fibula fracture. This relatively benign appearing proximal fibula fracture actually represents an unstable ankle injury that should not be missed as it requires surgical stabilization.

As long as the fracture does not involve the ankle joint, treatment is symptomatic—prescribe analgesia appropriately and provide crutches/walking stick as needed.

CLINICAL SPORTS MEDICINE
MASTERCLASSES
[W] www.clinicalsportsmedicine.com

- Listen to the podcast with the chapter authors.
- Watch the assessment of the patient with shin pain.
- See a video explanation of compartment pressure testing.

REFERENCES

1. Pedowitz R, Hargens A. Acute and chronic compartment syndromes. In: Garrett W, Speer K, Kirkendall D, eds. *Principles and practice of orthopaedic sports medicine*. Philadelphia: Lippincott Williams & Wilkins, 2000:87–97.

2. Blackman PG. A review of chronic exertional compartment syndrome in the lower leg. *Med Sci Sports Exerc* 2000;32(3 Suppl):S4–10.

3. Fredericson M, Bergman AG, Hoffman KL et al. Tibial stress reaction in runners. Correlation of clinical symptoms and scintigraphy with a new magnetic resonance imaging grading system. *Am J Sports Med* 1995;23(4):472–81.

4. Yao L, Johnson C, Gentili A et al. Stress injuries of bone: analysis of MR imaging staging criteria. *Acad Radiol* 1998;5(1):34–40.

5. Arendt E, Agel J, Heikes C et al. Stress injuries to bone in college athletes: a retrospective review of experience at a single institution. *Am J Sports Med* 2003;31(6):959–68.

6. Batt ME, Ugalde V, Anderson MW et al. A prospective controlled study of diagnostic imaging for acute shin splints. *Med Sci Sports Exerc* 1998;30(11):1564–71.

7. van den Brand JG, Nelson T, Verleisdonk EJ et al. The diagnostic value of intracompartmental pressure measurement, magnetic resonance imaging, and near-infrared spectroscopy in chronic exertional compartment syndrome: a prospective study in 50 patients. *Am J Sports Med* 2005;33(5):699–704.

8. Hislop M, Tierney P, Murray P et al. Chronic exertional compartment syndrome: the controversial "fifth" compartment of the leg. *Am J Sports Med* 2003;31(5):770–6.

9. Popp KL, Hughes JM, Smock AJ et al. Bone geometry, strength, and muscle size in runners with a history of stress fracture. *Med Sci Sports Exerc* 2009;41(12):2145–50.

10. Snyder RA, DeAngelis JP, Koester MC et al. Does shoe insole modification prevent stress fractures? A systematic review. *HSS Journal* 2009;5(2):92–8.

11. Zadpoor AA, Nikooyan AA. The relationship between lower-extremity stress fractures and the ground reaction force: a systematic review. *Clin Biomech* (Bristol, Avon) 2011;26(1):23–8.

12. Crowell HP, Davis IS. Gait retraining to reduce lower extremity loading in runners. *Clin Biomech* (Bristol, Avon) 2011;26(1):78–83.

13. Crowell HP, Milner CE, Hamill J et al. Reducing impact loading during running with the use of real-time visual feedback. *J Orthop Sports Phys Ther* 2010;40(4):206–13.

14. Edwards WB, Taylor D, Rudolphi TJ et al. Effects of stride length and running mileage on a probabilistic stress fracture model. *Med Sci Sports Exerc* 2009;41(12):2177–84.

15. Brent Edwards W, Taylor D, Rudolphi TJ et al. Effects of running speed on a probabilistic stress fracture model. *Clin Biomech* (Bristol, Avon) 2010;25(4):372–7.

16. Whitelaw GP, Wetzler MJ, Levy AS et al. A pneumatic leg brace for the treatment of tibial stress fractures. *Clin Orthop Relat Res* 1991(270):301–5.

17. Dickson TB, Kichline PD. Functional management of stress fractures in female athletes using a pneumatic leg brace. *Am J Sports Med* 1987;15(1):86–9.

18. Swenson EJ, DeHaven KE, Sebastianelli WJ et al. The effect of a pneumatic leg brace on return to play in athletes with tibial stress fractures. *Am J Sports Med* 1997;25(3):322–8.

19. Stewart GW, Brunet ME, Manning MR et al. Treatment of stress fractures in athletes with intravenous pamidronate. *Clin J Sport Med* 2005;15(2):92–4.

20. Brukner P, Bennell K, Matheson G. *Stress fractures*. Melbourne: Blackwells Scientific Asia, 1999.

21. Mollon B, da Silva V, Busse JW et al. Electrical stimulation for long-bone fracture-healing: a meta-analysis of randomized controlled trials. *J Bone Joint Surg Am* 2008;90(11):2322–30.

22. Batt ME, Kemp S, Kerslake R. Delayed union stress fractures of the anterior tibia: conservative management. *Br J Sports Med* 2001;35(1):74–7.

23. Chang PS, Harris RM. Intramedullary nailing for chronic tibial stress fractures. A review of five cases. *Am J Sports Med* 1996;24(5):688–92.

24. Detmer DE. Chronic shin splints. Classification and management of medial tibial stress syndrome. *Sports Med* 1986;3(6):436–46.

25. Tweed JL, Avil SJ, Campbell JA et al. Etiologic factors in the development of medial tibial stress syndrome: a review of the literature. *J Am Podiatr Med Assoc* 2008;98(2):107–11.

26. Moen MH, Tol JL, Weir A et al. Medial tibial stress syndrome: a critical review. *Sports Med* 2009;39(7): 523–46.

27. Craig DI. Current developments concerning medial tibial stress syndrome. *Phys Sportsmed* 2009;37(4): 39–44.

28. Bennett JE, Reinking MF, Pluemer B et al. Factors contributing to the development of medial tibial stress syndrome in high school runners. *J Orthop Sports Phys Ther* 2001;31(9):504–10.

29. Hubbard TJ, Carpenter EM, Cordova ML. Contributing factors to medial tibial stress syndrome: a prospective investigation. *Med Sci Sports Exerc* 2009;41(3): 490–6.

30. Pell RF, Khanuja HS, Cooley GR. Leg pain in the running athlete. *J Am Acad Orthop Surg* 2004;12(6): 396–404.

31. Magnusson HI, Westlin NE, Nyqvist F et al. Abnormally decreased regional bone density in athletes with medial tibial stress syndrome. *Am J Sports Med* 2001;29(6):712–5.

32. Magnusson HI, Ahlborg HG, Karlsson C et al. Low regional tibial bone density in athletes with medial tibial stress syndrome normalizes after recovery from symptoms. *Am J Sports Med* 2003;31(4):596–600.

33. Burne SG, Khan KM, Boudville PB et al. Risk factors associated with exertional medial tibial pain: a 12 month prospective clinical study. *Br J Sports Med* 2004;38(4):441–5.

34. Craig DI. Medial tibial stress syndrome: evidence-based prevention. *J Athl Train* 2008;43(3):316–8.

35. Holen KJ, Engebretsen L, Grontvedt T et al. Surgical treatment of medial tibial stress syndrome (shin splint) by fasciotomy of the superficial posterior compartment of the leg. *Scand J Med Sci Sports* 1995;5(1):40–3.

36. Fraipont M, Adamson G. Chronic exertional compartment syndrome. *J Am Acad Orthop Surg* 2003;11(4):268–76.

37. Barbour TD, Briggs CA, Bell SN et al. Histology of the fascial–periosteal interface in lower limb chronic deep posterior compartment syndrome. *Br J Sports Med* 2004;38(6):709–17.

38. Birtles DB, Rayson MP, Casey A et al. Venous obstruction in healthy limbs: a model for chronic compartment syndrome? *Med Sci Sports Exerc* 2003;35(10):1638–44.

39. Edmundsson D, Toolanen G, Thornell L et al. Evidence for low muscle capillary supply as a pathogenic factor in chronic compartment syndrome. *Scand J Med Sci Sports* 2010;20(6):805–13.

40. Balduini FC, Shenton DW, O'Connor KH et al. Chronic exertional compartment syndrome: correlation of compartment pressure and muscle ischemia utilizing 31P-NMR spectroscopy. *Clin Sports Med* 1993;12(1): 151–65.

41. Owens S, Edwards P, Miles K et al. Chronic compartment syndrome affecting the lower limb: MIBI perfusion imaging as an alternative to pressure monitoring: two case reports. *Br J Sports Med* 1999;33(1):49–51.

42. Edmundsson D, Svensson O, Toolanen G. Intermittent claudication in diabetes mellitus due to chronic exertional compartment syndrome of the leg: an observational study of 17 patients. *Acta Orthop* 2008;79(4):534–9.

43. Williams EH, Detmer DE, Guyton GP et al. Non-invasive neurosensory testing used to diagnose and confirm successful surgical management of lower extremity deep distal posterior compartment syndrome. *J Brachial Plex Peripher Nerve Inj* 2009;4:4.

44. Oturai PS, Lorenzen T, Norregaard J et al. Evaluation of Tc-99m-tetrofosmin single-photon emission computed tomography for detection of chronic exertional compartment syndrome of the leg. *Scand J Med Sci Sports* 2006;16(4):282–6.

45. Litwiller DV, Amrami KK, Dahm DL et al. Chronic exertional compartment syndrome of the lower extremities: improved screening using a novel dual birdcage coil and in-scanner exercise protocol. *Skeletal Radiol* 2007;36(11):1067–75.

46. Hutchinson MR, Bederka B, Kopplin M. Anatomic structures at risk during minimal-incision endoscopically assisted fascial compartment releases in the leg. *Am J Sports Med* 2003;31(5):764–9.

47. Wittstein J, Moorman CT, Levin LS. Endoscopic compartment release for chronic exertional compartment syndrome: surgical technique and results. *Am J Sports Med* 2010;38(8):1661–6.

48. Esmail AN, Flynn JM, Ganley TJ et al. Acute exercise-induced compartment syndrome in the anterior leg. A case report. *Am J Sports Med* 2001;29(4):509–12.

49. McKee M, Jupiter J. Acute-exercise-induced bilateral anterolateral leg compartment syndrome in a healthy young man. *Am J Orthop* 1995;24:862–4.

50. Howard JL, Mohtadi NG, Wiley JP. Evaluation of outcomes in patients following surgical treatment of chronic exertional compartment syndrome in the leg. *Clin J Sport Med* 2000;10(3):176–84.

51. Schepsis AA, Gill SS, Foster TA. Fasciotomy for exertional anterior compartment syndrome: is lateral

compartment release necessary? *Am J Sports Med* 1999;27(4):430–5.

52. Micheli L, Solomon R, Solomon J. Outcomes of fasciotomy for chronic exertional compartment syndrome. *Am J Sports Med* 1999;33(7):197–201.

53. Schepsis AA, Fitzgerald M, Nicoletta R. Revision surgery for exertional anterior compartment syndrome of the lower leg: technique, findings, and results. *Am J Sports Med* 2005;33(7):1040–7.

54. Slimmon D, Bennell K, Brukner P et al. Long-term outcome of fasciotomy with partial fasciectomy for chronic exertional compartment syndrome of the lower leg. *Am J Sports Med* 2002;30(4):581–8.

55. Bradshaw C. Exercise-related lower leg pain: vascular. *Med Sci Sports Exerc* 2000;32(3 Suppl):S34–6.

Chapter 36

Calf pain

with CHRIS BRADSHAW and MATT HISLOP

First it was frustrating, then it got beyond frustrating. It was very hard. In the past, I've never dealt with any injuries before. To sit out the whole season is very frustrating for a player. Sheryl Scanlan, New Zealand Silver Fern and world champion netball player who was stunned by a major calf strain in 2009 and then injured the same muscle in the other leg in 2010

Calf pain is a common presenting complaint and, if not managed appropriately, it can persist for months or recur and cause frustration for both sportsperson and clinician. Both acute and chronic calf pain can stem from injury to the calf muscle.

The term "calf muscle" refers to the triceps surae, which includes the gastrocnemius, the soleus, and the plantaris muscles. The more superficial muscle—the gastrocnemius—has medial and lateral heads that arise from the femoral condyles, whereas the deeper soleus arises from the upper fibula and the medial tibial border. The plantaris muscle arises just medial to the lateral head of the gastrocnemius and crosses the popliteal fossa.

These muscles have a joint tendon, the Achilles, which inserts onto the calcaneus. Together they act as a venous pump for the lower limb. Injuries to the Achilles tendon are discussed in Chapter 37. As a biarthrodial muscle extending over the knee and the ankle, the gastrocnemius is more susceptible to injury than a uniarthrodial muscle. The anatomy of the calf is shown in Figure 36.1.

Clinical perspective

Injuries to the musculotendinous complex are by far the most common causes of calf pain. Muscle strains occur most commonly in the medial head of the gastrocnemius, or near the musculotendinous junction. Acute calf muscle strains are common among middle-aged sportspeople, particularly in racquet sports.

An MRI study of calf injuries reported that gastrocnemius strains accompanied by other muscle strains may be more common than previously thought.[1] Other muscle strains included strains of soleus, plantaris,

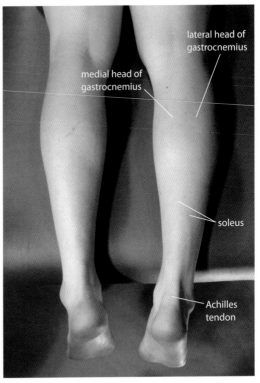

Figure 36.1 Anatomy of the calf
(a) Surface anatomy

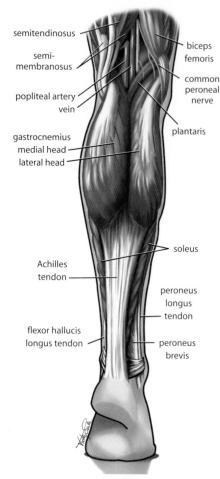

(b) Superficial calf muscles

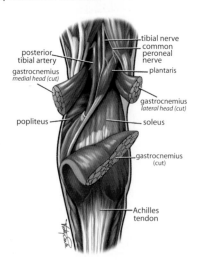

(c) Removal of the gastrocnemius showing the underlying soleus and plantaris muscles

tibialis posterior, flexor hallucis longus, and flexor digitorum longus. This highlights the importance of a thorough examination, as the presence of associated strains will change treatment and prognosis.

A sudden burst of acceleration (such as stretching to play a ball in squash or tennis) may precipitate a calf injury. The calf region is also a common site of contusion caused through contact with playing equipment or another player. Muscle strains and contusions are acute injuries that present with typical histories that are usually easily distinguishable.

Some patients present with intermittent episodes of cramping pain in the calf that may be due to recurrent minor calf muscle strain; this is often the a result of inadequately rehabilitated scar tissue.

The possibility of referred pain from the lumbar spine, or neural or myofascial structures should always be considered as this is sometimes the underlying basis of calf strains, especially in the older sportsperson.[2]

An observational study of pace bowlers in cricket has found an association between calf strains and a history of lumbar stress fractures.[3]

The calf is the most common site in the body for muscle cramps (Chapter 4). Cramps may occur at rest, or during or after exercise. Cramps are not specific to environmental conditions such as exercise in the cold or heat. They can occur in acclimatized and conditioned sportspeople. Cramps probably result from alterations in spinal neural reflex activity activated by fatigue in susceptible individuals.

The calf is also a common site of delayed onset muscle soreness (DOMS) (Chapter 4). This may occur after the first training session following a lay-off or a period of relative rest, or when excessive eccentric muscle contractions are performed, for example, during plyometrics.

Lateral calf pain may be due to a direct blow, referred pain from the superior tibiofibular joint, peroneal muscle strain, or fibula stress fracture.

The causes of calf pain are listed in Table 36.1.

Biomechanical factors may predispose a sportsperson to calf pain. Excessive subtalar pronation may overload the soleus and gastrocnemius muscles as they supinate and plantarflex the foot for propulsion. This can cause muscle tightness and soreness which will have an effect on shock absorption, and therefore may predispose a sportsperson to muscle strain or tendinopathy. Muscle overload can promote muscular hypertrophy, which can predispose to

Table 36.1 Causes of calf pain

Common	Less common	Not to be missed
Muscle strains	Superficial posterior compartment syndrome	Deep venous thrombosis
• Gastrocnemius	Deep posterior compartment syndrome (Chapter 35)	
• Soleus	Referred pain	
• Plantaris	• Lumbar spine	
Muscle contusion	• Myofascial structures	
• Gastrocnemius	• Superior tibiofibular joint	
Muscle cramp	• Knee (Baker's cyst, posterior cruciate ligament, posterior	
Delayed onset muscle	capsular sprain)	
soreness	Vascular entrapment	
	• Popliteal artery	
	• Endofibrosis of external iliac artery	
	Nerve entrapment	
	• Tibial	
	• Sural	
	Stress fracture of the fibula	
	Stress fracture of the posterior cortex of the tibia (Chapter 35)	
	Varicose veins (e.g. superficial thrombosis)	

the development of a compartment syndrome (Chapter 35) and muscle imbalances.

History

The most important aspect of the history is the description of the onset of pain. A sudden onset of a "tearing" or "popping" sensation in the calf is diagnostic of calf muscle strains. The patient is usually able to localize the site of the tear. The degree of disability, both immediately after the injury and subsequently, is a guide to the severity of the tear.

In sportspeople with chronic mild calf pain, a history of a previous acute injury may be significant and is a risk factor for chronic calf injury in marathon runners and soccer referees.[4, 5] The practitioner should ask about the treatment and rehabilitation of the previous injury, as inadequate rehabilitation will have an impact on recurrence rates.

A history of low back pain may be a clue to referred pain. The practitioner should also be alert to the possibility of referred pain if the calf pain is variable rather than constant. If there is no obvious precipitating cause of calf pain, the possibility of deep venous thrombosis after long car or airplane trips, or recent surgery, needs to be explored.

Claudicant pain that comes on with exertion and then disappears may indicate proximal vascular occlusion by atheroma or entrapment (e.g. femoral or iliac artery stenosis, Fig. 7.6) or exertional compartment syndrome. A ruptured Baker's cyst can also cause acute calf pain and swelling, and should be considered as a differential diagnosis (refer to Chapter 34).

A variety of contributing factors can predispose a sportsperson to calf injury. These include:

- foot biomechanics (excessive pronation/supination)
- muscle imbalances (quadriceps, hamstrings, ankle everters and inverters)
- poor jumping and landing technique
- change in sporting environment (terrain, weather)
- poor nutrition and hydration
- change in sporting activity (cycling and swimming compared with running)
- change in footwear
- reduced muscle power, endurance and muscle fatigue.

Examination

The aims of examination in the patient with acute calf strain are to determine the site and the severity of the injury as well as detecting any predisposing factors such as chronic calf tightness. Examination of a patient with chronic or intermittent calf pain requires not only palpation of muscles but also neurodynamic tests (e.g. slump test, Chapter 11), assessment of ankle reflexes, and examination of the lumbar spine. It is important to palpate the entire length and width of the muscle bellies and their associated aponeuroses for areas of muscle and fascial tightness and thickenings that may predispose to injury.

Clinical assessment should include both static and dynamic tests and should be performed in both knee flexion and extension. Comparing calf girth between left and right is also important. Foot alignment and biomechanics should also be considered.

1. Observation
   (a) standing (foot posture, calf girth, swelling)
   (b) walking (on toes, on heels)
   (c) prone
2. Active ankle movements
   (a) plantarflexion/dorsiflexion (standing) (Fig. 36.2a)
   (b) plantarflexion/dorsiflexion (prone)
3. Passive ankle movements
   (a) dorsiflexion (knee flexion) (Fig. 36.2b)
   (b) dorsiflexion (knee extension) (Fig. 36.2c)
   (c) muscle stretch
      (i) gastrocnemius (Fig. 36.2d)
      (ii) soleus (Fig. 36.2e)
4. Resisted movements
   (a) dorsiflexion
5. Functional tests
   (a) hop (on the spot, hop for distance)
   (b) jump (height, shock absorption)
   (c) run
   (d) calf raises (strength, endurance, power)
6. Palpation
   (a) gastrocnemius (Fig. 36.2f) (compare medial and lateral heads)

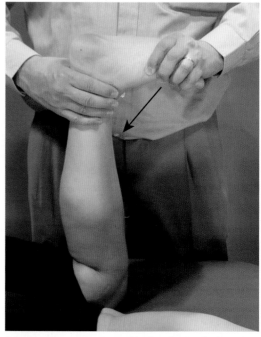

(b) Passive movement—ankle dorsiflexion (knee flexion). Examine with the knee flexed and add overpressure

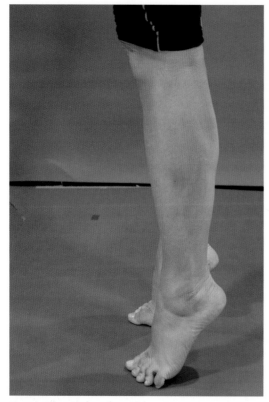

Figure 36.2 Examination of the patient with calf pain
(a) Active movement—plantarflexion/dorsiflexion (standing). The functional competence can be assessed during a bilateral or unilateral heel raise-and-drop until pain is reproduced

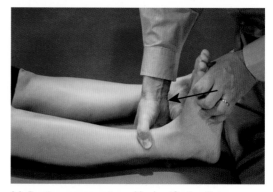

(c) Passive movement—ankle dorsiflexion (knee extension). Examine with the knee extended and add overpressure (Homan's sign)

(b)   soleus
(c)   posterior knee
(d)   superior tibiofibular joint
(e)   Achilles tendon
7. Special tests
(a)   Thompson's/Simmonds' test (Fig. 36.2g)
(b)   Homan's sign (Fig. 36.2c)

(c)   neurodynamic test—slump test (Fig. 36.2h overleaf)

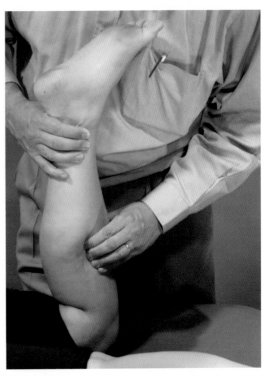

B

(d) Stretch—gastrocnemius (back leg)
Examine with the knee in full extension and the heel on the ground

(e) Stretch—soleus (lunge test)
The patient should flex the knee so that it passes vertically over the third toe to prevent excessive pronation. Record the range of motion and compare both sides

(f) Palpation
The patient should actively contract and relax the muscles and the ankle should be moved passively through dorsiflexion and plantarflexion during palpation. The gastrocnemius may be palpated in the relaxed position by placing the knee in flexion and the ankle in plantarflexion. Feel for swelling and defects in muscle or tendon tissue

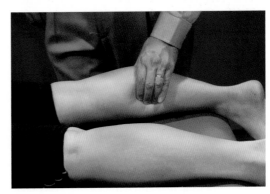

(g) Special test—Thompson's/Simmonds' test
The calf is squeezed. If no ankle plantarflexion occurs, there has been a complete tear of the Achilles tendon or musculotendinous junction

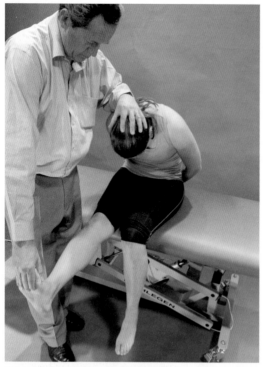

(h) Special test—neurodynamic test (slump test)

(d)   gluteal trigger points
(e)   lumbar spine (Chapter 26)
(f)   biomechanical examination (Chapter 8)
(g)   ankle jerk reflex

Investigations

Although investigations are generally not required in a sportsperson with calf pain, ultrasound or MRI may be useful either for evaluating an injury that is not responding to treatment, or for prognostic purposes in the case of an elite sportsperson. These imaging modalities can localize pathology, identify presence of hematoma and scar tissue, and differentiate between a muscle strain and a contusion if not clinically evident. If deep venous thrombosis is suspected, a Doppler scan may be required.

Gastrocnemius muscle strains

Acute strain

Acute strain of the gastrocnemius muscle occurs typically when the sportsperson attempts to accelerate by extending the knee from a stationary position with the ankle in dorsiflexion, or when lunging forward, such as while playing tennis or squash. Sudden eccentric overstretch, such as when a sportsperson runs onto a kerb and the ankle drops suddenly into dorsiflexion, is another common mechanism.

The medial head of the gastrocnemius has a greater proximal attachment and a longer distal insertion into the Achilles tendon than the lateral head.[1] Therefore the medial head may have a greater capacity for force generation and therefore may be more susceptible to injury compared with the lateral head.

The exact moment of injury was caught on video in the case of a famous Australian batsman whose gastrocnemius strain occurred when his entire body weight was over his foot on the injured side with the center of mass well in front of the leg.[6] The gastrocnemius muscle–tendon complex was at close to maximal length, and the muscle–tendon length was also constant at the time. Therefore, the injury probably occurred just as the muscle–tendon complex was moving from an eccentric to an isometric phase.

The sportsperson with gastrocnemius strain often complains of an acute, stabbing or tearing sensation, usually either in the medial belly of the gastrocnemius or at the musculotendinous junction.

Examination reveals tenderness at the site of muscle strain. Stretching the gastrocnemius reproduces pain (Fig. 36.2d), as does resisted plantarflexion with the knee extended. In grade III muscle tears, there may be a palpable defect.

The functional competence of the injured muscle is assessed by asking the patient to perform a bilateral heel raise. If necessary, a unilateral heel raise, or a heel drop or hop may be used to reproduce the pain and to assess for weakness. This places the muscle under progressively greater load concentrically and eccentrically.

Gastrocnemius strain can be graded as shown in Table 36.2.

The tightness of the muscle itself should be assessed, as overuse can often lead to palpable rope-like bands or local tissue thickening, which may predispose to further injury and compensatory movement patterns leading to muscle imbalances.

Treatment

Initial treatment of gastrocnemius strains aims to reduce pain and swelling. Treatment modalities include the use of ice, compression, electrotherapeutic modalities (e.g. TENS, magnetic field therapy, interferential stimulation) and analgesics. Crutches may be necessary if the sportsperson is unable to bear weight. A 6 mm (¼ in.) heel raise may be used

Table 36.2 Grading of calf strains

Grade	Symptoms	Signs	Average time to return to sport
I	Sharp pain at time of (or after) activity, may be able to continue	Pain on unilateral calf raise or hop	10–12 days
II	Unable to continue activity	Active plantarflexion pain Significant loss of dorsiflexion Bilateral calf raise pain	16–21 days
III	Immediate severe pain at musculotendinous junction	Thompson's test positive Defect palpable	6 months after surgery

(on both the injured and uninjured side) to initially reduce calf length and off-load calf structures.

Gentle stretching of the gastrocnemius to the level of a feeling of tightness (Fig. 36.3) can begin soon after the injury, as well as foot and ankle range of motion exercises. Muscle strengthening should start after 24 hours. This involves a progression of exercises, commencing with concentric bilateral calf raise, followed by unilateral calf raise with the

gradual addition of weights and, finally, eccentric calf lowering over a step gradually increasing speed, then adding weights (Fig. 36.4). Low-impact cross-training such as stationary cycling or swimming can be commenced as soon as pain allows.

When active weight-bearing muscle contraction is pain-free, sustained myofascial tension may be performed on the muscle belly (Fig. 36.5 overleaf) with digital ischemic pressure to focal areas of increased tone and/or tenderness. For favorable

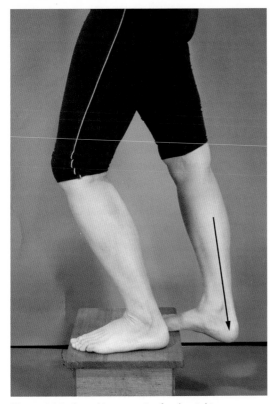

Figure 36.3 Stretching exercise for the right gastrocnemius muscle with the knee in full extension. This can be performed over a step or with the foot placed against a wall to increase the stretch

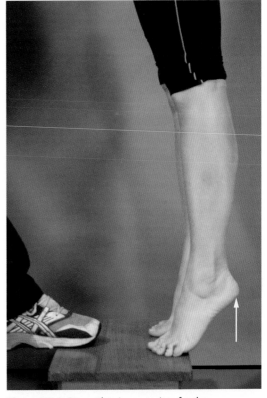

Figure 36.4 Strengthening exercises for the gastrocnemius muscle
(a) Bilateral calf raise

(b) Unilateral calf raise

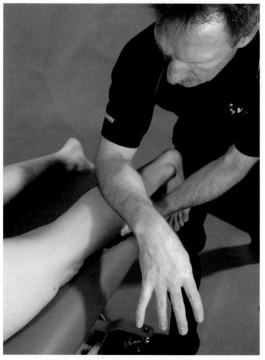

Figure 36.5 Soft tissue therapy—sustained myofascial tension to the muscle belly of the gastrocnemius

(c) Eccentric lowering

long-term results, treatment should address predisposing factors, such as calf muscle tightness, that may arise from poor biomechanics. Sportspeople should undergo a supervised, graduated return to sport program. Progression through weight-bearing activities to graduated running programs should be incorporated. Running programs should include sprint work, change of direction, and change of pace. Eccentric strength programs should be considered.

"Tennis leg"

The term "tennis leg" refers to the clinical presentation of a middle-aged sportsperson with a sports-related sudden onset of severe calf pain and significant disability. Mechanism of injury is forced knee extension with the foot in dorsiflexion.[7, 8] This injury is often associated with a characteristic popping sound, and has extensive bruising and swelling, especially in the first 24 hours.

Initially, tennis leg was attributed to the rupture of the plantaris muscle. However, surgical and ultrasound observational studies have reported a low incidence of plantaris muscle involvement (less than 2% of clinical presentations).[7–9]

Tennis leg represents partial or full rupture of the medial head of gastrocnemius, commonly at the musculotendinous junction.

Fluid collection between the gastrocnemius and the soleus aponeurosis is sometimes present and can be found on ultrasound investigation.[7, 8] Ultrasound investigation can rule out differential diagnoses such as deep vein thrombosis.

Treatment is conservative with the RICE method (Chapter 13) and analgesic medication, if indicated. Rehabilitation should then progress to strengthening and lengthening exercises of the calf complex. Return to sport may take a few months.

Fibrotic tissue between the gastrocnemius and soleus muscles has been described on follow-up ultrasound investigations.[8] This fibrotic tissue may increase the risk of recurrence. Surgical intervention is only indicated when the presentation is associated with compartment syndrome.[7]

Chronic strain

Chronic gastrocnemius muscle strain may occur as an overuse injury or following inadequate rehabilitation of an acute injury. Inadequate rehabilitation results in disorganized, weak scar tissue that is susceptible to further injury.

The key to successful treatment is progressive concentric and eccentric strengthening to promote tissue repair. For eccentric strengthening, patients should perform three sets of 15 heel drops (with a straight knee (Fig. 36.4c), and also with a bent knee) twice a day, seven days a week.[12] The intensity of the exercise can be progressed by adding hand weights.

Treatment should also include transverse friction and longitudinal gliding soft tissue therapy at the site of excessive scar tissue and along the entire musculotendinous unit. Stretching exercises will restore normal muscle length and should be held for at least 15 seconds.[10]

A systematic review of calf stretching on ankle dorsiflexion range of motion found an improvement of up to 2°–3°[11] but whether a 2°–3° change in range of motion is clinically relevant is not known.

Soleus muscle strains

The soleus muscle contains a high proportion of type II, slow-twitch muscle fibers, unlike the gastrocnemius, which contains a higher proportion of type I, fast-twitch muscle fibers. This allows the soleus muscle to have a significant role in posture control (especially in standing).

Strain of the soleus muscle is a relatively common sports injury and can be associated with gastrocnemius and other deep crural muscle strains.[1] Although patients with soleus strains can present with sudden onset pain, they commonly report a history of increasing calf tightness over a period of days or weeks. Often walking and jogging are more painful than sprinting.

The medial third of the fibers of the soleus and its aponeurosis are prone to becoming hard and inflexible, particularly in sportspeople with excessive subtalar pronation. This focal tissue can be more susceptible to strain, especially at its junction with adjacent "normal" tissue. Therefore, careful assessment by palpation as well as assessment of foot biomechanics is essential.

Examination often reveals tenderness deep to the gastrocnemius, usually in the lateral aspect of the soleus muscle, unlike isolated gastrocnemius strains which have a higher frequency of medial calf involvement. Often, both the soleus stretch (Fig. 36.2e) and resisted soleus contraction reproduce the sportsperson's pain. This can be differentiated from the stretch and contraction that provoke pain in gastrocnemius strains (Fig. 36.2d).

Treatment of soleus muscle strains is similar to gastrocnemius strains above. In the initial stages, the use of heel raises and stretching with the knee flexed (lunge position) are commonplace. After the initial acute stage, soft tissue therapy is often directed at the site of the lesion as well as tissue proximally and distally (Fig. 36.6 overleaf). Strengthening exercises are performed with the knee flexed (Fig. 36.7 overleaf). If foot biomechanics are assessed to be a predisposing factor to injury, orthoses may be required.

Accessory soleus

The soleus accessory muscle is a relatively rare (0.7–5.5%) anatomical variant and is bilateral in 10% of cases. It appears as a soft tissue mass bulging medially between the distal part of the tibia and the Achilles tendon, and may be mistaken for a tumor or an inflammatory lesion.[13] Sportspeople may have a fullness on inspection of their Achilles region from behind.

It may be asymptomatic (25%) or associated with chronic exertional compartment syndrome or posterior tibial nerve compression (tarsal tunnel

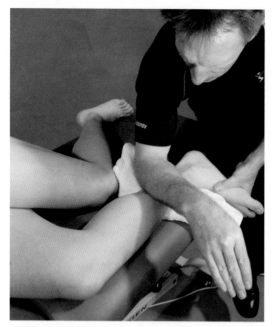

Figure 36.6 Soft tissue therapy—sustained myofascial tension to the soleus muscle

Figure 36.7 Strengthening exercises for the soleus muscle—calf raise with bent knee. This can be made more difficult by adding weights or having the patient drop down over the end of a step

syndrome). Sportspeople can present with ankle pain and soft tissue swelling.[14, 15]

Presentation is usually during adolescence—a stage of maturity associated with rapid muscle hypertrophy. Rapid muscle hypertrophy can lead to compartment type syndrome, posterior tibial nerve compression, tendinopathy, and/or partial accessory muscle strain.[14, 15]

X-ray generally shows soft tissue swelling between the deep compartment and the Achilles tendon, which obscures or obliterates Kager's triangle on a lateral radiograph of the ankle. The appearance of normal muscle on MRI allows the clinician to distinguish it from both abnormal muscle and soft tissue tumors.[14, 16] Additionally, MRI may show intrafascial fluid collection and perimuscular edema which have been associated with a symptomatic accessory soleus muscle.[15]

Asymptomatic cases require no treatment. If pain or discomfort is present, conservative treatment is trialed. Conservative treatment can include soft tissue therapy, stretching and strengthening of the calf muscles, and improvement of ankle range if it is limited.[14] Surgery (involving either fasciotomy alone or with excision of the accessory muscle) is recommended when conservative measures fail.[13, 14]

Less common causes
Vascular causes
Vascular causes of exercise-induced lower limb pain are uncommon and difficult to diagnose. The pain of vascular entrapment is difficult to differentiate from that caused by compartment syndrome and nerve entrapment, although there are subtle differences in the relationship of the pain to the bout of exercise. Post-exercise examination of the peripheral pulses and arterial bruits is vital and the diagnosis can be confirmed by Doppler ultrasound, ankle–brachial ratios and angiography. It may also be important to perform compartment pressure tests and nerve conduction studies to rule out coexisting conditions.

Popliteal artery entrapment
Popliteal artery entrapment syndrome is often not recognized, and so misdiagnosed as a compartment syndrome.[17, 18] The syndrome was first described as a cause of exercise-induced leg pain in 1879. There are two types of popliteal artery entrapment syndrome—anatomical and functional (acquired).

The classically described anatomical (congenital) abnormality is a variation in the anatomical relationship between the popliteal artery as it exits the popliteal fossa and the medial head of the gastrocnemius muscle. Popliteal artery entrapment syndrome can be classified into six categories according to the anatomical relationship between the popliteal artery and the adjacent muscular or fibrous bands in the popliteal fossa.[18-20]

The commonest abnormality describes an abnormal medial head of the gastrocnemius muscle, the accessory part of which is observed to pass behind the popliteal artery. Other observed abnormalities include a tendinous slip arising from the medial head of the muscle, an abnormal plantaris muscle, and multiple muscle abnormalities involving the lateral and medial heads of the gastrocnemius and the plantaris. Rarer anatomical variations of popliteal artery entrapment syndrome include entrapment of the artery at the level of the adductor hiatus, and an isolated entrapment of the anterior tibial artery as it passes through the interosseous membrane.

The term "functional" or "acquired" popliteal artery entrapment syndrome was first described by Rignault et al. in 1985,[21] and describes a situation where no anatomical abnormality is visible at surgical exploration. It is hypothesized that muscle contraction (active plantarflexion of the ankle) compresses the artery between muscle and the underlying bone. This may explain why the syndrome is commonly seen in healthy young sportspeople and military recruits with hypertrophied gastrocnemius muscles.[17, 19]

Differentiating artery entrapment from chronic compartment syndrome

With artery entrapment, cessation of exercise brings about rapid relief from the pain. This compares with the classic pain pattern of compartment syndrome, which is related to the volume of exercise and tends to settle over a period of approximately half an hour after stopping exercise. If exercise is attempted on consecutive days, the pain from a compartment syndrome is often more severe on the second day. The pain from popliteal artery entrapment syndrome is unaffected by the exercise on the previous day. The pain with artery entrapment can be paradoxically more severe on walking than on running. This is believed to be due to the more prolonged contraction of the gastrocnemius muscle while walking.

Clinically, sportspeople present with claudication-type pain in the calf or the anterior aspect of the leg, which can be bilateral. The pain is brought on by exercise, and the severity of the symptoms is related to the intensity of exercise. Approximately ten percent of sportspeople with popliteal artery entrapment syndrome present with signs and symptoms of either acute or chronic limb ischemia with paresthesia, discoloration of the foot and toes, temperature change, rest pain, and tissue necrosis.[22]

Examination of the distal pulses (dorsalis pedis and posterior tibial) may be unremarkable at rest. Assessing the pulses while the sportsperson actively plantarflexes or passively dorsiflexes the ankle may reveal a popliteal artery bruit; however, this may be unreliable.[19] Examining the sportsperson immediately post exercise is important in making the diagnosis. Immediately post exercise, a popliteal artery bruit may be heard and the peripheral pulses will be either weak, decreased or absent.

Non-invasive investigations include post-exercise ankle–brachial pressures and Doppler ultrasound; however, these investigations are limited in their identification of abnormalities of soft tissue constraints. Angiography can rule out differential diagnoses such as aneurysms and emboli, and can be performed while the sportsperson actively plantarflexes, and actively and passively dorsiflexes the ankle.[19, 20] There appears to be a significantly high rate of false positive tests using this method.

CT scans can quantify diameter of the popliteal artery and its relationship to adjacent structures. MRI and MR angiography may be more useful with multiplanar views, non-ionizing radiation, and high soft tissue contrast.[19]

There is some suggestion that the presence of chronic entrapment of the popliteal artery can lead to endothelial damage, which may lead to accelerated atherosclerotic disease in later life. Therefore, early surgical treatment is recommended to prevent the development of popliteal artery damage and the need for grafting.[23] Surgery aims to either release the entrapment or re-establish vascular patency and often involves open exploration of the popliteal fossa with division of the offending fascial or tendinous band.

Atherosclerotic vessel disease

Atherosclerotic vessel disease classically affects middle-aged sedentary patients. However, some sportspeople, particularly in the veteran or masters class, fall into the category of middle-aged or elderly, and possess risk factors that predispose them to atherosclerosis.

Pain may be felt in the thigh or the calf and is typically claudicant. With progression of the disease, less exercise is needed to produce symptoms. At rest, the peripheral pulses may be difficult to palpate or absent, and an arterial bruit may be heard. The presence of bruits may be enhanced by examining the patient post exercise.

Doppler ultrasound is the gold standard diagnostic test, although pre- and post-exercise ankle–brachial ratios can be used as a screening test. Angiography can confirm the diagnosis.

Surgical treatments include angiographic balloon catheter dilatation or stenting, open endarterectomy, or bypass surgery. Bypass surgery is the most commonly used surgical technique; its success depends on the extent of the disease and on the viability of the smaller distal vessels.

Endofibrosis

Endofibrotic disease can cause exercise-related calf pain, although more commonly the pain is felt in the thigh (Chapter 31 on page 621). Typically the lesion occurs in the proximal external iliac artery; however, it may extend distally towards the origin of the femoral artery beneath the inguinal ligament. It is bilateral in 15% of cases.

External iliac artery endofibrosis has been described in endurance sportspeople and professional cyclists, and causes exercise-related thigh or calf pain that is related to the intensity of cycling.[24, 25] The pain is therefore most commonly felt while racing, climbing a hill, or riding into a strong wind. The pain is typically relieved rapidly by a drop in the intensity of exercise.

In cyclists, it is postulated that the cycling position may cause repetitive stress and folding of the artery during high flow rates associated with extreme exercise. As a result, micro-traumatic lesions lead to thickening of arterial walls.[25] Hypertrophy of the psoas muscle may also have a direct effect on the stresses around the external iliac artery.

Examination at rest may reveal a positional bruit heard over the femoral artery, when the hip is held in flexion. The diagnosis is made clinically by examining the patient immediately post exercise, detecting a bruit over the femoral artery, and weak or absent distal pulses. Pre- and post-exercise ankle–brachial ratios screen for the diagnosis, which is anatomically confirmed with angiography. Arterial ultrasound

or echography can also be useful in visualizing the endofibrotic lesion.

Non-surgical techniques for the treatment of external iliac artery endofibrosis include angioplastic balloon catheter dilatation and stenting, which can be planned for and performed at the time of angiography. Surgical techniques include bypass surgery and open endarterectomy. In the short term, use of these techniques has allowed some sportspeople to return to top level cycling and triathlon;[26] however, long-term follow-up of such patients has not been reported.

The natural history of this pathology is not certain. Abraham et al. suggest that it is non-progressive once high-level sport is ceased.[27] They advise that a sportsperson who is reducing his or her sporting level and who is asymptomatic with activities of daily living and submaximal exercise should be managed conservatively but followed up regularly.

Referred pain

The neural component of calf pain can be assessed with the use of the slump test (Fig. 36.2h). This may reproduce the patient's calf pain. If pain is relieved by cervical extension, neural structures may be contributing to the patient's pain.

The most common source of referred pain is myofascial trigger points in the gluteal muscles. Myofascial pain may present as an episode of sudden sharp pain and mimic a calf strain, or may present as pain of more gradual onset accompanied by tightness, or as muscle cramps. Treatment consists of ischemic pressure or dry needling to the trigger points followed by muscle and neural stretching.

The joints of the lumbar spine may occasionally refer pain to the calf. This should be suspected clinically if the pain is somewhat variable in location or if there is a history of recurrent "calf strains."

The knee joint may also refer pain to the calf (Chapter 34). This may be due to a Baker's cyst, or a posterior cruciate ligament injury. Bleeding may track down into the calf from a strain of the posterior capsule of the knee joint or a popliteus muscle injury.

Nerve entrapments

Nerve entrapments around the calf include tibial nerve entrapment (rare) secondary to a Baker's cyst; popliteal artery aneurysm or ganglion resulting in ankle inverter and toe flexor weakness and paresthesia to the sole of the foot; and sural nerve entrapment, which may result from compression (ski boots, casts), mass lesions, trauma, or thrombophlebitis causing pain and paresthesia in the lateral heel and foot.

The sural nerve may be compressed in a fibrous arch that thickens the superficial sural aponeurosis around the opening through which the nerve passes. Intense physical training may lead to an increase in the sural muscle mass, which in turn compromises the sural nerve in its trajectory through the unyielding and inextensible superficial sural aponeurosis. The nerve may also become trapped in scar tissue.[28]

Investigations can include nerve conduction studies and MR imaging to look for a space-occupying lesion. Management includes conservative measures such as neural gliding, fascial massage, or corticosteroid injections. If conservative measures fail, surgical exploration and/or neurolysis can be considered.

Superficial compartment syndrome

Patients with superficial posterior compartment syndrome, the least common of the lower leg compartment syndromes, present with calf pain. The superficial compartment contains the gastrocnemius and soleus muscles enclosed in a fascial sheath. Symptoms are similar to those of the other compartment syndromes, with pain aggravated by activity and relieved by rest. An elevated compartment pressure confirms the diagnosis during and after exercise (Table 35.3). Treatment consists of soft tissue therapy or, if this is unsuccessful, surgery.

Patients with either deep posterior compartment syndrome or stress fracture involving the posterior cortex of the tibia may present with calf pain instead of, or as well as, shin pain (Chapter 35).

Conditions not to be missed

Deep venous thrombosis (DVT) occurs occasionally in association with calf injuries. The post-injury combination of lack of movement, disuse of the muscle pump, and the compressive effect of swelling may all lead to venous dilatation, pooling, and a decrease in the velocity of blood flow. Certainly sportspeople who sustain a calf muscle injury should avoid long airplane flights in the days after injury.

Deep venous thrombosis is seen rarely after arthroscopy.[29] After uncomplicated anterior cruciate ligament (ACL) knee reconstruction, deep venous thrombosis and pulmonary embolus proved fatal in an otherwise healthy 30-year-old.[29] The diagnosis should be suspected when the patient has constant calf pain, tenderness, increased temperature, and swelling. Homan's sign (passive dorsiflexion) is positive (Fig. 36.2c). The presence of deep venous thrombosis can be confirmed by Doppler scan and venography.

B

REFERENCES

1. Koulouris G, Ting AYI, Jhamb A et al. Magnetic resonance imaging findings of injuries to the calf muscle complex. *Skeletal Radiol* 2007;36:921–7.

2. Orchard JW, Farhart P, Leopold C. Lumbar spine region pathology and hamstring and calf injuries in athletes: is there a connection? *Br J Sports Med* 2004;38:502–4.

3. Orchard J, Farhart P, Kountouris A et al. Pace bowlers in cricket with history of lumbar stress fracture have increased risk of lower limb muscle strains, particularly calf strains. *Open Access J Sports Med* 2010;1:177–82.

4. Van Middelkoop M, Kolkman J, Van Ochten J et al. Risk factors for lower extremity injuries among male marathon runners. *Scand J Med Sci Sports* 2008;18(6):691–7.

5. Bizzini M, Junge A, Bahr R et al. Injuries and musculoskeletal complaints in referees and assistant referees selected for the 2006 FIFA World Cup: retrospective and prospective survey. *Br J Sports Med* 2009;43(7):490–7.

6. Orchard J, Alcott E, James T et al. Exact moment of a gastrocnemius muscle strain captured on video. *Br J Sports Med* 2002;36:222–3.

7. Delgado GJ, Chung CB, Lektrakul N et al. Tennis leg: clinical US study of 141 patients and anatomic investigation of four cadavers with MR imaging and US. *Radiology* 2002;224(1):112–19.

8. Kwak HS, Han YM, Lee SY et al. Diagnosis and follow-up US evaluation of ruptures of the medial head of the gastrocnemius ("tennis leg"). *Korean J Radiol* 2006;7(3):193–8.

9. Severance HJ, Basset FH. Rupture of the plantaris: does it exist? *J Bone Joint Surg Am* 1983;65:1387–8.

10. Roberts JM, Wilson K. Effects of stretching duration on active and passive range of motion in the lower extremity. *Br J Sports Med* 1999;33:259–63.

11. Radford JA, Burns J, Buchbinder R et al. Does stretching increase ankle dorsiflexion range of motion? A systematic review. *Br J Sports Med* 2006;40:870–5.

12. Alfredson H, Pietila T, Jonsson P et al. Heavy-load eccentric calf muscle training for the treatment of chronic achilles tendinosis. *Am J Sports Med* 1998;26(3):360–6.

13. Christodoulou A, Terzidis I, Natsis K et al. Soleus accessorius, an anomalous muscle in a young athlete: case report and analysis of the literature. *Br J Sports Med* 2004;38(6):e38.

14. Rossi R, Bonasia DE, Tron A et al. Accessory soleus in the athletes: literature review and case report of a massive muscle in a soccer player. *Knee Surg Sports Traumatol Arthrosc* 2009;17:990–5.

15. Doda N, Peh WC, Chawla A. Symptomatic accessory soleus muscle: diagnosis and follow-up on magnetic resonance imaging. *Br J Radiol* 2006;79(946): e129–32.

16. Buschmann WR, Cheung Y, Jahss MH. Magnetic resonance imaging of anomalous leg muscles: accessory soleus, peroneus quartus and the flexor digitorum longus accessorius. *Foot Ankle* 1991;12: 109–16.

17. Stager A, Clement D. Popliteal artery entrapment syndrome. *Sports Med* 1999;28(1):61–70.

18. Turnipseed WD. Functional popliteal artery entrapment syndrome: a poorly understood and often missed diagnosis that is frequently mistreated. *J Vasc Surg* 2009;49:1189–95.

19. O'Leary DP, O'Brien G, Fulton G. Popliteal artery entrapment syndrome. *Internat J Surg Case Rep* 2010;1(2):13–15.

20. McAree BJ, O'Donnell ME, Davison GW et al. Bilateral popliteal artery occlusion in a competitive bike rider: case report and clinical review. *Vasc Endovasc Surg* 2008;42(4):380–85.

21. Rignault DP, Pailler JL, Lunerl F. The "functional" popliteal entrapment syndrome. *Int Angiol* 1985;4: 341–8.

22. Barbaras AP. Popliteal artery entrapment syndrome. *Br J Hosp Med* 1985;34(5):304.

23. Baltopoulos P, Fillipou DK, Sigala F. Popliteal artery entrapment syndrome. Anatomic or functional syndrome? *Clin J Sport Med* 2004;14:8–12.

24. Willson TD, Revesz E, Podbielski FJ et al. External iliac artery dissection secondary to endofibrosis in a cyclist. *J Vasc Surg* 2010;52(1):219–21.

25. Smith WB, Olmsted KA, Zierler ER. Iliac artery endofibrosis in athletes: a case series. *J Vasc Ultrasound* 2008;32:193–99.

26. Giannoukas A, Berczi V, Anoop U et al. Endofibrosis of iliac arteries in high-performance athletes: diagnostic

approach and minimally invasive endovascular treatment. *CardioVasc Intervent Radiol* 2006;29(5): 866–9.

27. Abraham P, Bouye P, Quere I et al. Past, present and future of arterial endofibrosis in athletes. *Sports Med* 2004;34(7):419–25.

28. Fabre T, Montero C, Gaujard E et al. Chronic calf pain in athletes due to sural nerve entrapment. *Am J Sports Med*. 2000;28(5):679–82.

29. Jaureguito JW, Greenwald AE, Wilcox JF et al. The incidence of deep venous thrombosis after arthroscopic knee surgery. *Am J Sports Med* 1999;27:707–10.

B

Chapter 37

Pain in the Achilles region

with HÅKAN ALFREDSON, JILL COOK, KARIN SILBERNAGEL, and JON KARLSSON

Overcoming what was deemed impossible is what I will take with me and cherish the most ... That (coming back from injury) will be the number-one thing that stands out because I wasn't even able to walk. Olympic 100 meter sprint champion Donovan Bailey referring to his successful rehabilitation from Achilles tendon rupture—suffered playing pickup basketball. After rehabilitation, he ran sub-10 seconds for the 100 meters.
Modified from www.cbc.ca

The Achilles tendon is prone to injury with repeated high loads, and runners have a 15 times greater risk of Achilles tendon rupture, and 30 times greater risk of tendinopathy than do sedentary controls.[1] Potentially even more concerning, Achilles—the legendary warrior and hero of Homer's Iliad—died as a result of an injury to the midportion of his tendon. Despite these concerning facts, today's patient with a painful presentation in this region usually has a good long-term prognosis, even for demanding activities such as running and court sports.[2]

In this chapter, we review relevant anatomy, provide a clinical perspective (history, examination, investigation), and then share clinically useful, evidence-based treatments for pain in and about the Achilles region according to the following clinical scenarios:

- pain in the midportion region of the Achilles tendon
- pain at the insertion of the Achilles tendon and the calcaneum ("enthesis organ")
- Achilles tendon rupture
- posterior impingement (an important differential diagnosis).

Functional anatomy

The key areas of pain in the Achilles region (posterior heel and proximal toward the calf) are illustrated in Figure 37.1. The Achilles tendon, the thickest and strongest tendon in the human body,[3]

is the combined tendon of the gastrocnemius and soleus muscles. The tendon has no synovial sheath but has a posterior peritendon (also known as paratenon), which is continuous with the perimysium of the muscle and the periosteum of the calcaneus.

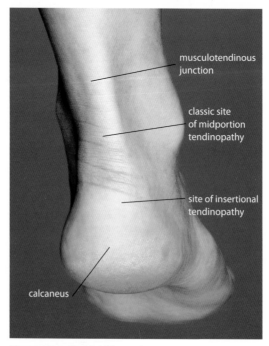

musculotendinous junction

classic site of midportion tendinopathy

site of insertional tendinopathy

calcaneus

Figure 37.1 The Achilles region
(a) Surface anatomy

talus approximates the Achilles, often with a bursa between. This area can become symptomatic (insertional Achilles pathology) if a person has a large and rather square-shaped calcaneum.

Clinical perspective

Overuse Achilles tendon injuries—tendinopathies—may arise with increased training volume or intensity; however, they can also arise insidiously among those who are relatively inactive. Chapter 5 details the pathology[4] that underlies the common tendinopathies. We recommend the reader review the "A contemporary model of a continuum of tendon pathology" outlined in Chapter 5 (Fig. 5.14 on page 36) which provides a clinical framework that helps to guide treatment options.

In patients presenting with Achilles region symptoms, the clinician should:

1. distinguish between midportion Achilles tendinopathy and insertional tendinopathy, as treatment differs slightly but importantly
2. consider the possibility of complete tendon rupture, and make that diagnosis, if appropriate
3. consider differential diagnoses (including systemic conditions and posterior impingement) (see Table 37.1 overleaf).

The site of pain and swelling can help the clinician distinguish midportion from insertional Achilles pathologies. Also, some functional tests are more painful for midportion than insertional disease and vice versa.

If the presentation is one of acute injury—a sudden severe sensation (sometimes pain) and loss of function—acute tendon rupture is the most likely diagnoses. This condition is most prevalent among men aged 30–50 years (mean age of occurrence is 40 years).

Many textbooks suggest that rupture prevents active weight-bearing plantarflexion of the affected leg—however, the patient can often plantarflex weakly when non-weight-bearing using intact accessory plantar flexors. The key diagnostic test is the "calf-squeeze test" (also called "Simmonds'" or "Thompson's" test) (Fig. 37.2i on page 782).

The main differential diagnoses of gradual-onset Achilles region pain arise from neighboring anatomy. These pathologies cause pain in and also *around* the Achilles tendon; true tendon pain is almost always confined to the tendon itself.

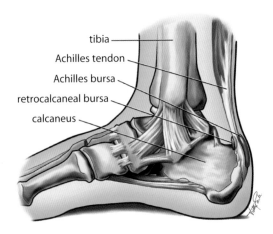

(b) Anatomy

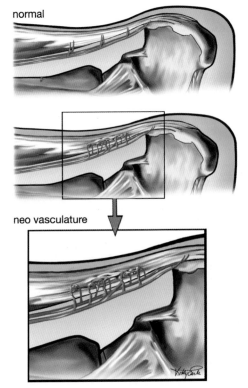

normal

neo vasculature

(c) Stylized and magnified depiction to illustrate abnormal vasculature in Achilles tendinopathy

Anteriorly, the deep surface of the tendon is supported by a fat pad through which the vessels and nerves enter the tendon (Fig. 37.1c). The sural nerve is close to the tendon through its length on the lateral side. The tendon attaches to the inferior half of the calcaneus. The posterosuperior process of the

The combination of morning stiffness and pain is a hallmark of Achilles tendinopathy. If this symptom is absent, the clinician should consider alternative diagnoses.

The Achilles bursa, which lies between the insertion of the Achilles tendon and the skin, can produce pain independent of Achilles tendon injury (Fig. 37.1b). The posterior process of the talus or a discrete anatomical variant, the os trigonum, can be involved in posterior impingement syndrome (p. 800). This occurs most commonly in ballet dancers and occasionally in sprinters and in football players. Other, much less common, differential diagnoses include dislocation of the peroneal tendons, an accessory soleus muscle, irritation or neuroma of the sural nerve, and systemic inflammatory disease. In adolescents, Sever's disease—apophysitis at the insertion of the Achilles tendon into the calcaneus—is the most common diagnosis (Chapter 42). Referred pain, without associated diffuse upper and/or lower leg pain, is a very rare cause of Achilles region pain.

History

The sportsperson with overuse tendinopathy notices a gradual development of symptoms and typically complains of pain and morning stiffness. "Inciting" factors (Chapter 9) include relatively sudden excessive overload (e.g. more distance, different surface, different training techniques). Less commonly, return to loading after a layoff for another injury is the catalyst for pain to start. Pain diminishes with walking about or applying heat (e.g. a hot shower). In most cases, pain diminishes during training, only to recur several hours afterwards.

The onset of pain is usually more sudden in a partial tear of the Achilles tendon. In this uncommon condition, pain and inhibition may be disabling for a shorter period. As partial tears occur in an area of overuse tendinopathy (i.e. in an area of existing pathology), we do not emphasize the distinction other than to suggest that recovery may take longer in cases of partial tear. A history of a sudden, severe pain in the Achilles region with marked disability suggests a complete rupture. The patient often reports hearing a noise like a shot or feeling like having been kicked on the tendon.

Examination

If the Achilles tendon seems to be the cause of pain, and you are confident that the tendon is intact, the examination should begin with the patient standing and the clinician assessing how the patient copes with tasks that load the tendon and likely provoke pain. In most patients, simple single-leg heel raises cause pain. In more active individuals, you may need to ask the patient to hop on the spot, or hop forward, to further load the tendon and reproduce pain. In some sportspeople, repeated loading tests (i.e. multiple hops, jumps) or examination after a training session may be needed to fully evaluate the tendon. It is critical to note not only the function of the calf and Achilles tendon, but also how the lower limb kinetic chain is performing. Longer-term symptoms can cause substantial unloading ("favoring" the unaffected side) and alter the function of the entire kinetic chain.

Functional tests provide a baseline against which to compare response to treatment response and to objectively monitor how the tendon copes with load. The Victorian Institute of Sport Assessment—Achilles (VISA-A) scale can be used to monitoring the clinical progress of Achilles tendinopathy[5] (Table 37.2). This simple questionnaire takes less than 5 minutes to complete and once patients are familiar with it they can complete it themselves. It is sensitive to longer term change and should be administered monthly rather than daily or weekly.

Table 37.1 Causes of pain in the Achilles region

Common	Less common	Not to be missed
Midportion Achilles tendinopathy (this includes tendinosis, paratendonitis, and partial tears)	Achilles bursitis	Achilles tendon rupture
	Accessory soleus muscle	Achilles tendinopathy
	Referred pain	due to the inflammatory
Posterior impingement syndrome	• Neural structures	arthropathies (Chapter 55)
Insertional Achilles tendinopathy including retrocalcaneal bursitis and Haglund's disease	• Lumbar spine	
Sever's disease (adolescents)		

Table 37.2 Victorian Institute of Sport Assessment—Achilles (VISA-A) questionnaire

1. For how many minutes do you have stiffness in the Achilles region on first getting up?   POINTS

    100 min | | | | | | | | | | | 0 min

    0   1   2   3   4   5   6   7   8   9   10

2. Once you have warmed up for the day, do you have pain when stretching the Achilles tendon fully over the edge of a step? (keeping knee straight)   POINTS

    Strong severe pain | | | | | | | | | | | No pain

    0   1   2   3   4   5   6   7   8   9   10

3. After walking on flat ground for 30 minutes, do you have pain within the next 2 hours? (If unable to walk on flat ground for 30 minutes because of pain, score 0 for this question.)   POINTS

    Strong severe pain | | | | | | | | | | | No pain

    0   1   2   3   4   5   6   7   8   9   10

4. Do you have pain walking down stairs with normal gait cycle?   POINTS

    Strong severe pain | | | | | | | | | | | No pain

    0   1   2   3   4   5   6   7   8   9   10

5. Do you have pain during or immediately after doing 10 (single-leg) heel raises from a flat surface?   POINTS

    Strong severe pain | | | | | | | | | | | No pain

    0   1   2   3   4   5   6   7   8   9   10

6. How many single-leg hops can you do without pain?   POINTS

    0 | | | | | | | | | | | 10

    0   1   2   3   4   5   6   7   8   9   10

7. Are you currently undertaking sport or other physical activity?   POINTS

    0 ☐ Not at all
    4 ☐ Modified training ± modified competition
    7 ☐ Full training ± competition but not at same level as when symptoms began
    10 ☐ Competing at the same or higher level as when symptoms began

8. Please complete *either* A, B or C in this question.
    - If you have no pain while undertaking Achilles tendon loading sports, please complete Q8A only.
    - If you have pain while undertaking Achilles tendon loading sports but it does not stop you from completing the activity, please complete Q8B only.
    - If you have pain that stops you from completing Achilles tendon loading sports, please complete Q8C only.

    A. If you have no pain while undertaking Achilles tendon loading sports, for how long can you train/practice?   POINTS

	Nil		1–10 min		11–20 min		21–30 min		>30 min
	0		7		14		21		30

    B. If you have some pain while undertaking Achilles tendon loading sports but it does not stop you from completing your training/practice, for how long can you train/practice?   POINTS

	Nil		1–10 min		11–20 min		21–30 min		>30 min
	0		4		10		14		20

    C. If you have pain that stops you from completing your training/practice in the Achilles tendon loading sports, for how long can you train/practice?   POINTS

	Nil		1–10 min		11–20 min		21–30 min		>30 min
	0		2		5		7		10

    TOTAL SCORE | | /100

After assessing function, seek possible predisposing factors, such as unilateral calf tightness, joint stiffness at the ankle or subtalar joints, and abnormal lower limb biomechanics (Chapter 8). Finally, palpate the painful area for tenderness, crepitus (a "crackling" feeling that arises because of the fibrinous exudate in the peritendon), and tendon thickening.

Thus, examination involves:

1. Observation
   (a) standing and walking
   (b) functional tests
       (i) plantarflexion—double- and single-leg calf raises
       (ii) hopping/forward hopping (if indicated) (Fig. 37.2a)
   (c) biomechanics (see also Chapter 8 for the general biomechanical assessment)
       (i) active dorsiflexion (lunge)
       (ii) gastrocnemius stretch (Fig. 37.2b)
       (iii) soleus stretch (Fig. 37.2c)
2. Supine/prone
   (a) active movements (only useful if rupture suspected)
       (i) plantarflexion and dorsiflexion
   (b) passive movements

(b) Passive movement—muscle stretch (gastrocnemius). The patient stands so that body weight causes overpressure. The knee must remain extended and the heel remains in contact with the floor. The foot remains in neutral by keeping the patella in line with the third metatarsal. Compare the stretch on both sides

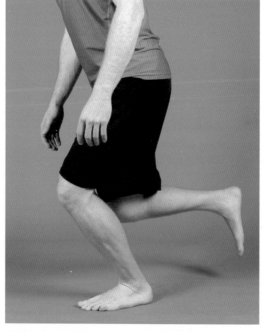

Figure 37.2 Examination of the patient with pain in the Achilles region
(a) Functional tests. These can be used to reproduce pain, if necessary, or to test strength. Tests include double-leg and single-leg calf raises, hops (illustrated), hops forward, eccentric drops and lunge

(c) Passive movement—muscle stretch (soleus) The patient stands upright and keeps the knee flexed. The foot should remain in a neutral position

(i) plantarflexion with and without overpressure (Fig. 37.2d)
(ii) subtalar joint

(iii) dorsiflexion
(iv) inversion and eversion (Fig. 37.2e)
(c) palpation
  (i) Achilles midtendon (Fig. 37.2f)
  (ii) Achilles insertion (Fig. 37.2g)
  (iii) posterior talus
  (iv) calf muscle
3. Special tests
  (a) inspection of resting tone for tendon rupture (Fig. 37.2h)
  (b) Thompson's/Simmonds' calf squeeze test[6] (Fig. 37.2i overleaf)

B

(d) Passive movement—plantarflexion
This will be painful if posterior impingement is present. Overpressure can be applied

(g) Palpation (prone)—Achilles insertion
Carefully palpate the tendon and the retrocalcaneal bursa(e) for tenderness

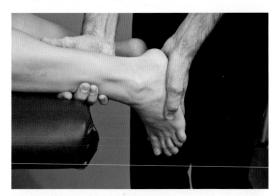

(e) Inversion and eversion

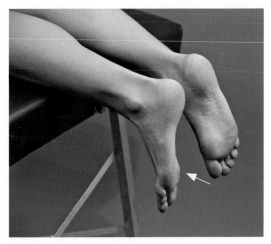

(h) Special test—inspect for Achilles tendon rupture
In many instances, Achilles tendon rupture is an "end of the bed" diagnosis. In many (but not all) cases of Achilles tendon rupture, the affected foot hangs more vertically when the patient is prone (arrow). The unaffected side is held in slight plantarflexion by resting calf tone—even when the patient is fully relaxed

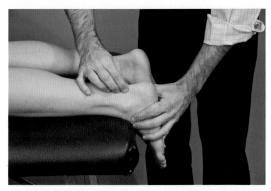

(f) Palpation (prone)—Achilles midtendon
Palpate the site of pain. Palpate the tendon and paratenon while the tendon moves to determine which structure is involved. Determine whether the focus of tenderness is in the midportion of the tendon

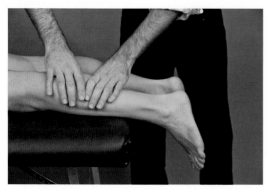 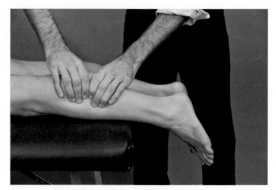

(i) Special test—Thompson's/Simmonds' calf squeeze test for Achilles tendon rupture.
The practitioner squeezes the fleshy part of the calf. The test is positive if the foot fails to plantarflex

Investigations

Plain radiographs are of limited value but, if symptoms are longstanding, radiographs may reveal a Haglund's deformity—a prominent superior projection of the calcaneus (Fig. 37.3a)—or spurs projecting into the tendon. This is associated with insertional tendinopathy and retrocalcaneal bursitis. Calcification in the tendon itself or at the insertion (Fig. 37.3b) can be asymptomatic; symptomatic patients can be managed according to the symptoms of tendinopathy. Posterior impingement can be shown on plain X-ray (Fig. 37.15 on page 800).

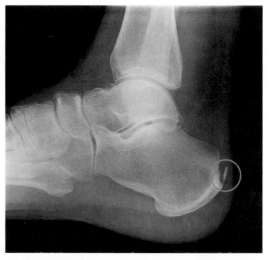

(b) Calcification in the insertion of the Achilles tendon

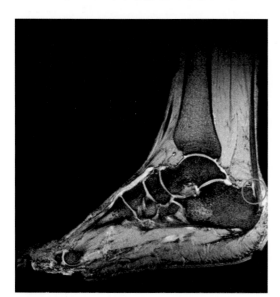

Figure 37.3 Imaging findings in patients presenting with Achilles pain
(a) MRI showing the prominent calcaneum of Haglund's deformity and associated tendon and bursal pathology

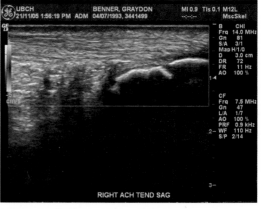

RIGHT ACH TEND SAG

(c) Grey-scale ultrasound appearance of a normal Achilles tendon

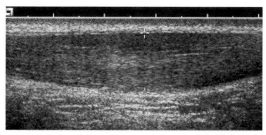

(d) Grey-scale ultrasound appearance of an tendon with mild morphological abnormality

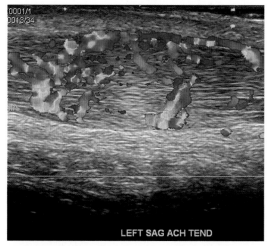

(e) Color Doppler ultrasound appearance showing abnormal vessels in symptomatic tendinopathy

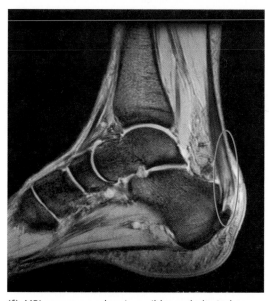

(f) MRI appearance showing mild morphological abnormality

In symptomatic patients, ultrasound and MRI (Fig. 37.3c–f) changes generally correspond with the histopathology of tendinopathy described below. Ultrasound and MRI can help distinguish different causes of Achilles region pain (e.g. highlight whether the Achilles or the peritendon or both have pathology). Color Doppler ultrasound provides information about the extent of abnormal vascularity. This may then serve as a target for sclerotherapy treatment. However, clinical outcomes are independent of imaging and changes in imaging.[7–10] Thus, imaging should not dominate clinical decision-making—treatment should be guided by how symptoms (e.g. morning stiffness, and pain with load) vary.

Midportion Achilles tendinopathy—basic science and clinical features

It is important to distinguish between midportion and insertional Achilles tendinopathy, as the treatments are different. We briefly review the pathology of Achilles tendinopathy, list expert opinion of factors that predispose to injury, and summarize the clinical features of the condition.

Histopathology and basic molecular biology

When operating on patients with chronic Achilles tendinopathy, the surgeon generally finds a degenerative lesion characterized by a poorly demarcated intratendinous dull-grayish discoloration of the tissue with a focal loss of normal fiber structure.[11] A partial tear or rupture, defined as a macroscopic discontinuity involving a small proportion of the tendon cross-section, is seen in approximately 20% of cases. These tears always occur in a region of pre-existing pathology and do not occur in normal tendon tissue.[12] The paratendinous structures are either normal or contain edema or scarring. When the symptomatic parts of such Achilles tendon tissue are examined under the light microscope, there is cell alteration, increases in ground substance, collagen fiber disarray, and increased vascularity as outlined in Chapter 5 (pp. 33–36 and Figs 5.11–5.13). This also applies to areas of partial tear, which show hypervascularity without signs of tissue repair.[11] These regions of tendon disarray correspond with areas of increased signal on MRI and hypoechoic regions on ultrasound[13] (Fig. 37.3d, e, f).

It has been proposed that there may be stages in tendon pathology—in the early stage, the main change is in the cell and ground substance; in later stages, the cell and ground substance changes persist with the addition of collagen disruption and increased vascularity[14, 15] (see Chapter 5). Cook and Purdam propose that early changes may be reversible but that, once the matrix is disorganized and abnormalities appear in collagen and vessels, these structural changes are more difficult to reverse.[14] How clinical signs and management principles align with the proposed "tendinopathy continuum model"[14] is shown in Table 37.3 (also Fig. 5.14 on page 36).

Inflammatory cells are absent in tendinosis. Also intratendinous microdialysis[16, 17] and molecular biology analysis of appropriately prepared biopsy tissue (cDNA-arrays, real-time quantitative polymerase chain reaction [PCR])[18] all fail to show evidence of prostaglandin-mediated inflammation. There are, however, signs of what Hart et al. have termed "neurogenic inflammation."[19] This is characterized by neuropeptides—such as substance P and calcitonin gene-related peptide (CGRP). It appears that peptidergic group IV nerve fibers release peptides from their terminals to start various pathophysiologic, and presumably painful, processes (see also Chapter 6 for pain). Activated tendon cells can produce substances that can cause pain.[20] The clinician's goal is to limit the onset and progression of pathology (and cell activation), by attending to load management and mitigating risk factors for Achilles tendinopathy.

Predisposing factors—clinical

Injury to the Achilles tendon occurs when the load applied to the tendon, either in a single episode or, more often, over a period of time, exceeds the ability of the tendon to withstand that load. The response of the tendon to load is moderated by a range of factors that can affect the tendon's response. (See Chapter 9 [Fig. 9.2] for distinction between "predisposing," "susceptibility," and "inciting" events.) Factors that may predispose to Achilles tendinopathy include:

- abnormal foot mechanics—excessive pronation[21] or supination (increased load on gastrocnemius–soleus complex to re-supinate the foot for toe-off) (Fig. 37.4)
- calf weakness
- altered tibial or femoral mechanics
- genetic predisposition[22]
- male sex
- central adiposity
- menopause
- type 2 diabetes mellitus.

Factors that increase susceptibility include:

- years of running
- poor muscle flexibility (e.g. tight gastrocnemius)
- joint range of motion (restricted dorsiflexion).

Events that may incite Achilles tendinopathy include:

- decrease in recovery time between training sessions
- change of surface
- change of footwear (e.g. lower-heeled spike, shoe with heel tab)
- poor footwear (e.g. inadequate heel counter, increased lateral flaring, decreased forefoot flexibility)
- increase in activity (mileage, speed, gradient).

Clinical features

The presentations of Achilles tendinopathy can vary, as listed in Table 37.4.

Table 37.3 How clinical signs and management principles align with the proposed "tendinopathy continuum model"[14]

Stage	Clinical signs	Management
Reactive tendinopathy/early tendon dysrepair	Acute overload Painful Swelling more general	Reduction in frequency +/– intensity of tendon load Medication to inhibit cell activity
Late tendon dysrepair/ degeneration	Chronic overload Pain tends to be "grumbly" Focal areas of swelling	Exercise with eccentric component Extracorporeal shockwave therapy (ESWT) Soft tissue treatment Therapeutic ultrasound Medication (often injection) to promote matrix structure

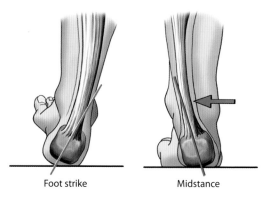

Figure 37.4 Although no "static" biomechanical measures (Chapter 8) predict Achilles tendinopathy; dynamic measures, including rapid subtalar joint eversion, are associated with an increased risk of symptoms

Practice tips relating to imaging Achilles tendinopathy

As there are various appearances of Achilles tendinopathy with imaging (Table 37.5), we recommend that the history and physical examination remain the keys to diagnosis. Until patients become familiar with the concept of tendinopathy, imaging may help illustrate that the abnormality is one of collagen disarray and abnormal vasculature; this will help the patient understand the lengthy time course of treatment.

Midportion Achilles tendinopathy—treatment

Experienced clinicians begin conservative treatment by identifying and correcting possible etiologic factors. This may include management of the patient's tendon load (either decrease or increase),

Table 37.4 Clinical features associated with presentation of overuse Achilles tendinopathy (i.e. not a complete rupture)

Clinical feature	Variability in presentation with overuse Achilles tendinopathy
History	
Onset of pain	May be sudden, gradual but noticeable, or insidious
Severity of pain	May range from a minor inconvenience to profound pain with activity
Duration	May range from days to years
Disability	May be minimal, moderate, or severe
Examination	
Extent of swelling/crepitus	Can range from being a major feature of the presentation to being absent
Extent of tenderness	May range from being pinpoint to extending throughout several centimeters of the tendon
Presence of a tender nodule	May or may not be present, and when present may vary in size

Table 37.5 Variations in imaging findings in patients with overuse Achilles tendinopathy (i.e. not a complete rupture). Symptoms and recovery are totally independent of imaging appearance

Imaging appearance	Variations seen in clinical practice
Ultrasound—extent of swelling	Tendon swelling can be associated with tendon fiber damage (see below) or it can occur without discontinuity (e.g. fusiform swelling). It is possible, but unusual, to have a normal ultrasound scan with symptoms and signs of Achilles tendinopathy; differential diagnoses must be fully evaluated and excluded.
Ultrasound—discontinuity of tendon fibers	Tendon fibers may appear intact or extensively damaged on ultrasonography ("hypoechogenicity"). This is usually associated with tendon swelling.
Ultrasound—evidence of vascularity	Vascularity may be extensive or absent. It can vary in amount when imaged on different days.
MRI appearance	The MRI appearance can vary from essentially normal to a marked increase in abnormal signal, best seen on T2-weighted sequences. Another feature of tendinopathy is increased tendon diameter without increased signal.

orthotic treatment (heel lift, change of shoes, corrections of malalignment), and amending biomechanical issues. Whether these "common sense" interventions contribute to outcome is unlikely to be tested. Level 2 evidence-based treatments for Achilles tendinopathy include targeted exercises (mechanotherapy, see Chapter 13), nitric oxide donor therapy (glyceryl trinitrate patches), and sclerosing injections (page 788).

Figure 37.5 illustrates a commonly used algorithm of progression of treatment.[23] The sequence of management options may need to vary in special cases such as the elite sportsperson, the person with acutely painful reactive tendon unable to walk properly, and the elderly patient who may be unable to complete the heel-drops. As always, the clinician should respond to individual patient needs and modify the algorithm appropriately.

Targeted eccentric exercise including the Alfredson program

In 1984, Curwin and Stanish[24, 25] pioneered what they termed "eccentric training" as therapy for tendon injuries. From this base, Alfredson and colleagues made three critical modifications.[26, 27]

First, they considered worsening pain a part of the normal recovery process; thus, they advised patients to continue with the full exercise program even as pain worsened on starting the program. Along those lines, if the patient experienced *no pain* doing the program, he or she was advised to increase the load until the exercises provoked pain (Fig. 37.6, Table 37.6 on pages 787 and 788).

The second innovation was to incorporate two types of heel drops into the program (details Fig. 37.6); traditionally only one type of heel-drop had been prescribed.

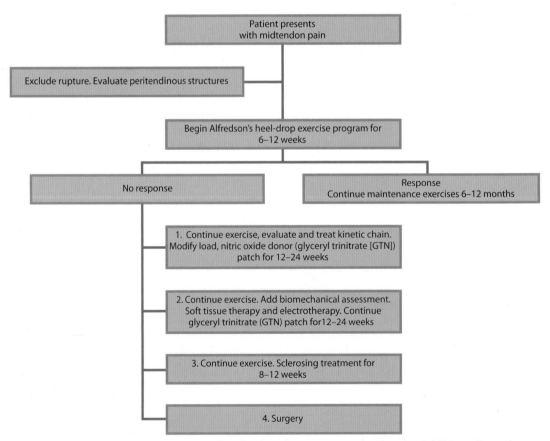

Figure 37.5 Flow chart showing one approach to the clinical management of midportion Achilles tendinopathy
MODIFIED FROM ALFREDSON ET AL.[23]

Håkan Alfredson's heel-drop protocol for Achilles tendinopathy

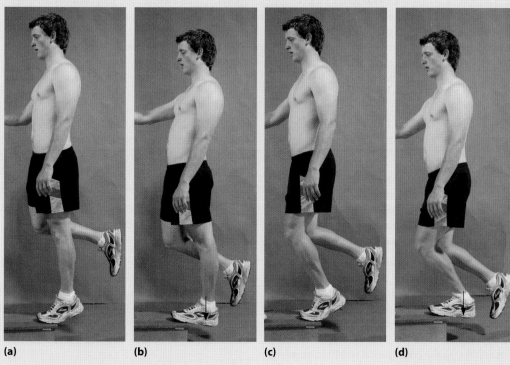

(a)   **(b)**   **(c)**   **(d)**

Figure 37.6 Alfredson's painful heel-drop protocol for Achilles tendinopathy. The heel-drop protocol consists of two key exercises—the "gastrocnemius drop" and the "soleus drop"

(a) For the gastrocnemius drop, the patient begins in a "demipointe" position, with the heel raised and the knee fully extended

(b) From this starting positions, the patient lowers the heel so that the foot is parallel with the ground

(c) For the soleus drop, the patient again adopts the "demipointe" position with the heel raised, but for this exercise the knee should be flexed to 45° so that the soleus is engaged

(d) The patient lowers the heel so that the foot is parallel with the ground

(e) To increase the load, additional weight can be added using a backpack or, where necessary, a weight machine

Table 37.6 Alfredson's painful heel-drop protocol (180 drops/day) (see also Fig. 37.6)

Number of exercises	Exercise specifics	Exercise progression
3 × 15 repetitions 2 times daily 7 days/week for 12 weeks	Do exercise both with knee straight (fully extended) (Fig. 37.6a, b) and knee bent (flexed 45°) (Fig. 37.6c, d) over edge of a step Lower only (heel drop) from standing on toes (i.e. raise back onto toes using unaffected leg or arms)	Do exercises until they become pain-free Add load until exercises are again painful (Fig. 37.6e) Progressively add load up to 60 kg

Finally, they prescribed 180 drops per day—a far greater number than had been recommended previously—but to do them all slowly.

In Alfredson's initial treatment trial,[27] the 12-week progressive program of 180 slow, heavy, eccentric heel-drops per day (using two different degrees of knee flexion) cured approximately 90% of those with midtendon pain and pathology.[27–29]

In the ensuing 14 years, clinicians the world over have reported high levels of success with this program in trials and in clinical practice. The program (Fig. 37.6 and Table 37.6 on pages 787 and 788) has saved many patients from needing Achilles tendon surgery.

In addition to the good clinical results, ultrasound and MRI follow-up demonstrated that patients' tendons returned toward normal appearance and thickness.[30] This program is standard treatment for Achilles tendinopathy and the exercise principles have been applied successfully to other tendons.

Variations on the heel-drop program may also be effective[31] but have not been as rigorously evaluated as patients in Alfredson's program. It is clear that eccentric exercise (heel-drops) promotes superior clinical recovery than does concentric exercise (heel-raises).[32] Exercise-based treatments in other tendons suggest that using both eccentric and concentric movements may be equally beneficial as concentrating on eccentric movements.[33, 34] Doing both may also promote muscle strength and endurance adaptations.[35] In addition, the inclusion of more dynamic exercise in addition to standard eccentric exercise may not affect outcome.[36]

Eccentric exercise appears to be ineffective as a prophylactic treatment to prevent Achilles tendinopathy, with soccer players who did eccentric exercise and stretches during the playing season being no more likely to be free of Achilles tendon injury than those who did not.[37]

Other interventions used in conjunction with targeted exercise therapy

Many interventions have been used in conjunction with an eccentric exercise program (Table 37.7 on page 790) with two factors of note:

- Exercise is excellent for tendons.
- Added interventions add minimally to exercise therapy.

The "exercise is medicine" message from public health[41] should be applied to tendon treatments. It is unfortunate that, among many patients and clinicians, exercise is incorrectly assumed to be less effective than traditional "medical" therapies such as medication or injection.

Nitric oxide donor therapy

There is conflicting evidence for nitric oxide donor therapy (glyceryl trinitrate [GTN] patches applied locally).[48] In mid-Achilles tendinopathy, GTN therapy reduced pain with activity by twelve weeks. Twenty-eight (78%) of thirty-six tendons in the glyceryl trinitrate group were asymptomatic with activities of daily living at six months, compared with twenty (49%) of forty-one tendons in the placebo group. A similar study from another group showed no better outcome in those treated with GTN, and, in those tendons that proceeded to surgery, biopsies of the tendon showed no improvement in healing in those who had used GTN.[43]

Injections

There are a range of substances that have been used both in and around the Achilles tendon. The basis for injection is often failure to respond to an exercise program or passive therapies.

Sclerosing

Sclerosing (Fig. 37.8 on page 793) consists of injecting a vascular sclerosant (polidocanol—an aliphatic

How does eccentric exercise promote recovery in tendinopathy?

There are several possible explanations for the effectiveness of eccentric exercise. In broad terms, exercise therapy can affect any tissue through the process of mechanotherapy[38] (also discussed in *Clinical Sports Medicine* masterclasses at www.clinicalsports medicine.com.) Specifically in this setting, heel drops probably have both an immediate and a longer-term influence on tendon.

In the short term, a single bout of exercise increases tendon volume and signal on MRI.[30] Heel drops affect type 1 collagen production and, in the absence of ongoing insult, may decrease tendon volume over the

longer term.[39] Thus, heel drops may increase tensile strength in the tendon over time. Repetitive loading and a lengthening of the muscle–tendon unit may improve the capacity of the musculotendinous unit to affectively absorb load (Fig. 37.7).

Eccentric exercise may be more beneficial than concentric exercise because of repeated stretching; however, it is unclear if the effect is mostly on tendon or on the muscle–tendon unit as a whole.[35] Eccentric exercise may also induce more force fluctuations in the tendon, adding greater load to the tendon.[40]

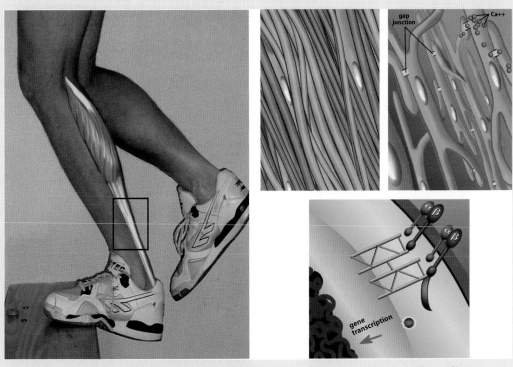

Figure 37.7 Heel drops (left panel), provide mechanical loading, which causes sliding of collagen fibers (microscopic view, top center panel) leading to intracellular communication via gap junctions (top right panel), and communication with the cell nucleus (lower right panel). Full details of this mechanotherapy process are in reference 38 and in *Clinical Sports Medicine* masterclasses at www.clinicalsportsmedicine.com.

nonionized nitrogen-free substance with a sclerosing and anesthetic effect) using ultrasound guidance (Fig. 37.8a on page 793) into the area of neovascularization anterior to the tendon (Fig. 37.8 b and c on page 793).

In a small double-blind randomized controlled study[50] comparing the effects of injections of a sclerosing and a nonsclerosing substance (lidocaine plus adrenaline), two doses of the sclerosing substance led to 5 of 10 participants being satisfied with

Table 37.7 Randomized trials that combined exercise and other interventions in treatment of Achilles tendinopathy

Comparative/additional intervention	Author, year	Outcome measure	Length of follow-up	Population (n [M/F] athletic level)	Conclusion	Notes
Eccentric exercise (EE) vs. concentric exercise (CE)	Silbernagel et al., 2001[31]	Pain (Visual Analog Scale [VAS]), self-assessments (level of recovery, satisfaction, pain during activity, return to activity), range of motion, toe-raise test, jumping test	6 weeks, 3, 6, and 12 months	n = 49 (36/13) 11 jog/run regularly, 36 participate in other activities regularly, 2 not regularly active	The EE group was observed to have a higher rate of full recovery, better range of motion, and less pain when compared with the CE group	The EE group performed their program under supervision The CE group was given a program to be completed at home (numerous follow-ups with the athletic therapist ensured compliance)
Low-level laser therapy (LLLT) + eccentric exercise (EE) vs. eccentric exercise + laser placebo	Stergioulas et al., 2008[42]	Pain intensity during activity, morning stiffness, crepitation, tenderness (all on a Visual Analog Scale [VAS]) and range of ankle dorsiflexion (goniometry)	4, 8, and 12 weeks	n = 52 (25/15; 12 dropped out) All recreational athletes	LLLT can accelerate clinical recovery in the short term (at 4 weeks) when used in conjunction with EE No benefit was found in the long term (at 12 weeks)	EE performed under supervision
Topical glyceryl trinitrate (GTN) + eccentric exercise (EE) vs. eccentric exercise	Kane et al., 2008[43]	Ankle Osteoarthritis Scale (AOS)	6 months	n = 40 (gender not disclosed) Activity level not disclosed	The GTN treatment showed no significant benefit over the standard EE rehabilitation program	Few details given about the implementation of the EE program
Low-energy shockwave treatment (SWT) + eccentric exercise (EE) vs. eccentric exercise	Rompe et al., 2009[44]	VISA-A, self-assessments (Pain [Numerical Rating Scale] and treatment success [Likert Scale])	6 weeks, 4 and 12 months	n = 68 (gender not disclosed) 21 performed sports on a weekly basis	Improved likeliness of recovery with SWT and EE after 4 months but no difference from just EE after 1 year	EE performed unsupervised All participants had previous Achilles tendinopathy treatment for >6 months (peritendonous injection, NSAIDs, or physiotherapy)

B

Comparative/additional intervention	Author, year	Outcome measure	Length of follow-up	Population (n [M/F] athletic level)	Conclusion	Notes
Eccentric exercise (EE) vs. low-energy shock-wave treatment (SWT) vs. wait-and-see policy	Rompe et al., 2007[45]	VISA-A, self-assessments (pain, tenderness [Numerical Rating Scale] and treatment success [Likert Scale]), tendon diameter	6 weeks and 4 months	n = 75 (29/46) 23 were considered athletic	No significant difference was found between the EE and SWT groups after 4 months. The wait-and-see group had very little improvement	EE not supervised but technique was evaluated after 6 weeks. All participants had previous Achilles tendinopathy treatment for >3 months (peritendinous injection, NSAIDs, or physiotherapy)
Platelet-rich plasma injection (PRP) + eccentric exercise (EE) vs. placebo injection + eccentric exercise	de Vos et al., 2010[46]	VISA-A, self-assessments (treatment success and return to sport [Likert Scale])	6, 12, and 24 weeks	n = 54 (26/28) 9 competitive sports, 37 recreational sports, 8 sedentary	The PRP injection showed no significant benefit over the standard EE rehabilitation program	The injection was guided by ultrasound imaging. EE was unsupervised
AirHeel bracing™ + eccentric exercise (EE) vs. eccentric exercise	Knobloch et al., 2008[47]	Foot and Ankle Outcome Score (FAOS) and pain (Visual Analog Scale [VAS])	12 weeks	n = 97 (63/34) 34 runners, 8 soccer, 17 other ball sports, 38 not specified	Although microcirculation was greatly better using the AirHeel™ Brace, no clinical advantages were found over EE alone	No supervision for the eccentric exercise program. Brace was worn all day, regardless of sports participation (not worn sleeping)
Night splint (NS) vs. eccentric exercise (EE) vs. night splint + eccentric exercise	Roos et al., 2004[29]	Foot and Ankle Outcome Score (FAOS), physical activity level (Likert Scale)	6 weeks, 3, 6, and 12 months	n = 45 (22/23) 29 active in sports	EE alone was observed to result in the best short-term and long-term outcomes. EE + NS resulted in the worst outcome both short- and long-term	EE was not supervised but a quality check was performed at 1 week from baseline. Night splints were custom formed for each patient and only worn at night
Running/jumping (R/J) (Achilles loading) + eccentric exercise vs. eccentric exercise	Silbernagel et al., 2007[36]	VISA-A-S, pain (Visual Analog Scale [VAS])	6 weeks, 3, 6, and 12 months	n = 38 (20/18) Based on the Physical Activity Score (1 [sedentary], 6 [extremely active]): mean = 4.45; range = 1–6	No significant differences were found between R/J + EE vs. EE at 12 months	EE program followed based on Silbernagel's "eccentric overload training". Running/jumping exercises restricted by a pain model

continues

Table 37.7 *continued*

Comparative/additional intervention	Author, year	Outcome measure	Length of follow-up	Population (n [M/F] athletic level)	Conclusion	Notes
Surgical treatment vs. eccentric exercise (EE)	Alfredson et al., 1998[2]	Muscle strength (Biodex Isokinetic Dynamometer), pain (Visual Analog Scale [VAS])	12 weeks	n = 30 (23/7) All recreational athletes	Surgical treatment was observed to have no benefit over EE and took double the amount of time to return to pre-injury level of activity	All patients who underwent surgery attempted conventional treatments and opted to have surgery EE was unsupervised but a quality check was done at 6 weeks
Topical glyceryl trinitrate (GTN) + eccentric exercise (EE) vs. placebo patch + eccentric exercise	Paoloni et al., 2004[48]	Pain scores (rest, activity, night), clinical assessment of tendon tenderness, functional hop test, ankle plantar flexor peak force and total work (Orthopaedic Research Institute – Ankle Strength Testing System)	2, 6, 12, and 24 weeks	n = 65 (40/25) Level of activity not disclosed	Treatment using GTN in conjunction with EE was observed to be a more effective treatment than EE alone Pain during activity and at night, functional measures and patient outcomes were all significantly better in the GTN treatment group	EE was not supervised. Patients administered their own GTN or placebo patches
Steroid injection + eccentric exercise (EE) vs. placebo injection + eccentric exercise	Fredberg et al., 2004[49]	Tendon thickness (ultrasound), pain detection threshold (Pressure algometry), walking pain (Numerical Rating Scale [NRSI)	1, 3, and 4 weeks and 3, 6, and 24 months	n = 48 (33/15) All athletes	Steroid injection was more effective than EE in reducing tendon thickness and pain but tendon atrophy was very frequent, which leaves the patient more susceptible to rupture 3–6 months of rehabilitation was suggested	Injections were ultrasonically guided. The eccentric exercise performed was described as "training and stretching of the calf muscle" (doesn't explicitly say eccentric exercise) All of the subjects were athletes and had attempted conservative treatment unsuccessfully prior to the study

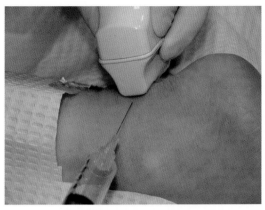

Figure 37.8 Sclerotherapy
(a) Ultrasound-guided sclerotherapy

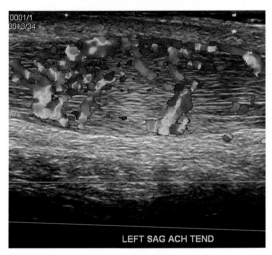

(b) Abnormal vessels—neovessels—before sclerotherapy

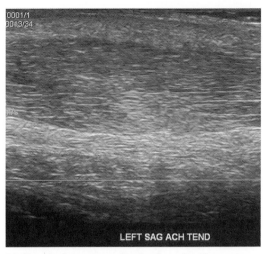

(c) Vessels absent immediately after sclerotherapy

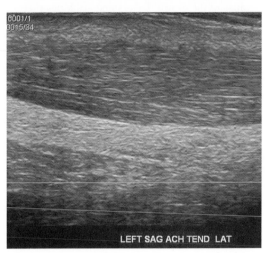

(d) Vessels still absent 12 months after treatment in a pain-free patient

treatment; a further open-label treatment (injection) led to all remaining patients being satisfied. The placebo group, on the other hand, saw no patients satisfied after two placebo injections, and 9 of 10 participants satisfied after open-label cross-over to the active agent.

Whether the sclerosant decreases vascularity or pain is not known. Short-term follow-up of tendons that have had vessels sclerosed demonstrate an increase in both short- and medium-term vascularity.[51] This, in combination with the anesthetic properties of polidocanol, suggests that a change in vascularity is not necessary for a change in pain.

Rehabilitation after sclerosing injection includes 1–3 days of rest, then light exercise (walk and bike) during the first two weeks. After two weeks, activities are increased gradually, returning to full loading as tolerated.

After treating 1000 Achilles tendons over 10 years, the pioneers of this treatment (Alfredson and colleagues) reported six total and three partial tendon ruptures in their center. Complications in other centers may be linked to using a non-standard protocol, such as not using ultrasound-guided injection, using too large a volume (more than 2 mL per session) and injecting into the tendon.

In summary, sclerosing therapy may have a role in patients who have extensive vascularity and who have failed to respond to exercise.

Corticosteroid injections

Corticosteroid injections are used peritendinously with or without ultrasound guidance. The pain-relieving effect of corticosteroid is likely to damp down cell response and limit protein production (i.e. settle a reactive tendon) rather than have an effect on inflammation. Using this intervention without concomitant exercise therapy is likely to give short-term relief without longer-term benefit.[51, 52] Longer-term clinical efficacy may be improved if corticosteroid injection is combined with exercise.

Autologous blood and platelet-rich plasma
with ROBERT-JAN DE VOS

Autologous blood and platelet-rich plasma (PRP) have become popular in recent years[53] (Fig. 37.9). They have been proposed to improve tendon healing because of the growth factors and cytokines present in blood—particularly in PRP. There are a variety of protocols for managing and injecting the blood and for the rehabilitation after injection—few have been rigorously investigated. A randomized trial of PRP and eccentric exercise with PRP or placebo injection showed no difference in clinical recovery or in tendon healing on ultrasound imaging.[46] Also, both groups had more pain and poorer function at six weeks than baseline, as measured on the VISA-A scale.

Injections designed to stimulate a healing response through irritation (such as prolotherapy) may have some benefit. A randomized trial that compared eccentric exercise to prolotherapy to a combination of both showed small benefits at different time points for prolotherapy and combined treatment.[54]

Medications

Nonsteroidal anti-inflammatory medications (NSAIDs) have not been shown to be effective in treating tendinopathy, either in reducing pain with loading or by improving tendon pathology. NSAIDs may affect the tendon in different ways and an acutely painful tendon may respond best to NSAIDs that limit cell activity and ground substance production. These include ibuprofen, naproxen, and celocoxib. Of these, ibuprofen affects tissue healing less than other NSAIDs.[55]

Adjunctive non-operative treatments

Biomechanical evaluation of the foot and leg is a clinically important part of Achilles tendon management. There is some empirical evidence to support the association between static foot posture and Achilles tendinopathy. A supinated foot seems more vulnerable to developing tendinopathy than a pronated foot, but that may be because a supinated foot is often associated with less dorsiflexion.[56] Modification of foot posture in some patients can reduce pain and increase the capacity to load the tendon.[21] A heel raise is a critical intervention in insertional tendinopathy.

Soft tissue therapy of the calf complex can assist rehabilitation (Fig. 37.10).[57] Deep tissue frictions increase protein output of tendon cells;[58] however, similar to the effect seen with ultrasound, greater amounts of collagen and ground substance may not improve pain or pathology.

Electrophysical agents

In one study,[44] extracorporeal shock wave therapy (ESWT) (see also Chapter 13) showed small benefits over eccentric exercise in treating midtendon tendin-

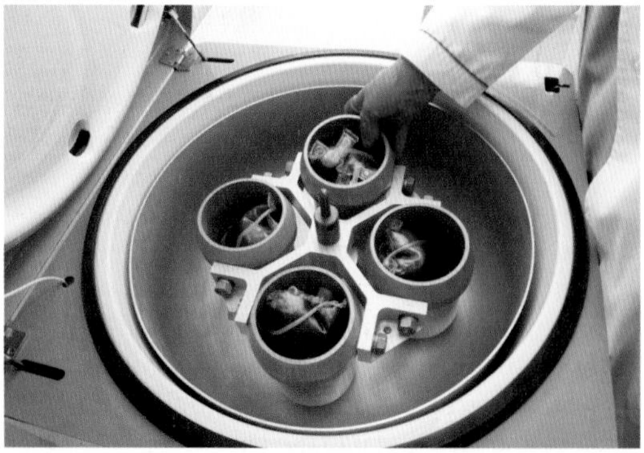

Figure 37.9 Platelet-rich plasma (PRP) failed to provide clinical benefits in a randomized trial of patients with Achilles tendinopathy[46]

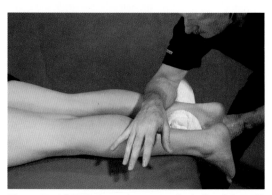

Figure 37.10 Soft tissue therapy to the belly of the calf muscles

opathy. (ESWT is discussed further under insertional tendinopathy, below.)

Therapeutic ultrasound increases protein synthesis in tendons,[59] but, as there is an oversupply of poor-quality protein in tendon pathology, ultrasound may not improve clinical outcome to further increase this substance.

There is limited evidence for laser and microwave therapies. For laser, where both groups did eccentric exercise, outcomes improved for those in the laser therapy group compared with the placebo group.[42] Microwave alone, without exercise, showed superior outcome after one month[60] in patients who had undergone hyperthermia with low-frequency microwave compared with those treated with traditional ultrasound after treatment and one month later. Microcurrent applied for two weeks decreased pain at 12 months compared with conventional treatment.[61]

Surgical treatment

Alfredson has pioneered minimally invasive surgery that surgically separates the ventral soft tissues including the vessels and nerves from the tendon, which reduces pain in the tendon for several months.[62] Compared with sclerosing injections, a similar number of patients in both groups (6/9 sclerosing group, 8/10 surgery group) were satisfied at three months, with slightly more improved at six months in the surgery group (6/9 sclerosing group, 10/10 surgery group).

Because of the plethora of successful conservative treatments now available for overuse Achilles tendinopathy, surgical treatments have received less attention recently. Aside from the minimally invasive surgery mentioned, procedures range from simple percutaneous tenotomy[63] to removal of tendon pathology via an open procedure. Percutaneous tenotomy resulted in 75% of patients reporting good or excellent results after 18 months.[64] The outcome of open surgery for Achilles tendinopathy was superior among patients whose tendons had diffuse disease, compared with those whose tendons had a focal area of tendinopathy.[65] At seven months post-surgery, 88% of those with diffuse disease had returned to physical activity, as had 50% of those with a focal lesion.

There are several important clinical issues with surgery that should influence clinical decision making:

- Post-surgical complications, especially infection, are common; 11% of 432 patients who had surgery had one or more complication.[66] Those with risk factors such as diabetes or who smoke are at higher risk for these complications.
- The tendon can remain thickened for many years after surgery, despite good clinical outcomes. Thirteen years after surgery, mean AP diameter was 9.3 mm, well above a normal tendon thickness of 5 mm[67]
- Surgery had more complications and poorer outcome for sedentary people[68]
- Full recovery of strength and function can also be compromised for many years.[69]

Achilles tendon surgery requires early postoperative rehabilitation and this needs to continue for 6–12 months, as final clinical results rely on the return of strength and functional capacity. Wise patients continue with a maintenance program of physiotherapist-prescribed rehabilitation exercises even after having returned to training and competition.

Insertional Achilles tendinopathy, retrocalcaneal bursitis, and Haglund's disease

Insertional Achilles tendinopathy, retrocalcaneal bursitis, and Haglund's disease are discussed together as they are intimately related in pathogenesis and clinical presentation.[70–73]

Relevant anatomy and pathogenesis

The Achilles tendon insertion, the fibrocartilaginous walls of the retrocalcaneal bursa that extend into the tendon (Fig. 37.1b), and adjacent cartilage-covered calcaneum form an "enthesis organ"[74] (Fig. 37.11 overleaf). The key concept is that, at this site, the tendon, the bursa, and the bone are so intimately related that a prominence of the calcaneum greatly predisposes to mechanical irritation of the bursa and the tendon just proximal to the insertion, through both compression and tensile loads. Also, the mechanical load on this area is greater with dorsiflexion when the calcaneus impinges on the bursa and tendon.[73] These mechanical loads lead to a change in the nature of those tissues, consistent with the biological process of mechanotransduction[38] (page 789).

"Haglund-type calcaneus" is a descriptive label for prominence of the posterolateral calcaneum. "Haglund's disease" is a label for the clinical syndrome of a prominent, painful lateral portion of the tendon/bursa/calcaneus interface associated with a prominent superolateral superior calcaneus.[3] Thus,

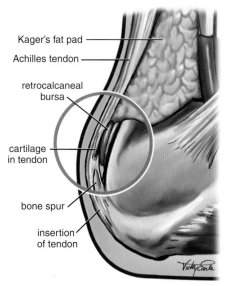

Kager's fat pad

Achilles tendon

retrocalcaneal
bursa

cartilage
in tendon

bone spur

insertion
of tendon

Figure 37.11 The "enthesis organ" illustrates why insertional Achilles tendinopathy is often associated with retrocalcaneal bursitis and calcaneal prominence. A prominence of the calcaneum greatly predisposes to mechanical irritation of the bursa, development of excess fibrocartilaginous tissue, and tendon pathology just proximal to the insertion

an asymptomatic patient may be found to have a Haglund-type calcaneus on radiographs taken for another reason. This is important as the morphology *per se* is not an indication for treatment.

We must also distinguish between the actual tendon insertion, which is onto the lower half of the calcaneus (which is occasionally pathological and a true enthesopathy), and where much of the pathology is seen—the upper calcaneal/bursa/tendon interface.

Insertional Achilles tendinopathy is not as common, or as well-researched, as midportion tendinopathy. The pathology is "tendinosis," not inflammation[75] and there is some local neovascularization inside and outside the distal tendon.

Clinical assessment

Good clinical practice includes evaluation of the tendon, bursa, and calcaneum by careful history, functional tests, and inspection and palpation of the region for bony prominence and local swelling. Discriminating between pain with tensile, and compressive and combined, loads can help with diagnosis. For example, hopping on the toes (tensile loads)

may give some pain, but a hop lunge into dorsiflexion (compression and tensile loads) may be more painful at the enthesis.

Ultrasound and MRI can help to assess the extent of pathology in the tendon and the bursa. Symptoms of insertional Achilles tendinopathy, as with any enthesopathy, should raise suspicion about the possibility of the diagnosis of rheumatoid arthritis or spondyloarthopathy; this is particularly true if symptoms are bilateral (Chapter 55).

Treatment

This is a challenging condition to treat. Treatment must consider the enthesis organ as a unit. Isolated treatment of a bursitis is generally unsuccessful. Alfredson's painful heel-drop protocol (very effective in *midportion* tendinopathy) only achieves good clinical results in approximately 30% of cases of *insertional* tendinopathy.[76] A modified treatment that used the Alfredson protocol but only did heel drops to the floor (rather than over the edge of a step) showed greatly increased efficacy (70% of patients with long-term symptoms were satisfied and returned to sport)[77] (Fig. 37.12). This simple modification of treatment merely reduces repeated compressive loads onto the enthesis organ and therefore reduces irritation of the structures. A heel-raise is a good practical way of reducing compressive loads on the region. Using similar reasoning, repeated stretching may not be beneficial for insertional Achilles pain.

Alternative treatments for chronic insertional tendinopathy include sclerosing of local neovessels with polidocanol. Both exercise and sclerosing treatment were successful even in those patients with multiple pathology (thickened retrocalcaneal bursae, calcification, loose fragment).[76, 77]

Treatment of insertional tendinopathy with extracorporeal shock wave therapy (ESWT) showed more benefit than exercise,[78] but the eccentric program used was designed for mid-Achilles tendinopathy, and better benefits from exercise are evident when using the specific insertional protocol.[77]

Spondyloarthropathy needs to be considered as a differential diagnosis in insertional tendinopathies. If this is the underlying condition, treatment needs to be directed to the causative condition (e.g. psoriatic arthritis, rheumatoid arthritis).

If conservative management fails in Haglund's disease where a deformity is present, surgery may be indicated. Only a few case series have reported

B

Figure 37.12 Variation of the Alfredson tendon loading program for insertional tendinopathy. The patient only lowers the heel to the level of the floor (or, in the early stages, onto a small heel raise) to limit irritation of the Achilles tendon against local structures

outcome after surgery for insertional Achilles tendinopathy.[79–81]

Achilles tendon rupture (complete)—diagnosis and initial management

Complete rupture of the Achilles tendon classically occurs in sportspeople in their 30s or 40s. The typical patient is a 40-year-old sports-active male; the male:female ratio is 10:1. The incidence is on the rise, especially in the last 10 years. The majority of patients have not had any symptoms from the Achilles tendon prior to injury. Whether or not the location of rupture is associated with a "watershed" area of poor blood supply is still an issue of debate.

Usually the rupture occurs during some kind of sport activity, when the person performs a quick change of direction and the ankle is forced into dorsiflexion while the calf muscle contracts. In most cases, the rupture does not occur at the start of the activity, but rather after about 30–40 minutes, and therefore general or localized fatigue might be a risk factor. The patient describes feeling "as if I was hit or kicked in the back of the leg"—pain might not always be the strongest sensation. This is immediately followed by grossly diminished function. A snap or tear may be audible and the patient has difficulties walking. However, he or she is usually able to resume walking within a short time, but without power in the push-off phase.

The patient usually has an obvious limp but may have surprisingly good function through the use of compensatory muscles. That is, the patient may be able to walk, but not on the toes with any strength.

Four clinical tests can greatly simplify examination for complete Achilles tendon rupture:

1. On careful inspection with the patient prone and both ankles fully relaxed (hanging off the end of the table), the foot on the side with the ruptured tendon hangs straight down (because of the absence of tendon tone); the foot on the non-ruptured side is in a plantarflexed position; approximately 15–25° (Fig. 37.2h).
2. Immediately after injury there is a palpable gap in the tendon, approximately 3–6 cm proximal to the insertion into the calcaneus. This gap might not be palpable because of swelling, especially after a few days. This might be an important reason why the diagnosis is sometimes delayed.
3. The strength of plantarflexion is markedly reduced.
4. Thompson's/Simmonds' calf squeeze test is positive (Fig. 37.2i).[6]

Rehabilitation after initial management of Achilles tendon rupture

Historically, clinicians feared loading the Achilles tendon during the first 6–8 weeks after rupture because of dogma that loading would cause

Treatment of the acutely ruptured Achilles tendon: to operate or not to operate?

Until the early 2000s, surgical repair of Achilles tendon rupture was essentially an "automatic" choice for healthy individuals who had no contraindications for surgery and who wanted to return to an active lifestyle. Several randomized trials and an increasing understanding of the therapeutic effect of tissue loading (mechanotherapy on page 789) mean that clinicians now need to consider both the operative and the non-operative options.

Surgical management

Open surgical treatment of Achilles tendon rupture (Fig. 37.13a) is associated with approximately 10% lower risk of rerupture compared with non-surgical treatment.[82–84] However, open operative treatment is associated with an increased risk of complications, including infection, adhesions, and disturbed skin sensitivity.[66] Another approach to reduce these operative complications is to perform surgery "percutaneously," but this does not eliminate the risk of complications.

The postoperative treatment regimen has a significant effect on the outcome. Comparisons of rigid cast immobilization with a short period of rigid cast and then use of a functional brace (Fig. 37.13b), after surgical intervention, indicates that early mobilization decreases re-rupture rates without a negative effect on other complications.[85, 86] Furthermore, a consistent finding is that the patient satisfaction is higher with a functional brace.[87]

Postoperative management depends on the type of surgery and the surgeon's postoperative protocols. Usually a cast or brace is used for the first 6–8 weeks; however, the period of postoperative immobilization may not need to be that long—recent studies[84] have reported success with minimal (2 weeks), or no, immobilization after surgery. Because range of movement and strength can be difficult to regain after rupture repair, we recommend the earliest possible mobilization and rehabilitation.

Non-surgical management

Historically, non-surgical management of an Achilles tendon rupture has only been recommended in older patients, or patients with low level of activity.[83] However, in a high-quality recent study where both surgically and non-surgically treated (Fig. 37.13b) patients received identical mobilization protocols (cast for 2 weeks and then a functional brace), there was no difference in the patient-reported outcomes.[84] Thus, non-surgical treatment leads to a high success rate, provided no re-rupture occurs, and may therefore be considered a valid option for all patients.

New studies are investigating the possibility of treating the ruptured Achilles tendon with early range of motion without any surgical intervention. The preliminary results are promising.

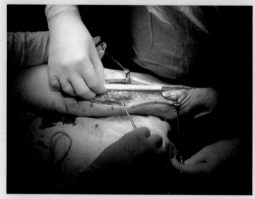

Figure 37.13 Management of Achilles tendon rupture

(a) Intra-operative photograph showing the ruptured Achilles tendon. The surgeon is showing that the gap between the torn tendon ends exceeds 5 cm

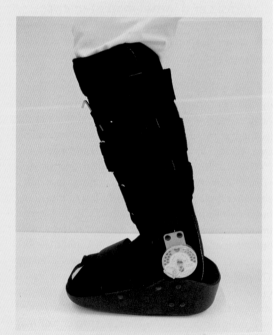

(b) There is increasing evidence that non-surgical management with appropriate rehabilitation can also be effective[84]

re-rupture and other complications. Thus, patients rarely started rehabilitation prior to the removal of the functional brace. However, research disproved that belief—early mobilization using a functional brace actually improved outcomes.[84] Thus, patients who are in a brace should move their toes and perform light plantar flexion isometrics or active range of motion (if the brace allows for it) during the brace/cast period.

"Formal" rehabilitation often starts after the removal of the brace/cast. The goal is for the patient to regain calf muscle strength and achieve normal gait while minimizing the risk of re-rupture. As the load on the Achilles tendon can be increased both by increasing the external load and also through increasing the speed of movement, slower and controlled movements during this initial 4-week period of rehabilitation are recommended. All the muscles around the ankle need to be strengthened and this can be progressed by the use of rubber tubing such as theraband (Fig. 37.14). Furthermore, the calf muscle is strengthened by progressively increasing the load through sitting heel raises and bilateral heel raises, and ultimately the patient should be able to perform a single-leg heel raise (Fig. 37.14).

> Achieving full ankle range of motion (compared with the healthy side) is important, but this should not be achieved by stretching the calf muscles early in the rehabilitation period, this leaves the Achilles tendon to heal in an elongated position.[84] Instead, full ankle range of motion can be achieved through joint mobilization and stretching into dorsiflexion with the knee in a flexed position.

Figure 37.14 Calf muscle strengthening after Achilles tendon rupture
(a) Early rehabilitation includes low-load ankle plantarflexion with knee extended (e.g., with Theraband)

Timing the return to jogging and sports

Often a time-based criterion is used for the recommendation of return to jogging and sports. Traditional recommendations are that jogging can be started after 12–16 weeks, return to non-contact sport after 16–20 weeks, and to contact sports after 20–24 weeks. We recommend adding functional criteria for return to jogging and sports, such as the recovery of calf muscle strength, ankle range of motion, and other more sport-specific tests. The injured side should be compared with the uninjured side. The normal number of single-leg heel raises is regarded to be 25 but can range from 6 to 70 in healthy individuals.[88] In the clinic, we require that the patient should be at least 12 weeks post injury and able to perform at least 5 single-leg heel raises at 90% of the available heel-raise height prior to initiating a jogging/running progression program.

Longer term rehabilitation issues

Regardless of whether initial treatment was surgical or non-surgical, complications such as calf muscle weakness, tendon elongation, and gait abnormalities can persist for at least a year after injury. Because

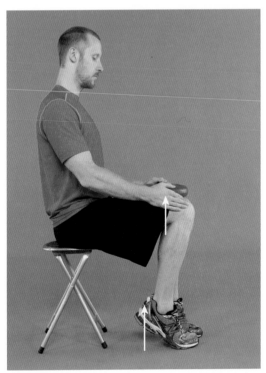

(b) Seated heel raise against resistance loads the soleus preferentially of individual differences, rehabilitation should be tailored to each patient's deficits. Often the patient cannot raise his or her heel as high on the injured side as on the uninjured side. The clinician should test whether this is due to tendon elongation, weakness, or both. This does not appear to limit return to physical activity in the majority of patients, and whether it leads to any long-term implications is not known.

About 50% of patients can perform a single-leg heel raise three months after their injury. Between 3 and 6 months after injury, the majority of the patients achieve this milestone. However, it is common to have a strength deficit of 10–30% in the calf musculature on the injured side compared with the healthy side, and this commonly becomes permanent.

Thus, it is important to encourage the patient to persist with a comprehensive functional rehabilitation program and, ideally, return to full activity. The clinician needs to be alert to identifying any specific factors that are barriers to this successful return to activity.

Additional studies are needed to garner better evidence regarding what the appropriate and most beneficial type of exercises are both in the initial "immobilization" period (if any) and during rehabilitation.

Posterior impingement syndrome

Posterior impingement syndrome of the ankle refers to impingement of the posterior talus by the adjacent aspect of the posterior aspect of the tibia in extremes of plantarflexion. An enlarged posterior tubercle of the talus (Fig. 37.15a) or an os trigonum (Fig. 37.15b) may be present. This condition is commonly found in ballet dancers, gymnasts, and footballers, all of whom maximally plantarflex their ankles. It is also seen secondary to ankle plantarflexion/inversion injuries.

The os trigonum represents an unfused ossific center in the posterior process of the talus. This is a normal anatomic variant present in approximately 10% of the population. The space-occupying nature of the bone causes pain irrespective of whether the bone is fused or united.

The diagnosis of posterior impingement syndrome is suggested by pain and tenderness at the posterior aspect of the ankle. It is confirmed by a positive posterior impingement test—pain is reproduced on passive plantarflexion of the ankle (Fig. 37.2d). If

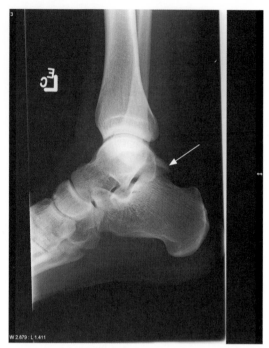

Figure 37.15 Anatomy that can be associated with posterior impingement

(a) A prominent posterior process of the talus (arrow)

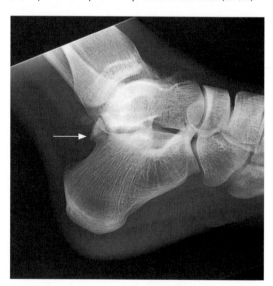

(b) The os trigonum (arrow)

further confirmation is required, a small amount of a local anesthetic agent can be injected around the posterior talus and the impingement test performed again—this time without pain. Ideally, this test would be done under radiographic guidance so that there is certainty about the location of the injection. In practice, this is not always feasible, and the test relies on the clinical accuracy of the practitioner.

Treatments that expert clinicians have used for posterior impingement syndrome include relative rest, manual mobilization of the subtalar, talocrural, and midfoot joints, as well as NSAIDs or acetaminophen (paracetamol) for symptomatic relief. In ballet dancers, forcing turnout and/or sickling the foot can predispose to this condition, so technique assessment is essential.

If the condition persists, a corticosteroid injection around the area of maximal tenderness may reduce pain. This is best done from the lateral side, as the medial aspect of the ankle contains the neurovascular bundle.

 Clinical Sports Medicine masterclasses contain a demonstration of how to perform this injection. www.clinicalsportsmedicine.com

Frequently, this condition does not respond to conservative management and requires surgical removal of the posterior process or the os trigonum. This can be done through a mini-incision. Dancers can return to full performance about three months after such an operation.

Sever's disease

Sever's disease, or calcaneal apophysitis, is a common insertional enthesopathy among adolescents (Chapter 42). It can be considered the Achilles tendon equivalent of Osgood-Schlatter's disease at the patellar tendon insertion.

Less common causes

Accessory soleus

Although it is considered a "rare" cause of Achilles region pain, anatomical studies suggest that an accessory soleus is present in about 6% of people. This was mirrored in an Italian study of 650 athletes—18 had an accessory soleus (2.7%).[89] The condition is more common among men than women, and the average age of presentation is 20 years.

The primary presenting patterns are pain in the Achilles region during exercise (a "compartment" type pain) with swelling, or painless swelling. When pain is present, it arises in the Achilles area.

Imaging findings are characteristic—plain radiographs show a soft-tissue shadow posterior to the tibia obscuring the pre-Achilles fat pad. Ultrasound, CT, and MRI can each confirm a mass the same texture as muscle.

In symptomatic patients, observation is an appropriate treatment; however, if symptoms warrant management, surgical removal of the accessory soleus is probably the best treatment.[90]

Other causes of pain in the Achilles region

Achilles bursitis (Fig. 37.1b) is generally caused by excessive friction, such as by heel tabs, or wearing shoes that are too tight or too large. Various types of rather stiff boots (e.g. skating, cricket, bowling) can cause such friction, and the pressure can often be relieved by using a punch to widen the heel of the boot and providing "donut" protection to the area of bursitis as it resolves.

Referred pain to this region from the lumbar spine or associated neural structures is unusual, and always warrants consideration in challenging cases (Chapters 6 and 40).

CLINICAL SPORTS MEDICINE MASTERCLASSES

[W] www.clinicalsportsmedicine.com

- A demonstration of how to perform an injection for posterior impingement syndrome.

REFERENCES

1. Kujala UM, Sarna S, Kaprio J. Cumulative incidence of Achilles tendon rupture and tendinopathy in male former elite athletes. *Clin J Sport Med* 2005;15(3):133–5.

2. Paavola M, Kannus P, Paakkala T et al. Long-term prognosis of patients with Achilles tendinopathy. An observational 8-year follow-up study. *Am J Sports Med* 2000;28(5):634–42.

3. O'Brien M. The anatomy of the Achilles tendon. *Foot Ankle Clin* 2005;10(2):225–38.

4. Alfredson H. Chronic midportion Achilles tendinopathy: an update on research and treatment. *Clin Sports Med* 2003;22(4):727–41.

5. Robinson JM, Cook JL, Purdam C et al. The VISA-A questionnaire: a valid and reliable index of the clinical severity of Achilles tendinopathy. *Br J Sports Med* 2001;35(5):335–41.

6. Simmonds FA. The diagnosis of the ruptured Achilles tendon. *Practitioner* 1957;179(1069):56–8.

7. Zanetti M, Metzdorf A, Kundert HP et al. Achilles tendons: clinical relevance of neovascularization diagnosed with power Doppler US. *Radiology* 2003;227(2):556–60.

8. Khan KM, Forster BB, Robinson J et al. Are ultrasound and magnetic resonance imaging of value in assessment of Achilles tendon disorders? A two year prospective study. *Br J Sports Med* 2003;37(2):149–53.

9. Cook JL, Khan KM, Kiss ZS et al. Asymptomatic hypoechoic regions on patellar tendon ultrasound: a 4-year clinical and ultrasound followup of 46 tendons. *Scand J Med Sci Sports* 2001;11(6):321–7.

10. Khan KM, Visentini PJ, Kiss ZS et al. Correlation of ultrasound and magnetic resonance imaging with clinical outcome after patellar tenotomy: prospective and retrospective studies. Victorian Institute of Sport Tendon Study Group. *Clin J Sport Med* 1999;9(3): 129–37.

11. Astrom M, Rausing A. Chronic Achilles tendinopathy. A survey of surgical and histopathologic findings. *Clin Orthop Relat Res* 1995(316):151–64.

12. Kannus P, Jozsa L. Histopathological changes preceding spontaneous rupture of a tendon. A controlled study of 891 patients. *J Bone Joint Surg Am* 1991;73(10):1507–25.

13. Astrom M, Gentz CF, Nilsson P et al. Imaging in chronic Achilles tendinopathy: a comparison of ultrasonography, magnetic resonance imaging and surgical findings in 27 histologically verified cases. *Skeletal Radiol* 1996;25(7):615–20.

14. Cook JL, Purdam CR. Is tendon pathology a continuum? A pathology model to explain the clinical presentation of load-induced tendinopathy. *Br J Sports Med* 2009;43(6):409–16.

15. Cook JL, Feller JA, Bonar SF et al. Abnormal tenocyte morphology is more prevalent than collagen disruption in asymptomatic athletes' patellar tendons. *J Orthop Res* 2004;22(2):334–8.

16. Alfredson H, Forsgren S, Thorsen K et al. Glutamate NMDAR1 receptors localised to nerves in human Achilles tendons. Implications for treatment? *Knee Surg Sports Traumatol Arthrosc* 2001;9(2):123–6.

17. Alfredson H, Thorsen K, Lorentzon R. In situ microdialysis in tendon tissue: high levels of glutamate, but not prostaglandin E2 in chronic Achilles tendon pain. *Knee Surg Sports Traumatol Arthrosc* 1999;7(6):378–81.

18. Alfredson H, Lorentzon M, Backman S et al. cDNA-arrays and real-time quantitative PCR techniques in the investigation of chronic Achilles tendinosis. *J Orthop Res* 2003;21(6):970–5.

19. Hart DA, Frank CB, Bray RC. Inflammatory processes in repetitive motion and overuse syndromes: potential role of neurogenic mechanisms in tendons and ligaments. In: Gordon SL, Blair SJ, Fine LJ, eds. *Repetive Motion Disorders of the Upper Extremity*. Rosemont: American Academy of Orthopaedic Surgeons; 1995:247–62.

20. Danielson P. Reviving the "biochemical" hypothesis for tendinopathy: new findings suggest the involvement of locally produced signal substances. *Br J Sports Med* 2009;43(4):265–8.

21. McCrory JL, Martin DF, Lowery RB et al. Etiologic factors associated with Achilles tendinitis in runners. *Med Sci Sports Exerc* 1999;31(10):1374–81.

22. Mokone GG, Gajjar M, September AV et al. The guanine-thymine dinucleotide repeat polymorphism within the tenascin-C gene is associated with Achilles tendon injuries. *Am J Sports Med* 2005;33(7):1016–21.

23. Alfredson H, Cook J. A treatment algorithm for managing Achilles tendinopathy: new treatment options. *Br J Sports Med* 2007;41(4):211–6.

24. Stanish WD, Curwin KS. *Tendinitis. Its etiology and treatment*. Toronto: Collamore Press, 1984.

25. Curwin S, Williams C, Stanish WD, et al. The aetiolgy and treatment of tendinitis. In: Harries M, Ed, *Oxford textbook of sports medicine* 2nd ed. Oxford: Oxford University Press 1998:610–632.

26. Alfredson H, Lorentzon R. Chronic Achilles tendinosis—recommendations for treatment and prevention. *Sports Med* 2000;29(2):135–46.

27. Alfredson H, Pietila T, Jonsson P et al. Heavy-load eccentric calf muscle training for the treatment of chronic Achilles tendinosis. *Am J Sports Med* 1998;26(3):360–6.

28. Fahlstrom M, Jonsson P, Lorentzon R et al. Chronic Achilles tendon pain treated with eccentric calf-muscle training. *Knee Surg Sports Traumatol Arthrosc* 2003;11(5):327–33.

29. Roos EM, Engstrom M, Lagerquist A et al. Clinical improvement after 6 weeks of eccentric exercise in patients with mid-portion Achilles tendinopathy – a randomized trial with 1-year follow-up. *Scand J Med Sci Sports* 2004;14(5):286–95.

30. Shalabi A, Kristoffersen-Wilberg M, Svensson L et al. Eccentric training of the gastrocnemius-soleus complex in chronic Achilles tendinopathy results in decreased tendon volume and intratendinous signal as evaluated by MRI. *Am J Sports Med* 2004;32(5):1286–96.

31. Silbernagel KG, Thomee R, Thomee P et al. Eccentric overload training for patients with chronic Achilles tendon pain – a randomized controlled study with reliability testing of the evaluation methods. *Scand J Med Sci Sports* 2001;11(4):197–206.

32. Niesen-Vertommen SL, Taunton JE, Clement DB et al. The effect of eccentric versus concentric exercise in the management of Achilles tendonitis. *Clin J Sport Med* 1992;2(2):109–13.

33. Kongsgaard M, Kovanen V, Aagaard P et al. Corticosteroid injections, eccentric decline squat training and heavy slow resistance training in patellar tendinopathy. *Scand J Med Sci Sports* 2009;19(6): 790–802.

34. Frohm A, Saartok T, Halvorsen K et al. Eccentric treatment for patellar tendinopathy: a prospective randomised short-term pilot study of two rehabilitation protocols. *Br J Sports Med* 2007;41(7):e7.

35. Allison GT, Purdam C. Eccentric loading for Achilles tendinopathy—strengthening or stretching? *Br J Sports Med* 2009;43(4):276–9.

36. Silbernagel KG, Thomee R, Eriksson BI et al. Continued sports activity, using a pain-monitoring model, during rehabilitation in patients with Achilles tendinopathy – a randomized controlled study. *Am J Sports Med* 2007;35(6):897–906.

37. Fredberg U, Bolvig L, Andersen NT. Prophylactic training in asymptomatic soccer players with ultrasonographic abnormalities in Achilles and patellar tendons – the Danish super league study. *Am J Sports Med* 2008;36(3):451–60.

38. Khan KM, Scott A. Mechanotherapy: how physical therapists' prescription of exercise promotes tissue repair. *Br J Sports Med* 2009;43(4):247–52.

39. Kjaer M, Langberg H, Miller BF et al. Metabolic activity and collagen turnover in human tendon in response to physical activity. *J Musculoskelet Neuronal Interact* 2005;5(1):41–52.

40. Rees JD, Lichtwark GA, Wolman RL et al. The mechanism for efficacy of eccentric loading in Achilles tendon injury; an in vivo study in humans. *Rheumatology* (Oxford) 2008;47(10):1493–7.

41. Sallis RE. Exercise is medicine and physicians need to prescribe it! *Br J Sports Med* 2009;43(1):3–4.

42. Stergioulas A, Stergioula M, Aarskog R et al. Effects of low-level laser therapy and eccentric exercises in the treatment of recreational athletes with chronic achilles tendinopathy. *Am J Sports Med* 2008;36(5):881–7.

43. Kane TP, Ismail M, Calder JD. Topical glyceryl trinitrate and noninsertional Achilles tendinopathy: a clinical and cellular investigation. *Am J Sports Med* 2008;36(6):1160–3.

44. Rompe JD, Furia J, Maffulli N. Eccentric loading versus eccentric loading plus shock-wave treatment for midportion achilles tendinopathy: a randomized controlled trial. *Am J Sports Med* 2009;37(3):463–70.

45. Rompe JD, Nafe B, Furia JP et al. Eccentric loading, shock-wave treatment, or a wait-and-see policy for tendinopathy of the main body of tendo Achillis: a randomized controlled trial. *Am J Sports Med* 2007;35(3):374–83.

46. de Vos RJ, Weir A, van Schie HT et al. Platelet-rich plasma injection for chronic Achilles tendinopathy a randomized controlled trial. *JAMA* 2010;303(2):144–9.

47. Knobloch K, Schreibmueller L, Longo UG et al. Eccentric exercises for the management of tendinopathy of the main body of the Achilles tendon with or without the AirHeel Brace. A randomized controlled trial. A: Effects on pain and microcirculation. *Disabil Rehabil* 2008;30(20–22):1685–91.

48. Paoloni JA, Appleyard RC, Nelson J et al. Topical glyceryl trinitrate treatment of chronic noninsertional achilles tendinopathy. A randomized, double-blind,

B

placebo-controlled trial. *J Bone Joint Surg Am* 2004; 86-A(5):916–22.

49. Fredberg U, Bolvig L, Pfeiffer-Jensen M et al. Ultrasonography as a tool for diagnosis, guidance of local steroid injection and, together with pressure algometry, monitoring of the treatment of athletes with chronic jumper's knee and Achilles tendinitis: a randomized, double-blind, placebo-controlled study. *Scand J Rheumatol* 2004;33(2):94–101.

50. Alfredson H, Ohberg L. Sclerosing injections to areas of neo-vascularisation reduce pain in chronic Achilles tendinopathy: a double-blind randomised controlled trial. *Knee Surg Sports Traumatol Arthrosc* 2005;13(4):338–44.

51. McLauchlan GJ, Handoll HH. Interventions for treating acute and chronic Achilles tendinitis. *Cochrane Database Syst Rev* 2001(2):CD000232.

52. Shrier I, Matheson GO, Kohl HW 3rd. Achilles tendonitis: are corticosteroid injections useful or harmful? *Clin J Sport Med* 1996;6(4):245–50.

53. Engebretsen L, Steffen K. To PRP or not? *Br J Sports Med* 2010;44(15):1071.

54. Yelland MJ, Sweeting KR, Lyftogt JA et al. Prolotherapy injections and eccentric loading exercises for painful Achilles tendinosis: a randomised trial. *Br J Sports Med* 2011;45(5):421–8.

55. Ferry ST, Dahners LE, Afshari HM et al. The effects of common anti-inflammatory drugs on the healing rat patellar tendon. *Am J Sports Med* 2007;35(8): 1326–33.

56. Astrom M, Arvidson T. Alignment and joint motion in the normal foot. *J Orthop Sports Phys Ther* 1995;22(5):216–22.

57. Hunter G. The conservative management of Achilles tendinopathy. *Phys Ther Sport* 2000;1(1):6–14.

58. Davidson CJ, Ganion LR, Gehlsen GM et al. Rat tendon morphologic and functional changes resulting from soft tissue mobilization. *Med Sci Sports Exerc* 1997;29(3):313–9.

59. Parvizi J, Wu CC, Lewallen DG et al. Low-intensity ultrasound stimulates proteoglycan synthesis in rat chondrocytes by increasing aggrecan gene expression. *J Orthop Res* 1999;17(4):488–94.

60. Giombini A, Di Cesare A, Casciello G et al. Hyperthermia at 434 MHz in the treatment of overuse sport tendinopathies: A randomised controlled clinical trial. *Int J Sports Med* 2002;23(3):207–11.

61. Chapman-Jones D, Hill D. Novel microcurrent treatment is more effective than conventional therapy for chronic Achilles tendinopathy: randomised comparative trial. *Physiotherapy* 2002;88(8):471–80.

62. Alfredson H, Ohberg L, Zeisig E et al. Treatment of midportion Achilles tendinosis: similar clinical results with US and CD-guided surgery outside the tendon and sclerosing polidocanol injections. *Knee Surg Sports Traumatol Arthrosc* 2007;15(12):1504–9.

63. Testa V, Capasso G, Maffulli N et al. Ultrasound-guided percutaneous longitudinal tenotomy for the management of patellar tendinopathy. *Med Sci Sports Exerc* 1999;31(11):1509–15.

64. Testa V, Capasso G, Benazzo F et al. Management of Achilles tendinopathy by ultrasound-guided percutaneous tenotomy. *Med Sci Sports Exerc* 2002;34(4):573–80.

65. Paavola M, Kannus P, Orava S et al. Surgical treatment for chronic Achilles tendinopathy: a prospective seven month follow up study. *Br J Sports Med* 2002;36(3): 178–82.

66. Paavola M, Orava S, Leppilahti J et al. Chronic Achilles tendon overuse injury: complications after surgical treatment – an analysis of 432 consecutive patients. *Am J Sports Med* 2000;28(1):77–82.

67. Alfredson H, Zeisig E, Fahlstrom M. No normalisation of the tendon structure and thickness after intratendinous surgery for chronic painful midportion Achilles tendinosis. *Br J Sports Med* 2009;43(12): 948–9.

68. Maffulli N, Testa V, Capasso G et al. Surgery for chronic Achilles tendinopathy yields worse results in nonathletic patients. *Clin J Sport Med* 2006;16(2): 123–8.

69. Alfredson H, Pietila T, Ohberg L et al. Achilles tendinosis and calf muscle strength. The effect of short-term immobilization after surgical treatment. *Am J Sports Med* 1998;26(2):166–71.

70. Benjamin M, Moriggl B, Brenner E et al. The "enthesis organ" concept: why enthesopathies may not present as focal insertional disorders. *Arthritis Rheum* 2004;50(10):3306–13.

71. de Palma L, Marinelli M, Meme L et al. Immunohistochemistry of the enthesis organ of the human Achilles tendon. *Foot Ankle Int* 2004;25(6): 414–18.

72. Canoso JJ. The premiere enthesis. *J Rheumatol* 1998;25(7):1254–6.

73. Lyman J, Weinhold PS, Almekinders LC. Strain behavior of the distal Achilles tendon – implications for insertional Achilles tendinopathy. *Am J Sports Med* 2004;32(2):457–61.

74. Rufai A, Ralphs JR, Benjamin M. Structure and histopathology of the insertional region of the human Achilles-tendon. *J Orthop Res* 1995;13(4):585–93.

75. McGarvey WC, Palumbo RC, Baxter DE et al. Insertional Achilles tendinosis: Surgical treatment through a central tendon splitting approach. *Foot Ankle Int* 2002;23(1):19–25.

76. Ohberg L, Alfredson H. Sclerosing therapy in chronic Achilles tendon insertional pain: results of a pilot study. *Knee Surg Sports Traumatol Arthros* 2003;11(5):339–43.

77. Jonsson P, Alfredson H, Sunding K et al. New regimen for eccentric calf-muscle training in patients with chronic insertional Achilles tendinopathy: results of a pilot study. *Br J Sports Med* 2008;42(9):746–9.

78. Rompe JD, Furia J, Maffulli N. Eccentric loading compared with shock wave treatment for chronic insertional achilles tendinopathy. A randomized, controlled trial. *J Bone Joint Surg Am* 2008;90(1):52–61.

79. Fridrich F. [Tendon-splitting approach for the surgical treatment of Haglund's deformity and associated condition. Evaluation and results]. *Acta Chir Orthop Traumatol Cech* 2009;76(3):212–7.

80. DeVries JG, Summerhays B, Guehlstorf DW. Surgical correction of Haglund's triad using complete detachment and reattachment of the Achilles tendon. *J Foot Ankle Surg* 2009;48(4):447–51.

81. Anderson JA, Suero E, O'Loughlin PF et al. Surgery for retrocalcaneal bursitis: a tendon-splitting versus a lateral approach. *Clin Orthop Rel Res* 2008;466(7):1678–82.

82. Bhandari M, Guyatt GH, Siddiqui F et al. Treatment of acute Achilles tendon ruptures: a systematic overview and meta-analysis. *Clin Orthop Relat Res* 2002(400):190–200.

83. Khan RJK, Fick D, Keogh A et al. Treatment of acute Achilles tendon ruptures, A meta-analysis of randomized, controlled trials. *J Bone Joint Surg Am* 2005;87(10):2202–10.

84. Nilsson-Helander K, Silbernagel KG, Thomee R et al. Acute achilles tendon rupture: a randomized, controlled study comparing surgical and nonsurgical treatments using validated outcome measures. *Am J Sports Med* 2010;38(11):2186–93.

85. Cetti R, Henriksen LO, Jacobsen KS. A new treatment of ruptured Achilles tendons. A prospective randomized study. *Clin Orthop Relat Res* 1994(308):155–65.

86. Kangas J, Pajala A, Siira P et al. Early functional treatment versus early immobilization in tension of the musculotendinous unit after Achilles rupture repair: a prospective, randomized, clinical study. *J Trauma* 2003;54(6):1171–80; discussion 1180–1.

87. Suchak AA, Spooner C, Reid DC et al. Postoperative rehabilitation protocols for Achilles tendon ruptures: a meta-analysis. *Clin Orthop Relat Res* 2006;445:216–21.

88. Lunsford BR, Perry J. The standing heel-rise test for ankle plantar flexion: criterion for normal. *Phys Ther* 1995;75(8):694–8.

89. Rossi F, Dragoni S. Symptomatic accessory soleus muscle: report of 18 cases in athletes. *J Sports Med Phys Fitness* 2005;45(1):93–7.

90. Leswick DA, Chow V, Stoneham GW. Resident's corner. Answer to case of the month #94. Accessory soleus muscle. *Can Assoc Radiol J* 2003;54(5):313–15.

B

Chapter 38

Acute ankle injuries

with EVERT VERHAGEN and JON KARLSSON

Unbeknownst to most historians, Einstein started down the road of professional basketball before an ankle injury diverted him to science. Gary Larson (cartoonist, creator of The Far Side) http://thinkexist.com/quotes/gary_larson/

Ankle injury is arguably the most common sport injury. It ranked number 1 among 24 of the 70 sports for which there are quality data.[1] In sports such as volleyball, ankle injuries make up almost half of all injuries.[1]

Ankle injuries include, but are not limited to, "ankle sprains." The first half of this chapter focuses on anatomy, clinical assessment, and management of lateral ligament injuries after ankle sprain. We also discuss two less common sequelae of ankle sprain—medial ligament injury and Pott's fracture.

The presentation of a "sprained ankle" can mask damage to other structures—such as subtle fractures around the ankle joint, osteochondral fractures of the dome of the talus, and dislocation or longitudinal rupture of the peroneal tendons. Such injuries persist much longer than would be expected with a straightforward lateral ligament sprain. This is often referred to as "the problem ankle"—it is discussed in the second half of this chapter.

Functional anatomy

The ankle contains three joints (Fig. 38.1):

- talocrural (ankle) joint
- inferior tibiofibular joint
- subtalar joint.

The talocrural or ankle joint (Fig. 38.1a) is a hinge joint formed between the inferior surface of the tibia and the superior surface of the talus. The medial and lateral malleoli provide additional articulations and stability to the ankle joint. The ankle joint can plantarflex and dorsiflex. Because the joint is least stable in plantarflexion, injuries are more common

when the foot is in this position, and most stability is provided by the ankle ligaments alone.

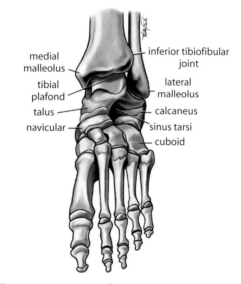

Figure 38.1 Anatomy of the ankle
(a) Talocrural (ankle) joint

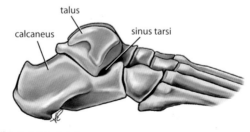

(b) Subtalar joint

Acute ankle injuries   Chapter 38

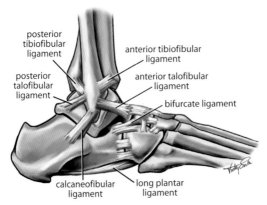

posterior tibiofibular ligament
anterior tibiofibular ligament
posterior talofibular ligament
anterior talofibular ligament
bifurcate ligament
calcaneofibular ligament
long plantar ligament

(c) Ligaments of the ankle joint—lateral view

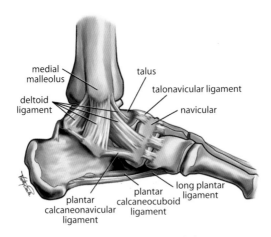

medial malleolus
talus
talonavicular ligament
deltoid ligament
navicular
long plantar ligament
plantar calcaneocuboid ligament
plantar calcaneonavicular ligament

(d) Ligaments of the ankle joint—medial view

The distal parts of the fibula and tibia articulate at the inferior tibiofibular joint where they are supported by the inferior tibiofibular ligament or syndesmosis. The small amount of movement present at this joint is extremely important for normal walking and running. Injuries to this joint are more common than previously thought.

The subtalar joint (Fig. 38.1b), between the talus and calcaneus, is divided into an anterior and posterior articulation separated by the sinus tarsi. The subtalar joint provides shock absorption, permits the foot to adjust to uneven ground, and allows the foot to remain flat on the ground when the leg is at an angle to the surface. Inversion and eversion occur at the subtalar joint.

The ligaments of the ankle joint are shown in Figures 38.1c and d. The lateral ligament consists of three parts—the anterior talofibular ligament (ATFL), which passes as a flat and rather thin band

from the tip of the fibula anteriorly to the lateral talar neck; the calcaneofibular ligament (CFL), which is a cord-like structure directed inferiorly and posteriorly; and the short posterior talofibular ligament (PTFL), which runs posteriorly from the fibula to the talus. The medial or deltoid ligament of the ankle is a fan-shaped ligament extending from the medial malleolus anteriorly to the navicular and talus, inferiorly to the calcaneus, and posteriorly to the talus. This strong ligament is composed of two layers, one deep and the other more superficial. It is injured only infrequently.

Clinical perspective

An ankle sprain is the most common acute sport trauma, accounting for about 14% of all sport-related injuries. Among these, 80% are ligamentous sprains caused by explosive inversion or supination.[1] Inversion injuries are four times more common than eversion injuries, due to the relative instability of the lateral joint and weakness of the lateral ligaments compared with the medial ligament.[1,2] The injury often occurs at the subtalar joint and tears the anterior talofibular ligament, which possesses the lowest ultimate load among the lateral ligaments at the ankle.

As the strong medial ligament requires a greater force to be injured, these sprains almost always take longer to rehabilitate. The differential diagnoses that must be considered after an ankle injury are listed in Table 38.1 overleaf. The aim of the initial clinical assessment is to rule out an ankle fracture, if possible, and to diagnose the site of abnormality as accurately as possible.

History

The mechanism of the ankle sprain is an important clue to diagnosis. An inversion injury suggests lateral ligament damage; an eversion injury suggests medial ligament damage. If the injury involved ankle compression, consider osteochondral injury.

The onset of pain is very important. A history of being able to weight-bear immediately after an injury followed by a subsequent increase in pain and swelling as the patient continues to play sport or walk about, suggests a sprain (ligament injury) rather than a fracture. The location of pain and swelling generally indicates which ligaments were injured. The most common site is over the anterolateral aspect of the ankle involving the anterior talofibular ligament, which occurs in approximately two-thirds

Table 38.1 Acute ankle injuries

Common	Less common	Not to be missed
Lateral ligament sprains (Fig. 38.1c) • ATFL • CFL • PTFL	Osteochondral lesion of the talus Ligament sprain/rupture • Medial ligament injury (Fig. 38.1d) • AITFL injury Fractures • Lateral/medial/posterior malleolus (Pott's) • Tibial plafond • Base of the fifth metatarsal • Anterior process of the calcaneus • Lateral process of the talus • Posterior process of the talus • Os trigonum Dislocated ankle (fracture/dislocation) Tendon rupture/dislocation • Tibialis posterior tendon • Peroneal tendons (longitudinal rupture)	Complex regional pain syndrome type I (post-injury) Greenstick fractures (children) Sprained syndesmosis Tarsal coalition (may come to light as a result of an ankle sprain)

ATFL = anterior talofibular ligament; CFL = calcaneofibular ligament; PTFL = posterior tibiofibular ligament; AITFL = anteroinferior tibiofibular ligament

of all injuries. In severe injuries, medial and lateral ligaments may both be damaged; however, this is infrequent. The degree of swelling and bruising is usually, but not always, an indication of the severity of injury.

The degree of disability, both immediately following the injury and subsequently, indicates the severity of the injury. Ask about initial management, the use of the RICE (rest, ice, compression, elevation) regimen, and the duration of restricted weight-bearing after the injury, as a poorly managed injury will appear "more significant" in terms of swelling and long-term disability than a similar injury that has been managed adroitly.

The practitioner should ask about a previous history of ankle injury and assess whether the post-injury rehabilitation was adequate. Did the sportsperson use protective tape or braces for the first three to six months after previous injury, or until the end of season?

Examination

Aims of ankle examination are to:

• assess the degree of instability present (i.e. grade the ligamentous injury)
• detect functional deficits (i.e. loss of range of motion, reduced strength, reduced proprioception)

• detect any associated injuries (e.g. avulsion fracture of the base of the fifth metatarsal is commonly overlooked but is easily detected by palpation; injury to the peroneal tendons may lead to longstanding disability and is easily missed during the acute phase).

Examination involves:

1. Observation
   (a) standing
   (b) supine
2. Active movements
   (a) plantarflexion/dorsiflexion (Fig. 38.2a)
   (b) inversion/eversion
3. Passive movements
   (a) plantarflexion/dorsiflexion
   (b) inversion/eversion (Fig. 38.2b)
4. Resisted movements
   (a) eversion (Fig. 38.2c)
5. Functional tests
   (a) lunge test (Fig. 38.2d)
   (b) hopping
6. Palpation
   (a) distal—and proximal—fibula
   (b) lateral malleolus
   (c) lateral ligaments (Fig. 38.2e on page 810)
   (d) talus
   (e) peroneal tendon(s)

(f) base of fifth metatarsal

(g) anterior joint line

(h) dome of talus (often difficult, not easily accessible and swelling may be marked)

(i) medial ligament

(j) sustentaculum tali

(k) sinus tarsi

(l) anteroinferior tibiofibular ligament (AITFL)

7. Special tests (comparison with other side necessary; however, it should be borne in mind that there is no obvious correlation between increased anterior drawer and/or lateral talar tilt and symptoms of ankle insufficiency)

(a) anterior drawer (Fig. 38.2f overleaf)

(b) lateral talar tilt (Fig. 38.2g overleaf)

(c) proprioception (Fig. 38.2h overleaf)

(c) Resisted movement—eversion. In acute, painful ankle injuries, resisted movements may not be possible. In cases of persistent pain following ankle injury, weakness of the ankle evertors (peroneal muscles) should be assessed

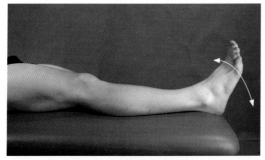

Figure 38.2 Examination of the patient with an acute ankle injury

(a) Active movement—plantarflexion/dorsiflexion. Assessment of dorsiflexion is important as restriction results in a functional deficit. Range of motion can be compared with the uninjured side. Tight calf muscles may restrict dorsiflexion. This can be eliminated by placing the knee in slight flexion

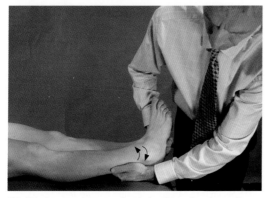

(b) Passive movement—inversion/eversion. Inversion is frequently painful and restricted in lateral ligament injury, while eversion is painful following injuries to the medial ligament. Increased pain on combined plantarflexion and inversion suggests anterior talofibular ligament injury

(d) Functional test—lunge test. Assess ankle dorsiflexion compared with the uninjured side. Note any pain. Other functional tests may be performed to reproduce the patient's pain if appropriate (e.g. single-leg standing, hopping)

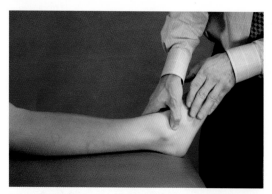

(e) Palpation—lateral ligament

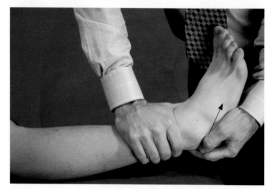

(f) Ligament testing—anterior drawer test. The ankle is placed in slight plantarflexion and grasped as shown. Pressure is exerted upwards and the degree of excursion (anterior drawer) is noted and compared with the uninjured side. This test assesses the integrity of the anterior talofibular ligament and calcaneofibular ligament. Pain on this test should also be noted; if painful it may indeed mask injury to the ligament. Then the test should be repeated within five days. The most optimal time to test the integrity of the lateral ligaments is on the fifth post-injury day

Investigations

Should I order an X-ray? Clinicians not yet confident in physical examination benefit from the Ottawa ankle rules (Fig. 38.3).[2, 3] X-rays of the ankle joint should include the base of the fifth metatarsal to exclude avulsion fracture. If damage to the lower tibiofibular syndesmosis (anteroinferior tibiofibular ligament [AITFL]) is suspected, special ankle mortise or syndesmosis views are required. Experienced sports medicine clinicians can distinguish tenderness to palpation on bone (lateral or medial malleolus) or on ligament tissue itself.

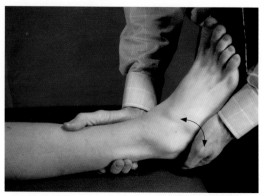

(g) Ligament testing—talar tilt. This tests integrity of the anterior talofibular and calcaneofibular ligaments laterally and the deltoid ligament medially. The ankle is grasped as shown, and the medial and lateral movement of the talus and calcaneus are assessed in relation to the tibia and fibula. Pain on this test must also be noted

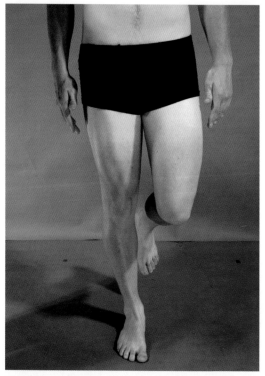

(h) Special test—proprioception. Single-leg standing with eyes closed may demonstrate impaired proprioception compared with the uninjured side

An osteochondral lesion of the talus—especially the medial side—may not be apparent on initial X-ray. If significant pain and disability persist despite

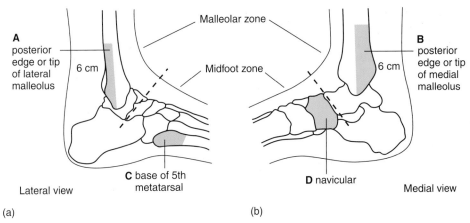

Figure 38.3 Ankle X-ray—Ottawa Rules 1: ankle X-rays are only required if there is any pain in the malleolar zone and any one of these findings—bone tenderness at A, or bone tenderness at B, or inability to bear weight both immediately and at the clinical assessment (four steps). Foot X-ray—recommendation 2: foot X-rays are only required if there is any pain in the midfoot zone, and any one of these findings—bone tenderness at C, or bone tenderness at D, or inability to bear weight both immediately and at the clinical assessment (four steps)

appropriate treatment four to six weeks after an apparent "routine" ankle sprain, MRI is the investigation of choice to exclude an osteochondral lesion, especially when dealing with the "problem ankle" (i.e. longstanding pain/disability without obvious cause or pathology [page 817]). If this is not readily available, radioisotopic bone scan or CT can be used.

Lateral ligament injuries

Lateral ligament injuries occur in activities requiring rapid changes in direction, especially if these take place on uneven surfaces (e.g. grass fields). They also occur when a player, having jumped, lands on another competitor's feet. They are very common in basketball, volleyball, netball, and most football codes.

The usual mechanism of lateral ligament injury is inversion and plantarflexion, and this damages the anterior talofibular ligament before the calcaneofibular ligament.[4] This occurs because the anterior talofibular ligament is taut in plantarflexion and the calcaneofibular ligament is relatively loose (Fig. 38.4). Also, the anterior talofibular ligament can only tolerate half the strain of the calcaneofibular ligament before tearing.

Complete tear of the anterior talofibular ligament, calcaneofibular ligament, and posterior talofibular ligament, results in a dislocation of the ankle joint and is frequently associated with a fracture. Such an injury is infrequent, however. Isolated ligament rup-

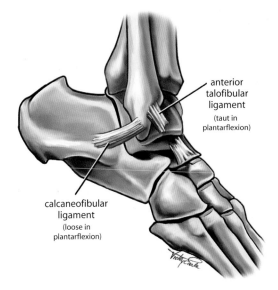

Figure 38.4 A plantarflexion injury can lead to injury of the anterior talofibular ligament before the calcaneofibular ligament

tures of the calcaneofibular ligament and especially the posterior talofibular ligament are also rare.

Ankle sprain may be accompanied by an audible snap, crack, or tear, which, although often of great concern to the sportsperson and onlookers, has no particular diagnostic significance (unlike the case in knee ligament injuries where it has profound implications [Chapter 32]). Depending on the severity of the injury, the sportsperson may continue to play or may rest immediately. Swelling usually appears rapidly, although occasionally it may be delayed some hours.

To assess lateral ligament injuries, examine all three components of the ligament and determine the degree of ankle instability. In a grade I tear there is no abnormal ligament laxity. It is important to compare both sides (assuming the other side has not been injured) as there is a large inter-individual variation in normal ankle laxity. Grade II injuries reveal some degree of laxity, however with a firm end point. Grade III injuries show gross laxity without a discernible end point. All three grades are associated with pain and tenderness, although grade III tears may be least painful after the initial episode has settled.

The grades may be useful in terms of rehabilitation, and they also affect the selection of the acute treatment. Note that in the acute phase the reliability and validity of manual stress tests (e.g. anterior drawer or talar-tilt test) are low; manual stress tests are only reliable with good validity when performed 4–7 days post injury.

Treatment and rehabilitation of lateral ligament injuries

The management of lateral ligament injuries of all three grades follows the same principles. After minimizing initial hemorrhage and reducing pain, the aims are to restore range of motion, muscle strength and proprioception, and then prescribe a progressive, sport-specific exercise program.

Initial management

Lateral ligament injuries require RICE treatment (Chapter 13). This essential treatment limits the hemorrhage and subsequent edema that would otherwise cause an irritating synovial reaction and restrict joint range of motion for a long period of time. The injured sportsperson must avoid factors that promote blood flow and swelling (such as hot showers, heat rubs, or excessive weight-bearing). Gradually increasing weight-bearing, however, helps reduce the swelling and increase the ankle motion, and enhances the rehabilitation.

Reduction of pain and swelling

Analgesics and/or nonsteroidal anti-inflammatory drugs (NSAIDs) may be required. After 48 hours, gentle soft tissue therapy and mobilization may reduce pain. By reducing pain and swelling, muscle inhibition around the joint is minimized, permitting the patient to begin range of motion exercises.

The indications for the use of NSAIDs in ankle injuries are unclear. The majority of practitioners tend to prescribe these drugs after lateral ligament sprains although their efficacy has not been proven (Chapter 13). The rationale for commencing NSAIDs two to three days after injury is to reduce the risk of joint synovitis with early return to weight-bearing.

Restoration of full range of motion

If necessary, the patient may be non-weight-bearing on crutches for the first 24 hours, but then should commence partial weight-bearing in normal heel–toe gait. This can be achieved while still using crutches or, in less severe cases, by protecting the damaged joint with strapping or bracing.[5] Thus, partial and, ultimately, full weight-bearing can take place without aggravating the injury. Lunge stretches and accessory and physiological mobilization of the ankle (Fig. 38.5a), subtalar (Fig. 38.5b), and midtarsal joints should begin early in rehabilitation. As soon as pain allows, the clinician should prescribe active range of motion exercises (e.g. stationary cycling).

Muscle conditioning

Active strengthening exercises, including plantarflexion, dorsiflexion, inversion, and eversion (Fig. 38.6), should begin as soon as pain allows. They should be progressed by increasing resistance (a common method is to use rubber tubing). Strengthening eversion with the ankle fully plantarflexed is particularly important to prevent future lateral ligament injuries. Weight-bearing exercises (e.g. shuttle [Fig. 38.6b], wobble board exercises) are encouraged as soon as pain permits, preferably the first or second day after injury.

Proprioception

Proprioception is invariably impaired after ankle ligament injuries. The assessment of proprioception is shown in Figure 38.2h. The patient should begin proprioceptive retraining (Chapter 15) early in rehabilitation and these exercises should gradually progress in difficulty. An example of a common progression is balancing on one leg, then using the rocker board (Fig. 38.7a on page 814) or mini-trampoline, and ultimately performing functional activities while balancing (Fig. 38.7b on page 814). Mobilization is recommended In order to reduce stiffness of the joint.

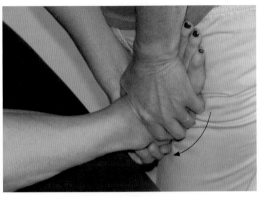

Figure 38.5 Mobilization of the ankle joint
(a) Ankle dorsiflexion. The calcaneus and foot are grasped to passively dorsiflex the ankle

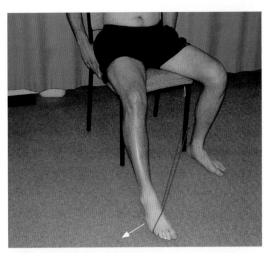

Figure 38.6 Strengthening exercises—eversion
(a) Using a rubber tube as resistance

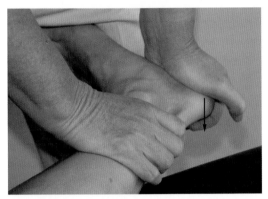

(b) Eversion mobilization techniques to restore subtalar joint movement after ankle sprain

Functional exercises

Functional exercises (e.g. jumping, hopping, twisting, figure-of-eight running) can be prescribed when the sportsperson is pain-free, has full range of motion, and adequate muscle strength and proprioception. Specific technical training not only accelerates a player's return to sport but can also substantially reduce the risk of re-injury.[6-8] It should be remembered that approximately 75% of those who sustain an ankle ligament injury have had a previous injury, often one that has not been fully rehabilitated. In other words, the risk of recurrent injury means that all lateral ligament ankle ligament injuries should be rehabilitated completely.

Return to sport

Return to sport is permitted when functional exercises can be performed without pain during or after activity. However, any sportsperson who has had a

(b) Shuttle exercises

significant lateral ligament injury has an increased risk of injury recurrence post-injury for a minimum of six to 12 months.[9-11] There are a number of methods to protect against these subsequent inversion injuries. Both external prophylactic measures (i.e. tape or brace), and neuromuscular training are arguably equally effective in reducing this increased risk for ankle sprain recurrences after an initial ankle

B

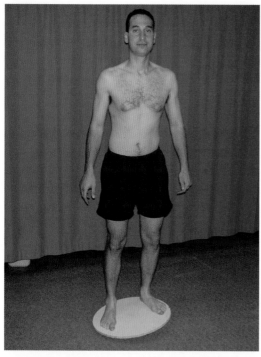

Figure 38.7 Proprioceptive retraining following acute ankle injury

(a) Rocker board

(b) Functional activity while balancing

sprain.[12, 13] However, both have seemingly different pathways through which they achieve this secondary preventive effect.

The relative advantages of taping and bracing have been discussed in Chapter 9. As both seem equally effective, the choice of taping or bracing depends on patient preference, cost, availability, and expertise in applying tape.[14]

The three main methods of tape application are stirrups (Fig. 38.8a), heel lock (Fig. 38.8b) and the figure of six (Fig. 38.8c). Usually at least two of these methods are used together.

 See a demonstration of ankle taping in the *Clinical Sports Medicine* masterclasses at www.clinicalsportsmedicine.com.

Braces have the advantage of ease of fitting and adjustment, lack of skin irritation, and reduced cost compared with taping for a lengthy period. There are a number of different ankle braces available (Fig. 38.9).[11]

Clinical and mechanical studies teach that external measures act to support neuromuscular function after an ankle sprain—their role in restricting ankle

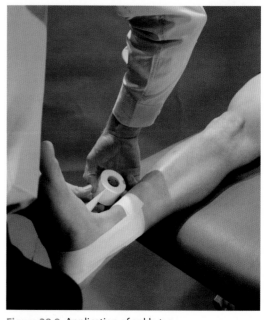

Figure 38.8 Application of ankle tape

(a) Stirrups. After preparation of the skin, anchors are applied circumferentially. The ankle should be in the neutral position. Stirrups are applied from medial to lateral, and repeated several times until functional stability is achieved

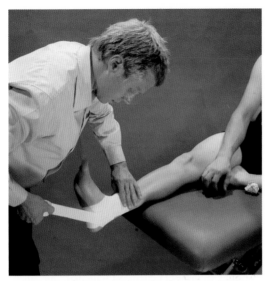

(b) Heel lock. One method used to limit inversion is taping commenced at the front of the ankle and then angled inferiorly across the medial longitudinal arch, then diagonally and posteriorly across the lateral aspect of the heel, and then continued medially over the back of the Achilles tendon to loop back anteriorly. Tape direction is thereafter reversed to restrict eversion

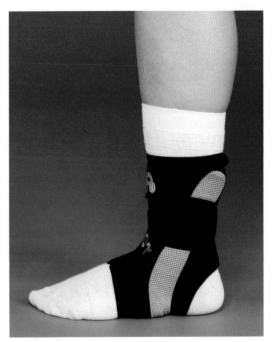

Figure 38.9 Ankle brace

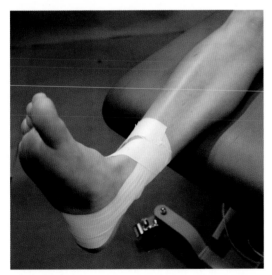

(c) Figure of six
This is applied over stirrups. Tape runs longitudinally along the lateral ankle, under the heel and is pulled up to loop back around the medial ankle as shown

range of motion is less important.[15-17] This support is immediately available when wearing external measures. Nonetheless, external measures only support the

impaired ankle and do not stimulate rehabilitation/retraining of the underlying impaired neuromuscular function. As such, their preventive effects are limited to the period when the sportsperson is wearing the external device. This means that an sportsperson should brace or tape for the entire 1 to 2 year period during which an increased risk is present in order to fully benefit from any preventive effects.

In contrast, neuromuscular training targets the underlying impairment by re-establishing and strengthening the ligament, muscles, and protective reflexes of the ankle.[18, 19] After completion of the training, the sportsperson's increased recurrence risk is reduced and, in theory, no further preventive means are necessary. However, these exercises do not reduce injury risk immediately with the first training session. Based on current available evidence, it takes between eight to ten weeks for more intensive training programs to achieve an effect.[6, 20]

It takes between 8 to 10 weeks for more intensive training programs to achieve an effect.

When external measures are employed during a period of intensive neuromuscular training after return to sport, the patient benefits from an immediate risk-reducing effect while targeting the underlying causes of an increased recurrence risk. This results in full reduction of the risk of a recurrent sprain within 10 weeks of return to sport.

Treatment of grade III injuries

A 2002 Cochrane systematic review concluded that there was insufficient information from randomized trials to recommend surgery over conservative treatment of grade III ankle sprains.[21] They found that functional recovery (as measured by return to work) was quicker in those treated with rehabilitation, subsequent rate of ankle sprains was no different between groups, and there was more ankle stiffness in those treated surgically.[21]

Finnish researchers compared surgical treatment (primary repair plus early controlled mobilization) with early controlled mobilization alone in a prospective study of 60 patients with grade III lateral ankle ligament injuries.[22] Of the patients treated with rehabilitation alone, 87% had excellent or good outcomes compared with 60% of patients treated surgically. Thus, early mobilization alone provided a better outcome than surgery plus mobilization in patients with complete tears of the lateral ankle ligaments.

Dutch investigators have reported better long-term outcomes after surgery for lateral ligament rupture compared with rehabilitation; however, this conclusion was controversial.[23] Differences in "rehabilitation" protocols can explain such contradictory study results.

In clinical practice, it is widely agreed that all grade III ankle injuries warrant a trial of initial conservative management over at least a six- to twelve-week period, irrespective of the caliber of the sportsperson.

If, despite appropriate rehabilitation and protection, the patient complains of recurrent episodes of instability or persistent pain, then surgical reconstruction of the lateral ligament is indicated.

The preferred surgical method is anatomical reconstruction using the damaged ligaments; this produces good functional results, with low risk of complications. The ligaments are shortened and reinserted to bone, and only if the ligament tissue is extremely damaged or even absent may other methods such as tenodesis, in most cases using the peroneus brevis tendon, be considered.

Following surgery, it is important to undertake a comprehensive rehabilitation program to restore full joint range of motion, strength, and proprioception. The principles of rehabilitation outlined on page 812

are appropriate. The anatomical reconstruction produces good clinical results in more than 90% of patients. There is, however, increased risk of inferior results in cases of very longstanding ligament insufficiency and generalized joint laxity. In case of anatomic reconstruction, both the anterior talofibular ligament and calcaneofibular ligament should be reconstructed simultaneously. Post-operatively, early range of motion training, e.g. using Aircast stirrup, is recommended.

Less common ankle joint injuries

Medial (deltoid) ligament injuries

Because the deltoid ligament is stronger than the lateral ligament, and probably because eversion is a less common mechanism of ankle sprain, medial ankle ligament injuries are less common than lateral ligament injuries. Occasionally, medial and lateral ligament injuries occur in the same ankle sprain, however, not commonly. Medial ligament injuries may occur together with fractures (e.g. medial malleolus, talar dome, articular surfaces). Medial ligament sprains should be treated in the same manner as lateral ligament sprains, although return to activity takes about twice as long (or more) as would be predicted were the injury on the lateral side.

Pott's fracture

A fracture affecting one or more of the malleoli (lateral, medial, posterior) is known as a Pott's fracture. It can be difficult to distinguish a fracture from a moderate-to-severe ligament sprain, as both conditions may result from similar mechanisms of injury and cause severe pain and inability to weight-bear. Careful and gentle palpation can generally localize the greatest site of tenderness to either the malleoli (fracture) or just distal to the malleolus to the ligament attachment (sprain). X-ray is often required—the Ottawa rules (Fig. 38.3) are useful in these cases.

The management of Pott's fractures requires restoration of the normal anatomy between the superior surface of the talus and the ankle mortise (inferior margins of the tibia and fibula). If this relationship has been disrupted with dislocation of the joint surface, internal fixation is almost always required. Stable internal fixation is used; early range of motion training is recommended.

Isolated undisplaced spiral fractures of the lateral malleolus (without medial ligament instability) and posterior malleolar fractures involving less than 25% of the articular surface are usually stable. These fractures can be treated symptomatically with early mobilization, using crutches only in the early stages for pain relief.

Lateral malleolar fractures associated with medial instability, hairline medial malleolar fractures, and larger undisplaced posterior malleolar fractures are potentially unstable, but may be treated conservatively with six weeks of immobilization using a below-knee cast with extension to include the metatarsal heads. In cases of undisplaced or minimally displaced fractures, the immobilization time may be shortened considerably, using an ankle brace and early range of motion training. A walking heel may be applied after swelling has subsided (3–5 days).

Displaced medial malleolar, large posterior malleolar, bimalleolar or trimalleolar fractures, or any displaced fracture that involves the ankle mortise require orthopedic referral for open reduction and internal fixation. A comprehensive rehabilitation program should be undertaken following surgical fixation or removal of the cast. The aims of the rehabilitation program are to restore full range of motion, strengthen the surrounding muscles and improve proprioception. Guidelines for ankle rehabilitation are provided on page 812.

Maisonneuve fracture

Maisonneuve fractures are found more commonly in patients presenting to emergency departments than in the sports setting, but occasionally high-impact sports injuries can cause this variant of the syndesmosis sprain. The injury involves complete rupture of the medial ligament, the anteroinferior tibiofibular ligament (see below) and interosseous membrane, as well as a proximal fibular fracture. Surprisingly, non-weight-bearing X-rays may not demonstrate the fracture, as the unstable ankle can reduce spontaneously. Urgent referral to an orthopedic surgeon is necessary.[24]

Persistent pain after ankle sprain—"the problem ankle"

Most cases of ankle ligament sprain resolve satisfactorily with treatment—pain and swelling settle and function improves. However, as ankle sprain is such a common condition, there remains a substantial number of patients who do not progress well and complain of pain, recurrent instability, swelling, and impaired function three to six weeks after injury, or even longer.

This is a very common presentation in a sports medicine practice and the key to successful management is accurate diagnosis. The ankle may continue to cause problems because of an undiagnosed fracture or other bony abnormality (Table 38.2). Alternatively, there may be ligament, tendon, synovial, or neurological dysfunction (Table 38.3 overleaf). In the remainder of this chapter, we discuss a clinical approach to managing patients with this presentation, and then detail management of specific conditions.

Clinical approach to the problem ankle

The clinician should take a detailed history that clarifies whether the problem has arisen following an ankle sprain (the true "problem ankle") or whether the patient has longstanding ankle pain that arose without a history of injury (see Chapter 39).

The patient who has had inadequate rehabilitation usually complains of persistent pain, reduced range of motion, and limitation of function with increasing activity. Determine whether the rehabilitation was adequate by asking the patient to show you the exercises he or she performed in rehabilitation. Did therapy include range of motion exercises

---

Table 38.2 Fractures and impingements that may cause persistent ankle pain after ankle injury

Fractures and chondral lesions	Bony impingements[a]
Anterior process calcaneus	Anterior impingement
Lateral process talus	Posterior impingement
Posterior process talus (or, rare, os trigonum fracture)	Anterolateral impingement
Osteochondral lesion	
Tibial plafond chondral lesion	
Base of fifth metatarsal	

[a] Although impingements are included here in the bony causes, pain commonly arises from soft tissue impingement between bony prominences. Also, impingements most commonly present as ankle pain of gradual onset but are included here as they can present and fail to resolve after acute injuries

Table 38.3 Ligamentous, tendon, and neurological causes of persistent ankle pain after ankle injury

Atypical sprains	Tendon injuries	Other soft tissue and neural abnormalities
Chronic ligamentous instability	Chronic peroneal tendon weakness	Inadequate rehabilitation
Medial ligament sprain	Peroneal tendon subluxation/rupture	Chronic synovitis
Syndesmosis sprain (AITFL sprain)	Tibialis posterior tendon subluxation/	Sinus tarsi syndrome
Subtalar joint sprain	rupture	Complex regional pain syndrome type 1

(particularly dorsiflexion), strengthening exercises (with the foot fully plantarflexed to engage the peroneal tendons/muscles) and possibly proprioceptive retraining?[25]

Examination of the inadequately rehabilitated ankle reveals decreased range of motion in the ankle joint (especially dorsiflexion), weak peroneal muscles, and impaired proprioception. These findings can be reversed with active and passive mobilization of the ankle joint (Fig. 38.5), peroneal muscle strengthening (Fig. 38.6), and proprioception training (Fig. 38.7). Other abnormalities can also cause this constellation of examination findings—remember that the ankle may be inadequately rehabilitated because of the pain of an osteochondral lesion of the talus.

If rehabilitation has been appropriate and symptoms persist, it is necessary to consider the presence of other abnormalities. Was it a high-energy injury that may have caused a fracture? Symptoms of intra-articular abnormalities include clicking, locking, and joint swelling. The clinician should palpate all the sites of potential fracture very carefully to exclude that condition.

Soft tissue injuries that can cause persistent ankle pain after sprain include chronic ligament instability, complex regional pain syndrome type 1 (formerly known as reflex sympathetic dystrophy [RSD]) and, rarely, tendon dislocation or subluxation, or even tendon rupture (partial or total). Inflammation of the sinus tarsi (sinus tarsi syndrome) can be a cause of persistent ankle pain, but this syndrome can also occur secondary to associated fractures. Thus, even if the patient has features of the sinus tarsi syndrome, the clinician should still seek other injuries too.

Appropriate investigation is a key part of management of patients with the problem ankle. Both radio-isotopic bone scan and MRI are able to distinguish soft tissue damage from bony injury; MRI is preferred in most cases. In soft tissue injuries, isotope activity in the bone phase is normal. If bony damage is present, isotope activity in the bone phase is increased. MRI can detect bony and soft tissue abnormalities but the clinician must remember that a subluxing tendon can appear normal on MRI. The conditions that are associated with the various findings on MRI and bone scan are listed in Figure 38.10.

Osteochondral lesions of the talar dome

It is not uncommon for osteochondral fractures of the talar dome to occur in association with ankle sprains, particularly when there is a compressive component to the inversion injury, such as when landing from a jump. The talar dome is compressed by the tibial plafond, causing damage to the osteochondral surface. The lesions occur most commonly in the superomedial corner of the talar dome, and much less commonly on the superolateral part.

Large fractures may be recognized at the time of injury. The fracture site will be tender and may be evident on X-ray. Usually, the lesion is not detected initially and the patient presents some time later with unremitting ankle aching and locking or catching, despite appropriate treatment for an ankle sprain.

 The patient with a talar dome lesion often gives a history of progressing well following a sprain but then develops symptoms of increasing pain and swelling, stiffness, and perhaps catching or locking as activity is increased. Reduced range of motion is often a prominent symptom.

Examination with the patient's foot plantarflexed at 45° to rotate the talus out of the ankle mortise may reveal tenderness of the dome of the talus. This may, however, be difficult due to pain. If this diagnosis is suspected, the practitioner should image the ankle with MRI (Fig. 38.11a on page 821) or isotopic bone scan (Fig. 38.11b on page 821). A positive bone scan should be supplemented with a CT scan (Fig. 38.11c on page 821) to determine the exact degree of skeletal injury. MRI alone provides anatomical and pathological data, and is as the investigation of choice. The

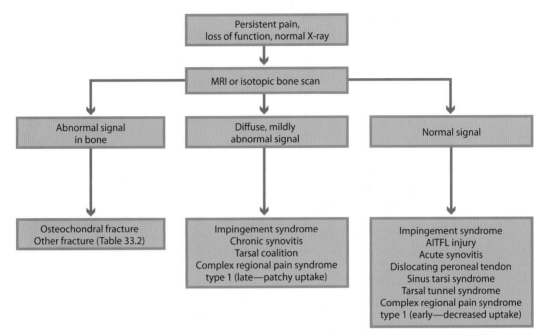

Figure 38.10 Investigation pathway in the patient with persistent ankle pain following an acute injury. When MRI is readily available it serves as an ideal first-line investigation for persistent ankle pain

grading of osteochondral fractures of the talar dome is shown in Table 38.4 overleaf.

Chronic grade I and II lesions should be treated conservatively. The patient should avoid activities that cause pain and be encouraged to pedal an exercise bicycle with low resistance. Formerly, cast immobilization was advocated for these injuries, but joint motion without significant loading is now encouraged to promote articular cartilage healing as early as possible. If there is pain, or symptoms of clicking, locking, or giving way persist beyond two to three months of this conservative management, ankle arthroscopy is indicated in order to remove or fixate loose bodies. A grade IIa, III, or IV lesion also requires arthroscopic removal of the separated fragment or cyst, and curetting and drilling of the fracture bed down to bleeding bone. After treatment of osteochondral lesions, a comprehensive rehabilitation program is required. Tibial plafond chondral lesions (see below) are managed identically.

Avulsion fracture of the base of the fifth metatarsal

Inversion injury may result in an avulsion fracture of the base of the fifth metatarsal either in isolation or, more commonly, in association with a lateral ligament sprain. This fracture results from avulsion of the peroneus brevis tendon from its attachment to the base of the fifth metatarsal.

X-rays should be examined closely. Avulsion fracture is characterized by its involvement of the joint surface of the base of the fifth metatarsal (Fig. 38.12 overleaf). A potentially confusing fracture is the fracture of the proximal diaphysis of the fifth metatarsal that does not involve any joint surfaces. This fracture is known as the Jones' fracture and usually requires internal fixation (Chapter 40). Although the mechanism can appear to be one of "acute" injury, in most cases the Jones' fracture is a result of repetitive overuse (i.e. a stress fracture) of the proximal diaphysis of the fifth metatarsal.

Fracture of the base of the fifth metatarsal may be treated conservatively with immobilization for pain relief followed after one to two weeks by protected mobilisation and rehabilitation. Therefore it is important to distinguish between fracture of the base of the fifth metatarsal and a Jones' fracture.

Other fractures

A number of other fractures may occasionally be seen as a result of acute ankle injuries (Fig. 38.13 overleaf), alone or in association with ligamentous injury. They may appear quite subtle on plain X-ray.

Table 38.4 Grading of osteochondral fracture of the talar dome

Grade	Description	Investigation	Appearance
I	Subchondral fracture	MRI	
II	Chondral fracture	CT/MRI	
IIa	Subchondral cyst	CT/MRI	
III	Chondral fracture with separated but not displaced fragment(s)	CT/MRI	
IV	Chondral fracture with separated and displaced fragment(s)	X-ray/CT/MRI	

Fractured lateral talar process

The lateral talar process is a prominence of the lateral talar body with an articular surface dorsolaterally for the fibula and inferomedially for the anterior portion of the posterior calcaneal facet (Fig. 38.13).

Patients with a fracture of this process may present with ankle pain, swelling and inability to weight-bear for long periods. Examination reveals swelling and bruising over the lateral aspect of the ankle and tenderness over the lateral process, immediately

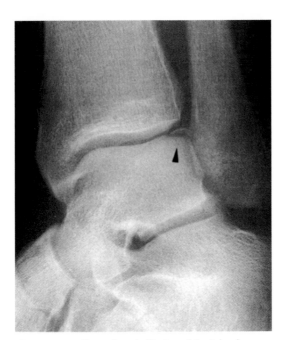

Figure 38.11 Osteochondral lesion of the talar dome
(a) MRI (grade I)

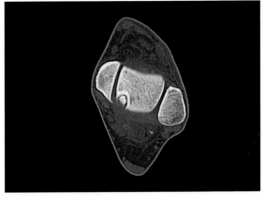

(c) CT scan (grade IV)

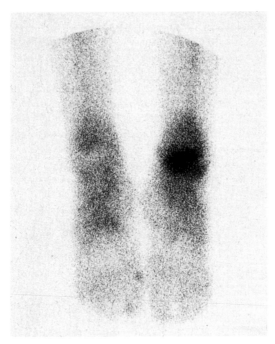

(b) Radioisotopic bone scan

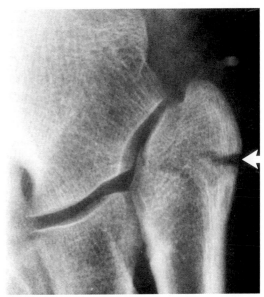

Figure 38.12 Avulsion fracture of the base of the fifth metatarsal

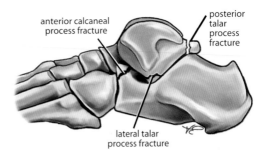

anterior calcaneal process fracture

posterior talar process fracture

lateral talar process fracture

Figure 38.13 Fractures around the talus and calcaneus

anterior and inferior to the tip of the lateral malleolus. The fracture is best seen on the mortise view X-ray of the ankle.

Undisplaced fractures may be treated in a short leg cast. Fractures displaced more than 2 mm (0.1 in.) require either primary excision or reduction and internal fixation. Comminuted fractures may require primary excision, which is a safe treatment, followed by short immobilization only.

Fractured anterior calcaneal process

Fractures of the anterior calcaneal process may cause persistent pain after an ankle sprain. Palpation of the anterior calcaneal process, just anterior to the opening of the sinus tarsi (Fig. 38.13), is painless in patients with a tear of the anterior talofibular ligament, but causes considerable pain in those with a fracture of the anterior process. If plain X-rays (including oblique foot views) fail to show a fracture that is suspected clinically, isotopic bone scan or MRI/CT is indicated.

If the fracture is small, symptomatic treatment may suffice. If large, it requires four weeks of non-weight-bearing cast immobilization or surgical excision of the fragment, which may be the best treatment.

Tibial plafond chondral lesions

Tibial plafond (the inferior tibial articular surface [Fig. 38.1a]) injuries may occur with vertical compression forces, such as a fall from a height. However, they can also complicate otherwise straightforward ankle sprains.

The patient complains of difficulty weight-bearing, and examination reveals swelling and restricted dorsiflexion. As with talar dome lesions, X-ray is generally normal, so MRI is the investigation of choice. CT/isotopic bone are alternatives if MRI is not available.

If imaging and clinical features are consistent with bony damage, arthroscopic debridement, including micro-fracturing, is indicated. Ankle pain can persist for months to a year, even after treatment.

Fractured posterior process of the talus

Acute fractures of the posterior process of the talus (Fig. 38.13) occasionally occur and are often the result of an acute plantarflexion injury in kicking, and have been seen in fencing. The fracture may require up to six weeks of cast immobilization or surgical excision depending on the size of the fragment (see also Chapter 39).

Impingement syndromes

The impingement syndromes of the ankle are usually the result of overuse but are occasionally present as persistent pain following an acute ankle injury. For example, ballet dancers often suffer posterior impingement following lateral ankle sprain, due to os trigonum, processus posterior of the talus, and/or posterior osteophytes. Posterior impingement syndrome was discussed in Chapter 37. Anterior and anterolateral impingement syndromes are discussed in Chapter 39.

Tendon dislocation or rupture

Dislocation or longitudinal rupture of the peroneal tendons (in most cases peroneus brevis tendon) can cause lateral ankle symptoms of the "problem ankle," and tibialis posterior injury can cause similar symptoms medially.

Dislocation of the peroneal tendons

The peroneal tendons are situated behind the lateral malleolus and fixed by the superior peroneal retinaculum. They are occasionally dislocated as a result of forceful passive dorsiflexion with disruption of the retinaculum from the posterior edge of the lateral malleolus. This may occur when a skier catches a tip and falls forward over the ski. The peroneal retinaculum is then ripped off the posterior edge of the lateral malleolus and one or both of the tendons slip out of their groove. This dislocated tendon(s) may remain in its dislocated position or spontaneously relocate and subsequently become prone to recurrent subluxation.

Examination reveals tender peroneal tendons that can be dislocated by the examiner, especially with ankle plantarflexion.

Treatment of dislocation of peroneal tendons is surgical replacement of the tendons in the peroneal groove and repair of the retinaculum, using bone anchors or drill holes. If the peroneal groove is shallow (which occurs in a few cases), retinacular repair should be accompanied by deepening of the groove or rotation of the malleolus (not often recommended) to better secure the tendons. Soft tissue repair, however, produces a good result in most cases.

Dislocation of the tibialis posterior tendon

Dislocation of the tibialis posterior tendon is extremely rare in sport. However, it occurs with ankle dorsiflexion and inversion, so that strong contraction

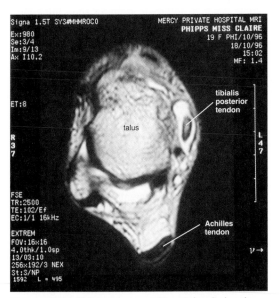

B

of the tibialis posterior muscle pulls the tendon out of its retinaculum using the malleolus as a fulcrum.

The patient may complain of moderate, not exquisite, medial ankle pain and inability to weight-bear. Examination reveals swelling and bruising of the medial ankle above and about the medial malleolus with tenderness along the path of the tibialis posterior tendon. The tendon can be subluxed anteriorly and subsequently relocated posteriorly with the foot in the fully plantarflexed position. The diagnosis is clinical but ultrasonography or MRI (Fig. 38.14) may reveal fluid around the tendon.

Immediate surgical treatment is indicated to minimize the time that the tendon is dislocated while permitting primary repair of the flexor retinaculum and reattachment of the tibialis posterior sheath.[26] Postoperatively the ankle is immobilized in a below-knee plaster cast with a total of six weeks non-weight-bearing on the affected ankle. After the cast is removed, an ankle brace can be used to immobilize the ankle, but active ankle motion is permitted three times daily while taking care to avoid resisted inversion. Weight-bearing can recommence at six

Figure 38.14 MRI appearance (T2-weighted) shortly after tibialis posterior tendon dislocation shows the tibialis posterior tendon (dark) in cross-section surrounded by abnormal fluid (high signal intensity). The tendon is in its normal position during this examination. If imaging had been delayed sufficiently, fluid would have been absent and the MRI appearance may have been normal

weeks under physiotherapy/physical therapy supervision followed by strengthening and functional rehabilitation.

Rupture of the tibialis posterior tendon

A sportsperson with a ruptured tibialis posterior tendon presents with pain in the region of the tubercle of the navicular extending to the posterosuperior border of the medial malleolus and along the posteromedial tibial border. This condition is also common among older people—it should not be waved off as 'arthritis' of the midfoot.

Examination reveals thickening or absence (less frequent) of the tibialis posterior tendon and inability to raise the heel. A flattened medial arch is a classic sign.

MRI is the investigation of choice; ultrasound may also be helpful. However, it should be borne in mind that there is low correlation between MRI findings and symptoms.

Surgical repair, reconstructing the anatomy, is indicated as the tibialis posterior tendon is essential to maintain the normal medial arch of the foot.

Anteroinferior tibiofibular ligament injury

The tibiofibular syndesmosis (Fig. 38.15 overleaf), consisting of the anterior and posterior inferior tibiofibular ligaments, the interosseous ligament, and the interosseous membrane, maintains the joint between the distal tibia and fibula. It plays a dynamic role in ankle function.

Mechanisms

Diastasis (separation) occurs with partial or complete rupture of the syndesmosis ligament, almost always in conjunction with ankle fracture. Ruptures of the syndesmosis are rarely isolated injuries, but generally occur in association with deltoid ligament injuries or, more frequently, with fractures of either the fibula or the posterior and medial malleoli. It should be strongly suspected if there is a Maisonneuve fracture (page 817).

It is increasingly recognized that isolated syndesmosis injury—without a fracture—is also more common than previously anticipated. Anteroinferior tibiofibular ligament (AITFL) injury should be suspected in cases where there is marked medial swelling, and swelling and pain more proximal than the typical anterior talofibular ligament (ATFL) injury.

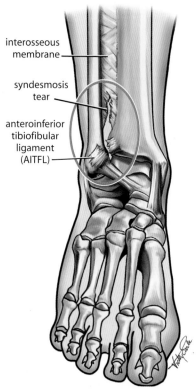

interosseous membrane

syndesmosis tear

anteroinferior tibiofibular ligament (AITFL)

Figure 38.15 Anatomy of a syndesmosis sprain. This injury may be associated with medial malleolar fracture (not illustrated)

Clinical features

- anterior and medial ankle pain following a moderate-to-severe ankle injury
- tenderness at the anterior aspect of the syndesmosis and interosseous membrane (Fig 38.15); there is usually also medial tenderness and bleeding/ swelling
- pain on active external rotation of the foot in relation to the lower leg
- if there is severe disruption of the syndesmosis, the squeeze test is positive (i.e. proximal compression produces distal pain in the region of the interosseous membrane).

Investigations

Initial plain X-rays are recommended to exclude fractures and bony avulsions. Mortise views may reveal widening of the syndesmosis and an increased space between the talus and the medial malleolus (clear space medially). Stress X-rays in external rotation

should demonstrate a diastasis, but in practice are difficult to perform and interpret. MRI is the investigation of choice for suspected AITFL injury. CT/ isotopic bone scan can help to exclude osteochondral lesions if MRI is not available.

Treatment

Provided there is no widening of the distal tibiofibular joint, conservative management consists of relative rest and gradual progression of loading, range of motion exercises, and proprioceptive retraining under physiotherapist supervision. In more severe cases, when there is widening of the distal tibiofibular joint, surgery is indicated. The syndesmosis and deltoid ligament are repaired and the region is stabilised with a temporary syndesmosis screw. With correct early diagnosis and appropriate treatment, the clinical outcome can be very good.

Post-traumatic synovitis

Some degree of synovitis occurs with any ankle injury due to the presence of blood within the joint. This usually resolves in a few days but may persist if there is excessive early weight-bearing, typically in sportspeople eager to return to training soon after their ankle sprain, or due to insufficient rehabilitation. These sportspeople often develop persistent ankle pain aggravated by activity and associated with swelling. Synovitis of the ankle joint is also seen in sportspeople who have chronic mild instability because of excessive accessory movement of the ankle joint during activity.

Treatment of synovitis includes NSAIDs, rest from aggravating activity and local electrotherapy. A corticosteroid injection into the ankle joint (Fig. 38.16) may be required. Injection should be followed by 48 hours of limited weight-bearing and gradual resumption of activity. Sometimes arthroscopy with synovectomy may be indicated.

When synovitis is associated with a degree of chronic instability, treatment involves taping or bracing. Such a patient can gain significant relief by wearing a brace for activities of daily living as well as sport. These patients may also benefit from ankle ligament reconstructive surgery.

Sinus tarsi syndrome

The sinus tarsi syndrome may occur as an overuse injury secondary to excessive subtalar pronation (Chapter 39) or as a sequel to an ankle sprain. Pain occurs at the lateral opening of the sinus tarsi

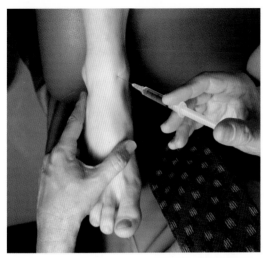

Figure 38.16 Corticosteroid injection into the ankle joint in the treatment of post-traumatic synovitis. The needle is inserted medial to the tibialis anterior tendon and directed posterolaterally

(Fig. 38.1b). The pain is often more severe in the morning and improves as the patient warms up.

Forced passive inversion and eversion may both be painful. The most appropriate aid to diagnosis is to monitor the effect of injection of a local anesthetic agent into the sinus tarsi under fluoroscopy (Fig. 38.17).

Treatment consists of relative rest, NSAIDs, electrotherapeutic modalities, subtalar joint mobilization, and taping to correct excessive pronation if present. If conservative management is unsuccessful,

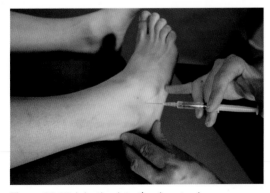

Figure 38.17 Injection into the sinus tarsi. The lateral opening of the sinus is maintained when the foot is inverted. The needle is directed towards the tip of the medial malleolus

injection of corticosteroid and local anesthetic agents may help resolve the inflammation.

Complex regional pain syndrome type 1

Complex regional pain syndrome (CRPS) type 1, formerly known as "reflex sympathetic dystrophy" (RSD) (Chapters 6, 7), may occasionally complicate ankle injury. Initially, it appears that the patient with a "sprained ankle" is improving, but then symptoms begin to relapse. The patient complains of increased pain, swelling recurs, and the skin may become hot or, more frequently, very cold. There may also be localized sweating, discoloration, and hypersensitivity.

As early treatment substantially improves the prognosis in CRPS type 1, early diagnosis is imperative. Initial X-rays are normal. Later, patchy demineralization occurs and this can be seen as regions of decreased opacity on X-ray and areas of increased uptake on bone scan—the investigation of choice.[27] Tests of sympathetic function (Chapter 12) may confirm the diagnosis.[27]

It is most important that the specific nature of the condition be explained to the patient as it may be a particularly painful condition, even at rest. It remains very difficult to treat and there have been few controlled treatment trials for established CRPS type 1.[28]

PRACTICE PEARL

Rest is contraindicated. The patient should be as active as can be tolerated.

Physiotherapy may play a role[29] and ultrasound and hydrotherapy may facilitate range of movement exercises. Gabapentin, an anticonvulsant with a proven analgesic effect in various neuropathic pain syndromes, has shown mild efficacy as treatment for pain in patients with CRPS type 1.[30] Because CRPS type 1 is associated with regional osteoclastic overactivity (excessive bone turnover, as shown by increased uptake on radionuclide bone scan), a bisphosphonate medication (alendronate) was trialed in 39 patients.[31] In contrast to placebo-treated patients, all of the alendronate-treated patients had substantially reduced pain and improved joint mobility as early as the fourth week of treatment.

If the pain does not settle, chemical or surgical blockade is indicated. However, a Cochrane systematic review failed to support this therapy for relieving pain.[32] CRPS type 1 remains a very difficult condition to treat.

📄 RECOMMENDED READING

Bachmann LM, Kolb E, Koller MT et al. Accuracy of Ottawa ankle rules to exclude fractures of the ankle and midfoot: systematic review. *BMJ* 2003;326(7386):417.

Chan KM, Karlsson J. ISAKOS-FIMS World Consensus Conference on Ankle Instability. Stockholm: International Society of Arthroscopy, Knee surgery and orthopaedic sports medicine, 2005.

Kannus P, Renstrom P. Treatment for acute tears of the lateral ligament of the ankle. *J Bone Joint Surg Am* 1991;73A:305–12. *(Classic reference)*

Osborne MD, Rizzo TD Jr. Prevention and treatment of ankle sprain in athletes. *Sports Med* 2003;33(15): 1145–50.

Quisel A, Gill JM, Witherell P. Complex regional pain syndrome underdiagnosed. *J Fam Pract* 2005;54(6):524–32. Available online: http://www. jfponline.com/Pages.asp?AID=1947.

📋 REFERENCES

1. Fong DT, Chan YY, Mok KM et al. Understanding acute ankle ligamentous sprain injury in sports. *Sports Med Arthrosc Rehabil Ther Technol* 2009;1:14.

2. Morrison KE, Kaminski TW. Foot characteristics in association with inversion ankle injury. *J Athl Train* 2007;42(1):135–42.

3. Bachmann LM, Kolb E, Koller MT et al. Accuracy of Ottawa ankle rules to exclude fractures of the ankle and mid-foot: systematic review. *BMJ* 2003;326(7386):417.

4. Dimmick S, Kennedy D, Daunt N. Evaluation of thickness and appearance of anterior talofibular and calcaneofibular ligaments in normal versus abnormal ankles with MRI. *J Med Imaging Radiat Oncol* 2008;52(6):559–63.

5. Jain N, Symes T, Doorgakant A et al. Clinical audit of the management of stable ankle fractures. *Ann R Col Surg Engl* 2008;90(6):483–7.

6. Holme E, Magnusson SP, Becher K et al. The effect of supervised rehabilitation on strength, postural sway, position sense and re-injury risk after acute ankle ligament sprain. *Scand J Med Sci Sports* 1999;9(2): 104–9.

7. Verhagen E, van der Beek A, Twisk J et al. The effect of a proprioceptive balance board training program for the prevention of ankle sprains: a prospective controlled trial. *Am J Sports Med* 2004;32(6):1385–93.

8. Verhagen EA, van Tulder M, van der Beek AJ et al. An economic evaluation of a proprioceptive balance board training programme for the prevention of ankle sprains in volleyball. *Br J Sports Med* 2005;39(2):111–15.

9. Bahr R, Bahr IA. Incidence of acute volleyball injuries: a prospective cohort study of injury mechanisms and risk factors. *Scand J Med Sci Sports* 1997;7(3):166–71.

10. Beynnon BD, Renstrom PA, Alosa DM et al. Ankle ligament injury risk factors: a prospective study of college athletes. *J Orthop Res* 2001;19(2):213–20.

11. Verhagen EA, Van der Beek AJ, Bouter LM et al. A one season prospective cohort study of volleyball injuries. *Br J Sports Med* 2004;38(4):477–81.

12. Verhagen EA, Bay K. Optimising ankle sprain prevention: a critical review and practical appraisal of the literature. *Br J Sports Med* 2010;44(15):1082–8.

13. McKeon PO, Hertel J. Systematic review of postural control and lateral ankle instability, part II: is balance training clinically effective? *J Athl Train* 2008;43(3): 305–15.

14. Abian-Vicen J, Alegre LM, Fernandez-Rodriguez JM et al. Prophylactic ankle taping: elastic versus inelastic taping. *Foot Ankle Int* 2009;30(3):218–25.

15. Hupperets MD, Verhagen EA, van Mechelen W. Effect of sensorimotor training on morphological, neurophysiological and functional characteristics of the ankle: a critical review. *Sports Med* 2009;39(7):591–605.

16. Verhagen EA, van Mechelen W, de Vente W. The effect of preventive measures on the incidence of ankle sprains. *Clin J Sport Med* 2000;10(4):291–6.

17. Verhagen EA, van der Beek AJ, van Mechelen W. The effect of tape, braces and shoes on ankle range of motion. *Sports Med* 2001;31(9):667–77.

18. Karlsson J, Lansinger O. Chronic lateral instability of the ankle in athletes. *Sports Med* 1993;16(5):355–65.

19. Lephart S, Conley K. The role of proprioception in chronic ankle instability. In: Schmidt R, Benesch S, Lipke K, eds. *Chronic ankle instability: manuscripts of the International Ankle Symposium.* Ulm: Libri Verlag, 2000:254–67.

20. Hupperets MD, Verhagen EA, van Mechelen W. Effect of unsupervised home based proprioceptive training on recurrences of ankle sprain: randomised controlled trial. *BMJ* 2009;339:b2684.

21. Kerkhoffs GM, Handoll HH, de Bie R et al. Surgical versus conservative treatment for acute injuries of the lateral ligament complex of the ankle in adults. *Cochrane Database Syst Rev* 2002(3):CD000380.

22. Kaikkonen A, Kannus P, Jarvinen M. Surgery versus functional treatment in ankle ligament tears. A prospective study. *Clin Orthop Relat Res* 1996(326): 194–202.

23. Pijnenburg ACM, Bogaard K, Krips R et al. Operative and functional treatment of rupture of the lateral ligament of the ankle: a randomised, prospective trial. *J Bone Joint Surg Br* 2003;85B(4):525–30.

24. Babis GC, Papagelopoulos PJ, Tsarouchas J et al. Operative treatment for Maisonneuve fracture of the proximal fibula. *Orthopedics* 2000;23(7): 687–90.

25. Wikstrom EA, Naik S, Lodha N et al. Bilateral balance impairments after lateral ankle trauma: a systematic review and meta-analysis. *Gait Posture* 2010;31(4): 407–14.

26. Rolf C, Guntner P, Ekenman I et al. Dislocation of the tibialis posterior tendon: diagnosis and treatment. *J Foot Ankle Surg* 1997;36(1):63–5.

27. Shehab D, Elgazzar A, Collier BD et al. Impact of three-phase bone scintigraphy on the diagnosis and treatment of complex regional pain syndrome type I or reflex sympathetic dystrophy. *Med Princ Pract* 2006;15(1):46–51.

28. Forouzanfar T, Koke AJ, van Kleef M et al. Treatment of complex regional pain syndrome type I. *Eur J Pain* 2002;6(2):105–22.

29. Oerlemans HM, Oostendorp RA, de Boo T et al. Adjuvant physical therapy versus occupational therapy in patients with reflex sympathetic dystrophy/complex regional pain syndrome type I. *Arch Phys Med Rehabil* 2000;81(1):49–56.

30. van de Vusse AC, Stomp-van den Berg SG, Kessels AH et al. Randomised controlled trial of gabapentin in complex regional pain syndrome type 1 [ISRCTN84121379]. *BMC Neurol* 2004;4:13.

31. Manicourt DH, Brasseur JP, Boutsen Y et al. Role of alendronate in therapy for posttraumatic complex regional pain syndrome type I of the lower extremity. *Arthritis Rheum* 2004;50(11):3690–7.

32. Cepeda MS, Carr DB, Lau J. Local anesthetic sympathetic blockade for complex regional pain syndrome. *Cochrane Database Syst Rev* 2005(4): CD004598.

B

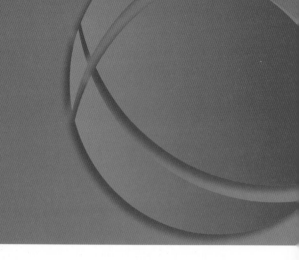

Chapter 39

Ankle pain

with KAREN HOLZER and JON KARLSSON

There are three steps you have to complete to become a professional dancer: learn to dance, learn to perform and learn how to cope with injuries.   David Gere

Sportspeople, particularly ballet dancers, footballers, and high jumpers, may complain of ankle pain that is not related to an acute ankle injury (Chapter 38). Clinical management is simplified if the presentations are further divided into:

- medial ankle pain
- lateral ankle pain
- anterior ankle pain.

The region that might be considered "posterior ankle" pain is defined as the "Achilles region" in this book (Chapter 37). Note that, in real life, patients present with combinations of pain, such as lateral and anterior pain in soccer players. In those circumstances, the systematic clinical approach outlined below still aids in diagnosis and management.

Medial ankle pain

Clinical experience suggests that the most common cause of medial ankle pain is tibialis posterior tendinopathy.[1] Posterior impingement syndrome of the ankle (Chapter 37) may occasionally present as medial ankle pain. Flexor hallucis longus tendinopathy is not uncommon and may occur together with posterior impingement syndrome. In the case of flexor hallucis longus tendinopathy, the patient is often suffering from loud—and painful—crepitation, behind not only the medial malleolus; but also may be projected further down the foot on the medial side. In some cases, patients feel that the crepitation is located in the big toe. The therapist should always look for tendinopathy in the region behind the medial malleolus. Flexor hallucis longus tendinopathy almost always needs surgery, which can be done with the aid of the arthroscope (i.e. hindfoot arthroscopy). Tarsal tunnel syndrome, in which the posterior tibial nerve is compressed behind the medial malleolus, may present as medial ankle pain with sensory symptoms distally. Causes of medial ankle pain are listed in Table 39.1. The anatomy of the region is illustrated in Figure 39.1.

Clinical perspective
History
In patients with medial ankle pain there is usually a history of overuse, especially running or excessive walking (tibialis posterior tendinopathy), toe flexion in ballet dancers and high jumpers (flexor hallucis longus tendinopathy), or plantarflexion in dancers and footballers (posterior impingement syndrome). Pain may radiate along the line of the tibialis posterior tendon to its insertion on the navicular tubercle or into the arch of the foot (with tarsal tunnel syndrome). Sensory symptoms such as pins and needles or numbness may suggest tarsal tunnel syndrome. Crepitus is commonly associated with pain in flexor hallucis longus tendinopathy.

Examination
Careful palpation and testing of resisted movements is the key to examination of this region. Examination includes:

1. Observation
   (a) standing
   (b) walking
   (c) supine
2. Active movements
   (a) ankle plantarflexion/dorsiflexion

Table 39.1 Causes of medial ankle pain

Common	Less common	Not to be missed
Tibialis posterior tendinopathy	Medial calcaneal nerve entrapment	Navicular stress fracture (Chapter 40)
Flexor hallucis longus tendinopathy	Calcaneal stress fracture	Complications of acute ankle injuries
	Tarsal tunnel syndrome	(Chapter 38)
	Talar stress fracture	Complex regional pain syndrome
	Medial malleolar stress fracture	type 1 (following knee or ankle injury)
	Posterior impingement syndrome	
	(Chapter 37)	
	Referred pain from lumbar spine	

B

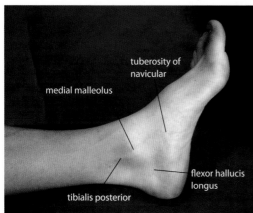

Figure 39.1 Medial aspect of the ankle
(a) Surface anatomy

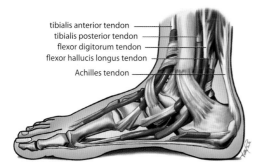

(b) Anatomy of the medial ankle

    (b)   ankle inversion/eversion
    (c)   flexion of the first metatarsophalangeal joint
3. Passive movements
    (a)   as for active movements
    (b)   subtalar joint
    (c)   midtarsal joint
    (d)   muscle stretches
        (i)   gastrocnemius
        (ii)   soleus

4. Resisted movement
    (a)   inversion (Fig. 39.2a)
    (b)   first toe flexion; check for crepitation (Fig. 39.2b overleaf)
5. Functional tests
    (a)   hop
    (b)   jump
6. Palpation
    (a)   tibialis posterior tendon (Fig. 39.2c overleaf)
    (b)   flexor hallucis longus; behind the medial malleolus
    (c)   navicular tubercle
    (d)   ankle joint
    (e)   midtarsal joint
    (f)   Achilles tendon
7. Special tests
    (a)   Tinel's test (Fig. 39.2d overleaf)
    (b)   sensory examination, especially for nerve entrapment of the calcanear branches (Baxter's nerve) (Fig. 39.2e overleaf)
    (c)   biomechanical examination (Chapter 8)
    (d)   lumbar spine examination (Chapter 26)

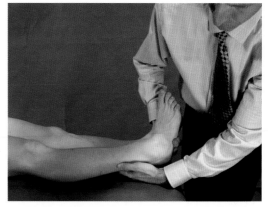

Figure 39.2 Examination of the patient with medial ankle pain
(a) Resisted movement—inversion (tibialis posterior)

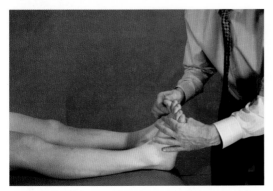

(b) Resisted movement—toe flexion (flexor hallucis longus)

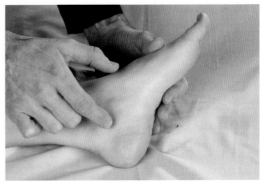

(d) Special tests—Tinel's test.
Tapping over the posterior tibial nerve in the tarsal tunnel may reproduce symptoms

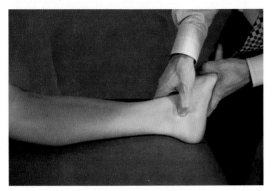

(c) Palpation—tibialis posterior tendon.
The tibialis posterior tendon is palpated from posteromedial to the medial malleolus to its insertion at the navicular tubercle

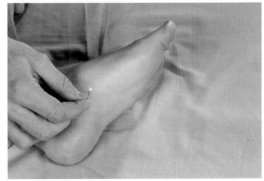

(e) Special tests—sensory examination especially for nerve entrapment of the calcanear branches (Baxter's nerve)

Investigations

Plain X-ray should be performed when posterior impingement is suspected, to confirm the presence of either a large posterior process of the talus, a fracture of the posterior process of the talus, or an os trigonum. A lateral view with the foot in a maximally plantarflexed position (posterior impingement view) can be useful to determine if bony impingement is occurring.

A radioisotopic bone scan may show an area of mildly increased uptake at the posterior aspect of the talus in cases of chronic posterior impingement.

In suspected cases of tendinopathy, ultrasonography or MRI may be indicated if pain has been longstanding or if there is doubt about the diagnosis. Nerve conduction studies should be obtained if tarsal tunnel syndrome is the likely diagnosis.

Tibialis posterior tendinopathy

The tibialis posterior tendon functions to invert the subtalar joint and is the main dynamic stabilizer of the hindfoot against valgus (eversion) forces, in addition to providing stability to the plantar arch. It is the most anterior structure that passes behind the medial malleolus; it then divides and sends attachments to the navicular tuberosity, the cuboid, the cuneiforms, the bases of the second to fourth metatarsals, and the spring ligament.

Causes

The etiology of tibialis posterior tendinopathy is usually related to an overuse injury rather than an acute traumatic injury.[2] Tibialis posterior tendinopathy is infrequent in young persons other than ballet dancers; it is most often seen in middle-aged women. It comes on slowly, and is not self-limiting. Causes include:

- Overuse—often related to:
  - excessive walking, running or jumping
  - excessive subtalar pronation—this increases eccentric tendon loading during supination for toe-off
- Acute
  - direct trauma—laceration
  - indirect trauma—eversion ankle sprain, ankle fracture
  - acute avulsion fracture
- Inflammatory conditions
  - tenosynovitis secondary to rheumatoid arthritis, seronegative arthropathies.

Chronic tendinopathy is characterized by collagen disarray and interstitial tears, and may eventually lead to total tendon rupture.

Clinical features

- Medial ankle pain behind the medial malleolus and extending towards the insertion of the tendon at the navicular bone.
- Swelling is very unusual at the beginning—if present, it suggests substantial tendon injury or an underlying seronegative arthropathy. In later stages, swelling is often pronounced; often diffuse around and below the medial malleolus
- Tenderness along the tendon is prominent posterior and inferior to the medial malleolus.
- Crepitus is only present occasionally.
- Resisted inversion (Fig. 39.2a) elicits pain and relative weakness compared with the contralateral side.
- A single heel raise test also viewed from behind reveals lack of inversion of the hindfoot and, if severe, the patient may have difficulty performing a heel raise. In the normal ankle, the calcaneus moves into varus position during a single heel raise; in patients with tibialis posterior tendinopathy, this does not happen and the heel remains in the valgus position.

Investigations

MRI or ultrasound may confirm the diagnosis and reveal the extent of tendinopathy. However, the correlation between tibialis posterior tendinopathy and MRI findings is often low. MRI is highly sensitive and specific for the detection of a tendon rupture.[3, 4] When compared with MRI, ultrasonography had a sensitivity of 80% and specificity of 90%.[5]

In cases of suspected inflammatory tenosynovitis, blood tests for serological and inflammatory markers should be performed.

Treatment

Conservative care consists of controlling pain where needed with ice, and prescribing concentric and eccentric tendon loading exercises (Fig. 39.3).[2, 6]

 PRACTICE PEARL **A rigid orthotic may prove effective if the patient has excessive pronation.**

Experienced clinicians often administer soft tissue therapy to the tibialis posterior muscle and tendon.

In severe cases, a period of immobilization in an Aircast has been prescribed to provide short-term symptom relief, but this would be an extreme measure.

If an inflammatory arthropathy is present, anti-inflammatory medications are sometimes indicated. However, anti-inflammatory medication is not very effective in most cases and should be used only to control pain. Corticosteroid injections should be used with caution, due to the risk of total tendon rupture.

If there is tendon rupture (Chapter 38), or if conservative management fails to settle the condition, surgery is recommended. In the case of tenosynovitis, a synovectomy may be performed; in cases of severe tendinopathy or tendon rupture, a reconstruction may be required.

There is often need for large corrective surgery, which may include alignment of the heel, with tendon transfer, calcaneus osteotomy, and/or midfoot corrective osteotomy/arthrodesis.

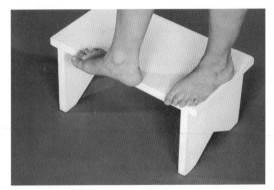

Figure 39.3 Eccentric exercises—tibialis posterior. Patient stands on the edge of a step and drops down into eversion, eccentrically contracting the tibialis posterior muscle

There is often need for large corrective surgical treatment.

A major problem in patients with tibialis posterior tendinopathy is the long time from injury to final treatment; this can result from delayed presentation or delay in diagnosis.

Flexor hallucis longus tendinopathy

The flexor hallucis longus tendon flexes the big toe and assists in plantarflexion of the ankle. It passes posterior to the medial malleolus, and runs between the two sesamoid bones to insert into the base of the distal phalanx of the big toe.

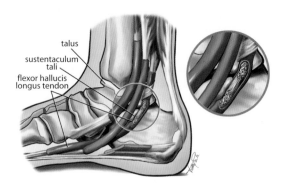

Figure 39.4 Flexor hallucis longus tendinopathy showing the tendon irritated near the medial malleolus

Causes

Flexor hallucis longus tendinopathy may occur secondary to:

- overuse, often in ballet dancers, as dancers repetitively go from flat-foot stance to the *en pointe* position, which requires extreme plantarflexion
- a stenosing tenosynovitis
- pseudocyst
- tendon tear, which may be partial or total
- "toe-grip" in athletes wearing shoes that are too big.

This condition is often associated with posterior impingement syndrome (Chapter 37) as the flexor hallucis tendon lies in a fibro-osseous tunnel between the lateral and medial tubercles of the posterior process of the talus. Enlargement or medial displacement of the posterior process of the talus or os trigonum puts pressure on the flexor hallucis longus at the point where the tendon changes direction from a vertical course dorsal to the talus to a horizontal course beneath the talus (Fig. 39.4). This can cause tendon thickening and may result in "triggering" of the tendon with loud and painful crepitation, when partial tearing and subsequent healing of the tendon produce excessive scar tissue.

Clinical features

- Pain on toe-off or forefoot weight-bearing (e.g. rising in ballet), maximal over the posteromedial aspect of the medial malleolus and the calcaneus around the sustentaculum tali.
- Pain may be aggravated by resisted flexion of the first toe or stretch into full dorsiflexion of the hallux.
- In more severe cases, there may be "triggering" of the first toe, both with rising onto the balls of the foot (e.g. in ballet) and in lowering from this

position. Triggering occurs when the foot is placed in plantarflexion and the athlete is unable to flex the hallux, but then with forcible active contraction of the flexor hallucis longus, is able to extend the interphalangeal or metatarsophalangeal joints of the toe. A snap or pop (creptitus) occurs in the posteromedial aspect of the ankle when this happens. The crepitus may be present with every step. Subsequent passive flexion or extension of the interphalangeal joint produces a painless snap posterior to the medial malleolus.

Investigations

MRI or ultrasound may both reveal pathology; however, the diagnosis is primarily based on clinical investigation. The correlation between MRI findings and symptoms is often limited. The characteristic MRI sign in case of tendon pathology (such as partial rupture) is abrupt fluid cut-off in the tendon sheath; excessive fluid is found loculated around a normal-appearing tendon proximal to the fibro-osseous canal.[7]

Treatment

In the acute phase, treatment may include:[8]

- ice
- avoidance of activities that stress the flexor hallucis longus tendon (e.g. dancer can work at the barre but not rise *en pointe*)
- flexor hallucis longus strength and stretching exercises
- soft tissue therapy proximally in the muscle belly
- correction of subtalar joint hypomobility with manual mobilization and orthotic

- control of excessive pronation during toe-off with tape or orthoses—this may be helpful but is difficult to achieve in dancers.

Prevention of recurrences should focus on a reduction in the amount of hip turnout, thus ensuring that the weight is directly over the hip, avoidance of hard floors, and using firm, well-fitting pointe shoes, so that the foot is well supported and no additional strain is placed on the tendon. Technique correction is important in ballet dancers with this condition, as it is thought to arise not only from excessive ankle eversion or inversion with pointe work, but also from proximal weakness such as poor trunk control.[9]

 Technique correction is important in ballet dancers with flexor hallucis longus tendinopathy.

Surgical treatment should be considered when persistent synovitis or triggering prevents dancing *en pointe*. Surgery involves exploration of the tendon and release of the tendon sheath. This can be accomplished in almost all cases using the arthroscope, with a posterior approach. The fibrous band around the tendon is cleaned off and the tendon released.

Tarsal tunnel syndrome

Tarsal tunnel syndrome occurs as a result of entrapment of the posterior tibial nerve in the tarsal tunnel where the nerve winds around the medial malleolus.[10] It may also involve only one of its terminal branches distal to the tarsal tunnel. Pain and sensory disturbance are felt in the medial part of the heel.

Causes

The causes of tarsal tunnel syndrome are:

- idiopathic—in approximately 50% of cases
- trauma (e.g. inversion injury to the ankle, or direct blow to the ankle with large bleeding, for instance in soccer)
- overuse associated with excessive pronation
- less common causes
  - ganglion
  - talonavicular coalition
  - varicose veins
  - synovial cyst
  - lipoma
  - accessory muscle—flexor digitorum accessorius longus

- tenosynovitis—often correlated with arthritis (seronegative rheumatoid arthritis)
- fracture of the distal tibia or calcaneus.

Clinical features

- Poorly defined burning, tingling, or numb sensation on the plantar aspect of the foot, often radiating into the toes.
- Pain is usually aggravated by activity and relieved by rest. Pain is usually the reason patients seek help; the location of the pain can be diffuse and poorly defined.
- In some patients the symptoms are worse in bed at night and relieved by getting up and moving or massaging the foot.
- Swellings, varicosities, or thickenings may be found on examination around the medial ankle or heel.
- A ganglion or cyst may be palpable in the tendon sheaths around the medial ankle.
- Tenderness in the region of the tarsal tunnel is common.
- Tapping over the posterior tibial nerve (Tinel's sign [Fig 39.2d]) may elicit the patient's pain and very occasionally cause fasciculations; however, this "classic" sign is not commonly seen.
- There may be altered sensation along the arch of the foot.
- The distribution of the sensory changes in the foot needs to be differentiated from the typical dermatomal distribution of S1 nerve root compression.

Investigations

Nerve conduction studies should be performed.[11, 12] These not only help to confirm the diagnosis but they can also guide the surgeon as to the location of the nerve compression. Nevertheless tarsal tunnel syndrome is primarily a clinical diagnosis and nerve conduction studies are negative in approximately 50% of patients.

Ultrasound or MRI may be required to assess for a space-occupying lesion as a cause of the syndrome.

An X-ray and, if required, a CT scan should be performed in the case of excessive pronation or if a tarsal coalition is suspected.

Differential diagnosis

Differential diagnosis includes entrapment of the medial and/or lateral plantar nerves, or both, plantar fasciitis, intervertebral disk degeneration and other causes of nerve inflammation or degeneration.

The diagnosis of tarsal tunnel is often difficult and the symptoms and signs are often vague. This is important to bear in mind, at least before surgical intervention is decided upon.

Treatment

Non-surgical treatment should be attempted in those with either an idiopathic or biomechanical cause. If neurodynamic tests prove positive, appropriate neural gliding treatments are indicated. If excessive pronation is present, an orthotic may prove helpful.

Surgical treatment is required if there is mechanical pressure on the nerve. A decompression of the posterior tibial nerve and its branches may be indicated in selected cases, but only after both the diagnosis and site of nerve entrapment have been confirmed.

 Surgery should be reserved as the last resort.

Surgery should be reserved as the last resort, if all other treatment fails, symptoms are severe, and the clinician is confident of mechanical pressure on the nerve. Results of surgery have not been encouraging,[13] with a high perioperative complication rate.[14]

Stress fracture of the medial malleolus

Stress fracture of the medial malleolus is an unusual injury but should be considered in the runner or soccer player presenting with persistent medial ankle pain aggravated by activity.[15, 16] Although the fracture line is frequently vertical from the junction of the tibial plafond and the medial malleolus, it may arch obliquely from the junction to the distal tibial metaphysis.

Clinical features

Sportspeople classically present with anterior and medial ankle pain that progressively increases with running and jumping activities. Often they experience an acute episode, which leads to their seeking medical attention. Examination reveals tenderness overlying the medial malleolus, frequently in conjunction with a mild ankle effusion. Symptoms may also develop slowly over a period of weeks to months.

Investigations

In the early stages, X-rays may be normal, but with time a linear area of hyperlucency may be apparent, progressing to a lytic area and fracture line

(Fig. 39.5a). If the X-ray is normal, a radioisotopic bone scan, MRI is the preferred investigation and CT scan is also good for imaging bony lesions (Fig. 39.5b).

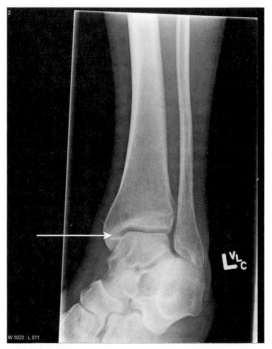

Figure 39.5 (a) X-ray of stress fracture of medial malleolus

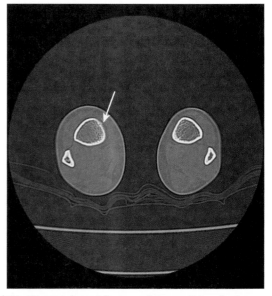

(b) CT scan of stress fracture of the medial malleolus

Treatment

If X-ray reveals no fracture or an undisplaced fracture, treatment requires non-weight-bearing rest with an Aircast brace until local tenderness resolves, a period of approximately six weeks.

If, however, a displaced fracture or a fracture that has progressed to non-union is present, surgery with internal fixation is required. Following fracture healing, the practitioner should assess biomechanics and footwear. A graduated return to activity is required and usually takes around 12 weeks.[17] Even in the case of undisplaced fracture, surgical intervention with internal screw fixation (percutaneous screw fixation) followed by immobilization in plaster for three weeks and Aircast for a further three weeks is advisable.

Medial calcaneal nerve entrapment

The medial calcaneal nerve is a branch of the posterior tibial nerve arising at the level of the medial malleolus or below and passing superficially to innervate the skin of the heel. Occasionally it may arise from the lateral plantar nerve, a branch of the posterior tibial nerve. It has been theorized that a valgus hindfoot may predispose joggers to compression of this nerve branch. This nerve entrapment is often termed "Baxter's nerve."

Clinical features

- Pain is burning; it is over the inferomedial aspect of the calcaneus.
- Pain often radiates into the arch of the foot.
- Pain is aggravated by running.
- Tenderness over the medial calcaneus.
- Tinel's sign is positive (Fig. 39.2d).
- There is often associated excessive pronation of the hindfoot.

Investigations

Nerve conduction studies can help confirm the diagnosis. Injection of local anesthetic at the point of maximal tenderness with a resultant disappearance of pain will confirm the diagnosis. The diagnosis may often be difficult to establish.

Treatment

Treatment involves minimizing the trauma to the nerve with a change of footwear or the use of a pad over the area to protect the nerve. Use of local electrotherapeutic modalities and transverse friction to the painful site may help to settle the pain.

If this is not successful, injection of corticosteroid and local anesthetic agents into the area of point tenderness may be helpful.

Surgery may, in selected cases, be required to decompress the nerve.

Other causes of medial ankle pain

Two conditions that generally cause foot pain but may present as medial ankle pain are stress fractures of the calcaneus and the navicular bone (Chapter 40). Referred pain from neural structures may occasionally present as medial ankle pain. Entrapment of the medial plantar nerve generally causes midfoot pain but may present as medial ankle pain.

Lateral ankle pain

Lateral ankle pain is generally associated with a biomechanical abnormality. The two most common causes are peroneal tendinopathy and sinus tarsi syndrome. The causes of lateral ankle pain are listed in Table 39.2. The anatomy of the region is illustrated in Figure 39.6 overleaf.

Table 39.2 Causes of lateral ankle pain

Common	Less common	Not to be missed
Peroneal tendinopathy	Impingement syndrome	Stress fracture of the distal fibula
Sinus tarsi syndrome	• Anterolateral	Cuboid syndrome
	• Posterior	Complex regional pain syndrome
	Recurrent dislocation of peroneal	type 1 (following knee or ankle
	tendons	trauma)
	Stress fracture of the talus	
	Referred pain	
	• Lumbar spine	
	• Peroneal nerve	
	• Superior tibiofibular joint	

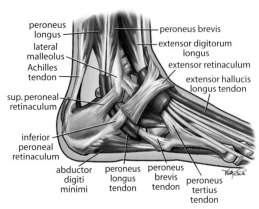

Figure 39.6 Lateral aspect of the ankle
(a) Anatomy of the lateral ankle

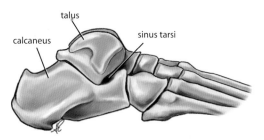

(b) Sinus tarsi

Examination

Examination is as for the patient with acute ankle injury (Chapter 38), with particular attention to testing resisted eversion of the peroneal tendons (Fig. 39.7a) and careful palpation for tenderness, swelling and crepitus (Fig. 39.7b).

Peroneal tendinopathy

The most common overuse injury causing lateral ankle pain is peroneal tendinopathy—almost always peroneus brevis tendinopathy. The peroneus longus and peroneus brevis tendons cross the ankle joint within a fibro-osseous tunnel, posterior to the lateral malleolus. The peroneus brevis tendon inserts into the tuberosity on the lateral aspect of the base of the fifth metatarsal. The peroneus longus tendon passes under the plantar surface of the foot to insert into the lateral side of the base of the first metatarsal and medial cuneiform. The peroneal tendons share a common tendon sheath proximal to the distal tip of the fibula, after which they have their own tendon sheaths. The peroneal muscles serve as ankle dorsiflexors in addition to being the primary evertors of the ankle.

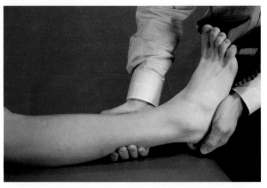

Figure 39.7 Examination of the patient with lateral ankle pain
(a) Resisted movement—eversion (peroneal muscles)

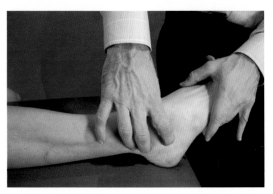

(b) Palpation—the peroneal tendons are palpated for tenderness and crepitus

Causes

Peroneal tendinopathy may occur either as a result of an acute or recurrent ankle inversion injury, or secondary to an overuse injury. Soft footwear may predispose to the development of peroneal tendinopathy.

Common causes of an overuse injury include:

- excessive eversion of the foot, such as occurs when running on slopes or cambered surfaces[18]
- excessive pronation of the foot
- secondary to tight ankle plantarflexors (most commonly soleus) resulting in excessive load on the lateral muscles
- excessive action of the peroneals (e.g. dancing, basketball, volleyball).

An inflammatory arthropathy may also result in the development of a peroneal tenosynovitis and subsequent peroneal tendinopathy.

It has been suggested that peroneal tendinopathy may be due to the excessive pulley action of, and abrupt change in direction of, the peroneal tendons at the lateral malleolus (e.g. in skiers and soccer players). In some cases, peroneal tendinopahy is correlated with peroneal tendon instability in the retromalleolar groove of the lateral malleolus.

There are three main sites of peroneal tendinopathy:

- posterior to the lateral malleolus (most common)
- at the peroneal trochlea
- at the plantar surface of the cuboid.

Clinical features

- Lateral ankle or heel pain and typical retromalleolar swelling, which is aggravated by activity and relieved by rest.
- Local tenderness over the peroneal tendons on examination, sometimes associated with swelling and crepitus (a true paratenonitis).
- Painful passive inversion and resisted eversion, although in some cases eccentric contraction may be required to reproduce the pain.
- Calf muscle tightness may be present.
- Excessive subtalar pronation or stiffness of the subtalar or midtarsal joints is demonstrated on biomechanical examination.

Investigations

MRI is the recommended investigation and shows characteristic features of tendinopathy—increased signal and tendon thickening and longitudinal rupture (Fig. 39.8).[19] If MRI is unavailable, an ultrasound may be performed, with similar good results. If an underlying inflammatory arthropathy is suspected, obtain blood tests to assess for rheumatological and inflammatory markers.

Treatment

Treatment initially involves settling the pain with rest from aggravating activities, analgesic medication if needed, and soft tissue therapy. Stretching in conjunction with mobilization of the subtalar and midtarsal joints may help. Footwear should be assessed and the use of lateral heel wedges or orthoses may be required to correct biomechanical abnormalities. Strengthening exercises should include resisted eversion (e.g. rubber tubing, rotagym), especially in plantarflexion as this position maximally engages the peroneal muscles.

In severe cases, surgery may be required, which may involve a synovectomy, tendon debridement, or

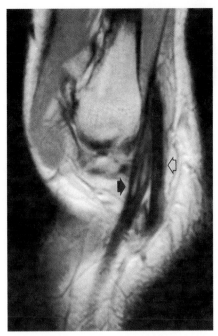

Figure 39.8 Sagittal oblique MR image of a longitudinal rupture of the peroneus brevis tendon at the lateral malleolus level. The rupture causes high signal (two bright regions) in black tendon (solid arrowhead points to peroneus brevis). The peroneus longus tendon (open arrowhead) is normal (homogenous black signal on MR)

repair of the tendon in case of longitudinal rupture.[20] If peroneal tendinopathy is associated with tendon instability, ligament reconstruction should address the instability of the tendon at the same time as the tendon is repaired.

Sinus tarsi syndrome

The sinus tarsi (Fig. 39.6b) is a small osseous canal running from an opening anterior and inferior to the lateral malleolus in a posteromedial direction to a point posterior to the medial malleolus. The interosseous ligament occupies the sinus tarsi and divides it into an anterior portion, which is part of the talocalcaneonavicular joint, and a posterior part, which represents the subtalar joint. It is lined by a synovial membrane and in addition to the ligament, it contains small blood vessels, fat and connective tissue.

Causes

Although injury to the sinus tarsi may result from chronic overuse secondary to poor biomechanics (especially excessive pronation), approximately 70%

of all patients with sinus tarsi syndrome have had a single or repeated inversion injury to the ankle. It may also occur after repeated forced eversion to the ankle, such as high-jump take off.

The sinus tarsi contains abundant synovial tissue that is prone to synovitis and inflammation when injured. An influx of inflammatory cells may result in the development of a low-grade and longstanding inflammatory synovitis.

Other causes of sinus tarsi syndrome include chronic inflammation in conditions such as gout, inflammatory arthropathies, and osteoarthritis.

Clinical features

- Pain may be poorly localized and vague but is most often centered just anterior to the lateral malleolus.
- Pain is often more severe in the morning and may diminish with exercise.
- Pain may be exacerbated by running on a curve in the direction of the affected ankle—the patient may also complain of ankle and foot stiffness, a feeling of instability of the hindfoot, and occasionally weakness.
- Difficulty, often marked, walking on uneven ground.
- Full range of pain-free ankle movement on examination, but the subtalar joint may be stiff.
- Pain occurs on forced passive eversion of the subtalar joint; forced passive inversion may also be painful due to damage to the subtalar ligaments.
- Tenderness of the lateral aspect of the ankle at the opening of the sinus tarsi and occasionally also over the anterior talofibular ligament; there may be minor localized swelling.

Diagnosis

The most appropriate diagnostic test is injection of 1 mL of a short-acting local anesthetic agent (e.g. 1% lignocaine [lidocaine]) into the sinus tarsi; this can be done using fluoroscopic to ensure correct location (Fig. 39.9). In sinus tarsi syndrome, this injection will relieve pain so that functional tests, such as hopping on the affected leg, can be performed comfortably (for diagnosis).

An ankle X-ray may be performed to exclude so-called "four-corner syndrome" or degenerative changes of the subtalar joint. MRI may show an increased signal and fluid in the sinus tarsi, but is not often helpful.

Treatment

Non-surgical management includes relative rest, ice, and electrotherapeutic modalities. Mobilization of the

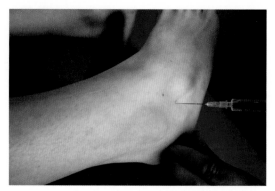

Figure 39.9 Local anesthetic injection under fluoroscopic guidance. The needle is introduced into the lateral opening of the sinus tarsi with the foot in passive inversion. The needle should be directed medially and slightly posteriorly

subtalar joint is essential (Fig. 39.10). Rehabilitation involves proprioception and strength training. Biomechanical correction may be indicated.

Direct infiltration of the sinus tarsi with corticosteroid and local anesthetic agents may prove therapeutic; however, it is important that all underlying abnormalities are also corrected. Surgery is rarely indicated.

Anterolateral impingement

Causes

Repeated minor ankle sprains or a major sprain involving the anterolateral aspect of the ankle may cause anterolateral impingement. An inversion sprain to the anterior talofibular ligament may

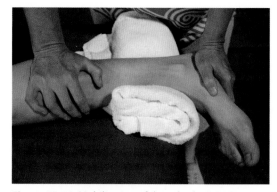

Figure 39.10 Mobilization of the subtalar joint is performed by medial-to-lateral transverse glide of the calcaneus on the talus with the patient side-lying and the ankle dorsiflexed

promote synovial thickening and exudation. Usually this is subsequently resorbed, but sometimes this is incomplete and the residual tissue becomes hyalinized and molded by pressure from the articular surfaces of the talus and fibula, where it may be trapped during ankle movements. A meniscoid lesion thus develops in the anterolateral gutter.

It has also been suggested that meniscoid lesions may result from tears of the anterior talofibular ligament (or aberrant ligament structure) in which the torn fragment becomes interposed between the lateral malleolus and the lateral aspect of the talus.

Another postulated cause of anterolateral ankle impingement is chondromalacia of the lateral wall of the talus with an associated synovial reaction.

Clinical features

The classic presentation is pain at the anterior aspect of the lateral malleolus and an intermittent catching sensation in the ankle in a sportsperson with a previous history of a single ankle inversion injury, or multiple inversion injuries (such as in soccer players).

Examination may reveal tenderness in the region of the anteroinferior border of the fibula and anterolateral surface of the talus. The pain is relieved by tightening the tibialis posterior tendon and releasing the peroneal tendons. Proprioception may be poor.[21]

Investigations

Clinical assessment is more reliable than MRI to diagnose this lesion.[22] An arthroscopic examination confirms the diagnosis.

Treatment

Corticosteroid injection may be helpful initially but, frequently, arthroscopic removal of the fibrotic, meniscoid lesion is required.

Generally results after arthroscopic removal of the impinged tissue are encouraging, and soccer players return to sport after a short period (three to four weeks) of rehabilitation. Even though anterolateral impingement limits dorsiflexion, it takes ballet dancers about three months to regain full pointe position (plantarflexion) after this operation.

Posterior impingement syndrome

Posterior impingement syndrome sometimes presents as lateral ankle pain but more commonly as pain in the posterior ankle (Chapter 37).

Stress fracture of the talus

Stress fractures of the posterolateral aspect of the talus have been described in track and field athletes, triathletes, and Australian Rules footballers.[23]

Causes

These stress fractures may develop secondary to excessive subtalar pronation and plantarflexion, resulting in impingement of the lateral process of the calcaneus on the posterolateral corner of the talus.[16] In pole vaulters, this injury is usually acute and is attributed to "planting" the pole too late.

Clinical features

- Lateral ankle pain of gradual onset.
- Pain is made worse by running and weight-bearing.
- Marked tenderness and occasionally swelling in the region of the sinus tarsi or posterior aspect of the ankle.

Diagnosis

Typical isotopic bone scan and CT scan appearances are shown in Figure 39.11 overleaf. MRI will also reveal the fracture, with the STIR (short TI inversion recovery) sequence being most helpful.

Treatment

Treatment requires cast immobilization for six to eight weeks, and then a supervised graduated rehabilitation. In elite sportspeople, when a rapid recovery is required in a few selected cases, or in the case of failure of non-surgical management, surgical removal of the lateral process has been shown to produce good results.

Biomechanical correction with orthoses is required before activity is resumed.

As this injury is invariably associated with excessive pronation, biomechanical correction with orthoses is required before activity is resumed.

Referred pain

A variation of the slump test (Chapter 11) with the ankle in plantarflexion and inversion can be performed to detect increased neural mechanosensitivity in the peroneal nerve. If the test is positive, this position can be used as a stretch in addition to soft tissue therapy to possible areas of restriction (e.g. around the head of the fibula).

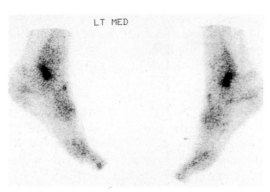

Figure 39.11 Stress fracture of the talus
(a) Isotopic bone scan

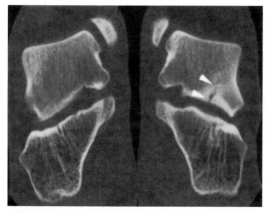

(b) CT scan

Anterior ankle pain

Pain over the anterior aspect of the ankle joint without a history of acute injury is usually due to either tibialis anterior tendinopathy or anterior impingement of the ankle. The surface anatomy of the anterior ankle is shown in Figure 39.12.

Anterior impingement of the ankle

Anterior impingement of the ankle joint (anterior tibiotalar impingement) is a condition in which additional soft or bony tissue is trapped between the tibia and talus during dorsiflexion; it may be the cause of chronic ankle pain or may result in pain and disability persisting after an ankle sprain. Although this syndrome has been called "footballer's ankle," it is also seen commonly in ballet dancers.

Causes

Anterior impingement occurs secondary to the development of exostoses (bone spurs) on the anterior rim of the tibia and on the upper anterior surface of the

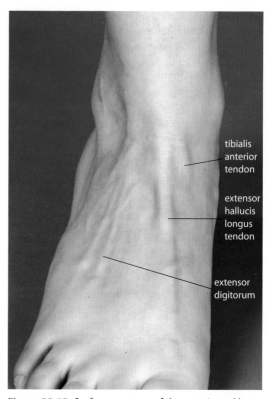

Figure 39.12 Surface anatomy of the anterior ankle showing tendons

tibialis anterior tendon

extensor hallucis longus tendon

extensor digitorum

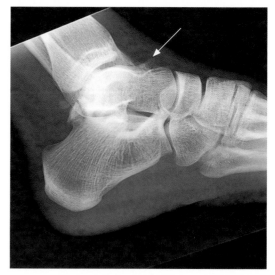

Figure 39.13 X-ray showing bony exostosis on the anterior talus

neck of talus (Fig. 39.13). The exostoses were initially described in ballet dancers and were thought to be secondary to a traction injury of the joint capsule of the ankle that occurs whenever the foot is repeatedly forced into extreme plantarflexion. Subsequently the development of the exostoses has been attributed to direct osseous impingement during extremes of dorsiflexion, as occurs with kicking in football and performing the *plié* (lunge) in ballet. As these exostoses become larger, they impinge on overlying soft tissue and cause pain.

Ligamentous injuries and thus instability following inversion injuries to the ankle may also result in anterior ankle impingement; it has been shown that the distal fascicle of the anterior inferior tibiofibular ligament may impinge on the anterolateral aspect of the talus and cause local pain.

Clinical features

- Anterior ankle pain initially starts as a vague discomfort.
- Pain ultimately becomes sharper and more localized to the anterior aspect of the ankle and foot—especially on dorsiflexion of the foot.
- Pain is worse with activity, particularly with running, descending *plié* (lunge) in classical ballet, kicking in football, and other activities involving dorsiflexion.
- Ankle stiffness occurs as the impingement develops.
- Loss of take-off speed is noticed as the impingement develops.
- Tenderness along the anterior margin of the talocrural joint.
- Palpable exostoses (if they are large).
- Restricted dorsiflexion.
- Painful dorsiflexion.
- The anterior impingement test (Fig. 39.14a), where the patient lunges forward maximally with the heel remaining on the floor, reproduces the pain.

Investigations

Lateral ankle X-rays in flexion and extension show exostoses and abnormal tibiotalar contact. Ideally performed weight-bearing in the lunge position, X-ray shows bone-on-bone impingement that confirms the diagnosis (Fig. 39.14b).

Treatment

In milder cases, non-surgical treatment consists of a heel lift, rest, modification of activities to limit dorsiflexion, nonsteroidal anti-inflammatory drugs (NSAIDs), and physiotherapy, including accessory anteroposterior glides of the talocrural joint at the

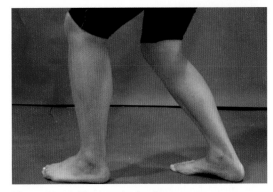

Figure 39.14 The anterior impingement test
(a) The patient lunges forward maximally and, if this reproduces the pain, the test is positive and suggests the diagnosis of anterior impingement

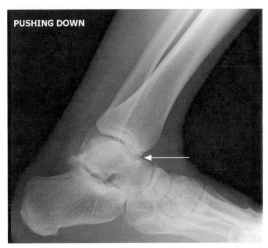

PUSHING DOWN

(b) The same position is used to take a lateral X-ray. A positive test reveals bone-on-bone impingement (arrowed) when the patient adopts the lunge position that reproduces pain

end of range of dorsiflexion. Taping or orthoses may help control the pain if they restrict ankle dorsiflexion or improve joint instability (as joint instability has been shown to contribute to the development of anterior impingement).

More prominent exostoses may require surgical removal arthroscopically. The clinical results after arthroscopic removal are encouraging and the majority of patients become pain-free, with increased range of ankle motion.

Tibialis anterior tendinopathy

The tibialis anterior tendon is the primary dorsiflexor of the foot; it also adducts and supinates (inverts) the foot. It passes medially over the anterior ankle joint and runs to insert into the medial and plantar aspects of the medial cuneiform bone and the adjacent base of the first metatarsal.

Causes

Tendinopathy of the tibialis anterior may result from:

- overuse of the ankle dorsiflexors secondary to;
  - restriction in joint range of motion (as may occur with a stiff ankle)
  - downhill running
- playing racquet sports involving constant change of direction
- excessive tightness of strapping or shoelaces over the tibialis anterior tendon.

Clinical features

The main symptoms are pain, swelling, and stiffness in the anterior ankle, which are aggravated by activity, especially running, and walking up hills or stairs.

On examination, there is localized tenderness, swelling, and occasionally crepitus along the tibialis anterior tendon, especially over the anterior joint line. There is pain on resisted dorsiflexion and eccentric inversion.

Longstanding and non-treated tendinopathy may eventually lead to partial or even total rupture of the tendon (under the extensor retinaculum).

Investigations

Ultrasound or MRI may be used to confirm the diagnosis and exclude tears of the tendon.

Treatment

Eccentric strengthening, soft tissue therapy and mobilization of the ankle joint are common treatments. Correction of biomechanics with orthoses may be helpful. In case of partial or total rupture, surgical reconstruction may be required.

Anteroinferior tibiofibular joint injury (AITFL)

This injury is discussed in Chapter 38 (pages 823–4) because it results from an acute ankle injury (and often a fracture). If missed, it will present as persistent pain and loss of function after an ankle sprain.

REFERENCES

1. Gluck GS, Heckman DS, Parekh SG. Tendon disorders of the foot and ankle, part 3: the posterior tibial tendon. *Am J Sports Med* 2010;38(10):2133–44.

2. Bowring B, Chockalingam N. Conservative treatment of tibialis posterior tendon dysfunction—a review. *Foot (Edinb)* 2010;20(1):18–26.

3. Hutchinson BL, O'Rourke EM. Tibialis posterior tendon dysfunction and peroneal tendon subluxation. *Clin Podiatr Med Surg* 1995;12(4):703–23.

4. Landorf K. Tibialis posterior tendon dysfunction. Early identification is the key to success. *Aust Podiatr* 1995;29:9–14.

5. Premkumar A, Perry MB, Dwyer AJ et al. Sonography and MR imaging of posterior tibial tendinopathy. *AJR Am J Roentgenol* 2002;178(1):223–32.

6. Kulig K, Lederhaus ES, Reischl S et al. Effect of eccentric exercise program for early tibialis posterior tendinopathy. *Foot Ankle Int* 2009;30(9):877–85.

7. Lo LD, Schweitzer ME, Fan JK et al. MR imaging findings of entrapment of the flexor hallucis longus tendon. *AJR Am J Roentgenol* 2001;176(5):1145–8.

8. Simpson MR, Howard TM. Tendinopathies of the foot and ankle. *Am Fam Physician* 2009;80(10):1107–14.

9. Khan K, Brown J, Way S et al. Overuse injuries in classical ballet. *Sports Med* 1995;19(5):341–57.

10. Rodriguez D, Devos Bevernage B, Maldague P et al. Tarsal tunnel syndrome and flexor hallucis longus tendon hypertrophy. *Orthop Traumatol Surg Res* 2010;96(7):829–31.

11. Patel AT, Gaines K, Malamut R et al. Usefulness of electrodiagnostic techniques in the evaluation of suspected tarsal tunnel syndrome: an evidence-based review. *Muscle Nerve* 2005;32(2):236–40.

12. Oh SJ, Meyer RD. Entrapment neuropathies of the tibial (posterior tibial) nerve. *Neurol Clin* 1999;17(3):593–615, vii.

13. Skalley TC, Schon LC, Hinton RY et al. Clinical results following revision tibial nerve release. *Foot Ankle Int* 1994;15(7):360–7.

14. Pfeiffer WH, Cracchiolo A, 3rd. Clinical results after tarsal tunnel decompression. *J Bone Joint Surg Am* 1994;76(8):1222–30.

15. Brukner P, Bennell K, Matheson G. *Stress fractures.* Melbourne: Blackwells Scientific Asia, 1999.

16. Kor A, Saltzman AT, Wempe PD. Medial malleolar stress fractures. Literature review, diagnosis, and treatment. *J Am Podiatr Med Assoc* 2003;93(4):292–7.

17. Jowett AJ, Birks CL, Blackney MC. Medial malleolar stress fracture secondary to chronic ankle impingement. *Foot Ankle Int* 2008;29(7):716–21.

18. Clarke HD, Kitaoka HB, Ehman RL. Peroneal tendon injuries. *Foot Ankle Int* 1998;19(5):280–8.

19. Tjin A, Ton ER, Schweitzer ME et al. MR imaging of peroneal tendon disorders. *AJR Am J Roentgenol* 1997;168(1):135–40.

20. Maffulli N, Ferran NA, Oliva F et al. Recurrent subluxation of the peroneal tendons. *Am J Sports Med* 2006;34(6):986–92.

21. Highet RM. Diagnosis of anterolateral ankle impingement: comparison between magnetic resonance imaging and clinical examination (Letter). *Am J Sports Med* 1998;26:152–3.

22. Liu SH, Nuccion SL, Finerman G. Diagnosis of anterolateral ankle impingement. Comparison between magnetic resonance imaging and clinical examination [see comments]. *Am J Sports Med* 1997;25(3):389–93.

23. Bradshaw C, Khan K, Brukner P. Stress fracture of the body of the talus in athletes demonstrated with computer tomography. *Clin J Sport Med* 1996;6(1):48–51.

Chapter 40

Foot pain

with JASON AGOSTA and KAREN HOLZER

Houston Rockets center Yao Ming has elected to have extensive surgery on his fractured left foot ... After consultation with a battery of doctors, Yao, 28, has decided to undergo a bone graft to heal the existing fracture and have his arch surgically lowered to reduce the stress on his foot. ESPN NBA news reporting Yao Ming's navicular stress fracture management plan. July 18, 2009. Yao Ming announced his retirement from basketball, July 8, 2011.

Many practitioners consider the foot a difficult region to treat, largely because the anatomy seems rather complex (Figs 40.1, 40.2). If the foot is considered in its three distinct regions (Fig. 40.1)—the rear foot (calcaneus and talus), the midfoot (the cuneiforms and navicular medially, the cuboid laterally), and the forefoot (the metatarsals and phalanges)—the bony anatomy is greatly simplified. Soft tissue anatomy can be superimposed on the regional division of the foot (Figs 40.2c–e).

In keeping with this anatomical division of the foot, clinical assessment of foot pain is most conveniently considered in three anatomical regions (Fig. 40.1):

- heel pain (arising from the rear foot)
- midfoot pain
- forefoot pain.

Rear foot pain

The most common cause of rear foot (inferior heel) pain is plantar fasciitis. A lay term for this condition is "heel spur(s)." This condition occurs mainly in runners and the older adult, and is often associated with a biomechanical abnormality, such as excessive pronation or supination. In non-athletic populations, limited ankle dorsiflexion range of motion and high body mass index (BMI) should be considered predisposing factors.[1] Another common cause of heel pain is the fat pad syndrome or fat pad contusion. This is also known as a "bruised heel" or a "stone bruise."

Less common causes of heel pain are stress fracture of the calcaneus and conditions that refer pain to this area such as tarsal tunnel syndrome (Chapter 39) or medial calcaneal nerve entrapment (Chapter 39). Causes of rear foot pain are listed in Table 40.1 overleaf.

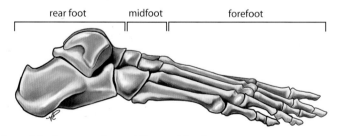

Figure 40.1 The regions of the foot—rear foot, midfoot and forefoot

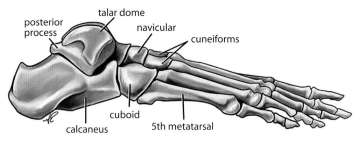

talar dome
posterior process
navicular
cuneiforms
cuboid
calcaneus
5th metatarsal

Figure 40.2 Anatomy of the foot
(a) Lateral view of the bones of the foot

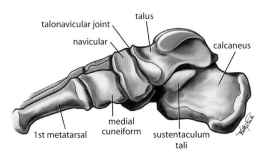

talonavicular joint
talus
navicular
calcaneus
1st metatarsal
medial cuneiform
sustentaculum tali

(b) Medial view of the bones of the foot

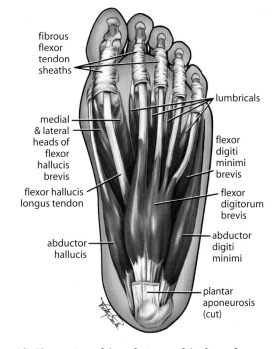

fibrous flexor tendon sheaths
lumbricals
medial & lateral heads of flexor hallucis brevis
flexor digiti minimi brevis
flexor hallucis longus tendon
flexor digitorum brevis
abductor hallucis
abductor digiti minimi
plantar aponeurosis (cut)

(d) Plantar view of the soft tissues of the foot—first layer

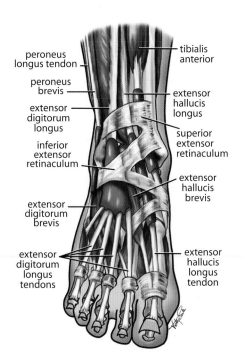

peroneus longus tendon
tibialis anterior
peroneus brevis
extensor hallucis longus
extensor digitorum longus
superior extensor retinaculum
inferior extensor retinaculum
extensor hallucis brevis
extensor digitorum brevis
extensor digitorum longus tendons
extensor hallucis longus tendon

(c) Dorsal view of the soft tissues of the foot

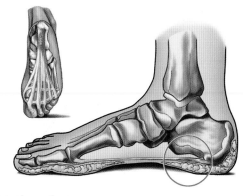

(e) Plantar fascia

Table 40.1 Causes of rear foot and inferior heel pain

Common	Less common	Not to be missed
Plantar fasciitis	Calcaneal fractures	Spondyloarthropathies
Fat pad contusion	• Traumatic	Osteoid osteoma
	• Stress fracture	Regional complex pain syndrome type 1
	Medial calcaneal nerve entrapment (Chapter 39)	(after knee or ankle injury)
	Lateral plantar nerve entrapment	
	Tarsal tunnel syndrome (Chapter 39)	
	Talar stress fracture (Chapter 39)	
	Retrocalcaneal bursitis (Chapter 37)	

Clinical perspective

History

The pain of plantar fasciitis is usually of insidious onset, whereas fat pad damage may occur either as a result of a single traumatic episode (e.g. jumping from a height onto the heel) or from repeated heel strike (e.g. on hard surfaces with inadequate heel support). Plantar fasciitis pain is typically worse in the morning, improves with exercise at first and is aggravated by standing.

Examination

Examination of the rearfoot is shown in Figure 40.3. The windlass (or Jack's) test (passive dorsiflexion of the first metatarsophalangeal joint) is a quick and highly specific test for the plantar fascia[2] (Fig. 40.3c).

Biomechanical assessment is an important component of the examination and must include ankle, subtalar, and midtarsal joint range of motion. Functional assessment of forefoot and first metatarsophalangeal joint range of motion can provide information on overall foot function. Inspection of footwear is also important. Close inspection of the soles of shoes can highlight asymmetrical wear, which may indicate biomechanical problems.

Investigations

X-ray only contributes to the clinical work-up of rearfoot pain in a small proportion of cases. It may reveal a calcaneal spur but, as this may or may not be symptomatic, it does not add clinical utility. Plain X-ray is generally normal in stress fractures of the calcaneus, but if the injury has been present for many weeks, there may be a line of sclerosis (increased opacity). This appearance is characteristic of stress fracture in trabecular bone.

Isotopic bone scan or MRI are the investigations of choice for stress fracture. MRI and ultrasound can each be used to confirm the presence and severity of plantar fasciitis. MRI reveals increased signal intensity and thickening at the attachment of the plantar fascia to the calcaneus (Fig. 42.d on page 845) at the medial calcaneal tuberosity, often with edema in the adjacent bone. Ultrasound reveals a characteristic region of hypoechogenicity. In plantar fasciitis, bone

Figure 40.3 Examination of the rear foot
(a) Palpation—medial process of calcaneal tuberosity. Palpate plantar fascia attachment

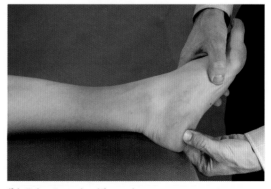

(b) Palpation—heel fat pad

(c) The windlass (or Jack's) test—passive dorsiflexion of the first metatarsalphalangeal joint

scan may demonstrate an increased uptake at the attachment of the plantar fascia at the medial calcaneal tuberosity as an incidental finding; it is not usually done for that purpose.

Plantar fasciitis

The plantar fascia plays an important role in normal foot biomechanics. The plantar fascia is composed of three segments, all arising from the calcaneus. The central, and clinically most important, segment arises from the plantar aspect of the posteromedial calcaneal tuberosity and inserts into the toes to form the longitudinal arch of the foot.

The fascia provides static support for the longitudinal arch and dynamic shock absorption. Normal walking and running biomechanics involve subtalar joint supination at heel contact, pronation at midstance (to allow shock absorption), and re-supination at late stance. Tension in the plantar fascia in late stance, caused by dorsiflexion of the metatarsophalangeal (MTP) joints, helps to stabilize the foot and reduce tension in plantar ligaments and neural structures.

Plantar fasciitis, an overuse condition of the plantar fascia at its attachment to the calcaneus, is due to collagen disarray in the absence of inflammatory cells.

Thus, the pathology resembles that of tendinosis/tendinopathy (Chapter 5) and the condition should be more correctly referred to as "plantar fasciosis"[3] or "fasciopathy." However, as neither of these terms is in common usage, we continue to use the traditional term, "plantar fasciitis," in this book.

Causes

Individuals with pes planus (low arches or flat feet) or pes cavus (high arches) are at increased risk of developing plantar fasciitis. Pes planus places an increased strain on the origin of the plantar fascia at the calcaneus, as the plantar fascia attempts to maintain a stable arch during the propulsive phase of the gait. Excessive movement into pronation, or a lack of re-supination in late stance may also predispose to plantar fasciitis.[4] In the cavus foot, there may be excessive strain on the heel area because the foot lacks the ability to evert, absorb shock, and adapt itself to the ground.

Plantar fasciitis commonly results from activities that require maximal plantarflexion of the ankle and simultaneous dorsiflexion of the MTP joints (e.g. running, dancing). In the older patient, it may be related to excessive walking in inappropriate or non-supportive footwear.[5]

The American Physical Therapy Association's 2008 guidelines on heel pain and plantar fasciitis state that clinicians should consider reduced ankle dorsiflexion and increased BMI as risk factors for plantar fasciitis, especially in non-athletic populations.[1] Obesity and work-related weight-bearing are also independent risk factors.[5]

Plantar fasciitis is commonly associated with tightness in the proximal myofascial structures, especially the calf, hamstring, and gluteal regions.[5] Tightness in these muscle groups can predispose to plantar fasciitis by altering the normal foot biomechanics outlined above. Hip muscle strength imbalances can also predispose to plantar fasciitis. A case-control study of 30 recreational runners with unilateral overuse injuries including plantar fasciitis, found significant reductions in hip flexor and abductor strength compared with the uninjured side.[6] No significant side-to-side differences were found in uninjured control subjects.

Clinical features

The pain is usually of gradual onset and felt classically on the medial aspect of the heel. Initially, it is worse in the morning and decreases with activity, often to ache post-activity. Periods of inactivity during the day are generally followed by an increase in pain as activity is recommenced. As the condition becomes more severe, the pain may be present when weight-bearing and worsen with activity. There may be a history of contralateral leg or foot problems in patients with abnormal biomechanics.

Examination reveals acute tenderness along the medial tuberosity of the calcaneus, and this may extend some centimeters along the medial border of the plantar fascia. The plantar fascia is generally tight, and stretching the plantar fascia may reproduce pain, such as during the windlass test (Fig. 40.3c).

Assessment of the patient's gait may reveal excessive supination or pronation. Both an abducted gait and calf tightness may reduce the sportsperson's ability to supinate, increasing the strain on the plantar fascia. Assessment of the patient's motor control through the single-leg squat test may reveal excessive subtalar and midfoot pronation, tibial internal rotation, and internal rotation and abduction of the hip. Individual assessment of lower limb muscle strength may reveal weakness in the tibialis posterior, calf, and hip abductor musculature. Assessment of the patient's single-leg balance may reveal toe clawing or reduced proximal muscle control. Toe clawing (excessive activity of the long toe flexors) can be an indication of weak intrinsic foot musculature or foot instability.

Investigations

Ultrasound is the gold standard diagnostic investigation for plantar fasciitis, with swelling of the plantar fascia the typical feature. The thickness of the fascia may also be measured.

X-rays are often performed but are not essential for the diagnosis. X-ray may show a calcaneal spur (Fig. 40.4); however, Lu et al. have confirmed that the spurs are not causally related to pain.[7] X-ray appearances were unrelated to pain; it is important to explain these findings to patients.

Treatment

Treatment options for plantar fasciitis can be divided into two groups—those for the short term, and those for the long term.

Treatment options for the short term include:

- avoidance of aggravating activity
- cryotherapy after activity
- stretching of the plantar fascia (Fig. 40.5a),[8] gastrocnemius, and soleus

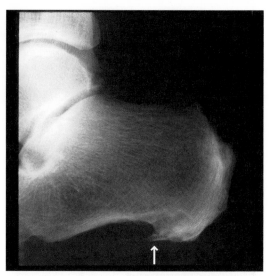

Figure 40.4 Although calcaneal spurs can be rather large, they are not causally associated with plantar fasciitis. They are also found in asymptomatic individuals, as in this case, on both feet when only one is symptomatic, and they can enlarge even after symptoms have resolved

- self-massage with a frozen bottle or golf ball (Fig. 40.5b)
- nonsteroidal anti-inflammatory drugs (NSAIDs), which provide pain relief in some patients[9]
- taping—two types of taping have been advocated:
  - taping the foot into inversion (Fig. 40.5c)
  - low-Dye taping (Fig. 40.5d) involves the application of rigid tape to the plantar aspect of the foot, with the aim of supporting the plantar fascia. Low-Dye taping can provide good

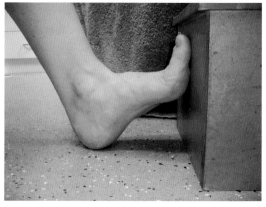

Figure 40.5 Treatment of plantar fasciitis
(a) Stretching the plantar fascia

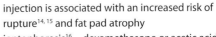

short-term pain relief and improved function for plantar fasciitis [10, 11]

- silicone gel heel pad (Fig. 40.5e)
- corticosteroid injection[12] (Fig. 40.5f)—level 2 evidence supports the use of corticosteroid injection in the short term.[13] It must be combined with other treatments such as stretching, biomechanical correction, and motor control re-education to prevent recurrence; there is some concern that injection is associated with an increased risk of rupture[14, 15] and fat pad atrophy

- iontophoresis[16]—dexamethasone or acetic acid administered via iontophoresis can provide short-term improvements to pain and function
- extracorporeal shock wave therapy—this has been used for chronic cases but research evidence of its efficacy has been conflicting.[17–20]

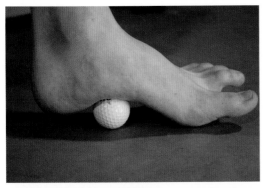

(b) Self-massage with a golf ball

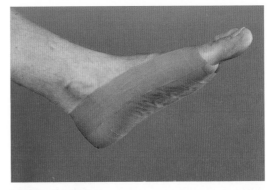

(d) Low-Dye taping

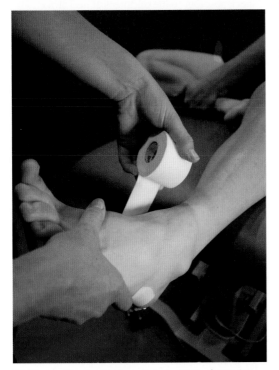

(c) Taping. The foot is placed into inversion by taping from the lateral aspect of the dorsum of the foot and across the plantar aspect before anchoring the tape to the skin over the medial arch

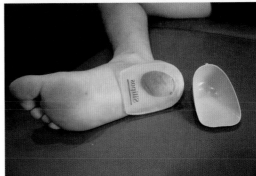

(e) A silicone gel heel pad and heel cup

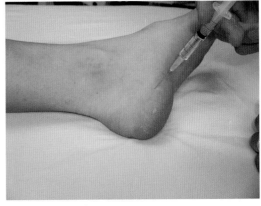

(f) Corticosteroid injection

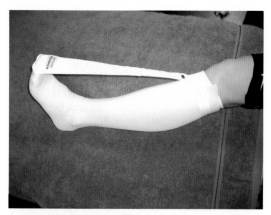

(g) Strasbourg sock

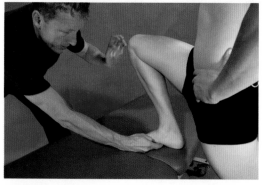

(h) Soft tissue therapy

Treatment options for the long term include:

- strengthening exercises[21]—strengthening exercises for the intrinsic muscles of the foot are designed to improve longitudinal arch support and decrease stress on the plantar fascia;[22] a simple technique is to raise the toes and press them each individually to the floor
- strengthening exercises for proximal muscle groups (e.g. tibialis posterior and hip abductors/external rotators)
- motor control re-education, technique modification
- footwear with well-supported arches and midsoles[4, 21]
- biomechanical correction with orthoses[23, 24]
- night splints[25–27] or Strasbourg sock should be considered for patients with pain of over six months in duration[1] (Fig. 40.5g)
- soft tissue therapy, both to the plantar fascia and also the proximal myofascial regions including calf, hamstring, and gluteals (Fig. 40.5h)

- surgery—this is sometimes required in patients who remain symptomatic despite appropriate treatment; this is needed more in patients with a rigid, cavus foot whose plantar fascia tends to be shortened and thickened rather than in those with a pes planus foot type.
  - plantar fasciectomy—in an uncontrolled case series of plantar fasciectomy with neurolysis of the nerve to the abductor digiti quinti muscle, 92% of patients had a "satisfactory functional outcome"; time from surgery to return to work averaged nine weeks[28]
  - minimally invasive endoscopic plantar fascia release—this is a promising procedure that is gaining acceptance among foot surgeons.[29, 30]

PRACTICE PEARL

The finding of a calcaneal spur on X-ray is not an indication for surgery.

Fat pad contusion

The fat pad, which is composed of an elastic fibrous tissue septa separating closely packed fat cells, acts as a shock absorber to the calcaneus at heel strike.

Causes

Fat pad contusion, or fat pad syndrome, may develop either acutely after a fall onto the heels from a height, or chronically because of excessive heel strike with poor heel cushioning or repetitive stops, starts, and changes in direction.

Clinical features

The patient complains of marked heel pain, particularly during weight-bearing activities. The pain is often felt laterally in the heel due to the pattern of heel strike, which may help differentiate this condition from plantar fasciitis. Examination generally reveals tenderness in the posterolateral heel region. There may be an area of redness.

Investigations

MRI often demonstrates edematous changes in the fat pad, with ill-defined areas of decreased signal intensity on T_1-weighted images that increase in signal intensity on T_2-weighted images.

Treatment

Treatment consists primarily of avoidance of aggravating activities, in particular, excessive weight-bearing.

RICE (rest, ice, compression, elevation) (Chapter 13) and NSAIDs may be required for short-term pain management. Sportspeople can maintain cardiovascular fitness by cross training with low impact activities such as cycling and swimming. Running or training on soft surfaces can assist athletes with returning to sport.

As the pain settles, the use of a silicone gel heel pad (Fig. 40.5e) and good footwear are important as the sportsperson resumes activity. A well-fitting heel counter in athletic footwear can reduce shear stress and tension in the fat pad, potentially reducing the risk of injury and recurrence.[31] Heel lock taping (Fig. 38.8b) often provides symptomatic relief.

Calcaneal stress fractures

Calcaneal stress fractures[32] are the second most common tarsal stress fracture, after the navicular. They occur most commonly at two main sites—the upper posterior margin of the os calcis, and adjacent to the medial tuberosity at the point where calcaneal spurs occur.

Causes

Calcaneal stress fractures were first described among the military and are related to marching; they also occur in runners, ballet dancers, and jumpers. Calcaneal stress fractures may be caused by heavy landing, over-striding, or poor heel cushioning.

Clinical features

Patients give a history of insidious onset of heel pain that is aggravated by weight-bearing activities, especially running.

Examination reveals localized tenderness over the medial or lateral aspects of the posterior calcaneus, and pain that is produced by squeezing the posterior aspect of the calcaneus from both sides simultaneously.

Investigations

Plain X-ray may show a typical sclerotic appearance on the lateral X-ray, parallel to the posterior margin of the calcaneus (Fig. 40.6). Isotopic bone scan reveals a focal area of increased uptake; MRI reveals an area of high signal on a T2-weighted image.

Treatment

Treatment involves a reduction in activity and, for those with marked pain, a short period of non-weight-

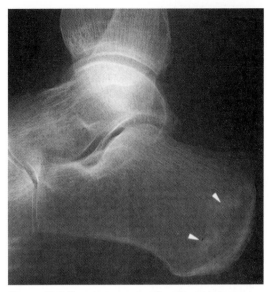

Figure 40.6 X-ray appearance of a calcaneal stress fracture

bearing. Once pain-free, a program of gradually increased weight-bearing can occur.

Stretching of the calf muscles and plantar fascia, and joint mobilization are important for long-term recovery. Soft heel pads, in conjunction with orthoses if required, are recommended. Coaching may be required to improve technique.

Lateral plantar nerve entrapment

An entrapment of the first branch of the lateral plantar nerve (one of the terminal branches of the posterior tibial nerve after it passes through the tarsal tunnel) occurs between the deep fascia of the abductor hallucis longus and the medial caudal margin of the quadratus planus muscle.[33]

Pain radiates to the medial inferior aspect of the heel and proximally into the medial ankle region. Patients do not normally complain of numbness in the heel or foot.

A diagnostic injection with local anesthetic will confirm the diagnosis. Nerve conduction tests may be helpful.

Treatment

Treatment consists of arch support using tape, or an orthotic is helpful in sportspeople with excessive pronation.

A corticosteroid injection may be helpful and occasionally surgical release may be necessary.[33]

Midfoot pain

The midfoot is comprised of the three cuneiform bones, the cuboid, and the navicular bones as well as the surrounding soft tissues (Figs 40.1, 40.2).

The most *common* cause of midfoot pain is midtarsal joint sprain after ankle injury but the most *important* cause of midfoot pain is a stress fracture of the navicular bone. Tendinopathy of the extensor tendons is another common cause of midfoot pain. The causes of midfoot pain are listed in Table 40.2.

Clinical perspective

History

Acute onset of midfoot pain occurs with a sprain of the midtarsal joint or plantar fascia. Gradual pain is a sign of overuse injury, such as extensor tendinopathy, tibialis posterior tendinopathy, or navicular stress fracture. In most conditions, pain is well localized to the site of the injury, but in navicular stress fracture pain is poorly localized.

Examination

Examination involves palpation of the area of tenderness and a biomechanical examination to detect factors that predispose to injury. Examination of the midfoot is shown in Figure 40.7.

Investigations

If there is a clinical suspicion of a stress fracture of the navicular or the cuneiform, an X-ray should be performed. This rarely reveals a fracture, even if one is present, but it is useful to rule out tarsal coalition (page 861), to show bony abnormalities such as talar beaking (osteophytes at the talonavicular joint) and accessory ossicles, and to exclude bony tumors.

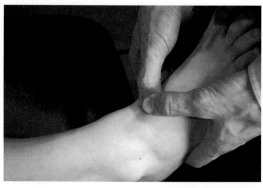

Figure 40.7 Examination of the midfoot
(a) Palpation—"N spot." The proximal dorsal surface of the navicular is tender when a stress fracture is present

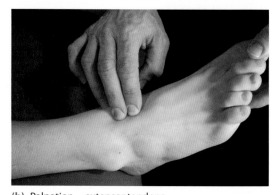

(b) Palpation—extensor tendons.
These may be tender as they pass under the extensor retinaculum. The midtarsal joint and bones should be palpated

X-ray followed by MRI is the routine method of investigation. An isotopic bone scan (with CT scan if positive) was the standard before MRI became widely available. An isotopic bone scan (with CT scan if positive).

Table 40.2 Causes of midfoot pain

Common	Less common	Not to be missed
Navicular stress fracture	Cuneiform stress fracture	Lisfranc joint injury (fracture or
Midtarsal joint sprain	Cuboid stress fracture	dislocation)
Extensor tendinopathy	Stress fracture base second metatarsal	Osteoid osteoma
Tibialis posterior tendinopathy	Peroneal tendinopathy	Complex regional pain syndrome
Plantar fascia strain	Abductor hallucis strain	type 1 (after knee or ankle injury)
	Cuboid syndrome	
	Tarsal coalition (in adolescents)	
	Köhler's disease (in young children)	
	Accessory navicular bone	

Stress fracture of the navicular

Stress fractures of the navicular are among the most common stress fractures seen in the athlete, especially in sports that involve sprinting, jumping, or hurdling.[34] The stress fracture commonly occurs in the middle third of the navicular bone, a relatively avascular region of the bone. Stress fractures in this region are thus susceptible to delayed union.

Cause

A combination of overuse and training errors plays a significant role in the development of navicular stress fractures. Although the exact cause of a navicular stress fracture is not known, it is believed that impingement of the navicular bone occurs between the proximal and distal tarsal bones. This impingement and compression is increased by muscle activity. Reduced ankle dorsiflexion range of motion may increase the risk of developing navicular stress fracture, because compensatory dorsiflexion occurs through the midfoot.[35]

Clinical features

The onset of symptoms is usually insidious, consisting of a poorly localized midfoot ache associated with activity. The pain typically radiates along the medial aspect of the longitudinal arch or the dorsum of the foot. The symptoms abate rapidly with rest.

Examination reveals localized tenderness at the "N-spot," located at the proximal dorsal portion of the navicular. If palpation confirms tenderness over the "N spot" (Fig. 40.7a), the sportsperson should be considered to have a navicular stress fracture until proven otherwise.

Investigations

Sensitivity of X-ray in navicular stress fracture is poor.[36] Thus, either isotopic bone scan (Fig. 40.8a) (with CT scan if positive [Figs 40.8b, c]) or MRI (Fig. 40.8d overleaf) is required if clinical features suggest stress fracture. Poor positioning and scanning technique can lead to a navicular stress fracture being missed on CT scan.[37] Appropriate views require correct angling of the CT gantry and thin (2 mm [0.1 in.]) slices extending from the distal talus to the distal navicular.

Treatment

The treatment of a navicular stress *reaction* (no cortical breach) is weight-bearing rest, often in an Aircast,

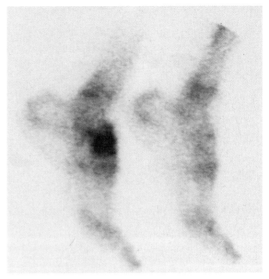

Figure 40.8 Navicular stress fracture
(a) Isotopic bone scan

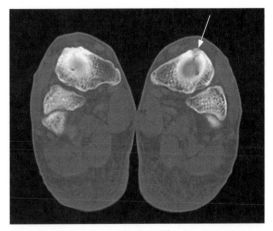

(b) CT scan showing undisplaced fracture (arrow)

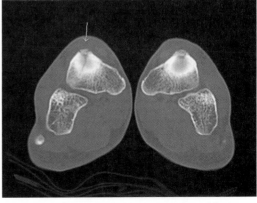

(c) CT scan showing more extensive Y-shaped fracture

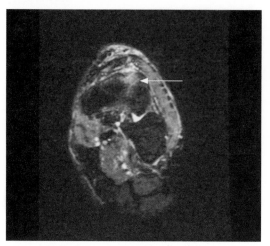

(d) T2-weighted MRI showing bone marrow edema

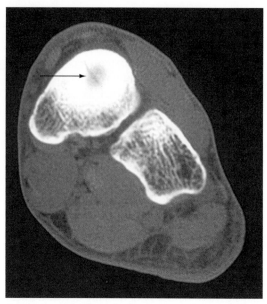

Figure 40.9 Imaging of navicular stress fracture does not necessarily mirror clinical recovery. This CT scan of a 26-year-old runner shows that the fracture line is still evident (arrow) but the patient had returned pain-free to all competition and had no further recurrences of stress fracture

until symptoms and signs have resolved, followed by a graduated return to activity.

PRACTICE PEARL Treatment of navicular stress fracture is strict non-weight-bearing immobilization in a cast or non-weight-bearing fiberglass boot for 6–8 weeks.[36]

Clinicians experienced in treating this condition tend to encourage the eight weeks over the six weeks unless the injury was diagnosed extremely soon after pain began.

At the end of the period of non-weight-bearing immobilization, the cast should be removed and the "N spot" palpated for tenderness. Generally, the "N spot" will be non-tender; however, if tenderness is present, the patient should have the cast reapplied for a further two weeks of non-weight-bearing immobilization. Management must be based on the clinical assessment, as there is poor CT and MRI correlation with clinical union of the stress fracture (Fig. 40.9).[36-38]

Often, patients with a stress fracture of the navicular present after a long period of pain or after a period of weight-bearing rest. All patients, even if they have been unsuccessfully treated with prolonged weight-bearing rest or short-term cast immobilization, should undergo cast immobilization for a six week period. This method of treatment is associated with an 80% successful return-to-sport rate[36] and may be successful even in longstanding cases.

Some clinicians advocate surgical treatment with the insertion of a screw where there is significant separation of the fracture (Fig. 40.8c). In cases of delayed or non-union, surgical internal fixation

with or without bone grafting is required. However, in most cases surgery is not indicated. A recent systematic review and meta-analysis found no significant difference between non-weight-bearing conservative treatment and surgical treatment in terms of pain reduction and return to previous activity level.[39] A retrospective case study found no difference in terms of pain, function, or abnormality on CT between surgical management and conservative management after two years.[40]

Post-cast rehabilitation and prevention of recurrence

Following removal of the cast, it is essential to mobilize the stiff ankle, and subtalar and midtarsal joints. The calf muscles require soft tissue therapy and exercise to regain strength. These must be done before resuming running. Activity must be begun gradually, slowly building up to full training over a period of six weeks. Predisposing factors to navicular stress fractures may include tarsal coalition, excessive pronation, and restricted dorsiflexion of the ankle. These factors need to be corrected before resuming activity.

Extensor tendinopathy

The extensor (dorsiflexor) muscles of the foot comprise the tibialis anterior, extensor hallucis longus and brevis, as well as extensor digitorum longus and brevis. The insertions in the foot and actions of the extensor muscles are shown in Table 40.3.

Tibialis anterior tendinopathy is the most common tendinopathy occurring in the extensor muscles of the foot. Tendinopathies of the extensor hallucis longus and brevis and extensor digitorum longus and brevis muscles are rare.

Causes

The tibialis anterior muscle resists plantarflexion and eversion of the foot at heel strike and its tendon is therefore susceptible to overuse injury. Tendinopathy may be related to extensor muscle weakness or, alternatively, it may occur secondary to a recent increase in the training load or compression by excessively tight shoelaces. Stiffness of the first MTP joint and midfoot joints may contribute.

Clinical features

Generally after a period of overuse, the patient with extensor tendinopathy complains of an aching dorsal aspect of the midfoot.

Examination may reveal tenderness, often with mild swelling, at the insertion of the tibialis anterior tendon at the base of the first metatarsal and the cuneiform. Resisted dorsiflexion and eccentric inversion may elicit pain. Functional assessment may reveal excessive heel strike or over-striding during running.

Both ultrasound and MRI may reveal swelling of the tendon at its insertion and exclude the presence of a degenerative tear.

Treatment

Popular clinical treatment involves relative rest and soft tissue therapy to the extensor muscles. Extensor muscle strengthening is advocated as is the case with other tendinopathies.

The underlying precipitating cause needs to be addressed. This may include mobilization of the first ray, and tarsometatarsal and midtarsal joints, if the first MTP joint and midfoot is stiff. A change of lacing pattern or placing adhesive foam to the underside of the tongue of the shoe will help if compression by the shoelaces is the cause. Modification of running technique may be required. Rarely, footwear will need to be replaced.

Midtarsal joint sprains

The midtarsal joint (Chopart's joint) consists of the talonavicular and calcaneocuboid joints. Other joints in the midtarsal area are the naviculocuneiform, cuboid cuneiform, and intercuneiform joints. Injuries to the midtarsal joints are most commonly seen in gymnasts, jumpers, and footballers.

Individual ligamentous sprains to the midtarsal joints are uncommon; they usually affect the dorsal calcaneocuboid or the bifurcate ligament (comprising the calcaneonavicular and calcaneocuboid ligament).

Dorsal calcaneocuboid ligament injury

Patients present with pain in the lateral midfoot following an inversion injury. Examination reveals localized tenderness and swelling at the dorsolateral aspect of the calcaneocuboid joint. Stress inversion of the foot elicits pain.

X-ray is required to exclude fracture. MRI may confirm the diagnosis.

Table 40.3 Extensor muscles, their insertions at the foot, and their actions

Muscle	Insertion in foot	Action
Tibialis anterior	Medial cuneiform and base of 1st metatarsal	Dorsiflexes foot at ankle Inverts foot at subtalar and transverse tarsal joints Maintains medial longitudinal arch
Extensor digitorum longus	Extensor expansion of lateral four toes	Extends toes and dorsiflexes foot
Extensor hallucis longus	Base of distal phalanx of big toe	Extends big toe Dorsiflexes foot Inverts foot at subtalar and transverse tarsal joints
Extensor digitorum brevis	Long extensor tendons to second, third, and fourth toes	Extends toes
Extensor hallucis brevis	Proximal phalanx of big toe	Extends big toe

Taping may provide additional support and help relieve pain. Orthoses may be required. Following a joint sprain, joint inflammation occasionally develops. This generally responds well to NSAIDs but, if it persists, the patient may benefit from a corticosteroid injection into one of the midtarsal joints.

Bifurcate ligament injuries

Injury to the bifurcate ligament (comprising the calcaneonavicular and calcaneocuboid ligament) may be associated with fractures of the anterior process of the calcaneus and may occur secondary to violent dorsiflexion, forceful plantarflexion, and inversion injuries.

Patients present with lateral midfoot pain and swelling, usually following an ankle sprain or injury. Examination reveals local tenderness and occasionally swelling overlying the ligament, with pain elicited at the site with simultaneous forefoot supination and plantarflexion.

X-rays are required to assess for a fracture of the anterior process of the calcaneus. If a fracture is present, a CT scan may be required for further assessment. An MRI scan can be used to confirm the joint/ligament sprain.

Treatment is similar to the dorsal calcaneocuboid sprain mentioned above. If there is a non-displaced or mildly displaced fracture of the anterior process of the calcaneum, four weeks' immobilization is required. If the fracture is displaced, surgery is required.

Lisfranc joint injuries

The eponymous Lisfranc joint refers to the tarsometatarsal joints—the bases of the five metatarsals with their corresponding three cuneiforms and cuboid (Fig. 40.10). Injuries to these joints are given this eponym after Jacques Lisfranc, a surgeon in Napoleon's army, who described an operation for amputation through the tarsometatarsal joint.

The spectrum of injuries of the Lisfranc joint complex ranges from partial sprains with no displacement, to complete tears with separation (diastasis) of the first and second metatarsal bones and, depending on the severity, different patterns of tarsal and metatarsal displacement (Fig. 40.11). Although Lisfranc joint injuries ("midfoot sprains") are not common in the general population, they are the second most common foot injury in sportspeople. They generally occur as a consequence of a low-velocity indirect

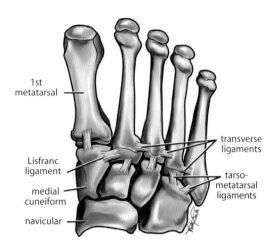

Figure 40.10 Ligamentous attachments of the Lisfranc joint articulation

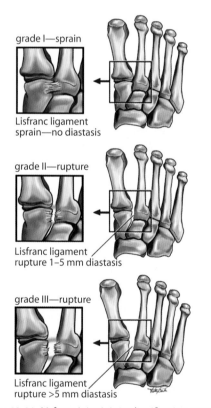

Figure 40.11 Lisfranc joint injury classification system

force, in contrast to the general population, where they occur as a consequence of a high-velocity force.

Lisfranc joint fracture–dislocation is rare in sport, but, because of its disastrous consequences if untreated, the diagnosis must be considered in all cases of "midfoot sprain" in the sportsperson.

Causes

There are two main mechanisms of injury:

- Direct—this injury is relatively uncommon and occurs as a simple crush injury to the tarsometatarsal joint region. There is no specific pattern of damage or distinctive appearance with a direct injury.
- Indirect—this mechanism is more common and generally occurs secondary to a longitudinal force sustained while the foot is plantarflexed and slightly rotated. There are three common injury situations: longitudinal compression (Fig. 40.12), a backward fall with the foot entrapped, and a fall on the point of the toes.[41]

The extent of the damage depends on the severity of the injury—in milder injuries, the weak dorsal tarsometatarsal ligaments are ruptured; with more severe injuries, there may also be fractures of the plantar aspect of the metatarsal base, or the plantar

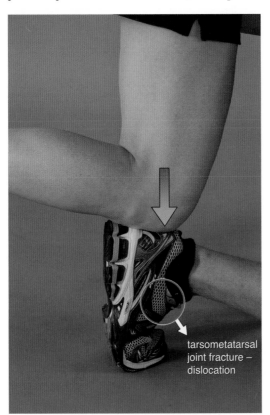

Figure 40.12 Mechanism of injury to Lisfranc joint— longitudinal compression

capsule may rupture and the metatarsal may displace dorsally. Thus, a fracture at the plantar base of a metatarsal can be a clue to a subtle Lisfranc joint injury.

Clinical features

A patient with Lisfranc joint injury may complain of midfoot pain and difficulty weight-bearing, following an acute injury by the mechanisms described above. Pain is classically aggravated by forefoot weight-bearing—the patient is unable to run on the toes and feels pain on the push-off phase of running and sometimes during walking and on calf raises.

Often the presentation may be delayed, and the patient presents with ongoing midfoot pain and swelling, aggravated by running.

 Midfoot pain that persists for more than five days post-injury should raise suspicion of a Lisfranc joint injury.

Examination reveals:

- tenderness with or without swelling on the dorsal midfoot, often with associated bruising in this region
- pain with combined eversion and abduction of the forefoot while the calcaneus is held still.

Neurovascular examination is mandatory as the dorsalis pedis artery can be compromised in the initial injury or by subsequent swelling of the foot.[41]

Investigations

Plain X-rays while weight-bearing are recommended. Diastasis between the first and second metatarsal bases of greater than 2 mm (0.1 in.) (Fig. 40.13a overleaf) suggests a Lisfranc joint injury, although in patients with a metatarsus adductus a 3 mm (0.15 in.) separation may be normal. In such cases, it is essential to take comparative weight-bearing X-rays of the non-injured side, as a difference in diastasis of greater than 1 mm (0.05 in.) between the two sides is considered diagnostic.

Other radiological signs that may indicate an injury to the Lisfranc joint include a "fleck sign," which appears as a fleck fracture near the base of the second metatarsal or medial cuneiform or, in the lateral view, either dorsal displacement of the metatarsal bases relative to the tarsus or flattening of the medial longitudinal arch. However, a dislocation may reduce spontaneously, and the foot may appear normal on plain X-rays despite the presence of severe soft tissue disruption.

MRI scans are sensitive in detecting tears of the Lisfranc ligament when plain X-rays appear normal, and should be performed if there is a possible midfoot injury.

A study compared MRI findings to intraoperative stability in 20 patients with Lisfranc joint injury.[42] There was a high correlation between rupture or grade 2 sprain of the plantar ligament between the first cuneiform and the bases of the second and third metatarsals, and true midfoot instability. Isotopic bone scan in conjunction with weight-bearing plain X-rays and/or CT scans (Fig. 40.13b) also detect Lisfranc joint injuries.

Treatment

The treatment of a Lisfranc joint injury depends on the degree of instability present.[43]

In grade 1 injuries, where there is no instability (diastasis), conservative management is recommended with non-weight-bearing in a cast or Aircast for six weeks. The goal of this treatment is to restore the integrity of the tarsometatarsal ligaments and hence the stability of the midfoot. Following removal of the cast, mobilization of the ankle and a calf strengthening program are required. Orthoses may be needed to correct the intrinsic alignment of the foot and to support the second metatarsal base. A graded return to activity is required.

If there is evidence of instability present, as in grade 2 and grade 3 injuries, surgical reduction and fixation is required. This may be performed percutaneously or, in more difficult cases, an open operation may be needed. In the situation of a delay in diagnosis, similar treatment protocols are required.

A grade 2 or grade 3 Lisfranc injury is a significant injury that has a much better prognosis if managed correctly initially, rather than being salvaged once there is prolonged joint malalignment and nonunion. A delay in diagnosis has been associated with a poor outcome, a prolonged absence from sport, and

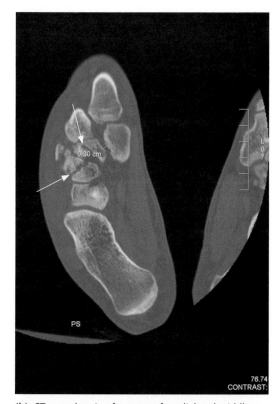

Figure 40.13 Lisfranc fracture–dislocation
(a) Plain X-ray

(b) CT scan showing fractures of medial and middle cuneiforms (arrows) with 0.30 cm of diastasis in the Lisfranc joint

chronic disability due to ligamentous instability of the tarsometatarsal joint.

Less common causes of midtarsal joint pain

First tarsometatarsal joint pain

In the excessively pronating foot, retrograde forces on the first ray result in the build-up of exostoses at the first metatarsal–cuneiform joint. These bone spurs may cause joint impingement and midfoot pain. The resultant limitation of dorsiflexion of the first ray subjects the second ray to an increased load that can damage the second metatarsal–cuneiform joint.

Treatment consists of correction of the abnormal foot mechanics with the use of orthoses and mobilization of restricted joint range of movement. Occasionally, surgery may be required to remove the bony exostoses.

Tibialis posterior tendinopathy

Tibialis posterior tendinopathy may present with medial foot pain when there is partial avulsion (tendinosis) at the insertion of the tendon into the navicular tuberosity. As with other overuse tendon injuries (Chapter 5), this condition has recently been shown to be a degenerative tendinosis rather than an inflammatory "tendonitis." This presentation can be more difficult to treat than the more common presentation of medial ankle pain arising from irritation of the tendon as it passes behind the medial malleolus (Chapter 39).

Treatment principles for both presentations are outlined in Chapter 39. In younger patients, the accessory ossicle, the os navicularis (Fig. 40.14), may be avulsed. This requires orthoses and gradual return to activity. Occasionally, surgery is indicated for failure of conservative management.

Peroneal tendinopathy

Peroneal tendinopathy is an overuse injury commonly associated with excessive pronation during the toe-off phase of gait. Peroneal tenosynovitis and partial tendon tears are included under the umbrella term of "peroneal tendinopathy."[44] Pathology may develop in the peroneal tendons or tendon sheath at the lateral aspect of the fibula (Chapter 39). The peroneus longus tendon may develop pathology in the peroneal groove of the cuboid.

Clinically, resisted eversion and hopping reproduce pain. Peroneal tendinopathy is often associated

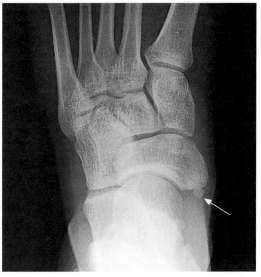

Figure 40.14 The os navicularis (arrow)

with chronic lateral ankle instability, so the ankle joint should be assessed.[44]

A retrospective study compared MRI findings in patients with peroneal tendinopathy with patients with no symptoms. Intermediate T2 signal within the peroneal tendons was a highly specific indicator of peroneal tendinopathy.[45] Fluid greater than 3 mm within the peroneal sheath was a highly specific indicator of peroneal tenosynovitis.

Management includes correction of excessive pronation with orthoses, and treatment of any underlying ankle instability. Resistance exercises are prescribed as for other tendinopathies. Soft tissue massage proximal to the site of pain—in the muscle bellies in the mid-calf—can be very helpful.

Cuboid syndrome

Peroneal tendinopathy is often associated with the development of the cuboid syndrome.[46] Due to excessive traction of the peroneus longus, the cuboid becomes subluxated. Cuboid syndrome may also manifest following plantarflexion and inversion ankle injury, and is common among professional ballet dancers.[47] Pain is experienced with lateral weight-bearing. Most patients with this syndrome have excessively pronated feet, but it is also seen in patients with lateral ankle instability.

Treatment involves a single manipulation to reverse the subluxation.[48] The cuboid should be pushed upward and laterally from the medial plantar aspect of the cuboid, as shown in Figure 40.15. A case series has demonstrated that athletes can return to sport immediately following cuboid manipulation with no recurrence of symptoms.[49]

Plantar fascia strain

Acute strains of the plantar fascia in the midfoot region are relatively common and respond more quickly to treatment than does plantar fasciitis at the calcaneal attachment. There may be a history of either one significant injury or repeated trauma. They have been reported to be more common following corticosteroid injection. The risk of plantar fascia rupture may be greatest in the first two weeks following injection.[13]

Examination reveals well-localized tenderness over the plantar fascia that is aggravated by extension of the MTP joints. A palpable nodule may indicate a partial rupture of the plantar fascia.

A short period of non-weight-bearing, a cast boot, soft tissue therapy and taping (Figs 40.5c, d) are all beneficial, and the condition generally resolves in two to six weeks depending on the severity.

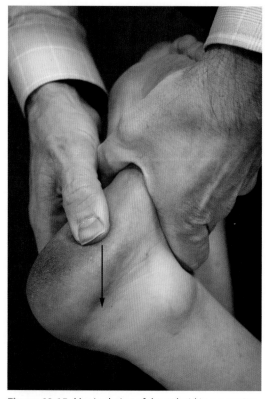

Figure 40.15 Manipulation of the cuboid in a superior and lateral direction in cuboid syndrome

Abductor hallucis strain

Abductor hallucis strains result in pain along the medial longitudinal arch and are often associated with excessive pronation. The abductor hallucis tendon is tender to palpate. Initial treatment consists of symptomatic management and taping.

Stress fracture of the cuboid

Stress fractures of the cuboid are not common and are thought to occur secondary to compression of the cuboid between the calcaneus and the fourth and fifth metatarsal bones when exaggerated plantarflexion is undertaken with or without inversion.[48]

Treatment, in the absence of displacement, is non-weight-bearing for four to six weeks, followed by a graduated return to activity. If displacement is present, surgical reduction and fixation with or without a bone graft may be required.

Stress fracture of the cuneiforms

Stress fractures of the cuneiform bones are rare, but have been described in military recruits and athletes.[50] They may be more common in heavier athletes or athletes with plantar fasciitis.[51]

Management depends on the cuneiform bone involved—limited weight-bearing rest is treatment for medial cuneiform stress fractures; however, stress fractures of the intermediate cuneiform require surgical reduction and fixation for adequate healing.[52]

Köhler's disease

Köhler's disease, or osteochondritis of the navicular, is found in children aged 2–8 years (Chapter 42).

Tarsal coalition

Congenital fusions of the foot bones usually present as midfoot pain. Tarsal coalitions[53] may be osseous, cartilaginous (synchondrosis), fibrous (syndesmosis), or a combination. A fibrous coalition is relatively mobile and therefore may not cause any pain on limited motion. As fibrous or cartilaginous coalitions ossify during adolescence, rear foot or midfoot joint range of motion decreases, placing additional stress on the talocrural (ankle) joint. The two most common tarsal coalitions occur at the calcaneonavicular joint and the talocalcaneal joint; 50–60% occur bilaterally.

Common presentations include an adolescent beginning sports participation or the person in their 20s complaining of pain after vigorous physical activity. Patients can also present after an ankle sprain when pain does not settle (Chapter 38). Because tarsal coalition alters foot biomechanics, it can present in adults with painful bony spurs at sites distant from the coalition (Fig. 40.16).

Examination often reveals reduced range of subtalar and midtarsal joint movement that may be painful at the end of range.

Plain X-rays are the most useful diagnostic tool for osseous coalitions. MRI may be required to visualize

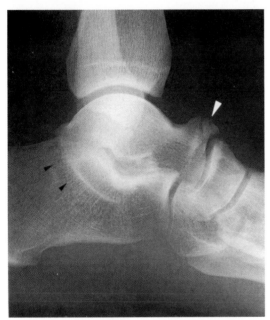

Figure 40.16 X-ray showing talocalcaneal coalition (black arrows) with a continuous cortical line joining the talus and sustentaculum tali, and talar beaking (white arrow) that results from abnormal subtalar movement

a fibrous coalition—these are not evident on plain X-ray or CT scan.

Conservative management includes mobilization of surrounding joints to optimize foot function and referral to a podiatrist. Surgery may be required.

Forefoot pain

Forefoot problems range from corns, calluses, and nail problems to bone and joint abnormalities. Forefoot pain is especially common in sportspeople participating in kicking sports and among ballet dancers. The causes of forefoot pain are listed in Table 40.4.

Clinical perspective

History

Most causes of forefoot pain result from overuse and thus have an insidious onset. Occasionally, acute forefoot pain may result from a sprain of the first MTP joint ("turf toe"). The type of activity performed provides a clue to the cause of the patient's forefoot pain. The presence of sensory symptoms may indicate that a neuroma is present.

Examination

The key to examination of the patient with forefoot pain is careful palpation to determine the site of maximal tenderness. Biomechanical examination is necessary.

1. Observation (Fig. 40.17a overleaf)
2. Palpation
   (a) metatarsals (Fig. 40.17b overleaf)
   (b) first MTP joint (Fig. 40.17c overleaf)
   (c) sesamoid bone of the foot (Fig. 40.17d overleaf)
   (d) space between third and fourth metatarsal (Fig. 40.17e overleaf)

Table 40.4 Causes of forefoot pain

Common	Less common	Not to be missed
Corns, calluses	Freiberg's osteochondritis	Complex regional pain syndrome
Onychocryptosis	Joplin's neuritis	type 1 (after ankle or knee injury)
Synovitis of the MTP joints	Stress fracture of the sesamoid	
First MTP joint sprain	Toe clawing	
Subungual hematoma	Plantar wart	
Hallux abducto-valgus	Subungual exostosis	
Hallux limitus	Stress fracture of the base of the	
Morton's neuroma	second metatarsal	
Sesamoid pathology	Synovitis of the metatarsal–cuneiform	
Stress fracture of the metatarsal	joint	
Fracture of the fifth metatarsal		

MTP = metatarsophalangeal

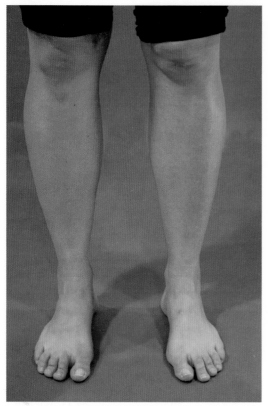

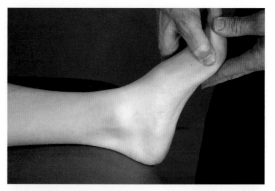

(c) Palpation—first MTP joint

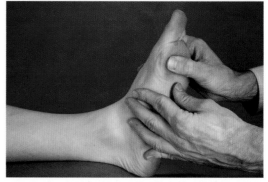

(d) Palpation—sesamoid

Figure 40.17 Examination of the patient with forefoot pain

(a) Observation for the presence of obvious abnormalities (e.g. hallux abducto-valgus, claw toes, Morton's foot, plantar warts, onychocryptosis, corns, callus)

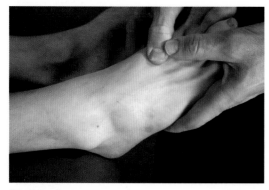

(b) Palpation—metatarsals

Investigations

X-ray may show evidence of a healing stress fracture or acute fracture, the presence of hallux abducto-valgus, hallux limitus, or a subungual exostosis.

Isotopic bone scan or MRI may confirm the diagnosis of a stress fracture. An MRI or ultrasound can be used to determine the presence of a neuroma.

Stress fractures of the metatarsals

Stress fractures of the metatarsals[32] are very common. Excessive loading of the forefoot is thought to be the main contributing factor.[54] Excessive activity and fatigue (particularly of the gastrocnemius muscle) increase forefoot loading.[55, 56]

A shift in pressure from the toes to forefoot was seen in a study of 200 marathon runners following a race.[55] This is thought to increase the risk of metatarsal stress fracture. Fatigue of the toe flexors (flexor digitorum, flexor hallucis longus, and intrinsic foot muscles) may be responsible for this change of loading.

The most common metatarsal stress fracture is at the neck of the second metatarsal. This occurs in the pronating foot, when the first ray is dorsiflexed, resulting in the second metatarsal being subjected to greater load.

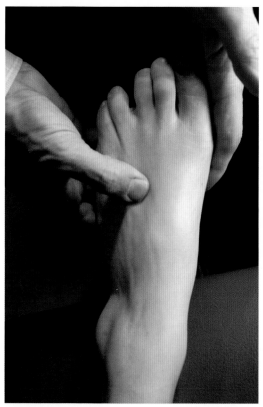

(e) Palpation—space between third and fourth metatarsal for neuroma

The second metatarsal is also susceptible to stress fracture in the case of a Morton's foot, where the first ray is shorter than the second (Fig. 40.18). The base of the second metatarsal is firmly fixed in position next to the cuneiform bones, further increasing the likelihood of fracture. Stress fracture of the second metatarsal is common in ballet dancers.

Stress fractures of the other metatarsals also occur, particularly in the third metatarsal if it is longer than the second.

 Two stress fractures require special treatment—fractures of the base of the second metatarsal and fractures of the fifth metatarsal; these are discussed overleaf.

Clinical features

The patient with a metatarsal stress fracture complains of forefoot pain aggravated by activity such as running or dancing. The pain is not severe initially but gradually worsens with activity. Examination

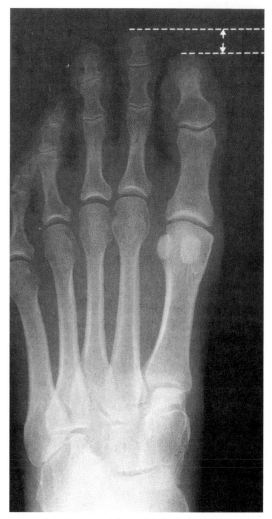

Figure 40.18 Morton's foot with the first ray shorter than the second

reveals the presence of focal tenderness overlying the metatarsal.

Investigation

X-rays may reveal a radiolucent line or periosteal thickening if the fracture has been present for a few weeks (Fig. 40.19a overleaf). If the X-ray is negative, an isotopic bone scan (Fig. 40.19b overleaf) or MRI may confirm the diagnosis.

Treatment

The management of most stress fractures is straightforward, involving rest from weight-bearing aggravating activities for approximately four weeks, and

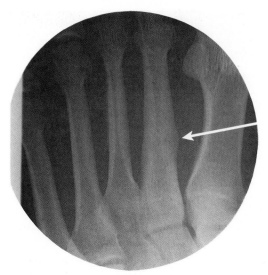

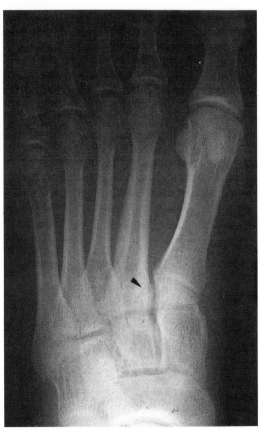

Figure 40.19 Stress fracture of the second metatarsal **(a)** X-ray appearance—note the generalized cortical hypertrophy, as seen in ballet dancers

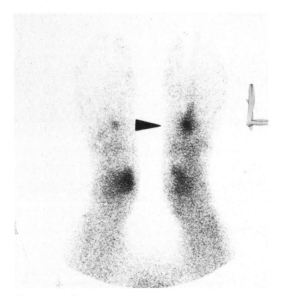

(b) Isotopic bone scan appearance

(c) Stress fracture of the base of the second metatarsal involving the joint

addressing any underlying contributing factors. If the patient is required to be on his or her feet excessively, the use of an Aircast may be required for one to two weeks until pain settles.

The sportsperson should be allowed to recommence activity when there is no pain when walking and there is no local tenderness at the fracture site. A graduated exercise program should be instituted to return the sportsperson to full training and competition.

Orthoses may be required to control abnormal foot mechanics; however, it is still unclear from current research whether orthoses can prevent metatarsal stress fractures.[57]

Any instability during forefoot weight-bearing may predispose to the development of a stress fracture. Motor control exercises to improve the function of the intrinsic and extrinsic foot muscles may help prevent recurrence.

Stress fractures of the base of the second metatarsal

A common stress fracture in ballet dancers occurs at the base of the second metatarsal [32, 58–60] (Fig. 40.19c). The differential diagnosis is chronic joint synovitis MRI is the investigation of choice.

PRACTICE PEARL This fracture should be treated by having the dancer remain non-weight-bearing on crutches until tenderness settles, usually at least four weeks.

Prevention strategies address Achilles tightness, low bone mass and high training loads.[61] Soft tissue therapy for the calf may help reduce strain on the metatarsals. Motor control exercises to strengthen peroneus longus may help unload the second metatarsal, as peroneus longus helps to plantarflex and stabilize the first ray for propulsion.[62]

Fractures of the fifth metatarsal

Three different fractures affect the fifth metatarsal.[32, 63] The fracture of the tuberosity at the base of the fifth metatarsal (Fig. 38.12) has been described in Chapter 38 and is usually an avulsion injury that results from an acute ankle sprain. This uncomplicated fracture heals well with a short period of immobilization for pain relief.

Jones' fracture

A serious fracture of the fifth metatarsal is the fracture of the diaphysis known as a Jones' fracture (Fig. 40.20a). This may be the result of an inversion plantarflexion injury or, more commonly, as a result of overuse (i.e. a stress fracture).

A Jones' fracture requires six to eight weeks of non-weight-bearing cast immobilization,[64] or immediate surgical fixation with the percutaneous insertion of a screw.

More recently, there has been a tendency to favor early screw fixation to manage Jones' fracture.

More recently there has been a tendency to favor early screw fixation due to concerns regarding the high incidence of failure of cast treatment. High patient satisfaction, good healing, and return to sport have been reported following intramedullary screw fixation.[65] Surgical fixation normally allows an earlier return to full weight-bearing (two to four weeks) which is a significant advantage over non-weight-bearing immobilization (six to eight weeks).[65]

Non-union may occur with this type of fracture because of the location of the nutrient artery (Fig. 40.21 overleaf).[66] Non-union may be treated by bone grafting or screw fixation. In one study, early screw fixation resulted in quicker times to union and return to sport compared with cast treatment.[67] The average time to return to sport after this procedure for non-union appears to be approximately eight weeks. Early return to sport may predispose the sportsperson to re-fracture[68] and it may be wise to wait for full radiographic healing before return to sport.[69]

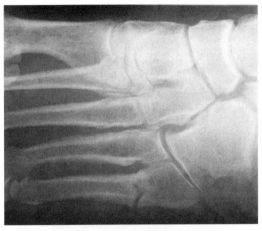

Figure 40.20 Fractures of the fifth metatarsal
(a) Diaphysis or Jones' fracture with slight separation. Sclerosis of the fracture margins suggests delayed union

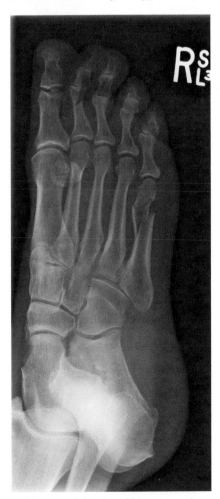

(b) Spiral fracture of the distal fifth metatarsal

- clawing or hammer toes
- tight extensor tendons of the toes
- prominent metatarsal heads
- Morton's foot—there is a shortened first metatarsal, which results in an abnormal subtalar joint, and increased weight going through the second MTP joint.

Clinical features

The patient complains of pain aggravated by forefoot weight-bearing, particularly in the midstance and propulsion phases of walking. The pain is usually gradual in onset.

Examination reveals local tenderness on palpation. Pain is aggravated by passive forced flexion of the toe. It most commonly affects the second MTP joint, occasionally the first or third. The "V" sign is sometimes seen in the early stages of metatarsal joint synovitis. A separation of the toes can create a V shape that may be indicative of underlying dysfunction (Fig. 40.22).[71]

There may be an associated skin lesion (e.g. a callus) over the plantar surface of the affected joint due to the excessive load. This injury may be caused by uneven distribution of load, especially with excessive pronation.

X-rays should be performed to assess the degree of degeneration of the joint.

Treatment

Treatment involves addressing the most likely biomechanical contributing factors, as well as providing symptomatic relief.

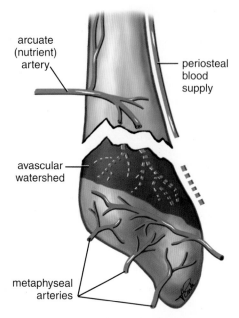

Figure 40.21 Arterial supply to the base of the fifth metatarsal

FROM DEN HARTOG.[66] ADAPTED FROM DAMERON TB JR. FRACTURES OF THE PROXIMAL FIFTH METATARSAL: SELECTING THE BEST TREATMENT OPTION. *J AM ACAD ORTHOP SURG* 1995;3:110–14

Spiral fracture (distal third)

An acute spiral fracture of the distal third of the fifth metatarsal is seen, especially in dancers who suffer this fracture when they lose their balance while on demi pointe and roll over the outer border of the foot—"fouette fracture" (Fig. 40.20b). Undisplaced fractures of this type may be treated with weight-bearing rest, while displaced fractures may require four to six weeks of cast immobilization.

Metatarsophalangeal joint synovitis

MTP joint synovitis (commonly referred to as "metatarsalgia") is a common inflammatory condition occurring most frequently in the second, third, and/or fourth MTP joints, or isolated in the first MTP joints. Tenosynovitis of the flexor tendon sheath is a potential differential diagnosis.[70]

Causes

The synovium of the MTP joints becomes inflamed, usually due to excessive pressure over a prolonged period. It is often related to:

- pes cavus or high arched foot
- excessive pronation of the foot

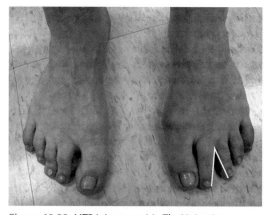

Figure 40.22 MTP joint synovitis. The V-sign is highlighted between the 2nd and 3rd toes on the left foot

FROM *PANCHBHAVI, AND TREVINO*[71]

Padding to redistribute weight from the painful areas can provide short-term relief. Footwear that has adequate midsole cushioning is essential. NSAIDs may help provide symptomatic relief. Corticosteroid injection is occasionally required; the joint is injected via the dorsal surface, while longitudinal traction is placed on the toe to open the joint space.

First metatarsophalangeal joint sprain ("turf toe")

A sprain to the first MTP, otherwise known as a "turf toe," is a common injury occurring in sportspeople in which the plantar capsule and ligament of the first MTP joint is damaged.

The classic mechanism of injury is usually that of a forced hyperextension to the first MTP joint, although occasionally a plantarflexion injury to the joint may result in this injury.

Turf toe injuries are classified on the basis of their severity into grade 1 (mild), grade 2 (partial plantar capsule and ligament disruption), and grade 3 (complete plantar capsule and ligament disruption) (Table 40.5). Grade 3 injuries are often associated with injury of other structures such as the plantar plate or the flexor hallucis longus/flexor hallucis brevis tendons.[72]

Predisposing risk factors include:

- competing or training on artificial turf
- pes planus or excessive pronation
- decreased preinjury ankle range of motion
- decreased preinjury MTP range of motion
- soft flexible footwear.

Clinical features

The sportsperson usually complains of localized pain, swelling, and occasional redness at the first MTP joint following a "bending" injury to the joint. The pain is classically aggravated by weight-bearing or movement of the big toe.

Examination reveals localized swelling and tenderness at the first MTP joint. In mild injuries, plantar or plantar medial tenderness is present; in more severe injuries, dorsal tenderness also occurs. Passive plantarflexion and dorsiflexion of the first MTP joint are generally painful, and there may be a reduction in the range of movement in both directions. Passive gliding of the joint in a dorsal to plantar direction can be used to evaluate the plantar plate. Resisted plantarflexion and dorsiflexion can be used to evaluate the integrity of the flexor and extensor tendons.[72]

Plain X-rays are generally unremarkable, although occasionally small periarticular flecks of bone are noted, most likely indicating avulsion of the MTP capsule or ligamentous complex. If injury to the plantar plate is suspected, lateral views in forced dorsiflexion can be used. This view may demonstrate a lack of distal sesamoid excursion, which is indicative of complete disruption of the plantar ligament structures.[72]

Isotopic bone scans, although not generally performed, may demonstrate increased uptake in spite of normal X-rays. MRI may be appropriate for elite sportspeople with grade 2 and grade 3 injuries to outline the extent of ligamentous, osseous, and cartilage damage.[73]

Table 40.5 Turf toe grading and treatment

Grade	Description/findings	Treatment	Return to play
1	Attenuation of plantar structures Localized swelling Minimal ecchymosis	Symptomatic	Return as tolerated
2	Partial tear of plantar structures	Walking boot Crutches as needed	Up to 2 weeks May need taping on return to play
3	Complete disruption of plantar structures Significant swelling/ecchymosis Hallux flexion weakness Frank instability of hallux MTP joint	Long-term immobilization in boot or cast OR Surgical reconstruction	6–10 weeks, depending on sport and position Likely need taping on return to play

FROM MCCORMICK & ANDERSON[72]

Treatment

Treatment consists of ice, NSAIDs, electrotherapeutic modalities, and decreased weight-bearing for at least 72 hours. Additional treatment may include taping (Fig. 40.23) and the use of stiff-soled shoes or a Cam walker boot to protect the first MTP joint from further injury. Treatment of the various grades of injury is summarized in Table 40.5. Recovery from grade 1 and grade 2 turf toe injury generally takes three to four weeks. Surgical indications for grade 3 injuries include:[72]

- large capsular avulsion and vertical instability
- retraction of sesamoids
- loose body
- chondral injury.

A possible long-term sequel to this injury is the development of hallux limitus.

Hallux limitus

Hallux limitus is defined as a restriction in dorsiflexion of the hallux at the first MTP joint secondary to exostoses or osteoarthritis of the joint. Often the term "hallux rigidus" is used to describe the final progression of hallux limitus as ankylosis of the joint occurs.

The primary role of the hallux is to enable dorsiflexion of the first metatarsal during the propulsive phase of gait. Approximately 60° of dorsiflexion is required for normal gait. Limitation of this range of motion results in problems with gait. Normal dorsiflexion is achieved via the action of peroneus longus, which helps to stabilize and maintain plantarflexion of the first ray.[74]

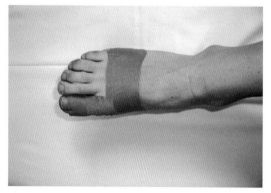

Figure 40.23 Taping to protect an injured first MTP joint

Causes

- Trauma—secondary to chondral damage.
- Excessive pronation of the foot may increase the stresses on the joint and promote development of exostoses.
- Repetitive weight-bearing dorsiflexion of the first MTP joint.
- Autoimmune arthropathy or metabolic conditions (e.g. rheumatoid arthritis, psoriatic arthritis, ankylosing spondylitis, gout).[74]
- Aberration of the first metatarsal or proximal phalanx.
- Hypomobile first ray (e.g. reduced plantarflexion of the first ray can increase compressive forces in the joint during propulsion).[74]
- Muscle imbalance.

Clinical features

The main presenting symptom is usually that of pain around the first MTP joint. The pain is often described as a deep aching sensation that is aggravated by walking, especially in high heels, or activities involving forefoot weight-bearing. Dorsal joint hypertrophy can be a source of irritation from footwear and may lead to pain secondary to skin or soft tissue irritation.

In patients with longstanding hallux limitus, a distinct shoe wear pattern is seen: the sole demonstrates wear beneath the second MTP joint and the first interphalangeal joint.

Examination reveals tenderness of the first MTP joint, especially over the dorsal aspect, often with palpable dorsal exostoses. There is a painful limitation of joint motion, the degree of limitation reflecting the severity of the arthrosis. Some sportspeople may develop chronic subungual hematoma due to repetitive compensatory dorsiflexion in the interphalangeal joint.[74]

Plain X-rays display the classic characteristics of degenerative osteoarthritis, and the degree of degeneration observed reflects the duration and severity of the condition. Features include joint space narrowing, sclerosis of the subchondral bone plate, osteophytic proliferation, flattening of the joint, sesamoid displacement, and free bony fragments.

Treatment

Conservative management consists of an initial reduction in activity, NSAIDs, a corticosteroid injection if required, physiotherapy, correction of biomechanical factors with orthoses and/or footwear, and dynamic splinting.[75] Conservative treatment often fails when hallux dorsiflexion is less than 50°.

In extreme cases, cheilectomy (resection of all bony prominences of the metatarsal head and base of the proximal phalanx) is required. Occasionally, arthroplasty of the first MTP joint is indicated.

Hallux valgus ("bunion")

Hallux valgus is a progressive foot deformity defined as a static subluxation of the first MTP joint. It is characterized by valgus (lateral) deviation of the great toe and varus (medial) deviation of the first metatarsal (Fig. 40.24). Bony exostoses develop around the first MTP joint, often with an overlying bursitis. In severe cases, exostoses limit first MTP joint range of motion and cause pain with the pressure of footwear. Hallux valgus is common, affecting 23% of adults aged between 18 and 65 years.[76] It is more common in females. Although it is more common in older people, it can also develop in adolescence.[77]

The development of hallux valgus appears to occur secondary to a combination of intrinsic and extrinsic causes. Recognized causative factors include:

- constricting footwear (e.g. high heels)
- excessive pronation—increased pressure on the medial border of the hallux, resulting in deformation of the medial capsular structures
- increased length of the first metatarsal and hallux[78]
- trauma to the medial and plantar ligament complex and medial sesamoid bone[72]
- other causes, including cystic degeneration of the medial capsule, Achilles tendon contracture, neuromuscular disorders, collagen deficient diseases.

Clinical features

In the early phases, hallux valgus is often asymptomatic; however, as the deformity develops, pain over the medial eminence occurs. The pain is typically relieved by removing the shoes or by wearing soft, flexible wide-toed shoes. Blistering of the skin or development of an inflamed bursa over the medial eminence may occur. In severe deformity, lateral metatarsalgia may occur due to the diminished weight-bearing capacity of the first ray.

Examination reveals the hallux valgus deformity often with a tender swelling overlying the medial eminence.

Plain X-rays should be performed to assess both the severity of the deformity and the degree of first MTP joint degeneration.

Treatment

Initial treatment involves appropriate padding and footwear to reduce friction over the medial eminence. Correction of foot function with orthoses is essential. In more severe cases, surgery may be required to reconstruct the first MTP joint and remove the bony exostoses.

Minimally invasive surgical techniques for hallux valgus have been developed, but research to support the routine use of these techniques is limited.[79] Orthoses are often required after surgery and gait re-education is needed to restore normal weight-bearing through the first ray.[80]

Sesamoid injuries

The first MTP joint is characterized by the two sesamoid bones, which play a significant part in the function of the great toe. Embedded within the two tendons of the flexor hallucis brevis, they function to:

- protect the tendon of flexor hallucis longus
- absorb most of the weight-bearing on the medial aspect of the forefoot
- increase the mechanical advantage of the intrinsic musculature of the hallux.

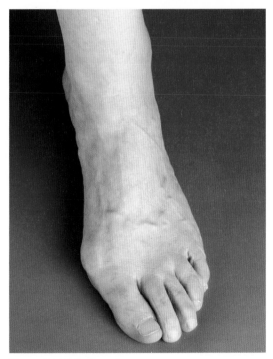

Figure 40.24 Hallux valgus

In approximately 30% of individuals, a bipartite medial or lateral sesamoid is present.

Causes

The sesamoid bones may be injured by traumatic fracture, stress fracture, sprain of a bipartite sesamoid, and sprain of the sesamoid–metatarsal articulation. Sesamoid stress fractures occur particularly in basketballers, tennis players, and dancers.[32]

Sesamoid abnormality involves inflammatory changes and osteonecrosis around the sesamoid. The medial sesamoid is usually affected. Inflammation may be caused by landing after a jump, increased forefoot weight-bearing activities (e.g. sprinting and dancing), or after traumatic dorsiflexion of the hallux.

Pronation may cause lateral displacement or subluxation of the sesamoids within the plantar grooves of the first metatarsal. This subluxation of the sesamoids may lead to erosion of the plantar aspect of the first metatarsal, resulting in pain underneath the first metatarsal head, arthritic changes, and ultimately decreased dorsiflexion.

Clinical features

The patient complains of pain with forefoot weight-bearing and will often walk with weight laterally to compensate. Examination reveals marked local tenderness and swelling overlying the medial or lateral sesamoid. Movement of the first MTP joint is usually painful and often restricted. Resisted plantarflexion of the great toe elicits both pain and weakness.

Plain X-rays including an axial sesamoid view should be performed to assess for a sesamoid fracture. Isotopic bone scan or MRI scan is often required to detect early stress fractures and to differentiate between a bipartite sesamoid sprain or inflammation and a fracture.

Treatment

Treatment of sesamoid inflammation is with ice, NSAIDs, and electrotherapeutic modalities to reduce inflammation. Padding can distribute weight away from the sesamoid bones (Fig. 40.25), and technique correction is mandatory in activities such as dance. In ballet, this injury arises because of excessive rolling in of the foot, which is commonly due to "forcing turnout."

Corticosteroid injection into the joint space between the sesamoid and metatarsal may prove effective if underlying abnormalities have been

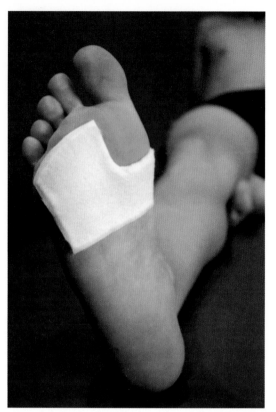

Figure 40.25 Sesamoiditis—padding

corrected. Orthoses are required if foot mechanics are abnormal.

Treatment of sesamoid stress fractures involves up to six weeks of non-weight-bearing in an Aircast or short leg cast. These stress fractures are prone to non-union and, in the elite athlete or in those who have non-union, percutaneous fixation with a screw may be indicated.

The surgical removal of a sesamoid bone should be avoided if possible, as removal causes significant muscle imbalances and may contribute to a hallux abducto-valgus deformity. However, excision is required in cases of significant osteonecrosis. Partial sesamoidectomy has had limited success and can be performed arthroscopically.[81]

Plantar plate tear
with KENT SWEETING

Tears of the plantar plate may be the most common cause of pain under the second MTP joint, although it can occur at any of the MTP joints. It is also referred to as "predislocation syndrome," "crossover toe deformity," and "floating toe syndrome." The plantar plate is a fibrocartilaginous thickening of the MTP joint (Fig. 40.26), which serves to:

- stabilize the MTP joint
- assist in the windlass mechanism due to its attachment to the plantar fascia
- resist hyperextension of the MTP joint
- absorb compressive loads.

Cause
The second MTP joint is most likely to be affected, as it is the longest metatarsal and has unopposed lumbricals and no plantar interossei insertions. Plantar plate tears usually result from repetitive overload from abnormal forefoot loading patterns resulting from hallux valgus, excessive pronation, short first metatarsal, or long second metatarsal. The tear usually arises from the base of the proximal phalanx.[82]

Clinical features
The sportsperson usually complains of localized pain under the MTP joint. Swelling may be present, extending to the dorsal aspect of the joint. Pain is aggravated by dorsiflexion of the affected joint. Neuroma-like symptoms may be experienced by patients due to irritation of the plantar digital nerve from the localized edema.

Examination reveals pain at the base of the proximal phalanx, which may be aggravated by dorsiflexion of the joint. In relaxed stance, a dorsiflexion deformity of the toe may be noted. This is often accompanied by a crossover deformity. The modified Lachman's test (A-P drawer) can also be utilized—the metatarsal head is stabilized and the proximal phalanx is dorsally translocated (Fig. 40.27). A 2 mm or 50% joint displacement is a positive sign of plantar plate laxity.

An ultrasound may reveal a hypoechoic defect in the plantar plate, usually at the distal attachment. An arthrogram may demonstrate synovial hypertrophy and extravasation of dye into the flexor tendon sheath. MRI may also demonstrate a tear of the plantar plate with increased signal intensity within the plate, along with a loss of continuity.[83]

Treatment
Treatment initially consists of ice, NSAIDs, relative rest, plantarflexion strapping of the digit (Fig. 40.28 overleaf), and accommodative padding to reduce loads under the affected MTP joint. Orthoses and a stiff-soled or rocker-bottom shoe are also required.

An extra-articular corticosteroid injection may also be useful. Primary repair of the plantar plate with or without a flexor tendon transfer may be required in patients who do not respond to conservative measures.

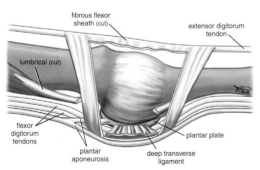

Figure 40.26 Anatomy of the MTP joint demonstrating the plantar plate

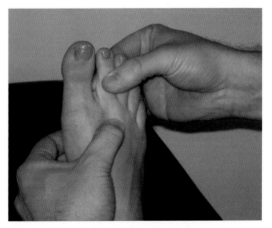

Figure 40.27 Modified Lachmans A-P drawer test— The metatarsal head is stabilized and the proximal phalanx is dorsally translocated. A 2 mm or 50% joint displacement is a positive sign of plantar plate laxity

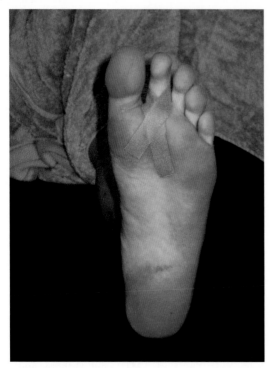

Figure 40.28 Taping—plantarflexion strapping of the digit

because of irritation from footwear and is common in patients with hallux abducto-valgus or exostoses around the first MTP joint. The patient complains of pain radiating along the first ray into the hallux.

Wearing appropriate footwear and using foam and felt to redistribute the load from the affected area generally provide relief. Orthoses may be required to prevent excessive pronation.

Morton's interdigital neuroma

So-called Morton's neuroma is not a true neuroma, but a swelling of nerve and scar tissue arising from compression of the interdigital nerve, usually between the third and fourth metatarsals (Fig. 40.29a). Excessive pronation contributes to metatarsal hypermobility and impingement of the interdigital nerve.

The patient complains of pain radiating into the toes, often associated with pins and needles, and numbness. Pain is increased by forefoot weight-bearing activities and with narrow-fitting footwear.

Examination reveals localized tenderness and, in cases of extensive chronic proliferation, there may be a palpable click on compression of the metatarsal heads. Web space tenderness and toe tip sensation deficit may be present.[86]

Treatment consists initially of ice to alleviate acute tenderness. Plantar metatarsal padding is used to spread the load over the metatarsals (Fig. 40.29b). However, in chronic cases, little improvement is seen with padding.

Injection of corticosteroid and local anesthetic agents in conjunction with the padding may provide lasting relief. Intrinsic and extrinsic foot muscle strengthening exercises are indicated to maintain or improve the transverse arch and control of foot pronation. The use of orthoses is essential if excessive pronation is present.

If the patient obtains no relief, radiofrequency ablation of the nerve appears to be a promising new therapy.[87]

Toe clawing

Toe clawing occurs secondary to short, tight long flexor tendons (Fig. 40.30). During the propulsive phase of gait, the long flexors contract to stabilize the toes. In the unstable foot, the long flexors contract excessively during the propulsive phase and the toes claw the surface in an attempt to maintain stability.

Stress fracture of the great toe

Stress fractures of the proximal phalanx of the great toe have been reported in adolescent sportspeople.[32, 84] Stress fractures in the distal phalanx can occur in ballet dancers.[85] There appears to be an association with hallux valgus.

Treatment involves a period of non-weight-bearing rest of four to six weeks, followed by graduated return to activity.

Freiberg's osteochondritis

Freiberg's disease or osteochondritis of the metatarsal head affects adolescents between the ages of 14 and 18 years (Chapter 42). The metatarsal head appears fragmented on X-ray.

Offloading of the metatarsal heads using padding and orthoses is essential to prevent permanent metatarsal head flattening that may predispose to adult osteoarthritis.

Joplin's neuritis

Joplin's neuritis involves compression and irritation of the dorsal medial cutaneous nerve over the first metatarsal and first MTP joint. It usually occurs

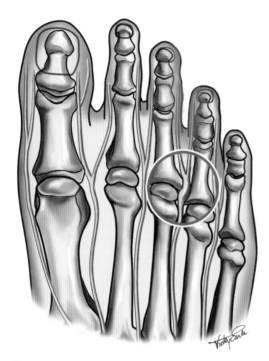

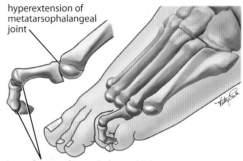

hyperextension of metatarsophalangeal joint

hyperflexion of interphalangeal joints

Figure 40.30 Toe clawing

B

Corns and calluses

Excessive pressure on the skin may cause hypertrophy of the squamous cell layer of the epidermis, which manifests as corns and calluses. In the feet, corns and calluses result from uneven weight distribution and thus indicate abnormal foot biomechanics or poorly fitting footwear.

Treatment involves the removal of circumscribed corns and diffuse areas of callus with a scalpel, the wearing of well-fitting footwear and, if abnormal foot mechanics are present, orthoses. Petroleum jelly over the corn or callus and on the outside of the sock can also help.

Plantar warts

The papovavirus causes plantar warts when it enters the skin. The warts can be particularly painful on weight-bearing. They should be differentiated from corns.

Applying lateral pressure or pinching will be painful in warts, whereas corns are more painful with direct pressure. Gentle paring with a scalpel will also reveal the characteristic appearance of a plantar wart with fine black dots within a defined margin of white or brown tissue.

Plantar warts are best treated with chemical solutions containing salicylic acid. The overlying hyperkeratosis should be removed weekly to allow the chemicals to penetrate the wart. Blistering and abscess formation occur and require debridement with a scalpel and the application of a dressing.

Subungual hematoma

Subungual hematoma occurs when direct trauma or repetitive pressure from footwear leads to bleeding under the toenails. Pain arises from increased pressure under the nail and, in cases of repetitive trauma,

Figure 40.29 Morton's neuroma
(a) Location of nerve entrapment in Morton's neuroma

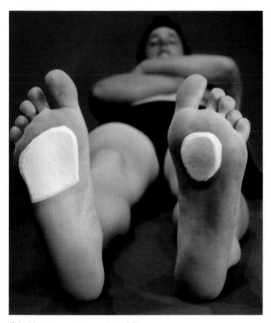

(b) Plantar metatarsal padding

Clawing of toes does not result in pain itself; however, excessive pressure on the prominent joints and ends of toes often causes painful skin lesions.

the nails appear black. The nails may eventually loosen from the nail bed.

Treatment of an acute subungual hematoma involves using a heated needle or paper clip to perforate the nail and release the collection of blood. Cover with a small dressing. Correctly fitting footwear and appropriate lacing techniques may prevent recurrence.

Subungual exostosis

A subungual exostosis develops because of direct trauma. The patient presents with pain on direct pressure to the nail. The nail plate may be displaced from the nail bed due to elevation from the exostosis.

Treatment requires the wearing of loose-fitting footwear, cutting of the nail appropriately, and padding. Surgery may be required to remove the bony exostosis.

Onychocryptosis

Onychocryptosis (ingrown toenail) arises from abnormal nail growth or poor nail cutting. Patients often present in acute pain with tenderness on gentle palpation. Nails are often infected.

Treatment with local and oral antibiotic therapy is required. Conservative treatment involves elevating the offending corner of the nail plate from the soft tissue, cutting a small "V" into the middle of the nail distally (to take pressure off the edges) and stretching the soft tissue away from the nail with a cotton bud.

Surgical management consists of resection of the outer aspect of the nail to prevent the nail border injuring the soft tissue. Resection involves anesthetizing the toe and removing the nail border with appropriate nail splitters and forceps. All abnormal tissue is removed, and the nail matrix is treated with phenol to prevent regrowth.

REFERENCES

1. McPoil TG, Martin RRL, Cornwall MW et al. Heel pain—plantar fasciitis: clinical practice guidelines linked to the international classification of functioning, disability, and health from the orthopedic section of the American Physical Therapy Association. *J Orthop Sports Phys Ther* 2008;38(4):A1–18.

2. De Garceau D, Dean D, Requejo SM et al. The association between diagnosis of plantar fasciitis and Windlass test results. *Foot Ankle Int.* 2003;24(3):251–5.

3. Lemont H, Ammirati KM, Ulsen N. Plantar fasciitis: a degenerative process (fasciosis) without inflammation. *J Am Podiatr Med Assoc* 2003;93(3):234–37.

4. Yamashita MH. Evaluation and selection of shoe wear and orthoses for the runner. *Phys Med Rehabil Clin N Am* 2005;16 801–29.

5. Riddle DL, Pulisic M, Pidcoe P et al. Risk factors for plantar fasciitis: a matched case-control study. *J Bone Joint Surg Br* 2003;85-A(5):872–7.

6. Niemuth PE, Johnson RJ, Myers MJ et al. Hip muscle weakness and overuse injuries in recreational runners. *Clin J Sport Med* 2005;15(1):14–21.

7. Lu H, Gu G, Zhu S. [Heel pain and calcaneal spurs]. *Chung Hua Wai Ko Tsa Chih* 1996;34:294–6.

8. DiGiovanni BF, Nawoczenski DA, Lintal ME et al. Tissue-specific plantar fascia-stretching exercise enhances outcomes in patients with chronic heel pain. A prospective randomized study. *J Bone Joint Surg Am* 2003;85-A(7):1270–7.

9. Wolgin M, Cook C, Graham CM et al. Conservative treatment of plantar heel pain: long term follow up. *Foot Ankle Int* 1994;15:97–102.

10. Landorf KB, Radford JA, Keenan A-M et al. Effectiveness of low-Dye taping for the short-term management of plantar fasciitis. *J Am Podiatr Med Assoc* 2005;95(6):525–30.

11. Radford JA, Landorf KB, Buchbinder R et al. Effectiveness of low-Dye taping for the short-term treatment of plantar heel pain: a randomised trial. *BMC Musculoskel Dis* 2006;7:64–70.

12. Crawford E, Atkins D, Young P et al. Steroid injection for heel pain: evidence of short term effectiveness: a randomized controlled trial. *Rheumatology* 1999;38(10): 974–7.

13. Tatli YZ, Kapasi S. The real risks of steroid injection for plantar fasciitis, with a review of conservative therapies. *Curr Rev Musculoskelet Med* 2009;2:3–9.

14. Sellman JR. Plantar fascia rupture associated with corticosteroid injection. *Foot Ankle Int* 1994;15(7): 376–81.

15. Acevedo JI, Beskin JL. Complications of plantar fascia rupture associated with corticosteroid injection. *Foot Ankle Int* 1998;19:91–7.

16. Gudeman SD, Eisele SA, Heidt Jr RS et al. Treatment of plantar fasciitis by iontophoresis of 0.4% dexamethasone. *Am J Sports Med* 1997;25(3):312–16.

17. Crawford F, Thomas C. Interventions for treating plantar heel pain. *Cochrane Database Syst Rev* 2003;3:CD000416.

18. Buchbinder R, Ptasznik R, Gordon J et al. Ultrasound-guided extracorporeal shock wave therapy for plantar fasciitis: a randomized controlled trial. *JAMA* 2002;288(11):1364–72.

19. Gollwitzer H, Diehl P, von Korff A et al. Extracorporeal shock wave therapy for chronic painful heel syndrome: a prospective, double blind, randomized trial assessing the efficacy of a new electromagnetic shock wave device. *J Foot Ankle Surg* 2007;46(5):348–57.

20. Malay DS, Pressman MM, Assili A et al. Extracorporeal shockwave therapy versus placebo for the treatment of chronic proximal plantar fasciitis: results of a randomized, placebo-controlled, double-blinded, multicenter intervention trial. *J Foot Ankle Surg* 2006;45(4):196–210.

21. Martin RL, Irrgang JJ, Cionti SF. Outcome study of subjects with insertional plantar fasciitis. *Foot Ankle Int* 1998;19:803–11.

22. Dyck DD, Boyajian-O'Neill LA. Plantar fasciitis. *Clin J Sport Med* 2004;14:305–9.

23. Pfeffer G, Bacchetti P, Deland J et al. Comparison of custom and prefabricated orthoses in the initial treatment of proximal plantar fasciitis. *Foot Ankle Int* 1999;20(4):214–21.

24. Gross MT, Byers JM, Krafft JL et al. The impact of custom semirigid foot orthotics on pain and disability for individuals with plantar fasciitis. *J Orthop Sports Phys Ther* 2002;32:149-57.

25. Batt ME, Tanji JL, Skattum N. Plantar fasciitis: a prospective randomized clinical trial of the tension night splint. *Clin J Sport Med* 1996;6:158–62.

26. Powell M, Post WR, Keener J et al. Effective treatment of chronic plantar fasciitis with dorsiflexion night splints: a crossover prospective randomised outcome study. *Foot Ankle Int* 1998;19(1):10–18.

27. Probe RA, Baca M, Adams R et al. Night splint treatment for plantar fasciitis. A prospective randomized study. *Clin Orthop* 1999;368:190–5.

B

28. Sammarco GJ, Helfrey RB. Surgical treatment of recalcitrant plantar fasciitis. *Foot Ankle Int* 1996;17: 520–6.

29. Jerosch J, Schunck J, Liebsch D et al. Indication, surgical technique and results of endoscopic fascial release in plantar fasciitis (EFRPF). *Knee Surg Sports Traumatol Arthrosc* 2004;12:471–7.

30. O'Malley MJ, Page A, Cook R. Endoscopic plantar fasciotomy for chronic heel pain. *Foot Ankle Int* 2000;21:505–10.

31. Spears IR, Miller-Young JE, Sharma J et al. The potential influence of the heel counter on internal stress during static standing: a combined finite element and positional MRI investigation. *J Biomech* 2007;40(12):2774–80.

32. Brukner PD, Bennell KL, Matheson GO. *Stress fractures.* Melbourne: Blackwells Scientific Asia, 1999.

33. Baxter D, Pfeffer G. Treatment of chronic heel pain by surgical release of the first branch of the lateral plantar nerve. *Clin Orthop* 1992;279:229–36.

34. Khan KM, Brukner PD, Kearney C et al. Tarsal navicular stress fracture in athletes. *Sports Med* 1994;17:65–76.

35. Karas MA, Hoy DJ. Compensatory midfoot dorsiflexion in the individual with heelcord tightness: implications for orthotic device designs. *J Prosthet Orthot* 2002;14:82–93.

36. Khan KM, Fuller PJ, Brukner PD et al. Outcome of conservative and surgical management of navicular stress fracture in athletes. Eighty-six cases proven with computerized tomography. *Am J Sports Med* 1992;20(6):657–66.

37. Kiss ZA, Khan KM, Fuller PJ. Stress fractures of the tarsal navicular bone: CT findings in 55 cases. *AmJ Roentgenol* 1993;160:111–15.

38. Burne SG, Mahoney CM, Forster BB et al. Tarsal navicular stress injury: long term outcome and clinico-radiological correlation using both computed tomograghy and magnetic resonance imaging. *Am J Sports Med* 2005;33:1875–81.

39. Torg JS, Moyer J, Gaughan JP et al. Management of tarsal navicular stress fractures. *Am J Sports Med* 2010;38(5):1048–53.

40. Potter NJ, Brukner PD, Makdissi M et al. Navicular stress fractures: outcomes of surgical and conservative management. *Br J Sports Med* 2006;40(8):692–5.

41. Lattermann C, Goldstein J, Wukich D et al. Practical management of Lisfranc injuries in athletes. *Clin J Sport Med* 2007;17(4):311–15.

42. Raikin SM, Elias I, Dheer S et al. Prediction of midfoot instability in the subtle Lisfranc injury. Comparison of magnetic resonance imaging with intraoperative findings. *J Bone Joint Surg Am* 2009;91(4):892–9.

43. Nunley JA, Vertullo CJ. Classification, investigation, and management of midfoot sprains. Lisfranc injuries in the athlete. *Am J Sports Med.* 2002;30(6):871–8.

44. Park HJ, Cha SD, Kim HS et al. Reliability of MRI findings of peroneal tendinopathy in patients with lateral chronic ankle instability. *Clin Orth Surg* 2010;2:237–43.

45. Kijowski R, De Smet A, Mukharjee R. Magnetic resonance imaging findings in patients with peroneal tendinopathy and peroneal tenosynovitis. *Skeletal Radiol* 2007;36(2):105–14.

46. Marshall P, Hamilton WG. Cuboid subluxation in ballet dancers. *Am J Sports Med* 1992;20(2):169–75.

47. Patterson SM. Cuboid syndrome: a review of the literature. *J Sports Sci Med* 2006;5:597–606.

48. Hermel MB, Gershon-Cohen J. The nutcracker fracture of the cuboid by indirect violence. *Radiology* 1953;60:850–4.

49. Jennings J, Davies GJ. Treatment of cuboid syndrome secondary to lateral ankle sprains: a case series. *J Orthop Sports PhysTher* 2005;35:409–15.

50. Khan KM, Brukner PD, Bradshaw C. Stress fracture of the medial cuneiform bone in a runner. *Clin J Sport Med* 1993;3(4):262–4.

51. Bui-Mansfield LT, Thomas WR. Magnetic resonance imaging of stress injury of the cuneiform bones in patients with plantar fasciitis. *J Comput Assist Tomogr* 2009;33(4):593–6.

52. Creighton R, Sonogar A, Gordon G. Stress fracture of the tarsal middle cuneiform bone. A case report. *J Am Podiatr Med Assoc* 1990;80:489–95.

53. Sakellariou A, Claridge RJ. Tarsal coalition. *Orthopedics* 1999;22:1066–73.

54. Bennell K, Matheson G, Meeuwisse W et al. Risk factors for stress fractures. *Sports Med* 1999;28(2):91–122.

55. Nagel A, Fernholz F, Kibele C et al. Long distance running increases plantar pressures beneath the metatarsal heads: A barefoot walking investigation of 200 marathon runners. *Gait Posture* 2008;27(1):152–5.

56. Weist R, Eils E, Rosenbaum D. The influence of muscle fatigue on electromyogram and plantar pressure patterns as an explanation for the incidence of metatarsal stress fractures. *Am J Sports Med* 2004;32(8):1893–8.

57. Snyder R, DeAngelis J, Koester M et al. Does shoe insole modification prevent stress fractures? A systematic review. *HSS J* 2009;5(2):92–8.

B

58. Harrington T, Crichton KJ, Anderson IF. Overuse ballet injury of the base of the second metatarsal. *Am J Sports Med* 1993;21:591–8.

59. Micheli LJ, Sohn RS, Soloman R. Stress fractures of the second metatarsal involving Lisfranc's joint in ballet dancers: a new overuse of the foot. *J Bone Joint Surg* 1985;67A:1372–5.

60. O'Malley MJ, Hamilton WG, Munyak J et al. Stress fractures at the base of the second metatarsal in ballet dancers. *Foot Ankle Intl* 1996;17(2):89–94.

61. Chuckpaiwong B, Cook C, Pietrobon R et al. Second metatarsal stress fracture in sport: comparative risk factors between proximal and non-proximal locations. *Br J Sports Med* 2007;41:510–14.

62. Johnson CH, Christensen JC. Biomechanics of the first ray part I. The effects of peroneus longus function: a three-dimensional kinematic study on a cadaver model. *J Foot Ankle Surg* 1999;38(5):313–21.

63. Yu WD, Shapiro MS. Fractures of the fifth metatarsal. Careful identification for optimum treatment. *Phys Sportsmed* 1998;26(2):47–64.

64. DeLee JC, Evans JP, Julian J. Stress fracture of the fifth metatarsal. *Am J Sports Med* 1983;11:349–53.

65. Leumann A, Pagenstert G, Fuhr P et al. Intramedullary screw fixation in proximal fifth-metatarsal fractures in sports: clinical and biomechanical analysis. *Arch Orthop Trauma Surg* 2008;128:1425–30.

66. Den Hartog BD. Fracture of the proximal fifth metatarsal. *J Am Acad Orthop Surg* 2009;17(7): 458–64.

67. Mologne TS, Lundeen JM, Clapper MF et al. Early screw fixation versus casting in the treatment of acute jones fractures. *Am J Sports Med* 2005;33(7):970–5.

68. Wright R, Fischer D, Shively R et al. Refracture of proximal fifth metatarsal (Jones) fracture after intramedullary screw fixation in athletes. *Am J Sports Med* 2000;28(5):732–6.

69. Larson CM, Almekinders LC, Taft TN et al. Intramedullary screw fixation of Jones fractures. Analysis of failure. *Am J Sports Med* 2002; 30(1): 55–60.

70. Perez HR, Roberts J. Flexor tendon sheath as a source of pain in lesser metatarsal overload. *J Am Podiatr Med Assoc* 2009;99(2):129–34.

71. Panchbhavi VK, Trevino S. Clinical tip: a new clinical sign associated with metatarsophalangeal joint synovitis of the lesser toes. *Foot Ankle Int* 2007;28(5):640–1.

72. McCormick JJ, Anderson RB. Rehabilitation following turf toe injury and plantar plate repair. *Clin Sports Med* 2010;29:313–23.

73. Anderson RB. Turf toe injuries of the hallux metatarsophalangeal joint. *Tech Foot Ankle Surg* 2002;1(2):102–11.

74. Grady JF, Axe TM, Zager EJ et al. A retrospective analysis of 772 patients with hallux limitus. *J Am Podiatr Med Assoc* 2002;92(2):102–8.

75. Kalish SR, Willis FB. Hallux limitus and dynamic splinting: a retrospective series. *Foot Ankle Online J* 2009;2(4):1.

76. Nix S, Smith M, Vicenzino B. Prevalence of hallux valgus in the general population: a systematic review and meta-analysis. *J Foot Ankle Res* 2010;3:21.

77. Shine J, Weil L, Weil LS et al. Scarf osteotomy for the correction of adolescent hallux valgus. *Foot Ankle Spec* 2010; 3:10–14.

78. Munuera PV, Polo J, Rebollo J. Length of the first metatarsal and hallux in hallux valgus in the initial stage. *Int Orth(SICOT)* 2008;32:489–95.

79. Maffulli N, Longo UG, Marinozzi A et al. Hallux valgus: effectiveness and safety of minimally invasive surgery. A systematic review. *Br Med Bull* 2011;97(1):149–67.

80. Schuh R, Hofstaetter SG, Adams SB et al. Rehabilitation after hallux valgus surgery: importance of physical therapy to restore weight bearing of the first ray during the stance phase. *Phys Ther* 2009;89(9):934–45.

81. Carro LP, Llata JI, Agueros JA. Arthroscopic medial bipartite sesamoidectomy of the great toe. *Arthroscopy* 1999;15(3):321–3.

82. Yu GV, Judge MS, Hudson JR et al. Predislocation syndrome. *J Am Podiatr Med Assoc.* 2002;92; 182-199.

83. Keir R, Abrahamian H, Caminear D et al. MR arthrography of the second and third metatarsophalangeal joints for the detection of tears of plantar plate and joint capsule. *Am J Roentgenol* 2010;194;1079-1081.

84. Pitsis GC, Best JP, Sullivan MR. Unusual stress fractures of the proximal phalanx of the great toe: a report of two cases. *Br J Sports Med* 2004;38(6):e31.

85. Lo SL, Zoga AC, Elias I et al. Stress fracture of the distal phalanx of the great toe in a professional ballet dancer. *Am J Sports Med* 2007;35(9):1564–6.

86. Owens R, Gougoulias N, Guthrie H et al. Morton's neuroma: clinical testing and imaging in 76 feet, compared to a control group. *Foot Ankle Surg* 2011; 17(3):197–200.

87. Genon MP, Chin TY, Bedi HS, et al. Radio-frequency ablation for the treatment of Morton's neuroma. *ANZ J Surg* 2010;80(9):583–5.

Chapter 41

The patient with longstanding symptoms: clinical pearls

with JIM MACINTYRE and JONAS KWIATKOWSKI

I messed my left knee up in my freshman year, and my right knee in my sophomore year [both in soccer]. A year and a half after the injuries, I finally couldn't take it anymore. My doctors originally thought my quads were weak, causing patella subluxation. After four months of therapy and getting worse, my doctors decided to check an MRI, after they decided I had meniscus tears. When the results came in, they realized I had double anterior cruciate ligament tears. The symptoms are very alike, from what they've said, so they can't be blamed for me getting worse. Make sure your doctors are at least 90% sure. "Guest China" at http://sportsmedicine.about.com

A regular presentation in sports medicine is that of a patient who has already consulted a number of practitioners for diagnosis and treatment about what appears to be a musculoskeletal problem but whose symptoms remain unresolved.

Presentations of patients with longstanding symptoms may include:

- chronic low back pain or neck pain
- persistent tendinopathies
- multiple painful sites
- a persistent joint problem
- a non-healing fracture
- persistent foot pain.

Longstanding symptoms may be due to a multitude of other conditions that masquerade as sports injuries (Chapter 7), but they may also be true musculoskeletal problems. We also suggest that the reader review Chapter 6, which discusses the perception of pain.

The purpose of this chapter is to provide a clinical approach to the "difficult" presentation. We do not suggest we have the answers for all, or even most, such presentations. Nevertheless, a systematic approach to this presentation improves the chances of a successful clinical outcome. We use case histories (boxed items) to illustrate our suggestions.

Unresolved problems generally present as (i) a diagnostic challenge, or (ii) a therapeutic challenge, so the chapter structure reflects this.

Diagnosis—is it correct?

There are several possibilities to consider in a patient who fails to get better. Most importantly, is the diagnosis correct? Patients will only completely respond to management when the proper diagnosis has been reached and the proper treatment has been given (and followed). A careful re-assessment is always indicated in the patient who has failed to improve. This will include reviewing the history and physical examination, as well as personally reviewing the pertinent imaging studies, in consultation with the radiologist if necessary.

Some conditions that can be easily misdiagnosed are listed in Table 41.1. On some occasions, patients are presumed to have a straightforward case of the condition listed as an "obvious" diagnosis when they actually are suffering from the condition listed in the second column of the table.

It is also important to look for factors that may have predisposed the patient to the injury. Overuse injuries are not random events, and occur when there is functional overload to the presenting painful structure (the "victim"). This overload may occur

Table 41.1 Some conditions that are not what they appear at first

"Obvious" diagnosis	True diagnosis
Migraine headache	Upper cervical zygapophyseal joint hypomobility
Shoulder pain	Scapular pain caused by rib dysfunction or referred pain from the cervical spine
Rotator cuff tendinopathy	Glenohumeral joint instability (in the younger sportsperson) Acromioclavicular joint osteoarthritis (in the older sportsperson)
Tennis elbow	Cervical disk abnormality
Wrist "tendonitis"	Cervical abnormality
Hip osteoarthritis	Upper lumbar spine disk degeneration
Persistent hamstring strain	Abnormal neural mechanosensitivity
Patellofemoral pain/knee osteoarthritis	Referred pain from hip
Bucket handle tear of the meniscus	Referred pain from a ruptured L4–5 disk
Patellar dislocation	Anterior cruciate ligament rupture
Osgood-Schlatter lesion (Chapter 42)	Osteoid osteoma of the tibial tuberosity
"Shin splints" (periostitis, tendinopathy)	Chronic compartment syndrome or stress fracture
Compartment syndrome	Popliteal artery entrapment syndrome
Achilles tendinopathy	Posterior impingement Retrocalcaneal bursitis
Plantar fasciitis	Medial plantar nerve entrapment
Morton's neuroma	Referred pain from an L5–S1 disk prolapse
Persistent lateral midfoot pain following sprain	Cuboid subluxation

because of dysfunction originating at a distant site (the "culprit," e.g. weakness, hypomobility, or hypermobility) that has caused the presenting symptoms. Failure to identify and correct the "culprit" will lead to persistent symptoms in the "victim" (see also Chapter 21, "Shoulder pain").

Clinical scenario 1: Persistent anterior knee pain—look above and below too!

This is a frequent problem with anterior knee pain. Dysfunctions proximal or distal to the knee can cause patellofemoral pain. Thus, it is critical to examine the entire kinetic chain and not just the injured structure. This should include dynamic functional tests of joint motion while performing sport-specific movements, such as a single-legged squat. Identifying the underlying factors will allow treatment to be directed at the underlying causes, rather than giving simple "cookbook" treatment of the symptoms.

History

Ensure there is enough time

When you are referred a patient known to have a long history of problems, you may wish to schedule extra time when making the appointment to permit a thorough evaluation. If there is no forewarning that the patient has longstanding symptoms, we suggest explaining to the patient the need to revisit the entire history, examination, and investigations thoroughly and that an additional appointment time will be needed. In this way, the initial consultation can be used to emphasize the chronicity and complexity of the problem, and the importance of treating it differently from a straightforward new problem.

Go back to square one

By definition, the problem began a long time earlier, so it is crucial to obtain details of the earliest symptoms in the patient's own words rather than from a referral letter or discharge summary. For example, what has been evaluated as chronic knee pain for the

Ask the patient to identify the site of maximal pain precisely. You may be surprised to have the patient with "shoulder" pain indicate that the pain is actually in the trapezius or scapula. These are not referral sites for true shoulder pain, and are more likely to indicate neck or rib or thoracic spine pain.

Similarly, patients with knee pain might localize the pain to the pes anserine tendons and bursa. Exact localization can help you investigate the proper structures and correct a previously missed diagnosis.

past few years may have begun with a childhood knee injury that had been overlooked.

After a thorough assessment of the presenting complaint, its time course, and its response to therapy, remember to ask about the past medical history and the past family history. Associated musculoskeletal symptoms may provide a clue to an underlying systemic disorder that is only identified through specific questioning.

Clinical scenario 3: Going back to square one—key to diagnosis

Wrist pain the key to rheumatoid arthritis

A 33-year-old woman who presented with chronic wrist pain unresponsive to physical therapies eventually recalled several episodes of joint swelling and pain in childhood that were attributed to playing sport. The history provided a vital clue to her final diagnosis of rheumatoid arthritis.

Neck pain the key to "shoulder" injury

A stockbroker with longstanding shoulder pain was surprised to be asked about previous neck pain. She had fallen from her horse two years earlier but an X-ray of her neck was normal at that time and, as her neck pain settled, she no longer gave it any consideration. Failed therapy to her shoulder, including several corticosteroid injections, led to a review. The history of neck injury, together with the discovery of C3–4 tenderness on palpation, led to the diagnosis of a significant facet joint hypomobility with pain referred to the shoulder.

Is the injury work-related?

The clinician should also ask about the demands of work, as active individuals often attribute symptoms to sport when this may not always be the case.

Clinical scenario 4: Work-related telephoning aggravated shoulder pain—not the weight training

An executive attributed his shoulder pain to weight training, particularly to resting the squat bar on his shoulders. Careful history taking revealed that he spent more than five hours a day with his neck side-flexed holding the phone in the crook of his shoulder while he typed on his computer. Examination revealed loss of triceps jerk and weakness in the C6/7 distribution. MR scan confirmed a lateral disk bulge that impinged the nerve root at its foraminal exit (Figure 41.1). Treatment consisted of a telephone headset and physiotherapy to the neck, rather than avoidance of squats with weight on the neck.

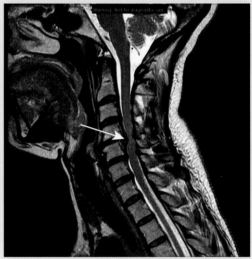

Figure 41.1 MR scan of neck showing lateral disk pathology in a patient who had presented to many clinicians with shoulder pain

Is it systemic?

A history of non-musculoskeletal symptoms may provide evidence of a systemic condition manifesting itself with long-term pain.

Clinical scenario 5: Joint pain linked to a systemic disease

A 42-year-old basketball coach was surprised to learn that his years of recalcitrant, but intermittent, midfoot pain could be linked to his psoriasis. These two aspects of his history had not been linked previously, as he had provided the information about each in isolation when he saw different health professionals about these problems. Similarly, patients with inflammatory bowel disease or celiac sprue may present with extra-intestinal symptoms, including joint pain and swelling.

Examination
Be thorough

In cases of longstanding symptoms, the physical examination must be systematic and thorough in scope, and meticulous in attention to subtle details. Always consider and examine the spine, as referred pain is commonly undiagnosed. It is not uncommon to have referred pain from a radiculopathy present with pain in a limb without back or neck symptoms. Peripheral nerve entrapments can also produce pain and should always be considered, especially if there is no tenderness of the painful site with local palpation (see also Chapter 6, "Pain").

Similarly, mechanical rib dysfunction can refer pain to the chest wall or costochondral region.

> **Clinical scenario 6: Not all chest pain is cardiac in origin!**
>
> A 44-year-old police officer who presented to the sports and exercise medicine clinic because of persistent chest pain had undergone a number of cardiac and gastrointestinal investigations. Examination was able to reproduce his chest pain precisely by palpation of the mid-thoracic costo-transverse joints. Careful, thorough physical examination and evaluation of his response to treatment confirmed that the ribs were the source of his pain (see Chapter 25, page 458, for more on referred pain to chest).

Continue to examine the patient thoroughly even if one abnormality has been found, as a combination of factors may contribute to the current problem. A full examination of the entire kinetic chain is required to identify and treat dysfunctions. This is especially important in cases where the patient has been immobilized, has limped, or has used crutches for a prolonged period. Joint restrictions and instability due to weakness are common, and can perpetuate the patient's symptoms.

> **Clinical scenario 7: Multiple shoulder problems**
>
> A 65-year-old retired executive had an obvious clinical case of rupture of the proximal head of biceps. He functioned well but complained of persisting shoulder pain while sleeping. Examination revealed wasting of the infraspinatus and weakness of shoulder external rotation. Ultrasound confirmed a torn rotator cuff that may, or may not, have pre-dated his biceps rupture. A strengthening program focused on the rotator cuff relieved his shoulder pain.

Limitations of the physical examination

The routine physical examination may not be a very sensitive test for pain in athletic individuals, particularly elite performers, due to their strength and flexibility. This is particularly true in ballet dancers and gymnasts.

> **Clinical scenario 8: In a dancer, limited flexion may be hard to find**
>
> The diagnosis of a large central lumbar disk herniation was overlooked for months in a principal dancer with calf pain, as he had "full" flexion and "normal" straight leg raise on examination. However, he was unable to lift his partners and, on closer examination, his straight leg raise was significantly reduced for him, although still greater than that for most patients.

Thus, neurodynamic tests including straight leg raise and seated slump (page 150) are an essential part of the examination, particularly if it is not possible to reproduce the patient's pain otherwise. Remember that static testing may not reveal problems that become symptomatic with dynamic activity. If a patient has exercise-associated leg pain that only comes on after running or riding, he or she should be encouraged to come to the consultation prepared to reproduce the pain by undertaking the activity. In this situation, provocative tests such as prolonged passive dorsiflexion and active plantarflexion may be useful in assessing for popliteal artery entrapment syndrome as a cause for exercise-related lower leg pain.

Is there a role for diagnostic injection in the sport and exercise medicine clinic?

When pain is vague, diagnostic injections may help distinguish between several possible sources of pain. A patient with thigh pain that may be arising from hip or knee osteoarthritis or from a lumbar radiculopathy might benefit from a lignocaine (lidocaine) injection to the knee or hip to determine which component is the most prominent source of pain.

Investigations

Functional imaging

X-rays should always be performed in a weight-bearing position, especially if degenerative changes are in the differential diagnosis. When looking for osteoarthritis in the lumbosacral spine, hip, knee, or ankle, radiographs should be performed in a weight-bearing position, as subtle joint space narrowing may not be apparent otherwise. In older patients, many knee MRIs would be unnecessary if weight-bearing radiographs had been performed. Furthermore, when investigating spinal stenosis or instability, standing radiographs will reveal the slip in an X-ray, while MRIs done in the supine position may allow for spondylolisthesis to naturally correct, masking any visible stenosis. Both MRI and standing X-rays are necessary when considering these diagnoses (see also Chapter 12, "Investigations and imaging").

Reassess the results of investigations

If an investigation provides a false negative result or is not interpreted correctly, it may lead to misdiagnosis and prolonged symptoms.[1] Thus, clinicians must be prepared to re-examine investigation results, or repeat tests, where clinical suspicion demands.

Clinical scenario 9: Reassess and investigate further

A 25-year-old woman with a classic longstanding history of traumatic rupture of her rotator cuff had undergone an ultrasound scan by very skilled ultrasound technicians that was reported correctly by the radiologist as being normal. Upon presentation as a patient with longstanding symptoms, MRI was performed, which revealed a full thickness tear of the cuff.

When ordering a shoulder MRI, an arthrogram should be considered, as plain MRI will frequently miss labral abnormalities and cuff tears that are quite apparent using an arthrogram. Sports and exercise medicine clinicians must have a close working relationship with the radiologist[1] (see also Chapter 12).

Furthermore, it is possible for radiologists to miss subtle diagnoses, particularly if the clinical notes are brief or inaccurate. Remember, you have seen the patient and know what you are looking for. You should always personally review the actual images, and not blindly rely on the radiologist's report. If the clinical picture suggests that imaging should reveal an abnormality, you should review the films with the radiologist if necessary. There are countless examples where this has provided the solution for a patient with significant symptoms.

Because of the wonderful advances that MRI has brought, there is a danger of accepting the myth that a normal MRI scan rules out an abnormality of any kind, or that an MRI abnormality actually represents the true source of the patient's complaints. Physicians should always treat patients, not MRIs.

MRIs should be ordered to answer a specific question based on the history and examination (e.g. Does this patient have a meniscal tear?, rather than an open-ended question such as "Why does the patient's knee hurt?"). It is important to remember that there are age-related MRI changes, and that meniscal tears, degenerative disc disease, and rotator cuff tears are all common MRI findings in older asymptomatic individuals, and that these changes are not necessarily the cause of the patient's pain.

The practitioner must also remember that MRI will not detect most nerve-related abnormalities, such as referred pain or nerve entrapments. For example, MRI of the groin will be normal if the pain comes from obturator neuropathy; tendon and joint subluxations may appear normal if the MRI is performed when the tissue is normally located.

There are also technical aspects of MRI windowing and sequence selection that can cause abnormalities to escape detection. Low field and open scanners may produce suboptimal images that fail to identify significant pathology. As introduced in Chapter 12, MRI provides much very useful diagnostic information but, as with all imaging, the clinician and the radiologist should collaborate to optimize the outcome for the patient.

Additionally, in patients with longstanding symptoms, you must consider other appropriate tests that have not yet been performed.

Clinical scenario 10: Consider a wide range of diagnoses

A 40-year-old retired ballet dancer had had years of shooting medial ankle pain that had been investigated with X-ray and bone scan, which were both consistent with early osteoarthritis. However, these appearances are common in former dancers. Careful clinical evaluation suggested the possibility of tarsal tunnel syndrome, and nerve conduction tests confirmed the diagnosis.

Is the test really needed?

Don't order a rash of tests just because the patient has had long-term problems. It is important to think about what you plan to do with the test results. If a test result will not change your management, then consider not performing it. Remember that tests can also have unintended consequences for patients. Insurance companies may use an MRI showing a disk bulge to refuse future coverage, even if it was not the pain generator and the pain has completely resolved. This is especially important in younger patients who may not have stable jobs and full quotients of life, health, and disability insurance.

Time to revisit treatment

In some cases of longstanding symptoms, the diagnosis appears straightforward but the patient does not benefit from treatment. In these cases, the experienced practitioner will:

- review details of the past treatment
- attempt to elicit the underlying cause of the problem
- consider a broad range of treatment options
- resist the temptation to resort to surgical intervention unless the indications for surgery are met.

Is there a persisting cause?

Assuming the diagnosis is correct, the practitioner must ask why the condition occurred. Persistent biomechanical problems are often culprits (Chapter 8). Examples of biomechanical errors that prevent treatment from being successful are given in Table 41.2.

Obtain details of treatment

The practitioner must discover the specific details of treatment. Even though Achilles tendinopathy may have been treated by several other clinicians, this does not guarantee that the appropriate eccentric strength training has ever been prescribed.

 We have seen many patients with tendinopathies whose treatment regimens have included ultrasound therapy, laser, shortwave diathermy, interferential stimulation, ice, heat, and rest but whose strength training was limited to 10 concentric exercises once daily.

The point here is not about tendon treatment *per se* but about the need to determine whether the

Table 41.2 Common biomechanical causes of persistent symptoms

Symptom	Biomechanical fault that may be present
Shoulder pain in a volleyball player	Poor scapular stability
Shoulder pain in a swimmer	Limited trunk rotation
Elbow pain in a throwing sportsperson	Letting the elbow "hang" because of trunk and lower limb weakness
Back pain in a tennis player	Failing to control lumbar hyperextension when serving
Anterior knee pain in a runner	Vastus medialis wasting and poor gluteal control of the pelvis (this might be best seen on a video of the athlete running)
Shin pain in ballet dancer	"Forcing turnout"—excessive tibial external rotation in an attempt to improve lower leg alignment
Achilles tendinopathy in a runner	Excessive rear foot varus that needs to be corrected with orthoses
Patellofemoral pain	Hip weakness
Back, neck, and shoulder pain	Poor posture
Iliotibial band friction syndrome	Sacroiliac joint dysfunction and weakness of the hip abductors

patient's treatment follows evidence-based practice principles.

It is possible that the patient's perception of the treatment is not at all what the treating physician intended, and that the patient has been doing the wrong exercises the wrong way.

 Always ask the patient to demonstrate the exercises they have been doing.

Inability to perform exercises at all suggests that the exercises were inappropriate (unlikely) or the patient has not been doing them at home.

Similarly, the patient may have been doing the exercises, but in an inappropriate fashion that in no way resembles the one that was intended. A printed handout with photos and descriptions of the exercises, or a video link (or sample) can help immensely. Various commercial products are available to provide this to the patient with the clinician's customization.

The therapist must spend time to experiment with various tape patterns. Clinical scenario 12 demonstrates that the details of past therapy must be known so that appropriate treatments can be prescribed.

Many patients have had their backs "treated" but never received targeted manual mobilization of hypomobile joints combined with an adequate lumbar stabilization program. This is particularly the case in those countries where high-quality manual therapy is not readily available.

Many patients have improved with targeted therapy, but then returned to sport in an overly aggressive fashion, resulting in a recurrence of symptoms. They may then re-present saying that they were no better at all. Unless the inappropriate resumption of training is identified, the "failure to improve" may suggest that the diagnosis or treatment was otherwise incorrect. For rehabilitation success, it is critical to stress that a more gradual return to activity is needed and that attention needs to be paid to the patient's pain levels.

Make the multidisciplinary team available

A therapy that is commonly overlooked is that of soft tissue massage. Fortunately, the evidence supporting, and the acceptance of, massage is growing, and many patients with chronic musculoskeletal pain have benefited from deep, focused soft tissue therapy combined with an appropriate rehabilitation program.[2]

Manual therapy is a highly effective treatment for neck and back pain (Chapters 20, 26).[3] It is also important in treating kinetic chain dysfunctions that are a critical factor in overuse injuries. Joint mobilization and restoration of functional mechanics are essential in treating foot and other lower extremity disorders. Treatment modalities such as trigger point therapy, extracorporeal shock wave therapy, and pro-lotherapy may be indicated for specific patients (see also Chapter 13). Rehabilitation may need to include exercise programs such as the Pilates' method, Feldenkrais, the Alexander method, and forms of yoga or tai chi (Chapter 15).

Appropriate referral

It is essential for the sports and exercise clinician to know the capabilities of the fellow clinician to whom patients are referred, to ensure that they possess the requisite expertise to treat the patient's problem. That is because physicians, physiothera-pists and soft-tissue therapists[2] have variable skill-sets to identify and treat difficult kinetic chain dysfunctions.

Physiotherapists who utilize modalities instead of mobilizations and therapeutic exercise seem to be falling out of favor in clinical practice, and there is little evidence for such treatments. Electrotherapeutic modalities have been described as merely "an illusion of treatment" as they fail to address patients' symptoms, which arise from underlying biomechanical problems. Similarly, physicians who have limited physical examination skills, poor understanding of the utility of investigations, and a penchant for prescribing nonsteroidal anti-inflammatory drugs (NSAIDs) as the predominant treatment are best eschewed.

Surgeons are critical members of the clinical team (Chapters 2, 13, and others). Non-surgical clinicians (particularly physicians and physical therapists) should do everything possible to know whether a surgical opinion is needed or not. This is both cost-effective and provides the patient with an impartial informed perspective. If surgery is indicated, aim to refer to a surgeon who has particular expertise in that problem rather than to a generalist.

Sports and exercise clinicians also need to be familiar with a range of other experts, including pain management practitioners with expertise in treating complex regional pain syndrome, a rheumatologist who understands sports and exercise medicine, and clinicians who are expert in treating special groups (e.g. the elderly active person, the young sports-person, the dancer).

Keeping professional ethics in mind

Patients with longstanding symptoms may have visited many physicians before seeing you, and may carry some resentment for not yet being cured.

 PRACTICE PEARL Avoid criticizing another physician's management—even if it is tempting!

As famed college football coach, Lou Holtz (retired American football coach) expressed, "If you burn your neighbor's house down, it doesn't make your house look any better!" Remember that you were not present at earlier visits to talk to and examine the patient, and that what the patient recalls having been told may be inaccurate. Remember also that many disorders evolve and progress with time, and what is obvious to you may not have been evident at the original presentation.

Summary

This chapter deals with a difficult presentation that is frustrating for patient and clinician. We believe that taking the time to acknowledge the genuine nature of the patient's problem, obtaining a thorough history, and performing a detailed physical examination all contribute to the patient's realization that they are being well cared for. If the clinician reviews all the previous findings, he or she may discover a flaw in the assumption that has underpinned diagnosis or treatment to date.

A critical review of the previous investigations including a formal review of the actual imaging studies is essential. Further investigations may be required if indicated by subtleties discovered on repeat history and examination. To discover why treatment has been unsuccessful may require critical biomechanical assessment and a detailed analysis of what has already taken place. Broad consultation with multidisciplinary colleagues may provide novel insights, and modern-day technologies allow for easy consultation with national and international experts.

📄 RECOMMENDED READING

Fauci AS, Braunwald E, Kasper DL et al. eds. The practice of medicine. In: *Harrison's Principles of internal medicine*. 17th edn. New York: McGraw-Hill, 2008:1–5.

📑 REFERENCES

1. Forster BB, Cresswell M. Musculoskeletal ultrasound: changing times, changing practice? *Br J Sports Med* 2010;44(16):1136–7.

2. Walach H, Guthlin C, Konig M. Efficacy of massage therapy in chronic pain: a pragmatic randomized trial. *J Altern Complement Med* 2003;9(6):837–46.

3. Sherrington C, Moseley AM, Herbert RD et al. Ten years of evidence to guide physiotherapy interventions: Physiotherapy Evidence Database (PEDro). *Br J Sports Med* 2010;44(12):836–7.

Part C

Special groups
of participants

Chapter 42

The younger athlete

with NICOLA MAFFULLI and DENNIS CAINE

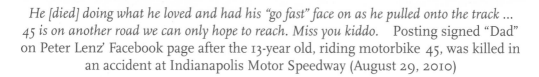

He [died] doing what he loved and had his "go fast" face on as he pulled onto the track …
45 is on another road we can only hope to reach. Miss you kiddo. Posting signed "Dad"
on Peter Lenz' Facebook page after the 13-year old, riding motorbike 45, was killed in
an accident at Indianapolis Motor Speedway (August 29, 2010)

Participation in youth (i.e. child and adolescent) sports is increasingly popular and widespread in Western culture. Many of these youngsters initiate year-round training and specialization in their sports in childhood, and during adolescence some may reach peak performance and compete nationally or internationally. It is not uncommon today for preteens to train 20 or more hours each week at regional training centers in tennis or gymnastics, to compete in triathlons, or for youngsters as young as six to eight years of age to play organized hockey or soccer and travel with select teams to compete against other teams of similar caliber. Thus, knowledge about specific physiologic characteristics, management of orthopedic conditions, injury prevention guidelines, and information regarding non-orthopedic concerns is imperative for all individuals involved in the medical care of young sportspeople.

The uniqueness of the young athlete

Engaging in sports activities at a young age has numerous health benefits, but also involves risk of injury. Indeed, the young athlete may be particularly vulnerable to sport injury due to the physical and physiological processes of growth. Injury risk factors that are unique to the young athlete include nonlinearity of growth, maturity-associated variation, the adolescent growth spurt, and unique response to skeletal injury.[1] They might also be at increased risk because of immature or underdeveloped coordination, skills, and perception.[2] Although problems do

not ordinarily arise at normal levels of activity, the more frequent and intense training and competition of young sportspeople today may create conditions under which this susceptibility exerts itself.

Nonlinearity of growth

The normal growth pattern is nonlinear; that is, differential growth of the body segments (head, trunk, and lower extremities) occurs throughout growth and influences body proportions accordingly.[3] At birth, the relative contribution of head and trunk to total stature is highest and this declines through childhood into adolescence. Thus, the child is characterized by a proportionately larger head and trunk, and shorter legs compared with an adult. In some events, for example rodeo "mutton busting," one can anticipate that a young "top-heavy" child would be at increased risk of falling off a sheep compared with an older child with proportional longer legs.

It could also be argued that, under a given physical load, for example over a distance run, a child's locomotor apparatus would be exposed to greater stress—hence to a higher risk of overuse injury than that of an adult. Yet, often these child athletes progress rapidly to training regimens, skills, and stunts that were originally introduced and intended for more mature individuals.

Maturity-associated variation

Children of the same chronological age may vary considerably in biological maturity status, and individual differences in maturity status influence measures of

growth and performance during childhood and adolescence.[3] For example, the structural, functional,
and performance advantages of early-maturity boys
in sports requiring size, strength, and power are well
known.

Children of the same age may vary considerably in biological maturity status.

Chronological age may add yet another dimension of individual variation given that most youth
sports are categorized by chronological age.
Within a single age group (e.g. 12 years of age), for
example, the child who is 12.9 years of age is likely
taller, heavier, and stronger than the child who is
12.0 years of age, even though both are classified as
12 years of age.

The fear is that an unbalanced competition
between early- and late-maturing and/or older and
younger boys in contact sports such as martial arts
and wrestling contributes to at least some of the
serious injuries in these sports. A matching system,
although logistically difficult to implement, may be
beneficial to equalizing competition, to maintaining
interest in participation, and to reducing potential for
injury.[4]

Unique response to skeletal injury

Younger sportspeople suffer many of the same injuries as their adult counterparts. However, there are
also some significant differences in the type of injuries sustained by children and adolescents because of
the differences in the structure of growing bone compared with adult bone. The different components of
growing bone are indicated in Figure 42.1.

The differences between adult and growing bone
(Fig. 42.2 overleaf) are summarized below:

- The articular cartilage of growing bone is a thicker
  layer than in adult bone and can remodel.
- The junction between the epiphyseal plate and the
  metaphysis is vulnerable to disruption, especially
  from shearing forces.
- Tendon attachment sites—apophyses—provide
  a relatively weak cartilaginous attachment,
  predisposing to the development of avulsion
  injuries.
- The metaphysis of long bones in children is more
  resilient and elastic than adult bone, withstanding
  greater deflection without fracture. Thus, children
  tend to suffer incomplete fractures of the greenstick
  type, which do not occur in adults.

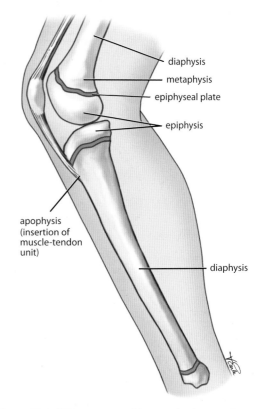

Figure 42.1 Different parts of the growing bone—the
metaphysis, epiphysis, diaphysis, and articular cartilage

- During the adolescent growth spurt, structural
  changes in physeal cartilage occur that result in a
  thicker and more fragile epiphyseal plate.[5] Studies
  of the incidence of physeal fractures indicate
  an increased occurrence of fractures during
  pubescence.[6, 7]
- It has been proposed that the adolescent growth
  spurt may also increase susceptibility to physeal
  injury by causing an increase in muscle-tendon
  tightness about the joints and an accompanying
  loss of flexibility.[8] However, this concept is
  controversial.[9]

As a result of these differences, a particular mechanism of injury may result in different pathological
conditions in the younger athlete compared with the
mature adult. The younger athlete is more likely to
injure cartilage and bone, or completely avulse an
apophysis than to have a significant ligament sprain.
Some examples of different injuries in children and
adults that are the result of similar mechanisms are
shown in Table 42.1 overleaf.

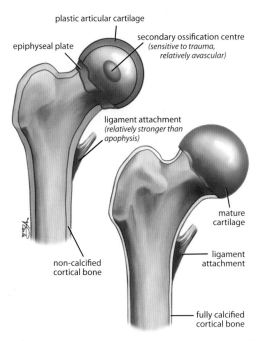

plastic articular cartilage

secondary ossification centre
*(sensitive to trauma,
relatively avascular)*

epiphyseal plate

ligament attachment
*(relatively stronger than
apophysis)*

mature
cartilage

ligament
attachment

non-calcified
cortical bone

fully calcified
cortical bone

Figure 42.2 Contrasting features of growing bone (left) and adult bone (right)

Management of musculoskeletal conditions

In children, traumatic injuries may result in fractures of the long bones or the growth plates. Strong, incoordinate muscle contractions are more likely to lead to an avulsion fracture at the site of attachment of the muscle or tendon rather than a tear of the muscle or tendon itself.

The osteochondroses are a group of conditions affecting the growth plates. Although the etiology of the osteochondroses is not well understood, non-articular osteochondroses may well be related to overuse (Table 42.2).

The following common pediatric injury presentations are discussed in this chapter—acute fractures, shoulder pain, elbow pain, wrist pain, back pain or postural abnormality, hip pain, knee pain, painless abnormalities of gait, and foot pain.

Acute fractures

Fractures occur in the young athlete due to the line of weakness between the epiphyseal plate and the formed bone, and the relative weakness of apophyseal cartilage compared with the musculotendinous complex. Three types of fractures are seen in the younger athlete—metaphyseal, epiphyseal growth plate, and apophyseal avulsion fractures.

Table 42.1 Comparison of injuries that occur with similar mechanisms in children and adults

Site	Mechanism	Injury in adult	Injury in child
Thumb	Valgus force as in "skier's thumb"	Sprain of ulnar collateral ligament	Fracture of proximal phalangeal physis (usually Salter–Harris type III)
Distal interphalangeal joint of finger	Hyperflexion injury	Mallet finger	Fracture of distal phalangeal epiphysis (type II or III)
Hand	Punching injury as in boxing	Fracture of metacarpal head	Fracture of metacarpal epiphysis (type II)
Shoulder	Fall on point of shoulder	Acromioclavicular joint sprain	Fracture of distal clavicle epiphysis
	Abduction and external rotation force	Dislocated shoulder	Fracture of proximal humeral epiphysis (type I or II)
Thigh/hip	Acute flexor muscle strain or extensor strain	Quadriceps strain or hamstring strain	Apophyseal avulsion of anterior inferior iliac spine or ischial tuberosity
Knee	Overuse injury	Patellar tendinopathy	Osgood-Schlatter lesion or Sinding-Larsen–Johansson lesion
	Acute trauma (e.g. skiing) injury	Meniscal or ligament injury	Fractured distal femoral or proximal tibial epiphysis, avulsion of tibial spine
Heel	Overuse	Achilles tendinopathy	Sever's apophysitis

Table 42.2 Types of osteochondrosis

Type	Condition	Site
Articular	Perthes' disease	Femoral head
	Kienböck's lesion	Lunate
	Kohler's lesion	Navicular
	Freiberg's lesion	Second metatarsal
	Osteochondritis dissecans	Medial femoral condyle, capitellum, talar dome
Non-articular	Osgood-Schlatter lesion	Tibial tubercle
	Sinding-Larsen–Johansson lesion	Inferior pole of patella
	Sever's lesion	Calcaneus
Physeal	Sheuermann's lesion	Thoracic spine
	Blount's lesion	Proximal tibia

Metaphyseal fractures

Metaphyseal fractures occur especially in the forearm and lower leg. The most common type of fracture seen is a buckling of one side of the bone. This incomplete fracture is often referred to as a "greenstick" fracture. Most fractures of the shaft of long bones that do not involve growth plates can be treated by simple immobilization and will heal quickly, usually within three weeks. Occasionally, angular or rotational deformity is present, and requires open reduction and internal fixation.

Epiphyseal plate fractures

Approximately 15% of all fractures in children involve the physis;[10] more than a third of these occur in organized sport settings. Fractures of the growth plate are of particular concern because of the dangers of interruption to the growth process via injury to the cells in the zone of hypertrophy.

Although more elaborate systems for describing acute physeal injuries are available,[10] the system most widely used was developed by Salter and Harris[11] (Fig. 42.3). Salter–Harris type I and II fractures usually heal well. However, these injuries are not as innocuous as originally described and may occasionally be associated with local growth plate closure and osseous bridging.[10]

Type III and IV fractures involve the joint surface as well as the growth plate and have a high complication rate. If these fractures are not recognized, they can produce permanent injury to the growth plate, resulting in growth disturbances. When recognized, accurate anatomical reduction must be performed to reduce the possibility of interference in growth and

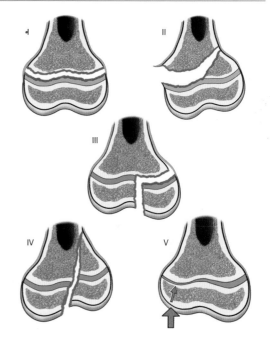

Figure 42.3 Salter–Harris classification of growth plate fractures. V represents compression of the growth plate (green in the figure) as shown by the region arrowed

to minimize the possibility of long-term degenerative change. However, occasionally the initial insult can produce permanent growth arrest despite subsequent anatomical reduction.

The common sites of growth plate fractures in the younger athlete, with recommended management and potential complications, are shown in Table 42.3 overleaf.

It is most important to recognize an epiphyseal fracture. Radiographs should be obtained of both

Table 42.3 Management and possible complications of growth plate fractures in young athletes

Site	Management	Potential complications
Distal radius fracture	Cast immobilization (3–4 weeks)	Not recognized, growth disturbance
Supracondylar fracture of the elbow	Sling (3 weeks)	Vascular compromise of brachial artery, median nerve damage, malalignment
Distal fibular fracture	Cast, non-weight-bearing (4–6 weeks)	Growth disturbance can occur up to 18 months later
Distal tibial fracture	Cast, non-weight-bearing (4–6 weeks)	Premature closure of physis can lead to angulation and leg length discrepancy
Distal femur fracture	Anatomical reduction	Greater incidence of growth discrepancies than in other fractures; Salter–Harris type I and II fractures must be observed closely

limbs (for comparison) if clinical features suggest growth plate injury. A normal radiograph does not exclude a growth plate fracture. A history of severe rotational or shear force with accompanying localized swelling, bony tenderness, and loss of function should be regarded as a growth plate fracture until proven otherwise. If there is any doubt regarding the diagnosis or management of these injuries, specialist orthopedic referral is mandatory.

Avulsion fractures

Avulsion fractures occur at the attachments of ligaments or, more commonly, large tendons to bones.

One site of an avulsion fracture at a ligamentous attachment is at the attachment of the anterior cruciate ligament to the tibia. An acute rotational injury to the knee may present with the symptoms and signs of an anterior cruciate ligament tear. Instead of the in-substance tear common in adults, the more common injury in children is avulsion of the tibial spine or distal femoral attachment. Radiographs should be performed in all cases of acute knee injuries accompanied by hemarthrosis. Management involves surgical reattachment of the avulsed fragment and ligament.

More commonly, avulsion fractures occur at the apophyseal attachment of large musculotendinous units.

The common sites in the lower extremity are at the attachment of:

- the sartorius muscle to the anterior superior iliac spine
- the rectus femoris muscle to the anterior inferior iliac spine
- the hamstring muscles to the ischial tuberosity
- the iliopsoas tendon to the lesser trochanter of the femur.

The most commonly reported acute apophyseal sport injuries in the upper extremity involve the olecranon and medial epicondyle of the humerus. The vertebral ring apophysis is the site most often mentioned in the spine.

In the younger athlete, apophyseal fractures are the equivalent of acute muscle strains in the adult. Instead of a tear of the muscle fibers in the mid-substance of the muscle or at the musculotendinous junction, the tendon is pulled away with its apophyseal attachment. Many patients will describe a "pop" with the onset of discomfort. This is confirmed on plain radiographs (Fig. 27.13). Even though injury involving the apophyseal growth plate does not normally result in length discrepancy, angular deformity, or altered joint mechanics, it may adversely affect training and performance, and long-term health of young athletes.

Management

Management of avulsion fractures is identical to that for grade III tears of the muscle. It involves initial reduction of the pain and swelling, restoration of full range of motion with passive stretching, and active range of motion exercises as symptoms settle, as well as a graduated program of muscle strengthening. Any biomechanical abnormalities that may have predisposed the athlete to this injury should be corrected. Reattachment of the avulsed fragment is rarely necessary.

Shoulder pain
Acute trauma

Acute trauma to the shoulder may result in fracture of the proximal humerus, the clavicle, the acromion, or the coracoid process. Dislocation of the gleno-humeral joint is common in the adolescent but uncommon in the younger child. Dislocations in adolescents are associated with a high incidence of recurrence and development of post-traumatic instability. The management of acute dislocation of the shoulder is discussed in Chapter 21.

Stress fracture

Stress fracture of the proximal humeral epiphyseal plate was first observed in young pitchers, but has since been reported in young athletes representing a variety of sports, including cricket, gymnastics, badminton, swimming, and volleyball.[12] Radiographs characteristically show widening of the proximal humeral physis. Metaphyseal sclerosis and demineralization or fragmentation of the epiphysis may also be present.[13] In most cases, subjects improve with rest and are able to return to their sport.

Shoulder impingement

Shoulder impingement is also seen in the younger athlete. In the young athlete involved in throwing sports, the impingement is usually secondary to atraumatic instability, which develops because of repetitive stress to the anterior capsule of the shoulder joint at the end range of movement (Chapter 21). Impingement and rotator cuff tendinopathy also occur in swimmers, where excessive internal rotation causes a tendency to impinge. The etiology of these problems in throwers and swimmers is discussed in Chapter 8.

Elbow pain

Delineating injury patterns to the elbow in children can be challenging, given the cartilaginous composition of the distal humerus and the multiple secondary ossification centers which appear and unite with the epiphysis at defined ages.

Forceful valgus stress

The pitching motion in baseball, serving in tennis, spiking in volleyball, passing in American football, and launching in javelin throwing can all produce elbow pathology caused by forceful valgus stress, with medial stretching, lateral compression, and posterior impingement.

The valgus forces generated during the acceleration phase of throwing (Chapter 8) result in traction on the medial elbow structures and compression to the lateral side of the joint. This may injure a number of structures on the medial aspect of the joint; injuries include chronic apophysitis of the medial epicondyle, chronic strain of the medial (ulnar) collateral ligament, and avulsion fracture of the medial epicondylar apophysis. The ulnar nerve may also be damaged.

The lateral compressive forces may damage the articular cartilage of the capitellum or radial head. The long-term sequelae of these repetitive valgus forces include bony thickening, loose body formation, and contractures.

Flexion contractures can occur because of repeated hyperextension. The majority of these contractures are relatively minor (less than 15°). Significant contractures (greater than 30°) should be treated with active and active-assisted range of motion exercises accompanied by a lengthy period of rest (e.g. three months).

Osteochondritis dissecans

Osteochondritis dissecans of the capitellum is also seen in pitchers and, more commonly, in gymnasts. Osteochondritis dissecans is a localized area of avascular necrosis on the anterolateral aspect of the capitellum. Initially, the articular surface softens and this may be followed by subchondral collapse and formation of loose bodies in the elbow. The early stages of osteochondritis dissecans may respond well to rest. Surgery is required to remove loose bodies. Joint debridement is usually performed at the same time. The results of surgical management of this condition are variable.

Panner's lesion

The younger child (under 11 years) may develop Panner's lesion. This self-limiting condition is characterized by fragmentation of the entire ossific center of the capitellum. Loose bodies are not seen in Panner's lesion and surgery is not required.

Wrist pain

Dorsal wrist pain is commonly seen in gymnasts where pain is aggravated by weight-bearing with the wrist extended. The gymnast complains of tenderness over the dorsum of the hand and perhaps swelling.

A common cause is compromise of the metaphyseal and/or the epiphyseal blood supply at the distal radial physis.[14] When longstanding, such injuries are associated with radiographic changes that include widening, irregularity, haziness, or cystic changes of the growth plate.

Other causes of dorsal wrist pain include scaphoid impaction syndrome, dorsal impingement syndrome/capsulitis, tear of the triangular fibrocartilage complex, and stress fractures.

Kienböck's lesion of the wrist (Chapter 23) is an osteochondrosis of the lunate bone. It occurs generally in older patients (20 years old) and is rarely in adolescents.

Management

Management of the younger gymnast with dorsal wrist pain includes relative rest, splinting, electrotherapeutic modalities, and nonsteroidal anti-inflammatory drugs (NSAIDs). Strengthening of the wrist flexors may also be useful in association with tape and pads to decrease hyperextension of the wrist. Most gymnasts with stress injuries involving the distal radial physis recover with rest; however, there are also reports of stress-related premature closure of the distal radial growth plate leading to positive ulnar variance.[15]

Back pain and postural abnormalities

Younger athletes may present with pain or postural abnormalities such as "curvature" of the spine (or both).

Low back pain

Common causes of back pain in the younger athlete are similar to those in the mature adult. Minor soft tissue injuries to the intervertebral disc, the apophyseal joints and associated ligaments, and muscle strains in the paravertebral muscles usually respond well to reduction in activity. Manipulative treatment in the management of these conditions in the younger athlete is probably contraindicated.

Back pain is more common among young athletes participating in sports with high demands on the back, such as wrestling, gymnastics, and American football, than in other athletes or non-athletes.[16] Back pain in the young athlete may be associated with:

- spondylolysis
- spondylolisthesis
- disc degeneration
- disc herniation
- Schmorl's nodes
- vertebral end-plate fracture
- atypical Scheuermann's lesion (vertebral apophysitis).

Severe disc injuries and tumors are occasionally seen in the lumbar spine of the adolescent athlete. The spine, as with the rest of the skeleton, is at greater risk of injury during the adolescent growth spurt.[16]

Biomechanical abnormalities such as leg length discrepancy, pelvic instability and excessive subtalar pronation may also indirectly lead to low back pain.

Spondylolysis

The high prevalence of spondylolysis among athletes has received particular attention. This condition may also occur in the younger athlete, particularly because of repeated hyperextension of the lumbar spine. This injury is typically seen as a result of participation in ballet, gymnastics, diving, volleyball, fast bowling in cricket, and serving in tennis. The management of this condition is discussed in Chapter 26. The amount of hyperextension activity must be reduced and this may involve some alteration in technique.

There is considerable debate whether these defects in the pars interarticularis are congenital or acquired. They are probably acquired, even though this may occur at an extremely young age. A fibrous union develops across the defect and this is susceptible to injury. The presence of a pars interarticularis defect does not automatically mean that this is the cause of the patient's pain.

MRI or isotopic bone scan may confirm that the pars interarticularis defect is the site of an acute fracture.

Scheuermann's lesion

The commonest postural abnormality of the spine in the younger athlete is excessive kyphosis of the spine due to an osteochondrosis (Scheuermann's lesion). This condition occurs typically in the thoracic spine, but is also seen at the thoracolumbar junction. The thoracolumbar form of Scheuermann's, which encompasses both the thoracic and lumbar regions of the spine, is more common in athletes than non-athletes and is associated more frequently with back pain.[16] Children can present with acute pain. It usually presents in later years as an excessive thoracic kyphosis in association with a compensatory excessive lumbar lordosis.

The typical radiographic appearance of Scheuermann's lesion is shown in Figure 42.4. This demonstrates irregularity of the growth plates of the vertebrae. The radiological diagnosis of Scheuermann's lesion is made on the presence of wedging of 5° or more at three adjacent vertebrae.

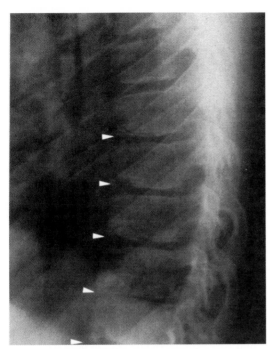

Figure 42.4 Radiographic appearance of Scheuermann's lesion

Management

Management of Scheuermann's lesion is aimed at preventing progression of the postural deformity and involves a combination of joint mobilization, massage therapy to the thoracolumbar fascia, stretching of the hamstring muscles, and abdominal muscle strengthening. A brace may be worn to decrease the thoracic kyphosis and lumbar lordosis. Surgery may be indicated if the kyphosis is greater than 50° or if signs of spinal cord irritation are present.

Hip pain

Hip pain is a more common presenting symptom in the younger athlete than the mature adult. The causes of hip pain in the younger athlete are shown in Figure 42.5. There are a number of possible causes of persistent hip pain and decreased range of motion in the younger athlete.

Apophysitis

A number of large musculotendinous units attach around the hip joint. Excessive activity can result in a traction apophysitis at one of these sites, usually the anterior inferior iliac spine at the attachment of the rectus femoris, the anterior superior iliac spine at the attachment of the sartorius, or the iliopsoas

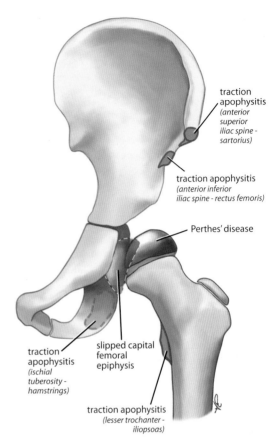

Figure 42.5 Causes of hip pain in children

attachment to the lesser trochanter. Conservative therapy, including rest, RICE (rest, ice, compression, elevation), modification of the athlete's activity level, stretching, and strengthening is usually effective.[17]

Perthes' disease

Perthes' disease is an osteochondrosis affecting the femoral head. It presents as a limp or low-grade ache in the thigh, groin, or knee. On examination there may be limited abduction and internal rotation of the hip. Perthes' disease is usually unilateral. It typically affects children between the ages of 4 and 10 years, is more common in males, and may be associated with delayed skeletal maturation. Radiographs vary with the stage of the disease, but may show increased density and flattening of the femoral capital epiphysis (Fig. 42.6 overleaf).

Management consists of rest from aggravating activity and range of motion exercises, particularly to maintain abduction and internal rotation. The age of the child and the severity of the condition will

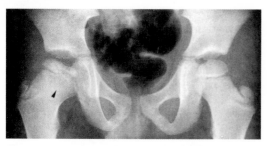

Figure 42.6 Radiographic appearance of Perthes' disease

affect the intensity of the management. Rest, the use of a brace, and even surgery may be required. Recently arthroscopic chondroplasty and loose body excision has shown good short term results.[18]

The condition usually resolves and return to sport is possible when the athlete is symptom-free and radiographs show some improvement. The main long-term concern is the development of osteoarthritis due to irregularity of the joint surface.

Slipped capital femoral epiphysis

A slipped capital femoral epiphysis may occur in older children, particularly between 12 and 15 years. This is similar to a Salter–Harris type I fracture. It occurs typically in overweight boys who tend to be late-maturing, and thus is of increased concern given the trend toward adolescent obesity and selection for heavy boys in sports like American football and rugby. A recent report suggests that increased physical stress associated with intense sports participation may precipitate this condition.[19]

The slip may occur suddenly or, more commonly, as a gradual process. There is sometimes associated pain, frequently in the knee, but the most common presenting symptom is a limp.

Examination reveals shortening and external rotation of the affected leg. Hip abduction and internal rotation are reduced. During flexion the hip moves into abduction and external rotation. Radiographs show widening of the growth plate and a line continued from the superior surface of the neck of the femur does not intersect the growth plate (Fig. 42.7). Bilateral involvement is common.

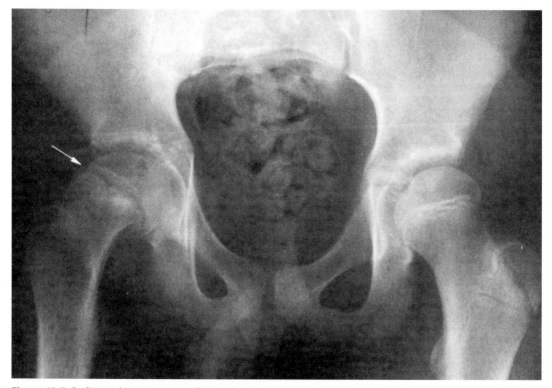

Figure 42.7 Radiographic appearance of slipped capital femoral epiphysis

Slips are a matter of considerable concern because they may compromise the vascular supply to the femoral head and lead to avascular necrosis. These require orthopedic assessment.

A gradually progressing slip is an indication for surgery. An acute severe slip occurs occasionally. This is a surgical emergency.

Irritable hip

"Irritable hip" is common in children, but should be a diagnosis of exclusion. The child presents with a limp and pain that may not be well localized. Examination reveals painful restriction of motion of the hip joint, particularly in extension and/or abduction in flexion. In the majority of cases, a specific cause is never identified and the pain settles after a period of bed rest and observation.

Radiographs, bone scanning and blood tests are usually normal, and the child is treated with rest.[20]

Knee pain

Knee pain, especially anterior knee pain, is a common presentation in the younger athlete. Common causes of anterior knee pain include:

- Osgood-Schlatter lesion
- Sinding-Larsen–Johansson lesion
- patellofemoral joint pain (Chapter 33)
- patellar tendinopathy (Chapter 33)
- referred pain from the hip.

Osgood-Schlatter lesion

Osgood-Schlatter lesion is an osteochondritis that occurs at the growth plate of the tibial tuberosity. Repeated contraction of the quadriceps muscle mass may cause softening and partial avulsion of the developing secondary ossification center.

This condition is extremely common in adolescents at the time of the growth spurt. It is usually associated with repeated forced knee extension, especially in sports involving running and jumping (such as basketball, football, or gymnastics). Pain around the tibial tuberosity is aggravated by exercise.

Examination reveals tenderness over the tibial tuberosity (Fig. 42.8). There may be associated tightness of the surrounding muscles, especially the quadriceps. The presence of excessive subtalar pronation may predispose to the development of this condition.

The diagnosis of Osgood-Schlatter lesion is clinical, and radiographs are usually not required. In

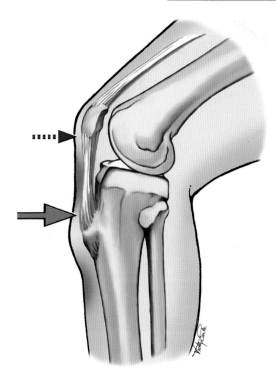

Figure 42.8 Sites of maximal tenderness in Sinding-Larsen–Johansson lesion (black arrow) and Osgood-Schlatter lesion (red arrow)

cases of severe anterior knee pain with more swelling than expected, a radiograph may be indicated to exclude bony tumor. Although all bone tumors are rare, the knee is a site of osteogenic sarcoma in the 10–30 year age group.

The typical radiographic appearance of Osgood-Schlatter lesion is shown in Figure 42.9 overleaf.

Osgood-Schlatter lesion is a self-limiting condition that settles at the time of bony fusion of the tibial tubercle. Its long-term sequel may be a thickening and prominence of the tubercle. Occasionally, a separate fragment develops at the site of the tibial tubercle. Athletes and parents need to understand the nature of the condition, as symptoms may persist for up to two years.

Management

Management of this condition requires activity modification. While there is no evidence that rest accelerates the healing process, a reduction in activity reduces the pain. As this condition occurs in young athletes with a high level of physical activity, it may be useful to suggest they eliminate one or two of the large number of sports they generally play. There is

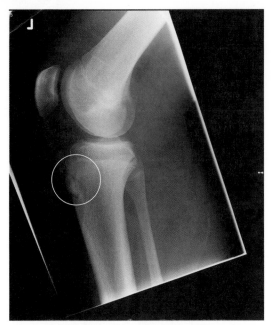

Figure 42.9 Radiographic appearance of Osgood-Schlatter lesion

no need to rest completely. Pain should be the main guide as to the limitation of activity.

Symptomatic management includes applying ice to the region. A trial of local electrotherapy may be warranted, but should be ceased if there is no noticeable improvement within two or three treatments as it is unhelpful in many cases.

Tightness of the quadriceps muscles may predispose to this condition. The athlete should commence a stretching program and, if possible, some massage therapy to the quadriceps muscle. Muscle strengthening can be introduced as pain allows.

Correction of any predisposing biomechanical abnormality, such as excessive subtalar pronation, is necessary. Neither injection of a corticosteroid agent nor surgery is required.

Very occasionally, the skeletally mature person may continue to have symptoms due to non-union. The separate fragment should then be excised.

Sinding-Larsen–Johansson lesion

Sinding-Larsen–Johansson lesion is a similar condition to Osgood-Schlatter lesion. It affects the inferior pole of the patella at the superior attachment of the patellar tendon (Fig. 42.8). It is much less common than Osgood-Schlatter lesion, but the same principles of management apply.

Patellar tendinopathy

Although symptomatic tendinopathy was thought to be rare in children, there is now evidence that patellar tendinopathy is prevalent in junior basketball players.[21, 22] Management is as for tendinopathy in adults, although healing may be quicker in the adolescent years.

Referred pain from the hip

Conditions affecting the hip, such as a slipped capital femoral epiphysis or Perthes' disease, commonly present as knee pain. Examination of the hip joint is mandatory in the assessment of any young athlete presenting with knee pain.

Less common causes of knee pain

Osteochondritis dissecans

Osteochondritis dissecans may affect the knee. This generally presents with intermittent pain and swelling of gradual onset. Occasionally, it may present as an acute painful locked knee. This acute presentation is associated with hemarthrosis and loose body formation.

Radiographs may reveal evidence of a defect at the lateral aspect of the medial femoral condyle. Osteochondritis dissecans requires orthopedic referral for possible fixation of the loosened fragment or removal of the detached fragment.

Juvenile rheumatoid arthritis (Still's disease)

In juvenile rheumatoid arthritis (Still's disease) of the knee, there is persistent intermittent effusion with increased temperature and restricted range of motion. There may be a family history of rheumatoid arthritis.

Investigation requires serological examination, including measuring the level of rheumatoid factor and the erythrocyte sedimentation rate (ESR) and, if indicated, serological examination of joint aspirate.

The child's activity should be adapted to avoid using the painful joints while exercising other body parts and promoting cardiovascular fitness.

Acute rheumatic fever

A differential diagnosis in pediatric arthritis that is relatively rare but is increasing in the developed world is acute rheumatic fever.[23] As there may be no history of sore throat and carditis may be silent, the diagnosis can only be made if the practitioner maintains an index of suspicion for this condition.

Investigations should include markers of inflammation (ESR, C-reactive protein), serology for streptococci (anti-streptolysin-O titer, anti-DNaseB titers) and echocardiography. Penicillin and aspirin taken orally remain the mainstays of management.

Discoid meniscus
A partial discoid meniscus may cause persistent knee pain and swelling in the adolescent athlete. There is usually marked joint line tenderness. Arthroscopy may be diagnostic and therapeutic.

A complete discoid meniscus is characterized by a history of clunking in the younger child (4 years).

Adolescent tibia vara (Blount's disease)
Adolescent tibia vara (Blount's disease) is an uncommon osteochondrosis that affects the proximal tibial growth plate. It usually affects tall, obese children around the age of 9 years. It is generally unilateral and radiographs show a reduced height of the medial aspect of the proximal tibial growth plate.

Surgery may be required to correct any resultant mechanical abnormality.

Anterior cruciate ligament injuries
Over the last few years there has been an apparent increase in the number of anterior cruciate ligament (ACL) injuries reported in young athletes secondary to higher participation levels, greater awareness, and improved imaging modalities. In some sports, such as basketball, girls have higher rates of anterior cruciate ligament injuries than their male counterparts.[24]

Risk factors for female athletes suffering anterior cruciate ligament injury include (i) being in the preovulatory phase of the menstrual cycle compared with the postovulatory phase; (ii) having decreased intercondylar notch width on plain radiography; and (iii) developing increased knee abduction moment during impact on landing.[25]

Anterior cruciate ligament injuries usually present with an acute history of a "pop" in the knee, with an inability to return to play, followed by swelling in the knee within six to twelve hours. Children with chronic anterior cruciate ligament insufficiency will present with functional instability in the knee when pivoting. The anterior drawer and Lachmann's test are usually positive (Chapter 32).

Caution must be taken in interpreting the findings of these tests given the inherent laxity present in the pediatric knee. Thus, before reaching a clinical diagnosis, the contralateral knee should be examined. MRI scans of the knee should be undertaken to confirm the diagnosis, and to rule out the presence of any associated meniscal tears.

Management
The management of anterior cruciate ligament injuries in the younger athlete is still controversial. Non-operative management is usually reserved for younger children who have not yet reached skeletal maturity (Tanner stage 1 and 2 [prepubertal children]). However, non-operative management has a poor outcome.[26, 27]

Surgery is usually performed in children who are either non-compliant to conservative management, or in those demonstrating functional instability with activities of daily living. When the child has associated meniscal pathology, anterior cruciate ligament surgery is strongly recommended irrespective of the child's Tanner stage.[24] In skeletally immature children, physeal sparing combined with intra-articular and extra-articular reconstruction of the anterior cruciate ligament using autologous iliotibial band graft has shown promising results.[28]

Painless abnormalities of gait
It is not uncommon for a child to present with an abnormality of gait. The child is typically brought in by a parent who has noticed an unusual appearance of the lower limb or an abnormal gait while walking or running. The child may complain of foot pain (see below). However, in many instances, the abnormal gait is painless.

It is not sufficient to say that the child will "grow out of it." The child requires a thorough biomechanical assessment, which may reveal a structural abnormality. The most common biomechanical problems in children are rotational abnormalities originating from the hip and the tibia causing either in-toed or out-toed gait.

Management
If the child is asymptomatic and biomechanical abnormalities are not marked, no treatment is indicated.

If abnormalities are marked or if the child is symptomatic, management may involve the use of braces or night splints when the child is very young. In the older child, orthotics can be used to compensate for the deformity.

Foot pain

Foot pain of gradual onset is a common presenting symptom in the younger athlete. The causes of foot pain are related to either abnormal biomechanics or the development of an osteochondrosis. Examination of younger athletes with foot pain requires precise determination of the site of maximal tenderness.

Sever's lesion

Heel pain is a common complaint in the skeletally immature athlete. Sever originally described this condition as an inflammatory condition to the apophysis (Sever's apophysitis). However, in keeping with similar trends for tendinopathy, MRI confirms that this condition is a noninflammatory chronic (repetitive) injury to the actively remodeling trabecular metaphyseal bone.[29]

The patient complains of activity-related pain, and examination reveals localized tenderness and swelling at the site of insertion of the Achilles tendon. There may be tightness of the gastrocnemius or soleus muscles, and dorsiflexion at the ankle is limited. Biomechanical examination is necessary. Radiographic examination is usually not required except in persistent cases.

Management

Management consists of activity modification so that the child becomes pain-free.

The patient should be advised that the condition will typically settle, usually within six to 12 months, but occasionally symptoms will persist for as long as two years.

A heel raise should be inserted in shoes. Stretching of the calf muscles is also advisable. Any biomechanical abnormalities should be corrected. Orthoses may be required.

Strengthening exercises for the ankle plantarflexors should be commenced when pain-free and progressed as symptoms permit. Corticosteroid injections and surgery are contraindicated.

Tarsal coalitions

Congenital fusions of the bones of the foot may be undetected until the child begins participation in sports. The most common form is a bony or cartilaginous bar between the calcaneus and navicular bone. The second most common coalition is between the calcaneus and talus. Calcaneocuboid coalition is the least common form. There is often a family history.

The adolescent may present with midfoot pain, after recurrent ankle sprains, or after repetitive running and jumping. The pain may be associated with a limp.

Examination reveals restriction of subtalar joint motion. There may be a rigid flat foot deformity. Radiographs taken at 45° oblique to the foot may confirm the diagnosis (Fig. 40.16 on page 861), but if these are normal and clinical suspicion persists, a CT scan or MRI should be obtained.

Management may require orthotic therapy. Surgical excision may be necessary in a young patient with severe symptoms or after failure of conservative therapy. The bar may recur after surgery.

Köhler's lesion

Köhler's lesion is a form of osteochondrosis affecting the navicular bone seen in young children, especially between the ages of 2 and 8 years. The child complains of pain over the medial aspect of the navicular bone and often develops a painful limp. Tenderness is localized to the medial aspect of the navicular bone.

Radiographs reveal typical changes of increased density and narrowing of the navicular bone.

Management in a walking cast for six weeks may accelerate relief of the symptoms. Orthoses should be used if biomechanical abnormalities are present.

Apophysitis of the tarsal navicular bone

Pain on the medial aspect of the tarsal navicular in the older child may result from a traction apophysitis at the insertion of the tibialis posterior tendon to the navicular. This condition is often associated with the presence of an accessory navicular (Fig. 40.14) or a prominent navicular tuberosity. Management involves modification of activity, local electrotherapy, and NSAIDs, with orthoses to control excessive pronation if this is present.

Apophysitis of the fifth metatarsal

A traction apophysitis at the insertion of the peroneus brevis tendon to the base of the fifth metatarsal is occasionally seen. Examination reveals local tenderness and pain on resisted eversion of the foot. Management consists of modification of activity, stretching, and progressive strengthening of the peroneal muscles.

Freiberg's lesion

Freiberg's lesion is an osteochondrosis causing collapse of the articular surface and adjacent bone of the metatarsal head. The second metatarsal is most commonly involved (especially in ballet dancers), the third occasionally, and the fourth rarely. It occurs most frequently in adolescents over the age of 12 years.

Standing on the forefoot aggravates pain. The head of the second metatarsal is tender and there is swelling around the second metatarsal joint.

Radiographs reveal a flattened head of the metatarsal with fragmentation of the growth plate. However, these changes may lag well behind the symptoms. Isotopic bone scan or MRI are more sensitive investigations.

If Freiberg's lesion is diagnosed early, management with activity modification, padding under the second metatarsal, and footwear modification to reduce the pressure over the metatarsal heads may prove successful. If the symptoms persist, surgical intervention may be necessary.

Guidelines for participation and injury prevention

Young athletes may be particularly vulnerable to injury due to such growth-related factors as susceptibility to growth plate injury, the adolescent growth spurt, differences in maturity status, and non-linearity of growth. There is also evidence that children's physiological response to concussion is different from adults' and that they may take longer to recover from these injuries.[30] The concern is that the frequent and more intensive training and competition of young athletes now may create conditions under which these potential risk factors can more readily exert their influence.[31]

A recent systematic review indicates that few modifiable injury risk factors have been subjected to statistical tests for correlation or evaluated for predictive value in studies of children's and youth sports injuries.[32] Compared with boys, girls have been shown to be at greater risk of sustaining injury, particularly knee injury, in several sports, and knee injury is more likely to require surgery or to involve the anterior cruciate ligament. There is also some evidence that periods of rapid growth, poor coaching, poor dynamic balance, previous injury, and heavier weight or high BMI are associated with an increased risk of injury in children's and youth sports.[32]

There is a paucity of epidemiological research testing preventive measures in children's and youth sports.[32] However, initial results are promising. Multiple interventions using warm-up, balance training, and neuromuscular control strategies have proven effective in reducing injuries among young athletes. Balance training appears to decrease the risk of lower extremity injuries, particularly ankle injuries. And the use of breakaway bases, mouth guards, helmets, and face shields results in a decrease in sports injuries.[32, 33]

Future research is needed to identify modifiable risk factors and evaluate promising interventions in children's and youth sports. In the meantime, however, safety guidelines have been provided by Sports Medicine Australia which provide clear and practical advice to people involved in sport to introduce uniform safety practices based on good preparation, correct techniques, appropriate equipment, safe sports areas, protective equipment, and modifying rules for children within community sport.[34] A summary of key elements of these safety guidelines is provided in the box (overleaf).

Injury is a known barrier to participation in sport and it is estimated that 50% of children's and youth sports injuries are preventable.

Resistance training: a special case

Resistance training refers to a method of physical conditioning that involves the progressive use of resistive loads, different movement velocities, and a variety of training modalities including weight machines, free weights (barbells and dumbbells), elastic bands, medicine balls, and plyometrics."[35] Resistance training differs from weightlifting and power-lifting, sports where individuals periodically train with heavy loads and attempt to lift maximal amounts of weight during competition, and from body-building in which the goal is increasing muscle size and definition.

Although some clinicians once considered resistance training unsafe and potentially injurious to the developing musculoskeletal system, there is more recently a qualified acceptance of the benefits of supervised and well-designed youth resistance training programs by medical, fitness, and sport organizations internationally.[35-38] For example, it is the current position of the National Strength and Conditioning Association (NCSA)[36] that a properly designed and supervised resistance training program is relatively safe for youth.

A properly designed and supervised resistance training program can:

- enhance the muscular strength and power of youth
- improve the cardiovascular risk profile of youth

Safety guidelines for children's and youth sports

1. Clubs, schools, and providers should ensure that they identify, manage, and monitor the risks involved in sport and recreation activities.
2. An estimated 50% of all sports injuries are preventable.
3. Coaches should have at least an entry-level qualification from a coaching course conducted by the national or state organization of their sport.
4. A first aider, sports/athletic trainer should be present at all sporting events with participants under 16 years of age. A sports/athletic trainer should be present at all sporting events with participants over 16 years of age. Any complaint of pain, tenderness, limitation of movement, or disability should be promptly referred to a qualified sports first aider, sports/athletic trainer or medical professional for management.
5. Appropriate and properly fitted protective equipment, clothing, and footwear should be used at all times.
6. The environment and facilities should be inspected and made safe before participation.
7. All coaches and teachers must be aware of the medical history and other commitments of participants. A pre-season medical and activity questionnaire should be completed by all participants, and the current medical state of individuals should be taken into consideration prior and during participation. A medical clearance must be obtained from the treating doctor before any child or young person taking prescription medication participates in sport or physical activity.
8. Warm-up, cool-down, and stretching should be included before and after all participation.
9. Activities for children and young people should be well planned and progress from easy to more difficult. Strength training can be safely introduced to young people provided it is carefully supervised. It should involve low resistance and high repetitions to avoid maximal lifts.
10. To reduce the likelihood of injury, match the physical and mental maturity of the child to the level of participation, complexity of the task, and game rules.

- improve motor skill performance and may contribute to enhanced sports performance of youth
- increase a young athlete's resistance to sports-related injuries
- help improve the psychosocial wellbeing of youth
- help promote and develop exercise habits during childhood and adolescence.

Detailed youth resistance training guidelines are provided by both the NCSA[36] and the Australian Strength and Conditioning Association (ASCA).[37] The reader is directed to their websites (see "Recommended websites" at end of chapter) for further information.

Nutrition for the younger athlete

At no time in life is nutrition more important than during childhood and adolescence. Adolescence, in particular, is a time of rapid growth and, frequently, high levels of activity. Eating and drinking practices established at this stage often form the foundation of dietary habits practiced through life.

A healthy diet consisting of a variety of foods from all food groups with sufficient energy to support growth, daily physical activities, and sport activities is critical, not only for athletic success but, more importantly, for growth, development, and overall health.[39] However, most dietary surveys suggest that many young athletes, particularly elite athletes involved in weight-controlled sports, do not consume adequate or healthy diets.[40] For example, nutrition studies on female gymnasts consistently report mean energy intakes that are 275–1200 kilocalories lower than national recommendations.[41] Female gymnasts also have correspondingly inadequate intakes of essential micronutrients such as zinc, iron, and calcium, which may have an impact on growth and skeletal development.[41] Even after accounting for the differences in precision of the various forms of self-reported food intakes, it is clear that many elite female gymnasts eat too little.

One area of major concern has been the increased pressure on young elite athletes to aim to achieve low levels of body fat, particularly where extreme thinness is prized (e.g. ballet dancing, gymnastics, endurance running). Losing weight to enhance performance is an important reason for dieting among adolescent elite athletes.[42] Eating disorders such as anorexia nervosa and bulimia are most commonly seen in adolescence; however, self-reported disordered eating prevalence may be no greater among controls than adolescent elite athletes.[42] An obvious concern associated with eating disorders in young athletes is risk of permanent growth deficits. Inadequate nutrition may negatively affect growth and maturation.

Energy
Children and adolescents involved in sport have high energy requirements.[43] During the growth spurt, children engaging in physically demanding sports may find it difficult to satisfy their energy needs. This may be due to a small stomach capacity, poor appetite, or food being a low priority. Fortunately, adolescents are great snackers. For some, snacks may provide the majority of their energy needs. Therefore, it is vital that these snacks are highly nutritious but low in fat. Snack ideas for young athletes are shown in the box (below).

Protein
During childhood and adolescence, protein needs per kilogram of body weight are higher than at later stages of life. This is due to the increased needs of growth.

In the case of athletes, exact protein requirements remain controversial. However, it is now widely accepted that exercise does increase protein requirements. An intake of 2.0 g protein/kg body weight per day is recommended for children and adolescents. Providing the total daily energy intake is adequate and protein represents 12% of the total energy, it seems unlikely that young athletes will not meet their protein needs. Good sources of protein are lean meat, low fat cheese, chicken without skin, milk, fish, legumes, rice, eggs, nuts, and seeds.

Carbohydrates
The benefits of a high carbohydrate diet on athletic performance have been well documented. However, young athletes may have difficulty in eating enough to fulfill their requirements. In most cases, it is necessary to incorporate some refined carbohydrates such as sugar in the diets of young athletes to help meet their energy needs.

A very high carbohydrate diet is not recommended for children and adolescents as it may reduce protein intake. This may be detrimental to growth and development in the long term. Good sources of carbohydrates are rice, pasta, breads and cereals, fruit, starchy vegetables, and legumes.

Fat
The fat intake of most schoolchildren is 40% of their energy needs. All children should be encouraged to reduce their fat intake to less than 30% of their total energy intake.

Snack ideas for young athletes

- Wholemeal dry biscuits topped with:
  - a slice of low fat cheese and tomato
  - peanut butter and celery strips
  - honey and banana
  - ricotta cheese and dried figs
- Wholegrain toast topped with ricotta cheese and jam
- Toasted English muffin spread with golden syrup/maple syrup
- Fruit loaf
- Pita bread (toasted) with "healthy" dips (e.g. yoghurt and cucumber)
- Warm tacos with hummus and salad
- Frozen banana
- Fresh fruit salad
- Half a rockmelon (cantaloupe) filled with blueberries
- Frozen yoghurt
- Low fat muesli bar
- Baked apple
- Low fat fruit yoghurt
- Low fat ice-cream with fresh or frozen berries
- Milk smoothies—blend low fat milk and yoghurt with fruit
- Baked custard (made with low fat milk)
- Low fat "creamy rice"
- Baked potato topped with flavored cottage cheese
- Rice salad
- Pumpkin soup and toast
- Baked beans with wholemeal toast
- Wholemeal pancakes with stewed apple and cinnamon or maple syrup
- Corn on the cob with freshly ground black pepper
- Boiled noodles
- Raisin bread with honey

Vitamins and minerals

Vitamin deficiencies adversely affect athletic performance. Diets that include excessive consumption of simple sugars may not only result in an inadequate intake of energy, but may result in vitamin deficiencies, especially the B group. B group vitamins are needed for the conversion of sugar to energy. As simple sugars do not supply B group vitamins, excessive intake may exhaust the body's store.

While indiscriminate use of vitamin supplements in athletes should be discouraged, especially in the absence of dietary change, supplements may be appropriate for vulnerable groups of young athletes e.g. those on low energy diets, or those who exhibit signs of possible vitamin deficiency (e.g. excessive tiredness). Calcium and iron are particularly important for the young athlete.

Calcium

Aside from pregnancy and lactation, calcium requirements are highest during childhood and adolescence.[44] Calcium is required for the formation of bones, and is essential for nerve and muscle function, blood clotting, and hormonal regulation. Although the body can increase calcium retention when intake is low, an inadequate calcium intake may compromise attainment of peak bone mass and, thus, increase risk of osteoporosis (Chapter 43).

Girls tend to be particularly at risk of inadequate calcium intake. This is at a time when it is essential for females to develop peak bone mass. The combination of inadequate calcium and amenorrhea, often found in athletic girls, may increase the long-term risk of osteoporosis.

Iron

Iron deficiency, with or without anemia, is known to have a deleterious effect on athletic performance. Female athletes are at greater risk of iron deficiency because of increased iron losses through menstruation, in addition to the gastrointestinal, bladder, and sweat losses, and decreased iron absorption common to all athletes.

Management of iron deficiency in athletes consists of regular screening (including serum ferritin levels), nutrition education, and, in some cases, iron supplementation.

Thermoregulation and hydration

Heat injury occurs when excessive thermal energy is generated or absorbed by the human body (Chapter 58).[45, 46] Between 1995 and 2008, 29 high school football players in the US died from heat stroke.[47] In autumn 2008 alone, there were four heat-related deaths in high school football in the US. In the US, more than 9 000 high school athletes each year are treated for heat-related injury.[48] These occurred most commonly in football and during the month of August. Unlike musculoskeletal sports injuries, all heat injuries are reversible—if they are detected in time and whole-body cooling is initiated.[45]

Exercising children are not as efficient as adults when it comes to thermoregulation. Thermoregulatory disadvantages faced by children when compared with adults include:[49]

- Children gain heat faster from the environment because of their greater surface area–body mass ratio than adults.
- Children produce more heat per mass unit than adults during activities that involve walking or running.
- The sweating capacity of children is considerably lower than adults', which reduces their ability to dissipate body heat by evaporation.
- Children acclimatize to exercising in hot weather at a slower rate than adults.

However, the exercise physiology literature lacks definitive well-controlled adult–child comparisons,[50] and thus it is difficult to assess the validity of these long-held tenets of exercise physiology. Rather than these physiologic reasons, it may be that children and adolescents are at increased risk simply because they are more likely to be exposed to vigorous physical exercise during the warm summer months.[45]

Maintenance of adequate hydration helps to prevent heat stress. During exercise, children may fail to ingest sufficient fluid to prevent dehydration, because they often do not feel the urge to drink enough to replenish the fluid loss before or following exercise.[51] Thus, attention to adequate hydration is essential. All these factors combine to increase the risk of heat illness in children. The recommended fluid intakes for children of various ages are shown in Table 42.4. Water appears to be the best fluid. Further guidelines for the prevention of heat illness are contained in Chapter 58.

Violence in youth sport

An aspect of the youth sports social environment that has been linked to injury, but not extensively studied from an epidemiological perspective or widely recognized as a public health concern, is violence. Sports-related violence, which includes incidents of foul play and brawling, occurs frequently in relation to a variety of sports, and has resulted in both physical and emotional injury to participants, parents, referees, and fans.[52]

Recent examples of sport-related violence which have attracted media attention include fistfights involving parents at children's sporting events, brawling among opponents, coaches and fans attacking referees, players fighting with fans, coaches deliberately encouraging players to foul opponents, and the "hazing" (initiation) of younger new players by older players and coaches.

In the US, a number of colleges, schools, communities, and sporting organizations have enacted policies to limit sport-related violence (e.g. anti-hazing laws, parents signing contracts, "silent game days"). However, while reports of sport-related violence are common, and earnest efforts have been taken to control it, few studies have examined the prevalence of sports-related violence or measures of the resultant morbidity and mortality, let alone the efficacy of preventive measures.

The "ugly parent" syndrome

Although parents generally aspire to provide the best sporting experience for their children, it does not always turn out that way. Parental interference and pressure are among the main reasons that children (and coaches) drop out of sport. Children competing under excessive parental pressure may display physical ailments ranging from headaches to stomach aches and muscle pains. In addition, stress may cause sleep disturbances, emotional volatility, fatigue, and prolonged depression. Guidelines for parents supporting their child's sporting interest are in the box overleaf.

Coaches' role

Coaches may have long-lasting positive influences on a child's enjoyment of sport. Unfortunately, many children feel ignored by coaches, are never given instructions about their faults, and never made aware of their progress[32–34] It must be remembered that, for a number of children, experience in a particular sport will be brief and the coach should aim to make the child the better for it. A code of behavior to assist coaches in achieving a beneficial influence on their athletes is listed in the box overleaf.

Table 42.4 Sports Medicine Australia guidelines for fluid replacement (water) for children and adolescents[34]

Age (years)	Time (min)	Volume (mL)[a]
~15	45 (before exercise)	300–400
	20 (during exercise)	150–200
	As soon as possible after exercise	Liberal until urination
~10	45 (before exercise)	150–200
	20 (during exercise)	75–100
	As soon as possible after exercise	Liberal until urination

[a] In hot environments, fluid intake may need to be more frequent

Guidelines for parents supporting their child's sporting interest

1. Encourage children to participate if they are interested. However, if a child is not willing, do not force him or her.
2. Focus on the child's efforts and performance rather than on the overall outcome of the event. This assists the child in setting realistic goals related to his or her ability by reducing the emphasis on winning.
3. Teach children that an honest effort is as important as victory, so that the result of each game is accepted without undue disappointment.
4. Encourage children to always participate according to the rules, and settle disagreements without resorting to hostility or violence.
5. Never ridicule a child for making a mistake or losing a competition.
6. Remember that children are involved in organized sports for their own enjoyment, not for their parents' enjoyment.
7. Remember that children learn best from example. Applaud good plays by all teams.
8. Respect officials' decisions and teach children to do likewise.
9. If you disagree with an official, raise the issue through the appropriate channels rather than questioning the official's judgment and honesty in public. Remember, most officials volunteer their time and effort to help children.
10. Support all efforts to remove verbal and physical abuse from sporting activities.
11. Recognize the value and importance of volunteer coaches. They give their time and resources to provide recreational activities for the children.
12. Respect the rights, dignity and worth of every young person regardless of their gender, ability, cultural background, or religion.

A code of behavior for coaches

1. Be reasonable in demands on young players' time, energy, and enthusiasm.
2. Teach players that rules of the sport are mutual agreements that no one should evade or break.
3. Whenever possible, group players to give a reasonable chance of success.
4. Avoid overplaying the talented players. The "just average" players need and deserve equal time.
5. Remember that children participate for fun and enjoyment, and that winning is only part of their motivation. Never ridicule or yell at children for making mistakes.
6. Ensure that equipment and facilities meet safety standards, and are appropriate to the age and ability of the players.
7. Take into consideration the maturity level of the children when scheduling and determining the length of practice times and competition.
8. Develop team respect for the ability of opponents as well as for the judgment of officials and opposing coaches.
9. Follow the advice of a sports medicine practitioner when determining when an injured player is ready to recommence training or competition.
10. Remain informed of sound coaching principles and the principles of growth and development of children.
11. Avoid use of derogatory language based on gender.

🌐 RECOMMENDED WEBSITES

National Strength and Conditioning Association position statement—youth resistance training. www.nsca-lift.org/Publications/YouthresistanceTrainingUpdatedPosition2.pdf

Australian Strength and Conditioning Association. The ASCA Position Stand—Resistance Training for Children and Adolescents, 2008: www.strengthandconditioning.org/content.aspx?clID=/default.aspx&ID=195

📄 REFERENCES

1. Caine DJ, Maffulli N. Epidemiology of pediatric sports injuries. An important area of medicine and sports science research. In: Caine DJ, Maffulli N, eds *Epidemiology of pediatric sports injuries. Individual sports.* Basel: Karger, 2005, vol 48, pp 1–7.

2. National Center for Injury Prevention and Control. CDC Injury Research Agenda 2009–2018. Atlanta (GA): Centers for Disease Control and Prevention, accessed 31 Oct 2009, www.cdc.gov/injury/ResearchAgenda/CDC_Injury_Research_Agenda-a.pdf.

3. Malina RM, Bouchard C, Bar-Or O. *Growth, maturation and physical activity*, 2nd ed. Champaign, Human Kinetics, 2004.

4. Beunen G, Malina RM. Growth and biologic maturation: relevance to athletic performance. In: Hebestreit H, Bar-Or O, eds. *The young athlete. Encyclopaedia of sports medicine*, 2008, vol. XIII, pp. 3–17.

5. Alexander CJ. Effect of growth rate on the strength of the growth plate-shaft function. *Skeletal Radiol* 1976;1:67–76.

6. Bailey DA, Wedge JH, McCulloch RG et al. Epidemiology of fractures of the distal end of the radius in children as associated with growth. *J Bone Joint Surg Am* 1989;71:1225–31.

7. Peterson CA, Peterson HA. Analysis of the incidence of injuries to the epiphyseal growth plate. *J Trauma* 1972; 12:275–81.

8. Micheli LJ, Fehlandt AF Jr. Overuse injuries to tendons and apophyses in children and adolescents. *Clin Sports Med* 1992;11(4):713–26.

9. Feldman D, Shrier I, Rossignol M et al. Adolescent growth is not associated with changes in flexibility. *Clin J Sport Med* 1999;9(1):24–9.

10. Ogden JA. *Skeletal injury in the child.* New York: Springer-Verlag, 2000.

11. Salter RB, Harris WR. Injuries involving the epiphyseal plate. *J Bone Joint Surg Am* 1963; 45:587–662.

12. Caine D, DeFiori J, Maffulli N. Physeal injuries in children's and youth sports: reasons for concern? *Br J Sports Med* 2006;40:749–60.

13. Frush TG, Lindenfeld TN. Peri-epiphyseal and overuse injuries in adolescent athletes. *Sports Health* 2009;1:201–10.

14. DiFiori JP, Caine DJ, Malina RM. Wrist pain, distal radial physeal injury, and ulnar variance in the young gymnast. *Am J Sports Med* 2006;34:840–9.

15. Caine D, Howe W, Ross W et al. Does repetitive physical loading inhibit radial growth in female gymnasts? *Clin J Sport Med* 1997;7(4):302–8.

16. Sward L. The thoracolumbar spine in young elite athletes. Current concepts on the effects of physical training. *Sports Med* 1992;13:357–64.

17. Peck DM. Apophyseal injuries in the young athlete. *Am Family Physician* 1995;51:1891–8.

18. Kocher MS, Kim YJ, Millis MB et al. Hip arthroscopy in children and adolescents. *J Pediatr Orthop* 2005;25(5): 680–6.

19. Kasper JC, Gerhardt MB, Mandelbaum BR. Stress injury leading to slipped capital femoral epiphysis in a competitive adolescent tennis player: a case report. *Clin J Sport Med* 2007;17:72–4.

20. Maffulli N, Bruns W. Injuries in young athletes. *Eur J Pediatr* 2000;159(1–2):59–63.

21. Cook JL, Khan KM, Kiss ZS et al. Patellar tendinopathy in junior basketball players: a controlled clinical and ultrasonographic study of 268 patellar tendons in players aged 14–18 years. *Scand J Med Sci Sports* 2000;10(4):216–20.

22. Cook JL, Kiss ZS, Khan KM et al. Anthropometry, physical performance, and ultrasound patellar tendon abnormality in elite junior basketball players: a cross-sectional study. *Br J Sports Med* 2004;38(2):206–9.

23. Williamson L, Bowness P, Mowat A et al. Difficulties in diagnosing acute rheumatic fever—arthritis may be short lived and carditis silent. *BMJ* 2000;320:362–5.

24. Messina DF, Farney WC, DeLee JC. The incidence of injury in Texas high school basketball. A prospective study among male and female athletes. *Am J Sports Med* 1999;27:294–9.

25. Renstrom P, Ljungqvist A, Arendt E et al. Non-contact ACL injuries in female athletes: an International Olympic Committee current concepts statement. *Br J Sports Med* 2008;42:394–412.

26. Kannus P, Jarvinen M. Knee ligament injuries in adolescents. Eight year follow-up of conservative management. *J Bone Joint Surg Br* 1988;70(5):772–6.

27. Mizuta H, Kubota K, Shiraishi M et al. The conservative treatment of complete tears of the anterior cruciate ligament in skeletally immature patients. *J Bone Joint Surg Br* 1995;77(6):890–4.

28. Kocher MS, Garg S, Micheli LJ. Physeal sparing reconstruction of the anterior cruciate ligament in skeletally immature prepubescent children and adolescents. *J Bone Joint Surg Am* 2005;87(11): 2371–9.

29. Ogden JA, Ganey TM, Hill JD et al. Sever's injury: a stress fracture of the immature calcaneal metaphysis. *J Pediatr Orthop* 2004; 24:488–93.

30. McCrory P, Meeuwisse W, Johnston K et al. Consensus statement on concussion in sport: the 3rd International Conference on Concussion in Sport held in Zurich, November 2008. *Br J Sports Med* 2009;43;i76–84.

31. Caine DJ. Are kids having a rough time of it in sports? *Br J Sports Med* 2010;44:1–3.

32. Caine D, Maffulli N. Caine C. Epidemiology of pediatric and adolescent sports injuries *Clin Sports Med* 2008;27(1):19–50.

33. Schiff M, Caine D, O'Halloran R. Injury prevention in sports. *Am J Lifestyle Med* 2010;4:42–64

34. Sports Medicine Australia. *Safety guidelines for children and young people in sport and recreation*, 2008. Accessed 2 December 2010 at: http://sma.org.au/wp-content/ uploads/2009/05/childrensafetyguidelines-fulldoc.pdf.

35. Faigenbaum AD, Myer GD. Resistance training among young athletes: safety, efficacy and injury prevention effects. *Br J Sports Med* 2010;44:56–63.

36. Faigenbaum AD, Kraemer WJ, Blimkie JR et al. Youth resistance training: updated position statement paper from the National Strength and Conditioning Association. *J Strength Cond Res* 2009;23(suppl 5): S60–79.

37. Australian Strength and Conditioning Association. *The ASCA Position Stand—Resistance Training for Children and Adolescents*, 2008, accessed 2 December 2010, www.strengthandconditioning.org/content. aspx?clID=/default.aspx&ID=195.

38. Council on Sports Medicine and Fitness (American Academy of Pediatrics). Strength training by children and adolescents. *Pediatr* 2008;121:835–40.

39. American Academy of Pediatrics. Promotion of healthy weight-control practices in young athletes. *Pediatr* 2005;116:1557–64.

40. Williams MV. Nutrition for the school-aged child athlete. In: Hebestreit H, Bar-Or O, eds. *The young athlete. Encyclopaedia of sports medicine* (v. XIII) Blackwell Publishing, 2008.

41. Caine D, Lewis R, O'Connor P et al. Does gymnastics training inhibit growth of females? *Clin J Sport Med* 2001; 11:260–70

42. Martinson M, Bratland-Sanda S, Eriksson AK et al. Dieting to win or to be thin? A study of dieting and disordered eating among adolescent elite athletes and non-athlete controls. *Br J Sports Med* 2010;44: 70–6.

43. Bass S, Inge K. Nutrition for special populations: children and young athletes. In: Burke L, Deakin V, eds. *Clinical sports nutrition*. 3rd ed. Sydney, McGraw-Hill Publishers, 2006.

44. Bailey DA, Martin AD, McKay HA et al. Calcium accretion in girls and boys during puberty: a longitudinal analysis. *J Bone Min Res* 2000; 15(11): 2245–50

45. Marshall SW. Heat injury in youth sport. *Br J Sports Med* 2010;44:8–12.

46. Howe AS, Boden BP. Heat-related illness in athletes. *Am J Sports Med* 2007;35:1384–95.

47. Mueller FO, Colgate B. *Annual survey of football injury research, 1931–2008*. National Center for Catastrophic Sports Injury Research, University of North Carolina at Chapel Hill, February, 2009.

48. Gilchrist J, Haileyesus T, Murphy M et al. Heat illness among high school athletes – United States, 2005–2009. *Morb Mortal Wkly Rep* 2010;59: 1009–13.

49. Malina RM, Bouchard C, Bar-Or O. *Growth, Maturation and physical activity*, 2nd ed. Champaign, Human Kinetics, 2004; pp 267–73.

50. Rowland T. Thermoregulation during exercise in the heat in children: old concepts revisited. *J Appl Physiol* 2008;105:718–24.

51. Walker SM, Casa DJ, Levreault ML et al. Children participating in summer sports camps are chronically dehydrated. *Med Sci Sports Excer* 2004; 36(suppl 5): 180–1.

52. Fields SK, Collins CL, Comstock RD. Violence in youth sports: hazing, brawling and foul play. *Br J Sports Med* 2010;44:32–7.

C

Chapter 43

Women and activity-related issues across the lifespan

with JULIA ALLEYNE and KIM BENNELL

Girls playing sports is not about winning gold medals. It's about self-esteem, learning to compete and learning how hard you have to work in order to achieve your goals.
Jackie Joyner-Kersee, member of the International Women's Sports Hall of Fame, three-time Olympic Gold Medalist in track and field

Overview

The history of women and sport is one filled with both glorious achievements and debatable myths. We have seen women embrace physical activity as they entered higher educational institutions and participated in many sports from lawn bowling to gymnastics, eventually taking their place proudly in national and international competition in both winter and summer Olympic sports. We have also seen women limited in their participation by their role in society, like the "Bloomer Girls" baseball teams of the early 20th century who played professional baseball but only until the war years were over and men could once again "play the game."

Myths related to understanding the differences between the sexes have also held women back from equal participation in sport. The first modern marathon Olympic race was held in 1896 with only male participants, as it was believed that women were not strong enough to complete a marathon and that the endurance would damage their reproductive organs. It took 88 years before women were allowed to participate in an Olympic marathon and rightly took their place in the 1984 Summer Olympics.

Understanding women's health requires an understanding of both sex and gender aspects of health:

- Sex refers to the anatomical and physiological differences that characterize men and women.
- Gender refers to the sociological, environmental, and psychological influences that affect a woman's opportunities and access to sport and health services.

Sex and gender differences

Although differences exist between the sexes, there are far more similarities between men and women than between males and females in many other species.

Sex differences

Sex differences include anatomical and physiological characteristics such as female organs, smaller bone structure, hormonal differences, and body composition differences in fat and muscle mass. Sex characteristics contribute to differences in prevalence and incidence of injury or disease throughout the lifespan. Some physiological differences between the sexes from the female perspective in relation to exercise performance are shown in Table 43.1.

Women's average body fat composition is approximately 26% compared with 14% in men. Women have lower lean body mass, indicating less muscle mass. The greater muscle mass in males is due to the predominant effect of the androgen hormones, whereas estrogen, predominant in females, results in increased body fat. In males, the subcutaneous fat is found mainly in the abdominal and upper regions of the body, whereas the female has a greater concentration of body fat in the hips and thighs. The other key sex differences are physiological, such as estrogen and progesterone hormone levels and lower testosterone levels.

Table 43.1 Some physiological differences between the sexes from the female perspective in relation to exercise performance

Difference	Result
Lower blood volume Fewer red blood cells (~6%) Less hemoglobin (~15%)	Lower total oxygen-carrying capacity of blood
Smaller heart	Higher heart rate, smaller stroke volume
Lower maximum cardiac output	Lower maximum aerobic capacity (~20%)
Smaller thorax	Lower vital capacity, lower tidal volume, lower residual volume, lower maximal breathing capacity
Less lung tissue	Lower minute ventilation
Less muscle mass (fewer fibers and smaller fibers)	40% weaker upper body strength; when strength expressed relative to lean body mass, no difference in some instances

Gender differences

Gender differences relate to society's norms and trends that affect access to opportunities in economical, social, cultural, and emotional spheres. This can manifest as barriers to physical conditioning for sport preparation, role definitions for sport participation, and psychological differences such as body image perceptions.

North American research has consistently revealed that girls as young as five years of age feel pressure to lose weight, and equate healthy eating with the selection of diet foods and healthy exercise as a means of weight loss.[1] This perception is rooted in our society from the fashion, food, and fitness sectors, where the models demonstrate ultra-thinness and where the female consumer is targeted with body image sales.

Girls and women have traditionally gravitated toward physical activity that is deemed by society to be more feminine, such as dance and esthetic sports. Team sports such as volleyball have witnessed striking difference in sport attire between men and women playing the same game, with women wearing tight skimpy shorts and men wearing loose baggy shorts.

Conditioning programs for sport are often determined by the coach and his or her experience or education on the attainment of physical fitness. However, since men have been involved more consistently in sport, there is a greater number of male coaches who have themselves been coached in a male environment and by male coaches. This leads to a gender bias in coaching and conditioning where a female athlete may not have a program customized to her physical or psychological needs and therefore may not be reaching optimal performance.

The lifespan approach to women and physical activity

In this chapter we examine women's health issues according to their progression through the lifespan—we focus first on young girls, then adolescents, then adult women, and finally on the needs of older women. At the appropriate stage we pay particular attention to clinical issues relating to the menstrual cycle, breast care, pregnancy, common female injuries, and menopause.

Some examples of issues that arise at different stages of the lifespan and whether they relate to sex or gender are shown in Table 43.2 overleaf.

Girlhood

Girlhood is characterized by bony growth which is similar to males' until approximately 9 or 10 years of age. Girls tend to commence their adolescent growth spurt around the age of 11 years and surge ahead of boys in height and weight. Boys begin their adolescent growth spurt, on average, two years later, around the age of 13 years. The rate of linear growth in girls usually decelerates with menarche (beginning of menstruation), between 12 and 14 years. After menarche, girls will usually gain approximately 5 cm and reach their maximal height by 16 or 17 years. The growth spurt in boys usually occurs between 12 and 15 years and full maturation may not occur until 20 to 21 years of age.

The pattern of body weight development is similar to that of height. The earlier growth spurt gives females an increased weight in the early teenage years. However, by 15 years of age, boys' weight usually exceeds that of girls. At full sexual maturity, the male

Table 43.2 Examples of issues that arise at different stages of the lifespan and whether they relate to sex or gender

Lifespan stage	Sex issues	Gender issues
Girlhood	Onset of Osgood-Schlatter disease is earlier in girls than boys due to growth patterns.	Municipal policies have restricted girls from competitive ice hockey or prime ice time.
Adolescence	Incidence of stress fractures is increased if estrogen levels are low.	Increased body image concern is prevalent and may be a barrier to sport participation.
Adult woman	Pregnancy and breast feeding affect physical activity and incidence of ligament strain.	Domestic violence affects women more than men and often is associated with musculoskeletal injuries.
Older woman	Increased incidence of osteoarthritis in medial knee.	Lack of lifespan role models and personal exercise experience make it challenging for women to start exercise at this age despite the proven benefits.

outweighs the female by approximately 11 kg. This is due to additional bone and muscle mass.

Males usually have wide shoulders and narrow hips, whereas a female generally has a wide pelvis in relation to the width of her shoulders. Because the woman is shorter and has a wider pelvis, she has a lower center of gravity and possibly greater stability. This may lead to superior balance. The wider pelvis leads to an increased inward slant of the thigh and, therefore, an increased Q angle at the knee. Women have shorter limbs, especially the upper arm, and thus have less lever action with a resultant loss of power. Females have an increased carrying angle at the elbow.[2]

Girls become very sensitive and aware of their bodies prior to the onset of actual pubertal changes. This heightened self-awareness should be respected in the locker room and clinic, and used as an opportunity to educate girls about their bodies and exercise.

Adolescence

Adolescence is marked by substantial development of bone density and the onset of menstruation. As much bone mineral is laid down during the adolescent years as most women will lose during their entire adult lives.[3] The timing of peak gains in bone accrual occurs approximately one year after the age of peak linear growth and is earlier in girls than boys, consistent with earlier onset of sexual maturation. This dissociation between linear growth and bone mineral accrual suggests a transient period of relative weakness during the adolescent growth spurt[2] and may partially explain the increase in fractures seen in children around the time of peak linear

growth.[4] Women, on average, have a smaller peak bone mass than men because their skeletons are physically smaller. However, a difference in bone density related to sex is not nearly as clear-cut and probably varies from site to site.[5]

Over the last hundred years, the average age of onset of menstruation has decreased from 17 years of age to the current 11 to 12.5 years of age. There is emerging evidence that menarche is becoming more common as young as 9 years of age. This shift is thought to be related to improved nutrition and caloric balance. Menarche, or the onset of menstrual bleeding, usually occurs one to two years after the commencement of the pubertal growth spurt and breast budding in girls.

The age of menarche appears to be correlated with athletic performance—with high-performance athletes tending to have a later age of menarche than the normal population.[6] These high-performance athletes fall into two groups—a group that commenced intense physical training prior to menarche, and a group that commenced training after menarche. The presence of a delayed onset of menarche in both groups indicates that there may be a combination of factors causing this condition.

Intense training in pre-menarcheal years, as occurs commonly in early specialization sport such as gymnastics and figure skating, is associated with a delayed onset of menarche. This association does not necessarily imply cause and effect. It may be that thinness, which may occur as a result of intense training, may be the most important factor preventing the onset of menses.[6] The combination of intensive exercise and low body weight may affect the hypothalamic secretion of hormones, thus delaying the onset of menarche. While breast development and menarche are delayed in this group of intensively exercising pre-pubertal athletes, the development of pubic hair is not delayed.

The observation that high-performance female athletes give a history of delayed onset of menarche, even without a history of intense training prior to menarche, suggests that delayed menarche may confer some athletic advantage. Athletes may inherit a tendency for a slower rate of maturation.

Late maturation may lead to prolonged bony growth due to delayed closure of the epiphyseal growth plates. Late maturity is associated with longer legs, narrower hips, less weight per unit height, and less relative body fat than the early maturer. These factors would be advantageous to athletic performance. There may also be a sociological component to this process. Current research emphasizes the primary role of constitutional factors in the selection process of athletes at relatively young ages.[7]

Whether delayed menarche has clinical consequences is unclear. A later age of menarche is associated with a lower rate of bone mineral accretion during adolescence and hence decreased peak bone mass.[8] This could have implications for the risk of osteoporotic fractures in later life. There have also been some reports of a greater incidence of stress fractures in athletes with delayed menarche[8, 9] although this is not a consistent finding.[10]

The female sex hormones exert a range of effects on many metabolic, thermoregulatory, cardiovascular, and respiratory parameters that may influence athletic performance. These are summarized in the boxes below.[11]

Actions of estrogen

Effects on cardiovascular system
- Altered plasma fibrinolytic activity and platelet aggregation—increase in thrombosis
- Decreased total cholesterol and low-density lipoprotein levels and increased high-density lipoprotein levels—protection against atherosclerosis
- Vasodilatory effect on vascular smooth muscle

Effects on regulation of substrate metabolism
- Increased intramuscular and hepatic glycogen storage and uptake—possibly increased endurance performance

- Glycogen-sparing effect through increased lipid synthesis, muscle lipolysis, and greater use of free fatty acids
- Decreased insulin-binding capacity—decreased glucose tolerance and insulin resistance

Other effects
- Deposition of fat in breast, buttocks, and thighs
- Increased blood pressure
- Increased calcium uptake in bone
- Change in neurotransmitters—possible improved cognitive function and memory

Actions of progesterone

- Increased core body temperature 0.3–0.5°C
- Increased minute ventilation
- Augmented ventilatory response to hypoxia and hypercapnia
- Post-ovulatory fluid retention via effects on aldosterone and the renin–angiotensin system
- Actions on insulin receptors leading to peripheral insulin resistance
- Metabolic effects resulting in a greater dependence on fat as a substrate

Before discussing other phases of the lifespan (adulthood, older age) we focus on menstrual irregularities and dysmenorrhea—a phenomenon that is prevalent between adolescence and adulthood.

Effect of the menstrual cycle on performance

The measurement of athletic performance is difficult and encompasses physical fitness (aerobic fitness, anaerobic fitness, muscle strength, flexibility, body composition) as well as neuromotor, cognitive, and psychological factors. Most research has failed to find a link between fluctuations in female reproductive hormones throughout the menstrual cycle, and muscle contractile characteristics or determinants of maximal oxygen consumption. This suggests that performance in strength-specific sports and intense anaerobic/aerobic sports is not affected.[12] For prolonged exercise performance, some research has found a higher cardiovascular strain in the mid-luteal phase and a reduced time to exhaustion in hot conditions.[12]

Dysmenorrhea

Dysmenorrhea refers to the painful uterine cramps experienced by many women during menstruation. In a sportswoman, these symptoms may adversely affect training or competition. Although many women who exercise have a reduced incidence of dysmenorrhea, some find that pain and cramping interferes with physical activity. Sportswomen suffering from dysmenorrhea should be treated with simple analgesics, and prostaglandin inhibitors such as naproxen (500 mg every 12 hours); sometimes the oral contraceptive pill (OCP) is used for significant dysmenorrhea.

Premenstrual syndrome

Premenstrual syndrome is defined as the presence of emotional and/or physical symptoms occurring cyclically 7–10 days prior to menstruation. Symptoms may include anxiety, depression, mood swings, headaches, fluid retention, breast soreness, and breast enlargement.

 Exercise may reduce the severity of premenstrual symptoms.

Treatments of premenstrual syndrome that are supported with evidence, particularly in cases with severe symptoms, include consumption of soy isoflavones,[13] selective serotonin reuptake inhibitors,[14] a low-dose oral contraceptive with drospirenone,[15] and luteal phase dosing with controlled release paroxetine.[16]

Menstrual cycle manipulation

Menstrual cycle manipulation is a method of stopping the monthly bleed by the use of hormonal manipulation. Those sportswomen who are, or perceive that they are, adversely affected during the premenstrual and/or menstrual phases may wish to manipulate their menstrual cycle to avoid that stage of the cycle coinciding with a major event. If a sportswoman wishes to manipulate her cycle only occasionally for a yearly event, then the most effective means of altering the cycle is by the use of the OCP. This can be done in one of two ways.

The OCP can be ceased 10 days prior to the planned activity, which will usually induce a withdrawal bleed. A new packet of the pill can either be resumed at the end of menstruation or following the completion of the sporting event. If this method is used, suppression of ovulation may fail and additional barrier methods of contraception (e.g. condoms) should be considered until two weeks after recommencing the pill.

Alternatively, the sportswoman may omit the seven day tablet-free interval (or sugar pills) and continue taking the OCP throughout the sporting event to prevent menstruation from occurring prior to or during the event. This method is simpler to use with monophasic pills than with triphasic pills.

Continuous OCPs or extended-cycle OCPs are currently available in worldwide markets for women who choose to induce amenorrhea. The first regimens introduced in clinical practice were an 84-day regimen that results in bleeding only 4 times a year. Women reported significantly fewer bleeding days requiring protection and were more likely to have amenorrhea. In addition they also reported significantly fewer days of bloating and menstrual pain.[17] Continuous OCPs have not demonstrated any additional adverse effects compared with the cyclic OCPs.

Over seventy per cent of women taking the continuous OCP have amenorrhea and this improves with the increase in the duration of use.[18] The sportswoman should have a medication trial for at least three months prior to key competitions to determine susceptibility to breakthrough bleeding.

Injectable progesterone, as Depo-Provera, is another form of contraception that eliminates the menstrual cycle; however, it requires administration of injection every three months. Progesterone-only contraception is associated with increased risk of premenopausal osteoporosis and should be cautioned for use in sportswomen with risk of fracture or stress fracture.[19, 20]

Menstrual irregularities associated with exercise

Menstrual irregularity associated with exercise is a common problem during the early adolescent years and it can be prolonged, particularly if there is an associated problem of disordered eating.

Luteal phase defects

Abnormal luteal function is common among sportswomen.[21] The luteal phase extends from the time of ovulation to the onset of menstruation. It is normally associated with high levels of estrogen and progesterone, and its normal length is 14 days. A shortened luteal phase of less than 10 days is commonly found in exercising women. This is usually associated with lower than normal levels of progesterone during the luteal phase and anovulatory cycles. This abnormality of the luteal phase is often not recognized, as women still menstruate regularly, and it may be associated with a slightly prolonged follicular phase resulting in normal or near-normal lengths of the menstrual cycle (28 days).

There appears to be a direct relationship between the amount of exercise and the development of luteal phase defects.[22, 23] It is uncertain whether this luteal insufficiency is a stage in a continuum of menstrual cycle irregularity preceding to oligomenorrhea or amenorrhea, or whether it is a separate entity. The main effect of luteal phase defects is infertility or sub-fertility as well as spontaneous habitual miscarriage. Bone loss is associated with luteal phase defects. Recurrent short luteal phase cycles and anovulation were associated with spinal bone loss of approximately 2–4% per year in physically active women.[24]

Oligomenorrhea and amenorrhea

The incidence of oligomenorrhea (irregular menstruation, three to six cycles per year) and amenorrhea (absent menstruation, fewer than three cycles per year or no cycles for the past six months) is increased in the athletic population.

The incidence of these conditions in sportswomen is between 10% and 20%, while the incidence in the general population may be around 5%.[25–27] The incidence in runners and ballet dancers is particularly high compared with swimmers and cyclists. As many as 50% of competitive distance runners have reduced or absent periods. Menstrual disturbances are higher in sports emphasizing leanness.[6]

Oligomenorrhea and amenorrhea are associated with a disruption of the hypothalamic–pituitary–ovarian axis, which manifests itself as low amplitude and irregular and infrequent luteinizing hormone pulsatility and low levels of estrogen and progesterone. This is known as "hypothalamic amenorrhea." Other neuroendocrine abnormalities associated with oligomenorrhea and amenorrhea include lower levels of thyroid hormones, insulin-like growth factor 1, and leptin (expressed mainly in adipose tissue) together with an increase in stress hormones (cortisol).

Causes of exercise-associated menstrual cycle irregularities

"Energy drain" appears to be the most critical final step in exercise-associated menstrual cycle irregularities. The initiating factor is restricted energy availability as a result of reduced energy intake and/or increased energy expenditure. This leads to low leptin levels[28] and stimulates compensatory mechanisms such as weight loss, metabolic hormone alterations, or energy conservation, which subsequently causes a central suppression of reproductive function and concomitant hypoestrogenism (Fig. 43.1).[29] Other factors that have been implicated are discussed briefly below.

Low body fat

There is an association between a reduced amount of body fat and the incidence of menstrual cycle

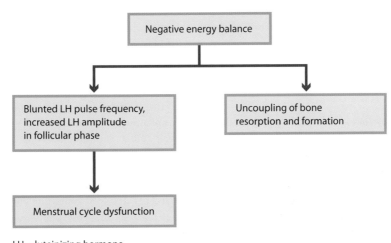

LH = luteinizing hormone

Figure 43.1 The causes of menstrual cycle irregularities

irregularity. This is not to say that there is a critical level of body fat below which menstrual cycle irregularities develop, as was once thought. There is considerable individual variation and there may be a critical level in each individual. Numerous examples have been reported where amenorrheic sportswomen have increased their percentage body fat for some reason (e.g. reduction in activity or injury) and normal menstruation has resumed.

Psychological stress

It is well established that psychological stress can affect hypothalamic function. Many sportswomen suffer high levels of psychological stress either related to their sporting activity or to outside factors such as work, family, or relationships.

Psychological stress may be a contributory factor in the development of menstrual irregularities in sportswomen but, as yet, there is no convincing evidence from the few studies researching this issue.

Level of exercise

There appears to be a relationship between menstrual irregularities and the level of exercise performed. The level of exercise may be the total amount of exercise or the intensity of the exercise.

Normal menstruation often resumes with cessation of the athletic activity due to injury, retirement, or a reduction of exercise during a pre-competition taper or in the off-season. Frequently, menstruation ceases again on resumption of the previous level of exercise.

The level of exercise is most likely related to menstrual disturbances via its contribution to an energy imbalance. A higher level of exercise expends greater energy. It is also feasible that exercise, as a form of stress, may have a direct effect on the hypothalamus or, alternatively, have its effect through the actions of one or more of the hormones whose levels are elevated by exercise.

Two hormones that are elevated during exercise and may affect the hypothalamus are cortisol and the opioid peptides. Cortisol levels have been shown to increase with exercise. This may be associated with increased corticotropin and corticotropin releasing hormone (CRH). It is possible that CRH may inhibit the secretion of luteinizing hormone from the pituitary gland. Opioid peptides, such as beta-endorphins, are elevated with exercise and may have a negative feedback effect on the hypothalamus.

"Immature" reproductive system

The above factors may all interact to affect hypothalamic and pituitary function in sportswomen; however, only certain sportswomen develop menstrual cycle irregularities. It may be that certain women have a susceptibility to developing these irregularities, possibly associated with immaturity of the reproductive system. This may explain why the incidence of menstrual cycle irregularities is more common in younger women, women who have not been pregnant, women with a history of menstrual irregularity, and those with a history of delayed menarche.

Complications of exercise-associated menstrual cycle irregularities

The major complications associated with menstrual cycle irregularities include reduced fertility and the risk of low bone mass.

Reduced fertility

Fertility is reduced among intensely exercising females compared with their sedentary counterparts. Anovulatory cycles are common in sportswomen and may be associated with amenorrhea, oligomenorrhea, or luteal phase defects, or even occur in normally menstruating athletes.

A good indication that ovulation has occurred in a particular cycle is the presence of either pre-menstrual symptoms at the end of the cycle or mid-cycle ovulation pain. Ovulation may be confirmed by measuring the basal body temperature. This rises between 0.3°C and 0.5°C (0.5°F and 0.9°F) at the time of ovulation and remains elevated during the luteal phase. It may also be confirmed using commercially available urine dip-sticks which detect the surge of luteinizing hormone just prior to ovulation.

The sportswoman should not automatically assume that, because she has been amenorrheic for some time, she is necessarily infertile. There have been many examples of sportswomen with long histories of amenorrhea becoming pregnant. The cause of their amenorrhea then becomes pregnancy rather than exercise.

If pregnancy is desired, ovulation and a normal menstrual cycle can usually be induced by reducing the level of exercise or increasing the level of body fat. If this does not induce ovulation, the sportswoman should be referred for gynecological assessment and, if necessary, induction of ovulation by pharmacological means.

Reduced bone mass

Energy imbalance related to poor nutritional intake and high activity output can have a significant impact on lifelong bone health. The detrimental effects of athletic amenorrhea on bone mass were first identified in the 1980s.[30–33] Since then, numerous authors have shown lower axial bone density in sportswomen with amenorrhea or oligomenorrhea compared with their eumenorrheic counterparts.[31, 34–36] Appendicular bone density may also be affected[39] but this has been a less consistent finding. Thus, some sports that apply high loads to bone (such as gymnastics) may be able to partly offset the negative skeletal effects of amenorrhea.[40]

Bone is lost rapidly in the first two or three years following menstrual disturbances at a rate of approximately 4% per year. After the first few years, the loss continues, but at a slower rate. This is an important consideration in the treatment of amenorrheic sportswomen.

Osteopenia/osteoporosis is one of the components of the female athlete triad. The triad description was revised by the American College of Sport Medicine in 2007 (Fig. 43.2) to be defined as a continuum of interrelated factors including low energy availability (i.e. disordered eating, eating disorder), hypothalamic menstrual disorder (i.e. ammenorrhea, oligomenorrhea, or anovulatory dysfunction) and low bone mineral density (i.e. osteopenia, osteoporosis, presence of stress fracture).[41]

The prevalence of the triad is still being determined, but when considered as a continuum where two or more factors determine diagnosis, we identify a greater number of sportswomen at risk.

 A Norwegian study of the prevalence of the triad found that fewer than 5% of elite female athletes met all the triad criteria and that this prevalence was comparable to that seen in normally active girls and young women.[42]

When evaluating the presence of two of the components of the triad, prevalence ranged from 5.4% to 26.9% in the athletes. This implies that a significant proportion of female athletes suffer from components of the triad rather than the triad itself, and that this is not just confined to elite athletes.

The mechanisms responsible for the deleterious effects of menstrual disturbances on bone density are probably multifactorial. Previously, the main cause was thought to be low circulating estrogens.[31, 43, 44]

However, this primary mechanism for bone loss is now questioned because[45, 46] amenorrheic sportswomen appear to be less responsive to estrogen therapy[47–50] than women with ovarian failure.

The postmenopausal state is characterized by increased bone turnover with an excess of bone resorption.[51] Conversely, the pattern of bone remodeling in amenorrheic athletes is atypical of an estrogen deficient state, with either no change[44, 52] or an apparent reduction in bone turnover and reduced bone formation.[53]

 It appears that undernutrition and its metabolic consequences (reduced levels of insulin-like growth factor 1 and leptin) may underlie the bone remodeling imbalance and bone loss in active, amenorrheic women.[46, 54, 55]

A recent experiment showed that bone formation is impaired at much higher levels of energy

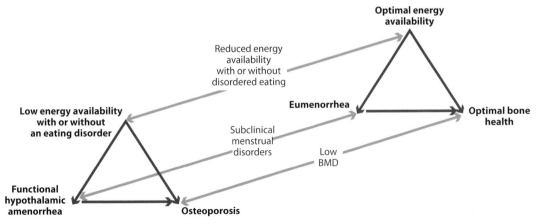

Figure 43.2 American College of Sport Medicine position stand: the female athlete triad

availability than is bone resorption[56] and at levels that may not manifest as amenorrhea.

Reduction in bone mass in sportswomen is particularly important for two reasons. In the short term, it increases susceptibility to the development of stress fractures; in the long term, there is the risk of osteoporosis.

Stress fractures

The incidence of stress fractures in amenorrheic females is higher than in normally menstruating females.[9, 57–61] This could be related to lower bone density, as female sportswomen who developed a stress fracture had lower bone density than those who did not have a stress fracture.[9, 59, 62] However, bone density may not necessarily be lower than that of less active non-sportswomen, which suggests that the level of bone density required by physically active individuals for short-term bone health may be greater than that required by the general population.

Another mechanism by which menstrual disturbances could increase the risk of stress fracture is via alterations in bone formation independent of reductions in bone density. Sportswomen with menstrual disturbances also often present with other factors, such as low calcium intake,[27] greater training load, and lower body fat or body mass index,[55, 63] all of which could impact on stress fracture development.

Postmenopausal osteoporosis

Reduced bone mass may increase the susceptibility of sportswomen to the development of postmenopausal osteoporosis if bone loss cannot be reversed once menses return. The most important means of prevention of postmenopausal osteoporosis is the attainment of a high peak bone mass. Peak bone mass, which is usually attained around the late-teens–early-twenties, depends on a number of interrelated factors, including genetics, nutrition (especially calcium intake, Vitamin D_3 and energy balance), exercise, and hormonal status.

The reversibility of bone loss observed with amenorrhea has been a concern due to the long-term consequences on bone mass. Drinkwater et al. followed up sportswomen with amenorrhea 15 months after they regained menses and showed a 6% increase in vertebral bone density.[64] The resumption of menses was also associated with an increase in body weight and a reduction in exercise level. However, the gain ceased after two years,[65] suggesting that bone mass may never fully recover. Despite resumption of menses, previously irregularly menstruating runners still have reduced vertebral bone mass compared with regularly menstruating runners.[8, 66, 67] A history of menstrual irregularity is therefore detrimental to the attainment and maintenance of peak bone mass.

Treatment of exercise-associated menstrual cycle irregularities

The OCP is now used by many sportswomen and can be administered safely from the age of 16 years or three years past menarche. OCPs have numerous beneficial effects for the sportswoman in addition to contraception and cycle control—reduction in dysmenorrhea, premenstrual syndrome, menorrhagia, and iron deficiency anemia secondary to excessive monthly blood loss.[11]

Women taking the OCP have decreased frequency of dysfunctional uterine bleeding, functional ovarian cysts, pelvic inflammatory disease, benign breast disease, and ectopic pregnancies. The risks of ovarian and endometrial cancers are also reduced. However, optimal levels of bone density are achieved through natural menstruation physiology.

Initial high-dose pills were associated with a high incidence of adverse effects, such as weight gain. The advent of low-dose pills reduced adverse effects. Most population studies indicate no overall effect on body weight while taking the OCP[68, 69] although individual responses to the hormones may involve some weight gain either due to fluid retention or possibly appetite stimulation. Sportswomen should be counseled about the misconception of weight gain as an inevitable consequence of OCP use. There is also no convincing evidence that the OCP affects performance.[70–73]

Safe prescribing of the OCP includes screening for high blood pressure and cardiovascular risk factors. Absolute and relative contraindications to estrogen therapy are shown in the box.

When a woman presents with menstrual cycle irregularities including amenorrhea, oligomenorrhea, or menstrual cycle length disorders, the physician should take a history (including dietary intake), complete a focused physical examination, and investigate the serum hormonal profile.

If menstrual dysfunction is identified and linked to low body weight or increased exercise intensity (i.e. energy imbalance[74]), treatment should aim to normalize nutritional intake and provide better balance of training, exercise intensity, and recovery strategies.

This should be monitored and supported through education and review of training logs for at least a six-month period prior to initiation of the OCP for menstrual dysfunction.

It is quite common that the menstrual cycle can remain irregular while the player regains cycles over the first year. A key clinical indicator of recovery is the patient reporting greater energy and more consistent performance.

Eating disorders and intense athletic activity

There has been considerable discussion regarding the relationship between eating disorders and intense athletic activity. While a direct relationship is unlikely, the emphasis on thinness and reduction in body fat in particular sports, such as gymnastics, endurance running, and ballet dancing, may lead to an increased incidence of eating disorders in susceptible individuals.[75] Pressure from coaches, parents, or fellow competitors regarding ideal body shape may lead to abnormal eating patterns. Other psychological risk factors include low self-esteem, poor coping skills, perfectionism, obsessive compulsive traits, and anxiety.

Disordered eating is defined as an inadequate energy consumption, which may be related to poor quality, quantity, frequency, or awareness of appropriate sports nutrition. This can be compounded by restrictive eating patterns and a drive for thinness. *Eating disorders* are psychiatric conditions where pathologic weight control measures are instituted that lead to eating disorders such as anorexia nervosa and bulimia nervosa.

Clinicians should have a high index of suspicion of the presence of eating disorders and disordered eating in young females who appear excessively thin, who have a distorted body image (i.e. they are convinced they are too fat when in fact they are extremely thin), or who present with amenorrhea, stress fracture, or fatigue.[31]

Amenorrhea related to anorexia nervosa seems to have a more marked effect on reduction of bone density than does exercise-associated amenorrhea.[76, 77] Patients presenting with unusual stress fractures, such as fractures of the pubic ramus, may have severely reduced bone density secondary to anorexia nervosa.

 A comprehensive evaluation should include assessment of exercise behaviors, nutritional intake, weight control measures, psychological factors, and laboratory or diagnostic testing as appropriate.

Adult women

The adult woman exerciser obtains numerous health benefits from her activity; however, she should be aware of some injuries that she is at increased risk of, and also should be aware of ongoing maintenance of care for specific women's issues.

Injuries

Musculoskeletal injuries

Three musculoskeletal injuries that occur more frequently in females than males are stress fractures, patellofemoral problems, and anterior cruciate ligament reputure.

Stress fractures

Stress fractures occur more frequently in amenorrheic women than in those who are menstruating normally, and menstrual status should be assessed in all sportswomen who present with stress fractures. However, stress fractures can also be related to training error, overuse, malalignment, and hard running surfaces. (See also Chapter 5 and discussion of stress fractures at specific skeletal sites, e.g. navicular stress fracture in Chapter 40.)

Patellofemoral pain syndrome

The increased Q angle at the knee caused by slanting of the femur may increase susceptibility of sportswomen to patellofemoral pain. This biomechanical abnormality may also increase susceptibility to the development of other overuse injuries of the lower leg (e.g. medial tibial stress syndrome).

 See detailed discussion of patellofemoral pain syndrome in Chapter 33 as well in the *Clinical Sports Medicine* masterclasses at www. clinicalsportsmedicine.com.

Anterior cruciate ligament rupture

Women are two to eight times more likely to sustain an anterior cruciate ligament rupture than males.[78] There are many theories as to why this difference in injury rate exists. These include both intrinsic and extrinsic factors. Intrinsic factors include joint laxity, hormonal influences, limb alignment, notch dimensions, and ligament size; extrinsic factors include type of sport, conditioning, and equipment.[78]

Female athletes may be more predisposed to anterior cruciate ligament injuries during the ovulatory phase of the menstrual cycle.[79, 80] Sportswomen taking oral contraceptives demonstrate lower impact forces and reduced torques at the knee, increased hamstring to quadriceps strength ratios, increased stability on one leg, and decreased knee laxity relative to sportswomen not using the OCP. The use of the OCP in combination with neuromuscular training may increase the dynamic stability of the knee joint and may decrease injury risk in female athletes. Interventional measures such as these may perhaps reduce the risk of anterior cruciate ligament injury in this high-risk population.[79, 80] Chapter 32 has a detailed discussion of this problem and relevant preventive strategies.[78]

Vulval injuries

Injuries to the female genital organs occur occasionally and usually are associated with blunt trauma or repetitive impact. Vulval contusions and lacerations can occur from trauma related to falls and traumatic impact. Women performing sports requiring equipment that is in close contact with the body (such as gymnastics) are vulnerable, as are women performing sports such as water-skiing where sudden impact can lead to tissue damage.

Contusions should be treated with the application of ice; lacerations may require surgical repair.

Breast care

The breast is composed primarily of fatty tissue. Breast size and shape is largely determined by genetic predisposition but may be affected by general weight loss or weight gain. Breast changes are common in the premenstrual period, when the breast may increase in size up to 40%. The nipple contains smooth muscle fibers that respond to cold or tactile stimulation. Recommendations for breast care in sport are shown in Table 43.3.

Trauma

Breast trauma is not common but a contusion may occur as a result of a direct blow from a ball, racquet, or opponent. The contusion is associated with bleeding and swelling. It should be treated with ice, analgesics, and support. Occasionally, a deep hematoma will require aspiration. It is important to reassure the sportswoman that there is no evidence that trauma to the breast causes tumors.

Nipple problems

"Runners' nipples" is a common condition in which the nipples are irritated by rubbing against clothing during prolonged activity. This condition is common in both men and women, and is more likely to occur in cold weather where the nipple is more prominent and harder. It may be prevented by the use of petroleum jelly, tape over the nipples, or a seamless bra.

Cyclists also commonly develop nipple problems as a result of a combination of perspiration and cold. This can be prevented by the use of appropriate clothing, especially a wind-breaking material over the chest.

Sports bras

Excessive movement of the breasts, particularly in an up-and-down motion, can occur during exercise. This may lead to pain and discomfort, and affect sports performance. A number of specialized sports bras are now available.

Sports bras should give support from above, below, and the sides. They should be made of a material that is firm, mostly non-elastic, non-abrasive, and of good absorptive quality. The straps should be of non-stretch material and, ideally, crossed or Y-shaped at the back. There should be no seams or ridges in the nipple area, and no fasteners or hooks. The sports bra should be individually fitted and be comfortable both at rest and with vigorous activity. There should

Table 43.3 Recommendations for breast care in sport

Issue	Garment solution	Healthcare practitioner role
Increased physical activity	Advise garment suited to type of exercise: • impact—supportive, compression, seamless, sweat absorbent • endurance—ventilated, scapular reinforcement, porous fabric • contact—protective padding	Advise exercise for health: • include bra advice • awareness that chaffing, bruising, irritation, and pain are not normal and should be addressed • refer to physician if further evaluation required
Bruising • shoulder strap • anterior breast	Shoulder strap: • wider shoulder straps, can add strap pads Anterior breast: • less anterior compression, separate cup style may help	Address the contact component of sport: • technique changes • shell chest protectors • game conduct
Nipple chafing	Bra cups: • seamless cups • ensure proper size and fit • sweat absorbent material	Hygiene issues: • dry nipples (change out of sweaty or wet garments) • air dry after showering • moisturizers such as vitamin E cream or lanolin • lubricants such as Bodyglide or Vaseline • educate on signs of infection
Controlling breast movement	Compression style garment: • full figure support • Spandex body suit for additional support • proper sizing and fit	Advise proper posture: • rhomboid and scapular stabilization, and strengthening to reduce forward posture • gait and footwear to ensure correct movement patterns

also be provision for the insertion of padding for use in contact sports.

Various degrees of padding can be added to the bra. In certain sports, such as martial arts and football, a plastic cup bra may be placed over the normal sports bra. Protective chest pads should be worn in softball and ice hockey, and are available in designs specific for women.

A large proportion of women living with breast cancer experience bra discomfort while they exercise.[81] The chest band has been identified as the bra component which causes the most discomfort to the patient with breast cancer. Band tightness is usually the acute cause of this discomfort, particularly for lumpectomy patients. Women living with a breast cancer diagnosis are particularly susceptible to fluctuating tissue edema during both treatment and exercise. A woman undergoing a lumpectomy experiences the partial removal of a breast, which can lead to asymmetrical breast mass. As bras are fitted to the larger breast, the smaller, treated breast frequently does not adequately fill the bra cup, and may experience greater motion and consequently greater breast pain. This may be addressed by having bras personally customized. Breast sensitivity may also be seen in women with other conditions, such as following traumatic injury to the thorax or following open heart surgery.

Posture and therapeutic exercise

It is not uncommon clinically to see women, particularly younger women, with poor posture related to breast size. Anecdotally this is particularly common in swimmers and women with larger breasts. The women may present clinically with insidious onset of back or neck pain; alternatively they may present with an injury or other medical condition. Posture may be related in part to psychosocial factors. They may be presenting for treatment of back pain, or they may report increased sensitivity to the wearing of a bra. In all of these situations, practitioners play a key role in educating women about posture and related breast care.

For many women, education and exercise alone are sufficient to correct posture. Further assessment of mobility and movement through the thorax, including ribs and thoracic vertebrae, should be undertaken if a woman is reporting pain or dysfunction. Trigger points within the intercostal muscles may benefit from soft tissue techniques to restore normal muscle tone and function. Manual therapy can restore joint mobility and rib mechanics. Breathing disorders or abnormal breathing mechanics must be addressed in order to normalize movement and any reported sensitivity.

Education and individualized exercise prescription should be provided for posture, scapulothoracic stability, and normal breathing. Women recovering from any condition that involves the thorax (e.g. breast cancer, post–open heart surgery, post-thoracotomy) can benefit from such therapeutic interventions.

Most women, including those with large breasts, can maintain a healthy active lifestyle with the correct fitting of a supportive sports bra. Despite this, some women report discomfort with high-impact exercises such as running. Deep-water running is a strenuous but more comfortable form of exercise for women with large breasts relative to running on a treadmill. This is sometimes part of the exercise prescription for women with large breasts.[82]

Exercise and pregnancy

The prescription of exercise during pregnancy is an effective tool for improving general emotional well-being, maintaining optimal weight management, and controlling blood glucose. The PARmed-X is a validated screening tool to assess readiness for physical activity and screen for contraindications while providing current exercise education.[83] The current guidelines for exercise prescription during pregnancy refer to low-risk single pregnancies.[84] The guidelines are listed on pages 923–24, after the box on the contraindications to exercise in pregnancy.

In general there is good evidence to support regular moderate low-impact exercise in a low-risk pregnancy. Contact sports carry a high risk in the second and third trimester because direct trauma to the pelvis and lower abdominal area may occur. At that time the uterus is thinning with fetal growth and migrating to the abdominal cavity where there is less protection. For this reason, contact sports or sports with a high risk of collision should be avoided after the first trimester.

Potential risks of maternal exercise to the fetus

Changes in fetal heart rate may occur in response to exercise; this seems to be related to gestational age and the duration, intensity, and type of exercise. Blood flow to the uterus during exercise is maximal at the area of attachment of the placenta, therefore minimizing the hypoxic effect on the fetus. Generally, increases in fetal heart rate of between 10 and 30 beats per minute are found following maternal exercise.[85] Occasionally, bradycardia (slowing of the heart rate) is observed.[86] The clinical significance of fetal tachycardia or bradycardia is uncertain.

The average birth weight of babies whose mothers have exercised intensively and very frequently during pregnancy is lower than that of babies born to sedentary mothers.[87] There do not appear to be any short- or long-term adverse sequelae as a result of this difference in weight between groups. There is a theoretical risk of premature labor associated with maternal exercise due to increased levels of noradrenalin (norepinephrine), which may cause increased uterine irritability and subsequent premature labor. This has not been observed in practice.

The other major area of concern for the health of the fetus with maternal exercise is the risk of hyperthermia. Animal data suggests that a core temperature in excess of 39°C (102°F) may result in neural tube defects in the fetus. This malformation is the result of failure of closure of the neural tube, a process that occurs approximately 25 days after conception. This has not been confirmed in humans.

 Pregnant women, however, should avoid hyperthermia during the first weeks of their pregnancy. Moderate exercise in normal environmental conditions results in only minimal increases in core temperature.

Risks to the mother

The pregnant woman shows an increased susceptibility to musculoskeletal pain, especially the development of pain in the low back, sacroiliac region, or pubic symphysis. The mechanism of the development of low back and pelvic girdle pain in the pregnant woman probably relates to a combination of factors, including a change in the center of gravity upwards and forwards associated with forward tilting of the pelvis, an increase in lumbar lordosis, and loosening of ligaments associated with increased levels of the hormone relaxin.[88] The incidence of low back pain can be reduced by careful attention to posture and avoidance of sudden movements as well as strengthening of the abdominal and back muscles. Pelvic girdle pain can be reduced by advice, and the use of a sacroiliac belt, stabilizing exercise, and acupuncture.[89, 90]

Another possible problem affecting the pregnant woman is hypotension. Postural hypotension results from prolonged standing whereby there is a decrease in cardiac output due to slowed venous return. Supine hypotension can occur with lying or exercising in the supine position. In the supine position, the uterus compresses the major blood vessels, resulting in reduced blood return to the heart and thus hypotension.

Advantages of exercise during pregnancy

The advantages of exercise during pregnancy relate more to the general physical and psychological well-being of the mother rather than to effects on the pregnancy itself.

Women who exercise prior to pregnancy and continue to do so during pregnancy, weigh less, gain less weight, and deliver slightly smaller babies than sedentary women. Increased fitness may enable women to cope better with labor. Even overweight pregnant women who commence an aerobic exercise program can improve fitness throughout pregnancy.[91] There is no evidence that women who have exercised during pregnancy have shorter or easier labors.

Exercise during pregnancy is also valuable for the prevention and treatment of conditions such as gestational diabetes. The activation of large groups of muscles allows for an improved glucose utilization while simultaneously increasing insulin sensitivity.[92]

 It appears that women who engage in recreational physical activity during pregnancy have approximately 50% reduction in the risk for gestational diabetes compared with inactive women.[93]

Active women also have approximately 40% reduction in pre-eclampsia risk.[93–95]

Contraindications to exercise during pregnancy

Exercise is contraindicated in women with any serious or potentially serious complication of pregnancy. A list of these contraindications is shown in the box.[96]

Contraindications to aerobic exercise during pregnancy[(a) (b)]

Absolute contraindications
Hemodynamically significant heart disease
Restrictive lung disease
Incompetent cervix/cerclage
Multiple gestations at risk for premature labor
Persistent 2nd or 3rd trimester bleeding
Placenta previa after 26 weeks of gestation
Premature labor during the current pregnancy
Ruptured membranes
Pre-eclampsia/pregnancy-induced hypertension

Relative contraindications
Severe anemia
Unevaluated maternal cardiac arrhythmia
Chronic bronchitis
Poorly controlled type 1 diabetes
Morbid obesity
Extreme underweight (BMI<12)
History of extremely sedentary lifestyle
Intrauterine growth restriction in current pregnancy
Poorly controlled hypertension
Orthopedic limitations
Poorly controlled seizure disorder
Poorly controlled hyperthyroidism
Heavy smoker

[(a)]As listed in the American College of Obstetricians and Gynecologists COG Committee Opinion No. 267. Exercise during pregnancy and the postpartum period 2002[96]
[(b)]Additional contraindications should be left for the physician to individualize

---

Guidelines for exercise during pregnancy

The majority of women are able to perform exercise during pregnancy to benefit their health and well-being. Serious sportswomen who wish to continue intense training during pregnancy should be counseled on an individual basis. In most cases, providing the pregnancy progresses normally, they are able to maintain a reasonably high level of training until discomfort forces them to reduce their training, usually around the sixth month. Guidelines for exercise during pregnancy are listed below:[96, 97]

1. Prior to participating in an exercise program, it is recommended that women meet with their healthcare provider to fill out the PARmed-X for Pregnancy[83] to determine any possible contraindications to exercise.

2. Accumulate 30 minutes or more of moderate exercise between three and five times a week. If a woman has been sedentary prior to pregnancy, then new exercise regimens should be avoided until the second trimester. All exercise should be gradually introduced and self-paced in low-impact aerobic forms.

3. Avoid prolonged exercise in the supine position after the first trimester.

4. Avoid exercise in hot weather.

5. It is recommended that an additional 1250 kJ (300 kcal) of nutrition be consumed for every exercise session including 250 mL (8 oz.) of fluid intake.

6. Perform a good warm-up and cool-down.

7. Avoid excessive or ballistic stretching.

8. Wear a firm supportive bra.

9. Cease activity immediately if any abnormal symptoms develop (see Table 43.4).

Type of exercise

There is no one recommended type of exercise during pregnancy. Readers are referred to published guidelines for safe exercise during pregnancy.[96, 98, 99] The pregnant woman should continue performing the exercise she enjoys most unless she wishes to change for reasons of comfort, such as changing from jogging to water exercises late in pregnancy.

Jogging is an extremely popular form of exercise and may be continued but not commenced during pregnancy. Many pregnant women reduce the distance run during pregnancy, particularly in the later stages. Particular care must be taken to avoid exercise in hot and humid conditions, and close attention should be paid to fluid intake. Running on softer surfaces and wearing running shoes with adequate support reduce the impact of jogging and may prevent musculoskeletal injuries, particularly sacro-iliac joint strain.

Aerobics classes may be continued, but modification of certain exercises may be required. Exercises involving lying supine or hyperextension of the lumbar spine should be avoided, especially after the fourth month. A pillow or towel placed under the right hemi-pelvis can help shift the weight of the uterus off the inferior vena cava, which can enable many women to tolerate exercises in a semi-supine position. Low-impact aerobics is preferable to high-impact aerobics during pregnancy. Bouncing or ballistic movements should be avoided.

Yoga is an excellent means of maintaining flexibility and relaxation. Excessive stretching should be avoided because the hormone relaxin loosens ligaments.

Cycling has the advantage of being a non-weight-bearing activity. In the middle and later stages of pregnancy, it may be advisable to use a stationary bike because of balance problems caused by the shift in the center of gravity. Cycling should be avoided in high temperatures or humidity.

Water activities are popular during pregnancy because of the support provided by the buoyancy of the water.

 Swimming, walking, or running in the water, and water aerobics are all excellent forms of exercise during pregnancy.

Pelvic floor exercises are important to provide women with a good understanding of the function of the pelvic floor and its vital role in continence, structural support of the pelvic organs, and sexual satisfaction. Performing the exercises also creates an awareness of the muscle group, so that women can increase their control over the pelvic floor and their ability to relax it during the second stage of labor.[94]

Trunk stability is of prime importance during pregnancy and in the postnatal period due to increased load of the fetus on the spine, decreased strength of the rectus abdominis, and the postural changes.[94] Exercises concentrating specifically on the internal obliques and transversus abdominis should be performed. If a diastasis of the abdominal muscles (separation of the rectus abdominis) occurs, physical activities that increase the visible herniation should be avoided. Manual support (e.g. a hand on each side of the linea alba and drawing medially) during abdominal strengthening exercises can help prevent or minimize the extent of diastasis during pregnancy. A support belt/binder may also be helpful in reducing strain to the area. The diastasis generally corrects itself over time after delivery.

Certain sports such as parachute jumping should be avoided during pregnancy. Anecdotal and survey evidence suggests that shallow scuba diving not requiring decompression (in less than 10 m [30 feet] in which the risk of venous air embolism is low) is not associated with an abnormal outcome unless it is frequent and occupationally related.[100, 101] Contact sports or those involving a high risk of collision are not recommended. Water skiing is also not recommended due to potential trauma during a fall and vaginal douching.

Exercising at high altitudes above 3000 m (10 000 feet) may not be wise due to the fact that the rates of pregnancy complications are much higher and birth weights lower at these altitudes.[102] At moderate altitudes, there have been no reports of injury, pregnancy complications, or losses associated with exercise at altitude (skiing, running, hiking, mountain biking).[101]

Weight training may be continued by the experienced sportswoman but heavy weights should be avoided. Concentration on high repetition, low weight exercises is advisable. During training, the Valsalva maneuver should be avoided.

Regular, light-intensity resistance exercise can be continued during the second half of pregnancy, as it does not increase the risk of maternal anemia nor does it alter hematological variables.[103]

The American College of Obstetricians and Gynecologists' warning signs for a pregnant woman to terminate exercise, and obtain medical advice are listed in Table 43.4.

Postpartum exercise

After a normal vaginal delivery, gentle exercises such as walking or stretching may be commenced as early as the mother is comfortable. The changes invoked by pregnancy may take some time to return to normal, so care should be taken in the first six weeks after delivery to avoid sudden high impact or contact. Avoidance of excessive stretching or lifting anything heavier than the newborn is advisable in this period.

After a Cesarean section, strenuous activity should be avoided for six weeks and heavy weight training for 12 weeks. Attention should be paid to restoring pelvic floor muscle strength and control in preparation for return to sport activities.

It is common for women to experience musculoskeletal pain throughout pregnancy and following delivery. Common locations include low back, upper back, sacroiliac joint, pubic symphysis, and coccyx. Diastasis recti occurs in up to two-thirds of women during pregnancy, a gap larger than 2.5 cm is clinically important. Pelvic floor muscle damage is common in vaginal delivery. Abdominal incision during Cesarean section affects transversus abdominis and subsequently influences posture and stability of the lumbar spine and pelvis.

Lactating women need to pay special attention to adequate fluid and caloric intake. A good supportive bra is also important for exercise during this period. Lactation and exercise can be successfully combined without any disruption of milk production or flow.

Table 43.4 Warning signs for a pregnant woman to stop exercising—American College of Obstetricians and Gynecologists[96]

System	Specific symptoms and signs that may be "red flags"
Obstetric	Amniotic fluid leakage
	Decreased fetal movement
	Uterine contractions
	Pre-term labor
	Vaginal bleeding
Cardiovascular/neurological	Dyspnea prior to exertion
	Palpations or tachycardia
	Chest pain
	Dizziness
	Headache
	Paresthesia
	Numbness
	Visual disturbances
	Nausea or vomiting
Musculoskeletal	Muscle weakness
	Calf pain or swelling (until DVT is ruled out)

Older adult

Many older women live rich, active, high-quality lives. In this section, the changes associated with menopause, bone health issues including falls prevention, and other specific conditions relating to sport and exercise are discussed.

Menopause

"Menopause" is defined as the time of cessation of menstruation. The exact timing of menopause can only be determined retrospectively, as a period of 12 months must occur without any evidence of menstruation. The time of hormonal change before and after the menopause is known as the "climacteric." This is associated with a gradual reduction in endocrine function of the ovarian follicle, which commences some years before the actual menopause. The average age of menopause in women in Western societies is approximately 50 years.

The changes of the menopause and climacteric are due to the decreased ability of the ovaries to respond to stimulation by the pituitary gonadotropins. The alteration in ovarian function initially causes dysfunctional (irregular) uterine bleeding in the premenopausal stage. Hormone-dependent symptoms such as hot flushes and vaginal dryness are also associated with a decrease of estradiol production, and may occur prior to and around the time of menopause. Some time after the menopause, symptoms of chronic estrogen deprivation may occur; these include chronic atrophic vaginitis and urinary incontinence.

With the steadily increasing life expectancy in most Western societies, increased attention is being paid to the problems of the menopause and the postmenopausal years. A woman who reaches the age of 65 years can now expect to live into her 80s. There is a steadily increasing percentage of the population in the postmenopausal years. There are two major health concerns related to the hormonal changes occurring around the time of menopause—an increased incidence of osteoporosis and coronary heart disease.

Osteoporosis

Osteoporosis is a major health problem in Western societies. Its major complications—fractures, especially of the spine, neck of the femur, and wrist—are associated with a high morbidity and mortality. Diagnostic criteria have been established by the World Health Organization based on bone mineral density (BMD) from dual-energy X-ray absorptiometry[104] (Table 43.5) as well as according to fracture history.

To reduce the risk of osteoporosis, women need to acquire as much bone mass as possible prior to menopause and reduce the rate at which bone is lost after menopause. Women attain their peak bone mass during the second decade of life. From then until the time of menopause, there is a very slow rate of bone loss. This is accelerated at menopause, and for a few years following the menopause the rate of bone loss may be as high as 5% per year. Later, the rate of loss slows. Decreasing the risk of falling substantially reduces the likelihood of fracture (page 928).[105]

Maximizing bone mass

The greater the bone mineral content at the time of peak bone mass, the more bone an individual can afford to lose. Thus, the period of early adolescence is a window of opportunity to maximize bone mass. While genetic factors are an important contributor to peak bone mass, there are a number of ways in which women can maximize their bone mass.

Animal studies have demonstrated that bone responds best to activities that generate high strain magnitudes, high strain rates, and strains that are different to what the bone is normally accustomed to. Fewer loading cycles are needed and better responses are gained if the loading bout is broken up with rest

Table 43.5 Diagnostic criteria for osteoporosis

Classification	Dual-energy X-ray absorptiometry result
Normal	BMD within 1 standard deviation (SD) below the mean of young adults (T score: > –1)
Osteopenia	BMD between 1 and 2.5 SD below the mean of young adults (T score: –1 to –2.5)
Osteoporosis	BMD more than 2.5 SD below the mean of young adults (T score: < –2.5)
Severe or established osteoporosis	BMD more than 2.5 SD below the mean of young adults plus one or more fragility fractures

BMD = bone mineral density

intervals in between.[106] Thus, a variety of weight-bearing, high-impact activities should be encouraged (Table 43.6). Even modest amounts of jump training[107] incorporated into the school curriculum can have beneficial effects on bone density.[108] Based on the principle of breaking the load up into smaller bouts, 10 jumps three times a day when the school bell rang was found to improve bone density.[108] Non-weight-bearing exercise such as swimming or cycling has not been shown to improve bone mass.[109]

The effects of exercise on bone appear to be maximized with adequate calcium intake. In adolescents, exercise together with calcium supplementation was more effective than exercise alone.[110, 111] The period from early childhood to young adulthood is important for calcium intake. It is recommended that a daily intake of 1200 mg of calcium be consumed during that time.

Excessive exercise associated with energy imbalance and menstrual irregularity may have a negative effect on bone mass as discussed previously (page 916). Lengthy periods of bed rest should be avoided if possible. Loss of bone mass associated with bed rest is approximately 4% per month. Reversal of this bone loss takes a relatively long period of time.

Minimizing bone loss

The second principle of prevention of osteoporosis is to reduce the rate at which bone is lost after menopause. As bone is lost more rapidly in the years immediately after menopause, it is important to institute measures to reduce the loss of bone prior to and at the time of menopause. A variety of moderate-impact exercises and strength training reduces the rate of loss of bone mass in the postmenopausal period[113, 114] even in those with low bone density.[115] Walking programs of up to a year have generally not been effective in preventing bone loss in healthy ambulant individuals. This is not surprising, as walking does not impart high loading forces onto bone nor does it represent a unique loading stimulus. However, this does not exclude the possibility that long-term habitual walking for many years helps to preserve bone mass. (Exercise guidelines are shown in Table 43.6.)

Smoking increases bone loss. Moderate alcohol consumption is associated with increased bone mass; excessive alcohol should be avoided.

In postmenopausal women, greater calcium intake is needed to retain calcium balance because of increased urinary calcium losses associated with low estrogen levels.[116] The recommended daily intake of calcium in postmenopausal women is 1200 mg per day. A 2008 amendment to a 2004 Cochrane review states that calcium supplementation alone has only a small positive effect on bone density.[117] The data show a trend toward reduction in vertebral fractures, but it is unclear if calcium reduces the incidence of non-vertebral fractures.[117]

Vitamin D is also important for bone health. Vitamin D is obtained through the skin via sunlight and thus Vitamin D deficiency can be a problem in particular climates and in those whose exposure to sunlight is minimal.

 Oral vitamin D supplementation between 700 to 800 IU/day appears to reduce the risk of hip and non-vertebral fractures in ambulatory or institutionalized elderly persons.

Table 43.6 Recommendations for exercise prescription for bone health in children and adolescents, and in adults[112]

Exercise prescription	Children and adolescents	Adults
Mode	Impact activities (e.g. gymnastics, plyometrics, jumping) and moderate intensity resistance training; participation in sports that involve running and jumping (e.g. soccer, basketball)	Weight-bearing endurance activities (e.g. tennis, stair climbing, jogging at least intermittently during walking); activities that involve jumping and resistance training
Intensity	High in terms of bone loading forces; for safety reasons, resistance training should be <60% of 1 repetition maximum	Moderate to high in terms of bone loading forces
Frequency	At least 3 times per week	Weight-bearing endurance activities 3–5 times per week; resistance exercises 2–3 times per week
Duration	10–20 mins (2 times per day may be more effective)	30–60 mins per day of a combination of activities

An oral vitamin D dose of 400 IU/day is insufficient for fracture prevention.[118]

Reducing falls risk

Falling is an important risk factor for fracture and risk of falling increases rapidly with age.[119] One in three individuals over the age of 65 years will suffer a fall each year. Risk factors for falling include visual impairment, neurological and musculoskeletal disabilities, muscle weakness, certain medications, postural hypotension, poor balance, environmental hazards, cognitive impairment, and stumbling gait. Assessment and treatment of modifiable factors should be included to reduce the risk of osteoporotic fracture[105] including the implementation of proprioceptive and balance training combined with toning programs.

Exercise may reduce falls, because high levels of habitual activity in the elderly are associated with a lower prevalence of many of the risk factors.[121, 122] The types of exercise found to be effective for reducing falls and falls risk include balance and strengthening activities[123] and Tai Chi.[124] In older women with low bone mass, the beneficial effects of group-based exercises on fall risk profile persist at least one year without any formal exercise intervention.[125]

Resistance training exercises once or twice a week improve the performance of executive cognitive functions in senior women.[126] Executive cognitive functions are highly associated with mobility and the ability to perform instrumental activities of daily living.[126] Exercises are detailed in Chapter 60.

Pharmacotherapy

Various medications are effective in reducing fracture rates among osteoporotic women (and men).[127] Therapy for postmenopausal osteoporosis includes bisphosphonates,[128] selective estrogen receptor modulators (SERMS), and parathyroid hormone (PTH). Bisphosphonates halve the relative risk of osteoporotic fracture, including hip fracture. Selective estrogen modulators include raloxifene, which can prevent vertebral fractures. Adverse effects of raloxifene include hot flushes and muscle cramps. Thus, it is most popular among those women well beyond the menopause who may be less likely to have recurrence of hot flushes. Patients at risk for vitamin D deficiency or deficient on the basis of low 25-hydroxyvitamin D levels should be given oral vitamin D in the order of 800 IU daily.

Coronary heart disease

There appears to be an increased risk of coronary artery disease in women after menopause. In particular, the severity of coronary artery disease appears to increase, as is evidenced by an increase in the presentation of myocardial infarction and sudden death, but no change in the frequency of patients presenting with angina. This increase in coronary artery disease may be due to an increase in total plasma cholesterol level and a decrease in high-density lipoprotein cholesterol level.

Physical activity reduces the risk of coronary heart disease in postmenopausal women. As little as 30 minutes of moderate-intensity activity per day can reduce risk.

Protective mechanisms of physical activity include the regulation of body weight; the reduction of insulin resistance, hypertension, atherogenic dyslipidemia, and inflammation; and the enhancement of insulin sensitivity, glycemic control, and fibrinolytic and endothelial function.[129] Women with coronary artery disease, peripheral vascular disease, or diabetes mellitus must be considered individually when prescribing exercise and a pre-participation medical evaluation is recommended.[130]

The pelvic floor and continence issues

Pelvic floor dysfunction can influence a woman's participation and performance in sport throughout the lifespan. Pelvic pain can be caused by many systems, including gynecological, gastrointestinal, neuropathic, vascular, urological, and orthopedic. Pain may be felt in the perineum, lower abdomen, groin, coccygeal or sacroiliac joint regions, and may refer into the low back or thighs. Other symptoms may include dyspareunia (painful intercourse), urinary frequency and urgency, urinary stress incontinence, or changes in bowel movements. Many conditions affecting the pelvis result in increased tone of the pelvic floor musculature (e.g. vulvar vestibulitis, vulvodynia), while others involve a lowering in tone, or relaxing, of the pelvic floor musculature (e.g. obesity, pregnancy). Hormonal changes with age lead to genital atrophy as well as loss of pelvic floor muscle tone and strength. Weakening of the vaginal walls may permit prolapse of the urethra, bladder, uterus, or rectum. Weakness can also result in stress urinary incontinence.

Continence

Two of the more common types of incontinence include urge incontinence, and stress incontinence, and it is not uncommon to have both. Factors that can lead to incontinence include hormonal changes, weakness of the pelvic floor and abdominal musculature, bladder dysfunction, prolapse, pregnancy, and incorrect lifting habits including the Valsalva maneuver. There is a positive correlation between incontinence and the number of vaginal deliveries a woman has had.

Stress incontinence typically involves a smaller amount of involuntary leakage of the bladder associated with activities of strain such as coughing, sneezing, or laughing. Changes associated with menopause commonly lead to development of stress incontinence.[131]

Stress urinary incontinence is a not uncommon problem for the female athlete, even in younger women where 28% of nulliparous athletes (average age 19 years) reported episodes of incontinence during their sport, most commonly in high-impact activities[131, 132]

Urge incontinence is somewhat less prevalent and involves larger amounts of leakage associated with a strong urge and inadequate ability to prevent subsequent voiding of the bladder.

Pelvic floor exercises

Exercises can be prescribed to improve pelvic floor strength, endurance, and motor control. Physiotherapy, including therapeutic exercise prescription, is recommended in the case of mild (Stage 1 or 2) prolapse and, through appropriate intervention, surgery may be avoided. Exercises are also indicated following childbirth and for the treatment of weakness resulting in back or pelvic pain, or incontinence. Depending on the complexity of the individual's condition, consider referring to a physiotherapist with an extended scope of practice in women's health.[107]

Exercises commonly target improved function of both pelvic floor and abdominal (transversus abdominis and diaphragm) muscles. It is important to ensure that the exercises are done correctly, as it is common for people with poor control of these muscles to attempt to compensate with strategies such as Valsalva maneuver (breath holding or forceful increase in intra-abdominal pressure) which can have detrimental effects on their rehabilitation.

Exercises should involve a combination of sustained holds for endurance, and quick contractions and relaxations for strength, timing, and control. Exercises are easiest to initiate in the supine position, with a gradual progression to sitting, standing, and functional/sport-related exercises.

Exercise guidelines
Aerobic fitness

For many years aerobic fitness was thought to steadily decrease with age. It was also thought that this decrease was accelerated at the onset of menopause. It now appears that any decrease in aerobic fitness is related more to a decrease in activity than age. Postmenopausal women are able to increase their aerobic fitness as measured by VO_2max. The less fit the woman is prior to commencement of exercise, the greater the gain in aerobic fitness.

Women should be encouraged to continue, resume, or commence exercise in the postmenopausal period. For those wishing to commence an exercise program, a comprehensive pre-exercise evaluation is necessary. A thorough history and examination should be performed, paying particular attention to cardiovascular risk factors. Blood measurements of hemoglobin, glucose, electrolyte, and cholesterol levels may also be performed. A graded exercise ECG/EKG should be performed prior to commencing an exercise program in the presence of abnormal symptoms (e.g. chest pain) or cardiovascular risk factors (e.g. family history).

It is important to tailor the exercise for the individual, taking into consideration fitness level, associated medical problems, and, most importantly, individual enjoyment (see also Chapter 16). The American College of Sports Medicine (ACSM) position stands on exercise and physical activity for older adults[133] and exercise and osteoporosis[112] provide information about exercise prescription in this age group.

Exercise involving large muscle groups, such as walking, swimming, cycling, or dancing, is recommended together with balance exercises. Some form of weight-bearing exercises should be included. For a positive health benefit, exercise should be performed between three and five times per week for a period of 30 minutes each. The individual should aim to attain a heart rate equivalent to 70% of the maximum heart rate, which can be estimated by subtracting their age from 220. For individuals with known cardiovascular conditions, maximum heart rate should be obtained from a graded exercise stress test, and intensity of aerobic exercise should be determined on an individual basis according to ACSM guidelines and under the recommendations of their monitoring specialist.

Progressive strength training is also important to prevent the muscle weakness that is a universal characteristic of advancing age. Given an adequate training stimulus, older women (and men) show similar or greater strength gains as a result of strength training compared with young individuals.[135] Each workout should consist of up to 15 repetitions of 8 to 10 different exercises that train the major muscle groups. Sets of one to two can be performed, two or three times per week. The weight lifted should be up to 85% of one repetition maximum.[136, 137] An appropriate warm-up and warm-down should be performed, and attention should be paid to good quality shoes and equipment as well as personal safety.

Risks of exercise

The main concern of exercise in this age group is cardiovascular disorders, such as angina, myocardial infarction, and sudden death. Careful clinical assessment is required prior to the commencement of an exercise program.[138] The patient must be counseled to cease activity immediately and report to her doctor if any abnormal symptoms such as chest pain, irregular heart beats, dizziness, shortness of breath, or excessive fatigue should occur (Chapter 49). In many cases, people who have a serious cardiovascular episode (e.g. myocardial infarction) while exercising have ignored previous symptoms.

REFERENCES

1. Abramovitz BA, Birch LL. Five-year-old girls' ideas about dieting are predicted by their mothers' dieting. *J Am Diet Assoc* 2000;100(10):1157–63.

2. Wang Q J, Alen M, Nicholson P et al. Growth patterns at distal radius and tibial shaft in pubertal girls: a 2-year longitudinal study. *J Bone Miner Res* 2005;20(6):954–61.

3. Bailey DA, Heather AD, McKay HA et al. Calcium accretion in girls and boys during puberty: a longitudinal analysis. *J Bone Miner Res* 2000;15(11): 2245–50.

4. Bailey DA, Wedge JH, McCulloch RG et al. Epidemiology of fractures of the distal end of the radius in children as associated with growth. *J Bone Joint Surg Am* 1989;71A(8):1225–31.

5. Faulkner RA, McCulloch RG, Fyke SL et al. Comparison of areal and estimated volumetric bone density values between older men and women. *Osteoporosis Int* 1995;5(4):271–5.

6. Torstveit MK, Sundgot-Borgen J. Participation in leanness sports but not training volume is associated with menstrual dysfunction: a national survey of 1276 elite athletes and controls. *Br J Sports Med* 2005;39(3):141–7.

7. Thomis M, Claessens AL, Lefevre J et al. Adolescent growth spurts in female gymnasts. *J Pediatr* 2005;146(2):239–44.

8. Warren MP, Brooks-Gunn J, Fox RP et al. Osteopenia in exercise-associated amenorrhea using ballet dancers as a model: a longitudinal study. *J Clin Endocrinol Metab* 2002;87(7):3162–8.

9. Bennell KL, Malcolm SA, Thomas SA et al. Risk factors for stress fractures in track and field athletes – a twelve-month prospective study. *Am J Sports Med* 1996;24(6):810–18.

10. Loud KJ, Gordon CM, Micheli LJ et al. Correlates of stress fractures among preadolescent and adolescent girls. *Pediatrics* 2005;115(4):e399–406.

11. Frankovich RJ, Lebrun CM. Menstrual cycle, contraception, and performance. *Clin Sports Med* 2000;19(2):251–71.

12. Janse de Jonge XA. Effects of the menstrual cycle on exercise performance. *Sports Med* 2003;33(11):833–51.

13. Bryant M, Cassidy A, Hill C et al. Effect of consumption of soy isoflavones on behavioural, somatic and affective symptoms in women with premenstrual syndrome. *Br J Nutr* 2005;93(5):731–9.

14. Wyatt KM, Dimmock PW, O'Brien PM. Selective serotonin reuptake inhibitors for premenstrual syndrome. *Cochrane Database Syst Rev* 2009;4(2): CD001396.

15. Yonkers KA, Brown C, Pearlstein TB et al. Efficacy of a new low-dose oral contraceptive with drospirenone in premenstrual dysphoric disorder. *Obstet Gynecol* 2005;106(3):492–501.

16. Steiner M, Hirschberg AL, Bergeron R et al. Luteal phase dosing with paroxetine controlled release (CR) in the treatment of premenstrual dysphoric disorder. *Am J Obste Gynecol* 2005;193(2):352–60.

17. Benagiano G, Carrara S, Filippi V. Safety, efficacy and patient satisfaction with continuous daily administration of levonorgestrel/ethinylestradiol oral contraceptives. *Patient Prefer Adherence* 2009;3: 131–43.

18. Krishnan S, Kiley J. The lowest-dose, extended-cycle combined oral contraceptive pill with continuous ethinyl estradiol in the United States: a review of the literature on ethinyl estradiol 20 µg/levonorgestrel 100 µg + ethinyl estradiol 10 µg. *Int J Womens Health* 2010;2:235–9.

19. Wanichsetakul P, Kamudhamas A, Watanaruangkovit P et al. Bone mineral density at various anatomic bone sites in women receiving combined oral contraceptives and depot-medroxyprogesterone acetate for contraception. *Contraception* 2002;65(6):407–10.

20. Rome E, Ziegler J, Secic M et al. Bone biochemical markers in adolescent girls using either depot medroxyprogesterone acetate or an oral contraceptive. *J Pediatr Adoles Gynecol* 2004;17(6):373–7.

21. De Souza MJ. Menstrual disturbances in athletes: a focus on luteal phase defects. *Med Sci Sports Exerc* 2003;35(9):1553–63.

22. Prior JC, Vigna YM. Ovulation disturbances and exercise training. *Clin Obstet Gynecol* 1991;34(1): 180–90.

23. Williams NI, Bullen BA, McArthur JW et al. Effects of short-term strenuous endurance exercise upon corpus luteum function. *Med Sci Sports Exerc* 1999;31(7): 949–58.

24. Petit MA, Prior JC, Barr SI. Running and ovulation positively change cancellous bone in premenopausal women. *Med Sci Sports Exerc* 1999;31(6):780–7.

25. Malina RM, Spirduso WW, Tate C et al. Age at menarche and selected menstrual characteristics in athletes at different competitive levels and in different sports. *Med Sci Sports Exerc* 1978;10(3):218–22.

26. Nattiv A, Puffer JC, Green GA. Lifestyles and health risks of collegiate athletes: a multi-center study. *Clin J Sport Med* 1997;7(4):262–72.

C

27. Kaiserauer S, Snyder AC, Sleeper M et al. Nutritional, physiological, and menstrual status of distance runners. *Med Sci Sports Exerc* 1989;21(2):120–5.

28. Chan JL, Mantzoros CS. Role of leptin in energy-deprivation states: normal human physiology and clinical implications for hypothalamic amenorrhoea and anorexia nervosa. *Lancet* 2005;366(9479):74–85.

29. De Souza MJ, Williams NI. Beyond hypoestrogenism in amenorrheic athletes: energy deficiency as a contributing factor for bone loss. *Curr Sports Med Rep* 2005;4(1):38–44.

30. Cann CE, Martin MC, Genant HK et al. Decreased spinal mineral-content in amenorrheic women. *JAMA* 1984;251(5):626–9.

31. Drinkwater BL, Nilson K, Chesnut CH 3rd et al. Bone mineral content of amenorrheic and eumenorrheic athletes. *N Engl J Med* 1984;311:277–81.

32. Linnell SL, Stager JM, Blue PW et al. Bone mineral content and menstrual regularity in female runners. *Med Sci Sports Exerc* 1984;16(4):343–8.

33. Marcus R, Cann C, Madvig P et al. Menstrual function and bone mass in elite women distance runners. Endocrine and metabolic features. *Ann Intern Med* 1985;102(2):158–63.

34. Rutherford OM. Spine and total body bone mineral density in amenorrheic endurance athletes. *J Appl Physiol* 1993;74(6):2904–8.

35. Micklesfield LK, Lambert EV, Fataar AB et al. Bone mineral density in mature, premenopausal ultramarathon runners. *Med Sci Sports Exerc* 1995;27(5):688–96.

36. Tomten SE, Falch A, Birkeland KI et al. Bone mineral density and menstrual irregularities. A comparative study on cortical and trabecular bone structures in runners with alleged normal eating behavior. *Int J Sports Med* 1998;19(2):92–7.

37. Pettersson U, Stålnacke BM, Ahlénius GM et al. Low bone mass density at multiple skeletal sites, including the appendicular skeleton in amenorrheic runners. *Calcif Tissue Int* 1999;64(2):117–25.

38. To WW, Wong MW, Lam IY. Bone mineral density differences between adolescent dancers and non-exercising adolescent females. *J Pediatr Adolesc Gynecol* 2005;18(5):337–42.

39. Morris FL, Payne WR, Wark JD. The impact of intense training on endogenous estrogen and progesterone concentrations and bone mineral acquisition in adolescent rowers. *Osteoporosis Int* 1999;10(5):361–8.

40. Robinson TL, Snowharter C, Taaffe DR et al. Gymnasts exhibit higher bone mass than runners despite similar prevalence of amenorrhea and oligomenorrhea. *J Bone Miner Res* 1995;10(1):26–35.

41. Nattiv A, Loucks AB, Manore MM et al. American College of Sports Medicine position stand. The female athlete triad. *Med Sci Sports Exerc* 2007;39(10):1867–82.

42. Torstveit MK, Sundgot-Borgen J. The female athlete triad exists in both elite athletes and controls. *Med Sci Sports Exerc* 2005;37(9):1449–59.

43. Myerson M, Gutin B, Warren MP et al. Total body bone density in amenorrheic runners. *Obstet Gynecol* 1992;79(6):973–8.

44. Hetland ML, Haarbo J, Christiansen C et al. Running induces menstrual disturbances but bone mass is unaffected, except in amenorrheic women. *Am J Med* 1993;95(1):53–60.

45. Zanker CL. Bone metabolism in exercise associated amenorrhoea: the importance of nutrition. *Br J Sports Med* 1999;33(4):228–9.

46. Zanker CL, Swaine IL. Relation between bone turnover, oestradiol, and energy balance in women distance runners. *Br J Sports Med* 1998;32(2):167–71.

47. Hergenroeder AC. Bone mineralization, hypothalamic amenorrhea, and sex steroid therapy in female adolescents and young adults. *J Pediatr* 1995;126(5):683–89.

48. Hergenroeder AC, Smith EOB, Shypailo R et al. Bone mineral changes in young women with hypothalamic amenorrhea treated with oral contraceptives, medroxyprogesterone, or placebo over 12 months. *Am J Obstet Gynecol* 1997;176(5):1017–25.

49. Rickenlund A, Carlstrom K, Ekblom B et al. Effects of oral contraceptives on body composition and physical performance in female athletes. *J Clin Endocrinol Metab* 2004;89(9):4364–70.

50. Braam LA, Knapen MH, Geusens P et al. Factors affecting bone loss in female endurance athletes. *Am J Sports Med* 2003;31(6):889–95.

51. Prince RL, Dick I, Devine A et al. The effects of menopause and age on calcitropic hormones: a cross-sectional study of 655 healthy women aged 35 to 90. *J Bone Miner Res* 1995;10(6):835–42.

52. Stacey E, Korkia P, Hukkanen MV et al. Decreased nitric oxide levels and bone turnover in amenorrheic athletes with spinal osteopenia. *J Clin Endocrinol Metab* 1998;83(9):3056–61.

53. Zanker CL, Swaine IL. Bone turnover in amenorrhoeic and eumenorrhoeic women distance runners. *Scand J Med Sci Sports* 1998;8(1):20–6.

54. Thissen J-P, Ketelslegers J-M, Underwood LE. Nutritional regulation of the insulin-like growth factors. *Endocr Rev* 1994;15(1):80–101.

55. De Souza MJ, Miller BE, Loucks AB et al. High frequency of luteal phase deficiency and anovulation in recreational women runners: blunted elevation in follicle-stimulating hormone observed during luteal-follicular transition. *J Clin Endocrinol Metab* 1998;83(12):4220–32.

56. Ihle R, Loucks AB. Dose response relationships between energy availability and bone turnover in young exercising women. *J Bone Miner Res* 2004;19(8): 1231–40.

57. Carbon R, Sambrook PN, Deakin V et al. Bone-density of elite female athletes with stress-fractures. *Med J Aust* 1990;153(7):373–6.

58. Frusztajer NT, Dhuper S, Warren MP et al. Nutrition and the incidence of stress fractures in ballet dancers. *Am J Clin Nutr* 1990;51(5):779–83.

59. Myburgh KH, Hutchins J, Fataar AB et al. Low bone density is an etiologic factor for stress fractures in athletes. *Ann Intern Med* 1990;113(10):754–9.

60. Kadel NJ, Teitz CC, Kronmal RA. Stress fractures in ballet dancers. *Am J Sports Med* 1992;20(4):445–9.

61. Tomten SE. Prevalence of menstrual dysfunction in Norwegian long-distance runners participating in the Oslo Marathon games. *Scand J Med Sci Sports* 1996;6(3):164–71.

62. Vinther A, Kanstrup IL, Christiansen E et al. Exercise-induced rib stress fractures: influence of reduced bone mineral density. *Scand J Med Sci Sports* 2005;15(2): 95–9.

63. Rosetta L, Harrison GA, Read GF. Ovarian impairments of female recreational distance runners during a season of training. *Ann Hum Biol* 1998;25(4):345–57.

64. Drinkwater BL, Nilson K, Ott S et al. Bone mineral density after resumption of menses in amenorrheic athletes. *JAMA* 1986;256(3):380–2.

65. Drinkwater BL, Bruemner B, Chesnut CH. Menstrual history as a determinant of current bone density in young athletes. *JAMA* 1990;263(4):545–8.

66. Keen AD, Drinkwater BL. Irreversible bone loss in former amenorrheic athletes. *Osteoporosis Int* 1997;7(4):311–15.

67. Micklesfield LK, Reyneke L, Fataar A et al. Long-term restoration of deficits in bone mineral density is inadequate in premenopausal women with prior menstrual irregularity. *Clin J Sport Med* 1998;8(3): 155–63.

68. Loucks AB. Energy availability, not body fatness, regulates reproductive function in women. *Ex Sport Sci Rev* 2003;31(3):144–8.

69. Dusterberg B, Ellman H, Muller U et al. A three year clinical investigation into efficacy, cycle control and tolerability of a new low-dose monophasic oral contraceptive containing gestodene. *Gynecol Endocrinol* 1996;10(1):33–9.

70. Rosenberg M. Weight change with oral contraceptive use and during the menstrual cycle: results of daily measurements. *Contraception* 1998;58(6):345–9.

71. Lynch NJ, Nimmo MA. Effects of menstrual cycle phase and oral contraceptive use on intermittent exercise. *Eur J Appl Physiol* 1998;78(6):565–72.

72. De Bruyn-Prevost P, Masset C, Sturbois X. Physiological response from 18–25 years women to aerobic and anaerobic physical fitness tests at different periods during the menstrual cycle. *J Sports Med Phys Fitness* 1984;24(2):144–8.

73. Lebrun CM. Effect of the different phases of the menstrual cycle and oral contraceptives on athletic performance. *Sports Med* 1993;16(6):400–30.

74. Scholes D, LaCroix AZ, Ichikawa LE et al. Change in bone mineral density among adolescent women using and discontinuing depot medroxyprogesterone acetate contraception. *Arch Pediatr Adolesc Med* 2005;159(2):139–44.

75. Johnson C, Powers PS, Dick R. Athletes and eating disorders: the National Collegiate Athletic Association study. *Int J Eat Disord* 1999;26(2):179–88.

76. Grinspoon S, Miller K, Coyle C et al. Severity of osteopenia in estrogen-deficient women with anorexia nervosa and hypothalamic amenorrhea. *J Clin Endocrinol Metab* 1999;84(6):2049–55.

77. Soyka LA, Grinspoon S, Levitsky LL et al. The effects of anorexia nervosa on bone metabolism in female adolescents. *J Clin Endocrinol Metab* 1999;84(12): 4489–96.

78. Harmon KG, Ireland ML. Gender differences in noncontact anterior cruciate ligament injuries. *Clin Sports Med* 2000;19(2):287–302.

79. Hewett TE, Zazulak BT, Myer GD. Effects of the menstrual cycle on anterior cruciate ligament injury risk. *Am J Sports Med* 2007;35(4):659–68.

80. Adachi N, Nawata K, Maeta M et al. Relationship of the menstrual cycle phase to anterior cruciate ligament injuries in teenaged female athletes. *Arch Orth Traum Surg* 2008;128(5):473–8.

81. Gho S, Steele J, Munro B. Is bra discomfort a barrier to

exercise for breast cancer patients? *Support Care Cancer* 2010;18(6):735–41.

82. McGhee DE, Power BM, Steele JR. Does deep water running reduce exercise-induced breast discomfort? *Br J Sports Med* 2007;41(12):879–83.

83. Physical Activity Readiness Medical Examination for Pregnancy [PARmed-X for pregnancy]. *Canadian Society for Exercise Physiology* 2002, www.csep.ca/forms.asp, viewed Feb 1, 2011.

84. Hartman S, Bung P. Physical exercise during pregnancy—physiological changes and recommendations. *J Perinat Med* 1999;27(3):204–15.

85. Clapp JF 3rd, Little KD, Capeless EL. Fetal heart-rate response to sustained recreational exercise. *Am J Obstet Gynecol* 1993;168(1):198–206.

86. Bung P, Huch R, Huch A. Maternal and fetal heart rate patterns: a pregnant athlete during training and laboratory exercise tests; a case report. *Eur J Obstet Gynecol Reprod Biol* 1991;39(1):59–62.

87. Clapp JF 3rd, Capeless EL. Neonatal morphometrics after endurance exercise during pregnancy. *Am J Obstet Gynecol* 1990;163(6 Part 1):1805–11.

88. Rungee J. Low back pain during pregnancy. *Orthopedics* 1993;16(12):1339–44.

89. Elden H, Ladfors L, Olsen MF et al. Effects of acupuncture and stabilising exercises as adjunct to standard treatment in pregnant women with pelvic girdle pain: randomised single blind controlled trial. *BMJ* 2005;330(7494):761.

90. Nilsson-Wikmar L, Holm K, Oijerstedt R et al. Effect of three different physical therapy treatments on pain and activity in pregnant women with pelvic girdle pain: a randomized clinical trial with 3, 6, and 12 months follow-up postpartum. *Spine* 2005;30(8):850–6.

91. Santos IA, Stein R, Fuchs SC et al. Aerobic exercise and submaximal functional capacity in overweight pregnant women: a randomized trial. *Obstet Gynecol* 2005;106(2):243–9

92. Hartmann S, Bung P. Physical exercise during pregnancy—physiological considerations and recommendations. *J Perinat Med* 1999;27(3):204–15.

93. Dempsey FC, Butler FL, Williams FA. No need for a pregnant pause: physical activity may reduce the occurrence of gestational diabetes mellitus and preeclampsia. *Exerc Sport Sci Rev* 2005;33(3):141–9.

94. Horsely K. Fitness in the child-bearing years. In: Sapsford R, Bullock-Saxton J, Markwell S, eds. *Women's health. A textbook for physiotherapists*. London: WB Saunders, 1998:168–91.

95. Weissgerber TL, Wolfe LA, Davies GAL. The role of

regular physical activity in pre-eclampsia prevention. *Med Sci Sports Exerc* 2004;36(12):2024–31.

96. ACOG Committee opinion. Number 267, January 2002: exercise during pregnancy and the postpartum period. *Obstet Gynecol* 2002;99(1):171–3.

97. American College of Sports Medicine. *ACSM's Guidelines for exercise testing and prescription*. 7th ed. Hagerstown, MD: Lipoincott Williams & Wilkins, 2005.

98. Carl De Crée. Safety guidelines for exercise during pregnancy. *Lancet* 1998;351(9119):1889–90.

99. Davies GAL, Wolfe LA, Mottola MF et al. Joint SOGC/CSEP Clinical Practice Guideline: exercise in pregnancy and the postpartum period. *Can J Appl Physiol* 2003;28(3):329–41.

100. Camporesi EM. Diving and pregnancy. *Semin Perinatol* 1996;20(4):292–302.

101. Clapp JF 3rd. Exercise during pregnancy. A clinical update. *Clin Sports Med* 2000;19(2):273–86.

102. Jensen GM, Moore LG. The effect of high altitude and other risk factors on birthweight: independent or interactive effects? *Am J Public Health* 1997;87(6):1003–7.

103. Barakat R, Ruiz JR, Lucia A. Exercise during pregnancy and risk of maternal anaemia: a randomised controlled trial. *Br J Sports Med* 2009;43(12):954–6.

104. Kanis JA, Melton LJ, Christiansen C et al. The diagnosis of osteoporosis. *J Bone Miner Res* 1994;9(8):1137–41.

105. Jarvinen TLN, Sievanen H, Khan KM et al. Shifting the focus in fracture prevention from osteoporosis to falls. *BMJ* 2008;336(7636):124–6.

106. Turner CH, Robling AG. Designing exercise regimens to increase bone strength. *Exerc Sport Sci Rev* 2003;31(1):45–50.

107. Kato T, Terashima T, Yamashita T et al. Effect of low-repetition jump training on bone mineral density in young women. *J Appl Physiol* 2006;100(3):839–43.

108. McKay HA, MacLean L, Petit M et al. "Bounce at the bell": a novel program of short bouts of exercise improves proximal femur bone mass in early pubertal children. *Br J Sports Med* 2005;39(8):521–6.

109. Hind K, Burrows M. Weight-bearing exercise and bone mineral accrual in children and adolescents: a review of controlled trials. *Bone* 2007;40(1):14–27.

110. Courteix D, Jaffre C, Lespessailles E et al. Cumulative effects of calcium supplementation and physical activity on bone accretion in premenarchal children: a double-blind randomised placebo-controlled trial. *Int J Sports Med* 2005;26(5):332–8.

111. Iuliano-Burns S, Saxon L, Naughton G et al. Regional specificity of exercise and calcium during skeletal growth in girls: a randomized controlled trial. *J Bone Miner Res* 2003;18(1):156–62.

112. Kohrt WM, Bloomfield SA, Little KD et al. American College of Sports Medicine. Position stand: physical activity and bone health. *Med Sci Sports Exerc* 2004;36(11):1985–96.

113. Kerr D, Morton A, Dick I et al. Exercise effects on bone mass in postmenopausal women are site-specific and load-dependent. *J Bone Miner Res* 1996;11(2):218–25.

114. Engelke K, Kemmler W, Lauber D et al. Exercise maintains bone density at spine and hip EFOPS: a 3-year longitudinal study in early postmenopausal women. *Osteoporosis Int* 2006;17(1):133–42.

115. Korpelainen R, Keinänen-Kiukaanniemi S, Heikkinen J et al. Effect of impact exercise on bone mineral density in elderly women with low BMD: a population-based randomized controlled 30-month intervention. *Osteoporosis Int* 2006;17(1):109–18.

116. Delaney MF. Strategies for the prevention and treatment of osteoporosis during early postmenopause. *Am J Obstet Gynecol* 2006;194 (2, Supplement 1):S12–23.

117. Shea B, Wells G, Cranney A et al. Calcium supplementation on bone loss in postmenopausal women. *Cochrane Database Syst Rev* 2008(1): CD004526.

118. Bischoff-Ferrari HA, Willett WC, Wong JB et al. Fracture prevention with vitamin D supplementation – a meta-analysis of randomized controlled trials. *JAMA* 2005;293(18):2257–64.

119. Ngugyen TV, Eisman JA, Kelly PJ et al. Risk factors for osteoporotic fractures in elderly men. *Am J Epidemiol* 1996;144(3):255–63.

120. Kannus P, Sievänen H, Palvanen M et al. Prevention of falls and consequent injuries in elderly people. *Lancet* 2005;366(9500):1885–93.

121. Henderson NK, White CP, Eisman JA. The roles of exercise and fall risk reduction in the prevention of osteoporosis. *Endocrinol Metab Clin North Am* 1998;27(2):369–87.

122. Gillespie LD, Gillespie WJ, Robertson MC et al. Interventions for preventing falls in elderly people. *Cochrane Database Syst Rev* 2003(4):CD000340.

123. Liu-Ambrose T, Khan KM, Eng JJ et al. Resistance and agility training reduce fall risk in women aged 75 to 85 with low bone mass: a 6-month randomized, controlled trial. *J Am Geriatr Soc* 2004;52(5):657–65.

124. Li F, Harmer P, Fisher KJ et al. Tai Chi: improving functional balance and predicting subsequent falls in older persons. *Med Sci Sports Exerc* 2004;36(12): 2046–52.

125. Liu-Ambrose TYL, Khan KM, Eng JJ et al. The beneficial effects of group-based exercises on fall risk profile and physical activity persist 1 year postintervention in older women with low bone mass: follow-up after withdrawal of exercise. *J Am Geriatr Soc* 2005;53(10):1767–73.

126. Liu-Ambrose T, Nagamatsu LS, Graf P et al. Resistance training and executive functions: a 12-month randomized controlled trial. *Arch Intern Med* 2010;170(2):170–8.

127. Häuselmann HJ, Rizzoli R. A comprehensive review of treatments for postmenopausal osteoporosis. *Osteoporosis Int* 2003;14(1):2–12.

128. Papapoulos SE, Quandt SA, Liberman UA et al. Meta-analysis of the efficacy of alendronate for the prevention of hip fractures in postmenopausal women. *Osteoporosis Int* 2005;16(5):468–74.

129. Bassuk SS, Manson JE. Epidemiological evidence for the role of physical activity in reducing risk of type 2 diabetes and cardiovascular disease. *J Appl Physiol* 2005;99(3):1193–204.

130. Armen J, Smith BW. Exercise considerations in coronary artery disease, peripheral vascular disease, and diabetes mellitus. *Clin Sports Med* 2003;22(1): 123–33.

131. Bo K. Urinary incontinence, pelvic floor dysfunction, exercise and sport. *Sports Med* 2004;34(7):451–64.

132. Nygaard IE, Thompson FL, Svengalis SL et al. Urinary incontinence in elite nulliparous athletes. *Obstet Gynecol* 1994;84(2):183–7.

133. American College of Sports Medicine. Position stand: exercise and physical activity for older adults. *Med Sci Sports Exerc* 1998;30(6):992–1008.

134. Jarvinen TL, Sievanen H, Kannus P et al. The true cost of pharmacological disease prevention *BMJ* 2011; 342:d2175.

135. Miszko TA, Cress ME. A lifetime of fitness: exercise in the perimenopausal and postmenopausal woman. *Clin Sports Med* 2000;19(2):215–32.

136. Evans WJ. Exercise training guidelines for the elderly. *Med Sci Sports Exerc* 1999;31(1):12–17.

137. Feigenbaum MS, Pollock ML. Prescription of resistance training for health and disease. *Med Sci Sports Exerc* 1999;31(1):38–45.

138. Campbell AJ. Assertive screening: health checks prior to exercise programmes in older people. *Br J Sports Med* 2009;43(1):5.

Chapter 44

The older person who exercises

with JACK TAUNTON, WENDY COOK, CALLISTA HAGGIS, and JACQUELINE CLOSE

We don't stop playing because we grow old; we grow old because we stop playing.
George Bernard Shaw

Increasing numbers of older people perform regular physical activity that ranges from recreational walking and swimming or lawn bowls, to vigorous and/or competitive activity. The Veterans or Masters sports movements have grown rapidly and now provide competition at local, national, and international levels for an increasing number of older athletes. Variability in health and functional status among those of a similar age makes defining "older" by chronology difficult.

The American College of Sports Medicine and the American Heart Association use 65+ or 50–64 with clinically significant chronic conditions and/or functional limitation to define the "older" person.[1]

While the cut-off point is relatively arbitrary, a prominent characteristic of relevance to older people and exercise is functional limitation. Physical limitations often prevent older people from engaging in vigorous high-intensity aerobic training.[1, 2] Health benefits are apparent with less intense forms of exercise and virtually all older adults are recommended to be physically active.[2]

This chapter focuses on:

- successful aging with the evidence for the considerable physiological and psychological benefits of exercise in the older person
- how to minimize certain risks associated with exercise for older people
- the potential interactions between medications commonly used by the elderly and exercise.

Exercise program prescription for older people is discussed in Chapter 60.

Successful aging

Physical activity benefits all body organs as well as the psyche.[3–6] Observational studies suggest that exercise and physical activity levels may have an important role in successful aging.

Definitions of "successful aging" vary among studies. Elements include longevity, as well as survival free of chronic disease, impaired physical and cognitive functioning, and incident disability.[7–9]

Midlife physical activity levels are inversely associated with survival and overall health status into old age.[8, 9] Other important health outcomes that impact on independence in old age (such as functional status and disability) are also linked with physical activity.[10–13]

Among older adults at risk for disability, exercise interventions improve physical performance and measures of mobility disability,[14] and benefits are sustained beyond the intervention period.[15] These findings raise the possibility that exercise even at moderate levels (in particular, avoiding sedentary behavior) may prevent or delay disability and improve survival into older age. Achieving meaningful health benefits for older adults may require a less intense exercise stimulus compared with the general population.[12]

The cardiovascular system

The most dramatic benefits of exercise are on the cardiovascular system.[16, 17] Exercise interventions in older people with coronary heart disease are associated with decreased morbidity, mortality, and symptoms, and reduced cardiac rehospitalizations.[18]

Numerous mechanisms may contribute to these benefits.[19] Increased demand on the myocardium improves oxygen utilization. Capillaries dilate and multiply to improve the delivery of oxygen and other nutrients to muscles. The myoglobin content of muscle is increased, thus improving the transfer of oxygen from the red blood cells to muscle cells. Inside the cell, the number of mitochondria increases, enhancing aerobic metabolism. There is also an increase in the glycogen storage sites of muscle. Exercise tends to lower the resting heart rate, and the resultant increased diastolic time allows improved coronary blood flow. Stroke volume increases.

Exercise also has an effect on blood lipid levels, raising levels of high-density lipoprotein cholesterol (the "cardioprotective" lipid) and lowering levels of low-density lipoprotein cholesterol. Exercise lowers blood pressure[12] and reduces obesity. A combination of these two factors, in addition to the reduction in cholesterol, decreases the risk of developing ischemic heart disease as well as the morbidity and mortality associated with the disease.

The respiratory system

Exercise as part of a pulmonary rehabilitation program improves physical status and quality of life in older people with chronic obstructive pulmonary disease.[20] Activity may increase the older person's exercise tolerance and produce the associated benefits of improved aerobic fitness.

Diabetes

Exercise in combination with dietary modification reduces the risk of developing type 2 diabetes across a wide age range. It may also improve blood sugar control in people with diabetes by decreasing insulin resistance, and may reduce the need for medication.[21]

Osteoarthritis

An exercise program may also be beneficial for older people with osteoarthritis by improving joint mobility and increasing muscle strength.[22]

Bone health and prevention of fall-related fractures

Resistance training and high-impact activities help maintain bone mass in the elderly.[23, 24] Exercise in the form of strength and balance training reduces an older person's risk of falling.[25, 40] The specially designed Otago Exercise Programme is a cost-effective way of reducing falls among community-dwelling older adults aged 65+.[41]

Psychological function

Along with the physical benefits of exercise, cognitive function, sleep, and mood patterns may also improve.[26, 27] The mechanisms by which exercise affects cognitive function are still being explored and include effects on insulin-like growth factor (IGF-I), which promotes neuronal growth, and the regulation of homocysteine, which prevents cognitive decline.[28] A review of randomized trials suggested that 6–12 months of regular resistance training or a combination of strength and balance training results in improved cognitive function for the elderly cohort.[28-30] Further investigations are necessary to gain a more detailed understanding of the relationship between different types of exercise (i.e. resistance and/or aerobic) and cognitive function.

Psychological benefits of exercise are also associated with muscle control and weight loss. Better physical health may lead to improvements in body image and reverse the older person's fear of activity.[31] Further, exercise reduces anxiety in older patients, especially in those recovering from illness. Exercise can lessen depressive symptoms[32] and perhaps even reduce the risk of developing depression.[33]

Risks of exercise in the older person

The risks associated with a sedentary lifestyle are well known. However, they are difficult to quantify and objectively compare to the risks associated with exercise in older populations. Underlying co-morbidity is often cited as a reason to preclude exercise despite the overwhelming evidence to support the benefits of exercise in many common chronic diseases.[1]

From a safety standpoint, clinicians prescribing exercise for older people are concerned that exercise may precipitate a significant cardiac event. Gill and colleagues have provided recommendations regarding precautions that may minimize the risk of serious adverse cardiac events among previously sedentary older persons who do not have symptomatic cardiovascular disease and are interested in starting an exercise program.[2] They argue, at a population level, that an overcautious perspective or policy will deter large numbers of older people from engaging in a program of exercise from which they stand to benefit.

Reducing the risks of exercise

Before starting an exercise program, older people should be encouraged to talk to a physician and undergo a physical examination where indicated.[34]

Contraindications to exercise outside of a monitored environment include:

- myocardial infarction within six months
- angina or physical signs and symptoms of congestive heart failure
- a resting systolic blood pressure of 200 mmHg or higher.

A simple test of cardiac capacity is to ask the patient to walk 15 m (50 ft) or climb a flight of stairs.[2] A resting ECG/EKG should be reviewed for new Q waves, ST segment depressions, or T-wave inversion. If the patient has no overt cardiovascular disease, and no other medical or orthopedic contraindications to exercise, he or she can begin a low-intensity exercise program as discussed below.[34] Adhering to the principles outlined in Chapter 9 reduces the risk of injury.

Exercise prescription for the older person

The inactive older person

For older adults who undertake no physical activity, the first goal of exercise prescription is simply to reduce their sitting time. Thus, an action plan might be to find engaging activities that reduce the amount of time spent watching television or other sedentary activity. Strategies may also involve creating more opportunities for brief physical activity. Exercises that are functional, task-specific, relevant to the individual, and incorporated into daily activities are best to consider.

Preliminary evidence of a "Lifestyle approach to reducing Falls through Exercise (LiFE)," which involves embedding balance and lower limb strength training in habitual daily routines, has shown benefit in terms of reducing recurrent falls.[35]

 Practical suggestions for the older person include parking further away at malls and shopping centers, taking the stairs instead of the elevator, or taking a 5- to 10-minute walk several times a day.

The aphorism "start low, go slow" applies in this population as it does in exercise prescription in general. The clinician should set easily attainable short-term goals and increase time spent performing moderate activities by no more than 5% per week. The eventual goal is to accumulate 30 minutes a day of moderately intense physical activity on most days of the week (see also Chapters 16 and 60) that includes a combination of aerobic, strength, and balance training.

The generally active older person

For older people who are generally active, begin by increasing the volume of aerobic exercise or resistance training. Aerobic exercises that are particularly attractive to older individuals are cycling on a stationary bicycle, brisk walking, swimming, and water aquatics. The person should warm up (e.g. slow walking) for 5 minutes and stretch slowly for 5–10 minutes before exercising at a moderate level—one at which a conversation can be easily maintained.

The person about to undertake resistance training should also perform a warm-up and stretch first. Free weights and commercially available equipment are suitable for the older person exercising. Proper breathing consists of exhaling during the lift for 2–4 seconds followed by inhaling during the lowering of the weight for 4–6 seconds, working through the entire range of motion (or as tolerated for those with arthritis). The Valsalva maneuver should be avoided, particularly in older people who are more prone to postural hypotension and syncope than their younger counterparts.

The lifts should be separated by 2 seconds of rest. The goal is to perform one or two sets of 8–15 repetitions per set with 1–2 minutes of rest between sets. The patient should aim to lift a weight that is 70–80% of a one repetition maximum (1RM) or the most that he or she can lift through a full range of motion at one time. The resistance should be increased no more frequently than monthly. Strength exercises should be followed by a cool-down and a stretch. Current evidence suggests that participants who undertake this type of program twice weekly or more obtain benefits. Only the very unfit benefit from a once-weekly program.[36]

The principles of follow-up and praise for progress, as outlined in the principles of exercise prescription (Chapter 16), apply particularly to older people, who may feel less confident about their capacity for activity.

Please also see Chapter 54 (for exercise prescription for neurological conditions) and Chapter 60 (for exercise prescription for various other conditions), which have relevance to the older person.

Interaction between medication and exercise in the older person

Many older people have at least one chronic medical condition, and many have multiple chronic conditions for which medication is warranted. As a result, many older people consume multiple medications. There are potential problems associated with exercise and some of these drugs.

Medications affecting the renin–angiotensin system

Drugs affecting the renin–angiotensin system (such as angiotensin-converting enzyme [ACE] inhibitors and angiotensin II receptor blockers) lower peripheral vascular resistance. They are widely used to treat hypertension, systolic heart failure, and chronic kidney disease.

These drugs are suitable for the hypertensive athlete as they do not limit maximal oxygen uptake. Although the risk of dehydration among young people may have been over-represented in recent years (Chapter 58), older people who are taking these medications may have an increased susceptibility to the effects of exercise-related dehydration. The vasodilator effect may combine with fluid losses to cause hypotension and dizziness.

Beta blockers

Beta blockers are used to treat hypertension, angina, heart failure, and cardiac dysrhythmias, as well as tremor and migraine; however, they may be less effective in older people than in middle-aged patients. These drugs are often prescribed after acute myocardial infarction.

Beta blockers reduce cardiac rate and output, and attenuate the normal physiological response to exercise. The lack of a tachycardia induced by exercise bothers some people—they dislike the absence of the "adrenalin surge." Older athletes who are taking beta blockers have a restricted exercise capacity, particularly in endurance events.

Adverse effects include postural hypotension, exacerbation of peripheral vascular disease, excessive tiredness, impotence, and hyperkalemia, as well as the potential of masking hypoglycemia in people with diabetes taking older nonselective agents.

Diuretics

Systematic reviews and clinical guidelines recommend thiazide diuretics as a first-line therapy for hypertension.[37, 38] Diuretics are also used in the treatment of heart failure and fluid retention to increase urinary excretion of excess salt and fluid.

Older athletes who exercise in warm-to-hot conditions and take diuretics are at a particular risk of dehydration. Less common adverse effects of thiazide diuretics include increased blood sugar levels[39] and increased uric acid levels, which can be sufficient to precipitate gout.

A combination of antihypertensive medication and vigorous exercise with associated dehydration may decrease the intravascular volume and cause postural hypotension, which may manifest itself as lightheadedness or fainting. Prevention includes maintaining adequate hydration and avoiding standing still immediately after exertion. Alternatively, other medications may be available.

By definition, diuretics lead to increased fluid excretion through the renal tract and the diuresis occurs in relatively close proximity to oral ingestion. Older exercise participants attending classes or undertaking exercise outdoors may wish to delay the intake of their diuretic until after exercise to avoid the need to urinate excessively. This should be undertaken in consultation with their medical practitioner.

Other cardiac drugs

Calcium-channel blockers and nitrates (glyceryl trinitrate/nitroglycerin) are used to treat hypertension and angina. They may impair cardiac output in exercise and cause peripheral vasodilatation, thus reducing performance. Peripheral venous pooling and the vasodilatation can lead to postural hypotension, particularly during the cool-down period of exercise. These adverse effects should, however, be weighed up against the drug's direct effect on improving exercise tolerance by improving blood flow to the heart. Antiarrhythmic drugs may also reduce cardiac output.

Nonsteroidal anti-inflammatory drugs

Nonsteroidal anti-inflammatory drugs (NSAIDs) are commonly used for the treatment of arthritis and musculoskeletal problems in the older athlete. Adverse effects of these medications include hypertension, fluid retention, renal impairment, and the development of peptic ulceration and bleeding.

The risk of bleeding is greatly increased when NSAIDs are prescribed in conjunction with warfarin. The risk of cardiac events in those taking certain NSAIDs was discussed in Chapter 13. The drugs should be used cautiously in older people and discontinued if the patient complains of adverse effects. To minimize the risk of gastric irritation, these medications should be taken with food or an acid-lowering medication (Chapter 13).

Topical anti-inflammatory medications may be a useful alternative.

Medications affecting the central nervous system

Hypnotic medications such as the benzodiazepines (including nitrazepam, diazepam, oxazepam, and temazepam) may affect fine motor skills, coordination, reaction time, and thermoregulation. This may lead to an increased risk of injury, especially in contact sports.

Often, people who commence exercise can reduce their need for these medications, as exercise can improve sleep patterns.

Insulin and oral hypoglycemic drugs

The dosages of insulin and the oral hypoglycemic drugs may need to be reduced prior to exercise to avoid hypoglycemia (Chapter 53). Early symptoms of insulin resistance in older people can be postprandial hyperglycemia.

Close monitoring of glycemic control and symptoms during exercise is necessary when initiating an exercise regimen in order to minimize the risk of hypoglycemia during exercise.

REFERENCES

1. Nelson ME, Rejeski WJ, Blair SN et al. Physical activity and public health in older adults: recommendation from the American College of Sports Medicine and the American Heart Association. *Med Sci Sports Exerc* 2007;39(8):1435–45.

2. Gill TM, DiPietro L, Krumholz HM. Role of exercise stress testing and safety monitoring for older persons starting an exercise program. *JAMA* 2000;284(3):342–9.

3. Galloway MT, Jokl P. Aging successfully: the importance of physical activity in maintaining health and function. *J Am Acad Orthop Surg* 2000;8(1):37–44.

4. Timiras P, ed. *Physiological basis of aging and geriatrics.* 3rd ed. Boca Raton, FL: CRC Press, 2003.

5. Christmas C, Andersen RA. Exercise and older patients: guidelines for the clinician. *J Am Geriatr Soc* 2000;48(3):318–24.

6. Daley MJ, Spinks WL. Exercise, mobility and aging. *Sports Med* 2000;29(1):1–12.

7. Rowe JW, Kahn RL. Successful aging. *Gerontologist* 1997;37(4):433–40.

8. Sun Q, Hu FB, Grodstein F. Invited commentary—physical activity benefits various aspects of healthy aging: comment on "Physical activity at midlife and health-related quality of life in older men." *Arch Intern Med* 2010;170(13):1172–3.

9. Newman AB, Arnold AM, Naydeck BL et al. "Successful aging": effect of subclinical cardiovascular disease. *Arch Intern Med* 2003;163(19):2315–22.

10. Meisner BA, Dogra S, Logan AJ et al. Do or decline? Comparing the effects of physical inactivity on biopsychosocial components of successful aging. *J Health Psychol* 2010;15(5):688–96.

11. Leveille SG, Guralnik JM, Ferrucci L et al. Aging successfully until death in old age: opportunities for increasing active life expectancy. *Am J Epidemiol* 1999;149(7):654–64.

12. Simonsick EM, Guralnik JM, Volpato S et al. Just get out the door! Importance of walking outside the home for maintaining mobility: findings from the women's health and aging study. *J Am Geriatr Soc* 2005;53(2):198–203.

13. Keysor JJ. Does late-life physical activity or exercise prevent or minimize disablement? A critical review of the scientific evidence. *Am J Prev Med* 2003;25 (3 Suppl 2):129–36.

14. Pahor M, Blair SN, Espeland M et al. Effects of a physical activity intervention on measures of physical performance: results of the Lifestyle Interventions and Independence for Elders Pilot (LIFE-P) study. *J Gerontol A Biol Sci Med Sci* 2006;61(11):1157–65.

15. Rejeski WJ, Marsh AP, Chmelo E et al. The Lifestyle Interventions and Independence for Elders Pilot (LIFE-P): 2-year follow-up. *J Gerontol A Biol Sci Med Sci* 2009;64(4):462–7.

16. American College of Sports Medicine. Position stand: the recommended quantity and quality of exercise for developing and maintaining cardiorespiratory and muscular fitness in healthy adults. *Med Sci Sports Exerc* 1990;22(2):265–74.

17. Ades PA, Coello CE. Effects of exercise and cardiac rehabilitation on cardiovascular outcomes. *Med Clin North Am* 2000;84(1):251–65, x–xi.

18. Jolliffe JA, Rees K, Taylor RS et al. Exercise-based rehabilitation for coronary heart disease. *Cochrane Database Syst Rev* 2001(1):CD001800.

19. Booth FW, Gordon SE, Carlson CJ et al. Waging war on modern chronic diseases: primary prevention through exercise biology. *J Appl Physiol* 2000;88(2):774–87.

20. Lacasse Y, Goldstein R, Lasserson TJ et al. Pulmonary rehabilitation for chronic obstructive pulmonary disease. *Cochrane Database Syst Rev* 2006(4):CD003793.

21. Nylen ES, Kokkinos P, Myers J et al. Prognostic effect of exercise capacity on mortality in older adults with diabetes mellitus. *J Am Geriatr Soc;* 58(10):1850–4.

22. Messier SP, Royer TD, Craven TE et al. Long-term exercise and its effect on balance in older, osteoarthritic adults: results from the Fitness, Arthritis, and Seniors Trial (FAST). *J Am Geriatr Soc* 2000;48(2):131–8.

23. von Stengel S, Kemmler W, Kalender WA et al. Differential effects of strength versus power training on bone mineral density in postmenopausal women: a 2-year longitudinal study. *Br J Sports Med* 2007;41(10):649–55; discussion 655.

24. Tolomio S, Ermolao A, Travain G et al. Short-term adapted physical activity program improves bone quality in osteopenic/osteoporotic postmenopausal women. *J Phys Act Health* 2008;5(6):844–53.

25. Sherrington C, Whitney JC, Lord SR et al. Effective exercise for the prevention of falls: a systematic review and meta-analysis. *J Am Geriatr Soc* 2008;56(12):2234–43.

26. Reid KJ, Baron KG, Lu B et al. Aerobic exercise improves self-reported sleep and quality of life in older adults with insomnia. *Sleep Med* 2010;11(9):934–40.

27. Li F, Fisher KJ, Harmer P et al. Tai chi and self-rated quality of sleep and daytime sleepiness in older adults: a randomized controlled trial. *J Am Geriatr Soc* 2004;52(6):892–900.

28. Liu-Ambrose T, Donaldson MG. Exercise and cognition in older adults: is there a role for resistance training programmes? *Br J Sports Med* 2009;43(1):25–7.

29. Kramer AF, Colcombe SJ, McAuley E et al. Fitness, aging and neurocognitive function. *Neurobiol Aging* 2005;26 Suppl 1:124–7.

30. Colcombe S, Kramer AF. Fitness effects on the cognitive function of older adults: a meta-analytic study. *Psychol Sci* 2003;14(2):125–30.

31. Blankevoort CG, van Heuvelen MJ, Boersma F et al. Review of effects of physical activity on strength, balance, mobility and ADL performance in elderly subjects with dementia. *Dement Geriatr Cogn Disord* 2010;30(5):392–402.

32. Singh NA, Stavrinos TM, Scarbek Y et al. A randomized controlled trial of high versus low intensity weight training versus general practitioner care for clinical depression in older adults. *J Gerontol A Biol Sci Med Sci* 2005;60(6):768–76.

33. Salminen M, Isoaho R, Vahlberg T et al. Effects of a health advocacy, counselling, and activation programme on depressive symptoms in older coronary heart disease patients. *Int J Geriatr Psychiatry* 2005;20(6):552–8.

34. Campbell AJ. Assertive screening: health checks prior to exercise programmes in older people. *Br J Sports Med* 2009;43(1):5.

35. Clemson L, Singh MF, Bundy A et al. LiFE Pilot Study: A randomised trial of balance and strength training embedded in daily life activity to reduce falls in older adults. *Aust Occup Ther J* 2010;57(1):42–50.

36. Stiggelbout M, Popkema DY, Hopman-Rock M et al. Once a week is not enough: effects of a widely implemented group based exercise programme for older adults; a randomised controlled trial. *J Epidemiol Community Health* 2004;58(2):83–8.

37. Williams B, Poulter NR, Brown MJ et al. Guidelines for management of hypertension: report of the fourth working party of the British Hypertension Society, 2004-BHS IV. *J Hum Hypertens* 2004;18(3):139–85.

38. Rosendorff C, Black HR, Cannon CP et al. Treatment of hypertension in the prevention and management of ischemic heart disease: a scientific statement from the American Heart Association Council for High Blood Pressure Research and the Councils on Clinical Cardiology and Epidemiology and Prevention. *Circulation* 2007;115(21):2761–88.

39. Mason JM, Dickinson HO, Nicolson DJ et al. The diabetogenic potential of thiazide-type diuretic and beta-blocker combinations in patients with hypertension. *J Hypertens* 2005;23(10):1777–81.

40. Thomas S, Mackintosh S, Halbert J. Does the 'Otago exercise programme' reduce mortality and falls in older adults? A systematic review and meta-analysis. *Age Ageing* 2010;39(6):681–7.

41. Davis JC, Robertson MC, Ashe MC et al. Does a home-based strength and balance programme in people aged ≥80 years provide the best value for money to prevent falls? A systematic review of economic evaluations of falls prevention interventions. *Br J Sports Med* 2010;44:80–89.

Chapter 45

Military personnel

with STEPHAN RUDZKI, TONY DELANEY, and ERIN MACI

Pain is weakness leaving the body.   US Marine Corps

The principles of sport and exercise medicine apply to a large extent when caring for military personnel. However, there are also important differences between military and athletic populations (Fig. 45.1). In this chapter, we discuss additional issues that are relevant when taking care of military personnel. For those inexperienced in working in this setting we introduce:

- the special culture of the military environment
- the epidemiology of military injuries
- common military injuries.

ISTOCKPHOTO

Figure 45.1 Physical training in the military takes place within a unique culture and environment

Special military culture

Providing primary care in a military setting offers unique challenges to the clinician. With regards to sports medicine, there are many special features which influence the type and severity of injuries seen, and multiple factors which have an impact on the rehabilitation process. The clinician must become well versed in these unique factors in order to ensure appropriate diagnosis, treatment, and, ultimately, timely and effective return to full duties.

One of the most important differences between civilian and military practice is the compulsory nature of physical training. To prepare a recruit for the ultimate goal of being fit for deployment, all military recruits undergo exercise regimens that are designed not only to improve their fitness, but also to prepare them physically and psychologically for extreme environments, discomfort, and pain. Furthermore, trainees have not always had a background of physical training, unlike an elite sportsperson who has come up through the junior ranks. With training in the military, it is the same goal whether a soldier is training to become a paratrooper, a weapons technician, or an administrator.

It follows that most militaries encourage personnel to continue exercising despite early warning signs of pain that would normally cause civilian sportspeople to stop or slow down. Many recruits conceal the nature and extent of their injuries until graduation, for fear of medical "back squadding" (recruits held back in training), and a degree of derision from fellow recruits and their superiors. A soldier who finishes a forced march by walking on a broken ankle for 12 miles with a fully weighted rucksack receives accolades and respect from peers and superiors.

Further to the drive toward pushing through pain, soldiers with a history of previous injury or who are diagnosed with post-traumatic stress demonstrate an increased threshold of pain—meaning they feel less pain for a given stimulus compared with controls.[1, 2] Pain thresholds may be related to environmental and psychological factors (for example, the common experience of WWII soldiers reporting no pain during the heat of battle despite severe injuries).[3]

As a consequence of these changes in experiencing or reporting of pain, military members often present to military clinics with musculoskeletal injuries that are severe and debilitating, requiring longer periods of rehabilitation. Clinicians must keep this in mind when assessing injured patients, who may present stoically, making it challenging to determine the severity of pain or injury.

A general tendency in medicine is to attribute a patient's symptoms to a unifying, single diagnosis. Because of the cultural overlay and late presentation, it is common for military patients to present with multiple concurrent pathologies. It is therefore very important to perform a thorough history and examination at the initial presentation, although time pressures may mitigate against this. Concurrent pathology should always be considered in a patient whose progress is slow or who does not respond to treatment considered appropriate for the initial diagnosis.

Epidemiology of military injuries

Military populations undertake strenuous physical training and have high rates of injury compared with most sportspeople. Recruit populations have especially high incidence of injury and attrition. In New Zealand, the injury rate for recruits was more than five times that of trained personnel.[4] High attrition rates represent a significant cost and a reduced return on investment. An injured soldier cannot perform his or her duties even if physically fit, and a moderate level of injury can impinge on the combat readiness of individual units.

US military studies have shown that injury incidence rates range from 120 to 144 injuries/100 soldiers/year[5] in infantry, special forces, and Ranger units, and 360/100/year for Naval Special Warfare training.[6] A comparison of injury incidence and annual injury rates between different military recruit populations is shown in Table 45.1. Types and incidence of injuries by country are shown in Table 45.2, and cause of injuries in Table 45.3.

Injuries are not just a problem within a barracks setting. Non-battle injuries in US service personnel have been a major cause of medical evacuation from Iraq and Afghanistan. As at December 2006, 35% of all medical evacuations from Iraq and 36% from Afghanistan were due to non-battle injury.[7] These constituted the largest single category of evacuations for both operations.

Historically, lower limb comprised the bulk of

Table 45.1 Comparison of injury incidence and annual injury rates between different military recruit populations

Year	Military	N	Weeks	Gender	Incidence	Rate per 100/year
1982	US Army	767	8	Female	42%	252
1982	US Army	3437	8	Male	23%	138
1994	South African Army	1261	9	Male	31%	179
1995	US Navy	4415	9	Female	22%	127
1995	US Navy	9500	9	Male	11%	63
1995	US Marine Corps	1498	11	Female	49%	232
1995	US Marine Corps	396	11	Male	29%	137
1995	US Air Force	5250	6	Female	33%	285
1995	US Air Force	8656	6	Male	15%	130
1999	Australian Army	154	12	Female	35%	140
1999	Australian Army	554	12	Male	22.5%	90
2008	British Army	1480	12	Female	13.6%	58
2008	British Army	11937	12	Male	4.6%	19

Table 45.2 Types and incidence of injuries by country

Body part	US infantry[8]	US military[14]	Australian recruits[9]	Australian army[9]	South African recruits[10]	New Zealand recruits[4]
Ankle/foot	11.6%/20.8%	13%	18.3%/11.9%			35%
Knee/lower leg	17.6% /15.1%	22%	32.1%/7.3%			16%
Low back	10.2%	20%				
Spine				15.2%		
Lower limb				39.6%	80%	
Upper limb				19.4%		

Table 45.3 Cause of injuries by country

Cause	US infantry[8]	Afghanistan/Iraq medical evacuations[11]	Australian recruits[9]	Norwegian recruits[12]	New Zealand recruits[4]
Training-related	47%	19–21%	19.2%		
Falls/jumps		18%			
Motor vehicle–related		12–16%			
Running			36.6%		28%
Obstacle course			14.6%		
Basic training				20–25%	
Acute overexertion					37%
Team sports					25%

injuries (Table 45.2), but in Afghanistan and Iraq the back, knee, and wrist/hand were the most common body regions affected in those medically evacuated. This pattern of military injuries (i.e. being primarily lower limb in nature) presents in contrast to the Australian civilian workplace, where back injury is reported as the most common single injury (25%), followed by other injuries (37%), the hand (14.3%) and, finally, lower limb injuries (10.8%).[13] Overuse is the most common cause of military training injuries reported in the literature.[5, 6, 9, 10]

Injuries cause disproportionate morbidity in young military populations. In a US military population, injuries accounted for 56% of sick-call diagnoses, but caused nearly 10 times the number of limited-duty days as illness. Soldiers with lower extremity running injuries spent seven times more days on a restricted duty profile than those with non-running injuries.[14] In outpatient clinics, between 80–90% of all limited-duty days accrued by US Army trainees and infantry soldiers were the result of training-related injuries.[5] Australian studies have similarly found morbidity to be proportionately larger than the percentage of injuries.[15]

Common military injuries

The range of injury and illness facing clinicians who serve the military greatly exceeds that usually seen in civilian medicine. Military members may be exposed to anything from extremes in temperature to biological and chemical agents, to communicable disease—including sexually transmitted and tropical illnesses. Traumatic injuries can result in concussion or traumatic brain injury, spinal cord injury, limb amputation, and a myriad of other injuries that can affect multiple systems and often require urgent care. For example, significant risk for injury occurs in diving operations, including submariner evacuation and rescue. However, the majority of the injuries tend to be related to environmental exposure (e.g. barotrauma, decompression illness, cold exposure, marine life exposure) rather than to mechanical mechanisms of injury, and thus most injuries are of a non-musculoskeletal nature.[16, 17]

Psychosocial factors can influence the recovery trajectory of military sports injuries. Experiencing deployment can affect emotional and psychological health, even in situations of peace-keeping missions, resulting in anything from fatigue and exhaustion to depression, post-traumatic stress disorders, and suicidal ideation. Counter insurgency and peace-keeping operations have confused lines between friend and foe. Decisions affecting the lives of civilians, soldiers' team members, and the enemy may have to be made rapidly and in confused situations. The stress of the battle situation and *post hoc* analysis of alternative outcomes add to the risk of post-traumatic stress disorders. Coping strategies may involve high rates of substance use, such as smoking and alcohol dependency. Social support networks can be affected. These and other complicating factors may not be obvious but need to be considered when assessing and treating members presenting to the clinic.

The following discussion addresses musculoskeletal and sports injuries; however, the reader is encouraged to maintain a broad perspective when assessing sports injuries, as often these other factors present comorbidly. Many "injury" chapters (Part B) in this book are relevant to the military population; the focus of this chapter is to highlight common specific military issues, and to highlight treatment approaches that are particular to this population.

Overuse injuries of the lower limb

There are three peaks of overuse lower limb injuries in the military. The first and greatest is among recruits, the second in trained soldiers preparing for special forces selection, and a third in older soldiers training to pass annual fitness assessments.

The syndromes of medial tibal stress syndrome, exertional compartment syndromes, and bone stress spectrum can coexist. All personnel presenting with lower limb injuries should be evaluated for spinal or discogenic pathology as well.

The most common lower limb overuse injury is "leg pain due to medial tibial stress syndrome" (MTSS) (Chapters 5 and 35). Early identification with correction of training errors and biomechanical factors often leads to rapid resolution. Recalcitrant MTSS may require appropriate orthoses, corticosteroid injection, and rarely medial tibial fascial release.

A significant proportion of recalcitrant MTSS has underlying exertional compartment syndrome. We have encountered resting compartment pressures >50 mmHg (normal resting <15 mmHg) in military trainees with medial tibial pain and tenderness.

The incidence of stress fracture in military recruits varies in the literature between 0.9% and 31%, with female rates generally higher than male (Table 45.4).[10, 18–22] The most common sites

Figure 45.2 Running is a predominant source of exercise in many forces. Competition is high and environments are usually extreme compared with recreational running programs

of stress fracture are the tibia, metatarsals, pelvis, and femur.[23, 24] The distinction between bone stress changes and incipient fracture can be difficult in military populations.[24] One of the major factors in preventing stress fractures, as well as other injuries, is to ensure that the individual enters physical training with a reasonable level of fitness (as measured by the "shuttle run"). The issue of fitness at entry, and injuries, is discussed in more detail below (page 950). Correction of biomechanical faults, and reduction of training to 60–70% of the injury-causing load contribute to rapid recovery and resumption of full training. Complete rest is contraindicated, as this leads to loss of cardiorespiratory fitness and also often to depression. Training should change from large marching and running volumes to cycling, rowing, and swimming-pool work.

(For more detailed information on treating specific stress fractures, see regional chapters (Part B) or the index.)

Blister injuries

Blister injury from endurance marching has been a major problem for infantry soldiers throughout

Table 45.4 The incidence of stress fractures in male and female military trainees

Study	Year	Population	Duration	Incidence		Relative risk F:M
				Female	Male	
Protzman[18]	1977	West Point cadets	8 wks	10.0%	1.0%	10.0
Reinker[19]	1979	Army recruits	8 wks	12.0%	2.0%	6.0
Brudvig[20]	1983	Army recruits	8 wks	3.4%	0.9%	3.8
Jones[21]	1989	Army recruits	8 wks	13.9%	3.2%	4.3

history. A Canadian study reported a 43% incidence during a 56-km night march carrying an 11-kg load.[25, 26] High rates of blister injury have also been reported in US Marine recruits and US Navy recruits.[27] The morbidity associated with blisters should not be underestimated.

Blisters are caused by shear forces acting on the skin, mainly due to friction while braking. This causes a mechanical split in the skin layers, which subsequently fills with fluid. Moist (sweaty) skin is most prone to blister formation because of increased friction and softening of the hard outer layer of skin (stratum corneum).[28] Braking forces on the foot increase with increased rucksack load.[29]

Sock type reduces the incidence of blisters. During a 3-day UK road march, soldiers wearing a nylon inner sock had fewer blisters per person than those with either a single or a double woolen sock.[30] A study in runners[28] suggests that an acrylic sock results in fewer and smaller blisters than a cotton sock. A joint US military task force recommended the use of synthetic blend socks to prevent blisters.[31]

In addition to type of sock, use of an inner sock can reduce the severity and associated morbidity of blister injuries compared with a single sock.[32] Foot powder does little to reduce blister incidence in recruits and may even increase the incidence of blister formation.[33]

Boots have traditionally been blamed for the problem of blisters but changes in boot fit, style, and composition have had little effect on blister incidence.[30, 34, 35] Nevertheless, the following strategies are recommended for boot fitting and blister prevention:[32]

- Wear a sock, sock liner, and insoles (if applicable).
- Have a load on your back when fitting boots.
- Measure both feet–length and width.
- Fit length first.
- Push foot forward in unlaced boot; ensure 1.5 cm (0.5 in.) space behind the heel.

- Push foot back; ensure 1.5 cm (0.5 in.) from the longest toe to the end of boot.
- Ensure the boot width over the arch is snug but not tight.
- Fit the boots at the end of a day's activity, when the foot has spread.

In addition to a well-fitting boot, other factors may help prevent blisters:

- Direct application of sports tape to the feet before a long march may prevent blisters.
- Use off-the-shelf heat-moldable orthoses to reduce shearing loads to the sole of the foot.
- To reduce heel lift and blistering, tighten boot laces over the dorsum of the foot and tie a reef knot to lock the lace at the anterior ankle joint.

Parachuting injuries

Military parachuting has the potential to cause severe injuries.[36] Unlike sports parachuting, most military parachutists use static line parachutes with limited maneuverability. In conditions where the prevailing winds exceed 5–8 knots, the parachutist has limited ability to reduce speed on landing. Dirt landing strips and airports tend to be more hazardous landing areas than fields and water. Night descents have a particular propensity to cause a greater rate and severity of injury.[36] Paratrooper body weight influences risk of injury, particularly when the drop zone is on land.[37] There appears to be a relatively high rate of thoracic spine injuries in military parachutists jumping with operational loads.

Military round parachutes should not be used in wind conditions over 10 knots for trainees and 13 knots for trained static line paratroopers. If the wind on a drop zone is a steady 10 knots, there is a high probability of 15–18 knot gusts every 10–15 minutes. A 20-knot wind carries a parachutist into an obstacle at 4 times the force of a 10-knot wind (i.e. $F = 0.5\, mv^2$).

Figure 45.3 Landing with military-style parachutes requires considerable skill and is inherently risky

There is often real or perceived pressure to complete training or military exercise jumps in marginal wind conditions. Most military mass parachuting injuries occur when a strong wind gust comes through after the jump has been initiated. Our experience is that the cost of aborting a jump due to wind is dwarfed by the financial and human cost of injuring highly trained paratroopers or special forces operators, many of whom will not be able to return to pre-injury duties.

 Prophylactic ankle bracing reduces ankle injuries in paratroopers.

Prophylactic ankle bracing significantly reduced ankle sprains and fractures in US Army paratroopers[38] and it also reduced the amount of time spent on medically restricted duties.[39] It has been estimated that, for every dollar expended on a parachute ankle brace, a saving of between $7 and $9 could be achieved in medical and personnel costs.[40]

The aging defense forces

Retirement ages are extending to 60 for full-time defense personnel and up to 65 for some reservists. With aging, incidence of injury may increase, as may risk of central obesity, insulin resistance, hyper-

lipidemia, hypertension, cardiovascular disease, and neoplasia. Attention to lifestyle, exercise, and diet is equally important for defense personnel as for the general population.

Injury prevention strategies in the military

This chapter extends the principles of injury prevention outlined in Chapter 9 and in specific injury chapters (e.g. Chapter 32 for prevention of anterior cruciate ligament injuries) to focus on prevention in the military setting. As in the civilian setting, risk factors for injury can be divided into intrinsic (specific to an individual, e.g. age, height, foot shape, gender, and body weight) or extrinsic (training errors, footwear, or environmental considerations such as weather or running surface). This distinction is important in a military context, because military forces must recruit from a civilian pool with a wide range of physical and athletic abilities, and seek to train these new members to achieve and maintain a standard of fitness relevant to the physical demands of the profession. This differs starkly from the sports and exercise medicine setting, where elite athletes naturally rise to the top due to a combination of genetic make-up, training, and the ability to avoid debilitating injury.

During recruit training, very high rates of injury lead to medical discharge and a loss of manpower. Australian recruits who developed an injury during recruit training were 10 times more likely to fail to complete training than those who were not injured.[41] A US study found that male recruits who were discharged during training sustained injuries at a rate of 3.4 times more than those not discharged. Discharged females sustained injuries at a rate 1.8 times greater than non-discharged females.[42]

As it is costly to attract and process new recruits into military forces, minimizing recruit attrition during basic training is an important objective for all military forces. Preventing injuries from occurring would appear to be the key objective in achieving this. Addressing all modifiable intrinsic and extrinsic factors can provide the greatest yield in terms of decreasing injury levels and allowing the broadest range of entrants to successfully enter into a military career.

Injury surveillance

Injury surveillance is the necessary precursor to injury prevention; it allows for the identification of incidence, location, nature, and cause of injury.

948

Population-based data is necessary in order to target interventions appropriately.

Ideally, military services adopt a public health approach to injury prevention as a framework.[43] The public health approach is characterized by four steps—surveillance, risk factor identification, intervention implementation, and evaluation.[44] Surveillance data is fundamental to priority setting, but is dependent on reliable and valid data collection and dissemination. Without such data it is nearly impossible to measure the impact of interventions.[43]

The aim of any military injury surveillance system should be to provide commanders with accurate and reliable information on the type, nature, and cause of injury, in conjunction with well thought out strategies for injury prevention. The army dictum "Do not come to me with problems, just solutions" is especially pertinent in military settings.

The public health approach to injury prevention was utilized to identify and eliminate anterior cruciate ligament ruptures at an Australian Army Recruit Training Centre as detailed below[45, 46] (Fig. 45.4):

1. Surveillance data identified a greater than expected number of anterior cruciate ligament ruptures occurring in an obstacle course landing area.
2. Risk factor analysis found that rubber matting installed to provide shock absorption was causing anterior cruciate ligament injuries due to increased friction and "stickiness" on landing.
3. Intervention was the removal of the rubber matting and its replacement with river pebbles.
4. Evaluation found there were no further anterior cruciate ligament ruptures at this particular location after removal of the rubber matting.

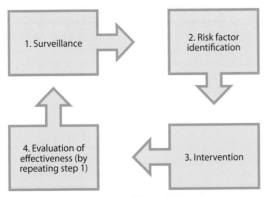

Figure 45.4 The public health model that is appropriate for the military setting (note the similarities with the injury prevention model outlined in Chapter 9)

The success of this approach highlights the utility of following a public health approach. A similar approach has been adopted with other key risk factors including initial level of aerobic fitness and running mileage (see relevant sections below).

Despite evidence to support strategies to prevent injuries in a military setting, effecting change is challenging (as in all walks of life).[47] Officers and non-commissioned officers (NCOs) alike may feel strongly about maintaining and honoring traditions, and may resist changes in training regimens or minimum fitness standards. For example, there are conflicting opinions within the military as to whether fitness standards should be different for men and women if they are working in the same trade. One argument is that a combat engineer needs to meet the standards for being a combat engineer regardless of gender.

A second example occurred many years ago at an army base in Canada, where a rule was passed down that no soldier was allowed to do double time (i.e. a shuffling run) while wearing combat boots. NCOs and recruits alike were puzzled at how they could be expected to train for active duty while not being able to run in their government-issued footwear. The order was therefore virtually ignored in practice.

To summarize, the implementation of changes must consider the cultural environment of the military, and a strategic plan must be implemented in order to ensure a smooth and effective transition. Harvard Professor John Kotter has written extensively on the subject of transformational change in various settings.[48]

Females and injury risk

Studies of Australian, British, and American troops have reported higher rates of injury and illness among female soldiers compared with their male counterparts.[49–52] Morbidity of injury in women is also greater.[53] Medical discharge rates are higher among women in both Australia and Britain.[50, 52]

An increased risk of injury was first identified in 1976 at West Point (US) with the introduction of female cadets.[54] On average, women had lower aerobic fitness than men (VO$_2$max, 46 mL/kg/min compared with 59 mL/kg/min) and this variable was associated with injury incidence.[55]

When stratified by 1-mile (1.6 km) run time, the risk of injury between men and women was comparable, with the highest risk of injury in the slowest group.[53] Of note was that 51% of the women were in the group with the longest run time compared with

1% of the men. Lower max VO$_2$ is also an independent risk factor for time-loss injury.[56] For a standardized level of physical activity, UK male recruits worked at a lower cardiovascular strain than females (24% compared with 33% of heart rate reserve), and this additional cardiovascular strain in females is believed to increase fatigue, thus predisposing to injury.[51] Gender is therefore not an independent risk factor for injury when controlled for aerobic fitness levels among recruits.[52] (For more detailed considerations of sex differences in relation to injury risk, see Chapter 43.)

Aerobic fitness

The initial level of aerobic fitness of a recruit has been shown to be a predictor of both injury and successful completion. In an Australian Army recruit cohort, aerobic fitness was measured using the 20 m shuttle run test (20 mSRT).[57, 58] Lower scores on the 20 mSRT were related to increased risk of attrition (Fig. 45.5a) as well as increased risk of injury (Fig. 45.5b).[41] The least fit soldiers (20 mSRT score 3.5) were 20 times more likely not to complete training than the fittest recruits (score 13.5). If injured, fit subjects were 25 times more likely to recover from their injury than the least fit subjects with an injury. Similar relationships between fitness, injury rates, and attrition have been seen in British Navy and Army recruits.[52, 59]

Both 1- and 2-mile run times (both proxies for aerobic fitness) are significant predictors of injury in US Army and Infantry recruits, respectively.[8, 53, 61] Table 45.5 shows the difference in injury risk between male and female recruits, stratified by 1-mile run time. As mentioned above, recruits of equivalent aerobic capacity have similar rates of injury. However, in a female cohort of US Marine recruits, a slower 2-mile run time was associated with increased incidence of stress fractures. It was suggested that stress fractures may be reduced if women participate in pre-training activities designed to improve aerobic fitness.[23]

It should not surprise that faster runners get fewer injuries. They are, almost by definition, good runners and therefore less likely to sustain a running-related injury. Fitter individuals also do not experience the same level of physiological strain during recruit training as those with lower levels of aerobic fitness. Less fit individuals work closer to their maximum workload during recruit training and thus are at increased risk of injury.

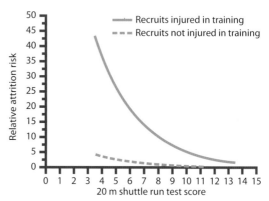

Figure 45.5 (a) The risk of recruit attrition based on 20 m shuttle run test (20 m SRT)
FROM POPE;[60] REPRODUCED WITH PERMISSION

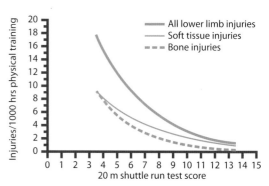

(b) The rate of recruit injury based on 20 m SRT score
FROM POPE;[60] REPRODUCED WITH PERMISSION

Table 45.5 Risk of injury for female versus male recruits by tertiles of run times

Run time for 1 mile (minutes)	Incidence of injury (%)		Risk ratio (F:M)
	Male	Female	
5.9–7.9	17.5%	20.0%	1.1
8.0–9.7	46.7%	37.3%	0.8
>9.7	0.0%	57.7%	–

From Blacker et al.[53]

The situation of a variable aerobic fitness start point and fixed endpoint could be viewed as a recipe for injury.[41, 53] Ensuring that recruits arrive at training centers with a minimum level of aerobic fitness is a logical strategy to reduce the risk of injury and subsequent attrition. This has been supported by the literature. A screening 20 mSRT test was introduced at all Australian Army recruiting centers in 1997, and only recruits who scored higher than level 7.5 on the 20 m SRT were allowed to proceed to the recruit training battalion. The Royal Navy used a 2.4 km treadmill run to assess initial aerobic fitness.[62] Following introduction of the screening test, the pass rate in recruit training increased by 10%. The number of recruits applying for voluntary release decreased from 15% to 6%. Overall, pre-enlistment aerobic testing positively impacted on recruit training pass rates.

The US Army tried a slightly different approach, in which they identified recruits with poor aerobic fitness at entry and then provided them with an in-service remedial physical fitness program before starting basic combat training. Women who undertook this remedial training then began basic combat training with similar mean 2-mile run times compared with non-remedial women, and had similar graduation success and time-loss injury rates.

Men with poor aerobic fitness (slower 2-mile run times) also undertook remedial training, but they did not improve their fitness to the level of normal entry male recruits. These men began basic combat training with considerably slower mean 2-mile run times than normal entry male recruits, and were ultimately less likely to graduate and more likely to suffer a time-loss injury.[42] Thus, the remedial program improved initial fitness levels in female, but not male recruits within a predetermined time period.

These data suggest to us that encouraging potential recruits to achieve a minimum level of aerobic fitness before presenting to a recruit training center may result in better outcomes than investing in remedial training once enlisted. Regardless of the method employed, overall evidence suggests that improving aerobic fitness levels prior to basic training could help to decrease the risk for injury and attrition, especially among women, who are generally slower on these timed run tests.[23]

Body composition

As aerobic fitness level influences risk of injury and subsequent attrition rates in the military, it might be wondered if body composition would also be a contributing factor? In the US Army's view, "obesity is associated with being unfit and unsoldierly."[53] This is a view shared by many military forces, and most have programs in place to assist members to maintain their weight within prescribed ranges of body mass index (BMI) or % body fat.

The US Army's weight control program has the stated aims of ensuring that soldiers are physically fit for their combat mission and that they present "a trim military appearance." US Army regulations consider body composition to be a subcomponent of fitness.[53] Using defined body fat standards, it has been estimated that 5% of eligible men and 30% of eligible women would be excluded from enlistment in the US military based on failing to meet these standards.

There is a clear relationship between body composition and performance on run tests, with 1- and 2-mile run times increasing dramatically with increased % body fat.[53] For males, the highest % body fat group had more injuries; however, in females, the reverse was true, with the leanest having more injuries.[53]

With this clear relationship between body composition and performance, it is no surprise that concerns exist regarding today's obesity epidemic in the US. Current cohorts of young adults are less fit than previous generations of young adults entering military service in the US, as mean times for 1- and 2-mile (1.6 and 3.2 km) runs have increased since 1987.[63] US Army recruit height, weight, and BMI values have progressively increased, with increases of both body fat and fat-free mass in male recruits. Body composition data on female recruits does not show a consistent trend.[63]

In Norwegian recruits, BMI was found to be an independent risk factor for injury, whereas height and weight were not associated with injury.[12] In Australian recruits, however, none of these measures could significantly predict injury.[41] Also, despite the US Army's views on obesity, studies have found no significant differences in attrition between Army recruits who met body weight standards and those who did not, regardless of gender, provided they met physical fitness standards on entry.[64]

 In considering the conflicting evidence available regarding BMI as an independent risk factor for injury, it is best to focus on overall fitness levels rather than body composition measures *per se* in assessing suitability for entry into the forces.

Previous injury

Many studies have found a link between history of injury and likelihood of a new injury. After adjusting for weekly distance, one study found a 65% increased risk of injury in runners with a history of previous injury.[65] Another study found a doubling of the risk in those with previous injury.[66] After adjusting for age and gender, previous injury was a strong predictor of injury with an odds ratio of 1.5.[67] One study of runners training for a marathon found that half of the participants who reported an injury had sustained a previous injury, with 42% reporting they were not completely rehabilitated before starting a training program.[68, 69] Controlled rehabilitation has been shown to reduce the number of injuries in soccer.[70]

Previous injury and incomplete rehabilitation is therefore a strong risk factor for recurrent injury. Rehabilitation is complete when an athlete is free from pain, muscle strength has returned to the pre-injury level, and joint range of motion is restored.[70] Clinicians responsible for the care of soldiers have a responsibility to ensure that complete recovery from injury has occurred before clearing them to return to full, unrestricted duties.

Musculoskeletal injuries can only recover fully with adequate functional training to encourage excellent scar remodeling, general reconditioning, and restoration of full strength, endurance, and motor control.

Consistent with the principle of specificity, a soldier will only recover sufficiently to return to full duties if given a functional training regimen that prepares him or her for full duties.[71]

Keeping a soldier on restricted duties without a plan in place to transition him or her to full duties will result in unnecessary time lost, in addition to the soldier's demoralization and subsequent loss of motivation.

Weekly running distance

Overtraining, and, in particular, excessive running distance, is the most significant underlying cause of lower limb injuries in athletic populations.[72, 73] There is an almost linear relationship between increasing weekly distance and the incidence of injury in both men and women.[65, 66, 74–77] A sudden increase in weekly distance without a gradual build-up is considered a training error.[77, 78] Training errors such as

running too frequently, too fast, or for too long are major causes of injury in both beginner and experienced runners, accounting for up to 60% of injuries.[72, 77, 79, 80]

Reducing weekly run distance

Most military forces use run tests ranging from 1.6 km (1 mile) to 5 km (3 miles) to assess physical fitness. There is a strong belief that running is an essential means of acquiring aerobic fitness. It also has the benefit of being a simple activity requiring little preparation and no equipment. These factors drive training regimens and consequently there is a heavy preponderance of running in most military physical training programs. The distance of the Australian Army physical training test has been reduced from 5 km to 2.4 km on the basis that reducing the test distance might reduce the training distances and result in a concomitant reduction in overtraining. However, attempts such as these have met with varying degrees of success worldwide.

US studies spanning Marine Corps, Army, and Navy found that recruits given lower mileage running programs sustained significantly fewer injuries with no subsequent differences in performance on run tests or other physical fitness tests.[81–84] The US Department of Defense estimated in 1995 that the reduction in running mileage had saved $4.5 million in medical care costs and nearly 15 000 training days annually by preventing stress fractures alone.[85]

Cross-training and other program modifications

Besides reducing mileage, there are alternatives to running that are effective in conditioning recruits. In fact, before running became fashionable in the 1960s, pack marching was the standard method of developing endurance and aerobic capacity in soldiers (Fig. 45.6). Marching with rucksacks in place of running was investigated in Australia, with subsequent reduction in injury rates and morbidity, while improvements in performance on run tests and VO_2max were as good as a group given a traditional running program.[66] Load-bearing or pack marching is more occupation-specific to the military environment than distance running in a singlet, shorts, and shoes. There is considerable gain in aerobic conditioning from shorter high-intensity training.

There is a huge variety of careers in the military, with varying physical and intellectual demands. Imposing a single rigid training regimen on all

iSTOCKPHOTO

Figure 45.6 Marching has historically been a mainstay of military forces both in training and in active deployments

recruits, regardless of physique, sex, age, and aspiration, is unrealistic.

Some level of running will always be found in military training programs, but the design of running programs may reduce the risk of injury. Interval training and periodization are other training modifications that have been successfully used to reduce injuries.[50, 83, 86] In Australia, one study examined the effect of discontinuing road runs as formed groups, introducing 400–800 m interval training, reducing test run distance from 5 km to 2.4 km, standardizing route march speed, and introducing deep-water running as an alternate aerobic activity. The incidence of injuries decreased by 10% in men and 12% in women.[50]

In a US study, recruits were divided into ability groups based on initial 2-mile run times.[87] Running speed was managed to keep effort at between 70% and 83% of VO_2max. This modified program was compared with a traditional training program. The proportion of recruits who failed the Army Physical Fitness Test (APFT) was lower in the modified program than the traditional training group (1.7% compared with 3.3%, p = 0.03). After adjustment for initial fitness levels, age, and body mass index, the relative risk of an injury in the traditional training group was 1.6 for men and 1.5 in women.

Training modifications have been found to nearly abolish the incidence of pelvic stress fractures in female recruits.[86] Interventions included a reduction in route march speed from 7.5 km/h to 5 km/h, and placing shorter women at the head of the column to reduce stride length. Individual step length was promoted instead of marching in step, march and run formations were more widely spaced, and interval-running training replaced traditional middle-distance runs. The rate of pelvic stress fractures fell from 11.2% to 0.6%.[86]

Deep-water running has been utilized as an aerobic activity that can rest the lower limbs and periodize impact loading.[88] It is performed in the deep end of a swimming pool, normally with the aid of a flotation vest or belt. Aerobic performance can be maintained with deep-water running for up to six weeks in trained endurance athletes. Previously sedentary individuals benefit more than sportspeople in improving maximal oxygen uptake.[89]

To summarize, a comprehensive review of injuries in the US Forces stated that "Military and civilian research indicates that high running volume significantly increases the risk for lower extremity injury. During initial military training, about 25% of men and about 50% of women incur one or more physical training–related injuries. About 80% of these injuries are in the lower extremities and are of the overuse type—a condition brought about by physical training volume overload (generally excessive running relative to initial fitness level and running capability of the individual)."[31] The literature overwhelmingly supports reductions in running distances among recruits as a strategy to reduce injury rates while still attaining minimal physical fitness standards.

Running experience

Despite the above research regarding the benefits of lower mileage running programs, the risk of running injuries does appear to decline with increased exposure time; that is, the longer a person has been a runner, the fewer injuries.[65] This appears contradictory in the context of the clear association between running distance and injury, but may be related to experience (i.e. chronic adaptation of tissues to long-term running programs, improved running mechanics with experience, etc.) and/or the "healthy runner" effect.[72, 80] Either way, runners with less than three years of regular running experience have been reported to have twice the risk of lower limb injury than those with greater than three years.[66]

The theory of the "healthy runner" is that only those without injury can continue with a running program on a long-term basis. If this is true, then the rate of injury among chronic runners may not be indicative of the general population, but, rather, suggests that "healthy runners" have the intrinsic characteristics required to become long-term runners in the first place, while others stop running due to inability to tolerate the sport. Alternatively, if experience is the cause of reduced injury rates over time, then military recruits may have higher injury rates is due to the fact that they are new to the intensity of the training regimen; long-term military members may have simply adapted to the exercise load.

Competitive behaviors

Injury incidence is significantly associated with motivation score,[90, 91] with higher scores correlating to higher incidence of injury. In addition, runners who compete have higher injury rates than recreational runners, even when adjusting for mileage.[65, 67] More motivated runners may ignore the first signs of injury, with their priorities on their outcomes in the heat of performance, rather than heeding discomfort.

In military populations every activity is highly competitive. The US Army places great emphasis on the Army Physical Fitness Test (APFT). Better scores influence prospects for promotion and most US soldiers strive to achieve the maximum possible score. The Australian Army now utilizes a pass/fail result instead of a score, with the intention of reducing competitive behaviors and subsequent risk of injury.

Warm-up/stretching

The use of stretches as a component of a pre-activity warm-up, and understanding of their role in preventing injuries in the military, are unclear. In the general population, an acute bout of stretching prior to activity results in short-term loss of strength, power, and endurance,[92, 93] and does not reduce overall injury risk.[94] In the military, a randomized controlled study in Australian recruits found no significant effect of pre-exercise static stretches on all-injury risk, soft-tissue injury risk, or bone injury risk.[95] A study of Japanese recruits found the total injury rate was the same between those who conducted static stretches and those who did not; however, the incidence of muscle/tendon injury and low back pain was significantly lower in the stretching group.[96]

As it is clear that traditional static stretches do not reduce overall injury rate, warm-ups today should be incorporating light cardiovascular activities such as jogging, dynamic range of motion activities, and progress to sport-specific drills.[92, 97, 98, 99]

Conclusion

Injury is a major problem for most Western military forces. While incidence varies significantly, female recruits ubiquitously bear a disproportionate burden.

Military recommendations for injury prevention

The evidence base for injury prevention has been reviewed by a joint US military task force.[31] Six interventions had strong enough evidence to be recommended for implementation in the military services and two interventions were not recommended due to evidence of ineffectiveness or harm.

Recommended interventions (sufficient scientific evidence)

(1) Prevent overtraining.
(2) Perform multiaxial, neuromuscular, proprioceptive, and agility training.
(3) Wear mouth-guards during high-risk activities.
(4) Wear semi-rigid ankle braces for high-risk activities.
(5) Consume nutrients to restore energy balance within 1 hour following high-intensity activity. (High carbohydrate/protein replacement within 15–30 minutes of finishing high-intensity exercise leads to more rapid muscle and liver glycogen restoration and preservation of muscle mass.)
(6) Wear synthetic-blend socks to prevent blisters.

Interventions not recommended (evidence of ineffectiveness or harm)

(1) Wear back braces, harnesses, or support belts.
(2) Take anti-inflammatory medication prior to exercise. While physical training is necessary to condition soldiers for their occupational tasks, the authors noted that "in classic military tradition, however, efforts to exceed the standards have contributed to the injury epidemic present today."

From Bullock et el.[31]

Overuse type injuries, especially of the lower limbs, predominate. In addition, although the military population usually is fit and has access to high-quality healthcare, they can still have the systemic, metabolic, infective, and neoplastic disease found in the wider population. The wise military physician should never assume that all apparent musculoskeletal pain in the young soldier is due to overuse injury.

Reducing running distance has been shown to reduce both the incidence and the severity of injury in military recruit populations, without affecting overall physical performance. The entry level of aerobic fitness has been identified as a key modifiable risk factor, and screening for physical fitness prior to clearing to participate in basic training programs has helped to reduce both injury and attrition rates. Early identification of injuries and counseling trainees about achievable career paths are an important part of rehabilitation. Not all somatotypes or psyches are suited for infantry, marines or special forces, regardless of pre-recruitment dreams. Modern military training programs have to incorporate scientifically validated principles and flexibility.

Injury prevention strategies should be based on robust surveillance systems using a public health approach to accurately identify risk factors, implement interventions, and evaluate outcomes. While the nature of the profession comes with inherent risk, it is clear that, through an evidence-based approach, it is possible to reduce injury, improve retention, and thus create strong and healthy forces.

REFERENCES

1. Geuze E, Westenberg HG, Jochims A et al. Altered pain processing in veterans with post-traumatic stress disorder. *Arch Gen Psychiatry* 2007;64(1):76–85.

2. Dar R, Ariely D, Frenk H. The effect of past injury on pain threshold and tolerance. *Pain* 1995;60(2):189–93.

3. Harper P. No pain, no gain: pain behaviour in the armed forces. *Br J Nurs* 2006;15(10):548–51.

4. Davidson PL, Chalmers DJ, Wilson BD et al. Lower limb injuries in New Zealand Defence Force personnel: descriptive epidemiology. *Aust N Z J Public Health* 2008;32(2):167–73.

5. Jones BH, Knapik JJ. Physical training and exercise-related injuries. Surveillance, research and injury prevention in military populations. *Sports Med* 1999;27(2):111–25.

6. Kaufman KR, Brodine S, Shaffer R. Military training-related injuries: surveillance, research, and prevention. *Am J Prev Med* 2000;18(3 Suppl):54–63.

7. Hauret KG, Taylor BJ, Clemmons NS et al. Frequency and causes of nonbattle injuries air evacuated from operations Iraqi Freedom and Enduring Freedom, U.S. Army, 2001–2006. *Am J Prev Med* 2010;38 (1 Suppl):S94–107.

8. Reynolds KL, Heckel HA, Witt CE et al. Cigarette smoking, physical fitness, and injuries in infantry soldiers. *Am J Prev Med* 1994;10(3):145–50.

9. Rudzki SJ. Injuries in Australian Army recruits. Part I: Decreased incidence and severity of injury seen with reduced running distance. *Mil Med* 1997;162:472–6.

10. Jordaan G, Schwellnus MP. The incidence of overuse injuries in military recruits during basic military training. *Mil Med* 1994;159(6):421–6.

11. Hauret KG, Jones BH, Bullock SH et al. Musculoskeletal injuries; description of an under-recognized injury problem among military personnel. *Am J Prev Med* 2010;38(1 Suppl)):S61–70.

12. Heir T, Eide G. Age, body composition, aerobic fitness and health condition as risk factors for musculoskeletal injuries in conscripts. *Scand J Med Sci Sports* 1996;6(4): 222–7.

13. Workcover Authority New South Wales Workers Compensation statistical bulletin. Sydney, Australia: Workcover, 1998.

14. Smith TA, Cashman TM. The incidence of injury in light infantry soldiers. *Mil Med* 2002;167(2):104–8.

15. Rudzki SJ. Injuries in the Australian Army 1987–91. A comparison to the US Army experience. Canberra: Australian Defence Directorate of Publishing, 1994.

16. Vann RD, Vorosmarti J. Military diving operations and medical support. In: Kelly Col P, ed. *Military preventive medicine: mobilization and deployment*: Department of Defense, Office of The Surgeon General, US Army, Borden Institute, 2003:955–94.

17. Broadhurst RS, Morrison LJ, Howsare CR et al. Military diving medicine. In: Kelly Col. P, ed. *Military preventive medicine: mobilization and deployment*: Department of Defense, Office of The Surgeon General, US Army, Borden Institute, 2003:575–610.

18. Protzman RR, Griffis CC. Comparative stress fracture incidence in males and females in an equal training environment. *Athletic Train* 1977;12:126–130.

19. Reinker KA, Ozbourne S. A comparison of male and female basic orthopedic pathology in basic training. *Mil Med* 1979;144:532–6.

20. Brudvig TJ, Gudjer TD, Obermeyer L. Stress fractures in 259 trainees: a one-year study of incidence as related to age, sex and race. *Mil Med* 1983;148:666–9.

21. Jones BH, Harris JM, Tuyethoa NV et al. Exercise induced stress fractures and stress reactions of bone: epidemiology, etiology and classification. In: Pandolf K, ed. *Exercise and sport science review* Baltimore: Williams and Wilkins, 1989:379–422.

22. Wentz L, Liu PY, Haymes E et al. Females have a greater incidence of stress fractures than males in both military and athletic populations: a systemic review. *Mil Med* 2011;176(4):420–30.

23. Shaffer RA, Rauh MJ, Brodine SK et al. Predictors of stress fracture susceptibility in young female recruits. *Am J Sports Med* 2006;34(1):108–15.

24. Milgrom C, Giladi M, Stein M et al. Stress fractures in military recruits. A prospective study showing an unusually high incidence. *J Bone Joint Surg Br* 1985;67(5):732–5.

25. Research into foot lesions among Canadian field forces. 13th Commonwealth Defence Conference on Operational Clothing and Combat Equipment; 1981; Malaysia.

26. Dalen A, Nilsson J, Thorstensson A. Factors influencing a prolonged foot march. Stockholm, Sweden: Karolinska Institute, 1978.

27. Bensel CK, Kish R. Lower extremity disorders among men and women in Army Basic training and the effects of two types of boots. *US Army Natick Research & Development Laboratories*, Natick, Massachusetts:pp1–99 (1983).

28. Herring KM, Richie DH. Friction blisters and sock fiber composition. *J Am Podiatr Med Assoc* 1990;80:63–71.

29. Kinoshita H. Effects of different loads and carrying systems on selected biomechanical parameters describing gait. *Ergonomics* 1985;28:1347–62.

30. Allan JR. A study of foot blisters. United Kingdom: Army Operational Research Establishment (AORE), 1964.

31. Bullock SH, Jones BH, Gilchrist J et al. Prevention of physical training-related injuries recommendations for the military and other active populations based on expedited systematic reviews. *Am J Prev Med* 2010;38(1):S156–81.

32. Thompson KJ, Hamlet MP, Jones BH et al. Impact of sock systems on frequency and severity of blister injury in a Marine recruit population. Natick MA: USARIEM, 1993.

33. Quinn J. The effects of two new foot powders on the incidence of foot infection and blisters in recruits during basic training. Farnborough UK: Army Personnel Research Establishment (APRE), 1967.

34. Military footwear and the occurence of blisters. *8th Commonwealth Defence Conference on clothing and general stores*; 1965; Melbourne, Australia.

35. Whittingham DG. A further investigation of marching in flying boots: Exercise Orthopod II. Farnborough UK: RAF Institute of Aviation Medicine, 1951.

36. Kragh JF Jr, Jones BH, Amaroso PJ et al. Parachuting injuries among Army Rangers: a prospective survey of an elite airborne battalion. *Mil Med* 1996;161(7): 416–19.

37. Hughes CD, Weinrauch PC. Military static line parachute injuries in an Australian commando battalion. *ANZ J Surg* 2008;78(10):848–52.

38. Amoroso PJ, Ryan JB, Bickley B et al. Braced for impact: reducing military paratroopers' ankle sprains using outside-the-boot braces. *J Trauma* 1998;45(3): 575–80.

39. Schumacher JT Jr, Creedon JF, Pope RW. The effectiveness of the parachutist ankle brace in reducing ankle injuries in an airborne ranger battalion. *Mil Med* 2000;165(12):944–8.

40. Knapik JJ, Spiess A, Swedler DI et al. Systematic review of the parachute ankle brace: injury risk reduction and cost effectiveness. *Am J Prev Med* 2010;38(1 Suppl): S182–8.

41. Pope RP, Herbert R, Kirwan JD et al. Predicting attrition in basic military training. *Mil Med* 1999a;164(10):710–4.

42. Knapik JJ, Canham-Chervak M, Hauret KG et al. Discharges during U.S. Army basic training: injury rates and risk factors. *Mil Med* 2001;166(7):641–7.

43. Pointer S, Harrison J, Bradley C. National Injury Prevention Plan priorities for 2004 and beyond. Canberra Australia: Australian Institute of Health and Welfare, 2003.

44. National Center for Injury Prevention and Control. Violence prevention: a public health study. Geneva: WHO Collaborating Center on Injury Control, 1998.

45. Pope RP. Injury surveillance and systematic investigation identify a rubber matting hazard for anterior cruciate ligament rupture on an obstacle course. *Mil Med* 2002;167(4):359–62.

46. Pope RP. Rubber matting on an obstacle course causes anterior cruciate ligament ruptures and its removal eliminates them. *Mil Med* 2002;167(4):355–8.

47. Langton N, Khan KM, Lusina SJ. FIFA's Football for Health: applying Kotter's eight-step programme for transformational change to a mass participation activity. *Br J Sports Med* 2010;44(8):537–9.

48. Kotter J. Leading change: why transformation efforts fail. *Harvard Bus Rev* 2007:96–103.

49. Darakjy S, Marin RE, Knapik JJ et al. Injuries and illnesses among armor brigade soldiers during operational training. *Mil Med* 2006;171(11):1051–6.

50. Rudzki SJ, Cunningham MJ. The effect of a modified physical training program in reducing injury and medical discharge rates in Australian Army recruits. *Mil Med* 1999;164(9):648–52.

51. Blacker S, Wilkinson D, Rayson M. Gender differences in the physical demands of British Army recruit training. *Mil Med* 2009 2009;174(8):811–16.

52. Blacker SD, Wilkinson DM, Bilzon JL et al. Risk factors for training injuries among British Army recruits. *Mil Med* 2008;173(3):278–86.

53. Jones BH, Bovee M, Knapik J. Associations among body composition, Physical fitness and injury in men and women Army Trainees. *Body Composition and Physical Performance: Applications for the Military Services.* Washington DC: National Academy Press, 1992:141–173.

54. Tomasi LF, Peterson JH, Pettit GP et al. Women's response to Army training. *Phys Sportsmed* 1977;5(6): 32–7.

55. Daniels WL, Kowal DM, Vogel JA et al. Physiological effects of a military training program on male and female cadets. *Aviat Space Environ Med* 1979;50(6): 562–6.

56. Knapik JJ, Sharp MA, Canham-Chervak M et al. Risk factors for training-related injuries among men and

women in basic combat training. *Med Sci Sports Exerc* 2001;33(6):946–54.

57. Leger LA, Gadoury C. Validity of the 20 m shuttle run test with 1 min stages to predict VO$_2$max in adults. *Can J Sport Sci* 1989;14:21–6.

58. Paliczka VJ, Nichols AK, Boreham CA. A multi-stage shuttle run as a predictor of running performance and maximal oxygen uptake in adults. *Br Sports Med* 1987;21:163–5.

59. Allsopp AJ, Scarpello EG, Andrews S et al. Survival of the fittest? The scientific basis for the Royal Navy pre-joining fitness test. *J R Nav Med Serv* 2003;89(1):11–18.

60. Pope RP. Prediction and prevention of lower limb injuries and attrition in Army recruits. Charles Sturt University, 2002.

61. Burke BG, Sauser WT, Kemery ER et al. Intelligence and physical fitness as predictors of success in early infantry training. *Percept Mot Skills* 1989;69:263–71.

62. Lunt H. A pre-joining fitness test improves pass rates of Royal Navy recruits. *Occup Med (Lond)* 2007;57(5): 377–9.

63. Knapik JJ, Sharp MA, Darakjy S et al. Temporal changes in the physical fitness of US Army recruits. *Sports Med* 2006;37(7):613–34.

64. Niebuhr DW, Scott CT, Li Y et al. Preaccession fitness and body composition as predictors of attrition in U.S. Army recruits. *Mil Med* 2009;174(7):695–701.

65. Marti B, Vader JP, Minder CE et al. On the epidemiology of running injuries. *Am J Sports Med* 1988;16:285–94.

66. Macera CA, Pate RR, Powell KE et al. Predicting lower extremity injuries among habitual runners. *Arch Int Med* 1989;149:2565–8.

67. Walter SD, Hart LE, McIntosh JM et al. The Ontario Cohort study of running related injuries. *Archives Int Med* 1989;149:2561–4.

68. Taunton JE, Ryan MB, Clement DB et al. A prospective study of running injuries: the Vancouver Sun Run "In Training" clinics. *Br J Sports Med* 2003;37(3): 329–44.

69. Powell KE, Kohl HW, Casperson CJ et al. An epidemiological perspective on the causes of running injuries. *Phys Sportsmed* 1986;14(6):100–14.

70. Ekstrand J. Soccer injuries and their prevention. [Medical Dissertations no 130]. Linkoping University, 1982.

71. Goss DL, Christopher GE, Faulk RT et al. Functional training program bridges rehabilitation and return to duty. *J Spec Oper Med* 2009;9(2):29–48.

72. Van Mechelen W. Running injuries: a review of the epidemiological literature. *Sports Med* 1992;14(5): 320–35.

73. Yeung EW, Yeung SS. Interventions for preventing lower limb soft-tissue injuries in runners. *Cochrane Database Syst Rev* 2011;7(CD001256).

74. Koplan JP, Powell KE, Sikes RK et al. An epidemiological study of the benefits and risks of running. *JAMA* 1982;248:3118–21.

75. Jacobs SJ, Berson BL. Injuries to runners: a study of entrants to a 10,000m race. *Am J Sports Med* 1986;14:151–5.

76. Bovens AM, Janssen GM, Vermeer HG et al. Occurrence of running injuries in adults following a supervised training programme. *Int J Sports Med* 1989;10:S186–190.

77. Lysholm J, Wiklander J. Injuries in runners. *Am J Sports Med* 1987;15:168–71.

78. Kowal DM. Nature and causes of injuries in women resulting from an endurance training programme. *Am J Sports Med* 1980;8:265–9.

79. Andrews JR. Overuse syndromes of the lower extremity. *Clin Sports Med* 1983;2:137–48.

80. Pollock ML, Gettman LR, Milesis LA et al. Effects of frequency and duration of training on attrition and incidence of injury. *Med Sci Sport Exerc* 1977;9:31–6.

81. Knapik JJ, Scott SJ, Sharp MA et al. The basis for prescribed ability group run speeds and distances in U.S. Army basic combat training. *Mil Med* 2006;171(7):669–77.

82. Trank TV, Ryman DH, Minagawa RY et al. Running mileage, movement mileage, and fitness in male U.S. Navy recruits. *Med Sci Sports Exerc* 2001;33(6): 1033–8.

83. Knapik JJ, Hauret KG, Arnold S et al. Injury and fitness outcomes during implementation of physical readiness training. *Int J Sports Med* 2003;24(5):372–81.

84. Jones BH, Cowan DN, Tomlinson JP et al. Epidemiology of injuries associated with physical training among young men in the Army. *Med Sci Sport Ex* 1993;25(1):197–203.

85. UASCHPPM. Recommendations for the prevention of physical training (PT)—related injuries: Results of a systematic evidence based review by the Joint Services Physical Training Injury Prevention Working Group (JSPTIPWG). Aberdeen Proving Ground MD: United States Army Center for Health Promotion and Preventative Medicine. 2008.

86. Pope RP. Prevention of pelvic stress fractures in female army recruits. *Mil Med* 1999;164(5):370–3.

87. Knapik JJ, Darakjy S, Scott SJ et al. Evaluation of a standardized physical training program for basic combat training. *J Strength Cond Res* 2005;19(2):246–53.

88. Burns AS, Lauder TD. Deep water running: an effective non-weightbearing exercise for the maintenance of land-based running performance. *Mil Med* 2001;166(3):253–8.

89. Reilly T, Dowzer CN, Cable NT. The physiology of deep-water running. *J Sports Sci* 2003;21(12):959–72.

90. Fields KB, Sykes JC, Walker KM et al. Prevention of running injuries. *Curr Sports Med Rep* 2010;9(3):176–82.

91. Yzerman JC, VanGalen WC. Blessures bij lange afstandlopers: KNAU, 1987.

92. McHugh MP, Cosgrave CH. To stretch or not to stretch; the role of stretching in injury prevention and performance. *Scand J Med Sci Sport* 2010;20(1):169–81.

93. Shrier I. Does stretching improve performance? A systematic and critical review of the literature. *Clin J Sport Med* 2004;14(5):267–73.

94. Small K, Mc Naughton L, Matthews M. A systematic review into the efficacy of static stretching as part of a warm-up for the prevention of exercise-related injury. *Res Sports Med* 2008;16(3):213–31.

95. Pope RP, Herbert RD, Kirwan JD et al. A randomized trial of preexercise stretching for prevention of lower-limb injury. *Med Sci Sports Exerc* 2000;32(2):271–7.

96. Amako M, Oda T, Masuoka K et al. Effect of static stretching on prevention of injuries for military recruits. *Mil Med* 2003;168(6):442–6.

97. Fletcher IM, Jones BH. The effect of different warm-up stretch protocols on 20 meter sprint performance in trained rugby union players. *J Strength Cond Res* 2004;18(4):885–8.

98. Jaggers JR, Swank AM, Frost KL et al. The acute effects of dynamic and ballistic stretching on vertical jump height, force, and power. *J Strength Cond Res* 2008;22(6):1844–9.

99. Fletcher IM, Anness R. The acute effects of combined static and dynamic stretch protocols on fifty-meter sprint performance in track-and-field athletes. *J Strength Cond Res* 2007;21(3):784–7.

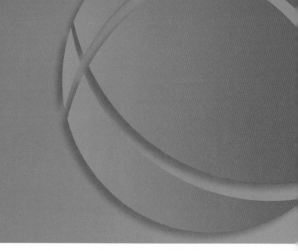

Chapter 46

The athlete with a disability

with NICK WEBBORN and LARISSA TREASE

It's not the disability that defines you, it's how you deal with the challenges the disability presents you with. We have an obligation to the abilities we do have, not the disability.
Jim Abbott, former one-handed baseball pitcher, www.jimabbott.info

Participation in sports by people with disabilities increased significantly over the latter half of the last century. In 1948, 16 competitors took part in the first Stoke Mandeville Games, a sporting competition for people with disabilities. Today, almost 4000 athletes from more than 146 countries compete in the summer Paralympic Games.

In this chapter we:

- provide a brief history of how people with disabilities have gained opportunities to be physically active
- discuss the challenges that people with disability face to achieve the benefits of physical activity
- discuss common clinical concerns of the person with various major physical disabilities (e.g. spinal cord injury, limb deficiency, cerebral palsy, visual impairment, Les Autres)
- introduce recent events to promote sport among people with intellectual disability
- outline the classification system that categorizes persons with disabilities to permit fair competition
- provide practical tips relating to
  - winter sports for disabled persons
  - anti-doping
  - travel with teams.

Historical perspective

At the start of the 20th century, sports participation among people with disabilities was very limited. A most significant figure in the history of disability sport was Sir Ludwig Guttman, who ran the Spinal Injuries Unit at Stoke Mandeville Hospital in England. He introduced sporting activity as part of the rehabilitation process for those with spinal cord injury. On the opening day of the 1948 Olympic Games in London, he arranged an archery contest on the lawns of the hospital between two spinal injury units. Thus began the Stoke Mandeville Games; four years later, the games became the International Stoke Mandeville Games with the inclusion of a team of spinally injured patients from Holland.

Guttman believed that "by restoring activity in mind and body—by instilling self-respect, self-discipline, a competitive spirit and comradeship—sport develops mental attitudes that are essential for social reintegration." The inclusion of other sports such as athletics, swimming, table tennis, and basketball increased the diversity of opportunities for people with disabilities. Participation improved slowly, and in 1960 the International Stoke Mandeville Games were held in Rome after the Olympic Games, with a plan to hold these quadrennial games in the Olympic Games host city where possible. In 1976 people with vision impairment and limb deficiencies were included and those with cerebral palsy joined in 1980.

Initially the term "Olympics for the Disabled" was used, but this was not acceptable to the International Olympic Committee (IOC), and in 1985 the term "Paralympic" was devised to describe a games "parallel to the Olympics" (not "paraplegic," a common misconception). In 1989, the International Paralympic Committee (IPC) was formed, and since then the games have truly been the Paralympic Games; cities bid to host the Olympics and Paralympic Games together. In the 12-day Beijing 2008 Paralympic Games, almost 4000 athletes represented

146 countries and competed before 1.8 million ticket holders. In the Vancouver 2010 Winter Paralympics, 500 athletes, 24% of which were women, competed in five sports.

The different disability groups are organized by various national and international organizations. The IPC is the international representative body for elite sports for athletes with disabilities, which are primarily physical disabilities, but also includes visual impairment. Hearing-impaired athletes participate in the "Deaflympics" organized by the international organization Comité International Sports des Sourds (CISS). The International Sports Federation for Persons with Intellectual Disability (INAS-FID) is affiliated with the IPC and represents solely elite athletes with intellectual disabilities. The Special Olympics is an organization for people with a full range of intellectual disability and focuses on participation at all ability levels. Its motto is "Let me win. But if I cannot win, let me be brave in the attempt."

Health benefits of physical activity

The health benefits of physical activity are well known,[1] but people with disabilities have fewer opportunities to participate in regular physical activity for reasons that include physiological restrictions associated with the disability, access to facilities, as well as sociocultural factors. Up to 10% of young people with spinal cord injury are at moderate-to-high long-term risk of cardiac events; this is increased with tetraplegia. Common risk factors include obesity and hyperlipidemia.[2]

On the other hand, disabled people who are regularly physically active have fewer healthcare costs, including fewer visits to physicians and hospitalizations, than their inactive counterparts. In addition to the musculoskeletal benefits of regular physical activity, social and psychological benefits include improvement in self-esteem and social integration.

It is challenging for a person with a disability to perform a sufficient intensity of exercise to optimize health benefits. For example, a person using a standard wheelchair will find it difficult to push with sufficient intensity to raise heart rate and blood pressure to the level required to reduce coronary risk factors and prevent type 2 diabetes. Thus, other modes of exercise are needed to provide more intense and prolonged activity.

An activity such as hand cycling or stationary hand crank can permit higher intensity exercise. Another approach to greater duration and intensity

of exercise is to use functional electrical stimulation of paralyzed muscles. For example, this can be used on a paralyzed leg to permit a rowing action. Both pieces of equipment have costs.

Choosing a suitable sport

The clinician who advises a disabled person should realize that people with disabilities take part in a wide range of sports—even high-risk activities such as mountain climbing and diving. For some sports, such as swimming, the rules and facilities require little or no adaptation. Other sports have modified equipment or rules to accommodate persons with disability (e.g. wheelchair basketball).

Certain sports have been developed with specific disability groups in mind; for example, goalball, a court-based ball sport developed for the visually impaired, and boccia, an adaptation of boules for people with severe cerebral palsy. Today, people with disabilities engage in all sports.

Some sports are designed for one disability group (e.g. those with tetraplegia in wheelchair rugby), whereas other sports (e.g. swimming) have competitions categorized by disability. The sports available to people with disabilities depend on a variety of aspects that include access to facilities and equipment, coaching, and local competition. For some disabled people, sport is a way of obtaining physical activity for health benefit or disease modification, whereas others aim for events such as the Paralympic Games (Table 46.1 overleaf).

Competitive sports have certain physiological requirements, such as aerobic or anaerobic fitness, skill, or strength. Some sports include a risk of trauma. Not all sports, however, need to be organized or competitive—the focus may be on building self-esteem and facilitating social benefits.

Sports prescription for patients with a disability is in line with exercise prescription for any patient with an ongoing medical condition and includes determining the:

- personal preference of the patient—enjoyment and achievement foster participation
- characteristics of the sport—physiological demands, coordination requirements, collision potential, preference for team or individual sport
- medical condition of the individual—exercise may be beneficial or detrimental to the disability

Table 46.1 Sports of the 2012 and 2010 Paralympic Games

Summer (2012)	Winter (2010)
Archery	Biathlon
Athletics	Cross-country (Nordic)
Basketball	skiing
Boccia (*not in 2008, but back*	Downhill (Alpine) skiing
in for London 2012)	Sledge hockey
Cycling (road and track)	Wheelchair curling
Equestrian	
Wheelchair fencing	
Football (CP, VI) (5 a-side	
and 7 a-side)	
Goalball	
Judo	
Power lifting	
Rowing	
Sailing	
Shooting	
Swimming	
Table tennis	
Wheelchair tennis	
Volleyball	
Wheelchair rugby	
Para canoe and	
Paratriathlon will be	
included in Rio 2016	

CP = cerebral palsy; VI = visually impaired

- cognitive ability and social skills—these determine whether a person can follow rules and interact with others
- facilities for training and competition
- availability of coaching and support staff
- availability of equipment—this may be expensive (e.g. specialist wheelchairs are used in road racing, wheelchair tennis, rugby, and basketball; prosthetics aids can be used by amputees for sprinting).

In Australia, "Come and try days" organized by disabled sporting organizations in each state allow people with disabilities to sample a range of sports, where equipment is provided.

For elite competition (e.g. the Paralympic Games), athletes are categorized as having:

- a physical disability
- visual impairment; or
- intellectual impairment.

We discuss each of these categories in turn.

The sportsperson with a physical disability

To permit fair competition, persons with physical disabilities are subcategorized into those with:

1. spinal cord injury, either congenital or acquired
2. limb deficiency or amputation
3. cerebral palsy
4. Les Autres (French for "the others")—physical disabilities such as muscular dystrophies, syndromic conditions, and ankylosis, or arthritis of major joints that do not fit within the other three categories.

The sports clinician needs to be familiar with the different sports risks, and capacities, of each disability group.

Spinal cord injury and sports medicine

The spinal cord lesion may be a congenital lesion (such as spina bifida) or an acquired lesion (through disease or trauma). Of those with a traumatic spinal cord injury, approximately 80% are men and the majority of these are aged between 16 and 30 years. Most spinal cord injuries occur as a result of motor vehicle accidents but about 15% occur during sporting activity. Spinal cord injury databases usually include diving into shallow water (often under the influence of alcohol) as a sporting injury.

 The sports where spinal cord injury is more likely and, thus, require vigilant prevention efforts include equestrian activities, gymnastics and trampolining, Rugby Union, American football, and skiing.

Sports-related spinal cord injuries can result in paraplegia or quadriplegia with different degrees of completeness. There are approximately equal percentages of complete and incomplete quadriplegias and paraplegias. Although the loss of motor function in spinal cord injury is immediately apparent, sensory impairment also has a major impact, with loss of light touch, proprioception, or pain sensation. Also, autonomic dysfunction alters thermoregulation, and impairs bladder and bowel function.[3]

A high thoracic spinal injury, around T1–4, causes sympathectomy of the myocardium, which reduces the maximal heart rate to between 110–130 beats per minute.[4] This means that training intensity scales that rely on percentages of heart rate maximum or heart rate reserve are inappropriate; however, rating of perceived exertion (Borg scale) remains useful.[5]

Overall, exercise prescription principles in persons with spinal cord injury parallel those offered to the general population.[6–8] Functional electrical stimulation can activate contraction of paralyzed muscles of some persons with spinal cord injury. Coordinated patterns of stimulation allow purposeful exercise movements, including recumbent cycling, rowing,[9, 10] and upright ambulation.

Exercise activity in persons with spinal cord injury is not without risks that relate to systemic dysfunction, such as autonomic dysreflexia, low bone mass[11] and altered geometry,[12] joint contractures, and problems with thermoregulation (see below). The benefit of exercise activities,[13] can be enhanced and the relative risks reduced with accurate classification of the spinal injury (page 966).

Thermoregulation

People with spinal cord injury are vulnerable to heat injury[14] due to a reduction in peripheral receptor and cooling mechanisms; sweating is impaired below the level of the spinal injury. Sportspeople need to hydrate appropriately and acclimatize. Cooling and pre-cooling strategies offset the risk of heat illness and enhance endurance of performance.[15] These techniques include misting fans on the bench, ice packs to axillae and neck, and pre-cooling with iced "slurpee" drinks or ice baths.

There is also an increased inability to maintain body temperature in a cold environment because of lack of sensory input and shivering response. Thus, adequate preventive measures, including appropriate clothing, are particularly important for the person with disabilities. (Chapters 58 and 59 have more information on exercising in hot and cold climates.)

Pressure sores

The insensible areas of skin below the level of the lesion are susceptible to unnoticed skin abrasions or pressure sores from prolonged sitting. Once established, a pressure sore can entail months out of normal activities for the individual.

 The key to prevention is regular inspection of the skin after activity or travel, particularly international or long haul flying, looking for telltale red areas and abrasions.

Involvement of a wound care specialist or nurse to facilitate early and aggressive management with a range of modern dressings can minimize time out of both sport and daily living due to skin problems.

Autonomic dysreflexia (boosting)

An injury such as a fracture below the level of the lesion may fail to trigger the normal pain response, but instead induce a phenomenon known as "autonomic dysreflexia." Any nociceptive input below the level of the lesion can be the catalyst, such as a blocked catheter causing bladder distension, constipation, urinary calculi, or ingrowing toenails. The nociceptive stimulus results in inappropriate levels of noradrenalin (norepinephrine) secretion, producing hypertension, sweating, and skin blotching above the level of the lesion, and a pounding headache.

Case reports have documented hypertension severe enough to cause cerebral hemorrhage, fits, and death.

 Autonomic dysreflexia is a medical emergency with urgent attention required to remove the nociceptive stimulus and reduce blood pressure with medication such as sublingual nifedipine.

Some wheelchair athletes have found that when they were in the dysreflexic state while exercising, it appeared to reduce their rating of perceived exertion. Hence, some athletes started to induce this state intentionally to improve their performance by as much as 10%. The technique became known as "boosting."[16]

In 1994, inducing the dysreflexic state was considered doping and was banned by the IPC. However, as the condition may occur without intent and the athletes cannot be assessed during competition, boosting was removed as a doping method. Athletes may, however, have their blood pressure taken in a pre-competition setting, and, if a systolic blood pressure is 180 mmHg or greater, then they may be removed from competition on safety grounds. No sanction is imposed but the sportsperson is unable to compete in that event.

Osteopenia

The paralysis and consequent immobility associated with spinal cord injury can promote osteopenic or osteoporotic changes in the lower limbs and spine. This may result in fractures caused by minimal trauma, or from impact collisions in sports such as ice sledge hockey, or a fall from a chair in basketball. The sports clinician needs to raise his or her index of suspicion for fractures in the wheelchair sportsperson. Even though the limbs are not used for ambulation, fracture healing is important, as persistent deformity may result in increased difficulty with transferring to and from the chair and performing activities of daily living.

Overuse shoulder injuries

Upper limb overuse injuries are common among wheelchair users because of repetitive use of the arms for propulsion as well as transferring in and out of the chair. Whether such shoulder pain is more common in sedentary wheelchair users than among those who are regularly active remains unclear. Nevertheless, in sports such as swimming or those involving overhead activities (e.g. tennis), the person with disability is prone to additional sport-specific risk factors for shoulder injuries.

Shoulder pain may be referred from the cervical or thoracic spine because of the underlying spinal pathologies. Factors such as scoliosis, poor seating position, and muscle imbalance that results from pushing techniques may all contribute to alterations in scapula stabilization and abnormal patterns of movement (Chapter 21).

As reducing the load on an injured shoulder in a wheelchair sportsperson involves bed rest or loss of independence with ADLs, prevention is very important and should include:

- progression of training loads
- correctly fitted and maintained equipment
- scapular and rotator cuff strengthening
- flexibility—focusing on tight pectorals and scalenes
- early reporting and assessment of injuries.

Upper limb nerve entrapments

The two most common nerve entrapments in wheelchair sportspeople are carpal tunnel syndrome involving the median nerve, and ulnar nerve entrapment at the wrist (Guyons canal) or elbow (cubital tunnel).[17] Both are associated with the mechanical trauma associated with propulsion of a wheelchair, and can be prevented with appropriate wheelchair fit and maintenance, and with protecting the volar surface of the wrist with gloves or guards (see also Chapters 23 and 24).

Urinary tract infection

Neurogenic bladder is a common result of spinal cord injury and increases the frequency of urinary tract infections from incomplete voiding, elevated intravesical pressure and/or catheter use.[18] Subtle clinical signs and symptoms may be the only indication of infection. Reduced sporting performance, malaise, reduced appetite, or "not feeling quite right" are common presenting complaints.

 Traveling clinicians, should carry a supply of urine dipsticks to detect infection—leucocytes, nitrates, and blood.

Prevention is important, and excellent hydration, cranberry juice, and aseptic catheter technique are appropriate strategies. Many individuals with spinal cord injury have bacteruria; therefore routine antibiotic prophylaxis is not recommended in asymptomatic patients as this promotes development of drug-resistant bacteria. Symptomatic athletes should have urine cultured and be treated with appropriate antibiotic therapy.

The sportsperson with a limb deficiency

Limb deficiencies may be congenital or acquired, and persons may compete with or without a prosthesis, or in a wheelchair. A single-leg amputee has exceeded 2 m (6 ft) in the high jump. Some amputee athletes use a wheelchair to play sports such as tennis and basketball. These athletes have full muscular strength and proprioceptive capability, which may not be the case for their spinal cord–injured counterparts.

A lower limb amputee who uses a prosthetic limb for running now has the opportunity of using equipment that enhances performance (Fig. 46.1). The flexible carbon-fiber lower portion of the prosthesis now absorbs and returns energy to the runner in much the same way as the human Achilles tendon does. The best 100 m sprint time with the prosthesis is now about 11 seconds.

Advances in technologies permit control of the swing of the prosthetic knee to aid sporting performance and also day-to-day life. Microprocessor technology is used to detect movement patterns and the joint can be programmed from a laptop computer to adapt to different situations.[19] Upper limb adaptations can be useful in sports such as lawn bowls and equestrian riding, and target sports such as archery.

Clinical issues

The impact of running at these speeds on the residual limb can result in skin chafing, abrasion, and bone bruising. Skin infections can occur in hot environments, with excessive sweating. Cool clothing, appropriate liners for prosthesis, and talcum powder can prevent problems. The residual limb must be inspected regularly and cared for diligently to avoid

iSTOCKPHOTO

Figure 46.1 Example of a prosthetic limb used by a runner

injury; crutches or a wheelchair may be necessary for the resting of stump pressure areas (although many amputees are loath to use them).

Given the increased walking load associated with international travel,[20] using bikes for transport may be an alternative method of reducing weight-bearing load.

Because the prosthetic limb is shorter than the unaffected limb to allow it to swing through, there is a side-to-side discrepancy that may cause pelvic or low back pain, and this should be addressed with preventive lumbopelvic stability training (Chapter 14). Video analysis of gait and running can be helpful in addressing inefficient and injury-prone running styles.

The sportsperson with cerebral palsy

Cerebral palsy is a complex condition characterized by a variety of movement disorders. It is a "non-progressive but not unchanging disorder of movement or posture due to an insult or anomaly of the developing brain." Classification is often by the number of affected limbs (e.g. diplegia, hemiplegia, monoplegia) or, alternatively, by the type of movement disorder (e.g. spastic cerebral palsy with increased tone, choreo-athetoid cerebral palsy with large amounts of involuntary movement and poor coordination, a hypotonia, or a mixture of these patterns).

This may result in classifying a particular person's disability with terms such as a "spastic diplegia." Approximately 50% of people participating in

Paralympic sports with cerebral palsy will do so in a wheelchair, with the others being ambulant.

Cerebral palsy is also commonly associated with a variety of other problems as well as movement impairment. These include epilepsy, visual defects, deafness, and intellectual impairment; they can occur in combination.

Muscle spasticity presents a variety of problems. It may cause discomfort and poor posture that may predispose the sportsperson to other injuries. Spasticity may provide joint stabilization so excessive stretching of these muscles may inhibit performance, particularly in the ambulant sportsperson. Thus, although flexibility exercises are performed to maintain range of motion in joints, the timing of this relative to competition needs to be reviewed with individual sportspeople.

The sportsperson classified as Les Autres

The group of sportspeople with disabilities classified as Les Autres consists of people with physical impairments that do not fit into any other particular physical disability category. Numerous rare syndromic conditions cause physical restrictions and, as is common with syndromic conditions, there may be a variety of concurrent medical problems other than the physical limitation.

It is important that the clinician serving any of these sportspeople is familiar with the other aspects of the condition. For example, Stickler syndrome affects collagen synthesis and is a congenital condition associated with myopia, retinal detachment, cataracts, and glaucoma. The sportsperson, therefore, may be competing in a visually impaired category but the collagen abnormality will result in hypermobility of joints, poor healing, and the risk of early onset of osteoarthritis.

The sportsperson with visual impairment

Sportspeople are classified by an accredited ophthalmologist according to three levels of visual impairment (see box overleaf).

Visually impaired sportspeople can take part in a variety of sports with different degrees of adaptation of the sport. For example, in judo, the competitors start by holding onto each other's tunic. In athletics, a guide runner runs alongside the visually impaired athlete, sometimes attached by a cord or leash.

Some sports such as goalball have been developed specifically for the visually impaired. Goalball, a

Levels of visual impairment

B1: Athletes have either a total absence of perception of light in both eyes or some perception of light but are unable to recognize the form of a hand at any distance and in any direction.

B2: Athletes have the ability to recognize the form of a hand to a visual acuity of 2/60 and/or a visual field of less than 5°.

B3: Athletes have a visual acuity of above 2/60 to a visual acuity of 6/60 and/or a visual field of more than 5° and less than 20°.

court-based sport, has a large goal and is played with a ball with a bell. Players on one team hurl the ball towards the opponent's goal and the opponents hear where the ball is going and try to block it from entering their goal.

In swimming, a method is used to indicate to the swimmers when they are approaching the end of the lane to initiate a turn or to finish; this is achieved by tapping them on the head or shoulders as they approach the end using a long stick with a padded end.

Visual impairment may result in alterations in gait that may cause overuse injuries. Sportspeople with a visual impairment are also subject to collisions and falls. This risk is increased in foreign environments, such as accommodation and competition venues while on tour; this can be minimized by familiarizing sportspeople on arrival or allocating a sighted guide.

The sportsperson with an intellectual impairment

Sportspeople with an intellectual impairment have been included at the elite level of competition since 1989 but verification of the classification has proven challenging. The Sydney 2000 Paralympics included events for sportspeople with an intellectual disability and the Spanish men's basketball team won the gold medal. It was later discovered, however, that 10 of the 12 players had no learning difficulties. The team was stripped of its title and the scandal led to the IPC scrapping the "athletes with an intellectual disability" category on the grounds that athlete eligibility was too difficult.

In November 2009 the IPC General Assembly voted to re-include athletes with intellectual disabilities in the London 2012 Paralympic Games and

beyond. The increased requirements for classification of athletes with an intellectual disability will include sport-specific testing. Swimming, athletics, table tennis, and rowing are the sports forecasted to be included in the intellectual disability program at the London 2012 Paralympics.

The most common disability in the intellectual disability group is Down syndrome; other common disorders include autism, Asperger syndrome, and Fragile X syndrome. In all of these groups, congenital heart disease, ocular and visual problems are common.[21] Team physicians must ensure appropriate screening including echocardiography and visual screening.

Atlantoaxial instability is associated with Down syndrome and allows increased mobility at the first and second cervical vertebrae; most individuals are asymptomatic. Diagnosis can be made with flexion and extension lateral views of the cervical spine; a separation of the odontoid and the atlas of greater than 4–5 mm is suggestive of instability. The need for yearly screening is controversial.

 Sportspeople with evidence of atlantoaxial instability should be restricted from competing in any sport that requires excessive neck movements.[22]

Sportspeople with an intellectual disability may also have coexisting medical conditions depending on the cause of the impairment. For example, following head injury there may be epilepsy.

Classification

The traditional system of classification for physical disabilities was based on a medical model. There is now an increasing push away from purely medical criteria toward functional performance and sport-specific testing.

The medical model classified sportspeople by their disability. For example, sportspeople with a similar level of spinal cord injury were grouped together and would compete against each other; this resulted in multiple races within each event (e.g. 100 m sprint). Then some sports started to move to a more functional classification, so that sportspeople of different disability groups were classified according to factors such as muscle strength, range of motion, and proprioception, and also dynamically by sport performance. For example, a single race may contain competitors with paraplegia, cerebral palsy, and multiple limb deficiencies. This approach has led to improved competition, fewer classes, and improved public understanding of the sports.

Some sports (e.g. basketball) use a system to encourage sportspeople with different levels of disability to play together. This means that people with tetraplegia, paraplegia, or an amputation can play together as a team. It uses a points system where sportspeople are awarded points according to their degree of disability, with eight classes from 1 point going up in half points to 4.5 points; a higher classification number represents a greater ability to perform basketball-specific skills. The coach is only allowed players who contribute to a maximum of 14 points on the court at any one time.

The classification includes sport-specific tests such as shooting, passing, pushing, and dribbling, rather than any medical examination of muscle function. This allows on-court assessment during practice and competition to verify the players' capability. The process of classification is evolving in all sports to seek the fairest and most sport-specific way to classify for each individual sport.

The classification of intellectually impaired sportspeople is challenging (as described above). To qualify as intellectually impaired, an athlete must:

1. have significant impairment of intellectual functioning as indicated by a full scale score of 75 or lower on an internationally recognized and professionally administered IQ test
2. show significant limitations in adapted behavior as expressed in conceptual, social, and practical adapted skills—this includes communication difficulties, problems with self-care, and social and interpersonal skills; the limitations in adapted behavior can be established with the use of standardized measures that have been referenced against the general population
3. have had evidence of intellectual disability during the developmental period—from conception to age 18 years.

These requirements are necessary for sportspeople undertaking elite sport and not for the Special Olympics.

A practical implication for the sports clinician working with the intellectually disabled is that consent to medical treatment should be agreed with the guardian or parent.

Adapting performance testing and training for disabled sportspeople

Within able-bodied sport, there are well-established physiological profiles and scientific literature on the performance capability of sportspeople. Within disability sport, research has been limited.[23] A challenge in disabled sport is that physiological responses to exercise vary in different sportspeople. For example, heart rate response differs between paraplegic and quadriplegic sportspeople because the maximal heart rate is restricted in the quadriplegic athlete.[24, 25] People with cerebral palsy have different capacities to clear lactate because of hypertonia.

The base of knowledge within disability sport has traditionally come from the rehabilitation or exercise therapy setting rather than from performance, so the base of knowledge focuses on this aspect rather than on elite sport performance. There has also been limited exposure to good-quality coaching. All these factors lead to difficulties in performance profiling.

Methods of assessment of fitness also need to be different. Arm crank ergometry has been used for wheelchair users, but is not specific to the normal action used in propelling a wheelchair. Wheelchair-usable treadmills and roller systems are used to assess aerobic capacity. Wheelchair propulsion is akin to cycling and running, and so VO_2 max peak measures are expressed as liters per minute.

Modifications to field tests that serve sportspeople with a disability include a multi-staged "shuttle" fitness test adapted to, and performed around, an octagonal circuit to avoid the abrupt forwards and backwards turning of a regular "shuttle" run.[26]

The standard principles of strength training need to be adapted according to the disability. The wheelchair user may be unable to stabilize the trunk to perform the action; however, the equipment can be adapted to allow the exercise to take place. Although there has been concern that sportspeople with cerebral palsy may suffer increased muscle tone from strength training, there is little evidence for this.

The standard principles of biomechanics also need to be re-examined where, for example, stroke technique in swimming, symmetry of running,[27] or javelin throwing techniques must be re-evaluated in the light of the disability. Efforts can be made to improve streamlining in the water or to improve range of motion in a joint, for example, but normal models of "correct technique" may have to be re-evaluated.

Winter sports and common injuries

Winter sports exist in a variety of disciplines for people with disabilities, and participation can include the competitive Paralympic level (Table 46.1). The alpine events cater for the visually impaired, spinally injured, or the limb-deficient sportsperson. Guide skiers are used for the visually impaired and a sitting monoski is used for paraplegic sportspeople.

Standing sportspeople are at risk of the usual skiing injuries (e.g. head injury or anterior cruciate ligament rupture). In the sitting classes, small outriggers are used with a ski on the end to control the ski, so forceful impact landing on the outrigger can cause wrist fracture or shoulder injury. The cross-country events are associated with overuse injuries, and the sit-skier may suffer shoulder and elbow problems. Biathlon (skiing and shooting) can be performed by the visually impaired using a sighting mechanism that utilizes an audible signal with increasing tone as the competitor points toward the center of the target.

Sledge hockey is an adapted form of ice hockey. Competitors sit on the sledge and skate by pushing two sticks, which are also used to strike the puck. A variety of disability groups participate in this sport as there are only minimal disability entry criteria. Injuries occur by direct contact between players, use of the stick (intentionally or accidentally), or by being hit by the puck. Sportspeople with spinal cord injury–induced low bone mass are susceptible to fracture in this sport. Wheelchair curling was introduced to the Paralympic Winter Games in Torino in 2006 and caused few injuries.

Anti-doping issues

The IOC is a signatory to the World Anti-Doping Code (WADA) (Chapter 66). The list of prohibited substances is the same for Paralympic athletes as for able-bodied athletes. Because of the nature of athletes' disabilities, it is more likely that they may need to take medications on the prohibited list to manage medical conditions. To do this, they must complete a therapeutic use exemption (TUE) application process that is outlined in Chapter 66. A successful application has to meet the same criteria as for able-bodied athletes:

1. that the athlete would experience a significant impairment to health if the prohibited substance or method was to be withheld in the course of treating an acute or chronic medical condition

2. that the therapeutic use of the prohibited substance would not produce additional enhancement of performance other than that which might be anticipated by a return to a state of normal health

3. that there are no reasonable therapeutic alternatives to the use of the prohibited substance or method

4. that the necessity for the use of the prohibited substance or method is not as a consequence of prior non-therapeutic use of the prohibited substance.

There are some differences to the sample collection process which vary according to the disability. Sportspeople who use intermittent catheterization are permitted to use their own catheter to collect the urine sample. For sportspeople who use a condom and leg bag drainage system, the contents of the leg bag must first be emptied, and a fresh sample of urine collected. This is to avoid the potential for inserting a "clean" sample of urine into the leg bag prior to competition.

Sportspeople who are visually impaired receive help to complete forms and are supervised by their own observer in the sample collection process. The sportsperson's representative observes the Doping Control Officer during the sample collection process to ensure that there is no tampering of the sample during the collection process. Sportspeople with an intellectual disability need to be accompanied by a representative who understands the process.

Disability sport does not appear to be rife with abuse of prohibited substances. However, as in able-bodied sport, power lifting has been tainted by anabolic steroid use. Understandably, there have been claims of inadvertent use of diuretics or beta blockers to treat hypertension. It is challenging for sportspeople to be aware of the anti-doping restrictions on medication used to manage their medical conditions; this population requires particularly skilled sports medicine care.

Travel with teams

Although Chapter 64 is devoted to travel with teams, sportspeople with disability have specific needs. Firstly, the simple logistics of boarding a team of wheelchair users on and off an aircraft takes additional time and may require lifting and handling. Toileting on board aircraft using a small-wheeled aisle chair is difficult and is likely to decrease the fluid intake of wheelchair users, leading to dehydration. Transportation at the destination needs to be accessible. The team clinician should aim to be familiar with the accessibility of toilets, rooms, and sports facilities in advance.

Prolonged sitting without the use of the normal pressure cushion may result in pressure areas on the skin. Sportspeople should try to take pressure-relieving measures during the journey and check pressure areas on arrival. The risk of deep vein thrombosis exists for all long-haul passengers. Dependent edema can be a particular problem among individuals who do not have the capacity to use the active muscle pump. Compression stockings can be appropriate.

REFERENCES

1. Booth FW, Gordon SE, Carlson CJ et al. Waging war on modern chronic diseases: primary prevention through exercise biology. *J Appl Physiol* 2000;88(2):774–87.

2. Groah SL, Nash MS, Ward EA et al. Cardiometabolic risk in community-dwelling persons with chronic spinal cord injury. *J Cardiopulm Rehabil Prev* 2011;31(2): 73–80.

3. Schmid A, Schmidt-Trucksass A, Huonker M et al. Catecholamines response of high performance wheelchair athletes at rest and during exercise with autonomic dysreflexia. *Int J Sports Med* 2001;22(1):2–7.

4. Dela F, Mohr T, Jensen CM et al. Cardiovascular control during exercise: insights from spinal cord-injured humans. *Circulation* 2003;107(16):2127–33.

5. Hopman MT, Houtman S, Groothuis JT et al. The effect of varied fractional inspired oxygen on arm exercise performance in spinal cord injury and able-bodied persons. *Arch Phys Med Rehabil* 2004;85(2): 319–23.

6. Jacobs PL, Nash MS. Exercise recommendations for individuals with spinal cord injury. *Sports Med* 2004;34(11):727–51.

7. Nash MS. Exercise as a health-promoting activity following spinal cord injury. *J Neurol Phys Ther* 2005;29(2):87–103,106.

8. Myslinski MJ. Evidence-based exercise prescription for individuals with spinal cord injury. *J Neurol Phys Ther* 2005;29(2):104–6.

9. Wheeler GD, Andrews B, Lederer R et al. Functional electric stimulation-assisted rowing: increasing cardiovascular fitness through functional electric stimulation rowing training in persons with spinal cord injury. *Arch Phys Med Rehabil* 2002;83(8):1093–9.

10. Halliday SE, Zavatsky AB, Hase K. Can functional electric stimulation-assisted rowing reproduce a race-winning rowing stroke? *Arch Phys Med Rehabil* 2004;85(8):1265–72.

11. Shields RK, Dudley-Javoroski S, Law LA. Electrically induced muscle contractions influence bone density decline after spinal cord injury. *Spine* 2006;31(5):548–53.

12. Giangregorio LM, Craven BC, Webber CE. Musculoskeletal changes in women with spinal cord injury: a twin study. *J Clin Densitom* 2005;8(3):347–51.

13. de Groot PC, Hjeltnes N, Heijboer AC et al. Effect of training intensity on physical capacity, lipid profile and insulin sensitivity in early rehabilitation of spinal cord injured individuals. *Spinal Cord* 2003;41(12):673–9.

14. Webborn AD. Heat-related problems for the Paralympic Games, Atlanta. *Br J Ther Rehabil* 1996;3:429–36.

15. Webborn N, Price MJ, Castle PC et al. Effects of two cooling strategies on thermoregulatory responses of tetraplegic athletes during repeated intermittent exercise in the heat. *J Appl Physiol* 2005;98(6):2101–7.

16. Webborn AD. 'Boosting' performance in disability sport. *Br J Sports Med* 1999;33(2):74–5.

17. Klenck C, Gebke K. Practical management: common medical problems in disabled athletes. *Clin J Sport Med* 2007;17:55–60.

18. Garcia ME, Esclarin De Ruz A. Management of urinary tract infection in patients with spinal cord injuries. *Clin Microbiol Infect* 2003;9:780–5.

19. Agarwal S, Triolo RJ, Kobetic R et al. Long-term user perceptions of an implanted neuroprosthesis for exercise, standing, and transfers after spinal cord injury. *J Rehabil Res Dev* 2003;40(3):241–52.

20. Burkett B. Is daily walking when living in the Paralympic village different to the typical home environment? *Br J Sports Med* 2010;44:533–6

21. Klenck C, Gebke K. Practical management: common medical problems in disabled athletes. *Clin J Sport Med* 2007;17(1):55–60.

22. Malanga GA. Athletes with disabilities. *Emedicine* 2005. Available at: www.emedicine.com

23. Tasiemski T, Bergstrom E, Savic G et al. Sports, recreation and employment following spinal cord injury—a pilot study. *Spinal Cord* 2000;38(3):173–84.

24. Bhambhani Y. Physiology of wheelchair racing in athletes with spinal cord injury. *Sports Med* 2002; 32(1):23–51.

25. van der Woude LH, Bouten C, Veeger HE et al. Aerobic work capacity in elite wheelchair athletes: a cross-sectional analysis. *Am J Phys Med Rehabil* 2002;81(4):261–71.

26. Vanderthommen M, Francaux M, Colinet C et al. A multistage field test of wheelchair users for evaluation of fitness and prediction of peak oxygen consumption. *J Rehabil Res Dev* 2002;39(6):685–92.

27. Burkett B, Smeathers J, Barker T. Walking and running inter-limb asymmetry for Paralympic trans-femoral amputees: a biomechanical analysis. *Prosthet Orthot Int* 2003;27(1):36–47.

Part D

Management of medical problems

Chapter 47

Medical emergencies in the sporting context

with SHANE BRUN

Fortune favors the prepared mind.   Louis Pasteur

This chapter addresses emergencies—the life- or limb-threatening situations that require more advanced medical knowledge, skills, and equipment. As with many elements of sport and exercise medicine (Chapter 2) these situations are best managed using a team approach (if possible). Because athletes and their accompanying clinical teams travel widely both nationally and internationally, not all athlete emergency care occurs near high-level definitive services. We were aware of this when writing this chapter.

Because emergencies are infrequent, it is tempting not to prepare and practice for such events because of all the other pressing demands on clinicians' time. Unfortunately, life- and limb-threatening conditions require immediate and expert care. Are you and your clinical team well prepared and rehearsed in the skills, knowledge, and equipment required? Clinicians with the responsibility of caring for athletes at any level should undertake a recognized and accredited medical emergency care course.

The role of the physiotherapist in emergency care

Most sporting situations take place in the absence of a physician trained in the management of sporting emergencies. Thus, the responsibility of preparing for, and managing, an emergency may fall to other clinicians such as the physiotherapist or athletic trainer. All clinicians must be aware of the limits of their practice, as determined by their national credentialing organization. Those responsible for sporting teams or athletes are strongly encouraged to gain further training in emergency care.

Although there are skills and procedures described in this chapter that are legally restricted to medical practitioners, the chapter is also relevant for physiotherapists. The physiotherapist performs a vital role in the management of sporting emergencies either as the team leader or team member. As a member of an emergency team, the physiotherapist assists the physician in preparing for an emergency situation, and in the overall immediate management of the patient with a life- or limb-threatening condition. If the physiotherapist is the emergency team leader, he or she has the responsibility for preparing for and managing the emergency situation.

Emergency care principles

When an emergency occurs, the onus is on the most senior clinician present to perform a rapid assessment of the situation and the patient and initiate life- and/or limb-saving management. Leadership and team roles must be clearly defined and outlined well in advance, and the skills related to each role rehearsed as a team. The sequence of events for emergency care is outlined in the box below.

Sequence of events for emergency care

1. Preparation
2. Triage
3. Primary survey
4. Resuscitate and stabilize
5. Focused history
6. Secondary survey
7. Continuous reassessment
8. Definitive care

Preparation

The two components of preparation are:

- pre-situation preparation
- situation preparation.

Pre-situation preparation

The clinical team must prepare and rehearse its approach to possible emergencies. A clinical team responsible for motor sports will have different emergency priorities and preparation than a team responsible for swimmers. Similarly, preparation is very different for a clinical team managing athletes in a major capital city with ready access to Pre-hospital Emergency Medical Services (PHEMS) such as a well-developed and professionally run ambulance service and nearby major medical facilities, compared with the clinical team taking care of sportspeople in a rural area (see also Chapter 63, "Providing team care," and Chapter 64, "Traveling with a team").

Pre-situation preparation comprises:

- emergency medical knowledge
- emergency medical skills
- emergency medical equipment/adjuncts
- clinical team rehearsal
- ensuring your clinical team, sportspeople, and officials are aware of emergency response procedures, exit points, and assembly points at the venues where they train and participate.

Situation preparation

When the emergency occurs, the clinical team leader should:

- survey the scene
- oversee universal precautions
- organize the clinical team.

Surveying the scene requires ensuring your and your clinical team's safety as an absolute priority. Establish that the environment is safe for you and the team to enter before proceeding. The biggest risk is for the medical team to rush into a situation without surveying the scene first, thereby compromising the safety of all concerned.

Universal precautions are for the safety of the clinical team—clinical team safety must remain a priority. As an absolute minimum each team member should be issued with and wear gloves, goggles or glasses, and protective footwear. Depending on the sport and situation, more extensive protective gear

may be necessary; this must be determined in the pre-situation phase.

Organizing the clinical team requires confirming roles previously assigned as well as which members will be responsible for which pieces of medical equipment to be brought to the scene.

Triage

Triage is the sorting of patients based on their need for treatment and the resources available. For this chapter we assume the clinical team will be confronted with either a single-casualty emergency or a multiple-casualty emergency where the number of casualties and the severity of their injuries do not overwhelm the clinical team or the resources available. Even where there are multiple casualties, the triage priorities remain: Airway, Breathing, Circulation and Disability. The topic of sporting event disasters preparedness—events with mass casualties—is outside the scope of this chapter.

> At the time of triage, the clinical team leader may wish to delegate the role of notifying the Pre-hospital Emergency Medical Services (PHEMS) (also widely known as ambulance service or emergency medical service (EMS)) of the situation. It is always better to notify early rather than late.

Primary survey

The primary survey is when life-threatening conditions are identified and treated simultaneously. Although the primary survey (Fig. 47.1 overleaf) is divided into system priorities for teaching purposes, in reality several life-threatening issues may be identified and treated at the same time. There are subsequent "surveys" to the primary survey, although this chapter only focuses on the "primary" and "secondary" surveys as these are the times to identify and treat life-threatening conditions (primary survey) as well as limb-threatening conditions (secondary survey).

The primary survey (Fig. 47.1) is somewhat different from how a physician would usually assess and treat a patient. In the primary survey, compromise or life threat is rapidly identified and treated. Parts of the patient history are often deferred until after the primary survey is complete, and when examinations are performed they are very specific and focused. In the pre-hospital setting very few medical investigations are performed, with the exception of obtaining vital signs, oxygen saturation, and electrocardiograph (ECG/EKG).

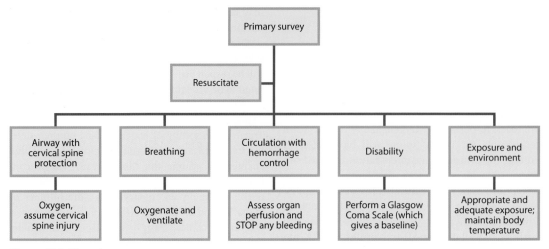

Figure 47.1 The primary survey

At the time of the primary survey, the patient is positioned to facilitate assessment and treatment. In most situations, the supine position best allows the clinical team to assess, observe, and treat the patient with minimal movement and delay.

The key priorities for each system in the primary survey are as follows (these are expanded later in this chapter):

A. Airway and cervical spine control:
   1. The first priority in any emergency situation is to establish a patent airway.
   2. In any emergency that has resulted from trauma or has involved an event in which the patient may have sustained a spinal injury, ensure cervical spine stabilization at the time of establishing airway patency.
   3. At this time, high-flow oxygen may be administered to the patient. In the critically ill or injured patient, in the acute stages, assume that there is no absolute contraindication to the administration of oxygen.
B. Breathing and ventilation:
   1. Airway patency does not ensure adequate ventilation.
   2. Once the airway is patent and the cervical spine stabilized, assess the patient's breathing to determine if it is adequate or if conditions exist which may compromise breathing.
   3. The aim is that the patient will be breathing effectively alone (active ventilation). If the patient is unable to breathe, the clinical team should ventilate the patient (passive ventilation).

C. Circulation and hemorrhage control:
   1. In patients who have sustained trauma and demonstrate signs and symptoms of shock, assume that the cause of shock is hypovolemia. Bleeding is a major cause of preventable death following trauma. Thus any external bleeding must be immediately controlled by direct and firm pressure.
   2. The shocked state in the patient who has not been involved in trauma is likely to be as a result of marked peripheral vasodilation, pump failure, and/or inadequate heart rate.
   3. In the primary survey, both traumatic shock and atraumatic shock are treated similarly.
   4. Don't underestimate the importance of splinting fractures as part of hemorrhage control. Significant blood loss can occur internally especially at femoral fracture sites. Early and appropriate fracture immobilization may be indicated during this phase of assessment.
D. Disability:
   1. This refers to neurological assessment and is usually performed toward the end of the primary survey. This important assessment provides
      (a) an early measure of neurological function—essential as a baseline against which to compare change as time progresses
      (b) in the absence of head injury, an altered level of consciousness indicates cerebral hypoxia or hypoperfusion—this should

immediately alert the clinician to reassess Airway, Breathing, and Circulation.

2. It is best assessed by performing a Glasgow Coma Scale (GCS) and pupillary size and response (see under the Disability section later in this chapter).

E. Exposure/environment control:

1. One of the major pitfalls in emergency care is not looking. Never assume that the injuries or compromise you initially see are all that is to be found.

2. Adequate and appropriate exposure of the patient is essential. The privacy provided on a sporting field or arena is indeed limited and must be kept in mind by the clinical team. Ensure as much patient privacy and confidentiality as is possible without compromising inspection of all body surfaces.

3. Environment control is an aspect of care that is often neglected. One must remember that a critically ill or injured patient may lose the ability to thermoregulate, thereby becoming poikilothermic, adopting the surrounding temperature. The natural inclination is to "keep the patient warm" but the ideal plan is to "keep the patient normothermic." Keep core temperature as close to 37°C (98.6°F) as possible. Note that your own comfort level may not be accurate or appropriate as a monitor of environmental condition.

Resuscitate and stabilize

In the clinical setting, the resuscitation and stabilization of the patient are performed at the same time in the primary survey. However, this phase is differentiated because an important aspect of emergency medical management is the use of drugs[a] and adjuncts. Adjuncts include intercostal catheters, intravenous catheters and fluids, pulse oximetry, and cardiac monitoring. Because legally a physician can use emergency drugs and medical adjuncts, the physician is an important member of the clinical team in an emergency.

Focused history

The history allows the clinical team to identify injuries or potential for compromise that might otherwise

be missed. Depending on the circumstances it may be appropriate to change the sequence of events between "focused history" and "secondary survey," thereby performing the secondary survey prior to or simultaneously with the focused history. Initially, at the time of the primary survey and resuscitation, history-taking may be very basic. Apply the A MIST acronym:

A **A**ge and sex of patient
M **M**echanism of injury or circumstances surrounding the event
I **I**njuries sustained or problems identified
S **S**igns and **S**ymptoms
T **T**reatment given so far

This acronym is also useful when handing a patient over to PHEMS (ambulance, emergency care) or definitive medical care.

Once the primary survey is complete and the patient stabilized, a more focused history may be performed. Apply the AMPLE acronym:

A **A**llergies
M **M**edications
P **P**ast illnesses/**P**regnancy
L **L**ast oral intake (solids and liquids)
E **E**vents/**E**nvironment related to the situation

Secondary survey

Depending on the distance of the emergency to definitive care, the severity of the condition, and the response time of the PHEMS, a secondary survey may not be performed. The primary objective in emergency care is to prevent loss of life; then to identify and prevent potential compromise and limb-threatening conditions. It is only when the clinical team leader is satisfied that the patient is stable and that all aspects of the primary survey are complete and have been addressed that attention should move to the secondary survey.

The secondary survey is a complete assessment of the patient—essentially a full systems review, with assessment of all body surfaces. A Glasgow Coma Scale should also be performed if it has not been performed earlier. Also perform a log roll, so the back and spine may be more adequately assessed. It is during this stage that non-life-threatening conditions are identified and treated. If at any time the patient's condition changes, the priority is to recommence the primary survey and reassess Airway, Breathing, Circulation, and Disability.

---

[a] Throughout this chapter all drug doses will assume an adult patient unless otherwise specified.

Reassessment

Reassessment is one of the most important aspects of emergency management. You must be continuously vigilant for changes in the patient's condition and have a very low threshold for reviewing and reassessing all components of the primary survey.

 If at any time the patient's condition changes, the patient is moved, or you are feeling overwhelmed by the situation, recommence the primary survey starting with reassessment of the airway.

It is important not to consider emergency care as a linear progression. The continuum of care should be considered as a continuous cycle of assessment and reassessment (Fig. 47.2).

Definitive care

Most patients who require out-of-hospital emergency care will require transfer to definitive medical care. In many situations this is done by a well-coordinated PHEMS; in most countries this is a highly skilled and professional paramedic ambulance service. In all situations, but particularly in rural and remote sporting locations, an important responsibility of the clinical team leader is to be familiar with the medical resources, facilities, availability, and skills of the PHEMS and the distance these are from the sporting venue and athlete accommodation. (This responsibility also applies with home events.)

The primary survey in detail

In this section we discuss basic life support, then each component of the primary survey. We also outline how to assess and manage each system and we discuss the use of appropriate primary survey adjuncts. At the end of each section we discuss how to identify and manage some common clinical emergency scenarios.

Basic life support

In most countries and regions it is a community and legal expectation that a person accepting the responsibility of clinical care for a sporting team or athletes is familiar and competent with performing basic life support. It is also an expectation that all physicians are familiar and competent with advanced life support techniques. This expectation is greater when the clinician is charged with the responsibility of care outside a hospital or clinic environment when the clinician is most likely to be the initial responder in an emergency situation.

Each member of the clinical team should be familiar, skilled, and practiced in basic life support techniques, such as those a recognized and accredited training provider may offer. An essential component of basic life support is the immediate management of a cardiac arrest and the effective performance of cardio-pulmonary resuscitation (CPR). A basic life support flowchart (Drs ABCD) is outlined in Figure 47.3; the chart is available through the Australian Resuscitation Council (www.resus.org.au/). Details of basic life support are not within

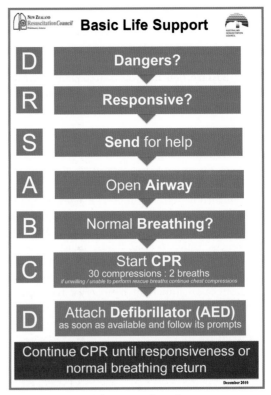

Figure 47.3 Basic life support flow chart

FROM AUSTRALIAN RESUSCITATION COUNCIL, WWW.RESUS.ORG.AU

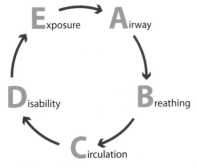

Figure 47.2 The cycle of emergency management

the scope of this chapter. Each member of the clinical team should recertify in basic life support skills annually.[1]

A very important skill for clinical team members to be confident and competent with, especially the physician, is performing bag-valve-mask (BVM) ventilation.

The mask is held onto the face using the jaw thrust technique (Fig. 47.4). When positioning and holding the mask it is important to remember that the concept is to bring the patient's face into the mask rather than forcing the mask onto the patient's face. The latter causes unnecessary operator finger fatigue and has the potential of flexing the patient's head, thereby risking an occluded airway.

Once the mask is positioned, the operator is able to perform either mouth-to-mask ventilation or BVM ventilation with supplemental oxygen (if available). For the inexperienced operator, BVM ventilation is best performed by two operators, one securing the mask to the patient's face and the other compressing the bag firmly.

Airway with cervical spine control

The first priority in any emergency is to establish a patent airway. The quickest way to identify the patency of the airway is to ask the patient their name and how they are. This 10-second assessment provides the clinical team with four valuable pieces of information:

- the patency of the airway
    - if the patient is unable to answer it may imply unconsciousness or an occluded airway
    - presence of stridor or noises coming from the airway suggests a degree of obstruction

Figure 47.4 Applying a face mask using the jaw thrust technique. Bring the patient's face into the mask

- the effectiveness and ease of breathing
- the hemodynamic status of the patient, as adequate cerebral perfusion is required to respond
- the neurological status of the patient.

If the patient is maintaining his or her own airway, all that is required is constant monitoring of its patency. In many instances airway patency is relatively easy to achieve using basic airway techniques, which are discussed below (pp. 978–82).

Oxygen is one of the most valuable drugs used in the emergency situation. Along with establishing and maintaining a patent airway, the patient should have oxygen administered (if it is available). In most initial situations, oxygen should be administered in high concentrations although oxygen delivery devices providing lesser concentrations may be more appropriate to maintain optimal oxygen saturation. Initially, oxygen delivery is best achieved using a non-rebreather face mask aiming for an oxygen saturation of at least 94–98% in patients without a history of lung disease.[2]

With any critically ill or injured person, it is safe to assume that there are no absolute contraindications to the administration of oxygen. Apply the mask as soon as possible and initially set the oxygen flow rate to 15 L per minute. Titrate the flow against the patient's oxygen saturation (aiming for at least 94–98%).

Cervical spine management

In any patient who has sustained significant trauma, an associated cervical spine injury or potential injury should be considered to be present. Thus, maintaining cervical spine control is an essential aspect of care. Each member of the clinical team must be competent at both sizing and fitting a cervical collar. Cervical collars are available in both fixed and adjustable collar sizes. The adjustable semi-rigid collars are most appropriate in the sporting context as they are compact and negate the need to carry multiple collars of various sizes (Fig. 47.5a overleaf). Adjusting the collar to the correct size is imperative; this is demonstrated in Figure 47.5b–e overleaf.

Initially the cervical spine is held stable by one member of the clinical team (Fig. 47.5f overleaf), the head and spine should remain in line, with the head in the neutral position. Then slide the correctly sized collar behind the patient's neck, position it correctly, and secure it quite firmly to prevent excessive movement (Fig. 47.5g–j on page 979). It is important to remember that a cervical collar does not "immobilize"

Figure 47.5 Cervical spine management
(a) Laerdel style adjustable semi-rigid cervical collar

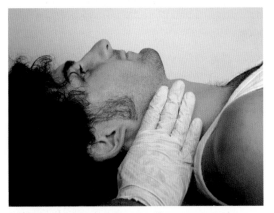

(b) Sizing a cervical collar using fingers as a guide

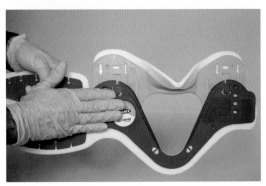

(c) Use this predetermined distance to measure from the blue plastic edge to nearest hole

the cervical spine; it merely assists in stabilization and helps remind the patient and the clinical team to assume spinal injury and manage accordingly.

Airway management technique adjuncts
How the patient is positioned and where the clinician stands are important initial steps. In most situations the patient is positioned supine and the clinician is either at the top or to the side of the patient's head.

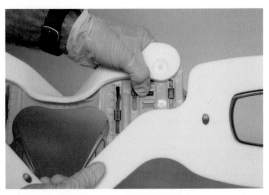

(d) Release locking lug and adjust collar so red marker (Fig. 47.5e) aligns with the correct measured hole

(e) Red marker positioned at sizing hole

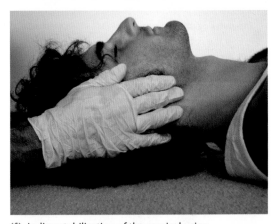

(f) In-line stabilization of the cervical spine

The priority in airway management is to maintain patency. Another priority in airway management (although less important than ensuring the patency of the airway) is protecting the airway and preventing the passage of blood or vomitus.

(g) Positioning and securing of cervical collar—step 1

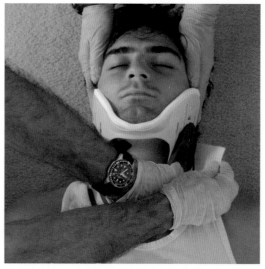

(i) Positioning and securing of cervical collar—step 3

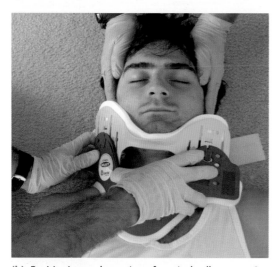

(h) Positioning and securing of cervical collar—step 2

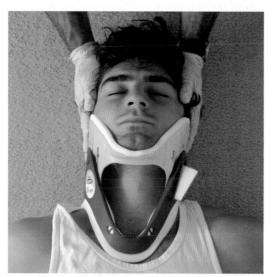

(j) Positioning and securing of cervical collar—step 4

Maintaining a patent airway can be achieved using one or a combination of several techniques. Inspect the mouth and upper airway for obstruction (teeth, blood, vomitus, a mouth guard). Remove any obstruction using gloved fingers, long forceps, and/or suction. Once foreign matter has been removed from the airway, the next possible obstruction is the tongue and soft tissues at the back of the throat.

To address this possibility use the "jaw lift" or "pistol grip" (Fig. 47.6 overleaf). This is achieved by grasping the lower jaw of the patient firmly and, while keeping the fingers clear of the throat, moving the jaw anteriorly so as to lift the tongue from the back of the throat. This is usually combined with head tilt which is obtained by tilting the head, not the neck, back.

A more effective technique is "jaw thrust" (Fig. 47.7 overleaf). This technique is performed by placing the fourth and fifth fingers behind the angles of the jaw and moving the entire mandible anteriorly. This subluxes the jaw anteriorly and moves the tongue well clear of the back of the throat.

Oropharyngeal airway

A useful adjunct for maintaining airway patency is the oropharyngeal airway (Fig. 47.8a overleaf). This curved piece of hollow plastic is placed into the airway

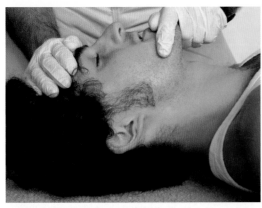

Figure 47.6 Jaw lift to clear the tongue from the back of the throat

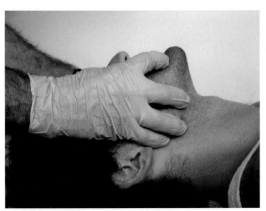

Figure 47.7 Jaw thrust—a more effective technique than the jaw lift
(a) Lateral view

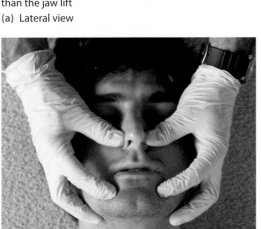

(b) Anterior view

and sits posterior to the tongue. It provides passage for air to flow. The lumen of an oropharyngeal airway is relatively narrow and the tube remains mobile in the airway and unsecured, so airway patency cannot be assumed. Frequent reassessment is essential.

Inserting the correct size of oropharyngeal airway is essential so as not to obstruct the airway. To size an oropharangeal airway, align the airway to the outside of the patient's mouth, so that the flange sits just anterior to the front teeth and the tail curves around the angle of the jaw (Fig. 47.8b).

To insert the airway use some lubricant or water on the tube. With the patient's mouth held slightly opened, insert the tube so the distal part of the tube, or its tail, is pointing toward the patient's nose (Fig. 47.9a). It is then passed over the tongue and

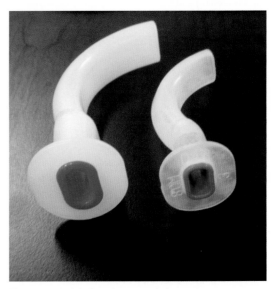

Figure 47.8 (a) Oropharyngeal airways

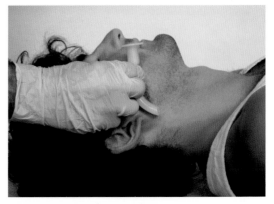

(b) Sizing the oropharyngeal airway

when the tail of the tube is at the back of the patient's throat, it is rotated 180° to rest in the posterior pharynx. The flange should sit anterior to the front teeth so as the reinforced bite area of the tube sits between the front teeth (Fig. 47.9b).

Endotracheal tube
Although patency is the first priority, providing the patient with both a patent and a protected airway is ideal. This can be achieved with a cuffed tube in the trachea—an endotracheal tube (ETT). The technique requires skill and training that must be practiced on a regular basis (as there is the potential for substantial risks in inexperienced operators' hands). Inserting an ETT is made significantly more difficult when attempted in an uncontrolled environment such as in the middle of a sporting field. It also requires the use of other instruments—such as a laryngoscope, which is costly and requires skill to use. Endotracheal intubation should only be performed by practitioners

skilled and practiced in the technique. The technique of ETT insertion is beyond the scope of this book.

Airway patency is the priority.

Laryngeal mask airway
A laryngeal mask airway (LMA) (Fig. 47.10) consists of an inflatable mask and a connecting tube. It is inserted into the pharynx. The use of a laryngeal mask airway (LMA) requires skills and training that are within the scope of many physicians. Insertion of the LMA may be simplified as a three-step process (Fig. 47.11 overleaf).

The LMA, once inserted and the cuff inflated, provides for a patent airway and offers partial airway protection. The patient may be ventilated through the LMA using the same technique as that used with an ETT.

Essential airway adjuncts

- Non-rebreather mask initially connected to high-flow oxygen
- Cervical collar—sized correctly and positioned securely

Potentially life-threatening airway problems
Three potentially fatal airway problems require vigilance—choking, anaphylaxis, and inability to clear the airway.

Choking—airway blockage
A common cause of partial or complete airway blockage is a foreign body. If the airway cannot be cleared by the procedures outlined above, then follow the

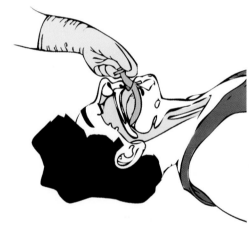

BROOKE FOWLER

Figure 47.9 (a) Inserting the oropharyngeal airway in an adult (with the tail pointing toward the nose)

BROOKE FOWLER

(b) Final position of oropharyngeal airway (after rotating 180°)

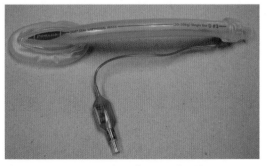

Figure 47.10 Laryngeal mask airway (LMA)

Figure 47.11 Inserting a laryngeal mask airway in three stages

algorithm on choking as outlined by the Australian Resuscitation Council (Fig. 47.12).

Anaphylaxis

Anaphylaxis can occur at any time in response to allergens to which the person has been previously sensitized (e.g. bee sting, peanuts). Ideally, the clinician should be aware of any adverse, allergic, or anaphylactic reactions which a sportsperson has previously experienced. Plan appropriate management to prevent it occurring again.

Signs and symptoms of anaphylaxis are outlined in the box below.

Anaphylaxis is likely when all of the following are present:
- There is life-threatening airway, breathing, or circulation compromise.
- There are skin and/or mucosal changes (although these may be subtle).
- These features are of sudden onset and the progression is rapid.

The immediate management of anaphylaxis is:[3]

- Follow an emergency management plan that has been previously developed for the patient.
- Remove any residual traces of the causative substance if possible (e.g. the bee's stinger).
- Administer oxygen, titrated to maintain saturation of at least 94%.
- Give adrenaline (intramuscular)
  - 0.3–0.5 mg IM[1] injection for adult
  - 0.01 mg/kg IM injection for child
  - Repeat every three to five minutes if there is inadequate response

Signs and symptoms of anaphylaxis

Anaphylaxis, although also a shock state, may cause significant airway compromise. Signs and symptoms of anaphylaxis may include:
- wheezing
- stridor
- flushed, red, and/or itchy skin
- hives
- swelling of the throat, tongue, and/or lips
- tachycardia
- extreme anxiety
- collapse followed by unconsciousness if not immediately treated.

AUSTRALIAN
RESUSCITATION
COUNCIL

MANAGEMENT OF FOREIGN BODY AIRWAY OBSTRUCTION (CHOKING)

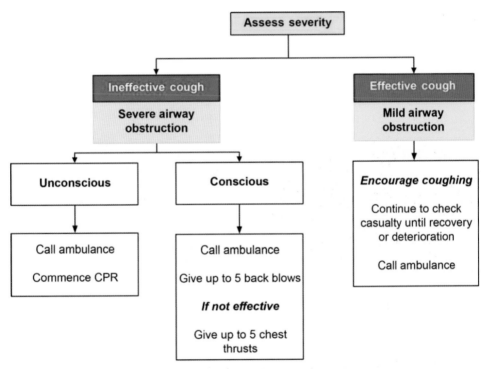

Figure 47.12 Flow chart for the management of foreign body airway obstruction

FROM AUSTRALIAN RESUSCITATION COUNCIL, www.resus.org.au

- The patient may have his or her own adrenaline for self-administration which contains a predetermined dose (Epipen).
- Give inhaled salbutamol if there is evidence of bronchospasm (e.g. wheeze).
- Obtain an intravenous access if possible.
- Fluid resuscitation if there is hemodynamic compromise.

- Administer both histamine H_1 (e.g. loratadine) and H_2 receptor antagonists (e.g. ranitidine), preferably by the intravenous route, if the drug is able to be administered this way, or orally.
- Give hydrocortisone 4 mg/kg IV six-hourly followed by prednisone 1 mg/kg up to a maximum of 50 mg orally daily for four days.

Oxygen and adrenaline are the first drugs to be administered during anaphylaxis. Note that the adrenaline is administered IMI—intramuscular injection. Intravenous access is not immediately required. As adrenaline will only work for a certain period, corticosteroid (hydrocortisone) administration should be commenced early. The dose of adrenalin should be repeated if there is ongoing compromise.

As anaphylaxis is a serious medical event, any patient who has experienced it must be educated appropriately, given strict instructions to always avoid the offending substance, have a well understood and regularly reviewed management plan, and have close medical follow-up after the event. Any patient who has experienced anaphylaxis should be assessed in a hospital emergency department after the event, even if initially managed successfully.

Significant facial swelling, facial trauma, or inability to clear a complete airway obstruction

Inability to clear a complete airway obstruction is a rare event, but potentially fatal. All initial interventions, as previously outlined, should be attempted first. If all attempts are unsuccessful and airway obstruction cannot be relieved, a needle cricothyroidotomy should be performed. This, although only temporizing, is a life-saving procedure. It is a relatively easy technique to perform, although the physician must be rehearsed in both identifying anatomical landmarks and also the technique of needle insertion, and it should only be performed by those who are trained and legally qualified.

The purpose of this procedure is to oxygenate the patient who is attempting to breathe for him or herself on a short-term (usually no longer than 30–40 minutes) basis, until a more definitive airway can be achieved. The administration of oxygen must be provided by jet insufflation as outlined below. See box below for issues relating to cricothyroidotomy.

Emergency cricothyroidotomy

Equipment to prepare for needle cricothyroidotomy

- A 12G or 14G standard intravenous cannula, the lower the gauge the less airflow resistance
- A 5 mL or 10 mL syringe
- Standard oxygen therapy tubing
- A skin preparation solution or swabs
- Oxygen supply, although the delivery of expired air via the cannula may be performed if oxygen is unavailable
- A 3-way tap

Anatomical landmarks and technique for performing needle cricothyroidotomy

- Palpate the thyroid cartilage and thyroid notch (Adam's apple).
- Slide your fingers inferiorly until you are in the space between the thyroid and cricoid cartilages; this is the cricothyroid membrane.
- With the region of the cricothyroid membrane identified (Fig. 47.13a), stabilize the trachea firmly with your thumb, second, and third fingers.
- If time permits, clean the overlying skin.

- Assemble the cannula onto the syringe (Fig. 47.13b).
- Insert the cannula into the center of the cricothyroid membrane (Fig. 47.13a) and angle the cannula 45° in the caudal direction while aspirating the syringe.
- Aspiration of air identifies entry into the trachea; at this point insert the cannula several millimeters further.
- Withdraw the syringe and stylet and at the same time advance the cannula sheath into the trachea.
- Secure the cannula sheath and connect the 3-way tap with the oxygen tubing attached, ensuring all three ports of the tap are open (Fig. 47.13c).
- While holding the cannula sheath and 3-way tap securely with one hand, with the thumb of the other hand occlude the third port of the tap for one second to allow for oxygen flow into the trachea (Fig. 47.13d); release your thumb for four seconds to allow for expiration (Fig. 47.13e).

Remember this is a temporary life-saving measure; urgent definitive medical care must be arranged.

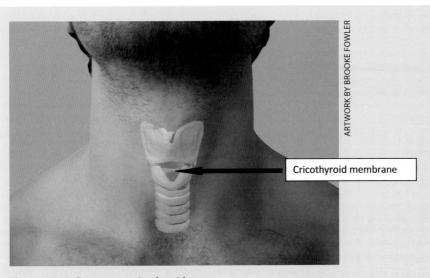

ARTWORK BY BROOKE FOWLER

Cricothyroid membrane

Figure 47.13 Emergency cricothyroidotomy
(a) Cricothyroid membrane—position for needle cricothyroidotomy

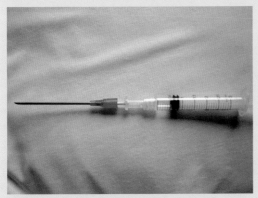

(b) Large-bore cannula attached to a syringe in preparation for a needle cricothyroidotomy

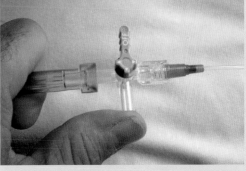

(d) Ensure all three ports are open and connected as shown and the oxygen turned on. Occlude the port open to the atmosphere with your thumb for one second to deliver oxygen to the patient

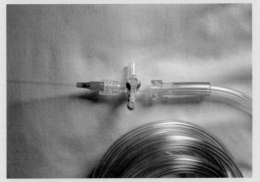

(c) Once the cannula sheath is inserted and secured in the trachea, attach the three-way tap with oxygen tubing

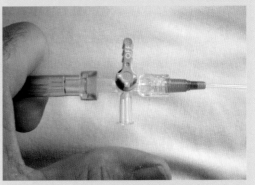

(e) Release the thumb over the port for four seconds to allow for exhalation

Breathing and ventilation

Breathing assessment and adjuncts are shown in the box below.

Breathing assessment and adjuncts

- Stethoscope
- Pulse oximetry if available

Once the airway is patent and secured, assess the patient's breathing and ventilation (note that performing auscultation and percussion at a noisy sporting venue can be difficult):

1. Inspection
   (a) While positioned at the head of the patient with the patient's chest exposed, inspect for:
      (i) rate, effort, and symmetry of breathing
      (ii) the presence of wounds or bruising to the chest or neck, which may suggest significant underlying airway or lung damage
      (iii) evidence of distended neck veins suggesting a tension pneumothorax or cardiac tamponade.
2. Palpation
   (a) With the patient's head in the neutral position, palpate trachea to ensure it is midline. Deviation of the trachea may suggest a tension pneumothorax.
   (b) Palpate the face, neck, and chest for evidence of subcutaneous emphysema suggesting a pneumothorax.
   (c) Palpate the anterior chest to check for symmetry and degree of expansion.
3. Auscultation
   (a) Using the stethoscope auscultate the chest at the apices, in the axillae, and towards the bases, noting:
      (i) equality of air entry
      (ii) degree of presence of breath sounds. Decreased breath sounds may suggest a pneumothorax or hemothorax, whereas completely absent breath sounds may suggest a tension pneumothorax
      (iii) any added sounds such as wheezes.
4. Percussion
   (a) Percuss all accessible regions of the chest, because much information is gained from the "feel" of the percussion as with the sound.
   (b) Dullness to percussion may suggest a hemothorax, especially if it is identified toward the lung bases or toward the posterior aspect in the supine patient.

If there is no compromise to breathing or ventilation, move to the next stage of assessment, always having a low threshold for reassessment.

Potentially life-threatening breathing and ventilation problems

Potentially life-threatening breathing and ventilation problems include pneumothorax and acute severe asthma. Pneumothorax—the presence of air within the pleural space—can become rapidly life-threatening. A pneumothorax can be closed (simple or tension) or open.

Simple pneumothorax

 Rib fractures are a common cause of pneumothorax.

In most cases a simple pneumothorax can be managed by the administration of oxygen until definitive medical care is reached. Occasionally a spontaneous pneumothorax can become life-threatening if it develops into a tension pneumothorax.

Open pneumothorax

An open pneumothorax results from a penetrating chest wound where the pleural space communicates directly with the outside. This situation is best managed by applying plastic wrap over the wound and taping the wrap on three sides only so as to produce a one-way flutter-valve effect. As the patient exhales, air from the pleural space is forced out under the wrap, and when the patient inhales, the plastic wrap is sucked onto the wound, thereby preventing air entering the pleural space.

Tension pneumothorax

A tension pneumothorax is an emergency. It may develop rapidly or gradually. If untreated, a tension pneumothorax is generally fatal. Tension pneumothoracies are made worse by active ventilation of the patient; occasionally they are the result of active ventilation. Keep this uppermost in your mind if you need to ventilate a patient. Signs and symptoms of a tension pneumothorax are shown in the box opposite.

Tension pneumothorax management

Management of a tension pneumothorax requires a needle thorocentesis to relieve the tension immediately (see box opposite). This, however, does not treat the resultant simple pneumothorax. A needle thorocentesis should only be performed by those appropriately trained and licenced.

Signs and symptoms of tension pneumothorax

- Tachypnea
- Patient anxiety and distress
- Distended neck veins (if not hypovolemic)
- Tachycardia
- Low oxygen saturation (although high-flow oxygen may mask this to some extent)
- Tracheal deviation to the *opposite* side of the pneumothorax, although this may be a late sign
- Absent breath sounds on *same* side as the pneumothorax
- Hyperresonance on the *same* side as the pneumothorax
- Cyanosis may be a late sign
- If being passively ventilated, the patient may become progressively more difficult to ventilate

Acute severe asthma

As outlined in Chapter 50, the clinician must be aware of all sportspeople under his or her care who have a diagnosis of asthma. Know the medications prescribed and the asthma action plan for the sportsperson. This chapter focuses on management of a severe asthma attack.

The signs and symptoms of severe asthma are outlined in the box below.

Signs and symptoms of severe asthma

- Marked dyspnea
- Inability to speak or only speak in single words
- Developing exhaustion
- Use of respiratory accessory muscles
- The chest may be "silent" to auscultation (this is an ominous sign)

Steps for a needle thoracentesis

- Identify the appropriate anatomical landmarks (Fig. 47.14a) on the side with the suspected tension. The site where the needle should be inserted is the intersection of the mid-clavicular line and the second intercostal space. (This is best found by palpating for the angle of Louis, which is where the manubrium joins the body of the sternum. Slide your finger parallel with this joint toward the side of the suspected tension; you will meet the second rib where it articulates with the sternum. Go just below this rib and this is the second intercostal space.)

- A 12G or 14G long intravenous cannula may be used and inserted its full length into the lower half of this space so as to avoid the neurovascular bundle which runs inferior to each rib. A standard intravenous cannula may be too short and not enter the pleural space; subsequently a longer and more specific cannula may be required (Fig. 47.14b).
- Remove the stylet and leave the cannula sheath open to the atmosphere.

ARTWORK BY BROOKE FOWLER

Angle of Louis

Mid-clavicular line

2nd rib

2nd intercostal space

Figure 47.14 **(a)** Anatomical landmarks for needle thorocentesis

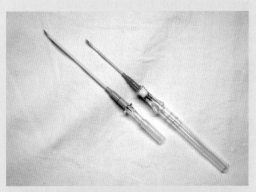

(b) The cannula designed for needle thoracentesis is on the left (blue) compared with a standard 14G intravenous cannula (orange)

Management of severe asthma

The management of severe asthma is as follows:

- Unless contraindicated, the patient should be positioned sitting up.
- Commence high-flow oxygen via a non-rebreather mask.
- If a nebulizer mask and oxygen supply are available, commence
  - salbutamol 5 mg diluted with 3 mL of normal saline
    - If there is no response to the initial dose, repeat immediately, then every 15–30 minutes or give continuously depending on patient response
  - ipratropium bromide 500 micrograms 2- to 4-hourly.[4–6]
- If a nebulizer mask or oxygen supply are not available, use the following metered dose inhalers via a large volume spacer[7, 8]
  - salbutamol 100 micrograms 4 to 10 inhalations repeated as necessary
  - ipratropium bromide 500 micrograms 2- to 4-hourly.[4–6]
- Give prednisone 50 mg orally
  OR
  hydrocortisone 100 mg IV.[5]
- Start inhaled corticosteroids as soon as possible.

Circulation and hemorrhage control

If the cause of circulatory compromise or life threat is bleeding, it must be stopped. The most effective means of controlling external hemorrhage is by direct pressure to and elevation of the bleeding site.

Signs and symptoms of blood loss

Signs and symptoms of blood loss are listed in the box below.

 Hypotension is not an early reliable sign of blood loss.

Signs and symptoms of shock due to blood loss

The most reliable early indicators of shock are:

- tachycardia
- pale, cold, and diaphoretic skin (i.e. peripheral shut down)
- confusion (in the absence of head injury, drugs, or alcohol).

The patient usually needs to have lost up to 25% of circulating blood volume before a substantial drop in systolic blood pressure is noted. This is particularly so in a supine patient and a very fit athlete (Fig. 47.15).

Sites of blood loss

Some sites of hemorrhage are easy to address, while others are impossible to manage outside an operating room. Possible sites of blood loss and what to do are shown in Table 47.1.

Circulation management principles

The priorities must always be Airway, Breathing, and then Circulation. The only exception to this is life-threatening external hemorrhage likely to result in rapid exsanguination, such as from a carotid or femoral artery. In that case, initiate hemorrhage control immediately.

The basic principles of hemorrhage control have been outlined above. As part of the circulatory management, insert two large-bore intravenous cannulae (14G or 16G). The ideal position for these is in large veins in or around the cubital fossae but any venous access is acceptable.

If the patient is exhibiting features of shock (see box below left), immediately infuse a bolus of crystalloid solution, either compound sodium lactate or sodium chloride (0.9%) (normal saline) at a dose of 20 mL/kg. Carefully monitor the patient's response. If blood loss continues or there is inadequate or only transient response to the fluid, repeat the bolus once or twice and continue to call for urgent assistance. For patients who have ongoing and uncontrolled hemorrhage it is safer to maintain a systolic blood pressure of around 90 mmHg (rather than higher

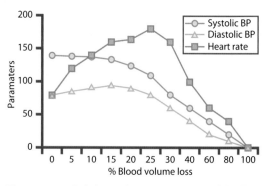

Figure 47.15 Early hemodynamic response to blood loss. Tachycardia is a much earlier sign of blood loss than hypotension

Table 47.1 Possible sites of blood loss and what to do

Sites	Management
External bleeding (e.g. major lacerations)	Direct pressure and elevation of the bleeding part above heart height (if not contraindicated)
Long bones, especially the femur, which may result in 1–2 liters of internal blood loss	Immobilize and splint the fractured limb; this significantly contributes to the control of hemorrhage
Pelvic fractures, which have the potential for a devastating outcome	Minimize movement and handling of the pelvis Stabilize the pelvis if possible by binding the pelvis with a towel or sheet (Fig. 47.16a–d) Internally rotate and secure the legs so as to decrease pelvic volume
Chest, abdominal, or retroperitoneal bleeds	Requires urgent transfer to an operating room

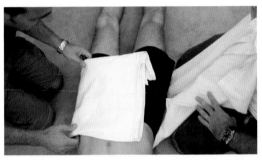

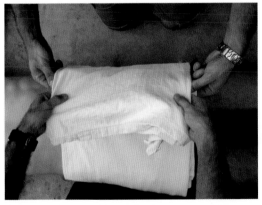

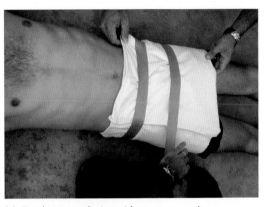

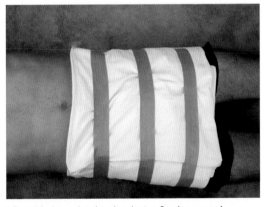

Figure 47.16 Application of a pelvic binding device
(a) Center the towel or sheet over the femoral greater trochanters

(c) Firmly secure device with sports strapping tape or ratcheted metal clamps

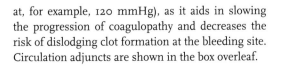

(b) Pull both ends of device firmly so as to compress the pelvis circumferentially

(d) With the pelvic binder device firmly secured, internally rotate the legs and secure together

at, for example, 120 mmHg), as it aids in slowing the progression of coagulopathy and decreases the risk of dislodging clot formation at the bleeding site. Circulation adjuncts are shown in the box overleaf.

Ischemic chest pain

The team clinician has medical responsibility for not only the sportspeople but also team coaches and officials. These persons may be at risk of ischemic heart

Circulation adjuncts

- 2 large-bore cannulae
- Intravenous giving sets
- Intravenous fluids
  - Compound sodium lactate
  - Normal saline (0.9%)
- Pads of automated external defibrillator (AED)
- Pulse oximeter
- Bandages and pads to control hemorrhage

disease and myocardial infarction or cardiac arrest. Chest pain in any person, especially those with risks for ischemic heart disease (IHD), should be assumed to be ischemic heart pain until proven otherwise (see also Chapter 49).

Thus, the clinical team must be competent with, and well rehearsed in, basic life support (Fig. 47.3) and the physician also in advanced life support (Fig. 47.17).

In the event of a cardiac arrest, the priorities remain Airway, Breathing, and Circulation. At the same time, applying the automated external defibrillator (AED) (Fig. 47.18) and following the AED instructions are an urgent consideration and should be performed while also assessing the airway. In patients with ventricular fibrillation (VF) or pulseless ventricular tachycardia (VT), urgent defibrillation provides the patient with the best chance of survival (see also Chapter 48).[9]

Therefore every physician must have rapid accessibility to an AED and accurate knowledge of the use of the device whenever they have responsibility for the care of sportspeople, coaches, or officials. Recognized and accredited courses in the use of AEDs for non-physicians are also available in many centers. It is essential that at least one member of the clinical team is trained and accredited to apply and use an AED in an emergency.

Advanced life support for adults

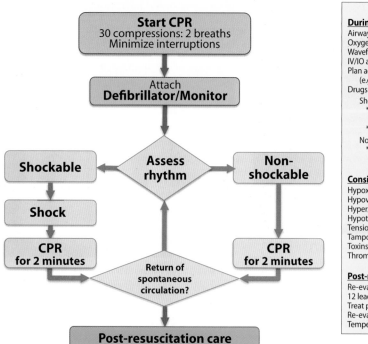

Figure 47.17 Adult advanced life support algorithm FROM AUSTRALIAN RESUSCITATION COUNCIL, www.resus.org.au

Management of ischemic chest pain

The golden rules of Airway, Breathing, Circulation remain constant and each of these are checked and established as in all other emergency care situations. In addition, the following apply:

- Unless contraindicated, have the patient in a sitting or semi-sitting position.
- Administer oxygen and ideally titrate the flow to an oxygen saturation of 94–98%.
- Attach AED pads and check monitor (Fig. 47.18).
- Obtain early intravenous access.
- Administer sublingual glyceryl trinitrate, one metered dose or one tablet. This may be repeated every 5 minutes if pain persists or to a maximum of 3 doses. Extreme caution should be observed if the patient has
  - a systolic BP of <100 mmHg or there is evidence of hemodynamic compromise
  - ingested medications such as Viagra® (sildenafil citrate) within the previous 12–24 hours.
- For persisting pain, administer cautiously 2.5–5 mg intravenous morphine.

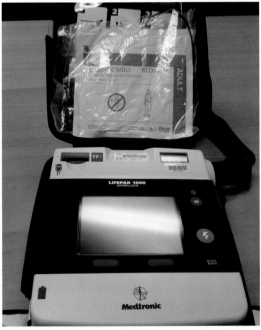

Figure 47.18 Automated external defibrillator (AED). This is an essential piece of emergency medical equipment. The clinical team leader must ensure that there is ready access to an AED (see also Chapter 48 for discussion of the importance of AEDs in public places including sporting venues)

- Give aspirin 300 mg, either chewed and swallowed or dissolved in water and swallowed.
- Urgent transfer to more definitive medical care is essential.

Disability (and neurological status)

A brief disability assessment is included as part of the primary survey to obtain a baseline measure. Neurological assessment is best assessed in the emergency setting by the Glasgow Coma Scale (GCS)[10] (Table 47.2) as well as assessing pupillary response (size, shape, and response to light). The GCS assessment should be standard practice with any head-injured athlete, no matter what the degree. A GCS score sheet should be kept in the team clinician's bag. When scoring a GCS, record the best patient response.

A normal GCS equals 15, with progressive deterioration as the score approaches a minimum of 3. A patient is usually unable to maintain or protect their airway with a GCS score of 8 or less.

Criteria for imaging the cervical spine

Any significantly injured sportsperson must always be assumed to have a cervical spine injury, so many injured sportspeople are fitted with a cervical collar. The next two steps related to the cervical collar can be difficult:

- Is it safe to take the collar off?
- Should the patient undergo cervical spine imaging?

Table 47.2 The Glasgow Coma Scale[10]

	Score
Best eye opening	
Spontaneous	4
To voice	3
To pain	2
None	1
Best verbal response	
Orientated	5
Confused/disorientated	4
Inappropriate words	3
Incomprehensible sounds	2
None	1
Best motor response	
Obeys commands	6
Localizes to pain	5
Withdraws to pain	4
Abnormal flexion to pain	3
Extension to pain	2
None	1

The National Emergency X-Radiography Utilization Study (NEXUS) cervical spine X-ray criteria[11-13] (box below) identify those who require further investigation of a possible cervical spine injury. Patients who meet all five criteria have a very low probability of clinically significant injury to the cervical spine,[13] in which case those fulfilling all criteria do not need radiological imaging and the cervical collar may be removed.

NEXUS cervical spine X-ray criteria[11-13]

- No tenderness at the posterior midline of the cervical spine
- No focal neurological deficit
- Normal level of alertness (GCS = 15)
- No evidence of intoxication
- No clinically apparent painful distracting injury

Criteria for performing a CT scan of the brain

Where a patient has sustained multisystem or moderate or severe trauma or where there is clinical concern, the patient must always be transferred to definitive medical care for further assessment and management.

For those patients with an isolated head injury, where the clinician is uncertain as to the need for further investigation, the Canadian Head CT Rule[14, 15] may prove useful. This states that a patient should undergo a head CT if he or she has any of:

- GCS<15 at two hours after the injury
- suspected open or depressed skull fracture
- any sign of basal skull fracture
  - hemotympanum (blood in the middle ear)
  - periorbital ecchymosis ("racoon" eyes)
  - cerebrospinal fluid (CSF) otorrhea or rhinorrhea
  - bruising of the mastoid process (Battle's sign)
- more than one episode of vomiting
- age >64 years old
- pre-impact amnesia of ≥ 30 minutes.
- dangerous mechanism of injury (e.g. fall >1 m).

If the clinician is in any doubt as to the presence or absence of the above features, it is prudent to adopt a cautious approach and refer for further investigation and care.

Exposure and environment control

Although often overlooked, this part of the primary survey is as important as any other. Clinicians should adopt the mantra "never assume." Never assume that what you see or what the patient identifies are the only priorities needing attention. Thus, the secondary survey includes the process of a closer inspection of the patient for life-threatening problems as well as taking action to ensure normothermia. This must be done while being mindful of ensuring patient confidentiality and privacy.

If not already performed, it is at this stage that the clinician performs a close inspection of the body parts covered by clothing and sporting gear. This also includes the back of the patient, for up until now the clinician has essentially only had vision and access to the front of the patient. It is at this time also that arrangements be made to perform a "log roll" (Fig. 47.19a–d).

Log roll

The log roll is an important skill which must be employed with any patient suspected of having a spinal injury. The technique described is also the procedure employed when moving an injured patient with the potential for spinal injury, to position a spine board.

Performing the log roll for a close inspection of the patient's back or to insert a spine board requires at least five people:

- The team leader or delegate takes control of the head and cervical spine and is responsible for coordinating the roll (Fig. 47.19a).
- Three members of the team are positioned on one side of the patient with one being positioned alongside the patient's chest, the next alongside the

Figure 47.19 The log roll
(a) Preparing for the log roll

(b) The roll is coordinated by the person controlling the cervical spine. Hand positions of the team members are demonstrated

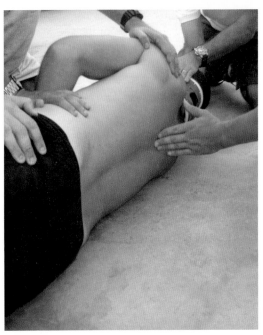

(d) Inspecting and examining the patient's back in the log roll position

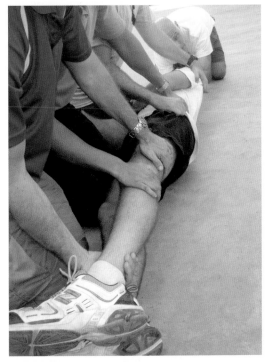

(c) The patient is rolled in one single and smooth motion so the spine and legs remain in line

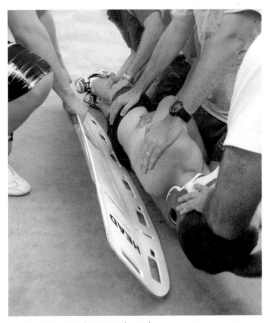

(e) Positioning the spine board

patient's hips, and the third alongside the region of the patient's knees.

- The fifth member of the team is responsible for inspecting the entire posterior aspect of the patient for injuries or objects which may result in life threat or compromise.

It is appropriate at this time to insert a spine board or appropriate field stretcher so as to assist with transfer of the patient (Fig. 47.19e). The roll must be controlled and coordinated; it is strongly advised that the log roll be rehearsed by the team on a regular basis with their other clinical drills.

A spine board is required to stabilize and move the seriously injured sportsperson. It is not meant as a transport device and is used in most situations to move the injured athlete or the sportsperson suspected of spinal injury from the site where the injury occurred to an appropriate transport stretcher. Leaving a patient on a spine board for extended periods of time results in compromise to skin integrity and the potential for pressure area sores.

Ensuring normothermia

A critically ill or critically injured patient often loses his or her ability to appropriately thermoregulate. Subsequently, the patient will rapidly adopt the surrounding environmental temperature. Unless ambient temperature is 37°C (98.6°F) there is the potential for further compromise. The aim is normothermia; therefore the clinician should aim to maintain the patient's body temperature as close to 37°C (98.6°F) as possible. This may mean applying blankets or warmers and sheltering the patient from the environment or perhaps taking measures to decrease surrounding temperature so a core temperature of approximately 37°C (98.6°F) is maintained.

Appropriate use of analgesia in trauma

The use of analgesia is important when managing emergencies, and the type of analgesia and the timing are critical. In any situation when the physician is prescribing and administering medication, it is the absolute responsibility of the physician to understand the risks and benefits associated with administering the medication as well as the indications, contraindications, and appropriate dosages. It is also considered best practice to have appropriate medication available in the event of a subsequent allergic or anaphylactic reaction.

The physician may consider several routes of administration for analgesia in the emergency situation:

1. Subcutaneous or intramuscular: These routes are easy for the physician to use; however, because of variable and unpredictable absorption (especially in emergencies), these routes are usually not advised. Although these routes are not used for analgesia, adrenaline (which is used for anaphylaxis) is one of the very few drugs used via the intramuscular route in an emergency situation.

2. Intravenous: In most settings this is the preferred route to use for analgesia. Action of onset is rapid and doses can be titrated reasonably accurately. Obtaining intravenous access may be a challenge in certain circumstances. The use of intravenous narcotics, in some situations, may be associated with patient nausea and vomiting, in which case administering an intravenous anti-emetic prior to the narcotic may be appropriate.

3. Regional blocks: Using a local anesthetic for a nerve block is a very effective form of analgesia, especially in limb trauma. However, many regional blocks require the physician to have undertaken further training to be able to perform these safely and effectively. For those trained, this is an exceptionally effective modality for pain relief.

4. Inhalational analgesia: most inhaled analgesics are self-administered by the patient. The onset and offset of action are quite rapid and the analgesic properties are usually predictable and reliable. These can be administered as a compressed gas in cylinders, or as a solution (e.g. methoxyflurane) inserted into a dispensing device. In Australasia, the latter has become the most popular in the pre-hospital care setting and in particular as an analgesic for serious sporting injuries.

The physician should be familiar and comfortable with using at least two separate forms of analgesia. It must be recognized that different countries have different rules and regulations relating to the use and possession of certain drugs. The physician must be aware of these restrictions and ensure they are not in breach with any medications that may be in their possession (see also Chapter 64 "Traveling with a team").

Recommended general and emergency medical equipment

The medical resources, drugs, and supplies required by the clinician responsible for the medical care of sportspeople depend at least somewhat on whether a physician is also part of the clinical team, and the sport which is being covered. However, there is basic equipment which spans all sports and situations, and equipment which may be effectively and safely used by non-physicians. Please see Chapters 63 and 64 for advice on how to prepare a kit bag when working with a team and when traveling to deliver team care.

 It is critical for the clinical team to have ready and easy access to both an AED and a spine board.

In this chapter, we emphasize that it is *critical* for the clinical team to have ready and easy access to both an automated external defibrillator (AED) (Fig. 47.18) and a spine board (Fig. 47.19e). Both are essential medical equipment when caring for sporting teams or athletes.

⊕ RECOMMENDED WEBSITES

Australian Resuscitation Council: www.resus.org.au

▤ REFERENCES

1. Consensus on resuscitation science and treatment recommendations. Part 8: Interdisciplinary topics. *Resuscitation* 2005;67(2):305–14.

2. O'Driscoll BR, Howard LS, Davison AG. BTS guideline for emergency oxygen use in adult patients. British Thoracic Society. *Thorax* 2008;63 Suppl 6:vi 1–68.

3. Brown SG. Anaphylaxis: clinical concepts and research priorities. *Emerg Med Australas* 2006;18(2):155–69.

4. Rodrigo GJ, Castro-Rodriguez JA. Anticholinergics in the treatment of children and adults with acute asthma: a systematic review with meta-analysis. *Thorax* 2005;60(9):740–6.

5. Rodrigo GJ, Rodrigo C. Triple inhaled drug protocol for the treatment of acute severe asthma. *Chest* 2003;123(6):1908–15.

6. Balanag VM, Yunus F, Yang PC et al. Efficacy and safety of budesonide/formoterol compared with salbutamol in the treatment of acute asthma. *Pulm Pharmacol Ther* 2006;19(2):139–47.

7. Cates C, Bara A, Crilly J et al. Holding chambers (spacers) versus nebulizers for beta-agonist treatment of acute asthma. *Cochrane Database Syst Rev* 2006;(2):CD000052.

8. Dolovich MB, Ahrens RC, Hess DR et al. Device selection and outcomes of aerosol therapy: evidence-based guidelines. *Chest* 2005;127(1):335–71.

9. Larsen MP, Eisenberg MS, Cummins RO et al. Predicting survival from out-of-hospital cardiac arrest: a graphic model. *Ann Emerg Med* 1993;22(11):1652–8.

10. Teasdale G, Jennett B. Assessment of coma and impaired consciousness. A practical scale. *Lancet* 1974;2:81–4.

11. Hoffman JR, Wolfson AB, Todd K et al. Selective cervical spine radiography in blunt trauma: methodology of the National Emergency X-Radiography Utilization Study (NEXUS). *Ann Emerg Med* 1998;32(4):461–9.

12. Hoffman JR, Mower WR, Wolfson AB et al. Validity of a set of clinical criteria to rule out injury to the cervical spine in patients with blunt trauma. National Emergency X-Radiography Utilization Study Group. *N Engl J Med* 2000;343(2):94–9.

13. Hoffman JR, Schriger DL, Mower W et al. Low-risk criteria for cervical-spine radiography in blunt trauma: a prospective study. *Ann Emerg Med* 1992;21(12):1454–60.

14. Stiell IG, Wells GA, Vandemheen K et al. The Canadian CT Head Rule for patients with minor head injury. *Lancet* 2001;357(9266):1391–6.

15. Ropper AH, Gorson KC. Concussion. *N Engl J Med* 2007;356(2):166–72.

D

Chapter 48

Sudden cardiac death in sport

with JONATHAN DREZNER, NAVIN CHANDRA, and SANJAY SHARMA

On 26 June 2003, Marc-Vivien Foé from Cameroon collapsed on the pitch during the 72nd minute of the FIFA Confederations Cup semi-final against Colombia. A national hero and international soccer star, his sudden death from hypertrophic cardiomyopathy came as a shock to the worldwide sporting community. His stunning death, an example of the tragic loss of any young athlete, reminds us all of the fragility of life. Adapted from report in *Br J Sports Med 2009;43:628*

The sudden death of a young sportsperson on the playing field is a most devastating event. Sudden cardiac death (SCD) is the leading cause of mortality in young athletes during exercise and typically is the result of undiagnosed structural or electrical cardiovascular disease.[1-5] SCD is always tragic, and it profoundly impacts the community, school, and team where it occurs.

Athletes are viewed as the healthiest segment of our society, and exercise and sport are widely encouraged to prevent illness and promote health. However, intense exercise and physical conditioning also may trigger an acute cardiovascular event or sudden cardiac arrest (SCA) in young individuals harboring silent hereditary or congenital heart disease. This "exercise paradox" is highlighted by the sudden death of a young athlete during training or competition.

Because of the importance of this topic, and the large number of advances in recent years, SCD has a dedicated chapter. The clinical approach to other cardiac symptoms (such as chest pain, syncope, dyspnea) is addressed in Chapter 49. The main goals in this chapter are to:

- review the incidence of SCD in young athletes—this is not a "rare" occurrence
- clarify the etiology of SCD—sports physicians should have a detailed understanding of the various pathologies that underpin SCD, and all clinicians

should be interested in the various ways the heart can fail:
  - structural (page 1000)
  - electrical (page 1005)
  - acquired (page 1008)
- outline how to evaluate an athlete for conditions that may cause SCD
- address three common diagnostic conundrums that need practical solutions
- briefly review the purpose of pre-participation cardiovascular screening (see also Chapters 61 and 62)
- discuss the contemporary approach to primary and secondary prevention of SCD in sport.

Incidence of sudden cardiac death

The true incidence of SCD in sportspeople is widely debated. Accurate calculation of the incidence of SCD in athletes requires a precise numerator (number of deaths per year), and an exact denominator (number of athlete participants per year) in the population studied. The reported incidence of SCD in young athletes varies widely, and it is challenging to compare studies which have vastly different methodology and originate from different geographic regions (Table 48.1).

In the US, there is no mandatory reporting system for juvenile sudden death, and incidence reports have relied heavily on case identification through searches

Table 48.1 Incidence of sudden cardiac death in children and young sportspeople

Study	Population	Methods and reporting system	Incidence
Van Camp (1995)[5]	High school and college athletes; age 13–24 (US)	Public media reports and other reported cases	1:300 000
Maron (1998)[6]	High school athletes in Minnesota; age 13–19 (US)	Catastrophic insurance claims	1:200 000
Eckart (2004)[8]	Military recruits; age 18–35 (US)	Mandatory, autopsy-based	1:9 000
Drezner (2005)[9]	College athletes; age 18–23 (US)	Retrospective survey	1:67 000
Corrado (2006)[7]	Competitive athletes; age 12–35 (Italy)	Mandatory registry for SCD	1:25 000
Maron (2009)[1]	Competitive athletes; age 12–35 (US)	Public media reports and other electronic databases	1:166 000
Atkins (2009)[10]	Adolescents and young adults; age 12–24 (US & Canada)	Prospective, population-based, EMS reports	1:27 000
Chugh (2009)[11]	Children in Oregon; age 10–14 (US)	Prospective, population-based, EMS/hospital reports	1:58 000
Drezner (2009)[12]	High school athletes; age 14–17 (US)	Cross-sectional survey	1:23 000
Solberg (2010)[13]	Competitive athletes and physically active adults; age 15–34 (Norway)	Retrospective review of mandatory national forensic registry	1:111 000
Harmon (2011)[3]	College athletes; age 17–24 (US)	NCAA Resolutions database, public media reports, and catastrophic insurance claims	1:44 000

EMS = emergency medical service; NCAA = National Collegiate Athletic Association

of public media reports, catastrophic insurance claims, and other electronic databases. Estimates of SCD in the US range from 1:160 000 to 1:300 000 deaths per year in young competitive sportspeople (age 12–35).[1, 5, 6] These studies risk underestimating the incidence of SCD due to the lack of a mandatory reporting system and potential for incomplete identification of all cases.

Other studies have reported a higher incidence of SCD than those initial estimates in the US.[7–12] The Veneto region of Italy utilizes a regional registry for juvenile sudden death and reported an SCD incidence of 1:28 000 for young competitive sportspeople (age 12–35 years) prior to implementing a national screening program.[7]

In US military recruits (age 18–35), the incidence of non-traumatic exercise-related SCA was 1:9 000.[8] A prospective population-based study conducted at 11 US and Canadian cities and utilizing rigorous methodology with all cases of SCA collected through the emergency medical services system reported an incidence of SCA from cardiovascular disease of 1:27 000 in children and young adults (age 14–24).[10] Another US population-based study found the incidence of SCA in children age 10–14 to be 1:58 000.[11]

Recently, a five-year review was conducted on the etiology and incidence of sudden death in National Collegiate Athletic Association (NCAA) athletes (age 17–24) in the US from 2004 to 2008.[3] Cases were identified primarily through the NCAA Resolutions database—a recommended reporting system for institutions to the NCAA Director of Health and Safety on the death of any NCAA athlete. Forty-five cardiovascular-related sudden deaths were identified during this period with an average of 400 000 individual athlete participants per year. Cardiovascular-related sudden death represented 75% of fatalities during exertion; this was far greater than the number of deaths from heat stroke, sickle cell trait, and head/neck trauma combined.[3] The incidence of SCD in NCAA athletes was 1:44 000 per year.[3]

Sex and race as risk factors

Certain populations of sportspeople also seem to be at greater risk. SCD occurs more commonly in males, with initial reports of male to female gender differences ranging from 5:1 to 9:1.[1, 2, 12] In the NCAA, male college athletes had 2.3 times the risk of SCD than female athletes (1:33 000 versus 1:76 000).[3] The incidence of SCD also seems to be disproportionately high in black/African-American sportspeople. In the NCAA, African-American athletes had over three times greater risk of SCD than Caucasian athletes (1:17 000 versus 1:58 000), and the risk of SCD in male African-American athletes was 1:13 000 per year.[3]

Some geographic areas have demonstrated a lower risk of SCD in young sportspeople, perhaps due to differences in the prevalence of certain inheritable cardiovascular disorders. In Norway, a retrospective study examined the rate of SCD in athletes age 15–34 years using a mandatory national forensic registry and reported the incidence of SCD among physically active young men as 1:111 000.[13]

Which sports carry the highest risk?

Although SCD can occur in any sport, these deaths occur most frequently in North America in basketball, American football, and soccer (sports that have the highest levels of participation). In the NCAA, basketball was by far the highest risk sport, with an overall annual death rate of 1:11 000 (male and female), 1:7000 (male), and 1:4000 (male, African-American).[3] The risk in American football was 1:38 000 overall and 1:14 000 in African-American athletes.[3] The higher incidence of SCD found in NCAA athletes may promote earlier detection of silent cardiovascular disease through more rigorous pre-participation screening.

Additional questions exist regarding the relative risk of SCA/SCD in competitive sportspeople versus the general population, and whether this risk justifies a separate, more advanced cardiovascular screening program in sportspeople. It is generally accepted that exercise and intense physical exertion through athletic participation increase the likelihood of sudden death for many disorders predisposing to SCA.

Corrado et al.[14] identified a 2.5 times relative risk for SCD due to sports activity in athletes versus an age-matched non-athletic population. Exercise is considered the exposure (risk factor) for SCA in individuals with an underlying cardiovascular disorder, and athletes may be at elevated risk of SCD compared to non-athletes due to the frequency of their exercise, perhaps justifying a more intensive screening program.

On the other hand, not all children are competitive athletes but most children are active and exercise in some way. According to statistics from the Centers for Disease Control (CDC), cardiovascular disease is second only to malignancy as the leading medical cause of death in individuals younger than 24 years old; it accounts for more than 2400 fatalities annually in the US.[15] Thus, if specific preventive measures are valuable for children and young adults who participate in organized sports, is it time for these tests to be considered for all children?[16]

Etiology of sudden cardiac death in sportspeople

Overview

The age of an athlete is strongly associated with the etiology of SCD. In athletes ≥35 years, more than 80% of all SCDs are due to atheromatous coronary artery disease.[17–19] The majority of deaths from coronary artery disease occur in competitive long-distance racing, jogging, and other vigorous sports such as rugby and squash.

Approximately 50% of sportspeople who die suddenly have prodromal symptoms suggestive of myocardial ischemia and many have significant risk factors for coronary artery disease including smoking, hypertension, diabetes mellitus, hypercholesterolemia, and a family history of premature myocardial infarction. Pathological findings in joggers and marathon runners dying suddenly reveal severe and extensive coronary atherosclerosis involving two or more large coronary arteries in over 70% of cases. Myocardial scarring is evident in approximately 40% and fresh infarcts are seen in 15% of cases.[19]

In contrast, SCD in younger sportspeople (<35 years old) is most commonly due to a variety of hereditary or congenital structural and electrical cardiac abnormalities, although a plethora of acquired conditions are also implicated (Fig. 48.1 and Table 48.2).[1–8] Most deaths occur during or immediately after

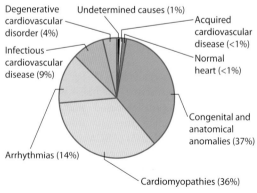

Figure 48.1 Causes of sudden cardiac death in young sportspeople[1]

Table 48.2 Causes of sudden cardiac death (SCD) in young sportspeople

Congenital/genetic pathology	
Disease of the myocardium	Hypertrophic cardiomyopathy (HCM)
	Arrhythmogenic ventricular cardiomyopathy (ARVC)
	Dilated cardiomyopathy (DCM)
Coronary artery disease/anomalies	Congenital coronary artery anomalies (CCAA)
	Premature atheromatous coronary artery disease
Cardiac conduction tissue abnormalities	Wolff–Parkinson–White syndrome
	Right ventricular outflow tachycardia
Valvular heart disease and disorders of the aorta	Mitral valve prolapse
	Congenital aortic stenosis
	Marfan syndrome
Ion channelopathies	Congenital long QT syndrome (LQTS)
	Catecholaminergic polymorphic ventricular tachycardia (CPVT)
Acquired causes	
Infections (myocarditis)	
Drugs (cocaine, amphetamine)	
Electrolyte disturbances (hypokalemia or hyperkalemia)	
Hypothermia	
Hyperthermia	
Trauma (commotio cordis)	

exercise.[20] Potential triggers for exercise-induced fatal arrhythmias include surges in catecholamine levels, dehydration, electrolyte imbalances, and increased platelet aggregation.

The cardiomyopathies are the commonest cause of SCD in young sportspeople; these collectively account for almost 50% of all deaths reported in the literature (this condition and other pathologies that underpin SCD are detailed overleaf). The main cardiomyopathies implicated in sudden death during sport are hypertrophic cardiomyopathy (HCM) and arrhythmogenic right ventricular cardiomyopathy (ARVC).

Reports from the US indicate that the commonest cause of SCD is HCM, accounting for 36% of all deaths (Fig. 48.1),[1] whereas data from northern Italy suggest that the leading cause of sudden death is ARVC. In one Italian study of 22 SCDs in young athletes, ARVC accounted for 22% of all deaths whereas HCM was responsible for only 2% of deaths (Fig. 48.2 overleaf).[21]

The difference between the US and Italian series may be partly explained by the fact that individuals with HCM are identified early in the mandatory Italian pre-participation screening program and subsequently disqualified from sport.[22] SCD rates from HCM in Italian athletes had been significantly lower than in American athletes even prior to the development of the Italian screening program, suggesting that the lower HCM-related SCD rate is partly explained by the lower genetic cluster of HCM in the relatively homogenous population of northern Italy.

Congenital coronary artery anomalies (CCAA) and premature coronary artery atherosclerosis account for one-fifth of cases of SCD. Sudden deaths associated with a structurally normal heart are usually attributable to ion channelopathies including congenital long or short QT syndrome, Brugada syndrome, and catecholaminergic polymorphic ventricular tachycardia as well as congenital accessory electrical pathways (Table 48.3 overleaf); collectively, these disorders account for at least 4% of all exercise-related SCDs. Data from a tertiary pathology center in the UK showed that although the cardiomyopathies accounted from the greatest number of SCDs in young athletes, one fifth of the athletes had structurally normal hearts.[4]

Most conditions predisposing to sudden death in athletes result in the same final common denominator (cardiac arrest) on presentation on the athletic field. Primary ventricular tachyarrhythmias are the predominant mechanisms of SCD in these inherited conditions, except in Marfan syndrome where death is often from aortic rupture or dissection.

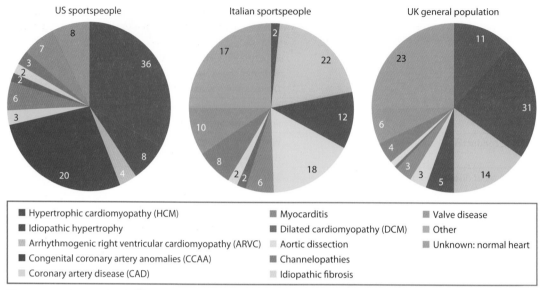

US sportspeople

Italian sportspeople

UK general population

- ■ Hypertrophic cardiomyopathy (HCM)
- ■ Idiopathic hypertrophy
- ■ Arrhythmogenic right ventricular cardiomyopathy (ARVC)
- ■ Congenital coronary artery anomalies (CCAA)
- ■ Coronary artery disease (CAD)

- ■ Myocarditis
- ■ Dilated cardiomyopathy (DCM)
- ■ Aortic dissection
- ■ Channelopathies
- ■ Idiopathic fibrosis

- ■ Valve disease
- ■ Other
- ■ Unknown: normal heart

Figure 48.2 Geographical differences in the etiology of sudden cardiac death in young sportspeople (<35 years) between the US, Italy, and the general population (<35 years) in UK (percentages)

Table 48.3 Causes of sudden cardiac deaths in structurally normal hearts

Congenital long QT syndrome

Brugada syndrome

Catecholaminergic polymorphic ventricular tachycardia

Short QT syndrome

Wolff–Parkinson–White syndrome

Right ventricular outflow tachycardia

Coronary vasospasm

Commotio cordis

Electrolyte disturbances

Hypothermia or hyperthermia

Drugs (amphetamine or cocaine)

Figure 48.3 Macroscopic specimen of hypertrophic cardiomyopathy

SCD due to congenital or genetic structural heart disease

We discuss cardiomyopathies, congenital coronary artery anomalies, and congenital valvular heart diseases.

The cardiomyopathies

Hypertrophic cardiomyopathy

Hypertrophic cardiomyopathy (HCM) is the commonest cause of exercise-related SCD in young sportspeople.[1] It is a primary myocardial disorder, predominantly caused by mutations within genes encoding sarcomeric contractile proteins; it is inherited as an autosomal dominant trait. The condition is characterized by left ventricular hypertrophy (LVH) (Fig. 48.3) in the absence of a cardiac or systemic cause, and myocardial disarray on histology. Approximately 25% of affected individuals exhibit dynamic left ventricular outflow obstruction due to systolic anterior motion of the mitral valve leaflet against the interventricular septum, although this figure may rise to almost 70% during exercise.

The prevalence of HCM in the general population is 0.2%;[23] however, data in sportspeople reveal a significantly lower prevalence of 0.06–0.07%.[22, 24] Increased left ventricular mass, small left ventricular cavity size, impaired myocardial filling in diastole, dynamic left ventricular outflow obstruction in systole, myocardial ischemia, and cardiac arrhythmias are likely to preclude augmentation of stroke volume for prolonged periods and prevent most affected individuals from competing at the elite level, particularly in endurance sports such as long distance running, cycling, and rowing. The same mechanisms may be associated with angina, dyspnea that is disproportional to the amount of exercise being performed, palpitations, exertional dizziness, or syncope. (Management of cardiac symptoms other than sudden death is discussed in Chapter 49).

HCM, however, is renowned for its clinical and morphologic heterogeneity and many affected individuals can compete at national level without experiencing any symptoms.[25] In such athletes, sudden death is commonly the first presentation and usually occurs during or immediately after exercise.[20] Deaths are most commonly observed in male athletes in start–stop sports such as football and basketball, which rely heavily on skill and are predominantly confined to male athletes.[26]

The diagnosis of HCM is established primarily from trans-thoracic echocardiography, but more than 95% of individuals with the condition also demonstrate an abnormal resting 12-lead electrocardiogram (ECG/EKG) (Fig. 48.9 on page 1006).[27]

Once a diagnosis is established, the risk of fatal arrhythmias during normal life activity can be predicted through a risk-stratification process that includes inquiring about symptoms and family history, exercise stress test, and 24-hour Holter monitor.[28] Markers high risk for SCD are shown in the box below. Individuals exhibiting two or more risk factors warrant prophylactic insertion of implantable cardioverter defibrillators (ICD).[29]

Unfortunately, it is difficult to extrapolate the information derived from such a risk stratification algorithm derived in controlled laboratory conditions to the athletic arena since intensive exercise

Markers of high risk for SCD

- Unheralded syncope
- Family history of HCM or SCD (<40 years of age)
- Severe LVH (>30 mm)
- Non-sustained ventricular tachycardia
- Attenuated or decreased blood pressure response to exercise

for prolonged periods generates its own specific metabolic stresses, which may trigger arrhythmias even in individuals usually considered to be at low risk. Therefore, the recommendations from the 36th Bethesda Conference and the European Society of Cardiology are conservative and relatively homogeneous, stating that athletes identified with HCM are disqualified from all competitive sports other than those of low dynamic intensity, regardless of age, gender, ethnicity, and the presence/absence of symptoms or the response to medical therapy.[30, 31]

The guidelines concede that many affected athletes may not fall victim to SCD in the event of continued participation in high-dynamic and high-intensity sporting disciplines; however, the aim is to identify/capture/ensure the safety of all individuals with preventable premature deaths.

Idiopathic left ventricular hypertrophy

Idiopathic left ventricular hypertrophy is a term used to describe increased left ventricular mass of greater than 500 mg in the absence of myocyte disarray (the histological hallmark of HCM).[1] Most deaths from idiopathic LVH are described in sportspeople of African/Afro-Caribbean origin.[1, 2, 4] It is unclear whether idiopathic LVH is a variant of HCM or whether it represents a situation whereby confounding genetic variables in black athletes result in the well-recognized exaggerated hypertrophic response,[32] which itself may become pathologic and predispose to arrhythmias. Conversely, the increased left ventricular mass identified in the athlete may represent a benign innocent bystander where the true cause of death from a potential ion channel disorder or accessory pathway has not been identified.

Arrhythmogenic right ventricular cardiomyopathy

Arrhythmogenic right ventricular cardiomyopathy (ARVC) is the commonest cause of SCD in young sportspeople in Italy.[21, 22] It is a familial disorder that is inherited as an autosomal dominant trait and is caused by mutations in genes encoding several cardiac desmosomal proteins. The disorder predominantly affects the right ventricle,[33] although left ventricular involvement is also recognized[34] in isolation and co-existent with right ventricular involvement in advanced cases. It is characterized histologically by progressive loss of myocardial cells with subsequent fibro-fatty replacement. The condition manifests with arrhythmias of right ventricular origin and morphological changes affecting the right ventricle.

Most deaths in athletes occur during sport, particularly soccer, and predominantly affect males. It is postulated that under conditions of mechanical stress, the inherent weakness of cell–cell junctions due to abnormal desmosomal proteins results in myocyte detachment and predisposes the athlete to fatal ventricular arrhythmias and SCD. The myocardium is subsequently repaired by fibro-fatty replacement, which forms further substrate for ventricular arrhythmias and subsequent right heart failure.[35, 36] Most athletes are asymptomatic and SCD is usually the first presentation, although a small number present with palpitation, dizziness, and exertional syncope.[21]

The prevalence of ARVC in the general population is between 1 in 1000 and 1 in 5000;[33] however, the prevalence of ARVC in sportspeople is unknown. There is some evidence that intensive ultra-endurance exercise may promote changes within the right ventricle that are identical to ARVC, indicating that ARVC might be acquired through intensive exercise in a small proportion of athletes.[37–41]

The diagnosis of ARVC usually requires a combination of clinical suspicion from personal symptoms or family history together with a plethora of electrocardiographic and imaging studies. These include 12-lead ECG/EKG, signal averaging where indicated, 24-hour Holter monitoring, exercise ECG/EKG, echocardiography with contrast to improve endocardial definition, and cardiac magnetic resonance.[42] The diagnosis of ARVC can be difficult to make, especially in the concealed form of the disease, when the ECG/EKG may exhibit very subtle changes that overlap with electrical manifestations of athletic training and cardiac imaging tests appear normal.[43]

Although the right ventricle is amenable to endocardial biopsy, histological diagnosis of ARVC is rarely possible and is potentially dangerous for several reasons—the disease is patchy, characteristically affects the thinnest portions of the right ventricle (notably the right ventricular inflow and outflow tract), and transmural tissue sampling is required for definitive diagnosis.

Phenotypic manifestations of ARVC on the 12-lead ECG/EKG include T-wave inversions and prolonged QRS duration in right ventricular leads (V1–V3), epsilon waves (delayed repolarization), and ventricular extrasystoles of right ventricular origin (manifest with left bundle branch block morphology) (Fig. 48.4). Holter monitoring and exercise testing are useful for identifying sustained or non-sustained

ventricular arrhythmias with left bundle branch block morphology (Fig. 48.5).

Echocardiography reveals thinning of the akinetic and dyskinetic segments affecting the right ventricle or overt right ventricular dilatation and hypokinesia, but may be normal in the early phases of the disease. The sensitivity of echocardiographic diagnosis is improved with contrast agents. Cardiac magnetic resonance imaging (cardiac MRI) may be more sensitive than echocardiography for the diagnosis of ARVC provided it is performed by an experienced operator.[43]

PRACTICE PEARL The diagnosis of ARVC in an athlete is an indication for disqualification from all competitive sports other than those of low intensity.[30, 31]

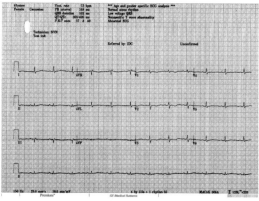

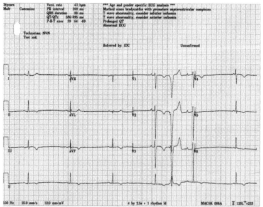

Figure 48.4 ECG/EKG in two individuals with arrhythmogenic right ventricular cardiomyopathy (ARVC) demonstrating T-wave inversion in leads V1–V3 (top panel) and a widespread T-wave inversion (more pronounced in V1–V4) and a ventricular extrasystole of right ventricular origin (conducts with left bundle branch morphology) (bottom panel)

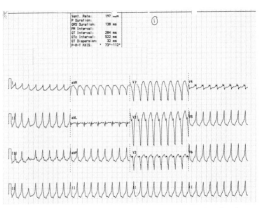

Figure 48.5 Ventricular tachycardia in an individual with arrhythmogenic right ventricular cardiomyopathy (ARVC)

Athletes at high risk of SCD even after abstinence from sport include those with a previous history of cardiac arrest, unheralded syncope, ventricular tachycardia with hemodynamic compromise and progressive deterioration of right ventricular function and left ventricular involvement. This small group should be offered implantable cardioverter defibrillator (ICD) implantation to minimize the risk of SCD.[44]

Dilated cardiomyopathy

Dilated cardiomyopathy (DCM) is a rare cause of SCD in young sportspeople, accounting for approximately 4% of all SCDs.[1, 2, 4, 5, 7, 22] This is probably because most affected individuals have relatively low exercise capacity due to markedly impaired systolic function. The disorder can be either congenital or acquired secondary to metabolic disorders, infection, inflammation or toxic substances. A congenital etiology should be considered in young individuals without identifiable underlying pathology and a family history of DCM or SCD below 40 years of age.

The prevalence of DCM is reported as 1 in 2500 and it is characterized morphologically by left ventricular dilatation and impaired systolic function. A diagnosis of DCM is an indication for abstinence from strenuous exertion and this usually translates to disqualification from most sports.[30, 31] However, gentle exercise for up to 30 minutes per day (moderately brisk walk or gentle cycling) may offer prognostic benefit. Pharmacological therapies in the form of ACE inhibitors and beta blockers are advised in all sportspeople with DCM.

Disorders of the coronary arteries and aorta

Congenital coronary artery anomalies

Congenital coronary artery anomalies (CCAA) are reported as a cause of SCD in 12–33% of athletes who have SCD.[1–6] A main coronary artery originating from the opposite sinus of Valsalva is the most common anomaly associated with SCD in athletes (Fig. 48.6) and is present in approximately 1% of the general population.[45, 46] Anomalous origin of the left coronary artery from the right sinus of Valsalva is less prevalent in the general population (0.2%) but is more serious than origin of the right coronary artery from the left sinus of Valsalva.[47]

Mechanisms of SCD associated with CCAAs include myocardial ischemia precipitated by exercise due to impaired coronary blood flow because of an abnormal ostium of the anomalous vessel, compression of the anomalous artery as it courses between the pulmonary artery and ascending aorta, or, possibly, coronary spasm triggered by endothelial dysfunction. In the majority of cases SCD is the first presentation, although some athletes may experience exertional chest pain associated with pre-syncope or syncope.[48]

Diagnosis of CCAA from a resting ECG/EKG, transthoracic echocardiography, and even exercise stress testing is notoriously difficult; most cases do not exhibit inducible myocardial ischemia during exercise stress testing even at high workloads. CT coronary angiography or magnetic resonance angiography (Fig. 49.1 on page 1028) are the imaging modalities of choice when clinical suspicion is raised.[49]

Recommendations state that athletes with anomalous coronary origins are disqualified from all competitive sports; however, participation three months

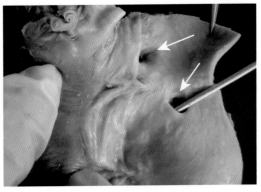

Figure 48.6 Origins of both main coronary arteries arising from the same sinus of Valsalva[36]

after surgical correction is permitted in cases without prior myocardial infarction, left ventricular dysfunction, or ventricular tachycardia during maximal exertion.[30, 31]

Premature coronary artery disease

Premature coronary artery disease accounts for 3–4% of all SCDs in young sportspeople in large series from the US and Italy;[1–6] however, it has been reported more commonly in Japan, Australia, and the UK.[4] The disorder is a common manifestation of familial hypercholesterolemia, which has a prevalence of 1 in 500. Sudden death is almost always the first presentation in young athletes. Prodromal symptoms of myocardial ischemia may be absent; however, peripheral stigmata of hypercholesterolemia including xanthelasma, corneal arcus, palmer, and eruptive xanthomata are common and their presence should raise the suspicion of the disorder (Fig. 48.7).

Marfan syndrome

Marfan syndrome is a collagen disorder caused by mutations in the gene encoding fibrillin. It is inherited as an autosomal dominant trait and has a prevalence of 1 in 5000. The condition is characterized by skeletal, cardiac, and ocular abnormalities (Fig. 48.8). Cystic medial necrosis in the tuna media of the aorta results in aortic dilatation and rupture or aortic dissection. The disorder accounts for approximately 3% of all exercise-related SCDs in young sportspeople.

Affected patients are excessively tall and, by virtue of this trait, usually excel in basketball or volleyball. Exercise-related increases in aortic pressure may expedite aortic root dilatation, dissection, and rupture causing instantaneous death during sport.[50]

 PRACTICE PEARL Participation in sporting disciplines where isometric stress is a significant component is prohibited (e.g. powerlifting, wrestling, judo, sprinting, rowing, and canoeing).[51]

In the past, beta blockers were considered to retard progressive aortic dilatation, but recent analyses have cast doubt on this claim.[52] Preliminary studies with angiotensin receptor blockers (losartan) hold great promise in preventing aortic complications in Marfan syndrome.[53] Annual aortic surveillance is recommended and prophylactic aortic root replacement should be considered when the aortic root diameter exceeds 50 mm.

Marfan syndrome is discussed further in Chapter 49.

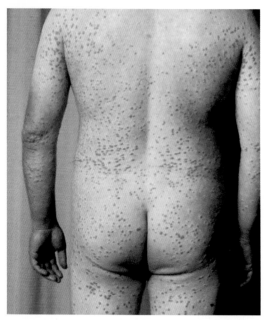

Figure 48.7 Peripheral stigmata of premature coronary artery disease

(a) Eruptive xanthomata

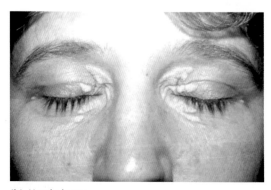

(b) Xanthelasma

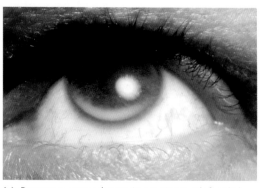

(c) Premature corneal arcus in a patient with familial hypercholesterolemia

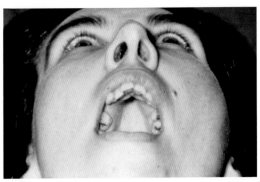

Figure 48.8 Features of Marfan syndrome
(a) High-arched palate

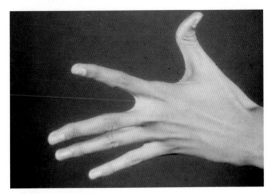

(b) Arachnodactyly

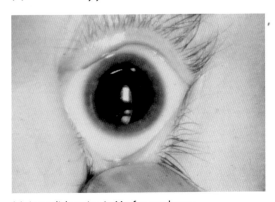

(c) Lens dislocation in Marfan syndrome

Valvular heart disease

Mitral valve prolapse

Mitral valve prolapse (MVP) is probably the commonest congenital valvular disorder; it affects 3–5% of the general population. Most individuals are asymptomatic, but in rare instances the condition is associated with ventricular tachycardia.[54] The exact mechanism for ventricular tachycardia is unknown. Fewer than 100 cases of sudden death have been

reported where MVP was the only abnormality identified in the literature and only three occurred during physical exertion.[55] Because of the relatively high frequency of MVP in the general population, it is not known whether the identification of MVP in a victim of SCD is causal or coincidental.

> The current guidelines state that an athlete with MVP is at low risk of SCD unless there is a history of syncope or documented ventricular arrhythmias, family history of premature SCD, disabling and protracted chest pain during sport, or associated moderate to severe mitral regurgitation.

Athletes with MVP as part of the spectrum of Marfan syndrome or coexistent long QT are precluded from participating in strenuous physical exertion.[51]

Aortic stenosis

Aortic stenosis due to a congenital bicuspid aortic valve is a rare but recognized cause of SCD in young athletes which can be identified through basic screening efforts involving cardiovascular physical examination.

Individuals with mild aortic stenosis may compete in sporting disciplines of low to moderate dynamic intensity or static sports if there are no symptoms and arrhythmias, and if left ventricular function is normal at rest and during an exercise echocardiogram.[51]

SCD due to congenital or genetic abnormalities predisposing to primary electrical disorders of the heart

Up to 4% of athletes who die suddenly have no identifiable cause at postmortem examination.

> This phenomenon—autopsy negative sudden unexplained death—is referred to as sudden adult death syndrome.[56]

Experience from studies in first-degree relatives of victims of sudden adult death syndrome indicates that a proportion of these deaths are attributable to inherited ion channelopathies. Fatal tachyarrhythmias due to undiagnosed accessory pathways comprise other potential causes (Table 48.3).

Congenital long QT syndromes

The congenital long QT syndromes (LQTS) are inherited as autosomal dominant or recessive traits and characterized by abnormalities in cardiac sodium or potassium ion channels. Abnormal shifts in electrical currents result in membrane instability during cardiac repolarization and predispose to polymorphic ventricular tachycardia and ventricular fibrillation.

There are currently 12 different identified loci accounting for the disorder; these are termed LQTS-1–LQTS-12 respectively. LQTS-1 (potassium ion channel), LQTS-2 (potassium ion channel), and LQTS-3 (sodium ion channel) account for approximately 95% of all known cases of the disorder.[57]

Adrenergic surges provoke ventricular arrhythmias, particularly in individuals with the LQTS-1 genotype.[58] Many deaths in sport occur in young females during swimming and are attributed to the adrenergic surge associated with diving suddenly into cold water. Affected sportspeople may present with palpitations, dizziness, and unheralded syncope secondary to polymorphic ventricular tachycardia. The latter may be associated with brief myoclonic movements, resulting in a misdiagnosis of epilepsy in recurrent cases.

Long QT syndrome is usually diagnosed on a resting ECG/EKG, which reveals a long QT interval (Fig. 48.9C) in approximately 60% of cases (QTc >440 ms in males and QTc >460 ms in females).

Exercise testing is recommended in all patients with suspected LQTS and often exhibits paradoxical prolongation of the QT interval in LQTS-1 and occasionally LQTS-2.[59] Holter monitoring is also recommended to evaluate the possibility of associated episodes of polymorphic ventricular tachycardia.[58]

The prevalence of congenital LQTS in the general population is approximately 1 in 2500.[57] However, based on the findings from screening programs in athletes, a long QT interval is identified in 0.42% of elite athletes.[60] The low death rate from sudden adult death syndrome in athletes in the context of a relatively high prevalence of long QT observed in this group suggests that the vast number of athletes with a slightly prolonged QT interval probably do not harbor gene mutations for LQTS. However, calculating the QTc accurately in this group is difficult because of profound bradycardia, sinus arrhythmia, slightly wide QRS complexes, and prominent U waves associated with athletic training.

In the absence of symptoms or a family history of LQTS or premature SCD, clear diagnosis of

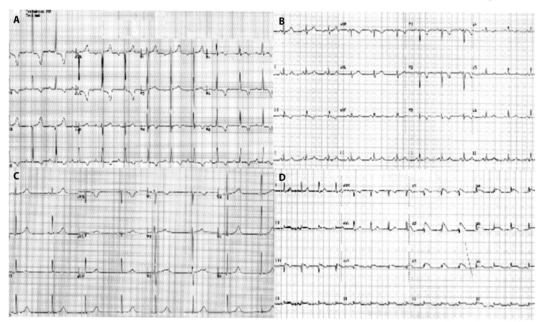

Figure 48.9 ECG/EKG changes in common structural and electrical cardiac abnormalities associated with sudden cardiac death

Panel A HCM—left ventricular hypertrophy associated with left axis deviation, ST-segment depression in leads I and aVL, and deep T-wave inversion in leads I, aVL, V5 and V6

Panel B ARVC—inverted T waves in V1–V4

Panel C LQTS—a prolonged QT interval of >500 msec

Panel D Brugada syndrome—incomplete right bundle branch block and coved ST-segment elevation in several leads but most marked in leads V1–V3

the disorder can occur only in athletes with a QTc >500 msec, or in athletes with a shorter QT interval in the presence of exercise-related paradoxical QT prolongation, the demonstration of polymorphic ventricular tachycardia, or the identification of a long QT interval in a first-degree relative.[60] Genetic testing is recommended in all cases as it may facilitate clinical management; however, the diagnostic yield from genetic analysis is only 70%. Athletes diagnosed with LQTS are recommended to avoid all sports associated with adrenergic surges.[61] All affected individuals should be treated with a beta blocker unless contraindicated. High-risk individuals include those with a QTc >500 msec, unheralded syncope, and LQTS-2 and LQTS-3 genotypes.[62]

Wolff–Parkinson–White syndrome (WPW)

Wolff-Parkinson-White syndrome (WPW) is characterized by the presence of an accessory conduction pathway between the atria and ventricles with a predilection to re-entrant supraventricular tachyarrhythmias, which may degenerate to ventricular fibrillation. It is a rare cause of SCD in sportspeople. The prevalence of WPW syndrome is 1 in 750 persons. The risk of SCD in WPW syndrome is believed to be approximately 0.4%.

Most deaths occur in athletes with previous symptoms of palpitation, dizziness, or syncope. The accessory pathway can be identified by the presence of a delta wave and a short PR interval on the 12-lead ECG/EKG (Fig. 48.10). Electrophysiological studies to assess the refractory period of the pathway are essential to gauge the risk of atrial fibrillation with high ventricular rates.

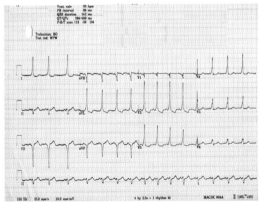

Figure 48.10 Short PR interval and slurred upstroke to the QRS complex (delta wave) in Wolff–Parkinson–White syndrome

Radiofrequency ablation is the definitive treatment in athletes with high-risk pathways who wish to continue to participate in competitive sport.[31, 61] Return to sport after successful ablation is possible after three months.

Brugada syndrome

Brugada syndrome (BrS) is an autosomal dominant sodium ion channelopathy with an incidence reported between 1 in 2000 and 1 in 5000.[63] The condition is characterized by a partial right bundle branch block pattern with associated coved ST-segment elevation (Fig. 48.9 panel D) and a propensity to fatal ventricular arrhythmias.

Affected individuals may present with unheralded syncope or SCD. Mixed phenotypic expressions of the disease, ranging from distinct repolarization abnormalities to subclinical cardiac conduction defects, also occur. Most deaths from Brugada syndrome occur at slow heart rates with deaths typically occurring during sleep, and theoretically, the condition should not preclude high-intensity sport.[64] However, chronic intensive exercise promotes increased cardiac vagal tone with subsequent resting bradycardia. Furthermore, prolonged exercise is associated with high core temperatures of >40°C (104°F), which is a recognized trigger in BrS.[65]

Affected individuals are advised to abstain from chronic or prolonged intensive exercise. The ICD is the only established treatment to prevent SCD and is reserved for survivors of aborted SCD, and those with sustained ventricular arrhythmias and unheralded syncope.

Catecholaminergic polymorphic ventricular tachycardia

Catecholaminergic polymorphic ventricular tachycardia (CPVT) is a hereditary ion channel disorder characterized by adrenergically mediated polymorphic ventricular tachycardia due to mutations within genes encoding the ryanodine receptor calsequestrin or the ankyrin-B proteins.

Intensive physical exercise (e.g. swimming) or emotional stress are well recognized triggers for SCD particularly in childhood and adolescent sportspeople.[67] Stress-induced syncope is one clinically recognized manifestation.[67, 68]

Typically, the baseline ECG/EKG is normal; however, exercise stress testing may demonstrate multifocal ventricular premature beats, which, in the context of unheralded syncope, should raise clinical suspicion of the condition in individuals with a structurally normal heart. Ventricular tachycardia with a beat-to-beat 180° alternating QRS axis (bi-directional ventricular tachycardia) is considered to be highly characteristic of CPVT; however, this is an exceptionally rare manifestation of the disorder. Prevention of SCD includes medical therapy with beta blockers and avoidance of moderate- to high-intensity exercise.[68]

SCD due to acquired cardiac abnormalities
Myocarditis
Myocarditis is usually due to a viral illness. It accounts for 7% of all SCDs in sportspeople. The inflammation and subsequent focal necrosis of the myocardium is thought to be the substrate for malignant ventricular tachyarrhythmias causing sudden death.

Most affected individuals experience coryzal symptoms and a mild febrile illness; however, sudden death in a relatively asymptomatic athlete is the commonest presentation. Overt cardiac symptoms are rare and include chest pain, dyspnea, and palpitation.

The ECG/EKG usually reveals non-specific ST and T wave abnormalities but may be normal. Echocardiography may also be normal in mild cases. A raised serum cardiac troponin is useful in confirming the diagnosis in an athlete with a febrile illness associated with chest pain, palpitation, and non-specific ECG/EKG abnormalities.[69]

Athletes with proven myocarditis should abstain from strenuous exertion and competitive sport for six months.[30, 31]

Commotio cordis
Commotio cordis refers to SCD from ventricular fibrillation resulting from blunt trauma to the chest wall. The precise frequency of the problem is unknown but it has been reported with increasing frequency in the past decade. The incidence is more common in children and adolescents due to their relatively thin and compliant chest walls. Sports usually associated with commotio cordis include baseball, field hockey, lacrosse, ice hockey, karate, and judo. The victim is often struck by an innocent-appearing blow or a projectile object regarded as a standard implement of the game. Sudden death due to ventricular fibrillation is instantaneous.[70]

Animal experiments in a juvenile swine model have provided insights into the mechanism responsible for ventricular fibrillation. Induction of ventricular fibrillation occurs following chest wall blows during a vulnerable window just before the peak of the T wave. A rapid rise in left ventricular pressure follows which is thought to activate ion channels via mechano-electric coupling. The generation of an inward current via mechanosensitive ion channels results in augmentation of repolarization and non-uniform myocardial activation, and is the cause of premature ventricular depolarizations that trigger ventricular fibrillation in commotio cordis.

Survival after commotio cordis is only 15% and only possible with prompt cardiac defibrillation. The velocity and hardness of the projectile object are recognized determinants of ventricular fibrillation. Several measures to prevent commotio cordis have been suggested, which include use of softer balls than traditional standard hard balls in hockey and baseball, and the use of chest barriers in sports vulnerable to commotio cordis.[71] Use of automated external defibrillators (AEDs) in young athletic individuals vulnerable to such trauma has saved lives.

Evaluation of an athlete for conditions causing sudden cardiac death
History, examination, and investigations help in the evaluation of an athlete at risk of sudden cardiac death. The box on pages 1010–12 contain three common diagnostic conundrums facing the clinician.

History
Most athletes are evaluated as part of cardiovascular programs implemented by sporting organizations to exclude potentially lethal inherited or congenital cardiac disorders prior to clearance for competition. Rarely, cardiovascular evaluation may be triggered because of symptoms of cardiovascular disease or a family history of premature cardiovascular disease or SCD in a first-degree relative (parent, sibling). In many situations, athletes are investigated at centers with expertise in conditions capable of causing SCD in athletes (particularly cardiomyopathy) as well as knowledge regarding the impact of cardiovascular training on cardiac size in order to enable the differentiation between physiological adaptation and cardiac pathology (see Chapter 49 for more information on the differentiation).

Most athletes are asymptomatic but the presence of chest pain, dyspnea disproportionate to the exercise performed, palpitations, dizziness, or syncope during exercise are ominous symptoms and warrant thorough evaluation (Chapter 49). It is prudent to ascertain any family history of premature cardiac disease or SCD in first-degree relatives as most conditions discussed above are hereditary. Ventricular arrhythmias in family members may present as syncope, epilepsy, or unexplained drowning, and inquiry into these circumstances may provide further important information regarding serious familial cardiac disease. Where possible, it is important to obtain post-mortem reports on first-degree relatives who suffered premature SCD as this may prove useful in differentiating death from a hereditary disorder (such as HCM) and a sporadic disorder (such as CCAA).

Physical examination

General physical examination may prove useful in identifying signs of Marfan syndrome (Fig. 48.7) and peripheral stigmata of familial hypercholesterolemia (Fig. 48.8). Cardiac auscultation may raise suspicion of aortic stenosis and HCM (of which approximately 25% have resting left ventricular outflow obstruction).

12-lead ECG/EKG

The 12-lead ECG/EKG permits the diagnosis of WPW and congenital LQTS, and the presence of certain repolarization patterns provides vital information regarding the possibility of an underlying cardiomyopathy; the ECG/EKG is abnormal in over 90% of individuals with HCM.

The presence of deep (>−0.2 mV) T-wave inversions in leads other than III, aVR, and V1 should result in further investigation for cardiomyopathy. Contrary to previously published literature, our experience suggests that deep T-wave inversions are a rare manifestation of cardiovascular adaptation in adult and adolescent athletes[72] but are common in HCM and may be present in almost any lead (Fig. 48.9 panel A). Additional electrocardiographic abnormalities in HCM include voltage criteria for left atrial enlargement, extreme leftward axis, ST-segment depression, pathological Q waves, and left bundle branch block. Although individuals with HCM commonly exhibit high voltage QRS complexes, the presence of isolated Sokolow–Lyon voltage criterion for left ventricular hypertrophy is rare in HCM and more suggestive of physiological cardiac adaptation.

T-wave inversion beyond V1 (and up to V4) may be normal in juvenile athletes and Afro-Caribbean athletes but their persistence in Caucasian athletes aged >16 years should prompt further investigation for ARVC (Fig. 48.9 panel B).[73] T-wave inversion may also be identified in athletes with dilated cardiomyopathy and LQTS.

Echocardiography

Echocardiography is the gold standard investigation for the diagnosis of HCM and valvular heart disease; however, it only proves diagnostic in relatively advanced cases of ARVC. The echocardiographic assessment of an athlete with chest pain or syncope should also involve identification of the origins of the coronary ostia to rule out the diagnosis of anomalous coronary origins, as exercise testing lacks sensitivity and is invariably normal in these conditions.

Further investigations

Some sportspeople require further electrocardiographic, imaging, and invasive electrophysiological investigations for the purposes of diagnostic clarification and risk stratification for SCD. Exercise testing and 24-hour Holter monitoring provide prognostic information in HCM and diagnostic information in ARVC and LQTS. Cardiac magnetic resonance facilitates the diagnosis of ARVC and HCM, and magnetic resonance coronary angiography is the investigation of choice for confirming the diagnosis of CCAA. Electrophysiological studies provide prognostic information in WPW.

In the past two decades, there have been major advances in the molecular genetics of HCM, ARVC, and LQTS. However, marked genetic heterogeneity and incomplete knowledge of causal mutations do not currently allow timely diagnosis in the majority of affected individuals. Additionally, failure to identify a genetic abnormality when screening for known mutations for a particular disorder such as HCM cannot be regarded as exclusion, as many mutations are yet to be identified. Continuing advances in molecular genetics and refinement of genetic analytic techniques hold promise and may prove invaluable in facilitating diagnoses in difficult clinical scenarios.

Three common diagnostic conundrums facing the clinician

Athlete's heart vs hypertrophic cardiomyopathy (HCM)

Regular participation in sport is associated with modest increases in ventricular wall thickness and cavity size as well as enhanced diastolic filling. This reversible physiological cardiac remodeling enables enhanced left ventricular filling and the augmentation of a large stroke volume even at rapid heart rates for sustained increases in cardiac output.[74]

A small proportion of male athletes, predominantly involved in endurance sports, demonstrate extreme physiological adaptation with left ventricular wall thickness measurements of 13–15 mm.[75] Although the majority of individuals with HCM have a mean left ventricular wall thickness of 18–20 mm, approximately 8% have morphologically mild hypertrophy in a lower range. Therefore a male athlete with a wall thickness of 13–15 mm falls into a grey zone where the differentiation between physiological left ventricular hypertrophy (LVH) is crucial, since diagnostic errors have the potential for serious consequences

In the majority of athletes, the differentiation between athlete's heart and HCM is possible with echocardiography alone. Physiological LVH is homogeneous and associated with enlarged chamber size and normal indices of diastolic function. In contrast, individuals with HCM often show bizarre patterns of LVH, small chamber size, and impaired diastolic function. End-diastolic LV dimensions (LVEDD) >55 mm are common in trained athletes but rare in HCM where LV cavity size is most often <45 mm. In contrast, a diagnosis of HCM is favored by abnormal pulsed and tissue Doppler indices of LV diastolic filling with impaired relaxation.

More detailed imaging in the form of cardiac MRI may have considerable value in selected athletes by virtue of its superiority over echocardiography in detecting segmental LVH in the anterolateral free wall, posterior ventricular septum, or apex, or the demonstration of delayed gadolinium enhancement, indicative of myocardial fibrosis.

In equivocal cases, the presence of a family history of HCM or SCD and low peak oxygen consumption (<50 mL/kg/min) on cardiopulmonary exercise testing favor HCM. Genetic analysis has a high positive-predictive accuracy but low negative-predictive accuracy and remains costly and time-consuming. In rare cases re-evaluation with ECG/EKG and echocardiography following a period (8–12 weeks) of de-training may be the only practical method of differentiating between the two entities[76] (Fig. 48.11).

Athlete's heart vs arrhythmogenic right ventricular cardiomyopathy (ARVC)

The diagnosis of ARVC in athletes is particularly challenging due to an early "concealed phase" of the disease and requires a high level of expertise (Fig. 48.11). Minor ECG/EKG abnormalities in right ventricular leads—infrequent ventricular extrasystoles of right ventricular origin, and subtle morphological changes of the right ventricle—may be the only objective manifestations of the disorder, and these overlap with physiological adaptation of the right ventricle with regular exercise.[77]

Right ventricular size alone (both inflow and outflow measurements) cannot reliably differentiate between athlete's heart and ARVC since almost 50% of endurance athletes exhibit enlarged right ventricular dimensions and 6% fulfill criteria for the diagnosis of ARVC according to the recent Task Force criteria.[78] However, the presence of epsilon waves or late potential on the signal averaged ECG/EKG, non-sustained ventricular tachycardia of left bundle branch block morphology, and regional wall motion abnormalities of the right ventricle favor the diagnosis of ARVC.

Electrical repolarization changes in athletes of African/Afro-Caribbean origin (black athletes)

The interpretation of repolarization changes in athletes of African/Afro-Caribbean origin can be challenging and often results in a diagnostic dilemma. Experience in these athletes indicates a high prevalence of repolarization changes including T-wave inversion,[79] which is a marker of cardiac pathology (particularly cardiomyopathy) in Caucasians and a definite recommendation for further investigation to exclude pathology.

Studies in black British and French athletes suggests that 23% of black male athletes exhibit T-wave inversion; these are deep (T wave >–0.2 mV) in 12% and overlap with those observed in cardiomyopathy.[80, 81] The scenario is compounded by the fact that black athletes exhibit a greater magnitude of left ventricular hypertrophy compared with Caucasian

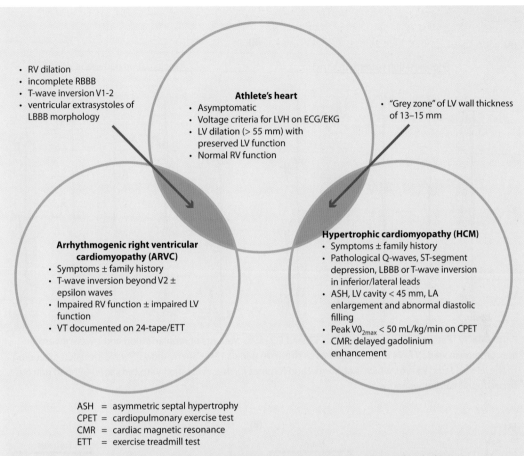

- RV dilation
- incomplete RBBB
- T-wave inversion V1-2
- ventricular extrasystoles of LBBB morphology

Athlete's heart
- Asymptomatic
- Voltage criteria for LVH on ECG/EKG
- LV dilation (> 55 mm) with preserved LV function
- Normal RV function

- "Grey zone" of LV wall thickness of 13–15 mm

Arrhythmogenic right ventricular cardiomyopathy (ARVC)
- Symptoms ± family history
- T-wave inversion beyond V2 ± epsilon waves
- Impaired RV function ± impaired LV function
- VT documented on 24-tape/ETT

Hypertrophic cardiomyopathy (HCM)
- Symptoms ± family history
- Pathological Q-waves, ST-segment depression, LBBB or T-wave inversion in inferior/lateral leads
- ASH, LV cavity < 45 mm, LA enlargement and abnormal diastolic filling
- Peak VO_{2max} < 50 mL/kg/min on CPET
- CMR: delayed gadolinium enhancement

ASH = asymmetric septal hypertrophy
CPET = cardiopulmonary exercise test
CMR = cardiac magnetic resonance
ETT = exercise treadmill test

Figure 48.11 Differentiation of physiological changes in "athlete's heart" from those of pathology in hypertrophic cardiomyopathy (HCM) and arrhythmogenic right ventricular cardiomyopathy (ARVC)

athletes participating in similar sports,[32] and black males appear to be more prone to exercise-related SCD from HCM according to studies in the US.[1]

Not surprisingly, the identification of deep T-wave inversion in a black athlete generates anxiety among sports physicians and cardiologists. However, the experience of the authors suggests that T-wave inversion in black athletes is most commonly confined to leads V1–V4 and is often preceded by convex ST-segment elevation or an isoelectric ST segment. The T waves in these leads may be asymmetrical or biphasic (Fig. 48.12 overleaf) and are not associated with left ventricular hypertrophy exceeding 16 mm (Fig. 48.13 overleaf), myocardial fibrosis on cardiac magnetic resonance imaging, or exercise-induced cardiac arrhythmias. Such T-wave patterns resolve rapidly (within six weeks of cessation of training) and follow-up of such athletes for over five years has not resulted in any fatalities.

In contrast, HCM has been identified in athletes with contiguous T-wave inversion in the inferior and lateral leads. Based on these findings we would not consider T-wave inversion in leads V1–V4 to represent cardiac pathology in the absence of symptoms or outside the context of familial cardiomyopathy. In contrast, we recommend investigation of all black athletes with T-wave inversion in contiguous inferior and lateral leads even though the precise significance of T-wave inversion in the inferior leads in isolation is presently unknown.

Black female athletes also exhibit a greater prevalence of T-wave inversion and left ventricular hypertrophy (Fig. 48.13 panel B) compared with Caucasian females; however, the differences between the two ethnicities are less marked than in male athletes (Fig. 48.13 panel A).[82]

continued

continued

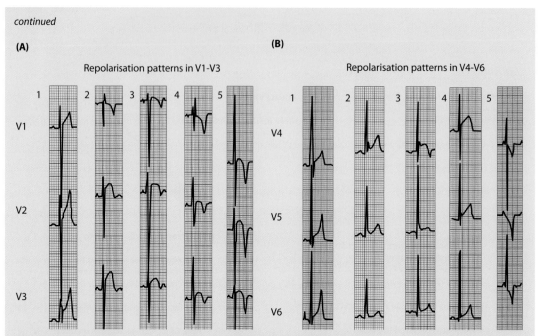

Figure 48.12 Patterns of repolarization on 12-lead ECG/EKG. Variants of repolarization and T-wave inversion are common in leads V1–V4 in black athletes as shown in panels 1–4. Panel 5 shows T-wave inversion extending to the lateral leads (V5–V6), which is abnormal and requires further evaluation with cardiac imaging to rule out hypertrophic cardiomyopathy

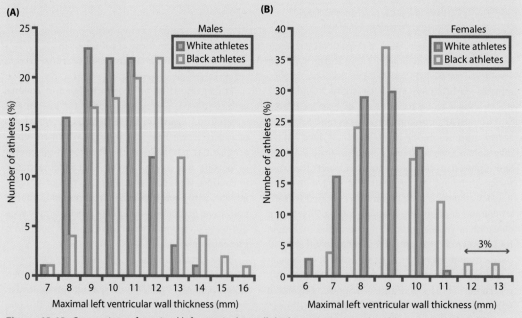

Figure 48.13 Comparison of maximal left ventricular wall thickness (mm) in male athletes (panel A[24]) and female athletes (panel B[82]). A small but important proportion of black athletes have ventricular thickness exceeding the upper limit of that seen among white athletes

Purpose of screening

Is the purpose of pre-participation cardiovascular screening purely to prevent SCD, or is the goal of screening to identify young sportspeople with cardiovascular conditions at risk for SCD? The American Heart Association (AHA) states that the principal objective of screening is to reduce the cardiovascular risks associated with physical activity and enhance the safety of athletic participation.[83] The American College of Cardiology contends that the ultimate objective of pre-participation screening of athletes is the detection of "silent" cardiovascular abnormalities that can lead to SCD,[84] and the Pre-participation Physical Evaluation Monograph states the primary objective of screening is to detect potentially life-threatening or disabling conditions before undergoing specific athletic participation.[85]

Therefore, perhaps it is the prevalence of cardiovascular conditions with the potential for sudden death, rather than the incidence of SCD itself, that should influence the rigor of pre-participation screening procedures. The goal of screening is early detection of occult cardiovascular disorders, as many of these conditions can be effectively managed through activity modification and medical intervention (pharmacotherapy, radiofrequency ablation, implantable cardioverter defibrillator [ICD], or even surgery) to reduce the risk of sudden death.

The AHA estimates the combined disease prevalence of all cardiovascular disorders that potentially predispose young sportspeople to SCD is 0.3%.[83] In contrast to the wide range of estimates for SCD incidence, the prevalence of potentially lethal cardiovascular diseases in athletes has consistently ranged between 0.2% and 0.7% in studies using non-invasive cardiovascular testing (Table 48.4).[7, 86–90] In other words, approximately 1 in 500 young sportspeople or more may harbor an occult cardiovascular condition that places them at risk for SCD.

Primary prevention of SCD in athletes—pre-participation cardiovascular screening

Pre-participation screening (PPS) of young sportspeople has been recommended by the American Heart Association, the American College of Cardiology, and the European Society of Cardiology (ESC); however, there remains controversy on the most suitable methodology.[16, 91, 92] In the US, PPS using a 12-point screening protocol encompassing personal symptoms, family history, and physical examination is recommended.[18] Important limitations to this include the fact that most deaths occur in individuals without antecedent symptoms and with an entirely normal cardiovascular examination.

In Italy, a mandatory state-sponsored screening program exists, incorporating the 12-lead ECG/EKG in conjunction with personal and family history as well as physical examination. Over a 25-year follow-up period a significant reduction (approximately 90%) in the incidence of SCD was demonstrated in screened athletes compared with unscreened non-athletic individuals.[6] Consequently, the ESC recommends PPS with ECG/EKG as part of its screening protocol[27]—a recommendation also endorsed by the IOC[93] and FIFA. However, such a recommendation remains controversial as the majority of countries do not have the infrastructure to cope with such large-scale screening programs. There are also concerns regarding the cost-effectiveness, efficacy, and impact of false-positive results.

Numerous sportspeople would need to be screened to identify a few who might die suddenly. Whereas the 12-lead ECG/EKG would identify the suspicion of an underlying cardiomyopathy in the vast majority of

Table 48.4 Prevalence of cardiovascular disorders at risk for sudden cardiac death

Study	Population	Prevalence
AHA (2007)[17]	Estimate in competitive athletes; age 12–35 (US)	0.3%
Fuller (1997)[20]	5617 high school athletes (US)	0.4%
Corrado (2006)[6]	42 386 athletes; age 12–35 (Italy)	0.2%
Wilson (2008)[21]	2720 athletes and children; age 10–17 (UK)	0.3%
Bessem (2009)[22]	428 athletes; age 12–35 (Netherlands)	0.7%
Hevia (2009)[24]	1220 amateur athletes (Spain)	0.16%
Baggish (2010)[23]	510 college athletes (US)	0.6%

athletes, it would fail to reveal anomalous coronary arteries, premature coronary disease, and a considerable number of cases of ion channel disease.

Up to 40% of sportspeople exhibit electrocardiographic findings that may be deemed abnormal for the general population.[94] In some cases, certain repolarization changes may overlap with phenotypic expressions of cardiomyopathy and electrical disorders, raising concerns about false-positive diagnoses and unfair disqualification from sport.[91, 92]

Pre-participation screening of older sportspeople (aged over 40 years old) to identify coronary disease, the commonest cause of SCD in this age group, is less straightforward since a routine ECG/EKG would fail to identify almost all asymptomatic athletes, and an exercise stress test is associated with low sensitivity in such individuals.[95] CT coronary angiography is more specific but it is expensive and associated with radiation.

Both the AHA and the European Association of Cardiovascular Prevention and Rehabilitation (EACPR) have taken a pragmatic approach in this regard and recommended initial evaluation with a health questionnaire relating to symptoms of coronary disease and the presence of specific risk factors.[96, 97] Only sportspeople with symptoms and recognized risk factors for coronary disease should be evaluated with an exercise test or CT coronary angiography on the understanding that neither test can predict rupture of a small atheromatous plaque and subsequent myocardial infarction during exercise.

Secondary prevention—responding when an athlete has collapsed

No screening program offers absolute prevention against SCA, and every school, club, and organization that sponsors athletic activities should be prepared to respond to a collapsed athlete with an acute cardiac emergency. Treatment of SCA begins with early recognition, early cardiopulmonary resuscitation (CPR), and early defibrillation. A comprehensive emergency response plan for SCA including access to an automated external defibrillator (AED) increases the likelihood of bystander CPR, reduces the time to defibrillation, and improves survival from SCA in the athletic setting.[9,12] Successful programs require an organized and practiced response, an established communication method to activate the emergency medical services (EMS) system, and rescuers trained and equipped to provide CPR and defibrillation.

Recognition of sudden cardiac arrest

Prompt recognition of SCA is the first step to an efficient emergency response. Sports medicine professionals and other anticipated first responders to SCA in an athlete, such as coaches and conditioning trainers, must maintain a high index of suspicion for SCA in any collapsed and unresponsive athlete. Delayed recognition of SCA by first responders can lead to critical delays or even failure to activate the EMS system, initiate CPR, and provide early defibrillation.

Resuscitation can be delayed because SCA is commonly mistaken for a seizure. Brief seizure-like activity or involuntary myoclonic jerks have been reported in over 50% of young athletes with SCA.[12, 98] Another challenge to recognizing SCA in athletes includes inaccurate rescuer assessment of pulse or respirations. Occasional or agonal gasping can occur in the first minutes after SCA and can be misinterpreted as normal breathing.[99] Occasional gasping does not represent adequate breathing and if present should not prevent rescuers from initiating CPR. Lay rescuers and even healthcare professionals can be inaccurate in assessing signs of circulation and the presence of a pulse.

In studies, rescuers with basic CPR training failed to recognize the absence of a pulse in 10% of pulseless victims, failed to correctly identify a pulse in 45% of victims with a pulse, and accurately identified pulselessness in only 2% of pulseless victims within 10 seconds.[100, 101] In high school and college athletes with SCA, perceived ongoing respirations or a pulse after collapse were reported in approximately half the cases.[12, 98]

Management of sudden cardiac arrest

Public access to defibrillators and first-responder AED programs improve survival from SCA by increasing the likelihood that SCA victims receive bystander CPR and early defibrillation. These programs require an organized and practiced response plan with rescuers trained and equipped to recognize SCA, activate the EMS system, provide CPR, and use an AED.[102] The AHA emphasizes the time-sensitive interventions for victims of SCA and has outlined four critical steps in a "chain of survival" to save lives in the event of a cardiovascular emergency:[103]

1. Early recognition of the emergency and activation of the local emergency response system
2. Early cardiopulmonary resuscitation (CPR)
3. Early defibrillation (AED)

4. Early advanced life support and cardiovascular care (hospital)

Every school, club, and organization that sponsors athletic activities should have an emergency response plan for SCA with written policies and procedures to ensure an efficient and structured response to a cardiac emergency.[104, 105] Essential elements of emergency planning include training of anticipated responders in CPR and AED use, establishing an effective communication system, ensuring access to early defibrillation, integrating on-site responder and AED programs with the local EMS system, and practicing and reviewing the response plan (Table 48.5).[105]

Consensus guidelines and several public access defibrillation studies uniformly support access to early defibrillation, targeting a time interval of less than 3–5 minutes from collapse to first shock.[105–107]

Cardiopulmonary resuscitation

CPR provides a small but critical amount of blood flow to the heart and brain and increases the likelihood that defibrillation will restore a normal rhythm in time to prevent neurological damage. Resuming CPR immediately after shock delivery is also critical. Many victims can have pulseless electric activity or asystole for several minutes after defibrillation, and CPR is needed to provide perfusion.[108–110] Unfortunately, bystander CPR is initiated in less than one-third of cases of witnessed SCA[111, 112] and, if initiated, more than 40% of chest compressions are of insufficient quality.[113]

Recent efforts have focused on ways to simplify CPR recommendations and emphasize the fundamental importance of high-quality CPR. Recommended changes in the compression–ventilation ratio

Table 48.5 Key components to emergency planning for sudden cardiac arrest

Develop a written emergency response plan for SCA.
Establish an effective and efficient communication
    system.
Identify and train likely responders in CPR and AED use.
Access to early defibrillation through on-site AED(s).
Integrate and register the AED with the local EMS system.
Practice and review the response plan with potential first
    responders at least annually.

SCA = sudden cardiac arrest; AED = automated external defibrillator; CPR = cardiopulmonary resuscitation; EMS = emergency medical services

(from 15:2 to 30:2) and in the defibrillation sequence (from 3 stacked shocks to 1 shock followed by immediate CPR) have been made to minimize interruptions in chest compressions. Minimizing the interval between stopping chest compressions and delivering a shock (i.e. the pre-shock pause) also improves the chances of shock success and patient survival. For most adults with out-of-hospital cardiac arrest, bystander CPR with chest compression only (hands-only CPR) appears to achieve outcomes similar to those of conventional CPR (compressions with rescue breathing).[114, 115]

Recently, CPR recommendations were updated in the 2010 AHA Guidelines for cardiopulmonary resuscitation and emergency cardiovascular care, and the 2010 International consensus on cardiopulmonary resuscitation and emergency cardiovascular care science with treatment recommendations.[115–117]

The newest development in the guidelines is a change in the basic life support sequence of steps from "A-B-C" (Airway, Breathing, Chest compressions) to "C-A-B" (Chest compressions, Airway, Breathing). In the A-B-C sequence, chest compressions are often delayed while the responder opens the airway to give mouth-to-mouth breaths or retrieves a barrier device or other ventilation equipment.

By changing the sequence to C-A-B, chest compressions are initiated sooner and ventilation only minimally delayed until completion of the first cycle of chest compressions. Starting with chest compressions may ensure that more victims receive CPR and that rescuers who are unable or unwilling to provide ventilations will at least perform chest compressions.

Immediate activation of the emergency response system and chest compressions should be started in any unresponsive victim with no breathing or no normal breathing (i.e. only gasps). Hands-only (compression only) CPR is encouraged for the untrained lay rescuer. Adequate chest compressions include:

- compressing to a depth of compression of at least 5 cm (2 in.)
- allowing complete recoil of the chest after each compression
- minimizing any pauses in compressions
- avoiding excessive ventilation.[116]

Early defibrillation

The single greatest factor affecting survival from SCA is the time interval from cardiac arrest to defibrillation.[103] In the US, historical survival rates from out-of-hospital cardiac arrest are <5%.[118–120] Drezner et al. reported a 7-year analysis of survival trends in the US following exercise-related SCA in youth. During the 7-year period 2000–2006, 486 total cases of exercise-related SCA were identified in individuals aged 5–22 with an overall survival rate of 11% (range 4–21%) per year.[121] Survival following SCA has been greatly improved by lay rescuer and public access defibrillation programs designed to shorten the time interval from SCA to shock delivery.[9, 102, 122–128] These programs train lay rescuers and non-traditional first responders in CPR and AED use and place AEDs in public locations where risk for SCA is high.

Rapid defibrillation in public settings such as casinos, airlines, and airports has led to survival rates ranging from 41% to 74% if bystander CPR is provided and defibrillation occurs within 3–5 minutes of collapse.[9, 102, 122–128] Once transported to a setting for advanced cardiac life support, rapid cooling (induced hypothermia) for victims with ventricular fibrillation arrest has been shown to improve survival and decrease neurological complications.[129]

Limited research is available regarding early defibrillation programs in the athletic setting. Questions also exist as to whether early defibrillation in young athletes who suffer SCA from a diverse etiology of structural and electrical cardiac diseases can provide the same survival benefit as demonstrated in the older general population with a predominance of coronary artery disease as the cause of SCA. Initial research on AED utilization at college athletic venues found an overall immediate resuscitation rate of 54% in older non-students but did not identify a survival benefit in a small number of intercollegiate athletes with SCA.[9, 98, 130]

Recent research suggests (for the first time) an improved survival rate for young athletes with SCA if early defibrillation is achieved. Drezner et al.[12] reported on a cohort of 1710 US high schools with an on-site AED program. Thirty-six cases of SCA were described, including 14 cases of high school student-athletes (mean age 16; range 14–17) and 22 cases of older non-students (mean age 57; range 42–71) such as employees and spectators. All but one case of SCA was witnessed, 94% received bystander CPR, and an AED deployed a shock in 30 of 36 (83%) cases. Twenty-three of the 36 SCA victims (64%) survived to hospital discharge including 9 of the 14 student-athletes (64%) and 14 of the 22 older non-students (64%). Although this was a retrospective cohort study, the consistent reported use of on-site school-based

AEDs makes this the largest study of early defibrillation to treat SCA in the school or athletic setting, and the first study to suggest a survival benefit for early defibrillation in young athletes with SCA.

A goal of less than 3–5 minutes from collapse to shock delivery (time it takes to recognize an emergency, notify designated responders, access the AED, reach the victim, apply the electrodes, and deliver the first shock) is recommended.[106, 131] If a facility has only one AED, it should be centrally located so it can be brought to the site of SCA through activation of the emergency response plan. Consideration should be given to the most populated areas and proximity to athletic facilities. For larger venues and schools with distant or multiple athletic facilities, duplicate equipment may be needed.

The AED should be highly visible and near a telephone or other means of activating the EMS system and on-site response team. All staff should be instructed on the location of the AED. The AED should be easily accessible during all hours the facility is open, including any sponsored event after usual working hours. The AED should be secured but not placed in a locked box, cabinet, or room that is inaccessible at the time of an emergency.

To avoid potentially fatal delays in resuscitation, a collapsed and unresponsive sportsperson should be treated as having had a cardiac arrest until a non-cardiac cause of collapse can be clearly determined or the athlete becomes responsive (Table 48.6). Brief seizure-like activity in a collapsed athlete should be assumed due to SCA. Young athletes who collapse shortly after being struck in the chest should be suspected of having commotio cordis and emergency procedures for SCA initiated.

 A high suspicion of SCA must be maintained for any collapsed and unresponsive athlete and an AED applied as soon as possible for rhythm analysis and defibrillation if indicated.[121]

Summary

- SCD is the leading cause of death in young athletes during sport and is usually caused by an inherited or congenital cardiac disorder.
- The incidence of SCD is substantially higher than is generally recognized and the risk is appreciably higher in males and black/African athletes.
- Greater efforts should be made toward more rigorous pre-participation screening and emergency

preparations at athletic venues. ECG/EKG screening substantially increases the sensitivity to detect conditions predisposing to SCD and can be performed with a low false-positive rate when contemporary criteria are used to guide ECG/EKG interpretation.
- Emergency response planning for SCA and prompt availability to AEDs are recommended for all organized athletic settings.
- Early recognition of SCA is based on assessing responsiveness and the absence of normal breathing.

Victims of SCA may initially have gasping respirations or even appear to be having a seizure. These atypical presentations may confuse a rescuer, causing a delay in calling for help or beginning CPR.
- All efforts should be made to minimize interruptions in chest compressions both before and after defibrillation.
- SCA in athletes can be effectively treated through prompt recognition of SCA, a coordinated emergency response, early CPR, and early defibrillation.

Table 48.6 Management of sudden cardiac arrest in sportspeople

1. Prompt recognition of SCA
  (a) Brief seizure-like activity after collapse is common in athletes with SCA
  (b) No breathing or no normal breathing (i.e. gasping) in an unresponsive victim
2. Early activation of the EMS system and call for additional rescuer assistance
3. Early CPR
  (a) C-A-B (Chest compressions–Airway–Breathing)
  (b) Chest compressions—push hard, push fast—100 per minute.
  (c) Hands-only (compression only) CPR for the untrained lay rescuer
	4. Immediate retrieval of the AED
	5. Application of the AED as soon as possible for rhythm analysis and shock delivery if indicated
	  (a) If no shock is recommended, a non-shockable SCA (i.e. asystole or pulseless electrical activity) is still possible, and CPR and life support measures should be continued until the patient becomes responsive or a non-cardiac etiology can be clearly established
	6. Transport of the SCA victim to a hospital facility capable of advanced cardiac life support
	7. Rapid cooling (induced hypothermia) for SCA victims with VF arrest has been shown to improve survival and decrease neurological complications[56]

SCA = sudden cardiac arrest; AED = automated external defibrillator; CPR = cardiopulmonary resuscitation; EMS = emergency medical services; VF = ventricular fibrillation

REFERENCES

1. Maron BJ, Doerer JJ, Haas TS et al. Sudden deaths in young competitive athletes: analysis of 1866 deaths in the United States, 1980–2006. *Circulation* 2009;119(8):1085–92.

2. Maron BJ. Sudden death in young athletes. *N Engl J Med* 2003;349(11):1064–75.

3. Harmon K, Asif I, Klossner D et al. Incidence and etiology of sudden death in NCAA athletes. *Circulation* 2011;123(15):1594–600.

4. de Noronha SV, Sharma S, Papadakis M et al. Aetiology of sudden cardiac death in athletes in the United Kingdom: a pathological study. *Heart* 2009;95: 1409–14.

5. Van Camp SP, Bloor CM, Mueller FO et al. Nontraumatic sports death in high school and college athletes. *Med Sci Sports Exerc* 1995;27(5):641–7.

6. Maron BJ, Gohman TE, Aeppli D. Prevalence of sudden cardiac death during competitive sports activities in Minnesota high school athletes. *J Am Coll Cardiol* 1998;32(7):1881–4.

7. Corrado D, Basso C, Pavei A et al. Trends in sudden cardiovascular death in young competitive athletes after implementation of a preparticipation screening program. *JAMA* 2006;296(13):1593–601.

8. Eckart RE, Scoville SL, Campbell CL et al. Sudden death in young adults: a 25-year review of autopsies in military recruits. *Ann Intern Med* 2004;141(11): 829–34.

9. Drezner JA, Rogers KJ, Zimmer RR et al. Use of automated external defibrillators at NCAA Division I universities. *Med Sci Sports Exerc* 2005;37(9): 1487–92.

10. Atkins DL, Everson-Stewart S, Sears GK et al. Epidemiology and outcomes from out-of-hospital cardiac arrest in children: the Resuscitation Outcomes Consortium Epistry-Cardiac Arrest. *Circulation* 2009;119(11):1484–91.

11. Chugh SS, Reinier K, Balaji S et al. Population-based analysis of sudden death in children: The Oregon Sudden Unexpected Death Study. *Heart Rhythm* 2009;6(11):1618–22.

12. Drezner JA, Rao AL, Heistand J et al. Effectiveness of emergency response planning for sudden cardiac arrest in United States high schools with automated external defibrillators. *Circulation* 2009;120(6):518–25.

13. Solberg EE, Gjertsen F, Haugstad E et al. Sudden death in sports among young adults in Norway. *Eur J Cardiovasc Prev Rehabil* 2010;17(3):337–41.

14. Corrado D, Basso C, Rizzoli G et al. Does sports activity enhance the risk of sudden death in adolescents and young adults? *J Am Coll Cardiol* 2003;42(11):1959–63.

15. Heron M, Hoyert D, Murphy S et al. Deaths: final data for 2006. *National Vital Statistics Reports* 2009;57(14): 1–136.

16. Drezner J, Berger S, Campbell R. Current controversies in the cardiovascular screening of athletes. *Curr Sports Med Rep* 2010;9(2):86–92.

17. Waller BF, Roberts WC. Sudden death whilst running in conditioned runners aged 40 years or over. *Am J Cardiology* 1980;45:1292–300.

18. Noakes TD, Opie HL, Rose AG. Autopsy proved coronary atherosclerosis in marathon runners. *N Engl J Med* 1979;310:86–95.

19. Thompson PD, Funk EJ, Carleton RA. Incidence of death during jogging in Rhode Island from 1975 through 1980. *JAMA* 1982;247:2535–8.

20. Maron BJ, Shirani J, Poliac LC et al. Sudden death in young competitive athletes. Clinical, demographic, and pathological profiles. *JAMA* 1996;276(3):199–204.

21. Corrado D, Thiene G, Nava A et al. Sudden death in young competitive athletes: clinicopathological correlation in 22 cases. *Am J Med* 1990;89:588.

22. Corrado D, Basso C, Schiavon M. Screening for hypertrophic cardiomyopathy in young athletes. *N Engl J Med* 1998;339 (6):364–9.

23. Maron BJ, Gardin JM, Flack JM et al. Prevalence of hypertrophic cardiomyopathy in a general population of young adults: echocardiographic analysis of 4111 subjects in the CARDIA study. Circulation 1995;92:785–9.

24. Basavarajaiah S, Wilson M, Whyte G et al. Prevalence of hypertrophic cardiomyopathy in elite athletes: relevance to pre-participation screening. *J Am Coll Cardiol* 2008;51(10):1033–9.

25. Maron BJ, Klues H. Surviving competitive athletics with hypertrophic cardiomyopathy. *Am J Cardiol* 1994;73:1098–104.

26. Maron BJ, Carney KP, Lever HM et al. Relationship of race to sudden cardiac death in competitive athletes with hypertrophic cardiomyopathy. *J Am Coll Cardiol* 2003;41(6):974–80.

27. Corrado D, Pelliccia A, Bjørnstad HH et al. Cardiovascular pre-participation screening of young competitive athletes for prevention of sudden death: proposal for a common European protocol. Consensus Statement of the Study Group of Sport Cardiology of the Working Group of Cardiac Rehabilitation and Exercise Physiology and the Working Group of

Myocardial and Pericardial Diseases of the European Society of Cardiology. *Eur Heart J* 2005;26(5):516–24.

28. Elliott PM, Poloniecki J, Dickie S et al. Sudden death in hypertrophic cardiomyopathy: identification of high risk patients. *J Am Coll Cardiol* 2000;36:2212–18.

29. Maron BJ, Shen W-K, Link MS et al. Efficacy of implantable cardioverter-defibrillators for the prevention of sudden death in patients with hypertrophic cardiomyopathy. *N Engl J Med* 2000;342:365–73.

30. Maron BJ, Isner JM, McKenna WJ. 26th Bethesda conference: recommendations for determining eligibility for competition in athletes with cardiovascular abnormalities. Task force 3: Hypertrophic cardiomyopathy, myocarditis and other myopericardial diseases, and mitral valve prolapse. *J Am Coll Cardiol* 1994;4:880–5.

31. Pelliccia A, Fagard R, Bjornstad HH et al. Recommendations for competitive sports participation in athletes with cardiovascular disease: a consensus document from the Study Group of Sports Cardiology of the Working Group of Cardiac Rehabilitation and Exercise Physiology and the Working Group of Myocardial and Pericardial Diseases of the European Society of Cardiology. *Eur Heart J* 2005;14:1422–45.

32. Basavarajaiah S, Boraita A, Whyte G et al. Ethnic differences in left ventricular remodeling in highly-trained athletes: relevance to differentiating physiologic left ventricular hypertrophy from hypertrophic cardiomyopathy. *J Am Coll Cardiol* 2008;51(23):2256–62.

33. Sen-Chowdhry S, Lowe MD, Sporton S et al. Arrhythmogenic right ventricular cardiomyopathy: clinical presentation, diagnosis, and management. *Am J Med* 2004;117:685–95.

34. Norman M, Simpson M, Mogensen J et al. Novel mutation in desmoplakin causes arrhythmogenic left ventricular cardiomyopathy. *Circulation* 2005;112:636–42.

35. Delmar M, McKenna WJ. The cardiac desmosome and arrhythmogenic cardiomyopathies: from gene to disease. *Circ Res* 2010;107(6):700–14.

36. Corrado D, Basso C, Pilichou K et al. Molecular biology and the clinical management of arrhythmogenic right ventricular cardiomyopathy/dysplasia. *Heart* 2011;97(7):530–9.

37. Heidbuchel H, Hoogsteen J, Fagard R et al. High prevalence of right ventricular involvement in endurance athletes with ventricular arrhythmias. Role of an electrophysiologic study in risk stratification. *Eur Heart J* 2003;24:1473–80.

38. Ector J, Ganame J, van der Merwe N et al. Reduced right ventricular ejection fraction in endurance athletes presenting with ventricular arrhythmias: a quantitative angiographic assessment. *Eur Heart J* 2007;28:345–53.

39. La Gerche A, Connelly KA, Mooney DJ et al. Biochemical and functional abnormalities of left and right ventricular function after ultra-endurance exercise. *Heart* 2008;94:860–6.

40. La Gerche A, Robberecht C, Kuiperi C et al. Lower than expected desmosomal gene mutation prevalence in endurance athletes with complex ventricular arrhythmias of right ventricular origin. *Heart* 2010;96(16):1268–74.

41. Sharma S, Papadakis M and Whyte G. Chronic ultra-endurance exercise: implications in arrhythmogenic substrates in previously normal hearts. *Heart* 2010;96:1255–6.

42. Marcus FI, McKenna WJ, Sherrill D et al. Diagnosis of arrhythmogenic right ventricular cardiomyopathy/dysplasia: proposed modification of the task force criteria. *Circulation* 2010;121(13):1533–41.

43. Sen-Chowdhry S, Morgan RD, Chambers JC et al. Arrhythmogenic cardiomyopathy: etiology, diagnosis, and treatment *Ann Rev Med* 2010;61:233–53.

44. Corrado D, Calkins H, Link MS et al. Prophylactic implantable defibrillator in patients with arrhythmogenic right ventricular cardiomyopathy/dysplasia and no prior ventricular fibrillation or sustained ventricular tachycardia. *Circulation* 2010;122(12):1144–52.

45. Taylor AJ, Rogan KM, Virmani R. Sudden cardiac death with isolated congenital coronary artery anomalies. *J Am Coll Cardiol* 1992;20:640–7.

46. Taylor AJ, Byers JP, Cheitlin MD et al. Anomalous right or left coronary artery from the contralateral coronary sinus: "high-risk" abnormalities in the initial coronary artery course and heterogeneous clinical outcomes. *Am Heart J* 1997;133:428–35.

47. Basso C, Maron BJ, Corrado D et al. Clinical profile of congenital coronary artery anomalies with origin from the wrong aortic sinus leading to sudden death in young competitive athletes. *J Am Coll Cardiol* 2000;35:1493–501.

48. Edwards CP, Yavari A, Sheppard MN et al. Anomalous coronary origin: the challenge in preventing exercise-related sudden cardiac death. *Br J Sports Med* 2010;44(12):895–7.

49. Prakken NH, Cramer MJ, Olimulder MA et al. Screening for proximal coronary artery anomalies with 3-dimensional MR coronary angiography. *Int J Cardiovasc Imaging* 2010;26(6):701–10.

D

50. Yetman AT, Bornemeier RA, McCrindle BW. Long-term outcome in patients with Marfan syndrome: is aortic dissection the only cause of sudden death? *J Am Coll Cardiol* 2003;41:329–32.

51. Maron BJ, Ackerman MJ, Nishimura RA et al. Task force 4: HCM and other cardiomyopathies, mitral valve prolapse, myocarditis, and Marfan syndrome. *J Am Coll Cardiol* 2005;45:1340–5.

52. Gersony DR, McClaughlin MA, Jin Z et al. The effect of beta-blocker therapy on clinical outcome in patients with Marfan's syndrome: a meta-analysis. *Int J Cardiol* 2007;114(3):303–8.

53. Brooke BS, Habashi JP, Judge DP et al. Angiotensin II blockade and aortic-root dilation in Marfan's syndrome *N Engl J Med* 2008;358(26):2787–95.

54. Kligfield P, Levy D, Devereux RB et al. Arrhythmias and sudden death in mitral valve prolapse. *Am Heart J* 1987;113:1298–307.

55. Jeresaty RM. Mitral valve prolapse: definition and implications in athletes. *J Am Coll Cardiol* 1986;7(1):231–6.

56. Behr E, Wood DA, Wright M et al. Sudden Arrhythmic Death Syndrome Steering Group: cardiological assessment of first-degree relatives in sudden arrhythmic death syndrome. *Lancet* 2003;362:1457–9.

57. Hedley PL, Jørgensen P, Schlamowitz S et al. The genetic basis of long QT and short QT syndromes: a mutation update. *Hum Mutat* 2009;30(11):1486–511.

58. Schwartz PJ, Priori SG, Spazzolini C et al. Genotype-phenotype correlation in the long-QT syndrome: gene-specific triggers for life-threatening arrhythmias. *Circulation* 2001;103:89–95.

59. Takenaka K, Ai T, Shimizu W et al. Exercise stress test amplifies genotype-phenotype correlation in the LQT1 and LQT2 forms of the long-QT syndrome. *Circulation* 2003; 107:838–46.

60. Basavarajaiah S, Wilson M, Whyte G et al. Prevalence and significance of an isolated long QT interval in athletes. *Eur Heart J* 2007;28;2944–9.

61. Zipes DP, Ackerman MJ, Estes NA 3rd et al. Task force 7: Arrhythmias. *J Am Coll Cardiol* 2005;45:1354–63.

62. Schwartz PJ, Spazzolini C, Priori SG et al. Who are the long-QT syndrome patients who receive an implantable cardioverter-defibrillator and what happens to them? Data from the European Long-QT Syndrome Implantable Cardioverter-Defibrillator (LQTS ICD) Registry. *Circulation*. 2010;122(13):1272–82.

63. Antzelevitch C, Brugada P, Borggrefe M et al. Brugada syndrome: report of the second consensus conference: endorsed by the Heart Rhythm Society and the European Heart Rhythm Association. *Circulation* 2005;111:659–70.

64. Corrado D, Basso C, Buja G et al. Right bundle branch block, right precordial ST-segment elevation, and sudden death in young people. *Circulation* 2001;103:710–17.

65. Antzelevitch C, Brugada R. Fever and Brugada syndrome. *Pacing Clin Electrophysiol* 2002;25(11): 1537–9.

66. Priori SG, Napolitano C, Memmi M et al. Clinical and molecular characterization of patients with catecholaminergic polymorphic ventricular tachycardia. *Circulation* 2002;106:69–74.

67. Choi G, Kopplin LJ, Tester DJ et al. Spectrum and frequency of cardiac channel defects in swimming-triggered arrhythmia syndromes. *Circulation* 2004;110:2119–24.

68. Haugaa KH, Leren IS, Berge KE et al. High prevalence of exercise-induced arrhythmias in catecholaminergic polymorphic ventricular tachycardia mutation-positive family members diagnosed by cascade genetic screening. *Europace* 2010;12(3):417–23.

69. Basso C, Carturan E, Corrado D et al. Myocarditis and dilated cardiomyopathy in athletes: diagnosis, management, and recommendations for sport activity. *Cardiol Clin* 2007;25(3):423–9, vi.

70. Madias C, Maron BJ, Weinstock J et al. Commotio cordis—sudden cardiac death with chest wall impact. *J Cardiovasc Electophysiolol* 2007;1:115–22.

71. Classie JA, Distel LM, Borchers JR. Safety baseballs and chest protectors: a systematic review on the prevention of commotio cordis. *Phys Sportsmed* 2010;38(1):83–90.

72. Sharma S, Whyte G, Elliott PM et al. Electrocardiographic changes in 1000 highly trained elite athletes. *Br J Sports Med* 1999;30(5):319–24.

73. Papadakis M, Basavarajaiah S, Rawlins J et al. Prevalence and significance of T wave inversions in predominantly Caucasian adolescent athletes. *Eur Heart J* 2009;30(14)1728–35.

74. Maron BJ, Pelliccia A. The heart of trained athletes: cardiac remodeling and the risks of sports, including sudden death. *Circulation* 2006;114(15):1633–44.

75. Pellicia A, Maron BJ, Spataro A et al. The upper limit of physiological hypertrophy in highly trained elite athletes. *N Engl J Med* 1991;324:295–301.

76. Rawlins J, Bhan A, Sharma S. Left ventricular hypertrophy in athletes. *Eur J Echocardiogr* 2009;10(3):350–6.

77. Bauce B, Frigo G, Benini G et al. Differences and similarities between arrhythmogenic right ventricular

cardiomyopathy and athlete's heart adaptations. *Br J Sports Med* 2010;44(2):148–54.

78. Marcus FI, McKenna WJ, Sherrill D et al. Diagnosis of of arrhythmogenic right ventricular cardiomyopathy/dysplasia: proposed modification of the Task Force Criteria. *Circulation* 2010;121(13):1533–41.

79. Magalski A, Maron BJ, Main ML et al. Relation of race to electrocardiographic patterns in elite American football players. *J Am Coll Cardiol* 2008;51(23):2250–5.

80. Papadakis M, Carre F, Kervio G et al. The prevalence, distribution, and clinical outcomes of electrocardiographic repolarization patterns in male athletes of African/Afro-Caribbean origin. *Eur Heart J* 2011; May 25. [Epub ahead of print].

81. Chandra N, Papadakis M, Sharma S. Cardiac adaptations to intense physical exercise in African/Afro-Carribean athletes. E-Journal of the ESC Council for Cardiology Practice. 2010;8(34)

82. Rawlins J, Carre F, Kervio G et al. Ethnic differences in physiological cardiac adaptation to intense physical exercise in highly trained female athletes. *Circulation* 2010;121(9):1078–85.

83. Maron BJ, Thompson PD, Ackerman MJ et al. Recommendations and considerations related to preparticipation screening for cardiovascular abnormalities in competitive athletes: 2007 update: a scientific statement from the American Heart Association Council on Nutrition, Physical Activity, and Metabolism: endorsed by the American College of Cardiology Foundation. *Circulation* 2007;115(12):1643–55.

84. Maron BJ, Zipes DP. 36th Bethesda Conference: Eligibility recommendations for competitive athletes with cardiovascular abnormalities. *J Am Coll Cardiol* 2005;45(8):1312–77.

85. American Academy of Family Physicians, American Academy of Pediatrics, American College of Sports Medicine, American Medical Society for Sports Medicine, American Orthopaedic Society for Sports Medicine, American Osteopathic Academy of Sports Medicine. Preparticipation Physical Evaluation, 4th ed. *American Academy of Pediatrics.* 2010.

86. Fuller CM, McNulty CM, Spring DA et al. Prospective screening of 5,615 high school athletes for risk of sudden cardiac death. *Med Sci Sports Exerc* 1997;29(9):1131–8.

87. Wilson MG, Basavarajaiah S, Whyte GP et al. Efficacy of personal symptom and family history questionnaires when screening for inherited cardiac pathologies:

the role of electrocardiography. *Br J Sports Med* 2008;42(3):207–11.

88. Bessem B, Groot FP, Nieuwland W. The Lausanne recommendations: a Dutch experience. *Br J Sports Med* 2009;43(9):708–715.

89. Baggish AL, Hutter AM Jr, Wang F et al. Cardiovascular screening in college athletes with and without electrocardiography: a cross-sectional study. *Ann Intern Med* 2010;152(5):269–75.

90. Hevia AC, Fernandez MM, Palacio JM et al. ECG as a part of the preparticipation screening programme: an old and still present international dilemma. *Br J Sports Med* 2011;45(10):776–9.

91. Papadakis M, Whyte G, Sharma S. Preparticipation screening for cardiovascular abnormalities in young competitive athletes. *BMJ* 2008;337:806–11.

92. Chandra N, Papadakis M, Sharma S. Preparticipation screening of young competitive athletes for cardiovascular disorders. *Phys Sportsmed* 2010;38(1):54–63.

93. Bille K, Figueiras D, Schamasch P et al. Sudden cardiac death in athletes: the Lausanne Recommendations. *Eur J Cardiovasc Prev Rehabil* 2006;13(6):859–75.

94. Pelliccia A, Maron BJ, Culasso F et al. Clinical significance of abnormal electrocardiographic patterns in trained athletes. *Circulation* 2000;102(3):278–84.

95. Lahav D, Leshno M, Brezis M. Is an exercise tolerance test indicated before beginning regular exercise? A decision analysis. *J Gen Intern Med* 2009;24:934–8.

96. Maron BJ, Araujo CG, Thompson PD et al. Recommendations for preparticipation screening and the assessment of cardiovascular disease in master athletes: an advisory for healthcare professionals from the working groups of the World Heart Federation, the International federation of Sports Medicine and the American Heart Association committe on Exercise, Cardiac Rehabilitation and Prevention. *Circulation* 2001;103:327–34.

97. Borjesson M, Urhausen A, Kouidi E et al. Cardiovascular evaluation of middle-aged/senior individuals engaged in leisure-time sport activities: position stand from the sections of exercise physiology and sports cardiology of the European Association of Cardiovascular Prevention and Rehabilitation. *Eur J Cardiovasc Prev Rehabil* 2011 Jan 28. [Epub ahead of print].

98. Drezner JA, Rogers KJ. Sudden cardiac arrest in intercollegiate athletes: detailed analysis and

outcomes of resuscitation in nine cases. *Heart Rhythm* 2006;3(7):755–9.

99. Ruppert M, Reith MW, Widmann JH et al. Checking for breathing: evaluation of the diagnostic capability of emergency medical services personnel, physicians, medical students, and medical laypersons. *Ann Emerg Med* 1999;34(6):720–9.

100. ECC committee, subcommittees and task forces of the American Heart Association. 2005 American Heart Association guidelines for cardiopulmonary resuscitation and emergency cardiovascular care. Part 4: Adult basic life support. *Circulation* 2005;112(24 Suppl):IV19–34.

101. Eberle B, Dick WF, Schneider T et al. Checking the carotid pulse check: diagnostic accuracy of first responders in patients with and without a pulse. *Resuscitation* 1996;33(2):107–16.

102. Hallstrom AP, Ornato JP, Weisfeldt M et al. Public-access defibrillation and survival after out-of-hospital cardiac arrest. *N Engl J Med* 2004;351(7):637–46.

103. The American Heart Association in Collaboration with the International Liaison Committee on Resuscitation. Guidelines 2000 for cardiopulmonary resuscitation and emergency cardiovascular care. Part 4: the automated external defibrillator: key link in the chain of survival. *Circulation* 2000;102(8 Suppl):I60–76.

104. Andersen J, Courson RW, Kleiner DM et al. National Athletic Trainers' Association Position statement: emergency planning in athletics. *J Athl Train* 2002;37(1):99–104.

105. Drezner JA, Courson RW, Roberts WO et al. Inter-association task force recommendations on emergency preparedness and management of sudden cardiac arrest in high school and college athletic programs: a consensus statement. *Heart Rhythm* 2007;4(4): 549–65.

106. Hazinski MF, Markenson D, Neish S et al. Response to cardiac arrest and selected life-threatening medical emergencies: the medical emergency response plan for schools: a statement for healthcare providers, policymakers, school administrators, and community leaders. *Circulation* 2004;109(2):278–91.

107. Myerburg RJ, Estes NA 3rd, Fontaine JM et al. Task force 10: Automated external defibrillators. *J Am Coll Cardiol* 2005;45(8):1369–71.

108. White RD, Russell JK. Refibrillation, resuscitation and survival in out-of-hospital sudden cardiac arrest victims treated with biphasic automated external defibrillators. *Resuscitation* 2002;55(1):17–23.

109. Berg MD, Clark LL, Valenzuela TD et al. Post-shock chest compression delays with automated external defibrillator use. *Resuscitation* 2005;64(3):287–91.

110. Carpenter J, Rea TD, Murray JA et al. Defibrillation waveform and post-shock rhythm in out-of-hospital ventricular fibrillation cardiac arrest. *Resuscitation* 2003;59(2):189–96.

111. Herlitz J, Ekstrom L, Wennerblom B et al. Effect of bystander initiated cardiopulmonary resuscitation on ventricular fibrillation and survival after witnessed cardiac arrest outside hospital. *Br Heart J* 1994;72(5):408–12.

112. Stiell I, Nichol G, Wells G et al. Health-related quality of life is better for cardiac arrest survivors who received citizen cardiopulmonary resuscitation. *Circulation* 2003;108(16):1939–44.

113. Wik L, Kramer-Johansen J, Myklebust H et al. Quality of cardiopulmonary resuscitation during out-of-hospital cardiac arrest. *JAMA* 2005;293(3):299–304.

114. Rea TD, Fahrenbruch C, Culley L et al. CPR with chest compression alone or with rescue breathing. *N Engl J Med* 2010;363(5):423–33.

115. Field JM, Hazinski MF, Sayre MR et al. Part 1: Executive summary: 2010 American Heart Association guidelines for cardiopulmonary resuscitation and emergency cardiovascular care. *Circulation* 2010;122(18 Suppl 3):S640–56.

116. Travers AH, Rea TD, Bobrow BJ et al. Part 4: CPR Overview: 2010 American Heart Association guidelines for cardiopulmonary resuscitation and emergency cardiovascular care. *Circulation* 2010;122(18 Suppl 3):S676–84.

117. Hazinski MF, Nolan JP, Billi JE et al. Part 1: Executive summary: 2010 International consensus on cardiopulmonary resuscitation and emergency cardiovascular care science with treatment recommendations. *Circulation* 2010;122(16 Suppl 2): S250–75.

118. Becker LB, Ostrander MP, Barrett J et al. Outcome of CPR in a large metropolitan area—where are the survivors? *Ann Emerg Med* 1991;20(4):355–61.

119. Gallagher EJ, Lombardi G, Gennis P. Effectiveness of bystander cardiopulmonary resuscitation and survival following out-of-hospital cardiac arrest. *JAMA* 1995;274(24):1922–5.

120. Bobrow BJ, Clark LL, Ewy GA et al. Minimally interrupted cardiac resuscitation by emergency medical services for out-of-hospital cardiac arrest. *JAMA* 2008;299(10):1158–65.

121. Drezner JA, Chun JS, Harmon KG et al. Survival trends in the United States following exercise-related sudden cardiac arrest in the youth: 2000–2006. *Heart Rhythm* 2008;5(6):794–9.

122. Caffrey SL, Willoughby PJ, Pepe PE et al. Public use of automated external defibrillators. *N Engl J Med* 2002;347(16):1242–7.

123. Page RL, Joglar JA, Kowal RC et al. Use of automated external defibrillators by a US airline. *N Engl J Med* 2000;343(17):1210–16.

124. Valenzuela TD, Roe DJ, Nichol G et al. Outcomes of rapid defibrillation by security officers after cardiac arrest in casinos. *N Engl J Med* 2000;343(17): 1206–9.

125. Weaver WD, Hill D, Fahrenbruch CE et al. Use of the automatic external defibrillator in the management of out-of-hospital cardiac arrest. *N Engl J Med* 1988;319(11):661–6.

126. White RD, Asplin BR, Bugliosi TF et al. High discharge survival rate after out-of-hospital ventricular fibrillation with rapid defibrillation by police and paramedics. *Ann Emerg Med* 1996;28(5): 480–5.

127. Myerburg RJ, Fenster J, Velez M et al. Impact of community-wide police car deployment of automated external defibrillators on survival from out-of-hospital cardiac arrest. *Circulation* 2002;106(9):1058–64.

128. White RD, Bunch TJ, Hankins DG. Evolution of a community-wide early defibrillation programme experience over 13 years using police/fire personnel and paramedics as responders. *Resuscitation* 2005;65(3):279–83.

129. Kim F, Carlbom D. Therapeutic hypothermia for cardiac arrest: yes, we can. *Rev Esp Cardiol* 2009;62(7):726–8.

130. Coris EE, Miller E, Sahebzamani F. Sudden cardiac death in Division I collegiate athletics: analysis of automated external defibrillator utilization in National Collegiate Athletic Association Division I athletic programs. *Clin J Sport Med* 2005;15(2):87–91.

131. Drezner JA, Courson RW, Roberts WO et al. Inter-association task force recommendations on emergency preparedness and management of sudden cardiac arrest in high school and college athletic programs: a consensus statement. *Clin J Sport Med* 2007;17(2): 87–103.

D

Chapter 49

Managing cardiovascular symptoms in sportspeople

with JONATHAN DREZNER and MARK LINK

It was like rowing through mud. 2000 Olympic gold medalist Rob Waddell describes the consequences of developing atrial fibrillation partway through a 2000 m trial race for the New Zealand men's single sculls berth at the Beijing 2008 Olympics. Waddell suffered a relapse of atrial fibrillation, having previously been free for some seven years. He fell rapidly behind and lost the race.

As discussed in Chapter 48, sudden cardiac death is the leading cause of death in young athletes during sport, and is typically the result of undiagnosed structural or electrical cardiovascular disease.[1-3] Some sportspeople present with symptoms that can alert the clinician to underlying cardiac pathologies. This chapter focuses on the clinical approach to those symptoms.

In this chapter we:

- highlight that certain symptoms can point to significant cardiovascular problems
- discuss the management of five symptoms
  - syncope
  - seizures
  - exertional chest pain
  - palpitations
  - fatigue/excessive dyspnea
- discuss physical examination findings that may be relevant to cardiovascular health

Abbreviations used in this chapter	
ARVC	Arrhythmogenic right ventricular cardiomyopathy
CCAA	Congenital coronary artery anomalies
CPVT	Catecholaminergic polymorphic ventricular tachycardia
LQTS	Long QT syndrome
HCM	Hypertrophic cardiomyopathy

- provide an overview of contemporary investigations for cardiovascular disease which now include genetic testing, as well as the traditional investigations such as electrocardiogram (ECG/EKG) and echocardiography
- discuss the approach to temporary and permanent disqualification from sport because of cardiac diagnoses.

Cardiovascular symptoms: potentially life or death decisions

Some athletes who later suffer sudden cardiac arrest have warning symptoms or signs but others do not.[4] For example, in studies, only 21% of athletes who died from HCM[5] and 44% of athletes who died of an CCAA[6] had any signs or symptoms of cardiovascular disease prior to death. Similarly only 10–20% of autopsy-negative sudden unexplained death had previous symptoms.[7, 8]

Symptoms are present in some other cardiovascular disorders. In a review of sudden cardiac death from ARVC, 68% of athletes had prodromal symptoms which included syncope, chest pain, or palpitations.[9] Ion channel disorders, such as LQTS and CPVT, also commonly present with recurrent syncope or unexplained seizure activity triggered by vigorous physical exertion or acute emotion (Table 49.1).[10, 11]

In the general athletic population, cardiovascular symptoms are uncommon and perhaps influenced by underreporting at the time of screening. In pre-

Table 49.1 Symptoms associated with certain cardiac ion channel disorders

Disorder	Trigger	Clinical event
LQTS-1	Emotional stress, physical exercise, swimming, and diving into water	Syncope, sudden death, seizure, drowning or near-drowning, motor vehicle accident
LQTS-2	Emotional stress, physical exercise, loud noises	Syncope, sudden death, seizure, motor vehicle accident
LQTS-3	Rest or sleep	Sudden death or sudden infant death
CPVT	Emotional stress, physical exercise	Syncope, sudden death, seizure, drowning or near-drowning

participation screenings, only a small percentage (1–8%) of athletes report cardiovascular symptoms that require further evaluation.[12–16] However, the sensitivity of cardiovascular symptoms identified during screening as a predictor of potentially lethal cardiovascular disease remains low (range 0–30%).[17]

Cardiovascular symptoms in sportspeople may be misinterpreted or disregarded by medical providers. A 1996 report summarized nine publications detailing 469 sudden deaths from cardiac causes in young persons.[18] These studies collectively reported preceding symptoms of dizziness, chest pain, syncope, palpitations, dyspnea, and/or a family history of sudden death from a cardiac cause in 25–61% in their study populations.[18] In a Swedish cohort of 15–35 year olds having suffered sudden cardiac death, investigators reported that 92 of 162 (57%) individuals had preceding symptoms that were often misinterpreted.[19] In 20 of 21 patients found to have CPVT, syncope was found to be a presenting symptom, although the diagnosis of CPVT was generally delayed due to the misdiagnosis of epilepsy or vasovagal events.[10]

 Warning symptoms such as syncope must be evaluated to rule out potentially lethal cardiac disorders.

Up to 20% of patients who have LQTS and present with syncope (but are not diagnosed and treated) will experience sudden death in the first year after their syncope, and 50% will have sudden cardiac death by five years.[11]

The clinical approach to potentially important cardiac symptoms

Before addressing each of the critical cardiovascular symptoms that clinicians need to evaluate, we review which symptoms to ask about in the clinical assessment. Patients often fail to volunteer cardiac "symp-

Specific question to ask during cardiovascular screening

Has there been any:

- exertional chest pain/discomfort
- unexplained syncope/near-syncope
- excessive exertional and/or unexplained dyspnea/fatigue associated with exercise
- prior recognition of a heart murmur
- history of elevated systemic blood pressure.

toms" so some symptoms need to be asked about specifically.

During pre-participation cardiovascular screening, the past medical history should focus on exertion-related symptoms that may suggest the presence of underlying cardiovascular disease. The American Heart Association recommends asking specific questions about specific symptoms when taking the personal medical history.[20] These are outlined in the box overleaf.

In addition to the five questions outlined in the box, a history of palpitations or an irregular heart beat related to exercise is also relevant. Other questions regarding cardiovascular risks include current or past illicit drug use, ergogenic supplement use (i.e. anabolic steroids, human growth hormone, and stimulants), and a recent acute viral syndrome (risk of myocarditis). In older patients (>35 years old), risk factors for coronary artery atherosclerosis such as hypertension, diabetes, hyperlipidemia, tobacco use, and a family history of premature atherosclerotic disease should be investigated.

Clinical approach to symptoms associated with cardiac conditions

In this section we outline the clinical approach to five common "cardiovascular" symptoms (syncope/near-syncope, unexplained seizure activity, exertional chest pain, palpitations, and excessive fatigue/ dyspnea) and the red flag of family history of early sudden cardiac death (Table 49.2).

Syncope/near-syncope

Syncope is common in young individuals, including sportspeople. The lifetime prevalence of syncope approaches 40–50%.[21, 22] In a review of 474 athletes with a history of syncope or near-syncope detected during pre-participation screening, 33% whose syncope occurred during exercise were found to have structural cardiac disease known to be capable of causing sudden cardiac death.[23]

The diagnostic workup of exertional syncope is usually performed in consultation with a cardiologist and should include ECG/EKG (electrocardiogram),

echocardiogram, stress ECG/EKG, and possibly advanced cardiac imaging (such as MRI or CT) to rule out rare structural abnormalities (such as ARVC and CCAAs) that are associated with syncope. If all these studies are normal, prolonged monitoring with an external ambulatory monitor should be considered. A small percentage of individuals may even require an implantable loop monitor. The specific cardiac causes of syncope and near-syncope are discussed below.

Neurogenic syncope (vasovagal syncope)

In the young the most common underlying disorder of syncope or near-syncope is neurocardiogenic syncope, also known as vasovagal syncope.[24] Neurocardiogenic syncope is more common in the

Table 49.2 Associated disorders and recommended evaluation in sportspeople with cardiovascular symptoms

Symptom	Potential cardiac disorders	Evaluation and testing to consider
Syncope/near-syncope during exercise	Cardiomyopathy (HCM, ARVC, LVNC)	ECG/EKG, echocardiography, consider cardiac MRI to evaluate cardiac morphology and presence of delayed gadolinium enhancement that indicates myocardial fibrosis
	Congenital coronary artery anomalies (CCAA)	Echocardiography, consider cardiac CT or MRI if coronary artery origins not well visualized
	Ion channel disorder (LQTS, CPVT, SQTS, Brugada syndrome)	ECG/EKG, stress ECG/EKG, ambulatory monitoring
	Critical aortic stenosis	Echocardiography
Unexplained seizure activity	Ion channel disorders, cardiomyopathy, and all potential causes of SCD	ECG/EKG, echocardiography, stress ECG/EKG, cardiac MRI, consider EEG if not performed
Exertional chest pain	Coronary artery atherosclerosis	ECG/EKG, stress ECG/EKG
	Congenital coronary artery anomalies (CCAA)	Echocardiography, consider cardiac CT or MRI if coronary artery origins not well visualized
	Cardiomyopathy	ECG/EKG, echocardiography, consider cardiac MRI
	Critical aortic stenosis	Echocardiography
Palpitations	Supraventricular tachyarrhythmias, ventricular arrhythmias, premature atrial and ventricular contractions, sinus tachycardia	ECG/EKG, echocardiography, stress ECG/EKG, ambulatory monitoring, consultation with electrophysiologist
Excessive dyspnea/ fatigue during exertion	Cardiomyopathy, myocarditis	ECG/EKG, echocardiography, stress ECG/EKG, consider pulmonary function testing

ARVC = arrhythmogenic right ventricular cardiomyopathy; CPVT = catecholaminergic polymorphic ventricular tachycardia; ECG/EKG = electrocardiogram; EEG = electroencephalogram; HCM = hypertrophic cardiomyopathy; LQTS = long QT syndrome; LVNC = left ventricular noncompoetion (outside the scope of this book); SCD = sudden cardiac death; SQTS = short QT syndrome

young than in the old, and children plagued by this syndrome tend to grow out of it by age 30–40 years.

Neurocardiogenic syncope is often triggered by certain events such as fear, pain, excitement, venepuncture, or prolonged standing. It nearly always occurs while the patient is standing. It is unusual for this type of syncope to occur with sitting and nearly impossible for it to occur while lying down.

Premonitory symptoms are common and include lightheadedness, dizziness, flushing, nausea, tunnel vision, and profuse sweating. The individual typically slumps to the ground and is not completely unconscious and, therefore, is usually able to avoid injury. Once the individual is on the ground, blood flow is restored to the brain, so typically the syncope episodes are short-lived. However, following the episode individuals often have a prolonged period of nausea and fatigue, and occasionally individuals may feel ill until they have had some sleep.

Exertional syncope

Exertional syncope is always a concern. Exertional syncope can occur because of outflow obstruction (e.g. in HCM or aortic stenosis) or arrhythmias. Exercise typically triggers arrhythmias in individuals with ARVC, HCM, CPVT, and LQTS (conditions that are outlined in Chapter 48).

The syncope associated with exertional outflow obstruction is during peak exercise with a brief period of lightheadedness followed by syncope.

Syncope caused by arrhythmic disorders often occurs during exertion (not post-exertion) with abrupt loss of consciousness or only a very brief period of lightheadedness prior to the syncope. Secondary injury is common as individuals are unconscious before they hit the ground and, therefore, cannot protect their head.

Syncope due to a ventricular arrhythmia (such as ventricular tachycardia or ventricular fibrillation) is a life-threatening event. In some cases, the ventricular arrhythmia self-terminates and the individual regains consciousness, usually within seconds of collapse.

Prolonged syncope should be treated as a sudden cardiac arrest (Chapter 48).

Exertional syncope is frequently due to a cardiac cause and should be thoroughly investigated. Post-exertional syncope is usually benign.

Post-exertional syncope

Post-exertional syncope, occurring while standing in a huddle or at the finish line, is typically neurocardiogenic (see also Chapter 58 for more on exercise-associated collapse after the finish line).[25-28] Exercise-associated collapse, commonly observed at endurance events, refers to sportspeople who are unable to stand or walk unaided after exertion because of weakness, lightheadedness, faintness, or dizziness.[29]

During exercise, increases in heart rate and stroke volume result in a substantial rise in cardiac output and offset diminished systemic vascular resistance from vasodilatation to exercising muscles. After exercise, without the muscular activity (muscle pump) to maintain venous return, cardiac filling may reduce dramatically. Forceful ventricular contractions against a diminished ventricular volume are postulated to excessively stimulate ventricular mechanoreceptors causing reflex vasodilatation and bradycardia, and subsequent hypotension and possibly syncope.[30]

Adverse effects from anti-hypertensive medications such as diuretics and beta blockers may also cause syncope in older individuals (Chapter 44).

Unexplained seizure activity

Seizures can be difficult to distinguish from syncope, and thus should be part of the differential diagnosis. Myoclonic movements caused by cerebral hypoperfusion can mimic true seizures. The clinical difference between the two is that if cerebral hypoperfusion is causing the myoclonic movements, the individual would faint first and 5 to 10 seconds later the involuntary body movements would start, whereas with a true seizure the myoclonic movements would begin concurrently with the loss of postural tone and consciousness (see also Chapter 17).[31] In addition, seizure patients may have an aura prior to the episode (not to be confused with tunnel vision, which is seen in cerebral hypoperfusion), and are post-ictal after the episodes.

The post-ictal state is characterized by prolonged confusion, whereas in syncope there may be only brief confusion about what occurred. Patients suffering neurocardiogenic syncope are often profoundly fatigued after the event. Tongue biting, incontinence, and injury are not sufficiently specific to aid in the differential diagnosis of most patients.

Any patient with an unexplained seizure episode should also have a cardiovascular work-up including at minimum a 12-lead ECG/EKG and an echocardiogram. In individuals who have classic seizures and a confirmatory encephalogram, the cardiac work-up may be limited; however, if there is still any doubt, then long-term cardiac monitoring should be performed in order to ensure that arrhythmias are not triggering the seizure activity.

Exertional chest pain

Chest pain is common in individuals of all ages and is often secondary to musculoskeletal processes.

 Chest pain *associated with exertion* is an important symptom that may reflect an underlying cardiovascular disorder.

Diseases such as CCAA, myocarditis, HCM, dilated cardiomyopathy, and atherosclerotic coronary disease often present with chest pain that is "dull" or "pressing" in nature and is usually exertional and relieved by rest.

Chest pain that is pleuritic (increases with deep inspiration) may be due to pericarditis, but is not typically due to the other cardiac causes of chest pain. In most cases, pleuritic chest pain is secondary to musculoskeletal syndromes or pulmonary conditions such as pulmonary embolism or pneumonias, which are unusual in the young sportsperson.

Investigations

Any young sportsperson with exertional chest pain should be evaluated for the presence of CCAA and HCM.

A transthoracic echocardiogram (explained on page 1034) is usually sufficient to rule out HCM, but in some cases it cannot be relied on to rule out anomalous coronary arteries.

Cardiac MRI has a high sensitivity and specificity for anomalous coronary arteries and should be undertaken when there is a question of anomalous coronary arteries.

Older sportspeople with exertional chest pain should undergo cardiac stress testing to evaluate for ischemic heart disease.

Palpitations

Palpitations are common in young individuals and in many cases are secondary to sinus tachycardia or not related to a cardiac process at all. However, palpitations may be due to supraventricular tachycardias or ventricular tachycardias.

 Palpitations that come on suddenly or are associated with other symptoms such as lightheadedness, chest pain, or dyspnea are potentially lethal and require expert cardiac evaluation.

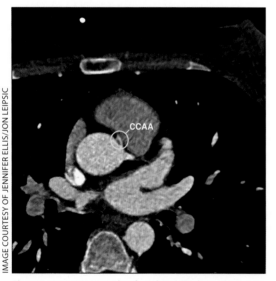
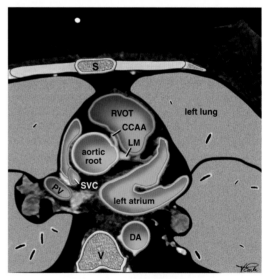

IMAGE COURTESY OF JENNIFER ELLIS/JON LEIPSIC

Figure 49.1 An example of cardiac MRI showing a congenital coronary artery anomaly (CCAA), which can be a "silent" presentation or may be associated with the five "cardiac symptoms" discussed in this section. The panel on the right provides orientation. (S = sternum, RVOT = right ventricular outflow tract, LM = left main coronary artery, SVC = superior vena cava, DA = descending aorta, V = thoracic vertebral body)

Investigation

The only method to truly diagnose the cause of palpitations is to capture an ECG/EKG while the patient is having symptoms. Typically this requires ambulatory monitoring and a stress test. In general, ambulatory monitoring should be undertaken in individuals with palpitations unless they are so benign as to be barely noticeable.

Treatment

Supraventricular tachycardias are not generally associated with sudden cardiac death, but usually need to be treated. Treatment may consist of abortive maneuvers such as Valsalva, preventive measures such as beta blockers or calcium channel blockers, or curative measures such as radiofrequency ablation.

Referral to a cardiologist should be considered when symptoms interfere with the patient's quality of life.

Ventricular arrhythmias are more concerning, and are frequently associated with syncope or severe lightheadedness. Patients require referral to a cardiologist.

Excessive fatigue or dyspnea with exertion

Fatigue is expected with sports, but excessive fatigue or dyspnea on exertion is unusual. A helpful method to assess these symptoms is to compare current symptoms to an individual's previous energy level, or to compare the sportsperson to his or her peers of a similar conditioning level.

Fatigue is rarely a cardiac symptom but can be seen with dilated cardiomyopathies. Excessive fatigue or dyspnea on exertion is especially troubling if of recent onset or worsening with time. Excessive fatigue following a viral syndrome may suggest myocarditis.

Dyspnea on exertion can be seen with heart disease such as HCM, aortic stenosis, subaortic membranes, and dilated cardiomyopathies. It can also be seen in individuals with congenital heart block or acquired heart block such as that observed in Lyme disease.

Investigations

The evaluation of patients with exertional fatigue and dyspnea includes an ECG/EKG and echocardiography. In some circumstances, stress ECG/EKG, cardiopulmonary exercise testing, or pulmonary function tests may be indicated.

Clinical approach to physical examination findings

The physical examination is rarely as illuminating as the history. Most cardiac diseases that place the the sportsperson at risk for sudden cardiac death are not associated with an abnormal physical examination. An exception is a systolic ejection murmur of the left ventricular outflow tract which can be due to HCM, subaortic membranes, or bicuspid aortic valve with stenosis. Murmurs are present in only one-third of individuals with HCM because at rest only one-third of individuals with hypertrophic cardiomyopathy have outflow tract obstruction; however, with exertion more than two-thirds develop obstruction.[32]

Other important aspects of the physical examination include recognizing the physical stigmata of Marfan syndrome (Fig. 48.8) such as a high-arched palate, tall height, and long arm/wing span.

Screening for hypertension and assessing for coarctation of the aorta with right and left blood pressure measurements and femoral artery palpation are also important aspects of the examination.

Patients with HCM, ARVC, LQTS, CPVT, Brugada syndrome and dilated cardiomyopathies generally have normal physical examinations. These conditions cannot be ruled out by physical examination.

See the box for an indication of which patients should be referred to a cardiologist.

> **When should patients be referred to a cardiologist?**
>
> Patients should be referred for concerning symptoms and findings on examination.
>
> In patients with syncope, if the symptoms are classic for neurocardiogenic syncope, the patient does not need referral to a specialist but, at minimum, an ECG/EKG should be performed.
>
> However, in patients with syncope that is unexplained or concerning, referral to a cardiologist is indicated.
>
> Patients with exertional syncope should always be referred, even if there are no findings on preliminary work-up.
>
> Exertional chest pain is an uncommon syndrome and often needs an extensive evaluation.
>
> Palpitations can generally be diagnosed by prolonged ambulatory monitoring:
> - If the prolonged ambulatory monitoring shows that the symptoms are not associated with a
>
> *continued*

continued

supraventricular or ventricular tachycardia, then, in general, no referral is needed, and reassurance is warranted.

- However, if palpitations are due to premature ventricular contractions, supraventricular tachycardias, or ventricular tachycardias, referral to a cardiologist is warranted.
- Occasionally, even patients with atrial premature beats will require cardiology referral, even though atrial premature beats are typically benign.

Excessive fatigue or dyspnea on exertion is equally likely to be noncardiac in etiology. A cardiac echocardiogram is reasonable to exclude HCM or a dilated cardiomyopathy and then patients should have a work-up for anemia, asthma, or other medical causes of fatigue and dyspnea as indicated.

Specific physical examination findings

Hypertension

Hypertension is a common cardiovascular disorder encountered in the athletic population, with an elevated blood pressure found in approximately 6% of athletes presenting for routine pre-participation screening.[33] Athletes with persistently elevated blood pressure should be questioned about a family history of hypertension and the use of stimulants (such as caffeine, nicotine, and ephedrine) or anabolic steroids.

The Seventh Report of the Joint National Committee on Prevention, Detection, Evaluation, and Treatment of High Blood Pressure (JNC 7)[34] has established a blood pressure classification for adults as in the box below.

The Fourth Report on the Diagnosis, Evaluation, and Treatment of High Blood Pressure in Children and Adolescents[35] has established BP standards for pediatric and adolescent patients based on gender, age, and height. The Fourth Report also classifies hypertension in athletes under 18 years as pre-hypertension, stage 1 hypertension, and stage 2 hypertension, which mirrors the taxonomy used for adults.[35]

Blood pressure classification for adults

Normal <120/80
Pre-hypertension 120–139 / 80–89
Stage 1 hypertension 140–159 / 90–99
Stage 2 hypertension ≥160/100

The diagnosis of hypertension in athletes under 18 years requires at least three blood pressure measurements; values between the 90th and 95th percentiles of the age-, gender-, and height-based norms defined as pre-hypertension, values between the 95th percentile and 5 mmHg above the 99th percentile are defined as stage 1 hypertension; values greater than 5 mmHg above the 99th percentile are defined as stage 2 hypertension.

 PRACTICE PEARL All children and adolescents diagnosed with hypertension require a careful evaluation for secondary causes of hypertension and target organ disease.

Evaluation includes blood chemistries (glucose, creatinine, electrolytes, lipid profile, and thyroid function), hematocrit, urinalysis, and ECG/EKG. A renal ultrasound is also recommended for all children with stage 1 or stage 2 hypertension.

Evaluation of target organ disease including an echocardiogram is recommended in all sportspeople diagnosed with stage 1 or stage 2 hypertension.[35]

Sportspeople found to have stage 2 hypertension or findings of end-organ damage should not be allowed to participate in any competitive sport until their blood pressure is further evaluated, treated, and under control, at which time eligibility for participation can be reevaluated.[36]

Management of hypertension in sportspeople

Pharmacologic therapy may be required in some sportspeople with hypertension. The drugs of choice for the exercising individual are usually angiotensin converting enzyme (ACE) inhibitors or angiotensin receptor blockers. These drugs control blood pressure without an associated decrease in aerobic capacity. Occasionally, sportspeople may notice an exaggeration of a tendency to postural hypotension when they cease aerobic exercise; this is a good reason to gradually cool down. This allows sufficient return of blood pressure to the right side of the heart to maintain pressure while upright without fainting (see also Chapter 58).

If ACE inhibitors or angiotensin receptor blockers are contraindicated or poorly tolerated, dihydropyridine calcium channel blockers should be considered in a competitive sportsperson as they do not cause any reduction in maximum aerobic capacity. For those sportspeople who exercise in cold conditions, the highly vascular selective calcium antagonist felodipine is a good choice as it enhances peripheral blood flow and may thereby reduce the tendency to frostbite.

Beta blockers and diuretics are commonly used to control blood pressure in the general population. However, both drugs reduce maximum exercise capacity, which is not desirable for most competitive sportspeople. Diuretics reduce plasma volume, which may make the the sportsperson more prone to heat illness (Chapter 58). For the elite sportsperson with hypertension, both diuretics and beta blockers are banned drugs in various sports and therefore may be contraindicated.

Heart murmur

Auscultation of the heart should be performed in both the supine and standing positions (or with Valsalva maneuver), specifically to identify murmurs of dynamic left ventricular outflow tract obstruction. Standing is preferred to sitting because the diagnostic murmur of hypertrophic cardiomyopathy (if present) becomes louder when the patient is standing due to decreased venous return. Only about 25% of patients with hypertrophic cardiomyopathy have a murmur.[37]

Significant murmurs that may indicate left ventricular outflow tract obstruction are typically early systolic, harsh, and heard best at the right upper sternal border; the murmur increases with maneuvers that decrease venous return such as Valsalva or moving from squatting to standing. In contrast, the murmur of aortic stenosis typically diminishes with maneuvers that decrease venous return, and increases with maneuvers that increase venous return (i.e. squatting). Both pathologic entities are important to recognize.

A pansystolic (holosystolic) murmur heard best at the apex with radiation to the axilla may indicate mitral valve regurgitation and could be related to a dilated cardiomyopathy. Systolic ejection or midsystolic clicks are typically abnormal at any age.

A diastolic murmur heard at the right upper sternal border may represent aortic regurgitation and indicate an incompetent aortic valve, such as that present in Marfan syndrome, or, sometimes, present with a bicuspid aortic valve. If aortic regurgitation is suspected, it can be accentuated by hand grip, which increases systemic vascular resistance.

 Any diastolic murmur should be considered pathologic. An echocardiogram should be requested to clarify the etiology of any concerning murmur.

A common murmur in well-trained sportspeople is a hyperdynamic "flow" murmur. These are characterized by a grade 1/6 or 2/6 soft early systolic murmur heard best at the upper sternal border. The murmur results from an overall increase in plasma volume and thus stroke volume that occurs as a physiologic adaptation to regular physical training. Often the murmur is only heard when the the sportsperson is supine (increased venous return), and is absent when the sportsperson is standing or sitting; the murmur should diminish with the strain phase of a Valsalva maneuver. In the absence of concerning symptoms or family history, innocent murmurs require no further investigation.

Marfan syndrome

Cardiovascular complications are the major cause of morbidity and mortality in patients with Marfan syndrome. Marfan syndrome causes a progressive dilatation and weakness (cystic medial necrosis) of the proximal aorta that can lead to rupture and sudden death. Myxomatous degeneration of the mitral and aortic valves may also lead to valvular dysfunction. Marfan syndrome is caused by mutations in the fibrillin-1 gene, with 75% of cases inherited through autosomal dominant transmission with variable expression and 25% of cases from *de novo* mutations.[38]

The risk of aortic rupture or dissection increases during adolescence and 50% of undiagnosed patients with Marfan syndrome die by 40 years of age.[38]

Symptoms of aortic dissection typically include sudden excruciating chest or thoracic pain, often described as tearing or ripping. Heart failure also occurs secondary to aortic valve incompetence.

Physical examination findings include highly variable clinical features usually manifested in adolescence and young adulthood (Fig. 48.8). An international expert panel has established a revised Ghent nosology, which puts more weight on the cardiovascular manifestations and the presence of aortic root aneurysm and ectopia lentis as cardinal clinical features.[39] In the absence of any family history, the presence of these two manifestations is sufficient for the unequivocal diagnosis of Marfan syndrome. In the absence of either of these two, the presence of a bonafide FBN1 mutation or a combination of systemic manifestations is required. For the latter a new scoring system has been designed.[39]

Non-invasive cardiovascular testing

Sportspeople with cardiovascular symptoms should undergo specific testing with the intent to rule out (or rule in) cardiac disorders known to cause sudden cardiac death. In this section we discuss ECG/EKGs, echocardiography, cardiac MRI, and CT, as well as the genetic investigations that are appropriate when there is a family history of early cardiac death. Table 49.3 shows a summary of non-invasive cardiovascular testing.

Electrocardiogram (ECG/EKG)

ECG/EKGs in athletes should be interpreted using contemporary criteria to assist in distinguishing physiologic changes commonly found in an athlete's heart from abnormalities suggesting a pathologic disorder.

Training-related ECG/EKG alterations are common, physiologic adaptations to regular exercise and are considered normal variants in sportspeople. These variants include:

- sinus bradycardia
- sinus arrhythmia

Table 49.3 Non-invasive cardiovascular testing

Test	What the test involves and what it measures
Electrocardiography (ECG/EKG)	ECG/EKG measures the electrical activity and function of the heart via surface electrodes. A number of recognizable electrical deflections (P wave, QRS complex, T wave) are observed. Characteristic ECG/EKG abnormalities may reflect underlying cardiac disease.
Ambulatory ECG/EKG monitoring	Ambulatory ECG/EKG monitoring is the long-term ECG/EKG monitoring of patients during normal daily activity. The patient wears a portable monitor that records the ECG/EKG changes. The ambulatory monitors allow for patient documentation of symptoms; some also have auto triggered modes which will automatically record tachycardias or bradycardias. This technique may be useful in the diagnosis of arrhythmias or abnormal premature ventricular contractions.
Stress electrocardiography	Stress or exercise ECG/EKG is performed by monitoring the patient electrocardiographically while exercising. It is used to investigate ischemic heart disease or coronary artery anomalies that may cause ischemia during exercise. It can also be useful in the work-up of exertional syncope or palpitations.
Echocardiography	Echocardiography is the clinical application of ultrasound to the diagnosis of heart disease. Ultrasound waves reflected from the different parts of the heart can map out the anatomical structure of the heart in two dimensions. Doppler echo techniques enable accurate measurements of intracardiac blood velocity and, therefore, enable the clinician to determine the gradients across valves or shunts.
Cardiac magnetic resonance imaging (MRI)	Cardiac MRI provides accurate assessment of cardiac morphology, clear delineation of proximal coronary arteries, and characterization of the subvalvular apparatus of the mitral valve. The additional value of delayed gadolinium enhancement for the detection of myocardial fibrosis or infiltrative disease makes cardiac MRI very valuable in the evaluation for cardiomyopathy.
Cardiac computed tomography (CT) angiography	Cardiac CT angiography provides an accurate assessment of the course of the proximal coronary arteries; it also can evaluate coronary artery calcium scores used in the evaluation of atherosclerotic coronary artery disease. Cardiac CT does provide radiation exposure to the chest that should be considered when performed in children and women.

- first degree atrioventricular (AV) block
- incomplete right bundle branch block (RBBB)
- early repolarization
- isolated QRS voltage criteria for left ventricular hypertrophy.

Isolated increases in QRS amplitude are common in trained sportspeople. However, QRS voltage criteria for left ventricular hypertrophy + any non-voltage criteria for left ventricular hypertrophy (such as atrial enlargement, left axis deviation, a "strain" pattern of repolarization, ST-segment depression, T-wave inversion, or pathologic Q waves) are abnormal and require further evaluation.

ECG/EKGs are readily accessible, and should be performed for all cardiovascular symptoms; they can suggest structural cardiac disorders or diagnose primary electrical disease (Table 49.4 overleaf).

An ECG/EKG is abnormal in up to 95% of patients with hypertrophic cardiomyopathy,[40, 41] with prominent Q waves, deep negative T waves, or dramatic increases in QRS voltage associated with ST depression or T-wave inversion.

In ARVC, the ECG/EKG may show right precordial T-wave inversion (beyond V1), an epsilon wave (small terminal notch seen just beyond the QRS in V1 or V2), prolongation of QRS duration (>120 ms), or a right bundle branch block pattern. Calculation of the QT interval corrected for heart rate (QTc) can be variable with some overlap of normal and abnormal values. The 99th percentile upper limit of normal is 0.47 seconds in men and 0.48 seconds in women.[42]

Patients with LQTS may also have bizarre, flat, or peaked T-wave morphology, alternating T-wave polarity (T wave alternans), or prominent U waves or T-U wave complexes.[43]

A QTc >0.5 seconds regardless of symptoms or family history distinguishes individuals most at risk for sudden cardiac death.[11]

Echocardiography and associated tests for structural disease (cardiac CT, MRI)

Echocardiography remains the standard to evaluate for structural cardiac disease such as hypertrophic cardiomyopathy. The diagnosis is suggested by pathologic, asymmetric left ventricular wall thickening (>16 mm) usually involving the intraventricular septum, a non-dilated left ventricle, and impaired diastolic function. In cases where the diagnosis of hypertrophic cardiomyopathy is uncertain (i.e. borderline left ventricularventricular wall thickness

of 13–15 mm), cardiac MRI (Fig. 49.1) can provide accurate estimations of left ventricularventricular morphology and evaluate for delayed gadolinium enhancement from myocardial fibrosis/scar which would support a diagnosis of hypertrophic cardiomyopathy.

Alternatively, repeat echocardiography after 4–6 weeks of deconditioning may resolve hypertrophy related to the athlete's heart and help distinguish pathologic hypertrophy from physiologic adaptations. Cardiac MRI also may be helpful in sportspeople with marked T-wave inversion in the inferior and lateral leads on ECG/EKG to rule out apical-variant hypertrophic cardiomyopathy that may not be easily identified by echocardiography.

Echocardiogram, cardiac MRI, or computed tomography (CT) may demonstrate right ventricular dilatation and wall thinning, reduced right ventricular ejection fraction, focal right ventricular wall motion abnormalities, or right ventricular aneurysms suggestive of ARVC. Fibro-fatty infiltration of the right ventricle consistent with a diagnosis of ARVC is best seen on cardiac MRI.

In evaluation of the coronary artery origins, transthoracic echocardiography can reliably identify the coronary ostia in about 95% of patients. Advanced cardiac imaging such as CT angiography, cardiac MRI, or coronary angiography may be needed in some cases to detect anomalous origins and can also identify other coronary anomalies such as an acute angled take-off, intramyocardial course, and hypoplastic coronary arteries.

Genetic testing when there is a family history of early sudden cardiac death

Many of the diseases that put a patient at risk of sudden cardiac death have a genetic origin. Thus, a family history of sudden cardiac death, especially if the relative died when they were younger than 50 years, should heighten awareness about the potential for an inheritable cardiac disease. Most of the cardiac diseases that cause sudden cardiac death are autosomal dominant; thus, only one parent need be affected. These diseases, including hypertrophic cardiomyopathy, ARVC, Brugada syndrome, CPVT and LQTS, can be diagnosed with genetic testing, although the exact role of genetic testing in sportspeople remains to be determined.

In hypertrophic cardiomyopathy, approximately 65% of the individuals have an identified gene mutation, and a small percentage have multiple mutations.

Table 49.4 ECG/EKG interpretation in sportspeople—abnormal findings

Any abnormal finding is considered training-unrelated and suggests the possibility of underlying pathologic cardiac disease, requiring further diagnostic work-up.

Abnormal ECG/EKG finding	Definition
T-wave inversion[a]	>1 mm in depth from baseline in two or more adjacent leads not including aVR or V1
ST-Segment depression	≥1 mm in depth in two or more adjacent leads
Pathologic Q waves	>3 mm in depth or >0.04 sec in duration in two or more leads
Complete left bundle branch block	QRS >0.12 sec, predominantly negative QRS complex in lead V1 (QS or rS), and upright monophasic R wave in leads I and V6
Complete right bundle branch block	QRS >0.12 sec, terminal R wave in lead V1 (rsR'), and wide terminal S wave in leads I and V6
Intra-ventricular conduction delay	Non-specific, QRS >0.12 sec
Left atrial enlargement	Prolonged P wave duration of >0.12 sec in leads I or II with negative portion of the P wave ≥1 mm in depth and ≥0.04 sec in duration in lead V1
Left axis deviation	−30° to −90°
Right atrial enlargement	High/pointed P wave ≥2.5 mm in leads II and III or V$_1$
Right ventricular hypertrophy	Right axis deviation ≥120°, tall R wave in V1 + persistent precordial S waves (R in V1 + S in V5 >10.5 mm)
Mobitz Type II second degree AV block	Intermittently non-conducted P waves not preceded by PR prolongation and not followed by PR shortening
Third degree AV block	Complete heart block
Ventricular pre-excitation	PR interval <0.12 sec with a delta wave (slurred upstroke in the QRS complex)
Long QT interval	QTc ≥0.47 sec (99% males) QTc ≥0.48 sec (99% females) QTc ≥0.50 sec (unequivocal LQTS)
Short QT interval	QTc ≤0.34 sec
Brugada-like ECG pattern	High take-off and downsloping ST-segment elevation in V1–V3
Epsilon wave	Small negative deflection just beyond the QRS in V1 or V2
Profound sinus bradycardia	<30 BPM or sinus pauses ≥3 sec
Atrial tachyarrhythmias	Supraventricular tachycardia, atrioventricular nodal re-entrant tachycardia, atrial fibrillation, atrial flutter
Premature ventricular contractions	≥2 per tracing
Ventricular arrhythmias	Couplets, triplets, non-sustained ventricular tachycardia

[a]Exception to T-wave inversion: elevated ST segment with an upward ("domed") convexity, followed by a negative T wave in V2–V4 is a common pattern of early repolarization seen in athletes of African-Caribbean descent and should be considered normal. This should not to be confused with the downsloping ST-segment elevation in V1–V3 found in a Brugada-like ECG/EKG pattern which is abnormal

Currently over 900 mutations have been identified. including many on the myosin heavy chain and myosin binding protein C.[44, 45] Less commonly, hypertrophic cardiomyopathy is caused by abnormalities in troponin T, troponin I, tropomyosin, myosin light chains and actin genes. Multiple mutations are thought to put the individual at an increased risk of sudden death.[46]

Abnormalities in the desmosome, including plakoglobin, desmoplakin, and plakophilin, are the cause of most ARVC.[47] However, ARVC genetic testing is still primarily a test of specialized research centers; none of the current commercially available genetic tests include panels for this condition.

Only about 20% of patients with Brugada syndrome carry an identified gene.[48] In LQTS, commercially available testing evaluates for types 1 to 5; approximately 75% are type 1, 2 or 3.[49]

In CPVT, approximately one-half test positive for an abnormality in the ryanodine receptor gene and this test is carried out by most commercial genetic testing.[50]

Genetic screening is expensive and the clinical significance of abnormalities found at screening is often unclear.

Genetic screening in the the sportsperson should be limited to those who have a borderline diagnosis or in whom there is a documented genetic disease in the family.

Temporary and permanent disqualification from sports

Careful activity recommendations involving temporary or permanent sports disqualification for sportspeople with identified cardiovascular disease should be made in consultation with a cardiologist. Exercise recommendations in sportspeople with underlying cardiovascular disease susceptible to sudden cardiac death are predicated on the likelihood that intense athletic training and competition act as a trigger to increase the risk of death or disease progression.[36]

The 36th Bethesda Conference sponsored by the American College of Cardiology[36] and the European Society of Cardiology[51] provide eligibility recommendations for competitive sportspeople with cardiovascular abnormalities. These expert consensus recommendations provide a framework on which to base clearance decisions once a cardiovascular abnormality is identified, taking into account the severity of disease, potential for sudden death or disease progression, and the type and intensity of exercise involved in a particular sport. Withdrawal from athletic training and competition can reduce

the exposure risk in sportspeople who have disorders predisposing them to sudden cardiac death.[52] Low intensity competitive sports such as golf and bowling are still allowed.

Individuals disqualified from competitive sports should be guided to engage in recreational exercise considered to be safe in order to maintain general health. The American Heart Association provides recommendations for physical activity and recreational sports participation for young patients with genetic cardiovascular diseases, which is a useful starting point.[53] Many experts suggest that the level of exertion be guided by the ability to converse during the activity. If an individual is so dyspneic that they can no longer talk, the level of exertion is too intense.

In some cases, early detection of clinically significant cardiovascular disease may permit timely therapeutic interventions, such as implantable cardioverter-defibrillators (ICD), that alter clinical course and significantly prolong life. Although there is controversy about sportspeople with ICDs competing, the Bethesda guidelines do not advise it.[36] The implantation of an ICD should not allow a return to sport in those with underlying structural heart disease that would otherwise prohibit competition. There is concern about sports triggering ventricular arrhythmias, heightened sympathetic tone which may make arrhythmias more resistant to defibrillation, and damage to the ICD system.

Summary

Cardiovascular symptoms in sportspeople warrant a comprehensive diagnostic evaluation to rule out conditions that predispose to sudden death. While not all sportspeople with underlying heart disease manifest symptoms, prodromal symptoms such as syncope, exertional chest pain, excessive dyspnea/fatigue, and unexplained seizure activity may occur in some sportspeople as warning events prior to sudden cardiac death. Careful evaluation of sportspeople with cardiovascular symptoms can detect potentially lethal cardiovascular disease and, through appropriate treatment and activity modification, reduce the risk for sudden death in sport.

REFERENCES

1. Maron BJ, Doerer JJ, Haas TS et al. Sudden deaths in young competitive athletes: analysis of 1866 deaths in the United States, 1980–2006. *Circulation* 2009;119(8):1085–92.

2. Maron BJ. Sudden death in young athletes. *N Engl J Med* 2003;349(11):1064–75.

3. Asif I, Harmon K, Drezner J et al. Incidence and etiology of sudden death in NCAA athletes. *Clin J Sport Med* 2010;20(2):136.

4. Campbell RM, Berger S, Drezner J. Sudden cardiac arrest in children and young athletes: the importance of a detailed personal and family history in the pre-participation evaluation. *Br J Sports Med* 2009;43(5):336–41.

5. Maron BJ, Shirani J, Poliac LC et al. Sudden death in young competitive athletes. Clinical, demographic, and pathological profiles. *JAMA* 1996;276(3):199–204.

6. Basso C, Maron BJ, Corrado D et al. Clinical profile of congenital coronary artery anomalies with origin from the wrong aortic sinus leading to sudden death in young competitive athletes. *J Am Coll Cardiol* 2000;35(6):1493–501.

7. Tester DJ, Spoon DB, Valdivia HH et al. Targeted mutational analysis of the RyR2-encoded cardiac ryanodine receptor in sudden unexplained death: a molecular autopsy of 49 medical examiner/coroner's cases. *Mayo Clin Proc* 2004;79(11):1380–4.

8. Eckart RE, Scoville SL, Campbell CL et al. Sudden death in young adults: a 25-year review of autopsies in military recruits. *Ann Intern Med* 2004;141(11):829–34.

9. Corrado D, Basso C, Fontaine G. Clinical profile of young competitive athletes who died suddenly of arrhythmogenic right ventricular cardiomyopathy/dysplasia: a multicenter study. *Pacing Clin Electrophysiol* 2002;25:544.

10. Leenhardt A, Lucet V, Denjoy I et al. Catecholaminergic polymorphic ventricular tachycardia in children. A 7-year follow-up of 21 patients. *Circulation* 1995;91(5):1512–9.

11. Hobbs JB, Peterson DR, Moss AJ et al. Risk of aborted cardiac arrest or sudden cardiac death during adolescence in the long-QT syndrome. *JAMA* 2006;296(10):1249–54.

12. Fuller CM, McNulty CM, Spring DA et al. Prospective screening of 5,615 high school athletes for risk of sudden cardiac death. *Med Sci Sports Exerc* 1997;29(9):1131–8.

13. Wilson MG, Basavarajaiah S, Whyte GP et al. Efficacy of personal symptom and family history questionnaires when screening for inherited cardiac pathologies: the role of electrocardiography. *Br J Sports Med* 2008;42(3):207–11.

14. Bessem B, Groot FP, Nieuwland W. The Lausanne recommendations: a Dutch experience. *Br J Sports Med* 2009;43(9):708–15.

15. Hevia AC, Fernandez MM, Palacio JM et al. ECG as a part of the preparticipation screening programme: an old and still present international dilemma. *Br J Sports Med* 2011;45(10):776–9.

16. Baggish AL, Hutter AM Jr, Wang F et al. Cardiovascular screening in college athletes with and without electrocardiography: a cross-sectional study. *Ann Intern Med* 2010;152(5):269–75.

17. Drezner J, Corrado D. Is there evidence for recommending ECG as part of the pre-participation examination? *Clin J Sport Med* 2011;21(1):13–17.

18. Liberthson RR. Sudden death from cardiac causes in children and young adults. *N Engl J Med* 1996;334(16):1039–44.

19. Wisten A, Messner T. Symptoms preceding sudden cardiac death in the young are common but often misinterpreted. *Scand Cardiovasc J* 2005;39(3):143–9.

20. Maron BJ, Thompson PD, Ackerman MJ et al. Recommendations and considerations related to preparticipation screening for cardiovascular abnormalities in competitive athletes: 2007 update: a scientific statement from the American Heart Association Council on Nutrition, Physical Activity, and Metabolism: endorsed by the American College of Cardiology Foundation. *Circulation* 2007;115(12):1643–455.

21. Kapoor WN. Syncope. *N Engl J Med* 2000;343(25):1856–62.

22. Strickberger SA, Benson DW, Biaggioni I et al. AHA/ACCF Scientific statement on the evaluation of syncope: from the American Heart Association Councils on Clinical Cardiology, Cardiovascular Nursing, Cardiovascular Disease in the Young, and Stroke, and the Quality of Care and Outcomes Research Interdisciplinary Working Group; and the American College of Cardiology Foundation: in collaboration with the Heart Rhythm Society: endorsed by the American Autonomic Society. *Circulation* 2006;113(2):316–27.

23. Colivicchi F, Ammirati F, Santini M. Epidemiology and prognostic implications of syncope in young competing athletes. *Eur Heart J* 2004;25(19):1749–53.

24. Grubb BP. Clinical practice. Neurocardiogenic syncope. *N Engl J Med* 2005;352(10):1004–10.

25. Sneddon JF, Scalia G, Ward DE et al. Exercise induced vasodepressor syncope. *Br Heart J* 1994;71(6):554–7.

26. Sakaguchi S, Shultz JJ, Remole SC et al. Syncope associated with exercise, a manifestation of neurally mediated syncope. *Am J Cardiol* 1995;75(7):476–81.

27. Calkins H, Seifert M, Morady F. Clinical presentation and long-term follow-up of athletes with exercise-induced vasodepressor syncope. *Am Heart J* 1995;129(6):1159–64.

28. Kosinski D, Grubb BP, Kip K et al. Exercise-induced neurocardiogenic syncope. *Am Heart J* 1996;132(2 Pt 1): 451–2.

29. Roberts WO. Exercise-associated collapse care matrix in the marathon. *Sports Med* 2007;37(4–5):431–3.

30. O'Connor FG, Oriscello RG, Levine BD. Exercise-related syncope in the young athlete: reassurance, restriction or referral? *Am Fam Physician* 1999;60(7): 2001–8.

31. Link MS, Estes NA 3rd. How to manage athletes with syncope. *Cardiol Clin* 2007;25(3):457–66, vii.

32. Maron MS, Olivotto I, Zenovich AG et al. Hypertrophic cardiomyopathy is predominantly a disease of left ventricular outflow tract obstruction. *Circulation* 2006;114(21):2232–9.

33. DiFiori J, Haney S. Preparticipation evaluation of collegiate athletes. *Med Sci Sports Exerc* 2004;36(5): S102.

34. Chobanian AV, Bakris GL, Black HR et al. The Seventh Report of the Joint National Committee on Prevention, Detection, Evaluation, and Treatment of High Blood Pressure: the JNC 7 report. *JAMA* 2003;289(19): 2560–72.

35. The fourth report on the diagnosis, evaluation, and treatment of high blood pressure in children and adolescents. *Pediatrics* 2004;114(2 Suppl 4th Report): 555–76.

36. Maron BJ, Zipes DP. 36th Bethesda Conference: Eligibility recommendations for competitive athletes with cardiovascular abnormalities. *J Am Coll Cardiol* 2005;45(8):1312–77.

37. Maron BJ. Hypertrophic cardiomyopathy. *Lancet* 1997;350(9071):127–33.

38. Ammash NM, Sundt TM, Connolly HM. Marfan syndrome: diagnosis and management. *Curr Probl Cardiol* 2008;33(1):7–39.

39. Loeys BL, Dietz HC, Braverman AC et al. The revised Ghent nosology for the Marfan syndrome. *J Med Genet* 2010;47:476–85.

40. Maron BJ, Roberts WC, Epstein SE. Sudden death in hypertrophic cardiomyopathy: a profile of 78 patients. *Circulation* 1982;65(7):1388–94.

41. Melacini P, Cianfrocca C, Calore C et al. Abstract 3390: Marginal overlap between electrocardiographic abnormalities in patients with hypertrophic cardiomyopathy and trained athletes: implications for preparticipation screening. *Circulation* 2007;116(II): 765.

42. Goldenberg I, Moss AJ, Zareba W. QT interval: how to measure it and what is "normal." *J Cardiovasc Electrophysiol* 2006;17(3):333–6.

43. Vetter VL. Clues or miscues? How to make the right interpretation and correctly diagnose long-QT syndrome. *Circulation* 2007;115(20):2595–8.

44. Ho CY. Genetics and clinical destiny: improving care in hypertrophic cardiomyopathy. *Circulation* 2010;122(23): 2430–40.

45. Landstrom AP, Ackerman MJ. Mutation type is not clinically useful in predicting prognosis in hypertrophic cardiomyopathy. *Circulation* 2010;122(23):2441–50.

46. Van Driest SL, Vasile VC, Ommen SR et al. Myosin binding protein C mutations and compound heterozygosity in hypertrophic cardiomyopathy. *J Am Coll Cardiol* 2004;44(9):1903–10.

47. Sen-Chowdhry S, Syrris P, McKenna WJ. Role of genetic analysis in the management of patients with arrhythmogenic right ventricular dysplasia/ cardiomyopathy. *J Am Coll Cardiol* 2007;50(19):1813–21.

48. Antzelevitch C, Brugada P, Borggrefe M et al. Brugada syndrome: report of the second consensus conference: endorsed by the Heart Rhythm Society and the European Heart Rhythm Association. *Circulation* 2005;111(5):659–70.

49. Goldenberg I, Moss AJ. Long QT syndrome. *J Am Coll Cardiol* 2008;51(24):2291–300.

50. Napolitano C, Priori SG. Diagnosis and treatment of catecholaminergic polymorphic ventricular tachycardia. *Heart Rhythm* 2007;4(5):675–8.

51. Pelliccia A, Fagard R, Bjornstad HH et al. Recommendations for competitive sports participation in athletes with cardiovascular disease: a consensus document from the Study Group of Sports Cardiology of the Working Group of Cardiac Rehabilitation and Exercise Physiology and the Working Group of Myocardial and Pericardial Diseases of the European Society of Cardiology. *Eur Heart J* 2005;26(14):1422–45.

52. Corrado D, Basso C, Pavei A et al. Trends in sudden cardiovascular death in young competitive athletes after implementation of a preparticipation screening program. *JAMA* 2006;296(13):1593–601.

53. Maron BJ, Chaitman BR, Ackerman MJ et al. Recommendations for physical activity and recreational sports participation for young patients with genetic cardiovascular diseases. *Circulation* 2004;109(22):2807–16.

Chapter 50

Respiratory symptoms during exercise

with KAREN HOLZER

You have to think of asthma the same way you think of diabetes. You wouldn't just take your insulin once in a while. Susan Auch, speed skater, Olympic medal winner. Quoted by Dakshana Bascaramurty in *Globe and Mail,* 3 December 2009

The normal functioning of the respiratory system is critical to athletic performance. The integrity of this system results in the delivery of oxygen to the blood (and subsequently to exercising muscles) and the elimination of waste products such as carbon dioxide. Any dysfunction of these processes results in impaired performance. A number of medical conditions (such as asthma and respiratory infections) may affect performance.

Common respiratory symptoms

There are a number of symptoms with which a sportsperson may present that indicate the presence of respiratory disease. These include:

- shortness of breath (dyspnea)
- wheeze
- cough
- chest pain or tightness.

Shortness of breath and wheeze

Some degree of breathlessness (dyspnea) is a normal physiological response to exercise. Often occurring during intense exercise, it may represent the reaching of maximal exercise and ventilatory capacity. However, an individual complaining of excessive shortness of breath, chest tightness, and/or wheezing, particularly during rest or low-intensity exercise, may be suffering from a respiratory or cardiac condition.

Breathlessness is a subjective symptom that can be defined as "an increased difficulty in breathing." Despite the frequency of this complaint, the exact physiological mechanism is unknown. The most important cause from an athletic point of view is asthma (exercise-induced bronchospasm). In the older sportsperson, especially with a history of smoking, chronic obstructive pulmonary disease (COPD) and cardiac ischemia should be considered. Dyspnea may be classified clinically as acute, chronic, or intermittent (see box).

Causes of dyspnea in sportspeople

Acute
Asthma
Cardiac causes
Infections
Spontaneous pneumothorax
Pulmonary embolism (rare)
Aspiration of foreign body (can occur in sportspeople with dental prosthesis or those who chew gum)

Chronic
Asthma
Chronic obstructive pulmonary disease (COPD)
Cardiac dysfunction—cardiac failure, ischemia, valvular
Anemia
Metabolic disorders (e.g. diabetes mellitus)
Pulmonary dysfunction
Obesity

Intermittent
Asthma (most likely)
Left ventricular dysfunction
Mitral stenosis
Psychological

Examination of the patient together with the history of the dyspnea may indicate the likely cause of the dyspnea. It is important to remember that examination of both the patient with exercise-induced bronchospasm and the patient with cardiac ischemia may be normal at rest.

A musculoskeletal examination should be performed to assess for the presence of thoracic stiffness and/or costochondritis.

Investigations

Respiratory function tests (e.g. spirometry) are required to further assess dyspnea. Spirometry pre- and post-bronchodilator should be performed, and if required a bronchial provocation challenge test.

If a cardiac cause is suspected, an exercise ECG/EKG and echocardiogram are required, often combined in a stress echocardiogram. A chest X-ray is essential to assess for a respiratory tract infection, cardiac failure, carcinoma, COPD, and a pneumothorax.

Blood tests, in particular the hemoglobin level and iron studies, may be required to exclude anemia or severe iron deficiency. Gastroscopy may be required to assess for gastroesophageal reflux.

Psychological factors, such as anxiety, are considered once other diagnoses are excluded and may require further assessment.

Cough

Coughing is such a common symptom that its presence and severity may be underestimated by both patients and clinicians.

From the clinical history, it is important to determine the nature of the cough, whether the cough is acute or chronic, productive or non-productive, and the nature and color of any sputum. The timing of the cough, whether it occurs during the day or night and whether it occurs before or after exercise, is important. Any associated disease such as sinusitis or gastroesophageal reflux should also be noted. It is important to establish whether the patient is or has been a smoker or exposed to passive smoking.

From this clinical history the etiology of the cough may be established. A guide to the causes of acute and chronic cough is shown in Table 50.1.

The treatment of cough is more likely to succeed if a specific diagnosis is made and treated appropriately. The treatment of asthma and respiratory tract infections are discussed below. Non-specific treatment for cough (e.g. pholcodine, 10 mg 6-hourly) may be

Table 50.1 Causes of cough

Acute	Chronic
Upper respiratory tract infection	Post-nasal drip
Asthma	Asthma
Bronchitis	Chronic bronchitis
Bronchogenic carcinoma	Gastroesophageal reflux
Foreign body inhalation	Post-infective cough
Left ventricular failure	Psychogenic
	Carcinoma
	Interstitial lung disease
	Benign tumors of the lung
	Drugs (e.g. ACE inhibitors)

ACE = angiotensin-converting enzyme

helpful when the symptoms are distressing. Perhaps more effective than any medication is an adequate explanation and reassurance when appropriate.

Chest pain or tightness

When considering respiratory symptoms, chest pain or tightness are not usually considered; however, many people with asthma may present with a subjective feeling of chest tightness alone. As well as the respiratory causes of chest tightness, there are other important and even life-threatening causes of chest tightness (such as cardiac ischemia). Hence, this symptom must be investigated appropriately.

The causes of chest pain are set out in Table 50.2. Successful treatment depends on the correct diagnosis being made. Prompt investigation of patients with this symptom is essential because of a number of potentially life-threatening causes.

Investigation of the sportsperson with chest pain or tightness is very similar to that of the sportsperson with dyspnea, and may include chest X-ray, spirometry, bronchial provocation challenge tests, exercise ECG/EKG, echocardiogram, blood tests, or

Table 50.2 Causes of chest pain or tightness in the athlete

Common causes	Conditions not to be missed
Asthma	Cardiac ischemia
Exercise-induced bronchoconstriction	Carcinoma
Infection	Interstitial lung disease
Chest wall injuries	Herpes zoster (shingles)
Referred pain from thoracic spine	

gastroscopy. The investigations should be guided by the history and examination findings.

Asthma

Asthma is a chronic inflammatory disorder of the airways in which many inflammatory cells and cellular elements play a role—in particular, mast cells, eosinophils, T lymphocytes, macrophages, neutrophils, and epithelial cells. In susceptible individuals, this inflammation causes recurrent episodes of widespread but variable airflow obstruction that is usually reversible, either spontaneously or with treatment. The inflammation also causes an increase in existing bronchial hyperresponsiveness to a variety of stimuli. Common stimuli or triggers include upper respiratory tract infections, cigarette smoke, exercise, inhaled allergens (e.g. dust mite, pollens), emotional triggers (e.g. stress, laughter), changes in temperature and weather, and environmental factors (e.g. dust, bush fires, pollution).

Epidemiology

The incidence and prevalence of asthma depends on the age of the population studied, the nature of the population, and the criteria used for diagnosis.

 Although 20–30% of people have experienced wheezing in the last 12 months, this is usually transient in response to a viral infection.

Asthma is more prevalent in developed countries, and it is thought by some that the "clean" lifestyle in these countries may contribute. Australia has the third highest prevalence of asthma in the world, with a prevalence of 10–11%. Other countries with significantly high prevalences are New Zealand, UK, and Ireland. Asthma is more common in children than adults, with over half the cases developing in childhood and another third before the age of 40. Genetic factors are thought to play a role.

Clinical features

The characteristic symptoms of asthma are:

- cough—dry, irritating and persistent, often worse in the early morning or late at night
- wheeze
- shortness of breath
- chest tightness.

However, since the degree of airway narrowing and obstruction varies with the condition and treatment, the symptoms can also vary from being absent or

not recognized, to low grade and occasional, through to severe and persistent. The symptoms are usually reversible, either spontaneously or with treatment.

Types of asthma

Historically, a distinction was made between intrinsic (non-allergic) and extrinsic (allergic) asthma in the International Disease Classification. This distinction is now rarely applied as it has been shown that the two types of asthma share many of the same pathological features.

Most existing guidelines classify patients with asthma as having intermittent or persistent asthma based on the severity of asthma, as determined by the patient's symptoms and spirometry before treatment is commenced. Importantly, the classification may change with time, and a severe episode of asthma may occur in any of the groups.[1] The current classification of asthma is outlined below.

1. Mild intermittent asthma:
   - Symptoms occur less than twice a week and are not present between asthma episodes.
   - Asthma episodes are brief (a few hours to a few days) and may vary from mild to severe.
   - Night-time symptoms occur less than twice a month.
   - Spirometry when not having an asthma episode is 80% or greater than predicted, and the peak expiratory flow rate (PEFR) varies little from morning to afternoon.

2. Mild persistent asthma:
   - Symptoms occur more than twice a week but less than once a day.
   - Asthma episodes interfere with daily activities.
   - Night-time symptoms occur more than twice a month.
   - Spirometry when not having an asthma episode is 80% or greater than predicted, and the PEFR varies little from morning to afternoon.

3. Moderate persistent asthma:
   - Symptoms occur daily and inhaled short-acting asthma medications are used every day.
   - Episodes interfere with daily activities, and occur more than twice a week and last for days.
   - Night-time symptoms occur more than once a week.
   - Spirometry is abnormal, and is more than 60% but less than 80% of predicted value; the PEFR varies more than 30% between morning and afternoon readings.

4. Severe persistent asthma:
   - Symptoms occur all the time during the day.
   - Daily physical activities are limited.
   - Asthma episodes occur frequently.
   - Night-time symptoms occur frequently.
   - Spirometry is abnormal and less than or equal to 60% of predicted value; the PEFR varies more than 30% between morning and afternoon readings.

Precipitating factors

Airway inflammation appears to be an important factor leading to the development of increased airway reactivity. A series of immunological and cellular events occurs in response to airway "triggers." Exposure to specific individualized triggers leads to mast cell degranulation, resulting in the release of a number of mediators such as histamine, prostaglandins, leukotrienes, and cytokines, with a subsequent influx of inflammatory cells into the airways.

As a consequence, inflammation of the airways results, with mucosal edema due to the increased permeability of the airway epithelium, mucus production, and contraction of the airway smooth muscle. The cumulative result is narrowing of the airways, which is the pathophysiological hallmark of asthma. Neurological factors, possibly mediated by the autonomic nervous system via the action of neuropeptides, have also been shown to play a role. This bronchial hyperreactivity may persist and become permanent.

Bronchial hyperreactivity may occur in response to specific stimuli, such as house dust mite (*Dermatophagoides pteronyssinus*) or fungal spores (e.g. *Aspergillus fumigatus*). It may also occur in response to non-specific stimuli such as cold, dust, smoke, and exercise. The role of food allergy in asthma remains controversial. Food intolerance does not necessarily indicate an allergic mechanism.

Most cases of asthma induced by specific food intolerance are evident from a carefully taken history, so elaborate exclusive diets are not warranted and have generally been disappointing. Skin prick tests and radioallergosorbent tests (RAST) may be helpful in confirming the patient's atopic status and also in establishing certain allergies (e.g. to house dust mite) but have no role in the diagnosis of "food allergies."

Drugs may be implicated in the production of asthma, especially beta-blocking agents and prostaglandin inhibitors such as aspirin (ASA) and nonsteroidal anti-inflammatory drugs (NSAIDs). Occasionally, drugs used to treat asthma (such as ipratropium bromide) have been responsible for provoking bronchoconstriction.

Psychological factors also can induce asthmatic episodes, although they do not produce asthma in subjects without underlying airway reactivity. Therefore, stress and emotional disturbance need to be taken into account in the overall management of asthmatic patients.

Risk factors

The main risk factors for the development of and worsening of asthma are:

1. *Genetic predisposition.* Atopy is characterized by the body's production of immunoglobulin E (IgE) after exposure to common environmental allergens. A person with high levels of IgE in the blood is more likely to have an allergic response when exposed to certain allergens in the environment. If a person has a parent with asthma, he or she is three to six times more likely to develop asthma.

2. *Environmental exposures.* The US Institute of Medicine[2] studied components in the environment that affected both the development of asthma and the exacerbation of the symptoms in someone who already has the disease:
   (a) Causal relationship between exposure to any of the following and the *development of asthma* in susceptible children:
      - house dust mite
      - environmental tobacco smoke—both prenatal exposure to maternal smoking and environmental exposure after birth
      - cockroach allergen
      - respiratory syncytial virus
   (b) Four exposures are considered causes of *asthma exacerbations*:
      - cat
      - cockroach
      - house dust mite
      - environmental tobacco smoke
   (c) Four additional exposures are associated with *worsening of the disease*:
      - dog allergen
      - fungi or moulds
      - rhinoviruses
      - high level of nitrous oxides

Asthma management

The general principles of asthma management are listed below:

1. Asthma is an inflammatory disease and treatment should be primarily directed against this inflammatory component.
2. Bronchodilators should be used for the relief of symptoms only. Increased use of bronchodilators indicates the need for increased anti-inflammatory treatment.
3. Recognition of symptoms and objective assessment of airflow obstruction by regular peak flow rate measurements are essential for optimal asthma management.
4. The patient must take responsibility for the initial assessment and treatment of worsening asthma through the use of a predetermined self-management plan.

The assessment of the severity of an asthma attack may be affected by its speed of onset. In some cases, severe episodes can occur within minutes with little or no warning. All patients should be educated to respond appropriately if they fail to obtain relief from their usual treatment or if peak flow rates fall significantly.

The patient's inability to assess and appreciate the severity of an asthma attack can result in a delay in commencing appropriate treatment. This occurs because patients determine the severity of their asthma by symptoms alone. Symptoms are a poor indicator of severity. Patients can assess airway function themselves on a regular basis with the use of a peak flow meter (Fig. 50.1).

While it is impossible to lay down strict criteria for hospital admission, the severity of the attack and the previous history of response to treatment are the main guides. Continued observation is essential once admitted.

Exercise-induced bronchospasm

Exercise-induced asthma or exercise-induced bronchospasm is described as a transitory increase in airway resistance that occurs following vigorous exercise.[3]

Epidemiology

Although exercise-induced bronchospasm occurs mainly in those with clinically recognized asthma—in 80% of asthmatics not taking inhaled corticosteroids and in 50% of those who do—it has

Figure 50.1 Peak flow meter

also been documented in healthy asymptomatic persons—schoolchildren, defense force recruits, highly trained sportspeople, and skaters. One study reported that 10% of Australian schoolchildren with no suggestive history of asthma had exercise-induced bronchospasm.[4] The prevalence of exercise-induced bronchospasm in the total Australian population is thought to be 12% with equal distribution in both sexes. In elite sportspeople, the prevalence has also been shown to be significantly higher, particularly in endurance-based, cold weather, and swimming pool-based sports.

The prevalence of exercise-induced bronchospasm in elite sportspeople has progressively increased over the years. In the 1976 and 1980 Summer Olympic games, 9.7% and 8.5% respectively of the Australian Olympic athletes reported asthma in a physical examination.[5] However, in the 2000 Australian Summer Olympic team 21% of the athletes reported asthma or exercise-induced bronchospasm.[6] Similarly, in the 1984 US Summer Olympic team, 11% reported on a medical history that they had asthma,[7] whereas in the 1996 Summer Olympic Games, 17% of the athletes had asthma, as defined by athlete-reported use of medication and/or previous diagnosis of asthma by a physician.[8]

A similar high prevalence of exercise-induced bronchospasm was seen in the 1998 US Winter Olympic team; 22% had asthma defined as athlete-reported use of asthma medication and/or previous diagnosis of asthma by a physician.[9] With the advent of required formalized laboratory testing, the prevalence of asthma/exercise-induced asthma was reduced for the subsequent international sporting competitions. The occurrence of asthma was highest in athletes performing in endurance sports, such as cycling, running, rowing, and triathlons, in swimming, and in winter sports such as cross-country skiing and figure skating.

Pathophysiology

In most cases, bronchoconstriction does not occur during the first few minutes of exercise but rather begins during the first few minutes of recovery. Two separate theories have been proposed to explain how the airway is protected from bronchoconstriction during exercise but is susceptible after exercise. In both theories, the primary stimulus for bronchoconstriction is the evaporation of water lining the airways secondary to the increased level of ventilation.

Gilbert et al. suggested that airway cooling during exercise and subsequent warming, with reactive hyperemia of the airway tissues after exercise, is responsible for the major component of the post-exercise bronchoconstriction.[10] In an alternative hypothesis—the osmotic hypothesis—Anderson suggested that it is the increased osmolarity of the airway tissues subsequent to the evaporation of water that occurs with hyperventilation that results in mast cell degranulation and the release of bronchoconstrictor mediators.[11]

The osmotic hypothesis has now been accepted, as a number of subsequent studies have shown that it is changes in the water content of the inspired air, and not temperature during exercise and recovery, that modifies the magnitude of EIA.[12, 13] Furthermore, bronchoconstriction may be induced by inhaling hypotonic and hypertonic aerosols of saline solution, dextrose, and urea.[14–16]

The protection against bronchoconstriction throughout the exercise period is attributed to the bronchodilating effect of circulating catecholamines;[17] however, this explanation fails to account for why the bronchoconstriction associated with eucapnic voluntary hyperpnea is often delayed until ventilation returns to normal.

Etiology

The actual etiology of exercise-induced bronchospasm in elite sportspeople appears to vary depending on the type of sport that the person is involved in and regularly performs. Exercise-induced bronchospasm is thought to develop as a consequence of injury to the airways secondary to exposure of the airways to large volumes of cold air, allergens, pollens, pollutants, smoke, or dust. Elite sportspeople may increase their ventilation during intense exercise to up to 200 L/min, and thus the load of such substances delivered to the airways may be extremely large.

In summer sports, exposure to and inhalation of allergens play a major role in the development of exercise-induced bronchospasm.[18–21] In winter sports, inhalation of cold air,[22] and in swimmers, inhalation of the gases of chlorine and its metabolites, which form a layer on the water surface of all pools, play a role.[23]

Clinical features

During exercise, flow rates and volumes actually improve in many subjects, in both those with and without exercise-induced bronchospasm. When exercise is continued for 6–8 minutes, the flow rates begin to fall in those with exercise-induced bronchospasm. The lowest rates are usually, but not always, observed 5–12 minutes following exercise cessation. It is the falling flow rates and volumes that are characteristic of the "asthmatic response."

Siblings of asthmatics, hay fever sufferers, and patients with cystic fibrosis may also increase their flow rates during exercise, but only those with exercise-induced bronchospasm show a reduction in excess of 10% after cessation of exercise.[24] When establishing a history of exercise-induced bronchospasm, it is important to confirm that the patient had symptoms after exercise ceased, not only during exercise.

Most sportspeople with mild exercise-induced bronchospasm recover spontaneously within minutes or soon after treatment with a bronchodilator; however, more severe bronchoconstriction may persist for up to an hour without treatment. In 50% of sportspeople who suffer from exercise-induced bronchospasm, there is a period after an episode of bronchoconstriction where further exercise is followed by either less severe or no bronchoconstriction at all. This "refractory period" may persist for up to four hours following the initial episode of exercise-induced bronchospasm.

Diagnosis

A clinical suspicion of exercise-induced bronchospasm may be indicated by symptoms of:

D

- shortness of breath
- chest tightness
- wheeze
- a dry cough post exercise
- poor performance
- fatigue.

Often the symptoms are made worse when exercising during the pollen season, indoors, or in the cold air. A firm diagnosis of exercise-induced bronchospasm, however, cannot be made on symptoms alone as these have been shown to be poor indicators of exercise-induced bronchospasm. A number of studies have shown that a diagnosis based purely on a history of exercise-related respiratory symptoms has a high level of misdiagnosis, both over- and under-diagnosis.[25, 26]

Diagnosis depends on demonstrating a deterioration in lung function, in particular the forced expiratory volume in one second (FEV_1), measured by lung spirometry (Figs 50.2, 50.3) following a recognized

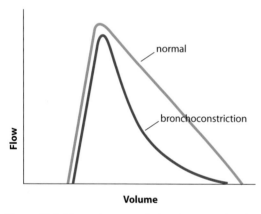

Figure 50.2 Flow volume graph showing normal and bronchoconstriction pattern

Figure 50.3 Lung spirometry

bronchial provocation challenge test. Previously, reductions in PEFR or forced expiratory flow (FEF_{25-75}) were also accepted, but these are now discouraged due to problems with reliability and reproducibility.

Until 2010, the International Olympic Committee Medical Commission (IOC-MC) and other major sporting bodies required objective evidence of asthma or exercise-induced bronchospasm for sportspeople to be permitted to use certain permitted beta agonists. The use of these medications required submission of Abbreviated Therapeutic Use Exemption forms (aTUEs). However this requirement was removed in 2010 for two of the more commonly used asthma medications—inhaled salbutamol and salmeterol—and now a simple Declaration of Use at the time of the drug test is sufficient (Chapter 66).

The World Anti Drug Association (WADA) still requires objective evidence of asthma or exercise-induced bronchospasm for sportspeople to be permitted to use particular asthma medications (some types of short- and long-acting inhaled beta-2 agonists). Use of these medications requires submission of Therapeutic Use Exemption forms (TUEs) for all sportspeople at state level or above, as dictated by the WADA in January 2010.

Bronchial provocation challenge tests

The challenge tests are classified as being either direct or indirect.

Direct challenge tests

Direct challenge tests, otherwise known as pharmacological challenge tests, involve the administration of increasing doses of a drug, usually histamine or methacholine, which acts directly on the airway smooth muscle receptors to elicit bronchoconstriction. The main problem with this type of challenge test is that although they have a high sensitivity for detecting bronchial hyperresponsiveness, they have a low specificity for exercise-induced bronchospasm, as both healthy subjects and those with other lung diseases may also have a positive response. Another disadvantage is that direct challenge tests, in contrast to indirect challenge tests, cannot be used to assess the response of a patient to treatment.

Indirect challenge tests

Indirect challenge tests act indirectly by provoking mast cell degranulation and thus the release of mediators, which then act on the receptors to elicit narrowing of the airways (see box opposite). They

Indirect challenge tests used for exercise-induced bronchospasm

Exercise challenge test

The exercise challenge test involves exercising the patient on the exercise bike or treadmill for a minimum of 4 minutes, but preferably for up to 8 minutes, at an intensity sufficient to raise ventilation to approximately 50% of the predicted maximum voluntary ventilation for the duration of the exercise.

This test has the disadvantage that in elite athletes a sufficient level of ventilation cannot be achieved.[27]

Eucapnic voluntary hyperpnea challenge test

The eucapnic voluntary hyperpnea (EVH) challenge test (Fig. 50.4) requires the voluntary hyperventilation of dry air containing 4.9% carbon dioxide. One of two protocols may be used:

- The progressive protocol involves the patient ventilating at each of 30%, 60%, and 90% of his or her maximum voluntary ventilation for a period of 3 minutes.
- The steady state protocol involves the patient ventilating at 80% maximum voluntary ventilation for 6 minutes.

The progressive protocol is recommended for clinically recognized asthmatics, while the steady state protocol is recommended for asymptomatic subjects, elite sportspeople, defense force recruits, and persons with no recent history of asthma, or in those in whom no airway narrowing was elicited in the progressive protocol.

This challenge test is the current gold standard for the diagnosis of exercise-induced bronchospasm.[27, 28]

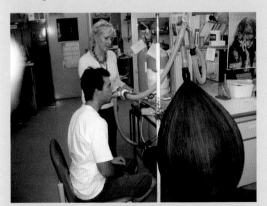

Figure 50.4 Eucapnic voluntary hyperpnea (EVH) challenge test

Hyperosmolar saline challenge test

The hyperosmolar saline challenge test requires the administration of increasing doses of inhaled 4.5% saline, which is thought to increase the osmolarity of the airways and, in susceptible individuals, leads to mast cell degranulation and release of mediators. These mediators then act to provoke airway narrowing. After each dose of saline, measurements of lung function are recorded. The test is aborted when the lung function falls by greater than 15% from pre-testing levels or when the full dose of 22 mL is reached. The response is said to be mild when the dose causing a fall of 15% is greater than 6 mL, moderate at 2.1–6.0 mL, and severe at less than 2 mL.

This test is particularly valuable for assessing a subject's suitability for scuba diving.[27]

Mannitol challenge test

The mannitol challenge test is similar to the hyperosmolar challenge test. This test requires the administration of doubling doses of inhaled mannitol, which acts to increase the osmolarity of the airways, thus leading to mast cell degranulation and subsequent airway narrowing in those with bronchial hyperresponsiveness. Again after each dose, airway function is measured. The test is continued until a greater than 15% fall in lung function occurs or a cumulative dose of 635 mg of mannitol is given.

This test has been shown to have a high sensitivity and specificity for the diagnosis of exercise-induced bronchospasm in sportspeople.[29] This test has the advantages of not being laboratory dependent (unlike those above), being safe, not being time-consuming, and being inexpensive.[30]

Diagnostic criteria

Each of the above challenge tests involves the measurement of lung function, in particular the FEV_1, PEFR, or FEF_{25-75} for up to 20 minutes following the challenge. The FEV_1 is the most sensitive and reliable measure of lung function, and is universally accepted. The FEF_{25-75}, which measures the flow through the mid-portions of the vital capacity, was previously considered important in the diagnosis of exercise-induced bronchospasm; however, similar to the PEFR, it has high variability and is dependent on the vital capacity, which can change

continued

continued

from pre- to post-exercise. Thus, the diagnosis of exercise-induced bronchospasm based on changes in the PEFR or FEF_{25-75} is not recommended.

Depending on the type of challenge test, the accepted fall in the FEV_1 for a positive challenge varies from 10% to 20% and must occur within a specified period following the administration of the challenge dose, or within a specific cumulative dose of administered agent. The IOC-MC accepts a fall of 10% in FEV_1 from baseline on two consecutive measurements for the eucapnic voluntary hyperpnea challenge test and the exercise challenge tests, both in the field and laboratory, of 15% for the hypertonic saline challenge test, and of 20% for the methacholine challenge test (Table 50.3).

Table 50.3 Diagnostic criteria for exercise-induced bronchospasm as guided by the IOC-MC

Bronchial provocation challenge test	Change in FEV_1 from baseline values
Post-bronchodilator	Increase by ≥12%
Eucapnic voluntary hyperpnea challenge	Decrease by ≥10%
Laboratory exercise challenge	Decrease by ≥10%
Field exercise challenge	Decrease by ≥10%
Methacholine challenge	Decrease by ≥20%
Hypertonic saline challenge	Decrease by ≥15%

It is important that on the day of testing, patients do not undertake any form of exercise prior to the challenge, and that they withhold their usual asthmatic medication, for a duration (as instructed) depending on the type of medication.

The severity of the exercise-induced bronchospasm can be assessed either by the percentage fall in the FEV_1 in response to a standard challenge (e.g. exercise or hyperventilation) (Table 50.4) or the dose of an agent required to induce a 15% fall in FEV_1 (e.g. hypertonic saline or mannitol) (Table 50.5).

The factors influencing the severity of exercise-induced bronchospasm are:[31]

1. type of exercise—endurance sports, cold weather sports, and swimming (Table 50.6)
2. duration of exercise
3. intensity of exercise—in general, the more strenuous the exercise, the more likely exercise-induced bronchospasm will occur
4. environmental factors:
   (a) cold more than warm
   (b) dry more than humid
   (c) air pollutants (e.g. sulfur dioxide and ozone)
5. interval since last episode of exercise-induced bronchospasm (refractory period)
6. underlying bronchial hyperreactivity.

Table 50.4 Severity of exercise-induced bronchospasm—exercise/hyperpnea challenge test

Severity	Fall in FEV_1
Mild	10–25%
Moderate	25.1–50%
Severe	>50%

Table 50.5 Severity of exercise-induced bronchospasm—hypertonic saline challenge test

Severity	Saline (mg)
Mild	>6
Moderate	2.1–6.0
Severe	<2.1

Table 50.6 Sports likely to be associated with exercise-induced bronchospasm

Middle/long-distance running
Cross-country skiing
Figure skating
Swimming
Aerobics
Cycling
Dancing
Basketball
Soccer
Rugby

have been found to have both a high sensitivity and specificity for exercise-induced bronchospasm.

Treatment
The treatment of exercise-induced bronchospasm is summarized in the flow chart given in Figure 50.5.

Non-pharmacological treatment
Most principles of non-pharmacological treatment are based on the theory that the primary stimulus for exercise-induced bronchospasm is the respiratory water loss.

Masks
Masks capture some of the heat and water on expiration so that it is inhaled in the next inspiration. They have been found to be successful in reducing the severity of exercise-induced bronchospasm.[32]

Nose breathing
Nose breathing during exercise has a similar effect to that of wearing masks.[33] However, nose breathing is not effective in everyone or during vigorous exercise. In addition, in some sportspeople the nasal mucosa is as sensitive as the lower airways, leading to nasal stuffiness, increased secretions, and sneezing.

Exercise training
The results of exercise training have been controversial. Training has been shown to increase the threshold at which exercise-induced bronchospasm occurs.[34] There are a few reports of a reduced severity in exercise-induced bronchospasm symptoms post training, but the majority of studies demonstrate no change in the occurrence or degree of exercise-induced bronchospasm.[35, 36]

Warm-up
Both submaximal work and short sprints have been shown to facilitate marked reductions in exercise-induced bronchospasm for subsequent exercise.[37–39] It is felt that such warm-ups increase bronchial blood flow and thus improve water delivery to the airways.

Refractory period
The refractory period occurs after exercise in more than 50% of subjects and may be used to lessen the severity of exercise-induced bronchospasm.[40] The exact mechanism whereby a person becomes refractory is not known but may be secondary to an improved delivery of water to the airways during the second episode of exercise. This effect is short-lived (a few hours) and can be inhibited by the use of NSAIDs.

Pharmacological treatment
Sodium cromoglycate (cromolyn sodium)
Sodium cromoglycate (cromolyn) is a prophylactic aerosol medication administered in a dose of 20–40 mg, 5–10 minutes prior to exercise. Its mode of action is thought to be that of stabilization of the basement membrane of the mast cell, preventing the release of the mediators for exercise-induced bronchospasm. It also acts to decrease vagal nerve afferent activity. It is most effective within two hours of administration and has been shown to prevent both the early- and late-phase asthmatic reactions. It has no bronchodilating effects so cannot be used in the treatment of acute symptoms. It has minimal adverse effects.[41]

Nedocromil sodium
Like sodium cromoglycate, nedocromil sodium has a membrane-stabilizing effect, preventing the release

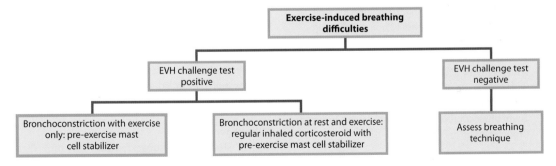

EVH = eucapnic voluntary hyperpnea

Figure 50.5 Management of exercise-induced bronchospasm

of mediators from mast cells and other inflammatory cells. It is administered in an inhaled dose of 4 mg, 5–10 minutes prior to exercise, with a duration of action of up to four hours. It, too, is effective in preventing the early- and late-phase asthmatic reactions but it is ineffective when used to treat acute symptoms.[42–44] Although it has minimal adverse effects, some patients do complain of the taste of this medication.

Beta-2 agonists

Inhaled beta-2 agonists are the most effective drugs available for the relief of acute asthma symptoms. They induce bronchodilation, prevent the release of mediators from mast cells, and modify the effects of the mediators on both the contractility of smooth muscle and the permeability of mucosal cells. Although it is effective in providing rapid symptomatic improvement to exercise-induced bronchospasm, regular use of beta-2 agonists leads to tolerance to the effects of these medications and may result in a reduction in baseline lung function, poor asthma control, and increased bronchial hyper-responsiveness.[45] Two main types of beta-2 agonists are available:

- Short-acting agents (e.g. salbutamol [albuterol], terbutaline). These agents have a rapid onset of action, usually within 5 minutes, with peak bronchodilation occurring within 15 minutes. Duration of action varies but effectiveness against exercise-induced bronchospasm usually lasts 3–6 hours. These agents are the gold standard for the treatment of symptoms of exercise-induced bronchospasm but are not recommended for use in the prevention of exercise-induced bronchospasm.
- Long-acting agents (e.g. salmeterol, formoterol). These agents have a slower onset of action and, as such, cannot be used in the treatment of symptoms of exercise-induced bronchospasm. The onset of action usually occurs within 20 minutes and the duration of action is at least 12 hours. Formoterol has been shown to induce bronchodilation at both 15 minutes and 4 hours post-administration.[46] In addition to the above complications associated with regular use of beta-2 agonists, salmeterol has the additional problem of a reduction in the acute bronchoprotection against exercise-induced bronchospasm.[47]

Leukotriene antagonists

Leukotrienes are potent bronchoconstrictors that also act to stimulate bronchial secretion of mucus and increase venopermeability, leading to airway edema. They are present in the airways of asthmatics but not normal subjects. Leukotriene antagonists (montelukast, zafirlukast) given orally prior to exercise attenuate the bronchoconstrictor and inflammatory response that would otherwise occur in response to the exercise.[48] One study showed that montelukasts provided superior protection compared with inhaled salmeterol (a long-acting beta-2 agonist).[49]

Inhaled corticosteroids

Inhaled corticosteroids improve asthma symptoms by reducing airway inflammation and bronchial hyperreactivity. They do not have an immediate bronchodilator effect and are not effective if used as prophylaxis just prior to exercise. The main role of corticosteroids is that of a maintenance therapy to help control asthma, but in doing so they also act to reduce bronchial responsiveness to exercise, thereby reducing the propensity for exercise-induced bronchospasm. They are often used on a regular basis, with sodium cromoglycate (cromolyn) or nedocromil sodium given prior to exercise.

Inhaled corticosteroids have been shown to reduce the incidence and severity of exercise-induced bronchospasm.[50, 51] The main adverse effects are oral candidiasis and dysphonia, both of which can be reduced by rinsing the mouth following administration.[47]

Theophylline

The role of theophylline in the management of asthma has changed profoundly over recent years, as research into the inflammatory etiology of asthma has led to the development of medications aimed to minimize this inflammation. Theophylline should not be used as intermittent prophylaxis for exercise-induced bronchospasm as it is not a potent bronchodilator. In addition, the intermittent use increases the likelihood of adverse effects such as headaches, nausea, vomiting, tachycardia, and central nervous system stimulation. The use of theophylline is, therefore, now limited to those with moderate–severe chronic asthma not controlled by main-line anti-asthmatic medications.

Other agents

Recent studies have suggested that fish oil,[52] diets low in sodium,[53] and diets high in vitamin C[54] may all play a protective role in the development of exercise-induced bronchospasm.

Treatment model

It is important to note that some drugs used to treat asthma are banned by the WADA (Chapter 66). In athletes subject to drug-testing procedures, clinicians are urged to check current banned drug listings. A treatment model for those athletes with exercise-induced bronchospasm is shown in Table 50.7. In athletes who are prone to developing exercise-induced bronchospasm, the regular use of medication prior to exercise is advised.

Conditions that may mimic exercise-induced bronchospasm

Vocal cord dysfunction

Vocal cord dysfunction is a psychogenic disorder of breathing, resulting in exercise-induced breathing difficulties. During normal breathing the true vocal cords abduct during inspiration and expiration; however, during vocal cord dysfunction, the true vocal cords adduct inappropriately during inspiration, resulting in airflow obstruction. Less commonly, severe narrowing of the vocal cords may occur during expiration.

The condition commonly occurs in 20- to 40-year-old women, although it may also occur in men and adolescents. Although in some situations it is related to an underlying psychiatric illness, such as generalized anxiety, depression, post-traumatic stress disorder, or a history of sexual abuse, in many cases there is no underlying psychological condition.

Clinical features

The classic symptoms of vocal cord dysfunction commonly occur during exercise and resolve within five minutes of cessation. They consist of a marked throat tightness or choking, in conjunction with severe dyspnea and an inspiratory stridor—the hallmark feature of vocal cord dysfunction. The symptoms are variable and not necessarily reproducible when exercising under identical conditions. Both acute or prophylactic treatment with inhaled beta-2 agonists is ineffective. The symptoms may be worse during times of stress or moderate-to-severe lethargy.

Vocal cord dysfunction should be considered in all sportspeople complaining of exercise-induced dyspnea, especially when either a diagnosis of exercise-induced bronchospasm has been excluded or, alternatively, made but the athlete has failed to respond to appropriate treatment.

The features of vocal cord dysfunction are shown in Table 50.8 overleaf.

Investigations

The diagnosis is often one of exclusion. An appropriate bronchial provocation challenge test should be performed, preferably an EVH challenge test, to exclude underlying exercise-induced bronchospasm. Ideally, reproduction of the symptoms during an exercise challenge or, in some situations, participation in normal competition is required as it is essential for the treating physician to witness the sportsperson when experiencing the symptoms. Typically the sportsperson struggles to breathe, with rapid shallow breaths and a loud inspiratory stridor; the sportsperson often leans forward, complaining of severe tightness of the throat.

Spirometry should be performed at the time of symptoms, when a flattening or truncation of the inspiratory limb of the flow–volume loop is usually seen.[55] However, in some cases, spirometry may miss the diagnosis.[56]

 In a patient with loud inspiratory stridor but with a normal EVH, the diagnosis of vocal cord dysfunction should be considered, especially in a young female.

Direct laryngoscopy is required to exclude other causes of upper airway obstruction such as vocal cord paralysis, glottic or tracheal stenosis, laryngeal polyps, and other laryngeal abnormalities. Although difficult, it is essential to perform direct laryngoscopy

Table 50.7 Pharmacological treatment of exercise-induced bronchospasm

Severity	Pre-exercise treatment	Regular treatment	Symptom treatment
Mild	Sodium cromoglycate (cromolyn)/nedocromil sodium		Short-acting beta-2 agonist
Moderate	Sodium cromoglycate (cromolyn)/nedocromil sodium	Low-dose inhaled corticosteroids	Short-acting beta-2 agonist
Severe	Sodium cromoglycate (cromolyn) and/or nedocromil sodium	Higher dose inhaled corticosteroids	Short-acting beta-2 agonist

Table 50.8 Comparative features of exercise-induced bronchoconstriction, vocal cord dysfunction, and exercise-induced hyperventilation

Feature	Exercise-induced bronchospasm	Vocal chord dysfunction	Hyperventilation
During or after exercise	Worse in first 12 minutes following cessation of exercise	Worse during exercise Resolves within 5 minutes of cessation	Worse during exercise Resolves within 5 minutes of cessation
Reproducibility under controlled situations	Reproducible	Often not reproducible	Often not reproducible
Classic symptoms	Chest tightness Dyspnea Cough Expiratory wheeze	Throat tightness/choking Dyspnea Inspiratory stridor	Throat tightness Dyspnea
Site of tightness	Chest	Throat	Throat
Bronchial provocation challenge tests	Abnormal	Normal	Normal
Spirometry	May be abnormal at rest	Normal at rest; abnormal during episode	Normal at all times
Laryngoscopy	Normal	Abnormal	Normal
Effect of beta-2 agonists	Prophylactic—prevents episode Therapeutic—resolves symptoms	Prophylactic—nil effect Therapeutic—nil effect	Prophylactic—nil effect Therapeutic—nil effect
Symptoms outside exercise	May be present	Absent	Absent

while the acute symptoms are present to visualize laryngeal closure.

Treatment

Treatment revolves around speech and relaxation therapy. It is essential that the speech therapist has experience with patients with vocal cord dysfunction. The focus of speech therapy is on respiratory control and diaphragmatic breathing patterns. As the sportsperson gains control over breathing patterns, he or she may realize a sense of control of this condition and reduce the emotional stress associated with dyspnea.

Consultation with a psychologist is recommended to help the sportsperson to recognize and come to terms with stress. It is also important for the psychologist to assess for, and manage, any other underlying psychological condition.

Speech therapy, alone or in combination with other treatment interventions, has proven to be successful in reducing or eliminating the paroxysms of wheezing, stridor, and dyspnea.[57] With appropriate

treatment, nearly all sportspeople who have vocal cord dysfunction should be able to exercise and compete unimpeded.[58]

Exercise-induced hyperventilation

Exercise-induced hyperventilation is a common condition occurring in both sportspeople with underlying exercise-induced bronchospasm and also those without. Often during intense exercise the sportsperson loses control of his or her breathing, resulting in rapid shallow breaths—the abdominal muscles are not used. The patient typically presents with shortness of breath and throat tightness occurring while exercising, and resolving immediately with rest.

The features of exercise-induced hyperventilation are shown in Table 50.8.

Bronchial provocation challenge tests, preferably a eucapnic voluntary hyperpnea challenge test, should be performed to exclude underlying exercise-induced bronchospasm. In those with known exercise-induced bronchospasm not responding to treatment the challenge test should be performed while the sportsperson is on medication to confirm adequate control. An exercise challenge test should be performed to allow the treating physician to assess the sportsperson while he or she is experiencing the symptoms. Laryngoscopy is required to exclude vocal cord dysfunction.

Treatment involves educating the sportsperson to breathe, especially during times of stress or intense exercise. Consultation with a psychologist with experience in this area is essential. Training is required and appropriate exercises are given. Concentration on the use of abdominal muscles during breathing is required. Principles similar to the Butyeko method of breathing may be used.

Sinus-related symptoms

Sinusitis is a common disorder in both sportspeople and non-sportspeople. While acute infections are easily diagnosed, chronic sinusitis may be far more subtle in its presentation. The paranasal sinuses are air-filled spaces within the skull that communicate with the nose. Most commonly, the maxillary sinus is affected.

Clinical features of acute sinusitis may include facial pain, headache, toothache, post-nasal drip, cough, rhinorrhea, nasal obstruction, pyrexia, and epistaxis. It is important to establish whether these symptoms are evidence of infective sinusitis or, alternatively, inflammation that is causing pain in the absence of infection. Inflammatory sinus pain may accompany acute exacerbations of rhinitis and is often short-lived. Features of chronic sinusitis are vague facial pain, post-nasal drip, cough, nasal obstruction, dental pain, malaise, and halitosis.

General and local factors may predispose toward sinusitis. General factors include diabetes, immune deficiency, mucus abnormalities, and disturbances in cilia function. Specific or local factors that may predispose sportspeople to this condition include anatomical deformities, polyps, foreign bodies, dental infections, cigarette smoking, barotraumas, and local tumors. Failure to respond to therapy or recurrent episodes should prompt the search for a complicating condition (e.g. fracture, tumor, or other abnormality).

Investigations

When investigating these patients, assessment may be difficult due to the degree of edema. This may obscure the relevant abnormality. Full examination sometimes must be delayed until treatment has been effective. The use of plain X-rays should be interpreted with caution since up to 1 cm (0.5 in.) of mucoid thickening may be regarded as normal. In children, a number of developmental changes also make radiological interpretation almost impossible. Useful findings that may be seen on plain X-ray include the presence of a fluid level and/or opacification of a sinus.

PRACTICE PEARL

CT scan is the investigation of choice in sinus-related conditions.

In the patient with infective sinusitis, microbiological culture of nasal pus may be useful; however, the presence of normal bacterial flora makes interpretation difficult. Approximately 50% of infections are due to *Hemophilus influenzae* or *Streptococcus pneumoniae* but there are a variety of other organisms that may play a role, including *Branhamella catarrhalis* (most common organism in children) and other mixed oral anaerobes.

Management of sinusitis

The principles of management of sinusitis are:

1. appropriate antibiotic therapy
2. the establishment of sinus drainage through the release of obstruction and the stimulation of mucus flow
3. the control of any predisposing factors.

The antibiotic of first choice is amoxicillin, either alone or in combination with clavulanic acid. Penicillin-allergic patients should use cefaclor, cotrimoxazole, or doxycycline. If a dental infection is the primary source, then anaerobic cover should be added (e.g. metronidazole).

Systemically administered decongestants, including pseudoephedrine, are of some value in the treatment of acute sinusitis. However, a topical decongestant is more effective and will have fewer systemic adverse effects.

Antihistamines usually slow mucociliary function but may have a role, especially if sinusitis is the result of nasal allergy. The use of topical steroids is widely advocated in the acute situation but there is often a latent period before these are effective. The maintenance of hydration in the treatment of these patients is critical.

There may well be a role for surgery in either the acute or chronic condition where there is an

D

anatomical deformity, polyps, or a failure to respond to medical treatment.

Other exercise-related conditions

Exercise-induced anaphylaxis

Approximately 500 cases of exercise-induced anaphylaxis have been reported, mostly occurring in sportspeople.[59, 60] Numerous attacks may occur before the diagnosis is correctly made.

The condition is characterized by a sensation of warmth, pruritis, cutaneous erythema, angioedema, urticaria (greater than 1 cm [0.5 in.] diameter), upper respiratory tract obstruction, and, occasionally, vascular collapse. It is considered a distinct entity from other exertion-related phenomena.

Risk factors include:

- previous atopic history (50%)
- family atopic history (67%)
- food ingestion (e.g. shellfish, celery, nuts, alcohol)
- weather conditions (e.g. heat, high humidity)
- drug ingestion (e.g. aspirin [ASA], NSAIDs).

The management of this condition involves:

1. prevention through modification of the exercise program to:
   (a) decrease intensity
   (b) avoid exercise during warm and humid days
   (c) stop exercise at the earliest sign of itching
   (d) avoid meals 4 hours before exercise
2. drugs/therapy
   (a) antihistamines
   (b) cromoglycate (cromolyn)
   (c) adrenalin (epinephrine)—should have an injection available
   (d) pre-treatment does not prevent onset.

Cholinergic urticaria

Cholinergic urticaria is an exaggerated cholinergic response to rapid elevation of the core body temperature through a mechanism such as exercise (most commonly), hot showers, fever, or anxiety.[61] It is characterized by generalized flushing, tan urticarial rash, and pruritus. Generally, the urticarial papules appear first within 10 minutes of starting exercise on the neck or upper thorax and spread to the limbs.[62] Systemic reactions such as syncope, abdominal pain, and wheezing are rare. Cholinergic symptoms such as lacrimation, salivation, and diarrhea may be observed. Recovery usually occurs spontaneously in 2–4 hours provided there are no systemic symptoms.[61] Antihistamines are generally used in treatment (e.g. hydroxyzine, 250 mg/day or cyproheptadine, 4 mg/day).

Exercise-induced angioedema

Angioedema is a non-itchy swelling occurring in the deep dermis and subcutaneous tissue. Although angioedema can affect any body region, it tends to involve the face and oral region. Occasional visceral manifestations occur. Attacks may be life-threatening if the airway is involved. Frank asthmatic attacks rarely occur in the setting of exercise-induced angioedema.[63]

Prevention may be achieved with modification of the exercise program and/or the use of antihistamines (e.g. diphenhydramine). The selective histamine H_2-receptor blockers (e.g. cimetidine) have been used in the treatment of this condition.

RECOMMENDED READING

Anderson SD. Indirect challenge tests: airway hyperresponsiveness in asthma: its measurement and clinical significance. *Chest* 2010;138(2 Suppl):25S–30S.

Carlsen KH, Anderson SD, Bjermer L et al Exercise-induced asthma, respiratory and allergic disorders in elite athletes: epidemiology, mechanisms and diagnosis: part I of the report from the Joint Task Force of the European Respiratory Society (ERS) and the European Academy of Allergy and Clinical Immunology (EAACI) in cooperation with GA2LEN. *Allergy* 2008;63(4): 387–403.

Carlsen KH, Anderson SD, Bjermer L et al Exercise-induced asthma, respiratory and allergic disorders in elite athletes: epidemiology, mechanisms and diagnosis: part II of the report from the Joint Task Force of the European Respiratory Society (ERS) and the European Academy of Allergy and Clinical Immunology (EAACI) in cooperation with GA2LEN. *Allergy* 2008; 63(5): 492–505.

Cockcroft DW. Direct challenge tests: Airway hyperresponsiveness in asthma: its measurement and clinical significance. *Chest* 2010 Aug;138(2 Suppl): 18S–24S

Fitch KD, Sue-Chu M, Anderson SD et al. Asthma and the elite athlete: summary of the International Olympic Committee's consensus conference, Lausanne, Switzerland, January 22–24, 2008. *J Allergy Clin Immunol* 2008;122(2):254–60

Holzer K, Brukner P, Douglass J. Evidence-based management of exercise-induced asthma. *Curr Sports Med Rep* 2002;1:86–92.

Millward DT, Tanner LG, Brown MA. Treatment options for the management of exercise-induced asthma and bronchoconstriction. *Phys Sportsmed* 2010; 38(4):74–80.

REFERENCES

1. National Institutes of Health. *Practical guide for the diagnosis and management of asthma.* Bethesda, MD: NIH Publication, 1997.

2. Institute of Medicine. *Clearing the air: asthma and indoor air exposure.* Washington, DC: National Academy of Press, 2000.

3. Anderson SD. Exercise-induced asthma. In: Middleton E, Reed C, Ellis E et al., eds. *Allergy: principles and practice.* 4th ed. St Louis: CV Mosby, 1993:1343–67.

4. Anderson S. Exercise-induced asthma. In: Carlsen K-H, Ibsen T, eds. *Exercise-induced asthma and sports in asthma.* Copenhagen: Munksgaard Press, 1999:11–17.

5. Fitch KD. Management of allergic Olympic athletes. *J Allergy Clin Immunol* 1984;73:722–7.

6. Corrigan B, Kazlaukas R. Medication use in athletes selected for doping control at the Sydney Olympics (2000). *Clin J Sport Med* 2003;13:33–40.

7. Voy RO. The US Olympic committee experience with exercise-induced bronchospasm, 1984. *Med Sci Sports Exerc* 1986;18(3):328–30.

8. Weiler JM, Layton T, Hunt M. Asthma in United States Olympic athletes who participated in the 1996 summer games. *J Allergy Clin Immunol* 1998;102(5):722–6.

9. Weiler JM, Ryan EJ 3rd. Asthma in United States Olympic athletes who participated in the 1998 Olympic winter games. *J Allergy Clin Immunol* 2000;106(2):267–71.

10. Gilbert IA, McFadden ER. Airway cooling and rewarming. The second reaction sequence in exercise-induced asthma. *J Clin Invest* 1992;90:699–704.

11. Anderson SD. Is there a unifying hypothesis for exercise-induced asthma? *J Allergy Clin Immunol* 1984;73:660–5.

12. Godfrey S, Bar-Yishay E. Exercise-induced asthma revisited. *Respir Med* 1993;87:331–44.

13. Argyros GJ, Phillips YY, Rayburn DB et al. Water loss without heat flux in exercise-induced bronchospasm. *Am Rev Respir Dis* 1993;147:1419–24.

14. Schmidt A, Bundgaard A. Exercise-induced asthma after inhalation of aerosols with different osmolarities. *Eur J Respir Dis Suppl* 1986;143:57–61.

15. Anderson SD, Smith CM. Osmotic challenges in the assessment of bronchial hyperresponsiveness. *Am Rev Respir Dis* 1991;143:S43–6.

16. Burge PS, Harries MG, Lam WK et al. Occupational asthma due to formaldehyde. *Thorax* 1985;40:255–60.

17. Godfrey S. Exercise-induced asthma. In: Barnes PJ, Grunstein MM, Leff AR et al., eds. *Asthma.* Philadelphia: Lippincott-Raven, 1997:1105–20.

18. Boulet L-P, Turcotte H, Laprise C. Comparative degree and type of sensitisation to common indoor and outdoor allergens in subjects with allergic rhinitis and/or asthma. *Clin Exp Allergy* 1997;27:52–9.

19. Helenius IJ, Tikkanen HO, Haahtela T. Association between type of training and risk of asthma in elite athletes. *Thorax* 1997;52:157–60.

20. Holzer K, Anderson SD, Douglass J. Exercise in elite summer athletes: challenges for diagnosis. *J Allergy Clin Immunol* 2002;110(3):374–80.

21. Warner JO. Bronchial hyperresponsiveness, atopy, airway inflammation and asthma. *Pediatr Allergy Immunol* 1998;9:56–60.

5

6

22. Langdeau JB, Boulet LP. Prevalence and mechanisms of development of asthma and airway hyperresponsiveness in athletes. *Sports Med* 2001;31(8):601–16.

23. Drobnic F, Freixa A, Casan P et al. Assessment of chlorine exposure in swimmers during training. *Med Sci Sports Exerc* 1996;28(2):271–4.

24. Anderson SD, Silverman M, Konig P et al. Exercise-induced asthma. A review. *Br J Dis Chest* 1975;69:1–39.

25. Rundell KW, Im J, Mayers LB et al. Self-reported symptoms and exercise-induced asthma in the elite athlete. *Med Sci Sports Exerc* 2001;33(2):208–13.

26. Holzer K, Douglass J, Anderson SD. Methacholine has a low sensitivity to identify elite athletes with a positive response to eucapnic voluntary hyperpnea and should not be used to exclude potential exercise-induced bronchoconstriction. *Respirology* 2002;7(suppl.):A28.

27. Anderson SD. Exercise-induced asthma. In: Kay AB, ed. *Allergy and allergic diseases*. Oxford: Blackwell Scientific Publications, 1997;692–711.

28. Anderson SD, Argyros GJ, Magnussen H et al. Provocation by eucapnic voluntary hyperpnoea to identify exercise induced bronchoconstriction. *Br J Sports Med* 2001;35:344–7.

29. Holzer K, Anderson SD, Chan H-K et al. Mannitol as a challenge test to identify exercise-induced bronchoconstriction in elite athletes. *Am J Respir Crit Care Med* 2003;167(4):534–47.

30. Anderson SD, Brannan J, Spring J et al. A new method for bronchial-provocation testing in asthmatic subjects using a dry powder of mannitol. *Am J Respir Crit Care Med* 1997;156:758–65.

31. Mahler DA. Exercise-induced asthma. *Med Sci Sports Exercise* 1993;25(5):554–61.

32. Nisar M, Spence DPS, West D et al. A mask to modify inspired air temperature and humidity and its effect on exercise induced asthma. *Thorax* 1992;47:446–50.

33. Shturman-Ellstein R, Zeballos RJ, Buckley JM et al. The beneficial effect of nasal breathing on exercise-induced bronchoconstriction. *Am Rev Respir Dis* 1978;118:65–73.

34. Fitch KD, Blitvich JD, Morton AR. The effect of running training on exercise-induced asthma. *Ann Allergy Asthma Immunol* 1986;7:90–4.

35. Welsh L, Kemp JG, Roberts RG. Effects of physical conditioning on children and adolescents with asthma. *Sports Med* 2005;35(2):127–41.

36. Ram FS, Robinson SM, Black PN. Effects of physical training in asthma: a systematic review. *Br J Sports Med* 2000;34(3):162–7.

37. de Bisschop C, Guenard H, Desnot P et al. Reduction of exercise-induced asthma in children by short, repeated warm ups. *Br J Sports Med* 1999;33:100–4.

38. Schnall RP, Landau LI. Protective effects of repeated short sprints in exercise-induced asthma. *Thorax* 1980;35:828–32.

39. McKenzie DC, McLuckie SL, Stirling DR. The protective effects of continuous and interval exercise in athletes with exercise-induced asthma. *Med Sci Sports Exerc* 1994;26(8):951–6.

40. Edmunds A, Tooley M, Godfrey S. The refractory period after exercise-induced asthma: its duration and relation to the severity of exercise. *Am Rev Respir Dis* 1978;117:247–54.

41. Anderson SD. Exercise-induced asthma: stimulus, mechanism, and management. In: Barnes PJ, Rodger I, Thomson NC, eds. *Asthma: basic mechanisms and clinical management*. London: Academic Press, 1988:503–22.

42. Speelberg B, Verhoeff NPLG, van den Berg NJ et al. Nedocromil sodium inhibits the early and late asthmatic response to exercise. *Eur Respir J* 1992;5:430–7.

43. Spooner C, Rowe BH, Saunders LD. Nedocromil sodium in the treatment of exercise-induced asthma: a meta-analysis. *Eur Respir J* 2000;16(1):30–7.

44. Spooner CH, Saunders LD, Rowe BH. Nedocromil sodium for preventing exercise-induced bronchoconstriction (Cochrane review). *Cochrane Database Syst Rev* 2002;1:CD001183.

45. Bhagat R, Kalra S, Swystun A. Rapid onset of tolerance to the bronchoprotective effect of salmeterol. *Chest* 1995;108:1235–9.

46. Ferrari M, Balestreri F, Baratieri S et al. Evidence of the rapid protective effect of formoterol dry-powder inhalation against exercise-induced bronchospasm in athletes with asthma. *Clin Invest Med* 2000;67:510–13.

47. Rupp NT. Diagnosis and management of exercise-induced asthma. *Phys Sportsmed* 1996;24(1):77–87.

48. Makker HK, Lau LC, Thomson HW et al. The protective effect of inhaled leukotriene D_4 receptor antagonist ICI 204,219 against exercise-induced asthma. *Am Rev Respir Dis* 1993;147:1413–18.

49. Ferrari M, Segattini C, Zanon R et al. Comparison of the protective effect of salmeterol against exercise-induced bronchospasm when given immediately before a cycloergometric test. *Respiration* 2002;69(6):509–12.

50. Henriksen JM, Dahl R. Effects of inhaled budesonide alone and in combination with low-dose terbutaline in children with exercise-induced asthma. *Am Rev Respir Dis* 1983;128:993–7.

51. Waalkans HJ, van Essen-Zandvliet EE, Gerritsen J et al. The effect of an inhaled corticosteroid (budesonide) on exercise-induced asthma in children. *Eur Respir J* 1993;6:652–6.

52. Mickleborough TD, Lindley MR, Ionescu AA et al. Protective effect of fish oil supplementation on exercise-induced bronchoconstriction in asthma. *Chest* 2006;129(1):39–49.

53. Mickleborough TD. Salt intake, asthma, and exercise-induced bronchoconstriction: a review. *Phys Sportsmed* 2010;38(1):118–31.

54. Tecklenburg SL, Mickleborough TD, Fly AD et al. Ascorbic acid supplementation attenuates exercise-induced bronchoconstriction in patients with asthma. *Resp Med* 2007;101(8):1770–8.

55. Newman KB, Mason III UG, Schmaling KB. Clinical features of vocal cord dysfunction. *Am J Respir Crit Care Med* 1995;152(4 Pt 1):1382–6.

56. Morris MJ, Deal L, Bean DR et al. Vocal cord dysfunction in patients with exertional dyspnea. *Chest* 1999;116(6):1676–82.

57. Sullivan MD, Heywood BM, Beukelman DR. A treatment for vocal cord dysfunction in female athletes: an outcome study. *Laryngoscope* 2001;111(10):1751–5.

58. Newshaun KR, Claben DK, Miller DJ et al. Paradoxical vocal cord dysfunction management in athletes. *J Athl Train* 2002;37:325–8.

59. Castells MC, Horan RS, Sheffer AL. Exercise induced anaphylaxis. *Clin Rev Allergy Immunol* 1999;17:413–24.

60. Castells MC, Horan RS, Sheffer AL. Exercise induced anaphylaxis. *Curr Allergy Asthma Rep* 2003;3:15–21.

61. Volcheck GW, Li JT. Exercise-induced urticaria and anaphylaxis. *Mayo Clin Proc* 1997;72(2):140–7.

62. Sweeney TM, Dexter WW. Cholinergic urticaria in a jogger: ruling out exercise-induced anaphylaxis. *Phys Sportsmed* 2003;31(6):32–6.

63. Leung AKC, Hedge HR. Exercise-induced angiodema and asthma. *Am J Sports Med* 1989;17(3):442–3.

D

Chapter 51

Gastrointestinal symptoms during exercise

with CHRIS MILNE

In 1997 during the Hawaiian Ironman I pushed my body to the limit. I was vomiting, had diarrhea and stomach cramps, but I just had to finish the race. Just 50 metres from the finish line I collapsed. Shortly after, I had to have surgery to remove one third of my large bowel, as it had died. Chris Legh, quoted from www.coolrunning.com.au/general/2003/2003e013.shtml

The gut is not an athletic organ. During exercise, blood is directed away from the splanchnic vessels and to the exercising muscles. The gut therefore becomes relatively ischemic, and it is this which causes the majority of gastrointestinal symptoms during exercise. These symptoms may be divided into those relating to the upper gut and those relating to the lower gut (Table 51.1). Bleeding is another important clinical presentation, as discussed below.

Physiological changes that alter gastrointestinal function during exercise include reduced blood flow to the abdominal viscera, gastrointestinal hormonal changes, and alterations to gastric emptying rates and intestinal motility. Also, vigorous diaphragmatic movements, abdominal contractions, and intestinal jarring can all cause abdominal symptoms.[1]

Although the incidence of gastrointestinal symptoms is increased with exercise, the presence of symptoms in a sportsperson should not automatically be assumed to be solely related to exercise. Sportspeople as well as non-sportspeople suffer from common conditions, such as hiatus hernia and peptic ulceration, inflammatory bowel disease, polyps, and cancer. Physical activity confers a 25% reduction in colon cancer risk.[2] Clinical judgment is required to appreciate when these conditions must be considered in the sportsperson with gastrointestinal symptoms.

A summary of the management of common gastrointestinal symptoms is shown in Table 51.2.

Table 51.1 Gastrointestinal symptoms associated with exercise

Upper gastrointestinal tract	Lower gastrointestinal tract
Heartburn	Cramping
Reflux	Urge to defecate
Nausea	Diarrhea
Vomiting	Rectal bleeding
Bloating	Flatulence
Epigastric pain	

Table 51.2 Treatment of common gastrointestinal problems

Symptoms	Treatment
Heartburn, reflux, epigastric pain	Avoid solid foods prior to exercise Antacid medication Histamine H_2-receptor antagonist (rarely necessary)
Gastrointestinal bleeding	Ensure adequate hydration Reduce jarring (e.g. food, shoes, soft surfaces)
Abdominal "stitch"	Reassurance Avoid pre-exercise meal
Runner's diarrhea	Reduce fiber content of food 24 hours prior to run Antidiarrheal medication (e.g. loperamide)

Upper gastrointestinal symptoms

Heartburn, reflux, nausea, vomiting, and upper abdominal pain are the most common upper gastrointestinal tract symptoms related to exercise. Gastroesophageal reflux is a common complaint among sportspeople and can even cause asthma-like symptoms.[3] Twenty per cent of patients with established reflux consider exercise to be the major contributor to their symptoms.

The mechanism by which exercise causes reflux is not well understood, as reflux is normally associated with relaxation of the lower esophageal sphincter. This has not been described with exercise. Reflux appears to be more common when exercise is performed after a meal. Importantly, exercise does not appear to have any effect on gastric acid secretion.

Distinguishing between chest pain due to gastroesophageal reflux or esophageal muscular spasm, and chest pain due to chest wall or cardiac causes can be difficult. Any sportsperson presenting with chest pain on exertion must be thoroughly assessed to exclude cardiac causes.

Much attention has been paid to the factors that may affect the gastric emptying rate. Exercise at a very high intensity reduces the gastric emptying rate. However, as this level of exercise intensity cannot be maintained for long periods, its effect on the gastric emptying rate may be fairly insignificant. Increased volume in the stomach results in an initial rapid emptying, followed by a phase of reduced emptying once the volume of the stomach has decreased to about 30% of its initial content.

Until recently, it was thought that osmolality was an important factor in the rate of gastric emptying. While it is true that liquids empty more quickly than solids, there does not appear to be significant differences in the gastric emptying rate for liquids of different osmolality.[4, 5] Other factors that may be involved include gastrointestinal hormone levels, particle size, meal volume, dietary fiber, gastric acidity, and the sportsperson's anxiety level.

Treatment

The treatment of upper gastrointestinal symptoms associated with exercise is aimed at reducing the contents of the stomach during exercise. This is achieved by avoiding solid foods for at least three hours before intense exercise. The pre-exercise meal should be high in carbohydrate and low in fat and protein.

If additional measures are required, the use of antacid medication, in either tablet or liquid form, may reduce the incidence of heartburn and upper abdominal pain. Antacids usually remain in the stomach for 30 minutes. If this is not sufficient, the use of histamine H_2-receptor antagonists (such as ranitidine and cimetidine) may occasionally be necessary. Domperidone 10–20 mg 1 hour before meals may also be effective.

Sportspeople in prolonged endurance events (over 4 hours' duration), who need to consume food while exercising, are particularly susceptible to upper gastrointestinal symptoms. Chewing gum is a mechanical means of stimulating gastric emptying and avoids possible complications of medications. Always trial any chosen intervention before "race day."

Gastrointestinal bleeding

An occasional bloody stool is frequently noted by runners[6] and the incidence of occult bleeding is high.[7] As the amount of bleeding in most cases is small, most sportspeople are not affected clinically; however, occasionally iron-deficiency anemia may occur. Reduced iron stores are denoted by a low serum ferritin level.

The most frequently reported site of exercise-associated gastrointestinal hemorrhage is the fundus of the stomach. The mechanism underpinning this transitory hemorrhagic gastritis is uncertain. Ischemia may play a role, as may direct trauma from the diaphragm. In susceptible individuals, the gastritis may result in part from the general stress of competition along with the associated rise in key stress hormones such as adrenalin (epinephrine) and cortisol. Nonsteroidal anti-inflammatory drugs (NSAIDs) contribute to gastrointestinal bleeding in runners.[6, 7] A Mallory-Weiss tear secondary to forceful vomiting may present with signs of upper gastrointestinal bleeding.

No examples of bleeding from the small intestine have been reported. However, colonic bleeding has been observed, particularly from the proximal colon.

The etiology of gastrointestinal bleeding associated with exercise is uncertain and is likely to be multifactorial. During exercise, blood flow is diverted from the splanchnic bed to the exercising muscles. Blood flow to the gastrointestinal tract may be reduced by as much as 75% during intense exercise.[8] A number of other factors may contribute to a reduction of blood flow. Such factors include exercise in the fasted state, as the absence of nutrients within the intestine reduces the blood flow to that area. Also, high thermal stress, dehydration, and high exercise intensity play a role.

It must be remembered that gastrointestinal bleeding in a sportsperson is not necessarily associated with exercise, and the sportsperson with obvious gastrointestinal bleeding should be fully investigated to determine the source of the bleeding.

Treatment

If no obvious cause of the bleeding is established, ensure adequate hydration to prevent aggravation of the relative ischemia. As the mechanical effect of jarring while running is thought by some to be a contributory factor to gastrointestinal bleeding, the amount of jarring should be reduced by using appropriate footwear and avoiding running on hard surfaces.

Those sportspeople with a known tendency for gastrointestinal bleeding and those who complain of fatigue should have the state of their iron stores assessed by measurement of their serum ferritin levels. Serum ferritin levels of less than 30 ng/mL in women and 50 ng/mL in men indicate reduced iron stores.

Abdominal pain

Many sportspeople complain of a sharp, colicky pain in the left or right upper quadrant during strenuous exercise. This is commonly referred to as a "stitch." The exact cause of this common phenomenon is unknown but it may be due to muscle spasm of the diaphragm or trapping of gas in the hepatic or splenic flexure of the colon. This condition has often been thought to be associated with exercise undertaken soon after eating a solid meal. There is no proof of this; however, avoiding a solid meal prior to exercise may be an appropriate treatment. Exhaling on foot-strike on the opposite side to the pain may be helpful.

Occasionally, athletes get a "claudication-type" abdominal pain. This occurs in association with intense, endurance exercise and is thought to occur as a consequence of relative ischemia due to shunting of blood away from the gastrointestinal tract to the exercising muscles.[8] This effect is aggravated by dehydration.

A rare cause of abdominal pain is "cecal slap" on the right psoas muscle.

The possibility of abdominal pain being referred from the thoracic spine should always be considered.

A thorough examination of the thoracic spine should be performed in any sportsperson who complains of abdominal pain. Hypomobility detected in one or more intervertebral segments should be corrected by manual therapy techniques, and the effect on the sportsperson's symptoms noted.

Diarrhea

Diarrhea appears to be more frequent with exercise,[9] especially with long-distance running; as a result the terms "runner's trots" and "runner's diarrhea" have been coined to describe the condition. Sportspeople may complain of an urge to defecate while running, and approximately half of those who experience this urge to defecate actually complain of episodes of diarrhea during running.

The incidence of runner's diarrhea seems to be related to the intensity of the exercise and occurs more commonly in competition than in training. The anxiety associated with competition may be a contributory factor.

The exact cause of runner's diarrhea is uncertain. Relative intestinal ischemia, described previously, may be a contributory factor. An increase in intestinal motility may also contribute. Studies of the relationship between intestinal transit time and exercise have shown conflicting results; however, it would appear that intestinal motility is increased with intense exercise. This increase in gut motility and changes in intestinal secretion and absorption may be related to the increased level of endorphins associated with exercise.

When faced with a patient with diarrhea, the clinician should also seek a history of vitamin and mineral supplementation, or ingestion of caffeine or artificial sweeteners prior to exercise. Each of these may contribute to runner's diarrhea.

 Acute diarrhea is usually due to an infective cause and may be viral or bacterial.

Acute diarrhea is a particular problem for sportspeople when they are traveling away from home and is further considered in Chapter 64. In the 24 hours prior to major competition, team physicians generally prescribe norfloxacin (800 mg) or ciprofloxacin (1 g) with loperamide (4 mg) to try to provide rapid symptom relief.

Sportspeople with chronic diarrhea should be fully investigated to exclude any other abnormality (e.g. inflammatory bowel disease, malabsorptive disorders).

Treatment

The treatment of sportspeople with exercise-related diarrhea is often difficult. Dietary changes should include reduction of the fiber content of the diet in the 24 hours prior to intense competitive exercise. If the problem persists, prophylactic antidiarrheal medication (such as loperamide) may be used; however, this should not be used on a regular basis. Antispasmodics (e.g. mebeverine) may be useful.

Exercise and gastrointestinal diseases

Lactose intolerance

A limited number of people lack the enzyme lactase, which is necessary for the digestion of lactose or milk sugar. Asian and African populations typically display an absence of lactase. Also, adult lactase has only about 5% of the activity of childhood lactase. Lactose intolerance leads to gastrointestinal disorders resulting in cramps, flatulence, and diarrhea.

Sportspeople suffering from lactose intolerance need to avoid dairy products, with the possible exception of yoghurt. The lactose in yoghurt is largely broken down by the bacterial cultures present. It is important that sportspeople who avoid lactose ensure an adequate dietary intake of calcium and protein via alternative sources such as soy-based products (including milks, yoghurts, cheeses, and ice-creams). An often unrecognized source of lactose is high-protein drinks and sports supplements.

Also, temporary lactose intolerance may follow acute infective diarrhea (particularly if caused by rotavirus). Therefore, milk-based products should be among the last to be reintroduced to the sportsperson's diet after such an episode.

Celiac disease

Celiac disease is characterized by abnormal mucosa in the small intestine induced by a component of the gluten protein of wheat. Barley, rye, and oats also contain gluten. Anemia is often seen in sportspeople with celiac disease due to malabsorption of iron and folate. Howell-Jolly bodies may be seen on the blood film due to folate deficiency.

Prevalence data suggest that symptomatic or latent celiac disease affects up to 1 in 200 people in most Western countries. It may not always present with the classic symptoms of diarrhea and bloating; tiredness is a common presentation (Chapter 57).[10] Laboratory testing may show high levels of IgA antiendomysial and IgA tissue transglutaminase antibodies. However, any of the IgA tests may be falsely negative in up to 3–5% of celiac patients, mainly in those with associated IgA deficiency.[11] Definitive diagnosis is via multiple small bowel biopsy, showing typical mucosal changes of subtotal villous atrophy.

Sportspeople diagnosed with celiac disease are given comprehensive lists of alternative high-carbohydrate food sources and should consult a dietitian for assistance in planning a nutritionally adequate diet. Unfortunately, many people self-diagnose their symptoms as being due to gluten intolerance. They may reduce their gluten intake and note an improvement. It then becomes very difficult to convince these people that they need to go back onto a diet containing gluten for one month prior to having a small bowel biopsy to definitely prove the diagnosis.

Irritable bowel syndrome

Irritable bowel syndrome is a very common gastrointestinal disorder that causes lower abdominal pain and constipation alternating with diarrhea. The cause is not known but there seems to be a strong association between this condition and the intestinal response to emotional stress (e.g. sporting competition). Treatment includes a balanced fiber diet together with antispasmodic agents (e.g. dicyclomine).

Non-steroidal anti-inflammatory drugs (NSAIDs) and the gastrointestinal tract

NSAIDs are used by up to 35% of sportspeople in competition.[12] During exercise, the reduction of gastrointestinal blood flow increases the potential for gut toxicity. Gastrointestinal adverse effects are the most common reason for cessation of use of these medicines both in the general and the athletic population. They can affect any portion of the gastrointestinal tract as indicated in Table 51.3 overleaf.

There are two groups of sportspeople who present for clinical evaluation. By far the most common are healthy individuals who experience dyspepsia with NSAID use. This affects about 10% of the population. Strategies which can be implemented include:

- using a traditional (non-specific) NSAID under cover of a proton pump inhibitor (PPI)[13]
- using a cyclooxygenase (COX)-2 agent

Table 51.3 Gastrointestinal related adverse effects of NSAIDs

Site	Adverse effects
Oesophagus (common)	Reflux, upper gastrointestinal bleeding
Stomach and duodenum (common)	Gastritis, upper gastrointestinal bleeding Perforation
Small intestine (rare)	Increased permeability
Large intestine (uncommon)	Increased permeability Lower gastrointestinal bleeding

- using a COX-2 agent plus PPI—for patients at high risk
- avoiding NSAIDs altogether and using paracetamol (acetaminophen)—where analgesia alone is required (i.e. pain but no significant inflammation).

Less common, but more serious, are the adverse effects of NSAIDs in those patients with known risk factors (age over 60 years, previous gastrointestinal bleeding, taking corticosteroids, or having diabetes or vascular disease). These people have over twice the risk of gastrointestinal adverse effects when taking NSAIDs. Over 80% of adverse events (gastrointestinal bleeding, perforation) are asymptomatic in this patient group, at least in the early phase. Because they are occurring in older, sicker people, they can be life-threatening. With the growing numbers of Masters athletes, clinicians need to be alert to these conditions.

It was the high frequency of dyspepsia with the use of NSAIDs that prompted the development of COX-2 agents. Clinicians need to advise patients that, despite all the marketing hype, these agents are no more potent than traditional NSAIDs. Their main therapeutic advantage is in the patient who cannot tolerate traditional NSAIDs due to gastrointestinal upset.

COX-2 agents do not reduce the risk of gastrointestinal upset to zero. Various tables of COX-2 selectivity have been published.[14] However, COX-2 selectivity is only relative, and other factors (e.g. drug dosage) also interact to contribute to the overall toxicity risk.

There is increasing recognition that inflammation plays much less of a role in sports injuries (e.g. tendinopathies) than previously thought.[15] Only use NSAIDs for conditions with inflammation.

 PRACTICE PEARL Reserve NSAID use for those injury problems where a significant inflammation is present (e.g. joint effusion).

Prevention of gastrointestinal symptoms that occur with exercise

Many of the gut complaints experienced by runners are a direct result of the physical activity of running, which causes jolting of the gastrointestinal tract and reduced blood supply to the cells. However, some relief can be gained by a number of dietary modifications. See box below for advice on minimizing gastrointestinal symptoms.

Limit dietary fiber intake prior to competition

To ensure that the gut has minimal food content prior to racing, it is necessary to reduce the fiber content of the diet in the days preceding the race. This means, in the two days prior to the competition, change from wholemeal and wholegrain varieties of rice, breads, and cereals to the more refined alternatives. Avoid fresh fruit and vegetables with skin, legumes, and heavy seasonings such as garlic, pepper, and curry.

Runners who regularly suffer from diarrhea or the urge to use their bowels regularly during a race may

---

Minimizing gastrointestinal tract symptoms when exercising—advice for sportspeople

1. Train and compete with your upper gut as empty as possible (at least 3 hours after a meal).
2. Limit the fat and protein content of your last meal before exercising.
3. Prevent dehydration—get used to drinking during training and long events.
4. Avoid high-fiber foods prior to competition.
5. Only take anti-inflammatory tablets (NSAIDs) on the advice of a doctor, if you have an injury where inflammation plays a large role. Otherwise, use paracetamol (acetaminophen).
6. Always take NSAIDs on a full stomach.
7. If you have a family history of bowel or stomach cancer, consider regular screening examinations.
8. If you develop "red flag" symptoms (e.g. upper or lower gastrointestinal bleeding, unintended weight loss), see your doctor and get these properly evaluated.
9. If pre-race nerves are a likely cause of gut symptoms, consult a sports psychologist.

benefit from a liquid nutrition supplement during the last days preceding the competition. This will ensure that the gastrointestinal contents are minimized prior to the race. An alternative approach is to consume only fluids prior to competition on the day of the event.

Avoid solid foods during the last three hours prior to the race

To ensure that the stomach is empty, it is important that the pre-event meal is consumed at least three hours before the race begins. However, in some sportspeople with a low gastric emptying rate, the pre-event meal may need to be accompanied by a prokinetic agent (e.g. domperidone) and eaten up to four to six hours prior to competition. Fluids, however, should still be consumed in the period leading up to the race.

Select the pre-event meal carefully

The pre-event meal should contain negligible amounts of fat and protein so that it will be easily digested by the time the event begins. Select from low-fiber high-carbohydrate foods such as white rice, white bread, plain pastas, plain breakfast cereals (e.g. cornflakes, rice bubbles), and avoid adding any fats such as margarine, butter, or creamy sauces. Simple carbohydrates such as honey, jam, and syrup may be used to increase the energy value of the meal. Note that high-fructose foods (e.g. dried fruit, fruit juices, jam, soft drinks/pop) are absorbed slowly, so large volumes may not be well tolerated if the sportsperson has a tendency for gastrointestinal upset.

Prevent dehydration

It is important to drink small amounts frequently during the event, aiming to prevent thirst. During long events (more than 90 minutes) the sportsperson should choose a drink that contains some carbohydrate (up to 10% solution) and low concentrations of sodium and potassium. Concentrated drinks are more likely to cause symptoms. Practice drinking during training so that it becomes a habit in competitions.

Avoid fat and protein intake during exercise

During ultra-endurance events where food may be consumed during the event, select items that contain minimum quantities of protein and fat. Fiber intake needs to be kept low and some runners may find liquid meal replacements a useful option. Boiled white rice, pasta, pancakes with syrup, canned fruit, peeled potatoes, plain dry biscuits, and plain rolls or bread all make good choices. Practice food intake during training.

Sample pre-event diet

A sample 24-hour pre-race diet that will help minimize gastrointestinal problems during a race is shown in the box below. This plan provides approximately 14 700 kJ (3500 kcal) with 76% of the energy from carbohydrate and less than 20 g of dietary fiber.

Consult a sports psychologist

If pre-race nerves are a likely cause of gastrointestinal problems, it may be helpful to discuss race build-up with a sports psychologist. Proper management of anxiety can not only improve stomach and bowel problems but may also help maximize race performance.

A sample 24-hour pre-race diet

Breakfast
1 large bowl (2 cups) breakfast cereal with skim milk
2 slices white toast spread with honey
1 cup canned peaches
1 glass 100% apple juice

Snack
3 pancakes (made with low-fat milk) topped with golden syrup
300 mL flavored mineral water

Lunch
2 white bread rolls filled with low-fat cheese
1 tub low-fat fruit yoghurt
2 glasses water

Snack
2 toasted crumpets spread with honey
1 glass 100% pineapple juice

Dinner
2 cups boiled white pasta topped with sauce made from tomato paste and fresh mushrooms
1 slice white bread
1 serve rice pudding (white rice)
3 glasses water

Snack
300 mL nutrition supplement
1 glass lemonade

📄 RECOMMENDED READING

Peters HP, De Vries WR, Vanberge-Henegouwen GP et al. Potential benefits and hazards of physical activity and exercise on the gastrointestinal tract. *Gut* 2001;48: 435–9.

Carter MJ, Lobo AJ, Travis SP, IBD section, British Society of Gastroenterology. Guidelines for the management of inflammatory bowel disease in adults. *Gut* 2004;53(suppl. 5):V1–16.

Ng V, Millard WM. Competing with Crohn's disease. Management issues in active patients. *Phys Sportsmed* 2005;33(11):47–53.

Pitsis GC, Fallon KE, Fallon SK et al. Response of soluble transferrin receptor and iron-related parameters to iron supplementation in elite, iron-depleted, nonanemic female athletes. *Clin J Sport Med* 2004;14(5):300–4.

📋 REFERENCES

1. Casey E, Mistry DJ, MacKnight JM. Training room management of medical conditions: sports gastroenterology. *Clin Sports Med* 2005;24(3): 525–40,viii.

2. de Vries E, Soerjomataram I, Lemmens VE et al. Lifestyle changes and reduction of colon cancer incidence in Europe: a scenario study of physical activity promotion and weight reduction. *Eur J Cancer* 2010;46(14):2605–16.

3. Shawdon A. Gastro-oesophageal reflux and exercise. Important pathology to consider in the athletic population. *Sports Med* 1995;20(2):109–16.

4. Brouns F, Senden J, Beckers EJ et al. Osmolarity does not affect the gastric emptying rate of oral rehydration solutions. *J Parenter Enteral Nutr* 1995;19(5): 403–6.

5. Rogers J, Summers RW, Lambert GP. Gastric emptying and intestinal absorption of a low-carbohydrate sport drink during exercise. *Int J Sport Nutr Exerc Metab* 2005;15(3):220–35.

6. Simons SM, Kennedy RG. Gastrointestinal problems in runners. *Curr Sports Med Rep* 2004;3(2):112–16.

7. Smetanka RD, Lambert GP, Murray R et al. Intestinal permeability in runners in the 1996 Chicago marathon. *Int J Sport Nutr* 1999;9(4):426–33.

8. van Nieuwenhoven MA, Brouns F, Brummer RJ. Gastrointestinal profile of symptomatic athletes at rest and during physical exercise. *Eur J Appl Physiol* 2004;91(4):429–34.

9. Rao SS, Beaty J, Chamberlain M et al. Effects of acute graded exercise on human colonic motility. *Am J Physiol* 1999;276(5 Pt 1):G1221–6.

10. Green HR, Cellier C. Celiac disease. *New Engl J Med* 2007;357:1731–43.

11. Gastroenterological Society of Australia. Professional guidelines. Coeliac disease. Available online: http://gesa.blissmedia.com.au/files/editor_upload/File/Professional/Coeliac_Disease4Ed07.pdf.

12. Tscholl P, Junge A, Dvorak J. The use of medication and nutritional supplements during FIFA World Cups 2002 and 2006. *Br J Sports Med* 2008;42:725–30.

13. Gupta M, Eisen GM. NSAIDs and the gastrointestinal tract. *Current Gastroenterol Rep* 2009;11:345–53.

14. Riendeau D, Percival MD, Brideau C et al. Etoricoxib (MK-0663): preclinical profile and comparison with other agents that selectively inhibit cyclooxygenase-2. *J Pharmacol Exp Therap* 2001;296:558–66.

15. Paoloni JA, Milne C, Orchard J et al. Non-steroidal anti-inflammatory drugs in sports medicine: guidelines for practical but sensible use. *Br J Sports Med* 2009;43:863–5.

Chapter 52

Renal symptoms during exercise

with CHRIS MILNE

If you want this jersey, you've got to piss blood for it. Attributed to All Black rugby player
Mark Shaw in conversation with his successor Mike Brewer

The kidneys are important but often neglected organs. Exercise can have significant effects on renal function. The most serious renal problem is rhabdomyolysis. Other common renal problems include post-exercise protein/hemoglobinuria, and non-steroidal anti-inflammatory drug (NSAID)–induced renal dysfunction and/or injury. Renal trauma can result from sports-related abdominal injury.

Clinical anatomy and physiology

Ordinarily, the kidneys are paired organs that lie under well-developed flank muscles.[1,2] Kidneys receive high blood flow (approximately 20% of the total cardiac output at rest) and are composed of metabolically active cells. These cells are susceptible to hypoxia, and tolerate this poorly. The tubular arrangement within the kidney uses a countercurrent mechanism to produce hypertonic urine.

The four major functions of kidneys are:

* to maintain salt and water balance
* to excrete nitrogen, mainly as urea
* to produce erythropoeitin and the vitamin D metabolite 1,25-dihydroxycholecalciferol
* to regulate blood pressure via the renin-angiotensin-aldosterone system.

Normal values for renal function at rest and with exercise are listed in Table 52.1.

Table 52.1 Renal function—normal values

	At rest	During exercise
Renal blood flow mL/min^{-1}	1200	300
Glomerular filtration rate (GFR) mL/min^{-1}	120	60

Concentrating ability:
Urine osmolality   100–1200 mOsmol/kg water^{-1}
Serum osmolality   280–295 mOsmol/kg water^{-1}
Daily urine volume 400–4000 mL
Obligatory water loss 840 mL*

*Assumptions:
* For each 3 g of protein ingested, about 1 g of urea will be produced.
* 1 g of urea equals approximately 17 mmol.
* Urine osmolality can be up to three times that of plasma.
It follows that 120 g of protein ingested per day provides 40 g of urea for excretion. This is about 680 mmol. At a urine osmolality three times that of plasma, 840 mL of obligatory water loss per day is required to excrete that nitrogen.

During exercise, physiological changes that have been observed are:

- increased glomerular permeability
- increased excretion of red blood cells and protein into the urine
- renal vasoconstriction, especially of efferent arterioles
- increased filtration pressure
- relative stasis of blood in glomerular capillaries.

Collectively, these changes result in a degree of hypoxic damage to the nephron.

In addition to the above, there is also:

- decreased urine flow, mainly due to antidiuretic hormone (ADH) secretion.

Exercise-related renal impairment

Exercise-related renal impairment usually occurs as a result of dehydration. Exercise results in fluid losses of 1–2 L/hr, particularly in hot conditions. Replacement rarely matches this fluid loss, so a cascade of events may occur as depicted in Figure 52.1.

In some cases, overly aggressive fluid replacement during exercise, especially in events lasting over four hours, can result in hyponatremia. Prolonged exercise is known to cause non-osmotic release of ADH. The non-osmotic release of ADH in combination with salt loss from sweat and excessive fluid intake causes hyponatremia.

Hyponatremia occurs in slow athletes in long events. Up to 30% of long-distance runners may develop mild hyponatremia (serum sodium in range 125–135 mmol/L). This is usually asymptomatic, but more severe drops (below 120 mmol/L) can result in

cerebral edema, seizures, and even death. Until quite recently, sportspeople were encouraged to drink according to a predetermined schedule in endurance events. The obsessional sportspeople that rigorously stuck to these schedules were consequently at the greatest risk of developing hyponatremia.

Current expert opinion on hydration is based on the proceedings of the Second World Conference on Hyponatremia in 2007.[3] Recommendations suggest starting any event well hydrated, and drinking according to thirst rather than to a predetermined schedule (see also Chapter 58).

Rhabdomyolysis and myoglobinuria

Rhabdomyolysis is the most serious renal condition associated with exercise. It is characterized as "muscle cell meltdown."[4] As a consequence of the breakdown of muscle cells, plus increased glomerular permeability, myoglobin (an oxygen transport protein) leaks into the urine. Serious sequelae may occur; in some cases the condition is fatal. More commonly, acute renal failure with associated hyperkalemia may ensue. Acute compartment syndrome is another recognized complication.

Rhabdomyolysis is predictable to some degree. Recognized risk factors include unaccustomed extreme exertion, especially in the heat, where dehydration and hypovolemia are more common. Eccentric exercise is associated with greater damage to muscle fibers and Z bands, and in military reports the condition is referred to as the "squat jump syndrome." Viral illnesses, metabolic disorders (e.g. diabetes), and certain drugs (e.g. statins, diuretics), are associated with the condition. It is more common in sportspeople with the sickle cell trait.[5]

Awareness of the above risk factors can be used to guide training to ensure an orderly progressive introduction of any eccentric exercise. Repeated bouts of the same type of exercise provoke less damage than the first bout.

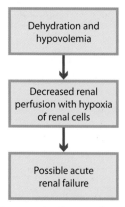

Figure 52.1 The cascade of events that can lead to renal impairment

Rhabdomyolysis is a potentially fatal condition, and requires hospital admission for close observation and active management.

Diagnosis relies on the history including risk factors listed above, plus examination findings which include marked tenderness of the affected muscle groups, and possibly hypovolemia. Signs of serious causes of exercise-related collapse include altered mental status, systolic blood pressure less than 100 mmHg, and heart rate greater then 100 bpm. The characteristic laboratory findings are of a grossly elevated serum creatine kinase (CK) level (over 10 000 IU/L) and myoglobin in the urine with a positive dipstick test.

Management consists of hospital admission, aggressive fluid replacement (4–11 L in the first 24 hours), cation exchange resins, forced diuresis, and careful alkalinization of the urine. Phosphate binders are also of benefit. In some cases, dialysis may be needed. Fasciotomy is indicated if associated compartment syndrome is present.

Other exercise-related renal impairment
Footstrike hemolysis
Hemoglobinuria may occur as a result of footstrike hemolysis when running, and also with karate. Solutions for runners include well cushioned shoes, use of viscoelastic inserts, and running on soft surfaces. Karate exponents may need to modify their training.

Athletic pseudonephritis
Gardner identified a condition he termed "athletic pseudonephritis."[6] Up to 20% of marathon runners presented with transient microhematuria and proteinuria. In football players, red blood cells were identified in post-match urine samples. Repeat urine testing a few days later usually shows resolution of any abnormality.

Abrasions of the bladder wall in long-distance runners
A seminal investigation by Blacklock in 1977 reported hematuria in long-distance runners.[7] Cystoscopy showed abrasions of the bladder wall around the trigone. The postulated mechanism of damage was repeated impact of the flaccid posterior bladder wall against the trigone. The observed time course was of recovery over several days. Preventive strategies include exercising with a partially full bladder, and attention to pre-exercise fluid intake.

Renal trauma
Renal trauma can occur from a direct blow in boxing or a collision sport such as Rugby Union. Running can also cause transmitted shock to the kidneys. Most renal trauma can be managed non-surgically, but damage to the pedicle requires urgent surgical treatment to restore an adequate blood supply to the kidney.[8]

Clinical approach to the athlete presenting with hematuria
The presence of blood in the urine is an alarming symptom for any sportsperson. When assessing a patient, ask about any recent trauma in the flank or urethral area, and any past history of renal stones. The sportsperson should be questioned about any recent sore throat that could be a precursor of poststreptococcal glomerulonephritis. On examination, look for evidence of edema or hypotension. Check for flank tenderness or evidence of urethral trauma. Investigations can usually be confined to urinalysis to check for cell casts and urine culture. No other investigations are required unless the clinical picture suggests it.

At follow-up two to three days from the first sighting of blood in the urine, in most cases the hematuria will have settled. This tends to suggest that the hematuria is related to a benign exercise-related cause (see above).

Further evaluation should be reserved for those with persistent urinary abnormalities or a suspicious history. Testing should aim to identify the site of bleeding and the nature of the pathology causing bleeding. Relevant investigations include renal ultrasound (or intravenous urography [IVU] in some circumstances), urine cytology, and cystoscopy.

The sportsperson with microscopic hematuria can resume normal activity. If macroscopic hematuria is present, the individual should rest until it clears. Management of renal disorders depends on the particular condition present. A discussion of management strategies is beyond the scope of this chapter.

Clinical approach to the sportsperson presenting with proteinuria
Proteinuria in sportspeople is typically picked up at a periodic medical screening examination. A small amount of proteinuria is normal (up to 200 mg/day). Dipstick testing usually registers "trace" proteinuria at urinary protein levels of 100 mg/L. Orthostatic proteinuria is common in patients below the age of 30 (i.e. the majority of those sportspeople having their first medical screening). If the protein:creatinine ratio is less than 0.2, and urinalysis is otherwise normal, then the diagnosis of orthostatic proteinuria is confirmed.[9]

With exercise, there is increased filtration of macro-molecules, especially albumin, and decreased tubular reabsorption of small molecular weight proteins. However, in most cases the proteinuria is transient, and resolves within four hours of stopping exercise. Standard protocols recommend a repeat urinalysis 24–48 hours later. If the urine still contains protein then a 24-hour urine should be collected for protein, creatine, and protein electrophoresis. Serum creatinine, urea, electrolytes, and glucose should be checked. If proteinuria exceeds 3 g/day, nephrology referral is indicated, as the likelihood of serious renal disease is high.

Lesser grades of exercise-related proteinuria are thought to be due to a variety of factors. These may include metabolic acidosis, some renal hypoxia, renal arteriole vasoconstriction, and loss of the negative charge on the glomerular membrane.[10] Proteinuria appears to be proportional to exercise intensity, and is more common with running than cycling or swimming at a given exercise intensity.[11]

Non-steroidal anti-inflammatory drugs (NSAIDs) and the kidney

The effects of NSAIDs on the kidney are outlined in the box below.

Exercise and the patient with renal impairment

People with varying degrees of renal impairment can benefit from exercise provided they adhere to a few simple rules:

- Firstly, depending on the degree of renal impairment, there will be some reduction in the homeostatic functions of the kidneys. The ability

---

Non-steroidal anti-inflammatory drugs (NSAIDs) and the kidney

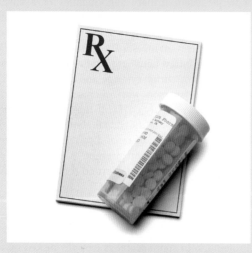

The renal effects of NSAIDs are often overlooked, but exercise can amplify them and cause clinical problems. NSAIDs inhibit prostaglandin synthesis. This in turn causes renal vasoconstriction, with reduced urine output, and salt and water retention. The sportsperson who becomes dehydrated and is taking NSAIDs is at special risk. The prostaglandin inhibition may abolish the normal protective vasodilatation of afferent arterioles and contribute to acute oliguric renal failure. In addition, there is potassium retention due to decreased plasma renin activity and decreased aldosterone.[12]

Rarely, NSAIDs can cause interstitial nephritis and the nephrotic syndrome. It can occur from 2–75 weeks after commencing the NSAID, and resolves up to one year after stopping it. There is no evidence that NSAIDs cause papillary necrosis, which is typically associated with phenacetin. Low-dose aspirin decreases platelet aggregation, and this could conceivably contribute to hematuria.

The counsel of perfection is to never use NSAIDs when exercising. The fact that NSAIDs are in widespread use by people who exercise, with *relatively* few serious adverse consequences, attests to their relative safety. However, the clinician should be mindful that, the longer and more intense the exercise bout, and the hotter the environmental conditions, the more risky it is to use NSAIDs when exercising.

 The risk of renal impairment following exercise is exacerbated by NSAID use. Risks are greater with prolonged or high-intensity exercise, both of which significantly compromise renal blood flow.

Any decision to use NSAIDs should be made by a well-informed sportsperson after discussion with their doctor, and will depend on the clinical scenario and a careful consideration of the benefits and risks. If NSAID use is justified, then a preparation with a short half-life (e.g. ibuprofen) is likely to be safer than one with a long half-life.

to excrete nitrogen and compensate for extremes decreases in proportion to the decline in renal function. We therefore advise against protein supplementation in any exercising individual with renal impairment.

- Secondly, as renal function decreases there may be associated hypertension. This needs good control, otherwise there will be an accelerated loss of the remaining functioning nephrons.
- Thirdly, with significant renal impairment there is a drop in erythropoietin production, which will result in anemia. This, in turn, will restrict exercise capacity.

Renal impairment reduces protein excretion and therefore we advise against protein supplementation in exercising individuals with this condition.

The most common cause of renal function decline is increase in age. Most organ systems, including the renal system, function at an optimal level in young adulthood (age 20–30 years). With each passing decade over 30 years there is approximately a 10% loss of function. Additional pathology such as hypertension or diabetes (type 1 or type 2) can accelerate this age-related decline. Collectively, these changes mean that the average 80-year-old has an estimated one-quarter of the renal function of a young adult.

Advanced renal disease is associated with fluid overload, electrolyte disturbances, muscle weakness, cardiac dysfunction, peripheral neuropathy, and renal osteodystrophy. Dialysis may ameliorate some of these, but the definitive treatment is renal transplantation.

Exercise for patients with renal transplantation

Most nephrologists encourage regular exercise after kidney transplantation. The Cleveland Clinic Foundation (CFC)[13] recommends warm-up stretches followed by aerobic activity that progressively increases in duration and intensity as physical capabilities improve. That foundation also suggests that more vigorous activities are followed by a proper cooldown. They counsel against exercising in extreme climatic conditions or in the presence of intercurrent illness. Chest pain, weakness, and lightheadedness are indications to stop exercising and rest.

Most transplant units encourage participation in a wide variety of sports but counsel against boxing, martial arts, and collision sports (e.g. rugby or American football).[14] There are reported cases of professional sportspeople in collision sports making a successful return to play, and these sportspeople are managed on a case-by-case basis in consultation with their nephrologist and transplant surgeon.

For sportspeople wishing to return to collision sports, the transplanted kidney should be placed in a less vulnerable position (e.g. up under the ribcage). Immunosuppressive drugs will need to be continued on a lifelong basis.

Similar to recommendations for exercise after kidney transplantation, traditional expert advice for individuals with one kidney has been to avoid contact (collision) sports.[15] However, more recent investigations indicate that individuals with one kidney have a low risk of further renal injury from contact sports and their restriction from play is unsupported by available evidence.[1] Patients' participation in contact sports remains a controversial issue and may be best determined by a thorough, individualized assessment.[2]

Prevention of renal complications of exercise

Most causes of exercise-related renal impairment are preventable. Simple measures that athletes can adopt to minimize their risk are listed in the box (below).

Prevention of renal complications of exercise

- Remain well hydrated from day to day. Know your "wet weight," particularly in hot weather, and regard any sudden weight loss as an indication of dehydration.
- Start any exercise bout well hydrated.
- During exercise, drink according to thirst.
- After exercise, drink freely in the first hour or two to replace fluids lost.
- Avoid anti-inflammatory drugs in the 48 hours prior to prolonged strenuous exercise.
- Weigh yourself daily.
- If you do not pass any urine in the 12 hours after an exercise bout, seek urgent medical advice.
- Do not ignore blood in the urine—it may have a serious cause.
- If traveling from a cool to a hot environment, acclimatize gradually to the conditions. Exercise initially in the coolest part of the day.
- If you exercise vigorously, do not restrict your salt intake.

D

Case study: Jonah Lomu

Jonah Lomu (Fig. 52.2) All Black international rugby player from New Zealand of Tongan descent developed nephrotic syndrome at the height of his career.

Despite treatment with immunosuppressive drugs, he developed progressive renal impairment with anemia. He received dialysis treatment, but developed severe peripheral neuropathy and had to stop playing rugby. Subsequently he received a live donor kidney transplant and the peripheral neuropathy resolved.

He was able to return to playing professional rugby and has been a very public supporter of initiatives to reduce the effect of kidney disease, particularly in children.

Figure 52.2 Jonah Lomu of New Zealand eludes an England player on his way to the tryline during the Rugby World Cup before he developed nephrotic syndrome

🌐 RECOMMENDED WEBSITES

Cleveland Clinic Foundation. Exercise guidelines after kidney transplant: http://my.clevelandclinic.org/services/Kidney_Transplantation/hic_Exercise_Guidelines_after_Kidney_Transplant.aspx

📄 RECOMMENDED READING

Poortmans JR. Exercise and renal function. *Sports Med* 1984;1:125–53

Rayner B, Schwellnus MP. Exercise and the kidney. In: Schwellnus M, ed. *Olympic textbook of medicine in sport.* London: Blackwell, 2008: 375–89

📑 REFERENCES

1. Grinsell MM, Showalter S, Gordon KA et al. Single kidney and sports participation: perception versus reality. *Pediatrics* 2006;118(3):1019–27.
2. Holmes FC, Hunt JJ, Sevier TL. Renal injury in sport. *Curr Sports Med Rep* 2003;2(2):103–9.
3. Hew-Butler T, Ayus JC, Kipps C et al. Statement of the Second International Exercise-Associated Hyponatremia Consensus Development Conference, New Zealand, 2007. *Clin J Sport Med* 2008;18(2):111–21.
4. Knochel J. Risks and benefits and myoglobinuria. *Semin Nephrol* 1981;18:75–86.
5. Eichner ER. Sickle cell trait in sports. *Curr Sports Med Rep* 2010;9(6):347–51.
6. Gardner KD, Jr. Athletic pseudonephritis; alteration of urine sediment by athletic competition. *J Am Med Assoc* 1956;161(17):1613–7.
7. Blacklock NJ. Bladder trauma in the long-distance runner: "10,000 metres haematuria." *Br J Urol* 1977;49(2):129–32.
8. Bernard JJ. Renal trauma: evaluation, management, and return to play. *Curr Sports Med Rep* 2009;8(2):98–103.
9. Batt M. Nephrology in sportspeople. In: Fields K, Fricker P, eds. *Medical problems in athletes.* Malden: Blackwell Science, 1997:209–15.
10. Rayner B. Exercise and the kidney. In: Schwellnus M, ed. *Olympic textbook of medicine in sport.* London: Blackwell, 2008:375–89.
11. Poortmans JR. Exercise and renal function. *Sports Med* 1984;1(2):125–53.
12. Walker RJ, Fawcett JP, Flannery EM et al. Indomethacin potentiates exercise-induced reduction in renal hemodynamics in athletes. *Med Sci Sports Exerc* 1994;26(11):1302–6.
13. Cleveland Clinic Foundation. Exercise guidelines after kidney transplant, 2009. Available: http://my.clevelandclinic.org/services/Kidney_Transplantation/hic_Exercise_Guidelines_after_Kidney_Transplant.aspx.
14. Heffernan A, Gill D. Sporting activity following kidney transplantation. *Pediatr Nephrol* 1998;12(6):447–8.
15. Dyment PG, Goldberg B, Haefele SB et al. American Academy of Pediatrics Committee on Sports Medicine. Recommendations for participation in competitive sports. *Pediatrics* 1988;81:737–9.

Chapter 53

Diabetes mellitus

with SANDY HOFFMANN, MATT HISLOP, and CAMERON STUART

It took me about 12 months to come to terms with diabetes. It was very frustrating. You want your body to do what you tell it to do.   Sir Stephen Redgrave, English rower who won his fifth Olympic gold medal in 2000, three years after being diagnosed with diabetes

In this chapter we examine two aspects of the relationship between diabetes mellitus and exercise:

- the adjustments the person with diabetes might make if he or she wishes to exercise
- short-term and long-term risks and benefits of exercise to the patient with diabetes.

British rower Sir Steven Redgrave (chapter opening quote) provides a remarkable story of sporting success despite having diabetes mellitus.[1] Many other athletes with diabetes have also been extremely successful: Jay Cutler, a National Football League (NFL) quarterback who was diagnosed with type 1 diabetes in 2008, continued his successful playing career.

There are two distinct types of diabetes mellitus—type 1 and type 2.

Types of diabetes

Type 1 diabetes

Type 1 diabetes, previously known as "juvenile-onset diabetes," is thought to be an inherited autoimmune disease in which antibodies are produced against the beta cells of the pancreas. This ultimately results in the absence of endogenous insulin production, which is the characteristic feature of type 1 diabetes.

The incidence of type 1 diabetes varies throughout the world but represents approximately 10–15% of diabetic cases in the Western world.

The onset commonly occurs in childhood and adolescence but can become symptomatic at any age. Insulin administration is essential to prevent ketosis, coma, and death. The aims of treatment are tight control of blood glucose levels and prevention of microvascular and macrovascular complications.

Type 2 diabetes

Type 2 diabetes, previously known as "maturity-onset" or "adult-onset" diabetes, is a disease of later onset, linked to both genetic and lifestyle factors. It is characterized by diminished insulin secretion relative to serum glucose levels, in conjunction with peripheral insulin resistance, both of which result in chronic hyperglycemia.

Approximately 90% of individuals with diabetes have type 2 diabetes and it is thought to affect 3–7% of people in Western countries. The prevalence of type 2 diabetes increases with age. The pathogenesis of type 2 diabetes remains unknown but it is believed to be a heterogeneous disorder with a strong genetic factor. Approximately 80% of individuals with type 2 diabetes are obese.

Type 2 diabetes is characterized by three major metabolic abnormalities:

- impairment in pancreatic beta cell insulin secretion in response to a glucose stimulus
- reduced sensitivity to the action of insulin in major organ systems such as muscle, liver, and adipose tissue
- excessive hepatic glucose production in the basal state.

Clinical perspective

Diagnosis

Both type 1 and type 2 diabetes are diagnosed by detection of a fasting (>8 hours) plasma glucose level that exceeds 7 mmol/L (126 mg/dL), a plasma glucose level greater than 11 mmol/L (200 mg/dL) at 2 hours after an oral glucose challenge (oral glucose tolerance test), a glycosylated HbA1c level of 6.5% or higher, or by the appearance of other classic symptoms of diabetes.[2]

Pre-exercise screening for people with diabetes

Prior to the commencement of, or an increase in the intensity of, an exercise program in patients with diabetes, a full clinical examination should be performed with particular attention to the potential sites of diabetic complications—the cardiovascular system, the feet, and the eyes.

Ideally patients should have reasonable diabetic control before considering exercise. Long-term diabetic control indicators such as glycosylated hemoglobin (HbA1c) and fructosamine allow an objective measure. The HbA1c level allows assessment of the diabetes control in the preceding two to three months, and fructosamine in the preceding three weeks. The actual levels of these markers that indicate reasonable control depend on the laboratory used.

The ideal HbA1c level for participating in competitive sports should be ≤7% for adults and ≤7.5% for adolescents. A blood glucose level diary should be kept, with measurements taken at variable times during the day. Fasting cholesterol and triglyceride levels should also be measured. Assessment of renal function measuring urea, creatinine, and electrolyte levels, and urinary protein excretion and creatinine clearance, should also be performed.

Examination should focus on:

- cardiovascular system—blood pressure including postural drop, heart, presence of carotid or renal bruits, peripheral pulses
- eyes—retinopathy, glaucoma, cataracts
- peripheral neuropathy—with emphasis on the feet.

Pre-exercise cardiac screening should be thorough. Ischemic heart disease is present in up to 50% of patients with type 2 diabetes at the time of diagnosis. Chest pain is not always present in diabetic patients because silent ischemia can occur secondary to autonomic neuropathy. Exercise stress testing should be performed if the patient:

- will be undergoing vigorous activity (heart rate >60% of maximum)
- has had type 2 diabetes for more than 10 years

- has had type 1 diabetes for more than 15 years
- is over 35 years of age
- has any coronary artery disease risk factors
- has any microvascular or macrovascular disease, or peripheral vascular disease.

Complications

Both type 1 and type 2 diabetes may result in complications that affect multiple end-organ systems. In particular, diabetes is associated with accelerated atherosclerosis formation, which results in the risk of acute myocardial infarction increasing by two to three times.[3] Peripheral arterial disease incidence is elevated dramatically and the risk of cerebral stroke doubles.

In addition, diabetes can cause retinopathy, nephropathy, and autonomic neuropathy (leading to complications 'such as impaired gastric emptying, altered sweating, and potential silent myocardial ischemia), all of which can have serious implications for exercise. The risk of such complications is associated with both the duration of the diabetes and the diabetic control.

Treatment

The treatment of both type 1 and type 2 diabetes focuses on the maintenance of near normal blood glucose levels. For those patients with type 1 diabetes, exogenous insulin is essential, in conjunction with management through diet and close monitoring of blood glucose levels.

In contrast, only patients with poorly controlled type 2 diabetes require insulin, the majority being managed with a combination of diet, exercise, and weight loss. If, however, this is not adequate, a patient with type 2 diabetes may require the use of oral hypoglycemic agents. These agents are used in preference to insulin—insulin being reserved only for patients in whom adequate control cannot be achieved.

For people with either type 1 or type 2 diabetes, a low-fat, carbohydrate-controlled diet with an emphasis on an increased intake of complex carbohydrates and reduced simple carbohydrates is recommended.

Pharmacotherapy in diabetes

Four principal types of insulin are available for patients with type 1 diabetes:

- rapid acting—very fast onset (within 5–15 minutes with a peak of action within 1 hour) and short duration (3–5 hours). Examples include insulin lispro, aspart, and glulisine

- short acting—rapid onset of action (within 30 minutes with peak of action between 2–3 hours) and longer duration (5–8 hours). Examples include regular insulin
- intermediate acting—slower onset (may take 1–2 hours with peak of action between 4–10 hours) and longer duration (6–18 hours). Examples include lente (Monotard), NPH, and Protophane
- long acting—slow onset (2+ hours with peak at 6–20 hours) and long duration (at least 24 hours) allowing a background level of insulin (e.g. ultralente). Insulin glargine and detimir are other long-acting insulins that are "peakless," with onset in about 1.5 hours and a maximum effect at 4–5 hours that is maintained for 17–24 hours.

Only patients with poorly controlled type 2 diabetes require insulin. If a trial of a healthy lifestyle for two to three months is unsuccessful in controlling the blood glucose level, oral agents can be used. Several classes of oral agents are available, each with different pharmacologic properties.[4] If weight continues to be lost while exercising, the dose may be reduced or even stopped. If an HbA1c of less than 7% is not achieved after three months of monotherapy, combination therapy should be considered.

Dietary management

The importance of a high-carbohydrate, low-fat diet for optimal diabetic control is now well established. Fortunately, this conforms to the guidelines for maximizing athletic performance.

Carbohydrate requirements for exercise vary considerably among individuals. People with diabetes should monitor their blood glucose levels to determine their carbohydrate needs before, during, and after exercise (Table 53.1).

Individuals vary considerably in their responses to exercise. Only blood glucose monitoring before, during, and after training determines individual needs. Table 53.1 should be used as a starting point or guide only.

Sportspeople involved in endurance events who are carbohydrate-loading prior to competition may need to increase their insulin dosage to cope with the increased carbohydrate intake. It is then important that carbohydrate is ingested before, during, and after the event.

Table 53.1 Adjustment of food intake recommended to permit the person with diabetes to exercise

Activity	Duration of exercise	Blood glucose level (mmol/L [mg/dL])	Adjustment
Low level	½ hour	<5.5 (<100)	10 g CHO (small serve fruit, bread, biscuits, yoghurt, or milk)
		>5.5 (>100)	No extra food
Moderate intensity	1 hour	<5.5 (<100)	20–30 g CHO (1.5–2 serves fruit, bread, biscuits, yoghurt, and/or milk)
		5.5–10 (100–180)	10 g CHO (small serve fruit, bread, biscuits, yoghurt, or milk)
		10–16.5 (180–300)	No extra food (in most cases)
		>16.5 (>300)	No extra food. Preferably do not exercise as blood glucose level may go up
Strenuous activity	1–2 hours	<5.5 (<100)	45–60 g CHO (1 sandwich and fruit, and/or milk or yoghurt)
		5.5–10 (100–180)	25–50 g CHO (½ sandwich and fruit, and/or milk or yoghurt)
		10–16.5 (180–300)	15 g CHO (1 serve fruit, bread, biscuits, yoghurt, or milk)
		>16.5 (>300)	Preferably do not exercise as blood glucose level may go up
Varying intensity	Long duration		Insulin may be decreased (conservatively estimate the decrease in insulin peaking at time of activity by 10%. A 50% reduction is not common)
	½–1 day		Increase carbohydrate before, during, and after activity 10–50 g CHO per hour, such as diluted fruit juice

CHO = carbohydrate

While it is advised that all insulin-dependent diabetic sportspeople seek individual counseling from appropriate clinicians to arrange a specific dietary and training program, there are some important points that all diabetic sportspeople should be aware of:

- Sportspeople need to learn the effects of different types of exercise, under different environmental conditions, on their blood glucose levels.
- It is important to always have carbohydrate foods available such as fruit, fruit juice, barley sugar, or biscuits.
- After vigorous exercise, blood glucose levels may continue to drop for a number of hours. It is important that carbohydrate is ingested when exercise is completed to ensure replenishment of glycogen stores and to prevent hypoglycemia.
- Diabetic sportspeople have similar micronutrient needs to non-diabetic sportspeople.[5] A sports nutritionist can assist in creating an eating plan that ensures adequate amounts of calcium, vitamin D, and micronutirents.

The box below can be used by patients as a reminder of dietary tips.

Exercise and diabetes

All clinicians engaged with a patient with diabetes should work together closely when considering exercise prescription for the diabetic patient. The target for an adult should be to achieve *at least* 30 minutes of continuous or intermittent moderate aerobic activity, equivalent to brisk walking, five or six days a week for a total of 150 minutes of aerobic activity per week.[6] Additionally, 2–3 sessions of resistance exercise per week should be included.[7,8] In long-standing diabetics, heart rate may be an unreliable indicator of exertion because of autonomic neuropathy, and the rating of perceived exertion scales may be more useful.

Although exercise in conjunction with a proper diet and medications is the cornerstone in the treatment of diabetes, special care must be taken in those taking insulin. Both insulin and exercise *independently* facilitate glucose transport across the mitochondrial membrane by promoting GLUT4 transporter proteins from intracellular vesicles.[9] The action of insulin and exercise is also *cumulative*. As such, an exercising type 1 diabetic will have lowered insulin requirements, and may notice up to a 30% reduction in insulin requirements with exercise. Importantly, in

For diabetic patients: important dietary points to consider when exercising

Before exercise	During exercise	After exercise
Know the effects of different types of exercise, and different environments, on your blood glucose level.	When exercising intermittently, ingest carbohydrates in between to control blood glucose levels.	After vigorous exercise, blood glucose levels may continue to drop. Ingest carbohydrate when exercise is complete to replenish glycogen stores.
Have quick-digesting carbohydrates available (e.g. barley sugar, fruit juice etc.).	Regular carbohydrate intake is usually necessary for long-duration exercise.	Alcohol consumption is discouraged after exercise as it dehydrates and lowers the blood glucose level.
Eat 1–2 hours prior to exercise to ensure ideal glucose levels.	Hydrate.	Hydrate.
Hydrate (dehydration can be confused with hypoglycemia).		
If insulin is injected prior to exercise, use a site away from the muscle group being exercised so that it is not metabolized too quickly.		

the person with type 1 diabetes, glycemic control may not be improved with regular exercise if changes in the individual's diet and insulin dosage do not appropriately match exercise requirements. In the absence of exercise, even for a few days, the increased insulin sensitivity begins to decline.

It is of extreme importance that those with diabetes monitor their blood glucose levels before and after every work-out. If the work-out is prolonged, or symptoms occur, the blood sugar level should also be taken during the exercise session. If no means exist to identify blood glucose levels before a work-out, then the work-out should be of short duration and low intensity with a glucose supply readily available.

Certain environmental conditions, such as extreme heat or strong winds, should be taken into consideration, as supplemental glucose may be required while exercising under such conditions. In contrast, if exercising when unwell or with a low-grade infection, glucose levels need to be monitored as relative hyperglycemia may occur.

All patients with diabetes should carry an identification card or bracelet identifying themselves as having diabetes. They should be educated to be alert to the early signs of hypoglycemia for up to 24 hours after exercise. It is essential that they carry glucose tablets or an alternative source of glucose with them at all times. Dehydration during exercise should be prevented by adequate fluid consumption. It is also recommended that the diabetic sportsperson exercise with somebody else, if possible, in case of adverse reactions.

Benefits of exercise

The benefits of exercise in type 1 diabetics include improved insulin sensitivity, improved blood lipids, decreased resting heart rate and blood pressure, decreased body weight, and possibly decreased risk of coronary heart disease.[10] In type I diabetes, exercise does not improve glycemic control *per se*, but it reduces the risk factors for development of cardiovascular disease.

It is well recognized that exercise reduces the risk of developing type 2 diabetes. There are also considerable benefits for those with type 2 diabetes.[11] A program of regular aerobic and resistance exercise can reverse many of the defects in metabolism of both fat and glucose that occur in people with type 2 diabetes; this will improve the HbA1c.[7]

Exercise and type 1 diabetes

Control of blood glucose is achieved in a patient with type 1 diabetes through a balance in the carbohydrate intake, exercise, and insulin dosage. The meal plan and insulin dosage should be adjusted according to the patient's response to exercise. A degree of trial and error is necessary for people with type 1 diabetes taking up new activities. Frequent self-monitoring should occur, at least until a balance is achieved among diet, exercise, and insulin parameters. The ideal pre-exercise blood level is 6.6–10 mmol/L (120–180 mg/dL).[4] Sportspeople who have blood glucose concentrations exceeding 11 mmol/L (200 mg/dL) and ketones in their urine, or a blood glucose level of more than 16.5 mmol/L (300 mg/dL) regardless of ketone status, should postpone exercise and take supplemental insulin. Those with blood glucose levels less than 5.5 mmol/L (100 mg/dL) require a pre-exercise carbohydrate snack (e.g. sports drink, juice, glucose tablet, fruit).

Exercise of 20–30 minutes at less than 70% VO_2max (e.g. walking, golf, table tennis) requires a rapidly absorbable carbohydrate (15 g fruit exchange or 60 calories) before exercise, but needs minimal insulin dosing adjustments.

More vigorous activity of less than 1 hour (e.g. jogging, swimming, cycling, skiing, tennis) often requires a 25% reduction in pre-exercise insulin and 15–30 g of rapidly absorbed carbohydrate before and every 30 minutes after the onset of activity.

Strenuous activity of longer than 1 hour (e.g. marathon running, triathlon, cross-country skiing) may require a 30–80% reduction in pre-exercise insulin and ingestion of two fruit exchanges (30 g or 100–120 calories) every 30 minutes.

If early morning activity is to be performed, the basal insulin from the evening dose of intermediate-acting insulin may need to be reduced by 20–50%. The morning regular-acting insulin dose may also need to be reduced by 30–50% before breakfast, or even omitted if exercise is performed before food. Depending on the intensity and duration of the initial activity and likelihood of further activity, a reduction of 30–50% may be needed with each subsequent meal.

Post-exercise hyperglycemia will occur, especially after high-intensity, short-burst activity,[12] but insulin should still be decreased by 25–50% (because insulin sensitivity is increased for 12–15 hours after activity has ceased). Consuming carbohydrates within 30 minutes of exhaustive, glycogen-depleting exercise allows for more efficient restoration of muscle glycogen. This will also help prevent post-exercise, late-onset hypoglycemia, which can occur up to 24 hours following such exercise.

If exercise is unexpected, insulin adjustment may be impossible. Instead, supplementation with 20–30 g of carbohydrate, at the onset of exercise and every 30 minutes thereafter, may prevent hypoglycemia. In elite sportspeople and with intense bouts of exercise, reductions in insulin dosage may be even higher than those listed above. During periods of inactivity (e.g. holidays, recovery from injury), increased insulin requirements are to be expected.

A practical guide for patients with diabetes is shown in the box overleaf.

Exercise and type 2 diabetes

Those patients with type 2 diabetes who are managed with diet therapy alone do not usually need to make any adjustments for exercise.

Patients taking oral hypoglycemic drugs may need to halve their doses on days of prolonged exercise or withhold them altogether, depending on their blood glucose levels. They are also advised to carry some glucose with them and to be able to recognize the symptoms of hypoglycemia. Hypoglycemia is a particular risk in those people with diabetes taking sulfonylureas due to their long half-lives and increased endogenous insulin production.

Diabetes and competition

Every diabetic sportsperson should develop an individual diabetes care plan for both training and competition.[13] As competition may require interstate travel and altered eating patterns, the diabetic sportsperson should practice the match day routine at home and have snacks available as necessary. Good control of blood glucose levels may require regular access to carbohydrate-containing drinks. This not only serves to improve the glucose profile but also aids rehydration during prolonged exercise.

Diabetes and travel

A physician's letter should accompany diabetic travelers stating that they carry insulin, needles, and blood glucose testing equipment. Copies of prescriptions should be taken, with medications in their original packaging. Insulin should not be packed into checked luggage as there is a risk of it being misplaced, and freezing and thawing in the luggage hold. Insulin will generally keep for a month at room temperature. Additional supplies should include those needed to treat hypoglycemia (including snacks), supplies for urine or blood ketone testing, a sharps container for used needles, and spare batteries and parts for meters and pumps. General recommendations for travel can be reviewed at several websites.[14]

Traveling in a north–south direction generally requires no alteration to insulin doses. East to west travel of more than five hours generally requires insulin dose adjustment. East-bound travel results in a shorter day, and west-bound travel a longer one. Travelers should check blood glucose levels at least every six hours on the flight. Omitting long-acting insulin for the flight duration and using quick-acting insulin approximately every six hours around average meal times is one technique. Once at the destination, quick-acting insulin is used until bedtime, when long-acting insulin is recommenced. Continuous insulin pumps usually require no adjustment, with the pump's clock being adjusted to the destination time on arrival.

High-risk sports

Diabetic patients are at increased risk of complications while participating in high-risk sports. Hypoglycemic attacks, characterized by inattention or lack of concentration, in sports such as rock and mountain climbing and skydiving have the potential for serious if not fatal injury.

The suitability of scuba diving for diabetics has been studied. Military diving is not allowed in Great Britain for those with type 1 diabetes, and in the US, people with diabetes cannot join the military at all.[9] Scuba diving may be safe with adequate preparation and a skilled partner who can handle trouble with diabetes during the dive.

Exercise and the complications of diabetes

Exercise is often neglected when the secondary complications of diabetes occur. Some unique concerns for the patient with diabetes that warrant close scrutiny include autonomic and peripheral neuropathy, retinopathy, and nephropathy.

Autonomic neuropathy

Abnormal autonomic function is common among those with diabetes of long duration. The risks of exercise when autonomic neuropathy is present include hypoglycemia, abnormal heart rate and blood pressure responses (e.g. postural drop), impaired

Do you have diabetes? Practical tips for a patient starting a physical activity program

Preparation

It is very important prior to exercise that a full assessment by a healthcare professional is performed to identify possible risks associated with diabetes while exercising. Special attention should be paid to understanding how your body and blood glucose levels respond to different types of physical activity. Previously sedentary individuals are recommended to gradually build into an exercise regime.

Nutrition

- Exercise 1–2 hours after eating a meal to ensure ideal glucose level during activity.
- Hydration before, during, and after exercise is important as dehydration can be confused with hypoglycemia.
- Have fast-acting carbohydrates (food/fluid) accessible during and immediately after exercise.
- Generally, carbohydrates should be ingested following exercise, but depending on the intensity and duration, adjustments may be required (Table 53.1 outlines a general guide for blood glucose adjustments, but it is advised that individual blood glucose is tested before, during, and after to identify personal nutrition needs):
  - short-burst high-intensity—carbohydrate may not be necessary after exercise as glucose production may exceed uptake
  - endurance or intermittent exercise—carbohydrate should be consumed before, during, and after. Be sure to understand personal insulin requirements when ingesting more carbohydrate than usual (i.e. "carb" loading prior to an event).

Insulin and blood glucose monitoring

- Individuals differ greatly in their insulin requirements. Duration and intensity of exercise, as well as type of diabetes, should all be considered. A personal protocol should be developed with a healthcare professional; this can be modified based on experience and consistency of exercise. If possible, avoid injecting insulin into the body part that will be exercised.
- Monitor blood glucose before, during, and immediately after exercising.

- Additional blood glucose monitoring 4–6 hours after aerobic exercise should be performed to monitor for low blood sugar (hypoglycemia).

Physical activity/exercise

A combination of aerobic and resistance exercises provides the most benefit to those with diabetes.

A healthcare professional and exercise specialist will be able to tailor a program to suit each individual, but general recommendations follow.

- Aerobic
  - A minimum of 150 minutes per week (spread over at least 3 days) of moderate to vigorous aerobic exercise. Exercise may be split into smaller time increments (3×10 minutes compared to 30 minutes continuous).

Intensity	Example
Moderate—50–70% of maximum heart rate	Biking, walking, swimming, dancing, water aerobics
Vigorous— >70% of maximum heart rate	Jogging, aerobics, hockey, basketball, hiking

- Resistance
  - Resistance exercise 2–3 times per week has been proven to improve insulin sensitivity and glycemic control (see Figures 53.1 and 53.2 for examples).
  - Initial instruction and periodic supervision by an exercise specialist is recommended.

Progression	Exercises
2–3 times per week[a]	Shoulder press
• Start with 1 set/10–12 reps with moderate weight	Bicep curls
	Push-ups
• Progress to 2 sets/10–12 reps	Leg press
• Progress to 3 sets/8–10 reps with heavier weight	Knee extension
	Hamstring curl

[a]Physical activity and diabetes, Canadian Diabetes Association, 2008

Figure 53.1 Shoulder press

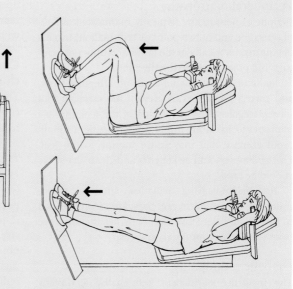

Figure 53.2 Leg press

Things to bring/wear

- Insulin medication
- Fast-digesting carbohydrates (e.g. fruit, barley sugar, biscuits, sport drinks)
- Medical ID bracelet
- Water
- Glucose monitor
- Comfortable shoes and socks

Sticking with it for health!

Some people find it very difficult to incorporate exercise into their daily lives. Below are a few techniques to help adhere to your lifestyle changes:

- Exercise with a friend or partner.
- Educate yourself about diabetes and know the benefits associated with physical activity and proper nutrition.
- Search out community exercise programs or exercise counseling.
- Vary the activities to keep it interesting.

Beware! Signs of hypoglycemia

- Headache
- Sweating
- Confusion (can be severe)
- Nervousness
- Tremors
- Hunger
- Loss of consciousness (severe cases)
- Abnormal behavior
- Convulsions

- Focus on regular physical activity rather than intense exercise episodes to avoid frustration.

Other things to consider

Be sure to take all factors into account when exercising and adjust accordingly. This may include environment temperature, exercise duration, and intensity of activity.

- Monitor blood sugars frequently.
- Most important, have fun!

sympathetic and parasympathetic nervous system activity, and abnormal thermoregulation.

Patients with autonomic neuropathy are at high risk of developing complications during exercise. Sudden death and myocardial infarction have been attributed to autonomic neuropathy and diabetes.

In diabetic patients with autonomic neuropathy, high-intensity activity should be avoided, as should rapid changes in body position and extremes in temperature. Water activities and stationary cycling are recommended.

Peripheral neuropathy

Peripheral neuropathy (typically manifested as loss of sensation and of two-point discrimination) usually begins symmetrically in the lower and upper extremities and progresses proximally.

Podiatric review should occur on a regular basis, and correct footwear can prevent the onset of foot ulcers. Regular close inspection of the feet and use of proper footwear are important. The patient should avoid exercise that may cause trauma to the feet. Feet and toes should be kept dry and clean, dry socks should be used.

Non-weight-bearing activities, such as swimming, cycling, and arm exercises, are recommended in those with insensitive feet. Activities that improve balance are also appropriate choices.

Diabetic retinopathy

The incidence of diabetic retinopathy is directly proportional to the severity and duration of the diabetes—98% of cases of type 1 and 78% of type 2 diabetes will progress to detectable retinopathy in 15 years from the diagnosis. Exercise that increases blood pressure may worsen retinopathy. Therefore, patients with proliferative retinopathy should avoid exercise that increases systolic blood pressures to 170 mmHg, and prolonged Valsalva-like activities. Exercise that results in a large increase in systolic pressure (such as weightlifting) can cause retinal hemorrhage.

Exercise for these patients could include stationary cycling, walking, and swimming. If possible, blood pressure should be monitored during the exercise program. Exercise is contraindicated if the individual has had recent photocoagulation treatment or surgery. Jarring of the head in contact sports may cause detachment of the retina.

Diabetic nephropathy can be classified according to urinary albumin excretion rates— <20 µg/min (normoalbuminuria); 20–200 µg/min (microalbuminuria); >200 µg/min (overt nephropathy).

Patients with microalbuminuria and overt renal disease should undertake light-to-moderate exercise only. Vigorous exercise that results in marked changes in hemodynamics should be avoided. This includes lifting heavy weights and high-intensity aerobic activities. Activities that are weight-bearing yet low impact are preferable.

Renal patients should be fully evaluated before commencing an exercise program. Fluid replacement is extremely important in these patients.

Specific training programs for patients undergoing hemodialysis should be developed in conjunction with a nephrologist.

Complications of exercise in the diabetic sportsperson

The diabetic sportsperson may suffer numerous complications associated with exercise, including hypoglycemia and ketoacidosis.

Hypoglycemia

Hypoglycemia (blood glucose level <3.6 mmol/L [<65 mg/dL]) is the major concern among sportspeople with type 1 diabetes[15] and has been shown to impair sports skill performance. The use of excessive exogenous insulin will prevent hepatic glucose production, and cause increased glucose uptake into skeletal muscle with a subsequent risk of exercise-induced hypoglycemia.

After exercise there is increased insulin sensitivity and reduced glycogen stores, and excess insulin will increase the risk of post-exercise hypoglycemia. Post-exercise hypoglycemia can occur up to 4 hours after exercise, and delayed-onset hypoglycemia up to 24 hours after exercise. The effects are commonly nocturnal with disturbed sleep patterns, altered recovery, and impaired performance the following day.

The initial symptoms of hypoglycemia include sweating, headache, nervousness, tremor, and hunger. The symptoms of impending hypoglycemia may be difficult to differentiate from symptoms experienced during vigorous exercise. If the hypoglycemia is not corrected, confusion, abnormal behavior, loss of consciousness, and convulsions may occur.

At the first indication of hypoglycemia, the sportsperson should ingest oral carbohydrate in solid or liquid form. Diabetic sportspeople should carry quickly digestible forms of carbohydrate (e.g. glucose tablets, barley sugar) or have a glucose–electrolyte solution available. The semiconscious or unconscious diabetic patient requires urgent intravenous glucose administration (50 mL of 50% solution) or glucagon injection.

Nocturnal hypoglycemia may occur following late afternoon or evening training or competition. Symptoms may include night sweats, unpleasant dreams, and early morning headaches.

Prevention of hypoglycemia depends on adjustment of the carbohydrate intake and insulin dosage to meet the individual sportsperson's needs, as discussed above. A continual source of glucose must be available during exercise and, as a rule of thumb, sportspeople usually require 15–30 g of glucose per half hour of vigorous exercise. Nocturnal hypoglycemia may be prevented by exercising earlier in the day, reducing the evening insulin dose,[16] or by consuming a complex carbohydrate prior to going to bed.

Diabetic ketoacidosis in the sportsperson

Despite increased glucose uptake that occurs in exercise independent of insulin, a relative deficiency of insulin can lead to hyperglycemia, and possible diabetic ketoacidosis. Individuals with blood glucose levels of 20–25 mmol/L (364–455 mg/dL) and above are especially at risk of precipitating diabetic ketoacidosis if they exercise vigorously. This occurs because the counter-regulatory hormone response (glucagon, catecholamines, growth hormone, and glucocorticoids) to exercise pushes the glucose levels higher and there is insufficient insulin to prevent ketosis. Therefore, a sportsperson must be aware of his or her glucose control before exercise. In addition, sportspeople with so-called brittle diabetes must be very cautious in reducing their insulin dose before exercise.

The presence of ketones in the urine confirms the presence of hypoinsulinemia and thus increases the risk of hyperglycemia and ketosis. Hyperglycemia may manifest as poor concentration, dehydration, or even under-performance, and sportspeople need to be aware of these signs. If the blood glucose level is >17 mmol/L (>309 mg/dL), or >14 mmol/L (255 mg/dL) with the presence of ketones on urinalysis, then exercise should be avoided until insulin has been administered and metabolic control is re-established. Sportspeople should not exercise as a way to control high blood glucose levels.

Musculoskeletal manifestations of diabetes

A number of musculoskeletal disorders are found in a higher prevalence in diabetic patients compared with the normal population.[17] The diagnosis of diabetes should always be considered in the patient presenting with the conditions listed below; the prevalence of these is summarized in Table 53.2 overleaf.

Frozen shoulder (adhesive capsulitis)

Frozen shoulder (adhesive capsulitis)[18, 19] appears at a younger age and is usually less painful in patients with diabetes. It is associated with the duration

of diabetes and with age. The use of corticosteroid injections may increase blood sugar levels in people with diabetes over the 24–48 hour period after the injection.

Achilles tendinopathy

Structural changes in the Achilles tendon due to glycation may contribute to pain; they are also postulated to cause biomechanical changes that are a precursor to development of foot problems such as diabetic pressure ulcers.[20]

Limited joint mobility

Limited joint mobility is also known as "diabetic cheiroarthropathy." It is characterized by thick, tight, waxy skin, mainly on the dorsal aspect of the hands, with flexion deformities of the metacarpophalangeal and interphalangeal joints.[21] In the early stages paresthesias and mild pain may develop with symptoms increasing slowly. Treatment consists of optimizing diabetic control and individualized hand therapy.

Dupuytren's contracture

Dupuytren's contracture is characterized by palmar or digital thickening, tethering, or contracture of the hands. In diabetics the ring and middle finger are more commonly affected, compared with the fifth finger in non-diabetics.[18, 19] Treatment consists of optimizing glycemic control, physiotherapy, and surgery if severe.

Carpal tunnel syndrome

Carpal tunnel syndrome has a prevalence of 11–16% in patients with diabetes.[18, 19]

 As 5–8% of patients with carpal tunnel syndrome have diabetes, the clinician should consider this diagnosis and test for it.

Flexor tenosynovitis

Fibrous tissue proliferation in the tendon sheath leads to limitation of the normal movement of the tendon. It is associated with the duration of diabetes, but not age.[18, 19] A corticosteroid injection is often curative.

Complex regional pain syndrome type 1

Complex regional pain syndrome type 1 is characterized by continuing pain out of proportion to stimuli and vasomotor dysfunction. As well as diabetes, other predisposing conditions include hyperthyroidism, hyperparathyroidism, and type IV hyperlipidemia.[22]

Diffuse idiopathic skeletal hyperostosis (DISH)

Diffuse idiopathic skeletal hyperostosis (DISH) is characterized by new bone formation, particularly in the thoracolumbar spine. New bone appears to flow from one vertebra to the next, and is more prominent on the right side of the thoracic vertebra. Ossification of ligaments and tendons can occur elsewhere, including the skull, pelvis, heels, and elbows. Of patients with DISH 12–80% have diabetes or impaired glucose tolerance.[23] Management consists of education, diabetic control, and physiotherapy.

Neuropathic (Charcot's) joints

Neuropathic (Charcot's) joints[24] result from diabetic peripheral neuropathy and are seen usually in patients over 50 years of age who have had diabetes for many years. The joints affected are weight-bearing joints. Management includes optimizing glycemic control, regular foot care and review, and occasionally surgery.

Diabetic amyotrophy

Diabetic amyotrophy[25] is distinct from other forms of diabetic neuropathy and is characterized by muscle weakness/wasting and by diffuse, proximal lower limb muscle pain, and asymmetrical loss of tendon jerks. The shoulder girdle may be affected but less commonly. It occurs most often in older men with type 2 diabetes and is a diagnosis of exclusion (sinister causes must be sought). Management consists of stabilizing glycemic control and physiotherapy.

Conclusion

The sportsperson with diabetes needs to have a good understanding of the effects of exercise on blood glucose levels. With regular monitoring and appropriate adjustments to medications, insulin dosing, and carbohydrate intake, the sportsperson with diabetes should be able to develop a diabetes care plan and participate fully in sporting activities.

Table 53.2 Prevalence of musculoskeletal disorders in patients with and without diabetes[10]

Musculoskeletal disorder	With diabetes	Without diabetes
Frozen shoulder (adhesive capsulitis)	11–30%	2–10%
Limited joint mobility	8–50%	0–26%
Dupuytren's contracture	20–63%	13%
Carpal tunnel syndrome	11–16%	0.125%
Flexor tenosynovitis	11%	<1%
Diffuse idiopathic skeletal hyperostosis (DISH)	13–49%	1.6–13%

📑 REFERENCES

1. Gallen IW, Redgrave A, Redgrave S. Olympic diabetes. *Clin Med* 2003;3(4):333–7.

2. American Diabetes Association. Diagnosis and classification of diabetes mellitus. *Diabetes Care* 2010; 33 Suppl 1:S62–9.

3. Garcia M, McNamara P, Gordon T et al. Morbidity and mortality in diabetes in the Framingham population. A sixteen year follow up study. *Diabetes Care* 1974;23: 105–11.

4. MacKnight JM, Mistry DJ, Pastors JG et al. The daily management of athletes with diabetes. *Clin Sports Med* 2009;28(3):479–95.

5. Colberg S. *The diabetic athlete*. Champaign, IL: Human Kinetics, 2001.

6. Haskell W, Lee I, Pate R et al. Physical activity and public health: updated recommendations for adults from the American College of Sports Medicine and the American Heart Association. *Med Sci Sports Exerc* 2007;39(8):1423–34.

7. Sigal RJ, Kenny GP, Boule NG et al. Effects of aerobic training, resistance training, or both on glycemic control in type 2 diabetes—a randomized trial. *Ann Intern Med* 2007;147(6):357–69.

8. Church TS, Blair SN, Cocreham S et al. Effects of aerobic and resistance training on hemoglobin A(1c) levels in patients with type 2 diabetes—a randomized controlled trial. *JAMA* 2010;304(20):2253–62.

9. Wang Y, Simar D, Fiatarone Singh MA. Adaptations to exercise training within skeletal muscle in adults with type 2 diabetes or impaired glucose tolerance: a systematic review. *Diabetes Metab Res Rev* 2009;25(1):13–40.

10. Peirce NS. Diabetes and exercise. *Br J Sports Med* 1999;33(3):161–72.

11. American College of Sports Medicine and the American Diabetes Association: joint position statement. Exercise and type 2 diabetes. *Med Sci Sports Exerc* 2010;42(12):2282–303.

12. Guelfi K, Jones T, Fournier P. New insights into managing the risk of hypoglycemia associated with intermittent high-intensity exercise in individuals with type 1 diabetes mellitus: implications for existing guidelines. *Sports Med* 2007;37:937–46.

13. Jimenez C, Corcoran M, Crawley J et al. National Athletic Trainers' Association: position statement. Management of the athlete with type 1 diabetes mellitus. *J Athl Train* 2007;42(4):536–45.

14. American Diabetes Association. Traveling with diabetes supplies, http://www.diabetes.org/assets/pdfs/ know-your-rights/public-accommodations/fact-sheet- tsa-12-2010.pdf.

15. Kirk SE. Hypoglycemia in athletes with diabetes. *Clin Sports Med* 2009;28(3):455–68.

16. Taplin CE, Cobry E, Messer L et al. Preventing post- exercise nocturnal hypoglycemia in children with type 1 diabetes. *J Pediatr* 2010;157(5):784–8.e1.

17. Smith LL, Burnet SP, McNeil JN. Musculoskeletal manifestations of diabetes mellitus. *Br J Sports Med* 2003;37(1):30–5.

18. Fitzgibbons PG, Weiss APC. Hand manifestations of diabetes mellitus. *J Hand Surg Am* 2008;33A(5):771–5.

19. Chammas M, Bousquet P, Renard E et al. Dupuytren's disease, carpal tunnel syndrome, trigger finger, and diabetes mellitus. *J Hand Surg Am* 1995;20A(1):109–14.

20. Batista F, Nery C, Pinzur M et al. Achilles tendinopathy in diabetes mellitus. *Foot Ankle Int* 2008;29(5): 498–501.

21. Buckingham BA, Uitto J, Sandborg C et al. Scleroderma-like changes in insulin-dependent diabetes mellitus: clinical and biochemical studies. *Diabetes Care* 1984;7(2):163–9.

22. Marshall AT, Crisp AJ. Reflex sympathetic dystrophy. *Rheumatology* 2000;39(7):692–5.

23. Forgacs SS. Diabetes mellitus and rheumatic disease. *Clin Rheum Dis* 1986;12(3):729–53.

24. Bayne O, Lu EJ. Diabetic Charcot's arthropathy of the wrist: case report and literature review. *Clin Orthop Rel Res* 1998;357:122–6.

25. Sander HW, Chokroverty S. Diabetic amyotrophy: current concepts. *Semin Neurol* 1996;16(2):173–8.

D

Chapter 54

Exercise to treat neurological diseases and improve mental health

with PAUL McCRORY and TERESA LIU-AMBROSE

I just came to the end of my hope. I felt depressed and I cut myself with scissors and I got desperate for things to go right for once. Everything in my life at the time was wrong. When you're in it, you don't see a way out. Kelly Holmes, before becoming the Olympic 800 m and 1500 m champion

The role of exercise and physical activity as a means of either preventing or treating neurological disease has received little interest from physicians in spite of decades of research showing clear benefits to this treatment approach. Some areas, such as stroke and depression, are well studied whereas other areas, such as multiple sclerosis, have lower levels of evidence (see Chapter 3 for levels of evidence). Unfortunately, as is also the case in other areas of clinical care, exercise is underprescribed for neurological conditions and for those with impaired mental health.

In this chapter we discuss exercise prescription in stroke, Parkinson's disease, multiple sclerosis, cognitive impairment/dementia and epilepsy, as well as in depression and anxiety. Also refer to Chapter 1 to review the importance of exercise for health and Chapter 16 for more instruction as to how to prescribe exercise.

> ### The ACSM physical activity guidelines— an appropriate foundation
>
> The population health physical activity guidelines of approximately 150 minutes per week of aerobic activity and one to two sessions of strength-based training are an appropriate foundation for patients with all the conditions discussed in this chapter. Flexibility and functional training (e.g. balance, transfers) are also important. Determining the correct type of aerobic activity (e.g. walking, arm cycling, water exercises) will depend on the neurological deficit and other factors such as balance.

Stroke

Stroke is a condition characterized by rapidly developing neurological symptoms that last for more than 24 hours or lead to death, with no apparent cause other than that of vascular origin. The two main causes of stroke are brain infarction (which is thromboembolic) and hemorrhage.

Effects of physical activity on stroke mortality

Physically active men and women have a 25–30% reduced risk of stroke when compared with inactive men and women. Various physical activities provide benefits—leisure time activity, occupational movement, and walking. The benefits are not influenced by age or gender.

Key data come from observational studies as well as two meta-analyses of physical activity and stroke.[1, 2] The magnitude of the effect of those studies is shown in Table 54.1. The beneficial effects of higher levels of occupational physical activity are similar in extent to those seen in general physical activities, such as walking.

Table 54.1 Dose-response for the benefit of exercise in stroke. Relative risks below 1.0 reflect relative protection against stroke

Median relative risk—all strokes	Men	Women
Moderate activity vs no/light activity	0.65	0.82
High activity vs no/light activity	0.72	0.72

Because the incidence of stroke is low for those younger than age 55 years, very few reports are available on the relation between physical activity and stroke morbidity or mortality in younger and middle-aged populations.

Effect of physical activity in the treatment of stroke patients

Once stroke patients have gone through the initial period of acute hospitalization and subsequent inpatient/outpatient rehabilitation, their transition to home or community care can be improved through exercise to improve fitness and function, and by prescribing physical activity. Hospitalization generally causes deconditioning, and the "rehabilitation," while improving function, is usually lacking in aerobic intensity. In part, this may relate to the fear of causing further cerebrovascular problems and, to date, only a small number of studies have adequately addressed this issue.[3-5]

Greater aerobic fitness, muscle strength, and physical endurance improve functional abilities such as walking. Treadmill and cycle training have also proven effective in this regard. An additional and important benefit of fitness training is improved self-confidence and general wellbeing. Increased endurance also seems to give individuals more confidence and energy to improve other activities as well.

What exercise or physical activity program should be used?

The ACSM physical activity guidelines (see box on page 1082 and also Chapter 60) apply to patients with stroke. Table 54.2 summarizes this basic exercise prescription.

Note that some medications will affect an individual's ability to exercise, particularly in hot environments. Similarly, many patients with stroke also have cardiac and/or vascular comorbidities that may influence the exercise prescription. A cardiological clearance may be necessary.

Parkinson's disease

Parkinson's disease is a degenerative neurological condition characterized by tremor, muscular rigidity, bradykinesia, gait impairment, and impaired postural reflexes. The physical features usually develop unilaterally and progress steadily. In late stages of the disease, patients develop a postural change (kyphoscoliosis) and fixed hip flexion, which further impairs their gait and balance difficulties. They may also experience motor fluctuations, depression, and dementia (30%). The prevalence of Parkinson's disease is approximately 0.2% of the population; it is more common in the elderly.

Physical activity is critical to the wellbeing of patients and should be introduced in the early stages of the disease. Patients are recommended to follow the general physical activity guidelines (see box on page 1082) and particularly focus on balance and strength exercises to prevent falls. Because physical inactivity is common and reduces fitness and functional capacity, exercise prescription is essential.

Does physical activity prevent the onset of Parkinson's disease?

No published studies have examined specifically whether physical activity prevents the onset of Parkinson's disease, although there is a trend toward a lower risk of developing Parkinson's disease among those with high levels of physical activity.[6]

Does physical activity reduce symptoms of Parkinson's disease?

Only a few studies have examined the physical capacity of patients with Parkinson's disease.[7, 8] Patients with mild to moderate Parkinson's disease usually have normal physiological fitness parameters and the standard Parkinson's disease therapy with levodopa improves functional muscular activity in patients. The overall findings of various studies suggest that physical capacity and activities of daily

Table 54.2 Guidelines for exercise prescription in patients with stroke, Parkinson's disease or multiple sclerosis

Type of exercise	Minimum length of program	Intensity	Frequency	Time
Aerobic	4 months	Moderate-vigorous 60–80% HR$_{max}$ Borg RPE 13–15	2–5 days/week	10–60 mins/ session
Strength	4 months	Start with 50% RM Borg RPE 9–11	1–5	1–3 sets 7–10 reps

HR$_{max}$ = maximum heart rate; RM = repetition max; RPE = rating of perceived exertion

living functions benefit from regular physical exercise. Surprisingly, some studies have also found that exercise training assists patients to manage dyskinesias (a complication of levodopa therapy) and stabilize autonomic dysfunction in mild to moderate Parkinson's disease.

No adverse events related to the exercise exposure in people with Parkinson's disease have occurred in the various published controlled studies. Only one study examined high-force eccentric resistance exercise in Parkinson's disease and did not find evidence of muscle damage.[9]

What exercise or physical activity program should be used?

The ACSM physical activity guidelines (see the box on page 1082, and also Chapter 60) apply to patients with Parkinson's disease. Table 54.2 summarizes this basic exercise prescription.

Parkinson's disease medication affects an individual's ability to exercise, particularly in hot environments. Many patients with Parkinson's disease also have cardiac and/or vascular comorbidities that may influence the exercise prescription. A cardiological clearance may be necessary. In the latter stages of Parkinson's disease, the risk of falling increases and orthostatic hypotension may occur. This may necessitate modification of the type of aerobic exercise prescribed. Strength and balance training reduces falls in healthy seniors and in those with previous falls;[10] however, we know of no study that has shown that patients with PD can prevent falls with exercise training.

Multiple sclerosis

Multiple sclerosis is a lifelong chronic demyelinating disease of the central nervous system that is thought largely to be an autoimmune response of the body triggered by an unknown factor that results in an immune-mediated attack on the myelin sheath around nerve fibers. These attacks occur intermittently and variably. They result in a gradual accumulation of damage to the nervous system and resultant functional impairment. It is more common in the young (20–40 years), females, and also more common with increasing distance from the equator. The incidence is approximately 5 per 100 000 of the population with substantial regional variation. Medical treatment reduces the frequency and severity of attacks.

Developing and maintaining muscle activity, strength, and aerobic fitness are just as important for people with multiple sclerosis as for healthy people. As the disease progresses over time, the need for improved functional capacity increases. After 15 years, 50% of patients with multiple sclerosis will require a walking aid to walk 100 meters; after 25 years, 50% will be confined to a wheelchair. There is strong evidence that exercise improves muscle function, aerobic fitness, mobility, and quality of life. The difficulty is that many patients with multiple sclerosis will have reduced aerobic capacity for a variety of reasons.

Does physical activity prevent the onset of multiple sclerosis or cause exacerbations?

No published studies have examined whether multiple sclerosis can be prevented with exercise. A recent review of studies of exercise in multiple sclerosis[11] found no evidence that exercise imposes a higher risk of exacerbation or harm in people with multiple sclerosis.

Does physical activity reduce symptoms of multiple sclerosis?

Numerous published studies have shown the benefits of regular physical activity in patients with multiple sclerosis and there is strong evidence of improvements in muscle function, aerobic fitness, quality of life, and mobility.[12] One study[13] compared neurological rehabilitation with aerobic exercise using the outcomes of distance and walking speed, and concluded that aerobic exercise generated greater improvements than formal rehabilitation programs. It is clear that exercise, regardless of whether it is similar to exercise for healthy individuals or is modified to maintain function, is of great benefit to those with multiple sclerosis and therefore should be widely recommended. There is, however, only limited evidence as to the level of exercise required in order to improve muscle strength.

Compared with people without multiple sclerosis, individuals with multiple sclerosis have lower levels of physical activity. This can lead to reduced muscle mass, weakness, and reduced endurance, as a secondary effect of inactivity. Reduced physical activity may in turn lead to less social interaction, restricted leisure activities, and depression, generally affecting the quality of life.

What exercise or physical activity program should be used?

The ACSM physical activity guidelines (see box on page 1082, and Chapter 60) apply to patients with multiple sclerosis. Table 54.2 summarizes this basic exercise prescription.

It is important to be aware that multiple sclerosis medication may affect an individual's ability to exercise, particularly in hot environments. Clinicians should be aware of this when prescribing exercise. Similarly, many patients with multiple sclerosis also have medical comorbidities that may influence the exercise prescription.

Special considerations for exercise in patients with multiple sclerosis

In patients with multiple sclerosis, neurological function deteriorates sharply if core body temperature rises (Uhthoff effect),[14] due to the negative effect of temperature on the conduction velocity of demyelinated nerves. Thus environmental evaluation is important and practical advice can include having a cool shower before and after exercise; wearing a cooling vest may be worthwhile.

Fatigue can strongly influence exercise adherence and approximately 90% of patients with multiple sclerosis experience fatigue; even in mild disease the symptom may be severe. The increased level of muscular fatigue is not correlated with muscular weakness, although muscular strength is also affected following a short period of exertion. This tiredness or fatigue affects all daily activities and the quality of life. Management is complex and may include a longer period of recovery following exertion, planned rest, use of aids, short breaks to gain new strength during the exercise regimen, assessment of sleep patterns, and the use of pharmacological medication.

Dizziness

Human locomotion requires an intact neural system involving input from vision, proprioceptive, and labyrinthine components of the neuraxis. Reduced, lost, or disturbed function in one or more of these aspect results in disturbed balance and the perception of motion illusions (e.g. vertigo). We focus on the vestibular aspects of dizziness that are the most common cause of this presentation.

Dizziness is an extremely common problem that can be caused either by central problems (10%), peripheral vestibular dysfunction (approximately 50%), psychiatric problems (15%), medical problems (26%) such as illness or medication, or by age-related changes to the balance systems. The prevalence of dizziness increases with age and by 75 years, approximately 40% of women and 30% of men report dizziness or disequilibrium symptoms.

One of the key elements in the management of dizziness is determining the cause of the patient's symptoms. This may involve sophisticated vestibular or otolithic neurophysiological investigation such as nystagmography. Clinical tests such as a Dix-Hallpike maneuver can be used to localize the site of the lesion; it may require Fresnel lenses to detect subtle nystagmus. Medications may be used to minimize symptoms temporarily; chronic use of such medications is to be avoided.

Table 54.3 Exercise protocols for patients with dizziness

Type of exercise	Minimum length of program	Intensity	Frequency	Time
Aerobic	4 months	Moderate-vigorous 60–80% HR_{max} Borg RPE 13–15	2–5 days/week	Total of 150 mins/week
Strength	4 months	Start with 50% RM Borg RPE 9–11	1–5	1–3 sets 7–10 reps
Habituation training	1–2 weeks	To induce dizziness	2 times per day minimum	20–60 mins
Balance training	1 month	"Challenging exercise"	2 or more days/week	20–60 mins

HR_{max} = maximum heart rate; RM = repetition max; RPE = rating of perceived exertion

Does physical activity prevent the onset of dizziness?

No published studies have examined specifically whether physical activity prevents the onset of dizziness.

Does physical activity reduce dizziness symptoms?

In acute peripheral vestibular loss, recovery is stimulated with eye and head movements and balance exercises of gradually increasing intensity, which assist in activating central compensation mechanisms. The most well-known of these rehabilitation exercises are the Cawthorne-Cooksey exercises,[15] which are widely used in physiotherapy settings for the treatment of benign positional postural vertigo.[16] This habituation training is clinically extremely effective, although patients may require additional balance training as well, because patients with benign positional postural vertigo have poor dynamic and static balance even after successful treatment of their vertigo. An alternative approach is otoconial repositioning or maneuver treatment, which is usually done as a single episode of treatment. In the case of injury to the central nervous system, balance and coordination training is necessary and a certain degree of compensation may be achieved through mobility training.

The effects of mobility training in patients with injuries to the central nervous system are still insufficiently described and evaluated. In a small randomized study of older patients with central dizziness and/or disequilibrium, improved balance function and subjective rating of symptoms were noted following balance training.[17]

What exercise or physical activity program should be used?

The ACSM physical activity guidelines (see box on page 1082, and Chapter 60) apply to patients with dizziness. Table 54.3 summarizes the basic exercise prescription.

Mild cognitive impairment and dementia

Mild cognitive impairment is a clinical entity characterized by cognitive decline greater than that expected for an individual's age and education level but that *does not interfere notably* with everyday function.

Mild cognitive impairment sits along the continuum between normality and dementia. It is distinct from dementia, in which cognitive deficits are severe, widespread, and substantially affect everyday function.

Mild cognitive impairment is a well-recognized risk factor for dementia.

Dementia is a broad descriptive term that encompasses a number of slowly progressive degenerative conditions characterized by a decline in cognitive function and higher levels of neurological function (e.g. executive function, motor planning, memory, emotion). The prevalence of the condition increases with age from 1% at 65 years to over 50% at 90 years of age. The most widely known form of dementia is Alzheimer's disease, which accounts for approximately 50% of patients with dementia.

Vascular dementia is the second most common type of dementia[18–20] and is the result of cerebrovascular disease and cardiovascular pathologic changes. Vascular dementia is possibly the most under-diagnosed and under-treated form of cognitive dysfunction in older adults.[21] Concepts of vascular dementia have historically been based on stroke and the multi-infarct model.[22]

There is now recognition that cognitive impairment associated with cerebrovascular disease extends well beyond the traditional concept of multi-infarct dementia. The growing consensus is that small vessel disease has an important role in vascular dementia.[23, 24] Small vessel disease is associated with white matter lesions, small infarcts, and cortical brain atrophy.[23, 24]

There is also growing recognition of a close relationship between Alzheimer's disease and vascular dementia including several vascular risk factors,[24] vascular pathology in the brain,[25, 26] and common pathogenic mechanisms such as neurotransmitter abnormalities.[27]

Alzheimer's disease accounts for approximately 50% of cases, followed by cerebrovascular disease (multi-infarct dementia), fronto-temporal dementia, and a variety of less common causes (e.g. dementia with Lewy bodies, prion diseases). A number of genetic risk factors are also associated with the propensity to develop dementia, particularly in younger individuals.

Does physical activity prevent the onset of cognitive impairment and dementia?

Physical activity has a protective effect against the risk of developing cognitive impairment (i.e. mild cognitive impairment and dementia).[28–32] Even in the oldest subjects (over 85 years), regular physical activity protects against the development of dementia.

Does physical activity minimize the progression of cognitive impairment and reduce dementia symptoms?

Exercise has cognitive benefits for older adults with mild cognitive impairment.[33, 34] However, much more research is needed to evaluate the effectiveness of exercise in delaying the progression of mild cognitive impairment.[35] As such, there is also insufficient evidence on whether or not physical activity programs are beneficial for cognitive function in people with dementia.[36]

However, older people with dementia have the same need for physical activity as other older persons. A key trial showed that a three-month exercise training program combined with behavioral therapy improved both physical health and depression.[37] Importantly, the intervention group showed a trend for less institutionalization due to behavioral disturbances at follow-up.

Other studies have shown that structured exercise training leads to an increase in physical fitness and function in daily life in people with mild to moderate dementia. In more severe cases of dementia (older patients admitted to nursing homes), there is a positive effect on mobility, but there are contradictory results when it comes to more functional aspects such as walking, activities of daily life, balance, and endurance.[38] Physical activity programs improve aspects of attention, memory, the ability to communicate and to perform practical tasks, as well as overall mental function.[38]

These studies indicate that older persons with different degrees of declining mental health, both those still living at home and in nursing homes, can benefit from exercise training.

One particular issue in patients with cognitive impairment is fall risk. While physical exercise that focuses on muscle strength and balance prevents falls in elderly subjects still living at home,[17] the same benefits are not seen in people with dementia, suggesting that cognitive factors have a substantial role to play in this risk.

Mechanisms that underpin the effect of exercise

Both animal and human studies strongly suggest that increased levels of growth factors, such as brain-derived neurotrophic factor (BDNF) and insulin-growth factor I (IGF-I), are a primary physiological mechanism underlying the benefit of exercise on cognitive function. Exercise may also have a neuroprotective effect by increasing mental wellness (i.e. reducing stress, anxiety, and depression) through the release of endorphins. Exercise may also increase mental wellness through increased socialization.

Tips for good verbal communication about exercise

The Swedish book *Physical activity in the prevention and treatment of disease* (Figure 54.1) provides useful tips for working with persons with dementia:[39]

- Give the person time to respond.
- Express yourself clearly and simply—one instruction or piece of information at a time.
- Use words and expressions that the patient is very familiar with.

Figure 54.1 Source for exercise prescription related not to only dementia, but for more than 60 medical conditions.[39] A free PDF copy can be downloaded for personal use from www.fyss.se REPRODUCED WITH PERMISSION FROM THE PROFESSIONAL ASSOCIATIONS FOR PHYSICAL ACTIVITY

- Repeat things often, and paraphrase if the patient does not understand.
- Avoid giving instruction for movements; have the patient solve the tasks instead.

This resource also encourages non-verbal communication including gestures, physical contact, visual reinforcement, audio amplification, and demonstrating the activity.

Epilepsy

Epilepsy is a neurological disorder of the brain characterized by recurrent (more than two) seizures. Approximately 10–30% of the population will have a seizure at some time in their lives.[40]

 Neither single episodes of seizures during adolescence or adult life, nor febrile convulsions in infancy, constitute a diagnosis of epilepsy.

The terms "seizure," "epilepsy," "convulsion," and "fit" are often used interchangeably. We use the term seizure to refer to an epileptic seizure and the term convulsion to describe the movements during an episode without implying a specific etiology.

Exercise prescription

Regular physical activity is advocated for individuals with epilepsy.[41] In general, people with epilepsy report better seizure control when exercising regularly.[42] Occasionally, some individuals will have more seizures with exercise,[43] hence every case must be treated individually. Persons with epilepsy have no higher injury rate in sport than those without epilepsy, and sport participation does not affect serum drug levels.

In a sample of more than 200 patients with epilepsy in Norway, exercise patterns were similar to those of the average population.[41] In the majority of patients, physical exercise had no adverse effects, and more than a third of patients claimed that regular exercise contributed to better seizure control. In 10% of patients, exercise appeared to be a seizure precipitant and this applied particularly to those with symptomatic partial epilepsy (i.e. underlying structural brain lesion). The risk of sustaining serious seizure-related injuries while exercising in this population was modest.[41]

Absolute and relative contraindications to sporting activities are shown in Table 54.4.

Table 54.4 Absolute and relative contraindications to sporting activities in people with epilepsy

Absolute	Relative (with supervision)
Rock climbing	Swimming
Flying	Cross-country skiing
Hang gliding	Backpacking
Pistol shooting	Cycling
Scuba diving	
Archery	
Sky diving, parachuting	
Motor racing	

Management of a seizure in the sport setting

Seizures always terminate spontaneously; they are rarely life threatening. The patient usually does not feel pain or remember the seizure. As a clinician observing or supervising a seizure you should have two aims. Firstly, protect the individual from injury. Secondly, observe the seizure closely to give an accurate description to the patient's physician. Do not put a knotted sheet or spoon in the patient's mouth and do not physically restrain the patient. After the seizure, the patient breathes normally and appears sleepy. The patient should be managed as for an unconscious patient (Chapter 47).

Overall, people with epilepsy are able to participate in sport with few limitations. Family, friends, teammates, and coaches must be aware of the epilepsy and understand what to do in the event of a seizure. This will contribute to removing unnecessary barriers to a normal active lifestyle for those with epilepsy.

Depression

The American Psychiatric Association in the DSM4 manual recognizes four categories of mood disorders:

1. depression (including a mild chronic form, dysthymia, and a more severe form—major depressive disorder)
2. bipolar or manic-depressive disorder
3. mood disorders due to a medical condition
4. substance-induced mood disorders.

Depression has an lifetime prevalence of between 6% and 20% worldwide. The rate of major depression has increased steadily over the past half century, and in 2000 the World Health Organization ranked depressive disorders as the fourth largest health problem in the world. Individuals are labeled as having a major depressive episode when they have depressed mood or lose interest or pleasure in normal activities most of the time for at least 2 weeks. These may be associated with symptoms such as abnormalities in appetite, libido, sleep, energy levels, concentration, and, often, suicidal thoughts. Occasionally, anxiety and agitation can be more prominent symptoms than depressed mood. Depression is not considered a major depressive episode if it is caused by grief (less than 2 months), drug abuse, or medication, or a medical condition such as heart disease, diabetes, and/or multiple sclerosis.

Does physical activity prevent the onset of mood disorders?

More than 100 cohort studies over many decades demonstrate that regular physical activity is effective in reducing the onset of depression; however, there is insufficient evidence about the effect of exercise on other types of mood disorders.

In the published studies of depression from around the world, there is a consistent reduction in the onset of depression with an odds ratio of 0.82 (95% CI, 0.78–0.86) when comparing active to inactive adults after adjustment for risk factors such as age, income, smoking, medical comorbidity.

Does physical activity reduce depression symptoms?

Physical activity has a positive effect on depression in preventing the onset of depressive episodes as well as the acute and long-term treatment of episodes that do occur. The physical training is beneficial when conducted parallel to customary treatment with drugs and other forms of therapy, such as cognitive and interpersonal therapy. Whether this beneficial effect is mediated through positive thoughts and emotions, increased confidence and self-control, or

through improved physical functional capacity and/or changes in brain neurotransmitters or endorphins is not known.

The findings of randomized controlled trials and other cohort studies demonstrate that exercise reduces the number and severity of symptoms of depression in both depressed patients as well as non-depressed adults. The magnitude of effect is generally about 40–50% greater than placebo or other non-pharmacological treatments (e.g. bright light therapy). Reductions were smaller for active men than for women, but men have been less studied. Studies of healthy adults and adults with medical conditions other than depression or disabling conditions that limit physical function (i.e. spinal cord injury, multiple sclerosis) demonstrated that exercise was also beneficial in reducing depressive symptoms.

What exercise or physical activity program should be used?

In general, the physical activity guidelines of approximately 150 minutes per week of aerobic activity and 12 sessions of strength-based training are appropriate for patients with depressive symptoms. See Table 54.5 for exercise program for patients with depression.

It is important to be aware that some antidepressant medications affect an individual's ability to exercise, particularly in hot environments. Clinicians should be aware of this when prescribing exercise. Similarly, where depression occurs in the setting of body image or eating disorders, the use of exercise, as a therapeutic modality, needs to be considered carefully in the overall management.

Anxiety

Anxiety includes a broad range of feelings; however, it is characterized by apprehensive or worrisome thoughts and may be accompanied by agitation,

Table 54.5 Exercise program for patients with depression and anxiety

Type of exercise	Minimum length of program	Intensity	Frequency	Time
Aerobic	9 weeks	Moderate–vigorous 60–80% HR max Borg RPE 13–15	2–3 sessions/ week	30–45 mins
Strength	9 weeks	Start with 50% RM Borg RPE 9–11	2–3 sessions/ week	30–60 mins 8–10 exercises, 1–3 sets, 8–12 reps

RM = repetition max; RPE = rating of perceived exertion

feelings of tension, and activation of the autonomic nervous system. A distinction is made between transient anxiety symptoms, persistent symptoms, and a group of disabling conditions characterized by excessive chronic anxiety that are known as anxiety disorders. The anxiety disorders broadly include phobias, panic disorder, obsessive-compulsive disorder, post-traumatic stress disorder, as well as the generalized anxiety disorders.

Anxiety disorders are common, affecting approximately 4% of women and 2% of men—however, nearly 20% of people will experience anxiety disorders at some time in their lives. Anxiety disorders begin at a median age of 15 years, often persist throughout life, and are associated with numerous physical and mental comorbidities, especially depression.

Does physical activity prevent the onset of anxiety disorders/symptoms?

Published cross-sectional and prospective cohort studies demonstrate that regular physical activity protects against the onset of anxiety disorders and anxiety symptoms.[37] Results of the US National Co-morbidity Study found that regular physical activity reduced the odds of a diagnosed anxiety disorder by an average of 43%.[45] After controlling for sociodemographic and illness variables, regular physical activity reduced the odds of an anxiety disorder by an average of 28%. These findings are supported by epidemiological studies from Australia and Germany.[46, 47]

Does physical activity reduce anxiety symptoms?

A number of studies involving subjects with normal or elevated anxiety levels who do not fulfill the DSM4 criteria for a psychiatric diagnosis have shown that physical activity reduces anxiety symptoms, at least transiently, after a bout of exercise.[44] Many controlled studies have shown beneficial effects with clinically meaningful effect sizes. Whether physical activity affects chronic anxiety remains uncertain, as only a few controlled studies with relatively small numbers of subjects have been carried out on patients with diagnosed anxiety disorders. There are a number of studies on panic disorder and agoraphobia, but only one study on generalized anxiety disorder and social phobia. There is an absence of evidence from prospective cohort studies that examine whether anxiety symptoms vary according to intensity or frequency of physical activity exposure.

What exercise or physical activity program should be used

In general, the physical activity guidelines of approximately 150 minutes per week of aerobic activity and 1–2 sessions of strength-based training are appropriate for patients with anxiety symptoms, although only a single study[48] has studied different forms of exercise prescription. See Table 54.5 for guidelines for exercise prescription in patient with anxiety.

It is important to be aware that some anti-anxiety medications affect an individual's ability to exercise, particularly in hot environments. Clinicians should be aware of this when prescribing exercise. It is also important to note that many patients experience an increase in anxiety symptoms when they begin a training program, presumable due to a sympathetic nervous system response. Patients should be warned of this and counseled as to how to deal with these feelings when they arise.

📄 RECOMMENDED READING

Professional Associations for Physical Activity (Sweden), ed. *Physical activity in the prevention and treatment of disease*. Stockholm: Swedish National Institute of Public Health, 2010 (ISBN: 978-91-7257-715-2). A free PDF copy can be downloaded for personal use from www.fyss.se.

Physical Activity Guidelines Advisory Committee. *Physical activity guidelines advisory committee report, 2008*. Washington, DC: US Department of Health and Human Services, 2008

📄 REFERENCES

1. Lee CD, Folsom AR, Blair SN. Physical activity and stroke risk—a meta-analysis. *Stroke* 2003;34(10): 2475–81.
2. Wendel-Vos GW, Schuit AJ, Feskens EM et al. Physical activity and stroke. A meta-analysis of observational data. *Int J Epidemiol* 2004;33(4):787–98.
3. Saunders DH, Greig CA, Young A et al. Physical fitness training for stroke patients. *Cochrane Database Syst Rev* 2004(1):CD003316.
4. Pang MC, Eng JJ, Dawson AS et al. The use of aerobic exercise training in improving aerobic capacity in individuals with stroke: a meta-analysis. *Clin Rehabil* 2006;20(2):97–111.
5. Gordon NF, Gulanick M, Costa F et al. Physical activity and exercise recommendations for stroke survivors—an American Heart Association scientific statement from the Council on Clinical Cardiology, Subcommittee on Exercise, Cardiac Rehabilitation, and Prevention; the Council on Cardiovascular Nursing; the Council on Nutrition, Physical Activity, and Metabolism; and the Stroke Council. *Stroke* 2004;35(5):1230–40.
6. Chen H, Zhang SM, Schwarzschild MA et al. Physical activity and the risk of Parkinson's disease. *Neurology* 2005;64(4):664–9.
7. Crizzle AM, Newhouse IJ. Is physical exercise beneficial for persons with Parkinson's disease? *Clin J Sport Med* 2006;16(5):422–5.
8. Dibble LE, Hale TF, Marcus RL et al. High intensity eccentric resistance training decreases bradykinesia and improves quality of life in persons with Parkinson's disease: a preliminary study. *Parkinsonism Relat Disord* 2009;15(10):752–7.
9. Dibble LE, Hale T, Marcus RL et al. The safety and feasibility of high-force eccentric resistance exercise in persons with Parkinson's disease. *Arch Phys Med Rehabil* 2006;87(9):1280–2.
10. Sherrington C, Whitney JC, Lord SR et al. Effective exercise for the prevention of falls: a systematic review and meta-analysis. *J Am Geriatr Soc* 2008;56(12): 2234–43.
11. Ginis KAM, Hicks AL. Considerations for the development of a physical activity guide for Canadians with physical disabilities. *Can J Public Health* 2007;98 Suppl 2:S135–47.
12. White LJ, Dressendorfer RH. Exercise and multiple sclerosis. *Sports Med* 2004;34(15):1077–100.
13. Rampello A, Franceschini M, Piepoli M et al. Effect of aerobic training on walking capacity and maximal exercise tolerance in patients with multiple sclerosis: a randomized crossover controlled study. *Phys Ther* 2007;87(5):545–55.
14. Davis SL, Frohman TC, Crandall CG et al. Modeling Uhthoff's phenomenon in MS patients with internuclear ophthalmoparesis. *Neurology* 2008; 70(13 Pt 2):1098–106.
15. Schubert MC, Whitney SL. From Cawthorne-Cooksey to biotechnology: where we have been and where we are headed in vestibular rehabilitation. *J Neurol Phys Ther* 2010;34(2):62–3.
16. Hillier SL, Hollohan V. Vestibular rehabilitation for unilateral peripheral vestibular dysfunction. *Cochrane Database Syst Rev* 2007(4):CD005397.
17. Gillespie LD, Robertson MC, Gillespie WJ et al. Interventions for preventing falls in older people living in the community. *Cochrane Database Syst Rev* 2009(2):CD007146.
18. Rockwood K, Wentzel C, Hachinski V et al. Prevalence and outcomes of vascular cognitive impairment. Vascular Cognitive Impairment Investigators of the Canadian Study of Health and Aging. *Neurology* 2000;54(2):447–51.
19. Desmond DW, Erkinjuntti T, Sano M et al. The cognitive syndrome of vascular dementia: implications for clinical trials. *Alzheimer Dis Assoc Disord* 1999; 13 Suppl 3:S21–9.
20. Erkinjuntti T, Bowler JV, DeCarli CS et al. Imaging of static brain lesions in vascular dementia: implications for clinical trials. *Alzheimer Dis Assoc Disord* 1999; 13 Suppl 3:S81–90.
21. Roman GC. Vascular dementia may be the most common form of dementia in the elderly. *J Neurol Sci* 2002;203–204:7–10.
22. Erkinjuntti T, Kurz A, Gauthier S et al. Efficacy of galantamine in probable vascular dementia and Alzheimer's disease combined with

cerebrovascular disease: a randomised trial. *Lancet* 2002;359(9314):1283–90.

23. Moorhouse P, Rockwood K. Vascular cognitive impairment: current concepts and clinical developments. *Lancet Neurol* 2008;7(3):246–55.

24. O'Brien JT, Erkinjuntti T, Reisberg B et al. Vascular cognitive impairment. *Lancet Neurol* 2003;2(2): 89–98.

25. Leys D, Erkinjuntti T, Desmond DW et al. Vascular dementia: the role of cerebral infarcts. *Alzheimer Dis Assoc Disord* 1999;13 Suppl 3:S38–48.

26. Snowdon DA, Greiner LH, Mortimer JA et al. Brain infarction and the clinical expression of Alzheimer disease. The nun study. *JAMA* 1997;277(10):813–7.

27. Kalaria RN, Ballard C. Overlap between pathology of Alzheimer disease and vascular dementia. *Alzheimer Dis Assoc Disord* 1999;13 Suppl 3:S115–23.

28. Geda YE, Roberts RO, Knopman DS et al. Physical exercise, aging, and mild cognitive impairment: a population-based study. *Arch Neurol* 2010;67(1): 80–6.

29. Etgen T, Sander D, Huntgeburth U et al. Physical activity and incident cognitive impairment in elderly persons: the INVADE study. *Arch Intern Med* 2010;170(2):186–93.

30. Hamer M, Chida Y. Walking and primary prevention: a meta-analysis of prospective cohort studies. *Br J Sports Med* 2008;42(4):238–43.

31. Weuve J, Kang JH, Manson JE et al. Physical activity, including walking, and cognitive function in older women. *JAMA* 2004;292(12):1454–61.

32. Larson EB, Wang L, Bowen JD et al. Exercise is associated with reduced risk for incident dementia among persons 65 years of age and older. *Ann Int Med* 2006;144(2):73–81.

33. Baker LD, Frank LL, Foster-Schubert K et al. Effects of aerobic exercise on mild cognitive impairment: a controlled trial. *Arch Neurol* 2010;67(1):71–9.

34. Lautenschlager NT, Cox KL, Flicker L et al. Effect of physical activity on cognitive function in older adults at risk for Alzheimer disease: a randomized trial. *JAMA* 2008;300(9):1027–37.

35. Orgeta V, Regan C, Orrell M. Physical activity for improving cognition in older people with mild cognitive impairment. *Cochrane Database Syst Rev* 2010(1):CD008198.

36. Forbes D, Forbes S, Morgan DG et al. Physical activity programs for persons with dementia. *Cochrane Database Syst Rev* 2008(3):CD006489.

37. Goodwin RD. Association between physical activity and mental disorders among adults in the United States. *Prev Med* 2003;36(6):698–703.

38. McDonnell MN, Smith AE, Mackintosh SF. Aerobic exercise to improve cognitive function in adults with neurological disorders: a systematic review. *Arch Phys Med Rehabil* 2011;92(7):1044–52.

39. Professional Associations for Physical Activity (Sweden), ed. *Physical activity in the prevention and treatment of disease.* Stockholm: Swedish National Institute of Public Health, 2010.

40. Sander JW, Hart YM, Johnson AL et al. National General Practice Study of Epilepsy: newly diagnosed epileptic seizures in a general population. *Lancet* 1990;336:1267–71.

41. Nakken KO. Physical exercise in outpatients with epilepsy. *Epilepsia* 1999;40:643–51.

42. Arida RM, Cavalheiro EA, da Silva AC et al. Physical activity and epilepsy: proven and predicted benefits. *Sports Med* 2008;38(7):607–15.

43. Howard GM, Radloff M, Sevier TL. Epilepsy and sports participation. *Curr Sports Med Rep* 2004;3(1):15–9.

44. Windle G, Hughes D, Linck P et al. Is exercise effective in promoting mental well-being in older age? A systematic review. *Aging and Mental Health* 2010;14(6):652–69.

45. Byers AL, Yaffe K, Covinsky KE et al. High occurrence of mood and anxiety disorders among older adults: The National Comorbidity Survey Replication. *Arch Gen Psychiatry* 2010;67(5):489–96.

46. Pasco JA, Williams LJ, Jacka FN et al. Habitual physical activity and the risk for depressive and anxiety disorders among older men and women. *Int Psychogeriatr* 2011;23(2):292–8.

47. Wolff E, Strohle A. Causal associations of physical activity/exercise and symptoms of depression and anxiety. *Arch Gen Psychiatry* 2010;67(5):540–1.

48. Knapen J, Van de Vliet P, Van Coppenolle H et al. Comparison of changes in physical self-concept, global self-esteem, depression and anxiety following two different psychomotor therapy programs in nonpsychotic psychiatric inpatients. *Psychother Psychosom* 2005;74(6):353–61.

Chapter 55

Joint-related symptoms without acute injury

with NICK CARTER

I don't deserve this award, but I have arthritis and I don't deserve that either.   Jack Benny

Not everything that presents to the sports clinic is sports medicine! In daily practice, sports clinicians see many patients who have mechanical joint injuries, so it can be tempting to attribute a mechanical diagnosis to every patient who presents with a painful or swollen joint. It is, however, wise to maintain an index of suspicion for inflammatory joint disease masquerading as a mechanical condition.

Consider the case of a 30-year-old runner who presents with recurrent knee swelling without history of injury. Swelling is very uncommon in patellofemoral pain (Chapter 33) and a meniscal injury is rare without trauma at that age. The clinician should be alert to the possibility that this swollen knee may be caused by an inflammatory condition.

In this chapter, we discuss the clinical approach to diagnosing patients with the following four common presentations:

* the single swollen joint
* low back pain and stiffness
* multiple joint symptoms
* joint pain and "pain all over."

We also discuss when to use rheumatological investigations and how to interpret them.

The patient with a single swollen joint

In the sportsperson with a single swollen joint without a history of trauma, a possible inflammatory cause should be considered. Table 55.1 summarizes the differential diagnosis of a single swollen joint.

Clinical perspective

The key to accurate diagnosis of a swollen joint is taking a careful history, performing a physical examination, and having an appropriate index of suspicion. Inflammatory joint problems are characterized by pain, swelling, warmth, redness, night pain, and prominent morning stiffness. In all sportspeople, and especially in children and adolescents, inflammatory, infective, or neoplastic conditions should be considered in the light of these symptoms.

History

Many of the inflammatory diseases are associated with extra-articular features that may provide additional clues as to the diagnosis:

* Psoriatic arthritis may be associated with rash, nail dystrophy, tendon insertion pain (enthesopathy), or low back pain.

Table 55.1 Differential diagnosis in the sportsperson presenting with a single swollen joint without a clear history of trauma

Common conditions	Less common conditions
Reactive arthritis	Pigmented villonodular synovitis
Septic arthritis	Juxta-articular bone tumors
Psoriatic arthritis	Synovial sarcoma
Gout/pseudogout	Monoarticular rheumatoid arthritis
Peripheral ankylosing spondylitis	Acute sarcoidosis
Osteoarthritis	Peripheral enteric arthritis

- A history of inflammatory bowel disease (ulcerative colitis, Crohn's disease, or celiac disease) suggests enteropathic arthritis.
- Urethral discharge or eye inflammation may suggest a reactive arthritis.
- Rheumatoid arthritis is characteristically a small joint (hands, wrists, and feet), symmetrical polyarthritis but can present as a single swollen joint in 15% of cases.
- Hypothyroidism, hyperparathyroidism, and hemochromatosis may be associated with calcium pyrophosphate dihydrate deposition in articular tissues that may manifest as an acute gout-like presentation ("pseudogout") or may have a subacute or chronic course. With chronic pyrophosphate arthropathy, changes of osteoarthritis are often seen. In older sportspeople with anterior knee pain, the presence of subchondral patellar cysts in the absence of tibio-femoral osteoarthritic change may represent chronic pyrophosphate deposition disease.

- Previous renal disease or diuretic use may give clues to diagnosing gout.
- Septic arthritis is uncommon in the normal joint but the possibility should be considered in joints recently aspirated or in patients with arthritis, diabetes, or impaired immune function.
- A family history of inflammatory arthritis is significant as first-degree relatives of patients with rheumatoid arthritis are four times more likely to develop the condition than the general population.[1]

The clinician must ask about these features as the sportsperson is unlikely to volunteer them.

Examination

In addition to examining the symptomatic joint, the clinician should perform a general physical examination. This may provide clues to indicate an underlying inflammatory cause. Table 55.2 summarizes important extra-articular signs that may be associated with an acutely swollen joint.

Table 55.2 Extra-articular signs that may be associated with an acutely swollen joint

System	Sign	Disease
General	Fever	Septic arthritis, acute gout
	Lymphadenopathy	Septic arthritis, malignant bone/soft tissue tumor
Skin/mucous membranes	Psoriasis, nail dystrophy	Psoriatic arthritis
	Erythema nodosum	Acute sarcoidosis
	Tophi	Gout
	Nail fold infarcts, splinter hemorrhages	RA (vasculitis)
	Circinate balanitis, keratoderma blennorrhagica (Fig. 55.1)	ReA
	Pyoderma gangrenosum	EnA
	Erythema chronicum migrans	Lyme disease
Eyes	Conjunctivitis	ReA
	Iritis	AS, psoriatic arthritis, EnA
	Dry eyes (and mouth)	Sjogren's syndrome (often associated with RA)
Locomotor system	Small hand (MCP, PIP) and foot (MTP) synovitis	RA, psoriatic arthritis, chondrocalcinosis
	Hand (DIP, 1st CMC joints)	Nodal osteoarthritis
	Large (lower limb) joint synovitis	ReA, AS, psoriatic arthritis, EnA
	Restricted lumbar range of motion/sacroiliac tenderness	AS, ReA, psoriatic arthritis, EnA
	Tender, swollen entheses	AS, ReA, psoriatic arthritis, EnA
	Tenosynovitis	RA, gout
Neurological	Carpal tunnel syndrome	RA

AS = ankylosing spondylitis; CMC = carpometacarpal; DIP = distal interphalangeal; EnA = enteropathic arthritis; MCP = metacarpophalangeal; MTP = metatarsophalangeal; PIP = proximal interphalangeal; RA = rheumatoid arthritis; ReA = reactive arthritis

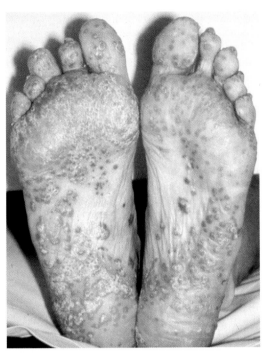

Figure 55.1 Keratoderma blennorrhagica in reactive arthritis

Investigations

Laboratory tests and imaging should be guided by the clinical findings to help confirm or refute a suspected diagnosis. The clinician should avoid blanket screening. Infectious or inflammatory conditions may be associated with elevation of acute-phase reactants e.g. erythrocyte sedimentation rate (ESR), C-reactive protein (CRP).

Synovial fluid aspiration should be considered mandatory in cases of acute monoarthritis. If septic arthritis is suspected, the aspiration must be performed before antibiotics are given. The choice of antibiotic can be adjusted depending on the results of the Gram stain and culture of synovial fluid and blood culture. Uric acid (gout) or calcium pyrophosphate dihydrate (pseudogout) crystals may be detected under polarized light microscopy. It is important to remember that acute crystal arthropathy can be associated with fever and leukocytosis and may mimic septic arthritis. Furthermore, these conditions may coexist.

In cases of suspected reactive arthritis, symptoms of urethral discharge should prompt referral to a genitourinary specialist. Stool culture may help identify gut infection (e.g. *Shigella*, *Salmonella*, or *Campylobacter*).

For non-traumatic acute presentations of a swollen joint, plain radiographs are not indicated as they seldom show more than soft tissue swelling or joint effusion. Plain films may, however, be helpful in identifying bone tumors, erosions, or osteoarthritis. Chest X-ray may reveal bilateral hilar lymphadenopathy in acute sarcoidosis.

Ultrasound is useful to detect synovitis and early erosions (more sensitive than radiographs) in suspected rheumatoid arthritis.

MRI is a powerful tool for patients with traumatic lesions, bone, and soft tissue tumors, pigmented villonodular synovitis (Fig. 55.2), and osteomyelitis (Fig. 55.3), and for the early detection of erosions.

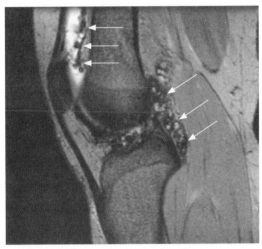

Figure 55.2 MRI scan of pigmented villonodular synovitis of the knee

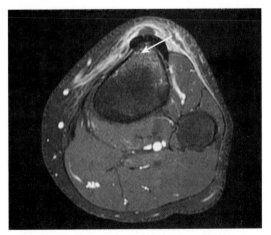

Figure 55.3 MRI scan of osteomyelitis (arrow to abnormal high signal in bone) that caused swelling of the knee

The patient with low back pain and stiffness

A systemic illness is present in up to 10% of patients who present with low back pain. Because patients with low back pain gravitate to sports clinicians for management, it is important that clinicians have an index of suspicion for those patients with a non-mechanical cause for their back pain.

Clinical perspective

The differential diagnosis of low back pain is broad and is documented in Chapter 26. This differential diagnosis includes inflammatory arthritis of the spine and sacroiliac joints, known as "spondyloarthropathy," Spondyloarthropathy is a generic term applied to the clinical, radiological, and immunological features shared by the following diseases:

- ankylosing spondylitis
- reactive arthritis following genitourinary or gut infection
- psoriatic arthritis
- enteropathic arthritis (Crohn's disease, ulcerative colitis, or celiac disease).

Although patients with these conditions have an increased likelihood of being positive for HLA B27 (see below), a negative result does not eliminate the diagnosis. Spondyloarthropathy has its greatest prevalence in young men and usually achieves near full disease expression by age 35 years; thus, patients commonly present to the sports clinician.

History

Patients with back pain due to spondyloarthropathy complain of pain that is worse at night, with prominent morning stiffness (of 2 hours or more), which is eased with gentle exercise and nonsteroidal anti-inflammatory drugs (NSAIDs). This pain pattern is very different from the typical pain pattern of mechanical low back pain (Chapter 26). Buttock or posterior thigh pain may be present, so this symptom does not distinguish inflammatory back pain (i.e. spondyloarthropathy) from back pain of mechanical origin.

When the patient describes morning back pain with prominent stiffness, the physician should ask whether there is a past history of psoriasis or nail dystrophy (psoriatic arthritis), inflammatory bowel disease (enteropathic arthritis), or recent genitourinary or gut infection (reactive arthritis). Spondyloarthropathy is characterized by inflam-

mation of the entheses, commonly at the patellar tendon, Achilles tendon, and the plantar fascia.

Peripheral joints may be involved with spondyloarthropathy, particularly an asymmetric, lower limb, large joint inflammation. The shoulder or hip is involved in 30% of patients with ankylosing spondylitis.

A history of extra-articular involvement such as anterior uveitis (iritis) and the rash of keratoderma blennorrhagica (Fig. 55.1) or circinate balanitis (reactive arthritis) may provide clues to the specific cause of back pain.

It is important that the clinician actively seeks these associations as the sportsperson may not find them noteworthy to mention. There is often a strong family history of spondyloarthropathy; for example, approximately 6% of siblings of patients with ankylosing spondylitis will develop the condition.[2]

Examination

When examining the patient with back pain and a suspected inflammatory etiology, the clinician should seek tenderness over the sacroiliac joints and pain on sacroiliac springing. Restriction of lumbosacral spine movement becomes evident first in lateral flexion.

The clinician should also examine the appendicular skeleton for evidence of enthesopathy or peripheral joint involvement.

Thorough inspection of the skin may detect previously unrecognized plaques of psoriasis (Fig. 55.4). The umbilicus, natal cleft, and scalp are common sites, and these changes may be subtle.[3]

Figure 55.4 Subtle psoriatic plaques. Examine for psoriasis if spondyloarthropathy is in the differential diagnosis

Investigations

The diagnosis of spondyloarthropathy is essentially clinical. Investigations may help confirm or refute a suspected diagnosis but should not be used as a blanket screening tool. There may be a non-specific elevation of acute-phase reactants (ESR, CRP), particularly with peripheral joint involvement, but only one-third to two-thirds of patients with active ankylosing spondylitis have an acute-phase response. HLA B27 (see below) is associated with ankylosing spondylitis in up to 95% of cases, and approximately 70% of patients with reactive arthritis and axial involvement. The association is weaker in patients with enteropathic arthritis and psoriatic arthritis, with only about 50% of these patients being HLA B27 positive. As 7% of the general population is positive for HLA B27, there is no place for requesting HLA B27 as a screening tool for back pain.[4]

The diagnosis of ankylosing spondylitis requires sacroiliitis to be evident on plain X-ray. Early changes include sclerosis and erosion of the sacroiliac joints progressing to ankylosis (spontaneous fusion). Concurrently, there may be erosion at the edges of, and squaring of (Fig. 55.5), the vertebral bodies in the thoracolumbar spine progressing to syndesmophyte (bone spur) formation and bony bridging ("bamboo spine"). As these changes may take up to 10 years to develop,[5] plain radiography is relatively insensitive

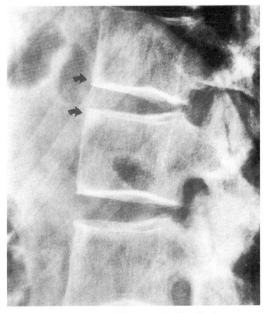

Figure 55.5 Squaring of the vertebral bodies in ankylosing spondylitis

in identifying inflammatory spine and sacroiliac lesions in sportspeople with a short history of symptoms. MRI, however, may detect up to 84% of cases of X-ray-negative early sacroiliitis and this may be considered in such cases.[6] When inflammatory back pain is suspected, sagittal and coronal view short T1 inversion recovery (STIR) images of the spine as well as the sacroiliac joints should be requested.

The patient presenting with multiple painful joints

Occasionally patients attend the sports medicine clinic with multiple joint pain (polyarthralgia) or multiple joint pain with synovitis (polyarthritis). A systematic approach is vital to make an accurate diagnosis. Table 55.3 summarizes the differential diagnosis of the patient presenting with a polyarthritis.

Clinical perspective

History

The practitioner should begin by distinguishing polyarthritis with joint pain, stiffness, and swelling from polyarthralgia alone. Joint inflammation is characterized by night pain, prominent morning stiffness (of at least 60 minutes but often for hours), swelling, warmth, and loss of function. In many of these conditions the diagnosis is clinical. A key diagnostic feature is the onset and pattern of joint involvement.

Rheumatoid arthritis symmetrically affects the small joints of the hands (Fig. 55.6 overleaf), wrists and feet (proximal interphalangeal joints, metacarpophalangeal joints, metatarsophalangeal) and in the majority of patients onset occurs over weeks or months.[7]

Table 55.3 Conditions that must be considered when a patient presents with polyarthritis

Common conditions	Less common conditions
Rheumatoid arthritis	Lyme disease
Viral arthritis	Viral arthritis
• Parvovirus B19	• Hepatitis B, C
• Epstein-Barr virus	• Rubella
Polyarticular psoriatic arthritis	Rheumatic fever
	Enteropathic polyarthritis
Polyarticular reactive arthritis	Overlap syndrome (with inflammatory myositis,
Inflammatory osteoarthritis	scleroderma)
Systemic lupus erythematosus	Polyarticular gout/ pseudogout

Reactive arthritis (following genitourinary or gastrointestinal infection) is often more rapid in onset and has a propensity to asymmetric involvement of the large joints of the lower limb together with enthesitis (inflammation at the insertions of tendons, ligaments, or capsules) or dactylitis (sausage digits). The duration of symptoms should be recorded.

Parvovirus B19 polyarthritis frequently affects young women who care for small children (mothers or school teachers) who develop parvovirus B19 infection (fifth disease or "slapped cheek" syndrome). This condition may be indistinguishable from early rheumatoid arthritis. Symptoms and signs of parvovirus B19 polyarthritis usually settle within six weeks, whereas rheumatoid arthritis often follows a chronic and progressive course. The presence or absence of extra-articular manifestations of rheumatological conditions may also aid accurate diagnosis (Table 55.2).

The pattern of joint involvement in polyarticular pseudogout or psoriatic arthritis often resembles rheumatoid arthritis but without nodulosis, vasculitis, or other systemic features seen in rheumatoid arthritis.

Examination

Clinical examination requires thorough evaluation of all systems. Many of the extra-articular features are summarized in Table 55.2.

The polyarthritis of systemic lupus erythematosus may be associated with alopecia, mouth ulceration, cutaneous vasculitis (local hemorrhages), or a lacy purplish rash referred to as livido reticularis in the young female sportsperson. The characteristic photosensitive facial rash (Fig. 55.7) in systemic lupus erythematosus is often follicular or sometimes itchy. The overlap connective tissue disorders may be

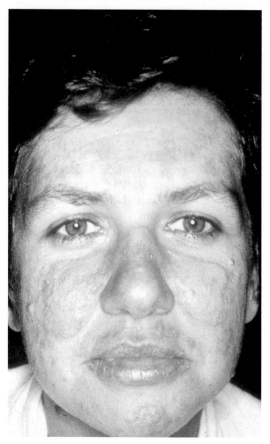

Figure 55.7 Urticarial photosensitive rash in systemic lupus erythematosus

associated with Raynaud's phenomenon, dyspepsia due to esophageal dysmotility, scleroderma of the hands and face, and soft tissue calcification.

Investigations

Investigations should only be requested to help confirm or refute a suspected diagnosis and must be guided by the clinical findings. As with other presentations discussed in this chapter, there is no place for blanket screening tests as these are likely to lead to a high number of false positive results.

There may be a non-specific elevation of acute-phase reactants (ESR, CRP). Aggressive rheumatoid arthritis is often associated with a highly elevated ESR in the early stages of disease. The clinical utility of rheumatoid factor and antinuclear antibody tests is discussed below. Rising immunoglobulin M (IgM) antibody titers to *Borrelia burgdorferi* may aid in the diagnosis of Lyme disease when suspected. Likewise, antibody screening may help with the diagnosis of

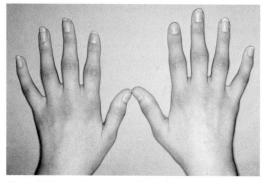

Figure 55.6 Early rheumatoid hands

viral arthropathies (parvovirus B19, Epstein-Barr virus, and hepatitis).

When crystal arthropathy is suspected, the physician should aspirate the joint and arrange for crystal microscopy under polarized light. Radiographs of the hands and feet may detect early erosive change in patients with rheumatoid arthritis (Fig. 55.8) or psoriatic arthritis, a feature rarely seen in systemic lupus erythematosus. A polyarthritis with radiological changes of osteoarthritis and chondrocalcinosis in the menisci or triangular fibrocartilage complex of the wrist may represent calcium pyrophosphate dihydrate deposition disease.

Specialist management of rheumatological conditions

The management of rheumatological conditions is not within the scope of this chapter. The treatment of inflammatory arthritis has changed hugely over the last decade. The outcome for patients with conditions such as rheumatoid arthritis and the spondyloarthropathies has improved dramatically. This is largely due to the introduction of biologic agents directed against tumor necrosis factor alpha (TNF α) and other pro-inflammatory cytokines. Prompt referral and treatment is the key, and so early referral to a rheumatology service is encouraged when a diagnosis of an inflammatory musculoskeletal condition is suspected.

The patient with joint pain who "hurts all over"

A challenging presentation for any clinician is the evaluation of the sportsperson with widespread joint or muscle pain who "hurts all over." These patients are often frequent attendees and it can be extremely rewarding to provide a diagnosis and the help they need. In many cases, patients with this presentation have little to find on clinical examination. The differential diagnosis of this presentation is broad and includes the conditions listed in Table 55.3. Table 55.4 highlights other possible diagnoses and directs the practitioner toward appropriate clinical evaluation.

Investigations must be directed toward a specific diagnosis but may include blood count with differential white cell count, ESR, plasma immunoglobulin assay and electrophoresis, calcium, phosphate, thyroid function, and creatine kinase tests.

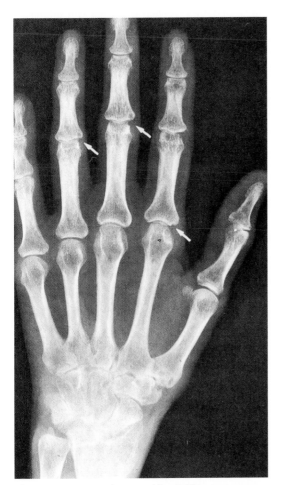

Figure 55.8 Erosive rheumatoid arthritis

Table 55.4 Conditions in patients presenting with polyarthralgia

System	Cause
Drug-induced	Quinolones, acyclovir, vitamin A, clofibrate, beta blockers, statins
Infectious	Viral syndromes, vaccines
Endocrine	Hyper/hypothyroidism, hyperparathyroidism, corticosteroid withdrawal
Autoimmune	Polymyalgia rheumatica, inflammatory myositis
Neoplastic	Leukemia, lymphoma, multiple myeloma, bone metastasis
Psychiatric	Depression, somatization disorder
Other	Fibromyalgia (chronic fatigue syndrome), silicone implant syndrome

1099

Ordering and interpreting rheumatological tests

The indication for and interpretation of the results of commonly requested rheumatological tests can cause confusion. In this section we consider five frequently requested investigations—rheumatoid factor (RhF), erythrocyte sedimentation rate (ESR), antinuclear antibodies (ANA), HLA B27, and serum uric acid.

Rheumatoid factor

Rheumatoid factors (RhF) are autoantibodies that react, principally, with a specific Fc antigen of normal IgG. Approximately 80% of patients with rheumatoid arthritis are RhF positive. Vasculitis, nodules, and more rapidly progressive erosive disease are all features of patients with high RhF titers. Note that both patients with other conditions and also up to 5% of healthy young individuals may be RhF positive (15% in the older adult) (Table 55.5). Blanket screening for RhF may therefore yield a high rate of false positives and the request for an RhF test should be reserved for patients with clinical features consistent with rheumatoid arthritis. More recently, additional antibodies such as anti-CCP (anti-cyclic citrullinated peptide) have been identified that are as sensitive as RhF in rheumatoid arthritis patients though far more specific for the condition. A positive anti-CCP result will yield fewer false-positive results[8] and may predict disease severity.[9]

Erythrocyte sedimentation rate

The ESR is simple and cheap to perform. It is a non-specific acute- and chronic-phase reactant, and while very high elevations (>100 mm/h) may indicate malignancy, sepsis, or vasculitis (e.g. giant cell arteritis), normal levels do not exclude disease. Confounding factors in the interpretation of the ESR include anemia, polycythemia, abnormal red cell morphology, and congestive heart failure. ESR testing is not useful as a screening test in asymptomatic individuals.

Antinuclear antibodies

Autoantibodies that react with various components of the cell nucleus are called "antinuclear antibodies" (ANAs). Almost 100% of patients with systemic lupus erythematosus will be ANA positive but, as with RhF, ANAs are found in individuals with other conditions, such as scleroderma, Sjogren's syndrome, rheumatoid arthritis, inflammatory myositis, Hashimoto's thyroiditis, chronic liver or lung disease, drug-induced lupus, and in 15% of healthy older persons. The ANA test should not be used to screen patients with joint pain or presumed systemic illness.

HLA B27

HLA B27 is a gene found in up to 7% of normal individuals. HLA B27 is often associated with ankylosing spondylitis, reactive arthritis, psoriatic arthritis, and enteropathic arthritis (the spondyloarthropathies). The prevalence of this allele in different populations is shown in Table 55.6.

Also, 12% of HLA B27 positive siblings of patients with ankylosing spondylitis will develop the condition.[2] In sportspeople with low back pain, HLA B27 should not be ordered routinely as there is a 7% prevalence of HLA B27 positive alleles in the general population, whereas the prevalence in patients with spondyloarthropathy is approximately 95%. Given these pre-test probabilities, the test is more likely to produce a false positive than a true positive result. It is diagnostically valuable when the incomplete syndrome is present or when the pre-test probability that

Table 55.5 Conditions with an RhF association

Condition	RhF association (%)
Sjogren's syndrome	90
Rheumatoid arthritis	75–80
Systemic lupus erythematosus	25–50
Pulmonary diseases	10–25
Ankylosing spondylitis/gout	5–10
Healthy young individuals	<5
Healthy older adults	<15

Table 55.6 Prevalence of the HLA B27 allele

Population	Frequency of HLA B27 (%)
Ankylosing spondylitis	90
Ankylosing spondylitis with iritis	>95
Reactive arthritis (Reiter's syndrome)	75–80
Psoriatic arthritis	
• Spondylitis	50
• Peripheral arthritis	<10
Enteropathic arthritis	
• Spondylitis	50
• Peripheral arthritis	<10
General population	<7

the sportsperson has the condition lies between 30% and 70%. It has no value for screening (low pre-test probability) or in patients with classic presentations (high pre-test probability).[10]

Serum uric acid

Serum uric acid estimation is primarily used in the diagnosis of gout. Abnormal levels are taken at two standard deviations either side of the mean (range, 150–425 μmol/L [2.5–7 mg/dL]) and therefore 5% of the normal population will have abnormally low or high uric acid levels. Uric acid will reach saturation level in extra-cellular tissues over approximately 380 μmol/L (6 mg/dL) and serum uric acid levels greater than this are associated with an increased risk of gout and kidney stones. During 40% of acute attacks of gout, the uric acid level will, however, fall within the reference range. The diagnosis of acute gout cannot be made merely because of the presence of an acutely swollen joint and a high serum uric acid level. The diagnosis depends on the demonstration of uric acid crystals in synovial fluid. Serial uric acid estimations are useful to monitor the effect of hypo-uricemic drugs.

REFERENCES

1. Alamanos Y, Drosos AA. Epidemiology of adult rheumatoid arthritis. *Autoimmun Rev* 2005;4(3):130–6.
2. Carter N, Williamson L, Kennedy L et al. Susceptibility to ankylosing spondylitis. *Rheumatology* 2000;39(4):445.
3. Gladman DD, Antoni C, Mease P et al. Psoriatic arthritis: epidemiology, clinical features, course, and outcome. *Ann Rheum Dis* 2005;64(Suppl 2):ii, 14–17.
4. Kim TH, Uhm WS, Inman RD. Pathogenesis of ankylosing spondylitis and reactive arthritis. *Curr Opin Rheumatol* 2005;17(4):400–5.
5. Baraliakos X, Landewe R, Hermann KG et al. Inflammation in ankylosing spondylitis: a systematic description of the extent and frequency of acute spinal changes using magnetic resonance imaging. *Ann Rheum Dis* 2005;64(5):730–4.
6. Bennett AN, McGonagle D, O'Connor P et al. Severity of baseline magnetic resonance imaging-evident sacroiliitis and HLA-B27 status in early inflammatory back pain predict radiographically evident ankylosing spondylitis at eight years. *Arthritis Rheum* 2008;58(11):3413–8.
7. Harris E, ed. *Clinical features of rheumatoid arthritis.* Philadelphia: WB Saunders, 2001.
8. Lee DM, Schur PH. Clinical utility of the anti-CCP assay in patients with rheumatic diseases. *Ann Rheum Dis* 2003;62(9):870–4.
9. Riedemann JP, Munoz S, Kavanaugh A. The use of second generation anti-CCP antibody (anti-CCP2) testing in rheumatoid arthritis—a systematic review. *Clin Exp Rheumatol* 2005;23(5 Suppl 39):S69–76.
10. Brown M, Wordsworth P. Predisposing factors to spondyloarthropathies. *Curr Opin Rheumatol* 1997;9(4):308–14.

D

Chapter 56

Common sports-related infections

with ZAFAR IQBAL and HASAN TAHIR

I've been feeling ill for four weeks. We thought originally it was just a virus but found out through tests that it is malaria. I don't know when I caught it but am very glad I'm over the worst of it. I'm hoping to be back to full fitness in the next couple of weeks. Ivory Coast and Chelsea striker Didier Drogba, quoted in www.thesun.co.uk, November 2010

Sportspeople are subject to the same infections as the rest of the community; however, certain circumstances in sport may increase the susceptibility of sportspeople to infections. Sportspeople involved in team sports have close contact with teammates, which increases the likelihood of spread of infection. In addition, team members often share food and drink, particularly since the increased use of squeeze bottles during exercise.

In this chapter we:

- review the relationships between exercise/activity and infections
- discuss whether sportspeople should exercise/train when suffering an infection
- discuss management of a range of specific infections in athletes according to the region of presentation—skin, respiratory, gastrointestinal and liver etc.
- outline national infection prevention strategy guidelines.

Exercise and infection

There is considerable debate regarding the relationship between exercise and infection. It is important to, firstly, consider the relationship between exercise and the immune system, and then examine whether there is an increased incidence of infection associated with intense exercise. Finally we discuss when an athlete can train and play with an infection.

Exercise and the immune system

The immune system can be considered as two complementary parts.[1] First is the innate immune system, which is non-specific regarding host defense. Its components include the skin, mucous membranes, phagocytes, natural killer (NK) cells, cytokines, and complement factors. The latter two elements control and mediate immune function and help activate T- and B-lymphocytes, key parts of the acquired immune system. In contrast to the innate system, the acquired system protects the body against specific infectious agents during both initial and subsequent attacks.[1]

The body's first line of defense consists of skin and mucous membranes, which can be impaired by temperature, wind, sun, humidity, and trauma. Many upper respiratory pathogens are airborne and affected by airflow patterns, mechanical barriers, and ciliary action in the respiratory tract.[1]

During exercise, the sportsperson switches from nasal to mouth breathing, and this can increase deposition of harmful articles in the lower respiratory tract. It also causes increased cooling and drying of the respiratory mucosa, which slows ciliary movement and increases mucous viscosity.[2]

NK cells express spontaneous cytolytic activity against cells infected with viruses.[1] NK cell counts increase 150–300% immediately after high-intensity exercise lasting less than 1 hour. Within 30 minutes of the end of such high-intensity exercise, however, NK cell counts fall below pre-exercise levels.[3] NK cell activity increases by 40–100% in response to acute exercise of less than 1 hour in duration, and falls to 25–40% below pre-exercise levels 1–2 hours into recovery time. Intense exercise lasting longer than 1 hour causes no rise in NK cell activity. There is, however, a more pro-found and sustained drop in NK cell activity in recovery, which is likely to be a cortisol-induced effect.[4]

Macrophages phagocytose foreign particles, present antigens to lymphocytes, and produce lymphocyte-stimulating cytokines.[2] Acute strenuous exercise increases the macrophage count and several aspects of macrophage function. Long-term training seems to attenuate the macrophage response to acute exercise, but the resulting macrophage function is still greater than in untrained subjects.[3]

Cytokines are produced by and mediate communication between immune and non-immune cells, and are divided into pro-inflammatory and anti-inflammatory types. Pro-inflammatory cytokines such as tumor necrosis factor (TNF)-α, interleukin (IL)-1 and IL-6 are increased with acute exercise. IL-6 levels can increase up to 100-fold after a marathon. Anti-inflammatory cytokines such as IL-10 and IL-1 receptor antagonist (IL-1ra) also increase with exercise.

Neutrophils are capable of phagocytosis both alone and in response to antigen-dependent defenses.[1] Neutrophil counts increase with acute exercise, most likely due to demargination, and several hours after exercise, a cortisol-induced phenomenon. Acute moderate exercise increases neutrophil activity, but acute intense exercise suppresses it.[3] Endurance training reduces several aspects of neutrophil function compared with being sedentary. It seems that long-term moderate training increases neutrophil counts whereas intense training decreases them.[3]

The acquired portion of the immune system has the ability to form a memory and attack specific foreign particles that have invaded the body previously. The main components of this system are T- and B-lymphocytes and plasma cell–secreted antibodies. Overall, lymphocyte counts increase with acute exercise. Lymphocyte counts and B-cell function are decreased after intense exercise, but not after moderate exercise.

Antibody production, most notably IgA, is impaired by intense prolonged exercise.[1] Cross-country skiers have low baseline salivary IgA levels, which further decline after racing. Studies of longitudinal changes in salivary IgA levels in swimmers have yielded conflicting results.[1] IgG does not seem to be affected as much by intense training, although some elite sportspeople show a small decrease during peak training.[2]

Among T-lymphocytes are the CD4+ (T-helper) and CD8+ (T-suppressor) cells. A ratio of CD4+ to

CD8+ cells of 1.5:1 is considered necessary for proper cellular immune function. Heavy exercise decreases this ratio by decreasing CD4+ cells and increasing CD8+ cells. A decreased CD4+ count also diminishes cytokine output, which decreases NK cell and macrophage activation, and B-cell proliferation.[2]

The brief period of immunosuppression after acute intense physical activity, when ciliary action, mucosal IgA levels, NK cell count and activity, T-lymphocyte count, and CD4+ to CD8+ ratio are decreased, is an immunological "open window" during which a sportsperson may be more susceptible to infection.

Exercise and clinical infections

Given the measurable changes in the immune system with exercise, are sportspeople more susceptible to infections? A number of studies have been performed examining the incidence of upper respiratory tract infection and exercise. The results are conflicting, although there is some evidence that intense training is associated with a higher level of infection.[1]

Nieman[5] has proposed the J curve (Fig. 56.1). According to this theory, regular moderate exercise decreases the risk of upper respiratory tract infection to below that of sedentary individuals, whereas strenuous intense exercise increases the risk above that of sedentary individuals. The exact frequency, duration, type, and intensity of exercise required to optimally lower one's risk of infection, or to adversely increase the risk of infection, remain to be determined.[1]

Foster[6] proposed identifiable parameters of training which related to illness. He related the incidence of common illness to indices of training load and noted a correspondence between spikes in the indices

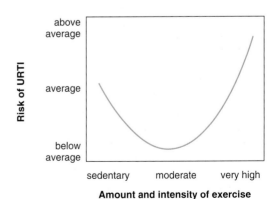

Figure 56.1 The association between exercise and susceptibility to upper respiratory tract infection
FROM NIEMAN[5]

of training and subsequent (within 10 days) illness, and computed individual thresholds that allowed for optimal explanation of illnesses. On these calculations, 84% of illnesses could be explained by a preceding spike in training load above the individual training threshold. However, 55% of the excursions above the threshold were accomplished without a related illness. A subsequent study failed to support Foster's theory.[7]

Infection and athletic performance

Infection or subclinical infection is commonly used to explain poor athletic performance. Infection may compromise muscle enzyme activity and muscle strength. Impaired muscle metabolism has also been demonstrated using MRI. Exercise performed during illness also requires greater cardiopulmonary effort. These findings may theoretically lead to a detrimental effect of infection on performance.

See the box below for a discussion of the issue of whether a sportsperson should train during illness.

A number of studies have been performed at the Australian Institute of Sport in Canberra examining the relationship between mild illness and sporting performance. An initial study in elite swimmers did not show any statistically significant decrease in performance in competition in those who had suffered a minor illness in the month leading up to competition.[8]

In a group of elite middle-distance and distance runners, illness-affected runners reported a higher perceived training intensity. However, laboratory-based measures of performance showed little change in physical work capacity.[7] A third study in another group of elite swimmers suggested that mild illness had a trivial effect on the competitive performances of female swimmers, and a substantial though small harmful effect in male swimmers. In this study it was noted that, although the mean harmful effects were trivial to small, the chances of harm for individuals were substantial.[9]

Should a sportsperson train during illness?

One of the most difficult dilemmas facing the clinician and the sportsperson is to decide whether or not to train and/or compete in the presence of a viral illness.

It is important to differentiate those sportspeople suffering from viral illness into two groups—those with symptoms restricted to one system, usually the upper respiratory tract, and those with generalized symptoms. A sportsperson with an upper respiratory tract infection manifesting itself as a sore throat, runny nose, or headache, who is afebrile, should be allowed to continue with mild-to-moderate training below 80% of Vo_2max.

Exercise in moderately fit and active people with an upper respiratory tract infection does not prolong or intensify the illness.[10]

Modification of the training program may involve increased skill training with less anaerobic or endurance training for the period of the illness.

Those sportspeople with systemic symptoms of general malaise, excessive fatigue, muscle pains and tenderness, temperature in excess of 38°C (100°F), or a resting heart rate greater than 10 beats above normal should avoid any athletic activity until the systemic symptoms and signs return to normal or near normal. Activity should then be gradually resumed.

Engaging in intense exercise during an infection has been associated with an increased risk of heat exhaustion,[11] post-viral fatigue syndrome,[12, 13] and viral myocarditis.[14]

This differentiation between the two forms of viral illness is known as the "neck check."[11, 15]

PRACTICE PEARL

If symptoms are above the neck (runny nose, nasal congestion, sore throat) and not associated with symptoms below the neck (fever, malaise, muscle aches, severe cough, gastrointestinal), then the athlete may commence training at half-intensity for 10 minutes. If symptoms do not worsen, then the training session can continue as tolerated.

There is no evidence that exercise will affect the severity or duration of an illness.[16] If symptoms of viral illness are generalized, sportspeople should not train intensely or compete. If they are confined to one area (e.g. sore throat), then they can train moderately.

Common infections in sportspeople

Sportspeople are subject to the same infections as those suffered by the rest of the community; however, in certain circumstances in sport there may be an increase in the susceptibility to infections. The accurate diagnosis, management, and prevention of infections is important to limit disruption of training and subsequent performance. Sports-related infections can cause serious complications and even epidemics that sideline entire teams.

We review infections according to their clinical presentation—those affecting skin, the respiratory system, the gastrointestinal tract.

Skin infections

Skin infections occur more commonly in sportspeople than sedentary individuals.[17] Sportspeople are at risk for skin infections because of several factors. These include skin-to-skin contact with other sportspeople and athletic equipment, and an increased likelihood of skin trauma such as abrasions and lacerations. Further, increased sweating and occlusive clothing form the perfect environment for skin infections. Skin infections may be due to viruses (e.g. herpes simplex, molluscum contagiosum, warts), bacteria (e.g. impetigo, folliculitis, otitis externa) or fungi (e.g. tinea, scabies, lice).

Viral skin infections

Contact sports such as wrestling or rugby have a higher rate of viral skin infections than non-contact sports.[17] Training environments may promote the transmission of some viral infections via fomites, such as weights, mats, weight benches, pool decks and communal showers.[18] The three main viral infections that affect sportspeople are herpes simplex, molluscum contagiosum, and warts (verrucae).

Herpes simplex virus infections

Herpes simplex virus (HSV-1) skin infections occur in sportspeople, particularly among wrestlers (herpes gladiatorum) and rugby forwards (herpes rugbeiorum or "scrum pox"). The virus is transmitted through skin-to-skin contact. Outbreaks have been reported particularly among wrestlers. A review of a recent outbreak suggested that there is a 33% probability of transmission if herpes develops on a sparring partner.[19]

In contact sports, lesions are common on the head and may involve the eyes, leading to conjunctivitis or blepharitis (infection of the eyelids). HSV infections can be extremely painful and may be accompanied by systemic symptoms such as fever and malaise. These symptoms represent the prodrome, but not every episode of HSV has a prodrome.

After an incubation period of 5–10 days, asymptomatic shedding of viral particles and the development of clinical lesions may occur. The vesicles rupture quickly and crust over within a few days. Crusted lesions last five to seven days, and may take two to three weeks to heal completely.[17] The diagnosis is made on the typical appearance of the herpes lesions and can be confirmed with viral cultures.

Herpes labialis (cold sores) typically appear at mucocutaneous junctions, especially on the lip. They may affect snow skiers and others who are exposed to cold stress or to increased ultraviolet solar radiation at high altitudes. In healthy patients, the infection is self-limited and does not usually require treatment. However, one may consider systemic treatment if lesions are noticed within 72 hours, to reduce outbreaks and suppress herpes recurrences.

Treatment of HSV is with oral acyclovir or valaciclovir immediately with the onset of prodromal symptoms for seven to ten days. Topical acyclovir is not helpful. The earlier the antiviral is taken, the more effective it is.

HSV is highly contagious and no one should compete in a contact sport until the scabs have dried and there are no further vesicles, ulcers, or drainage. In the US where high school and college wrestling is a popular sport, organizations have imposed strict rules. The National Collegiate Athletic Association's (NCAA) rules include the following:[20]

- The athlete must be free of systemic symptoms (fever, malaise).
- The athlete must be free of any new lesions for 72 hours.
- No moist lesions, and all lesions must have a firm, adherent crust.
- The athlete must be using appropriate antiviral medication for 120 hours (five days) before competition.
- Covering active lesions is not acceptable.

As HSV is not eliminated, recurrences may occur, particularly at times of undue physical or psychological stress. Recurrent attacks are usually milder, lasting only five days. Treatment is the same but a shorter course.

None of these recommendations, however, are evidence-based. On the basis of virus shedding studies in herpes genitalis, the sportsperson can probably return to competition four to seven days after a recurrent outbreak,[19] whereas others recommend removing the sportsperson from practice and competition for eight days.[21]

Molluscum contagiosum

Molluscum contagiosum is characterized by discrete white to skin-colored, umbilicated papules that are 3–5 mm (~0.2 in.) in diameter, which mainly affect children. It is caused by a virus from the Poxviridae family.[17] The papules are more common in swimmers, gymnasts, and wrestlers, and are commonly seen on the hands, forearms, and face. They are generally asymptomatic and spread by skin-to-skin contact.

Treatment is generally recommended, particularly if a sportsperson participates in a contact sport. The infection is self-limited but may take months or even years to resolve without treatment.[17] The most common method of treatment is application of liquid nitrogen or curettage. Lesions should be covered while playing contact sport. Patients should be educated about prevention of spread of the disease—by use of separate towels and other measures of basic hygiene.

Warts (verrucae)

Warts, or verrucae, are caused by infection with various forms of the human papilloma virus (HPV). They are commonly seen on the hands and feet and tend to be hard and have a verrucous surface. Infectivity is low, but warts are transmitted either by direct skin-to-skin contact or through fomites such as swimming pool decks and showers. Warts are frequently spread by autoinoculation from shaving, scratching, or other skin trauma. Plantar warts can be painful and should be treated.

Visual inspection is usually sufficient for diagnosis. The main challenge is distinguishing a wart from a callus. Warts do not retain the normal fingerprint lines on the hands and feet that corns and calluses do. A wart on the surface of the foot can also be distinguished from a callus by paring the lesion down with a no.15 blade. Warts will have 10 to 15 pinpoint black spots that are thrombosed capillaries. Once the wart has been pared down it can be treated with liquid nitrogen.

Sportspeople can return to competition as soon as warts have been treated, but the warts should remain covered until completely resolved.[17]

Bacterial skin infections

Staphylococci and streptococci are the most common bacterial organisms causing skin infections. They may present as various conditions such as impetigo, folliculitis, furunculosis, and boils.[22]

Impetigo

Impetigo is a skin infection that is easily spread from person to person; it is particularly common in sports with close skin-to-skin contact, such as wrestling and the various football codes. Impetigo has two different presentations—bullous and non-bullous—with multiple lesions affecting the face or extremities.

The bullous form typically begins as multiple fluid-filled vesicles that either coalesce or individually enlarge, forming blister-like lesions that eventually collapse centrally. The center has a classic honey-crusted lesion that, when removed, reveals erythematous plaques draining serous fluid.

Non-bullous impetigo originates as small vesicles or pustules with erythematous bases and honey-colored crusts which also drain fluid. Breaks in the skin provide an avenue for bacterial invasion. Patients are typically afebrile, but enlarged lymph glands may be present.[23]

In most cases the diagnosis is made clinically; it can be confirmed with bacterial cultures when necessary. Impetigo may resolve spontaneously but when the disorder is widespread treatment should be implemented, either with topical (fucidic acid [fusidate sodium] or mupirocin) or oral (flucloxacillin, cephalexin) antibiotics for 7–10 days.[24]

Scratching should be resisted because of the highly contagious nature of the infection; an antihistamine is sometimes prescribed. All lesions should be covered during contact sport. The NCAA wrestling guidelines state that the sportsperson must take antibiotics for 72 hours before competition and be free from any new skin lesion for 48 hours.[20]

Folliculitis, furunculosis (boils), and carbuncles

Folliculitis is a superficial infection of the upper portion of the hair follicle and surrounding areas, characterized by mildly tender papules or pustules surrounded by erythema.

Furunculosis (boil) is an infection of the deeper hair follicle cavity; the lesions usually contain pus and present as large, well-defined erythematous and fluctuant nodules that commonly occur in areas of increased sweating and friction, such as the buttock, belt line, anterior thigh, and axilla.[23]

A carbuncle describes confluent infection of multiple, contiguous hair follicles like multiple boils, in which the infection is limited to the subcutaneous tissue.

Local treatment of these infections includes using chlorhexidine and applying saline or aluminum subacetate soaks/compresses for 15 minutes, twice daily. Widespread infection should be treated with anti-staphylococcal antibiotics (e.g. flucloxacillin 500 mg four times a day for 7–14 days). Boils and abscesses may require incision and drainage.

Pseudomonas or "hot tub" folliculitis is usually contracted in spas or hot tubs. Symptoms appear from 6 hours to five days after bathing in contaminated water and include generalized malaise, low-grade fever, and headache, accompanied by a pustular rash commonly appearing in the axilla, perineum, or buttocks. The rash is usually self-limiting and disappears after seven to 14 days. These infections are prevented by adequate filtration and chlorination of the baths.

Folliculitis may also occur after a vigorous massage (especially when insufficient lubricants are used) or after leg waxing or shaving.

Fungal skin infections

Fungal skin infections are common among sportspeople because of the presence of sweat and occlusive clothing or footwear.

Tinea

The most common fungal skin infections are tinea pedis ("athlete's foot") and tinea cruris ("jock itch"). Topical antifungal cream (e.g. clotrimazole, miconazole, ketoconazole) is effective in most cases of tinea pedis and cruris. This should be applied two to three times per day over the affected areas for two to four weeks. Moist infections between the toes resolve more quickly with the addition of drying powders.

 Preventive measures include regular changes of socks, shorts, and underwear, the use of foot powders, and regular cleaning of shower facilities.

Resistant cases should be referred to a dermatologist for alternative medications. Oral therapy (e.g. terbinafine, griseofulvin, or itraconazole) is generally required, after confirmation of diagnosis, for tinea infections of the scalp, hair, and nails.

Tinea gladiatorum is a fungal infection that is transmitted through skin-to-skin contact in wrestlers. It is the second most common skin infection in wrestlers after herpes, with a prevalence of between 20% and 75%. Although it is fairly benign, it can have major effects on the ability of the wrestler to compete. Screening of all wrestlers and disinfection of mats can help reduce spread.[25]

Onychomycosis

Onychomycosis is a fungal nail infection, typically caused by *Tricophyton rubrum* or *Tricophyton mentagrophytes*. It is common among sportspeople, particularly those who swim in pools, use communal showers, or have chronic tinea pedis and wear occlusive footwear.[26] The infection results from migration of the fungus under the distal nail plate leading to a nail bed infection that results in discoloration of the nail plate. Subungual debris then forms and the nail plate becomes distorted, thickened, and separated from the nail bed. Over time the nail plate becomes brittle and crumbles.[27] Treatment requires a long-term commitment with either an oral antifungal agent or topical nail lacquer.[28]

Scabies

Scabies mites are easily transmitted through skin-to-skin contact. Once on the skin surface the mite burrows into the epidermis, but symptoms may not arise until three to four weeks after exposure.[27]

Infestation manifests as small linear burrows and/or vesicles characteristically in axillary skin folds, finger and toe web spaces, the flexor surface of the wrists, the extensor surface of the elbows and knees, periumbilicus, genitalia, buttocks, and lateral foot. The most prominent symptom is severe itching.

Confirmation of the diagnosis can be made by direct microscopic visualization of mites from an infected papule. Topical therapy with acarides such as permethrin 5% cream or malathion 0.5% liquid is very effective if applied twice, a week apart. It is also important to treat close contacts.

Pediculosis (lice)

Lice can occur on the body (pediculosis corporis), head (pediculosis capitis), and genitalia (pediculosis pubis); they are spread by close physical contact.[27] Once a person is infested, it can take up to 10 days for the nit (louse egg) to hatch. Patients may describe night-time itching and may develop an inflammatory reaction to scratching. As bites emerge, they appear as 2–4 mm (<0.25 in.) red papules on an erythematous base. Diagnosis can be confirmed by direct visualization. Various over-the-counter medications are available for head lice. Most involve application to the scalp once and, if required, again seven days later. In addition, a fine comb should be used to remove nits, and all clothing, bed linen, and sporting equipment should be washed and dried in a hot dryer or discarded.

Respiratory and ear, nose, and throat infections

The major ear, nose, and throat infections include various forms of influenza and infectious mononucleosis (IM). IM brings with it the risk of splenic enlargement and, thus, splenic rupture in sportspeople (see below). Ear infections are a common problem in water sports.

Viral

Infections of the upper and lower respiratory tracts are common, especially during winter months. In the vast majority of cases these are due to viruses. Over 200 different viruses can cause upper respiratory tract infections; those commonly involved are the adenovirus, influenza virus, echovirus, cytomegalovirus, and rhinovirus. They may cause rhinitis, pharyngitis, bronchitis, or pneumonia.

Treatment is usually aimed at controlling the accompanying fever and reducing the symptoms. Some symptomatic treatments are on the list of substances banned by the World Anti-Doping Agency (WADA) (Chapter 66). Antibiotics should not be used unless bacterial infection is suspected.

Influenza

Influenza ("flu") is a common viral infection occurring in winter months. The flu season typically begins in November until April in the temperate northern hemisphere and April to October in the southern hemisphere. There are a number of strains of influenza virus; the predominant strain tends to vary from year to year.

Influenza can be a debilitating illness with systemic symptoms such as fever, malaise, and myalgia. It is recommended that susceptible individuals, such as the elderly and those with a chronic illness, have annual influenza immunization.

Sportspeople may wish to have annual influenza immunization as the illness may result in their missing a considerable period of competition and training. Sportspeople involved in team sports may wish to be immunized because of the possibility of spread among team members. However, there is conflicting evidence for the effectiveness of influenza immunization in healthy adults.

A 2010 Cochrane review noted that "influenza vaccines have a modest effect in reducing influenza symptoms and working days lost" in healthy adults but found no evidence of prevention of complications, such as pneumonia, or transmission.[29] Some recently developed anti-influenza drugs are showing promise as a possible treatment for those who are in the early stages of the illness.

Infectious mononucleosis

The Epstein-Barr virus (EBV) causes infectious mononucleosis, also known as "glandular fever" or "mono." The incidence of infectious mononucleosis is highest in adolescence and early adulthood with 1–3% of American college students reported to become infected each year.[30] Many clinicians believe that the incidence of infectious mononucleosis is higher in sportspeople who are training intensely but there are no studies to support (or refute) this claim.

Clinical perspective

The severity of the infection appears to increase with age. Children infected by the Epstein-Barr virus develop a flu-like illness. Adolescents and young adults typically develop symptoms of fatigue, sore throat, malaise, headache, and, less commonly, myalgia, nausea and vomiting.

Examination of the typical 15- to 19-year-old patient reveals an exudative pharyngitis and swollen cervical lymph nodes. A fever of 39–40°C (102–104°F) is common. Splenomegaly due to lymphocyte infiltration occurs in about 50% of cases and peaks in the second or third week of the illness. A similar clinical picture may be seen with cytomegalovirus infection, toxoplasmosis, and primary infection with HIV.

Patients with infectious mononucleosis who are treated with ampicillin or amoxicillin often develop a diffuse macular rash. Older patients have an increased tendency to develop complications of infectious mononucleosis, such as hepatitis or thrombocytopenia (reduced platelet count).

The virus is spread through close contact, especially saliva (kissing). The incubation period is usually between 30 and 50 days after exposure to the virus, and the illness lasts between five and 15 days.

However, tiredness may be more prolonged and, in some patients, may continue for a number of months.

Investigations

Investigations usually reveal a moderately raised white cell count ($10-20 \times 10^9$/L) with an increase in the number of lymphocytes (50% or more of total white blood cell count). Between 10% and 20% of these lymphocytes are usually described as "atypical." Mild thrombocytopenia (platelet count <140×10^9/L) occurs in approximately 50% of patients. Liver function test abnormalities occur in approximately 75% of patients. The development of jaundice, however, is uncommon. Enlargement of the spleen may be confirmed on ultrasound.

Confirmation of infectious mononucleosis is usually made serologically. The presence of heterophile antibodies can be seen in 85–90% of acute EBV infections. Most clinical laboratories use some form of latex agglutination method such as the Monospot and Paul Bunnell tests. These tests are usually positive in the second week of illness. False negative results occur but other diagnoses (e.g. cytomegalovirus, HIV, toxoplasmosis) should be considered in the presence of a negative Monospot result.

In the 10–15% who never develop a positive Monospot test result, EBV-specific antibodies are measured. Most laboratories provide IgM and IgG antibody results. The IgM assay is positive in an acute infection and remains so for one to two months. The IgG antibodies tend to persist for life so are not indicative of current infection, only that a previous infection has occurred.

Treatment

Treatment of infectious mononucleosis involves symptomatic treatment to reduce fever and sore throat. Infectious mononucleosis is not particularly contagious despite the relatively high incidence in adolescents and young adults. There is no need for isolation of the sportsperson with infectious mononucleosis. Many people have adequate antibody levels because of childhood exposure.

The sportsperson with infectious mononucleosis should rest from sporting activity until all acute symptoms have resolved.

Risk of splenic rupture in infectious mononucleosis

The incidence of splenic rupture in cases of infectious mononucleosis is thought to be between only 0.1% and 0.2%.[31, 32] Contact and collision sports should be avoided while the spleen is enlarged as splenic rupture can be fatal. Most reports of splenic ruptures have occurred during the first three weeks of illness and so it is thought that spleen vulnerability peaks in this period.[32] The dilemma for the treating physician is how to determine that the spleen size has returned to normal. If the spleen is palpable, then it is clearly enlarged. However, many enlarged spleens are not palpable.

Ultrasound is used to measure spleen size. Simple linear ultrasonographic measurements are often used, but there is uncertainty as to the normal size. An upper limit of normal of 12 cm (6 in.) length, 7 cm (3.5 in.) width and 4 cm (2 in.) thickness has been proposed, but spleen size varies considerably between individuals, although it correlates reasonably well with body size. Unfortunately, very few individuals have previous ultrasonic measurement of the spleen with which to compare the post-infective size.

As the majority of spleen ruptures have occurred within 21 days of the onset of symptoms, most expert clinicians advise allowing return to play after that period of time, remembering that there is still a slight possibility of rupture at a later date; these risks should be clearly outlined to the patient. See Putukain et al.[32] for a detailed discussion of this issue.

 Peak splenic enlargement by ultrasound occurred within 2–3½ weeks and splenomegaly resolved within 4–6 weeks of the onset of symptoms of infectious mononucleosis.[32]

Otitis externa

Otitis externa is a diffuse inflammation of the skin lining the external auditory meatus which can be caused by either *Pseudomonas* or *Staphlococcal aureus* infection. This is sometimes known as "swimmer's ear" as it is exacerbated by moisture but also by trauma of the ear canal with cotton buds or finger nails.

Otitis externa presents as a painful itch or discharge from the external ear. Pain is aggravated by traction on the tragus of the ear. The external auditory canal is usually swollen and tender and may be filled with debris.

Treatment is by irrigation to remove purulent debris, protection from exposure to water and mechanical trauma (e.g. avoiding ear plugs), and application of antibiotic and steroid combination drops (e.g. Gentisone HC, Sofradex, Kenacomb). There is a high incidence of recurrent infection.

Recurrences may be limited by the use of drying agents such as 5% acetic acid (Aquaear) before and after swimming and the insertion of water-resistant ear plugs. Another simple preventive measure is shaking water out of the ear after swimming and drying the area with a hair dryer.

Otitis media

Otitis media is inflammation of the middle ear and is sometimes associated with upper respiratory tract infections, which may be viral or bacterial. Clinical feature include ear pain, and inflamed or bulging ear drum. Most (80%) recover without antibiotics; nasal decongestants may help.[33] Diving should be avoided until there is normal tympanic membrane movement by as indicated by Valsava or tympanometry due to risk of membrane rupture at depths greater than 1.5 m. Swimming should only be resumed if there is an intact tympanic membrane.

Gastrointestinal and liver infections

Acute gastroenteritis

Acute gastroenteritis remains a major public health concern worldwide. The norovirus (an RNA virus) causes approximately 90% of epidemic non-bacterial outbreaks of gastroenteritis around the world.[34] The viruses are transmitted by contaminated food or water surfaces and person-to-person contact. Because outbreaks of norovirus infection often occur in closed or semi-closed communities (such as hospitals and hotels), it can quickly spread among sports teams where sportspeople are in close contact. Many norovirus outbreaks have been traced to food that was handled by one infected person.[35]

The symptoms of a norovirus gastroenteritis usually start between 12 and 48 hours after the initial infection; the first symptom is usually nausea, followed by projectile vomiting and watery diarrhea. The symptoms normally last 12–60 hours. Norovirus is rapidly inactivated by either sufficient heating or by chlorine-based disinfectants. For the affected individual it is important to ensure good hydration and paracetamol for any fever. It is important to limit spread and to isolate the player as soon as symptoms appear; he or she should not be in contact with other players until having been symptom-free for at least 48 hours.

Travelers' diarrhea

Diarrhea is commonly associated with travel to foreign countries. Limited attacks of diarrhea occur frequently among sportspeople in international competition. Agents that may cause travelers' diarrhea include *Escherichia coli*, *Campylobacter*, rotavirus, *Salmonella*, *Shigella*, and *Giardia lamblia*.

The high incidence of diarrhea among travelers is thought to be due to changes in the normal bacterial flora of the food and water in foreign countries. The traveler is exposed to different bacteria to which he or she is not already immune.

The attack of diarrhea usually occurs in the first week after arrival, and commonly lasts between 24 and 48 hours. It is often associated with mild fever, abdominal pain, and malaise. Although the majority of these illnesses settle quickly, athletic performance may be affected during the attack and for some time afterwards.

Because of the potential effect on performance, attention has been paid to possible methods of preventing travelers' diarrhea. Avoidance of local water and raw foods that may have been washed in water (e.g. salads) is recommended. However, in spite of these precautions infection may still occur.

Prophylaxis

The use of freeze-dried cultures or yoghurt may reduce the possibility of infection.

Antibiotic prophylaxis remains controversial.[36] When deciding whether or not to use this approach, the sportsperson and physician must take into account any underlying medical illnesses, the importance of the competition, compliance of the traveler with food precautions, and individual preference. Antibiotics may cause mild, or in some cases serious, allergic reactions.

For prophylaxis, recommended antibiotics include norfloxacin (400 mg/day) and ciprofloxacin (500 mg/day). These should be commenced on arrival in the foreign country and continued until the athlete has been back home for 48 hours.

Trimethoprim+sulfamethoxazole and doxycycline were popular for prophylaxis in the 1990s but resistance is common now. Bismuth subsalicylate is less effective than antibiotic prophylaxis.

Treatment

Treatment of travelers' diarrhea includes appropriate fluid and electrolyte replacement. Antidiarrheal medications (e.g. loperamide) can be used. Antibiotics can shorten symptoms but they are only indicated if diarrhea is severe, bloody, or persists for more than

48 hours. Choice of antibiotic depends on local practice and resistance. If diarrhea persists for more than five to seven days, infections such as giardiasis should be considered; this can be treated with a single dose of tinidazole (2 g). More persistent diarrhea should be investigated.

Hepatitis

Viral hepatitis is neither a single disease condition nor is it caused by a single viral agent. There are a multitude of viral causes including hepatitis A, B, C, D, E, cytomegalovirus, Epstein-Barr, herpes simplex, and adenovirus to name but a few.

The commonest group is the hepatitis group of viruses of which at least five distinct types have been identified: hepatitis A (HAV), hepatitis B (HBV), hepatitis C (HCV), hepatitis delta or D (HDV), and hepatitis E (HEV).

The sport-specific risks of hepatitis are discussed in the box overleaf.

Hepatitis A

Hepatitis A virus (HAV) infection occurs worldwide. HAV is spread via the fecal–oral route, and is more prevalent in low socioeconomic areas in which a lack of adequate sanitation and poor hygienic practices facilitate spread of the infection. HAV infection usually results in an acute, self-limiting illness and only rarely leads to fulminant hepatic failure.[37]

The diagnosis of acute HAV infection is made by the detection of anti-HAV antibodies in a patient with the typical clinical presentation. Treatment is supportive. Approximately 85% of individuals who are infected with HAV have full clinical and biochemical recovery within three months, and nearly all have complete recovery by six months.[38]

Safe and effective vaccines against HAV are available and sportspeople working or traveling in countries that have a high or intermediate rate of HAV infection should be immunized.

Hepatitis B

Hepatitis B virus (HBV) infection is a global public health problem, and it is estimated that there are more than 350 million HBV carriers in the world, of whom roughly one million die annually from HBV-related liver disease.[39] The predominant mode of transmission of HBV varies in different geographical areas. Perinatal infection is the predominant mode of transmission in high prevalence areas.[40]

In comparison, horizontal transmission, particularly in early childhood, accounts for most cases of chronic HBV infection in intermediate prevalence areas, while unprotected sexual intercourse and intravenous drug use in adults are the major routes of spread in low prevalence areas.[41]

The spectrum of clinical manifestations of HBV infection varies in both acute and chronic disease. During the acute phase, manifestations range from subclinical or anicteric hepatitis to icteric hepatitis and, in some cases, fulminant hepatitis. During the chronic phase, manifestations range from an asymptomatic carrier state to chronic hepatitis, cirrhosis, and hepatocellular carcinoma. Extrahepatic manifestations can also occur with both acute and chronic infection.

The percentage of patients who progress from acute to chronic hepatitis B is determined primarily by the age at infection. The rate is approximately 90% for a perinatally acquired infection, 20–50% for infections acquired between the age of one and five years, and less than 5% for an adult-acquired infection.[39] Chronic carriers of hepatitis B pose a problem regarding their current infectivity risk to others. They should be assessed regularly by a hepatitis specialist for further tests including hepatitis B DNA load to determine how active their condition and thus infectivity is.

Treatment for acute hepatitis B is mainly supportive. In addition, appropriate measures should be taken to prevent infection in exposed contacts. The main aim of treatment for chronic hepatitis B is to suppress replication before there is irreversible liver damage. Treatment strategies for chronic hepatitis B include interferon, lamivudine, adefovir, dipivoxil, telbivudine, entecavir, and tenofovir. Many new treatments are undergoing testing. Thus, an approach to the care of patients with HBV is evolving rapidly.

There are safe and effective vaccines against HBV. Until recently it was only those at increased risk were advised to have an HBV immunization course, but recently HBV immunization has been recommended in all children.[42]

 PRACTICE PEARL Any athlete involved in a contact or collision sport should be immunized against HBV.

Any sportsperson involved in a contact or collision sport should be immunized against HBV. The hepatitis B vaccine (Engerix-B) has a zero-, one- and six-month schedule. Immunity should be assessed 1–4 months after the last course of the vaccine by means of a blood test. If the sportsperson does not produce an adequate response then he or she may need a booster or testing to exclude past or current hepatitis B infection.

Sportspeople and risk of hepatitis

Sportspeople are at risk of developing hepatitis mainly as a result of non-sports-related activity (e.g. sexual contact, sharing needles); however, a small theoretical risk of virus contamination during certain types of athletic activity does exist. The mode of transmission of viral hepatitis from an infected individual varies depending upon the specific viral agent, although some overlap does exist (Table 56.1).

Infection with HAV or HEV is likely to occur as a result of exposure to contaminated food or beverages. The risk of infection is particularly high during international travel to areas with poor hygienic conditions where HAV and HEV are endemic.[43] Direct transmission of HAV or HEV during sports participation has not been described;[44] however, outbreaks of hepatitis among groups of sportspeople have been reported, the most famous of which involved 90 members of an American college football team after an infected group of children contaminated the drinking water used during practice.[45]

For sportspeople, exposure to blood-borne pathogens such as HBV and HCV is also much more likely to occur during non-sports-related activities such as unprotected sexual activity, using injectable drugs such as anabolic steroids, sharing personal items such as razors, and tattooing and body piercing. However, there is the potential for horizontal transmission of HBV and HCV while playing sports, especially contact or collision sports. In a study in wrestlers who were found to be chronic carriers of hepatitis B, it was discovered that sweat may be another way of hepatitis B transmission as the hepatitis B DNA load was similar in the sweat to that of the serum.[46]

The concentration of HBV in blood is higher than of HIV, and HBV is also more stable in the environment; therefore the risk of transmission of HBV is much (actually 50–100 times) greater than the risk of transmission of HIV.[47]

The blood of an infected sportsperson may contaminate the skin or mucous membranes of other sportspeople or staff. Two reports of transmission of HBV among Japanese sportspeople have been described, one in sumo wrestling[48] and the other in American footballers at the University of Okayama.[49]

There has been only one report of HBV transmission in a non-contact sport.[50] Between 1957 and 1963, 568 cases of hepatitis B were reported among Swedish athletes participating in the sport of orienteering. It was thought that the most likely route of contamination was the use of water contaminated with infected blood to clean the wounds on multiple individuals who were cut by thorns and bushes during the competition.

There have been no documented cases of HCV transmission during sporting activity,[44] but there has been a documented case during bloody fisticuffs which was thought to have occurred when the two participants shared a common handkerchief to wipe their bleeding wounds.[51] There has also been a report of three soccer players from one amateur club contracting HCV as a result of sharing a syringe to inject intravenous vitamin complexes.[52]

It is clear that the risk of transmission of both HBV and HCV during sport is very low, and there is no reason why infected individuals should not be allowed to compete. All carriers should have regular follow-up by specialists to monitor viral activity and any systemic effects. There is the dilemma of allowing infected sportspeople to compete without disclosing their status to team members and opposition (Chapter 67).

Table 56.1 Transmission of viral hepatitis[2]

Transmission	HAV	HBV	HCV	HDV	HEV
Fecal–oral	Yes	No	No	No	Yes
Percutaneous	Yes (unusual)	Yes	Yes	Yes	No
Perinatal	No	Yes	Yes	Yes	No
Sexual	Yes (homosexual men)	Yes	Yes	Yes	No

Approximately 90% of people become immune after a course of three injections. If immunity is not present, a further injection should be given. This increases the chance of developing immunity to approximately 95%.

In those who have not been immunized and who experience a known or high-risk exposure to HBV, post-exposure prophylaxis with immune globulin should be administered. Post-exposure immunization with HBV vaccine can attenuate or prevent acute HBV.

Hepatitis C

Infection with the hepatitis C virus (HCV) can result in both acute and chronic hepatitis. The acute process is most often asymptomatic; if symptoms are present, they usually abate within a few weeks. Acute infection rarely causes hepatic failure. Acute hepatitis C typically leads to chronic infection; 60–80% develop chronic hepatitis (abnormal liver enzymes). Chronic hepatitis C is usually slowly progressive; it may not result in clinically apparent liver disease in many patients if the infection is acquired later in life. Approximately 20–30% of chronically infected individuals develop cirrhosis over a 20- to 30-year period.

Chronic hepatitis C is the most common cause of chronic liver disease and the most frequent indication for liver transplantation in the US. The decision to offer antiviral therapy to a treatment-naïve patient is usually straightforward when there is a detectable viral load, significant chronic hepatitis and fibrosis on liver biopsy, and an absence of contraindications to treatment.

Treatment is with combination therapy with peginterferon plus ribavirin. The duration of therapy depends on the patient's HCV genotype. Genotypes 1 and 4 have lower response rates and require longer courses of treatment (48 weeks) compared with HCV genotypes 2 or 3 (24 weeks).

Hepatitis D

Hepatitis D virus (HDV) is often referred to as "hepatitis delta virus" or "delta agent." Although HDV can replicate autonomously, the simultaneous presence of HBV is required for complete virion assembly and secretion. As a result, individuals with hepatitis D are always dually infected with HDV and HBV. Acute HBV and HDV co-infection tends to be more severe than acute HBV infection alone and is more likely to result in fulminant hepatitis.

Hepatitis E

Hepatitis E virus (HEV) is an enterically-transmitted acute viral hepatitis. The epidemiology of HEV is similar to that of HAV. HEV generally causes a self-limiting acute infection, although fulminant hepatitis can develop. The clinical signs and symptoms in patients with typical hepatitis E are similar to those seen with other forms of acute viral hepatitis, although the disease appears to be relatively more severe than hepatitis A.

The diagnosis of HEV is based on the detection HEV in serum or stool by PCR (polymerase chain reaction) or by the detection of IgM antibodies to HEV. Treatment is supportive.

An effective vaccine against HEV has been developed but is not yet commercially available. Travelers to endemic areas (i.e. Asia, Africa, Middle East, and Central America) should engage in practices that may prevent infection, such as avoiding drinking water of unknown purity, uncooked shellfish, and uncooked fruits or vegetables.

Acute viral hepatitis and physical activity

In those patients with acute viral hepatitis, strict bed rest and avoidance of all physical activity are no longer thought to be necessary. Acute hepatitis infection should be viewed just as other viral infections, and the ability to play should be based on clinical signs and symptoms such as fever, fatigue, or hepatomegaly.[53] Hepatomegaly (80%) and splenomegaly (10–20%) may persist after other symptoms have settled. Contact and collision sports should be avoided until the organomegaly has resolved.[43]

Other infections

Human immunodeficiency virus (HIV)

The human immunodeficiency virus (HIV) pandemic has spread to every country in the world and has infected 59 million persons worldwide, including 20 million who have already died.[54] HIV infection is usually acquired through sexual intercourse, exposure to contaminated blood, or perinatal transmission. Risk factors for HIV transmission include viral load, lack of circumcision, sexual risk, presence of ulcerative sexually transmitted diseases, nitrate inhalant use, and host and genetic factors.[55-57]

Infection with HIV initially causes a flu-like illness. This is followed by an asymptomatic period characterized by replication of the HIV virus and antibody formation. The length of this period is variable but may last months or years. This is followed by the development of acquired immunodeficiency syndrome (AIDS), which may present as a variety of diseases associated with the suppression of immunity. These include *Pneumocystis carinii* pneumonia, Kaposi's sarcoma, cytomegalovirus infection, cryptosporidiosis, and lymphoma.

The presence of HIV antibodies can be detected a short time (usually within three months) after the initial exposure. Practicing safe sex and avoiding direct contact with blood or blood products can reduce the risk of HIV infection. There is an extremely slight risk of acquiring HIV from a contact on the sporting field, from an HIV carrier bleeding from an open wound or from bloodstained clothing. This risk has been described as being "exceedingly low" and is estimated to be between one per million and one per 85 million game contacts.[58]

There are no confirmed reports of HIV transmission during sport, although there has been one possible transmission during a football match[59] and a number of reports of transmission during bloody street fights.[60, 61]

Attention to the guidelines described in the box opposite will reduce this risk. Medical personnel attending bleeding players must make every attempt to stop the bleeding and remove all exposed blood. If bleeding cannot be controlled, the player should be removed from the field of play. Medical staff should always wear gloves when treating a bleeding wound.

The optimal level of participation and competition in an HIV-affected sportsperson remains unknown. Healthy, asymptomatic sportspeople with HIV may continue in competition and exercise without restriction but should avoid overtraining. Sportspeople with AIDS may remain physically active and continue training on a symptom-related basis but should avoid strenuous exercise and reduce activity during acute illness.

Sexually transmitted infections

More than 20 different sexually transmitted infections have been identified and should be considered with any patient with testicular pain, penile/uretharal discharge, prostatitis, urethritis, dyspareunia, dysuria, or genital warts.

It should be noted that patients may have more than one sexually transmitted disease and should be screened and tested accordingly. This is particularly important in sportspeople, who need to be aware that sexually transmitted infections have been shown to also cause other symptoms that could affect their athletic performance. These include reactive arthritis, which is an autoimmune condition that develops in response to an infection in another part of the body. By the time the patient presents with symptoms of arthritis, the "trigger" infection has been cured or is in remission in chronic cases, thus making determination of the initial cause difficult. It was reported in a case study of 10 professional sportsmen with persistent knee injuries that eight had sexually acquired reactive arthritis.[62]

Tetanus

Tetanus is caused by *Clostridium tetani* which is normally found in soil and feces; it only flourishes in dead tissue and produces a toxin that targets anterior horn cells (in the spinal cord). A tetanus-prone injury is defined as "an injury where there has been a puncture type of wound, significant devitalized tissue or contact with soil or manure," which is something that should be considered with all open wound injuries in sportspeople especially on the playing field. The incubation period is 2–24 days. Initially there is muscle spasm at injury site; the spasm then progress to the muscles of the face, neck, and spine. It can also cause autonomic dysfunction.

Diagnosis is by clinical assessment with no definitive laboratory test. The single most important step in preventing tetanus infection is good wound cleaning with debridement of dead tissue. Human antitetanus immunoglobulin is given intramuscularly, together with parenteral penicillin. Wound toilet should also be carried out.

If the immune status of a patient is not known, the patient should be assumed to be non-immune. For tetanus a total of 5 doses of vaccine at the appropriate intervals are considered to give lifelong immunity. If the risk of tetanus is especially high (e.g. the wound is contaminated with soil), human tetanus immunoglobulin should be given to provide immediate additional protection.

Preventive measures and reducing risk of infections

As with any medical condition, prevention is better than cure and so it is important that all sportspeople are advised to report any illness immediately to their doctor. By isolating the infected individual, or preventing him or her from mixing with others, the risk of spread is reduced. Where possible, the sportsperson's doctor should consider screening for sexually transmitted infections and conditions for which vaccines may be available.

Sportspeople should also be educated about good hygiene procedures, such as hand-washing, or using antibacterial hand gels, and trying not to share drink bottles (or at least not making direct contact with the mouth and instead squirting the fluid into the mouth). See the national guidelines in the box below.

As sportspeople may compete or reside around the globe, one should consider the appropriate travel immunizations and malaria chemoprophylaxis if required (as illustrated by this chapter's opening quote). The clinician should always enquire about the travel history, in case the player has been in contact with an "exotic" illness. See also Chapters 63 and 64, relating to clinicians working with and traveling with a team.

National position statements on infectious diseases

Sports medicine authorities in Australia, the US and Canada have all produced national position statements on infectious diseases, with particular reference to HIV and hepatitis B. These are summarized below.

A number of blood-borne infectious diseases can be transmitted during body contact and collision sports. The more serious include HIV (AIDS) and hepatitis infections. These diseases may be spread by contact with infected:

- blood
- saliva (not for HIV)
- perspiration (not for HIV)
- semen and vaginal fluids.

The following recommendations will reduce the risk of disease transmission. All open cuts and abrasions must be reported and treated immediately.

Players

1. It is the players' responsibility to maintain strict personal hygiene, as this is the best method of controlling the spread of these diseases.
2. It is strongly recommended that all participants involved in contact sport be vaccinated with hepatitis B vaccine.
3. Players with prior evidence of these diseases must obtain advice and clearance from a physician prior to participation.

Team areas

1. It is the clubs' responsibility to ensure that the dressing rooms be clean and tidy. Particular attention should be paid to hand basins, toilets, and showers. Adequate soap, paper hand towels, brooms, and disinfectants must be available at all times.
2. Communal bathing areas (e.g. spas) should be strongly discouraged.
3. Spitting or urinating in team areas must not be permitted.

4. All clothing, equipment and surfaces contaminated by blood must be considered potentially infectious and treated accordingly. Clothing soiled with blood and other body fluids should be washed in hot, soapy water.
5. Sharing of towels, face washers, and drink containers should be avoided.
6. All personnel working in team areas should be vaccinated against hepatitis B.
7. In all training areas, open cuts and abrasions must be reported and treated immediately.

Referees and game officials

1. These officials must report all open cuts and abrasions at the first available opportunity.
2. Those who officiate in body contact and collision sports should be vaccinated against hepatitis B.
3. All contaminated clothing and equipment must be replaced prior to the player being allowed to resume play.
4. If bleeding should recur, the above procedure must be repeated.
5. If bleeding cannot be controlled and the wound securely covered, the player must not continue in the game.

Education

1. There is an obligation upon all relevant sporting organizations to provide suitable information on associated risk factors and prevention strategies for these diseases.
2. The safe handling of contaminated clothing, equipment, and surfaces must be brought to the attention of all players and ancillary staff.
3. In the event of a player, official, or member of the ancillary staff being found to be suffering from such a blood-borne disease (e.g. hepatitis B, HIV), that person cannot resume training or play, nor be involved in any team or match, until cleared by his or her local medical officer or the team physician.

REFERENCES

1. Metz JP. Upper respiratory tract infections: who plays, who sits? *Curr Sports Med Rep* 2003;2:84–90.

2. Shepard RJ, Shek PN. Exercise, immunity, and susceptibility to infection. A J-shaped relationship? *Phys Sportsmed* 1999;27(6):47–71.

3. Woods J, Davis J, Smith J et al. Exercise and cellular innate immune function. *Med Sci Sports Exerc* 1999;31:57–66.

4. Nieman D. Nutrition, exercise and immune system function. *Clin Sports Med* 1999;18:537–48.

5. Nieman D. Is infection risk linked to exercise workload? *Med Sci Sports Exerc* 2000;32(7):S406–11.

6. Foster C. Monitoring training in athletes with reference to overtraining syndrome. *Med Sci Sports Exerc* 1998;30:1164–8.

7. Fricker PA, Pyne DB, Saunders PU et al. Influence of training loads on patterns of illness in elite distance runners. *Clin J Sport Med* 2005;15(4):246–52.

8. Pyne DB, McDonald W, Gleeson M et al. Mucosal immunity, respiratory illness, and competitive performance in elite swimmers. *Med Sci Sports Exerc* 2001;33:348–53.

9. Pyne DB, Hopkins WG, Batterham AM et al. Characterising the individual performance responses to mild illness in international swimmers. *Br J Sports Med* 2005;39(10):752–6.

10. Nieman DC, Henson DA, Austin MD et al. Upper respiratory tract infection is reduced in physically fit and active adults. *Br J Sports Med* 2011;45(12)987–92.

11. Primos JR WA. Sports and exercise during acute illness. Recommending the right course for patients. *Phys Sportsmed* 1996;24(1):44–54.

12. Budgett R. Fatigue and underperformance in athletes: the overtraining syndrome. *Br J Sports Med* 1998;32:107–10.

13. Parker S, Brukner P. Chronic fatigue syndrome and the athlete. *Sports Med Train Rehab* 1996;6:269–78.

14. Friman G, Wesslen L. Infections and exercise in the high-performance athlete. *Immunol Cell Biol* 2000;78:510–22.

15. Eichner E. Infection, immunity, and exercise: what to tell your patients. *Phys Sportsmed* 1993;21:125.

16. Weidner T, Schurr T. Effect of exercise on upper respiratory tract infecion in sedentary subjects. *Br J Sports Med* 2003;37:304–6.

17. Cyr PR. Viral skin infections. Preventing outbreaks in sports settings. *Phys Sportsmed* 2004;32(7):33–8.

18. Rush S. Sports dermatology. *ACSM Health Fitness J* 2002;6(4):24–6.

19. Anderson BJ. The effectiveness of valacyclovir in preventing reactivation of herpes gladiatorum in wrestlers. *Clin J Sport Med* 1999;9(2):86–90.

20. Bubb RG. *Wrestling rules and interpretations.* Indianapolis: The National Collegiate Athletic Association, 2002.

21. Johnson R. Herpes gladiatorum and other skin diseases. *Clin Sports Med* 2004;23:473–84.

22. Adams BB. Transmission of cutaneous infections in athletes. *Br J Sports Med* 2000;34:413–14.

23. Levy JA. Common bacterial dermatoses. *Phys Sportsmed* 2004;32(6):33–9.

24. Koning S, Verhagen AP, van Suijlekom-Smit LW et al. Interventions for impetigo. *Cochrane Database Syst Rev* 2004(2):CD003261.

25. Hedayati MT, Afshar P, Shokohi T et al. A study on tinea gladiatorum in young wrestlers and dermatophyte contamination of wrestling mats from Sari, Iran. *Br J Sports Med* 2007;41:332–4.

26. Seraly MF, Fuerst ML. Diagnosing and treating onychomycosis. *Phys Sportsmed* 1998;26(8):58–67.

27. Winokur RC, Dexter WM. Fungal infections and parasitic infestations in sports. *Phys Sportsmed* 2004;32(10):23–33.

28. De Berker D. Fungal nail disease. *New Eng J Med* 2009;360:2108–16.

29. Jefferson T, Di Pietrantonj C, Rivetti A et al. Vaccines for preventing influenza in healthy adults. *Cochrane Database Syst Rev* 2010;Jul 7(7):CD001269.

30. Brodski AL, Heath CW. Infectious mononucleosis: epidemiological patterns at United States colleges and universities. *Am J Epidemiol* 1972;96:87–93.

31. Hosey RG, Kriss V, Uhl TL et al. Ultrasonographic evaluation of splenic enlargement in athletes with acute infectious mononucleosis. *Br J Sports Med* 2008;42:974–7.

32. Putukain M, O'Connor F, Stricker P et al. Mononucleousis and atheletic participation: an evidence-based subject review. *Clin J Sport Med* 2008;18(4):309–15.

33. Ramakrishnan K, Sparks RA, Berryhill WE. Diagnosis and treatment of otitis media. *Am Fam Physician* 2007;76(11):1650–8.

34. Lindesmith L, Moe C, Marionneau S et al. Human susceptibility and resistance to Norwalk virus infection. *Nat Med* 2003;9(5):548–53.

35. Koopmans M, Duizer E. Foodborne viruses: an emerging problem. *Int J Food Microbiol* 2004;90(1):23–41.

36. Young MA, Fricker PA, Maughan RJ et al. The traveling athlete: issues relating to the Commonwealth Games, Malaysia, 1998. *Clin J Sport Med* 1998;8:130–5.

37. Taylor RM, Davern T, Munoz S et al. Fulminant hepatitis A virus infection in the United States: incidence, prognosis, and outcomes. *Hepatology* 2006;44:1589–97.

38. Koff RS. Review article: vaccination and viral hepatitis—current status and future prospects. *Aliment Pharm Ther* 2007;26(10):1285–92.

39. Lok AS, McMahon BJ. Chronic hepatitis B: update 2009. *Hepatology* 2009;50:661.

40. Wiseman E, Fraser MA, Holden S et al. Perinatal transmission of hepatitis B virus: an Australian experience. *Med J Aust* 2009;190(9):489–92.

41. Kim WR. Epidemiology of hepatitis B in the United States. *Curr Hep Rep* 2007;6(1):3–8.

42. World Health Organization. Hepatitis B. *www.who.int/mediacentre/factsheets/fs204/en* 2002.

43. Harrington DW. Viral hepatitis and exercise. *Med Sci Sports Exerc* 2000;32:S422–30.

44. Anish EJ. Viral hepatitis: sports-related risk. *Curr Sports Med Rep* 2004;3:100–6.

45. Morse LJ, Bryan JA, Hurley JP et al. The Holy Cross college football team hepatitis outbreak. *JAMA* 1972;219:706–8.

46. Bereket-Yücel S. Risk of hepatitis B infections in Olympic wrestling. *Br J Sports Med* 2007;41(5):306–10.

47. Kordi R, Wallace WA. Blood borne infections in sport: risks of transmission, methods of prevention, and recommendations for hepatitis B vaccination. *Br J Sports Med* 2004;38:678–84.

48. Kashiwagi S, Hayashi J, Ikematsu H et al. An outbreak of hepatitis B in members of a high school sumo wrestling club. *JAMA* 1982;248:213–14.

49. Tobe K, Matsuura K, Ogura T et al. Horizontal transmission of hepatitis B virus among players of an American football team. *Arch Intern Med* 2000;160:2541–5.

50. Ringertz O, Zetterberg B. Serum hepatitis among Swedish track finders. *N Engl J Med* 1967;276:540–6.

51. Bourliere M, Halfon P, Quenin Y et al. Covert transmission of hepatitis C virus during fisticuffs. *Gastroenterology* 2000;119(2):507–11.

52. Parana R, Lyra L, Trepo C. Intravenous vitamin complexes used in sporting activities and transmission of HCV in Brazil. *Am J Gastroenterol* 1999;94:857–8.

53. American Medical Society for Sports Medicine. Human immunodeficiency virus and other blood-borne pathogens in sports. *Clin J Sport Med* 1995;5(3):199–204.

54. UNAIDS. Report on the global AIDS epidemic, 2004. Bangkok, Thailand, 2004.

55. Quinn TC, Wawer MJ, Sewankambo N et al. Viral load and heterosexual transmission of human immunodeficiency virus type 1. Rakai Project Study Group. *N Engl J Med* 2000;342(13):921–9.

56. Gray RH, Wawer MJ, Brookmeyer R et al. Probability of HIV-1 transmission per coital act in monogamous, heterosexual, HIV-1-discordant couples in Rakai, Uganda. *Lancet* 2001;357(9263):1149–53.

57. Dorak MT, Tang J, Penman-Aguilar A et al. Transmission of HIV-1 and HLA-B allele-sharing within serodiscordant heterosexual Zambian couples. *Lancet* 2004;363(9427):2137–9.

58. Brown L, Drotman P, Chu A, Brown CL Jr et al. Bleeding injuries in professional football: estimates of the risk of HIV transmission. *Ann Intern Med* 1995;122:271–5.

59. Torre D. Transmission of HIV-1 infection via a sports injury. *Lancet* 1990;335:1105.

60. Ippolito G, Del Paggio P, Arici C et al. Transmission of zidovudine-resistant HIV during a bloody fight. *JAMA* 1994;272:433–4.

61. O'Farrell N, Tovey SJ. Transmission of HIV-1 infection after a fight. *Lancet* 1992;339:246.

62. Coghlan A. Shagged out. *New Scientist* 1999;5–7.

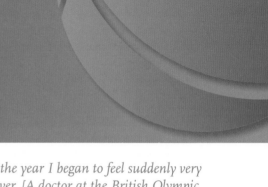

Chapter 57

The tired athlete

with KAREN HOLZER

It all started to go wrong in 2003. From the start of the year I began to feel suddenly very tired during training and would not be able to recover. [A doctor at the British Olympic Association] said that I had unexplained underperformance syndrome, a polite way of saying I'd overtrained.   Anna Hemmings, world champion canoeist, from *The Observer*, 2 April 2006

Persistent tiredness, often accompanied by a feeling of lethargy and impaired sporting performance, is a frequent presenting symptom to a sports and exercise medicine practitioner. These symptoms may be the primary reason for a visit to the practitioner, or they may be an additional complaint of a sportsperson presenting with an injury, commonly an overuse injury.

There are many possible causes of persistent tiredness and/or impaired performance in sportspeople. A list of possible causes is shown in Table 57.1. Sportspeople in heavy training are constantly tired but can usually differentiate between normal, "healthy," tiredness and abnormal tiredness, particularly when this is accompanied by a deterioration in training and competition performance. "Healthy" tiredness is usually easily reversed with a day or two of reduced training or rest. This chapter addresses the problem

Table 57.1 Causes of persistent tiredness in sportspeople

Common	Less common	Not to be missed
Overtraining syndrome	Dehydration	Malignancy
Viral illness	Asthma/exercise-induced asthma	Cardiac problems
• Upper respiratory tract infection	Deficiency—magnesium, zinc,	Bacterial endocarditis
• Infectious mononucleosis	vitamin B, vitamin D	Cardiac failure
(glandular fever or "mono")	Allergic disorders	Diabetes
Inadequate carbohydrate intake	Jet lag	Renal failure
Depletion of iron stores	Anemia	Neuromuscular disorders
Inadequate protein intake	Psychological stress	Malabsorption
Insufficient sleep	• Anxiety	Infections
Chronic fatigue syndrome	• Depression	• Hepatitis A, B, C
	Medications	• HIV
	• Beta blockers	• Malaria
	• Anxiolytics	Eating disorders
	• Antihistamines	• Anorexia
	Spondyloarthropathies	• Bulimia
	Hypothyroidism	Pregnancy
		Post-concussive syndrome

of the sportsperson with persistent tiredness whose symptoms do not disappear after a brief period of rest.

Clinical perspective

A summary of the history, examination, and investigations used in the diagnosis of the tired athlete is shown in the box on p. 1121.

History

The degree of tiredness should be established from the history:

- Does the patient fall asleep during the day?
- Is there a constant feeling of fatigue or does tiredness occur only during or after training?
- Is the tiredness constant or intermittent? If it is intermittent, does it occur only at a particular venue (which may indicate an allergy) or only in hot weather (which may indicate dehydration)?
- How long has tiredness been present?
- Was the onset of tiredness related to any particular event, such as an associated viral illness or an overseas trip?
- Are there associated symptoms such as a sore throat or discomfort with swallowing (which may indicate an upper respiratory tract infection or infectious mononucleosis)?
- Are there respiratory symptoms, such as a post-exercise cough or chest tightness (which may indicate exercise-induced asthma or a lower respiratory tract infection)?

Training diary

A comprehensive training history is a crucial diagnostic aid. Note the volume and intensity of training and, in particular, any recent changes in either of these parameters. It is important to take a weekly training history to judge whether or not there is sufficient recovery time between intense training sessions. The sportsperson should be asked whether any active recovery is undertaken (Chapter 10). Also, it is essential to examine the overall training cycle over a period of weeks or months. The concept of periodization is discussed in Chapter 9. Discover what stage of the cycle the sportsperson is at, and what the forthcoming program entails.

Other factors to note include:

- the amount of sleep and bed rest—swimmers, who tend to rise early to train, are particularly susceptible to lack of sleep, and many sportspeople, especially those studying or in employment, find it difficult to get adequate rest and sleep
- the sportperson's social life, which may regularly intrude on sleep
- other commitments (such as sponsors' functions)—it is difficult for many sportspeople to combine training with the demands of a job, study, and social life.

Psychological factors

Any psychosocial factors that may be contributing to the sportsperson's tiredness should also be noted. These may be related to either the sportsperson's sporting performance or to other aspects of his or her life.

Typical sport-related problems are a fear of a major impending competition, concern about poor training performance, and a fear of failure. Factors unrelated to sport may include anxiety or depression related to work, study, or relationships.

Nutrition diary

Inadequate fluid intake may contribute to the development of fatigue, especially in hot weather. Fluid intake before, during, and after training should be noted.

There are a number of possible dietary causes of persistent tiredness and, thus, a full dietary history should be taken. This involves the sportsperson completing a seven-day food diary, which is subsequently analyzed to ensure an adequate carbohydrate, protein, and iron intake.

The sportsperson should also be questioned about eating habits to detect eating disorders (e.g. anorexia, bulimia).

Medical causes

In addition to the multitude of sport-related causes of persistent tiredness, there are numerous medical causes of this symptom. A full medical history should include:

- past history, history of allergies, and current medications
- attention to any cardiac symptoms such as palpitation, ankle edema, or chest pain (which may indicate the presence of bacterial endocarditis or cardiac failure)
- cough, shortness of breath, or wheeze (which suggest asthma or respiratory infection)
- gastrointestinal symptoms such as diarrhea (which raise the possibility of malabsorption)
- muscle weakness (which may indicate a neuromuscular problem)

- a history of travel within the previous few months (which may indicate a tropical infection such as malaria)
- a history of frequent, heavy menstrual bleeding (which suggests iron deficiency and anemia)
- a history of absent periods (which may be due to pregnancy [and an unrecognized cause of tiredness] or weight loss [which is suggestive of an eating disorder]).

Examination

A full physical examination must be performed to exclude any of the possible medical causes of persistent tiredness. Inspection should determine the presence of anemia or jaundice. Examination includes:

- assessment of the upper respiratory tract and cervical lymph nodes
- a thorough cardiovascular examination, including resting pulse, blood pressure, and examination of the heart
- respiratory examination to exclude the presence of a chest infection or asthma
- examination of the abdomen with particular attention to palpation of the liver and spleen
- examining for any evidence of endocrine disease, such as hypothyroidism or diabetes
- neurological examination if indicated by the history.

Investigations

Although the history and examination are the most important contributors to the diagnosis of the tired sportsperson, a number of investigations are performed as part of the routine work-up of this sportsperson. Other investigations may be indicated from the history or examination.

Routine tests include:

- urine, for the presence of glucose, blood, and protein
- full blood examination, including a blood film
- iron studies (iron, ferritin, and transferrin receptor saturation)
- vitamin B12, vitamin D, and folate levels.

Other tests that may be indicated include:

- zinc and magnesium
- urea and electrolyte levels
- liver function tests
- thyroid function tests
- if a viral illness is suspected
  - a Paul Bunnell test or Monospot test for infectious mononucleosis
  - serological examination for cytomegalovirus and Epstein-Barr virus
  - hepatitis and HIV serological examination
- chest X-ray may be performed if there is a clinical suspicion of a cardiac or respiratory tract abnormality
- lung spirometry, if exercise-induced asthma is suspected from the clinical history and examination. Comparison of lung function tests pre- and post-exercise or other challenge tests for exercise-induced asthma should be performed
- skin sensitivity tests and RAST blood tests, if an allergy is suspected.

Overtraining syndrome

The overtraining syndrome is a common cause of persistent tiredness in sportspeople. It may have disastrous consequences for the serious sportsperson. It is important to clarify exactly what is meant by certain terms. The terms "overtraining," "overreaching," "overtraining syndrome," "burnout," and "staleness" have all been used in association with this condition and need to be clarified.

Overtraining is a process of excessive training in high performance sportspeople that may lead to persistent fatigue, performance decrements, neuroendocrine changes, alterations in mood states, and frequent illness, especially upper respiratory tract infections.

The *overtraining syndrome* is a neuroendocrine disorder that may result from the process of overtraining and reflects accumulated fatigue during periods of excessive training with inadequate recovery.

The term *overreaching* describes similar symptoms (fatigue, performance decrements, mood state changes) but of a more transitory nature. Thus, overreaching is resolved with short periods of rest or recovery training, usually within a two-week period, whereas overtraining may require months or occasionally years.

Burnout and *staleness* are other terms previously used to describe overtraining.

Development of the overtraining syndrome

Overreaching is often utilized by sportspeople during a typical training cycle to enhance performance. Intense training, in the short term, can result in a decline in performance; however, when incorporated with appropriate periods of recovery, a

Summary of history, examination, and investigations of the tired sportsperson

History

Full medical history including:

- duration of tiredness
- degree of tiredness
- timing of symptoms
- association with viral illness
- associated symptoms
- training diary
- amount of sleep and rest
- time commitments
- psychological problems
- fluid intake
- dietary history
- menstrual history
- work/personal stress
- associated medical problems
- medications
- allergies

Examination

Full medical examination including:

- pallor
- resting pulse
- blood pressure
- upper respiratory tract including sinuses
- heart
- lungs
- liver/spleen/lymph nodes

- thyroid
- others as indicated

Investigations

Urine testing:

- blood
- glucose
- protein

Routine blood tests:

- hemoglobin
- white cell count
- blood film
- erythrocyte sedimentation rate (ESR)
- C-reactive protein (CRP)
- urea, electrolytes
- serum ferritin/transferrin receptor saturation level
- vitamin B_{12} and folate
- vitamin D
- thyroid function tests

Selective blood tests:

- infectious mononucleosis (Paul Bunnell, Monospot)
- vitamins and minerals (zinc, magnesium)
- serology (Epstein-Barr virus, cytomegalovirus, hepatitis, HIV)

Chest X-ray

ECG/EKG, echocardiography

Lung spirometry/eucapnic voluntary hyperpnea (pre- and post-exercise)

"supercompensation" effect may occur, with the sportsperson exhibiting an enhanced performance when compared with the baseline level.[1]

The overtraining syndrome develops when there is failed adaptation to overload training (Chapter 9) due to inadequate regeneration. A combination of excessive training load and inadequate recovery time results in short-term overtraining or overreaching. The overreaching is associated with impaired performance. If, at this stage, the sportsperson rests and has time to regenerate, the symptoms disappear and supercompensation may occur.

Unfortunately, some sportspeople react to impaired performance by increasing the intensity of their training. This leads to further impairment of performance, which may, in turn, result in the sportsperson increasing training further. A vicious cycle develops and leads to the overtraining syndrome. This progression is demonstrated in Figure 57.1 overleaf.

Clinical perspective

The initial symptom of the overtraining syndrome is usually fatigue but, in time, other symptoms develop. There are a large number of symptoms associated with the overtraining syndrome, although few of these have been clearly documented as reliable and valid indicators of the syndrome.[2]

Some of the physiological variables used as indicators of overtraining include:

- performance decrements despite continued training
- decreased economy of effort during exercise or decreased work rate at lactate threshold
- persistent fatigue

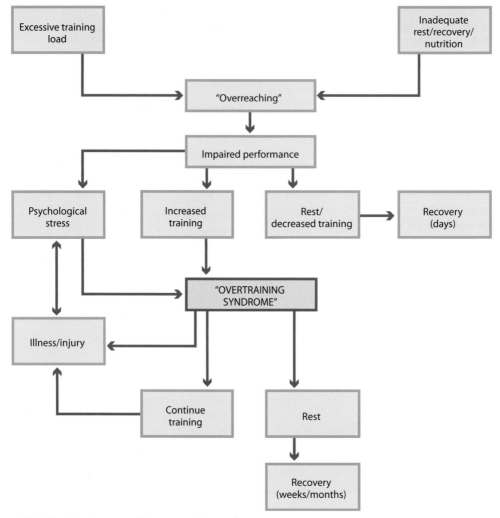

Figure 57.1 The development of the overtraining syndrome

- cardiovascular changes, such as increased early morning heart rate or resting blood pressure
- hematological changes, such as decreased serum ferritin concentration
- hormonal changes, such as decreased catecholamine production or alterations in the ratio of serum free testosterone to cortisol
- frequent illness, such as upper respiratory tract infection
- persistent muscle soreness
- loss of body mass.

Psychological and behavioral variables often associated with the overtraining syndrome include:

- mood state changes as shown by the Profile of Mood States (POMS)[3]

- apathy, lack of motivation
- loss of appetite
- sleep disturbances
- high self-reported stress levels
- irritability or depression.

The only parameters consistently shown in scientific studies[2] to be associated with overtraining are:

- performance decrements
- persistent high fatigue ratings
- decreased maximal heart rate
- changes in the blood lactate threshold, lactate concentration at a given work rate, or maximal blood lactate level
- neuroendocrine changes such as elevated resting plasma noradrenaline (norepinephrine) levels, and

decreased noradrenaline (norepinephrine) excretion
- high self-reported stress levels and sleep disturbances.

Physiological changes

Performance decrements of 10% as well as an inability to maintain training loads are not unusual. In one large study, training pace decreased 11–15%, competition pace decreased 6–17%, and training distance decreased 43–71% in overtrained distance runners.[4] Deterioration in performance is an essential criterion for the diagnosis of overtraining; it is not sufficient as a single marker of the syndrome because performance also may be adversely affected by short-term fatigue.[2] In general, measurements of time to fatigue show greater changes in exercise capacity as a result of overreaching and overtraining;[1] however, these tests are not an accurate performance indicator as they do not truly reflect the demands of competition.

Although many sportspeople and coaches have found the early morning heart rate or resting heart rate useful indicators of overtraining,[5] most scientific studies have failed to confirm this relationship.[6] However, there is good evidence that maximal heart rate (measured at maximal work rate in a progressive exercise test) decreases by 5–10 beats per minute during overreaching/overtraining in endurance sportspeople.[7] "Heart rate variability," the term used to describe the oscillation in the interval between consecutive heart beats, has also been suggested as an indicator of overtraining, but limited research has thus far failed to confirm this correlation.[1]

Biochemical changes

Resting blood lactate levels do not appear to change in overtrained sportspeople; however, decreased blood lactate concentrations at maximal work rate have been consistently noted in overreached/overtrained sportspeople.[8]

Skeletal muscle glycogen depletion has been associated with overtraining in swimmers;[7] however, a study in cyclists showed no evidence of depletion.[8]

Other biochemical markers such as creatine kinase, urea, and iron levels have been considered as possible indicators of overtraining, although findings have been inconsistent.[1]

Overreaching and overtraining can also occur in power athletes, such as weightlifters. Decreases in muscle strength and endurance may be seen in association with fatigue.[9]

Hormonal changes

Basal urinary catecholamine excretion has been reported to be significantly reduced in overtrained sportspeople,[10] and catecholamine excretion has been negatively correlated to fatigue ratings. Furthermore, following a period of recovery, catecholamine excretion returned to baseline values.[10] Both Hooper et al.[6] and Lehmann et al.[11] observed increased resting noradrenaline levels in sportspeople who were thought to be overtrained, or who had undergone a period of increased training that resulted in performance incompetence.

Although resting cortisol levels do not appear to change with overtraining, maximal cortisol responses appear to be reduced. Both Snyder et al.[8] and Urhausen et al.[12] have reported reduced maximal cortisol levels in overreached sportspeople.

The response of both total and free testosterone levels in overreached sportspeople is contradictory. Flynn et al.[13] observed decreased total and free testosterone levels in conjunction with a decease in performance following a period of intensive training. However, Vervoorn et al.,[14] although also reporting lower testosterone levels in rowers following an intense period of training, found these changes in the absence of overtraining. A further study found no significant differences in resting testosterone levels during normal training and a state of overreaching, with an associated reduction in performance.[12]

Testosterone and cortisol are thought to have opposing effects on muscle metabolism, protein synthesis, and growth.[2] The ratio of free testosterone to cortisol is suggested to indicate the balance between androgenic–anabolic activity (testosterone) and catabolic activity (cortisol), and has been suggested as a diagnostic tool for overtraining. Both cortisol and testosterone are released in response to high-intensity aerobic and anaerobic exercise, and it is believed that the ratio of testosterone to cortisol is an indicator of the positive and negative effects of training due to the opposing effects that the hormones have on growth, protein synthesis, and muscle metabolism.[15]

A decrease in the testosterone:cortisol ratio of 30% or more has been suggested as an indicator of overtraining. However, studies have failed to support the usefulness of this ratio; the ratio has been shown to be unchanged in overreached sportspeople,[12] and decreased in sportspeople who show no performance decrements following intensive training.[14] It has been suggested, however, that if followed over time in individual sportspeople, the ratio of these hormones may give an indication of the sportsperson's adaptive response to short-term physiological strain.[16]

Immunological changes

Although there are numerous anecdotal reports of increased susceptibility to illness and infections in sportspeople who are overtrained, there is little scientific evidence to substantiate this.

A number of studies have been performed measuring peripheral leukocyte counts, both during periods of intense training that have resulted in overreaching, and in sportspeople diagnosed as overtrained. In all but one of these studies, a change in leukocyte count has not been demonstrated in overtrained individuals.[1] The single study that demonstrated a change found a significant decline in the leukocyte count when training was increased.[17]

Although resting peripheral blood lymphocyte counts also do not appear to be influenced by overtraining, it has been suggested that the activation of the lymphocytes may be increased.[1] Neutrophil numbers have been reported to be both unchanged and also increased during periods of intensified training; however, neutrophil function has not been assessed in overreached sportspeople, so the role of the neutrophil in immune dysfunction is not known. Natural killer cell numbers appear to be unaltered in sportspeople showing symptoms of overreaching.[1]

Salivary IgA, an important factor in host defense, has been used to study the mucosal immune system response to overtraining. Salivary IgA levels have been shown to be reduced in sportspeople with symptoms of overtraining compared with those sportspeople who were well trained.[18] A further study also reported lower, but not statistically significant, levels of IgA after intensified training.[19]

The production of glutamine, an important substrate for cells of the immune system, especially lymphocytes, macrophages, and, possibly, natural killer cells, is usually increased during periods of immunological challenge.[20] Plasma glutamine levels have been found to be lowered in overtrained sportspeople,[21, 22] although a lowered glutamine level was not associated with any increase in upper respiratory tract infections in overtrained swimmers.[21] It has been suggested that low glutamine levels after prolonged exercise may result in a reduction in immune function and a subsequent increased risk of infection; however, there is still no evidence to link low glutamine levels with impaired immune function and increased susceptibility to illness or infection.[1]

Psychological changes

Psychological symptoms associated with overtraining include anxiety, depression, apathy, lack of motivation, irritability, inability to relax, and lack of self-confidence. In sportspeople, the Profile of Mood States (POMS)[3] has been used to quantify total mood disturbance. The specific POMS scores of tension and depression have been shown to be higher in overtrained swimmers,[23] but also in swimmers after increased training without any evidence of overtraining.[24, 25] Self-ratings of wellbeing have correlated well with overtraining and may be a predictor of its onset.

Central fatigue and overtraining

Although the exact biochemical and metabolic changes fundamental to the development of the overtraining syndrome have not been clearly established, changes within the central nervous system appear to play an important role in the development of chronic fatigue and many of the other common signs and symptoms that are frequently seen in the overtraining syndrome, such as disrupted sleep, changes in appetite and weight, irritability, impaired concentration, decreased motivation, and depressed mood. It has been suggested that alterations in brain neurotransmitters (e.g. serotonin) and the central effects of peripherally released inflammatory mediators (e.g. cytokines) are important in the development of the overtraining syndrome.[26]

Serotonin has been shown to influence central fatigue and depression, and it has been suggested that it may also play a role in the overtraining syndrome. It has been proposed that overtraining can result in chronically diminished concentrations of branched-chain amino acids and increased plasma free tryptophan levels.[26] Tryptophan is a metabolic precursor to serotonin.

The central nervous system, in turn, influences the peripheral neuroendocrine milieu through two hormonal axes—the hypothalamic–pituitary–adrenocortical (HPA) axis and the sympathetic–adrenal medullary (SAM) axis.[27] The end products of these axes—catecholamines and glucocorticoids—have been implicated in the overtraining syndrome.[28]

As a consequence of the hypothalamic and pituitary dysfunction, overtrained sportspeople may experience decreased pituitary release of thyroid-stimulating hormone, reduced pituitary adrenocorticotrophic response to corticotropin-releasing hormone, and alterations in growth hormone. There is also evidence of reduced intrinsic activity of the sympathetic nervous system in the later stages of the overtraining syndrome.[29]

Ultimately it may be changes in noradrenergic, serotonergic, or dopaminergic activity in the hypothalamus and pituitary gland that occur with the prolonged stress of overtraining that lead to alterations in the HPA and SAM axes.[30] Circulating cytokines, released in association with a state of chronic systemic inflammation induced by overtraining, may also bind to receptors in the hypothalamus and also have an impact on the HPA and SAM axes.[28]

Many of the signs and symptoms that characterize the overtraining syndrome are remarkably similar to those of clinical depression, and unfavorable changes in global mood, behavior, and cognition are a consistent finding in sportspeople with the overtraining syndrome. It may be difficult to clinically distinguish between the two conditions.[26] Armstrong et al.[27] have proposed using an antidepressant such as the selective serotonin reuptake inhibitor (SSRI) fluoxetine as a treatment for the overtraining syndrome and they describe the dramatic effect the use of such a medication had on the running fortunes of the great American distance runner Alberto Salazar who had suffered from the overtraining syndrome for more than a decade.

Monitoring of overtraining

Unfortunately, no single test can detect overtraining in the sportsperson. However, there are a number of parameters, both clinical and laboratory, which in combination may enable the sportsperson to be monitored in order to prevent the development of full-blown overtraining syndrome.

Probably the simplest and most effective means of monitoring overtraining is self-analysis by sportspeople themselves. Daily documentation should include sources and ratings of stress, fatigue, muscle soreness, quality of sleep, irritability, and perceived exertion during training or standardized exercise. An example of the contents of a daily diary is shown in the box on this page.

Blood parameters such as red and white blood cell counts, hemoglobin level, hematocrit, urea, and ammonia levels are not usually abnormal during overtraining. Changes in exercise blood lactate concentration and blood lactate threshold have been shown to be good indicators of overtraining but are influenced by many other factors and are probably

> **Recommended items for daily logbook self-analysis by sportspeople[2]**
>
> - Training details—distance, duration, pace, perceived intensity, heart rate responses, resistance work
> - Space for sportsperson's comments on training—enjoyment, coping
> - Wellbeing ratings on a quantifiable scale (1–7)—fatigue, stress, quality of sleep, muscle soreness, irritability
> - Causes of stress/dissatisfaction
> - Illness, injury, menstruation (female sportspeople)

only useful if assessed repeatedly. The POMS test (as mentioned above) may be a useful predictor of overtraining but is not a reliable diagnostic tool.

Prevention of overtraining

The prevention of overtraining is discussed in previous chapters. It requires maintenance of the correct balance between training load (Chapter 9) and recovery/regeneration (Chapter 10). The most important component of prevention is awareness of the problem, particularly among coaches. Education of coaches in the science of training will lead to fewer sportspeople developing this syndrome. Periodization of training, allowing sufficient regeneration time within the training program, and the use of regenerative techniques such as massage, hydrotherapy, and relaxation, as well as higher fluid and carbohydrate intakes are all being used increasingly by serious sportspeople to enable them to cope with high training loads.

Certain groups of sportspeople appear to be at an increased risk of developing the overtraining syndrome. A sportsperson new to a particular sport may train overzealously, and a sportsperson who is achieving some initial success may be encouraged to train even harder. A sportsperson may be led into overtraining by trying to train with better sportspeople. It may also be dangerous to follow the training program of an established "champion" whose training log may have been published in a magazine or passed into sporting folklore.

The sportsperson who does not have a coach or training group to set training programs is far more likely to overtrain. The support of a sensible, experienced coach or training partner is the best means of maximizing performance and avoiding overtraining.

Early recognition that a sportsperson may be developing the overtraining syndrome may enable the practitioner or coach to take the immediate measures to avoid further progression. Close liaison between the coach and the clinician is essential (Chapter 2). The coach can provide feedback on the sportsperson's condition and details of the past, present, and intended training program.

Treatment of the overtrained sportsperson

In patients who present with a relatively brief history of overtraining, complete rest is recommended in the short term, and the sportsperson is advised to get as much sleep as possible over the next 48 hours. Often this can be done over a weekend. If the syndrome is not severe, this may be sufficient, and the sportsperson may recover and begin the week with renewed vigor.

If this brief period of rest does not reduce the sportsperson's fatigue, the overtraining syndrome has developed. This may take weeks or months to resolve. Treatment includes rest, attention to dietary and fluid intake, and psychological support.

Viral illness

Viral illness is a common cause of persistent tiredness in the sportsperson. The immunological changes that occur as a result of prolonged intense training may result in the sportsperson having an increased susceptibility to viral illness, especially upper respiratory tract infections.

The sportsperson with a viral illness presents the sports and exercise medicine practitioner with a number of dilemmas.

- Should the sportsperson be allowed to continue intense training?
- Will continued intense training result in aggravation of the symptoms and the development of a more serious illness?
- If the decision is made to avoid intense training, is *light* training or *no* training preferable?
- If the sportsperson is about to compete, will performance be impaired as a result of this viral illness and, in team sports, will this affect the performance of the team and should a replacement be sought?
- If the sportsperson does have time off from training due to a viral illness, when is it appropriate to resume training, and at what level?

In these situations, each case must be considered on its merits. However, when a sportsperson presents with a viral illness and has an elevated temperature, intense training is contraindicated as there may be

the potential for serious illness to develop (e.g. myocarditis), or the sportsperson may prolong the illness or develop post-viral fatigue syndrome. In a sportsperson with a mild temperature, light training is permissible and may, in fact, have a positive effect. In this case, the pulse rate should be kept below 70% of the maximum heart rate. When the viral illness is accompanied by systemic symptoms (e.g. muscle pain), training is contraindicated.

The conundrum of whether or not to compete with a viral illness is almost impossible to solve. In most cases, performance will be impaired when a sportsperson has a viral illness. However, there are anecdotal reports of excellent sporting performances in sportspeople who apparently competed while ill.

Recurrent viral illnesses may indicate a specific immune deficiency, most commonly an IgG3 subclass deficiency.[31] IgA and IgM deficiencies are less common.[32] Specific viral infections (e.g. infectious mononucleosis, hepatitis, HIV) are considered in Chapter 56.

Nutritional deficiencies

Depletion of iron stores

Depletion of body stores of iron is a common cause of tiredness, particularly in swimmers and endurance sportspeople. Sportspeople are susceptible to iron deficiency for a number of reasons, including inadequate iron intake, increased iron loss, and inadequate absorption of dietary iron. Special groups with a greater risk of iron deficiency are menstruating females, any sportsperson who diets, and adolescent sportspeople.

Runners and endurance sportspeople are at high risk of iron deficiency due to a combination of increased gastrointestinal and genitourinary blood loss and loss of iron in sweat, as well as increased hemolysis in runners, swimmers, and rowers. The hemolysis is due to increased destruction of older, more fragile red blood cells during vigorous sports and an increase in body temperature.

Iron deficiency is further contributed to by an inadequate dietary intake, commonly seen in distance runners and vegetarians.

Sportspeople rarely develop frank anemia, which will clearly result in tiredness and impaired performance due to a reduced oxygen-carrying capacity in the blood. However, some sportspeople with hemoglobin levels within the normal range may have relative anemia, in other words, their hemoglobin level is too low for them and they have mild anemia.

An earlier stage of iron deficiency involves depletion of iron stores, primarily from the bone marrow. This can also result in tiredness and impaired performance, probably because of the important role of iron as a cofactor in muscle metabolism.

Serum ferritin measurement is a good indicator of body iron stores and serum transferrin receptor levels are a good indicator of the transmission of iron-bearing transferrin to cells. Elevated levels of ferritin represent increased iron stores; elevated transferrin receptor levels are a reflection of tissue iron needs. The combination of both ferritin and transferrin receptor levels provides the most sensitive measurement of the iron status of a sportsperson.[33] Both ferritin and transferrin receptor levels should be measured regularly in sportspeople who train intensely.

 Female endurance athletes who eat little or no red meat are particularly susceptible to depletion of iron stores.

Serum ferritin levels of less than 30 µg/L (30 ng/mL) in females and less than 50 µg/L (50 ng/mL) in males, and/or the transferrin receptor level of greater than 2.4 mg/L are evidence of reduced body iron stores and thus a possible cause of tiredness and impaired performance.

Sportspeople with symptoms of lethargy and poor performance who have low ferritin levels and/or increased transferrin receptor levels should attempt to increase their iron intake. Referral to a dietitian may be required. Exclusion of a gastrointestinal or genitourinary cause of iron loss is important. Oral supplementation with ferrous gluconate, sulfate, or lactate may be required and appears to be effective.[34, 35] Absorption is best between meals and may be improved with the intake of vitamin C. Often gastrointestinal intolerance or poor absorption of oral iron may necessitate the administration of intramuscular iron.

Glycogen depletion

Chronic glycogen depletion is an important cause of fatigue in the sportsperson. Glycogen is the storage form of carbohydrate and the major source of energy for the sportsperson. Glycogen stores are depleted after an intense bout of exercise, such as a heavy training session. If the glycogen stores are not adequately replenished prior to the next training session, they will become further depleted. Over a period of intense training and inadequate glycogen repletion,

a state of chronic glycogen depletion will develop. In this state there is inadequate energy available for intense exercise, resulting in fatigue and impaired performance.

Replenishment of glycogen stores is achieved with a diet high in complex carbohydrates, as described in Chapter 10. The sooner carbohydrate is taken following the bout of exercise, the more effective is the replenishment of glycogen stores. Therefore, sportspeople should replenish their glycogen stores immediately after exercise with a source of complex carbohydrate such as fruit, cereal, or high-carbohydrate drinks.

Inadequate protein intake

Inadequate protein intake is another potential cause of persistent tiredness in the sportsperson, although the mechanism by which this tiredness is produced is not clear.

Protein is an energy source providing 10% of the body's energy needs through conversion of amino acids to glucose. Adequate protein is essential to replace protein broken down by muscle contraction. Good sources of protein in the diet include lean meat, poultry, fish, and eggs. Protein intake is discussed further in Chapter 10.

Chronic fatigue syndrome

Chronic fatigue syndrome (CFS) is a controversial condition, the existence of which is hotly debated within the medical profession. The term itself was first used in 1988 but the syndrome has existed for much longer. It has previously been known as "neurasthenia" and "myalgic encephalomyelitis" (ME). The term "chronic fatigue syndrome" has been adopted to define a sufficiently homogeneous group of patients to allow research into etiology, pathogenesis, natural history and management. As the word "syndrome" suggests, CFS is not recognized as a distinct disease process.

Definition

A number of definitions of CFS have been proposed. All include the concept of fatigue that interferes with activities of daily living of at least six months' duration. The Center for Disease Control (CDC) in Atlanta has defined CFS as the presence of:[36]

- clinically evaluated, unexplained, persistent, or relapsing fatigue that is of new or definite onset; is not the result of ongoing exertion; is not alleviated by rest; and results in a substantial reduction of previous levels of occupational, educational, social, or personal activities and

- four or more of the following symptoms that persist or recur during six or more consecutive months of illness and that do not predate the fatigue:
  - self-reported impairment in short-term memory or concentration
  - sore throat
  - tender cervical or axillary nodes
  - muscle pain
  - multijoint pain without redness or swelling
  - headaches of a new pattern or severity
  - unrefreshing sleep
  - post-exertional malaise of at least 24 hours.

Etiology

CFS is more common in females, high achievers, and professionals, and more common in young adults. CFS is widespread in affluent settings and virtually unreported in developing countries.

Research to date has not identified any clear etiology for CFS. It is unlikely that CFS has a single etiology in an individual patient. There are likely to be predisposing states, predisposing factors, and perpetuating factors all operating to produce abnormal prolonged pathological fatigue. Predisposing states might include a positive family history, trait anxiety, depression, coping styles, and family factors. Fatigue symptoms might be perpetuated by secondary gain or learned behavior.

Acute infectious illnesses are clearly important precipitating factors in many cases, more often a viral respiratory tract illness than infectious mononucleosis. Orthostatic hypotension has been associated with CFS; however, this may be a product of the deconditioning associated with the syndrome rather than a causative factor.

Studies have reported immunological abnormalities such as decreased T-cell responses to mitogens *in vitro* and immunological subclass G abnormalities in cases of CFS; however, as immune abnormalities have been found in psychological disorders, these findings are non-specific.

Symptoms

The most prominent symptom of CFS is usually overwhelming fatigue, especially after exercise. Other common symptoms include headaches, sore throat, enlarged lymph nodes, muscle pain especially after exercise, unrefreshing sleep, and chest and abdominal pains.

The diagnosis of CFS is difficult to confirm in the absence of any definitive sign or test. It is often a diagnosis of exclusion. The other problem with the diagnosis of CFS is that there are a number of conditions whose symptoms overlap with those of CFS. The two most significant are fibromyalgia and depression.

The major presenting symptom in fibromyalgia is usually widespread muscle and joint pain, but fatigue is nearly always present. Fibromyalgia is characterized by the presence of multiple tender points in the muscles; however, trigger points are also frequently seen in patients with CFS and form an important part of the treatment.

Fatigue is often the primary presenting symptom in patients with depression and many of the symptoms described in CFS are found in depressive patients.

Management

Management of the patient with CFS (and fibromyalgia and depression) is a considerable challenge for the practitioner. The natural history of CFS is of a very gradual improvement over a period of months and sometimes years. Treatment should be oriented toward psychological support and symptom relief. It is essential that the treating practitioner acknowledges that the patient has a real problem and is prepared to give the patient a diagnosis. It is important to give the patient plenty of time, and both the patient and those close to her (or him) will have many questions. We recommend seeing the patient at least weekly in the initial treatment phase and later on a less frequent but still regular basis.

 Exercise is the cornerstone of treatment of chronic fatigue.[37]

This may seem strange when one considers that post-exercise fatigue and muscle pain are two of the most significant features of the disease; however, a slow, graduated increase in activity is an essential part of management. The exercise program may have to commence at a "ridiculously" low level considering the history of some sportspeople. But it should commence at a level that the patient can achieve comfortably with minimal or no adverse effects in the 24–48 hours post-exercise. The increase in activity should be very gradual and if adverse symptoms develop, the patient should return to the previous level of activity and build up even more slowly.

In a six-month randomized blinded prospective trial[38] in 96 individuals with CFS, it was found that a graded exercise program significantly improved both health perceptions and the sense of fatigue whereas the use of an antidepressant (fluoxetine) improved depression only. Another study of 66 patients with CFS also demonstrated a positive effect with graded aerobic exercise.[39]

Many drug treatments have been advocated but with little evidence of their efficacy. Simple analgesics may be helpful, and also a tricyclic antidepressant (e.g. amitriptyline 10–25 mg) in a single dose at night. This drug seems to improve sleep quality, and patients usually wake up more refreshed as a result.

Many nutritional supplements have also been advocated, but there is no evidence of their efficacy. We have found that the treatment of muscle trigger points with dry needling to be helpful in reducing muscle pains and headaches in a number of patients with CFS.

Chronic fatigue syndrome and the sportsperson

It has been suggested that the incidence of CFS is higher in sportspeople than in the normal population.[40] Certainly a number of high-profile sportspeople have been diagnosed with the condition. One problem in sportspeople is the overlap in symptoms between the overtraining syndrome and CFS.[41] It may be that the etiology of the two conditions is similar, with both having a neurotransmitter effect on central fatigue.

Sportspeople who appear to be particularly prone to developing CFS are those who are attempting to combine a high level of commitment to their sport with full-time work, social, and family commitments. The other group who appear vulnerable are those sportspeople who continue to train and/or compete at an intense level when they are suffering from a viral illness. We have seen a number of sportspeople with debilitating CFS whose onset appears to have coincided with such an episode.

Other causes of tiredness

A number of psychological problems are associated with a feeling of excessive tiredness. The two most common states are anxiety and depression. These problems may be related to the sportsperson's sporting endeavors or, alternatively, may be quite unrelated. The presence of eating disorders such as anorexia nervosa and bulimia should also be considered.

Hypothyroidism is more common than most realize, occurring in 1% of adults, with subclinical disease in 5%. The condition can affect any organ system. Hypothyroidism is characterized by a general slowing of body processes and can present as chronic fatigue, cold intolerance, weight gain, and, in women, menorrhagia.[42] It is often associated with high cholesterol levels. An elevated serum thyroid stimulating hormone level is a sensitive indicator, and patients with this condition generally respond well to treatment with levothyroxine.

Diabetes, neuromuscular disorders, and cardiac problems are all associated with excessive tiredness. Exercise-induced asthma may occasionally present with tiredness as the major symptom rather than the more typical cough, chest tightness, or shortness of breath post-exercise.

A number of medications may cause excessive tiredness. These include beta blockers, antihistamines, diuretics, anticonvulsants, sedatives, and muscle relaxants.

Summary

Excessive tiredness is a common problem among sportspeople in hard training. While overtraining, a viral illness or a nutritional deficiency (especially iron) are the most likely causes; other causes should always be considered. A thorough history, comprehensive examination, and appropriate use of investigations will usually lead to the correct diagnosis.

RECOMMENDED READING

Beard J, Tobin B. Iron status and exercise. *Am J Clin Nutr* 2000;72(suppl.):594S–597S.

Halson SL, Jeukendrup AE. Does overtraining exist? An analysis of overreaching and overtraining research. *Sports Med* 2004;34(14):967–81.

Hawley CJ, Schoene RB. Overtraining syndrome. A guide to diagnosis, treatment and prevention. *Phys Sportsmed* 2003;31(6):25–31.

Moeller JL. The athlete with fatigue. *Curr Sports Med Rep* 2004;3:304–9.

Purvis D, Gonsalves S, Deuster PA. Physiological and psychological fatigue in extreme conditions: overtraining and elite athletes. *PM R* 2010;2(5):442–50.

Silverman MN, Heim CM, Nater UM et al. Neuroendocrine and immune contributors to fatigue. *PM R* 2010;2(5):338–46.

REFERENCES

1. Halson SL, Jeukendrup AE. Does overtraining exist? An analysis of overreaching and overtraining research. *Sports Med* 2004;34(14):967–81.

2. Mackinnon LT, Hooper SL. Overtraining and overreaching: causes, effects, and prevention. In: Garrett WE, Kirkendall DT, eds. *Exercise and sports science*. Philadelphia: Lippincott, Williams & Wilkins, 2000.

3. McNair BM, Lorr M, Doppleman LE. *Profile of mood states manual*. San Diego: Educational & Industrial Testing Service, 1971.

4. Barron JL, Noakes TD, Levy W et al. Hypothalamic dysfunction in overtrained athletes. *J Clin Endocrinol Metab* 1985;60:803–6.

5. Dressendorfer RH, Wade CE, Scaff JH Jr. Increased morning heart rate in runners: a valid sign of overtraining? *Phys Sportsmed* 1985;13(8):77–92.

6. Hooper SL, Mackinnon LT, Gordon RD et al. Hormonal responses of elite swimmers to overtraining. *Med Sci Sports Exerc* 1993;25(6):741–7.

7. Costill DL, Flynn MG, Kirwan JP et al. Effects of repeated days of intensified training on muscle glycogen and swimming performance. *Med Sci Sports Exerc* 1988;20:249–54.

8. Snyder AC, Kuipers H, Cheng B et al. Overtraining followed intensified training with normal muscle glycogen. *Med Sci Sports Exerc* 1995;27:1063–70.

9. Fry AC, Kraemer WJ, van Borselen F et al. Performance decrements with high-intensity resistance exercise overtraining. *Med Sci Sports Exerc* 1994;26:255–9.

10. Lehmann MJ, Foster C, Dickhuth HH et al. Autonomic imbalance hypothesis and overtraining syndrome. *Med Sci Sports Exerc* 1998;30(7):1140–5.

11. Lehmann M, Schnee W, Scheu R et al. Decreased nocturnal catecholamine excretion: parameter for an overtraining syndrome in athletes. *Int J Sports Med* 1992;13:236–42.

12. Urhausen A, Gabriel HH, Kindermann W. Impaired pituitary hormonal response to exhaustive exercise in overtrained endurance athletes. *Med Sci Sports Exerc* 1998;30(3):407–14.

13. Flynn MG, Pizza FX, Boone JB Jr et al. Indices of training stress during competitive running and swimming seasons. *Int J Sports Med* 1994;15:21–6.

14. Vervoon C, Quist AM, Vermulst LJ et al. The behaviour of the plasma free testosterone/cortisol ratio during a season of elite rowing training. *Int J Sports Med* 1991;12(3):257–63.

15. Mackinnon LT, Hooper SL, Jones S et al. Hormonal, immunological and hematological responses to intensified training in swimmers. *Med Sci Sports Exerc* 1997;29:1637–45.

16. Urhausen A, Gabriel H, Kindermann W. Blood hormones as markers of training stress and overtraining. *Sports Med* 1995;20:251–76.

17. Lehmann MJ, Wieland H, Gastmann U. Influence of an unaccustomed increase in training volume vs intensity on performance, hematological and blood chemical parameters in distance runners. *J Sports Med Phys Fitness* 1997;37(2):110–16.

18. Mackinnon LT, Hooper S. Mucosal (secretory) immune system responses to exercise of varying intensity and during overtraining. *Int J Sports Med* 1994;15:S179–83.

19. Halson SL, Lancaster GI, Jeukendrup AE et al. Immunological responses to overreaching in cyclists. *Med Sci Sports Exerc* 2003;35(5):854–61.

20. Rowbottom DG, Keast D, Morton AR. The emerging role of glutamine as an indicator of exercise stress and overtraining. *Sports Med* 1996;21(2):80–97.

21. Mackinnon LT, Hooper SL. Plasma glutamine and upper respiratory tract infection during intensified training in swimmers. *Med Sci Sports Exerc* 1996;28(3):285–90.

22. Parry-Billings M, Budgett R, Koutedakis Y et al. Plasma amino acid concentrations in the overtraining syndrome: possible effects on the immune system. *Med Sci Sports Exerc* 1992;24(12):1353–8.

23. Hooper SL, Mackinnon LT, Hanrahan SJ. Mood states as an indication of staleness and recovery. *Int J Sport Psych* 1997;28:1–12.

24. O'Connor PJ, Morgan WP, Raglin JS. Psychobiologic effects of 3 d of increased training in female and male swimmers. *Med Sci Sports Exerc* 1991;23(9):1055–61.

25. Morgan WP, Costill DL, Flynn MG et al. Mood disturbance following increased training in swimmers. *Med Sci Sports Exerc* 1988;20(4):408–14.

26. Anish EJ. Exercise and its effects on the central nervous system. *Curr Sports Med Rep* 2005;4:18–23.

27. Armstrong LE, VanHeest JL. The unknown mechanism of the overtraining syndrome: clues from depression and psychoneuroimmunology. *Sports Med* 2002;32(3):185–209.

28. Smith LL. Cytokine hypothesis of overtraining: a physiological adaptation to excessive stress? *Med Sci Sports Exerc* 2000;32:317–31.

29. Uusitalo AL. Overtraining: making a difficult diagnosis and implementing targeted treatment. *Phys Sportsmed* 2001;29(5):35–50.

30. Budgett R. Fatigue and underperformance in athletes: the overtraining syndrome. *Br J Sports Med* 1998;32:107–10.

31. Reid VL, Gleeson M, Williams N et al. Clinical investigation of athletes with persistent fatigue and/or recurrent infections. *Br J Sports Med* 2004;38:42–5.

32. Fallon KE. Inability to train, recurrent infection, and selective IgM deficiency. *Clin J Sport Med* 2004;14: 357–9.

33. Feelders RA, Kuiper-Kramer EP, Van Eijk HG. Structure, function and clinical significance of transferrin receptors. *Clin Chem Lab Med* 1999;37:1–10.

34. Brutsaert TD, Hernandez-Cordero S, Rivera J et al. Iron supplementation improves progressive fatigue resistance during dynamic knee extensor exercise in iron-depleted, nonanemic women. *Am J Clin Nutr* 2003;77:441–8.

35. Verdon F, Burnand B, Stubi CL et al. Iron depletion without anaemia and physical performance in young women. *BMJ* 2003;326:1124–31.

36. Fukuda K, Straus SE, Hickie I et al. The chronic fatigue syndrome: a comprehensive approach to its definition and study. International chronic fatigue syndrome study group. *Ann Intern Med* 1994;121:953–9.

37. McCully KK, Sisto SA, Natelson BH. Use of exercise for treatment of chronic fatigue syndrome. *Sports Med* 1996;21(1):35–48.

38. Wearden AJ, Morriss RK, Mullis R et al. Randomised, double-blind, placebo-controlled treatment trial of fluoxetine and graded exercise for chronic fatigue syndrome. *Br J Psychiatry* 1998;172:485–90.

39. Fulcher KY, White PD. Randomised controlled trial of graded exercise in patients with the chronic fatigue syndrome. *BMJ* 1997;314:1647–52.

40. Parker S, Brukner P. Is your sportsperson suffering from chronic fatigue syndrome? *Sport Health* 1994;12(1):15–17.

41. Shephard R. Chronic fatigue syndrome: an update. *Sports Med* 2001;31(3):167–94.

42. Lathan SR. Chronic fatigue? Consider hypothyroidism. *Phys Sportsmed* 1991;19(10):67–70.

D

Chapter 58

Exercise in the heat

with TIMOTHY NOAKES

Whenever one's body temperature rises, even for physiological reasons, we enter into danger and anything that interferes with physiological cooling, or adds to the internal heat load, exacerbates that danger. The wonder is, not that anyone gets hyperpyrexia, but that so few of us do. Ladell WS Disorders due to heat. *Trans R Soc Trop Med Hyg* 1957;51:189–207

Because sporting activity can occur in hot conditions, sports medicine clinicians must be well versed in both prevention and management of heat-associated illness. Humans can only survive core temperatures greater than 41°C (106°F) for short periods, and protein denatures at a body temperature of 45°C (113°F).

Fortunately, of all mammals, humans have developed an almost unmatched capacity to sweat, providing our species with one of the greatest capacities to lose heat during exercise and thus safely regulate our body temperatures even during exercise of long duration in environmental conditions that would otherwise be considered extreme. This was brilliantly shown by the performance of the 40 kg Japanese runner, Mizuki Noguchi, who won the 2004 Athens Olympic Marathon for women in a time of 2 hr 26 min 20 sec despite the extreme environmental conditions—35°C with moderate humidity.

Some have argued that this remarkable sweating capacity of humans must have developed for some evolutionary purpose. Thus, Heinrich has proposed that as humans are savanna-adapted animals, the reason for our highly developed sweating response is because it provides us with an advantage, most likely to perform prolonged exercise in the heat.[1] According to Heinrich, "We don't need a sweating response to outrun predators, because that requires relatively short, fast sprinting, where accumulating a heat load is, like a lactic acid load, acceptable. What we do need sweating for is to *sustain* running in the heat of the day—the time when most predators retire into the shade."[1] Heinrich also notes that

modern hunter-gatherers, like the !Kung Bushmen (San) of Southern Africa, do not carry food or water with them (on 30 km hunts in the heat) because that "hinders their ability to travel."[1] The first documentation of just such a hunt recorded that the !Kung San do not begin these long hunts lasting 4–6 hours unless the desert temperature is in excess of 40°C (104°F) with low humidity;[2] the preferred hunting temperature is 42–45°C (108–113°F). Recently, highly trained members of the South African Special Forces were able to race march over 25 km in a temperature of 43°C while fully clothed in battle dress carrying rifles and full packs without ill effect while drinking only according to the dictates of thirst.[3]

Despite this remarkable ability of some humans to exercise in such heat without health risk, on occasion, heat injury, in particular heatstroke, occurs to persons exercising in much less severe environmental conditions when the total heat load cannot explain why heatstroke developed. This suggests that individual susceptibility, rather than the environmental conditions, plays a much more important role in the development of this condition than has previously been acknowledged.

For example, there was a case of heatstroke in the last official finisher in a 56 km ultramarathon.[4] This sportsperson, whose average running/walking speed was only 8 km/h, required 10 hours of active cooling before his temperature stabilized in the normal range. The sole explanation for this unusual response was a continuous state of abnormal heat production that must have begun during exercise and which continued for the first 10 hours after the termination of exercise.

This condition bears some resemblance to the well-recognized condition of malignant hyperthermia, in which exposure to a specific anesthetic agent, halothane, produces an explosive and sustained state of accelerated heat production leading to heatstroke if not treated with the specific antidote, dantrolene.

In this chapter, we briefly review the physiology of heat gain and heat loss before discussing the diagnosis and management of three common presentations in the heat—heatstroke, exercise-associated collapse, and cramps. As these names suggest, only the former is truly related to heat! Finally, we discuss an important differential diagnosis of heatstroke—hyponatremia. This condition results from fluid overload.[5-8]

 Listen to Tim Noakes discuss the management of sportspeople in the heat in the *Clinical Sports Medicine* masterclasses at www.clinicalsportsmedicine.com.

Mechanisms of heat gain and loss

Heat is produced by both endogenous sources (muscle activity and metabolism) and exogenous sources (transfer to the body when environmental temperature exceeds body temperature). The rate of heat production and the risk of heatstroke should be greatest in those who run the fastest and have the highest work rate (i.e. in short-distance rather than marathon events). Heat loss occurs by conduction, convection, radiation, or evaporation. At rest, when environmental temperature is below body temperature, thermal balance is maintained by convection of heat to the skin surface and radiation of heat to the environment.

As an individual starts to exercise and produce more heat, sweating provides compensatory heat loss through evaporation. When the environmental temperature equals or exceeds body temperature, sweating is the predominant mechanism of heat loss;[9] sportspeople exercising in these conditions rely almost exclusively on evaporative heat loss to regulate body temperature.

The effectiveness of sweating to cool the body is affected by humidity. In a dry environment, sweat is evaporated. A humid environment, in which there is a high level of water vapor in the air, limits the evaporation of sweat and its cooling effect. Therefore, the combination of high temperature and high humidity is particularly dangerous. Sportspeople should avoid

exercising in these conditions if possible. In extreme environmental conditions, when the humidity is high and the temperature is in excess of about 33°C (91°F), core temperature can increase substantially even in relatively short-distance races (6–15 km).

Heavier sportspeople are particularly at risk because they produce more heat and have greater difficulty losing that heat adequately than do lighter sportspeople when both exercise at the same velocity in humid conditions.[10] In contrast, because they produce less heat when exercising at the same velocity as heavier sportspeople, small sportspeople are especially advantaged when competing in prolonged events in the heat.[10-12]

For example, the 52 kg world marathon record holder Paula Radcliffe was unable to finish the Athens 2004 Olympic Marathon, which was won by a sportsperson who was 12 kg lighter and whose best marathon time in cooler conditions was substantially slower than Radcliffe's best. It is suggested that when running in those conditions Radcliffe was unable both to run at the pace of the smaller woman and to maintain thermal homeostasis. Instead her core temperature continued to rise progressively until it reached about 42°C at which time she would have become temporarily paralyzed and unable to continue running—the paralysis of hyperthermia.

The effects of humidity as well as the effects of solar and ground radiation, air temperature, and wind speed are included in the wet bulb globe temperature (WBGT) index. This index is used to determine the amount of activity that should be undertaken in hot conditions. It is recommended that endurance events, especially those involving high intensities of exercise (4–21 km), should not be held when the WBGT index exceeds 28°C (82°F).[13] In practical terms, a WBGT index of 28°C (82°F) approximates a dry bulb temperature of 28°C (82°F) with 100% humidity. Activities in which the rate of heat production is less (golf) or in which activity is intermittent (American football and tennis) can be played at higher temperatures provided adequate rest intervals are allowed between bouts of activity.

Clinical perspective

Appropriate clinical assessment of the sportsperson who presents after exercising in the heat is the cornerstone of good management. In the past, there has been a tendency to initiate treatment before making a rational diagnosis. This position was taken partly because of the problem of high rates of admission to the medical tent at major events and partly because it was assumed that all sportspeople who collapsed were dehydrated and needed immediate intravenous hydration. The former problem can be overcome by a system of triage at events (Chapter 65), and the latter assumption is not evidence-based.[14]

Thus, the emergency treatment of life-threatening conditions, including heatstroke and hyponatremia, can safely be delayed for one or two minutes while the rectal temperature and the blood sodium concentration are measured and a reasonable working diagnosis is established. The obvious exception is cardiac arrest, which occurs uncommonly, and the diagnosis of which is unambiguous.

The criteria for determining the severity of collapse are shown in Table 58.1. The initial assessment is based on the sportsperson's level of consciousness and knowledge of where in the race the sportsperson collapsed.

 Patients who are seriously ill show alterations in their level of consciousness and almost always collapse before completion of the race (Fig. 58.1).

In addition, the cause of illness in persons who collapse during the race is usually quite easily determined and forms part of the physician's standard medical training.

Measuring rectal temperature, blood pressure, and heart rate provides additional diagnostic information. However, the level of "dehydration" during exercise cannot be determined accurately by clinical examination;[15] only the measurement of the body weight loss provides some measure of the likely fluid loss during prolonged exercise like marathon running. In longer

Figure 58.1 Collapse *before* the finish line suggests a serious cause of collapse. Exercise-associated collapse occurs *after* the sportsperson has completed the race, crosses the finish line, and stops voluntarily

races (>25 km) when hypoglycemia is more likely, a glucometer should also be used.

In mass events of much longer duration (>4 hours), including ultramarathons, equipment for measuring the serum sodium concentration *must* be available so that potentially lethal exercise-induced hyponatremia (EAH) can be diagnosed expeditiously. Intravenous therapy should only be considered after a serum

Table 58.1 Guidelines for determining the severity of the collapsed sportperson's condition

Non-severe	Severe
Immediate assessment	
Conscious	Unconscious or altered mental state
Alert	Confused, disoriented, aggressive
Rectal temperature: <40°C (104°F)	Rectal temperature: >40°C (104°F)
Systolic blood pressure: >100 mmHg	Systolic blood pressure: <100 mmHg
Heart rate: <100 beats/min	Heart rate: >100 beats/min
Specialized assessment	
Blood glucose level: 4–10 mmol/L (72–180 mg/dL)	Blood glucose level: <4 or >10 mmol/L (<72 or >180 mg/dL)
Serum sodium concentration: 135–148 mmol/L (135–148 mEq/L)	Serum sodium concentration: <135 or >148 mmol/L (<135 or >148 mEq/L)
Body weight loss: 0–5%	Body weight loss: >10%
	Body weight gain: >2%

sodium concentration greater than 135 mmol/L (>135 mEq/L) has been measured. It is no longer defensible *not* to measure the serum sodium concentration in a sportsperson admitted to a medical tent after a sporting event of four or more hours and in whom there is evidence of some alteration in the level of consciousness.[16]

 Whether or not the sportsperson is conscious or unconscious is the most important sign guiding the differential diagnosis.

If the sportsperson is unconscious, the initial differential diagnosis is between a medical condition not necessarily related to exercise (e.g. cardiac arrest, grand mal epilepsy, subarachnoid hemorrhage, or diabetic coma) and an exercise-related disorder, most especially heatstroke, hyponatremia, or severe hypoglycemia. The latter is an uncommon cause of exercise-related coma in non-diabetic subjects. If the sportsperson is unconscious, the crucial initial measurement is the rectal temperature, followed by heart rate and blood pressure. If the rectal temperature is above 41°C (106°F), the diagnosis is heatstroke and the patient must be cooled immediately (see below) and the cooling continued until the rectal temperature stabilizes at 38°C (100°F) or lower.

If the rectal temperature is below 40°C (104°F) in an unconscious patient, the blood pressure and pulse rate are not grossly abnormal, and there is no other obvious medical condition, the probability is that the sportsperson has EAH or, rarely, another electrolyte abnormality such as hypochloremia also causing cerebral edema.

 Note that "dehydration" in the range measured in athletes during marathon and other endurance or ultraendurance events does not cause unconsciousness.

Heatstroke—a temperature above 41°C (106°F)

When running, the metabolic rate is a function of running speed and body mass; thus, the highest rectal temperatures are usually seen in the fastest runners competing in events of 8–21 km. In such runners, the rectal temperatures may increase to 40.5°C (104.9°F) without symptoms or evidence of heat-related illness.[17, 18] Higher rectal temperatures are usually associated with symptoms that include dizziness, weakness, nausea, headache, confusion, disorientation, and irrational behavior, including aggressive combativeness or drowsiness progressing to coma. Examination reveals the patient is hypotensive and has tachycardia. The presence or absence of sweating does not influence the diagnosis. The tachycardia and hypotension are initially due to a low peripheral resistance in the face of an elevated cardiac output.[19] Recovery of cardiovascular function occurs with normalization of the cardiac output and with an increase in peripheral vascular resistance.

If, during exercise, a previously healthy sportsperson shows marked changes in mental functioning (e.g. collapse with unconsciousness or a reduced level of consciousness [stupor, coma] or mental stimulation [irritability, convulsions]), in association with a rectal temperature above 41°C (106°F), the diagnosis of heatstroke is confirmed and warrants immediate initiation of cooling.

Management of heatstroke

The more rapidly the rectal temperature is reduced to 38°C (100°F) the better the prognosis. The patient should be placed in a bath of ice water for 5–10 minutes. The body temperature should decrease to 38°C (100°F) within this time.[20] Care must be taken to avoid inducing hypothermia as rectal temperature lags behind the core temperature. Shivering indicates that core temperature has decreased to 37°C (99°F) or below.

Although there is no evidence that dehydration is the single critical factor causing heatstroke, intravenous fluids may be given to correct the expected dehydration and to assist in stabilizing the hyperkinetic circulation. Thus, 1–1.5 L of a 0.5% or 0.9% saline solution can be given initially, in part to ensure rapid venous access should this be required. However, cardiac function is compromised in hyperthermia and aggressive fluid therapy can induce pulmonary edema.

Mortality from heatstroke should be zero in healthy sportspeople who are cooled promptly. Indeed, it is usual for sportspeople to be fully recovered and ambulatory within 30–60 minutes of collapse, providing they are correctly and expeditiously treated and they do not have a predisposing medical condition that explains their increased individual susceptibility to heatstroke (exercise-induced malignant hyperpyrexia).

 Any delay in initiating cooling can convert an uncomplicated case of heatstroke into a potentially fatal condition. However, some cases of heatstroke follow a malignant course with a fatal outcome occurring within a few hours despite appropriate medical care.

It seems logical to assume that such cases are caused by unusual circumstances including a potential genetic contribution similar to that found in cases of malignant hyperthermia and related conditions.

Is hospital admission indicated?

The medical team must decide whether or not to admit the sportsperson to hospital for further observation after his or her temperature has been reduced to below 38°C (100°F). There is a tendency for rectal temperature to increase after cooling; this increase may not be noticed if the patient returns home without appropriate supervision. An increasing rectal temperature after cessation of exercise and appropriate cooling indicates ongoing heat-generating biochemical processes in muscle unrelated to exercise that may be related to conditions such as malignant hyperthermia.

Hospital admission is always required if the patient fails to regain consciousness within 30 minutes of appropriate therapy that returns the rectal temperature to 38°C (100°F). Patients who regain consciousness rapidly, whose cardiovascular system is stable, and whose rectal temperature does not increase in the first hour after active cooling ceases usually do not need hospital admission. Thus, the decision as to whether hospital admission is needed can usually be made within an hour of the patient reaching medical treatment.

An absolute indication for hospital admission would be a failure to achieve cardiovascular stability during that time. A persisting tachycardia and hypotension in the supine head-down position suggests that cardiogenic shock is developing. As heatstroke is such an uncommon complication of exercise, its presence should raise the possibility that other factors may be operative. These include genetic predisposition, unaccustomed drug use, or subclinical viral infection. Indeed, in such cases the following must be asked: "Is the hyperthermia the cause of the condition or merely a sign of another potentially more serious condition?"

Complications of heatstroke

Heatstroke may be associated with damage to one or more body systems, as shown in Table 58.2. Whether the hyperthermia of heatstroke directly causes this damage or whether it is merely an accompanying feature of another disease syndrome that has yet to be properly described needs to be considered.[5] It appears that there is an individual susceptibility to heatstroke.

Table 58.2 Complications of heatstroke

System	Abnormality
Cardiovascular	Arrhythmias
	Myocardial infarction
	Pulmonary edema
Neurological	Coma
	Convulsion
	Stroke
Gastrointestinal	Liver damage
	Gastric bleeding
Hematological	Disseminated intravascular coagulation
Muscular	Rhabdomyolysis
Renal	Renal failure

Malignant hyperthermia, which is usually activated by certain general anesthetic agents, may also be triggered by other stimuli, perhaps including exercise. The biochemical abnormality resides in skeletal muscle, where it may activate uncontrolled metabolism and hyperthermia and, ultimately, an extensive, and potentially fatal, rhabdomyolysis (degeneration of skeletal muscle). The process can only be reversed by a specific drug, dantrolene sodium, or, less often, by rapid whole-body cooling.

A number of deaths among high-profile professional sportspeople in the US who died within 16–24 hours of the onset of "heatstroke" despite receiving appropriate medical care raises the strong possibility that:

1. they were not suffering from heatstroke but from some other condition of which the hyperthermia was merely a diagnostic "red herring"
2. because of a hereditary or acquired predisposition, exercise may be one factor that triggers the development of this fatal condition in susceptible individuals
3. focusing solely on lowering the body temperature may not be enough to save the lives of predisposed individuals—rather, attempts must be made to prevent the rhabdomyolysis, which appears to be the immediate cause of the critical complications (acute renal failure and cardiac arrest) that ultimately cause death.

Patients suffering rhabdomyolysis present with brown-colored urine accompanied by muscle weakness, swelling, and pain. The skin may become discolored because of hemorrhages and the muscles have a "doughy" feel. The urine contains high levels of myoglobin, which causes the brown discoloration and granular casts. Serum creatine kinase activity is also high. Laboratory tests may reveal elevated levels of potassium and uric acid and, in severe cases, evidence of disseminated intravascular coagulation. This condition requires urgent intensive care treatment.

Exercise-associated collapse

Exercise-associated collapse describes the common type of collapse that occurs in sportspeople who successfully complete endurance events without distress but who suddenly develop symptoms and signs of postural hypotension when they stop exercising. This condition has been referred to as "heat syncope" and "heat exhaustion;" however, we avoid these terms as the condition is benign and the rectal temperature is never sufficiently elevated to suggest a diagnosis of heatstroke. If the rectal temperature is elevated and the patient has an altered level of consciousness, heatstroke is the correct diagnosis.

The largest modern study of subjects who required medical attention after long-distance events found that only a very small proportion of participants had markedly elevated rectal temperatures, indicating heatstroke, and few without heatstroke required hospitalization.[21]

The phenomenon of collapse after completing a sporting event in the heat occurs because the sudden cessation of exercise induces postural hypotension by causing blood to "pool" in the dilated capacitance veins in the lower limb when the "second heart" action of the lower limb musculature stops.

In addition, there may be abnormal perfusion of the splanchnic circulation, with loss of a large fluid volume into the highly compliant splanchnic veins. The problem is a precipitous fall in the central (rather than circulating) blood volume and, hence, atrial filling pressures.[22–24] Since sportspeople collapse after exercise, dehydration cannot be a factor as fluid loss sufficient to impair cardiovascular function must produce its effects before the sportsperson completes the race and not after the race has been completed when the stress on the cardiovascular function is reducing.

The early publications referring to this condition did not find elevated rectal temperatures and used the terms "heat exhaustion," "heat prostration," or "heat syncope" to describe the condition of collapse due to postural hypotension that develops in people who exercise in the heat. Unfortunately, this terminology has been misinterpreted to indicate that the collapse is caused by elevated body temperature and failure of heat regulation due to "cardiac strain" often caused by "dehydration," which is not the case.

Rather the condition is caused by the persistence into recovery of the low state of peripheral vascular resistance present during exercise—hence exercise-associated postural hypotension (EAPH). In addition, Noakes has drawn attention to the possible action of the Barcroft–Edholm reflex in this condition.[25] In 1945 Barcroft and Edholm showed that a sudden reduction in the right atrial pressure, in their case induced by venesection but analogous to the sudden reduction in atrial pressure that will result when the muscle pump becomes inactive on the cessation of exercise, induced a sudden and atavistic reduction in peripheral vascular resistance leading to hypotension and syncope.[26] Restoration of the right atrial filling pressure reversed this vasodilation by increasing the peripheral vascular resistance.

The diagnosis of exercise-associated collapse/EAPH can be made on the basis of a typical history, findings of a postural hypotension reversed by lying supine with the pelvis and legs elevated (Trendelenberg position), and the exclusion of readily identifiable medical syndromes such as diabetes and heatstroke (Chapter 44).

Management of exercise-associated collapse/exercise-associated postural hypotension (EAPH)

As patients with EAPH are conscious, they can be encouraged to ingest fluids orally during recovery. Sports drinks containing both glucose (4–8%) and electrolytes (Na: 10–20 mM) are appropriate, provided the sportsperson does not also have evidence of fluid overload. The patients should lie with their pelvis and legs elevated. Nursing patients in this head-down position is always dramatically effective, producing a more stable cardiovascular system within 30–90 seconds and, usually, instant reversal of symptoms as a result of reversal of the Barcroft–Edholm reflex. The symptoms of dizziness, nausea, and vomiting associated with this condition may result simply from a sudden reduction in blood pressure, especially as there is a dramatic fall from the elevated blood pressure maintained during exercise.

Generally, recovery occurs within 10–20 minutes in persons nursed in the head-down position. Most sportspeople with exercise-associated collapse are able to stand and walk unaided within 10–30 minutes of appropriate treatment, and can be encouraged to leave the facility at that time. Indeed a recent clinical trial has shown that recovery from EAPH is not expedited by the provision of intravenous fluids.[27] Instead "endurance athletes with EAPH can be treated effectively using the Trendelenburg position and oral fluids."[27, 47]

Few, if any, sportspeople with exercise-associated collapse are sufficiently dehydrated to show the usual clinical signs of dry mucous membranes, loss of skin turgor, sunken eyeballs, and an inability to spit. Some clinicians advocate intravenous therapy when these signs are present but we only use intravenous therapy in sportspeople who continue to have increased heart rates (>100 beats/min) and hypotension (<110 mmHg) when lying supine with the legs and pelvis elevated above the level of the heart. In such cases the possibility of an underlying cardiac condition causing a reduced cardiac output must be considered.

Cramps

Heat cramps were first described among coal miners in 1923, eventually becoming known as "miner's," "fireman's," "stoker's," "cane-cutter's," or simply "heat" cramps. The popular belief that cramps are caused by severe dehydration and large sodium chloride losses that develop during hot conditions has no scientific basis.[28–30] After a lifetime studying sodium balance in persons exercising in desert heat, Epstein and Sohar concluded that salt-deficiency heat cramps had never been proven to exist and illustrated "christening by conjecture."[31]

Cramps can occur at rest or during or after exercise undertaken in any environmental conditions; they are specific neither to exercise, nor to exercise in the heat. The more modern hypothesis proposes that cramps probably result from alterations in spinal neural reflex activity activated by fatigue in susceptible individuals (Chapter 5).[28–30] The term "heat cramps" should be abandoned as it clouds understanding of the possible neural nature of this connection.

Management of cramps

Stretching out the muscle to length is one effective therapy. Application of ice and physiotherapy of the affected muscle may also help. The Boston Marathon medical team treats muscle cramps with intravenous normal saline, and intravenous magnesium therapy has been used in the Hawaiian Ironman Triathlon; however, clinical trials of either treatment have yet to be published. More recently, evidence has accumulated that the ingestion of pickle juice may expedite recovery from cramps by a central neural mechanism,[32] since recovery occurs before there is any chance that the ingredients could have acted at a peripheral site (e.g. in the skeletal muscles).[33]

Fluid overload: hyponatremia

Hyponatremia is perhaps the most important differential diagnosis in sportspeople who seek medical attention at an event undertaken in the heat, particularly in endurance events lasting four or more hours. Thus, any sportsperson who becomes unconscious during or after ultra-distance running or triathlon races and whose rectal temperature is not elevated should be considered to have symptomatic hyponatremia (exercise associated hyponatremic encephalopathy—EAHE) until measurement of the serum sodium concentration refutes the diagnosis.

We emphasize that dehydration does not cause unconsciousness until it is associated with renal failure with uremia or hepatic failure.[14] To achieve such a weight loss as a result of dehydration, a 50 kg sportsperson would require 10 hours of high-intensity exercise at a sweat rate of 1 L per hour without any fluid replacement. Such a performance seems improbable in modern sporting events in which fluid is provided usually every 1–3 km and sportspeople are typically advised to drink "as much as tolerable during exercise."

In contrast, the !Kung San have been known to exercise for six hours in 45°C (113°F) desert heat without fluid replacement and without obvious detrimental effects other than some evidence of fatigue.[2] Indeed a recent study found that the current world record in the 42 km marathon was set by a sportsperson who lost 10% of his body weight during his record-setting performance.[34] It is much more likely that sportspeople encouraged to drink "as much as tolerable" during exercise in order to prevent "dehydration" will present with fluid overload.[5–8, 35–40]

Sportspeople with EAHE and serum sodium concentrations below 129 mmol/L (129 mEq/L) are overhydrated by between 2 L and 6 L.[7, 36] The physician should be alerted to this diagnosis in a patient with an altered level of consciousness. If the patient is conscious, he or she may complain of feeling bloated or "swollen." A helpful clinical sign is that rings, race identification bracelets, and watchstraps feel and are noticeably tighter. The race bracelet is a particularly useful indicator, as it is usually loose fitting before a race. A feeling of intestinal fullness or vomiting of clear fluid is another indicator of prolonged excessive fluid ingestion.

Management of exercise-induced hyponatremia (EAH) and exercise-associated postural hypotension (EAHE)

Under no circumstances should any hypotonic or isotonic fluids be given to unconscious or semiconscious sportspeople with EAH or EAHE. Rather, patients with EAH require some or all of the following interventions dependent on the degree to which they have developed encephalopathy secondary to cerebral edema:

- fluid restriction
- diuretics
- intravenous hypertonic (3–5%) saline at rates of about 100 mL/hr.[16]

As the condition is due in part (see below) to abnormal secretion of arginine/vasopressin (antidiuretic hormone [ADH]) in the face of hypotonicity and fluid overload, diuresis may be delayed even in patients with quite mild EAH. The use of a diuretic may be justified to initiate diuresis. Providing hypotonic or isotonic fluids to patients who are unconscious because of cerebral edema delays recovery and may produce a fatal result, as appears to have happened in isolated cases in recent years.[37–39]

In summary, it is essential that physicians caring for sportspeople with EAH and EAHE are aware of the correct management of this condition. The current management includes:

- bladder catheterization to monitor the rate of urine production during recovery—spontaneous recovery will occur if adequate amounts of urine (>500 mL/hr) are passed. (Note: A high urine sodium concentration in the face of EAH is diagnostic of inappropriate secretion of arginine/vasopressin [ADH], one of the three cardinal requirements for the development of this condition, see below)
- no fluids by mouth—salt tablets and sodium-containing foods can be given
- high sodium (3–5%) solutions given intravenously provided they are infused slowly (50–100 mL/hr)
- use of diuretics.

Etiology of EAH and EAHE

The 1985 seminal paper describing the first cases of exercise-associated hyponatremia concluded, on the basis of the history, the clinical findings, and the estimated sodium and water balance during exercise in those athletes, that the etiology of EAH was due to overhydration.[6]

The article also concluded that the intake of hypotonic fluids in excess of that required to balance sweat and urine losses may be hazardous in some individuals.

A second study published in 1991[7] unambiguously resolved the issue of what causes EAHE. In that study, each of eight sportspeople who collapsed with either EAH or EAHE was fluid overloaded by 1.22–5.92 L. The sportspeople conservatively estimated that their fluid intakes during exercise ranged from 0.8 to 1.3 L/hr, compared with maximum values of 0.6 L/hr in sportspeople with normal serum sodium concentrations.

It was also found that the sportspeople's sodium losses (153 ± 35 mmol) were not larger than those of sportspeople who maintained normonatremia during exercise. Thus, this study concluded that EAH and EAHE result from fluid retention in sportspeople who consume abnormally large fluid volumes during prolonged exercise. It was also noted that because the potential dangers of severe dehydration and, thus, the need to drink adequately during prolonged exercise have been so well publicized, some sportspeople may consume dangerously large volumes of water during prolonged exercise.

Despite this unequivocal evidence presented 20 years earlier,[7] and subsequently confirmed by a large prospective clinical trial,[35] a number of influential sports medicine organizations began to advocate that sportspeople should drink "as much as tolerable" during exercise. At the same time the theory evolved that EAH was due to large unreplaced sodium losses in sweat and that the condition could therefore be prevented by the ingestion of sports drinks during exercise.

However, the first international consensus statement on exercise-associated hyponatremia[16] has concluded that the role of sodium loss in the development of exercise-associated hyponatremia has yet to be established. Rather, the study of Noakes et al.[5] identifies three factors that can explain why the range of serum sodium concentrations after exercise is so variable even when the weight change is the same. Thus, to develop EAH subjects must:

1. over-drink, usually by drinking in excess of 750 mL per hour for at least four hours during exercise
2. fail adequately to suppress the inappropriate secretion of the water-retaining hormone arginine/vasopressin (ADH) and
3. either inappropriately osmotically inactivate circulating serum ionized sodium or fail to mobilize osmotically inactive sodium to maintain a normal serum sodium concentration in an expanded total body water.

The conclusion of these findings is that the avoidance of over-drinking is the sole factor required to prevent exercise-associated hyponatremia.[5–8, 16, 35, 40] Furthermore, the ingestion of sports drinks plays no role in prevention of EAH because:

1. sports drinks are markedly hypotonic with a low sodium concentration (about one-seventh the serum sodium concentration). Thus, their ingestion adds substantially more water than sodium to the body. Since EAH is due to fluid overload, the inappropriate ingestion of large volumes of sports drinks will compound the hyponatremia

2. exercise-associated hyponatremia is always also due to inappropriate secretion of arginine/vasopressin (ADH). The action of ADH on the kidney is to produce water retention and sodium diuresis[5] especially when there is also cerebral edema. Thus, the ingestion of any fluid regardless of its sodium content will cause further fluid retention, with excretion of all the sodium present in the ingested fluid

3. the internal osmotically inactive sodium stores exceed, by an order of magnitude, the amount of sodium that might be ingested from a sports drink during prolonged exercise. Thus, appropriate mobilization of these stores will prevent EAH, regardless of how much sodium is ingested by mouth during exercise.

More recently, a study funded by the sports drink industry has established that the change in body mass explains about 96% of the variance of the blood sodium concentration during exercise[8] and that sodium ingestion during exercise produced no significant effect. This confirmed that the 1985 predictions of Noakes et al.,[6] proven in their 1991 study[7] were correct.

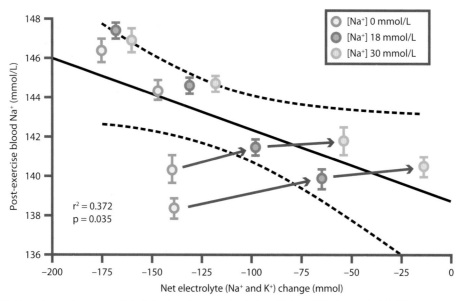

Figure 58.2 Post-exercise serum Na+ plotted against net electrolyte (Na+ and K+) change in 12 different experimental combinations of weight loss and sodium ingestion during exercise. Arrows indicate the effects of the ingestion of drinks with progressively higher Na+ on reducing the extent of the fall of serum Na+ in those who over-drink during exercise. This effect is trivial compared with the effect of overdrinking and weight gain (Fig. 58.3)

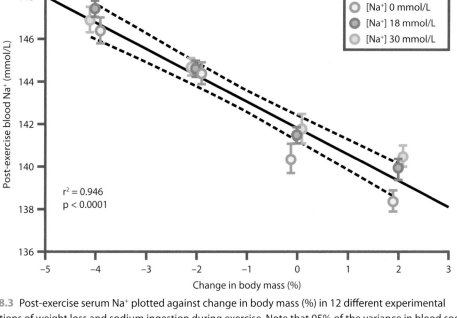

Figure 58.3 Post-exercise serum Na⁺ plotted against change in body mass (%) in 12 different experimental combinations of weight loss and sodium ingestion during exercise. Note that 95% of the variance in blood sodium concentrations in these experiments is explained by the change in body mass alone. This confirms the earlier findings and assumptions of Noakes et al.[6,7]

Other causes of exercise-related collapse in hot weather

Heatstroke and exercise-associated collapse due to EAPH are the most likely causes of distress or collapse while exercising in hot weather. It is, however, important to consider other possible causes of distress or collapse that may also occur in these conditions. Causes of collapse and the likely circumstances surrounding collapse are shown in Table 58.3. This highlights the importance of determining the rectal temperature as the first step in assessing the collapsed sportsperson in hot weather. A rectal temperature above 40°C (104°F) indicates that heat illness is the most likely cause of collapse. A rectal temperature below 40°C (104°F) should encourage the clinician to consider other causes of collapse.

Sportspeople suffering from hyperthermia and sportspeople suffering from hypothermia may present in the same event. The faster runners with their increased heat production may present with hyperthermia, while slower competitors, particularly those who have walked, may present later in the day with hypothermia. The possibility of hypothermia is increased if rain or a cold wind or both are present, or if the temperature drops over the dura-

Table 58.3 Other causes of collapse

Cause	Associated features
Hypoglycemia	Diabetic using medication Poor carbohydrate loading and intake High alcohol intake prior to event
Hyponatremia	Ultra-endurance event Large amounts of fluid, either plain water or sports drink
Hypothermia	Slow athlete in endurance event Cold wind (change of weather)
Drug toxicity	Athlete using social or performance-enhancing drugs (e.g. cocaine, amphetamines)
Ischemic heart disease/ arrhythmia	Previous history of cardiac disease Family history High risk factor profile
Stroke	Older athlete Hypertensive athlete
Convulsions/ coma	Epilepsy Head injury Hyponatremia
Head injury	Contact sport

tion of the event. Cold-related illness is discussed in Chapter 59.

Heat acclimatization

Sportspeople are able to cope much better with hot or humid conditions if they are acclimatized.[41, 42] The human body adjusts to exposure to hot conditions by increasing blood volume and venous tone and, particularly, by alterations to the sweating mechanism. The main ways in which the sweating mechanism is affected are by:

- earlier onset of sweating
- increased amount of sweating
- increased dilution of the sweat (lower sodium concentration).

These changes result in increased heat loss for a given set of environmental conditions and a smaller rise in body temperature.

There is considerable dispute regarding the ideal length of time required for heat acclimatization, although a minimum of two weeks is probably required when coming from a cool climate to a hot or humid climate. One problem that reduces the effectiveness of heat acclimatization is that in the week or two prior to a major event, the sportsperson is often tapering (i.e. reducing the amount of training). While there is some effect on heat acclimatization in the rested state, it may be necessary to perform relatively intensive exercise to maximize acclimatization. Therefore, exposure to the warmer environment should occur for a minimum of two weeks.

A number of other factors affect acclimatization. If the sportsperson wishes to compete in a hot and humid environment, it is necessary to acclimatize for both heat and humidity. Training in a hot, dry environment provides only partial acclimatization for a hot, humid environment. Another factor affecting heat acclimatization is the presence or absence of air conditioning. To maximize acclimatization, the sportsperson should be exposed to the environmental conditions 24 hours a day. If the only exposure to the hot conditions is during training and the sportsperson then returns to an air-conditioned environment, the effectiveness of acclimatization is reduced. Therefore, it is recommended that sportspeople spend a minimum of two weeks acclimatizing at the site of competition or in an environment very similar to that anticipated for competition. Some intense training should be performed during this period and air conditioning should be restricted to night-time for sleeping and adequate recovery.

Although it is possible to assist the acclimatization process by exercising in a heat chamber for three hours per day prior to departure, it is only partially effective and should be used only as an adjunct to, rather than as a replacement for, full acclimatization. Wearing impermeable clothing while exercising may also make a small contribution to acclimatization.

 Listen to Tim Noakes discuss the management of sportspeople in the heat in the *Clinical Sports Medicine* masterclasses at www.clinicalsportsmedicine.com

Guidelines for the prevention of heat illness

Most cases of heat illness could be prevented if the following guidelines are followed.

1. Perform adequate conditioning. The sportsperson must have trained appropriately and be conditioned for the planned activity.
2. Undergo acclimatization if competing in unaccustomed heat or humidity.
3. Avoid adverse conditions. Event organizers should ensure that high intensity or endurance events should not take place in adverse conditions of heat or humidity. If events are to occur in hot climates, they should take place in the early morning before conditions deteriorate.

4. Alter training times. Unless trying to acclimatize, the sportsperson should avoid exercise at the hottest time of the day.
5. Wear appropriate clothing. In hot conditions, sportspeople should wear a minimal amount of loose-fitting, light-colored clothing. An open weave or mesh top is ideal. Many sportspeople choose to remove their top during training in hot conditions. This has the advantage of allowing better heat loss from sweating but is counterbalanced by an increased heat gain from the environment.
6. Drink appropriate amounts of fluids before the event. There is no evidence that "dehydration" or

that drinking to stay ahead of thirst either before or during exercise play any role in the prevention of heat illness. Sportspeople should drink according to the dictates of thirst before and during exercise and will remain optimally hydrated.

7. There is no evidence that fluid ingestion during exercise can prevent heatstroke in those predisposed to develop the condition. Nor is there any published evidence that dehydration is an important factor predisposing to heatstroke or the development of illness in sportspeople who have some access to such fluids during exercise.[3, 14] It has been shown that fluid ingestion during exercise in the laboratory may reduce the rectal temperature somewhat[43] but that this effect may be a result of the inadequate convective cooling usually present in indoor exercise.[44] When exercise is undertaken in the laboratory in environmental conditions that reproduce the conditions in out-of-door exercise, high rates of fluid ingestion are not required to prevent this additional increase in rectal temperature. Rather, drinking to the dictates of thirst produces an optimum result.[44, 45]

8. To minimize the uncomfortable sensations of thirst and so to optimize performance during exercise, sportspeople can be assured that they need drink only according to the dictates of their thirst.[46] This rate may vary between 200 and 800 mL per hour; much higher amounts are not uncommon

in sportspeople who develop exercise-associated hyponatremia.[5, 7] Elite sportspeople appear to drink sparingly during exercise, suggesting that superior athletic ability may be associated with a reduced dipsogenic drive during exercise. This would clearly be an advantageous evolutionary adaptation in early human hunter-gathers like the !Kung San who, since they have no access to fluid during hunting, will not be disabled by the development of intolerable thirst and hence have to terminate their hunt prematurely. For exercise up to one hour in duration, plain water is appropriate. For exercise lasting longer than one hour, a dilute glucose and electrolyte solution should be used. At longer distances and durations it may become increasingly necessary also to eat calorie-dense foods according to individual choice.

9. Ensure sportspeople and officials are well educated. It is important that event organizers, coaches, and sportspeople understand the importance of adequate hydration, the danger of water intoxication, and the need to avoid excessive environmental conditions.

10. Provide proficient medical support. A well-equipped, well-trained medical team should be present at all endurance events occurring in hot or humid conditions. The guidelines for the medical coverage of an endurance event are discussed in Chapter 65.

RECOMMENDED READING

Noakes TD. *Lore of running*. 4th ed. Champaign, IL: Human Kinetics, 2003.

Noakes TD. *Waterlogged. Why the science of hydration fails to fit the facts*. 2012; Human Kinetics. Champaign, Il, USA (in press).

Asplund CA, O'Connor FG, Noakes, TD. Exercise-associated collapse: an evidence-based review and primer for clinicians. *Br J Sports Med* 2011;45(14) in press.

REFERENCES

1. Heinrich B. *Racing the antelope*. New York: Harper Collins, 2001.
2. Foster D, Foster D. *Africa. Speaking with earth and sky*. Cape Town: David Philip Publishers, 2005.
3. Nolte HW, Noakes TD, Van Vuuren B. Trained humans can exercise safely in extreme dry heat when drinking water ad libitum. *J Sports Sci* 2011;29(12):1233–41.
4. Rae DE, Knobel GJ, Mann T et al. Heatstroke during endurance exercise: is there evidence for excessive endothermy? *Med Sci Sports Exerc* 2008 Jul;40(7):1193–204.
5. Noakes TD, Sharwood K, Speedy D et al. Three independent biological mechanisms cause exercise-associated hyponatremia: evidence from 2,135 weighed competitive athletic performances. *Proc Natl Acad Sci USA* 2005;102(51):18550–5.
6. Noakes TD, Goodwin N, Rayner BL et al. Water intoxication: a possible complication during endurance exercise. *Med Sci Sports Exerc* 1985 Jun;17(3):370–5.
7. Irving RA, Noakes TD, Buck R et al. Evaluation of renal function and fluid homeostasis during recovery from exercise-induced hyponatremia. *J Appl Physiol* 1991;70(1):342–8.
8. Noakes TD. Changes in body mass alone explain almost all of the variance in the serum sodium concentrations during prolonged exercise. Has commercial influence impeded scientific endeavour? *Br J Sports Med* 2011;45(6):475–7.
9. Bracker MD. Environmental and thermal injury. *Clin Sports Med* 1992;11(2):419–36.
10. Dennis SC, Noakes TD. Advantages of a smaller bodymass in humans when distance-running in warm, humid conditions. *Eur J Appl Physiol Occup Physiol* 1999;79(3):280–4.
11. Marino FE, Mbambo Z, Kortekaas E et al. Advantages of smaller body mass during distance running in warm, humid environments. *Pflugers Arch* 2000;441(2-3):359–67.
12. Marino FE, Lambert MI, Noakes TD. Superior performance of African runners in warm, humid but not in cool environmental conditions. *J Appl Physiol* 2004;96(1):124–30.
13. Armstrong L, Epstein Y, Greenleaf J et al. American College of Sports Medicine position stand. Heat and cold illnesses during distance running. *Med Sci Sports Exerc* 1996;28(12):i–x.
14. Noakes TD. Hyperthermia, hypothermia and problems of hydration. In: Shepard RJ, Astrand PO, eds. *Endurance in sport*. Oxford: Blackwell Scientific, 2000:591–613.
15. McGarvey J, Thompson J, Hanna C et al. Sensitivity and specificity of clinical signs for assessment of dehydration in endurance athletes. *Br J Sports Med* 2010;44(10):716–19.
16. Hew-Butler T, Almond C, Ayus JC et al. Consensus statement of the 1st International Exercise-Associated Hyponatremia Consensus Development Conference, Cape Town, South Africa 2005. *Clin J Sport Med* 2005;15(4):208–13.
17. Maughan RJ. Thermoregulation in marathon competition at low ambient temperature. *Int J Sports Med* 1985;6(1):15–19.
18. Noakes TD, Myburgh KH, Duplessis J et al. Metabolic rate, not percent dehydration, predicts rectal temperature in marathon runners. *Med Sci Sports Exerc* 1991;23(4):443–9.
19. O'Donnell TF Jr, Clowes GH Jr. The circulatory requirements of heat stroke. *Surg Forum* 1971;22:12–14.
20. Armstrong LE, Crago AE, Adams R et al. Whole-body cooling of hyperthermic runners: comparison of two field therapies. *Am J Emerg Med* 1996;14(4):355–8.
21. Roberts WO. A 12-year summary of twin cities marathon injury. *Med Sci Sports Exerc* 1996;28(5 Suppl.):S123.
22. Holtzhausen LM, Noakes TD, Kroning B et al. Clinical and bioclinical characteristics of collapsed ultramarathon runners. *Med Sci Sports Exerc* 1994;26(9):1095–101.
23. Holtzhausen LM, Noakes TD. The prevalence and significance of post-exercise (postural) hypotension in ultramarathon runners. *Med Sci Sports Exerc* 1995;27(12):1595–601.
24. Holtzhausen LM, Noakes TD. Collapsed ultraendurance athlete: proposed mechanisms and an approach to management. *Clin J Sport Med* 1997;7(4):292–301.

25. Noakes TD. The forgotten Barcroft/Edholm reflex: potential role in exercise associated collapse. *Br J Sports Med* 2003;37(3):277–8.

26. Barcroft H, Edholm OG. On the vasodilatation in human skeletal muscle during post-haemorrhagic fainting. *J Physiol* 1945;104(2):161–75.

27. Anley C, Noakes T, Collins M et al. A comparison of two treatment protocols in the management of exercise-associated postural hypotension: a randomised clinical trial. *Br J Sports Med* 2010 Jun 28 Epub.

28. Schwellnus MP. Skeletal muscle cramps during exercise. *Phys Sportsmed* 1999;27(12):109–15.

29. Schwellnus MP, Nicol J, Laubscher R et al. Serum electrolyte concentrations and hydration status are not associated with exercise associated muscle cramping (EAMC) in distance runners. *Br J Sports Med* 2004;38(4):488–92.

30. Sulzer NU, Schwellnus MP, Noakes TD. Serum electrolytes in ironman triathletes with exercise-associated muscle cramping. *Med Sci Sports Exerc* 2005;37(7):1081–5.

31. Epstein Y, Sohar E. Fluid balance in hot climates: sweating, water intake, and prevention of dehydration. *Public Health Rev* 1985;13(1–2):115–38.

32. Miller KC, Mack GW, Knight KL et al. Reflex inhibition of electrically induced muscle cramps in hypohydrated humans. *Med Sci Sports Exerc* 2010;42(5):953–61

33. Miller KC, Mack G, Knight KL. Electrolyte and plasma changes after ingestion of pickle juice, water, and a common carbohydrate-electrolyte solution. *J Athl Train* 2009;44(5):454–61.

34. Beis L, Fudge BW, Noakes TD et al. Drinking behaviours of elite male runners during marathon competition. *BASES Annual Conference* 2010; Glasgow, University of Glasgow.

35. Almond CSD, Shin AY, Fortescue EB et al. Hyponatremia among runners in the Boston Marathon. *N Engl J Med* 2005;352(15):1550–6.

36. Speedy DB, Noakes TD, Rogers IR et al. Hyponatremia in ultradistance triathletes. *Med Sci Sports Exerc* 1999;31(6):809–15.

37. Garigan TP, Ristedt DE. Death from hyponatremia as a result of acute water intoxication in an army basic trainee. *Mil Med* 1999;164(3):234–8.

38. Noakes TD. Perpetuating ignorance: intravenous fluid therapy in sport. *Br J Sports Med* 1999;33(5):296–7.

39. Thompson J-A, Wolff AJ. Hyponatremic encephalopathy in a marathon runner. *Chest* 2003;124(4):313S.

40. Noakes TD, Speedy DB. Case proven: exercise associated hyponatraemia is due to overdrinking. So why did it take 20 years before the original evidence was accepted? *Br J Sports Med* 2006;40(7):567–72.

41. Sparling PB. Expected environmental conditions for the 1996 Summer Olympic Games in Atlanta. *Clin J Sport Med* 1995;5(4):220–2.

42. Sparling PB. Environmental conditions during the 1996 Olympic Games: a brief follow-up report. *Clin J Sport Med* 1997;7(3):159–61.

43. Montain SJ, Coyle EF. Influence of graded dehydration on hyperthermia and cardiovascular drift during exercise. *J Appl Physiol* 1992;73(4):1340–50.

44. Saunders AG, Dugas JP, Tucker R et al. The effects of different air velocities on heat storage and body temperature in humans cycling in a hot, humid environment. *Acta Physiol Scand* 2005;183(3):241–55.

45. Dugas JP, Oosthuizen U, Tucker R et al. Rates of fluid ingestion alter pacing but not thermoregulatory responses during prolonged exercise in hot and humid conditions with appropriate convective cooling. *Eur J Appl Physiol* 2009;105(1):69–80.

46. Goulet ED. Effect of exercise-induced dehydration on time-trial exercise performance: a meta-analysis. *Br J Sports Med* 2011 Apr 4. [Epub ahead of print]

47. Asplund CA, O'Connor FG, Noakes, TD. Exercise-associated collapse: an evidence-based review and primer for clinicians. *Br J Sports Med* 2011;45(14) in press.

Chapter 59

Exercise at the extremes of cold and altitude

with MICHAEL KOEHLE

There are only three real sports: bullfighting, motor racing, and mountaineering.
All the others are merely games.   Commonly attributed to Ernest Hemingway

The five primary areas of focus in the first half of this chapter are:

- a brief review of thermoregulation—how the body generates heat and how heat is lost
- strategies for measuring body temperature—a key to clinical assessment
- how hypothermia affects major body systems
- management of hypothermia and its complication, frostbite
- prevention of cold injuries.

The second half of this chapter focuses on exercise at altitude.

Generation of body heat

Humans function optimally in a relatively narrow temperature range. At ambient air temperatures above 28°C (82°F), heat produced by basal metabolism maintains the core temperature at 37°C (99°F). In conditions below this temperature, the body must produce additional heat to remain thermoneutral. Such heat production can be achieved by greater physical activity and autonomically mediated shivering, a physiological response of healthy individuals in a moderate environment.

Shivering involves involuntary muscular contractions in response to cold and uses energy stores quickly. The capacity to shiver lessens as local glycogen stores are depleted. The intensity of shivering is generally related to the rate of change of temperature. Shivering results in decreased muscular coordination and, therefore, impairs sporting performance. Non-shivering thermogenesis occurs in young children because of metabolism of brown fat; however, this mechanism is not available to adults.

Heat loss

Heat transfer occurs mainly from the skin and is therefore regulated by the circulation, the amount of insulation, and perspiration. Heat loss occurs through conduction, convection, radiation, and evaporation.

Conduction occurs because of direct contact with a cold object or air. Heat transfer is related to the area of contact and the relative heat conductance of the objects. Conduction is most important in water immersion, as the conductivity of water is approximately 23 times that of air. Conduction may also be important when lying on cold, wet ground.

Convection relates to the movement of air close to the body. Convection becomes important in windy conditions with temperatures up to 20°C (68°F). It is also significant in sports such as cycling and running.

Radiation involves the emission of heat energy to nearby objects. This occurs from uncovered skin and is the greatest source of heat loss under normal conditions. In cold conditions, however, the amount of heat loss through radiation is less as the skin temperature approximates the environmental temperature.

Heat lost as sweat on the external skin or clothing is converted from liquid to gas by evaporation. Evaporation forms part of the body's insensible water losses. Evaporation is increased in dry, windy conditions and may go unnoticed. Heat is also lost through feces, urine, and respiration.

Minimizing heat loss

Several factors help minimize heat loss. Peripheral vasoconstriction reduces external heat loss and increases the thickness of the shell of insulation but it is not effective in the head and scalp. Clothing helps reduce heat loss and curling the body into a ball to reduce the exposed surface area may minimize this even further. Keeping still also prevents heat loss. Lean athletes may be at a disadvantage with exposure to cold due to decreased insulation from body fat.

Measurement of body temperature

Direct measurement of core temperature is often inconvenient in the field. Thus, for convenience, indirect measures are substituted for direct measures of core temperature, although each method has significant limitations.

Oral temperature may be affected by wind, rain, external temperature, and recent ingestion of food. It may, however, be a useful screening exercise as the core temperature will never be lower than the oral temperature. If the oral temperature is above 35°C (95°F), hypothermia can be excluded.

When measuring temperature orally, leave the thermometer in the mouth for at least three minutes. Temperature should not be taken within 30 minutes of ingestion of hot or cold food.

Measurement of axillary temperature is also not reliable as it may be affected by skin temperature. Axillary temperature is usually 1–1.5°C (1.8–2.7°F) below core temperature, and becomes less reliable in cold conditions.

Tympanic membrane temperature may be affected by water or wax in the ear as well as the surrounding skin temperature.[1] Rectal temperature is more reliable than all other indirect methods of measuring core temperature but its changes can lag behind core temperature changes.

In an outdoor emergency, if a thermometer is not available, the best means of assessing body temperature is to feel an area of the body that is not normally cold (e.g. axilla). It is important to remember that skin temperature is a poor guide to core temperature. Skin temperatures can drop to as low as 21–23°C (70–73°F) before any decrease in core temperature is detected.

Effects of hypothermia

Cardiovascular effects

Vasoconstriction may lead to fluid shifts by increasing the central blood volume, thus causing a cold diuresis. This diuresis, in conjunction with the increased fluid loss from respiration and sweat during exercise, may reduce total circulating volume. On rewarming, peripheral vessels dilate and cause a fluid shift to the periphery with a further reduction in central circulation. Decreased cardiac output occurs because of a combination of reduced circulatory volume, myocardial depression, and impaired electrical conductance.

Impaired conductance results in a decreased heart rate and ECG/EKG changes with prolongation of all intervals. The presence of a J wave in the ST segment is indicative of hypothermia.

Atrial fibrillation may occur and usually reverts with rewarming. Ventricular fibrillation may occur and may be refractory to treatment at very low temperatures.

Respiratory effects

Cold exposure results in hyperventilation with a resultant respiratory heat and water loss. This may contribute to dehydration and bronchospasm.

A decrease in core temperature is also associated with a reduction in airway protective mechanisms with subsequent increased risk of aspiration. There is, however, no direct damage to the lung from exposure to cold, because of the effective heating and humidifying mechanism of the upper airway.

Other effects

Delayed nerve conduction and neuromuscular transmission cause numbness, and impaired coordination and cognition. This may persist for some hours or even days after the core temperature returns to normal.

Muscle stiffness and weakness associated with mild hypothermia may lead to an increased risk of muscle tears. Adequate warm-up and stretching should be performed prior to muscular activity in cold conditions.

Excessive shivering may lead to poor voluntary muscular control and increased fatigue. Hypothermia may inhibit glycolysis and fat metabolism, affecting both speed and endurance. Renal function can be impaired due to decreased renal blood flow,[2] and coagulopathies can occur.[3]

General principles of managing hypothermia

Management of the hypothermic sportsperson requires:

- recognition of the problem by appreciating the clinical features

- removal from cold, windy, or wet conditions
- gentle and minimal handling
- measurement of the core temperature
- insulation to prevent further heat loss
- provision of nutritional and fluid support
- assessment for the presence of other conditions (e.g. frostbite)
- possible passive or active rewarming
- possible transportation to a medical facility.

Clinical features of hypothermia

The clinical features of hypothermia vary depending on the degree of reduction in core temperature. These are listed in Table 59.1.

Methods to achieve rewarming

Passive rewarming

Passive rewarming involves insulating the patient adequately to allow metabolic heat to rewarm slowly from within. If the patient can be removed from the cold environment, it is advisable to remove all wet clothing and cover the whole body, including the head, with dry blankets.

If removal from the cold environment is not possible, wet clothing should only be removed if it can be done in a gentle fashion without exposing the bare patient to wind or rain. If the wet clothing is not removed, the patient should be placed in a plastic bag from the neck downwards to prevent any evaporative loss and to avoid wetting the dry insulation placed over the wet clothes. A second plastic bag placed over the dry insulation will keep it dry from subsequent exposure to rain. If none of the above is possible, a group of fully clothed people closely surrounding the patient is helpful ("penguin effect").[4]

In cases of moderate and severe hypothermia, passive rewarming is the safest way to rewarm[5]

unless the patient is in a highly monitored intensive care unit with experienced skilled staff.

Metabolic heat production initially increases with shivering and then decreases with decreasing temperature to 50% of a normal rate at 24°C (75°F). This heat production can rewarm the patient at 0.5–1°C (1–1.8°F) per hour even in profound hypothermia.

Active rewarming

Active rewarming may be by external or internal methods.

External

External active rewarming is recommended in cases of mild hypothermia but should be avoided in severe hypothermia. There are a number of different means of external active rewarming, including a hot air or water-circulating blanket, hot packs to the axillae, groin, and torso, or a hot tub. Warming should be ideally directed to the trunk to reduce the risk of core temperature afterdrop, a phenomenon caused by cold blood returning from the extremities to the core.

Internal

Internal active rewarming can be performed in a hospital setting. Techniques that can be used include extracorporeal blood warming, cardiopulmonary bypass, airway warming, and warm intravenous infusion. In severe hypothermia, active rewarming in a highly monitored intensive care unit with experienced staff can increase survival; however, in circumstances less than that, active rewarming may be both dangerous and counterproductive.

Other rewarming methods

Drugs play little or no role in the treatment of complicated hypothermia.

Table 59.1 Clinical features of hypothermia

Mild (33–35°C [91–95°F])	Moderate (31–32°C [88–90°F])	Severe (<31°C [<88°F])
Cold extremities	Apathy, poor judgment	Inappropriate behavior
Shivering	Reduced shivering	Total loss of shivering
Tachycardia	Weakness and drowsiness	Cardiac arrhythmias
Tachypnea	Slurred speech and amnesia	Pulmonary edema
Urinary urgency	Dehydration	Hypotension and bradycardia
Mild incoordination	Increased incoordination and clumsiness	Reduced level of consciousness
	Fatigue	Muscle rigidity

Exercise is not helpful in anything but very mild hypothermia. Exercise depletes glycogen and therefore eventually inhibits shivering. Exercise can also increase the rate of heat loss.

Treatment of hypothermia in sport

Although sporting activity generally provides sufficient body heat to keep the sportsperson warm, hypothermia may occur as a result of:

- an accident or injury
- exhaustion
- dehydration
- immersion (accidental or deliberate).

Sports with a particularly high risk of cold injury include endurance running, skiing, cycling, mountaineering, hiking, caving, windsurfing, kayaking, and scuba diving. Insufficient clothing may provide inadequate protection from the environment, particularly near the end of a long race when running speed and heat production are reduced. Frostbite can occur in low temperatures, especially when combined with high wind speed.

The risk of hypothermia in sportspeople is increased by a lack of knowledge, lack of communication, pushing oneself to exhaustion, ignoring early warning signs, poor psychological and physical preparation, and inadequate protection from the weather. Cold wind increases heat loss in proportion to wind speed, that is, wind chill factor. For example, if the temperature is −1°C (30°F) in still air, wind speeds of 16, 32 and 48 km/hr reduce the temperature to −9°C (16°F), −14°C (7°F) and −19°C (−2°F), respectively.[6] Cyclists and skiers can generate these wind chill factors on a still day.

Hypothermia is a medical emergency, and therapy should be instituted at once. Sportspeople presenting with hypothermia must have their temperature measured with a low-reading thermometer and managed according to whether they have mild, moderate, or severe hypothermia, or hypothermia associated with cold-water immersion.

Treatment of mild hypothermia

A patient with mild hypothermia (33–35°C [91–95°F]) should be removed from the cold, insulated appropriately, and given a warm, sweet drink. Alcohol should be avoided. This patient will safely rewarm with or without active rewarming. The application of external heat may make him or her feel more comfortable. Heat should be applied to the torso, axillae, and groin only, and the patient should be continually monitored. Mild activity may be performed provided the rectal temperature remains close to 35°C.

Treatment of moderate hypothermia

The patient with moderate hypothermia (31–32°C [88–90°F]) should also be removed from the cold and insulated appropriately. In the field setting, the patient should not be rewarmed actively until the rectal temperature is rising and is above 34°C (93°F). The patient should be continually monitored, if possible, for the presence of hypotension and arrhythmias. Active rewarming can be performed in the hospital setting with continuous monitoring, intravenous rehydration, and the availability of resuscitation equipment. Moderate hypothermia is not usually life-threatening itself; however, these patients are at risk of progressing to severe hypothermia, which has a significant mortality.

Treatment of severe hypothermia

The patient with severe hypothermia (<31°C [<88°F]) should be handled as little and as gently as possible as the risk of ventricular fibrillation is increased. The treatment of the severely hypothermic patient depends on the availability of appropriate facilities. If the patient can be transported quickly and safely with minimal handling, he or she should be transferred to a hospital equipped with an intensive care unit. In this setting, active rewarming can begin.

The severely hypothermic patient may often appear dead but on closer observation may have an extremely slow heart rate (as low as six beats per minute) and a slow respiration rate. These patients must not be mistaken for being in asystole, as cardiopulmonary resuscitation may precipitate ventricular fibrillation.

 Patients suffering from severe hypothermia should never be considered to be dead until they are warm and dead.[7,8]

Treatment of immersion hypothermia

Immersion hypothermia usually results from rapid cooling in a non-exhausted patient. Other major dangers to a victim of immersion hypothermia are impaired swimming performance and immediate cardiorespiratory responses due to cold. The patient should be gently removed, in the horizontal position if possible, from the water, with particular attention paid to signs of cardiovascular collapse when the hydrostatic support of the patient's blood pressure is removed. If the rectal temperature is below 31°C, the patient should be treated in the same way as any patient with severe hypothermia. If the rectal temperature is above 32°C and the patient has been in the water less than three hours, rapid rewarming can begin, as significant fluid shifts should not have occurred.[9] It is important to remember when insulating the patient that sweat may reduce the effectiveness of the insulating material and that evaporation from the outer surface of a wetsuit may cause considerable heat loss.

Space blankets are commonly used in the treatment of hypothermia. However, in cold conditions, radiant heat loss is minimal compared with conductive loss, especially with poor insulation and high winds. Space blankets, therefore, provide little added protection;, also they are easily torn by twigs, they shred easily, and they are highly flammable.

Frostbite

Frostbite involves crystallization of fluids in the skin or subcutaneous tissue after exposure to subfreezing temperatures (<–0.6°C [<31°F]). With low skin temperature and dehydration, cutaneous blood vessels constrict and limit circulation because the viscosity of blood increases. Water is drawn out of the cells and ice crystals cause mechanical destruction of skin and subcutaneous tissues. Frostbite most commonly occurs in the periphery, with the fingers and toes being most affected.[10] The tips of the nose and ears and the tissue of the cheek are also affected.

Frostbite can be classified as:

- superficial or mild, involving the skin and subcutaneous tissue only
- deep or severe, involving the full skin thickness and deeper tissues.

Superficial frostbite—management

Patients with superficial frostbite complain of a burning local pain with numbness. On examination, the skin is initially pale and grey, and becomes red after thawing. Superficial serous bullae (blisters) may be present; hemorrhagic blisters represent subdermal damage.

Local thawing by contact with direct body heat can treat superficial frostbite. The injured part should not be directly rubbed as sloughing may occur. No attempt should be made to thaw the injured part

unless it is certain that refreezing will be prevented. Refreezing results in a far more serious injury.

Deep frostbite—management

Deep frostbite is initially extremely painful and then becomes numb. The body part affected appears as a frozen block of hard, white tissue with areas of gangrene and deep hemoserous blisters if the frostbite is severe. The affected part should be rapidly rewarmed in a hot water bath of temperature 39–41°C (102–106°F). A whirlpool bath with added antiseptic is ideal. The rewarming process is often acutely painful and requires analgesia. Radiant heat from a fire or radiator should not be used as skin burns may occur. The tissue should continue to be warmed until it becomes soft and pliable, and normal sensation returns. Appropriate tetanus prophylaxis is indicated.[11]

The serous blisters contain thromboxanes and prostaglandins that damage underlying tissue. These serous blisters should be debrided and treated topically with aloe. Hemorrhagic blisters should be left intact. Ibuprofen 400 mg orally twice a day is recommended to prevent further prostaglandin-mediated tissue damage.[11]

Intravenous infusion of low-molecular-weight dextran may help reduce swelling and maintain vasodilatation. Prophylactic parenteral penicillin should be administered for 72 hours.[11] It is important to salvage as much tissue as possible.

Debridement should be delayed for days to weeks, until obvious demarcation has occurred. Contractures and compartment syndromes may develop and should be treated appropriately.

Prevention of cold injuries

The majority of cold injuries are preventable if general guidelines (box opposite) are followed and the sportsperson benefits from the specific strategies that have been developed for cold weather activities.

Sportspeople should wear appropriate clothing for the particular environmental conditions. It is advisable to wear a number of layers of clothing rather than one thick layer. This strategy enables the sportsperson to remove layers of clothing when exercising in warmer conditions and therefore reduce sweating. It also enables the sportsperson to put on additional clothing if the temperature or level of activity drops. Clothing should be made of a good insulating material such as wool, synthetic fleece, or polypropylene. Use of cotton garments should be avoided.

In rain or snow, adequate waterproof outer clothing should be worn. The outer jacket should also offer adequate protection against wind. Recommended materials include nylon and Gore-Tex. In cold conditions, extremities such as the head, face, and hands should be covered. Synthetic or wool socks should be worn instead of cotton.

Exercise and physical activity at altitude

Many active people enjoy traveling to altitude for recreation or competition. One of the potential concerns for travelers to altitude is the risk of getting altitude illness. The term "altitude illness" refers to all conditions that can occur as a result of exposure to altitude, including acute mountain sickness, high-altitude pulmonary edema, and high-altitude cerebral edema.

Altitude illness usually occurs at altitudes above 3000 m (10 000 ft) and can cause significant morbidity. The life-threatening manifestations of altitude illness—high-altitude cerebral edema and high-altitude pulmonary edema—occur in 0.1–4.0% of visitors to altitude.[13, 14] A larger proportion of travelers experience acute mountain sickness, which typically presents as headache, nausea, vomiting, dizziness, fatigue, and insomnia. Although these milder symptoms are not life-threatening, they can be severe enough to interfere with trip participation and enjoyment. Fortunately, altitude illness is preventable, and

proper pre-trip planning can reduce morbidity and mortality at altitude. In this section we discuss:

- the critical issue of the trip itinerary
- the patient's past history with respect to altitude and certain relevant medical conditions
- prevention of altitude illness.

Itinerary—ascent rate

One of the most important determinants of an individual's risk of altitude illness is the itinerary.

PRACTICE PEARL Rate of ascent is a strong predictor for acute mountain sickness.[13] Those who ascend slowly, allowing for gradual acclimatization, have a lower likelihood of developing acute mountain sickness.[13]

Sleeping altitude is monitored when assessing the rate of ascent, as large increases in sleeping altitude pose the greatest risk of altitude illness.

Various guidelines have been proposed for graded ascent, ranging from 300 m to 600 m (1000–2000 ft) of ascent per night[14, 15] when above 3000 m (10 000 ft). Additionally, at least one night at an intermediate altitude (1500–2500 m [5000–8000 ft]) on the way to very high altitude is recommended for acclimatization.[12] No controlled studies have been conducted that demonstrate an ideal ascent rate. A recommended ascent rate of no more than approximately 500 m (1600 ft) per night should be followed.[16] Approximately every 1000 m (3200 ft), an additional rest day is recommended where the traveler sleeps at the same altitude for two consecutive nights.

Daytime acclimatization hikes to higher altitudes are permitted and encouraged in travelers who are not exhibiting signs and symptoms of altitude illness. This "climb high, sleep low" approach accelerates acclimatization by intermittently exposing the individual to a higher dose of hypoxia.

Travelers with more rigid itineraries often ascend too quickly, or while symptomatic or sick, in order to meet external deadlines. Although only 40% of trekkers in the Nepal Himalayas are in organized groups, they account for 80% of medical evacuations.[17] Patients should be encouraged to have a flexible itinerary, with room for extra rest days to allow for illness or other setbacks.

Previous altitude history

Patients with a previous history of altitude illness are at increased risk of recurrence.[13, 18] Susceptible individuals should follow a more conservative itinerary, aiming for 300 m (1000 ft) increments in sleeping altitude. These individuals should also strongly consider chemoprophylaxis, especially if they are returning to an altitude at which they were previously ill (page 1154).

The effect of recent previous altitude exposure is a matter of much debate. In laboratory models of deacclimatization,[19] hypoxic ventilatory response seems to recede after only one week. However, observational studies suggest that altitude exposure in the previous two months provides a significant degree of protection from acute mountain sickness.[13]

The protection from high-altitude pulmonary edema seems to be much shorter lasting. Re-entry high-altitude pulmonary edema[20, 21] is a phenomenon whereby high-altitude residents develop pulmonary edema after a brief trip to low altitude. These residents would presumably be well acclimatized to their home altitude, but apparently do not retain any protection from high-altitude pulmonary edema when they briefly descend. It therefore appears that previous altitude exposure may provide some protection from acute mountain sickness, but not from high-altitude pulmonary edema.

Patient characteristics and previous medical history

Gender is not believed to be a risk factor for acute mountain sickness.[22, 23] However, there appears to be a slight overrepresentation of male patients with high-altitude pulmonary edema.[12] Although early work suggested that older travelers might have some slight protection from acute mountain sickness, there is insufficient data using current definitions of altitude illness to confirm this finding.[24]

High-altitude pulmonary edema has some unique medical risk factors. The pathophysiology of high-altitude pulmonary edema involves increased pulmonary vascular pressures, possibly related to heterogeneous hypoxic pulmonary vasoconstriction. Therefore, conditions that increase pulmonary vascular pressure, such as unilateral pulmonary artery hypertension[25, 26] and primary pulmonary hypertension,[26] increase the risk of an individual developing high-altitude pulmonary edema.

Asthma

Asthma is not a risk factor for altitude illness. Persons with asthma tend to have fewer symptoms while at moderate altitude. The improvement in

clinical status is believed to be due to thinner air and a relative dearth of pollutants and lung irritants in the air.[27] However, at extreme altitude, airway heat loss may aggravate asthma. Before intense physical efforts, patients should medicate with bronchodilators (and possibly inhaled corticosteroids), especially if they have known exercise-induced bronchospasm.[28] Rapid ascent to an altitude of 3000 m (10 000 ft) or more should be avoided in those with moderate or severe asthma.[28]

Refractive eye surgery

Patients who have had refractive eye surgery may have visual difficulties while traveling at altitude, especially above 5000 m (16 400 ft). There are several reports of visual disturbances at high altitude in individuals who have had scalpel radial keratotomy.[29, 30] The more recent laser procedures (laser photorefractive keratectomy [laser PRK] and laser-assisted in-situ keratomileusis [LASIK]) have resulted in fewer complications; however, mountaineers with LASIK can have symptoms such as blurring and dry eyes while traveling above 5000 m (16 400 ft).[31]

 Patients with a previous history of refractive eye surgery should be cautioned about possible visual problems and should bring artificial tears for daily instillation while at moderate altitude and above. If visual blurring occurs, they should not ascend any further.

Oral contraceptive pill and pregnancy

The effectiveness of oral contraceptive pill regimens is not believed to be altered at altitude.[23] Mountain travelers often suffer diarrhea or other conditions requiring concurrent medication therapy that may interfere with the efficacy of oral contraceptive pills.

 Women should be cautioned to use a second method of contraception when diarrhea or the need for concurrent medication may affect the efficacy of oral contraceptive pills.

Theoretically, combination oral contraceptive pills have the potential of increasing the risk of thrombosis at altitude (especially when combined with dehydration, polycythemia, and stasis, which commonly occur at high altitude). To date, there have been no reports of deep vein thrombosis in this group.[23] At sea level, third-generation oral contraceptive pills (containing desorgestrel or gestodene) are associated with a higher risk of thrombosis than second-generation oral contraceptive pills (relative risk 1.7);[32] consequently, second-generation oral contraceptive pills may be preferable for sojourners to altitude.

There are some specific concerns for pregnant women at altitude. With travel at altitude, comprehensive medical care is often unavailable. Furthermore, medication options for acute mountain sickness prevention are more limited in pregnant women (e.g. sulfonamides [such as acetazolamide] are contraindicated in the first trimester and after 36 weeks of pregnancy). Pregnancy-specific conditions that may be affected by altitude include spontaneous abortion, pre-eclampsia, gestational hypertension, placental abruption, and intrauterine growth restriction. The data relevant to these conditions are limited and usually derived from studies of high-altitude residents (as opposed to sojourners), who may have different risk profiles. The Union Internationale des Associations d'Alpinisme (UIAA) consensus paper[23] has the following recommendations regarding pregnant women:

- Those at risk of spontaneous abortion, pre-eclampsia, intrauterine growth restriction, and placental abruption should avoid high-altitude exposure.
- Pregnant women should allow two to three days for acclimatization prior to exercising at altitude, waiting two weeks before performing strenuous exercise.
- Chronic hypertension, anemia, smoking, and cardiopulmonary disease are contraindications for travel to altitude after 20 weeks' gestation.

General preventive measures

Exertion

Exertion is an independent risk factor for acute mountain sickness.[33] Because both exertion and cold can increase pulmonary vascular pressure, they are both believed to worsen high-altitude pulmonary edema.[34] Travelers are therefore encouraged to adopt a regular, even pace and avoid overexertion while at altitude. They should also be encouraged to bring appropriate clothing and equipment for the cold weather.

Hydration

Some recent research indicates that dehydration may also potentiate acute mountain sickness.[35] The air at altitude is dry, respiratory rate is higher, and mouth breathing is more common. These factors increase insensible losses at altitude. Travelers

should therefore consume at least 3–4 L of water and clear, non-caffeinated, non-alcoholic beverages per day while trekking or climbing. On rest days, fluid requirements would be slightly less. A good guideline is to aim for the urine to be clear.

Infections

Upper respiratory tract infections are extremely common at altitude. There is some evidence that these infections may increase the risk of acute mountain sickness[36] and high-altitude pulmonary edema.[37] At altitude, upper respiratory tract infections may also increase the potential for dehydration (through increased insensible losses). Travelers should be counseled to modify their rate of ascent when they contract an upper respiratory tract infection, allowing more time for rest and acclimatization. They should also be monitoring their fluid intake to avoid dehydration.

Diet

A high-carbohydrate diet is recommended for altitude travelers.[38] The benefit from this diet is related to an elevated respiratory quotient (V_{CO_2}/V_{O_2}) from the metabolism of carbohydrates over fats. Increasing carbon dioxide production leads to increased ventilation and improved arterial oxygen saturation.

One of the later manifestations of altitude acclimatization is increased red blood cell production. Adequate iron stores are required to allow for the new heme pigment production. Those who may have low iron stores (e.g. vegetarians, menstruating women) should consider iron supplementation to facilitate this process.[39]

Ultraviolet light

With ascent, ultraviolet light exposure increases by approximately 4% per 300 m (1000 ft).[15] By this formula, there would be approximately 70% more ultraviolet radiation at Everest Base Camp than at sea level. This increased radiation is compounded by radiation reflected off snow, if it is present. This reflected radiation can cause sunburns in unlikely places, such as the underside of the nose or chin.

Travelers should be advised of the increased risk of sunburn and snow blindness (ultraviolet keratitis) at altitude. They should bring appropriate sun-protective clothing, hats, sunblock, and lip balm. Sunglasses with adequate face protection (glacier glasses or wraparound glasses are best) are essential for the prevention of snow blindness.

Figure 59.1 Ultraviolet light exposure increase with altitude and this is compounded by radiation reflected off snow. Thus, porters working snowy peaks are at particular risk of ultraviolet keratitis (seen here after treatment in the clinic) PHOTO COURTESY OF DR CHRIS GOOCH

If traveling with guides or porters, the traveler should ensure that they are also adequately equipped for sun and cold protection. As many cases of snow blindness occur after the patient's sunglasses have been broken or lost, it is a good idea to bring an extra pair of sunglasses for the traveling group.

Prophylactic medications

In certain conditions, prophylactic medications may be warranted. Individuals who are at higher risk of altitude illness should consider taking medications for prophylaxis. These individuals are those with a previous history of an altitude illness, with an aggressive itinerary, or with other risk factors mentioned above. Different medication regimens are used for prevention of acute mountain sickness/high-altitude cerebral edema than for high-altitude pulmonary edema.

Acute mountain sickness

Acetazolamide (a sulfonamide) is a medication that is legendary among climbers and trekkers.

PRACTICE PEARL

Several high-quality studies have demonstrated the efficacy of acetazolamide in preventing acute mountain sickness.[40–43] The currently recommended dose for prevention is 125 mg orally twice daily and started prior to the onset of ascent.[16]

Acetazolamide is contraindicated in many travelers to altitude, including those with an allergy to sulfonamides and those with glucose-6-phosphate dehydrogenase deficiency. Pregnant and breast-feeding women should also avoid this medication. Furthermore, acetazolamide should not be taken in conjunction with salicylates as there is an increased risk of central nervous system depression and metabolic acidosis.

Dexamethasone is an appropriate alternative for acute mountain sickness prophylaxis in those who cannot tolerate acetazolamide. The prophylactic dose is 8 mg daily (usually divided into two or four doses daily).[44] For prophylaxis, these medications need only be taken until the traveler reaches a stable altitude (and is asymptomatic at that altitude). Once descent has begun, these medications are not required.

Some xenobiotics have been proposed for acute mountain sickness prophylaxis. Ginkgo biloba initially showed some promise in smaller initial studies, but two recent high-quality studies have shown no benefit over placebo.[41, 45] Both coca and garlic have been proposed as possible prophylactic therapies. There have been no published studies of either intervention. Coca can also increase the risk of acute coronary syndrome among users,[46] a devastating complication in a remote area. None of these alternative therapies can be recommended for the prevention of acute mountain sickness.

High-altitude pulmonary edema

Several medications prevent recurrent high-altitude pulmonary edema (Table 59.2). Unfortunately, no quality studies have yet been performed to compare

Table 59.2 Medications used to prevent pulmonary edema and the level of evidence* of the study

Medication	Dose	Level of evidence
Nifedipine[47]	20 mg sustained-release preparation three times daily	1
Dexamethasone[48]	8 mg twice daily	2
Tadalafil[48]	10 mg twice daily	2
Salmeterol[49]	Two puffs twice daily	3

* Centre for Evidence-based Medicine (Oxford) system (see Chapter 3 for more on evidence-based practice)

each of these four therapies. The decision of which medication to prescribe should probably be based on tolerance and mitigation of adverse events.

Sleep at altitude

Visitors to high altitude often have poor sleep marked by frequent arousals and periodic breathing.[50] Sleep quality and periodicity improve with acclimatization at moderate altitudes, but may persist at extreme elevations.[50] Both acetazolamide and benzodiazepines have been used effectively to improve sleep quality at altitude.

Acetazolamide reduces respiratory alkalosis, and hence respiratory periodicity. It has long been used to improve the sleep quality at high altitude.[51] The standard dose of acetazolamide for improving sleep is 125 mg orally.

Temazepam (10 mg orally) improves both subjective[52, 53] and objective measures of sleep quality in travelers to altitude.[53] It is an appropriate alternative in those patients unable to take acetazolamide.

Specific issues for sportspeople

Although sporting events can often take place at moderate altitude (e.g. the Mexico City Olympics were held at 2240 m [7300 ft]), it is rare that they would occur above 3000 m (10 000 ft) where altitude illness is a risk. However, some ski resorts (e.g. in Colorado) are high enough to cause altitude illness among visitors.

Altitude presents a few unique challenges to competing sportspeople. Hypobaric hypoxia can cause decrements in performance, particularly in endurance events. With drier air and more ultraviolet light exposure, sportspeople can be at an increased risk of dehydration and sunburn. Full acclimatization can take weeks to months, but a short acclimatization period at the altitude of competition prior to the event is beneficial for performance. This should be of at least 48 hours in duration and preferably longer if scheduling permits.[54] During this acclimatization period, rest and hydration status should be prioritized. A high-carbohydrate diet may also be beneficial (as discussed above).

Summary

In summary, exposure to altitude can lead to altitude illness and/or exacerbation of pre-existing medical conditions. Many of these situations are preventable through appropriate planning or pharmaceutical intervention. A thorough medical history combined with analysis of the itinerary is a key step to prevent medical problems at altitude. Altitude also provides unique challenges to the competing sportsperson that can be mitigated with appropriate preparation and acclimatization.

CLINICAL SPORTS MEDICINE
MASTERCLASSES
[W] www.clinicalsportsmedicine.com

- See podcast with chapter author Dr Michael Koehle.
  Topics include:
  - Management of hypothermia in sport—clinical scenarios
  - Practical tips for the first-time visitor to altitude.

RECOMMENDED READING

Auerbach P, ed. *Wilderness medicine: management of wilderness and environmental emergencies*. 4th ed. St Louis: Mosby, 2007.

West JB, Schoene RB, Milledge JS. *High altitude medicine and physiology*, 4th ed. London: Hodder Arnold, 2007.

Bezruchka S. *Altitude illness: prevention and treatment*, 2nd ed. Seattle: The Mountaineers Outdoor Expert, 2005.

REFERENCES

1. Cattaneo CG, Frank SM, Hesel TW et al. The accuracy and precision of body temperature monitoring methods during regional and general anesthesia. *Anesth Analg* 2000;90(4):938–45.

2. Yoshitomi Y, Kojima S, Ogi M et al. Acute renal failure in accidental hypothermia of cold water immersion. *Am J Kidney Dis* 1998;31(5):856–9.

3. Ulrich AS, Rathlev NK. Hypothermia and localized cold injuries. *Emerg Med Clin North Am* 2004;22(2): 281–98.

4. Blows WT. Crowd physiology: the "penguin effect." *Accid Emerg Nurs* 1998;6(3):126–9.

5. Nielsen HK, Toft P, Koch J et al. Hypothermic patients admitted to an intensive care unit: a fifteen year survey. *Dan Med Bull* 1992;39(2):190–3.

6. Armstrong LE, Epstein Y, Greenleaf JE et al. American College of Sports Medicine position stand. Heat and cold illnesses during distance running. *Med Sci Sports Exerc* 1996;28(12):i–x.

7. Bolte RG, Black PG, Bowers RS et al. The use of extracorporeal rewarming in a child submerged for 66 minutes. *JAMA* 1988;260(3):377–9.

8. Southwick FS, Dalglish PH Jr. Recovery after prolonged asystolic cardiac arrest in profound hypothermia. A case report and literature review. *JAMA* 1980;243(12):1250–3.

9. Golden FS, Tipton MJ, Scott RC. Immersion, near-drowning and drowning. *Br J Anaesth* 1997;79(2): 214–25.

10. Cattermole TJ. The epidemiology of skiing injuries in Antarctica. *Injury* 1999;30(7):491–5.

11. Murphy JV, Banwell PE, Roberts AH et al. Frostbite: pathogenesis and treatment. *J Trauma* 2000;48(1): 171–8.

12. Basnyat B, Murdoch DR. High-altitude illness. *Lancet* 2003;361(9373):1967–74.

13. Schneider M, Bernasch D, Weymann J et al. Acute mountain sickness: influence of susceptibility, preexposure, and ascent rate. *Med Sci Sports Exerc* 2002;34(12):1886–91.

14. Murdoch D. How fast is too fast? Attempts to define a recommended ascent rate to prevent acute mountain sickness. *Int Soc Mountain Med Newsletter* 1999;9(1): 3–6.

15. Hackett P, Roach R. High-altitude medicine. In: Auerbach P, ed. *Wilderness medicine: management of wilderness and environmental emergencies*. 4th ed. St Louis: Mosby, 2001:1–37.

16. Luks, AM, McIntosh, SE, Grissom, CK et al. Wilderness Medical Society consensus guidelines for the prevention and treatment of acute altitude illness. *Wilderness Environ Med J* 2010;21(2):146–55.

17. Shlim DR, Gallie J. The causes of death among trekkers in Nepal. *Int J Sports Med* 1992;13(suppl. 1):S74–6.

18. Bartsch P, Bailey DM, Berger MM et al. Acute mountain sickness: controversies and advances. *High Alt Med Biol* 2004;5(2):110–24.

19. Katayama K, Sato Y, Shima N et al. Enhanced chemosensitivity after intermittent hypoxic exposure does not affect exercise ventilation at sea level. *Eur J Appl Physiol* 2002;87(2):187–91.

20. Hultgren HN, Marticorena EA. High altitude pulmonary edema. Epidemiologic observations in Peru. *Chest* 1978;74(4):372–6.

21. Scoggin CH, Hyers TM, Reeves JT et al. High-altitude pulmonary edema in the children and young adults of Leadville, Colorado. *N Engl J Med* 1977;297(23): 1269–72.

22. Gaillard S, Dellasanta P, Loutan L et al. Awareness, prevalence, medication use, and risk factors of acute mountain sickness in tourists trekking around the Annapurnas in Nepal: a 12-year follow-up. *High Alt Med Biol* 2004;5(4):410–19.

23. Jean D, Leal C, Kriemler S et al. Medical recommendations for women going to altitude. *High Alt Med Biol* 2005;6(1):22–31.

24. Honigman B, Theis MK, Koziol-McLain J et al. Acute mountain sickness in a general tourist population at moderate altitudes. *Ann Intern Med* 1993;118(8):587–92.

25. Hackett PH, Roach RC. High altitude cerebral edema. *High Alt Med Biol* 2004;5(2):136–46.

26. Naeije R, De Backer D, Vachiery JL et al. High-altitude pulmonary edema with primary pulmonary hypertension. *Chest* 1996;110(1):286–9.

27. Smith JM. The use of high altitude treatment for childhood asthma. *Practitioner* 1981;225(1361):1663–6.

28. Cogo A, Fischer R, Schoene R. Respiratory diseases and high altitude. *High Alt Med Biol* 2004;5(4):435–44.

29. Mader TH, White LJ. Refractive changes at extreme altitude after radial keratotomy. *Am J Ophthalmol* 1995;119(6):733–7.

30. White LJ, Mader TH. Refractive changes with increasing altitude after radial keratotomy. *Am J Ophthalmol* 1993;115(6):821–3.

31. Dimmig JW, Tabin G. The ascent of Mount Everest following laser in situ keratomileusis. *J Refract Surg* 2003;19(1):48–51.

32. Kemmeren JM, Algra A, Grobbee DE. Third generation oral contraceptives and risk of venous thrombosis: meta-analysis. *BMJ* 2001;323(7305):131–4.

33 Roach RC, Maes D, Sandoval D et al. Exercise exacerbates acute mountain sickness at simulated high altitude. *J Appl Physiol* 2000;88(2):581–5.

34. Reeves JT, Wagner J, Zafren K et al. Seasonal variation in barometric pressure and temperature in Summit County: effect on altitude illness. In: Sutton JR, Houston CS, Coates G, eds. *Hypoxia and molecular medicine.* Burlington VT: Queen City Printers, 1993:275–81.

35. Cumbo TA, Basnyat B, Graham J et al. Acute mountain sickness, dehydration, and bicarbonate clearance: preliminary field data from the Nepal Himalaya. *Aviat Space Environ Med* 2002;73(9):898–901.

36. Murdoch DR. Symptoms of infection and altitude illness among hikers in the Mount Everest region of Nepal. *Aviat Space Environ Med* 1995;66(2):148–51.

37. Durmowicz AG, Noordeweier E, Nicholas R et al. Inflammatory processes may predispose children to high-altitude pulmonary edema. *J Pediatr* 1997;130(5):838–40.

38. Hansen JE, Hartley LH, Hogan RP 3rd. Arterial oxygen increase by high-carbohydrate diet at altitude. *J Appl Physiol* 1972;33(4):441–5.

39. Hannon JP, Chinn KS, Shields JL. Effects of acute high-altitude exposure on body fluids. *Fed Proc* 1969;28(3):1178–84.

40. Dumont L, Mardirosoff C, Tramer MR. Efficacy and harm of pharmacological prevention of acute mountain sickness: quantitative systematic review. *BMJ* 2000;321(7256):267–72.

41. Gertsch JH, Basnyat B, Johnson EW et al. Randomised, double blind, placebo controlled comparison of ginkgo biloba and acetazolamide for prevention of acute mountain sickness among Himalayan trekkers: the prevention of high altitude illness trial (PHAIT). *BMJ* 2004;328(7443):797.

42. Basnyat B, Gertsch JH, Johnson EW et al. Efficacy of low-dose acetazolamide (125 mg bid) for the prophylaxis of acute mountain sickness: a prospective, double-blind, randomized, placebo-controlled trial. *High Alt Med Biol* 2003;4(1):45–52.

43. Carlsten C, Swenson ER, Ruoss S. A dose-response study of acetazolamide for acute mountain sickness prophylaxis in vacationing tourists at 12,000 feet (3630 m). *High Alt Med Biol* 2004;5(1):33–9.

44. Rock PB, Johnson TS, Larsen RF et al. Dexamethasone as prophylaxis for acute mountain sickness. Effect of dose level. *Chest* 1989;95(3):568–73.

45. Chow T, Browne V, Heileson HL et al. Ginkgo biloba and acetazolamide prophylaxis for acute mountain sickness: a randomized, placebo-controlled trial. *Arch Intern Med* 2005;165(3):296–301.

46. Mittleman MA, Mintzer D, Maclure M et al. Triggering of myocardial infarction by cocaine. *Circulation* 1999;99(21):2737–41.

47. Oelz O, Maggiorini M, Ritter M et al. Prevention and treatment of high altitude pulmonary edema by a calcium channel blocker. *Int J Sports Med* 1992;13 (suppl. 1):S65–8.

48. Maggiorini M, Brunner-La Rocca HP et al. Both tadalafil and dexamethasone may reduce the incidence of high-altitude pulmonary edema: a randomized trial. *Ann Intern Med* 2006;145(7): 497–506.

49. Sartori C, Allemann Y, Duplain H et al. Salmeterol for the prevention of high-altitude pulmonary edema. *N Engl J Med* 2002;346(21):1631–6.

50. Weil JV. Sleep at high altitude. *High Alt Med Biol* 2004;5(2):180–9.

51. Sutton JR, Houston CS, Mansell AL et al. Effect of acetazolamide on hypoxemia during sleep at high altitude. *N Engl J Med* 1979;301(24):1329–31.

52. Dubowitz G. Effect of temazepam on oxygen saturation and sleep quality at high altitude: randomised placebo controlled crossover trial. *BMJ* 1998;316(7131): 587–9.

53. Nickol AH, Leverment J, Richards P et al. Temazepam at high altitude reduces periodic breathing without impairing next-day performance: a randomized cross-over double-blind study. *J Sleep Res* 2006;4:445–54.

54. Weston AR, Mackenzie G, Tufts MA et al. Optimal time of arrival for performance at moderate altitude (1700 m). *Med Sci Sports Exerc* 2001;33(2):298–302.

Chapter 60

Quick exercise prescriptions for specific medical conditions

with VANESSA YOUNG, PEKKA KANNUS, WILLEM VAN MECHELEN, and STEVEN N BLAIR

Better to hunt in fields for health unbought
Than fee the doctor for a nauseous draught.
The wise for cure on exercise depend;
God never made his work for man to mend.
John Dryden (1631–1700)

Introduction

Physical inactivity is the biggest public health problem of the 21st century (Chapter 1).[1] This chapter supplements Chapter 16, which outlines the principles of exercise prescription and potential health benefits of exercise. It also complements Chapter 54, which provides exercise prescription for neurological conditions and mental health. Our aim is to provide clinicians with a quick reference exercise prescription guide for common medical conditions.

 For clinicians' convenience in sharing these prescriptions, they are included in PDF form in the *Clinical Sports Medicine* masterclasses at www.clinicalsportsmedicine.com.

Primary care clinicians play an important role in influencing their patient's physical activity behaviors.[2] We argue that ministries of health and health authorities should place a book of exercise prescriptions on every physician's desk. We acknowledge the various superb resources that already provide base standards on physical activity and health. These include:

- World Health Organization. *Global recommendations on physical activity for health*[3]
- Swedish National Institute of Public Health. *Physical activity in the prevention and treatment of disease*[4] (Fig. 60.1 on p. 1160) (available in English, Swedish, and Vietnamese)

- the US National Physical Activity Plan section on clinical medicine, *www.physicalactivityplan.org/healthcare.php*[5]
- the White Paper on physical activity in clinical practice, developed for the US national plan[6]
- US Department of Health and Human Services. The *Physical activity guidelines for Americans*[7] (www.health.gov/paguidelines)
- the Canadian consensus reports on physical activity and childhood obesity: Canadian physical activity guidelines 2011.[8]

Thus, a breadth of information is available on exercise prescription. However, recommended doses of activity (frequency, intensity, duration, and type of exercise) vary considerably, in part due to the range in scientific rigor applied across publications. Evidence ranges from level 1 to level 5 (Chapter 3). The tables below are collated from a number of published sources to amalgamate the best of the currently available evidence. The essential components of exercise prescription are aerobic and resistance training exercises;[9] flexibility exercises are also recommended.[10] As this field evolves, guidelines will be updated via the *Clinical Sports Medicine* masterclasses (www.clinicalsportsmedicine.com). For the primary prevention of chronic illness, Tables 60.1 and 60.2 serve as an excellent guideline.[9]

Any increase in activity improves health, regardless of baseline fitness, and regardless of body weight (at least up to Class 3 obesity defined as

Table 60.1 Physical activity recommendations for healthy adults ≤65 years

Exercise type	Frequency	Intensity	Time
Aerobic (e.g. walking, cycling, swimming, cross-country skiing)	≥5 days/week	Moderate, RPE 5–6/10	30–60 mins/day or 150–300 mins/week
	At least 3 days/week	Vigorous, RPE 7–8/10	20–30 mins/day or 75–100 mins/week
	3–5 days/week	Combination of moderate and vigorous	Equivalent combination of above
Resistance (e.g. circuit training, free weights, stair climbing, calisthenics)	2–3 days/week with 48 hours separating training sessions for the same muscle group	Moderate–vigorous	2–4 sets of 8–12 reps 8–10 major muscle groups 2–3 mins rest in between sets
Flexibility (e.g. static stretches)	Following warm-up or cool-down at least 2–3 days/week	To the point of tension, before discomfort	10–30 seconds 4 or more repetitions

From *ACSM's Guidelines for exercise testing and prescription*. 8th ed[9]
RPE = rating of perceived exertion

Table 60.2 Physical activity guidelines for adults 65 years and over[9]

Exercise type	Frequency	Intensity	Time
Aerobic (e.g. walking, cycling, swimming, cross-country skiing, Nordic pole walking, adult age dancing)	≥5 days/week	Moderate, RPE 5–6/10	30–60 mins/day or 150–300 mins/week
	3 days/week	Vigorous, RPE 7–8/10	20–30 mins/day or 75–100 mins/week
	3–5 days/week	Combination of moderate and vigorous	Equivalent combination of above
Resistance (e.g. circuit training, free weights, stair climbing, calisthenics)	At least 2 days/week with 48 hours separating training sessions for the same muscle group	Moderate, 60–70% 1RM	One or more sets of 10–15 reps 8–10 major muscle groups 2–3 min rest in between sets
Flexibility (e.g. static stretches) Upper/lower body ROM	At least 2 days/week	To the point of tension, before discomfort	10–30 seconds
Balance training[9]*	At least 3 days/week	To challenge balance safety	At least 10 minutes

From *ACSM's Guidelines for exercise testing and prescription*[9] * Balance prescription is based on the *Otago Exercise Program*[65]
RM = repetition max; RPE = rating of perceived exertion

BMI 35.0–39.9). In addition, physical fitness prevents loss of function as people age.[11, 12] In fact, not only does physical activity prevent loss of function, it actually improves function, as measured by the Short Performance Physical Battery, in older adults at risk for disability.[13]

All adults across the lifespan should strive to achieve the guidelines for healthy adults (Tables 60.1 and 60.2). The sections and tables that follow are guidelines for commencing exercise programs in individuals with underlying medical conditions who are new to exercise. Clinical judgment needs to be applied to adapt the information presented here to each patient. A guiding principle is to concentrate on improving functional abilities first and then on achieving a level of fitness. All individuals deserve to be physically active, to the level of their own abilities.

Figure 60.1 Also highlighted in Chapters 16 and 54, this Swedish book, featured here on the cover of the *British Journal of Sports Medicine*, is a tremendous resource for exercise prescription for over 60 conditions. We recommend a copy be placed in every consulting room. A free PDF copy of the book can be downloaded for personal use from www.fyss.se. A podcast with the authors can be heard in the *Clinical Sports Medicine* masterclasses at www.clinicalsportsmedicine.com

Obesity

The role that obesity plays as a risk factor for comorbidity varies across studies. Although standard risk assessment tools for cardiovascular disease include obesity as a risk factor,[9] many experts contend that obesity is not an independent risk factor for mortality. Specifically, a "fit and fat" person has lower risk of death than an unfit thin person,[1] suggesting that body composition is ultimately not as important as participation in a regular exercise program. However, it *is* known that obesity links strongly with the development of osteoarthritis. Further, BMI has been shown to be predictive of all-cause cancer mortality in women.[14]

Thus, regular exercise with a goal of weight management has the potential to prevent significant pain and disability as one ages. Consequently exercise should focus not only on body weight management (for the prevention of osteoarthritis), but rather on enhancing overall health through the same mechanisms that benefit all individuals regardless of body composition.[1, 15, 16]

The amount of exercise required to achieve a healthy, stable body weight varies among individuals. Exercise prescription targeting weight loss is generally orientated toward maximum energy expenditure. Therefore, individuals who aim to lose weight must increase activity above the recommended guidelines for healthy adults (Table 60.1). In this context, aerobic exercise will provide the bulk of energy expenditure. However, resistance exercise also has an important role in maintaining overall health and has been linked to improved mortalities in men.[16, 17] Resistance training can influence body composition favorably with improved lean body mass, despite not having direct influence on body weight.[18] Table 60.3 serves as a guide to people living with obesity who wish to reduce their body weight. Note that with regards to resistance training, the guide suggests beginning with "low intensity" training. However, clinicians should consider patients individually, as many will both tolerate and enjoy higher intensities of training.

Cardiovascular disease

If an individual with cardiovascular disease (CVD) risk factors or known CVD is ready to begin an exercise program, a thorough pre-screening is indicated. This includes a detailed history, medical examination, and risk stratification. Relevant investigations should be reviewed, particularly if a graded exercise stress test has been completed. The results should be used to help guide initial exercise prescription.

It is of particular importance that exercise programs are done under supervision or guidance of appropriately qualified clinicians, and for some individuals it is recommended that programs be completed in a facility with access to appropriately trained medical staff and varying levels of monitoring (e.g. ECG monitoring). Patients should be educated early on methods for monitoring their exercise intensity (e.g. perceived exertion, the talk test, heart rate monitor) and should be aware of specific signs and symptoms pertaining to their individual condition.

Table 60.3 Exercise prescription: obesity

Exercise type	Frequency	Intensity	Time
Aerobic (e.g. large-muscle activities such as walking, swimming, cycling)	≥5 days/week to maximize energy expenditure	Low–moderate progressing to moderate–vigorous 1–11/20 RPE, 40–60% HRR	50–60 minutes/day, or as tolerated for weight loss 30–60 min/day for health benefits Emphasize duration rather than intensity
Resistance[a] (e.g. free weights, weight machines, isokinetic machines)	3 days/week with 48 hours between sessions that use the same muscle groups	Low intensity	1–3 sets of 10–12 reps Involving 8–10 muscle groups Depending on patient tolerance
Flexibility (e.g. stretching/ yoga)	5–7 days/week	To level of tension, before discomfort	10–30 seconds/stretch

[a]In this context, resistance exercise is less important. When coupled with dietary change it improves lean body mass, but does not affect body weight[18]

Resources: *ACSM's Exercise management for persons with chronic diseases and disabilities;*[19] *ACSM's Guidelines for exercise testing and prescription;*[9] ACSM position stand for weight loss and maintenance of weight etc.[20]

RPE = rating of perceived exertion; HRR = heart rate reserve

The following discussion provides basic information to guide the clinician prescribing exercise for a variety of cardiovascular conditions. It is not a comprehensive tool for individual exercise prescription and individual clinicians will vary in their confidence to prescribe exercise in this setting. Referral to an exercise specialist or a clinical specialist who is knowledgeable about prescribing exercise may be part of the management plan.

Myocardial infarction

Inpatient cardiac rehabilitation ideally begins 48 hours following a myocardial infarction. Orthostatic stress and postural changes are undertaken initially and patients are mobilized as tolerated. Following discharge from hospital, outpatient cardiac rehabilitation programs target secondary prevention (i.e. lifestyle modification) and most often include exercise programs. Over time, exercise can positively influence risk factors for atherosclerosis.[21]

Barriers to exercise following a myocardial infarction include dyspnea, angina, and acute cardiac events. Exercising through discomfort is not indicated, so it is important to modify or curtail an exercise session if the patient reports perceived exertion or discomfort that exceeds their individually recommended intensity levels. Type of exercise should be based on individual preferences and abilities.

For example, if a person's angina is induced in cold weather, an outdoor walking program in cold climates may be inappropriate.

If patients have been prescribed glyceryl trinitrate, ensure they keep it within reach at all times when exercising. Often patients will lock it in a dressing room locker or leave it at home, confident that they will not need it. The benefits of glyceryl trinitrate can only be achieved if it is taken at the onset of symptoms of angina, and minutes can make a difference in the prevention of an acute event, and buy time if waiting for the arrival of paramedics. Table 60.4 overleaf shows exercise prescriptions for patients following myocardial infarction.

Post–cardiac surgery

Exercise prescription following coronary artery bypass grafting (CABG) or percutaneous transluminal coronary angioplasty (PTCA) is similar to that prescribed for those who have had a myocardial infarction. Cardiac rehabilitation two weeks postoperatively usually focuses on aerobic exercises and distances are gradually increased as tolerated. In those who have had a sternotomy, upper limb resistance training should be avoided for 12 weeks postoperatively to allow for sternal healing. Once safe to begin resistance training, light weights can be used and increased gradually over time. It is important to

Table 60.4 Exercise prescription: following myocardial infarction

Exercise type	Frequency	Intensity	Time
Aerobic (e.g. arm/leg ergometry)	≥3 days/week	Moderate–vigorous: RPE 11–16/20 or 40–80% HRR	20–60 minutes/session 5–10 mins/warm-up and cool-down Begin with 5–10 min sessions and increase by 1–5 mins/session or as tolerated symptomatically
Resistance (e.g. circuit training)	2–3 days/week	Lower body: 50–60% 1RM Upper body: 30–40% 1RM	2–4 sets of 12–15 reps
Flexibility (e.g. static stretches) Upper/lower body ROM	2–3 days/week	To the point of tension, before discomfort	10–30 seconds

Resources: *ACSM's Guidelines for exercise testing and prescription;*[9] *ACSM's Exercise management for persons with chronic diseases and disabilities;*[19] *ACSM's Resource manual for guidelines for exercise testing and prescription*[22]

RM = repetition max; RPE = rating of perceived exertion; HRR = heart rate reserve

avoid the Valsalva maneuver as it causes profound increases in blood pressure.

Some studies have compared exercise programs to surgery and have actually found comparable long-term results with exercise alone when compared with percutaneous coronary intervention.[23] Table 60.5 shows exercise prescriptions for patients post-CABG and post-PCTA.

Cardiac insufficiency

The American College of Cardiology Foundation and American Heart Association both encourage clinicians to identify those *at risk* of developing heart failure (HF) and those who are asymptomatic and have current left ventricular functional impairment or hypertrophy, *in addition* to those living with symptomatic heart insufficiency.[24] Several studies have investigated the effects of exercise on heart insufficiency/heart failure. Results have varied, not surprisingly given the broad category of conditions leading to heart insufficiencies and the range of severity that presents with this diagnosis. Overall, however, studies show many benefits of exercise both physiologically (e.g. increased VO_2max, improved

Table 60.5 Exercise prescription: post-CABG and post-PCTA

Exercise type	Frequency	Intensity	Time
Aerobic (e.g. arm/leg ergometry)	4–7 days/week	RPE 11–16/20 or 40–80% HRR Keep below ischemic threshold	20–60 minutes/session 5–10 minutes of warm-up and cool-down
Resistance (e.g. circuit training, elastic bands, light free weights)	2–3 days/week	40–50% 1RM, 0.5–0.9 kg until 12 wks post-CABG, then increase resistance gradually	2–4 sets of 12–15 reps One set to volitional fatigue is effective in the first 12 weeks post-procedure
Flexibility (e.g. static stretches) Upper/lower body ROM	2–3 days/week	To the level of tension, before discomfort	10–30 seconds

Resources: *ACSM's Guidelines for exercise testing and prescription;*[9] *ACSM's Exercise management for persons with chronic diseases and disabilities*[19]

CAGB = coronary artery bypass grafting; PCTA = percutaneous transluminal coronary angioplasty; RM = repetition max; RPE = rating of perceived exertion; HRR = heart rate reserve

endothelial function) and functionally (e.g. improved walking speed and tolerance).[25, 26] It is therefore recommended that exercise be included as adjunctive treatment for people with reduced left ventricular ejection fraction whether or not the patient is currently symptomatic.[24]

The Heart Failure Society of America, in its 2010 guideline,[26] recommends that exercise testing be done prior to beginning a program, in order to determine whether the patient will tolerate exercise and to what extent. Exercise is contraindicated in the presence of uncontrolled congestive heart failure.[9] If the patient does not develop significant ischemia or arrhythmias during exercise testing, then exercising is likely safe for the patient and an exercise program can be prescribed.

Aerobic exercise programs should start conservatively and progress gradually toward a goal of up to 30 minutes of moderate activity, 5 days per week with appropriate warm-up and cool-down. Patients should not exercise if they have had a major event or procedure within the past six weeks, if they are receiving cardiac devices that limit the ability to achieve target heart rates, or if they developed significant ischemia or arrhythmia during exercise testing.[26]

With regards to intensity, it is not appropriate to calculate target heart rate based on age, as the individual may be taking medication (such as beta blockers) which has a ceiling effect on heart rate, or they may become symptomatic at a lower intensity than would be predicted by age alone. Therefore, it is best to consider the results of initial graded exercise stress testing (while on medication) to determine the intensity at which the individual develops signs or symptoms.

Intensity should remain at least 10 beats per minute below onset of symptoms or signs of ischemia. If the individual does not become symptomatic during exercise testing, then a prescription of 40–80% of VO_2 max is appropriate.[9, 25] In the absence of baseline exercise tolerance testing, it is recommended that maximum heart rate not exceed 20 bpm above the individual's resting heart rate.[9] Interval training is a good way to begin a program, allowing periods of rest throughout the exercise session. Rate of perceived exertion should be incorporated into the training program to help the individual to self-monitor intensity.

Individuals with an implantable cardioverter defibrillator (ICD) require specific review of the type of implantation (i.e. 4 letter code) in order to ensure a safe target heart rate range that does not inappropriately trigger the pacemaker.[9] Individuals recovering from cardiac transplant also require special consideration with regard to establishing appropriate intensity. These individuals will exhibit elevated resting heart rate and abnormal heart rate response to exercise, including delayed increase in heart rate with onset of exercise.[9] It is important to incorporate a long warm-up for these patients. Perceived exertion is especially important in the absence of a reliable heart rate response.

Hypertension

Aerobic exercise is beneficial in the management of hypertension.[27] Table 60.6 shows the program recommended for individuals with controlled hypertension. Exercise is generally contraindicated in cases where resting systolic blood pressure is greater than 200 mmHg, or where resting diastolic

Table 60.6 Exercise prescription: hypertension

Exercise type	Frequency	Intensity	Time
Aerobic (e.g. large-muscle activities)	4–7 days/week	RPE 11–13/20 or 40–80% HRR	30–60 minutes/session (continuous or accumulated in 10 minute periods)
Resistance (e.g. circuit training)	2–3 days/week	60–80% 1RM or 11–13/20 RPE	1 set of 8–12 reps
Flexibility (e.g. static stretches) Upper/lower body ROM	2–3 days/week	To the level of tension, before discomfort	10–30 seconds ≥4 per muscle group

Resources: *ACSM's Guidelines for exercise testing and prescription;*[9] *ACSM's Exercise management for persons with chronic diseases and disabilities*[19]

RM = repetition max; RPE = rating of perceived exertion; HRR = heart rate reserve

blood pressure is greater than 110 mmHg diastolic. Antihypertensive medications may cause adverse effects. Beta blockers typically reduce exercise capacity due to the ceiling effect they have on heart rate, so target heart rate is not ideal for monitoring intensity in these individuals.

A target heart rate can be calculated if the individual has had a graded exercise stress test while on their medications. Rating of perceived exertion (RPE) is useful as a tool for self-monitoring intensity levels. Alpha blockers, calcium channel blockers, and vasodilators may lead to sudden drops in blood pressure during or after exercise. An adequate warm-up and cool-down period can improve blood pressure response to exercise. Exercise should be discontinued if the systolic blood pressure drops more than 10 mmHg during exercise.[9] With resistance training exercises, it is imperative to educate patients to avoid the Valsalva maneuver.

Table 60.6 has exercise prescriptions for patients with hypertension.

Hyperlipidemia

Exercise is an important lifestyle intervention for minimizing the effect of risk factors including hyperlipidemia/hypercholesterolemia.[28,29,30] Achieving and maintaining a healthy body weight may also be beneficial in this clinical population.[31] Table 60.7 has exercise prescriptions for patients with hyperlipidemia.

Chronic obstructive pulmonary disease

Chronic obstructive pulmonary disease (COPD) is typically characterized by dyspnea and reduced exercise tolerance. During exercise, increased work of breathing leads to exertional shortness of breath. Some individuals experience oxyhemoglobin desaturation when exercising, and may need supplemental oxygen or an increase in supplemental oxygen when engaging in physical activity. In advanced stages of COPD, pulmonary hypertension can lead to right heart failure, further compromising exercise tolerance.

A program including both aerobic exercise and strength training is recommended for people with COPD, which can improve exercise capacity, dyspnea, and quality of life.[32] Some patients may find stationary cycling or using the arm rests on a treadmill to be a more comfortable form of exercise, as holding the handlebars may allow the individual to use accessory respiratory muscles during exercise to assist with breathing.[33]

Table 60.8 has exercise prescriptions for patients with COPD.

Asthma

An exercise program is encouraged as an adjunct to pharmacological treatment in all individuals living with asthma due to the beneficial effects of exercise on cardiovascular fitness and disease severity.[35] Exercise prescription is similar for patients with asthma and mild COPD though the two conditions are very different. Ensure an adequate warm-up, take

Table 60.7 Exercise prescription: hyperlipidemia

Exercise type	Frequency	Intensity	Time
Aerobic (e.g. large-muscle activities such as walking, swimming, cycling)	≥5 days/week	Moderate–vigorous 40–80% HRR	30–60 mins/day Either continuous or intermittent periods of 10–30 mins
Resistance (e.g. free weights, isokinetic/isotonic machines)	2–3 days/week	60–80% 1RM	2–4 sets of 8–12 reps
Flexibility (e.g. upper and lower body ROM exercises)	2–3 days/week	To level of tension, before discomfort	10–30 seconds per stretch

Resources: ACSM's Guidelines for exercise testing and prescription;[9] ACSM's Exercise management for persons with chronic diseases and disabilities[19]

RM = repetition max; RPE = rating of perceived exertion; HRR = heart rate reserve

Table 60.8 Exercise prescription: moderate–severe COPD[a]

Exercise type	Frequency	Intensity	Time
Aerobic (e.g. large-muscle activities such as walking, swimming, cycling)	3–5 days/week	RPE 11–13/20 Monitor dyspnea	30 minutes/session as tolerated Emphasize longer duration, rather than increased intensity
Resistance (e.g. free weights, isokinetic/isotonic machines)	2–3 days/week	Low resistance	1 or more sets of 12–15 reps
Flexibility (e.g. static stretches) Upper/lower body ROM	3 days/week	To level of tension, before discomfort	20–60 seconds per stretch

[a] For mild disease, refer to ACSM guidelines for healthy adults, Table 60.1

Resources: *ACSM's Guidelines for exercise testing and prescription;*[9] *ACSM's Exercise management for persons with chronic diseases and disabilities;*[19] Nelson et al. *Physical activity and public health in older adults;*[10] Nici et al. ATS/ERS Statement on pulmonary rehabilitation[34]

COPD = chronic obstructive pulmonary disease; RPE = rating of perceived exertion

bronchodilators if needed before exercise, and avoid triggers that lead to exercise-induced bronchoconstriction (cold climate, dust). Ensure patients know how to properly administer their bronchodilators for optimal benefits. Individuals with well-controlled asthma may be capable of high levels of physical activity, as evidenced by the high percentage of elite sportspeople diagnosed and performing with asthma.

Table 60.9 has exercise prescriptions for patients with asthma.

Diabetes

In type 2 diabetes a central focus is on achieving or maintaining a healthy body weight and adequate cardiorespiratory fitness, resulting in increased insulin sensitivity, decreased Hemoglobin A1c (HbA1c), decreased insulin requirements, and decreased cardiovascular risk factors. Recent randomized clinical trials show the value of combining aerobic and resistance training for patients with type 2 diabetes.[36, 37] In both type 1 and type 2 diabetes, a primary aim is to

Table 60.9 Exercise prescription: asthma

Exercise type	Frequency	Intensity	Time
Aerobic (e.g. large-muscle activities such as walking, swimming, cycling)	3–5 days/week	RPE 11–13/20 Monitor dyspnea	20–60 minutes/day Either continuous or intermittent periods of 10 mins Emphasize longer duration, rather than increased intensity
Resistance (e.g. free weights, isokinetic/isotonic machines)	2–3 days/week	Low resistance, progress as tolerated	1 or more sets of 12–15 reps
Flexibility (e.g. static stretches, tai chi)	3 days/week	To level of tension, before discomfort	20–60 seconds per stretch

Resources: *ACSM's Guidelines for exercise testing and prescription;*[9] *ACSM's Exercise management for persons with chronic diseases and disabilities*[19]

RPE = rating of perceived exertion

increase cardiorespiratory fitness.[38, 39] Table 60.10 outlines an exercise prescription that is appropriate for both type 1 and type 2 diabetes. Note that while recommendations are for four days or more per week, some individuals manage their blood sugar best with consistent, daily exercise.

Be aware of hypoglycemia in those on oral hypoglycemic agents or insulin. Blood sugar levels should be taken pre- and post-exercise, the timing of peak insulin action should be considered, and the diet should incorporate adequate carbohydrates. Injecting into an abdominal site, rather than into a limb, may help to avoid exercise induced hypoglycemia. Trainers should ensure patients are competent and diligent at monitoring their condition, and simple sugars should be located in the facility's first aid kit as it is not uncommon for individuals to develop symptoms such as lightheadedness, mood change, or unusual sweating. Most individuals with diabetes recognize these signs early on. However, trainers and clinicians should be prepared to initiate first aid, particularly with those who are new to exercise or who present with multiple risk factors.

End-stage renal disease

Physical activity is safe for patients on dialysis; however some modifications may be necessary. Clinicians recommend that patients with renal disease participate in physical activity as there are widespread health benefits to this general population.

As with other clinical populations, the ideal exercise prescription has not yet been developed. For patients on hemodialysis, training on non-dialysis days or during the first half of treatment is recommended to try to avoid hypotensive episodes. We note that as evidence accumulates to have more frequent dialysis days (6/week), patients and clinicians will need to use creativity to fit in the therapeutic exercise programs. Those on peritoneal dialysis may drain abdominal fluid if they become uncomfortable while exercising.

Table 60.11 has exercise prescriptions for patients with renal disease.

Cancer

Cancer treatments may cause longstanding adverse effects, such as fatigue and pain.[42] More than fifty percent of cancer survivors report physical limitations five years later.[43] In this population, physical activity leads to the usual positive effects of exercise (quality of life, body composition, cardiovascular fitness).[44] In addition, individuals with breast and colon cancers have more successful clinical outcomes if they undertake exercise programs after treatment.[45-47] The evidence for exercise on other cancer types is limited and the ideal exercises for this population are yet to be determined; however, it is clear that cardiorespiratory fitness has positive influences on all-cause cancer mortality.[14]

The exercise prescription recommendations in Table 60.12 are for those with cancer (before, during, and after treatment). Although it is currently recommended that resistance exercises be of low intensity, increasingly studies are demonstrating that progressing intensity level is safe and appropriate. This is slowly changing the fears clinicians once had

Table 60.10 Exercise prescription: diabetes

Exercise type	Frequency	Intensity	Time
Aerobic (e.g. large-muscle activities such as walking, swimming, cycling)	≥4 days/week	Moderate–vigorous 12–16/20 RPE, 50–80% HR_{max}	30–60 minutes/day Either continuous or intermittent periods of 10–30 mins
Resistance (e.g. free weights, weight machines, elastic bands)	2–3 days/week with 48 hours between sessions that use the same muscle groups	60–80% 1RM	2–3 sets of 8–12 reps Involving 8–10 muscle groups
Flexibility (e.g. stretching/ yoga)	Daily	To level of tension, before discomfort	6–20 seconds, as tolerated

Resources: *ACSM's Guidelines for exercise testing and prescription;*[9] *ACSM's Exercise management for persons with chronic diseases and disabilities;*[19] American diabetes Association: Standards of medical care in diabetes[40]

RM = repetition max; RPE = rating of perceived exertion; HR_{max} = maximum heart rate

Table 60.11 Exercise prescription: renal disease

Exercise type	Frequency	Intensity	Time
Aerobic (e.g. large-muscle activities such as walking, swimming, cycling)	≥4 days/week	Low–moderate 11–13/20 RPE, 50–80% HR_{max}	30–60 minutes/day, or as tolerated Either continuous or intermittent periods of 10–30 mins
Resistance (e.g. free weights, weight machines, isokinetic machines)	3 days/week with 48 hours between sessions that use the same muscle groups	Moderate 60–75% 1RM	1–3 sets of 10–15 reps Involving 8–10 muscle groups Depending on patient tolerance
Flexibility (e.g. stretching, yoga)	3 days/week	To level of tension, before discomfort	10–30 seconds/stretch

Resources: *ACSM's Guidelines for exercise testing and prescription;*[9] *ACSM's Exercise management for persons with chronic diseases and disabilities;*[19] Johansen KL. Exercise and chronic kidney disease: current recommendations[41]
RM = repetition max; RPE = rating of perceived exertion; HR_{max} = maximum heart rate

Table 60.12 Exercise prescription: cancer

Exercise type	Frequency	Intensity	Time
Aerobic (e.g. large-muscle activities such as walking, swimming, cycling)	3–5 days per week	Low–moderate 40–60% HRR	20–60 minutes/session Symptom-limited
Resistance (e.g. free weights, weight machines, isokinetic machines)	3 days/week with 48 hours between sessions that use the same muscle groups	Low intensity	1–3 sets of 10–12 reps Involving 8–10 muscle groups Depending on patient tolerance
Flexibility (e.g. stretching, balance exercise, yoga)	5–7 days/week	To level of tension, before discomfort	10–30 seconds/stretch Total stretch time 2 minutes 4 repetitions per stretch

Resources: *ACSM's Guidelines for exercise testing and prescription;*[9] *ACSM's Exercise management for persons with chronic diseases and disabilities;*[19] *ACSM's resources for clinical exercise physiology: musculoskeletal, neuromuscular, neoplastic, immunologic, and hematologic conditions;*[51] Kushi et al.;[50] McNeely et al.;[42] Ness KK et al.;[43] Schmitz et al.[52]
HRR = heart rate reserve

regarding risk of developing lymphedema, particularly in breast cancer survivors.[48, 49]

Flexibility exercises can be particularly beneficial to cancer survivors. These exercises can be individually prescribed with a goal of restoring length of muscle and soft tissue which may have become shortened or sclerotic as a result of surgery, longstanding postural changes, or other treatment effects. Flexibility exercises should be combined with targeted resistance exercises to restore posture, range of motion, and function.

Arthritis

Table 60.13 overleaf is based on resources for individuals living with osteoarthritis and rheumatoid arthritis. However, clinicians are encouraged to adapt these recommendations for other rheumatological conditions in consultation with an individual's consulting specialist(s). In patients with arthritis, exercise reduces pain, inflammation, muscle weakness, and fatigue, and it can help the patient regain range of motion. It may also slow progression of the disease.[53] An exercise program should initially concentrate on

Table 60.13 Exercise prescription: arthritis

Exercise type	Frequency	Intensity	Time
Aerobic (e.g. large-muscle activities such as walking, swimming, cycling)	3–5 days/week	11–16/20 RPE, 60–80% HR_{max} Limited by symptoms	Starting with 5–10 minutes/session, increasing to 30 minutes/session Emphasize duration over intensity
Resistance (e.g. free weights, weight machines, isokinetic machines)	2–3 days/week with 48 hours between sessions that use the same muscle groups	10% 1RM to 40–60% 1RM	1–3 sets of 2–10 reps, building slowly depending on patient tolerance Involving 8–10 muscle groups
Flexibility (e.g. stretching, ROM)	Daily	To level of tension, before discomfort	10–30 seconds/stretch 4 repetitions per stretch 5–10 minutes per ROM exercise

Resources: *ACSM's Guidelines for exercise testing and prescription;*[9] *ACSM's Exercise management for persons with chronic diseases and disabilities;*[19] *ACSM's resources for clinical exercise physiology: musculoskeletal, neuromuscular, neoplastic, immunologic, and hematologic conditions*[51]

RM = repetition max; RPE = rating of perceived exertion; HR_{max} = maximum heart rate

flexibility and resistance training, although aerobic training also benefits rheumatic conditions, as well as improves overall health of the individual. Managing obesity should be an important focus for individuals with osteoarthritis, particularly of the lower limbs.

Patients should be advised that discomfort may increase during exercise; however, if pain continues for more than two hours following exercise, exercise intensity should be decreased. Vigorous exercise should be avoided during bouts of acute inflammation, although individuals are encouraged to continue gentle range of motion exercises.[9] Selection of exercises should be targeted towards the individual with a goal of optimizing posture, alignment, and joint health. (Diagnosis of patients with osteoarthritis is discussed in Chapter 55.)

Low back pain

Graded exercise is recommended for individuals with both acute and chronic non-specific back pain. A detailed assessment (including history, red flags, and physical examination) will guide the clinician towards an effective, individualized exercise prescription (see Chapter 26). Managing low back pain should be done within a biopsychosocial model of care, particularly in cases of chronic pain or pain disorders where multiple barriers may exist that

prevent full participation in an exercise-based intervention. Current guidelines indicate that education and keeping active improve clinical outcomes.[54, 55] Detailed management of low back pain is discussed in Chapter 26. Pain is discussed in Chapter 6.

Table 60.14 has exercise prescriptions for patients with low back pain.

Promotion of bone health and prevention of fall-related fractures (for patients diagnosed with osteoporosis)

Strength and balance training is an effective way of reducing falls.[56–58] Jarvinen and colleagues emphasized that the focus for preventing fractures should be by addressing falls.[59] Appropriate exercise prescription includes balance training, aerobic weight-bearing exercise, and resistance training.[60–63]

As with other clinical populations, the ideal program for managing osteoporosis has not been determined.[61] Moderate intensity exercise that does not cause pain should be encouraged. In people with osteoporosis, exercises that cause heavy twisting or bending of the spine may cause compression fractures.[9] The Otago Exercise Program can help guide clinicians in developing a tailored exercise program for the prevention of falls.[64, 65]

Table 60.14 Exercise prescription: low back pain (acute and chronic)

Exercise type	Frequency	Intensity	Time
Aerobic (e.g. low-impact large-muscle activities such as walking, swimming, cycling, rowing, water aerobics)	5–7 days/week	11–16/20 RPE, 60–80% HR_{max} Limited by symptoms	150–300 mins/week Emphasize duration over intensity
Resistance (e.g. abdominal strengthening/back extensions)	Daily	As tolerated	Age <50, 10–15 reps/day Age >50, 8–12 reps/day Involving 8–10 muscle groups
Flexibility (e.g. exercise not exacerbating low back pain)	Daily	To level of tension, before discomfort	2 min/muscle group, 3 reps

Resources: *ACSM's Guidelines for exercise testing and prescription;*[9] *ACSM's Exercise management for persons with chronic diseases and disabilities;*[19] *ACSM's resources for clinical exercise physiology: musculoskeletal, neuromuscular, neoplastic, immunologic, and hematologic conditions*[51]

RPE = rating of perceived exertion; HR_{max} = maximum heart rate

Table 60.15 overleaf has exercise prescriptions for bone health and fracture prevention.

Parkinson's disease

The effect of exercise in people with Parkinson's disease is variable due to the varying disease states. Because of the chronic, progressive nature of Parkinson's disease, it is particularly important to evaluate exercise programs regularly. As outlined in Chapter 54, exercise in people with Parkinson's disease improves cognitive, motor, and functional ability.[66] Exercise prescription targets range of motion and flexibility exercises, balance and gait training, mobility, and/or coordination exercises to assist with functional ability. Evidence for aerobic activities and resistance training remains limited.[67, 68]

Specific exercise training that targets speech and motor deficits in Parkinson's disease appears to be beneficial.[69] Techniques that can improve the ability to initiate movements or resume movements during bouts of akinesia include rocking (side to side), rhythm, use of music, or counting.

Depressive symptoms

Studies have also shown links between exercise and mental wellbeing (Chapter 54). Dunn et al.[70] studied the effects of exercise on major depressive disorders and found that meeting recommended doses of aerobic exercise was as effective as medication or cognitive behavioral therapy in treating mild to moderate major depressive disorders. Exercise that did not meet recommended doses was ineffective.[70, 71]

Table 60.15 Exercise prescription: bone health, fracture prevention

Exercise type	Frequency	Intensity	Time
Aerobic (e.g. large-muscle activities such as walking, swimming, cycling, rowing, water aerobics)	3–5 days/week	11–16/20 RPE 60–80% HR_{max} Limited by symptoms	150–300 mins/week Emphasize duration over intensity
Resistance (e.g. free weights, machine weights, calisthenics)	2–3 days/week	60–80% 1RM	8–12 reps/day Involving 8–10 muscle groups
		80–90% 1RM	5–6 reps/day Involving 8–10 muscle groups
Flexibility (e.g. ROM exercises)	3–7 days/week	To level of tension, before discomfort	1 min/muscle group, 3 reps
Balance training (static and dynamic)	4–7 days/week	Safe but individually challenging	2–4 exercises, 3 reps each

Resources: *ACSM's Guidelines for exercise testing and prescription;*[9] *ACSM's Exercise management for persons with chronic diseases and disabilities;*[19] *ACSM's resources for clinical exercise physiology: musculoskeletal, neuromuscular, neoplastic, immunologic, and hematologic conditions*[51]

RM = repetition max; RPE = rating of perceived exertion; HR_{max} = maximum heart rate

CLINICAL SPORTS MEDICINE MASTERCLASSES

 www.clinicalsportsmedicine.com

- Listen to the podcast by Karim Khan on exercise prescription for bone health and falls prevention.

RECOMMENDED READING

Bouchard C, Blair SN, Haskell WL, eds. *Physical activity and health*. 2nd ed. Human Kinetics 2011.

Thompson WR, ed. *ACSM's Guidelines for exercise testing and prescription*. 8th ed. Philadelphia PA: Lippincott Williams & Wilkins, 2010.

Myers J, Nieman D, eds. *ACSM's Resources for clinical exercise physiology: musculoskeletal, neuromuscular, neoplastic, immunologic, and hematologic conditions*. 2nd ed. Philadelphia PA: Lippincott Williams & Wilkins, 2010.

Papaioannou A, Morin S, Cheung AM et al. 2010 clinical practice guidelines for the diagnosis and management of osteoporosis in Canada: summary. *CMAJ* 2010;182(17):1864–73.

REFERENCES

1. Blair SN. Physical inactivity: the biggest public health problem of the 21st century. *Br J Sports Med* 2009;43(1): 1–2.

2. Sallis R. Developing healthcare systems to support exercise: exercise as the fifth vital sign. *Br J Sports Med* 2011;45(6):473–4.

3. World Health Organization. Global recommendations on physical activity for health. Switzerland: World Health Organization, 2010.

4. FYSS The Swedish National Institute of Public Health. *Physical activity in the prevention and treatment of disease* (in Swedish). 2008.

5. Health USP. National physical activity plan. *www.physicalactivityplan.org/healthcare.php*, 2010.

6. Patrick K, Pratt M, Sallis RE. The healthcare sector's role in the US national physical activity plan. *J Phys Act Health* 2009;6(Suppl 2):S211–19.

7. US Department of Health and Human Services. Physical activity guidelines for Americans. *www.health.gov/paguidelines/*, 2008.

8. Tremblay MS, Warburton DE, Janssen I et al. New Canadian physical activity guidelines. *Appl Physiol Nutr Metab* 2011;36(1):36–46; 47–58.

9. Thompson WR, ed. *ACSM's Guidelines for exercise testing and prescription*. 8th ed. Philadelphia PA: Lippincott Williams & Wilkins, 2010.

10. Nelson ME, Rejeski WJ, Blair SN et al. Physical activity and public health in older adults: recommendation from the American College of Sports Medicine and the American Heart Association. *Med Sci Sports Exerc* 2007;39(8):1435–45.

11. Huang Y, Macera CA, Blair SN et al. Physical fitness, physical activity, and functional limitation in adults aged 40 and older. *Med Sci Sports Exerc* 1998;30(9):1430–5.

12. Brill PA, Macera CA, Davis DR et al. Muscular strength and physical function. *Med Sci Sports Exerc* 2000;32: 412–16.

13. LIFE Study Investigators, Pahor M, Blair SN et al. Effects of a physical activity intervention on measures of physical performance: results of the lifestyle interventions and independence for elders pilot (LIFE-P) study. *J Gerontol A Biol Sci Med Sci Med Sci* 2006;61(11):1157–65.

14. Evenson KR, Stevens J, Cai J et al. The effect of cardiorespiratory fitness and obesity on cancer mortality in women and men. *Med Sci Sports Exerc* 2003;35(2):270–7.

15. Lee DC, Sui X, Blair SN. Does physical activity ameliorate the health hazards of obesity? *Br J Sports Med* 2009;43(1):49–51.

16. Ruiz JR, Sui X, Lobelo F et al. Muscular strength and adiposity as predictors of adulthood cancer mortality in men. *Cancer Epidemiol Biomarkers Prev* 2009;18(5): 1468–76.

17. Ruiz JR, Sui X, Lobelo F et al. Association between muscular strength and mortality in men: prospective cohort study. *BMJ* 2008;337:a439.

18. Donnelly JE, Smith B, Jacobsen DJ et al. The role of exercise for weight loss and maintenance. *Best Pract Res Clin Gastroenterol* 2004;18(6):1009–29.

19. Durstine JL, Moore GE, Painter PL et al., eds. *ACSM's Exercise management for persons with chronic diseases and disabilities*. 3rd ed: Human Kinetics, 2009.

20. Donnelly JE, Blair SN, Jakicic JM et al. American College of Sports Medicine position stand. Appropriate physical activity intervention strategies for weight loss and prevention of weight regain for adults. *Med Sci Sports Exerc* 2009;41(2):459–71.

21. Taylor RS, Brown A, Ebrahim S et al. Exercise-based rehabilitation for patients with coronary heart disease: systematic review and meta-analysis of randomized controlled trials. *Am J Med* 2004;116(10): 682–92.

22. Ehrman J et al., eds. *ACSM's Resource manual for guidelines for exercise testing and prescription*. 6th ed:

Philadelphia PA: Lippincott Williams & Wilkins, 2009.

23. Hambrecht R, Walther C, Mobius-Winkler S et al. Patients with stable coronary artery disease: a randomized trial percutaneous coronary angioplasty compared with exercise training. *Circulation* 2004;109:1371–8.

24. Jessup M, Abraham WT, Casey DE et al. 2009 Focused update: ACCF/AHA Guidelines for the diagnosis and management of heart failure in adults: a report of the American College of Cardiology Foundation/American Heart Association Task Force on Practice Guidelines: developed in collaboration with the international society for heart and lung transplantation. *Circulation* 2009;119:1977–2016.

25. Piña IL, Apstein CS, Balady GJ et al. Exercise and heart failure: a statement from the American Heart Association committee on exercise, rehabilitation, and prevention. *Circulation* 2003;107:1210–6.

26. Heart Failure Society of America (HFSA). 2010 comprehensive heart failure practice guideline. *J Card Fail* 2010;16:e1–194.

27. Whelton SP, Chin A, Xin X et al. Effect of aerobic exercise on blood pressure: a meta-analysis of randomized, controlled trials. *Ann Int Med* 2002;136(7):493–503.

28. Carvalho J, Marques E, Ascensao A et al. Multicomponent exercise program improves blood lipid profile and antioxidant capacity in older women. *Arch Gerontol Geriatr* 2010;51(1):1–5.

29. Kelly RB. Diet and exercise in the management of hyperlipidemia. *Am Fam Phys* 2010;81(9):1097–102.

30. Wilund KR, Feeney LA, Tomayko EJ et al. Effects of endurance exercise training on markers of cholesterol absorption and synthesis. *Physiol Res* 2009;58(4):545–52.

31. Fletcher B, Berra K, Ades P et al. Managing abnormal blood lipids: a collaborative approach. *Circulation* 2005;112(20):3184–209.

32. O'Donnell DE, Aaron S, Bourbeau J et al. Canadian Thoracic Society recommendations for management of chronic obstructive pulmonary disease—2007 update. *Can Respir J* 2007;14(Suppl B):5–32B.

33. Reid WD, Chung F. *Clinical management notes and case histories in cardiopulmonary physical therapy.* Thorofare, NJ: SLACK Incorporated, 2004.

34. Nici L, Donner C, Wouters E et al. American Thoracic Society/European Respiratory Society Statement on pulmonary rehabilitation. *Am J Respir Crit Care Med* 2006;173(12):1390–413.

35. Lucas SR, Platts-Mills TAE. Physical activity and exercise in asthma: relevance to etiology and treatment. *J Allergy Clin Immunol* 2005;115(5):928–34.

36. Church TS, Blair SN, Cocreham S et al. Effects of aerobic and resistance training on hemoglobin A1c levels in patients with type 2 diabetes: a randomized controlled trial. *JAMA* 2010;304(20):2253–62.

37. Sigal RJ, Kenny GP, Boule NG et al. Effects of aerobic training, resistance training, or both on glycemic control in type 2 diabetes: a randomized trial. *Ann Intern Med* 2007;147(6):357–69.

38. Church TS, Cheng YJ, Earnest CP et al. Exercise capacity and body composition as predictors of mortality among men with diabetes. *Diabetes Care* 2004;27(1):83–8.

39. Church TS, LaMonte MJ, Barlow CE et al. Cardiorespiratory fitness and body mass index as predictors of cardiovascular disease mortality among men with diabetes. *Arch Intern Med* 2005;165(18):2114–20.

40. American Diabetes Association: Standards of medical care in diabetes—2007. *Diabetes Care* 2007;30 Suppl 1:S4–41.

41. Johansen KL. Exercise and chronic kidney disease: current recommendations. *Sports Med* 2005;35(6):485–99.

42. McNeely ML, Peddle CJ, Parliament M et al. Cancer rehabilitation: recommendations for integrating exercise programming in the clinical practice setting. *Curr Cancer Ther Rev* 2006;2:351–60.

43. Ness KK, Wall MM, Oakes JM et al. Physical performance limitations and particpation restrictions among cancer survivors: a population-based study. *Ann Epidemiol* 2006;16:197–205.

44. Bicego D, Brown K, Ruddick M et al. Effects of exercise on quality of life in women living with breast cancer: a systematic review. *Breast J* 2009;15(1):45–51.

45. Holmes MD, Chen WY, Feskanich D et al. Physical activity and survival after breast cancer diagnosis. *JAMA* 2005;293(20):2479–86.

46. Meyerhardt JA, Giovannucci EL, Holmes MD et al. Physical activity and survival after colorectal cancer diagnosis. *J Clin Oncol* 2006;24(22):3527–34.

47. Meyerhardt JA, Heseltine D, Niedzwiecki D et al. Impact of physical activity on cancer recurrence and survival in patients with stage III colon cancer: findings from CALGB 89803. *J Clin Oncol* 2006;24(22):3535–41.

48. Schmitz KH, Ahmed RL, Troxel AB et al. Weight lifting for women at risk for breast cancer–

related lymphedema: a randomized trial. *JAMA* 2010;304(24):2699–705.

49. Bicego D, Brown K, Ruddick M et al. Exercise for women with or at risk for breast cancer-related lymphedema. *Phys Ther* 2006;86:1398–405.

50. Kushi LH, Byers T, Doyle C et al. American Cancer Society guidelines on nutrition and physical activity for cancer prevention: reducing the risk of cancer with healthy food choices and physical activity. *CA Cancer J Clin* 2006;56(5):254–81; quiz 313–4.

51. Myers J, Nieman D, eds. *ACSM's resources for clinical exercise physiology: musculoskeletal, neuromuscular, neoplastic, immunologic, and hematologic conditions.* 2nd ed. Philadelphia PA: Lippincott Williams & Wilkins, 2010.

52. Schmitz KH, Courneya KS, Matthews C et al. American College of Sports Medicine roundtable on exercise guidelines for cancer survivors. *Med Sci Sports Exerc* 2010;42(7):1409–26.

53. Bennell K, Hinman R. Exercise as a treatment for osteoarthritis. *Curr Opin Rheumatol* 2005;17(5):634–40.

54. Fritz JM, Cleland JA, Brennan GP. Does adherence to the guideline recommendation for active treatments improve the quality of care for patients with acute low back pain delivered by physical therapists? *Med Care* 2007;45(10):973–80.

55. Airaksinen O, Brox JI, Cedraschi C et al. Chapter 4. European guidelines for the management of chronic nonspecific low back pain. *Eur Spine J* 2006;15 Suppl 2: S192–300.

56. Gillespie LD, Robertson MC, Gillespie WJ et al. Interventions for preventing falls in older people living in the community. *Cochrane Database of Systc Rev* 2009(2):CD007146.

57. Robertson MC, Campbell AJ, Gardner MM et al. Preventing injuries in older people by preventing falls: a meta-analysis of individual-level data. *J Am Geriatr Soc* 2002;50(5):905–11.

58. Kannus P, Sievanen H, Palvanen M et al. Prevention of falls and consequent injuries in elderly people. *Lancet* 2005;366(9500):1885–93.

59. Jarvinen TLN, Sievanen H, Khan KM et al. Shifting the focus in fracture prevention from osteoporosis to falls. *BMJ* 2008;336(7636):124–6.

60. Li WC, Chen YC, Yang RS et al. Effects of exercise programmes on quality of life in osteoporotic and osteopenic postmenopausal women: a systematic review and meta-analysis. *Clin Rehabil* 2009;23(10):888–96.

61. Papaioannou A, Morin S, Cheung AM et al. 2010 clinical practice guidelines for the diagnosis and management of osteoporosis in Canada: summary. *CMAJ* 2010;182(17):1864–73.

62. Rhodes EC, Martin AD, Taunton JE et al. Effects of one year of resistance training on the relation between muscular strength and bone density in elderly women. *Br J Sports Med* 2000;34(1):18–22.

63. Sherrington C, Whitney JC, Lord SR et al. Effective exercise for the prevention of falls: a systematic review and meta-analysis. *J Am Geriatr Soc* 2008;56(12): 2234–43.

64. Thomas S, Mackintosh S, Halbert J. Does the "Otago exercise programme" reduce mortality and falls in older adults?: a systematic review and meta-analysis. *Age Ageing* 2010;39(6):681–7.

65. Campbell AJ, Robertson MC. Otago exercise programme provider book. In: Campbell AJ, Robertson MC, eds. *Otago exercise programme: to prevent falls in older adults.* Dunedin, NZ: ACC Publications, 2003.

66. de Goede CJ, Keus SH, Kwakkel G et al. The effects of physical therapy in Parkinson's disease: a research synthesis. *Arch Phys Med Rehabil* 2001;82(4):509–15.

67. Falvo MJ, Schilling BK, Earhart GM. Parkinson's disease and resistive exercise: rationale, review, and recommendations. *Mov Disord* 2008;23(1):1–11.

68. Goodwin VA, Richards SH, Taylor RS et al. The effectiveness of exercise interventions for people with Parkinson's disease: a systematic review and meta-analysis. *Mov Disord* 2008;23:631–40.

69. Ebersbach G, Ebersbach A, Edler D et al. Comparing exercise in Parkinson's disease—the Berlin LSVT(R) BIG study. *Mov Disord* 2010;25(12):1902–8.

70. Dunn AL, Trivedi MH, Kampert JB et al. Exercise treatment for depression: efficacy and dose response. *Am J Prev Med* 2005;28(1):1–8.

71. Martin CK, Church TS, Thompson AM et al. Exercise dose and quality of life: a randomized controlled trial. *Arch Intern Med* 2009;169(3):269–78.

Practical sports medicine

Chapter 61

The preparticipation physical evaluation

with SANDY HOFFMANN and ERIN MACRI

The preparticipation physical examination (PPE) is ideally done as part of routine health screening examinations by an athlete's primary physician and should be considered a part of the preventive health examination for all children and adolescents to encourage safe physical activity of any kind on a regular basis. Preparticipation Physical Evaluation Working Group. *Preparticipation physical evaluation monograph.* Sandy Hoffman and Erin Macri[1]

At a time when various elements of clinical practice are under appropriate scrutiny, the preparticipation physical evaluation (PPE)[1] has gone from the routine to a part of sports and exercise medicine that is garnering a great deal of interest.

The most fundamental question is—what is the purpose of the PPE? In this chapter we begin by addressing that question and we then discuss:

- who benefits from a PPE
- who is best qualified and appropriate to conduct a PPE
- ideal times for conducting the assessment
- location considerations
- selecting a format and appropriate content
- considerations for clearing a sportsperson for participation.

A PPE is often a mandatory administrative requirement of an athletic association for organized sports participation. There is enormous variation throughout the world in how these examinations are performed, including questions asked, physical examination components performed, and the level of training required of practitioners conducting these examinations. The ensuing discussion will clarify key components and considerations for developing and conducting evaluations that best meet the needs of specific sportspeople, teams, or leagues.

The reader is referred to Chapters 42, 43, 44, and 46 for details regarding special populations. such as the older and younger sportsperson, the female sportsperson, and the disabled sportsperson.

Objectives

Setting the tone

The physical, psychological, and social benefits of physical activity and sports participation for people of all ages and abilities are vast and well recognized. These benefits should serve as an underlying tenet guiding the development and implementation of PPEs. It is important that clinicians, coaches, and league administrators uphold the message that a PPE is designed to be valuable, enjoyable, and educational for the sportsperson.

The information gained from the PPE should encourage the sportsperson toward improved self-care, and should never feel like a "test" or make the sportsperson feel ill at ease about being evaluated. To facilitate this, the environment should be positive and the clinician should focus the evaluation around optimizing health, safety, performance, and participation for the sportsperson.

To summarize, the overall experience for both clinician and sportsperson should be constructive, motivating, and enjoyable.

Specific objectives

Conducting pre-participation physical evaluations can achieve several key objectives (see box opposite).

Objectives of pre-participation physical evaluations

- To provide an entry point for medical care
- To screen for potentially life-threatening conditions
- To review injury history and identify relevant ongoing sequelae (e.g. concussion)
- To identify current illnesses, injuries, or chronic medical conditions that may endanger the health and safety of the sportsperson or of those with whom they practice and compete.[1]
- To guide sportspeople with chronic conditions toward optimal participation in sport/identify suitable sports given individual abilities/impairments
- To identify factors that increase risk of future injury or illness
- To identify factors that may affect performance
- To review medications to ensure compliance with relevant doping regulations
- To provide education or advice
- To provide medical clearance to participate in sport
- To develop rapport between sportsperson and sports medicine team

For many sportspeople the PPE serves as an entry point into a healthcare system, especially for adolescents, who may have limited contact with the healthcare system and thus may not have seen a physician. Therefore, in many cases, the PPE allows an opportunity to provide quality and cost-effective healthcare, determine general health, and initiate discussion on health-related topics.

In addition, the PPE affords the opportunity to screen for conditions that may currently be asymptomatic yet could be potentially life-threatening. Sudden cardiac death (SCD), while rare, is known to happen more often in sportspeople compared to those who do not play competitive sports.[2] In sportspeople SCD is most often related to cardiac conditions such as hypertrophic cardiomyopathy (HCM) (Chapter 48). Detection of such conditions is difficult and may depend on the level of experience of the healthcare practitioner or the conditions under which the examination is performed. In a case series of 158 sportspeople with sudden death, the cardiovascular abnormality responsible for death was prospectively identified in only one sportsperson.[3] Developing worldwide uniformity in the approach to a comprehensive PPE may help define and improve the ability to achieve the goal of identifying these conditions in a typically younger and "healthier" population.[1, 4–9]

The evaluator should review the sportsperson's medical history in addition to evaluating the present illness or injury. Previous musculoskeletal injuries may not have been adequately rehabilitated, resulting in ongoing weakness, joint laxity, or poor neuromotor control. Identifying such factors enables the evaluator to develop an effective rehabilitation plan for any pre-existing injury.

Concussions can leave the sportsperson with ongoing symptoms, vulnerable to more serious brain injury if continuing to participate in athletics, in particular in contact sports. The evaluator may use this information to determine if the sportsperson is suitable for a certain sport or would benefit from appropriate protective gear to minimize risk.

Inadequate management of chronic conditions such as asthma can leave a sportsperson with specific impairments that appropriate intervention can target toward improved sport performance. The PPE can provide a forum for clinicians to advise participants on appropriate sports in which to participate, especially for those sportspeople with disabilities.[10]

 One of the primary objectives of the PPE is to screen for conditions that may predispose a competitive sportspeople to injury or illness.

There is no literature to support the concept that performance of a PPE predicts who will develop an orthopedic injury, or prevents or reduces the severity of an orthopedic injury in a sportsperson.[11]

However, despite this, there is research regarding individual components that could be included in a PPE that could guide training in an effort to reduce risk of future injury. For example, in female sportspeople, dynamic knee valgus when landing during a jump was shown to be predictive of anterior cruciate ligament injury.[12] Training programs to improve motor control in tasks such as jumping and cutting decrease the incidence of anterior cruciate ligament injuries.[13, 14] Thus, early recognition and treatment of factors such as abnormal biomechanics may minimize time lost from training and competition, an important goal of a competitive sportsperson.

At higher levels of competition, consider assessing psychological, social, and nutritional factors that may affect performance. Since the list of doping agents changes regularly, the assessor should review the sportsperson's medications, if any, to ensure compliance with regulations or to identify a need to request exemption.

The PPE affords the opportunity for the sports and exercise medicine team and sportspeople to meet and develop a working relationship. The clinician can initiate counseling and education regarding injury and illness prevention, high-risk behaviors, nutrition and hydration, environmental issues, as well as other aspects of training and performance.

The PPE can serve as a vehicle to meet administrative requirements of an athletic association or governing body for eligibility to participate in competitive athletics. In the US, a PPE is required in order to participate in organized sports at the high school and collegiate levels. Italy requires compulsory annual medical clearance to compete in organized sports at many levels.[7] The PPE requirements are different in Australia.[4] In addition, there are numerous country-specific legal statutes that govern the rights of sportspeople to participate, as well as the confidentiality of medical records obtained during performance of a PPE. Generally, unless explicit signed consent has been provided by the sportsperson to release medical information to a coach or team administrator, details within the PPE are confidential beyond whether or not the sportsperson is cleared for participation.

Overall, the PPE provides considerable information that is relevant, practical, and beneficial for the sportsperson in optimizing both sport performance and overall health. The breadth and depth of information available will depend on the design of the evaluation and the context in which the examination is conducted, which is discussed in greater depth below.

Who should undergo the PPE?

In the broadest context, all persons who begin a new activity program should have a "PPE" tailored to their age, ability, and anticipated "athletic" endeavor. This chapter, however, will focus on the competitive sportsperson.

The PPE was developed for competitive sportspeople at the high school, college, and elite amateur and professional levels. Recently Maron et al.[15] have proposed recommendations for pre-participation screening and assessment of cardiovascular disease at the masters athlete level. Ideally, PPEs should take place for competitive sportspeople of all ages, genders, and levels of organized sports competition.

Who should perform the PPE?

The Team Physician Consensus Statement from the American College of Sports Medicine makes recommendations at the collegiate level for which practitioners should perform the PPE.[16] Skills in both musculoskeletal evaluation and cardiac auscultation may require that more than one clinician perform components of the examination. In the US, laws vary from state to state as to the educational and experiential skills that a practitioner needs to perform a PPE. International and professional sportspeople are governed by their athletic organizations as to who is considered qualified to perform a PPE.

When to perform the PPE?

Timing of the PPE ideally should occur in the off-season, at least six to eight weeks prior to the beginning of the practice season, to allow time for appropriate rehabilitation of injuries or to evaluate and treat medical conditions.

The required frequency of the PPE varies according to the governing bodies of various athletic organizations and the age of the sportsperson.[4, 6, 8] Generally it is recommended that a comprehensive PPE be performed at least at entry to middle school, high school, and college. After an initial comprehensive PPE, they can be repeated any time a sportsperson transfers to a new school; afterwards, frequency varies by state, generally yearly for college level, every two years in younger sportspeople, and every two to three years in older sportspeople.[1]

Yearly assessments are valuable during the years of increased growth and development, or in cases where a sportsperson does not otherwise have access to primary healthcare. If PPEs are done less than annually, an interim evaluation should include a comprehensive history incorporating the integral components of the American Heart Association screening guidelines,[17] height, weight, blood pressure, and a problem-focused examination. The optimal frequency for elite amateur, professional, and masters sportspeople has yet to be determined.

Where to conduct the PPE?

Office-based examinations are more costly but provide privacy and the opportunity for continuity of care, especially if there is a previously established provider–patient relationship. If the provider, however, has not had adequate training in components of the PPE, particularly in musculoskeletal and cardiac examination, the visit may end up focusing more on health maintenance and developmental concerns than on a particular athletic endeavor. Further, offices may not have the tools needed to perform detailed clinical assessments such as proprioception testing, evaluation of cardiovascular fitness, or equipment for measuring ECG/EKG.

A station-based examination is inexpensive and designed to have a sports focus, but lacks continuity of care and often does not allow a sportsperson an opportunity to explore developmental issues or risk-taking behaviors. The PPE working group has developed tips to improve the coordinated medical team approach to a PPE, including having the team physician coordinate the process, and having clinicians with various expertise available.[1] The evaluation may best be split up so that parts of the assessment are done on-field or at a suitable facility, while others are done in the privacy of an office/clinic.

What to include in the PPE?

History

A thorough medical history is crucial to the pre-participation evaluation of competitive sportspeople. Various questionnaires have been developed for sportspeople of all ages and levels of competition. Controversy exists as to whether the PPE should cover a broad range of topics, including health promotion and risk behaviors, or be limited to orthopedic and cardiac conditions.

The Preparticipation Evaluation Working Group has developed an evaluation form that includes most conditions that could affect the health and safety of sportspeople.[1] This form also includes follow-up questions on substance use, mental health, and general safety issues that it recommends be discussed face-to-face with the clinician performing the examination.

Younger sportspeople are encouraged to complete the history form prior to the evaluation with an adult to help ensure accuracy. A web-based PPE has been used on a small scale with collegiate and high school sportspeople in the US,[18, 19] and has the potential to facilitate research on the effectiveness of the PPE as currently performed.

The essential components of the history include a thorough system review for acute or chronic medical and orthopedic conditions (Table 61.1 overleaf). This should include:[1, 2]

- cardiovascular symptoms
- pulmonary symptoms
- musculoskeletal symptoms
- hematological symptoms
- allergies
- infection/immunology

- ear/nose/throat symptoms
- dermatological symptoms
- genitourinary symptoms
- gastrointestinal symptoms
- neurological symptoms
- endocrine/metabolic symptoms
- ophthalmologic symptoms
- dental symptoms.

Review the sportsperson's sports participation history, including the use of protective equipment, use of medications and supplements, allergies, and a menstrual history for female sportspeople. Questions regarding immunization status, dietary status, and health-risk behaviors are often included (Table 61.1).

Physical examination

The physical examination component of the PPE should be performed by skilled clinicians with a particular focus on cardiovascular, neurological, and orthopedic abnormalities that would identify sportspeople at high risk of injury, disability, or death. Baseline data should also be obtained on blood pressure, weight, height, and organ function in case of injury or illness (Table 61.2 on page 1181).

Diagnostic tests

Cardiovascular testing

The prevalence of cardiovascular diseases capable of causing sudden death in young sportspeople is estimated to be very low, although it differs in various parts of the world.[19, 20] A thorough history and physical examination based on the American Heart Association screening recommendations remains the cornerstone of the cardiac pre-participation screening.[17, 21] Reviews of high school[6] and collegiate[8] PPE forms used in the US, however, demonstrate a significant lack of essential components in most questionnaires.

Much interest has been generated in the use of diagnostic testing to assist in screening for cardiovascular conditions that may predispose a sportsperson to sudden cardiac death. Routine diagnostic testing with an ECG/EKG has been performed as part of the PPE in Italy for many years and has been found useful in identifying sportspeople with hypertrophic cardiomyopathy in that population. For a more thorough review of this subject the reader is referred to Chapter 48. Atherosclerotic coronary disease is the most common form of heart disease in Masters athletes and a routine screening ECG/EKG

Table 61.1 Important components of the history

Past history
• Ever been denied participation
• Chronic medical conditions
• Hospitalizations, surgeries
• Unpaired organ (eye, testicle, kidney)
• Medications, supplements

Allergies
• Medications
• Foods
• Bees, wasps, other

Cardiovascular
• Syncope, near-syncope (during or after activity)
• Chest pain
• Palpitations
• Heart murmur
• High blood pressure
• Fatigue
• Shortness of breath with exertion
• Family history of sudden cardiac death (or unexpected drowning)
• Family history of premature coronary disease

Orthopedic
• Injury (sprain, strain)
• Broken bones, dislocated joints, or stress fracture
• Brace

Respiratory
• Exercise-related wheezing, cough, difficulty breathing

Infectious diseases
• Recent infectious mononucleosis (glandular fever)
• Herpes skin infection

Neurological
• Head, facial, or dental injury
• Confusion or memory loss after a head injury
• Numbness, tingling, or inability to move arms or legs after being hit
• Headaches with or immediately after exercise

Eyes
• Glasses or contact lenses
• Use of protective eyewear

General
• History of heat illness
• History of sickle-cell trait or disease

Dietary
• Weight loss/gain
• Satisfaction with current weight
• Dietary habits

Females
• When menstruation commenced
• How many menses in last 12 months
• Last menstrual period, prior menstrual period

Immunizations
• Tetanus
• Hepatitis A, B
• Meningococcal
• Influenza
• Others (dependent on travel history)

Health-risk behaviors
• Tobacco, alcohol, drugs
• Sexual history

is recommended for this population as part of their PPE.[15]

Echocardiography and exercise stress testing are not suggested for routine screening; however, these diagnostic tests may be indicated in certain populations such as Masters athletes, particularly if they are undertaking sudden vigorous training,[15] and for sportspeople with abnormalities on a resting ECG/EKG.

It is important to recognize that further testing and referral should be considered for any sportsperson who has a personal or family history of sudden cardiac death or premature coronary disease. Symptoms of syncope, unexplained exertional dyspnea, or chest pain should be thoroughly evaluated[22] as they may be an early sign of one of the genetic cardiovascular diseases (Table 61.3). Additional testing should also be undertaken if the sportsperson has a heart murmur, hypertension, or abnormalities suggestive of Marfan syndrome or coarctation of the aorta.

Neurological testing

No evidence-based guidelines exist as to the requirements for assessment of a previous head injury during the PPE.[23] Consensus expert recommendations exist, however, for the use of a baseline cognitive assessment such as the Prague sport concussion assessment tool (SCAT) as well as baseline neuro-

Table 61.2 Important components of the physical examination

General

- Height
- Weight

Eyes, ears, nose, throat

- Visual acuity
- Pupil symmetry
- Ear canals and tympanic membranes
- Nasal septum, polyps
- Teeth
- Throat lesions

Lungs

- Breath sounds
- Chest expansion
- Contour of thoracic cage

Cardiovascular system

- Blood pressure in both arms
- Radial and femoral pulses
- Heart rate, rhythm
- Murmurs (systolic/diastolic and grade)
- Stigmata of Marfan syndrome

Abdomen

- Tenderness
- Organomegaly
- Masses

Skin

- Rashes
- Lesions

Genitalia (males only)

- Testicles, masses
- Hernia

Musculoskeletal (symmetry, range of motion, strength, flexibility, balance, proprioception, motor control, joint stability)

- Neck, back
- Shoulder
- Elbow, wrist, hand
- Hip
- Knee
- Ankle, foot
- Gait

Table 61.3 Genetic cardiovascular diseases

Hypertrophic cardiomyopathy (HCM)
Arrhythmogenic right ventricular cardiomyopathy (ARVC)
Marfan syndrome
Ion channel diseases
Long-QT syndrome (LQTS)
Brugada syndrome
Catecholaminergic polymorphic ventricular tachycardia (CPVT)

psychological testing, particularly for those sportspeople in high-risk sports such as rugby, soccer, ice hockey, and the various football codes.[24]

Other diagnostic tests

Other diagnostic tests may be appropriate for selected sportspeople (Table 61.4). See Chapter 62 for further discussion and examples of where various tests would be appropriate.

What is "clearance"?

The objective of the PPE is to ensure sportspeople are medically fit to participate in their sport of choice safely, without harm to themselves or others. In the rare event that findings suggest that participation in sport should be modified or restricted, it is imperative that the sportsperson (and care giver if appropriate) be fully informed of findings and associated risks. The sportsperson should be involved in the decision-making process wherever possible regarding participation options given the relative risks affecting his or her health or safety.[1] Suggestions regarding conditions precluding sport participation are available;[1] however, each sportsperson's situation is unique and therefore should be considered individually, considering both the PPE findings, sport of choice, and in

Table 61.4 Investigations as indicated

Urinalysis
ECG/EKG, echocardiograph (see Chapters 48 and 49)
Hemoglobin and ferritin levels
Hepatitis B, C, and HIV antibodies
Bone mineral density
Peak flow and pulmonary function
Body fat composition
Isokinetic muscle testing
Biomechanical analysis and gait assessment
Video analysis of technique

E

consultation with appropriate medical specialists and caregivers where appropriate.

If a sportsperson cannot safely participate in his or her chosen sport despite treatment of a medical or orthopedic condition, even on a limited basis, determination should be made as to what activities he or she *can* compete in. Classification of activities based on dynamic (volume load) or static (pressure load) demands on the left ventricle[25] and degree of physical contact[26] can help the clinician guide sportspeople into appropriate activities based on their general health and cardiovascular status.

Tables 61.5 and 61.6 provide examples of sports based on strenuousness and degree of contact. Detailed recommendations that contain expert consensus regarding "clearance" for a particular competitive sport have been developed by several groups.[1, 15, 22, 26–28] As in all aspects of medicine, reliance on current consensus guidelines, good medical practice, and the sportsperson's overall health should be considered when making individual decisions about participation.[29]

Conclusions

The PPE as currently performed may not be an ideal evidence-based screening tool for prevention of illness and injury in sportspeople. Some authors suggest a move toward a history and examination that contain an overview of a sportsperson's entire health status, including age-appropriate preventive health services (such as tobacco cessation). The PPE, however, should not replace comprehensive health maintenance visits for sportspeople unless it incorporates components of such into its format.[30]

Research continues to elucidate important relationships between an individual sportsperson and factors affecting his or her fitness to participate, optimal performance, and risk of injury or illness, thus guiding the drive toward an ever better PPE. For example, injury and illness surveillance is becoming more prevalent among various organizations, including the International Olympic Committee, and FIFA. Findings are revealing valuable data on injury and illness relating to various sporting events.[31]

This knowledge regarding relative risk of specific sports and the nature of injury and illness relating to specific sports, combined with better knowledge regarding specific predictive indicators and valid screening tools (see also Chapter 62), continues to shape PPEs. As this field matures, cost-effectiveness will enter the equation as well.[32]

Considerations for improving the way a PPE is performed include developing a common format, determining optimal frequency, and measuring the effectiveness of the delivery of healthcare services performed during a PPE.[1, 4, 7, 9] Electronic implementation of a PPE questionnaire has been attempted at the high school and collegiate levels in the US,[18, 19]

Table 61.5 Examples of sports classified by strenuousness; based on dynamic (volume load) and static (pressure load) demands on the left ventricle

High/moderate dynamic and static	High/moderate dynamic and low static	High/moderate static and low dynamic	Low static and low dynamic
Rugby	Soccer	Gymnastics	Curling
Downhill skiing	Swimming	Sailing	Golf
Wrestling	Table tennis	Archery	Bowling
Ice hockey	Volleyball	Diving	Cricket
Water polo	Squash	Auto racing	

Table 61.6 Examples of sports classified by contact

Contact/collision	Limited contact	Non-contact
Rugby	Gymnastics	Curling
Ice hockey	Snowboarding	Golf
Soccer	Skiing	Swimming
Water polo	Volleyball	Bowling
Wrestling	Handball	Table tennis

providing the beginning of a database from which we may gather information, measure effectiveness of our current process, and develop a PPE that focuses on how sports participation influences an individual sportsperson's short– and long-term health.

A more focused, systematic, standardized PPE, tailored to specific populations, that is age and developmentally specific is a goal of sports and exercise medicine practitioners throughout the world.

REFERENCES

1. Preparticipation Physical Evaluation Working Group. *Preparticipation physical evaluation monograph*. 4th ed, American College of Sports Medicine 2010.

2. Ljungqvist A, Jenoure P, Engebretsen L et al. The International Olympic Committee (IOC) Consensus statement on periodic health evaluation of elite athletes March 2009. *Br J Sports Med* 2009;43(9):631–43.

3. Maron BJ, Shirani J, Poliac LC et al. Sudden death in young competitive athletes—clinical, demographic, and pathological profiles. *JAMA* 1996;276(3):199–204.

4. Brukner P, White S, Shawdon A et al. Screening of athletes—Australian experience. *Clin J Sport Med* 2004;14(3):169–77.

5. Corrado D, Basso C, Schiavon M et al. Screening for hypertrophic cardiomyopathy in young athletes. *N Engl J Med* 1998;339(6):364–9.

6. Glover DW, Maron BJ. Profile of preparticipation cardiovascular screening for high school athletes. *JAMA* 1998;279(22):1817–19.

7. Pelliccia A, Maron B. Preparticipation cardiovascular examination of the competitive athlete: perspectives from the 30-year Italian experience. *Am J Cardiol* 1995;75.

8. Pfister GC, Puffer JC, Maron BJ. Preparticipation cardiovascular screening for US collegiate student-athletes. *JAMA* 2000;283(12):1597–9.

9. Wingfield K, Matheson GO, Meeuwisse WH. Preparticipation evaluation—an evidence-based review. *Clin J Sport Med* 2004;14(3):109–22.

10. Patel DR, Greydanus DE. The pediatric athlete with disabilities. *Pediatr Clin North Am* 2002;49(4):803–27.

11. Hulkower S, Fagan B, Watts J et al. Do preparticipation clinical exams reduce morbidity and mortality for athletes? *J Fam Pract* 2005; 54:28–32.

12. Hewett TE, Myer GD, Ford KR et al. Biomechanical measures of neuromuscular control and valgus loading of the knee predict anterior cruciate ligament injury risk in female athletes. *Am J Sports Med* 2005;33(4):492–501.

13. Mandelbaum BR, Silvers HJ, Watanabe DS et al. Effectiveness of a neuromuscular and proprioceptive training program in preventing anterior cruciate ligament injuries in female athletes. *Am J Sports Med* 2005;33(7):1003–10.

14. Labella C, Carl R. Preventing knee ligament injuries in young athletes. *Pediatr Ann* 2010;39(11):714–20.

15. Maron BJ, Araujo CGS, Thompson PD et al. Recommendations for preparticipation screening and the assessment of cardiovascular disease in Masters athletes: an advisory for healthcare professionals from the working groups of the World Heart Federation, the International Federation of Sports Medicine, and the American Heart Association Committee on Exercise, Cardiac Rehabilitation, and Prevention. *Circulation* 2001;103(2):327–34.

16. American College of Sports Medicine. Issues in injury and illness prevention and the team physician: a consensus statement. *Med Sci Sports Exerc* 2007;39(11):2058–68.

17. Maron BJ, Thompson PD, Puffer JC et al. Cardiovascular preparticipation screening of competitive athletes: a statement for health professionals from the Sudden Death Committee (clinical cardiology) and Congenital Cardiac Defects Committee (cardiovascular disease in the young), American Heart Association. *Circulation* 1996; 94:850–6.

18. Meeuwisse W, Matheson G. Prevalence of positive responses on sports participation screening in Ohio students. *Clin J Sport Med* 2003;13:381.

19. Peltz JE, Haskell WL, Matheson GO. A comprehensive and cost-effective preparticipation exam implemented on the World Wide Web. *Med Sci Sports Exerc* 1999;31(12):1727–40.

20. Maron BJ. Sudden death in young athletes. *N Engl J Med* 2003;349(11):1064–75.

21. Maron BJ, Douglas PS, Graham TP et al. 36th Bethesda Conference. Task Force 1: Preparticipation screening and diagnosis of cardiovascular disease in athletes. *J Am Coll Cardiol* 2005;45(8):1322–6.

E

22. Maron BJ, Chaitman BR, Ackerman MJ et al. Recommendations for physical activity and recreational sports participation for young patients with genetic cardiovascular diseases. *Circulation* 2004;109(22): 2807–16.

23. McCrory P. Preparticipation assessment for head injury. *Clin J Sport Med* 2004;14(3):139–44.

24. McCrory P, Johnston K, Meeuwisse W et al. Summary and agreement statement of the 2nd International Conference on Concussion in Sport, Prague 2004. *Br J Sports Med* 2005;39:196–204.

25. Mitchell JH, Haskell WL, Raven PB. Classification of sports. *Med Sci Sports Exerc* 1994;26(10):S242–5.

26. American Academy of Pediatrics: Medical conditions affecting sports participation. *Pediatrics* 2001;107(5):1205–9.

27. Pelliccia A, Fagard R, Bjornstad HH et al. Recommendations for competitive sports participation in athletes with cardiovascular disease—a consensus document from the Study Group of Sports Cardiology of the Working Group of Cardiac Rehabilitation and Exercise Physiology and the Working Group of Myocardial and Pericardial Diseases of the European Society of Cardiology. *Eur Heart J* 2005;26(14):1422–45.

28. Maron BJ, Zipes DP. 36th Bethesda Conference. Introduction: eligibility recommendations for competitive athletes with cardiovascular abnormalities—general considerations. *J Am Coll Cardiol* 2005;45(8):1318–21.

29. Mitten MJ, Maron BJ, Zipes DP. Task force 12: Legal aspects of the 36th Bethesda Conference recommendations. *J Am Coll Cardiol* 2005;45(8):1373–5.

30. US Department of Health and Human Services, Centers for Disease Control and Prevention: Assessing health risk behaviors among young people: Youth Risk Behavior Surveillance System 2004. www.cdc.gov/yrbss.

31. Engebretsen L, Steffen K, Alonso JM et al. Sports injuries and illnesses during the Winter Olympic Games 2010. *Br J Sports Med* 2010;44(11):772–80.

32. Wheeler MT, Heidenreich PA, Froelicher VF et al. Cost-effectiveness of preparticipation screening for prevention of sudden cardiac death in young athletes. *Ann Intern Med* 2010;152(5):276–96.

Chapter 62

Screening the elite sportsperson

with ZAFAR IQBAL and PHIL COLES

What price screening the elite athlete? Dutch national Ruud van Nistelrooy "failed" his screening examination with Manchester United in April 2000. Within days, he ruptured his ACL training with a leading Dutch club. We hope the clinician got a cut of the cost-saving to Manchester United! (At the time average player salaries were £409 000 per season.)

Screening the competitive sportsperson is an important component of the sports medicine team's job. It involves taking a comprehensive history, performing a complete examination, and utilizing additional tests if appropriate. Screening differs from a pre-participation examination (Chapter 61) in that it is oriented toward both health and performance.

Aims of screening an elite sportsperson

The screening of high performance sportspeople has a number of aims.

1. Ensure optimal medical health:
   (a) Recognize previously undiagnosed medical problems, such as cardiac disorders, exercise-induced asthma, anorexia nervosa, Marfan syndrome, depression.
   (b) Assess the status of known medical problems (such as asthma, diabetes, epilepsy).
   (c) Identify family history of inheritable medical disorders.
2. Ensure optimal musculoskeletal health:
   (a) Assess any current injury.
   (b) Assess the deficit(s) resulting from any previous injury.
   (c) Identify unrecognized injury.
3. Optimize performance:
   (a) Obtain information that will help improve factors that may affect performance (i.e. physical characteristics such as strength and

joint range) as well as more holistic factors (such as nutrition, psychology, biomechanics).
4. Injury prevention:
   (a) Assess the presence of any predisposing factors to future musculoskeletal injury.
5. Baseline data collection:
   (a) Establish clinical baselines on musculoskeletal tests that can be used for reference during any future rehabilitation.
   (b) Establish functional baselines that can be used for reference as part of any testing prior to return to play post-injury.
   (c) Establish medical baselines (including blood tests, psychological testing, etc.) that can be used for reference while monitoring general health throughout the year.
   (d) Establish accurate medical records on medications and vaccinations so appropriate future planning can occur.
6. Develop professional relationship with sportsperson.
7. Education.

Additional benefits of screening

There are a number of advantages of screening the sportsperson in addition to the abovementioned aims. Screening provides an opportunity for the sportsperson to be examined by a physician, sometimes for the first time in many years. Young sportspeople are usually healthy and rarely seek assistance from a medical practitioner. The athletic screening may be the first time that a physician has listened to the sportsperson's heart since birth. It may be the first time the sportsperson's blood pressure has been measured or urine has been tested.

The screening process gives the clinical team an opportunity to develop a relationship with the sportsperson that may stand them in good stead in the future. A knowledge of the sportsperson's personal details, including family, job, and other personal habits, may provide useful information in the future management of the sportsperson.

Screening also gives the opportunity for the clinical team to offer advice regarding the prevention of injuries (e.g. the need for warm-up), to emphasize the importance of early reporting of injuries and appropriate initial management, to discuss possible symptoms of overtraining and the various methods of preventing overtraining, and to give advice regarding diet and psychological techniques.

When should sportspeople be screened?

Sportspeople should be screened at the earliest opportunity. This may be prior to or immediately after they join a high-level squad or team. A full screening should be performed initially. Subsequent modified screening, usually concentrating on musculoskeletal problems, injuries that may have proved a problem in the preceding season, and new medical complaints (such as exertional chest pain or lightheadedness) should be performed each year between the end of one season and the commencement of training for the following season. This allows adequate time for any specific treatment (such as surgery or rehabilitation) to be performed before the resumption of intense training.

The screening protocol

The three components of the elite sportsperson screening process are:

1. medical screening
2. musculoskeletal screening
3. performance screening.

The proposed protocol is shown in the box opposite.

This protocol is also available as a downloadable PDF file in the *Clinical Sports Medicine* masterclasses at www.clinicalsportsmedicine.com.

The first two parts contain the athlete's personal details and consent form, and a brief summary. This is followed by the review of systems, family history, and vaccinations, which can be filled in by the sports-

person. Previous injuries are noted in the next section. A general medical examination follows, then the various tests are performed. This is followed by an example of a lower limb musculoskeletal screening protocol.

The medical screening

Cardiovascular screening

The important subject of sudden cardiac death (SCD) in sport has been addressed in a previous chapter (Chapter 48). A comprehensive cardiovascular history and physical examination should be included in the screening protocol. Unfortunately the history and examination generally fail to detect many causes of SCD including cardiomyopathies which are, in many countries, the most common cause of sudden cardiac death in young sportspeople. As a result it has been proposed that a 12-lead electrocardiograph (ECG/EKG) be included in the screening protocol as has been the case in Italy for the past 25 years.[1]

While this is not able to detect all cardiomyopathies, 95% of individuals with hypertrophic cardiomyopathy (HCM)[2] and 80% of individuals with arrhythmogenic right ventricular cardiomyopathy (ARVC)[3] exhibit electrocardiographic abnormalities. The experience in Italy is that since the inclusion of EKG in the screening protocol, there has been a 90% reduction in mortality from SCD in competitive sportspeople.[4]

Whether or not to include an ECG/EKG in the screening program is still a matter of considerable debate. Borjesson and Dellborg[5] recently addressed the question "Is there evidence for mandating electrocardiogram as part of the pre-participation examination?" They concluded that there are firm scientific grounds to state that the sensitivity of screening with ECG/EKG is vastly superior to, and the cost-effectiveness significantly better than, screening without ECG/EKG. Furthermore they stated that cardiac screening without ECG/EKG is not cost-effective and may be only marginally better than no screening at all and at a considerably higher cost. The difficulties in feasibility and liability issues for recommending ECG/EKGs in some countries need to be acknowledged but must be dealt with within those countries/systems.

Borjesson and Dellborg[5] proposed that, on ethical grounds, the reasons (logistical, legal, economic) for not screening individual sportspeople should be clearly stated as the current evidence suggests that the

Screening protocol

ATHLETE MEDICAL INFORMATION
(Athlete to complete)

Name.. Date of birth...

Address ....

Home phone .... Mobile ....

Email..

Next of kin... Relationship to you ....

Contact number...

Local doctor's name and contact details ....

Examination by .... Date..

Consent

- I agree to undertake this procedure in order to enable medical staff to ensure that I am fit to train/compete.
- I am aware that medical fitness issues may be discussed with the coaching staff/ physiotherapist.
- I understand that the information contained in this form is otherwise confidential and can only be released with my consent.
- I confirm that no medical information has been knowingly withheld that could affect the decision as to whether I am medically fit to train and compete.

Consent to discuss with coaching staff/phsyio   Yes/No

Received advice re drug doping procedures + informing whereabouts   Yes/No

Name..

Signature .... Date ....

PHYSICIAN USE ONLY

Outcome of screening

Yes	No	
☐	☐	Is the athlete medically fit to compete and train in a high-performance program?
☐	☐	Are there any medical issues that warrant further assessment?
☐	☐	Are any further vaccinations required?

FURTHER EXAMINATIONS/RECOMMENDATIONS ....

....

....

....

....

....

....

....

....

Name of doctor... Date ....

Signature ....

E

REVIEW OF SYSTEMS

Yes   No   Unsure

Cardiovascular system

❏ ❏ ❏   Any history of chest pain/dizziness/passing out during/after exercise?

❏ ❏ ❏   Anyone in family died suddenly under age of 50?

❏ ❏ ❏   Ever had heart abnormality/murmur diagnosed by a doctor?

❏ ❏ ❏   Any abnormal heart rate/palpitations/irregular heartbeat?

❏ ❏ ❏   Ever had high BP/cholesterol?

❏ ❏ ❏   Any restrictions in sport due to heart problems?

❏ ❏ ❏   Any relatives with heart problems—arrhythmia/HOCM?

Respiratory system

❏ ❏ ❏   Any current or history of asthma/chest tightness/coughing spells during/after exercise?

❏ ❏ ❏   Any history of recurrent chest infections/bronchitis?

Neurological system

❏ ❏ ❏   Any history of concussion/fits/faints?

❏ ❏ ❏   Any history of loss of consciousness/head injury requiring time off training/playing?

❏ ❏ ❏   Any problems with your vision—need glasses/contact lenses?

Gastrointestinal and genitourinary systems

❏ ❏ ❏   Any problems with bowels—constipation/diarrhea/GI upset?

❏ ❏ ❏   Any problems with passing urine/urine infections?

Female athletes only

❏ ❏ ❏   Have you started your periods? If so, at what age ....

          What is the date of your last gynecological examination/PAP smear? .../.../...

❏ ❏ ❏   Have you ever missed your period for more than 6 months?

❏ ❏ ❏   Does your menstruation affect your performance?

General health

❏ ❏ ❏   Any history of recurrent infections?

❏ ❏ ❏   Any loss of appetite/weight loss?

❏ ❏ ❏   Any recurrent ear/nose/throat/sinus infections?

❏ ❏ ❏   Any skin problems—eczema/psoriasis/dermatitis?

❏ ❏ ❏   Any sleeplessness/muscle aches?

❏ ❏ ❏   Do you have any chronic illnesses/see a physician regularly for a medical problem?

          ....

          ....

❏ ❏ ❏   Do you take any prescribed medication or supplements?

          ....

          ....

❏ ❏ ❏   Do you have any allergies? ....

❏ ❏ ❏   Any history of smoking, and quantity? ....

❏ ❏ ❏   Any history of alcohol intake, and quantity? ....

❏ ❏ ❏   Any TUEs in past 12 months? ....

          ....

Family medical history

Is there any family history of the following (parents/brothers/sisters):

❑ ❑ ❑ heart disease/stroke/hypertension?
❑ ❑ ❑ cancer/blood disease?
❑ ❑ ❑ vascular problems/DVT?
❑ ❑ ❑ arthritis/chronic joint or muscle problems?
❑ ❑ ❑ diabetes?
❑ ❑ ❑ allergies/asthma?
❑ ❑ ❑ hormonal problems e.g. thyroid dysfunction?

Infections/vaccinations

❑ ❑ ❑ Any history of infections requiring treatment in hospital?
❑ ❑ ❑ Any history of infections caught outside the UK?
❑ ❑ ❑ Any history of blood transfusions?
❑ ❑ ❑ Any history of hepatitis A/B/C?

Date of any of following infections/vaccinations

Tetanus:	Rubella:	Influenza:	Polio:
Typhoid:	Hep A:	Hep B:	
Yellow fever:	Chicken Pox:	Men C:	

Other vaccinations: ....

....

❑ ❑ ❑ Any history of hospital admission other than for a sports-related injury?

....
....
....

❑ ❑ ❑ Any history where unable to play due to a medical illness other than injury?

....
....
....
....

Any other issues?

....
....
....
....
....

E

HISTORY OF INJURIES SUSTAINED DURING TRAINING/PLAYING

	Previous season	Two seasons ago	Three seasons ago	Four seasons ago
Games played				
Started				
Substituted				
Minutes on pitch				
Games missed due to injury				

Date of injury	Nature of injury	Management and time off from training/ playing

GENERAL MEDICAL EXAMINATION

Weight ....kg   Height .... m

Preferred dominant side .... Usual position played...................................

Cardiovascular
Pulse rate .... Rhythm ....
HS .... Apex.................................... BP ..../...............

Respiratory
RR .... Peak flow rate ....

	Right	Left
Gastrointestinal		
Hernias		
External inguinal ring palpation		
ENT		
Eyes		
Fundoscopy		
Visual acuity		

Skin
Any evidence of abnormal moles?..
Any evidence of eczema/dermatitis/psoriases?..

Neurological

	Right side		Left side	
Tone				
Upper limb	✓	x	✓	x
Lower limb	✓	x	✓	x
Power				
Upper limb	✓	x	✓	x
Lower limb	✓	x	✓	x
Coordination				
Upper limb	✓	x	✓	x
Lower limb	✓	x	✓	x
Reflexes				
Ankle	✓	x	✓	x
Knee	✓	x	✓	x
Triceps	✓	x	✓	x
Biceps	✓	x	✓	x
Supinator	✓	x	✓	x

E

INVESTIGATIONS

I give my consent to the following further investigations.

Name..

Signature .... DATE..

	Normal	Abnormal	Comment
Bloods			
FBC/U+E	✓	x	....
LFT/TFT	✓	x	....
Glucose	✓	x	....
Clotting	✓	x	....
Lipids	✓	x	....
Vit B12/folate	✓	x	....
Iron/ferritin	✓	x	....
RBC Mg/zinc	✓	x	....
Calcium/phosphate/vit D	✓	x	....
Uric acid	✓	x	....
ESR/CRP	✓	x	....
Sickle cell/thalassemia	✓	x	....
Creatine kinase	✓	x	....
Hep A/B/C	✓	x	....
HIV	✓	x	....
Urine dipstick	✓	x	....
Blood group	✓	x	....
ECG/EKG	✓	x	....
Echocardiogram	✓	x	....
MRI/X-rays/Ultrasound			
Lumbar	✓	x	....
			....
Hips	✓	x	....
			....
Knees	✓	x	....
			....
Ankles	✓	x	....
			....
Shoulders	✓	x	....
			....

LOWER LIMB MUSCULOSKELETAL EXAM

	RIGHT SIDE	LEFT SIDE
Feet and ankles		
Foot posture index (FPI): *score −12 to +12*	....	....
Ankle DF lunge: *big toe to wall*	.... cm	.... cm
Calf endurance: *no of reps*	....	....
Achilles palpation: *pain*	✓ x	✓ x
thickening	✓ x	✓ x
Ankle antero-lat drawer:	Norm/mild/mod/severe	Norm/mild/mod/severe
Inversion stress test:	Norm/mild/mod/severe	Norm/mild/mod/severe
Ankle plantarflexion: *range*	.... deg	.... deg
Star excursion balance test	.... cm	.... cm
Posterior impingement sign	✓ x	✓ x
Mid-foot/bifurcate ligament test (*pain/no pain*)	✓ x	✓ x
Syndesmosis/Foot ER (*pain/no pain*)	✓ x	✓ x
General observation		
General palpation...		
Knees		
Effusion: brush/swipe test	✓ x	✓ x
Passive ROM: Flexion	.... deg	.... deg
Extension	.... deg	.... deg
Patellar apprehension	✓ x	✓ x
ACL laxity (Lachman's)	✓ x	✓ x
PCL laxity (Post drawer)	✓ x	✓ x
MCL laxity (0 and 30°)	✓ x	✓ x
LCL laxity (0 and 30°)	✓ x	✓ x
Joint line tenderness	✓ x	✓ x
Waddle walk (Full WB, deep knee flex, ext rot) *pain*	✓ x	✓ x
General observation		
General palpation		
Hamstrings		
Hamstring length—active knee extension (AKE)	.... deg	.... deg
90/90 Hip flex strength—dynamometer	.... n	.... n
Single leg hamstring bridges: *no of reps*	....	
General observation		
General palpation		
Quadriceps		
Prone knee bend	.... deg	.... deg
General observation		
General palpation		

ISOKINETIC TESTING

		60 degrees	120 degrees	240 degrees
HAMSTRINGS	Left			
	Right			
	Contra-lateral difference			
QAUDRICEPS	Left			
	Right			
	Contra-lateral difference			
	H/Q ratio			

Hips and groins   RIGHT SIDE   LEFT SIDE

Adductor squeeze: 45° with dynamometer   .... n   .... n
Hip IR (sitting off bed)   .... deg   .... deg
Hip ER (sitting off bed)   .... deg   .... deg
Thomas test—hip flexor   above/level/below neutral   above/level/below neutral
Hip flexion impingement test (*pain/no pain*)   ✓   x   ✓   x
FABER's (*pain/no pain*)   ✓   x   ✓   x
Bent knee fall out (BNFO)—*fibula head to plinth*   .... cm   .... cm
Anterior hip capsule—ASIS to plinth   .... cm   .... cm
General observation ....
General palpation ....

Lumbar spine

Forward flexion (Schobers)   .... cm   .... cm
Extension (Schobers)   .... cm   .... cm
Quadrant—L/R (*pain/no pain*)   ✓   x   ✓   x
Back muscle endurance—Biering-Sorensen > *2 mins*   ✓   x   ✓   x
Slump neural test   ✓   x   ✓   x
SIJ pain positive tests   ✓   x   ✓   x
SIJ ASLR & SIJ closure   ✓   x   ✓   x
General observation ....
General palpation ....

Inner core

TA/multifidus/pelvic floor—activation with RTUS   ....
Inner core—most effective cues   ....

Functional testing

3 × hop for distance   .... cm   .... cm
Single-leg hop for height   .... cm   .... cm
Multi-hop test (*no of balance corrections*)   ....

Quality of movement testing

Single-leg deep squats (comment on quality)   ....
Single-leg "running man" × 5 (comment on quality) ....
Dynamic lunges (comment on quality)   ....
Hip/pelvis dissociation exercises (comment on quality) ....
Jump landing posture—varus knee position
    (comment on quality)   ....

ECG/EKG should be mandatory in pre-participation screening of sportspeople.

In the same journal issue, Drezner and Corrado agreed that the pool of scientific evidence supports the efficacy and cost-effectiveness of ECG/EKG screening for sportspeople.[6] They also acknowledge that in most countries there are still feasibility issues and practical concerns regarding false-positive results, cost-effectiveness, physician infrastructure, and healthcare resources for large-scale implementation of ECG/EKG screening. These issues should be addressed through physician education and use of contemporary standards for ECG/EKG interpretation in young sportspeople. A particular emphasis must be in distinguishing physiologic cardiac adaptations from underlying pathology to minimize false-positive results (Chapter 49, Tables 49.4b-c).[6] Similarly, a *British Medical Journal* head-to-head debate highlighted divergent opinions among two eminent sports medicine groups on the value of ECG/EKG in preventing sudden cardiac death.[7, 8]

A number of sporting bodies now require an ECG/EKG to be performed prior to participation. For the 2010 FIFA World Cup, both ECG/EKG and echocardiograph were mandatory. The questions relating to cardiovascular problems in our questionnaire are adapted from those recommended by the American Heart Association (see box below).[4]

Questions relating to cardiovascular problems

- Have you ever passed out, become dizzy, or had chest pain during or after exercise?
- Has anyone in the family died suddenly and unexpectedly before the age of 50?
- Have you ever had a heart abnormality or murmur diagnosed by a doctor?
- Have you ever had an abnormal heart rate, palpitations, or irregular heartbeats?
- Have you had high blood pressure or high cholesterol?
- Has a physician ever denied or restricted your participation in sport because of heart problems?
- Have any of your relatives ever had cardiomyopathy, Marfan syndrome, long QT syndrome, or a significant heart arrhythmia?

Adapted from those recommended by the American Heart Association[4]

Medical health

Generally, fit, young sportspeople have very little occasion to visit a physician. Some of the sportspeople will not have been to see a physician for many years and may not have a regular general practitioner, especially if their sporting prowess has resulted in them moving from their hometown. The examining physician should not assume that basic medical procedures such as auscultation of the heart and blood pressure measurement have ever been performed on the sportsperson. The screening questionnaire necessarily focuses on the more common conditions affecting young sportspeople.

Asthma and exercise-induced asthma have a significant prevalence of both under- and over-diagnosis, as well as under- and over-treatment. The efficacy of different methods of screening[9] for the presence of asthma and exercise-induced asthma are described in Chapter 50. The standard questions in our protocol are:

- Do you have asthma, chest tightness, wheezing, or coughing spells during or after exercise?
- Have you been tested in an accredited laboratory?

Obviously, many items could be included in a health questionnaire in an attempt to detect some abnormality. Apart from the cardiovascular and respiratory questions mentioned above, we include the following questions in our questionnaire:

- Do you have a history of concussion, fits, or faints?
- Do you have any history of loss of consciousness or head injury requiring time off training/playing?
- Any problems with your vision? Do you require glasses or contact lenses?
- Do you have any problems with your bowels such as constipation, diarrhea, GI upset?
- Do you have any problems with passing urine, or urine infections?
- Do you have any history of recurrent infections?
- Do you have any recent loss of appetite or weight loss?
- Do you have any recurrent ear, nose, throat, or sinus problems?
- Do you have any skin problems—eczema, psoriasis, dermatitis?
- Do you have any chronic illnesses or see a physician regularly for a medical problem?
- Do you take prescribed medication or supplements?
- Do you have any allergies?
- Have you ever been a smoker? If so, when and how much?

- What is your weekly alcohol intake?
- Does anyone in your family have any of the following medical problems—heart disease, stroke, hypertension, cancer, blood disease, vascular problems, DVT, arthritis, chronic joint or muscle problems, diabetes, allergies, asthma, hormonal problems (e.g. thyroid)?
- Have you ever had an infection that has required treatment in hospital?
- Have you had infections while overseas?
- Have you ever had a blood transfusion?
- Have you had hepatitis?
- Have you ever had surgery or required hospitalization?

In our clinical experience, the incidence of mild depression among high-level sportspeople is quite significant. The medical screening presents an opportunity for the sportsperson to discuss their depression. If the sportsperson complains of excessive fatigue, depression should be considered among other possible causes of the fatigue:

- Have you, or a close relative, ever suffered from depression?
- Have you ever suffered from excessive fatigue or overtraining?

Menstrual abnormalities are commonly associated with intense athletic activity in females and may lead to significant bone loss resulting in stress fractures and osteoporosis. Therefore, it is important to include questions designed to detect abnormal menstruation in the questionnaire:

- Have you started your periods? _____
  If so, what age _____?
- Date of your last gynecological examination/PAP smear? _____ / _____ / _____
- Have you ever missed your period for more than 6 months?
- Does your menstruation affect your performance?

The screening also presents an opportunity to check the vaccination status of the sportsperson:

- Vaccinations (please put dates if you have had any of the following):
  - Tetanus
  - Rubella (German measles)
  - Influenza
  - Typhoid
  - Hepatitis A
  - Hepatitis B
  - Yellow fever
  - Chickenpox
  - Meningitis C
  - Polio

Hepatitis A and B may be in a combination vaccine, usually a series of three injections over 6 months. Measles, mumps, and rubella is a combination vaccine, part of the usual childhood series.

Baseline data collection

In certain sports, particularly at the elite level, regular monitoring of hematological and biochemical parameters is performed to detect early evidence of deficiencies. An example is the monitoring of serum ferritin levels in female endurance sportspeople.

Table 62.1 on pages 1198–1200 lists the possible blood and biochemical tests that can be performed in a comprehensive screening of a professional sportsperson.

Blood and biochemical tests that may be included in the medical screening of a sportsperson are:

- FBC/U+E
- LFT/TFT
- Glucose
- Clotting
- Lipids
- Vit B_{12}/folate
- Iron/ferritin
- RBC Mg/zinc
- Calcium/phosphate/vit D
- Uric acid
- ESR/CRP
- Sickle cell/thalassemia
- Creatine kinase
- Hep A/B/C
- HIV
- Urine dipstick
- Blood group.

In contact sports such as football, team physicians are increasingly using neuropsychological testing to monitor recovery from concussion (Chapter 17). A team physician might wish to perform baseline testing before the season to use as a comparison in the recovery process.

Musculoskeletal screening

A full injury history should be taken and any deficits remaining post-injury should be fully assessed with a view to designing a rehabilitation program to restore full function. This is important as athletes will often resume athletic participation following a significant injury and yet still have considerable limitations in strength, range of movement, proprioception, etc.

The questionnaire asks the sportsperson to describe the nature and date of any previous injury and list any residual problems. They are asked to describe the nature, date, and symptoms of any current injury.

Which tests?

Every musculoskeletal screening should be individually developed to address the specific risks involved in each sport or each sportsperson. Before deciding whether to include any specific tests to your screening, you must consider what you are trying to achieve with each test. There are multiple reasons for wanting do musculoskeletal screening. These are:

* to prevent injury
* to establish a clinical baseline
* to establish a functional baseline
* to achieve a holistic picture of the sportsperson.

The box below shows information about these reasons.

When planning a musculoskeletal screening one should start with a spreadsheet that clearly outlines which tests are to be included and why (some tests may fit into more than one category). Ideally this would be supported by references to the supporting literature. See Table 62.1 overleaf for an example of this process—a musculoskeletal screening tool for footballers, where the primary concern is the lower limb.

Imaging

As a result of the musculoskeletal history and examination, imaging may be appropriate to help determine the current state of a region (e.g. knee) that has been previously injured. As part of "pre-signing" medicals in high-level sports, the team doctor may deem it appropriate to perform MRI of all vulnerable joints, both to detect any abnormality and to use as a baseline in case of future injury. This is obviously an expensive exercise.

Injury prevention

There is limited research evidence showing associations between the presence of certain risk factors and

Reasons for including the various tests in musculoskeletal screening

Prevent injury

There is limited evidence to support any one musculoskeletal screening protocol in terms of preventing injury. There is, however, reasonably good evidence to support a number of different individual tests that may highlight risk of injury and this is the primary goal of screening. It is achieved by finding any physical deficits that may pre-dispose a sportsperson to injury and then implementing appropriate rehabilitation programs to correct them.

For a test to be included on this basis, there should be evidence to show that it is reliable, valid, and predictive of injury.

A clinical baseline

Having a "normative" value on a test when a sportsperson is fully fit makes a subsequent test far more relevant when the player is re-examined after any injury. The second test results can be seen in context of that particular sportsperson and how he or she presents when uninjured.

For a test to be included on this basis, there should be evidence to show that it is both reliable and valid.

A functional baseline

It is often difficult to decide when a sportsperson who is going through the injury rehabilitation process should be allowed to return to play. Reliable information from functional tests taken when that sportsperson was uninjured gives a good baseline for comparison and may help you in clearing the person to return to play.

For a test to be included on this basis, there only needs to be evidence to show that it is likely to be reliable.

A holistic picture of the sportsperson

There are many tests that you may consider worthwhile to gain a full insight into an individual player. These may include tests that involve making judgments on the "quality of movement," on the "feel" of a test, or simply clinical tests that have not yet been proven reliable or involve significant levels of subjective observations.

These tests may be included in your screening as part of a holistic approach. However it must be recognized that without any proof of reliability or validity, their results must be taken as part of a general holistic appraisal and not as reliable measures for comparison.

Table 62.1 Musculoskeletal screening tests

Football pre-season screening

	Possibly predicts injury	Clinical baseline measure	Functional baseline measure	Holistic picture
Personal details				
Age	*			
Games played in past 3 seasons	*		*	
Regular strappings		*		
Orthotics		*		
Dominant foot				*
Position				*
Detailed past history of injury	*			*
Feet and ankles				
Foot Posture Index	*			
Ankle dorsiflexion lunge	*	*		
Calf endurance (repeated raises)	*		*	
Achilles palpation		*		
Anterolateral drawer		*		
Inversion stress test		*		
Ankle plantarflexion range		*		
Star excursion balance test			*	
Posterior impingement sign				*
Midfoot/bifurcate ligament test				*
Syndesmosis test (foot external rotation + ankle dorsiflexion)				*
General observation				*
General palpation				*
Knees				
Effusion—brush/swipe test		*		
Passive knee ROM		*		
Patellar apprehension test		*		
ACL laxity (Lachman's)		*		
PCL laxity (Posterior drawer)		*		
MCL laxity (0° and 30°)		*		
LCL laxity (0° and 30°)		*		
Joint line tenderness		*		
Waddle walk (deep flexion/rotation/FWB)				*
General observation				*
General palpation				*

Football pre-season screening

	Possibly predicts injury	Clinical baseline measure	Functional baseline measure	Holistic picture
Hamstrings				
Isokinetic testing	*			
Hamstring length—active knee extension		*		
90/90 Hip flexion strength—with dynamometer		*		
Single-leg hamstring bridges			*	
General observation				*
General palpation				*
Quadriceps				
Isokinetic testing	*			
General observation				*
General palpation				*
Hips and groins				
Adductor squeeze power—with dynamometer at 45° knee flexion	*	*		
Hip internal rotation—sitting off bed	*	*		
Hip external rotation—sitting off bed		*		
Thomas test		*		
Hip flexion impingement sign		*		
FABER's sign		*		
Adductor length—bent knee fall out		*		
Anterior hip capsule tightness		*		
General observation				*
General palpation				*
Lumbar spine/sacroiliac joint				
Flexion (Schober's)		*		
Extension (Schober's)		*		
Quadrant pain provocation testing		*		
Back muscle endurance—Biering-Sorensen	*	*		
Slump neurodynamic test		*		
SIJ pain positive tests		*		
SIJ ASLR +/− SIJ closure		*		
General observation				*

continues

Table 62.1 Musculoskeletal screening tests *continued*

Football pre-season screening

	Possibly predicts injury	Clinical baseline measure	Functional baseline measure	Holistic picture
General palpation				*
Inner core				
Transvere abdominus/multifidus/ pelvic floor—activation with real-time ultrasound		*		
Inner core—most effective cues				*
Functional testing				
3 × hop for distance			*	
Single-leg hop for height			*	
Multiple hop test			*	
Bridging hold test			*	
Quality of movement testing				
Single-leg deep squats				*
Single leg "running man x 10"—active Trendelenburgs				*
¼ decline squat single-leg—active Trendelenburgs				*
Dynamic lunges				*
Hip/pelvis dissociation exercises				*
Jump landing posture—varus knee control				*

DF = dorsiflexion; ER = external rotation; IR = internal rotation; ROM = range of movement; SIJ = sacroiliac joint; FABER = flexion abduction external rotation; ASLR = active straight leg raise; RTUS = real-time ultrasound; ACL = anterior cruciate ligament; PCL = posterior cruciate ligament; MCL = medial collateral ligament; LCL = lateral collateral ligament; FWB = full weight bear

particular injuries. One example of an association is the presence of menstrual abnormalities or an eating disorder leading to the development of stress fractures. Clinical experience suggests other possible relationships. The medical screening process is an opportunity to identify potentially correctable risk factors and implement measures designed to reduce that risk. It is also an opportunity to ensure that appropriate equipment (such as helmets, mouth guards, and shin pads) is used in relevant sports by asking questions such as:

* Do you wear orthoses?
* Do you wear any protective equipment when playing your sport?

Performance screening

The screening process is an opportunity to assess areas that may not necessarily have an impact on health but may affect performance. There are components of both the medical and musculoskeletal screening that will highlight deficiencies that may directly affect performance. From the medical screen, issues are nutrition, psychology, and biomechanics. A brief assessment of these areas may suggest a problem that can then be followed up by an appropriate expert.

Sports in which competitors have to be under a specified weight (e.g. wrestling, boxing) or where being thin is thought to have some aesthetic (gymnastics) or performance (distance running) advantage provide an additional risk to consider during medical screening. Athletes in these sports may be at an increased risk of unhealthy eating habits or the development of an eating disorder. If you are wary of this, common questions that should be included are:

- Do you have problems making weight for your sport?
- Do you follow any special diet (e.g. vegetarian, weight loss)?
- Have you ever had a nutritional deficiency diagnosed (e.g. iron, vitamin B$_{12}$)?

From the musculoskeletal screen issues such as decreased muscle strength, joint range, poor joint stability, or poor performance on functional testing may all highlight areas that contribute to suboptimal performance. Any issue that could be suspected of contributing to decreased performance should be discussed in detail among the sports science and medicine teams to achieve the appropriate multidisciplinary solutions.

The final part of screening to optimize performance may also require the input of sports scientists and/or coaches. There are likely to be simple, reliable, sport-specific tests that can be done on players in pre-season to identify weak areas. Team clinicians and coaches can then develop specific programs to address those weaknesses and improve athletic performance. These programs need to be developed in a sport- and athlete-specific way.

Advantages and disadvantages of screening

Professional relationship with the sportsperson

The medical screening process on entry into a professional team or institute program gives an opportunity for the team physician to commence his or her professional relationship with the sportsperson. It enables the physician to become fully aware of the person's past history and gives an insight into the person. The sportsperson is given the opportunity to list on the form any issues that he or she would like to discuss with the physician.

Education

The medical screening presents an opportunity for the physician to educate the sportsperson on many issues, such as injury prevention (stretching, warm-up), immediate injury management (RICE),

nutrition, appropriate equipment, the use of medications and supplements, and vaccinations.

Problems

There are a number of problems inherent in the medical screening program.

There is no uniformity of protocols. Some are very long (up to 40 pages of questionnaire, with full muscle and joint examinations) and are therefore time-consuming for both sportsperson and physician, resulting in compliance issues. In some cases multiple screenings are performed by different organizations on the same person. For example, an elite 18-year-old basketballer in Australia may have screenings as part of his professional team, his state or national institute of sport, the national basketball team, and the Australian Olympic team. All will probably be slightly different and this represents a waste of time and resources.

Another issue is that of follow-up. Often an extensive screening is performed with various recommendations emanating from it. Unfortunately there is frequently no mechanism for follow-up. We recommend that the examining physician or Chief Medical Officer (CMO) follows up with the sportsperson either by telephone or in person approximately six weeks after the screening to ensure that the recommended actions have taken place.

Who has access to the data from the screening? The sportsperson? The team or organization? The examining physician? The information obtained from medical screening is bound by the same confidentiality restrictions as any medical information. Certainly, the sportsperson has the right to the information. How the information is presented to the sportsperson is another area of controversy. Sportspeople who are traveling constantly (e.g. tennis players or golfers on international circuits) should have the screening information in their possession at all times so that the treating practitioner can be made aware of any problems. One suggestion is that traveling sportspeople have a "medical passport" (hard copy and CD-ROM) containing all relevant information.

The confidential medical information obtained at the screening should not be distributed to the team or institute administration. It should be held by the CMO of the organization and forwarded to relevant medical and paramedical practitioners only as necessary and appropriate for the optimal management of the athlete, and only with the athlete's consent (see also Chapter 67).

📄 RECOMMENDED READING

Best TM. The preparticipation evaluation: an opportunity for change and consensus. *Clin J Sport Med* 2004;14(3):107–8.

Brukner PD, White S, Shawdon A et al. Screening of athletes—the Australian experience. *Clin J Sport Med* 2004;14(3):169–77.

Fallon KE. Utility of hematological and iron-related screening in elite athletes. *Clin J Sport Med* 2004;14(3):145–52.

Gabbe BJ, Bennell KL, Wajswelner H et al. Reliability of common lower extremity musculoskeletal screening tests. *Phys Ther Sport* 2004;5:90–7.

📑 REFERENCES

1. Corrado D, Pelliccia A, Bjornstad HH et al. Cardiovascular pre-participation screening of young competitive athletes for prevention of sudden death: proposal for a common European protocol. Consensus Statement of the Study Group of Sport Cardiology of the Working Group of Cardiac Rehabilitation and Exercise Physiology and the Working Group of Myocardial and Pericardial Diseases of the European Society of Cardiology. *Eur Heart J* 2005;26(5):516–24.

2. Maron BJ. Hypertrophic cardiomyopathy. *Phys Sportsmed* 2002;30(1):19–24.

3. Marcus FI. Electrocardiographic features of inherited diseases that predispose to the development of cardiac arrhythmias, long QT syndrome, arrhythmogenic right ventricular cardiomyopathy/dysplasia, and Brugada syndrome. *J Electrocardiol* 2000;33(Suppl):1–10.

4. Corrado D, Basso C, Pavei A et al. Trends in sudden cardiovascular death in young competitive athletes after implementation of a pre-participation screening program. *JAMA* 2006;296(13):1593–601.

5. Borjesson B, Dellborg M. Is there evidence for mandating electrocardiogram as part of the pre-participation examination? *Clin J Sport Med* 2011;21:13–17.

6. Drezner J, Corrado D. Is there evidence for recommending electrocardiogram as part of the pre-participation examination? *Clin J Sport Med* 2011;21(1):18–24.

7. Pelliccia A, Corrado D. Can electrocardiographic screening prevent sudden death in athletes? Yes. *BMJ* 2010;341:c4923.

8. Bahr R. Can electrocardiographic screening prevent sudden death in athletes? No. *BMJ*. 2010;341:c4919.

9. Holzer K, Brukner PD. Screening of athletes for exercise-induced asthma. *Clin J Sport Med* 2004;14(3):134–8.

Chapter 63

Providing team care

with JILL COOK, PETER HARCOURT and CHRIS MILNE

Contrary to popular belief, there most certainly is an "I" in "team." It is the same "I" that appears three times in "responsibility."   Amber Harding

One of the most challenging yet enjoyable aspects of sports medicine is involvement in team care. Working with a team provides opportunities to:

- belong to a team and share in its successes and failures
- work closely with athletes on a regular basis
- implement preventive strategies
- manage acute injuries from the time of injury
- closely monitor the progress of injuries
- learn and develop decision-making skills in a competitive environment
- work closely with other clinicians and disciplines and thereby develop your own skills (e.g. massage, nutrition advice)
- liaise closely with coaching and fitness staff
- better understand the demands of the particular sport
- understand the psychological pressures on the players
- fully appreciate the importance of team dynamics.

Many of the skills gained in the team environment can be incorporated into everyday practice.

The off-field team

The size and make-up of the medical support team often depends on the size of the sporting team, the standard of competition, and financial considerations. Frequently, the support team will consist of just one individual, who may be either a physiotherapist, physician, massage therapist, or trainer. Specialists from various branches of medicine can contribute to the sports and exercise medicine team.[1-3] A solo clinician should develop a network of supporting colleagues who can assist where additional specialized management is indicated.

Support teams for professional sports often consist of representatives of different health disciplines. Whoever is responsible for assembling such a team must ensure that all the individuals have high professional standards and work well collectively.[4] The ethical issues facing professional teams' clinicians are different from those of volunteer clinicians' (see also Chapter 67).[5-8] If possible, the professional sporting team should have access to the services of a sports physician, physiotherapist, massage therapist, podiatrist, dietitian, psychologist, orthopedic surgeon, and sports trainer as well as the coaching and fitness staff. Clearly defining roles may help avoid conflict. Ideally, one member of this team should be the leader and take ultimate responsibility for difficult management decisions and the smooth running of the group.

Coaching and fitness staff

Clinicians caring for a team have multiple responsibilities. Although their primary responsibility is to the sportspeople, they also have responsibilities to the coach, the team management, and fellow support staff. Thus, the medical team should liaise closely with the coaching and fitness staff for the sportspeople's benefit. Fitness staff should be included in the regular sports and exercise medicine team meetings to maintain a coordinated approach. This enables the clinicians and fitness staff to have input into injury prevention training programs (Chapter 9). It is particularly important that medical and fitness staff collaborate closely in injury rehabilitation so that a player's post-injury rehabilitation transfers seamlessly from the physiotherapist/athletic trainer's care to that of the conditioning coach. Unfortunately, cases have arisen where the player receives conflicting instructions from "competing" members of the rehabilitation team!

Pre-season assessment

As team sports have a distinct playing season, all players should be reviewed at the end of a season to plan appropriate individual treatment and off-season rehabilitation. Arrangements for how this will be monitored by the sports clinician should also be made. Similarly, there should be full assessment of all team members at the beginning of pre-season training. New recruits should be evaluated as soon as possible.

The pre-season assessment consists of a comprehensive history and examination. The purpose of this assessment is to look for evidence of medical illness and evaluate musculoskeletal conditions. Further tests may be performed if necessary. The assessment is described further in Chapters 61 and 62 and is often carried out in conjunction with a fitness assessment.

Educate team members—health literacy

Working with a team provides an ideal opportunity to educate sportspeople and coaches. Pre-season assessment provides one opportunity. Other teaching moments arise during follow-up consultations or treatments and in regular brief talks given to the team by the sports medicine practitioners. Experienced team clinicians have found that relevant topics of education include:

- injury prevention strategies (e.g. appropriate warm-up, stretching, strength programs, protective equipment)
- the importance of players reporting injuries early
- the importance of the first 24 hours in acute injury management
- a request that the players report any other treatment being received for their injuries
- nutritional advice
- advice regarding permitted and banned medications—team members should be told that it is essential that they do not take any medication without checking first with the medical staff.[9]

In many cases the most important education for athletes in sports that are subject to drug testing is advice regarding permitted and banned medications—team members should be told that it is essential that they do not take any medication without checking first with the medical staff.[9]

Other essentials

Issues such as the quality of the medical facilities, thorough record-keeping, respect for athletes' confidentiality, availability of equipment, and having an active presence around the team all contribute to being a successful team clinician.

Facilities

Adequate facilities are essential. If possible, there should be a separate, well-equipped room at training and competition venues to enable proper assessment and treatment of injuries. This room should have a door to enclose it from the training venue when privacy and confidentiality are required. The room should contain a good light source, a couch, and appropriate equipment and medications.

It is the responsibility of the sports medicine team to ensure that adequate first-aid equipment is present at both training and competition venues (Chapter 47). This includes:

- stretchers (including an appropriate stretcher for the transport of spinal injuries)
- resuscitation equipment, such as an automatic external defibrillator (Chapter 48)
- an Air-Viva for oxygen
- splints, bandages, and crutches
- an adequate supply of ice.

There should also be easy access for an ambulance if required, and a telephone with emergency numbers (ambulance, nearest hospital) must be readily available.

Record-keeping

As in all medical practice, records are important for patient care and medico-legal purposes. It becomes particularly important when more than one member of the medical team is involved in the treatment of a patient. Excellent software programs allow practitioners to maintain records on a laptop computer. This is particularly useful when there are various training venues or when traveling with the team (Chapter 64).

Confidentiality

It is essential that members of the sports medicine team do not discuss a player's medical problems with other team members, officials, or the media without the player's express permission.[10] The British Olympic Association has published a position statement on athlete confidentiality that clearly tells coaches, managers, administrators, and other team officials that the athlete comes first![11, 12] A key platform of the code of conduct states: "Coaches wish to be informed of athletes' problems. This can only occur with the consent of the individual athlete." The British Olympic Association has produced a consent form (see box) that other sporting bodies may consider using. The code emphasizes that even if the athlete has signed a consent form, he or she may still withhold consent for any specific consultation, test, or treatment.

The "team clinician's bag"

The contents of the "team clinician's bag" will vary depending on the type of sport, access to other facilities, and the clinician's own preferences. Some suggested contents for the "team clinician's bag" for a sports clinician responsible for a contact sport team without immediate access to more sophisticated facilities are listed in the box.

Athlete consent form as proposed by the British Olympic Association[12]

Athlete consent form

I agree/do not agree to relevant details from consultations, test or treatments undertaken by

.... in (year/season)

.... being released to (e.g. coach/performance director/member of support staff) ....

I realize that refusal to give consent for the release of details will not affect my access to medical care, treatment, or testing. It cannot be guaranteed that others will not use this refusal of consent in relation to selection.

Consent can be withdrawn at any time, and only notice of its withdrawal will be released to those specified above.

I have read the notes on informed consent and fully understand them.

Signed..

Date..

(to be signed also by parent or guardian for those under 18 years)

The "team clinician's bag"

Diagnostic instruments

Oral/rectal thermometer

Stethoscope

Blood pressure cuff

Ophthalmoscope

Otoscope

Pencil torch

Sutures/dressings

Needle holders

Forceps

Scissors (nail clippers, small sharp scissors, and tape scissors)

Scalpel

Scalpel blades

Syringes (2 mL, 5 mL, 10 mL)

Needles (23G, 21G, 16G)

Sutures (nylon 3/0, 4/0, 5/0, 6/0; dexon 3/0)

Suture cutters

Local anesthetics (1% lignocaine [lidocaine], 1% lignocaine [lidocaine] with adrenalin [epinephrine], marcaine)

Steri-strips (3 mm [0.12 in.], 6 mm [0.25 in.])

Alcohol swabs

Gauze swabs

Dressing packs

Antiseptic solution (povidone iodine)

Tincture of benzoin

Melolin dressing pads

Dressing strips

Bandaid plastic strips

Crepe bandages

Tube gauze

Medications

Oral analgesics (e.g. paracetamol [acetaminophen], aspirin)

Injectable analgesics (e.g. pethidine [meperidine], morphine)

Nonsteroidal anti-inflammatory drugs (NSAIDs)

Antibiotics (e.g. amoxycillin [amoxicillin], erythromycin, flucloxacillin, doxycycline, metronidazole)

Antacid tablets

Antinausea (e.g. prochlorperazine [oral/IM])

Antidiarrheal (e.g. loperamide)

Fecal softeners

Antihistamines

Bronchodilators (e.g. salbutamol inhaler, beclomethasone inhaler)   *continued*

E

continued

50% glucose solution	Adhesive spray
Sedatives	Coolant spray
Throat lozenges	Finger splints
Cough mixture (e.g. senega and ammonia)	Cervical collar (soft and hard)
Creams/ointments (antifungal, antibiotic, corticosteroid, anti-inflammatory)	Sterile gloves, goggles, mask
Eye/otic antibiotic drops	Eye kit including irrigation solution, fluorescein, eye patches, local anesthetic and antibiotic eye drops, contact lens container (Chapter 19)
Tetanus toxoid	Sunscreen
Equipment	Massage oil/heat rubs
Oral airway	Intravenous fluid and giving sets
Bolt cutters/screwdriver	
Air splints	**Other**
Triangular bandage (sling)	Urine reagent strips
Tongue depressors	Safety pins
Cotton-tipped applicators	Tampons
Rigid sports tape (2.5 cm [1 in.], 3.8 cm [1.5 in.], 5 cm [2 in.])	Contaminated needle container
Hypoallergenic tape	Spare shoelaces
Dressing retention tape	Batteries
Elastic adhesive bandage (2.5 cm [1 in.], 5 cm [2 in.])	Safety razor
Compression bandage (5 cm [2 in.], 7.5 cm [3 in.], 10 cm [4 in.])	Plastic bags (for ice)
Adhesive felt	Heel raises
Adhesive foam	Heel wedges
Blister pads	Arch supports
	List of banned substances

Being part of the "team chemistry"

To be effective, the members of the sports and exercise medicine team must attend training sessions and competition. In this way, the medical team members gain an understanding of the physical and psychological demands placed on sportspeople. It also enables them to observe specific training routines and techniques, which in turn may lead to an increased understanding of the mechanism of injury.

This assists the clinician in devising a sport-specific rehabilitation program. Regular attendance also means that the clinician is likely to be present when an acute injury occurs and is therefore able to institute appropriate therapy. The final advantage of being in constant attendance is an increased acceptance by the team members and officials of the clinician as a valuable part of the team.

📄 RECOMMENDED READING

Anderson L. Writing a new code of ethics for sports physicians: principles and challenges. *Br J Sports Med* 2009;43(13):1079–82.

Anderson L. Contractual obligations and the sharing of confidential health information in sport. *J Med Ethics* 2008;34(9):e6.

Apple D. Team physician—bad ethics, bad business, or both? *Orthopedics* 2002;25(1):16,26.

American College of Sports Medicine. Mass participation event management for the team physician: a consensus statement. *Med Sci Sports Exerc* 2004;36(11):2004–8.

McFarland EG, Dobrowolski PA, Srikumaran U et al. Lessons in sports medicine: advice from experience. *Clin Sports Med* 2007;26(2):265–83.

Woods CB, Moynihan A. General practitioners' knowledge, practice and training requirements in relation to doping in sport. *Ir Med J* 2009;102(1):8–10.

📑 REFERENCES

1. Batt ME, Maryon-Davis A. Sport and exercise medicine: a timely specialty development. *Clin J Sport Med* 2007;17(2):85–6.

2. Dubey SG, Roberts C, Adebajo AO et al. Rheumatology training in the United Kingdom: the trainees' perspective. *Rheumatology (Oxford)* 2004;43(7):896–900.

3. Speed C, Jaques R. High-performance sports medicine: an ancient but evolving field. *Br J Sports Med* 2011;45(2):81–3.

4. Fu FH, Tjoumakaris FP, Buoncristiani A. Building a sports medicine team. *Clin Sports Med* 2007;26(2):173–9.

5. Goforth M, Almquist J, Matney M et al. Understanding organization structures of the college, university, high school, clinical, and professional settings. *Clin Sports Med* 2007;26(2):201–26.

6. Menetrey J. [Medical supervision of sports events and the role of the team physician]. *Rev Med Suisse* 2008;4(166):1717–18, 1720–2.

7. Anderson L. Contractual obligations and the sharing of confidential health information in sport. *J Med Ethics* 2008;34(9):e6.

8. Tucker AM. Ethics and the professional team physician. *Clin Sports Med* 2004;23(2):227–41, vi.

9. Woods CB, Moynihan A. General practitioners' knowledge, practice and training requirements in relation to doping in sport. *Ir Med J* 2009;102(1):8–10.

10. Dunn WR, George MS, Churchill L et al. Ethics in sports medicine. *Am J Sports Med* 2007;35(5):840–4.

11. British Olympic Association. The British Olympic Association's position statement on athlete confidentiality. *Br J Sports Med* 2000;34:71–2.

12. MacAuley D, Bartlett R. The British Olympic Association's position statement on athlete confidentiality. *Br J Sports Med* 2000;34:1–2.

E

Chapter 64

Traveling with a team

with JILL COOK, PETER HARCOURT, CHRIS MILNE,
and HASHEL AL-TUNAIJI

We may run, walk, stumble, drive, or fly, but let us never lose sight of the reason for the journey,
or miss a chance to see a rainbow on the way. Gloria Gaither

Traveling with a team presents the sports medicine clinician with a considerable challenge.[1] Providing quality medical support for a traveling team requires far more than good professional skills. Successful practitioners develop multiple treatment skills, strong interpersonal skills, and effective personal coping mechanisms.

The traveling sports clinician often has to fill a number of roles. These may include physician, physiotherapist, massage therapist, podiatrist, trainer, fitness adviser, dietitian, psychologist, assistant team manager, assistant coach, statistician, travel coordinator, and baggage supervisor. Traveling with a team often involves working long hours in less than ideal conditions with sportspeople and coaches who are under great stress due to the demands of competition and travel.[2]

Preparation

Adequate planning is fundamental for a successful trip. Preparation includes researching the destination, providing advice for team members, and obtaining supplies. It also requires thorough self-preparation.

Things to do before travel

- Be well-versed about the travel destination. Climate, altitude, level of pollution, accommodation, food, water, vaccination requirements, security, and the level of medical support at the destination must all be anticipated.[3–5] If the competition is at altitude or in the heat, acclimatization will be necessary (Chapter 58). This may entail arriving well before the competition begins.

- Obtain details about the team's accommodation. In hot climates, air-conditioning may be an advantage for comfort although it may delay heat acclimatization. Sleeping arrangements must be adequate. Particularly tall sportspeople require extra-long beds. Try to guarantee a dedicated medical room when traveling with a large team. If this is not possible, the clinician should have a hotel room to himself or herself which doubles as a treatment room and permits players to be treated with privacy and confidentiality as needed.

- Research the type of food available at the venue. If there is not sufficient high-carbohydrate food available or if the food is likely to be unfamiliar and unappetizing, have appropriate meals prepared. It may be necessary to bring food and drink from home.

- Discover whether the water supply is of good quality and if there is a risk of gastrointestinal infections, especially "traveler's diarrhea." This will affect planning and determination of whether precautionary measures are needed.

- Vaccination requirements vary considerably between countries. Cholera and typhoid vaccinations are required in certain countries, particularly in Asia, South America, and Africa.[6,7] Travel to tropical areas may require malaria prophylaxis. Immunizations for the sportsperson are listed in Table 64.1. The vaccination and malaria prophylaxis requirements are constantly changing and up-to-date information should be obtained from local or national travel advisory services and from databases such as the websites of the World Health Organization and the Centers for Disease Control and Prevention in Atlanta

Table 64.1 Immunizations for the sportsperson according to the World Health Organization in January 2011

Routine vaccination	Selective use for travelers	Mandatory vaccination in particular countries
• Diphtheria, tetanus, and pertussis • Hepatitis B • Haemophilus influenzae type b • Human papillomavirus • Influenza • Measles, mumps, and rubella • Pneumococcal disease • Poliomyelitis • Rotavirus A • Tuberculosis (BCG) • Varicella	• Cholera • Hepatitis A • Japanese encephalitis • Meningococcal disease • Rabies • Tick-borne encephalitis • Typhoid fever • Yellow fever	• Yellow fever (depending on the country) • Meningococcal disease and polio (required by Saudi Arabia for pilgrims; updates are available on www.who.int/wer)

(see Recommended websites at the end of the chapter). This is particularly important for illnesses where the disease pattern is rapidly evolving.[8]

• Assess medical support services such as ambulance and hospitals at the destination. Travel insurance, including medical cover, should be arranged for all team members.

Assessing team members' fitness prior to departure

• Contact all team members, including coaches and officials, to ask about present and past injuries and illnesses. Often officials can cause anxiety for a traveling clinician because of their medical conditions such as coronary artery disease. Attempts must be made to treat injuries prior to departure. This benefits the sportsperson and reduces the subsequent load on the medical team. It may be necessary to liaise with the player's own treating clinician.

• In many cases the team will assemble at a pre-departure camp. The medical support team should attend the camp to meet sportspeople and officials, perform comprehensive assessments, and initiate treatment for any medical or musculoskeletal problem.

• The clinician should ask whether the coach and officials expect non-medical tasks to be performed during the forthcoming trip. This may include responsibility for warm-ups, nutrition advice, and attention to strength and conditioning. Videotaping has been needed at times!

Advice for team members

A vital part of the preparation is to provide advice for the team members about air travel, jet lag,

precautions required with food and drink during the tour, heat acclimatization, drugs, and sexual activity. This advice may be given prior to departure by hand-outs, emails, or via team websites. Written background information is most effective when supplemented by team or individual discussions at the pre-departure camp or at a meeting soon after arrival at the destination.

Nutrition

It is not easy for sportspeople to maintain good dietary practices when traveling. In some situations, it may be difficult to obtain sufficient amounts of appropriate foods. Sportspeople should be advised about wise food choices.[9] Fast food outlets are convenient but often supply high-fat foods inadequate in carbohydrate. In addition, sportspeople often eat in village dining rooms or restaurants where buffet-style food is offered. They may overeat if this situation is unfamiliar. Since the sportsperson may also be tapering and so burning fewer calories, weight gain can occur. Swimmers seem to be particularly susceptible to this problem.

Sportspeople should be advised about the importance of maintaining an adequate fluid intake in hot climates.[5] If there is uncertainty about the quality of the water, tap water and ice should be avoided and fluid intake restricted to bottled water. To minimize the risk of traveler's diarrhea, sportspeople should wash their hands carefully before meals (using bottled water where necessary) or use an antiseptic hand wash/wipe. They should eat only food that has been cooked, and avoid shellfish, salads, unpasteurized milk products, and unpeeled fruits.

E

Gender verification

Gender verification is no longer required at most World Championships or the Olympic Games. Staff should check with the relevant international federation.

Drug testing

If drug testing is to be performed, team members must be reminded that certain medications, including many over-the-counter medications used in the treatment of coughs and colds, are banned (Chapter 66). It is vital that sportspeople do not take any medications without checking with the medical support team. It is also important to explain the drug testing procedure as this may be stressful, particularly for younger or inexperienced sportspeople. If possible, a member of the medical team should accompany the sportsperson to the drug test, both to provide emotional support and to ensure that the correct testing procedure is followed.

Up-to-date information about drug testing and banned substances can be obtained from national sporting organizations and Olympic Federations. Telephone inquiry hotlines have been established in many countries and some are listed in Table 64.2. Remember to discuss illicit drug use, such as marijuana and ecstasy, and how this may be detected in drug testing.

Sexual activity

Team members should be warned of the dangers of acquiring sexually transmitted infections such as gonorrhea, chlamydia, hepatitis B, or HIV. Abstinence guarantees prevention, but condoms should be made available.

The medical bag

The next step in the preparation for travel is to assemble the medical kit of equipment and supplies. The contents of the medical kit will vary depending on the make-up of the medical support team, the size of the overall team, the destination, and the local facilities available. It is advisable to be as self-sufficient as possible. Obtaining equipment and medications in a foreign country may be difficult, time-consuming, and expensive.

The suggested contents for a medical kit for a sports clinician accompanying a team to overseas competition are shown in the box opposite. Sportspeople should be advised that it is their responsibility to provide any supplements (e.g. vitamin, mineral, or carbohydrate supplements) they may wish to take. However, the clinician should ensure that banned substances are not inadvertently included by a sportsperson.

Table 64.2 Contact details for obtaining drug information in various countries

Country	Drug information hotline telephone number and/or website address
World Anti-Doping Agency (WADA)	www.wada-ama.org/ www.wada-ama.org/en/Anti-Doping-Community/NADOs/List-of-NADOs/ lists all of the anti-doping organizations in alphabetical order by country
Australia	Australian Sports Anti-Doping Authority, (02) 6206 0200, www.asada.org.au
Brazil	Brazilian Agency for Doping Control, (21) 3433-5777, www.cob.org.br
Canada	Canadian Centre for Ethics in Sport, 1800 672 7775, www.cces.ca, (613) 748 5755
France	Agence française de lutte contre le dopage, (0) 1 40 62 76 76, www.afld.fr
United Kingdom	0171 380 8029 (UK Sports Council), 0181 864 0609 or 0181 992 1963 (British Olympic Association Medical Centre), www.ukad.org.uk, 0800 032 2332
India	National Anti-Doping Agency, India, www.nada.nic.in
Japan	Japan Anti-Doping Agency, www.anti-doping.or.jp/
New Zealand	Drug Free Sport NZ, 0800 DRUGFREE = 0800 378 437, www.drugfreesport.org.nz/
South Africa	SA Institute for Drug-Free Sport, (12) 841 2686/2639, www.drugfreesport.org.za/
Spain	Agencia Estatal Antidopaje, www.aea.gob.es/
United States	US Anti-Doping Agency (USADA), (800) 233 0393, www.usada.org

Contents of the medical bag for interstate and international travel

Diagnostic instruments
Oral/rectal thermometer
Stethoscope
Blood pressure cuff
Ophthalmoscope
Otoscope (auroscope)
Pencil torch

Sutures/dressings
Needle holders
Forceps
Scissors: nail clippers, small sharp scissors, and tape
    scissors
Scalpel
Scalpel blades
Syringes (2 mL, 5 mL, 10 mL)
Needles (23G, 21G, 16G)
Sutures: nylon 3/0, 4/0, 5/0, 6/0; dexon 3/0
Suture cutters
Local anesthetics:
    1% lignocaine (lidocaine)
    1% lignocaine (lidocaine) with adrenalin
    (epinephrine)
    marcaine
Steri-strips (3 mm [0.12 in.], 6 mm [0.25 in.])
Alcohol swabs
Gauze swabs
Dressing packs
Antiseptic solution (povidone iodine)
Tincture of benzoin
Melolin dressing pads
Dressing strips
Band-Aid plastic strips
Crepe bandages
Tube gauze

Medications
Oral analgesics (e.g. paracetamol [acetaminophen],
    aspirin)
Adrenalin (epinephrine) for anaphylaxis
NSAIDs (nonsteroidal anti-inflammatory drugs)
Tramadol
Antibiotics (e.g. amoxycillin [amoxicillin],
    erythromycin, flucloxacillin, doxycycline,
    metronidazole)
Antacid tablets
Antinausea agent (e.g. prochlorperazine [oral/IM])
Antidiarrheal agent (e.g. loperamide)
Oral contraceptive pill
Fecal softeners
Antihistamines
Bronchodilators (e.g. salbutamol inhaler,
    beclomethasone inhaler)
50% glucose solution
Sedatives and hypnotics

Throat lozenges
Cough mixture (e.g. senega and ammonia)
Creams/ointments: antifungal, antibiotic,
    corticosteroid, anti-inflammatory
Eye/otic antibiotic drops
Tetanus toxoid

Equipment
Oral airway
Bolt cutters/screwdriver
Air splints
Triangular bandage (sling)
Tongue depressors
Cotton-tipped applicators
Rigid sports tape (2.5 cm [1 in.], 3.8 cm [1.5 in.],
    5 cm [2 in.])
Hypoallergenic tape
Dressing retention tape
Elastic adhesive bandage (2.5 cm [1 in.], 5 cm [2 in.])
Compression bandage (5 cm [2 in.], 7.5 cm [3 in.],
    10 cm [4 in.])
Adhesive felt
Adhesive foam
Blister pads
Adhesive spray
Coolant spray
Finger splints
Cervical collar, soft and hard
Sterile gloves, goggles, mask
Eye kit including irrigation solution, fluorescein, eye
    patches, local anesthetic and antibiotic eye drops,
    contact lens container (Chapter 19)
Sunscreen
Massage oil/heat rubs
Electrotherapy (e.g. TENS, portable laser)
Portable couch
Alarm clock
Intravenous fluid and giving sets

Other
Urine reagent strips
Safety pins
Tampons
Contaminated needle container
Spare shoelaces
Flexible orthoses
Batteries
Safety razor
Plastic bags (for ice)
Heel raises
Heel wedges
Arch supports
List of banned substances
Transformer and dual voltage connector
    (if appropriate)

When traveling internationally, take a written inventory of the contents of each bag for customs purposes. A non-confrontational response to customs checks usually works best! Do not carry narcotic analgesics; tramadol is effective for severe pain and is subject to fewer restrictions in most countries.

Clinician's hip bag

A small hip bag[10] is a useful way to carry small quantities of basic medical supplies when traveling by plane; this contains the essentials to provide team members symptom relief until hold baggage can be accessed. Note that even small nail scissors are not permitted in cabin baggage.

The precise contents will vary according to individual team needs, but consider including:

- simple analgesics (e.g. paracetamol [acetaminophen], soluble aspirin)
- adhesive plasters (e.g. bandaids)
- nose spray (e.g. oxymetazoline)
- throat lozenges

Guidelines for preparation for travel with a team

1. Information
   (a) Venue
      (i)   climate
      (ii)   altitude
      (iii) pollution
      (iv)   accommodation
      (v)   food
      (vi)   security
      (vii) water
      (viii) vaccination requirements
      (ix)   malaria prophylaxis
      (x)   available medical support
   (b) Team members
      (i)   past and present illnesses and injuries
2. Advice
   (a) air travel
   (b) jet lag
   (c) food
   (d) drink
   (e) drugs
   (g) infectious diseases
3. Medical kit
   (a) medication
   (b) tape, bandages etc.
   (c) other (e.g. nutritional supplements)

- antiemetic (e.g. metoclopramide, prochlorperazine buccal tablets)
- antidiarrheal (e.g. loperamide)
- sedatives (e.g. triazolam) on long night flights.

Self-preparation

Finally, it is important for the clinician to prepare himself or herself for travel. Because trips are always extremely busy, it is important to be well rested and in good health prior to departure. It is also important to spend time with loved ones prior to departure, especially for lengthy trips.

Air travel and jet lag

Air travel is an important part of professional and international sport. Short-distance air travel (up to three hours) does not appear to present any problems for the sportsperson.[11] However, extended air travel, often required for major events such as Olympic Games or World Championships, can provide significant problems.[12] Thus, high-level traveling sportspeople, team officials, and team physicians will benefit from education and action to ameliorate the effects of long-distance travel, such as jet lag, on optimal performance.

Jet lag occurs when the body is unable to adapt rapidly to a time zone shift and normal body rhythms lose synchrony with the environment. In general, it is a benign and self-limited condition. The major symptoms of the condition are poor sleep, daytime fatigue, and poor performance.[13] The sleep deprivation secondary to the flight can be mostly made up in a day whereas jet lag lasts much longer.[14] A number of factors influence the severity of jet lag symptoms.[15, 16] These include individual difference, number and direction of time zones crossed, temporal and seasonal timing of flight, age, impaired health, lack of previous travel experience, sleep deprivation, dehydration, stress, alcohol and excessive food intake.[17]

Pathophysiology

The suprachiasmatic nuclei (SNC), located in the hypothalamus, produce a timing signal that modulates circadian rhythms of sleep and alertness, core body temperature, and certain hormonal secretions, such as melatonin and cortisol. The SNC, via the eyes, senses darkness and sends a timing signal to the pineal gland. This maintains the nocturnal secretion of melatonin for 10–12 hours. Beta blockers can inhibit melatonin secretion. Although the SNC signal is essential, melatonin secretion requires darkness.

Light intensity of >50 lux (lx) can cause some melatonin inhibition and light intensity of >2000 lx completely suppresses it. Therefore, summer's long days and short nights will suppress melatonin secretion despite the 12-hour SNC "on" signal.

The 12-hour SNC "on" signal despite melatonin inhibition by light is considered an operational definition for biological night. Therefore, the nocturnal SNC signal synchronized to home night time (biological night) may result in melatonin secretion if an un-adapted jet traveler is placed in a dimly lit room. Melatonin can be measured in saliva, plasma, and urine.[13]

The circadian rhythm is regularly synchronized to the 24-hour day by the environmental time cues termed "zeitgebers," such as alternation of light and darkness, ingestion of melatonin, sleep/awake schedules, as well as activity and meal timing.[13, 17]

Traveling across multiple time zones (>3 time zones) causes a temporary misalignment between the circadian clock (lag) and the sleep/wake schedule at the destination time zone that is slow to reset

(Fig. 64.1). The symptoms of jet lag dissipate as the circadian clock gradually resets (adjusts) to the time cues at the new destination time zone.[7, 8, 13, 14] Although there is considerable individual variability, it is estimated that it takes about one day per time zone for the biological clock to resynchronize with the sleep/wake schedule.[9, 13]

Prevention of jet lag

The faster the biological clock adapts to the new time zone the shorter the symptomatic period. Thus speeding up the adaptation is the primary goal.[17] Traveling (>3 time zone) for a stay longer than five days, circadian adaptation is desirable.[17, 18] Preflight adjustment to travel may speed up adaptation.[20] A summary of the general guidelines and principles are presented in Table 64.3 and Table 64.4 overleaf.

PRACTICE PEARL Athletes should spend time outdoors, rather than indoors, during the sunlight hours particularly on arrival at the destination. Natural light resets circadian rhythm.

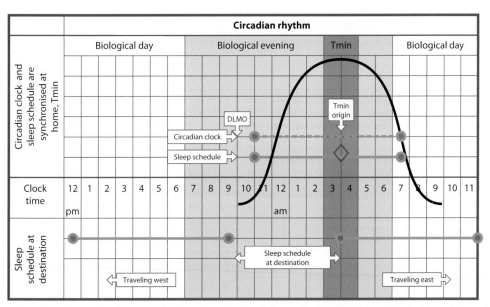

Figure 64.1 The relationship between the circadian clock and sleep schedule for an individual with an 8-hour sleep episode (11 pm–7 am) and the lag effect induced by east or west travel
Top: Biological evening is the time during which melatonin is secreted ~9 pm (DLMO: dim light melatonin onset) and lasts for 8–12 hours. **Tmin origin** is minimum core temperature estimated to occur at 3–5 am (hours before wake-up time) for most individuals, 2–4 am for larks (morning type, M-type), and 5–7 am for owls (evening type, E-type) based on the sleep pattern for the last week. Tmin coincides roughly with the maximum circulating nocturnal melatonin level
Bottom: Sleep schedule at destination where there has been abrupt east or west travel. The biological evening will be situated during the day after an 8–12 hour time zone shift (the largest possible shift).

Table 64.3 General guidelines for adaptation strategies based on the length of stay at destination and numbers of zones crossed[17]

Length of stay at destination	Recommended strategy
Long (>5 days)	• Pre-travel sleep schedule to destination • Timed light exposure and avoidance • Timed melatonin intake
Intermediate (3–4 days) OR Short (1–2 days) OR Game aligned with circadian time of peak performance	• Work around sleep and alertness times • Schedule critical activity to daytime in the departure zone • Airplane light exposure/avoidance strategy • Short-term measure to maintain alertness (caffeine) and sleep (naps and short-acting hypnotics)

Table 64.4 General principles to help clinicians customize jet travel schedules for sportspeople traveling in any directions across multiple time zones

Goal: Get Tmin within sleeping episodes and avoid being awake at the sleepiest time (Tmin)

Eastward jet lag (Fig. 64.3 on page 1216)	Westward jet lag (Fig. 64.4 on page 1217)
Differences	
• Requires advancing the circadian clock • Harder and slower to adjust (1-hr/day) • Abrupt 12-hour time zone shift, takes 8–9 days to adjust • Destination Tmin = origin Tmin + number of time zones crossed	• Requires delaying the circadian clock • Easier and quicker to adjust (1.5 to 2 hr/day) • Abrupt 12-hour time zone shift, takes 4–5 days to adjust • Destination Tmin = origin Tmin – number of time zones crossed
Similarities	
• Maximum or largest shift is 12-hour time zones • Traveler feels sleepy in hours surrounding Tmin and difficulty sleeping at hours far from Tmin • Traveler will experience impaired daytime activity near Tmin • Phase shifting needs to be applied daily for several days to produce results	

Tmin origin = minimum core temperature, estimated to occur at 3–5 am (hours before wake-up time) for most individuals, 2–4 am for larks (morning type, M-type), and 5–7 am for owls (evening type, E-type) based on the sleep pattern for the last week. Tmin coincides roughly with the maximum nocturnal melatonin level in the circulation

Experienced practitioners and many successful sportspeople also suggest that low-intensity physical activity early after arrival helps promote adjustment to the new time zone. Seasoned air travelers have developed a series of guidelines to minimize the adverse effects of long-distance travel. These are shown in the tables; these may be photocopied and given to sportspeople.

Timed light exposure and avoidance

Light intensity and timing are the two important factors that influence phase shift the most. Exposure to bright light (sunlight ~3000 to 100 000 lx, light box ~1500 to 3500 lx or room light 100 to 550 lx) for 1–2 hours (continuous or intermittent) can help phase shifting. The magnitude of shift is greater as the light exposure gets closer to the Tmin (the minimum core temperature, which is estimated to occur at 3–5 am in most individuals). Light has more shifting effect at night when bright light is absent.

> Light exposure late in the sleep episode or in the early morning (i.e. after the Tmin phase advances) will promote phase shifting. The same light stimulus, when applied early in the sleep episode (i.e. before the Tmin) will delay phase shifting.[13, 14, 17, 19]

Timed light avoidance is equally important. Light avoidance can be achieved by staying in a dim light room (<10 lux) or wearing dark sunglasses.[19]

Light exposure should be augmented with light avoidance during flight or on arrival to a new destination as it ensures a unidirectional phase shifting. For instance, an eastward traveling sportsperson needs to maximize light exposure after Tmin and avoid or minimize light before Tmin to ensure phase advancement of the circadian clock (Fig. 64.2, top) and vice versa for the westward traveling sportsperson (Fig. 64.2, middle).[20] On the other hand, exposure to light before and after Tmin would result in no phase shifting (Fig. 64.2, bottom).

Timed melatonin pills

Despite being marketed as an over-the-counter sleeping aid, melatonin is not associated with sleep or increased sleepiness. Instead melatonin is considered a darkness signal. The timing of melatonin pills is more important than dose. It has more phase-shifting effect when there is less endogenous melatonin in the circulation. Therefore, the timed melatonin pills (3 mg) can help produce the greatest phase advance of the circadian clock when taken in the afternoon (~5 hours before dim light melatonin onset (DLMO) or 12 hours before Tmin), while phase delays occur when it is taken in the morning (Fig. 64.2).[14, 17]

Pre-travel sleeping schedule

Adjusting sleep schedules in 1–2 days (depending on number of zones crossed) prior to travel to gradually match the destination schedule could help with phase shifting. Sleep on flights should be avoided unless it is night at the destination.[21]

Synergistic approach

When combined with the pre-travel sleep schedule for the destination, timed light exposure/avoidance and melatonin pills can have a synergistic phase-shifting effect (Fig. 64.2, Fig. 64.3, and Fig. 64.4).

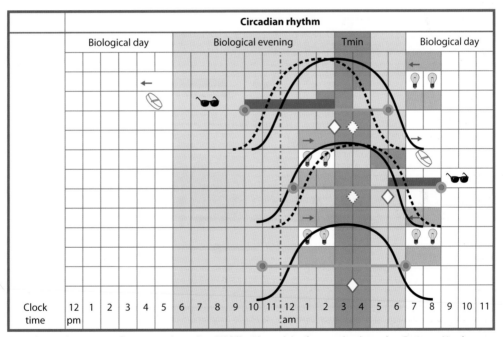

Top: Phase advancement for eastward traveler. **Middle:** Phase delay for westward traveler. **Bottom:** No phase shift.

Dark rectangle represents light avoidance period by staying in a dim light room or wearing dark sunglasses

⊘ = take melatonin   ◇ = Tmin

🕶 = wear dark glasses to avoid sun exposure   💡 = light/sun exposure

Figure 64.2 The augmentive effect of timed light avoidance and timed melatonin to timed light exposure around the Tmin

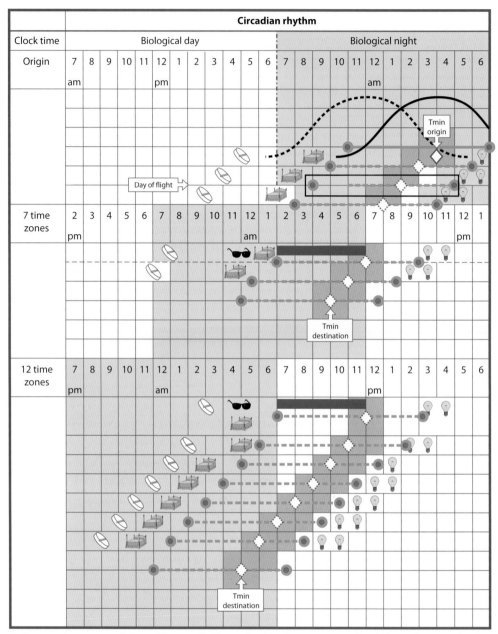

Dark rectangles represent light avoidance period by staying in a dim room or wearing dark sunglasses on the day of arrival

= take melatonin   ◇ = Tmin

= wear dark glasses to avoid sun exposure   💡 = light/sun exposure

= bedtime

Figure 64.3 Synergistic approach for a traveler planning to cross seven time zones (intermediate shift) or continue to twelve time zones (large shift) east. To avoid circadian clock lag (misalignment), the traveler's biological clock needs to be gradually advanced (1 hour/day)

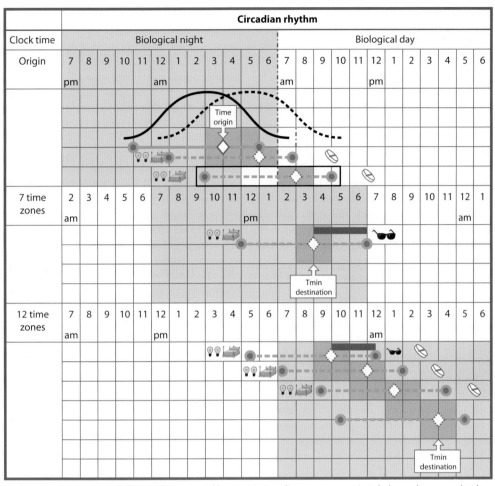

Dark rectangle represents light avoidance period by staying in a dim room or wearing dark sunglasses on the day of arrival

= take melatonin	◇ = Tmin
= wear dark glasses to avoid sun exposure	💡 = light/sun exposure
= bedtime	

Figure 64.4 The same traveler after his or her circadian clock has been adjusted to the sleep schedule at the destination is returning to destination of origin crossing seven time zones (intermediate shift) or twelve time zones (large shift) west. Now, the traveler's circadian clocked needs to be gradually delayed (2 hour/day)

Symptomatic treatment for jet lag

If the traveling sportsperson still suffers jet lag symptoms, despite the gradual shifting, stimulants such as slow-release caffeine 300 mg could be helpful to induce daytime alertness, and hypnotics such as zolpidem 10 mg could be used to counteract night insomnia.

The medical room

A medical room should be established soon after arrival. Ideally, this should be a large room separated from any bedrooms. Hours of treatment should be specified so that the practitioner has adequate time for meal and exercise breaks. This must be strictly enforced as sportspeople have a tendency to extend these hours. An appointment sheet enables sports-people to plan their treatment. The clinician should ensure that sportspeople know the room number of the medical staff in case of emergencies at night. It is important that the team manager knows how to contact the medical staff if the medical room is unattended. It also helps if the medical staff obtains a room list for the sportspeople.

For trips involving a single venue, a portable examination couch (treatment table) is valuable for the comfort of both the sportsperson and treating clinician. A low, soft bed may not be an appropriate site for massage or spinal mobilization. On trips involving multiple venues, the advantages of having a treatment couch must be weighed against the inconvenience of transporting the couch. When traveling with two clinicians, a compromise is often to take one portable table and to use the hotel bed as a second treatment site.

Illness

Travelers' diarrhea

Traveler's diarrhea, the most common infectious illness encountered when on the road with a team, is generally due to non-viral pathogens such as enterotoxigenic *Escherichia coli*, *Salmonella*, *Shigella*, *Campylobacter*, or *Giardia lamblia*.[22] Prevention and management of travelers' diarrhea are discussed in Chapter 56.

Upper respiratory tract infections

Upper respiratory tract infections are common among traveling sportspeople. Moving from one environment to another exposes the sportsperson to different strains of respiratory viruses. Air travel and accommodation in air-conditioned hotels also increase the risk of upper respiratory tract infections. At events where drug testing is taking place, therapeutic options for the treatment of these infections are limited. Antihistamines may be helpful. Throat lozenges and corticosteroid nasal sprays can provide symptomatic relief. Early intervention with antibiotics should be considered.

There is some concern in a team situation of the possibility of cross-infection between teammates. Any team member with a significant viral or bacterial infection should be isolated to minimize the risk of the infection spreading.[23] This may involve the infected team member sleeping in a room away from other sportspeople and taking care when handling water bottles and towels.

Injury

A good time to implement injury prevention strategies is when a team is on the road. Strategies may include warm-up, stretching, strength maintenance, and soft tissue therapy. Traveling with a team also permits early intensive treatment of injuries, which, in conjunction with the high motivation of sportspeople, often results in some dramatic responses.

While on tour, the sports clinician may need to provide the services of other health professionals. For instance, if the sole clinician is a physician, he or she needs to be able to use electrotherapeutic modalities, and provide soft tissue therapy and spinal mobilization in the treatment of soft tissue injury. Similarly, a physiotherapist traveling with a team needs to have a broader understanding of medical issues than one who works exclusively in an office/clinic. Every opportunity should be taken to acquire the necessary skills before going on tour. However, the clinician who travels with a team cannot be an expert in all areas of knowledge. If faced with a problem beyond one's knowledge and experience, it is advisable to seek assistance, either locally or from a colleague at home.

Drug testing

The sports clinician must be familiar with the drug-testing rules for the particular competition, including the list of banned drugs and the testing procedure (Chapter 66). The clinician should attempt to meet the chief medical officer in charge of drug testing prior to the event. The medical support team needs to remind sportspeople constantly that they must not take any medication without approval.[24]

Sometimes a conflict arises when the clinician needs to decide whether to stay with a sportsperson who is undergoing drug testing (which may involve a wait of some hours) or to return to the location to treat other sportspeople. This should be discussed with players and the coaching staff prior to the situation. However, decisions may alter depending on the specific needs of each situation.

Local contacts

It is best to contact local medical officials before arrival. National consulates and embassies may provide useful sources of information about the quality of local medical personnel and facilities. On arrival and before competition begins, the traveling practitioner should meet local medical support staff.

In addition to facilitating immediate care of the competitors, this provides an opportunity to exchange ideas with clinicians from different backgrounds.

Psychological skills

One of the main roles of the medical team while on tour is to provide psychological support to the rest of the team. Travel can be extremely stressful for team members and this may be compounded by the stress of high-level competition. There is a tendency for team members, coaches, and officials alike to unburden their problems onto the medical staff. These problems may be related to poor performance or they may be personal problems. Personal conflicts within a team are common, particularly when the team is unsuccessful. It is important that the members of the medical support team retain a positive and professional attitude at all times.

The medical support team is expected to adopt a leadership role in team situations. The most difficult situation for medical team members is situations of conflict, particularly between the coach and one or more team members. It is essential that the medical team gives the coach its full support, while at the same time using its psychological and interpersonal skills for conflict resolution.

Personal coping skills—sustainability

The medical support team should adopt certain personal skills to enable it to cope with the stresses of traveling with a team.[15] It is also important to control the hours of work to ensure adequate time for meals, exercise, and sleep. It may also, on occasion, be necessary to give priority to certain team members who may play more important roles in a team sport. This needs to be explained to all team members. It is important at all times to adopt a positive mental attitude in spite of any excessive physical or emotional demands of the job.

On return from traveling with a team, it is time to rest and spend quality time with family and friends. This is the ideal time to review the tour and submit a tour report. It is also important to consider ways in which performance could be improved if further travel opportunities arise.

E

🌐 RECOMMENDED WEBSITES

Communicable Diseases Australia:
www9.health.gov.au/cda/Source/CDA-index.cfm;
www.healthinsite.gov.au/topics/Infectious_Diseases

US Centers for Disease Prevention and Control:
www.cdc.gov

World Health Organization (WHO):
www.who.int/topics/en/

WHO site on avian influenza:
www.who.int/csr/disease/avian_influenza/en/

📄 RECOMMENDED READING

Simon LM, Rubin AL. Traveling with the team. *Curr Sports Med Rep* 2008;7(3):138–43.

Tuli K. The Commonwealth Games and "Delhi belly": what India can learn from LA. *BMJ* 2010;341:c4507.

Succo G, Crosetti E, Mattiazzo A et al. 2006 XX Olympic and IX Paralympic Winter Games: the ENT experience. *Acta Otorhinolaryngol Ital* 2008;28(3):101–9.

Zuckerman JN, Bröker M, Worth C. 2010 FIFA World Cup South Africa: travel health issues and new options for protection against meningococcal disease. *Travel Med Infect Dis* 2010;8(2):68–73.

📋 REFERENCES

1. Milne C. New Zealand Olympic experience—Sydney 2000. *Br J Sports Med* 2001;35(4):281.
2. Waterhouse J, Reilly T, Edwards B. The stress of travel. *J Sports Sci* 2004;22(10):946–65.
3. Blumberg LH, de Frey A, Frean J et al. The 2010 FIFA World Cup: communicable disease risks and advice for visitors to South Africa. *J Travel Med* 2010;17(3):150–2.
4. Muza SR, Beidleman BA, Fulco CS. Altitude preexposure recommendations for inducing acclimatization. *High Alt Med Biol* 2010;11(2):87–92.
5. Igreja RP. Olympics in the tropics and infectious diseases. *Clin Infect Dis* 2010;50(4):616–17.
6. Pollack RJ, Marcus LC. A travel medicine guide to arthropods of medical importance. *Infect Dis Clin North Am* 2005;19(1):169–83.
7. Siedenburg J, Perry I, Stuben U. Tropical medicine and travel medicine: medical advice for aviation medical examiners concerning flight operations in tropical areas. *Aviat Space Environ Med* 2005;76(3 Suppl):A1–30.
8. Khan K, Freifeld CC, Wang J et al. Preparing for infectious disease threats at mass gatherings: the case of the Vancouver 2010 Olympic Winter Games. *CMAJ* 2010;182(6):579–83.
9. Reilly T, Waterhouse J, Burke LM et al. Nutrition for travel. *J Sports Sci* 2007;25 Suppl 1:S125–34.
10. Milne C. The doctor's hip bag: advice sheet. *NZ J Sports Med* 2003;31.
11. Samuels C. Sleep, recovery, and performance: the new frontier in high-performance athletics. *Phys Med Rehabil Clin N Am* 2009;20(1):149–59, ix.
12. Geertsema C, Williams AB, Dzendrowskyj P et al. Effect of commercial airline travel on oxygen saturation in athletes. *Br J Sports Med* 2008;42(11):577–81.
13. Sack RL. The pathophysiology of jet lag. *Travel Med Infect Dis* 2009;7(2):102–10.
14. Eastman CI, Burgess HJ. How to travel the world without jet lag. *Sleep Med Clin* 2009;4(2):241–55.
15. Winter WC, Hammond WR, Green NH et al. Measuring circadian advantage in Major League Baseball: a 10-year retrospective study. *Int J Sports Physiol Perform* 2009;4(3):394–401.
16. Reilly T, Edwards B. Altered sleep-wake cycles and physical performance in athletes. *Physiol Behav* 2007;90(2-3):274–84.
17. Arendt J. Managing jet lag: some of the problems and possible new solutions. *Sleep Med Rev* 2009;13(4):249–56.
18. Waterhouse J, Reilly T. Managing jet lag. *Sleep Med Rev* 2009;13(4):247–8.
19. Postolache TT, Hung TM, Rosenthal RN et al. Sports chronobiology consultation: from the lab to the arena. *Clin Sports Med* 2005;24(2):415–56, xiv.
20. Reilly T, Waterhouse J, Edwards B. Jet lag and air travel: implications for performance. *Clin Sports Med* 2005;24(2):367–80.
21. Waterhouse J, Reilly T, Atkinson G et al. Jet lag: trends and coping strategies. *Lancet* 2007;369(9567):1117–29.
22. Boggess BR. Gastrointestinal infections in the traveling athlete. *Curr Sports Med Rep* 2007;6(2):125–9.
23. Ewald AJ, McKeag DB. Meningitis in the athlete. *Curr Sports Med Rep* 2008;7(1):22–7.
24. Maughan RJ. Contamination of dietary supplements and positive drug tests in sport. *J Sports Sci* 2005;23(9):883–9.

Chapter 65

Medical coverage of endurance events

with TIMOTHY NOAKES

Three months ago, this seemed like a good idea! On the back of a t-shirt during a marathon

The organizers of endurance events are obliged to provide medical coverage both to enable competitors to have immediate access to optimal management of medical problems and to relieve the burden on local medical services. These endurance events include marathons, ultramarathons, triathlons and ironman triathlon events, as well as long-distance events such as walking, swimming, cycling, and cross-country skiing. Many of these events have large numbers of competitors with varying degrees of fitness.

Blisters, bruises, lacerations, and muscle cramps are the cause of a large number of presentations to the medical tent at these events. Overuse injuries may develop or be aggravated in sportspeople during an endurance event, and traumatic injuries may occur (e.g. as a result of a fall in a crowded running field or from a bike). Thermal injuries (heatstroke or hypothermia) are common (Chapters 58 and 59). As there is the possibility of cardiovascular collapse during such events, appropriate facilities, including an automatic external defibrillator (AED), must be available.

The precise medical services required depend on the particular sport, the duration and intensity of the activity, and the prevailing environmental conditions.[1] Experienced medical teams for endurance events are able to predict the expected numbers of casualties. It is vital to keep medical records for all sportspeople treated at a particular event, and to analyze these data for historical trends (Table 65.1).

In this chapter, we consider a marathon foot race with 1000 competitors as the basis for our recommendations. The figures should be adjusted according to the type of events and the number of competitors.

Table 65.1 The expected percentage of race starters at a sporting event with 1000 competitors likely to be admitted to the central medical care facility[1]

Activity	Percentage of race starters
Running	
• 42 km	2–20
• 21 km	1–5
Ultratriathlon >200 km	15–30
Cycling	5
Cross-country skiing	5

Race organization

Specific pre-race strategies to enhance the safety of the competitors include the following:

1. Schedule the race at a time of year and day when environmental conditions will not adversely affect performance or health. The medical director of the race should have the authority to cancel the race should adverse weather conditions prevail. The American College of Sports Medicine position statement recommends that if the wet bulb globe temperature index is above 28°C (82°F) or if the ambient dry bulb temperature is below –20°C (–4°F), organizers should consider canceling or rescheduling the event.[2]

2. Ensure adequate provision of carbohydrate-containing fluids en route, as this is essential.

3. Plan the race course so that the start and finish are in an area large enough to accommodate all spectators, participants, and medical facilities, and allow quick get-away routes for emergency vehicles. Place first-aid stations along the route

at points allowing for rapid access by emergency vehicles and ideally about 3–5 km apart.

4. Set pre-participation screening and qualification standards to ensure that unfit and inexperienced sportspeople do not place themselves at undue medical risk during the event.

5. Provide pre-race seminars for participants by medical personnel, as this can reduce the number of casualties. Advice may include:
   (a) correct training
   (b) consumption of sufficient carbohydrate before the race
   (c) eating a pre-race breakfast and drinking approximately 500–800 mL of a 4–7% carbohydrate solution every hour during the race
   (d) warning of the dangers of competing during or shortly after a febrile illness or while taking medications.

6. Ensure registration forms include questions regarding past and present medical history. This enables identification of, for example, sportspeople with diabetes, asthma, or coronary artery disease. Such sportspeople could be sent specific information advising them on safety precautions such as wearing a medical bracelet.

7. Implement an "impaired competitor" strategy. Strategically positioned first-aid helpers should be permitted to stop sportspeople who appear ill and unable to finish the course. There should be vehicles to transport these competitors to the finish line.

8. Advise the local hospital emergency department of the forthcoming race and the likely number and nature of casualties.

9. Hold meetings between the various members of the medical team (see below).

10. Ensure an emergency transport service is available to bring problem cases to the central medical facility or to the nearest hospital emergency facility. Helicopter evacuation has proven invaluable for prompt treatment of sportspeople suffering cardiac arrest and other life-threatening conditions.

The medical team

A medical director with appropriate expertise should be appointed a number of months prior to the staging of an endurance event to work closely with the event director. Early appointment of a medical director permits him or her to implement the pre-race strategies outlined above.

The medical director is responsible for the preparation of medical services and the supervision of the medical team on the day of the event. As endurance events are commonly held over a large area, communication between the different members of the medical team is the highest priority. The medical director should ensure adequate means of communication are available through the use of a two-way radio system or cellular network system.

The medical team should consist of appropriately trained doctors (sporting injuries and medical emergencies), physiotherapists, sports/athletic trainers, nurses, podiatrists, and masseurs. For an endurance event with 1000 competitors, the medical team should number approximately 20, of which at least one-third should be doctors. Approximately 60% of the medical team should be situated in the medical areas near the finishing line, 10% of the medical team should be at the finish line itself, 20% of the medical team should be distributed at the first-aid stations along the route, and 10% of the medical team should be patrolling the route in road cars, bicycles, or ambulances. In shorter events, a greater proportion of the medical team should be situated near the finish line.

The medical team should practice performing emergency procedures, sportsperson evacuation, and rapid assessment of the collapsed sportsperson prior to the event.

At peak periods in a large race of 10 000–20 000 competitors, it is common to have four to six sportspeople requiring attention every minute—a much faster rate of admission than even the busiest inner-city trauma centers. Thus, the medical team must have procedures well rehearsed. The preparation period also provides the medical director with the opportunity to ensure that all caregivers are using the most recent, evidence-based guidelines for the management of casualties.[3] In large events (>3000 competitors) and in adverse environmental conditions, at least one fully equipped mobile intensive care ambulance should be in attendance near the finish line. In small events, the ambulance service should be notified that the event is taking place.

First-aid stations

First-aid stations should be placed en route at strategic positions, providing a stretch and massage facility for cramping muscles, first aid (sticking plasters) for chafing skin and blistered feet, and identification of the at-risk runner who is confused or delirious. These stations provide a center from which sportspeople can be transported to the central medical facility or to a nearby hospital emergency department. Thus, stations should be positioned in areas that have good access to exit routes as needed.

In running events, first-aid stations should be about 3–5 km apart. Clinicians skilled in treating common musculoskeletal problems and administering emergency first aid should staff these. All first-aid stations should be in communication with the medical director. In larger events, a road car or ambulance should patrol the course with a doctor in attendance.

Drink stations are usually situated next to first-aid stations. It is important that the two be separated by at least 50 m so that the large crowds passing through the drink stations do not interfere with first-aid management. Additional drink stations should be situated at approximately 2–2.5 km intervals in events such as a marathon. For events lasting less than one hour, water is the fluid of choice for rehydration. For longer events, a glucose–electrolyte drink is preferred in order to improve endurance and to prevent hypoglycemia.

Medical facility at the race finish

The layout of the central medical station depends on the facilities available to the race organizers. Figure 65.1 shows the floor plan of the medical facility at the end of the 56 km Two Oceans ultramarathon foot race held annually in Cape Town, South Africa.[1] The green and red zones are for non-severe and severe cases, respectively. Other areas are allocated for the diagnostic laboratory, physiotherapy, medical supplies, and toilets.

Note that the red zone for emergencies such as cardiovascular collapse, hypothermia, and heatstroke is best located immediately adjacent to the triage station. The red zone can be constructed to afford a degree of privacy for distressed or seriously ill patients and permit discreet measurement of rectal temperatures. This area should be staffed by emergency-trained doctors and nurses. An ambulance should be located next to the red zone to allow rapid transport of emergency cases.

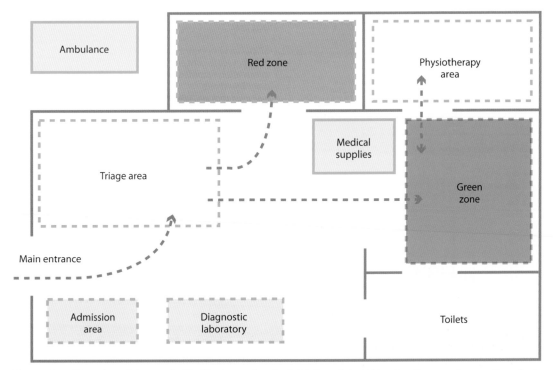

Figure 65.1 Floor plan of the medical facility located at the finish line of the 56-km Two Oceans ultramarathon foot race held in Cape Town, South Africa

The benefit of this type of system over the undifferentiated medical tent that was prevalent in the past is that potentially lethal emergencies are much less likely to be overlooked in the general hustle and bustle of sportspeople with numerous important but not life-threatening musculoskeletal problems. Figure 65.2 provides guidelines for the activities that need to be completed in each of the areas.

The equipment needs for a race medical center include the following:

1. Chairs and tables for the computer operator at the admission area, the laboratory technologist and the diagnostic equipment, and for the other medical equipment and drugs.

2. Stretchers for transporting collapsed sportspeople from the race finish to the medical facilities. These are also used for sportspeople to lie on in the green and red zones. Stretchers must be rigid so the foot can be elevated and so collapsed sportspeople can be nursed, at least initially, in the head-down position (Chapter 58). Some A-frame stands are needed to elevate the foot of the stretcher. These are removed once the sportsperson's cardiovascular status has normalized.

3. Blankets for each stretcher. These allow for discreet measurement of rectal temperature (Chapter 58) and treatment of hypothermia (Chapter 59).

4. Plastic baths large enough to accommodate the torso of 40–90 kg (6.3–14.5 stone) sportspeople. These are filled with ice water and are used to treat heatstroke (Chapter 58).

5. Refrigerator facility—a mobile refrigerator truck is ideal for large races.

6. Computer terminal linked to the race finish.

7. Blood electrolyte and sodium analyzers. Ideally, serum sodium and potassium concentrations should be measured in all patients; however, this is *essential* in all subjects who are diagnosed as "dehydrated" and in need of intravenous fluids. A serum sodium concentration below 130 mmol/L (130 mEq/L) indicates that the sportsperson is more likely overhydrated rather than underhydrated.[3–5]

8. Bins for rubbish and "sharps."

9. Toilet facilities.

10. Medications and equipment. Table 65.2 lists the resuscitation and medical equipment and Table 65.3 lists the medications required to

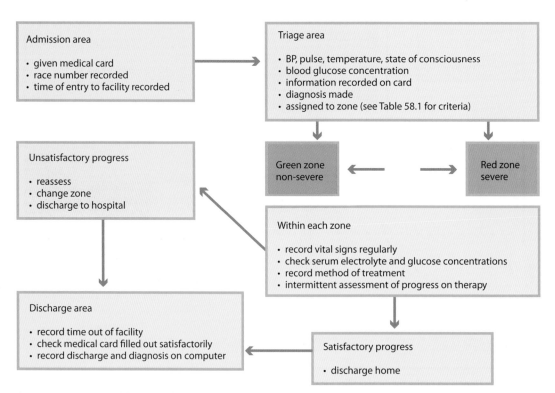

Figure 65.2 Suggested flow chart for the management of sportspeople once they enter the central medical facility

Table 65.2 Essential resuscitation and diagnostic tools for an endurance sporting event with 1000 competitors

Resuscitation tools	Diagnostic tools
Oral airways (sizes 6–8)	Stethoscopes (5)
Resuscitation masks (disposable)	Sphygmomanometers for blood pressure measurement (5)
Defribrillator	Rectal thermometers (5; with disinfectant)
Oxygen cylinder/mask (2)	Torches
	Ophthalmoscope and otoscope
	Glucometers for blood monitoring (2)
	Reflex hammer
	Blood electrolyte analyzer
	Urine sticks
	Peak flow meter (1)

cope with the expected emergency conditions. A pharmacist should be present to control the distribution of medications.

11. Given that over 60% of runners requiring attention after a marathon require physiotherapy services, it is ideal if a separate physiotherapy area can be set aside from the central medical facility. Many endurance events also provide a massage tent for sportspeople. As there are often a large number of minor foot injuries associated with endurance running events, the presence of a podiatrist is also of great assistance.

Additional supplies required for the medical tents and first-aid stations are shown in the boxes overleaf.

Conclusion

The risks associated with endurance events can be reduced with adequate preparation, good medical coverage on the day of the event, and, most importantly, education of the competitors. Educating the competitors regarding some of the pitfalls of competing in an endurance event improves their performance and reduces the risk of any major problems.

Table 65.3 Basic medications required in the medical facility at an endurance sporting event with 1000 competitors

Mode of administration	Medication
Injectable	Atropine (0.4 mg/mL)
	Dexamethasone (4 mg/mL)
	Morphine sulfate (15 mg/mL)
	Dextrose 50%
	Adrenalin (epinephrine) (1:1000) (1 mg/mL)
	Salbutamol for nebulizer
	Metoclopramide
	Cardiac resuscitation drugs—atropine, lignocaine (lidocaine), frusemide
	Xylocaine (local anesthetic)
	Tetanus toxoid
Inhalation	Salbutamol inhaler
Oral	Paracetamol (acetaminophen) (500 mg)
	Sublingual glyceryl trinitrate (nitroglycerin) (0.4 mg)
	Isordil spray
	Chlorzoxazone tablets (500 mg)
	Loperamide capsules (2 mg)
Topical	Propacaine (0.5%) eye anesthetic
	Water-soluble lubricant
	Povidone iodine
	Tincture of benzoin

E

Supplies required for medical stations at the finish line of a marathon with 1000 competitors

Surgical instruments and disposables
Scissors
Latex gloves
Syringes (3 mL, 5 mL, 10 mL)
Needles (18, 21, 25 gauge)
Steri-strips, sticking plasters
Skin disinfectant
Adhesive bandages
Gauze pads
Suture equipment (disposable)
Fluid administration sets; cannulas, poles, giving sets (10)
Normal saline for intravenous use (10×1 L)
5% dextrose for intravenous use (2×1 L)
Haemaccel for intravenous use (2×1 L)

Supplies required at a first-aid station along a marathon course with 1000 competitors

Stretchers (5)
Blankets (5)
10 cm (4 in.) and 15 cm (7.5 in.) elastic bandages (6 each)
Gauze pads
Rigid strapping tape
Dressing packs (5)
Skin disinfectant
Inflatable arm and leg splints (1 each)
Athletic trainer's kit
Petroleum jelly
Pen and paper for record collection

Other equipment

Ice and plastic bags (100 kg of ice)
Water (500 L)
Glucose–electrolyte drink (to make 250 L)
Cups (2000)
Towels
Blankets (10)
Rigid-frame stretchers (10)
Nebulizer (2)
Inflatable arm and leg splints (2 each)
Slings (5)
Rigid strapping tape (various sizes)
Elastic bandages (various sizes)
Tape scissors
Dressing packs (10)
Eye pads
Petroleum jelly
Pens and paper for record collection
Laptop computer for data entry
Athletic trainer's kit
Podiatrist's kit (scalpel, sharp scissors, disinfectant, skin care pad, adhesive felt)

Medical input into the planning of the event is essential. The risk of thermal injury is reduced if the event is held at a time that is likely to avoid extremes of heat or cold. Events held in warmer climates should be commenced early in the morning or in the evening. Adequate facilities and equipment should be provided with well-stocked, regular drink stations along the route.

The presence of experienced, trained medical and paramedical staff to deal with any emergency dramatically reduces the risk of serious problems. A functional layout of the medical facility can permit rapid, appropriate care of all race participants.

RECOMMENDED READING

McGarvey J, Thompson J, Hanna C et al. Sensitivity and specificity of clinical signs for assessment of dehydration in endurance athletes. *Br J Sports Med* 2010;44(10):716–19.

Maughan RJ, Watson P, Shirreffs SM. Heat and cold: what does the environment do to the marathon runner? *Sports Med* 2007;37(4-5):396–9.

Noakes T, Mekler J, Pedoe DT. Jim Peters' collapse in the 1954 Vancouver Empire Games marathon. *S Afr Med J* 2008 Aug;98(8):596–600.

Noakes TD. *The lore of running.* 4th ed. Champaign, Il: Human Kinetics Publishers, 2003.

Noakes TD. *Waterlogged. Why the science of hydration fails to fit the facts.* Champaign, Il: Human Kinetics Publishers, 2012 (in press).

Speedy DB, Noakes TD, Kimber NE et al. Fluid balance during and after an ironman triathlon. *Clin J Sport Med* 2001; 11(1): 44–50.

Speedy DB, Noakes TD, Boswell T et al. Response to a fluid load in athletes with a history of exercise induced hyponatremia. *Med Sci Sports Exerc* 2001; 33(9): 1434–42.

Winger JM, Dugas JP, Dugas LR. Beliefs about hydration and physiology drive drinking behaviours in runners. *Bri J Sports Med.* 2011 (45)8;646–9.

REFERENCES

1. Holtzhausen LM, Noakes TD. Collapsed ultraendurance athlete: proposed mechanisms and an approach to management. *Clin J Sport Med* 1997;7(4):292–301.

2. Armstrong LE, Epstein Y, Greenleaf JE et al. American College of Sports Medicine position stand. Heat and cold illnesses during distance running. *Med Sci Sports Exerc* 1996;28(12):i–x.

3. Hew-Butler T, Almond C, Ayus JC et al. Consensus statement of the 1st International Exercise-Associated Hyponatremia Consensus Development Conference, Cape Town, South Africa 2005. *Clin J Sport Med* 2005;15(4):208–13.

4. Speedy DB, Rogers IR, Noakes TD et al. Diagnosis and prevention of hyponatremia at an ultradistance triathlon. *Clin J Sport Med* 2000;10(1):52–8.

5. Reid SA, Speedy DB, Thompson JM et al. Study of hematological and biochemical parameters in runners completing a standard marathon. *Clin J Sport Med* 2004;14(6):344–53.

E

Chapter 66

Drugs and the athlete

I don't know. I never smoked AstroTurf. Tug McGraw, when asked if he preferred grass or artificial turf, 1974

The use of performance-enhancing drugs is probably the major problem facing sport today. Despite intense efforts by sporting bodies and the medical profession to eliminate the problem, drug-taking to assist sports performance remains widespread.

The International Olympic Committee's (IOC) definition of doping is:

> The use of an expedient (substance or method) which is potentially harmful to an athlete's health and/or capable of enhancing their performance, or the presence in the athlete's body of a prohibited substance or evidence of the use thereof or evidence of the use of a prohibited method.

The World Anti-Doping Agency (WADA) is responsible for producing and maintaining the World Anti-Doping Code containing the Prohibited List of Substances—substances and methods that are banned either at all times or in-competition only. Substances will be added to the list if they satisfy any two of the following three criteria:

1. the potential for enhanced performance
2. the potential for being detrimental to health
3. they violate the spirit of sport.

The list is reviewed annually and an updated list commences on 1 January each year. The list that took effect on 1 January 2011 contains five classes of *substances* that are prohibited both in and out of competition, another four classes of substances prohibited in competition only, three *methods* prohibited in and out of competition, and two substances prohibited in particular sports (see box at top of page 1229).

In addition, WADA monitors certain other substances (in 2011, stimulants and narcotics) to detect patterns of misuse; this may lead to these substances being added to the prohibited list in the future.

Athletes may have illnesses or conditions that require them to take banned medications. In these cases, the athlete may apply for a Therapeutic Use Exemption (TUE) from their National Anti-Doping Organization or their International Federation to obtain authority to use the substance. WADA does not grant TUEs but may consider appeals related to the granting or denying of a TUE.

The prohibited list is shown in the box opposite. A summary of the prohibited classes of drugs, and their medical usage, effect on performance, and adverse effects is shown in Table 66.1 on pages 1230 to 1232.

Non-approved substances at all times (in and out of competition)

S0: Non-approved substances[1]

Any pharmacological substance which is not addressed by any of the subsequent sections of the List and with no current approval by any governmental regulatory health authority for human therapeutic use (i.e. drugs under pre-clinical or clinical development or discontinued) is prohibited at all times.

Prohibited substances all times (in and out of competition)

Anabolic agents

Prohibited anabolic agents are shown in the box.

S1: Anabolic agents[1]

Anabolic agents are prohibited.
1. Anabolic androgenic steroids (AAS)
   (a) Exogenous AAS including: 1-androstenediol, 1-androstenedione, bolandiol, bolasterone, boldenone, boldione, calusterone, clostebol, danazol, dehydrochlormethyltestosterone, desoxymethyltestosterone, drostanolone, ethylestrenol, fluoxymesterone, formebolone, furazabol, gestrinone, 4-hydroxytestosterone, mestanolone, mesterolone, metenolone, methandienone, methandriol, methasterone, methyldienolone, methyl-1-testosterone, methylnortestosterone, methyltestosterone, metribolone, mibolerone, nandrolone, 19-norandrostenedione, norboletone, norclostebol, norethandrolone, oxabolone, oxandrolone, oxymesterone, oxymetholone, prostanozol, quinbolone, stanozolol, stenbolone, 1-testosterone, tetrahydrogestrinone, trenbolone, and other substances with a similar chemical structure or similar biological effect(s)
   (b) Endogenous AAS when administered exogenously: androstenediol, androstenedione, dihydrotestosterone, prasterone, testosterone, and their metabolites and isomers
2. Other anabolic agents: e.g. clenbuterol, selective androgen receptor modulators (SARMs), tibolone, zeranol, zilpaterol.

Anabolic androgenic steroids

Androgens are steroid hormones that are secreted primarily by the testes but also by the adrenal glands and ovaries. Testosterone is the principal androgen responsible for the development of the primary sexual characteristics *in utero* and during the neonatal period. It is also responsible for the development of the pubertal secondary sexual characteristics and it contributes to the increase in height and amount of skeletal muscle at that time. Testosterone promotes aggressive behavior, which is possibly due to direct stimulation of brain receptors. It also plays a role in sexual orientation.

Anabolic androgenic steroid (AAS) hormones are derivatives of testosterone. The structure of the testosterone molecule can be adjusted to maximize either the androgenic or the anabolic effect. Athletes generally abuse those agents that have maximum anabolic effect while minimizing the androgenic adverse effects. A large number of different AAS hormones have been synthesized.

Examples of prohibited AASs are shown in the box on the left. The exogenous AASs are synthetic analogs of testosterone; the endogenous ones are naturally occurring and are involved in the metabolic pathways of testosterone.

The clinical uses of anabolic steroids are limited. They may be used as hormone replacement for primary and secondary hypogonadism, Klinefelter's syndrome, and, occasionally, delayed puberty. They have also been used to treat disturbances of nitrogen balance and muscular development, and several other non-endocrine diseases, including forms of

Table 66.1 Prohibited drugs and their effects

Type of drug	Examples	Medical usage	Effect on performance	Adverse effects
Anabolic steroids	Methandrostenolone Stanozolol Nandrolone	Hypogonadism Severe osteoporosis Breast carcinoma	Increased muscle bulk Increased muscle strength Possibly improving anticatabolic effect, recovery	Acne Baldness Gynecomastia Decreased sperm production, testes size, and sex drive Increased aggression Liver abnormalities Hypertension Hypercholesterolemia
Peptide hormones, growth factors, and related substances	Erythropoietin (EPO)	Anemia secondary to chronic renal disease	Increased endurance	Increased blood viscosity Myocardial infarction
	Human growth hormone (hGH)	Dwarfism Short stature	Anecdotal evidence only	Allergic reactions Diabetogenic effect Acromegaly
	Insulin-like growth factor (IGF-1)	Dwarfism Diabetes mellitus type 2	Anecdotal evidence only	Acromegaly Organomegaly Hypoglycemia
	Insulin	Diabetes	Anecdotal evidence only	Hypoglycemia
	Human chorionic gonadotrophin (HCG)	Hypogonadism	May increase endogenous production of steroids	Gynecomastia
	Adrenocorticotropic hormone (ACTH)	Steroid-responsive conditions	Euphoria	As in glucocorticosteroids
Beta-2 agonists	Salbutamol (oral) Terbutaline	Asthma Exercise-induced bronchospasm	Possible anabolic effects	Tachycardia Tremor Palpitations

Type of drug	Examples	Medical usage	Effect on performance	Adverse effects
Hormone anatgonists and modulators	Aromatase inhibitors (anastrozole, aminoglutethamide)	Breast cancer	Used to counter gynecomastia	Joint aches Stiffness
	Selective estrogen receptor modulators (SERMS) (tamoxifen)	Breast cancer, osteoporosis	Males: used with AAS to prevent gynecomastia Females: muscle bulk (anecdotal evidence)	Females: masculinization Deep venous thrombosis
	Clomiphene Cyclofenil	Anovulatory infertility	Increases gonadotrophin-releasing hormone (GnRH) and endogenous testosterone (anecdotal evidence)	Bloating Stomach pains Blurred vision Headaches Nausea Dizziness
Diuretics and other masking agents	Frusemide Hydrochlorothiazide Chlorothiazide	Hypertension Edema Congestive cardiac failure	Rapid weight loss Decreases concentration of drugs in urine	Electrolyte imbalance Dehydration Muscle cramps
Stimulants	Amphetamines (dexamphetamine, dimethylamphetamine)	Narcolepsy ADHD (attention deficit hyperactivity disorder)	May delay fatigue Increased alertness	Anxiety Insomnia Dizziness Euphoria Headache Nausea and vomiting Confusion Psychosis Hypertension Addiction
	Ephedra	Dietary supplements for weight loss	Large doses improve cycling performance Additive effect with caffeine	Hypertension Arrythmias Seizure Cerebrovascular accident
	Cocaine	Nasal anesthetic	Increased alertness	Impaired hand–eye coordination, aggression, cardiac and cerebral abnormalities

continued

Table 66.1 Prohibited drugs and their effects *continued*

Type of drug	Examples	Medical usage	Effect on performance	Adverse effects
Narcotics	Pethidine Morphine	Moderate-to-severe pain	No evidence of improved performance May be able to compete with injury	Nausea and vomiting Dizziness Respiratory depression Addiction
Cannabinoids	Marijuana Hashish	Palliative care Chronic pain	Negative effect	Impaired psychomotor skills Altered perception of time Impaired concentration
Glucocorticosteroids	Prednisolone	Widely used anti-inflammatory Severe asthma	Euphoria Some evidence of performance enhancement	Cushingoid symptoms
Enhancement of oxygen transfer	Blood doping	Nil	Improves endurance	Transfusion reaction Increased blood viscosity
	Artificial oxygen carriers (hemoglobin oxygen carriers, perfluorocarbon emissions)	Provide rapid blood volume expansion following acute blood loss	Improved endurance (no evidence as yet)	

AAS = anabolic androgenic steroids

anemia, hereditary angioneurotic edema, and breast carcinoma. Steroids increase lean body mass in patients with chronic obstructive pulmonary disease (COPD) and HIV, and they may have a role in the treatment of muscular dystrophy and several dermatological diseases.[2]

The use of AASs in certain sports, particularly power sports such as weightlifting, power lifting,[3] sprinting, and throwing, is widespread, as is their use by body builders.[4] The use of AASs in footballers varies in the different codes of football. There would appear to be a high incidence of use in players of American football, with a lower incidence in players of other football codes.

 While the incidence of AAS use is highest in elite athletes, there is a disturbingly high incidence among recreational and high school athletes.[5–8]

This may be related to a desire to increase sporting performance or to improve body image. In 1987, the first US national study of AAS use at a high school level found that 6.6% of male seniors had used the drugs; 38% of those users had commenced before turning 16 years of age.[5] Subsequent studies have confirmed that 4–6% (range 3–12%) of US high school boys have used AASs at some time, as have 1–2% of US high school girls.[9]

AASs are taken orally or by intramuscular injection. More recently, transdermal patches, buccal tablets, nasal sprays, gels, and creams are being used as the delivery mechanisms.[10]

AASs are usually used in a cyclical manner with periods of heavy use, generally lasting six to 12 weeks, alternating with drug-free periods lasting from one to 12 months. The aim of the drug-free periods is to reduce the adverse effects of the drugs; whether this is the case remains unknown.

AAS users follow a "pyramid" regimen, which commences with a low daily dose and gradually increases to a high dose then back down to a lower dose, and/or a "stacking" regimen, in which several different types of anabolic steroids, oral and/or injectable, are taken simultaneously. The purpose behind the "stacking" regimen is to achieve receptor saturation with a lower total androgen dose than would be required if only one compound were used. Users hope that this regimen may reduce the incidence of adverse effects. Commonly, a combination known as "pyramid stacking" is used. The dosages taken by AAS users varies but those wishing to bulk up frequently use dosages 10–100 times the physiological dose.

Different AASs are used at different times of the training program depending on the phase of activity being performed. Certain AASs are regarded by their users (e.g. body builders) as more appropriate for specific aims, such as increased muscle definition. AAS users may use other drugs (e.g. diuretics, anti-estrogens, human chorionic gonadotrophin [HCG] and anti-acne medications) to counteract the common adverse effects of AAS.

Most AASs are obtained through a black market that exists through gymnasiums, health centers, and, increasingly, on the internet. Information (and misinformation!) is readily available in pamphlets, niche-market magazines, and, of course, on the internet.

Testosterone precursors (e.g. dehydroepiandrosterone [DHEA]) and designer steroids (e.g. tetrahydrogestrinone [THG]) have recently received considerable publicity (page 1236).

Effect on performance

Anabolic steroids have a threefold effect:

1. *Anabolic effect.* This is due to the induction of protein synthesis in skeletal muscle cells. AASs attach to specific cytoplasmic receptors in muscle cells and this complex then activates the nucleus to synthesize ribosomal and messenger RNA and initiate the process of protein synthesis. This anabolic effect continues during steroid treatment. An additional anabolic effect may occur indirectly through increased levels of endogenous growth hormone associated with AAS administration.

2. *Anticatabolic effect.* This is mediated in two ways. AASs may reverse the catabolic effects of glucocorticosteroids released at times of training stress, and they may improve the utilization of ingested protein, thereby increasing nitrogen retention. This effect depends on adequate protein intake. Athletes in heavy training, especially weight training, are in a catabolic state. This is associated with the release of glucocorticosteroids and increased nitrogen utilization. When intense training is combined with insufficient recovery time or inadequate protein intake, a chronic catabolic state may develop. This can be associated with impaired training and competition performance and the development of overuse injuries. Anabolic steroids may reverse this catabolic state, and permit an increased training load.

    AAS use appears to increase muscle size and muscle strength but only when certain conditions are met. For anabolic steroids to be effective in increasing muscle size and strength, the athlete taking the steroids must perform intense weight training and have an adequate protein intake. If these conditions are met, an increase in muscle size and strength will result.

3. *Enhancement of aggressive behavior.* Increased aggression may encourage a greater training intensity and may also be advantageous during competition in sports such as weightlifting and contact sports. However, there may also be negative psychological effects (as discussed below).

There is considerable evidence that testosterone administration combined with weight training leads to an increase in lean body mass and a decrease in body fat.[11-13] This effect appears to be dose-related. The change in muscle mass with testosterone use is due to muscle fiber hypertrophy and increased numbers of myonuclei.[14]

Studies have demonstrated a 5–20% increase in baseline strength, depending on the drugs and dose used as well as the administration period.[2]

While the majority of anabolic steroid use has been by athletes in power events, there is anecdotal evidence of a positive effect of anabolic steroids on endurance exercise. Firstly, the anti-catabolic effect may improve recovery from heavy training, thus reducing the likelihood of injury and allowing the athlete to undertake a greater volume and intensity of training. Secondly, anabolic steroids have a stimulatory effect on bone marrow, which may result in an increased production of red blood cells, thus improving the oxygen-carrying capacity of the blood.

Long-term treatment of certain anemias with AASs has shown an increase in hemoglobin concentrations, but the majority of studies have failed to show any improvement in endurance performance with AAS.[2]

The above effects of anabolic steroids occur in both males and females.

Adverse effects

Adverse effects of anabolic steroid usage are extremely common and can be particularly significant in women.

The majority of adverse effects are reversible on cessation of the drug(s). However, a number of serious adverse effects have been reported with anabolic steroid use, in some cases leading to death. The mortality rate among elite power lifters suspected of

steroid abuse was significantly higher (12.9%) than that of a control population (3.1%).[15] Another study investigating the deaths of 34 known users of the drugs concluded that AAS use was associated with an increased risk of violent death from impulsive, aggressive behavior or depressive symptoms.[16]

An additional health risk associated with the use of AASs is that of infection associated with needle sharing.[2] HIV, hepatitis B and C, and abscesses have been documented among anabolic steroid injectors who share needles[17] and one study found that 25% of adolescent AAS users shared needles.[17]

The long-term effects of prolonged anabolic steroid usage are unknown. However, as athletes who abuse these compounds often administer doses as high as 100 times the usual therapeutic dose, there is a high risk of adverse effects and toxicity.

As well as this, a number of violent crimes, including domestic violence, which have resulted in death, have been attributed to "roid rage." A list of the common and less common adverse effects of anabolic steroid usage is shown in Table 66.2.

Toxicity in both sexes

Liver

As many as 80% of individuals using those androgens that have a 17-methyl substitution on the steroid molecule have developed liver disorders, including hyperbilirubinemia and elevated liver enzyme levels.[18] These changes can be reversed with cessation of the drug. However, continued administration can lead to biliary obstruction and jaundice. This may take up to three months to reverse when steroid use is ceased.

The responsible steroid compounds are mainly oral and include stanozolol and oxymethalone. Intermittent administration of these compounds has been shown to lower the incidence of these symptoms. The carbon-17 esters, such as testosterone and nandrolone, are not associated with these liver problems as these substances are administered by injection and bypass the liver. The use of anabolic steroids to treat various medical illnesses has been occasionally associated with the development of other liver abnormalities, such as peliosis hepatis (blood-filled cysts in the liver),[19, 20] and benign and malignant hepatic tumors.[21, 22]

Tumors

There have been occasional cases of tumors reported in athletes using anabolic steroids. These include

Table 66.2 Adverse effects of anabolic steroids

Common	Less common
Both sexes	
Acne	Peliosis hepatis
Alopecia	Hepatoma/
Abnormal liver enzymes	hepatocarcinoma
Lowered HDL level	Wilms' tumor
Raised LDL level	Coronary artery disease
Elevated triglyceride level	Tendon ruptures
Hypertension	Psychosis
Reduced humoral immunity	Acute schizophrenia
Irritability	Addiction
Aggression	? Leukemia
Mood swings	
Changes in libido	
Males	
Decreased sperm	? Cancer of the prostate
production	
Decreased testicle size	
Decreased FSH, LH	
Gynecomastia	
Females	
Menstrual irregularities	Deepening of voice
	Male pattern baldness
	Hirsuitism
	Clitoromegaly
	Breast shrinkage
Adolescents	
Increased facial/body hair	Phallic enlargement
Acne	Male pattern baldness
Premature closure of	Deepening of voice
epiphyses	Abnormal psychosocial
	maturation

FSH = follicle stimulating hormone; HDL = high-density lipoprotein; LDL = low-density lipoprotein; LH = luteinizing hormone

Wilms' tumor, carcinoma of the prostate, and leukemia. It is not possible to prove a direct relationship between the development of these tumors and anabolic steroid usage.

Lipids

Changes in lipid profiles are commonly seen with anabolic steroid usage.[23-26] Lowered levels of high-density lipoprotein (HDL) cholesterol and raised levels of low-density lipoprotein (LDL) cholesterol are seen. A lowered HDL:LDL ratio is a risk factor for the development of coronary heart disease, but as yet there is no convincing evidence of an increased incidence of coronary heart disease in anabolic steroid users.[27] These lipid changes appear to be reversed on cessation of the drug(s).[28]

Hypertension

Raised blood pressure is commonly seen in association with anabolic steroid usage,[25, 29] although the changes are not consistent. The increase in blood pressure also usually reverts to normal on cessation of use. The elevation in blood pressure may be secondary to sodium and water retention.

Cardiovascular effects

Isolated cases of myocardial infarction[30, 31] and cerebrovascular accident[30-32] have been reported in association with anabolic steroid use. Long-term use is associated with left ventricular dysfunction.[33] There is serious concern about the possible long-term sequelae of anabolic steroid use—in particular, the possibility of an increased incidence of coronary artery disease in the light of the persistent findings of elevated blood pressure, decreased HDL levels, and increased LDL levels. Whether or not these transient effects are negated by the return to normal values in times of steroid abstinence remains to be seen.

Immunity

There is evidence that humoral immunity is reduced with steroid use. Lowered levels of IgG, IgM, and IgA have been noted. The clinical significance of these changes is uncertain.

Skin changes

Skin changes are common with anabolic steroid usage and are related to excessive sebum production.[34, 35] These changes include acne, rosacea, sebaceous cysts, furunculosis, folliculitis, and increased body and facial hair. Care should be taken with the treatment of severe acne with either tetracyclines or isotretinoin as these drugs may aggravate pre-existent liver damage.

Psychological

Mild psychological effects, such as irritability, mood swings, changes in libido, and increased aggression, are common with anabolic steroid usage.[36, 37] AAS use directly causes significant disturbances in personality profile.[38] One study showed that AAS users reported being significantly less in control of their aggression than did controls.[39]

1235

Violent behavior may occur in susceptible individuals, and psychiatric abnormalities such as acute schizophrenia and transient psychoses are not uncommon.[40] It would appear that anabolic steroids may also become both psychologically and physically addictive.[41] Withdrawal may lead to depression, fatigue, decreased sex drive, insomnia, and anorexia.

Toxicity in males

A reduction in testicular size and sperm volume appears to be common with anabolic steroid use due to a negative feedback effect resulting in decreased pituitary production of follicle stimulating hormone (FSH) and luteinizing hormone (LH).[42] Testicular volume is reduced on average by 20%, and sperm production is severely reduced and commonly ceases altogether. The popular usage of human chorionic gonadotrophin (HCG) in conjunction with anabolic steroids to avoid testicular atrophy does not appear to be effective, although it has been suggested that clomiphene may successfully restore AAS-induced pituitary–gonadal dysfunction.[43]

These adverse effects appear to be reversible on cessation of anabolic steroids. However, decreased sperm production may take three months to return to normal.

 Ironically, one of the adverse effects of anabolic steroid usage is feminization. This occurs as a result of peripheral conversion of AAS to estrogens.

Plasma estradiol levels rise considerably with anabolic steroid usage. This feminization manifests itself as gynecomastia (development of breast tissue in males). Body-builders use tamoxifen to counteract this estrogen effect and, as a result, increase the androgenic adverse effects, but there is no evidence for its effectiveness.[44]

Toxicity in females

In female athletes, menstrual irregularities frequently occur with anabolic steroid use. Other symptoms can include deepening of the voice, male pattern baldness, hirsutism, altered libido, uterine atrophy, and an enlarged clitoris. These changes may be irreversible. Anabolic steroids taken in pregnancy can cause fetal abnormalities or miscarriage.

Toxicity in adolescents

Anabolic steroid usage during adolescence in both sexes is commonly associated with acne, increased facial and body hair, and premature closing of the epiphyseal plates.[45, 46] Other changes that may be seen during adolescence include phallic enlargement, male pattern baldness, deepening of the voice, and abnormal psychosocial maturation.

Testosterone precursors

It has been suggested that testosterone precursors or pro-hormones such as androstenedione ("andro") and dehydroepiandrosterone (DHEA) may have an ergogenic effect by increasing testosterone levels.

Androstenedione

Androstenedione is a relatively weak steroid available in many over-the-counter nutritional supplements. It is an immediate precursor to testosterone as well as estradiol and estrone. Its anabolic activity is one-fifth to one-tenth of testosterone. Although some studies have shown that androstenedione use will lead to increased testosterone levels, there is no evidence that it will significantly increase strength or lean body mass.[10] Adverse effects include gynecomastia and increased risk of cardiovascular disease secondary to increased levels of estrogen, and a significant reduction of HDL cholesterol.

Dehydroepiandrosterone (DHEA)

Dehydroepiandrosterone (DHEA) is a testosterone precursor and secreted by the adrenal gland.[47] It has been promoted to increase muscle mass and weight loss. Its use was publicized by the US baseballer Mark McGwire, who admitted to using DHEA during the season in which he set the home run scoring record. DHEA does not enhance serum testosterone concentration or increase strength.[48] Although there is some evidence of a weight loss effect in rats, the only human study into the effectiveness of DHEA in weight loss failed to show any benefit.[49] Due to the potential for androgenic effects, DHEA is not recommended for young children and women.[10]

Designer steroids

In order to try to evade detection, athletes who continue to "dope" are having to resort to the use of a far more dangerous form of drug—the designer steroid.[50] These steroids are manufactured to closely resemble existing known compounds, but with sufficient chemical diversity to ensure that their detection by the WADA accredited laboratories is more difficult. A worrying feature of the use of these compounds is that no data are available to evaluate either the efficacy or the safety of these substances.

Many such drugs are now being made in clandestine ways (as demonstrated by the recent Bay Area Laboratory Co-operative [BALCO] case) and passed on to athletes who become the guinea pigs determining the potential of the substances as doping agents. Methods for the detection of these new compounds are being developed using emerging techniques such as gas chromatography or liquid chromatography using a variety of mass spectrometry instruments.[50]

The first designer steroids were norbolethone in 2002, tetrahydrogestrinone (THG) in 2003, and "madol" (17-methyl-5-androst-2-ene-17-ol) in 2004.[51] THG was discovered when a track and field coach gave the contents of a used syringe to drug testing authorities. The drug was subsequently analyzed and its chemical structure determined. A test to detect the presence of THG was developed and past urine samples of a number of elite track athletes were analyzed and found to be positive.[52]

THG was created with the dual purpose of imparting anabolic steroid effects to athletes, and allowing those athletes to avoid detection by standard doping control drug testing. The primary reason THG went undetected in urine samples was that it tends to break down when the urine is prepared for analysis by the standard anabolic steroid screen.[53] Once it was suspected that the steroid was disintegrating during standard testing, a more sensitive assay process was used.

THG has been shown to be chemically and pharmacologically related to the specifically listed anabolic steroids gestrinone and trenbolone on the WADA Prohibited List. *In vitro* studies have suggested that THG may be a potent anabolic agent, although the *in vivo* potency will depend on the steroid's circulating half-life and its binding to the sex hormone–binding globulin.[54]

Clenbuterol

Clenbuterol, which is considered both an anabolic agent and a beta-2 agonist, has been used as an ergogenic aid but there is no scientific evidence in humans to support the animal studies that showed increased lean mass.[55] Adverse effects include tremor and tachycardia. There are anecdotal reports of sudden death in two body builders.[55]

Peptide hormones, growth factors, and related substances

The peptide hormones, growth factors, and related substances are shown in the box.

S2: Peptide hormones, growth factors, and related substances[1]

The following substances and their releasing factors are prohibited:

1. Erythropoiesis-stimulating agents (e.g. erythropoietin [EPO], darbepoetin [dEPO], hypoxia-inducible factor stabilizers [HIF], methoxy polyethylene glycol-epoetin beta [CERA], peginesatide [Hematide])
2. Human chorionic gonadotrophin (HCG) and luteinizing hormone (LH) in males
3. Insulins
4. Corticotrophins
5. Growth hormone (GH), insulin-like growth factor-1 (IGF-1), fibroblast growth factors, hepatocyte growth factors (HGF), mechano growth factors (MGFs), platelet-derived growth factor, vascular-endothelial growth factor as well as any other growth factors affecting muscle, tendon, or ligament protein synthesis/degradation, vascularization, energy utilization, regenerative capacity or fiber-type switching

and other substances with similar chemical structure or similar biological effect(s).

Erythropoiesis-stimulating agents

Erythropoietin (EPO) is a naturally occurring hormone secreted by the kidney. It stimulates the bone marrow and increases red blood cell production. This leads to an increase in red blood cell mass, hemoglobin, and hematocrit. Its main therapeutic use has been in patients with anemia due to conditions such as chronic renal failure, cancer chemotherapy, or HIV (patients on zidovudine), and also for surgical patients to minimize the need for blood transfusions.[56]

There have been incidents in the past two decades in which athletes have either admitted taking or tested positive to EPO, particularly in cycling and cross-country skiing, the most publicized being the 1998 Tour de France where the Festina team was caught with huge amounts of EPO.

As EPO causes an increased red cell mass, an extra oxygen-carrying capacity is created, which permits an increase in energy production by aerobic oxidation of glucose and free fatty acids.[57, 58] This is the most efficient means of energy production and limits anaerobic production, which is inefficient and leads to fatigue. Aerobic oxidation is the most important energy source for endurance athletes. EPO provides the benefits of blood doping without the risk of blood transfusion.

EPO has been shown to increase hemoglobin levels by 11%[59] and improve VO_2max (7%)[60] and exercise tolerance (17% increased time for run to exhaustion).[61]

The main adverse effect of EPO is hyperviscosity of the blood due to a raised hematocrit. This raises the risk of myocardial infarction and cerebrovascular accident, the risk being increased with dehydrating endurance exercise.[62] The unexplained death of 18 otherwise healthy cyclists between 1997 and 2000 has been linked to EPO, but there is no concrete evidence to support this theory.[56]

Less serious adverse effects of EPO use include fever, nausea, headache, anxiety, and lethargy. Seizures have been reported in 2–3% of patients in the first 90 days of therapy.[56]

Some sports have introduced safety cut-offs for hematocrit levels (e.g. 50%) as an indirect means of restricting the use of EPO.[63] This is unsatisfactory due to the wide variations in "normal" hematocrit levels and the number of factors that can affect the value.[64] Also athletes may then manipulate their drug intake to ensure that they are just below the allowed limit.

 It is now possible to detect the use of EPO by athletes. Testing for EPO was introduced at the 2000 Sydney Olympics and involved a combination of blood and urine tests.[65]

Two cross-country skiers were stripped of their medals at the 2002 Winter Olympic Games in Salt Lake City after testing positive for darbepoetin, at the time a new recombinant version of EPO.

Recombinant erythropoietins are produced by transfection of the erythropoietin gene into mammalian cells in culture or activation of the gene in human cells.[66] The first recombinant erythropoietins that were commercially available were epoetin alfa and epoetin beta, which were released in 1989 and 1990 respectively. These came to be known as the first-generation epoietins. They both had short serum half-lives of approximately eight hours when administered intravenously, so in therapeutic use the frequency of administration was between one and three times per week.

Since the late 1990s a multitude of producers in the emerging world have started to produce copies of the first-generation epoetins. At present around 80 different epoetin analogs are being produced in Eastern Europe, Asia, Africa, and the Americas. Currently none of these are licensed by the Food and Drug Administration (FDA) in the US or by the European Medicines Agency.

These epoetins very often show not only a great variation in biological activity in comparison to other products but also wide intra-batch variability due to the absence of strict standardization of cultivation and purification procedures. In some products contamination with bacterial endotoxins or other contaminants has been described.

To overcome the pharmacokinetic limitations of the first-generation of epoetins, research was targeted to develop molecules with a longer serum half-life and to achieve longer application intervals. The first candidate to achieve these goals was darbepoetin alfa. The addition of two side chains resulted in an increase of the serum half-life to about 24 and 48 hours when administered intravenously or subcutaneously, respectively. This increase in half-life results in a prolongation of administration intervals to once weekly or once every second week. In selected patient populations, dosing intervals of up to once monthly have been described.[66]

A next step toward more physiological pharmacokinetics was the development of methoxy polyethylene glycol-epoetin beta, named "continuous erythropoietin receptor activator" (CERA). In clinical practice, the pharmacokinetics of CERA allow the routine administration of the drug once monthly or even less frequently. Due to its high molecular weight (60 kDa), CERA is not readily filtered in the kidney. Therefore CERA is detectable only on blood tests.

Two classes of non-epoetin erythropoiesis-stimulating substances are most likely to become commercially available in the near future—EPO mimetic peptides (Hematide) and HIF-stabilizers;[66] these are already suspected of being used by athletes.

Human chorionic gonadotrophin

Human chorionic gonadotrophin (HCG) is produced by the placenta and is a glycoprotein hormone produced in large amounts during pregnancy, and also by certain types of tumors. It has a very similar structure to luteinizing hormone (LH) and has the same biological activity except that it has a much longer half-life. HCG mainly stimulates sex steroid hormone biosynthesis in the gonads. Thus, in the female, HCG can substitute for the ovulatory surge of LH and ovulation and also maintain the corpus luteum for the production of progesterone, mainly in pregnancy. In the male, HCG can replace LH in stimulation of the interstitial cells within the testes to produce testosterone.

The therapeutic uses of HCG are limited. It can be used to stimulate ovulation in females and has been used to induce puberty in adolescent males who have delayed sexual development. It is mainly abused by male athletes as it increases the endogenous production of both testosterone and epitestosterone without increasing the urinary testosterone-to-epitestosterone ratio above the normal levels. Its other main use is to attempt to maintain testicular volume in the male athlete using anabolic steroids, which leads to inhibition of pituitary LH and follicle stimulating hormone (FSH) secretion and consequently loss of testicular volume. However, as it is FSH that maintains testicular volume, using HCG is unlikely to be effective. In the female athlete it is unlikely to give any benefit.

The main adverse effect of HCG is gynecomastia, probably from raised estrogen secretion from the testes. The drug combination of HCG and an anabolic steroid causes headaches, depression, and edema.

HCG and LH were prohibited in all athletes, but following problems with elevated HCG levels in females who were either currently pregnant or had recently miscarried, since 2006 they are prohibited in male athletes only. An elevated level of HCG in the male is a doping offence unless it can be shown to be due to a physiological or (very rarely) a pathological condition such as a tumor.

Insulins

Insulin is a small hormone produced in the pancreas; its main role is in carbohydrate metabolism. Insulin is anabolic in nature, causing cell growth, increasing both glucose and amino acid uptake by cells, and increasing protein synthesis. It decreases protein catabolism. Insulin also increases lipogenesis by promoting fatty acid synthesis and storage in adipose tissue. The main clinical use for insulin is for treating people with diabetes mellitus type 1.

The first suggestions of insulin as an anabolic agent were published in two body-building magazines in 1996. The most graphic account of doping with insulin came from Victor Conte, the founder and owner of BALCO, who alleged that he personally provided Marion Jones and other athletes with various performance enhancing concoctions that included a number of peptide hormones including insulin, erythropoietin, and human GH.[67] He described how insulin was used after strenuous weight training sessions during the off-season. Three units of the fast-acting insulin lispro were injected immediately after the workout sessions together with a glucose and protein drink, with the purpose of replenishing glycogen and adenosine triphosphate (ATP) quickly and promoting protein synthesis and muscle growth.

 Athletic use of insulin is mainly found in the power sports—weightlifting and body building.

In one report, 25% of AAS users concurrently used insulin.[68] As insulin has a half-life of 4 minutes in the human body, it vanishes rapidly and would be very difficult to detect. Even when detected it is impossible to distinguish from the athlete's own insulin.

The anabolic properties of insulin used in the hypoinsulinemic state (diabetic) are well recognized; however, the concept of a hyperinsulinemia-induced anabolic state is much less well supported.[69] Physiological hyperinsulinemia reportedly stimulates amino acid transport in human skeletal muscle. Although insulin inhibits protein breakdown, stimulation of bulk protein synthesis during hyperinsulinemia is observed only when concomitant hyperaminoacidemia occurs.[70]

The use of insulin in this situation is potentially very dangerous. Unrecognized hypoglycemic attacks can cause permanent neurological deficit and even death.[69]

Corticotrophins

Adrenocorticotropic hormone (ACTH) is also known as "corticotrophin" or "adrenocorticotrophin;" it is secreted by the anterior pituitary gland. Its main effect is on the adrenal cortex. Three major steroid hormones are produced in the adrenal cortex; these are:

- aldosterone (mineral corticoid)
- cortisol (glucocorticoid effect)
- DHEA (androgenic effect) (page 1236).

ACTH stimulates secretory activity in those cells that produce cortisol and androgens. It is abused in sport to increase the secretion of the adrenal androgens, which are moderately active male sex hormones. These are converted to testosterone in extra-adrenal tissues, which accounts for much of their androgenic activity. ACTH abuse also increases cortisol levels and this in turn stimulates gluconeogenesis, which raises blood glucose levels. This is achieved by mobilization of amino acids, mainly from muscle for conversion to glucose in the liver, and also by decreasing glucose utilization by the cells. Thus, the ergogenic effect of ACTH is negligible as its catabolic effects cancel out its anabolic effects. In fact, ACTH has no ergogenic benefit and is detrimental to performance. It is because of a belief in increased performance within the athletic community that it is placed on the prohibited list.

Human growth hormone

Human growth hormone (hGH) is a polypeptide hormone produced by the anterior pituitary. It is also called somatotrophic hormone and somatotrophin. It is essential for normal growth and development.

hGH exerts its effect on all cells in the body. It is anabolic in nature and causes an increased rate of protein synthesis and concurrent reduction in protein catabolism. It produces mobilization and increased use of fatty acids for energy and thus increases lean tissue mass and decreases fat mass. It causes a decreased rate of glucose utilization. hGH also produces accelerated growth. In the skeletally immature, stature is increased and prolonged treatment results in gigantism. When the epiphyses are closed, linear growth ceases and hGH produces acromegaly.

Another important action of hGH is the stimulation of the insulin-like growth factor-1 (IGF-1) in the liver, which synergizes with hGH to produce many of its effects. Exercise stimulates the production of hGH five- to ten-fold, whereas starvation decreases its production.[71]

hGH is species-specific and bovine and porcine hormones have no effect in humans. Since 1985 recombinant hGH has been produced. Prior to this, hGH was derived from cadavers and this led to several cases of Creutzfeldt–Jakob disease in the recipients.

The medical use of hGH is limited to the treatment of "dwarfism" and replacement therapy in growth-deficient children. It may have a role for children with Turner's syndrome and for people with chronic renal insufficiency. It is only available in the injectable form.

 Athletes use hGH because of its alleged anabolic effects—increased muscle mass and decreased fat mass.[72]

Use of hGH in athletes was first described by Dan Duchaine in the *Underground steroid handbook*

published in 1982. In 1988 Ben Johnson's coach admitted that he had given his athletes hGH in addition to anabolic steroids. In that year also, a large quantity of hGH was found in a team car at the Tour de France.

In 1989 the IOC added hGH to its list of banned substances despite not having a test that could detect its use. At the 1998 World Swimming Championships, Yuan Yuan, a Chinese swimmer, was stopped on entry into Perth with a suitcase full of GH that had been exported to China for therapeutic reasons. Six months before the Sydney Olympic Games, 1575 vials of hGH were stolen from an importer's warehouse in Sydney. More recently, Victor Conte, the owner of BALCO, claimed that he had supplied hGH to many high-profile American athletes including Tim Montgomery and Marion Jones.[73]

The effect of hGH on physical performance in healthy adults has not been studied rigorously. Most of the studies available have evaluated hGH effects in small groups of subjects and almost exclusively in men. Liu and colleagues[74] have undertaken a systematic review of the effects of hGH on various measures of athletic performance—such as muscle strength and endurance. Twenty-seven studies comprising a total number of 303 physically fit participants with mean age of 27 years and mean body mass index (BMI) of 24 kg/m² were considered suitable for analyses. Participants from seven studies received hGH as only one injection; the other 20 studies used hGH treatment for an average of 20 days with average daily dose of 36 µg/kg. Change in strength was evaluated in two studies and exercise capacity outcomes were measured in six studies.

 The claims that hGH enhances physical performance are not supported by the scientific literature.

However, these studies include very small sample sizes and use doses of hGH which are probably considerably less than those used by athletes; no studies have evaluated the use of a combination of hGH and AAS, a common practice among athletes. In a recent Australian study,[75] hGH significantly reduced fat mass, increased lean body mass through an increase in extracellular water, and increased body cell mass in men when co-administered with testosterone. It also significantly increased sprint capacity in men and women combined, alone, and with testosterone. Further studies must be done before we can finally determine whether hGH has an anabolic effect.

Adverse reactions are well documented and include gigantism in the younger athlete, acromegaly in the adult athlete, hypothyroidism, hypercholesterolemia, ischemic heart disease, congestive cardiac failure, cardiomyopathy, myopathies, arthritis, diabetes mellitus, impotence, osteoporosis, menstrual irregularities, and Creutzfeldt–Jakob disease. Although recombinant hGH has no risk of Creutzfeldt–Jakob disease, "black market" sources of hGH are often derived from cadavers.

In 1996 the IOC launched a program called Human Growth Hormone 2000 (HGH 2000) with the aim of developing a reliable screening test to detect exogenous hGH by the time of the Sydney Olympic Games in 2000. Despite considerable funding, the difficulties proved insurmountable and the test was not ready by the Sydney Games. There were a number of reasons for the difficulty. Firstly, hGH is a naturally occurring hormone, with varying levels between individuals of different ages, sexes, and activity levels. Secondly, hGH release is stimulated by exercise and varies in concentration throughout the day in each individual, and, thirdly, no reliable marker for hGH level is excreted in the urine, therefore a blood test must be used.[65] Since 2000 further progress has been made and it is now possible to perform a blood test to detect the presence of hGH.

Insulin-like growth factors

Growth hormone effects on the growth of bones and cartilage and on protein metabolism are brought about indirectly by stimulation of the liver and other tissue to release somatomedins (growth factors). The principal somatomedin is insulin-like growth factor (IGF-1/somatomedin C). IGF-1 results in an increase in glucose and amino acid uptake, and it inhibits apoptosis (programmed cell death). It enhances lipolysis indirectly by insulin suppression, and it may be linked to carcinogenesis (increased IGF-1 receptors have been found in tumors of the lung, breast, and Wilms' tumor of the kidney).

Clinical applications are limited but include some types of dwarfism and growth problems in children, and in people with diabetes mellitus type 2. It may have a role in kidney disease, catabolic states, osteoporosis, atherosclerosis, and osteoarthritis.

Little is known, however, about the prevalence of abuse with exogenous IGF-1. IGF-1 has effects on carbohydrate, lipid, and protein metabolism and some of these actions could prove beneficial to competitive athletes. No studies have demonstrated a positive effect of IGF-1 on physical performance in healthy individuals but this has not yet been studied in appropriately designed trials.[76]

In addition, supplementation of IGF-1 appears to be associated with moderate-to-severe hypoglycemia, decreased growth hormone secretion, a shift from lipid to carbohydrate oxidation for energy, and a general disruption of the insulin–glucagon system.[77] In the clinical trials, the commonest short-term adverse effects are edema, headache, arthralgia, jaw pain, and hypoglycemia.[78]

Two pharmaceutical preparations of IGF-1 have recently become available for the treatment of growth disorders in children. This availability is likely to increase the prevalence of IGF-1 abuse. Combining IGF-1 with its binding protein IGFBP-3 in one preparation has the potential to reduce the adverse effect profile, but the adverse effects of long-term IGF-1 abuse are currently unknown. Detection of abuse with IGF-1 is a major challenge for anti-doping authorities. It is extremely difficult to distinguish the exogenous recombinant form of the hormone from endogenously produced IGF-1. One approach currently being investigated is based on measuring markers of GH and IGF-1 action.[76]

Beta-2 agonists

The rules applying to beta-2 agonists are shown in the box below.

The prevalence of asthma is higher in elite athletes than in the general population. The risk of developing asthmatic symptoms is the highest in endurance athletes and swimmers. Asthma seems particularly

---

S3: Beta-2 agonists[1]

All beta-2 agonists (including both optical isomers where relevant) are prohibited except salbutamol (maximum 1600 micrograms over 24 hours) and salmeterol when taken by inhalation in accordance with the manufacturers' recommended therapeutic regime.

The presence of salbutamol in urine in excess of 1000 ng/mL is presumed not to be an intended therapeutic use of the substance and will be considered as an adverse analytical finding unless the athlete proves, through a controlled pharmacokinetic study, that the abnormal result was the consequence of the use of a therapeutic dose (maximum 1600 micrograms over 24 hours) of inhaled salbutamol.

widespread in winter-sport athletes such as cross-country skiers. Asthmatic athletes commonly use inhaled beta-2 agonists to prevent and treat asthmatic symptoms.

When given systemically by tablet or injection, beta-2 agonists may have anabolic effects and their use is therefore prohibited. Only salbutamol and salmeterol by inhalation are permitted.

In 17 of 19 randomized placebo-controlled trials in non-asthmatic competitive athletes, performance-enhancing effects of the inhaled beta-2 agonists formoterol, salbutamol, salmeterol, and terbutaline could not be proved. This is particularly true for endurance performance, anaerobic power and strength performance. In three of four studies, even supratherapeutic doses of salbutamol (800–1200 µg) had no ergogenic effect.[79]

Adverse effects include:

- nervousness
- tremor
- tachycardia
- palpitation
- headache
- nausea
- vomiting
- sweating.

The adverse effects are minimized when the drugs are given by inhalation.

Hormone antagonists and modulators

Prohibited hormone antagonists and modulators are shown in the box below.

Aromatase inhibitors lower the amount of estrogen in the body, whereas drugs such as the selective estrogen receptor modulators (SERMs) block the estrogen receptors.

The anti-estrogen drugs such as tamoxifen and clomiphene are used by both male and female athletes for different reasons. Male athletes primarily use tamoxifen in conjunction with AASs to prevent the development of gynecomastia. Tamoxifen also increases testosterone levels in males and is advertised as a body fat reducer.

In females, there is evidence that tamoxifen is used as an ergogenic agent, particularly by body builders.[80] By blocking the estrogen receptors in a woman's body, tamoxifen leaves testosterone unopposed. This could lead to masculinization.

Tamoxifen has a number of harmful effects in females. It has been shown to increase the risk of venous thromboembolic events. As it is related to diethylstilbestrol (DES), women who became pregnant while taking the drug may be at increased risk of giving birth to a child with congenital defects.

Diuretics and other masking agents

The rules applying to diuretics and other masking agents are shown in the box below.

S4: Hormone antagonists and modulators[1]

The following classes are prohibited:

1. Aromatase inhibitors including, but not limited to, aminoglutethimide, anostrozole, androsta-1,4,6-triene-3,17-dione (androstatrienedione), 4-androstene-3,6,17 trione (6-oxo), exemestane, formestane, letrozole, testolactone.
2. Selective estrogen receptor modulators (SERMs) including, but not limited to, raloxifene, tamoxifen, toremifene.
3. Other anti-estrogenic substances, including, but not limited to, clomiphene, cyclofenil, fulvestrant.
4. Agents modifying myostatin function(s) including, but not limited to, myostatin inhibitors.

S5: Diuretics and other masking agents[1]

Masking agents are prohibited. They include:

diuretics, desmopressin, plasma expanders (e.g. glycerol; intravenous administration of albumin, dextran, hydroxyethyl starch and mannitol), probenecid; and other substances with similar biological effect(s).

Diuretics include:

acetazolamide, amiloride, bumetanide, canrenone, chlorthalidone, ethacrynic acid, frusemide, indapamide, metolazone, spironolactone, thiazides (e.g. bendroflumethiazide, chlorothiazide, hydrochlorothiazide), triamterene and other substances with a similar chemical structure or similar biological effect(s) (except drosperinone, pamabrom, and topical dorzolamide and brinzolamide, which are not prohibited).

The use in and out of competition, as applicable, of any quantity of a substance subject to threshold limits (i.e. salbutamol, morphine, cathine, ephedrine, methylephedrine, and pseudoephedrine) in conjunction with a diuretic or other masking agent requires the deliverance of a specific Therapeutic Use Exemption (TUE) for that substance in addition to the one granted for the diuretic or other masking agent.

Diuretics

Clinically, diuretics are used in the treatment of hypertension, fluid retention, and congestive cardiac failure. Adverse effects from their use include dehydration, hypotension, muscle cramps, and electrolyte disturbances. Athletes use diuretics in order to lose weight rapidly prior to competition in sports where weight limits are set. These sports include boxing, wrestling, weightlifting, judo, and light-weight rowing; they are also used by jockeys.

The use of diuretics may be combined with other dehydration techniques such as use of a sauna, exercise in hot conditions, and food and water restrictions. These practices may result in rapid dehydration and electrolyte imbalances, which may be harmful to the athlete, particularly if practiced on a regular basis. Diuretics are also used to aid the excretion of or to dilute the presence of illegal substances in the urine.

Masking agents

Probenecid is a drug used clinically to increase the uptake of penicillin administered intramuscularly. It is used by athletes to accelerate the excretion of prohibited substances. Plasma volume expanders such as hydroxyethyl starch (HES) dilute the concentration of hemoglobin and erythrocytes. A number of Finnish cross-country skiers were found to be using HES at the 2001 World Championships and were subsequently disqualified.

Prohibited methods at all times (in and out of competition)

Enhancement of oxygen transfer

The rules applying to the use of oxygen transfer enhancement are shown in the box below.

M1: Enhancement of oxygen transfer[1]

The following are prohibited:
1. Blood doping, including the use of autologous, homologous, or heterologous blood, or red blood cell products of any origin.
2. Artificially enhancing the uptake, transport, or delivery of oxygen, including, but not limited to, perfluorochemicals, efaproxiral (RSR13) and modified hemoglobin products (e.g. hemoglobin-based blood substitutes, microencaspsulated hemoglobin products), excluding supplemental oxygen.

Blood doping

Blood doping is the administration of blood or red blood cells to an athlete to increase the red blood cell mass. This may be autologous (infusion with the athlete's own blood) or homologous (infusion with appropriately cross-matched donated blood).

The usual method of blood doping is to withdraw two units of an athlete's own blood four to six weeks prior to competition. This allows time for the red blood cell count to return to normal prior to re-infusing the blood a day or two before competition. The aim of this procedure is to increase the red blood cell mass and therefore increase the oxygen-carrying capacity of the blood. Improved endurance may occur as a result of blood doping.[81, 82]

Blood doping has been prohibited since 1984 but its use dropped dramatically when recombinant erythropoietin (EPO) became available in 1987.[83] Recently with the advent of testing for EPO, blood doping has again become popular. Only recently has a reliable method been developed for its detection. The American cyclist Tyler Hamilton was one of the first athletes to be found guilty of blood doping, in 2004.

Adverse effects do occur with blood doping as they do with any transfusion, especially if donated blood is used. Allergic reactions may occur and there is an increased risk of blood-borne diseases such as hepatitis B and C, and HIV. In addition, blood doping has been reported to increase the blood viscosity significantly and this may lead to some serious health risks due to sludging of blood, particularly in the cerebral circulation.

Artificial oxygen carriers

Artificial oxygen carriers or "blood substitutes" are being developed to serve as a temporary replacement for transfused red blood cells in the prevention of ischemic tissue damage and hypovolemic shock. Two main types are available—hemoglobin oxygen carriers (HBOCs) and perfluorocarbons (PFCs).

Hemoglobin oxygen carriers

Hemoglobin oxygen carriers (HBOCs) have been developed as hemoglobin substitutes in recent years for use when a rapid expansion of blood volume is needed in acute blood loss following severe injury, surgery, or severe hemolytic anemia when human blood is unavailable, time necessary to undertake a proper cross-match is short, or the risk of blood infection is high.[84]

As the free hemoglobin molecule is inherently unstable, biochemical modifications have been made to the molecule. Three principal approaches have been used to stabilize and modify tetramic hemoglobin—polymerization using polyaldehydes, conjugation of polymers to the surface of the hemoglobin, and cross-linking the alpha- and beta-dimers of the protein.[85]

Hemoglobin is available from three different sources—bovine blood, human blood, and genetic engineering. Bovine blood is cross-linked by glutaraldehyde, thus preventing the breakdown of hemoglobin. It can readily release oxygen into the tissues and is relatively inexpensive. One study of its effect on exercise performance, although significantly flawed, showed increased oxygen uptake and lowered lactate levels compared with autologous transfusion.[86]

HBOCs have several advantages. They can be pasteurized and ultrafiltered and so are safe from infection; they are readily available and easy to store with a long shelf-life of up to two years; all blood types are compatible, and they have only one-third the viscosity of blood.[84] The main disadvantage is that they only last 12–48 hours in the body, compared with 120 days for blood cells. There is some evidence of high pulmonary and peripheral blood pressure associated with their use.[85] There have been rumors of their use in sport but no definitive evidence.

Perfluorocarbon emulsions

Perfluorocarbon emulsions (PFCs), a group of synthetic compounds similar to teflon, are hydrocarbons to which fluorine atoms have been added. They are extremely inert, inexpensive to produce, and are made up in a sponge-like emulsion containing very small particles (0.2 μm in diameter) that can deliver oxygen to the tissues through very small blood vessels. They are capable of physically dissolving large amounts of oxygen in plasma.[84]

Unlike hemoglobin, PFCs do not bind oxygen. The amount of oxygen that can be carried in solution is directly proportional to the gas partial pressure. A high partial pressure gradient is required to dissolve a large quantity of oxygen in the PFCs, and such gradients are also necessary between PFC and tissue in order to achieve a biologically useful degree of oxygen unloading. This precludes their use where supplemental oxygen is not available.[85]

The first-generation PFCs (e.g. Fluosol-DA) proved unsatisfactory, but the second-generation products (Oxygent, Oxyfluor), using improved technology and

containing higher concentrations of the active agent in the emulsion, show promise.

As yet, no study has investigated the performance-enhancing effects of PFCs; however, they *have* been found to improve oxygen delivery to the tissue under many conditions.

Detection

It would be futile to analyze urine samples in search of PFCs and most HBOCs since they are not processed by the kidney and/or the urinary excretion is too low and variable. The presence of an artificial oxygen carrier in the blood will be easily detected as long as the sample is taken soon after competition.[85]

Chemical and physical manipulation

The rules applying to manipulation of samples taken for testing are shown in the box below.

Chemical and physical manipulation is the use of substances and/or methods that alter, attempt to alter, or may reasonably be expected to alter the integrity and validity of urine samples used in doping controls. These include, but are not limited to:

- catheterization
- sample substitution and/or tampering.

The success or failure of the use of a prohibited substance or method is not material. It is sufficient that the said substance or procedure was used or attempted for the infraction to be considered as consummated.

WADA has prohibited procedures that interfere with the content or collection of urine samples used for drug testing, such as the use of catheters to substitute urine. There have been a number of cases of athletes who have been disqualified from competition

---

M2: Chemical and physical manipulation[1]

The following is prohibited:

1. Tampering, or attempting to tamper, in order to alter the integrity and validity of samples collected during doping control is prohibited. These include, but are not limited to, catheterization, urine substitution and/or adulteration (e.g. proteases).
2. Intravenous infusions are prohibited, except for those legitimately received in the course of hospital admissions or clinical investigation.
3. Sequential withdrawal, manipulation, and reinfusion of whole blood into the circulatory system.

when they have been caught substituting urine from a coach, relative, or fellow athlete in order to avoid having their own urine tested. This use of surrogate urine is prohibited and there have been examples where the athlete has subsequently been caught out because the surrogate urine has contained a prohibited substance that was being used by a friend or relative at the time of the test!

Current testing procedures are structured in such a way that the risk of substituting surrogate urine is minimal. The athlete is accompanied by a chaperone (of the same gender) so that the urine sample is provided under direct observation and the chance of substituting alternative urine is virtually impossible. However, athletes still use ingenious methods to avoid detection.

Gene doping
with MALCOLM COLLINS

The rules applying to gene doping are shown in the box below.

Gene doping or gene transfer technology to improve athletic performance is a serious threat to the integrity of elite sport. The principle of gene therapy is based on the delivery to a cell of a therapeutic gene that may compensate for an absent or abnormal gene. In general, DNA is used as the genetic material. This genetic material encodes for a therapeutic protein and needs to be delivered to the cell nucleus to be active.

Gene delivery

To facilitate the introduction of a gene into the cells of the recipient, a delivery vehicle is required. These delivery systems can be either biologic or physical.

M3: Gene doping[1]

The following, with the potential to enhance performance, are prohibited:

1. The transfer of nucleic acids or nucleic acid sequences.
2. The use of normal or genetically modified cells.
3. The use of agents that directly or indirectly affect functions known to influence performance by altering gene expression. For example, peroxisome proliferator-activated receptor δ (PPARδ), agonists (e.g. GW 1516) and PPARδ-AMP-activated protein kinase (AMPK) axis agonists (e.g. AICAR) are prohibited.

The use of a biologic vector is the most common delivery mode for gene therapy. Viral vectors such as retroviruses, adenoviruses, and adeno-associated viruses (AAVs) are commonly used as they function to integrate into host cells and use this cell to replicate their own genetic material. In gene therapy, these viruses are modified to reduce the potential for viral infection while carrying the ability to be delivered to specific cells for expression.

Plasmid DNA (pDNA) is an alternative biologic vector but differs from viral vectors in that pDNA is synthetic and may be grown in bacteria, then purified. Although pDNA is more inefficient than viral vectors, it has the advantage of avoiding a possible immune response.

Plasmid delivery can also be improved by combining the plasmid with lipid vesicles that aid penetration of the cell membrane. These plasmid/liposome complexes can be enhanced by the addition of proteins to target specific cell surface receptors, essentially creating an artificial virus.

In comparison with gene delivery with viral vectors, pDNA is very inefficient, but its efficiency can be markedly increased by modifying the means of delivery to add a physical component. The application of a series of electrical pulses following intramuscular injection (*in vivo* electroporation) can increase the efficiency of pDNA delivery more than 1000-fold and genetically modify the majority of the target muscle fibers. Other methods of physically enhancing plasmid-based gene delivery include ultrasound, laser, and magnetic particles.

Gene therapy and gene doping

The fundamental difference, physically, biochemically, and ethically, between gene therapy and gene doping is that the goal of gene doping is not to replace an absent or dysfunctional protein in an unhealthy individual but rather to artificially alter gene expression in an otherwise healthy individual. The evolution of gene therapy from a strictly medical tool to a performance-enhancement mechanism has significant ramifications both in the competitive sports world and in the general population.

What makes a gene a good candidate for doping? Obviously, the targets for gene doping would depend on the desired effect. Overexpression or underexpression of the gene product should enhance traits that are desirable for peak athletic performance.

For endurance sports, such as long-distance running or swimming, genes that bolster oxygen production or usage and delay fatigue would be the likely candidates. For sports in which strength or agility provide the competitive advantage, genes involved in muscle mass stimulation and injury recovery are the more likely targets.

Genes for endurance
Erythropoietin
Erythropoietin (EPO) is a hormone produced in response to decreased oxygen levels in the blood that signals the body to increase hemoglobin production. EPO-stimulating agents have long been a part of performance-enhancing doping.[87] Overexpression of EPO by gene doping would increase endogenous hemoglobin production and thereby oxygen distribution to muscles.

Peroxisome proliferator-activated receptor delta
Peroxisome proliferator-activated receptor delta (PPARδ) and its family of hormones are involved in changing type I (fast twitch) skeletal muscle fibers to type II (slow twitch) muscle fibers. Upregulation of this gene could produce an increase in the number of type II muscle fibers desired for endurance sports, even in the absence of endurance training. The WADA 2011 Prohibited List bans PPARδ-d agonists (e.g. GW1516) and PPARδ-adenosine monophosphate–activated protein kinase axis agonists (e.g. AICAR), the only genes specifically mentioned under the gene doping section.[1]

Phosphoenolpyruvate carboxykinase
The role of phosphoenolpyruvate carboxykinase (PEPCK) in skeletal muscle is somewhat unclear, but overexpression in mice increases endurance and longevity and leads to decreased body fat.[88]

Vascular endothelial growth factor
Vascular endothelial growth factor is instrumental in the development of new blood vessels and also appears to be important in some injury-healing molecular pathways.

Genes for strength
There are two agents capable of strength enhancement:

- Insulin-like growth factor 1 (IGF-1) is the primary target of growth hormone action. Increased gene expression leads to increased muscle mass

and power. In addition to promoting muscle hypertrophy, IGF-1 also hastens muscle repair.[89]
- Myostatin—unlike many other candidate genes for gene doping, myostatin would be targeted to promote decreased expression of this gene. Myostatin is a negative regulator of muscle growth, and by impeding its actions, increased muscle mass would be expected.[90]

Genes for tissue repair/other
There are two agents capable of enhancing tissue repair:

- Bone morphogenetic protein (BMP)—the BMP family of growth factors enhances bone repair and would theoretically shorten recovery time from injury. In the absence of an injury, these growth factors have the potential to increase bone, cartilage, or tendon strength in an effort to stave off potential career-ending injuries.[91]
- Endorphins—endorphins are important components of pain management, fatigue delay, and endurance. Genes that increase endorphins would increase pain threshold both acutely during competition by reducing lactic acid–related pain and chronically by dulling the effects of prior injury. These effects make genes related to endorphin production, expression, and release reasonable targets for gene doping.[90]

Animal studies
Examples of potential areas for gene doping to improve athletic performance are EPO for endurance performance and IGF-1 for muscle strength. An adenovirus was used to deliver the EPO gene in mice and monkeys and this boosted the hematocrit from 49% to 81% in the mice and from 40% to 70% in the monkeys. The effects lasted over a year in the mice and for 12 weeks in the monkeys.[92] Mice injected with the IGF-1 gene showed a 15% increase in muscle bulk.[93]

However, in addition to shedding light on the potential enhancement effects of gene doping in humans, animal studies have also uncovered concerns that may directly affect human subjects.[90] It is perhaps unsurprising that artificially overexpressing genes to promote athletic prowess may lead to unwanted and negative side effects.

Some studies reported an increase in hyperactivity, aggressiveness, and other behavioral sequelae in treated mice. Overexpression of EPO in macaques has been reported to increase blood viscosity, with effects on cardiac functioning.[88] Clearly, although animal models may demonstrate the promise of gene doping, the perils of this procedure cannot be ignored because its use is contemplated in humans.

Risks of gene doping

The risks associated with gene therapy in a regulated, controlled setting are still being defined.[90] Results of gene therapy trials performed in the 1990s indicated both a substantial variability in response to vectors and a nonlinear relationship between vector dose and toxicity.

The death of an 18-year-old volunteer in a pilot study of gene therapy was attributed to systemic inflammatory response syndrome caused by an immune response to the adenoviral vector used.[94] Therefore, the risks associated with taking a new procedure and illegally abusing it in otherwise healthy individuals are real and concerning. The most significant risks are associated with both the unregulated delivery of the gene therapy by dopers and the effects of this doping on a cellular and functional level in the athlete.

The illicit production and administration of gene doping products would compound these risks. The safety, quality, and contents of a gene doping product would be unregulated, and the secretive nature of doping in general may hinder appropriate medical follow-up if needed.

The risks secondary to altered gene expression include:

- an immune response to a viral vector
- an autoimmune response to a recombinant protein
- insertional mutagenesis
- lack of expression control and the sequelae related to an artificial overproduction of a protein in a healthy subject.

The immune response to a viral vector can be mild (such as a fever or inflammation), but can also be overwhelming and fatal. If a protein produced differs from that which is endogenously produced, autoimmune responses are possible.[90]

The prospect of insertional mutagenesis is concerning in that the vector could insert itself into the host genome and disrupt oncogenes, leading to tumor development. In some cases, the risk of germline integration, or permanent, heritable genetic changes being introduced adds another serious ethical consideration to gene doping.

EPO overexpression leads to increased blood viscosity, which can increase the risk for heart failure or stroke. Overexpression of a growth factor, such as IGF-1, can cause cardiac hypertrophy and stimulate growth of cancerous cells. Increasing muscle mass by manipulating myostatin, IGF-1, or other factors is also likely to put extra stress on supporting bones and tendons, which could actually increase the risk of injury.

Detection

Detecting gene doping will be very difficult.

 PRACTICE PEARL To be successful, doping detection needs to be accessible, fast, and reliable—three significant challenges when dealing with gene doping.

For example, if a gene doping product is produced by introducing genes to make more proteins endogenously, how can it be distinguished from the naturally produced protein? Can evidence of gene doping be reliably assessed using body fluids?

Studies have shown that gene therapy with IGF-1, while increasing the detectable levels in muscle cells, did not show an increase in circulating IGF-1 levels in the blood.[95] A muscle biopsy, although more sensitive, is not practical.

Detection strategies can be categorized into direct (evidence of doping agent) and indirect (evidence of consequences of gene doping).[90]

Direct approach

Direct detection of gene doping would involve identification of the vector used or a recombinant protein that differs from naturally occurring protein.[90] Vectors have been identified in blood after gene therapy, but the window of opportunity for detection seems to be short, which poses obvious limitations.[91] There is some evidence that some proteins produced by gene therapy undergo slightly different post-translational modification, which opens a possible detection.

Some genes may be regulated by promoters that need to be activated. Detection of activating substances such as rapamycin, tetracycline, and antiprogestins would indicate gene doping but may also be present for therapeutic reasons.[95] Although direct evidence of gene doping may be preferred, especially if legally challenged, the technical limitations of these processes may not make it the most likely solution for gene doping detection.

Indirect approach

Indirect detection of gene doping would involve the identification of the consequences of this procedure on the athlete. Various fields of study are being investigated as a potential "biologic profile" to distinguish normal standards from those indicating gene doping.

For example, transcriptomics (the profiling of gene expression) measures changes in the concentration of messenger RNA for thousands of genes. Proteomics (protein profiling) evaluates the set of proteins expressed from the genome and provides qualitative and quantitative analysis of their variants. Metabolomics (the profiling of nonprotein low-molecular-weight metabolites) can also provide a possible measure of gene-doping activities.[96]

Although these are promising approaches, the development of normal standards, individual "passports," and variability parameters is expected to be costly, time-consuming, and open to legal interpretation if a gene-doping charge is made. As illustrated in the testosterone metabolism studies, natural genetic variation in the population can lead to extremely variable enzyme activity under normal circumstances and may provide enough reasonable doubt to discount a suspected case of gene doping.[90]

Prohibited substances in-competition

Stimulants

Information about stimulants is provided in the box.

The stimulants are a broad group of substances and include central nervous system stimulants, sympathomimetic agents, and cocaine. Until 2004 all stimulants were on the prohibited list. In 2004 bupropion, caffeine, phenylephrine, phenylpropanolamine, pipadrol, pseudoephedrine, and synephrine were removed from the list and placed on the Monitoring Program. Pseudoephedrine was reintroduced on the banned list in 2010 due to evidence of abuse in some sports and scientific proof of its performance enhancing effects at certain doses. The major stimulants remaining on the banned list are the amphetamines, cocaine, ephedrine, and modafinil.

Amphetamines

Amphetamines were first used clinically in the 1930s for their stimulatory effects in the treatment of narcolepsy. Their clinical use nowadays is restricted to the treatment of narcolepsy and childhood hyperactive syndromes such as attention deficit hyper-

---

S6: Stimulants[1]

All stimulants (including both optical isomers where relevant) are prohibited in competition, except imidazole derivatives for topical use and those stimulants included in the 2011 monitoring program.[a]

Stimulants include:

1. Non-specified stimulants—adrafinil, amfepramone, amiphenazole, amphetamine, amphetaminil, benfluorex, benzphetamine, benzylpiperazine, bromantan, clobenzorex, cocaine, cropopamide, crotetamide, dimethylamphetamine, etilamphetamine, famprofazone, fencamine, fenetylline, fenfluramine, fenproporex, furfenorex, mefenorex, mephentermine, mesocarb, methamphetamine(D-), p-methylamphetamine, methylenedioxyamphetamine, methylenedioxymethamphetamine, modafinil, norflenfluramine, phendimetrazine, phenmetrazine, phentermine, 4-phenylpiracetam (carphedon), prenylamine, prolintane.

A stimulant not expressly listed in this section is a specified substance.

2. Specified stimulants (examples)—adrenaline (epinephrine),[b] cathine,[c] ephedrine,[d] etamivan, etilefrine, fenbutrazate, fencamfamine, heptaminol, isometheptene, levmethamfetamine, meclofenoxate, methylephedrine,[d] methylhexaneamine (dimethylpentylamine), methylphenidate, nikethamide, norfenefrine, octopamine, oxilofrine, parahydroxyamphetamine, pemoline, pentetrazol, phenpromethamine, propylhexedrine, pseudoephedrine,[e] selegiline, sibutramine, strychnine, tuaminoheptane, and other substances with a similar chemical structure or similar biological effect(s).

[a] The following substances included in the 2011 monitoring program (bupropion, caffeine, phenyepherine, phenylpropanolamine, pipradol, synephrine) are not considered prohibited substances

[b] Adrenaline (epinephrine) associated with local anesthetic agents or by local administration (e.g. nasal, ophthalmological) is not prohibited

[c] Cathine is prohibited when its concentration in urine is greater than 5 μg/mL

[d] Each of ephedrine and methylephedrine is prohibited when its concentration in urine is greater than 10 μg/mL

[e] Pseudoephedrine is prohibited when its concentration in urine is greater than 150 μg/mL

activity disorder (ADHD).[97] They have been widely used in sport to delay fatigue and increase alertness, although their use appears to have diminished in recent years, possibly due to adverse publicity regarding adverse effects. There is some evidence that the use of amphetamines may enhance speed, power, endurance, and concentration.

The "benefits" of amphetamine use must be weighed against the adverse effects. Acute behavioral adverse effects are common with the use of amphetamines. These include central nervous system excitation as demonstrated by irritability, insomnia, restlessness, dizziness, or a tremor. Occasionally, more severe effects such as confusion, paranoia, delirium, and uncontrolled aggression occur. Systemic adverse effects include hypertension, angina, vomiting, abdominal pain, and occasionally cerebral hemorrhage.

Some deaths of sportspeople have resulted, even when "normal" doses of amphetamines have been used, when undertaking maximal physical activity. Chronic use of amphetamines is associated with central nervous system–related symptoms such as uncontrolled involuntary movements. Amphetamines are addictive and withdrawal is associated with fatigue, lethargy, and depression.

There has been considerable controversy over the granting of TUEs for amphetamines on the basis of required treatment for ADHD. The granting of TUEs in ADHD is mostly confined to children. The previous requirements involved requiring children to cease their ADHD treatment on weekends or other occasions to allow them to compete but this was considered unreasonable after expert advice deemed it to have negative effects on symptom control. Currently, the granting of TUEs for children with ADHD is well documented and accepted.

The use of stimulants in the treatment of adult-onset ADHD remains controversial, primarily because recognition of the clinical entity itself is relatively recent. It appears that with the release of a new non-stimulating medication (e.g. atoxematine) for adult ADHD, the problem of no alternative treatment may be solved.

Ephedra and pseudoephedrine

Ephedra is a shrub that grows mainly in desert or arid regions and is native to northern China and inner Mongolia. Different species vary in the amount of ephedrine alkaloids they contain, the content of which produces the pharmacological effects of ephedra. The most common alkaloid is ephedrine, which generally constitutes 40–90% of the alkaloid content. This is the major ephedra alkaloid found in over-the-counter supplements.

Pseudoephedrine is the next most common alkaloid and is less potent. It is produced synthetically and is used in many over-the-counter and prescription medications as a nasal decongestant. Norephedrine and norpseudoephedrine are minor alkaloid components.

The main use of ephedra, especially in the US, is in dietary supplements. A review of case reports showed that 60% of users of ephedra-containing supplements were women and that the major reasons for its use were weight loss (59%), improved athletic performance (16%), and increased energy (6%).[98] There is some physiological basis for the use of ephedra as a weight loss medication and some data showing a modest increase in weight loss, although only over a six-month period.[99]

The performance-enhancing effects of ephedrine and pseudoephedrine have been extensively studied. Normal dosages of both substances do not appear to enhance performance.[100]

 Large doses of pseudoephedrine enhance cycling performance;[101] the combination of ephedrine and caffeine enhances performance[102] and carries the most risk.

Following an increasing number of reports of adverse events, including hypertension, arrhythmias, myocardial infarction, seizure, cerebrovascular accidents, and death, the US Food and Drug Administration (FDA) made it illegal for manufacturers to sell dietary supplements containing ephedrine.

Similarly, phenylpropanolamine, another commonly used dietary supplement, was voluntarily withdrawn from the market after its use was found to be an independent risk factor for hemorrhagic stroke in females.

Until the end of 2003, pseudoephedrine was prohibited in sports when a threshold value of 25 mg/mL of urine was exceeded. The threshold level for pseudoephedrine was initially set to 10 mg/mL, then increased to 25 mg/mL in 2000. In January 2004 the presence of this drug in doping control urine samples and its use in sports were no longer banned. Hence, pseudoephedrine represents an interesting object to outline a possible effect of lifting a ban for a drug, the ergogenic properties of which are controversially discussed.[103]

Following the lifting of the ban, the use of pseudoephedrine was monitored by WADA and its incidence in testing samples increased dramatically especially among cyclists.

While only 0.2% of specimens measured between 2001 and 2003 yielded pseudoephedrine levels greater than 25 mg/mL, 3.9% of all samples analyzed in 2007/2008 were found to contain more than the formerly existing threshold value.[103]

These data suggest that the misuse of the stimulating agent pseudoephedrine was rather limited as long as the substance was prohibited and that lifting the ban resulted in a much more frequent use aiming for performance enhancement. Consequently, a new threshold value for urinary pseudoephedrine of 150 mg/mL becoming effective in January 2010.

Cocaine

Cocaine is more a community drug problem than a drug for performance enhancement. It emerged in the 1960s to become a major health problem. Recently, the introduction of "crack," a purer form of cocaine, has increased the risks associated with its use.

Cocaine has a minimal performance-enhancing effect because of the brief duration of its action. Decreased fatigue has been noticed and cocaine use causes increased activity and talkativeness. The main feeling produced by cocaine is one of euphoria and a sense of wellbeing.

The mood elevation appears similar to that produced by amphetamines but is far more transient. The feeling of euphoria is usually followed soon after by a feeling of dysphoria and craving. This may be overcome by another dose of cocaine. Tachyphylaxis (rapid decrease in the response to a drug due to previous exposure to that drug) occurs following repeated use.

The positive effects on athletic performance are minimal, and may be associated with heightened arousal and increased alertness with low doses. Detrimental effects on performance are reported more frequently and include impaired hand–eye coordination, distorted sense of time, and inappropriate aggression.

The adverse effects of cocaine are numerous and include:

- serious cardiovascular problems, such as myocardial infarction, cardiac arrhythmia
- cerebral hemorrhage
- convulsions
- similar behavioral changes as occur with the use of amphetamines (page 1248).

The normal clinical use of cocaine is restricted to its use as a topical anesthetic agent in eye and nose surgery but it cannot be used in sport as a topical anesthetic. Its use is illegal in most countries and possession of cocaine can carry heavy penalties.

Modafinil

In the 2003 World Track and Field Championships, Kelli White was disqualified after her victories in the 100 m and 200 m sprints when she tested positive for the presence of modafinil, which she claimed she was taking for the treatment of narcolepsy. At the time modafinil was not specifically listed on the prohibited list, but the International Association of Athletics Federations (IAAF) considered that modafinil fell under the category "and related substances" for stimulants and recommended that she be stripped of her medals. Modafinil is not a classic psychostimulant and it is not clear if it is a performance-enhancing agent.[104] Those who are prescribed modafinil in the treatment of narcolepsy should apply for a TUE, which requires the diagnosis of narcolepsy to be confirmed by one of the accepted methods (e.g. sleep studies in an accredited institution).

Narcotics

Narcotics prohibited in competition are listed in the box below.

Narcotics are derivatives of the opium poppy and include morphine, pethidine, and diamorphine (heroin). They are commonly used in the management of moderate-to-severe pain.

In addition to their analgesic effect, narcotics may cause:

- mood disturbances
- drowsiness

S7: Narcotics[1]

The following narcotics are prohibited in competition—buprenorphine, dextromoramide, diamorphine (heroin), fentanyl and its derivatives, hydromorphone, methadone, morphine, oxycodone, oxymorphone, pentazocine, pethidine.

- mental clouding
- constipation
- nausea
- vomiting.

In high doses they may cause:

- respiratory depression
- hypotension
- muscle rigidity
- addiction
- significant withdrawal effects.

Narcotics have no ergogenic effect but have the potential to mask pain and permit athletes to compete with musculoskeletal injuries. For this reason, they are included on the list of prohibited substances.

Codeine, dextromethorphan, dextropropoxyphene, dihydrocodeine, diphenoxylate, ethylmorphine, pholcodine, propoxyphene, and tramadol are permitted.

Cannabinoids

Cannabinoids that are prohibited in competition are listed in the box below.

The products of the cannabis plant such as marijuana, hashish, hash oil, sensemilla, and others are considered to be the most popular illicit drug in the world. The most important compound contained in the plant is the cannabinoids, in which the substance delta-9-tetrahydrocannabinol (THC) is the most significant compound because of its psychoactive properties. The rate of absorption of THC by the lungs is very high. Maximal blood concentrations are obtained after 3–8 minutes; the onset of action on the central nervous system is observed in approximately 20 minutes, and the peak effect in 2–4 hours. Duration of action for psychoactive effects is 4–6 hours.

For occasional users cannabinoid metabolites can be detected in urine up to five to seven days after the exposure. In chronic users it may be detected for as long as 30 days after the last exposure.

Since 1989, cannabis has been included on the list of drugs subject to certain restrictions. A concentration in the urine of carboxy-THC greater than 15 ng/mL has been used to allow for the possible effect of passive smoking. In the 1998 Nagano Winter Olympics, snowboarder Ross Rebagliati tested positive for cannabinoids, was suspended, and was subsequently reinstated.

Cannabinoids have a negative effect on sports performance through impairment of psychomotor skills, altered perception of time, and impaired concentration. They may also have a negative effect on exercise performance.[105] The well-recognized "amotivational" syndrome associated with long-term marijuana use may be particularly damaging to a sporting career.

Glucocorticosteroids

All glucocorticosteroids are prohibited in competition (see box).

Glucocorticosteroids (GCs) exert many beneficial actions in exercising humans. Glucocorticosteroids increase the availability of metabolic substrates for energy needs of muscles (increased lipolysis and plasma free fatty acids [FFA], increased glycogen synthesis) and maintain normal vascular integrity and responsiveness during exercise. In addition, glucocorticosteroids prevent an overreaction of the immune system as a result of exercise-induced muscle damage (immunosuppressive and anti-inflammatory effects).

Cortisol also prepares the organism for the next bout of exercise, explaining why, when an acute bout of endurance-exercise is stopped, cortisol levels may return to pre-exercise values with a delay (<2 hours post-exercise).[106]

These physiologic properties of glucocorticosteroids suggest that they could enhance performance, and this explains why they are in such widespread use in the sporting world. Indeed, the expected effects of the use and abuse of glucocorticosteroids are numerous—neurostimulatory effects at cerebral glucocorticosteroid receptors could attenuate central impressions of fatigue, and anti-inflammatory and analgesic effects could inhibit sensations of muscle pain on effort and raise the fatigue threshold.

The metabolic effects of these compounds consolidate glycogen reserves in muscle tissue and accelerate lipolysis and glycolysis mechanisms induced

---

S8: Cannabinoids[1]

Natural (e.g. cannabis, hashish, marijuana) or synthetic delta 9-tetrahydrocannabinol (THC) and cannabimimetics (e.g. "Spice" [containing JWH018, JWH073], HU-210) are prohibited.

S9: Glucocorticosteroids[1]

All glucocorticosteroids are prohibited in competition when administered by oral, intravenous, intramuscular, or rectal routes.

E

by catecholamines and growth hormone, thereby leading to more efficient use of energy sources by the muscles in the course of exercise.[106]

Research reveals inconsistencies regarding the ergogenic effect of glucocorticosteroid administrations in humans. These inconsistencies may be attributed to:

- the glucocorticosteroid administration dosage, route, and mode (acute or short term)
- the type, duration, and intensity (submaximal, maximal) of exercise tested
- the participants (highly trained or professional versus recreationally trained)
- the differences in diet, such as whether or not experiments are food-controlled and whether or not subjects fasted
- glucocorticosteroid intake coupled or not with intensive training.[106]

Arlettaz et al.[107] found that after short-term prednisolone (a glucocorticosteroid) administration (60 mg for 7 days) there was a significant improvement of performance (154% compared with placebo) measured by time to exhaustion at 70% to 75% VO_2max in healthy, recreationally trained men. To determine if the effects of glucocorticosteroid treatment could be extrapolated to elite athletes, Collomp et al.[108] investigated the influence of short-term prednisolone administration (60 mg for 7 days) combined with standardized training (2 hours per day) on performance measured by time to exhaustion at 70% to 75% VO_2max. Compared with the placebo condition, strenuous training associated with the glucocorticosteroid treatment resulted in a marked improvement in endurance performance (average increase of about 80% compared with an average increase of 54% in their previous study without training).

The health risks of using glucocorticosteroids are well characterized. Long-term glucocorticosteroid use may lead to complications, notably on bone tissue (osteoporosis), metabolism (insulin resistance), and the cardiovascular system (hypertension and atherosclerosis). While the inclusion of corticosteroids on the WADA Prohibited List is controversial, there would appear to be sufficient evidence of performance enhancement and health risk to justify their presence. Some[106] would argue that systemic use of glucocorticosteroids should be prohibited at all times (in and out of competition) and not just in-competition as in the current WADA legislation.[1]

Substances prohibited in particular sports in-competition

Alcohol

The prohibitions relating to alcohol and competitive sport are shown in the box below.

Alcohol generally has a negative effect on sports performance, impairing reaction time, hand–eye coordination, accuracy, balance, gross motor skills, and strength.[109]

> **P1: Alcohol[1]**
>
> Alcohol (ethanol) is prohibited in-competition only, in the following sports. Detection will be conducted by analysis of breath and/or blood. The doping violation threshold (hematological values) is 0.10 g/L.
> - Aeronautic (FAI)
> - Archery (FGITA, IPC)
> - Automobile (FIA)
> - Karate (WKF)
> - Motorcycling (FIM)
> - Ninepin and tenpin bowling (FIQ)
> - Powerboating (UIM).

Beta blockers

The prohibitions relating to beta blockers and competitive sport are shown in the box opposite.

Beta blockers are drugs commonly used in the treatment of hypertension, angina, arrhythmia, migraine, anxiety, and tremor; they are also used following myocardial infarction. Their anxiolytic and anti-tremor effects resulted in their use in the sports of shooting and archery where steadiness of hand and arm is important.

Beta blockers do not show any other positive effect on performance; in fact, they may have negative effects on both anaerobic and aerobic endurance. Adverse effects may include fatigue, depression, nightmares, bronchospasm, and sexual dysfunction. Alternative treatments to beta blockers are available for most clinical conditions they are indicated for.

Therapeutic use of a prohibited substance (therapeutic use exemption)

Athletes may have illnesses or conditions that require them to take particular medications. If the medication an athlete is required to take to treat an illness or condition happens to fall under the Prohibited List, a therapeutic use exemption (TUE) may give

P2: Beta blockers[1]

Unless otherwise specified, beta blockers are prohibited, in competition only, in the following sports:

- Aeronautic (FAI)
- Archery (FGITA, IPC) (also prohibited out of competition)
- Automobile (FIA)
- Billiards and snooker (WCBS)
- Bobsleigh and skeleton (FIBT)
- Boules (CMSB)
- Bridge (FMB)
- Curling (WCF)
- Darts (WDF)
- Golf (IGF)
- Motorcycling (FIM)
- Modern pentathlon (UIPM) (for disciplines involving shooting)
- Ninepin and tenpin bowling (FIQ)
- Powerboating (UIM)
- Sailing (ISAF) (for match race helms only)
- Shooting (ISSF, IPC) (also prohibited out of competition)
- Skiing/snowboarding (FIS) in ski jumping, freestyle aerials/halfpipe and snowboard halfpipe/big air
- Wrestling (FILA).

Beta blockers include, but are not limited to, the following—acebutolol, alprenolol, atenolol, betaxolol, bisoprolol, bunolol, carteolol, carvedilol, celiprolol, esmolol, labetalol, levobunolol, metipranolol, metoprolol, nadolol, oxyprenolol, pindolol, propranolol, sotalol, timolol.

athletes with documented medical conditions can request a TUE, and have such a request appropriately dealt with by a panel of independent physicians called a Therapeutic Use Exemption Committee (TUEC).

Those athletes wishing to take a prohibited substance can begin treatment only after receiving the authorization notice from the relevant organization. TUEs are granted for a specific medication with a defined dosage and specific length of time.

Permitted substances

Drug groups permitted by WADA are listed in the box below.

Recently deleted drugs

As mentioned above, a number of drugs have been removed from the prohibited list over the past few years and are now being monitored by WADA to detect possible patterns of misuse. The most controversial omission is caffeine.

Caffeine

Caffeine is the most commonly used drug in the world. It occurs naturally in more than 60 plants and is contained in coffee, tea, chocolate, cola, and various beverages. Until 2004, caffeine was on the prohibited list with urine levels above 12 µg/mL deemed illegal. This was thought to be the equivalent of six to eight cups of coffee. A typical cup of brewed coffee contains about 100 mg of caffeine, the same amount as an Australian No-Doz tablet. (A US No-Doz tablet contains 200 mg of caffeine.) For many years athletes in various sports have been using caffeine in doses below the banned level. A list of the amounts

that athlete the authorization to take the needed medicine.

The criteria necessary to be fulfilled to grant "therapeutic use" are all three of:

- the athlete would experience significant health problems without taking the prohibited substance or method
- the therapeutic use of the substance would not produce significant enhancement of performance
- there is no reasonable therapeutic alternative to the use of the otherwise prohibited substance or method.

WADA has issued an International Standard for the granting of TUEs. The standard states that all international federations and national anti-doping organizations must have a process in place whereby

Drug groups permitted by WADA

Antibiotics
Antidepressants
Antidiarrheals
Antihistamines
Antihypertensives (excluding beta blockers)
Antinauseants
Aspirin (ASA), paracetamol (acetaminophen), codeine, dextropropoxyphene
Eye medications
Nonsteroidal anti-inflammatory drugs (NSAIDs)
Oral contraceptives
Skin creams and ointments
Sleeping tablets

of caffeine contained in various foods and drinks is shown in Table 66.3.

There is clear evidence that caffeine is an ergogenic aid for a variety of sports, although studies involving elite athletes and field situations are lacking. Further research is needed to define the range of caffeine protocols and sports activities that show evidence of performance enhancement, as well as the benefits or harm to other issues underpinning recovery after exercise or preparation for an event.[110]

Newer evidence suggests, at least in endurance sports, that the maximal benefits of caffeine are seen at small to moderate caffeine doses (2–3 mg.kg^{-1}), which are well within the normal daily caffeine intakes of the general population. This makes the recent decision to remove caffeine from the list of prohibited substances in sports a pragmatic choice.

To date, there is little evidence that this change has increased the use or misuse of caffeine by athletes, at least within the levels of elite and sub-elite sport, where anti-doping codes apply. Caffeine use may also enhance the performance of sport in recreational athletes, but it is inappropriate and unnecessary for use by young adults.[110]

Non-intentional doping in sports

When athletes test positive for a banned substance, they frequently deny the claim and allege circumstances other than intentional doping. Typical defenses include that their drink had been spiked,

Table 66.3 Caffeine contained in various foods and drinks

Food or drink	Serve	Caffeine content (mg)
Instant coffee	250 mL	60
Brewed coffee	250 mL	80–100 (variable)
Tea	250 mL	30
Hot chocolate	250 mL	5–10
Chocolate	60 g bar	50
Coca-Cola	375 mL can	50
Red Bull energy drink	250 mL can	80
V energy drink	250 mL can	50
Lift Plus	250 mL can	36
Black Stallion	250 mL can	80

passive inhalation of drug smoke, or inadvertent taking of a nutritional supplement or food that contained a prohibited substance.

Studies have shown that it is possible that an individual could produce detectable levels of cannabinoids in urine samples only after extremely severe conditions of passive exposure to marijuana smoke. Similarly, only individuals exposed to passive cocaine smoke under extremely harsh conditions would show cocaine metabolites in a urine sample.

Research has indicated that both poppy seed–containing food[111] and herbal cocoa tea[112, 113] can produce levels of morphine and cocaine metabolites above the allowed limit. Studies have also shown that it is possible to yield illegal positive results for anabolic agents after consumption of meat originating from animals treated with anabolic agents.[114]

A number of studies have shown that there is a significant number of "nutritional supplements" that contain substances other than those described on the label, and that a number of these are prohibited substances such as pro-hormones or anabolic steroids.[115]

The IOC has reported that 14.8% of some 650 products sampled contained levels of banned substances sufficient to result in a positive urine sample. None of the substances carried warnings or product information on the contents.[116] Athletes should be wary of ingesting these supplements.

Biotransformation products of permitted substances can also cause an athlete to test positive. One example is the permitted analgesic codeine, which is metabolized to morphine at levels above the threshold.

Drug testing

Drug testing has become commonplace in both amateur and professional sport. The clinician providing services to the team or individual must be familiar with the list of prohibited substances and the drug testing procedure itself. The athlete is entitled to have a representative present to confirm that the correct testing procedures have taken place. Often the representative is the team clinician.

Testing procedure
Selection
An athlete can be selected for a drug test at any time (including while injured and/or postoperatively).

Notification

An athlete can be notified of their selection for a drug test by a drug control official either:

- in person (at any time, in or out of competition)
- by telephone (out of competition)
- by written notice (out of competition).

The criteria for deciding which athlete is tested vary from event to event. At some competitions, place-getters are tested; at others, competitors are selected randomly; while at other times, certain events may be targeted for testing.

Presenting for a drug test

The drug control official records the athlete's details on a notification form, which is then signed by the athlete. A copy is kept by the athlete for his/her records.

In the presence of the chaperone, the athlete may:

- receive necessary medical attention
- attend a victory ceremony
- fulfill media commitments
- compete in further events
- warm-down
- eat or drink (at his/her own risk)—during competition events sealed drinks are provided and it is recommended that athletes only consume these fluids until after the testing is completed.

Sample collection

The athlete is required to provide a urine sample in the direct view of a drug control official who is the same gender as the athlete. The athlete's representative is not permitted to observe the actual collection of the sample, only the testing procedures and paperwork.

A minimum of 90 mL of urine is required for a competition test and 60 mL for an out-of-competition test. If there is insufficient sample, the initial sample will be sealed with a temporary seal and additional urine sample(s) will be collected and mixed with the original sample until there is sufficient. Following the collection of the sample, the athlete will return to the doping control area, where a second doping control official will be present, as well as the athlete's representative (if there is one), to complete the sealing of the sample and paperwork.

The athlete will be asked to select a sample collection kit, which consists of two bottles (labeled "A" and "B" with identifying numbers) housed in a sealed polystyrene outer case. It is important that the athlete, and his or her representative, checks that the kits are sealed correctly, that the bottles are clean, and that the lids are suitable.

Splitting, sealing, and labeling of the sample

The athlete will be asked to pour a measured amount of urine into both the A and B bottles, leaving a small amount behind for the drug control official to test the specific gravity. The athlete will seal the bottles with the self-sealing, one-use only lids provided. The sample code number of the kit will be identified and recorded on the drug testing form.

Checking the concentration of sample

The drug control official will check the specific gravity of the sample. If the urine has a specific gravity of less than 1.005, a further specimen is required.

Final paperwork

At this stage, the competitor provides the medical declaration. The medical declaration is extremely important. The competitor is asked to list all medications taken in the previous week, including over-the-counter medications, prescription drugs, and other substances taken by mouth, injection, inhalation, or suppository.

This list should include all vitamins, amino acids, and other supplements. It is vitally important that this list be completed accurately as all substances taken in that period are likely to show up in the laboratory test.

The competitor, his or her representative, and the drug control officer then check all the written information and, if satisfied, sign the drug testing form. The competitor is given a copy of the form.

The sealed samples and the section of paperwork that does not disclose the athlete's name are then sent in a sealed bag to an accredited laboratory where the sample is analyzed using gas chromatography and mass spectrometry.

Initially only the A sample is analyzed. If the laboratory finds a possible positive test result in the sample in the A bottle, it informs the drug testing agency, which then informs the competitor that a possible positive test result has been recorded. The competitor, or a representative, is then entitled to be present at the unsealing and testing of the B sample. If the B sample also proves positive, the relevant sporting organizations are informed. It is the responsibility of the relevant sporting organization to determine what penalty/sanctions are to be applied following a report of a positive test result. The testing agency does not determine the penalty to apply. WADA has designated penalties to which most sporting bodies now adhere.

The role of the team clinician

The team clinician has an extremely important role to play in the prevention and management of doping problems. The primary role of the team clinician should be education of team members. This should involve regular briefings, especially prior to the season. Topics covered should include:

- the Prohibited List (available at < http://www.wada-ama.org/en/World-Anti-Doping-Program/Sports-and-Anti-Doping-Organizations/International-Standards/Prohibited-List/>)
- prescription drugs
  - athletes must inform clinicians that they are subject to drug testing and ensure that the

clinician confirms that the medication being prescribed does not contain any banned substance
  - if the clinician is uncertain, suggest contacting the national anti-doping agency for confirmation
- inadvertent doping
  - checking the contents of all medications, especially over-the-counter substances and supplements
  - if uncertain, contact the national anti-doping agency for confirmation
- drug testing protocols
  - especially the importance of listing all medications including supplements
- travel
  - be aware while traveling in foreign countries that drugs with the same or similar brand names may have a different composition in different countries
  - always ensure that you take your own regular medications with you.

REFERENCES

1. WADA. www.wada-ama.org/en/World-Anti-Doping-Program/Sports-and-Anti-Doping-Organizations/International-Standards/Prohibited-List, 2011.

2. Hartgens F, Kuipers H. Effects of androgenic-anabolic steroids in athletes. *Sports Med* 2004;34(8):513–54.

3. Yesalis III CE, Herrick RT, Buckley WE et al. Self-reported use of anabolic-androgenic steroids by elite power lifters. *Phys Sportsmed* 1988;16(12):91–8.

4. Lindstrom M, Nilsson AL, Katzman PL et al. Use of anabolic-androgenic steroids among body builders—frequency and attitudes. *J Intern Med* 1990;227:407–11.

5. Buckley WE, Yesalis CE, Friedl KE et al. Estimated prevalence of anabolic-androgenic steroid use among male high school seniors. *JAMA* 1988;260:3441–5.

6. Corbin CB, Feyrer-Melk SA, Phelps C et al. Anabolic steroids: a study of high school athletes. *Ped Exerc Sci* 1994;6:149–58.

7. Melia P, Pipe A, Greenberg L. The use of anabolic-androgenic steroids by Canadian students. *Clin J Sport Med* 1996;6:9–14.

8. Terney R, McLain LG. The use of anabolic steroids in high school students. *AmJ Dis Child* 1990;144:99–103.

9. Thiblin I, Petersson A. Pharmacoepidemiology of anabolic androgenic steroids: a review. *Fund Clin Pharmacol* 2004;19:27–44.

10. Yesalis CE, Bahrke MS. Anabolic-androgenic steroids and related substances. *Curr Sports Med Rep* 2002;4:246–52.

11. Bhasin S, Storer TW, Berman N et al. The effects of supraphysiologic doses of testosterone on muscle size and strength in normal men. *N Engl J Med* 1996;335:1–7.

12. Forbes GB, Porta CR, Herr BE et al. Sequence of changes in body composition induced by testosterone and reversal of changes after drug is stopped. *JAMA* 1992;267:397–9.

13. Giorgi A, Weatherby RP, Murphy PW. Muscular strength, body composition, and health responses to the use of testosterone enanthate: a double blind study. *J Sci Med Sport* 1999;2:341–55.

14. Sinha-Hikim I, Artaza J, Woodhouse L et al. Testosterone-induced increase in muscle size in healthy young men is associated with muscle fiber hypertrophy. *Am J Physiol Endocrinol Metab* 2002;283:E154–64.

15. Parssinen M, Kujala U, Vartiainen E et al. Increased premature mortality of competitive power lifters suspected to have used anabolic agents. *Int J Sports Med* 2000;21:225–7.

16. Thiblin I, Lindquist O, Rais J. Cause and manner of death among users of anabolic androgenic steroids. *J Forensic Sci* 2000;45:16–23.

17. Rich JD, Dickinson BP, Feller A et al. The infectious complications of anabolic-androgenic steroid injection. *Int J Sports Med* 1999;20:563–6.

18. Ishak KG, Zimmerman HJ. Hepatotoxic effects of the anabolic/androgenic steroids. *Sem Liver Dis* 1987;7(3):230–6.

19. Bagheri SA, Boyer JL. Peliosis hepatis associated with androgenic-anabolic steroid therapy. A severe form of hepatic injury. *Ann Intern Med* 1971;81:610–18.

20. Cabasso A. Peliosis hepatis in a young adult bodybuilder. *Med Sci Sports Exerc* 1994;26(1):2–4.

21. Creagh TM, Rubin A, Evans DJ. Hepatic tumours induced by anabolic steroids in an athlete. *J Clin Path* 1988;41:441–3.

22. Klava A, Super P, Aldridge M et al. Body builder's liver. *J R Soc Med* 1994;87:43–44.

23. Cohen LI, Hartford CG, Rogers GG. Lipoprotein (a) and cholesterol in body builders using anabolic androgenic steroids. *Med Sci Sports Exerc* 1996;28(2):176–9.

24. Ebenbichler CF, Sturm W, Ganzer H et al. Flow-mediated endothelium-dependent vasodilatation is impaired in male body builders taking anabolic-androgenic steroids. *Atherosclerosis* 2001;158:483–90.

25. Kuipers H, Wijnen JA, Hartgens F et al. Influence of anabolic steroids on body composition, blood pressure, lipid profile, and liver functions in body builders. *Int J Sports Med* 1991;12:413–18.

26. Achar S, Rostamian A, Narayan SM. Cardiac and metabolic effects of anabolic-androgenic steroid abuse on lipids, blood pressure, left ventricular dimensions, and rhythm. *Am J Cardiol* 2010;106(6):893–901.

27. Melchert RB, Welder AA. Cardiovascular effects of androgenic-anabolic steroids. *Med Sci Sports Exerc* 1995;27(9):1252–62.

28. Hartgens F, Kuipers H. Body composition, cardiovascular risk factors and liver function in long-term androgenic-anabolic steroids using body builders three months after drug withdrawal. *Int J Sports Med* 1996;17:429–33.

29. Riebe D, Fernhall B, Thompson PD. The blood pressure response to exercise in anabolic steroid users. *Med Sci Sports Exerc* 1992;24(6):633–7.

30. Ferenchick GS, Adelman S. Myocardial infarction associated with anabolic steroid use in a previously healthy 37-year-old weight lifter. *Am Heart J* 1992;124(2):507–8.

E

31. Sullivan ML, Martinez CM, Gennis P et al. The cardiac toxicity of anabolic steroids. *Prog Cardiovasc Dis* 1998;41:1–15.

32. Mochizuki RM, Richter KJ. Cardiomyopathy and cerebrovascular accident associated with anabolic-androgenic steroid use. *Phys Sportsmed* 1988;18(11):109–14.

33. Baggish AL, Weiner RB, Kanayama G et al. Long-term anabolic-androgenic steroid use is associated with left ventricular dysfunction. *Circ Heart Fail* 2010;3(4):472–6.

34. Kiraly CL. Androgenic-anabolic steroid effects on serum and skin surface lipids, on red cells, and on liver enzymes. *Int J Sports Med* 1988;9:249–52.

35. Walker J, Adams B. Cutaneous Manifestations of anabolic-androgenic steroid use in athletes. *Int J Dermatol* 2009;48(10):1044–8.

36. Bahrke MS, Yesalis III CE, Wright JE. Psychological and behavioural effects of endogenous testosterone levels and anabolic-androgenic steroids among males. *Sports Med* 1990;10(5):303–37.

37. Trenton AJ, Currier GW. Behavior Manifestations of anabolic steroid use. *CNS Drugs* 2005;19(7):571–95.

38. Cooper CJ, Noakes T, Dunne T et al. A high prevalence of personality traits in chronic users of anabolic-androgenic steroid users. *Br J Sports Med* 1996;30:246–50.

39. Midgley SJ, Heather N, Davies JB. Levels of aggression among a group of anabolic-androgenic steroid users. *Med Sci Law* 2001;41:309–14.

40. Lubell A. Does steroid abuse cause—or excuse—violence? *Phys Sportsmed* 1989;17(2):176–85.

41. Kashkin KB, Kleber HD. Hooked on hormones? An anabolic steroid addiction hypothesis. *JAMA* 1989;262(22):3166–70.

42. Jarow JP, Lipshultz LI. Anabolic steroid-induced hypogonadotropic hypogonadism. *Am J Sports Med* 1990;18(4):429–31.

43. Tan RS, Vasudevan D. Use of clomiphene citrate to reverse premature andropause secondary to steroid abuse. *Fertil Steril* 2003;79:203–5.

44. Friedl KE, Yesalis CE. Self-treatment of gynecomastia in bodybuilders who use anabolic steroids. *Phys Sportsmed* 1989;17(3):67–79.

45. Rogol AD, Yesalis CE 3rd. Anabolic-androgenic steroids and athletes: what are the issues? *J Clin Endocrin Metabol* 1992;74(3):465–69.

46. Wilson JD. Androgen abuse by athletes. *Endocr Rev* 1988;9(2):181–99.

47. Corrigan B. DHEA and Sport. *Clin J Sport Med* 2002;12:236–41.

48. Brown GA, Vukovich MD, Reifenrath TA et al. Effects of anabolic precursors on serum testosterone concentrations and adaptations to resistance training in young men. *Int J Sport Nutr Exerc Metab* 2001;10:340–59.

49. Welle S, Jozefowicz R, Statt M. Failure of dehydroepiandrosterone to influence energy and protein metabolism in humans. *J Clin Endocrinol Metab* 1990;71:1259–64.

50. Kazlauskas R. Designer steroids. *Handb Exp Pharmacol* 2010;195:155–85.

51. Van Eenoo P, Delbeke FT. Metabolism and excretion of anabolic steroids in doping control—new steroids and new insights. *J Steroid Biochem Mol Biol* 2006;101:161–78.

52. Caitlin DH, Sekera MH, Ahrens BH et al. Tetrahydrogestrinone discovery, synthesis, and detection in urine *Rapid Commun Mass Spectrom* 2004;18:1245–9.

53. Malvey TC, Armsey TD. Tetrahydrogestrinone: the discovery of a designer steroid. *Curr Sports Med Rep* 2005;4:227–30.

54. Death AK, McGrath KCY, Kazlauskas R et al. Tetrahydrogestrinone is a potent androgen and progestin. *J Clin Endocrinol Metab* 2004;89:2498–500.

55. Prather ID, Brown DE, North P et al. Clenbuterol: a substitute for anabolic steroids? *Med Sci Sports Exerc* 1995;27(8):1118–21.

56. Scott J, Phillips GC. Erythropoietin in sports: a new look at an old problem. *Curr Sports Med Rep* 2005;4:224–6.

57. Audran M, Gareau R, Matecki S et al. Effects of erythropoietin administration in training athletes and possible indirect detection in doping control. *Med Sci Sports Exerc* 1999;31(5):639–45.

58. Ekblom B. Blood doping and erythropoietin. The effects of variation in hemoglobin concentration and other related factors on physical performance. *Am J Sports Med* 1996;24(6):S40–2.

59. Berglund B, Ekblom B. Effect of recombinant erythropoietin treatment on blood pressure and some hematological parameters in healthy men. *J Intern Med* 1991;229:125–30.

60. Birkeland KI, Stray-Gundersen J, Hemmersbach P et al. Effect of rhEPO administration on serum levels of sTfR and cycling performance. *Med Sci Sports Exerc* 2000;32:1238–43.

61. Ekblom B, Berglund B. Effect of erythropoietin administration on maximal aerobic power. *Scand J Med Sci Sports* 1991;1:88–93.

62. Lippi G, Franchini M, Salvagno GL et al. Biochemistry, physiology and complications of blood doping: facts and speculation. *Crit Rev Clin Lab Sci* 2006;43:349–91.

63. O'Toole ML, Douglas PS, Hiller WD et al. Hematocrits of triathletes: is monitoring useful? *Med Sci Sports Exerc* 1999;31(3):372–7.

64. Scumacher YO, Schmid A, Lenz T et al. Blood testing in sports: hematological profile of a convicted athlete. *Clin J Sport Med* 2001;11:115–17.

65. Kazlauskas R, Howe C, Trout G. Strategies for rhEPO detection in sport. *Clin J Sport Med* 2002;12:229–35.

66. Franz SE. Erythropoiesis-stimulating agents: development, detection and dangers. *Drug Test Anal* 2009;1:245–9.

67. Erotokritou-Mulligan I, Holt RIG. Insulin-like growth factor I and insulin and their abuse in sport. *Endocrinol Metab Clin N Am* 2010;39:33–43.

68. Rich JD, Dickinson BP, Merriman MA et al. Insulin use by bodybuilders. *JAMA* 1998;279:161–3.

69. Evans PJ, Lynch RM. Insulin as a drug of abuse in body building. *Br J Sports Med* 2003;37:356–7.

70. Banadonna RC, Saccomani MP, Cobelli C et al. Effect of insulin on system A anmino acid transport in human skeletal muscle. *J Clin Invest* 1993;91:514–21.

71. Dean H. Does exogenous growth hormone improve athletic performance? *Clin J Sport Med* 2002;12:250–3.

72. Crist DM, Peake GT, Egan PA et al. Body composition response to exogenous GH during training in highly conditioned adults. *J App Physiol* 1988;65(2):579–84.

73. Holt RI, Erotokritou-Mulligan I, Sönksen PH. The history of doping and growth hormone abuse in sport. *Growth Horm IGF Res* 2009;19(4):320–6.

74. Liu H, Bravata DM, Olkin I et al. Systematic review: the effects of growth hormone on athletic performance. *Ann Intern Med* 2008;148(10):747–58.

75. Meinhardt U, Nelson AE, Hansen JL et al. The effects of growth hormone on body composition and physical performance in recreational athletes: a randomized trial. *Ann Intern Med* 2010;152(9):568–77.

76. Guha N, Dashwood A, Thomas NJ et al. IGF-1 abuse in sport. *Curr Drug Abuse Rev* 2009;2(3):263–72.

77. Adams G. Insulin-like growth factor in muscle growth and its potential abuse by athletes. *Br J Sports Med* 2000;34:412–13.

78. Kemp SF, Fowlkes JL, Thrailkill KM. Efficacy and safety of mecasermin rinfabate. *Expert Opin Biol Ther* 2006;6:533–8.

79. Kindermann W. Do inhaled beta(2)-agonists have an ergogenic potential in non-asthmatic competitive athletes? *Sports Med* 2007;37(2):95–102.

80. Seeheusen DA, Glorioso JE. Tamoxifen as an ergogenic agent in women body builders. A case report. *Clin J Sport Med* 2002;12:313–14.

81. Jones M, Pedoe DS. Blood doping—a literature review. *Br J Sports Med* 1989;23(2):84–8.

82. Sawka MN, Joyner MJ, Miles DS et al. American College of Sports Medicine position stand. The use of blood doping as an ergogenic aid. *Med Sci Sports Exerc* 1996;28(6):i–viii.

83. Leigh-Smith S. Blood boosting. *Br J Sports Med* 2004;38:99–101.

84. Corrigan B. Beyond EPO. *Clin J Sport Med* 2002;12:242–4.

85. Schumacher YO, Ashenden M. Doping with artificial oxygen carriers. *Sports Med* 2004;34(3):141–50.

86. Hughes GS, Yancey EP, Albrecht R et al. Hemoglobin-based oxygen carrier preserves submaximal exercise capacity in humans. *Clin Pharmacol Ther* 1995;58:434–43.

87. Varlet-Marie E, Audran M, Ashenden M et al. Modification of gene expression: help to detect doping with erythropoiesis-stimulating agents. *Am J Hematol* 2009;84(11):755–9.

88. Azzazy HM, Mansour MM, Christenson RH. Gene doping: of mice and men. *Clin Biochem* 2009;42:435–41.

89. Harridge SD, Velloso CP. IGF-1 and GH: potential use in gene doping. *Growth Horm IGF Res* 2009;19:378–82.

90. McKanna TA, Toriello HV. Gene doping: the hype and the harm. *Pediatr Clin North Am* 2010;57(3):719–27.

91. Wells DJ. Gene doping: possibilities and practicalities. *Med Sport Sci* 2009;54:166–75.

92. Svensson E, Black H, Dugger D et al. Long term erythropoietin expression in rodents and non-human primates following intramuscular ingestion of a replication-defective adenoviral vector. *Hum Gene Ther* 1997;8:1797–806.

93. Barton-Davis E, Shoturma D, Musaro A et al. Viral mediated expression of insulin like growth factor 1 blocks the ageing-related loss of skeletal muscle function. *Proc Natl Acad Sci USA* 1998;95:15603–7.

94. Raper SE, Chirmule N, Lee FS et al. Fatal systemic inflammatory response syndrome in an ornithine transcarbamylase deficient patient following adenoviral gene transfer. *Mol Genet Metab* 2003;80:148–58.

95. Wells DJ. Gene doping: the hype and the reality. *Br J Pharmacol* 2008;154:623–31.

96. Baoutina A, Alexander IE, Rasko JE et al. Developing strategies for detection of gene doping. *J Gene Med* 2008;10:3–20.

97. Hickey G, Fricker P. Attention deficit hyperactivity disorder, CNS stimulants and sport. *Sports Med* 1999;27(1):11–21.

98. Geiger JD. Adverse effects associated with supplements containing ephedra alkaloids. *Clin J Sport Med* 2002;12:263.

99. Shekelle P, Hardy MA, Morton S et al. Efficacy and safety of ephedra and ephedrine for weight loss and athletic performance: a meta-analysis. *JAMA* 2003;289:1537–45.

100. Bohn AM, Khodaee M, Schwenk TL. Ephedrine and other stimulants as ergogenic aids. *Curr Sports Med Rep* 2003;2:220–5.

101. Pritchard-Peschek KR, Jenkins DG, Osborne MA et al. Pseudoephedrine ingestion and cycling time-trial performance. *Int J Sport Nutr Exerc Metab* 2010;20(2):132–8.

102. Bell DG, Jacobs I, Zamecnik J. Effects of caffeine, ephedrine, and their combination on time to exhaustion during high intensity exercise. *Eur J Appl Physiol* 1996;81:428–33.

103. Thevis M, Sigmund G, Geyer H et al. Stimulants and doping in sport. *Endocrinol Metab Clin North Am* 2010;39(1):89–105.

104. Kaufman KR, Gerner R. Modafinil in sports: ethical considerations. *Br J Sports Med* 2005;39(4):241–4.

105. Renaud AM, Cormier Y. Acute effects of marihuana smoking on maximal exercise performance. *Med Sci Sports Exerc* 1986;18(6):685–9.

106. Duclos M, Gouarne C, Bonnemaison D. Acute and chronic effects of exercise on tissue sensitivity to glucocorticoids. *J Appl Physiol* 2003;94:869–75.

107. Arlettaz A, Portier H, Lecoq AM et al. Effects of short-term prednisolone intake during submaximal exercise. *Med Sci Sports Exerc* 2007;39(9):1672–8.

108. Collomp K, Arlettaz A, Portier H et al. Short-term glucocorticoid intake combined with intense training on performance and hormonal responses. *Br J Sports Med* 2008;42(12):983–8.

109. O'Brien CP. Alcohol and sport. Impact of social drinking on recreational and competitive sports performance. *Sports Med* 1993;15(2):71–7.

110. Burke LM. Caffeine and sports performance. *Appl Physiol Nutr Metab* 2008;33(6):1319–34.

111. elSohly HN, elSohly MA, Stanford DF. Poppy seed ingestion and opiates urinalysis: a closer look. *J Anal Toxicol* 1990;14:308–10.

112. Jackson GF, Saady JJ, Poklis A. Urinary excretion of benzoylecgonine following ingestion of health inca tea. *Forensic Sci Int* 1991;49(1):57–64.

113. Jenkins AJ, llosa T, Montoya I et al. Identification and quantitation of alkaloids in cocoa tea. *Forensic Sci Int* 1996;77:179–86.

114. Kicman AT, Cowan DA, Myhre L et al. Effect on sports drug tests of ingesting meat from steroid (methenolone)-treated livestock. *Clin Chem* 1994;40(11):2084–7.

115. Yonamine M, Garcia PR, Moreau RL. Non-intentional doping in sports. *Sports Med* 2004;34(11):697–704.

116. Geyer H, Parr MK, Mareck U et al. Analysis of non-hormonal nutritional supplements for anabolic-androgenic steroids—results of an international study. *Int J Sports Med* 2004;25:124–9.

Chapter 67

Ethics and sports medicine

I know that a football club doctor would never have the audacity to tell you the truth … Front up in the medical room with severe internal bleeding and they will say something like "it's just a scratch—you'll be right." I guess that's why they have football club doctors and why players should never go to anyone else. A 1970s Australian Rules football star quoted in *The Age* (Melbourne), 6 July 1979

The broad goal of medical ethics is to improve the quality of patient care by identifying, analyzing, and attempting to resolve the ethical problems that arise in the practice of clinical medicine.[1] In addition, the increased professionalism of sport has raised numerous significant ethical issues in sports medicine. Influences such as the clinician's employer (sports team or organization), the athlete's desire to play with pain and injury, and the economic consequences of playing or not playing all complicate medical decisions.[2, 3]

Five of those contentious areas are discussed below:

- conflict of interest
- confidentiality
- performance-enhancing drugs
- infectious diseases
- ethics in sport.

In 1993 the Federation International de Sports Medicine (FIMS) espoused three principles to guide the clinician treating athletes:[4]

1. Always make the athlete a priority.
2. Never do harm.
3. Never impose your authority in a way that impinges on the individual right of the athlete to make his or her own decision.

Conflict of interest

The goal of most clinicians is to reduce suffering and prolong healthy life. Athletes, especially professional athletes, have as their priority a desire to perform. A major objective for a sports clinician is to support athletic achievement.[2] As a result of the dynamics of professional sports, medical decision making can be affected by a host of factors not normally encountered in standard practice.

Decision making can potentially be affected by pressures exerted from a variety of sources that may influence both clinicians and the patient/players. A professional team clinician should recognize these potential influences and their effect on ethical medical decision making. These pressures may come from players, management and coaches, and the clinicians themselves.[5]

The team clinician may come under pressure to allow the athlete to play from a number of different sources. The players themselves are usually the greatest potential source of pressure on the clinician. Athletes are highly motivated. An athlete may prefer to risk his or her health for the sake of participation and success in the game, motivated by machismo, peer pressure, pride, institutional pressures, and also economic considerations.[6]

Pressure may also come also from the coach, team mates, parents, or team administration. This can take several forms, including pressuring the athlete who will in turn attempt to influence the clinician's decision making. Other forms of pressure may come about from direct or indirect questioning of the clinician's decisions, or scrutinizing the medical care of the team with comments to the media.[3] Management could directly attempt to affect decisions by threatening replacement of the team clinician.[5] Team clinicians must keep those powerful motivators in mind when determining the extent of an injury and the time needed for recovery.

A danger that may befall the unwary team clinician is the "fan syndrome."[7] Its principal symptom is the distortion of proper clinical judgment when the clinician may be influenced by his or her desire to see the team succeed. This can be manifested in many ways. The clinician's desire to see the team succeed may propel a decision to declare a leading player fit for a crucial competition when further recuperation from injury is in order. Such may be the clinician's desire to remain on good terms with the team's management that he or she is influenced to provide advice which accords with what will please rather than what may be dispassionately appropriate. The insidious nature of the "fan syndrome" is such that very rarely will a clinician be aware that his or her behavior is affected by it.

Team clinicians inevitably benefit from team success. There may be financial benefits as the staff earn bonuses for success and may have their contracts increased for the following season; they may get the opportunity for travel to play-off games and end-of-season trips based on success; they may get increased media exposure if the team progresses to a high-profile game and their professional reputation may be enhanced (rightly or wrongly) if the team is successful.

The sum of these pressures may affect a clinician's judgment and lead to a vulnerability to litigation.

Bloodgate

The term "Bloodgate" was given to events occurring in April 2009 during a rugby match, in the semifinals of the European Rugby Cup between Leinster and Harlequins. Normally in Rugby Union, players cannot return to play once they have been substituted, except to replace a player who has a "blood injury." A Harlequins player (Tom Williams) appeared to suffer a "blood injury" through the use of a fake blood capsule so that a specialist goal kicker could be brought back on to the field to try to secure victory in the last few minutes. At the behest of the head coach, the team physiotherapist had purchased fake blood capsules in advance of the game and had delivered one to the player during the match. The team doctor cut the inside of Williams' mouth to "demonstrate a real injury."

At the European Rugby Cup hearing, the physiotherapist admitted having done this on four previous occasions. The physiotherapist received a two-year worldwide ban from the sport, and in September 2010, the Health Professions Council (HPC) struck off the physiotherapist. The doctor admitted "reluctantly" cutting the inside of Williams' mouth to "demonstrate a real injury." In August 2010, the doctor was given a warning by the General Medical Council (GMC) which was listed on her registration.

At first glance the penalties for each seemed inequitable. The doctor caused physical harm, and both she and the physiotherapist engaged in deception after the event, yet the doctor emerged with a lighter penalty. However, the HPC decided the physiotherapist displayed a degree of premeditation in his actions by purchasing the blood capsules. He also "took an active role in the drafting of false witness statements" to sustain the deception.

Further underhand practices have emerged since the Rugby Union incident. Players have told of the deceptive use of blood soaked towels and the opening up of stitches in previous minor wounds to obtain an illicit blood injury substitution.

Figure 67.1 Harlequins Rugby Union team player Tom Williams, who was at the heart of the "Bloodgate" scandal

There have been instances in a number of countries of team clinicians being sued.

The clinician's duty: the team or the athlete?

The clinician employed by the professional team, either on a salary or, more commonly, on a contract, has an inherent conflict of interest. Is the primary duty of the clinician to the athlete or the team?

In most situations, the interests of the team and the athlete coincide. What is best for the athlete is usually best for the team. However, situations may arise where there may be short-term benefit to the team to the detriment of the athlete's health. This conflict is considered further below under the heading "Confidentiality."

The overriding duty of the team clinician is always to the athlete. This is true regardless of how much pressure the team clinician feels under from the coaches, other members of the team, and parents. The team clinician is required to give full disclosure to the athlete (and the parents if appropriate) regarding the extent of the injury, the nature of the injury, proper rehabilitation, and the consequences of injuries.[8]

If the wellbeing of the athlete is in conflict with an interest of a third party, the wellbeing of the athlete is always paramount.[6] Instituting a policy that the team clinician has the final say regarding any player's participation minimizes potential conflicts between the medical team, and coaches and other members of the team administration.

The coaches and other members of the administration associated with the team should all be aware that the team clinician makes the ultimate determination regarding the decision of whether an injured athlete can return to play. If, after full disclosure, the legally competent athlete (or the parents in the case of an athlete who is a minor) insists on contravening the clinician's recommendation, the team clinician should ask the player (or parent) to sign an exculpatory waiver.

Holm et al.[9] advocated securing the independence of healthcare professionals from the club and other sporting organizations that employ them. They also promoted the establishment of a forum between healthcare professionals from different organizations to facilitate discourse on ethical and professional issues in a non-judgmental setting.

Devitt et al.[10] recommend that a team doctor should report to a clinical colleague outside the team-management structure. This will protect not only the player, but also the team management, the team doctor, and, ultimately, the sporting organization, when ethical conflicts arise in future.

Local anesthetic injection and administration of analgesics

In professional sport, local anesthetic administration is commonplace, but there has been a reluctance to disclose the extent of the prevalence of these injections (Scenario 1).[11] The most common way of administering these drugs such as lignocaine (lidocaine) is by injection into or around the painful area. The most common site and conditions for which local anesthetics are used are acromioclavicular joint injury, iliac crest contusion (hip pointer), a rib contusion or fracture, or an undisplaced finger fracture. Other conditions for which local anesthetic injections have been used include the plantar fascia (Scenario 1), stress fractures, ankle ligament sprains, tennis elbow, and adductor muscle tears.

Analgesics are commonly used in professional sport. These range from simple oral analgesics (e.g. paracetamol (acetaminophen)) to more powerful oral medications (e.g. codeine) to injectable analgesics (e.g. ketorolac). A survey of National Football League team clinicians documented that 28 of the 30 responding teams used ketorolac during the season. Medical staff that used the drug treated an average of 15 different players over the course of the season, with the range from 2 to 35.[12]

There are at least two issues at stake in these situations. The clinician must firstly consider whether playing with the injury may make the injury worse. In most cases the answer is "yes." Also, the clinician must consider whether playing with an injury would place the player at an increased risk of other injuries. Also, whether a player "carrying" an injury would place other players at increased risk of injury.

Issues that make decision making complex are whether the situation changes:

- if the team clinician has an employment agreement with the team or not
- if the player is professional or amateur
- if it is an important/less important game
- if the player is a key player/lesser player
- if the request comes from the athlete or the coach or the team administration
- if the athlete is under-age.

What if the athlete is under-age? What is the role of the parents in the decision making? Can we assume that they are acting in the best interests of the child? What if the player wants to rest and the parents insist he or she plays on?

Without pain from the injured area acting as a warning symptom, players will not be aware that they may be aggravating the injury until the effect of the injection wears off. The clinician and the athlete must weigh up the potential advantages and disadvantages of playing.

In professional sport, this may be affected by the importance of the occasion, and whether it is a one-off game such as the final game of the season, after which the player may have an extended time to recover, or whether the injury will require weekly anesthetic injections for a number of weeks to enable the player to continue playing. It may be that continuing to play after an injection may prevent the injury from healing.

The other concern is the long-term effects of continuing to play after an anesthetic or analgesic. Pain may be considered the body's mechanism to alert patients to the potential for damage.

Short-term gain, long-term pain

Frequently there is a conflict between short-term advantage and the potential for long-term problems. Scenarios 2 and 3 are typical examples.

Scenario 3 is a common one which provides a significant ethical dilemma for team clinicians and orthopedic surgeons. There is a general acceptance in the sporting and medical communities that a torn anterior cruciate ligament is no longer a career-ending injury and that the athlete should be able to return to high-level competition somewhere between four and 12 months after anterior cruciate ligament reconstruction. However, we[13] and others[14] have expressed concern about the long-term consequences of facilitating return to sport after these injuries.

As described previously, the incidence of long-term osteoarthritis following injuries such as a torn meniscus and torn ACL is significant. It is likely that returning to high-level, high-intensity sport following these injuries would accelerate this process. Clinicians need to discuss these possible adverse effects with the athlete prior to them returning to sport. This emphasizes the importance of informed consent.

Informed consent

Informed consent is of vital importance throughout medicine, particularly in the light of ethical and legal concerns. Informed consent is "the voluntary agreement by a patient to a proposed healthcare management approach after proper and adequate information is conveyed to the patient about the proposed management, including potential risks and benefits and alternative management options."[15]

The potential risks and benefits of a particular course of action need to be explained in a relaxed atmosphere away from distractions. When practical, the clinician should always give players an opportunity to go away and think about it, preferably with some relevant written material, and offer the opportunity of another discussion to answer any queries they may have.

Informed consent in the context of a professional athlete has its particular challenges. It is complicated by some of the issues already mentioned, pressure from coaches, management, agent, family, and others who stand to benefit from the athlete's continued participation in their sport. The injured athlete is under pressure to "do what is best for the team." An athlete who acts contrary to this, seeks outside advice, chooses non-traditional therapies, refuses to play while still hurting or otherwise attempts to act autonomously is considered petulant, uncommitted, and indifferent to the goals of the team. Within professional sports, the number of injured players who have been so labeled is legion.[16]

The athlete invariably receives information about the possible courses of action from a variety of sources. The internet is now a major source of medical information for patients. Unfortunately, there is no means of separating unscientific information from that which is based on good scientific evidence. Personal testimonials carry a lot of weight with athletes, who will often be more influenced by the experience of a colleague, or a well-publicized experience of a high-profile player, than the advice given by their practitioner. The athlete usually does not appreciate that every case is different.

Another potential difficulty is decisions being made in the middle of a game—such as whether or not to have an injection. Fully informed consent is not practical in this circumstance, but this does not excuse the clinician from making a good faith attempt at educating the player on the risks and benefits, and documenting the discussion in the medical record.

Documentation is essential. Ideally, documentation should be provided to the athlete explaining the risks and benefits of a particular course of action. The athlete and the clinician should both sign a document stating that the athlete has been given certain information and advice.

Occasionally the athlete will decide not to heed the advice of the clinician and go ahead with a course of action contrary to what has been advised. Of course, this is the right of the athlete as it is the right of any patient. However, it is essential that it be documented that the athlete is acting against the advice of the practitioner.

Guidelines for resolution of conflict of interest

The guidelines for a clinician to follow for the resolution of conflict of interest include:

- player's health is paramount
- informed consent
- full disclosure

- exculpatory waiver
- team clinician's contract
- player contract
- care with the media.

Confidentiality

Patient confidentiality is fundamental to the practice of medicine. The professional codes of conduct of medical and paramedical practitioners limits their freedom to report injuries, illnesses, and other problems to anyone other than the individual directly concerned. How does this affect the team clinician? Scenarios 4 and 5 provide examples.

The athlete and the team clinician have a confidential clinician–patient relationship. But when management pays a team clinician, this may change the relationship between clinician and athlete. The team clinician has two masters to serve—the athlete-patient and the team management.

The American Medical Association admonishes clinicians "not to reveal confidences entrusted to them unless required to do so by law or, if necessary, to protect the welfare of the individual or community."[17]

In the case of professional or collegiate team clinicians, because of the salaries or scholarships received by the athletes, management may have access to their records. This access is deemed by some to be appropriate. Therefore, discussing the condition of the athlete with management would also probably be viewed as appropriate.

Before examining the athlete, the team clinician should remind the athlete that he or she is acting on behalf of the team. Permission must be sought from

Scenario 4

During the last training session before a major game, a player sustains a mild hamstring strain, which is not noticed by the coaching staff. The player presents for treatment, tells the clinician "in confidence," and begs the clinician not to inform the coach.

How would you advise the clinician?

Scenario 5

A professional player has a career-threatening injury. You are asked by team management to help conceal the injury as the club wishes to trade the player.

What should you do?

the athlete to disclose relevant information regarding his or her medical or physical condition to appropriate team officials.[18] However, what if the athlete asks to speak to the clinician "in confidence," or, after telling the clinician some information, the athlete asks that it be kept confidential?

While it is clear that team clinicians have the right to inform team management of relevant injuries, there is a gray area about what is appropriate. Issues such as drug or alcohol use, personal issues, and psychiatric or psychological problems may all impact on the player's performance, and yet the consequences of revealing these problems to the team management may impact negatively on the careers of the players.

It is strongly advised that all players and medical staff sign written agreements prior to the season which make it absolutely clear that the team clinician has the player's permission to divulge information to the team coach/management if appropriate. This has the unfortunate consequence that the player is more likely to seek advice and/or treatment away from the team medical staff.

The British Olympic Association (BOA) has a different view on this question. Just prior to the Sydney Olympic Games, the BOA published a position statement on athlete confidentiality.[19] This argues that coaches can only be informed of an athlete's problems with the consent of the individual athlete. In relation to contracts, the BOA statement said that medical support staff who sign a contract with the governing body may be in breach of their professional code of conduct if they breach their duties of confidentiality. It suggested that athletes who had signed a general consent form could still withhold consent for any specific consultation, test, or treatment.

The media

Relationships with the media are another potential problem for the team clinician as sports medicine information can be personally and/or financially damaging to the athlete. The team clinician should always have the permission of the player and, if appropriate, team management before divulging details of injuries to the media.

It is much safer for the clinicians not to talk to the media at all and leave all communication regarding injuries to the team media spokesperson.

Performance-enhancing drugs

It is clear that since the 1980s a significant minority of sports clinicians have played a role in administering performance-enhancing drugs to athletes. The most extreme example occurred in the systemized doping practices of the East German regime of the 1970s and 1980s.[20] Other prominent examples of clinicians mediating doping were the Ben Johnson steroid case at the 1988 Olympics, and the 1998 Tour de France erythropoietin (EPO) scandal. There has always been a small number of clinicians who encouraged the use of drugs—particularly anabolic steroids.

There were a number of different rationales for this support. Some used the patient autonomy notion that the non-medical use of drugs is simply a matter of personal liberty and individual experimentation and that if athletes are aware of possible adverse reactions and are willing to accept the risks in the hope of other rewards, there should be no reason not to prescribe the drugs.

Some argued that as other performance-enhancing techniques were allowed, drugs were no different; others argued that given that steroid use was widespread, there was no point trying to prevent it; others argued the harm minimization line that clinicians have an obligation to monitor the effects of steroids in the same way as they monitor the potential harmful effects of alcohol and smoking. It is possible that others were influenced by their desire to become associated with elite athletes.

The comments of Californian clinician Robert Kerr, who was a well-known supplier of anabolic steroids in the 1980s, are interesting. Kerr ceased prescribing steroids, stating that while his intention was to steer athletes clear of black-market steroids of dubious quality and to minimize the medical risks of taking steroids by prescribing so-called safe types and dosages, he was duped by his patients because they went to the black market for additional steroids and used far more than the dosages he prescribed.[21]

While it is now illegal to prescribe anabolic steroids in a number of countries, it is not illegal to give advice about how to alleviate some of the harmful effects of steroid use, just as clinicians and other healthcare providers give information to intravenous drug users about how to avoid becoming infected with the human immunodeficiency virus (HIV).

By monitoring are you giving de facto approval? Are you facilitating this player's drug use? Scenario 6 provides an example. Monitoring steroid use may allow a clinician to develop a relationship with an athlete that will give the opportunity to help the athlete stop using anabolic steroids. Clinicians are much more effective in changing attitudes about steroid use if they give balanced information about the potential benefits as well as the risks of using anabolic steroids.

A team clinician should be careful not to give the athlete the impression that he or she condones the use of steroids or other performance-enhancing drugs, and should make it clear that the opposite is true. This information should be documented in the athlete's record.

We concur with Kennedy's advice[20] that the proper medical response to a request to prescribe or monitor drug use is to provide accurate information and advice in a non-judgmental manner.

The athlete will not seek help or advice about drugs from a team clinician whom they cannot trust to keep their confidence. However, the confidentiality of the clinician–patient relationship allows the clinician to assure the athlete that disclosures, discussions, and treatments will remain confidential. Clinicians, however, have a duty to warn third parties of impending harm related to an athlete's drug use, and a team clinician's public duty to warn may override the private duty of confidentiality.

McNamee et al.[22] have noted a conflict between the issue of patient confidentiality and the World Anti-Doping Code (WADC) regulations. Article 2.8 states that a doping offence may be deemed to have occurred if a healthcare professional acts so as to satisfy any or all of the following conditions: "administration or attempted administration to any athlete in-competition of any prohibited method or prohibited substance, or administration or attempted administration to any athlete out-of-competition of any prohibited method or any prohibited substance that is prohibited out of-competition; or assisting, encouraging, aiding, abetting, covering up or any other type of complicity involving an anti-doping rule violation or any attempted anti-doping rule violation."

McNamee et al.[22] believe dialogue between World Anti-Doping Agency (WADA), (inter)national sports governing bodies, and relevant (inter)national healthcare professions is urgently needed to protect healthcare professionals who are committed both to their clients', their own, and their employers' requirements for doping-free sport. Clearly, more precise guidelines on how such conflicts will be interpreted by both WADA and the relevant bodies should be made public to prevent professional dilemmas such as this from occurring.

Scenario 7 provides another example. The situation in this scenario places the team clinician in a difficult position. Let us assume, firstly, that the player himself/herself has told you he/she is taking steroids. Does your duty to the team to prevent the adverse effects of a positive drug test result override patient confidentiality? Is the situation different if a third party has informed you? If so, do you approach the player and say that you have heard a rumor and offer advice regarding the personal dangers and the implications for the team?

According to the BOA's position statement, "a refusal to consent to disclosure must be respected even in the event of an athlete taking a prohibited substance."[19]

Or, if you confront the player and he/she refuses to stop taking the steroids, what should you do? There are two components to this question. Firstly, it is the clinician's duty to counsel the athlete regarding the dangers of taking anabolic steroids. The second, more difficult, ethical question is whether the clinician should inform team management of the player's anabolic drug use on the basis that a positive drug test may have disastrous implications for the player, the team, and team management (possibly including the team clinician if it is known that the clinician was aware of the drug taking).

We believe that patient confidentiality is paramount; however, attempts should be made to encourage the player to admit his or her drug-taking.

What about the situation in Scenario 8 where a new "undetectable" drug becomes available. How is this situation different from Scenario 7 now that there is no risk of testing positive for a drug? There is no longer the risk of embarrassment/shame/penalty that would result from a positive drug test result, but you are still aware that one of the players in your care is acting against the laws of the game. Again, patient confidentiality is paramount unless the physical health of another person is endangered.

Infectious diseases

Several questions arise in this contentious area. Can an athlete with HIV, hepatitis B, or hepatitis C compete? Is this a medical, ethical or legal problem? This is probably a decision for the sporting body with input from medical, legal, and advocacy groups.[23]

In the 1990s in Melbourne, an amateur Australian Rules footballer who admitted to being HIV positive was refused permission to play. The player's appeal on the grounds of discrimination was heard at the state Civil and Administrative Tribunal. The Australian *Equal Opportunity Act 1995* provides that a person must not discriminate against another person by excluding such other person from participating in a sporting activity. However, another section of the Act provides that discrimination on the basis of impairment may be permitted if such discrimination is reasonably necessary to protect the health or safety of any person.

The tribunal found that although there was a statistical risk of transmission of HIV from the player to another player or official, the prospects of such transmission were so low that the tribunal granted the player permission to play with the proviso that appropriate precautions be taken to protect players from such transmission as far as possible.[24]

Scenario 9 raises similar confidentiality issues to those discussed previously. The clinician must determine whether the public interest outweighs patient confidentiality. The infected player may be a risk to both team mates and opponents.

The type of sport being played influences the risk of bleeding and may, thus, affect the decision. Sports are divided into combat (e.g. boxing), contact (e.g. football), collision (e.g. basketball), and non-contact (e.g. tennis, golf). Combat, contact, and collision sports have higher risks of transmission than non-contact sports.

Ethics in sport

The sports clinician has an important role to play in sport in providing quality medical care. The clinician can also play an important role in sport in general. Currently, many condemnable practices are associated with sport. These include violence, hazardous training practices, drug use, emotional, physical, and sexual abuse, cheating, and antisocial behavior.

In the battle to eradicate drug use in sport, the team clinician plays an important role,[25] although until society's attitude toward success changes markedly, it is doubtful whether the use of education and widespread drug testing will ever eradicate the problem.[26]

As sports and exercise medicine clinicians, we have unique ethical responsibilities for the athlete in our care, the sports organizations we work for, and the ideals of fair play and fair competition.[27] It is easy at times, when caught up in the pressure of competition, to lose sight of the full range of responsibilities. Sports clinicians are in a unique position to intervene with patients, speak out with respect to rules, drugs, and violence, and develop and adhere to a sports medicine code of ethics.

RECOMMENDED WEBSITES

American College of Sports Medicine. Code of ethics for ACSM certified and registered professionals: www.acsm.org/AM/Template.cfm?Section=Search&TEMPLATE=/CM/HTMLDisplay.cfm&CONTENTID=2385

Australasian College of Sports Physicians (ACSP) Code of Ethics: https://acsp.org.au/uploads/ACSP%20Code%20of%20Ethics%20April%202008.pdf

International Federation of Sports Medicine (FIMS) Code of ethics: www.fims.org/en/general/code-of-ethics/.

Olympic Movement Medical Code 2009: www.olympic.org/PageFiles/61597/Olympic_Movement_Medical_Code_eng.pdf

World Medical Association Declaration on Principles of Health Care for Sports Medicine 1999: www.wma.net/en/30publications/10policies/h14/index.html.

World Medical Association International Code of Medical Ethics, 2006: www.wma.net/en/30publications/10policies/c8/index.html.

RECOMMENDED READING

Anderson L. Contractual obligations and the sharing of confidential health information in sport. *J Med Ethics* 2008;34:e6

Anderson L. Writing a new code of ethics for sports physicians: principles and challenges *Br J Sports Med* 2009;43:1079–82

British Olympic Association's position statement on athlete confidentiality. *Br J Sports Med* 2000;34:71–2.

Bunch WH, Dvonch VM. Informed consent in sports medicine. *Clin Sports Med* 2004;23:183–93.

Dunn WR, George MS, Churchill L Et al. Ethics in sports medicine. *Am J Sports Med* 2007;35:840–4.

Foddy B, Savulescu J. Ethics of performance enhancement in sport: drugs and gene doping. In: Ashcroft RE, Dawson A, Draper H, McMillan J, eds. *Principles of healthcare ethics*, 2nd ed. London: Wiley, 2007:511–20.

Gallup EM. *Law and the team physician.* Champaign, IL: Human Kinetics, 1995.

Grayson E. *Ethics, injuries and the law in sports medicine.* Oxford: Butterworth Heinemann, 1999.

Holm S, McNamee M. Ethics in sports medicine. *BMJ* 2009;339:b3898.

Johnson R. The unique ethics of sports medicine. *Clin Sports Med* 2004;23:175–82

McCrory P. No pain, no gain. The dilemma of a team physician [editorial]. *Br J Sports Med* 2001;35:141–2.

McNamee MJ. Doctors' duties and doping dilemmas In: Moller V, McNamee MJ, Dimeo P, eds. *Elite sport, doping and public health.* Odense: University of Southern Denmark Press, 2009:179–90.

Matheson G. Can team physicians buy credibility? *Phys Sportsmed* 2001;29(12):3.

Mitten M. Emerging legal issues in sports medicine: a synthesis, summary and analysis. *St Johns Law Rev* 2002;76(1):5–86.

Opie H. Medico-legal issues in sport: the view from the grandstand. *Sydney Law Rev* 2001;375:375–6.

Pipe A, Best T. Drugs, sport, and medical practice. *Clin J Sport Med* 2002; 12: 201–2.

Rubin A. Team physician or athlete's doctor. *Phys Sportsmed* 1998;26(7):27–9.

Salomon B. Ethics in the locker room: the challenges for team physicians. *Occupat Med* 2002;17:693.

Tucker AM. Ethics and the professional team physician. *Clin Sports Med* 2004;23:227–41.

Waddington I, Roderick M. Management of medical confidentiality in English professional football clubs: some ethical problems and issues. *Br J Sports Med* 2002;36:118–23.

REFERENCES

1. Singer PA. Recent advances. Medical ethics. *BMJ* 2000;321:282–5.
2. Bernstein J, Perlis C, Bartolozzi AR. Normative ethics in sports medicine. *Clin Orthop* 2004;420:309–18.
3. Polsky SD. Winning medicine: professional sports team doctors' conflicts of interest. *J Contemp Health Law Policy* 1998;14(2):503–29.
4. FIMS. FIMS code of ethics in sports medicine 1997, *www.fims.org/en/general/code-of-ethics/.*
5. Tucker AM. Ethics and the professional team physician. *Clin Sports Med* 2004;23:227–41.
6. King JHJ. The duty and standards of care for team physicians. *Houston L Rev* 1981;18(4):657–704.
7. Opie H. The team doctor/athlete legal relationship. *Sports Train Med Rehab* 1991;2:287–99.
8. Gallup EM. *Law and the team physician.* Champaign, IL: Human Kinetics, 1995.
9. Holm S, McNamee M. Ethics in sports medicine. *BMJ* 2009;339:b3898.
10. Devitt BM, McCarthy C. 'I am in blood Stepp'd in so far ...": ethical dilemmas and the sports team doctor. *Br J Sports Med* 2010 44: 175–8
11. Orchard J. The use of local anaesthetic injections in professional football. *Br J Sports Med* 2001;35:212–13.

12. Tokisk JM, Powell ET, Schlegel TF et al. Ketorolac use in the National Football League. *Phys Sportsmed* 2002;30(9):19–25.

13. Brukner P. Return to play. A personal perspective. *Clin J Sport Med* 2005;15:459.

14. Myklebust G, Bahr R. Return to play guidelines after anterior cruciate ligament surgery. *Br J Sports Med* 2005;39(3):127–31.

15. MDAV. *Medicine and the law. A practical guide for doctors.* Melbourne: Medical Defence Association of Victoria, 2005.

16. Bunch WH, Dvonch VM. Informed consent in sports medicine. *Clin Sports Med* 2004;23:183–93.

17. American Medical Association. Year end review, medicine by the book. *AMA News* 1989;6:1–28.

18. Mitten MJ. Emerging legal issues in sports medicine: a synthesis, summary and analysis. *St Johns Law Rev* 2002;76(1):5–86.

19. British Olympic Association. The British Olympic Association's position statement on athlete confidentiality. *Br J Sports Med* 2000;34:71–2.

20. Kennedy MC, Kennedy JR. Ethics of prescribing drugs to enhance sporting performance. *Med J Aust* 1999;171: 204–5.

21. Duda M. Do anabolic steroids pose an ethical dilemma for US physicians? *Phys Sportsmed* 1986;14(11):173–5.

22. McNamee M, Phillips N. Confidentiality, disclosure and doping in sports medicine. *Br J Sports Med* 2011;45(3): 174–7.

23. Magnusson R, Opie H. HIV and hepatitis in sport: a legal framework for resolving hard cases. *Monash Univ Law Rev* 1994;214:243–4.

24. Opie H. Medico-legal issues in sport: the view from the grandstand. *Sydney Law Rev* 2001;375:375–6.

25. Pipe A. Drugs, sport and the new millenium. *Clin J Sport Med* 2000;10:7–8.

26. Yesalis CE, Bahrke MS, Wright JE. Societal alternatives to anabolic steroid use. *Clin J Sport Med* 2000;10:1–6.

27. Pipe A. Reviving ethics in sport. Time for physicians to act. *Phys Sportsmed* 1998;26(6):39–40.